C.B. '96

THE COLLINS
PAPERBACK
FRENCH
DICTIONARY

THE COLLINS PAPERBACK FRENCH DICTIONARY

FRENCH · ENGLISH   ENGLISH · FRENCH

Pierre-Henri Cousin
Lorna Sinclair   Jean-François Allain
Catherine E. Love

HarperCollins*Publishers*

First published in this edition 1988

© William Collins Sons & Co. Ltd. 1988

Latest reprint 1993

ISBN 0 00 433446 9

contributors/avec la collaboration de
Claude Nimmo, Renée Birks,
Hélène Lewis, Philippe Patry,
Elisabeth Campbell, Vivian Marr

editorial staff/secrétariat de rédaction
Elspeth Anderson, Angela Campbell,
Lesley Robertson

All rights reserved

*Printed in Great Britain by
HarperCollins Manufacturing, Glasgow*

TABLE DES MATIÈRES

CONTENTS

Introduction	vii	Introduction	vii
Abréviations employées dans le texte	viii	Abbreviations used in the dictionary	viii
Symboles phonétiques	x	Phonetic symbols	x
Le verbe français	xii	French verb forms	xii
Le verbe anglais	xiv	English verb forms	xiv
Les nombres	xvi	Numbers	xvi
FRANÇAIS-ANGLAIS		FRENCH-ENGLISH	
ANGLAIS-FRANÇAIS		ENGLISH-FRENCH	

Les marques déposées

Les termes qui constituent à notre connaissance une marque déposée ont été désignés comme tels. La présence ou l'absence de cette désignation ne peut toutefois être considérée comme ayant valeur juridique.

Note on trademarks

Words which we have reason to believe constitute trademarks have been designated as such. However, neither the presence nor the absence of such designation should be regarded as affecting the legal status of any trademark.

INTRODUCTION

Pour comprendre l'anglais

Ce dictionnaire nouveau, résolument tourné vers le monde moderne, rend compte de l'usage actuel de la langue anglaise, y compris dans les domaines du commerce et de la micro-informatique, et contient un choix étendu d'abréviations, sigles et noms géographiques fréquemment rencontrés dans la presse. Pour faciliter les recherches, les formes irrégulières des verbes et substantifs anglais font l'objet d'une entrée séparée qui renvoie à la forme de base suivie de sa traduction.

Pour vous exprimer en anglais

Pour vous aider à vous exprimer dans un anglais correct et idiomatique, de nombreuses indications précisant le sens ou le domaine d'emploi sont là pour vous guider et vous orienter vers la traduction la mieux adaptée à votre contexte. Tous les termes courants sont traités en détail et illustrés d'exemples.

Un compagnon de travail

Par le soin apporté à sa confection, ce nouveau dictionnaire Collins constitue un outil fiable et facile d'emploi qui saura répondre à vos besoins linguistiques et se montrer un fidèle compagnon de route dans vos études ou votre travail.

Understanding French

This new and thoroughly up-to-date dictionary provides the user with wide-ranging, practical coverage of current usage, including terminology relevant to business and office automation, and a comprehensive selection of abbreviations, acronyms and geographical names commonly found in the press. You will also find, for ease of consultation, irregular forms of French verbs and nouns with a cross-reference to the basic form where a translation is given.

Self-expression in French

To help you express yourself correctly and idiomatically in French, numerous indications — think of them as signposts — guide you to the most appropriate translation for your context. All the most commonly used words are given detailed treatment, with many examples of typical usage.

A working companion

Much care has been taken to make this new Collins dictionary thoroughly reliable, easy to use and relevant to your work and study. We hope it will become a long-serving companion for all your foreign language needs.

ABRÉVIATIONS

ABBREVIATIONS

adjectif, locution adjective	**a**	adjective, adjectival phrase
abréviation	**ab(b)r**	abbreviation
adverbe, locution adverbiale	**ad**	adverb, adverbial phrase
administration	**ADMIN**	administration
agriculture	**AGR**	agriculture
anatomie	**ANAT**	anatomy
architecture	**ARCHIT**	architecture
l'automobile	**AUT(O)**	the motor car and motoring
aviation, voyages aériens	**AVIAT**	flying, air travel
biologie	**BIO(L)**	biology
botanique	**BOT**	botany
anglais de Grande-Bretagne	**Brit**	British English
conjonction	**cj**	conjunction
langue familière (! emploi vulgaire)	**col(!)**	colloquial usage (! particularly offensive)
commerce, finance, banque	**COMM**	commerce, finance, banking
informatique	**COMPUT**	computing
construction	**CONSTR**	building
nom utilisé comme adjectif, ne peut s'employer ni comme attribut, ni après le nom qualifié	**cpd**	compound element: noun used as an adjective and which cannot follow the noun it qualifies
cuisine, art culinaire	**CULIN**	cookery
déterminant: article, adjectif démonstratif ou indéfini etc	**dét, det**	determiner: article, demonstrative etc.
économie	**ECON**	economics
électricité, électronique	**ELEC**	electricity, electronics
exclamation, interjection	**excl**	exclamation, interjection
féminin	**f**	feminine
langue familière (! emploi vulgaire)	**fam (!)**	colloquial usage (! particularly offensive)
emploi figuré	**fig**	figurative use
(verbe anglais) dont la particule est inséparable du verbe	**fus**	(phrasal verb) where the particle cannot be separated from main verb
dans la plupart des sens; généralement	**gén, gen**	in most or all senses; generally
géographie, géologie	**GEO**	geography, geology
géométrie	**GEOM**	geometry
histoire	**HIST**	history
informatique	**INFORM**	computing
invariable	**inv**	invariable
irrégulier	**irg**	irregular
domaine juridique	**JUR**	law
grammaire, linguistique	**LING**	grammar, linguistics
masculin	**m**	masculine
mathématiques, algèbre	**MATH**	mathematics, calculus
médecine	**MED**	medical term, medicine
masculine ou féminin, suivant le sexe	**m/f**	either masculine or feminine depending on sex
domaine militaire, armée	**MIL**	military matters
musique	**MUS**	music
nom	**n**	noun

ABRÉVIATIONS

ABBREVIATIONS

ABRÉVIATIONS		ABBREVIATIONS
navigation, nautisme	**NAVIG, NAUT**	sailing, navigation
adjectif ou nom numérique	**num**	numeral adjective or noun
	o.s.	oneself
péjoratif	**péj, pej**	derogatory, pejorative
photographie	**PHOT(O)**	photography
physiologie	**PHYSIOL**	physiology
pluriel	**pl**	plural
politique	**POL**	politics
participe passé	**pp**	past participle
préposition	**prép, prep**	preposition
psychologie, psychiatrie	**PSYCH**	psychology, psychiatry
temps du passé	**pt**	past tense
nom non comptable: ne peut s'utiliser au pluriel	**q**	collective (uncountable) noun: is not used in the plural
quelque chose	**qch**	
quelqu'un	**qn**	
religions, domaine ecclésiastique	**REL**	religions, church service
	sb	somebody
enseignement, système scolaire et universitaire	**SCOL**	schooling, schools and universities
singulier	**sg**	singular
	sth	something
subjonctif	**sub**	subjunctive
sujet (grammatical)	**su(b)j**	(grammatical) subject
techniques, technologie	**TECH**	technical term, technology
télécommunications	**TEL**	telecommunications
télévision	**TV**	television
typographie	**TYP(O)**	typography, printing
anglais des USA	**US**	American English
verbe	**vb**	verb
verbe ou groupe verbal à fonction intransitive	**vi**	verb or phrasal verb used intransitively
verbe ou groupe verbal à fonction transitive	**vt**	verb or phrasal verb used transitively
zoologie	**ZOOL**	zoology
marque déposée	**®**	registered trademark
indique une équivalence culturelle	**≈**	introduces a cultural equivalent

TRANSCRIPTION PHONÉTIQUE

CONSONNES

CONSONANTS

NB. **p, b, t, d, k, g** sont suivis d'une aspiration en anglais.

NB. **p, b, t, d, k, g** are not aspirated in French.

poupée	p	*puppy*
bombe	b	*baby*
*tente the*rmal	t	*tent*
dinde	d	*daddy*
*coq qui ké*pi	k	*cork kiss chord*
gag bague	g	*gag guess*
sale ce nation	s	*so rice kiss*
zéro rose	z	*cousin buzz*
tache chat	ʃ	*sheep sugar*
gilet juge	ʒ	*pleasure beige*
	tʃ	*church*
	dʒ	*judge general*
fer phare	f	*farm raffle*
valve	v	*very rev*
	θ	*thin maths*
	ð	*that other*
lent salle	l	*little ball*
rare rentrer	ʀ	
	r	*rat rare*
maman femme	m	*mummy comb*
non nonne	n	*no ran*
agneau vigne	ɲ	
	ŋ	*singing bank*
hop!	h	*hat reheat*
yeux paille pied	j	*yet*
nouer oui	w	*wall bewail*
huile lui	ɥ	
	x	*loch*

DIVERS

MISCELLANEOUS

pour l'anglais: le r final se prononce en liaison devant une voyelle	*	in French wordlist: no liaison
pour l'anglais: précède la syllabe accentuée	'	in French transcription: no liaison

En règle générale, la prononciation est donnée entre crochets après chaque entrée. Toutefois, du côté anglais-français et dans le cas des expressions composées de deux ou plusieurs mots non réunis par un trait d'union et faisant l'objet d'une entrée séparée, la prononciation doit être cherchée sous chacun des mots constitutifs de l'expression en question.

PHONETIC TRANSCRIPTION

VOYELLES

NB. La mise en équivalence de certains sons n'indique qu'une ressemblance approximative.

VOWELS

NB. The pairing of some vowel sounds only indicates approximate equivalence.

*i*ci *vie* l*y*re	i iː	heel bead
	ɪ	hit pity
jou*er* ét*é*	e	
la*i*t jou*et* merc*i*	ɛ	set tent
pl*a*t *a*mour	a æ	bat apple
b*a*s p*â*te	ɑ ɑː	after car calm
	ʌ	fun cousin
l*e* pr*e*mier	ə	over above
b*eu*rre p*eu*r	œ	
p*eu* d*eu*x	ø əː	urn fern work
*o*r h*o*mme	ɔ	wash pot
m*o*t *eau* g*au*che	o ɔː	born cork
gen*ou* r*ou*e	u	full soot
	uː	boon lewd
r*ue* *u*rne	y	

DIPHTONGUES

DIPHTHONGS

	ɪə	beer tier
	ɛə	tear fair there
	eɪ	date plaice day
	aɪ	life buy cry
	au	owl foul now
	əu	low no
	ɔɪ	boil boy oily
	uə	poor tour

NASALES

NASAL VOWELS

mat*in* pl*ein*	ɛ̃
br*un*	œ̃
s*an*g *an* d*an*s	ɑ̃
n*on* p*on*t	ɔ̃

In general, we give the pronunciation of each entry in square brackets after the word in question. However, on the English-French side, where the entry is composed of two or more unhyphenated words, each of which is given elsewhere in this dictionary, you will find the pronunciation of each word in its alphabetical position.

FRENCH VERB FORMS

1 Participe présent *2* Participe passé *3* Présent *4* Imparfait *5* Futur *6* Conditionnel
7 Subjonctif présent

acquérir *1* acquérant *2* acquis *3* acquiers, acquérons, acquièrent *4* acquérais *5* acquerrai *7* acquière
ALLER *1* allant *2* allé *3* vais, vas, va, allons, allez, vont *4* allais *5* irai *6* irais *7* aille
asseoir *1* asseyant *2* assis *3* assieds, asseyons, asseyez, asseyent *4* asseyais *5* assiérai *7* asseye
atteindre *1* atteignant *2* atteint *3* atteins, atteignons *4* atteignais *7* atteigne
AVOIR *1* ayant *2* eu *3* ai, as, a, avons, avez, ont *4* avais *5* aurai *6* aurais *7* aie, aies, ait, ayons, ayez, aient
battre *1* battant *2* battu *3* bats, bat, battons *4* battais *7* batte
boire *1* buvant *2* bu *3* bois, buvons, boivent *4* buvais *7* boive
bouillir *1* bouillant *2* bouilli *3* bous, bouillons *4* bouillais *7* bouille
conclure *1* concluant *2* conclu *3* conclus, concluons *4* concluais *7* conclue
conduire *1* conduisant *2* conduit *3* conduis, conduisons *4* conduisais *7* conduise
connaître *1* connaissant *2* connu *3* connais, connaît, connaissons *4* connaissais *7* connaisse
coudre *1* cousant *2* cousu *3* couds, cousons, cousez, cousent *4* cousais *7* couse
courir *1* courant *2* couru *3* cours, courons *4* courais *5* courrai *7* coure
couvrir *1* couvrant *2* couvert *3* couvre, couvrons *4* couvrais *7* couvre
craindre *1* craignant *2* craint *3* crains, craignons *4* craignais *7* craigne
croire *1* croyant *2* cru *3* crois, croyons, croient *4* croyais *7* croie
croître *1* croissant *2* crû, crue, crus, crues *3* croîs, croissons *4* croissais *7* croisse
cueiller *1* cueillant *2* cueilli *3* cueille, cueillons *4* cueillais *5* cueillerai *7* cueille
devoir *1* devant *2* dû, due, dus, dues *3* dois, devons, doivent *4* devais *5* devrai *7* doive
dire *1* disant *2* dit *3* dis, disons, dites, disent *4* disais *7* dise
dormir *1* dormant *2* dormi *3* dors, dormons *4* dormais *7* dorme
écrire *1* écrivant *2* écrit *3* écris, écrivons *4* écrivais *7* écrive
ÊTRE *1* étant *2* été *3* suis, es, est, sommes, êtes, sont *4* étais *5* serai *6* serais *7* sois, sois, soit, soyons, soyez, soient
FAIRE *1* faisant *2* fait *3* fais, fais, fait, faisons, faites, font *4* faisais *5* ferai *6* ferais *7* fasse
falloir *3* fallu *4* fallait *5* faudra *7* faille
FINIR *1* finissant *2* fini *3* finis, finis, finit, finissons, finissez, finissent *4* finissais *5* finirai *6* finirais *7* finisse
fuir *1* fuyant *2* fui *3* fuis, fuyons, fuient *4* fuyais *7* fuie
joindre *1* joignant *2* joint *3* joins, joignons *4* joignais *7* joigne
lire *1* lisant *2* lu *3* lis, lisons *4* lisais *7* lise
luire *1* luisant *2* lui *3* luis, luisons *4* luisais *7* luise
maudire *1* maudissant *2* maudit *3* maudis, maudissons *4* maudissait *7* maudisse
mentir *1* mentant *2* menti *3* mens, mentons *4* mentais *7* mente
mettre *1* mettant *2* mis *3* mets, metons *4* mettais *7* mette
mourir *1* mourant *2* mort *3* meurs, mourons, meurent *4* mourais *5* mourrai *7* meure
naître *1* naissant *2* né *3* nais, naît, naissons *4* naissais *7* naisse
offrir *1* offrant *2* offert *3* offre, offrons *4* offrais *7* offre
PARLER *1* parlant *2* parlé *3* parle, parles, parle, parlons, parlez, parlent *4* parlais, parlais, parlait, parlions, parliez, parlaient *5* parlerai, parleras, parlera, parlerons, parlerez, parleront *6* parlerais, parlerais, parlerait, parlerions, parleriez, parleraient *7* parle, parles, parle, parlions, parliez, parlent *impératif* parle! parlez!
partir *1* partant *2* parti *3* pars, partons *4* partais *7* parte
plaire *1* plaisant *2* plu *3* plais, plaît, plaisons *4* plaisais *7* plaise
pleuvoir *1* pleuvant *2* plu *3* pleut, pleuvent *4* pleuvait *5* pleuvra *7* pleuve
pourvoir *1* pourvoyant *2* pourvu *3* pourvois, pourvoyons, pourvoient *4* pourvoyais *7* pourvoie
pouvoir *1* pouvant *2* pu *3* peux, peut, pouvons, peuvent *4* pouvais *5* pourrai *7* puisse
prendre *1* prenant *2* pris *3* prends, prenons, prennent *4* prenais *7* prenne
prévoir *like voir 5* prévoirai

RECEVOIR *1* recevant *2* reçu *3* reçois, reçois, reçoit, recevons, recevez, reçoivent *4* recevais *5* recevrai *6* recevrais *7* reçoive

RENDRE *1* rendant *2* rendu *3* rends, rends, rend, rendons, rendez, rendent *4* rendais *5* rendrai *6* rendrais *7* rende

résoudre *1* résolvant *2* résolu *3* résous, résolvons *4* résolvais *7* résolve

rire *1* riant *2* ri *3* ris, rions *4* riais *7* rie

savoir *1* sachant *2* su *3* sais, savons, savent *4* savais *5* saurai *7* sache *impératif* sache, sachons, sachez

servir *1* servant *2* servi *3* sers, servons *4* servais *7* serve

sortir *1* sortant *2* sorti *3* sors, sortons *4* sortais *7* sorte

souffrir *1* souffrant *2* souffert *3* souffre, souffrons *4* souffrais *7* souffre

suffire *1* suffisant *2* suffi *3* suffis, suffisons *4* suffisais *7* suffise

suivre *1* suivant *2* suivi *3* suis, suivons *4* suivais *7* suive

taire *1* taisant *2* tu *3* tais, taisons *4* taisais *7* taise

tenir *1* tenant *2* tenu *3* tiens, tenons, tiennent *4* tenais *5* tiendrai *7* tienne

vaincre *1* vainquant *2* vaincu *3* vaincs, vainc, vainquons *4* vainquais *7* vainque

valoir *1* valant *2* valu *3* vaux, vaut, valons *4* valais *5* vaudrai *7* vaille

venir *1* venant *2* venu *3* viens, venons, viennent *4* venais *5* viendrai *7* vienne

vivre *1* vivant *2* vécu *3* vis, vivons *4* vivais *7* vive

voir *1* voyant *2* vu *3* vois, voyons, voient *4* voyais *5* verrai *7* voie

vouloir *1* voulant *2* voulu *3* veux, veut, voulons, veulent *4* voulais *5* voudrai *7* veuille *impératif* veuillez

LE VERBE ANGLAIS

present	pt	pp	present	pt	pp
arise (arising)	arose	arisen	fall	fell	fallen
awake (awaking)	awoke	awaked	feed	fed	fed
			feel	felt	felt
be (am, is, are, being)	was, were	been	fight	fought	fought
			find	found	found
bear	bore	born(e)	flee	fled	fled
beat	beat	beaten	fling	flung	flung
become (becoming)	became	become	fly (flies)	flew	flown
			forbid (forbidding)	forbade	forbidden
befall	befell	befallen	forecast	forecast	forecast
begin (beginning)	began	begun	forego	forewent	foregone
behold	beheld	beheld	foresee	foresaw	foreseen
bend	bent	bent	foretell	foretold	foretold
beseech	besought	besought	forget (forgetting)	forgot	forgotten
beset (besetting)	beset	beset	forgive (forgiving)	forgave	forgiven
bet (betting)	bet (also betted)	bet (also betted)	forsake (forsaking)	forsook	forsaken
bid (bidding)	bid (also bade)	bid (also bidden)	freeze (freezing)	froze	frozen
bind	bound	bound	get (getting)	got	got, (US) gotten
bite (biting)	bit	bitten			
bleed	bled	bled	give (giving)	gave	given
blow	blew	blown	go (goes)	went	gone
break	broke	broken	grind	ground	ground
breed	bred	bred	grow	grew	grown
bring	brought	brought	hang	hung (also hanged)	hung (also hanged)
build	built	built			
burn	burnt (also burned)	burnt (also burned)	have (has; having)	had	had
burst	burst	burst	hear	heard	heard
buy	bought	bought	hide (hiding)	hid	hidden
can	could	(been able)	hit (hitting)	hit	hit
cast	cast	cast	hold	held	held
catch	caught	caught	hurt	hurt	hurt
choose (choosing)	chose	chosen	keep	kept	kept
cling	clung	clung	kneel	knelt (also kneeled)	knelt (also kneeled)
come (coming)	came	come			
			know	knew	known
cost	cost	cost	lay	laid	laid
creep	crept	crept	lead	led	led
cut (cutting)	cut	cut	lean	leant (also leaned)	leant (also leaned)
deal	dealt	dealt			
dig (digging)	dug	dug	leap	leapt (also leaped)	leapt (also leaped)
do (3rd person: he/she/it does)	did	done	learn	learnt (also learned)	learnt (also learned)
draw	drew	drawn	leave (leaving)	left	left
dream	dreamed (also dreamt)	dreamed (also dreamt)	lend	lent	lent
drink	drank	drunk	let (letting)	let	let
drive (driving)	drove	driven	lie (lying)	lay	lain
			light	lit (also lighted)	lit (also lighted)
dwell	dwelt	dwelt			
eat	ate	eaten	lose (losing)	lost	lost

present	pt	pp	present	pt	pp
make (making)	made	made	spell	spelt (*also* spelled)	spelt (*also* spelled)
may	might	—	spend	spent	spent
mean	meant	meant	spill	spilt (*also* spilled)	spilt (*also* spilled)
meet	met	met	spin (spinning)	spun	spun
mistake (mistaking)	mistook	mistaken	spit (spitting)	spat	spat
mow	mowed	mown (*also* mowed)	split (splitting)	split	split
must	(had to)	(had to)	spoil	spoiled (*also* spoilt)	spoiled (*also* spoilt)
pay	paid	paid	spread	spread	spread
put (putting)	put	put	spring	sprang	sprung
quit (quitting)	quit (*also* quitted)	quit (*also* quitted)	stand	stood	stood
read	read	read	steal	stole	stolen
rend	rent	rent	stick	stuck	stuck
rid (ridding)	rid	rid	sting	stung	stung
ride (riding)	rode	ridden	stink	stank	stunk
ring	rang	rung	stride (striding)	strode	stridden
rise (rising)	rose	risen	strike (striking)	struck	struck (*also* stricken)
run (running)	ran	run	strive (striving)	strove	striven
saw	sawed	sawn	swear	swore	sworn
say	said	said	sweep	swept	swept
see	saw	seen	swell	swelled	swollen (*also* swelled)
seek	sought	sought	swim (swimming)	swam	swum
sell	sold	sold	swing	swung	swung
send	sent	sent	take (taking)	took	taken
set (setting)	set	set	teach	taught	taught
shake (shaking)	shook	shaken	tear	tore	torn
shall	should	—	tell	told	told
shear	sheared	shorn (*also* sheared)	think	thought	thought
shed (shedding)	shed	shed	throw	threw	thrown
shine (shining)	shone	shone	thrust	thrust	thrust
shoot	shot	shot	tread	trod	trodden
show	showed	shown	wake (waking)	woke (*also* waked)	woken (*also* waked)
shrink	shrank	shrunk	waylay	waylaid	waylaid
shut (shutting)	shut	shut	wear	wore	worn
sing	sang	sung	weave (weaving)	wove (*also* weaved)	woven (*also* weaved)
sink	sank	sunk	wed (wedding)	wedded (*also* wed)	wedded (*also* wed)
sit (sitting)	sat	sat	weep	wept	wept
slay	slew	slain	win (winning)	won	won
sleep	slept	slept	wind	wound	wound
slide (sliding)	slid	slid	withdraw	withdrew	withdrawn
sling	slung	slung	withhold	withheld	withheld
slit (slitting)	slit	slit	withstand	withstood	withstood
smell	smelt (*also* smelled)	smelt (*also* smelled)	wring	wrung	wrung
sow	sowed	sown (*also* sowed)	write (writing)	wrote	written
speak	spoke	spoken			
speed	sped (*also* speeded)	sped (*also* speeded)			

LES NOMBRES

un (une)	**1**	one
deux	**2**	two
trois	**3**	three
quatre	**4**	four
cinq	**5**	five
six	**6**	six
sept	**7**	seven
huit	**8**	eight
neuf	**9**	nine
dix	**10**	ten
onze	**11**	eleven
douze	**12**	twelve
treize	**13**	thirteen
quatorze	**14**	fourteen
quinze	**15**	fifteen
seize	**16**	sixteen
dix-sept	**17**	seventeen
dix-huit	**18**	eighteen
dix-neuf	**19**	nineteen
vingt	**20**	twenty
vingt et un (une)	**21**	twenty-one
vingt-deux	**22**	twenty-two
trente	**30**	thirty
quarante	**40**	forty
cinquante	**50**	fifty
soixante	**60**	sixty
soixante-dix	**70**	seventy
soixante et onze	**71**	seventy-one
soixante-douze	**72**	seventy-two
quatre-vingts	**80**	eighty
quatre-vingt-un (-une)	**81**	eighty-one
quatre-vingt-dix	**90**	ninety
quatre-vingt-onze	**91**	ninety-one
cent	**100**	a hundred
cent un (une)	**101**	a hundred and one
trois cents	**300**	three hundred
trois cent un (une)	**301**	three hundred and one
mille	**1 000**	a thousand
un million	**1 000 000**	a million

NUMBERS

xvi

LES NOMBRES

NUMBERS

premier (première), 1er	first, 1st
deuxième, 2e or 2ème	second, 2nd
troisième, 3e or 3ème	third, 3rd
quatrième	fourth, 4th
cinquième	fifth, 5th
sixième	sixth, 6th
septième	seventh
huitième	eighth
neuvième	ninth
dixième	tenth
onzième	eleventh
douzième	twelfth
treizième	thirteenth
quatorzième	fourteenth
quinzième	fifteenth
seizième	sixteenth
dix-septième	seventeenth
dix-huitième	eighteenth
dix-neuvième	nineteenth
vingtième	twentieth
vingt-et-unième	twenty-first
vingt-deuxième	twenty-second
trentième	thirtieth
centième	hundredth
cent-unième	hundred-and-first
millième	thousandth

FRANÇAIS-ANGLAIS
FRENCH-ENGLISH

A

A, a [ɑ] *nm inv* A, a ♦ *abr* = **anticyclone, are**; (= *ampère*) amp; (= *autoroute*) ≈ M (*Brit*); **A comme Anatole** A for Andrew (*Brit*) *ou* Able (*US*); **de a à z** from a to z; **prouver qch par a + b** to prove sth conclusively.

a [a] *vb voir* **avoir**.

à [a] (*à + le* = **au**, *à + les* = **aux**) [a, o] *prép* (*situation*) at, in; (*direction, attribution*) to; (*provenance*) from; (*moyen*) with, by; **donner qch à qn** to give sb sth, give sth to sb; **prendre de l'eau à la fontaine** to take some water from the fountain; **payé au mois** paid by the month; **100 km/unités à l'heure** 100 km/units per hour; **à 3 heures/minuit** at 3 o'clock/midnight; **il habite à 5 minutes de la gare** he lives 5 minutes (away) from the station; **ils vivent à deux heures de Paris, par la route** they live two hours' drive (away) from Paris; **au mois de juin** in the month of June; **au départ** at the start, at the outset; **se chauffer au gaz/à l'électricité** to heat one's house with gas/electricity, to have gas/electric heating; **à la main/machine** by hand/machine; **à bicyclette** by bicycle *ou* on a bicycle; **à pied** by *ou* on foot; **être/aller à la campagne** to be in/go to the country; **l'homme aux yeux bleus/à la veste rouge** the man with the blue eyes/with *ou* in the red jacket; **un ami à moi** a friend of mine; **cinq à six heures** five to six hours; **à demain/la semaine prochaine!** see you tomorrow/next week!; **à la russe** the Russian way, in the Russian fashion; **à bien réfléchir** if you think about it; **maison à vendre** house for sale; **à sa grande surprise** to his great surprise; **à ce qu'il prétend** according to him, from what he says; **tasse à café** coffee cup.

Å *abr* (= *Angstrom*) A *ou* Å.

A2 *abr* (= *Antenne 2*) French TV channel.

abaissement [abɛsmɑ̃] *nm* lowering; pulling down.

abaisser [abese] *vt* to lower, bring down; (*manette*) to pull down; (*fig*) to debase; to humiliate; **s'~** *vi* to go down; (*fig*) to demean o.s.; **s'~ à faire/à qch** to stoop *ou* descend to doing/to sth.

abandon [abɑ̃dɔ̃] *nm* abandoning; deserting; giving up; withdrawal; surrender, relinquishing; (*fig*) lack of constraint; relaxed pose *ou* mood; **être à l'~** to be in a state of neglect; **laisser à l'~** to abandon.

abandonné, e [abɑ̃dɔne] *a* (*solitaire*) deserted; (*route, usine*) disused; (*jardin*) abandoned.

abandonner [abɑ̃dɔne] *vt* to leave, abandon, desert; (*projet, activité*) to abandon, give up; (*SPORT*) to retire *ou* withdraw from; (*céder*) to surrender, relinquish; **s'~** *vi* to let o.s. go; **s'~ à** (*paresse, plaisirs*) to give o.s. up to; **~ qch à qn** to give sth up to sb.

abasourdir [abazuʀdiʀ] *vt* to stun, stagger.

abat [aba] *etc vb voir* **abattre**.

abat-jour [abaʒuʀ] *nm inv* lampshade.

abats [aba] *vb voir* **abattre** ♦ *nmpl* (*de bœuf, porc*) offal *sg* (*Brit*), entrails (*US*); (*de volaille*) giblets.

abattage [abataʒ] *nm* cutting down, felling.

abattant [abatɑ̃] *vb voir* **abattre** ♦ *nm* leaf, flap.

abattement [abatmɑ̃] *nm* (*physique*) enfeeblement; (*moral*) dejection, despondency; (*déduction*) reduction; **~ fiscal** ≈ tax allowance.

abattis [abati] *vb voir* **abattre** ♦ *nmpl* giblets.

abattoir [abatwaʀ] *nm* abattoir (*Brit*), slaughterhouse.

abattre [abatʀ(ə)] *vt* (*arbre*) to cut down, fell; (*mur, maison*) to pull down; (*avion, personne*) to shoot down; (*animal*) to shoot, kill; (*fig: physiquement*) to wear out, tire out; (*: moralement*) to demoralize; **s'~** *vi* to crash down; **s'~ sur** (*suj: pluie*) to beat down on; (*: coups, injures*) to rain down on; **~ ses cartes** (*aussi fig*) to lay one's cards on the table; **~ du travail** *ou* **de la besogne** to get through a lot of work.

abattu, e [abaty] *pp de* **abattre** ♦ *a* (*déprimé*) downcast.

abbaye [abei] *nf* abbey.

abbé [abe] *nm* priest; (*d'une abbaye*) abbot; **M l'~** Father.

abbesse [abɛs] *nf* abbess.

abc, ABC [abese] *nm* alphabet primer; (*fig*) rudiments *pl*.

abcès [apsɛ] *nm* abscess.

abdication [abdikɑsjɔ̃] *nf* abdication.

abdiquer [abdike] *vi* to abdicate ♦ *vt* to renounce, give up.

abdomen [abdɔmɛn] *nm* abdomen.

abdominal, e, aux [abdɔminal, -o] *a* abdominal ♦ *nmpl*: **faire des abdominaux** to do exercises for the stomach muscles.

abécédaire [abesedɛʀ] *nm* alphabet primer.

abeille [abɛj] *nf* bee.

aberrant, e [abeʀɑ̃, -ɑ̃t] *a* absurd.

aberration [abeʀɑsjɔ̃] *nf* aberration.

abêtir [abetiʀ] *vt* to make morons (*ou* a moron) of.

abhorrer [abɔʀe] *vt* to abhor, loathe.

abîme [abim] *nm* abyss, gulf.

abîmer [abime] *vt* to spoil, damage; **s'~** *vi* to get spoilt *ou* damaged; (*fruits*) to spoil; (*tomber*) to sink, founder; **s'~ les yeux** to ruin one's eyes *ou* eyesight.

abject, e [abʒɛkt] *a* abject, despicable.

abjurer [abʒyʀe] *vt* to abjure, renounce.

ablation [ablɑsjɔ̃] *nf* removal.
ablutions [ablysjɔ̃] *nfpl*: **faire ses** ~ to perform one's ablutions.
abnégation [abnegɑsjɔ̃] *nf* (self-)abnegation.
aboie [abwa] *etc vb voir* **aboyer**.
aboiement [abwamɑ̃] *nm* bark, barking *q*.
aboierai [abwajəʀe] *etc vb voir* **aboyer**.
abois [abwa] *nmpl*: **aux** ~ at bay.
abolir [abɔliʀ] *vt* to abolish.
abolition [abɔlisjɔ̃] *nf* abolition.
abolitionniste [abɔlisjɔnist(ə)] *a*, *nm/f* abolitionist.
abominable [abɔminabl(ə)] *a* abominable.
abomination [abɔminɑsjɔ̃] *nf* abomination.
abondamment [abɔ̃damɑ̃] *ad* abundantly.
abondance [abɔ̃dɑ̃s] *nf* abundance; *(richesse)* affluence; **en** ~ in abundance.
abondant, e [abɔ̃dɑ̃, -ɑ̃t] *a* plentiful, abundant, copious.
abonder [abɔ̃de] *vi* to abound, be plentiful; ~ **en** to be full of, abound in; ~ **dans le sens de qn** to concur with sb.
abonné, e [abɔne] *nm/f* subscriber; season ticket holder ♦ *a*: **être** ~ **à un journal** to subscribe to *ou* have a subscription to a periodical; **être** ~ **au téléphone** to be on the (tele)phone.
abonnement [abɔnmɑ̃] *nm* subscription; *(pour transports en commun, concerts)* season ticket.
abonner [abɔne] *vt*: **s'**~ **à** to subscribe to, take out a subscription to.
abord [abɔʀ] *nm*: **être d'un** ~ **facile** to be approachable; **être d'un** ~ **difficile** *(personne)* to be unapproachable; *(lieu)* to be hard to reach *ou* difficult to get to; **de prime** ~, **au premier** ~ at first sight; **d'**~ *ad* first; **tout d'**~ first of all.
abordable [abɔʀdabl(ə)] *a* *(personne)* approachable; *(marchandise)* reasonably priced; *(prix)* affordable, reasonable.
abordage [abɔʀdaʒ] *nm* boarding.
aborder [abɔʀde] *vi* to land ♦ *vt* *(sujet, difficulté)* to tackle; *(personne)* to approach; *(rivage etc)* to reach; *(NAVIG: attaquer)* to board; *(: heurter)* to collide with.
abords [abɔʀ] *nmpl* surroundings.
aborigène [abɔʀiʒɛn] *nm* aborigine, native.
Abou Dhabî, Abu Dhabî [abudabi] *nm* Abu Dhabi.
aboulique [abulik] *a* totally lacking in willpower.
aboutir [abutiʀ] *vi* *(négociations etc)* to succeed; *(abcès)* to come to a head; ~ **à/ dans/sur** to end up at/in/on.
aboutissants [abutisɑ̃] *nmpl voir* **tenants**.
aboutissement [abutismɑ̃] *nm* success; *(de concept, projet)* successful realization; *(d'années de travail)* successful conclusion.
aboyer [abwaje] *vi* to bark.
abracadabrant, e [abʀakadabʀɑ̃, -ɑ̃t] *a* incredible, preposterous.
abrasif, ive [abʀazif, -iv] *a*, *nm* abrasive.
abrégé [abʀeʒe] *nm* summary; **en** ~ in a shortened *ou* abbreviated form.
abréger [abʀeʒe] *vt* *(texte)* to shorten, abridge; *(mot)* to shorten, abbreviate; *(réunion, voyage)* to cut short, shorten.
abreuver [abʀœve] *vt* to water; *(fig)*: ~ **qn de** to shower *ou* swamp sb with; *(injures etc)* to shower sb with; **s'**~ *vi* to drink.
abreuvoir [abʀœvwaʀ] *nm* watering place.
abréviation [abʀevjɑsjɔ̃] *nf* abbreviation.
abri [abʀi] *nm* shelter; **à l'**~ under cover; **être/se mettre à l'**~ to be/get under cover *ou* shelter; **à l'**~ **de** sheltered from; *(fig)* safe from.
abricot [abʀiko] *nm* apricot.
abricotier [abʀikɔtje] *nm* apricot tree.
abrité, e [abʀite] *a* sheltered.
abriter [abʀite] *vt* to shelter; *(loger)* to accommodate; **s'**~ to shelter, take cover.
abrogation [abʀɔgɑsjɔ̃] *nf* *(JUR)* repeal, abrogation.
abroger [abʀɔʒe] *vt* to repeal, abrogate.
abrupt, e [abʀypt] *a* a sheer, steep; *(ton)* abrupt.
abruti, e [abʀyti] *nm/f* *(fam)* idiot, moron.
abrutir [abʀytiʀ] *vt* to daze; *(fatiguer)* to exhaust; *(abêtir)* to stupefy.
abrutissant, e [abʀytisɑ̃, -ɑ̃t] *a* *(bruit, travail)* stupefying.
abscisse [apsis] *nf* X axis, abscissa.
absence [apsɑ̃s] *nf* absence; *(MÉD)* blackout; *(distraction)* mental blank; **en l'**~ **de** in the absence of.
absent, e [apsɑ̃, -ɑ̃t] *a* absent; *(chose)* missing, lacking; *(distrait: air)* vacant, faraway ♦ *nm/f* absentee.
absentéisme [apsɑ̃teism(ə)] *nm* absenteeism.
absenter [apsɑ̃te]: **s'**~ *vi* to take time off work; *(sortir)* to leave, go out.
abside [apsid] *nf* *(ARCHIT)* apse.
absinthe [apsɛ̃t] *nf* *(boisson)* absinth(e); *(BOT)* wormwood, absinth(e).
absolu, e [apsɔly] *a* absolute; *(caractère)* rigid, uncompromising ♦ *nm* *(PHILOSOPHIE)*: **l'**~ the Absolute; **dans l'**~ in the absolute, in a vacuum.
absolument [apsɔlymɑ̃] *ad* absolutely.
absolution [apsɔlysjɔ̃] *nf* absolution; *(JUR)* dismissal *(of case)*.
absolutisme [apsɔlytism(ə)] *nm* absolutism.
absolvais [apsɔlve] *etc vb voir* **absoudre**.
absorbant, e [apsɔʀbɑ̃, -ɑ̃t] *a* absorbent; *(tâche)* absorbing, engrossing.
absorbé, e [apsɔʀbe] *a* absorbed, engrossed.
absorber [apsɔʀbe] *vt* to absorb; *(gén MÉD: manger, boire)* to take; *(ÉCON: firme)* to take over, absorb.
absorption [apsɔʀpsjɔ̃] *nf* absorption.
absoudre [apsudʀ(ə)] *vt* to absolve; *(JUR)* to dismiss.
absous, oute [apsu, -ut] *pp de* **absoudre**.
abstenir [apstəniʀ]: **s'**~ *vi* *(POL)* to abstain; **s'**~ **de qch/de faire** to refrain from sth/from doing.
abstention [apstɑ̃sjɔ̃] *nf* abstention.
abstentionniste [apstɑ̃sjɔnist(ə)] *nm* abstentionist.
abstenu, e [apstəny] *pp de* **abstenir**.
abstiendrai [apstjɛ̃dʀe], **abstiens** [apstjɛ̃] *etc voir* **abstenir**.
abstinence [apstinɑ̃s] *nf* abstinence; **faire** ~ to abstain *(from meat on Fridays)*.
abstint [apstɛ̃] *etc vb voir* **abstenir**.
abstraction [apstʀaksjɔ̃] *nf* abstraction; **faire** ~ **de** to set *ou* leave aside; ~ **faite de** ...

leaving aside ....

abstraire [apstʀɛʀ] *vt* to abstract; **s'~** *vi*: **s'~ (de)** (*s'isoler*) to cut o.s. off (from).

abstrait, e [apstʀɛ, -ɛt] *pp de* **abstraire** ♦ *a* abstract ♦ *nm*: **dans l'~** in the abstract.

abstraitement [apstʀɛtmɑ̃] *ad* abstractly.

abstrayais [apstʀɛjɛ] *etc vb voir* **abstraire**.

absurde [apsyʀd(ə)] *a* absurd ♦ *nm* absurdity; (*PHILOSOPHIE*): **l'~** absurd; **par l'~** *ad* absurdio.

absurdité [apsyʀdite] *nf* absurdity.

abus [aby] *nm* (*excès*) abuse, misuse; (*injustice*) abuse; **~ de confiance** breach of trust; (*détournement de fonds*) embezzlement; **~ de pouvoir** abuse of power.

abuser [abyze] *vi* to go too far, overstep the mark ♦ *vt* to deceive, mislead; **s'~** *vi* (*se méprendre*) to be mistaken; **~ de** *vt* (*force, droit*) to misuse; (*alcool*) to take to excess; (*violer, duper*) to take advantage of.

abusif, ive [abyzif, -iv] *a* exorbitant; (*punition*) excessive; (*pratique*) improper.

abusivement [abyzivmɑ̃] *ad* exorbitantly; excessively; improperly.

AC *sigle f* (= *appellation contrôlée*) *guarantee of quality of wine*.

acabit [akabi] *nm*: **du même ~** of the same type.

acacia [akasja] *nm* (*BOT*) acacia.

académicien, ne [akademisjɛ̃, -ɛn] *nm/f* academician.

académie [akademi] *nf* (*société*) learned society; (*école: d'art, de danse*) academy; (*ART: nu*) nude; (*SCOL: circonscription*) ≈ regional education authority; **l'A~ (française)** the French Academy.

académique [akademik] *a* academic.

Acadie [akadi] *nf*: **l'~** the Maritime Provinces.

acadien, ne [akadjɛ̃, -ɛn] *a* Acadian, of *ou* from the Maritime Provinces.

acajou [akaʒu] *nm* mahogany.

acariâtre [akaʀjɑtʀ(ə)] *a* sour(-tempered) (*Brit*), cantankerous.

accablant, e [akɑblɑ̃, -ɑt] *a* (*témoignage, preuve*) overwhelming.

accablement [akɑbləmɑ̃] *nm* deep despondency.

accabler [akɑble] *vt* to overwhelm, overcome; (*suj: témoignage*) to condemn, damn; **~ qn d'injures** to heap *ou* shower abuse on sb; **~ qn de travail** to overburden sb with work; **accablé de dettes/soucis** weighed down with debts/cares.

accalmie [akalmi] *nf* lull.

accaparant, e [akapaʀɑ̃, -ɑt] *a* that takes up all one's time *ou* attention.

accaparer [akapaʀe] *vt* to monopolize; (*suj: travail etc*) to take up (all) the time *ou* attention of.

accéder [aksede]: **~ à** *vt* (*lieu*) to reach; (*fig: pouvoir*) to accede to; (*: poste*) to attain; (*accorder: requête*) to grant, accede to.

accélérateur [akseleʀatœʀ] *nm* accelerator.

accélération [akseleʀɑsjɔ̃] *nf* speeding up; acceleration.

accéléré [akseleʀe] *nm*: **en ~** (*CINÉMA*) speeded up.

accélérer [akseleʀe] *vt* (*mouvement, travaux*) to speed up ♦ *vi* (*AUTO*) to accelerate.

accent [aksɑ̃] *nm* accent; (*inflexions expressives*) tone (of voice); (*PHONÉTIQUE, fig*) stress; **aux ~s de** (*musique*) to the strains of; **mettre l'~ sur** (*fig*) to stress; **~ aigu/grave/circonflexe** acute/grave/circumflex accent.

accentuation [aksɑ̃tɥɑsjɔ̃] *nf* accenting; stressing.

accentué, e [aksɑ̃tɥe] *a* marked, pronounced.

accentuer [aksɑ̃tɥe] *vt* (*LING: orthographe*) to accent; (*: phonétique*) to stress, accent; (*fig*) to accentuate, emphasize; (*: effort, pression*) to increase; **s'~** *vi* to become more marked *ou* pronounced.

acceptable [akseptabl(ə)] *a* satisfactory, acceptable.

acceptation [akseptɑsjɔ̃] *nf* acceptance.

accepter [aksepte] *vt* to accept; (*tolérer*): **~ que qn fasse** to agree to sb doing; **~ de faire** to agree to do.

acception [aksɛpsjɔ̃] *nf* meaning, sense; **dans toute l'~ du terme** in the full sense *ou* meaning of the word.

accès [aksɛ] *nm* (*à un lieu, INFORM*) access; (*MÉD*) attack; (*: de toux*) fit, bout ♦ *nmpl* (*routes etc*) means of access, approaches; **d'~ facile/malaisé** easily/not easily accessible; **donner ~ à** (*lieu*) to give access to; (*carrière*) to open the door to; **avoir ~ auprès de qn** to have access to sb; **l'~ aux quais est interdit aux personnes non munies d'un billet** ticket-holders only on platforms, no access to platforms without a ticket; **~ de colère** fit of anger; **~ de joie** burst of joy.

accessible [aksesibl(ə)] *a* accessible; (*personne*) approachable; (*livre, sujet*): **~ à qn** within the reach of sb; (*sensible*): **~ à la pitié/l'amour** open to pity/love.

accession [aksesjɔ̃] *nf*: **~ à** accession to; (*à un poste*) attainment of; **~ à la propriété** home-ownership.

accessit [aksesit] *nm* (*SCOL*) ≈ certificate of merit.

accessoire [akseswaʀ] *a* secondary, of secondary importance; (*frais*) incidental ♦ *nm* accessory; (*THÉÂTRE*) prop.

accessoirement [akseswaʀmɑ̃] *ad* secondarily; incidentally.

accessoiriste [akseswaʀiste(ə)] *nm/f* (*TV, CINÉMA*) property man/woman.

accident [aksidɑ̃] *nm* accident; **par ~** by chance; **~ de parcours** mishap; **~ de la route** road accident; **~ du travail** accident at work; industrial injury *ou* accident; **~s de terrain** unevenness of the ground.

accidenté, e [aksidɑ̃te] *a* damaged *ou* injured (in an accident); (*relief, terrain*) uneven; hilly.

accidentel, le [aksidɑ̃tɛl] *a* accidental.

accidentellement [aksidɑ̃tɛlmɑ̃] *ad* (*par hasard*) accidentally; (*mourir*) in an accident.

accidenter [aksidɑ̃te] *vt* (*personne*) to injure; (*véhicule*) to damage.

accise [aksiz] *nf*: **droit d'~(s)** excise duty.

acclamation [aklamɑsjɔ̃] *nf*: **par ~** (*vote*) by acclamation; **~s** *nfpl* cheers, cheering *sg*.

acclamer [aklame] *vt* to cheer, acclaim.

acclimatation [aklimatɑsjɔ̃] *nf* acclimatization.

acclimater [aklimate] *vt* to acclimatize; **s'~** *vi* to become acclimatized.

accointances [akwɛ̃tɑ̃s] *nfpl*: **avoir des ~ avec** to have contacts with.

accolade [akɔlad] *nf* (*amicale*) embrace; (*signe*) brace; **donner l'~ à qn** to embrace sb.

accoler [akɔle] *vt* to place side by side.

accommodant, e [akɔmɔdɑ̃, -ɑ̃t] *a* accommodating, easy-going.

accommodement [akɔmɔdmɑ̃] *nm* compromise.

accommoder [akɔmɔde] *vt* (*CULIN*) to prepare; (*points de vue*) to reconcile; **~ qch à** (*adapter*) to adapt sth to; **s'~ de** to put up with; (*se contenter de*) to make do with; **s'~ à** (*s'adapter*) to adapt to.

accompagnateur, trice [akɔ̃paɲatœʀ, -tʀis] *nm/f* (*MUS*) accompanist; (*de voyage*) guide; (*: de voyage organisé*) courier; (*d'enfants*) accompanying adult.

accompagnement [akɔ̃paɲmɑ̃] *nm* (*MUS*) accompaniment; (*MIL*) support.

accompagner [akɔ̃paɲe] *vt* to accompany, be *ou* go *ou* come with; (*MUS*) to accompany; **s'~ de** to bring, be accompanied by.

accompli, e [akɔ̃pli] *a* accomplished.

accomplir [akɔ̃pliʀ] *vt* (*tâche, projet*) to carry out; (*souhait*) to fulfil; **s'~** *vi* to be fulfilled.

accomplissement [akɔ̃plismɑ̃] *nm* carrying out; fulfilment (*Brit*), fulfillment (*US*).

accord [akɔʀ] *nm* (*entente, convention, LING*) agreement; (*entre des styles, tons etc*) harmony; (*consentement*) agreement, consent; (*MUS*) chord; **donner son ~** to give one's agreement; **mettre 2 personnes d'~** to make 2 people come to an agreement, reconcile 2 people; **se mettre d'~** to come to an agreement (with each other); **être d'~** to agree; **être d'~ avec qn** to agree with sb; **d'~!** OK!, right!; **d'un commun ~** of one accord; **~ parfait** (*MUS*) tonic chord.

accord-cadre, *pl* **accords-cadres** [akɔʀkadʀ(ə)] *nm* framework *ou* outline agreement.

accordéon [akɔʀdeɔ̃] *nm* (*MUS*) accordion.

accordéoniste [akɔʀdeɔnist(ə)] *nm/f* accordionist.

accorder [akɔʀde] *vt* (*faveur, délai*) to grant; (*attribuer*): **~ de l'importance/de la valeur à qch** to attach importance/value to sth; (*harmoniser*) to match; (*MUS*) to tune; **s'~** to get on together; (*être d'accord*) to agree; (*couleurs, caractères*) to go together, match; (*LING*) to agree; **je vous accorde que ...** I grant you that ....

accordeur [akɔʀdœʀ] *nm* (*MUS*) tuner.

accoster [akɔste] *vt* (*NAVIG*) to draw alongside; (*personne*) to accost ♦ *vi* (*NAVIG*) to berth.

accotement [akɔtmɑ̃] *nm* (*de route*) verge (*Brit*), shoulder; **~ stabilisé/non stabilisé** hard shoulder/soft verge *ou* shoulder.

accoter [akɔte] *vt*: **~ qch contre/à** to lean *ou* rest sth against/on; **s'~ contre/à** to lean against/on.

accouchement [akuʃmɑ̃] *nm* delivery, (child)birth; (*travail*) labour (*Brit*), labor

(*US*); **~ à terme** delivery at (full) term; **~ sans douleur** natural childbirth.

accoucher [akuʃe] *vi* to give birth, have a baby; (*être en travail*) to be in labour (*Brit*) *ou* labor (*US*) ♦ *vt* to deliver; **~ d'un garçon** to give birth to a boy.

accoucheur [akuʃœʀ] *nm*: (**médecin**) **~** obstetrician.

accoucheuse [akuʃøz] *nf* midwife.

accouder [akude]: **s'~** *vi*: **s'~ à/contre/sur** to rest one's elbows on/against/on; **accoudé à la fenêtre** leaning on the windowsill.

accoudoir [akudwaʀ] *nm* armrest.

accouplement [akupləmɑ̃] *nm* coupling; mating.

accoupler [akuple] *vt* to couple; (*pour la reproduction*) to mate; **s'~** to mate.

accourir [akuʀiʀ] *vi* to rush *ou* run up.

accoutrement [akutʀəmɑ̃] *nm* (*péj*) getup (*Brit*), outfit.

accoutrer [akutʀe] (*péj*) *vt* to do *ou* get up; **s'~** to do *ou* get o.s. up.

accoutumance [akutymɑ̃s] *nf* (*gén*) adaptation; (*MÉD*) addiction.

accoutumé, e [akutyme] *a* (*habituel*) customary, usual; **comme à l'~e**, as is customary *ou* usual.

accoutumer [akutyme] *vt*: **~ qn à qch/faire** to accustom sb to sth/to doing; **s'~ à** to get accustomed *ou* used to.

accréditer [akʀedite] *vt* (*nouvelle*) to substantiate; **~ qn (auprès de)** to accredit sb (to).

accro [akʀo] *nm/f* (*fam*: = *accroché(e)*) addict.

accroc [akʀo] *nm* (*déchirure*) tear; (*fig*) hitch, snag; **sans ~** without a hitch; **faire un ~ à** (*vêtement*) to make a tear in, tear; (*fig: règle etc*) to infringe.

accrochage [akʀoʃaʒ] *nm* hanging (up); hitching (up); (*AUTO*) (minor) collision; (*MIL*) encounter, engagement; (*dispute*) clash, brush.

accroche-cœur [akʀoʃkœʀ] *nm* kiss-curl.

accrocher [akʀoʃe] *vt* (*suspendre*): **~ qch à** to hang sth (up) on; (*attacher: remorque*): **~ qch à** to hitch sth (up) to; (*heurter*) to catch; to hit; (*déchirer*): **~ qch (à)** to catch sth (on); (*MIL*) to engage; (*fig*) to catch, attract ♦ *vi* to stick, get stuck; (*fig: pourparlers etc*) to hit a snag; (*plaire: disque etc*) to catch on; **s'~** (*se disputer*) to have a clash *ou* brush; (*ne pas céder*) to hold one's own, hang on in (*fam*); **s'~ à** (*rester pris à*) to catch on; (*agripper, fig*) to hang on *ou* cling to.

accrocheur, euse [akʀoʃœʀ, -øz] *a* (*vendeur, concurrent*) tenacious; (*publicité*) eye-catching; (*titre*) catchy, eye-catching.

accroire [akʀwaʀ] *vt*: **faire** *ou* **laisser ~ à qn qch/que** to give sb to believe sth/that.

accrois [akʀwa], **accroissais** [akʀwasɛ] *etc vb voir* **accroître**.

accroissement [akʀwasmɑ̃] *nm* increase.

accroître [akʀwatʀ(ə)] *vt*, **s'~** *vi* to increase.

accroupi, e [akʀupi] *a* squatting, crouching (down).

accroupir [akʀupiʀ]: **s'~** *vi* to squat, crouch (down).

accru, e [akʀy] *pp de* **accroître**.

accu [aky] *nm* (*fam*: = *accumulateur*) accumulator, battery.

accueil [akœj] *nm* welcome; (*endroit*) reception (desk); (: *dans une gare*) information kiosk; **comité/centre d'~** reception committee/centre.

accueillant, e [akœjã, -ãt] *a* welcoming, friendly.

accueillir [akœjiʀ] *vt* to welcome; (*loger*) to accommodate.

acculer [akyle] *vt*: **~ qn à** *ou* **contre** to drive sb back against; **~ qn dans** to corner sb in; **~ qn à** (*faillite*) to drive sb to the brink of.

accumulateur [akymylatœʀ] *nm* accumulator, battery.

accumulation [akymylɔsjɔ̃] *nf* accumulation; **chauffage/radiateur à ~** (night-)storage heating/heater.

accumuler [akymyle] *vt* to accumulate, amass; **s'~** *vi* to accumulate; to pile up.

accusateur, trice [akyzatœʀ, -tʀis] *nm/f* accuser ♦ *a* accusing; (*document, preuve*) incriminating.

accusatif [akyzatif] *nm* (*LING*) accusative.

accusation [akyzasjɔ̃] *nf* (*gén*) accusation; (*JUR*) charge; (*partie*): **l'~** the prosecution; **mettre en ~** to indict; **acte d'~** bill of indictment.

accusé, e [akyze] *nm/f* accused; (*prévenu(e)*) defendant ♦ *nm*: **~ de réception** acknowledgement of receipt.

accuser [akyze] *vt* to accuse; (*fig*) to emphasize, bring out; (: *montrer*) to show; **s'~** *vi* (*s'accentuer*) to become more marked; **~ qn de** to accuse sb of; (*JUR*) to charge sb with; **~ qn/qch de qch** (*rendre responsable*) to blame sb/sth for sth; **s'~ de qch/d'avoir fait qch** to admit sth/having done sth; to blame o.s. for sth/for having done sth; **~ réception de** to acknowledge receipt of; **~ le coup** (*aussi fig*) to be visibly affected.

acerbe [asɛʀb(ə)] *a* caustic, acid.

acéré, e [aseʀe] *a* sharp.

acétate [asetat] *nm* acetate.

acétique [asetik] *a*: **acide ~** acetic acid.

acétone [aseton] *nf* acetone.

acétylène [asetilɛn] *nm* acetylene.

ACF *sigle m* (= *Automobile Club de France*) ≈ AA (*Brit*), ≈ AAA (*US*).

ach. *abr* = *achète*.

achalandé, e [aʃalɑ̃de] *a*: **bien/mal ~** well-/poorly stocked.

acharné, e [aʃaʀne] *a* (*lutte, adversaire*) fierce, bitter; (*travail*) relentless, unremitting.

acharnement [aʃaʀnəmɑ̃] *nm* fierceness; relentlessness.

acharner [aʃaʀne]: **s'~** *vi*: **s'~ sur** to go at fiercely, hound; **s'~ contre** to set o.s. against; to dog, pursue; (*suj: malchance*) to hound; **s'~ à faire** to try doggedly to do; to persist in doing.

achat [aʃa] *nm* buying *q*; (*article acheté*) purchase; **faire l'~ de** to buy, purchase; **faire des ~s** to do some shopping, buy a few things.

acheminement [aʃminmɑ̃] *nm* conveyance.

acheminer [aʃmine] *vt* (*courrier*) to forward, dispatch; (*troupes*) to convey, transport;

(*train*) to route; **s'~ vers** to head for.

acheter [aʃte] *vt* to buy, purchase; (*soudoyer*) to buy, bribe; **~ qch à** (*marchand*) to buy *ou* purchase sth from; (*ami etc: offrir*) to buy sth for; **~ à crédit** to buy on credit.

acheteur, euse [aʃtœʀ, -øz] *nm/f* buyer; shopper; (*COMM*) buyer; (*JUR*) vendee, purchaser.

achevé, e [aʃve] *a*: **d'un ridicule ~** thoroughly *ou* absolutely ridiculous; **d'un comique ~** absolutely hilarious.

achèvement [aʃɛvmɑ̃] *nm* completion, finishing.

achever [aʃve] *vt* to complete, finish; (*blessé*) to finish off; **s'~** *vi* to end.

achoppement [aʃɔpmɑ̃] *nm*: **pierre d'~** stumbling block.

acide [asid] *a* sour, sharp; (*ton*) acid, biting; (*CHIMIE*) acid(ic) ♦ *nm* acid.

acidifier [asidifje] *vt* to acidify.

acidité [asidite] *nf* sharpness; acidity.

acidulé, e [asidyle] *a* slightly acid; **bonbons ~s** acid drops (*Brit*), ≈ lemon drops (*US*).

acier [asje] *nm* steel; **~ inoxydable** stainless steel.

aciérie [asjeʀi] *nf* steelworks *sg*.

acné [akne] *nf* acne.

acolyte [akɔlit] *nm* (*péj*) associate.

acompte [akɔ̃t] *nm* deposit; (*versement régulier*) instalment; (*sur somme due*) payment on account; (*sur salaire*) advance; **un ~ de 100 F** 100 F on account.

acoquiner [akɔkine]: **s'~ avec** *vt* (*péj*) to team up with.

Açores [asɔʀ] *nfpl*: **les ~** the Azores.

à-côté [akote] *nm* side-issue; (*argent*) extra.

à-coup [aku] *nm* (*du moteur*) (hic)cough; (*fig*) jolt; **sans ~s** smoothly; **par ~s** by fits and starts.

acoustique [akustik] *nf* (*d'une salle*) acoustics *pl*; (*science*) acoustics *sg* ♦ *a* acoustic.

acquéreur [akeʀœʀ] *nm* buyer, purchaser; **se porter/se rendre ~ de qch** to announce one's intention to purchase/to purchase sth.

acquérir [akeʀiʀ] *vt* to acquire; (*par achat*) to purchase, acquire; (*valeur*) to gain; (*résultats*) to achieve; **ce que ses efforts lui ont acquis** what his efforts have won *ou* gained (for) him.

acquiers [akjɛʀ] *etc vb voir* **acquérir**.

acquiescement [akjɛsmɑ̃] *nm* acquiescence, agreement.

acquiescer [akjese] *vi* (*opiner*) to agree; (*consentir*): **~ (à qch)** to acquiesce *ou* assent (to sth).

acquis, e [aki, -iz] *pp de* **acquérir** ♦ *nm* (accumulated) experience; (*avantage*) gain ♦ *a* (*voir acquérir*) acquired; gained; achieved; **être ~ à** (*plan, idée*) to be in full agreement with; **son aide nous est ~e** we can count on *ou* be sure of his help; **tenir qch pour ~** to take sth for granted.

acquisition [akizisjɔ̃] *nf* acquisition; (*achat*) purchase; **faire l'~ de** to acquire; to purchase.

acquit [aki] *vb voir* **acquérir** ♦ *nm* (*quittance*) receipt; **pour ~** received; **par ~ de conscience** to set one's mind at rest.

acquittement [akitmɑ̃] *nm* acquittal; payment, settlement.

acquitter |akite| *vt* (*JUR*) to acquit; (*facture*) to pay, settle; **s'~ de** to discharge; (*promesse, tâche*) to fulfil (*Brit*), fulfill (*US*), carry out.

âcre |ɑkʀ(ə)| *a* acrid, pungent.

âcreté |ɑkʀəte| *nf* acridness, pungency.

acrobate |akʀɔbat| *nm/f* acrobat.

acrobatie |akʀɔbasi| *nf* (*art*) acrobatics *sg*; (*exercice*) acrobatic feat; **~ aérienne** aerobatics *sg*.

acrobatique |akʀɔbatik| *a* acrobatic.

acronyme |akʀɔnim| *nm* acronym.

Acropole |akʀɔpɔl| *nf*: **l'~** the Acropolis.

acrylique |akʀilik| *a*, *nm* acrylic.

acte |akt(ə)| *nm* act, action; (*THÉÂTRE*) act; **~s** *nmpl* (*compte-rendu*) proceedings; **prendre ~ de** to note, take note of; **faire ~ de présence** to put in an appearance; **faire ~ de candidature** to submit an application; **~ d'accusation** charge (*Brit*), bill of indictment; **~ de baptême** baptismal certificate; **~ de mariage/naissance** marriage/birth certificate; **~ de vente** bill of sale.

acteur |aktœʀ| *nm* actor.

actif, ive |aktif, -iv| *a* active ♦ *nm* (*COMM*) assets *pl*; (*LING*) active (voice); (*fig*): **avoir à son ~** to have to one's credit; **~s** *nmpl* people in employment; **mettre à son ~** to add to one's list of achievements; **l'~ et le passif** assets and liabilities; **prendre une part active à qch** to take an active part in sth; **population active** working population.

action |aksjɔ̃| *nf* (*gén*) action; (*COMM*) share; **une bonne/mauvaise ~** a good/an unkind deed; **mettre en ~** to put into action; **passer à l'~** to take action; **sous l'~ de** under the effect of; **l'~ syndicale** (the) union action; **un film d'~** an action film *ou* movie; **~ en diffamation** libel action; **~ de grâce(s)** (*REL*) thanksgiving.

actionnaire |aksjɔnɛʀ| *nm/f* shareholder.

actionner |aksjɔne| *vt* to work; to activate; to operate.

active |aktiv| *af voir* **actif**.

activement |aktivmɑ̃| *ad* actively.

activer |aktive| *vt* to speed up; (*CHIMIE*) to activate; **s'~** *vi* (*s'affairer*) to bustle about; (*se hâter*) to hurry up.

activisme |aktivism(ə)| *nm* activism.

activiste |aktivist(ə)| *nm/f* activist.

activité |aktivite| *nf* activity; **en ~** (*volcan*) active; (*fonctionnaire*) in active life; (*militaire*) on active service.

actrice |aktʀis| *nf* actress.

actualiser |aktɥalize| *vt* to actualize; (*mettre à jour*) to bring up to date.

actualité |aktɥalite| *nf* (*d'un problème*) topicality; (*événements*): **l'~** current events; **les ~s** (*CINÉMA, TV*) the news; **l'~ politique/sportive** the political/sports *ou* sporting news; **les ~s télévisées** the television news; **d'~** topical.

actuel, le |aktɥɛl| *a* (*présent*) present; (*d'actualité*) topical; (*non virtuel*) actual; **à l'heure ~le** at this moment in time, at the moment.

actuellement |aktɥɛlmɑ̃| *ad* at present, at the present time.

acuité |akɥite| *nf* acuteness.

acuponcteur, acupuncteur |akypɔ̃ktœʀ| *nm* acupuncturist.

acuponcture, acupuncture |akypɔ̃ktyʀ| *nf* acupuncture.

adage |adaʒ| *nm* adage.

adaptable |adaptabl(ə)| *a* adaptable.

adaptateur, trice |adaptatœʀ, -tʀis| *nm/f* adapter.

adaptation |adaptasjɔ̃| *nf* adaptation.

adapter |adapte| *vt* to adapt; **s'~ (à)** (*suj: personne*) to adapt (to); (*: objet, prise etc*) to apply (to); **~ qch à** (*approprier*) to adapt sth to (fit); **~ qch sur/dans/à** (*fixer*) to fit sth on/into/to.

addenda |adɛ̃da| *nm inv* addenda.

Addis-Ababa |adisababa|, **Addis-Abeba** |adisabəba| *n* Addis Ababa.

additif |aditif| *nm* additional clause; (*substance*) additive; **~ alimentaire** food additive.

addition |adisjɔ̃| *nf* addition; (*au café*) bill.

additionnel, le |adisjɔnɛl| *a* additional.

additionner |adisjɔne| *vt* to add (up); **s'~** *vi* to add up; **~ un produit d'eau** to add water to a product.

adduction |adyksjɔ̃| *nf* (*de gaz, d'eau*) conveyance.

ADEP *sigle f* (= *Agence nationale pour le développement de l'éducation permanente*) national body which promotes adult education.

adepte |adɛpt(ə)| *nm/f* follower.

adéquat, e |adekwa, -at| *a* appropriate, suitable.

adéquation |adekwasjɔ̃| *nf* appropriateness; (*LING*) adequacy.

adhérence |adeʀɑ̃s| *nf* adhesion.

adhérent, e |adeʀɑ̃, -ɑ̃t| *nm/f* (*de club*) member.

adhérer |adeʀe| *vi* (*coller*) to adhere, stick; **~ à** (*coller*) to adhere *ou* stick to; (*se rallier à: parti, club*) to join; to be a member of; (*: opinion, mouvement*) to support.

adhésif, ive |adezif, -iv| *a* adhesive, sticky ♦ *nm* adhesive.

adhésion |adezjɔ̃| *nf* (*à un club*) joining; membership; (*à une opinion*) support.

ad hoc |adɔk| *a* ad hoc.

adieu, x |adjø| *excl* goodbye ♦ *nm* farewell; **dire ~ à qn** to say goodbye *ou* farewell to sb; **dire ~ à qch** (*renoncer*) to say *ou* wave goodbye to sth.

adipeux, euse |adipø, -øz| *a* bloated, fat; (*ANAT*) adipose.

adjacent, e |adʒasɑ̃, -ɑ̃t| *a*: **~ (à)** adjacent (to).

adjectif |adʒɛktif| *nm* adjective; **~ attribut** adjectival complement; **~ épithète** attributive adjective.

adjoignais |adʒwaɲɛ| *etc vb voir* **adjoindre**.

adjoindre |adʒwɛ̃dʀ(ə)| *vt*: **~ qch à** to attach sth to; (*ajouter*) to add sth to; **~ qn à** (*personne*) to appoint sb as an assistant to; (*comité*) to appoint sb to, attach sb to; **s'~** *vt* (*collaborateur etc*) to take on, appoint.

adjoint, e |adʒwɛ̃, -wɛ̃t| *pp de* **adjoindre** ♦ *nm/f* assistant; **directeur ~** assistant manager.

adjonction [adʒɔ̃ksjɔ̃] *nf* (*voir adjoindre*) attaching; addition; appointment.

adjudant [adʒydɑ̃] *nm* (*MIL*) warrant officer; **~-chef** ≈ warrant officer 1st class (*Brit*), ≈ chief warrant officer (*US*).

adjudicataire [adʒydikatɛʀ] *nm/f* successful bidder, purchaser; (*pour travaux*) successful tenderer (*Brit*) *ou* bidder (*US*).

adjudicateur, trice [adʒydikatœʀ, -tʀis] *nm/f* (*aux enchères*) seller.

adjudication [adʒydikɑsjɔ̃] *nf* sale by auction; (*pour travaux*) invitation to tender (*Brit*) *ou* bid (*US*).

adjuger [adʒyʒe] *vt* (*prix, récompense*) to award; (*lors d'une vente*) to auction (off); **s'~** *vt* to take for o.s; **adjugé!** (*vendu*) gone!, sold!

adjurer [adʒyʀe] *vt*: **~ qn de faire** to implore *ou* beg sb to do.

adjuvant [adʒyvɑ̃] *nm* (*médicament*) adjuvant; (*additif*) additive; (*stimulant*) stimulant.

admettre [admɛtʀ(ə)] *vt* (*visiteur, nouveau-venu*) to admit, let in; (*candidat: SCOL*) to pass; (*TECH: gaz, eau, air*) to admit; (*tolérer*) to allow, accept; (*reconnaître*) to admit, acknowledge; (*supposer*) to suppose; **j'admets que ...** I admit that ...; **je n'admets pas que tu fasses cela** I won't allow you to do that; **admettons que ...** let's suppose that ...; **admettons** let's suppose so.

administrateur, trice [administʀatœʀ, -tʀis] *nm/f* (*COMM*) director; (*ADMIN*) administrator; **~ délégué** managing director; **~ judiciaire** receiver.

administratif, ive [administʀatif, -iv] *a* administrative ♦ *nm* person in administration.

administration [administʀɑsjɔ̃] *nf* administration; **l'A~** ≈ the Civil Service.

administré, e [administʀe] *nm/f* ≈ citizen.

administrer [administʀe] *vt* (*firme*) to manage, run; (*biens, remède, sacrement etc*) to administer.

admirable [admiʀabl(ə)] *a* admirable, wonderful.

admirablement [admiʀabləmɑ̃] *ad* admirably.

admirateur, trice [admiʀatœʀ, -tʀis] *nm/f* admirer.

admiratif, ive [admiʀatif, -iv] *a* admiring.

admiration [admiʀɑsjɔ̃] *nf* admiration; **être en ~ devant** to be lost in admiration before.

admirativement [admiʀativmɑ̃] *ad* admiringly.

admirer [admiʀe] *vt* to admire.

admis, e [admi, -iz] *pp de* **admettre**.

admissibilité [admisibilite] *nf* eligibility; admissibility, acceptability.

admissible [admisibl(ə)] *a* (*candidat*) eligible; (*comportement*) admissible, acceptable; (*JUR*) receivable.

admission [admisjɔ̃] *nf* admission; **tuyau d'~** intake pipe; **demande d'~** application for membership; **service des ~s** admissions.

admonester [admɔneste] *vt* to admonish.

ADN *sigle m* (= *acide désoxyribonucléique*) DNA.

ado [ado] *nm/f* (*fam*: = *adolescent(e)*) adolescent, teenager.

adolescence [adɔlesɑ̃s] *nf* adolescence.

adolescent, e [adɔlesɑ̃, -ɑ̃t] *nm/f* adolescent, teenager.

adonner [adɔne]: **s'~ à** *vt* (*sport*) to devote o.s. to; (*boisson*) to give o.s. over to.

adopter [adɔpte] *vt* to adopt; (*projet de loi etc*) to pass.

adoptif, ive [adɔptif, -iv] *a* (*parents*) adoptive; (*fils, patrie*) adopted.

adoption [adɔpsjɔ̃] *nf* adoption; **son pays/sa ville d'~** his adopted country/town.

adorable [adɔʀabl(ə)] *a* adorable.

adoration [adɔʀɑsjɔ̃] *nf* adoration; (*REL*) worship; **être en ~ devant** to be lost in adoration before.

adorer [adɔʀe] *vt* to adore; (*REL*) to worship.

adosser [adose] *vt*: **~ qch à** *ou* **contre** to stand sth against; **s'~ à** *ou* **contre** to lean with one's back against; **être adossé à** *ou* **contre** to be leaning with one's back against.

adoucir [adusiʀ] *vt* (*goût, température*) to make milder; (*avec du sucre*) to sweeten; (*peau, voix, eau*) to soften; (*caractère, personne*) to mellow; (*peine*) to soothe, allay; **s'~** *vi* to become milder; to soften; to mellow.

adoucissement [adusismɑ̃] *nm* becoming milder; sweetening; softening; mellowing; soothing.

adoucisseur [adusisœʀ] *nm*: **~ (d'eau)** water softener.

adr. *abr* = **adresse, adresser**.

adrénaline [adʀenalin] *nf* adrenaline.

adresse [adʀɛs] *nf* (*voir adroit*) skill, dexterity; (*domicile, INFORM*) address; **à l'~ de** (*pour*) for the benefit of.

adresser [adʀese] *vt* (*lettre: expédier*) to send; (: *écrire l'adresse sur*) to address; (*injure, compliments*) to address; **~ qn à un docteur/bureau** to refer *ou* send sb to a doctor/an office; **~ la parole à qn** to speak to *ou* address sb; **s'~ à** (*parler à*) to speak to, address; (*s'informer auprès de*) to go and see, go and speak to; (: *bureau*) to enquire at; (*suj: livre, conseil*) to be aimed at.

Adriatique [adʀijatik] *nf*: **l'~** the Adriatic.

adroit, e [adʀwa, -wat] *a* (*joueur, mécanicien*) skilful (*Brit*), skillful (*US*), dext(e)rous; (*politicien etc*) shrewd, skilled.

adroitement [adʀwatmɑ̃] *ad* skilfully (*Brit*), skillfully (*US*), dext(e)rously; shrewdly.

AdS *sigle f* = *Académie des Sciences*.

aduler [adyle] *vt* to adulate.

adulte [adylt(ə)] *nm/f* adult, grown-up ♦ *a* (*personne, attitude*) adult, grown-up; (*chien, arbre*) fully-grown, mature; **l'âge ~** adulthood; **formation/film pour ~s** adult training/film.

adultère [adyltɛʀ] *a* adulterous ♦ *nm/f* adulterer/adulteress ♦ *nm* (*acte*) adultery.

adultérin, e [adylteʀɛ̃, -in] *a* born of adultery.

advenir [advəniʀ] *vi* to happen; **qu'est-il advenu de?** what has become of?; **quoi qu'il advienne** whatever befalls *ou* happens.

adventiste [advɑ̃tist(ə)] *nm/f* (*REL*) Adventist.

adverbe [advɛʀb(ə)] *nm* adverb; **~ de manière** adverb of manner.

adverbial, e, aux [advɛʀbjal, -o] *a* adverbial.

adversaire [advɛʀsɛʀ] *nm/f* (*SPORT, gén*) opponent, adversary; (*MIL*) adversary, en-

emy.
adverse [advɛʀs(ə)] *a* opposing.
adversité [advɛʀsite] *nf* adversity.
AE *sigle m* (= *adjoint d'enseignement*) non-certificated teacher.
AELE *sigle f* (= *Association européenne de libre échange*) EFTA (= *European Free Trade Association*).
AEN *sigle f* (= *Agence pour l'énergie nucléaire*) ≈ AEA (= *Atomic Energy Authority*).
aérateur [aeʀatœʀ] *nm* ventilator.
aération [aeʀasjɔ̃] *nf* airing; (*circulation de l'air*) ventilation; **conduit d'~** ventilation shaft; **bouche d'~** air vent.
aéré, e [aeʀe] *a* (*pièce, local*) airy, well-ventilated; (*tissu*) loose-woven; **centre ~** outdoor centre.
aérer [aeʀe] *vt* to air; (*fig*) to lighten; **s'~** *vi* to get some (fresh) air.
aérien, ne [aeʀjɛ̃, -ɛn] *a* (*AVIAT*) air *cpd*, aerial; (*câble, métro*) overhead; (*fig*) light; **compagnie ~ne** airline (company); **ligne ~ne** airline.
aérobic [aeʀɔbik] *nm* aerobics *sg*.
aérobie [aeʀɔbi] *a* aerobic.
aéro-club [aeʀɔklœb] *nm* flying club.
aérodrome [aeʀodʀɔm] *nm* airfield, aerodrome.
aérodynamique [aeʀodinamik] *a* aerodynamic, streamlined ♦ *nf* aerodynamics *sg*.
aérogare [aeʀogaʀ] *nf* airport (buildings); (*en ville*) air terminal.
aéroglisseur [aeʀoglisœʀ] *nm* hovercraft.
aérogramme [aeʀogʀam] *nm* air letter, aerogram(me).
aéromodélisme [aeʀomodelism(ə)] *nm* model aircraft making.
aéronaute [aeʀonot] *nm/f* aeronaut.
aéronautique [aeʀonotik] *a* aeronautical ♦ *nf* aeronautics *sg*.
aéronaval, e [aeʀonaval] *a* air and sea *cpd* ♦ *nf*: **l'A~e** ≈ the Fleet Air Arm (*Brit*), ≈ the Naval Air Force (*US*).
aéronef [aeʀonɛf] *nm* aircraft.
aérophagie [aeʀofaʒi] *nf* aerophagy.
aéroport [aeʀopɔʀ] *nm* airport; **~ d'embarquement** departure airport.
aéroporté, e [aeʀopɔʀte] *a* airborne, airlifted.
aéroportuaire [aeʀopɔʀtɥɛʀ] *a* of an *ou* the airport, airport *cpd*.
aéropostal, e, aux [aeʀopɔstal, -o] *a* airmail *cpd*.
aérosol [aeʀosɔl] *nm* aerosol.
aérospatial, e, aux [aeʀospasjal, -o] *a* aerospace ♦ *nf* aerospace industry.
aérostat [aeʀosta] *nm* aerostat.
aérotrain [aeʀotʀɛ̃] *nm* hovertrain.
AF *sigle fpl* = **allocations familiales** ♦ *sigle f* (*Suisse*) = *Assemblée fédérale*.
AFAT [afat] *sigle m* (= *Auxiliaire féminin de l'armée de terre*) *member of the women's army*.
affable [afabl(ə)] *a* affable.
affabulateur, trice [afabylatœʀ, -tʀis] *nm/f* storyteller.
affabuler [afabyle] *vi* to make up stories.
affacturage [afaktyʀaʒ] *nm* factoring.
affadir [afadiʀ] *vt* to make insipid *ou* tasteless.

affaiblir [afebliʀ] *vt* to weaken; **s'~** *vi* to weaken, grow weaker; (*vue*) to grow dim.
affaiblissement [afeblismɑ̃] *nm* weakening.
affaire [afɛʀ] *nf* (*problème, question*) matter; (*criminelle, judiciaire*) case; (*scandaleuse etc*) affair; (*entreprise*) business; (*marché, transaction*) (business) deal, (piece of) business *q*; (*occasion intéressante*) good deal, bargain; **~s** *nfpl* affairs; (*activité commerciale*) business *sg*; (*effets personnels*) things, belongings; **tirer qn/se tirer d'~** to get sb/o.s. out of trouble; **ceci fera l'~** this will do (nicely); **avoir ~ à** (*comme adversaire*) to be faced with; (*en contact*) to be dealing with; **tu auras ~ à moi!** (*menace*) you'll have me to contend with!; **c'est une ~ de goût/d'argent** it's a question *ou* matter of taste/money; **c'est l'~ d'une minute/heure** it'll only take a minute/an hour; **ce sont mes ~s** (*cela me concerne*) that's my business; **toutes ~s cessantes** forthwith; **les ~s étrangères** (*POL*) foreign affairs.
affairé, e [afeʀe] *a* busy.
affairer [afeʀe]: **s'~** *vi* to busy o.s., bustle about.
affairisme [afeʀism(ə)] *nm* (political) racketeering.
affaissement [afɛsmɑ̃] *nm* subsidence, collapse.
affaisser [afese]: **s'~** *vi* (*terrain, immeuble*) to subside, sink; (*personne*) to collapse.
affaler [afale]: **s'~** *vi*: **s'~ dans/sur** to collapse *ou* slump into/onto.
affamé, e [afame] *a* starving, famished.
affamer [afame] *vt* to starve.
affectation [afɛktɑsjɔ̃] *nf* (*voir affecter*) allotment; appointment; posting; (*voir affecté*) affectedness.
affecté, e [afɛkte] *a* affected.
affecter [afɛkte] *vt* (*émouvoir*) to affect, move; (*feindre*) to affect, feign; (*telle ou telle forme etc*) to take on, assume; **~ qch à** to allocate *ou* allot sth to; **~ qn à** to appoint sb to; (*diplomate*) to post sb to; **~ qch de** (*de coefficient*) to modify sth by.
affectif, ive [afɛktif, -iv] *a* emotional, affective.
affection [afɛksjɔ̃] *nf* affection; (*mal*) ailment; **avoir de l'~ pour** to feel affection for; **prendre en ~** to become fond of.
affectionner [afɛksjɔne] *vt* to be fond of.
affectueusement [afɛktɥøzmɑ̃] *ad* affectionately.
affectueux, euse [afɛktɥø, -øz] *a* affectionate.
afférent, e [afeʀɑ̃, -ɑ̃t] *a*: **~ à** pertaining *ou* relating to.
affermir [afɛʀmiʀ] *vt* to consolidate, strengthen.
affichage [afiʃaʒ] *nm* billposting, billsticking; (*électronique*) display; **"~ interdit"** "stick no bills", "billsticking prohibited"; **~ à cristaux liquides** liquid crystal display, LCD; **~ numérique** *ou* **digital** digital display.
affiche [afiʃ] *nf* poster; (*officielle*) (public) notice; (*THÉÂTRE*) bill; **être à l'~** (*THÉÂTRE*) to be on; **tenir l'~** to run.
afficher [afiʃe] *vt* (*affiche*) to put up, post up;

(*réunion*) to put up a notice about; (*électroniquement*) to display; (*fig*) to exhibit, display; **s'~** (*péj*) to flaunt o.s.; **"défense d'~"** "stick no bills".

affichette [afiʃɛt] *nf* small poster *ou* notice.

affilé, e [afile] *a* sharp.

affilée [afile]: **d'~** *ad* at a stretch.

affiler [afile] *vt* to sharpen.

affiliation [afiljɑsjɔ̃] *nf* affiliation.

affilié, e [afilje] *a*: **être ~ à** to be affiliated to ♦ *nm/f* affiliated party *ou* member.

affilier [afilje] *vt*: **s'~ à** to become affiliated to.

affiner [afine] *vt* to refine; **s'~** *vi* to become (more) refined.

affinité [afinite] *nf* affinity.

affirmatif, ive [afiʀmatif, -iv] *a* affirmative ♦ *nf*: **répondre par l'affirmative** to reply in the affirmative; **dans l'affirmative** (*si oui*) if (the answer is) yes, if he does (*ou* you do *etc*).

affirmation [afiʀmɑsjɔ̃] *nf* assertion.

affirmativement [afiʀmativmɑ̃] *ad* affirmatively, in the affirmative.

affirmer [afiʀme] *vt* (*prétendre*) to maintain, assert; (*autorité etc*) to assert; **s'~** to assert o.s.; to assert itself.

affleurer [aflœʀe] *vi* to show on the surface.

affliction [afliksjɔ̃] *nf* affliction.

affligé, e [afliʒe] *a* distressed, grieved; **~ de** (*maladie, tare*) afflicted with.

affligeant, e [afliʒɑ̃, -ɑ̃t] *a* distressing.

affliger [afliʒe] *vt* (*peiner*) to distress, grieve.

affluence [aflyɑ̃s] *nf* crowds *pl*; **heures d'~** rush hour *sg*; **jours d'~** busiest days.

affluent [aflyɑ̃] *nm* tributary.

affluer [aflye] *vi* (*secours, biens*) to flood in, pour in; (*sang*) to rush, flow.

afflux [afly] *nm* flood, influx; rush.

affolant, e [afɔlɑ̃, -ɑ̃t] *a* terrifying.

affolé, e [afɔle] *a* panic-stricken, panicky.

affolement [afɔlmɑ̃] *nm* panic.

affoler [afɔle] *vt* to throw into a panic; **s'~** *vi* to panic.

affranchir [afʀɑ̃ʃiʀ] *vt* to put a stamp *ou* stamps on; (*à la machine*) to frank (*Brit*), meter (*US*); (*esclave*) to enfranchise, emancipate; (*fig*) to free, liberate; **s'~ de** to free o.s. from; **machine à ~** franking machine, postage meter.

affranchissement [afʀɑ̃ʃismɑ̃] *nm* franking (*Brit*), metering (*US*); freeing; (*POSTES: prix payé*) postage; **tarifs d'~** postage rates.

affres [afʀ(ə)] *nfpl*: **dans les ~ de** in the throes of.

affréter [afʀete] *vt* to charter.

affreusement [afʀøzmɑ̃] *ad* dreadfully, awfully.

affreux, euse [afʀø, -øz] *a* dreadful, awful.

affriolant, e [afʀijɔlɑ̃, -ɑ̃t] *a* tempting, enticing.

affront [afʀɔ̃] *nm* affront.

affrontement [afʀɔ̃tmɑ̃] *nm* (*MIL, POL*) clash, confrontation.

affronter [afʀɔ̃te] *vt* to confront, face; **s'~** to confront each other.

affubler [afyble] *vt* (*péj*): **~ qn de** to rig *ou* deck sb out in; (*surnom*) to attach to sb.

affût [afy] *nm* (*de canon*) gun carriage; **à l'~ (de)** (*gibier*) lying in wait (for); (*fig*) on the look-out (for).

affûter [afyte] *vt* to sharpen, grind.

afghan, e [afgɑ̃, -an] *a* Afghan.

Afghanistan [afganistɑ̃] *nm*: **l'~** Afghanistan.

afin [afɛ̃]: **~ que** *cj* so that, in order that; **~ de faire** in order to do, so as to do.

AFNOR [afnɔʀ] *sigle f* (= *Association française de normalisation*) *industrial standards authority*.

a fortiori [afɔʀsjɔʀi] *ad* all the more, a fortiori.

AFP *sigle f* = *Agence France-Presse*.

AFPA *sigle f* = *Association pour la formation professionnelle des adultes*.

africain, e [afʀikɛ̃, -ɛn] *a* African ♦ *nm/f*: **A~, e** African.

afrikaans [afʀikɑ̃] *nm, a inv* Afrikaans.

Afrikaner [afʀikanɛʀ], **Afrikander** [afʀikɑ̃dɛʀ] *nm/f* Afrikaner.

Afrique [afʀik] *nf*: **l'~** Africa; **l'~ australe/du Nord/du Sud** southern/North/South Africa.

afro [afʀo] *a inv*: **coupe ~** afro hairstyle ♦ *nm/f*: **A~** Afro.

afro-américain, e [afʀoameʀikɛ̃, -ɛn] *a* Afro-American.

afro-asiatique [afʀoazjatik] *a* Afro-Asian.

AG *sigle f* = *assemblée générale*.

ag. *abr* = **agence**.

agaçant, e [agasɑ̃, -ɑ̃t] *a* irritating, aggravating.

agacement [agasmɑ̃] *nm* irritation, aggravation.

agacer [agase] *vt* to pester, tease; (*involontairement*) to irritate, aggravate; (*aguicher*) to excite, lead on.

agapes [agap] *nfpl* (*humoristique*: *festin*) feast.

agate [agat] *nf* agate.

AGE *sigle f* = *assemblée générale extraordinaire*.

âge [ɑʒ] *nm* age; **quel ~ as-tu?** how old are you?; **une femme d'un certain ~** a middle-aged woman, a woman who is getting on (in years); **bien porter son ~** to wear well; **prendre de l'~** to be getting on (in years), grow older; **limite d'~** age limit; **dispense d'~** special exemption from age limit; **troisième ~** (*période*) retirement; (*personnes âgées*) senior citizens; **l'~ ingrat** the awkward *ou* difficult age; **~ légal** legal age; **~ mental** mental age; **l'~ mûr** maturity, middle age; **~ de raison** age of reason.

âgé, e [ɑʒe] *a* old, elderly; **~ de 10 ans** 10 years old.

agence [aʒɑ̃s] *nf* agency, office; (*succursale*) branch; **~ immobilière** estate agent's (office) (*Brit*), real estate office (*US*); **~ matrimoniale** marriage bureau; **~ de placement** employment agency; **~ de publicité** advertising agency; **~ de voyages** travel agency.

agencé, e [aʒɑ̃se] *a*: **bien/mal ~** well/badly put together; well/badly laid out *ou* arranged.

agencement [aʒɑ̃smɑ̃] *nm* putting together; arrangement, laying out.

agencer [aʒɑ̃se] *vt* to put together; (*local*) to arrange, lay out.

agenda [aʒɛ̃da] *nm* diary.

agenouiller [aʒnuje]: **s'~** *vi* to kneel (down).

agent [aʒɑ̃] *nm* (*aussi*: ~ **de police**) police-man; (*ADMIN*) official, officer; (*fig: élément, facteur*) agent; ~ **d'assurances** insurance broker; ~ **de change** stockbroker; ~ **commercial** sales representative; ~ **immobilier** estate agent (*Brit*), realtor (*US*); ~ **(secret)** (secret) agent.

agglomérat [aglɔmeʀa] *nm* (*GÉO*) agglomer-ate.

agglomération [aglɔmeʀɑsjɔ̃] *nf* town; (*AUTO*) built-up area; **l'~ parisienne** the urban area of Paris.

aggloméré [aglɔmeʀe] *nm* (*bois*) chipboard; (*pierre*) conglomerate.

agglomérer [aglɔmeʀe] *vt* to pile up; (*TECH: bois, pierre*) to compress; **s'~** *vi* to pile up.

agglutiner [aglytine] *vt* to stick together; **s'~** *vi* to congregate.

aggravant, e [agʀavɑ̃, -ɑ̃t] *a*: **circonstances ~es** aggravating circumstances.

aggravation [agʀavɑsjɔ̃] *nf* worsening, ag-gravation; increase.

aggraver [agʀave] *vt* to worsen, aggravate; (*JUR: peine*) to increase; **s'~** *vi* to worsen; ~ **son cas** to make one's case worse.

agile [aʒil] *a* agile, nimble.

agilité [aʒilite] *nf* agility, nimbleness.

agio [aʒjo] *nm* (bank) charges *pl*.

agir [aʒiʀ] *vi* (*se comporter*) to behave, act; (*faire quelque chose*) to act, take action; (*avoir de l'effet*) to act; **il s'agit de** it's a matter *ou* question of; it is about; (*il importe que*): **il s'agit de faire** we (*ou* you *etc*) must do; **de quoi s'agit-il?** what is it about?

agissements [aʒismɑ̃] *nmpl* (*gén péj*) schemes, intrigues.

agitateur, trice [aʒitatœʀ, -tʀis] *nm/f* agitator.

agitation [aʒitɑsjɔ̃] *nf* (hustle and) bustle; (*trouble*) agitation, excitement; (*politique*) unrest, agitation.

agité, e [aʒite] *a* (*remuant*) fidgety, restless; (*troublé*) agitated, perturbed; (*journée*) hec-tic; (*mer*) rough; (*sommeil*) disturbed, broken.

agiter [aʒite] *vt* (*bouteille, chiffon*) to shake; (*bras, mains*) to wave; (*préoccuper, exciter*) to trouble, perturb; **s'~** *vi* to bustle about; (*dormeur*) to toss and turn; (*enfant*) to fidget; (*POL*) to grow restless; **"~ avant l'emploi"** "shake before use".

agneau, x [aɲo] *nm* lamb; (*toison*) lambswool.

agnelet [aɲlɛ] *nm* little lamb.

agnostique [agnɔstik] *a*, *nm/f* agnostic.

agonie [agɔni] *nf* mortal agony, death pangs *pl*; (*fig*) death throes *pl*.

agonir [agɔniʀ] *vt*: ~ **qn d'injures** to hurl abuse at sb.

agoniser [agɔnize] *vi* to be dying; (*fig*) to be in its death throes.

agrafe [agʀaf] *nf* (*de vêtement*) hook, fastener; (*de bureau*) staple; (*MÉD*) clip.

agrafer [agʀafe] *vt* to fasten; to staple.

agrafeuse [agʀaføz] *nf* stapler.

agraire [agʀɛʀ] *a* agrarian; (*mesure, surface*) land *cpd*.

agrandir [agʀɑ̃diʀ] *vt* (*magasin, domaine*) to extend, enlarge; (*trou*) to enlarge, make bigger; (*PHOTO*) to enlarge, blow up; **s'~** *vi*

to be extended; to be enlarged.

agrandissement [agʀɑ̃dismɑ̃] *nm* extension; enlargement; (*photographie*) enlargement.

agrandisseur [agʀɑ̃disœʀ] *nm* (*PHOTO*) en-larger.

agréable [agʀeabl(ə)] *a* pleasant, nice.

agréablement [agʀeabləmɑ̃] *ad* pleasantly.

agréé, e [agʀee] *a*: **concessionnaire ~** reg-istered dealer; **magasin ~** registered dealer('s).

agréer [agʀee] *vt* (*requête*) to accept; ~ **à** *vt* to please, suit; **veuillez ~ ...** (*formule épistolaire*) yours faithfully.

agrég [agʀɛg] *nf* (*fam*) = **agrégation**.

agrégat [agʀega] *nm* aggregate.

agrégation [agʀegɑsjɔ̃] *nf highest teaching di-ploma in France (competitive examination)*.

agrégé, e [agʀeʒe] *nm/f* holder of the *agréga-tion*.

agréger [agʀeʒe] *vt*: **s'~** *vi* to aggregate.

agrément [agʀemɑ̃] *nm* (*accord*) consent, approval; (*attraits*) charm, attractiveness; (*plaisir*) pleasure; **voyage/jardin d'~** pleasure trip/garden.

agrémenter [agʀemɑ̃te] *vt*: ~ **(de)** to embel-lish (with), adorn (with).

agrès [agʀɛ] *nmpl* (gymnastics) apparatus *sg*.

agresser [agʀese] *vt* to attack.

agresseur [agʀesœʀ] *nm* aggressor.

agressif, ive [agʀesif, -iv] *a* aggressive.

agression [agʀesjɔ̃] *nf* attack; (*POL, MIL, PSYCH*) aggression.

agressivement [agʀesivmɑ̃] *ad* aggressively.

agressivité [agʀesivite] *nf* aggressiveness.

agreste [agʀɛst(ə)] *a* rustic.

agricole [agʀikɔl] *a* agricultural, farm *cpd*.

agriculteur, trice [agʀikyltœʀ, -tʀis] *nm/f* farmer.

agriculture [agʀikyltyʀ] *nf* agriculture; farm-ing.

agripper [agʀipe] *vt* to grab, clutch; (*pour arracher*) to snatch, grab; **s'~ à** to cling (on) to, clutch, grip.

agro-alimentaire [agʀoalimɑ̃tɛʀ] *a* farming *cpd* ♦ *nm*: **l'~** agribusiness.

agronomique [agʀonɔmik] *a* agronomic(al).

agrumes [agʀym] *nmpl* citrus fruit(s).

aguerrir [ageʀiʀ] *vt* to harden; **s'~ (contre)** to become hardened (to).

aguets [agɛ]: **aux ~** *ad*: **être aux ~** to be on the look-out.

aguichant, e [agiʃɑ̃, -ɑ̃t] *a* enticing.

aguicher [agiʃe] *vt* to entice.

aguicheur, euse [agiʃœʀ, -øz] *a* enticing.

ah [ɑ] *excl* ah!; ~ **bon?** really?, is that so?; ~ **mais ...** yes, but ...; ~ **non!** oh no!

ahuri, e [ayʀi] *a* (*stupéfait*) flabbergasted; (*idiot*) dim-witted.

ahurir [ayʀiʀ] *vt* to stupefy, stagger.

ahurissant, e [ayʀisɑ̃, -ɑ̃t] *a* stupefying, staggering.

ai [e] *vb voir* **avoir**.

aide [ɛd] *nm/f* assistant ♦ *nf* assistance, help; (*secours financier*) aid; **à l'~ de** with the help *ou* aid of; **aller à l'~ de qn** to go to sb's aid, go to help sb; **venir en ~ à qn** to help sb, come to sb's assistance; **appeler (qn) à l'~** to call for help (from sb); **à l'~!** help!; ~ **de camp** *nm* aide-de-camp; ~ **comptable** *nm* accountant's assistant; ~ **électricien** *nm* electrician's mate; ~ **familiale** *nf* mother's help, ≈ home help; ~ **judiciaire** *nf* legal aid; ~ **de laboratoire** *nm/f* laboratory assistant; ~ **ménagère** *nf* ≈ home help; ~ **sociale** *nf* (*assistance*) state aid; ~ **soignant, e** *nm/f* auxiliary nurse; ~ **technique** *nf* ≈ VSO (*Brit*), ≈ Peace Corps (*US*).

aide-mémoire [ɛdmemwaʀ] *nm inv* (key facts) handbook.

aider [ede] *vt* to help; ~ **à qch** to help (towards) sth; ~ **qn à faire qch** to help sb to do sth; **s'~ de** (*se servir de*) to use, make use of.

aie [ɛ] *etc vb voir* **avoir**.

aïe [aj] *excl* ouch!

AIEA *sigle f* (= *Agence internationale de l'énergie nucléaire*) IAEA (= *International Atomic Energy Agency*).

aïeul, e [ajœl] *nm/f* grandparent, grandfather/grandmother; (*ancêtre*) forebear.

aïeux [ajø] *nmpl* grandparents; forebears, forefathers.

aigle [ɛgl(ə)] *nm* eagle.

aiglefin [ɛgləfɛ̃] *nm* = **églefin**.

aigre [ɛgʀ(ə)] *a* sour, sharp; (*fig*) sharp, cutting; **tourner à l'~** to turn sour.

aigre-doux, -douce [ɛgʀədu, -dus] *a* (*fruit*) bitter-sweet; (*sauce*) sweet and sour.

aigrefin [ɛgʀəfɛ̃] *nm* swindler.

aigrelet, te [ɛgʀəlɛ, -ɛt] *a* (*taste*) sourish; (*voix, son*) sharpish.

aigrette [ɛgʀɛt] *nf* (*plume*) feather.

aigreur [ɛgʀœʀ] *nf* sourness; sharpness; **~s d'estomac** heartburn *sg*.

aigri, e [ɛgʀi] *a* embittered.

aigrir [ɛgʀiʀ] *vt* (*personne*) to embitter; (*caractère*) to sour; **s'~** *vi* to become embittered; to sour; (*lait etc*) to turn sour.

aigu, ë [egy] *a* (*objet, arête*) sharp, pointed; (*son, voix*) high-pitched, shrill; (*note*) high (-pitched); (*douleur, intelligence*) acute, sharp.

aigue-marine, *pl* **aigues-marines** [ɛgmaʀin] *nf* aquamarine.

aiguillage [eguija3] *nm* (*RAIL*) points *pl*.

aiguille [eguij] *nf* needle; (*de montre*) hand; ~ **à tricoter** knitting needle.

aiguiller [eguije] *vt* (*orienter*) to direct; (*RAIL*) to shunt.

aiguillette [eguijɛt] *nf* (*CULIN*) aiguillette.

aiguilleur [eguijœʀ] *nm* (*RAIL*) pointsman; ~ **du ciel** air traffic controller.

aiguillon [eguijɔ̃] *nm* (*d'abeille*) sting; (*fig*) spur, stimulus.

aiguillonner [eguijone] *vt* to spur *ou* goad on.

aiguiser [egize] *vt* to sharpen, grind; (*fig*) to stimulate; (: *esprit*) to sharpen; (: *sens*) to excite.

aïkido [ajkido] *nm* aikido.

ail [aj] *nm* garlic.

aile [ɛl] *nf* wing; (*de voiture*) wing (*Brit*), fender (*US*); **battre de l'~** (*fig*) to be in a sorry state; **voler de ses propres ~s** to stand on one's own two feet; ~ **libre** hang-glider.

ailé, e [ele] *a* winged.

aileron [ɛlʀɔ̃] *nm* (*de requin*) fin; (*d'avion*) aileron.

ailette [ɛlɛt] *nf* (*TECH*) fin; (: *de turbine*) blade.

ailier [elje] *nm* (*SPORT*) winger.

aille [aj] *etc vb voir* **aller**.

ailleurs [ajœʀ] *ad* elsewhere, somewhere else; **partout/nulle part** ~ everywhere/nowhere else; **d'~** *ad* (*du reste*) moreover, besides; **par** ~ *ad* (*d'autre part*) moreover, furthermore.

ailloli [ajɔli] *nm* garlic mayonnaise.

aimable [ɛmabl(ə)] *a* kind, nice; **vous êtes bien** ~ that's very nice *ou* kind of you, how kind (of you)!

aimablement [ɛmabləmã] *ad* kindly.

aimant [ɛmã] *nm* magnet.

aimant, e [ɛmã, -ãt] *a* loving, affectionate.

aimanté, e [ɛmãte] *a* magnetic.

aimanter [ɛmãte] *vt* to magnetize.

aimer [eme] *vt* to love; (*d'amitié, affection, par goût*) to like; (*souhait*): **j'aimerais ... I would like ...**; **s'~** to love each other; to like each other; **je n'aime pas beaucoup Paul** I don't like Paul much, I don't care much for Paul; ~ **faire qch** to like doing sth, like to do sth; **aimeriez-vous que je vous accompagne?** would you like me to come with you?; **j'aimerais (bien) m'en aller** I should (really) like to go; **bien** ~ **qn/qch** to like sb/sth; **j'aime mieux Paul (que Pierre)** I prefer Paul (to Pierre); **j'aime mieux** *ou* **autant vous dire que** I may as well tell you that; **j'aimerais autant** *ou* **mieux y aller maintenant** I'd sooner *ou* rather go now; **j'aime assez aller au cinéma** I quite like going to the cinema.

aine [ɛn] *nf* groin.

aîné, e [ene] *a* elder, older; (*le plus âgé*) eldest, oldest ♦ *nm/f* oldest child *ou* one, oldest boy *ou* son/girl *ou* daughter; **~s** *nmpl* (*fig: anciens*) elders; **il est mon** ~ **(de 2 ans)** he's (2 years) older than me, he's 2 years my senior.

aînesse [enɛs] *nf*: **droit d'~** birthright.

ainsi [ɛ̃si] *ad* (*de cette façon*) like this, in this way, thus; (*ce faisant*) thus ♦ *cj* thus, so; ~ **que** (*comme*) (just) as; (*et aussi*) as well as; **pour** ~ **dire** so to speak, as it were; ~ **donc** and so; ~ **soit-il** (*REL*) so be it; **et** ~ **de suite** and so on (and so forth).

aïoli [ajɔli] *nm* = **ailloli**.

air [ɛʀ] *nm* air; (*mélodie*) tune; (*expression*) look, air; (*atmosphère, ambiance*): **dans l'~** in the air (*fig*); **prendre de grands ~s (avec qn)** to give o.s. airs (with sb); **en l'~** (up) into the air; **tirer en l'~** to fire shots in the air; **paroles/menaces en l'~** idle words/threats; **prendre l'~** to get some (fresh) air; (*avion*) to take off; **avoir l'~ triste** to look *ou* seem sad; **avoir l'~ de qch** to look like sth; **avoir l'~ de faire** to look as though one is doing, appear to be doing; **courant d'~** draught (*Brit*), draft (*US*); **le grand** ~ the open air; **mal de l'~** air-sickness; **tête en l'~** scatterbrain; ~ **comprimé** compressed air; ~ **conditionné** air-conditioning.

aire [ɛʀ] *nf* (*zone, fig, MATH*) area; (*nid*) eyrie (*Brit*), aerie (*US*); ~ **d'atterrissage** landing strip; landing patch; ~ **de jeu** play area; ~ **de lancement** launching site; ~ **de**

stationnement parking area.

airelle [εʀεl] *nf* bilberry.

aisance [εzɑ̃s] *nf* ease; *(COUTURE)* easing, freedom of movement; *(richesse)* affluence; **être dans l'~** to be well-off *ou* affluent.

aise [εz] *nf* comfort ♦ *a*: **être bien ~ de/que** to be delighted to/that; **~s** *nfpl*: **aimer ses ~s** to like one's *(creature)* comforts; **prendre ses ~s** to make o.s. comfortable; **frémir d'~** to shudder with pleasure; **être à l'~** *ou* **à son ~** to be comfortable; *(pas embarrassé)* to be at ease; *(financièrement)* to be comfortably off; **se mettre à l'~** to make o.s. comfortable; **être mal à l'~** *ou* **à son ~** to be uncomfortable; *(gêné)* to be ill at ease; **mettre qn à l'~** to put sb at his *(ou* her*)* ease; **mettre qn mal à l'~** to make sb feel ill at ease; **à votre ~** please yourself, just as you like; **en faire à son ~** to do as one likes; **en prendre à son ~ avec qch** to be free and easy with sth, do as one likes with sth.

aisé, e [eze] *a* easy; *(assez riche)* well-to-do, well-off.

aisément [ezemɑ̃] *ad* easily.

aisselle [εsεl] *nf* armpit.

ait [ε] *vb voir* **avoir**.

ajonc [aʒɔ̃] *nm* gorse *q*.

ajouré, e [aʒuʀe] *a* openwork *cpd*.

ajournement [aʒuʀnəmɑ̃] *nm* adjournment; deferment, postponement.

ajourner [aʒuʀne] *vt (réunion)* to adjourn; *(décision)* to defer, postpone; *(candidat)* to refer; *(conscrit)* to defer.

ajout [aʒu] *nm* addition.

ajouter [aʒute] *vt* to add; *(INFORM)* to append; **~ à** *vt (accroître)* to add to; **s'~ à** to add to; **~ que** to add that; **~ foi à** to lend *ou* give credence to.

ajustage [aʒystaʒ] *nm* fitting.

ajusté, e [aʒyste] *a*: **bien ~** *(robe etc)* close-fitting.

ajustement [aʒystəmɑ̃] *nm* adjustment.

ajuster [aʒyste] *vt (régler)* to adjust; *(vêtement)* to alter; *(arranger)*: **~ sa cravate** to adjust one's tie; *(coup de fusil)* to aim; *(cible)* to aim at; *(adapter)*: **~ qch à** to fit sth to.

ajusteur [aʒystœʀ] *nm* metal worker.

al *abr* = **année-lumière**.

alaise [alεz] *nf* = **alèse**.

alambic [alɑ̃bik] *nm* still.

alambiqué, e [alɑ̃bike] *a* convoluted, over-complicated.

alangui, e [alɑ̃gi] *a* languid.

alanguir [alɑ̃giʀ]: **s'~** *vi* to grow languid.

alarme [alaʀm(ə)] *nf* alarm; **donner l'~** to give *ou* raise the alarm; **jeter l'~** to cause alarm.

alarmer [alaʀme] *vt* to alarm; **s'~** *vi* to become alarmed.

alarmiste [alaʀmist(ə)] *a* alarmist.

Alaska [alaska] *nm*: **l'~** Alaska.

albanais, e [albanε, -εz] *a* Albanian ♦ *nm (LING)* Albanian ♦ *nm/f*: **A~, e** Albanian.

Albanie [albani] *nf*: **l'~** Albania.

albâtre [albɑtʀ(ə)] *nm* alabaster.

albatros [albatʀos] *nm* albatross.

albigeois, e [albiʒwa, -waz] *a* of *ou* from Albi.

albinos [albinos] *nm/f* albino.

album [albɔm] *nm* album; **~ à colorier** colouring book; **~ de timbres** stamp album.

albumen [albymεn] *nm* albumen.

albumine [albymin] *nf* albumin; **avoir** *ou* **faire de l'~** to suffer from albuminuria.

alcalin, e [alkalε̃, -in] *a* alkaline.

alchimiste [alʃimist(ə)] *nm* alchemist.

alcool [alkɔl] *nm*: **l'~** alcohol; **un ~** a spirit, a brandy; **~ à brûler** methylated spirits *(Brit)*, wood alcohol *(US)*; **~ à 90°** surgical spirit; **~ camphré** camphorated alcohol; **~ de prune** *etc* plum *etc* brandy.

alcoolémie [alkɔlemi] *nf* blood alcohol level.

alcoolique [alkɔlik] *a, nm/f* alcoholic.

alcoolisé, e [alkɔlize] *a* alcoholic.

alcoolisme [alkɔlism(ə)] *nm* alcoholism.

alco(o)test [alkɔtεst] *nm* ® *(objet)* Breathalyser ®; *(test)* breath-test; **faire subir l'~ à qn** to Breathalyze ® sb.

alcôve [alkov] *nf* alcove, recess.

aléas [alea] *nmpl* hazards.

aléatoire [aleatwaʀ] *a* uncertain; *(INFORM, STATISTIQUE)* random.

alentour [alɑ̃tuʀ] *ad* around (about); **~s** *nmpl* surroundings; **aux ~s de** in the vicinity *ou* neighbourhood of, around about; *(temps)* around about.

Aléoutiennes [aleusjεn] *nfpl*: **les (îles) ~** the Aleutian Islands.

alerte [alεʀt(ə)] *a* agile, nimble; *(style)* brisk, lively ♦ *nf* alert; warning; **donner l'~** to give the alert; **à la première ~** at the first sign of trouble *ou* danger.

alerter [alεʀte] *vt* to alert.

alèse [alεz] *nf (drap)* undersheet, drawsheet.

aléser [aleze] *vt* to ream.

alevin [alvε̃] *nm* alevin, young fish.

alevinage [alvinaʒ] *nm* fish farming.

Alexandrie [alεksɑ̃dʀi] *n* Alexandria.

alexandrin [alεksɑ̃dʀε̃] *nm* alexandrine.

alezan, e [alzɑ̃, -an] *a* chestnut.

algarade [algaʀad] *nf* row, dispute.

algèbre [alʒεbʀ(ə)] *nf* algebra.

Alger [alʒe] *n* Algiers.

Algérie [alʒeʀi] *nf*: **l'~** Algeria.

algérien, ne [alʒeʀjε̃, -εn] *a* Algerian ♦ *nm/f*: **A~, ne** Algerian.

algérois, e [alʒeʀwa, -waz] *a* of *ou* from Algiers ♦ *nm*: **l'A~** *(région)* the Algiers region.

algorithme [algɔʀitm(ə)] *nm* algorithm.

algue [alg(ə)] *nf (gén)* seaweed *q*; *(BOT)* alga *(pl* -ae*)*.

alias [aljas] *ad* alias.

alibi [alibi] *nm* alibi.

aliénation [aljenasjɔ̃] *nf* alienation.

aliéné, e [aljene] *nm/f* insane person, lunatic *(péj)*.

aliéner [aljene] *vt* to alienate; *(bien, liberté)* to give up; **s'~** *vt* to alienate.

alignement [aliɲmɑ̃] *nm* alignment, lining up; **à l'~** in line.

aligner [aliɲe] *vt* to align, line up; *(idées, chiffres)* to string together; *(adapter)*: **~ qch sur** to bring sth into alignment with; **s'~** *(soldats etc)* to line up; **s'~ sur** *(POL)* to align o.s. with.

aliment [alimɑ̃] *nm* food; **~ complet** whole food.

alimentaire [alimɑ̃tɛʀ] *a* food *cpd*; (*péj: besogne*) done merely to earn a living; **produits ~s** foodstuffs, foods.

alimentation [alimɑ̃tasjɔ̃] *nf* feeding; supplying, supply; (*commerce*) food trade; (*produits*) groceries *pl*; (*régime*) diet; (*INFORM*) feed; ~ **(générale)** (general) grocer's; ~ **de base** staple diet; ~ **en feuilles/en continu/en papier** form/stream/sheet feed.

alimenter [alimɑ̃te] *vt* to feed; (*TECH*): ~ **(en)** to supply (with), feed (with); (*fig*) to sustain, keep going.

alinéa [alinea] *nm* paragraph; **"nouvel ~"** "new line".

aliter [alite]: **s'~** *vi* to take to one's bed; **infirme alité** bedridden person *ou* invalid.

alizé [alize] *a, nm*: **(vent)** ~ trade wind.

allaitement [alɛtmɑ̃] *nm* feeding; ~ **maternel/au biberon** breast-/bottle-feeding; ~ **mixte** mixed feeding.

allaiter [alete] *vt* (*suj: femme*) to (breast-)feed, nurse; (*suj: animal*) to suckle; ~ **au biberon** to bottle-feed.

allant [alɑ̃] *nm* drive, go.

alléchant, e [alefɑ̃, -ɑ̃t] *a* tempting, enticing.

allécher [alefe] *vt*: ~ **qn** to make sb's mouth water; to tempt sb, entice sb.

allée [ale] *nf* (*de jardin*) path; (*en ville*) avenue, drive; **~s et venues** comings and goings.

allégation [alegasjɔ̃] *nf* allegation.

alléger [aleʒe] *vt* (*voiture*) to make lighter; (*chargement*) to lighten; (*souffrance*) to alleviate, soothe.

allégorie [alegɔʀi] *nf* allegory.

allégorique [alegɔʀik] *a* allegorical.

allègre [alɛgʀ(ə)] *a* lively, jaunty (*Brit*); (*personne*) gay, cheerful.

allégresse [alegʀɛs] *nf* elation, gaiety.

alléguer [alege] *vt* to put forward (as proof *ou* an excuse).

Allemagne [aləmaɲ] *nf*: **l'~** Germany; **l'~ de l'Est/Ouest** East/West Germany; **l'~ fédérale (RFA)** the Federal Republic of Germany (FRG).

allemand, e [almɑ̃, -ɑ̃d] *a* German ♦ *nm* (*LING*) German ♦ *nm/f*: **A~, e** German; **A~ de l'Est/l'Ouest** East/West German.

aller [ale] *nm* (*trajet*) outward journey; (*billet*): ~ **(simple)** single (*Brit*) *ou* one-way ticket; ~ **(et) retour (AR)** (*trajet*) return trip *ou* journey (*Brit*), round trip (*US*); (*billet*) return (*Brit*) *ou* round-trip (*US*) ticket ♦ *vi* (*gén*) to go; ~ **à** (*convenir*) to suit; (*suj: forme, pointure etc*) to fit; **cela me va** (*couleur*) that suits me; (*vêtement*) that suits me; that fits me; (*projet, disposition*) that suits me, that's fine *ou* OK by me; ~ **à la chasse/pêche** to go hunting/fishing; ~ **avec** (*couleurs, style etc*) to go (well) with; **je vais le faire/me fâcher** I'm going to do it/to get angry; ~ **voir/chercher qn** to go and see/look for sb; **comment allez-vous?** how are you?; **comment ça va?** how are you?; (*affaires etc*) how are things?; **ça va? — oui (ça va)**how are things? — fine!; **ça va (comme ça)**that's fine (as it is); **il va bien/mal** he's well/not well, he's fine/ill; **ça va bien/mal** (*affaires etc*) it's going well/not going well;

tout va bien everything's fine; **ça ne va pas!** (*mauvaise humeur etc*) that's not on!, hey, come on!; **ça ne va pas sans difficultés** it's not without difficulties; ~ **mieux** to be better; **il y a va de leur vie** their lives are at stake; **se laisser** ~ to let o.s. go; **s'en** ~ *vi* (*partir*) to be off, go, leave; (*disparaître*) to go away; ~ **jusqu'à** to go as far as; **ça va de soi, ça va sans dire** that goes without saying; **tu y vas un peu fort** you're going a bit (too) far; **allez!** go on!; come on!; **allons-y!** let's go!; **allez, au revoir** right *ou* OK then, bye-bye!

allergie [alɛʀʒi] *nf* allergy.

allergique [alɛʀʒik] *a* allergic; ~ **à** allergic to.

allez [ale] *vb voir* **aller**.

alliage [aljaʒ] *nm* alloy.

alliance [aljɑ̃s] *nf* (*MIL, POL*) alliance; (*mariage*) marriage; (*bague*) wedding ring; **neveu par** ~ nephew by marriage.

allié, e [alje] *nm/f* ally; **parents et ~s** relatives and relatives by marriage.

allier [alje] *vt* (*métaux*) to alloy; (*POL, gén*) to ally; (*fig*) to combine; **s'~** to become allies; (*éléments, caractéristiques*) to combine; **s'~ à** to become allied to *ou* with.

alligator [aligatɔʀ] *nm* alligator.

allitération [aliteʀasjɔ̃] *nf* alliteration.

allô [alo] *excl* hullo, hallo.

allocataire [alɔkatɛʀ] *nm/f* beneficiary.

allocation [alɔkasjɔ̃] *nf* allowance; ~ **(de) chômage** unemployment benefit; ~ **(de) logement** rent allowance; **~s familiales** ≈ child benefit *q*; **~s de maternité** maternity allowance.

allocution [alɔkysjɔ̃] *nf* short speech.

allongé, e [alɔ̃ʒe] *a* (*étendu*): **être** ~ to be stretched out *ou* lying down; (*long*) long; (*étiré*) elongated; (*oblong*) oblong; **rester** ~ to be lying down; **mine ~e** long face.

allonger [alɔ̃ʒe] *vt* to lengthen, make longer; (*étendre: bras, jambe*) to stretch (out); (*sauce*) to spin out, make go further; **s'~** *vi* to get longer; (*se coucher*) to lie down, stretch out; ~ **le pas** to hasten one's step(s).

allouer [alwe] *vt*: ~ **qch à** to allocate sth to, allot sth to.

allumage [alymaʒ] *nm* (*AUTO*) ignition.

allume-cigare [alymsigaʀ] *nm inv* cigar lighter.

allume-gaz [alymgaz] *nm inv* gas lighter.

allumer [alyme] *vt* (*lampe, phare, radio*) to put *ou* switch on; (*pièce*) to put *ou* switch the light(s) on in; (*feu, bougie, cigare, pipe, gaz*) to light; (*chauffage*) to put on; **s'~** *vi* (*lumière, lampe*) to come *ou* go on; ~ **(la lumière** *ou* **l'électricité)** to put on the light.

allumette [alymɛt] *nf* match; (*morceau de bois*) matchstick; (*CULIN*): ~ **au fromage** cheese straw; ~ **de sûreté** safety match.

allumeuse [alymøz] *nf* (*péj*) tease (*woman*).

allure [alyʀ] *nf* (*vitesse*) speed; (: *à pied*) pace; (*démarche*) walk; (*maintien*) bearing; (*aspect, air*) look; **avoir de l'~** to have style *ou* a certain elegance; **à toute** ~ at top *ou* full speed.

allusion [alyzjɔ̃] *nf* allusion; (*sous-entendu*) hint; **faire** ~ **à** to allude *ou* refer to; to hint at.

alluvions [alyvjɔ̃] *nfpl* alluvial deposits,

alluvium *sg.*

almanach [almana] *nm* almanac.

aloès [alɔɛs] *nm* (*BOT*) aloe.

aloi [alwa] *nm*: **de bon/mauvais** ~ of genuine/ doubtful worth *ou* quality.

alors [alɔʀ] *ad* then, at that time ♦ *cj* then, so; ~, **Paul?** well, Paul?; ~**? quoi de neuf?** well *ou* so? what's new?; **et** ~**?** and then (what)?; (*indifférence*) so?; **jusqu'**~ up till *ou* until then; **ça** ~**!** well really!; ~ **que** *cj* (*au moment où*) when, as; (*pendant que*) while, when; (*opposition*) whereas, while.

alouette [alwɛt] *nf* (sky)lark.

alourdir [aluʀdiʀ] *vt* to weigh down, make heavy; **s'**~ *vi* to grow heavy *ou* heavier.

aloyau [alwajo] *nm* sirloin.

alpaga [alpaga] *nm* (*tissu*) alpaca.

alpage [alpaʒ] *nm* high mountain pasture.

Alpes [alp(ə)] *nfpl*: **les** ~ the Alps.

alpestre [alpɛstʀ(ə)] *a* alpine.

alphabet [alfabɛ] *nm* alphabet; (*livre*) ABC (book), primer.

alphabétique [alfabetik] *a* alphabetic(al); **par ordre** ~ in alphabetical order.

alphabétisation [alfabetizasjɔ̃] *nf* literacy teaching.

alphabétiser [alfabetize] *vt* to teach to read and write; (*pays*) to eliminate illiteracy in.

alphanumérique [alfanymeʀik] *a* alphanumeric.

alpin, e [alpɛ̃, -in] *a* (*plante etc*) alpine; (*club*) climbing.

alpinisme [alpinism(ə)] *nm* mountaineering, climbing.

alpiniste [alpinist(ə)] *nm/f* mountaineer, climber.

Alsace [alzas] *nf*: **l'**~ Alsace.

alsacien, ne [alzasjɛ̃, -ɛn] *a* Alsatian.

altercation [altɛʀkasjɔ̃] *nf* altercation.

alter ego [altɛʀego] *nm* alter ego.

altérer [alteʀe] *vt* (*faits, vérité*) to falsify, distort; (*qualité*) to debase, impair; (*données*) to corrupt; (*donner soif à*) to make thirsty; **s'**~ *vi* to deteriorate; to spoil.

alternance [altɛʀnɑ̃s] *nf* alternation; **en** ~ alternately; **formation en** ~ sandwich course.

alternateur [altɛʀnatœʀ] *nm* alternator.

alternatif, ive [altɛʀnatif, -iv] *a* alternating ♦ *nf* alternative.

alternativement [altɛʀnativmɑ̃] *ad* alternately.

alterner [altɛʀne] *vt* to alternate ♦ *vi*: ~ (**avec**) to alternate (with); (**faire**) ~ **qch avec qch** to alternate sth with sth.

Altesse [altɛs] *nf* Highness.

altier, ière [altje, -jɛʀ] *a* haughty.

altimètre [altimɛtʀ(ə)] *nm* altimeter.

altiport [altipɔʀ] *nm* mountain airfield.

altiste [altist(ə)] *nm/f* viola player, violist.

altitude [altityd] *nf* altitude, height; **à 1000 m d'**~ at a height *ou* an altitude of 1000 m; **en** ~ at high altitudes; **perdre/prendre de l'**~ to lose/gain height; **voler à haute/basse** ~ to fly at a high/low altitude.

alto [alto] *nm* (*instrument*) viola ♦ *nf* (*contr*)alto.

altruisme [altʀɥism(ə)] *nm* altruism.

altruiste [altʀɥist(ə)] *a* altruistic.

aluminium [alyminjɔm] *nm* aluminium (*Brit*), aluminum (*US*).

alun [alœ̃] *nm* alum.

alunir [alyniʀ] *vi* to land on the moon.

alvéole [alveɔl] *nf* (*de ruche*) alveolus.

alvéolé, e [alveɔle] *a* honeycombed.

AM *sigle f* = **assurance maladie**.

amabilité [amabilite] *nf* kindness; **il a eu l'**~ **de** he was kind *ou* good enough to.

amadou [amadu] *nm* touchwood, amadou.

amadouer [amadwe] *vt* to coax, cajole; (*adoucir*) to mollify, soothe.

amaigrir [amegʀiʀ] *vt* to make thin *ou* thinner.

amaigrissant, e [amegʀisɑ̃, -ɑ̃t] *a*: **régime** ~ slimming (*Brit*) *ou* weight-reduction (*US*) diet.

amalgame [amalgam] *nm* amalgam; (*fig: de gens, d'idées*) hotch-potch, mixture.

amalgamer [amalgame] *vt* to amalgamate.

amande [amɑ̃d] *nf* (*de l'amandier*) almond; (*de noyau de fruit*) kernel; **en** ~ (*yeux*) almond *cpd*, almond-shaped.

amandier [amɑ̃dje] *nm* almond (tree).

amant [amɑ̃] *nm* lover.

amarre [amaʀ] *nf* (*NAVIG*) (mooring) rope *ou* line; ~**s** *nfpl* moorings.

amarrer [amaʀe] *vt* (*NAVIG*) to moor; (*gén*) to make fast.

amaryllis [amaʀilis] *nf* amaryllis.

amas [ama] *nm* heap, pile.

amasser [amase] *vt* to amass; **s'**~ *vi* to pile up, accumulate; (*foule*) to gather.

amateur [amatœʀ] *nm* amateur; **en** ~ (*péj*) amateurishly; **musicien/sportif** ~ amateur musician/sportsman; ~ **de musique/sport** *etc* music/sport *etc* lover.

amateurisme [amatœʀism(ə)] *nm* amateurism; (*péj*) amateurishness.

Amazone [amazon] *nf*: **l'**~ the Amazon; **en a**~ sidesaddle.

Amazonie [amazoni] *nf*: **l'**~ Amazonia.

ambages [ɑ̃baʒ]: **sans** ~ *ad* without beating about the bush, plainly.

ambassade [ɑ̃basad] *nf* embassy; (*mission*): **en** ~ on a mission.

ambassadeur, drice [ɑ̃basadœʀ, -dʀis] *nm/f* ambassador/ambassadress.

ambiance [ɑ̃bjɑ̃s] *nf* atmosphere; **il y a de l'**~ everyone's having a good time.

ambiant, e [ɑ̃bjɑ̃, -ɑ̃t] *a* (*air, milieu*) surrounding; (*température*) ambient.

ambidextre [ɑ̃bidɛkstʀ(ə)] *a* ambidextrous.

ambigu, ë [ɑ̃bigy] *a* ambiguous.

ambiguïté [ɑ̃bigɥite] *nf* ambiguousness *q*, ambiguity.

ambitieux, euse [ɑ̃bisjø, -øz] *a* ambitious.

ambition [ɑ̃bisjɔ̃] *nf* ambition.

ambitionner [ɑ̃bisjɔne] *vt* to have as one's aim *ou* ambition.

ambivalent, e [ɑ̃bivalɑ̃, -ɑ̃t] *a* ambivalent.

amble [ɑ̃bl(ə)] *nm*: **aller l'**~ to amble.

ambre [ɑ̃bʀ(ə)] *nm*: ~ (**jaune**) amber; ~ **gris** ambergris.

ambré, e [ɑ̃bʀe] *a* (*couleur*) amber; (*parfum*) ambergris-scented.

ambulance [ɑ̃bylɑ̃s] *nf* ambulance.

ambulancier, ière [ɑ̃bylɑ̃sje, -jɛʀ] ambulanceman/woman (*Brit*), paramedic (*US*).

ambulant, e [ãbylã, -ãt] *a* travelling, itinerant.

âme [ɑm] *nf* soul; **rendre l'~** to give up the ghost; **bonne ~** *(aussi ironique)* kind soul; **un joueur/tricheur dans l'~** a gambler/cheat through and through; **~ sœur** kindred spirit.

amélioration [ameljɔʀasjɔ̃] *nf* improvement.

améliorer [ameljɔʀe] *vt* to improve; **s'~** *vi* to improve, get better.

aménagement [amenaʒmã] *nm* fitting out; laying out; development; **~s** *nmpl* developments; **l'~ du territoire** ≈ town and country planning; **~s fiscaux** tax adjustments.

aménager [amenaʒe] *vt (agencer: espace, local)* to fit out; *(: terrain)* to lay out; *(: quartier, territoire)* to develop; *(installer)* to fix up, put in; **ferme aménagée** converted farmhouse.

amende [amãd] *nf* fine; **mettre à l'~** to penalize; **faire ~ honorable** to make amends.

amendement [amãdmã] *nm (JUR)* amendment.

amender [amãde] *vt (loi)* to amend; *(terre)* to enrich; **s'~** *vi* to mend one's ways.

amène [amɛn] *a* affable; **peu ~** unkind.

amener [amne] *vt* to bring; *(causer)* to bring about; *(baisser: drapeau, voiles)* to strike; **s'~** *vi (fam)* to show up, turn up; **~ qn à qch/à faire** to lead sb to sth/to do.

amenuiser [amənɥize]: **s'~** *vi* to dwindle; *(chances)* to grow slimmer, lessen.

amer, amère [amɛʀ] *a* bitter.

amèrement [amɛʀmã] *ad* bitterly.

américain, e [ameʀikɛ̃, -ɛn] *a* American ♦ *nm (LING)* American (English) ♦ *nm/f*: **A~, e** American; **en vedette ~e** as a special guest (star).

américaniser [ameʀikanize] *vt* to Americanize.

américanisme [ameʀikanism(ə)] *nm* Americanism.

amérindien, ne [ameʀɛ̃djɛ̃, -ɛn] *a* Amerindian, American Indian.

Amérique [ameʀik] *nf* America; **l'~ centrale** Central America; **l'~ latine** Latin America; **l'~ du Nord** North America; **l'~ du Sud** South America.

amerloque [amɛʀlɔk] *n (péj)* Yank, Yankee.

amerrir [ameʀiʀ] *vi* to land (on the sea); *(capsule spatiale)* to splash down.

amerrissage [ameʀisaʒ] *nm* landing (on the sea); splash-down.

amertume [amɛʀtym] *nf* bitterness.

améthyste [ametist(ə)] *nf* amethyst.

ameublement [amœbləmã] *nm* furnishing; *(meubles)* furniture; **articles d'~** furnishings; **tissus d'~** soft furnishings, furnishing fabrics.

ameuter [amøte] *vt (badauds)* to draw a crowd of; *(peuple)* to rouse, stir up.

ami, e [ami] *nm/f* friend; *(amant/maîtresse)* boyfriend/girlfriend ♦ *a*: **pays/groupe ~** friendly country/group; **être (très) ~ avec qn** to be (very) friendly with sb; **être ~ de l'ordre** to be a lover of order; **un ~ des arts** a patron of the arts; **un ~ des chiens** a dog lover; **petit ~/petite ~e** *(fam)* boyfriend/girlfriend.

amiable [amjabl(ə)]: **à l'~** *ad (JUR)* out of court; *(gén)* amicably.

amiante [amjãt] *nm* asbestos.

amibe [amib] *nf* amoeba *(pl -ae)*.

amical, e, aux [amikal, -o] *a* friendly ♦ *nf (club)* association.

amicalement [amikalmã] *ad* in a friendly way; *(formule épistolaire)* regards.

amidon [amidɔ̃] *nm* starch.

amidonner [amidɔne] *vt* to starch.

amincir [amɛ̃siʀ] *vt (objet)* to thin (down); **s'~** *vi* to get thinner *ou* slimmer; **~ qn** to make sb thinner *ou* slimmer.

aminé, e [amine] *a*: **acide ~** amino acid.

amiral, aux [amiʀal, -o] *nm* admiral.

amirauté [amiʀote] *nf* admiralty.

amitié [amitje] *nf* friendship; **prendre en ~** to take a liking to; **faire** *ou* **présenter ses ~s à qn** to send sb one's best wishes; **~s** *(formule épistolaire)* (with) best wishes.

ammoniac [amɔnjak] *nm*: **(gaz) ~** ammonia.

ammoniaque [amɔnjak] *nf* ammonia (water).

amnésie [amnezi] *nf* amnesia.

amniocentèse [amnjosɛ̃tɛz] *nf* amniocentesis.

amnistie [amnisti] *nf* amnesty.

amnistier [amnistje] *vt* to amnesty.

amoindrir [amwɛ̃dʀiʀ] *vt* to reduce.

amollir [amɔliʀ] *vt* to soften.

amonceler [amɔ̃sle] *vt*, **s'~** *vi* to pile *ou* heap up; *(fig)* to accumulate.

amoncellement [amɔ̃sɛlmã] *nm* piling *ou* heaping up; accumulation; *(tas)* pile, heap; accumulation.

amont [amɔ̃]: **en ~** *ad* upstream; *(sur une pente)* uphill; **en ~ de** *prép* upstream from; uphill from, above.

amoral, e, aux [amɔʀal, -o] *a* amoral.

amorce [amɔʀs(ə)] *nf (sur un hameçon)* bait; *(explosif)* cap; *(tube)* primer; *(: contenu)* priming; *(fig: début)* beginning(s), start.

amorcer [amɔʀse] *vt* to bait; to prime; *(commencer)* to begin, start.

amorphe [amɔʀf(ə)] *a* passive, lifeless.

amortir [amɔʀtiʀ] *vt (atténuer: choc)* to absorb, cushion; *(bruit, douleur)* to deaden; *(COMM: dette)* to pay off, amortize; *(: mise de fonds, matériel)* to write off; **~ un abonnement** to make a season ticket pay (for itself).

amortissable [amɔʀtisabl(ə)] *a (COMM)* that can be paid off.

amortissement [amɔʀtismã] *nm (de matériel)* writing off; *(d'une dette)* paying off.

amortisseur [amɔʀtisœʀ] *nm* shock absorber.

amour [amuʀ] *nm* love; *(liaison)* love affair; love; *(statuette etc)* cupid; **un ~ de** a lovely little; **faire l'~** to make love.

amouracher [amuʀaʃe]: **s'~ de** *vt (péj)* to become infatuated with.

amourette [amuʀɛt] *nf* passing fancy.

amoureusement [amuʀøzmã] *ad* lovingly.

amoureux, euse [amuʀø, -øz] *a (regard, tempérament)* amorous; *(vie, problèmes)* love *cpd*; *(personne)*: **~ (de qn)** in love (with sb) ♦ *nm/f* lover ♦ *nmpl* courting couple(s); **tomber ~ de qn** to fall in love with sb; **être ~ de qch** to be passionately fond of sth; **un ~ de la nature** a nature lover.

amour-propre, *pl* **amours-propres** [amuʀpʀɔpʀ(ə)] *nm* self-esteem.

amovible [amɔvibl(ə)] *a* removable, detachable.

ampère [ɑ̃pɛʀ] *nm* amp(ere).

ampèremètre [ɑ̃pɛʀmɛtʀ(ə)] *nm* ammeter.

amphétamine [ɑ̃fetamin] *nf* amphetamine.

amphi [ɑ̃fi] *nm* (*SCOL fam*: = *amphithéâtre*) lecture hall *ou* theatre.

amphibie [ɑ̃fibi] *a* amphibious.

amphibien [ɑ̃fibjɛ̃] *nm* (*ZOOL*) amphibian.

amphithéâtre [ɑ̃fiteɑtʀ(ə)] *nm* amphitheatre; (*d'université*) lecture hall *ou* theatre.

amphore [ɑ̃fɔʀ] *nf* amphora.

ample [ɑ̃pl(ə)] *a* (*vêtement*) roomy, ample; (*gestes, mouvement*) broad; (*ressources*) ample; **jusqu'à plus ~ informé** (*ADMIN*) until further details are available.

amplement [ɑ̃pləmɑ̃] *ad* amply; **~ suffisant** ample, more than enough.

ampleur [ɑ̃plœʀ] *nf* scale, size; extent, magnitude.

ampli [ɑ̃pli] *nm* (*fam*: = *amplificateur*) amplifier, amp.

amplificateur [ɑ̃plifikatœʀ] *nm* amplifier.

amplification [ɑ̃plifikasjɔ̃] *nf* amplification; expansion, increase.

amplifier [ɑ̃plifje] *vt* (*son, oscillation*) to amplify; (*fig*) to expand, increase.

amplitude [ɑ̃plityd] *nf* amplitude; (*des températures*) range.

ampoule [ɑ̃pul] *nf* (*électrique*) bulb; (*de médicament*) phial; (*aux mains, pieds*) blister.

ampoulé, e [ɑ̃pule] *a* (*péj*) pompous, bombastic.

amputation [ɑ̃pytɑsjɔ̃] *nf* amputation.

amputer [ɑ̃pyte] *vt* (*MÉD*) to amputate; (*fig*) to cut *ou* reduce drastically; **~ qn d'un bras/pied** to amputate sb's arm/foot.

Amsterdam [amstɛʀdam] *n* Amsterdam.

amulette [amylɛt] *nf* amulet.

amusant, e [amyzɑ̃, -ɑ̃t] *a* (*divertissant, spirituel*) entertaining, amusing; (*comique*) funny, amusing.

amusé, e [amyze] *a* amused.

amuse-gueule [amyzgœl] *nm inv* appetizer, snack.

amusement [amyzmɑ̃] *nm* (*voir amusé*) amusement; (*voir amuser*) entertaining, amusing; (*jeu etc*) pastime, diversion.

amuser [amyze] *vt* (*divertir*) to entertain, amuse; (*égayer, faire rire*) to amuse; (*détourner l'attention de*) to distract; **s'~** *vi* (*jouer*) to amuse o.s., play; (*se divertir*) to enjoy o.s., have fun; (*fig*) to mess around; **s'~ de qch** (*trouver comique*) to find sth amusing; **s'~ avec** *ou* **de qn** (*duper*) to make a fool of sb.

amusette [amyzɛt] *nf* idle pleasure, trivial pastime.

amuseur [amyzœʀ] *nm* entertainer; (*péj*) clown.

amygdale [amidal] *nf* tonsil; **opérer qn des ~s** to take sb's tonsils out.

amygdalite [amidalit] *nf* tonsillitis.

AN *sigle f* = **Assemblée nationale.**

an [ɑ̃] *nm* year; **être âgé de** *ou* **avoir 3 ~s** to be 3 (years old); **en l'~ 1980** in the year 1980; **le jour de l'~**, **le premier de l'~**, **le nouvel ~** New Year's Day.

anabolisant [anabɔlizɑ̃] *nm* anabolic steroid.

anachronique [anakʀɔnik] *a* anachronistic.

anachronisme [anakʀɔnism(ə)] *nm* anachronism.

anaconda [anakɔda] *nm* (*ZOOL*) anaconda.

anagramme [anagʀam] *nf* anagram.

ANAH *sigle f* = *Agence nationale pour l'amélioration de l'habitat.*

anal, e, aux [anal, -o] *a* anal.

analgésique [analʒezik] *nm* analgesic.

anallergique [analɛʀʒik] *a* hypoallergenic.

analogie [analɔʒi] *nf* analogy.

analogique [analɔʒik] *a* (*LOGIQUE*: *raisonnement*) analogical; (*calculateur, montre etc*) analogue; (*INFORM*) analog.

analogue [analɔg] *a*: **~ (à)** analogous (to), similar (to).

analphabète [analfabɛt] *nm/f* illiterate.

analphabétisme [analfabetism(ə)] *nm* illiteracy.

analyse [analiz] *nf* analysis; (*MÉD*) test; **faire l'~ de** to analyse; **une ~ approfondie** an in-depth analysis; **en dernière ~** in the last analysis; **avoir l'esprit d'~** to have an analytical turn of mind; **~ grammaticale** grammatical analysis, parsing (*SCOL*).

analyser [analize] *vt* to analyse; (*MÉD*) to test.

analyste [analist(ə)] *nm/f* analyst; (*psychanalyste*) (psycho)analyst.

analyste-programmeur, euse, *pl* **analystes-programmeurs, euses** [analist-pʀɔgʀamœʀ, -øz] *nm/f* systems analyst.

analytique [analitik] *a* analytical.

analytiquement [analitikmɑ̃] *ad* analytically.

ananas [anana] *nm* pineapple.

anarchie [anaʀʃi] *nf* anarchy.

anarchique [anaʀʃik] *a* anarchic.

anarchisme [anaʀʃism(ə)] *nm* anarchism.

anarchiste [anaʀʃist(ə)] *a* anarchistic ♦ *nm/f* anarchist.

anathème [anatɛm] *nm*: **jeter l'~ sur, lancer l'~ contre** to anathematize, curse.

anatomie [anatɔmi] *nf* anatomy.

anatomique [anatɔmik] *a* anatomical.

ancestral, e, aux [ɑ̃sɛstʀal, -o] *a* ancestral.

ancêtre [ɑ̃sɛtʀ(ə)] *nm/f* ancestor; (*fig*): **l'~ de** the forerunner of.

anche [ɑ̃ʃ] *nf* reed.

anchois [ɑ̃ʃwa] *nm* anchovy.

ancien, ne [ɑ̃sjɛ̃, -ɛn] *a* old; (*de jadis, de l'antiquité*) ancient; (*précédent, ex-*) former, old ♦ *nm* (*mobilier ancien*): **l'~** antiques *pl* ♦ *nm/f* (*dans une tribu etc*) elder; **un ~ ministre** a former minister; **mon ~ne voiture** my previous car; **être plus ~ que qn dans une maison** to have been in a firm longer than sb; (*dans l'hiérarchie*) to be senior to sb in a firm; **~ combattant** ex-serviceman; **~ (élève)** (*SCOL*) ex-pupil (*Brit*), alumnus (*US*).

anciennement [ɑ̃sjɛnmɑ̃] *ad* formerly.

ancienneté [ɑ̃sjɛnte] *nf* oldness; antiquity; (*ADMIN*) (length of) service; seniority.

ancrage [ɑ̃kʀaʒ] *nm* anchoring; (*NAVIG*) anchorage; (*CONSTR*) anchor.

ancre [ɑ̃kʀ(ə)] *nf* anchor; **jeter/lever l'~** to cast/weigh anchor; **à l'~** at anchor.

ancrer [ɑ̃kʀe] *vt* (*CONSTR*) to anchor; (*fig*) to fix firmly; **s'~** *vi* (*NAVIG*) to (cast) anchor.

andalou, ouse [ãdalu, -uz] *a* Andalusian.

Andalousie [ãdaluzi] *nf*: **l'~** Andalusia.

andante [ãdãt] *ad, nm* andante.

Andes [ãd] *nfpl*: **les ~** the Andes.

Andorre [ãdɔʀ] *n* Andorra.

andouille [ãduj] *nf* (*CULIN*) *sausage made of chitterlings*; (*fam*) clot, nit.

andouillette [ãdujɛt] *nf small andouille*.

âne [ɑn] *nm* donkey, ass; (*péj*) dunce, fool.

anéantir [aneãtiʀ] *vt* to annihilate, wipe out; (*fig*) to obliterate, destroy; (*déprimer*) to overwhelm.

anecdote [anɛkdɔt] *nf* anecdote.

anecdotique [anɛkdɔtik] *a* anecdotal.

anémie [anemi] *nf* anaemia.

anémié, e [anemje] *a* anaemic; (*fig*) enfeebled.

anémique [anemik] *a* anaemic.

anémone [anemɔn] *nf* anemone; **~ de mer** sea anemone.

ânerie [ɑnʀi] *nf* stupidity; (*parole etc*) stupid *ou* idiotic comment *etc*.

anéroïde [aneʀɔid] *a voir* **baromètre**.

ânesse [ɑnɛs] *nf* she-ass.

anesthésie [anɛstezi] *nf* anaesthesia; **sous ~** under anaesthetic; **~ générale/locale** general/local anaesthetic; **faire une ~ locale à qn** to give sb a local anaesthetic.

anesthésier [anɛstezje] *vt* to anaesthetize.

anesthésique [anɛstezik] *a* anaesthetic.

anesthésiste [anɛstezist(ə)] *nm/f* anaesthetist.

anfractuosité [ãfʀaktɥozite] *nf* crevice.

ange [ãʒ] *nm* angel; **être aux ~s** to be over the moon; **~ gardien** guardian angel.

angélique [ãʒelik] *a* angelic(al) ♦ *nf* angelica.

angelot [ãʒlo] *nm* cherub.

angélus [ãʒelys] *nm* angelus; (*cloches*) evening bells *pl*.

angevin, e [ãʒvɛ̃, -in] *a* of *ou* from Anjou; of *ou* from Angers.

angine [ãʒin] *nf* sore throat, throat infection; **~ de poitrine** angina (pectoris).

angiome [ãʒjom] *nm* angioma.

anglais, e [ãglɛ, -ez] *a* English ♦ *nm* (*LING*) English ♦ *nm/f*: **A~, e** Englishman/woman; **les A~** the English; **filer à l'~e** to take French leave; **à l'~e** (*CULIN*) boiled.

anglaises [ãglɛz] *nfpl* (*cheveux*) ringlets.

angle [ãgl(ə)] *nm* angle; (*coin*) corner; **~ droit/obtus/aigu/mort** right/obtuse/acute/dead angle.

Angleterre [ãglətɛʀ] *nf*: **l'~** England.

anglican, e [ãglikã, -an] *a, nm/f* Anglican.

anglicisme [ãglisism(ə)] *nm* anglicism.

angliciste [ãglisist(ə)] *nm/f* English scholar; (*étudiant*) student of English.

anglo... [ãglo] *préfixe* Anglo-, anglo(-).

anglo-américain, e [ãgloameʀikɛ̃, -ɛn] *a* Anglo-American ♦ *nm* (*LING*) American English.

anglo-arabe [ãgloaʀab] *a* Anglo-Arab.

anglo-canadien, ne [ãglokanadjɛ̃, -ɛn] *a* Anglo-Canadian ♦ *nm* (*LING*) Canadian English.

anglo-normand, e [ãglonɔʀmã, -ãd] *a* Anglo-Norman; **les îles ~es** the Channel Islands.

anglophile [ãglofil] *a* anglophilic.

anglophobe [ãglofɔb] *a* anglophobic.

anglophone [ãglofɔn] *a* English-speaking.

anglo-saxon, ne [ãglosaksɔ̃, -ɔn] *a* Anglo-Saxon.

angoissant, e [ãgwasã, -ãt] *a* harrowing.

angoisse [ãgwas] *nf*: **l'~** anguish *q*.

angoissé, e [ãgwase] *a* anguished; (*personne*) full of anxieties *ou* hang-ups (*fam*).

angoisser [ãgwase] *vt* to harrow, cause anguish to ♦ *vi* to worry, fret.

Angola [ãgɔla] *nm*: **l'~** Angola.

angolais, e [ãgɔlɛ, -ɛz] *a* Angolan.

angora [ãgɔʀa] *a, nm* angora.

anguille [ãgij] *nf* eel; **~ de mer** conger (eel); **il y a ~ sous roche** (*fig*) there's something going on, there's something beneath all this.

angulaire [ãgylɛʀ] *a* angular.

anguleux, euse [ãgylø, -øz] *a* angular.

anicroche [anikʀɔʃ] *nf* hitch, snag.

animal, e, aux [animal, -o] *a, nm* animal; **~ domestique/sauvage** domestic/wild animal.

animalier [animalje] *a*: **peintre ~** animal painter.

animateur, trice [animatœʀ, -tʀis] *nm/f* (*de télévision*) host; (*de music-hall*) compère; (*de groupe*) leader, organizer; (*CINÉMA: technicien*) animator.

animation [animasjɔ̃] *nf* (*voir animé*) busyness; liveliness; (*CINÉMA: technique*) animation; (*activité*): **~s** activities; **centre d'~** ≈ community centre.

animé, e [anime] *a* (*rue, lieu*) busy, lively; (*conversation, réunion*) lively, animated; (*opposé à inanimé, aussi LING*) animate.

animer [anime] *vt* (*ville, soirée*) to liven up, enliven; (*mettre en mouvement*) to drive; (*stimuler*) to drive, impel; **s'~** *vi* to liven up, come to life.

animosité [animozite] *nf* animosity.

anis [ani] *nm* (*CULIN*) aniseed; (*BOT*) anise.

anisette [anizɛt] *nf* anisette.

Ankara [ãkaʀa] *n* Ankara.

ankyloser [ãkiloze]: **s'~** *vi* to get stiff, ankylose.

annales [anal] *nfpl* annals.

anneau, x [ano] *nm* ring; (*de chaîne*) link; (*SPORT*): **exercices aux ~x** ring exercises.

année [ane] *nf* year; **souhaiter la bonne ~ à qn** to wish sb a Happy New Year; **tout au long de l'~** all year long; **d'une ~ à l'autre** from one year to the next; **d'~ en ~** from year to year; **l'~ scolaire/fiscale** the school/tax year.

année-lumière,   *pl*   **années-lumières** [anelymjɛʀ] *nf* light year.

annexe [anɛks(ə)] *a* (*problème*) related; (*document*) appended; (*salle*) adjoining ♦ *nf* (*bâtiment*) annex(e); (*de document, ouvrage*) annex, appendix; (*jointe à une lettre, un dossier*) enclosure.

annexer [anɛkse] *vt* to annex; **s'~** (*pays*) to annex; **~ qch à** (*joindre*) to append sth to.

annexion [anɛksjɔ̃] *nf* annexation.

annihiler [aniile] *vt* to annihilate.

anniversaire [anivɛʀsɛʀ] *nm* birthday; (*d'un événement, bâtiment*) anniversary ♦ *a*: **jour ~** anniversary.

annonce [anɔ̃s] *nf* announcement; (*signe, indice*) sign; (*aussi*: **~ publicitaire**) advertisement; (*CARTES*) declaration; **~ personnelle** personal message; **les petites ~s** the small *ou* classified ads.

annoncer [anɔ̃se] *vt* to announce; (*être le signe de*) to herald; (*CARTES*) to declare; **je vous annonce que** ... I wish to tell you that ...; **s'~ bien/difficile** to look promising/difficult; **~ la couleur** (*fig*) to lay one's cards on the table.

annonceur, euse [anɔ̃sœʀ, -øz] *nm/f* (*TV, RADIO: speaker*) announcer; (*publicitaire*) advertiser.

annonciateur, trice [anɔ̃sjatœʀ, -tʀis] *a:* ~ **d'un événement** presaging an event.

Annonciation [anɔ̃sjasjɔ̃] *nf:* **l'~** (*REL*) the Annunciation; (*jour*) Annunciation Day.

annotation [anɔtasjɔ̃] *nf* annotation.

annoter [anɔte] *vt* to annotate.

annuaire [anɥɛʀ] *nm* yearbook, annual; ~ **téléphonique** (telephone) directory, phone book.

annuel, le [anɥɛl] *a* annual, yearly.

annuellement [anɥɛlmɑ̃] *ad* annually, yearly.

annuité [anɥite] *nf* annual instalment.

annulaire [anɥlɛʀ] *nm* ring *ou* third finger.

annulation [anylasjɔ̃] *nf* cancellation; annulment; quashing, repeal.

annuler [anyle] *vt* (*rendez-vous, voyage*) to cancel, call off; (*mariage*) to annul; (*jugement*) to quash (*Brit*), repeal (*US*); (*résultats*) to declare void; (*MATH, PHYSIQUE*) to cancel out; **s'~** to cancel each other out.

anoblir [anɔbliʀ] *vt* to ennoble.

anode [anɔd] *nf* anode.

anodin, e [anɔdɛ̃, -in] *a* harmless; (*sans importance*) insignificant, trivial.

anomalie [anɔmali] *nf* anomaly.

ânon [anɔ̃] *nm* baby donkey; (*petit âne*) little donkey.

ânonner [anɔne] *vi, vt* to read in a drone; (*hésiter*) to read in a fumbling manner.

anonymat [anɔnima] *nm* anonymity; **garder l'~** to remain anonymous.

anonyme [anɔnim] *a* anonymous; (*fig*) impersonal.

anonymement [anɔnimmɑ̃] *ad* anonymously.

anorak [anɔʀak] *nm* anorak.

anorexie [anɔʀɛksi] *nf* anorexia.

anormal, e, aux [anɔʀmal, -o] *a* abnormal; (*insolite*) unusual, abnormal.

anormalement [anɔʀmalmɑ̃] *ad* abnormally; unusually.

ANPE *sigle f* (= *Agence nationale pour l'emploi*) national employment agency (*functions include job creation*).

anse [ɑ̃s] *nf* handle; (*GÉO*) cove.

antagonisme [ɑ̃tagɔnism(ə)] *nm* antagonism.

antagoniste [ɑ̃tagɔnist(ə)] *a* antagonistic ♦ *nm* antagonist.

antan [ɑ̃tɑ̃]: **d'~** *a* of yesteryear, of long ago.

antarctique [ɑ̃taʀktik] *a* Antarctic ♦ *nm:* **l'A~** the Antarctic; **le cercle A~** the Antarctic Circle; **l'océan A~** the Antarctic Ocean.

antécédent [ɑ̃tesedɑ̃] *nm* (*LING*) antecedent; ~**s** *nmpl* (*MÉD etc*) past history *sg*; ~**s professionnels** record, career to date.

antédiluvien, ne [ɑ̃tedilyvjɛ̃, -ɛn] *a* (*fig*) ancient, antediluvian.

antenne [ɑ̃tɛn] *nf* (*de radio, télévision*) aerial; (*d'insecte*) antenna (*pl* -ae), feeler; (*poste avancé*) outpost; (*petite succursale*) sub-

branch; **sur l'~** on the air; **passer à/avoir l'~** to go/be on the air; **2 heures d'~** 2 hours' broadcasting time; **hors** ~ off the air; ~ **chirurgicale** (*MIL*) advance surgical unit.

antépénultième [ɑ̃tepenyltjɛm] *a* antepenultimate.

antérieur, e [ɑ̃teʀjœʀ] *a* (*d'avant*) previous, earlier; (*de devant*) front; ~ **à** prior *ou* previous to; **passé/futur** ~ (*LING*) past/future anterior.

antérieurement [ɑ̃teʀjœʀmɑ̃] *ad* earlier; (*précédemment*) previously; ~ **à** prior *ou* previous to.

antériorité [ɑ̃teʀjɔʀite] *nf* precedence (*in time*).

anthologie [ɑ̃tɔlɔʒi] *nf* anthology.

anthracite [ɑ̃tʀasit] *nm* anthracite ♦ *a:* (*gris*) ~ **charcoal** (grey).

anthropologie [ɑ̃tʀɔpɔlɔʒi] *nf* anthropology.

anthropologue [ɑ̃tʀɔpɔlɔg] *nm/f* anthropologist.

anthropomorphisme [ɑ̃tʀɔpɔmɔʀfism(ə)] *nm* anthropomorphism.

anthropophagie [ɑ̃tʀɔpɔfaʒi] *nf* cannibalism, anthropophagy.

anti... [ɑ̃ti] *préfixe* anti....

antiaérien, ne [ɑ̃tiaeʀjɛ̃, -ɛn] *a* anti-aircraft; **abri** ~ air-raid shelter.

antialcoolique [ɑ̃tialkɔlik] *a* anti-alcohol; **ligue** ~ temperance league.

antiatomique [ɑ̃tiatɔmik] *a:* **abri** ~ fallout shelter.

antibiotique [ɑ̃tibjɔtik] *nm* antibiotic.

antibrouillard [ɑ̃tibʀujaʀ] *a:* **phare** ~ fog lamp.

antibruit [ɑ̃tibʀɥi] *a inv:* **mur** ~ (*sur autoroute*) sound-muffling wall.

antibuée [ɑ̃tibɥe] *a inv:* **dispositif** ~ demister; **bombe** ~ demister spray.

anticancéreux, euse [ɑ̃tikɑ̃seʀø, -øz] *a* cancer *cpd*.

anticasseur(s) [ɑ̃tikɑsœʀ] *a:* **loi/mesure** ~ law/measure against damage done by demonstrators.

antichambre [ɑ̃tiʃɑ̃bʀ(ə)] *nf* antechamber, anteroom; **faire** ~ to wait (for an audience).

antichar [ɑ̃tiʃaʀ] *a* anti-tank.

antichoc [ɑ̃tiʃɔk] *a* shockproof.

anticipation [ɑ̃tisipasjɔ̃] *nf* anticipation; (*COMM*) payment in advance; **par** ~ in anticipation, in advance; **livre/film d'~** science fiction book/film.

anticipé, e [ɑ̃tisipe] *a* (*règlement, paiement*) early, in advance; (*joie etc*) anticipated, early; **avec mes remerciements** ~**s** thanking you in advance *ou* anticipation.

anticiper [ɑ̃tisipe] *vt* to anticipate, foresee; (*paiement*) to pay *ou* make in advance ♦ *vi* to look *ou* think ahead; (*en racontant*) to jump ahead; (*prévoir*) to anticipate; ~ **sur** to anticipate.

anticlérical, e, aux [ɑ̃tikleʀikal, -o] *a* anticlerical.

anticoagulant, e [ɑ̃tikɔagylɑ̃, -ɑ̃t] *a, nm* anticoagulant.

anticonceptionnel, le [ɑ̃tikɔ̃sɛpsjɔnɛl] *a* contraceptive.

anticonformisme [ɑ̃tikɔ̃fɔʀmism(ə)] *nm* nonconformism.

anticonstitutionnel, le [ãtikõstitysjɔnɛl] *a* unconstitutional.

anticorps [ãtikɔʀ] *nm* antibody.

anticyclone [ãtisiklon] *nm* anticyclone.

antidater [ãtidate] *vt* to backdate, predate.

antidémocratique [ãtidemɔkʀatik] *a* antidemocratic; (*peu démocratique*) undemocratic.

antidérapant, e [ãtideʀapɑ̃, -ãt] *a* non-skid.

antidopage [ãtidɔpaʒ], **antidoping** [ãtidɔpiŋ] *a* (*lutte*) anti-doping; (*contrôle*) dope *cpd*.

antidote [ãtidɔt] *nm* antidote.

antienne [ãtjɛn] *nf* (*fig*) chant, refrain.

antigang [ãtigãg] *a inv*: **brigade** ~ commando unit.

antigel [ãtiʒɛl] *nm* antifreeze.

antigène [ãtiʒɛn] *nm* antigen.

antigouvernemental, e, aux [ãtiguvɛʀnəmãtal, -o] *a* anti-government.

Antigua et Barbude [ãtigaebaʀbyd] *nf* Antigua and Barbuda.

antihistaminique [ãtiistaminik] *nm* antihistamine.

anti-inflammatoire [ãtiẽflamatwaʀ] *a* anti-inflammatory.

anti-inflationniste [ãtiẽflasjɔnist(ə)] *a* anti-inflationary.

antillais, e [ãtije, -ɛz] *a* West Indian.

Antilles [ãtij] *nfpl*: **les** ~ the West Indies; **les Grandes/Petites** ~ the Greater/Lesser Antilles.

antilope [ãtilɔp] *nf* antelope.

antimilitariste [ãtimilitaʀist(ə)] *a* antimilitarist.

antimissile [ãtimisil] *a* antimissile.

antimite(s) [ãtimit] *a*, *nm*: (**produit**) ~ mothproofer, moth repellent.

antinucléaire [ãtinykleɛʀ] *a* antinuclear.

antioxydant [ãtiɔksidã] *nm* antioxidant.

antiparasite [ãtipaʀazit] *a* (*RADIO, TV*) anti-interference; **dispositif** ~ suppressor.

antipathie [ãtipati] *nf* antipathy.

antipathique [ãtipatik] *a* unpleasant, disagreeable.

antipelliculaire [ãtipelikylɛʀ] *a* anti-dandruff.

antiphrase [ãtifʀɑz] *nf*: **par** ~ ironically.

antipodes [ãtipɔd] *nmpl* (*GÉO*): **les** ~ the antipodes; (*fig*): **être aux** ~ **de** to be the opposite extreme of.

antipoison [ãtipwazõ] *a inv*: **centre** ~ poison centre.

antipoliomyélitique [ãtipɔljɔmjelitik] *a* polio *cpd*.

antiprotectionniste [ãtipʀɔtɛksjɔnist(ə)] *a* free-trade.

antiquaire [ãtikɛʀ] *nm/f* antique dealer.

antique [ãtik] *a* antique; (*très vieux*) ancient, antiquated.

antiquité [ãtikite] *nf* (*objet*) antique; **l'A~** Antiquity; **magasin/marchand d'~s** antique shop/dealer.

antirabique [ãtiʀabik] *a* rabies *cpd*.

antiraciste [ãtiʀasist(ə)] *a* antiracist, antiracialist.

antirépublicain, e [ãtiʀepyblikẽ, -ɛn] *a* antirepublican.

antirides [ãtiʀid] *a* (*crème*) anti-wrinkle.

antirouille [ãtiʀuj] *a inv*: **peinture** ~ anti-rust paint; **traitement** ~ rustproofing.

antisémite [ãtisemit] *a* anti-semitic.

antisémitisme [ãtisemitism(ə)] *nm* anti-semitism.

antiseptique [ãtisɛptik] *a*, *nm* antiseptic.

antisocial, e, aux [ãtisɔsjal, -o] *a* antisocial.

antisportif, ive [ãtispɔʀtif, -iv] *a* unsporting; (*hostile au sport*) against sport, anti-sport.

antitétanique [ãtitetanik] *a* tetanus *cpd*.

antithèse [ãtitɛz] *nf* antithesis.

antitrust [ãtitʀœst] *a inv* (*loi, mesures*) anti-monopoly.

antituberculeux, euse [ãtitybɛʀkylø, -øz] *a* tuberculosis *cpd*.

antitussif, ive [ãtitysif, -iv] *a* antitussive, cough *cpd*.

antivariolique [ãtivaʀjɔlik] *a* smallpox *cpd*.

antivol [ãtivɔl] *a*, *nm*: (**dispositif**) ~ anti-theft device; (*pour vélo*) padlock.

antonyme [ãtɔnim] *nm* antonym.

antre [ãtʀ(ə)] *nm* den, lair.

anus [anys] *nm* anus.

Anvers [ãvɛʀ] *n* Antwerp.

anxiété [ãksjete] *nf* anxiety.

anxieusement [ãksjøzmã] *ad* anxiously.

anxieux, euse [ãksjø, -øz] *a* anxious, worried; **être** ~ **de faire** to be anxious to do.

AOC *sigle f* (= *Appellation d'origine contrôlée*) guarantee of quality of wine.

aorte [aɔʀt(ə)] *nf* aorta.

août [u] *nm* August; *voir aussi* **juillet**.

aoûtien, ne [ausjẽ, -ɛn] *nm/f* August holiday-maker.

AP *sigle f* = **Assistance publique**.

apaisement [apɛzmã] *nm* calming; soothing; (*aussi POL*) appeasement; ~**s** *nmpl* soothing reassurances; (*pour calmer*) pacifying words.

apaiser [apeze] *vt* (*colère*) to calm, quell, soothe; (*faim*) to appease, assuage; (*douleur*) to soothe; (*personne*) to calm (down), pacify; **s'**~ *vi* (*tempête, bruit*) to die down, subside.

apanage [apanaʒ] *nm*: **être l'**~ **de** to be the privilege *ou* prerogative of.

aparté [apaʀte] *nm* (*THÉÂTRE*) aside; (*entretien*) private conversation; **en** ~ *ad* in an aside (*Brit*); (*entretien*) in private.

apartheid [apaʀtɛd] *nm* apartheid.

apathie [apati] *nf* apathy.

apathique [apatik] *a* apathetic.

apatride [apatʀid] *nm/f* stateless person.

Apennins [apɛnẽ] *nmpl*: **les** ~ the Apennines.

apercevoir [apɛʀsəvwaʀ] *vt* to see; **s'**~ **de** *vt* to notice; **s'**~ **que** to notice that; **sans s'en** ~ without realizing *ou* noticing.

aperçu, e [apɛʀsy] *pp de* **apercevoir** ♦ *nm* (*vue d'ensemble*) general survey; (*intuition*) insight.

apéritif, ive [apeʀitif, -iv] *a* which stimulates the appetite ♦ *nm* (*boisson*) aperitif; (*réunion*) (pre-lunch *ou* -dinner) drinks *pl*; **prendre l'**~ to have drinks (before lunch *ou* dinner) *ou* an aperitif.

apesanteur [apəzãtœʀ] *nf* weightlessness.

à-peu-près [apøpʀɛ] *nm inv* (*péj*) vague approximation.

apeuré, e [apœʀe] *a* frightened, scared.

aphone [afɔn] *a* voiceless.

aphorisme [afɔʀism(ə)] *nm* aphorism.

aphrodisiaque [afʀɔdizjak] *a*, *nm* aphrodisiac.

aphte [aft(ə)] nm mouth ulcer.

aphteuse [aftøz] af: **fièvre** ~ foot-and-mouth disease.

apicole [apikɔl] a beekeeping cpd.

apiculture [apikyltyʀ] nf beekeeping, apiculture.

apitoiement [apitwamã] nm pity, compassion.

apitoyer [apitwaje] vt to move to pity; ~ **qn sur qn/qch** to move sb to pity for sb/over sth; **s'~ (sur qn/qch)** to feel pity ou compassion (for sb/over sth).

ap. J.-C. abr (= après Jésus-Christ) AD.

APL sigle f (= aide personnalisée au logement) type of loan for house purchase.

aplanir [aplaniʀ] vt to level; (fig) to smooth away, iron out.

aplati, e [aplati] a flat, flattened.

aplatir [aplatiʀ] vt to flatten; **s'~** vi to become flatter; (écrasé) to be flattened; (fig) to lie flat on the ground; (: fam) to fall flat on one's face; (: péj) to grovel.

aplomb [aplɔ̃] nm (équilibre) balance, equilibrium; (fig) self-assurance; (: péj) nerve; **d'~** ad steady; (CONSTR) plumb.

apocalypse [apɔkalips(ə)] nf apocalypse.

apocalyptique [apɔkaliptik] a (fig) apocalyptic.

apocryphe [apɔkʀif] a apocryphal.

apogée [apɔʒe] nm (fig) peak, apogee.

apolitique [apɔlitik] a (indifférent) apolitical; (indépendant) unpolitical, non-political.

apologie [apɔlɔʒi] nf praise; (JUR) vindication.

apoplexie [apɔplɛksi] nf apoplexy.

a posteriori [apɔsteʀjɔʀi] ad after the event, with hindsight, a posteriori.

apostolat [apɔstɔla] nm (REL) apostolate, discipleship; (gén) evangelism.

apostolique [apɔstɔlik] a apostolic.

apostrophe [apɔstʀɔf] nf (signe) apostrophe; (appel) interpellation.

apostropher [apɔstʀɔfe] vt (interpeller) to shout at, address sharply.

apothéose [apɔteoz] nf pinnacle (of achievement); (MUS etc) grand finale.

apothicaire [apɔtikɛʀ] nm apothecary.

apôtre [apotʀ(ə)] nm apostle, disciple.

Appalaches [apalaʃ] nmpl: **les** ~ the Appalachian Mountains.

appalachien, ne [apalaʃjɛ̃, -ɛn] a Appalachian.

apparaître [apaʀɛtʀ(ə)] vi to appear ♦ vb avec attribut to appear, seem.

apparat [apaʀa] nm: **tenue/dîner d'~** ceremonial dress/dinner.

appareil [apaʀɛj] nm (outil, machine) piece of apparatus, device; (électrique etc) appliance; (politique, syndical) machinery; (avion) (aero)plane (Brit), (air)plane (US), aircraft inv; (téléphonique) telephone; (dentier) brace (Brit), braces (US); ~ **digestif/ reproducteur** digestive/reproductive system ou apparatus; **l'~ productif** the means of production; **qui est à l'~?** who's speaking?; **dans le plus simple** ~ in one's birthday suit; ~ **(photographique)** camera; ~ **24 x 36** ou **petit format** 35 mm camera.

appareillage [apaʀɛjaʒ] nm (appareils) equipment; (NAVIG) casting off, getting under way.

appareiller [apaʀeje] vi (NAVIG) to cast off, get under way ♦ vt (assortir) to match up.

appareil-photo, pl **appareils-photos** [apaʀɛjfɔtɔ] nm camera.

apparemment [apaʀamã] ad apparently.

apparence [apaʀãs] nf appearance; **malgré les** ~s despite appearances; **en** ~ apparently, seemingly.

apparent, e [apaʀã, -ãt] a visible; (évident) obvious; (superficiel) apparent; **coutures** ~es topstitched seams; **poutres** ~es exposed beams.

apparenté, e [apaʀãte] a: ~ **à** related to; (fig) similar to.

apparenter [apaʀãte]: **s'~ à** vt to be similar to.

apparier [apaʀje] vt (gants) to pair, match.

appariteur [apaʀitœʀ] nm attendant, porter (in French universities).

apparition [apaʀisjɔ̃] nf appearance; (surnaturelle) apparition; **faire son** ~ to appear.

appartement [apaʀtəmã] nm flat (Brit), apartment (US).

appartenance [apaʀtənãs] nf: ~ **à** belonging to, membership of.

appartenir [apaʀtəniʀ]: ~ **à** vt to belong to; (faire partie de) to belong to, be a member of; **il lui appartient de** it is up to him to.

appartiendrai [apaʀtjɛ̃dʀe], **appartiens** [apaʀtjɛ̃] etc voir **appartenir**.

apparu, e [apaʀy] pp de **apparaître**.

appas [apɑ] nmpl (d'une femme) charms.

appât [apɑ] nm (PÊCHE) bait; (fig) lure, bait.

appâter [apate] vt (hameçon) to bait; (poisson, fig) to lure, entice.

appauvrir [apovʀiʀ] vt to impoverish; **s'~** vi to grow poorer, become impoverished.

appauvrissement [apovʀismã] nm impoverishment.

appel [apɛl] nm call; (nominal) roll call; (: SCOL) register; (MIL: recrutement) call-up; (JUR) appeal; **faire** ~ **à** (invoquer) to appeal to; (avoir recours à) to call on; (nécessiter) to call for, require; **faire** ou **interjeter** ~ (JUR) to appeal, lodge an appeal; **faire l'~** to call the roll; to call the register; **indicatif d'~** call sign; **numéro d'~** (TÉL) number; **produit d'~** (COMM) loss leader; **sans** ~ (fig) final, irrevocable; ~ **d'air** in-draught; ~ **d'offres** (COMM) invitation to tender; **faire un** ~ **de phares** to flash one's headlights; ~ **(téléphonique)** (tele)phone call.

appelé [aple] nm (MIL) conscript.

appeler [aple] vt to call; (TÉL) to call, ring; (faire venir: médecin etc) to call, send for; (fig: nécessiter) to call for, demand; ~ **au secours** to call for help; ~ **qn à l'aide** ou **au secours** to call to sb to help; ~ **qn à un poste/des fonctions** to appoint sb to a post/ assign duties to sb; **être appelé à** (fig) to be destined to; ~ **qn à comparaître** (JUR) to summon sb to appear; **en** ~ **à** to appeal to; **s'~**: **elle s'appelle Gabrielle** her name is Gabrielle, she's called Gabrielle; **comment ça s'appelle?** what is it ou that called?

appellation [apelɑsjɔ̃] nf designation, appellation; **vin d'~ contrôlée** 'appellation contrôlée' wine, *wine guaranteed of a certain quality.*

appelle [apel] *etc vb voir* **appeler.**

appendice [apɛ̃dis] *nm* appendix.

appendicite [apɑ̃disit] *nf* appendicitis.

appentis [apɑ̃ti] *nm* lean-to.

appert [apɛʀ] *vb:* **il ~ que** it appears that, it is evident that.

appesantir [apzɑ̃tiʀ]: **s'~** *vi* to grow heavier; **s'~ sur** *(fig)* to dwell at length on.

appétissant, e [apetisɑ̃, -ɑ̃t] *a* appetizing, mouth-watering.

appétit [apeti] *nm* appetite; **couper l'~ à qn** to take away sb's appetite; **bon ~!** enjoy your meal!

applaudimètre [aplodimɛtʀ(ə)] *nm* applause meter.

applaudir [aplodiʀ] *vt* to applaud ♦ *vi* to applaud, clap; **~ à** *vt (décision)* to applaud, commend.

applaudissements [aplodismɑ̃] *nmpl* applause *sg,* clapping *sg.*

applicable [aplikabl(ə)] *a* applicable.

applicateur [aplikatœʀ] *nm* applicator.

application [aplikasjɔ̃] *nf* application; *(d'une loi)* enforcement; **mettre en ~** to implement.

applique [aplik] *nf* wall lamp.

appliqué, e [aplike] *a (élève etc)* industrious, assiduous; *(science)* applied.

appliquer [aplike] *vt* to apply; *(loi)* to enforce; *(donner: gifle, châtiment)* to give; **s'~** *vi (élève etc)* to apply o.s.; **s'~ à** *(loi, remarque)* to apply to; **s'~ à faire qch** to apply o.s. to doing sth, take pains to do sth; **s'~ sur** *(coïncider avec)* to fit over.

appoint [apwɛ̃] *nm* (extra) contribution *ou* help; **avoir/faire l'~** *(en payant)* to have/give the right change *ou* money; **chauffage d'~** extra heating.

appointements [apwɛ̃tmɑ̃] *nmpl* salary *sg,* stipend *(surtout REL).*

appointer [apwɛ̃te] *vt:* **être appointé à l'année/au mois** to be paid yearly/monthly.

appontement [apɔ̃tmɑ̃] *nm* landing stage, wharf.

apponter [apɔ̃te] *vi (avion, hélicoptère)* to land.

apport [apɔʀ] *nm* supply; *(argent, biens etc)* contribution.

apporter [apɔʀte] *vt* to bring; *(preuve)* to give, provide; *(modification)* to make; *(suj: remarque)* to contribute, add.

apposer [apoze] *vt* to append; *(sceau etc)* to affix.

apposition [apozisjɔ̃] *nf* appending; affixing; *(LING):* **en ~** in apposition.

appréciable [apʀesjabl(ə)] *a (important)* appreciable, significant.

appréciation [apʀesjasjɔ̃] *nf* appreciation; estimation, assessment; **~s** *nfpl (avis)* assessment *sg,* appraisal *sg.*

apprécier [apʀesje] *vt* to appreciate; *(évaluer)* to estimate, assess; **j'apprécierais que tu ... I** should appreciate it if you ....

appréhender [apʀeɑ̃de] *vt (craindre)* to dread; *(arrêter)* to apprehend; **~ que** to fear that; **~ de faire** to dread doing.

appréhensif, ive [apʀeɑ̃sif, -iv] *a* apprehensive.

appréhension [apʀeɑ̃sjɔ̃] *nf* apprehension.

apprendre [apʀɑ̃dʀ(ə)] *vt* to learn; *(événement, résultats)* to learn of, hear of; **~ qch à qn** *(informer)* to tell sb (of) sth; *(enseigner)* to teach sb sth; **tu me l'apprends!** that's news to me!; **~ à faire qch** to learn to do sth; **~ à qn à faire qch** to teach sb to do sth.

apprenti, e [apʀɑ̃ti] *nm/f* apprentice; *(fig)* novice, beginner.

apprentissage [apʀɑ̃tisaʒ] *nm* learning; *(COMM, SCOL: période)* apprenticeship; **école** *ou* **centre d'~** training school *ou* centre; **faire l'~ de qch** *(fig)* to be initiated into sth.

apprêt [apʀɛ] *nm (sur un cuir, une étoffe)* dressing; *(sur un mur)* size; *(sur un papier)* finish; **sans ~** *(fig)* without artifice, unaffectedly.

apprêté, e [apʀete] *a (fig)* affected.

apprêter [apʀete] *vt* to dress, finish; **s'~** *vi:* **s'~ à qch/à faire qch** to prepare for sth/for doing sth. ·

appris, e [apʀi, -iz] *pp de* **apprendre.**

apprivoisé, e [apʀivwaze] *a* tame, tamed.

apprivoiser [apʀivwaze] *vt* to tame.

approbateur, trice [apʀɔbatœʀ, -tʀis] *a* approving.

approbatif, ive [apʀɔbatif, -iv] *a* approving.

approbation [apʀɔbasjɔ̃] *nf* approval; **digne d'~** *(conduite, travail)* praiseworthy, commendable.

approchant, e [apʀɔʃɑ̃, -ɑ̃t] *a* similar, close; **quelque chose d'~** something similar.

approche [apʀɔʃ] *nf* approaching; *(arrivée, attitude)* approach; **~s** *nfpl (abords)* surroundings; **à l'~ du bateau/de l'ennemi** as the ship/enemy approached *ou* drew near; **l'~ d'un problème** the approach to a problem; **travaux d'~** *(fig)* manoeuvrings.

approché, e [apʀɔʃe] *a* approximate.

approcher [apʀɔʃe] *vi* to approach, come near ♦ *vt (vedette, artiste)* to come close to, approach; *(rapprocher):* **~ qch (de qch)** to bring *ou* put *ou* move sth near (to sth); **~ de** *vt* to draw near to; *(quantité, moment)* to approach; **s'~ de** *vt* to approach, go *ou* come *ou* move near to; **approchez-vous** come *ou* go nearer.

approfondi, e [apʀɔfɔ̃di] *a* thorough, detailed.

approfondir [apʀɔfɔ̃diʀ] *vt* to deepen; *(question)* to go further into; **sans ~** without going too deeply into it.

appropriation [apʀɔpʀijasjɔ̃] *nf* appropriation.

approprié, e [apʀɔpʀije] *a:* **~ (à)** appropriate (to), suited to.

approprier [apʀɔpʀije] *vt (adapter)* adapt; **s'~** *vt* to appropriate, take over.

approuver [apʀuve] *vt* to agree with; *(autoriser: loi, projet)* to approve, pass; *(trouver louable)* to approve of; **je vous approuve entièrement/ne vous approuve pas** I agree with you entirely/don't agree with you; **lu et approuvé** (read and) approved.

approvisionnement [apʀɔvizjɔnmɑ̃] *nm* supplying; *(provisions)* supply, stock.

approvisionner [apʀɔvizjɔne] *vt* to supply; *(compte bancaire)* to pay funds into; **~ qn en** to supply sb with; **s'~** *vi:* **s'~ dans un certain magasin/au marché** to shop in a certain shop/at the market; **s'~ en** to stock up with.

approximatif, ive [apʀɔksimatif, -iv] *a* approximate, rough; (*imprécis*) vague.

approximation [apʀɔksimasjɔ̃] *nf* approximation.

approximativement [apʀɔksimativmɑ̃] *ad* approximately, roughly; vaguely.

appt *abr* = **appartement**.

appui [apɥi] *nm* support; **prendre ~ sur** to lean on; (*objet*) to rest on; **point d'~** fulcrum; (*fig*) something to lean on; **à l'~ de** (*pour prouver*) in support of; **à l'~** *ad* to support one's argument; **l'~ de la fenêtre** the windowsill, the window ledge.

appuie [apɥi] *etc vb voir* **appuyer**.

appui-tête, appuie-tête [apɥitɛt] *nm inv* headrest.

appuyé, e [apɥije] *a* (*regard*) meaningful; (: *insistant*) intent, insistent; (*excessif: politesse, compliment*) exaggerated, over-done.

appuyer [apɥije] *vt* (*poser*): **~ qch sur/contre/à** to lean *ou* rest sth on/against/on; (*soutenir: personne, demande*) to support, back (up) ♦ *vi*: **~ sur** (*bouton, frein*) to press, push; (*mot, détail*) to stress, emphasize; (*suj: chose: peser sur*) to rest (heavily) on, press against; **s'~ sur** *vt* to lean on; (*compter sur*) to rely on; **s'~ sur qn** to lean on sb; **~ contre** (*toucher: mur, porte*) to lean *ou* rest against; **~ à droite** *ou* **sur sa droite** to bear (to the) right; **~ sur le champignon** to put one's foot down.

apr. *abr* = **après**.

âpre [ɑpʀ(ə)] *a* acrid, pungent; (*fig*) harsh; (*lutte*) bitter; **~ au gain** grasping, greedy.

après [apʀɛ] *prép* after ♦ *ad* afterwards; **2 heures ~** 2 hours later; **~ qu'il est** *ou* **soit parti/avoir fait** after he left/having done; **courir ~ qn** to run after sb; **crier ~ qn** to shout at sb; **être toujours ~ qn** (*critiquer etc*) to be always on at sb; **~ quoi** after which; **d'~** *prép* (*selon*) according to; **d'~ lui** according to him; **d'~ moi** in my opinion; **~ coup** *ad* after the event, afterwards; **~ tout** *ad* (*au fond*) after all; **et (puis) ~?** so what?

après-demain [apʀɛdmɛ̃] *ad* the day after tomorrow.

après-guerre [apʀɛgɛʀ] *nm* post-war years *pl*; **d'~** *a* post-war.

après-midi [apʀɛmidi] *nm ou nf inv* afternoon.

après-rasage [apʀɛʀazaʒ] *nm inv*: **(lotion) ~** after-shave (lotion).

après-ski [apʀɛski] *nm inv* (*chaussure*) snow boot; (*moment*) après-ski.

après-vente [apʀɛvɑ̃t] *a inv* after-sales *cpd*.

âpreté [ɑpʀəte] *nf* (*voir âpre*) pungency; harshness; bitterness.

à-propos [apʀopo] *nm* (*d'une remarque*) aptness; **faire preuve d'~** to show presence of mind, do the right thing; **avec ~** suitably, aptly.

apte [apt(ə)] *a*: **~ à qch/faire qch** capable of sth/doing sth; **~ (au service)** (*MIL*) fit (for service).

aptitude [aptityd] *nf* ability, aptitude.

apurer [apyʀe] *vt* (*COMM*) to clear.

aquaplanage [akwaplanaʒ] *nm* (*AUTO*) aqua-planing.

aquaplane [akwaplan] *nm* (*planche*) aqua-plane; (*sport*) aquaplaning.

aquarelle [akwaʀɛl] *nf* (*tableau*) watercolour (*Brit*), watercolor (*US*); (*genre*) water-colo(u)rs *pl*, aquarelle.

aquarium [akwaʀjɔm] *nm* aquarium.

aquatique [akwatik] *a* aquatic, water *cpd*.

aqueduc [akdyk] *nm* aqueduct.

aqueux, euse [akø, -øz] *a* aqueous.

aquilin [akilɛ̃] *am*: **nez ~** aquiline nose.

AR *sigle m* (= *accusé de réception*): **lettre/paquet avec ~** ≈ recorded delivery letter/parcel; (*AVIAT, RAIL etc*) = **aller (et) retour** ♦ *abr* (*voir*) = **arrière**.

arabe [aʀab] *a* Arabic; (*désert, cheval*) Ara-bian; (*nation, peuple*) Arab ♦ *nm* (*LING*) Ar-abic ♦ *nm/f*: **A~** Arab.

arabesque [aʀabɛsk(ə)] *nf* arabesque.

Arabie [aʀabi] *nf*: **l'~** Arabia; **l'~ Saoudite** *ou* **Séoudite** Saudi Arabia.

arable [aʀabl(ə)] *a* arable.

arachide [aʀaʃid] *nf* groundnut (plant); (*graine*) peanut, groundnut.

araignée [aʀeɲe] *nf* spider; **~ de mer** spider crab.

araser [aʀaze] *vt* to level; (*en rabotant*) to plane (down).

aratoire [aʀatwaʀ] *a*: **instrument ~** ploughing implement.

arbalète [aʀbalɛt] *nf* crossbow.

arbitrage [aʀbitʀaʒ] *nm* refereeing; umpiring; arbitration.

arbitraire [aʀbitʀɛʀ] *a* arbitrary.

arbitrairement [aʀbitʀɛʀmɑ̃] *ad* arbitrarily.

arbitre [aʀbitʀ(ə)] *nm* (*SPORT*) referee; (: *TENNIS, CRICKET*) umpire; (*fig*) arbiter, judge; (*JUR*) arbitrator.

arbitrer [aʀbitʀe] *vt* to referee; to umpire; to arbitrate.

arborer [aʀbɔʀe] *vt* to bear, display; (*avec ostentation*) to sport.

arborescence [aʀbɔʀesɑ̃s] *nf* tree structure.

arboriculture [aʀbɔʀikyltyʀ] *nf* arboriculture; **~ fruitière** fruit (tree) growing.

arbre [aʀbʀ(ə)] *nm* tree; (*TECH*) shaft; **~ à cames** (*AUTO*) camshaft; **~ fruitier** fruit tree; **~ généalogique** family tree; **~ de Noël** Christmas tree; **~ de transmission** (*AUTO*) driveshaft.

arbrisseau, x [aʀbʀiso] *nm* shrub.

arbuste [aʀbyst(ə)] *nm* small shrub, bush.

arc [aʀk] *nm* (*arme*) bow; (*GÉOM*) arc; (*ARCHIT*) arch; **~ de cercle** arc of a circle; **en ~ de cercle** *a* semi-circular.

arcade [aʀkad] *nf* arch(way); **~s** *nfpl* arcade *sg*, arches; **~ sourcilière** arch of the eye-brows.

arcanes [aʀkan] *nmpl* mysteries.

arc-boutant, pl arcs-boutants [aʀkbutɑ̃] *nm* flying buttress.

arc-bouter [aʀkbute]: **s'~** *vi*: **s'~ contre** to lean on press against.

arceau, x [aʀso] *nm* (*métallique etc*) hoop.

arc-en-ciel, pl arcs-en-ciel [aʀkɑ̃sjɛl] *nm* rain-bow.

archaïque [aʀkaik] *a* archaic.

archaïsme [aʀkaism(ə)] *nm* archaism.

archange [aʀkɑ̃ʒ] *nm* archangel.
arche [aʀʃ(ə)] *nf* arch; ~ **de Noé** Noah's Ark.
archéologie [aʀkeɔlɔʒi] *nf* arch(a)eology.
archéologique [aʀkeɔlɔʒik] *a* arch(a)e-ological.
archéologue [aʀkeɔlɔg] *nm/f* arch(a)eologist.
archer [aʀʃe] *nm* archer.
archet [aʀʃɛ] *nm* bow.
archétype [aʀketip] *nm* archetype.
archevêché [aʀʃəveʃe] *nm* archbishopric; (*palais*) archbishop's palace.
archevêque [aʀʃəvɛk] *nm* archbishop.
archi... [aʀʃi] *préfixe* (*très*) dead, extra.
archibondé, e [aʀʃibɔ̃de] *a* chock-a-block (*Brit*), packed solid.
archiduc [aʀʃidyk] *nm* archduke.
archiduchesse [aʀʃidyʃɛs] *nf* archduchess.
archipel [aʀʃipɛl] *nm* archipelago.
archisimple [aʀʃisɛ̃pl(ə)] *a* dead easy *ou* simple.
architecte [aʀʃitɛkt(ə)] *nm* architect.
architectural, e, aux [aʀʃitɛktyʀal, -o] *a* architectural.
architecture [aʀʃitɛktyʀ] *nf* architecture.
archive [aʀʃiv] *nf* file; ~**s** *nfpl* archives.
archiver [aʀʃive] *vt* to file.
archiviste [aʀʃivist(ə)] *nm/f* archivist.
arçon [aʀsɔ̃] *nm voir* **cheval**.
arctique [aʀktik] *a* Arctic ♦ *nm*: **l'A~** the Arctic; **le cercle A~** the Arctic Circle; **l'océan A~** the Arctic Ocean.
ardemment [aʀdamɑ̃] *ad* ardently, fervently.
ardent, e [aʀdɑ̃, -ɑ̃t] *a* (*soleil*) blazing; (*fièvre*) raging; (*amour*) ardent, passionate; (*prière*) fervent.
ardeur [aʀdœʀ] *nf* blazing heat; (*fig*) fervour, ardour.
ardoise [aʀdwaz] *nf* slate.
ardu, e [aʀdy] *a* arduous, difficult; (*pente*) steep, abrupt.
are [aʀ] *nm* are, 100 square metres.
arène [aʀɛn] *nf* arena; (*fig*): **l'~ politique/littéraire** the political/literary arena; ~**s** *nfpl* bull-ring *sg*.
arête [aʀɛt] *nf* (*de poisson*) bone; (*d'une montagne*) ridge; (*GÉOM etc*) edge (*where two faces meet*).
arg. *abr* = **argus**.
argent [aʀʒɑ̃] *nm* (*métal*) silver; (*monnaie*) money; (*couleur*) silver; **en avoir pour son ~** to get value for money; **gagner beaucoup d'~** to earn a lot of money; ~ **comptant** (hard) cash; ~ **liquide** ready money, (ready) cash; ~ **de poche** pocket money.
argenté, e [aʀʒɑ̃te] *a* silver(y); (*métal*) silver-plated.
argenter [aʀʒɑ̃te] *vt* to silver(-plate).
argenterie [aʀʒɑ̃tʀi] *nf* silverware; (*en métal argenté*) silver plate.
argentin, e [aʀʒɑ̃tɛ̃, -in] *a* (*son*) silvery; (*d'Argentine*) Argentinian, Argentine ♦ *nm/f*: **A~, e** Argentinian, Argentine.
Argentine [aʀʒɑ̃tin] *nf*: **l'~** Argentina, the Argentine.
argile [aʀʒil] *nf* clay.
argileux, euse [aʀʒilø, -øz] *a* clayey.
argot [aʀgo] *nm* slang.
argotique [aʀgɔtik] *a* slang *cpd*; (*très familier*) slangy.

arguer [aʀgɥe]: ~ **de** *vt* to put forward as a pretext *ou* reason; ~ **que** to argue that.
argument [aʀgymɑ̃] *nm* argument.
argumentaire [aʀgymɑ̃tɛʀ] *nm* list of sales points; (*brochure*) sales leaflet.
argumenter [aʀgymɑ̃te] *vi* to argue.
argus [aʀgys] *nm guide to second-hand car etc prices*.
arguties [aʀgysi] *nfpl* pettifoggery *sg* (*Brit*), quibbles.
aride [aʀid] *a* arid.
aridité [aʀidite] *nf* aridity.
arien, ne [aʀjɛ̃, -ɛn] *a* Arian.
aristocrate [aʀistɔkʀat] *nm/f* aristocrat.
aristocratie [aʀistɔkʀasi] *nf* aristocracy.
aristocratique [aʀistɔkʀatik] *a* aristocratic.
arithmétique [aʀitmetik] *a* arithmetic(al) ♦ *nf* arithmetic.
armagnac [aʀmaɲak] *nm* armagnac.
armateur [aʀmatœʀ] *nm* shipowner.
armature [aʀmatyʀ] *nf* framework; (*de tente etc*) frame; (*de corset*) bone; (*de soutien-gorge*) wiring.
arme [aʀm(ə)] *nf* weapon; (*section de l'armée*) arm; ~**s** *nfpl* weapons, arms; (*blason*) (coat of) arms; **les** ~**s** (*profession*) soldiering *sg*; **à** ~**s égales** on equal terms; **en** ~**s** up in arms; **passer par les** ~**s** to execute (by firing squad); **prendre/présenter les** ~**s** to take up/present arms; **se battre à l'**~ **blanche** to fight with blades; ~ **à feu** firearm.
armé, e [aʀme] *a* armed; ~ **de** armed with.
armée [aʀme] *nf* army; ~ **de l'air** Air Force; **l'**~ **du Salut** the Salvation Army; ~ **de terre** Army.
armement [aʀməmɑ̃] *nm* (*matériel*) arms *pl*, weapons *pl*; (*: d'un pays*) arms *pl*, armament; (*action d'équiper: d'un navire*) fitting out; ~**s nucléaires** nuclear armaments; **course aux** ~**s** arms race.
Arménie [aʀmeni] *nf*: **l'~** Armenia.
arménien, ne [aʀmenjɛ̃, -ɛn] *a* Armenian ♦ *nm* (*LING*) Armenian ♦ *nm/f*: **A~, ne** Armenian.
armer [aʀme] *vt* to arm; (*arme à feu*) to cock; (*appareil-photo*) to wind on; ~ **qch de** to fit sth with; (*renforcer*) to reinforce sth with; ~ **qn de** to arm *ou* equip sb with; **s'**~ **de** to arm o.s. with.
armistice [aʀmistis] *nm* armistice; **l'A~** ≈ Remembrance (*Brit*) *ou* Veterans (*US*) Day.
armoire [aʀmwaʀ] *nf* (tall) cupboard; (*penderie*) wardrobe (*Brit*), closet (*US*); ~ **à pharmacie** medicine chest.
armoiries [aʀmwaʀi] *nfpl* coat of arms *sg*.
armure [aʀmyʀ] *nf* armour *q*, suit of armour.
armurerie [aʀmyʀʀi] *nf* arms factory; (*magasin*) gunsmith's (shop).
armurier [aʀmyʀje] *nm* gunsmith; (*MIL, d'armes blanches*) armourer.
ARN *sigle m* (= *acide ribonucléique*) RNA.
arnaque [aʀnak] *nf*: **de l'**~ daylight robbery.
arnaquer [aʀnake] *vt* to do (*fam*), swindle; **se faire** ~ to be had (*fam*) *ou* done.
arnaqueur [aʀnakœʀ] *nm* swindler.
arnica [aʀnika] *nm*: **(teinture d')**~ arnica.
aromates [aʀɔmat] *nmpl* seasoning *sg*, herbs (and spices).
aromatique [aʀɔmatik] *a* aromatic.

aromatiser [aʀɔmatize] *vt* to flavour.
arôme [aʀom] *nm* aroma; *(d'une fleur etc)* fragrance.
arpège [aʀpɛʒ] *nm* arpeggio.
arpentage [aʀpɑ̃taʒ] *nm* (land) surveying.
arpenter [aʀpɑ̃te] *vt* to pace up and down.
arpenteur [aʀpɑ̃tœʀ] *nm* land surveyor.
arqué, e [aʀke] *a* arched; *(jambes)* bow *cpd*, bandy.
arr. *abr* = **arrondissement**.
arrachage [aʀaʃaʒ] *nm*: ~ **des mauvaises herbes** weeding.
arraché [aʀaʃe] *nm* (SPORT) snatch; **obtenir à l'~** *(fig)* to snatch.
arrache-pied [aʀaʃpje]: **d'~** *ad* relentlessly.
arracher [aʀaʃe] *vt* to pull out; *(page etc)* to tear off, tear out; *(déplanter: légume)* to lift; *(: herbe, souche)* to pull up; *(bras etc: par explosion)* to blow off; *(: par accident)* to tear off; **s'~** *vt (article très recherché)* to fight over; ~ **qch à qn** to snatch sth from sb; *(fig)* to wring sth out of sb, wrest sth from sb; ~ **qn à** *(solitude, rêverie)* to drag sb out of; *(famille etc)* to tear ou wrench sb away from; **se faire ~ une dent** to have a tooth out ou pulled (US); **s'~ de** *(lieu)* to tear o.s. away from; *(habitude)* to force o.s. out of.
arraisonner [aʀɛzɔne] *vt* to board and search.
arrangeant, e [aʀɑ̃ʒɑ̃, -ɑ̃t] *a* accommodating, obliging.
arrangement [aʀɑ̃ʒmɑ̃] *nm* arrangement.
arranger [aʀɑ̃ʒe] *vt* to arrange; *(réparer)* to fix, put right; *(régler)* to settle, sort out; *(convenir à)* to suit, be convenient for; **s'~** *(se mettre d'accord)* to come to an agreement ou arrangement; *(s'améliorer: querelle, situation)* to be sorted out; *(se débrouiller)*: **s'~ pour que ...** to arrange things so that ...; **je vais m'~** I'll manage; **ça va s'~** it'll sort itself out; **s'~ pour faire** to make sure that ou see to it that one can do.
arrangeur [aʀɑ̃ʒœʀ] *nm* (MUS) arranger.
arrestation [aʀɛstasjɔ̃] *nf* arrest.
arrêt [aʀɛ] *nm* stopping; *(de bus etc)* stop; *(JUR)* judgment, decision; *(FOOTBALL)* save; **~s** *nmpl* (MIL) arrest *sg*; **être à l'~** to be stopped, have come to a halt; **rester** ou **tomber en ~ devant** to stop short in front of; **sans ~** without stopping, non-stop; *(fréquemment)* continually; ~ **d'autobus** bus stop; ~ **facultatif** request stop; ~ **de mort** capital sentence; ~ **de travail** stoppage (of work).
arrêté, e [aʀɛte] *a (idées)* firm, fixed ♦ *nm* order, decree; ~ **municipal** ≈ bylaw, byelaw.
arrêter [aʀɛte] *vt* to stop; *(chauffage etc)* to turn off, switch off; *(COMM: compte)* to settle; *(COUTURE: point)* to fasten off; *(fixer: date etc)* to appoint, decide on; *(criminel, suspect)* to arrest; **s'~** *vi* to stop; *(s'interrompre)* to stop o.s.; ~ **de faire** to stop doing; **arrête de te plaindre** stop complaining; **ne pas ~ de faire** to keep on doing; **s'~ de faire** to stop doing; **s'~ sur** *(suj: choix, regard)* to fall on.
arrhes [aʀ] *nfpl* deposit *sg*.
arrière [aʀjɛʀ] *nm* back; *(SPORT)* fullback ♦ *a inv*: **siège/roue ~** back ou rear seat/wheel; **~s** *nmpl (fig)*: **protéger ses ~s** to protect

the rear; **à l'~** *ad* behind, at the back; **en ~** *ad* behind; *(regarder)* back, behind; *(tomber, aller)* backwards; **en ~ de** *prép* behind.
arriéré, e [aʀjeʀe] *a (péj)* backward ♦ *nm (d'argent)* arrears *pl*.
arrière-boutique [aʀjɛʀbutik] *nf* back shop.
arrière-cour [aʀjɛʀkuʀ] *nf* backyard.
arrière-cuisine [aʀjɛʀküizin] *nf* scullery.
arrière-garde [aʀjɛʀgaʀd(ə)] *nf* rearguard.
arrière-goût [aʀjɛʀgu] *nm* aftertaste.
arrière-grand-mère, *pl* **arrière-grand-mères** [aʀjɛʀgʀɑ̃mɛʀ] *nf* great-grandmother.
arrière-grand-père, *pl* **arrière-grands-pères** [aʀjɛʀgʀɑ̃pɛʀ] *nm* great-grandfather.
arrière-grands-parents [aʀjɛʀgʀɑ̃paʀɑ̃] *nmpl* great-grandparents.
arrière-pays [aʀjɛʀpei] *nm inv* hinterland.
arrière-pensée [aʀjɛʀpɑ̃se] *nf* ulterior motive; *(doute)* mental reservation.
arrière-petite-fille, *pl* **arrière-petites-filles** [aʀjɛʀpətitfij] *nf* great-granddaughter.
arrière-petit-fils, *pl* **arrière-petits-fils** [aʀjɛʀpətifis] *nm* great-grandson.
arrière-petits-enfants [aʀjɛʀpətizɑ̃fɑ̃] *nmpl* great-grandchildren.
arrière-plan [aʀjɛʀplɑ̃] *nm* background; **d'~** *a* (INFORM) background *cpd*.
arriérer [aʀjeʀe]: **s'~** *vi* (COMM) to fall into arrears.
arrière-saison [aʀjɛʀsɛzɔ̃] *nf* late autumn.
arrière-salle [aʀjɛʀsal] *nf* back room.
arrière-train [aʀjɛʀtʀɛ̃] *nm* hindquarters *pl*.
arrimer [aʀime] *vt* to stow; *(fixer)* to secure, fasten securely.
arrivage [aʀivaʒ] *nm* arrival.
arrivant, e [aʀivɑ̃, -ɑ̃t] *nm/f* newcomer.
arrivée [aʀive] *nf* arrival; *(ligne d'arrivée)* finish; ~ **d'air/de gaz** air/gas inlet; **courrier à l'~** incoming mail; **à mon ~** when I arrived.
arriver [aʀive] *vi* to arrive; *(survenir)* to happen, occur; **j'arrive!** (I'm) just coming!; **il arrive à Paris à 8h** he gets to ou arrives in Paris at 8; ~ **à destination** to arrive at one's destination; ~ **à** *(atteindre)* to reach; ~ **à (faire) qch** *(réussir)* to manage (to do) sth; ~ **à échéance** to fall due; **en ~ à faire** to end up doing, get to the point of doing; **il arrive que** it happens that; **il lui arrive de faire** he sometimes does.
arrivisme [aʀivism(ə)] *nm* ambition, ambitiousness.
arriviste [aʀivist(ə)] *nm/f* go-getter.
arrogance [aʀɔgɑ̃s] *nf* arrogance.
arrogant, e [aʀɔgɑ̃, -ɑ̃t] *a* arrogant.
arroger [aʀɔʒe]: **s'~** *vt* to assume (without right); **s'~ le droit de ...** to assume the right to ....
arrondi, e [aʀɔ̃di] *a* round ♦ *nm* roundness.
arrondir [aʀɔ̃diʀ] *vt (forme, objet)* to round; *(somme)* to round off; **s'~** *vi* to become round(ed); ~ **ses fins de mois** to supplement one's pay.
arrondissement [aʀɔ̃dismɑ̃] *nm* (ADMIN) ≈ district.
arrosage [aʀozaʒ] *nm* watering; **tuyau d'~** hose(pipe).
arroser [aʀoze] *vt* to water; *(victoire etc)* to celebrate (over a drink); *(CULIN)* to baste.

arroseur [aʀozœʀ] *nm* (*tourniquet*) sprinkler.
arroseuse [aʀozøz] *nf* water cart.
arrosoir [aʀozwaʀ] *nm* watering can.
arrt *abr* = **arrondissement**.
arsenal, aux [aʀsənal, -o] *nm* (*NAVIG*) naval dockyard; (*MIL*) arsenal; (*fig*) gear, paraphernalia.
arsenic [aʀsənik] *nm* arsenic.
art [aʀ] *nm* art; **avoir l'~ de faire** (*fig*: *personne*) to have a talent for doing; **les ~s** the arts; **livre/critique d'~** art book/critic; **objet d'~** objet d'art; **~ dramatique** dramatic art; **~s et métiers** applied arts and crafts; **~s ménagers** home economics *sg*; **~s plastiques** plastic arts.
art. *abr* = **article**.
artère [aʀtɛʀ] *nf* (*ANAT*) artery; (*rue*) main road.
artériel, le [aʀteʀjɛl] *a* arterial.
artériosclérose [aʀteʀjoskleʀoz] *nf* arteriosclerosis.
arthrite [aʀtʀit] *nf* arthritis.
arthrose [aʀtʀoz] *nf* (degenerative) osteoarthritis.
artichaut [aʀtiʃo] *nm* artichoke.
article [aʀtikl(ə)] *nm* article; (*COMM*), item, article; (*INFORM*) record, item; **faire l'~** (*COMM*) to do one's sales spiel; **faire l'~ de** (*fig*) to sing the praises of; **à l'~ de la mort** at the point of death; **~ défini/indéfini** definite/indefinite article; **~ de fond** (*PRESSE*) feature article; **~s de bureau** office equipment; **~s de voyage** travel goods *ou* items.
articulaire [aʀtikylɛʀ] *a* of the joints, articular.
articulation [aʀtikylasjɔ̃] *nf* articulation; (*ANAT*) joint.
articulé, e [aʀtikyle] *a* (*membre*) jointed; (*poupée*) with moving joints.
articuler [aʀtikyle] *vt* to articulate; **s'~** (**sur**) (*ANAT*, *TECH*) to articulate (with); **s'~ autour de** (*fig*) to centre around *ou* on, turn on.
artifice [aʀtifis] *nm* device, trick.
artificiel, le [aʀtifisjɛl] *a* artificial.
artificiellement [aʀtifisjɛlmɑ̃] *ad* artificially.
artificier [aʀtifisje] *nm* pyrotechnist.
artificieux, euse [aʀtifisjø, -øz] *a* guileful, deceitful.
artillerie [aʀtijʀi] *nf* artillery, ordnance.
artilleur [aʀtijœʀ] *nm* artilleryman, gunner.
artisan [aʀtizɑ̃] *nm* artisan, (self-employed) craftsman; **l'~ de la victoire/du malheur** the architect of victory/of the disaster.
artisanal, e, aux [aʀtizanal, -o] *a* of *ou* made by craftsmen; (*péj*) cottage industry *cpd*, unsophisticated.
artisanat [aʀtizana] *nm* arts and crafts *pl*.
artiste [aʀtist(ə)] *nm/f* artist; (*THÉÂTRE*, *MUS*) artist, performer; (*: de variétés*) entertainer.
artistique [aʀtistik] *a* artistic.
artistiquement [aʀtistikmɑ̃] *ad* artistically.
aryen, ne [aʀjɛ̃, -ɛn] *a* Aryan.
AS *sigle fpl* (*ADMIN*) = **assurances sociales** ♦ *sigle f* (*SPORT*: = *Association sportive*) ≈ FC (= *Football Club*).
as *vb* [a] *voir* avoir ♦ *nm* [ɑs] ace.
a/s *abr* (= *aux soins de*) c/o.
ASBL *sigle f* (= *association sans but lucratif*) non-profit-making organization.

asc. *abr* = **ascenseur**.
ascendance [asɑ̃dɑ̃s] *nf* (*origine*) ancestry; (*ASTROLOGIE*) ascendant.
ascendant, e [asɑ̃dɑ̃, -ɑ̃t] *a* upward ♦ *nm* influence; **~s** *nmpl* ascendants.
ascenseur [asɑ̃sœʀ] *nm* lift (*Brit*), elevator (*US*).
ascension [asɑ̃sjɔ̃] *nf* ascent; climb; **l'A~** (*REL*) the Ascension; **(île de) l'A~** Ascension Island.
ascète [asɛt] *nm/f* ascetic.
ascétisme [asetism(ə)] *nm* asceticism.
ascorbique [askɔʀbik] *a*: **acide ~** ascorbic acid.
ASE *sigle f* (= *Agence spatiale européenne*) ESA (= *European Space Agency*).
asepsie [asɛpsi] *nf* asepsis.
aseptique [asɛptik] *a* aseptic.
aseptiser [asɛptize] *vt* to sterilize; (*plaie*) to disinfect.
Asiate [azjat] *nm/f* Asian.
asiatique [azjatik] *a* Asian, Asiatic ♦ *nm/f*: **A~** Asian.
Asie [azi] *nf*: **l'~** Asia.
asile [azil] *nm* (*refuge*) refuge, sanctuary; (*POL*): **droit d'~** (political) asylum; (*pour malades, vieillards etc*) home; **accorder l'~ politique à qn** to grant *ou* give sb political asylum; **chercher/trouver ~ quelque part** to seek/find refuge somewhere.
asocial, e, aux [asɔsjal, -o] *a* antisocial.
aspect [aspɛ] *nm* appearance, look; (*fig*) aspect, side; (*LING*) aspect; **à l'~ de** at the sight of.
asperge [aspɛʀʒ(ə)] *nf* asparagus *q*.
asperger [aspɛʀʒe] *vt* to spray, sprinkle.
aspérité [aspeʀite] *nf* excrescence, protruding bit (of rock *etc*).
aspersion [aspɛʀsjɔ̃] *nf* spraying, sprinkling.
asphalte [asfalt(ə)] *nm* asphalt.
asphyxie [asfiksi] *nf* suffocation, asphyxia, asphyxiation.
asphyxier [asfiksje] *vt* to suffocate, asphyxiate; (*fig*) to stifle; **mourir asphyxié** to die of suffocation *ou* asphyxiation.
aspic [aspik] *nm* (*ZOOL*) asp; (*CULIN*) aspic.
aspirant, e [aspiʀɑ̃, -ɑ̃t] *a*: **pompe ~e** suction pump ♦ *nm* (*NAVIG*) midshipman.
aspirateur [aspiʀatœʀ] *nm* vacuum cleaner, hoover ®.
aspiration [aspiʀasjɔ̃] *nf* inhalation; sucking (up); drawing up; **~s** *nfpl* (*ambitions*) aspirations.
aspirer [aspiʀe] *vt* (*air*) to inhale; (*liquide*) to suck (up); (*suj: appareil*) to suck *ou* draw up; **~ à** *vt* to aspire to.
aspirine [aspiʀin] *nf* aspirin.
assagir [asaʒiʀ] *vt*, **s'~** *vi* to quieten down, sober down.
assaillant, e [asajɑ̃, -ɑ̃t] *nm/f* assailant, attacker.
assaillir [asajiʀ] *vt* to assail, attack; **~ qn de** (*questions*) to assail *ou* bombard sb with.
assainir [aseniʀ] *vt* to clean up; (*eau, air*) to purify.
assainissement [asenismɑ̃] *nm* cleaning up; purifying.
assaisonnement [asɛzɔnmɑ̃] *nm* seasoning.
assaisonner [asɛzɔne] *vt* to season; **bien**

assaisonné highly seasoned.

assassin [asasɛ̃] *nm* murderer; assassin.

assassinat [asasina] *nm* murder; assassination.

assassiner [asasine] *vt* to murder; (*surtout POL*) to assassinate.

assaut [aso] *nm* assault, attack; **prendre d'~** to (take by) storm, assault; **donner l'~ (à)** to attack; **faire ~ de** (*rivaliser*) to vie with *ou* rival each other in.

assèchement [asɛʃmɑ̃] *nm* draining, drainage.

assécher [aseʃe] *vt* to drain.

ASSEDIC [asedik] *sigle f* (= *Association pour l'emploi dans l'industrie et le commerce*) unemployment insurance scheme.

assemblage [asɑ̃blaʒ] *nm* assembling; (*MENUISERIE*) joint; **un ~ de** (*fig*) a collection of; **langage d'~** (*INFORM*) assembly language.

assemblée [asɑ̃ble] *nf* (*réunion*) meeting; (*public, assistance*) gathering; assembled people; (*POL*) assembly; **l'~ des fidèles** the congregation; **l'A~ nationale (AN)** the (French) National Assembly.

assembler [asɑ̃ble] *vt* (*joindre, monter*) to assemble, put together; (*amasser*) to gather (together), collect (together); **s'~** *vi* to gather, collect.

assembleur [asɑ̃blœʀ] *nm* assembler, fitter; (*INFORM*) assembler.

assener, asséner [asene] *vt*: **~ un coup à qn** to deal sb a blow.

assentiment [asɑ̃timɑ̃] *nm* assent, consent; (*approbation*) approval.

asseoir [aswaʀ] *vt* (*malade, bébé*) to sit up; (*personne debout*) to sit down; (*autorité, réputation*) to establish; **s'~** *vi* to sit (o.s.) up; to sit (o.s.) down; **faire ~ qn** to ask sb to sit down; **~ qch sur** to build sth on; (*appuyer*) to base sth on.

assermenté, e [asɛʀmɑ̃te] *a* sworn, on oath.

assertion [asɛʀsjɔ̃] *nf* assertion.

asservir [asɛʀviʀ] *vt* to subjugate, enslave.

assesseur [asesœʀ] *nm* (*JUR*) assessor.

asseyais [aseje] *etc vb voir* **asseoir**.

assez [ase] *ad* (*suffisamment*) enough, sufficiently; (*passablement*) rather, quite, fairly; **~!** enough!, that'll do!; **~/pas ~ cuit** well enough done/underdone; **est-il ~ fort/rapide?** is he strong/fast enough *ou* sufficiently strong/fast?; **il est passé ~ vite** he went past rather *ou* quite *ou* fairly fast; **~ de pain/livres** enough *ou* sufficient bread/books; **vous en avez ~?** have you got enough?; **en avoir ~ de qch** (*en être fatigué*) to have had enough of sth; **travailler ~** to work sufficiently (hard), work (hard) enough.

assidu, e [asidy] *a* assiduous, painstaking; (*régulier*) regular; **~ auprès de qn** attentive towards sb.

assiduité [asidɥite] *nf* assiduousness, painstaking; regularity; attentiveness; **~s** *nfpl* assiduous attentions.

assidûment [asidymɑ̃] *ad* assiduously, painstakingly; attentively.

assied [asje] *etc vb voir* **asseoir**.

assiéger [asjeʒe] *vt* to besiege, lay siege to; (*suj: foule, touristes*) to mob, besiege.

assiérai [asjeʀe] *etc vb voir* **asseoir**.

assiette [asjɛt] *nf* plate; (*contenu*) plate(ful); (*équilibre*) seat; (*de colonne*) seating; (*de navire*) trim; **~ anglaise** assorted cold meats; **~ creuse** (soup) dish, soup plate; **~ à dessert** dessert *ou* side plate; **~ de l'impôt** basis of (tax) assessment; **~ plate** (dinner) plate.

assiettée [asjete] *nf* plateful.

assignation [asiɲasjɔ̃] *nf* assignation; (*JUR*) summons; (*: de témoin*) subpoena; **~ à résidence** compulsory order of residence.

assigner [asiɲe] *vt*: **~ qch à** to assign *ou* allot sth to; (*valeur, importance*) to attach sth to; (*somme*) to allocate sth to; (*limites*) to set *ou* fix sth to; (*cause, effet*) to ascribe *ou* attribute sth to; **~ qn à** (*affecter*) to assign sb to; **~ qn à résidence** (*JUR*) to give sb a compulsory order of residence.

assimilable [asimilabl(ə)] *a* easily assimilated *ou* absorbed.

assimilation [asimilasjɔ̃] *nf* assimilation, absorption.

assimiler [asimile] *vt* to assimilate, absorb; (*comparer*): **~ qch/qn à** to liken *ou* compare sth/sb to; **s'~** *vi* (*s'intégrer*) to be assimilated *ou* absorbed; **ils sont assimilés aux infirmières** (*ADMIN*) they are classed as nurses.

assis, e [asi, -iz] *pp de* **asseoir** ♦ *a* sitting (down), seated ♦ *nf* (*CONSTR*) course; (*GÉO*) stratum (*pl* -a); (*fig*) basis (*pl* bases), foundation; **~ en tailleur** sitting cross-legged.

assises [asiz] *nfpl* (*JUR*) assizes; (*congrès*) (annual) conference.

assistanat [asistana] *nm* assistantship; (*à l'université*) probationary lectureship.

assistance [asistɑ̃s] *nf* (*public*) audience; (*aide*) assistance; **porter *ou* prêter ~ à qn** to give sb assistance; **A~ publique (AP)** *public health service*; **enfant de l'A~ (publique)** (*formerly*) child in care; **~ technique** technical aid.

assistant, e [asistɑ̃, -ɑ̃t] *nm/f* assistant; (*d'université*) probationary lecturer; **les ~s** *nmpl* (*auditeurs etc*) those present; **~e sociale** social worker.

assisté, e [asiste] *a* (*AUTO*) power assisted ♦ *nm/f* person receiving aid from the State.

assister [asiste] *vt* to assist; **~ à** *vt* (*scène, événement*) to witness; (*conférence, séminaire*) to attend, be (present) at; (*spectacle, match*) to be at, see.

association [asɔsjasjɔ̃] *nf* association; (*COMM*) partnership; **~ d'idées/images** association of ideas/images.

associé, e [asɔsje] *nm/f* associate; (*COMM*) partner.

associer [asɔsje] *vt* to associate; **~ qn à** (*profits*) to give sb a share of; (*affaire*) to make sb a partner in; (*joie, triomphe*) to include sb in; **~ qch à** (*joindre, allier*) to combine sth with; **s'~** *vi* to join together; (*COMM*) to form a partnership ♦ *vt* (*collaborateur*) to take on (as a partner); **s'~ à** to be combined with; (*opinions, joie de qn*) to share in; **s'~ à *ou* avec qn pour faire** to join (forces) *ou* join together with sb to do.

assoie [aswa] *etc vb voir* **asseoir**.

assoiffé, e [aswafe] *a* thirsty; *(fig)*: ~ **de** *(sang)* thirsting for; *(gloire)* thirsting after.

assoirai [asware], **assois** [aswa] *etc vb voir* **asseoir**.

assolement [asɔlmɑ̃] *nm* (systematic) rotation of crops.

assombrir [asɔ̃briʀ] *vt* to darken; *(fig)* to fill with gloom; **s'~** *vi* to darken; *(devenir nuageux, fig: visage)* to cloud over; *(fig)* to become gloomy.

assommer [asɔme] *vt (étourdir, abrutir)* to knock out, stun; *(fam: ennuyer)* to bore stiff.

Assomption [asɔ̃psjɔ̃] *nf*: **l'~** the Assumption.

assorti, e [asɔrti] *a* matched, matching; **fromages/légumes ~s** assorted cheeses/vegetables; ~ **à** matching; ~ **de** accompanied with; *(conditions, conseils)* coupled with; **bien/mal** ~ well/ill-matched.

assortiment [asɔrtimɑ̃] *nm (choix)* assortment, selection; *(harmonie de couleurs, formes)* arrangement; *(COMM: lot, stock)* selection.

assortir [asɔrtiʀ] *vt* to match; **s'~** to go well together, match; ~ **qch à** to match sth with; ~ **qch de** to accompany sth with; **s'~ de** to be accompanied by.

assoupi, e [asupi] *a* dozing, sleeping; *(fig)* (be)numbed; *(sens)* dulled.

assoupir [asupiʀ]: **s'~** *vi (personne)* to doze off; *(sens)* to go numb.

assoupissement [asupismɑ̃] *nm (sommeil)* dozing; *(fig: somnolence)* drowsiness.

assouplir [asupliʀ] *vt* to make supple, soften; *(membres, corps)* to limber up, make supple; *(fig)* to relax; *(: caractère)* to soften, make more flexible; **s'~** *vi* to soften; to limber up; to relax; to become more flexible.

assouplissement [asuplismɑ̃] *nm* softening; limbering up; relaxation; **exercices d'~** limbering up exercises.

assourdir [asurdiʀ] *vt (bruit)* to deaden, muffle; *(suj: bruit)* to deafen.

assourdissant, e [asurdisɑ̃, -ɑ̃t] *a (bruit)* deafening.

assouvir [asuviʀ] *vt* to satisfy, appease.

assoyais [aswajɛ] *etc vb voir* **asseoir**.

ASSU [asy] *sigle f* = **Association du sport scolaire et universitaire**.

assujetti, e [asyʒeti] *a*: ~ **(à)** subject (to); *(ADMIN)*: ~ **à l'impôt** subject to tax(ation).

assujettir [asyʒetiʀ] *vt* to subject, subjugate; *(fixer: planches, tableau)* to secure, fix securely; ~ **qn à** *(règle, impôt)* to subject sb to.

assujettissement [asyʒetismɑ̃] *nm* subjection, subjugation.

assumer [asyme] *vt (fonction, emploi)* to assume, take on; *(accepter: conséquence, situation)* to accept.

assurance [asyrɑ̃s] *nf (certitude)* assurance; *(confiance en soi)* (self-)confidence; *(contrat)* insurance (policy); *(secteur commercial)* insurance; **prendre une ~ contre** to take out insurance *ou* an insurance policy against; ~ **contre l'incendie** fire insurance; ~ **contre le vol** insurance against theft; **société d'~, compagnie d'~s** insurance company; ~ **maladie (AM)** health insurance; ~ **au tiers** third party insurance; ~ **tous risques** *(AUTO)* comprehensive insurance; **~s sociales (AS)** ≈ National Insurance *(Brit)*, ≈ Social Security *(US)*.

assurance-vie, *pl* **assurances-vie** [asyrɑ̃svi] *nf* life assurance *ou* insurance.

assurance-vol, *pl* **assurances-vol** [asyrɑ̃svɔl] *nf* insurance against theft.

assuré, e [asyre] *a (victoire etc)* certain, sure; *(démarche, voix)* assured, (self-)confident; *(certain)*: ~ **de** confident of; *(ASSURANCES)* insured ♦ *nm/f* insured (person); ~ **social** ≈ member of the National Insurance *(Brit)* *ou* Social Security *(US)* scheme.

assurément [asyremɑ̃] *ad* assuredly, most certainly.

assurer [asyre] *vt (COMM)* to insure; *(stabiliser)* to steady, stabilize; *(victoire etc)* to ensure, make certain; *(frontières, pouvoir)* to make secure; *(service, garde)* to provide, operate; ~ **qch à qn** *(garantir)* to secure *ou* guarantee sth for sb; *(certifier)* to assure sb of sth; ~ **à qn que** to assure sb that; **je vous assure que non/si** I assure you that that is not the case/is the case; ~ **qn de** to assure sb of; ~ **ses arrières** *(fig)* to be sure one has something to fall back on; **s'~** *(contre)* *(COMM)* to insure o.s. (against); **s'~ de/que** *(vérifier)* to make sure of/that; **s'~ (de)** *(aide de qn)* to secure; **s'~ sur la vie** to take out a life insurance; **s'~ le concours/la collaboration de qn** to secure sb's aid/collaboration.

assureur [asyrœʀ] *nm* insurance agent; *(société)* insurers *pl*.

Assyrie [asiri] *nf*: **l'~** Assyria.

assyrien, ne [asirjɛ̃, -ɛn] *a* Assyrian.

astérisque [asterisk(ə)] *nm* asterisk.

asthmatique [asmatik] *a* asthmatic.

asthme [asm(ə)] *nm* asthma.

asticot [astiko] *nm* maggot.

astigmate [astigmat] *a (MÉD: personne)* astigmatic, having an astigmatism.

astiquer [astike] *vt* to polish, shine.

astrakan [astrakɑ̃] *nm* astrakhan.

astral, e, aux [astral, -o] *a* astral.

astre [astr(ə)] *nm* star.

astreignant, e [astreɲɑ̃, -ɑ̃t] *a* demanding.

astreindre [astrɛ̃dr(ə)] *vt*: ~ **qn à qch** to force sth upon sb; ~ **qn à faire** to compel *ou* force sb to do; **s'~ à** to compel *ou* force o.s. to.

astringent, e [astrɛ̃ʒɑ̃, -ɑ̃t] *a* astringent.

astrologie [astrɔlɔʒi] *nf* astrology.

astrologique [astrɔlɔʒik] *a* astrological.

astrologue [astrɔlɔg] *nm/f* astrologer.

astronaute [astrɔnot] *nm/f* astronaut.

astronome [astrɔnɔm] *nm/f* astronomer.

astronomie [astrɔnɔmi] *nf* astronomy.

astronomique [astrɔnɔmik] *a* astronomic(al).

astrophysicien, ne [astrɔfizisjɛ̃, -ɛn] *nm/f* astrophysicist.

astuce [astys] *nf* shrewdness, astuteness; *(truc)* trick, clever way; *(plaisanterie)* wisecrack.

astucieusement [astysjøzmɑ̃] *ad* shrewdly, cleverly, astutely.

astucieux, euse [astysjø, -øz] *a* shrewd,

clever, astute.
asymétrique [asimetʀik] *a* asymmetric(al).
AT *sigle m* (= *Ancien Testament*) OT.
atavisme [atavism(ə)] *nm* atavism, heredity.
atelier [atəlje] *nm* workshop; (*de peintre*) studio.
atermoiements [atɛʀmwamɑ̃] *nmpl* procrastination *sg*.
atermoyer [atɛʀmwaje] *vi* to temporize, procrastinate.
athée [ate] *a* atheistic ♦ *nm/f* atheist.
athéisme [ateism(ə)] *nm* atheism.
Athènes [atɛn] *n* Athens.
athénien, ne [atenjɛ̃, -ɛn] *a* Athenian.
athlète [atlɛt] *nm/f* (*SPORT*) athlete; (*costaud*) muscleman.
athlétique [atletik] *a* athletic.
athlétisme [atletism(ə)] *nm* athletics *sg*; **faire de l'~** to do athletics; **tournoi d'~** athletics meeting.
Atlantide [atlɑ̃tid] *nf*: **l'~** Atlantis.
atlantique [atlɑ̃tik] *a* Atlantic ♦ *nm*: **l'(océan) A~** the Atlantic (Ocean).
atlantiste [atlɑ̃tist(ə)] *a, nm/f* Atlanticist.
Atlas [atlɑs] *nm*: **l'~** the Atlas Mountains.
atlas [atlɑs] *nm* atlas.
atmosphère [atmɔsfɛʀ] *nf* atmosphere.
atmosphérique [atmɔsferik] *a* atmospheric.
atoll [atɔl] *nm* atoll.
atome [atom] *nm* atom.
atomique [atɔmik] *a* atomic, nuclear; (*usine*) nuclear; (*nombre, masse*) atomic.
atomiseur [atɔmizœʀ] *nm* atomizer.
atomiste [atɔmist(ə)] *nm/f* (*aussi*: **savant, ingénieur** *etc* ~) atomic scientist.
atone [atɔn] *a* lifeless; (*LING*) unstressed, unaccented.
atours [atuʀ] *nmpl* attire *sg*, finery *sg*.
atout [atu] *nm* trump; (*fig*) asset; (: *plus fort*) trump card; **"~ pique/trèfle"** "spades/clubs are trumps".
ATP *sigle f* (= *Association des tennismen professionnels*) ATP (= *Association of Tennis Professionals*) ♦ *sigle mpl* (= *arts et traditions populaires*): **musée des ~** ≈ folk museum.
âtre [ɑtʀ(ə)] *nm* hearth.
atroce [atʀɔs] *a* atrocious, horrible.
atrocement [atʀɔsmɑ̃] *ad* atrociously, horribly.
atrocité [atʀɔsite] *nf* atrocity.
atrophie [atʀɔfi] *nf* atrophy.
atrophier [atʀɔfje]: **s'~** *vi* to atrophy.
atropine [atʀɔpin] *nf* (*CHIMIE*) atropine.
attabler [atable]: **s'~** *vi* to sit down at (the) table; **s'~ à la terrasse** to sit down (at a table) on the terrace.
attachant, e [ataʃɑ̃, -ɑ̃t] *a* engaging, likeable.
attache [ataʃ] *nf* clip, fastener; (*fig*) tie; **~s** *nfpl* (*relations*) connections; **à l'~** (*chien*) tied up.
attaché, e [ataʃe] *a*: **être ~ à** (*aimer*) to be attached to ♦ *nm* (*ADMIN*) attaché; **~ de presse/d'ambassade** press/embassy attaché; **~ commercial** commercial attaché.
attaché-case [ataʃekɛz] *nm inv* attaché case (*Brit*), briefcase.
attachement [ataʃmɑ̃] *nm* attachment.
attacher [ataʃe] *vt* to tie up; (*étiquette*) to

attach, tie on; (*souliers*) to do up ♦ *vi* (*poêle, riz*) to stick; **s'~** (*robe etc*) to do up; **s'~ à** (*par affection*) to become attached to; **s'~ à faire qch** to endeavour to do sth; **~ qch à** to tie *ou* fasten *ou* attach sth to; **~ qn à** (*fig: lier*) to attach sb to; **~ du prix/de l'importance à** to attach great value/attach importance to.
attaquant [atakɑ̃] *nm* (*MIL*) attacker; (*SPORT*) striker, forward.
attaque [atak] *nf* attack; (*cérébrale*) stroke; (*d'épilepsie*) fit; **être/se sentir d'~** to be/feel on form; **~ à main armée** armed attack.
attaquer [atake] *vt* to attack; (*en justice*) to bring an action against, sue; (*travail*) to tackle, set about ♦ *vi* to attack; **s'~ à** to attack; (*épidémie, misère*) to tackle, attack.
attardé, e [ataʀde] *a* (*passants*) late; (*enfant*) backward; (*conceptions*) old-fashioned.
attarder [ataʀde]: **s'~** *vi* (*sur qch, en chemin*) to linger; (*chez qn*) to stay on.
atteignais [atɛɲɛ] *etc vb voir* **atteindre**.
atteindre [atɛ̃dʀ(ə)] *vt* to reach; (*blesser*) to hit; (*contacter*) to reach, contact, get in touch with; (*émouvoir*) to affect.
atteint, e [atɛ̃, -ɛ̃t] *pp de* **atteindre** ♦ *a* (*MÉD*): **être ~ de** to be suffering from ♦ *nf* attack; **hors d'~e** out of reach; **porter ~e à** to strike a blow at, undermine.
attelage [atlaʒ] *nm* (*de remorque etc*) coupling (*Brit*), (trailer) hitch (*US*); (*animaux*) team; (*harnachement*) harness; (: *de bœufs*) yoke.
atteler [atle] *vt* (*cheval, bœufs*) to hitch up; (*wagons*) to couple; **s'~ à** (*travail*) to buckle down to.
attelle [atɛl] *nf* splint.
attenant, e [atnɑ̃, -ɑ̃t] *a*: **~ (à)** adjoining.
attendant [atɑ̃dɑ̃]: **en ~** *ad* (*dans l'intervalle*) meanwhile, in the meantime.
attendre [atɑ̃dʀ(ə)] *vt* to wait for; (*être destiné ou réservé à*) to await, be in store for ♦ *vi* to wait; **je n'attends plus rien (de la vie)** I expect nothing more (from life); **attendez que je réfléchisse** wait while I think; **s'~ à (ce que)** (*escompter*) to expect (that); **je ne m'y attendais pas** I didn't expect that; **ce n'est pas ce à quoi je m'attendais** that's not what I expected; **~ un enfant** to be expecting a baby; **~ de pied ferme** to wait determinedly; **~ de faire/d'être** to wait until one does/is; **~ que** to wait until; **~ qch de** to expect sth of; **faire ~ qn** to keep sb waiting; **se faire ~** to keep people (*ou us etc*) waiting; **en attendant** *ad voir* **attendant**.
attendri, e [atɑ̃dʀi] *a* tender.
attendrir [atɑ̃dʀiʀ] *vt* to move (to pity); (*viande*) to tenderize; **s'~ (sur)** to be moved *ou* touched (by).
attendrissant, e [atɑ̃dʀisɑ̃, -ɑ̃t] *a* moving, touching.
attendrissement [atɑ̃dʀismɑ̃] *nm* (*tendre*) emotion; (*apitoyé*) pity.
attendrisseur [atɑ̃dʀisœʀ] *nm* tenderizer.
attendu, e [atɑ̃dy] *pp de* **attendre** ♦ *a* a long-awaited; (*prévu*) expected ♦ *nm*: **~s** reasons adduced for a judgment; **~ que** *cj* considering that, since.
attentat [atɑ̃ta] *nm* (*contre une personne*)

assassination attempt; (*contre un bâtiment*) attack; ~ **à la bombe** bomb attack; ~ **à la pudeur** (*exhibitionnisme*) indecent exposure *q*; (*agression*) indecent assault *q*.

attente [atɑ̃t] *nf* wait; (*espérance*) expectation; **contre toute** ~ contrary to (all) expectations.

attenter [atɑ̃te]: ~ **à** *vt* (*liberté*) to violate; ~ **à la vie de qn** to make an attempt on sb's life; ~ **à ses jours** to make an attempt on one's life.

attentif, ive [atɑ̃tif, -iv] *a* (*auditeur*) attentive; (*soin*) scrupulous; (*travail*) careful; ~ **à paying attention to**; (*devoir*) mindful of; ~ **à faire** careful to do.

attention [atɑ̃sjɔ̃] *nf* attention; (*prévenance*) attention, thoughtfulness *q*; **mériter** ~ to be worthy of attention; **à l'~ de** for the attention of; **porter qch à l'~ de qn** to bring sth to sb's attention; **attirer l'~ de qn sur qch** to draw sb's attention to sth; **faire** ~ **(à)** to be careful (of); **faire** ~ **(à ce) que** to be *ou* make sure that; **~!** careful!, watch!, watch *ou* mind (*Brit*) out!; **~, si vous ouvrez cette lettre** (*sanction*) just watch out, if you open that letter; **~, respectez les consignes de sécurité** be sure to observe the safety instructions.

attentionné, e [atɑ̃sjɔne] *a* thoughtful, considerate.

attentisme [atɑ̃tism(ə)] *nm* wait-and-see policy.

attentiste [atɑ̃tist(ə)] *a* (*politique*) wait-and-see ♦ *nm/f* believer in a wait-and-see policy.

attentivement [atɑ̃tivmɑ̃] *ad* attentively.

atténuant, e [atenɥɑ̃, -ɑ̃t] *a*: **circonstances ~es** extenuating circumstances.

atténuer [atenɥe] *vt* to alleviate, ease; (*diminuer*) to lessen; (*amoindrir*) to mitigate the effects of; **s'~** *vi* to ease; (*violence etc*) to abate.

atterrer [atere] *vt* to dismay, appal.

atterrir [ateʀiʀ] *vi* to land.

atterrissage [ateʀisaʒ] *nm* landing; ~ **sur le ventre/sans visibilité/forcé** belly/blind/forced landing.

attestation [atɛstɑsjɔ̃] *nf* certificate, testimonial; ~ **médicale** doctor's certificate.

attester [atɛste] *vt* to testify to, vouch for; (*démontrer*) to attest, testify to; ~ **que** to testify that.

attiédir [atjediʀ]: **s'~** *vi* to become lukewarm; (*fig*) to cool down.

attifé, e [atife] *a* (*fam*) got up (*Brit*), decked out.

attifer [atife] *vt* to get (*Brit*) *ou* do up, deck out.

attique [atik] *nm*: **appartement en ~** penthouse (flat (*Brit*) *ou* apartment (*US*)).

attirail [atiʀaj] *nm* gear; (*péj*) paraphernalia.

attirance [atiʀɑ̃s] *nf* attraction; (*séduction*) lure.

attirant, e [atiʀɑ̃, -ɑ̃t] *a* attractive, appealing.

attirer [atiʀe] *vt* to attract; (*appâter*) to lure, entice; ~ **qn dans un coin/vers soi** to draw sb into a corner/towards one; ~ **l'attention de qn** to attract sb's attention; ~ **l'attention de qn sur qch** to draw sb's attention to sth; ~ **des ennuis à qn** to make trouble for sb;

s'~ des ennuis to bring trouble upon o.s., get into trouble.

attiser [atize] *vt* (*feu*) to poke (up), stir up; (*fig*) to fan the flame of, stir up.

attitré, e [atitʀe] *a* qualified; (*agréé*) accredited, appointed.

attitude [atityd] *nf* attitude; (*position du corps*) bearing.

attouchements [atuʃmɑ̃] *nmpl* touching *sg*; (*sexuels*) fondling *sg*, stroking *sg*.

attraction [atʀaksjɔ̃] *nf* attraction; (*de cabaret, cirque*) number.

attrait [atʀɛ] *nm* appeal, attraction; (*plus fort*) lure; **~s** *nmpl* attractions; **éprouver de l'~ pour** to be attracted to.

attrape [atʀap] *nf voir* **farce**.

attrape-nigaud [atʀapnigo] *nm* con.

attraper [atʀape] *vt* to catch; (*habitude, amende*) to get, pick up; (*fam: duper*) to take in (*Brit*), con.

attrayant, e [atʀɛjɑ̃, -ɑ̃t] *a* attractive.

attribuer [atʀibɥe] *vt* (*prix*) to award; (*rôle, tâche*) to allocate, assign; (*imputer*): ~ **qch à** to attribute sth to, ascribe sth to, put sth down to; **s'~** *vt* (*s'approprier*) to claim for o.s.

attribut [atʀiby] *nm* attribute; (*LING*) complement.

attribution [atʀibysjɔ̃] *nf* (*voir* **attribuer**) awarding; allocation, assignment; attribution; **~s** *nfpl* (*compétence*) attributions; **complément d'~** (*LING*) indirect object.

attrister [atʀiste] *vt* to sadden; **s'~ de qch** to be saddened by sth.

attroupement [atʀupmɑ̃] *nm* crowd, mob.

attrouper [atʀupe]: **s'~** *vi* to gather.

au [o] *prép* + *dét voir* **à**.

aubade [obad] *nf* dawn serenade.

aubaine [obɛn] *nf* godsend; (*financière*) windfall; (*COMM*) bonanza.

aube [ob] *nf* dawn, daybreak; (*REL*) alb; **à l'~** at dawn *ou* daybreak; **à l'~ de** (*fig*) at the dawn of.

aubépine [obepin] *nf* hawthorn.

auberge [obɛʀʒ(ə)] *nf* inn; ~ **de jeunesse** youth hostel.

aubergine [obɛʀʒin] *nf* aubergine (*Brit*), eggplant (*US*).

aubergiste [obɛʀʒist(ə)] *nm/f* inn-keeper, hotel-keeper.

auburn [obœʀn] *a inv* auburn.

aucun, e [okœ̃, -yn] *dét no, tournure négative* + *any*; (*positif*) *any* ♦ *pronom* none, *tournure négative* + *any*; (*positif*) *any(one)*; **il n'y a ~ livre** there's no book, there is no book; **je n'en vois ~ qui** I can't see any which, I (can) see none which; ~ **homme** no man; **sans ~ doute** without any doubt; **sans ~e hésitation** without hesitation; **plus qu'~ autre** more than any other; **plus qu'~ de ceux qui** ... more than any of those who ...; **en ~e façon** in no way at all; ~ **des deux** neither of the two; ~ **d'entre eux** none of them; **d'~s** (*certains*) some.

aucunement [okynmɑ̃] *ad* in no way, not in the least.

audace [odas] *nf* daring, boldness; (*péj*) audacity; **il a eu l'~ de ...** he had the audacity to ...; **vous ne manquez pas d'~!**

you're not lacking in nerve *ou* cheek!
audacieux, euse [odasjø, -øz] *a* daring, bold.
au-dedans [odədɑ̃] *ad, prép* inside.
au-dehors [odəɔr] *ad, prép* outside.
au-delà [odla] *ad* beyond ♦ *nm*: **l'~** the here-after; **~ de** *prép* beyond.
au-dessous [odsu] *ad* underneath; below; **~ de** *prép* under(neath), below; (*limite, somme etc*) below, under; (*dignité, condition*) below.
au-dessus [odsy] *ad* above; **~ de** *prép* above.
au-devant [odvɑ̃]: **~ de** *prép*: **aller ~ de** to go (out) and meet; (*souhaits de qn*) to antici-pate.
audible [odibl(ə)] *a* audible.
audience [odjɑ̃s] *nf* audience; (*JUR*: *séance*) hearing; **trouver ~ auprès de** to arouse much interest among, get the (interested) attention of.
audiogramme [odjɔgram] *nm* audiogramme.
audio-visuel, le [odjɔvizɥɛl] *a* audio-visual ♦ *nm* (*équipement*) audio-visual aids *pl*; (*méthodes*) audio-visual methods *pl*; **l'~** radio and television.
auditeur, trice [oditœr, -tris] *nm/f* (*à la radio*) listener; (*à une conférence*) member of the audience, listener; **~ libre** unregistered student (*attending lectures*), auditor (*US*).
auditif, ive [oditif, -iv] (*mémoire*) auditory; **appareil ~** hearing aid.
audition [odisjɔ̃] *nf* (*ouïe, écoute*) hearing; (*JUR*: *de témoins*) examination; (*MUS, THÉÂTRE*: *épreuve*) audition.
auditionner [odisjɔne] *vt, vi* to audition.
auditoire [oditwar] *nm* audience.
auditorium [oditɔrjɔm] *nm* (public) studio.
auge [oʒ] *nf* trough.
augmentation [ɔgmɑ̃tasjɔ̃] *nf* (*action*) in-creasing; raising; (*résultat*) increase; **~ (de salaire)** rise (in salary) (*Brit*), (pay) raise (*US*).
augmenter [ɔgmɑ̃te] *vt* to increase; (*salaire, prix*) to increase, raise, put up; (*employé*) to increase the salary of, give a (salary) rise (*Brit*) *ou* (pay) raise (*US*) to ♦ *vi* to in-crease; **~ de poids/volume** to gain (in) weight/volume.
augure [ɔgyr] *nm* soothsayer, oracle; **de bon/mauvais ~** of good/ill omen.
augurer [ɔgyre] *vt*: **~ qch de** to foresee sth (coming) from *ou* out of; **~ bien de** to augur well for.
auguste [ɔgyst(ə)] *a* august, noble, majestic.
aujourd'hui [oʒurdɥi] *ad* today; **~ en huit/quinze** a week/two weeks today, a week/two weeks from now; **à dater** *ou* **partir d'~** from today('s date).
aumône [omon] *nf* alms *sg* (*pl inv*); **faire l'~ (à qn)** to give alms (to sb); **faire l'~ de qch à qn** (*fig*) to favour sb with sth.
aumônerie [omonri] *nf* chaplaincy.
aumônier [omonje] *nm* chaplain.
auparavant [oparavɑ̃] *ad* before(hand).
auprès [oprɛ]: **~ de** *prép* next to, close to; (*recourir, s'adresser*) to; (*en comparaison de*) compared with, next to; (*dans l'opinion de*) in the opinion of.
auquel [okɛl] *prép* + *pronom voir* **lequel**.
aurai [ɔre] *etc vb voir* **avoir**.
auréole [ɔreɔl] *nf* halo; (*tache*) ring.

auréolé, e [ɔreɔle] *a* (*fig*): **~ de gloire** crowned with *ou* in glory.
auriculaire [ɔrikylɛr] *nm* little finger.
aurore [ɔrɔr] *nf* dawn, daybreak; **~ boréale** northern lights *pl*.
ausculter [ɔskylte] *vt* to sound.
auspices [ɔspis] *nmpl*: **sous les ~ de** under the patronage *ou* auspices of; **sous de bons/mauvais ~** under favourable/unfavourable auspices.
aussi [osi] *ad* (*également*) also, too; (*comparaison*) as ♦ *cj* therefore, consequently; **~ fort que** as strong as; **lui ~** (*sujet*) he too; (*objet*) him too; **~ bien que** (*de même que*) as well as.
aussitôt [osito] *ad* straight away, immediately; **~ que** as soon as; **~ envoyé** as soon as it is (*ou* was) sent; **~ fait** no sooner done.
austère [ɔstɛr] *a* austere; (*sévère*) stern.
austérité [ɔsterite] *nf* austerity; **plan/budget d'~** austerity plan/budget.
austral, e [ɔstral] *a* southern; **l'océan A~** the Antarctic Ocean; **les Terres A~es** Antarctica.
Australie [ɔstrali] *nf*: **l'~** Australia.
australien, ne [ɔstraljɛ̃, -ɛn] *a* Australian ♦ *nm/f*: **A~, ne** Australian.
autant [otɑ̃] *ad* so much; (*comparatif*): **~ (que)** as much (as); (*nombre*) as many (as); **~ (de)** so much (*ou* many); as much (*ou* many); **n'importe qui aurait pu en faire ~** anyone could have done the same *ou* as much; **~ partir we** (*ou* you *etc*) may as well leave; **~ ne rien dire** best not say anything; **~ dire que** ... one might as well say that ...; **fort ~ que courageux** as strong as he is brave; **il n'est pas découragé pour ~** he isn't discouraged for all that; **pour ~ que** *cj* assuming, as long as; **d'~ ad** accordingly, in proportion; **d'~ plus/mieux (que)** all the more/the better (since).
autarcie [otarsi] *nf* autarky, self-sufficiency.
autel [otɛl] *nm* altar.
auteur [otœr] *nm* author; **l'~ de cette remarque** the person who said that; **droit d'~** copyright.
authenticité [otɑ̃tisite] *nf* authenticity.
authentifier [otɑ̃tifje] *vt* to authenticate.
authentique [otɑ̃tik] *a* authentic, genuine.
auto [oto] *nf* car; **~s tamponneuses** bumper cars, dodgems.
auto... [oto] *préfixe* auto..., self-.
autobiographie [otɔbjɔgrafi] *nf* autobiog-raphy.
autobiographique [otɔbjɔgrafik] *a* autobio-graphical.
autobus [otɔbys] *nm* bus.
autocar [otɔkar] *nm* coach.
autochtone [otɔktɔn] *nm/f* native.
autocollant, e [otɔkɔlɑ̃, -ɑ̃t] *a* self-adhesive; (*enveloppe*) self-seal ♦ *nm* sticker.
auto-couchettes [otɔkuʃɛt] *a inv*: **train ~** car sleeper train, motorail ® train (*Brit*).
autocratique [otɔkratik] *a* autocratic.
autocritique [otɔkritik] *nf* self-criticism.
autocuiseur [otɔkwizœr] *nm* (*CULIN*) pressure cooker.
autodéfense [otɔdefɑ̃s] *nf* self-defence;

groupe d'~ vigilante committee.

autodétermination [ɔtɔdetɛrminasjɔ̃] *nf* self-determination.

autodidacte [ɔtɔdidakt(ə)] *nm/f* self-taught person.

autodiscipline [ɔtɔdisiplin] *nf* self-discipline.

autodrome [ɔtɔdrom] *nm* motor-racing stadium.

auto-école [ɔtɔekɔl] *nf* driving school.

autofinancement [ɔtɔfinɑ̃smɑ̃] *nm* self-financing.

autogéré, e [ɔtɔʒere] *a* self-managed, managed internally.

autographe [ɔtɔgraf] *nm* autograph.

autoguidé, e [ɔtɔgide] *a* self-guided.

automate [ɔtɔmat] *nm* (*robot*) automaton; (*machine*) (automatic) machine.

automatique [ɔtɔmatik] *a*, *nm* automatic; **l'~** (*TÉL*) ≈ direct dialling.

automatiquement [ɔtɔmatikmɑ̃] *ad* automatically.

automatiser [ɔtɔmatize] *vt* to automate.

automatisme [ɔtɔmatism(ə)] *nm* automatism.

automédication [ɔtɔmedikasjɔ̃] *nf* self-medication.

automitrailleuse [ɔtɔmitrajøz] *nf* armoured car.

automnal, e, aux [ɔtɔnal, -o] *a* autumnal.

automne [ɔtɔn] *nm* autumn (*Brit*), fall (*US*).

automobile [ɔtɔmɔbil] *a* motor *cpd* ♦ *nf* (motor) car; **l'~** motoring; (*industrie*) the car *ou* automobile (*US*) industry.

automobiliste [ɔtɔmɔbilist(ə)] *nm/f* motorist.

autonettoyant, e [ɔtɔnɛtwajɑ̃, -ɑ̃t] *a*: **four ~** self-cleaning oven.

autonome [ɔtɔnɔm] *a* autonomous; (*INFORM*) stand-alone; **(en mode) ~** off line.

autonomie [ɔtɔnɔmi] *nf* autonomy; (*POL*) self-government, autonomy; **~ de vol** range.

autoportrait [ɔtɔpɔrtrɛ] *nm* self-portrait.

autopsie [ɔtɔpsi] *nf* post-mortem (examination), autopsy.

autopsier [ɔtɔpsje] *vt* to carry out a post-mortem *ou* an autopsy on.

autoradio [ɔtɔradjo] *nf* car radio.

autorail [ɔtɔraj] *nm* railcar.

autorisation [ɔtɔrizasjɔ̃] *nf* permission, authorization; (*papiers*) permit; **donner à qn l'~ de** to give sb permission to, authorize sb to; **avoir l'~ de faire** to be allowed *ou* have permission to do, be authorized to do.

autorisé, e [ɔtɔrize] *a* (*opinion, sources*) authoritative; (*permis*): **~ à faire** authorized *ou* permitted to do; **dans les milieux ~s** in official circles.

autoriser [ɔtɔrize] *vt* to give permission for, authorize; (*fig*) to allow (of), sanction; **~ qn à faire** to give permission to sb to do, authorize sb to do.

autoritaire [ɔtɔritɛr] *a* authoritarian.

autoritarisme [ɔtɔritarism(ə)] *nm* authoritarianism.

autorité [ɔtɔrite] *nf* authority; **faire ~** to be authoritative; **~s constituées** constitutional authorities.

autoroute [ɔtɔrut] *nf* motorway (*Brit*), expressway (*US*).

autoroutier, ière [ɔtɔrutje, -jɛr] *a* motorway *cpd* (*Brit*), expressway *cpd* (*US*).

autosatisfaction [ɔtɔsatisfaksjɔ̃] *nf* self-satisfaction.

auto-stop [ɔtɔstɔp] *nm*: **l'~** hitch-hiking; **faire de l'~** to hitch-hike; **prendre qn en ~** to give sb a lift.

auto-stoppeur, euse [ɔtɔstɔpœr, -øz] *nm/f* hitch-hiker, hitcher (*Brit*).

autosuffisant, e [ɔtɔsyfizɑ̃, -ɑ̃t] *a* self-sufficient.

autosuggestion [ɔtɔsygʒɛstjɔ̃] *nf* autosuggestion.

autour [otur] *ad* around; **~ de** *prép* around; (*environ*) around, about; **tout ~** *ad* all around.

autre [otr(ə)] *a* other; **un ~ verre** (*supplémentaire*) one more glass, another glass; (*différent*) another glass, a different glass; **un ~** another (one); **l'~** the other (one); **les ~s** (*autrui*) others; **l'un et l'~** both (of them); **se détester** *etc* **l'un l'~/les uns les ~s** to hate *etc* each other/one another; **ni l'un ni l'~** neither (one) of them; **d'une semaine à l'~** from one week to the next; (*incessamment*) any week now; **de temps à ~** from time to time; **d'~s** others; **d'~s verres** other glasses; **j'en ai vu d'~s** I've seen worse; **à d'~s!** tell that to the marines!; **se sentir ~** to feel different; **la difficulté est ~** the difficulty is not there, that's not the difficulty; **~ chose** something else; **~ part** *ad* somewhere else; **d'~ part** *ad* on the other hand; **entre ~s** (*gens*) among others; (*choses*) among other things; **nous/vous ~s** us/you.

autrefois [otrəfwa] *ad* in the past.

autrement [otrəmɑ̃] *ad* differently; (*d'une manière différente*) in another way; (*sinon*) otherwise; **je n'ai pas pu faire ~** I couldn't do anything else, I couldn't do otherwise; **~ dit** in other words; (*c'est-à-dire*) that is to say.

Autriche [otriʃ] *nf*: **l'~** Austria.

autrichien, ne [otriʃjɛ̃, -ɛn] *a* Austrian ♦ *nm/f*: **A~, ne** Austrian.

autruche [otryʃ] *nf* ostrich; **faire l'~** (*fig*) to bury one's head in the sand.

autrui [otrui] *pronom* others.

auvent [ovɑ̃] *nm* canopy.

auvergnat, e [ovɛrɲa, -at] *a* of *ou* from the Auvergne.

Auvergne [ovɛrɲ(ə)] *nf*: **l'~** the Auvergne.

aux [o] *prép* + *dét voir* **à**.

auxiliaire [ɔksiljɛr] *a*, *nm/f* auxiliary.

auxquels, auxquelles [okɛl] *prép* + *pronom voir* **lequel**.

AV *sigle m* (*BANQUE*: = *avis de virement*) advice of bank transfer ♦ *abr* (*AUTO*) = **avant**.

av. *abr* (= *avenue*) Av(e).

avachi, e [avaʃi] *a* limp, flabby; (*chaussure, vêtement*) out-of-shape; (*personne*): **~ sur qch** slumped on *ou* across sth.

avais [avɛ] *etc vb voir* **avoir**.

aval [aval] *nm* (*accord*) endorsement, backing; (*GÉO*): **en ~** downstream, downriver; (*sur une pente*) downhill; **en ~ de** downstream *ou* downriver from; downhill from.

avalanche [avalɑ̃ʃ] *nf* avalanche; **~ poudreuse** powder snow avalanche.

avaler [avale] *vt* to swallow.

avaliser [avalize] *vt* (*plan, entreprise*) to back, support; (*COMM, JUR*) to guarantee.

avance [avɑ̃s] *nf* (*de troupes etc*) advance; (*progrès*) progress; (*d'argent*) advance; (*opposé à retard*) lead; being ahead of schedule; **~s** *nfpl* overtures; (*amoureuses*) advances; **une ~ de 300 m/4 h** (*SPORT*) a 300 m/4 hour lead; (**être**) **en ~** (to be) early; (*sur un programme*) (to be) ahead of schedule; **on n'est pas en ~!** we're kind of late!; **être en ~ sur qn** to be ahead of sb; **d'~, à l'~, par ~** in advance; **~ (du) papier** (*INFORM*) paper advance.

avancé, e [avɑ̃se] *a* advanced; (*travail etc*) well on, well under way; (*fruit, fromage*) overripe ♦ *nf* projection; overhang; **il est ~ pour son âge** he is advanced for his age.

avancement [avɑ̃smɑ̃] *nm* (*professionnel*) promotion; (*de travaux*) progress.

avancer [avɑ̃se] *vi* to move forward, advance; (*projet, travail*) to make progress; (*être en saillie*) to overhang; to project; (*montre, réveil*) to be fast; (: *d'habitude*) to gain ♦ *vt* to move forward, advance; (*argent*) to advance; (*montre, pendule*) to put forward; (*faire progresser: travail etc*) to advance, move on; **s'~** *vi* to move forward, advance; (*fig*) to commit o.s.; (*faire saillie*) to overhang; to project; **j'avance (d'une heure)** I'm (an hour) fast.

avanies [avani] *nfpl* snubs (*Brit*), insults.

avant [avɑ̃] *prép* before ♦ *ad*: **trop/plus ~** too far/further forward ♦ *a inv*: **siège/roue ~** front seat/wheel ♦ *nm* front; (*SPORT: joueur*) forward; **~ qu'il parte/de partir** before he leaves/leaving; **~ qu'il (ne) pleuve** before it rains (*ou* rained); **~ tout** (*surtout*) above all; **à l'~** (*dans un véhicule*) in (the) front; **en ~** *ad* forward(s); **en ~ de** *prép* in front of; **aller de l'~** to steam ahead (*fig*), make good progress.

avantage [avɑ̃taʒ] *nm* advantage; (*TENNIS*): **~ service/dehors** advantage *ou* van (*Brit*) *ou* ad (*US*) in/out; **tirer ~ de** to take advantage of; **vous auriez ~ à faire** you would be well-advised to do, it would be to your advantage to do; **à l'~ de qn** to sb's advantage; **être à son ~** to be at one's best; **~s en nature** benefits in kind; **~s sociaux** fringe benefits.

avantager [avɑ̃taʒe] *vt* (*favoriser*) to favour; (*embellir*) to flatter.

avantageux, euse [avɑ̃taʒø, -øz] *a* attractive; (*intéressant*) attractively priced; (*portrait, coiffure*) flattering; **conditions avantageuses** favourable terms.

avant-bras [avɑ̃bra] *nm inv* forearm.

avant-centre [avɑ̃sɑ̃tʀ(ə)] *nm* centre-forward.

avant-coureur [avɑ̃kuʀœʀ] *a inv* (*bruit etc*) precursory; **signe ~** advance indication *ou* sign.

avant-dernier, ière [avɑ̃dɛʀnje, -jɛʀ] *a, nm/f* next to last, last but one.

avant-garde [avɑ̃gaʀd(ə)] *nf* (*MIL*) vanguard; (*fig*) avant-garde; **d'~** avant-garde.

avant-goût [avɑ̃gu] *nm* foretaste.

avant-hier [avɑ̃tjɛʀ] *ad* the day before yesterday.

avant-poste [avɑ̃pɔst(ə)] *nm* outpost.

avant-première [avɑ̃pʀəmjɛʀ] *nf* (*de film*) preview; **en ~** as a preview, in a preview showing.

avant-projet [avɑ̃pʀɔʒɛ] *nm* preliminary draft.

avant-propos [avɑ̃pʀɔpo] *nm* foreword.

avant-veille [avɑ̃vɛj] *nf*: **l'~** two days before.

avare [avaʀ] *a* miserly, avaricious ♦ *nm/f* miser; **~ de compliments** stingy *ou* sparing with one's compliments.

avarice [avaʀis] *nf* avarice, miserliness.

avaricieux, euse [avaʀisjø, -øz] *a* miserly, niggardly.

avarié, e [avaʀje] *a* (*viande, fruits*) rotting, going off (*Brit*); (*NAVIG: navire*) damaged.

avaries [avaʀi] *nfpl* (*NAVIG*) damage *sg.*

avatar [avataʀ] *nm* misadventure; (*transformation*) metamorphosis (*pl* -phoses).

avec [avɛk] *prép* with; (*à l'égard de*) to(wards), with ♦ *ad* (*fam*) with it' (*ou* him *etc*); **~ habileté/lenteur** skilfully/slowly; **~ eux/ces maladies** with them/these diseases; **~ ça** (*malgré ça*) for all that; **et ~ ça?** (*dans un magasin*) anything *ou* something else?

avenant, e [avnɑ̃, -ɑ̃t] *a* pleasant ♦ *nm* (*ASSURANCES*) additional clause; **à l'~** *ad* in keeping.

avènement [avɛnmɑ̃] *nm* (*d'un roi*) accession, succession; (*d'un changement*) advent; (*d'une politique, idée*) coming.

avenir [avniʀ] *nm*: **l'~** the future; **à l'~** in future; **sans ~** with no future, without a future; **carrière/politicien d'~** career/politician with prospects *ou* a future.

Avent [avɑ̃] *nm*: **l'~** Advent.

aventure [avɑ̃tyʀ] *nf*: **l'~** adventure; **une ~** an adventure; (*amoureuse*) an affair; **partir à l'~** to go off in search of adventure; (*au hasard*) to go where one's fancy takes one; **roman/film d'~** adventure story/film.

aventurer [avɑ̃tyʀe] *vt* (*somme, réputation, vie*) to stake; (*remarque, opinion*) to venture; **s'~** *vi* to venture; **s'~ à faire qch** to venture into sth.

aventureux, euse [avɑ̃tyʀø, -øz] *a* adventurous, venturesome; (*projet*) risky, chancy.

aventurier, ière [avɑ̃tyʀje, -jɛʀ] *nm/f* adventurer ♦ *nf* (*péj*) adventuress.

avenu, e [avny] *a*: **nul et non ~** null and void.

avenue [avny] *nf* avenue.

avéré, e [aveʀe] *a* recognized, acknowledged.

avérer [aveʀe]: **s'~** *vb avec attribut*: **s'~ faux/coûteux** to prove (to be) wrong/expensive.

averse [avɛʀs(ə)] *nf* shower.

aversion [avɛʀsjɔ̃] *nf* aversion, loathing.

averti, e [avɛʀti] *a* (well-)informed.

avertir [avɛʀtiʀ] *vt*: **~ qn (de qch/que)** to warn sb (of sth/that); (*renseigner*) to inform sb (of sth/that); **~ qn de ne pas faire qch** to warn sb not to do sth.

avertissement [avɛʀtismɑ̃] *nm* warning.

avertisseur [avɛʀtisœʀ] *nm* horn, siren; **~ (d'incendie)** (fire) alarm.

aveu, x [avø] *nm* confession; **passer aux ~x** to make a confession; **de l'~ de** according to.

aveuglant, e [avœglɑ̃, -ɑ̃t] *a* blinding.

aveugle [avœgl(ə)] *a* blind ♦ *n* blind person; **les ~s** the blind; **test en (double) ~** (double) blind test.

aveuglement [avœgləmɑ̃] *nm* blindness.

aveuglément [avœglemɑ̃] *ad* blindly.

aveugler [avœgle] *vt* to blind.

aveuglette [avœglɛt]: **à l'~** groping one's way along; *(fig)* in the dark, blindly.

avez [ave] *vb voir* avoir.

aviateur, trice [avjatœr, -tris] *nm/f* aviator, pilot.

aviation [avjɑsjɔ̃] *nf* (secteur commercial) aviation; (sport, métier de pilote) flying; *(MIL)* air force; **terrain d'~** airfield; **~ de chasse** fighter force.

aviculteur, trice [avikyltœr, -tris] *nm/f* poultry farmer; bird breeder.

avide [avid] *a* eager; *(péj)* greedy, grasping; **~ de** (sang etc) thirsting for; **~ d'honneurs/d'argent** greedy for honours/money; **~ de connaître/d'apprendre** eager to know/learn.

avidité [avidite] *nf* eagerness; greed.

avilir [avilir] *vt* to debase.

avilissant, e [avilisɑ̃, -ɑ̃t] *a* degrading.

aviné, e [avine] *a* drunken.

avion [avjɔ̃] *nm* (aero)plane (Brit), (air)plane (US); **aller (quelque part) en ~** to go (somewhere) by plane, fly (somewhere); **par ~** by airmail; **~ de chasse** fighter; **~ de ligne** airliner; **~ à réaction** jet (plane).

avion-cargo [avjɔ̃kargo] *nm* air freighter.

avion-citerne [avjɔ̃sitɛrn(ə)] *nm* air tanker.

aviron [avirɔ̃] *nm* oar; *(sport)*: **l'~** rowing.

avis [avi] *nm* opinion; (notification) notice; *(COMM)*: **~ de crédit/débit** credit/debit advice; **à mon ~** in my opinion; **je suis de votre ~** I share your opinion, I am of your opinion; **être d'~ que** to be of the opinion that; **changer d'~** to change one's mind; **sauf ~ contraire** unless you hear to the contrary; **sans ~ préalable** without notice; **jusqu'à nouvel ~** until further notice; **~ de décès** death announcement.

avisé, e [avize] *a* sensible, wise; **être bien/mal ~ de faire** to be well-/ill-advised to do.

aviser [avize] *vt* (voir) to notice, catch sight of; (informer): **~ qn de/que** to advise ou inform ou notify sb of/that ♦ *vi* to think about things, assess the situation; **s'~ de qch/que** to become suddenly aware of sth/that; **s'~ de faire** to take it into one's head to do.

aviver [avive] *vt* (douleur, chagrin) to intensify; (intérêt, désir) to sharpen; (colère, querelle) to stir up; (couleur) to brighten up.

av. J.-C. *abr* (= avant Jésus-Christ) BC.

avocat, e [avɔka, -at] *nm/f* (JUR) ≈ barrister (Brit), lawyer; *(fig)* advocate, champion ♦ *nm* (CULIN) avocado (pear); **se faire l'~ du diable** to be the devil's advocate; **l'~ de la défense/partie civile** the counsel for the defence/plaintiff; **~ d'affaires** business lawyer; **~ général** assistant public prosecutor.

avocat-conseil, *pl* **avocats-conseils** [avɔkakɔ̃sɛj] *nm* ≈ barrister (Brit).

avocat-stagiaire, *pl* **avocats-stagiaires** [avɔkastaʒjɛr] *nm* ≈ barrister doing his articles (Brit).

avoine [avwan] *nf* oats *pl*.

avoir [avwar] *nm* assets *pl*, resources *pl*; *(COMM)*: **~ (fiscal)** (tax) credit ♦ *vt* (gén) to have; (fam: duper) to do, have ♦ *vb auxiliaire* to have; **vous avez du sel?** do you have any salt?, have you got any salt?; **~ à faire qch** to have to do sth; **tu n'as pas à me poser de questions** it's not for you to ask me questions; **il a 3 ans** he is 3 (years old); *voir* faim, peur *etc*; **~ 3 mètres de haut** to be 3 metres high; **~ les cheveux blancs/un chapeau rouge** to have white hair/a red hat; **~ mangé/dormi** to have eaten/slept; **il y a** there is + *sg*, there are + *pl*; *(temporel)*: **il y a 10 ans** 10 years ago; **il y a 10 ans/longtemps que je le sais** I've known (it) for 10 years/a long time; **il y a 10 ans qu'il est arrivé** it's 10 years since he arrived; **qu'y-a-t-il?, qu'est-ce qu'il y a?** what is it?, what's the matter?; **il doit y ~** there must be; **il ne peut y en ~ qu'un** there can only be one; **il n'y a qu'à ...** we (ou you etc) will just have to ...; **en ~ à ou contre qn** to have a down on sb; **en ~ assez** to be fed up; **j'en ai pour une demi-heure** it'll take me half an hour; **n'~ que faire de qch** to have no use for sth.

avoisinant, e [avwazinɑ̃, -ɑ̃t] *a* neighbouring.

avoisiner [avwazine] *vt* to be near ou close to; *(fig)* to border ou verge on.

avons [avɔ̃] *vb voir* avoir.

avortement [avɔrtəmɑ̃] *nm* abortion.

avorter [avɔrte] *vi* (MÉD) to have an abortion; *(fig)* to fail; **faire ~** to abort; **se faire ~** to have an abortion.

avorton [avɔrtɔ̃] *nm* (péj) little runt.

avoué, e [avwe] *a* avowed ♦ *nm* (JUR) ≈ solicitor (Brit), lawyer.

avouer [avwe] *vt* (crime, défaut) to confess (to) ♦ *vi* (se confesser) to confess; (admettre) to admit; **~ avoir fait/que** to admit ou confess to having done/that; **~ que oui/non** to admit that that is so/not so; **s'~ vaincu** to admit defeat.

avril [avril] *nm* April; *voir aussi* juillet.

avt *abr* = avant.

axe [aks(ə)] *nm* axis (pl axes); (de roue etc) axle; (prolongement): **dans l'~ de** directly in line with; *(fig)* main line; **~ routier** trunk road, main road.

axer [akse] *vt*: **~ qch sur** to centre sth on.

axial, e, aux [aksjal, -o] *a* axial.

axiome [aksjom] *nm* axiom.

ayant [ejɑ̃] *vb voir* avoir ♦ *nm*: **~ droit** assignee; **~ droit à** (pension etc) person eligible for ou entitled to.

ayons [ejɔ̃] *etc vb voir* avoir.

azalée [azale] *nf* azalea.

azimut [azimyt] *nm* azimuth; **tous ~s** *a* *(fig)* omnidirectional.

azote [azɔt] *nm* nitrogen.

azoté, e [azɔte] *a* nitrogenous.

aztèque [aztɛk] *a* Aztec.

azur [azyr] *nm* (couleur) azure, sky blue; (ciel) sky, skies *pl*.

azyme [azim] *a*: **pain ~** unleavened bread.

B

B, b [be] *nm inv* B, b ♦ *abr* (= *bien*) g (= *good*); **B comme Bertha** B for Benjamin (*Brit*) ou Baker (*US*).
BA *sigle f* (= *bonne action*) good deed.
baba [baba] *a inv*: **en être ~** (*fam*) to be flabbergasted ♦ *nm*: **~ au rhum** rum baba.
babil [babi] *nm* prattle.
babillage [babijaʒ] *nm* chatter.
babiller [babije] *vi* to prattle, chatter; (*bébé*) to babble.
babines [babin] *nfpl* chops.
babiole [babjɔl] *nf* (*bibelot*) trinket; (*vétille*) trifle.
bâbord [babɔʀ] *nm*: **à** ou **par ~** to port, on the port side.
babouin [babwɛ̃] *nm* baboon.
baby-foot [babifut] *nm inv* table football.
Babylone [babilɔn] *n* Babylon.
babylonien, ne [babilɔnjɛ̃, -ɛn] *a* Babylonian.
baby-sitter [babisitœʀ] *nm/f* baby-sitter.
baby-sitting [babisitiŋ] *nm* baby-sitting.
bac [bak] *nm* (*SCOL*) = **baccalauréat**; (*bateau*) ferry; (*récipient*) tub; (*: PHOTO etc*) tray; (*: INDUSTRIE*) tank; **~ à glace** ice-tray; **~ à légumes** vegetable compartment ou rack.
baccalauréat [bakalɔʀea] *nm* ≈ GCE A-levels *pl* (*Brit*), ≈ high school diploma (*US*).
bâche [baʃ] *nf* tarpaulin, canvas sheet.
bachelier, ière [baʃəlje, -jɛʀ] *nm/f* holder of the *baccalauréat*.
bâcher [baʃe] *vt* to cover (with a canvas sheet ou a tarpaulin).
bachot [baʃo] *nm* = **baccalauréat**.
bachotage [baʃɔtaʒ] *nm* (*SCOL*) cramming.
bachoter [baʃɔte] *vi* (*SCOL*) to cram (for an exam).
bacille [basil] *nm* bacillus (*pl* -i).
bâcler [bakle] *vt* to botch (up).
bactéricide [bakteʀisid] *nm* (*MÉD*) bactericide.
bactérie [bakteʀi] *nf* bacterium (*pl* -ia).
bactériologie [bakteʀjɔlɔʒi] *nf* bacteriology.
bactériologique [bakteʀjɔlɔʒik] *a* bacteriological.
bactériologiste [bakteʀjɔlɔʒist(ə)] *nm/f* bacteriologist.
badaud, e [bado, -od] *nm/f* idle onlooker, stroller.
baderne [badɛʀn(ə)] *nf* (*péj*): **(vieille) ~** old fossil.
badge [badʒ(ə)] *nm* badge.
badigeon [badiʒɔ̃] *nm* distemper; colourwash.
badigeonner [badiʒɔne] *vt* to distemper; to colourwash; (*péj: barbouiller*) to daub; (*MÉD*) to paint.
badin, e [badɛ̃, -in] *a* light-hearted, playful.
badinage [badinaʒ] *nm* banter.
badine [badin] *nf* switch (*stick*).
badiner [badine] *vi*: **~ avec qch** to treat sth lightly; **ne pas ~ avec qch** not to trifle with sth.
badminton [badmintɔn] *nm* badminton.
BAFA [bafa] *sigle m* (= *Brevet d'aptitude aux fonctions d'animation*) *diploma for youth leaders and workers*.
baffe [baf] *nf* (*fam*) slap, clout.
Baffin [bafin] *nf*: **terre de ~** Baffin Island.
baffle [bafl(ə)] *nm* baffle (board).
bafouer [bafwe] *vt* to deride, ridicule.
bafouillage [bafujaʒ] *nm* (*fam: propos incohérents*) jumble of words.
bafouiller [bafuje] *vi, vt* to stammer.
bâfrer [bafʀe] *vi, vt* (*fam*) to guzzle, gobble.
bagage [bagaʒ] *nm*: **~s** luggage *sg*, baggage *sg*; (*littéraire*) (stock of) literary knowledge; **~s à main** hand-luggage.
bagarre [bagaʀ] *nf* fight, brawl; **il aime la ~** he loves a fight, he likes fighting.
bagarrer [bagaʀe]: **se ~** *vi* to (have a) fight.
bagarreur, euse [bagaʀœʀ, -øz] *a* pugnacious ♦ *nm/f*: **il est ~** he loves a fight.
bagatelle [bagatɛl] *nf* trifle, trifling sum (ou matter).
Bagdad, Baghdâd [bagdad] *n* Baghdad.
bagnard [baɲaʀ] *nm* convict.
bagne [baɲ] *nm* penal colony; **c'est le ~** (*fig*) it's forced labour.
bagnole [baɲɔl] *nf* (*fam*) car, wheels *pl* (*Brit*).
bagout [bagu] *nm* glibness; **avoir du ~** to have the gift of the gab.
bague [bag] *nf* ring; **~ de fiançailles** engagement ring; **~ de serrage** clip.
baguenauder [bagnode]: **se ~** *vi* to trail around, loaf around.
baguer [bage] *vt* to ring.
baguette [bagɛt] *nf* stick; (*cuisine chinoise*) chopstick; (*de chef d'orchestre*) baton; (*pain*) stick of (French) bread; (*CONSTR: moulure*) beading; **mener qn à la ~** to rule sb with a rod of iron; **~ magique** magic wand; **~ de sourcier** divining rod; **~ de tambour** drumstick.
Bahamas [baamas] *nfpl*: **les (îles) ~** the Bahamas.
Bahrein [baʀɛn] *nm* Bahrain ou Bahrein.
bahut [bay] *nm* chest.
bai, e [bɛ] *a* (*cheval*) bay.
baie [bɛ] *nf* (*GÉO*) bay; (*fruit*) berry; **~ (vitrée)** picture window.
baignade [bɛɲad] *nf* (*action*) bathing; (*baiɲ*) bathe; (*endroit*) bathing place.
baigné, e [beɲe] *a*: **~ de** bathed in; (*trempé*) soaked with; (*inondé*) flooded with.
baigner [beɲe] *vt* (*bébé*) to bath ♦ *vi*: **~ dans son sang** to lie in a pool of blood; **~ dans la brume** to be shrouded in mist; **se ~** *vi* to go swimming ou bathing; (*dans une baignoire*) to have a bath; **ça baigne!** (*fam*) everything's great!
baigneur, euse [bɛɲœʀ, -øz] *nm/f* bather ♦ *nm* (*poupée*) baby doll.
baignoire [beɲwaʀ] *nf* bath (tub); (*THÉÂTRE*) ground-floor box.
bail, baux [baj, bo] *nm* lease; **donner** ou **prendre qch à ~** to lease sth.
bâillement [bajmã] *nm* yawn.
bâiller [baje] *vi* to yawn; (*être ouvert*) to

gape.

bailleur [bajœʀ] *nm*: ~ **de fonds** sponsor, backer; (*COMM*) sleeping *ou* silent partner.

bâillon [bɑjɔ̃] *nm* gag.

bâillonner [bɑjɔne] *vt* to gag.

bain [bɛ̃] *nm* (*dans une baignoire, PHOTO, TECH*) bath; (*dans la mer, une piscine*) swim; **costume de** ~ bathing costume (*Brit*), swimsuit; **prendre un** ~ to have a bath; **se mettre dans le** ~ (*fig*) to get into (the way of) it *ou* things; ~ **de bouche** mouthwash; ~ **de foule** walkabout; ~ **de pieds** footbath; (*au bord de la mer*) paddle; ~ **de siège** hip bath; ~ **de soleil** sunbathing *q*; **prendre un** ~ **de soleil** to sunbathe; ~**s de mer** sea bathing *sg*; ~**s(-douches) municipaux** public baths.

bain-marie, *pl* **bains-marie** [bɛ̃maʀi] *nm* double boiler; **faire chauffer au** ~ (*boîte etc*) to immerse in boiling water.

baïonnette [bajɔnɛt] *nf* bayonet; (*ÉLEC*): **douille à** ~ bayonet socket; **ampoule à** ~ bulb with a bayonet fitting.

baisemain [bɛzmɛ̃] *nm* kissing a lady's hand.

baiser [beze] *nm* kiss ♦ *vt* (*main, front*) to kiss; (*fam!*) to screw (*!*).

baisse [bɛs] *nf* fall, drop; (*COMM*): "~ **sur la viande**" "meat prices down"; **en** ~ (*cours, action*) falling; **à la** ~ downwards.

baisser [bese] *vt* to lower; (*radio, chauffage*) to turn down; (*AUTO: phares*) to dip (*Brit*), lower (*US*) ♦ *vi* to fall, drop, go down; **se** ~ *vi* to bend down.

bajoues [baʒu] *nfpl* chaps, chops.

bal [bal] *nm* dance; (*grande soirée*) ball; ~ **costumé/masqué** fancy-dress/masked ball; ~ **musette** dance (*with accordion accompaniment*).

balade [balad] *nf* walk, stroll; (*en voiture*) drive; **faire une** ~ to go for a walk *ou* stroll; to go for a drive.

balader [balade] *vt* (*traîner*) to trail around; **se** ~ *vi* to go for a walk *ou* stroll; to go for a drive.

baladeur [baladœʀ] *nm* personal stereo.

baladeuse [baladøz] *nf* inspection lamp.

baladin [baladɛ̃] *nm* wandering entertainer.

balafre [balafʀ(ə)] *nf* gash, slash; (*cicatrice*) scar.

balafrer [balafʀe] *vt* to gash, slash.

balai [balɛ] *nm* broom, brush; (*AUTO: d'essuie-glace*) blade; (*MUS: de batterie etc*) brush; **donner un coup de** ~ to give the floor a sweep; ~ **mécanique** carpet sweeper.

balai-brosse, *pl* **balais-brosses** [balɛbʀɔs] *nm* (long-handled) scrubbing brush.

balance [balɑ̃s] *nf* (*à plateaux*) scales *pl*; (*de précision*) balance; (*COMM, POL*): ~ **des comptes** *ou* **paiements** balance of payments; (*signe*): **la B**~ Libra, the Scales; **être de la B**~ to be Libra; ~ **commerciale** balance of trade; ~ **des forces** balance of power; ~ **romaine** steelyard.

balancelle [balɑ̃sɛl] *nf* garden hammock-seat.

balancer [balɑ̃se] *vt* to swing; (*lancer*) to fling, chuck; (*renvoyer, jeter*) to chuck out ♦ *vi* to swing; **se** ~ *vi* to swing; (*bateau*) to rock; (*branche*) to sway; **se** ~ **de qch** (*fam*) not to give a toss about sth.

balancier [balɑ̃sje] *nm* (*de pendule*) pendulum; (*de montre*) balance wheel; (*perche*) (balancing) pole.

balançoire [balɑ̃swaʀ] *nf* swing; (*sur pivot*) seesaw.

balayage [balɛjaʒ] *nm* sweeping; scanning.

balayer [balɛje] *vt* (*feuilles etc*) to sweep up, brush up; (*pièce, cour*) to sweep; (*chasser*) to sweep away *ou* aside; (*suj: radar*) to scan; (*: phares*) to sweep across.

balayette [balɛjɛt] *nf* small brush.

balayeur, euse [balɛjœʀ, -øz] *nm/f* road-sweeper ♦ *nf* (*engin*) roadsweeper.

balayures [balɛjyʀ] *nfpl* sweepings.

balbutiement [balbysimɑ̃] *nm* (*paroles*) stammering *q*; ~**s** *nmpl* (*fig: débuts*) first faltering steps.

balbutier [balbysje] *vi*, *vt* to stammer.

balcon [balkɔ̃] *nm* balcony; (*THÉÂTRE*) dress circle.

baldaquin [baldakɛ̃] *nm* canopy.

Bâle [bɑl] *n* Basle *ou* Basel.

Baléares [baleaʀ] *nfpl*: **les** ~ the Balearic Islands.

baleine [balɛn] *nf* whale; (*de parapluie*) rib; (*de corset*) bone.

baleinier [balɛnje] *nm* (*NAVIG*) whaler.

baleinière [balɛnjɛʀ] *nf* whaleboat.

balisage [balizaʒ] *nm* (*signaux*) beacons *pl*; buoys *pl*; runway lights *pl*; signs *pl*, markers *pl*.

balise [baliz] *nf* (*NAVIG*) beacon, (marker) buoy; (*AVIAT*) runway light, beacon; (*AUTO, SKI*) sign, marker.

baliser [balize] *vt* to mark out (with beacons *ou* lights *etc*).

balistique [balistik] *a* (*engin*) ballistic ♦ *nf* ballistics.

balivernes [balivɛʀn(ə)] *nfpl* twaddle *sg* (*Brit*), nonsense *sg*.

balkanique [balkanik] *a* Balkan.

Balkans [balkɑ̃] *nmpl*: **les** ~ the Balkans.

ballade [balad] *nf* ballad.

ballant, e [balɑ̃, -ɑ̃t] *a* dangling.

ballast [balast] *nm* ballast.

balle [bal] *nf* (*de fusil*) bullet; (*de sport*) ball; (*du blé*) chaff; (*paquet*) bale; (*fam: franc*) franc; ~ **perdue** stray bullet.

ballerine [balʀin] *nf* ballet dancer; (*chaussure*) pump, ballerina.

ballet [balɛ] *nm* ballet; (*fig*): ~ **diplomatique** diplomatic to-ings and fro-ings.

ballon [balɔ̃] *nm* (*de sport*) ball; (*jouet, AVIAT, de bande dessinée*) balloon; (*de vin*) glass; ~ **d'essai** (*météorologique*) pilot balloon; (*fig*) feeler(s); ~ **de football** football; ~ **d'oxygène** oxygen bottle.

ballonner [balɔne] *vt*: **j'ai le ventre ballonné** I feel bloated.

ballon-sonde, *pl* **ballons-sondes** [balɔ̃sɔ̃d] *nm* sounding balloon.

ballot [balo] *nm* bundle; (*péj*) nitwit.

ballottage [balɔtaʒ] *nm* (*POL*) second ballot.

ballotter [balɔte] *vi* to roll around; (*bateau etc*) to toss ♦ *vt* to shake *ou* throw about; to toss; **être ballotté entre** (*fig*) to be shunted between; (*: indécis*) to be torn between.

ballottine [balɔtin] *nf* (*CULIN*): ~ **de volaille** meat loaf made with poultry.

ball-trap [baltʀap] *nm* (*appareil*) trap; (*tir*) clay pigeon shooting.

balluchon [balyʃɔ̃] *nm* bundle (of clothes).

balnéaire [balneɛʀ] *a* seaside *cpd*.

balnéothérapie [balneɔteʀapi] *nf* spa bath therapy.

BALO *sigle m* (= *Bulletin des annonces légales obligatoires*) ≈ Public Notices (*in newspapers etc*).

balourd, e [baluʀ, -uʀd(ə)] *a* clumsy ♦ *nm/f* clodhopper.

balourdise [baluʀdiz] *nf* clumsiness; (*gaffe*) blunder.

balte [balt] *a* Baltic ♦ *nm/f*: **B~** native of the Baltic States.

baltique [baltik] *a* Baltic ♦ *nf*: **la (mer) B~** the Baltic (Sea).

baluchon [balyʃɔ̃] *nm* = **balluchon**.

balustrade [balystʀad] *nf* railings *pl*, handrail.

bambin [bɑ̃bɛ̃] *nm* little child.

bambou [bɑ̃bu] *nm* bamboo.

ban [bɑ̃] *nm* round of applause, cheer; **être/mettre au ~ de** to be outlawed/to outlaw from; **le ~ et l'arrière-~ de sa famille** every last one of his relatives; **~s (de mariage)** banns, bans.

banal, e [banal] *a* banal, commonplace; (*péj*) trite; **four/moulin ~** village oven/mill.

banalisé, e [banalize] *a* (*voiture de police*) unmarked.

banalité [banalite] *nf* banality; (*remarque*) truism, trite remark.

banane [banan] *nf* banana.

bananeraie [bananʀɛ] *nf* banana plantation.

bananier [bananje] *nm* banana tree; (*bateau*) banana boat.

banc [bɑ̃] *nm* seat, bench; (*de poissons*) shoal; **~ des accusés** dock; **~ d'essai** (*fig*) testing ground; **~ de sable** sandbank; **~ des témoins** witness box.

bancaire [bɑ̃kɛʀ] *a* banking, bank *cpd*.

bancal, e [bɑ̃kal] *a* wobbly; (*personne*) bow-legged; (*fig: projet*) shaky.

bandage [bɑ̃daʒ] *nm* bandaging; (*pansement*) bandage; **~ herniaire** truss.

bande [bɑ̃d] *nf* (*de tissu etc*) strip; (*MÉD*) bandage; (*motif, dessin*) stripe; (*CINÉMA*) film; (*INFORM*) tape; (*RADIO, groupe*) band; (*péj*): **une ~** a bunch *ou* crowd of; **par la ~ in** a roundabout way; **donner de la ~** to list; **faire ~ à part** to keep to o.s.; **~ dessinée (BD)** strip cartoon (*Brit*), comic strip; **~ magnétique** magnetic tape; **~ perforée** punched tape; **~ de roulement** (*de pneu*) tread; **~ sonore** sound track; **~ de terre** strip of land; **~ Velpeau** ® (*MÉD*) crêpe bandage.

bandé, e [bɑ̃de] *a* bandaged; **les yeux ~s** blindfold.

bande-annonce, *pl* **bandes-annonces** [bɑ̃danɔ̃s] *nf* (*CINÉMA*) trailer.

bandeau, x [bɑ̃do] *nm* headband; (*sur les yeux*) blindfold; (*MÉD*) head bandage.

bandelette [bɑ̃dlɛt] *nf* strip of cloth, bandage.

bander [bɑ̃de] *vt* to bandage; (*muscle*) to tense; (*arc*) to bend ♦ *vi* (*fam!*) to have a hard on (!); **~ les yeux à qn** to blindfold sb.

banderole [bɑ̃dʀɔl] *nf* banderole; (*dans un défilé etc*) streamer.

bande-son, *pl* **bandes-son** [bɑ̃dsɔ̃] *nf* (*CINÉMA*) soundtrack.

bande-vidéo, *pl* **bandes-vidéo** [bɑ̃dvideo] *nf* video tape.

bandit [bɑ̃di] *nm* bandit.

banditisme [bɑ̃ditism(ə)] *nm* violent crime, armed robberies *pl*.

bandoulière [bɑ̃duljɛʀ] *nf*: **en ~** (slung *ou* worn) across the shoulder.

Bangkok [bɑ̃gkɔk] *n* Bangkok.

Bangla Desh [bɑ̃gladɛʃ] *nm*: **le ~** Bangladesh.

banjo [bɑ̃(d)ʒo] *nm* banjo.

banlieue [bɑ̃ljø] *nf* suburbs *pl*; **lignes/quartiers de ~** suburban lines/areas; **trains de ~** commuter trains.

banlieusard, e [bɑ̃ljøzaʀ, -aʀd(ə)] *nm/f* suburbanite.

bannière [banjɛʀ] *nf* banner.

bannir [baniʀ] *vt* to banish.

banque [bɑ̃k] *nf* bank; (*activités*) banking; **~ des yeux/du sang** eye/blood bank; **~ d'affaires** merchant bank; **~ de dépôt** deposit bank; **~ de données** (*INFORM*) data bank; **~ d'émission** bank of issue.

banqueroute [bɑ̃kʀut] *nf* bankruptcy.

banquet [bɑ̃kɛ] *nm* (*de club*) dinner; (*de noces*) reception; (*d'apparat*) banquet.

banquette [bɑ̃kɛt] *nf* seat.

banquier [bɑ̃kje] *nm* banker.

banquise [bɑ̃kiz] *nf* ice field.

bantou, e [bɑ̃tu] *a* Bantu.

baptême [batɛm] *nm* (*sacrement*) baptism; (*cérémonie*) christening, baptism; (*d'un navire*) launching; (*d'une cloche*) consecration, dedication; **~ de l'air** first flight.

baptiser [batize] *vt* to christen; to baptize; to launch; to consecrate, dedicate.

baptismal, e, aux [batismal, -o] *a*: **eau ~e** baptismal water.

baptiste [batist(ə)] *a, nm/f* Baptist.

baquet [bakɛ] *nm* tub, bucket.

bar [baʀ] *nm* bar; (*poisson*) bass.

baragouin [baʀagwɛ̃] *nm* gibberish.

baragouiner [baʀagwine] *vi* to gibber, jabber.

baraque [baʀak] *nf* shed; (*fam*) house; **~ foraine** fairground stand.

baraqué, e [baʀake] *a* well-built, hefty.

baraquements [baʀakmɑ̃] *nmpl* huts (*for refugees, workers etc*).

baratin [baʀatɛ̃] *nm* (*fam*) smooth talk, patter.

baratiner [baʀatine] *vt* to chat up.

baratte [baʀat] *nf* churn.

Barbade [baʀbad] *nf*: **la ~** Barbados.

barbant, e [baʀbɑ̃, -ɑ̃t] *a* (*fam*) deadly (boring).

barbare [baʀbaʀ] *a* barbaric ♦ *nm/f* barbarian.

Barbarie [baʀbaʀi] *nf*: **la ~** the Barbary Coast.

barbarie [baʀbaʀi] *nf* barbarism; (*cruauté*) barbarity.

barbarisme [baʀbaʀism(ə)] *nm* (*LING*) barbarism.

barbe [baʀb(ə)] *nf* beard; **(au nez et) à la ~ de qn** (*fig*) under sb's very nose; **quelle ~!** (*fam*) what a drag *ou* bore!; **~ à papa** candy-floss (*Brit*), cotton candy (*US*).

barbecue [baʀbəkju] *nm* barbecue.

barbelé [baʀbəle] *nm* barbed wire *q*.

barber [baʀbe] vt (fam) to bore stiff.
barbiche [baʀbiʃ] nf goatee.
barbichette [baʀbiʃɛt] nf small goatee.
barbiturique [baʀbityʀik] nm barbiturate.
barboter [baʀbɔte] vi to paddle, dabble ♦ vt (fam) to filch.
barboteuse [baʀbɔtøz] nf rompers pl.
barbouiller [baʀbuje] vt to daub; (péj: écrire, dessiner) to scribble; **avoir l'estomac barbouillé** to feel queasy ou sick.
barbu, e [baʀby] a bearded.
barbue [baʀby] nf (poisson) brill.
Barcelone [baʀsəlɔn] n Barcelona.
barda [baʀda] nm (fam) kit, gear.
barde [baʀd(ə)] nf (CULIN) piece of fat bacon ♦ nm (poète) bard.
bardé, e [baʀde] a: ~ **de médailles** etc bedecked with medals etc.
bardeaux [baʀdo] nmpl shingle q.
barder [baʀde] vt (CULIN: rôti, volaille) to bard ♦ vi (fam): **ça va** ~ sparks will fly, things are going to get hot.
barème [baʀɛm] nm scale; (liste) table; ~ **des salaires** salary scale.
barguigner [baʀgiɲe] vi: **sans** ~ without (any) humming and hawing ou shilly-shallying.
baril [baʀil] nm (tonneau) barrel; (de poudre) keg.
barillet [baʀijɛ] nm (de revolver) cylinder.
bariolé, e [baʀjɔle] a many-coloured, rainbow-coloured.
barman [baʀman] nm barman.
baromètre [baʀɔmɛtʀ(ə)] nm barometer; ~ **anéroïde** aneroid barometer.
baron [baʀɔ̃] nm baron.
baronne [baʀɔn] nf baroness.
baroque [baʀɔk] a (ART) baroque; (fig) weird.
baroud [baʀud] nm: ~ **d'honneur** gallant last stand.
baroudeur [baʀudœʀ] nm (fam) fighter.
barque [baʀk(ə)] nf small boat.
barquette [baʀkɛt] nf small boat-shaped tart; (récipient: en aluminium) tub; (: en bois) basket.
barracuda [baʀakyda] nm barracuda.
barrage [baʀaʒ] nm dam; (sur route) road-block, barricade; ~ **de police** police road-block.
barre [baʀ] nf (de fer etc) rod, bar; (NAVIG) helm; (écrite) line, stroke; (DANSE) barre; (JUR): **comparaître à la** ~ to appear as a witness; **être à** ou **tenir la** ~ (NAVIG) to be at the helm; **coup de** ~ (fig): **c'est le coup de** ~! it's daylight robbery!; **j'ai le coup de** ~! I'm all in!; ~ **fixe** (GYM) horizontal bar; ~ **de mesure** (MUS) bar line; ~ **à mine** crowbar; ~**s parallèles/asymétriques** (GYM) parallel/asymmetric bars.
barreau, x [baʀo] nm bar; (JUR): **le** ~ the Bar.
barrer [baʀe] vt (route etc) to block; (mot) to cross out; (chèque) to cross (Brit); (NAVIG) to steer; **se** ~ vi (fam) to clear off.
barrette [baʀɛt] nf (pour cheveux) (hair) slide (Brit) ou clip (US); (REL: bonnet) biretta; (broche) brooch.
barreur [baʀœʀ] nm helmsman; (aviron) coxswain.

barricade [baʀikad] nf barricade.
barricader [baʀikade] vt to barricade; **se** ~ **chez soi** (fig) to lock o.s. in.
barrière [baʀjɛʀ] nf fence; (obstacle) barrier; (porte) gate; **la Grande B**~ the Great Barrier Reef; (ADMIN: on road-signs) no heavy vehicles - road liable to subsidence due to thaw; ~**s douanières** trade barriers.
barrique [baʀik] nf barrel, cask.
barrir [baʀiʀ] vi to trumpet.
baryton [baʀitɔ̃] nm baritone.
BAS sigle m (= bureau d'aide sociale) ≈ social security office (Brit), ≈ Welfare office (US).
bas, basse [ba, bas] a low; (action) low, ignoble ♦ nm (vêtement) stocking; (partie inférieure): **le** ~ **de** the lower part ou foot ou bottom of ♦ nf (MUS) bass ♦ ad low; (parler) softly; **plus** ~ lower down; more softly; (dans un texte) further on, below; **la tête basse** with lowered head; (fig) with head hung low; **avoir la vue basse** to be short-sighted; **au** ~ **mot** at the lowest estimate; **enfant en** ~ **âge** infant, young child; **en** ~ down below; at (ou to) the bottom; (dans une maison) downstairs; **en** ~ **de** at the bottom of; **de** ~ **en haut** upwards; from the bottom to the top; **des hauts et des** ~ ups and downs; **un** ~ **de laine** (fam: économies) money under the mattress (fig); **mettre** ~ vi to give birth; **à** ~ **la dictature!** down with dictatorship!; ~ **morceaux** (viande) cheap cuts.
basalte [bazalt(ə)] nm basalt.
basané, e [bazane] a tanned, bronzed; (immigré etc) swarthy.
bas-côté [bakote] nm (de route) verge (Brit), shoulder (US); (d'église) (side) aisle.
bascule [baskyl] nf: (jeu de) ~ seesaw; (balance à) ~ scales pl; **fauteuil à** ~ rocking chair; **système à** ~ tip-over device; rocker device.
basculer [baskyle] vi to fall over, topple (over); (benne) to tip up ♦ vt (aussi: **faire** ~) to topple over; to tip out, tip up.
base [baz] nf base; (POL): **la** ~ the rank and file, the grass roots; (fondement, principe) basis (pl bases); **jeter les** ~**s de** to lay the foundations of; **à la** ~ **de** (fig) at the root of; **sur la** ~ **de** (fig) on the basis of; **de** ~ basic; **à** ~ **de café** etc coffee etc -based; ~ **de données** (INFORM) database; ~ **de lancement** launching site.
base-ball [bezbol] nm baseball.
baser [baze] vt: ~ **qch sur** to base sth on; **se** ~ **sur** (données, preuves) to base one's argument on; **être basé à/dans** (MIL) to be based at/in.
bas-fond [bafɔ̃] nm (NAVIG) shallow; ~**s** nmpl (fig) dregs.
BASIC [bazik] nm BASIC.
basilic [bazilik] nm (CULIN) basil.
basilique [bazilik] nf basilica.
basket(-ball) [basket(bol)] nm basketball.
baskets [basket] nmpl (chaussures) trainers (Brit), sneakers (US).
basketteur, euse [basketœʀ, -øz] nm/f basketball player.

basquaise [baskɛz] *af* Basque ♦ *nf*: **B~** Basque.

basque [bask(ə)] *a, nm* (*LING*) Basque ♦ *nm/f*: **B~** Basque; **le Pays ~** the Basque country.

basques [bask(ə)] *nfpl* skirts; **pendu aux ~ de qn** constantly pestering sb; (*mère etc*) hanging on sb's apron strings.

bas-relief [baRəljɛf] *nm* bas-relief.

basse [bas] *af, nf voir* **bas**.

basse-cour, *pl* **basses-cours** [baskuR] *nf* farmyard; (*animaux*) farmyard animals.

bassement [basmã] *ad* basely.

bassesse [basɛs] *nf* baseness; (*acte*) base act.

basset [basɛ] *nm* (*ZOOL*) basset (hound).

bassin [basɛ̃] *nm* (*cuvette*) bowl; (*pièce d'eau*) pond, pool; (*de fontaine, GÉO*) basin; (*ANAT*) pelvis; (*portuaire*) dock; **~ houiller** coalfield.

bassine [basin] *nf* basin; (*contenu*) bowl, bowlful.

bassiner [basine] *vt* (*plaie*) to bathe; (*lit*) to warm with a warming pan; (*fam: ennuyer*) to bore; (: *importuner*) to bug, pester.

bassiste [basist(ə)] *nm/f* (double) bass player.

basson [basɔ̃] *nm* bassoon.

bastide [bastid] *nf* (*maison*) country house (*in Provence*); (*ville*) walled town (*in SW France*).

bastingage [bastɛ̃gaʒ] *nm* (ship's) rail.

bastion [bastjɔ̃] *nm* (*aussi fig, POL*) bastion.

bas-ventre [bavɑ̃tR(ə)] *nm* (lower part of the) stomach.

bât [ba] *nm* packsaddle.

bataille [bataj] *nf* battle; **en ~** (*en travers*) at an angle; (*en désordre*) awry; **~ rangée** pitched battle.

bataillon [batajɔ̃] *nm* battalion.

bâtard, **e** [bataʀ, -aʀd(ə)] *a* (*enfant*) illegitimate; (*fig*) hybrid ♦ *nm/f* illegitimate child, bastard (*péj*) ♦ *nm* (*BOULANGERIE*) ≈ Vienna loaf; **chien ~** mongrel.

batavia [batavja] *nf* ≈ Webb lettuce.

bateau, **x** [bato] *nm* boat; (*grand*) ship ♦ *a inv* (*banal, rebattu*) hackneyed; **~ de pêche/à moteur** fishing/motor boat.

bateau-citerne [batositɛRn(ə)] *nm* tanker.

bateau-mouche [batomuʃ] *nm* (passenger) pleasure boat (*on the Seine*).

bateau-pilote [batopilɔt] *nm* pilot ship.

bateleur, **euse** [batlœR, -øz] *nm/f* street performer.

batelier, **ière** [batəlje, -jɛR] *nm/f* ferryman/woman.

bat-flanc [baflɑ̃] *nm inv raised boards for sleeping, in cells, army huts etc.*

bâti, **e** [bati] *a* (*terrain*) developed ♦ *nm* (*armature*) frame; (*COUTURE*) tacking; **bien ~** (*personne*) well-built.

batifoler [batifɔle] *vi* to frolic *ou* lark about.

batik [batik] *nm* batik.

bâtiment [batimã] *nm* building; (*NAVIG*) ship, vessel; (*industrie*): **le ~** the building trade.

bâtir [batiR] *vt* to build; (*COUTURE: jupe, ourlet*) to tack; **fil à ~** (*COUTURE*) tacking thread.

bâtisse [batis] *nf* building.

bâtisseur, **euse** [batisœR, -øz] *nm/f* builder.

batiste [batist(ə)] *nf* (*COUTURE*) batiste, cambric.

bâton [batɔ̃] *nm* stick; **mettre des ~s dans les roues à qn** to put a spoke in sb's wheel; **à ~s rompus** informally; **~ de rouge (à lèvres)** lipstick; **~ de ski** ski stick.

bâtonnet [batɔnɛ] *nm* short stick *ou* rod.

bâtonnier [batɔnje] *nm* (*JUR*) ≈ President of the Bar.

batraciens [batRasjɛ̃] *nmpl* amphibians.

battage [bataʒ] *nm* (*publicité*) (hard) plugging.

battant, **e** [batɑ̃, -ɑ̃t] *vb voir* **battre** ♦ *a*: **pluie ~e** lashing rain ♦ *nm* (*de cloche*) clapper; (*de volets*) shutter, flap; (*de porte*) side; (*fig: personne*) fighter; **porte à double ~** double door; **tambour ~** briskly.

batte [bat] *nf* (*SPORT*) bat.

battement [batmã] *nm* (*de cœur*) beat; (*intervalle*) interval (*between classes, trains etc*); **~ de paupières** blinking *q* (of eyelids); **un ~ de 10 minutes**, **10 minutes de ~** 10 minutes to spare.

batterie [batRi] *nf* (*MIL, ÉLEC*) battery; (*MUS*) drums *pl*, drum kit; **~ de cuisine** kitchen utensils *pl*; (*casseroles etc*) pots and pans *pl*; **une ~ de tests** a string of tests.

batteur [batœR] *nm* (*MUS*) drummer; (*appareil*) whisk.

batteuse [batøz] *nf* (*AGR*) threshing machine.

battoir [batwaR] *nm* (*à linge*) beetle (*for laundry*); (*à tapis*) (carpet) beater.

battre [batR(ə)] *vt* to beat; (*suj: pluie, vagues*) to beat *ou* lash against; (*œufs etc*) to beat up, whisk; (*blé*) to thresh; (*cartes*) to shuffle; (*passer au peigne fin*) to scour ♦ *vi* (*cœur*) to beat; (*volets etc*) to bang, rattle; **se ~** *vi* to fight; **~ la mesure** to beat time; **~ en brèche** (*MIL: mur*) to batter; (*fig: théorie*) to demolish; (: *institution etc*) to attack; **~ son plein** to be at its height, be going full swing; **~ pavillon britannique** to fly the British flag; **~ des mains** to clap one's hands; **~ des ailes** to flap its wings; **~ de l'aile** (*fig*) to be in a bad way *ou* in bad shape; **~ la semelle** to stamp one's feet; **~ en retraite** to beat a retreat.

battu, **e** [baty] *pp de* **battre** ♦ *nf* (*chasse*) beat; (*policière etc*) search, hunt.

baud [bo(d)] *nm* baud.

baudruche [bodRyʃ] *nf*: **ballon en ~** (toy) balloon; (*fig*) windbag.

baume [bom] *nm* balm.

bauxite [boksit] *nf* bauxite.

bavard, **e** [bavaR, -aRd(ə)] *a* (very) talkative, gossipy.

bavardage [bavaRdaʒ] *nm* chatter *q*; gossip *q*.

bavarder [bavaRde] *vi* to chatter; (*indiscrètement*) to gossip; (: *révéler un secret*) to blab.

bavarois, **e** [bavaRwa, -waz] *a* Bavarian ♦ *nm ou nf* (*CULIN*) bavarois.

bave [bav] *nf* dribble; (*de chien etc*) slobber, slaver (*Brit*), drool (*US*); (*d'escargot*) slime.

baver [bave] *vi* to dribble; to slobber, slaver (*Brit*), drool (*US*); (*encre, couleur*) to run; **en ~** (*fam*) to have a hard time (of it).

bavette [bavɛt] *nf* bib.

baveux, **euse** [bavø, -øz] *a* dribbling; (*omelette*) runny.

Bavière [bavjɛR] *nf*: **la ~** Bavaria.

bavoir [bavwaʀ] *nm* (*de bébé*) bib.
bavure [bavyʀ] *nf* smudge; (*fig*) hitch; blunder.
bayer [baje] *vi*: ~ **aux corneilles** to stand gaping.
bazar [bazaʀ] *nm* general store; (*fam*) jumble.
bazarder [bazaʀde] *vt* (*fam*) to chuck out.
BCBG *sigle a* (= *bon chic bon genre*) ≈ preppy.
BCG *sigle m* (= *bacille Calmette-Guérin*) BCG.
bcp *abr* = **beaucoup**.
BD *sigle f* = **bande dessinée**; (= *base de données*) DB.
bd *abr* = **boulevard**.
b.d.c. *abr* (*TYPO*: = *bas de casse*) l.c.
béant, e [beã, -ãt] *a* gaping.
béarnais, e [beaʀnɛ, -ɛz] *a* of *ou* from the Béarn.
béat, e [bea, -at] *a* showing open-eyed wonder; (*sourire etc*) blissful.
béatitude [beatityd] *nf* bliss.
beau (**bel**), **belle, beaux** [bo, bɛl] *a* beautiful, lovely; (*homme*) handsome ♦ *nf* (*SPORT*) decider ♦ *ad*: **il fait** ~ the weather's fine ♦ *nm*: **avoir le sens du** ~ to have a aesthetic sense; **le temps est au** ~ the weather is set fair; **un** ~ **geste** (*fig*) a fine gesture; **un** ~ **salaire** a good salary; **un** ~ **gâchis/rhume** a fine mess/nasty cold; **en faire/dire de belles** to do/say (some) stupid things; **le** ~ **monde** high society; ~ **parleur** smooth talker; **un** ~ **jour** one (fine) day; **de plus belle** more than ever, even more; **bel et bien** well and truly; (*vraiment*) really (and truly); **le plus** ~ **c'est que ...** the best of it is that ...; **c'est du** ~! that's great, that is!; **on a** ~ **essayer** however hard *ou* no matter how hard we try; **il a** ~ **jeu de protester** *etc* it's easy for him to protest *etc*; **faire le** ~ (*chien*) to sit up and beg.
beauceron, ne [bosʀɔ̃, -ɔn] *a* of *ou* from the Beauce.
beaucoup [boku] *ad* a lot; much (*gén en tournure négative*); **il ne boit pas** ~ he doesn't drink much *ou* a lot; ~ **de** (*nombre*) many, a lot of; (*quantité*) a lot of, much; **pas** ~ **de** not much *ou* not a lot of; ~ **plus/trop** far *ou* much more/too much; **de** ~ *ad* by far.
beau-fils, *pl* **beaux-fils** [bofis] *nm* son-in-law; (*remariage*) stepson.
beau-frère, *pl* **beaux-frères** [bofʀɛʀ] *nm* brother-in-law.
beau-père, *pl* **beaux-pères** [bopɛʀ] *nm* father-in-law; (*remariage*) stepfather.
beauté [bote] *nf* beauty; **de toute** ~ beautiful; **en** ~ *ad* with a flourish, brilliantly.
beaux-arts [bozaʀ] *nmpl* fine arts.
beaux-parents [bopaʀã] *nmpl* wife's/husband's family *sg ou pl*, in-laws.
bébé [bebe] *nm* baby.
bébé-éprouvette, *pl* **bébés-éprouvette** [bebeepʀuvɛt] *nm* test-tube baby.
bec [bɛk] *nm* beak, bill; (*de plume*) nib; (*de cafetière etc*) spout; (*de casserole etc*) lip; (*d'une clarinette etc*) mouthpiece; (*fam*) mouth; **clouer le** ~ **à qn** (*fam*) to shut sb up; **ouvrir le** ~ (*fam*) to open one's mouth; ~ **de gaz** (street) gaslamp; ~ **verseur** pour-

ing lip.
bécane [bekan] *nf* (*fam*) bike.
bécarre [bekaʀ] *nm* (*MUS*) natural.
bécasse [bekas] *nf* (*ZOOL*) woodcock; (*fam*) silly goose.
bec-de-cane, *pl* **becs-de-cane** [bɛkdəkan] *nm* (*poignée*) door handle.
bec-de-lièvre, *pl* **becs-de-lièvre** [bɛkdəljɛvʀ(ə)] *nm* harelip.
béchamel [beʃamɛl] *nf*: (**sauce**) ~ white sauce, bechamel sauce.
bêche [bɛʃ] *nf* spade.
bêcher [beʃe] *vt* (*terre*) to dig; (*personne: critiquer*) to slate; (*: snober*) to look down on.
bêcheur, euse [beʃœʀ, -øz] *a* (*fam*) stuck-up ♦ *nm/f* fault-finder; (*snob*) stuck-up person.
bécoter [bekɔte]: **se** ~ *vi* to smooch.
becquée [beke] *nf*: **donner la** ~ **à** to feed.
becqueter [bekte] *vt* (*fam*) to eat.
bedaine [bədɛn] *nf* paunch.
bédé [bede] *nf* (*fam*: = *bande dessinée*) strip cartoon (*Brit*), comic strip.
bedeau, x [bədo] *nm* beadle.
bedonnant, e [bədɔnã, -ãt] *a* paunchy, potbellied.
bée [be] *a*: **bouche** ~ gaping.
beffroi [befʀwa] *nm* belfry.
bégaiement [begɛmã] *nm* stammering.
bégayer [begeje] *vt, vi* to stammer.
bégonia [begɔnja] *nm* (*BOT*) begonia.
bègue [bɛg] *nm/f*: **être** ~ to have a stammer.
bégueule [begœl] *a* prudish.
béguin [begɛ̃] *nm*: **avoir le** ~ **de** *ou* **pour** to have a crush on.
beige [bɛʒ] *a* beige.
beignet [bɛɲɛ] *nm* fritter.
bel [bɛl] *am voir* **beau**.
bêler [bele] *vi* to bleat.
belette [bəlɛt] *nf* weasel.
belge [bɛlʒ(ə)] *a* Belgian ♦ *nm/f*: **B~** Belgian.
Belgique [bɛlʒik] *nf*: **la** ~ Belgium.
Belgrade [bɛlgʀad] *n* Belgrade.
bélier [belje] *nm* ram; (*engin*) (battering) ram; (*signe*): **le B~** Aries, the Ram; **être du B~** to be Aries.
Bélize [beliz] *nm*: **le** ~ Belize.
bellâtre [belɑtʀ(ə)] *nm* dandy.
belle [bɛl] *af, nf voir* **beau**.
belle-famille, *pl* **belles-familles** [bɛlfamij] *nf* (*fam*) in-laws *pl*.
belle-fille, *pl* **belles-filles** [bɛlfij] *nf* daughter-in-law; (*remariage*) stepdaughter.
belle-mère, *pl* **belles-mères** [bɛlmɛʀ] *nf* mother-in-law; (*remariage*) stepmother.
belle-sœur, *pl* **belles-sœurs** [bɛlsœʀ] *nf* sister-in-law.
belliciste [belisist(ə)] *a* warmongering.
belligérance [beliʒeʀãs] *nf* belligerence.
belligérant, e [beliʒeʀã, -ãt] *a* belligerent.
belliqueux, euse [belikø, -øz] *a* aggressive, warlike.
belote [bəlɔt] *nf* belote (*card game*).
belvédère [belvedɛʀ] *nm* panoramic viewpoint (*or small building there*).
bémol [bemɔl] *nm* (*MUS*) flat.
ben [bɛ̃] *excl* (*fam*) well.
bénédiction [benediksjɔ̃] *nf* blessing.
bénéfice [benefis] *nm* (*COMM*) profit; (*avan-*

tage) benefit; **au** ~ **de** in aid of.
bénéficiaire [benefisjɛʀ] *nm/f* beneficiary.
bénéficier [benefisje] *vi*: ~ **de** to enjoy; *(profiter)* to benefit by *ou* from; *(obtenir)* to get, be given.
bénéfique [benefik] *a* beneficial.
Bénélux [benelyks] *nm*: **le** ~ Benelux, the Benelux countries.
benêt [bɔnɛ] *nm* simpleton.
bénévolat [benevɔla] *nm* voluntary service *ou* work.
bénévole [benevɔl] *a* voluntary, unpaid.
bénévolement [benevɔlmɑ̃] *ad* voluntarily.
Bengale [bɛ̃gal] *nm*: **le** ~ Bengal; **le golfe du** ~ the Bay of Bengal.
bengali [bɛ̃gali] *a* Bengali, Bengalese ♦ *nm* (*LING*) Bengali.
Bénin [benɛ̃] *nm*: **le** ~ Benin.
bénin, igne [benɛ̃, -iɲ] *a* minor, mild; *(tumeur)* benign.
bénir [beniʀ] *vt* to bless.
bénit, e [beni, -it] *a* consecrated; **eau** ~**e** holy water.
bénitier [benitje] *nm* stoup, font *(for holy water)*.
benjamin, e [bɛ̃ʒamɛ̃, -in] *nm/f* youngest child; *(SPORT)* under-13.
benne [bɛn] *nf* skip; *(de téléphérique)* (cable) car; ~ **basculante** tipper *(Brit)*, dump *ou* dumper truck.
benzine [bɛ̃zin] *nf* benzine.
béotien, ne [beɔsjɛ̃, -ɛn] *nm/f* philistine.
BEP *sigle m* (= *Brevet d'études professionnelles*) *school-leaving diploma, taken at approx. 18 years.*
BEPA [bepa] *sigle m* (= *Brevet d'études professionnelles agricoles*) *school-leaving diploma in agriculture, taken at approx. 18 years.*
BEPC *sigle m* (= *Brevet d'études du premier cycle*) *former school certificate (taken at approx. 16 years).*
béquille [bekij] *nf* crutch; *(de bicyclette)* stand.
berbère [bɛʀbɛʀ] *a* Berber ♦ *nm* (*LING*) Berber ♦ *nm/f*: **B**~ Berber.
bercail [bɛʀkaj] *nm* fold.
berceau, x [bɛʀso] *nm* cradle, crib.
bercer [bɛʀse] *vt* to rock, cradle; *(suj: musique etc)* to lull; ~ **qn de** *(promesses etc)* to delude sb with.
berceur, euse [bɛʀsœʀ, -øz] *a* soothing ♦ *nf (chanson)* lullaby.
béret (basque) [beʀɛ(bask(ə))] *nm* beret.
bergamote [bɛʀgamɔt] *nf* (*BOT*) bergamot.
berge [bɛʀʒ(ə)] *nf* bank.
berger, ère [bɛʀʒe, -ɛʀ] *nm/f* shepherd/shepherdess; ~ **allemand** *(chien)* alsatian (dog) *(Brit)*, German shepherd (dog) *(US)*.
bergerie [bɛʀʒəʀi] *nf* sheep pen.
béribéri [beʀibeʀi] *nm* beriberi.
Berlin [bɛʀlɛ̃] *n* Berlin; ~**-Est/-Ouest** East/West Berlin.
berline [bɛʀlin] *nf* (*AUTO*) saloon (car) *(Brit)*, sedan *(US)*.
berlingot [bɛʀlɛ̃go] *nm* *(emballage)* carton *(pyramid shaped)*; *(bonbon)* lozenge.
berlinois, e [bɛʀlinwa, -waz] *a* of *ou* from Berlin ♦ *nm/f*: **B**~, **e** Berliner.

berlue [bɛʀly] *nf*: **j'ai la** ~ I must be seeing things.
bermuda [bɛʀmyda] *nm* *(short)* Bermuda shorts.
Bermudes [bɛʀmyd] *nfpl*: **les (îles)** ~ Bermuda.
Berne [bɛʀn(ə)] *n* Bern.
berne [bɛʀn(ə)] *nf*: **en** ~ at half-mast; **mettre en** ~ to fly at half-mast.
berner [bɛʀne] *vt* to fool.
bernois, e [bɛʀnwa, -waz] *a* Bernese.
berrichon, ne [beʀiʃɔ̃, -ɔn] *a* of *ou* from the Berry.
besace [bəzas] *nf* beggar's bag.
besogne [bəzɔɲ] *nf* work *q*, job.
besogneux, euse [bəzɔɲø, -øz] *a* hard-working.
besoin [bəzwɛ̃] *nm* need; *(pauvreté)*: **le** ~ need, want; **le** ~ **d'argent/de gloire** the need for money/glory; ~**s (naturels)** nature's needs; **faire ses** ~**s** to relieve o.s.; **avoir** ~ **de qch/faire qch** to need sth/to do sth; **il n'y a pas** ~ **de (faire)** there is no need to (do); **au** ~, **si** ~ **est** if need be; **pour les** ~**s de la cause** for the purpose in hand.
bestial, e, aux [bɛstjal, -o] *a* bestial, brutish ♦ *nmpl* cattle.
bestiole [bɛstjɔl] *nf* (tiny) creature.
bétail [betaj] *nm* livestock, cattle *pl*.
bétaillère [betajɛʀ] *nf* livestock truck.
bête [bɛt] *nf* animal; *(bestiole)* insect, creature ♦ *a* stupid, silly; **les** ~**s** (the) animals; **chercher la petite** ~ to nit-pick; ~ **noire** pet hate, bugbear *(Brit)*; ~ **sauvage** wild beast; ~ **de somme** beast of burden.
bêtement [bɛtmɑ̃] *ad* stupidly; **tout** ~ quite simply.
Bethléem [bɛtleɛm] *n* Bethlehem.
bêtifier [betifje] *vi* to talk nonsense.
bêtise [betiz] *nf* stupidity; *(action, remarque)* stupid thing (to say *ou* do); *(bonbon)* type of mint sweet *(Brit)* *ou* candy *(US)*; **faire/dire une** ~ to do/say something stupid.
béton [betɔ̃] *nm* concrete; **(en)** ~ *(fig: alibi, argument)* cast iron; ~ **armé** reinforced concrete; ~ **précontraint** prestressed concrete.
bétonner [betɔne] *vt* to concrete (over).
bétonnière [betɔnjɛʀ] *nf* cement mixer.
bette [bɛt] *nf* (*BOT*) Chinese leaves *pl*.
betterave [bɛtʀav] *nf* *(rouge)* beetroot *(Brit)*, beet *(US)*; ~ **fourragère** mangel-wurzel; ~ **sucrière** sugar beet.
beugler [bøgle] *vi* to low; *(péj: radio etc)* to blare ♦ *vt (péj: chanson etc)* to bawl out.
Beur [bœʀ] *a*, *nm/f* second-generation Arab immigrant.
beurre [bœʀ] *nm* butter; **mettre du** ~ **dans les épinards** *(fig)* to add a little to the kitty; ~ **de cacao** cocoa butter; ~ **noir** brown butter (sauce).
beurrer [bœʀe] *vt* to butter.
beurrier [bœʀje] *nm* butter dish.
beuverie [bœvʀi] *nf* drinking session.
bévue [bevy] *nf* blunder.
Beyrouth [beʀut] *n* Beirut.
Bhoutan [butɑ̃] *nm*: **le** ~ Bhutan.
bi... [bi] *préfixe* bi..., two-.
biais [bjɛ] *nm* *(moyen)* device, expedient; *(aspect)* angle; *(bande de tissu)* piece of

cloth cut on the bias; **en ~, de ~** (*obliquement*) at an angle; (*fig*) indirectly.
biaiser [bjeze] *vi* (*fig*) to sidestep the issue.
bibelot [biblo] *nm* trinket, curio.
biberon [bibʁɔ̃] *nm* (feeding) bottle; **nourrir au ~** to bottle-feed.
bible [bibl(ə)] *nf* bible.
bibliobus [biblijɔbys] *nm* mobile library van.
bibliographie [biblijɔgʁafi] *nf* bibliography.
bibliophile [biblijɔfil] *nm/f* book-lover.
bibliothécaire [biblijɔtekɛʁ] *nm/f* librarian.
bibliothèque [biblijɔtɛk] *nf* library; (*meuble*) bookcase; **~ municipale** public library.
biblique [biblik] *a* biblical.
bicarbonate [bikaʁbɔnat] *nm*: **~ (de soude)** bicarbonate of soda.
bicentenaire [bisãtnɛʁ] *nm* bicentenary.
biceps [bisɛps] *nm* biceps.
biche [biʃ] *nf* doe.
bichonner [biʃɔne] *vt* to groom.
bicolore [bikɔlɔʁ] *a* two-coloured (*Brit*), two-colored (*US*).
bicoque [bikɔk] *nf* (*péj*) shack, dump.
bicorne [bikɔʁn(ə)] *nm* cocked hat.
bicyclette [bisiklɛt] *nf* bicycle.
bide [bid] *nm* (*fam: ventre*) belly; (*THÉÂTRE*) flop.
bidet [bidɛ] *nm* bidet.
bidirectionnel, le [bidiʁɛksjɔnɛl] *a* bidirectional.
bidon [bidɔ̃] *nm* can ♦ *a inv* (*fam*) phoney.
bidonville [bidɔ̃vil] *nm* shanty town.
bidule [bidyl] *nm* (*fam*) thingamajig.
bielle [bjɛl] *nf* connecting rod; (*AUTO*) track rod.
bien [bjɛ̃] *nm* good; (*patrimoine*) property *q*; **le ~ public** the public good; **faire du ~ à qn** to do sb good; **dire/penser du ~ de** to speak/think well of; **changer en ~** to turn to the good; **~s de consommation/d'équipement** consumer/capital goods; **~s durables** durables ♦ *ad* (*travailler*) well; (*approximativement*): **il y a ~ 2 ans** at least 2 years ago; (*intensif*): **~ jeune** rather young; **~ assez** quite enough; **~ mieux** very much better; **~ du temps/des gens** quite a time/a number of people; **j'espère ~ y aller** I do hope to go; **il semble ~ que** it seems that; **je veux ~ le faire** I'm (quite) willing *ou* happy to do it; **il faut ~ le faire** it has to be done; **tu as eu ~ raison de faire ça** you were quite right to do that; **~ sûr**, **entendu** certainly, of course; **c'est ~ fait** (*mérité*) it serves him (*ou* her *etc*) right; **croyant ~ faire** thinking he *etc* was doing the right thing; **faire ~ de ...** to be right to ...; **peut-être ~** it could well be; **aimer ~** to like; **aller ~** to be well; **eh ~!** well!; **si ~ que** with the result that ♦ *excl* right!, OK!, fine! ♦ *a inv* good; (*joli*) good-looking; (*à l'aise*): **être ~** to be fine; **ce n'est pas ~ de** it's not right to; **c'est (très) ~ (comme ça)** it's fine (like that); **ce n'est pas si ~ que ça** it's not as good *ou* great as all that; **c'est ~?** is that all right?; **des gens ~** respectable people; **être ~ avec qn** to be on good terms with sb.
bien-aimé, e [bjɛ̃neme] *a, nm/f* beloved.
bien-être [bjɛ̃nɛtʁ(ə)] *nm* well-being.

bienfaisance [bjɛ̃fəzɑ̃s] *nf* charity.
bienfaisant, e [bjɛ̃fəzɑ̃, -ɑ̃t] *a* (*chose*) beneficial.
bienfait [bjɛ̃fɛ] *nm* act of generosity, benefaction; (*de la science etc*) benefit.
bienfaiteur, trice [bjɛ̃fɛtœʁ, -tʁis] *nm/f* benefactor/benefactress.
bien-fondé [bjɛ̃fɔ̃de] *nm* soundness.
bien-fonds [bjɛ̃fɔ̃] *nm* property.
bienheureux, euse [bjɛ̃nœʁø, -øz] *a* happy; (*REL*) blessed, blest.
biennal, e, aux [bjenal, -o] *a* biennial.
bien-pensant, e [bjɛ̃pɑ̃sɑ̃, -ɑ̃t] *a* right-thinking ♦ *nm/f*: **les ~s** right-minded people.
bien que [bjɛ̃k(ə)] *cj* although.
bienséance [bjɛ̃seɑ̃s] *nf* propriety, decorum *q*; **les ~s** (*convenances*) the proprieties.
bienséant, e [bjɛ̃seɑ̃, -ɑ̃t] *a* proper, seemly.
bientôt [bjɛ̃to] *ad* soon; **à ~** see you soon.
bienveillance [bjɛ̃vejɑ̃s] *nf* kindness.
bienveillant, e [bjɛ̃vejɑ̃, -ɑ̃t] *a* kindly.
bienvenu, e [bjɛ̃vny] *a* welcome ♦ *nm/f*: **être le ~/la ~e** to be welcome ♦ *nf*: **souhaiter la ~e à** to welcome; **~e à** welcome to.
bière [bjɛʁ] *nf* (*boisson*) beer; (*cercueil*) bier; **~ blonde** lager; **~ brune** brown ale; **~ (à la) pression** draught beer.
biffer [bife] *vt* to cross out.
bifteck [biftɛk] *nm* steak.
bifurcation [bifyʁkasjɔ̃] *nf* fork (*in road*); (*fig*) new direction.
bifurquer [bifyʁke] *vi* (*route*) to fork; (*véhicule*) to turn off.
bigame [bigam] *a* bigamous.
bigamie [bigami] *nf* bigamy.
bigarré, e [bigaʁe] *a* multicoloured (*Brit*), multicolored (*US*); (*disparate*) motley.
bigarreau, x [bigaʁo] *nm* *type of* cherry.
bigorneau, x [bigɔʁno] *nm* winkle.
bigot, e [bigo, -ɔt] (*péj*) *a* bigoted ♦ *nm/f* bigot.
bigoterie [bigɔtʁi] *nf* bigotry.
bigoudi [bigudi] *nm* curler.
bigrement [bigʁəmɑ̃] *ad* (*fam*) fantastically.
bijou, x [biʒu] *nm* jewel.
bijouterie [biʒutʁi] *nf* (*magasin*) jeweller's (shop) (*Brit*), jewelry store (*US*); (*bijoux*) jewellery, jewelry.
bijoutier, ière [biʒutje, -jɛʁ] *nm/f* jeweller (*Brit*), jeweler (*US*).
bikini [bikini] *nm* bikini.
bilan [bilɑ̃] *nm* (*COMM*) balance sheet(s); (*annuel*) end of year statement; (*fig*) (net) outcome; (*: de victimes*) toll; **faire le ~ de** to assess; to review; **déposer son ~** to file a bankruptcy statement; **~ de santé** (*MÉD*) check-up; **~ social** *statement of a firm's policies towards its employees*.
bilatéral, e, aux [bilateʁal, -o] *a* bilateral.
bilboquet [bilbɔkɛ] *nm* (*jouet*) cup-and-ball game.
bile [bil] *nf* bile; **se faire de la ~** (*fam*) to worry o.s. sick.
biliaire [biljɛʁ] *a* biliary.
bilieux, euse [biljø, -øz] *a* bilious; (*fig: colérique*) testy.
bilingue [bilɛ̃g] *a* bilingual.
bilinguisme [bilɛ̃gɥism(ə)] *nm* bilingualism.
billard [bijaʁ] *nm* billiards *sg*; (*table*) billiard

table; **c'est du ~** *(fam)* it's a cinch; **passer sur le ~** *(fam)* to have an *(ou* one's) operation; **~ électrique** pinball.

bille [bij] *nf* ball; *(du jeu de billes)* marble; *(de bois)* log; **jouer aux ~s** to play marbles.

billet [bijɛ] *nm (aussi:* **~ de banque)** (bank)note; *(de cinéma, de bus etc)* ticket; *(courte lettre)* note; **~ à ordre** *ou* **de commerce** *(COMM)* promissory note, IOU; **~ d'avion/de train** plane/train ticket; **~ circulaire** round-trip ticket; **~ doux** love letter; **~ de faveur** complimentary ticket; **~ de loterie** lottery ticket; **~ de quai** platform ticket.

billetterie [bijɛtRi] *nf* ticket office; *(distributeur)* ticket dispenser; *(BANQUE)* cash dispenser.

billion [biljɔ̃] *nm* billion *(Brit)*, trillion *(US)*.

billot [bijo] *nm* block.

BIMA *sigle m = Bulletin d'information du ministère de l'agriculture.*

bimbeloterie [bɛ̃blɔtRi] *nf (objets)* fancy goods.

bimensuel, le [bimɑ̃sɥɛl] *a* bimonthly, twice-monthly.

bimestriel, le [bimɛstRijɛl] *a* bimonthly, two-monthly.

bimoteur [bimɔtœR] *a* twin-engined.

binaire [binɛR] *a* binary.

biner [bine] *vt* to hoe.

binette [binɛt] *nf (outil)* hoe.

binoclard, e [binɔklaR, -aRd(ə)] *a (fam)* specky ♦ *nm/f* four-eyes.

binocle [binɔkl(ə)] *nm* pince-nez.

binoculaire [binɔkylɛR] *a* binocular.

binôme [binom] *nm* binomial.

bio... [bjɔ] *préfixe* bio...

biochimie [bjɔʃimi] *nf* biochemistry.

biochimique [bjɔʃimik] *a* biochemical.

biochimiste [bjɔʃimist(ə)] *nm/f* biochemist.

biodégradable [bjɔdegRadabl(ə)] *a* biodegradable.

biographe [bjɔgRaf] *nm/f* biographer.

biographie [bjɔgRafi] *nf* biography.

biographique [bjɔgRafik] *a* biographical.

biologie [bjɔlɔʒi] *nf* biology.

biologique [bjɔlɔʒik] *a* biological.

biologiste [bjɔlɔʒist(ə)] *nm/f* biologist.

biopsie [bjɔpsi] *nf (MÉD)* biopsy.

biosphère [bjɔsfɛR] *nf* biosphere.

bipartisme [bipaRtism(ə)] *nm* two-party system.

bipède [biped] *nm* biped, two-footed creature.

biphasé, e [bifaze] *a (ÉLEC)* two-phase.

biplace [biplas] *a, nm (avion)* two-seater.

biplan [biplɑ̃] *nm* biplane.

bique [bik] *nf* nanny goat; *(péj)* old hag.

biquet, te [bikɛ, -ɛt] *nm/f:* **mon ~** *(fam)* my lamb.

biréacteur [biReaktœR] *nm* twin- engined jet.

birman, e [biRmɑ̃, -an] *a* Burmese.

Birmanie [biRmani] *nf:* **la ~** Burma.

bis, e [bi, biz] *a (couleur)* greyish brown ♦ *ad* [bis]: **12 ~ 12a** *ou* **A** ♦ *excl, nm* [bis] encore ♦ *nf (baiser)* kiss; *(vent)* North wind.

bisaïeul, e [bizajœl] *nm/f* great-grandfather/great-grandmother.

bisannuel, le [bizanɥɛl] *a* biennial.

bisbille [bisbij] *nf:* **être en ~ avec qn** to be at

loggerheads with sb.

Biscaye [biskɛ] *nf:* **le golfe de ~** the Bay of Biscay.

biscornu, e [biskɔRny] *a* crooked; *(bizarre)* weird(-looking).

biscotte [biskɔt] *nf* (breakfast) rusk.

biscuit [biskɥi] *nm* biscuit *(Brit)*, cookie *(US)*; *(gateau)* sponge cake; **~ à la cuiller** sponge finger.

biscuiterie [biskɥitRi] *nf* biscuit manufacturing.

bise [biz] *af, nf voir* **bis**.

biseau, x [bizo] *nm* bevelled edge; **en ~** bevelled.

biseauter [bizote] *vt* to bevel.

bisexué, e [bisɛksɥe] *a* bisexual.

bismuth [bismyt] *nm* bismuth.

bison [bizɔ̃] *nm* bison.

bisou [bizu] *nm (fam)* kiss.

bisque [bisk(ə)] *nf:* **~ d'écrevisses** shrimp bisque.

bissectrice [bisɛktRis] *nf* bisector.

bisser [bise] *vt (faire rejouer: artiste, chanson)* to encore; *(rejouer: morceau)* to give an encore of.

bissextile [bisɛkstil] *a:* **année ~** leap year.

bistouri [bisturi] *nm* lancet.

bistre [bistR(ə)] *a (couleur)* bistre; *(peau, teint)* tanned.

bistro(t) [bistRo] *nm* bistro, café.

BIT *sigle m (= Bureau international du travail)* ILO.

bit [bit] *nm (INFORM)* bit.

biterrois, e [bitɛRwa, -waz] *a* of *ou* from Béziers.

bitte [bit] *nf:* **~ d'amarrage** bollard *(NAUT)*.

bitume [bitym] *nm* asphalt.

bitumer [bityme] *vt* to asphalt.

bivalent, e [bivalɑ̃, -ɑ̃t] *a* bivalent.

bivouac [bivwak] *nm* bivouac.

bizarre [bizaR] *a* strange, odd.

bizarrement [bizaRmɑ̃] *ad* strangely, oddly.

bizarrerie [bizaRRi] *nf* strangeness, oddness.

blackbouler [blakbule] *vt (à une élection)* to blackball.

blafard, e [blafaR, -aRd(ə)] *a* wan.

blague [blag] *nf (propos)* joke; *(farce)* trick; **sans ~!** no kidding!; **~ à tabac** tobacco pouch.

blaguer [blage] *vi* to joke ♦ *vt* to tease.

blagueur, euse [blagœR, -øz] *a* teasing ♦ *nm/f* joker.

blair [blɛR] *nm (fam)* conk.

blaireau, x [blɛRo] *nm (ZOOL)* badger; *(brosse)* shaving brush.

blairer [blɛRe] *vt:* **je ne peux pas le ~** I can't bear *ou* stand him.

blâmable [blɑmabl(ə)] *a* blameworthy.

blâme [blɑm] *nm* blame; *(sanction)* reprimand.

blâmer [blɑme] *vt (réprouver)* to blame; *(réprimander)* to reprimand.

blanc, blanche [blɑ̃, blɑ̃ʃ] *a* white; *(non imprimé)* blank; *(innocent)* pure ♦ *nm/f* white, white man/woman ♦ *nm (couleur)* white; *(linge)* **le ~** whites *pl*; *(espace non écrit)* blank; *(aussi:* **~ d'œuf)** (egg-)white; *(aussi:* **~ de poulet)** breast, white meat; *(aussi:* **vin ~)** white wine ♦ *nf (MUS)* minim

(*Brit*), half-note (*US*); **d'une voix blanche** in a toneless voice; **aux cheveux** ~s white-haired; **le** ~ **de l'œil** the white of the eye; **laisser en** ~ to leave blank; **chèque en** ~ blank cheque; **à** ~ *ad* (*chauffer*) white-hot; (*tirer, charger*) with blanks; **saigner à** ~ to bleed white; ~ **cassé** off-white.

blanc-bec, *pl* **blancs-becs** [blɑ̃bɛk] *nm* green-horn.

blanchâtre [blɑ̃ʃɑtʀ(ə)] *a* (*teint, lumière*) whitish.

blancheur [blɑ̃ʃœʀ] *nf* whiteness.

blanchir [blɑ̃ʃiʀ] *vt* (*gén*) to whiten; (*linge, fig: argent*) to launder; (*CULIN*) to blanch; (*fig: disculper*) to clear ♦ *vi* to grow white; (*cheveux*) to go white; **blanchi à la chaux** whitewashed.

blanchissage [blɑ̃ʃisaʒ] *nm* (*du linge*) laundering.

blanchisserie [blɑ̃ʃisʀi] *nf* laundry.

blanchisseur, euse [blɑ̃ʃisœʀ, -øz] *nm/f* launderer.

blanc-seing, *pl* **blancs-seings** [blɑ̃sɛ̃] *nm* signed blank paper.

blanquette [blɑ̃kɛt] *nf* (*CULIN*): ~ **de veau** veal in a white sauce, blanquette de veau.

blasé, e [blɑze] *a* blasé.

blaser [blɑze] *vt* to make blasé.

blason [blɑzɔ̃] *nm* coat of arms.

blasphémateur, trice [blasfematœʀ, -tʀis] *nm/f* blasphemer.

blasphématoire [blasfematwaʀ] *a* blasphemous.

blasphème [blasfɛm] *nm* blasphemy.

blasphémer [blasfeme] *vi* to blaspheme ♦ *vt* to blaspheme against.

blatte [blat] *nf* cockroach.

blazer [blazɛʀ] *nm* blazer.

blé [ble] *nm* wheat; ~ **en herbe** wheat on the ear; ~ **noir** buckwheat.

bled [blɛd] *nm* (*péj*) hole; (*en Afrique du Nord*): **le** ~ the interior.

blême [blɛm] *a* pale.

blêmir [blemiʀ] *vi* (*personne*) to (turn) pale; (*lueur*) to grow pale.

blennorragie [blenɔʀaʒi] *nf* blennorrhoea.

blessant, e [blesɑ̃, -ɑ̃t] *a* hurtful.

blessé, e [blese] *a* injured ♦ *nm/f* injured person, casualty; **un** ~ **grave, un grand** ~ a seriously injured *ou* wounded person.

blesser [blese] *vt* to injure; (*délibérément: MIL etc*) to wound; (*suj: souliers etc, offenser*) to hurt; **se** ~ to injure o.s.; **se** ~ **au pied** *etc* to injure one's foot *etc*.

blessure [blesyʀ] *nf* injury; wound.

blet, te [blɛ, blɛt] *a* overripe.

blette [blɛt] *nf* = **bette**.

bleu, e [blø] *a* blue; (*bifteck*) very rare ♦ *nm* (*couleur*) blue; (*novice*) greenhorn; (*contusion*) bruise; (*vêtement: aussi* ~s) overalls *pl* (*Brit*), coveralls *pl* (*US*); **avoir une peur** ~**e** to be scared stiff; **zone** ~**e** ≈ restricted parking area; **fromage** ~ blue cheese; **au** ~ (*CULIN*) au bleu; ~ (**de lessive**) ≈ blue bag; ~ **de méthylène** (*MÉD*) methylene blue; ~ **marine/nuit/roi** navy/midnight/royal blue.

bleuâtre [bløɑtʀ(ə)] *a* (*fumée etc*) bluish, blueish.

bleuet [bløɛ] *nm* cornflower.

bleuir [blœiʀ] *vt, vi* to turn blue.

bleuté, e [bløte] *a* blue-shaded.

blindage [blɛ̃daʒ] *nm* armour-plating.

blindé, e [blɛ̃de] *a* armoured (*Brit*), armored (*US*); (*fig*) hardened ♦ *nm* armoured *ou* armored car; (*char*) tank.

blinder [blɛ̃de] *vt* to armour (*Brit*), armor (*US*); (*fig*) to harden.

blizzard [blizaʀ] *nm* blizzard.

bloc [blɔk] *nm* (*de pierre etc, INFORM*) block; (*de papier à lettres*) pad; (*ensemble*) group, block; **serré à** ~ tightened right down; **en** ~ as a whole; wholesale; **faire** ~ to unite; ~ **opératoire** operating *ou* theatre block; ~ **sanitaire** toilet block; ~ **sténo** shorthand notebook.

blocage [blɔkaʒ] *nm* (*voir bloquer*) blocking; jamming; freezing; (*PSYCH*) hang-up.

bloc-cuisine, *pl* **blocs-cuisines** [blɔkkɥizin] *nm* kitchen unit.

bloc-cylindres, *pl* **blocs-cylindres** [blɔksilɛ̃dʀ(ə)] *nm* cylinder block.

bloc-évier, *pl* **blocs-éviers** [blɔkevje] *nm* sink unit.

bloc-moteur, *pl* **blocs-moteurs** [blɔkmɔtœʀ] *nm* engine block.

bloc-notes, *pl* **blocs-notes** [blɔknɔt] *nm* note pad.

blocus [blɔkys] *nm* blockade.

blond, e [blɔ̃, -ɔ̃d] *a* fair; (*plus clair*) blond; (*sable, blés*) golden ♦ *nm/f* fair-haired *ou* blond man/woman; ~ **cendré** ash blond.

blondeur [blɔ̃dœʀ] *nf* fairness; blondness.

blondin, e [blɔ̃dɛ̃, -in] *nm/f* fair-haired *ou* blond child *ou* young person.

blondinet, te [blɔ̃dinɛ, -ɛt] *nm/f* blondy.

blondir [blɔ̃diʀ] *vi* (*personne, cheveux*) to go fair *ou* blond.

bloquer [blɔke] *vt* (*passage*) to block; (*pièce mobile*) to jam; (*crédits, compte*) to freeze; (*personne, négociations etc*) to hold up; (*regrouper*) to group; ~ **les freins** to jam on the brakes.

blottir [blɔtiʀ]: **se** ~ *vi* to huddle up.

blousant, e [bluzɑ̃, ɑ̃t] *a* blousing out.

blouse [bluz] *nf* overall.

blouser [bluze] *vi* to blouse out.

blouson [bluzɔ̃] *nm* blouson (jacket); ~ **noir** (*fig*) ≈ rocker.

blue-jean(s) [bludʒin(s)] *nm* jeans.

blues [bluz] *nm* blues *pl*.

bluet [blyɛ] *nm* = **bleuet**.

bluff [blœf] *nm* bluff.

bluffer [blœfe] *vi, vt* to bluff.

BN *sigle f* = Bibliothèque nationale.

BNP *sigle f* = Banque nationale de Paris.

boa [bɔa] *nm* (*ZOOL*): ~ (**constricteur**) boa (constrictor); (*tour de cou*) (feather *ou* fur) boa.

bobard [bɔbaʀ] *nm* (*fam*) tall story.

bobèche [bɔbɛʃ] *nf* candle-ring.

bobine [bɔbin] *nf* (*de fil*) reel; (*de machine à coudre*) spool; (*de machine à écrire*) ribbon; (*ÉLEC*) coil; ~ (**d'allumage**) (*AUTO*) coil; ~ **de pellicule** (*PHOTO*) roll of film.

bobo [bɔbo] *nm* (*aussi fig*) sore spot.

bob(sleigh) [bɔb(slɛg)] *nm* bob(sleigh).

bocage [bɔkaʒ] *nm* (*GÉO*) bocage, *farmland criss-crossed by hedges and trees*; (*bois*) grove, copse (*Brit*).

bocal, aux [bɔkal, -o] *nm* jar.

bock [bɔk] *nm* (beer) glass; (*contenu*) glass of beer.

bœuf [bœf, *pl* bø] *nm* ox (*pl* oxen), steer; (*CULIN*) beef.

bof [bɔf] *excl* (*fam*: *indifférence*) don't care!; (*: pas terrible*) nothing special.

Bogotá [bɔgɔta] *n* Bogotá.

Bohême [bɔɛm] *nf*: **la ~** Bohemia.

bohème [bɔɛm] *a* happy-go-lucky, unconventional.

bohémien, ne [bɔemjɛ̃, -ɛn] *a* Bohemian ♦ *nm/f* gipsy.

boire [bwaʀ] *vt* to drink; (*s'imprégner de*) to soak up; **~ un coup** to have a drink.

bois [bwa] *vb voir* **boire** ♦ *nm* wood; (*ZOOL*) antler; (*MUS*): **les ~** the woodwind; **de ~, en ~** wooden; **~ vert** green wood; **~ mort** deadwood; **~ de lit** bedstead.

boisé, e [bwaze] *a* woody, wooded.

boiser [bwaze] *vt* (*galerie de mine*) to timber; (*chambre*) to panel; (*terrain*) to plant with trees.

boiseries [bwazʀi] *nfpl* panelling *sg*.

boisson [bwasɔ̃] *nf* drink; **pris de ~** drunk, intoxicated; **~s alcoolisées** alcoholic beverages *ou* drinks; **~s non alcoolisées** soft drinks.

boit [bwa] *vb voir* **boire.**

boîte [bwat] *nf* box; (*fam*: *entreprise*) firm, company; **aliments en ~** canned *ou* tinned (*Brit*) foods; **~ de sardines/petits pois** can *ou* tin (*Brit*) of sardines/peas; **mettre qn en ~** (*fam*) to have a laugh at sb's expense; **~ d'allumettes** box of matches; (*vide*) matchbox; **~ de conserves** can *ou* tin (*Brit*) of food); **~ crânienne** cranium; **~ à gants** glove compartment; **~ aux lettres** letter box, mailbox (*US*); (*INFORM*) mailbox; **~ à musique** musical box; **~ noire** (*AVIAT*) black box; **~ de nuit** night club; **~ à ordures** dustbin (*Brit*), trash can (*US*); **~ postale (BP)** PO box; **~ de vitesses** gear box.

boiter [bwate] *vi* to limp; (*fig*) to wobble; (*raisonnement*) to be shaky.

boiteux, euse [bwatø, -øz] *a* lame; wobbly; shaky.

boîtier [bwatje] *nm* case; (*d'appareil-photo*) body; **~ de montre** watch case.

boitiller [bwatije] *vi* to limp slightly, have a slight limp.

boive [bwav] *etc vb voir* **boire.**

bol [bɔl] *nm* bowl; (*contenu*): **un ~ de café** *etc* a bowl of coffee *etc*; **un ~ d'air** a breath of fresh air; **en avoir ras le ~** (*fam*) to have had a bellyful.

bolée [bɔle] *nf* bowlful.

bolet [bɔle] *nm* boletus (mushroom).

bolide [bɔlid] *nm* racing car; **comme un ~** like a rocket.

Bolivie [bɔlivi] *nf*: **la ~** Bolivia.

bolivien, ne [bɔlivjɛ̃, -ɛn] *a* Bolivian ♦ *nm/f*: **B~, ne** Bolivian.

bolognais, e [bɔlɔɲɛ, -ɛz] *a* Bolognese.

Bologne [bɔlɔɲ] *n* Bologna.

bombance [bɔ̃bɑ̃s] *nf*: **faire ~** to have a feast, revel.

bombardement [bɔ̃baʀdəmɑ̃] *nm* bombing.

bombarder [bɔ̃baʀde] *vt* to bomb; **~ qn de**

(*cailloux, lettres*) to bombard sb with; **~ qn directeur** to thrust sb into the director's seat.

bombardier [bɔ̃baʀdje] *nm* (*avion*) bomber; (*aviateur*) bombardier.

bombe [bɔ̃b] *nf* bomb; (*atomiseur*) (aerosol) spray; (*ÉQUITATION*) riding cap; **faire la ~** (*fam*) to go on a binge; **~ atomique** atomic bomb; **~ à retardement** time bomb.

bombé, e [bɔ̃be] *a* rounded; (*mur*) bulging; (*front*) domed; (*route*) steeply cambered.

bomber [bɔ̃be] *vi* to bulge; (*route*) to camber ♦ *vt*: **~ le torse** to swell out one's chest.

bon, bonne [bɔ̃, bɔn] *a* good; (*charitable*): **~ (envers)** good (to), kind (to); (*juste*): **le ~ numéro/moment** the right number/moment; (*intensif*): **un ~ nombre** a good number; (*approprié*): **~ à/pour** fit to/for ♦ *nm* (*billet*) voucher; (*aussi*: **~ cadeau**) gift coupon *ou* voucher ♦ *nf* (*domestique*) maid ♦ *ad*: **il fait ~** it's *ou* the weather's fine ♦ *excl* right!, good!; **vous êtes trop ~** you are too kind; **avoir ~ goût** to taste nice *ou* good; (*fig*) to have good taste; **avoir ~ dos** to be always willing to shoulder responsibility; (*chose*) to be a good excuse; **de bonne heure** early; **sentir ~** to smell good; **tenir ~** to stand firm, hold out; **pour de ~** for good; **à quoi ~ (...)?** what's the good *ou* use of (...)?; **juger ~ de faire ...** to think fit to do ...; **ah ~?** (oh) really?; **il y a du ~ dans cela** there are some advantages in it; **il y a du ~ dans ce qu'il dit** there is some sense in what he says; **~ anniversaire!** happy birthday!; **~ voyage!** have a good journey!, enjoy your trip!; **bonne chance!** good luck!; **bonne année!** happy New Year!; **bonne nuit!** good night!; **~ de caisse** cash voucher; **~ enfant** *a inv* accommodating, easy-going; **~ d'essence** petrol coupon; **~ marché** *a inv, ad* cheap; **~ mot** witticism; **~ sens** common sense; **~ à tirer** pass for press; **~ du Trésor** Treasury bond; **~ vivant** jovial chap; **bonne d'enfant** nanny; **bonne femme** (*péj*) woman; female (*péj*); **bonne sœur** nun; **bonne à tout faire** general help; **bonnes œuvres** charitable works; charities.

bonasse [bɔnas] *a* soft, meek.

bonbon [bɔ̃bɔ̃] *nm* (boiled) sweet.

bonbonne [bɔ̃bɔn] *nf* demijohn; carboy.

bonbonnière [bɔ̃bɔnjɛʀ] *nf* sweet (*Brit*) *ou* candy (*US*) box.

bond [bɔ̃] *nm* leap; (*d'une balle*) rebound, ricochet; **faire un ~** to leap in the air; **d'un seul ~** in one bound, with one leap; **~ en avant** (*fig*: *progrès*) leap forward.

bonde [bɔ̃d] *nf* (*d'évier etc*) plug; (*: trou*) plughole; (*de tonneau*) bung; bunghole.

bondé, e [bɔ̃de] *a* packed (full).

bondieuserie [bɔ̃djøzʀi] *nf* (*péj*: *objet*) religious knick-knack.

bondir [bɔ̃diʀ] *vi* to leap; **~ de joie** (*fig*) to jump for joy; **~ de colère** (*fig*) to be hopping mad.

bonheur [bɔnœʀ] *nm* happiness; **avoir le ~ de** to have the good fortune to; **porter ~ (à qn)** to bring (sb) luck; **au petit ~** haphazardly; **par ~** fortunately.

bonhomie [bɔnɔmi] *nf* goodnaturedness.

bonhomme [bɔnɔm], *pl* **bonshommes**

[bɔ̃zɔm] *nm* fellow ♦ *a* good-natured; **un vieux ~** an old chap; **aller son ~ de chemin** to carry on in one's own sweet way; **~ de neige** snowman.

boni [bɔni] *nm* profit.

bonification [bɔnifikasjɔ̃] *nf* bonus.

bonifier [bɔnifje] *vt*, **se ~** *vi* to improve.

boniment [bɔnimɑ̃] *nm* patter *q*.

bonjour [bɔ̃ʒuʀ] *excl, nm* hello; (*selon l'heure*) good morning (*ou* afternoon); **donner** *ou* **souhaiter le ~ à qn** to bid sb good morning *ou* afternoon.

Bonn [bɔn] *n* Bonn.

bonne [bɔn] *af, nf voir* **bon**.

bonne-maman, *pl* **bonnes-mamans** [bɔnmamɑ̃] granny, grandma, gran.

bonnement [bɔnmɑ̃] *ad*: **tout ~** quite simply.

bonnet [bɔnɛ] *nm* bonnet, hat; (*de soutien-gorge*) cup; **~ d'âne** dunce's cap; **~ de bain** bathing cap; **~ de nuit** nightcap.

bonneterie [bɔnɛtʀi] *nf* hosiery.

bon-papa, *pl* **bons-papas** [bɔ̃papa] *nm* grandpa, grandad.

bonsoir [bɔ̃swaʀ] *excl* good evening.

bonté [bɔ̃te] *nf* kindness *q*; **avoir la ~ de** to be kind *ou* good enough to.

bonus [bɔnys] *nm* (*assurances*) no-claims bonus.

bonze [bɔ̃z] *nm* (*REL*) bonze.

boomerang [bumʀɑ̃g] *nm* boomerang.

borborygme [bɔʀbɔʀigm(ə)] *nm* rumbling noise.

bord [bɔʀ] *nm* (*de table, verre, falaise*) edge; (*de rivière, lac*) bank; (*de route*) side; (*de vêtement*) edge, border; (*de chapeau*) brim; (**monter**) **à ~** (to go) on board; **jeter par-dessus ~** to throw overboard; **le commandant/les hommes du ~** the ship's master/crew; **du même ~** (*fig*) of the same opinion; **au ~ de la mer/route** at the seaside/roadside; **être au ~ des larmes** to be on the verge of tears; **virer de ~** (*NAVIG*) to tack; **sur les ~s** (*fig*) slightly; **de tous ~s** on all sides; **~ du trottoir** kerb (*Brit*), curb (*US*).

bordage [bɔʀdaʒ] *nm* (*NAVIG*) planking *q*; plating *q*.

bordeaux [bɔʀdo] *nm* Bordeaux ♦ *a inv* maroon.

bordée [bɔʀde] *nf* broadside; **une ~ d'injures** a volley of abuse; **tirer une ~** to go on the town.

bordel [bɔʀdɛl] *nm* brothel; (*fam!*) bloody (*Brit*) *ou* goddamn (*US*) mess (!) ♦ *excl* hell!

bordelais, e [bɔʀdəlɛ, -ɛz] *a* of *ou* from Bordeaux.

border [bɔʀde] *vt* (*être le long de*) to border, line; (*garnir*): **~ qch de** to line sth with; to trim sth with; (*qn dans son lit*) to tuck up.

bordereau, x [bɔʀdəʀo] *nm* docket, slip.

bordure [bɔʀdyʀ] *nf* border; (*sur un vêtement*) trim(ming), border; **en ~ de** on the edge of.

boréal, e, aux [bɔʀeal, -o] *a* boreal, northern.

borgne [bɔʀɲ(ə)] *a* one-eyed; **hôtel ~** shady hotel; **fenêtre ~** obstructed window.

bornage [bɔʀnaʒ] *nm* (*d'un terrain*) demarcation.

borne [bɔʀn(ə)] *nf* boundary stone; (*aussi:* **~**

kilométrique) kilometre-marker, ≈ milestone; **~s** *nfpl* (*fig*) limits; **dépasser les ~s** to go too far; **sans ~(s)** boundless.

borné, e [bɔʀne] *a* narrow; (*obtus*) narrow-minded.

Bornéo [bɔʀneo] *nm*: **le ~** Borneo.

borner [bɔʀne] *vt* (*délimiter*) to limit; (*limiter*) to confine; **se ~ à faire** to content o.s. with doing; to limit o.s. to doing.

bosniaque [bɔznjak] *a* Bosnian.

bosnien, ne [bɔznjɛ̃, -ɛn] *a* Bosnian.

Bosphore [bɔsfɔʀ] *nm*: **le ~** the Bosphorus.

bosquet [bɔskɛ] *nm* copse (*Brit*), grove.

bosse [bɔs] *nf* (*de terrain etc*) bump; (*enflure*) lump; (*du bossu, du chameau*) hump; **avoir la ~ des maths** *etc* to have a gift for maths *etc*; **il a roulé sa ~** he's been around.

bosseler [bɔsle] *vt* (*ouvrer*) to emboss; (*abîmer*) to dent.

bosser [bɔse] *vi* (*fam*) to work; (: *dur*) to slog (hard) (*Brit*), slave (away).

bosseur, euse [bɔsœʀ, -øz] *nm/f* (hard) worker, slogger (*Brit*).

bossu, e [bɔsy] *nm/f* hunchback.

bot [bo] *am*: **pied ~** club foot.

botanique [bɔtanik] *nf* botany ♦ *a* botanic(al).

botaniste [bɔtanist(ə)] *nm/f* botanist.

Botswana [bɔtswana] *nm*: **le ~** Botswana.

botte [bɔt] *nf* (*soulier*) (high) boot; (*ESCRIME*) thrust; (*gerbe*): **~ de paille** bundle of straw; **~ de radis/d'asperges** bunch of radishes/asparagus; **~s de caoutchouc** wellington boots.

botter [bɔte] *vt* to put boots on; (*donner un coup de pied à*) to kick; (*fam*): **ça me botte** I fancy that.

bottier [bɔtje] *nm* bootmaker.

bottillon [bɔtijɔ̃] *nm* bootee.

bottin [bɔtɛ̃] *nm* ® directory.

bottine [bɔtin] *nf* ankle boot.

botulisme [bɔtylism(ə)] *nm* botulism.

bouc [buk] *nm* goat; (*barbe*) goatee; **~ émissaire** scapegoat.

boucan [bukɑ̃] *nm* din, racket.

bouche [buʃ] *nf* mouth; **une ~ à nourrir** a mouth to feed; **les ~s inutiles** the non-productive members of the population; **faire le ~ à ~ à qn** to give sb the kiss of life (*Brit*), give sb mouth-to-mouth resuscitation; **de ~ à oreille** confidentially; **pour la bonne ~** (*pour la fin*) till last; **faire venir l'eau à la ~** to make one's mouth water; **~ cousue!** mum's the word!; **~ d'aération** air vent; **~ de chaleur** hot air vent; **~ d'égout** manhole; **~ d'incendie** fire hydrant; **~ de métro** métro entrance.

bouché, e [buʃe] *a* (*flacon etc*) stoppered; (*temps, ciel*) overcast; (*carrière*) blocked; (*péj: personne*) thick; (*trompette*) muted; **avoir le nez ~** to have a blocked(-up) nose.

bouchée [buʃe] *nf* mouthful; **faire qu'une ~ de** (*fig*) to make short work of; **pour une ~ de pain** (*fig*) for next to nothing; **~s à la reine** chicken vol-au-vents.

boucher [buʃe] *nm* butcher ♦ *vt* (*pour colmater*) to stop up; to fill up; (*obstruer*) to block (up); **se ~** (*tuyau etc*) to block up, get blocked up; **se ~ le nez** to hold one's nose.

bouchère [buʃɛʀ] *nf* butcher; (*femme du*

boucher) butcher's wife.
boucherie [buʃʀi] *nf* butcher's (shop); (*métier*) butchery; (*fig*) slaughter, butchery.
bouche-trou [buʃtʀu] *nm* (*fig*) stop-gap.
bouchon [buʃɔ̃] *nm* (*en liège*) cork; (*autre matière*) stopper; (*fig: embouteillage*) hold-up; (*PÊCHE*) float; ~ **doseur** measuring cap.
bouchonner [buʃɔne] *vt* to rub down ♦ *vi* to form a traffic jam.
bouchot [buʃo] *nm* mussel bed.
bouclage [buklaʒ] *nm* sealing off.
boucle [bukl(ə)] *nf* (*forme, figure, aussi IN-FORM*) buckle; (*objet*) buckle; ~ (**de cheveux**) curl; ~ **d'oreilles** earring.
bouclé, e [bukle] *a* curly; (*tapis*) uncut.
boucler [bukle] *vt* (*fermer: ceinture etc*) to fasten; (: *magasin*) to shut; (*terminer*) to finish off; (: *circuit*) to complete; (*budget*) to balance; (*enfermer*) to shut away; (: *condamné*) to lock up; (: *quartier*) to seal off ♦ *vi* to curl; **faire** ~ (*cheveux*) to curl; ~ **la boucle** (*AVIAT*) to loop the loop.
bouclette [buklɛt] *nf* small curl.
bouclier [buklije] *nm* shield.
bouddha [buda] *nm* Buddha.
bouddhisme [budism(ə)] *nm* Buddhism.
bouddhiste [budist(ə)] *nm/f* Buddhist.
bouder [bude] *vi* to sulk ♦ *vt* (*chose*) to turn one's nose up at; (*personne*) to refuse to have anything to do with.
bouderie [budʀi] *nf* sulking *q*.
boudeur, euse [budœʀ, -øz] *a* sullen, sulky.
boudin [budɛ̃] *nm* (*CULIN*) black pudding; (*TECH*) roll; ~ **blanc** white pudding.
boudiné, e [budine] *a* (*doigt*) podgy; (*serré*): ~ **dans** (*vêtement*) bulging out of.
boudoir [budwaʀ] *nm* boudoir; (*biscuit*) sponge finger.
boue [bu] *nf* mud.
bouée [bwe] *nf* buoy; (*de baigneur*) rubber ring; ~ (**de sauvetage**) lifebuoy; (*fig*) life-line.
boueux, euse [bwø, -øz] *a* muddy ♦ *nm* ref-use (*Brit*) *ou* garbage (*US*) collector.
bouffant, e [bufɑ̃, -ɑ̃t] *a* puffed out.
bouffe [buf] *nf* (*fam*) grub, food.
bouffée [bufe] *nf* puff; ~ **de chaleur** blast of hot air; ~ **de fièvre/de honte** flush of fever/shame; ~ **d'orgueil** fit of pride.
bouffer [bufe] *vi* (*fam*) to eat; (*COUTURE*) to puff out ♦ *vt* (*fam*) to eat.
bouffi, e [bufi] *a* swollen.
bouffon, ne [bufɔ̃, -ɔn] *a* farcical, comical ♦ *nm* jester.
bouge [buʒ] *nm* (*bar louche*) (low) dive; (*taudis*) hovel.
bougeoir [buʒwaʀ] *nm* candlestick.
bougeotte [buʒɔt] *nf*: **avoir la** ~ to have the fidgets.
bouger [buʒe] *vi* to move; (*dent etc*) to be loose; (*changer*) to alter; (*agir*) to stir ♦ *vt* to move; **se** ~ (*fam*) to move (oneself).
bougie [buʒi] *nf* candle; (*AUTO*) spark(ing) plug.
bougon, ne [bugɔ̃, -ɔn] *a* grumpy.
bougonner [bugɔne] *vi*, *vt* to grumble.
bougre [bugʀ(ə)] *nm* chap; (*fam*): **ce** ~ **de ...** that confounded ....
bouillabaisse [bujabɛs] *nf type of fish soup*.

bouillant, e [bujɑ̃, -ɑ̃t] *a* (*qui bout*) boiling; (*très chaud*) boiling (hot); (*fig: ardent*) hot-headed; ~ **de colère** *etc* seething with anger *etc*.
bouilleur [bujœʀ] *nm*: ~ **de cru** (home) distiller.
bouillie [buji] *nf* gruel; (*de bébé*) cereal; **en** ~ (*fig*) crushed.
bouillir [bujiʀ] *vi* to boil ♦ *vt* (*aussi*: **faire** ~: *CULIN*) to boil; ~ **de colère** *etc* to seethe with anger *etc*.
bouilloire [bujwaʀ] *nf* kettle.
bouillon [bujɔ̃] *nm* (*CULIN*) stock *q*; (*bulles, écume*) bubble; ~ **de culture** culture medium.
bouillonnement [bujɔnmɑ̃] *nm* (*d'un liquide*) bubbling; (*des idées*) ferment.
bouillonner [bujɔne] *vi* to bubble; (*fig*) to bubble up; (*torrent*) to foam.
bouillotte [bujɔt] *nf* hot-water bottle.
boulanger, ère [bulɑ̃ʒe, -ɛʀ] *nm/f* baker ♦ *nf* (*femme du boulanger*) baker's wife.
boulangerie [bulɑ̃ʒʀi] *nf* bakery, baker's (shop); (*commerce*) bakery; ~ **industrielle** bakery.
boulangerie-pâtisserie, *pl* **boulangeries-pâtisseries** [bulɑ̃ʒʀipɑtisʀi] *nf* baker's and confectioner's (shop).
boule [bul] *nf* (*gén*) ball; (*pour jouer*) bowl; (*de machine à écrire*) golf ball; **roulé en** ~ curled up in a ball; **se mettre en** ~ (*fig*) to fly off the handle, blow one's top; **perdre la** ~ (*fig: fam*) to go off one's rocker; ~ **de gomme** (*bonbon*) gum(drop), pastille; ~ **de neige** snowball; **faire** ~ **de neige** (*fig*) to snowball.
bouleau, x [bulo] *nm* (silver) birch.
bouledogue [buldɔg] *nm* bulldog.
boulet [bulɛ] *nm* (*aussi*: ~ **de canon**) cannon-ball; (*de bagnard*) ball and chain; (*charbon*) (coal) nut.
boulette [bulɛt] *nf* ball.
boulevard [bulvaʀ] *nm* boulevard.
bouleversant, e [bulvɛʀsɑ̃, -ɑ̃t] *a* (*récit*) deeply distressing; (*nouvelle*) shattering.
bouleversé, e [bulvɛʀse] *a* (*ému*) deeply distressed; shattered.
bouleversement [bulvɛʀsəmɑ̃] *nm* (*politique, social*) upheaval.
bouleverser [bulvɛʀse] *vt* (*émouvoir*) to over-whelm; (*causer du chagrin à*) to distress; (*pays, vie*) to disrupt; (*papiers, objets*) to turn upside down, upset.
boulier [bulje] *nm* abacus; (*de jeu*) scoring board.
boulimie [bulimi] *nf* compulsive eating.
boulingrin [bulɛ̃gʀɛ̃] *nm* lawn.
bouliste [bulist(ə)] *nm/f* bowler.
boulocher [bulɔʃe] *vi* (*laine etc*) to develop little snarls.
boulodrome [bulɔdʀɔm] *nm* bowling pitch.
boulon [bulɔ̃] *nm* bolt.
boulonner [bulɔne] *vt* to bolt.
boulot [bulo] *nm* (*fam: travail*) work.
boulot, te [bulo, -ɔt] *a* plump, tubby.
boum [bum] *nm* bang ♦ *nf* party.
bouquet [bukɛ] *nm* (*de fleurs*) bunch (of flowers), bouquet; (*de persil etc*) bunch; (*parfum*) bouquet; (*fig*) crowning piece; **c'est**

le ~! that's the last straw!; **~ garni** (*CULIN*) bouquet garni.
bouquetin [buktɛ̃] *nm* ibex.
bouquin [bukɛ̃] *nm* (*fam*) book.
bouquiner [bukine] *vi* (*fam*) to read.
bouquiniste [bukinist(ə)] *nm/f* bookseller.
bourbeux, euse [buʀbø, -øz] *a* muddy.
bourbier [buʀbje] *nm* (quag)mire.
bourde [buʀd(ə)] *nf* (*erreur*) howler; (*gaffe*) blunder.
bourdon [buʀdɔ̃] *nm* bumblebee.
bourdonnement [buʀdɔnmɑ̃] *nm* buzzing *q*, buzz; **avoir des ~s d'oreilles** to have a buzzing (noise) in one's ears.
bourdonner [buʀdɔne] *vi* to buzz; (*moteur*) to hum.
bourg [buʀ] *nm* small market town (*ou* village).
bourgade [buʀgad] *nf* township.
bourgeois, e [buʀʒwa, -waz] *a* (*péj*) ≈ (upper) middle class; bourgeois; (*maison etc*) very comfortable ♦ *nm/f* (*autrefois*) burgher.
bourgeoisie [buʀʒwazi] *nf* ≈ upper middle classes *pl*; bourgeoisie; **petite ~** middle classes.
bourgeon [buʀʒɔ̃] *nm* bud.
bourgeonner [buʀʒɔne] *vi* to bud.
Bourgogne [buʀgɔɲ] *nf*: **la ~** Burgundy ♦ *nm*: **b~** burgundy (wine).
bourguignon, ne [buʀgiɲɔ̃, -ɔn] *a* of *ou* from Burgundy, Burgundian; **bœuf ~** bœuf bourguignon.
Bourkina [buʀkina] *nm*: **le ~** Burkina Faso.
bourlinguer [buʀlɛ̃ge] *vi* to knock about a lot, get around a lot.
bourrade [buʀad] *nf* shove, thump.
bourrage [buʀaʒ] *nm* (*papier*) jamming; **~ de crâne** brainwashing; (*SCOL*) cramming.
bourrasque [buʀask(ə)] *nf* squall.
bourratif, ive [buʀatif, -iv] *a* filling, stodgy.
bourre [buʀ] *nf* (*de coussin, matelas etc*) stuffing.
bourré, e [buʀe] *a* (*rempli*): **~ de** crammed full of; (*fam: ivre*) pickled, plastered.
bourreau, x [buʀo] *nm* executioner; (*fig*) torturer; **~ de travail** workaholic, glutton for work.
bourrelé, e [buʀle] *a*: **être ~ de remords** to be racked with remorse.
bourrelet [buʀlɛ] *nm* draught (*Brit*) *ou* draft (*US*) excluder; (*de peau*) fold *ou* roll (of flesh).
bourrer [buʀe] *vt* (*pipe*) to fill; (*poêle*) to pack; (*valise*) to cram (full); **~ de** to cram (full) with, stuff with; **~ de coups** to hammer blows on, pummel; **~ le crâne à qn** to pull the wool over sb's eyes; (*endoctriner*) to brainwash sb.
bourricot [buʀiko] *nm* small donkey.
bourrique [buʀik] *nf* (*âne*) ass.
bourru, e [buʀy] *a* surly, gruff.
bourse [buʀs(ə)] *nf* (*subvention*) grant; (*porte-monnaie*) purse; **sans ~ délier** without spending a penny; **la B~** the Stock Exchange; **~ du travail** ≈ trades union council (regional headquarters).
boursicoter [buʀsikɔte] *vi* (*COMM*) to dabble on the Stock Market.

boursier, ière [buʀsje, -jɛʀ] *a* (*COMM*) Stock Market *cpd* ♦ *nm/f* (*SCOL*) grant-holder.
boursouflé, e [buʀsufle] *a* swollen, puffy; (*fig*) bombastic, turgid.
boursoufler [buʀsufle] *vt* to puff up, bloat; **se ~** *vi* (*visage*) to swell *ou* puff up; (*peinture*) to blister.
boursouflure [buʀsuflyʀ] *nf* (*du visage*) swelling, puffiness; (*de la peinture*) blister; (*fig: du style*) pomposity.
bous [bu] *vb voir* **bouillir**.
bousculade [buskylad] *nf* (*hâte*) rush; (*poussée*) crush.
bousculer [buskyle] *vt* to knock over; to knock into; (*fig*) to push, rush.
bouse [buz] *nf*: **~ (de vache)** (cow) dung *q* (*Brit*), manure *q*.
bousiller [buzije] *vt* (*fam*) to wreck.
boussole [busɔl] *nf* compass.
bout [bu] *vb voir* **bouillir** ♦ *nm* bit; (*extrémité: d'un bâton etc*) tip; (: *d'une ficelle, table, rue, période*) end; **au ~ de** at the end of, after; **au ~ du compte** at the end of the day; **pousser qn à ~** to push sb to the limit (of his patience); **venir à ~ de** to manage to finish (off) *ou* overcome; **~ à ~** end to end; **à tout ~ de champ** at every turn; **d'un ~ à l'autre, de ~ en ~** from one end to the other; **à ~ portant** at point-blank range; **un ~ de chou** (*enfant*) a little tot; **~ d'essai** (*CINÉMA etc*) screen test; **~ filtre** filter tip.
boutade [butad] *nf* quip, sally.
boute-en-train [butɑ̃tʀɛ̃] *nm inv* live wire (*fig*).
bouteille [butɛj] *nf* bottle; (*de gaz butane*) cylinder.
boutiquaire [butikɛʀ] *a*: **niveau ~** shopping level.
boutique [butik] *nf* shop (*Brit*), store (*US*); (*de grand couturier, de mode*) boutique.
boutiquier, ière [butikje, -jɛʀ] *nm/f* shopkeeper (*Brit*), storekeeper (*US*).
boutoir [butwaʀ] *nm*: **coup de ~** (*choc*) thrust; (*fig: propos*) barb.
bouton [butɔ̃] *nm* (*de vêtement, électrique etc*) button; (*BOT*) bud; (*sur la peau*) spot; (*de porte*) knob; **~ de manchette** cuff-link; **~ d'or** buttercup.
boutonner [butɔne] *vt* to button up, do up; **se ~** to button one's clothes up.
boutonneux, euse [butɔnø, -øz] *a* spotty.
boutonnière [butɔnjɛʀ] *nf* buttonhole.
bouton-poussoir, *pl* **boutons-poussoirs** [butɔ̃puswaʀ] *nm* pushbutton.
bouton-pression, *pl* **boutons-pression** [butɔ̃pʀesjɔ̃] *nm* press stud, snap fastener.
bouture [butyʀ] *nf* cutting; **faire des ~s** to take cuttings.
bouvreuil [buvʀœj] *nm* bullfinch.
bovidé [bɔvide] *nm* bovine.
bovin, e [bɔvɛ̃, -in] *a* bovine ♦ *nm*: **~s** cattle.
bowling [bɔliŋ] *nm* (tenpin) bowling; (*salle*) bowling alley.
box [bɔks] *nm* lock-up (garage); (*de salle, dortoir*) cubicle; (*d'écurie*) loose-box; **le ~ des accusés** the dock.
box(-calf) [bɔks(kalf)] *nm inv* box calf.
boxe [bɔks(ə)] *nf* boxing.
boxer [bɔkse] *vi* to box ♦ *nm* [bɔksɛʀ] (*chien*)

boxer.

boxeur [bɔksœʀ] *nm* boxer.

boyau, x [bwajo] *nm* (*corde de raquette etc*) (cat) gut; (*galerie*) passage(way); (narrow) gallery; (*pneu de bicyclette*) tubeless tyre ♦ *nmpl* (*viscères*) entrails, guts.

boycottage [bɔjkɔtaʒ] *nm* (*d'un produit*) boycotting.

boycotter [bɔjkɔte] *vt* to boycott.

BP *sigle f* = **boîte postale.**

BPAL *sigle f* (= *base de plein air et de loisir*) open-air leisure centre.

BPF *sigle* (= *bon pour francs*) *printed on cheques before space for amount to be inserted.*

brabançon, ne [bʀabɑ̃sɔ̃, -ɔn] *a* of *ou* from Brabant.

Brabant [bʀabɑ̃] *nm*: **le ~** Brabant.

bracelet [bʀaslɛ] *nm* bracelet.

bracelet-montre [bʀaslɛmɔ̃tʀ(ə)] *nm* wristwatch.

braconnage [bʀakɔnaʒ] *nm* poaching.

braconner [bʀakɔne] *vi* to poach.

braconnier [bʀakɔnje] *nm* poacher.

brader [bʀade] *vt* to sell off, sell cheaply.

braderie [bʀadʀi] *nf* clearance sale; (*par des particuliers*) ≈ car boot sale (*Brit*), ≈ garage sale (*US*); (*magasin*) discount store; (*sur marché*) cut-price (*Brit*) *ou* cut-rate (*US*) stall.

braguette [bʀagɛt] *nf* fly, flies *pl* (*Brit*), zipper (*US*).

braille [bʀaj] *nm* Braille.

braillement [bʀajmɑ̃] *nm* (*cri*) bawling *q*, yelling *q*.

brailler [bʀaje] *vi* to bawl, yell ♦ *vt* to bawl out, yell out.

braire [bʀɛʀ] *vi* to bray.

braise [bʀɛz] *nf* embers *pl*.

braiser [bʀeze] *vt* to braise; **bœuf braisé** braised steak.

bramer [bʀame] *vi* to bell; (*fig*) to wail.

brancard [bʀɑ̃kaʀ] *nm* (*civière*) stretcher; (*bras, perche*) shaft.

brancardier [bʀɑ̃kaʀdje] *nm* stretcher-bearer.

branchages [bʀɑ̃ʃaʒ] *nmpl* branches, boughs.

branche [bʀɑ̃ʃ] *nf* branch; (*de lunettes*) side (-piece).

branché, e [bʀɑ̃ʃe] *a* (*fam*) switched-on, trendy ♦ *nm/f* (*fam*) trendy.

branchement [bʀɑ̃ʃmɑ̃] *nm* connection.

brancher [bʀɑ̃ʃe] *vt* to connect (up); (*en mettant la prise*) to plug in; **~ qn/qch sur** (*fig*) to get sb/sth launched onto.

branchies [bʀɑ̃ʃi] *nfpl* gills.

brandade [bʀɑ̃dad] *nf* brandade (*cod dish*).

brandebourgeois, e [bʀɑ̃dəbuʀʒwa, -waz] *a* of *ou* from Brandenburg.

brandir [bʀɑ̃diʀ] *vt* (*arme*) to brandish, wield; (*document*) to flourish, wave.

brandon [bʀɑ̃dɔ̃] *nm* firebrand.

branlant, e [bʀɑ̃lɑ̃, -ɑ̃t] *a* (*mur, meuble*) shaky.

branle [bʀɑ̃l] *nm*: **mettre en ~** to set swinging; **donner le ~ à** to set in motion.

branle-bas [bʀɑ̃lba] *nm inv* commotion.

branler [bʀɑ̃le] *vi* to be shaky, be loose ♦ *vt*: **~ la tête** to shake one's head.

braquage [bʀakaʒ] *nm* (*fam*) stick-up, hold-

up; (*AUTO*): **rayon de ~** turning circle.

braque [bʀak] *nm* (*ZOOL*) pointer.

braquer [bʀake] *vi* (*AUTO*) to turn (the wheel) ♦ *vt* (*revolver etc*): **~ qch sur** to aim sth at, point sth at; (*mettre en colère*): **~ qn** to antagonize sb, put sb's back up; **~ son regard sur** to fix one's gaze on; **se ~** *vi*: **se ~ (contre)** to take a stand (against).

bras [bʀa] *nm* arm; (*de fleuve*) branch ♦ *nmpl* (*fig: travailleurs*) labour *sg* (*Brit*), labor *sg* (*US*), hands; **~ dessus ~ dessous** arm in arm; **à ~ raccourcis** with fists flying; **à tour de ~** with all one's might; **baisser les ~** to give up; **~ droit** (*fig*) right hand man; **~ de fer** arm-wrestling; **une partie de ~ de fer** (*fig*) a trial of strength; **~ de levier** lever arm; **~ de mer** arm of the sea, sound.

brasero [bʀazeʀo] *nm* brazier.

brasier [bʀazje] *nm* blaze, (blazing) inferno; (*fig*) inferno.

Brasilia [bʀazilja] *n* Brasilia.

bras-le-corps [bʀalkɔʀ]: **à ~** *ad* (a)round the waist.

brassage [bʀasaʒ] *nm* (*de la bière*) brewing; (*fig*) mixing.

brassard [bʀasaʀ] *nm* armband.

brasse [bʀas] *nf* (*nage*) breast-stroke; (*mesure*) fathom; **~ papillon** butterfly (-stroke).

brassée [bʀase] *nf* armful; **une ~ de** (*fig*) a number of.

brasser [bʀase] *vt* (*bière*) to brew; (*remuer: salade*) to toss; (: *cartes*) to shuffle; (*jig*) to mix; **~ l'argent/les affaires** to handle a lot of money/business.

brasserie [bʀasʀi] *nf* (*restaurant*) bar (*selling food*), brasserie; (*usine*) brewery.

brasseur [bʀasœʀ] *nm* (*de bière*) brewer; **~ d'affaires** big businessman.

brassière [bʀasjɛʀ] *nf* (*baby's*) vest (*Brit*) *ou* undershirt (*US*); (*de sauvetage*) life jacket.

bravache [bʀavaʃ] *nm* blusterer, braggart.

bravade [bʀavad] *nf*: **par ~** out of bravado.

brave [bʀav] *a* (*courageux*) brave; (*bon, gentil*) good, kind.

bravement [bʀavmɑ̃] *ad* bravely; (*résolument*) boldly.

braver [bʀave] *vt* to defy.

bravo [bʀavo] *excl* bravo! ♦ *nm* cheer.

bravoure [bʀavuʀ] *nf* bravery.

BRB *sigle f* (*POLICE*): = *Brigade de répression du banditisme*) ≈ serious crime squad.

break [bʀɛk] *nm* (*AUTO*) estate car (*Brit*), station wagon (*US*).

brebis [bʀəbi] *nf* ewe; **~ galeuse** black sheep.

brèche [bʀɛʃ] *nf* breach, gap; **être sur la ~** (*fig*) to be on the go.

bredouille [bʀəduj] *a* empty-handed.

bredouiller [bʀəduje] *vi, vt* to mumble, stammer.

bref, brève [bʀɛf, bʀɛv] *a* short, brief ♦ *ad* in short ♦ *nf* (*voyelle*) short vowel; (*information*) brief news item; **d'un ton ~** sharply, curtly; **en ~** in short, in brief; **à ~ délai** shortly.

brelan [bʀəlɑ̃] *nm*: **un ~** three of a kind; **un ~ d'as** three aces.

breloque [bʀəlɔk] *nf* charm.

brème [bʀɛm] *nf* bream.

Brésil [bʀezil] *nm*: le ~ Brazil.
brésilien, ne [bʀeziljɛ̃, -ɛn] *a* Brazilian ♦ *nm/f*: B~, **ne** Brazilian.
bressan, e [bʀesɑ̃, -an] *a* of *ou* from Bresse.
Bretagne [bʀətaɲ] *nf*: la ~ Brittany.
bretelle [bʀətɛl] *nf* (*de fusil etc*) sling; (*de vêtement*) strap; (*d'autoroute*) slip road (*Brit*), entrance *ou* exit ramp (*US*); ~**s** *nfpl* (*pour pantalon*) braces (*Brit*), suspenders (*US*); ~ **de contournement** (*AUTO*) bypass; ~ **de raccordement** (*AUTO*) access road.
breton, ne [bʀətɔ̃, -ɔn] *a* Breton ♦ *nm* (*LING*) Breton ♦ *nm/f*: B~, **ne** Breton.
breuvage [bʀœvaʒ] *nm* beverage, drink.
brève [bʀɛv] *af*, *nf voir* **bref**.
brevet [bʀəvɛ] *nm* diploma, certificate; ~ (**d'invention**) patent; ~ **d'apprentissage** certificate of apprenticeship; ~ (**des collèges**) *school certificate, taken at approx. 16 years.*
breveté, e [bʀəvte] *a* patented; (*diplômé*) qualified.
breveter [bʀəvte] *vt* to patent.
bréviaire [bʀevjɛʀ] *nm* breviary.
BRGM *sigle m = Bureau de recherches géologiques et minières.*
briard, e [bʀijaʀ, -aʀd(ə)] *a* of *ou* from Brie ♦ *nm* (*chien*) briard.
bribes [bʀib] *nfpl* bits, scraps; (*d'une conversation*) snatches; **par** ~ piecemeal.
bric [bʀik]: **de** ~ **et de broc** *ad* with any old thing.
bric-à-brac [bʀikabʀak] *nm inv* bric-a-brac, jumble.
bricolage [bʀikɔlaʒ] *nm*: **le** ~ do-it-yourself (jobs); (*péj*) patched-up job.
bricole [bʀikɔl] *nf* (*babiole, chose insignifiante*) trifle; (*petit travail*) small job.
bricoler [bʀikɔle] *vi* to do odd jobs; (*en amateur*) to do DIY jobs; (*passe-temps*) to potter about ♦ *vt* (*réparer*) to fix up; (*mal réparer*) to tinker with; (*trafiquer: voiture etc*) to doctor, fix.
bricoleur, euse [bʀikɔlœʀ, -øz] *nm/f* handyman/woman, DIY enthusiast.
bride [bʀid] *nf* bridle; (*d'un bonnet*) string, tie; **à** ~ **abattue** flat out, hell for leather; **tenir en** ~ to keep in check; **lâcher la** ~ **à**, **laisser la** ~ **sur le cou à** to give free rein to.
bridé, e [bʀide] *a*: **yeux** ~**s** slit eyes.
brider [bʀide] *vt* (*réprimer*) to keep in check; (*cheval*) to bridle; (*CULIN: volaille*) to truss.
bridge [bʀidʒ(ə)] *nm* bridge.
brie [bʀi] *nm* Brie (*cheese*).
brièvement [bʀijɛvmɑ̃] *ad* briefly.
brièveté [bʀijɛvte] *nf* brevity.
brigade [bʀigad] *nf* squad; (*MIL*) brigade.
brigadier [bʀigadje] *nm* (*POLICE*) ≈ sergeant; (*MIL*) bombardier; corporal.
brigadier-chef, *pl* **brigadiers-chefs** [bʀigadjeʃɛf] *nm* ≈ lance-sergeant.
brigand [bʀigɑ̃] *nm* brigand.
brigandage [bʀigɑ̃daʒ] *nm* robbery.
briguer [bʀige] *vt* to aspire to; (*suffrages*) to canvass.
brillamment [bʀijamɑ̃] *ad* brilliantly.
brillant, e [bʀijɑ̃, -ɑ̃t] *a* brilliant; bright; (*luisant*) shiny, shining ♦ *nm* (*diamant*) brilliant.

briller [bʀije] *vi* to shine.
brimade [bʀimad] *nf* vexation, harassment *q*; bullying *q*.
brimbaler [bʀɛ̃bale] *vb* = **bringuebaler**.
brimer [bʀime] *vt* to harass; to bully.
brin [bʀɛ̃] *nm* (*de laine, ficelle etc*) strand; (*fig*): **un** ~ **de** a bit of; **un** ~ **mystérieux** *etc* (*fam*) a weeny bit mysterious *etc*; ~ **d'herbe** blade of grass; ~ **de muguet** sprig of lily of the valley; ~ **de paille** wisp of straw.
brindille [bʀɛ̃dij] *nf* twig.
bringue [bʀɛ̃g] *nf* (*fam*): **faire la** ~ to go on a binge.
bringuebaler [bʀɛ̃gbale] *vi* to shake (about) ♦ *vt* to cart about.
brio [bʀijo] *nm* brilliance; (*MUS*) brio; **avec** ~ brilliantly, with panache.
brioche [bʀijɔʃ] *nf* brioche (bun); (*fam*: *ventre*) paunch.
brioché, e [bʀijɔʃe] *a* brioche-style.
brique [bʀik] *nf* brick; (*fam*) 10,000 francs ♦ *a inv* brick red.
briquer [bʀike] *vt* (*fam*) to polish up.
briquet [bʀikɛ] *nm* (*cigarette*) lighter.
briqueterie [bʀiktʀi] *nf* brickyard.
bris [bʀi] *nm*: ~ **de clôture** (*JUR*) breaking in; ~ **de glaces** (*AUTO*) breaking of windows.
brisant [bʀizɑ̃] *nm* reef; (*vague*) breaker.
brise [bʀiz] *nf* breeze.
brisé, e [bʀize] *a* broken; ~ (**de fatigue**) exhausted; **d'une voix** ~**e** in a voice broken with emotion; **pâte** ~**e** shortcrust pastry.
brisées [bʀize] *nfpl*: **aller** *ou* **marcher sur les** ~ **de qn** to compete with sb in his own province.
brise-glace [bʀizglas] *nm inv* icebreaker.
brise-jet [bʀizʒɛ] *nm inv* tap swirl.
brise-lames [bʀizlam] *nm inv* breakwater.
briser [bʀize] *vt* to break; **se** ~ *vi* to break.
brise-tout [bʀiztu] *nm inv* wrecker.
briseur, euse [bʀizœʀ, -øz] *nm/f*: ~ **de grève** strike-breaker.
brise-vent [bʀizvɑ̃] *nm inv* windbreak.
bristol [bʀistɔl] *nm* (*carte de visite*) visiting card.
britannique [bʀitanik] *a* British ♦ *nm/f*: B~ Briton, British person; **les** B~**s** the British.
broc [bʀo] *nm* pitcher.
brocante [bʀɔkɑ̃t] *nf* (*objets*) secondhand goods *pl*, junk; (*commerce*) secondhand trade; junk dealing.
brocanteur, euse [bʀɔkɑ̃tœʀ, -øz] *nm/f* junkshop owner; junk dealer.
brocart [bʀɔkaʀ] *nm* brocade.
broche [bʀɔʃ] *nf* brooch; (*CULIN*) spit; (*fiche*) spike, peg; (*MÉD*) pin; **à la** ~ spit-roasted, roasted on a spit.
broché, e [bʀɔʃe] *a* (*livre*) paper-backed; (*tissu*) brocaded.
brochet [bʀɔʃɛ] *nm* pike *inv*.
brochette [bʀɔʃɛt] *nf* skewer; ~ **de décorations** row of medals.
brochure [bʀɔʃyʀ] *nf* pamphlet, brochure, booklet.
brocoli [bʀɔkɔli] *nm* broccoli.
brodequins [bʀɔdkɛ̃] *nmpl* (*de marche*) (lace-up) boots.
broder [bʀɔde] *vt* to embroider ♦ *vi*: ~ (**sur des faits** *ou* **une histoire**) to embroider the

facts.

broderie [bʀɔdʀi] *nf* embroidery.

bromure [bʀɔmyʀ] *nm* bromide.

broncher [bʀɔ̃ʃe] *vi*: **sans ~** without flinching, without turning a hair.

bronches [bʀɔ̃ʃ] *nfpl* bronchial tubes.

bronchite [bʀɔ̃ʃit] *nf* bronchitis.

broncho-pneumonie [bʀɔ̃kɔpnømɔni] *nf* broncho-pneumonia *q*.

bronzage [bʀɔ̃zaʒ] *nm* (*hâle*) (sun)tan.

bronze [bʀɔ̃z] *nm* bronze.

bronzé, e [bʀɔ̃ze] *a* tanned.

bronzer [bʀɔ̃ze] *vt* to tan ♦ *vi* to get a tan; **se ~** to sunbathe.

brosse [bʀɔs] *nf* brush; **donner un coup de ~ à qch** to give sth a brush; **coiffé en ~** with a crewcut; **~ à cheveux** hairbrush; **~ à dents** toothbrush; **~ à habits** clothesbrush.

brosser [bʀɔse] *vt* (*nettoyer*) to brush; (*fig: tableau etc*) to paint; to draw; **se ~** to brush one's clothes; **se ~ les dents** to brush one's teeth; **tu peux te ~**! (*fam*) you can sing for it!

brou [bʀu] *nm*: **~ de noix** (*pour bois*) walnut stain; (*liqueur*) walnut liqueur.

brouette [bʀuɛt] *nf* wheelbarrow.

brouhaha [bʀuaa] *nm* hubbub.

brouillage [bʀujaʒ] *nm* (*d'une émission*) jamming.

brouillard [bʀujaʀ] *nm* fog; **être dans le ~** (*fig*) to be all at sea.

brouille [bʀuj] *nf* quarrel.

brouillé, e [bʀuje] *a* (*fâché*): **il est ~ avec ses parents** he has fallen out with his parents; (*teint*) muddy.

brouiller [bʀuje] *vt* to mix up; to confuse; (*RADIO*) to cause interference to; (*: délibérément*) to jam; (*rendre trouble*) to cloud; (*désunir: amis*) to set at odds; **se ~** *vi* (*ciel, vue*) to cloud over; (*détails*) to become confused; **se ~** (**avec**) to fall out (with); **~ les pistes** to cover one's tracks; (*fig*) to confuse the issue.

brouillon, ne [bʀujɔ̃, -ɔn] *a* disorganized, unmethodical ♦ *nm* (first) draft; **cahier de ~** rough (work) book.

broussailles [bʀusaj] *nfpl* undergrowth *sg*.

broussailleux, euse [bʀusajø, -øz] *a* bushy.

brousse [bʀus] *nf*: **la ~** the bush.

brouter [bʀute] *vt* to graze on ♦ *vi* to graze; (*AUTO*) to judder.

broutille [bʀutij] *nf* trifle.

broyer [bʀwaje] *vt* to crush; **~ du noir** to be down in the dumps.

bru [bʀy] *nf* daughter-in-law.

brucelles [bʀysɛl] *nfpl*: (**pinces**) **~** tweezers.

brugnon [bʀyɲɔ̃] *nm* nectarine.

bruine [bʀɥin] *nf* drizzle.

bruiner [bʀɥine] *vb impersonnel*: **il bruine** it's drizzling, there's a drizzle.

bruire [bʀɥiʀ] *vi* (*eau*) to murmur; (*feuilles, étoffe*) to rustle.

bruissement [bʀɥismɑ̃] *nm* murmuring; rustling.

bruit [bʀɥi] *nm*: **un ~** a noise, a sound; (*fig: rumeur*) a rumour (*Brit*), a rumor (*US*); **le ~** noise; **pas/trop de ~** no/too much noise; **sans ~** without a sound, noiselessly; **faire du ~** to make a noise; **~ de fond** background

noise.

bruitage [bʀɥitaʒ] *nm* sound effects *pl*.

bruiteur, euse [bʀɥitœʀ, -øz] *nm/f* sound-effects engineer.

brûlant, e [bʀylɑ̃, -ɑ̃t] *a* burning (hot); (*liquide*) boiling (hot); (*regard*) fiery; (*sujet*) red-hot.

brûlé, e [bʀyle] *a* (*fig: démasqué*) blown; (*: homme politique etc*) discredited ♦ *nm*: **odeur de ~** smell of burning.

brûle-pourpoint [bʀylpuʀpwɛ̃]: **à ~** *ad* point-blank.

brûler [bʀyle] *vt* to burn; (*suj: eau bouillante*) to scald; (*consommer: électricité, essence*) to use; (*feu rouge, signal*) to go through (without stopping) ♦ *vi* to burn; (*jeu*): **tu brûles** you're getting warm *ou* hot; **se ~** to burn o.s.; to scald o.s.; **se ~ la cervelle** to blow one's brains out; **~ les étapes** to make rapid progress; (*aller trop vite*) to cut corners; **~ (d'impatience) de faire qch** to burn with impatience to do sth, be dying to do sth.

brûleur [bʀylœʀ] *nm* burner.

brûlot [bʀylo] *nm* (*CULIN*) flaming brandy; **un ~ de contestation** (*fig*) a hotbed of dissent.

brûlure [bʀylyʀ] *nf* (*lésion*) burn; (*sensation*) burning *q*, burning sensation; **~s d'estomac** heartburn *sg*.

brume [bʀym] *nf* mist.

brumeux, euse [bʀymø, -øz] *a* misty; (*fig*) hazy.

brun, e [bʀœ̃, -yn] *a* brown; (*cheveux, personne*) dark ♦ *nm* (*couleur*) brown.

brunâtre [bʀynɑtʀ(ə)] *a* brownish.

Brunei [bʀynei] *nm*: **le ~** Brunei.

brunir [bʀyniʀ] *vi* (*aussi*: **se ~**) to get a tan ♦ *vt* to tan.

brushing [bʀœʃiŋ] *nm* blow-dry.

brusque [bʀysk(ə)] *a* (*soudain*) abrupt, sudden; (*rude*) abrupt, brusque.

brusquement [bʀyskəmɑ̃] *ad* (*soudainement*) abruptly, suddenly.

brusquer [bʀyske] *vt* to rush.

brusquerie [bʀyskəʀi] *nf* abruptness, brusqueness.

brut, e [bʀyt] *a* raw, crude, rough; (*diamant*) uncut; (*soie, minéral, INFORM: données*) raw; (*COMM*) gross ♦ *nf* brute; (**champagne**) **~ brut** champagne; (**pétrole**) **~ crude** (oil).

brutal, e, aux [bʀytal, -o] *a* brutal.

brutalement [bʀytalmɑ̃] *ad* brutally.

brutaliser [bʀytalize] *vt* to handle roughly, manhandle.

brutalité [bʀytalite] *nf* brutality *q*.

brute [bʀyt] *af*, *nf voir* **brut**.

Bruxelles [bʀysɛl] *n* Brussels.

bruxellois, e [bʀyselwa, -waz] *a* of *ou* from Brussels ♦ *nm/f*: **B~, e** inhabitant *ou* native of Brussels.

bruyamment [bʀɥijamɑ̃] *ad* noisily.

bruyant, e [bʀɥijɑ̃, -ɑ̃t] *a* noisy.

bruyère [bʀyjɛʀ] *nf* heather.

BT *sigle m* (= *Brevet de technicien*) *vocational training certificate, taken at approx. 18 years*.

BTA *sigle m* (= *Brevet de technicien agricole*) *agricultural training certificate, taken at approx. 18 years*.

BTP *sigle mpl* (= *Bâtiments et travaux publics*) *public buildings and works sector*.

BTS *sigle m* (= *Brevet de technicien supérieur*) *vocational training certificate taken at end of 2-year higher education course.*

BU *sigle f* = *Bibliothèque universitaire.*

bu, e [by] *pp de* **boire.**

buanderie [buɑ̃dʀi] *nf* laundry.

Bucarest [bykaʀɛst] *n* Bucharest.

buccal, e, aux [bykal, -o] *a*: **par voie ~e** orally.

bûche [byʃ] *nf* log; **prendre une ~** *(fig)* to come a cropper *(Brit)*, fall flat on one's face; **~ de Noël** Yule log.

bûcher [byʃe] *nm* pyre; bonfire ♦ *vi (fam: étudier)* to swot *(Brit)*, grind *(US)* ♦ *vt* to swot up *(Brit)*, cram.

bûcheron [byʃʀɔ̃] *nm* woodcutter.

bûchette [byʃɛt] *nf (de bois)* stick, twig; *(pour compter)* rod.

bûcheur, euse [byʃœʀ, -øz] *nm/f (fam: étudiant)* swot *(Brit)*, grind *(US)*.

bucolique [bykɔlik] *a* bucolic, pastoral.

Budapest [bydapɛst] *n* Budapest.

budget [bydʒɛ] *nm* budget.

budgétaire [bydʒeteʀ] *a* budgetary, budget *cpd.*

budgétiser [bydʒetize] *vt* to budget (for).

buée [bɥe] *nf (sur une vitre)* mist; *(de l'haleine)* steam.

Buenos Aires [bwenɔzeʀ] *n* Buenos Aires.

buffet [byfɛ] *nm (meuble)* sideboard; *(de réception)* buffet; **~ (de gare)** (station) buffet, snack bar.

buffle [byfl(ə)] *nm* buffalo.

buis [bɥi] *nm* box tree; *(bois)* box(wood).

buisson [bɥisɔ̃] *nm* bush.

buissonnière [bɥisɔnjɛʀ] *af*: **faire l'école ~** to play truant *(Brit)*, skip school.

bulbe [bylb(ə)] *nm (BOT, ANAT)* bulb; *(coupole)* onion-shaped dome.

bulgare [bylgaʀ] *a* Bulgarian ♦ *nm (LING)* Bulgarian ♦ *nm/f*: **B~** Bulgarian, Bulgar.

Bulgarie [bylgaʀi] *nf*: **la ~** Bulgaria.

bulldozer [buldozœʀ] *nm* bulldozer.

bulle [byl] *a, nm*: **(papier) ~** manil(l)a paper ♦ *nf* bubble; *(de bande dessinée)* balloon; *(papale)* bull; **~ de savon** soap bubble.

bulletin [byltɛ̃] *nm (communiqué, journal)* bulletin; *(papier)* form; *(: de bagages)* ticket; *(SCOL)* report; **~ d'informations** news bulletin; **~ météorologique** weather report; **~ de naissance** birth certificate; **~ de salaire** pay slip; **~ de santé** medical bulletin; **~ (de vote)** ballot paper.

buraliste [byʀalist(ə)] *nm/f (de bureau de tabac)* tobacconist; *(de poste)* clerk.

bure [byʀ] *nf* homespun; *(de moine)* frock.

bureau, x [byʀo] *nm (meuble)* desk; *(pièce, service)* office; **~ de change** (foreign) exchange office *ou* bureau; **~ d'embauche** ≈ job centre; **~ d'études** design office; **~ de location** box office; **~ de placement** employment agency; **~ de poste** post office; **~ de tabac** tobacconist's (shop), smoke shop *(US)*; **~ de vote** polling station.

bureaucrate [byʀokʀat] *nm* bureaucrat.

bureaucratie [byʀokʀasi] *nf* bureaucracy.

bureaucratique [byʀokʀatik] *a* bureaucratic.

bureautique [byʀotik] *nf* office automation.

burette [byʀɛt] *nf (de mécanicien)* oilcan; *(de chimiste)* burette.

burin [byʀɛ̃] *nm* cold chisel; *(ART)* burin.

buriné, e [byʀine] *a (fig: visage)* craggy, seamed.

burlesque [byʀlɛsk(ə)] *a* ridiculous; *(LITTÉRATURE)* burlesque.

burnous [byʀnu(s)] *nm* burnous.

Burundi [buʀundi] *nm*: **le ~** Burundi.

BUS *sigle m* = *Bureau universitaire de statistiques.*

bus *vb* [by] *voir* **boire** ♦ *nm* [bys] *(véhicule, aussi INFORM)* bus.

busard [byzaʀ] *nm* harrier.

buse [byz] *nf* buzzard.

busqué, e [byske] *a*: **nez ~** hook(ed) nose.

buste [byst(ə)] *nm (ANAT)* chest; *(: de femme)* bust; *(sculpture)* bust.

bustier [bystje] *nm (soutien-gorge)* long-line bra.

but [by] *vb voir* **boire** ♦ *nm (cible)* target; *(fig)* goal, aim; *(FOOTBALL etc)* goal; **de ~ en blanc** point-blank; **avoir pour ~ de faire** to aim to do; **dans le ~ de** with the intention of.

butane [bytan] *nm* butane; *(domestique)* calor gas ® *(Brit)*, butane.

buté, e [byte] *a* stubborn, obstinate ♦ *nf (TECH)* stop; *(ARCHIT)* abutment.

buter [byte] *vi*: **~ contre** *ou* **sur** to bump into; *(trébucher)* to stumble against ♦ *vt* to antagonize; **se ~** *vi* to get obstinate, dig in one's heels.

buteur [bytœʀ] *nm* striker.

butin [bytɛ̃] *nm* booty, spoils *pl*; *(d'un vol)* loot.

butiner [bytine] *vi* to gather nectar.

butor [bytɔʀ] *nm (fig)* lout.

butte [byt] *nf* mound, hillock; **être en ~ à** to be exposed to.

buvable [byvabl(ə)] *a (eau, vin)* drinkable; *(MÉD: ampoule etc)* to be taken orally; *(fig: roman etc)* reasonable.

buvais [byvɛ] *etc vb voir* **boire.**

buvard [byvaʀ] *nm* blotter.

buvette [byvɛt] *nf* refreshment room *ou* stall; *(comptoir)* bar.

buveur, euse [byvœʀ, -øz] *nm/f* drinker.

buvons [byvɔ̃] *etc vb voir* **boire.**

BVP *sigle m* (= *Bureau de vérification de la publicité*) *advertising standards authority.*

Byzance [bizɑ̃s] *n* Byzantium.

byzantin, e [bizɑ̃tɛ̃, -in] *a* Byzantine.

BZH *abr* (= *Breizh*) Brittany.

C

C, c [se] *nm inv* C, c ♦ *abr* (= *centime*) c; (= *Celsius*) C; **C comme Célestin** C for Charlie.

c' [s] *dét voir* **ce.**

CA *sigle m* = **chiffre d'affaires, conseil d'administration, corps d'armée** ♦ *sigle f* = **chambre d'agriculture.**

ca *abr* (= *centiare*) *1 m².*

ça [sa] *pronom* (*pour désigner*) this; (*: plus loin*) that; (*comme sujet indéfini*) it; ~ **m'étonne que** it surprises me that; ~ **va?** how are you?; how are things?; (*d'accord?*) OK?, all right?; ~ **alors!** (*désapprobation*) well!, really!; (*étonnement*) heavens!; **c'est** ~ that's right.

çà [sa] *ad:* ~ **et là** here and there.

cabale [kabal] *nf* (THÉÂTRE, POL) cabal, clique.

caban [kabɑ̃] *nm* reefer jacket, donkey jacket.

cabane [kaban] *nf* hut, cabin.

cabanon [kabanɔ̃] *nm* chalet; (*country*) cottage.

cabaret [kabaʀɛ] *nm* night club.

cabas [kaba] *nm* shopping bag.

cabestan [kabɛstɑ̃] *nm* capstan.

cabillaud [kabijo] *nm* cod *inv.*

cabine [kabin] *nf* (*de bateau*) cabin; (*de plage*) (beach) hut; (*de piscine etc*) cubicle; (*de camion, train*) cab; (*d'avion*) cockpit; ~ (**d'ascenseur**) lift cage; ~ **d'essayage** fitting room; ~ **de projection** projection room; ~ **spatiale** space capsule; ~ (**téléphonique**) call *ou* (tele)phone box, (tele)phone booth.

cabinet [kabinɛ] *nm* (*petite pièce*) closet; (*de médecin*) surgery (*Brit*), office (*US*); (*de notaire etc*) office; (*: clientèle*) practice; (*POL*) cabinet; (*d'un ministre*) advisers *pl*; ~**s** *nmpl* (*w.-c.*) toilet *sg*, loo *sg* (*fam Brit*); ~ **d'affaires** business consultants' (*bureau*), business partnership; ~ **de toilette** toilet; ~ **de travail** study.

câble [kɑbl(ə)] *nm* cable.

câblé, e [kɑble] *a* (*fam*) switched on; (*TECH*) linked to cable television.

câbler [kɑble] *vt* to cable.

câblogramme [kɑblɔgʀam] *nm* cablegram.

cabosser [kabɔse] *vt* to dent.

cabot [kabo] *nm* (*péj: chien*) mutt.

cabotage [kabɔtaʒ] *nm* coastal navigation.

caboteur [kabɔtœʀ] *nm* coaster.

cabotin, e [kabɔtɛ̃, -in] *nm/f* (*péj: personne maniérée*) poseur; (*: acteur*) ham ♦ *a* dramatic, theatrical.

cabotinage [kabɔtinaʒ] *nm* playacting; third-rate acting, ham acting.

cabrer [kabʀe] *nm*: **se** ~ *vi* (*cheval*) to rear up; (*avion*) to nose up; (*fig*) to revolt, rebel; to jib.

cabri [kabʀi] *nm* kid.

cabriole [kabʀijɔl] *nf* caper; (*gymnastique etc*) somersault.

cabriolet [kabʀijɔlɛ] *nm* convertible.

CAC [kak] *sigle f* (= *Compagnie des agents de change*): **indice** ~ ≈ FT index (*Brit*), ≈ Dow Jones average (*US*).

caca [kaka] *nm* (*langage enfantin*) pooh; (*couleur*): ~ **d'oie** greeny-yellow; **faire** ~ (*fam*) to do a pooh.

cacahuète [kakaɥɛt] *nf* peanut.

cacao [kakao] *nm* cocoa (powder); (*boisson*) cocoa.

cachalot [kaʃalo] *nm* sperm whale.

cache [kaʃ] *nm* mask, card (*for masking*) ♦ *nf* hiding place.

cache-cache [kaʃkaʃ] *nm*: **jouer à** ~ to play hide-and-seek.

cache-col [kaʃkɔl] *nm* scarf (*pl* scarves).

cachemire [kaʃmiʀ] *nm* cashmere ♦ *a*: **dessin** ~ paisley pattern; **le C**~ Kashmir.

cache-nez [kaʃne] *nm inv* scarf (*pl* scarves), muffler.

cache-pot [kaʃpo] *nm inv* flower-pot holder.

cache-prise [kaʃpʀiz] *nm inv* socket cover.

cacher [kaʃe] *vt* to hide, conceal; ~ **qch à qn** to hide *ou* conceal sth from sb; **se** ~ to hide; to be hidden *ou* concealed; **il ne s'en cache pas** he makes no secret of it.

cache-sexe [kaʃsɛks] *nm inv* G-string.

cachet [kaʃɛ] *nm* (*comprimé*) tablet; (*sceau: du roi*) seal; (*: de la poste*) postmark; (*rétribution*) fee; (*fig*) style, character.

cacheter [kaʃte] *vt* to seal; **vin cacheté** vintage wine.

cachette [kaʃɛt] *nf* hiding place; **en** ~ on the sly, secretly.

cachot [kaʃo] *nm* dungeon.

cachotterie [kaʃɔtʀi] *nf* mystery; **faire des** ~**s** to be secretive.

cachottier, ière [kaʃɔtje, -jɛʀ] *a* secretive.

cachou [kaʃu] *nm*: (**pastille de**) ~ cachou (*sweet*).

cacophonie [kakɔfɔni] *nf* cacophony, din.

cactus [kaktys] *nm* cactus.

c-à-d *abr* (= *c'est-à-dire*) i.e.

cadastre [kadastʀ(ə)] *nm* land register.

cadavéreux, euse [kadaveʀø, -øz] *a* (*teint, visage*) deathly pale.

cadavérique [kadaveʀik] *a* deathly (pale), deadly pale.

cadavre [kadavʀ(ə)] *nm* corpse, (dead) body.

caddie [kadi] *nm* (supermarket) trolley.

cadeau, x [kado] *nm* present, gift; **faire un** ~ **à qn** to give sb a present *ou* gift; **faire** ~ **de qch à qn** to make a present of sth to sb, give sb sth as a present.

cadenas [kadna] *nm* padlock.

cadenasser [kadnase] *vt* to padlock.

cadence [kadɑ̃s] *nf* (MUS) cadence; (*: rythme*) rhythm; (*de travail etc*) rate; ~**s** *nfpl* (*en usine*) production rate *sg*; **en** ~ rhythmically; in time.

cadencé, e [kadɑ̃se] *a* rhythmic(al); **au pas** ~ (MIL) in quick time.

cadet, te [kadɛ, -ɛt] *a* younger; (*le plus jeune*) youngest ♦ *nm/f* youngest child *ou* one, youngest boy *ou* son/girl *ou* daughter; **il est mon** ~ **de deux ans** he's 2 years younger than me, he's 2 years my junior; **les** ~**s** (SPORT) the minors (*15 - 17 years*); **le** ~ **de mes soucis** the least of my worries.

cadran [kadʀɑ̃] *nm* dial; ~ **solaire** sundial.

cadre [kadʀ(ə)] *nm* frame; (*environnement*) surroundings *pl*; (*limites*) scope ♦ *nm/f* (ADMIN) managerial employee, executive ♦ *a*: **loi** ~ outline *ou* blueprint law; ~ **moyen/supérieur** (ADMIN) middle/senior management employee, junior/senior executive; **rayer qn des** ~**s** to discharge sb; to dismiss sb; **dans le** ~ **de** (*fig*) within the framework *ou* context of.

cadrer [kadʀe] *vi*: ~ **avec** to tally *ou* correspond with ♦ *vt* (CINÉMA) to centre.

cadreur, euse [kadʀœʀ, -øz] *nm/f* (CINÉMA) cameraman/woman.

caduc, uque [kadyk] *a* obsolete; (BOT) deciduous.

CAF *sigle f* (= *Caisse d'allocations familiales*) family allowance office.

caf *abr* (= *coût, assurance, fret*) cif.

cafard [kafaʀ] *nm* cockroach; **avoir le ~** to be down in the dumps, be feeling low.

cafardeux, euse [kafaʀdø, -øz] *a* (*personne, ambiance*) depressing, melancholy.

café [kafe] *nm* coffee; (*bistro*) café ♦ *a inv* coffee *cpd*; **~ crème** coffee with cream; **~ au lait** white coffee; **~ noir** black coffee; **~ en grains** coffee beans; **~ en poudre** instant coffee; **~ tabac** *tobacconist's or newsagent's also serving coffee and spirits*; **~ liégeois** *coffee ice cream with whipped cream*.

café-concert, *pl* **cafés-concerts** [kafekɔ̃sɛʀ] *nm* (*aussi*: **caf'conc'**) *café with a cabaret*.

caféine [kafein] *nf* caffeine.

cafétéria [kafeteʀja] *nf* cafeteria.

café-théâtre, *pl* **cafés-théâtres** [kafeteatʀ(ə)] *nm café used as a venue by (experimental) theatre groups*.

cafetier, ière [kaftje, -jɛʀ] *nm/f* café-owner ♦ *nf* (*pot*) coffee-pot.

cafouillage [kafujaʒ] *nm* shambles *sg*.

cafouiller [kafuje] *vi* to get in a shambles; (*machine etc*) to work in fits and starts.

cage [kaʒ] *nf* cage; **~ (des buts)** goal; **en ~** in a cage, caged up *ou* in; **~ d'ascenseur** lift shaft; **~ d'escalier** (stair)well; **~ thoracique** rib cage.

cageot [kaʒo] *nm* crate.

cagibi [kaʒibi] *nm* shed.

cagneux, euse [kaɲø, -øz] *a* knock-kneed.

cagnotte [kaɲɔt] *nf* kitty.

cagoule [kagul] *nf* cowl; hood; (*SKI etc*) cagoule.

cahier [kaje] *nm* notebook; (*TYPO*) signature; (*revue*): **~s** journal; **~ de revendications/doléances** list of claims/grievances; **~ de brouillons** roughbook, jotter; **~ des charges** specification; **~ d'exercices** exercise book.

cahin-caha [kaɛ̃kaa] *ad*: **aller ~** to jog along; (*fig*) to be so-so.

cahot [kao] *nm* jolt, bump.

cahoter [kaɔte] *vi* to bump along, jog along.

cahoteux, euse [kaɔtø, -øz] *a* bumpy.

cahute [kayt] *nf* shack, hut.

caïd [kaid] *nm* big chief, boss.

caillasse [kajas] *nf* (*pierraille*) loose stones *pl*.

caille [kɑj] *nf* quail.

caillé, e [kaje] *a*: **lait ~** curdled milk, curds *pl*.

caillebotis [kajbɔti] *nm* duckboard.

cailler [kaje] *vi* (*lait*) to curdle; (*sang*) to clot; (*fam*) to be cold.

caillot [kajo] *nm* (blood) clot.

caillou, x [kaju] *nm* (little) stone.

caillouter [kajute] *vt* (*chemin*) to metal.

caillouteux, euse [kajutø, -øz] *a* stony; pebbly.

cailloutis [kajuti] *nm* (*petits graviers*) gravel.

caïman [kaimɑ̃] *nm* cayman.

Caïmans [kaimɑ̃] *nfpl*: **les ~** the Cayman Islands.

Caire [kɛʀ] *nm*: **le ~** Cairo.

caisse [kɛs] *nf* box; (*où l'on met la recette*) cashbox; (: *machine*) till; (*où l'on paye*) cash desk (*Brit*), checkout counter; (: *au supermarché*) checkout; (*de banque*)

cashier's desk; (*TECH*) case, casing; **faire sa ~** (*COMM*) to count the takings; **~ claire** (*MUS*) side *ou* snare drum; **~ éclair** express checkout; **~ enregistreuse** cash register; **~ d'épargne (CE)** savings bank; **~ noire** slush fund; **~ de retraite** pension fund; **~ de sortie** checkout; *voir* **grosse**.

caissier, ière [kesje, -jɛʀ] *nm/f* cashier.

caisson [kɛsɔ̃] *nm* box, case.

cajoler [kaʒɔle] *vt* to wheedle, coax; to surround with love and care, make a fuss of.

cajoleries [kaʒɔlʀi] *nfpl* coaxing *sg*, flattery *sg*.

cajou [kaʒu] *nm* cashew nut.

cake [kɛk] *nm* fruit cake.

CAL *sigle m* (= *Comité d'action lycéen*) *pupils' action group seeking to reform school system*.

cal [kal] *nm* callus.

cal. *abr* = **calorie**.

calamar [kalamaʀ] *nm* = **calmar**.

calaminé, e [kalamine] *a* (*AUTO*) coked up.

calamité [kalamite] *nf* calamity, disaster.

calandre [kalɑ̃dʀ(ə)] *nf* radiator grill; (*machine*) calender, mangle.

calanque [kalɑ̃k] *nf* rocky inlet.

calcaire [kalkɛʀ] *nm* limestone ♦ *a* (*eau*) hard; (*GÉO*) limestone *cpd*.

calciné, e [kalsine] *a* burnt to ashes.

calcium [kalsjɔm] *nm* calcium.

calcul [kalkyl] *nm* calculation; **le ~** (*SCOL*) arithmetic; **~ différentiel/intégral** differential/integral calculus; **~ mental** mental arithmetic; **~ (biliaire)** (gall)stone; **~ (rénal)** (kidney) stone; **d'après mes ~s** by my reckoning.

calculateur [kalkylatœʀ] *nm*, **calculatrice** [kalkylatʀis] *nf* calculator.

calculé, e [kalkyle] *a*: **risque ~** calculated risk.

calculer [kalkyle] *vt* to calculate, work out, reckon; (*combiner*) to calculate; **~ qch de tête** to work sth out in one's head.

calculette [kalkylɛt] *nf* (pocket) calculator.

cale [kal] *nf* (*de bateau*) hold; (*en bois*) wedge, chock; **~ sèche** *ou* **de radoub** dry dock.

calé, e [kale] *a* (*fam*) clever, bright.

calebasse [kalbɑs] *nf* calabash, gourd.

calèche [kalɛʃ] *nf* horse-drawn carriage.

caleçon [kalsɔ̃] *nm* pair of underpants, trunks *pl*; **~ de bain** bathing trunks *pl*.

calembour [kalɑ̃buʀ] *nm* pun.

calendes [kalɑ̃d] *nfpl*: **renvoyer aux ~ grecques** to postpone indefinitely.

calendrier [kalɑ̃dʀije] *nm* calendar; (*fig*) timetable.

cale-pied [kalpje] *nm inv* toe clip.

calepin [kalpɛ̃] *nm* notebook.

caler [kale] *vt* to wedge, chock up; **~ (son moteur/véhicule)** to stall (one's engine/vehicle); **se ~ dans un fauteuil** to make o.s. comfortable in an armchair.

calfater [kalfate] *vt* to caulk.

calfeutrer [kalføtʀe] *vt* to (make) draughtproof (*Brit*) *ou* draftproof (*US*); **se ~** to make o.s. snug and comfortable.

calibre [kalibʀ(ə)] *nm* (*d'un fruit*) grade; (*d'une arme*) bore, calibre (*Brit*), caliber

(US); (fig) calibre, caliber.

calibrer [kalibʀe] vt to grade.

calice [kalis] nm (REL) chalice; (BOT) calyx.

calicot [kaliko] nm (tissu) calico.

Californie [kalifɔʀni] nf: la ~ California.

californien, ne [kalifɔʀnjɛ̃, -ɛn] a Californian.

califourchon [kalifuʀʃɔ̃]: à ~ ad astride; à ~ sur astride, straddling.

câlin, e [kalɛ̃, -in] a cuddly, cuddlesome; tender.

câliner [kaline] vt to fondle, cuddle.

câlineries [kalinʀi] nfpl cuddles.

calisson [kalisɔ̃] nm diamond-shaped sweet or candy made with ground almonds.

calleux, euse [kalø, -øz] a horny, callous.

calligraphie [kaligʀafi] nf calligraphy.

callosité [kalozite] nf callus.

calmant [kalmɑ̃] nm tranquillizer, sedative; (contre la douleur) painkiller.

calmar [kalmaʀ] nm squid.

calme [kalm(ə)] a calm, quiet ♦ nm calm(ness), quietness; **sans perdre son ~** without losing one's cool ou calmness; ~ **plat** (NAVIG) dead calm.

calmer [kalme] vt to calm (down); (douleur, inquiétude) to ease, soothe; **se ~** to calm down.

calomniateur, trice [kalɔmnjatœʀ, -tʀis] nm/f slanderer; libeller.

calomnie [kalɔmni] nf slander; (écrite) libel.

calomnier [kalɔmnje] vt to slander; to libel.

calomnieux, euse [kalɔmnjø, -øz] a slanderous; libellous.

calorie [kalɔʀi] nf calorie.

calorifère [kalɔʀifɛʀ] nm stove.

calorifique [kalɔʀifik] a calorific.

calorifuge [kalɔʀify3] a (heat-)insulating, heat-retaining.

calot [kalo] nm forage cap.

calotte [kalɔt] nf (coiffure) skullcap; (gifle) slap; **la ~** (péj) clergé) the cloth, the clergy; ~ **glaciaire** icecap.

calque [kalk(ə)] nm (aussi: **papier ~**) tracing paper; (dessin) tracing; (fig) carbon copy.

calquer [kalke] vt to trace; (fig) to copy exactly.

calvados [kalvados] nm Calvados (apple brandy).

calvaire [kalvɛʀ] nm (croix) wayside cross, calvary; (souffrances) suffering, martyrdom.

calvitie [kalvisi] nf baldness.

camaïeu [kamajø] nm: (**motif en**) ~ monochrome motif.

camarade [kamaʀad] nm/f friend, pal; (POL) comrade.

camaraderie [kamaʀadʀi] nf friendship.

camarguais, e [kamaʀgɛ, -ɛz] a of ou from the Camargue.

Camargue [kamaʀg] nf: la ~ the Camargue.

cambiste [kãbist(ə)] nm (COMM) foreign exchange dealer, exchange agent.

Cambodge [kãbɔdʒ] nm: le ~ Cambodia.

cambodgien, ne [kãbɔdʒjɛ̃, -ɛn] a Cambodian ♦ nm/f: **C~, ne** Cambodian.

cambouis [kãbwi] nm dirty oil ou grease.

cambré, e [kãbʀe] a: **avoir les reins ~s** to have an arched back; **avoir le pied très ~** to have very high arches ou insteps.

cambrer [kãbʀe] vt to arch; **se ~** to arch

one's back; ~ **la taille** ou **les reins** to arch one's back.

cambriolage [kãbʀijɔlaʒ] nm burglary.

cambrioler [kãbʀijɔle] vt to burgle (Brit), burglarize (US).

cambrioleur, euse [kãbʀijɔlœʀ, -øz] nm/f burglar.

cambrure [kãbʀyʀ] nf (du pied) arch; (de la route) camber; ~ **des reins** small of the back.

cambuse [kãbyz] nf storeroom.

came [kam] nf: **arbre à ~s** camshaft; **arbre à ~s en tête** overhead camshaft.

camée [kame] nm cameo.

caméléon [kameleɔ̃] nm chameleon.

camélia [kamelja] nm camellia.

camelot [kamlo] nm street pedlar.

camelote [kamlɔt] nf rubbish, trash, junk.

camembert [kamãbɛʀ] nm Camembert (cheese).

caméra [kameʀa] nf (CINÉMA, TV) camera; (d'amateur) cine-camera.

Cameroun [kamʀun] nm: le ~ Cameroon.

camerounais, e [kamʀunɛ, -ɛz] a Cameroonian.

camescope [kamskɔp] nm camcorder.

camion [kamjɔ̃] nm lorry (Brit), truck; (plus petit, fermé) van; (charge): ~ **de sable/cailloux** lorry-load (Brit) ou truck-load of sand/stones; ~ **de dépannage** breakdown (Brit) ou tow (US) truck.

camion-citerne, pl **camions-citernes** [kamjɔ̃sitɛʀn(ə)] nm tanker.

camionnage [kamjɔnaʒ] nm haulage (Brit), trucking (US); **frais/entreprise de ~** haulage costs/business.

camionnette [kamjɔnɛt] nf (small) van.

camionneur [kamjɔnœʀ] nm (entrepreneur) haulage contractor (Brit), trucker (US); (chauffeur) lorry (Brit) ou truck driver; van driver.

camisole [kamizɔl] nf: ~ (**de force**) straitjacket.

camomille [kamɔmij] nf camomile; (boisson) camomile tea.

camouflage [kamuflaʒ] nm camouflage.

camoufler [kamufle] vt to camouflage; (fig) to conceal, cover up.

camouflet [kamuflɛ] nm (fam) snub.

camp [kã] nm camp; (fig) side; ~ **de nudistes/vacances** nudist/holiday camp; ~ **de concentration** concentration camp.

campagnard, e [kãpaɲaʀ, -aʀd(ə)] a country cpd ♦ nm/f countryman/woman.

campagne [kãpaɲ] nf country, countryside; (MIL, POL, COMM) campaign; **en ~** (MIL) in the field; **à la ~** in/to the country; **faire ~ pour** to campaign for; ~ **électorale** election campaign; ~ **de publicité** advertising campaign.

campé, e [kãpe] a: **bien ~** (personnage, tableau) well-drawn.

campement [kãpmã] nm camp, encampment.

camper [kãpe] vi to camp ♦ vt (chapeau etc) to pull ou put on firmly; (dessin) to sketch; **se ~ devant** to plant o.s. in front of.

campeur, euse [kãpœʀ, -øz] nm/f camper.

camphre [kãfʀ(ə)] nm camphor.

camphré, e [kãfʀe] a camphorated.

camping [kɑ̃piŋ] *nm* camping; **(terrain de)** ~ campsite, camping site; **faire du** ~ to go camping; **faire du** ~ **sauvage** to camp rough.

camping-car [kɑ̃piŋkaʀ] *nm* caravanette, camper (*US*).

campus [kɑ̃pys] *nm* campus.

camus, e [kamy, -yz] *a*: **nez** ~ pug nose.

Canada [kanada] *nm*: **le** ~ Canada.

canadair [kanadɛʀ] *nm* ® fire-fighting plane.

canadien, ne [kanadjɛ̃, -ɛn] *a* Canadian ♦ *nm/f*: **C~, ne** Canadian ♦ *nf* (*veste*) fur-lined jacket.

canaille [kanɑj] *nf* (*péj*) scoundrel; (*populace*) riff-raff ♦ *a* raffish, rakish.

canal, aux [kanal, -o] *nm* canal; (*naturel*) channel; (*ADMIN*): **par le** ~ **de** through (the medium of), via; ~ **de distribution/télévision** distribution/television channel; ~ **de Panama/Suez** Panama/Suez Canal.

canalisation [kanalizɑsjɔ̃] *nf* (*tuyau*) pipe.

canaliser [kanalize] *vt* to canalize; (*fig*) to channel.

canapé [kanape] *nm* settee, sofa; (*CULIN*) canapé, open sandwich.

canapé-lit, *pl* **canapés-lits** [kanapeli] *nm* sofa bed.

canaque [kanak] *a* of *ou* from New Caledonia ♦ *nm/f*: **C~** native of New Caledonia.

canard [kanaʀ] *nm* duck.

canari [kanaʀi] *nm* canary.

Canaries [kanaʀi] *nfpl*: **les (îles)** ~ the Canary Islands, the Canaries.

cancaner [kɑ̃kane] *vi* to gossip (maliciously); (*canard*) to quack.

cancanier, ière [kɑ̃kanje, -jɛʀ] *a* gossiping.

cancans [kɑ̃kɑ̃] *nmpl* (malicious) gossip *sg*.

cancer [kɑ̃sɛʀ] *nm* cancer; (*signe*): **le C~** Cancer, the Crab; **être du C~** to be Cancer; **il a un** ~ he has cancer.

cancéreux, euse [kɑ̃seʀø, -øz] *a* cancerous; (*personne*) suffering from cancer.

cancérigène [kɑ̃seʀiʒɛn] *a* carcinogenic.

cancérologue [kɑ̃seʀɔlɔg] *nm/f* cancer specialist.

cancre [kɑ̃kʀ(ə)] *nm* dunce.

cancrelat [kɑ̃kʀəla] *nm* cockroach.

candélabre [kɑ̃delabʀ(ə)] *nm* candelabrum; (*lampadaire*) street lamp, lamppost.

candeur [kɑ̃dœʀ] *nf* ingenuousness, guilelessness.

candi [kɑ̃di] *a inv*: **sucre** ~ (sugar-)candy.

candidat, e [kɑ̃dida, -at] *nm/f* candidate; (*à un poste*) applicant, candidate.

candidature [kɑ̃didatyʀ] *nf* candidacy; application; **poser sa** ~ to submit an application, apply.

candide [kɑ̃did] *a* ingenuous, guileless, naïve.

cane [kan] *nf* (female) duck.

caneton [kantɔ̃] *nm* duckling.

canette [kanɛt] *nf* (*de bière*) (flip-top) bottle; (*de machine à coudre*) spool.

canevas [kanva] *nm* (*COUTURE*) canvas (for tapestry work); (*fig*) framework, structure.

caniche [kaniʃ] *nm* poodle.

caniculaire [kanikylɛʀ] *a* (*chaleur, jour*) scorching.

canicule [kanikyl] *nf* scorching heat; midsummer heat, dog days *pl*.

canif [kanif] *nm* penknife, pocket knife.

canin, e [kanɛ̃, -in] *a* canine ♦ *nf* canine (tooth), eye tooth; **exposition** ~**e** dog show.

caniveau, x [kanivo] *nm* gutter.

cannabis [kanabis] *nm* cannabis.

canne [kan] *nf* (walking) stick; ~ **à pêche** fishing rod; ~ **à sucre** sugar cane; **les** ~**s blanches** (*les aveugles*) the blind.

canné, e [kane] *a* (*chaise*) cane *cpd*.

cannelé, e [kanle] *a* fluted.

cannelle [kanɛl] *nf* cinnamon.

cannelure [kanlyʀ] *nf* fluting *q*.

canner [kane] *vt* (*chaise*) to make *ou* repair with cane.

cannibale [kanibal] *nm/f* cannibal.

canoë [kanɔe] *nm* canoe; (*sport*) canoeing; ~ **(kayak)** kayak.

canon [kanɔ̃] *nm* (*arme*) gun; (*HIST*) cannon; (*d'une arme: tube*) barrel; (*fig*) model; (*MUS*) canon ♦ *a*: **droit** ~ canon law; ~ **rayé** rifled barrel.

cañon [kaɲɔ̃] *nm* canyon.

canonique [kanɔnik] *a*: **âge** ~ respectable age.

canoniser [kanɔnize] *vt* to canonize.

canonnade [kanɔnad] *nf* cannonade.

canonnier [kanɔnje] *nm* gunner.

canonnière [kanɔnjɛʀ] *nf* gunboat.

canot [kano] *nm* boat, ding(h)y; ~ **pneumatique** rubber *ou* inflatable ding(h)y; ~ **de sauvetage** lifeboat.

canotage [kanɔtaʒ] *nm* rowing.

canoter [kanɔte] *vi* to go rowing.

canoteur, euse [kanɔtœʀ, -øz] *nm/f* rower.

canotier [kanɔtje] *nm* boater.

Cantal [kɑ̃tal] *nm*: **le** ~ Cantal.

cantate [kɑ̃tat] *nf* cantata.

cantatrice [kɑ̃tatʀis] *nf* (opera) singer.

cantilène [kɑ̃tilɛn] *nf* (*MUS*) cantilena.

cantine [kɑ̃tin] *nf* canteen; (*réfectoire d'école*) dining hall.

cantique [kɑ̃tik] *nm* hymn.

canton [kɑ̃tɔ̃] *nm* district *consisting of several communes*; (*en Suisse*) canton.

cantonade [kɑ̃tɔnad]: **à la** ~ *ad* to everyone in general; (*crier*) from the rooftops.

cantonais, e [kɑ̃tɔnɛ, -ɛz] *a* Cantonese ♦ *nm* (*LING*) Cantonese.

cantonner [kɑ̃tɔne] *vt* (*MIL*) to billet (*Brit*), quarter; to station; **se** ~ **dans** to confine o.s. to.

cantonnier [kɑ̃tɔnje] *nm* roadmender.

canular [kanylaʀ] *nm* hoax.

CAO *sigle f* (= *conception assistée par ordinateur*) CAD.

caoutchouc [kautʃu] *nm* rubber; ~ **mousse** foam rubber; **en** ~ rubber *cpd*.

caoutchouté, e [kautʃute] *a* rubberized.

caoutchouteux, euse [kautʃutø, -øz] *a* rubbery.

CAP *sigle m* (= *Certificat d'aptitude professionnelle*) *vocational training certificate taken at secondary school*.

cap [kap] *nm* (*GÉO*) cape; headland; (*fig*) hurdle; watershed; (*NAVIG*): **changer de** ~ to change course; **mettre le** ~ **sur** to head *ou* steer for; **doubler** *ou* **passer le** ~ (*fig*) to get over the worst; **Le C~** Cape Town; **le** ~ **de Bonne Espérance** the Cape of Good Hope; **le**

~ Horn Cape Horn; **les îles du C~ Vert** (*aussi*: **le C~-Vert**) the Cape Verde Islands.

capable [kapabl(ə)] *a* able, capable; **~ de qch/faire** capable of sth/doing; **il est ~ d'oublier** he could easily forget; **spectacle/livre ~ d'intéresser** show/book liable *ou* likely to be of interest.

capacité [kapasite] *nf* (*compétence*) ability; (*JUR, INFORM, d'un récipient*) capacity; **~ (en droit)** basic legal qualification.

caparaçonner [kaparasɔne] *vt* (*fig*) to clad.

cape [kap] *nf* cape, cloak; **rire sous ~** to laugh up one's sleeve.

capeline [kaplin] *nf* wide-brimmed hat.

CAPES [kapɛs] *sigle m* (= *Certificat d'aptitude au professorat de l'enseignement du second degré*) secondary teaching diploma.

capésien, ne [kapesjɛ̃, -ɛn] *nm/f* person who holds the CAPES.

CAPET [kapɛt] *sigle m* (= *Certificat d'aptitude au professorat de l'enseignement technique*) technical teaching diploma.

capharnaüm [kafarnaɔm] *nm* shambles *sg*.

capillaire [kapilɛr] *a* (*soins, lotion*) hair *cpd*; (*vaisseau etc*) capillary; **artiste ~** hair artist *ou* designer.

capillarité [kapilarite] *nf* capillary action.

capilliculteur [kapilikyltœr] *nm* hair-care specialist.

capilotade [kapilɔtad]: **en ~** *ad* crushed to a pulp; smashed to pieces.

capitaine [kapitɛn] *nm* captain; **~ des pompiers** fire chief (*Brit*), fire marshal (*US*); **~ au long cours** master mariner.

capitainerie [kapitɛnri] *nf* (*du port*) harbour (*Brit*) *ou* harbor (*US*) master's (office).

capital, e, aux [kapital, -o] *a* major; of paramount importance; fundamental; (*JUR*) capital ♦ *nm* capital; (*fig*) stock; asset ♦ *nf* (*ville*) capital; (*lettre*) capital (letter); ♦ *nmpl* (*fonds*) capital *sg*, money *sg*; **les sept péchés capitaux** the seven deadly sins; **peine ~e** capital punishment; **~ (social)** authorized capital; **~ d'exploitation** working capital.

capitaliser [kapitalize] *vt* to amass, build up; (*COMM*) to capitalize ♦ *vi* to save.

capitalisme [kapitalism(ə)] *nm* capitalism.

capitaliste [kapitalist(ə)] *a, nm/f* capitalist.

capiteux, euse [kapitø, -øz] *a* (*vin, parfum*) heady; (*sensuel*) sensuous, alluring.

capitonné, e [kapitɔne] *a* padded.

capitulation [kapitylasjɔ̃] *nf* capitulation.

capituler [kapityle] *vi* to capitulate.

caporal, aux [kapɔral, -o] *nm* lance corporal.

caporal-chef, *pl* **caporaux-chefs** [kapɔralʃɛf, kapɔro-] *nm* corporal.

capot [kapo] *nm* (*AUTO*) bonnet (*Brit*), hood (*US*) ♦ *a inv* (*CARTES*): **être ~** to lose without taking a single trick.

capote [kapɔt] *nf* (*de voiture*) hood (*Brit*), top (*US*); (*de soldat*) greatcoat; **~ (anglaise)** (*fam*) rubber, condom.

capoter [kapɔte] *vi* to overturn; (*négociations*) to founder.

câpre [kɑpr(ə)] *nf* caper.

caprice [kapris] *nm* whim, caprice; passing fancy; **~s** *nmpl* (*de la mode etc*) vagaries; **faire un ~** to throw a tantrum; **faire des ~s** to be temperamental.

capricieux, euse [kaprisjø, -øz] *a* capricious; whimsical; temperamental.

Capricorne [kaprikɔrn] *nm*: **le ~** Capricorn, the Goat; **être du ~** to be Capricorn.

capsule [kapsyl] *nf* (*de bouteille*) cap; (*amorce*) primer; cap; (*BOT etc, spatiale*) capsule.

capter [kapte] *vt* (*ondes radio*) to pick up; (*eau*) to harness; (*fig*) to win, capture.

capteur [kaptœr] *nm*: **~ solaire** solar collector.

captieux, euse [kapsjø, -øz] *a* specious.

captif, ive [kaptif, -iv] *a, nm/f* captive.

captiver [kaptive] *vt* to captivate.

captivité [kaptivite] *nf* captivity; **en ~** in captivity.

capture [kaptyr] *nf* capture, catching *q*; catch.

capturer [kaptyre] *vt* to capture, catch.

capuche [kapyʃ] *nf* hood.

capuchon [kapyʃɔ̃] *nm* hood; (*de stylo*) cap, top.

capucin [kapysɛ̃] *nm* Capuchin monk.

capucine [kapysin] *nf* (*BOT*) nasturtium.

caquelon [kaklɔ̃] *nm* (*ustensile de cuisson*) fondue pot.

caquet [kakɛ] *nm*: **rabattre le ~ à qn** to bring sb down a peg or two.

caqueter [kakte] *vi* (*poule*) to cackle; (*fig*) to prattle.

car [kar] *nm* coach (*Brit*), bus ♦ *cj* because, for; **~ de police** police van; **~ de reportage** broadcasting *ou* radio van.

carabine [karabin] *nf* carbine, rifle; **~ à air comprimé** airgun.

carabiné, e [karabine] *a* violent; (*cocktail, amende*) stiff.

Caracas [karakas] *n* Caracas.

caracoler [karakɔle] *vi* to caracole, prance.

caractère [karaktɛr] *nm* (*gén*) character; **en ~s gras** in bold type; **en petits ~s** in small print; **en ~s d'imprimerie** in block capitals; **avoir du ~** to have character; **avoir bon/mauvais ~** to be good-/ill-natured *ou* tempered; **~ de remplacement** wild card (*INFORM*); **~s/seconde (cps)** characters per second (cps).

caractériel, le [karakterjɛl] *a* (*enfant*) (emotionally) disturbed ♦ *nm/f* problem child; **troubles ~s** emotional problems.

caractérisé, e [karakterize] *a*: **c'est une grippe/de l'insubordination ~e** it is a clear(-cut) case of flu/insubordination.

caractériser [karakterize] *vt* to characterize; **se ~ par** to be characterized *ou* distinguished by.

caractéristique [karakteristik] *a, nf* characteristic.

carafe [karaf] *nf* decanter; carafe.

carafon [karafɔ̃] *nm* small carafe.

caraïbe [karaib] *a* Caribbean; **les C~s** *nfpl* the Caribbean (Islands); **la mer des C~s** the Caribbean Sea.

carambolage [karãbɔlaʒ] *nm* multiple crash, pileup.

caramel [karamɛl] *nm* (*bonbon*) caramel, toffee; (*substance*) caramel.

caraméliser [karamelize] *vt* to caramelize.

carapace [karapas] *nf* shell.

carapater [kaʀapate]: **se ~** *vi* to take to one's heels, scram.

carat [kaʀa] *nm* carat; **or à 18 ~s** 18-carat gold.

caravane [kaʀavan] *nf* caravan.

caravanier [kaʀavanje] *nm* caravanner.

caravaning [kaʀavaniŋ] *nm* caravanning; *(emplacement)* caravan site.

caravelle [kaʀavɛl] *nf* caravel.

carbonate [kaʀbɔnat] *nm* (*CHIMIE*): **~ de soude** sodium carbonate.

carbone [kaʀbɔn] *nm* carbon; *(feuille)* carbon, sheet of carbon paper; *(double)* carbon (copy).

carbonique [kaʀbɔnik] *a*: **gaz ~** carbon dioxide; **neige ~** dry ice.

carbonisé, e [kaʀbɔnize] *a* charred; **mourir ~** to be burned to death.

carboniser [kaʀbɔnize] *vt* to carbonize; *(brûler complètement)* to burn down, reduce to ashes.

carburant [kaʀbyʀɑ̃] *nm* (motor) fuel.

carburateur [kaʀbyʀatœʀ] *nm* carburettor.

carburation [kaʀbyʀasjɔ̃] *nf* carburation.

carburer [kaʀbyʀe] *vi* (*moteur*): **bien/mal ~** to be well/badly tuned.

carcan [kaʀkɑ̃] *nm* (*fig*) yoke, shackles *pl*.

carcasse [kaʀkas] *nf* carcass; *(de véhicule etc)* shell.

carcéral, e, aux [kaʀseʀal, -o] *a* prison *cpd*.

carcinogène [kaʀsinɔʒɛn] *a* carcinogenic.

cardan [kaʀdɑ̃] *nm* universal joint.

carder [kaʀde] *vt* to card.

cardiaque [kaʀdjak] *a* cardiac, heart *cpd* ♦ *nm/f* heart patient; **être ~** to have a heart condition.

cardigan [kaʀdigɑ̃] *nm* cardigan.

cardinal, e, aux [kaʀdinal, -o] *a* cardinal ♦ *nm* (*REL*) cardinal.

cardiologie [kaʀdjɔlɔʒi] *nf* cardiology.

cardiologue [kaʀdjɔlɔg] *nm/f* cardiologist, heart specialist.

cardio-vasculaire [kaʀdjɔvaskylɛʀ] *a* cardio-vascular.

cardon [kaʀdɔ̃] *nm* cardoon.

carême [kaʀɛm] *nm*: **le C~** Lent.

carence [kaʀɑ̃s] *nf* incompetence, inadequacy; *(manque)* deficiency; **~ vitaminique** vitamin deficiency.

carène [kaʀɛn] *nf* hull.

caréner [kaʀene] *vt* (*NAVIG*) to careen; *(carrosserie)* to streamline.

caressant, e [kaʀesɑ̃, -ɑ̃t] *a* affectionate; caressing, tender.

caresse [kaʀes] *nf* caress.

caresser [kaʀese] *vt* to caress, stroke, fondle; *(fig: projet, espoir)* to toy with.

cargaison [kaʀgɛzɔ̃] *nf* cargo, freight.

cargo [kaʀgo] *nm* cargo boat, freighter; **~ mixte** cargo and passenger ship.

cari [kaʀi] *nm* = **curry**.

caricatural, e, aux [kaʀikatyʀal, -o] *a* caricatural, caricature-like.

caricature [kaʀikatyʀ] *nf* caricature; *(politique etc)* (satirical) cartoon.

caricaturer [kaʀikatyʀe] *vt* (*personne*) to caricature; *(politique etc)* to satirize.

caricaturiste [kaʀikatyʀist(ə)] *nm/f* caricaturist; (satirical) cartoonist.

carie [kaʀi] *nf*: **la ~ (dentaire)** tooth decay; **une ~** a bad tooth.

carié, e [kaʀje] *a*: **dent ~e** bad *ou* decayed tooth.

carillon [kaʀijɔ̃] *nm* (*d'église*) bells *pl*; *(de pendule)* chimes *pl*; *(de porte)*: **~ (électrique)** (electric) door chime *ou* bell.

carillonner [kaʀijɔne] *vi* to ring, chime, peal.

carlingue [kaʀlɛ̃g] *nf* cabin.

carmin [kaʀmɛ̃] *a inv* crimson.

carnage [kaʀnaʒ] *nm* carnage, slaughter.

carnassier, ière [kaʀnasje, -jɛʀ] *a* carnivorous ♦ *nm* carnivore.

carnation [kaʀnasjɔ̃] *nf* complexion; **~s** *nfpl* (*PEINTURE*) flesh tones.

carnaval [kaʀnaval] *nm* carnival.

carné, e [kaʀne] *a* meat *cpd*, meat-based.

carnet [kaʀnɛ] *nm* (*calepin*) notebook; *(de tickets, timbres etc)* book; *(d'école)* school report; *(journal intime)* diary; **~ d'adresses** address book; **~ de chèques** cheque (*Brit*) *ou* check (*US*) book; **~ de commandes** order book; **~ de notes** (*SCOL*) (school) report; **~ à souches** counterfoil book.

carnier [kaʀnje] *nm* gamebag.

carnivore [kaʀnivɔʀ] *a* carnivorous ♦ *nm* carnivore.

Carolines [kaʀɔlin] *nfpl*: **les ~** the Caroline Islands.

carotide [kaʀɔtid] *nf* carotid (artery).

carotte [kaʀɔt] *nf* (*aussi fig*) carrot.

Carpates [kaʀpat] *nfpl*: **les ~** the Carpathians, the Carpathian Mountains.

carpe [kaʀp(ə)] *nf* carp.

carpette [kaʀpɛt] *nf* rug.

carquois [kaʀkwa] *nm* quiver.

carre [kaʀ] *nf* (*de ski*) edge.

carré, e [kaʀe] *a* square; *(fig: franc)* straightforward ♦ *nm* (*de terrain, jardin*) patch, plot; (*NAVIG: salle*) wardroom; (*MATH*) square; (*CARTES*): **~ d'as/de rois** four aces/kings; **élever un nombre au ~** to square a number; **mètre/kilomètre ~** square metre/kilometre; **~ de soie** silk headsquare *ou* headscarf; **~ d'agneau** loin of lamb.

carreau, x [kaʀo] *nm* (*en faïence etc*) (floor) tile; (wall) tile; *(de fenêtre)* (window) pane; *(motif)* check, square; (*CARTES: couleur*) diamonds *pl*; (*: carte*) diamond; **tissu à ~x** checked fabric; **papier à ~x** squared paper.

carrefour [kaʀfuʀ] *nm* crossroads *sg*.

carrelage [kaʀlaʒ] *nm* tiling; (tiled) floor.

carreler [kaʀle] *vt* to tile.

carrelet [kaʀlɛ] *nm* (*poisson*) plaice.

carreleur [kaʀlœʀ] *nm* (floor) tiler.

carrément [kaʀemɑ̃] *ad* (*franchement*) straight out, bluntly; (*sans détours, sans hésiter*) straight; (*nettement*) definitely; **il l'a ~ mis à la porte** he threw him straight out.

carrer [kaʀe]: **se ~** *vi*: **se ~ dans un fauteuil** to settle o.s. comfortably *ou* ensconce o.s. in an armchair.

carrier [kaʀje] *nm*: **(ouvrier) ~** quarryman, quarrier.

carrière [kaʀjɛʀ] *nf* (*de roches*) quarry; *(métier)* career; **militaire de ~** professional soldier; **faire ~ dans** to make one's career in.

carriole [kaʀjɔl] *nf* (*péj*) old cart.

carrossable [kaʀɔsabl(ə)] *a* suitable for (motor) vehicles.

carrosse [kaʀɔs] *nm* (horse-drawn) coach.

carrosserie [kaʀɔsʀi] *nf* body, bodywork *q* (*Brit*); (*activité, commerce*) coachwork (*Brit*), (car) body manufacturing; **atelier de ~** (*pour réparations*) body shop, panel beaters' (yard) (*Brit*).

carrossier [kaʀɔsje] *nm* coachbuilder (*Brit*), (car) body repairer; (*dessinateur*) car designer.

carrousel [kaʀuzɛl] *nm* (*ÉQUITATION*) carousel; (*fig*) merry-go-round.

carrure [kaʀyʀ] *nf* build; (*fig*) stature.

cartable [kaʀtabl(ə)] *nm* (*d'écolier*) satchel, (school)bag.

carte [kaʀt(ə)] *nf* (*de géographie*) map; (*marine, du ciel*) chart; (*de fichier, d'abonnement etc, à jouer*) card; (*au restaurant*) menu; (*aussi:* **~ postale**) (post)card; (*aussi:* **~ de visite**) (visiting) card; **avoir/donner ~ blanche** to have/give carte blanche *ou* a free hand; **tirer les ~s à qn** to read sb's cards; **jouer aux ~s** to play cards; **jouer ~s sur table** (*fig*) to put one's cards on the table; **à la ~** (*au restaurant*) à la carte; **~ bancaire** cash card; **~ à circuit imprimé** printed circuit; **~ de crédit** credit card; **~ d'état-major** ≈ Ordnance (*Brit*) *ou* Geological (*US*) Survey map; **la ~ grise** (*AUTO*) ≈ the (car) registration document; **~ d'identité** identity card; **~ perforée** punch(ed) card; **~ de séjour** residence permit; **~ routière** road map; **la ~ verte** (*AUTO*) the green card; **la ~ des vins** the wine list.

cartel [kaʀtɛl] *nm* cartel.

carte-lettre, *pl* **cartes-lettres** [kaʀtəlɛtʀ(ə)] *nf* letter-card.

carte-mère, *pl* **cartes-mères** [kaʀtəmɛʀ] *nf* (*INFORM*) mother board.

carter [kaʀtɛʀ] *nm* (*AUTO: d'huile*) sump (*Brit*), oil pan (*US*); (*: de la boîte de vitesses*) casing; (*de bicyclette*) chain guard.

carte-réponse, *pl* **cartes-réponses** [kaʀt(ə)ʀepɔ̃s] *nf* reply card.

Carthage [kaʀtaʒ] *n* Carthage.

carthaginois, e [kaʀtaʒinwa, -waz] *a* Carthaginian.

cartilage [kaʀtilaʒ] *nm* (*ANAT*) cartilage.

cartilagineux, euse [kaʀtilaʒinø, -øz] *a* (*viande*) gristly.

cartographe [kaʀtɔgʀaf] *nm/f* cartographer.

cartographie [kaʀtɔgʀafi] *nf* cartography, map-making.

cartomancie [kaʀtɔmɑ̃si] *nf* fortune-telling, card-reading.

cartomancien, ne [kaʀtɔmɑ̃sjɛ̃, -ɛn] *nm/f* fortune-teller (*with cards*).

carton [kaʀtɔ̃] *nm* (*matériau*) cardboard; (*boîte*) (cardboard) box; (*d'invitation*) invitation card; (*ART*) sketch; cartoon; **en ~** cardboard *cpd*; **faire un ~** (*au tir*) to have a go at the rifle range; to score a hit; **~ (à dessin)** portfolio.

cartonnage [kaʀtɔnaʒ] *nm* cardboard (packing).

cartonné, e [kaʀtɔne] *a* (*livre*) hardback, cased.

carton-pâte [kaʀtɔ̃pɑt] *nm* pasteboard; **de ~** (*fig*) cardboard *cpd*.

cartouche [kaʀtuʃ] *nf* cartridge; (*de cigarettes*) carton.

cartouchière [kaʀtuʃjɛʀ] *nf* cartridge belt.

cas [kɑ] *nm* case; **faire peu de ~/grand ~ de** to attach little/great importance to; **le ~ échéant** if need be; **en aucun ~** on no account, under no circumstances (whatsoever); **au ~ où** in case; **dans ce ~** in that case; **en ~ de** in case of, in the event of; **en ~ de besoin** if need be; **en ~ d'urgence** in an emergency; **en ce ~** in that case; **en tout ~** in any case, at any rate; **~ de conscience** matter of conscience; **~ de force majeure** case of absolute necessity; (*ASSURANCES*) act of God; **~ limite** borderline case; **~ social** social problem.

Casablanca [kazablɑ̃ka] *n* Casablanca.

casanier, ière [kazanje, -jɛʀ] *a* stay-at-home.

casaque [kazak] *nf* (*de jockey*) blouse.

cascade [kaskad] *nf* waterfall, cascade; (*fig*) stream, torrent.

cascadeur, euse [kaskadœʀ, -øz] *nm/f* stuntman/girl.

case [kɑz] *nf* (*hutte*) hut; (*compartiment*) compartment; (*pour le courrier*) pigeonhole; (*de mots croisés, d'échiquier*) square; (*sur un formulaire*) box.

casemate [kazmat] *nf* blockhouse.

caser [kɑze] *vt* (*mettre*) to put; (*loger*) to put up; (*péj*) to find a job for; to marry off; **se ~** (*personne*) to settle down.

caserne [kazɛʀn(ə)] *nf* barracks.

casernement [kazɛʀnəmɑ̃] *nm* barrack buildings *pl*.

cash [kaʃ] *ad*: **payer ~** to pay cash down.

casier [kɑzje] *nm* (*à journaux etc*) rack; (*de bureau*) filing cabinet; (*: à cases*) set of pigeonholes; (*case*) compartment; pigeonhole; (*: à clef*) locker; (*PÊCHE*) lobster pot; **~ à bouteilles** bottle rack; **~ judiciaire** police record.

casino [kazino] *nm* casino.

casque [kask(ə)] *nm* helmet; (*chez le coiffeur*) (hair-)drier; (*pour audition*) (head-)phones *pl*, headset; **les C~s bleus** the UN peace-keeping force.

casquer [kaske] *vi* (*fam*) to cough up, stump up (*Brit*).

casquette [kaskɛt] *nf* cap.

cassable [kɑsabl(ə)] *a* (*fragile*) breakable.

cassant, e [kɑsɑ̃, -ɑ̃t] *a* brittle; (*fig*) brusque, abrupt.

cassate [kasat] *nf*: **(glace) ~** cassata.

cassation [kɑsasjɔ̃] *nf*: **se pourvoir en ~** to lodge an appeal; **recours en ~** appeal to the Supreme Court.

casse [kɑs] *nf* (*pour voitures*): **mettre à la ~** to scrap, send to the breakers (*Brit*); (*dégâts*): **il y a eu de la ~** there were a lot of breakages; (*TYPO*): **haut/bas de ~** upper/lower case.

cassé, e [kɑse] *a* (*voix*) cracked; (*vieillard*) bent.

casse-cou [kɑsku] *a inv* daredevil, reckless; **crier ~ à qn** to warn sb (*against a risky undertaking*).

casse-croûte [kɑskʀut] *nm inv* snack.

casse-noisette(s) [kɑsnwazɛt], **casse-noix**

[kɑsnwa] *nm inv* nutcrackers *pl.*

casse-pieds [kɑspje] *a, nm/f inv (fam)*: **il est ~, c'est un ~** he's a pain (in the neck).

casser [kɑse] *vt* to break; *(ADMIN: gradé)* to demote; *(JUR)* to quash; *(COMM)*: **~ les prix** to slash prices; **se ~ *vi*** to break; *(fam)* to go, leave ♦ *vt*: **se ~ la jambe/une jambe** to break one's leg/a leg; **à tout ~** fantastic, brilliant; **se ~ net** to break clean off.

casserole [kɑsRɔl] *nf* saucepan; **à la ~** *(CULIN)* braised.

casse-tête [kɑstɛt] *nm inv (fig)* brain teaser; *(difficultés)* headache *(fig)*.

cassette [kasɛt] *nf (bande magnétique)* cassette; *(coffret)* casket.

casseur [kɑsœR] *nm* hooligan; rioter.

cassis [kasis] *nm* blackcurrant; *(de la route)* dip, bump.

cassonade [kasɔnad] *nf* brown sugar.

cassoulet [kasulɛ] *nm* sausage and bean hot-pot.

cassure [kɑsyR] *nf* break, crack.

castagnettes [kastaɲɛt] *nfpl* castanets.

caste [kast(ə)] *nf* caste.

castillan, e [kastijɑ̃, -an] *a* Castilian ♦ *nm (LING)* Castilian.

Castille [kastij] *nf*: **la ~** Castile.

castor [kastɔR] *nm* beaver.

castrer [kastRe] *vt (mâle)* to castrate; *(femelle)* to spay; *(cheval)* to geld; *(chat, chien)* to doctor *(Brit)*, fix *(US)*.

cataclysme [kataklism(ə)] *nm* cataclysm.

catacombes [katakɔ̃b] *nfpl* catacombs.

catadioptre [katadjɔptR(ə)] *nm* = **cataphote**.

catafalque [katafalk(ə)] *nm* catafalque.

catalan, e [katalɑ̃, -an] *a* Catalan, Catalonian ♦ *nm (LING)* Catalan.

Catalogne [katalɔɲ] *nf*: **la ~** Catalonia.

catalogue [katalɔg] *nm* catalogue.

cataloguer [katalɔge] *vt* to catalogue, list; *(péj)* to put a label on.

catalyse [kataliz] *nf* catalysis.

catalyseur [katalizœR] *nm* catalyst.

catamaran [katamaRɑ̃] *nm (voilier)* catamaran.

cataphote [katafɔt] *nm* reflector.

cataplasme [kataplasm(ə)] *nm* poultice.

catapulte [katapylt(ə)] *nf* catapult.

catapulter [katapylte] *vt* to catapult.

cataracte [kataRakt(ə)] *nf* cataract; **opérer qn de la ~** to operate on sb for a cataract.

catarrhe [kataR] *nm* catarrh.

catarrheux, euse [kataRø, -øz] *a* catarrhal.

catastrophe [katastRɔf] *nf* catastrophe, disaster; **atterrir en ~** to make an emergency landing; **partir en ~** to rush away.

catastropher [katastRɔfe] *vt (personne)* to shatter.

catastrophique [katastRɔfik] *a* catastrophic, disastrous.

catch [katʃ] *nm* (all-in) wrestling.

catcheur, euse [katʃœR, -øz] *nm/f* (all-in) wrestler.

catéchiser [kateʃize] *vt* to indoctrinate; to lecture.

catéchisme [kateʃism(ə)] *nm* catechism.

catéchumène [katekymɛn] *nm/f* catechumen, *person attending religious instruction prior to baptism.*

catégorie [kategɔRi] *nf* category; *(BOUCHER-IE)*: **morceaux de première/deuxième ~** prime/second cuts.

catégorique [kategɔRik] *a* categorical.

catégoriquement [kategɔRikmɑ̃] *ad* categorically.

catégoriser [kategɔRize] *vt* to categorize.

caténaire [katenɛR] *nf (RAIL)* catenary.

cathédrale [katedRal] *nf* cathedral.

cathéter [katetɛR] *nm (MÉD)* catheter.

cathode [katɔd] *nf* cathode.

cathodique [katɔdik] *a*: **rayons ~s** cathode rays; **tube/écran ~** cathode-ray tube/screen.

catholicisme [katɔlisism(ə)] *nm* (Roman) Catholicism.

catholique [katɔlik] *a, nm/f* (Roman) Catholic; **pas très ~** a bit shady *ou* fishy.

catimini [katimini]: **en ~** *ad* on the sly, on the quiet.

catogan [katɔgɑ̃] *nm* bow *(tying hair on neck)*.

Caucase [kɔkɑz] *nm*: **le ~** the Caucasus (Mountains).

caucasien, ne [kɔkazjɛ̃, -ɛn] *a* Caucasian.

cauchemar [kɔʃmaR] *nm* nightmare.

cauchemardesque [kɔʃmaRdɛsk(ə)] *a* nightmarish.

caudal, e, aux [kodal, -o] *a* caudal, tail *cpd*.

causal, e [kozal] *a* causal.

causalité [kozalite] *nf* causality.

cause [koz] *nf* cause; *(JUR)* lawsuit, case; brief; **faire ~ commune avec qn** to take sides with sb; **être ~ de** to be the cause of; **à ~ de** because of, owing to; **pour ~ de** on account of; owing to; **(et) pour ~** and for (a very) good reason; **être en ~** *(intérêts)* to be at stake; *(personne)* to be involved; *(qualité)* to be in question; **mettre en ~** to implicate; to call into question; **remettre en ~** to challenge, call into question; **c'est hors de ~** it's out of the question; **en tout état de ~** in any case.

causer [koze] *vt* to cause ♦ *vi* to chat, talk.

causerie [kozRi] *nf* talk.

causette [kozɛt] *nf*: **faire la** *ou* **un brin de ~** to have a chat.

caustique [kostik] *a* caustic.

cauteleux, euse [kotlø, -øz] *a* wily.

cautériser [koteRize] *vt* to cauterize.

caution [kosjɔ̃] *nf* guarantee, security; deposit; *(JUR)* bail (bond); *(fig)* backing, support; **payer la ~ de qn** to stand bail for sb; **se porter ~ pour qn** to stand security for sb; **libéré sous ~** released on bail; **sujet à ~** unconfirmed.

cautionnement [kosjɔnmɑ̃] *nm (somme)* guarantee, security.

cautionner [kosjɔne] *vt* to guarantee; *(soutenir)* to support.

cavalcade [kavalkad] *nf (fig)* stampede.

cavale [kaval] *nf*: **en ~** on the run.

cavalerie [kavalRi] *nf* cavalry.

cavalier, ière [kavalje, -jɛR] *a (désinvolte)* offhand ♦ *nm/f* rider; *(au bal)* partner ♦ *nm (ÉCHECS)* knight; **faire ~ seul** to go it alone; **allée** *ou* **piste cavalière** riding path.

cave [kav] *nf* cellar; *(cabaret)* (cellar) nightclub ♦ *a*: **yeux ~s** sunken eyes; **joues ~s** hollow cheeks.

caveau, x [kavo] *nm* vault.

caverne [kavɛʀn(ə)] *nf* cave.

caverneux, euse [kavɛʀnø, -øz] *a* cavernous.

caviar [kavjaʀ] *nm* caviar(e).

cavité [kavite] *nf* cavity.

Cayenne [kajɛn] *n* Cayenne.

CB [sibi] *sigle f* (= *citizens' band, canaux banalisés*) CB.

CC *sigle m* = **corps consulaire, compte courant**.

CCI *sigle f* = **Chambre de commerce et d'industrie**.

CCP *sigle m* = **compte chèque postal**.

CD *sigle m* (= *chemin départemental*) secondary road, ≈ B road (*Brit*); (= *compact disc*) CD; (= *comité directeur*) steering committee; (*POL*) = **corps diplomatique**.

CDF, CdF *sigle mpl* (= *Charbonnages de France*) national coal board.

CDI *sigle m* (= *Centre de documentation et d'information*) school library.

CDS *sigle m* (= *Centre des démocrates sociaux*) political party.

CE *sigle f* (= *Communauté européenne*) EC; (*COMM*) = **caisse d'épargne** ♦ *sigle m* (*INDUSTRIE*) = **comité d'entreprise**; (*SCOL*) = **cours élémentaire**.

ce (**c'**), **cet, cette, ces** [sə, sɛt, se] *dét* (*gén*) this; these *pl*; (*non-proximité*) that; those *pl*; **cette nuit** (*qui vient*) tonight; (*passée*) last night ♦ *pronom:* ~ **qui**, ~ **que** what; (*chose qui ...*): **il est bête,** ~ **qui me chagrine** he's stupid, which saddens me; **tout** ~ **qui bouge** everything that *ou* which moves; **tout** ~ **que je sais** all I know; ~ **dont j'ai parlé** what I talked about; ~ **que c'est grand!** how big it is!, what a size it is!; **c'est: c'est petit/grand/un livre** it's *ou* it is small/big/a book; **c'est un peintre** he's *ou* he is a painter; ~ **sont des livres/ peintres** they're *ou* they are books/painters; **c'est le facteur** *etc* (*à la porte*) it's the postman *etc*; **qui est-~?** who is it?; (*en désignant*) who is he/she?; **qu'est-~?** what is it?; **c'est ça** (*correct*) that's it, that's right; **c'est qu'il n'a pas faim** the fact is he's not hungry; **ce n'est pas à moi de faire** it's not up to me to do; *voir aussi* **-ci, est-ce que, n'est-ce pas, c'est-à-dire**.

CEA *sigle m* (= *Commissariat à l'énergie atomique*) ≈ AEA (= *Atomic Energy Authority*) (*Brit*), ≈ AEC (= *Atomic Energy Commission*) (*US*).

CECA [seka] *sigle f* (= *Communauté européenne du charbon et de l'acier*) ECSC (= *European Coal and Steel Community*).

ceci [səsi] *pronom* this.

cécité [sesite] *nf* blindness.

céder [sede] *vt* to give up ♦ *vi* (*pont, barrage*) to give way; (*personne*) to give in; ~ **à** to yield to, give in to.

CEDEX [sedɛks] *sigle m* (= *courrier d'entreprise à distribution exceptionnelle*) accelerated postal service for bulk users.

cédille [sedij] *nf* cedilla.

cèdre [sɛdʀ(ə)] *nm* cedar.

CEE *sigle f* (= *Communauté économique européenne*) EEC.

CEG *sigle m* (= *Collège d'enseignement général*) ≈ junior secondary school (*Brit*), ≈

junior high school (*US*).

ceindre [sɛ̃dʀ(ə)] *vt* (*mettre*) to put on, don; (*entourer*): ~ **qch de qch** to put sth round sth.

ceinture [sɛ̃tyʀ] *nf* belt; (*taille*) waist; (*fig*) ring; belt; circle; ~ **de sauvetage** lifebelt; ~ **de sécurité** safety *ou* seat belt; ~ **(de sécurité) à enrouleur** inertia reel seat belt; ~ **verte** green belt.

ceinturer [sɛ̃tyʀe] *vt* (*saisir*) to grasp (round the waist); (*entourer*) to surround.

ceinturon [sɛ̃tyʀɔ̃] *nm* belt.

cela [səla] *pronom* that; (*comme sujet indéfini*) it; ~ **m'étonne que** it surprises me that; **quand/où ~?** when/where (was that)?

célébrant [selebʀɑ̃] *nm* (*REL*) celebrant.

célébration [selebʀasjɔ̃] *nf* celebration.

célèbre [selɛbʀ(ə)] *a* famous.

célébrer [selebʀe] *vt* to celebrate; (*louer*) to extol.

célébrité [selebʀite] *nf* fame; (*star*) celebrity.

céleri [sɛlʀi] *nm:* ~**(-rave)** celeriac; ~ **(en branche)** celery.

célérité [seleʀite] *nf* speed, swiftness.

céleste [selɛst(ə)] *a* celestial; heavenly.

célibat [seliba] *nm* celibacy; bachelor/ spinsterhood.

célibataire [selibatɛʀ] *a* single, unmarried ♦ *nm/f* bachelor/unmarried *ou* single woman; **mère** ~ single *ou* unmarried mother.

celle, celles [sɛl] *pronom voir* **celui**.

cellier [selje] *nm* storeroom.

cellophane [seləfan] *nf* ® cellophane.

cellulaire [selylɛʀ] *a* (*BIO*) cell *cpd*, cellular; **voiture** *ou* **fourgon** ~ prison *ou* police van; **régime** ~ confinement.

cellule [selyl] *nf* (*gén*) cell; ~ **(photo- électrique)** electronic eye.

cellulite [selylit] *nf* cellulite.

celluloïd [selyləid] *nm* ® Celluloid.

cellulose [selyloz] *nf* cellulose.

celte [sɛlt(ə)], **celtique** [sɛltik] *a* Celt, Celtic.

celui, celle, ceux, celles [səlɥi, sɛl, sø] *pronom* the one; ~ **qui bouge** the one which *ou* that moves; (*personne*) the one who moves; ~ **que je vois** the one (which *ou* that) I see; the one (whom) I see; ~ **dont je parle** the one I'm talking about; ~ **qui veut** (*valeur indéfinie*) whoever wants, the one *ou* person who wants; ~ **du salon/du dessous** the one in (*ou* from) the lounge/below; ~ **de mon frère** my brother's; **celui-ci/-là, celle-ci/-là** this/that one; the latter/former; **ceux-ci, celles-ci** these ones; the latter; **ceux-là, celles-là** those (ones); the former.

cénacle [senakl(ə)] *nm* (*literary*) coterie *ou* set.

cendre [sɑ̃dʀ(ə)] *nf* ash; ~**s** (*d'un foyer*) ash(es), cinders; (*volcaniques*) ash *sg*; (*d'un défunt*) ashes; **sous la** ~ (*CULIN*) in (the) embers.

cendré, e [sɑ̃dʀe] *a* (*couleur*) ashen; (*piste*) ~**e** cinder track.

cendreux, euse [sɑ̃dʀø, -øz] *a* (*terrain, substance*) cindery; (*teint*) ashen.

cendrier [sɑ̃dʀije] *nm* ashtray.

cène [sɛn] *nf:* **la** ~ (Holy) Communion; (*ART*) the Last Supper.

censé, e [sɑ̃se] *a:* **être** ~ **faire** to be supposed to do.

censément |sãscmã| *ad* supposedly.

censeur |sãsœr| *nm* (*SCOL*) deputy-head (*Brit*), vice-principal (*US*); (*CINÉMA*, *POL*) censor.

censure |sãsyr| *nf* censorship.

censurer |sãsyrc| *vt* (*CINÉMA*, *PRESSE*) to censor; (*POL*) to censure.

cent |sã| *num* a hundred, one hundred; **pour ~ (%)** per cent (*%*); **faire les ~ pas** to pace up and down.

centaine |sãtɛn| *nf*: **une ~ (de)** about a hundred, a hundred or so; (*COMM*) a hundred; **plusieurs ~s (de)** several hundred; **des ~s (de)** hundreds (of).

centenaire |sãtnɛr| *a* hundred-year-old ♦ *nm/f* centenarian ♦ *nm* (*anniversaire*) centenary.

centième |sãtjɛm| *num* hundredth.

centigrade |sãtigrad| *nm* centigrade.

centigramme |sãtigram| *nm* centigramme.

centilitre |sãtilitr(ə)| *nm* centilitre (*Brit*), centiliter (*US*).

centime |sãtim| *nm* centime.

centimètre |sãtimɛtr(ə)| *nm* centimetre (*Brit*), centimeter (*US*); (*ruban*) tape measure, measuring tape.

centrafricain, e |sãtrafrikɛ̃, -ɛn| *a* of *ou* from the Central African Republic.

central, e, aux |sãtral, -o| *a* central ♦ *nm*: **~ (téléphonique)** (telephone) exchange ♦ *nf*: **~e d'achat** (*COMM*) central buying service; **~e électrique/nucléaire** electric/nuclear power station; **~e syndicale** group of af-filiated trade unions.

centralisation |sãtralizasjɔ̃| *nf* centralization.

centraliser |sãtralize| *vt* to centralize.

centraméricain, e |sãtramerikɛ̃, -ɛn| *a* Central American.

centre |sãtr(ə)| *nm* centre (*Brit*), center (*US*); **~ commercial/sportif/culturel** shopping/sports/arts centre; **~ aéré** outdoor centre; **~ d'apprentissage** training college; **~ d'at-traction** centre of attraction; **~ de gravité** centre of gravity; **~ hospitalier** hospital complex; **~ de tri** (*POSTES*) sorting office; **~s nerveux** (*ANAT*) nerve centres.

centrer |sãtre| *vt* to centre ♦ *vi* (*FOOTBALL*) to centre the ball.

centre-ville, *pl* **centres-villes** |sãtrəvil| *nm* town centre (*Brit*) *ou* center (*US*), downtown (area) (*US*).

centrifuge |sãtrify3| *a*: **force ~** centrifugal force.

centrifuger |sãtrify3e| *vt* to centrifuge.

centrifugeuse |sãtrify3øz| *nf* (*pour fruits*) juice extractor.

centripète |sãtripɛt| *a*: **force ~** centripetal force.

centriste |sãtrist(ə)| *a*, *nm/f* centrist.

centuple |sãtypl(ə)| *nm*: **le ~ de qch** a hundred times sth; **au ~** a hundredfold.

centupler |sãtyple| *vi*, *vt* to increase a hundredfold.

CEP *sigle m* = **Certificat d'études (primaires)**.

cep |sɛp| *nm* (vine) stock.

cépage |sepa3| *nm* (type of) vine.

cèpe |sɛp| *nm* (edible) boletus.

cependant |səpãdã| *ad* however, nevertheless.

céramique |seramik| *a* ceramic ♦ *nf* ceramic; (*art*) ceramics *sg*.

céramiste |seramist(ə)| *nm/f* ceramist.

cerbère |sɛrbɛr| *nm* (*fig*: *péj*) bad-tempered doorkeeper.

cerceau, x |sɛrso| *nm* (*d'enfant, de tonnelle*) hoop.

cercle |sɛrkl(ə)| *nm* circle; (*objet*) band, hoop; **décrire un ~** (*avion*) to circle; (*projectile*) to describe a circle; **~ d'amis** circle of friends; **~ de famille** family circle; **~ vicieux** vicious circle.

cercler |sɛrkle| *vt*: **lunettes cerclées d'or** gold-rimmed glasses.

cercueil |sɛrkœj| *nm* coffin.

céréale |sereal| *nf* cereal.

céréalier, ière |serealje, -jɛr| *a* (*production, cultures*) cereal *cpd*.

cérébral, e, aux |serebral, -o| *a* (*ANAT*) cer-ebral, brain *cpd*; (*fig*) mental, cerebral.

cérémonial |seremɔnjal| *nm* ceremonial.

cérémonie |seremɔni| *nf* ceremony; **~s** *nfpl* (*péj*) fuss *sg*, to-do *sg*.

cérémonieux, euse |seremɔnjø, -øz| *a* cer-emonious, formal.

CERES |sɛrɛs| *sigle m* (= *Centre d'études, de recherches et d'éducation socialiste*) (*formerly*) *intellectual section of the French Socialist party*.

cerf |sɛr| *nm* stag.

cerfeuil |sɛrfœj| *nm* chervil.

cerf-volant |sɛrvɔlã| *nm* kite; **jouer au ~** to fly a kite.

cerisaie |sərize| *nf* cherry orchard.

cerise |səriz| *nf* cherry.

cerisier |sərizje| *nm* cherry (tree).

CERN |sɛrn| *sigle m* (= *Conseil européen pour la recherche nucléaire*) CERN.

cerné, e |sɛrne| *a*: **les yeux ~s** with dark rings *ou* shadows under the eyes.

cerner |sɛrne| *vt* (*MIL etc*) to surround; (*fig*: *problème*) to delimit, define.

cernes |sɛrn(ə)| *nfpl* (dark) rings, shadows (under the eyes).

certain, e |sɛrtɛ̃, -ɛn| *a* certain; (*sûr*): **~ (de/que)** certain *ou* sure (of/ that) ♦ *dét* certain; **d'un ~ âge** past one's prime, not so young; **un ~ temps** (quite) some time; **sûr et ~** absolutely certain; **~s** *pronom* some.

certainement |sɛrtɛnmã| *ad* (*probablement*) most probably *ou* likely; (*bien sûr*) certainly, of course.

certes |sɛrt(ə)| *ad* admittedly; of course; in-deed (yes).

certificat |sɛrtifika| *nm* certificate; **C~ d'études (primaires) (CEP)** *former school leaving certificate* (*taken at the end of primary education*); **C~ de fin d'études secondaires (CFES)** school leaving certificate.

certifié, e |sɛrtifje| *a*: **professeur ~** qualified teacher; (*ADMIN*): **copie ~e conforme (à l'original)** certified copy (of the original).

certifier |sɛrtifje| *vt* to certify, guarantee; **~ à qn que** to assure sb that, guarantee to sb that; **~ qch à qn** to guarantee sth to sb.

certitude |sɛrtityd| *nf* certainty.

cérumen |serymɛn| *nm* (ear)wax.

cerveau, x |sɛrvo| *nm* brain; **~ électronique** electronic brain.

cervelas [sɛʀvəla] nm saveloy.

cervelle [sɛʀvɛl] nf (ANAT) brain; (CULIN) brain(s); **se creuser la ~** to rack one's brains.

cervical, e, aux [sɛʀvikal, -o] a cervical.

cervidés [sɛʀvide] nmpl cervidae.

CES sigle m (= Collège d'enseignement secondaire) ≈ (junior) secondary school (Brit), ≈ junior high school (US).

ces [se] dét voir **ce**.

césarienne [sezaʀjɛn] nf caesarean (section).

cessantes [sesɑ̃t] afpl: **toutes affaires ~** forthwith.

cessation [sesasjɔ̃] nf: **~ des hostilités** cessation of hostilities; **~ de paiements/commerce** suspension of payments/trading.

cesse [sɛs]: **sans ~** ad continually, constantly; continuously; **il n'avait de ~ que** he would not rest until.

cesser [sese] vt to stop ♦ vi to stop, cease; **~ de faire** to stop doing; **faire ~** (bruit, scandale) to put a stop to.

cessez-le-feu [seselfø] nm inv ceasefire.

cession [sesjɔ̃] nf transfer.

c'est [sɛ] pronom + vb voir **ce**.

c'est-à-dire [sɛtadiʀ] ad that is (to say); (demander de préciser): **~?** what does that mean?; **~ que ...** (en conséquence) which means that ...; (manière d'excuse) well, in fact ....

CET sigle m (= Collège d'enseignement technique) formerly technical school.

cet [sɛt] dét voir **ce**.

cétacé [setase] nm cetacean.

cette [sɛt] dét voir **ce**.

ceux [sø] pronom voir **celui**.

cévenol, e [sevnɔl] a of ou from the Cévennes region.

cf. abr (= confer) cf, cp.

CFAO sigle f (= conception de fabrication assistée par ordinateur) CAM.

CFDT sigle f (= Confédération française et démocratique du travail) trade union.

CFES sigle m = **Certificat de fin d'études secondaires**.

CFF sigle m (= Chemin de fer fédéral) Swiss railways.

CFL sigle m (= Chemin de fer luxembourgeois) Luxembourg railways.

CFP sigle m = Centre de formation professionnelle ♦ sigle f = Compagnie française des pétroles.

CFTC sigle f (= Confédération française des travailleurs chrétiens) trade union.

CGC sigle f (= Confédération générale des cadres) management union.

CGPME sigle f = Confédération générale des petites et moyennes entreprises.

CGT sigle f (= Confédération générale du travail) trade union.

CH abr (= Confédération helvétique) CH.

ch. abr = **charges, chauffage, cherche**.

chacal [ʃakal] nm jackal.

chacun, e [ʃakœ̃, -yn] pronom each; (indéfini) everyone, everybody.

chagrin, e [ʃagʀɛ̃, -in] a morose ♦ nm grief, sorrow; **avoir du ~** to be grieved ou sorrowful.

chagriner [ʃagʀine] vt to grieve, distress; (contrarier) to bother, worry.

chahut [ʃay] nm uproar.

chahuter [ʃayte] vt to rag, bait ♦ vi to make an uproar.

chahuteur, euse [ʃaytœʀ, -øz] nm/f rowdy.

chai [ʃɛ] nm wine and spirit store(house).

chaîne [ʃɛn] nf chain; (RADIO, TV) channel; **~s** nfpl (liens, asservissement) fetters, bonds; **travail à la ~** production line work; **réactions en ~** chain reactions; **faire la ~** to form a (human) chain; **~ d'entraide** mutual aid association; **~ haute-fidélité** ou **hi-fi**) hi-fi system; **~ (de montage** ou **de fabrication)** production ou assembly line; **~ (de montagnes)** (mountain) range; **~ de solidarité** solidarity network; **~ (stéréo** ou **audio)** stereo (system).

chaînette [ʃɛnɛt] nf (small) chain.

chaînon [ʃɛnɔ̃] nm link.

chair [ʃɛʀ] nf flesh ♦ a: **(couleur) ~** flesh-coloured; **avoir la ~ de poule** to have goosepimples ou gooseflesh; **bien en ~** plump, well-padded; **en ~ et en os** in the flesh; **~ à saucisses** sausage meat.

chaire [ʃɛʀ] nf (d'église) pulpit; (d'université) chair.

chaise [ʃɛz] nf chair; **~ de bébé** high chair; **~ électrique** electric chair; **~ longue** deck-chair.

chaland [ʃalɑ̃] nm (bateau) barge.

châle [ʃɑl] nm shawl.

chalet [ʃalɛ] nm chalet.

chaleur [ʃalœʀ] nf heat; (fig) warmth; fire, fervour (Brit), fervor (US); heat; **en ~** (ZOOL) on heat.

chaleureusement [ʃalœʀøzmɑ̃] ad warmly.

chaleureux, euse [ʃalœʀø, -øz] a warm.

challenge [ʃalɑ̃ʒ] nm contest, tournament.

challenger [ʃalɑ̃ʒɛʀ] nm (SPORT) challenger.

chaloupe [ʃalup] nf launch; (de sauvetage) lifeboat.

chalumeau, x [ʃalymo] nm blowlamp, blowtorch.

chalut [ʃaly] nm trawl (net); **pêcher au ~** to trawl.

chalutier [ʃalytje] nm trawler; (pêcheur) trawlerman.

chamade [ʃamad] nf: **battre la ~** to beat wildly.

chamailler [ʃamaje]: **se ~** vi to squabble, bicker.

chamarré, e [ʃamaʀe] a richly brocaded.

chambard [ʃɑ̃baʀ] nm rumpus.

chambardement [ʃɑ̃baʀdəmɑ̃] nm: **c'est le grand ~** everything has been (ou is being) turned upside down.

chambarder [ʃɑ̃baʀde] vt to turn upside down.

chamboulement [ʃɑ̃bulmɑ̃] nm disruption.

chambouler [ʃɑ̃bule] vt to disrupt, turn upside down.

chambranle [ʃɑ̃bʀɑl] nm (door) frame.

chambre [ʃɑ̃bʀ(ə)] nf bedroom; (TECH) chamber; (POL) chamber, house; (JUR) court; (COMM) chamber; federation; **faire ~ à part** to sleep in separate rooms; **stratège/alpiniste en ~** armchair strategist/mountaineer; **~ à un lit/deux lits** single/twin-bedded room; **~ pour une/deux personne(s)** single/double room; **~**

d'accusation court of criminal appeal; ~ **d'agriculture** *body responsible for the agricultural interests of a département*; ~ **à air** *(de pneu)* (inner) tube; ~ **d'amis** spare *ou* guest room; ~ **de combustion** combustion chamber; ~ **de commerce et d'industrie (CCI)** chamber of commerce and industry; ~ **à coucher** bedroom; **la C~ des députés** the Chamber of Deputies, ≈ the House (of Commons) *(Brit)*, ≈ the House of Representatives *(US)*; ~ **forte** strongroom; ~ **froide** *ou* **frigorifique** cold room; ~ **à gaz** gas chamber; ~ **d'hôte** ≈ bed and breakfast *(in private home)*; ~ **des machines** engine-room; ~ **des métiers (CM)** *chamber of commerce for trades*; ~ **meublée** bedsit(ter) *(Brit)*, furnished room; ~ **noire** *(PHOTO)* dark room.

chambrée [ʃɑ̃bʀe] *nf* room.

chambrer [ʃɑ̃bʀe] *vt (vin)* to bring to room temperature.

chameau, x [ʃamo] *nm* camel.

chamois [ʃamwa] *nm* chamois ♦ *a:* **(couleur)** ~ fawn, buff.

champ [ʃɑ̃] *nm (aussi INFORM)* field; *(PHOTO)*: **dans le** ~ in the picture; **prendre du** ~ to draw back; **laisser le** ~ **libre à qn** to leave sb a clear field; ~ **d'action** sphere of operation(s); ~ **de bataille** battlefield; ~ **de courses** racecourse; ~ **d'honneur** field of honour; ~ **de manœuvre** *(MIL)* parade ground; ~ **de mines** minefield; ~ **de tir** shooting *ou* rifle range; ~ **visuel** field of vision.

Champagne [ʃɑ̃paɲ] *nf:* **la** ~ Champagne, the Champagne region.

champagne [ʃɑ̃paɲ] *nm* champagne.

champenois, e [ʃɑ̃pənwa, -waz] *a* of *ou* from Champagne; *(vin)*: **méthode** ~**e** champagne-type.

champêtre [ʃɑ̃pɛtʀ(ə)] *a* country *cpd*, rural.

champignon [ʃɑ̃piɲɔ̃] *nm* mushroom; *(terme générique)* fungus *(pl* -i); *(fam: accélérateur)* accelerator, gas pedal *(US)*; ~ **de couche** *ou* **de Paris** button mushroom; ~ **vénéneux** toadstool, poisonous mushroom.

champion, ne [ʃɑ̃pjɔ̃, -ɔn] *a, nm/f* champion.

championnat [ʃɑ̃pjɔna] *nm* championship.

chance [ʃɑ̃s] *nf:* **la** ~ luck; **une** ~ a stroke *ou* piece of luck *ou* good fortune; *(occasion)* a lucky break; ~**s** *nfpl (probabilités)* chances; **avoir de la** ~ to be lucky; **il a des** ~**s de gagner** he has a chance of winning; **il y a de fortes** ~**s pour que Paul soit malade** it's highly probable that Paul is ill; **bonne** ~**!** good luck!; **encore une** ~ **que tu viennes!** it's lucky you're coming; **je n'ai pas de** ~ I'm out of luck; *(toujours)* I never have any luck; **donner sa** ~ **à qn** to give sb a chance.

chancelant, e [ʃɑ̃slɑ̃, -ɑ̃t] *a (personne)* tottering; *(santé)* failing.

chanceler [ʃɑ̃sle] *vi* to totter.

chancelier [ʃɑ̃səlje] *nm (allemand)* chancellor; *(d'ambassade)* secretary.

chancellerie [ʃɑ̃sɛlʀi] *nf (en France)* ministry of justice; *(en Allemagne)* chancellery; *(d'ambassade)* chancery.

chanceux, euse [ʃɑ̃sø, -øz] *a* lucky, fortunate.

chancre [ʃɑ̃kʀ(ə)] *nm* canker.

chandail [ʃɑ̃daj] *nm* (thick) jumper *ou* sweater.

Chandeleur [ʃɑ̃dlœʀ] *nf:* **la** ~ Candlemas.

chandelier [ʃɑ̃dəlje] *nm* candlestick; *(à plusieurs branches)* candelabra.

chandelle [ʃɑ̃dɛl] *nf (tallow)* candle; *(TENNIS)*: **faire une** ~ to lob; *(AVIAT)*: **monter en** ~ to climb vertically; **tenir la** ~ to play gooseberry; **dîner aux** ~**s** candlelight dinner.

change [ʃɑ̃ʒ] *nm (COMM)* exchange; **opérations de** ~ (foreign) exchange transactions; **contrôle des** ~**s** exchange control; **gagner/perdre au** ~ to be better/worse off (for it); **donner le** ~ **à qn** *(fig)* to lead sb up the garden path.

changeant, e [ʃɑ̃ʒɑ̃, -ɑ̃t] *a* changeable, fickle.

changement [ʃɑ̃ʒmɑ̃] *nm* change; ~ **de vitesse** *(dispositif)* gears *pl*; *(action)* gear change.

changer [ʃɑ̃ʒe] *vt (modifier)* to change, alter; *(remplacer, COMM, rhabiller)* to change ♦ *vi* to change, alter; **se** ~ to change (o.s.); ~ **de** *(remplacer: adresse, nom, voiture etc)* to change one's; *(échanger, alterner: côté, place, train etc)* to change + *npl*; ~ **d'air** to get a change of air; ~ **de couleur/direction** to change colour/direction; ~ **d'idée** to change one's mind; ~ **de place avec qn** to change places with sb; ~ **de vitesse** *(AUTO)* to change gear; ~ **qn/qch de place** to move sb/sth to another place; ~ **(de train** *etc)* to change (trains *etc)*; ~ **qch en** to change sth into.

changeur [ʃɑ̃ʒœʀ] *nm (personne)* money-changer; ~ **automatique** change machine; ~ **de disques** record changer, autochange.

chanoine [ʃanwan] *nm* canon.

chanson [ʃɑ̃sɔ̃] *nf* song.

chansonnette [ʃɑ̃sɔnɛt] *nf* ditty.

chansonnier [ʃɑ̃sɔnje] *nm* cabaret artist *(specializing in political satire)*; *(recueil)* song book.

chant [ʃɑ̃] *nm* song; *(art vocal)* singing; *(d'église)* hymn; *(de poème)* canto; *(TECH)*: **posé de** *ou* **sur** ~ placed edgeways; ~ **de Noël** Christmas carol.

chantage [ʃɑ̃taʒ] *nm* blackmail; **faire du** ~ to use blackmail; **soumettre qn à un** ~ to blackmail sb.

chantant, e [ʃɑ̃tɑ̃, -ɑ̃t] *a (accent, voix)* sing-song.

chanter [ʃɑ̃te] *vt, vi* to sing; ~ **juste/faux** to sing in tune/out of tune; **si cela lui chante** *(fam)* if he feels like it *ou* fancies it.

chanterelle [ʃɑ̃tʀɛl] *nf* chanterelle *(edible mushroom)*.

chanteur, euse [ʃɑ̃tœʀ, -øz] *nm/f* singer; ~ **de charme** crooner.

chantier [ʃɑ̃tje] *nm* (building) site; *(sur une route)* roadworks *pl*; **mettre en** ~ to start work on; ~ **naval** shipyard.

chantilly [ʃɑ̃tiji] *nf voir* **crème**.

chantonner [ʃɑ̃tɔne] *vi, vt* to sing to oneself, hum.

chantre [ʃɑ̃tʀ(ə)] *nm (fig)* eulogist.

chanvre [ʃɑ̃vʀ(ə)] *nm* hemp.

chaos [kao] *nm* chaos.

chaotique [kaɔtik] *a* chaotic.

chap. *abr* (= *chapitre*) ch.

chapardage [ʃapaʀdaʒ] *nm* pilfering.

chaparder [ʃapaʀde] *vt* to pinch.

chapeau, x [ʃapo] *nm* hat; (*PRESSE*) introductory paragraph; **~!** well done!; **~ melon** bowler hat; **~ mou** trilby; **~x de roues** hub caps.

chapeauter [ʃapote] *vt* (*ADMIN*) to head, oversee.

chapelain [ʃaplɛ̃] *nm* (*REL*) chaplain.

chapelet [ʃaplɛ] *nm* (*REL*) rosary; (*fig*) **un ~ de** a string of; **dire son ~** to tell one's beads.

chapelier, ière [ʃapəlje, -jɛʀ] *nm/f* hatter; milliner.

chapelle [ʃapɛl] *nf* chapel; **~ ardente** chapel of rest.

chapelure [ʃaplyʀ] *nf* (dried) bread-crumbs *pl*.

chaperon [ʃapʀɔ̃] *nm* chaperon.

chaperonner [ʃapʀɔne] *vt* to chaperon.

chapiteau, x [ʃapito] *nm* (*ARCHIT*) capital; (*de cirque*) marquee, big top.

chapitre [ʃapitʀ(ə)] *nm* chapter; (*fig*) subject, matter; **avoir voix au ~** to have a say in the matter.

chapitrer [ʃapitʀe] *vt* to lecture, reprimand.

chapon [ʃapɔ̃] *nm* capon.

chaque [ʃak] *dét* each, every; (*indéfini*) every.

char [ʃaʀ] *nm* (*à foin etc*) cart, waggon; (*de carnaval*) float; **~ (d'assaut)** tank.

charabia [ʃaʀabja] *nm* (*péj*) gibberish, gobbledygook (*Brit*).

charade [ʃaʀad] *nf* riddle; (*mimée*) charade.

charbon [ʃaʀbɔ̃] *nm* coal; **~ de bois** charcoal.

charbonnage [ʃaʀbɔnaʒ] *nm:* **les ~s de France** the (French) Coal Board *sg*.

charbonnier [ʃaʀbɔnje] *nm* coalman.

charcuterie [ʃaʀkytʀi] *nf* (*magasin*) butcher's shop and delicatessen; (*produits*) cooked pork meats *pl*.

charcutier, ière [ʃaʀkytje, -jɛʀ] *nm/f* pork butcher.

chardon [ʃaʀdɔ̃] *nm* thistle.

chardonneret [ʃaʀdɔnʀɛ] *nm* goldfinch.

charentais, e [ʃaʀɑ̃tɛ, -ɛz] *a* of *ou* from Charente ♦ *nf* (*pantoufle*) slipper.

charge [ʃaʀʒ(ə)] *nf* (*fardeau*) load; (*explosif, ÉLEC, MIL, JUR*) charge; (*rôle, mission*) responsibility; **~s** *nfpl* (*du loyer*) service charges; **à la ~ de** (*dépendant de*) dependent upon, supported by; (*aux frais de*) chargeable to, payable by; **j'accepte, à ~ de revanche** I accept, provided I can do the same for you (in return) one day; **prendre en ~** to take charge of; (*suj: véhicule*) to take on; (*dépenses*) to take care of; **~ utile** (*AUTO*) live load; (*COMM*) payload; **~s sociales** social security contributions.

chargé [ʃaʀʒe] *a* (*voiture, animal, personne*) laden; (*fusil, batterie, caméra*) loaded; (*occupé: emploi du temps, journée*) busy, full; (*estomac*) heavy, full; (*langue*) furred; (*décoration, style*) heavy, ornate ♦ *nm:* **~ d'affaires** chargé d'affaires; **~ de cours** ≈ lecturer; **~ de** (*responsable de*) responsible for.

chargement [ʃaʀʒəmɑ̃] *nm* (*action*) loading; charging; (*objets*) load.

charger [ʃaʀʒe] *vt* (*voiture, fusil, caméra, INFORM*) to load; (*batterie*) to charge ♦ *vi* (*MIL etc*) to charge; **se ~ de** vt to see to, take care of; **~ qn de qch/faire qch** to give sb the responsibility for sth/of doing sth; to put sb in charge of sth/doing sth; **se ~ de faire qch** to take it upon o.s. to do sth.

chargeur [ʃaʀʒœʀ] *nm* (*dispositif: d'arme à feu*) magazine; (*: PHOTO*) cartridge; **~ de batterie** (*ÉLEC*) battery charger.

chariot [ʃaʀjo] *nm* trolley; (*charrette*) waggon; (*de machine à écrire*) carriage; **~ élévateur** fork-lift truck.

charisme [kaʀism(ə)] *nm* charisma.

charitable [ʃaʀitabl(ə)] *a* charitable; kind.

charité [ʃaʀite] *nf* charity; **faire la ~** to give to charity; to do charitable works; **faire la ~ à qn** to give (something) to; **fête/vente de ~** fête/sale in aid of charity.

charivari [ʃaʀivaʀi] *nm* hullabaloo.

charlatan [ʃaʀlatɑ̃] *nm* charlatan.

charmant, e [ʃaʀmɑ̃, -ɑ̃t] *a* charming.

charme [ʃaʀm(ə)] *nm* charm; **~s** *nmpl* (*appas*) charms; **c'est ce qui en fait le ~** that is its attraction; **faire du ~** to be charming, turn on the charm; **aller** *ou* **se porter comme un ~** to be in the pink.

charmer [ʃaʀme] *vt* to charm; **je suis charmé de** I'm delighted to.

charmeur, euse [ʃaʀmœʀ, -øz] *nm/f* charmer; **~ de serpents** snake charmer.

charnel, le [ʃaʀnɛl] *a* carnal.

charnier [ʃaʀnje] *nm* mass grave.

charnière [ʃaʀnjɛʀ] *nf* hinge; (*fig*) turning-point.

charnu, e [ʃaʀny] *a* fleshy.

charogne [ʃaʀɔɲ] *nf* carrion *q*; (*fam!*) bastard (!).

charolais, e [ʃaʀɔlɛ, -ɛz] *a* of *ou* from the Charolais.

charpente [ʃaʀpɑ̃t] *nf* frame(work); (*fig*) structure, framework; (*carrure*) build, frame.

charpenté, e [ʃaʀpɑ̃te] *a:* **bien** *ou* **solidement ~** (*personne*) well-built; (*texte*) well-constructed.

charpenterie [ʃaʀpɑ̃tʀi] *nf* carpentry.

charpentier [ʃaʀpɑ̃tje] *nm* carpenter.

charpie [ʃaʀpi] *nf:* **en ~** (*fig*) in shreds *ou* ribbons.

charretier [ʃaʀtje] *nm* carter; **de ~** (*péj: langage, manières*) uncouth.

charrette [ʃaʀɛt] *nf* cart.

charrier [ʃaʀje] *vt* to carry (along); to cart, carry ♦ *vi* (*fam*) to exaggerate.

charrue [ʃaʀy] *nf* plough (*Brit*), plow (*US*).

charte [ʃaʀt(ə)] *nf* charter.

charter [tʃaʀtœʀ] *nm* (*vol*) charter flight; (*avion*) charter plane.

chasse [ʃas] *nf* hunting; (*au fusil*) shooting; (*poursuite*) chase; (*aussi: ~ d'eau*) flush; **la ~ est ouverte** the hunting season is open; **la ~ est fermée** it is the close (*Brit*) *ou* closed (*US*) season; **aller à la ~** to go hunting; **prendre en ~, donner la ~ à** to give chase to; **tirer la ~ (d'eau)** to flush the toilet, pull the chain; **~ aérienne** aerial pursuit; **~ à courre** hunting; **~ à l'homme** manhunt; **~ gardée** private hunting grounds *pl*; **~ sous-**

marine underwater fishing.

châsse [ʃɑs] *nf* reliquary, shrine.

chassé-croisé, *pl* **chassés-croisés** [ʃasekʀwaze] *nm* (*DANSE*) chassé-croisé; (*fig*) mix-up (*where people miss each other in turn*).

chasse-neige [ʃasnɛʒ] *nm inv* snowplough (*Brit*), snowplow (*US*).

chasser [ʃase] *vt* to hunt; (*expulser*) to chase away *ou* out, drive away *ou* out; (*dissiper*) to chase *ou* sweep away; to dispel, drive away.

chasseur, euse [ʃasœʀ, -øz] *nm/f* hunter ♦ *nm* (*avion*) fighter; (*domestique*) page (boy), messenger (boy); ~ **d'images** roving photographer; ~ **de têtes** (*fig*) headhunter; ~**s alpins** mountain infantry.

chassieux, euse [ʃasjø, -øz] *a* sticky, gummy.

châssis [ʃɑsi] *nm* (*AUTO*) chassis; (*cadre*) frame; (*de jardin*) cold frame.

chaste [ʃast(ə)] *a* chaste.

chasteté [ʃastəte] *nf* chastity.

chasuble [ʃazybl(ə)] *nf* chasuble; **robe** ~ pinafore dress (*Brit*), jumper (*US*).

chat [ʃa] *nm* cat; ~ **sauvage** wildcat.

châtaigne [ʃatɛɲ] *nf* chestnut.

châtaignier [ʃatɛɲe] *nm* chestnut (tree).

châtain [ʃatɛ̃] *a inv* chestnut (brown); (*personne*) chestnut-haired.

château, x [ʃɑto] *nm* castle; ~ **d'eau** water tower; ~ **fort** stronghold, fortified castle; ~ **de sable** sandcastle.

châtelain, e [ʃɑtlɛ̃, -ɛn] *nm/f* lord/lady of the manor ♦ *nf* (*ceinture*) chatelaine.

châtier [ʃatje] *vt* to punish, castigate; (*fig: style*) to polish, refine.

chatière [ʃatjɛʀ] *nf* (*porte*) cat flap.

châtiment [ʃatimɑ̃] *nm* punishment, castigation; ~ **corporel** corporal punishment.

chatoiement [ʃatwamɑ̃] *nm* shimmer(ing).

chaton [ʃatɔ̃] *nm* (*ZOOL*) kitten; (*BOT*) catkin; (*de bague*) bezel; stone.

chatouiller [ʃatuje] *vt* to tickle; (*l'odorat, le palais*) to titillate.

chatouilleux, euse [ʃatujø, -øz] *a* ticklish; (*fig*) touchy, over-sensitive.

chatoyant, e [ʃatwajɑ̃, -ɑ̃t] *a* (*reflet, étoffe*) shimmering; (*couleurs*) sparkling.

chatoyer [ʃatwaje] *vi* to shimmer.

châtrer [ʃɑtʀe] *vt* (*mâle*) to castrate; (*femelle*) to spay; (*cheval*) to geld; (*chat, chien*) to doctor (*Brit*), fix (*US*); (*fig*) to mutilate.

chatte [ʃat] *nf* (she-)cat.

chatterton [ʃatɛʀtɔn] *nm* (*ruban isolant: ÉLEC*) (adhesive) insulating tape.

chaud, e [ʃo, -od] *a* (*gén*) warm; (*très chaud*) hot; (*fig: félicitations*) hearty; (*discussion*) heated; **il fait** ~ it's warm; it's hot; **manger** ~ to have something hot to eat; **avoir** ~ to be warm; to be hot; **tenir** ~ to keep hot; **ça me tient** ~ it keeps me warm; **tenir au** ~ to keep in a warm place; **rester au** ~ to stay in the warm.

chaudement [ʃodmɑ̃] *ad* warmly; (*fig*) hotly.

chaudière [ʃodjɛʀ] *nf* boiler.

chaudron [ʃodʀɔ̃] *nm* cauldron.

chaudronnerie [ʃodʀɔnʀi] *nf* (*usine*) boiler-works; (*activité*) boilermaking; (*boutique*) coppersmith's workshop.

chauffage [ʃofaʒ] *nm* heating; ~ **au gaz/à l'électricité/au charbon** gas/electric/solid fuel heating; ~ **central** central heating; ~ **par le sol** underfloor heating.

chauffagiste [ʃofaʒist(ə)] *nm* (*installateur*) heating engineer.

chauffant, e [ʃofɑ̃, -ɑ̃t]: **couverture** ~**e** electric blanket; **plaque** ~**e** hotplate.

chauffard [ʃofaʀ] *nm* (*péj*) reckless driver; roadhog; (*après un accident*) hit-and-run driver.

chauffe-bain [ʃofbɛ̃] *nm* = **chauffe-eau**.

chauffe-biberon [ʃofbibʀɔ̃] *nm* (baby's) bottle warmer.

chauffe-eau [ʃofo] *nm inv* water heater.

chauffe-plats [ʃofpla] *nm inv* dish warmer.

chauffer [ʃofe] *vt* to heat ♦ *vi* to heat up; warm up; (*trop chauffer: moteur*) to overheat; **se** ~ (*se mettre en train*) to warm up; (*au soleil*) to warm o.s.

chaufferie [ʃofʀi] *nf* boiler room.

chauffeur [ʃofœʀ] *nm* driver; (*privé*) chauffeur; **voiture avec/sans** ~ chauffeur-driven/self-drive car.

chauffeuse [ʃoføz] *nf* fireside chair.

chauler [ʃole] *vt* (*mur*) to whitewash.

chaume [ʃom] *nm* (*du toit*) thatch; (*tiges*) stubble.

chaumière [ʃomjɛʀ] *nf* (thatched) cottage.

chaussée [ʃose] *nf* road(way); (*digue*) causeway.

chausse-pied [ʃospje] *nm* shoe-horn.

chausser [ʃose] *vt* (*bottes, skis*) to put on; (*enfant*) to put shoes on; (*suj: soulier*) to fit; ~ **du 38/42** to take size 38/42; ~ **grand/bien** to be big-/well-fitting; **se** ~ to put one's shoes on.

chausse-trappe [ʃostʀap] *nf* trap.

chaussette [ʃosɛt] *nf* sock.

chausseur [ʃosœʀ] *nm* (*marchand*) footwear specialist, shoemaker.

chausson [ʃosɔ̃] *nm* slipper; (*de bébé*) bootee; ~ **(aux pommes)** (apple) turnover.

chaussure [ʃosyʀ] *nf* shoe; (*commerce*): **la** ~ the shoe industry *ou* trade; ~**s basses** flat shoes; ~**s montantes** ankle boots; ~**s de ski** ski boots.

chaut [ʃo] *vb*: **peu me** ~ it matters little to me.

chauve [ʃov] *a* bald.

chauve-souris, *pl* **chauves-souris** [ʃovsuʀi] *nf* bat.

chauvin, e [ʃovɛ̃, -in] *a* chauvinistic; jingoistic.

chauvinisme [ʃovinism(ə)] *nm* chauvinism; jingoism.

chaux [ʃo] *nf* lime; **blanchi à la** ~ white-washed.

chavirer [ʃaviʀe] *vi* to capsize, overturn.

chef [ʃɛf] *nm* head, leader; (*patron*) boss; (*de cuisine*) chef; **au premier** ~ extremely, to the nth degree; **de son propre** ~ on his *ou* her own initiative; **général/commandant en** ~ general-/commander-in-chief; ~ **d'accusation** (*JUR*) charge, count (of indictment); ~ **d'atelier** (shop) foreman; ~ **de bureau** head clerk; ~ **de clinique** senior hospital lecturer; ~ **d'entreprise** company head; ~ **d'équipe** team leader; ~ **d'état**

head of state; ~ **de famille** head of the family; ~ **de file** *(de parti etc)* leader; ~ **de gare** station master; ~ **d'orchestre** conductor *(Brit)*, leader *(US)*; ~ **de rayon** department(al) supervisor; ~ **de service** departmental head.

chef-d'œuvre, *pl* **chefs-d'œuvre** [ʃɛdœvʀ(ə)] *nm* masterpiece.

chef-lieu, *pl* **chefs-lieux** [ʃɛfljø] *nm* county town.

cheftaine [ʃɛftɛn] *nf* (guide) captain.

cheik [ʃɛk] *nm* sheik.

chemin [ʃəmɛ̃] *nm* path; *(itinéraire, direction, trajet)* way; **en** ~, ~ **faisant** on the way; ~ **de fer** railway *(Brit)*, railroad *(US)*; **par** ~ **de fer** by rail; **les** ~**s de fer** the railways *(Brit)*, the railroad *(US)*; ~ **de terre** dirt track.

cheminée [ʃəmine] *nf* chimney; *(à l'intérieur)* chimney piece, fireplace; *(de bateau)* funnel.

cheminement [ʃəminmɑ̃] *nm* progress; course.

cheminer [ʃəmine] *vi* to walk (along).

cheminot [ʃəmino] *nm* railwayman *(Brit)*, railroad worker *(US)*.

chemise [ʃəmiz] *nf* shirt; *(dossier)* folder; ~ **de nuit** nightdress.

chemiserie [ʃəmizʀi] *nf* (gentlemen's) outfitters'.

chemisette [ʃəmizɛt] *nf* short-sleeved shirt.

chemisier [ʃəmizje] *nm* blouse.

chenal, aux [ʃənal, -o] *nm* channel.

chenapan [ʃənapɑ̃] *nm (garnement)* rascal; *(péj: vaurien)* rogue.

chêne [ʃɛn] *nm* oak (tree); *(bois)* oak.

chenet [ʃənɛ] *nm* fire-dog, andiron.

chenil [ʃənil] *nm* kennels *pl*.

chenille [ʃənij] *nf* *(ZOOL)* caterpillar; *(AUTO)* caterpillar track; **véhicule à** ~**s** tracked vehicle, caterpillar.

chenillette [ʃənijɛt] *nf* tracked vehicle.

cheptel [ʃɛptɛl] *nm* livestock.

chèque [ʃɛk] *nm* cheque *(Brit)*, check *(US)*; **faire/toucher un** ~ to write/cash a cheque; **par** ~ by cheque; ~ **barré/sans provision** crossed *(Brit)*/bad cheque; ~ **en blanc** blank cheque; ~ **au porteur** cheque to bearer; ~ **postal** post office cheque, ≈ giro cheque *(Brit)*; ~ **de voyage** traveller's cheque.

chèque-cadeau, *pl* **chèques-cadeaux** [ʃɛkkado] *nm* gift token.

chèque-repas, *pl* **chèques-repas** [ʃɛkʀəpa], **chèque-restaurant**, *pl* **chèques-restaurant** [ʃɛkʀɛstɔʀɑ̃] *nm* ≈ luncheon voucher.

chéquier [ʃekje] *nm* cheque book *(Brit)*, check book *(US)*.

cher, ère [ʃɛʀ] *a (aimé)* dear; *(coûteux)* expensive, dear ♦ *ad:* **coûter/payer** ~ to cost/pay a lot; **cela coûte** ~ it's expensive, it costs a lot of money ♦ *nf:* **la bonne chère** good food; **mon** ~, **ma chère** my dear.

chercher [ʃɛʀʃe] *vt* to look for; *(gloire etc)* to seek; *(INFORM)* to search; ~ **des ennuis/la bagarre** to be looking for trouble/a fight; **aller** ~ to go for, go and fetch; ~ **à faire** to try to do.

chercheur, euse [ʃɛʀʃœʀ, -øz] *nm/f* researcher, research worker; ~ **de** seeker of; hunter of; ~ **d'or** gold digger.

chère [ʃɛʀ] *af*, *nf voir* **cher**.

chèrement [ʃɛʀmɑ̃] *ad* dearly.

chéri, e [ʃeʀi] *a* beloved, dear; **(mon)** ~ darling.

chérir [ʃeʀiʀ] *vt* to cherish.

cherté [ʃɛʀte] *nf:* **la** ~ **de la vie** the high cost of living.

chérubin [ʃeʀybɛ̃] *nm* cherub.

chétif, ive [ʃetif, -iv] *a* puny, stunted.

cheval, aux [ʃəval, -o] *nm* horse; *(AUTO):* ~ **(vapeur) (CV)** horsepower *q*; **50 chevaux (au frein)** 50 brake horsepower, 50 b.h.p.; **10 chevaux (fiscaux)** 10 horsepower *(for tax purposes)*; **faire du** ~ to ride; **à** ~ on horseback; **à** ~ **sur** astride, straddling; *(fig)* overlapping; ~ **d'arçons** vaulting horse; ~ **à bascule** rocking horse; ~ **de bataille** charger; *(fig)* hobby-horse; ~ **de course** race horse; **chevaux de bois** *(des manèges)* wooden (fairground) horses; *(manège)* merry-go-round.

chevaleresque [ʃəvalʀɛsk(ə)] *a* chivalrous.

chevalerie [ʃəvalʀi] *nf* chivalry; knighthood.

chevalet [ʃəvalɛ] *nm* easel.

chevalier [ʃəvalje] *nm* knight; ~ **servant** escort.

chevalière [ʃəvaljɛʀ] *nf* signet ring.

chevalin, e [ʃəvalɛ̃, -in] *a* of horses, equine; *(péj)* horsy; **boucherie** ~**e** horse-meat butcher's.

cheval-vapeur, *pl* **chevaux-vapeur** [ʃəvalvapœʀ, ʃəvo-] *nm voir* **cheval**.

chevauchée [ʃəvoʃe] *nf* ride; cavalcade.

chevauchement [ʃəvoʃmɑ̃] *nm* overlap.

chevaucher [ʃəvoʃe] *vi (aussi:* **se** ~) to overlap (each other) ♦ *vt* to be astride, straddle.

chevaux [ʃəvo] *nmpl voir* **cheval**.

chevelu, e [ʃəvly] *a* with a good head of hair, hairy *(péj)*.

chevelure [ʃəvlyʀ] *nf* hair *q*.

chevet [ʃəvɛ] *nm:* **au** ~ **de qn** at sb's bedside; **lampe de** ~ bedside lamp.

cheveu, x [ʃəvø] *nm* hair ♦ *nmpl (chevelure)* hair *sg*; **avoir les** ~**x courts/en brosse** to have short hair/a crew cut; **se faire couper les** ~**x** to get *ou* have one's hair cut; **tiré par les** ~**x** *(histoire)* far-fetched.

cheville [ʃəvij] *nf (ANAT)* ankle; *(de bois)* peg; *(pour enfoncer une vis)* plug; **être en** ~ **avec qn** to be in cahoots with sb; ~ **ouvrière** *(fig)* kingpin.

chèvre [ʃɛvʀ(ə)] *nf* (she-)goat; **ménager la** ~ **et le chou** to try to please everyone.

chevreau, x [ʃəvʀo] *nm* kid.

chèvrefeuille [ʃɛvʀəfœj] *nm* honeysuckle.

chevreuil [ʃəvʀœj] *nm* roe deer *inv*; *(CULIN)* venison.

chevron [ʃəvʀɔ̃] *nm (poutre)* rafter; *(motif)* chevron, v(-shape); **à** ~**s** chevron-patterned; *(petits)* herringbone.

chevronné, e [ʃəvʀɔne] *a* seasoned, experienced.

chevrotant, e [ʃəvʀɔtɑ̃, -ɑ̃t] *a* quavering.

chevroter [ʃəvʀɔte] *vi (personne, voix)* to quaver.

chevrotine [ʃəvʀɔtin] *nf* buckshot *q*.

chewing-gum [ʃwiŋɡɔm] *nm* chewing gum.

chez [ʃe] *prép (à la demeure de):* ~ **qn** at *(ou* to) sb's house *ou* place; *(parmi)* among; ~

moi at home; *(avec direction)* home; ~ **le boulanger** *(à la boulangerie)* at the baker's; ~ **les Français** *(dans leur caractère)* among the French; ~ **ce musicien/poète** *(dans ses œuvres)* in this musician/poet.

chez-soi [ʃeswa] *nm inv* home.

Chf. cent. *abr* (= *chauffage central*) c.h.

chic [ʃik] *a inv* chic, smart; *(généreux)* nice, decent ♦ *nm* stylishness; **avoir le ~ de** *ou* **pour** to have the knack of *ou* for; **de ~** *ad* off the cuff; **~!** great!, terrific!

chicane [ʃikan] *nf (obstacle)* zigzag; *(querelle)* squabble.

chicaner [ʃikane] *vi (ergoter)*: ~ **sur** to quibble about.

chiche [ʃiʃ] *a (mesquin)* niggardly, mean; *(pauvre)* meagre *(Brit)*, meager *(US)* ♦ *excl (en réponse à un défi)* you're on!; **tu n'es pas ~ de lui parler!** you wouldn't (dare) speak to her!

chichement [ʃiʃmɑ̃] *ad (pauvrement)* meagrely *(Brit)*, meagerly *(US)*; *(mesquinement)* meanly.

chichi [ʃiʃi] *nm (fam)* fuss; **faire des ~s** to make a fuss.

chicorée [ʃikɔʀe] *nf (café)* chicory; *(salade)* endive; ~ **frisée** curly endive.

chicot [ʃiko] *nm* stump.

chien [ʃjɛ̃] *nm* dog; *(de pistolet)* hammer; **temps de ~** rotten weather; **vie de ~** dog's life; **couché en ~ de fusil** curled up; ~ **d'aveugle** guide dog; ~ **de chasse** gun dog; ~ **de garde** guard dog; ~ **policier** police dog; ~ **de race** pedigree dog; ~ **de traîneau** husky.

chiendent [ʃjɛ̃dɑ̃] *nm* couch grass.

chien-loup, *pl* **chiens-loups** [ʃjɛ̃lu] *nm* wolfhound.

chienne [ʃjɛn] *nf* (she-)dog, bitch.

chier [ʃje] *vi (fam!)* to crap *(!)*, shit *(!)*; **faire ~ qn** *(importuner)* to bug sb; *(causer des ennuis à)* to piss sb around *(!)*; **se faire ~** *(s'ennuyer)* to be bored rigid.

chiffe [ʃif] *nf*: **il est mou comme une ~, c'est une ~ molle** he's spineless *ou* wet.

chiffon [ʃifɔ̃] *nm* (piece of) rag.

chiffonné, e [ʃifɔne] *a (fatigué: visage)* worn-looking.

chiffonner [ʃifɔne] *vt* to crumple, crease; *(tracasser)* to concern.

chiffonnier [ʃifɔnje] *nm* ragman, rag-and-bone man; *(meuble)* chiffonier.

chiffrable [ʃifʀabl(ə)] *a* numerable.

chiffre [ʃifʀ(ə)] *nm (représentant un nombre)* figure; numeral; *(montant, total)* total, sum; *(d'un code)* code, cipher; **~s romains/arabes** roman/arabic figures *ou* numerals; **en ~s ronds** in round figures; **écrire un nombre en ~s** to write a number in figures; ~ **d'affaires** (CA) turnover; ~ **de ventes** sales figures.

chiffrer [ʃifʀe] *vt (dépense)* to put a figure to, assess; *(message)* to (en)code, cipher ♦ *vi*: ~ **à, se ~ à** to add up to.

chignole [ʃiɲɔl] *nf* drill.

chignon [ʃiɲɔ̃] *nm* chignon, bun.

Chili [ʃili] *nm*: **le ~** Chile.

chilien, ne [ʃiljɛ̃, -ɛn] *a* Chilean ♦ *nm/f*: **C~, ne** Chilean.

chimère [ʃimɛʀ] *nf* (wild) dream; pipe dream,

idle fancy.

chimérique [ʃimeʀik] *a (utopique)* fanciful.

chimie [ʃimi] *nf* chemistry.

chimio [ʃimjo], **chimiothérapie** [ʃimjoteʀapi] *nf* chemotherapy.

chimique [ʃimik] *a* chemical; **produits ~s** chemicals.

chimiste [ʃimist(ə)] *nm/f* chemist.

chinchilla [ʃɛ̃ʃila] *nm* chinchilla.

Chine [ʃin] *nf*: **la ~** China; **la ~ libre, la république de ~** the Republic of China, Nationalist China *(Taiwan)*.

chine [ʃin] *nm* rice paper; *(porcelaine)* china *(vase)*.

chiné, e [ʃine] *a* flecked.

chinois, e [ʃinwa, -waz] *a* Chinese; *(fig: péj)* pernickety, fussy ♦ *nm (LING)* Chinese ♦ *nm/f*: **C~, e** Chinese.

chinoiserie(s) [ʃinwazʀi] *nf(pl) (péj)* red tape, fuss.

chiot [ʃjo] *nm* pup(py).

chiper [ʃipe] *vt (fam)* to pinch.

chipie [ʃipi] *nf* shrew.

chipolata [ʃipolata] *nf* chipolata.

chipoter [ʃipote] *vi (manger)* to nibble; *(ergoter)* to quibble, haggle.

chips [ʃips] *nfpl (aussi*: **pommes ~**) crisps *(Brit)*, (potato) chips *(US)*.

chique [ʃik] *nf* quid, chew.

chiquenaude [ʃiknod] *nf* flick, flip.

chiquer [ʃike] *vi* to chew tobacco.

chiromancie [kiʀɔmɑ̃si] *nf* palmistry.

chiromancien, ne [kiʀɔmɑ̃sjɛ̃, -ɛn] *nm/f* palmist.

chiropracteur [kiʀɔpʀaktœʀ] *nm*, **chiropracticien, ne** [kiʀɔpʀaktisjɛ̃, -ɛn] *nm/f* chiropractor.

chirurgical, e, aux [ʃiʀyʀʒikal, -o] *a* surgical.

chirurgie [ʃiʀyʀʒi] *nf* surgery; ~ **esthétique** cosmetic *ou* plastic surgery.

chirurgien [ʃiʀyʀʒjɛ̃] *nm* surgeon; ~ **dentiste** dental surgeon.

chiure [ʃjyʀ] *nf*: **~s de mouche** fly specks.

ch.-l. *abr* = **chef-lieu**.

chlore [klɔʀ] *nm* chlorine.

chloroforme [klɔʀɔfɔʀm(ə)] *nm* chloroform.

chlorophylle [klɔʀɔfil] *nf* chlorophyll.

chlorure [klɔʀyʀ] *nm* chloride.

choc [ʃɔk] *nm* impact; shock; crash; *(moral)* shock; *(affrontement)* clash ♦ *a*: **prix ~** amazing *ou* incredible price/prices; **de ~** *(troupe, traitement)* shock *cpd*; *(patron etc)* high-powered; ~ **opératoire/nerveux** postoperative/nervous shock; ~ **en retour** return shock; *(fig)* backlash.

chocolat [ʃɔkɔla] *nm* chocolate; *(boisson)* (hot) chocolate; ~ **à cuire** cooking chocolate; ~ **au lait** milk chocolate; ~ **en poudre** drinking chocolate.

chocolaté, e [ʃɔkɔlate] *a* chocolate *cpd*, chocolate-flavoured.

chocolaterie [ʃɔkɔlatʀi] *nf (fabrique)* chocolate factory.

chocolatier, ière [ʃɔkɔlatje, -jɛʀ] *nm/f* chocolate maker.

chœur [kœʀ] *nm (chorale)* choir; *(OPÉRA, THÉÂTRE)* chorus; *(ARCHIT)* choir, chancel; **en ~** in chorus.

choir [ʃwaʀ] *vi* to fall.

choisi, e [ʃwazi] a (de premier choix) carefully chosen; select; **textes** ~**s** selected writings.

choisir [ʃwaziʀ] vt to choose; (entre plusiers) to choose, select; ~ **de faire qch** to choose ou opt to do sth.

choix [ʃwa] nm choice; selection; **avoir le** ~ to have the choice; **je n'avais pas le** ~ I had no choice; **de premier** ~ (COMM) class ou grade one; **de** ~ choice cpd, selected; **au** ~ as you wish ou prefer; **de mon/son** ~ of my/his ou her choosing.

choléra [kɔleʀa] nm cholera.

cholestérol [kɔlɛsteʀɔl] nm cholesterol.

chômage [ʃomaʒ] nm unemployment; **mettre au** ~ to make redundant, put out of work; **être au** ~ to be unemployed ou out of work; ~ **partiel** short-time working; ~ **structurel** structural unemployment; ~ **technique** lay-offs pl.

chômer [ʃome] vi to be unemployed, be idle; **jour chômé** public holiday.

chômeur, euse [ʃomœʀ, -øz] nm/f unemployed person, person out of work.

chope [ʃɔp] nf tankard.

choquant, e [ʃɔkɑ̃, -ɑ̃t] a shocking.

choquer [ʃɔke] vt (offenser) to shock; (commotionner) to shake (up).

choral, e [kɔʀal] a choral ♦ nf choral society, choir.

chorégraphe [kɔʀegʀaf] nm/f choreographer.

chorégraphie [kɔʀegʀafi] nf choreography.

choriste [kɔʀist(ə)] nm/f choir member; (OPÉRA) chorus member.

chorus [kɔʀys] nm: **faire** ~ **(avec)** to voice one's agreement (with).

chose [ʃoz] nf thing ♦ nm (fam: machin) thingamajig ♦ a inv: **être/se sentir tout** ~ (bizarre) to be/feel a bit odd; (malade) to be/feel out of sorts; **dire bien des** ~**s à qn** to give sb's regards to sb; **parler de** ~**(s) et d'autre(s)** to talk about one thing and another; **c'est peu de** ~ it's nothing much.

chou, x [ʃu] nm cabbage ♦ a inv cute; **mon petit** ~ (my) sweetheart; **faire** ~ **blanc** to draw a blank; **feuille de** ~ (fig: journal) rag; ~ **à la crème** cream bun (made of choux pastry); ~ **de Bruxelles** Brussels sprout.

choucas [ʃuka] nm jackdaw.

chouchou, te [ʃuʃu, -ut] nm/f (SCOL) teacher's pet.

chouchouter [ʃuʃute] vt to pet.

choucroute [ʃukʀut] nf sauerkraut; ~ **garnie** sauerkraut with cooked meats and potatoes.

chouette [ʃwɛt] nf owl ♦ a (fam) great, smashing.

chou-fleur, pl choux-fleurs [ʃuflœʀ] nm cauliflower.

chou-rave, pl choux-raves [ʃuʀav] nm kohlrabi.

choyer [ʃwaje] vt to cherish; to pamper.

CHR sigle m = Centre hospitalier régional.

chrétien, ne [kʀetjɛ̃, -ɛn] a, nm/f Christian.

chrétiennement [kʀetjɛnmɑ̃] ad in a Christian way ou spirit.

chrétienté [kʀetjɛ̃te] nf Christendom.

Christ [kʀist] nm: **le** ~ Christ; **c~** (crucifix etc) figure of Christ; **Jésus** ~ Jesus Christ.

christianiser [kʀistjanize] vt to convert to Christianity.

christianisme [kʀistjanism(ə)] nm Christianity.

Christmas [kʀistmas] nf: **(l'île)** ~ Christmas Island.

chromatique [kʀɔmatik] a chromatic.

chrome [kʀom] nm chromium; (revêtement) chrome, chromium.

chromé, e [kʀome] a chrome-plated, chromium-plated.

chromosome [kʀɔmozom] nm chromosome.

chronique [kʀɔnik] a chronic ♦ nf (de journal) column, page; (historique) chronicle; (RADIO, TV): **la** ~ **sportive/théâtrale** the sports/theatre review; **la** ~ **locale** local news and gossip.

chroniqueur [kʀɔnikœʀ] nm columnist; chronicler.

chronologie [kʀɔnɔlɔʒi] nf chronology.

chronologique [kʀɔnɔlɔʒik] a chronological.

chronomètre [kʀɔnɔmɛtʀ(ə)] nm stopwatch.

chronométrer [kʀɔnɔmetʀe] vt to time.

chronométreur [kʀɔnɔmetʀœʀ] nm timekeeper.

chrysalide [kʀizalid] nf chrysalis.

chrysanthème [kʀizɑ̃tɛm] nm chrysanthemum.

CHU sigle m (= Centre hospitalo-universitaire) ≈ (teaching) hospital.

chu, e [ʃy] pp de **choir**.

chuchotement [ʃyʃɔtmɑ̃] nm whisper.

chuchoter [ʃyʃɔte] vt, vi to whisper.

chuintement [ʃɥɛ̃tmɑ̃] nm hiss.

chuinter [ʃɥɛ̃te] vi to hiss.

chut excl [ʃyt] sh! ♦ vb [ʃy] voir **choir**.

chute [ʃyt] nf fall; (de bois, papier: déchet) scrap; **la** ~ **des cheveux** hair loss; **faire une** ~ **(de 10 m)** to fall (10 m); ~**s de pluie/neige** rain/snowfalls; ~ **(d'eau)** waterfall; ~ **du jour** nightfall; ~ **libre** free fall; ~ **des reins** small of the back.

Chypre [ʃipʀ] nm: **le** ~ Cyprus.

chypriote [ʃipʀiɔt] a, nm/f = **cypriote**.

-ci, ci- [si] ad voir **par**, **ci-contre**, **ci-joint** etc ♦ dét: **ce garçon-ci/-là** this/that boy; **ces femmes-ci/-là** these/those women.

CIA sigle f CIA.

cial abr = **commercial**.

ciao [tʃao] excl (fam) (bye-)bye.

ci-après [siapʀɛ] ad hereafter.

cibiste [sibist(ə)] nm CB enthusiast.

cible [sibl(ə)] nf target.

cibler [sible] vt to target.

ciboire [sibwaʀ] nm ciborium (vessel).

ciboule [sibul] nf (large) chive.

ciboulette [sibulɛt] nf (small) chive.

cicatrice [sikatʀis] nf scar.

cicatriser [sikatʀize] vt to heal; **se** ~ to heal (up), form a scar.

ci-contre [sikɔ̃tʀ(ə)] ad opposite.

ci-dessous [sidəsu] ad below.

ci-dessus [sidəsy] ad above.

ci-devant [sidəvɑ̃] nm/f inv aristocrat who lost his/her title in the French Revolution.

CIDEX sigle m (= Courrier individuel à distribution exceptionnelle) system which groups letter boxes in country areas, rather than each house having its letter box at its front door.

CIDJ sigle m (= Centre d'information et de documentation de la jeunesse) careers advisory service.

cidre [sidʀ(ə)] nm cider.

CIDUNATI [sidynati] sigle m (= Comité interprofessionnel de défense de l'union nationale des artisans et travailleurs indépendants) union of self-employed craftsmen.

Cie abr (= compagnie) Co.

ciel [sjɛl] nm sky; (REL) heaven; ~s nmpl (PEINTURE etc) skies; **cieux** nmpl sky sg, skies; (REL) heaven sg; **à ~ ouvert** open-air; (mine) opencast; **tomber du ~** (arriver à l'improviste) to appear out of the blue; (être stupéfait) to be unable to believe one's eyes; **C~!** good heavens!; **~ de lit** canopy.

cierge [sjɛʀʒ(ə)] nm candle; **~ pascal** Easter candle.

cieux [sjø] nmpl voir **ciel**.

cigale [sigal] nf cicada.

cigare [sigaʀ] nm cigar.

cigarette [sigaʀɛt] nf cigarette; **~ (à) bout filtre** filter cigarette.

ci-gît [siʒi] ad here lies.

cigogne [sigɔɲ] nf stork.

ciguë [sigy] nf hemlock.

ci-inclus, e [siɛkly, -yz] a, ad enclosed.

ci-joint, e [siʒwɛ̃, -ɛt] a, ad enclosed; **veuillez trouver ~** please find enclosed.

cil [sil] nm (eye)lash.

ciller [sije] vi to blink.

cimaise [simɛz] nf picture rail.

cime [sim] nf top; (montagne) peak.

ciment [simɑ̃] nm cement; **~ armé** reinforced concrete.

cimenter [simɑ̃te] vt to cement.

cimenterie [simɑ̃tʀi] nf cement works sg.

cimetière [simtjɛʀ] nm cemetery; (d'église) churchyard; **~ de voitures** scrapyard.

cinéaste [sineast(ə)] nm/f film-maker.

ciné-club [sineklœb] nm film club; film society.

cinéma [sinema] nm cinema; **aller au ~** to go to the cinema ou pictures ou movie; **~ d'animation** cartoon (film).

cinémascope [sinemaskɔp] nm ® Cinemascope (film).

cinémathèque [sinematɛk] nf film archives pl ou library.

cinématographie [sinematɔgʀafi] nf cinematography.

cinématographique [sinematɔgʀafik] a film cpd, cinema cpd.

cinéphile [sinefil] nm/f film buff.

cinérama [sineʀama] nm ®: **en ~** in Cinerama ®.

cinétique [sinetik] a kinetic.

cing(h)alais, e [sɛ̃galɛ, -ɛz] a Sin(g)halese.

cinglant, e [sɛ̃glɑ̃, -ɑ̃t] a (propos, ironie) scathing, biting; (échec) crushing.

cinglé, e [sɛ̃gle] a (fam) crazy.

cingler [sɛ̃gle] vt to lash; (fig) to sting ♦ vi (NAVIG): **~ vers** to make ou head for.

cinq [sɛ̃k] num five.

cinquantaine [sɛ̃kɑ̃tɛn] nf: **une ~ (de)** about fifty; **avoir la ~** (âge) to be around fifty.

cinquante [sɛ̃kɑ̃t] num fifty.

cinquantenaire [sɛ̃kɑ̃tnɛʀ] a, nm/f fifty-year-old.

cinquantième [sɛ̃kɑ̃tjɛm] num fiftieth.

cinquième [sɛ̃kjɛm] num fifth.

cinquièmement [sɛ̃kjɛmmɑ̃] ad fifthly.

cintre [sɛ̃tʀ(ə)] nm coat-hanger; (ARCHIT) arch; **plein ~** semicircular arch.

cintré, e [sɛ̃tʀe] a curved; (chemise) fitted, slim-fitting.

CIO sigle m (= Comité international olympique) IOC (= International Olympic Committee).

cirage [siʀaʒ] nm (shoe) polish.

circoncis, e [siʀkɔ̃si, -iz] a circumcized.

circoncision [siʀkɔ̃sizjɔ̃] nf circumcision.

circonférence [siʀkɔ̃feʀɑ̃s] nf circumference.

circonflexe [siʀkɔ̃flɛks(ə)] a: **accent ~** circumflex accent.

circonscription [siʀkɔ̃skʀipsjɔ̃] nf district; **~ électorale** (d'un député) constituency; **~ militaire** military area.

circonscrire [siʀkɔ̃skʀiʀ] vt to define, delimit; (incendie) to contain; (propriété) to mark out; (sujet) to define.

circonspect, e [siʀkɔ̃spɛkt] a circumspect, cautious.

circonspection [siʀkɔ̃spɛksjɔ̃] nf circumspection, caution.

circonstance [siʀkɔ̃stɑ̃s] nf circumstance; (occasion) occasion; **œuvre de ~** occasional work; **air de ~** fitting air; **tête de ~** appropriate demeanour (Brit) ou demeanor (US); **~s atténuantes** mitigating circumstances.

circonstancié, e [siʀkɔ̃stɑ̃sje] a detailed.

circonstanciel, le [siʀkɔ̃stɑ̃sjɛl] a: **complément/proposition ~(le)** adverbial phrase/clause.

circonvenir [siʀkɔ̃vniʀ] vt to circumvent.

circonvolutions [siʀkɔ̃vɔlysjɔ̃] nfpl twists, convolutions.

circuit [siʀkɥi] nm (trajet) tour, (round) trip; (ÉLEC, TECH) circuit; **~ automobile** motor circuit; **~ de distribution** distribution network; **~ fermé** closed circuit; **~ intégré** integrated circuit.

circulaire [siʀkylɛʀ] a, nf circular.

circulation [siʀkylasjɔ̃] nf circulation; (AUTO): **la ~** (the) traffic; **bonne/mauvaise ~** good/bad circulation; **mettre en ~** to put into circulation.

circulatoire [siʀkylatwaʀ] a: **avoir des troubles ~s** to have problems with one's circulation.

circuler [siʀkyle] vi to drive (along); to walk along; (train etc) to run; (sang, devises) to circulate; **faire ~** (nouvelle) to spread (about), circulate; (badauds) to move on.

cire [siʀ] nf wax; **~ à cacheter** sealing wax.

ciré [siʀe] nm oilskin.

cirer [siʀe] vt to wax, polish.

cireur [siʀœʀ] nm shoeshine-boy.

cireuse [siʀøz] nf floor polisher.

cireux, euse [siʀø, -øz] a (fig: teint) sallow, waxen.

cirque [siʀk(ə)] nm circus; (arène) amphitheatre (Brit), amphitheater (US); (GÉO) cirque; (fig: désordre) chaos, bedlam; (: chichis) carry-on.

cirrhose [siʀoz] nf: **~ du foie** cirrhosis of the

liver.

cisailler [sizaje] *vt* to clip.

cisaille(s) [sizaj] *nf(pl)* (gardening) shears *pl*.

ciseau, x [sizo] *nm*: ~ **(à bois)** chisel ♦ *nmpl* (pair of) scissors; **sauter en** ~**x** to do a scissors jump; ~ **à froid** cold chisel.

ciseler [sizle] *vt* to chisel, carve.

ciselure [sizlyʀ] *nf* engraving; *(bois)* carving.

Cisjordanie [sisʒɔʀdani] *nf*: **la** ~ the West Bank (of Jordan).

citadelle [sitadɛl] *nf* citadel.

citadin, e [sitadɛ̃, -in] *nm/f* city dweller ♦ *a* town *cpd*, city *cpd*, urban.

citation [sitasjɔ̃] *nf* *(d'auteur)* quotation; *(JUR)* summons *sg*; *(MIL: récompense)* mention.

cité [site] *nf* town; *(plus grande)* city; ~ **ou-vrière** (workers') housing estate; ~ **universitaire** students' residences *pl*.

cité-dortoir, *pl* **cités-dortoirs** [sitedɔʀtwaʀ] *nf* dormitory town.

cité-jardin, *pl* **cités-jardins** [siteʒaʀdɛ̃] *nf* garden city.

citer [site] *vt* *(un auteur)* to quote (from); *(nommer)* to name; *(JUR)* to summon; ~ **(en exemple)** *(personne)* to hold up (as an example); **je ne veux** ~ **personne** I don't want to name names.

citerne [sitɛʀn(ə)] *nf* tank.

cithare [sitaʀ] *nf* zither.

citoyen, ne [sitwajɛ̃, -ɛn] *nm/f* citizen.

citoyenneté [sitwajɛnte] *nf* citizenship.

citrique [sitʀik] *a*: **acide** ~ citric acid.

citron [sitʀɔ̃] *nm* lemon; ~ **pressé** (fresh) lemon juice; ~ **vert** lime.

citronnade [sitʀɔnad] *nf* lemonade.

citronné, e [sitʀɔne] *a* *(boisson)* lemon-flavoured *(Brit)* ou -flavored *(US)*; *(eau de toilette)* lemon-scented.

citronnier [sitʀɔnje] *nm* lemon tree.

citrouille [sitʀuj] *nf* pumpkin.

cive(s) [siv] *nf(pl)* *(BOT)* chive(s); *(CULIN)* chives.

civet [sivɛ] *nm* stew; ~ **de lièvre** jugged hare.

civette [sivɛt] *nf* *(BOT)* chives *pl*; *(ZOOL)* civet (cat).

civière [sivjɛʀ] *nf* stretcher.

civil, e [sivil] *a* *(JUR, ADMIN, poli)* civil; *(non militaire)* civilian ♦ *nm* civilian; **en** ~ in civilian clothes; **dans le** ~ in civilian life.

civilement [sivilmɑ̃] *ad* *(poliment)* civilly; **se marier** ~ to have a civil wedding.

civilisation [sivilizasjɔ̃] *nf* civilization.

civilisé, e [sivilize] *a* civilized.

civiliser [sivilize] *vt* to civilize.

civilité [sivilite] *nf* civility; **présenter ses** ~**s** to present one's compliments.

civique [sivik] *a* civic; **instruction** ~ *(SCOL)* civics *sg*.

civisme [sivism(ə)] *nm* public-spiritedness.

cl. *abr* (= *centilitre*) cl.

clafoutis [klafuti] *nm* batter pudding *(containing fruit)*.

claie [klɛ] *nf* grid, riddle.

clair, e [klɛʀ] *a* light; *(chambre)* light, bright; *(eau, son, fig)* clear ♦ *ad*: **voir** ~ to see clearly ♦ *nm*: **mettre au** ~ *(notes etc)* to tidy up; **tirer qch au** ~ to clear sth up, clarify sth; **bleu** ~ light blue; **pour être** ~ so as to make it plain; **y voir** ~ *(comprendre)* to

understand, see; **le plus** ~ **de son temps/argent** the better part of his time/money; **en** ~ *(non codé)* in clear; ~ **de lune** moonlight.

claire [klɛʀ] *nf*: **(huître de)** ~ fattened oyster.

clairement [klɛʀmɑ̃] *ad* clearly.

claire-voie [klɛʀvwa]: **à** ~ *a* letting the light through; openwork *cpd*.

clairière [klɛʀjɛʀ] *nf* clearing.

clair-obscur, *pl* **clairs-obscurs** [klɛʀɔpskyʀ] *nm* half-light; *(fig)* uncertainty.

clairon [klɛʀɔ̃] *nm* bugle.

claironner [klɛʀɔne] *vt* *(fig)* to trumpet, shout from the rooftops.

clairsemé, e [klɛʀsəme] *a* sparse.

clairvoyant, e [klɛʀvwajɑ̃, -ɑ̃t] *a* perceptive, clear-sighted.

clam [klam] *nm* *(ZOOL)* clam.

clamer [klame] *vt* to proclaim.

clameur [klamœʀ] *nf* clamour *(Brit)*, clamor *(US)*.

clandestin, e [klɑ̃dɛstɛ̃, -in] *a* clandestine, covert; *(POL)* underground, clandestine; **passager** ~ stowaway.

clandestinité [klɑ̃dɛstinite] *nf*: **dans la** ~ *(en secret)* under cover; *(en se cachant: vivre)* underground; **entrer dans la** ~ to go underground.

clapet [klapɛ] *nm* *(TECH)* valve.

clapier [klapje] *nm* (rabbit) hutch.

clapotement [klapɔtmɑ̃] *nm* lap(ping).

clapoter [klapɔte] *vi* to lap.

clapotis [klapɔti] *nm* lap(ping).

claquage [klakaʒ] *nm* pulled *ou* strained muscle.

claque [klak] *nf* *(gifle)* slap; *(THÉÂTRE)* claque ♦ *nm* *(chapeau)* opera hat.

claquement [klakmɑ̃] *nm* *(de porte: bruit ré-pété)* banging; *(: bruit isolé)* slam.

claquemurer [klakmyʀe]: **se** ~ *vi* to shut o.s. away, closet o.s.

claquer [klake] *vi* *(drapeau)* to flap; *(porte)* to bang, slam; *(coup de feu)* to ring out ♦ *vt* *(porte)* to slam, bang; *(doigts)* to snap; **elle claquait des dents** her teeth were chattering; **se** ~ **un muscle** to pull *ou* strain a muscle.

claquettes [klakɛt] *nfpl* tap-dancing *sg*.

clarification [klaʀifikasjɔ̃] *nf* *(fig)* clarification.

clarifier [klaʀifje] *vt* *(fig)* to clarify.

clarinette [klaʀinɛt] *nf* clarinet.

clarinettiste [klaʀinetist(ə)] *nm/f* clarinettist.

clarté [klaʀte] *nf* lightness; brightness; *(d'un son, de l'eau)* clearness; *(d'une explication)* clarity.

classe [klɑs] *nf* class; *(SCOL: local)* class(room); *(: leçon)* class; *(: élèves)* class, form; **1ère/2ème** ~ 1st/2nd class; **un (soldat de) deuxième** ~ *(MIL: armée de terre)* ≈ private (soldier); *(: armée de l'air)* ≈ air-craftman *(Brit)*, ≈ airman basic *(US)*; **de** ~ luxury *cpd*; **faire ses** ~**s** *(MIL)* to do one's (recruit's) training; **faire la** ~ *(SCOL)* to be the teacher; to teach; **aller en** ~ to go to school; **aller en** ~ **verte/de neige/de mer** to go to the countryside/skiing/to the seaside with the school; ~ **ouvrière** working class; ~ **sociale** social class; ~ **touriste** economy class.

classement [klɑsmɑ̃] *nm* classifying; filing; grading; closing; *(rang: SCOL)* place; *(:*

SPORT) placing; (*liste: SCOL*) class list (in order of merit); (*: SPORT*) placings *pl*; **premier au ~ général** (*SPORT*) first overall.

classer [klɑse] *vt* (*idées, livres*) to classify; (*papiers*) to file; (*candidat, concurrent*) to grade; (*personne: juger: péj*) to rate; (*JUR: affaire*) to close; **se ~ premier/dernier** to come first/last; (*SPORT*) to finish first/last.

classeur [klɑsœʀ] *nm* (*cahier*) file; (*meuble*) filing cabinet; **~ à feuillets mobiles** ring binder.

classification [klasifikɑsjɔ̃] *nf* classification.

classifier [klɑsifje] *vt* to classify.

classique [klɑsik] *a* classical; (*sobre: coupe etc*) classic(al); (*habituel*) standard, classic ♦ *nm* classic; classical author; **études ~s** classical studies, classics.

claudication [klodikɑsjɔ̃] *nf* limp.

clause [kloz] *nf* clause.

claustrer [klostʀe] *vt* to confine.

claustrophobie [klostʀɔfɔbi] *nf* claustrophobia.

clavecin [klavsɛ̃] *nm* harpsichord.

claveciniste [klavsinist(ə)] *nm/f* harpsichordist.

clavicule [klavikyl] *nf* clavicle, collarbone.

clavier [klavje] *nm* keyboard.

clé *ou* **clef** [kle] *nf* key; (*MUS*) clef; (*de mécanicien*) spanner (*Brit*), wrench (*US*) ♦ *a*: **problème/position** ~ key problem/position; **mettre sous** ~ to place under lock and key; **prendre la** ~ **des champs** to run away, make off; **prix ~s en main** (*d'une voiture*) on-the-road price; (*d'un appartement*) price with immediate entry; **~ de sol/de fa/d'ut** treble/bass/alto clef; **livre/film** *etc* **à** ~ book/film *etc* in which real people are depicted under fictitious names; **à la** ~ (*à la fin*) at the end of it all; **~ anglaise = ~ à molette**; **~ de contact** ignition key; **~ à molette** adjustable spanner (*Brit*) *ou* wrench, monkey wrench; **~ de voûte** keystone.

clématite [klematit] *nf* clematis.

clémence [klemɑ̃s] *nf* mildness; leniency.

clément, e [klemɑ̃, -ɑ̃t] *a* (*temps*) mild; (*indulgent*) lenient.

clémentine [klemɑ̃tin] *nf* (*BOT*) clementine.

clenche [klɑ̃ʃ] *nf* latch.

cleptomane [klɛptɔman] *nm/f* = **kleptomane**.

clerc [klɛʀ] *nm*: **~ de notaire** *ou* **d'avoué** lawyer's clerk.

clergé [klɛʀʒe] *nm* clergy.

clérical, e, aux [kleʀikal, -o] *a* clerical.

cliché [kliʃe] *nm* (*PHOTO*) negative; print; (*TYPO*) (printing) plate; (*LING*) cliché.

client, e [klijɑ̃, -ɑ̃t] *nm/f* (*acheteur*) customer, client; (*d'hôtel*) guest, patron; (*du docteur*) patient; (*de l'avocat*) client.

clientèle [klijɑ̃tɛl] *nf* (*du magasin*) customers *pl*, clientèle; (*du docteur, de l'avocat*) practice; **accorder sa** ~ **à** to give one's custom to; **retirer sa** ~ **à** to take one's business away from.

cligner [kliɲe] *vi*: **~ des yeux** to blink (one's eyes); **~ de l'œil** to wink.

clignotant [kliɲɔtɑ̃] *nm* (*AUTO*) indicator.

clignoter [kliɲɔte] *vi* (*étoiles etc*) to twinkle; (*lumière: à intervalles réguliers*) to flash; (*: vaciller*) to flicker; (*yeux*) to blink.

climat [klima] *nm* climate.

climatique [klimatik] *a* climatic.

climatisation [klimatizɑsjɔ̃] *nf* air conditioning.

climatisé, e [klimatize] *a* air-conditioned.

climatiseur [klimatizœʀ] *nm* air conditioner.

clin d'œil [klɛ̃dœj] *nm* wink; **en un** ~ in a flash.

clinique [klinik] *a* clinical ♦ *nf* nursing home, (*private*) clinic.

clinquant, e [klɛ̃kɑ̃, -ɑ̃t] *a* flashy.

clip [klip] *nm* (*pince*) clip; (*vidéo*) pop (*ou* promotional) video.

clique [klik] *nf* (*péj: bande*) clique, set; **prendre ses ~s et ses claques** to pack one's bags.

cliqueter [klikte] *vi* to clash; (*ferraille, clefs, monnaie*) to jangle, jingle; (*verres*) to chink.

cliquetis [klikti] *nm* jangle, jingle; chink.

clitoris [klitɔʀis] *nm* clitoris.

clivage [klivaʒ] *nm* cleavage; (*fig*) rift, split.

cloaque [klɔak] *nm* (*fig*) cesspit.

clochard, e [klɔʃaʀ, -aʀd(ə)] *nm/f* tramp.

cloche [klɔʃ] *nf* (*d'église*) bell; (*fam*) clot; (*chapeau*) cloche (hat); **~ à fromage** cheese-cover.

cloche-pied [klɔʃpje]: **à** ~ *ad* on one leg, hopping (along).

clocher [klɔʃe] *nm* church tower; (*en pointe*) steeple ♦ *vi* (*fam*) to be *ou* go wrong; **de** ~ (*péj*) parochial.

clocheton [klɔʃtɔ̃] *nm* pinnacle.

clochette [klɔʃɛt] *nf* bell.

clodo [klɔdo] *nm* (*fam*: = *clochard*) tramp.

cloison [klwazɔ̃] *nf* partition (wall); **~ étanche** (*fig*) impenetrable barrier, brick wall (*fig*).

cloisonner [klwazɔne] *vt* to partition (off); to divide up; (*fig*) to compartmentalize.

cloître [klwatʀ(ə)] *nm* cloister.

cloîtrer [klwatʀe] *vt*: **se** ~ to shut o.s. up *ou* away; (*REL*) to enter a convent *ou* monastery.

clone [klɔn] *nm* clone.

clope [klɔp] *nm* (*fam*) fag (*Brit*), cigarette.

clopin-clopant [klɔpɛ̃klɔpɑ̃] *ad* hobbling along; (*fig*) so-so.

clopiner [klɔpine] *vi* to hobble along.

cloporte [klɔpɔʀt(ə)] *nm* woodlouse (*pl* -lice).

cloque [klɔk] *nf* blister.

cloqué, e [klɔke] *a*: **étoffe ~e** seersucker.

cloquer [klɔke] *vi* (*peau, peinture*) to blister.

clore [klɔʀ] *vt* to close; **~ une session** (*INFORM*) to log out.

clos, e [klo, -oz] *pp de* **clore** ♦ *a voir* **maison, huis, vase** ♦ *nm* (enclosed) field.

clôt [klo] *vb voir* **clore**.

clôture [klotyʀ] *nf* closure, closing; (*barrière*) enclosure, fence.

clôturer [klotyʀe] *vt* (*terrain*) to enclose, close off; (*festival, débats*) to close.

clou [klu] *nm* nail; (*MÉD*) boil; **~s** *nmpl* = **passage clouté**; **pneus à ~s** studded tyres; **le** ~ **du spectacle** the highlight of the show; **~ de girofle** clove.

clouer [klue] *vt* to nail down (*ou* up); (*fig*): **~ sur/contre** to pin to/against.

clouté, e [klute] *a* studded.

clown [klun] *nm* clown; **faire le** ~ (*fig*) to

clown (about), play the fool.

CLT sigle f = Compagnie Luxembourgeoise de Télévision.

club [klœb] nm club.

CM sigle f = **chambre des métiers** ♦ sigle m = **conseil municipal**; (SCOL) = **cours moyen**.

cm. abr (= centimètre) cm.

CNAT sigle f (= Commission nationale d'aménagement du territoire) national development agency.

CNC sigle m (= Conseil national de la consommation) national consumers' council.

CNCL sigle f (= Commission nationale de la communication et des libertés) independent broadcasting authority.

CNDP sigle m = Centre national de documentation pédagogique.

CNE sigle f (= Caisse nationale d'épargne) national savings bank.

CNEC sigle m (= Centre national de l'enseignement par correspondance) ≈ Open University.

CNIL sigle f (= Commission nationale de l'informatique et des libertés) board which enforces law on data protection.

CNIT sigle m (= Centre national des industries et des techniques) exhibition centre in Paris.

CNJA sigle m (= Centre national des jeunes agriculteurs) farmers' union.

CNL sigle f (= Confédération nationale du logement) consumer group for housing.

CNP sigle f (= Caisse nationale de prévoyance) savings bank.

CNPF sigle m (= Conseil national du patronat français) national council of French employers.

CNRS sigle m = Centre national de la recherche scientifique.

c/o abr (= care of) c/o.

coagulant [kɔagylɑ̃] nm (MÉD) coagulant.

coaguler [kɔagyle] vi, vt, **se** ~ vi to coagulate.

coaliser [kɔalize]: **se** ~ vi to unite, join forces.

coalition [kɔalisjɔ̃] nf coalition.

coasser [kɔase] vi to croak.

coauteur [kɔotœʀ] nm co-author.

cobalt [kɔbalt] nm cobalt.

cobaye [kɔbaj] nm guinea-pig.

COBOL ou **Cobol** [kɔbɔl] nm COBOL.

cobra [kɔbʀa] nm cobra.

coca [kɔka] nm ® Coke ®.

cocagne [kɔkaɲ] nf: **pays de** ~ land of plenty; **mât de** ~ greasy pole (fig).

cocaïne [kɔkain] nf cocaine.

cocarde [kɔkaʀd(ə)] nf rosette.

cocardier, ière [kɔkaʀdje, -jɛʀ] a jingoistic, chauvinistic; militaristic.

cocasse [kɔkas] a comical, funny.

coccinelle [kɔksinɛl] nf ladybird (Brit), ladybug (US).

coccyx [kɔksis] nm coccyx.

cocher [kɔʃe] nm coachman ♦ vt to tick off; (entailler) to notch.

cochère [kɔʃɛʀ] af: **porte** ~ carriage entrance.

cochon, ne [kɔʃɔ̃, -ɔn] nm pig ♦ nm/f (péj: sale) (filthy) pig; (: méchant) swine ♦ a (fam) dirty, smutty; ~ **d'Inde** guinea-pig; ~ **de lait** (CULIN) sucking pig.

cochonnaille [kɔʃɔnaj] nf (péj: charcuterie) (cold) pork.

cochonnerie [kɔʃɔnʀi] nf (fam: saleté) filth; (: marchandises) rubbish, trash.

cochonnet [kɔʃɔnɛ] nm (BOULES) jack.

cocker [kɔkɛʀ] nm cocker spaniel.

cocktail [kɔktɛl] nm cocktail; (réception) cocktail party.

coco [kɔko] nm voir **noix**; (fam) bloke (Brit), dude (US).

cocon [kɔkɔ̃] nm cocoon.

cocorico [kɔkɔʀiko] excl, nm cock-a-doodle-do.

cocotier [kɔkɔtje] nm coconut palm.

cocotte [kɔkɔt] nf (en fonte) casserole; **ma** ~ (fam) sweetie (pie); ~ **(minute)** ® pressure cooker; ~ **en papier** paper shape.

cocu [kɔky] nm cuckold.

code [kɔd] nm code; **se mettre en** ~**(s)** to dip (Brit) ou dim (US) one's (head)lights; ~ **à barres** bar code; ~ **de caractère** (INFORM) character code; ~ **civil** Common Law; ~ **machine** machine code; ~ **pénal** penal code; ~ **postal** (numéro) postcode (Brit), zip code (US); ~ **de la route** highway code; ~ **secret** cipher.

codéine [kɔdein] nf codeine.

coder [kɔde] vt to (en)code.

codétenu, e [kɔdetny] nm/f fellow prisoner ou inmate.

codicille [kɔdisil] nm codicil.

codifier [kɔdifje] vt to codify.

codirecteur, trice [kɔdiʀɛktœʀ, -tʀis] nm/f co-director.

coéditeur, trice [kɔeditœʀ, -tʀis] nm/f co-publisher; (rédacteur) co-editor.

coefficient [kɔefisjɑ̃] nm coefficient; ~ **d'erreur** margin of error.

coéquipier, ière [kɔekipje, -jɛʀ] nm/f teammate, partner.

coercition [kɔɛʀsisjɔ̃] nf coercion.

cœur [kœʀ] nm heart; (CARTES: couleur) hearts pl; (: carte) heart; (CULIN): ~ **de laitue/d'artichaut** lettuce/artichoke heart; (fig): ~ **du débat** heart of the debate; ~ **de l'été** height of summer; ~ **de la forêt** depths pl of the forest; **affaire de** ~ love affair; **avoir bon** ~ to be kind-hearted; **avoir mal au** ~ to feel sick; **contre** ou **sur son** ~ to one's breast; **opérer qn à** ~ **ouvert** to perform open-heart surgery on sb; **recevoir qn à** ~ **ouvert** to welcome sb with open arms; **parler à** ~ **ouvert** to open one's heart; **de tout son** ~ with all one's heart; **avoir le** ~ **gros** ou **serré** to have a heavy heart; **en avoir le** ~ **net** to be clear in one's own mind (about it); **par** ~ by heart; **de bon** ~ willingly; **avoir à** ~ **de faire** to be very keen to do; **cela lui tient à** ~ that's (very) close to his heart; **prendre les choses à** ~ to take things to heart; **à** ~ **joie** to one's heart's content; **être de tout** ~ **avec qn** to be (completely) in accord with sb.

coexistence [kɔɛgzistɑ̃s] nf coexistence.

coexister [kɔɛgziste] vi to coexist.

coffrage [kɔfʀaʒ] nm (CONSTR: dispositif) form(work).

coffre [kɔfʀ(ə)] nm (meuble) chest; (coffre-fort) safe; (d'auto) boot (Brit), trunk (US); **avoir du** ~ (fam) to have a lot of puff.

coffre-fort, pl **coffres-fortes** [kɔfʀəfɔʀ] nm safe.

coffrer [kɔfʀe] vt (fam) to put inside, lock up.

coffret [kɔfʀɛ] nm casket; ~ **à bijoux** jewel box.

cogérant, e [kɔʒeʀɑ̃, -ɑ̃t] nm/f joint manager/manageress.

cogestion [kɔʒɛstjɔ̃] nf joint management.

cogiter [kɔʒite] vi to cogitate.

cognac [kɔɲak] nm brandy, cognac.

cognement [kɔɲmɑ̃] nm knocking.

cogner [kɔɲe] vi to knock, bang; **se** ~ to bump o.s.

cohabitation [kɔabitɑsjɔ̃] nf living together; (POL, JUR) cohabitation.

cohabiter [kɔabite] vi to live together.

cohérence [kɔeʀɑ̃s] nf coherence.

cohérent, e [kɔeʀɑ̃, -ɑ̃t] a coherent.

cohésion [kɔezjɔ̃] nf cohesion.

cohorte [kɔɔʀt(ə)] nf troop.

cohue [kɔy] nf crowd.

coi, coite [kwa, kwat] a: **rester** ~ to remain silent.

coiffe [kwaf] nf headdress.

coiffé, e [kwafe] a: **bien/mal** ~ with tidy/untidy hair; ~ **d'un béret** wearing a beret; ~ **en arrière** with one's hair brushed ou combed back; ~ **en brosse** with a crew cut.

coiffer [kwafe] vt (fig) to cover, top; ~ **qn** to do sb's hair; ~ **qn d'un béret** to put a beret on sb; **se** ~ to do one's hair; to put on a ou one's hat.

coiffeur, euse [kwafœʀ, -øz] nm/f hairdresser ♦ nf (table) dressing table.

coiffure [kwafyʀ] nf (cheveux) hairstyle, hairdo; (chapeau) hat, headgear q; (art): **la** ~ hairdressing.

coin [kwɛ̃] nm corner; (pour graver) die; (pour coincer) wedge; (poinçon) hallmark; **l'épicerie du** ~ the local grocer; **dans le** ~ (aux alentours) in the area, around about; locally; **au** ~ **du feu** by the fireside; **du** ~ **de l'œil** out of the corner of one's eye; **regard en** ~ side(ways) glance; **sourire en** ~ half-smile.

coincé, e [kwɛ̃se] a stuck, jammed; (fig: inhibé) inhibited, with hang-ups.

coincer [kwɛ̃se] vt to jam; (fam) to catch (out); to nab; **se** ~ to get stuck ou jammed.

coïncidence [kɔɛ̃sidɑ̃s] nf coincidence.

coïncider [kɔɛ̃side] vi: ~ **(avec)** to coincide (with); (correspondre: témoignage etc) to correspond ou tally (with).

coin-coin [kwɛ̃kwɛ̃] nm inv quack.

coing [kwɛ̃] nm quince.

coït [kɔit] nm coitus.

coite [kwat] af voir **coi**.

coke [kɔk] nm coke.

col [kɔl] nm (de chemise) collar; (encolure, cou) neck; (de montagne) pass; ~ **du fémur** neck of the thighbone; ~ **roulé** polo-neck; ~ **de l'utérus** cervix.

coléoptère [kɔleɔptɛʀ] nm beetle.

colère [kɔlɛʀ] nf anger; **une** ~ a fit of anger; **être en** ~ **(contre qn)** to be angry (with sb); **mettre qn en** ~ to make sb angry; **se mettre en** ~ to get angry.

coléreux, euse [kɔleʀø, -øz] a, **colérique** [kɔleʀik] a quick-tempered, irascible.

colibacillose [kɔlibasiloz] nf colibacillosis.

colifichet [kɔlifiʃɛ] nm trinket.

colimaçon [kɔlimasɔ̃] nm: **escalier en** ~ spiral staircase.

colin [kɔlɛ̃] nm hake.

colin-maillard [kɔlɛ̃majaʀ] nm (jeu) blind man's buff.

colique [kɔlik] nf diarrhoea (Brit), diarrhea (US); (douleurs) colic (pains pl); (fam: personne ou chose ennuyeuse) pain.

colis [kɔli] nm parcel; **par** ~ **postal** by parcel post.

colistier, ière [kɔlistje, -jɛʀ] nm/f fellow candidate.

colite [kɔlit] nf colitis.

coll. abr = **collection**; (= collaborateurs): **et** ~ **et al.**

collaborateur, trice [kɔlabɔʀatœʀ, -tʀis] nm/f (aussi POL) collaborator; (d'une revue) contributor.

collaboration [kɔlabɔʀasjɔ̃] nf collaboration.

collaborer [kɔlabɔʀe] vi to collaborate; ~ **à** to collaborate on; (revue) to contribute to.

collage [kɔlaʒ] nm (ART) collage.

collant, e [kɔlɑ̃, -ɑ̃t] a sticky; (robe etc) clinging, skintight; (péj) clinging ♦ nm (bas) tights pl.

collatéral, e, aux [kɔlateʀal, -o] nm/f collateral.

collation [kɔlasjɔ̃] nf light meal.

colle [kɔl] nf glue; (à papiers peints) (wallpaper) paste; (devinette) teaser, riddle; (SCOL fam) detention; ~ **forte** superglue ®.

collecte [kɔlɛkt(ə)] nf collection; **faire une** ~ to take up a collection.

collecter [kɔlɛkte] vt to collect.

collecteur [kɔlɛktœʀ] nm (égout) main sewer.

collectif, ive [kɔlɛktif, -iv] a collective; (visite, billet etc) group cpd ♦ nm: ~ **budgétaire** mini-budget (Brit), mid-term budget; **immeuble** ~ block of flats.

collection [kɔlɛksjɔ̃] nf collection; (ÉDITION) series; **pièce de** ~ collector's item; **faire (la)** ~ **de** to collect; **(toute) une** ~ **de** ... (fig) a (complete) set of ....

collectionner [kɔlɛksjɔne] vt (tableaux, timbres) to collect.

collectionneur, euse [kɔlɛksjɔnœʀ, -øz] nm/f collector.

collectivement [kɔlɛktivmɑ̃] ad collectively.

collectiviste [kɔlɛktivist(ə)] a collectivist.

collectivité [kɔlɛktivite] nf group; **la** ~ the community, the collectivity; **les** ~**s locales** local authorities.

collège [kɔlɛʒ] nm (école) (secondary) school; (assemblée) body; ~ **électoral** electoral college; ~ **d'enseignement secondaire (CES)** ≈ junior secondary school (Brit), ≈ junior high school (US).

collégial, e, aux [kɔleʒjal, -o] a collegiate.

collégien, ne [kɔleʒjɛ̃, -ɛn] nm/f secondary school pupil (Brit), high school student (US).

collègue [kɔlɛg] nm/f colleague.

coller [kɔle] vt (papier, timbre) to stick (on); (affiche) to stick up; (appuyer, placer contre): ~ **son front à la vitre** to press one's face to the window; (enveloppe) to stick down; (morceaux) to stick ou glue together; (fam: mettre, fourrer) to stick, shove; (SCOL *fam*) to keep in, give detention to ♦ *vi* (*être collant*) to be sticky; (*adhérer*) to stick; ~ **qch sur** to stick (*ou* paste *ou* glue) sth on(to); ~ **à** to stick to; (*fig*) to cling to.

collerette [kɔlʀɛt] *nf* ruff; (*TECH*) flange.

collet [kɔlɛ] *nm* (*piège*) snare, noose; (*cou*): **prendre qn au** ~ to grab sb by the throat; ~ **monté** *a inv* straight-laced.

colleter [kɔlte] *vt* (*adversaire*) to collar, grab by the throat; **se** ~ **avec** to wrestle with.

colleur [kɔlœʀ] *nm*: ~ **d'affiches** bill-poster.

collier [kɔlje] *nm* (*bijou*) necklace; (*de chien, TECH*) collar; ~ (**de barbe**), **barbe en** ~ narrow beard along the line of the jaw; ~ **de serrage** choke collar.

collimateur [kɔlimatœʀ] *nm*: **être dans le** ~ (*fig*) to be in the firing line; **avoir qn/qch dans le** ~ (*fig*) to have sb/sth in one's sights.

colline [kɔlin] *nf* hill.

collision [kɔlizjɔ̃] *nf* collision, crash; **entrer en** ~ (**avec**) to collide (with).

colloque [kɔlɔk] *nm* colloquium, symposium.

collusion [kɔlyzjɔ̃] *nf* collusion.

collutoire [kɔlytwaʀ] *nm* (*MÉD*) oral medication; (*en bombe*) throat spray.

collyre [kɔliʀ] *nm* (*MÉD*) eye lotion.

colmater [kɔlmate] *vt* (*fuite*) to seal off; (*brèche*) to plug, fill in.

Cologne [kɔlɔɲ] *n* Cologne.

colombe [kɔlɔ̃b] *nf* dove.

Colombie [kɔlɔ̃bi] *nf*: **la** ~ Colombia.

colombien, ne [kɔlɔ̃bjɛ̃, -ɛn] *a* Colombian ♦ *nm/f*: **C~, ne** Colombian.

colon [kɔlɔ̃] *nm* settler; (*enfant*) boarder (*in children's holiday camp*).

côlon [kolɔ̃] *nm* colon (*MÉD*).

colonel [kɔlɔnɛl] *nm* colonel; (*armée de l'air*) group captain.

colonial, e, aux [kɔlɔnjal, -o] *a* colonial.

colonialisme [kɔlɔnjalism(ə)] *nm* colonialism.

colonie [kɔlɔni] *nf* colony; ~ (**de vacances**) holiday camp (*for children*).

colonisation [kɔlɔnizasjɔ̃] *nf* colonization.

coloniser [kɔlɔnize] *vt* to colonize.

colonnade [kɔlɔnad] *nf* colonnade.

colonne [kɔlɔn] *nf* column; **se mettre en** ~ **par deux/quatre** to get into twos/fours; **en** ~ **par deux** in double file; ~ **de secours** rescue party; ~ (**vertébrale**) spine, spinal column.

colonnette [kɔlɔnɛt] *nf* small column.

colophane [kɔlɔfan] *nf* rosin.

colorant [kɔlɔʀɑ̃] *nm* colo(u)ring.

coloration [kɔlɔʀasjɔ̃] *nf* colour(ing) (*Brit*), color(ing) (*US*); **se faire faire une** ~ (*chez le coiffeur*) to have one's hair dyed.

coloré, e [kɔlɔʀe] *a* (*fig*) colo(u)rful.

colorer [kɔlɔʀe] *vt* to colour (*Brit*), color (*US*); **se** ~ *vi* to turn red; to blush.

coloriage [kɔlɔʀjaʒ] *nm* colo(u)ring.

colorier [kɔlɔʀje] *vt* to colo(u)r (in); **album à** ~ colouring book.

coloris [kɔlɔʀi] *nm* colo(u)r, shade.

coloriste [kɔlɔʀist(ə)] *nm/f* colo(u)rist.

colossal, e, aux [kɔlɔsal, -o] *a* colossal, huge.

colosse [kɔlɔs] *nm* giant.

colostrum [kɔlɔstʀɔm] *nm* colostrum.

colporter [kɔlpɔʀte] *vt* to hawk, peddle.

colporteur, euse [kɔlpɔʀtœʀ, -øz] *nm/f* hawker, pedlar.

colt [kɔlt] *nm* revolver, Colt ®.

coltiner [kɔltine] *vt* to lug about.

colza [kɔlza] *nm* rape(seed).

coma [kɔma] *nm* coma; **être dans le** ~ to be in a coma.

comateux, euse [kɔmatø, -øz] *a* comatose.

combat [kɔ̃ba] *vb voir* **combattre** ♦ *nm* fight; fighting *q*; ~ **de boxe** boxing match; ~ **de rues** street fighting *q*; ~ **singulier** single combat.

combatif, ive [kɔ̃batif, -iv] *a* with a lot of fight.

combativité [kɔ̃bativite] *nf* fighting spirit.

combattant [kɔ̃batɑ̃] *vb voir* **combattre** ♦ *nm* combatant; (*d'une rixe*) brawler; **ancien** ~ war veteran.

combattre [kɔ̃batʀ(ə)] *vi* to fight ♦ *vt* to fight; (*épidémie, ignorance*) to combat, fight (against).

combien [kɔ̃bjɛ̃] *ad* (*quantité*) how much; (*nombre*) how many; (*exclamatif*) how; ~ **de** how much; how many; ~ **de temps** how long, how much time; ~ **coûte/pèse ceci?** how much does this cost/weigh?; **vous mesurez** ~? what size are you?; **ça fait** ~ **en largeur?** how wide is that?

combinaison [kɔ̃binɛzɔ̃] *nf* combination; (*astuce*) device, scheme; (*de femme*) slip; (*d'aviateur*) flying suit; (*d'homme-grenouille*) wetsuit; (*bleu de travail*) boilersuit (*Brit*), coveralls *pl* (*US*).

combine [kɔ̃bin] *nf* trick; (*péj*) scheme, fiddle (*Brit*).

combiné [kɔ̃bine] *nm* (*aussi*: ~ **téléphonique**) receiver; (*SKI*) combination (event); (*vêtement de femme*) corselet.

combiner [kɔ̃bine] *vt* to combine; (*plan, horaire*) to work out, devise.

comble [kɔ̃bl(ə)] *a* (*salle*) packed (full) ♦ *nm* (*du bonheur, plaisir*) height; ~**s** *nmpl* (*CONSTR*) attic *sg*, loft *sg*; **de fond en** ~ from top to bottom; **pour** ~ **de malchance** to cap it all; **c'est le** ~! that beats everything!, that takes the biscuit! (*Brit*); **sous les** ~**s** in the attic.

combler [kɔ̃ble] *vt* (*trou*) to fill in; (*besoin, lacune*) to fill; (*déficit*) to make good; (*satisfaire*) to gratify, fulfil (*Brit*), fulfill (*US*); ~ **qn de joie** to fill sb with joy; ~ **qn d'honneurs** to shower sb with honours.

combustible [kɔ̃bystibl(ə)] *a* combustible ♦ *nm* fuel.

combustion [kɔ̃bystjɔ̃] *nf* combustion.

COMECON [kɔmekɔn] *sigle m* Comecon.

comédie [kɔmedi] *nf* comedy; (*fig*) playacting *q*; **jouer la** ~ (*fig*) to put on an act; ~ **musicale** musical.

comédien, ne [kɔmedjɛ̃, -ɛn] *nm/f* actor/actress; (*comique*) comedy actor/actress, comedian/comedienne; (*fig*) sham.

COMES [kɔmɛs] *sigle m* = *Commissariat à l'énergie solaire*.

comestible [kɔmɛstibl(ə)] *a* edible; ~**s** *nmpl* foods.

comète [kɔmɛt] *nf* comet.

comice [kɔmis] *nm*: ~ **agricole** agricultural show.

comique [kɔmik] *a* (*drôle*) comical; (*THÉÂTRE*) comic ♦ *nm* (*artiste*) comic, comedian; **le ~ de qch** the funny *ou* comical side of sth.

comité [kɔmite] *nm* committee; **petit ~** select group; **~ directeur** management committee; **~ d'entreprise (CE)** works council; **~ des fêtes** festival committee.

commandant [kɔmɑ̃dɑ̃] *nm* (*gén*) commander, commandant; (*MIL: grade*) major; (*: armée de l'air*) squadron leader; (*NAVIG*) captain; **~ (de bord)** (*AVIAT*) captain.

commande [kɔmɑ̃d] *nf* (*COMM*) order; (*INFORM*) command; **~s** *nfpl* (*AVIAT etc*) controls; **passer une ~ (de)** to put in an order (for); **sur ~** to order; **~ à distance** remote control; **véhicule à double ~** vehicle with dual controls.

commandement [kɔmɑ̃dmɑ̃] *nm* command; (*ordre*) command, order; (*REL*) commandment.

commander [kɔmɑ̃de] *vt* (*COMM*) to order; (*diriger, ordonner*) to command; **~ à** (*MIL*) to command; (*contrôler, maîtriser*) to have control over; **~ à qn de faire** to command *ou* order sb to do.

commanditaire [kɔmɑ̃diteʀ] *nm* sleeping partner.

commandite [kɔmɑ̃dit] *nf*: **(société en) ~** limited partnership.

commanditer [kɔmɑ̃dite] *vt* (*COMM*) to finance, back; to commission.

commando [kɔmɑ̃do] *nm* commando (squad).

comme [kɔm] *prép* like; (*en tant que*) as ♦ *cj* as; (*parce que, puisque*) as, since ♦ *ad*: **~ il est fort/c'est bon!** how strong he is/good it is!; **donner ~ prix/heure** to give the price/ time as; **~ si** as if, as though; **~ quoi** (*disant que*) with the result that; (*d'où il s'ensuit que*) which shows that; **faites-le ~ cela** *ou* **ça** do it like this *ou* this way; **... ~ ça** *ou* **cela on n'aura pas d'ennuis** that way we won't have any problems; **comment ça va?** **— ~ ça** how are things? **— OK**; **~ ci ~ ça** so-so, middling; **joli ~ tout** ever so pretty; **on dit** as they say; **~ de juste** needlessly to say; **~ il faut** properly.

commémoration [kɔmemɔʀasjɔ̃] *nf* commemoration.

commémorer [kɔmemɔʀe] *vt* to commemorate.

commencement [kɔmɑ̃smɑ̃] *nm* beginning, start, commencement; **~s** *nmpl* (*débuts*) beginnings.

commencer [kɔmɑ̃se] *vt* to begin, start, commence; (*être placé au début de*) to begin ♦ *vi* to begin, start, commence; **~ à** *ou* **de faire** to begin *ou* start doing; **~ par qch** to begin with sth; **~ par faire qch** to begin by doing sth.

commensal, e, aux [kɔmɑ̃sal, -o] *nm/f* companion at table.

comment [kɔmɑ̃] *ad* how; **~?** (*que dites-vous*) (I beg your) pardon?; **~!** what! ♦ *nm*: **le ~ et le pourquoi** the whys and wherefores; **et ~!** and how!; **~ donc!** of course!; **~ faire?** how will we do it?; **~ se fait-il que?** how is it that?

commentaire [kɔmɑ̃teʀ] *nm* comment; remark; **~ (de texte)** (*SCOL*) commentary; **~**

sur image voice-over.

commentateur, trice [kɔmɑ̃tatœʀ, -tʀis] *nm/f* commentator.

commenter [kɔmɑ̃te] *vt* (*jugement, événement*) to comment (up)on; (*RADIO, TV: match, manifestation*) to cover, give a commentary on.

commérages [kɔmeʀaʒ] *nmpl* gossip *sg*.

commerçant, e [kɔmɛʀsɑ̃, -ɑ̃t] *a* commercial; trading; (*rue*) shopping *cpd*; (*personne*) commercially shrewd ♦ *nm/f* shopkeeper, trader.

commerce [kɔmɛʀs(ə)] *nm* (*activité*) trade, commerce; (*boutique*) business; **le petit ~** small shopowners *pl*, small traders *pl*; **faire ~ de** to trade in; (*fig: péj*) to trade on; **chambre de ~** Chamber of Commerce; **livres de ~** (account) books; **vendu dans le ~** sold in the shops; **vendu hors-~** sold directly to the public; **~ en** *ou* **de gros/détail** wholesale/retail trade; **~ intérieur/ extérieur** home/foreign trade.

commercer [kɔmɛʀse] *vi*: **~ avec** to trade with.

commercial, e, aux [kɔmɛʀsjal, -o] *a* commercial, trading; (*péj*) commercial ♦ *nm*: **les commerciaux** the commercial people.

commercialisation [kɔmɛʀsjalizasjɔ̃] *nf* marketing.

commercialiser [kɔmɛʀsjalize] *vt* to market.

commère [kɔmɛʀ] *nf* gossip.

commettant [kɔmetɑ̃] *vb voir* **commettre** ♦ *nm* (*JUR*) principal.

commettre [kɔmɛtʀ(ə)] *vt* to commit; **se ~** to compromise one's good name.

commis [kɔmi] *vb voir* **commettre** ♦ *nm* (*de magasin*) (shop) assistant (*Brit*), sales clerk (*US*); (*de banque*) clerk; **~ voyageur** commercial traveller (*Brit*) *ou* traveler (*US*).

commis, e [kɔmi, -iz] *pp de* **commettre**.

commisération [kɔmizeʀasjɔ̃] *nf* commiseration.

commissaire [kɔmisɛʀ] *nm* (*de police*) ≈ (police) superintendent (*Brit*), ≈ (police) captain (*US*); (*de rencontre sportive etc*) steward; **~ du bord** (*NAVIG*) purser; **~ aux comptes** (*ADMIN*) auditor.

commissaire-priseur, *pl* **commissaires-priseurs** [kɔmisɛʀpʀizœʀ] *nm* (official) auctioneer.

commissariat [kɔmisaʀja] *nm* police station; (*ADMIN*) commissionership.

commission [kɔmisjɔ̃] *nf* (*comité, pourcentage*) commission; (*message*) message; (*course*) errand; **~s** *nfpl* (*achats*) shopping *sg*; **~ d'examen** examining board.

commissionnaire [kɔmisjɔnɛʀ] *nm* delivery boy (*ou* man); messenger; (*TRANSPORTS*) (forwarding) agent.

commissure [kɔmisyʀ] *nf*: **les ~s des lèvres** the corners of the mouth.

commode [kɔmɔd] *a* (*pratique*) convenient, handy; (*facile*) easy; (*air, personne*) easygoing; (*personne*): **pas ~** awkward (to deal with) ♦ *nf* chest of drawers.

commodité [kɔmɔdite] *nf* convenience.

commotion [kɔmɔsjɔ̃] *nf*: **~ (cérébrale)** concussion.

commotionné, e [kɔmosjɔne] *a* shocked, shaken.

commuer [kɔmɥe] *vt* to commute.

commun, e [kɔmœ̃, -yn] *a* common; (*pièce*) communal, shared; (*réunion, effort*) joint ♦ *nf* (*ADMIN*) commune, ≈ district; (*: urbaine*) ≈ borough; ~**s** *nmpl* (*bâtiments*) outbuildings; **cela sort du ~** it's out of the ordinary; **le ~ des mortels** the common run of people; **sans ~e mesure** incomparable; **être ~ à** (*suj: chose*) to be shared by; **en ~** (*faire*) jointly; **mettre en ~** to pool, share; **peu ~** unusual; **d'un ~ accord** of one accord; **with one accord.**

communal, e, aux [kɔmynal, -o] *a* (*ADMIN*) of the commune, ≈ (district *ou* borough) council *cpd*.

communautaire [kɔmynotɛʀ] *a* community *cpd*.

communauté [kɔmynote] *nf* community; (*JUR*): **régime de la ~** communal estate settlement.

commune [kɔmyn] *af, nf voir* **commun**.

Communes [kɔmyn] *nfpl* (*Brit: parlement*) Commons.

communiant, e [kɔmynjɑ̃, -ɑ̃t] *nm/f* communicant; **premier ~** child taking his first communion.

communicant, e [kɔmynikɑ̃, -ɑ̃t] *a* communicating.

communicatif, ive [kɔmynikatif, -iv] *a* (*personne*) communicative; (*rire*) infectious.

communication [kɔmynikasjɔ̃] *nf* communication; ~ (**téléphonique**) (telephone) call; **avoir la ~** (**avec**) to get *ou* be through (to); **vous avez la ~** you're through; **donnez-moi la ~ avec** put me through to; **mettre qn en ~ avec qn** (*en contact*) to put sb in touch with sb; (*au téléphone*) to connect sb with sb; ~ **interurbaine** long-distance call; ~ **PCV** reverse charge (*Brit*) *ou* collect (*US*) call; ~ **avec préavis** personal call.

communier [kɔmynje] *vi* (*REL*) to receive communion; (*fig*) to be united.

communion [kɔmynjɔ̃] *nf* communion.

communiqué [kɔmynike] *nm* communiqué; ~ **de presse** press release.

communiquer [kɔmynike] *vt* (*nouvelle, dossier*) to pass on, convey; (*maladie*) to pass on; (*peur etc*) to communicate; (*chaleur, mouvement*) to transmit ♦ *vi* to communicate; ~ **avec** (*suj: salle*) to communicate with; **se ~ à** (*se propager*) to spread to.

communisant, e [kɔmynizɑ̃, -ɑ̃t] *a* communistic ♦ *nm/f* communist sympathizer.

communisme [kɔmynism(ə)] *nm* communism.

communiste [kɔmynist(ə)] *a, nm/f* communist.

commutateur [kɔmytatœʀ] *nm* (*ÉLEC*) (change-over) switch, commutator.

commutation [kɔmytasjɔ̃] *nf* (*INFORM*): ~ **de messages** message switching; ~ **de paquets** packet switching.

Comores [kɔmɔʀ] *nfpl*: **les (îles) ~** the Comoros (Islands).

comorien, ne [kɔmɔʀjɛ̃, -ɛn] *a* of *ou* from the Comoros.

compact, e [kɔ̃pakt] *a* dense; compact.

compagne [kɔ̃paɲ] *nf* companion.

compagnie [kɔ̃paɲi] *nf* (*firme, MIL*) company; (*groupe*) gathering; (*présence*): **la ~ de qn** sb's company; **homme/femme de ~** escort; **tenir ~ à qn** to keep sb company; **fausser ~ à qn** to give sb the slip, slip *ou* sneak away from sb; **en ~ de** in the company of; **Dupont et ~, Dupont et Cie** Dupont and Company, Dupont and Co; ~ **aérienne** airline (company).

compagnon [kɔ̃paɲɔ̃] *nm* companion; (*autrefois: ouvrier*) craftsman; journeyman.

comparable [kɔ̃paʀabl(ə)] *a*: ~ (**à**) comparable (to).

comparais [kɔ̃paʀe] *etc vb voir* **comparaître**.

comparaison [kɔ̃paʀɛzɔ̃] *nf* comparison; (*métaphore*) simile; **en ~ (de)** in comparison (with); **par ~ (à)** by comparison (with).

comparaître [kɔ̃paʀɛtʀ(ə)] *vi*: ~ (**devant**) to appear (before).

comparatif, ive [kɔ̃paʀatif, -iv] *a, nm* comparative.

comparativement [kɔ̃paʀativmɑ̃] *ad* comparatively; ~ **à** by comparison with.

comparé, e [kɔ̃paʀe] *a*: **littérature** *etc* ~**e** comparative literature *etc*.

comparer [kɔ̃paʀe] *vt* to compare; ~ **qch/qn à** *ou* **et** (*pour choisir*) to compare sth/sb with *ou* and; (*pour établir une similitude*) to compare sth/sb to *ou* and.

comparse [kɔ̃paʀs(ə)] *nm/f* (*péj*) associate, stooge.

compartiment [kɔ̃paʀtimɑ̃] *nm* compartment.

compartimenté, e [kɔ̃paʀtimɑ̃te] *a* partitioned; (*fig*) compartmentalized.

comparu, e [kɔ̃paʀy] *pp de* **comparaître**.

comparution [kɔ̃paʀysjɔ̃] *nf* appearance.

compas [kɔ̃pa] *nm* (*GÉOM*) (pair of) compasses *pl*; (*NAVIG*) compass.

compassé, e [kɔ̃pase] *a* starchy, formal.

compassion [kɔ̃pasjɔ̃] *nf* compassion.

compatibilité [kɔ̃patibilite] *nf* compatibility.

compatible [kɔ̃patibl(ə)] *a*: ~ (**avec**) compatible (with).

compatir [kɔ̃patiʀ] *vi*: ~ (**à**) to sympathize (with).

compatissant, e [kɔ̃patisɑ̃, -ɑ̃t] *a* sympathetic.

compatriote [kɔ̃patʀijɔt] *nm/f* compatriot, fellow countryman/woman.

compensateur, trice [kɔ̃pɑ̃satœʀ, -tʀis] *a* compensatory.

compensation [kɔ̃pɑ̃sasjɔ̃] *nf* compensation; (*BANQUE*) clearing; **en ~** in *ou* as compensation.

compensé, e [kɔ̃pɑ̃se] *a*: **semelle** ~**e** platform sole.

compenser [kɔ̃pɑ̃se] *vt* to compensate for, make up for.

compère [kɔ̃pɛʀ] *nm* accomplice; fellow musician *ou* comedian *etc*.

compétence [kɔ̃petɑ̃s] *nf* competence.

compétent, e [kɔ̃petɑ̃, -ɑ̃t] *a* (*apte*) competent, capable; (*JUR*) competent.

compétitif, ive [kɔ̃petitif, -iv] *a* competitive.

compétition [kɔ̃petisjɔ̃] *nf* (*gén*) competition; (*SPORT: épreuve*) event; **la ~** competitive sport; **être en ~ avec** to be competing with; **la ~ automobile** motor racing.

compétitivité [kɔ̃petitivite] *nf* competitiveness.

compilateur [kɔ̃pilatœʀ] *nm* (*INFORM*) compiler.

compiler [kɔ̃pile] *vt* to compile.

complainte [kɔ̃plɛ̃t] *nf* lament.

complaire [kɔ̃plɛʀ]: **se ~** *vi*: **se ~ dans/parmi** to take pleasure in/in being among.

complaisais [kɔ̃plɛzɛ] *etc vb voir* **complaire**.

complaisamment [kɔ̃plɛzamɑ̃] *ad* kindly; complacently.

complaisance [kɔ̃plɛzɑ̃s] *nf* kindness; (*péj*) indulgence; (: *fatuité*) complacency; **attestation de ~** *certificate produced to oblige a patient etc*; **pavillon de ~** flag of convenience.

complaisant, e [kɔ̃plɛzɑ̃, -ɑ̃t] *vb voir* **complaire** ♦ *a* (*aimable*) kind; obliging; (*péj*) accommodating; (: *fat*) complacent.

complaît [kɔ̃plɛ] *vb voir* **complaire**.

complément [kɔ̃plemɑ̃] *nm* complement; (*reste*) remainder; (*LING*) complement; **~ d'information** (*ADMIN*) supplementary *ou* further information; **~ d'agent** agent; **~ (d'objet) direct/indirect** direct/indirect object; **~ (circonstanciel) de lieu/temps** adverbial phrase of place/time; **~ de nom** possessive phrase.

complémentaire [kɔ̃plemɑ̃tɛʀ] *a* complementary; (*additionnel*) supplementary.

complet, ète [kɔ̃plɛ, -ɛt] *a* complete; (*plein: hôtel etc*) full ♦ *nm* (*aussi*: **~-veston**) suit; **au (grand) ~** all together.

complètement [kɔ̃plɛtmɑ̃] *ad* (*en entier*) completely; (*absolument: fou, faux etc*) absolutely; (*à fond: étudier etc*) fully, in depth.

compléter [kɔ̃plete] *vt* (*porter à la quantité voulue*) to complete; (*augmenter*) to complement, supplement; to add to; **se ~** (*personnes*) to complement one another; (*collection etc*) to become complete.

complexe [kɔ̃plɛks(ə)] *a* complex ♦ *nm* (*PSYCH*) complex, hang-up; (*bâtiments*): **~ hospitalier/industriel** hospital/industrial complex.

complexé, e [kɔ̃plɛkse] *a* mixed-up, hung-up.

complexité [kɔ̃plɛksite] *nf* complexity.

complication [kɔ̃plikasjɔ̃] *nf* complexity, intricacy; (*difficulté, ennui*) complication; **~s** *nfpl* (*MÉD*) complications.

complice [kɔ̃plis] *nm* accomplice.

complicité [kɔ̃plisite] *nf* complicity.

compliment [kɔ̃plimɑ̃] *nm* (*louange*) compliment; **~s** *nmpl* (*félicitations*) congratulations.

complimenter [kɔ̃plimɑ̃te] *vt*: **~ qn (sur ou de)** to congratulate *ou* compliment sb (on).

compliqué, e [kɔ̃plike] *a* complicated, complex, intricate; (*personne*) complicated.

compliquer [kɔ̃plike] *vt* to complicate; **se ~** *vi* (*situation*) to become complicated; **se ~ la vie** to make life difficult *ou* complicated for o.s.

complot [kɔ̃plo] *nm* plot.

comploter [kɔ̃plɔte] *vi, vt* to plot.

complu, e [kɔ̃ply] *pp de* **complaire**.

comportement [kɔ̃pɔʀtəmɑ̃] *nm* behaviour (*Brit*), behavior (*US*); (*TECH: d'une pièce, d'un véhicule*) behavio(u)r, performance.

comporter [kɔ̃pɔʀte] *vt* to be composed of, consist of, comprise; (*être équipé de*) to have; (*impliquer*) to entail, involve; **se ~** *vi* to behave; (*TECH*) to behave, perform.

composant [kɔ̃pozɑ̃] *nm* component, constituent.

composante [kɔ̃pozɑ̃t] *nf* component.

composé, e [kɔ̃poze] *a* (*visage, air*) studied; (*BIO, CHIMIE, LING*) compound ♦ *nm* (*CHIMIE, LING*) compound; **~ de** made up of.

composer [kɔ̃poze] *vt* (*musique, texte*) to compose; (*mélange, équipe*) to make up; (*faire partie de*) to make up, form; (*TYPO*) to (type)set ♦ *vi* (*SCOL*) to sit *ou* do a test; (*transiger*) to come to terms; **se ~ de** to be composed of, be made up of; **~ un numéro** (*au téléphone*) to dial a number.

composite [kɔ̃pozit] *a* heterogeneous.

compositeur, trice [kɔ̃pozitœʀ, -tʀis] *nm/f* (*MUS*) composer; (*TYPO*) compositor, typesetter.

composition [kɔ̃pozisjɔ̃] *nf* composition; (*SCOL*) test; (*TYPO*) (type)setting, composition; **de bonne ~** (*accommodant*) easy to deal with; **amener qn à ~** to get sb to come to terms; **~ française** (*SCOL*) French essay.

compost [kɔ̃pɔst] *nm* compost.

composter [kɔ̃pɔste] *vt* to date-stamp; to punch.

composteur [kɔ̃pɔstœʀ] *nm* date stamp; punch; (*TYPO*) composing stick.

compote [kɔ̃pɔt] *nf* stewed fruit *q*; **~ de pommes** stewed apples.

compotier [kɔ̃pɔtje] *nm* fruit dish *ou* bowl.

compréhensible [kɔ̃pʀeɑ̃sibl(ə)] *a* comprehensible; (*attitude*) understandable.

compréhensif, ive [kɔ̃pʀeɑ̃sif, -iv] *a* understanding.

compréhension [kɔ̃pʀeɑ̃sjɔ̃] *nf* understanding; comprehension.

comprendre [kɔ̃pʀɑ̃dʀ(ə)] *vt* to understand; (*se composer de*) to comprise, consist of; (*inclure*) to include; **se faire ~** to make o.s. understood; to get one's ideas across; **mal ~** to misunderstand.

compresse [kɔ̃pʀɛs] *nf* compress.

compresser [kɔ̃pʀese] *vt* to squash in, crush together.

compresseur [kɔ̃pʀesœʀ] *am voir* **rouleau**.

compressible [kɔ̃pʀesibl(ə)] *a* (*PHYSIQUE*) compressible; (*dépenses*) reducible.

compression [kɔ̃pʀesjɔ̃] *nf* compression; (*d'un crédit etc*) reduction.

comprimé, e [kɔ̃pʀime] *a*: **air ~** compressed air ♦ *nm* tablet.

comprimer [kɔ̃pʀime] *vt* to compress; (*fig: crédit etc*) to reduce, cut down.

compris, e [kɔ̃pʀi, -iz] *pp de* **comprendre** ♦ *a* (*inclus*) included; **~?** understood?, is that clear?; **~ entre** (*situé*) contained between; **la maison ~e/non ~e, y/non ~ la maison** including/excluding the house; **service ~** service (charge) included; **100 F tout ~** 100 F all inclusive *ou* all-in.

compromettre [kɔ̃pʀɔmɛtʀ(ə)] *vt* to compromise.

compromis [kɔ̃pʀɔmi] *vb voir* **compromettre** ♦ *nm* compromise.

compromission [kɔ̃prɔmisjɔ̃] *nf* compromise, deal.

comptabiliser [kɔ̃tabilize] *vt* (*valeur*) to post; (*fig*) to evaluate.

comptabilité [kɔ̃tabilite] *nf* (*activité*, *technique*) accounting, accountancy; (*d'une société: comptes*) accounts *pl*, books *pl*; (: *service*) accounts office *ou* department; ~ **à partie double** double-entry book-keeping.

comptable [kɔ̃tabl(ə)] *nm/f* accountant ♦ *a* accounts *cpd*, accounting.

comptant [kɔ̃tɑ̃] *ad*: **payer** ~ to pay cash; **acheter** ~ to buy for cash.

compte [kɔ̃t] *nm* count, counting; (*total, montant*) count, (*right*) number; (*bancaire, facture*) account; ~**s** *nmpl* accounts, books; (*fig*) explanation *sg*; **ouvrir un** ~ to open an account; **rendre des** ~**s à qn** (*fig*) to be answerable to sb; **faire le** ~ **de** to count up, make a count of; **tout** ~ **fait** on the whole; **à ce** ~**-là** (*dans ce cas*) in that case; (*à ce train-là*) at that rate; **en fin de** ~ (*fig*) all things considered, weighing it all up; **au bout du** ~ in the final analysis; **à bon** ~ at a favourable price; (*fig*) lightly; **avoir son** ~ (*fig: fam*) to have had it; **pour le** ~ **de** on behalf of; **pour son propre** ~ for one's own benefit; **sur le** ~ **de qn** (*à son sujet*) about sb; **travailler à son** ~ to work for oneself; **mettre qch sur le** ~ **de qn** (*le rendre responsable*) to attribute sth to sb; **prendre qch à son** ~ to take responsibility for sth; **trouver son** ~ **à qch** to do well out of sth; **régler un** ~ (*s'acquitter de qch*) to settle an account; (*se venger*) to get one's own back; **rendre** ~ (**à qn**) **de qch** to give (sb) an account of sth; **tenir** ~ **de qch** to take sth into account; ~ **tenu de** taking into account; ~ **chèque(s)** current account; ~ **chèque postal (CCP)** Post Office account; ~ **client** (*sur bilan*) accounts receivable; ~ **courant (CC)** current account; ~ **de dépôt** deposit account; ~ **d'exploitation** operating account; ~ **fournisseur** (*sur bilan*) accounts payable; ~ **à rebours** countdown; ~ **rendu** account, report; (*de film, livre*) review; *voir aussi* **rendre**.

compte-gouttes [kɔ̃tgut] *nm inv* dropper.

compter [kɔ̃te] *vt* to count; (*facturer*) to charge for; (*avoir à son actif, comporter*) to have; (*prévoir*) to allow, reckon; (*tenir compte de, inclure*) to include; (*penser, espérer*): ~ **réussir/revenir** to expect to succeed/return ♦ *vi* to count; (*être économe*) to economize; (*être non négligeable*) to count, matter; (*valoir*): ~ **pour** to count for; (*figurer*): ~ **parmi** to be *ou* rank among; ~ **sur** to count (up)on; ~ **avec qch/qn** to reckon with *ou* take account of sth/sb; ~ **sans qch/qn** to reckon without sth/sb; **sans** ~ **que** besides which; **à** ~ **du 10 janvier** (*COMM*) (as) from 10th January.

compte-tours [kɔ̃ttur] *nm inv* rev(olution) counter.

compteur [kɔ̃tœr] *nm* meter; ~ **de vitesse** speedometer.

comptine [kɔ̃tin] *nf* nursery rhyme.

comptoir [kɔ̃twar] *nm* (*de magasin*) counter; (*de café*) counter, bar; (*colonial*) trading post.

compulser [kɔ̃pylse] *vt* to consult.

comte, comtesse [kɔ̃t, kɔ̃tɛs] *nm/f* count/countess.

con, ne [kɔ̃, kɔn] *a* (*fam!*) bloody (*Brit*) *ou* damned stupid (*!*).

concasser [kɔ̃kɑse] *vt* (*pierre, sucre*) to crush; (*poivre*) to grind.

concave [kɔ̃kav] *a* concave.

concéder [kɔ̃sede] *vt* to grant; (*défaite, point*) to concede; ~ **que** to concede that.

concentration [kɔ̃sɑ̃trɑsjɔ̃] *nf* concentration.

concentrationnaire [kɔ̃sɑ̃trɑsjɔnɛr] *a* of *ou* in concentration camps.

concentré [kɔ̃sɑ̃tre] *nm* concentrate; ~ **de tomates** tomato purée.

concentrer [kɔ̃sɑ̃tre] *vt* to concentrate; **se** ~ to concentrate.

concentrique [kɔ̃sɑ̃trik] *a* concentric.

concept [kɔ̃sɛpt] *nm* concept.

concepteur, trice [kɔ̃sɛptœr, -tris] *nm/f* designer.

conception [kɔ̃sɛpsjɔ̃] *nf* conception; (*d'une machine etc*) design.

concernant [kɔ̃sɛrnɑ̃] *prép* (*se rapportant à*) concerning; (*en ce qui concerne*) as regards.

concerner [kɔ̃sɛrne] *vt* to concern; **en ce qui me concerne** as far as I am concerned; **en ce qui concerne ceci** as far as this is concerned, with regard to this.

concert [kɔ̃sɛr] *nm* concert; **de** ~ *ad* in unison; together.

concertation [kɔ̃sɛrtɑsjɔ̃] *nf* (*échange de vues*) dialogue; (*rencontre*) meeting.

concerter [kɔ̃sɛrte] *vt* to devise; **se** ~ *vi* (*collaborateurs etc*) to put our (*ou* their *etc*) heads together, consult (each other).

concertiste [kɔ̃sɛrtist(ə)] *nm/f* concert artist.

concerto [kɔ̃sɛrto] *nm* concerto.

concession [kɔ̃sesjɔ̃] *nf* concession.

concessionnaire [kɔ̃sesjɔnɛr] *nm/f* agent, dealer.

concevable [kɔ̃səvabl(ə)] *a* conceivable.

concevoir [kɔ̃səvwar] *vt* (*idée, projet*) to conceive (of); (*méthode, plan d'appartement, décoration etc*) to plan, design; (*enfant*) to conceive; **maison bien/mal conçue** well-/badly-designed *ou* -planned house.

concierge [kɔ̃sjɛrʒ(ə)] *nm/f* caretaker; (*d'hôtel*) head porter.

conciergerie [kɔ̃sjɛrʒəri] *nf* caretaker's lodge.

concile [kɔ̃sil] *nm* council, synod.

conciliable [kɔ̃siljabl(ə)] *a* (*opinions etc*) reconcilable.

conciliabules [kɔ̃siljabyl] *nmpl* (*private*) discussions, confabulations (*Brit*).

conciliant, e [kɔ̃siljɑ̃, -ɑ̃t] *a* conciliatory.

conciliateur, trice [kɔ̃siljatœr, -tris] *nm/f* mediator, go-between.

conciliation [kɔ̃siljɑsjɔ̃] *nf* conciliation.

concilier [kɔ̃silje] *vt* to reconcile; **se** ~ **qn/l'appui de qn** to win sb over/sb's support.

concis, e [kɔ̃si, -iz] *a* concise.

concision [kɔ̃sizjɔ̃] *nf* concision, conciseness.

concitoyen, ne [kɔ̃sitwajɛ̃, -ɛn] *nm/f* fellow citizen.

conclave [kɔ̃klav] *nm* conclave.

concluant, e [kɔ̃klyɑ̃, -ɑ̃t] *vb voir* **conclure** ♦ *a* conclusive.

conclure [kɔ̃klyʀ] *vt* to conclude; (*signer: accord, pacte*) to enter into; (*déduire*): ~ **qch de qch** to deduce sth from sth; ~ **à l'acquittement** to decide in favour of an acquittal; ~ **au suicide** to come to the conclusion (*ou* (*JUR*) to pronounce) that it is a case of suicide; ~ **un marché** to clinch a deal; **j'en conclus que** from that I conclude that.

conclusion [kɔ̃klyzjɔ̃] *nf* conclusion; ~**s** *nfpl* (*JUR*) submissions; findings; **en** ~ in conclusion.

concocter [kɔ̃kɔkte] *vt* to concoct.

conçois [kɔ̃swa], **conçoive** [kɔ̃swav] *etc vb voir* **concevoir**.

concombre [kɔ̃kɔ̃bʀ(ə)] *nm* cucumber.

concomitant, e [kɔ̃kɔmitɑ̃, -ɑ̃t] *a* concomitant.

concordance [kɔ̃kɔʀdɑ̃s] *nf* concordance; **la** ~ **des temps** (*LING*) the sequence of tenses.

concordant, e [kɔ̃kɔʀdɑ̃, -ɑ̃t] *a* (*témoignages, versions*) corroborating.

concorde [kɔ̃kɔʀd(ə)] *nf* concord.

concorder [kɔ̃kɔʀde] *vi* to tally, agree.

concourir [kɔ̃kuʀiʀ] *vi* (*SPORT*) to compete; ~ **à** *vt* (*effet etc*) to work towards.

concours [kɔ̃kuʀ] *vb voir* **concourir** ♦ *nm* competition; (*SCOL*) competitive examination; (*assistance*) aid, help; **recrutement par voie de** ~ recruitment by (competitive) examination; **apporter son** ~ **à** to give one's support to; ~ **de circonstances** combination of circumstances; ~ **hippique** horse show; *voir* **hors.**

concret, ète [kɔ̃kʀɛ, -ɛt] *a* concrete.

concrètement [kɔ̃kʀɛtmɑ̃] *ad* in concrete terms.

concrétiser [kɔ̃kʀetize] *vt* to realize; **se** ~ *vi* to materialize.

conçu, e [kɔ̃sy] *pp de* **concevoir.**

concubin, e [kɔ̃kybɛ̃, -in] *nm/f* (*JUR*) cohabitant.

concubinage [kɔ̃kybinaʒ] *nm* (*JUR*) cohabitation.

concupiscence [kɔ̃kypisɑ̃s] *nf* concupiscence.

concurremment [kɔ̃kyʀamɑ̃] *ad* concurrently; jointly.

concurrence [kɔ̃kyʀɑ̃s] *nf* competition; **jusqu'à** ~ **de** up to; ~ **déloyale** unfair competition.

concurrent, e [kɔ̃kyʀɑ̃, -ɑ̃t] *a* competing ♦ *nm/f* (*SPORT, ÉCON etc*) competitor; (*SCOL*) candidate.

conçus [kɔ̃sy] *vb voir* **concevoir.**

condamnable [kɔ̃danabl(ə)] *a* (*action, opinion*) reprehensible.

condamnation [kɔ̃danasjɔ̃] *nf* (*action*) condemnation; sentencing; (*peine*) sentence; conviction; ~ **à mort** death sentence.

condamné, e [kɔ̃dane] *nm/f* (*JUR*) convict.

condamner [kɔ̃dane] *vt* (*blâmer*) to condemn; (*JUR*) to sentence; (*porte, ouverture*) to fill in, block up; (*malade*) to give up (hope for); (*obliger*): ~ **qn à qch/faire** to condemn sb to sth/to do; ~ **qn à 2 ans de prison** to sentence sb to 2 years' imprisonment; ~ **qn à une amende** to impose a fine on sb.

condensateur [kɔ̃dɑ̃satœʀ] *nm* condenser.

condensation [kɔ̃dɑ̃sasjɔ̃] *nf* condensation.

condensé [kɔ̃dɑ̃se] *nm* digest.

condenser [kɔ̃dɑ̃se] *vt*, **se** ~ *vi* to condense.

condescendant, e [kɔ̃desɑ̃dɑ̃, -ɑ̃t] *a* (*personne, attitude*) condescending.

condescendre [kɔ̃desɑ̃dʀ(ə)] *vi*: ~ **à** to condescend to.

condiment [kɔ̃dimɑ̃] *nm* condiment.

condisciple [kɔ̃disipl(ə)] *nm/f* school fellow, fellow student.

condition [kɔ̃disjɔ̃] *nf* condition; ~**s** *nfpl* (*tarif, prix*) terms; (*circonstances*) conditions; **sans** ~ *a* unconditional ♦ *ad* unconditionally; **sous** ~ **que** on condition that; **à** ~ **de** *ou* **que** provided that; **en bonne** ~ in good condition; **mettre en** ~ (*SPORT etc*) to get fit; (*PSYCH*) to condition (mentally); ~**s de vie** living conditions.

conditionnel, le [kɔ̃disjɔnɛl] *a* conditional ♦ *nm* conditional (tense).

conditionnement [kɔ̃disjɔnmɑ̃] *nm* (*emballage*) packaging; (*fig*) conditioning.

conditionner [kɔ̃disjɔne] *vt* (*déterminer*) to determine; (*COMM: produit*) to package; (*fig: personne*) to condition; **air conditionné** air conditioning; **réflexe conditionné** conditioned reflex.

condoléances [kɔ̃dɔleɑ̃s] *nfpl* condolences.

conducteur, trice [kɔ̃dyktœʀ, -tʀis] *a* (*ÉLEC*) conducting ♦ *nm/f* (*AUTO etc*) driver; (*machine*) operator ♦ *nm* (*ÉLEC etc*) conductor.

conduire [kɔ̃dɥiʀ] *vt* (*véhicule, passager*) to drive; (*délégation, troupeau*) to lead; **se** ~ *vi* to behave; ~ **vers/à** to lead towards/to; ~ **qn quelque part** to take sb somewhere; to drive sb somewhere.

conduit, e [kɔ̃dɥi, -it] *pp de* **conduire** ♦ *nm* (*TECH*) conduit, pipe; (*ANAT*) duct, canal.

conduite [kɔ̃dɥit] *nf* (*en auto*) driving; (*comportement*) behaviour (*Brit*), behavior (*US*); (*d'eau, de gaz*) pipe; **sous la** ~ **de** led by; ~ **forcée** pressure pipe; ~ **à gauche** left-hand drive; ~ **intérieure** saloon (car).

cône [kon] *nm* cone; **en forme de** ~ cone-shaped.

conf. *abr* (= *confort*): **tt** ~ all mod cons.

confection [kɔ̃fɛksjɔ̃] *nf* (*fabrication*) making; (*COUTURE*): **la** ~ the clothing industry, the rag trade (*fam*); **vêtement de** ~ ready-to-wear *ou* off-the-peg garment.

confectionner [kɔ̃fɛksjɔne] *vt* to make.

confédération [kɔ̃federasjɔ̃] *nf* confederation.

conférence [kɔ̃feʀɑ̃s] *nf* (*exposé*) lecture; (*pourparlers*) conference; ~ **de presse** press conference; ~ **au sommet** summit (conference).

conférencier, ière [kɔ̃feʀɑ̃sje, -jɛʀ] *nm/f* lecturer.

conférer [kɔ̃feʀe] *vt*: ~ **à qn** (*titre, grade*) to confer on sb; ~ **à qch/qn** (*aspect etc*) to endow sth/sb with, give (to) sth/sb.

confesser [kɔ̃fese] *vt* to confess; **se** ~ *vi* (*REL*) to go to confession.

confesseur [kɔ̃fesœʀ] *nm* confessor.

confession [kɔ̃fesjɔ̃] *nf* confession; (*culte: catholique etc*) denomination.

confessionnal, aux [kɔ̃fesjɔnal, -o] *nm* confessional.

confessionnel, le [kɔ̃fesjɔnɛl] *a* denominational.

confetti [kɔ̃feti] *nm* confetti *q*.

confiance [kɔ̃fjɑ̃s] *nf* confidence, trust; faith; **avoir ~ en** to have confidence *ou* faith in, trust; **faire ~ à** to trust; **en toute ~** with complete confidence; **de ~** trustworthy, reliable; **mettre qn en ~** to win sb's trust; **vote de ~** (*POL*) vote of confidence; **inspirer ~ à** to inspire confidence in; **~ en soi** self-confidence; *voir* **question**.

confiant, e [kɔ̃fjɑ̃, -ɑ̃t] *a* confident; trusting.

confidence [kɔ̃fidɑ̃s] *nf* confidence.

confident, e [kɔ̃fidɑ̃, -ɑ̃t] *nm/f* confidant/confidante.

confidentiel, le [kɔ̃fidɑ̃sjɛl] *a* confidential.

confier [kɔ̃fje] *vt*: **~ à qn** (*objet en dépôt, travail etc*) to entrust to sb; (*secret, pensée*) to confide to sb; **se ~ à qn** to confide in sb.

configuration [kɔ̃figyʀɑsjɔ̃] *nf* configuration, layout; (*INFORM*) configuration.

confiné, e [kɔ̃fine] *a* enclosed; (*air*) stale.

confiner [kɔ̃fine] *vt*: **~ à** to confine to; (*toucher*) to border on; **se ~ dans** *ou* **à** to confine o.s. to.

confins [kɔ̃fɛ̃] *nmpl*: **aux ~ de** on the borders of.

confirmation [kɔ̃fiʀmɑsjɔ̃] *nf* confirmation.

confirmer [kɔ̃fiʀme] *vt* to confirm; **~ qn dans une croyance/ses fonctions** to strengthen sb in a belief/his duties.

confiscation [kɔ̃fiskɑsjɔ̃] *nf* confiscation.

confiserie [kɔ̃fizʀi] *nf* (*magasin*) confectioner's *ou* sweet shop (*Brit*), candy store (*US*); **~s** *nfpl* (*bonbons*) confectionery *sg*, sweets, candy *q*.

confiseur, euse [kɔ̃fizœʀ, -øz] *nm/f* confectioner.

confisquer [kɔ̃fiske] *vt* to confiscate.

confit, e [kɔ̃fi, -it] *a*: **fruits ~s** crystallized fruits ♦ *nm*: **~ d'oie** potted goose.

confiture [kɔ̃fityʀ] *nf* jam; **~ d'oranges** (orange) marmalade.

conflagration [kɔ̃flagʀɑsjɔ̃] *nf* cataclysm.

conflictuel, le [kɔ̃fliktɥɛl] *a* full of clashes *ou* conflicts.

conflit [kɔ̃fli] *nm* conflict.

confluent [kɔ̃flyɑ̃] *nm* confluence.

confondre [kɔ̃fɔ̃dʀ(ə)] *vt* (*jumeaux, faits*) to confuse, mix up; (*témoin, menteur*) to confound; **se ~** *vi* to merge; **se ~ en excuses** to offer profuse apologies, apologize profusely; **~ qch/qn avec qch/qn d'autre** to mistake sth/sb for sth/sb else.

confondu, e [kɔ̃fɔ̃dy] *pp de* **confondre** ♦ *a* (*stupéfait*) speechless, overcome; **toutes catégories ~es** taking all categories together.

conformation [kɔ̃fɔʀmɑsjɔ̃] *nf* conformation.

conforme [kɔ̃fɔʀm(ə)] *a*: **~ à** (*en accord avec*) in accordance with, in keeping with; (*identique à*) true to; **copie certifiée ~** (*ADMIN*) certified copy; **~ à la commande** as per order.

conformé, e [kɔ̃fɔʀme] *a*: **bien ~** well-formed.

conformément [kɔ̃fɔʀmemɑ̃] *ad*: **~ à** in accordance with.

conformer [kɔ̃fɔʀme] *vt*: **~ qch à** to model sth on; **se ~ à** to conform to.

conformisme [kɔ̃fɔʀmism(ə)] *nm* conformity.

conformiste [kɔ̃fɔʀmist(ə)] *a*, *nm/f* conformist.

conformité [kɔ̃fɔʀmite] *nf* conformity; agreement; **en ~ avec** in accordance with.

confort [kɔ̃fɔʀ] *nm* comfort; **tout ~** (*COMM*) with all mod cons (*Brit*) *ou* modern conveniences.

confortable [kɔ̃fɔʀtabl(ə)] *a* comfortable.

confortablement [kɔ̃fɔʀtabləmɑ̃] *ad* comfortably.

conforter [kɔ̃fɔʀte] *vt* to reinforce, strengthen.

confrère [kɔ̃fʀɛʀ] *nm* colleague; fellow member.

confrérie [kɔ̃fʀeʀi] *nf* brotherhood.

confrontation [kɔ̃fʀɔ̃tɑsjɔ̃] *nf* confrontation.

confronté, e [kɔ̃fʀɔ̃te] *a*: **~ à** confronted by, facing.

confronter [kɔ̃fʀɔ̃te] *vt* to confront; (*textes*) to compare, collate.

confus, e [kɔ̃fy, -yz] *a* (*vague*) confused; (*embarrassé*) embarrassed.

confusément [kɔ̃fyzemɑ̃] *ad* (*distinguer, ressentir*) vaguely; (*parler*) confusedly.

confusion [kɔ̃fyzjɔ̃] *nf* (*voir confus*) confusion; embarrassment; (*voir confondre*) confusion; mixing up; (*erreur*) confusion; **~ des peines** (*JUR*) concurrency of sentences.

congé [kɔ̃ʒe] *nm* (*vacances*) holiday; (*arrêt de travail*) time off *q*; leave *q*; (*MIL*) leave *q*; (*avis de départ*) notice; **en ~** on holiday; off (work); on leave; **semaine/jour de ~** week/day off; **prendre ~ de qn** to take one's leave of sb; **donner son ~ à** to hand *ou* give in one's notice to; **~ de maladie** sick leave; **~ de maternité** maternity leave; **~s payés** paid holiday *ou* leave.

congédier [kɔ̃ʒedje] *vt* to dismiss.

congélateur [kɔ̃ʒelatœʀ] *nm* freezer, deep freeze.

congeler [kɔ̃ʒle] *vt*, **se ~** *vi* to freeze.

congénère [kɔ̃ʒenɛʀ] *nm/f* fellow (bear *ou* lion *etc*), fellow creature.

congénital, e, aux [kɔ̃ʒenital, -o] *a* congenital.

congère [kɔ̃ʒɛʀ] *nf* snowdrift.

congestion [kɔ̃ʒɛstjɔ̃] *nf* congestion; **~ cérébrale** stroke; **~ pulmonaire** congestion of the lungs.

congestionner [kɔ̃ʒɛstjɔne] *vt* to congest; (*MÉD*) to flush.

conglomérat [kɔ̃ɡlɔmeʀa] *nm* conglomerate.

Congo [kɔ̃ɡo] *nm*: **le ~** (*pays, fleuve*) the Congo.

congolais, e [kɔ̃ɡɔlɛ, -ɛz] *a* Congolese ♦ *nm/f*: **C~, e** Congolese.

congratuler [kɔ̃ɡʀatyle] *vt* to congratulate.

congre [kɔ̃ɡʀ(ə)] *nm* conger (eel).

congrégation [kɔ̃ɡʀeɡɑsjɔ̃] *nf* (*REL*) congregation; (*gén*) assembly; gathering.

congrès [kɔ̃ɡʀɛ] *nm* congress.

congressiste [kɔ̃ɡʀɛsist(ə)] *nm/f* delegate, participant (at a congress).

congru, e [kɔ̃ɡʀy] *a*: **la portion ~e** the smallest *ou* meanest share.

conifère [kɔnifɛʀ] *nm* conifer.

conique [kɔnik] *a* conical.

conjecture [kɔ̃ʒɛktyʀ] *nf* conjecture, speculation *q*.

conjecturer [kɔ̃ʒɛktyʀe] *vt*, *vi* to conjecture.

conjoint, e [kɔ̃ʒwɛ̃, -wɛ̃t] *a* joint ♦ *nm/f* spouse.

conjointement [kɔ̃ʒwɛ̃tmɑ̃] *ad* jointly.

conjonctif, ive [kɔ̃ʒɔ̃ktif, -iv] *a*: **tissu ~** connective tissue.

conjonction [kɔ̃ʒɔ̃ksjɔ̃] *nf* (*LING*) conjunction.

conjonctivite [kɔ̃ʒɔ̃ktivit] *nf* conjunctivitis.

conjoncture [kɔ̃ʒɔ̃ktyʀ] *nf* circumstances *pl*; **la ~ (économique)** the economic climate *ou* situation.

conjugaison [kɔ̃ʒygɛzɔ̃] *nf* (*LING*) conjugation.

conjugal, e, aux [kɔ̃ʒygal, -o] *a* conjugal; married.

conjuguer [kɔ̃ʒyge] *vt* (*LING*) to conjugate; (*efforts etc*) to combine.

conjuration [kɔ̃ʒyʀasjɔ̃] *nf* conspiracy.

conjuré, e [kɔ̃ʒyʀe] *nm/f* conspirator.

conjurer [kɔ̃ʒyʀe] *vt* (*sort, maladie*) to avert; (*implorer*): **~ qn de faire qch** to beseech *ou* entreat sb to do sth.

connais [kɔnɛ], **connaissais** [kɔnɛsɛ] *etc vb voir* **connaître**.

connaissance [kɔnɛsɑ̃s] *nf* (*savoir*) knowledge *q*; (*personne connue*) acquaintance; (*conscience, perception*) consciousness; **~s** *nfpl* knowledge *q*; **être sans ~** to be unconscious; **perdre/reprendre ~** to lose/regain consciousness; **à ma/sa ~** to (the best of) my/his knowledge; **faire ~ avec qn** *ou* **la ~ de qn** (*rencontrer*) to meet sb; (*apprendre à connaître*) to get to know sb; **avoir ~ de** to be aware of; **prendre ~ de** (*document etc*) to peruse; **en ~ de cause** with full knowledge of the facts; **de ~** (*personne, visage*) familiar.

connaissant [kɔnɛsɑ̃] *etc vb voir* **connaître**.

connaissement [kɔnɛsmɑ̃] *nm* bill of lading.

connaisseur, euse [kɔnɛsœʀ, -øz] *nm/f* connoisseur ♦ *a* expert.

connaître [kɔnɛtʀ(ə)] *vt* to know; (*éprouver*) to experience; (*avoir*) to have; to enjoy; **~ de nom/vue** to know by name/sight; **se ~** to know each other; (*soi-même*) to know o.s.; **ils se sont connus à Genève** they (first) met in Geneva; **s'y ~ en qch** to know about sth.

connecté, e [kɔnɛkte] *a* (*INFORM*) on line.

connecter [kɔnɛkte] *vt* to connect.

connerie [kɔnʀi] *nf* (*fam*) (bloody) stupid (*Brit*) *ou* damn-fool (*US*) thing to do *ou* say.

connexe [kɔnɛks(ə)] *a* closely related.

connexion [kɔnɛksjɔ̃] *nf* connection.

connivence [kɔnivɑ̃s] *nf* connivance.

connu, e [kɔny] *pp de* **connaître** ♦ *a* (*célèbre*) well-known.

conquérant, e [kɔ̃keʀɑ̃, -ɑ̃t] *nm/f* conqueror.

conquérir [kɔ̃keʀiʀ] *vt* to conquer, win.

conquerrai [kɔ̃keʀʀe] *etc vb voir* **conquérir**.

conquête [kɔ̃kɛt] *nf* conquest.

conquiers, conquiers [kɔ̃kjɛʀ] *etc vb voir* **conquérir**.

conquis, e [kɔ̃ki, -iz] *pp de* **conquérir**.

consacrer [kɔ̃sakʀe] *vt* (*REL*): **~ qch (à)** to consecrate sth (to); (*fig: usage etc*) to sanction, establish; (*employer*): **~ qch à** to devote *ou* dedicate sth to; **se ~ à qch/faire** to dedicate *ou* devote o.s. to sth/to doing.

consanguin, e [kɔ̃sɑ̃gɛ̃, -in] *a* between blood relations; **frère ~** half-brother (*on father's* side); **mariage ~** intermarriage.

consciemment [kɔ̃sjamɑ̃] *ad* consciously.

conscience [kɔ̃sjɑ̃s] *nf* conscience; (*perception*) consciousness; **avoir/prendre ~ de** to be/become aware of; **perdre/reprendre ~** to lose/regain consciousness; **avoir bonne/mauvaise ~** to have a clear/guilty conscience; **en (toute) ~** in all conscience; **~ professionnelle** professional conscience.

consciencieux, euse [kɔ̃sjɑ̃sjø, -øz] *a* conscientious.

conscient, e [kɔ̃sjɑ̃, -ɑ̃t] *a* conscious; **~ de** aware *ou* conscious of.

conscription [kɔ̃skʀipsjɔ̃] *nf* conscription.

conscrit [kɔ̃skʀi] *nm* conscript.

consécration [kɔ̃sekʀasjɔ̃] *nf* consecration.

consécutif, ive [kɔ̃sekytif, -iv] *a* consecutive; **~ à** following upon.

consécutivement [kɔ̃sekytivmɑ̃] *ad* consecutively; **~ à** following upon.

conseil [kɔ̃sɛj] *nm* (*avis*) piece of advice, advice *q*; (*assemblée*) council; (*expert*): **~ en recrutement** recruitment consultant ♦ *a*: **ingénieur-~** consulting engineer, engineering consultant; **tenir ~** to hold a meeting; to deliberate; **donner un ~** *ou* **des ~s à qn** to give sb (a piece of) advice; **demander ~ à qn** to ask sb's advice; **prendre ~ (auprès de qn)** to take advice (from sb); **~ d'administration (CA)** board (of directors); **~ de classe** (*SCOL*) meeting of teachers, parents and class representatives to discuss pupils' progress; **~ de discipline** disciplinary committee; **~ général** regional council; **~ de guerre** court-martial; **le ~ des ministres** ≈ the Cabinet; **~ municipal (CM)** town council; **~ régional** regional board of elected representatives; **~ de révision** recruitment *ou* draft (*US*) board.

conseiller [kɔ̃seje] *vt* (*personne*) to advise; (*méthode, action*) to recommend, advise; **~ qch à qn** to recommend sth to sb; **~ à qn de faire qch** to advise sb to do sth.

conseiller, ère [kɔ̃seje, -ɛʀ] *nm/f* adviser; **~ matrimonial** marriage guidance counsellor; **~ municipal** town councillor.

consentement [kɔ̃sɑ̃tmɑ̃] *nm* consent.

consentir [kɔ̃sɑ̃tiʀ] *vt*: **~ (à qch/faire)** to agree *ou* consent (to sth/to doing); **~ qch à qn** to grant sb sth.

conséquence [kɔ̃sekɑ̃s] *nf* consequence, outcome; **~s** *nfpl* consequences, repercussions; **en ~** (*donc*) consequently; (*de façon appropriée*) accordingly; **ne pas tirer à ~** to be unlikely to have any repercussions; **sans ~** unimportant; **de ~** important.

conséquent, e [kɔ̃sekɑ̃, -ɑ̃t] *a* logical, rational; (*fam: important*) substantial; **par ~** consequently.

conservateur, trice [kɔ̃sɛʀvatœʀ, -tʀis] *a* conservative ♦ *nm/f* (*POL*) conservative; (*de musée*) curator.

conservation [kɔ̃sɛʀvasjɔ̃] *nf* retention; keeping; preserving; preservation.

conservatoire [kɔ̃sɛʀvatwaʀ] *nm* academy; (*ÉCOLOGIE*) conservation area.

conserve [kɔ̃sɛʀv(ə)] *nf* (*gén pl*) canned *ou* tinned (*Brit*) food; **~s de poisson** canned *ou* tinned (*Brit*) fish; **en ~** canned, tinned

(*Brit*); **de** ~ (*ensemble*) in concert; (*naviguer*) in convoy.

conservé, e [kɔ̃sɛʀve] *a*: **bien** ~ (*personne*) well-preserved.

conserver [kɔ̃sɛʀve] *vt* (*faculté*) to retain, keep; (*habitude*) to keep up; (*amis*, *livres*) to keep; (*préserver*, *aussi CULIN*) to preserve; **se** ~ *vi* (*aliments*) to keep; "~ **au frais**" "store in a cool place".

conserverie [kɔ̃sɛʀvəʀi] *nf* canning factory.

considérable [kɔ̃sideʀabl(ə)] *a* considerable, significant, extensive.

considération [kɔ̃sideʀasjɔ̃] *nf* consideration; (*estime*) esteem, respect; **~s** *nfpl* (*remarques*) reflections; **prendre en** ~ to take into consideration *ou* account; **ceci mérite** ~ this is worth considering; **en** ~ **de** given, because of.

considéré, e [kɔ̃sideʀe] *a* respected; **tout bien** ~ all things considered.

considérer [kɔ̃sideʀe] *vt* to consider; (*regarder*) to consider, study; ~ **qch comme** to regard sth as.

consigne [kɔ̃siɲ] *nf* (*COMM*) deposit; (*de gare*) left luggage (office) (*Brit*), checkroom (*US*); (*punition*: *SCOL*) detention; (*: MIL*) confinement to barracks; (*ordre*, *instruction*) instructions *pl*; ~ **automatique** left-luggage locker; **~s de sécurité** safety instructions.

consigné, e [kɔ̃siɲe] *a* (*COMM*: *bouteille*, *emballage*) returnable; **non** ~ non-returnable.

consigner [kɔ̃siɲe] *vt* (*note*, *pensée*) to record; (*marchandises*) to deposit; (*punir*: *MIL*) to confine to barracks; (*: élève*) to put in detention; (*COMM*) to put a deposit on.

consistance [kɔ̃sistɑ̃s] *nf* consistency.

consistant, e [kɔ̃sistɑ̃, -ɑ̃t] *a* thick; solid.

consister [kɔ̃siste] *vi*: ~ **en/dans/à faire** to consist of/in/in doing.

consœur [kɔ̃sœʀ] *nf* (lady) colleague; fellow member.

consolation [kɔ̃sɔlasjɔ̃] *nf* consolation *q*, comfort *q*.

console [kɔ̃sɔl] *nf* console; ~ **graphique** *ou* **de visualisation** (*INFORM*) visual display unit, VDU.

consoler [kɔ̃sɔle] *vt* to console; **se** ~ (**de qch**) to console o.s. (for sth).

consolider [kɔ̃sɔlide] *vt* to strengthen, reinforce; (*fig*) to consolidate; **bilan consolidé** consolidated balance sheet.

consommateur, trice [kɔ̃sɔmatœʀ, -tʀis] *nm/f* (*ÉCON*) consumer; (*dans un café*) customer.

consommation [kɔ̃sɔmasjɔ̃] *nf* consumption; (*JUR*) consummation; (*boisson*) drink; ~ **aux 100 km** (*AUTO*) (fuel) consumption per 100 km, ≈ miles per gallon (mpg), ≈ gas mileage (*US*); **de** ~ (*biens*, *société*) consumer *cpd*.

consommé, e [kɔ̃sɔme] *a* consummate ♦ *nm* consommé.

consommer [kɔ̃sɔme] *vt* (*suj: personne*) to eat *ou* drink, consume; (*suj: voiture*, *usine*, *poêle*) to use, consume; (*JUR*) to consummate ♦ *vi* (*dans un café*) to (have a) drink.

consonance [kɔ̃sɔnɑ̃s] *nf* consonance; **nom à** ~ **étrangère** foreign-sounding name.

consonne [kɔ̃sɔn] *nf* consonant.

consorts [kɔ̃sɔʀ] *nmpl*: **et** ~ (*péj*) and company, and his bunch *ou* like.

conspirateur, trice [kɔ̃spiʀatœʀ, -tʀis] *nm/f* conspirator, plotter.

conspiration [kɔ̃spiʀasjɔ̃] *nf* conspiracy.

conspirer [kɔ̃spiʀe] *vi* to conspire, plot; ~ **à** (*tendre à*) to conspire to.

conspuer [kɔ̃spɥe] *vt* to boo, shout down.

constamment [kɔ̃stamɑ̃] *ad* constantly.

constant, e [kɔ̃stɑ̃, -ɑ̃t] *a* constant; (*personne*) steadfast ♦ *nf* constant.

Constantinople [kɔ̃stɑ̃tinɔpl(ə)] *n* Constantinople.

constat [kɔ̃sta] *nm* (*d'huissier*) certified report (*by bailiff*); (*de police*) report; (*observation*) (observed) fact, observation; (*affirmation*) statement; ~ (**à l'amiable**) (*jointly agreed*) statement for insurance purposes.

constatation [kɔ̃statasjɔ̃] *nf* noticing; certifying; (*remarque*) observation.

constater [kɔ̃state] *vt* (*remarquer*) to note, notice; (*ADMIN*, *JUR*: *attester*) to certify; (*dégâts*) to note; ~ **que** (*dire*) to state that.

constellation [kɔ̃stelasjɔ̃] *nf* constellation.

constellé, e [kɔ̃stele] *a*: ~ **de** (*étoiles*) studded *ou* spangled with; (*taches*) spotted with.

consternation [kɔ̃stɛʀnasjɔ̃] *nf* consternation, dismay.

consterner [kɔ̃stɛʀne] *vt* to dismay.

constipation [kɔ̃stipasjɔ̃] *nf* constipation.

constipé, e [kɔ̃stipe] *a* constipated; (*fig*) stiff.

constituant, e [kɔ̃stitɥɑ̃, -ɑ̃t] *a* (*élément*) constituent; **assemblée ~e** (*POL*) constituent assembly.

constitué, e [kɔ̃stitɥe] *a*: ~ **de** made up *ou* composed of; **bien** ~ of sound constitution; well-formed.

constituer [kɔ̃stitɥe] *vt* (*comité*, *équipe*) to set up, form; (*dossier*, *collection*) to put together, build up; (*suj: éléments*, *parties*: *composer*) to make up, constitute; (*représenter*, *être*) to constitute; **se** ~ **prisonnier** to give o.s. up; **se** ~ **partie civile** to bring an independent action for damages.

constitution [kɔ̃stitysjɔ̃] *nf* setting up; building up; (*composition*) composition, make-up; (*santé*, *POL*) constitution.

constitutionnel, le [kɔ̃stitysjɔnɛl] *a* constitutional.

constructeur [kɔ̃stʀyktœʀ] *nm* manufacturer, builder.

constructif, ive [kɔ̃stʀyktif, -iv] *a* (*positif*) constructive.

construction [kɔ̃stʀyksjɔ̃] *nf* construction, building.

construire [kɔ̃stʀɥiʀ] *vt* to build, construct; **se** ~: **l'immeuble s'est construit très vite** the building went up *ou* was built very quickly.

consul [kɔ̃syl] *nm* consul.

consulaire [kɔ̃sylɛʀ] *a* consular.

consulat [kɔ̃syla] *nm* consulate.

consultatif, ive [kɔ̃syltatif, -iv] *a* advisory.

consultation [kɔ̃syltasjɔ̃] *nf* consultation; **~s** *nfpl* (*POL*) talks; **être en** ~ (*délibération*) to be in consultation; (*médecin*) to be consulting; **aller à la** ~ (*MÉD*) to go to the surgery (*Brit*) *ou* doctor's office (*US*); **heures de** ~ (*MÉD*) surgery (*Brit*) *ou* office (*US*) hours.

consulter [kɔ̃sylte] *vt* to consult ♦ *vi* (*médecin*) to hold surgery (*Brit*), be in (the office) (*US*); **se ~** to confer.

consumer [kɔ̃syme] *vt* to consume; **se ~** *vi* to burn; **se ~ de chagrin/douleur** to be consumed with sorrow/grief.

consumérisme [kɔ̃symeRism(ə)] *nm* consumerism.

contact [kɔ̃takt] *nm* contact; **au ~ de** (*air, peau*) on contact with; (*gens*) through contact with; **mettre/couper le ~** (*AUTO*) to switch on/off the ignition; **entrer en ~** (*fils, objets*) to come into contact, make contact; **se mettre en ~ avec** (*RADIO*) to make contact with; **prendre ~ avec** (*relation d'affaires, connaissance*) to get in touch *ou* contact with.

contacter [kɔ̃takte] *vt* to contact, get in touch with.

contagieux, euse [kɔ̃taʒjø, -øz] *a* contagious; infectious.

contagion [kɔ̃taʒjɔ̃] *nf* contagion.

container [kɔ̃tenɛR] *nm* container.

contaminer [kɔ̃tamine] *vt* to contaminate.

conte [kɔ̃t] *nm* tale; **~ de fées** fairy tale.

contemplation [kɔ̃tɑ̃plɑsjɔ̃] *nf* contemplation; (*REL, PHILOSOPHIE*) meditation.

contempler [kɔ̃tɑ̃ple] *vt* to contemplate, gaze at.

contemporain, e [kɔ̃tɑ̃pɔRɛ̃, -ɛn] *a, nm/f* contemporary.

contenance [kɔ̃tnɑ̃s] *nf* (*d'un récipient*) capacity; (*attitude*) bearing, attitude; **perdre ~** to lose one's composure; **se donner une ~** to give the impression of composure; **faire bonne ~ (devant)** to put on a bold front (in the face of).

conteneur [kɔ̃tnœR] *nm* container.

conteneurisation [kɔ̃tnœRizɑsjɔ̃] *nf* containerization.

contenir [kɔ̃niR] *vt* to contain; (*avoir une capacité de*) to hold; **se ~** (*se retenir*) to control o.s. *ou* one's emotions, contain o.s.

content, e [kɔ̃tɑ̃, -ɑ̃t] *a* pleased, glad; **~ de** pleased with; **je serais ~ que tu ...** I would be pleased if you ....

contentement [kɔ̃tɑ̃tmɑ̃] *nm* contentment, satisfaction.

contenter [kɔ̃tɑ̃te] *vt* to satisfy, please; (*envie*) to satisfy; **se ~ de** to content o.s. with.

contentieux [kɔ̃tɑ̃sjø] *nm* (*COMM*) litigation; (*: service*) litigation department; (*POL etc*) contentious issues *pl*.

contenu, e [kɔ̃tny] *pp de* **contenir** ♦ *nm* (*d'un bol*) contents *pl*; (*d'un texte*) content.

conter [kɔ̃te] *vt* to recount, relate; **en ~ de belles à qn** to tell tall stories to sb.

contestable [kɔ̃tɛstabl(ə)] *a* questionable.

contestataire [kɔ̃tɛstatɛR] *a* (*journal, étudiant*) anti-establishment ♦ *nm/f* (anti-establishment) protester.

contestation [kɔ̃tɛstɑsjɔ̃] *nf* questioning, contesting; (*POL*): **la ~** anti-establishment activity, protest.

conteste [kɔ̃tɛst(ə)]: **sans ~** *ad* unquestionably, indisputably.

contesté, e [kɔ̃tɛste] *a* (*roman, écrivain*) controversial.

contester [kɔ̃tɛste] *vt* to question, contest ♦ *vi*

(*POL, gén*) to protest, rebel (against established authority).

conteur, euse [kɔ̃tœR, -øz] *nm/f* story-teller.

contexte [kɔ̃tɛkst(ə)] *nm* context.

contiendrai [kɔ̃tjɛ̃dRe], **contiens** [kɔ̃tjɛ̃] *etc vb voir* **contenir**.

contigu, ë [kɔ̃tigy] *a*: **~ (à)** adjacent (to).

continent [kɔ̃tinɑ̃] *nm* continent.

continental, e, aux [kɔ̃tinɑtal, -o] *a* continental.

contingences [kɔ̃tɛ̃ʒɑ̃s] *nfpl* contingencies.

contingent [kɔ̃tɛ̃ʒɑ̃] *nm* (*MIL*) contingent; (*COMM*) quota.

contingenter [kɔ̃tɛ̃ʒɑ̃te] *vt* (*COMM*) to fix a quota on.

contins [kɔ̃tɛ̃] *etc vb voir* **contenir**.

continu, e [kɔ̃tiny] *a* continuous; **(courant) ~** direct current, DC.

continuation [kɔ̃tinɥɑsjɔ̃] *nf* continuation.

continuel, le [kɔ̃tinɥɛl] *a* (*qui se répète*) constant, continual; (*continu*) continuous.

continuellement [kɔ̃tinɥɛlmɑ̃] *ad* continually; continuously.

continuer [kɔ̃tinɥe] *vt* (*travail, voyage etc*) to continue (with), carry on (with), go on (with); (*prolonger: alignement, rue*) to continue ♦ *vi* (*pluie, vie, bruit*) to continue, go on; (*voyageur*) to go on; **se ~** *vi* to carry on; **~ à** *ou* **de faire** to go on *ou* continue doing.

continuité [kɔ̃tinɥite] *nf* continuity; continuation.

contondant, e [kɔ̃tɔ̃dɑ̃, -ɑ̃t] *a*: **arme ~e** blunt instrument.

contorsion [kɔ̃tɔRsjɔ̃] *nf* contortion.

contorsionner [kɔ̃tɔRsjɔne]: **se ~** *vi* to contort o.s., writhe about.

contour [kɔ̃tuR] *nm* outline, contour; **~s** *nmpl* (*d'une rivière etc*) windings.

contourner [kɔ̃tuRne] *vt* to bypass, walk (*ou* drive) round.

contraceptif, ive [kɔ̃tRasɛptif, -iv] *a, nm* contraceptive.

contraception [kɔ̃tRasɛpsjɔ̃] *nf* contraception.

contracté, e [kɔ̃tRakte] *a* (*muscle*) tense, contracted; (*personne: tendu*) tense, tensed up; **article ~** (*LING*) contracted article.

contracter [kɔ̃tRakte] *vt* (*muscle etc*) to tense, contract; (*maladie, dette, obligation*) to contract; (*assurance*) to take out; **se ~** *vi* (*métal, muscles*) to contract.

contraction [kɔ̃tRaksjɔ̃] *nf* contraction.

contractuel, le [kɔ̃tRaktɥɛl] *a* contractual ♦ *nm/f* (*agent*) traffic warden; (*employé*) contract employee.

contradiction [kɔ̃tRadiksjɔ̃] *nf* contradiction.

contradictoire [kɔ̃tRadiktwaR] *a* contradictory, conflicting; **débat ~** (open) debate.

contraignant, e [kɔ̃tRɛɲɑ̃, -ɑ̃t] *vb voir* **contraindre** ♦ *a* restricting.

contraindre [kɔ̃tRɛ̃dR(ə)] *vt*: **~ qn à faire** to force *ou* compel sb to do.

contraint, e [kɔ̃tRɛ̃, -ɛ̃t] *pp de* **contraindre** ♦ *a* (*mine, air*) constrained, forced ♦ *nf* constraint; **sans ~e** unrestrainedly, unconstrainedly.

contraire [kɔ̃tRɛR] *a, nm* opposite; **~ à** contrary to; **au ~** *ad* on the contrary.

contrairement [kɔ̃tRɛRmɑ̃] *ad*: **~ à** contrary to, unlike.

contralto [kɔ̃tralto] *nm* contralto.
contrariant, e [kɔ̃tRaRjɑ̃, -ɑ̃t] *a (personne)* contrary, perverse; *(incident)* annoying.
contrarier [kɔ̃tRaRje] *vt (personne)* to annoy, bother; *(fig)* to impede; to thwart, frustrate.
contrariété [kɔ̃tRaRjete] *nf* annoyance.
contraste [kɔ̃tRast(ə)] *nm* contrast.
contraster [kɔ̃tRaste] *vt, vi* to contrast.
contrat [kɔ̃tRa] *nm* contract; *(fig: accord, pacte)* agreement; ~ **de travail** employment contract.
contravention [kɔ̃tRavɑ̃sjɔ̃] *nf (infraction)*: ~ **à** contravention of; *(amende)* fine; *(PV pour stationnement interdit)* parking ticket; **dresser** ~ **à** *(automobiliste)* to book; to write out a parking ticket for.
contre [kɔ̃tR(ə)] *prép* against; *(en échange)* (in exchange) for; **par** ~ on the other hand.
contre-amiral, aux [kɔ̃tRamiRal, -o] *nm* rear admiral.
contre-attaque [kɔ̃tRatak] *nf* counter-attack.
contre-attaquer [kɔ̃tRatake] *vi* to counter-attack.
contre-balancer [kɔ̃tRəbalɑ̃se] *vt* to counterbalance; *(fig)* to offset.
contrebande [kɔ̃tRəbɑ̃d] *nf (trafic)* contraband, smuggling; *(marchandise)* contraband, smuggled goods *pl*; **faire la** ~ **de** to smuggle.
contrebandier, ière [kɔ̃tRəbɑ̃dje, -jɛR] *nm/f* smuggler.
contrebas [kɔ̃tRəba]: **en** ~ *ad* (down) below.
contrebasse [kɔ̃tRəbas] *nf* (double) bass.
contrebassiste [kɔ̃tRəbasist(ə)] *nm/f* (double) bass player.
contre-braquer [kɔ̃tRəbRake] *vi* to steer into a skid.
contrecarrer [kɔ̃tRəkaRe] *vt* to thwart.
contrechamp [kɔ̃tRəʃɑ̃] *nm (CINÉMA)* reverse shot.
contrecœur [kɔ̃tRəkœR]: **à** ~ *ad* (be)grudgingly, reluctantly.
contrecoup [kɔ̃tRəku] *nm* repercussions *pl*; **par** ~ as an indirect consequence.
contre-courant [kɔ̃tRəkuRɑ̃]: **à** ~ *ad* against the current.
contredire [kɔ̃tRədiR] *vt (personne)* to contradict; *(témoignage, assertion, faits)* to refute; **se** ~ to contradict o.s.
contredit, e [kɔ̃tRədi, -it] *pp de* **contredire** ♦ *nm*: **sans** ~ without question.
contrée [kɔ̃tRe] *nf* region; land.
contre-écrou [kɔ̃tRekRu] *nm* lock nut.
contre-espionnage [kɔ̃tRɛspjɔnaʒ] *nm* counter-espionage.
contre-expertise [kɔ̃tRɛkspɛRtiz] *nf* second (expert) assessment.
contrefaçon [kɔ̃tRəfasɔ̃] *nf* forgery; ~ **de brevet** patent infringement.
contrefaire [kɔ̃tRəfɛR] *vt (document, signature)* to forge, counterfeit; *(personne, démarche)* to mimic; *(dénaturer: sa voix etc)* to disguise.
contrefait, e [kɔ̃tRəfɛ, -ɛt] *pp de* **contrefaire** ♦ *a* misshapen, deformed.
contrefasse [kɔ̃tRəfas], **contreferai** [kɔ̃tRəfRe] *etc vb voir* **contrefaire**.
contre-filet [kɔ̃tRəfilɛ] *nm (CULIN)* sirloin.
contreforts [kɔ̃tRəfɔR] *nmpl* foothills.
contre-haut [kɔ̃tRəo]: **en** ~ *ad* (up) above.

contre-indication [kɔ̃tRɛ̃dikasjɔ̃] *nf* contra-indication.
contre-interrogatoire [kɔ̃tRɛ̃teRɔgatwaR] *nm*: **faire subir un** ~ **à qn** to cross-examine sb.
contre-jour [kɔ̃tRəʒuR]: **à** ~ *ad* against the light.
contremaître [kɔ̃tRəmɛtR(ə)] *nm* foreman.
contre-manifestation [kɔ̃tRəmanifɛstasjɔ̃] *nf* counter-demonstration.
contremarque [kɔ̃tRəmaRk(ə)] *nf (ticket)* pass-out ticket.
contre-offensive [kɔ̃tRɔfɑ̃siv] *nf* counter-offensive.
contre-ordre [kɔ̃tRɔRdR(ə)] *nm* = **contrordre**.
contrepartie [kɔ̃tRəpaRti] *nf* compensation; **en** ~ in compensation; in return.
contre-performance [kɔ̃tRəpɛRfɔRmɑ̃s] *nf* below-average performance.
contrepèterie [kɔ̃tRəpetRi] *nf* spoonerism.
contre-pied [kɔ̃tRəpje] *nm (inverse, opposé)*: **le** ~ **de ...** the exact opposite of ...; **prendre le** ~ **de** to take the opposing view of; to take the opposite course to; **prendre qn à** ~ *(SPORT)* to wrong-foot sb.
contre-plaqué [kɔ̃tRəplake] *nm* plywood.
contre-plongée [kɔ̃tRəplɔ̃ʒe] *nf* low-angle shot.
contrepoids [kɔ̃tRəpwa] *nm* counterweight, counterbalance; **faire** ~ to act as a counterbalance.
contrepoil [kɔ̃tRəpwal]: **à** ~ *ad* the wrong way.
contrepoint [kɔ̃tRəpwɛ̃] *nm* counterpoint.
contrepoison [kɔ̃tRəpwazɔ̃] *nm* antidote.
contrer [kɔ̃tRe] *vt* to counter.
contre-révolution [kɔ̃tRəRevɔlysjɔ̃] *nf* counter-revolution.
contresens [kɔ̃tRəsɑ̃s] *nm* misinterpretation; *(mauvaise traduction)* mistranslation; *(absurdité)* nonsense *q*; **à** ~ *ad* the wrong way.
contresigner [kɔ̃tRəsiɲe] *vt* to countersign.
contretemps [kɔ̃tRətɑ̃] *nm* hitch, contretemps; **à** ~ *ad (MUS)* out of time; *(fig)* at an inopportune moment.
contre-terrorisme [kɔ̃tRəteRɔRism(ə)] *nm* counter-terrorism.
contre-torpilleur [kɔ̃tRətɔRpijœR] *nm* destroyer.
contrevenant, e [kɔ̃tRəvnɑ̃, -ɑ̃t] *vb voir* **contrevenir** ♦ *nm/f* offender.
contrevenir [kɔ̃tRəvniR]: ~ **à** *vt* to contravene.
contrevoie [kɔ̃tRəvwa]: **à** ~ *ad (en sens inverse)* on the wrong track; *(du mauvais côté)* on the wrong side.
contribuable [kɔ̃tRibɥabl(ə)] *nm/f* taxpayer.
contribuer [kɔ̃tRibɥe]: ~ **à** *vt* to contribute towards.
contribution [kɔ̃tRibysjɔ̃] *nf* contribution; **les** ~**s** *(bureaux)* the tax office; **mettre à** ~ to call upon; ~**s directes/indirectes** direct/indirect taxation.
contrit, e [kɔ̃tRi, -it] *a* contrite.
contrôle [kɔ̃tRol] *nm* checking *q*, check; supervision; monitoring; *(test)* test, examination; **perdre le** ~ **de son véhicule** to lose control of one's vehicle; ~ **des changes** *(COMM)* exchange controls; ~ **continu**

(SCOL) continuous assessment; ~ **d'identité** identity check; ~ **des naissances** birth control; ~ **des prix** price control.

contrôler [kɔ̃tʀole] vt (vérifier) to check; (surveiller) to supervise; to monitor, control; (maîtriser, COMM: firme) to control; **se** ~ to control o.s.

contrôleur, euse [kɔ̃tʀolœʀ, -øz] nm/f (de train) (ticket) inspector; (de bus) (bus) conductor/tress; ~ **de la navigation aérienne** air traffic controller; ~ **financier** financial controller.

contrordre [kɔ̃tʀɔʀdʀ(ə)] nm counter-order, countermand; **sauf** ~ unless otherwise directed.

controverse [kɔ̃tʀɔvɛʀs(ə)] nf controversy.

controversé, e [kɔ̃tʀɔvɛʀse] a (personnage, question) controversial.

contumace [kɔ̃tymas]: **par** ~ ad in absentia.

contusion [kɔ̃tyzjɔ̃] nf bruise, contusion.

contusionné, e [kɔ̃tyzjɔne] a bruised.

conurbation [kɔnyʀbasjɔ̃] nf conurbation.

convaincant, e [kɔ̃vɛ̃kɑ̃, -ɑ̃t] vb voir **convaincre** ♦ a convincing.

convaincre [kɔ̃vɛ̃kʀ(ə)] vt: ~ **qn (de qch)** to convince sb (of sth); ~ **qn (de faire)** to persuade sb (to do); ~ **qn de** (JUR: délit) to convict sb of.

convaincu, e [kɔ̃vɛ̃ky] pp de **convaincre** ♦ a: **d'un ton** ~ with conviction.

convainquais [kɔ̃vɛ̃kɛ] etc vb voir **convaincre**.

convalescence [kɔ̃valesɑ̃s] nf convalescence; **maison de** ~ convalescent home.

convalescent, e [kɔ̃valesɑ̃, -ɑ̃t] a, nm/f convalescent.

convenable [kɔ̃vnabl(ə)] a suitable; (décent) acceptable, proper; (assez bon) decent, acceptable; adequate, passable.

convenablement [kɔ̃vnabləmɑ̃] ad (placé, choisi) suitably; (s'habiller, s'exprimer) properly; (payé, logé) decently.

convenance [kɔ̃vnɑ̃s] nf: **à ma/votre** ~ to my/your liking; ~**s** nfpl proprieties.

convenir [kɔ̃vniʀ] vi to be suitable; ~ **à** to suit; **il convient de** it is advisable to; (bienséant) it is right ou proper to; ~ **de** (bien-fondé de qch) to admit (to), acknowledge; (date, somme etc) to agree upon; ~ **que** (admettre) to admit that, acknowledge the fact that; ~ **de faire qch** to agree to do sth; **il a été convenu que** it has been agreed that; **comme convenu** as agreed.

convention [kɔ̃vɑ̃sjɔ̃] nf convention; ~**s** nfpl (convenances) convention sg, social conventions; **de** ~ conventional; ~ **collective** (ÉCON) collective agreement.

conventionné, e [kɔ̃vɑ̃sjɔne] a (ADMIN) applying charges laid down by the state.

conventionnel, le [kɔ̃vɑ̃sjɔnɛl] a conventional.

conventuel, le [kɔ̃vɑ̃tɥɛl] a monastic; monastery cpd; conventual, convent cpd.

convenu, e [kɔ̃vny] pp de **convenir** ♦ a agreed.

convergent, e [kɔ̃vɛʀʒɑ̃, -ɑ̃t] a convergent.

converger [kɔ̃vɛʀʒe] vi to converge; ~ **vers** ou **sur** to converge on.

conversation [kɔ̃vɛʀsasjɔ̃] nf conversation; **avoir de la** ~ to be a good conversationalist.

converser [kɔ̃vɛʀse] vi to converse.

conversion [kɔ̃vɛʀsjɔ̃] nf conversion; (SKI) kick turn.

convertible [kɔ̃vɛʀtibl(ə)] a (ÉCON) convertible; **(canapé)** ~ sofa bed.

convertir [kɔ̃vɛʀtiʀ] vt: ~ **qn (à)** to convert sb (to); ~ **qch en** to convert sth into; **se** ~ **(à)** to be converted (to).

convertisseur [kɔ̃vɛʀtisœʀ] nm (ÉLEC) converter.

convexe [kɔ̃vɛks(ə)] a convex.

conviction [kɔ̃viksjɔ̃] nf conviction.

conviendrai [kɔ̃vjɛ̃dʀe], **conviens** [kɔ̃vjɛ̃] etc vb voir **convenir**.

convier [kɔ̃vje] vt: ~ **qn à** (dîner etc) to (cordially) invite sb to; ~ **qn à faire** to urge sb to do.

convint [kɔ̃vɛ̃] etc vb voir **convenir**.

convive [kɔ̃viv] nm/f guest (at table).

convivial, e [kɔ̃vivjal] a (INFORM) user-friendly.

convocation [kɔ̃vɔkasjɔ̃] nf (voir convoquer) convening, convoking; summoning; invitation; (document) notification to attend; summons sg.

convoi [kɔ̃vwa] nm (de voitures, prisonniers) convoy; (train) train; ~ **(funèbre)** funeral procession.

convoiter [kɔ̃vwate] vt to covet.

convoitise [kɔ̃vwatiz] nf covetousness; (sexuelle) lust, desire.

convoler [kɔ̃vɔle] vi: ~ **(en justes noces)** to be wed.

convoquer [kɔ̃vɔke] vt (assemblée) to convene, convoke; (subordonné, témoin) to summon; (candidat) to ask to attend; ~ **qn (à)** (réunion) to invite sb to (attend).

convoyer [kɔ̃vwaje] vt to escort.

convoyeur [kɔ̃vwajœʀ] nm (NAVIG) escort ship; ~ **de fonds** security guard.

convulsé, e [kɔ̃vylse] a (visage) distorted.

convulsions [kɔ̃vylsjɔ̃] nfpl convulsions.

coopérant [kɔɔpeʀɑ̃] nm ≈ person doing Voluntary Service Overseas (Brit), ≈ member of the Peace Corps (US).

coopératif, ive [kɔɔpeʀatif, -iv] a, nf cooperative.

coopération [kɔɔpeʀasjɔ̃] nf co-operation; (ADMIN): **la C**~ ≈ Voluntary Service Overseas (Brit), ≈ the Peace Corps (US), done as alternative to military service.

coopérer [kɔɔpeʀe] vi: ~ **(à)** to co-operate (in).

coordination [kɔɔʀdinasjɔ̃] nf coordination.

coordonné, e [kɔɔʀdɔne] a coordinated ♦ nf (LING) coordinate clause; ~**s** nmpl (vêtements) coordinates; ~**es** nfpl (MATH) coordinates; (détails personnels) address, phone number, schedule etc; whereabouts.

coordonner [kɔɔʀdɔne] vt to coordinate.

copain, copine [kɔpɛ̃, kɔpin] nm/f mate (Brit), pal ♦ a: **être** ~ **avec** to be pally with.

copeau, x [kɔpo] nm shaving; (de métal) turning.

Copenhague [kɔpənag] n Copenhagen.

copie [kɔpi] nf copy; (SCOL) script, paper; exercise; ~ **certifiée conforme** certified copy; ~ **papier** (*INFORM*) hard copy.

copier |kɔpje| *vt, vi* to copy; ~ **sur** to copy from.

copieur |kɔpjœʀ| *nm* (photo)copier.

copieusement |kɔpjøzmɑ̃| *ad* copiously.

copieux, euse |kɔpjø, -øz| *a* copious, hearty.

copilote |kɔpilɔt| *nm* (*AVIAT*) co-pilot; (*AUTO*) co-driver, navigator.

copine |kɔpin| *nf voir* **copain**.

copiste |kɔpist(ə)| *nm/f* copyist, transcriber.

coproduction |kɔpʀɔdyksjɔ̃| *nf* coproduction, joint production.

copropriété |kɔpʀɔpʀijete| *nf* co-ownership, joint ownership; **acheter en** ~ to buy on a co-ownership basis.

copulation |kɔpylasjɔ̃| *nf* copulation.

coq |kɔk| *nm* cock, rooster ♦ *a inv* (*BOXE*): **poids** ~ bantamweight; ~ **de bruyère** grouse; ~ **du village** (*fig: péj*) ladykiller.

coq-à-l'âne |kɔkalɑn| *nm inv* abrupt change of subject.

coque |kɔk| *nf* (*de noix, mollusque*) shell; (*de bateau*) hull; **à la** ~ (*CULIN*) (soft-)boiled.

coquelet |kɔklɛ| *nm* (*CULIN*) cockerel.

coquelicot |kɔkliko| *nm* poppy.

coqueluche |kɔklyʃ| *nf* whooping-cough; (*fig*): **être la** ~ **de qn** to be sb's flavour of the month.

coquet, te |kɔkɛ, -ɛt| *a* appearance-conscious; (*joli*) pretty.

coquetier |kɔktje| *nm* egg-cup.

coquettement |kɔkɛtmɑ̃| *ad* (*s'habiller*) attractively; (*meubler*) prettily.

coquetterie |kɔkɛtʀi| *nf* appearance-conciousness.

coquillage |kɔkijaʒ| *nm* (*mollusque*) shellfish *inv*; (*coquille*) shell.

coquille |kɔkij| *nf* shell; (*TYPO*) misprint; ~ **de beurre** shell of butter; ~ **d'œuf** *a* (*couleur*) eggshell; ~ **de noix** nutshell; ~ **St Jacques** scallop.

coquillettes |kɔkijɛt| *nfpl* pasta shells.

coquin, e |kɔkɛ̃, -in| *a* mischievous, roguish; (*polisson*) naughty ♦ *nm/f* (*péj*) rascal.

cor |kɔʀ| *nm* (*MUS*) horn; (*MÉD*): ~ (**au pied**) corn; **réclamer à** ~ **et à cri** to clamour for; ~ **anglais** cor anglais; ~ **de chasse** hunting horn.

corail, aux |kɔʀaj, -o| *nm* coral *q*.

Coran |kɔʀɑ̃| *nm*: **le** ~ the Koran.

coraux |kɔʀo| *pl de* **corail**.

corbeau, x |kɔʀbo| *nm* crow.

corbeille |kɔʀbɛj| *nf* basket; (*BOURSE*): **la** ~ ≈ the floor (of the Stock Exchange); ~ **de mariage** (*fig*) wedding presents *pl*; ~ **à ouvrage** work-basket; ~ **à pain** bread-basket; ~ **à papier** waste paper basket *ou* bin.

corbillard |kɔʀbijaʀ| *nm* hearse.

cordage |kɔʀdaʒ| *nm* rope; ~**s** *nmpl* (*de voilure*) rigging *sg*.

corde |kɔʀd(ə)| *nf* rope; (*de violon, raquette, d'arc*) string; (*trame*): **la** ~ the thread; (*ATHLÉTISME, AUTO*): **la** ~ **les rails** *pl*; **les** ~**s** (*BOXE*) the ropes; **les (instruments à)** ~**s** (*MUS*) the strings, the stringed instruments; **semelles de** ~ rope soles; **tenir la** ~ (*ATHLÉTISME, AUTO*) to be in the inside lane; **tomber des** ~**s** to rain cats and dogs; **tirer sur la** ~ to go too far; **la** ~ **sensible** the

right chord; **usé jusqu'à la** ~ threadbare; ~ **à linge** washing *ou* clothes line; ~ **lisse** (climbing) rope; ~ **à nœuds** knotted climbing rope; ~ **raide** tight-rope; ~ **à sauter** skipping rope; ~**s vocales** vocal cords.

cordeau, x |kɔʀdo| *nm* string, line; **tracé au** ~ as straight as a die.

cordée |kɔʀde| *nf* (*d'alpinistes*) rope, roped party.

cordelière |kɔʀdəljɛʀ| *nf* cord (belt).

cordial, e, aux |kɔʀdjal, -o| *a* warm, cordial ♦ *nm* cordial, pick-me-up.

cordialement |kɔʀdjalmɑ̃| *ad* cordially, heartily; (*formule épistolaire*) (kind) regards.

cordialité |kɔʀdjalite| *nf* warmth, cordiality.

cordillère |kɔʀdijɛʀ| *nf*: **la** ~ **des Andes** the Andes cordillera *ou* range.

cordon |kɔʀdɔ̃| *nm* cord, string; ~ **sanitaire/de police** sanitary/police cordon; ~ **littoral** sandbank, sandbar; ~ **ombilical** umbilical cord.

cordon-bleu |kɔʀdɔ̃blø| *a, nm/f* cordon bleu.

cordonnerie |kɔʀdɔnʀi| *nf* shoe repairer's *ou* mender's (shop).

cordonnier |kɔʀdɔnje| *nm* shoe repairer *ou* mender, cobbler.

cordouan, e |kɔʀduɑ̃, -an| *a* Cordovan.

Cordoue |kɔʀdu| *n* Cordoba.

Corée |kɔʀe| *nf*: **la** ~ Korea; **la** ~ **du Sud/du Nord** South/North Korea; **la République (démocratique populaire) de** ~ the (Democratic People's) Republic of Korea.

coréen, ne |kɔʀeɛ̃, -ɛn| *a* Korean ♦ *nm* (*LING*) Korean ♦ *nm/f*: **C~, ne** Korean.

coreligionnaire |kɔʀəliʒɔnɛʀ| *nm/f* fellow Christian/Muslim/Jew *etc*.

Corfou |kɔʀfu| *n* Corfu.

coriace |kɔʀjas| *a* tough.

Corinthe |kɔʀɛ̃t| *n* Corinth.

cormoran |kɔʀmɔʀɑ̃| *nm* cormorant.

cornac |kɔʀnak| *nm* elephant driver.

corne |kɔʀn(ə)| *nf* horn; (*de cerf*) antler; (*de la peau*) callus; ~ **d'abondance** horn of plenty; ~ **de brume** (*NAVIG*) foghorn.

cornée |kɔʀne| *nf* cornea.

corneille |kɔʀnɛj| *nf* crow.

cornélien, ne |kɔʀneljɛ̃, -ɛn| *a* (*débat etc*) where love and duty conflict.

cornemuse |kɔʀnəmyz| *nf* bagpipes *pl*; **joueur de** ~ piper.

corner *nm* |kɔʀnɛʀ| (*FOOTBALL*) corner (kick) ♦ *vb* |kɔʀne| *vt* (*pages*) to make dog-eared ♦ *vi* (*klaxonner*) to blare out.

cornet |kɔʀnɛ| *nm* (paper) cone; (*de glace*) cornet, cone; ~ **à pistons** cornet.

cornette |kɔʀnɛt| *nf* cornet (*headgear*).

corniaud |kɔʀnjo| *nm* (*chien*) mongrel; (*péj*) twit, clot.

corniche |kɔʀniʃ| *nf* (*de meuble, neigeuse*) cornice; (*route*) coast road.

cornichon |kɔʀniʃɔ̃| *nm* gherkin.

Cornouailles |kɔʀnwaj| *nf(pl)* Cornwall.

cornue |kɔʀny| *nf* retort.

corollaire |kɔʀɔlɛʀ| *nm* corollary.

corolle |kɔʀɔl| *nf* corolla.

coron |kɔʀɔ̃| *nm* mining cottage; mining village.

coronaire |kɔʀɔnɛʀ| *a* coronary.

corporation |kɔʀpɔʀasjɔ̃| *nf* corporate body;

(au moyen-âge) guild.

corporel, le [kɔʀpɔʀɛl] *a* bodily; *(punition)* corporal; **soins ~s** care *sg* of the body.

corps [kɔʀ] *nm (gén)* body; *(cadavre)* (dead) body; **à son ~ défendant** against one's will; **à ~ perdu** headlong; **perdu ~ et biens** lost with all hands; **prendre ~** to take shape; **faire ~ avec** to be joined to; to form one body with; **~ d'armée (CA)** army corps; **~ de ballet** corps de ballet; **~ constitués** *(POL)* constitutional bodies; **le ~ consulaire (CC)** the consular corps; **~ à ~** *ad* hand-to-hand ♦ *nm* clinch; **le ~ du délit** *(JUR)* corpus delicti; **le ~ diplomatique (CD)** the diplomatic corps; **le ~ électoral** the electorate; **le ~ enseignant** the teaching profession; **~ étranger** *(MÉD)* foreign body; **~ expéditionnaire** task force; **~ de garde** guardroom; **~ législatif** legislative body; **le ~ médical** the medical profession.

corpulence [kɔʀpylɑ̃s] *nf* build; *(embonpoint)* stoutness *(Brit)*, corpulence; **de forte ~** of large build.

corpulent, e [kɔʀpylɑ̃, -ɑ̃t] *a* stout *(Brit)*, corpulent.

correct, e [kɔʀɛkt] *a (exact)* accurate, correct; *(bienséant, honnête)* correct; *(passable)* adequate.

correctement [kɔʀɛktəmɑ̃] *ad* accurately; correctly; adequately.

correcteur, trice [kɔʀɛktœʀ, -tʀis] *nm/f (SCOL)* examiner, marker; *(TYPO)* proofreader.

correctif, ive [kɔʀɛktif, -iv] *a* corrective ♦ *nm (mise au point)* rider, qualification.

correction [kɔʀɛksjɔ̃] *nf (voir corriger)* correction; marking; *(voir correct)* correctness; *(rature, surcharge)* correction, emendation; *(coups)* thrashing; **~ sur écran** *(INFORM)* screen editing; **~ (des épreuves)** proofreading.

correctionnel, le [kɔʀɛksjɔnɛl] *a (JUR)*: **tribunal ~** ≈ criminal court.

corrélation [kɔʀelasjɔ̃] *nf* correlation.

correspondance [kɔʀɛspɔ̃dɑ̃s] *nf* correspondence; *(de train, d'avion)* connection; **ce train assure la ~ avec l'avion de 10 heures** this train connects with the 10 o'clock plane; **cours par ~** correspondence course; **vente par ~** mail-order business.

correspondancier, ière [kɔʀɛspɔ̃dɑ̃sje, -jɛʀ] *nm/f* correspondence clerk.

correspondant, e [kɔʀɛspɔ̃dɑ̃, -ɑ̃t] *nm/f* correspondent; *(TÉL)* person phoning *(ou* being phoned).

correspondre [kɔʀɛspɔ̃dʀ(ə)] *vi (données, témoignages)* to correspond; *(chambres)* to communicate; **~ à** to correspond to; **~ avec qn** to correspond with sb.

corrida [kɔʀida] *nf* bullfight.

corridor [kɔʀidɔʀ] *nm* corridor, passage.

corrigé [kɔʀiʒe] *nm (SCOL)* correct version; fair copy.

corriger [kɔʀiʒe] *vt (devoir)* to correct, mark; *(texte)* to correct, emend; *(erreur, défaut)* to correct, put right; *(punir)* to thrash; **~ qn de** *(défaut)* to cure sb of; **se ~ de** to cure o.s. of.

corroborer [kɔʀɔbɔʀe] *vt* to corroborate.

corroder [kɔʀɔde] *vt* to corrode.

corrompre [kɔʀɔ̃pʀ(ə)] *vt (dépraver)* to corrupt; *(acheter: témoin etc)* to bribe.

corrompu, e [kɔʀɔ̃py] *a* corrupt.

corrosif, ive [kɔʀɔzif, -iv] *a* corrosive.

corrosion [kɔʀozjɔ̃] *nf* corrosion.

corruption [kɔʀypsjɔ̃] *nf* corruption; bribery.

corsage [kɔʀsaʒ] *nm (d'une robe)* bodice; *(chemisier)* blouse.

corsaire [kɔʀsɛʀ] *nm* pirate, corsair; privateer.

corse [kɔʀs(ə)] *a* Corsican ♦ *nm/f*: **C~** Corsican ♦ *nf*: **la C~** Corsica.

corsé, e [kɔʀse] *a* vigorous; *(café etc)* full-flavoured *(Brit) ou* -flavored *(US)*; *(goût)* full; *(fig)* spicy; tricky.

corselet [kɔʀsəlɛ] *nm* corselet.

corser [kɔʀse] *vt (difficulté)* to aggravate; *(intrigue)* to liven up; *(sauce)* to add spice to.

corset [kɔʀsɛ] *nm* corset; *(d'une robe)* bodice; **~ orthopédique** surgical corset.

corso [kɔʀso] *nm*: **~ fleuri** procession of floral floats.

cortège [kɔʀtɛʒ] *nm* procession.

cortisone [kɔʀtizon] *nf (MÉD)* cortisone.

corvée [kɔʀve] *nf* chore, drudgery *q*; *(MIL)* fatigue (duty).

cosignataire [kosiɲatɛʀ] *a, nm/f* co-signatory.

cosinus [kosinys] *nm (MATH)* cosine.

cosmétique [kɔsmetik] *nm (pour les cheveux)* hair-oil; *(produit de beauté)* beauty care product.

cosmique [kɔsmik] *a* cosmic.

cosmonaute [kɔsmɔnɔt] *nm/f* cosmonaut, astronaut.

cosmopolite [kɔsmɔpɔlit] *a* cosmopolitan.

cosmos [kɔsmɔs] *nm* outer space; cosmos.

cosse [kɔs] *nf (BOT)* pod, hull.

cossu, e [kɔsy] *a* opulent-looking, well-to-do.

Costa Rica [kɔstaʀika] *nm*: **le ~** Costa Rica.

costaricien, ne [kɔstaʀisjɛ̃, -ɛn] *a* Costa Rican ♦ *nm/f*: **C~, ne** Costa Rican.

costaud, e [kɔsto, -od] *a* strong, sturdy.

costume [kɔstym] *nm (d'homme)* suit; *(de théâtre)* costume.

costumé, e [kɔstyme] *a* dressed up.

costumier, ière [kɔstymje, -jɛʀ] *nm/f (fabricant, loueur)* costumier; *(THÉÂTRE)* wardrobe master/mistress.

cotangente [kotɑ̃ʒɑ̃t] *nf (MATH)* cotangent.

cotation [kotasjɔ̃] *nf* quoted value.

cote [kɔt] *nf (en Bourse etc)* quotation; quoted value; *(d'un cheval)*: **la ~ de** the odds *pl* on; *(d'un candidat etc)* rating; *(mesure: sur une carte)* spot height; *(: sur un croquis)* dimension; *(de classement)* (classification) mark; reference number; **avoir la ~** to be very popular; **inscrit à la ~** quoted on the Stock Exchange; **~ d'alerte** danger *ou* flood level; **~ mal taillée** *(fig)* compromise; **~ de popularité** popularity rating.

coté, e [kɔte] *a*: **être ~** to be listed *ou* quoted; **être ~ en Bourse** to be quoted on the Stock Exchange; **être bien/mal ~** to be highly/poorly rated.

côte [kot] *nf (rivage)* coast(line); *(pente)* slope; *(: sur une route)* hill; *(ANAT)* rib; *(d'un tricot, tissu)* rib, ribbing *q*; **~ à ~** *ad* side by side; **la C~ (d'Azur)** the (French) Riviera; **la C~ d'Ivoire** the Ivory Coast.

côté [kote] *nm* (*gén*) side; (*direction*) way, direction; **de chaque ~ (de)** on each side of; **de tous les ~s** from all directions; **de quel ~ est-il parti?** which way *ou* in which direction did he go?; **de ce/de l'autre ~** this/the other way; **d'un ~ ... de l'autre ~** (*alternative*) on (the) one hand ... on the other (hand); **du ~ de** (*provenance*) from; (*direction*) towards; **du ~ de Lyon** (*proximité*) near Lyons; **du ~ gauche** on the left-hand side; **de ~** *ad* sideways; on one side; on one side; aside; **laisser de ~** to leave on one side; **mettre de ~** to put on one side, put aside; **de mon ~** (*quant à moi*) for my part; **à ~** *ad* (*right*) nearby; beside; next door; (*d'autre part*) besides; **à ~ de** beside; next to; (*fig*) in comparison to; **à ~ de (de la cible)** off target, wide (of the mark); **être aux ~s de** to be by the side of.

coteau, x [kɔto] *nm* hill.

côtelé, e [kotle] *a* ribbed; **pantalon en velours ~** corduroy trousers *pl*.

côtelette [kotlɛt] *nf* chop.

coter [kote] *vt* (*BOURSE*) to quote.

coterie [kɔtʀi] *nf* set.

côtier, ière [kotje, -jɛʀ] *a* coastal.

cotisation [kɔtizasjɔ̃] *nf* subscription, dues *pl*; (*pour une pension*) contributions *pl*.

cotiser [kɔtize] *vi*: **~ (à)** to pay contributions (to); (*à une association*) to subscribe (to); **se ~** to club together.

coton [kɔtɔ̃] *nm* cotton; **~ hydrophile** cotton wool (*Brit*), absorbent cotton (*US*).

cotonnade [kɔtɔnad] *nf* cotton (fabric).

coton-tige [kɔtɔ̃tiʒ] *nm* ® cotton bud ®.

côtoyer [kotwaje] *vt* to be close to; (*rencontrer*) to rub shoulders with; (*longer*) to run alongside; (*fig: friser*) to be bordering *ou* verging on.

cotte [kɔt] *nf*: **~ de mailles** coat of mail.

cou [ku] *nm* neck.

couac [kwak] *nm* (*fam*) bum note.

couard, e [kwaʀ, -aʀd(ə)] *a* cowardly.

couchage [kuʃaʒ] *nm voir* **sac.**

couchant [kuʃɑ̃] *a*: **soleil ~** setting sun.

couche [kuʃ] *nf* (*strate: gén, GÉO*) layer, stratum (*pl* -a); (*de peinture, vernis*) coat; (*de poussière, crème*) layer; (*de bébé*) nappy (*Brit*), diaper (*US*); **~s** *nfpl* (*MÉD*) confinement *sg*; **~s sociales** social levels *ou* strata.

couché, e [kuʃe] *a* (*étendu*) lying down; (*au lit*) in bed.

couche-culotte, *pl* **couches-culottes** [kuʃkylɔt] *nf* (plastic-coated) disposable nappy (*Brit*) *ou* diaper (*US*).

coucher [kuʃe] *nm* (*du soleil*) setting ♦ *vt* (*personne*) to put to bed; (*: loger*) to put up; (*objet*) to lay on its side; (*écrire*) to inscribe, couch ♦ *vi* (*dormir*) to sleep, spend the night; **~ avec qn** to sleep with sb, go to bed with sb; **se ~** *vi* (*pour dormir*) to go to bed; (*pour se reposer*) to lie down; (*soleil*) to set, go down; **à prendre avant le ~** (*MÉD*) take at night *ou* before going to bed; **~ de soleil** sunset.

couchette [kuʃɛt] *nf* couchette; (*de marin*) bunk.

coucheur [kuʃœʀ] *nm*: **mauvais ~** awkward customer.

couci-couça [kusikusa] *ad* (*fam*) so-so.

coucou [kuku] *nm* cuckoo ♦ *excl* peek-a-boo.

coude [kud] *nm* (*ANAT*) elbow; (*de tuyau, de la route*) bend; **~ à ~** *ad* shoulder to shoulder, side by side.

coudée [kude] *nf*: **avoir ses ~s franches** (*fig*) to have a free rein.

cou-de-pied, *pl* **cous-de-pied** [kudpje] *nm* instep.

coudoyer [kudwaje] *vt* to brush past *ou* against; (*fig*) to rub shoulders with.

coudre [kudʀ(ə)] *vt* (*bouton*) to sew on; (*robe*) to sew (up) ♦ *vi* to sew.

couenne [kwan] *nf* (*de lard*) rind.

couette [kwɛt] *nf* duvet, (continental) quilt; **~s** *nfpl* (*cheveux*) bunches.

couffin [kufɛ̃] *nm* Moses basket; (straw) basket.

couilles [kuj] *nfpl* (*fam!*) balls (!).

couiner [kwine] *vi* to squeal.

coulage [kulaʒ] *nm* (*COMM*) loss of stock (*due to theft ou negligence*).

coulant, e [kulɑ̃, -ɑ̃t] *a* (*indulgent*) easy-going; (*fromage etc*) runny.

coulée [kule] *nf* (*de lave, métal en fusion*) flow; **~ de neige** snowslide.

couler [kule] *vi* to flow, run; (*fuir: stylo, récipient*) to leak; (*sombrer: bateau*) to sink ♦ *vt* (*cloche, sculpture*) to cast; (*bateau*) to sink; (*fig*) to ruin, bring down; (*: passer*): **~ une vie heureuse** to enjoy a happy life; **se ~ dans** (*interstice etc*) to slip into; **faire ~** (*eau*) to run; **faire ~ un bain** to run a bath; **il a coulé une bielle** (*AUTO*) his big end went; **~ de source** to follow on naturally; **~ à pic** to sink *ou* go straight to the bottom.

couleur [kulœʀ] *nf* colour (*Brit*), color (*US*); (*CARTES*) suit; **~s** *nfpl* (*du teint*) colo(u)r *sg*; **les ~s** (*MIL*) the colo(u)rs; **en ~s** (*film*) in colo(u)r; **télévision en ~s** colo(u)r television; **de ~** (*homme, femme*) colo(u)red; **sous ~ de** on the pretext of.

couleuvre [kulœvʀ(ə)] *nf* grass snake.

coulisse [kulis] *nf* (*TECH*) runner; **~s** *nfpl* (*THÉÂTRE*) wings; (*fig*): **dans les ~s** behind the scenes; **porte à ~** sliding door.

coulisser [kulise] *vi* to slide, run.

couloir [kulwaʀ] *nm* corridor, passage; (*de bus*) gangway; (*: sur la route*) bus lane; (*SPORT: de piste*) lane; (*GÉO*) gully; **~ aérien** air corridor *ou* lane; **~ de navigation** shipping lane.

coulpe [kulp(ə)] *nf*: **battre sa ~** to repent openly.

coup [ku] *nm* (*heurt, choc*) knock; (*affectif*) blow, shock; (*agressif*) blow; (*avec arme à feu*) shot; (*de l'horloge*) chime; stroke; (*SPORT*) stroke; shot; blow; (*fam: fois*) time; (*ÉCHECS*) move; **~ de coude/genou** nudge (with the elbow)/with the knee; **à ~s de hache/marteau** (hitting) with an axe/a hammer; **~ de tonnerre** clap of thunder; **~ de sonnette** ring of the bell; **~ de crayon/pinceau** stroke of the pencil/brush; **donner un ~ de balai** to sweep up, give the floor a sweep; **donner un ~ de chiffon** to go round with the duster; **avoir le ~** (*fig*) to have the knack; **être dans le/hors du ~** to be/not to be in on it; **boire un ~** to have a drink; **d'un seul ~** (*subitement*) suddenly; (*à la fois*) at one go; in one blow; **du ~** so (you see); **du premier ~** first time *ou* go, at the first attempt; **du même ~** at the same time; **à ~ sûr** definitely, without fail; **après ~** afterwards; **~ sur ~** in quick succession; **être sur un ~** to be on to something; **sur le ~** outright; **sous le ~ de** (*surprise etc*) under the influence of; **tomber sous le ~ de la loi** to constitute a statutory offence; **à tous les ~s** every time; **il a raté son ~** he missed his turn; **pour le ~** for once; **~ bas** (*fig*): **donner un ~ bas à qn** to hit sb below the belt; **~ de chance** stroke of luck; **~ de chapeau** (*fig*) pat on the back; **~ de couteau** stab (of a knife); **~ dur** hard blow; **~ d'éclat** (great) feat; **~ d'envoi** kick-off; **~ d'essai** first attempt; **~ d'état** coup d'état; **~ de feu** shot; **~ de filet** (*POLICE*) haul; **~ de foudre** (*fig*) love at first sight; **~ fourré** stab in the back; **~ franc** free kick; **~ de frein** (sharp) braking *q*; **~ de fusil** rifle shot; **~ de grâce** coup de grâce; **~ du lapin** (*AUTO*) whiplash; **~ de main**: **donner un ~ de main à qn** to give sb a (helping) hand; **~ de maître** master stroke; **~ d'œil** glance; **~ de pied** kick; **~ de poing** punch; **~ de soleil** sunburn *q*; **~ de téléphone** phone call; **~ de tête** (*fig*) (sudden) impulse; **~ de théâtre** (*fig*) dramatic turn of events; **~ de vent** gust of wind; **en ~ de vent** (*rapidement*) in a tearing hurry.

coupable [kupabl(ə)] *a* guilty; (*pensée*) guilty, culpable ♦ *nm/f* (*gén*) culprit; (*JUR*) guilty party; **~ de** guilty of.

coupant, e [kupɑ̃, -ɑ̃t] *a* (*lame*) sharp; (*fig: voix, ton*) cutting.

coupe [kup] *nf* (*verre*) goblet; (*à fruits*) dish; (*SPORT*) cup; (*de cheveux, de vêtement*) cut; (*graphique, plan*) (cross) section; **être sous la ~ de** to be under the control of; **faire des ~s sombres dans** to make drastic cuts in.

coupé, e [kupe] *a* (*communications, route*) cut, blocked; (*vêtement*): **bien/mal ~** well/badly cut ♦ *nm* (*AUTO*) coupé.

coupe-circuit [kupsirkɥi] *nm inv* cutout, circuit breaker.

coupée [kupe] *nf* (*NAVIG*) gangway.

coupe-feu [kupfø] *nm inv* firebreak.

coupe-gorge [kupgɔrʒ(ə)] *nm inv* cut-throats' den.

coupe-ongles [kupɔ̃gl(ə)] *nm inv* (*pince*) nail clippers; (*ciseaux*) nail scissors.

coupe-papier [kuppapje] *nm inv* paper knife.

couper [kupe] *vt* to cut; (*retrancher*) to cut (out), take out; (*route, courant*) to cut off; (*appétit*) to take away; (*fièvre*) to take down, reduce; (*vin, cidre*) to blend; (*: à table*) to dilute (with water) ♦ *vi* to cut; (*prendre un raccourci*) to take a short-cut; (*CARTES*): *diviser le paquet* to cut; (*: avec l'atout*) to trump; **se ~** (*se blesser*) to cut o.s.; (*en témoignant etc*) to give o.s. away; **~ l'appétit à qn** to spoil sb's appetite; **~ la parole à qn** to cut sb short; **~ les vivres à qn** to cut off sb's vital supplies; **~ le contact** *ou* **l'allumage** (*AUTO*) to turn off the ignition;

~ les ponts avec qn to break with sb; **se faire ~ les cheveux** to have *ou* get one's hair cut.

couperet [kuprɛ] *nm* cleaver, chopper.

couperosé, e [kuproze] *a* blotchy.

couple [kupl(ə)] *nm* couple; **~ de torsion** torque.

coupler [kuple] *vt* to couple (together).

couplet [kuplɛ] *nm* verse.

coupleur [kuplœr] *nm*: **~ acoustique** acoustic coupler.

coupole [kupɔl] *nf* dome; cupola.

coupon [kupɔ̃] *nm* (*ticket*) coupon; (*de tissu*) remnant; roll.

coupon-réponse, *pl* **coupons-réponses** [kupɔ̃repɔ̃s] *nm* reply coupon.

coupure [kupyr] *nf* cut; (*billet de banque*) note; (*de journal*) cutting; **~ de courant** power cut.

cour [kur] *nf* (*de ferme, jardin*) (court)yard; (*d'immeuble*) back yard; (*JUR, royale*) court; **faire la ~ à qn** to court sb; **~ d'appel** appeal court (*Brit*), appellate court (*US*); **~ d'assises** court of assizes, ≈ Crown Court (*Brit*); **~ de cassation** final court of appeal; **~ des comptes** (*ADMIN*) revenue court; **~ martiale** court-martial; **~ de récréation** (*SCOL*) schoolyard, playground.

courage [kuraʒ] *nm* courage, bravery.

courageux, euse [kuraʒø, -øz] *a* brave, courageous.

couramment [kuramɑ̃] *ad* commonly; (*parler*) fluently.

courant, e [kurɑ̃, -ɑ̃t] *a* (*fréquent*) common; (*COMM, gén: normal*) standard; (*en cours*) current ♦ *nm* current; (*fig*) movement; trend; **être au ~ (de)** (*fait, nouvelle*) to know (about); **mettre qn au ~ (de)** (*fait, nouvelle*) to tell sb (about); (*nouveau travail etc*) to teach sb the basics (of), brief sb (about); **se tenir au ~ (de)** (*techniques etc*) to keep o.s. up-to-date (on); **dans le ~ de** (*pendant*) in the course of; **~ octobre** *etc* in the course of October *etc*; **le 10 ~** (*COMM*) the 10th inst; **~ d'air** draught (*Brit*), draft (*US*); **~ électrique** (electric) current, power.

courbature [kurbatyr] *nf* ache.

courbaturé, e [kurbatyre] *a* aching.

courbe [kurb(ə)] *a* curved ♦ *nf* curve; **~ de niveau** contour line.

courber [kurbe] *vt* to bend; **~ la tête** to bow one's head; **se ~** *vi* (*branche etc*) to bend, curve; (*personne*) to bend (down).

courbette [kurbɛt] *nf* low bow.

coure [kur] *etc vb voir* **courir**.

coureur, euse [kurœr, -øz] *nm/f* (*SPORT*) runner (*ou* driver); (*péj*) womanizer/manhunter; **~ cycliste/automobile** racing cyclist/driver.

courge [kurʒ(ə)] *nf* (*BOT*) gourd; (*CULIN*) marrow.

courgette [kurʒɛt] *nf* courgette (*Brit*), zucchini (*US*).

courir [kurir] *vi* (*gén*) to run; (*se dépêcher*) to rush; (*fig: rumeurs*) to go round; (*COMM: intérêt*) to accrue ♦ *vt* (*SPORT: épreuve*) to compete in; (*risque*) to run; (*danger*) to face; **~ les cafés/bals** to do the rounds of the cafés/dances; **le bruit court que** the rumour is going round that; **par les temps qui courent** at the present time; ~ **après qn** to run after sb, chase (after) sb; **laisser** ~ to let things alone; **faire** ~ **qn** to make sb run around (all over the place); **tu peux (toujours)** ~! you've got a hope!

couronne [kuʀɔn] *nf* crown; (*de fleurs*) wreath, circlet; ~ **(funéraire** *ou* **mortuaire)** (funeral) wreath.

couronnement [kuʀɔnmɑ̃] *nm* coronation, crowning; (*fig*) crowning achievement.

couronner [kuʀɔne] *vt* to crown.

courons [kuʀɔ̃], **courrai** [kuʀe] *etc vb voir* **courir**.

courre [kuʀ] *vb voir* **chasse**.

courrier [kuʀje] *nm* mail, post; (*lettres à écrire*) letters *pl*; (*rubrique*) column; **qualité** ~ letter quality; **long/moyen** ~ *a* (*AVIAT*) long-/medium-haul; ~ **du cœur** problem page; ~ **électronique** electronic mail.

courroie [kuʀwa] *nf* strap; (*TECH*) belt; ~ **de transmission/de ventilateur** driving/fan belt.

courrons [kuʀɔ̃] *etc vb voir* **courir**.

courroucé, e [kuʀuse] *a* wrathful.

cours [kuʀ] *vb voir* **courir** ♦ *nm* (*leçon*) lesson; class; (*série de leçons*) course; (*cheminement*) course; (*écoulement*) flow; (*avenue*) walk; (*COMM*) rate; price; (*BOURSE*) quotation; **donner libre** ~ **à** to give free expression to; **avoir** ~ (*monnaie*) to be legal tender; (*fig*) to be current; (*SCOL*) to have a class *ou* lecture; **en** ~ (*année*) current; (*travaux*) in progress; **en** ~ **de route** on the way; **au** ~ **de** in the course of, during; **le** ~ **du change** the exchange rate; ~ **d'eau** waterway; ~ **élémentaire (CE)** *2nd and 3rd years of primary school*; ~ **moyen (CM)** *4th and 5th years of primary school*; ~ **préparatoire** ≈ infants' class (*Brit*), ≈ 1st grade (*US*); ~ **du soir** night school.

course [kuʀs(ə)] *nf* running; (*SPORT: épreuve*) race; (*trajet: du soleil*) course; (: *d'un projectile*) flight; (: *d'une pièce mécanique*) travel; (*excursion*) outing; climb; (*d'un taxi, autocar*) journey, trip; (*petite mission*) errand; ~s *nfpl* (*achats*) shopping *sg*; (*HIPPISME*) races; **faire les** *ou* **ses** ~s to go shopping; **jouer aux** ~s to bet on the races; **à bout de** ~ (*épuisé*) exhausted; ~ **automobile** car race; ~ **de côte** (*AUTO*) hill climb; ~ **par étapes** *ou* **d'étapes** race in stages; ~ **d'obstacles** obstacle race; ~ **à pied** walking race; ~ **de vitesse** sprint; ~s **de chevaux** horse racing.

court, e [kuʀ, kuʀt(ə)] *a* short ♦ *ad* short ♦ *nm*: ~ **(de tennis)** (tennis) court; **tourner** ~ to come to a sudden end; **couper** ~ **à** to cut short; **à** ~ **de** short of; **prendre qn de** ~ to catch sb unawares; **pour faire** ~ briefly, to cut a long story short; **ça fait** ~ that's not very long; **tirer à la** ~**e paille** to draw lots; **faire la** ~**e échelle à qn** to give sb a leg up; ~ **métrage** (*CINÉMA*) short (film).

court-bouillon, *pl* **courts-bouillons** [kuʀbujɔ̃] *nm* court-bouillon.

court-circuit, *pl* **courts-circuits** [kuʀsiʀkɥi] *nm* short-circuit.

court-circuiter [kuʀsiʀkɥite] *vt* (*fig*) to by-pass.

courtier, ière [kuʀtje, -jɛʀ] *nm/f* broker.

courtisan [kuʀtizɑ̃] *nm* courtier.

courtisane [kuʀtizan] *nf* courtesan.

courtiser [kuʀtize] *vt* to court, woo.

courtois, e [kuʀtwa, -waz] *a* courteous.

courtoisie [kuʀtwazi] *nf* courtesy.

couru, e [kuʀy] *pp de* **courir** ♦ *a* (*spectacle etc*) popular; **c'est** ~ **(d'avance)!** (*fam*) it's a safe bet!

cousais [kuzɛ] *etc vb voir* **coudre**.

couscous [kuskus] *nm* couscous.

cousin, e [kuzɛ̃, -in] *nm/f* cousin ♦ *nm* (*ZOOL*) mosquito; ~ **germain** first cousin.

cousons [kuzɔ̃] *etc vb voir* **coudre**.

coussin [kusɛ̃] *nm* cushion; ~ **d'air** (*TECH*) air cushion.

cousu, e [kuzy] *pp de* **coudre** ♦ *a*: ~ **d'or** rolling in riches.

coût [ku] *nm* cost; **le** ~ **de la vie** the cost of living.

coûtant [kutɑ̃] *am*: **au prix** ~ at cost price.

couteau, x [kuto] *nm* knife; ~ **à cran d'arrêt** flick-knife; ~ **de cuisine** kitchen knife; ~ **à pain** bread knife; ~ **de poche** pocket knife.

couteau-scie, *pl* **couteaux-scies** [kutosi] *nm* serrated(-edged) knife.

coutellerie [kutɛlʀi] *nf* cutlery shop; cutlery.

coûter [kute] *vt* to cost ♦ *vi*: ~ **à qn** to cost sb a lot; ~ **cher** to be expensive; ~ **cher à qn** (*fig*) to cost sb dear *ou* dearly; **combien ça coûte?** how much is it?, what does it cost?; **coûte que coûte** at all costs.

coûteux, euse [kutø, -øz] *a* costly, expensive.

coutume [kutym] *nf* custom; **de** ~ usual, customary.

coutumier, ière [kutymje, -jɛʀ] *a* customary: **elle est coutumière du fait** that's her usual trick.

couture [kutyʀ] *nf* sewing; dress-making; (*points*) seam.

couturier [kutyʀje] *nm* fashion designer, couturier.

couturière [kutyʀjɛʀ] *nf* dressmaker.

couvée [kuve] *nf* brood, clutch.

couvent [kuvɑ̃] *nm* (*de sœurs*) convent; (*de frères*) monastery; (*établissement scolaire*) convent (school).

couver [kuve] *vt* to hatch; (*maladie*) to be sickening for ♦ *vi* (*feu*) to smoulder (*Brit*), smolder (*US*); (*révolte*) to be brewing; ~ **qn/qch des yeux** to look lovingly at sb/sth; (*convoiter*) to look longingly at sb/sth.

couvercle [kuvɛʀkl(ə)] *nm* lid; (*de bombe aérosol etc, qui se visse*) cap, top.

couvert, e [kuvɛʀ, -ɛʀt(ə)] *pp de* **couvrir** ♦ *a* (*ciel*) overcast; (*coiffé d'un chapeau*) wearing a hat ♦ *nm* place setting; (*place à table*) place; (*au restaurant*) cover charge; ~s *nmpl* place settings; cutlery *sg*; ~ **de** covered with *ou* in; **bien** ~ (*habillé*) well wrapped up; **mettre le** ~ to lay the table; **à** ~ under cover; **sous le** ~ **de** under the shelter of; (*fig*) under cover of.

couverture [kuvɛʀtyʀ] *nf* (*de lit*) blanket; (*de bâtiment*) roofing; (*de livre, fig: d'un espion etc, ASSURANCES*) cover; (*PRESSE*) coverage; **de** ~ (*lettre etc*) covering; ~ **chauffante** electric blanket.

couveuse [kuvøz] *nf* (*à poules*) sitter,

brooder; (de maternité) incubator.

couvre [kuvʀ(ə)] etc vb voir **couvrir**.

couvre-chef [kuvʀəʃɛf] nm hat.

couvre-feu, x [kuvʀəfø] nm curfew.

couvre-lit [kuvʀəli] nm bedspread.

couvre-pieds [kuvʀəpje] nm inv quilt.

couvreur [kuvʀœʀ] nm roofer.

couvrir [kuvʀiʀ] vt to cover; (dominer, étouffer: voix, pas) to drown out; (erreur) to cover up; (ZOOL: s'accoupler à) to cover; **se ~** (ciel) to cloud over; (s'habiller) to cover up, wrap up; (se coiffer) to put on one's hat; (par une assurance) to cover o.s.; **se ~ de** (fleurs, boutons) to become covered in.

coyote [kɔjɔt] nm coyote.

CP sigle m = **cours préparatoire**.

CPAM sigle f (= Caisse primaire d'assurances maladie) health insurance office.

cps abr (= caractères par seconde) cps.

cpt abr = **comptant**.

CQFD abr (= ce qu'il fallait démontrer) QED (= quod erat demonstrandum).

CR sigle m = **compte rendu**.

crabe [kʀab] nm crab.

crachat [kʀaʃa] nm spittle q, spit q.

craché, e [kʀaʃe] a: **son père tout ~** the spitting image of his (ou her) father.

cracher [kʀaʃe] vi to spit ♦ vt to spit out; (fig: lave etc) to belch (out); **~ du sang** to spit blood.

crachin [kʀaʃɛ̃] nm drizzle.

crachiner [kʀaʃine] vi to drizzle.

crachoir [kʀaʃwaʀ] nm spittoon; (de dentiste) bowl.

crachoter [kʀaʃɔte] vi (haut-parleur, radio) to crackle.

crack [kʀak] nm (intellectuel) whizzkid; (sportif) ace; (poulain) hot favourite (Brit) ou favorite (US).

Cracovie [kʀakɔvi] n Cracow.

cradingue [kʀadɛ̃g] a (fam) disgustingly dirty, filthy-dirty.

craie [kʀɛ] nf chalk.

craignais [kʀɛɲɛ] etc vb voir **craindre**.

craindre [kʀɛ̃dʀ(ə)] vt to fear, be afraid of; (être sensible à: chaleur, froid) to be easily damaged by; **~ de/que** to be afraid of/that; **je crains qu'il (ne) vienne** I am afraid he may come.

crainte [kʀɛ̃t] nf fear; **de ~ de/que** for fear of/that.

craintif, ive [kʀɛ̃tif, -iv] a timid.

cramoisi, e [kʀamwazi] a crimson.

crampe [kʀɑ̃p] nf cramp; **~ d'estomac** stomach cramp.

crampon [kʀɑ̃pɔ̃] nm (de semelle) stud; (ALPINISME) crampon.

cramponner [kʀɑ̃pɔne]: **se ~** vi: **se ~ (à)** to hang ou cling on (to).

cran [kʀɑ̃] nm (entaille) notch; (de courroie) hole; (courage) guts pl; **~ d'arrêt** safety catch; **~ de mire** bead; **~ de sûreté** safety catch.

crâne [kʀɑn] nm skull.

crâner [kʀɑne] vi (fam) to swank, show off.

crânien, ne [kʀɑnjɛ̃, -ɛn] a cranial, skull cpd, brain cpd.

crapaud [kʀapo] nm toad.

crapule [kʀapyl] nf villain.

crapuleux, euse [kʀapylø, -øz] a: **crime ~** villainous crime.

craquelure [kʀaklyʀ] nf crack; crackle q.

craquement [kʀakmɑ̃] nm crack, snap; (du plancher) creak, creaking q.

craquer [kʀake] vi (bois, plancher) to creak; (fil, branche) to snap; (couture) to come apart, burst; (fig) to break down, fall apart; (: être enthousiasmé) to go wild ♦ vt: **~ une allumette** to strike a match.

crasse [kʀas] nf grime, filth ♦ a (fig: ignorance) crass.

crassier [kʀasje] nm slag heap.

cratère [kʀatɛʀ] nm crater.

cravache [kʀavaʃ] nf (riding) crop.

cravacher [kʀavaʃe] vt to use the crop on.

cravate [kʀavat] nf tie.

cravater [kʀavate] vt to put a tie on; (fig) to grab round the neck.

crawl [kʀol] nm crawl.

crawlé, e [kʀole] a: **dos ~** backstroke.

crayeux, euse [kʀɛjø, -øz] a chalky.

crayon [kʀɛjɔ̃] nm pencil; (de rouge à lèvres etc) stick, pencil; **écrire au ~** to write in pencil; **~ à bille** ball-point pen; **~ de couleur** crayon; **~ optique** light pen.

crayon-feutre, pl **crayons-feutres** [kʀɛjɔ̃føtʀ(ə)] nm felt(-tip) pen.

crayonner [kʀɛjɔne] vt to scribble, sketch.

CRDP sigle m (= Centre régional de documentation pédagogique) teachers' resource centre.

créance [kʀeɑ̃s] nf (COMM) (financial) claim, (recoverable) debt; **donner ~ à qch** to lend credence to sth.

créancier, ière [kʀeɑ̃sje, -jɛʀ] nm/f creditor.

créateur, trice [kʀeatœʀ, -tʀis] a creative ♦ nm/f creator; **le C~** (REL) the Creator.

créatif, ive [kʀeatif, -iv] a creative.

création [kʀeasjɔ̃] nf creation.

créativité [kʀeativite] nf creativity.

créature [kʀeatyʀ] nf creature.

crécelle [kʀesɛl] nf rattle.

crèche [kʀɛʃ] nf (de Noël) crib; (garderie) crèche, day nursery.

crédence [kʀedɑ̃s] nf (small) sideboard.

crédibilité [kʀedibilite] nf credibility.

crédible [kʀedibl(ə)] a credible.

CREDIF [kʀedif] sigle m (= Centre de recherche et d'étude pour la diffusion du français) official body promoting use of the French language.

crédit [kʀedi] nm (gén) credit; **~s** nmpl funds; **payer/acheter à ~** to pay/buy on credit ou on easy terms; **faire ~ à qn** to give sb credit; **~ municipal** pawnshop; **~ relais** bridging loan.

crédit-bail, pl **crédits-bails** [kʀedibaj] nm (ÉCON) leasing.

créditer [kʀedite] vt: **~ un compte (de)** to credit an account (with).

créditeur, trice [kʀeditœʀ, -tʀis] a in credit, credit cpd ♦ nm/f customer in credit.

credo [kʀedo] nm credo, creed.

crédule [kʀedyl] a credulous, gullible.

crédulité [kʀedylite] nf credulity, gullibility.

créer [kʀee] vt to create; (THÉÂTRE: pièce) to produce (for the first time); (: rôle) to create.

crémaillère [kʀemajɛʀ] *nf* (*RAIL*) rack; (*tige crantée*) trammel; **direction à ~** (*AUTO*) rack and pinion steering; **pendre la ~** to have a house-warming party.

crémation [kʀemasjɔ̃] *nf* cremation.

crématoire [kʀematwaʀ] *a*: **four ~** crematorium.

crème [kʀɛm] *nf* cream; (*entremets*) cream dessert ♦ *a inv* cream; **un (café) ~** ≈ a white coffee; **~ chantilly** whipped cream, crème Chantilly; **~ fouettée** whipped cream; **~ glacée** ice cream; **~ à raser** shaving cream.

crémerie [kʀemʀi] *nf* dairy; (*tearoom*) tea-shop.

crémeux, euse [kʀemø, -øz] *a* creamy.

crémier, ière [kʀemje, -jɛʀ] *nm/f* dairyman/ woman.

créneau, x [kʀeno] *nm* (*de fortification*) crenel(le); (*fig, aussi COMM*) gap, slot; (*AUTO*): **faire un ~** to reverse into a parking space (*between cars alongside the kerb*).

créole [kʀeɔl] *a, nm/f* Creole.

créosote [kʀeɔzɔt] *nf* creosote.

crêpe [kʀɛp] *nf* (*galette*) pancake ♦ *nm* (*tissu*) crêpe; (*de deuil*) black mourning crêpe; (*ruban*) black armband (*ou* hatband *ou* ribbon); **semelle (de) ~** crêpe sole; **~ de Chine** crêpe de Chine.

crêpé, e [kʀepe] *a* (*cheveux*) backcombed.

crêperie [kʀepʀi] *nf* pancake shop *ou* restaurant.

crépi [kʀepi] *nm* roughcast.

crépir [kʀepiʀ] *vt* to roughcast.

crépiter [kʀepite] *vi* to sputter, splutter, crackle.

crépon [kʀepɔ̃] *nm* seersucker.

CREPS [kʀɛps] *sigle m* (= *Centre régional d'éducation physique et sportive*) ≈ sports *ou* leisure centre.

crépu, e [kʀepy] *a* frizzy, fuzzy.

crépuscule [kʀepyskyl] *nm* twilight, dusk.

crescendo [kʀeʃɛndo] *nm, ad* (*MUS*) crescendo; **aller ~** (*fig*) to rise higher and higher, grow ever greater.

cresson [kʀesɔ̃] *nm* watercress.

Crète [kʀɛt] *nf*: **la ~** Crete.

crête [kʀɛt] *nf* (*de coq*) comb; (*de vague, montagne*) crest.

crétin, e [kʀetɛ̃, -in] *nm/f* cretin.

crétois, e [kʀetwa, -waz] *a* Cretan.

cretonne [kʀətɔn] *nf* cretonne.

creuser [kʀøze] *vt* (*trou, tunnel*) to dig; (*sol*) to dig a hole in; (*bois*) to hollow out; (*fig*) to go (deeply) into; **ça creuse** that gives you a real appetite; **se ~ (la cervelle)** to rack one's brains.

creuset [kʀøze] *nm* crucible; (*fig*) melting pot; (*severe*) test.

creux, euse [kʀø, -øz] *a* hollow ♦ *nm* hollow; (*fig: sur graphique etc*) trough; **heures creuses** slack periods; off-peak periods; **le ~ de l'estomac** the pit of the stomach.

crevaison [kʀəvɛzɔ̃] *nf* puncture, flat.

crevasse [kʀəvas] *nf* (*dans le sol*) crack, fissure; (*de glacier*) crevasse; (*de la peau*) crack.

crevé, e [kʀəve] *a* (*fam: fatigué*) worn out, dead beat.

crève-cœur [kʀɛvkœʀ] *nm inv* heartbreak.

crever [kʀəve] *vt* (*papier*) to tear, break; (*tambour, ballon*) to burst ♦ *vi* (*pneu*) to burst; (*automobiliste*) to have a puncture (*Brit*) *ou* a flat (tire) (*US*); (*abcès, outre, nuage*) to burst (open); (*fam*) to die; **cela lui a crevé un œil** it blinded him in one eye; **~ l'écran** to have real screen presence.

crevette [kʀəvet] *nf*: **~ (rose)** prawn; **~ grise** shrimp.

cri [kʀi] *nm* cry, shout; (*d'animal: spécifique*) cry, call; **à grands ~s** at the top of one's voice; **c'est le dernier ~** (*fig*) it's the latest fashion.

criant, e [kʀijɑ̃, -ɑ̃t] *a* (*injustice*) glaring.

criard, e [kʀijaʀ, -aʀd(ə)] *a* (*couleur*) garish, loud; (*voix*) yelling.

crible [kʀibl(ə)] *nm* riddle; (*mécanique*) screen, jig; **passer qch au ~** to put sth through a riddle; (*fig*) to go over sth with a fine-tooth comb.

criblé, e [kʀible] *a*: **~ de** riddled with.

cric [kʀik] *nm* (*AUTO*) jack.

cricket [kʀikɛt] *nm* cricket.

criée [kʀije] *nf*: **(vente à la) ~** (sale by) auction.

crier [kʀije] *vi* (*pour appeler*) to shout, cry (out); (*de peur, de douleur etc*) to scream, yell; (*fig: grincer*) to squeal, screech ♦ *vt* (*ordre, injure*) to shout (out), yell (out); **sans ~ gare** without warning; **~ grâce** to cry for mercy; **~ au secours** to shout for help.

crieur, euse [kʀijœʀ, -øz] *nm/f*: **~ de journaux** newspaper seller.

crime [kʀim] *nm* crime; (*meurtre*) murder.

Crimée [kʀime] *nf*: **la ~** the Crimea.

criminaliste [kʀiminalist(ə)] *nm/f* specialist in criminal law.

criminalité [kʀiminalite] *nf* criminality, crime.

criminel, le [kʀiminɛl] *a* criminal ♦ *nm/f* criminal; murderer; **~ de guerre** war criminal.

criminologiste [kʀiminɔlɔʒist(ə)] *nm/f* criminologist.

crin [kʀɛ̃] *nm* hair *q*; (*fibre*) horsehair; **à tous ~s, à tout ~** diehard, out-and-out.

crinière [kʀinjɛʀ] *nf* mane.

crique [kʀik] *nf* creek, inlet.

criquet [kʀike] *nm* grasshopper.

crise [kʀiz] *nf* crisis (*pl* crises); (*MÉD*) attack; fit; **~ cardiaque** heart attack; **~ de foi** crisis of belief; **~ de foie** bilious attack; **~ de nerfs** attack of nerves.

crispant, e [kʀispɑ̃, -ɑ̃t] *a* annoying, irritating.

crispation [kʀispasjɔ̃] *nf* (*spasme*) twitch; (*contraction*) contraction; tenseness.

crispé, e [kʀispe] *a* tense, nervous.

crisper [kʀispe] *vt* to tense; (*poings*) to clench; **se ~** to tense; to clench; (*personne*) to get tense.

crissement [kʀismɑ̃] *nm* crunch; rustle; screech.

crisser [kʀise] *vi* (*neige*) to crunch; (*tissu*) to rustle; (*pneu*) to screech.

cristal, aux [kʀistal, -o] *nm* crystal ♦ *nmpl* (*objets*) crystal(ware) *sg*; **~ de plomb** (lead) crystal; **~ de roche** rock-crystal; **cristaux de soude** washing soda *sg*.

cristallin, e [kʀistalɛ̃, -in] *a* crystal-clear ♦ *nm*

(*ANAT*) crystalline lens.

cristalliser [kʀistalize] *vi*, *vt*, **se** ~ *vi* to crystallize.

critère [kʀitɛʀ] *nm* criterion (*pl* -ia).

critiquable [kʀitikabl(ə)] *a* open to criticism.

critique [kʀitik] *a* critical ♦ *nm/f* (*de théâtre*, *musique*) critic ♦ *nf* criticism; (*THÉÂTRE etc*: *article*) review; **la** ~ (*activité*) criticism; (*personnes*) the critics *pl*.

critiquer [kʀitike] *vt* (*dénigrer*) to criticize; (*évaluer*, *juger*) to assess, examine (critically).

croasser [kʀɔase] *vi* to caw.

croate [kʀɔat] *a* Croatian ♦ *nm* (*LING*) Croat, Croatian.

Croatie [kʀɔasi] *nf*: **la** ~ Croatia.

croc [kʀo] *nm* (*dent*) fang; (*de boucher*) hook.

croc-en-jambe, *pl* **crocs-en-jambe** [kʀɔkɑ̃ʒɑ̃b] *nm*: **faire un** ~ **à qn** to trip sb up.

croche [kʀɔʃ] *nf* (*MUS*) quaver (*Brit*), eighth note (*US*); **double** ~ semiquaver (*Brit*), sixteenth note (*US*).

croche-pied [kʀɔʃpje] *nm* = **croc-en-jambe**.

crochet [kʀɔʃɛ] *nm* hook; (*clef*) picklock; (*détour*) detour; (*BOXE*): ~ **du gauche** left hook; (*TRICOT*: *aiguille*) crochet hook; (: *technique*) crochet; ~**s** *nmpl* (*TYPO*) square brackets; **vivre aux** ~**s de qn** to live ou sponge off sb.

crocheter [kʀɔʃte] *vt* (*serrure*) to pick.

crochu, e [kʀɔʃy] *a* hooked; claw-like.

crocodile [kʀɔkɔdil] *nm* crocodile.

crocus [kʀɔkys] *nm* crocus.

croire [kʀwaʀ] *vt* to believe; ~ **qn honnête** to believe sb (to be) honest; **se** ~ **fort** to think one is strong; ~ **que** to believe ou think that; **vous croyez?** do you think so?; ~ **être/faire** to think one is/does; ~ **à**, ~ **en** to believe in.

croîs [kʀwa] *etc vb voir* **croître**.

croisade [kʀwazad] *nf* crusade.

croisé, e [kʀwaze] *a* (*veston*) double-breasted ♦ *nm* (*guerrier*) crusader ♦ *nf* (*fenêtre*) window, casement; (*TISSU*): **à la** ~**e des chemins** at the crossroads.

croisement [kʀwazmɑ̃] *nm* (*carrefour*) crossroads *sg*; (*BIO*) crossing; crossbreed.

croiser [kʀwaze] *vt* (*personne*, *voiture*) to pass; (*route*) to cross, cut across; (*BIO*) to cross ♦ *vi* (*NAVIG*) to cruise; ~ **les jambes/bras** to cross one's legs/fold one's arms; **se** ~ (*personnes*, *véhicules*) to pass each other; (*routes*) to cross, intersect; (*lettres*) to cross (in the post); (*regards*) to meet; **se** ~ **les bras** (*fig*) to twiddle one's thumbs.

croiseur [kʀwazœʀ] *nm* cruiser (*warship*).

croisière [kʀwazjɛʀ] *nf* cruise; **vitesse de** ~ (*AUTO etc*) cruising speed.

croisillon [kʀwazijɔ̃] *nm*: **motif/fenêtre à** ~**s** lattice pattern/window.

croissais [kʀwasɛ] *etc vb voir* **croître**.

croissance [kʀwasɑ̃s] *nf* growing, growth; **troubles de la** ~ growing pains; **maladie de** ~ growth disease; ~ **économique** economic growth.

croissant, e [kʀwasɑ̃, -ɑ̃t] *vb voir* **croître** ♦ *a* growing ♦ *nm* (*à manger*) croissant; (*motif*) crescent; ~ **de lune** crescent moon.

croître [kʀwatʀ(ə)] *vi* to grow; (*lune*) to wax.

croix [kʀwa] *nf* cross; **en** ~ *a*, *ad* in the form

of a cross; **la C**~ **Rouge** the Red Cross.

croquant, e [kʀɔkɑ̃, -ɑ̃t] *a* crisp, crunchy ♦ *nm/f* (*péj*) yokel, (country) bumpkin.

croque-madame [kʀɔkmadam] *nm inv* toasted cheese sandwich with a fried egg on top.

croque-mitaine [kʀɔkmitɛn] *nm* bog(e)y-man (*pl* -men).

croque-monsieur [kʀɔkməsjø] *nm inv* toasted ham and cheese sandwich.

croque-mort [kʀɔkmɔʀ] *nm* (*péj*) pallbearer.

croquer [kʀɔke] *vt* (*manger*) to crunch; to munch; (*dessiner*) to sketch ♦ *vi* to be crisp ou crunchy; **chocolat à** ~ plain dessert chocolate.

croquet [kʀɔkɛ] *nm* croquet.

croquette [kʀɔkɛt] *nf* croquette.

croquis [kʀɔki] *nm* sketch.

cross(-country), *pl* **cross(-countries)** [kʀɔs(kuntʀi)] *nm* cross-country race ou run; cross-country racing ou running.

crosse [kʀɔs] *nf* (*de fusil*) butt; (*de revolver*) grip; (*d'évêque*) crook, crosier; (*de hockey*) hockey stick.

crotale [kʀɔtal] *nm* rattlesnake.

crotte [kʀɔt] *nf* droppings *pl*; ~**!** (*fam*) damn!

crotté, e [kʀɔte] *a* muddy, mucky.

crottin [kʀɔtɛ̃] *nm*: ~ (**de cheval**) (horse) dung ou manure.

croulant, e [kʀulɑ̃, -ɑ̃t] *nm/f* (*fam*) old fogey.

crouler [kʀule] *vi* (*s'effondrer*) to collapse; (*être délabré*) to be crumbling.

croupe [kʀup] *nf* croup, rump; **en** ~ pillion.

croupier [kʀupje] *nm* croupier.

croupir [kʀupiʀ] *vi* to stagnate.

CROUS [kʀus] *sigle m* (= *Centre régional des œuvres universitaires et scolaires*) students' representative body.

croustillant, e [kʀustijɑ̃, -ɑ̃t] *a* crisp; (*fig*) spicy.

croustiller [kʀustije] *vi* to be crisp ou crusty.

croûte [kʀut] *nf* crust; (*du fromage*) rind; (*de vol-au-vent*) case; (*MÉD*) scab; **en** ~ (*CULIN*) in pastry, in a pie; ~ **aux champignons** mushrooms on toast; ~ **au fromage** cheese on toast *q*; ~ **de pain** (*morceau*) crust (of bread); ~ **terrestre** earth's crust.

croûton [kʀutɔ̃] *nm* (*CULIN*) crouton; (*bout du pain*) crust, heel.

croyable [kʀwajabl(ə)] *a* believable, credible.

croyais [kʀwajɛ] *etc vb voir* **croire**.

croyance [kʀwajɑ̃s] *nf* belief.

croyant, e [kʀwajɑ̃, -ɑ̃t] *vb voir* **croire** ♦ *a*: **être/ne pas être** ~ to be/not to be a believer ♦ *nm/f* believer.

Crozet [kʀɔze] *n*: **les îles** ~ the Crozet Islands.

CRS *sigle fpl* (= *Compagnies républicaines de sécurité*) state security police force ♦ *sigle m* member of the CRS.

cru, e [kʀy] *pp de* **croire** ♦ *a* (*non cuit*) raw; (*lumière*, *couleur*) harsh; (*description*) crude; (*paroles*, *langage: franc*) blunt; (: *grossier*) crude ♦ *nm* (*vignoble*) vineyard; (*vin*) wine ♦ *nf* (*d'un cours d'eau*) swelling, rising; **de son (propre)** ~ (*fig*) of his own devising; **monter à** ~ to ride bareback; **du** ~ local; **en** ~**e** in spate.

crû [kʀy] *pp de* **croître**.

cruauté [kʀyote] nf cruelty.

cruche [kʀyʃ] nf pitcher, (earthenware) jug.

crucial, e, aux [kʀysjal, -o] a crucial.

crucifier [kʀysifje] vt to crucify.

crucifix [kʀysifi] nm crucifix.

crucifixion [kʀysifiksjɔ̃] nf crucifixion.

cruciforme [kʀysifɔʀm(ə)] a cruciform, cross-shaped.

cruciverbiste [kʀysivɛʀbist(ə)] nm/f crossword puzzle enthusiast.

crudité [kʀydite] nf crudeness q; harshness q; ~s nfpl (CULIN) mixed salads (as hors-d'œuvre).

crue [kʀy] nf voir cru.

cruel, le [kʀyɛl] a cruel.

cruellement [kʀyɛlmã] ad cruelly.

crûment [kʀymã] ad (voir cru) harshly; bluntly; crudely.

crus, crûs [kʀy] etc vb voir croire, croître.

crustacés [kʀystase] nmpl shellfish.

crypte [kʀipt(ə)] nf crypt.

cse abr = **cause.**

CSEN sigle f (= Confédération des syndicats de l'éducation nationale) group of teachers' unions.

Cte abr = **Comtesse.**

CU sigle f = communauté urbaine.

Cuba [kyba] nf: **la** ~ Cuba.

cubage [kybaʒ] nm cubage, cubic content.

cubain, e [kybɛ̃, -ɛn] a Cuban ♦ nm/f: **C~, e** Cuban.

cube [kyb] nm cube; (jouet) brick, building block; **gros** ~ powerful motorbike; **mètre** ~ cubic metre; **2 au** ~ **= 8** 2 cubed is 8; **élever au** ~ to cube.

cubique [kybik] a cubic.

cubisme [kybism(ə)] nm cubism.

cubitus [kybitys] nm ulna.

cueillette [kœjɛt] nf picking, gathering; harvest ou crop (of fruit).

cueillir [kœjiʀ] vt (fruits, fleurs) to pick, gather; (fig) to catch.

cuiller ou **cuillère** [kɥijɛʀ] nf spoon; ~ **à café** coffee spoon; (CULIN) ≈ teaspoonful; ~ **à soupe** soup spoon; (CULIN) ≈ tablespoonful.

cuillerée [kɥijʀe] nf spoonful; (CULIN): ~ **à soupe/café** tablespoonful/teaspoonful.

cuir [kɥiʀ] nm leather; (avant tannage) hide; ~ **chevelu** scalp.

cuirasse [kɥiʀas] nf breastplate.

cuirassé [kɥiʀase] nm (NAVIG) battleship.

cuire [kɥiʀ] vt (aliments) to cook; (au four) to bake; (poterie) to fire ♦ vi to cook; (picoter) to smart, sting, burn; **bien cuit** (viande) well done; **trop cuit** overdone; **pas assez cuit** underdone; **cuit à point** medium done; done to a turn.

cuisant, e [kɥizã, -ãt] vb voir **cuire** ♦ a (douleur) smarting, burning; (fig: souvenir, échec) bitter.

cuisine [kɥizin] nf (pièce) kitchen; (art culinaire) cookery, cooking; (nourriture) cooking, food; **faire la** ~ to cook.

cuisiné, e [kɥizine] a: **plat** ~ ready-made meal ou dish.

cuisiner [kɥizine] vt to cook; (fam) to grill ♦ vi to cook.

cuisinette [kɥizinɛt] nf kitchenette.

cuisinier, ière [kɥizinje, -jɛʀ] nm/f cook ♦ nf (poêle) cooker.

cuisis [kɥizi] etc vb voir **cuire.**

cuissardes [kɥisaʀd] nfpl (de pêcheur) waders; (de femme) thigh boots.

cuisse [kɥis] nf (ANAT) thigh; (CULIN) leg.

cuisson [kɥisɔ̃] nf cooking; (de poterie) firing.

cuissot [kɥiso] nm haunch.

cuistre [kɥistʀ(ə)] nm prig.

cuit, e [kɥi, -it] pp de **cuire.**

cuivre [kɥivʀ(ə)] nm copper; **les** ~s (MUS) the brass; ~ **rouge** copper; ~ **jaune** brass.

cuivré, e [kɥivʀe] a coppery; (peau) bronzed.

cul [ky] nm (fam!) arse (Brit !), ass (US !), bum (Brit); ~ **de bouteille** bottom of a bottle.

culasse [kylas] nf (AUTO) cylinder-head; (de fusil) breech.

culbute [kylbyt] nf somersault; (accidentelle) tumble, fall.

culbuter [kylbyte] vi to (take a) tumble, fall (head over heels).

culbuteur [kylbytœʀ] nm (AUTO) rocker arm.

cul-de-jatte, pl culs-de-jatte [kydʒat] nm/f legless cripple.

cul-de-sac, pl culs-de-sac [kydsak] nm cul-de-sac.

culinaire [kylinɛʀ] a culinary.

culminant, e [kylminã, -ãt] a: **point** ~ highest point; (fig) height, climax.

culminer [kylmine] vi to reach its highest point; to tower.

culot [kylo] nm (d'ampoule) cap; (effronterie) cheek, nerve.

culotte [kylɔt] nf (de femme) panties pl, knickers pl (Brit); (d'homme) underpants pl; (pantalon) trousers pl (Brit), pants pl (US); ~ **de cheval** riding breeches pl.

culotté, e [kylɔte] a (pipe) seasoned; (cuir) mellowed; (effronté) cheeky.

culpabiliser [kylpabilize] vt: ~ **qn** to make sb feel guilty.

culpabilité [kylpabilite] nf guilt.

culte [kylt(ə)] nm (religion) religion; (hommage, vénération) worship; (protestant) service.

cultivateur, trice [kyltivatœʀ, -tʀis] nm/f farmer.

cultivé, e [kyltive] a (personne) cultured, cultivated.

cultiver [kyltive] vt to cultivate; (légumes) to grow, cultivate.

culture [kyltyʀ] nf cultivation; growing; (connaissances etc) culture; **(champs de)** ~s land(s) under cultivation; ~ **physique** physical training.

culturel, le [kyltyʀɛl] a cultural.

culturisme [kyltyʀism(ə)] nm body-building.

culturiste [kyltyʀist(ə)] nm/f body-builder.

cumin [kymɛ̃] nm (CULIN) caraway seeds pl; cumin.

cumul [kymyl] nm (voir cumuler) holding (ou drawing) concurrently; ~ **de peines** sentences to run consecutively.

cumuler [kymyle] vt (emplois, honneurs) to hold concurrently; (salaires) to draw concurrently; (JUR: droits) to accumulate.

cupide [kypid] a greedy, grasping.

curable [kyʀabl(ə)] a curable.

Curaçao [kyʀaso] n Curaçao ♦ nm: **c~** curaçao.

curatif, ive [kyʀatif, -iv] *a* curative.

cure [kyʀ] *nf* (*MÉD*) course of treatment; (*REL*) cure, ≈ living; presbytery, ≈ vicarage; **faire une ~ de fruits** to go on a fruit cure *ou* diet; **faire une ~ thermale** to take the waters; **n'avoir ~ de** to pay no attention to; **~ d'amaigrissement** slimming course; **~ de repos** rest cure; **~ de sommeil** sleep therapy *q*.

curé [kyʀe] *nm* parish priest; **M le ~** ≈ Vicar.

cure-dent [kyʀdɑ̃] *nm* toothpick.

curée [kyʀe] *nf* (*fig*) scramble for the pickings.

cure-ongles [kyʀɔ̃gl(ə)] *nm inv* nail cleaner.

cure-pipe [kyʀpip] *nm* pipe cleaner.

curer [kyʀe] *vt* to clean out; **se ~ les dents** to pick one's teeth.

curieusement [kyʀjøzmɑ̃] *ad* oddly.

curieux, euse [kyʀjø, -øz] *a* (*étrange*) strange, curious; (*indiscret*) curious, inquisitive; (*intéressé*) inquiring, curious ♦ *nmpl* (*badauds*) onlookers, bystanders.

curiosité [kyʀjozite] *nf* curiosity, inquisitiveness; (*objet*) curio(sity); (*site*) unusual feature *ou* sight.

curiste [kyʀist(ə)] *nm/f person taking the waters at a spa.*

curriculum vitae (CV) [kyʀikylɔmvite] *nm inv* curriculum vitae (CV).

curry [kyʀi] *nm* curry; **poulet au ~** curried chicken, chicken curry.

curseur [kyʀsœʀ] *nm* (*INFORM*) cursor; (*de règle*) slide; (*de fermeture-éclair*) slider.

cursif, ive [kyʀsif, -iv] *a*: **écriture cursive** cursive script.

cursus [kyʀsys] *nm* degree course.

cutané, e [kytane] *a* cutaneous, skin *cpd*.

cuti-réaction [kytiʀeaksjɔ̃] *nf* (*MÉD*) skin-test.

cuve [kyv] *nf* vat; (*à mazout etc*) tank.

cuvée [kyve] *nf* vintage.

cuvette [kyvɛt] *nf* (*récipient*) bowl, basin; (*du lavabo*) (wash)basin; (*des w.-c.*) pan; (*GÉO*) basin.

CV *sigle m* (*AUTO*) = **cheval vapeur**; (*ADMIN*) = **curriculum vitae**.

CVS *sigle a* (= *corrigées des variations saisonnières*) seasonally adjusted.

cx *abr* (= *coefficient de pénétration dans l'air*) drag coefficient.

cyanure [sjanyʀ] *nm* cyanide.

cybernétique [sibɛʀnetik] *nf* cybernetics *sg*.

cyclable [siklabl(ə)] *a*: **piste ~** cycle track.

cyclamen [siklamɛn] *nm* cyclamen.

cycle [sikl(ə)] *nm* cycle; (*SCOL*): **premier/second ~** ≈ middle/upper school (*Brit*), ≈ junior/senior high school (*US*).

cyclique [siklik] *a* cyclic(al).

cyclisme [siklism(ə)] *nm* cycling.

cycliste [siklist(ə)] *nm/f* cyclist ♦ *a* cycle *cpd*; **coureur ~** racing cyclist.

cyclo-cross [siklɔkʀɔs] *nm* (*SPORT*) cyclo-cross; (*épreuve*) cyclo-cross race.

cyclomoteur [siklɔmɔtœʀ] *nm* moped.

cyclomotoriste [siklɔmɔtɔʀist(ə)] *nm/f* moped rider.

cyclone [siklon] *nm* hurricane.

cyclotourisme [siklɔtuʀism(ə)] *nm* (bi)cycle touring.

cygne [siɲ] *nm* swan.

cylindre [silɛ̃dʀ(ə)] *nm* cylinder; **moteur à 4 ~s en ligne** straight-4 engine.

cylindrée [silɛ̃dʀe] *nf* (*AUTO*) (cubic) capacity; **une (voiture de) grosse ~** a big-engined car.

cylindrique [silɛ̃dʀik] *a* cylindrical.

cymbale [sɛ̃bal] *nf* cymbal.

cynique [sinik] *a* cynical.

cynisme [sinism(ə)] *nm* cynicism.

cyprès [sipʀɛ] *nm* cypress.

cypriote [sipʀijɔt] *a* Cypriot ♦ *nm/f*: **C~** Cypriot.

cyrillique [siʀilik] *a* Cyrillic.

cystite [sistit] *nf* cystitis.

cytise [sitiz] *nm* laburnum.

cytologie [sitɔlɔʒi] *nf* cytology.

D

D, d [de] *nm inv* D, d ♦ *abr*: **D** (*MÉTÉO*: = *dépression*) low, depression; **D comme Désiré** D for David (*Brit*) *ou* Dog (*US*); *voir* **système**.

d' *prép, dét voir* **de**.

Dacca [daka] *n* Dacca.

dactylo [daktilo] *nf* (*aussi*: **~graphe**) typist; (*aussi*: **~graphie**) typing, typewriting.

dactylographier [daktilɔgʀafje] *vt* to type (out).

dada [dada] *nm* hobby-horse.

dadais [dadɛ] *nm* ninny, lump.

dague [dag] *nf* dagger.

dahlia [dalja] *nm* dahlia.

dahoméen, ne [daɔmeɛ̃, -ɛn] *a* Dahomean.

Dahomey [daɔme] *nm*: **le ~** Dahomey.

daigner [deɲe] *vt* to deign.

daim [dɛ̃] *nm* (fallow) deer *inv*; (*peau*) buckskin; (*imitation*) suede.

dais [dɛ] *nm* (*tenture*) canopy.

Dakar [dakaʀ] *n* Dakar.

dal. *abr* (= *décalitre*) dal.

dallage [dalaʒ] *nm* paving.

dalle [dal] *nf* slab; (*au sol*) paving stone, flag(stone); **que ~** nothing at all, damn all (*Brit*).

daller [dale] *vt* to pave.

dalmate [dalmat] *a* Dalmatian.

Dalmatie [dalmasi] *nf*: **la ~** Dalmatia.

dalmatien, ne [dalmasjɛ̃, -ɛn] *nm/f* (*chien*) Dalmatian.

daltonien, ne [daltɔnjɛ̃, -ɛn] *a* colour-blind (*Brit*), color-blind (*US*).

daltonisme [daltɔnism(ə)] *nm* colour (*Brit*) *ou* color (*US*) blindness.

dam [dam] *nm*: **au grand ~ de** much to the detriment (*ou* annoyance) of.

Damas [dama] *n* Damascus.

damas [dama] *nm* (*étoffe*) damask.

damassé, e [damase] *a* damask *cpd*.

dame [dam] *nf* lady; (*CARTES*, *ÉCHECS*) queen; **~s** *nfpl* (*jeu*) draughts *sg* (*Brit*), checkers *sg* (*US*); **les (toilettes des) ~s** the ladies' (toilets); ~ **de charité** benefactress; ~ **de compagnie** lady's companion.

dame-jeanne, *pl* **dames-jeannes** [damʒɑn] *nf* demijohn.

damer [dame] *vt* to ram *ou* pack down; ~ **le pion à** (*fig*) to get the better of.

damier [damje] *nm* draughtboard (*Brit*), checkerboard (*US*); (*dessin*) check (pattern); **en** ~ check.

damner [dane] *vt* to damn.

dancing [dɑ̃siŋ] *nm* dance hall.

dandiner [dɑ̃dine]: **se** ~ *vi* to sway about; (*en marchant*) to waddle along.

Danemark [danmaʀk] *nm*: **le** ~ Denmark.

danger [dɑ̃ʒe] *nm* danger; **mettre en** ~ to endanger, put in danger; **être en** ~ **de mort** to be in peril of one's life; **être hors de** ~ to be out of danger.

dangereusement [dɑ̃ʒʀøzmɑ̃] *ad* dangerously.

dangereux, euse [dɑ̃ʒʀø, -øz] *a* dangerous.

danois, e [danwa, -waz] *a* Danish ♦ *nm* (*LING*) Danish ♦ *nm/f*: **D~, e** Dane.

dans [dɑ̃] *prép* in; (*direction*) into, to; (*à l'intérieur de*) in, inside; **je l'ai pris** ~ **le tiroir/salon** I took it out of *ou* from the drawer/lounge; **boire** ~ **un verre** to drink out of *ou* from a glass; ~ **2 mois** in 2 months, in 2 months' time, 2 months from now; ~ **quelques instants** in a few minutes; ~ **quelques jours** in a few days' time; **il part** ~ **quinze jours** he's leaving in two weeks' (time); ~ **les 20 F** about 20 F.

dansant, e [dɑ̃sɑ̃, -ɑ̃t] *a*: **soirée** ~**e** evening of dancing; (*bal*) dinner dance.

danse [dɑ̃s] *nf*: **la** ~ dancing; (*classique*) (ballet) dancing; **une** ~ a dance; ~ **du ventre** belly dancing.

danser [dɑ̃se] *vi, vt* to dance.

danseur, euse [dɑ̃sœʀ, -øz] *nm/f* ballet dancer; (*au bal etc*) dancer; (*: cavalier*) partner; ~ **de claquettes** tap-dancer; **en danseuse** (*à vélo*) standing on the pedals.

Danube [danyb] *nm*: **le** ~ the Danube.

DAO *sigle m* (= *dessin assisté par ordinateur*) CAD.

dard [daʀ] *nm* sting (*organ*).

Dardanelles [daʀdanɛl] *nfpl*: **les** ~ the Dardanelles.

darder [daʀde] *vt* to shoot, send forth.

dare-dare [daʀdaʀ] *ad* in double quick time.

Dar-es-Salaam, Dar-es-Salam [daʀesalam] *n* Dar-es-Salaam.

darse [daʀs(ə)] *nf* sheltered dock (*in a Mediterranean port*).

datation [datasjɔ̃] *nf* dating.

date [dat] *nf* date; **faire** ~ to mark a milestone; **de longue** ~ *a* longstanding; ~ **de naissance** date of birth; ~ **limite** deadline; (*d'un aliment: aussi*: ~ **limite de vente**) sell-by date.

dater [date] *vt, vi* to date; ~ **de** to date from, go back to; **à** ~ **de** (as) from.

dateur [datœʀ] *nm* (*de montre*) date indicator; **timbre** ~ date stamp.

datif [datif] *nm* dative.

datte [dat] *nf* date.

dattier [datje] *nm* date palm.

daube [dob] *nf*: **bœuf en** ~ beef casserole.

dauphin [dofɛ̃] *nm* (*ZOOL*) dolphin; (*du roi*) dauphin; (*fig*) heir apparent.

Dauphiné [dofine] *nm*: **le** ~ the Dauphiné.

dauphinois, e [dofinwa, -waz] *a* of *ou* from the Dauphiné.

daurade [doʀad] *nf* sea bream.

davantage [davɑ̃taʒ] *ad* more; (*plus longtemps*) longer; ~ **de** more; ~ **que** more than.

DB *sigle f* (*MIL*) = *division blindée*.

DCT *sigle m* (= *diphtérie coqueluche tétanos*) DPT.

DDASS [das] *sigle f* (= *Direction départementale d'action sanitaire et sociale*) ≈ DHSS (= *Department of Health and Social Security*) (*Brit*), ≈ SSA (= *Social Security Administration*) (*US*).

DDT *sigle m* (= *dichloro-diphénol-trichloréthane*) DDT.

de (*de + le* = **du**, *de + les* = **des**) [də, dy, de] *prép* of; (*provenance*) from; (*moyen*) with; **la voiture d'Élisabeth/de mes parents** Elizabeth's/my parents' car; **un mur de brique/bureau d'acajou** a brick wall/mahogany desk; **augmenter** *etc* **de 10 F** to increase *etc* by 10 F; **une pièce de 2 m de large** *ou* **large de 2 m** a room 2 m wide *ou* in width, a 2 m wide room; **un bébé de 10 mois** a 10-month-old baby; **un séjour de 2 ans** a 2-year stay; **12 mois de crédit/travail** 12 months' credit/work; **de 14 à 18h** from 2pm till 6pm ♦ *dét*: **du vin, de l'eau, des pommes** (some) wine, (some) water, (some) apples; **des enfants sont venus** some children came; **a-t-il du vin?** has he got any wine?; **il ne veut pas de pommes** he doesn't want any apples; **il n'a pas d'enfants** he has no children, he hasn't (got) any children; **pendant des mois** for months.

dé [de] *nm* (*à jouer*) die *ou* dice (*pl* dice); (*aussi*: ~ **à coudre**) thimble; ~**s** *nmpl* (*jeu*) (game of) dice; **un coup de** ~**s** a throw of the dice; **couper en** ~**s** (*CULIN*) to dice.

DEA *sigle m* (= *Diplôme d'études approfondies*) *post-graduate diploma.*

déambuler [deɑ̃byle] *vi* to stroll about.

déb. *abr* = **débutant**; (*COMM*) = à débattre.

débâcle [debɑkl(ə)] *nf* rout.

déballer [debale] *vt* to unpack.

débandade [debɑ̃dad] *nf* scattering; (*déroute*) rout.

débander [debɑ̃de] *vt* to unbandage.

débaptiser [debatize] *vt* (*rue*) to rename.

débarbouiller [debaʀbuje] *vt* to wash; **se** ~ to wash (one's face).

débarcadère [debaʀkadɛʀ] *nm* landing stage (*Brit*), wharf.

débardeur [debaʀdœʀ] *nm* docker, stevedore; (*maillot*) slipover, tank top.

débarquement [debaʀkəmɑ̃] *nm* unloading, landing; disembarcation; (*MIL*) landing; **le D~** the Normandy landings.

débarquer [debaʀke] *vt* to unload, land ♦ *vi* to disembark; (*fig*) to turn up.

débarras [debaʀa] *nm* lumber room; (*placard*) junk cupboard; (*remise*) outhouse; **bon** ~! good riddance!

débarrasser [debaʀase] *vt* to clear ♦ *vi* (*enlever le couvert*) to clear away; ~ **qn de**

(*vêtements, paquets*) to relieve sb of; (*habitude, ennemi*) to rid sb of; ~ **qch de** (*fouillis etc*) to clear sth of; **se** ~ **de** *vt* to get rid of; to rid o.s. of.

débat [deba] *vb voir* **débattre** ♦ *nm* discussion, debate; ~**s** *nmpl* (*POL*) proceedings, debates.

débattre [debatʀ(ə)] *vt* to discuss, debate; **se** ~ *vi* to struggle.

débauche [deboʃ] *nf* debauchery; **une** ~ **de** (*fig*) a profusion of; (: *de couleurs*) a riot of.

débauché, e [deboʃe] *a* debauched ♦ *nm/f* profligate.

débaucher [deboʃe] *vt* (*licencier*) to lay off, dismiss; (*entraîner*) to lead astray, debauch; (*inciter à la grève*) to incite.

débile [debil] *a* weak, feeble; (*fam: idiot*) dim-witted ♦ *nm/f*: ~ **mental, e** mental defective.

débilitant, e [debilitā, -āt] *a* debilitating.

débilité [debilite] *nf* debility; (*fam: idiotie*) stupidity; ~ **mentale** mental debility.

débiner [debine]: **se** ~ *vi* to do a bunk (*Brit*), clear out.

débit [debi] *nm* (*d'un liquide, fleuve*) (rate of) flow; (*d'un magasin*) turnover (of goods); (*élocution*) delivery; (*bancaire*) debit; **avoir un** ~ **de 10 F** to be 10 F in debit; ~ **de boissons** drinking establishment; ~ **de tabac** tobacconist's (shop) (*Brit*), tobacco *ou* smoke shop (*US*).

débiter [debite] *vt* (*compte*) to debit; (*liquide, gaz*) to yield, produce, give out; (*couper: bois, viande*) to cut up; (*vendre*) to retail; (*péj: paroles etc*) to come out with, churn out.

débiteur, trice [debitœʀ, -tʀis] *nm/f* debtor ♦ *a* in debit; (*compte*) debit *cpd*.

déblai [deblɛ] *nm* earth (*moved*).

déblaiement [deblɛmɑ̃] *nm* clearing; **travaux de** ~ earth moving *sg*.

déblatérer [deblateʀe] *vi*: ~ **contre** to go on about.

déblayer [debleje] *vt* to clear; ~ **le terrain** (*fig*) to clear the ground.

débloquer [deblɔke] *vt* (*frein, fonds*) to release; (*prix*) to free ♦ *vi* (*fam*) to talk rubbish.

débobiner [debɔbine] *vt* to unwind.

déboires [debwaʀ] *nmpl* setbacks.

déboisement [debwazmɑ̃] *nm* deforestation.

déboiser [debwaze] *vt* to clear of trees; (*région*) to deforest; **se** ~ *vi* (*colline, montagne*) to become bare of trees.

déboîter [debwate] *vt* (*AUTO*) to pull out; **se** ~ **le genou** *etc* to dislocate one's knee *etc*.

débonnaire [debɔnɛʀ] *a* easy-going, good-natured.

débordant, e [debɔʀdɑ̃, -āt] *a* (*joie*) unbounded; (*activité*) exuberant.

débordé, e [debɔʀde] *a*: **être** ~ **de** (*travail, demandes*) to be snowed under with.

débordement [debɔʀdəmɑ̃] *nm* overflowing.

déborder [debɔʀde] *vi* to overflow; (*lait etc*) to boil over ♦ *vt* (*MIL, SPORT*) to outflank; ~ **(de) qch** (*dépasser*) to extend beyond sth; ~ **de** (*joie, zèle*) to be brimming over with *ou* bursting with.

débouché [debuʃe] *nm* (*pour vendre*) outlet;

(*perspective d'emploi*) opening; (*sortie*): **au** ~ **de la vallée** where the valley opens out (onto the plain).

déboucher [debuʃe] *vt* (*évier, tuyau etc*) to unblock; (*bouteille*) to uncork, open ♦ *vi*: ~ **de** to emerge from, come out of; ~ **sur** to come out onto; to open out onto; (*fig*) to arrive at, lead up to.

débouler [debule] *vi* to go (*ou* come) tumbling down; (*sans tomber*) to come careering down ♦ *vt*: ~ **l'escalier** to belt down the stairs.

déboulonner [debulɔne] *vt* to dismantle; (*fig: renvoyer*) to dismiss; (: *détruire le prestige de*) to discredit.

débours [debuʀ] *nmpl* outlay.

débourser [debuʀse] *vt* to pay out, lay out.

déboussoler [debusɔle] *vt* to disorientate, disorient.

debout [dəbu] *ad*: **être** ~ (*personne*) to be standing, stand; (: *levé, éveillé*) to be up (and about); (*chose*) to be upright; **être encore** ~ (*fig: en état*) to be still going; to be still standing; to be still up; **mettre qn** ~ to get sb to his feet; **mettre qch** ~ to stand sth up; **se mettre** ~ to get up (on one's feet); **se tenir** ~ to stand; ~! get up!; **cette histoire ne tient pas** ~ this story doesn't hold water.

débouter [debute] *vt* (*JUR*) to dismiss; ~ **qn de sa demande** to dismiss sb's petition.

déboutonner [debutɔne] *vt* to undo, unbutton; **se** ~ *vi* to come undone *ou* unbuttoned.

débraillé, e [debʀaje] *a* slovenly, untidy.

débrancher [debʀɑ̃ʃe] *vt* (*appareil électrique*) to unplug; (*téléphone, courant électrique*) to disconnect, cut off.

débrayage [debʀejaʒ] *nm* (*AUTO*) clutch; (: *action*) disengaging the clutch; (*grève*) stoppage; **faire un double** ~ to double-declutch.

débrayer [debʀeje] *vi* (*AUTO*) to declutch, disengage the clutch; (*cesser le travail*) to stop work.

débridé, e [debʀide] *a* unbridled, unrestrained.

débrider [debʀide] *vt* (*cheval*) to unbridle; (*CULIN: volaille*) to untruss.

débris [debʀi] *nm* (*fragment*) fragment ♦ *nmpl* (*déchets*) pieces, debris *sg*; rubbish *sg* (*Brit*), garbage *sg* (*US*).

débrouillard, e [debʀujaʀ, -aʀd(ə)] *a* smart, resourceful.

débrouillardise [debʀujaʀdiz] *nf* smartness, resourcefulness.

débrouiller [debʀuje] *vt* to disentangle, untangle; (*fig*) to sort out, unravel; **se** ~ *vi* to manage.

débroussailler [debʀusaje] *vt* to clear (of brushwood).

débusquer [debyske] *vt* to drive out (from cover).

début [deby] *nm* beginning, start; ~**s** *nmpl* beginnings; (*de carrière*) début *sg*; **faire ses** ~**s** to start out; **au** ~ in *ou* at the beginning, at first; **au** ~ **de** at the beginning *ou* start of; **dès le** ~ from the start.

débutant, e [debytā, -āt] *nm/f* beginner, novice.

débuter [debyte] *vi* to begin, start; (*faire ses*

débuts) to start out.

deçà [dəsa]: **en ~ de** *prép* this side of; **en ~ ad** on this side.

décacheter [dekaʃte] *vt* to unseal, open.

décade [dekad] *nf* (*10 jours*) (period of) ten days; (*10 ans*) decade.

décadence [dekadɑ̃s] *nf* decadence; decline.

décadent, e [dekadɑ̃, -ɑ̃t] *a* decadent.

décaféiné, e [dekafeine] *a* decaffeinated, caffeine-free.

décalage [dekalaʒ] *nm* move forward *ou* back; shift forward *ou* back; (*écart*) gap; (*désaccord*) discrepancy; **~ horaire** time difference (between time zones), time-lag.

décalaminer [dekalamine] *vt* to decoke.

décalcomanie [dekalkɔmani] *nf* transfer.

décaler [dekale] *vt* (*dans le temps: avancer*) to bring forward; (: *retarder*) to put back; (*changer de position*) to shift forward *ou* back; **~ de 10 cm** to move forward *ou* back by 10 cm; **~ de 2 h** to bring *ou* move forward 2 hours; to put back 2 hours.

décalitre [dekalitʀ(ə)] *nm* decalitre (*Brit*), decaliter (*US*).

décalquer [dekalke] *vt* to trace; (*par pression*) to transfer.

décamètre [dekamɛtʀ(ə)] *nm* decametre (*Brit*), decameter (*US*).

décamper [dekɑ̃pe] *vi* to clear out *ou* off.

décan [dekɑ̃] *nm* (*ASTROLOGIE*) decan.

décanter [dekɑ̃te] *vt* to (allow to) settle (and decant); **se ~** *vi* to settle.

décapage [dekapaʒ] *nm* stripping; scouring; sanding.

décapant [dekapɑ̃] *nm* acid solution; scouring agent; paint stripper.

décaper [dekape] *vt* to strip; (*avec abrasif*) to scour; (*avec papier de verre*) to sand.

décapiter [dekapite] *vt* to behead; (*par accident*) to decapitate; (*fig*) to cut the top off; (: *organisation*) to remove the top people from.

décapotable [dekapɔtabl(ə)] *a* convertible.

décapoter [dekapɔte] *vt* to put down the top of.

décapsuler [dekapsyle] *vt* to take the cap *ou* top off.

décapsuleur [dekapsylœʀ] *nm* bottle-opener.

décathlon [dekatlɔ̃] *nm* decathlon.

décati, e [dekati] *a* faded, aged.

décédé, e [desede] *a* deceased.

décéder [desede] *vi* to die.

déceler [desle] *vt* to discover, detect; (*révéler*) to indicate, reveal.

décélération [deselerɑsjɔ̃] *nf* deceleration.

décélérer [deselere] *vi* to decelerate, slow down.

décembre [desɑ̃bʀ(ə)] *nm* December; *voir aussi* **juillet**.

décemment [desamɑ̃] *ad* decently.

décence [desɑ̃s] *nf* decency.

décennal, e, aux [desenal, -o] *a* (*qui dure dix ans*) having a term of ten years, ten-year; (*qui revient tous les dix ans*) ten-yearly.

décennie [desni] *nf* decade.

décent, e [desɑ̃, -ɑ̃t] *a* decent.

décentralisation [desɑ̃tʀalizɑsjɔ̃] *nf* decentralization.

décentraliser [desɑ̃tʀalize] *vt* to decentralize.

décentrer [desɑ̃tʀe] *vt* to decentre; **se ~** to move off-centre.

déception [desɛpsjɔ̃] *nf* disappointment.

décerner [desɛʀne] *vt* to award.

décès [desɛ] *nm* death, decease; **acte de ~** death certificate.

décevant, e [desvɑ̃, -ɑ̃t] *a* disappointing.

décevoir [desvwaʀ] *vt* to disappoint.

déchaîné, e [deʃene] *a* unbridled, raging.

déchaîner [deʃene] *vt* (*passions, colère*) to unleash; (*rires etc*) to give rise to, arouse; **se ~** *vi* to be unleashed; (*rires*) to burst out; (*se mettre en colère*) to fly into a rage; **se ~ contre qn** to unleash one's fury on sb.

déchanter [deʃɑ̃te] *vi* to become disillusioned.

décharge [deʃaʀʒ(ə)] *nf* (*dépôt d'ordures*) rubbish tip *ou* dump; (*électrique*) electrical discharge; (*salve*) volley of shots; **à la ~ de** in defence of.

déchargement [deʃaʀʒəmɑ̃] *nm* unloading.

décharger [deʃaʀʒe] *vt* (*marchandise, véhicule*) to unload; (*ÉLEC*) to discharge; (*arme: neutraliser*) to unload; (: *faire feu*) to discharge, fire; **~ qn de** (*responsabilité*) to relieve sb of, release sb from; **~ sa colère (sur)** to vent one's anger (on); **~ sa conscience** to unburden one's conscience; **se ~ dans** (*se déverser*) to flow into; **se ~ d'une affaire sur qn** to hand a matter over to sb.

décharné, e [deʃaʀne] *a* bony, emaciated, fleshless.

déchaussé, e [deʃose] *a* (*dent*) loose.

déchausser [deʃose] *vt* (*personne*) to take the shoes off; (*skis*) to take off; **se ~** to take off one's shoes; (*dent*) to come *ou* work loose.

dèche [dɛʃ] *nf* (*fam*): **être dans la ~** to be flat broke.

déchéance [deʃeɑ̃s] *nf* (*déclin*) degeneration, decay, decline; (*chute*) fall.

déchet [deʃɛ] *nm* (*de bois, tissu etc*) scrap; (*perte: gén COMM*) wastage, waste; **~s** *nmpl* (*ordures*) refuse *sg*, rubbish *sg* (*Brit*), garbage *sg* (*US*); **~s radioactifs** radioactive waste.

déchiffrage [deʃifʀaʒ] *nm* sight-reading.

déchiffrer [deʃifʀe] *vt* to decipher.

déchiqueté, e [deʃikte] *a* jagged(-edged), ragged.

déchiqueter [deʃikte] *vt* to tear *ou* pull to pieces.

déchirant, e [deʃiʀɑ̃, -ɑ̃t] *a* heart-breaking, heart-rending.

déchiré, e [deʃiʀe] *a* torn; (*fig*) heart-broken.

déchirement [deʃiʀmɑ̃] *nm* (*chagrin*) wrench, heartbreak; (*gén pl: conflit*) rift, split.

déchirer [deʃiʀe] *vt* to tear, rip; (*mettre en morceaux*) to tear up; (*pour ouvrir*) to tear off; (*arracher*) to tear out; (*fig*) to tear apart; **se ~** *vi* to tear, rip; **se ~ un muscle/tendon** to tear a muscle/tendon.

déchirure [deʃiʀyʀ] *nf* (*accroc*) tear, rip; **~ musculaire** torn muscle.

déchoir [deʃwaʀ] *vi* (*personne*) to lower o.s., demean o.s.; **~ de** to fall from.

déchu, e [deʃy] *pp de* **déchoir** ♦ *a* fallen; (*roi*) deposed.

décibel [desibɛl] *nm* decibel.

décidé, e [deside] *a* (*personne, air*)

determined; **c'est** ~ it's decided; **être** ~ **à faire** to be determined to do.

décidément [desidemã] *ad* undoubtedly; really.

décider [deside] *vt*: ~ **qch** to decide on sth; ~ **de faire/que** to decide to do/that; ~ **qn (à faire qch)** to persuade *ou* induce sb (to do sth); ~ **de qch** to decide upon sth; *(suj: chose)* to determine sth; **se** ~ *vi (personne)* to decide, make up one's mind; *(problème, affaire)* to be resolved; **se** ~ **à qch** to decide on sth; **se** ~ **à faire** to decide *ou* make up one's mind to do; **se** ~ **pour qch** to decide on *ou* in favour of sth.

décilitre [desilitʀ(ə)] *nm* decilitre *(Brit)*, deciliter *(US)*.

décimal, e, aux [desimal, -o] *a, nf* decimal.

décimalisation [desimalizasjɔ̃] *nf* decimalization.

décimaliser [desimalize] *vt* to decimalize.

décimer [desime] *vt* to decimate.

décimètre [desimɛtʀ(ə)] *nm* decimetre *(Brit)*, decimeter *(US)*; **double** ~ (20 cm) ruler.

décisif, ive [desizif, -iv] *a* decisive; *(qui l'emporte)*: **le facteur/l'argument** ~ the deciding factor/argument.

décision [desizjɔ̃] *nf* decision; *(fermeté)* decisiveness, decision; **prendre une** ~ to make a decision; **prendre la** ~ **de faire** to take the decision to do; **emporter** *ou* **faire la** ~ to be decisive.

déclamation [deklamasjɔ̃] *nf* declamation; *(péj)* ranting, spouting.

déclamatoire [deklamatwaʀ] *a* declamatory.

déclamer [deklame] *vt* to declaim; *(péj)* to spout ♦ *vi*: ~ **contre** to rail against.

déclarable [deklaʀabl(ə)] *a (marchandise)* dutiable; *(revenus)* declarable.

déclaration [deklaʀasjɔ̃] *nf* declaration; registration; *(discours: POL etc)* statement; *(compte rendu)* report; **fausse** ~ misrepresentation; ~ **(d'amour)** declaration; ~ **de décès** registration of death; ~ **de guerre** declaration of war; ~ **(d'impôts)** statement of income, tax declaration, ≈ tax return; ~ **(de sinistre)** (insurance) claim; ~ **de revenus** statement of income.

déclaré, e [deklaʀe] *a (juré)* avowed.

déclarer [deklaʀe] *vt* to declare, announce; *(revenus, employés, marchandises)* to declare; *(décès, naissance)* to register; *(vol etc: à la police)* to report; **se** ~ *vi (feu, maladie)* to break out; ~ **la guerre** to declare war.

déclassé, e [deklase] *a* relegated, downgraded; *(matériel)* (to be) sold off.

déclassement [deklɑsmã] *nm* relegation, downgrading; *(RAIL etc)* change of class.

déclasser [deklɑse] *vt* to relegate, downgrade; *(déranger: fiches, livres)* to get out of order.

déclenchement [deklɑ̃ʃmã] *nm* release; setting off.

déclencher [deklɑ̃ʃe] *vt (mécanisme etc)* to release; *(sonnerie)* to set off, activate; *(attaque, grève)* to launch; *(provoquer)* to trigger off; **se** ~ *vi* to release itself; to go off.

déclencheur [deklɑ̃ʃœʀ] *nm* release mechanism.

déclic [deklik] *nm* trigger mechanism; *(bruit)* click.

déclin [deklɛ̃] *nm* decline.

déclinaison [deklinɛzɔ̃] *nf* declension.

décliner [dekline] *vi* to decline ♦ *vt (invitation)* to decline, refuse; *(responsabilité)* to refuse to accept; *(nom, adresse)* to state; *(LING)* to decline; **se** ~ *(LING)* to decline.

déclivité [deklivite] *nf* slope, incline; **en** ~ sloping, on the incline.

décloisonner [deklwazɔne] *vt* to decompartmentalize.

déclouer [deklue] *vt* to unnail.

décocher [dekɔʃe] *vt* to hurl; *(flèche, regard)* to shoot.

décoction [dekɔksjɔ̃] *nf* decoction.

décodage [dekɔdaʒ] *nm* deciphering, decoding.

décoder [dekɔde] *vt* to decipher, decode.

décodeur [dekɔdœʀ] *nm* decoder.

décoiffé, e [dekwafe] *a*: **elle est toute** ~**e** her hair is in a mess.

décoiffer [dekwafe] *vt*: ~ **qn** to disarrange *ou* mess up sb's hair; to take sb's hat off; **se** ~ to take off one's hat.

décoincer [dekwɛ̃se] *vt* to unjam, loosen.

déçois [deswa] *etc*, **déçoive** [deswav] *etc vb voir* **décevoir**.

décolérer [dekɔleʀe] *vi*: **il ne décolère pas** he's still angry, he hasn't calmed down.

décollage [dekɔlaʒ] *nm (AVIAT, ÉCON)* takeoff.

décollé, e [dekɔle] *a*: **oreilles** ~**es** sticking-out ears.

décollement [dekɔlmã] *nm (MÉD)*: ~ **de la rétine** retinal detachment.

décoller [dekɔle] *vt* to unstick ♦ *vi* to take off; *(projet, entreprise)* to take off, get off the ground; **se** ~ *vi* to come unstuck.

décolleté, e [dekɔlte] *a* low-necked, low-cut; *(femme)* wearing a low-cut dress ♦ *nm* low neck(line); *(épaules)* (bare) neck and shoulders; *(plongeant)* cleavage.

décolleter [dekɔlte] *vt (vêtement)* to give a low neckline to; *(TECH)* to cut.

décoloniser [dekɔlɔnize] *vt* to decolonize.

décolorant [dekɔlɔʀã] *nm* decolorant, bleaching agent.

décoloration [dekɔlɔʀasjɔ̃] *nf*: **se faire faire une** ~ *(chez le coiffeur)* to have one's hair bleached *ou* lightened.

décoloré, e [dekɔlɔʀe] *a (vêtement)* faded; *(cheveux)* bleached.

décolorer [dekɔlɔʀe] *vt (tissu)* to fade; *(cheveux)* to bleach, lighten; **se** ~ *vi* to fade.

décombres [dekɔ̃bʀ(ə)] *nmpl* rubble *sg*, debris *sg*.

décommander [dekɔmãde] *vt* to cancel; *(invités)* to put off; **se** ~ to cancel, cry off.

décomposé, e [dekɔ̃poze] *a (pourri)* decomposed; *(visage)* haggard, distorted.

décomposer [dekɔ̃poze] *vt* to break up; *(CHIMIE)* to decompose; *(MATH)* to factorize; **se** ~ *vi* to decompose.

décomposition [dekɔ̃pozisjɔ̃] *nf* breaking up; decomposition; factorization; **en** ~ *(organisme)* in a state of decay, decomposing.

décompresseur [dekɔ̃pʀesœʀ] *nm*

decompressor.

décompression [dekɔ̃presjɔ̃] *nf* decompression.

décomprimer [dekɔ̃prime] *vt* to decompress.

décompte [dekɔ̃t] *nm* deduction; *(facture)* breakdown (of an account), detailed account.

décompter [dekɔ̃te] *vt* to deduct.

déconcentration [dekɔ̃sɑ̃trasjɔ̃] *nf (des industries etc)* dispersal; ~ **des pouvoirs** devolution.

déconcentré, e [dekɔ̃sɑ̃tre] *a (sportif etc)* who has lost (his/her) concentration.

déconcentrer [dekɔ̃sɑ̃tre] *vt (ADMIN)* to disperse; **se** ~ *vi* to lose (one's) concentration.

déconcertant, e [dekɔ̃sɛrtɑ̃, -ɑ̃t] *a* disconcerting.

déconcerter [dekɔ̃sɛrte] *vt* to disconcert, confound.

déconfit, e [dekɔ̃fi, -it] *a* crestfallen, downcast.

déconfiture [dekɔ̃fityr] *nf* collapse, ruin; *(morale)* defeat.

décongélation [dekɔ̃ʒelasjɔ̃] *nf* defrosting, thawing.

décongeler [dekɔ̃ʒle] *vt* to thaw (out).

décongestionner [dekɔ̃ʒɛstjɔne] *vt (MÉD)* to decongest; *(rues)* to relieve congestion in.

déconnecter [dekɔnɛkte] *vt* to disconnect.

déconner [dekɔne] *vi (fam!: en parlant)* to talk (a load of) rubbish *(Brit)* ou garbage *(US)*; (*: faire des bêtises*) to muck about; **sans** ~ no kidding.

déconseiller [dekɔ̃seje] *vt*: ~ **qch (à qn)** to advise (sb) against sth; ~ **à qn de faire** to advise sb against doing; **c'est déconseillé** it's not advised ou advisable.

déconsidérer [dekɔ̃sidere] *vt* to discredit.

décontaminer [dekɔ̃tamine] *vt* to decontaminate.

décontenancer [dekɔ̃tnɑ̃se] *vt* to disconcert, discountenance.

décontracté, e [dekɔ̃trakte] *a* relaxed.

décontracter [dekɔ̃trakte] *vt*, **se** ~ *vi* to relax.

décontraction [dekɔ̃traksjɔ̃] *nf* relaxation.

déconvenue [dekɔ̃vny] *nf* disappointment.

décor [dekɔr] *nm* décor; *(paysage)* scenery; ~**s** *nmpl (THÉÂTRE)* scenery *sg*, decor *sg*; *(CINÉMA)* set *sg*; **changement de** ~ *(fig)* change of scene; **entrer dans le** ~ *(fig)* to run off the road; **en** ~ **naturel** *(CINÉMA)* on location.

décorateur, trice [dekɔratœr, -tris] *nm/f* (interior) decorator; *(CINÉMA)* set designer.

décoratif, ive [dekɔratif, -iv] *a* decorative.

décoration [dekɔrasjɔ̃] *nf* decoration.

décorer [dekɔre] *vt* to decorate.

décortiqué, e [dekɔrtike] *a* shelled; hulled.

décortiquer [dekɔrtike] *vt* to shell; *(riz)* to hull; *(fig)* to dissect.

décorum [dekɔrɔm] *nm* decorum; etiquette.

décote [dekɔt] *nf* tax relief.

découcher [dekuʃe] *vi* to spend the night away.

découdre [dekudr(ə)] *vt (vêtement, couture)* to unpick, take the stitching out of; *(bouton)* to take off; **se** ~ *vi* to come unstitched; *(bouton)* to come off; **en** ~ *(fig)* to fight, do battle.

découler [dekule] *vi*: ~ **de** to ensue ou follow from.

découpage [dekupaʒ] *nm* cutting up; carving; *(image)* cut-out (figure); ~ **électoral** division into constituencies.

découper [dekupe] *vt (papier, tissu etc)* to cut up; *(volaille, viande)* to carve; *(détacher: manche, article)* to cut out; **se** ~ **sur** *(ciel, fond)* to stand out against.

découplé, e [dekuple] *a*: **bien** ~ well-built, well-proportioned.

découpure [dekupyr] *nf*: ~**s** *(morceaux)* cut-out bits; *(d'une côte, arête)* indentations, jagged outline *sg*.

découragement [dekuraʒmɑ̃] *nm* discouragement, despondency.

décourager [dekuraʒe] *vt* to discourage, dishearten; *(dissuader)* to discourage, put off; **se** ~ *vi* to lose heart, become discouraged; ~ **qn de faire/de qch** to discourage sb from doing/from sth, put sb off doing/sth.

décousu, e [dekuzy] *pp de* **découdre** ♦ *a* unstitched; *(fig)* disjointed, disconnected.

découvert, e [dekuvɛr, -ɛrt(ə)] *pp de* **découvrir** ♦ *a (tête)* bare, uncovered; *(lieu)* open, exposed ♦ *nm (bancaire)* overdraft ♦ *nf* discovery; **à** ~ *ad (MIL)* exposed, without cover; *(fig)* openly ♦ *a (COMM)* overdrawn; **à visage** ~ openly; **aller à la** ~**e de** to go in search of.

découvrir [dekuvrir] *vt* to discover; *(apercevoir)* to see; *(enlever ce qui couvre ou protège)* to uncover; *(montrer, dévoiler)* to reveal; **se** ~ to take off one's hat; *(se déshabiller)* to take something off; *(au lit)* to uncover o.s.; *(ciel)* to clear; **se** ~ **des talents** to find hidden talents in o.s.

décrasser [dekrase] *vt* to clean.

décrêper [dekrepe] *vt (cheveux)* to straighten.

décrépi, e [dekrepi] *a* peeling; with roughcast rendering removed.

décrépit, e [dekrepi, -it] *a* decrepit.

décrépitude [dekrepityd] *nf* decrepitude; decay.

decrescendo [dekreʃɛndo] *nm (MUS)* decrescendo; **aller** ~ *(fig)* to decline, be on the wane.

décret [dekrɛ] *nm* decree.

décréter [dekrete] *vt* to decree; *(ordonner)* to order.

décret-loi [dekrɛlwa] *nm* statutory order.

décrié, e [dekrije] *a* disparaged.

décrire [dekrir] *vt* to describe; *(courbe, cercle)* to follow, describe.

décrisper [dekrispe] *vt* to defuse.

décrit, e [dekri, -it] *pp de* **décrire**.

décrivais [dekrive] *etc vb voir* **décrire**.

décrochement [dekrɔʃmɑ̃] *nm (d'un mur etc)* recess.

décrocher [dekrɔʃe] *vt (dépendre)* to take down; *(téléphone)* to take off the hook; *(: pour répondre)*: ~ **(le téléphone)** to pick up ou lift the receiver; *(fig: contrat etc)* to get, land ♦ *vi* to drop out; to switch off; **se** ~ *vi (tableau, rideau)* to fall down.

décrois [dekrwa] *etc vb voir* **décroître**.

décroiser [dekrwaze] *vt (bras)* to unfold; *(jambes)* to uncross.

décroissant, e [dekrwasɑ̃, -ɑ̃t] *vb voir* **décroi-**

tre ♦ a decreasing, declining, diminishing; **par ordre ~** in descending order.

décroître [dekʀwatʀ(ə)] vi to decrease, decline, diminish.

décrotter [dekʀɔte] vt (chaussures) to clean the mud from; **se ~ le nez** to pick one's nose.

décru, e [dekʀy] pp de **décroître**.

décrue [dekʀy] nf drop in level (of the waters).

décrypter [dekʀipte] vt to decipher.

déçu, e [desy] pp de **décevoir ♦** a disappointed.

déculotter [dekylɔte] vt: **~ qn** to take off ou down sb's trousers; **se ~** to take off ou down one's trousers.

déculpabiliser [dekylpabilize] vt (personne) to relieve of guilt; (chose) to decriminalize.

décuple [dekypl(ə)] nm: **le ~ de** ten times; **au ~** tenfold.

décupler [dekyple] vt, vi to increase tenfold.

déçut [desy] etc vb voir **décevoir**.

dédaignable [dedɛɲabl(ə)] a: **pas ~** not to be despised.

dédaigner [dedɛɲe] vt to despise, scorn; (négliger) to disregard, spurn; **~ de faire** to consider it beneath one to do, not deign to do.

dédaigneusement [dedɛɲøzmɑ̃] ad scornfully, disdainfully.

dédaigneux, euse [dedɛɲø, -øz] a scornful, disdainful.

dédain [dedɛ̃] nm scorn, disdain.

dédale [dedal] nm maze.

dedans [dədɑ̃] ad inside; (pas en plein air) indoors, inside ♦ nm inside; **au ~** on the inside; inside; **en ~** (vers l'intérieur) inwards; voir aussi **là**.

dédicace [dedikas] nf (imprimée) dedication; (manuscrite, sur une photo etc) inscription.

dédicacer [dedikase] vt: **~ (à qn)** to sign (for sb), autograph (for sb), inscribe (to sb).

dédié, e [dedje] a: **ordinateur ~** dedicated computer.

dédier [dedje] vt to dedicate.

dédire [dediʀ]: **se ~** vi to go back on one's word; (se rétracter) to retract, recant.

dédit, e [dedi, -it] pp de **dédire ♦** nm (COMM) forfeit, penalty.

dédommagement [dedɔmaʒmɑ̃] nm compensation.

dédommager [dedɔmaʒe] vt: **~ qn (de)** to compensate sb (for); (fig) to repay sb (for).

dédouaner [dedwane] vt to clear through customs.

dédoublement [dedubləmɑ̃] nm splitting; (PSYCH): **~ de la personnalité** split ou dual personality.

dédoubler [deduble] vt (classe, effectifs) to split (into two); (couverture etc) to unfold; (manteau) to remove the lining of; **~ un train/les trains** to run a relief train/additional trains; **se ~** vi (PSYCH) to have a split personality.

dédramatiser [dedʀamatize] vt (situation) to defuse; (événement) to play down.

déductible [dedyktibl(ə)] a deductible.

déduction [dedyksjɔ̃] nf (d'argent) deduction; (raisonnement) deduction, inference.

déduire [dedɥiʀ] vt: **~ qch (de)** (ôter) to

deduct sth (from); (conclure) to deduce ou infer sth (from).

déesse [deɛs] nf goddess.

DEFA sigle m (= Diplôme d'État relatif aux fonctions d'animation) diploma for senior youth leaders.

défaillance [defajɑ̃s] nf (syncope) blackout; (fatigue) (sudden) weakness q; (technique) fault, failure; (morale etc) weakness; **~ cardiaque** heart failure.

défaillant, e [defajɑ̃, -ɑ̃t] a defective; (JUR: témoin) defaulting.

défaillir [defajiʀ] vi to faint; to feel faint; (mémoire etc) to fail.

défaire [defɛʀ] vt (installation, échafaudage) to take down, dismantle; (paquet etc, nœud, vêtement) to undo; (bagages) to unpack; (ouvrage) to undo, unpick; (cheveux) to take out; **se ~** vi to come undone; **se ~ de** vt (se débarrasser de) to get rid of; (se séparer de) to part with; **~ le lit** (pour changer les draps) to strip the bed; (pour se coucher) to turn back the bedclothes.

défait, e [defɛ, -ɛt] pp de **défaire ♦** a (visage) haggard, ravaged ♦ nf defeat.

défaites [defɛt] vb voir **défaire**.

défaitisme [defetism(ə)] nm defeatism.

défaitiste [defetist(ə)] a, nm/f defeatist.

défalcation [defalkasjɔ̃] nf deduction.

défalquer [defalke] vt to deduct.

défasse [defas] etc vb voir **défaire**.

défausser [defose] vt to get rid of; **se ~** vi (CARTES) to discard.

défaut [defo] nm (moral) fault, failing, defect; (d'étoffe, métal) fault, flaw, defect; (manque, carence): **~ de** lack of; shortage of; (INFORM) bug; **~ de la cuirasse** (fig) chink in the armour (Brit) ou armor (US); **en ~** at fault; in the wrong; **faire ~** (manquer) to be lacking; **à ~** ad failing that; **à ~ de** for lack ou want of; **par ~** (JUR) in his (ou her etc) absence.

défaveur [defavœʀ] nf disfavour (Brit), disfavor (US).

défavorable [defavɔʀabl(ə)] a unfavourable (Brit), unfavorable (US).

défavoriser [defavɔʀize] vt to put at a disadvantage.

défectif, ive [defɛktif, -iv] a: **verbe ~** defective verb.

défection [defɛksjɔ̃] nf defection, failure to give support ou assistance; failure to appear; **faire ~** (d'un parti etc) to withdraw one's support, leave.

défectueux, euse [defɛktɥø, -øz] a faulty, defective.

défectuosité [defɛktɥozite] nf defectiveness q; (défaut) defect, fault.

défendable [defɑ̃dabl(ə)] a defensible.

défendeur, eresse [defɑ̃dœʀ, -dʀɛs] nm/f (JUR) defendant.

défendre [defɑ̃dʀ(ə)] vt to defend; (interdire) to forbid; **~ à qn qch/de faire** to forbid sb sth/to do; **il est défendu de cracher** spitting (is) prohibited ou is not allowed; **c'est défendu** it is forbidden; **se ~ to defend o.s.; il se défend** (fig) he can hold his own; **ça se défend** (fig) it holds together; **se ~ de/contre** (se protéger) to protect o.s. from/

against; **se ~ de** (*se garder de*) to refrain from; (*nier*): **se ~ de vouloir** to deny wanting.

défenestrer [defənɛstʀe] *vt* to throw out of the window.

défense [defɑ̃s] *nf* defence (*Brit*), defense (*US*); (*d'éléphant etc*) tusk; **ministre de la ~** Minister of Defence (*Brit*), Defence Secretary; **la ~ nationale** defence, the defence of the realm (*Brit*); **la ~ contre avions** anti-aircraft defence; "**~ de fumer/cracher**" "no smoking/spitting", "smoking/spitting prohibited"; **prendre la ~ de qn** to stand up for sb; **~ des consommateurs** consumerism.

défenseur [defɑ̃sœʀ] *nm* defender; (*JUR*) counsel for the defence.

défensif, ive [defɑ̃sif, -iv] *a*, *nf* defensive; **être sur la défensive** to be on the defensive.

déferai [defʀe] *etc vb voir* **défaire**.

déférence [defeʀɑ̃s] *nf* deference.

déférent, e [defeʀɑ̃, -ɑ̃t] *a* (*poli*) deferential, deferent.

déférer [defeʀe] *vt* (*JUR*) to refer; **~ à** *vt* (*requête, décision*) to defer to; **~ qn à la justice** to hand sb over to justice.

déferlant, e [defeʀlɑ̃, -ɑ̃t] *a*: **vague ~e** breaker.

déferlement [defeʀləmɑ̃] *nm* breaking; surge.

déferler [defeʀle] *vi* (*vagues*) to break; (*fig*) to surge.

défi [defi] *nm* (*provocation*) challenge; (*bravade*) defiance; **mettre qn au ~ de faire qch** to challenge sb to do sth; **relever un ~** to take up *ou* accept a challenge.

défiance [defjɑ̃s] *nf* mistrust, distrust.

déficeler [defisle] *vt* (*paquet*) to undo, untie.

déficience [defisjɑ̃s] *nf* deficiency.

déficient, e [defisjɑ̃, -ɑ̃t] *a* deficient.

déficit [defisit] *nm* (*COMM*) deficit; (*PSYCH etc: manque*) defect; **~ budgétaire** budget deficit; **être en ~** to be in deficit.

déficitaire [defisitɛʀ] *a* (*année, récolte*) bad; **entreprise/budget ~** business/budget in deficit.

défier [defje] *vt* (*provoquer*) to challenge; (*fig*) to defy, brave; **se ~ de** (*se méfier de*) to distrust, mistrust; **~ qn de faire** to challenge *ou* defy sb to do; **~ qn à** to challenge sb to; **~ toute comparaison/concurrence** to be incomparable/unbeatable.

défigurer [defigyʀe] *vt* to disfigure; (*suj: boutons etc*) to mar *ou* spoil (the looks of); (*fig: œuvre*) to mutilate, deface.

défilé [defile] *nm* (*GÉO*) (narrow) gorge *ou* pass; (*soldats*) parade; (*manifestants*) procession, march; **un ~ de** (*voitures, visiteurs etc*) a stream of.

défiler [defile] *vi* (*troupes*) to march past; (*sportifs*) to parade; (*manifestants*) to march; (*visiteurs*) to pour, stream; **se ~ vi** (*se dérober*) to slip away, sneak off; **faire ~** (*bande, film*) to put on; (*INFORM*) to scroll.

défini, e [defini] *a* definite.

définir [definiʀ] *vt* to define.

définissable [definisabl(ə)] *a* definable.

définitif, ive [definitif, -iv] *a* (*final*) final, definitive; (*pour longtemps*) permanent, definitive; (*sans appel*) final, definite ♦ *nf*: **en**

définitive eventually; (*somme toute*) when all is said and done.

définition [definisjɔ̃] *nf* definition; (*de mots croisés*) clue; (*TV*) (picture) resolution.

définitivement [definitivmɑ̃] *ad* definitively; permanently; definitely.

défit [defi] *etc vb voir* **défaire**.

déflagration [deflagʀasjɔ̃] *nf* explosion.

déflation [deflɑsjɔ̃] *nf* deflation.

déflationniste [deflɑsjɔnist(ə)] *a* deflationist, deflationary.

déflecteur [deflɛktœʀ] *nm* (*AUTO*) quarterlight (*Brit*), deflector (*US*).

déflorer [defloʀe] *vt* (*jeune fille*) to deflower; (*fig*) to spoil the charm of.

défoncé, e [defɔ̃se] *a* smashed in; broken down; (*route*) full of potholes ♦ *nm/f* addict.

défoncer [defɔ̃se] *vt* (*caisse*) to stave in; (*porte*) to smash in *ou* down; (*lit, fauteuil*) to burst (the springs of); (*terrain, route*) to rip *ou* plough up; **se ~ vi** (*se donner à fond*) to give it all one's got.

défont [defɔ̃] *vb voir* **défaire**.

déformant, e [defɔʀmɑ̃, -ɑ̃t] *a*: **glace** *ou* **miroir ~(e)** distorting mirror.

déformation [defɔʀmɑsjɔ̃] *nf* loss of shape; deformation; distortion; **~ professionnelle** conditioning by one's job.

déformer [defɔʀme] *vt* to put out of shape; (*corps*) to deform; (*pensée, fait*) to distort; **se ~ vi** to lose its shape.

défoulement [defulmɑ̃] *nm* release of tension; unwinding.

défouler [defule]: **se ~ vi** (*PSYCH*) to work off one's tensions, release one's pent-up feelings; (*gén*) to unwind, let off steam.

défraîchi, e [defʀeʃi] *a* faded; (*article à vendre*) shop-soiled.

défraîchir [defʀeʃiʀ]: **se ~ vi** to fade; to become shop-soiled.

défrayer [defʀeje] *vt*: **~ qn** to pay sb's expenses; **~ la chronique** to be in the news; **~ la conversation** to be the main topic of conversation.

défrichement [defʀiʃmɑ̃] *nm* clearance.

défricher [defʀiʃe] *vt* to clear (for cultivation).

défriser [defʀize] *vt* (*cheveux*) to straighten; (*fig*) to annoy.

défroisser [defʀwase] *vt* to smooth out.

défroque [defʀɔk] *nf* cast-off.

défroqué [defʀɔke] *nm* former monk (*ou* priest).

défroquer [defʀɔke] *vi* (*aussi*: **se ~**) to give up the cloth, renounce one's vows.

défunt, e [defœ̃, -œ̃t] *a*: **son ~ père** his late father ♦ *nm/f* deceased.

dégagé, e [degaʒe] *a* clear; (*ton, air*) casual, jaunty.

dégagement [degaʒmɑ̃] *nm* emission; freeing; clearing; (*espace libre*) clearing; passage; clearance; (*FOOTBALL*) clearance; **voie de ~** slip road; **itinéraire de ~** alternative route (*to relieve traffic congestion*).

dégager [degaʒe] *vt* (*exhaler*) to give off, emit; (*délivrer*) to free, extricate; (*MIL: troupes*) to relieve; (*désencombrer*) to clear; (*isoler, mettre en valeur*) to bring out; (*crédits*) to release; **se ~ vi** (*odeur*) to emanate, be given off; (*passage, ciel*) to clear; ~ **qn de** (*engagement, parole etc*) to release *ou* free sb from; **se ~ de** (*fig: engagement etc*) to get out of; (*: promesse*) to go back on.

dégaine [degɛn] *nf* awkward way of walking.

dégainer [degene] *vt* to draw.

dégarni, e [degaʀni] *a* bald.

dégarnir [degaʀniʀ] *vt* (*vider*) to empty, clear; **se ~** to empty; to be cleaned out *ou* cleared; (*tempes, crâne*) to go bald.

dégâts [degɑ] *nmpl* damage *sg*; **faire des ~** to damage.

dégazer [degɑze] *vi* (*pétrolier*) to clean its tanks.

dégel [deʒɛl] *nm* thaw; (*fig: des prix etc*) unfreezing.

dégeler [deʒle] *vt* to thaw (out); (*fig*) to unfreeze ♦ *vi* to thaw (out); **se ~** *vi* (*fig*) to thaw out.

dégénéré, e [deʒeneʀe] *a, nm/f* degenerate.

dégénérer [deʒeneʀe] *vi* to degenerate; (*empirer*) to go from bad to worse; (*devenir*): **~ en** to degenerate into.

dégénérescence [deʒeneʀesɑ̃s] *nf* degeneration.

dégingandé, e [deʒɛ̃gɑ̃de] *a* gangling, lanky.

dégivrage [deʒivʀaʒ] *nm* defrosting; de-icing.

dégivrer [deʒivʀe] *vt* (*frigo*) to defrost; (*vitres*) to de-ice.

dégivreur [deʒivʀœʀ] *nm* defroster; de-icer.

déglinguer [deglɛ̃ge] *vt* to bust.

déglutir [deglytiʀ] *vt, vi* to swallow.

déglutition [deglytisjɔ̃] *nf* swallowing.

dégonflé, e [degɔ̃fle] *a* (*pneu*) flat; (*fam*) chicken ♦ *nm/f* (*fam*) chicken.

dégonfler [degɔ̃fle] *vt* (*pneu, ballon*) to let down, deflate ♦ *vi* (*désenfler*) to go down; **se ~** *vi* (*fam*) to chicken out.

dégorger [degɔʀʒe] *vi* (*CULIN*): **faire ~** to leave to sweat; (*aussi*: **se ~**: *rivière*): **~ dans** to flow into ♦ *vt* to disgorge.

dégoter [degɔte] *vt* (*fam*) to dig up, find.

dégouliner [deguline] *vi* to trickle, drip; **~ de** to be dripping with.

dégoupiller [degupije] *vt* (*grenade*) to take the pin out of.

dégourdi, e [deguʀdi] *a* smart, resourceful.

dégourdir [deguʀdiʀ] *vt* to warm (up); **se ~ (les jambes)** to stretch one's legs.

dégoût [degu] *nm* disgust, distaste.

dégoûtant, e [degutɑ̃, -ɑ̃t] *a* disgusting.

dégoûté, e [degute] *a* disgusted; **~ de** sick of.

dégoûter [degute] *vt* to disgust; **cela me dégoûte** I find this disgusting *ou* revolting; **~ qn de qch** to put sb off sth; **se ~ de** to get *ou* become sick of.

dégoutter [degute] *vi* to drip; **~ de** to be dripping with.

dégradant, e [degʀadɑ̃, -ɑ̃t] *a* degrading.

dégradation [degʀadɑsjɔ̃] *nf* reduction in rank; defacement; degradation, debasement; deterioration; (*aussi*: **~s**: *dégâts*) damage *q*.

dégradé, e [degʀade] *a* (*couleur*) shaded off; (*teintes*) faded; (*cheveux*) layered ♦ *nm* (*PEINTURE*) gradation.

dégrader [degʀade] *vt* (*MIL: officier*) to degrade; (*abîmer*) to damage, deface; (*avilir*) to degrade, debase; **se ~** *vi* (*relations, situa-*

tion) to deteriorate.

dégrafer [degʀafe] *vt* to unclip, unhook, unfasten.

dégraissage [degʀesaʒ] *nm* (*ÉCON*) cutbacks *pl*; **~ et nettoyage à sec** dry cleaning.

dégraissant [degʀesɑ̃] *nm* spot remover.

dégraisser [degʀese] *vt* (*soupe*) to skim; (*vêtement*) to take the grease marks out of; (*ÉCON*) to cut back; (*: entreprise*) to slim down.

degré [dəgʀe] *nm* degree; (*d'escalier*) step; **brûlure au 1er/2ème ~** 1st/2nd degree burn; **équation du 1er/2ème ~** linear/quadratic equation; **le premier ~** (*SCOL*) primary level; **alcool à 90 ~s** surgical spirit; **vin de 10 ~s** 10° wine (*on Gay-Lussac scale*); **par ~(s)** *ad* by degrees, gradually.

dégressif, ive [degʀesif, -iv] *a* on a decreasing scale, degressive; **tarif ~** decreasing rate of charge.

dégrèvement [degʀɛvmɑ̃] *nm* tax relief.

dégrever [degʀəve] *vt* to grant tax relief to; to reduce the tax burden on.

dégriffé, e [degʀife] *a* (*vêtement*) sold without the designer's label.

dégringolade [degʀɛ̃gɔlad] *nf* tumble; (*fig*) collapse.

dégringoler [degʀɛ̃gɔle] *vi* to tumble (down); (*fig: prix, monnaie etc*) to collapse.

dégriser [degʀize] *vt* to sober up.

dégrossir [degʀosiʀ] *vt* (*bois*) to trim; (*fig*) to work out roughly; (*: personne*) to knock the rough edges off.

déguenillé, e [degnije] *a* ragged, tattered.

déguerpir [degɛʀpiʀ] *vi* to clear off.

dégueulasse [degœlas] *a* (*fam*) disgusting.

dégueuler [degœle] *vi* (*fam*) to puke, throw up.

déguisé, e [degize] *a* disguised; dressed up; **~ en** disguised (*ou* dressed up) as.

déguisement [degizmɑ̃] *nm* disguise; (*habits: pour s'amuser*) dressing-up clothes; (*: pour tromper*) disguise.

déguiser [degize] *vt* to disguise; **se ~ (en)** (*se costumer*) to dress up (as); (*pour tromper*) to disguise o.s. (as).

dégustation [degystɑsjɔ̃] *nf* tasting; sampling; savouring (*Brit*), savoring (*US*); (*séance*): **~ de vin(s)** wine-tasting.

déguster [degyste] *vt* (*vins*) to taste; (*fromages etc*) to sample; (*savourer*) to enjoy, savour (*Brit*), savor (*US*).

déhancher [deɑ̃ʃe]: **se ~** *vi* to sway one's hips; to lean (one's weight) on one hip.

dehors [dəɔʀ] *ad* outside; (*en plein air*) outdoors, outside ♦ *nm* outside ♦ *nmpl* (*apparences*) appearances, exterior *sg*; **mettre** *ou* **jeter ~** to throw out; **au ~** outside; (*en apparence*) outwardly; **au ~ de** outside; **de ~** from outside; **en ~** outside; outwards; **en ~ de** apart from.

déifier [deifje] *vt* to deify.

déjà [deʒa] *ad* already; (*auparavant*) before, already; **as-tu ~ été en France?** have you been to France before?; **c'est ~ pas mal** that's not too bad (at all); **c'est ~ quelque chose** (at least) it's better than nothing; **quel nom, ~?** what was the name again?

déjanter [deʒɑ̃te]: **se ~** *vi* (*pneu*) to come off the rim.

déjà-vu [deʒavy] *nm*: **c'est du** ~ there's nothing new in that.

déjeté, e [deʒte] *a* lop-sided, crooked.

déjeuner [deʒœne] *vi* to (have) lunch; (*le matin*) to have breakfast ♦ *nm* lunch; (*petit déjeuner*) breakfast; ~ **d'affaires** business lunch.

déjouer [deʒwe] *vt* to elude; to foil, thwart.

déjuger [deʒyʒe]: **se** ~ *vi* to go back on one's opinion.

delà [dəla] *ad*: **par** ~, **en** ~ **(de)**, **au** ~ **(de)** beyond.

délabré, e [delabʀe] *a* dilapidated, broken-down.

délabrement [delabʀəmã] *nm* decay, dilapidation.

délabrer [delabʀe]: **se** ~ *vi* to fall into decay, become dilapidated.

délacer [delase] *vt* to unlace, undo.

délai [delɛ] *nm* (*attente*) waiting period; (*sursis*) extension (of time); (*temps accordé*: *aussi*: ~**s**) time limit; **sans** ~ without delay; **à bref** ~ shortly, very soon; at short notice; **dans les** ~**s** within the time limit; **un** ~ **de 30 jours** a period of 30 days; **comptez un** ~ **de livraison de 10 jours** allow 10 days for delivery.

délaissé, e [delese] *a* abandoned, deserted; neglected.

délaisser [delese] *vt* (*abandonner*) to abandon, desert; (*négliger*) to neglect.

délassant, e [delasã, -ãt] *a* relaxing.

délassement [delasmã] *nm* relaxation.

délasser [delase] *vt* (*reposer*) to relax; (*divertir*) to divert, entertain; **se** ~ *vi* to relax.

délateur, trice [delatœʀ, -tʀis] *nm/f* informer.

délation [delasjɔ̃] *nf* denouncement, informing.

délavé, e [delave] *a* faded.

délayage [delejaʒ] *nm* mixing; thinning down.

délayer [deleje] *vt* (*CULIN*) to mix (with water *etc*); (*peinture*) to thin down; (*fig*) to pad out, spin out.

delco [dɛlko] *nm* ® (*AUTO*) distributor; **tête de** ~ distributor cap.

délectation [delɛktasjɔ̃] *nf* delight.

délecter [delɛkte]: **se** ~ *vi*: **se** ~ **de** to revel *ou* delight in.

délégation [delegasjɔ̃] *nf* delegation; ~ **de pouvoir** delegation of power.

délégué, e [delege] *a* delegated ♦ *nm/f* delegate; representative; **ministre** ~ **à** minister with special responsibility for.

déléguer [delege] *vt* to delegate.

délestage [delɛstaʒ] *nm*: **itinéraire de** ~ alternative route (*to relieve traffic congestion*).

délester [delɛste] *vt* (*navire*) to unballast; ~ **une route** to relieve traffic congestion on a road by diverting traffic.

Delhi [dɛli] *n* Delhi.

délibérant, e [delibeʀã, -ãt] *a*: **assemblée** ~**e** deliberative assembly.

délibératif, ive [delibeʀatif, -iv] *a*: **avoir voix délibérative** to have voting rights.

délibération [delibeʀasjɔ̃] *nf* deliberation.

délibéré, e [delibeʀe] *a* (*conscient*) deliberate; (*déterminé*) determined, resolute; **de propos** ~ (*à dessein, exprès*) intentionally.

délibérément [delibeʀemã] *ad* deliberately;

(*résolument*) resolutely.

délibérer [delibeʀe] *vi* to deliberate.

délicat, e [delika, -at] *a* delicate; (*plein de tact*) tactful; (*attentionné*) thoughtful; (*exigeant*) fussy, particular; **procédés peu** ~**s** unscrupulous methods.

délicatement [delikatmã] *ad* delicately; (*avec douceur*) gently.

délicatesse [delikatɛs] *nf* delicacy; tactfulness; thoughtfulness; ~**s** *nfpl* attentions, consideration *sg*.

délice [delis] *nm* delight.

délicieusement [delisjøzmã] *ad* deliciously; delightfully.

délicieux, euse [delisjø, -øz] *a* (*au goût*) delicious; (*sensation, impression*) delightful.

délictueux, euse [deliktɥø, -øz] *a* criminal.

délié, e [delje] *a* nimble, agile; (*mince*) slender, fine ♦ *nm*: **les** ~**s** the upstrokes (*in handwriting*).

délier [delje] *vt* to untie; ~ **qn de** (*serment etc*) to free *ou* release sb from.

délimitation [delimitasjɔ̃] *nf* delimitation.

délimiter [delimite] *vt* to delimit.

délinquance [delɛ̃kãs] *nf* criminality; ~ **juvénile** juvenile delinquency.

délinquant, e [delɛ̃kã, -ãt] *a, nm/f* delinquent.

déliquescence [delikesãs] *nf*: **en** ~ in a state of decay.

déliquescent, e [delikesã, -ãt] *a* decaying.

délirant, e [deliʀã, -ãt] *a* (*MÉD*: *fièvre*) delirious; (*imagination*) frenzied; (*fam*: *déraisonnable*) crazy.

délire [deliʀ] *nm* (*fièvre*) delirium; (*fig*) frenzy; (: *folie*) lunacy.

délirer [deliʀe] *vi* to be delirious; (*fig*) to be raving.

délit [deli] *nm* (criminal) offence; ~ **de droit commun** violation of common law; ~ **de fuite** failure to stop after an accident; ~ **de presse** violation of the press laws.

délivrance [delivʀãs] *nf* freeing, release; (*sentiment*) relief.

délivrer [delivʀe] *vt* (*prisonnier*) to (set) free, release; (*passeport, certificat*) to issue; ~ **qn de** (*ennemis*) to set sb free from, deliver *ou* free sb from; (*fig*) to rid sb of.

déloger [delɔʒe] *vt* (*locataire*) to turn out; (*objet coincé, ennemi*) to dislodge.

déloyal, e, aux [delwajal, -o] *a* (*personne, conduite*) disloyal; (*procédé*) unfair.

Delphes [dɛlf] *n* Delphi.

delta [dɛlta] *nm* (*GÉO*) delta.

deltaplane [dɛltaplan] *nm* ® hang-glider.

déluge [delyʒ] *nm* (*biblique*) Flood, Deluge; (*grosse pluie*) downpour, deluge; (*grand nombre*): ~ **de** flood of.

déluré, e [delyʀe] *a* smart, resourceful; (*péj*) forward, pert.

démagogie [demagɔʒi] *nf* demagogy.

démagogique [demagɔʒik] *a* demagogic, popularity-seeking; (*POL*) vote-catching.

démagogue [demagɔg] *a* demagogic ♦ *nm* demagogue.

démaillé, e [demaje] *a* (*bas*) laddered (*Brit*), with a run (*ou* runs).

demain [dəmɛ̃] *ad* tomorrow; ~ **matin/soir** tomorrow morning/evening; ~ **midi** tomorrow at midday; **à** ~! see you tomorrow!

demande [dəmɑ̃d] *nf* (*requête*) request; (*revendication*) demand; (*ADMIN, formulaire*) application; (*ÉCON*): **la ~** demand; **"~s d'emploi"** "situations wanted"; **à la ~ générale** by popular request; **~ en mariage** (marriage) proposal; **faire sa ~** (**en mariage**) to propose (marriage); **~ de naturalisation** application for naturalization; **~ de poste** job application.

demandé, e [dəmɑ̃de] *a* (*article etc*): **très ~** (very) much in demand.

demander [dəmɑ̃de] *vt* to ask for; (*question: date, heure, chemin*) to ask; (*requérir, nécessiter*) to require, demand; **~ qch à qn** to ask sb for sth, ask sb sth; **ils demandent 2 secrétaires et un ingénieur** they're looking for 2 secretaries and an engineer; **~ la main de qn** to ask for sb's hand (in marriage); **~ pardon à qn** to apologize to sb; **~ à ou de voir/faire** to ask to see/ask if one can do; **~ à qn de faire** to ask sb to do; **~ que/pourquoi** to ask that/why; **se ~ si/pourquoi** *etc* to wonder if/why *etc*; (*sens purement réfléchi*) to ask o.s. if/why *etc*; **on vous demande au téléphone** you're wanted on the phone, there's someone for you on the phone; **il ne demande que ça** that's all he wants; **je ne demande pas mieux** I'm asking nothing more; **il ne demande qu'à faire** all he wants is to do.

demandeur, euse [dəmɑ̃dœʀ, -øz] *nm/f*: **~ d'emploi** job-seeker.

démangeaison [demɑ̃ʒɛzɔ̃] *nf* itching.

démanger [demɑ̃ʒe] *vi* to itch; **la main me démange** my hand is itching; **l'envie** *ou* **ça me démange de faire** I'm itching to do.

démanteler [demɑ̃tle] *vt* to break up; to demolish.

démaquillant [demakijɑ̃] *nm* make-up remover.

démaquiller [demakije] *vt*: **se ~** to remove one's make-up.

démarcage [demaʀkaʒ] *nm* = **démarquage**.

démarcation [demaʀkasjɔ̃] *nf* demarcation.

démarchage [demaʀʃaʒ] *nm* (*COMM*) door-to-door selling.

démarche [demaʀʃ(ə)] *nf* (*allure*) gait, walk; (*intervention*) step; approach; (*fig: intellectuelle*) thought processes *pl*; approach; **faire** *ou* **entreprendre des ~s** to take action; **faire des ~s auprès de qn** to approach sb.

démarcheur, euse [demaʀʃœʀ, -øz] *nm/f* (*COMM*) door-to-door salesman/woman; (*POL etc*) canvasser.

démarquage [demaʀkaʒ] *nm* marking down.

démarque [demaʀk(ə)] *nf* (*COMM: d'un article*) mark-down.

démarqué, e [demaʀke] *a* (*FOOTBALL*) unmarked; (*COMM*) reduced; **prix ~s** marked-down prices.

démarquer [demaʀke] *vt* (*prix*) to mark down; (*joueur*) to stop marking; **se ~** *vi* (*SPORT*) to shake off one's marker.

démarrage [demaʀaʒ] *nm* starting *q*, start; **~ en côte** hill start.

démarrer [demaʀe] *vt* to start up ♦ *vi* (*conducteur*) to start (up); (*véhicule*) to move off; (*travaux, affaire*) to get moving; (*coureur: accélérer*) to pull away.

démarreur [demaʀœʀ] *nm* (*AUTO*) starter.

démasquer [demaske] *vt* to unmask; **se ~** to unmask; (*fig*) to drop one's mask.

démâter [demate] *vt* to dismast ♦ *vi* to be dismasted.

démêlant, e [demelɑ̃, -ɑ̃t] *a*: **baume ~, crème ~e** (hair) conditioner.

démêler [demele] *vt* to untangle, disentangle.

démêlés [demele] *nmpl* problems.

démembrer [demɑ̃bʀe] *vt* to slice up, tear apart.

déménagement [demenaʒmɑ̃] *nm* (*du point de vue du locataire etc*) move; (*: du déménageur*) removal (*Brit*), moving (*US*); **entreprise/camion de ~** removal (*Brit*) *ou* moving (*US*) firm/van.

déménager [demenaʒe] *vt* (*meubles*) to (re)move ♦ *vi* to move (house).

déménageur [demenaʒœʀ] *nm* removal man (*Brit*), (*furniture*) mover (*US*); (*entrepreneur*) furniture remover.

démence [demɑ̃s] *nf* madness, insanity; (*MÉD*) dementia.

démener [demne]: **se ~** *vi* to thrash about; (*fig*) to exert o.s.

dément, e [demɑ̃, -ɑ̃t] *vb voir* **démentir** ♦ *a* (*fou*) mad (*Brit*), crazy; (*fam*) brilliant, fantastic.

démentiel, le [demɑ̃sjɛl] *a* insane.

démentir [demɑ̃tiʀ] *vt* (*nouvelle, témoin*) to refute; (*suj: faits etc*) to belie, refute; **~ que** to deny that; **ne pas se ~** not to fail, keep up.

démerder [demɛʀde]: **se ~** *vi* (*fam!*) to bloody well manage for o.s.

démériter [demeʀite] *vi*: **~ auprès de qn** to come down in sb's esteem.

démesure [deməzyʀ] *nf* immoderation, immoderateness.

démesuré, e [deməzyʀe] *a* immoderate, disproportionate.

démesurément [deməzyʀemɑ̃] *ad* disproportionately.

démettre [demɛtʀ(ə)] *vt*: **~ qn de** (*fonction, poste*) to dismiss sb from; **se ~** (**de ses fonctions**) to resign (from) one's duties; **se ~ l'épaule** *etc* to dislocate one's shoulder *etc*.

demeurant [dəmœʀɑ̃]: **au ~** *ad* for all that.

demeure [dəmœʀ] *nf* residence; **dernière ~** (*fig*) last resting place; **mettre qn en ~ de faire** to enjoin *ou* order sb to do; **à ~** *ad* permanently.

demeuré, e [dəmœʀe] *a* backward ♦ *nm/f* backward person.

demeurer [dəmœʀe] *vi* (*habiter*) to live; (*séjourner*) to stay; (*rester*) to remain; **en ~ là** (*suj: personne*) to leave it at that; (*: choses*) to be left at that.

demi, e [dəmi] *a*: **et ~**: **trois heures/bouteilles et ~es** three and a half hours/bottles, three hours/bottles and a half ♦ *nm* (*bière*) ≈ half-pint (*.25 litre*); (*FOOTBALL*) half-back; **il est 2 heures/midi et ~e** it's half past 2/12; **~ de mêlée/d'ouverture** (*RUGBY*) scrum/fly half; **à ~** *ad* half-; **ouvrir à ~** to half-open; **faire les choses à ~** to do things by halves; **à la ~e** (*heure*) on the half-hour.

demi... [dəmi] *préfixe* half-, semi..., demi-.

demi-bas [dəmibɑ] *nm inv* (*chaussette*) knee-sock.

demi-bouteille [dəmibutɛj] *nf* half-bottle.

demi-cercle [dəmisɛrkl(ə)] *nm* semicircle; **en ~ a** semicircular ♦ *ad* in a semicircle.

demi-douzaine [dəmiduzɛn] *nf* half-dozen, half a dozen.

demi-finale [dəmifinal] *nf* semifinal.

demi-finaliste [dəmifinalist(ə)] *nm/f* semifinalist.

demi-fond [dəmifɔ̃] *nm* (*SPORT*) medium-distance running.

demi-frère [dəmifʀɛʀ] *nm* half-brother.

demi-gros [dəmigʀo] *nm inv* wholesale trade.

demi-heure [dəmijœʀ] *nf*: **une ~ a** half-hour, half an hour.

demi-jour [dəmiʒuʀ] *nm* half-light.

demi-journée [dəmiʒuʀne] *nf* half-day, half a day.

démilitariser [demilitaʀize] *vt* to demilitarize.

demi-litre [dəmilitʀ(ə)] *nm* half-litre (*Brit*), half-liter (*US*), half a litre *ou* liter.

demi-livre [dəmilivʀ(ə)] *nf* half-pound, half a pound.

demi-longueur [dəmilɔ̃gœʀ] *nf* (*SPORT*) half-length, half a length.

demi-lune [dəmilyn]: **en ~ a** *inv* semi-circular.

demi-mal [dəmimal] *nm*: **il n'y a que ~** there's not much harm done.

demi-mesure [dəmimzyʀ] *nf* half-measure.

demi-mot [dəmimo]: **à ~ ad** without having to spell things out.

déminer [demine] *vt* to clear of mines.

démineur [deminœʀ] *nm* bomb disposal expert.

demi-pension [dəmipɑ̃sjɔ̃] *nf* half-board; **être en ~** (*SCOL*) to take school meals.

demi-pensionnaire [dəmipɑ̃sjɔnɛʀ] *nm/f* (*SCOL*) half-boarder.

demi-place [dəmiplas] *nf* half-price; (*TRANSPORTS*) half-fare.

démis, e [demi, -iz] *pp de* **démettre** ♦ *a* (*épaule etc*) dislocated.

demi-saison [dəmisɛzɔ̃] *nf*: **vêtements de ~** spring *ou* autumn clothing.

demi-sel [dəmisɛl] *a inv* slightly salted.

demi-sœur [dəmisœʀ] *nf* half-sister.

demi-sommeil [dəmisɔmɛj] *nm* doze.

demi-soupir [dəmisupiʀ] *nm* (*MUS*) quaver (*Brit*) *ou* eighth note (*US*) rest.

démission [demisjɔ̃] *nf* resignation; **donner sa ~** to give *ou* hand in one's notice, hand in one's resignation.

démissionnaire [demisjɔnɛʀ] *a* outgoing ♦ *nm/f* person resigning.

démissionner [demisjɔne] *vi* (*de son poste*) to resign, give *ou* hand in one's notice.

demi-tarif [dəmitaʀif] *nm* half-price; (*TRANSPORTS*) half-fare.

demi-ton [dəmitɔ̃] *nm* (*MUS*) semitone.

demi-tour [dəmituʀ] *nm* about-turn; **faire un ~** (*MIL etc*) to make an about-turn; **faire ~** to turn (and go) back; (*AUTO*) to do a U-turn.

démobilisation [demɔbilizasjɔ̃] *nf* demobilization; (*fig*) demotivation, demoralization.

démobiliser [demɔbilize] *vt* to demobilize; (*fig*) to demotivate, demoralize.

démocrate [demɔkʀat] *a* democratic ♦ *nm/f* democrat.

démocrate-chrétien, ne [demɔkʀatkʀetjɛ̃, -ɛn] *nm/f* Christian Democrat.

démocratie [demɔkʀasi] *nf* democracy; **~ populaire/libérale** people's/liberal democracy.

démocratique [demɔkʀatik] *a* democratic.

démocratiquement [demɔkʀatikmɑ̃] *ad* democratically.

démocratiser [demɔkʀatize] *vt* to democratize.

démodé, e [demɔde] *a* old-fashioned.

démoder [demɔde]: **se ~ vi** to go out of fashion.

démographie [demɔgʀafi] *nf* demography.

démographique [demɔgʀafik] *a* demographic; **poussée ~** increase in population.

demoiselle [dəmwazɛl] *nf* (*jeune fille*) young lady; (*célibataire*) single lady, maiden lady; **~ d'honneur** bridesmaid.

démolir [demɔliʀ] *vt* to demolish; (*fig: personne*) to do for.

démolisseur [demɔlisœʀ] *nm* demolition worker.

démolition [demɔlisjɔ̃] *nf* demolition.

démon [demɔ̃] *nm* demon, fiend; evil spirit; (*enfant turbulent*) devil, demon; **le ~ du jeu/des femmes** a mania for gambling/women; **le D~** the Devil.

démonétiser [demɔnetize] *vt* to demonetize.

démoniaque [demɔnjak] *a* fiendish.

démonstrateur, trice [demɔ̃stʀatœʀ, -tʀis] *nm/f* demonstrator.

démonstratif, ive [demɔ̃stʀatif, -iv] *a, nm* (*aussi LING*) demonstrative.

démonstration [demɔ̃stʀasjɔ̃] *nf* demonstration; (*aérienne, navale*) display.

démontable [demɔ̃tabl(ə)] *a* folding.

démontage [demɔ̃taʒ] *nm* dismantling.

démonté, e [demɔ̃te] *a* (*fig*) raging, wild.

démonte-pneu [demɔ̃təpnø] *nm* tyre lever (*Brit*), tire iron (*US*).

démonter [demɔ̃te] *vt* (*machine etc*) to take down, dismantle; (*pneu, porte*) to take off; (*cavalier*) to throw, unseat; (*fig: personne*) to disconcert; **se ~ vi** (*personne*) to lose countenance.

démontrable [demɔ̃tʀabl(ə)] *a* demonstrable.

démontrer [demɔ̃tʀe] *vt* to demonstrate, show.

démoralisant, e [demɔʀalizɑ̃, -ɑ̃t] *a* demoralizing.

démoralisateur, trice [demɔʀalizatœʀ, -tʀis] *a* demoralizing.

démoraliser [demɔʀalize] *vt* to demoralize.

démordre [demɔʀdʀ(ə)] *vi*: **ne pas ~ de** to refuse to give up, stick to.

démouler [demule] *vt* (*gâteau*) to turn out.

démoustiquer [demustike] *vt* to clear of mosquitoes.

démultiplication [demyltiplikasjɔ̃] *nf* reduction; reduction ratio.

démuni, e [demyni] *a* (*sans argent*) impoverished; **~ de** without, lacking in.

démunir [demyniʀ] *vt*: **~ qn de** to deprive sb of; **se ~ de** to part with, give up.

démuseler [demyzle] *vt* to unmuzzle.

démystifier [demistifje] *vt* to demystify.

démythifier [demitifje] *vt* to demythologize.

dénatalité [denatalite] *nf* fall in the birth rate.
dénationalisation [denasjɔnalizasjɔ̃] *nf* denationalization.
dénationaliser [denasjɔnalize] *vt* to denationalize.
dénaturé, e [denatyʀe] *a* (*alcool*) denaturized; (*goûts*) unnatural.
dénaturer [denatyʀe] *vt* (*goût*) to alter (completely); (*pensée, fait*) to distort, misrepresent.
dénégations [denegasjɔ̃] *nfpl* denials.
déneigement [denɛʒmã] *nm* snow clearance.
déneiger [deneʒe] *vt* to clear snow from.
déni [deni] *nm*: ~ (**de justice**) denial of justice.
déniaiser [denjeze] *vt*: ~ **qn** to teach sb about life.
dénicher [deniʃe] *vt* to unearth.
dénicotinisé, e [denikɔtinize] *a* nicotine-free.
denier [dənje] *nm* (*monnaie*) formerly, a coin of small value; (*de bas*) denier; ~ **du culte** contribution to parish upkeep; ~**s publics** public money; **de ses (propres)** ~**s** out of one's own pocket.
dénier [denje] *vt* to deny; ~ **qch à qn** to deny sb sth.
dénigrer [denigʀe] *vt* to denigrate, run down.
dénivelé, e [denivle] *a* (*chaussée*) on a lower level ♦ *nm* difference in height.
déniveler [denivle] *vt* to make uneven; to put on a lower level.
dénivellation [denivelasjɔ̃] *nf*, **dénivellement** [denivɛlmã] *nm* difference in level; (*pente*) ramp; (*creux*) dip.
dénombrer [denɔ̃bʀe] *vt* (*compter*) to count; (*énumérer*) to enumerate, list.
dénominateur [denɔminatœʀ] *nm* denominator; ~ **commun** common denominator.
dénomination [denɔminasjɔ̃] *nf* designation, appellation.
dénommé, e [denɔme] *a*: **le** ~ **Dupont** the man by the name of Dupont.
dénommer [denɔme] *vt* to name.
dénoncer [denɔ̃se] *vt* to denounce; **se** ~ to give o.s. up, come forward.
dénonciation [denɔ̃sjasjɔ̃] *nf* denunciation.
dénoter [denɔte] *vt* to denote.
dénouement [denumã] *nm* outcome, conclusion; (*THÉÂTRE*) dénouement.
dénouer [denwe] *vt* to unknot, undo.
dénoyauter [denwajote] *vt* to stone; **appareil à** ~ stoner.
dénoyauteur [denwajotœʀ] *nm* stoner.
denrée [dãʀe] *nf* commodity; (*aussi*: ~ **alimentaire**) food (stuff).
dense [dãs] *a* dense.
densité [dãsite] *nf* denseness; (*PHYSIQUE*) density.
dent [dã] *nf* tooth (*pl* teeth); **avoir/garder une** ~ **contre qn** to have/hold a grudge against sb; **se mettre qch sous la** ~ to eat sth; **être sur les** ~**s** to be on one's last legs; **faire ses** ~**s** to teethe, cut (one's) teeth; **en** ~**s de scie** serrated; (*irrégulier*) jagged; **avoir les** ~**s longues** (*fig*) to be ruthlessly ambitious; ~ **de lait/sagesse** milk/wisdom tooth.
dentaire [dãtɛʀ] *a* dental; **cabinet** ~ dental surgery; **école** ~ dental school.
denté, e [dãte] *a*: **roue** ~**e** cog wheel.

dentelé, e [dãtle] *a* jagged, indented.
dentelle [dãtɛl] *nf* lace *q*.
dentelure [dãtlyʀ] *nf* (*aussi*: ~**s**) jagged outline.
dentier [dãtje] *nm* denture.
dentifrice [dãtifʀis] *a, nm*: (**pâte**) ~ toothpaste; **eau** ~ mouthwash.
dentiste [dãtist(ə)] *nm/f* dentist.
dentition [dãtisjɔ̃] *nf* teeth *pl*, dentition.
dénucléariser [denyklearize] *vt* to make nuclear-free.
dénudé, e [denyde] *a* bare.
dénuder [denyde] *vt* to bare; **se** ~ (*personne*) to strip.
dénué, e [denɥe] *a*: ~ **de** lacking in; (*intérêt*) devoid of.
dénuement [denymã] *nm* destitution.
dénutrition [denytʀisjɔ̃] *nf* undernourishment.
déodorant [deɔdɔʀã] *nm* deodorant.
déodoriser [deɔdɔʀize] *vt* to deodorize.
déontologie [deɔ̃tɔlɔʒi] *nf* code of ethics; (*professionnelle*) (professional) code of practice.
dép. *abr* (*ADMIN*: = *département*) dept; (= *départ*) dep.
dépannage [depanaʒ] *nm*: **service/camion de** ~ (*AUTO*) breakdown service/truck.
dépanner [depane] *vt* (*voiture, télévision*) to fix, repair; (*fig*) to bail out, help out.
dépanneur [depanœʀ] *nm* (*AUTO*) breakdown mechanic; (*TV*) television engineer.
dépanneuse [depanøz] *nf* breakdown lorry (*Brit*), tow truck (*US*).
dépareillé, e [depaʀeje] *a* (*collection, service*) incomplete; (*gant, volume, objet*) odd.
déparer [depaʀe] *vt* to spoil, mar.
départ [depaʀ] *nm* leaving *q*, departure; (*SPORT*) start; (*sur un horaire*) departure; **à son** ~ when he left; **au** ~ (*au début*) initially, at the start; **courrier au** ~ outgoing mail.
départager [depaʀtaʒe] *vt* to decide between.
département [depaʀtəmã] *nm* department.
départemental, e, aux [depaʀtəmãtal, -o] *a* departmental.
départementaliser [depaʀtəmãtalize] *vt* to devolve authority to.
départir [depaʀtiʀ]: **se** ~ **de** *vt* to abandon, depart from.
dépassé, e [depase] *a* superseded, outmoded; (*fig*) out of one's depth.
dépassement [depasmã] *nm* (*AUTO*) overtaking *q*.
dépasser [depase] *vt* (*véhicule, concurrent*) to overtake; (*endroit*) to pass, go past; (*somme, limite*) to exceed; (*fig: en beauté etc*) to surpass, outshine; (*être en saillie sur*) to jut out above (*ou* in front of); (*dérouter*): **cela me dépasse** it's beyond me ♦ *vi* (*AUTO*) to overtake; (*jupon*) to show; **se** ~ to excel o.s.
dépassionner [depasjɔne] *vt* (*débat etc*) to take the heat out of.
dépaver [depave] *vt* to remove the cobblestones from.
dépaysé, e [depeize] *a* disorientated.
dépaysement [depeizmã] *nm* disorientation; change of scenery.
dépayser [depeize] *vt* (*désorienter*) to disorientate; (*changer agréablement*) to provide

with a change of scenery.

dépecer [depəse] *vt* (*suj: boucher*) to joint, cut up; (*suj: animal*) to dismember.

dépêche [depɛʃ] *nf* dispatch; ~ (**télégraphique**) telegram, wire.

dépêcher [depeʃe] *vt* to dispatch; **se** ~ *vi* to hurry; **se** ~ **de faire qch** to hasten to do sth, to hurry (in order) to do sth.

dépeindre [depɛ̃dʀ(ə)] *vt* to depict.

dépendance [depɑ̃dɑ̃s] *nf* (*interdépendance*) dependence *q*, dependency; (*bâtiment*) outbuilding.

dépendant, e [depɑ̃dɑ̃, -ɑ̃t] *vb voir* **dépendre** ♦ *a* (*financièrement*) dependent.

dépendre [depɑ̃dʀ(ə)] *vt* (*tableau*) to take down; ~ **de** *vt* to depend on; (*financièrement etc*) to be dependent on; (*appartenir*) to belong to.

dépens [depɑ̃] *nmpl*: **aux** ~ **de** at the expense of.

dépense [depɑ̃s] *nf* spending *q*, expense, expenditure *q*; (*fig*) consumption; (*: de temps, de forces*) expenditure; **pousser qn à la** ~ to make sb incur an expense; ~ **physique** (physical) exertion; ~ **de temps** investment of time; ~**s de fonctionnement** revenue expenditure; ~**s d'investissement** capital expenditure; ~**s publiques** public expenditure.

dépenser [depɑ̃se] *vt* to spend; (*gaz, eau*) to use; (*fig*) to expend, use up; **se** ~ (*se fatiguer*) to exert o.s.

dépensier, ière [depɑ̃sje, -jɛʀ] *a*: **il est** ~ he's a spendthrift.

déperdition [depɛʀdisjɔ̃] *nf* loss.

dépérir [depeʀiʀ] *vi* (*personne*) to waste away; (*plante*) to wither.

dépersonnaliser [depɛʀsɔnalize] *vt* to depersonalize.

dépêtrer [depetʀe] *vt*: **se** ~ **de** (*situation*) to extricate o.s. from.

dépeuplé, e [depœple] *a* depopulated.

dépeupler [depœple] *vt* to depopulate; **se** ~ to be depopulated.

déphasage [defazaʒ] *nm* (*fig*) being out of touch.

déphasé, e [defaze] *a* (*ÉLEC*) out of phase; (*fig*) out of touch.

déphaser [defaze] *vt* (*fig*) to put out of touch.

dépilation [depilasjɔ̃] *nf* hair loss; hair removal.

dépilatoire [depilatwaʀ] *a* depilatory, hair-removing.

dépiler [depile] *vt* (*épiler*) to depilate, remove hair from.

dépistage [depistaʒ] *nm* (*MÉD*) screening.

dépister [depiste] *vt* to detect; (*MÉD*) to screen; (*voleur*) to track down; (*poursuivants*) to throw off the scent.

dépit [depi] *nm* vexation, frustration; **en** ~ **de** *prép* in spite of; **en** ~ **du bon sens** contrary to all good sense.

dépité, e [depite] *a* vexed, frustrated.

dépiter [depite] *vt* to vex, frustrate.

déplacé, e [deplase] *a* (*propos*) out of place, uncalled-for; **personne** ~**e** displaced person.

déplacement [deplasmɑ̃] *nm* moving; shifting; transfer; (*voyage*) trip, travelling *q* (*Brit*), traveling *q* (*US*); **en** ~ away (on a trip); ~ **d'air** displacement of air; ~ **de vertèbre** slipped disc.

déplacer [deplase] *vt* (*table, voiture*) to move, shift; (*employé*) to transfer, move; **se** ~ *vi* (*objet*) to move; (*organe*) to become displaced; (*personne: bouger*) to move, walk; (*: voyager*) to travel ♦ *vt* (*vertèbre etc*) to displace.

déplaire [deplɛʀ] *vi*: **ceci me déplaît** I don't like this, I dislike this; **il cherche à nous** ~ he's trying to displease us *ou* be disagreeable to us; **se** ~ **quelque part** to dislike it *ou* be unhappy somewhere.

déplaisant, e [deplɛzɑ̃, -ɑ̃t] *vb voir* **déplaire** ♦ *a* disagreeable, unpleasant.

déplaisir [deplɛziʀ] *nm* displeasure, annoyance.

déplaît [deplɛ] *vb voir* **déplaire**.

dépliant [deplijɑ̃] *nm* leaflet.

déplier [deplije] *vt* to unfold; **se** ~ (*parachute*) to open.

déplisser [deplise] *vt* to smooth out.

déploiement [deplwamɑ̃] *nm* (*voir déployer*) deployment; display.

déplomber [deplɔ̃be] *vt* (*caisse, compteur*) to break (open) the seal of.

déplorable [deplɔʀabl(ə)] *a* deplorable; lamentable.

déplorer [deplɔʀe] *vt* (*regretter*) to deplore; (*pleurer sur*) to lament.

déployer [deplwaje] *vt* to open out, spread; (*MIL*) to deploy; (*montrer*) to display, exhibit.

déplu [deply] *pp de* **déplaire**.

dépointer [depwɛ̃te] *vi* to clock out.

dépoli, e [depɔli] *a*: **verre** ~ frosted glass.

dépolitiser [depɔlitize] *vt* to depoliticize.

déportation [depɔʀtasjɔ̃] *nf* deportation.

déporté, e [depɔʀte] *nm/f* deportee; (*1939-45*) concentration camp prisoner.

déporter [depɔʀte] *vt* (*POL*) to deport; (*dévier*) to carry off course; **se** ~ *vi* (*voiture*) to swerve.

déposant, e [depozɑ̃, -ɑ̃t] *nm/f* (*épargnant*) depositor.

dépose [depoz] *nf* taking out; taking down.

déposé, e [depoze] *a* registered; *voir aussi* **marque**.

déposer [depoze] *vt* (*gén: mettre, poser*) to lay down, put down, set down; (*à la banque, à la consigne*) to deposit; (*caution*) to put down; (*passager*) to drop (off), set down; (*démonter: serrure, moteur*) to take out; (*: rideau*) to take down; (*roi*) to depose; (*ADMIN: faire enregistrer*) to file; to register ♦ *vi* to form a sediment *ou* deposit; (*JUR*): ~ (**contre**) to testify *ou* give evidence (against); **se** ~ *vi* to settle; ~ **son bilan** (*COMM*) to go into (voluntary) liquidation.

dépositaire [depoziteʀ] *nm/f* (*JUR*) depository; (*COMM*) agent; ~ **agréé** authorized agent.

déposition [depozisjɔ̃] *nf* (*JUR*) deposition.

déposséder [deposede] *vt* to dispossess.

dépôt [depo] *nm* (*à la banque, sédiment*) deposit; (*entrepôt, réserve*) warehouse, store; (*gare*) depot; (*prison*) cells *pl*; ~ **d'ordures** rubbish (*Brit*) *ou* garbage (*US*) dump, tip (*Brit*); ~ **de bilan** (voluntary) liquidation; ~ **légal** registration of copyright.

dépoter [depɔte] vt (plante) to take from the pot, transplant.

dépotoir [depɔtwaʀ] nm dumping ground, rubbish (Brit) ou garbage (US) dump; ~ **nucléaire** nuclear (waste) dump.

dépouille [depuj] nf (d'animal) skin, hide; (humaine): ~ **(mortelle)** mortal remains pl.

dépouillé, e [depuje] a (fig) bare, bald; ~ **de** stripped of; lacking in.

dépouillement [depujmã] nm (de scrutin) count, counting q.

dépouiller [depuje] vt (animal) to skin; (spolier) to deprive of one's possessions; (documents) to go through, peruse; ~ **qn/qch de** to strip sb/sth of; ~ **le scrutin** to count the votes.

dépourvu, e [depuʀvy] a: ~ **de** lacking in, without; **au** ~ ad: **prendre qn au** ~ to catch sb unawares.

dépoussiérer [depusjeʀe] vt to remove dust from.

dépravation [depʀavasjɔ̃] nf depravity.

dépravé, e [depʀave] a depraved.

dépraver [depʀave] vt to deprave.

dépréciation [depʀesjasjɔ̃] nf depreciation.

déprécier [depʀesje] vt, **se** ~ vi to depreciate.

déprédations [depʀedasjɔ̃] nfpl damage sg.

dépressif, ive [depʀesif, -iv] a depressive.

dépression [depʀesjɔ̃] nf depression; ~ **(nerveuse)** (nervous) breakdown.

déprimant, e [depʀimã, -ãt] a depressing.

déprime [depʀim] nf (fam): **la** ~ depression.

déprimé, e [depʀime] a (découragé) depressed.

déprimer [depʀime] vt to depress.

déprogrammer [depʀɔgʀame] vt (supprimer) to cancel.

DEPS sigle (= dernier entré premier sorti) LIFO (= last in first out).

dépt abr (= département) dept.

dépuceler [depysle] vt (fam) to take the virginity of.

depuis [dəpɥi] prép (temps: date) since; (: période) for; (lieu) since, from; (quantité, rang) from ♦ ad (ever) since; ~ **que** (temps) (ever) since; **je le connais** ~ **3 ans** I've known him for 3 years; **il est parti** ~ **mardi** he has been gone since Tuesday; ~ **quand le connaissez-vous?** how long have you known him?; **elle a téléphoné** ~ **Valence** she phoned from Valence; ~ **lors** since then.

dépuratif, ive [depyʀatif, -iv] a depurative, purgative.

députation [depytasjɔ̃] nf deputation; (fonction) position of deputy, ≈ parliamentary seat (Brit), ≈ seat in Congress (US).

député, e [depyte] nm/f (POL) deputy, ≈ Member of Parliament (Brit), ≈ Congressman/woman (US).

députer [depyte] vt to delegate; ~ **qn auprès de** to send sb (as a representative) to.

déraciner [deʀasine] vt to uproot.

déraillement [deʀajmã] nm derailment.

dérailler [deʀaje] vi (train) to be derailed, go off ou jump the rails; (fam) to be completely off the track; **faire** ~ to derail.

dérailleur [deʀajœʀ] nm (de vélo) dérailleur gears pl.

déraison [deʀezɔ̃] nf unreasonableness.

déraisonnable [deʀezɔnabl(ə)] a unreasonable.

déraisonner [deʀezɔne] vi to talk nonsense, rave.

dérangement [deʀãʒmã] nm (gêne, déplacement) trouble; (gastrique etc) disorder; (mécanique) breakdown; **en** ~ (téléphone) out of order.

déranger [deʀãʒe] vt (personne) to trouble, bother, disturb; (projets) to disrupt, upset; (objets, vêtements) to disarrange; **se** ~ to put o.s. out; (se déplacer) to (take the trouble to) come (ou go) out; **est-ce que cela vous dérange si ...?** do you mind if ...?; **ça te dérangerait de faire ...?** would you mind doing ...?; **ne vous dérangez pas** don't go to any trouble; don't disturb yourself.

dérapage [deʀapaʒ] nm skid, skidding q; going out of control.

déraper [deʀape] vi (voiture) to skid; (personne, semelles, couteau) to slip; (fig: économie etc) to go out of control.

dératé, e [deʀate] nm/f: **courir comme un** ~ to run like the clappers.

dératiser [deʀatize] vt to rid of rats.

déréglé, e [deʀegle] a (mœurs) dissolute.

dérèglement [deʀegləmã] nm upsetting q, upset.

dérégler [deʀegle] vt (mécanisme) to put out of order, cause to break down; (estomac) to upset; **se** ~ vi to break down, go wrong.

dérider [deʀide] vt, **se** ~ vi to brighten ou cheer up.

dérision [deʀizjɔ̃] nf derision; **tourner en** ~ to deride; **par** ~ in mockery.

dérisoire [deʀizwaʀ] a derisory.

dérivatif [deʀivatif] nm distraction.

dérivation [deʀivasjɔ̃] nf derivation; diversion.

dérive [deʀiv] nf (de dériveur) centre-board; **aller à la** ~ (NAVIG, fig) to drift; ~ **des continents** (GÉO) continental drift.

dérivé, e [deʀive] a derived ♦ nm (LING) derivative; (TECH) by-product ♦ nf (MATH) derivative.

dériver [deʀive] vt (MATH) to derive; (cours d'eau etc) to divert ♦ vi (bateau) to drift; ~ **de** to derive from.

dériveur [deʀivœʀ] nm sailing dinghy.

dermatite [deʀmatit] nf dermatitis.

dermato [deʀmato] nm/f (fam: = dermatologue) dermatologist.

dermatologie [deʀmatɔlɔʒi] nf dermatology.

dermatologue [deʀmatɔlɔg] nm/f dermatologist.

dermite [deʀmit] nf = **dermatite**.

dernier, ière [deʀnje, -jɛʀ] a (dans le temps, l'espace) last; (le plus récent: gén avant n) latest, last; (final, ultime: effort) final; (échelon, grade) top, highest ♦ nm (étage) top floor; **lundi/le mois** ~ last Monday/month; **du** ~ **chic** extremely smart; **le** ~ **cri** the last word (in fashion); **les** ~**s honneurs** the last tribute; **le** ~ **soupir**: **rendre le** ~ **soupir** to breathe one's last; **en** ~ ad last; **ce** ~, **cette dernière** the latter.

dernièrement [deʀnjɛʀmã] ad recently.

dernier-né, dernière-née [deʀnjene, deʀnjɛʀne] nm/f (enfant) last-born.

dérobade [deʀɔbad] nf side-stepping q.

dérobé, e [derɔbe] a (porte) secret, hidden; **à la ~e** surreptitiously.

dérober [derɔbe] vt to steal; (cacher): **~ qch à (la vue de) qn** to conceal ou hide sth from sb('s view); **se ~** vi (s'esquiver) to slip away; (fig) to shy away; **se ~ sous** (s'effondrer) to give way beneath; **se ~ à** (justice, regards) to hide from; (obligation) to shirk.

dérogation [derɔgasjɔ̃] nf (special) dispensation.

déroger [derɔʒe]: **~ à** vt to go against, depart from.

dérouiller [deruje] vt: **se ~ les jambes** to stretch one's legs.

déroulement [derulmɑ̃] nm (d'une opération etc) progress.

dérouler [derule] vt (ficelle) to unwind; (papier) to unroll; **se ~** vi to unwind; to unroll, come unrolled; (avoir lieu) to take place; (se passer) to go.

déroutant, e [derutɑ̃, -ɑ̃t] a disconcerting.

déroute [derut] nf (MIL) rout; (fig) total collapse; **mettre en ~** to rout; **en ~** routed.

dérouter [derute] vt (avion, train) to reroute, divert; (étonner) to disconcert, throw (out).

derrière [dɛrjɛr] ad, prép behind ♦ nm (d'une maison) back; (postérieur) behind, bottom; **les pattes de ~** the back legs, the hind legs; **par ~** from behind; (fig) in an underhand way, behind one's back.

des [de] dét, prép + dét voir **de**.

dès [dɛ] prép from; **~ que** cj as soon as; **~ à présent** here and now; **~ son retour** as soon as he was (ou is) back; **~ réception** upon receipt; **~ lors** ad from then on; **~ lors que** cj from the moment (that).

désabusé, e [dezabyze] a disillusioned.

désaccord [dezakɔr] nm disagreement.

désaccordé, e [dezakɔrde] a (MUS) out of tune.

désacraliser [desakralize] vt to deconsecrate; (fig: profession, institution) to take the mystique out of.

désaffecté, e [dezafɛkte] a disused.

désaffection [dezafɛksjɔ̃] nf: **~ pour** estrangement from.

désagréable [dezagreable(ə)] a unpleasant, disagreeable.

désagréablement [dezagreabləmɑ̃] ad disagreeably, unpleasantly.

désagrégation [dezagregasjɔ̃] nf disintegration.

désagréger [dezagreʒe]: **se ~** vi to disintegrate, break up.

désagrément [dezagremɑ̃] nm annoyance, trouble q.

désaltérant, e [dezalterɑ̃, -ɑ̃t] a thirst-quenching.

désaltérer [dezaltere] vt: **se ~** to quench one's thirst; **ça désaltère** it's thirst-quenching, it quenches your thirst.

désamorcer [dezamɔrse] vt to remove the primer from; (fig) to defuse; (: prévenir) to forestall.

désappointé, e [dezapwɛ̃te] a disappointed.

désapprobateur, trice [dezaprɔbatœr, -tris] a disapproving.

désapprobation [dezaprɔbasjɔ̃] nf disapproval.

désapprouver [dezapruve] vt to disapprove of.

désarçonner [dezarsɔne] vt to unseat, throw; (fig) to throw, nonplus (Brit), disconcert.

désargenté, e [dezarʒɑ̃te] a impoverished.

désarmant, e [dezarmɑ̃, -ɑ̃t] a disarming.

désarmé, e [dezarme] a (fig) disarmed.

désarmement [dezarməmɑ̃] nm disarmament.

désarmer [dezarme] vt (MIL, aussi fig) to disarm; (NAVIG) to lay up; (fusil) to unload; (: mettre le cran de sûreté) to put the safety catch on ♦ vi (pays) to disarm; (haine) to wane; (personne) to give up.

désarrimer [dezarime] vt to shift.

désarroi [dezarwa] nm helplessness, disarray.

désarticulé, e [dezartikyle] a (pantin, corps) dislocated.

désarticuler [dezartikyle] vt: **se ~** to contort (o.s.).

désassorti, e [dezasɔrti] a unmatching, unmatched; (magasin, marchand) sold out.

désastre [dezastr(ə)] nm disaster.

désastreux, euse [dezastrø, -øz] a disastrous.

désavantage [dezavɑ̃taʒ] nm disadvantage; (inconvénient) drawback, disadvantage.

désavantager [dezavɑ̃taʒe] vt to put at a disadvantage.

désavantageux, euse [dezavɑ̃taʒø, -øz] a unfavourable, disadvantageous.

désaveu [dezavø] nm repudiation; (déni) disclaimer.

désavouer [dezavwe] vt to disown, repudiate, disclaim.

désaxé, e [dezakse] a (fig) unbalanced.

désaxer [dezakse] vt (roue) to put out of true; (personne) to throw off balance.

desceller [desele] vt (pierre) to pull free.

descendance [desɑ̃dɑ̃s] nf (famille) descendants pl, issue; (origine) descent.

descendant, e [desɑ̃dɑ̃, -ɑ̃t] vb voir **descendre** ♦ nm/f descendant.

descendeur, euse [desɑ̃dœr, -øz] nm/f (SPORT) downhiller.

descendre [desɑ̃dr(ə)] vt (escalier, montagne) to go ou (come) down; (valise, paquet) to take ou get down; (étagère etc) to lower; (fam: abattre) to shoot down; (: boire) to knock back ♦ vi to go ou (come) down; (passager: s'arrêter) to get out, alight; (niveau, température) to go ou come down, fall, drop; (marée) to go out; **~ à pied/en voiture** to walk/drive down, go down on foot/by car; **~ de** (famille) to be descended from; **~ du train** to get out of ou off the train; **~ d'un arbre** to climb down from a tree; **~ de cheval** to dismount, get off one's horse; **~ à l'hôtel** to stay at a hotel; **~ dans la rue** (manifester) to take to the streets; **~ en ville** to go into town, go down town.

descente [desɑ̃t] nf descent, going down; (chemin) way down; (SKI) downhill (race); **au milieu de la ~** halfway down; **freinez dans les ~s** use the brakes going downhill; **~ de lit** bedside rug; **~ (de police)** (police) raid.

descriptif, ive [dɛskriptif, -iv] a descriptive ♦

nm explanatory leaflet.
description [dɛskripsjɔ̃] *nf* description.
désembourber [dezɑ̃buʀbe] *vt* to pull out of the mud.
désembourgeoiser [dezɑ̃buʀʒwaze] *vt*: ~ qn to get sb out of his (*ou* her) middle-class attitudes.
désembuer [dezɑ̃bɥe] *vt* to demist.
désemparé, e [dezɑ̃paʀe] *a* bewildered, distraught; (*bateau, avion*) crippled.
désemparer [dezɑ̃paʀe] *vi*: **sans** ~ without stopping.
désemplir [dezɑ̃pliʀ] *vi*: **ne pas** ~ to be always full.
désenchanté, e [dezɑ̃ʃɑ̃te] *a* disenchanted, disillusioned.
désenchantement [dezɑ̃ʃɑ̃tmɑ̃] *nm* disenchantment, disillusion.
désenclaver [dezɑ̃klave] *vt* to open up.
désencombrer [dezɑ̃kɔ̃bʀe] *vt* to clear.
désenfler [dezɑ̃fle] *vi* to become less swollen.
désengagement [dezɑ̃gaʒmɑ̃] *nm* (*POL*) disengagement.
désensabler [dezɑ̃sable] *vt* to pull out of the sand.
désensibiliser [desɑ̃sibilize] *vt* (*MÉD*) to desensitize.
désenvenimer [dezɑ̃vnime] *vt* (*plaie*) to remove the poison from; (*fig*) to take the sting out of.
désépaissir [dezepesiʀ] *vt* to thin (out).
déséquilibre [dezekilibʀ(ə)] *nm* (*position*): **être en** ~ to be unsteady; (*fig: des forces, du budget*) imbalance; (*PSYCH*) unbalance.
déséquilibré, e [dezekilibʀe] *nm/f* (*PSYCH*) unbalanced person.
déséquilibrer [dezekilibʀe] *vt* to throw off balance.
désert, e [dezɛʀ, -ɛʀt(ə)] *a* deserted ♦ *nm* desert.
déserter [dezɛʀte] *vi, vt* to desert.
déserteur [dezɛʀtœʀ] *nm* deserter.
désertion [dezɛʀsjɔ̃] *nf* desertion.
désertique [dezɛʀtik] *a* desert *cpd*; (*inculte*) barren, empty.
désescalade [dezeskalad] *nf* (*MIL*) de-escalation.
désespérant, e [dezɛspeʀɑ̃, -ɑ̃t] *a* hopeless, despairing.
désespéré, e [dezɛspeʀe] *a* desperate; (*regard*) despairing; **état** ~ (*MÉD*) hopeless condition.
désespérément [dezɛspeʀemɑ̃] *ad* desperately.
désespérer [dezɛspeʀe] *vt* to drive to despair ♦ *vi*, **se** ~ *vi* to despair; ~ **de** to despair of.
désespoir [dezɛspwaʀ] *nm* despair; **être** *ou* **faire le** ~ **de qn** to be the despair of sb; **en** ~ **de cause** in desperation.
déshabillé, e [dezabije] *a* undressed ♦ *nm* négligée.
déshabiller [dezabije] *vt* to undress; **se** ~ to undress (o.s.).
déshabituer [dezabitɥe] *vt*: **se** ~ **de** to get out of the habit of.
désherbant [dezɛʀbɑ̃] *nm* weed-killer.
désherber [dezɛʀbe] *vt* to weed.
déshérité, e [dezeʀite] *a* disinherited ♦ *nm/f*: **les** ~s (*pauvres*) the underprivileged, the

deprived.
déshériter [dezeʀite] *vt* to disinherit.
déshonneur [dezɔnœʀ] *nm* dishonour (*Brit*), dishonor (*US*), disgrace.
déshonorer [dezɔnɔʀe] *vt* to dishonour (*Brit*), dishonor (*US*), bring disgrace upon; **se** ~ to bring dishono(u)r on o.s.
déshumaniser [dezymanize] *vt* to dehumanize.
déshydratation [dezidʀatasjɔ̃] *nf* dehydration.
déshydraté, e [dezidʀate] *a* dehydrated.
déshydrater [dezidʀate] *vt* to dehydrate.
desiderata [dezideʀata] *nmpl* requirements.
design [dizajn] *a* (*mobilier*) designer *cpd* ♦ *nm* (*industrial*) design.
désignation [deziɲasjɔ̃] *nf* naming, appointment; (*signe, mot*) name, designation.
designer [dizajnɛʀ] *nm* designer.
désigner [deziɲe] *vt* (*montrer*) to point out, indicate; (*dénommer*) to denote, refer to; (*nommer: candidat etc*) to name, appoint.
désillusion [dezilyzjɔ̃] *nf* disillusion(ment).
désillusionner [dezilyzjɔne] *vt* to disillusion.
désincarné, e [dezɛ̃kaʀne] *a* disembodied.
désinence [dezinɑ̃s] *nf* ending, inflexion.
désinfectant, e [dezɛ̃fɛktɑ̃, -ɑ̃t] *a, nm* disinfectant.
désinfecter [dezɛ̃fɛkte] *vt* to disinfect.
désinformation [dezɛ̃fɔʀmasjɔ̃] *nf* disinformation.
désintégrer [dezɛ̃tegʀe] *vt*, **se** ~ *vi* to disintegrate.
désintéressé, e [dezɛ̃teʀese] *a* (*généreux, bénévole*) disinterested, unselfish.
désintéressement [dezɛ̃teʀesmɑ̃] *nm* (*générosité*) disinterestedness.
désintéresser [dezɛ̃teʀese] *vt*: **se** ~ **(de)** to lose interest (in).
désintérêt [dezɛ̃teʀe] *nm* (*indifférence*) disinterest.
désintoxication [dezɛ̃tɔksikasjɔ̃] *nf* treatment for alcoholism (*ou* drug addiction); **faire une cure de** ~ to have *ou* undergo treatment for alcoholism (*ou* drug addiction).
désintoxiquer [dezɛ̃tɔksike] *vt* to treat for alcoholism (*ou* drug addiction).
désinvolte [dezɛ̃vɔlt(ə)] *a* casual, off-hand.
désinvolture [dezɛ̃vɔltyʀ] *nf* casualness.
désir [deziʀ] *nm* wish; (*fort, sensuel*) desire.
désirer [deziʀe] *vt* to want, wish for; (*sexuellement*) to desire; **je désire** ... (*formule de politesse*) I would like ...; **il désire que tu l'aides** he would like *ou* he wants you to help him; ~ **faire** to want *ou* wish to do; **ça laisse à** ~ it leaves something to be desired.
désireux, euse [deziʀø, -øz] *a*: ~ **de faire** anxious to do.
désistement [dezistmɑ̃] *nm* withdrawal.
désister [deziste]: **se** ~ *vi* to stand down, withdraw.
désobéir [dezɔbeiʀ] *vi*: ~ **(à qn/qch)** to disobey (sb/sth).
désobéissance [dezɔbeisɑ̃s] *nf* disobedience.
désobéissant, e [dezɔbeisɑ̃, -ɑ̃t] *a* disobedient.
désobligeant, e [dezɔbliʒɑ̃, -ɑ̃t] *a* disagreeable, unpleasant.
désobliger [dezɔbliʒe] *vt* to offend.
désodorisant [dezɔdɔʀizɑ̃] *nm* air freshener,

deodorizer.

désodoriser [dezɔdɔʀize] *vt* to deodorize.

désœuvré, e [dezœvʀe] *a* idle.

désœuvrement [dezœvʀəmɑ̃] *nm* idleness.

désolant, e [dezɔlɑ̃, -ɑ̃t] *a* distressing.

désolation [dezɔlasjɔ̃] *nf* (*affliction*) distress, grief; (*d'un paysage etc*) desolation, devastation.

désolé, e [dezɔle] *a* (*paysage*) desolate; **je suis ~** I'm sorry.

désoler [dezɔle] *vt* to distress, grieve; **se ~** to be upset.

désolidariser [desɔlidaʀize] *vt*: **se ~ de** *ou* **d'avec** to dissociate o.s. from.

désopilant, e [dezɔpilɑ̃, -ɑ̃t] *a* screamingly funny, hilarious.

désordonné, e [dezɔʀdɔne] *a* untidy, disorderly.

désordre [dezɔʀdʀ(ə)] *nm* disorder(liness), untidiness; (*anarchie*) disorder; **~s** *nmpl* (POL) disturbances, disorder *sg*; **en ~** in a mess, untidy.

désorganiser [dezɔʀganize] *vt* to disorganize.

désorienté, e [dezɔʀjɑ̃te] *a* disorientated; (*fig*) bewildered.

désormais [dezɔʀmɛ] *ad* in future, from now on.

désosser [dezɔse] *vt* to bone.

despote [dɛspɔt] *nm* despot; (*fig*) tyrant.

despotique [dɛspɔtik] *a* despotic.

despotisme [dɛspɔtism(ə)] *nm* despotism.

desquamer [dɛskwame]: **se ~** *vi* to flake off.

desquels, desquelles [dekɛl] *prép* + *pronom voir* **lequel**.

DESS *sigle m* (= *Diplôme d'études supérieures spécialisées*) *post-graduate diploma*.

dessaisir [desɛziʀ] *vt*: **~ un tribunal d'une affaire** to remove a case from a court; **se ~ de** *vt* to give up, part with.

dessaler [desale] *vt* (*eau de mer*) to desalinate; (CULIN: *morue etc*) to soak; (*fig fam*: *délurer*): **~ qn** to teach sb a thing or two ♦ *vi* (*voilier*) to capsize.

Desse *abr* = **duchesse**.

desséché, e [desefe] *a* dried up.

dessèchement [desɛʃmɑ̃] *nm* drying out; dryness; hardness.

dessécher [desefe] *vt* (*terre, plante*) to dry out, parch; (*peau*) to dry out; (*volontairement*: *aliments etc*) to dry, dehydrate; (*fig*: *cœur*) to harden; **se ~** *vi* to dry out; (*peau, lèvres*) to go dry.

dessein [desɛ̃] *nm* design; **dans le ~ de** with the intention of; **à ~** intentionally, deliberately.

desserrer [desɛʀe] *vt* to loosen; (*frein*) to release; (*poing, dents*) to unclench; (*objets alignés*) to space out; **ne pas ~ les dents** not to open one's mouth.

dessert [desɛʀ] *vb voir* **desservir** ♦ *nm* dessert, pudding.

desserte [desɛʀt(ə)] *nf* (*table*) side table; (*transport*): **la ~ du village est assurée par autocar** there is a coach service to the village; **chemin de ~** *ou* **voie de ~** service road.

desservir [desɛʀviʀ] *vt* (*ville, quartier*) to serve; (: *suj: voie de communication*) to lead into; (*suj: vicaire: paroisse*) to serve; (*nuire*

à: *personne*) to do a disservice to; (*débarrasser*): **~ (la table)** to clear the table.

dessiller [desije] *vt* (*fig*): **~ les yeux à qn** to open sb's eyes.

dessin [desɛ̃] *nm* (*œuvre, art*) drawing; (*motif*) pattern, design; (*contour*) (out)line; **le ~ industriel** draughtsmanship (*Brit*), draftsmanship (US); **~ animé** cartoon (film); **~ humoristique** cartoon.

dessinateur, trice [desinatœʀ, -tʀis] *nm/f* drawer; (*de bandes dessinées*) cartoonist; (*industriel*) draughtsman (*Brit*), draftsman (US); **dessinatrice de mode** fashion designer.

dessiner [desine] *vt* to draw; (*concevoir*: *carrosserie, maison*) to design; (*suj: robe: taille*) to show off; **se ~** *vi* (*forme*) to be outlined; (*fig: solution*) to emerge.

dessoûler [desule] *vt, vi* to sober up.

dessous [dəsu] *ad* underneath, beneath ♦ *nm* underside; (*étage inférieur*): **les voisins du ~** the downstairs neighbours ♦ *nmpl* (*sousvêtements*) underwear *sg*; (*fig*) hidden aspects; **en ~** underneath; below; (*fig: en catimini*) slyly, on the sly; **par ~** underneath; below; **de ~ le lit** from under the bed; **au-~** *ad* below; **au-~ de** *prép* below; (*peu digne de*) beneath; **au-~ de tout** the (absolute) limit; **avoir le ~** to get the worst of it.

dessous-de-bouteille [dəsudbutɛj] *nm* bottle mat.

dessous-de-plat [dəsudpla] *nm inv* tablemat.

dessous-de-table [dəsudtabl(ə)] *nm* (*fig*) bribe, under-the-counter payment.

dessus [dəsy] *ad* on top; (*collé, écrit*) on it ♦ *nm* top; (*étage supérieur*): **les voisins/ l'appartement du ~** the upstairs neighbours/ flat; **en ~** above; **par ~** *ad* over it ♦ *prép* over; **au-~** above; **au-~ de** above; **avoir/ prendre le ~** to have/get the upper hand; **reprendre le ~** to get over it; **bras ~ bras dessous** arm in arm; **sens ~ dessous** upside down; *voir* **ci-, là-.**

dessus-de-lit [dəsydli] *nm inv* bedspread.

déstabiliser [destabilize] *vt* (POL) to destabilize.

destin [dɛstɛ̃] *nm* fate; (*avenir*) destiny.

destinataire [dɛstinatɛʀ] *nm/f* (POSTES) addressee; (*d'un colis*) consignee; (*d'un mandat*) payee; **aux risques et périls du ~** at owner's risk.

destination [dɛstinasjɔ̃] *nf* (*lieu*) destination; (*usage*) purpose; **à ~ de** (*avion etc*) bound for; (*voyageur*) bound for, travelling to.

destinée [dɛstine] *nf* fate; (*existence, avenir*) destiny.

destiner [dɛstine] *vt*: **~ qn à** (*poste, sort*) to destine sb for, intend sb to + *verbe*; **~ qn/ qch à** (*prédestiner*) to mark sb/sth out for, destine sb/sth to + *verbe*; **~ qch à** (*envisager d'affecter*) to intend to use sth for; **~ qch à qn** (*envisager de donner*) to intend to give sth to sb, intend sb to have sth; (*adresser*) to intend sth for sb; **se ~ à l'enseignement** to intend to become a teacher; **être destiné à** (*sort*) to be destined to + *verbe*; (*usage*) to be intended *ou* meant for; (*suj: sort*) to be in store for.

destituer [dɛstitɥe] *vt* to depose; ~ **qn de ses fonctions** to relieve sb of his duties.

destitution [dɛstitysjɔ̃] *nf* deposition.

destructeur, trice [dɛstryktœʀ, -tʀis] *a* destructive.

destructif, ive [dɛstryktif, -iv] *a* destructive.

destruction [dɛstryksjɔ̃] *nf* destruction.

déstructuré, e [destryktyʀe] *a*: **vêtements** ~**s** casual clothes.

déstructurer [destryktyʀe] *vt* to break down, take to pieces.

désuet, ète [desɥɛ, -ɛt] *a* outdated, outmoded.

désuétude [desɥetyd] *nf*: **tomber en** ~ to fall into disuse, become obsolete.

désuni, e [dezyni] *a* divided, disunited.

désunion [dezynjɔ̃] *nf* disunity.

désunir [dezyniʀ] *vt* to disunite; **se** ~ *vi* (*athlète*) to get out of one's stride.

détachable [detaʃabl(ə)] *a* (*coupon etc*) tear-off *cpd*; (*capuche etc*) detachable.

détachant [detaʃɑ̃] *nm* stain remover.

détaché, e [detaʃe] *a* (*fig*) detached ♦ *nm/f* (*représentant*) person on secondment (*Brit*) *ou* a posting.

détachement [detaʃmɑ̃] *nm* detachment; (*fonctionnaire, employé*): **être en** ~ to be on secondment (*Brit*) *ou* a posting.

détacher [detaʃe] *vt* (*enlever*) to detach, remove; (*délier*) to untie; (*ADMIN*): ~ **qn (auprès de** *ou* **à)** to send sb on secondment (to) (*Brit*), post sb (to); (*MIL*) to detail; (*vêtement: nettoyer*) to remove the stains from; **se** ~ *vi* (*tomber*) to come off; to come out; (*se défaire*) to come undone; (*SPORT*) to pull *ou* break away; (*se délier: chien, prisonnier*) to break loose; **se** ~ **sur** to stand out against; **se** ~ **de** (*se désintéresser*) to grow away from.

détail [detaj] *nm* detail; (*COMM*): **le** ~ retail; **prix de** ~ retail price; **au** ~ *ad* (*COMM*) retail; (*: individuellement*) separately; **donner le** ~ **de** to give a detailed account of; (*compte*) to give a breakdown of; **en** ~ in detail.

détaillant, e [detajɑ̃, -ɑ̃t] *nm/f* retailer.

détaillé, e [detaje] *a* (*récit*) detailed.

détailler [detaje] *vt* (*COMM*) to sell retail; to sell separately; (*expliquer*) to explain in detail; to detail; (*examiner*) to look over, examine.

détaler [detale] *vi* (*lapin*) to scamper off; (*fam: personne*) to make off, scarper (*fam*).

détartrant [detaʀtʀɑ̃] *nm* descaling agent (*Brit*), scale remover.

détartrer [detaʀtʀe] *vt* to descale; (*dents*) to scale.

détaxe [detaks(ə)] *nf* (*réduction*) reduction in tax; (*suppression*) removal of tax; (*remboursement*) tax refund.

détaxer [detakse] *vt* (*réduire*) to reduce the tax on; (*ôter*) to remove the tax on.

détecter [detɛkte] *vt* to detect.

détecteur [detɛktœʀ] *nm* detector, sensor; ~ **de mensonges** lie detector; ~ **(de mines)** mine detector.

détection [detɛksjɔ̃] *nf* detection.

détective [detɛktiv] *nm* (*Brit: policier*) detective; ~ **(privé)** private detective *ou* investigator.

déteindre [detɛ̃dʀ(ə)] *vi* to fade; (*fig*): ~ **sur** to rub off on.

déteint, e [detɛ̃, -ɛ̃t] *pp de* **déteindre**.

dételer [detle] *vt* to unharness; (*voiture, wagon*) to unhitch ♦ *vi* (*fig: s'arrêter*) to leave off (working).

détendeur [detɑ̃dœʀ] *nm* (*de bouteille à gaz*) regulator.

détendre [detɑ̃dʀ(ə)] *vt* (*fil*) to slacken, loosen; (*relaxer: personne, atmosphère*) to relax; (*: situation*) to relieve; **se** ~ to lose its tension; to relax.

détendu, e [detɑ̃dy] *a* relaxed.

détenir [detniʀ] *vt* (*fortune, objet, secret*) to be in possession of, have (in one's possession); (*prisonnier*) to detain, hold; (*record*) to hold; ~ **le pouvoir** to be in power.

détente [detɑ̃t] *nf* relaxation; (*POL*) détente; (*d'une arme*) trigger; (*d'un athlète qui saute*) spring.

détenteur, trice [detɑ̃tœʀ, -tʀis] *nm/f* holder.

détention [detɑ̃sjɔ̃] *nf* (*voir détenir*) possession; detention; holding; ~ **préventive** (pretrial) custody.

détenu, e [detny] *pp de* **détenir** ♦ *nm/f* prisoner.

détergent [detɛʀʒɑ̃] *nm* detergent.

détérioration [deteʀjɔʀasjɔ̃] *nf* damaging; deterioration.

détériorer [deteʀjɔʀe] *vt* to damage; **se** ~ *vi* to deteriorate.

déterminant, e [detɛʀminɑ̃, -ɑ̃t] *a*: **un facteur** ~ a determining factor ♦ *nm* (*LING*) determiner.

détermination [detɛʀminasjɔ̃] *nf* determining; (*résolution*) decision; (*fermeté*) determination.

déterminé, e [detɛʀmine] *a* (*résolu*) determined; (*précis*) specific, definite.

déterminer [detɛʀmine] *vt* (*fixer*) to determine; (*décider*): ~ **qn à faire** to decide sb to do; **se** ~ **à faire** to make up one's mind to do.

déterminisme [detɛʀminism(ə)] *nm* determinism.

déterré, e [deteʀe] *nm/f*: **avoir une mine de** ~ to look like death warmed up.

déterrer [deteʀe] *vt* to dig up.

détersif, ive [detɛʀsif, -iv] *a, nm* detergent.

détestable [detɛstabl(ə)] *a* foul, detestable.

détester [detɛste] *vt* to hate, detest.

détiendrai [detjɛ̃dʀe], **détiens** [detjɛ̃] *etc vb voir* **détenir**.

détonant, e [detɔnɑ̃, -ɑ̃t] *a*: **mélange** ~ explosive mixture.

détonateur [detɔnatœʀ] *nm* detonator.

détonation [detɔnasjɔ̃] *nf* detonation, bang, report (of a gun).

détoner [detɔne] *vi* to detonate, explode.

détonner [detɔne] *vi* (*MUS*) to go out of tune; (*fig*) to clash.

détordre [detɔʀdʀ(ə)] *vt* to untwist, unwind.

détour [detuʀ] *nm* detour; (*tournant*) bend, curve; (*fig: subterfuge*) roundabout means; **au** ~ **de chemin** at the bend in the path; **sans** ~ (*fig*) plainly.

détourné, e [detuʀne] *a* (*sentier, chemin, moyen*) roundabout.

détournement [detuʀnəmɑ̃] *nm* diversion, rerouting; **~ d'avion** hijacking; **~ (de fonds)** embezzlement *ou* misappropriation (of funds); **~ de mineur** corruption of a minor.

détourner [deturne] *vt* to divert; (*avion*) to divert, reroute; (: *par la force*) to hijack; (*yeux, tête*) to turn away; (*de l'argent*) to embezzle, misappropriate; **se ~** to turn away; **~ la conversation** to change the subject; **~ qn de son devoir** to divert sb from his duty; **~ l'attention (de qn)** to distract *ou* divert (sb's) attention.

détracteur, trice [detraktœr, -tris] *nm/f* disparager, critic.

détraqué, e [detrake] *a* (*machine, santé*) broken-down ♦ *nm/f* (*fam*): **c'est un ~** he's unhinged.

détraquer [detrake] *vt* to put out of order; (*estomac*) to upset; **se ~** *vi* to go wrong.

détrempe [detrɑ̃p] *nf* (*ART*) tempera.

détrempé, e [detrɑ̃pe] *a* (*sol*) sodden, waterlogged.

détremper [detrɑ̃pe] *vt* (*peinture*) to water down.

détresse [detrɛs] *nf* distress; **en ~** (*avion etc*) in distress; **appel/signal de ~** distress call/signal.

détriment [detrimɑ̃] *nm*: **au ~ de** to the detriment of.

détritus [detritys] *nmpl* rubbish *sg*, refuse *sg*, garbage *sg* (*US*).

détroit [detrwa] *nm* strait; **le ~ de Bering** *ou* **Behring** the Bering Strait; **le ~ de Gibraltar** the Straits of Gibraltar; **le ~ du Bosphore** the Bosphorus; **le ~ de Magellan** the Strait of Magellan, the Magellan Strait.

détromper [detrɔ̃pe] *vt* to disabuse; **se ~**: **détrompez-vous** don't believe it.

détrôner [detrone] *vt* to dethrone, depose; (*fig*) to oust, dethrone.

détrousser [detruse] *vt* to rob.

détruire [detruir] *vt* to destroy; (*fig: santé, réputation*) to ruin; (*documents*) to shred.

détruit, e [detrui, -it] *pp de* **détruire**.

dette [dɛt] *nf* debt; **~ publique** *ou* **de l'État** national debt.

DEUG [døg] *sigle m* = *Diplôme d'études universitaires générales*.

deuil [dœj] *nm* (*perte*) bereavement; (*période*) mourning; (*chagrin*) grief; **porter le ~** to wear mourning; **prendre le/être en ~** to go into/be in mourning.

DEUST [dœst] *sigle m* = *Diplôme d'études universitaires scientifiques et techniques*.

deux [dø] *num* two; **les ~** both; **ses ~ mains** both his hands, his two hands; **à ~ pas a** short distance away; **tous les ~ mois** every two months, every other month; **~ points** colon *sg*.

deuxième [døzjɛm] *num* second.

deuxièmement [døzjɛmmɑ̃] *ad* secondly, in the second place.

deux-pièces [døpjɛs] *nm inv* (*tailleur*) two-piece (suit); (*de bain*) two-piece (swimsuit); (*appartement*) two-roomed flat (*Brit*) *ou* apartment (*US*).

deux-roues [døru] *nm* two-wheeled vehicle.

deux-temps [døtɑ̃] *a* two-stroke.

devais [dəvɛ] *etc vb voir* **devoir**.

dévaler [devale] *vt* to hurtle down.

dévaliser [devalize] *vt* to rob, burgle.

dévalorisant, e [devalɔrizɑ̃, -ɑ̃t] *a* depreciatory.

dévalorisation [devalɔrizasjɔ̃] *nf* depreciation.

dévaloriser [devalɔrize] *vt*, **se ~** *vi* to depreciate.

dévaluation [devaluasjɔ̃] *nf* depreciation; (*ÉCON: mesure*) devaluation.

dévaluer [devalue] *vt*, **se ~** *vi* to devalue.

devancer [dəvɑ̃se] *vt* to be ahead of; (*distancer*) to get ahead of; (*arriver avant*) to arrive before; (*prévenir*) to anticipate; **~ l'appel** (*MIL*) to enlist before call-up.

devancier, ière [dəvɑ̃sje, -jɛr] *nm/f* precursor.

devant [dəvɑ̃] *vb voir* **devoir** ♦ *ad* in front; (*à distance: en avant*) ahead ♦ *prép* in front; ahead of; (*avec mouvement: passer*) past; (*fig*) before, in front of; (: *face à*) faced with, in the face of; (: *vu*) in view of ♦ *nm* front; **prendre les ~s** to make the first move; **de ~** (*roue, porte*) front; **les pattes de ~** the front legs, the forelegs; **par ~** (*boutonner*) at the front; (*entrer*) the front way; **par-~ notaire** in the presence of a notary; **aller au-~ de qn** to go out to meet sb; **aller au-~ de** (*désirs de qn*) to anticipate; **aller au-~ des ennuis** *ou* **difficultés** to be asking for trouble.

devanture [dəvɑ̃tyr] *nf* (*façade*) (shop) front; (*étalage*) display; (shop) window.

dévastateur, trice [devastatœr, -tris] *a* devastating.

dévastation [devastasjɔ̃] *nf* devastation.

dévaster [devaste] *vt* to devastate.

déveine [devɛn] *nf* rotten luck *q*.

développement [devlɔpmɑ̃] *nm* development.

développer [devlɔpe] *vt*, **se ~** *vi* to develop.

devenir [dəvnir] *vb avec attribut* to become; **~ instituteur** to become a teacher; **que sont-ils devenus?** what has become of them?

devenu, e [dəvny] *pp de* **devenir**.

dévergondé, e [devɛrgɔ̃de] *a* wild, shameless.

dévergonder [devɛrgɔ̃de] *vt*, **se ~** *vi* to get into bad ways.

déverminer [devɛrmine] *vt* (*INFORM*) to debug.

déverrouiller [devɛruje] *vt* to unbolt.

devers [dəvɛr] *ad*: **par ~ soi** to oneself.

déverser [devɛrse] *vt* (*liquide*) to pour (out); (*ordures*) to tip (out); **se ~ dans** (*fleuve, mer*) to flow into.

déversoir [devɛrswar] *nm* overflow.

dévêtir [devetir] *vt*, **se ~** *vi* to undress.

devez [dəve] *vb voir* **devoir**.

déviation [devjasjɔ̃] *nf* deviation; (*AUTO*) diversion (*Brit*), detour (*US*); **~ de la colonne (vertébrale)** curvature of the spine.

dévider [devide] *vt* to unwind.

dévidoir [devidwar] *nm* reel.

deviendrai [dəvjɛ̃dre], **deviens** [dəvjɛ̃] *etc vb voir* **devenir**.

dévier [devje] *vt* (*fleuve, circulation*) to divert; (*coup*) to deflect ♦ *vi* to veer (off course); **(faire) ~** (*projectile*) to deflect; (*véhicule*) to push off course.

devin [dəvɛ̃] *nm* soothsayer, seer.

deviner [dəvine] *vt* to guess; (*prévoir*) to foretell, foresee; (*apercevoir*) to distinguish.

devinette [dəvinɛt] *nf* riddle.

devint [dəvɛ̃] *etc vb voir* **devenir**.

devis [dəvi] *nm* estimate, quotation; ~ **descriptif/estimatif** detailed/preliminary estimate.

dévisager [devizaʒe] *vt* to stare at.

devise [dəviz] *nf (formule)* motto, watchword; *(ÉCON: monnaie)* currency; ~**s** *nfpl (argent)* currency *sg*.

deviser [dəvize] *vi* to converse.

dévisser [devise] *vt* to unscrew, undo; **se** ~ *vi* to come unscrewed.

de visu [dəvizy] *ad*: **se rendre compte de qch** ~ to see sth for o.s.

dévitaliser [devitalize] *vt (dent)* to remove the nerve from.

dévoiler [devwale] *vt* to unveil.

devoir [dəvwaʀ] *nm* duty; *(SCOL)* piece of homework, homework *q*; *(: en classe)* exercise ♦ *vt (argent, respect)*: ~ **qch (à qn)** to owe (sb) sth; *(suivi de l'infinitif: obligation)*: **il doit le faire** he has to do it, he must do it; *(: fatalité)*: **cela devait arriver un jour** it was bound to happen; *(: intention)*: **il doit partir demain** he is (due) to leave tomorrow; *(: probabilité)*: **il doit être tard** it must be late; **se faire un** ~ **de faire qch** to make it one's duty to do sth; ~**s de vacances** homework set for the holidays; **se** ~ **de faire qch** to be duty bound to do sth; **je devrais faire** I ought to *ou* should do; **tu n'aurais pas dû** you ought not to have *ou* shouldn't have; **comme il se doit** *(comme il faut)* as is right and proper.

dévolu, e [devɔly] *a*: ~ **à** allotted to ♦ *nm*: **jeter son** ~ **sur** to fix one's choice on.

devons [dəvɔ̃] *vb voir* **devoir**.

dévorant, e [devɔʀɑ̃, -ɑ̃t] *a (faim, passion)* raging.

dévorer [devɔʀe] *vt* to devour; *(suj: feu, soucis)* to consume; ~ **qn/qch des yeux** *ou* **du regard** *(fig)* to eye sb/sth intently; *(: convoitise)* to eye sb/sth greedily.

dévot, e [devo, -ɔt] *a* devout, pious ♦ *nm/f* devout person; **un faux** ~ a falsely pious person.

dévotion [devɔsjɔ̃] *nf* devoutness; **être à la** ~ **de qn** to be totally devoted to sb; **avoir une** ~ **pour qn** to worship sb.

dévoué, e [devwe] *a* devoted.

dévouement [devumɑ̃] *nm* devotion, dedication.

dévouer [devwe]: **se** ~ *vi (se sacrifier)*: **se** ~ **(pour)** to sacrifice o.s. (for); *(se consacrer)*: **se** ~ **à** to devote *ou* dedicate o.s. to.

dévoyé, e [devwaje] *a* delinquent.

dévoyer [devwaje] *vt* to lead astray; **se** ~ *vi* to go off the rails; ~ **l'opinion publique** to influence public opinion.

devrai [dəvʀe] *etc vb voir* **devoir**.

dextérité [dɛksteʀite] *nf* skill, dexterity.

dfc *abr (= désire faire connaissance) in personal column of newspaper*.

DG *sigle m = directeur général*.

dg. *abr (= décigramme)* dg.

DGE *sigle f (= Dotation globale d'équipement) state contribution to local government budget*.

DGSE *sigle f (= Direction générale des services extérieurs)* ≈ MI6 *(Brit)*, ≈ CIA *(US)*.

DI *sigle f (MIL)* = *division d'infanterie*.

dia [dja] *abr* = **diapositive**.

diabète [djabɛt] *nm* diabetes *sg*.

diabétique [djabetik] *nm/f* diabetic.

diable [djɑbl(ə)] *nm* devil; **une musique du** ~ an unholy racket; **il fait une chaleur du** ~ it's fiendishly hot; **avoir le** ~ **au corps** to be the very devil.

diablement [djɑbləmɑ̃] *ad* fiendishly.

diableries [djɑbləʀi] *nfpl (d'enfant)* devilment *sg*, mischief *sg*.

diablesse [djɑblɛs] *nf (petite fille)* little devil.

diablotin [djɑblɔtɛ̃] *nm* imp; *(pétard)* cracker.

diabolique [djɑbɔlik] *a* diabolical.

diabolo [djɑbɔlo] *nm (jeu)* diabolo; *(boisson)* lemonade and fruit cordial; ~**(-menthe)** lemonade and mint cordial.

diacre [djakʀ(ə)] *nm* deacon.

diadème [djadɛm] *nm* diadem.

diagnostic [djagnɔstik] *nm* diagnosis *sg*.

diagnostiquer [djagnɔstike] *vt* to diagnose.

diagonal, e, aux [djagɔnal, -o] *a, nf* diagonal; **en** ~**e** diagonally; **lire en** ~**e** *(fig)* to skim through.

diagramme [djagʀam] *nm* chart, graph.

dialecte [djalɛkt(ə)] *nm* dialect.

dialogue [djalɔg] *nm* dialogue; ~ **de sourds** dialogue of the deaf.

dialoguer [djalɔge] *vi* to converse; *(POL)* to have a dialogue.

dialoguiste [djalɔgist(ə)] *nm/f* dialogue writer.

diamant [djamɑ̃] *nm* diamond.

diamantaire [djamɑ̃tɛʀ] *nm* diamond dealer.

diamétralement [djametʀalmɑ̃] *ad* diametrically; ~ **opposés** *(opinions)* diametrically opposed.

diamètre [djamɛtʀ(ə)] *nm* diameter.

diapason [djapazɔ̃] *nm* tuning fork; *(fig)*: **être/se mettre au** ~ **(de)** to be/get in tune (with).

diaphane [djafan] *a* diaphanous.

diaphragme [djafʀagm(ə)] *nm (ANAT, PHOTO)* diaphragm; *(contraceptif)* diaphragm, cap; **ouverture du** ~ *(PHOTO)* aperture.

diapo [djapo], **diapositive** [djapozitiv] *nf* transparency, slide.

diaporama [djapɔʀama] *nm* slide show.

diapré, e [djapʀe] *a* many-coloured *(Brit)*, many-colored *(US)*.

diarrhée [djaʀe] *nf* diarrhoea *(Brit)*, diarrhea *(US)*.

diatribe [djatʀib] *nf* diatribe.

dichotomie [dikɔtɔmi] *nf* dichotomy.

dictaphone [diktafɔn] *nm* Dictaphone ®.

dictateur [diktatœʀ] *nm* dictator.

dictatorial, e, aux [diktatɔʀjal, -o] *a* dictatorial.

dictature [diktatyʀ] *nf* dictatorship.

dictée [dikte] *nf* dictation; **prendre sous** ~ to take down *(sth dictated)*.

dicter [dikte] *vt* to dictate.

diction [diksjɔ̃] *nf* diction, delivery; **cours de** ~ speech production lesson(s).

dictionnaire [diksjɔnɛʀ] *nm* dictionary; ~ **géographique** gazetteer.

dicton [diktɔ̃] *nm* saying, dictum.

didacticiel [didaktisjɛl] *nm* educational software.

didactique [didaktik] *a* didactic.

dièse [djɛz] *nm* (*MUS*) sharp.

diesel [djezɛl] *nm*, *a inv* diesel.

diète [djɛt] *nf* diet; **être à la ~** to be on a diet.

diététicien, ne [djetetisjɛ̃, -ɛn] *nm/f* dietician.

diététique [djetetik] *nf* dietetics *sg* ♦ *a*: **magasin ~** health food shop (*Brit*) *ou* store (*US*).

dieu, x [djø] *nm* god; **D~** God; **le bon D~** the good Lord; **mon D~!** good heavens!

diffamant, e [difamɑ̃, -ɑ̃t] *a* slanderous, defamatory; libellous.

diffamation [difamɑsjɔ̃] *nf* slander; (*écrite*) libel; **attaquer qn en ~** to sue sb for slander (*ou* libel).

diffamatoire [difamatwaʀ] *a* slanderous, defamatory; libellous.

diffamer [difame] *vt* to slander, defame; to libel.

différé [difeʀe] *a* (*INFORM*): **traitement ~** batch processing; **crédit ~** deferred credit ♦ *nm* (*TV*): **en ~** (pre-)recorded.

différemment [difeʀamɑ̃] *ad* differently.

différence [difeʀɑ̃s] *nf* difference; **à la ~ de** unlike.

différencier [difeʀɑ̃sje] *vt* to differentiate; **se ~ vi** (*organisme*) to become differentiated; **se ~ de** to differentiate o.s. from; (*être différent*) to differ from.

différend [difeʀɑ̃] *nm* difference (of opinion), disagreement.

différent, e [difeʀɑ̃, -ɑ̃t] *a*: **~ (de)** different (from); **~s objets** different *ou* various objects; **à ~es reprises** on various occasions.

différentiel, le [difeʀɑ̃sjɛl] *a, nm* differential.

différer [difeʀe] *vt* to postpone, put off ♦ *vi*: **~ (de)** to differ (from); **~ de faire** (*tarder*) to delay doing.

difficile [difisil] *a* difficult; (*exigeant*) hard to please, difficult (to please); **faire le** *ou* **la ~** to be hard to please, be difficult.

difficilement [difisilmɑ̃] *ad* (*marcher, s'expliquer etc*) with difficulty; **~ lisible/ compréhensible** difficult *ou* hard to read/ understand.

difficulté [difikylte] *nf* difficulty; **en ~** (*bateau, alpiniste*) in trouble *ou* difficulties; **avoir de la ~ à faire** to have difficulty (in) doing.

difforme [difɔʀm(ə)] *a* deformed, misshapen.

difformité [difɔʀmite] *nf* deformity.

diffracter [difʀakte] *vt* to diffract.

diffus, e [dify, -yz] *a* diffuse.

diffuser [difyze] *vt* (*chaleur, bruit, lumière*) to diffuse; (*émission, musique*) to broadcast; (*nouvelle, idée*) to circulate; (*COMM: livres, journaux*) to distribute.

diffuseur [difyzœʀ] *nm* diffuser; distributor.

diffusion [difyzjɔ̃] *nf* diffusion; broadcast(ing); circulation; distribution.

digérer [diʒeʀe] *vt* (*suj: personne*) to digest; (*: machine*) to process; (*fig: accepter*) to stomach, put up with.

digeste [diʒɛst(ə)] *a* easily digestible.

digestible [diʒɛstibl(ə)] *a* digestible.

digestif, ive [diʒɛstif, -iv] *a* digestive ♦ *nm* (after-dinner) liqueur.

digestion [diʒɛstjɔ̃] *nf* digestion.

digit [didʒit] *nm*: **~ binaire** binary digit.

digital, e, aux [diʒital, -o] *a* digital.

digitale [diʒital] *nf* digitalis, foxglove.

digne [diɲ] *a* dignified; **~ de** worthy of; **~ de foi** trustworthy.

dignitaire [diɲitɛʀ] *nm* dignitary.

dignité [diɲite] *nf* dignity.

digression [digʀesjɔ̃] *nf* digression.

digue [dig] *nf* dike, dyke; (*pour protéger la côte*) sea wall.

dijonnais, e [diʒɔnɛ, -ɛz] *a* of *ou* from Dijon ♦ *nm/f*: **D~, e** inhabitant *ou* native of Dijon.

dilapider [dilapide] *vt* to squander, waste; (*détourner: biens, fonds publics*) to embezzle, misappropriate.

dilater [dilate] *vt* to dilate; (*gaz, métal*) to cause to expand; (*ballon*) to distend; **se ~ vi** to expand.

dilemme [dilɛm] *nm* dilemma.

dilettante [diletɑ̃t] *nm/f* dilettante [dɪlɪ'tɑːntɪ]; **en ~** in a dilettantish way.

diligence [diliʒɑ̃s] *nf* stagecoach, diligence; (*empressement*) despatch; **faire ~** to make haste.

diligent, e [diliʒɑ̃, -ɑ̃t] *a* prompt and efficient; diligent.

diluant [dilɥɑ̃] *nm* thinner(s).

diluer [dilɥe] *vt* to dilute.

diluvien, ne [dilyvjɛ̃, -ɛn] *a*: **pluie ~ne** torrential rain.

dimanche [dimɑ̃ʃ] *nm* Sunday; **le ~ des Rameaux/de Pâques** Palm/Easter Sunday; *voir aussi* **lundi**.

dîme [dim] *nf* tithe.

dimension [dimɑ̃sjɔ̃] *nf* (*grandeur*) size; (*gén pl: cotes, MATH: de l'espace*) dimension.

diminué, e [diminɥe] *a* (*personne: physiquement*) run-down; (*: mentalement*) less alert.

diminuer [diminɥe] *vt* to reduce, decrease; (*ardeur etc*) to lessen; (*personne: physiquement*) to undermine; (*dénigrer*) to belittle ♦ *vi* to decrease, diminish.

diminutif [diminytif] *nm* (*LING*) diminutive; (*surnom*) pet name.

diminution [diminysjɔ̃] *nf* decreasing, diminishing.

dînatoire [dinatwaʀ] *a*: **goûter ~** ≈ high tea (*Brit*); **apéritif ~** ≈ evening buffet.

dinde [dɛ̃d] *nf* turkey; (*femme stupide*) goose.

dindon [dɛ̃dɔ̃] *nm* turkey.

dindonneau, x [dɛ̃dɔno] *nm* turkey poult.

dîner [dine] *nm* dinner ♦ *vi* to have dinner; **~ d'affaires/de famille** business/family dinner.

dînette [dinɛt] *nf* (*jeu*): **jouer à la ~** to play at tea parties.

dingue [dɛ̃g] *a* (*fam*) crazy.

dinosaure [dinozɔʀ] *nm* dinosaur.

diode [djɔd] *nf* diode.

diphasé, e [difaze] *a* (*ÉLEC*) two-phase.

diphtérie [difteʀi] *nf* diphtheria.

diphtongue [diftɔ̃g] *nf* diphthong.

diplomate [diplɔmat] *a* diplomatic ♦ *nm* diplomat; (*fig: personne habile*) diplomatist; (*CULIN: gâteau*) dessert made of sponge cake, candied fruit and custard, ≈ trifle (*Brit*).

diplomatie [diplɔmasi] *nf* diplomacy.

diplomatique [diplɔmatik] *a* diplomatic.

diplôme [diplom] *nm* diploma certificate; (*examen*) (diploma) examination.

diplômé, e [diplome] a qualified.

dire [diʀ] nm: **au ~ de** according to; **leur ~s** what they say ♦ vt to say; (secret, mensonge) to tell; **~ l'heure/la vérité** to tell the time/the truth; **dis pardon/merci** say sorry/thank you; **~ qch à qn** to tell sb sth; **~ à qn qu'il fasse** ou **de faire** to tell sb to do; **~ que** to say that; **on dit que** they say that; **comme on dit** as they say; **on dirait que** it looks (ou sounds etc) as though; **on dirait du vin** you'd ou one would think it was wine; **que dites-vous de** (penser) what do you think of; **si cela lui dit** if he feels like it, if he fancies it; **cela ne me dit rien** that doesn't appeal to me; **à vrai ~** truth to tell; **pour ainsi ~** so to speak; **cela va sans ~** that goes without saying; **dis donc!, dites donc!** (pour attirer l'attention) hey!; (au fait) by the way; **et ~ que** ... and to think that ...; **ceci** ou **cela dit** that being said; (à ces mots) whereupon; **c'est dit, voilà qui est dit** so that's settled; **il n'y a pas à ~** there's no getting away from it; **c'est ~ si** ... that just shows that ...; **c'est beaucoup/peu ~** that's saying a lot/not saying much; **se ~** (à soi-même) to say to oneself; (se prétendre): **se ~ malade** etc to say (that) one is ill etc; **ça se dit ... en anglais** that is ... in English; **cela ne se dit pas comme ça** you don't say it like that; **se ~ au revoir** to say goodbye (to each other).

direct, e [diʀɛkt] a direct ♦ nm (train) through train; **en ~** (émission) live; **train/ bus ~** express train/bus.

directement [diʀɛktəmɑ̃] ad directly.

directeur, trice [diʀɛktœʀ, -tʀis] nm/f (d'entreprise) director; (de service) manager/eress; (d'école) head(teacher) (Brit), principal (US); **comité ~** manage- ment ou steering committee; **~ général** gen- eral manager; **~ de thèse** ≈ Ph.D. super- visor.

direction [diʀɛksjɔ̃] nf management; conduct- ing; supervision; (AUTO) steering; (sens) direction; **sous la ~ de** (MUS) conducted by; **en ~ de** (avion, train, bateau) for; **"toutes ~s"** (AUTO) "all routes".

directive [diʀɛktiv] nf directive, instruction.

directorial, e, aux [diʀɛktɔʀjal, -o] a (bureau) director's; manager's; head teacher's.

directrice [diʀɛktʀis] af, nf voir **directeur**.

dirent [diʀ] vb voir **dire**.

dirigeable [diʀiʒabl(ə)] a, nm: (**ballon**) **~** dirigible.

dirigeant, e [diʀiʒɑ̃, -ɑ̃t] a managerial; (clas- ses) ruling ♦ nm/f (d'un parti etc) leader; (d'entreprise) manager, member of the management.

diriger [diʀiʒe] vt (entreprise) to manage, run; (véhicule) to steer; (orchestre) to con- duct; (recherches, travaux) to supervise, be in charge of; (braquer: regard, arme): **~ sur** to point ou level ou aim at; (fig: critiques): **~ contre** to aim at; **se ~** (s'orienter) to find one's way; **se ~ vers** ou **sur** to make ou head for.

dirigisme [diʀiʒism(ə)] nm (ÉCON) state inter- vention, interventionism.

dirigiste [diʀiʒist(ə)] a interventionist.

dis [di], **disais** [dizɛ] etc vb voir **dire**.

discal, e, aux [diskal, -o] a (MÉD): **hernie ~e** slipped disc.

discernement [disɛʀnəmɑ̃] nm discernment, judgment.

discerner [disɛʀne] vt to discern, make out.

disciple [disipl(ə)] nm/f disciple.

disciplinaire [disiplinɛʀ] a disciplinary.

discipline [disiplin] nf discipline.

discipliné, e [disipline] a (well-)disciplined.

discipliner [disipline] vt to discipline; (cheveux) to control.

discobole [diskɔbɔl] nm/f discus thrower.

discontinu, e [diskɔ̃tiny] a intermittent; (bande: sur la route) broken.

discontinuer [diskɔ̃tinɥe] vi: **sans ~** without stopping, without a break.

disconvenir [diskɔ̃vniʀ] vi: **ne pas ~ de qch/ que** not to deny sth/that.

discophile [diskɔfil] nm/f record enthusiast.

discordance [diskɔʀdɑ̃s] nf discordance; con- flict.

discordant, e [diskɔʀdɑ̃, -ɑ̃t] a discordant; conflicting.

discorde [diskɔʀd(ə)] nf discord, dissension.

discothèque [diskɔtek] nf (disques) record collection; (: dans une bibliothèque): **~ (de prêt)** record library; (boîte de nuit) dis- co(thèque).

discourais [diskuʀɛ] etc vb voir **discourir**.

discourir [diskuʀiʀ] vi to discourse, hold forth.

discours [diskuʀ] vb voir **discourir** ♦ nm speech; **~ direct/indirect** (LING) direct/ indirect ou reported speech.

discrédit [diskʀedi] nm: **jeter le ~ sur** to dis- credit.

discréditer [diskʀedite] vt to discredit.

discret, ète [diskʀɛ, -ɛt] a discreet; (fig: musique, style) unobtrusive; (: endroit) quiet.

discrètement [diskʀɛtmɑ̃] ad discreetly.

discrétion [diskʀesjɔ̃] nf discretion; **à la ~ de qn** at sb's discretion; in sb's hands; **à ~** (boisson etc) unlimited, as much as one wants.

discrétionnaire [diskʀesjɔnɛʀ] a discre- tionary.

discrimination [diskʀiminasjɔ̃] nf discrimina- tion; **sans ~** indiscriminately.

discriminatoire [diskʀiminatwaʀ] a dis- criminatory.

disculper [diskylpe] vt to exonerate.

discussion [diskysjɔ̃] nf discussion.

discutable [diskytabl(ə)] a (contestable) doubt- ful; (à débattre) debatable.

discuté, e [diskyte] a controversial.

discuter [diskyte] vt (contester) to question, dispute; (débattre: prix) to discuss ♦ vi to talk; (ergoter) to argue; **~ de** to discuss.

dise [diz] etc vb voir **dire**.

disert, e [dizɛʀ, -ɛʀt(ə)] a loquacious.

disette [dizɛt] nf food shortage.

diseuse [dizøz] nf: **~ de bonne aventure** fortuneteller.

disgrâce [disgʀɑs] nf disgrace; **être en ~** to be in disgrace.

disgracieux, euse [disgʀasjø, -øz] a ungainly, awkward.

disjoindre [disʒwɛ̃dʀ(ə)] vt to take apart; **se**

~ *vi* to come apart.

disjoint, e [disʒwɛ̃, -wɛt] *pp de* **disjoindre** ♦ *a* loose.

disjoncteur [disʒ5ktœR] *nm* (*ÉLEC*) circuit breaker.

dislocation [dislɔkasj5] *nf* dislocation.

disloquer [dislɔke] *vt* (*membre*) to dislocate; (*chaise*) to dismantle; (*troupe*) to disperse; **se** ~ *vi* (*parti, empire*) to break up; **se** ~ **l'épaule** to dislocate one's shoulder.

disparaître [dispaRɛtR(ə)] *vi* to disappear; (*à la vue*) to vanish, disappear; to be hidden *ou* concealed; (*être manquant*) to go missing, disappear; (*se perdre: traditions etc*) to die out; (*personne: mourir*) to die; **faire** ~ (*objet, tache, trace*) to remove; (*personne*) to get rid of.

disparate [dispaRat] *a* disparate; (*couleurs*) ill-assorted.

disparité [dispaRite] *nf* disparity.

disparition [dispaRisj5] *nf* disappearance.

disparu, e [dispaRy] *pp de* **disparaître** ♦ *nm/f* missing person; (*défunt*) departed; **être porté** ~ to be reported missing.

dispendieux, euse [dispɑ̃djø, -øz] *a* extravagant, expensive.

dispensaire [dispɑ̃sɛR] *nm* community clinic.

dispense [dispɑ̃s] *nf* exemption; (*permission*) special permission; ~ **d'âge** special exemption from age limit.

dispenser [dispɑ̃se] *vt* (*donner*) to lavish, bestow; (*exempter*): ~ **qn de** to exempt sb from; **se** ~ **de** *vt* to avoid, get out of.

disperser [dispɛRse] *vt* to scatter; (*fig: son attention*) to dissipate; **se** ~ *vi* to scatter; (*fig*) to dissipate one's efforts.

disponibilité [dispɔnibilite] *nf* availability; (*ADMIN*): **être en** ~ to be on leave of absence; ~**s** *nfpl* (*COMM*) liquid assets.

disponible [dispɔnibl(ə)] *a* available.

dispos [dispo] *am:* (**frais et**) ~ fresh (as a daisy).

disposé, e [dispoze] *a* (*d'une certaine manière*) arranged, laid-out; **bien/mal** ~ (*humeur*) in a good/bad mood; **bien/mal** ~ **pour** *ou* **envers qn** well/badly disposed towards sb; ~ **à** (*prêt à*) willing *ou* prepared to.

disposer [dispoze] *vt* (*arranger, placer*) to arrange; (*inciter*): ~ **qn à qch/faire qch** to dispose *ou* incline sb towards sth/to do sth ♦ *vi*: **vous pouvez** ~ you may leave; ~ **de** *vt* to have (at one's disposal); **se** ~ **à faire** to prepare to do, be about to do.

dispositif [dispozitif] *nm* device; (*fig*) system, plan of action; set-up; (*d'un texte de loi*) operative part; ~ **de sûreté** safety device.

disposition [dispozisj5] *nf* (*arrangement*) arrangement, layout; (*humeur*) mood; (*tendance*) tendency; ~**s** *nfpl* (*mesures*) steps, measures; (*préparatifs*) arrangements; (*de loi, testament*) provisions; (*aptitudes*) bent *sg*, aptitude *sg*; **à la** ~ **de qn** at sb's disposal.

disproportion [dispRopɔRsj5] *nf* disproportion.

disproportionné, e [dispRopɔRsjone] *a* disproportionate, out of all proportion.

dispute [dispyt] *nf* quarrel, argument.

disputer [dispyte] *vt* (*match*) to play;

(*combat*) to fight; (*course*) to run; **se** ~ *vi* to quarrel, have a quarrel; (*match, combat, course*) to take place; ~ **qch à qn** to fight with sb for *ou* over sth.

disquaire [diskɛR] *nm/f* record dealer.

disqualification [diskalifikasj5] *nf* disqualification.

disqualifier [diskalifje] *vt* to disqualify; **se** ~ *vi* to bring discredit on o.s.

disque [disk(ə)] *nm* (*MUS*) record; (*INFORM*) disk, disc; (*forme, pièce*) disc; (*SPORT*) discus; ~ **compact** compact disc; ~ **dur** hard disk; ~ **d'embrayage** (*AUTO*) clutch plate; ~ **laser** compact disc; ~ **de stationnement** parking disc; ~ **système** system disk.

disquette [diskɛt] *nf* diskette, floppy (disk); ~ (**à**) **simple/double densité** single/double density disk; ~ **une face/double face** single-/double-sided disk.

dissection [disɛksj5] *nf* dissection.

dissemblable [disɑ̃blabl(ə)] *a* dissimilar.

dissemblance [disɑ̃blɑ̃s] *nf* dissimilarity, difference.

disséminer [disemine] *vt* to scatter; (*chasser*) to disperse.

dissension [disɑ̃sj5] *nf* dissension; ~**s** *nfpl* dissension.

disséquer [diseke] *vt* to dissect.

dissertation [disɛRtasj5] *nf* (*SCOL*) essay.

disserter [disɛRte] *vi*: ~ **sur** to discourse upon.

dissident, e [disidɑ̃, -ɑ̃t] *a, nm/f* dissident.

dissimilitude [disimilityd] *nf* dissimilarity.

dissimulateur, trice [disimyltœR, -tRis] *a* dissembling ♦ *nm/f* dissembler.

dissimulation [disimylasj5] *nf* concealing; (*duplicité*) dissimulation; ~ **de bénéfices/de revenus** concealment of profits/income.

dissimulé, e [disimyle] (*personne: secret*) secretive; (: *fourbe, hypocrite*) deceitful.

dissimuler [disimyle] *vt* to conceal; **se** ~ to conceal o.s.; to be concealed.

dissipation [disipasj5] *nf* squandering; unruliness; (*débauche*) dissipation.

dissipé, e [disipe] *a* (*indiscipliné*) unruly.

dissiper [disipe] *vt* to dissipate; (*fortune*) to squander, fritter away; **se** ~ *vi* (*brouillard*) to clear, disperse; (*doutes*) to disappear, melt away; (*élève*) to become undisciplined *ou* unruly.

dissociable [disɔsjabl(ə)] *a* separable.

dissocier [disɔsje] *vt* to dissociate; **se** ~ *vi* (*éléments, groupe*) to break up, split up; **se** ~ **de** (*groupe, point de vue*) to dissociate o.s. from.

dissolu, e [disɔly] *a* dissolute.

dissoluble [disɔlybl(ə)] *a* (*POL: assemblée*) dissolvable.

dissolution [disɔlysj5] *nf* dissolving; (*POL, JUR*) dissolution.

dissolvant, e [disɔlvɑ̃, -ɑ̃t] *vb voir* **dissoudre** ♦ *nm* (*CHIMIE*) solvent; ~ (**gras**) nail polish remover.

dissonant, e [disɔnɑ̃, -ɑ̃t] *a* discordant.

dissoudre [disudR(ə)] *vt*, **se** ~ *vi* to dissolve.

dissous, oute [disu, -ut] *pp de* **dissoudre**.

dissuader [disɥade] *vt*: ~ **qn de faire/de qch** to dissuade sb from doing/from sth.

dissuasion [disɥazj5] *nf* dissuasion; **force de**

~ deterrent power.

distance [distãs] *nf* distance; (*fig: écart*) gap; **à** ~ at *ou* from a distance; (*mettre en marche, commander*) by remote control; (*situé*) **à** ~ (*INFORM*) remote; **tenir qn à** ~ to keep sb at a distance; **se tenir à** ~ to keep one's distance; **à une** ~ **de 10 km, à 10 km de** ~ 10 km away, at a distance of 10 km; **à 2 ans de** ~ with a gap of 2 years; **prendre ses** ~s to space out; **garder ses** ~s to keep one's distance; **tenir la** ~ (*SPORT*) to cover the distance, last the course; ~ **focale** (*PHOTO*) focal length.

distancer [distãse] *vt* to outdistance, leave behind.

distancier [distãsje]: **se** ~ *vi* to distance o.s.

distant, e [distã, -ãt] *a* (*réservé*) distant, aloof; (*éloigné*) distant, far away; ~ **de** (*lieu*) far away *ou* a long way from; ~ **de 5 km (d'un lieu)** 5 km away (from a place).

distendre [distãdR(ə)] *vt*, **se** ~ *vi* to distend.

distillation [distilasjõ] *nf* distillation, distilling.

distillé, e [distile] *a*: **eau** ~**e** distilled water.

distiller [distile] *vt* to distil; (*fig*) to exude; to elaborate.

distillerie [distilRi] *nf* distillery.

distinct, e [distẽ(kt), distẽkt(ə)] *a* distinct.

distinctement [distẽktəmã] *ad* distinctly.

distinctif, ive [distẽktif, -iv] *a* distinctive.

distinction [distẽksjõ] *nf* distinction.

distingué, e [distẽge] *a* distinguished.

distinguer [distẽge] *vt* to distinguish; **se** ~ *vi* (*s'illustrer*) to distinguish o.s.; (*différer*): **se** ~ **(de)** to distinguish o.s. *ou* be distinguished (from).

distinguo [distẽgo] *nm* distinction.

distraction [distRaksjõ] *nf* (*manque d'attention*) absent-mindedness; (*oubli*) lapse (in concentration *ou* attention); (*détente*) diversion, recreation; (*passe-temps*) distraction, entertainment.

distraire [distRER] *vt* (*déranger*) to distract; (*divertir*) to entertain, divert; (*détourner: somme d'argent*) to divert, misappropriate; **se** ~ to amuse *ou* enjoy o.s.

distrait, e [distRE, -εt] *pp de* **distraire** ♦ *a* absent-minded.

distraitement [distRεtmã] *ad* absent-mindedly.

distrayant, e [distRεjã, -ãt] *vb voir* **distraire** ♦ *a* entertaining.

distribanque [distRibãk] *nm* cash dispenser.

distribuer [distRibɥe] *vt* to distribute; to hand out; (*CARTES*) to deal (out); (*courrier*) to deliver.

distributeur [distRibytœR] *nm* (*AUTO, COMM*) distributor; (*automatique*) (vending) machine; ~ **de billets** (*RAIL*) ticket machine; (*BANQUE*) cash dispenser.

distribution [distRibysjõ] *nf* distribution; (*postale*) delivery; (*choix d'acteurs*) casting; **circuits de** ~ (*COMM*) distribution network; ~ **des prix** (*SCOL*) prize giving.

district [distRik(t)] *nm* district.

dit, e [di, dit] *pp de* **dire** ♦ *a* (*fixé*): **le jour** ~ the arranged day; (*surnommé*): **X,** ~ **Pierrot** X, known as *ou* called Pierrot.

dites [dit] *vb voir* **dire**.

dithyrambique [ditiRãbik] *a* eulogistic.

DIU *sigle m* (= *dispositif intra-utérin*) IUD.

diurétique [djyRetik] *a*, *nm* diuretic.

diurne [djyRn(ə)] *a* diurnal, daytime *cpd*.

divagations [divagasjõ] *nfpl* ramblings; ravings.

divaguer [divage] *vi* to ramble; (*malade*) to rave.

divan [divã] *nm* divan.

divan-lit [divãli] *nm* divan (bed).

divergent, e [divεRʒã, -ãt] *a* divergent.

diverger [divεRʒe] *vi* to diverge.

divers, e [divεR, -εRs(ə)] *a* (*varié*) diverse, varied; (*différent*) different, various ♦ *dét* (*plusieurs*) various, several; (*frais*) ~ (*COMM*) sundries, miscellaneous (expenses); "~" (*rubrique*) "miscellaneous".

diversement [divεRsəmã] *ad* in various *ou* diverse ways.

diversification [divεRsifikasjõ] *nf* diversification.

diversifier [divεRsifje] *vt*, **se** ~ *vi* to diversify.

diversion [divεRsjõ] *nf* diversion; **faire** ~ to create a diversion.

diversité [divεRsite] *nf* diversity, variety.

divertir [divεRtiR] *vt* to amuse, entertain; **se** ~ to amuse *ou* enjoy o.s.

divertissant, e [divεRtisã, -ãt] *a* entertaining.

divertissement [divεRtismã] *nm* entertainment; (*MUS*) divertimento, divertissement.

dividende [dividãd] *nm* (*MATH, COMM*) dividend.

divin, e [divẽ, -in] *a* divine; (*fig: excellent*) heavenly, divine.

divinateur, trice [divinatœR, -tRis] *a* perspicacious.

divinatoire [divinatwaR] *a* (*art, science*) divinatory; **baguette** ~ divining rod.

diviniser [divinize] *vt* to deify.

divinité [divinite] *nf* divinity.

divisé, e [divize] *a* divided.

diviser [divize] *vt* (*gén, MATH*) to divide; (*morceler, subdiviser*) to divide (up), split (up); **se** ~ **en** to divide into; ~ **par** to divide by.

diviseur [divizœR] *nm* (*MATH*) divisor.

divisible [divizibl(ə)] *a* divisible.

division [divizjõ] *nf* (*gén*) division; ~ **du travail** (*ÉCON*) division of labour.

divisionnaire [divizjonεR] *a*: **commissaire** ~ ≈ chief superintendent (*Brit*), ≈ police chief (*US*).

divorce [divɔRs(ə)] *nm* divorce.

divorcé, e [divɔRse] *nm/f* divorcee.

divorcer [divɔRse] *vi* to get a divorce, get divorced; ~ **de** *ou* **d'avec qn** to divorce sb.

divulgation [divylgasjõ] *nf* disclosure.

divulguer [divylge] *vt* to divulge, disclose.

dix [di, dis, diz] *num* ten.

dix-huit [dizɥit] *num* eighteen.

dix-huitième [dizɥitjεm] *num* eighteenth.

dixième [dizjεm] *num* tenth.

dix-neuf [diznœf] *num* nineteen.

dix-neuvième [diznœvjεm] *num* nineteenth.

dix-sept [disεt] *num* seventeen.

dix-septième [disεtjεm] *num* seventeenth.

dizaine [dizεn] *nf* (*10*) ten; (*environ 10*): **une** ~ **(de)** about ten, ten or so.

Djakarta [dʒakaRta] *n* Djakarta.

Djibouti [dʒibuti] *n* Djibouti.

DM *abr* (= *Deutschmark*) DM.

dm. *abr* (= *décimètre*) dm.

do [do] *nm* (*note*) C; (*en chantant la gamme*) do(h).

docile [dɔsil] *a* docile.

docilité [dɔsilite] *nf* docility.

dock [dɔk] *nm* dock; (*hangar, bâtiment*) warehouse.

docker [dɔkɛʀ] *nm* docker.

docte [dɔkt(ə)] *a* (*péj*) learned.

docteur [dɔktœʀ] *nm* doctor; ~ **en médecine** doctor of medicine.

doctoral, e, aux [dɔktɔʀal, -o] *a* pompous, bombastic.

doctorat [dɔktɔʀa] *nm*: ~ (**d'Université**) ≈ doctorate; ~ **d'État** ≈ PhD; ~ **de troisième cycle** ≈ doctorate.

doctoresse [dɔktɔʀɛs] *nf* lady doctor.

doctrinaire [dɔktʀinɛʀ] *a* doctrinaire; (*sententieux*) pompous, sententious.

doctrinal, e, aux [dɔktʀinal, o] *a* doctrinal.

doctrine [dɔktʀin] *nf* doctrine.

document [dɔkymɑ̃] *nm* document.

documentaire [dɔkymɑ̃tɛʀ] *a*, *nm* documentary.

documentaliste [dɔkymɑ̃talist(ə)] *nm/f* archivist; (*PRESSE, TV*) researcher.

documentation [dɔkymɑ̃tasjɔ̃] *nf* documentation, literature; (*PRESSE, TV: service*) research.

documenté, e [dɔkymɑ̃te] *a* well-informed, well-documented; well-researched.

documenter [dɔkymɑ̃te] *vt*: **se** ~ (**sur**) to gather information *ou* material (on *ou* about).

Dodécanèse [dɔdekanɛz] *nm* Dodecanese (Islands).

dodeliner [dɔdline] *vi*: ~ **de la tête** to nod one's head gently.

dodo [dɔdo] *nm*: **aller faire** ~ to go to beddy-byes.

dodu, e [dɔdy] *a* plump.

dogmatique [dɔgmatik] *a* dogmatic.

dogme [dɔgm(ə)] *nm* dogma.

dogue [dɔg] *nm* mastiff.

doigt [dwa] *nm* finger; **à deux** ~**s de** within an ace (*Brit*) *ou* an inch of; **un** ~ **de lait/whisky** a drop of milk/whisky; **désigner** *ou* **montrer du** ~ to point at; **au** ~ **et à l'œil** to the letter; **connaître qch sur le bout du** ~ to know sth backwards; **mettre le** ~ **sur la plaie** (*fig*) to find the sensitive spot; ~ **de pied** toe.

doigté [dwate] *nm* (*MUS*) fingering; (*fig: habileté*) diplomacy, tact.

doigtier [dwatje] *nm* fingerstall.

dois [dwa], **doive** [dwav] *etc vb voir* **devoir**.

doive [dwav] *etc vb voir* **devoir**.

doléances [dɔleɑ̃s] *nfpl* complaints; (*réclamations*) grievances.

dolent, e [dɔlɑ̃, -ɑ̃t] *a* doleful, mournful.

dollar [dɔlaʀ] *nm* dollar.

dolmen [dɔlmɛn] *nm* dolmen.

DOM [deɔɛm, dɔm] *sigle m ou mpl* = *Département(s) d'outre-mer*.

domaine [dɔmɛn] *nm* estate, property; (*fig*) domain, field; **tomber dans le** ~ **public** (*livre etc*) to be out of copyright; **dans tous les** ~**s** in all areas.

domanial, e, aux [dɔmanjal, -o] *a* national,

state *cpd*.

dôme [dom] *nm* dome.

domestication [dɔmɛstikasjɔ̃] *nf* (*voir domestiquer*) domestication; harnessing.

domesticité [dɔmɛstisite] *nf* (*domestic*) staff.

domestique [dɔmɛstik] *a* domestic ♦ *nm/f* servant, domestic.

domestiquer [dɔmɛstike] *vt* to domesticate; (*vent, marées*) to harness.

domicile [dɔmisil] *nm* home, place of residence; **à** ~ at home; **élire** ~ **à** to take up residence in; **sans** ~ **fixe** of no fixed abode; ~ **conjugal** marital home; ~ **légal** domicile.

domicilié, e [dɔmisilje] *a*: **être** ~ **à** to have one's home in *ou* at.

dominant, e [dɔminɑ̃, -ɑ̃t] *a* dominant; (*plus important*) predominant.

dominateur, trice [dɔminatœʀ, -tʀis] *a* dominating; (*qui aime à dominer*) domineering.

domination [dɔminasjɔ̃] *nf* domination.

dominer [dɔmine] *vt* to dominate; (*passions etc*) to control, master; (*surpasser*) to outclass, surpass; (*surplomber*) to tower above, dominate ♦ *vi* to be in the dominant position; **se** ~ to control o.s.

dominicain, e [dɔminikɛ̃, -ɛn] *a* Dominican.

dominical, e, aux [dɔminikal, -o] *a* Sunday *cpd*, dominical.

Dominique [dɔminik] *nf*: **la** ~ Dominica.

domino [dɔmino] *nm* domino; ~**s** *nmpl* (*jeu*) dominoes *sg*.

dommage [dɔmaʒ] *nm* (*préjudice*) harm, injury; (*dégâts, pertes*) damage *q*; **c'est** ~ **de faire/que** it's a shame *ou* pity to do/that; ~**s corporels** physical injury.

dommages-intérêts [dɔmaʒ(əz)ēteʀɛ] *nmpl* damages.

dompter [dɔ̃te] *vt* to tame.

dompteur, euse [dɔ̃tœʀ, -øz] *nm/f* trainer; (*de lion*) liontamer.

DOM-TOM [dɔmtɔm] *sigle m ou mpl* = *Département(s) d'outre-mer/Territoire(s) d'outre-mer.*

don [dɔ̃] *nm* (*cadeau*) gift; (*charité*) donation; (*aptitude*) gift, talent; **avoir des** ~**s pour** to have a gift *ou* talent for; **faire** ~ **de** to make a gift of; ~ **en argent** cash donation.

donateur, trice [dɔnatœʀ, -tʀis] *nm/f* donor.

donation [dɔnasjɔ̃] *nf* donation.

donc [dɔ̃k] *cj* therefore, so; (*après une digression*) so, then; (*intensif*): **voilà** ~ **la solution** so there's the solution; **je disais** ~ **que** ... as I was saying, ...; **venez** ~ **dîner à la maison** do come for dinner; **allons** ~! come now!; **faites** ~ go ahead.

donjon [dɔ̃ʒɔ̃] *nm* keep.

donnant, e [dɔnɑ̃, -ɑ̃t] *a*: ~, ~ fair's fair.

donne [dɔn] *nf* (*CARTES*): **il y a mauvaise** *ou* **fausse** ~ there's been a misdeal.

donné, e [dɔne] *a* (*convenu*) given; (*pas cher*) dirt cheap, very cheap ♦ *nf* (*MATH, INFORM, gén*) datum (*pl* data); **c'est** ~ it's a gift; **étant** ~ ... given ....

donner [dɔne] *vt* to give; (*vieux habits etc*) to give away; (*spectacle*) to put on; (*film*) to show; ~ **qch à qn** to give sb sth, give sth to sb; ~ **sur** (*suj: fenêtre, chambre*) to look (out) onto; ~ **dans** (*piège etc*) to fall into;

faire ~ l'infanterie (*MIL*) to send in the infantry; **~ l'heure à qn** to tell sb the time; **~ le ton** (*fig*) to set the tone; **~ à penser/ entendre que ...** to make one think/give one to understand that ...; **se ~ à fond (à son travail)** to give one's all (to one's work), devote o.s. heart and soul (to one's work); **se ~ du mal** *ou* **de la peine (pour faire qch)** to go to a lot of trouble (to do sth); **s'en ~ à cœur joie** (*fam*) to have a great time (of it).

donneur, euse [dɔnœʀ, -øz] *nm/f* (*MÉD*) donor; (*CARTES*) dealer; **~ de sang** blood donor.

dont [dɔ̃] *pronom relatif*: **la maison ~ je vois le toit** the house whose roof I can see, the house I can see the roof of; **la maison ~ le toit est rouge** the house whose roof is red *ou* the roof of which is red; **l'homme ~ je connais la sœur** the man whose sister I know; **10 blessés, ~ 2 grièvement** 10 injured, 2 of them seriously; **2 livres, ~ l'un est ...** 2 books, one of which is ...; **il y avait plusieurs personnes, dont Gabrielle** there were several people, among them Gabrielle; **le fils ~ il est si fier** the son he's so proud of; **ce ~ je parle** what I'm talking about; *voir adjectifs et verbes à complément prépositionnel*: **responsable de, souffrir de** *etc*.

donzelle [dɔ̃zɛl] *nf* (*péj*) young madam.

dopage [dɔpaʒ] *nm* doping.

dopant [dɔpɑ̃] *nm* dope.

doper [dɔpe] *vt* to dope; **se ~** to take dope.

doping [dɔpiŋ] *nm* doping; (*excitant*) dope.

dorade [dɔʀad] *nf* = **daurade**.

doré, e [dɔʀe] *a* golden; (*avec dorure*) gilt, gilded.

dorénavant [dɔʀenavɑ̃] *ad* from now on, henceforth.

dorer [dɔʀe] *vt* (*cadre*) to gild; **(faire) ~** (*CULIN*) to brown; (: *gâteau*) to glaze; **se ~ au soleil** to sunbathe; **~ la pilule à qn** to sugar the pill for sb.

dorloter [dɔʀlɔte] *vt* to pamper, cosset (*Brit*); **se faire ~** to be pampered *ou* cosseted.

dormant, e [dɔʀmɑ̃, -ɑ̃t] *a*: **eau ~e** still water.

dorme [dɔʀm(ə)] *etc vb voir* **dormir**.

dormeur, euse [dɔʀmœʀ, -øz] *nm/f* sleeper.

dormir [dɔʀmiʀ] *vi* to sleep; (*être endormi*) to be asleep; **~ à poings fermés** to sleep very soundly.

dorsal, e, aux [dɔʀsal, -o] *a* dorsal; *voir* **rouleau**.

dortoir [dɔʀtwaʀ] *nm* dormitory.

dorure [dɔʀyʀ] *nf* gilding.

doryphore [dɔʀifɔʀ] *nm* Colorado beetle.

dos [do] *nm* back; (*de livre*) spine; **"voir au ~"** "see over"; **robe décolletée dans le ~** low-backed dress; **de ~** from the back, from behind; **~ à ~** back to back; **sur le ~** on one's back; **à ~ de chameau** riding on a camel; **avoir bon ~** to be a good excuse; **se mettre qn à ~** to turn sb against one.

dosage [dozaʒ] *nm* mixture.

dos-d'âne [dodɑn] *nm* humpback; **pont en ~** humpbacked bridge.

dose [doz] *nf* (*MÉD*) dose; **forcer la ~** (*fig*) to overstep the mark.

doser [doze] *vt* to measure out; (*mélanger*) to mix in the correct proportions; (*fig*) to expend in the right amounts *ou* proportions; to strike a balance between.

doseur [dozœʀ] *nm* measure; **bouchon ~** measuring cap.

dossard [dosaʀ] *nm* number (*worn by competitor*).

dossier [dosje] *nm* (*renseignements, fichier*) file; (*enveloppe*) folder, file; (*de chaise*) back; (*PRESSE*) feature; **le ~ social/ monétaire** (*fig*) the social/financial question; **~ suspendu** suspension file.

dot [dɔt] *nf* dowry.

dotation [dɔtasjɔ̃] *nf* block grant; endowment.

doté, e [dɔte] *a*: **~ de** equipped with.

doter [dɔte] *vt*: **~ qn/qch de** to equip sb/sth with.

douairière [dwɛʀjɛʀ] *nf* dowager.

douane [dwan] *nf* (*poste, bureau*) customs *pl*; (*taxes*) (customs) duty; **passer la ~** to go through customs; **en ~** (*marchandises, entrepôt*) bonded.

douanier, ière [dwanje, -jɛʀ] *a* customs *cpd* ♦ *nm* customs officer.

doublage [dublaʒ] *nm* (*CINÉMA*) dubbing.

double [dubl(ə)] *a, ad* double ♦ *nm* (*2 fois plus*): **le ~ (de)** twice as much (*ou* many) (as), double the amount (*ou* number) (of); (*autre exemplaire*) duplicate, copy; (*sosie*) double; (*TENNIS*) doubles *sg*; **voir ~** to see double; **en ~ (exemplaire)** in duplicate; **faire ~ emploi** to be redundant; **à ~ sens** with a double meaning; **à ~ tranchant** two-edged; **~ carburateur** twin carburettor; **à ~s commandes** dual-control; **~ messieurs/ mixte** men's/mixed doubles *sg*; **~ toit** (*de tente*) fly sheet; **~ vue** second sight.

doublé, e [duble] *a* (*vêtement*): **~ (de)** lined (with).

doublement [dubləmɑ̃] *nm* doubling; twofold increase ♦ *ad* doubly; (*pour deux raisons*) in two ways, on two counts.

doubler [duble] *vt* (*multiplier par 2*) to double; (*vêtement*) to line; (*dépasser*) to overtake, pass; (*film*) to dub; (*acteur*) to stand in for ♦ *vi* to double, increase twofold; **se ~ de** to be coupled with; **~ (la classe)** (*SCOL*) to repeat a year; **~ un cap** (*NAVIG*) to round a cape; (*fig*) to get over a hurdle.

doublure [dublyʀ] *nf* lining; (*CINÉMA*) stand-in.

douce [dus] *af voir* **doux**.

douceâtre [dusɑtʀ(ə)] *a* sickly sweet.

doucement [dusmɑ̃] *ad* gently; (*à voix basse*) softly; (*lentement*) slowly.

doucereux, euse [dusʀø, -øz] *a* (*péj*) sugary.

douceur [dusœʀ] *nf* softness; sweetness; mildness; gentleness; **~s** *nfpl* (*friandises*) sweets (*Brit*), candy *sg* (*US*); **en ~** gently.

douche [duʃ] *nf* shower; **~s** *nfpl* shower room *sg*; **prendre une ~** to have *ou* take a shower; **~ écossaise** (*fig*), **~ froide** (*fig*) let-down.

doucher [duʃe] *vt*: **~ qn** to give sb a shower; (*mouiller*) to drench sb; (*fig*) to give sb a telling-off; **se ~** to have *ou* take a shower.

doudoune [dudun] *nf* padded jacket; (*fam*) boob.

doué, e [dwe] *a* gifted, talented; **~ de** endowed with; **être ~ pour** to have a gift for.

douille [duj] *nf* (*ÉLEC*) socket; (*de projectile*) case.

douillet, te [dujɛ, -ɛt] *a* cosy; (*péj*) soft.

douleur [dulœʀ] *nf* pain; (*chagrin*) grief, distress; **ressentir des ~s** to feel pain; **il a eu la ~ de perdre son père** he suffered the grief of losing his father.

douloureux, euse [duluʀø, -øz] *a* painful.

doute [dut] *nm* doubt; **sans ~** *ad* no doubt; (*probablement*) probably; **sans nul** *ou* **aucun ~** without (a) doubt; **hors de ~** beyond doubt; **nul ~ que** there's no doubt that; **mettre en ~** to call into question; **mettre en ~ que** to question whether.

douter [dute] *vt* to doubt; **~ de** *vt* (*allié*) to doubt, have (one's) doubts about; (*résultat*) to be doubtful of; **~ que** to doubt whether *ou* if; **j'en doute** I have my doubts; **se ~ de qch/que** to suspect sth/that; **je m'en doutais** I suspected as much; **il ne se doutait de rien** he didn't suspect a thing.

douteux, euse [dutø, -øz] *a* (*incertain*) doubtful; (*discutable*) dubious, questionable; (*péj*) dubious-looking.

douve [duv] *nf* (*de château*) moat; (*de tonneau*) stave.

Douvres [duvʀ(ə)] *n* Dover.

doux, douce [du, dus] *a* (*lisse, moelleux, pas vif: couleur, non calcaire: eau*) soft; (*sucré, agréable*) sweet; (*peu fort: moutarde etc, clément: climat*) mild; (*pas brusque*) gentle; **en douce** (*partir etc*) on the quiet.

douzaine [duzɛn] *nf* (*12*) dozen; (*environ 12*): **une ~ (de)** a dozen or so, twelve or so.

douze [duz] *num* twelve; **les D~** (*membres de la CEE*) the Twelve.

douzième [duzjɛm] *num* twelfth.

doyen, ne [dwajɛ̃, -ɛn] *nm/f* (*en âge, ancienneté*) most senior member; (*de faculté*) dean.

DPLG *sigle* (= *diplômé par le gouvernement*) *extra certificate for architects, engineers etc.*

Dr *abr* (= *docteur*) Dr.

dr. *abr* (= *droit(e)*) R, r.

draconien, ne [dʀakɔnjɛ̃, -ɛn] *a* draconian, stringent.

dragage [dʀagaʒ] *nm* dredging.

dragée [dʀaʒe] *nf* sugared almond; (*MÉD*) (sugar-coated) pill.

dragéifié, e [dʀaʒeifje] *a* (*MÉD*) sugar-coated.

dragon [dʀagɔ̃] *nm* dragon.

drague [dʀag] *nf* (*filet*) dragnet; (*bateau*) dredger.

draguer [dʀage] *vt* (*rivière: pour nettoyer*) to dredge; (*: pour trouver qch*) to drag; (*fam*) to try and pick up, chat up (*Brit*) ♦ *vi* (*fam*) to try and pick sb up, chat sb up (*Brit*).

dragueur [dʀagœʀ] *nm* (*aussi: ~ de mines*) minesweeper; (*fam*): **quel ~!** he's a great one for picking up girls!

drain [dʀɛ̃] *nm* (*MÉD*) drain.

drainage [dʀenaʒ] *nm* drainage.

drainer [dʀene] *vt* to drain; (*fig: visiteurs, région*) to drain off.

dramatique [dʀamatik] *a* dramatic; (*tragique*) tragic ♦ *nf* (*TV*) (television) drama.

dramatiser [dʀamatize] *vt* to dramatize.

dramaturge [dʀamatyʀʒ(ə)] *nm* dramatist, playwright.

drame [dʀam] *nm* (*THÉÂTRE*) drama; (*catastrophe*) drama, tragedy; **~ familial** family drama.

drap [dʀa] *nm* (*de lit*) sheet; (*tissu*) woollen fabric; **~ de plage** beach towel.

drapé [dʀape] *nm* (*d'un vêtement*) hang.

drapeau, x [dʀapo] *nm* flag; **sous les ~x** with the colours (*Brit*) *ou* colors (*US*), in the army.

draper [dʀape] *vt* to drape; (*robe, jupe*) to arrange.

draperies [dʀapʀi] *nfpl* hangings.

drap-housse, pl draps-housses [dʀaus] *nm* fitted sheet.

drapier [dʀapje] *nm* (woollen) cloth manufacturer; (*marchand*) clothier.

drastique [dʀastik] *a* drastic.

dressage [dʀesaʒ] *nm* training.

dresser [dʀese] *vt* (*mettre vertical, monter: tente*) to put up, erect; (*fig: liste, bilan, contrat*) to draw up; (*animal*) to train; **se ~** *vi* (*falaise, obstacle*) to stand; (*avec grandeur, menace*) to tower (up); (*personne*) to draw o.s. up; **~ l'oreille** to prick up one's ears; **~ la table** to set *ou* lay the table; **~ qn contre qn d'autre** to set sb against sb else; **~ un procès-verbal** *ou* **une contravention à qn** to book sb.

dresseur, euse [dʀesœʀ, -øz] *nm/f* trainer.

dressoir [dʀeswaʀ] *nm* dresser.

dribbler [dʀible] *vt, vi* (*SPORT*) to dribble.

drille [dʀij] *nm*: **joyeux ~** cheerful sort.

drogue [dʀɔg] *nf* drug; **la ~** drugs *pl*; **~ dure/douce** hard/soft drugs *pl*.

drogué, e [dʀɔge] *nm/f* drug addict.

droguer [dʀɔge] *vt* (*victime*) to drug; (*malade*) to give drugs to; **se ~** (*aux stupéfiants*) to take drugs; (*péj: de médicaments*) to dose o.s. up.

droguerie [dʀɔgʀi] *nf* ≈ hardware shop (*Brit*) *ou* store (*US*).

droguiste [dʀɔgist(ə)] *nm* ≈ keeper (*ou* owner) of a hardware shop *ou* store.

droit, e [dʀwa, dʀwat] *a* (*non courbe*) straight; (*vertical*) upright, straight; (*fig: loyal, franc*) upright, straight(forward); (*opposé à gauche*) right, right-hand ♦ *ad* straight ♦ *nm* (*prérogative, BOXE*) right; (*taxe*) duty, tax; (*: d'inscription*) fee; (*lois, branche*): **le ~** law ♦ *nf* (*POL*) right (wing); (*ligne*) straight line; **~ au but** *ou* **au fait/ cœur** straight to the point/heart; **avoir le ~ de** to be allowed to; **avoir ~ à** to be entitled to; **être en ~ de** to have a *ou* the right to; **faire ~ à** to grant, accede to; **être dans son ~** to be within one's rights; **à bon ~** (*justement*) with good reason; **de quel ~?** by what right?; **à qui de ~** to whom it may concern; **à ~e** on the right; (*direction*) (to the) right; **à ~e de** to the right of; **de ~e** (*POL*) rightwing; **~ d'auteur** copyright; **avoir ~ de cité (dans)** (*fig*) to belong (to); **~ coutumier** common law; **~ de regard** right of access *ou* inspection; **~ de réponse** right to reply; **~ de visite** (right of) access; **~ de vote** (right to) vote; **~s d'auteur** royalties; **~s d'inscription** enrolment *ou* registration fees.

droitement [dʀwatmɑ̃] *ad* (*agir*) uprightly.

droitier, ière [dʀwatje, -jɛʀ] *nm/f* right-handed person.

droiture [dʀwatyʀ] *nf* uprightness, straightness.

drôle [dʀol] *a* (*amusant*) funny, amusing; (*bizarre*) funny, peculiar; **un ~ de ...** (*bizarre*) a strange *ou* funny ...; (*intensif*) an incredible ..., a terrific ....

drôlement [dʀolmɑ̃] *ad* funnily; peculiarly; (*très*) terribly, awfully; **il fait ~ froid** it's awfully cold.

drôlerie [dʀolʀi] *nf* funniness; funny thing.

dromadaire [dʀɔmadɛʀ] *nm* dromedary.

dru, e [dʀy] *a* (*cheveux*) thick, bushy; (*pluie*) heavy ♦ *ad* (*pousser*) thickly; (*tomber*) heavily.

drugstore [dʀœgstɔʀ] *nm* drugstore.

druide [dʀɥid] *nm* Druid.

ds *abr* = **dans**.

DST *sigle f* (= *Direction de la surveillance du territoire*) *internal security service*, ≈ MI5 (*Brit*).

DT *sigle m* (= *diphtérie tétanos*) *vaccine*.

DTCP *sigle m* (= *diphtérie tétanos coqueluche polio*) *vaccine*.

DTP *sigle m* (= *diphtérie tétanos polio*) *vaccine*.

DTTAB *sigle m* (= *diphtérie tétanos typhoïde A et B*) *vaccine*.

du [dy] *prép* + *dét*, *dét voir* **de**.

dû, due [dy] *pp de* **devoir** ♦ *a* (*somme*) owing, owed; (: *venant à échéance*) due; (*causé par*): **~ à** due to ♦ *nm* due; (*somme*) dues *pl*.

Dubaï, Dubay [dybaj] *n* Dubai.

dubitatif, ive [dybitatif, -iv] *a* doubtful, dubious.

Dublin [dyblɛ̃] *n* Dublin.

duc [dyk] *nm* duke.

duché [dyʃe] *nm* dukedom, duchy.

duchesse [dyʃɛs] *nf* duchess.

DUEL [dɥɛl] *sigle m* = *Diplôme universitaire d'études littéraires*.

duel [dɥɛl] *nm* duel.

DUES [dyɛs] *sigle m* = *Diplôme universitaire d'études scientifiques*.

duffel-coat [dœfœlkot] *nm* duffelcoat.

dûment [dymɑ̃] *ad* duly.

dune [dyn] *nf* dune.

Dunkerque [dœ̃kɛʀk] *n* Dunkirk.

duo [dɥo] *nm* (*MUS*) duet; (*fig: couple*) duo, pair.

dupe [dyp] *nf* dupe ♦ *a*: (**ne pas) être ~ de** (not) to be taken in by.

duper [dype] *vt* to dupe, deceive.

duperie [dypʀi] *nf* deception, dupery.

duplex [dyplɛks] *nm* (*appartement*) split-level apartment, duplex; (*TV*): **émission en ~** link-up.

duplicata [dyplikata] *nm* duplicate.

duplicateur [dyplikatœʀ] *nm* duplicator; **~ à alcool** spirit duplicator.

duplicité [dyplisite] *nf* duplicity.

duquel [dykɛl] *prép* + *pronom voir* **lequel**.

dur, e [dyʀ] *a* (*pierre, siège, travail, problème*) hard; (*lumière, voix, climat*) harsh; (*sévère*) hard, harsh; (*cruel*) hard

(-*hearted*); (*porte, col*) stiff; (*viande*) tough ♦ *ad* hard ♦ *nf*: **à la ~e** rough; **mener la vie ~e à qn** to give sb a hard time; **~ d'oreille** hard of hearing.

durabilité [dyʀabilite] *nf* durability.

durable [dyʀabl(ə)] *a* lasting.

durablement [dyʀabləmɑ̃] *ad* for the long term.

durant [dyʀɑ̃] *prép* (*au cours de*) during; (*pendant*) for; **~ des mois, des mois ~** for months.

durcir [dyʀsiʀ] *vt, vi*, **se ~** *vi* to harden.

durcissement [dyʀsismɑ̃] *nm* hardening.

durée [dyʀe] *nf* length; (*d'une pile etc*) life; (*déroulement: des opérations etc*) duration; **pour une ~ illimitée** for an unlimited length of time; **de courte ~** (*séjour, répit*) brief, short-term; **de longue ~** (*effet*) long-term; **pile de longue ~** long-life battery.

durement [dyʀmɑ̃] *ad* harshly.

durent [dyʀ] *vb voir* **devoir**.

durer [dyʀe] *vi* to last.

dureté [dyʀte] *nf* (*voir dur*) hardness; harshness; stiffness; toughness.

durillon [dyʀijɔ̃] *nm* callus.

durit [dyʀit] *nf* ® (car radiator) hose.

DUT *sigle m* = *Diplôme universitaire de technologie*.

dut [dy] *etc vb voir* **devoir**.

duvet [dyvɛ] *nm* down; (**sac de couchage en**) **~** down-filled sleeping bag.

duveteux, euse [dyvtø, -øz] *a* downy.

dynamique [dinamik] *a* dynamic.

dynamiser [dinamize] *vt* to pep up, enliven; (*équipe, service*) to inject some dynamism into.

dynamisme [dinamism(ə)] *nm* dynamism.

dynamite [dinamit] *nf* dynamite.

dynamiter [dinamite] *vt* to (blow up with) dynamite.

dynamo [dinamo] *nf* dynamo.

dynastie [dinasti] *nf* dynasty.

dysenterie [disɑ̃tʀi] *nf* dysentery.

dyslexie [dislɛksi] *nf* dyslexia, word-blindness.

dyslexique [dislɛksik] *a* dyslexic.

dyspepsie [dispɛpsi] *nf* dyspepsia.

E

E, e [ə] *nm inv* E, e ♦ *abr* (= *Est*) E; **E comme Eugène** E for Edward (*Brit*) *ou* Easy (*US*).

EAO *sigle m* (= *enseignement assisté par ordinateur*) CAL (= *computer-aided learning*).

EAU *sigle mpl* (= *Émirats arabes unis*) UAE (= *United Arab Emirates*).

eau, x [o] *nf* water ♦ *nfpl* waters; **prendre l'~** (*chaussure etc*) to leak, let in water; **prendre les ~x** to take the waters; **faire ~** to leak; **tomber à l'~** (*fig*) to fall through; **à l'~ de rose** slushy, sentimental; **~ bénite** holy

water; ~ **de Cologne** eau de Cologne; ~
courante running water; ~ **distillée** distilled
water; ~ **douce** fresh water; ~ **de Javel**
bleach; ~ **lourde** heavy water; ~ **minérale**
mineral water; ~ **oxygénée** hydrogen peroxide; ~ **plate** still water; ~ **de pluie** rainwater; ~ **salée** salt water; ~ **de toilette** toilet water; ~**x ménagères** dirty water (*from
washing up etc*); ~**x territoriales** territorial
waters; ~**x usées** liquid waste.

eau-de-vie, pl **eaux-de-vie** [odvi] nf brandy.

eau-forte, pl **eaux-fortes** [ofɔrt(ə)] nf etching.

ébahi, e [ebai] a dumbfounded, flabbergasted.

ébahir [ebair] vt to astonish, astound.

ébats [eba] vb voir **ébattre** ♦ nmpl frolics,
gambols.

ébattre [ebatr(ə)]: **s'~** vi to frolic.

ébauche [eboʃ] nf (rough) outline, sketch.

ébaucher [eboʃe] vt to sketch out, outline;
(*fig*): ~ **un sourire/geste** to give a hint of a
smile/make a slight gesture; **s'~** vi to take
shape.

ébène [eben] nf ebony.

ébéniste [ebenist(ə)] nm cabinetmaker.

ébénisterie [ebenistri] nf cabinetmaking;
(*bâti*) cabinetwork.

éberlué, e [ebɛrlɥe] a astounded,
flabbergasted.

éblouir [ebluir] vt to dazzle.

éblouissant, e [ebluisã, -ãt] a dazzling.

éblouissement [ebluismã] nm dazzle;
(*faiblesse*) dizzy turn.

ébonite [ebɔnit] nf vulcanite.

éborgner [ebɔrɲe] vt: ~ **qn** to blind sb in one
eye.

éboueur [ebwœr] nm dustman (*Brit*),
garbageman (*US*).

ébouillanter [ebujãte] vt to scald; (*CULIN*) to
blanch; **s'~** to scald o.s.

éboulement [ebulmã] nm falling rocks pl,
rock fall; (*amas*) heap of boulders *etc*.

ébouler [ebule]: **s'~** vi to crumble, collapse.

éboulis [ebuli] nmpl fallen rocks.

ébouriffé, e [eburife] a tousled, ruffled.

ébouriffer [eburife] vt to tousle, ruffle.

ébranlement [ebrãlmã] nm shaking.

ébranler [ebrãle] vt to shake; (*rendre instable: mur, santé*) to weaken; **s'~** vi (*partir*)
to move off.

ébrécher [ebreʃe] vt to chip.

ébriété [ebrijete] nf: **en état d'~** in a state of
intoxication.

ébrouer [ebrue]: **s'~** vi (*souffler*) to snort;
(*s'agiter*) to shake o.s.

ébruiter [ebrɥite] vt, **s'~** vi to spread.

ébullition [ebylisjɔ̃] nf boiling point; **en** ~ boiling; (*fig*) in an uproar.

écaille [ekaj] nf (*de poisson*) scale; (*de
coquillage*) shell; (*matière*) tortoiseshell; (*de
roc etc*) flake.

écaillé, e [ekaje] a (*peinture*) flaking.

écailler [ekaje] vt (*poisson*) to scale; (*huître*)
to open; **s'~** vi to flake ou peel (off).

écarlate [ekarlat] a scarlet.

écarquiller [ekarkije] vt: ~ **les yeux** to stare
wide-eyed.

écart [ekar] nm gap; (*embardée*) swerve;
(*saut*) sideways leap; (*fig*) departure, devia-

tion; **à l'~** ad out of the way; **à l'~ de** prép
away from; (*fig*) out of; **faire le grand** ~
(*DANSE, GYM*) to do the splits; ~ **de
conduite** misdemeanour.

écarté, e [ekarte] a (*lieu*) out-of-the-way, remote; (*ouvert*): **les jambes** ~**es** legs apart;
les bras ~**s** arms outstretched.

écarteler [ekartəle] vt to quarter; (*fig*) to
tear.

écartement [ekartəmã] nm space, gap;
(*RAIL*) gauge.

écarter [ekarte] vt (*séparer*) to move apart,
separate; (*éloigner*) to push back, move
away; (*ouvrir: bras, jambes*) to spread,
open; (: *rideau*) to draw (back); (*éliminer:
candidat, possibilité*) to dismiss; (*CARTES*) to
discard; **s'~** vi to part; (*personne*) to move
away; **s'~ de** to wander from.

ecchymose [ekimoz] nf bruise.

ecclésiastique [eklezjastik] a ecclesiastical ♦
nm ecclesiastic.

écervelé, e [esɛrvəle] a scatterbrained,
featherbrained.

échafaud [eʃafo] nm scaffold.

échafaudage [eʃafodaʒ] nm scaffolding; (*fig*)
heap, pile.

échafauder [eʃafode] vt (*plan*) to construct.

échalas [eʃala] nm stake, pole; (*personne*)
beanpole.

échalote [eʃalɔt] nf shallot.

échancré, e [eʃãkre] a (*robe, corsage*) low-
necked; (*côte*) indented.

échancrure [eʃãkryr] nf (*de robe*) scoop
neckline; (*de côte, arête rocheuse*) indentation.

échange [eʃãʒ] nm exchange; **en** ~ in
exchange; **en** ~ **de** in exchange ou return
for; **libre** ~ free trade; ~ **de lettres/
politesses/vues** exchange of letters/civilities/
views; ~**s commerciaux** trade; ~**s culturels**
cultural exchanges.

échangeable [eʃãʒabl(ə)] a exchangeable.

échanger [eʃãʒe] vt: ~ **qch (contre)** to
exchange sth (for).

échangeur [eʃãʒœr] nm (*AUTO*) interchange.

échantillon [eʃãtijɔ̃] nm sample.

échantillonnage [eʃãtijɔnaʒ] nm selection of
samples.

échappatoire [eʃapatwar] nf way out.

échappée [eʃape] nf (*vue*) vista; (*CYCLISME*)
breakaway.

échappement [eʃapmã] nm (*AUTO*) exhaust;
~ **libre** cutout.

échapper [eʃape]: ~ **à** vt (*gardien*) to escape
(from); (*punition, péril*) to escape; ~ **à qn**
(*détail, sens*) to escape sb; (*objet qu'on tient:
aussi*: ~ **des mains de qn**) to slip out of sb's
hands; **laisser** ~ to let fall; (*cri etc*) to let
out; **s'~** vi to escape; **l'~ belle** to have a
narrow escape.

écharde [eʃard(ə)] nf splinter (of wood).

écharpe [eʃarp(ə)] nf scarf (pl scarves); (*de
maire*) sash; (*MÉD*) sling; **prendre en** ~
(*dans une collision*) to hit sideways on.

écharper [eʃarpe] vt to tear to pieces.

échasse [eʃas] nf stilt.

échassier [eʃasje] nm wader.

échauder [eʃode] vt: **se faire** ~ (*fig*) to get
one's fingers burnt.

échauffement [eʃofmɑ̃] nm overheating; (SPORT) warm-up.

échauffer [eʃofe] vt (métal, moteur) to overheat; (fig: exciter) to fire, excite; **s'~** vi (SPORT) to warm up; (discussion) to become heated.

échauffourée [eʃofuʀe] nf clash, brawl; (MIL) skirmish.

échéance [eʃeɑ̃s] nf (d'un paiement: date) settlement date; (: somme due) financial commitment(s); (fig) deadline; **à brève/ longue** ~ a short-/long-term ♦ ad in the short/long term.

échéancier [eʃeɑ̃sje] nm schedule.

échéant [eʃeɑ̃]: **le cas** ~ ad if the case arises.

échec [eʃɛk] nm failure; (ÉCHECS): ~ **et mat/au roi** checkmate/check; **~s** nmpl (jeu) chess sg; **mettre en** ~ to put in check; **tenir en** ~ to hold in check; **faire** ~ **à** to foil, thwart.

échelle [eʃɛl] nf ladder; (fig, d'une carte) scale; **à l'~ de** on the scale of; **sur une grande/petite** ~ on a large/small scale; **faire la courte** ~ **à qn** to give sb a leg up; ~ **de corde** rope ladder.

échelon [eʃlɔ̃] nm (d'échelle) rung; (ADMIN) grade.

échelonner [eʃlɔne] vt to space out, spread out; **(versement) échelonné** (payment) by instalments.

écheveau, x [ɛʃvo] nm skein, hank.

échevelé, e [eʃəvle] a tousled, dishevelled; (fig) wild, frenzied.

échine [eʃin] nf backbone, spine.

échiner [eʃine]: **s'~** vi (se fatiguer) to work o.s. to the bone.

échiquier [eʃikje] nm chessboard.

écho [eko] nm echo; **~s** nmpl (potins) gossip sg, rumours; (PRESSE: rubrique) 'news in brief'; **rester sans** ~ (suggestion etc) to come to nothing; **se faire l'~ de** to repeat, spread about.

échographie [ekɔgʀafi] nf ultrasound (scan).

échoir [eʃwaʀ] vi (dette) to fall due; (délais) to expire; ~ **à** vt to fall to.

échoppe [eʃɔp] nf stall, booth.

échouer [eʃwe] vi to fail; (débris etc : sur la plage) to be washed up; (aboutir: personne dans un café etc) to arrive ♦ vt (bateau) to ground; **s'~** vi to run aground.

échu, e [eʃy] pp de **échoir** ♦ a due, mature.

échut [eʃy] etc vb voir **échoir**.

éclabousser [eklabuse] vt to splash; (fig) to tarnish.

éclaboussure [eklabusyʀ] nf splash; (fig) stain.

éclair [eklɛʀ] nm (d'orage) flash of lightning, lightning q; (PHOTO: de flash) flash; (fig) flash, spark; (gâteau) éclair.

éclairage [eklɛʀaʒ] nm lighting.

éclairagiste [eklɛʀaʒist(ə)] nm/f lighting engineer.

éclaircie [eklɛʀsi] nf bright ou sunny interval.

éclaircir [eklɛʀsiʀ] vt to lighten; (fig) to clear up, clarify; (CULIN) to thin (down); **s'~** vi (ciel) to brighten up, clear; (cheveux) to go thin; (situation etc) to become clearer; **s'~ la voix** to clear one's throat.

éclaircissement [eklɛʀsismɑ̃] nm clearing up, clarification.

éclairer [eklɛʀe] vt (lieu) to light (up); (personne) to light the way for; (fig: instruire) to enlighten; (: rendre comprehensible) to shed light on ♦ vi: ~ **mal/bien** to give a poor/good light; **s'~** vi (phare, rue) to light up; (situation etc) to become clearer; **s'~ à la bougie/l'électricité** to use candlelight/have electric lighting.

éclaireur, euse [eklɛʀœʀ, -øz] nm/f (scout) (boy) scout/(girl) guide ♦ nm (MIL) scout; **partir en** ~ to go off to reconnoitre.

éclat [ekla] nm (de bombe, de verre) fragment; (du soleil, d'une couleur etc) brightness, brilliance; (d'une cérémonie) splendour; (scandale): **faire un** ~ to cause a commotion; **action d'** ~ outstanding action; **voler en ~s** to shatter; **des ~s de verre** broken glass; flying glass; ~ **de rire** burst ou roar of laughter; ~ **de voix** shout.

éclatant, e [eklatɑ̃, -ɑ̃t] a brilliant, bright; (succès) resounding; (revanche) devastating.

éclater [eklate] vi (pneu) to burst; (bombe) to explode; (guerre, épidémie) to break out; (groupe, parti) to break up; ~ **de rire/en sanglots** to burst out laughing/sobbing.

éclectique [eklɛktik] a eclectic.

éclipse [eklips(ə)] nf eclipse.

éclipser [eklipse] vt to eclipse; **s'~** vi to slip away.

éclopé, e [eklope] a lame.

éclore [eklɔʀ] vi (œuf) to hatch; (fleur) to open (out).

éclosion [eklozjɔ̃] nf blossoming.

écluse [eklyz] nf lock.

éclusier [eklyzje] nm lock keeper.

écœurant, e [ekœʀɑ̃, -ɑ̃t] a sickening; (gâteau etc) sickly.

écœurement [ekœʀmɑ̃] nm disgust.

écœurer [ekœʀe] vt: ~ **qn** to make sb feel sick; (fig: démoraliser) to disgust sb.

école [ekɔl] nf school; **aller à l'~** to go to school; **faire** ~ to collect a following; **les grandes ~s** prestige university-level colleges with competitive entrance examinations; ~ **maternelle** nursery school; ~ **primaire** primary (Brit) ou grade (US) school; ~ **secondaire** secondary (Brit) ou high (US) school; ~ **privée/publique/élémentaire** private/state/elementary school; ~ **de dessin/danse/musique** art/dancing/music school; ~ **hôtelière** catering college; ~ **normale (d'instituteurs) (ENI)** primary school teachers' training college; ~ **normale supérieure (ENS)** grande école for training secondary school teachers; ~ **de secrétariat** secretarial college.

écolier, ière [ekɔlje, -jɛʀ] nm/f schoolboy/girl.

écolo [ekɔlo] nm/f (fam) ecologist ♦ a ecological.

écologie [ekɔlɔʒi] nf ecology; (sujet scolaire) environmental studies pl.

écologique [ekɔlɔʒik] a ecological; environmental.

écologiste [ekɔlɔʒist(ə)] nm/f ecologist; environmentalist.

éconduire [ekɔ̃dɥiʀ] vt to dismiss.

économat [ekɔnɔma] nm (fonction) bursar-

ship (*Brit*), treasurership (*US*); (*bureau*) bursar's office (*Brit*), treasury (*US*).

économe [ekɔnɔm] *a* thrifty ♦ *nm/f* (*de lycée etc*) bursar (*Brit*), treasurer (*US*).

économétrie [ekɔnɔmetʀi] *nf* econometrics *sg*.

économie [ekɔnɔmi] *nf* (*vertu*) economy, thrift; (*gain: d'argent, de temps etc*) saving; (*science*) economics *sg*; (*situation économique*) economy; **~s** *nfpl* (*pécule*) savings; **une ~ de temps/d'argent** a saving in time/of money; **~ dirigée** planned economy.

économique [ekɔnɔmik] *a* (*avantageux*) economical; (*ÉCON*) economic.

économiquement [ekɔnɔmikmɑ̃] *ad* economically; **les ~ faibles** (*ADMIN*) the low-paid, people on low incomes.

économiser [ekɔnɔmize] *vt*, *vi* to save.

économiste [ekɔnɔmist(ə)] *nm/f* economist.

écoper [ekɔpe] *vi* to bale out; (*fig*) to cop it; **~ (de)** *vt* to get.

écorce [ekɔʀs(ə)] *nf* bark; (*de fruit*) peel.

écorcer [ekɔʀse] *vt* to bark.

écorché, e [ekɔʀʃe] *a*: **~ vif** flayed alive ♦ *nm* cut-away drawing.

écorcher [ekɔʀʃe] *vt* (*animal*) to skin; (*égratigner*) to graze; **~ une langue** to speak a language brokenly; **s'~ le genou** *etc* to scrape *ou* graze one's knee *etc*.

écorchure [ekɔʀʃyʀ] *nf* graze.

écorner [ekɔʀne] *vt* (*taureau*) to dehorn; (*livre*) to make dog-eared.

écossais, e [ekɔsɛ, -ɛz] *a* (*lacs, tempérament*) Scottish, Scots; (*whisky, confiture*) Scotch; (*écharpe, tissu*) tartan ♦ *nm* (*LING*) Scots; (: *gaélique*) Gaelic; (*tissu*) tartan (cloth); **É~** Scot, Scotsman; **les É~** the Scots ♦ *nf*: **É~e** Scot, Scotswoman.

Écosse [ekɔs] *nf*: **l'~** Scotland.

écosser [ekɔse] *vt* to shell.

écosystème [ekɔsistɛm] *nm* ecosystem.

écot [eko] *nm*: **payer son ~** to pay one's share.

écoulement [ekulmɑ̃] *nm* (*de faux billets*) circulation; (*de stock*) selling.

écouler [ekule] *vt* to dispose of; **s'~** *vi* (*eau*) to flow (out); (*foule*) to drift away; (*jours, temps*) to pass (by).

écourter [ekuʀte] *vt* to curtail, cut short.

écoute [ekut] *nf* (*NAVIG: cordage*) sheet; (*RADIO, TV*): **temps/heure d'~** (listening *ou* viewing) time/ hour; **heure de grande ~** peak listening *ou* viewing time; **prendre l'~** to tune in; **rester à l'~ (de)** to stay listening (to) *ou* tuned in (to); **~s téléphoniques** phone tapping *sg*.

écouter [ekute] *vt* to listen to.

écouteur [ekutœʀ] *nm* (*TÉL*) (additional) ear-piece; **~s** *nmpl* (*RADIO*) headphones, headset *sg*.

écoutille [ekutij] *nf* hatch.

écr. *abr* = **écrire**.

écrabouiller [ekʀabuje] *vt* to squash, crush.

écran [ekʀɑ̃] *nm* screen; (*INFORM*) VDU, screen; **~ de fumée/d'eau** curtain of smoke/water; **porter à l'~** (*CINÉMA*) to adapt for the screen; **le petit ~** television, the small screen.

écrasant, e [ekʀazɑ̃, -ɑ̃t] *a* overwhelming.

écraser [ekʀaze] *vt* to crush; (*piéton*) to run over; (*INFORM*) to overwrite; **se faire ~** to be run over; **écrase(-toi)!** shut up!; **s'~ (au sol)** to crash; **s'~ contre** to crash into.

écrémer [ekʀeme] *vt* to skim.

écrevisse [ekʀəvis] *nf* crayfish *inv*.

écrier [ekʀije]: **s'~** *vi* to exclaim.

écrin [ekʀɛ̃] *nm* case, box.

écrire [ekʀiʀ] *vt*, *vi* to write; **~ à qn que** to write and tell sb that; **s'~** to write to one another ♦ *vi*: **ça s'écrit comment?** how is it spelt?

écrit, e [ekʀi, -it] *pp de* **écrire** ♦ *a*: **bien/mal ~** well/badly written ♦ *nm* document; (*examen*) written paper; **par ~** in writing.

écriteau, x [ekʀito] *nm* notice, sign.

écritoire [ekʀitwaʀ] *nf* writing case.

écriture [ekʀityʀ] *nf* writing; (*COMM*) entry; **~s** *nfpl* (*COMM*) accounts, books; **l'É~ (sainte), les É~s** the Scriptures.

écrivain [ekʀivɛ̃] *nm* writer.

écrivais [ekʀive] *etc vb voir* **écrire**.

écrou [ekʀu] *nm* nut.

écrouer [ekʀue] *vt* to imprison; (*provisoirement*) to remand in custody.

écroulé, e [ekʀule] *a* (*de fatigue*) exhausted; (*par un malheur*) overwhelmed; **~ (de rire)** in stitches.

écroulement [ekʀulmɑ̃] *nm* collapse.

écrouler [ekʀule]: **s'~** *vi* to collapse.

écru, e [ekʀy] *a* (*toile*) raw, unbleached; (*couleur*) off-white, écru.

écu [eky] *nm* (*bouclier*) shield; (*monnaie: ancienne*) crown; (: *de la CEE*) ecu.

écueil [ekœj] *nm* reef; (*fig*) pitfall; stumbling block.

écuelle [ekɥɛl] *nf* bowl.

éculé, e [ekyle] *a* (*chaussure*) down-at-heel; (*fig: péj*) hackneyed.

écume [ekym] *nf* foam; (*CULIN*) scum; **~ de mer** meerschaum.

écumer [ekyme] *vt* (*CULIN*) to skim; (*fig*) to plunder ♦ *vi* (*mer*) to foam; (*fig*) to boil with rage.

écumoire [ekymwaʀ] *nf* skimmer.

écureuil [ekyʀœj] *nm* squirrel.

écurie [ekyʀi] *nf* stable.

écusson [ekysɔ̃] *nm* badge.

écuyer, ère [ekɥije, -ɛʀ] *nm/f* rider.

eczéma [ɛgzema] *nm* eczema.

éd. *abr* = **édition**.

édam [edam] *nm* (*fromage*) edam.

édelweiss [edɛlvajs] *nm inv* edelweiss.

éden [edɛn] *nm* Eden.

édenté, e [edɑ̃te] *a* toothless.

EDF *sigle f* (= *Électricité de France*) *national electricity company*.

édifiant, e [edifjɑ̃, -ɑ̃t] *a* edifying.

édifice [edifis] *nm* building, edifice.

édifier [edifje] *vt* to build, erect; (*fig*) to edify.

édiles [edil] *nmpl* city fathers.

Édimbourg [edɛ̃buʀ] *n* Edinburgh.

édit [edi] *nm* edict.

édit. *abr* = **éditeur**.

éditer [edite] *vt* (*publier*) to publish; (: *disque*) to produce; (*préparer: texte, INFORM*) to edit.

éditeur, trice [editœʀ, -tʀis] *nm/f* publisher; editor.

édition [edisjɔ̃] *nf* editing *q*; (*série d'exemplaires*) edition; (*industrie du livre*): **l'~** publishing; **~ sur écran** (*INFORM*) screen editing.

édito [edito] *nm* (*fam* = *éditorial*) editorial, leader.

éditorial, aux [editɔʀjal, -o] *nm* editorial, leader.

éditorialiste [editɔʀjalist(ə)] *nm/f* editorial *ou* leader writer.

édredon [edʀədɔ̃] *nm* eiderdown.

éducateur, trice [edykatœʀ, -tʀis] *nm/f* teacher; **~ spécialisé** specialist teacher.

éducatif, ive [edykatif, -iv] *a* educational.

éducation [edykasjɔ̃] *nf* education; (*familiale*) upbringing; (*manières*) (good) manners *pl*; **bonne/mauvaise ~** good/bad upbringing; **sans ~** bad-mannered, ill-bred; **l'É~ (nationale)** ≈ the Department of Education; **~ permanente** continuing education; **~ physique** physical education.

édulcorer [edylkɔʀe] *vt* to sweeten; (*fig*) to tone down.

éduquer [edyke] *vt* to educate; (*élever*) to bring up; (*faculté*) to train; **bien/mal éduqué** well/badly brought up.

effacé, e [efase] *a* (*fig*) retiring, unassuming.

effacer [efase] *vt* to erase, rub out; (*bande magnétique*) to erase; (*INFORM*: *fichier, fiche*) to delete, erase; **s'~** *vi* (*inscription etc*) to wear off; (*pour laisser passer*) to step aside; **~ le ventre** to pull one's stomach in.

effarant, e [efaʀɑ̃, -ɑ̃t] *a* alarming.

effaré, e [efaʀe] *a* alarmed.

effarement [efaʀmɑ̃] *nm* alarm.

effarer [efaʀe] *vt* to alarm.

effarouchement [efaʀuʃmɑ̃] *nm* alarm.

effaroucher [efaʀuʃe] *vt* to frighten *ou* scare away; (*personne*) to alarm.

effectif, ive [efɛktif, -iv] *a* real; effective ♦ *nm* (*MIL*) strength; (*SCOL*) total number of pupils, size; **~s** numbers, strength *sg*; (*COMM*) manpower *sg*.

effectivement [efɛktivmɑ̃] *ad* effectively; (*réellement*) actually, really; (*en effet*) indeed.

effectuer [efɛktɥe] *vt* (*opération, mission*) to carry out; (*déplacement, trajet*) to make, complete; (*mouvement*) to execute, make; **s'~** to be carried out.

efféminé, e [efemine] *a* effeminate.

effervescence [efɛʀvesɑ̃s] *nf* (*fig*): **en ~** in a turmoil.

effervescent, e [efɛʀvesɑ̃, -ɑ̃t] *a* (*cachet, boisson*) effervescent; (*fig*) agitated, in a turmoil.

effet [efɛ] *nm* (*résultat, artifice*) effect; (*impression*) impression; (*COMM*) bill; (*JUR*: *d'une loi, d'un jugement*): **avec ~ rétroactif** applied retrospectively; **~s** *nmpl* (*vêtements etc*) things; **~ de style/couleur/lumière** stylistic/colour/lighting effect; **~s de voix** dramatic effects with one's voice; **faire de l'~** (*médicament, menace*) to have an effect, be effective; **sous l'~ de** under the effect of; **donner de l'~ à une balle** (*TENNIS*) to put some spin on a ball; **à cet ~** to that end; **en ~** *ad* indeed; **~ (de commerce)** bill of exchange; **~s spéciaux** (*CINÉMA*) special effects.

effeuiller [efœje] *vt* to remove the leaves (*ou* petals) from.

efficace [efikas] *a* (*personne*) efficient; (*action, médicament*) effective.

efficacité [efikasite] *nf* efficiency; effectiveness.

effigie [efiʒi] *nf* effigy; **brûler qn en ~** to burn an effigy of sb.

effilé, e [efile] *a* slender; (*pointe*) sharp; (*carrosserie*) streamlined.

effiler [efile] *vt* (*cheveux*) to thin (out); (*tissu*) to fray.

effilocher [efilɔʃe]: **s'~** *vi* to fray.

efflanqué, e [eflɑ̃ke] *a* emaciated.

effleurement [eflœʀmɑ̃] *nm*: **touche à ~** touch-sensitive control *ou* key.

effleurer [eflœʀe] *vt* to brush (against); (*sujet*) to touch upon; (*suj: idée, pensée*): **~ qn** to cross sb's mind.

effluves [eflyv] *nmpl* exhalation(s).

effondré, e [efɔ̃dʀe] *a* (*abattu: par un malheur, échec*) overwhelmed.

effondrement [efɔ̃dʀəmɑ̃] *nm* collapse.

effondrer [efɔ̃dʀe]: **s'~** *vi* to collapse.

efforcer [efɔʀse]: **s'~ de** *vt*: **s'~ de faire** to try hard to do.

effort [efɔʀ] *nm* effort; **faire un ~** to make an effort; **faire tous ses ~s** to try one's hardest; **faire l'~ de ...** to make the effort to ...; **sans ~** *a* effortless ♦ *ad* effortlessly; **~ de mémoire** attempt to remember; **~ de volonté** effort of will.

effraction [efʀaksjɔ̃] *nf* breaking-in; **s'introduire par ~ dans** to break into.

effrangé, e [efʀɑ̃ʒe] *a* fringed; (*effiloché*) frayed.

effrayant, e [efʀɛjɑ̃, -ɑ̃t] *a* frightening, fearsome; (*sens affaibli*) dreadful.

effrayer [efʀeje] *vt* to frighten, scare; (*rebuter*) to put off; **s'~ (de)** to be frightened *ou* scared (by).

effréné, e [efʀene] *a* wild.

effritement [efʀitmɑ̃] *nm* crumbling; erosion; slackening off.

effriter [efʀite]: **s'~** *vi* to crumble; (*monnaie*) to be eroded; (*valeurs*) to slacken off.

effroi [efʀwa] *nm* terror, dread *q*.

effronté, e [efʀɔ̃te] *a* insolent.

effrontément [efʀɔ̃temɑ̃] *ad* insolently.

effronterie [efʀɔ̃tʀi] *nf* insolence.

effroyable [efʀwajabl(ə)] *a* horrifying, appalling.

effusion [efyzjɔ̃] *nf* effusion; **sans ~ de sang** without bloodshed.

égailler [egaje]: **s'~** *vi* to scatter, disperse.

égal, e, aux [egal, -o] *a* (*identique, ayant les mêmes droits*) equal; (*plan: surface*) even, level; (*constant: vitesse*) steady; (*équitable*) even ♦ *nm/f* equal; **être ~ à** (*prix, nombre*) to be equal to; **ça lui est ~** it's all the same to him, it doesn't matter to him, he doesn't mind; **c'est ~, ...** all the same, ...; **sans ~** matchless, unequalled; **à l'~ de** (*comme*) just like; **d'~ à ~** as equals.

également [egalmɑ̃] *ad* equally; evenly; steadily; (*aussi*) too, as well.

égaler [egale] *vt* to equal.

egalisateur, trice [egalizatœʀ, -tʀis] *a*

(*SPORT*): **but** ~ equalizing goal, equalizer.

égalisation [egalizɑsjɔ̃] *nf* (*SPORT*) equalization.

égaliser [egalize] *vt* (*sol, salaires*) to level (out); (*chances*) to equalize ♦ *vi* (*SPORT*) to equalize.

égalitaire [egalitɛʀ] *a* egalitarian.

égalitarisme [egalitaʀism(ə)] *nm* egalitarianism.

égalité [egalite] *nf* equality; evenness; steadiness; (*MATH*) identity; **être à ~ (de points)** to be level; ~ **de droits** equality of rights; ~ **d'humeur** evenness of temper.

égard [egaʀ] *nm*: ~**s** *nmpl* consideration *sg*; **à cet** ~ in this respect; **à certains** ~**s**/**tous** ~**s** in certain respects/all respects; **eu** ~ **à** in view of; **par** ~ **pour** out of consideration for; **sans** ~ **pour** without regard for; **à l'**~ **de** *prép* towards; (*en ce qui concerne*) concerning, as regards.

égaré, e [egaʀe] *a* lost.

égarement [egaʀmɑ̃] *nm* distraction; aberration.

égarer [egaʀe] *vt* (*objet*) to mislay; (*moralement*) to lead astray; **s'**~ *vi* to get lost, lose one's way; (*objet*) to go astray; (*fig: dans une discussion*) to wander.

égayer [egeje] *vt* (*personne*) to amuse; (: *remonter*) to cheer up; (*récit, endroit*) to brighten up, liven up.

Égée [eʒe] *a*: **la mer** ~ the Aegean (Sea).

égéen, ne [eʒeɛ̃, -ɛn] *a* Aegean.

égérie [eʒeʀi] *nf*: **l'**~ **de qn/qch** the brains behind sb/sth.

égide [eʒid] *nf*: **sous l'**~ **de** under the aegis of.

églantier [eglɑ̃tje] *nm* wild *ou* dog rose(-bush).

églantine [eglɑ̃tin] *nf* wild *ou* dog rose.

églefin [egləfɛ̃] *nm* haddock.

église [egliz] *nf* church.

égocentrique [egɔsɑ̃tʀik] *a* egocentric, self-centred.

égocentrisme [egɔsɑ̃tʀism(ə)] *nm* egocentricity.

égoïne [egɔin] *nf* handsaw.

égoïsme [egɔism(ə)] *nm* selfishness, egoism.

égoïste [egɔist(ə)] *a* selfish, egoistic ♦ *nm/f* egoist.

égoïstement [egɔistəmɑ̃] *ad* selfishly.

égorger [egɔʀʒe] *vt* to cut the throat of.

égosiller [egɔzije]: **s'**~ *vi* to shout o.s. hoarse.

égotisme [egɔtism(ə)] *nm* egotism, egoism.

égout [egu] *nm* sewer; **eaux d'**~ sewage.

égoutier [egutje] *nm* sewer worker.

égoutter [egute] *vt* (*linge*) to wring out; (*vaisselle, fromage*) to drain ♦ *vi*, **s'**~ *vi* to drip.

égouttoir [egutwaʀ] *nm* draining board; (*mobile*) draining rack.

égratigner [egʀatiɲe] *vt* to scratch; **s'**~ to scratch o.s.

égratignure [egʀatiɲyʀ] *nf* scratch.

égrener [egʀəne] *vt*: ~ **une grappe**, ~ **des raisins** to pick grapes off a bunch; **s'**~ *vi* (*fig: heures etc*) to pass by; (: *notes*) to chime out.

égrillard, e [egʀijaʀ, -aʀd(ə)] *a* ribald, bawdy.

Égypte [eʒipt] *nf*: **l'**~ Egypt.

égyptien, ne [eʒipsjɛ̃, -ɛn] *a* Egyptian ♦ *nm/f*:

É~, ne Egyptian.

égyptologue [eʒiptɔlɔg] *nm/f* Egyptologist.

eh [e] *excl* hey!; ~ **bien** well.

éhonté, e [eɔ̃te] *a* shameless, brazen (*Brit*).

éjaculation [eʒakylɑsjɔ̃] *nf* ejaculation.

éjaculer [eʒakyle] *vi* to ejaculate.

éjectable [eʒɛktabl(ə)] *a*: **siège** ~ ejector seat.

éjecter [eʒɛkte] *vt* (*TECH*) to eject; (*fam*) to kick *ou* chuck out.

éjection [eʒɛksjɔ̃] *nf* ejection.

élaboration [elabɔʀasjɔ̃] *nf* elaboration.

élaboré, e [elabɔʀe] *a* (*complexe*) elaborate.

élaborer [elabɔʀe] *vt* to elaborate; (*projet, stratégie*) to work out; (*rapport*) to draft.

élagage [elagaʒ] *nm* pruning.

élaguer [elage] *vt* to prune.

élan [elɑ̃] *nm* (*ZOOL*) elk, moose; (*SPORT: avant le saut*) run up; (*de véhicule ou objet en mouvement*) momentum; (*fig: de tendresse etc*) surge; **prendre son** ~/**de l'**~ to take a run up/gather speed; **perdre son** ~ to lose one's momentum.

élancé, e [elɑ̃se] *a* slender.

élancement [elɑ̃smɑ̃] *nm* shooting pain.

élancer [elɑ̃se]: **s'**~ *vi* to dash, hurl o.s.; (*fig: arbre, clocher*) to soar (upwards).

élargir [elaʀʒiʀ] *vt* to widen; (*vêtement*) to let out; (*JUR*) to release; **s'**~ *vi* to widen; (*vêtement*) to stretch.

élargissement [elaʀʒismɑ̃] *nm* widening; letting out.

élasticité [elastisite] *nf* (*aussi ÉCON*) elasticity; ~ **de l'offre/de la demande** flexibility of supply/demand.

élastique [elastik] *a* elastic ♦ *nm* (*de bureau*) rubber band; (*pour la couture*) elastic *q*.

élastomère [elastɔmɛʀ] *nm* elastomer.

Elbe [ɛlb] *nf*: **l'île d'**~ (the Island of) Elba; (*fleuve*): **l'**~ the Elbe.

eldorado [ɛldɔʀado] *nm* Eldorado.

électeur, trice [elɛktœʀ, -tʀis] *nm/f* elector, voter.

électif, ive [elɛktif, -iv] *a* elective.

élection [elɛksjɔ̃] *nf* election; ~**s** *nfpl* (*POL*) election(s); **sa terre/patrie d'**~ one's chosen land/country, the land/country of one's choice; ~ **partielle** ≈ by-election; ~**s législatives** general election *sg*.

électoral, e, aux [elɛktɔʀal, -o] *a* electoral, election *cpd*.

électoralisme [elɛktɔʀalism(ə)] *nm* electioneering.

électorat [elɛktɔʀa] *nm* electorate.

électricien, ne [elɛktʀisjɛ̃, -ɛn] *nm/f* electrician.

électricité [elɛktʀisite] *nf* electricity; **allumer/éteindre l'**~ to put on/off the light; ~ **statique** static electricity.

électrification [elɛktʀifikasjɔ̃] *nf* (*RAIL*) electrification; (*d'un village etc*) laying on of electricity.

électrifier [elɛktʀifje] *vt* (*RAIL*) to electrify.

électrique [elɛktʀik] *a* electric(al).

électriser [elɛktʀize] *vt* to electrify.

électro... [elɛktʀo] *préfixe* electro....

électro-aimant [elɛktʀoɛmɑ̃] *nm* electromagnet.

électrocardiogramme [elɛktʀokaʀdjɔgʀam]

nm electrocardiogram.

électrocardiographe [elɛktrɔkardjɔgraf] *nm* electrocardiograph.

électrochoc [elɛktrɔʃɔk] *nm* electric shock treatment.

électrocuter [elɛktrɔkyte] *vt* to electrocute.

électrocution [elɛktrɔkysjɔ̃] *nf* electrocution.

électrode [elɛktrɔd] *nf* electrode.

électro-encéphalogramme [elɛktrɔɑ̃sefalɔgram] *nm* electroencephalogram.

électrogène [elɛktrɔʒɛn] *a*: **groupe ~** generating set.

électrolyse [elɛktrɔliz] *nf* electrolysis *sg*.

électromagnétique [elɛktrɔmaɲetik] *a* electromagnetic.

électroménager [elɛktrɔmenaʒe] *a*: **appareils ~s** domestic (electrical) appliances ♦ *nm*: **l'~** household appliances.

électron [elɛktrɔ̃] *nm* electron.

électronicien, ne [elɛktrɔnisjɛ̃, -ɛn] *nm/f* electronics (*Brit*) *ou* electrical (*US*) engineer.

électronique [elɛktrɔnik] *a* electronic ♦ *nf* (*science*) electronics *sg*.

électronucléaire [elɛktrɔnykleɛr] *a* nuclear power *cpd* ♦ *nm*: **l'~** nuclear power.

électrophone [elɛktrɔfɔn] *nm* record player.

élégamment [elegamɑ̃] *ad* elegantly.

élégance [elegɑ̃s] *nf* elegance.

élégant, e [elegɑ̃, -ɑ̃t] *a* elegant; (*solution*) neat, elegant; (*attitude, procédé*) courteous, civilized.

élément [elemɑ̃] *nm* element; (*pièce*) component, part; **~s** *nmpl* (*aussi: rudiments*) elements.

élémentaire [elemɑ̃tɛr] *a* elementary; (*CHIMIE*) elemental.

éléphant [elefɑ̃] *nm* elephant; **~ de mer** elephant seal.

éléphanteau, x [elefɑ̃to] *nm* baby elephant.

éléphantesque [elefɑ̃tɛsk(ə)] *a* elephantine.

élevage [ɛlvaʒ] *nm* breeding; (*de bovins*) cattle breeding *ou* rearing; (*ferme*) cattle farm.

élévateur [elevatœr] *nm* elevator.

élévation [elevasjɔ̃] *nf* (*gén*) elevation; (*voir élever*) raising; (*voir s'élever*) rise.

élevé, e [ɛlve] *a* (*prix, sommet*) high; (*fig: noble*) elevated; **bien/mal ~** well-/ill-mannered.

élève [elɛv] *nm/f* pupil; **~ infirmière** student nurse.

élever [ɛlve] *vt* (*enfant*) to bring up, raise; (*bétail, volaille*) to breed; (*abeilles*) to keep; (*hausser: taux, niveau*) to raise; (*fig: âme, esprit*) to elevate; (*édifier: monument*) to put up, erect; **s'~** *vi* (*avion, alpiniste*) to go up; (*niveau, température, aussi: cri etc*) to rise; (*survenir: difficultés*) to arise; **s'~ à** (*suj: frais, dégâts*) to amount to, add up to; **s'~ contre** to rise up against; **~ une protestation/critique** to raise a protest/make a criticism; **~ la voix** to raise one's voice; **~ qn au rang de** to raise *ou* elevate sb to the rank of; **~ un nombre au carré/au cube** to square/cube a number.

éleveur, euse [ɛlvœr, -øz] *nm/f* stock breeder.

elfe [ɛlf(ə)] *nm* elf.

élidé, e [elide] *a* elided.

élider [elide] *vt* to elide.

éligibilité [eliʒibilite] *nf* eligibility.

éligible [eliʒibl(ə)] *a* eligible.

élimé, e [elime] *a* worn (thin), threadbare.

élimination [eliminasjɔ̃] *nf* elimination.

éliminatoire [eliminatwar] *a* eliminatory; (*SPORT*) disqualifying ♦ *nf* (*SPORT*) heat.

éliminer [elimine] *vt* to eliminate.

élire [elir] *vt* to elect; **~ domicile à** to take up residence in *ou* at.

élision [elizjɔ̃] *nf* elision.

élite [elit] *nf* elite; **tireur d'~** crack rifleman; **chercheur d'~** top-notch researcher.

élitiste [elitist(ə)] *a* elitist.

élixir [eliksir] *nm* elixir.

elle [ɛl] *pronom* (*sujet*) she; (: *chose*) it; (*complément*) her; it; **~s** (*sujet*) they; (*complément*) them; **~-même** herself; itself; **~s-mêmes** themselves; *voir* **il**.

ellipse [elips(ə)] *nf* ellipse; (*LING*) ellipsis *sg*.

elliptique [eliptik] *a* elliptical.

élocution [elɔkysjɔ̃] *nf* delivery; **défaut d'~** speech impediment.

éloge [elɔʒ] *nm* praise (*gén q*); **faire l'~ de** to praise.

élogieusement [elɔʒjøzmɑ̃] *ad* very favourably.

élogieux, euse [elɔʒjø, -øz] *a* laudatory, full of praise.

éloigné, e [elwaɲe] *a* distant, far-off.

éloignement [elwaɲmɑ̃] *nm* removal; putting off; estrangement; (*fig: distance*) distance.

éloigner [elwaɲe] *vt* (*objet*): **~ qch (de)** to move *ou* take sth away (from); (*personne*): **~ qn (de)** to take sb away *ou* remove sb (from); (*échéance*) to put off, postpone; (*soupçons, danger*) to ward off; **s'~ (de)** (*personne*) to go away (from); (*véhicule*) to move away (from); (*affectivement*) to become estranged (from).

élongation [elɔ̃gasjɔ̃] *nf* strained muscle.

éloquence [elɔkɑ̃s] *nf* eloquence.

éloquent, e [elɔkɑ̃, -ɑ̃t] *a* eloquent.

élu, e [ely] *pp de* **élire** ♦ *nm/f* (*POL*) elected representative.

élucider [elyside] *vt* to elucidate.

élucubrations [elykybrasjɔ̃] *nfpl* wild imaginings.

éluder [elyde] *vt* to evade.

élus [ely] *etc vb voir* **élire**.

élusif, ive [elyzif, -iv] *a* elusive.

Élysée [elize] *nm*: **(le palais de) l'~** the Élysée palace (*the French president's residence and offices*); **les Champs ~s** the Champs Élysées.

émacié, e [emasje] *a* emaciated.

émail, aux [emaj, -o] *nm* enamel.

émaillé, e [emaje] *a* enamelled; (*fig*): **~ de** dotted with.

émailler [emaje] *vt* to enamel.

émanation [emanasjɔ̃] *nf* emanation; **être l'~ de** to emanate from; to proceed from.

émancipation [emɑ̃sipasjɔ̃] *nf* emancipation.

émancipé, e [emɑ̃sipe] *a* emancipated.

émanciper [emɑ̃sipe] *vt* to emancipate; **s'~** (*fig*) to become emancipated *ou* liberated.

émaner [emane]: **~ de** *vt* to emanate from; (*ADMIN*) to proceed from.

émarger [emaʀʒe] *vt* to sign; ~ **de 1000 F à un budget** to receive 1000 F out of a budget.

émasculer [emaskyle] *vt* to emasculate.

emballage [ɑ̃balaʒ] *nm* wrapping; packing; (*papier*) wrapping; (*carton*) packaging.

emballer [ɑ̃bale] *vt* to wrap (up); (*dans un carton*) to pack (up); (*fig: fam*) to thrill (to bits); **s'~** *vi* (*moteur*) to race; (*cheval*) to bolt; (*fig: personne*) to get carried away.

emballeur, euse [ɑ̃balœʀ, -øz] *nm/f* packer.

embarcadère [ɑ̃baʀkadɛʀ] *nm* landing stage (*Brit*), pier.

embarcation [ɑ̃baʀkɑsjɔ̃] *nf* (small) boat, (small) craft *inv*.

embardée [ɑ̃baʀde] *nf* swerve; **faire une ~** to swerve.

embargo [ɑ̃baʀgo] *nm* embargo; **mettre l'~ sur** to put an embargo on, embargo.

embarquement [ɑ̃baʀkəmɑ̃] *nm* embarkation; loading; boarding.

embarquer [ɑ̃baʀke] *vt* (*personne*) to embark; (*marchandise*) to load; (*fam*) to cart off; (: *arrêter*) to nick ♦ *vi* (*passager*) to board; (*NAVIG*) to ship water; **s'~** *vi* to board; **s'~ dans** (*affaire, aventure*) to embark upon.

embarras [ɑ̃baʀa] *nm* (*obstacle*) hindrance; (*confusion*) embarrassment; (*ennuis*): **être dans l'~** to be in a predicament *ou* an awkward position; (*gêne financière*) to be in difficulties; ~ **gastrique** stomach upset.

embarrassant, e [ɑ̃baʀasɑ̃, -ɑ̃t] *a* cumbersome; embarrassing; awkward.

embarrassé, e [ɑ̃baʀase] *a* (*encombré*) encumbered; (*gêné*) embarrassed; (*explications etc*) awkward.

embarrasser [ɑ̃baʀase] *vt* (*encombrer*) to clutter (up); (*gêner*) to hinder, hamper; (*fig*) to cause embarrassment to; to put in an awkward position; **s'~ de** to burden o.s. with.

embauche [ɑ̃boʃ] *nf* hiring; **bureau d'~** labour office.

embaucher [ɑ̃boʃe] *vt* to take on, hire; **s'~ comme** to get (o.s.) a job as.

embauchoir [ɑ̃boʃwaʀ] *nm* shoetree.

embaumer [ɑ̃bome] *vt* to embalm; (*parfumer*) to fill with its fragrance; ~ **la lavande** to be fragrant with (the scent of) lavender.

embellie [ɑ̃beli] *nf* bright spell, brighter period.

embellir [ɑ̃beliʀ] *vt* to make more attractive; (*une histoire*) to embellish ♦ *vi* to grow lovelier *ou* more attractive.

embellissement [ɑ̃belismɑ̃] *nm* embellishment.

embêtant, e [ɑ̃bɛtɑ̃, -ɑ̃t] *a* annoying.

embêtement [ɑ̃bɛtmɑ̃] *nm* problem, difficulty; **~s** *nmpl* trouble *sg*.

embêter [ɑ̃bɛte] *vt* to bother; **s'~** *vi* (*s'ennuyer*) to be bored; **il ne s'embête pas!** (*ironique*) he does all right for himself!

emblée [ɑ̃ble]: **d'~** *ad* straightaway.

emblème [ɑ̃blɛm] *nm* emblem.

embobiner [ɑ̃bɔbine] *vt* (*enjôler*): ~ **qn** to get round sb.

emboîtable [ɑ̃bwatabl(ə)] *a* interlocking.

emboîter [ɑ̃bwate] *vt* to fit together; **s'~ dans** to fit into; **s'~ (l'un dans l'autre)** to fit

together; ~ **le pas à qn** to follow in sb's footsteps.

embolie [ɑ̃bɔli] *nf* embolism.

embonpoint [ɑ̃bɔ̃pwɛ̃] *nm* stoutness (*Brit*), corpulence; **prendre de l'~** to grow stout (*Brit*) *ou* corpulent.

embouché, e [ɑ̃buʃe] *a*: **mal ~** foul-mouthed.

embouchure [ɑ̃buʃyʀ] *nf* (*GÉO*) mouth; (*MUS*) mouthpiece.

embourber [ɑ̃buʀbe]: **s'~** *vi* to get stuck in the mud; (*fig*): **s'~ dans** to sink into.

embourgeoiser [ɑ̃buʀʒwaze]: **s'~** *vi* to adopt a middle-class outlook.

embout [ɑ̃bu] *nm* (*de canne*) tip; (*de tuyau*) nozzle.

embouteillage [ɑ̃butɛjaʒ] *nm* traffic jam, (traffic) holdup (*Brit*).

embouteiller [ɑ̃butɛje] *vt* (*suj: véhicules etc*) to block.

emboutir [ɑ̃butiʀ] *vt* (*TECH*) to stamp; (*heurter*) to crash into, ram.

embranchement [ɑ̃bʀɑ̃ʃmɑ̃] *nm* (*routier*) junction; (*classification*) branch.

embrancher [ɑ̃bʀɑ̃ʃe] *vt* (*tuyaux*) to join; ~ **qch sur** to join sth to.

embraser [ɑ̃bʀaze]: **s'~** *vi* to flare up.

embrassades [ɑ̃bʀasad] *nfpl* hugging and kissing *sg*.

embrasse [ɑ̃bʀas] *nf* (*de rideau*) tie-back, loop.

embrasser [ɑ̃bʀase] *vt* to kiss; (*sujet, période*) to embrace, encompass; (*carrière*) to embark on; (*métier*) to go in for, take up; ~ **du regard** to take in (*with eyes*); **s'~** to kiss (each other).

embrasure [ɑ̃bʀazyʀ] *nf*: **dans l'~ de la porte** in the door(way).

embrayage [ɑ̃bʀɛjaʒ] *nm* clutch.

embrayer [ɑ̃bʀeje] *vi* (*AUTO*) to let in the clutch ♦ *vt* (*fig: affaire*) to set in motion; ~ **sur qch** to begin on sth.

embrigader [ɑ̃bʀigade] *vt* to recruit.

embrocher [ɑ̃bʀɔʃe] *vt* to (put on a) spit (*ou* skewer).

embrouillamini [ɑ̃bʀujamini] *nm* (*fam*) muddle.

embrouillé, e [ɑ̃bʀuje] *a* (*affaire*) confused, muddled.

embrouiller [ɑ̃bʀuje] *vt* (*fils*) to tangle (up); (*fiches, idées, personne*) to muddle up; **s'~** *vi* to get in a muddle.

embroussaillé, e [ɑ̃bʀusaje] *a* overgrown, scrubby; (*cheveux*) bushy, shaggy.

embruns [ɑ̃bʀœ̃] *nmpl* sea spray *sg*.

embryologie [ɑ̃bʀijɔlɔʒi] *nf* embryology.

embryon [ɑ̃bʀijɔ̃] *nm* embryo.

embryonnaire [ɑ̃bʀijɔnɛʀ] *a* embryonic.

embûches [ɑ̃byʃ] *nfpl* pitfalls, traps.

embué, e [ɑ̃bɥe] *a* misted up; **yeux ~s de larmes** eyes misty with tears.

embuscade [ɑ̃byskad] *nf* ambush; **tendre une ~ à** to lay an ambush for.

embusqué, e [ɑ̃byske] *a* in ambush ♦ *nm* (*péj*) shirker, skiver (*Brit*).

embusquer [ɑ̃byske] *vt*: **s'~** *vi* to take up position (for an ambush).

éméché, e [emeʃe] *a* tipsy, merry.

émeraude [ɛmʀod] *nf* emerald ♦ *a inv* emerald-green.

émergence [emerʒɑ̃s] *nf* (*fig*) emergence.
émerger [emerʒe] *vi* to emerge; (*faire saillie, aussi fig*) to stand out.
émeri [emri] *nm*: **toile** *ou* **papier ~** emery paper.
émérite [emerit] *a* highly skilled.
émerveillement [emervejmɑ̃] *nm* wonderment.
émerveiller [emerveje] *vt* to fill with wonder; **s'~ de** to marvel at.
émet [eme] *etc vb voir* **émettre**.
émétique [emetik] *nm* emetic.
émetteur, trice [emetœr, -tris] *a* transmitting; (**poste**) **~** transmitter.
émettre [emetr(ə)] *vt* (*son, lumière*) to give out, emit; (*message etc*: *RADIO*) to transmit; (*billet, timbre, emprunt, chèque*) to issue; (*hypothèse, avis*) to voice, put forward; (*vœu*) to express ♦ *vi*: **~ sur ondes courtes** to broadcast on short wave.
émeus [emø] *etc vb voir* **émouvoir**.
émeute [emøt] *nf* riot.
émeutier, ière [emøtje, -jɛr] *nm/f* rioter.
émeuve [emœv] *etc vb voir* **émouvoir**.
émietter [emjete] *vt* (*pain, terre*) to crumble; (*fig*) to split up, disperse; **s'~** *vi* (*pain, terre*) to crumble.
émigrant, e [emigrɑ̃, -ɑ̃t] *nm/f* emigrant.
émigration [emigrasjɔ̃] *nf* emigration.
émigré, e [emigre] *nm/f* expatriate.
émigrer [emigre] *vi* to emigrate.
émincer [emɛ̃se] *vt* (*CULIN*) to slice thinly.
éminemment [eminamɑ̃] *ad* eminently.
éminence [eminɑ̃s] *nf* distinction; (*colline*) knoll, hill; **Son É~** His Eminence; **~ grise** éminence grise.
éminent, e [eminɑ̃, -ɑ̃t] *a* distinguished.
émir [emir] *nm* emir.
émirat [emira] *nm* emirate; **les É~s arabes unis (EAU)** the United Arab Emirates (UAE).
émis, e [emi, -iz] *pp de* **émettre**.
émissaire [emiser] *nm* emissary.
émission [emisjɔ̃] *nf* (*voir émettre*) emission; transmission; issue; (*RADIO, TV*) programme, broadcast.
émit [emi] *etc vb voir* **émettre**.
emmagasinage [ɑ̃magazinaʒ] *nm* storage; storing away.
emmagasiner [ɑ̃magazine] *vt* to (put into) store; (*fig*) to store up.
emmailloter [ɑ̃majote] *vt* to wrap up.
emmanchure [ɑ̃mɑ̃ʃyr] *nf* armhole.
emmêlement [ɑ̃mɛlmɑ̃] *nm* (*état*) tangle.
emmêler [ɑ̃mele] *vt* to tangle (up); (*fig*) to muddle up; **s'~** to get into a tangle.
emménagement [ɑ̃menaʒmɑ̃] *nm* settling in.
emménager [ɑ̃menaʒe] *vi* to move in; **~ dans** to move into.
emmener [ɑ̃mne] *vt* to take (with one); (*comme otage, capture*) to take away; **~ qn au concert** to take sb to a concert.
emment(h)al [emɛtal] *nm* (*fromage*) Emmenthal.
emmerder [ɑ̃mɛrde] (*fam!*) *vt* to bug, bother; **s'~** *vi* (*s'ennuyer*) to be bored stiff; **je t'emmerde!** to hell with you!
emmitoufler [ɑ̃mitufle] *vt* to wrap up (warmly); **s'~** to wrap (o.s.) up (warmly).
emmurer [ɑ̃myre] *vt* to wall up, immure.

émoi [emwa] *nm* (*agitation, effervescence*) commotion; (*trouble*) agitation; **en ~** (*sens*) excited, stirred.
émollient, e [emɔljɑ̃, -ɑ̃t] *a* (*MÉD*) emollient.
émoluments [emɔlymɑ̃] *nmpl* remuneration *sg*, fee *sg*.
émonder [emɔ̃de] *vt* (*arbre etc*) to prune; (*amande etc*) to blanch.
émotif, ive [emɔtif, -iv] *a* emotional.
émotion [emosjɔ̃] *nf* emotion; **avoir des ~s** (*fig*) to get a fright; **donner des ~s à** to give a fright to; **sans ~** without emotion, coldly.
émotionnant, e [emosjɔnɑ̃, -ɑ̃t] *a* upsetting.
émotionnel, le [emosjɔnɛl] *a* emotional.
émotionner [emosjɔne] *vt* to upset.
émoulu, e [emuly] *a*: **frais ~ de** fresh from, just out of.
émoussé, e [emuse] *a* blunt.
émousser [emuse] *vt* to blunt; (*fig*) to dull.
émoustiller [emustije] *vt* to titillate, arouse.
émouvant, e [emuvɑ̃, -ɑ̃t] *a* moving.
émouvoir [emuvwar] *vt* (*troubler*) to stir, affect; (*toucher, attendrir*) to move; (*indigner*) to rouse; (*effrayer*) to disturb, worry; **s'~** *vi* to be affected; to be moved; to be roused; to be disturbed *ou* worried.
empailler [ɑ̃paje] *vt* to stuff.
empailleur, euse [ɑ̃pajœr, -øz] *nm/f* (*d'animaux*) taxidermist.
empaler [ɑ̃pale] *vt* to impale.
empaquetage [ɑ̃paktaʒ] *nm* packing, packaging.
empaqueter [ɑ̃pakte] *vt* to pack up.
emparer [ɑ̃pare]: **s'~ de** *vt* (*objet*) to seize, grab; (*comme otage, MIL*) to seize; (*suj: peur etc*) to take hold of.
empâter [ɑ̃pɑte]: **s'~** *vi* to thicken out.
empattement [ɑ̃patmɑ̃] *nm* (*AUTO*) wheelbase; (*TYPO*) serif.
empêché, e [ɑ̃peʃe] *a* detained.
empêchement [ɑ̃peʃmɑ̃] *nm* (unexpected) obstacle, hitch.
empêcher [ɑ̃peʃe] *vt* to prevent; **~ qn de faire** to prevent *ou* stop sb (from) doing; **~ que qch (n')arrive/qn (ne) fasse** to prevent sth from happening/sb from doing; **il n'empêche que** nevertheless, be that as it may; **il n'a pas pu s'~ de rire** he couldn't help laughing.
empêcheur [ɑ̃peʃœr] *nm*: **~ de danser en rond** spoilsport, killjoy (*Brit*).
empeigne [ɑ̃pɛɲ] *nf* upper (*of shoe*).
empennage [ɑ̃penaʒ] *nm* (*AVIAT*) tailplane.
empereur [ɑ̃prœr] *nm* emperor.
empesé, e [ɑ̃pəze] *a* (*fig*) stiff, starchy.
empeser [ɑ̃pəze] *vt* to starch.
empester [ɑ̃peste] *vt* (*lieu*) to stink out ♦ *vi* to stink, reek; **~ le tabac/le vin** to stink *ou* reek of tobacco/wine.
empêtrer [ɑ̃petre] *vt*: **s'~ dans** (*fils etc, aussi fig*) to get tangled up in.
emphase [ɑ̃faz] *nf* pomposity, bombast; **avec ~** pompously.
emphatique [ɑ̃fatik] *a* emphatic.
empiècement [ɑ̃pjɛsmɑ̃] *nm* (*COUTURE*) yoke.
empierrer [ɑ̃pjere] *vt* (*route*) to metal.
empiéter [ɑ̃pjete]: **~ sur** *vt* to encroach upon.
empiffrer [ɑ̃pifre]: **s'~** *vi* (*péj*) to stuff o.s.

empiler [ɑ̃pile] *vt* to pile (up), stack (up); **s'~** *vi* to pile up.

empire [ɑ̃piʀ] *nm* empire; *(fig)* influence; **style E~** Empire style; **sous l'~ de** in the grip of.

empirer [ɑ̃piʀe] *vi* to worsen, deteriorate.

empirique [ɑ̃piʀik] *a* empirical.

empirisme [ɑ̃piʀism(ə)] *nm* empiricism.

emplacement [ɑ̃plasmɑ̃] *nm* site; **sur l'~ de** on the site of.

emplâtre [ɑ̃plɑtʀ(ə)] *nm* plaster; *(fam)* twit.

emplette [ɑ̃plɛt] *nf*: **faire l'~ de** to purchase; **~s** shopping *sg*; **faire des ~s** to go shopping.

emplir [ɑ̃pliʀ] *vt* to fill; **s'~ (de)** to fill (with).

emploi [ɑ̃plwa] *nm* use; *(COMM, ÉCON)*: **l'~** employment; *(poste)* job, situation; **d'~ facile** easy to use; **le plein ~** full employment; **~ du temps** timetable, schedule.

emploie [ɑ̃plwa] *etc vb voir* **employer**.

employé, e [ɑ̃plwaje] *nm/f* employee; **~ de bureau/banque** office/bank employee *ou* clerk; **~ de maison** domestic (servant).

employer [ɑ̃plwaje] *vt (outil, moyen, méthode, mot)* to use; *(ouvrier, main-d'œuvre)* to employ; **s'~ à qch/à faire** to apply *ou* devote o.s. to sth/to doing.

employeur, euse [ɑ̃plwajœʀ, -øz] *nm/f* employer.

empocher [ɑ̃pɔʃe] *vt* to pocket.

empoignade [ɑ̃pwaɲad] *nf* row, set-to.

empoigne [ɑ̃pwaɲ] *nf*: **foire d'~** free-for-all.

empoigner [ɑ̃pwaɲe] *vt* to grab; **s'~** *(fig)* to have a row *ou* set-to.

empois [ɑ̃pwa] *nm* starch.

empoisonnement [ɑ̃pwazɔnmɑ̃] *nm* poisoning; *(fam: ennui)* annoyance, irritation.

empoisonner [ɑ̃pwazɔne] *vt* to poison; *(empester: air, pièce)* to stink out; *(fam)*: **~ qn** to drive sb mad; **s'~** to poison o.s.; **~ l'atmosphère** *(aussi fig)* to poison the atmosphere; **il nous empoisonne l'existence** he's the bane of our life.

empoissonner [ɑ̃pwasɔne] *vt (étang, rivière)* to stock with fish.

emporté, e [ɑ̃pɔʀte] *a (personne, caractère)* fiery.

emportement [ɑ̃pɔʀtəmɑ̃] *nm* fit of rage, anger *q*.

emporte-pièce [ɑ̃pɔʀtəpjɛs] *nm inv (TECH)* punch; **à l'~** *a (fig)* incisive.

emporter [ɑ̃pɔʀte] *vt* to take (with one); *(en dérobant ou enlevant, emmener: blessés, voyageurs)* to take away; *(entraîner)* to carry away *ou* along; *(arracher)* to tear off; *(suj: rivière, vent)* to carry away; *(MIL: position)* to take; *(avantage, approbation)* to win; **s'~** *vi (de colère)* to fly into a rage, lose one's temper; **la maladie qui l'a emporté** the illness which caused his death; **l'~** to gain victory; **l'~ (sur)** to get the upper hand (of); *(méthode etc)* to prevail (over); **boissons à ~** take-away drinks.

empoté, e [ɑ̃pɔte] *a (maladroit)* clumsy.

empourpré, e [ɑ̃puʀpʀe] *a* crimson.

empreint, e [ɑ̃pʀɛ̃, -ɛ̃t] *a*: **~ de** marked with; tinged with ♦ *nf (de pied, main)* print; *(fig)* stamp, mark; **~e (digitale)** fingerprint.

empressé, e [ɑ̃pʀese] *a* attentive; *(péj)* overanxious to please, overattentive.

empressement [ɑ̃pʀesmɑ̃] *nm* eagerness.

empresser [ɑ̃pʀese]: **s'~** *vi*: **s'~ auprès de qn** to surround sb with attentions; **s'~ de faire** to hasten to do.

emprise [ɑ̃pʀiz] *nf* hold, ascendancy; **sous l'~ de** under the influence of.

emprisonnement [ɑ̃pʀizɔnmɑ̃] *nm* imprisonment.

emprisonner [ɑ̃pʀizɔne] *vt* to imprison, jail.

emprunt [ɑ̃pʀœ̃] *nm* borrowing *q*, loan *(from debtor's point of view)*; *(LING etc)* borrowing; **nom d'~** assumed name; **~ d'État** government *ou* state loan; **~ public à 5%** 5% public loan.

emprunté, e [ɑ̃pʀœ̃te] *a (fig)* ill-at-ease, awkward.

emprunter [ɑ̃pʀœ̃te] *vt* to borrow; *(itinéraire)* to take, follow; *(style, manière)* to adopt, assume.

emprunteur, euse [ɑ̃pʀœ̃tœʀ, -øz] *nm/f* borrower.

empuantir [ɑ̃pɥɑ̃tiʀ] *vt* to stink out.

EMT *sigle f* (= *éducation manuelle et technique)* handwork as a school subject.

ému, e [emy] *pp de* **émouvoir** ♦ *a* excited; touched; moved.

émulation [emylɑsjɔ̃] *nf* emulation.

émule [emyl] *nm/f* imitator.

émulsion [emylsjɔ̃] *nf* emulsion; *(cosmétique)* (water-based) lotion.

émut [emy] *etc vb voir* **émouvoir**.

en [ɑ̃] *prép* in; *(avec direction)* to; *(temps: durée)*: **~ 3 jours/20 ans** in 3 days/20 years; *(: moment)*: **~ mars/hiver** in March/winter; *(moyen)*: **~ avion/taxi** by plane/taxi; *(composition)*: **~ verre** made of glass, glass *cpd*; **~ deux volumes/une pièce** in two volumes/one piece; **se casser ~ deux/ plusieurs morceaux** to break in two/into several pieces; **~ dormant** while sleeping, as one sleeps; **~ sortant** on going out, as he *etc* went out; **fort ~ maths** good at maths; **~ bonne santé** in good *ou* sound health; **~ réparation** being repaired, under repair; **~ T/étoile** T-/star-shaped; **~ chemise/ chaussettes** in one's shirt/socks; **partir ~ vacances/voyage** to go (off) on holiday/on a journey; **peindre qch ~ rouge** to paint sth red; **~ soldat** as a soldier; **~ bon diplomate, il n'a rien dit** tactful as he is, he said nothing; **le même ~ plus grand** the same only *ou* but bigger ♦ *pronom (provenance)*: **j'~ viens** I've come from there; *(cause)*: **il ~ est malade** he's ill because of it; *(agent)*: **il ~ est aimé** he's loved by her; *(complément de nom)*: **j'~ connais les dangers** I know its dangers; *(indéfini)*: **j'~ ai/veux** I have/want some; **~ as-tu?** have you got any?; **je n'~ veux pas** I don't want any; **j'~ ai assez** I've got enough (of it *ou* them); *(fig)* I've had enough; **j'~ ai 2** I've got 2 (of them); **combien y ~ a-t-il?** how many (of them) are there?; **j'~ suis fier/ai besoin** I am proud of it/need it; **où ~ étais-je?** where was I?, where had I got to? : *voir le verbe ou l'adjectif lorsque 'en' correspond à 'de' introduisant un complément prépositionnel.*

ENA [ena] *sigle f* (= *École nationale*

d'administration) grande école for training civil servants.

énarque [enaʀk(ə)] nm/f former ENA student.

encablure [ɑ̃kablyʀ] nf (NAVIG) cable's length.

encadrement [ɑ̃kadʀəmɑ̃] nm framing; training; (de porte) frame; ~ du crédit credit restrictions.

encadrer [ɑ̃kadʀe] vt (tableau, image) to frame; (fig: entourer) to surround; (personnel, soldats etc) to train; (COMM: crédit) to restrict.

encadreur [ɑ̃kadʀœʀ] nm (picture) framer.

encaisse [ɑ̃kɛs] nf cash in hand; ~ or/ métallique gold/gold and silver reserves.

encaissé, e [ɑ̃kese] a (vallée) steep-sided; (rivière) with steep banks.

encaisser [ɑ̃kese] vt (chèque) to cash; (argent) to collect; (fig: coup, défaite) to take.

encaisseur [ɑ̃kesœʀ] nm collector (of debts etc).

encan [ɑ̃kɑ̃]: à l'~ ad by auction.

encanailler [ɑ̃kanaje]: s'~ vi to become vulgar ou common; to mix with the riff-raff.

encart [ɑ̃kaʀ] nm insert; ~ publicitaire publicity insert.

encarter [ɑ̃kaʀte] vt to insert.

en-cas [ɑ̃ka] nm inv snack.

encastrable [ɑ̃kastʀabl(ə)] a (four, élément) that can be built in.

encastré, e [ɑ̃kastʀe] a (four, baignoire) built-in.

encastrer [ɑ̃kastʀe] vt: ~ qch dans (mur) to embed sth in(to); (boîtier) to fit sth into; s'~ dans to fit into; (heurter) to crash into.

encaustiquage [ɑ̃kɔstikaʒ] nm polishing, waxing.

encaustique [ɑ̃kɔstik] nf polish, wax.

encaustiquer [ɑ̃kɔstike] vt to polish, wax.

enceinte [ɑ̃sɛ̃t] af: ~ (de 6 mois) (6 months) pregnant ♦ nf (mur) wall; (espace) enclosure; ~ (acoustique) speaker.

encens [ɑ̃sɑ̃] nm incense.

encenser [ɑ̃sɑ̃se] vt to (in)cense; (fig) to praise to the skies.

encensoir [ɑ̃sɑ̃swaʀ] nm thurible (Brit), censer.

encercler [ɑ̃sɛʀkle] vt to surround.

enchaîné [ɑ̃ʃene] nm (CINÉMA) link shot.

enchaînement [ɑ̃ʃɛnmɑ̃] nm (fig) linking.

enchaîner [ɑ̃ʃene] vt to chain up; (mouvements, séquences) to link (together) ♦ vi to carry on.

enchanté, e [ɑ̃ʃɑ̃te] a (ravi) delighted; (ensorcelé) enchanted; ~ (de faire votre connaissance) pleased to meet you, how do you do?

enchantement [ɑ̃ʃɑ̃tmɑ̃] nm delight; (magie) enchantment; comme par ~ as if by magic.

enchanter [ɑ̃ʃɑ̃te] vt to delight.

enchanteur, teresse [ɑ̃ʃɑ̃tœʀ, -tʀɛs] a enchanting.

enchâsser [ɑ̃ʃase] vt: ~ qch (dans) to set sth (in).

enchère [ɑ̃ʃɛʀ] nf bid; faire une ~ to (make a) bid; mettre/vendre aux ~s to put up for (sale by)/sell by auction; les ~s montent the bids are rising; faire monter les ~s (fig) to

raise the bidding.

enchérir [ɑ̃ʃeʀiʀ] vi: ~ sur qn (aux enchères, aussi fig) to outbid sb.

enchérisseur, euse [ɑ̃ʃeʀisœʀ, -øz] nm/f bidder.

enchevêtrement [ɑ̃ʃvɛtʀəmɑ̃] nm tangle.

enchevêtrer [ɑ̃ʃvɛtʀe] vt to tangle (up).

enclave [ɑ̃klav] nf enclave.

enclaver [ɑ̃klave] vt to enclose, hem in.

enclencher [ɑ̃klɑ̃ʃe] vt (mécanisme) to engage; (fig: affaire) to set in motion; s'~ vi to engage.

enclin, e [ɑ̃klɛ̃, -in] a: ~ à qch/à faire inclined ou prone to sth/to do.

enclore [ɑ̃klɔʀ] vt to enclose.

enclos [ɑ̃klo] nm enclosure; (clôture) fence.

enclume [ɑ̃klym] nf anvil.

encoche [ɑ̃kɔʃ] nf notch.

encoder [ɑ̃kɔde] vt to encode.

encodeur [ɑ̃kɔdœʀ] nm encoder.

encoignure [ɑ̃kɔɲyʀ] nf corner.

encoller [ɑ̃kɔle] vt to paste.

encolure [ɑ̃kɔlyʀ] nf (tour de cou) collar size; (col, cou) neck.

encombrant, e [ɑ̃kɔ̃bʀɑ̃, -ɑ̃t] a cumbersome, bulky.

encombre [ɑ̃kɔ̃bʀ(ə)]: sans ~ ad without mishap ou incident.

encombré, e [ɑ̃kɔ̃bʀe] a (pièce, passage) cluttered; (lignes téléphoniques) engaged; (marché) saturated.

encombrement [ɑ̃kɔ̃bʀəmɑ̃] nm (d'un lieu) cluttering (up); (d'un objet: dimensions) bulk.

encombrer [ɑ̃kɔ̃bʀe] vt to clutter (up); (gêner) to hamper; s'~ de (bagages etc) to load ou burden o.s. with; ~ le passage to block ou obstruct the way.

encontre [ɑ̃kɔ̃tʀ(ə)]: à l'~ de prép against, counter to.

encorbellement [ɑ̃kɔʀbɛlmɑ̃] nm: fenêtre en ~ oriel window.

encorder [ɑ̃kɔʀde] vt: s'~ (ALPINISME) to rope up.

encore [ɑ̃kɔʀ] ad (continuation) still; (de nouveau) again; (restriction) even then ou so; (intensif): ~ plus fort/mieux even louder/better; ~! (insatisfaction) not again!; pas ~ not yet; ~ que even though; ~ une fois (once) again; ~ deux jours still two days, two more days; ~ un effort just a little more effort; hier ~ ... even yesterday ...; non seulement ... mais ~ not only ... but also; (et puis) quoi ~? what else?; si ~ if only.

encourageant, e [ɑ̃kuʀaʒɑ̃, -ɑ̃t] a encouraging.

encouragement [ɑ̃kuʀaʒmɑ̃] nm encouragement; (récompense) incentive.

encourager [ɑ̃kuʀaʒe] vt to encourage; ~ qn à faire qch to encourage sb to do sth.

encourir [ɑ̃kuʀiʀ] vt to incur.

encrasser [ɑ̃kʀase] vt to foul up; (AUTO etc) to soot up.

encre [ɑ̃kʀ(ə)] nf ink; ~ de Chine Indian ink; ~ indélébile indelible ink; ~ sympathique invisible ink.

encrer [ɑ̃kʀe] vt to ink.

encreur [ɑ̃kʀœʀ] am: rouleau ~ inking roller.

encrier [ɑ̃kʀije] *nm* inkwell.

encroûter [ɑ̃kʀute]: **s'~** *vi* (*fig*) to get into a rut, get set in one's ways.

encyclique [ɑ̃siklik] *nf* encyclical.

encyclopédie [ɑ̃siklɔpedi] *nf* encyclopaedia (*Brit*), encyclopedia (*US*).

encyclopédique [ɑ̃siklɔpedik] *a* encyclopaedic (*Brit*), encyclopedic (*US*).

endémique [ɑ̃demik] *a* endemic.

endetté, e [ɑ̃dete] *a* in debt; (*fig*): **très ~ envers qn** deeply indebted to sb.

endettement [ɑ̃dɛtmɑ̃] *nm* debts *pl*.

endetter [ɑ̃dete] *vt*, **s'~** *vi* to get into debt.

endeuiller [ɑ̃dœje] *vt* to plunge into mourning; **manifestation endeuillée par** event over which a tragic shadow was cast by.

endiablé, e [ɑ̃djɑble] *a* furious; (*enfant*) boisterous.

endiguer [ɑ̃dige] *vt* to dyke (up); (*fig*) to check, hold back.

endimancher [ɑ̃dimɑ̃ʃe] *vt*: **s'~** to put on one's Sunday best; **avoir l'air endimanché** to be all done up to the nines (*fam*).

endive [ɑ̃div] *nf* chicory *q*.

endocrine [ɑ̃dɔkʀin] *af*: **glande ~** endocrine (gland).

endoctrinement [ɑ̃dɔktʀinmɑ̃] *nm* indoctrination.

endoctriner [ɑ̃dɔktʀine] *vt* to indoctrinate.

endolori, e [ɑ̃dɔlɔʀi] *a* painful.

endommager [ɑ̃dɔmaʒe] *vt* to damage.

endormant, e [ɑ̃dɔʀmɑ̃, -ɑ̃t] *a* dull, boring.

endormi, e [ɑ̃dɔʀmi] *pp de* **endormir** ♦ *a* (*personne*) asleep; (*fig: indolent, lent*) sluggish; (*engourdi: main, pied*) numb.

endormir [ɑ̃dɔʀmiʀ] *vt* to put to sleep; (*suj: chaleur etc*) to send to sleep; (*MÉD: dent, nerf*) to anaesthetize; (*fig: soupçons*) to allay; **s'~** *vi* to fall asleep, go to sleep.

endoscope [ɑ̃dɔskɔp] *nm* (*MÉD*) endoscope.

endoscopie [ɑ̃dɔskɔpi] *nf* endoscopy.

endosser [ɑ̃dose] *vt* (*responsabilité*) to take, shoulder; (*chèque*) to endorse; (*uniforme, tenue*) to put on, don.

endroit [ɑ̃dʀwa] *nm* place; (*localité*): **les gens de l'~** the local people; (*opposé à l'envers*) right side; **à cet ~** in this place; **à l'~** right side out; the right way up; (*vêtement*) the right way out; **à l'~ de** *prép* regarding, with regard to; **par ~s** in places.

enduire [ɑ̃dɥiʀ] *vt* to coat; **~ qch de** to coat sth with.

enduit, e [ɑ̃dɥi, -it] *pp de* **enduire** ♦ *nm* coating.

endurance [ɑ̃dyʀɑ̃s] *nf* endurance.

endurant, e [ɑ̃dyʀɑ̃, -ɑ̃t] *a* tough, hardy.

endurcir [ɑ̃dyʀsiʀ] *vt* (*physiquement*) to toughen; (*moralement*) to harden; **s'~** *vi* to become tougher; to become hardened.

endurer [ɑ̃dyʀe] *vt* to endure, bear.

énergétique [enɛʀʒetik] *a* (*ressources etc*) energy *cpd*; (*aliment*) energizing.

énergie [enɛʀʒi] *nf* (*PHYSIQUE*) energy; (*TECH*) power; (*fig: physique*) energy; (: *morale*) vigour, spirit.

énergique [enɛʀʒik] *a* energetic; vigorous; (*mesures*) drastic, stringent.

énergiquement [enɛʀʒikmɑ̃] *ad* energetically; drastically.

énergisant, e [enɛʀʒizɑ̃, -ɑ̃t] *a* energizing.

énergumène [enɛʀɡymɛn] *nm* rowdy character *ou* customer.

énervant, e [enɛʀvɑ̃, -ɑ̃t] *a* irritating.

énervé, e [enɛʀve] *a* nervy, on edge; (*agacé*) irritated.

énervement [enɛʀvəmɑ̃] *nm* nerviness; irritation.

énerver [enɛʀve] *vt* to irritate, annoy; **s'~** *vi* to get excited, get worked up.

enfance [ɑ̃fɑ̃s] *nf* (*âge*) childhood; (*fig*) infancy; (*enfants*) children *pl*; **c'est l'~ de l'art** it's child's play; **petite ~** infancy; **souvenir/ami d'~** childhood memory/friend; **retomber en ~** to lapse into one's second childhood.

enfant [ɑ̃fɑ̃] *nm/f* child (*pl* children); **~ adoptif/naturel** adopted/natural child; **bon ~** *a* good-natured, easy-going; **~ de chœur** *nm* (*REL*) altar boy; **~ prodige** child prodigy; **~ unique** only child.

enfanter [ɑ̃fɑ̃te] *vi* to give birth ♦ *vt* to give birth to.

enfantillage [ɑ̃fɑ̃tijaʒ] *nm* (*péj*) childish behaviour *q*.

enfantin, e [ɑ̃fɑ̃tɛ̃, -in] *a* childlike; (*péj*) childish; (*langage*) child *cpd*.

enfer [ɑ̃fɛʀ] *nm* hell; **allure/bruit d'~** horrendous speed/noise.

enfermer [ɑ̃fɛʀme] *vt* to shut up; (*à clef, interner*) to lock up; **s'~** to shut o.s. away; **s'~ à clé** to lock o.s. in; **s'~ dans la solitude/le mutisme** to retreat into solitude/silence.

enferrer [ɑ̃feʀe]: **s'~** *vi*: **s'~ dans** to tangle o.s. up in.

enfiévré, e [ɑ̃fjevʀe] *a* (*fig*) feverish.

enfilade [ɑ̃filad] *nf*: **une ~ de** a series *ou* line of; **prendre des rues en ~** to cross directly from one street into the next.

enfiler [ɑ̃file] *vt* (*vêtement*): **~ qch** to slip sth on, slip into sth; (*insérer*): **~ qch dans** to stick sth into; (*rue, couloir*) to take; (*perles*) to string; (*aiguille*) to thread; **s'~ dans** to disappear into.

enfin [ɑ̃fɛ̃] *ad* at last; (*en énumérant*) lastly; (*de restriction, résignation*) still; (*eh bien*) well; (*pour conclure*) in a word.

enflammé, e [ɑ̃flame] *a* (*torche, allumette*) burning; (*MÉD: plaie*) inflamed; (*fig: nature, discours, déclaration*) fiery.

enflammer [ɑ̃flame] *vt* to set fire to; (*MÉD*) to inflame; **s'~** *vi* to catch fire; to become inflamed.

enflé, e [ɑ̃fle] *a* swollen; (*péj: style*) bombastic, turgid.

enfler [ɑ̃fle] *vi* to swell (up); **s'~** *vi* to swell.

enflure [ɑ̃flyʀ] *nf* swelling.

enfoncé, e [ɑ̃fɔ̃se] *a* staved-in, smashed-in; (*yeux*) deep-set.

enfoncement [ɑ̃fɔ̃smɑ̃] *nm* (*recoin*) nook.

enfoncer [ɑ̃fɔ̃se] *vt* (*clou*) to drive in; (*faire pénétrer*): **~ qch dans** to push (*ou* drive) sth into; (*forcer: porte*) to break open; (: *plancher*) to cause to cave in; (*défoncer: côtes etc*) to smash; (*fam: surpasser*) to lick, beat (hollow) ♦ *vi* (*dans la vase etc*) to sink in; (*sol, surface porteuse*) to give way; **s'~** *vi* to sink; **s'~ dans** to sink into; (*forêt, ville*) to disappear into; ~ **un chapeau sur la tête** to cram *ou* jam a hat on one's head; ~ **qn dans la dette** to drag sb into debt.

enfouir [ɑ̃fwiʀ] *vt* (*dans le sol*) to bury; (*dans un tiroir etc*) to tuck away; **s'~ dans/sous** to bury o.s. in/under.

enfourcher [ɑ̃fuʀʃe] *vt* to mount; ~ **son dada** (*fig*) to get on one's hobby-horse.

enfourner [ɑ̃fuʀne] *vt* to put in the oven; (*poterie*) to put in the kiln; ~ **qch dans** to shove *ou* stuff sth into; **s'~ dans** (*suj: personne*) to dive into.

enfreignais [ɑ̃fʀɛɲɛ] *etc vb voir* **enfreindre**.

enfreindre [ɑ̃fʀɛ̃dʀ(ə)] *vt* to infringe, break.

enfuir [ɑ̃fɥiʀ]: **s'~** *vi* to run away *ou* off.

enfumer [ɑ̃fyme] *vt* to smoke out.

enfuyais [ɑ̃fɥijɛ] *etc vb voir* **enfuir**.

engagé, e [ɑ̃gaʒe] *a* (*littérature etc*) engagé, committed.

engageant, e [ɑ̃gaʒɑ̃, -ɑ̃t] *a* attractive, appealing.

engagement [ɑ̃gaʒmɑ̃] *nm* taking on, engaging; starting; investing; (*promesse*) commitment; (MIL: *combat*) engagement; (: *recrutement*) enlistment; (SPORT) entry; **prendre l'~ de faire** to undertake to do; **sans ~** (COMM) without obligation.

engager [ɑ̃gaʒe] *vt* (*embaucher*) to take on, engage; (*commencer*) to start; (*lier*) to bind, commit; (*impliquer, entraîner*) to involve; (*investir*) to invest, lay out; (*faire intervenir*) to engage; (SPORT: *concurrents, chevaux*) to enter; (*inciter*): ~ **qn à faire** to urge sb to do; (*faire pénétrer*): ~ **qch dans** to insert sth into; ~ **qn à qch** to urge sth on sb; **s'~** to get taken on; (MIL) to enlist; (*promettre, politiquement*) to commit o.s.; (*débuter*) to start (up); **s'~ à faire** to undertake to do; **s'~ dans** (*rue, passage*) to enter, turn into; (*s'emboîter*) to engage *ou* fit into; (*fig: affaire, discussion*) to enter into, embark on.

engazonner [ɑ̃gazɔne] *vt* to turf.

engeance [ɑ̃ʒɑ̃s] *nf* mob.

engelure [ɑ̃ʒlyʀ] *nf* chilblain.

engendrer [ɑ̃ʒɑ̃dʀe] *vt* to father; (*fig*) to create, breed.

engin [ɑ̃ʒɛ̃] *nm* machine; instrument; vehicle; (*péj*) gadget; (AVIAT: *avion*) aircraft *inv*; (: *missile*) missile; ~ **blindé** armoured vehicle; ~ **(explosif)** (explosive) device; **~s (spéciaux)** missiles.

englober [ɑ̃glɔbe] *vt* to include.

engloutir [ɑ̃glutiʀ] *vt* to swallow up; (*fig: dépenses*) to devour; **s'~** to be engulfed.

engoncé, e [ɑ̃gɔ̃se] *a*: ~ **dans** cramped in.

engorgement [ɑ̃gɔʀʒmɑ̃] *nm* blocking; (MÉD) engorgement.

engorger [ɑ̃gɔʀʒe] *vt* to obstruct, block; **s'~** *vi* to become blocked.

engouement [ɑ̃gumɑ̃] *nm* (sudden) passion.

engouffrer [ɑ̃gufʀe] *vt* to swallow up, devour; **s'~ dans** to rush into.

engourdi, e [ɑ̃guʀdi] *a* numb.

engourdir [ɑ̃guʀdiʀ] *vt* to numb; (*fig*) to dull, blunt; **s'~** *vi* to go numb.

engrais [ɑ̃gʀɛ] *nm* manure; ~ **(chimique)** (chemical) fertilizer; ~ **organique/ inorganique** organic/inorganic fertilizer.

engraisser [ɑ̃gʀese] *vt* to fatten (up); (*terre:*

fertiliser) to fertilize ♦ *vi* (*péj*) to get fat(ter).

engranger [ɑ̃gʀɑ̃ʒe] *vt* (*foin*) to bring in; (*fig*) to store away.

engrenage [ɑ̃gʀənaʒ] *nm* gears *pl*, gearing; (*fig*) chain.

engueuler [ɑ̃gœle] *vt* (*fam*) to bawl at *ou* out.

enguirlander [ɑ̃giʀlɑ̃de] *vt* (*fam*) to give sb a bawling out, bawl at.

enhardir [ɑ̃aʀdiʀ]: **s'~** *vi* to grow bolder.

ENI [eni] *sigle f* = **école normale (d'instituteurs)**.

énième [ɛnjɛm] *a* = **nième**.

énigmatique [enigmatik] *a* enigmatic.

énigmatiquement [enigmatikmɑ̃] *ad* enigmatically.

énigme [enigm(ə)] *nf* riddle.

enivrant, e [ɑ̃nivʀɑ̃, -ɑ̃t] *a* intoxicating.

enivrer [ɑ̃nivʀe] *vt*: **s'~** to get drunk; **s'~ de** (*fig*) to become intoxicated with.

enjambée [ɑ̃ʒɑ̃be] *nf* stride; **d'une ~** with one stride.

enjamber [ɑ̃ʒɑ̃be] *vt* to stride over; (*suj: pont etc*) to span, straddle.

enjeu, x [ɑ̃ʒø] *nm* stakes *pl*.

enjoindre [ɑ̃ʒwɛ̃dʀ(ə)] *vt*: ~ **à qn de faire** to enjoin *ou* order sb to do.

enjôler [ɑ̃ʒole] *vt* to coax, wheedle.

enjôleur, euse [ɑ̃ʒolœʀ, -øz] *a* (*sourire, paroles*) winning.

enjolivement [ɑ̃ʒolivmɑ̃] *nm* embellishment.

enjoliver [ɑ̃ʒolive] *vt* to embellish.

enjoliveur [ɑ̃ʒolivœʀ] *nm* (AUTO) hub cap.

enjoué, e [ɑ̃ʒwe] *a* playful.

enlacer [ɑ̃lase] *vt* (*étreindre*) to embrace, hug; (*suj: lianes*) to wind round, entwine.

enlaidir [ɑ̃lediʀ] *vt* to make ugly ♦ *vi* to become ugly.

enlevé, e [ɑ̃lve] *a* (*morceau de musique*) played brightly.

enlèvement [ɑ̃lɛvmɑ̃] *nm* removal; (*rapt*) abduction, kidnapping; **l'~ des ordures ménagères** refuse collection.

enlever [ɑ̃lve] *vt* (*ôter: gén*) to remove; (: *vêtement, lunettes*) to take off; (: MÉD: *organe*) to remove; (*emporter: ordures etc*) to collect, take away; (*prendre*): ~ **qch à qn** to take sth (away) from sb; (*kidnapper*) to abduct, kidnap; (*obtenir: prix, contrat*) to win; (MIL: *position*) to take; (*morceau de piano etc*) to execute with spirit *ou* brio; **s'~** *vi* (*tache*) to come out *ou* off; **la maladie qui nous l'a enlevé** (*euphémisme*) the illness which took him from us.

enliser [ɑ̃lize]: **s'~** *vi* to sink, get stuck; (*dialogue etc*) to get bogged down.

enluminure [ɑ̃lyminyʀ] *nf* illumination.

ENM *sigle f* (= *École nationale de la magistrature*) *grande école for law students.*

enneigé, e [ɑ̃neʒe] *a* snowy; (*col*) snowed-up; (*maison*) snowed-in.

enneigement [ɑ̃nɛʒmɑ̃] *nm* depth of snow, snowfall; **bulletin d'~** snow report.

ennemi, e [ɛnmi] *a* hostile; (MIL) enemy *cpd* ♦ *nm/f* enemy; **être ~ de** to be strongly averse *ou* opposed to.

ennième [ɛnjɛm] *a* = **nième**.

ennoblir [ɑ̃nɔbliʀ] *vt* to ennoble.

ennui [ɑ̃nɥi] *nm* (*lassitude*) boredom;

(difficulté) trouble *q*; **avoir des ~s** to have problems; **s'attirer des ~s** to cause problems for o.s.

ennuie [ɑ̃nɥi] *etc vb voir* **ennuyer**.

ennuyé, e [ɑ̃nɥije] *a (air, personne)* preoccupied, worried.

ennuyer [ɑ̃nɥije] *vt* to bother; *(lasser)* to bore; **s'~** *vi* to be bored; **s'~ de** *(regretter)* to miss; **si cela ne vous ennuie pas** if it's no trouble to you.

ennuyeux, euse [ɑ̃nɥijø, -øz] *a* boring, tedious; *(agaçant)* annoying.

énoncé [enɔ̃se] *nm* terms *pl*; wording; *(LING)* utterance.

énoncer [enɔ̃se] *vt* to say, express; *(conditions)* to set out, lay down, state.

énonciation [enɔ̃sjɑsjɔ̃] *nf* statement.

enorgueillir [ɑ̃nɔʀɡœjiʀ]: **s'~ de** *vt* to pride o.s. on; to boast.

énorme [enɔʀm(ə)] *a* enormous, huge.

énormément [enɔʀmemɑ̃] *ad* enormously, tremendously; **~ de neige/gens** an enormous amount of snow/number of people.

énormité [enɔʀmite] *nf* enormity, hugeness; *(propos)* outrageous remark.

enquérir [ɑ̃keʀiʀ]: **s'~ de** *vt* to inquire about.

enquête [ɑ̃ket] *nf (de journaliste, de police)* investigation; *(judiciaire, administrative)* inquiry; *(sondage d'opinion)* survey.

enquêter [ɑ̃kete] *vi* to investigate; to hold an inquiry; *(faire un sondage)*: **~ (sur)** to do a survey (on), carry out an opinion poll (on).

enquêteur, euse *ou* **trice** [ɑ̃ketœʀ, -øz, -tʀis] *nm/f* officer in charge of an investigation; person conducting a survey; pollster.

enquiers, enquière [ɑ̃kjeʀ] *etc vb voir* **enquérir**.

enquiquiner [ɑ̃kikine] *vt* to rile, irritate.

enquis, e [ɑ̃ki, -iz] *pp de* **enquérir**.

enraciné, e [ɑ̃ʀasine] *a* deep-rooted.

enragé, e [ɑ̃ʀaʒe] *a (MÉD)* rabid, with rabies; *(furieux)* furiously angry; *(fig)* fanatical; **~ de** wild about.

enrageant, e [ɑ̃ʀaʒɑ̃, -ɑ̃t] *a* infuriating.

enrager [ɑ̃ʀaʒe] *vi* to be furious, be in a rage; **faire ~ qn** to make sb wild with anger.

enrayer [ɑ̃ʀeje] *vt* to check, stop; **s'~** *vi (arme à feu)* to jam.

enrégimenter [ɑ̃ʀeʒimɑ̃te] *vt (péj)* to enlist.

enregistrement [ɑ̃ʀʒistʀɔmɑ̃] *nm* recording; *(ADMIN)* registration; **~ des bagages** *(à l'aéroport)* baggage check-in; **~ magnétique** tape-recording.

enregistrer [ɑ̃ʀʒistʀe] *vt (MUS, INFORM etc)* to record; *(remarquer, noter)* to note, record; *(COMM: commande)* to note, enter; *(fig: mémoriser)* to make a mental note of; *(ADMIN)* to register; *(aussi:* **faire ~:** *bagages: par train)* to register; *(: à l'aéroport)* to check in.

enregistreur, euse [ɑ̃ʀʒistʀœʀ, -øz] *a (machine)* recording *cpd* ♦ *nm (appareil):* **~ de vol** *(AVIAT)* flight recorder.

enrhumé, e [ɑ̃ʀyme] *a:* **il est ~** he has a cold.

enrhumer [ɑ̃ʀyme]: **s'~** *vi* to catch a cold.

enrichir [ɑ̃ʀiʃiʀ] *vt* to make rich(er); *(fig)* to enrich; **s'~** to get rich(er).

enrichissement [ɑ̃ʀiʃismɑ̃] *nm* enrichment.

enrober [ɑ̃ʀɔbe] *vt:* **~ qch de** to coat sth with; *(fig)* to wrap sth up in.

enrôlement [ɑ̃ʀolmɑ̃] *nm* enlistment.

enrôler [ɑ̃ʀole] *vt* to enlist; **s'~ (dans)** to enlist (in).

enroué, e [ɑ̃ʀwe] *a* hoarse.

enrouer [ɑ̃ʀwe]: **s'~** *vi* to go hoarse.

enrouler [ɑ̃ʀule] *vt (fil, corde)* to wind (up); **s'~** to coil up; **~ qch autour de** to wind sth (a)round.

enrouleur, euse [ɑ̃ʀulœʀ, -øz] *a (TECH)* winding ♦ *nm voir* **ceinture**.

enrubanné, e [ɑ̃ʀybane] *a* trimmed with ribbon.

ENS *sigle f* = **école normale supérieure**.

ensabler [ɑ̃sable] *vt (port, canal)* to silt up, sand up; *(embarcation)* to strand (on a sandbank); **s'~** *vi* to silt up; to get stranded.

ensacher [ɑ̃saʃe] *vt* to pack into bags.

ENSAM *sigle f (= École nationale supérieure des arts et métiers)* grande école for engineering students.

ensanglanté, e [ɑ̃sɑ̃ɡlɑ̃te] *a* covered with blood.

enseignant, e [ɑ̃sɛɲɑ̃, -ɑ̃t] *a* teaching ♦ *nm/f* teacher.

enseigne [ɑ̃sɛɲ] *nf* sign ♦ *nm:* **~ de vaisseau** lieutenant; **à telle ~ que** so much so that; **être logés à la même ~** *(fig)* to be in the same boat; **~ lumineuse** neon sign.

enseignement [ɑ̃sɛɲmɑ̃] *nm* teaching; **~ ménager** home economics; **~ primaire** primary *(Brit) ou* grade school *(US)* education; **~ secondaire** secondary *(Brit) ou* high school *(US)* education.

enseigner [ɑ̃sɛɲe] *vt, vi* to teach; **~ qch à qn/à qn que** to teach sb sth/sb that.

ensemble [ɑ̃sɑ̃bl(ə)] *ad* together ♦ *nm (assemblage, MATH)* set; *(totalité):* **l'~ du/ de la** the whole *ou* entire; *(vêtement féminin)* ensemble, suit; *(unité, harmonie)* unity; *(résidentiel)* housing development; **aller ~** to go together; **impression/idée d'~** overall *ou* general impression/idea; **dans l'~** *(en gros)* on the whole; **dans son ~** overall, in general; **~ vocal/musical** vocal/musical ensemble.

ensemblier [ɑ̃sɑ̃blije] *nm* interior designer.

ensemencer [ɑ̃smɑ̃se] *vt* to sow.

enserrer [ɑ̃seʀe] *vt* to hug (tightly).

ENSET [ɛnset] *sigle f (= École normale supérieure de l'enseignement technique)* grande école for training technical teachers.

ensevelir [ɑ̃səvliʀ] *vt* to bury.

ensilage [ɑ̃silaʒ] *nm (aliment)* silage.

ensoleillé, e [ɑ̃sɔleje] *a* sunny.

ensoleillement [ɑ̃sɔlɛjmɑ̃] *nm* period *ou* hours *pl* of sunshine.

ensommeillé, e [ɑ̃sɔmeje] *a* sleepy, drowsy.

ensorceler [ɑ̃sɔʀsəle] *vt* to enchant, bewitch.

ensuite [ɑ̃sɥit] *ad* then, next; *(plus tard)* afterwards, later; **~ de quoi** after which.

ensuivre [ɑ̃sɥivʀ(ə)]: **s'~** *vi* to follow, ensue; **il s'ensuit que ...** it follows that ...; **et tout ce qui s'ensuit** and all that goes with it.

entaché, e [ɑ̃taʃe] *a:* **~ de** marred by; **~ de nullité** null and void.

entacher [ɑ̃taʃe] *vt* to soil.

entaille [ɑ̃taj] *nf (encoche)* notch; *(blessure)*

cut; **se faire une ~** to cut o.s.

entailler [ɑ̃tɑje] *vt* to notch; to cut; **s'~ le doigt** to cut one's finger.

entamer [ɑ̃tame] *vt* to start; *(hostilités, pourparlers)* to open; *(fig: altérer)* to make a dent in; to damage.

entartrer [ɑ̃tartre]: **s'~** *vi* to fur up; *(dents)* to become covered with plaque.

entassement [ɑ̃tɑsmɑ̃] *nm (tas)* pile, heap.

entasser [ɑ̃tase] *vt (empiler)* to pile up, heap up; *(tenir à l'étroit)* to cram together; **s'~** *vi* to pile up; to cram; **s'~ dans** to cram into.

entendement [ɑ̃tɑ̃dmɑ̃] *nm* understanding.

entendre [ɑ̃tɑ̃dʀ(ə)] *vt* to hear; *(comprendre)* to understand; *(vouloir dire)* to mean; *(vouloir)*: **~ être obéi/que** to intend *ou* mean to be obeyed/that; **j'ai entendu dire que** I've heard (it said) that; **je suis heureux de vous l'~ dire** I'm pleased to hear you say it; **~ parler de** to hear of; **laisser ~ que, donner à ~ que** to let it be understood that; **~ raison** to see sense, listen to reason; **qu'est- ce qu'il ne faut pas ~!** whatever next!; **j'ai mal entendu** I didn't catch what was said; **je vous entends très mal** I can hardly hear you; **s'~** *vi (sympathiser)* to get on; *(se mettre d'accord)* to agree; **s'~ à qch/à faire** *(être compétent)* to be good at sth/doing; **ça s'entend** *(est audible)* it's audible; **je m'entends** I mean; **entendons-nous!** let's be clear what we mean.

entendu, e [ɑ̃tɑ̃dy] *pp de* **entendre** ♦ *a (réglé)* agreed; *(au courant: air)* knowing; **étant ~ que** since (it's understood *ou* agreed that); **(c'est) ~** all right, agreed; **c'est ~** *(concession)* all right, granted; **bien ~** of course.

entente [ɑ̃tɑ̃t] *nf (entre amis, pays)* understanding, harmony; *(accord, traité)* agreement, understanding; **à double ~** *(sens)* with a double meaning.

entériner [ɑ̃teʀine] *vt* to ratify, confirm.

entérite [ɑ̃teʀit] *nf* enteritis *q*.

enterrement [ɑ̃tɛʀmɑ̃] *nm* burying; *(cérémonie)* funeral, burial; *(cortège funèbre)* funeral procession.

enterrer [ɑ̃teʀe] *vt* to bury.

entêtant, e [ɑ̃tɛtɑ̃, -ɑ̃t] *a* heady.

entêté, e [ɑ̃tɛte] *a* stubborn.

en-tête [ɑ̃tɛt] *nm* heading; *(de papier à lettres)* letterhead; **papier à ~** headed notepaper.

entêtement [ɑ̃tɛtmɑ̃] *nm* stubbornness.

entêter [ɑ̃tɛte]: **s'~** *vi*: **s'~ (à faire)** to persist (in doing).

enthousiasmant, e [ɑ̃tuzjasmɑ̃, -ɑ̃t] *a* exciting.

enthousiasme [ɑ̃tuzjasm(ə)] *nm* enthusiasm; **avec ~** enthusiastically.

enthousiasmé, e [ɑ̃tuzjasme] *a* filled with enthusiasm.

enthousiasmer [ɑ̃tuzjasme] *vt* to fill with enthusiasm; **s'~ (pour qch)** to get enthusiastic (about sth).

enthousiaste [ɑ̃tuzjast(ə)] *a* enthusiastic.

enticher [ɑ̃tiʃe]: **s'~ de** *vt* to become infatuated with.

entier, ière [ɑ̃tje, -jɛʀ] *a (non entamé, en totalité)* whole; *(total, complet)* complete; *(fig: caractère)* unbending, averse to

compromise ♦ *nm (MATH)* whole; **en ~** totally; in its entirety; **se donner tout ~ à qch** to devote o.s. completely to sth; **lait ~** full-cream milk; **pain ~** wholemeal bread; **nombre ~** whole number.

entièrement [ɑ̃tjɛʀmɑ̃] *ad* entirely, completely, wholly.

entité [ɑ̃tite] *nf* entity.

entomologie [ɑ̃tɔmɔlɔʒi] *nf* entomology.

entonner [ɑ̃tɔne] *vt (chanson)* to strike up.

entonnoir [ɑ̃tɔnwaʀ] *nm (ustensile)* funnel; *(trou)* shell-hole, crater.

entorse [ɑ̃tɔʀs(ə)] *nf (MÉD)* sprain; *(fig)*: **~ à la loi/au règlement** infringement of the law/rule; **se faire une ~ à la cheville/au poignet** to sprain one's ankle/wrist.

entortiller [ɑ̃tɔʀtije] *vt (envelopper)*: **~ qch dans/avec** to wrap sth in/with; *(enrouler)*: **~ qch autour de** to twist *ou* wind sth (a)round; *(fam)*: **~ qn** to get (a)round sb; *(: duper)* to hoodwink sb *(Brit)*, trick sb; **s'~ dans** *(draps)* to roll o.s. up in; *(fig: réponses)* to get tangled up in.

entourage [ɑ̃tuʀaʒ] *nm* circle; family (circle); *(d'une vedette etc)* entourage; *(ce qui enclôt)* surround.

entouré, e [ɑ̃tuʀe] *a (recherché, admiré)* popular; **~ de** surrounded by.

entourer [ɑ̃tuʀe] *vt* to surround; *(apporter son soutien à)* to rally round; **~ de** to surround with; *(trait)* to encircle with; **s'~ de** to surround o.s. with; **s'~ de précautions** to take all possible precautions.

entourloupette [ɑ̃tuʀlupɛt] *nf* mean trick.

entournures [ɑ̃tuʀnyʀ] *nfpl*: **gêné aux ~** in financial difficulties; *(fig)* a bit awkward.

entracte [ɑ̃tʀakt(ə)] *nm* interval.

entraide [ɑ̃tʀɛd] *nf* mutual aid *ou* assistance.

entraider [ɑ̃tʀede]: **s'~** *vi* to help each other.

entrailles [ɑ̃tʀaj] *nfpl* entrails; *(humaines)* bowels.

entrain [ɑ̃tʀɛ̃] *nm* spirit; **avec ~** *(répondre, travailler)* energetically; **faire qch sans ~** to do sth half-heartedly *ou* without enthusiasm.

entraînant, e [ɑ̃tʀɛnɑ̃, -ɑ̃t] *a (musique)* stirring, rousing.

entraînement [ɑ̃tʀɛnmɑ̃] *nm* training; *(TECH)*: **~ à chaîne/galet** chain/wheel drive; **manquer d'~** to be unfit; **~ par ergots/friction** *(INFORM)* tractor/friction feed.

entraîner [ɑ̃tʀene] *vt (tirer: wagons)* to pull; *(charrier)* to carry *ou* drag along; *(TECH)* to drive; *(emmener: personne)* to take (off); *(mener à l'assaut, influencer)* to lead; *(SPORT)* to train; *(impliquer)* to entail; *(causer)* to lead to, bring about; **~ qn à faire** *(inciter)* to lead sb to do; **s'~** *(SPORT)* to train; **s'~ à qch/à faire** to train o.s. for sth/to do.

entraîneur [ɑ̃tʀɛnœʀ] *nm (SPORT)* coach, trainer; *(HIPPISME)* trainer.

entraîneuse [ɑ̃tʀɛnøz] *nf (de bar)* hostess.

entrapercevoir [ɑ̃tʀapɛʀsəvwaʀ] *vt* to catch a glimpse of.

entrave [ɑ̃tʀav] *nf* hindrance.

entraver [ɑ̃tʀave] *vt (circulation)* to hold up; *(action, progrès)* to hinder, hamper.

entre [ɑ̃tʀ(ə)] *prép* between; (*parmi*) among(st); **l'un d'~ eux/nous** one of them/us; **le meilleur d'~ eux/nous** the best of them/us; **ils préfèrent rester ~ eux** they prefer to keep to themselves; **~ autres (choses)** among other things; **~ nous, ...** between ourselves ..., between you and me ...; **ils se battent ~ eux** they are fighting among(st) themselves.

entrebâillé, e [ɑ̃tʀəbaje] *a* half-open, ajar.

entrebâillement [ɑ̃tʀəbajmɑ̃] *nm:* **dans l'~ (de la porte)** in the half-open door.

entrebâiller [ɑ̃tʀəbaje] *vt* to half open.

entrechat [ɑ̃tʀəʃa] *nm* leap.

entrechoquer [ɑ̃tʀəʃɔke]: **s'~** *vi* to knock *ou* bang together.

entrecôte [ɑ̃tʀəkot] *nf* entrecôte *ou* rib steak.

entrecoupé, e [ɑ̃tʀəkupe] *a* (*paroles, voix*) broken.

entrecouper [ɑ̃tʀəkupe] *vt:* **~ qch de** to intersperse sth with; **~ un récit/voyage de** to interrupt a story/journey with; **s'~** (*traits, lignes*) to cut across each other.

entrecroiser [ɑ̃tʀəkʀwaze] *vt,* **s'~** *vi* to intertwine.

entrée [ɑ̃tʀe] *nf* entrance; (*accès: au cinéma etc*) admission; (*billet*) (admission) ticket; (*CULIN*) first course; (*COMM: de marchandises*) entry; (*INFORM*) entry, input; **~s** *nfpl:* **avoir ses ~s chez** *ou* **auprès de** to be a welcome visitor to; **d'~** *ad* from the outset; **erreur d'~** input error; **"~ interdite"** "no admittance *ou* entry"; **~ des artistes** stage door; **~ en matière** introduction; **~ en scène** entrance; **~ de service** service entrance.

entrefaites [ɑ̃tʀəfɛt]: **sur ces ~** *ad* at this juncture.

entrefilet [ɑ̃tʀəfilɛ] *nm* (*article*) paragraph, short report.

entregent [ɑ̃tʀəʒɑ̃] *nm:* **avoir de l'~** to have an easy manner.

entre-jambes [ɑ̃tʀəʒɑ̃b] *nm inv* crotch.

entrelacement [ɑ̃tʀəlasmɑ̃] *nm:* **un ~ de ...** a network of ....

entrelacer [ɑ̃tʀəlase] *vt,* **s'~** *vi* to intertwine.

entrelarder [ɑ̃tʀəlaʀde] *vt* to lard; (*fig*): **entrelardé de** interspersed with.

entremêler [ɑ̃tʀəmele] *vt:* **~ qch de** to (inter)mingle sth with.

entremets [ɑ̃tʀəmɛ] *nm* (cream) dessert.

entremetteur, euse [ɑ̃tʀəmetœʀ, -øz] *nm/f* go-between.

entremettre [ɑ̃tʀəmetʀ(ə)]: **s'~** *vi* to intervene.

entremise [ɑ̃tʀəmiz] *nf* intervention; **par l'~ de** through.

entrepont [ɑ̃tʀəpɔ̃] *nm* steerage; **dans l'~** in steerage.

entreposer [ɑ̃tʀəpoze] *vt* to store, put into storage.

entrepôt [ɑ̃tʀəpo] *nm* warehouse.

entreprenant, e [ɑ̃tʀəpʀənɑ̃, -ɑ̃t] *vb voir* **entreprendre ♦** *a* (*actif*) enterprising; (*trop galant*) forward.

entreprendre [ɑ̃tʀəpʀɑ̃dʀ(ə)] *vt* (*se lancer dans*) to undertake; (*commencer*) to begin *ou* start (upon); (*personne*) to buttonhole; **~ qn sur un sujet** to tackle sb on a subject; **~ de faire** to undertake to do.

entrepreneur [ɑ̃tʀəpʀənœʀ] *nm:* **~ (en bâtiment)** (building) contractor; **~ de pompes funèbres** funeral director, undertaker.

entreprenne [ɑ̃tʀəpʀɛn] *etc vb voir* **entreprendre.**

entrepris, e [ɑ̃tʀəpʀi, -iz] *pp de* **entreprendre ♦** *nf* (*société*) firm, business; (*action*) undertaking, venture.

entrer [ɑ̃tʀe] *vi* to go (*ou* come) in, enter **♦** *vt* (*INFORM*) to input, enter; **(faire) ~ qch dans** to get sth into; **~ dans** (*gén*) to enter; (*pièce*) to go (*ou* come) into, enter; (*club*) to join; (*heurter*) to run into; (*partager: vues, craintes de qn*) to share; (*être une composante de*) to go into; (*faire partie de*) to form part of; **~ au couvent** to enter a convent; **~ à l'hôpital** to go into hospital; **~ dans le système** (*INFORM*) to log in; **~ en fureur** to become angry; **~ en ébullition** to start to boil; **~ en scène** to come on stage; **laisser ~ qn/qch** to let sb/sth in; **faire ~** (*visiteur*) to show in.

entresol [ɑ̃tʀəsɔl] *nm* entresol, mezzanine.

entre-temps [ɑ̃tʀətɑ̃] *ad* meanwhile, (in the) meantime.

entretenir [ɑ̃tʀətniʀ] *vt* to maintain; (*amitié*) to keep alive; (*famille, maîtresse*) to support, keep; **~ qn (de)** to speak to sb (about); **s'~ (de)** to converse (about); **~ qn dans l'erreur** to let sb remain in ignorance.

entretenu, e [ɑ̃tʀətny] *pp de* **entretenir ♦** *a* (*femme*) kept; **bien/mal ~** (*maison, jardin*) well/badly kept.

entretien [ɑ̃tʀətjɛ̃] *nm* maintenance; (*discussion*) discussion, talk; (*audience*) interview; **frais d'~** maintenance charges.

entretiendrai [ɑ̃tʀətjɛ̃dʀe], **entretiens** [ɑ̃tʀətjɛ̃] *etc vb voir* **entretenir.**

entretuer [ɑ̃tʀətɥe]: **s'~** *vi* to kill one another.

entreverrai [ɑ̃tʀəveʀe], **entrevit** [ɑ̃tʀəvi] *etc vb voir* **entrevoir.**

entrevoir [ɑ̃tʀəvwaʀ] *vt* (*à peine*) to make out; (*brièvement*) to catch a glimpse of.

entrevu, e [ɑ̃tʀəvy] *pp de* **entrevoir ♦** *nf* meeting; (*audience*) interview.

entrouvert, e [ɑ̃tʀuvɛʀ, -ɛʀt(ə)] *pp de* **entrouvrir ♦** *a* half-open.

entrouvrir [ɑ̃tʀuvʀiʀ] *vt,* **s'~** *vi* to half open.

énumération [enymeʀasjɔ̃] *nf* enumeration.

énumérer [enymeʀe] *vt* to list, enumerate.

énurésie [enyʀezi] *nf* enuresis.

envahir [ɑ̃vaiʀ] *vt* to invade; (*suj: inquiétude, peur*) to come over.

envahissant, e [ɑ̃vaisɑ̃, -ɑ̃t] *a* (*péj: personne*) interfering, intrusive.

envahissement [ɑ̃vaismɑ̃] *nm* invasion.

envahisseur [ɑ̃vaisœʀ] *nm* (*MIL*) invader.

envasement [ɑ̃vazmɑ̃] *nm* silting up.

envaser [ɑ̃vaze]: **s'~** *vi* to get bogged down (in the mud).

enveloppe [ɑ̃vlɔp] *nf* (*de lettre*) envelope; (*TECH*) casing; outer layer; **mettre sous ~** to put in an envelope; **~ autocollante** self-seal envelope; **~ budgétaire** budget; **~ à fenêtre** window envelope.

envelopper [ɑ̃vlɔpe] *vt* to wrap; (*fig*) to envelop, shroud; **s'~ dans un châle/une**

couverture to wrap o.s. in a shawl/blanket.

envenimer [ãvnime] *vt* to aggravate; **s'~** *vi* (*plaie*) to fester; (*situation*, *relations*) to worsen.

envergure [ãvɛʀgyʀ] *nf* (*d'un oiseau*, *avion*) wingspan; (*fig: étendue*) scope; (*: valeur*) calibre.

enverrai [ãvɛʀe] *etc vb voir* **envoyer.**

envers [ãvɛʀ] *prép* towards, to; ♦ *nm* other side; (*d'une étoffe*) wrong side; **à l'~** upside down; back to front; (*vêtement*) inside out; **~ et contre tous** *ou* **tout** against all opposition.

enviable [ãvjabl(ə)] *a* enviable; **peu ~** unenviable.

envie [ãvi] *nf* (*sentiment*) envy; (*souhait*) desire, wish; (*tache sur la peau*) birthmark; (*filet de peau*) hangnail; **avoir ~ de** to feel like; (*désir plus fort*) to want; **avoir ~ de faire** to feel like doing; to want to do; **avoir ~ que** to wish that; **donner à qn l'~ de faire** to make sb want to do; **ça lui fait ~** he would like that.

envier [ãvje] *vt* to envy; **~ qch à qn** to envy sb sth; **n'avoir rien à ~ à** to have no cause to be envious of.

envieux, euse [ãvjø, -øz] *a* envious.

environ [ãviʀɔ̃] *ad:* **~ 3 h/2 km, 3 h/2 km ~** (around) about 3 o'clock/2 km, 3 o'clock/2 km or so.

environnant, e [ãviʀɔnã, -ãt] *a* surrounding.

environnement [ãviʀɔnmã] *nm* environment.

environnementaliste [ãviʀɔnmãtalist(ə)] *nm/f* environmentalist.

environner [ãviʀɔne] *vt* to surround.

environs [ãviʀɔ̃] *nmpl* surroundings; **aux ~ de** around.

envisageable [ãvizaʒabl(ə)] *a* conceivable.

envisager [ãvizaʒe] *vt* (*examiner*, *considérer*) to view, contemplate; (*avoir en vue*) to envisage; **~ de faire** to consider *ou* contemplate doing.

envoi [ãvwa] *nm* sending; (*paquet*) parcel, consignment; **~ contre remboursement** (*COMM*) cash on delivery.

envoie [ãvwa] *etc vb voir* **envoyer.**

envol [ãvɔl] *nm* takeoff.

envolée [ãvɔle] *nf* (*fig*) flight.

envoler [ãvɔle]: **s'~** *vi* (*oiseau*) to fly away *ou* off; (*avion*) to take off; (*papier*, *feuille*) to blow away; (*fig*) to vanish (into thin air).

envoûtement [ãvutmã] *nm* bewitchment.

envoûter [ãvute] *vt* to bewitch.

envoyé, e [ãvwaje] *nm/f* (*POL*) envoy; (*PRESSE*) correspondent ♦ *a:* **bien ~** (*remarque*, *réponse*) well-aimed.

envoyer [ãvwaje] *vt* to send; (*lancer*) to hurl, throw; **~ une gifle/un sourire à qn** to aim a blow/flash a smile at sb; **~ les couleurs** to run up the colours; **~ chercher** to send for; **~ par le fond** (*bateau*) to send to the bottom.

envoyeur, euse [ãvwajœʀ, -øz] *nm/f* sender.

enzyme [ãzim] *nm* enzyme.

éolien, ne [eɔljɛ̃, -ɛn] *a* wind *cpd*; **pompe ~ne** windpump.

EOR *sigle m* (= *élève officier de réserve*) ≈ military cadet.

éosine [eɔzin] *nf* eosin (*antiseptic used in France to treat skin ailments*).

épagneul, e [epaɲœl] *nm/f* spaniel.

épais, se [epɛ, -ɛs] *a* thick.

épaisseur [epɛsœʀ] *nf* thickness.

épaissir [epesiʀ] *vt*, **s'~** *vi* to thicken.

épaississement [epesismã] *nm* thickening.

épanchement [epãʃmã] *nm:* **un ~ de sinovie** water on the knee; **~s** *nmpl* (*fig*) (sentimental) outpourings.

épancher [epãʃe] *vt* to give vent to; **s'~** *vi* to open one's heart; (*liquide*) to pour out.

épandage [epãdaʒ] *nm* manure spreading.

épanoui, e [epanwi] *a* (*éclos*, *ouvert*, *développé*) blooming; (*radieux*) radiant.

épanouir [epanwiʀ]: **s'~** *vi* (*fleur*) to bloom, open out; (*visage*) to light up; (*fig: se développer*) to blossom (out); (*: mentalement*) to open up.

épanouissement [epanwismã] *nm* blossoming; opening up.

épargnant, e [epaʀɲã, -ãt] *nm/f* saver, investor.

épargne [epaʀɲ(ə)] *nf* saving; **l'~-logement** property investment.

épargner [epaʀɲe] *vt* to save; (*ne pas tuer ou endommager*) to spare ♦ *vi* to save; **~ qch à qn** to spare sb sth.

éparpiller [epaʀpije] *vt* to scatter; (*pour répartir*) to disperse; (*fig: efforts*) to dissipate; **s'~** *vi* to scatter; (*fig*) to dissipate one's efforts.

épars, e [epaʀ, -aʀs(ə)] *a* (*maisons*) scattered; (*cheveux*) sparse.

épatant, e [epatã, -ãt] *a* (*fam*) super, splendid.

épaté, e [epate] *a:* **nez ~** flat nose (with wide nostrils).

épater [epate] *vt* to amaze; (*impressionner*) to impress.

épaule [epol] *nf* shoulder.

épaulé-jeté, *pl* **épaulés-jetés** [epoleʒəte] *nm* (*SPORT*) clean-and-jerk.

épaulement [epolmã] *nm* escarpment; (*mur*) retaining wall.

épauler [epole] *vt* (*aider*) to back up, support; (*arme*) to raise (to one's shoulder) ♦ *vi* to (take) aim.

épaulette [epolɛt] *nf* (*MIL*, *d'un veston*) epaulette; (*de combinaison*) shoulder strap.

épave [epav] *nf* wreck.

épée [epe] *nf* sword.

épeler [eple] *vt* to spell.

éperdu, e [epɛʀdy] *a* (*personne*) overcome; (*sentiment*) passionate; (*fuite*) frantic.

éperdument [epɛʀdymã] *ad* (*aimer*) wildly; (*espérer*) fervently.

éperlan [epɛʀlã] *nm* (*ZOOL*) smelt.

éperon [epʀɔ̃] *nm* spur.

éperonner [epʀɔne] *vt* to spur (on); (*navire*) to ram.

épervier [epɛʀvje] *nm* (*ZOOL*) sparrowhawk; (*PÊCHE*) casting net.

éphèbe [efɛb] *nm* beautiful young man.

éphémère [efemɛʀ] *a* ephemeral, fleeting.

éphéméride [efemeʀid] *nf* block *ou* tear-off calendar.

épi [epi] *nm* (*de blé*, *d'orge*) ear; **~ de cheveux** tuft of hair; **stationnement/se garer en ~** parking/to park at an angle to the kerb.

épice [epis] *nf* spice.

épicé, e [epise] *a* highly spiced, spicy; *(fig)* spicy.

épicéa [episea] *nm* spruce.

épicentre [episãtʀ(ə)] *nm* epicentre.

épicer [epise] *vt* to spice; *(fig)* to add spice to.

épicerie [episʀi] *nf (magasin)* grocer's shop; *(denrées)* groceries *pl*; ~ **fine** delicatessen (shop).

épicier, ière [episje, -jɛʀ] *nm/f* grocer.

épidémie [epidemi] *nf* epidemic.

épidémique [epidemik] *a* epidemic.

épiderme [epidɛʀm(ə)] *nm* skin, epidermis.

épidermique [epidɛʀmik] *a* skin *cpd*, epidermic.

épier [epje] *vt* to spy on, watch closely; *(occasion)* to look out for.

épieu, x [epjø] *nm* (hunting-)spear.

épigramme [epigʀam] *nf* epigram.

épilation [epilɑsjɔ̃] *nf* removal of unwanted hair.

épilatoire [epilatwaʀ] *a* depilatory, hair-removing.

épilepsie [epilɛpsi] *nf* epilepsy.

épileptique [epilɛptik] *a, nm/f* epileptic.

épiler [epile] *vt (jambes)* to remove the hair from; *(sourcils)* to pluck; **s'~ les jambes** to remove the hair from one's legs; **s'~ les sourcils** to pluck one's eyebrows; **se faire ~** to get unwanted hair removed; **crème à ~** hair-removing *ou* depilatory cream; **pince à ~** eyebrow tweezers.

épilogue [epilɔg] *nm (fig)* conclusion, dénouement.

épiloguer [epilɔge] *vi*: ~ **sur** to hold forth on.

épinard [epinaʀ] *nm (aussi: ~s)* spinach *sg*.

épine [epin] *nf* thorn, prickle; *(d'oursin etc)* spine, prickle; ~ **dorsale** backbone.

épineux, euse [epinø, -øz] *a* thorny, prickly.

épinglage [epɛ̃glaʒ] *nm* pinning.

épingle [epɛ̃gl(ə)] *nf* pin; **tirer son ~ du jeu** to play one's game well; **tiré à quatre ~s** well turned-out; **monter qch en ~** to build sth up, make a thing of sth *(fam)*; ~ **à chapeau** hatpin; ~ **à cheveux** hairpin; **virage en ~ à cheveux** hairpin bend; ~ **de cravate** tie pin; ~ **de nourrice** *ou* **de sûreté** *ou* **double** safety pin, nappy *(Brit) ou* diaper *(US)* pin.

épingler [epɛ̃gle] *vt (badge, décoration)*: ~ **qch sur** to pin sth on(to); *(COUTURE: tissu, robe)* to pin together; *(fam)* to catch, nick.

épinière [epinjɛʀ] *af voir* **moelle.**

Épiphanie [epifani] *nf* Epiphany.

épique [epik] *a* epic.

épiscopal, e, aux [episkɔpal, -o] *a* episcopal.

épiscopat [episkɔpa] *nm* bishopric, episcopate.

épisiotomie [epizjɔtɔmi] *nf (MÉD)* episiotomy.

épisode [epizɔd] *nm* episode; **film/roman à ~s** serialized film/novel, serial.

épisodique [epizɔdik] *a* occasional.

épissure [episyʀ] *nf* splice.

épistémologie [epistemɔlɔʒi] *nf* epistemology.

épistolaire [epistɔlɛʀ] *a* epistolary; **être en relations ~s avec qn** to correspond with sb.

épitaphe [epitaf] *nf* epitaph.

épithète [epitɛt] *nf (nom, surnom)* epithet; **adjectif ~** attributive adjective.

épître [epitʀ(ə)] *nf* epistle.

éploré, e [eplɔʀe] *a* in tears, tearful.

épluchage [eplyʃaʒ] *nm* peeling; *(de dossier etc)* careful reading *ou* analysis.

épluche-légumes [eplyʃlegym] *nm inv* potato peeler.

éplucher [eplyʃe] *vt (fruit, légumes)* to peel; *(comptes, dossier)* to go over with a fine-tooth comb.

éplucheur [eplyʃœʀ] *nm* (automatic) peeler.

épluchures [eplyʃyʀ] *nfpl* peelings.

épointer [epwɛ̃te] *vt* to blunt.

éponge [epɔ̃ʒ] *nf* sponge; **passer l'~ (sur)** *(fig)* to let bygones be bygones (with regard to); **jeter l'~** *(fig)* to throw in the towel; ~ **métallique** scourer.

éponger [epɔ̃ʒe] *vt (liquide)* to mop *ou* sponge up; *(surface)* to sponge; *(fig: déficit)* to soak up, absorb; **s'~ le front** to mop one's brow.

épopée [epɔpe] *nf* epic.

époque [epɔk] *nf (de l'histoire)* age, era; *(de l'année, la vie)* time; **d'~** *a (meuble)* period *cpd*; **à cette ~** at this *(ou* that) time *ou* period; **faire ~** to make history.

épouiller [epuje] *vt* to pick lice off; *(avec un produit)* to delouse.

époumoner [epumɔne]: **s'~** *vi* to shout *(ou* sing) o.s. hoarse.

épouse [epuz] *nf* wife *(pl* wives).

épouser [epuze] *vt* to marry; *(fig: idées)* to espouse; *(: forme)* to fit.

époussetage [epustaʒ] *nm* dusting.

épousseter [epuste] *vt* to dust.

époustouflant, e [epustuflɑ̃, -ɑ̃t] *a* staggering, mind-boggling.

époustoufler [epustufle] *vt* to flabbergast, astound.

épouvantable [epuvɑ̃tabl(ə)] *a* appalling, dreadful.

épouvantail [epuvɑ̃taj] *nm (à moineaux)* scarecrow; *(fig)* bog(e)y; bugbear.

épouvante [epuvɑ̃t] *nf* terror; **film d'~** horror film.

épouvanter [epuvɑ̃te] *vt* to terrify.

époux [epu] *nm* husband ♦ *nmpl*: **les ~** the (married) couple, the husband and wife.

éprendre [epʀɑ̃dʀ(ə)]: **s'~ de** *vt* to fall in love with.

épreuve [epʀœv] *nf (d'examen)* test; *(malheur, difficulté)* trial, ordeal; *(PHOTO)* print; *(TYPO)* proof; *(SPORT)* event; **à l'~ des balles/du feu** *(vêtement)* bulletproof/fireproof; **à toute ~** unfailing; **mettre à l'~** to put to the test; ~ **de force** trial of strength; *(fig)* showdown; ~ **de résistance** test of resistance; ~ **de sélection** *(SPORT)* heat.

épris, e [epʀi, -iz] *vb voir* **éprendre** ♦ *a*: ~ **de** in love with.

éprouvant, e [epʀuvɑ̃, -ɑ̃t] *a* trying.

éprouvé, e [epʀuve] *a* tested, proven.

éprouver [epʀuve] *vt (tester)* to test; *(mettre à l'épreuve)* to put to the test; *(marquer, faire souffrir)* to afflict, distress; *(ressentir)* to experience.

éprouvette [epʀuvet] *nf* test tube.

EPS *sigle f (= Éducation physique et sportive)* ≈ PE.

épuisant, e [epɥizɑ̃, -ɑ̃t] *a* exhausting.

épuisé, e [epɥize] *a* exhausted; *(livre)* out of print.

épuisement [epu̯izmã] *nm* exhaustion; **jusqu'à ~ des stocks** while stocks last.

épuiser [epu̯ize] *vt* (*fatiguer*) to exhaust, wear *ou* tire out; (*stock, sujet*) to exhaust; **s'~** *vi* to wear *ou* tire o.s. out, exhaust o.s.; (*stock*) to run out.

épuisette [epu̯izɛt] *nf* landing net; shrimping net.

épuration [epyʀasjɔ̃] *nf* purification; purging; refinement.

épurer [epyʀe] *vt* (*liquide*) to purify; (*parti, administration*) to purge; (*langue, texte*) to refine.

équarrir [ekaʀiʀ] *vt* (*pierre, arbre*) to square (off); (*animal*) to quarter.

équateur [ekwatœʀ] *nm* equator; **(la république de) l'É~** Ecuador.

équation [ekwasjɔ̃] *nf* equation; **mettre en ~** to equate; **~ du premier/second degré** simple/quadratic equation.

équatorial, e, aux [ekwatɔʀjal, -o] *a* equatorial.

équatorien, ne [ekwatɔʀjɛ̃, -ɛn] *a* Ecuadorian ♦ *nm/f*: **É~, ne** Ecuadorian.

équerre [ekɛʀ] *nf* (*à dessin*) (set) square; (*pour fixer*) brace; **en ~** at right angles; **à l'~, d'~** straight; **double ~** T-square.

équestre [ekɛstʀ(ə)] *a* equestrian.

équeuter [ekøte] *vt* (*CULIN*) to remove the stalk(s) from.

équidé [ekide] *nm* (*ZOOL*) member of the horse family.

équidistance [eku̯idistãs] *nf*: **à ~ (de)** equidistant (from).

équidistant, e [eku̯idistã, -ãt] *a*: **~ (de)** equidistant (from).

équilatéral, e, aux [eku̯ilateʀal, -o] *a* equilateral.

équilibrage [ekilibʀaʒ] *nm* (*AUTO*): **~ des roues** wheel balancing.

équilibre [ekilibʀ(ə)] *nm* balance; (*d'une balance*) equilibrium; **~ budgétaire** balanced budget; **garder/perdre l'~** to keep/lose one's balance; **être en ~** to be balanced; **mettre en ~** to make steady; **avoir le sens de l'~** to be well-balanced.

équilibré, e [ekilibʀe] *a* (*fig*) well-balanced, stable.

équilibrer [ekilibʀe] *vt* to balance; **s'~** (*poids*) to balance; (*fig: défauts etc*) to balance each other out.

équilibriste [ekilibʀist(ə)] *nm/f* tightrope walker.

équinoxe [ekinɔks] *nm* equinox.

équipage [ekipaʒ] *nm* crew; **en grand ~** in great array.

équipe [ekip] *nf* team; (*bande: parfois péj*) bunch; **travailler par ~s** to work in shifts; **travailler en ~** to work as a team; **faire ~ avec** to team up with; **~ de chercheurs** research team; **~ de secours** *ou* **de sauvetage** rescue team.

équipé, e [ekipe] *a* (*cuisine etc*) equipped, fitted(-out) ♦ *nf* escapade.

équipement [ekipmã] *nm* equipment; **~s** *nmpl* amenities, facilities; installations; **biens/dépenses d'~** capital goods/expenditure; **ministère de l'É~** department of public works; **~s sportifs/collectifs** sports/community facilities *ou* resources.

équiper [ekipe] *vt* to equip; (*voiture, cuisine*) to equip, fit out; **~ qn/qch de** to equip sb/sth with; **s'~** (*sportif*) to equip o.s., kit o.s. out.

équipier, ière [ekipje, -jɛʀ] *nm/f* team member.

équitable [ekitabl(ə)] *a* fair.

équitation [ekitasjɔ̃] *nf* (horse-)riding; **faire de l'~** to go (horse-)riding.

équité [ekite] *nf* equity.

équivaille [ekivaj] *etc vb voir* **équivaloir**.

équivalence [ekivalãs] *nf* equivalence.

équivalent, e [ekivalã, -ãt] *a, nm* equivalent.

équivaloir [ekivalwaʀ]: **~ à** *vt* to be equivalent to; (*représenter*) to amount to.

équivaut [ekivo] *etc vb voir* **équivaloir**.

équivoque [ekivɔk] *a* equivocal, ambiguous; (*louche*) dubious ♦ *nf* ambiguity.

érable [eʀabl(ə)] *nm* maple.

éradiquer [eʀadike] *vt* to eradicate.

érafler [eʀafle] *vt* to scratch; **s'~ la main/les jambes** to scrape *ou* scratch one's hand/legs.

éraflure [eʀaflyʀ] *nf* scratch.

éraillé, e [eʀaje] *a* (*voix*) rasping, hoarse.

ère [ɛʀ] *nf* era; **en l'an 1050 de notre ~** in the year 1050 A.D.

érection [eʀɛksjɔ̃] *nf* erection.

éreintant, e [eʀɛ̃tã, -ãt] *a* exhausting.

éreinté, e [eʀɛ̃te] *a* exhausted.

éreintement [eʀɛ̃tmã] *nm* exhaustion.

éreinter [eʀɛ̃te] *vt* to exhaust, wear out; (*fig: critiquer*) to slate; **s'~ (à faire qch/à qch)** to wear o.s. out (doing sth/with sth).

ergonomie [ɛʀgɔnɔmi] *nf* ergonomics *sg*.

ergonomique [ɛʀgɔnɔmik] *a* ergonomic.

ergot [ɛʀgo] *nm* (*de coq*) spur; (*TECH*) lug.

ergoter [ɛʀgɔte] *vi* to split hairs, argue over details.

ergoteur, euse [ɛʀgɔtœʀ, -øz] *nm/f* hair-splitter.

ériger [eʀiʒe] *vt* (*monument*) to erect; **~ qch en principe/loi** to make sth a principle/law; **s'~ en critique (de)** to set o.s. up as a critic (of).

ermitage [ɛʀmitaʒ] *nm* retreat.

ermite [ɛʀmit] *nm* hermit.

éroder [eʀode] *vt* to erode.

érogène [eʀɔʒɛn] *a* erogenous.

érosion [eʀozjɔ̃] *nf* erosion.

érotique [eʀɔtik] *a* erotic.

érotiquement [eʀɔtikmã] *ad* erotically.

érotisme [eʀɔtism(ə)] *nm* eroticism.

errance [eʀãs] *nf* wandering.

errant, e [eʀã, -ãt] *a*: **un chien ~** a stray dog.

erratum, a [eʀatɔm, -a] *nm* erratum (*pl* -a).

errements [eʀmã] *nmpl* misguided ways.

errer [eʀe] *vi* to wander.

erreur [eʀœʀ] *nf* mistake, error; (*INFORM: de programme*) bug; (*morale*): **~s** *nfpl* errors; **être dans l'~** to be wrong; **induire qn en ~** to mislead sb; **par ~** by mistake; **sauf ~** unless I'm mistaken; **faire ~** to be mistaken; **~ de date** mistake in the date; **~ de fait** error of fact; **~ d'impression** (*TYPO*) misprint; **~ judiciaire** miscarriage of justice; **~ de jugement** error of judgment; **~ matérielle** *ou* **d'écriture** clerical error; **~ tactique** tactical error.

erroné, e [eʀɔne] *a* wrong, erroneous.

éructer [erykte] *vi* to belch.

érudit, e [erydi, -it] *a* erudite, learned ♦ *nm/f* scholar.

érudition [erydisjɔ̃] *nf* erudition, scholarship.

éruptif, ive [eryptif, -iv] *a* eruptive.

éruption [erypsjɔ̃] *nf* eruption; *(cutanée)* outbreak; *(: boutons)* rash; *(fig: de joie, colère, folie)* outburst.

es [ɛ] *vb voir* **être**.

ès [ɛs] *prép:* **licencié ~ lettres/sciences** ≈ Bachelor of Arts/Science; **docteur ~ lettres** ≈ doctor of philosophy, PhD.

E/S *abr (= entrée/sortie)* I/O *(= in/out).*

esbroufe [ɛsbruf] *nf:* **faire de l'~** to have people on.

escabeau, x [ɛskabo] *nm (tabouret)* stool; *(échelle)* stepladder.

escadre [ɛskadr(ə)] *nf (NAVIG)* squadron; *(AVIAT)* wing.

escadrille [ɛskadrij] *nf (AVIAT)* flight.

escadron [ɛskadrɔ̃] *nm* squadron.

escalade [ɛskalad] *nf* climbing *q*; *(POL etc)* escalation.

escalader [ɛskalade] *vt* to climb, scale.

escale [ɛskal] *nf (NAVIG)* call; *(: port)* port of call; *(AVIAT)* stop(over); **faire ~ à** to put in at, call in at; to stop over at; **~ technique** *(AVIAT)* refuelling stop.

escalier [ɛskalje] *nm* stairs *pl*; **dans l'~** *ou* **les ~s** on the stairs; **descendre l'~** *ou* **les ~s** to go downstairs; **~ mécanique** *ou* **roulant** escalator; **~ de secours** fire escape; **~ de service** backstairs; **~ à vis** *ou* **en colimaçon** spiral staircase.

escalope [ɛskalɔp] *nf* escalope.

escamotable [ɛskamɔtabl(ə)] *a (train d'atterrissage, antenne)* retractable; *(table, lit)* fold-away.

escamoter [ɛskamɔte] *vt (esquiver)* to get round, evade; *(faire disparaître)* to conjure away; *(dérober: portefeuille etc)* to snatch; *(train d'atterrissage)* to retract; *(mots)* to miss out.

escapade [ɛskapad] *nf:* **faire une ~** to go on a jaunt; *(s'enfuir)* to run away *ou* off.

escarbille [ɛskarbij] *nf* bit of grit.

escarcelle [ɛskarsɛl] *nf:* **faire tomber dans l'~** *(argent)* to bring in.

escargot [ɛskargo] *nm* snail.

escarmouche [ɛskarmuʃ] *nf (MIL)* skirmish; *(fig: propos hostiles)* angry exchange.

escarpé, e [ɛskarpe] *a* steep.

escarpement [ɛskarpəmã] *nm* steep slope.

escarpin [ɛskarpɛ̃] *nm* flat(-heeled) shoe.

escarre [ɛskar] *nf* bedsore.

Escaut [ɛsko] *nm:* **l'~** the Scheldt.

escient [ɛsjã] *nm:* **à bon ~** advisedly.

esclaffer [ɛsklafe]: **s'~** *vi* to guffaw.

esclandre [ɛsklɑ̃dr(ə)] *nm* scene, fracas.

esclavage [ɛsklavaʒ] *nm* slavery.

esclave [ɛsklav] *nm/f* slave; **être ~ de** *(fig)* to be a slave of.

escogriffe [ɛskɔgrif] *nm (péj)* beanpole.

escompte [ɛskɔ̃t] *nm* discount.

escompter [ɛskɔ̃te] *vt (COMM)* to discount; *(espérer)* to expect, reckon upon; **~ que** to reckon *ou* expect that.

escorte [ɛskɔrt(ə)] *nf* escort; **faire ~ à** to escort.

escorter [ɛskɔrte] *vt* to escort.

escorteur [ɛskɔrtœr] *nm (NAVIG)* escort (ship).

escouade [ɛskwad] *nf* squad; *(fig: groupe de personnes)* group.

escrime [ɛskrim] *nf* fencing; **faire de l'~** to fence.

escrimer [ɛskrime]: **s'~** *vi:* **s'~ à faire** to wear o.s. out doing.

escrimeur, euse [ɛskrimœr, -øz] *nm/f* fencer.

escroc [ɛskro] *nm* swindler, con-man.

escroquer [ɛskrɔke] *vt:* **~ qn (de qch)/qch à qn** to swindle sb (out of sth)/sth out of sb.

escroquerie [ɛskrɔkri] *nf* swindle.

ésotérique [ezɔterik] *a* esoteric.

espace [ɛspas] *nm* space; **~ publicitaire** advertising space; **~ vital** living space.

espacé, e [ɛspase] *a* spaced out.

espacement [ɛspasmã] *nm:* **~ proportionnel** proportional spacing *(on printer).*

espacer [ɛspase] *vt* to space out; **s'~** *vi (visites etc)* to become less frequent.

espadon [ɛspadɔ̃] *nm* swordfish *inv.*

espadrille [ɛspadrij] *nf* rope-soled sandal.

Espagne [ɛspaɲ(ə)] *nf:* **l'~** Spain.

espagnol, e [ɛspaɲɔl] *a* Spanish ♦ *nm (LING)* Spanish ♦ *nm/f:* **E~, e** Spaniard.

espagnolette [ɛspaɲɔlɛt] *nf (window)* catch; **fermé à l'~** resting on the catch.

espalier [ɛspalje] *nm (arbre fruitier)* espalier.

espèce [ɛspɛs] *nf (BIO, BOT, ZOOL)* species *inv*; *(gén: sorte)* sort, kind, type; *(péj):* **~ de maladroit/de brute!** you clumsy oaf/you brute!; **~s** *nfpl (COMM)* cash *sg*; *(REL)* species; **de toute ~** of all kinds *ou* sorts; **en l'~** *ad* in the case in point; **payer en ~s** to pay (in) cash; **cas d'~** individual case; **l'~ humaine** humankind.

espérance [ɛsperãs] *nf* hope; **~ de vie** life expectancy.

espéranto [ɛsperãto] *nm* esperanto.

espérer [ɛspere] *vt* to hope for; **j'espère (bien)** I hope so; **~ que/faire** to hope that/to do; **~ en** to trust in.

espiègle [ɛspjɛgl(ə)] *a* mischievous.

espièglerie [ɛspjɛgləri] *nf* mischievousness; *(tour, farce)* piece of mischief, prank.

espion, ne [ɛspjɔ̃, -ɔn] *nm/f* spy; **avion ~** spy plane.

espionnage [ɛspjɔnaʒ] *nm* espionage, spying; **film/roman d'~** spy film/novel.

espionner [ɛspjɔne] *vt* to spy (up)on.

esplanade [ɛsplanad] *nf* esplanade.

espoir [ɛspwar] *nm* hope; **l'~ de qch/de faire qch** the hope of sth/of doing sth; **avoir bon ~ que ...** to have high hopes that ...; **garder l'~ que ...** to remain hopeful that ...; **un ~ de la boxe/du ski** one of boxing's/skiing's hopefuls, one of the hopes of boxing/skiing; **sans ~** hopeless.

esprit [ɛspri] *nm (pensée, intellect)* mind; *(humour, ironie)* wit; *(mentalité, d'une loi etc, fantôme etc)* spirit; **l'~ d'équipe/de compétition** team/competitive spirit; **faire de l'~** to try to be witty; **reprendre ses ~s** to come to; **perdre l'~** to lose one's mind; **avoir bon/mauvais ~** to be of a good/bad disposition; **avoir l'~ à faire qch** to have a mind to do sth; **avoir l'~ critique** to be critical; **~ de**

contradiction contrariness; **~ de corps** esprit de corps; **~ de famille** family loyalty; **l'~ malin** (*le diable*) the Evil One; **~s chagrins** faultfinders.

esquif [ɛskif] *nm* skiff.

esquimau, de, x [ɛskimo, -od] *a* Eskimo ♦ *nm* (*LING*) Eskimo; (*glace*): **E~** ® ice lolly (*Brit*), popsicle (*US*) ♦ *nm/f*: **E~, de** Eskimo; **chien ~** husky.

esquinter [ɛskɛ̃te] *vt* (*fam*) to mess up; **s'~** *vi*: **s'~ à faire qch** to knock o.s. out doing sth.

esquisse [ɛskis] *nf* sketch; **l'~ d'un sourire/ changement** a hint of a smile/of change.

esquisser [ɛskise] *vt* to sketch; **s'~** *vi* (*amélioration*) to begin to be detectable; **~ un sourire** to give a hint of a smile.

esquive [ɛskiv] *nf* (*BOXE*) dodging; (*fig*) sidestepping.

esquiver [ɛskive] *vt* to dodge; **s'~** *vi* to slip away.

essai [esɛ] *nm* trying; (*tentative*) attempt, try; (*RUGBY*) try; (*LITTÉRATURE*) essay; **~s** *nmpl* (*AUTO*) trials; **à l'~** on a trial basis; **~ gratuit** (*COMM*) free trial.

essaim [esɛ̃] *nm* swarm.

essaimer [eseme] *vi* to swarm; (*fig*) to spread, expand.

essayage [esɛjaʒ] *nm* (*d'un vêtement*) trying on, fitting; **salon d'~** fitting room; **cabine d'~** fitting room (*cubicle*).

essayer [eseje] *vt* (*gén*) to try; (*vêtement, chaussures*) to try (on); (*restaurant, méthode, voiture*) to try (out) ♦ *vi* to try; **~ de faire** to try *ou* attempt to do; **s'~ à faire** to try one's hand at doing; **essayez un peu!** (*menace*) just you try!

essayeur, euse [esɛjœʀ, -øz] *nm/f* (*chez un tailleur etc*) fitter.

ESSEC [esɛk] *sigle f* (= *École supérieure des sciences économiques et sociales*) *grande école for management and business studies.*

essence [esɑ̃s] *nf* (*de voiture*) petrol (*Brit*), gas(oline) (*US*); (*extrait de plante, PHILOSOPHIE*) essence; (*espèce: d'arbre*) species *inv*; **prendre de l'~** to get (some) petrol *ou* gas; **par ~** (*essentiellement*) essentially; **~ de citron/rose** lemon/rose oil; **~ de térébenthine** turpentine.

essentiel, le [esɑ̃sjɛl] *a* essential ♦ *nm*: **l'~ d'un discours/d'une œuvre** the essence of a speech/work of art; **emporter l'~** to take the essentials; **c'est l'~** (*ce qui importe*) that's the main thing; **l'~ de** (*la majeure partie*) the main part of.

essentiellement [esɑ̃sjɛlmɑ̃] *ad* essentially.

esseulé, e [esœle] *a* forlorn.

essieu, x [esjø] *nm* axle.

essor [esɔʀ] *nm* (*de l'économie etc*) rapid expansion; **prendre son ~** (*oiseau*) to fly off.

essorage [esɔʀaʒ] *nm* wringing out; spindrying; spinning; shaking.

essorer [esɔʀe] *vt* (*en tordant*) to wring (out); (*par la force centrifuge*) to spin-dry; (*salade*) to spin; (*: en secouant*) to shake dry.

essoreuse [esɔʀøz] *nf* mangle, wringer; (*à tambour*) spin-dryer.

essouffler [esufle] *vt* to make breathless; **s'~** *vi* to get out of breath; (*fig: économie*) to run

out of steam.

essuie [esɥi] *etc vb voir* **essuyer**.

essuie-glace [esɥiglas] *nm* windscreen (*Brit*) *ou* windshield (*US*) wiper.

essuie-mains [esɥimɛ̃] *nm inv* hand towel.

essuierai [esɥiʀe] *etc vb voir* **essuyer**.

essuie-tout [esɥitu] *nm inv* kitchen paper.

essuyer [esɥije] *vt* to wipe; (*fig: subir*) to suffer; **s'~** (*après le bain*) to dry o.s.; **~ la vaisselle** to dry up, dry the dishes.

est [ɛ] *vb voir* **être** ♦ *nm* [ɛst]: **l'~** the east ♦ *a inv* east; (*région*) east(ern); **à l'~** in the east; (*direction*) to the east, east(wards); **à l'~ de** (to the) east of; **les pays de l'E~** the eastern countries.

estafette [ɛstafɛt] *nf* (*MIL*) dispatch rider.

estafilade [ɛstafilad] *nf* gash, slash.

est-allemand, e [ɛstalmɑ̃, -ɑ̃d] *a* East German.

estaminet [ɛstaminɛ] *nm* tavern.

estampe [ɛstɑ̃p] *nf* print, engraving.

estamper [ɛstɑ̃pe] *vt* (*monnaies etc*) to stamp; (*fam: escroquer*) to swindle.

estampille [ɛstɑ̃pij] *nf* stamp.

est-ce que [ɛskə] *ad*: **~ c'est cher/c'était bon?** is it expensive/was it good?; **quand est-ce qu'il part?** when does he leave?, when is he leaving?; **où est-ce qu'il va?** where's he going?; **qui est-ce qui le connaît/a fait ça?** who knows him/did that?; *voir aussi* **que**.

este [ɛst(ə)] *a* Estonian ♦ *nm/f*: **E~** Estonian.

esthète [ɛstɛt] *nm/f* aesthete.

esthéticienne [ɛstetisjɛn] *nf* beautician.

esthétique [ɛstetik] *a* (*sens, jugement*) aesthetic; (*beau*) attractive, aesthetically pleasing ♦ *nf* aesthetics *sg*; **l'~ industrielle** industrial design.

esthétiquement [ɛstetikmɑ̃] *ad* aesthetically.

estimable [ɛstimabl(ə)] *a* respected.

estimatif, ive [ɛstimatif, -iv] *a* estimated.

estimation [ɛstimasjɔ̃] *nf* valuation; assessment; **d'après mes ~s** according to my calculations.

estime [ɛstim] *nf* esteem, regard; **avoir de l'~ pour qn** to think highly of sb.

estimer [ɛstime] *vt* (*respecter*) to esteem, hold in high regard; (*expertiser*) to value; (*évaluer*) to assess, estimate; (*penser*): **~ que/être** to consider that/o.s. to be; **s'~ satisfait/heureux** to feel satisfied/happy; **j'estime la distance à 10 km** I reckon the distance to be 10 km.

estival, e, aux [ɛstival, -o] *a* summer *cpd*; **station ~e** (summer) holiday resort.

estivant, e [ɛstivɑ̃, -ɑ̃t] *nm/f* (summer) holiday-maker.

estoc [ɛstɔk] *nm*: **frapper d'~ et de taille** to cut and thrust.

estocade [ɛstɔkad] *nf* death-blow.

estomac [ɛstɔma] *nm* stomach; **avoir mal à l'~** to have stomach ache; **avoir l'~ creux** to have an empty stomach.

estomaqué, e [ɛstɔmake] *a* flabbergasted.

estompe [ɛstɔ̃p] *nf* stump; (*dessin*) stumpdrawing.

estompé, e [ɛstɔ̃pe] *a* blurred.

estomper [ɛstɔ̃pe] *vt* (*ART*) to shade off; (*fig*) to blur, dim; **s'~** *vi* (*sentiments*) to soften; (*contour*) to become blurred.

Estonie [ɛstɔni] *nf:* **l'~** Estonia.

estonien, ne [ɛstɔnjɛ̃, -ɛn] *a* Estonian.

estrade [ɛstrad] *nf* platform, rostrum.

estragon [ɛstragɔ̃] *nm* tarragon.

estropié, e [ɛstrɔpje] *nm/f* cripple.

estropier [ɛstrɔpje] *vt* to cripple, maim; *(fig)* to twist, distort.

estuaire [ɛstɥɛr] *nm* estuary.

estudiantin, e [ɛstydjɑ̃tɛ̃, -in] *a* student *cpd*.

esturgeon [ɛstyrʒɔ̃] *nm* sturgeon.

et [e] *cj* and; **~ lui?** what about him?; **~ alors?, ~ (puis) après?** so what?; *(ensuite)* and then?

ét. *abr* = **étage.**

ETA [eta] *sigle m (POL)* ETA.

étable [etabl(ə)] *nf* cowshed.

établi, e [etabli] *a* established ♦ *nm* (work)bench.

établir [etablir] *vt (papiers d'identité, facture)* to make out; *(liste, programme)* to draw up; *(gouvernement, artisan etc: aider à s'installer)* to set up, establish; *(entreprise, atelier, camp)* to set up; *(réputation, usage, fait, culpabilité, relations)* to establish; *(SPORT: record)* to set; **s'~** *vi (se faire: entente etc)* to be established; **s'~ (à son compte)** to set up in business; **s'~ à/près de** to settle in/near.

établissement [etablismɑ̃] *nm* making out; drawing up; setting up, establishing; *(entreprise, institution)* establishment; **~ de crédit** credit institution; **~ hospitalier** hospital complex; **~ industriel** industrial plant, factory; **~ scolaire** school, educational establishment.

étage [etaʒ] *nm (d'immeuble)* storey *(Brit)*, story *(US)*, floor; *(de fusée)* stage; *(GÉO: de culture, végétation)* level; **au 2ème ~** on the 2nd *(Brit)* ou 3rd *(US)* floor; **à l'~** upstairs; **maison à deux ~s** two-storey *ou* -story house; **de bas ~** *a* low-born; *(médiocre)* inferior.

étager [etaʒe] *vt (cultures)* to lay out in tiers; **s'~** *vi (prix)* to range; *(zones, cultures)* to lie on different levels.

étagère [etaʒɛr] *nf (rayon)* shelf; *(meuble)* shelves *pl*, set of shelves.

étai [etɛ] *nm* stay, prop.

étain [etɛ̃] *nm* tin; *(ORFÈVRERIE)* pewter *q*.

étais [etɛ] *etc vb voir* **être.**

étal [etal] *nm* stall.

étalage [etalaʒ] *nm* display; *(vitrine)* display window; **faire ~ de** to show off, parade.

étalagiste [etalaʒist(ə)] *nm/f* window-dresser.

étale [etal] *a (mer)* slack.

étalement [etalmɑ̃] *nm* spreading; *(échelonnement)* staggering.

étaler [etale] *vt (carte, nappe)* to spread (out); *(peinture, liquide)* to spread; *(échelonner: paiements, dates, vacances)* to spread, stagger; *(exposer: marchandises)* to display; *(richesses, connaissances)* to parade; **s'~** *vi (liquide)* to spread out; *(fam)* to come a cropper *(Brit)*, fall flat on one's face; **s'~ sur** *(suj: paiements etc)* to be spread over.

étalon [etalɔ̃] *nm (mesure)* standard; *(cheval)* stallion; **l'~-or** the gold standard.

étalonner [etalɔne] *vt* to calibrate.

étamer [etame] *vt (casserole)* to tin(plate); *(glace)* to silver.

étamine [etamin] *nf (BOT)* stamen; *(tissu)* butter muslin.

étanche [etɑ̃ʃ] *a (récipient; aussi fig)* watertight; *(montre, vêtement)* waterproof; **~ à l'air** airtight.

étanchéité [etɑ̃ʃeite] *nf* watertightness; airtightness.

étancher [etɑ̃ʃe] *vt (liquide)* to stop (flowing); **~ sa soif** to quench *ou* slake one's thirst.

étançon [etɑ̃sɔ̃] *nm (TECH)* prop.

étançonner [etɑ̃sɔne] *vt* to prop up.

étang [etɑ̃] *nm* pond.

étant [etɑ̃] *vb voir* **être, donné.**

étape [etap] *nf* stage; *(lieu d'arrivée)* stopping place; *(: CYCLISME)* staging point; **faire ~ à** to stop off at; **brûler les ~s** *(fig)* to cut corners.

état [eta] *nm (POL, condition)* state; *(d'un article d'occasion etc)* condition, state; *(liste)* inventory, statement; *(condition professionnelle)* profession, trade; *(: sociale)* status; **en mauvais ~** in poor condition; **en ~ (de marche)** in (working) order; **remettre en ~** to repair; **hors d'~** out of order; **être en ~/hors d'~ de faire** to be in a state/in no fit state to do; **en tout ~ de cause** in any event; **être dans tous ses ~s** to be in a state; **faire ~ de** *(alléguer)* to put forward; **en ~ d'arrestation** under arrest; **~ de grâce** *(REL)* state of grace; *(fig)* honeymoon period; **en ~ de grâce** *(fig)* inspired; **en ~ d'ivresse** under the influence of drink; **~ de choses** *(situation)* state of affairs; **~ civil** civil status; *(bureau)* registry office; **~ d'esprit** frame of mind; **~ des lieux** inventory of fixtures; **~ de santé** state of health; **~ de siège/d'urgence** state of siege/emergency; **~ de veille** *(PSYCH)* waking state; **~s d'âme** moods; **les É~s barbaresques** the Barbary States; **les É~s du Golfe** the Gulf States; **~s de service** service record *sg*.

étatique [etatik] *a* state *cpd*, State *cpd*.

étatiser [etatize] *vt* to bring under state control.

étatisme [etatism(ə)] *nm* state control.

étatiste [etatist(ə)] *a (doctrine etc)* of state control ♦ *nm/f* partisan of state control.

état-major, pl états-majors [etamaʒɔr] *nm (MIL)* staff; *(d'un parti etc)* top advisers *pl*; *(d'une entreprise)* top management.

État-providence [etaprɔvidɑ̃s] *nm* welfare state.

États-Unis [etazyni] *nmpl:* **les ~ (d'Amérique)** the United States (of America).

étau, x [eto] *nm* vice *(Brit)*, vise *(US)*.

étayer [eteje] *vt* to prop *ou* shore up; *(fig)* to back up.

et c(a)etera [ɛtsetera], **etc.** *ad* et cetera, and so on, etc.

été [ete] *pp de* **être** ♦ *nm* summer; **en ~** in summer.

éteignais [etɛɲɛ] *etc vb voir* **éteindre.**

éteignoir [etɛɲwar] *nm* (candle) snuffer; *(péj)* killjoy, wet blanket.

éteindre [etɛ̃dr(ə)] *vt (lampe, lumière, radio, chauffage)* to turn *ou* switch off; *(cigarette, incendie, bougie)* to put out, extinguish;

(*JUR: dette*) to extinguish; **s'~** *vi* to go off;
to go out; (*mourir*) to pass away.
éteint, e [etɛ̃, -ɛ̃t] *pp de* **éteindre ♦** *a* (*fig*)
lacklustre, dull; (*volcan*) extinct; **tous feux
~s** (*AUTO: rouler*) without lights.
étendard [etɑ̃daʀ] *nm* standard.
étendre [etɑ̃dʀ(ə)] *vt* (*appliquer: pâte,
liquide*) to spread; (*déployer: carte etc*) to
spread out; (*sur un fil: lessive, linge*) to hang
up *ou* out; (*bras, jambes, par terre: blessé*)
to stretch out; (*diluer*) to dilute, thin; (*fig:
agrandir*) to extend; (*fam: adversaire*) to
floor; **s'~** *vi* (*augmenter, se propager*) to
spread; (*terrain, forêt etc*): **s'~ jusqu'à/de
...** à to stretch as far as/from ... to; **s'~ (sur)**
(*s'allonger*) to stretch out (upon); (*se
coucher*) to lie down (on); (*fig: expliquer*) (*se
coucher*) to lie down (on); (*fig: expliquer*) (*se
coucher*) to elaborate *ou* enlarge (upon).
étendu, e [etɑ̃dy] *a* extensive **♦** *nf* (*d'eau, de
sable*) stretch, expanse; (*importance*) extent.
éternel, le [etɛʀnɛl] *a* eternal; **les neiges
~les** perpetual snow.
éternellement [etɛʀnɛlmɑ̃] *ad* eternally.
éterniser [etɛʀnize]: **s'~** *vi* to last for ages;
(*personne*) to stay for ages.
éternité [etɛʀnite] *nf* eternity; **il y a** *ou* **ça fait
une ~ que** it's ages since; **de toute ~** from
time immemorial.
éternuement [etɛʀnymɑ̃] *nm* sneeze.
éternuer [etɛʀnɥe] *vi* to sneeze.
êtes [ɛt] *vb voir* **être**.
étêter [etete] *vt* (*arbre*) to poll(ard); (*clou,
poisson*) to cut the head off.
éther [etɛʀ] *nm* ether.
éthéré, e [etere] *a* ethereal.
Ethiopie [etjɔpi] *nf*: **l'~** Ethiopia.
éthiopien, ne [etjɔpjɛ̃, -ɛn] *a* Ethiopian.
éthique [etik] *a* ethical **♦** *nf* ethics *sg*.
ethnie [ɛtni] *nf* ethnic group.
ethnique [ɛtnik] *a* ethnic.
ethnographe [ɛtnɔgraf] *nm/f* ethnographer.
ethnographique [ɛtnɔgrafik] *a* ethno-
graphic(al).
ethnologique [ɛtnɔlɔʒik] *a* ethnological.
ethnologue [ɛtnɔlɔg] *nm/f* ethnologist.
éthylique [etilik] *a* alcoholic.
éthylisme [etilism(ə)] *nm* alcoholism.
étiage [etjaʒ] *nm* low water.
étiez [etje] *vb voir* **être**.
étincelant, e [etɛ̃slɑ̃, -ɑ̃t] *a* sparkling.
étinceler [etɛ̃sle] *vi* to sparkle.
étincelle [etɛ̃sɛl] *nf* spark.
étioler [etjɔle]: **s'~** *vi* to wilt.
étions [etjɔ̃] *vb voir* **être**.
étique [etik] *a* skinny, bony.
étiqueter [etikte] *vt* to label.
étiquette [etikɛt] *vb voir* **étiqueter ♦** *nf* label;
(*protocole*): **l'~** etiquette.
étirer [etire] *vt* to stretch; (*ressort*) to stretch
out; **s'~** *vi* (*personne*) to stretch; (*convoi,
route*): **s'~ sur** to stretch out over.
étoffe [etɔf] *nf* material, fabric; **avoir l'~ d'un
chef** *etc* to be cut out to be a leader *etc*;
avoir de l'~ to be a forceful personality.
étoffer [etɔfe] *vt*, **s'~** *vi* to fill out.
étoile [etwal] *nf* star **♦** *a*: **danseuse ou
danceur ~** leading dancer; **la bonne/
mauvaise ~ de qn** sb's lucky/unlucky star; **à
la belle ~** (out) in the open; **~ filante** shoot-

ing star; **~ de mer** starfish; **~ polaire** pole
star.
étoilé, e [etwale] *a* starry.
étole [etɔl] *nf* stole.
étonnant, e [etɔnɑ̃, -ɑ̃t] *a* surprising.
étonné, e [etɔne] *a* surprised.
étonnement [etɔnmɑ̃] *nm* surprise; **à mon
grand ~ ...** to my great surprise *ou* amazement ....
étonner [etɔne] *vt* to surprise; **s'~ que/de** to
be surprised that/at; **cela m'étonnerait (que)**
(*j'en doute*) I'd be (very) surprised (if).
étouffant, e [etufɑ̃, -ɑ̃t] *a* stifling.
étouffé, e [etufe] *a* (*asphyxié*) suffocated;
(*assourdi: cris, rires*) smothered **♦** *ad*: **à l'~e**
(*CULIN: poisson, légumes*) steamed; (*:
viande*) braised.
étouffement [etufmɑ̃] *nm* suffocation.
étouffer [etufe] *vt* to suffocate; (*bruit*) to
muffle; (*scandale*) to hush up **♦** *vi* to
suffocate; (*avoir trop chaud; aussi fig*) to feel
stifled; **s'~** *vi* (*en mangeant etc*) to choke.
étouffoir [etufwar] *nm* (*MUS*) damper.
étourderie [eturdəri] *nf* heedlessness *q*;
thoughtless blunder; **faute d'~** careless mistake.
étourdi, e [eturdi] *a* (*distrait*) scatterbrained,
heedless.
étourdir [eturdir] *vt* (*assommer*) to stun,
daze; (*griser*) to make dizzy *ou* giddy.
étourdissant, e [eturdisɑ̃, -ɑ̃t] *a* staggering.
étourdissement [eturdismɑ̃] *nm* dizzy spell.
étourneau, x [eturno] *nm* starling.
étrange [etrɑ̃ʒ] *a* strange.
étrangement [etrɑ̃ʒmɑ̃] *ad* strangely.
étranger, ère [etrɑ̃ʒe, -ɛr] *a* foreign; (*pas de
la famille, non familier*) strange **♦** *nm/f*
foreigner; stranger **♦** *nm*: **l'~** foreign countries; **à l'~** abroad; **de l'~** from abroad; **~ à**
(*mal connu*) unfamiliar to; (*sans rapport*)
irrelevant to.
étrangeté [etrɑ̃ʒte] *nf* strangeness.
étranglé, e [etrɑ̃gle] *a*: **d'une voix ~e** in a
strangled voice.
étranglement [etrɑ̃gləmɑ̃] *nm* (*d'une vallée
etc*) constriction, narrow passage.
étrangler [etrɑ̃gle] *vt* to strangle; (*fig: presse,
libertés*) to stifle; **s'~** *vi* (*en mangeant etc*)
to choke; (*se resserrer*) to make a bottleneck.
étrave [etrav] *nf* stem.
être [ɛtʀ(ə)] *nm* being **♦** *vb avec attribut, vi* to
be **♦** *vb auxiliaire* to have (*ou parfois be*); **il
est instituteur** he is a teacher; **~ à qn**
(*appartenir*) to be sb's, to belong to sb; **c'est
à moi/eux** it is *ou* it's mine/theirs; **c'est à lui
de le faire** it's up to him to do it; **il est à
Paris/au salon** he is *ou* he's in Paris/the
sitting room; **~ de** (*provenance, origine*) to
be from; (*appartenance*) to belong to; **~ de
Genève/de la même famille** to come from
Geneva/belong to the same family; **nous
sommes le 10 janvier** it's the 10th of January
(today); **il est 10 heures, c'est 10 heures** it
is *ou* it's 10 o'clock; **c'est à réparer** it needs
repairing; **c'est à essayer** it should be tried;
il est à espérer que it is to be hoped that; **~
fait par** to be made by; **il a été promu** he
has been promoted; **~ humain** human being;

voir aussi **est-ce que, n'est-ce pas, c'est-à-dire, ce.**

étreindre [etRɛ̃dR(ə)] *vt* to clutch, grip; *(amoureusement, amicalement)* to embrace; **s'~** to embrace.

étreinte [etRɛ̃t] *nf* clutch, grip; embrace; **resserrer son ~ autour de** *(fig)* to tighten one's grip on *ou* around.

étrenner [etRene] *vt* to use (*ou* wear) for the first time.

étrennes [etRɛn] *nfpl* *(cadeaux)* New Year's present; *(gratifications)* ≈ Christmas box *sg*, ≈ Christmas bonus.

étrier [etRije] *nm* stirrup.

étriller [etRije] *vt* *(cheval)* to curry; *(fam: battre)* to slaughter *(fig)*.

étriper [etRipe] *vt* to gut; *(fam)*: **~ qn** to tear sb's guts out.

étriqué, e [etRike] *a* skimpy.

étroit, e [etRwa, -wat] *a* narrow; *(vêtement)* tight; *(fig: serré)* close, tight; **à l'~** cramped; **~ d'esprit** narrow-minded.

étroitement [etRwatmɑ̃] *ad* closely.

étroitesse [etRwates] *nf* narrowness; **~ d'esprit** narrow-mindedness.

Étrurie [etRyRi] *nf*: **l'~** Etruria.

étrusque [etRysk(ə)] *a* Etruscan.

étude [etyd] *nf* studying; *(ouvrage, rapport, MUS)* study; *(de notaire: bureau)* office; *(: charge)* practice; *(SCOL: salle de travail)* study room; **~s** *nfpl (SCOL)* studies; **être à l'~** *(projet etc)* to be under consideration; **faire des ~s (de droit/médecine)** to study (law/medicine); **~s secondaires/supérieures** secondary/higher education; **~ de cas** case study; **~ de faisabilité** feasibility study; **~ de marché** *(ÉCON)* market research.

étudiant, e [etydjɑ̃, -ɑ̃t] *a, nm/f* student.

étudié, e [etydje] *a (démarche)* studied; *(système)* carefully designed; *(prix)* keen.

étudier [etydje] *vt, vi* to study.

étui [etɥi] *nm* case.

étuve [etyv] *nf* steamroom; *(appareil)* sterilizer.

étuvée [etyve] *nf*: **à l'~** *ad* braised.

étymologie [etimɔlɔʒi] *nf* etymology.

étymologique [etimɔlɔʒik] *a* etymological.

eu, eue [y] *pp de* **avoir.**

EU(A) *sigle mpl (= États-Unis (d'Amérique))* US(A).

eucalyptus [økaliptys] *nm* eucalyptus.

Eucharistie [økaRisti] *nf*: **l'~** the Eucharist, the Lord's Supper.

eugénique [øʒenik] *a* eugenic ♦ *nf* eugenics *sg*.

eugénisme [øʒenism(ə)] *nm* eugenics *sg*.

euh [ø] *excl* er.

eunuque [ønyk] *nm* eunuch.

euphémique [øfemik] *a* euphemistic.

euphémisme [øfemism(ə)] *nm* euphemism.

euphonie [øfɔni] *nf* euphony.

euphorbe [øfɔRb(ə)] *nf (BOT)* spurge.

euphorie [øfɔRi] *nf* euphoria.

euphorique [øfɔRik] *a* euphoric.

euphorisant, e [øfɔRizɑ̃, -ɑ̃t] *a* exhilarating.

Euphrate [øfRat] *nm*: **l'~** the Euphrates *sg*.

eurafricain, e [øRafRikɛ̃, -ɛn] *a* Eurafrican.

eurasiatique [øRazjatik] *a* Eurasiatic.

Eurasie [øRazi] *nf*: **l'~** Eurasia.

eurasien, ne [øRazjɛ̃, -ɛn] *a* Eurasian.

EURATOM [øRatɔm] *sigle f* Euratom.

eurent [yR(ə)] *vb voir* **avoir.**

eurocrate [øRɔkRat] *nm/f (péj)* Eurocrat.

eurodevise [øRɔdəviz] *nf* Eurocurrency.

euromonnaie [øRɔmɔnɛ] *nf* Eurocurrency.

Europe [øRɔp] *nf*: **l'~** Europe; **l'~ centrale** Central Europe; **l'~ verte** European agriculture.

européaniser [øRɔpeanize] *vt* to Europeanize.

européen, ne [øRɔpeɛ̃, -ɛn] *a* European ♦ *nm/f*: **E~, ne** European.

eus [y] *etc vb voir* **avoir.**

euthanasie [øtanazi] *nf* euthanasia.

eux [ø] *pronom (sujet)* they; *(objet)* them; **~, ils ont fait ...** THEY did ....

EV *abr (= en ville)* used on mail to be delivered by hand, courier etc within the same town.

évacuation [evakɥasjɔ̃] *nf* evacuation.

évacuer [evakɥe] *vt (salle, région)* to evacuate, clear; *(occupants, population)* to evacuate; *(toxine etc)* to evacuate, discharge.

évadé, e [evade] *a* escaped ♦ *nm/f* escapee.

évader [evade]: **s'~** *vi* to escape.

évaluation [evalɥasjɔ̃] *nf* assessment, evaluation.

évaluer [evalɥe] *vt* to assess, evaluate.

évanescent, e [evanesɑ̃, -ɑ̃t] *a* evanescent.

évangélique [evɑ̃ʒelik] *a* evangelical.

évangéliser [evɑ̃ʒelize] *vt* to evangelize.

évangéliste [evɑ̃ʒelist(ə)] *nm* evangelist.

évangile [evɑ̃ʒil] *nm* gospel; *(texte de la Bible)*: **É~** Gospel; **ce n'est pas l'É~** *(fig)* it's not gospel.

évanoui, e [evanwi] *a* in a faint; **tomber ~** to faint.

évanouir [evanwiR]: **s'~** *vi* to faint, pass out; *(disparaître)* to vanish, disappear.

évanouissement [evanwismɑ̃] *nm (syncope)* fainting fit; *(MÉD)* loss of consciousness.

évaporation [evapɔRasjɔ̃] *nf* evaporation.

évaporé, e [evapɔRe] *a* giddy, scatterbrained.

évaporer [evapɔRe]: **s'~** *vi* to evaporate.

évasé, e [evaze] *a (jupe etc)* flared.

évaser [evaze] *vt (tuyau)* to widen, open out; *(jupe, pantalon)* to flare; **s'~** *vi* to widen, open out.

évasif, ive [evazif, -iv] *a* evasive.

évasion [evazjɔ̃] *nf* escape; **littérature d'~** escapist literature; **~ des capitaux** *(ÉCON)* flight of capital; **~ fiscale** tax avoidance.

évasivement [evazivmɑ̃] *ad* evasively.

évêché [eveʃe] *nm (fonction)* bishopric; *(palais)* bishop's palace.

éveil [evɛj] *nm* awakening; **être en ~** to be alert; **mettre qn en ~, donner l'~ à qn** to arouse sb's suspicions; **activités d'~** early-learning activities.

éveillé, e [eveje] *a* awake; *(vif)* alert, sharp.

éveiller [eveje] *vt* to (a)waken; **s'~** *vi* to (a)waken; *(fig)* to be aroused.

événement [evɛnmɑ̃] *nm* event.

éventail [evɑ̃taj] *nm* fan; *(choix)* range; **en ~** fanned out; fan-shaped.

éventaire [evɑ̃tɛR] *nm* stall, stand.

éventé, e [evɑ̃te] *a (parfum, vin)* stale.

éventer [evɑ̃te] *vt (secret, complot)* to uncover; *(avec un éventail)* to fan; **s'~** *vi* *(parfum, vin)* to go stale.

éventrer [evɑ̃tʀe] *vt* to disembowel; *(fig)* to tear *ou* rip open.

éventualité [evɑ̃tɥalite] *nf* eventuality; possibility; **dans l'~ de** in the event of; **parer à toute ~** to guard against all eventualities.

éventuel, le [evɑ̃tɥɛl] *a* possible.

éventuellement [evɑ̃tɥɛlmɑ̃] *ad* possibly.

évêque [evɛk] *nm* bishop.

Everest [evʀɛst] *nm*: **(mont) ~** (Mount) Everest.

évertuer [evɛʀtɥe]: **s'~** *vi*: **s'~ à faire** to try very hard to do.

éviction [eviksjɔ̃] *nf* ousting, supplanting; *(de locataire)* eviction.

évidemment [evidamɑ̃] *ad* obviously.

évidence [evidɑ̃s] *nf* obviousness; *(fait)* obvious fact; **se rendre à l'~** to bow before the evidence; **nier l'~** to deny the evidence; **à l'~** evidently; **de toute ~** quite obviously *ou* evidently; **en ~** conspicuous; **mettre en ~** to bring to the fore.

évident, e [evidɑ̃, -ɑ̃t] *a* obvious, evident; **ce n'est pas ~** *(cela pose des problèmes)* it's not (all that) straightforward, it's not as simple as all that.

évider [evide] *vt* to scoop out.

évier [evje] *nm* (kitchen) sink.

évincement [evɛ̃smɑ̃] *nm* ousting.

évincer [evɛ̃se] *vt* to oust, supplant.

évitable [evitabl(ə)] *a* avoidable.

évitement [evitmɑ̃] *nm*: **place d'~** *(AUTO)* passing place.

éviter [evite] *vt* to avoid; **~ de faire/que qch ne se passe** to avoid doing/sth happening; **~ qch à qn** to spare sb sth.

évocateur, trice [evɔkatœʀ, -tʀis] *a* evocative, suggestive.

évocation [evɔkasjɔ̃] *nf* evocation.

évolué, e [evɔlɥe] *a* advanced; *(personne)* broad-minded.

évoluer [evɔlɥe] *vi* *(enfant, maladie)* to develop; *(situation, moralement)* to evolve, develop; *(aller et venir: danseur etc)* to move about, circle.

évolutif, ive [evɔlytif, -iv] *a* evolving.

évolution [evɔlysjɔ̃] *nf* development; evolution; **~s** *nfpl* movements.

évoquer [evɔke] *vt* to call to mind, evoke; *(mentionner)* to mention.

ex. *abr* (= *exemple*) ex.

ex- [ɛks] *préfixe* ex-.

exacerber [ɛgzasɛʀbe] *vt* to exacerbate.

exact, e [ɛgzakt] *a* *(précis)* exact, accurate, precise; *(correct)* correct; *(ponctuel)* punctual; **l'heure ~e** the right *ou* exact time.

exactement [ɛgzaktəmɑ̃] *ad* exactly, accurately, precisely; correctly; *(c'est cela même)* exactly.

exactions [ɛgzaksjɔ̃] *nfpl* exactions.

exactitude [ɛgzaktityd] *nf* exactitude, accurateness, precision.

ex aequo [ɛgzeko] *a* equally placed; **classé 1er ~** placed equal first.

exagération [ɛgzaʒeʀasjɔ̃] *nf* exaggeration.

exagéré, e [ɛgzaʒeʀe] *a* *(prix etc)* excessive.

exagérément [ɛgzaʒeʀemɑ̃] *ad* excessively.

exagérer [ɛgzaʒeʀe] *vt* to exaggerate ♦ *vi* *(abuser)* to go too far; *(déformer les bornes)*

to overstep the mark; *(déformer les faits)* to exaggerate; **s'~ qch** to exaggerate sth.

exaltation [ɛgzaltɑsjɔ̃] *nf* exaltation.

exalté, e [ɛgzalte] *a* (over)excited ♦ *nm/f* *(péj)* fanatic.

exalter [ɛgzalte] *vt* *(enthousiasmer)* to excite, elate; *(glorifier)* to exalt.

examen [ɛgzamɛ̃] *nm* examination; *(SCOL)* exam, examination; **à l'~** *(dossier, projet)* under consideration; *(COMM)* on approval; **~ blanc** mock exam(ination); **~ de la vue** sight test.

examinateur, trice [ɛgzaminatœʀ, -tʀis] *nm/f* examiner.

examiner [ɛgzamine] *vt* to examine.

exaspération [ɛgzaspeʀasjɔ̃] *nf* exasperation.

exaspéré, e [ɛgzaspeʀe] *a* exasperated.

exaspérer [ɛgzaspeʀe] *vt* to exasperate; *(aggraver)* to exacerbate.

exaucer [ɛgzose] *vt* *(vœu)* to grant, fulfil; **~ qn** to grant sb's wishes.

excavateur [ɛkskavatœʀ] *nm* excavator, mechanical digger.

excavation [ɛkskavasjɔ̃] *nf* excavation.

excavatrice [ɛkskavatʀis] *nf* = **excavateur**.

excédent [ɛksedɑ̃] *nm* surplus; **en ~** surplus; **payer 600 F d'~** *(de bagages)* to pay 600 francs excess luggage; **~ de bagages** excess luggage; **~ commercial** trade surplus.

excédentaire [ɛksedɑ̃tɛʀ] *a* surplus, excess.

excéder [ɛksede] *vt* *(dépasser)* to exceed; *(agacer)* to exasperate; **excédé de fatigue** exhausted; **excédé de travail** worn out with work.

excellence [ɛkselɑ̃s] *nf* excellence; *(titre)* Excellency; **par ~** par excellence.

excellent, e [ɛkselɑ̃, -ɑ̃t] *a* excellent.

exceller [ɛksele] *vi*: **~ (dans)** to excel (in).

excentricité [ɛksɑ̃tʀisite] *nf* eccentricity.

excentrique [ɛksɑ̃tʀik] *a* eccentric; *(quartier)* outlying ♦ *nm/f* eccentric.

excepté, e [ɛksɛpte] *a, prép*: **les élèves ~s, ~ les élèves** except for *ou* apart from the pupils; **~ si/quand** except if/when; **~ que** except that.

excepter [ɛksɛpte] *vt* to except.

exception [ɛksɛpsjɔ̃] *nf* exception; **faire ~** to be an exception; **faire une ~** to make an exception; **sans ~** without exception; **à l'~ de** except for, with the exception of; **d'~** *(mesure, loi)* special, exceptional.

exceptionnel, le [ɛksɛpsjɔnɛl] *a* exceptional; *(prix)* special.

exceptionnellement [ɛksɛpsjɔnɛlmɑ̃] *ad* exceptionally; *(par exception)* by way of an exception, on this occasion.

excès [ɛksɛ] *nm* surplus ♦ *nmpl* excesses; **à l'~** *(méticuleux, généreux)* to excess; **avec ~** to excess; **sans ~** in moderation; **tomber dans l'~ inverse** to go to the opposite extreme; **~ de langage** immoderate language; **~ de pouvoir** abuse of power; **~ de vitesse** speeding *q*, exceeding the speed limit; **~ de zèle** overzealousness *q*.

excessif, ive [ɛksesif, -iv] *a* excessive.

exciper [ɛksipe]: **~ de** *vt* to plead.

excipient [ɛksipjɑ̃] *nm* *(MÉD)* inert base, excipient.

exciser [ɛksize] *vt* *(MÉD)* to excise.

excitant, e [ɛksitɑ̃, -ɑ̃t] *a* exciting ♦ *nm* stimulant.

excitation [ɛksitasjɔ̃] *nf* (*état*) excitement.

excité, e [ɛksite] *a* excited.

exciter [ɛksite] *vt* to excite; (*suj: café etc*) to stimulate; **s'~** *vi* to get excited; **~ qn à** (*révolte etc*) to incite sb to.

exclamation [ɛksklamasjɔ̃] *nf* exclamation.

exclamer [ɛksklame]: **s'~** *vi* to exclaim.

exclu, e [ɛkskly] *pp de* **exclure** ♦ *a*: **il est/ n'est pas ~ que ...** it's out of the question/ not impossible that ...; **ce n'est pas exclu** it's not impossible, I don't rule that out.

exclure [ɛksklyʀ] *vt* (*faire sortir*) to expel; (*ne pas compter*) to exclude, leave out; (*rendre impossible*) to exclude, rule out.

exclusif, ive [ɛksklyzif, -iv] *a* exclusive; **avec la mission exclusive/ dans le but ~ de ...** with the sole mission/aim of ...; **agent ~** sole agent.

exclusion [ɛksklyzjɔ̃] *nf* expulsion; **à l'~ de** with the exclusion *ou* exception of.

exclusivement [ɛksklyzivmɑ̃] *ad* exclusively.

exclusivité [ɛksklyzivite] *nf* exclusiveness; (*COMM*) exclusive rights *pl*; **film passant en ~ à** film showing only at.

excommunier [ɛkskɔmynje] *vt* to excommunicate.

excréments [ɛkskʀemɑ̃] *nmpl* excrement *sg*, faeces.

excroissance [ɛkskʀwasɑ̃s] *nf* excrescence, outgrowth.

excursion [ɛkskyʀsjɔ̃] *nf* (*en autocar*) excursion, trip; (*à pied*) walk, hike; **faire une ~** to go on an excursion *ou* a trip; to go on a walk *ou* hike.

excursionniste [ɛkskyʀsjɔnist(ə)] *nm/f* tripper; hiker.

excuse [ɛkskyz] *nf* excuse; **~s** *nfpl* apology *sg*, apologies; **faire des ~s** to apologize; **faire ses ~s** to offer one's apologies; **mot d'~** (*SCOL*) note from one's parent(s) (*to explain absence etc*); **lettre d'~s** letter of apology.

excuser [ɛkskyze] *vt* to excuse; **~ qn de qch** (*dispenser*) to excuse sb from sth; **s'~ (de)** to apologize (for); **"excusez-moi"** "I'm sorry"; (*pour attirer l'attention*) "excuse me"; **se faire ~** to ask to be excused.

exécrable [ɛgzekʀabl(ə)] *a* atrocious.

exécrer [ɛgzekʀe] *vt* to loathe, abhor.

exécutant, e [ɛgzekytɑ̃, -ɑ̃t] *nm/f* performer.

exécuter [ɛgzekyte] *vt* (*prisonnier*) to execute; (*tâche etc*) to execute, carry out; (*MUS: jouer*) to perform, execute; (*INFORM*) to run; **s'~** *vi* to comply.

exécuteur, trice [ɛgzekytœʀ, -tʀis] *nm/f* (*testamentaire*) executor ♦ *nm* (*bourreau*) executioner.

exécutif, ive [ɛgzekytif, -iv] *a, nm* (*POL*) executive.

exécution [ɛgzekysjɔ̃] *nf* execution; carrying out; **mettre à ~** to carry out.

exécutoire [ɛgzekytwaʀ] *a* (*JUR*) (legally) binding.

exégèse [ɛgzeʒɛz] *nf* exegesis.

exemplaire [ɛgzɑ̃plɛʀ] *a* exemplary ♦ *nm* copy.

exemple [ɛgzɑ̃pl(ə)] *nm* example; **par ~** for instance, for example; (*valeur intensive*)

really!; **sans ~** (*bêtise, gourmandise etc*) unparalleled; **donner l'~** to set an example; **prendre ~ sur** to take as a model; **à l'~ de** just like; **pour l'~** (*punir*) as an example.

exempt, e [ɛgzɑ̃, -ɑ̃t] *a*: **~ de** (*dispensé de*) exempt from; (*sans*) free from; **~ de taxes** tax-free.

exempter [ɛgzɑ̃te] *vt*: **~ de** to exempt from.

exercé, e [ɛgzɛʀse] *a* trained.

exercer [ɛgzɛʀse] *vt* (*pratiquer*) to exercise, practise; (*faire usage de: prérogative*) to exercise; (*effectuer: influence, contrôle, pression*) to exert; (*former*) to exercise, train ♦ *vi* (*médecin*) to be in practice; **s'~** (*sportif, musicien*) to practise; (*se faire sentir: pression etc*): **s'~ (sur ou contre)** to be exerted (on); **s'~ à faire qch** to train o.s. to do sth.

exercice [ɛgzɛʀsis] *nm* practice; exercising; (*tâche, travail*) exercise; (*COMM, ADMIN: période*) accounting period; **l'~** (*sportive etc*) exercise; (*MIL*) drill; **en ~** (*juge*) in office; (*médecin*) practising; **dans l'~ de ses fonctions** in the discharge of his duties; **~s d'assouplissement** limbering-up (exercises).

exergue [ɛgzɛʀg(ə)] *nm*: **mettre en ~** (*inscription*) to inscribe; **porter en ~** to be inscribed with.

exhalaison [ɛgzalɛzɔ̃] *nf* exhalation.

exhaler [ɛgzale] *vt* (*parfum*) to exhale; (*souffle, son, soupir*) to utter, breathe; **s'~** *vi* to rise (up).

exhausser [ɛgzose] *vt* to raise (up).

exhaustif, ive [ɛgzostif, -iv] *a* exhaustive.

exhiber [ɛgzibe] *vt* (*montrer: papiers, certificat*) to present, produce; (*péj*) to display, flaunt; **s'~** (*personne*) to parade; (*suj: exhibitionniste*) to expose o.s.

exhibitionnisme [ɛgzibisjɔnism(ə)] *nm* exhibitionism.

exhibitionniste [ɛgzibisjɔnist(ə)] *nm/f* exhibitionist.

exhorter [ɛgzɔʀte] *vt*: **~ qn à faire** to urge sb to do.

exhumer [ɛgzyme] *vt* to exhume.

exigeant, e [ɛgziʒɑ̃, -ɑ̃t] *a* demanding; (*péj*) hard to please.

exigence [ɛgziʒɑ̃s] *nf* demand, requirement.

exiger [ɛgziʒe] *vt* to demand, require.

exigible [ɛgziʒibl(ə)] *a* (*COMM, JUR*) payable.

exigu, ë [ɛgzigy] *a* cramped, tiny.

exil [ɛgzil] *nm* exile; **en ~** in exile.

exilé, e [ɛgzile] *nm/f* exile.

exiler [ɛgzile] *vt* to exile; **s'~** to go into exile.

existant, e [ɛgzistɑ̃, -ɑ̃t] *a* (*actuel, présent*) existing.

existence [ɛgzistɑ̃s] *nf* existence; **dans l'~** in life.

existentialisme [ɛgzistɑ̃sjalism(ə)] *nm* existentialism.

existentiel, le [ɛgzistɑ̃sjɛl] *a* existential.

exister [ɛgziste] *vi* to exist; **il existe un/des** there is a/are (some).

exode [ɛgzɔd] *nm* exodus.

exonération [ɛgzɔneʀasjɔ̃] *nf* exemption.

exonéré, e [ɛgzɔneʀe] *a*: **~ de TVA** zero-rated (for VAT).

exonérer [ɛgzɔneʀe] *vt*: **~ de** to exempt from.

exorbitant, e [ɛgzɔʀbitɑ̃, -ɑ̃t] *a* exorbitant.

exorbité, e [ɛgzɔʀbite] *a*: **yeux ~s** bulging eyes.

exorciser [ɛgzɔʀsize] *vt* to exorcize.

exorde [ɛgzɔʀd(ə)] *nm* introduction.

exotique [ɛgzɔtik] *a* exotic.

exotisme [ɛgzɔtism(ə)] *nm* exoticism.

expansif, ive [ɛkspɑ̃sif, -iv] *a* expansive, communicative.

expansion [ɛkspɑ̃sjɔ̃] *nf* expansion.

expansionniste [ɛkspɑ̃sjɔnist(ə)] *a* expansionist.

expatrié, e [ɛkspatʀije] *nm/f* expatriate.

expatrier [ɛkspatʀije] *vt* (*argent*) to take *ou* send out of the country; **s'~** to leave one's country.

expectative [ɛkspɛktativ] *nf*: **être dans l'~** to be waiting to see.

expectorant, e [ɛkspɛktɔʀɑ̃, -ɑ̃t] *a*: **sirop ~** expectorant (syrup).

expédient [ɛkspedjɑ̃] *nm* (*parfois péj*) expedient; **vivre d'~s** to live by one's wits.

expédier [ɛkspedje] *vt* (*lettre, paquet*) to send; (*troupes, renfort*) to dispatch; (*péj: travail etc*) to dispose of, dispatch.

expéditeur, trice [ɛkspeditœʀ, -tʀis] *nm/f* (*POSTES*) sender.

expéditif, ive [ɛkspeditif, -iv] *a* quick, expeditious.

expédition [ɛkspedisjɔ̃] *nf* sending; (*scientifique, sportive, MIL*) expedition; **~ punitive** punitive raid.

expéditionnaire [ɛkspedisjɔnɛʀ] *a*: **corps ~** (*MIL*) task force.

expérience [ɛkspeʀjɑ̃s] *nf* (*de la vie, des choses*) experience; (*scientifique*) experiment; **avoir de l'~** to have experience, be experienced; **avoir l'~ de** to have experience of; **faire l'~ de qch** to experience sth; **~ de chimie/d'électricité** chemical/electrical experiment.

expérimental, e, aux [ɛkspeʀimɑ̃tal, -o] *a* experimental.

expérimenté, e [ɛkspeʀimɑ̃te] *a* experienced.

expérimenter [ɛkspeʀimɑ̃te] *vt* (*machine, technique*) to test out, experiment with.

expert, e [ɛkspɛʀ, -ɛʀt(ə)] *a*: **~ en expert in** ♦ *nm* (*spécialiste*) expert; **~ en assurances** insurance valuer.

expert-comptable, *pl* **experts-comptables** [ɛkspɛʀkɔ̃tabl(ə)] *nm* ≈ chartered (*Brit*) *ou* certified public (*US*) accountant.

expertise [ɛkspɛʀtiz] *nf* valuation; assessment; valuer's (*ou* assessor's) report; (*JUR*) (forensic) examination.

expertiser [ɛkspɛʀtize] *vt* (*objet de valeur*) to value; (*voiture accidentée etc*) to assess damage to.

expier [ɛkspje] *vt* to expiate, atone for.

expiration [ɛkspiʀasjɔ̃] *nf* expiry (*Brit*), expiration; breathing out *q*.

expirer [ɛkspiʀe] *vi* (*prendre fin, littéraire: mourir*) to expire; (*respirer*) to breathe out.

explétif, ive [ɛkspletif, -iv] *a* (*LING*) expletive.

explicable [ɛksplikabl(ə)] *a*: **pas ~** inexplicable.

explicatif, ive [ɛksplikatif, -iv] *a* (*mot, texte, note*) explanatory.

explication [ɛksplikasjɔ̃] *nf* explanation; (*discussion*) discussion; **~ de texte** (*SCOL*)

critical analysis (of a text).

explicite [ɛksplisit] *a* explicit.

explicitement [ɛksplisitmɑ̃] *ad* explicitly.

expliciter [ɛksplisite] *vt* to make explicit.

expliquer [ɛksplike] *vt* to explain; **~ (à qn) comment/que** to point out *ou* explain (to sb) how/that; **s'~** (*se faire comprendre: personne*) to explain o.s.; (*discuter*) to discuss things; (*se disputer*) to have it out; (*comprendre*): **je m'explique son retard/ absence** I understand his lateness/absence; **son erreur s'explique** one can understand his mistake.

exploit [ɛksplwa] *nm* exploit, feat.

exploitable [ɛksplwatabl(ə)] *a* (*gisement etc*) that can be exploited; **~ par une machine** machine-readable.

exploitant [ɛksplwatɑ̃] *nm* farmer.

exploitation [ɛksplwatasjɔ̃] *nf* exploitation; running; (*entreprise*): **~ agricole** farming concern.

exploiter [ɛksplwate] *vt* to exploit; (*entreprise, ferme*) to run, operate.

exploiteur, euse [ɛksplwatœʀ, -øz] *nm/f* (*péj*) exploiter.

explorateur, trice [ɛksplɔʀatœʀ, -tʀis] *nm/f* explorer.

exploration [ɛksplɔʀasjɔ̃] *nf* exploration.

explorer [ɛksplɔʀe] *vt* to explore.

exploser [ɛksploze] *vi* to explode, blow up; (*engin explosif*) to go off; (*fig: joie, colère*) to burst out, explode; (: *personne: de colère*) to explode, flare up; **faire ~** (*bombe*) to explode, detonate; (*bâtiment, véhicule*) to blow up.

explosif, ive [ɛksplozif, -iv] *a, nm* explosive.

explosion [ɛksplozjɔ̃] *nf* explosion; **~ de joie/ colère** outburst of joy/rage; **~ démographique** population explosion.

exponentiel, le [ɛkspɔnɑ̃sjɛl] *a* exponential.

exportateur, trice [ɛkspɔʀtatœʀ, -tʀis] *a* exporting ♦ *nm* exporter.

exportation [ɛkspɔʀtasjɔ̃] *nf* export.

exporter [ɛkspɔʀte] *vt* to export.

exposant [ɛkspozɑ̃] *nm* exhibitor; (*MATH*) exponent.

exposé, e [ɛkspoze] *nm* (*écrit*) exposé; (*oral*) talk ♦ *a*: **~ au sud** facing south, with a southern aspect; **bien ~** well situated; **très ~** very exposed.

exposer [ɛkspoze] *vt* (*montrer: marchandise*) to display; (: *peinture*) to exhibit, show; (*parler de: problème, situation*) to explain, expose, set out; (*mettre en danger, orienter: maison etc*) to expose; **~ qn/qch à** to expose sb/sth to; **~ sa vie** to risk one's life; **s'~ à** (*soleil, danger*) to expose o.s. to; (*critiques, punition*) to lay o.s. open to.

exposition [ɛkspozisjɔ̃] *nf* (*voir exposer*) displaying; exhibiting; explanation, exposition; exposure; (*voir exposé*) aspect, situation; (*manifestation*) exhibition; (*PHOTO*) exposure; (*introduction*) exposition.

exprès [ɛksprɛ] *ad* (*délibérément*) on purpose; (*spécialement*) specially; **faire ~ de faire qch** to do sth on purpose.

exprès, esse [ɛksprɛs] *a* (*ordre, défense*) express, formal ♦ *a inv, ad* (*POSTES*) express; **envoyer qch en ~** to send sth express.

express [ɛkspʀɛs] *a, nm*: (café) ~ espresso; (train) ~ fast train.

expressément [ɛkspʀɛsemã] *ad* expressly, specifically.

expressif, ive [ɛkspʀesif, -iv] *a* expressive.

expression [ɛkspʀɛsjɔ̃] *nf* expression; **réduit à sa plus simple** ~ reduced to its simplest terms; **liberté/moyens d'**~ freedom/means of expression; ~ **toute faite** set phrase.

exprimer [ɛkspʀime] *vt* (sentiment, idée) to express; (faire sortir: jus, liquide) to press out; **s'**~ *vi* (personne) to express o.s.

expropriation [ɛkspʀɔpʀijasjɔ̃] *nf* expropriation; **frapper d'**~ to put a compulsory purchase order on.

exproprier [ɛkspʀɔpʀije] *vt* to buy up (ou buy the property of) by compulsory purchase, expropriate.

expulser [ɛkspylse] *vt* (d'une salle, d'un groupe) to expel; (locataire) to evict; (FOOT-BALL) to send off.

expulsion [ɛkspylsjɔ̃] *nf* expulsion; eviction; sending off.

expurger [ɛkspyʀʒe] *vt* to expurgate, bowdlerize.

exquis, e [ɛkski, -iz] *a* (gâteau, parfum, élégance) exquisite; (personne, temps) delightful.

exsangue [ɛksãg] *a* bloodless, drained of blood.

exsuder [ɛksyde] *vt* to exude.

extase [ɛkstaz] *nf* ecstasy; **être en** ~ to be in raptures.

extasier [ɛkstazje]: **s'**~ *vi*: **s'**~ **sur** to go into raptures over.

extatique [ɛkstatik] *a* ecstatic.

extenseur [ɛkstãsœʀ] *nm* (SPORT) chest expander.

extensible [ɛkstãsibl(ə)] *a* extensible.

extensif, ive [ɛkstãsif, -iv] *a* extensive.

extension [ɛkstãsjɔ̃] *nf* (d'un muscle, ressort) stretching; (MÉD): **à l'**~ in traction; (fig) extension; expansion.

exténuant, e [ɛkstenɥã, -ãt] *a* exhausting.

exténuer [ɛkstenɥe] *vt* to exhaust.

extérieur, e [ɛksteʀjœʀ] *a* (de dehors: porte, mur etc) outer, outside; (: commerce, politique) foreign; (: influences, pressions) external; (au dehors: escalier, w.-c.) outside; (apparent: calme, gaieté etc) outer ♦ *nm* (d'une maison, d'un récipient etc) outside, exterior; (d'une personne: apparence) exterior; (d'un pays, d'un groupe social): **l'**~ the outside world; **à l'**~ (dehors) outside; (fig: à l'étranger) abroad.

extérieurement [ɛksteʀjœʀmã] *ad* (de dehors) on the outside; (en apparence) on the surface.

extérioriser [ɛksteʀjɔʀize] *vt* to exteriorize.

exterminer [ɛkstɛʀmine] *vt* to exterminate, wipe out.

externat [ɛkstɛʀna] *nm* day school.

externe [ɛkstɛʀn(ə)] *a* external, outer ♦ *nm/f* (MÉD) non-resident medical student, extern (US); (SCOL) day pupil.

extincteur [ɛkstɛ̃ktœʀ] *nm* (fire) extinguisher.

extinction [ɛkstɛ̃ksjɔ̃] *nf* extinction; (JUR: d'une dette) extinguishment; ~ **de voix** (MÉD) loss of voice.

extirper [ɛkstiʀpe] *vt* (tumeur) to extirpate; (plante) to root out, pull up; (préjugés) to eradicate.

extorquer [ɛkstɔʀke] *vt* (de l'argent, un renseignement): ~ **qch à qn** to extort sth from sb.

extorsion [ɛkstɔʀsjɔ̃] *nf*: ~ **de fonds** extortion of money.

extra [ɛkstʀa] *a inv* first-rate; (marchandises) top-quality ♦ *nm inv* extra help ♦ *préfixe* extra(-).

extraction [ɛkstʀaksjɔ̃] *nf* extraction.

extrader [ɛkstʀade] *vt* to extradite.

extradition [ɛkstʀadisjɔ̃] *nf* extradition.

extra-fin, e [ɛkstʀafɛ̃, -in] *a* extra-fine.

extra-fort, e [ɛkstʀafɔʀ] *a* extra strong.

extraire [ɛkstʀɛʀ] *vt* to extract.

extrait, e [ɛkstʀɛ, -ɛt] *pp de* **extraire** ♦ *nm* (de plante) extract; (de film, livre) extract, excerpt; ~ **de naissance** birth certificate.

extra-lucide [ɛkstʀalysid] *a*: **voyante** ~ clairvoyant.

extraordinaire [ɛkstʀaɔʀdinɛʀ] *a* extraordinary; (POL, ADMIN) special; **ambassadeur** ~ ambassador extraordinary; **assemblée** ~ extraordinary meeting; **par** ~ by some unlikely chance.

extraordinairement [ɛksʀaɔʀdinɛʀmã] *ad* extraordinarily.

extrapoler [ɛkstʀapɔle] *vt, vi* to extrapolate.

extra-sensoriel, le [ɛkstʀasãsɔʀjɛl] *a* extrasensory.

extra-terrestre [ɛkstʀateʀɛstʀ(ə)] *nm/f* extraterrestrial.

extra-utérin, e [ɛkstʀayteʀɛ̃, -in] *a* extra-uterine.

extravagance [ɛkstʀavagãs] *nf* extravagance *q*; extravagant behaviour *q*.

extravagant, e [ɛkstʀavagã, -ãt] *a* (personne, attitude) extravagant; (idée) wild.

extraverti, e [ɛkstʀavɛʀti] *a* extrovert.

extrayais [ɛkstʀɛjɛ] *etc vb voir* **extraire**.

extrême [ɛkstʀɛm] *a, nm* extreme; (intensif): **d'une** ~ **simplicité/brutalité** extremely simple/brutal; **d'un** ~ **à l'autre** from one extreme to another; **à l'**~ in the extreme; **à l'**~ **rigueur** in the absolute extreme.

extrêmement [ɛkstʀɛmmã] *ad* extremely.

extrême-onction, *pl* **extrêmes-onctions** [ɛkstʀɛmɔ̃ksjɔ̃] *nf* (REL) last rites *pl*, Extreme Unction.

Extrême-Orient [ɛkstʀɛmɔʀjã] *nm*: **l'**~ the Far East.

extrême-oriental, e, aux [ɛkstʀɛmɔʀjãtal, -o] *a* Far Eastern.

extrémiste [ɛkstʀemist(ə)] *a, nm/f* extremist.

extrémité [ɛkstʀemite] *nf* (bout) end; (situation) straits *pl*, plight; (geste désespéré) extreme action; ~**s** *nfpl* (pieds et mains) extremities; **à la dernière** ~ (à l'agonie) on the point of death.

extroverti, e [ɛkstʀɔvɛʀti] *a* = **extraverti**.

exubérant, e [ɛgzybeʀã, -ãt] *a* exuberant.

exulter [ɛgzylte] *vi* to exult.

exutoire [ɛgzytwaʀ] *nm* outlet, release.

ex-voto [ɛgzvɔto] *nm inv* ex-voto.

eye-liner [ajlajnœʀ] *nm* eyeliner.

F

F, f [ɛf] *nm inv* F, f ♦ *abr* = **féminin**; (= *franc*) fr.; (= *Fahrenheit*) F; (= *frère*) Br(o).; (= *femme*) W; (*appartement*): **un F2/F3** a 2-/3-roomed flat (*Brit*) *ou* apartment (*US*); **F comme François** F for Frederick (*Brit*) *ou* Fox (*US*).

fa [fa] *nm inv* (*MUS*) F; (*en chantant la gamme*) fa.

fable [fabl(ə)] *nf* fable; (*mensonge*) story, tale.

fabricant [fabʀikɑ̃] *nm* manufacturer, maker.

fabrication [fabʀikɑsjɔ̃] *nf* manufacture, making.

fabrique [fabʀik] *nf* factory.

fabriquer [fabʀike] *vt* to make; (*industriellement*) to manufacture, make; (*construire: voiture*) to manufacture, build; (*: maison*) to build; (*fig: inventer: histoire, alibi*) to make up; (*fam*): **qu'est-ce qu'il fabrique?** what is he up to?; ~ **en série** to mass-produce.

fabulateur, trice [fabylatœʀ, -tʀis] *nm/f*: **c'est un** ~ he fantasizes, he makes up stories.

fabulation [fabylɑsjɔ̃] *nf* (*PSYCH*) fantasizing.

fabuleusement [fabyløzmɑ̃] *ad* fabulously, fantastically.

fabuleux, euse [fabylø, -øz] *a* fabulous, fantastic.

fac [fak] *abr f* (*fam*: = *faculté*) Uni (*Brit fam*), ≈ college (*US*).

façade [fasad] *nf* front, façade; (*fig*) façade.

face [fas] *nf* face; (*fig: aspect*) side ♦ *a*: **le côté** ~ heads; **perdre/sauver la** ~ to lose/save face; **regarder qn en** ~ to look sb in the face; **la maison/le trottoir d'en** ~ the house/pavement opposite; **en** ~ **de** *prép* opposite; (*fig*) in front of; **de** ~ *ad* from the front; face on; ~ à *prép* facing; (*fig*) faced with, in the face of; **faire** ~ à to face; **faire** ~ à la **demande** (*COMM*) to meet the demand; ~ à ~ *ad* facing each other ♦ *nm inv* encounter.

face-à-main, *pl* **faces-à-main** [fasamɛ̃] *nm* lorgnette.

facéties [fasesi] *nfpl* jokes, pranks.

facétieux, euse [fasesjø, -øz] *a* mischievous.

facette [fasɛt] *nf* facet.

fâché, e [fɑʃe] *a* angry; (*désolé*) sorry.

fâcher [fɑʃe] *vt* to anger; **se** ~ *vi* to get angry; **se** ~ **avec** (*se brouiller*) to fall out with.

fâcherie [fɑʃʀi] *nf* quarrel.

fâcheusement [fɑʃøzmɑ̃] *ad* unpleasantly; (*impressionné etc*) badly; **avoir** ~ **tendance à** to have an irritating tendency to.

fâcheux, euse [fɑʃø, -øz] *a* unfortunate, regrettable.

facho [faʃo] *a, nm/f* (*fam*: = *fasciste*) fascist.

facial, e, aux [fasjal, -o] *a* facial.

faciès [fasjɛs] *nm* (*visage*) features *pl*.

facile [fasil] *a* easy; (*accommodant*) easygoing; ~ **d'emploi** (*INFORM*) user-friendly.

facilement [fasilmɑ̃] *ad* easily.

facilité [fasilite] *nf* easiness; (*disposition, don*) aptitude; (*moyen, occasion, possibilité*): **il a la** ~ **de rencontrer les gens** he has every opportunity to meet people; ~**s** *nfpl* facilities; (*COMM*) terms; ~**s de crédit** credit terms; ~**s de paiement** easy terms.

faciliter [fasilite] *vt* to make easier.

façon [fasɔ̃] *nf* (*manière*) way; (*d'une robe etc*) making-up; cut; (*: main-d'œuvre*) labour (*Brit*), labor (*US*); (*imitation*): **châle** ~ **cachemire** cashmere-style shawl; ~**s** *nfpl* (*péj*) fuss *sg*; **faire des** ~**s** (*péj: être affecté*) to be affected; (*: faire des histoires*) to make a fuss; **de quelle** ~? (in) what way?; **sans** ~ *ad* without fuss ♦ *a* unaffected; **d'une autre** ~ in another way; **en aucune** ~ in no way; **de** ~ à so as to; **de** ~ à **ce que**, **de (telle)** ~ **que** so that; **de toute** ~ anyway, in any case; **(c'est une)** ~ **de parler** it's a way of putting it; **travail à** ~ tailoring.

façonner [fasɔne] *vt* (*fabriquer*) to manufacture; (*travailler: matière*) to shape, fashion; (*fig*) to mould, shape.

fac-similé [faksimile] *nm* facsimile.

facteur, trice [faktœʀ, -tʀis] *nm/f* postman/woman (*Brit*), mailman/woman (*US*) ♦ *nm* (*MATH, gén*) factor; ~ **d'orgues** organ builder; ~ **de pianos** piano maker; ~ **rhésus** rhesus factor.

factice [faktis] *a* artificial.

faction [faksjɔ̃] *nf* (*groupe*) faction; (*MIL*) guard *ou* sentry (duty); watch; **en** ~ on guard; standing watch.

factionnaire [faksjɔnɛʀ] *nm* guard, sentry.

factoriel, le [faktɔʀjɛl] *a, nf* factorial.

factotum [faktɔtɔm] *nm* odd-job man, dogsbody (*Brit*).

factuel, le [faktɥɛl] *a* factual.

facturation [faktyʀɑsjɔ̃] *nf* invoicing; (*bureau*) invoicing (office).

facture [faktyʀ] *nf* (*à payer: gén*) bill; (*: COMM*) invoice; (*d'un artisan, artiste*) technique, workmanship.

facturer [faktyʀe] *vt* to invoice.

facturier, ière [faktyʀje, -jɛʀ] *nm/f* invoice clerk.

facultatif, ive [fakyltatif, -iv] *a* optional; (*arrêt de bus*) request cpd.

faculté [fakylte] *nf* (*intellectuelle, d'université*) faculty; (*pouvoir, possibilité*) power.

fadaises [fadɛz] *nfpl* twaddle *sg*.

fade [fad] *a* insipid.

fading [fadiŋ] *nm* (*RADIO*) fading.

fagot [fago] *nm* (*de bois*) bundle of sticks.

fagoté, e [fagɔte] *a* (*fam*): **drôlement** ~ oddly dressed.

faible [fɛbl(ə)] *a* weak; (*voix, lumière, vent*) faint; (*élève, copie*) poor; (*rendement, intensité, revenu etc*) low ♦ *nm* weak point; (*pour quelqu'un*) weakness, soft spot; ~ **d'esprit** feeble-minded.

faiblement [fɛbləmɑ̃] *ad* weakly; (*peu: éclairer etc*) faintly.

faiblesse [fɛblɛs] *nf* weakness.

faiblir [fɛbliʀ] *vi* to weaken; (*lumière*) to dim; (*vent*) to drop.

faïence [fajɑ̃s] *nf* earthenware *q*; (*objet*) piece of earthenware.

faignant, e [fɛɲɑ̃, -ɑ̃t] *nm/f* = **fainéant, e**.

faille [faj] *vb voir* **falloir** ♦ *nf* (*GÉO*) fault; (*fig*) flaw, weakness.

failli, e [faji] *a*, *nm/f* bankrupt.

faillible [fajibl(ə)] *a* fallible.

faillir [fajiʀ] *vi*: **j'ai failli tomber/lui dire** I almost *ou* nearly fell/told him; **~ à une promesse/un engagement** to break a promise/an agreement.

faillite [fajit] *nf* bankruptcy; (*échec: d'une politique etc*) collapse; **être en ~** to be bankrupt; **faire ~** to go bankrupt.

faim [fɛ̃] *nf* hunger; (*fig*): **~ d'amour/de richesse** hunger *ou* yearning for love/wealth; **avoir ~** to be hungry; **rester sur sa ~** (*aussi fig*) to be left wanting more.

fainéant, e [fɛnɛɑ̃, -ɑ̃t] *nm/f* idler, loafer.

fainéantise [fɛneɑ̃tiz] *nf* idleness, laziness.

faire [fɛʀ] *vt* to do; (*fabriquer, préparer*) to make; (*maison*) to build; (*produire*) to produce; **"vraiment?" fit-il** "really?" he said; **je n'ai pas pu ~ autrement** I couldn't do otherwise; **fait à la main/machine** hand-/machine-made; **~ du bruit/des taches** to make a noise/marks; **~ du droit/du français** to do law/French; **~ du rugby/du piano** to play rugby/play the piano; **~ le malade/l'ignorant** to act the invalid/the fool; **~ du diabète** to suffer from *ou* have diabetes; **~ de la tension** to have high blood pressure; **~ de la fièvre** to run a temperature; **~ les magasins** to go round *ou* do the shops; **~ de qn un frustré/avocat** to make sb frustrated/a lawyer; **ça ne me fait rien**, (*ça ne me fait ni chaud ni froid* (*m'est égal*) I don't care *ou* mind; (*me laisse froid*) it has no effect on me; (*ça ne me fait rien* it doesn't matter; **qu'est-ce que ça peut ~?** what does it matter?; **je vous le fais 10 F** I'll let you have it for 10 F; **que faites-vous?** (*quel métier etc*) what do you do?; (*quelle activité: au moment de la question*) what are you doing?; **que ~?** what are we going to do?, what can be done (about it)?; **tu as bien fait de me le dire** you did well *ou* right to tell me; **comment a-t-il fait pour ...?** how did he manage to ...?; **qu'a-t-il fait de sa valise?** what has he done with his case?; **n'avoir que ~ de qch** to have no need of sth; **2 et 2 font 4** 2 and 2 are *ou* make 4; **9 divisé par 3 fait 3** 9 divided by 3 makes *ou* gives *ou* is 3; **~ que** (*impliquer*) to mean that ♦ *vi* (*agir, s'y prendre*) to act; (*faire ses besoins*) to go (to the toilet); **faites comme chez vous** make yourself at home ♦ *vb avec attribut*: **ça fait 10 m/15 F** it's 10 m/15 F; **~ vieux/démodé** to look old/old-fashioned ♦ *vb substitut*: **remets-le en place — je viens de le ~** put it back in its place — I've just done so *ou* I just have (done); **faites!** please do!; **il ne fait que critiquer** (*sans cesse*) all he (ever) does is criticize; (*seulement*) he's only criticizing ♦ *vb impersonnel*: **il fait beau** *etc* the weather is fine *etc*; **voir jour, froid** *etc*; **ça fait 2 ans qu'il est parti** it's 2 years since he left; **ça fait 2 ans qu'il y est** he's been there for 2 years ♦ **~ faire**: **~ réparer qch** to get *ou* have sth repaired; **~ tomber/bouger qch** to make sth fall/move; **cela fait dormir** it makes you sleep; **~ travailler les enfants** to make

the children work, get the children to work; **~ punir les enfants** to have the children punished; **il m'a fait traverser la rue** (*aidé*) he helped me (to) cross the road, he helped me across the road; **~ démarrer un moteur/chauffer de l'eau** to start up an engine/heat some water; **se ~ couper les cheveux** to get *ou* have one's hair cut; **se ~ examiner la vue/opérer** to have one's eyes tested/have an operation; **il s'est fait aider (par qn)** he got sb to help him; **il va se ~ tuer/punir** he's going to get himself killed/get (himself) punished; **elle s'est fait expliquer le problème** she had the problem explained to her; **se ~ faire un vêtement** to get a garment made for o.s. ♦ **se ~** *vi* (*fromage, vin*) to mature; **se ~ à** (*s'habituer*) to get used to; **cela se fait beaucoup/ne se fait pas** it's done a lot/not done; **comment se fait-il que ...?** how is it that ...?; **il peut se ~ que ...** it can happen that ...; **se ~ vieux** to be getting old; **se ~ beau** to do o.s. up; **se ~ les yeux/ongles** to do one's eyes/nails; **se ~ une jupe** to make o.s. a skirt; **se ~ des amis** to make friends; **se ~ du souci** to worry; **il ne s'en fait pas** he doesn't worry; **sans s'en ~** without worrying.

faire-part [fɛʀpaʀ] *nm inv* announcement (*of birth, marriage etc*).

fair-play [fɛʀplɛ] *a inv* fair.

fais [fɛ] *vb voir* **faire**.

faisable [fəzabl(ə)] *a* feasible.

faisais [fəzɛ] *etc vb voir* **faire**.

faisan, e [fəzɑ̃, -an] *nm/f* pheasant.

faisandé, e [fəzɑ̃de] *a* high (*bad*); (*fig péj*) corrupt, decadent.

faisceau, x [fɛso] *nm* (*de lumière etc*) beam; (*de branches etc*) bundle.

faiseur, euse [fəzœʀ, -øz] *nm/f* (*gén: péj*): **~ de** maker of ♦ *nm* (*bespoke*) tailor; **~ d'embarras** fusspot; **~ de projets** schemer.

fait [fɛ] *vb voir* **faire** ♦ *nm* (*événement*) event, occurrence; (*réalité, donnée*) fact; **le ~ que/de manger** the fact that/of eating; **être le ~ de** (*causé par*) to be the work of; **être au ~ (de)** to be informed (of); **mettre qn au ~** to inform sb, put sb in the picture; **au ~** (*à propos*) by the way; **en venir au ~** to get to the point; **de ~** *a* (*opposé à: de droit*) de facto ♦ *ad* in fact; **du ~ de ceci/qu'il a menti** because of *ou* on account of this/his having lied; **de ce ~** therefore, for this reason; **en ~** in fact; **en ~ de repas** by way of a meal; **prendre ~ et cause pour qn** to support sb, side with sb; **prendre qn sur le ~** to catch sb in the act; **dire à qn son ~** to give sb a piece of one's mind; **hauts ~s** (*exploits*) exploits; **~ d'armes** feat of arms; **~ divers** (short) news item; **les ~s et gestes de qn** sb's actions *ou* doings.

fait, e [fɛ, fɛt] *pp de* **faire** ♦ *a* (*mûr: fromage, melon*) ripe; (*maquillé: yeux*) made-up; (*vernis: ongles*) painted, polished; **un homme ~** a grown man; **tout(e) ~(e)** (*préparé à l'avance*) ready-made; **c'en est ~ de notre tranquillité** that's the end of our peace; **c'est bien ~ (pour lui *ou* eux *etc*)** it serves him (*ou* them *etc*) right.

faîte [fɛt] *nm* top; (*fig*) pinnacle, height.

faites [fɛt] *vb voir* **faire**.
faîtière [fɛtjɛʀ] *nf* (*de tente*) ridge pole.
fait-tout *nm inv*, **faîtout** *nm* [fɛtu] stewpot.
fakir [fakiʀ] *nm* (*THÉÂTRE*) wizard.
falaise [falɛz] *nf* cliff.
falbalas [falbala] *nmpl* fripperies, frills.
fallacieux, euse [falasjø, -øz] *a* (*raisonnement*) fallacious; (*apparences*) deceptive; (*espoir*) illusory.
falloir [falwaʀ] *vb impersonnel*: **il faut faire les lits** we (*ou* you *etc*) have to *ou* must make the beds; **il faut que je fasse les lits** I have to *ou* must make the beds; **il a fallu qu'il parte** he had to leave; **il faudrait qu'elle rentre** she ought to go home; **il va ~ 100 F** we'll (*ou* I'll *etc*) need 100 F; **il doit ~ du temps** that must take time; **il vous faut tourner à gauche après l'église** you have to turn left past the church; **nous avons ce qu'il (nous) faut** we have what we need; **il faut qu'il ait oublié** he must have forgotten; **il a fallu qu'il l'apprenne** he would have to hear about it; **il ne fallait pas** (*pour remercier*) you shouldn't have (done); **faut le faire!** (it) takes some doing! ♦ **s'en ~**: **il s'en est fallu de 100 F/5 minutes** we (*ou* they *etc*) were 100 F short/5 minutes late (*ou* early); **il s'en faut de beaucoup qu'il soit ...** he is far from being ...; **il s'en est fallu de peu que cela n'arrive** it very nearly happened; **ou peu s'en faut** or just about, or as good as; **comme il faut** *a* proper ♦ *ad* properly.
fallu [faly] *pp de* **falloir**.
falot, e [falo, -ɔt] *a* a dreary, colourless (*Brit*), colorless (*US*) ♦ *nm* lantern.
falsifier [falsifje] *vt* to falsify; to doctor.
famé, e [fame] *a*: **mal ~** disreputable, of ill repute.
famélique [famelik] *a* half-starved.
fameux, euse [famø, -øz] *a* (*illustre: parfois péj*) famous; (*bon: repas, plat etc*) first-rate, first-class; (*intensif*): **un ~ problème** *etc* a real problem *etc*; **pas ~** not great, not much good.
familial, e, aux [familjal, -o] *a* family *cpd* ♦ *nf* (*AUTO*) estate car (*Brit*), station wagon (*US*).
familiariser [familjaʀize] *vt*: **~ qn avec** to familiarize sb with; **se ~ avec** to familiarize o.s. with.
familiarité [familjaʀite] *nf* familiarity; informality; **~s** *nfpl* familiarities; **~ avec** (*sujet, science*) familiarity with.
familier, ière [familje, -jɛʀ] *a* (*connu, impertinent*) familiar; (*dénotant une certaine intimité*) informal, friendly; (*LING*) informal, colloquial ♦ *nm* regular (visitor).
famille [famij] *nf* family; **il a de la ~ à Paris** he has relatives in Paris.
famine [famin] *nf* famine.
fan [fan] *nm/f* fan.
fana [fana] *a, nm/f* (*fam*) = **fanatique**.
fanal, aux [fanal, -o] *nm* beacon; lantern.
fanatique [fanatik] *a*: **~ (de)** fanatical (about) ♦ *nm/f* fanatic.
fanatisme [fanatism(ə)] *nm* fanaticism.
fane [fan] *nf* top.
fané, e [fane] *a* faded.
faner [fane]: **se ~** *vi* to fade.

faneur, euse [fanœʀ, -øz] *nm/f* haymaker ♦ *nf* (*TECH*) tedder.
fanfare [fɑ̃faʀ] *nf* (*orchestre*) brass band; (*musique*) fanfare; **en ~** (*avec bruit*) noisily.
fanfaron, ne [fɑ̃faʀɔ̃, -ɔn] *nm/f* braggart.
fanfaronnades [fɑ̃faʀɔnad] *nfpl* bragging *q*.
fanfreluches [fɑ̃fʀəlyʃ] *nfpl* trimming *q*.
fange [fɑ̃ʒ] *nf* mire.
fanion [fanjɔ̃] *nm* pennant.
fanon [fanɔ̃] *nm* (*de baleine*) plate of baleen; (*repli de peau*) dewlap, wattle.
fantaisie [fɑ̃tezi] *nf* (*spontanéité*) fancy, imagination; (*caprice*) whim; extravagance; (*MUS*) fantasia ♦ *a*: **bijou (de) ~** (piece of) costume jewellery (*Brit*) *ou* jewelry (*US*); **pain (de) ~** fancy bread.
fantaisiste [fɑ̃tezist(ə)] *a* (*péj*) unorthodox, eccentric ♦ *nm/f* (*de music-hall*) variety artist *ou* entertainer.
fantasme [fɑ̃tasm(ə)] *nm* fantasy.
fantasmer [fɑ̃tasme] *vi* to fantasize.
fantasque [fɑ̃task(ə)] *a* a whimsical, capricious; fantastic.
fantassin [fɑ̃tasɛ̃] *nm* infantryman.
fantastique [fɑ̃tastik] *a* fantastic.
fantoche [fɑ̃tɔʃ] *nm* (*péj*) puppet.
fantomatique [fɑ̃tɔmatik] *a* ghostly.
fantôme [fɑ̃tom] *nm* ghost, phantom.
FAO *sigle f* (= *Food and Agricultural Organization*) FAO.
faon [fɑ̃] *nm* fawn (*deer*).
faramineux, euse [faʀaminø, -øz] *a* (*fam*) fantastic.
farce [faʀs(ə)] *nf* (*viande*) stuffing; (*blague*) (practical) joke; (*THÉÂTRE*) farce; **faire une ~ à qn** to play a (practical) joke on sb; **~s et attrapes** jokes and novelties.
farceur, euse [faʀsœʀ, -øz] *nm/f* practical joker; (*fumiste*) clown.
farci, e [faʀsi] *a* (*CULIN*) stuffed.
farcir [faʀsiʀ] *vt* (*viande*) to stuff; (*fig*): **~ qch de** to stuff sth with; **se ~** (*fam*): **je me suis farci la vaisselle** I've got stuck *ou* landed with the washing-up.
fard [faʀ] *nm* make-up; **~ à joues** blusher.
fardeau, x [faʀdo] *nm* burden.
farder [faʀde] *vt* to make up; (*vérité*) to disguise; **se ~** to make o.s. up.
farfelu, e [faʀfəly] *a* a wacky (*fam*), harebrained.
farfouiller [faʀfuje] *vi* (*péj*) to rummage around.
fariboles [faʀibɔl] *nfpl* nonsense *q*.
farine [faʀin] *nf* flour; **~ de blé** wheatflour; **~ de maïs** cornflour (*Brit*), cornstarch (*US*); **~ lactée** (*pour bouillie*) gruel.
fariner [faʀine] *vt* to flour.
farineux, euse [faʀinø, -øz] *a* (*sauce, pomme*) floury ♦ *nmpl* (*aliments*) starchy foods.
farniente [faʀnjɛnte] *nm* idleness.
farouche [faʀuʃ] *a* shy, timid; (*sauvage*) savage, wild; (*violent*) fierce.
farouchement [faʀuʃmɑ̃] *ad* fiercely.
fart [faʀ(t)] *nm* (ski) wax.
farter [faʀte] *vt* to wax.
fascicule [fasikyl] *nm* volume.
fascinant, e [fasinɑ̃, -ɑ̃t] *a* fascinating.
fascination [fasinasjɔ̃] *nf* fascination.

fasciner [fasine] *vt* to fascinate.

fascisant, e [faʃizɑ̃, -ɑ̃t] *a* fascistic.

fascisme [faʃism(ə)] *nm* fascism.

fasciste [faʃist(ə)] *a, nm/f* fascist.

fasse [fas] *etc vb voir* **faire**.

faste [fast(ə)] *nm* splendour (*Brit*), splendor (*US*) ♦ *a*: **c'est un jour ~** it's his (*ou* our *etc*) lucky day.

fastidieux, euse [fastidjø, -øz] *a* tedious, tiresome.

fastueux, euse [fastɥø, -øz] *a* sumptuous, luxurious.

fat [fa] *am* conceited, smug.

fatal, e [fatal] *a* fatal; (*inévitable*) inevitable.

fatalement [fatalmɑ̃] *ad* inevitably.

fatalisme [fatalism(ə)] *nm* fatalism.

fataliste [fatalist(ə)] *a* fatalistic.

fatalité [fatalite] *nf* (*destin*) fate; (*coïncidence*) fateful coincidence; (*caractère inévitable*) inevitability.

fatidique [fatidik] *a* fateful.

fatigant, e [fatigɑ̃, -ɑ̃t] *a* tiring; (*agaçant*) tiresome.

fatigue [fatig] *nf* tiredness, fatigue; (*détérioration*) fatigue; **les ~s du voyage** the wear and tear of the journey.

fatigué, e [fatige] *a* tired.

fatiguer [fatige] *vt* to tire, make tired; (*TECH*) to put a strain on, strain; (*fig: importuner*) to wear out ♦ *vi* (*moteur*) to labour (*Brit*), labor (*US*), strain; **se ~** *vi* to get tired; to tire o.s. (out); **se ~ à faire qch** to tire o.s. out doing sth.

fatras [fatra] *nm* jumble, hotchpotch.

fatuité [fatɥite] *nf* conceitedness, smugness.

faubourg [fobuʀ] *nm* suburb.

faubourien, ne [fobuʀjɛ̃, -ɛn] *a* (*accent*) working-class.

fauché, e [foʃe] *a* (*fam*) broke.

faucher [foʃe] *vt* (*herbe*) to cut; (*champs, blés*) to reap; (*fig*) to cut down; to mow down; (*fam: voler*) to pinch, nick.

faucheur, euse [foʃœʀ, -øz] *nm/f* reaper, mower.

faucille [fosij] *nf* sickle.

faucon [fokɔ̃] *nm* falcon, hawk.

faudra [fodʀa] *etc vb voir* **falloir**.

faufil [fofil] *nm* (*COUTURE*) tacking thread.

faufilage [fofila3] *nm* (*COUTURE*) tacking.

faufiler [fofile] *vt* to tack, baste; **se ~** *vi*: **se ~ dans** to edge one's way into; **se ~ parmi/entre** to thread one's way among/between.

faune [fon] *nf* (*ZOOL*) wildlife, fauna; (*fig péj*) set, crowd ♦ *nm* faun; **~ marine** marine (*animal*) life.

faussaire [fosɛʀ] *nm/f* forger.

fausse [fos] *af voir* **faux**.

faussement [fosmɑ̃] *ad* (*accuser*) wrongly, wrongfully; (*croire*) falsely, erroneously.

fausser [fose] *vt* (*objet*) to bend, buckle; (*fig*) to distort; **~ compagnie à qn** to give sb the slip.

fausset [fosɛ] *nm*: **voix de ~** falsetto voice.

fausseté [foste] *nf* wrongness; falseness.

faut [fo] *vb voir* **falloir**.

faute [fot] *nf* (*erreur*) mistake, error; (*péché, manquement*) misdemeanour; (*FOOTBALL etc*) offence; (*TENNIS*) fault; (*responsabilité*): **par la ~ de** through the fault of, because of; **c'est de sa/ma ~** it's his/my fault; **être en ~** to be in the wrong; **prendre qn en ~** to catch sb out; **~ de** (*temps, argent*) for *ou* through lack of; **~ de mieux** for want of anything *ou* something better; **sans ~** without fail; **~ de frappe** typing error; **~ d'inattention** careless mistake; **~ d'orthographe** spelling mistake; **~ professionnelle** professional misconduct *q*.

fauteuil [fotœj] *nm* armchair; **~ à bascule** rocking chair; **~ club** (big) easy chair; **~ d'orchestre** seat in the front stalls (*Brit*) *ou* the orchestra (*US*); **~ roulant** wheelchair.

fauteur [fotœʀ] *nm*: **~ de troubles** trouble-maker.

fautif, ive [fotif, -iv] *a* (*incorrect*) incorrect, inaccurate; (*responsable*) at fault, in the wrong; (*coupable*) guilty ♦ *nm/f* culprit.

fauve [fov] *nm* wildcat; (*peintre*) Fauve ♦ *a* (*couleur*) fawn.

fauvette [fovɛt] *nf* warbler.

faux [fo] *nf* scythe.

faux, fausse [fo, fos] *a* (*inexact*) wrong; (*piano, voix*) out of tune; (*falsifié*) fake, forged; (*sournois, postiche*) false ♦ *ad* (*MUS*) out of tune ♦ *nm* (*copie*) fake, forgery; (*opposé au vrai*): **le ~** falsehood; **le ~ numéro/la fausse clé** the wrong number/key; **faire fausse route** to go the wrong way; **faire ~ bond à qn** to let sb down; **~ ami** (*LING*) faux ami; **~ col** detachable collar; **~ départ** (*SPORT, fig*) false start; **~ frais** *nmpl* extras, incidental expenses; **~ frère** (*fig péj*) false friend; **~ mouvement** awkward movement; **~ nez** false nose; **~ nom** assumed name; **~ pas** tripping *q*; (*fig*) faux pas; **~ témoignage** (*délit*) perjury; **fausse alerte** false alarm; **fausse clé** skeleton key; **fausse couche** (*MÉD*) miscarriage; **fausse joie** vain joy; **fausse note** wrong note.

faux-filet [fofilɛ] *nm* sirloin.

faux-fuyant [fofɥijɑ̃] *nm* equivocation.

faux-monnayeur [fomɔnɛjœʀ] *nm* counterfeiter, forger.

faux-semblant [fosɑ̃blɑ̃] *nm* pretence (*Brit*), pretense (*US*).

faux-sens [fosɑ̃s] *nm* mistranslation.

faveur [favœʀ] *nf* favour (*Brit*), favor (*US*); **traitement de ~** preferential treatment; **à la ~ de** under cover of; (*grâce à*) thanks to; **en ~ de** in favo(u)r of.

favorable [favoʀabl(ə)] *a* favo(u)rable.

favori, te [favoʀi, -it] *a, nm/f* favo(u)rite.

favoris [favoʀi] *nmpl* (*barbe*) sideboards (*Brit*), sideburns.

favoriser [favoʀize] *vt* to favour (*Brit*), favor (*US*).

favoritisme [favoʀitism(ə)] *nm* (*péj*) favo(u)ritism.

fayot [fajo] *nm* (*fam*) crawler.

FB *abr* (= *franc belge*) BF, FB.

FBI *sigle m* FBI.

FC *sigle m* (= *Football Club*) FC.

fébrile [febʀil] *a* feverish, febrile; **capitaux ~s** (*ÉCON*) hot money.

fébrilement [febʀilmɑ̃] *ad* feverishly.

fécal, e, aux [fekal, -o] *a voir* **matière**.

fécond, e [fekɔ̃, -ɔ̃d] *a* fertile.

fécondation [fekɔ̃dasjɔ̃] *nf* fertilization.

féconder [fekɔ̃de] *vt* to fertilize.

fécondité [fekɔ̃dite] *nf* fertility.

fécule [fekyl] *nf* potato flour.

féculent [fekylɑ̃] *nm* starchy food.

fédéral, e, aux [federal, -o] *a* federal.

fédéralisme [federalism(ə)] *nm* federalism.

fédération [federasjɔ̃] *nf* federation.

fée [fe] *nf* fairy.

féerie [feri] *nf* enchantment.

féerique [ferik] *a* magical, fairytale *cpd*.

feignant, e [fɛɲɑ̃, -ɑ̃t] *nm/f* = **fainéant, e**.

feindre [fɛ̃dr(ə)] *vt* to feign ♦ *vi* to dissemble; ~ **de faire** to pretend to do.

feint, e [fɛ̃, fɛ̃t] *pp de* **feindre** ♦ *a* feigned ♦ *nf* (*SPORT*) dummy.

fêler [fele] *vt* to crack.

félicitations [felisitasjɔ̃] *nfpl* congratulations.

félicité [felisite] *nf* bliss.

féliciter [felisite] *vt*: ~ **qn (de)** to congratulate sb (on).

félin, e [felɛ̃, -in] *a* feline ♦ *nm* (big) cat.

félon, ne [felɔ̃, -ɔn] *a* perfidious, treacherous.

félonie [feloni] *nf* treachery.

fêlure [felyr] *nf* crack.

femelle [fəmɛl] *a* (*aussi ÉLEC, TECH*) female ♦ *nf* female.

féminin, e [feminɛ̃, -in] *a* feminine; (*sexe*) female; (*équipe, vêtements etc*) women's; (*parfois péj: homme*) effeminate ♦ *nm* (*LING*) feminine.

féminiser [feminize] *vt* to feminize; (*rendre efféminé*) to make effeminate; **se** ~ *vi*: **cette profession se féminise** this profession is attracting more women.

féminisme [feminism(ə)] *nm* feminism.

féministe [feminist(ə)] *a, nf* feminist.

féminité [feminite] *nf* femininity.

femme [fam] *nf* woman; (*épouse*) wife (*pl* wives); **être très** ~ to be very much a woman; **devenir** ~ to attain womanhood; ~ **d'affaires** businesswoman; ~ **de chambre** chambermaid; ~ **fatale** femme fatale; ~ **au foyer** housewife; ~ **d'intérieur** (real) home-maker; ~ **de ménage** domestic help, cleaning lady; ~ **du monde** society woman; ~ **de tête** determined, intellectual woman.

fémur [femyr] *nm* femur, thighbone.

FEN [fɛn] *sigle f* (= *Fédération de l'éducation nationale*) *teachers' trades union.*

fenaison [fənɛzɔ̃] *nf* haymaking.

fendillé, e [fɑ̃dije] *a* (*terre etc*) crazed.

fendre [fɑ̃dr(ə)] *vt* (*couper en deux*) to split; (*fissurer*) to crack; (*fig: traverser*) to cut through; to push one's way through; **se** ~ *vi* to crack.

fendu, e [fɑ̃dy] *a* (*sol, mur*) cracked; (*jupe*) slit.

fenêtre [fənɛtr(ə)] *nf* window; ~ **à guillotine** sash window.

fenouil [fənuj] *nm* fennel.

fente [fɑ̃t] *nf* slit; (*fissure*) crack.

féodal, e, aux [feodal, -o] *a* feudal.

féodalisme [feodalism(ə)] *nm* feudalism.

fer [fɛr] *nm* iron; (*de cheval*) shoe; ~**s** *pl* (*MÉD*) forceps; **mettre aux** ~**s** (*enchaîner*) to put in chains; **au** ~ **rouge** with a red-hot iron; **santé/main de** ~ iron constitution/hand; ~ **à cheval** horseshoe; **en** ~ **à cheval** (*fig*) horseshoe-shaped; ~ **forgé** wrought

iron; ~ **à friser** curling tongs; ~ **de lance** spearhead; ~ **(à repasser)** iron; ~ **à souder** soldering iron.

ferai [fəre] *etc vb voir* **faire**.

fer-blanc [fɛrblɑ̃] *nm* tin(plate).

ferblanterie [fɛrblɑ̃tri] *nf* tinplate making; (*produit*) tinware.

ferblantier [fɛrblɑ̃tje] *nm* tinsmith.

férié, e [ferje] *a*: **jour** ~ public holiday.

férir [ferir]: **sans coup** ~ *ad* without meeting any opposition.

fermage [fɛrmaʒ] *nm* tenant farming.

ferme [fɛrm(ə)] *a* firm ♦ *ad* (*travailler etc*) hard; (*discuter*) ardently ♦ *nf* (*exploitation*) farm; (*maison*) farmhouse; **tenir** ~ to stand firm.

fermé, e [fɛrme] *a* closed, shut; (*gaz, eau etc*) off; (*fig: personne*) uncommunicative; (: *milieu*) exclusive.

fermement [fɛrməmɑ̃] *ad* firmly.

ferment [fɛrmɑ̃] *nm* ferment.

fermentation [fɛrmɑ̃tasjɔ̃] *nf* fermentation.

fermenter [fɛrmɑ̃te] *vi* to ferment.

fermer [fɛrme] *vt* to close, shut; (*cesser l'exploitation de*) to close down, shut down; (*eau, lumière, électricité, robinet*) to put off, turn off; (*aéroport, route*) to close ♦ *vi* to close, shut; to close down, shut down; **se** ~ *vi* (*yeux*) to close, shut; (*fleur, blessure*) to close up; ~ **à clef** to lock; ~ **au verrou** to bolt; ~ **les yeux (sur qch)** (*fig*) to close one's eyes (to sth); **se** ~ **à** (*pitié, amour*) to close one's heart *ou* mind to.

fermeté [fɛrməte] *nf* firmness.

fermette [fɛrmɛt] *nf* farmhouse.

fermeture [fɛrmətyr] *nf* (*voir fermer*) closing; shutting; closing *ou* shutting down; putting *ou* turning off; (*dispositif*) catch; fastening, fastener; **heure de** ~ (*COMM*) closing time; **jour de** ~ (*COMM*) day on which the shop (*etc*) is closed; ~ **éclair** ® *ou* **à glissière** zip (fastener) (*Brit*), zipper.

fermier, ière [fɛrmje, -jɛr] *nm/f* farmer ♦ *nf* (*femme de fermier*) farmer's wife ♦ *a*: **beurre/cidre** ~ farm butter/cider.

fermoir [fɛrmwar] *nm* clasp.

féroce [ferɔs] *a* ferocious, fierce.

férocement [ferɔsmɑ̃] *ad* ferociously.

férocité [ferɔsite] *nf* ferocity, ferociousness.

ferons [fərɔ̃] *etc vb voir* **faire**.

ferraille [fɛrɑj] *nf* scrap iron; **mettre à la** ~ to scrap; **bruit de** ~ clanking.

ferrailler [fɛrɑje] *vi* to clank.

ferrailleur [fɛrɑjœr] *nm* scrap merchant.

ferrant [fɛrɑ̃] *am voir* **maréchal**.

ferré, e [fɛre] *a* (*chaussure*) hobnailed; (*canne*) steel-tipped; ~ **sur** (*fam: savant*) well up on.

ferrer [fɛre] *vt* (*cheval*) to shoe; (*chaussure*) to nail; (*canne*) to tip; (*poisson*) to strike.

ferreux, euse [fɛrø, -øz] *a* ferrous.

ferronnerie [fɛrɔnri] *nf* ironwork; ~ **d'art** wrought iron work.

ferronnier [fɛrɔnje] *nm* craftsman in wrought iron; (*marchand*) ironware merchant.

ferroviaire [fɛrɔvjɛr] *a* rail *cpd*, railway *cpd* (*Brit*), railroad *cpd* (*US*).

ferrure [fɛryr] *nf* (ornamental) hinge.

ferry(-boat) [fɛre(bot)] *nm* ferry.

fertile [fɛrtil] a fertile; ~ **en incidents** eventful, packed with incidents.

fertilisant [fɛrtilizɑ̃] nm fertilizer.

fertiliser [fɛrtilize] vt to fertilize.

fertilité [fɛrtilite] nf fertility.

féru, e [fery] a: ~ **de** with a keen interest in.

férule [feryl] nf: **être sous la ~ de qn** to be under sb's (iron) rule.

fervent, e [fɛrvɑ̃, -ɑ̃t] a fervent.

ferveur [fɛrvœr] nf fervour (Brit), fervor (US).

fesse [fɛs] nf buttock; **les ~s** the bottom sg, the buttocks.

fessée [fese] nf spanking.

fessier [fesje] nm (fam) behind.

festin [fɛstɛ̃] nm feast.

festival [fɛstival] nm festival.

festivalier [fɛstivalje] nm festival-goer.

festivités [fɛstivite] nfpl festivities, merrymaking sg.

feston [fɛstɔ̃] nm (ARCHIT) festoon; (COUTURE) scallop.

festoyer [fɛstwaje] vi to feast.

fêtard [fɛtar] nm (péj) high liver, merrymaker.

fête [fɛt] nf (religieuse) feast; (publique) holiday; (en famille etc) celebration; (kermesse) fête, fair, festival; (du nom) feast day, name day; **faire la ~** to live it up; **faire ~ à qn** to give sb a warm welcome; **se faire une ~ de** to look forward to; to enjoy; **ça va être sa ~!** (fam) he's going to get it!; **jour de ~** holiday; **les ~s (de fin d'année)** the festive season; **la salle/le comité des ~s** the village hall/festival committee; **la ~ des Mères/Pères** Mother's/Father's Day; **~ de charité** charity fair ou fête; **~ foraine** (fun) fair; **mobile** movable feast (day); **la F~ Nationale** the national holiday.

Fête-Dieu [fɛtdjø] nf: **la ~** Corpus Christi.

fêter [fete] vt to celebrate; (personne) to have a celebration for.

fétiche [fetiʃ] nm fetish; **animal ~, objet ~** mascot.

fétichisme [fetiʃism(ə)] nm fetishism.

fétide [fetid] a fetid.

fétu [fety] nm: ~ **de paille** wisp of straw.

feu [fø] a inv: ~ **son père** his late father.

feu, x [fø] nm (gén) fire; (signal lumineux) light; (de cuisinière) ring; (sensation de brûlure) burning (sensation); ~**x** nmpl fire sg; (AUTO) (traffic) lights; **tous ~x éteints** (NAVIG, AUTO) without lights; **au ~!** (incendie) fire!; **à ~ doux/vif** over a slow/brisk heat; **à petit ~** (CULIN) over a gentle heat; (fig) slowly; **faire ~** to fire; **ne pas faire long ~** (fig) not to last long; **commander le ~** (MIL) to give the order to (open) fire; **tué au ~** (MIL) killed in action; **mettre à ~** (fusée) to fire off; **pris entre deux ~x** caught in the crossfire; **en ~** on fire; **être tout ~ tout flamme (pour)** (passion) to be aflame with passion (for); (enthousiasme) to be fired with enthusiasm (for); **prendre ~** to catch fire; **mettre le ~ à** to set fire to, set on fire; **faire du ~** to make a fire; **avez-vous du ~?** (pour cigarette) have you (got) a light?; ~ **rouge/vert/orange** (AUTO) red/green/amber (Brit) ou yellow (US) light; **donner le ~ vert**

à qch/qn (fig) to give sth/sb the go-ahead ou green light; ~ **arrière** (AUTO) rear light; ~ **d'artifice** firework; (spectacle) fireworks pl; ~ **de camp** campfire; ~ **de cheminée** chimney fire; ~ **de joie** bonfire; ~ **de paille** (fig) flash in the pan; ~**x de brouillard** (AUTO) fog lights ou lamps; ~**x de croisement** (AUTO) dipped (Brit) ou dimmed (US) headlights; ~**x de position** (AUTO) sidelights; ~**x de route** (AUTO) headlights (on full (Brit) ou high (US) beam); ~**x de stationnement** parking lights.

feuillage [fœjaʒ] nm foliage, leaves pl.

feuille [fœj] nf (d'arbre) leaf (pl leaves); ~ **(de papier)** sheet (of paper); **rendre ~ blanche** (SCOL) to give in a blank paper; ~ **d'or/de métal** gold/metal leaf; ~ **de chou** (péj: journal) rag; ~ **d'impôts** tax form; ~ **de maladie** medical expenses claim form; ~ **morte** dead leaf; ~ **de paye** pay slip; ~ **de présence** attendance sheet; ~ **de température** temperature chart; ~ **de vigne** (BOT) vine leaf; (sur statue) fig leaf; ~ **volante** loose sheet.

feuillet [fœjɛ] nm leaf (pl leaves), page.

feuilletage [fœjtaʒ] nm (aspect feuilleté) flakiness.

feuilleté, e [fœjte] a (CULIN) flaky; (verre) laminated.

feuilleter [fœjte] vt (livre) to leaf through.

feuilleton [fœjtɔ̃] nm serial.

feuillette [fœjɛt] etc vb voir **feuilleter**.

feuillu, e [fœjy] a leafy ♦ nm broad-leaved tree.

feulement [følmɑ̃] nm growl.

feutre [føtr(ə)] nm felt; (chapeau) felt hat; (stylo) felt-tip(ped pen).

feutré, e [føtre] a feltlike; (pas, voix) muffled.

feutrer [føtre] vt to felt; (fig: bruits) to muffle ♦ vi, **se ~** vi (tissu) to felt.

feutrine [føtrin] nf (lightweight) felt.

fève [fɛv] nf broad bean; (dans la galette des Rois) charm (hidden in cake eaten on Twelfth Night).

février [fevrije] nm February; voir aussi **juillet**.

fez [fɛz] nm fez.

FF abr (= franc français) FF.

FFA sigle fpl (= Forces françaises en Allemagne) French forces in Germany.

FFI sigle fpl = Forces françaises de l'intérieur (1942-45) ♦ sigle m member of the FFI.

FFL sigle fpl (= Forces françaises libres) Free French Army.

Fg abr = **faubourg**.

FGA sigle m (= Fonds de garantie automobile) fund financed through insurance premiums, to compensate victims of uninsured losses.

FGEN sigle f (= Fédération générale de l'éducation nationale) teachers' trade union.

fi [fi] excl: **faire ~ de** to snap one's fingers at.

fiabilité [fjabilite] nf reliability.

fiable [fjabl(ə)] a reliable.

fiacre [fjakr(ə)] nm (hackney) cab ou carriage.

fiançailles [fjɑ̃saj] nfpl engagement sg.

fiancé, e [fjɑ̃se] nm/f fiancé/fiancée ♦ a: **être**

~ **(à)** to be engaged (to).

fiancer [fjɑ̃se]: **se** ~ *vi*: **se** ~ **(avec)** to become engaged (to).

fiasco [fjasko] *nm* fiasco.

fibranne [fibʀan] *nf* bonded fibre *ou* fiber (*US*).

fibre [fibʀ(ə)] *nf* fibre, fiber (*US*); **avoir la** ~ **paternelle/militaire** to be a born father/ soldier; ~ **optique** optical fibre *ou* fiber; ~ **de verre** fibreglass (*Brit*), fiberglass (*US*), glass fibre *ou* fiber.

fibreux, euse [fibʀø, -øz] *a* fibrous; (*viande*) stringy.

fibrome [fibʀom] *nm* (*MÉD*) fibroma.

ficelage [fisla3] *nm* tying (up).

ficeler [fisle] *vt* to tie up.

ficelle [fisɛl] *nf* string *q*; (*morceau*) piece *ou* length of string; (*pain*) stick of French bread; ~**s** *pl* (*fig*) strings; **tirer sur la** ~ (*fig*) to go too far.

fiche [fiʃ] *nf* (*carte*) (index) card; (*INFORM*) record; (*formulaire*) form; (*ÉLEC*) plug; ~ **de paye** pay slip; ~ **signalétique** (*POLICE*) identification card; ~ **technique** data sheet, specification *ou* spec sheet.

ficher [fiʃe] *vt* (*dans un fichier*) to file; (: *POLICE*) to put on file; (*planter*): ~ **qch dans** to stick *ou* drive sth into; (*fam*) to do; (: *donner*) to give; (: *mettre*) to stick *ou* shove; ~ **qn à la porte** (*fam*) to chuck sb out; **fiche(-moi) le camp** (*fam*) clear off; **fiche-moi la paix** (*fam*) leave me alone; **se** ~ **dans** (*s'enfoncer*) to get stuck in, embed itself in; **se** ~ **de** (*fam*) to make fun of; not to care about.

fichier [fiʃje] *nm* (*gén*, *INFORM*) file; (*à cartes*) card index; ~ **actif** *ou* **en cours d'utilisation** (*INFORM*) active file; ~ **d'adresses** mailing list; ~ **d'archives** (*INFORM*) archive file.

fichu, e [fiʃy] *pp de* **ficher** (*fam*) *a* (*fam*: *fini, inutilisable*) bust, done for; (: *intensif*) wretched, darned ♦ *nm* (*foulard*) (head)scarf (*pl* -scarves); **être** ~ **de** to be capable of; **mal** ~ feeling lousy; useless; **bien** ~ great.

fictif, ive [fiktif, -iv] *a* fictitious.

fiction [fiksjɔ̃] *nf* fiction; (*fait imaginé*) invention.

fictivement [fiktivmɑ̃] *ad* fictitiously.

fidèle [fidɛl] *a*: ~ **(à)** faithful (to) ♦ *nmf* (*REL*): **les** ~**s** the faithful; (*à l'église*) the congregation.

fidèlement [fidɛlmɑ̃] *ad* faithfully.

fidélité [fidelite] *nf* faithfulness.

Fidji [fidʒi] *nfpl*: **(les îles)** ~ Fiji.

fief [fjɛf] *nm* fief; (*fig*) preserve; stronghold.

fieffé, e [fjefe] *a* (*ivrogne, menteur*) arrant, out-and-out.

fiel [fjɛl] *nm* gall.

fiente [fjɑ̃t] *nf* (*bird*) droppings *pl*.

fier [fje]: **se** ~ **à** *vt* to trust.

fier, fière [fjɛʀ] *a* proud; ~ **de** proud of; **avoir fière allure** to cut a fine figure.

fièrement [fjɛʀmɑ̃] *ad* proudly.

fierté [fjɛʀte] *nf* pride.

fièvre [fjɛvʀ(ə)] *nf* fever; **avoir de la** ~**/39 de** ~ to have a high temperature/a temperature of 39°C; ~ **typhoïde** typhoid fever.

fiévreusement [fjevʀøzmɑ̃] *ad* (*fig*) feverishly.

fiévreux, euse [fjevʀø, -øz] *a* feverish.

FIFA [fifa] *sigle f* (= *Fédération internationale de Football Association*) FIFA.

fifre [fifʀ(ə)] *nm* fife; (*personne*) fife-player.

figer [fiʒe] *vt* to congeal; (*fig*: *personne*) to freeze, root to the spot; **se** ~ *vi* to congeal; to freeze; (*institutions etc*) to become set, stop evolving.

fignoler [fiɲɔle] *vt* to put the finishing touches to.

figue [fig] *nf* fig.

figuier [figje] *nm* fig tree.

figurant, e [figyʀɑ̃, -ɑ̃t] *nm/f* (*THÉÂTRE*) walk-on; (*CINÉMA*) extra.

figuratif, ive [figyʀatif, -iv] *a* representational, figurative.

figuration [figyʀasjɔ̃] *nf* walk-on parts *pl*; extras *pl*.

figure [figyʀ] *nf* (*visage*) face; (*image, tracé, forme, personnage*) figure; (*illustration*) picture, diagram; **faire** ~ **de** to look like; **faire bonne** ~ to put up a good show; **faire triste** ~ to be a sorry sight; ~ **de rhétorique** figure of speech.

figuré, e [figyʀe] *a* (*sens*) figurative.

figurer [figyʀe] *vi* to appear ♦ *vt* to represent; **se** ~ **que** to imagine that; **figurez-vous que** ... would you believe that ...?

figurine [figyʀin] *nf* figurine.

fil [fil] *nm* (*brin, fig*: *d'une histoire*) thread; (*du téléphone*) cable, wire; (*textile de lin*) linen; (*d'un couteau*: *tranchant*) edge; **au** ~ **des années** with the passing of the years; **au** ~ **de l'eau** with the stream *ou* current; **de** ~ **en aiguille** one thing leading to another; **ne tenir qu'à un** ~ (*vie, réussite etc*) to hang by a thread; **donner du** ~ **à retordre à qn** to make life difficult for sb; **donner/recevoir un coup de** ~ to make/get a phone call; ~ **à coudre** (sewing) thread *ou* yarn; ~ **électrique** electric wire; ~ **de fer** wire; ~ **de fer barbelé** barbed wire; ~ **à pêche** fishing line; ~ **à plomb** plumbline; ~ **à souder** soldering wire.

filament [filamɑ̃] *nm* (*ÉLEC*) filament; (*de liquide*) trickle, thread.

filandreux, euse [filɑ̃dʀø, -øz] *a* stringy.

filant, e [filɑ̃, -ɑ̃t] *a*: **étoile** ~**e** shooting star.

filasse [filas] *a inv* white blond.

filature [filatyʀ] *nf* (*fabrique*) mill; (*policière*) shadowing *q*, tailing *q*; **prendre qn en** ~ to shadow *ou* tail sb.

fildefériste [fildəfeʀist(ə)] *nm/f* high-wire artist.

file [fil] *nf* line; ~ **(d'attente)** queue (*Brit*), line (*US*); **prendre la** ~ to join the (end of the) queue *ou* line; **prendre la** ~ **de droite** (*AUTO*) to move into the right-hand lane; **se mettre en** ~ to form a line; **stationner en double** ~ (*AUTO*) to double-park; **à la** ~ *ad* (*d'affilée*) in succession; (*à la suite*) one after another; **à la** *ou* **en** ~ **indienne** in single file.

filer [file] *vt* (*tissu, toile, verre*) to spin; (*dérouler*: *câble etc*) to pay *ou* let out; (*prendre en filature*) to shadow, tail; (*fam*: *donner*): ~ **qch à qn** to slip sb sth ♦ *vi* (*bas, maille, liquide, pâte*) to run; (*aller vite*) to fly past *ou* by; (*fam*: *partir*) to make off; ~ **à l'anglaise** to take French leave; ~ **doux** to behave o.s., toe the line; ~ **un mauvais coton** to be in a bad way.

filet [filɛ] *nm* net; (*CULIN*) fillet; (*d'eau, de sang*) trickle; **tendre un** ~ (*suj: police*) to set a trap; ~ **(à bagages)** (*RAIL*) luggage rack; ~ **(à provisions)** string bag.

filetage [filtaʒ] *nm* threading; thread.

fileter [filte] *vt* to thread.

filial, e, aux [filjal, -o] *a* filial ♦ *nf* (*COMM*) subsidiary; affiliate.

filiation [filjasjɔ̃] *nf* filiation.

filière [filjɛʀ] *nf*: **passer par la** ~ to go through the (administrative) channels; **suivre la** ~ to work one's way up (through the hierarchy).

filiforme [filifɔʀm(ə)] *a* spindly; threadlike.

filigrane [filigran] *nm* (*d'un billet, timbre*) watermark; **en** ~ (*fig*) showing just beneath the surface.

filin [filɛ̃] *nm* (*NAVIG*) rope.

fille [fij] *nf* girl; (*opposé à fils*) daughter; **vieille** ~ old maid; ~ **de joie** prostitute; ~ **de salle** waitress.

fille-mère, *pl* **filles-mères** [fijmɛʀ] *nf* unmarried mother.

fillette [fijɛt] *nf* (little) girl.

filleul, e [fijœl] *nm/f* godchild, godson/daughter.

film [film] *nm* (*pour photo*) (roll of) film; (*œuvre*) film, picture, movie; (*couche*) film; ~ **muet/parlant** silent/talking picture *ou* movie; ~ **d'animation** animated film; ~ **policier** thriller.

filmer [filme] *vt* to film.

filon [filɔ̃] *nm* vein, lode; (*fig*) lucrative line, moneyspinner.

filou [filu] *nm* (*escroc*) swindler.

fils [fis] *nm* son; ~ **de famille** moneyed young man; ~ **à papa** (*péj*) daddy's boy.

filtrage [filtʀaʒ] *nm* filtering.

filtrant, e [filtʀɑ̃, -ɑ̃t] *a* (*huile solaire etc*) filtering.

filtre [filtʀ(ə)] *nm* filter; **"~ ou sans ~?"** (*cigarettes*) "tipped or plain?"; ~ **à air** air filter.

filtrer [filtʀe] *vt* to filter; (*fig: candidats, visiteurs*) to screen ♦ *vi* to filter (through).

fin [fɛ̃] *nf* end; ~**s** *nfpl* (*but*) ends; **à (la)** ~ **mai**, ~ **mai** at the end of May; **en** ~ **de semaine** at the end of the week; **prendre** ~ to come to an end; **toucher à sa** ~ to be drawing to a close; **mettre** ~ **à** to put an end to; **mener à bonne** ~ to bring to a successful conclusion; **à cette** ~ to this end; **à toutes** ~**s utiles** for your information; **à la** ~ in the end, eventually; **sans** ~ *a* endless ♦ *ad* endlessly; ~ **de non-recevoir** (*JUR, ADMIN*) objection; ~ **de section** (*de ligne d'autobus*) (fare) stage.

fin, e [fɛ̃, fin] *a* (*papier, couche, fil*) thin; (*cheveux, poudre, pointe, visage*) fine; (*taille*) neat, slim; (*esprit, remarque*) subtle; shrewd ♦ *ad* (*moudre, couper*) finely ♦ *nm*: **vouloir jouer au plus** ~ **(avec qn)** to try to outsmart sb ♦ *nf* (*alcool*) liqueur brandy; **c'est** ~! (*ironique*) how clever!; ~ **prêt/soûl** quite ready/drunk; **un** ~ **gourmet** a gourmet; **un** ~ **tireur** a crack shot; **avoir la vue/l'ouïe** ~**e** to have sharp eyes/ears, have keen eyesight/hearing; **or/linge/vin** ~ fine gold/linen/wine; **le** ~ **fond de** the very depths of; **le** ~ **mot de** the real story behind; **la** ~**e fleur de** the flower of; **une** ~**e mouche** (*fig*) a sharp customer; ~**es herbes** mixed herbs.

final, e [final] *a, nf* final ♦ *nm* (*MUS*) finale; **quarts de** ~**e** quarter finals; **8èmes/16èmes de** ~**e** 2nd/1st round (*in 5 round knock-out competition*).

finalement [finalmɑ̃] *ad* finally, in the end; (*après tout*) after all.

finaliste [finalist(ə)] *nm/f* finalist.

finance [finɑ̃s] *nf* finance; ~**s** *nfpl* (*situation financière*) finances; (*activités financières*) finance *sg*; **moyennant** ~ for a fee *ou* consideration.

financement [finɑ̃smɑ̃] *nm* financing.

financer [finɑ̃se] *vt* to finance.

financier, ière [finɑ̃sje, -jɛʀ] *a* financial ♦ *nm* financier.

financièrement [finɑ̃sjɛʀmɑ̃] *ad* financially.

finasser [finase] *vi* (*péj*) to wheel and deal.

finaud, e [fino, -od] *a* wily.

fine [fin] *af*, *nf voir* **fin, e**.

finement [finmɑ̃] *ad* thinly; finely; neatly, slimly; subtly; shrewdly.

finesse [finɛs] *nf* thinness; fineness; neatness, slimness; subtlety; shrewdness; ~**s** *nfpl* (*subtilités*) niceties; finer points.

fini, e [fini] *a* finished; (*MATH*) finite; (*intensif*): **un menteur** ~ a liar through and through ♦ *nm* (*d'un objet manufacturé*) finish.

finir [finiʀ] *vt* to finish ♦ *vi* to finish, end; ~ **quelque part** to end *ou* finish up somewhere; ~ **de faire** to finish doing; (*cesser*) to stop doing; ~ **par faire** to end *ou* finish up doing; **il finit par m'agacer** he's beginning to get on my nerves; ~ **en pointe/tragédie** to end in a point/in tragedy; **en** ~ **avec** to be *ou* have done with; **à n'en plus** ~ (*route, discussions*) never-ending; **il va mal** ~ he will come to a bad end; **c'est bientôt fini?** (*reproche*) have you quite finished?

finish [finiʃ] *nm* (*SPORT*) finish.

finissage [finisaʒ] *nm* finishing.

finisseur, euse [finisœʀ, -øz] *nm/f* (*SPORT*) strong finisher.

finition [finisjɔ̃] *nf* finishing; finish.

finlandais, e [fɛ̃lɑ̃dɛ, -ɛz] *a* Finnish ♦ *nm/f*: **F~, e** Finn.

Finlande [fɛ̃lɑ̃d] *nf*: **la** ~ Finland.

finnois, e [finwa, -waz] *a* Finnish ♦ *nm* (*LING*) Finnish.

fiole [fjɔl] *nf* phial.

fiord [fjɔʀ(d)] *nm* = **fjord**.

fioriture [fjɔʀityʀ] *nf* embellishment, flourish.

fioul [fjul] *nm* fuel oil.

firent [fiʀ] *vb voir* **faire**.

firmament [fiʀmamɑ̃] *nm* firmament, skies *pl*.

firme [fiʀm(ə)] *nf* firm.

fis [fi] *vb voir* **faire**.

fisc [fisk] *nm* tax authorities *pl*, ≈ Inland Revenue (*Brit*), ≈ Internal Revenue Service (*US*).

fiscal, e, aux [fiskal, -o] *a* tax *cpd*, fiscal.

fiscaliser [fiskalize] *vt* to subject to tax.

fiscaliste [fiskalist] *nm/f* tax specialist.

fiscalité [fiskalite] *nf* tax system; (*charges*) taxation.

fission [fisjɔ̃] *nf* fission.

fissure [fisyʀ] *nf* crack.

fissurer [fisyʀe] *vt*, **se ~** *vi* to crack.

fiston [fistɔ̃] *nm* (*fam*) son, lad.

fit [fi] *vb voir* **faire**.

fixage [fiksaʒ] *nm* (*PHOTO*) fixing.

fixateur [fiksatœʀ] *nm* (*PHOTO*) fixer; (*pour cheveux*) hair cream.

fixatif [fiksatif] *nm* fixative.

fixation [fiksasjɔ̃] *nf* fixing; fastening; setting; (*de ski*) binding; (*PSYCH*) fixation.

fixe [fiks(ə)] *a* fixed; (*emploi*) steady, regular ♦ *nm* (*salaire*) basic salary; **à heure ~** at a set time; **menu à prix ~** set menu.

fixé, e [fikse] *a* (*heure, jour*) appointed; **être ~ (sur)** to have made up one's mind (about); to know for certain (about).

fixement [fiksəmɑ̃] *ad* fixedly, steadily.

fixer [fikse] *vt* (*attacher*): **~ qch (à/sur)** to fix *ou* fasten sth (to/onto); (*déterminer*) to fix, set; (*CHIMIE, PHOTO*) to fix; (*poser son regard sur*) to look hard at, stare at; **se ~** (*s'établir*) to settle down; **~ son choix sur qch** to decide on sth; **se ~ sur** (*suj: attention*) to focus on.

fixité [fiksite] *nf* fixedness.

fjord [fjɔʀ(d)] *nm* fjord, fiord.

fl. *abr* (= *fleuve*) r, R; (= *florin*) fl.

flacon [flakɔ̃] *nm* bottle.

flagellation [flaʒɛlasjɔ̃] *nf* flogging.

flageller [flaʒele] *vt* to flog, scourge.

flageoler [flaʒɔle] *vi* to have knees like jelly.

flageolet [flaʒɔle] *nm* (*MUS*) flageolet; (*CULIN*) dwarf kidney bean.

flagornerie [flagɔʀnəʀi] *nf* toadying, fawning.

flagorneur, euse [flagɔʀnœʀ, -øz] *nm/f* toady, fawner.

flagrant, e [flagʀɑ̃, -ɑ̃t] *a* flagrant, blatant; **en ~ délit** in the act, in flagrante delicto.

flair [flɛʀ] *nm* sense of smell; (*fig*) intuition.

flairer [flɛʀe] *vt* (*humer*) to sniff (at); (*détecter*) to scent.

flamand, e [flamɑ̃, -ɑ̃d] *a* Flemish ♦ *nm* (*LING*) Flemish ♦ *nm/f*: **F~, e** Fleming; **les F~s** the Flemish.

flamant [flamɑ̃] *nm* flamingo.

flambant [flɑ̃bɑ̃] *ad*: **~ neuf** brand new.

flambé, e [flɑ̃be] *a* (*CULIN*) flambé ♦ *nf* blaze; (*fig*) flaring-up, explosion.

flambeau, x [flɑ̃bo] *nm* (flaming) torch; **se passer le ~** (*fig*) to hand down the (*ou* a) tradition.

flambée [flɑ̃be] *nf* (*feu*) blaze; (*COMM*): **~ des prix** (sudden) shooting up of prices.

flamber [flɑ̃be] *vi* to blaze (up) ♦ *vt* (*poulet*) to singe; (*aiguille*) to sterilize.

flamboyant, e [flɑ̃bwajɑ̃, -ɑ̃t] *a* blazing; flaming.

flamboyer [flɑ̃bwaje] *vi* to blaze (up); (*fig*) to flame.

flamingant, e [flamɛ̃gɑ̃, -ɑ̃t] *a* Flemish-speaking ♦ *nm/f*: **F~, e** Flemish speaker; (*POL*) Flemish nationalist.

flamme [flam] *nf* flame; (*fig*) fire, fervour; **en ~s** on fire, ablaze.

flammèche [flamɛʃ] *nf* (flying) spark.

flammerole [flamʀɔl] *nf* will-o'-the-wisp.

flan [flɑ̃] *nm* (*CULIN*) custard tart *ou* pie.

flanc [flɑ̃] *nm* side; (*MIL*) flank; **à ~ de**

colline on the hillside; **prêter le ~ à** (*fig*) to lay o.s. open to.

flancher [flɑ̃ʃe] *vi* (*cesser de fonctionner*) to fail, pack up; (*armée*) to quit.

Flandre [flɑ̃dʀ(ə)] *nf*: **la ~** (*aussi*: **les ~s**) Flanders.

flanelle [flanɛl] *nf* flannel.

flâner [flɑne] *vi* to stroll.

flânerie [flɑnʀi] *nf* stroll.

flâneur, euse [flɑnœʀ, -øz] *a* idle ♦ *nm/f* stroller.

flanquer [flɑ̃ke] *vt* to flank; (*fam: jeter*): **~ par terre/à la porte** to fling to the ground/ chuck out; (*: donner*): **~ la frousse à qn** to put the wind up sb, give sb an awful fright.

flapi, e [flapi] *a* dog-tired.

flaque [flak] *nf* (*d'eau*) puddle; (*d'huile, de sang etc*) pool.

flash, pl flashes [flaʃ] *nm* (*PHOTO*) flash; **~ (d'information)** newsflash.

flasque [flask(ə)] *a* flabby ♦ *nf* (*flacon*) flask.

flatter [flate] *vt* to flatter; (*caresser*) to stroke; **se ~ de qch** to pride o.s. on sth.

flatterie [flatʀi] *nf* flattery.

flatteur, euse [flatœʀ, -øz] *a* flattering ♦ *nm/f* flatterer.

flatulence [flatylɑ̃s], **flatuosité** [flatɥozite] *nf* (*MÉD*) flatulence, wind.

FLB *abr* (= *franco long du bord*) FAS ♦ *sigle m* (*POL*) = *Front de libération de la Bretagne*.

FLC *sigle m* = *Front de libération de la Corse*.

fléau, x [fleo] *nm* scourge, curse; (*de balance*) beam; (*pour le blé*) flail.

fléchage [fleʃaʒ] *nm* (*d'un itinéraire*) signposting.

flèche [flɛʃ] *nf* arrow; (*de clocher*) spire; (*de grue*) jib; (*trait d'esprit, critique*) shaft; **monter en ~** (*fig*) to soar, rocket; **partir en ~** (*fig*) to be off like a shot; **à ~ variable** (*avion*) swing-wing *cpd*.

flécher [fleʃe] *vt* to arrow, mark with arrows.

fléchette [fleʃɛt] *nf* dart; **~s** *nfpl* (*jeu*) darts *sg*.

fléchir [fleʃiʀ] *vt* (*corps, genou*) to bend; (*fig*) to sway, weaken ♦ *vi* (*poutre*) to sag, bend; (*fig*) to weaken, flag; (*: baisser: prix*) to fall off.

fléchissement [fleʃismɑ̃] *nm* bending; sagging; flagging; (*de l'économie*) dullness.

flegmatique [flɛgmatik] *a* phlegmatic.

flegme [flɛgm(ə)] *nm* composure.

flemmard, e [flemaʀ, -aʀd(ə)] *nm/f* lazybones *sg*, loafer.

flemme [flɛm] *nf* (*fam*): **j'ai la ~ de faire** I can't be bothered to do.

flétan [fletɑ̃] *nm* (*ZOOL*) halibut.

flétrir [fletʀiʀ] *vt* to wither; (*stigmatiser*) to condemn in the most severe terms; **se ~** *vi* to wither.

fleur [flœʀ] *nf* flower; (*d'un arbre*) blossom; **être en ~** (*arbre*) to be in blossom; **tissu à ~s** flowered *ou* flowery fabric; **la (fine) ~ de** (*fig*) the flower of; **être ~ bleue** to be soppy *ou* sentimental; **à ~ de terre** just above the ground; **faire une ~ à qn** to do sb a favour (*Brit*) *ou* favor (*US*); **~ de lis** fleur-de-lis.

fleurer [flœʀe] *vt*: **~ la lavande** to have the scent of lavender.

fleuret 160 **fois**

fleuret [flœʀɛ] *nm* (*arme*) foil; (*sport*) fencing.

fleurette [flœʀɛt] *nf*: **conter ~ à qn** to whisper sweet nothings to sb.

fleuri, e [flœʀi] *a* in flower *ou* bloom; surrounded by flowers; (*fig: style*) flowery; (: *teint*) glowing.

fleurir [flœʀiʀ] *vi* (*rose*) to flower; (*arbre*) to blossom; (*fig*) to flourish ♦ *vt* (*tombe*) to put flowers on; (*chambre*) to decorate with flowers.

fleuriste [flœʀist(ə)] *nm/f* florist.

fleuron [flœʀɔ̃] *nm* jewel (*fig*).

fleuve [flœv] *nm* river; **roman-~** saga; **discours-~** interminable speech.

flexibilité [flɛksibilite] *nf* flexibility.

flexible [flɛksibl(ə)] *a* flexible.

flexion [flɛksjɔ̃] *nf* flexing, bending; (*LING*) inflection.

flibustier [flibystje] *nm* buccaneer.

flic [flik] *nm* (*fam: péj*) cop.

flipper *nm* [flipœʀ] pinball (machine) ♦ *vi* [flipe] (*fam: être déprimé*) to feel down, be on a downer; (: *être exalté*) to freak out.

flirt [flœʀt] *nm* flirting; (*personne*) boyfriend, girlfriend.

flirter [flœʀte] *vi* to flirt.

FLN *sigle m* = *Front de libération nationale* (*during the Algerian war*).

FLNKS *sigle m* (= *Front de libération nationale kanak et socialiste*) *political movement in New Caledonia*.

flocon [flɔkɔ̃] *nm* flake; (*de laine etc: boulette*) flock; **~s d'avoine** oatflakes, porridge oats.

floconneux, euse [flɔkɔnø, -øz] *a* fluffy, fleecy.

flonflons [flɔ̃flɔ̃] *nmpl* blare *sg.*

flopée [flɔpe] *nf*: **une ~ de** loads of.

floraison [flɔʀɛzɔ̃] *nf* (*voir fleurir*) flowering; blossoming; flourishing.

floral, e, aux [flɔʀal, -o] *a* floral, flower *cpd.*

floralies [flɔʀali] *nfpl* flower show *sg.*

flore [flɔʀ] *nf* flora.

Florence [flɔʀɑ̃s] *n* (*ville*) Florence.

florentin, e [flɔʀɑ̃tɛ̃, -in] *a* Florentine.

floriculture [flɔʀikyltyʀ] *nf* flower-growing.

florissant, e [flɔʀisɑ̃, -ɑ̃t] *vb voir fleurir* ♦ *a* flourishing; (*santé, teint, mine*) blooming.

flot [flo] *nm* flood, stream; (*marée*) flood tide; **~s** *nmpl* (*de la mer*) waves; **être à ~** (*NAVIG*) to be afloat; (*fig*) to be on an even keel; **à ~s** (*couler*) in torrents; **entrer à ~s** to stream *ou* pour in.

flottage [flɔtaʒ] *nm* (*du bois*) floating.

flottaison [flɔtɛzɔ̃] *nf*: **ligne de ~** waterline.

flottant, e [flɔtɑ̃, -ɑ̃t] *a* (*vêtement*) loose(-fitting); (*cours, barème*) floating.

flotte [flɔt] *nf* (*NAVIG*) fleet; (*fam*) water; rain.

flottement [flɔtmɑ̃] *nm* (*fig*) wavering, hesitation; (*ÉCON*) floating.

flotter [flɔte] *vi* to float; (*nuage, odeur*) to drift; (*drapeau*) to fly; (*vêtements*) to hang loose ♦ *vb impersonnel* (*fam: pleuvoir*): **il flotte** it's raining ♦ *vt* to float; **faire ~** to float.

flotteur [flɔtœʀ] *nm* float.

flottille [flɔtij] *nf* flotilla.

flou, e [flu] *a* fuzzy, blurred; (*fig*) woolly (*Brit*), vague; (*non ajusté: robe*) loose(-fitting).

flouer [flue] *vt* to swindle.

FLQ *abr* (= *franco long du quai*) FAQ.

fluctuation [flyktɥasjɔ̃] *nf* fluctuation.

fluctuer [flyktɥe] *vi* to fluctuate.

fluet, te [flyɛ, -ɛt] *a* thin, slight; (*voix*) thin.

fluide [flɥid] *a* fluid; (*circulation etc*) flowing freely ♦ *nm* fluid; (*force*) (mysterious) power.

fluidifier [flɥidifje] *vt* to make fluid.

fluidité [flɥidite] *nf* fluidity; free flow.

fluor [flyɔʀ] *nm* fluorine.

fluoré, e [flyɔʀe] *a* fluoridated.

fluorescent, e [flyɔʀesɑ̃, -ɑ̃t] *a* fluorescent.

flûte [flyt] *nf* (*aussi*: **~ traversière**) flute; (*verre*) flute glass; (*pain*) long loaf (*pl* loaves); **petite ~** piccolo (*pl* -s); **~!** drat it!; **~ (à bec)** recorder; **~ de Pan** panpipes *pl.*

flûtiste [flytist(ə)] *nm/f* flautist, flute player.

fluvial, e, aux [flyvjal, -o] *a* river *cpd*, fluvial.

flux [fly] *nm* incoming tide; (*écoulement*) flow; **le ~ et le reflux** the ebb and flow.

fluxion [flyksjɔ̃] *nf*: **~ de poitrine** pneumonia.

FM *sigle f* (= *frequency modulation*) FM.

Fme *abr* (= *femme*) W.

FMI *sigle m* (= *Fonds monétaire international*) IMF.

FN *sigle m* (= *Front national*) ≈ NF (= *National Front*).

FNAC [fnak] *sigle f* (= *Fédération nationale des achats des cadres*) *chain of discount shops* (*hi-fi, photo etc*).

FNAH *sigle m* = *Fonds national d'amélioration de l'habitat.*

FNEF [fnɛf] *sigle f* (= *Fédération nationale des étudiants de France*) *student union.*

FNSEA *sigle f* (= *Fédération nationale des syndicats d'exploitants agricoles*) *farmers' union.*

FO *sigle f* (= *Force ouvrière*) *trades union.*

foc [fɔk] *nm* jib.

focal, e, aux [fɔkal, -o] *a* focal ♦ *nf* focal length.

focaliser [fɔkalize] *vt* to focus.

foehn [føn] *nm* foehn, föhn.

fœtal, e, aux [fetal, -o] *a* fetal, foetal (*Brit*).

fœtus [fetys] *nm* fetus, foetus (*Brit*).

foi [fwa] *nf* faith; **sous la ~ du serment** under *ou* on oath; **ajouter ~ à** to lend credence to; **faire ~** (*prouver*) to be evidence; **digne de ~** reliable; **sur la ~ de** on the word *ou* strength of; **être de bonne/mauvaise ~** to be in good faith/not to be in good faith; **ma ~!** well!

foie [fwa] *nm* liver; **~ gras** foie gras.

foin [fwɛ̃] *nm* hay; **faire les ~s** to make hay; **faire du ~** (*fam*) to kick up a row.

foire [fwaʀ] *nf* fair; (*fête foraine*) (fun) fair; (*fig: désordre, confusion*) bear garden; **faire la ~** to whoop it up; **~ (exposition)** trade fair.

fois [fwa] *nf* time; **une/deux ~** once/twice; **trois/vingt ~** three/twenty times; **2 ~ 2** 2 times 2; **deux/quatre ~ plus grand (que)** twice/four times as big (as); **une ~** (*passé*) once; (*futur*) sometime; **une (bonne) ~ pour toutes** once and for all; **encore une ~** again, once more; **il était une ~** once upon a time;

une ~ que c'est fait once it's done; une ~ parti once he (ou I etc) had left; des ~ (parfois) sometimes; si des ~ ... (fam) if ever ...; non mais des ~! (fam) (now) look here!; à la ~ (ensemble) (all) at once; à la ~ grand et beau both tall and handsome.

foison [fwazɔ̃] nf: une ~ de an abundance of; à ~ ad in plenty.

foisonnant, e [fwazɔnɑ̃, -ɑ̃t] a teeming.

foisonnement [fwazɔnmɑ̃] nm profusion, abundance.

foisonner [fwazɔne] vi to abound; ~ en ou de to abound in.

fol [fɔl] am voir **fou**.

folâtre [fɔlɑtr(ə)] a playful.

folâtrer [fɔlɑtre] vi to frolic (about).

folichon, ne [fɔliʃɔ̃, -ɔn] a: ça n'a rien de ~ it's not a lot of fun.

folie [fɔli] nf (d'une décision, d'un acte) madness, folly; (état) madness, insanity; (acte) folly; la ~ des grandeurs delusions of grandeur; faire des ~s (en dépenses) to be extravagant.

folklore [fɔlklɔr] nm folklore.

folklorique [fɔlklɔrik] a folk cpd; (fam) weird.

folle [fɔl] af, nf voir **fou**.

follement [fɔlmɑ̃] ad (très) madly, wildly.

follet [fɔlɛ] am: feu ~ will-o'-the-wisp.

fomentateur, trice [fɔmɑ̃tatœr, -tris] nm/f agitator.

fomenter [fɔmɑ̃te] vt to stir up, foment.

foncé, e [fɔ̃se] a dark; **bleu ~** dark blue.

foncer [fɔ̃se] vt to make darker; (CULIN: moule etc) to line ♦ vi to go darker; (fam: aller vite) to tear ou belt along; ~ sur to charge at.

fonceur, euse [fɔ̃sœr, -øz] nm/f whizz kid.

foncier, ière [fɔ̃sje, -jɛr] a (honnêteté etc) basic, fundamental; (malhonnêteté) deeprooted; (COMM) real estate cpd.

foncièrement [fɔ̃sjɛrmɑ̃] ad basically, (absolument) thoroughly.

fonction [fɔ̃ksjɔ̃] nf (rôle, MATH, LING) function; (emploi, poste) post, position; ~s (professionnelles) duties; entrer en ~s to take up one's post ou duties; to take up office; voiture de ~ company car; être ~ de (dépendre de) to depend on; en ~ de (par rapport à) according to; faire ~ de to serve as; la ~ publique the state ou civil (Brit) service.

fonctionnaire [fɔ̃ksjɔnɛr] nm/f state employee ou official; (dans l'administration) ≈ civil servant (Brit).

fonctionnariser [fɔ̃ksjɔnarize] vt (ADMIN: personne) to give the status of a state employee to.

fonctionnel, le [fɔ̃ksjɔnɛl] a functional.

fonctionnellement [fɔ̃ksjɔnɛlmɑ̃] ad functionally.

fonctionnement [fɔ̃ksjɔnmɑ̃] nm working; functioning; operation.

fonctionner [fɔ̃ksjɔne] vi to work, function; (entreprise) to operate, function; faire ~ to work, operate.

fond [fɔ̃] nm voir aussi **fonds**; (d'un récipient, trou) bottom; (d'une salle, scène) back; (d'un tableau, décor) background; (opposé à la forme) content; (petite quantité): un ~ de verre a drop; (SPORT): le ~ long distance (running); course/épreuve de ~ long-distance race/trial; au ~ de at the bottom of; at the back of; aller au ~ des choses to get to the root of things; le ~ de sa pensée his (ou her) true thoughts ou feelings; sans ~ a bottomless; envoyer par le ~ (NAVIG: couler) to sink, scuttle; à ~ ad (connaître, soutenir) thoroughly; (appuyer, visser) right down ou home; à ~ (de train) ad (fam) full tilt; dans le ~, au ~ ad (en somme) basically, really; de ~ en comble ad from top to bottom; ~ sonore background noise; background music; ~ de teint (make-up) foundation.

fondamental, e, aux [fɔ̃damɑ̃tal, -o] a fundamental.

fondamentalement [fɔ̃damɑ̃talmɑ̃] ad fundamentally.

fondamentalisme [fɔ̃damɑ̃talism(ə)] nm fundamentalism.

fondant, e [fɔ̃dɑ̃, -ɑ̃t] a (neige) melting; (poire) that melts in the mouth; (chocolat) fondant.

fondateur, trice [fɔ̃datœr, -tris] nm/f founder; membre ~ founder (Brit) ou founding (US) member.

fondation [fɔ̃dasjɔ̃] nf founding; (établissement) foundation; ~s nfpl (d'une maison) foundations; travail de ~ foundation works pl.

fondé, e [fɔ̃de] a (accusation etc) wellfounded; mal ~ unfounded; être ~ à croire to have grounds for believing ou good reason to believe ♦ nm: ~ de pouvoir authorized representative.

fondement [fɔ̃dmɑ̃] nm (derrière) behind; ~s nmpl foundations; sans ~ a (rumeur etc) groundless, unfounded.

fonder [fɔ̃de] vt to found; (fig): ~ qch sur to base sth on; se ~ sur (suj: personne) to base o.s. on; ~ un foyer (se marier) to set up home.

fonderie [fɔ̃dri] nf smelting works sg.

fondeur, euse [fɔ̃dœr, -øz] nm/f (skieur) long-distance skier ♦ nm: (ouvrier) ~ caster.

fondre [fɔ̃dr(ə)] vt to melt; (dans l'eau: sucre, sel) to dissolve; (fig: mélanger) to merge, blend ♦ vi to melt; to dissolve; (fig) to melt away; (se précipiter): ~ sur to swoop down on; se ~ vi (se combiner, se confondre) to merge into each other; to dissolve; ~ en larmes to dissolve into tears.

fondrière [fɔ̃drijɛr] nf rut.

fonds [fɔ̃] nm (de bibliothèque) collection; (COMM): ~ (de commerce) business; (fig): ~ de probité etc fund of integrity etc ♦ nmpl (argent) funds; à ~ perdus ad with little or no hope of getting the money back; être en ~ to be in funds; mise de ~ investment, (capital) outlay; F~ Monétaire International (FMI) International Monetary Fund (IMF); ~ de roulement nm float.

fondu, e [fɔ̃dy] a (beurre, neige) melted; (métal) molten ♦ nm (CINÉMA): ~ (enchaîné) dissolve ♦ nf (CULIN) fondue.

fongicide [fɔ̃ʒisid] nm fungicide.

font [fɔ̃] *vb voir* faire.

fontaine [fɔ̃tɛn] *nf* fountain; (*source*) spring.

fonte [fɔ̃t] *nf* melting; (*métal*) cast iron; **la ~ des neiges** the (spring) thaw.

fonts baptismaux [fɔ̃batismo] *nmpl* (baptismal) font *sg*.

foot(ball) [fut(bol)] *nm* football, soccer.

footballeur, euse [futbolœʀ, -øz] *nm/f* footballer (*Brit*), football *ou* soccer player.

footing [futiŋ] *nm* jogging; **faire du ~** to go jogging.

for [fɔʀ] *nm*: **dans** *ou* **en son ~ intérieur** in one's heart of hearts.

forage [fɔʀaʒ] *nm* drilling, boring.

forain, e [fɔʀɛ̃, -ɛn] *a* fairground *cpd* ♦ *nm* (*marchand*) stallholder; (*acteur etc*) fairground entertainer.

forban [fɔʀbɑ̃] *nm* (*pirate*) pirate; (*escroc*) crook.

forçat [fɔʀsa] *nm* convict.

force [fɔʀs(ə)] *nf* strength; (*puissance: surnaturelle etc*) power; (*PHYSIQUE, MÉCANIQUE*) force; **~s** *nfpl* (*physiques*) strength *sg*; (*MIL*) forces; (*effectifs*): **d'importantes ~s de police** big contingents of police; **avoir de la ~** to be strong; **être à bout de ~** to have no strength left; **à la ~ du poignet** (*fig*) by the sweat of one's brow; **à ~ de faire** by dint of doing; **arriver en ~** (*nombreux*) to arrive in force; **cas de ~ majeure** case of absolute necessity; (*ASSURANCES*) act of God; **~ de la nature** natural force; **de ~** forcibly, by force; **de toutes mes/ses ~s** with all my/his strength; **par la ~** using force; **par la ~ des choses/d'habitude** by force of circumstances/habit; **à toute ~** (*absolument*) at all costs; **faire ~ de rames/voiles** to ply the oars/cram on sail; **être de ~ à faire** to be up to doing; **de première ~** first class; **la ~ armée** (*les troupes*) the army; **~ d'âme** fortitude; **~ de frappe** strike force; **~ d'inertie** force of inertia; **la ~ publique** the authorities responsible for public order; **~s d'intervention** (*MIL, POLICE*) peace-keeping force *sg*; **les ~s de l'ordre** the police.

forcé, e [fɔʀse] *a* forced; (*bain*) unintended; (*inévitable*): **c'est ~!** it's inevitable!, it HAS to be!

forcément [fɔʀsemɑ̃] *ad* necessarily; inevitably; (*bien sûr*) of course.

forcené, e [fɔʀsəne] *a* frenzied ♦ *nm/f* maniac.

forceps [fɔʀsɛps] *nm* forceps *pl*.

forcer [fɔʀse] *vt* (*contraindre*): **~ qn à faire** to force sb to do; (*porte, serrure, plante*) to force; (*moteur, voix*) to strain ♦ *vi* (*SPORT*) to overtax o.s.; **~ à faire qch** to force o.s. to do sth; **~ la dose/l'allure** to overdo it/increase the pace; **~ l'attention/le respect** to command attention/respect; **~ la consigne** to bypass orders.

forcing [fɔʀsiŋ] *nm* (*SPORT*): **faire le ~** to pile on the pressure.

forcir [fɔʀsiʀ] *vi* (*grossir*) to broaden out; (*vent*) to freshen.

forclore [fɔʀklɔʀ] *vt* (*JUR: personne*) to debar.

forclusion [fɔʀklyzjɔ̃] *nf* (*JUR*) debarment.

forer [fɔʀe] *vt* to drill, bore.

forestier, ière [fɔʀɛstje, -jɛʀ] *a* forest *cpd*.

foret [fɔʀɛ] *nm* drill.

forêt [fɔʀɛ] *nf* forest; **Office National des F~s** (*ADMIN*) ≈ Forestry Commission (*Brit*), ≈ National Forest Service (*US*); **la F~ Noire** the Black Forest.

foreuse [fɔʀøz] *nf* (electric) drill.

forfait [fɔʀfɛ] *nm* (*COMM*) fixed *ou* set price; all-in deal *ou* price; (*crime*) infamy; **déclarer ~** to withdraw; **gagner par ~** to win by a walkover; **travailler à ~** to work for a lump sum.

forfaitaire [fɔʀfɛtɛʀ] *a* set; inclusive.

forfait-vacances, *pl* **forfaits-vacances** [fɔʀfɛvakɑ̃s] *nm* package holiday.

forfanterie [fɔʀfɑ̃tʀi] *nf* boastfulness *q*.

forge [fɔʀʒ(ə)] *nf* forge, smithy.

forger [fɔʀʒe] *vt* to forge; (*fig: personnalité*) to form; (: *prétexte*) to contrive, make up; **être forgé de toutes pièces** to be a complete fabrication.

forgeron [fɔʀʒəʀɔ̃] *nm* (black)smith.

formaliser [fɔʀmalize]: **se ~** *vi*: **se ~ (de)** to take offence (at).

formalisme [fɔʀmalism(ə)] *nm* formality.

formalité [fɔʀmalite] *nf* formality.

format [fɔʀma] *nm* size; **petit ~** small size; (*PHOTO*) 35 mm (film).

formater [fɔʀmate] *vt* (*disque*) to format; **non formaté** unformatted.

formateur, trice [fɔʀmatœʀ, -tʀis] *a* formative.

formation [fɔʀmasjɔ̃] *nf* forming; (*éducation*) training; (*MUS*) group; (*MIL, AVIAT, GÉO*) formation; **la ~ permanente** *ou* **continue** continuing education; **la ~ professionnelle** vocational training.

forme [fɔʀm(ə)] *nf* (*gén*) form; (*d'un objet*) shape, form; **~s** *nfpl* (*bonnes manières*) proprieties; (*d'une femme*) figure *sg*; **en ~ de poire** pear-shaped, in the shape of a pear; **sous ~ de** in the form of; in the guise of; **sous ~ de cachets** in the form of tablets; **être en (bonne** *ou* **pleine) ~,** **avoir la ~** (*SPORT etc*) to be on form; **en bonne et due ~** in due form; **pour la ~** for the sake of form; **sans autre ~ de procès** (*fig*) without further ado; **prendre ~** to take shape.

formel, le [fɔʀmɛl] *a* (*preuve, décision*) definite, positive; (*logique*) formal.

formellement [fɔʀmɛlmɑ̃] *ad* (*interdit*) strictly.

former [fɔʀme] *vt* (*gén*) to form; (*éduquer: soldat, ingénieur etc*) to train; **se ~** to form; to train.

formidable [fɔʀmidabl(ə)] *a* tremendous.

formidablement [fɔʀmidabləmɑ̃] *ad* tremendously.

formol [fɔʀmɔl] *nm* formalin, formol.

formosan, e [fɔʀmozɑ̃, -an] *a* Formosan.

Formose [fɔʀmoz] *nm* Formosa.

formulaire [fɔʀmylɛʀ] *nm* form.

formule [fɔʀmyl] *nf* (*gén*) formula; (*formulaire*) form; **selon la ~ consacrée** as one says; **~ de politesse** polite phrase; (*en fin de lettre*) letter ending.

formuler [fɔʀmyle] *vt* (*émettre: réponse, vœux*) to formulate; (*expliciter: sa pensée*) to express.

forniquer [fɔʀnike] *vi* to fornicate.

fort, e [fɔʀ, fɔʀt(ə)] *a* strong; *(intensité, rendement)* high, great; *(corpulent)* large; *(doué)*: **être ~ (en)** to be good (at) ♦ *ad (serrer, frapper)* hard; *(sonner)* loud(ly); *(beaucoup)* greatly, very much; *(très)* very ♦ *nm (édifice)* fort; *(point fort)* strong point, forte; *(gén pl: personne, pays)*: **le ~, les ~s** the strong; **c'est un peu ~!** it's a bit much!; **à plus ~e raison** even more so, all the more reason; **avoir ~ à faire avec qn** to have a hard job with sb; **se faire ~ de faire** to claim one can do; **~ bien/peu** very well/few; **au plus ~ de** *(au milieu de)* in the thick of, at the height of; **~e tête** rebel.

fortement [fɔʀtəmɑ̃] *ad* strongly; *(s'intéresser)* deeply.

forteresse [fɔʀtəʀɛs] *nf* fortress.

fortifiant [fɔʀtifjɑ̃] *nm* tonic.

fortifications [fɔʀtifikasjɔ̃] *nfpl* fortifications.

fortifier [fɔʀtifje] *vt* to strengthen, fortify; *(MIL)* to fortify; **se ~** *vi (personne, santé)* to grow stronger.

fortin [fɔʀtɛ̃] *nm* (small) fort.

fortiori [fɔʀtjɔʀi]: **à ~** *ad* all the more so.

FORTRAN [fɔʀtʀɑ̃] *nm* FORTRAN.

fortuit, e [fɔʀtɥi, -it] *a* fortuitous, chance *cpd*.

fortuitement [fɔʀtɥitmɑ̃] *ad* fortuitously.

fortune [fɔʀtyn] *nf* fortune; **faire ~** to make one's fortune; **de ~** *a* makeshift; *(compagnon)* chance *cpd*.

fortuné, e [fɔʀtyne] *a* wealthy, well-off.

forum [fɔʀɔm] *nm* forum.

fosse [fos] *nf (grand trou)* pit; *(tombe)* grave; **la ~ aux lions/ours** the lions' den/bear pit; **~ commune** common *ou* communal grave; **~ (d'orchestre)** *(orchestra)* pit; **~ à purin** cesspit; **~s septique** septic tank; **~s nasales** nasal fossae.

fossé [fose] *nm* ditch; *(fig)* gulf, gap.

fossette [fosɛt] *nf* dimple.

fossile [fosil] *nm* fossil ♦ *a* fossilized, fossil *cpd*.

fossoyeur [foswajœʀ] *nm* gravedigger.

fou (fol), folle [fu, fɔl] *a* mad, crazy; *(déréglé etc)* wild, erratic; *(mèche)* stray; *(herbe)* wild; *(fam: extrême, très grand)* terrific, tremendous ♦ *nm/f* madman/woman ♦ *nm (du roi)* jester, fool; *(ÉCHECS)* bishop; **~ à lier, ~ furieux (folle furieuse)** raving mad; **être ~ de** to be mad *ou* crazy about; *(chagrin, joie, colère)* to be wild with; **faire le ~** to play *ou* act the fool; **avoir le ~ rire** to have the giggles.

foucade [fukad] *nf* caprice.

foudre [fudʀ(ə)] *nf* lightning; **~s** *nfpl (fig: colère)* wrath *sg*.

foudroyant, e [fudʀwajɑ̃, -ɑ̃t] *a* devastating; *(maladie, poison)* violent.

foudroyer [fudʀwaje] *vt* to strike down; **~ qn du regard** to look daggers at sb; **il a été foudroyé** he was struck by lightning.

fouet [fwɛ] *nm* whip; *(CULIN)* whisk; **de plein ~** *ad* head on.

fouettement [fwɛtmɑ̃] *nm* lashing *q*.

fouetter [fwete] *vt* to whip; to whisk.

fougasse [fugas] *nf type of flat pastry*.

fougère [fuʒɛʀ] *nf* fern.

fougue [fug] *nf* ardour *(Brit)*, ardor *(US)*, spirit.

fougueusement [fugøzmɑ̃] *ad* ardently.

fougueux, euse [fugø, -øz] *a* fiery, ardent.

fouille [fuj] *nf* search; **~s** *nfpl (archéologiques)* excavations; **passer à la ~** to be searched.

fouillé, e [fuje] *a* detailed.

fouiller [fuje] *vt* to search; *(creuser)* to dig; *(: suj: archéologue)* to excavate; *(approfondir: étude etc)* to go into ♦ *vi (archéologue)* to excavate; **~ dans/parmi** to rummage in/among.

fouillis [fuji] *nm* jumble, muddle.

fouine [fwin] *nf* stone marten.

fouiner [fwine] *vi (péj)*: **~ dans** to nose around *ou* about in.

fouineur, euse [fwinœʀ, -øz] *a* nosey ♦ *nm/f* nosey parker, snooper.

fouir [fwiʀ] *vt* to dig.

fouisseur, euse [fwisœʀ, -øz] *a* burrowing.

foulage [fulaʒ] *nm* pressing.

foulante [fulɑ̃t] *af*: **pompe ~** force pump.

foulard [fulaʀ] *nm* scarf *(pl* scarves).

foule [ful] *nf* crowd; **une ~ de** masses of; **venir en ~** to come in droves.

foulée [fule] *nf* stride; **dans la ~ de** on the heels of.

fouler [fule] *vt* to press; *(sol)* to tread upon; **se ~** *vi (fam)* to overexert o.s.; **se ~ la cheville** to sprain one's ankle; **~ aux pieds** to trample underfoot.

foulure [fulyʀ] *nf* sprain.

four [fuʀ] *nm* oven; *(de potier)* kiln; *(THÉÂTRE: échec)* flop; **allant au ~** oven-proof.

fourbe [fuʀb(ə)] *a* deceitful.

fourberie [fuʀbəʀi] *nf* deceit.

fourbi [fuʀbi] *nm (fam)* gear, junk.

fourbir [fuʀbiʀ] *vt*: **~ ses armes** *(fig)* to get ready for the fray.

fourbu, e [fuʀby] *a* exhausted.

fourche [fuʀʃ(ə)] *nf* pitchfork; *(de bicyclette)* fork.

fourcher [fuʀʃe] *vi*: **ma langue a fourché** it was a slip of the tongue.

fourchette [fuʀʃɛt] *nf* fork; *(STATISTIQUE)* bracket, margin.

fourchu, e [fuʀʃy] *a* split; *(arbre etc)* forked.

fourgon [fuʀgɔ̃] *nm* van; *(RAIL)* wag(g)on; **~ mortuaire** hearse.

fourgonnette [fuʀgɔnɛt] *nf* (delivery) van.

fourmi [fuʀmi] *nf* ant; **avoir des ~s** *(fig)* to have pins and needles.

fourmilière [fuʀmiljɛʀ] *nf* ant-hill; *(fig)* hive of activity.

fourmillement [fuʀmijmɑ̃] *nm (démangeaison)* pins and needles *pl*; *(grouillement)* swarming *q*.

fourmiller [fuʀmije] *vi* to swarm; **~ de** to teeming with, be swarming with.

fournaise [fuʀnɛz] *nf* blaze; *(fig)* furnace, oven.

fourneau, x [fuʀno] *nm* stove.

fournée [fuʀne] *nf* batch.

fourni, e [fuʀni] *a (barbe, cheveux)* thick; *(magasin)*: **bien ~ (en)** well stocked (with).

fournil [fuʀni] *nm* bakehouse.

fournir [fuʀniʀ] *vt* to supply; *(preuve, exemple)* to provide, supply; *(effort)* to put in; **~ qch à qn** to supply sth to sb, supply *ou* provide sb with sth; ~ **qn en** (*COMM*) to supply sb with; **se ~ chez** to shop at.

fournisseur, euse [furniscœr, -øz] *nm/f* supplier.

fourniture [furnityr] *nf* supply(ing); ~**s** *nfpl* supplies; ~**s de bureau** office supplies, stationery; ~**s scolaires** school stationery.

fourrage [fura3] *nm* fodder.

fourrager [fura3e] *vi*: ~ **dans/parmi** to rummage through/among.

fourrager, ère [fura3e, -ɛr] *a* fodder *cpd* ♦ *nf* (*MIL*) fourragère.

fourré, e [fure] *a* (*bonbon, chocolat*) filled; (*manteau, botte*) fur-lined ♦ *nm* thicket.

fourreau, x [furo] *nm* sheath; (*de parapluie*) cover; **robe/jupe** ~ figure-hugging dress/skirt.

fourrer [fure] *vt* (*fam*): ~ **qch dans** to stick *ou* shove sth into; **se ~ dans/sous** to get into/under; **se ~ dans** (*une mauvaise situation*) to land o.s. in.

fourre-tout [furtu] *nm inv* (*sac*) holdall; (*péj*) junk room (*ou* cupboard); (*fig*) rag-bag.

fourreur [furœr] *nm* furrier.

fourrière [furjɛr] *nf* pound.

fourrure [furyr] *nf* fur; (*sur l'animal*) coat; **manteau/col de** ~ fur coat/collar.

fourvoyer [furvwaje]: **se ~** *vi* to go astray, stray; **se ~ dans** to stray into.

foutre [futr(ə)] *vt* (*fam!*) = **ficher** (*fam*).

foutu, e [futy] *a* (*fam!*) = **fichu**.

foyer [fwaje] *nm* (*de cheminée*) hearth; (*fig*) seat, centre; (*famille*) family; (*domicile*) home; (*local de réunion*) (social) club; (*résidence*) hostel; (*salon*) foyer; (*OPTIQUE, PHOTO*) focus; **lunettes à double** ~ bi-focal glasses.

FP *sigle f* (= *franchise postale*) exemption *from postage*.

FPA *sigle f* (= *Formation professionnelle pour adultes*) adult education.

FPLP *sigle m* (= *Front populaire de la libération de la Palestine*) PFLP (= *Popular Front for the Liberation of Palestine*).

FR3 [ɛfɛrtrwa] *sigle f* (= *France Régions 3*) *TV channel*.

fracas [fraka] *nm* din; crash.

fracassant, e [frakasɑ̃, -ɑ̃t] *a* sensational, staggering.

fracasser [frakase] *vt* to smash; **se ~ contre** *ou* **sur** to crash against.

fraction [fraksjɔ̃] *nf* fraction.

fractionnement [fraksjɔnmɑ̃] *nm* division.

fractionner [fraksjɔne] *vt* to divide (up), split (up).

fracture [fraktyr] *nf* fracture; ~ **du crâne** fractured skull; ~ **de la jambe** broken leg.

fracturer [fraktyre] *vt* (*coffre, serrure*) to break open; (*os, membre*) to fracture.

fragile [fraʒil] *a* fragile, delicate; (*fig*) frail.

fragiliser [fraʒilize] *vt* to weaken, make fragile.

fragilité [fraʒilite] *nf* fragility.

fragment [fragmɑ̃] *nm* (*d'un objet*) fragment, piece; (*d'un texte*) passage, extract.

fragmentaire [fragmɑ̃tɛr] *a* sketchy.

fragmenter [fragmɑ̃te] *vt* to split up.

frai [frɛ] *nm* spawn; (*ponte*) spawning.

fraîche [frɛʃ] *af voir* **frais**.

fraîchement [frɛʃmɑ̃] *ad* (*sans enthousiasme*)

coolly; (*récemment*) freshly, newly.

fraîcheur [frɛʃœr] *nf* (*voir frais*) coolness; freshness.

fraîchir [frɛʃir] *vi* to get cooler; (*vent*) to freshen.

frais, fraîche [frɛ, frɛʃ] *a* (*air, eau, accueil*) cool; (*petit pois, œufs, nouvelles, couleur, troupes*) fresh; **le voilà** ~! he's in a (right) mess! (*récemment*) newly, fresh(ly); **il fait** ~ it's cool; **servir** ~ chill before serving, serve chilled ♦ *nm*: **mettre au** ~ to put in a cool place; **prendre le** ~ to take a breath of cool air ♦ *nmpl* (*débours*) expenses; (*COMM*) costs; charges; **faire des** ~ to spend; to go to a lot of expense; **faire les** ~ **de** to bear the brunt of; **faire les** ~ **de la conversation** (*parler*) to do most of the talking; (*en être le sujet*) to be the topic of conversation; **il en a été pour ses** ~ he could have spared himself the trouble; **rentrer dans ses** ~ to recover one's expenses; ~ **de déplacement** travel(ling) expenses; ~ **d'entretien** upkeep; ~ **généraux** overheads; ~ **de scolarité** school fees, tuition (*US*).

fraise [frɛz] *nf* strawberry; (*TECH*) countersink (bit); (*de dentiste*) drill; ~ **des bois** wild strawberry.

fraiser [frɛze] *vt* to countersink; (*CULIN*: *pâte*) to knead.

fraiseuse [frɛzøz] *nf* (*TECH*) milling machine.

fraisier [frɛzje] *nm* strawberry plant.

framboise [frɑ̃bwaz] *nf* raspberry.

framboisier [frɑ̃bwazje] *nm* raspberry bush.

franc, franche [frɑ̃, frɑ̃ʃ] *a* (*personne*) frank, straightforward; (*visage*) open; (*net: refus, couleur*) clear; (*: coupure*) clean; (*intensif*) downright; (*exempt*): ~ **de port** post free, postage paid; (*zone, port*) free; (*boutique*) duty-free ♦ *ad*: **parler** ~ to be frank *ou* candid ♦ *nm* franc.

français, e [frɑ̃sɛ, -ɛz] *a* French ♦ *nm* (*LING*) French ♦ *nm/f*: **F~, e** Frenchman/woman; **les F~** the French.

franc-comtois, e, *mpl* **francs-comtois** [frɑ̃kɔ̃twa, -waz] *a* of *ou* from (the) Franche-Comté.

France [frɑ̃s] *nf*: **la** ~ France; **en** ~ in France.

Francfort [frɑ̃kfɔr] *n* Frankfurt.

franche [frɑ̃ʃ] *af voir* **franc**.

franchement [frɑ̃ʃmɑ̃] *ad* (*voir franc*) frankly; clearly; (*tout à fait*) downright ♦ *excl* well, really!

franchir [frɑ̃ʃir] *vt* (*obstacle*) to clear, get over; (*seuil, ligne, rivière*) to cross; (*distance*) to cover.

franchisage [frɑ̃ʃizaʒ] *nm* (*COMM*) franchising.

franchise [frɑ̃ʃiz] *nf* frankness; (*douanière, d'impôt*) exemption; (*ASSURANCES*) excess; (*COMM*) franchise; ~ **de bagages** baggage allowance.

franchissable [frɑ̃ʃisabl(ə)] *a* (*obstacle*) surmountable.

franciscain, e [frɑ̃siskɛ̃, -ɛn] *a* Franciscan.

franciser [frɑ̃size] *vt* to gallicize, Frenchify.

franc-jeu [frɑ̃ʒø] *nm*: **jouer** ~ to play fair.

franc-maçon, *pl* **francs-maçons** [frɑ̃masɔ̃] *nm* Freemason.

franc-maçonnerie [fʀɑ̃masɔnʀi] *nf* Freemasonry.

franco [fʀɑ̃ko] *ad* (*COMM*): ~ **(de port)** postage paid.

franco... [fʀɑ̃ko] *préfixe* franco-.

franco-canadien [fʀɑ̃kɔkanadjɛ̃] *nm* (*LING*) Canadian French.

francophile [fʀɑ̃kɔfil] *a* francophile.

francophone [fʀɑ̃kɔfɔn] *a* French-speaking ♦ *nm/f* French speaker.

francophonie [fʀɑ̃kɔfɔni] *nf* French-speaking communities *pl*.

franco-québécois [fʀɑ̃kɔkebekwa] *nm* (*LING*) Quebec French.

franc-parler [fʀɑ̃paʀle] *nm inv* outspokenness.

franc-tireur [fʀɑ̃tiʀœʀ] *nm* (*MIL*) irregular; (*fig*) freelance.

frange [fʀɑ̃ʒ] *nf* fringe; (*cheveux*) fringe (*Brit*), bangs (*US*).

frangipane [fʀɑ̃ʒipan] *nf* almond paste.

franglais [fʀɑ̃ɡlɛ] *nm* Franglais.

franquette [fʀɑ̃kɛt]: **à la bonne** ~ *ad* without any fuss.

frappant, e [fʀapɑ̃, -ɑ̃t] *a* striking.

frappe [fʀap] *nf* (*d'une dactylo, pianiste, machine à écrire*) touch; (*BOXE*) punch; (*péj*) hood, thug.

frappé, e [fʀape] *a* (*CULIN*) iced; ~ **de panique** panic-stricken; ~ **de stupeur** thunderstruck, dumbfounded.

frapper [fʀape] *vt* to hit, strike; (*étonner*) to strike; (*monnaie*) to strike, stamp; **se** ~ *vi* (*s'inquiéter*) to get worked up; ~ **à la porte** to knock at the door; ~ **dans ses mains** to clap one's hands; ~ **du poing sur** to bang one's fist on; ~ **un grand coup** (*fig*) to strike a blow.

frasques [fʀask(ə)] *nfpl* escapades; **faire des** ~**s** to get up to mischief.

fraternel, le [fʀatɛʀnɛl] *a* brotherly, fraternal.

fraternellement [fʀatɛʀnɛlmɑ̃] *ad* in a brotherly way.

fraterniser [fʀatɛʀnize] *vi* to fraternize.

fraternité [fʀatɛʀnite] *nf* brotherhood.

fratricide [fʀatʀisid] *a* fratricidal.

fraude [fʀod] *nf* fraud; (*SCOL*) cheating; **passer qch en** ~ to smuggle sth in (*ou* out); ~ **fiscale** tax evasion.

frauder [fʀode] *vi*, *vt* to cheat; ~ **le fisc** to evade paying tax(es).

fraudeur, euse [fʀodœʀ, -øz] *nm/f* person guilty of fraud; (*candidat*) candidate who cheats; (*au fisc*) tax evader.

frauduleux, euse [fʀodylø, -øz] *a* fraudulent.

frayer [fʀeje] *vt* to open up, clear ♦ *vi* to spawn; (*fréquenter*): ~ **avec** to mix *ou* associate with; **se** ~ **un passage dans** to clear o.s. a path through, force one's way through.

frayeur [fʀejœʀ] *nf* fright.

fredaines [fʀədɛn] *nfpl* mischief *sg*, escapades.

fredonner [fʀədɔne] *vt* to hum.

freezer [fʀizœʀ] *nm* freezing compartment.

frégate [fʀeɡat] *nf* frigate.

frein [fʀɛ̃] *nm* brake; **mettre un** ~ **à** (*fig*) to put a brake on, check; **sans** ~ (*sans limites*) unchecked; ~ **à main** handbrake; ~ **moteur** engine braking; ~**s à disques** disc brakes;

~**s à tambour** drum brakes.

freinage [fʀenaʒ] *nm* braking; **distance de** ~ braking distance; **traces de** ~ tyre (*Brit*) *ou* tire (*US*) marks.

freiner [fʀene] *vi* to brake ♦ *vt* (*progrès etc*) to check.

frelaté, e [fʀəlate] *a* adulterated; (*fig*) tainted.

frêle [fʀɛl] *a* frail, fragile.

frelon [fʀəlɔ̃] *nm* hornet.

freluquet [fʀəlykɛ] *nm* (*péj*) whippersnapper.

frémir [fʀemiʀ] *vi* (*de froid, de peur*) to tremble, shiver; (*de joie*) to quiver; (*eau*) to (begin to) bubble.

frémissement [fʀemismɑ̃] *nm* shiver; quiver; bubbling *q*.

frêne [fʀɛn] *nm* ash (tree).

frénésie [fʀenezi] *nf* frenzy.

frénétique [fʀenetik] *a* frenzied, frenetic.

fréquemment [fʀekamɑ̃] *ad* frequently.

fréquence [fʀekɑ̃s] *nf* frequency.

fréquent, e [fʀekɑ̃, -ɑ̃t] *a* frequent.

fréquentable [fʀekɑ̃tabl(ə)] *a*: **il est peu** ~ he's not the type one can associate oneself with.

fréquentation [fʀekɑ̃tasjɔ̃] *nf* frequenting; seeing; ~**s** *nfpl* company *sg*.

fréquenté, e [fʀekɑ̃te] *a*: **très** ~ (very) busy; **mal** ~ patronized by disreputable elements.

fréquenter [fʀekɑ̃te] *vt* (*lieu*) to frequent; (*personne*) to see; **se** ~ to see a lot of each other.

frère [fʀɛʀ] *nm* brother ♦ *a*: **partis/pays** ~**s** sister parties/countries.

fresque [fʀɛsk(ə)] *nf* (*ART*) fresco.

fret [fʀɛ] *nm* freight.

fréter [fʀete] *vt* to charter.

frétiller [fʀetije] *vi* to wriggle; to quiver; ~ **de la queue** to wag its tail.

fretin [fʀətɛ̃] *nm*: **le menu** ~ the small fry.

freux [fʀø] *nm* (*ZOOL*) rook.

friable [fʀijabl(ə)] *a* crumbly.

friand, e [fʀijɑ̃, -ɑ̃d] *a*: ~ **de** very fond of ♦ *nm* (*CULIN*) small minced-meat (*Brit*) *ou* ground-meat (*US*) pie; (*: sucré*) small almond cake.

friandise [fʀijɑ̃diz] *nf* sweet.

fric [fʀik] *nm* (*fam*) cash, bread.

fricassée [fʀikase] *nf* fricassee.

fric-frac [fʀikfʀak] *nm* break-in.

friche [fʀiʃ]: **en** ~ *a*, *ad* (lying) fallow.

friction [fʀiksjɔ̃] *nf* (*massage*) rub, rub-down; (*chez le coiffeur*) scalp massage; (*TECH*, *fig*) friction.

frictionner [fʀiksjɔne] *vt* to rub (down); to massage.

frigidaire [fʀiʒidɛʀ] *nm* ® refrigerator.

frigide [fʀiʒid] *a* frigid.

frigidité [fʀiʒidite] *nf* frigidity.

frigo [fʀiɡo] *nm* (= *frigidaire*) fridge.

frigorifier [fʀiɡɔʀifje] *vt* to refrigerate; (*fig: personne*) to freeze.

frigorifique [fʀiɡɔʀifik] *a* refrigerating.

frileusement [fʀiløzmɑ̃] *ad* with a shiver.

frileux, euse [fʀilø, -øz] *a* sensitive to (the) cold; (*fig*) overcautious.

frimas [fʀima] *nmpl* wintry weather *sg*.

frime [fʀim] *nf* (*fam*): **c'est de la** ~ it's all put on; **pour la** ~ just for show.

frimer [fʀime] *vi* to put on an act.

frimeur, euse [fʀimœʀ, -øz] *nm/f* poser.

frimousse [fʀimus] *nf* (sweet) little face.

fringale [fʀɛ̃gal] *nf*: **avoir la ~** to be ravenous.

fringant, e [fʀɛ̃gɑ̃, -ɑ̃t] *a* dashing.

fringues [fʀɛ̃g] *nfpl* (*fam*) clothes, gear *q*.

fripé, e [fʀipe] *a* crumpled.

friperie [fʀipʀi] *nf* (*commerce*) secondhand clothes shop; (*vêtements*) secondhand clothes.

fripes [fʀip] *nfpl* secondhand clothes.

fripier, ière [fʀipje, -jɛʀ] *nm/f* secondhand clothes dealer.

fripon, ne [fʀipɔ̃, -ɔn] *a* roguish, mischievous ♦ *nm/f* rascal, rogue.

fripouille [fʀipuj] *nf* scoundrel.

frire [fʀiʀ] *vt* (*aussi*: **faire ~**), *vi* to fry.

frise [fʀiz] *nf* frieze.

frisé, e [fʀize] *a* curly, curly-haired ♦ *nf*: **(chicorée) ~e** curly endive.

friser [fʀize] *vt* to curl; (*fig: surface*) to skim, graze; (: *mort*) to come within a hair's breadth of; (: *hérésie*) to verge on ♦ *vi* (*cheveux*) to curl; (*personne*) to have curly hair; **se faire ~** to have one's hair curled.

frisette [fʀizɛt] *nf* little curl.

frisotter [fʀizɔte] *vi* (*cheveux*) to curl tightly.

frisquet [fʀiskɛ] *am* chilly.

frisson [fʀisɔ̃], **frissonnement** [fʀisɔnmɑ̃] *nm* shudder, shiver; quiver.

frissonner [fʀisɔne] *vi* (*personne*) to shudder, shiver; (*feuilles*) to quiver.

frit, e [fʀi, fʀit] *pp de* **frire** ♦ *a* fried ♦ *nf*: **(pommes) ~es** chips (*Brit*), French fries.

friterie [fʀitʀi] *nf* ≈ chip shop (*Brit*), ≈ hamburger stand (*US*).

friteuse [fʀitøz] *nf* chip pan (*Brit*), deep (fat) fryer.

friture [fʀityʀ] *nf* (*huile*) (deep) fat; (*plat*): **~ (de poissons)** fried fish; (*RADIO*) crackle, crackling *q*; **~s** *nfpl* (*aliments frits*) fried food *sg*.

frivole [fʀivɔl] *a* frivolous.

frivolité [fʀivɔlite] *nf* frivolity.

froc [fʀɔk] *nm* (*REL*) habit; (*fam: pantalon*) trousers *pl*, pants *pl*.

froid, e [fʀwa, fʀwad] *a* cold ♦ *nm* cold; (*absence de sympathie*) coolness *q*; **il fait ~** it's cold; **avoir ~** to be cold; **prendre ~** to catch a chill *ou* cold; **à ~** *ad* (*démarrer*) (from) cold; **(pendant) les grands ~s** (in) the depths of winter, (during) the cold season; **jeter un ~** (*fig*) to cast a chill; **être en ~ avec** to be on bad terms with; **battre ~ à qn** to give sb the cold shoulder.

froidement [fʀwadmɑ̃] *ad* (*accueillir*) coldly; (*décider*) coolly.

froideur [fʀwadœʀ] *nf* coolness *q*.

froisser [fʀwase] *vt* to crumple (up), crease; (*fig*) to hurt, offend; **se ~** *vi* to crumple, crease; to take offence (*Brit*) *ou* offense (*US*); **se ~ un muscle** to strain a muscle.

frôlement [fʀolmɑ̃] *nm* (*contact*) light touch.

frôler [fʀole] *vt* to brush against; (*suj: projectile*) to skim past; (*fig*) to come within a hair's breadth of, come very close to.

fromage [fʀɔmaʒ] *nm* cheese; **~ blanc** soft white cheese; **~ de tête** pork brawn.

fromager, ère [fʀɔmaʒe, -ɛʀ] *nm/f* cheese merchant ♦ *a* (*industrie*) cheese *cpd*.

fromagerie [fʀɔmaʒʀi] *nf* cheese dairy.

froment [fʀɔmɑ̃] *nm* wheat.

fronce [fʀɔ̃s] *nf* (*de tissu*) gather.

froncement [fʀɔ̃smɑ̃] *nm*: **~ de sourcils** frown.

froncer [fʀɔ̃se] *vt* to gather; **~ les sourcils** to frown.

frondaison [fʀɔ̃dɛzɔ̃] *nf* foliage.

fronde [fʀɔ̃d] *nf* sling; (*fig*) rebellion, rebelliousness.

frondeur, euse [fʀɔ̃dœʀ, -øz] *a* rebellious.

front [fʀɔ̃] *nm* forehead, brow; (*MIL, MÉTÉOROLOGIE, POL*) front; **avoir le ~ de faire** to have the effrontery *ou* front to do; **de ~** *ad* (*se heurter*) head-on; (*rouler*) together (*i.e. 2 or 3 abreast*); (*simultanément*) at once; **faire ~ à** to face up to; **~ de mer** (sea) front.

frontal, e, aux [fʀɔ̃tal, -o] *a* frontal.

frontalier, ière [fʀɔ̃talje, -jɛʀ] *a* border *cpd*, frontier *cpd* ♦ *nm/f*: **(travailleurs) ~s** workers who cross the border to go to work, commuters from across the border.

frontière [fʀɔ̃tjɛʀ] *nf* (*GÉO, POL*) frontier, border; (*fig*) frontier, boundary.

frontispice [fʀɔ̃tispis] *nm* frontispiece.

fronton [fʀɔ̃tɔ̃] *nm* pediment; (*de pelote basque*) (front) wall.

frottement [fʀɔtmɑ̃] *nm* rubbing, scraping; **~s** *nmpl* (*fig: difficultés*) friction *sg*.

frotter [fʀɔte] *vi* to rub, scrape ♦ *vt* to rub; (*pour nettoyer*) to rub (up); (: *avec une brosse*) to scrub; **~ une allumette** to strike a match; **se ~ à qn** to cross swords with sb; **se ~ à qch** to come up against sth; **se ~ les mains** (*fig*) to rub one's hands (gleefully).

frottis [fʀɔti] *nm* (*MÉD*) smear.

frottoir [fʀɔtwaʀ] *nm* (*d'allumettes*) friction strip; (*pour encaustiquer*) (long-handled) brush.

frou-frou, *pl* **frous-frous** [fʀufʀu] *nm* rustle.

frousse [fʀus] *nf* (*fam: peur*): **avoir la ~** to be in a blue funk.

fructifier [fʀyktifje] *vi* to yield a profit; **faire ~** to turn to good account.

fructueux, euse [fʀyktɥø, -øz] *a* fruitful; profitable.

frugal, e, aux [fʀygal, -o] *a* frugal.

fruit [fʀɥi] *nm* fruit *gén q*; **~s de mer** (*CULIN*) seafood(s); **~s secs** dried fruit *sg*.

fruité, e [fʀɥite] *a* (*vin*) fruity.

fruiterie [fʀɥitʀi] *nf* (*boutique*) greengrocer's (*Brit*), fruit (and vegetable) store (*US*).

fruitier, ière [fʀɥitje, -jɛʀ] *a*: **arbre ~** fruit tree ♦ *nm/f* fruiterer (*Brit*), fruit merchant (*US*).

fruste [fʀyst(ə)] *a* unpolished, uncultivated.

frustrant, e [fʀystʀɑ̃, -ɑ̃t] *a* frustrating.

frustration [fʀystʀasjɔ̃] *nf* frustration.

frustré, e [fʀystʀe] *a* frustrated.

frustrer [fʀystʀe] *vt* to frustrate; (*priver*): **~ qn de qch** to deprive sb of sth.

FS *abr* (= *franc suisse*) FS, SF.

FSE *sigle m* (= *foyer socio-éducatif*) community home.

FTP *sigle mpl* (= *Francs-tireurs et partisans*) Communist Resistance in 1940-45.

fuel(-oil) [fjul(ɔjl)] *nm* fuel oil; (*pour chauffer*) heating oil.

fugace [fygas] *a* fleeting.

fugitif, ive [fyʒitif, -iv] a (lueur, amour) fleeting; (prisonnier etc) runaway ♦ nm/f fugitive, runaway.

fugue [fyg] nf (d'un enfant) running away q; (MUS) fugue; **faire une ~** to run away, abscond.

fuir [fɥiʀ] vt to flee from; (éviter) to shun ♦ vi to run away; (gaz, robinet) to leak.

fuite [fɥit] nf flight; (écoulement) leak, leakage; (divulgation) leak; **être en ~** to be on the run; **mettre en ~** to put to flight; **prendre la ~** to take flight.

fulgurant, e [fylgyʀɑ̃, -ɑ̃t] a lightning cpd, dazzling.

fulminant, e [fylminɑ̃, -ɑ̃t] a (lettre, regard) furious; **~ de colère** raging with anger.

fulminer [fylmine] vi: **~ (contre)** to thunder forth (against).

fumant, e [fymɑ̃, -ɑ̃t] a smoking; (liquide) steaming; **un coup ~** (fam) a master stroke.

fumé, e [fyme] a (CULIN) smoked; (verre) tinted ♦ nf smoke; **partir en ~e** to go up in smoke.

fume-cigarette [fymsigaʀɛt] nm inv cigarette holder.

fumer [fyme] vi to smoke; (liquide) to steam ♦ vt to smoke; (terre, champ) to manure.

fumerie [fymʀi] nf: **~ d'opium** opium den.

fumerolles [fymʀɔl] nfpl gas and smoke (from volcano).

fûmes [fym] vb voir **être**.

fumet [fymɛ] nm aroma.

fumeur, euse [fymœʀ, -øz] nm/f smoker; **(compartiment) ~s** smoking compartment.

fumeux, euse [fymø, -øz] a (péj) woolly (Brit), hazy.

fumier [fymje] nm manure.

fumigation [fymigɑsjɔ̃] nf fumigation.

fumigène [fymiʒɛn] a smoke cpd.

fumiste [fymist(ə)] nm (ramoneur) chimney sweep ♦ nm/f (péj: paresseux) shirker; (charlatan) phoney.

fumisterie [fymistəʀi] nf (péj) fraud, con.

fumoir [fymwaʀ] nm smoking room.

funambule [fynãbyl] nm tightrope walker.

funèbre [fynɛbʀ(ə)] a funeral cpd; (fig) doleful; funereal.

funérailles [fyneʀɑj] nfpl funeral sg.

funéraire [fyneʀɛʀ] a funeral cpd, funerary.

funeste [fynɛst(ə)] a disastrous; deathly.

funiculaire [fynikylɛʀ] nm funicular (railway).

FUNU [fyny] sigle f (= Force d'urgence des Nations Unies) UNEF (= United Nations Emergency Forces).

fur [fyʀ]: **au ~ et à mesure** ad as one goes along; **au ~ et à mesure que** as; **au ~ et à mesure de leur progression** as they advance (ou advanced).

furax [fyʀaks] a inv (fam) livid.

furent [fyʀ] vb voir **être**.

furet [fyʀɛ] nm ferret.

fureter [fyʀte] vi (péj) to nose about.

fureur [fyʀœʀ] nf fury; (passion): **~ de** passion for; **faire ~** to be all the rage.

furibard, e [fyʀibaʀ, -aʀd(ə)] a (fam) livid, absolutely furious.

furibond, e [fyʀibɔ̃, -ɔ̃d] a livid, absolutely furious.

furie [fyʀi] nf fury; (femme) shrew, vixen; **en ~** (mer) raging.

furieusement [fyʀjøzmɑ̃] ad furiously.

furieux, euse [fyʀjø, -øz] a furious.

furoncle [fyʀɔ̃kl(ə)] nm boil.

furtif, ive [fyʀtif, -iv] a furtive.

fus [fy] vb voir **être**.

fusain [fyzɛ̃] nm (BOT) spindle-tree; (ART) charcoal.

fuseau, x [fyzo] nm (pantalon) (ski-)pants pl; (pour filer) spindle; **en ~** (jambes) tapering; (colonne) bulging; **~ horaire** time zone.

fusée [fyze] nf rocket; **~ éclairante** flare.

fuselage [fyzlaʒ] nm fuselage.

fuselé, e [fyzle] a slender; (galbé) tapering.

fuser [fyze] vi (rires etc) to burst forth.

fusible [fyzibl(ə)] nm (ÉLEC: fil) fuse wire; (: fiche) fuse.

fusil [fyzi] nm (de guerre, à canon rayé) rifle, gun; (de chasse, à canon lisse) shotgun, gun; **~ à deux coups** double-barrelled rifle ou shotgun; **~ sous-marin** spear-gun.

fusilier [fyzilje] nm (MIL) rifleman.

fusillade [fyzijad] nf gunfire q, shooting q; (combat) gun battle.

fusiller [fyzije] vt to shoot; **~ qn du regard** to look daggers at sb.

fusil-mitrailleur, pl **fusils-mitrailleurs** [fyzimitʀɑjœʀ] nm machine gun.

fusion [fyzjɔ̃] nf fusion, melting; (fig) merging; (COMM) merger; **en ~** (métal, roches) molten.

fusionnement [fyzjɔnmɑ̃] nm merger.

fusionner [fyzjɔne] vi to merge.

fustiger [fystiʒe] vt to denounce.

fut [fy] vb voir **être**.

fût [fy] vb voir **être** ♦ nm (tonneau) barrel, cask; (de canon) stock; (d'arbre) bole, trunk; (de colonne) shaft.

futaie [fytɛ] nf forest, plantation.

futé, e [fyte] a crafty.

fûtes [fyt] vb voir **être**.

futile [fytil] a (inutile) futile; (frivole) frivolous.

futilité [fytilite] nf futility; frivolousness; (chose futile) futile pursuit (ou thing etc).

futur, e [fytyʀ] a, nm future; **son ~ époux** her husband-to-be; **au ~** (LING) in the future.

futuriste [fytyʀist(ə)] a futuristic.

fuyant, e [fɥijɑ̃, -ɑ̃t] vb voir **fuir** ♦ a (regard etc) evasive; (lignes etc) receding; (perspective) vanishing.

fuyard, e [fɥijaʀ, -aʀd(ə)] nm/f runaway.

fuyons [fɥijɔ̃] etc vb voir **fuir**.

G

G, g [ʒe] nm inv G, g ♦ abr (= gramme) g; (= gauche) L, l; **G comme Gaston** G for George.

gabardine [gabaʀdin] nf gabardine.

gabarit [gabaʀi] nm (fig: dimension, taille) size; (: valeur) calibre; (TECH) template; **du**

même ~ (*fig*) of the same type, of that ilk.

gabegie [gabʒi] *nf* (*péj*) chaos.

Gabon [gabɔ̃] *nm*: **le** ~ Gabon.

gabonais, e [gabɔnɛ, -ɛz] *a* Gabonese.

gâcher [gɑʃe] *vt* (*gâter*) to spoil, ruin; (*gaspiller*) to waste; (*plâtre*) to temper; (*mortier*) to mix.

gâchette [gɑʃɛt] *nf* trigger.

gâchis [gɑʃi] *nm* (*désordre*) mess; (*gaspillage*) waste *q*.

gadget [gadʒɛt] *nm* thingumajig; (*nouveauté*) gimmick.

gadoue [gadu] *nf* sludge.

gaélique [gaelik] *a* Gaelic ♦ *nm* (*LING*) Gaelic.

gaffe [gaf] *nf* (*instrument*) boat hook; (*fam*: *erreur*) blunder; **faire** ~ (*fam*) to watch out.

gaffer [gafe] *vi* to blunder.

gaffeur, euse [gafœʀ, -øz] *nm/f* blunderer.

gag [gag] *nm* gag.

gaga [gaga] *a* (*fam*) gaga.

gage [gaʒ] *nm* (*dans un jeu*) forfeit; (*fig: de fidélité*) token; ~**s** *nmpl* (*salaire*) wages; (*garantie*) guarantee *sg*; **mettre en** ~ to pawn; **laisser en** ~ to leave as security.

gager [gaʒe] *vt*: ~ **que** to bet *ou* wager that.

gageure [gaʒyʀ] *nf*: **c'est une** ~ it's attempting the impossible.

gagnant, e [gaɲɑ̃, -ɑ̃t] *a*: **billet/numéro** ~ winning ticket/number ♦ *ad*: **jouer** ~ (*aux courses*) to be bound to win ♦ *nm/f* winner.

gagne-pain [gaɲpɛ̃] *nm inv* job.

gagne-petit [gaɲpəti] *nm inv* low wage earner.

gagner [gaɲe] *vt* (*concours, procès, pari*) to win; (*somme d'argent, revenu*) to earn; (*aller vers, atteindre*) to reach; (*s'emparer de*) to overcome; (*envahir*) to spread to; (*se concilier*): ~ **qn** to win sb over ♦ *vi* to win; (*fig*) to gain; ~ **du temps/de la place** to gain time/save space; ~ **sa vie** to earn one's living; ~ **du terrain** (*aussi fig*) to gain ground; ~ **qn de vitesse** (*aussi fig*) to outstrip sb; ~ **à faire** (*s'en trouver bien*) to be better off doing; **il y gagne** it's in his interest, it's to his advantage.

gagneur, e [gaɲœʀ] *nm* winner.

gai, e [ge] *a* cheerful; (*livre, pièce de théâtre*) light-hearted; (*un peu ivre*) merry.

gaieté [gete] *nf* cheerfulness; ~**s** *nfpl* (*souvent ironique*) delights; **de** ~ **de cœur** with a light heart.

gaillard, e [gajaʀ, -aʀd(ə)] *a* (*robuste*) sprightly; (*grivois*) bawdy, ribald ♦ *nm/f* (*strapping*) fellow/wench.

gaillardement [gajaʀdəmɑ̃] *ad* cheerfully.

gain [gɛ̃] *nm* (*revenu*) earnings *pl*; (*bénéfice: gén pl*) profits *pl*; (*au jeu: gén pl*) winnings *pl*; (*fig: de temps, place*) saving; (: *avantage*) benefit; (: *lucre*) gain; **avoir** ~ **de cause** to win the case; (*fig*) to be proved right; **obtenir** ~ **de cause** (*fig*) to win out.

gaine [gɛn] *nf* (*corset*) girdle; (*fourreau*) sheath; (*de fil électrique etc*) outer covering.

gaine-culotte, pl gaines-culottes [gɛnkylɔt] *nf* pantie girdle.

gainer [gene] *vt* to cover.

gala [gala] *nm* official reception; **soirée de** ~ gala evening.

galant, e [galɑ̃, -ɑ̃t] *a* (*courtois*) courteous, gentlemanly; (*entreprenant*) flirtatious, gallant; (*aventure, poésie*) amorous; **en** ~**e compagnie** (*homme*) with a lady friend; (*femme*) with a gentleman friend.

Galapagos [galapagos] *nfpl*: **les (îles)** ~ the Galapagos Islands.

galaxie [galaksi] *nf* galaxy.

galbe [galb(ə)] *nm* curve(s); shapeliness.

gale [gal] *nf* (*MÉD*) scabies *sg*; (*de chien*) mange.

galéjade [galeʒad] *nf* tall story.

galère [galɛʀ] *nf* galley.

galérer [galeʀe] *vi* (*fam*) to work hard, slave (away).

galerie [galʀi] *nf* gallery; (*THÉÂTRE*) circle; (*de voiture*) roof rack; (*fig: spectateurs*) audience; ~ **marchande** shopping mall; ~ **de peinture** (*private*) art gallery.

galérien [galeʀjɛ̃] *nm* galley slave.

galet [galɛ] *nm* pebble; (*TECH*) wheel; ~**s** *nmpl* pebbles, shingle *sg*.

galette [galɛt] *nf* (*gâteau*) flat pastry cake; (*crêpe*) savoury pancake; **la** ~ **des Rois** *cake traditionally eaten on Twelfth Night*.

galeux, euse [galø, -øz] *a*: **un chien** ~ a mangy dog.

Galice [galis] *nf*: **la** ~ Galicia (*in Spain*).

Galicie [galisi] *nf*: **la** ~ Galicia (*in Central Europe*).

galiléen, ne [galileɛ̃, -ɛn] *a* Galilean.

galimatias [galimatja] *nm* (*péj*) gibberish.

galipette [galipɛt] *nf*: **faire des** ~**s** to turn somersaults.

Galles [gal] *nfpl*: **le pays de** ~ Wales.

gallicisme [galisism(ə)] *nm* French idiom; (*tournure fautive*) gallicism.

gallois, e [galwa, -waz] *a* Welsh ♦ *nm* (*LING*) Welsh ♦ *nm/f*: **G~,** **e** Welshman/woman.

galoche [galɔʃ] *nf* clog.

galon [galɔ̃] *nm* (*MIL*) stripe; (*décoratif*) piece of braid; **prendre du** ~ to be promoted.

galop [galo] *nm* gallop; **au** ~ at a gallop; ~ **d'essai** (*fig*) trial run.

galopade [galɔpad] *nf* stampede.

galopant, e [galɔpɑ̃, -ɑ̃t] *a*: **inflation** ~**e** galloping inflation; **démographie** ~**e** exploding population.

galoper [galɔpe] *vi* to gallop.

galopin [galɔpɛ̃] *nm* urchin, ragamuffin.

galvaniser [galvanize] *vt* to galvanize.

galvauder [galvode] *vt* to debase.

gambade [gɑ̃bad] *nf*: **faire des** ~**s** to skip *ou* frisk about.

gambader [gɑ̃bade] *vi* to skip *ou* frisk about.

gamberger [gɑ̃bɛʀʒe] (*fam*) *vi* to (have a) think ♦ *vt* to dream up.

Gambie [gɑ̃bi] *nf*: **la** ~ (*pays*) Gambia; (*fleuve*) the Gambia.

gamelle [gamɛl] *nf* mess tin; billy can; (*fam*): **ramasser une** ~ to fall flat on one's face.

gamin, e [gamɛ̃, -in] *nm/f* kid ♦ *a* mischievous, playful.

gaminerie [gaminʀi] *nf* mischievousness, playfulness.

gamme [gam] *nf* (*MUS*) scale; (*fig*) range.

gammé, e [game] *a*: **croix** ~**e** swastika.

Gand [gɑ̃] *n* Ghent.

gang [gɑ̃g] *nm* gang.

Gange [gãʒ] *nm*: **le ~** the Ganges.

ganglion [gãglijɔ̃] *nm* ganglion; *(lymphatique)* gland; **avoir des ~s** to have swollen glands.

gangrène [gãgʀɛn] *nf* gangrene; *(fig)* corruption; corrupting influence.

gangster [gãgstɛʀ] *nm* gangster.

gangue [gãg] *nf* coating.

ganse [gãs] *nf* braid.

gant [gã] *nm* glove; **prendre des ~s** *(fig)* to handle the situation with kid gloves; **relever le ~** *(fig)* to take up the gauntlet; **~ de crin** massage glove; **~ de toilette** (face) flannel *(Brit)*, face cloth; **~s de boxe** boxing gloves; **~s de caoutchouc** rubber gloves.

ganté, e [gãte] *a*: **~ de blanc** wearing white gloves.

ganterie [gãtʀi] *nf* glove trade; *(magasin)* glove shop.

garage [gaʀaʒ] *nm* garage; **~ à vélos** bicycle shed.

garagiste [gaʀaʒist(ə)] *nm/f* *(propriétaire)* garage owner; *(mécanicien)* garage mechanic.

garant, e [gaʀã, -ãt] *nm/f* guarantor ♦ *nm* guarantee; **se porter ~ de** to vouch for; to be answerable for.

garantie [gaʀãti] *nf* guarantee, warranty; *(gage)* security, surety; **(bon de) ~** guarantee *ou* warranty slip; **~ de bonne exécution** performance bond.

garantir [gaʀãtiʀ] *vt* to guarantee; *(protéger)*: **~ de** to protect from; **je vous garantis que** I can assure you that; **garanti pure laine/2 ans** guaranteed pure wool/for 2 years.

garce [gaʀs(ə)] *nf* *(péj)* bitch.

garçon [gaʀsɔ̃] *nm* boy; *(célibataire)* bachelor; *(jeune homme)* boy, lad; *(aussi:* **~ de café)** waiter; **~ boucher/coiffeur** butcher's/hairdresser's assistant; **~ de courses** messenger; **~ d'écurie** stable lad; **~ manqué** tomboy.

garçonnet [gaʀsɔnɛ] *nm* small boy.

garçonnière [gaʀsɔnjɛʀ] *nf* bachelor flat.

garde [gaʀd(ə)] *nm* *(de prisonnier)* guard; *(de domaine etc)* warden; *(soldat, sentinelle)* guardsman ♦ *nf* guarding; looking after; *(soldats, BOXE, ESCRIME)* guard; *(faction)* watch; *(d'une arme)* hilt; *(TYPO: aussi:* **page** *ou* **feuille de ~)** flyleaf; *(: collée)* endpaper; **de ~** *a, ad* on duty; **monter la ~** to stand guard; **être sur ses ~s** to be on one's guard; **mettre en ~** to warn; **mise en ~** warning; **prendre ~ (à)** to be careful (of); **avoir la ~ des enfants** *(après divorce)* to have custody of the children; **~ champêtre** *nm* rural policeman; **~ du corps** *nm* bodyguard; **~ d'enfants** *nf* child minder; **~ forestier** *nm* forest warden; **~ mobile** *nm, nf* mobile guard; **~ des Sceaux** *nm* ≈ Lord Chancellor *(Brit)*, ≈ Attorney General *(US)*; **~ à vue** *nf* *(JUR)* ≈ police custody.

garde-à-vous [gaʀdavu] *nm inv*: **être/se mettre au ~** to be at/stand to attention; **~ (fixe)!** *(MIL)* attention!

garde-barrière, *pl* **gardes-barrière(s)** [gaʀdəbaʀjɛʀ] *nm/f* level-crossing keeper.

garde-boue [gaʀdəbu] *nm inv* mudguard.

garde-chasse, *pl* **gardes-chasse(s)** [gaʀdəʃas] *nm* gamekeeper.

garde-côte [gaʀdəkot] *nm* *(vaisseau)* coastguard boat.

garde-feu [gaʀdəfø] *nm inv* fender.

garde-fou [gaʀdəfu] *nm* railing, parapet.

garde-malade, *pl* **gardes-malade(s)** [gaʀdəmalad] *nf* home nurse.

garde-manger [gaʀdmãʒe] *nm inv* *(boîte)* meat safe; *(placard)* pantry, larder.

garde-meuble [gaʀdəmœbl(ə)] *nm* furniture depository.

garde-pêche [gaʀdəpɛʃ] *nm inv* *(personne)* water bailiff; *(navire)* fisheries protection ship.

garder [gaʀde] *vt* *(conserver)* to keep; *(: sur soi: vêtement, chapeau)* to keep on; *(surveiller: enfants)* to look after; *(: immeuble, lieu, prisonnier)* to guard; **se ~** *vi* *(aliment: se conserver)* to keep; **se ~ de faire** to be careful not to do; **~ le lit/la chambre** to stay in bed/indoors; **~ le silence** to keep silent *ou* quiet; **~ la ligne** to keep one's figure; **~ à vue** to keep in custody; **pêche/chasse gardée** private fishing/hunting (ground).

garderie [gaʀdəʀi] *nf* day nursery, crèche.

garde-robe [gaʀdəʀɔb] *nf* wardrobe.

gardeur, euse [gaʀdœʀ, -øz] *nm/f* *(de vaches)* cowherd; *(de chèvres)* goatherd.

gardian [gaʀdjã] *nm* cowboy *(in the Camargue)*.

gardien, ne [gaʀdjɛ̃, -ɛn] *nm/f* *(garde)* guard; *(de prison)* warder; *(de domaine, réserve)* warden; *(de musée etc)* attendant; *(de phare, cimetière)* keeper; *(d'immeuble)* caretaker; *(fig)* guardian; **~ de but** goalkeeper; **~ de nuit** night watchman; **~ de la paix** policeman.

gare [gaʀ] *nf* *(railway)* station, train station *(US)* ♦ *excl*: **~ à** ... mind ...!, watch out for ...!; **~ à ne pas** ... mind you don't ...; **~ à toi!** watch out!; **sans crier ~** without warning; **~ maritime** harbour station; **~ routière** coach *(Brit)* *ou* bus station; *(camions)* haulage *(Brit)* *ou* trucking *(US)* depot; **~ de triage** marshalling yard.

garenne [gaʀɛn] *nf voir* **lapin**.

garer [gaʀe] *vt* to park; **se ~** to park; *(pour laisser passer)* to draw into the side.

gargantuesque [gaʀgãtɥɛsk(ə)] *a* gargantuan.

gargariser [gaʀgaʀize]: **se ~** *vi* to gargle; **se ~ de** *(fig)* to revel in.

gargarisme [gaʀgaʀism(ə)] *nm* gargling *q*; *(produit)* gargle.

gargote [gaʀgɔt] *nf* cheap restaurant, greasy spoon *(fam)*.

gargouille [gaʀguj] *nf* gargoyle.

gargouiller [gaʀguje] *vi* *(estomac)* to rumble; *(eau)* to gurgle.

garnement [gaʀnəmã] *nm* rascal, scallywag.

garni, e [gaʀni] *a* *(plat)* served with vegetables *(and chips or pasta or rice)* ♦ *nm* *(appartement)* furnished accommodation *q* *(Brit)* *ou* accommodations *pl* *(US)*.

garnir [gaʀniʀ] *vt* to decorate; *(remplir)* to fill; *(recouvrir)* to cover; **se ~** *vi* *(pièce, salle)* to fill up; **~ qch de** *(orner)* to decorate sth with; to trim sth with; *(approvisionner)* to fill *ou* stock sth with; *(protéger)* to fit sth with; *(CULIN)* to garnish sth with.

garnison [garnizɔ̃] nf garrison.

garniture [garnityr] nf (CULIN: légumes) vegetables pl; (: persil etc) garnish; (: farce) filling; (décoration) trimming; (protection) fittings pl; ~ **de cheminée** mantelpiece ornaments pl; ~ **de frein** (AUTO) brake lining; ~ **intérieure** (AUTO) interior trim; ~ **périodique** sanitary towel (Brit) ou napkin (US).

garrigue [garig] nf scrubland.

garrot [garo] nm (MÉD) tourniquet; (torture) garrotte.

garrotter [garɔte] vt to tie up; (fig) to muzzle.

gars [ga] nm lad; (type) guy.

Gascogne [gaskɔɲ] nf: **la** ~ Gascony.

gascon, ne [gaskɔ̃, -ɔn] a Gascon ♦ nm: **G~** (hâbleur) braggart.

gas-oil [gazɔjl] nm diesel oil.

gaspillage [gaspijaʒ] nm waste.

gaspiller [gaspije] vt to waste.

gaspilleur, euse [gaspijœr, -øz] a wasteful.

gastrique [gastrik] a gastric, stomach cpd.

gastro-entérite [gastrɔ̃āterit] nf (MÉD) gastro-enteritis.

gastronome [gastrɔnɔm] nm/f gourmet.

gastronomie [gastrɔnɔmi] nf gastronomy.

gastronomique [gastrɔnɔmik] a: **menu** ~ gourmet menu.

gâteau, x [gato] nm cake ♦ a inv (fam: trop indulgent): **papa-/maman-**~ doting father/ mother; ~ **d'anniversaire** birthday cake; ~ **de riz** ≈ rice pudding; ~ **sec** biscuit.

gâter [gate] vt to spoil; **se** ~ vi (dent, fruit) to go bad; (temps, situation) to change for the worse.

gâterie [gatri] nf little treat.

gâteux, euse [gatø, -øz] a senile.

gâtisme [gatism(ə)] nm senility.

GATT [gat] sigle m (= General Agreement on Tariffs and Trade) GATT.

gauche [goʃ] a left, left-hand; (maladroit) awkward, clumsy ♦ nf (POL) left (wing); (BOXE) left; **à** ~ on the left; (direction) (to the) left; **à** ~ **de** (on ou to the) left of; **à la** ~ **de** to the left of; **de** ~ (POL) left-wing.

gauchement [goʃmā] ad awkwardly, clumsily.

gaucher, ère [goʃe, -εr] a left-handed.

gaucherie [goʃri] nf awkwardness, clumsiness.

gauchir [goʃir] vt (planche, objet) to warp; (fig: fait, idée) to distort.

gauchisant, e [goʃizā, -āt] a with left-wing tendencies.

gauchisme [goʃism(ə)] nm leftism.

gauchiste [goʃist(ə)] a, nm/f leftist.

gaufre [gofr(ə)] nf (pâtisserie) waffle; (de cire) honeycomb.

gaufrer [gofre] vt (papier) to emboss; (tissu) to goffer.

gaufrette [gofrεt] nf wafer.

gaufrier [gofrije] nm (moule) waffle iron.

Gaule [gol] nf: **la** ~ Gaul.

gaule [gol] nf (perche) (long) pole; (canne à pêche) fishing rod.

gaulliste [golist(ə)] a, nm/f Gaullist.

gaulois, e [golwa, -waz] a Gallic; (grivois) bawdy ♦ nm/f: **G~, e** Gaul.

gauloiserie [golwazri] nf bawdiness.

gausser [gose]: **se** ~ **de** vt to deride.

gaver [gave] vt to force-feed; (fig): ~ **de** to cram with, fill up with; (personne): **se** ~ **de** to stuff o.s. with.

gaz [gaz] nm inv gas; **mettre les** ~ (AUTO) to put one's foot down; **chambre/masque à** ~ gas chamber/mask; ~ **en bouteille** bottled gas; ~ **butane** Calor gas ® (Brit), butane gas; ~ **carbonique** carbon dioxide; ~ **hilarant** laughing gas; ~ **lacrymogène** tear gas; ~ **naturel** natural gas; ~ **de ville** town gas (Brit), manufactured domestic gas.

gaze [gaz] nf gauze.

gazéifié, e [gazeifje] a carbonated, aerated.

gazelle [gazεl] nf gazelle.

gazer [gaze] vt to gas ♦ vi (fam) to be going ou working well.

gazette [gazεt] nf news sheet.

gazeux, euse [gazø, -øz] a gaseous; (eau) sparkling; (boisson) fizzy.

gazoduc [gazɔdyk] nm gas pipeline.

gazole [gazɔl] nm = **gas-oil**.

gazomètre [gazɔmεtr(ə)] nm gasometer.

gazon [gazɔ̃] nm (herbe) turf, grass; (pelouse) lawn.

gazonner [gazɔne] vt (terrain) to grass over.

gazouiller [gazuje] vi (oiseau) to chirp; (enfant) to babble.

gazouillis [gazuji] nmpl chirp sg.

GB sigle f (= Grande Bretagne) GB.

gd abr (= grand) L.

GDF sigle m (= Gaz de France) national gas company.

geai [ʒε] nm jay.

géant, e [ʒeā, -āt] a gigantic, giant; (COMM) giant-size ♦ nm/f giant.

geignement [ʒεɲmā] nm groaning, moaning.

geindre [ʒɛ̃dr(ə)] vi to groan, moan.

gel [ʒεl] nm frost; (de l'eau) freezing; (fig: des salaires, prix) freezing; freezing; (produit de beauté) gel.

gélatine [ʒelatin] nf gelatine.

gélatineux, euse [ʒelatinø, -øz] a jelly-like, gelatinous.

gelé, e [ʒəle] a frozen ♦ nf jelly; (gel) frost; ~ **blanche** hoarfrost, white frost.

geler [ʒəle] vt, vi to freeze; **il gèle** it's freezing.

gélule [ʒelyl] nf capsule.

gelures [ʒəlyr] nfpl frostbite sg.

Gémeaux [ʒemo] nmpl: **les** ~ Gemini, the Twins; **être des** ~ to be Gemini.

gémir [ʒemir] vi to groan, moan.

gémissement [ʒemismā] nm groan, moan.

gemme [ʒεm] nf gem(stone).

gémonies [ʒemɔni] nfpl: **vouer qn aux** ~ to subject sb to public scorn.

gênant, e [ʒεnā, -āt] a (objet) awkward, in the way; (histoire, personne) embarrassing.

gencive [ʒāsiv] nf gum.

gendarme [ʒādarm(ə)] nm gendarme.

gendarmer [ʒādarme]: **se** ~ vi to kick up a fuss.

gendarmerie [ʒādarməri] nf military police force in countryside and small towns; their police station or barracks.

gendre [ʒādr(ə)] nm son-in-law.

gène [ʒεn] nm (BIO) gene.

gêne [ʒεn] nf (à respirer, bouger) discomfort,

difficulty; (*dérangement*) bother, trouble; (*manque d'argent*) financial difficulties *pl ou* straits *pl*; (*confusion*) embarrassment; **sans** ~ *a* inconsiderate.

gêné, e [ʒene] *a* embarrassed; (*dépourvu d'argent*) short (of money).

généalogie [ʒenealɔʒi] *nf* genealogy.

généalogique [ʒenealɔʒik] *a* genealogical.

gêner [ʒene] *vt* (*incommoder*) to bother; (*encombrer*) to hamper; (*bloquer le passage*) to be in the way of; (*déranger*) to bother; (*embarrasser*): ~ **qn** to make sb feel ill-at-ease; **se** ~ to put o.s. out; **ne vous gênez pas!** (*ironique*) go right ahead!, don't mind me!; **je vais me** ~! (*ironique*) why should I care?

général, e, aux [ʒeneʀal, -o] *a, nm* general ♦ *nf*: (**répétition**) ~**e** final dress rehearsal; **en** ~ usually, in general; **à la satisfaction** ~**e** to everyone's satisfaction.

généralement [ʒeneʀalmɑ̃] *ad* generally.

généralisable [ʒeneʀalizabl(ə)] *a* generally applicable.

généralisation [ʒeneʀalizɑsjɔ̃] *nf* generalization.

généraliser [ʒeneʀalize] *vt, vi* to generalize; **se** ~ *vi* to become widespread.

généraliste [ʒeneʀalist(ə)] *nm/f* (*MÉD*) general practitioner, GP.

généralité [ʒeneʀalite] *nf*: **la** ~ **des** ... the majority of ...; ~**s** *nfpl* generalities; (*introduction*) general points.

générateur, trice [ʒeneʀatœʀ, -tʀis] *a*: ~ **de** which causes *ou* brings about ♦ *nf* (*ÉLEC*) generator.

génération [ʒeneʀasjɔ̃] *nf* (*aussi INFORM*) generation.

généreusement [ʒeneʀøzmɑ̃] *ad* generously.

généreux, euse [ʒeneʀø, -øz] *a* generous.

générique [ʒeneʀik] *a* generic ♦ *nm* (*CINÉMA, TV*) credits *pl*, credit titles *pl*.

générosité [ʒeneʀozite] *nf* generosity.

Gênes [ʒɛn] *n* Genoa.

genèse [ʒənɛz] *nf* genesis.

genêt [ʒəne] *nm* (*BOT*) broom *q*.

généticien, ne [ʒenetisjɛ̃, -ɛn] *nm/f* geneticist.

génétique [ʒenetik] *a* genetic ♦ *nf* genetics *sg*.

gêneur, euse [ʒenœʀ, -øz] *nm/f* (*personne qui gêne*) obstacle; (*importun*) intruder.

Genève [ʒənɛv] Geneva.

genevois, e [ʒənəvwa, -waz] *a* Genevan.

genévrier [ʒənevʀije] *nm* juniper.

génial, e, aux [ʒenjal, -o] *a* of genius; (*fam*) fantastic, brilliant.

génie [ʒeni] *nm* genius; (*MIL*): **le** ~ ≈ the Engineers *pl*; **avoir du** ~ to have genius; ~ **civil** civil engineering.

genièvre [ʒənjɛvʀ(ə)] *nm* (*BOT*) juniper (tree); (*boisson*) geneva; **grain de** ~ juniper berry.

génisse [ʒenis] *nf* heifer; **foie de** ~ ox liver.

génital, e, aux [ʒenital, -o] *a* genital.

génitif [ʒenitif] *nm* genitive.

génocide [ʒenɔsid] *nm* genocide.

génois, e [ʒenwa, -waz] *a* Genoese ♦ *nf* (*gâteau*) ≈ sponge cake.

genou, x [ʒnu] *nm* knee; **à** ~**x** on one's knees; **se mettre à** ~**x** to kneel down.

genouillère [ʒənujɛʀ] *nf* (*SPORT*) kneepad.

genre [ʒɑ̃ʀ] *nm* (*espèce, sorte*) kind, type, sort; (*allure*) manner; (*LING*) gender; (*ART*) genre; (*ZOOL etc*) genus; **se donner du** ~ to give o.s. airs; **avoir bon** ~ to have style; **avoir mauvais** ~ to be ill-mannered.

gens [ʒɑ̃] *nmpl* (*f in some phrases*) people *pl*; **les** ~ **d'Église** the clergy; **les** ~ **du monde** society people; ~ **de maison** domestics.

gentiane [ʒɑ̃sjan] *nf* gentian.

gentil, le [ʒɑ̃ti, -ij] *a* kind; (*enfant: sage*) good; (*sympa: endroit etc*) nice; **c'est très** ~ **à vous** it's very kind *ou* nice of you.

gentilhommière [ʒɑ̃tijɔmjɛʀ] *nf* (small) manor house *ou* country seat.

gentillesse [ʒɑ̃tijɛs] *nf* kindness.

gentillet, te [ʒɑ̃tijɛ, -ɛt] *a* nice little.

gentiment [ʒɑ̃timɑ̃] *ad* kindly.

génuflexion [ʒenyflɛksjɔ̃] *nf* genuflexion.

géodésique [ʒeodezik] *a* geodesic.

géographe [ʒeɔgʀaf] *nm/f* geographer.

géographie [ʒeɔgʀafi] *nf* geography.

géographique [ʒeɔgʀafik] *a* geographical.

geôlier [ʒolje] *nm* jailer.

géologie [ʒeɔlɔʒi] *nf* geology.

géologique [ʒeɔlɔʒik] *a* geological.

géologue [ʒeɔlɔg] *nm/f* geologist.

géomètre [ʒeɔmɛtʀ(ə)] *nm/f*: (**arpenteur-)~** (land) surveyor.

géométrie [ʒeɔmetʀi] *nf* geometry; **à** ~ **variable** (*AVIAT*) swing-wing.

géométrique [ʒeɔmetʀik] *a* geometric.

géophysique [ʒeofizik] *nf* geophysics *sg*.

géopolitique [ʒeopolitik] *nf* geopolitics *sg*.

Géorgie [ʒeɔʀʒi] *nf*: **la** ~ (*URSS, USA*) Georgia; **la** ~ **du Sud** South Georgia.

géorgien, ne [ʒeɔʀʒjɛ̃, -ɛn] *a* Georgian.

géothermique [ʒeotɛʀmik] *a*: **énergie** ~ geothermal energy.

gérance [ʒeʀɑ̃s] *nf* management; **mettre en** ~ to appoint a manager for; **prendre en** ~ to take over (the management of).

géranium [ʒeʀanjɔm] *nm* geranium.

gérant, e [ʒeʀɑ̃, -ɑ̃t] *nm/f* manager/manageress; ~ **d'immeuble** managing agent.

gerbe [ʒɛʀb(ə)] *nf* (*de fleurs, d'eau*) spray; (*de blé*) sheaf (*pl* sheaves); (*fig*) shower, burst.

gercé, e [ʒɛʀse] *a* chapped.

gercer [ʒɛʀse] *vi*, **se** ~ *vi* to chap.

gerçure [ʒɛʀsyʀ] *nf* crack.

gérer [ʒeʀe] *vt* to manage.

gériatrie [ʒeʀjatʀi] *nf* geriatrics *sg*.

gériatrique [ʒeʀjatʀik] *a* geriatric.

germain, e [ʒɛʀmɛ̃, -ɛn] *a*: **cousin** ~ first cousin.

germanique [ʒɛʀmanik] *a* Germanic.

germaniste [ʒɛʀmanist(ə)] *nm/f* German scholar.

germe [ʒɛʀm(ə)] *nm* germ.

germer [ʒɛʀme] *vi* to sprout; (*semence, aussi fig*) to germinate.

gérondif [ʒeʀɔ̃dif] *nm* gerund; (*en latin*) gerundive.

gérontologie [ʒeʀɔ̃tɔlɔʒi] *nf* gerontology.

gésier [ʒezje] *nm* gizzard.

gésir [ʒeziʀ] *vi* to be lying (down); *voir aussi* **ci-gît**.

gestation [ʒɛstɑsjɔ̃] *nf* gestation.

geste [ʒɛst(ə)] *nm* gesture; move; motion; **il**

fit un ~ de la main pour m'appeler he signed to me to come over, he waved me over; **ne faites pas un ~** (ne bougez pas) don't move.

gesticuler [ʒɛstikyle] vi to gesticulate.

gestion [ʒɛstjɔ̃] nf management; **~ des disques** (INFORM) housekeeping; **~ de fichier(s)** (INFORM) file management.

gestionnaire [ʒɛstjɔnɛʀ] nm/f administrator; **~ de fichier** (INFORM) file manager.

geyser [ʒɛzɛʀ] nm geyser.

Ghana [gana] nm: **le ~** Ghana.

ghanéen, ne [ganeɛ̃, -ɛn] a Ghanaian.

ghetto [geto] nm ghetto.

gibecière [ʒibsjɛʀ] nf (de chasseur) gamebag; (sac en bandoulière) shoulder bag.

gibet [ʒibɛ] nm gallows pl.

gibier [ʒibje] nm (animaux) game; (fig) prey.

giboulée [ʒibule] nf sudden shower.

giboyeux, euse [ʒibwajø, -øz] a well-stocked with game.

Gibraltar [ʒibʀaltaʀ] nm Gibraltar.

gibus [ʒibys] nm opera hat.

giclée [ʒikle] nf spurt, squirt.

gicler [ʒikle] vi to spurt, squirt.

gicleur [ʒiklœʀ] nm (AUTO) jet.

GIE sigle m = **groupement d'intérêt économique**.

gifle [ʒifl(ə)] nf slap (in the face).

gifler [ʒifle] vt to slap (in the face).

gigantesque [ʒigɑ̃tɛsk(ə)] a gigantic.

GIGN sigle m (= Groupe d'intervention de la gendarmerie nationale) special crack force of the gendarmerie, ≈ SAS (Brit).

gigogne [ʒigɔɲ] a: **lits ~s** truckle (Brit) ou trundle (US) beds; **tables/poupées ~s** nest of tables/dolls.

gigot [ʒigo] nm leg (of mutton ou lamb).

gigoter [ʒigɔte] vi to wriggle (about).

gilet [ʒilɛ] nm waistcoat; (pull) cardigan; (de corps) vest; **~ pare-balles** bulletproof jacket; **~ de sauvetage** life jacket.

gin [dʒin] nm gin.

gingembre [ʒɛ̃ʒɑ̃bʀ(ə)] nm ginger.

girafe [ʒiʀaf] nf giraffe.

giratoire [ʒiʀatwaʀ] a: **sens ~** roundabout.

girofle [ʒiʀɔfl(ə)] nm: **clou de ~** clove.

giroflée [ʒiʀɔfle] nf wallflower.

girolle [ʒiʀɔl] nf chanterelle.

giron [ʒiʀɔ̃] nm (genoux) lap; (fig: sein) bosom.

Gironde [ʒiʀɔ̃d] nf: **la ~** the Gironde.

girophare [ʒiʀɔfaʀ] nm revolving (flashing) light.

girouette [ʒiʀwɛt] nf weather vane ou cock.

gis [ʒi], **gisais** [ʒizɛ] etc vb voir **gésir**.

gisement [ʒizmɑ̃] nm deposit.

gît [ʒi] vb voir **gésir**.

gitan, e [ʒitɑ̃, -an] nm/f gipsy.

gîte [ʒit] nm home; shelter; (du lièvre) form; **~ (rural)** (country) holiday cottage ou apartment.

gîter [ʒite] vi (NAVIG) to list.

givrage [ʒivʀaʒ] nm icing.

givrant, e [ʒivʀɑ̃, -ɑ̃t] a: **brouillard ~** freezing fog.

givre [ʒivʀ(ə)] nm (hoar) frost.

givré, e [ʒivʀe] a: **citron ~/orange ~e** lemon/orange sorbet (served in fruit skin).

glabre [glɑbʀ(ə)] a hairless; (menton) clean-shaven.

glace [glas] nf ice; (crème glacée) ice cream; (verre) sheet of glass; (miroir) mirror; (de voiture) window; **~s** nfpl (GÉO) ice sheets, ice sg; **de ~** (fig: accueil, visage) frosty, icy; **rester de ~** to remain unmoved.

glacé, e [glase] a icy; (boisson) iced.

glacer [glase] vt to freeze; (boisson) to chill, ice; (gâteau) to ice (Brit), frost (US); (papier, tissu) to glaze; (fig): **~ qn** to chill sb; (fig) to make sb's blood run cold.

glaciaire [glasjɛʀ] a (période) ice cpd; (relief) glacial.

glacial, e [glasjal] a icy.

glacier [glasje] nm (GÉO) glacier; (marchand) ice-cream maker.

glacière [glasjɛʀ] nf icebox.

glaçon [glasɔ̃] nm icicle; (pour boisson) ice cube.

gladiateur [gladjatœʀ] nm gladiator.

glaïeul [glajœl] nm gladiola.

glaire [glɛʀ] nf (MÉD) phlegm q.

glaise [glɛz] nf clay.

glaive [glɛv] nm two-edged sword.

gland [glɑ̃] nm (de chêne) acorn; (décoration) tassel; (ANAT) glans.

glande [glɑ̃d] nf gland.

glaner [glane] vt, vi to glean.

glapir [glapiʀ] vi to yelp.

glas [glɑ] nm knell, toll.

glauque [glok] a dull blue-green.

glissade [glisad] nf (par jeu) slide; (chute) slip; (dérapage) skid; **faire des ~s** to slide.

glissant, e [glisɑ̃, -ɑ̃t] a slippery.

glissement [glismɑ̃] nm sliding; (fig) shift; **~ de terrain** landslide.

glisser [glise] vi (avancer) to glide ou slide along; (coulisser, tomber) to slide; (déraper) to slip; (être glissant) to be slippery ♦ vt: **~ qch sous/dans/à** to slip sth under/into/to; **~ sur** (fig: détail etc) to skate over; **se ~ dans/entre** to slip into/between.

glissière [glisjɛʀ] nf slide channel; **à ~** (porte, fenêtre) sliding; **~ de sécurité** (AUTO) crash barrier.

glissoire [gliswaʀ] nf slide.

global, e, aux [glɔbal, -o] a overall.

globalement [glɔbalmɑ̃] ad taken as a whole.

globe [glɔb] nm globe; **sous ~** under glass; **~ oculaire** eyeball; **le ~ terrestre** the globe.

globule [glɔbyl] nm (du sang): **~ blanc/rouge** white/red corpuscle.

globuleux, euse [glɔbylø, -øz] a: **yeux ~** protruding eyes.

gloire [glwaʀ] nf glory; (mérite) distinction, credit; (personne) celebrity.

glorieux, euse [glɔʀjø, -øz] a glorious.

glorifier [glɔʀifje] vt to glorify, extol; **se ~ de** to glory in.

gloriole [glɔʀjɔl] nf vainglory.

glose [gloz] nf gloss.

glossaire [glɔsɛʀ] nm glossary.

glotte [glɔt] nf (ANAT) glottis.

glouglouter [gluglute] vi to gurgle.

glousser [gluse] vi to cluck; (rire) to chuckle.

glouton, ne [glutɔ̃, -ɔn] a gluttonous, greedy.

gloutonnerie [glutɔnʀi] nf gluttony.

glu [gly] nf birdlime.

gluant, e [glyɑ̃, -ɑ̃t] *a* sticky, gummy.
glucose [glykoz] *nm* glucose.
gluten [glytɛn] *nm* gluten.
glycérine [gliserin] *nf* glycerine.
glycine [glisin] *nf* wisteria.
GMT *sigle a* (= *Greenwich Mean Time*) GMT.
GNL *sigle m* (= *gaz naturel liquéfié*) LNG (= *liquefied natural gas*).
gnôle [njol] *nf* (*fam*) booze *q*; **un petit verre de ~** a drop of the hard stuff.
gnome [gnom] *nm* gnome.
GO *sigle fpl* (= *grandes ondes*) LW ♦ *sigle m* (= *gentil organisateur*) *title given to leaders on Club Méditerranée holidays; extended to refer to easy-going leader of any group.*
go [go]: **tout de ~** *ad* straight out.
goal [gol] *nm* goalkeeper.
gobelet [gɔblɛ] *nm* (*en métal*) tumbler; (*en plastique*) beaker; (*à dés*) cup.
gober [gɔbe] *vt* to swallow.
goberger [gɔbɛrʒe]: **se ~** *vi* to cosset o.s.
Gobi [gɔbi] *n*: **désert de ~** Gobi Desert.
godasse [gɔdas] *nf* (*fam*) shoe.
godet [gɔdɛ] *nm* pot; (*COUTURE*) unpressed pleat.
godiller [gɔdije] *vi* (*NAVIG*) to scull; (*SKI*) to wedeln.
goéland [gɔelɑ̃] *nm* (sea)gull.
goélette [gɔelɛt] *nf* schooner.
goémon [gɔemɔ̃] *nm* wrack.
gogo [gɔgo] *nm* (*péj*) mug, sucker; **à ~** *ad* galore.
goguenard, e [gɔgnar, -ard(ə)] *a* mocking.
goguette [gɔgɛt] *nf*: **en ~** on the binge.
goinfre [gwɛ̃fr(ə)] *nm* glutton.
goinfrer [gwɛ̃fre]: **se ~** *vi* to make a pig of o.s.; **se ~ de** to guzzle.
goitre [gwatr(ə)] *nm* goitre.
golf [gɔlf] *nm* (*jeu*) golf; (*terrain*) golf course; **~ miniature** crazy *ou* miniature golf.
golfe [gɔlf(ə)] *nm* gulf; bay; **le ~ d'Aden** the Gulf of Aden; **le ~ de Gascogne** the Bay of Biscay; **le ~ du Lion** the Gulf of Lions; **le ~ Persique** the Persian Gulf.
gominé, e [gɔmine] *a* slicked down.
gomme [gɔm] *nf* (*à effacer*) rubber (*Brit*), e-raser; (*résine*) gum; **boule** *ou* **pastille de ~** throat pastille.
gommé, e [gɔme] *a*: **papier ~** gummed paper.
gommer [gɔme] *vt* (*effacer*) to rub out (*Brit*), erase; (*enduire de gomme*) to gum.
gond [gɔ̃] *nm* hinge; **sortir de ses ~s** (*fig*) to fly off the handle.
gondole [gɔ̃dɔl] *nf* gondola; (*pour l'étalage*) shelves *pl*, gondola.
gondoler [gɔ̃dɔle]: **se ~** *vi* to warp, buckle; (*fam: rire*) to hoot with laughter; to be in stitches.
gondolier [gɔ̃dɔlje] *nm* gondolier.
gonflable [gɔ̃flabl(ə)] *a* inflatable.
gonflage [gɔ̃flaʒ] *nm* inflating, blowing up.
gonflé, e [gɔ̃fle] *a* swollen; (*ventre*) bloated; (*fam: culotté*): **être ~** to have a nerve.
gonfler [gɔ̃fle] *vt* (*pneu, ballon*) to inflate, blow up; (*nombre, importance*) to inflate ♦ *vi* (*pied etc*) to swell (up); (*CULIN: pâte*) to rise.
gonfleur [gɔ̃flœr] *nm* air pump.

gong [gɔ̃g] *nm* gong.
gonzesse [gɔ̃zɛs] *nf* (*fam*) chick, bird (*Brit*).
goret [gɔrɛ] *nm* piglet.
gorge [gɔrʒ(ə)] *nf* (*ANAT*) throat; (*poitrine*) breast; (*GÉO*) gorge; (*rainure*) groove; **avoir mal à la ~** to have a sore throat; **avoir la ~ serrée** to have a lump in one's throat.
gorgé, e [gɔrʒe] *a*: **~ de** filled with; (*eau*) saturated with ♦ *nf* mouthful; sip; gulp; **boire à petites/grandes ~es** to take little sips/big gulps.
gorille [gɔrij] *nm* gorilla; (*fam*) bodyguard.
gosier [gozje] *nm* throat.
gosse [gɔs] *nm/f* kid.
gothique [gɔtik] *a* gothic.
gouaille [gwaj] *nf* street wit, cocky humour (*Brit*) *ou* humor (*US*).
goudron [gudrɔ̃] *nm* (*asphalte*) tar(mac) (*Brit*), asphalt; (*du tabac*) tar.
goudronner [gudrɔne] *vt* to tar(mac) (*Brit*), asphalt.
gouffre [gufr(ə)] *nm* abyss, gulf.
goujat [guʒa] *nm* boor.
goujon [guʒɔ̃] *nm* gudgeon.
goulée [gule] *nf* gulp.
goulet [gulɛ] *nm* bottleneck.
goulot [gulo] *nm* neck; **boire au ~** to drink from the bottle.
goulu, e [guly] *a* greedy.
goupille [gupij] *nf* (metal) pin.
goupiller [gupije] *vt* to pin (together).
goupillon [gupijɔ̃] *nm* (*REL*) sprinkler; (*brosse*) bottle brush; **le ~** (*fig*) the cloth, the clergy.
gourd, e [gur, gurd(ə)] *a* numb (with cold); (*fam*) oafish.
gourde [gurd(ə)] *nf* (*récipient*) flask; (*fam*) (clumsy) clot *ou* oaf.
gourdin [gurdɛ̃] *nm* club, bludgeon.
gourmand, e [gurmɑ̃, -ɑ̃d] *a* greedy.
gourmandise [gurmɑ̃diz] *nf* greed; (*bonbon*) sweet (*Brit*), piece of candy (*US*).
gourmet [gurmɛ] *nm* epicure.
gourmette [gurmɛt] *nf* chain bracelet.
gourou [guru] *nm* guru.
gousse [gus] *nf* (*de vanille etc*) pod; **~ d'ail** clove of garlic.
gousset [gusɛ] *nm* (*de gilet*) fob.
goût [gu] *nm* taste; (*fig: appréciation*) taste, liking; **le (bon) ~** good taste; **de bon ~** in good taste, tasteful; **de mauvais ~** in bad taste, tasteless; **avoir bon/mauvais ~** (*aliment*) to taste nice/nasty; (*personne*) to have good/bad taste; **avoir du/manquer de ~** to have/lack taste; **avoir du ~ pour** to have a liking for; **prendre ~ à** to develop a taste *ou* a liking for.
goûter [gute] *vt* (*essayer*) to taste; (*apprécier*) to enjoy ♦ *vi* to have (afternoon) tea ♦ *nm* (afternoon) tea; **~ à** to taste, sample; **~ de** to have a taste of; **~ d'enfants/d'anniversaire** children's tea/ birthday party.
goutte [gut] *nf* drop; (*MÉD*) gout; (*alcool*) nip (*Brit*), tot (*Brit*), drop (*US*); **~s** *nfpl* (*MÉD*) drops; **~ à ~** *ad* a drop at a time; **tomber ~ à ~** to drip.
goutte-à-goutte [gutagut] *nm inv* (*MÉD*) drip; **alimenter au ~** to drip-feed.

gouttelette [gutlɛt] *nf* droplet.

goutter [gute] *vi* to drip.

gouttière [gutjɛʀ] *nf* gutter.

gouvernail [guvɛʀnaj] *nm* rudder; (*barre*) helm, tiller.

gouvernant, e [guvɛʀnɑ̃, -ɑ̃t] *a* ruling *cpd* ♦ *nf* housekeeper; (*d'un enfant*) governess.

gouverne [guvɛʀn(ə)] *nf*: **pour sa ~** for his guidance.

gouvernement [guvɛʀnəmɑ̃] *nm* government.

gouvernemental, e, aux [guvɛʀnəmɑ̃tal, -o] *a* (*politique*) government *cpd*; (*journal, parti*) pro-government.

gouverner [guvɛʀne] *vt* to govern; (*diriger*) to steer; (*fig*) to control.

gouverneur [guvɛʀnœʀ] *nm* governor; (*MIL*) commanding officer.

goyave [gɔjav] *nf* guava.

GPL *sigle m* (= *gaz de pétrole liquéfié*) LPG (= *liquefied petroleum gas*).

GQG *sigle m* (= *grand quartier général*) GHQ.

grabataire [gʀabatɛʀ] *a* bedridden ♦ *nm/f* bedridden invalid.

grâce [gʀɑs] *nf* grace; (*faveur*) favour; (*JUR*) pardon; **~s** *nfpl* (*REL*) grace *sg*; **de bonne/ mauvaise ~** with (a) good/bad grace; **dans les bonnes ~s de qn** in favour with sb; **faire ~ à qn de qch** to spare sb sth; **rendre ~(s) à** to give thanks to; **demander ~** to beg for mercy; **droit de ~** right of reprieve; **recours en ~** plea for pardon; **~ à** *prép* thanks to.

gracier [gʀasje] *vt* to pardon.

gracieusement [gʀasjøzmɑ̃] *ad* graciously, kindly; (*gratuitement*) freely; (*avec grâce*) gracefully.

gracieux, euse [gʀasjø, -øz] *a* (*charmant, élégant*) graceful; (*aimable*) gracious, kind; **à titre ~** free of charge.

gracile [gʀasil] *a* slender.

gradation [gʀadɑsjɔ̃] *nf* gradation.

grade [gʀad] *nm* (*MIL*) rank; (*SCOL*) degree; **monter en ~** to be promoted.

gradé [gʀade] *nm* (*MIL*) officer.

gradin [gʀadɛ̃] *nm* (*dans un théâtre*) tier; (*de stade*) step; **~s** *nmpl* (*de stade*) terracing *q* (*Brit*), standing area; **en ~s** terraced.

graduation [gʀadyɑsjɔ̃] *nf* graduation.

gradué, e [gʀadye] *a* (*exercices*) graded (for difficulty); (*thermomètre, verre*) graduated.

graduel, le [gʀadɥɛl] *a* gradual; progressive.

graduer [gʀadye] *vt* (*effort etc*) to increase gradually; (*règle, verre*) to graduate; (*exercices*) to increase in difficulty.

graffiti [gʀafiti] *nmpl* graffiti.

grain [gʀɛ̃] *nm* (*gén*) grain; (*de chapelet*) bead; (*NAVIG*) squall; (*averse*) heavy shower; (*fig: petite quantité*): **un ~ de** a touch of; **~ de beauté** beauty spot; **~ de café** coffee bean; **~ de poivre** peppercorn; **~ de poussière** speck of dust; **~ de raisin** grape.

graine [gʀɛn] *nf* seed; **mauvaise ~** (*mauvais sujet*) bad lot; **une ~ de voyou** a hooligan in the making.

grainetier, -ière [gʀɛntje, -jɛʀ] seed merchant.

graissage [gʀɛsaʒ] *nm* lubrication, greasing.

graisse [gʀɛs] *nf* fat; (*lubrifiant*) grease.

graisser [gʀese] *vt* to lubricate, grease; (*tacher*) to make greasy.

graisseux, euse [gʀesø, -øz] *a* greasy; (*ANAT*) fatty.

grammaire [gʀamɛʀ] *nf* grammar.

grammatical, e, aux [gʀamatikal, -o] *a* grammatical.

gramme [gʀam] *nm* gramme.

grand, e [gʀɑ̃, gʀɑ̃d] *a* (*haut*) tall; (*gros, vaste, large*) big, large; (*long*) long; (*sens abstraits*) great ♦ *ad*: **~ ouvert** wide open; **un ~ buveur** a heavy drinker; **un ~ homme** a great man; **son ~ frère** his big *ou* older brother; **avoir ~ besoin de** to be in dire *ou* desperate need of; **il est ~ temps de** it's high time to; **il est assez ~ pour** he's big *ou* old enough to; **voir ~** to think big; **en ~** on a large scale; **au ~ air** in the open (air); **les ~s blessés/brûlés** the severely injured/ burned; **de ~ matin** at the crack of dawn; **~ écart** splits *pl*; **~ ensemble** housing scheme; **~ jour** broad daylight; **~ livre** (*COMM*) ledger; **~ magasin** department store; **~ malade** very sick person; **~ public** general public; **~e personne** grown-up; **~e surface** hypermarket, superstore; **~es écoles** prestige university-level colleges with competitive entrance examinations; **~es lignes** (*RAIL*) main lines; **~es vacances** summer holidays.

grand-angle, *pl* **grands-angles** [gʀɑ̃tɑ̃gl(ə)] *nm* (*PHOTO*) wide-angle lens.

grand-angulaire, *pl* **grands-angulaires** [gʀɑ̃tɑ̃gylɛʀ] *nm* (*PHOTO*) wide-angle lens.

grand-chose [gʀɑ̃ʃoz] *nm/f inv*: **pas ~** not much.

Grande-Bretagne [gʀɑ̃dbʀətaɲ] *nf*: **la ~** (Great) Britain; **en ~** in (Great) Britain.

grandement [gʀɑ̃dmɑ̃] *ad* (*tout à fait*) greatly; (*largement*) easily; (*généreusement*) lavishly.

grandeur [gʀɑ̃dœʀ] *nf* (*dimension*) size; (*fig: ampleur, importance*) magnitude; (*: gloire, puissance*) greatness; **~ nature** a life-size.

grand-guignolesque [gʀɑ̃giɲɔlɛsk(ə)] *a* gruesome.

grandiloquent, e [gʀɑ̃dilɔkɑ̃, -ɑ̃t] *a* bombastic, grandiloquent.

grandir [gʀɑ̃diʀ] *vi* (*enfant, arbre*) to grow; (*bruit, hostilité*) to increase, grow ♦ *vt*: **~ qn** (*suj: vêtement, chaussure*) to make sb look taller; (*fig*) to make sb grow in stature.

grandissant, e [gʀɑ̃disɑ̃, -ɑ̃t] *a* growing.

grand-mère [gʀɑ̃mɛʀ] *nf* grandmother.

grand-messe [gʀɑ̃mɛs] *nf* high mass.

grand-peine [gʀɑ̃pɛn]: **à ~** *ad* with (great) difficulty.

grand-père, *pl* **grands-pères** [gʀɑ̃pɛʀ] *nm* grandfather.

grand-route [gʀɑ̃ʀut] *nf* main road.

grand-rue [gʀɑ̃ʀy] *nf* high street.

grands-parents [gʀɑ̃paʀɑ̃] *nmpl* grandparents.

grand-voile [gʀɑ̃vwal] *nf* mainsail.

grange [gʀɑ̃ʒ] *nf* barn.

granit(e) [gʀanit] *nm* granite.

granule [gʀanyl] *nm* small pill.

granulé [gʀanyle] *nm* granule.

granuleux, euse [gʀanylø, -øz] *a* granular.

graphe [gʀaf] *nm* graph.
graphie [gʀafi] *nf* written form.
graphique [gʀafik] *a* graphic ♦ *nm* graph.
graphisme [gʀafism(ə)] *nm* graphic arts *pl*; graphics *sg*; (*écriture*) handwriting.
graphiste [gʀafist(ə)] *nm/f* graphic designer.
graphologue [gʀafɔlɔg] *nm/f* graphologist.
grappe [gʀap] *nf* cluster; ~ **de raisin** bunch of grapes.
grappiller [gʀapije] *vt* to glean.
grappin [gʀapɛ̃] *nm* grapnel; **mettre le ~ sur** (*fig*) to get one's claws on.
gras, se [gʀɑ, gʀɑs] *a* (*viande, soupe*) fatty; (*personne*) fat; (*surface, main, cheveux*) greasy; (*terre*) sticky; (*toux*) loose, phlegmy; (*rire*) throaty; (*plaisanterie*) coarse; (*crayon*) soft-lead; (*TYPO*) bold ♦ *nm* (*CULIN*) fat; **faire la ~se matinée** to have a lie-in (*Brit*), sleep late; **matière ~se** fat (content).
gras-double [gʀɑdubl(ə)] *nm* (*CULIN*) tripe.
grassement [gʀɑsmɑ̃] *ad* (*généreusement*): ~ **payé** handsomely paid; (*grossièrement: rire*) coarsely.
grassouillet, te [gʀasujɛ, -ɛt] *a* podgy, plump.
gratifiant, e [gʀatifjɑ̃, -ɑ̃t] *a* gratifying, rewarding.
gratification [gʀatifikasjɔ̃] *nf* bonus.
gratifier [gʀatifje] *vt*: ~ **qn de** to favour sb with; to reward sb with; (*sourire etc*) to favour sb with.
gratin [gʀatɛ̃] *nm* (*CULIN*) cheese- (*ou* crumb-) topped dish; (*: croûte*) topping; **au** ~ **au** gratin; **tout le** ~ **parisien** all the best people of Paris.
gratiné, e [gʀatine] *a* (*CULIN*) au gratin; (*fam*) hellish ♦ *nf* (*soupe*) onion soup au gratin.
gratis [gʀatis] *ad, a* free.
gratitude [gʀatityd] *nf* gratitude.
gratte-ciel [gʀatsjɛl] *nm inv* skyscraper.
grattement [gʀatmɑ̃] *nm* (*bruit*) scratching (noise).
gratte-papier [gʀatpapje] *nm inv* (*péj*) penpusher.
gratter [gʀate] *vt* (*frotter*) to scrape; (*enlever*) to scrape off; (*bras, bouton*) to scratch; **se** ~ to scratch o.s.
grattoir [gʀatwaʀ] *nm* scraper.
gratuit, e [gʀatɥi, -ɥit] *a* (*entrée*) free; (*billet*) free, complimentary; (*fig*) gratuitous.
gratuité [gʀatɥite] *nf* being free (of charge); gratuitousness.
gratuitement [gʀatɥitmɑ̃] *ad* (*sans payer*) free; (*sans preuve, motif*) gratuitously.
gravats [gʀava] *nmpl* rubble *sg*.
grave [gʀav] *a* (*dangereux: maladie, accident*) serious, bad; (*sérieux: sujet, problème*) serious, grave; (*personne, air*) grave, solemn; (*voix, son*) deep, low-pitched ♦ *nm* (*MUS*) low register; **ce n'est pas** ~**!** it's all right, don't worry; **blessé** ~ seriously injured person.
graveleux, euse [gʀavlø, -øz] *a* (*terre*) gravelly; (*fruit*) gritty; (*contes, propos*) smutty.
gravement [gʀavmɑ̃] *ad* seriously; badly; gravely.
graver [gʀave] *vt* (*plaque, nom*) to engrave; (*fig*): ~ **qch dans son esprit/sa mémoire** to

etch sth in one's mind/memory.
graveur [gʀavœʀ] *nm* engraver.
gravier [gʀavje] *nm* (loose) gravel *q*.
gravillons [gʀavijɔ̃] *nmpl* gravel *sg*, loose chippings *ou* gravel.
gravir [gʀaviʀ] *vt* to climb (up).
gravité [gʀavite] *nf* (*voir grave*) seriousness; gravity; (*PHYSIQUE*) gravity.
graviter [gʀavite] *vi*: ~ **autour de** to revolve around.
gravure [gʀavyʀ] *nf* engraving; (*reproduction*) print; plate.
GRE *sigle f* (= *garantie contre les risques à l'exportation*) ≈ service provided by ECGD (= *Export Credit Guarantees Department*).
gré [gʀe] *nm*: **à son** ~ *a* to his liking; *ad* as he pleases; **au** ~ **de** according to, following; **contre le** ~ **de qn** against sb's will; **de son (plein)** ~ of one's own free will; **de** ~ **ou de force** whether one likes it or not; **de bon** ~ willingly; **bon** ~ **mal** ~ like it or not; willy-nilly; **de** ~ **à** ~ (*COMM*) by mutual agreement; **savoir (bien)** ~ **à qn de qch** to be (most) grateful to sb for sth.
grec, grecque [gʀɛk] *a* Greek; (*classique: vase etc*) Grecian ♦ *nm* (*LING*) Greek ♦ *nm/f*: **G~, Grecque** Greek.
Grèce [gʀɛs] *nf*: **la** ~ Greece.
gredin, e [gʀədɛ̃, -in] *nm/f* rogue, rascal.
gréement [gʀemɑ̃] *nm* rigging.
greffe [gʀɛf] *nf* graft; transplant ♦ *nm* (*JUR*) office.
greffer [gʀefe] *vt* (*BOT, MÉD: tissu*) to graft; (*MÉD: organe*) to transplant.
greffier [gʀefje] *nm* clerk of the court.
grégaire [gʀegɛʀ] *a* gregarious.
grège [gʀɛʒ] *a*: **soie** ~ raw silk.
grêle [gʀɛl] *a* (very) thin ♦ *nf* hail.
grêlé, e [gʀele] *a* pockmarked.
grêler [gʀele] *vb impersonnel*: **il grêle** it's hailing ♦ *vt*: **la région a été grêlée** the region was damaged by hail.
grêlon [gʀelɔ̃] *nm* hailstone.
grelot [gʀəlo] *nm* little bell.
grelotter [gʀəlɔte] *vi* (*trembler*) to shiver.
Grenade [gʀənad] *n* Granada ♦ *nf* (*île*) Grenada.
grenade [gʀənad] *nf* (*explosive*) grenade; (*BOT*) pomegranate; ~ **lacrymogène** teargas grenade.
grenadier [gʀənadje] *nm* (*MIL*) grenadier; (*BOT*) pomegranate tree.
grenadine [gʀənadin] *nf* grenadine.
grenat [gʀəna] *a inv* dark red.
grenier [gʀənje] *nm* (*de maison*) attic; (*de ferme*) loft.
grenouille [gʀənuj] *nf* frog.
grenouillère [gʀənujɛʀ] *nf* (*de bébé*) leggings; (*: combinaison*) sleepsuit.
grenu, e [gʀəny] *a* grainy, grained.
grès [gʀɛ] *nm* (*roche*) sandstone; (*poterie*) stoneware.
grésil [gʀezi] *nm* (fine) hail.
grésillement [gʀezijmɑ̃] *nm* sizzling; crackling.
grésiller [gʀezije] *vi* to sizzle; (*RADIO*) to crackle.
grève [gʀɛv] *nf* (*d'ouvriers*) strike; (*plage*) shore; **se mettre en/faire** ~ to go on/be on

strike; ~ **bouchon** partial strike (in key areas of a company); ~ **de la faim** hunger strike; ~ **perlée** go-slow (Brit), slowdown (US); ~ **sauvage** wildcat strike; ~ **de solidarité** sympathy strike; ~ **surprise** lightning strike; ~ **sur le tas** sit down strike; ~ **tournante** strike by rota; ~ **du zèle** work-to-rule (Brit), slowdown (US).

grever [gRəve] vt (budget, économie) to put a strain on; **grevé d'impôts** crippled by taxes; **grevé d'hypothèques** heavily mortgaged.

gréviste [gRevist(ə)] nm/f striker.

gribouillage [gRibujaʒ] nm scribble, scrawl.

gribouiller [gRibuje] vt to scribble, scrawl ♦ vi to doodle.

grief [gRijef] nm grievance; **faire ~ à qn de** to reproach sb for.

grièvement [gRijɛvmã] ad seriously.

griffe [gRif] nf claw; (fig) signature; (: d'un couturier, parfumeur) label, signature.

griffé, e [gRife] a designer(-label) cpd.

griffer [gRife] vt to scratch.

griffonnage [gRifɔnaʒ] nm scribble.

griffonner [gRifɔne] vt to scribble.

griffure [gRifyR] nf scratch.

grignoter [gRiɲɔte] vt, vi to nibble.

gril [gRil] nm steak ou grill pan.

grillade [gRijad] nf grill.

grillage [gRijaʒ] nm (treillis) wire netting; (clôture) wire fencing.

grille [gRij] nf (portail) (metal) gate; (clôture) railings pl; (d'égout) (metal) grate; (fig) grid.

grille-pain [gRijpɛ̃] nm inv toaster.

griller [gRije] vt (aussi: **faire ~**: pain) to toast; (: viande) to grill (Brit), broil (US); (: café) to roast; (fig: ampoule etc) to burn out, blow; ~ **un feu rouge** to jump the lights (Brit), run a stoplight (US) ♦ vi (brûler) to be roasting.

grillon [gRijɔ̃] nm (ZOOL) cricket.

grimace [gRimas] nf grimace; (pour faire rire): **faire des ~s** to pull ou make faces.

grimacer [gRimase] vi to grimace.

grimer [gRime] vt to make up.

grimpant, e [gRɛ̃pã, -ãt] a: **plante ~e** climbing plant, climber.

grimper [gRɛ̃pe] vi, vt to climb ♦ nm: **le ~** (SPORT) rope-climbing; ~ **à/sur** to climb (up)/climb onto.

grimpeur, euse [gRɛ̃pœR, -øz] nm/f climber.

grinçant, e [gRɛ̃sã, -ãt] a grating.

grincement [gRɛ̃smã] nm grating (noise); creaking (noise).

grincer [gRɛ̃se] vi (porte, roue) to grate; (plancher) to creak; ~ **des dents** to grind one's teeth.

grincheux, euse [gRɛ̃ʃø, -øz] a grumpy.

gringalet [gRɛ̃gale] am puny ♦ nm weakling.

griotte [gRijɔt] nf Morello cherry.

grippe [gRip] nf flu, influenza; **avoir la ~** to have (the) flu; **prendre qn/qch en ~** (fig) to take a sudden dislike to sb/sth.

grippé, e [gRipe] a: **être ~** to have (the) flu; (moteur) to have seized up (Brit) ou jammed.

gripper [gRipe] vt, vi to jam.

gris, e [gRi, gRiz] a grey (Brit), gray (US); (ivre) tipsy ♦ nm (couleur) grey (Brit), gray

(US); **il fait ~** it's a dull ou grey day; **faire ~e mine** to look miserable ou morose; **faire ~e mine à qn** to give sb a cool reception.

grisaille [gRizaj] nf greyness (Brit), grayness (US), dullness.

grisant, e [gRizã, -ãt] a intoxicating, exhilarating.

grisâtre [gRizatR(ə)] a greyish (Brit), grayish (US).

griser [gRize] vt to intoxicate; **se ~ de** (fig) to become intoxicated with.

grisonnant, e [gRizɔnã, -ãt] a greying (Brit), graying (US).

grisonner [gRizɔne] vi to be going grey (Brit) ou gray (US).

grisou [gRizu] nm firedamp.

grive [gRiv] nf (ZOOL) thrush.

grivois, e [gRivwa, -waz] a saucy.

Groenland [gRɔɛnlãd] nm: **le ~** Greenland.

groenlandais, e [gRɔɛnlãdɛ, -ɛz] a of ou from Greenland ♦ nm/f: **G~, e** Greenlander.

grog [gRɔg] nm grog.

grogne [gRɔɲ] nf grumble.

grogner [gRɔɲe] vi to growl; (fig) to grumble.

grognon, ne [gRɔɲɔ̃, -ɔn] a grumpy, grouchy.

groin [gRwɛ̃] nm snout.

grommeler [gRɔmle] vi to mutter to o.s.

grondement [gRɔ̃dmã] nm rumble; growl.

gronder [gRɔ̃de] vi (canon, moteur, tonnerre) to rumble; (animal) to growl; (fig: révolte) to be brewing ♦ vt to scold.

groom [gRum] nm page, bellhop (US).

gros, se [gRo, gRos] a big, large; (obèse) fat; (problème, quantité) great; (travaux, dégâts) extensive; (large: trait, fil) thick, heavy ♦ ad: **risquer/gagner ~** to risk/win a lot ♦ nm (COMM): **le ~** the wholesale business; **écrire ~** to write in big letters; **prix de ~** wholesale price; **par ~ temps/~se mer** in rough weather/heavy seas; **le ~ de** the main body of; (du travail etc) the bulk of; **en avoir ~ sur le cœur** to be upset; **en ~** roughly; (COMM) wholesale; ~ **intestin** large intestine; ~ **lot** jackpot; ~ **mot** coarse word, vulgarity; ~ **œuvre** shell (of building); ~ **plan** (PHOTO) close-up; ~ **porteur** wide-bodied aircraft, jumbo (jet); ~ **sel** cooking salt; ~ **titre** headline; ~**se caisse** big drum.

groseille [gRozɛj] nf: ~ **(rouge)/(blanche)** red/white currant; ~ **à maquereau** gooseberry.

groseillier [gRozeje] nm red ou white currant bush; gooseberry bush.

grosse [gRos] af voir **gros** ♦ nf (COMM) gross.

grossesse [gRosɛs] nf pregnancy; ~ **nerveuse** phantom pregnancy.

grosseur [gRosœR] nf size; fatness; (tumeur) lump.

grossier, ière [gRosje, -jɛR] a coarse; (travail) rough; crude; (évident: erreur) gross.

grossièrement [gRosjɛRmã] ad coarsely; roughly; crudely; (en gros) roughly.

grossièreté [gRosjɛRte] nf coarseness; rudeness.

grossir [gRosiR] vi (personne) to put on weight; (fig) to grow, get bigger; (rivière) to swell ♦ vt to increase; (exagérer) to exaggerate; (au microscope) to magnify, enlarge;

(suj: vêtement): ~ **qn** to make sb look fatter.

grossissant, e [grosisã, -ãt] *a* magnifying, enlarging.

grossissement [grosismã] *nm* *(optique)* magnification.

grossiste [grosist(ə)] *nm/f* wholesaler.

grosso modo [grosomɔdo] *ad* roughly.

grotesque [grɔtɛsk(ə)] *a* grotesque.

grotte [grɔt] *nf* cave.

grouiller [gruje] *vi* *(foule)* to mill about; *(fourmis)* to swarm about; ~ **de** to be swarming with.

groupe [grup] *nm* group; **cabinet de** ~ group practice; **médecine de** ~ group practice; ~ **électrogène** generator; ~ **de pression** pressure group; ~ **sanguin** blood group; ~ **scolaire** school complex.

groupement [grupmã] *nm* grouping; *(groupe)* group; ~ **d'intérêt économique (GIE)** ≈ trade association.

grouper [grupe] *vt* to group; *(ressources, moyens)* to pool; **se** ~ to get together.

groupuscule [grupyskyl] *nm* clique.

gruau [gryo] *nm*: **pain de** ~ wheaten bread.

grue [gry] *nf* crane; **faire le pied de** ~ *(fam)* to hang around (waiting), kick one's heels *(Brit)*.

gruger [gryʒe] *vt* to cheat, dupe.

grumeaux [grymo] *nmpl* *(CULIN)* lumps.

grumeleux, euse [grymlø, -øz] *a* *(sauce etc)* lumpy; *(peau etc)* bumpy.

grutier [grytje] *nm* crane driver.

gruyère [gryjɛʀ] *nm* gruyère *(Brit)* ou Swiss cheese.

Guadeloupe [gwadlup] *nf*: **la** ~ Guadeloupe.

guadeloupéen, ne [gwadlupeɛ̃, -ɛn] *a* Guadelupian.

Guatemala [gwatemala] *nm*: **le** ~ Guatemala.

guatémalien, ne [gwatemaljɛ̃, -ɛn] *a* Guatemalan.

guatémaltèque [gwatemaltɛk] *a* Guatemalan.

GUD [gyd] *sigle m* (= *Groupe Union Défense*) student union.

gué [ge] *nm* ford; **passer à** ~ to ford.

guenilles [gənij] *nfpl* rags.

guenon [gənɔ̃] *nf* female monkey.

guépard [gepaʀ] *nm* cheetah.

guêpe [gɛp] *nf* wasp.

guêpier [gepje] *nm* *(fig)* trap.

guère [gɛʀ] *ad* *(avec adjectif, adverbe)*: **ne** ... ~ hardly; *(avec verbe)*: **ne** ... ~ *tournure négative* + much; hardly ever; *tournure négative* + (very) long; **il n'y a** ~ **que/de** there's hardly anybody *(ou* anything) but/ hardly any.

guéridon [geʀidɔ̃] *nm* pedestal table.

guérilla [geʀija] *nf* guerrilla warfare.

guérillero [geʀijeʀo] *nm* guerrilla.

guérir [geʀiʀ] *vt* *(personne, maladie)* to cure; *(membre, plaie)* to heal ♦ *vi* *(personne)* to recover, be cured; *(plaie, chagrin)* to heal; ~ **de** to be cured of, recover from; ~ **qn de** to cure sb of.

guérison [geʀizɔ̃] *nf* curing; healing; recovery.

guérissable [geʀisabl(ə)] *a* curable.

guérisseur, euse [geʀisœʀ, -øz] *nm/f* healer.

guérite [geʀit] *nf* *(MIL)* sentry box; *(sur un*

chantier) *(workman's)* hut.

Guernesey [gɛʀnəze] *nf* Guernsey.

guernesiais, e [gɛʀnəzje, -ɛz] *a* of *ou* from Guernsey.

guerre [gɛʀ] *nf* war; *(méthode)*: ~ **atomique/de tranchées** atomic/trench warfare *q*; **en** ~ at war; **faire la** ~ **à** to wage war against; **de** ~ **lasse** *(fig)* tired of fighting *ou* resisting; **de bonne** ~ fair and square; ~ **civile/mondiale** civil/world war; ~ **froide/ sainte** cold/holy war; ~ **d'usure** war of attrition.

guerrier, ière [gɛʀje, -jɛʀ] *a* warlike ♦ *nm/f* warrior.

guerroyer [gɛʀwaje] *vi* to wage war.

guet [gɛ] *nm*: **faire le** ~ to be on the watch *ou* look-out.

guet-apens, pl guets-apens [gɛtapã] *nm* ambush.

guêtre [gɛtʀ(ə)] *nf* gaiter.

guetter [gete] *vt* *(épier)* to watch (intently); *(attendre)* to watch (out) for; *(: pour surprendre)* to be lying in wait for.

guetteur [getœʀ] *nm* look-out.

gueule [gœl] *nf* mouth; *(fam: visage)* mug; *(: bouche)* gob (!), mouth; **ta** ~! *(fam)* shut up!; ~ **de bois** *(fam)* hangover.

gueule-de-loup, pl gueules-de-loup [gœldəlu] *nf* snapdragon.

gueuler [gœle] *vi* *(fam)* to bawl.

gueux [gø] *nm* beggar; *(coquin)* rogue.

gui [gi] *nm* mistletoe.

guichet [giʃɛ] *nm* *(de bureau, banque)* counter, window; *(d'une porte)* wicket, hatch; **les** ~**s** *(à la gare, au théâtre)* the ticket office; **jouer à** ~**s fermés** to play to a full house.

guichetier, ière [giʃtje, -jɛʀ] *nm/f* counter clerk.

guide [gid] *nm* guide; *(livre)* guide(book) ♦ *nf* *(fille scout)* (girl) guide *(Brit)*, girl scout *(US)*; ~**s** *nfpl* *(d'un cheval)* reins.

guider [gide] *vt* to guide.

guidon [gidɔ̃] *nm* handlebars *pl*.

guignol [giɲɔl] *nm* ≈ Punch and Judy show; *(fig)* clown.

guillemets [gijmɛ] *nmpl*: **entre** ~ in inverted commas *ou* quotation marks; ~ **de répétition** ditto marks.

guilleret, te [gijʀɛ, -ɛt] *a* perky, bright.

guillotine [gijɔtin] *nf* guillotine.

guillotiner [gijɔtine] *vt* to guillotine.

guimauve [gimov] *nf* *(BOT)* marshmallow; *(fig)* sentimentality, sloppiness.

guimbarde [gɛ̃baʀd(ə)] *nf* old banger *(Brit)*, jalopy.

guindé, e [gɛ̃de] *a* stiff, starchy.

Guinée [gine] *nf*: **la (République de)** ~ (the Republic of) Guinea; **la** ~ **équatoriale** Equatorial Guinea.

Guinée-Bissau [ginebiso] *nf*: **la** ~ Guinea-Bissau.

guinéen, ne [gineɛ̃, -ɛn] *a* Guinean.

guingette [gɛ̃ʒɛt] *nf* open-air café or dance-hall.

guingois [gɛ̃gwa]: **de** ~ *ad* askew.

guirlande [giʀlãd] *nf* garland; *(de papier)* paper chain; ~ **lumineuse** (fairy *(Brit)*) lights *pl*; ~ **de Noël** tinsel *q*.

guise [giz] *nf*: **à votre ~** as you wish *ou* please; **en ~ de** by way of.

guitare [gitar] *nf* guitar.

guitariste [gitarist(ə)] *nm/f* guitarist, guitar player.

gustatif, ive [gystatif, -iv] *a* gustatory; *voir* **papille.**

guttural, e, aux [gytyral, -o] *a* guttural.

guyanais, e [gɥijanɛ, -ɛz] *a* Guyanese, Guyanan; *(français)* Guianese, Guianan.

Guyane [gɥijan] *nf*: **la ~** Guyana; **la ~ (française)** (French) Guiana.

gvt *abr* (= *gouvernement*) govt.

gymkhana [ʒimkana] *nm* rally; **~ motocycliste** (motorbike) scramble *(Brit)*, motocross.

gymnase [ʒimnaz] *nm* gym(nasium).

gymnaste [ʒimnast(ə)] *nm/f* gymnast.

gymnastique [ʒimnastik] *nf* gymnastics *sg*; *(au réveil etc)* keep-fit exercises *pl*; **~ corrective** remedial gymnastics.

gynécologie [ʒinekɔlɔʒi] *nf* gynaecology.

gynécologue [ʒinekɔlɔg] *nm/f* gynaecologist.

gypse [ʒips(ə)] *nm* gypsum.

gyrophare [ʒirɔfar] *nm* *(sur une voiture)* revolving (flashing) light.

H

H, h [aʃ] *nm inv* H, h ♦ *abr* (= *homme*) M; (= *hydrogène*) H; **bombe ~** H H bomb; (= *heure*): **à l'heure ~** at zero hour; **H comme Henri** H for Harry *(Brit)* ou How *(US)*.

ha. *abr* (= *hectare*) ha.

hab. *abr* = **habitant.**

habile [abil] *a* skilful; *(malin)* clever.

habilement [abilmã] *ad* skilfully; cleverly.

habileté [abilte] *nf* skill, skilfulness; cleverness.

habilité, e [abilite] *a*: **~ à faire** entitled to do, empowered to do.

habiliter [abilite] *vt* empower, entitle.

habillage [abijaʒ] *nm* dressing.

habillé, e [abije] *a* dressed; *(chic)* dressy; *(TECH)*: **~ de** covered with; encased in.

habillement [abijmã] *nm* clothes *pl*; *(profession)* clothing industry.

habiller [abije] *vt* to dress; *(fournir en vêtements)* to clothe; **s'~** to dress (o.s.); *(se déguiser, mettre des vêtements chic)* to dress up; **s'~ de/en** to dress in/dress up as; **s'~ chez/à** to buy one's clothes from/at.

habilleuse [abijøz] *nf* *(CINÉMA, THÉÂTRE)* dresser.

habit [abi] *nm* outfit; **~s** *nmpl* *(vêtements)* clothes; **~ (de soirée)** tails *pl*; evening dress; **prendre l'~** *(REL: entrer en religion)* to enter (holy) orders.

habitable [abitabl(ə)] *a* (in)habitable.

habitacle [abitakl(ə)] *nm* cockpit; *(AUTO)* passenger cell.

habitant, e [abitã, -ãt] *nm/f* inhabitant;

(d'une maison) occupant, occupier; **loger chez l'~** to stay with the locals.

habitat [abita] *nm* housing conditions *pl*; *(BOT, ZOOL)* habitat.

habitation [abitɑsjɔ̃] *nf* living; *(demeure)* residence, home; *(maison)* house; **~s à loyer modéré (HLM)** low-rent, state-owned housing, ≈ council housing *sg* *(Brit)*, ≈ public housing units *(US)*.

habité, e [abite] *a* inhabited; lived in.

habiter [abite] *vt* to live in; *(suj: sentiment)* to dwell in ♦ *vi*: **~ à/dans** to live in *ou* at/in; **~ chez** *ou* **avec qn** to live with sb; **~ 16 rue Montmartre** to live at number 16 rue Montmartre; **~ rue Montmartre** to live in rue Montmartre.

habitude [abityd] *nf* habit; **avoir l'~ de faire** to be in the habit of doing; **avoir l'~ des enfants** to be used to children; **prendre l'~ de faire qch** to get into the habit of doing sth; **perdre une ~** to get out of a habit; **d'~** usually; **comme d'~** as usual; **par ~** out of habit.

habitué, e [abitɥe] *a*: **être ~ à** to be used *ou* accustomed to ♦ *nm/f* regular visitor; *(client)* regular (customer).

habituel, le [abitɥɛl] *a* usual.

habituellement [abitɥɛlmã] *ad* usually.

habituer [abitɥe] *vt*: **~ qn à** to get sb used to; **s'~ à** to get used to.

'hâbleur, euse ['ablœr, -øz] *a* boastful.

'hache ['aʃ] *nf* axe.

'haché, e ['aʃe] *a* minced *(Brit)*, ground *(US)*; *(persil)* chopped; *(fig)* jerky.

'hache-légumes ['aʃlegym] *nm inv* vegetable chopper.

'hacher ['aʃe] *vt* *(viande)* to mince *(Brit)*, grind *(US)*; *(persil)* to chop; **~ menu** to mince *ou* grind finely; to chop finely.

'hachette ['aʃɛt] *nf* hatchet.

'hache-viande ['aʃvjãd] *nm inv* (meat) mincer *(Brit)* ou grinder *(US)*; *(couteau)* (meat) cleaver.

'hachis ['aʃi] *nm* mince *q* *(Brit)*, hamburger meat *(US)*; **~ de viande** minced *(Brit)* ou ground *(US)* meat.

'hachisch ['aʃiʃ] *nm* hashish.

'hachoir ['aʃwar] *nm* chopper; (meat) mincer *(Brit)* ou grinder *(US)*; *(planche)* chopping board.

'hachurer ['aʃyre] *vt* to hatch.

'hachures ['aʃyr] *nfpl* hatching *sg*.

'hagard, e ['agar, -ard(ə)] *a* wild, distraught.

'haie ['ɛ] *nf* hedge; *(SPORT)* hurdle; *(fig: rang)* line, row; **200 m ~s** 200 m hurdles; **~ d'honneur** guard of honour.

'haillons ['ajɔ̃] *nmpl* rags.

'haine ['ɛn] *nf* hatred.

'haineux, euse ['ɛnø, -øz] *a* full of hatred.

'haïr ['air] *vt* to detest, hate; **se ~** to hate each other.

'hais ['ɛ], **'haïs** ['ai] *etc vb voir* **haïr.**

'haïssable ['aisabl(ə)] *a* detestable.

Haïti [aiti] *n* Haiti.

haïtien, ne [aisjɛ̃, -ɛn] *a* Haitian.

'halage ['alaʒ] *nm*: **chemin de ~** towpath.

'hâle ['al] *nm* (sun)tan.

'hâlé, e ['ale] *a* (sun)tanned, sunburnt.

haleine [alɛn] *nf* breath; **perdre ~** to get out

of breath; **à perdre** ~ until one is gasping for breath; **avoir mauvaise** ~ to have bad breath; **reprendre** ~ to get one's breath back; **hors d'**~ out of breath; **tenir en** ~ to hold spellbound; (*en attente*) to keep in suspense; **de longue** ~ *a* long-term.

'haler ['ale] *vt* to haul in; (*remorquer*) to tow.

'haleter ['alte] *vi* to pant.

'hall ['ol] *nm* hall.

hallali [alali] *nm* kill.

'halle ['al] *nf* (covered) market; ~**s** *nfpl* central food market *sg*.

hallucinant, e [alysinɑ̃, -ɑ̃t] *a* staggering.

hallucination [alysinasjɔ̃] *nf* hallucination.

hallucinatoire [alysinatwar] *a* hallucinatory.

halluciné, e [alysine] *nm/f* person suffering from hallucinations; (*fou*) (raving) lunatic.

'halo ['alo] *nm* halo.

halogène [alɔʒɛn] *nm*: **lampe (à)** ~ halogen lamp.

'halte ['alt(ə)] *nf* stop, break; (*escale*) stopping place; (*RAIL*) halt ♦ *excl* stop!; **faire** ~ to stop.

'halte-garderie, *pl* **'haltes-garderies** ['altgardəri] *nf* crèche.

haltère [altɛr] *nm* (*à boules, disques*) dumbbell, barbell; (**poids et**) ~**s** weightlifting.

haltérophile [alterɔfil] *nm/f* weightlifter.

haltérophilie [alterɔfili] *nf* weightlifting.

'hamac ['amak] *nm* hammock.

'Hambourg ['ɑ̃bur] *n* Hamburg.

'hameau, x ['amo] *nm* hamlet.

hameçon [amsɔ̃] *nm* (fish) hook.

'hampe ['ɑ̃p] *nf* (*de drapeau etc*) pole; (*de lance*) shaft.

'hamster ['amstɛr] *nm* hamster.

'hanche ['ɑ̃ʃ] *nf* hip.

'hand-ball ['ɑ̃dbal] *nm* handball.

'handicap ['ɑ̃dikap] *nm* handicap.

'handicapé, e ['ɑ̃dikape] *a* handicapped ♦ *nm/f* physically (*ou* mentally) handicapped person; ~ **moteur** spastic.

'handicaper ['ɑ̃dikape] *vt* to handicap.

'hangar ['ɑ̃gar] *nm* shed; (*AVIAT*) hangar.

'hanneton ['antɔ̃] *nm* cockchafer.

'Hanovre ['anɔvr(ə)] *n* Hanover.

'hanovrien, ne ['anɔvrjɛ̃, -ɛn] *a* Hanoverian.

'hanter ['ɑ̃te] *vt* to haunt.

'hantise ['ɑ̃tiz] *nf* obsessive fear.

'happer ['ape] *vt* to snatch; (*suj: train etc*) to hit.

'haranguer ['arɑ̃ge] *vt* to harangue.

'haras ['ara] *nm* stud farm.

'harassant, e ['arasɑ̃, -ɑ̃t] *a* exhausting.

'harceler ['arsəle] *vt* (*MIL, CHASSE*) to harass, harry; (*importuner*) to plague.

'hardes ['ard(ə)] *nfpl* rags.

'hardi, e ['ardi] *a* bold, daring.

'hareng ['arɑ̃] *nm* herring.

'hargne ['arɲ(ə)] *nf* aggressivity, aggressiveness.

'haricot ['ariko] *nm* bean; ~ **blanc/rouge** haricot/kidney bean; ~ **vert** French (*Brit*) *ou* green bean.

harmonica [armɔnika] *nm* mouth organ.

harmonie [armɔni] *nf* harmony.

harmonieux, euse [armɔnjø, -øz] *a* harmonious.

harmonique [armɔnik] *a, nm ou nf* harmonic.

harmoniser [armɔnize] *vt* to harmonize; **s'**~ (*couleurs, teintes*) to go well together.

harmonium [armɔnjɔm] *nm* harmonium.

'harnaché, e ['arnaʃe] *a* (*fig*) rigged out.

'harnachement ['arnaʃmɑ̃] *nm* (*habillement*) rig-out; (*équipement*) harness, equipment.

'harnacher ['arnaʃe] *vt* to harness.

'harnais ['arnɛ] *nm* harness.

'haro ['aro] *nm*: **crier** ~ **sur qn/qch** to inveigh against sb/sth.

'harpe ['arp(ə)] *nf* harp.

'harpiste ['arpist(ə)] *nm/f* harpist.

'harpon ['arpɔ̃] *nm* harpoon.

'harponner ['arpɔne] *vt* to harpoon; (*fam*) to collar.

'hasard ['azar] *nm*: **le** ~ chance, fate; **un** ~ *a* coincidence; (*aubaine, chance*) a stroke of luck; **au** ~ (*sans but*) aimlessly; (*à l'aveuglette*) at random, haphazardly; **par** ~ by chance; **comme par** ~ as if by chance; **à tout** ~ on the off chance; (*en cas de besoin*) just in case.

'hasarder ['azarde] *vt* (*mot*) to venture; (*fortune*) to risk; **se** ~ **à faire** to risk doing, venture to do.

'hasardeux, euse ['azardø, -øz] *a* hazardous, risky; (*hypothèse*) rash.

'haschisch ['aʃiʃ] *nm* hashish.

'hâte ['ɑt] *nf* haste; **à la** ~ hurriedly, hastily; **en** ~ posthaste, with all possible speed; **avoir** ~ **de** to be eager *ou* anxious to.

'hâter ['ɑte] *vt* to hasten; **se** ~ to hurry; **se** ~ **de** to hurry *ou* hasten to.

'hâtif, ive ['ɑtif, -iv] *a* (*travail*) hurried; (*décision*) hasty; (*légume*) early.

'hâtivement ['ɑtivmɑ̃] *ad* hurriedly; hastily.

'hauban ['obɑ̃] *nm* (*NAVIG*) shroud.

'hausse ['os] *nf* rise, increase; (*de fusil*) back-sight adjuster; **à la** ~ upwards; **en** ~ rising.

'hausser ['ose] *vt* to raise; ~ **les épaules** to shrug (one's shoulders); **se** ~ **sur la pointe des pieds** to stand (up) on tiptoe *ou* tippy-toe (*US*).

'haut, e ['o, 'ot] *a* high; (*grand*) tall; (*son, voix*) high(-pitched) ♦ *ad* high ♦ *nm* top (part); **de 3m de** ~, ~ **de 3m** 3m high, 3m in height; **en** ~**e montagne** high up in the mountains; **en** ~ **lieu** in high places; **à** ~**e voix, (tout)** ~ aloud, out loud; **des** ~**s et des bas** ups and downs; **du** ~ **de** from the top of; **tomber de** ~ to fall from a height; (*fig*) to have one's hopes dashed; **dire qch bien** ~ to say sth plainly; **prendre qch de (très)** ~ to react haughtily to sth; **traiter qn de** ~ to treat sb with disdain; **de** ~ **en bas** from top to bottom; downwards; ~ **en couleur** (*chose*) highly coloured; (*personne*): **un personnage** ~ **en couleur** a colourful character; **plus** ~ higher up, further up; (*dans un texte*) above; (*parler*) louder; **en** ~ up above; **at** (*ou* to) the top; (*dans une maison*) upstairs; **en** ~ **de** at the top of; ~ **les mains!** hands up!, stick 'em up!; **la** ~**e couture/ coiffure** haute couture/coiffure; ~**e fidélité** hi-fi, high fidelity; **la** ~**e finance** high finance; ~**e trahison** high treason.

'hautain, e ['otɛ̃, -ɛn] *a* (*personne, regard*) haughty.

'hautbois ['obwa] *nm* oboe.

'**hautboïste** ['obɔist(ə)] *nm/f* oboist.
'**haut-de-forme,** *pl* '**hauts-de-forme** ['odfɔrm(ə)] *nm* top hat.
'**haute-contre,** *pl* '**hautes-contre** ['otkɔ̃tr(ə)] *nf* counter-tenor.
'**hauteur** ['otœr] *nf* height; (*GÉO*) height, hill; (*fig*) loftiness; haughtiness; **à ~ de** up to (the level of); **à ~ des yeux** at eye level; **à la ~ de** (*sur la même ligne*) level with; by; (*fig*) equal to; **à la ~** (*fig*) up to it, equal to the task.
'**Haute-Volta** ['otvɔlta] *nf*: **la ~** Upper Volta.
'**haut-fond,** *pl* '**hauts-fonds** ['ofɔ̃] *nm* shallow.
'**haut-fourneau,** *pl* '**hauts-fourneaux** ['ofurno] *nm* blast *ou* smelting furnace.
'**haut-le-cœur** ['olkœr] *nm inv* retch, heave.
'**haut-le-corps** ['olkɔr] *nm inv* start, jump.
'**haut-parleur,** *pl* '**haut-parleurs** ['oparlœr] *nm* (loud)speaker.
'**hauturier, ière** ['otyrje, -jɛr] *a* (*NAVIG*) deep-sea.
'**havanais, e** ['avanɛ, -ɛz] *a* of *ou* from Havana.
'**Havane** ['avan] *nf*: **la ~** Havana ♦ *nm*: '**h~** (*cigare*) Havana.
'**hâve** ['av] *a* gaunt.
'**havrais, e** ['avrɛ, -ɛz] *a* of *ou* from Le Havre.
'**havre** ['avr(ə)] *nm* haven.
'**havresac** ['avrəsak] *nm* haversack.
Hawaï *ou* **Hawaii** [awai] *n* Hawaii; **les îles ~** the Hawaiian Islands.
hawaïen, ne [awajɛ̃, -ɛn] *a* Hawaiian ♦ *nm* (*LING*) Hawaiian.
'**Haye** ['ɛ] *n*: **la ~** the Hague.
'**hayon** ['ɛjɔ̃] *nm* tailgate.
hdb. *abr* (= *heures de bureau*) o.h. (= *office hours*).
'**hé** ['e] *excl* hey!
hebdo [ɛbdo] *nm* (*fam*) weekly.
hebdomadaire [ɛbdɔmadɛr] *a, nm* weekly.
hébergement [ebɛrʒəmã] *nm* accommodation, lodging; taking in.
héberger [ebɛrʒe] *vt* to accommodate, lodge; (*réfugiés*) to take in.
hébété, e [ebete] *a* dazed.
hébétude [ebetyd] *nf* stupor.
hébraïque [ebraik] *a* Hebrew, Hebraic.
hébreu, x [ebrø] *am, nm* Hebrew.
Hébrides [ebrid] *nf*: **les ~** the Hebrides.
HEC *sigle fpl* (= *École des hautes études commerciales*) *grande école for management and business studies*.
hécatombe [ekatɔ̃b] *nf* slaughter.
hectare [ɛktar] *nm* hectare, 10,000 square metres.
hecto... [ɛkto] *préfixe* hecto....
hectolitre [ɛktɔlitr(ə)] *nm* hectolitre.
hédoniste [edɔnist(ə)] *a* hedonistic.
hégémonie [eʒemɔni] *nf* hegemony.
'**hein** ['ɛ̃] *excl* eh?; (*sollicitant l'approbation*): **tu m'approuves, ~?** so I did the right thing then?; **Paul est venu, ~?** Paul came, did he?; **que fais-tu, ~?** hey! what are you doing?
'**hélas** ['elɑs] *excl* alas! ♦ *ad* unfortunately.
'**héler** ['ele] *vt* to hail.
hélice [elis] *nf* propeller.
hélicoïdal, e, aux [elikɔidal, -o] *a* helical;
helicoid.
hélicoptère [elikɔptɛr] *nm* helicopter.
hélio(gravure) [eljɔgravyr] *nf* heliogravure.
héliomarin, e [eljɔmarɛ̃, -in] *a*: **centre ~** *centre offering sea and sun therapy*.
héliotrope [eljɔtrɔp] *nm* (*BOT*) heliotrope.
héliport [elipɔr] *nm* heliport.
héliporté, e [elipɔrte] *a* transported by helicopter.
hélium [eljɔm] *nm* helium.
hellénique [elenik] *a* Hellenic.
hellénisant, e [elenizã, -ãt], **helléniste** [elenist(ə)] *nm/f* hellenist.
Helsinki [ɛlzinki] *n* Helsinki.
helvète [ɛlvɛt] *a* Helvetian ♦ *nm/f*: **H~** Helvetian.
Helvétie [ɛlvesi] *nf*: **la ~** Helvetia.
helvétique [ɛlvetik] *a* Swiss.
hématologie [ematɔlɔʒi] *nf* (*MÉD*) haematology.
hématome [ematom] *nm* haematoma.
hémicycle [emisikl(ə)] *nm* semicircle; (*POL*): **l'~** the benches (in French parliament).
hémiplégie [emipleʒi] *nf* paralysis of one side, hemiplegia.
hémisphère [emisfɛr] *nf*: **~ nord/sud** northern/southern hemisphere.
hémisphérique [emisferik] *a* hemispherical.
hémoglobine [emɔglɔbin] *nf* haemoglobin (*Brit*), hemoglobin (*US*).
hémophile [emɔfil] *a* haemophiliac (*Brit*), hemophiliac (*US*).
hémophilie [emɔfili] *nf* haemophilia (*Brit*), hemophilia (*US*).
hémorragie [emɔraʒi] *nf* bleeding *q*, haemorrhage (*Brit*), hemorrhage (*US*); **~ cérébrale** cerebral haemorrhage; **~ interne** internal bleeding *ou* haemorrhage.
hémorroïdes [emɔrɔid] *nfpl* piles, haemorrhoids (*Brit*), hemorrhoids (*US*).
hémostatique [emostatik] *a* haemostatic (*Brit*), hemostatic (*US*).
'**henné** ['ene] *nm* henna.
'**hennir** ['enir] *vi* to neigh, whinny.
'**hennissement** ['enismã] *nm* neighing, whinnying.
'**hep** ['ɛp] *excl* hey!
hépatite [epatit] *nf* hepatitis, liver infection.
héraldique [eraldik] *a* heraldry.
herbacé, e [ɛrbase] *a* herbaceous.
herbage [ɛrbaʒ] *nm* pasture.
herbe [ɛrb(ə)] *nf* grass; (*CULIN, MÉD*) herb; **en ~** unripe; (*fig*) budding; **touffe/brin d'~** clump/blade of grass.
herbeux, euse [ɛrbø, -øz] *a* grassy.
herbicide [ɛrbisid] *nm* weed-killer.
herbier [ɛrbje] *nm* herbarium.
herbivore [ɛrbivɔr] *nm* herbivore.
herboriser [ɛrbɔrize] *vi* to collect plants.
herboriste [ɛrbɔrist(ə)] *nm/f* herbalist.
herboristerie [ɛrbɔristri] *nf* (*magasin*) herbalist's shop; (*commerce*) herb trade.
herculéen, ne [ɛrkyleɛ̃, -ɛn] *a* (*fig*) herculean.
'**hère** ['ɛr] *nm*: **pauvre ~** poor wretch.
héréditaire [ereditɛr] *a* hereditary.
hérédité [eredite] *nf* heredity.
hérésie [erezi] *nf* heresy.
hérétique [eretik] *nm/f* heretic.

'hérissé, e ['erise] *a* bristling; ~ **de** spiked with; (*fig*) bristling with.

'hérisser ['erise] *vt*: ~ **qn** (*fig*) to ruffle sb; **se** ~ *vi* to bristle, bristle up.

'hérisson ['erisɔ̃] *nm* hedgehog.

héritage [eritaʒ] *nm* inheritance; (*fig*) heritage; (: *legs*) legacy; **faire un (petit)** ~ to come into (a little) money.

hériter [erite] *vi*: ~ **de qch (de qn)** to inherit sth (from sb); ~ **de qn** to inherit sb's property.

héritier, ière [eritje, -jɛr] *nm/f* heir/heiress.

hermaphrodite [ermafrɔdit] *a* (*BOT*, *ZOOL*) hermaphrodite.

hermétique [ermetik] *a* (à *l'air*) airtight; (à *l'eau*) watertight; (*fig: écrivain, style*) abstruse; (: *visage*) impenetrable.

hermétiquement [ermetikmɑ̃] *ad* hermetically.

hermine [ermin] *nf* ermine.

hernie ['erni] *nf* hernia.

héroïne [erɔin] *nf* heroine; (*drogue*) heroin.

héroïnomane [erɔinɔman] *nm/f* heroin addict.

héroïque [erɔik] *a* heroic.

héroïquement [erɔikmɑ̃] *ad* heroically.

héroïsme [erɔism(ə)] *nm* heroism.

'héron ['erɔ̃] *nm* heron.

'héros ['ero] *nm* hero.

herpès [erpɛs] *nm* herpes.

'herse ['ers(ə)] *nf* harrow; (*de château*) portcullis.

hertz [erts] *nm* (*ÉLEC*) hertz.

hertzien, ne [ertsjɛ̃, -en] *a* (*ÉLEC*) Hertzian.

hésitant, e [ezitɑ̃, -ɑ̃t] *a* hesitant.

hésitation [ezitasjɔ̃] *nf* hesitation.

hésiter [ezite] *vi*: ~ **(à faire)** to hesitate (to do); ~ **sur qch** to hesitate over sth.

hétéro [etero] *a inv* (= *hétérosexuel(le)*) hetero.

hétéroclite [eterɔklit] *a* heterogeneous; (*objets*) sundry.

hétérogène [eterɔʒɛn] *a* heterogeneous.

hétérosexuel, le [eterɔsekɥɛl] *a* heterosexual.

'hêtre ['ɛtr(ə)] *nm* beech.

heure [œr] *nf* hour; (*SCOL*) period; (*moment, moment fixé*) time; **c'est l'**~ it's time; **pourriez-vous me donner l'**~, **s'il vous plaît?** could you tell me the time, please?; **quelle** ~ **est-il?** what time is it?; **2** ~**s (du matin)** 2 o'clock (in the morning); **à la bonne** ~! (*parfois ironique*) splendid!; **être à l'**~ to be on time; (*montre*) to be right; **le bus passe à l'**~ the bus runs on the hour; **mettre à l'**~ to set right; **100km à l'**~ ≈ 60 miles an ou per hour; **à toute** ~ at any time; **24** ~**s sur 24** round the clock, 24 hours a day; **à l'**~ **qu'il est** at this time (of day); (*fig*) now; **à l'**~ **actuelle** at the present time; **sur l'**~ at once; **pour l'**~ for the time being; **d'**~ **en** ~ from one hour to the next; (*régulièrement*) hourly; **d'une** ~ **à l'autre** from hour to hour; **de bonne** ~ early; **2** ~**s de marche/travail** 2 hours' walking/work; **une** ~ **d'arrêt** an hour's break ou stop; ~ **d'été** summer time (*Brit*), daylight saving time (*US*); ~ **de pointe** rush hour; ~**s de bureau** office hours; ~**s supplémentaires** overtime *sg*.

heureusement [œrøzmɑ̃] *ad* (*par bonheur*) fortunately, luckily; ~ **que** ... it's a good job that ..., fortunately ....

heureux, euse [œrø, -øz] *a* happy; (*chanceux*) lucky, fortunate; (*judicieux*) felicitous, fortunate; **être** ~ **de qch** to be pleased *ou* happy about sth; **être** ~ **de faire/que** to be pleased *ou* happy to do/that; **s'estimer** ~ **de qch/que** to consider o.s. fortunate with/that; **encore** ~ **que** ... just as well that ....

'heurt ['œr] *nm* (*choc*) collision; ~**s** *nmpl* (*fig*) clashes.

'heurté, e ['œrte] *a* (*fig*) jerky, uneven; (: *couleurs*) clashing.

'heurter ['œrte] *vt* (*mur*) to strike, hit; (*personne*) to collide with; (*fig*) to go against, upset; **se** ~ (*couleurs, tons*) to clash; **se** ~ **à** to collide with; (*fig*) to come up against; ~ **qn de front** to clash head-on with sb.

'heurtoir ['œrtwar] *nm* door knocker.

hévéa [evea] *nm* rubber tree.

hexagonal, e, aux [egzagɔnal, -o] *a* hexagonal; (*français*) French (*see note at hexagone*).

hexagone [egzagɔn] *nm* hexagon; (*la France*) France (*because of its roughly hexagonal shape*).

HF *sigle f* (= *haute fréquence*) HF.

hiatus [jatys] *nm* hiatus.

hibernation [ibernasjɔ̃] *nf* hibernation.

hiberner [iberne] *vi* to hibernate.

hibiscus [ibiskys] *nm* hibiscus.

'hibou, x ['ibu] *nm* owl.

'hic ['ik] *nm* (*fam*) snag.

'hideusement ['idøzmɑ̃] *ad* hideously.

'hideux, euse ['idø, -øz] *a* hideous.

hier [jɛr] *ad* yesterday; ~ **matin/soir/midi** yesterday morning/evening/at midday; **toute la journée d'**~ all day yesterday; **toute la matinée d'**~ all yesterday morning.

'hiérarchie ['jerarʃi] *nf* hierarchy.

'hiérarchique ['jerarʃik] *a* hierarchic.

'hiérarchiquement ['jerarʃikmɑ̃] *ad* hierarchically.

'hiérarchiser ['jerarʃize] *vt* to organize into a hierarchy.

'hiéroglyphe ['jerɔglif] *nm* hieroglyphic.

'hiéroglyphique ['jerɔglifik] *a* hieroglyphic.

hilarant, e [ilarɑ̃, -ɑ̃t] *a* hilarious.

hilare [ilar] *a* mirthful.

hilarité [ilarite] *nf* hilarity, mirth.

Himalaya [imalaja] *nm*: **l'**~ the Himalaya *pl*.

himalayen, ne [imalajɛ̃, -en] *a* Himalayan.

hindou, e [ɛ̃du] *a, nm/f* Hindu; (*Indien*) Indian.

hindouisme [ɛ̃duism(ə)] *nm* Hinduism.

Hindoustan [ɛ̃dustɑ̃] *nm*: **l'**~ Hindustan.

hippique [ipik] *a* equestrian, horse *cpd*.

hippisme [ipism(ə)] *nm* (horse) riding.

hippocampe [ipɔkɑ̃p] *nm* sea horse.

hippodrome [ipɔdrom] *nm* racecourse.

hippophagique [ipɔfaʒik] *a*: **boucherie** ~ horse butcher's.

hippopotame [ipɔpɔtam] *nm* hippopotamus.

hirondelle [irɔdɛl] *nf* swallow.

hirsute [irsyt] *a* (*personne*) hairy; (*barbe*) shaggy; (*tête*) tousled.

hispanique [ispanik] *a* Hispanic.

hispanisant, e [ispanizɑ̃, -ɑ̃t], **hispaniste** [ispanist(ə)] *nm/f* Hispanist.

hispano-américain, e [ispanɔamerikɛ̃, -ɛn] *a* Spanish-American.

hispano-arabe [ispanɔarab] *a* Hispano-Moresque.

'hisser ['ise] *vt* to hoist, haul up; **se ~ sur** to haul o.s. up onto.

histoire [istwar] *nf* (*science, événements*) history; (*anecdote, récit, mensonge*) story; (*affaire*) business *q*; (*chichis: gén pl*) fuss *q*; **~s** *nfpl* (*ennuis*) trouble *sg*; **l'~ de France** French history, the history of France; **l'~ sainte** biblical history; **une ~ de** (*fig*) a question of.

histologie [istɔlɔʒi] *nf* histology.

historien, ne [istɔrjɛ̃, -ɛn] *nm/f* historian.

historique [istɔrik] *a* historical; (*important*) historic ♦ *nm* (*exposé, récit*): **faire l'~ de** to give the background to.

historiquement [istɔrikmɑ̃] *ad* historically.

hiver [ivɛr] *nm* winter; **en ~** in winter.

hivernal, e, aux [ivɛrnal, -o] *a* (*de l'hiver*) winter *cpd*; (*comme en hiver*) wintry.

hivernant, e [ivɛrnɑ̃, -ɑ̃t] *n* winter holiday-maker.

hiverner [ivɛrne] *vi* to winter.

HLM *sigle m ou f* (= *habitations à loyer modéré*) low-rent, state-owned housing; **un(e) ~** ≈ a council flat (*ou* house) (*Brit*), ≈ a public housing unit (*US*).

Hme *abr* (= *homme*) M.

HO *abr* (= *hors œuvre*) labour not included (*on invoices*).

'hobby ['ɔbi] *nm* hobby.

'hochement ['ɔʃmɑ̃] *nm*: **~ de tête** nod; shake of the head.

'hocher ['ɔʃe] *vt*: **~ la tête** to nod; (*signe négatif ou dubitatif*) to shake one's head.

'hochet ['ɔʃɛ] *nm* rattle.

'hockey ['ɔkɛ] *nm*: **~ (sur glace/gazon)** (ice/field) hockey.

'hockeyeur, euse ['ɔkɛjœr, -øz] *nm/f* hockey player.

'hola ['ɔla] *nm*: **mettre le ~ à qch** to put a stop to sth.

'holding ['ɔldiŋ] *nm* holding company.

'hold-up ['ɔldœp] *nm inv* hold-up.

'hollandais, e ['ɔlɑ̃dɛ, -ɛz] *a* Dutch ♦ *nm* (*LING*) Dutch ♦ *nm/f*: **H~, e** Dutchman/woman; **les H~** the Dutch.

'Hollande ['ɔlɑ̃d] *nf*: **la ~** Holland ♦ *nm*: **h~** (*fromage*) Dutch cheese.

holocauste [ɔlɔkost(ə)] *nm* holocaust.

hologramme [ɔlɔgram] *nm* hologram.

'homard ['ɔmar] *nm* lobster.

homéopathe [ɔmeɔpat] *n* homoeopath.

homéopathie [ɔmeɔpati] *nf* homoeopathy.

homéopathique [ɔmeɔpatik] *a* homoeopathic.

homérique [ɔmerik] *a* Homeric.

homicide [ɔmisid] *nm* murder ♦ *nm/f* murderer/eress; **~ involontaire** manslaughter.

hommage [ɔmaʒ] *nm* tribute; **~s** *nmpl*: **présenter ses ~s** to pay one's respects; **rendre ~ à** to pay tribute *ou* homage to; **en ~ de** as a token of; **faire ~ de qch à qn** to present sb with sth.

homme [ɔm] *nm* man; (*espèce humaine*): **l'~** man, mankind; **~ d'affaires** businessman; **~ des cavernes** caveman; **~ d'Église** church-

man, clergyman; **~ d'État** statesman; **~ de loi** lawyer; **~ de main** hired man; **~ de paille** stooge; **l'~ de la rue** the man in the street; **~ à tout faire** odd-job man.

homme-grenouille, *pl* **hommes-grenouilles** [ɔmgrənuj] *nm* frogman.

homme-orchestre, *pl* **hommes-orchestres** [ɔmɔrkɛstr(ə)] *nm* one-man band.

homme-sandwich, *pl* **hommes-sandwichs** [ɔmsɑ̃dwitʃ] *nm* sandwich (board) man.

homogène [ɔmɔʒɛn] *a* homogeneous.

homogénéisé, e [ɔmɔʒeneize] *a*: **lait ~** homogenized milk.

homogénéité [ɔmɔʒeneite] *nf* homogeneity.

homologation [ɔmɔlɔgasjɔ̃] *nf* ratification; official recognition.

homologue [ɔmɔlɔg] *nm/f* counterpart, opposite number.

homologué, e [ɔmɔlɔge] *a* (*SPORT*) officially recognized, ratified; (*tarif*) authorized.

homologuer [ɔmɔlɔge] *vt* (*JUR*) to ratify; (*SPORT*) to recognize officially, ratify.

homonyme [ɔmɔnim] *nm* (*LING*) homonym; (*d'une personne*) namesake.

homosexualité [ɔmɔsɛksɥalite] *nf* homosexuality.

homosexuel, le [ɔmɔsɛksɥɛl] *a* homosexual.

'Honduras ['ɔ̃dyras] *nm*: **le ~** Honduras.

'hondurien, ne ['ɔ̃dyrjɛ̃, -ɛn] *a* Honduran.

'Hong Kong ['ɔ̃gkɔ̃g] *n* Hong Kong.

'hongre ['ɔ̃gr(ə)] *a* (*cheval*) gelded ♦ *nm* gelding.

'Hongrie ['ɔ̃gri] *nf*: **la ~** Hungary.

'hongrois, e ['ɔ̃grwa, -waz] *a* Hungarian ♦ *nm* (*LING*) Hungarian ♦ *nm/f*: **'H~, e** Hungarian.

honnête [ɔnɛt] *a* (*intègre*) honest; (*juste, satisfaisant*) fair.

honnêtement [ɔnɛtmɑ̃] *ad* honestly.

honnêteté [ɔnɛtte] *nf* honesty.

honneur [ɔnœr] *nm* honour; (*mérite*): **l'~ lui revient** the credit is his; **à qui ai-je l'~?** to whom have I the pleasure of speaking?; **"j'ai l'~ de ..."** "I have the honour of ..."; **en l'~ de** (*personne*) in honour of; (*événement*) on the occasion of; **faire ~ à** (*engagements*) to honour; (*famille, professeur*) to be a credit to; (*fig: repas etc*) to do justice to; **être à l'~** to be in the place of honour; **être en ~** to be in favour; **membre d'~** honorary member; **table d'~** top table.

Honolulu [ɔnɔlyly] *n* Honolulu.

honorable [ɔnɔrabl(ə)] *a* worthy, honourable; (*suffisant*) decent.

honorablement [ɔnɔrabləmɑ̃] *ad* honourably, decently.

honoraire [ɔnɔrɛr] *a* honorary; **~s** *nmpl* fees; **professeur ~** professor emeritus.

honorer [ɔnɔre] *vt* to honour; (*estimer*) to hold in high regard; (*faire honneur à*) to do credit to; **~ qn de** to honour sb with; **s'~ de** to pride o.s. upon.

honorifique [ɔnɔrifik] *a* honorary.

'honte ['ɔ̃t] *nf* shame; **avoir ~ de** to be ashamed of; **faire ~ à qn** to make sb (feel) ashamed.

'honteusement ['ɔ̃tøzmɑ̃] *ad* ashamedly, shamefully.

'honteux, euse ['ɔ̃tø, -øz] *a* ashamed; (*conduite, acte*) shameful, disgraceful.

hôpital, aux [ɔpital, -o] *nm* hospital.

'hoquet ['ɔke] *nm* hiccough; **avoir le ~** to have (the) hiccoughs.

'hoqueter ['ɔkte] *vi* to hiccough.

horaire [ɔRɛR] *a* hourly ♦ *nm* timetable, schedule; **~s** *nmpl* (*heures de travail*) hours; **~ flexible** *ou* **mobile** *ou* **à la carte** *ou* **souple** flex(i)time.

'horde ['ɔRd(ə)] *nf* horde.

'horions ['ɔRjɔ̃] *nmpl* blows.

horizon [ɔRizɔ̃] *nm* horizon; (*paysage*) landscape, view; **sur l'~** on the skyline *ou* horizon.

horizontal, e, aux [ɔRizɔ̃tal, -o] *a* horizontal ♦ *nf:* **à l'~e** on the horizontal.

horizontalement [ɔRizɔ̃talmɑ̃] *ad* horizontally.

horloge [ɔRlɔʒ] *nf* clock; **l'~ parlante** the speaking clock; **~ normande** grandfather clock.

horloger, ère [ɔRlɔʒe, -ɛR] *nm/f* watchmaker; clockmaker.

horlogerie [ɔRlɔʒRi] *nf* watch-making; watchmaker's (shop); clockmaker's (shop); **pièces d'~** watch parts *ou* components.

'hormis ['ɔRmi] *prép* save.

hormonal, e, aux [ɔRmɔnal, -o] *a* hormonal.

hormone [ɔRmɔn] *nf* hormone.

horodaté, e [ɔRɔdate] *a* (*ticket*) time- and date-stamped; (*stationnement*) automatically timed.

horodateur, trice [ɔRɔdatœR, -tRis] *a* (*appareil*) for stamping the time and date ♦ *nm/f* (*parking*) ticket machine.

horoscope [ɔRɔskɔp] *nm* horoscope.

horreur [ɔRœR] *nf* horror; **avoir ~ de** to loathe, detest; **quelle ~!** how awful!; **cela me fait ~** I find that awful.

horrible [ɔRibl(ə)] *a* horrible.

horriblement [ɔRibləmɑ̃] *ad* horribly.

horrifiant, e [ɔRifjɑ̃, -ɑ̃t] *a* horrifying.

horrifier [ɔRifje] *vt* to horrify.

horrifique [ɔRifik] *a* horrific.

horripiler [ɔRipile] *vt* to exasperate.

'hors ['ɔR] *prép* except (for); **~ de** out of; **~ ligne, ~ pair** outstanding; **~ de propos** inopportune; **~ série** (*sur mesure*) made-to-order; (*exceptionnel*) exceptional; **~ service (HS), ~ d'usage** out of service; **~ taxe (HT)** (*article, boutique*) duty-free; (*prix*) before tax; **être ~ de soi** to be beside o.s.

'hors-bord ['ɔRbɔR] *nm inv* outboard motor; (*canot*) speedboat (with outboard motor).

'hors-concours ['ɔRkɔ̃kuR] *a inv* ineligible to compete; (*fig*) in a class of one's own.

'hors-d'œuvre ['ɔRdœvR(ə)] *nm inv* hors d'œuvre.

'hors-jeu ['ɔRʒø] *nm inv* being offside *q*.

'hors-la-loi ['ɔRlalwa] *nm inv* outlaw.

'hors-piste(s) ['ɔRpist] *nm inv* (*SKI*) cross-country.

'hors-texte ['ɔRtɛkst(ə)] *nm inv* plate.

hortensia [ɔRtɑ̃sja] *nm* hydrangea.

horticole [ɔRtikɔl] *a* horticultural.

horticulteur, trice [ɔRtikyltœR, -tRis] *nm/f* horticulturalist (*Brit*), horticulturist (*US*).

horticulture [ɔRtikyltyR] *nf* horticulture.

hospice [ɔspis] *nm* (*de vieillards*) home; (*asile*) hospice.

hospitalier, ière [ɔspitalje, -jɛR] *a*

(*accueillant*) hospitable; (*MÉD: service, centre*) hospital *cpd*.

hospitalisation [ɔspitalizasjɔ̃] *nf* hospitalization.

hospitaliser [ɔspitalize] *vt* to take (*ou* send) to hospital, hospitalize.

hospitalité [ɔspitalite] *nf* hospitality.

hospitalo-universitaire [ɔspitalɔynivɛRsitɛR] *a:* **centre ~ (CHU)** ≈ (teaching) hospital.

hostie [ɔsti] *nf* host (*REL*).

hostile [ɔstil] *a* hostile.

hostilité [ɔstilite] *nf* hostility; **~s** *nfpl* hostilities.

hôte [ot] *nm* (*maître de maison*) host; (*invité*) guest; (*client*) patron; (*fig*) inhabitant, occupant; **~ payant** paying guest.

hôtel [otɛl] *nm* hotel; **aller à l'~** to stay in a hotel; **~ (particulier)** (private) mansion; **~ de ville** town hall.

hôtelier, ière [otəlje, -jɛR] *a* hotel *cpd* ♦ *nm/f* hotelier, hotel-keeper.

hôtellerie [otɛlRi] *nf* (*profession*) hotel business; (*auberge*) inn.

hôtesse [otɛs] *nf* hostess; **~ de l'air** air hostess (*Brit*) *ou* stewardess; **~ (d'accueil)** receptionist.

'hotte ['ɔt] *nf* (*panier*) basket (*carried on the back*); (*de cheminée*) hood; **~ aspirante** cooker hood.

'houblon ['ublɔ̃] *nm* (*BOT*) hop; (*pour la bière*) hops *pl*.

'houe ['u] *nf* hoe.

'houille ['uj] *nf* coal; **~ blanche** hydroelectric power.

'houiller, ère ['uje, -ɛR] *a* coal *cpd*; (*terrain*) coal-bearing ♦ *nf* coal mine.

'houle ['ul] *nf* swell.

'houlette ['ulɛt] *nf:* **sous la ~ de** under the guidance of.

'houleux, euse ['ulø, -øz] *a* heavy, swelling; (*fig*) stormy, turbulent.

'houppe ['up] *nf,* **'houppette** ['upɛt] *nf* powder puff; (*cheveux*) tuft.

'hourra ['uRa] *nm* cheer ♦ *excl* hurrah!

'houspiller ['uspije] *vt* to scold.

'housse ['us] *nf* cover; (*pour protéger provisoirement*) dust cover; (*pour recouvrir à neuf*) loose *ou* stretch cover; **~ (penderie)** hanging wardrobe.

'houx ['u] *nm* holly.

HS *abr* = **hors service.**

HT *abr* = **hors taxe.**

'hublot ['yblo] *nm* porthole.

'huche ['yʃ] *nf:* **~ à pain** bread bin.

'huées ['ɥe] *nfpl* boos.

'huer ['ɥe] *vt* to boo; (*hibou, chouette*) to hoot.

huile [ɥil] *nf* oil; (*ART*) oil painting; (*fam*) bigwig; **mer d'~** (*très calme*) glassy sea, sea of glass; **faire tache d'~** (*fig*) to spread; **~ d'arachide** groundnut oil; **~ essentielle** essential oil; **~ de foie de morue** cod-liver oil; **~ de ricin** castor oil; **~ solaire** suntan oil; **~ de table** salad oil.

huiler [ɥile] *vt* to oil.

huilerie [ɥilRi] *nf* (*usine*) oil-works.

huileux, euse [ɥilø, -øz] *a* oily.

huilier [ɥilje] *nm* (oil and vinegar) cruet.

huis [ɥi] *nm:* **à ~ clos** in camera.

huissier [ɥisje] *nm* usher; (*JUR*) ≈ bailiff.

'**huit** ['ɥi(t)] *num* eight; **samedi en** ~ a week on Saturday; **dans** ~ **jours** in a week('s time).

'**huitaine** ['ɥitɛn] *nf*: **une** ~ **de** about eight, eight or so; **une** ~ **de jours** a week or so.

'**huitante** ['ɥitɑ̃t] *num* (*Suisse*) eighty.

'**huitième** ['ɥitjɛm] *num* eighth.

huître [ɥitʀ(ə)] *nf* oyster.

'**hululer** ['ylyle] *vi* to hoot.

humain, e [ymɛ̃, -ɛn] *a* human; (*compatissant*) humane ♦ *nm* human (being).

humainement [ymɛnmɑ̃] *ad* humanly; humanely.

humaniser [ymanize] *vt* to humanize.

humaniste [ymanist(ə)] *nm/f* (*LING*) classicist; humanist.

humanitaire [ymanitɛʀ] *a* humanitarian.

humanitarisme [ymanitaʀism(ə)] *nm* humanitarianism.

humanité [ymanite] *nf* humanity.

humanoïde [ymanɔid] *nm/f* humanoid.

humble [œ̃bl(ə)] *a* humble.

humblement [œ̃bləmɑ̃] *ad* humbly.

humecter [ymɛkte] *vt* to dampen; **s'**~ **les lèvres** to moisten one's lips.

'**humer** ['yme] *vt* to inhale; (*pour sentir*) to smell.

humérus [ymeʀys] *nf* (*ANAT*) humerus.

humeur [ymœʀ] *nf* mood; (*tempérament*) temper; (*irritation*) bad temper; **de bonne/mauvaise** ~ in a good/bad mood; **être d'**~ **à faire qch** to be in the mood for doing sth.

humide [ymid] *a* (*linge*) damp; (*main, yeux*) moist; (*climat, chaleur*) humid; (*saison, route*) wet.

humidificateur [ymidifikatœʀ] *nm* humidifier.

humidifier [ymidifje] *vt* to humidify.

humidité [ymidite] *nf* humidity; dampness; **traces d'**~ traces of moisture *ou* damp.

humiliant, e [ymiljɑ̃, -ɑ̃t] humiliating.

humiliation [ymiljasjɔ̃] *nf* humiliation.

humilier [ymilje] *vt* to humiliate; **s'**~ **devant qn** to humble o.s. before sb.

humilité [ymilite] *nf* humility.

humoriste [ymɔʀist(ə)] *nm/f* humorist.

humoristique [ymɔʀistik] *a* humorous; humoristic.

humour [ymuʀ] *nm* humour; **avoir de l'**~ to have a sense of humour; ~ **noir** sick humour.

humus [ymys] *nm* humus.

'**huppé, e** ['ype] *a* crested; (*fam*) posh.

'**hurlement** ['yʀləmɑ̃] *nm* howling *q*, howl; yelling *q*, yell.

'**hurler** ['yʀle] *vi* to howl, yell; (*fig: vent*) to howl; (: *couleurs etc*) to clash; ~ **à la mort** (*suj: chien*) to bay at the moon.

hurluberlu [yʀlybɛʀly] *nm* (*péj*) crank ♦ *a* cranky.

'**hutte** ['yt] *nf* hut.

hybride [ibʀid] *a* hybrid.

hydratant, e [idʀatɑ̃, -ɑ̃t] *a* (*crème*) moisturizing.

hydrate [idʀat] *nm*: ~**s de carbone** carbohydrates.

hydrater [idʀate] *vt* to hydrate.

hydraulique [idʀolik] *a* hydraulic.

hydravion [idʀavjɔ̃] *nm* seaplane, hydroplane.

hydro... [idʀɔ] *préfixe* hydro....

hydrocarbure [idʀɔkaʀbyʀ] *nm* hydrocarbon.

hydrocution [idʀɔkysjɔ̃] *nf* immersion syncope.

hydro-électrique [idʀɔelektʀik] *a* hydro-electric.

hydrogène [idʀɔʒɛn] *nm* hydrogen.

hydroglisseur [idʀɔglisœʀ] *nm* hydroplane.

hydrographie [idʀɔgʀafi] *nf* (*fleuves*) hydrography.

hydrophile [idʀɔfil] *a voir* **coton**.

hyène [jɛn] *nf* hyena.

hygiène [iʒjɛn] *nf* hygiene; ~ **intime** personal hygiene.

hygiénique [iʒenik] *a* hygienic.

hymne [imn(ə)] *nm* hymn; ~ **national** national anthem.

hyper... [ipɛʀ] *préfixe* hyper....

hypermarché [ipɛʀmaʀʃe] *nm* hypermarket.

hypermétrope [ipɛʀmetʀɔp] *a* long-sighted.

hypernerveux, euse [ipɛʀnɛʀvø, -øz] *a* highly-strung.

hypersensible [ipɛʀsɑ̃sibl(ə)] *a* hypersensitive.

hypertendu, e [ipɛʀtɑ̃dy] *a* having high blood pressure, hypertensive.

hypertension [ipɛʀtɑ̃sjɔ̃] *nf* high blood pressure, hypertension.

hypertrophié, e [ipɛʀtʀɔfje] *a* hypertrophic.

hypnose [ipnoz] *nf* hypnosis.

hypnotique [ipnɔtik] *a* hypnotic.

hypnotiser [ipnɔtize] *vt* to hypnotize.

hypnotiseur [ipnɔtizœʀ] *nm* hypnotist.

hypnotisme [ipnɔtism(ə)] *nm* hypnotism.

hypocondriaque [ipɔkɔ̃dʀijak] *a* hypochondriac.

hypocrisie [ipɔkʀizi] *nf* hypocrisy.

hypocrite [ipɔkʀit] *a* hypocritical ♦ *nm/f* hypocrite.

hypocritement [ipɔkʀitmɑ̃] *ad* hypocritically.

hypotendu, e [ipɔtɑ̃dy] *a* having low blood pressure, hypotensive.

hypotension [ipɔtɑ̃sjɔ̃] *nf* low blood pressure, hypotension.

hypoténuse [ipɔtenyz] *nf* hypotenuse.

hypothécaire [ipɔtekɛʀ] *a* hypothecary; **garantie/prêt** ~ mortgage security/loan.

hypothèque [ipɔtɛk] *nf* mortgage.

hypothéquer [ipɔteke] *vt* to mortgage.

hypothermie [ipɔtɛʀmi] *nf* hypothermia.

hypothèse [ipɔtɛz] *nf* hypothesis; **dans l'**~ **où** assuming that.

hypothétique [ipɔtetik] *a* hypothetical.

hystérectomie [isteʀɛktɔmi] *nf* hysterectomy.

hystérie [isteʀi] *nf* hysteria; ~ **collective** mass hysteria.

hystérique [isteʀik] *a* hysterical.

Hz *abr* (= *Hertz*) Hz.

I

I, i [i] *nm inv* I, i; **I comme Irma** I for Isaac (*Brit*) *ou* Item (*US*).

IAC *sigle f* (= *insémination artificielle entre*

conjoints) AIH.

IAD *sigle f* (= *insémination artificielle par donneur extérieur*) AID.

ibère [ibɛʀ] *a* Iberian ♦ *nm/f*: **I~** Iberian.

ibérique [ibeʀik] *a*: **la péninsule ~** the Iberian peninsula.

iceberg [isbɛʀg] *nm* iceberg.

ici [isi] *ad* here; **jusqu'~** as far as this; (*temporel*) until now; **d'~ là** by then; (*en attendant*) in the meantime; **d'~ peu** before long.

icône [ikon] *nf* (*aussi INFORM*) icon.

iconoclaste [ikɔnɔklast(ə)] *nm/f* iconoclast.

iconographie [ikɔnɔgʀafi] *nf* iconography; (*illustrations*) (collection of) illustrations.

idéal, e, aux [ideal, -o] *a* ideal ♦ *nm* ideal; (*système de valeurs*) ideals *pl*.

idéalement [idealmɑ̃] *ad* ideally.

idéalisation [idealizasjɔ̃] *nf* idealization.

idéaliser [idealize] *vt* to idealize.

idéalisme [idealism(ə)] *nm* idealism.

idéaliste [idealist(ə)] *a* idealistic ♦ *nm/f* idealist.

idée [ide] *nf* idea; (*illusion*): **se faire des ~s** to imagine things, get ideas into one's head; **avoir dans l'~ que** to have an idea that; **mon ~, c'est que ...** I suggest that ..., I think that ...; **à l'~ de/que** at the idea of/that, at the thought of/that; **je n'ai pas la moindre ~** I haven't the faintest idea; **avoir ~ que** to have an idea that; **avoir des ~s larges/ étroites** to be broad-/narrow-minded; **venir à l'~ de qn** to occur to sb; **en voilà des ~s!** the very idea!; **~ fixe** idée fixe, obsession; **~s noires** black *ou* dark thoughts; **~s reçues** accepted ideas *ou* wisdom.

identification [idɑ̃tifikasjɔ̃] *nf* identification.

identifier [idɑ̃tifje] *vt* to identify; **~ qch/qn à** to identify sth/sb with; **s'~ avec** *ou* **à qn/qch** (*héros etc*) to identify with sb/sth.

identique [idɑ̃tik] *a*: **~ (à)** identical (to).

identité [idɑ̃tite] *nf* identity; **~ judiciaire** (*POLICE*) ≈ Criminal Records Office.

idéologie [ideɔlɔʒi] *nf* ideology.

idéologique [ideɔlɔʒik] *a* ideological.

idiomatique [idjɔmatik] *a*: **expression ~** idiom, idiomatic expression.

idiome [idjɔm] *nm* (*LING*) idiom.

idiot, e [idjo, idjɔt] *a* idiotic ♦ *nm/f* idiot.

idiotie [idjɔsi] *nf* idiocy; (*propos*) idiotic remark *etc*.

idiotisme [idjɔtism(ə)] *nm* idiom, idiomatic phrase.

idoine [idwan] *a* fitting.

idolâtrer [idɔlɑtʀe] *vt* to idolize.

idolâtrie [idɔlɑtʀi] *nf* idolatry.

idole [idɔl] *nf* idol.

IDS *sigle f* (= *Initiative de défense stratégique*) SDI.

idylle [idil] *nf* idyll.

idyllique [idilik] *a* idyllic.

if [if] *nm* yew.

IFOP [ifɔp] *sigle m* (= *Institut français d'opinion publique*) French market research institute.

IGF *sigle m* (= *Impôt sur les grandes fortunes*) wealth tax.

IGH *sigle m* = *immeuble de grande hauteur*.

igloo [iglu] *nm* igloo.

IGN *sigle m* = *Institut géographique national*.

ignare [iɲaʀ] *a* ignorant.

ignifuge [iɲify3] *a* fireproofing ♦ *nm* fireproofing (substance).

ignifuger [iɲify3e] *vt* to fireproof.

ignoble [iɲɔbl(ə)] *a* vile.

ignominie [iɲɔmini] *nf* ignominy; (*acte*) ignominious *ou* base act.

ignominieux, euse [iɲɔminjø, øz] *a* ignominious.

ignorance [iɲɔʀɑ̃s] *nf* ignorance; **dans l'~ de** in ignorance of, ignorant of.

ignorant, e [iɲɔʀɑ̃, -ɑ̃t] *a* ignorant ♦ *nm/f*: **faire l'~** to pretend one doesn't know; **~ de** ignorant of, not aware of; **~ en** ignorant of, knowing nothing of.

ignoré, e [iɲɔʀe] *a* unknown.

ignorer [iɲɔʀe] *vt* (*ne pas connaître*) not to know, be unaware *ou* ignorant of; (*être sans expérience de: plaisir, guerre etc*) not to know about, have no experience of; (*bouder: personne*) to ignore; **j'ignore comment/si** I do not know how/if; **~ que** to be unaware that, not to know that; **je n'ignore pas que ...** I'm not forgetting that ..., I'm not unaware that ...; **je l'ignore** I don't know.

IGPN *sigle f* (= *Inspection générale de la police nationale*) police disciplinary body.

IGS *sigle f* (= *Inspection générale des services*) police disciplinary body for Paris.

iguane [igwan] *nm* iguana.

il [il] *pronom* he; (*animal, chose, en tournure impersonnelle*) it; *NB: en anglais les navires et les pays sont en général assimilés aux femelles, et les bébés aux choses, si le sexe n'est pas spécifié*; **~** they; **~ neige** it's snowing; *voir aussi* **avoir**.

île [il] *nf* island; **les Î~s** the West Indies; **l'~ de Beauté** Corsica; **l'~ Maurice** Mauritius; **les ~s anglo- normandes** the Channel Islands; **les ~s Britanniques** the British Isles; **les ~s Cocos** *ou* **Keeling** the Cocos *ou* Keeling Islands; **les ~s Cook** the Cook Islands; **les ~s Scilly** the Scilly Isles, the Scillies; **les ~s Shetland** the Shetland Islands, Shetland; **les ~s Sorlingues = les ~s Scilly**; **les ~s Vierges** the Virgin Islands.

iliaque [iljak] *a* (*ANAT*): **os/artère ~** iliac bone/artery.

illégal, e, aux [ilegal, -o] *a* illegal, unlawful (*ADMIN*).

illégalement [ilegalmɑ̃] *ad* illegally.

illégalité [ilegalite] *nf* illegality; unlawfulness; **être dans l'~** to be outside the law.

illégitime [ileʒitim] *a* illegitimate; (*optimisme, sévérité*) unjustified, unwarranted.

illégitimement [ileʒitimmɑ̃] *ad* illegitimately.

illégitimité [ileʒitimite] *nf* illegitimacy; **gouverner dans l'~** to rule illegally.

illettré, e [iletʀe] *a*, *nm/f* illiterate.

illicite [ilisit] *a* illicit.

illicitement [ilisitmɑ̃] *ad* illicitly.

illico [iliko] *ad* (*fam*) pronto.

illimité, e [ilimite] *a* (*immense*) boundless, unlimited; (*congé, durée*) indefinite, unlimited.

illisible [ilizibl(ə)] *a* illegible; (*roman*) unreadable.

illisiblement [ilizibləmɑ̃] *ad* illegibly.

illogique [ilɔʒik] *a* illogical.

illogisme [iloʒism(ə)] *nm* illogicality.
illumination [ilyminɑsjɔ̃] *nf* illumination, floodlighting; (*inspiration*) flash of inspiration; **~s** *nfpl* illuminations, lights.
illuminé, e [ilymine] *a* lit up; illuminated, floodlit ♦ *nm/f* (*fig: péj*) crank.
illuminer [ilymine] *vt* to light up; (*monument, rue: pour une fête*) to illuminate, floodlight; **s'~** *vi* to light up.
illusion [ilyzjɔ̃] *nf* illusion; **se faire des ~s** to delude o.s.; **faire ~** to delude *ou* fool people; **~ d'optique** optical illusion.
illusionner [ilyzjone] *vt* to delude; **s'~** (**sur qn/qch**) to delude o.s. (about sb/sth).
illusionnisme [ilyzjonism(ə)] *nm* conjuring.
illusionniste [ilyzjonist(ə)] *nm/f* conjuror.
illusoire [ilyzwar] *a* illusory, illusive.
illustrateur [ilystratœr] *nm* illustrator.
illustratif, ive [ilystratif, -iv] *a* illustrative.
illustration [ilystrɑsjɔ̃] *nf* illustration; (*d'un ouvrage: photos*) illustrations *pl*.
illustre [ilystr(ə)] *a* illustrious, renowned.
illustré, e [ilystre] *a* illustrated ♦ *nm* illustrated magazine; (*pour enfants*) comic.
illustrer [ilystre] *vt* to illustrate; **s'~** to become famous, win fame.
îlot [ilo] *nm* small island, islet; (*de maisons*) block; (*petite zone*): **un ~ de verdure** an island of greenery, a patch of green.
ils [il] *pronom voir* **il**.
image [imaʒ] *nf* (*gén*) picture; (*comparaison, ressemblance, OPTIQUE*) image; **~ de** picture *ou* image of; **~ d'Épinal** (social) stereotype; **~ de marque** brand image; (*d'une personne*) (public) image; (*d'une entreprise*) corporate image; **~ pieuse** holy picture.
imagé, e [imaʒe] *a* full of imagery.
imaginable [imaʒinabl(ə)] *a* imaginable; **difficilement ~** hard to imagine.
imaginaire [imaʒinɛr] *a* imaginary.
imaginatif, ive [imaʒinatif, -iv] *a* imaginative.
imagination [imaʒinɑsjɔ̃] *nf* imagination; (*chimère*) fancy, imagining; **avoir de l'~** to be imaginative, have a good imagination.
imaginer [imaʒine] *vt* to imagine; (*croire*): **qu'allez-vous ~ là?** what on earth are you thinking of?; (*inventer: expédient, mesure*) to devise, think up; **s'~** *vt* (*se figurer: scène etc*) to imagine, picture; **s'~ à 60 ans** to picture *ou* imagine o.s. at 60; **s'~ que** to imagine that; **s'~ pouvoir faire qch** to think one can do sth; **j'imagine qu'il a voulu plaisanter** I suppose he was joking; **~ de faire** (*se mettre dans l'idée de*) to dream up the idea of doing.
imbattable [ɛ̃batabl(ə)] *a* unbeatable.
imbécile [ɛ̃besil] *a* idiotic ♦ *nm/f* idiot; (*MÉD*) imbecile.
imbécillité [ɛ̃besilite] *nf* idiocy; imbecility; idiotic action (*ou* remark *etc*).
imberbe [ɛ̃bɛrb(ə)] *a* beardless.
imbiber [ɛ̃bibe] *vt*: **~ qch de** to moisten *ou* wet sth with; **s'~ de** to become saturated with; **imbibé(e) d'eau** (*chaussures, étoffe*) saturated; (*terre*) waterlogged.
imbriqué, e [ɛ̃brike] *a* overlapping.
imbriquer [ɛ̃brike]: **s'~** *vi* to overlap (each other); (*fig*) to become interlinked *ou* interwoven.

imbu, e [ɛ̃by] *a*: **~ de** full of; **~ de soi-même/sa supériorité** full of oneself/one's superiority.
imbuvable [ɛ̃byvabl(ə)] *a* undrinkable.
imitable [imitabl(ə)] *a* imitable; **facilement ~** easily imitated.
imitateur, trice [imitatœr, -tris] *nm/f* (*gén*) imitator; (*MUSIC-HALL: d'une personnalité*) impersonator.
imitation [imitɑsjɔ̃] *nf* imitation; impersonation; **sac ~ cuir** bag in imitation *ou* simulated leather; **à l'~ de** in imitation of.
imiter [imite] *vt* to imitate; (*personne*) to imitate, impersonate; (*contrefaire: signature, document*) to forge, copy; (*ressembler à*) to look like; **il se leva et je l'imitai** he got up and I did likewise.
imm. *abr* = **immeuble.**
immaculé, e [imakyle] *a* spotless, immaculate; **l'I~e Conception** (*REL*) the Immaculate Conception.
immanent, e [imanɑ̃, -ɑ̃t] *a* immanent.
immangeable [ɛ̃mɑ̃ʒabl(ə)] *a* inedible, uneatable.
immanquable [ɛ̃mɑ̃kabl(ə)] *a* (*cible*) impossible to miss; (*fatal, inévitable*) bound to happen, inevitable.
immanquablement [ɛ̃mɑ̃kabləmɑ̃] *ad* inevitably.
immatériel, le [imaterjɛl] *a* ethereal; (*PHILOSOPHIE*) immaterial.
immatriculation [imatrikylɑsjɔ̃] *nf* registration.
immatriculer [imatrikyle] *vt* to register; **faire/se faire ~** to register; **voiture immatriculée dans la Seine** car with a Seine registration (number).
immature [imatyr] *a* immature.
immaturité [imatyrite] *nf* immaturity.
immédiat, e [imedja, -at] *a* immediate ♦ *nm*: **dans l'~** for the time being; **dans le voisinage ~ de** in the immediate vicinity of.
immédiatement [imedjatmɑ̃] *ad* immediately.
immémorial, e, aux [imemɔrjal, -o] *a* ancient, age-old.
immense [imɑ̃s] *a* immense.
immensément [imɑ̃semɑ̃] *ad* immensely.
immensité [imɑ̃site] *nf* immensity.
immerger [imɛrʒe] *vt* to immerse, submerge; (*câble etc*) to lay under water; (*déchets*) to dump at sea; **s'~** *vi* (*sous-marin*) to dive, submerge.
immérité, e [imerite] *a* undeserved.
immersion [imɛrsjɔ̃] *nf* immersion.
immettable [ɛ̃metabl(ə)] *a* unwearable.
immeuble [imœbl(ə)] *nm* building ♦ *a* (*JUR*) immovable, real; **~ locatif** block of rented flats (*Brit*), rental building (*US*); **~ de rapport** investment property.
immigrant, e [imigrɑ̃, -ɑ̃t] *nm/f* immigrant.
immigration [imigrɑsjɔ̃] *nf* immigration.
immigré, e [imigre] *nm/f* immigrant.
immigrer [imigre] *vi* to immigrate.
imminence [iminɑ̃s] *nf* imminence.
imminent, e [iminɑ̃, -ɑ̃t] *a* imminent, impending.
immiscer [imise]: **s'~** *vi*: **s'~ dans** to interfere in *ou* with.

immixtion [imiksjɔ̃] *nf* interference.

immobile [imɔbil] *a* still, motionless; *(pièce de machine)* fixed; *(fig)* unchanging; **rester/ se tenir ~** to stay/keep still.

immobilier, ière [imɔbilje, -jɛʀ] *a* property *cpd*, in real property ♦ *nm*: **l'~** the property *ou* the real estate business.

immobilisation [imɔbilizasjɔ̃] *nf* immobilization; **~s** *nfpl (JUR)* fixed assets.

immobiliser [imɔbilize] *vt (gén)* to immobilize; *(circulation, véhicule, affaires)* to bring to a standstill; **s'~** *(personne)* to stand still; *(machine, véhicule)* to come to a halt *ou* a standstill.

immobilisme [imɔbilism(ə)] *nm* strong resistance *ou* opposition to change.

immobilité [imɔbilite] *nf* immobility.

immodéré, e [imɔdeʀe] *a* immoderate, inordinate.

immodérément [imɔdeʀemɑ̃] *ad* immoderately.

immoler [imɔle] *vt* to sacrifice.

immonde [imɔ̃d] *a* foul; *(sale: ruelle, taudis)* squalid.

immondices [imɔ̃dis] *nmpl (ordures)* refuse *sg*; *(saletés)* filth *sg*.

immoral, e, aux [imɔʀal, -o] *a* immoral.

immoralité [imɔʀalite] *nf* immorality.

immortaliser [imɔʀtalize] *vt* to immortalize.

immortel, le [imɔʀtɛl] *a* immortal ♦ *nf (BOT)* everlasting (flower).

immuable [imɥabl(ə)] *a (inébranlable)* immutable; *(qui ne change pas)* unchanging; *(personne)*: **~ dans ses convictions** immoveable (in one's convictions).

immunisation [imynizasjɔ̃] *nf* immunization.

immuniser [imynize] *vt (MÉD)* to immunize; **~ qn contre** to immunize sb against; *(fig)* to make sb immune to.

immunité [imynite] *nf* immunity; **~ di- plomatique** diplomatic immunity; **~ parlementaire** parliamentary privilege.

immunologie [imynɔlɔʒi] *nf* immunology.

impact [ɛ̃pakt] *nm* impact; **point d'~** point of impact.

impair, e [ɛ̃pɛʀ] *a* odd ♦ *nm* faux pas, blunder; **numéros ~s** odd numbers.

impaludation [ɛ̃palydasjɔ̃] *nf* inoculation against malaria.

imparable [ɛ̃paʀabl(ə)] *a* unstoppable.

impardonnable [ɛ̃paʀdɔnabl(ə)] *a* unpardonable, unforgivable; **vous êtes ~ d'avoir fait cela** it's unforgivable of you to have done that.

imparfait, e [ɛ̃paʀfɛ, -ɛt] *a* imperfect ♦ *nm (LING)* imperfect (tense).

imparfaitement [ɛ̃paʀfɛtmɑ̃] *ad* imperfectly.

impartial, e, aux [ɛ̃paʀsjal, -o] *a* impartial, unbiased.

impartialité [ɛ̃paʀsjalite] *nf* impartiality.

impartir [ɛ̃paʀtiʀ] *vt*: **~ qch à qn** to assign sth to sb; *(dons)* to bestow sth upon sb; **dans les délais impartis** in the time allowed.

impasse [ɛ̃pɑs] *nf* dead-end, cul-de-sac; *(fig)* deadlock; **être dans l'~** *(négociations)* to have reached deadlock; **~ budgétaire** budget deficit.

impassibilité [ɛ̃pasibilite] *nf* impassiveness.

impassible [ɛ̃pasibl(ə)] *a* impassive.

impatiemment [ɛ̃pasjamɑ̃] *ad* impatiently.

impatience [ɛ̃pasjɑ̃s] *nf* impatience.

impatient, e [ɛ̃pasjɑ̃, -ɑ̃t] *a* impatient; **~ de faire qch** keen *ou* impatient to do sth.

impatienter [ɛ̃pasjɑ̃te] *vt* to irritate, annoy; **s'~** *vi* to get impatient; **s'~ de/contre** to lose patience at/with, grow impatient at/with.

impayable [ɛ̃pɛjabl(ə)] *a (drôle)* priceless.

impayé, e [ɛ̃pɛje] *a* unpaid, outstanding.

impeccable [ɛ̃pekabl(ə)] *a* faultless, impeccable; *(propre)* spotlessly clean; *(chic)* impeccably dressed; *(fam)* smashing.

impeccablement [ɛ̃pekabləmɑ̃] *ad* impeccably.

impénétrable [ɛ̃penetʀabl(ə)] *a* impenetrable.

impénitent, e [ɛ̃penitɑ̃, -ɑ̃t] *a* unrepentant.

impensable [ɛ̃pɑ̃sabl(ə)] *a* unthinkable, unbelievable.

imper [ɛ̃pɛʀ] *nm* (= *imperméable*) mac.

impératif, ive [ɛ̃peʀatif, -iv] *a* imperative; *(JUR)* mandatory ♦ *nm (LING)* imperative; **~s** *nmpl* requirements; demands.

impérativement [ɛ̃peʀativmɑ̃] *ad* imperatively.

impératrice [ɛ̃peʀatʀis] *nf* empress.

imperceptible [ɛ̃pɛʀsɛptibl(ə)] *a* imperceptible.

imperceptiblement [ɛ̃pɛʀsɛptibləmɑ̃] *ad* imperceptibly.

imperdable [ɛ̃pɛʀdabl(ə)] *a* that cannot be lost.

imperfectible [ɛ̃pɛʀfɛktibl(ə)] *a* which cannot be perfected.

imperfection [ɛ̃pɛʀfɛksjɔ̃] *nf* imperfection.

impérial, e, aux [ɛ̃peʀjal, -o] *a* imperial ♦ *nf* upper deck; **autobus à ~e** double-decker bus.

impérialisme [ɛ̃peʀjalism(ə)] *nm* imperialism.

impérialiste [ɛ̃peʀjalist(ə)] *a* imperialist.

impérieusement [ɛ̃peʀjøzmɑ̃] *ad*: **avoir ~ besoin de qch** to have urgent need of sth.

impérieux, euse [ɛ̃peʀjø, -øz] *a (caractère, ton)* imperious; *(obligation, besoin)* pressing, urgent.

impérissable [ɛ̃peʀisabl(ə)] *a* an undying, imperishable.

imperméabilisation [ɛ̃pɛʀmeabilizasjɔ̃] *nf* waterproofing.

imperméabiliser [ɛ̃pɛʀmeabilize] *vt* to waterproof.

imperméable [ɛ̃pɛʀmeabl(ə)] *a* waterproof; *(GÉO)* impermeable; *(fig)*: **~ à** impervious to ♦ *nm* raincoat; **~ à l'air** airtight.

impersonnel, le [ɛ̃pɛʀsɔnɛl] *a* impersonal.

impertinemment [ɛ̃pɛʀtinamɑ̃] *ad* impertinently.

impertinence [ɛ̃pɛʀtinɑ̃s] *nf* impertinence.

impertinent, e [ɛ̃pɛʀtinɑ̃, -ɑ̃t] *a* impertinent.

imperturbable [ɛ̃pɛʀtyʀbabl(ə)] *a (personne)* imperturbable; *(sang-froid)* unshakeable; **rester ~** to remain unruffled.

imperturbablement [ɛ̃pɛʀtyʀbabləmɑ̃] *ad* imperturbably; unshakeably.

impétrant, e [ɛ̃petʀɑ̃, -ɑ̃t] *nm/f (JUR)* applicant.

impétueux, euse [ɛ̃petɥø, -øz] *a* fiery.

impétuosité [ɛ̃petɥozite] *nf* fieriness.

impie [ɛ̃pi] *a* impious, ungodly.

impiété [ɛ̃pjete] *nf* impiety.

impitoyable [ɛ̃pitwajabl(ə)] *a* pitiless, merciless.

impitoyablement [ɛ̃pitwajabləmɑ̃] *ad* mercilessly.

implacable [ɛ̃plakabl(ə)] *a* implacable.

implacablement [ɛ̃plakabləmɑ̃] *ad* implacably.

implant [ɛ̃plɑ̃] *nm* (*MÉD*) implant.

implantation [ɛ̃plɑ̃tasjɔ̃] *nf* establishment; settling; implantation.

implanter [ɛ̃plɑ̃te] *vt* (*usine, industrie, usage*) to establish; (*colons etc*) to settle; (*idée, préjugé*) to implant; **s'~ dans** to be established in; to settle in; to become implanted in.

implication [ɛ̃plikasjɔ̃] *nf* implication.

implicite [ɛ̃plisit] *a* implicit.

implicitement [ɛ̃plisitmɑ̃] *ad* implicitly.

impliquer [ɛ̃plike] *vt* to imply; **~ qn (dans)** to implicate sb (in).

implorer [ɛ̃plɔre] *vt* to implore.

imploser [ɛ̃ploze] *vi* to implode.

implosion [ɛ̃plozjɔ̃] *nf* implosion.

impoli, e [ɛ̃poli] *a* impolite, rude.

impoliment [ɛ̃polimɑ̃] *ad* impolitely.

impolitesse [ɛ̃polites] *nf* impoliteness, rudeness; (*propos*) impolite *ou* rude remark.

impondérable [ɛ̃pɔ̃derabl(ə)] *nm* imponderable.

impopulaire [ɛ̃popylɛr] *a* unpopular.

impopularité [ɛ̃popylarite] *nf* unpopularity.

importable [ɛ̃pɔrtabl(ə)] *a* (*COMM: marchandise*) importable; (*vêtement: immettable*) unwearable.

importance [ɛ̃pɔrtɑ̃s] *nf* importance; **avoir de l'~** to be important; **sans ~** unimportant; **d'~** important, considerable; **quelle ~?** what does it matter?

important, e [ɛ̃pɔrtɑ̃, -ɑ̃t] *a* important; (*en quantité*) considerable, sizeable; (: *gamme, dégâts*) extensive; (*péj: airs, ton*) self-important ♦ *nm*: **l'~** the important thing.

importateur, trice [ɛ̃pɔrtatœr, -tris] *a* importing ♦ *nm/f* importer; **pays ~ de blé** wheat-importing country.

importation [ɛ̃pɔrtasjɔ̃] *nf* import; introduction; (*produit*) import.

importer [ɛ̃pɔrte] *vt* (*COMM*) to import; (*maladies, plantes*) to introduce ♦ *vi* (*être important*) to matter; **~ à qn** to matter to sb; **il importe de** it is important to; **il importe qu'il fasse** he must do, it is important that he should do; **peu m'importe** I don't mind, I don't care; **peu importe** it doesn't matter; **peu importe (que)** it doesn't matter (if); **peu importe le prix** never mind the price; *voir aussi* **n'importe**.

import-export [ɛ̃pɔrɛkspɔr] *nm* import-export business.

importun, e [ɛ̃pɔrtœ̃, -yn] *a* irksome, importunate; (*arrivée, visite*) inopportune, ill-timed ♦ *nm* intruder.

importuner [ɛ̃pɔrtyne] *vt* to bother.

imposable [ɛ̃pozabl(ə)] *a* taxable.

imposant, e [ɛ̃pozɑ̃, -ɑ̃t] *a* imposing.

imposé, e [ɛ̃poze] *a* (*soumis à l'impôt*) taxed; (*GYM etc: figures*) set.

imposer [ɛ̃poze] *vt* (*taxer*) to tax; (*REL*): **~ les mains** to lay on hands; **~ qch à qn** to impose sth on sb; **s'~** (*être nécessaire*) to be imperative; (*montrer sa proéminence*) to stand out, emerge; (*artiste: se faire connaître*) to win recognition, come to the fore; **en ~** to be imposing; **en ~ à** to impress; **ça s'impose** it's essential, it's vital.

imposition [ɛ̃pozisjɔ̃] *nf* (*ADMIN*) taxation.

impossibilité [ɛ̃pɔsibilite] *nf* impossibility; **être dans l'~ de faire** to be unable to do, find it impossible to do.

impossible [ɛ̃pɔsibl(ə)] *a* impossible ♦ *nm*: **l'~** the impossible; **~ à faire** impossible to do; **il m'est ~ de le faire** it is impossible for me to do it, I can't possibly do it; **faire l'~ (pour que)** to do one's utmost (so that); **si, par ~ ...** if, by some miracle ....

imposteur [ɛ̃pɔstœr] *nm* impostor.

imposture [ɛ̃pɔstyr] *nf* imposture, deception.

impôt [ɛ̃po] *nm* tax; (*taxes*) taxation, taxes *pl*; **~s** *nmpl* (*contributions*) (income) tax *sg*; **payer 1.000 F d'~s** to pay 1,000 F in tax; **~ direct/indirect** direct/indirect tax; **~ sur le chiffre d'affaires** tax on turnover; **~ foncier** land tax; **~ sur la fortune** wealth tax; **~ sur les plus-values** capital gains tax; **~ sur le revenu** income tax; **~ sur le RPP** personal income tax; **~ sur les sociétés** tax on companies; **~s locaux** rates.

impotence [ɛ̃potɑ̃s] *nf* disability.

impotent, e [ɛ̃potɑ̃, -ɑ̃t] *a* disabled.

impraticable [ɛ̃pratikabl(ə)] *a* (*projet*) impracticable, unworkable; (*piste*) impassable.

imprécation [ɛ̃prekasjɔ̃] *nf* imprecation.

imprécis, e [ɛ̃presi, -iz] *a* (*contours, souvenir*) imprecise, vague; (*tir*) inaccurate, imprecise.

imprécision [ɛ̃presizjɔ̃] *nf* imprecision.

imprégner [ɛ̃preɲe] *vt* (*tissu, tampon*): **~ (de)** to soak *ou* impregnate (with); (*lieu, air*): **~ (de)** to fill (with); (*suj: amertume, ironie*) to pervade; **s'~ de** to become impregnated with; to be filled with; (*fig*) to absorb.

imprenable [ɛ̃prənabl(ə)] *a* (*forteresse*) impregnable; **vue ~** unimpeded outlook.

impresario [ɛ̃presarjo] *nm* manager, impresario.

impression [ɛ̃presjɔ̃] *nf* impression; (*d'un ouvrage, tissu*) printing; (*PHOTO*) exposure; **faire bonne ~** to make a good impression; **donner une ~ de/l'~ que** to give the impression of/that; **avoir l'~ de/que** to have the impression of/that; **faire ~** to make an impression; **~s de voyage** impressions of one's journey.

impressionnable [ɛ̃presjɔnabl(ə)] *a* impressionable.

impressionnant, e [ɛ̃presjɔnɑ̃, -ɑ̃t] *a* impressive; upsetting.

impressionner [ɛ̃presjɔne] *vt* (*frapper*) to impress; (*troubler*) to upset; (*PHOTO*) to expose.

impressionnisme [ɛ̃presjɔnism(ə)] *nm* impressionism.

impressionniste [ɛ̃presjɔnist(ə)] *a, nm/f* impressionist.

imprévisible [ɛ̃previzibl(ə)] *a* unforeseeable; (*réaction, personne*) unpredictable.

imprévoyance [ɛ̃prevwajɑ̃s] *nf* lack of foresight.

imprévoyant, e [ɛ̃pʀevwajã, -ãt] a lacking in foresight; *(en matière d'argent)* improvident.

imprévu, e [ɛ̃pʀevy] a unforeseen, unexpected ♦ *nm* unexpected incident; **l'~** the unexpected; **en cas d'~** if anything unexpected happens; **sauf ~** barring anything unexpected.

imprimante [ɛ̃pʀimãt] *nf (INFORM)* printer; **~ à jet d'encre** ink-jet printer; **~ à laser** laser printer; **~ (ligne par) ligne** line printer; **~ à marguerite** daisy-wheel printer; **~ matricielle** dot-matrix printer; **~ thermique** thermal printer.

imprimé [ɛ̃pʀime] *nm (formulaire)* printed form; *(POSTES)* printed matter *q*; *(tissu)* printed fabric; **un ~ à fleurs/pois** *(tissu)* a floral/polka-dot print.

imprimer [ɛ̃pʀime] *vt* to print; *(INFORM)* to print (out); *(apposer: visa, cachet)* to stamp; *(empreinte etc)* to imprint; *(publier)* to publish; *(communiquer: mouvement, impulsion)* to impart, transmit.

imprimerie [ɛ̃pʀimʀi] *nf* printing; *(établissement)* printing works *sg*; *(atelier)* printing house, printery.

imprimeur [ɛ̃pʀimœʀ] *nm* printer; **imprimeur-éditeur/-libraire** printer and publisher/bookseller.

improbable [ɛ̃pʀɔbabl(ə)] a unlikely, improbable.

improductif, ive [ɛ̃pʀɔdyktif, -iv] a unproductive.

impromptu, e [ɛ̃pʀɔ̃pty] a impromptu; *(départ)* sudden.

imprononçable [ɛ̃pʀɔnɔ̃sabl(ə)] a unpronounceable.

impropre [ɛ̃pʀɔpʀ(ə)] a inappropriate; **~ à** unsuitable for.

improprement [ɛ̃pʀɔpʀəmã] *ad* improperly.

impropriété [ɛ̃pʀɔpʀijete] *nf*: **~ (de langage)** incorrect usage *q*.

improvisation [ɛ̃pʀɔvizasjɔ̃] *nf* improvization.

improvisé, e [ɛ̃pʀɔvize] a makeshift, improvized; *(jeu etc)* scratch, improvized; **avec des moyens ~s** using whatever comes to hand.

improviser [ɛ̃pʀɔvize] *vt, vi* to improvize; **s'~** *(secours, réunion)* to be improvized; **s'~ cuisinier** to (decide to) act as cook; **~ qn cuisinier** to get sb to act as cook.

improviste [ɛ̃pʀɔvist(ə)]: **à l'~** *ad* unexpectedly, without warning.

imprudemment [ɛ̃pʀydamã] *ad* carelessly; unwisely, imprudently.

imprudence [ɛ̃pʀydãs] *nf* carelessness *q*; imprudence *q*; act of carelessness; foolish *ou* unwise action.

imprudent, e [ɛ̃pʀydã, -ãt] a *(conducteur, geste, action)* careless; *(remarque)* unwise, imprudent; *(projet)* foolhardy.

impubère [ɛ̃pybɛʀ] a below the age of puberty.

impudemment [ɛ̃pydamã] *ad* impudently.

impudence [ɛ̃pydãs] *nf* impudence.

impudent, e [ɛ̃pydã, -ãt] a impudent.

impudeur [ɛ̃pydœʀ] *nf* shamelessness.

impudique [ɛ̃pydik] a shameless.

impuissance [ɛ̃pɥisãs] *nf* helplessness; ineffectualness; impotence.

impuissant, e [ɛ̃pɥisã, -ãt] a helpless; *(sans effet)* ineffectual; *(sexuellement)* impotent ♦ *nm* impotent man; **~ à faire qch** powerless to do sth.

impulsif, ive [ɛ̃pylsif, -iv] a impulsive.

impulsion [ɛ̃pylsjɔ̃] *nf (ÉLEC, instinct)* impulse; *(élan, influence)* impetus.

impulsivement [ɛ̃pylsivmã] *ad* impulsively.

impulsivité [ɛ̃pylsivite] *nf* impulsiveness.

impunément [ɛ̃pynemã] *ad* with impunity.

impuni, e [ɛ̃pyni] a unpunished.

impunité [ɛ̃pynite] *nf* impunity.

impur, e [ɛ̃pyʀ] a impure.

impureté [ɛ̃pyʀte] *nf* impurity.

imputable [ɛ̃pytabl(ə)] a *(attribuable)*: **~ à** imputable to, ascribable to; *(COMM: somme)*: **~ sur** chargeable to.

imputation [ɛ̃pytasjɔ̃] *nf* imputation, charge.

imputer [ɛ̃pyte] *vt (attribuer)*: **~ qch à** to ascribe *ou* impute sth to; *(COMM)*: **~ qch à ou sur** to charge sth to.

imputrescible [ɛ̃pytʀesibl(ə)] a rotproof.

in [in] a *inv* in, trendy.

INA [ina] *sigle m* (= *Institut national de l'audio-visuel*) library of television archives.

inabordable [inabɔʀdabl(ə)] a *(lieu)* inaccessible; *(cher)* prohibitive.

inaccentué, e [inaksãtɥe] a *(LING)* unstressed.

inacceptable [inaksɛptabl(ə)] a unacceptable.

inaccessible [inaksesibl(ə)] a inaccessible; *(objectif)* unattainable; *(insensible)*: **~ à** impervious to.

inaccoutumé, e [inakutyme] a unaccustomed.

inachevé, e [inaʃve] a unfinished.

inactif, ive [inaktif, -iv] a inactive, idle.

inaction [inaksjɔ̃] *nf* inactivity.

inactivité [inaktivite] *nf (ADMIN)*: **en ~** out of active service.

inadaptation [inadaptasjɔ̃] *nf (PSYCH)* maladjustment.

inadapté, e [inadapte] a *(PSYCH: adulte, enfant)* maladjusted ♦ *nm/f (péj: adulte: asocial)* misfit; **~ à** not adapted to, unsuited to.

inadéquat, e [inadekwa, wat] a inadequate.

inadéquation [inadekwasjɔ̃] *nf* inadequacy.

inadmissible [inadmisibl(ə)] a inadmissible.

inadvertance [inadvɛʀtãs]: **par ~** *ad* inadvertently.

inaliénable [inaljenabl(ə)] a inalienable.

inaltérable [inalteʀabl(ə)] a *(matière)* stable; *(fig)* unchanging; **~ à** unaffected by; **couleur ~ (au lavage/à la lumière)** fast colour/fade-resistant colour.

inamovible [inamɔvibl(ə)] a fixed; *(JUR)* irremovable.

inanimé, e [inanime] a *(matière)* inanimate; *(évanoui)* unconscious; *(sans vie)* lifeless.

inanité [inanite] *nf* futility.

inanition [inanisjɔ̃] *nf*: **tomber d'~** to faint with hunger (and exhaustion).

inaperçu, e [inapɛʀsy] a: **passer ~** to go unnoticed.

inappétence [inapetãs] *nf* lack of appetite.

inapplicable [inaplikabl(ə)] a inapplicable.

inapplication [inaplikasjɔ̃] *nf* lack of application.

inappliqué, e [inaplike] a lacking in application.

inappréciable [inapʀesjabl(ə)] *a* (*service*) invaluable; (*différence, nuance*) inappreciable.

inapte [inapt(ə)] *a*: ~ **à** incapable of; (*MIL*) unfit for.

inaptitude [inaptityd] *nf* inaptitude; unfitness.

inarticulé, e [inaʀtikyle] *a* inarticulate.

inassimilable [inasimilabl(ə)] *a* that cannot be assimilated.

inassouvi, e [inasuvi] *a* unsatisfied, unfulfilled.

inattaquable [inatakabl(ə)] *a* (*MIL*) unassailable; (*texte, preuve*) irrefutable.

inattendu, e [inatɑ̃dy] *a* unexpected ♦ *nm*: l'~ the unexpected.

inattentif, ive [inatɑ̃tif, -iv] *a* inattentive; ~ **à** (*dangers, détails*) heedless of.

inattention [inatɑ̃sjɔ̃] *nf* inattention; (*inadvertance*): **une minute d'**~ a minute of inattention, a minute's carelessness; **par** ~ inadvertently; **faute d'**~ careless mistake.

inaudible [inodibl(ə)] *a* inaudible.

inaugural, e, aux [inɔgyʀal, -o] *a* (*cérémonie*) inaugural, opening; (*vol, voyage*) maiden.

inauguration [inɔgyʀasjɔ̃] *nf* unveiling; opening; **discours/cérémonie d'**~ inaugural speech/ceremony.

inaugurer [inɔgyʀe] *vt* (*monument*) to unveil; (*exposition, usine*) to open; (*fig*) to inaugurate.

inauthenticité [inɔtɑ̃tisite] *nf* inauthenticity.

inavouable [inavwabl(ə)] *a* undisclosable; (*honteux*) shameful.

inavoué, e [inavwe] *a* unavowed.

INC *sigle m* (= *Institut national de la consommation*) *consumer research organization*.

inca [ɛ̃ka] *a inv* Inca ♦ *nm/f*: l'~ Inca.

incalculable [ɛ̃kalkylabl(ə)] *a* incalculable; **un nombre** ~ **de** countless numbers of.

incandescence [ɛ̃kɑ̃desɑ̃s] *nf* incandescence; **en** ~ incandescent, white-hot; **porter à** ~ to heat white-hot; **lampe/manchon à** ~ incandescent lamp/(gas) mantle.

incandescent, e [ɛ̃kɑ̃desɑ̃, -ɑ̃t] *a* incandescent, white-hot.

incantation [ɛ̃kɑ̃tasjɔ̃] *nf* incantation.

incapable [ɛ̃kapabl(ə)] *a* incapable; ~ **de faire** incapable of doing; (*empêché*) unable to do.

incapacitant, e [ɛ̃kapasitɑ̃, -ɑ̃t] *a* (*MIL*) incapacitating.

incapacité [ɛ̃kapasite] *nf* incapability; (*JUR*) incapacity; **être dans l'**~ **de faire** to be unable to do; ~ **permanente/de travail** permanent/industrial disablement; ~ **électorale** ineligibility to vote.

incarcération [ɛ̃kaʀseʀasjɔ̃] *nf* incarceration.

incarcérer [ɛ̃kaʀseʀe] *vt* to incarcerate.

incarnat, e [ɛ̃kaʀna, -at] *a* (*rosy*) pink.

incarnation [ɛ̃kaʀnasjɔ̃] *nf* incarnation.

incarné, e [ɛ̃kaʀne] *a* incarnate; (*ongle*) ingrown.

incarner [ɛ̃kaʀne] *vt* to embody, personify; (*THÉÂTRE*) to play; (*REL*) to incarnate; **s'**~ **dans** (*REL*) to be incarnate in.

incartade [ɛ̃kaʀtad] *nf* prank, escapade.

incassable [ɛ̃kasabl(ə)] *a* unbreakable.

incendiaire [ɛ̃sɑ̃djɛʀ] *a* incendiary; (*fig: discours*) inflammatory ♦ *nm/f* fire-raiser, arsonist.

incendie [ɛ̃sɑ̃di] *nm* fire; ~ **criminel** arson *q*;

~ **de forêt** forest fire.

incendier [ɛ̃sɑ̃dje] *vt* (*mettre le feu à*) to set fire to, set alight; (*brûler complètement*) to burn down.

incertain, e [ɛ̃sɛʀtɛ̃, -ɛn] *a* uncertain; (*temps*) uncertain, unsettled; (*imprécis: contours*) indistinct, blurred.

incertitude [ɛ̃sɛʀtityd] *nf* uncertainty.

incessamment [ɛ̃sɛsamɑ̃] *ad* very shortly.

incessant, e [ɛ̃sɛsɑ̃, -ɑ̃t] *a* incessant, unceasing.

incessible [ɛ̃sesibl(ə)] *a* (*JUR*) nontransferable.

inceste [ɛ̃sɛst(ə)] *nm* incest.

incestueux, euse [ɛ̃sɛstɥø, -øz] *a* incestuous.

inchangé, e [ɛ̃ʃɑ̃ʒe] *a* unchanged, unaltered.

inchauffable [ɛ̃ʃofabl(ə)] *a* impossible to heat.

incidemment [ɛ̃sidamɑ̃] *ad* in passing.

incidence [ɛ̃sidɑ̃s] *nf* (*effet, influence*) effect; (*PHYSIQUE*) incidence.

incident [ɛ̃sidɑ̃] *nm* incident; ~ **de frontière** border incident; ~ **de parcours** minor hitch *ou* setback; ~ **technique** technical difficulties *pl*, technical hitch.

incinérateur [ɛ̃sineʀatœʀ] *nm* incinerator.

incinération [ɛ̃sineʀasjɔ̃] *nf* (*d'ordures*) incineration; (*crémation*) cremation.

incinérer [ɛ̃sineʀe] *vt* (*ordures*) to incinerate; (*mort*) to cremate.

incise [ɛ̃siz] *nf* (*LING*) interpolated clause.

inciser [ɛ̃size] *vt* to make an incision in; (*abcès*) to lance.

incisif, ive [ɛ̃sizif, -iv] *a* incisive, cutting ♦ *nf* incisor.

incision [ɛ̃sizjɔ̃] *nf* incision; (*d'un abcès*) lancing.

incitation [ɛ̃sitasjɔ̃] *nf* (*encouragement*) incentive; (*provocation*) incitement.

inciter [ɛ̃site] *vt*: ~ **qn à** (*faire*) **qch** to prompt *ou* encourage sb to do sth; (*à la révolte etc*) to incite sb to do sth.

incivil, e [ɛ̃sivil] *a* uncivil.

incivilité [ɛ̃sivilite] *nf* incivility.

inclinable [ɛ̃klinabl(ə)] *a* (*dossier etc*) tilting; **siège à dossier** ~ reclining seat.

inclinaison [ɛ̃klinɛzɔ̃] *nf* (*déclivité: d'une route etc*) incline; (: *d'un toit*) slope; (*état penché: d'un mur*) lean; (: *de la tête*) tilt; (: *d'un navire*) list.

inclination [ɛ̃klinasjɔ̃] *nf* (*penchant*) inclination, tendency; **montrer de l'**~ **pour les sciences** *etc* to show an inclination for the sciences *etc*; ~**s égoïstes/altruistes** egoistic/altruistic tendencies; ~ **de (la) tête** nod (of the head); ~ **(de buste)** bow.

incliner [ɛ̃kline] *vt* (*bouteille*) to tilt; (*tête*) to incline; (*inciter*): ~ **qn à qch/à faire** to encourage sb towards sth/to do ♦ *vi*: ~ **à qch/à faire** (*tendre à, pencher pour*) to incline towards sth/doing, tend towards sth/to do; **s'**~ (*route*) to slope; (*toit*) to be sloping; **s'**~ **(devant)** to bow (before).

inclure [ɛ̃klyʀ] *vt* to include; (*joindre à un envoi*) to enclose; **jusqu'au 10 mars inclus** until 10th March inclusive.

inclus, e [ɛ̃kly, -yz] *pp de* **inclure** ♦ *a* (*joint à un envoi*) enclosed; (*compris: frais, dépense*) included; (*MATH: ensemble*): ~ **dans** included in; **jusqu'au troisième chapitre** ~ up to and including the third chapter.

inclusion [ɛ̃klyzjɔ̃] nf (voir inclure) inclusion; enclosing.

inclusivement [ɛ̃klyzivmɑ̃] ad inclusively.

inclut [ɛ̃kly] vb voir **inclure**.

incoercible [ɛ̃kɔɛʀsibl(ə)] a uncontrollable.

incognito [ɛ̃kɔɲito] ad incognito ♦ nm: **garder l'~** to remain incognito.

incohérence [ɛ̃kɔeʀɑ̃s] nf inconsistency; incoherence.

incohérent, e [ɛ̃kɔeʀɑ̃, -ɑ̃t] a inconsistent; incoherent.

incollable [ɛ̃kɔlabl(ə)] a (riz) that does not stick; (fam: personne): **il est ~** he's got all the answers.

incolore [ɛ̃kɔlɔʀ] a colourless.

incomber [ɛ̃kɔ̃be]: **~ à** vt (suj: devoirs, responsabilité) to rest ou be incumbent upon; (: frais, travail) to be the responsibility of.

incombustible [ɛ̃kɔ̃bystibl(ə)] a incombustible.

incommensurable [ɛ̃kɔmɑ̃syʀabl(ə)] a immeasurable.

incommodant, e [ɛ̃kɔmɔdɑ̃, -ɑ̃t] a (bruit) annoying; (chaleur) uncomfortable.

incommode [ɛ̃kɔmɔd] a inconvenient; (posture, siège) uncomfortable.

incommodément [ɛ̃kɔmɔdemɑ̃] ad (installé, assis) uncomfortably; (logé, situé) inconveniently.

incommoder [ɛ̃kɔmɔde] vt: **~ qn** to bother ou inconvenience sb; (embarrasser) to make sb feel uncomfortable ou ill at ease.

incommodité [ɛ̃kɔmɔdite] nf inconvenience.

incomparable [ɛ̃kɔ̃paʀabl(ə)] a not comparable; (inégalable) incomparable, matchless.

incomparablement [ɛ̃kɔ̃paʀabləmɑ̃] ad incomparably.

incompatibilité [ɛ̃kɔ̃patibilite] nf incompatibility; **~ d'humeur** (mutual) incompatibility.

incompatible [ɛ̃kɔ̃patibl(ə)] a incompatible.

incompétence [ɛ̃kɔ̃petɑ̃s] nf lack of expertise; incompetence.

incompétent, e [ɛ̃kɔ̃petɑ̃, -ɑ̃t] a (ignorant) inexpert; (incapable) incompetent, not competent.

incomplet, ète [ɛ̃kɔ̃plɛ, -ɛt] a incomplete.

incomplètement [ɛ̃kɔ̃plɛtmɑ̃] ad not completely, incompletely.

incompréhensible [ɛ̃kɔ̃pʀeɑ̃sibl(ə)] a incomprehensible.

incompréhensif, ive [ɛ̃kɔ̃pʀeɑ̃sif, -iv] a lacking in understanding, unsympathetic.

incompréhension [ɛ̃kɔ̃pʀeɑ̃sjɔ̃] nf lack of understanding.

incompressible [ɛ̃kɔ̃pʀesibl(ə)] a (PHYSIQUE) incompressible; (fig: dépenses) that cannot be reduced; (JUR: peine) irreducible.

incompris, e [ɛ̃kɔ̃pʀi, -iz] a misunderstood.

inconcevable [ɛ̃kɔ̃svabl(ə)] a (conduite etc) inconceivable; (mystère) incredible.

inconciliable [ɛ̃kɔ̃siljabl(ə)] a irreconcilable.

inconditionnel, le [ɛ̃kɔ̃disjɔnɛl] a unconditional; (partisan) unquestioning ♦ nm/f (partisan) unquestioning supporter.

inconditionnellement [ɛ̃kɔ̃disjɔnɛlmɑ̃] ad unconditionally.

inconduite [ɛ̃kɔ̃dɥit] nf bad ou unsuitable behaviour q.

inconfort [ɛ̃kɔ̃fɔʀ] nm lack of comfort, discomfort.

inconfortable [ɛ̃kɔ̃fɔʀtabl(ə)] a uncomfortable.

inconfortablement [ɛ̃kɔ̃fɔʀtabləmɑ̃] ad uncomfortably.

incongru, e [ɛ̃kɔ̃gʀy] a unseemly; (remarque) ill-chosen, incongruous.

incongruité [ɛ̃kɔ̃gʀyite] nf unseemliness; incongruity; (parole incongrue) ill-chosen remark.

inconnu, e [ɛ̃kɔny] a unknown; (sentiment, plaisir) new, strange ♦ nm/f stranger; unknown person (ou artist etc) ♦ nm: **l'~** the unknown ♦ nf (MATH) unknown; (fig) unknown factor.

inconsciemment [ɛ̃kɔ̃sjamɑ̃] ad unconsciously.

inconscience [ɛ̃kɔ̃sjɑ̃s] nf unconsciousness; recklessness.

inconscient, e [ɛ̃kɔ̃sjɑ̃, -ɑ̃t] a unconscious; (irréfléchi) reckless ♦ nm (PSYCH): **l'~** the subconscious, the unconscious; **~ de** unaware of.

inconséquence [ɛ̃kɔ̃sekɑ̃s] nf inconsistency; thoughtlessness; (action, parole) thoughtless thing to do (ou say).

inconséquent, e [ɛ̃kɔ̃sekɑ̃, -ɑ̃t] a (illogique) inconsistent; (irréfléchi) thoughtless.

inconsidéré, e [ɛ̃kɔ̃sideʀe] a ill-considered.

inconsidérément [ɛ̃kɔ̃sideʀemɑ̃] ad thoughtlessly.

inconsistant, e [ɛ̃kɔ̃sistɑ̃, -ɑ̃t] a flimsy, weak; (crème etc) runny.

inconsolable [ɛ̃kɔ̃sɔlabl(ə)] a inconsolable.

inconstance [ɛ̃kɔ̃stɑ̃s] nf inconstancy, fickleness.

inconstant, e [ɛ̃kɔ̃stɑ̃, -ɑ̃t] a inconstant, fickle.

inconstitutionnel, le [ɛ̃kɔ̃stitysjɔnɛl] a unconstitutional.

incontestable [ɛ̃kɔ̃tɛstabl(ə)] a unquestionable, indisputable.

incontestablement [ɛ̃kɔ̃tɛstabləmɑ̃] ad unquestionably, indisputably.

incontesté, e [ɛ̃kɔ̃tɛste] a undisputed.

incontinence [ɛ̃kɔ̃tinɑ̃s] nf (MÉD) incontinence.

incontinent, e [ɛ̃kɔ̃tinɑ̃, -ɑ̃t] a (MÉD) incontinent ♦ ad (tout de suite) forthwith.

incontournable [ɛ̃kɔ̃tuʀnabl(ə)] a unavoidable.

incontrôlable [ɛ̃kɔ̃tʀolabl(ə)] a unverifiable.

incontrôlé, e [ɛ̃kɔ̃tʀole] a uncontrolled.

inconvenance [ɛ̃kɔ̃vnɑ̃s] nf (parole, action) impropriety.

inconvenant, e [ɛ̃kɔ̃vnɑ̃, -ɑ̃t] a unseemly, improper.

inconvénient [ɛ̃kɔ̃venjɑ̃] nm (d'une situation, d'un projet) disadvantage, drawback; (d'un remède, changement etc) risk, inconvenience; **si vous n'y voyez pas d'~** if you have no objections; **y a-t-il un ~ à ...?** (risque) isn't there a risk in ...?; (objection) is there any objection to ...?

inconvertible [ɛ̃kɔ̃vɛʀtibl(ə)] a inconvertible.

incorporation [ɛ̃kɔʀpɔʀasjɔ̃] nf (MIL) call-up.

incorporé, e [ɛ̃kɔʀpɔʀe] a (micro etc) built-in.

incorporel, le [ɛ̃kɔʀpɔʀɛl] a (JUR): **biens ~s** intangible property.

incorporer [ɛ̃kɔʀpɔʀe] vt: **~ (à)** to mix in

(with); (*paragraphe etc*): ~ **(dans)** to incorporate (in); (*territoire, immigrants*): ~ **(dans)** to incorporate (into); (*MIL: appeler*) to recruit, call up; (: *affecter*): ~ **qn dans** to enlist sb into.

incorrect, e [ɛ̃kɔrɛkt] *a* (*impropre, inconvenant*) improper; (*défectueux*) faulty; (*inexact*) incorrect; (*impoli*) impolite; (*déloyal*) underhand.

incorrectement [ɛ̃kɔrɛktəmɑ̃] *ad* improperly; faultily; incorrectly; impolitely; in an underhand way.

incorrection [ɛ̃kɔrɛksjɔ̃] *nf* impropriety; incorrectness; underhand nature; (*terme impropre*) impropriety; (*action, remarque*) improper behaviour (*ou* remark).

incorrigible [ɛ̃kɔriʒibl(ə)] *a* incorrigible.

incorruptible [ɛ̃kɔryptibl(ə)] *a* incorruptible.

incrédibilité [ɛ̃kredibilite] *nf* incredibility.

incrédule [ɛ̃kredyl] *a* incredulous; (*REL*) unbelieving.

incrédulité [ɛ̃kredylite] *nf* incredulity; **avec** ~ incredulously.

increvable [ɛ̃krəvabl(ə)] *a* (*pneu*) punctureproof; (*fam*) tireless.

incriminer [ɛ̃krimine] *vt* (*personne*) to incriminate; (*action, conduite*) to bring under attack; (*bonne foi, honnêteté*) to call into question; **livre/article incriminé** offending book/article.

incrochetable [ɛ̃krɔʃtabl(ə)] *a* (*serrure*) that can't be picked, burglarproof.

incroyable [ɛ̃krwajabl(ə)] *a* incredible, unbelievable.

incroyablement [ɛ̃krwajabləmɑ̃] *ad* incredibly, unbelievably.

incroyant, e [ɛ̃krwajɑ̃, -ɑ̃t] *nm/f* non-believer.

incrustation [ɛ̃krystasjɔ̃] *nf* inlaying *q*; inlay; (*dans une chaudière etc*) fur *q*, scale *q*.

incruster [ɛ̃kryste] *vt* (*ART*): ~ **qch dans/qch de** to inlay sth into/sth with; (*radiateur etc*) to coat with scale *ou* fur; **s'~** *vi* (*invité*) to take root; (*radiateur etc*) to become coated with fur *ou* scale; **s'~ dans** (*suj: corps étranger, caillou*) to become embedded in.

incubateur [ɛ̃kybatœr] *nm* incubator.

incubation [ɛ̃kybasjɔ̃] *nf* incubation.

inculpation [ɛ̃kylpasjɔ̃] *nf* charging *q*; charge; **sous l'~ de** on a charge of.

inculpé, e [ɛ̃kylpe] *nm/f* accused.

inculper [ɛ̃kylpe] *vt*: ~ **(de)** to charge (with).

inculquer [ɛ̃kylke] *vt*: ~ **qch à** to inculcate sth in, instil sth into.

inculte [ɛ̃kylt(ə)] *a* uncultivated; (*esprit, peuple*) uncultured; (*barbe*) unkempt.

incultivable [ɛ̃kyltivabl(ə)] *a* (*terrain*) unworkable.

inculture [ɛ̃kyltyr] *nf* lack of education.

incurable [ɛ̃kyrabl(ə)] *a* incurable.

incurie [ɛ̃kyri] *nf* carelessness.

incursion [ɛ̃kyrsjɔ̃] *nf* incursion, foray.

incurvé, e [ɛ̃kyrve] *a* curved.

incurver [ɛ̃kyrve] *vt* (*barre de fer*) to bend into a curve; **s'~** *vi* (*planche, route*) to bend.

Inde [ɛ̃d] *nf*: **l'~** India.

indécemment [ɛ̃desamɑ̃] *ad* indecently.

indécence [ɛ̃desɑ̃s] *nf* indecency; (*propos, acte*) indecent remark (*ou* act *etc*).

indécent, e [ɛ̃desɑ̃, -ɑ̃t] *a* indecent.

indéchiffrable [ɛ̃deʃifrabl(ə)] *a* indecipherable.

indéchirable [ɛ̃deʃirabl(ə)] *a* tearproof.

indécis, e [ɛ̃desi, -iz] *a* indecisive; (*perplexe*) undecided.

indécision [ɛ̃desizjɔ̃] *nf* indecision, indecisiveness.

indéclinable [ɛ̃deklinabl(ə)] *a* (*LING: mot*) indeclinable.

indécomposable [ɛ̃dekɔ̃pozabl(ə)] *a* that cannot be broken down.

indéfectible [ɛ̃defɛktibl(ə)] *a* (*attachement*) indestructible.

indéfendable [ɛ̃defɑ̃dabl(ə)] *a* indefensible.

indéfini, e [ɛ̃defini] *a* (*imprécis, incertain*) undefined; (*illimité, LING*) indefinite.

indéfiniment [ɛ̃definimɑ̃] *ad* indefinitely.

indéfinissable [ɛ̃definisabl(ə)] *a* indefinable.

indéformable [ɛ̃defɔrmabl(ə)] *a* that keeps its shape.

indélébile [ɛ̃delebil] *a* indelible.

indélicat, e [ɛ̃delika, -at] *a* tactless; (*malhonnête*) dishonest.

indélicatesse [ɛ̃delikatɛs] *nf* tactlessness, dishonesty.

indémaillable [ɛ̃demajabl(ə)] *a* run-resist.

indemne [ɛ̃dɛmn(ə)] *a* unharmed.

indemnisable [ɛ̃dɛmnizabl(ə)] *a* entitled to compensation.

indemnisation [ɛ̃dɛmnizasjɔ̃] *nf* (*somme*) indemnity, compensation.

indemniser [ɛ̃dɛmnize] *vt*: ~ **qn (de)** to compensate sb (for); **se faire** ~ to get compensation.

indemnité [ɛ̃dɛmnite] *nf* (*dédommagement*) compensation *q*; (*allocation*) allowance; ~ **de licenciement** redundancy payment; ~ **de logement** housing allowance; ~ **parlementaire** ≈ M.P.'s (*Brit*) *ou* Congressman's (*US*) salary.

indémontable [ɛ̃demɔ̃tabl(ə)] *a* (*meuble etc*) that cannot be dismantled, in one piece.

indéniable [ɛ̃denjabl(ə)] *a* undeniable, indisputable.

indéniablement [ɛ̃denjabləmɑ̃] *ad* undeniably.

indépendamment [ɛ̃depɑ̃damɑ̃] *ad* independently; ~ **de** independently of; (*abstraction faite de*) irrespective of; (*en plus de*) over and above.

indépendance [ɛ̃depɑ̃dɑ̃s] *nf* independence; ~ **matérielle** financial independence.

indépendant, e [ɛ̃depɑ̃dɑ̃, -ɑ̃t] *a* independent; ~ **de** independent of; **chambre** ~**e** room with private entrance; **travailleur** ~ self-employed worker.

indépendantiste [ɛ̃depɑ̃dɑ̃tist(ə)] *a, nm/f* separatist.

indéracinable [ɛ̃derasinabl(ə)] *a* (*fig: croyance etc*) ineradicable.

indéréglable [ɛ̃dereglabl(ə)] *a* which will not break down.

indescriptible [ɛ̃dɛskriptibl(ə)] *a* indescribable.

indésirable [ɛ̃dezirabl(ə)] *a* undesirable.

indestructible [ɛ̃dɛstryktibl(ə)] *a* indestructible; (*marque, impression*) indelible.

indéterminable [ɛ̃detɛrminabl(ə)] *a* indeterminable.

indétermination [ɛ̃detɛrminasjɔ̃] *nf* indecision, indecisiveness.

indéterminé, e [ɛ̃detɛʁmine] *a* unspecified; indeterminate; indeterminable.

index [ɛ̃dɛks] *nm* (*doigt*) index finger; (*d'un livre etc*) index; **mettre à l'~** to blacklist.

indexation [ɛ̃dɛksasjɔ̃] *nf* indexing.

indexé, e [ɛ̃dɛkse] *a* (*ÉCON*): **~ (sur)** index-linked (to).

indexer [ɛ̃dɛkse] *vt* (*salaire, emprunt*): **~ (sur)** to index (on).

indicateur [ɛ̃dikatœʁ] *nm* (*POLICE*) informer; (*livre*) guide; (*: liste*) directory; (*TECH*) gauge; indicator; (*ÉCON*) indicator ♦ *a*: **poteau ~** signpost; **tableau ~** indicator (board); **~ des chemins de fer** railway timetable; **~ de direction** (*AUTO*) indicator; **~ immobilier** property gazette; **~ de niveau** level, gauge; **~ de pression** pressure gauge; **~ de rues** street directory; **~ de vitesse** speedometer.

indicatif, ive [ɛ̃dikatif, -iv] *a*: **à titre ~** for (your) information ♦ *nm* (*LING*) indicative; (*d'une émission*) theme *ou* signature tune; (*TÉL*) dialling code; **~ d'appel** (*RADIO*) call sign.

indication [ɛ̃dikasjɔ̃] *nf* indication; (*renseignement*) information *q*; **~s** *nfpl* (*directives*) instructions; **~ d'origine** (*COMM*) place of origin.

indice [ɛ̃dis] *nm* (*marque, signe*) indication, sign; (*POLICE*: *lors d'une enquête*) clue; (*JUR*: *présomption*) piece of evidence; (*SCIENCE, ÉCON, TECH*) index; (*ADMIN*) grading; rating; **~ du coût de la vie** cost-of-living index; **~ inférieur** subscript; **~ d'octane** octane rating; **~ des prix** price index; **~ de traitement** salary grading.

indicible [ɛ̃disibl(ə)] *a* inexpressible.

indien, ne [ɛ̃djɛ̃, -ɛn] *a* Indian ♦ *nm/f*: **I~, ne** (*d'Amérique*) (American *ou* Red) Indian; (*d'Inde*) Indian.

indifféremment [ɛ̃diferamɑ̃] *ad* (*sans distinction*) equally; indiscriminately.

indifférence [ɛ̃diferɑ̃s] *nf* indifference.

indifférencié, e [ɛ̃diferɑ̃sje] *a* undifferentiated.

indifférent, e [ɛ̃diferɑ̃, -ɑ̃t] *a* (*peu intéressé*) indifferent; **~ à** (*insensible à*) indifferent to, unconcerned about; (*peu intéressant pour*) indifferent to; immaterial to; **ça m'est ~ (que ...)** it doesn't matter to me (whether ...).

indifférer [ɛ̃difere] *vt*: **cela m'indiffère** I'm indifferent about it.

indigence [ɛ̃diʒɑ̃s] *nf* poverty; **être dans l'~** to be destitute.

indigène [ɛ̃diʒɛn] *a* native, indigenous; (*de la région*) local ♦ *nm/f* native.

indigent, e [ɛ̃diʒɑ̃, -ɑ̃t] *a* destitute, poverty-stricken; (*fig*) poor.

indigeste [ɛ̃diʒɛst(ə)] *a* indigestible.

indigestion [ɛ̃diʒɛstjɔ̃] *nf* indigestion *q*; **avoir une ~** to have indigestion.

indignation [ɛ̃diɲasjɔ̃] *nf* indignation; **avec ~** indignantly.

indigne [ɛ̃diɲ] *a*: **~ (de)** unworthy (of).

indigné, e [ɛ̃diɲe] *a* indignant.

indignement [ɛ̃diɲmɑ̃] *ad* shamefully.

indigner [ɛ̃diɲe] *vt* to make indignant; **s'~ (de/contre)** to be (*ou* become) indignant (at).

indignité [ɛ̃diɲite] *nf* unworthiness *q*; (*acte*) shameful act.

indigo [ɛ̃digo] *nm* indigo.

indiqué, e [ɛ̃dike] *a* (*date, lieu*) given, appointed; (*adéquat*) appropriate, suitable; (*conseillé*) advisable; (*remède, traitement*) appropriate.

indiquer [ɛ̃dike] *vt* (*désigner*): **~ qch/qn à qn** to point sth/sb out to sb; (*suj: pendule, aiguille*) to show; (*suj: étiquette, plan*) to show, indicate; (*faire connaître: médecin, restaurant*): **~ qch/qn à qn** to tell sb of sth/sb; (*renseigner sur*) to point out, tell; (*déterminer: date, lieu*) to give, state; (*dénoter*) to indicate, point to; **~ du doigt** to point out; **~ de la main** to indicate with one's hand; **~ du regard** to glance towards *ou* in the direction of; **pourriez-vous m'~ les toilettes/l'heure?** could you direct me to the toilets/tell me the time?

indirect, e [ɛ̃diʁɛkt] *a* indirect.

indirectement [ɛ̃diʁɛktəmɑ̃] *ad* indirectly; (*apprendre*) in a roundabout way.

indiscernable [ɛ̃disɛʁnabl(ə)] *a* indiscernable.

indiscipline [ɛ̃disiplin] *nf* lack of discipline.

indiscipliné, e [ɛ̃disipline] *a* undisciplined; (*fig*) unmanageable.

indiscret, ète [ɛ̃diskʁɛ, -ɛt] *a* indiscreet.

indiscrétion [ɛ̃diskʁesjɔ̃] *nf* indiscretion; **sans ~, ...** without wishing to be indiscreet, ...

indiscutable [ɛ̃diskytabl(ə)] *a* indisputable.

indiscutablement [ɛ̃diskytabləmɑ̃] *ad* indisputably.

indiscuté, e [ɛ̃diskyte] *a* (*incontesté: droit, chef*) undisputed.

indispensable [ɛ̃dispɑ̃sabl(ə)] *a* indispensable, essential; **~ à qn/pour faire qch** essential for sb/to do sth.

indisponibilité [ɛ̃disponibilite] *nf* unavailability.

indisponible [ɛ̃disponibl(ə)] *a* unavailable.

indisposé, e [ɛ̃dispoze] *a* indisposed, unwell.

indisposer [ɛ̃dispoze] *vt* (*incommoder*) to upset; (*déplaire à*) to antagonize.

indisposition [ɛ̃dispozisjɔ̃] *nf* (slight) illness, indisposition.

indistinct, e [ɛ̃distɛ̃, -ɛ̃kt(ə)] *a* indistinct.

indistinctement [ɛ̃distɛ̃ktəmɑ̃] *ad* (*voir, prononcer*) indistinctly; (*sans distinction*) without distinction, indiscriminately.

individu [ɛ̃dividy] *nm* individual.

individualiser [ɛ̃dividɥalize] *vt* to individualize; (*personnaliser*) to tailor to individual requirements; **s'~** to develop one's own identity.

individualisme [ɛ̃dividɥalism(ə)] *nm* individualism.

individualiste [ɛ̃dividɥalist(ə)] *nm/f* individualist.

individualité [ɛ̃dividɥalite] *nf* individuality.

individuel, le [ɛ̃dividɥɛl] *a* (*gén*) individual; (*opinion, livret, contrôle, avantages*) personal; **chambre ~le** single room; **maison ~le** detached house; **propriété ~le** personal *ou* private property.

individuellement [ɛ̃dividɥɛlmɑ̃] *ad* individually.

indivis, e [ɛ̃divi, -iz] *a* (*JUR: bien, propriété, succession*) indivisible; (*: cohéritiers,* *propriétaires*) joint.

indivisible [ɛ̃divizibl(ə)] *a* indivisible.

Indochine [ɛ̃dɔʃin] *nf*: **l'~** Indochina.

indochinois, e [ɛ̃dɔʃinwa, -waz] *a* Indochinese.

indocile [ɛ̃dɔsil] *a* unruly.

indo-européen, ne [ɛ̃dɔøʀɔpeɛ̃, -ɛn] *a* Indo-European ♦ *nm* (*LING*) Indo-European.

indolence [ɛ̃dɔlɑ̃s] *nf* indolence.

indolent, e [ɛ̃dɔlɑ̃, -ɑ̃t] *a* indolent.

indolore [ɛ̃dɔlɔʀ] *a* painless.

indomptable [ɛ̃dɔ̃tabl(ə)] *a* untameable; (*fig*) invincible, indomitable.

indompté, e [ɛ̃dɔ̃te] *a* (*cheval*) unbroken.

Indonésie [ɛ̃dɔnezi] *nf*: **l'~** Indonesia.

indonésien, ne [ɛ̃dɔnezjɛ̃, -ɛn] *a* Indonesian ♦ *nm/f*: **l'~, ne** Indonesian.

indu, e [ɛ̃dy] *a*: **à des heures ~es** at an ungodly hour.

indubitable [ɛ̃dybitabl(ə)] *a* indubitable.

indubitablement [ɛ̃dybitabləmɑ̃] *ad* indubitably.

induire [ɛ̃dɥiʀ] *vt*: **~ qch de** to induce sth from; **~ qn en erreur** to lead sb astray, mislead sb.

indulgence [ɛ̃dylʒɑ̃s] *nf* indulgence; leniency; **avec ~** indulgently; leniently.

indulgent, e [ɛ̃dylʒɑ̃, -ɑ̃t] *a* (*parent, regard*) indulgent; (*juge, examinateur*) lenient.

indûment [ɛ̃dymɑ̃] *ad* without due cause; (*illégitimement*) wrongfully.

industrialisation [ɛ̃dystʀijalizasjɔ̃] *nf* industrialization.

industrialiser [ɛ̃dystʀijalize] *vt* to industrialize; **s'~** to become industrialized.

industrie [ɛ̃dystʀi] *nf* industry; **~ automobile/textile** car/textile industry; **~ du spectacle** entertainment business.

industriel, le [ɛ̃dystʀijɛl] *a* industrial; (*produit industriellement: pain etc*) mass-produced, factory-produced ♦ *nm* industrialist; (*fabricant*) manufacturer.

industriellement [ɛ̃dystʀijɛlmɑ̃] *ad* industrially.

industrieux, euse [ɛ̃dystʀijø, -øz] *a* industrious.

inébranlable [inebʀɑ̃labl(ə)] *a* (*masse, colonne*) solid; (*personne, certitude, foi*) steadfast, unwavering.

inédit, e [inedi, -it] *a* (*correspondance etc*) (hitherto) unpublished; (*spectacle, moyen*) novel, original.

ineffable [inefabl(ə)] *a* inexpressible, ineffable.

ineffaçable [inefasabl(ə)] *a* indelible.

inefficace [inefikas] *a* (*remède, moyen*) ineffective; (*machine, employé*) inefficient.

inefficacité [inefikasite] *nf* ineffectiveness; inefficiency.

inégal, e, aux [inegal, -o] *a* unequal; (*irrégulier*) uneven.

inégalable [inegalabl(e)] *a* matchless.

inégalé, e [inegale] *a* unmatched, unequalled.

inégalement [inegalmɑ̃] *ad* unequally.

inégalité [inegalite] *nf* inequality; unevenness *q*; **~ de 2 hauteurs** difference *ou* disparity between 2 heights; **~s de terrain** uneven ground.

inélégance [inelegɑ̃s] *nf* inelegance.

inélégant, e [inelegɑ̃, -ɑ̃t] *a* inelegant; (*in-*

délicat) discourteous.

inéligible [ineliʒibl(ə)] *a* ineligible.

inéluctable [inelyktabl(ə)] *a* inescapable.

inéluctablement [inelyktabləmɑ̃] *ad* inescapably.

inemployable [inɑ̃plwajabl(ə)] *a* unusable.

inemployé, e [inɑ̃plwaje] *a* unused.

inénarrable [inenaʀabl(ə)] *a* hilarious.

inepte [inɛpt(ə)] *a* inept.

ineptie [inɛpsi] *nf* ineptitude; (*propos*) nonsense *q*.

inépuisable [inepɥizabl(ə)] *a* inexhaustible.

inéquitable [inekitabl(ə)] *a* inequitable.

inerte [inɛʀt(ə)] *a* lifeless; (*apathique*) passive, inert; (*PHYSIQUE, CHIMIE*) inert.

inertie [inɛʀsi] *nf* inertia.

inescompté, e [inɛskɔ̃te] *a* unexpected, unhoped-for.

inespéré, e [inɛspeʀe] *a* unhoped-for, unexpected.

inesthétique [inɛstetik] *a* unsightly.

inestimable [inɛstimabl(e)] *a* priceless; (*fig: bienfait*) invaluable.

inévitable [inevitabl(ə)] *a* unavoidable; (*fatal, habituel*) inevitable.

inévitablement [inevitabləmɑ̃] *ad* inevitably.

inexact, e [inɛgzakt] *a* inaccurate, inexact; (*non ponctuel*) unpunctual.

inexactement [inɛgzaktəmɑ̃] *ad* inaccurately.

inexactitude [inɛgzaktityd] *nf* inaccuracy.

inexcusable [inɛkskyzabl(ə)] *a* inexcusable, unforgivable.

inexécutable [inɛgzekytabl(ə)] *a* impracticable, unworkable; (*MUS*) unplayable.

inexistant, e [inɛgzistɑ̃, -ɑ̃t] *a* non-existent.

inexorable [inɛgzɔʀabl(ə)] *a* inexorable; (*personne: dur*): **~ (à)** unmoved (by).

inexorablement [inɛgzɔʀabləmɑ̃] *ad* inexorably.

inexpérience [inɛkspeʀjɑ̃s] *nf* inexperience, lack of experience.

inexpérimenté, e [inɛkspeʀimɑ̃te] *a* inexperienced; (*arme, procédé*) untested.

inexplicable [inɛksplikabl(ə)] *a* inexplicable.

inexpliqué, e [inɛksplike] *a* unexplained.

inexploité, e [inɛksplwate] *a* unexploited, untapped.

inexploré, e [inɛksplɔʀe] *a* unexplored.

inexpressif, ive [inɛkspʀesif, -iv] *a* inexpressive; (*regard etc*) expressionless.

inexpressivité [inɛkspʀesivite] *nf* expressionlessness.

inexprimable [inɛkspʀimabl(ə)] *a* inexpressible.

inexprimé, e [inɛkspʀime] *a* unspoken, unexpressed.

inexpugnable [inɛkspygnabl(ə)] *a* impregnable.

inextensible [inɛkstɑ̃sibl(ə)] *a* (*tissu*) nonstretch.

in extenso [inɛkstɛ̃so] *ad* in full.

inextinguible [inɛkstɛ̃gibl(ə)] *a* (*soif*) unquenchable; (*rire*) uncontrollable.

in extremis [inɛkstʀemis] *ad* at the last minute ♦ *a* last-minute; (*testament*) death bed *cpd*.

inextricable [inɛkstʀikabl(ə)] *a* inextricable.

inextricablement [inɛkstʀikabləmɑ̃] *ad* inextricably.

infaillible [ɛ̃fajibl(ə)] *a* infallible; *(instinct)* infallible, unerring.

infailliblement [ɛ̃fajibləmɑ̃] *ad* (*certainement*) without fail.

infaisable [ɛ̃fəzabl(ə)] *a* (*travail etc*) impossible, impractical.

infamant, e [ɛ̃famɑ̃, -ɑ̃t] *a* libellous, defamatory.

infâme [ɛ̃fɑm] *a* vile.

infamie [ɛ̃fami] *nf* infamy.

infanterie [ɛ̃fɑ̃tʀi] *nf* infantry.

infanticide [ɛ̃fɑ̃tisid] *nm/f* child-murderer/eress ♦ *nm* (*meurtre*) infanticide.

infantile [ɛ̃fɑ̃til] *a* (*MÉD*) infantile, child *cpd*; (*péj: ton, réaction*) infantile, childish.

infantilisme [ɛ̃fɑ̃tilism(ə)] *nm* infantilism.

infarctus [ɛ̃faʀktys] *nm*: ~ **(du myocarde)** coronary (thrombosis).

infatigable [ɛ̃fatigabl(ə)] *a* tireless, indefatigable.

infatué, e [ɛ̃fatɥe] *a* conceited; ~ **de** full of.

infécond, e [ɛ̃fekɔ̃, -ɔ̃d] *a* infertile, barren.

infect, e [ɛ̃fɛkt] *a* vile, foul; (*repas, vin*) revolting, foul.

infecter [ɛ̃fɛkte] *vt* (*atmosphère, eau*) to contaminate; (*MÉD*) to infect; **s'~** to become infected *ou* septic.

infectieux, euse [ɛ̃fɛksjø, -øz] *a* infectious.

infection [ɛ̃fɛksjɔ̃] *nf* infection.

inféoder [ɛ̃feɔde] *vt*: **s'~ à** to pledge allegiance to.

inférer [ɛ̃feʀe] *vt*: ~ **qch de** to infer sth from.

inférieur, e [ɛ̃feʀjœʀ] *a* lower; (*en qualité, intelligence*) inferior ♦ *nm/f* inferior; ~ **à** (*somme, quantité*) less *ou* smaller than; (*moins bon que*) inferior to; (*tâche: pas à la hauteur de*) unequal to.

infériorité [ɛ̃feʀjɔʀite] *nf* inferiority; ~ **en nombre** inferiority in numbers.

infernal, e, aux [ɛ̃fɛʀnal, -o] *a* (*chaleur, rythme*) infernal; (*méchanceté, complot*) diabolical.

infester [ɛ̃fɛste] *vt* to infest; **infesté de moustiques** infested with mosquitoes, mosquito-ridden.

infidèle [ɛ̃fidɛl] *a* unfaithful; (*REL*) infidel.

infidélité [ɛ̃fidelite] *nf* unfaithfulness *q*.

infiltration [ɛ̃filtʀasjɔ̃] *nf* infiltration.

infiltrer [ɛ̃filtʀe]: **s'~** *vi*: **s'~ dans** to penetrate into; (*liquide*) to seep into; (*fig: noyauter*) to infiltrate.

infime [ɛ̃fim] *a* minute, tiny; (*inférieur*) lowly.

infini, e [ɛ̃fini] *a* infinite ♦ *nm* infinity; **à l'~** (*MATH*) to infinity; (*discourir*) ad infinitum, endlessly; (*agrandir, varier*) infinitely; (*à perte de vue*) endlessly (into the distance).

infiniment [ɛ̃finimɑ̃] *ad* infinitely; ~ **grand/petit** (*MATH*) infinitely great/infinitesimal.

infinité [ɛ̃finite] *nf*: **une ~ de** an infinite number of.

infinitésimal, e, aux [ɛ̃finitezimal, -o] *a* infinitessimal.

infinitif, ive [ɛ̃finitif, -iv] *a, nm* infinitive.

infirme [ɛ̃fiʀm(ə)] *a* disabled ♦ *nm/f* disabled person; ~ **mental** mentally-handicapped person; ~ **moteur** spastic; ~ **de guerre** war cripple; ~ **du travail** industrially disabled person.

infirmer [ɛ̃fiʀme] *vt* to invalidate.

infirmerie [ɛ̃fiʀməʀi] *nf* sick bay.

infirmier, ière [ɛ̃fiʀmje, -jɛʀ] *nm/f* nurse ♦ *a*: **élève ~** student nurse; **infirmière chef** sister; **infirmière diplômée** registered nurse; **infirmière visiteuse** ≈ district nurse.

infirmité [ɛ̃fiʀmite] *nf* disability.

inflammable [ɛ̃flamabl(ə)] *a* (in)flammable.

inflammation [ɛ̃flamɑsjɔ̃] *nf* inflammation.

inflammatoire [ɛ̃flamatwaʀ] *a* (*MÉD*) inflammatory.

inflation [ɛ̃flɑsjɔ̃] *nf* inflation; ~ **rampante/galopante** creeping/galloping inflation.

inflationniste [ɛ̃flɑsjɔnist(ə)] *a* inflationist.

infléchir [ɛ̃fleʃiʀ] *vt* (*fig: politique*) to reorientate, redirect; **s'~** *vi* (*poutre, tringle*) to bend, sag.

inflexibilité [ɛ̃flɛksibilite] *nf* inflexibility.

inflexible [ɛ̃flɛksibl(ə)] *a* inflexible.

inflexion [ɛ̃flɛksjɔ̃] *nf* inflexion; ~ **de la tête** slight nod (of the head).

infliger [ɛ̃fliʒe] *vt*: ~ **qch (à qn)** to inflict sth (on sb); (*amende, sanction*) to impose sth (on sb).

influençable [ɛ̃flyɑ̃sabl(ə)] *a* easily influenced.

influence [ɛ̃flyɑ̃s] *nf* influence; (*d'un médicament*) effect.

influencer [ɛ̃flyɑ̃se] *vt* to influence.

influent, e [ɛ̃flyɑ̃, -ɑ̃t] *a* influential.

influer [ɛ̃flye]: ~ **sur** *vt* to have an influence upon.

influx [ɛ̃fly] *nm*: ~ **nerveux** (nervous) impulse.

infographie [ɛ̃fɔgʀafi] *nf* computer graphics *sg*.

informateur, trice [ɛ̃fɔʀmatœʀ, -tʀis] *nm/f* informant.

informaticien, ne [ɛ̃fɔʀmatisjɛ̃, -ɛn] *nm/f* computer scientist.

informatif, ive [ɛ̃fɔʀmatif, -iv] *a* informative.

information [ɛ̃fɔʀmɑsjɔ̃] *nf* (*renseignement*) piece of information; (*PRESSE, TV: nouvelle*) item of news; (*diffusion de renseignements, INFORM*) information; (*JUR*) inquiry, investigation; ~**s** *nfpl* (*TV*) news *sg*; **voyage d'~** fact-finding trip; **agence d'~** news agency; **journal d'~** quality (*Brit*) *ou* serious newspaper.

informatique [ɛ̃fɔʀmatik] *nf* (*technique*) data processing; (*science*) computer science ♦ *a* computer *cpd*.

informatisation [ɛ̃fɔʀmatizɑsjɔ̃] *nf* computerization.

informatiser [ɛ̃fɔʀmatize] *vt* to computerize.

informe [ɛ̃fɔʀm(ə)] *a* shapeless.

informé, e [ɛ̃fɔʀme] *a*: **jusqu'à plus ample ~** until further information is available.

informer [ɛ̃fɔʀme] *vt*: ~ **qn (de)** to inform sb (of) ♦ *vi* (*JUR*): ~ **contre qn/sur qch** to initiate inquiries about sb/sth; **s'~ (sur)** to inform o.s. (about); **s'~ (de qch/si)** to inquire *ou* find out (about sth/whether *ou* if).

informulé, e [ɛ̃fɔʀmyle] *a* unformulated.

infortune [ɛ̃fɔʀtyn] *nf* misfortune.

infos [ɛ̃fo] *nfpl* (= *informations*) news.

infraction [ɛ̃fʀaksjɔ̃] *nf* offence; ~ **à** violation *ou* breach of; **être en ~** to be in breach of the law.

infranchissable [ɛ̃fʀɑ̃ʃisabl(ə)] *a* impassable; (*fig*) insuperable.

infrarouge [ɛ̃fraruʒ] *a, nm* infrared.

infrason [ɛ̃frasɔ̃] *nm* infrasonic vibration.

infrastructure [ɛ̃frastryktyr] *nf* (*d'une route etc*) substructure; (*AVIAT, MIL*) ground installations *pl*; (*touristique etc*) facilities.

infréquentable [ɛ̃frekɑ̃tabl(ə)] *a* not to be associated with.

infroissable [ɛ̃frwasabl(ə)] *a* crease-resistant.

infructueux, euse [ɛ̃fryktɥø, -øz] *a* fruitless, unfruitful.

infus, e [ɛ̃fy, -yz] *a*: **avoir la science ~e** to have innate knowledge.

infuser [ɛ̃fyze] *vt* (*aussi*: **faire ~**: *thé*) to brew; (: *tisane*) to infuse ♦ *vi* to brew; to infuse; **laisser ~** (to leave) to brew.

infusion [ɛ̃fyzjɔ̃] *nf* (*tisane*) infusion, herb tea.

ingambe [ɛ̃gɑ̃b] *a* spry, nimble.

ingénier [ɛ̃ʒenje]: **s'~** *vi*: **s'~ à faire** to strive to do.

ingénierie [ɛ̃ʒeniri] *nf* engineering.

ingénieur [ɛ̃ʒenjœr] *nm* engineer; **~ agronome/chimiste** agricultural/chemical engineer; **~ conseil** consulting engineer; **~ du son** sound engineer.

ingénieusement [ɛ̃ʒenjøzmɑ̃] *ad* ingeniously.

ingénieux, euse [ɛ̃ʒenjø, -øz] *a* ingenious, clever.

ingéniosité [ɛ̃ʒenjozite] *nf* ingenuity.

ingénu, e [ɛ̃ʒeny] *a* ingenuous, artless ♦ *nf* (*THÉÂTRE*) ingénue.

ingénuité [ɛ̃ʒenɥite] *nf* ingenuousness.

ingénument [ɛ̃ʒenymɑ̃] *ad* ingenuously.

ingérence [ɛ̃ʒerɑ̃s] *nf* interference.

ingérer [ɛ̃ʒere]: **s'~** *vi*: **s'~ dans** to interfere in.

ingouvernable [ɛ̃guvɛrnabl(ə)] *a* ungovernable.

ingrat, e [ɛ̃gra, -at] *a* (*personne*) ungrateful; (*sol*) poor; (*travail, sujet*) arid, thankless; (*visage*) unprepossessing.

ingratitude [ɛ̃gratityd] *nf* ingratitude.

ingrédient [ɛ̃gredjɑ̃] *nm* ingredient.

inguérissable [ɛ̃gerisabl(ə)] *a* incurable.

ingurgiter [ɛ̃gyrʒite] *vt* to swallow; **faire ~ qch à qn** to make sb swallow sth; (*fig*: *connaissances*) to force sth into sb.

inhabile [inabil] *a* clumsy; (*fig*) inept.

inhabitable [inabitabl(ə)] *a* uninhabitable.

inhabité, e [inabite] *a* (*régions*) uninhabited; (*maison*) unoccupied.

inhabituel, le [inabitɥɛl] *a* unusual.

inhalateur [inalatœr] *nm* inhaler; **~ d'oxygène** oxygen mask.

inhalation [inalasjɔ̃] *nf* (*MÉD*) inhalation; **faire des ~s** to use an inhalation bath.

inhaler [inale] *vt* to inhale.

inhérent, e [inerɑ̃, -ɑ̃t] *a*: **~ à** inherent in.

inhiber [inibe] *vt* to inhibit.

inhibition [inibisjɔ̃] *nf* inhibition.

inhospitalier, ière [inɔspitalje, -jɛr] *a* inhospitable.

inhumain, e [inymɛ̃, -ɛn] *a* inhuman.

inhumation [inymasjɔ̃] *nf* interment, burial.

inhumer [inyme] *vt* to inter, bury.

inimaginable [inimaʒinabl(ə)] *a* unimaginable.

inimitable [inimitabl(ə)] *a* inimitable.

inimitié [inimitje] *nf* enmity.

ininflammable [inɛ̃flamabl(ə)] *a* nonflammable.

inintelligent, e [inɛ̃teliʒɑ̃, -ɑ̃t] *a* unintelligent.

inintelligible [inɛ̃teliʒibl(ə)] *a* unintelligible.

inintéressant, e [inɛ̃teresɑ̃, -ɑ̃t] *a* uninteresting.

ininterrompu, e [inɛ̃terɔ̃py] *a* (*file, série*) unbroken; (*flot, vacarme*) uninterrupted, nonstop; (*effort*) unremitting, continuous.

iniquité [inikite] *nf* iniquity.

initial, e, aux [inisjal, -o] *a, nf* initial; **~es** *nfpl* initials.

initialement [inisjalmɑ̃] *ad* initially.

initialiser [inisjalize] *vt* to initialize.

initiateur, trice [inisjatœr, -tris] *nm/f* initiator; (*d'une mode, technique*) innovator, pioneer.

initiation [inisjasjɔ̃] *nf* initiation.

initiatique [inisjatik] *a* (*rites, épreuves*) initiatory.

initiative [inisjativ] *nf* initiative; **prendre l'~ de qch/de faire** to take the initiative for sth/of doing; **avoir de l'~** to have initiative, show enterprise; **esprit/qualités d'~** spirit/qualities of initiative; **à** *ou* **sur l'~ de qn** on sb's initiative; **de sa propre ~** on one's own initiative.

initié, e [inisje] *a* initiated ♦ *nm/f* initiate.

initier [inisje] *vt* to initiate; **~ qn à** to initiate sb into; (*faire découvrir*: *art, jeu*) to introduce sb to; **s'~ à** (*métier, profession, technique*) to become initiated into.

injecté, e [ɛ̃ʒɛkte] *a*: **yeux ~s de sang** bloodshot eyes.

injecter [ɛ̃ʒɛkte] *vt* to inject.

injection [ɛ̃ʒɛksjɔ̃] *nf* injection; **à ~** (*AUTO*) fuel injection *cpd*.

injonction [ɛ̃ʒɔ̃ksjɔ̃] *nf* injunction, order; **~ de payer** (*JUR*) order to pay.

injouable [ɛ̃ʒwabl(ə)] *a* unplayable.

injure [ɛ̃ʒyr] *nf* insult, abuse *q*.

injurier [ɛ̃ʒyrje] *vt* to insult, abuse.

injurieux, euse [ɛ̃ʒyrjø, -øz] *a* abusive, insulting.

injuste [ɛ̃ʒyst(ə)] *a* unjust, unfair.

injustement [ɛ̃ʒystəmɑ̃] *ad* unjustly, unfairly.

injustice [ɛ̃ʒystis] *nf* injustice.

injustifiable [ɛ̃ʒystifjabl(ə)] *a* unjustifiable.

injustifié, e [ɛ̃ʒystifje] *a* unjustified, unwarranted.

inlassable [ɛ̃lasabl(ə)] *a* tireless, indefatigable.

inné, e [ine] *a* innate, inborn.

innocemment [inɔsamɑ̃] *ad* innocently.

innocence [inɔsɑ̃s] *nf* innocence.

innocent, e [inɔsɑ̃, -ɑ̃t] *a* innocent ♦ *nm/f* innocent person; **faire l'~** to play *ou* come the innocent.

innocenter [inɔsɑ̃te] *vt* to clear, prove innocent.

innocuité [inɔkɥite] *nf* innocuousness.

innombrable [inɔ̃brabl(ə)] *a* innumerable.

innommable [inɔmabl(ə)] *a* unspeakable.

innovateur, trice [inɔvatœr, -tris] *a* innovatory.

innovation [inɔvasjɔ̃] *nf* innovation.

innover [inɔve] *vi*: **~ en matière d'art** to break new ground in the field of art.

inobservance [inɔpsɛrvɑ̃s] *nf* non-observance.

inobservation [inɔpsɛrvasjɔ̃] *nf* nonobservation, inobservance.

inoccupé, e [inɔkype] *a* unoccupied.

inoculer [inɔkyle] *vt*: ~ **qch à qn** (*volontairement*) to inoculate sb with sth; (*accidentellement*) to infect sb with sth; ~ **qn contre** to inoculate sb against.

inodore [inɔdɔʀ] *a* (*gaz*) odourless; (*fleur*) scentless.

inoffensif, ive [inɔfɑ̃sif, -iv] *a* harmless, innocuous.

inondable [inɔ̃dabl(ə)] *a* (*zone etc*) liable to flooding.

inondation [inɔ̃dasjɔ̃] *nf* flooding *q*; (*torrent, eau*) flood.

inonder [inɔ̃de] *vt* to flood; (*fig*) to inundate, overrun; ~ **de** (*fig*) to flood *ou* swamp with.

inopérable [inɔpeʀabl(ə)] *a* inoperable.

inopérant, e [inɔpeʀɑ̃, -ɑ̃t] *a* inoperative, ineffective.

inopiné, e [inɔpine] *a* unexpected, sudden.

inopinément [inɔpinemɑ̃] *ad* unexpectedly.

inopportun, e [inɔpɔʀtœ̃, -yn] *a* ill-timed, untimely; inappropriate; (*moment*) inopportune.

inorganisation [inɔʀganizasjɔ̃] *nf* lack of organization.

inorganisé, e [inɔʀganize] *a* (*travailleurs*) non-organized.

inoubliable [inublijabl(ə)] *a* unforgettable.

inouï, e [inwi] *a* unheard-of, extraordinary.

inox [inɔks] *a, nm* (= *inoxydable*) stainless (steel).

inoxydable [inɔksidabl(ə)] *a* stainless; (*couverts*) stainless steel *cpd*.

inqualifiable [ɛ̃kalifjabl(ə)] *a* unspeakable.

inquiet, ète [ɛ̃kjɛ, -ɛt] *a* (*par nature*) anxious; (*momentanément*) worried; ~ **de qch/au sujet de qn** worried about sth/sb.

inquiétant, e [ɛ̃kjetɑ̃, -ɑ̃t] *a* worrying, disturbing.

inquiéter [ɛ̃kjete] *vt* to worry, disturb; (*harceler*) to harass; **s'~** to worry, become anxious; **s'~ de** to worry about; (*s'enquérir de*) to inquire about.

inquiétude [ɛ̃kjetyd] *nf* anxiety; **donner de l'~ ou des ~s à** to worry; **avoir de l'~ ou des ~s au sujet de** to feel anxious *ou* worried about.

inquisiteur, trice [ɛ̃kizitœʀ, -tʀis] *a* (*regards, questions*) inquisitive, prying.

inquisition [ɛ̃kizisjɔ̃] *nf* inquisition.

INR *sigle m* = *Institut national (belge) de radiodiffusion*.

INRA [inʀa] *sigle m* = *Institut national de la recherche agronomique*.

insaisissable [ɛ̃sezisabl(ə)] *a* elusive.

insalubre [ɛ̃salybʀ(ə)] *a* insalubrious, unhealthy.

insanité [ɛ̃sanite] *nf* madness *q*, insanity *q*.

insatiable [ɛ̃sasjabl(ə)] *a* insatiable.

insatisfaction [ɛ̃satisfaksjɔ̃] *nf* dissatisfaction.

insatisfait, e [ɛ̃satisfɛ, -ɛt] *a* (*non comblé*) unsatisfied; (: *passion, envie*) unfulfilled; (*mécontent*) dissatisfied.

inscription [ɛ̃skʀipsjɔ̃] *nf* (*sur un mur, écriteau etc*) inscription; (*à une institution: voir s'inscrire*) enrolment; registration.

inscrire [ɛ̃skʀiʀ] *vt* (*marquer: sur son calepin etc*) to note *ou* write down; (: *sur un mur, une affiche etc*) to write; (: *dans la pierre, le métal*) to inscribe; (*mettre: sur une liste, un*

budget *etc*) to put down; (*enrôler: soldat*) to enlist; ~ **qn à** (*club, école etc*) to enrol sb at; **s'~** (*pour une excursion etc*) to put one's name down; **s'~ (à)** (*club, parti*) to join; (*université*) to register *ou* enrol (at); (*examen, concours*) to register *ou* enter (for); **s'~ dans** (*se situer: négociations etc*) to come within the scope of; **s'~ en faux contre** to deny (strongly); (*JUR*) to challenge.

inscrit, e [ɛ̃skʀi, it] *pp de* **inscrire** ♦ *a* (*étudiant, électeur etc*) registered.

insecte [ɛ̃sɛkt(ə)] *nm* insect.

insecticide [ɛ̃sɛktisid] *nm* insecticide.

insécurité [ɛ̃sekyʀite] *nf* insecurity, lack of security.

INSEE [inse] *sigle m* (= *Institut national de la statistique et des études économiques*) national institute of statistical and economic information.

insémination [ɛ̃seminasjɔ̃] *nf* insemination.

insensé, e [ɛ̃sɑ̃se] *a* insane, mad.

insensibiliser [ɛ̃sɑ̃sibilize] *vt* to anaesthetize; (*à une allergie*) to desensitize; ~ **à qch** (*fig*) to cause to become insensitive to sth.

insensibilité [ɛ̃sɑ̃sibilite] *nf* insensitivity.

insensible [ɛ̃sɑ̃sibl(ə)] *a* (*nerf, membre*) numb; (*dur, indifférent*) insensitive; (*imperceptible*) imperceptible.

insensiblement [ɛ̃sɑ̃sibləmɑ̃] *ad* (*doucement, peu à peu*) imperceptibly.

inséparable [ɛ̃sepaʀabl(ə)] *a*: ~ **(de)** inseparable (from) ♦ *nmpl*: **~s** (*oiseaux*) lovebirds.

insérer [ɛ̃seʀe] *vt* to insert; **s'~ dans** to fit into; (*fig*) to come within.

INSERM [ɛ̃sɛʀm] *sigle m* (= *Institut national de la santé et de la recherche médicale*) national institute for medical research.

insert [ɛ̃sɛʀ] *nm* enclosed fireplace burning solid fuel.

insertion [ɛ̃sɛʀsjɔ̃] *nf* (*d'une personne*) integration.

insidieusement [ɛ̃sidjøzmɑ̃] *ad* insidiously.

insidieux, euse [ɛ̃sidjø, -øz] *a* insidious.

insigne [ɛ̃siɲ] *nm* (*d'un parti, club*) badge ♦ *a* distinguished; **~s** *nmpl* (*d'une fonction*) insignia *pl*.

insignifiant, e [ɛ̃siɲifjɑ̃, -ɑ̃t] *a* insignificant; (*somme, affaire, détail*) trivial, insignificant.

insinuant, e [ɛ̃sinɥɑ̃, -ɑ̃t] *a* ingratiating.

insinuation [ɛ̃sinɥasjɔ̃] *nf* innuendo, insinuation.

insinuer [ɛ̃sinɥe] *vt* to insinuate, imply; **s'~ dans** to seep into; (*fig*) to worm one's way into, creep into.

insipide [ɛ̃sipid] *a* insipid.

insistance [ɛ̃sistɑ̃s] *nf* insistence; **avec ~** insistently.

insistant, e [ɛ̃sistɑ̃, -ɑ̃t] *a* insistent.

insister [ɛ̃siste] *vi* to insist; (*s'obstiner*) to keep on; ~ **sur** (*détail, note*) to stress; ~ **pour qch/pour faire qch** to be insistent about sth/about doing sth.

insociable [ɛ̃sɔsjabl(ə)] *a* unsociable.

insolation [ɛ̃sɔlasjɔ̃] *nf* (*MÉD*) sunstroke *q*; (*ensoleillement*) period of sunshine.

insolence [ɛ̃sɔlɑ̃s] *nf* insolence *q*; **avec ~** insolently.

insolent, e [ɛ̃sɔlɑ̃, -ɑ̃t] *a* insolent.

insolite [ɛ̃sɔlit] *a* strange, unusual.

insoluble [ɛ̃sɔlybl(ə)] *a* insoluble.

insolvable [ɛ̃sɔlvabl(ə)] *a* insolvent.

insomniaque [ɛ̃sɔmnjak] *a*, *nm/f* insomniac.

insomnie [ɛ̃sɔmni] *nf* insomnia *q*, sleeplessness *q*; **avoir des ~s** to suffer from insomnia.

insondable [ɛ̃sɔ̃dabl(ə)] *a* unfathomable.

insonore [ɛ̃sɔnɔR] *a* soundproof.

insonorisation [ɛ̃sɔnɔRizasjɔ̃] *nf* sound-proofing.

insonoriser [ɛ̃sɔnɔRize] *vt* to soundproof.

insouciance [ɛ̃susjɑ̃s] *nf* carefree attitude; heedless attitude.

insouciant, e [ɛ̃susjɑ̃, -ɑ̃t] *a* carefree; (*imprévoyant*) heedless.

insoumis, e [ɛ̃sumi, -iz] *a* (*caractère, enfant*) rebellious, refractory; (*contrée, tribu*) unsubdued; (*MIL: soldat*) absent without leave ♦ *nm* (*MIL: soldat*) absentee.

insoumission [ɛ̃sumisjɔ̃] *nf* rebelliousness; (*MIL*) absence without leave.

insoupçonnable [ɛ̃supsɔnabl(ə)] *a* above suspicion.

insoupçonné, e [ɛ̃supsɔne] *a* unsuspected.

insoutenable [ɛ̃sutnabl(ə)] *a* (*argument*) untenable; (*chaleur*) unbearable.

inspecter [ɛ̃spɛkte] *vt* to inspect.

inspecteur, trice [ɛ̃spɛktœR, -tRis] *nm/f* inspector; (*des assurances*) assessor; **~ d'Académie** (regional) director of education; **~ (de l'enseignement) primaire** primary school inspector; **~ des finances** ≈ tax inspector (*Brit*), ≈ Internal Revenue Service agent (*US*); **~ (de police)** (police) inspector.

inspection [ɛ̃spɛksjɔ̃] *nf* inspection.

inspirateur, trice [ɛ̃spiRatœR, -tRis] *nm/f* (*instigateur*) instigator; (*animateur*) inspirer.

inspiration [ɛ̃spiRasjɔ̃] *nf* inspiration; breathing in *q*; (*idée*) flash of inspiration, brainwave; **sous l'~ de** prompted by.

inspiré, e [ɛ̃spiRe] *a*: **être bien/mal ~ de faire qch** to be well-advised/ill-advised to do sth.

inspirer [ɛ̃spiRe] *vt* (*gén*) to inspire ♦ *vi* (*aspirer*) to breathe in; **s'~ de** (*suj: artiste*) to draw one's inspiration from; (*suj: tableau*) to be inspired by; **~ qch à qn** (*œuvre, project, action*) to inspire sb with sth; (*dégoût, crainte, horreur*) to fill sb with sth; **ça ne m'inspire pas** I'm not keen on the idea.

instabilité [ɛ̃stabilite] *nf* instability.

instable [ɛ̃stabl(ə)] *a* (*meuble, équilibre*) unsteady; (*population, temps*) unsettled; (*paix, régime, caractère*) unstable.

installateur [ɛ̃stalatœR] *nm* fitter.

installation [ɛ̃stalasjɔ̃] *nf* installation; putting in *ou* up; fitting out; settling in; (*appareils etc*) fittings *pl*, installations *pl*; **~s** *nfpl* installations; (*industrielles*) plant *sg*; (*de loisirs*) facilities.

installé, e [ɛ̃stale] *a*: **bien/mal ~** well/poorly equipped; (*personne*) well/not very well set up *ou* organized.

installer [ɛ̃stale] *vt* (*loger*): **~ qn** to get sb settled, install sb; (*asseoir, coucher*) to settle (down); (*placer*) to put, place; (*meuble*) to put in; (*rideau, étagère, tente*) to put up; (*gaz, électricité etc*) to put in, install; (*appartement*) to fit out; (*aménager*): **~ une salle de bains dans une pièce** to fit out a

room with a bathroom suite; **s'~** (*s'établir: artisan, dentiste etc*) to set o.s. up; (*se loger*): **s'~ à l'hôtel/chez qn** to move into a hotel/in with sb; (*emménager*) to settle in; (*sur un siège, à un emplacement*) to settle (down); (*fig: maladie, grève*) to take a firm hold *ou* grip.

instamment [ɛ̃stamɑ̃] *ad* urgently.

instance [ɛ̃stɑ̃s] *nf* (*JUR: procédure*) (legal) proceedings *pl*; (*ADMIN: autorité*) authority; **~s** *nfpl* (*prières*) entreaties; **affaire en ~** matter pending; **courrier en ~** mail ready for posting; **être en ~ de divorce** to be awaiting a divorce; **train en ~ de départ** train on the point of departure; **tribunal de première ~** court of first instance; **en seconde ~** on appeal.

instant [ɛ̃stɑ̃] *nm* moment, instant; **dans un ~** in a moment; **à l'~** this instant; **je l'ai vu à l'~** I've just this minute seen him, I saw him a moment ago; **à l'~ (même) où** at the (very) moment that *ou* when, (just) as; **à chaque ~, à tout ~** at any moment; constantly; **pour l'~** for the moment, for the time being; **par ~s** at times; **de tous les ~s** perpetual; **dès l'~ où** *ou* **que ...** from the moment when ..., since that moment when ....

instantané, e [ɛ̃stɑ̃tane] *a* (*lait, café*) instant; (*explosion, mort*) instantaneous ♦ *nm* snapshot.

instantanément [ɛ̃stɑ̃tanemɑ̃] *ad* instantaneously.

instar [ɛ̃staR]: **à l'~ de** *prép* following the example of, like.

instaurer [ɛ̃stɔRe] *vt* to institute; **s'~** *vi* to set o.s. up; (*collaboration etc*) to be established.

instigateur, trice [ɛ̃stigatœR, -tRis] *nm/f* instigator.

instigation [ɛ̃stigasjɔ̃] *nf*: **à l'~ de qn** at sb's instigation.

instiller [ɛ̃stile] *vt* to instil, apply.

instinct [ɛ̃stɛ̃] *nm* instinct; **d'~** (*spontanément*) instinctively; **~ grégaire** herd instinct; **~ de conservation** instinct of self-preservation.

instinctif, ive [ɛ̃stɛ̃ktif, -iv] *a* instinctive.

instinctivement [ɛ̃stɛ̃ktivmɑ̃] *ad* instinctively.

instituer [ɛ̃stitɥe] *vt* to institute, set up; **s'~ défenseur d'une cause** to set o.s up as defender of a cause.

institut [ɛ̃stity] *nm* institute; **~ de beauté** beauty salon; **~ médico-légal** mortuary; **I~ universitaire de technologie (IUT)** technical college.

instituteur, trice [ɛ̃stitytœR, -tRis] *nm/f* (primary (*Brit*) *ou* grade (*US*) school) teacher.

institution [ɛ̃stitysjɔ̃] *nf* institution; (*collège*) private school.

institutionnaliser [ɛ̃stitysjɔnalize] *vt* to institutionalize.

instructeur, trice [ɛ̃stRyktœR, -tRis] *a* (*MIL*): **sergent ~** drill sergeant; (*JUR*): **juge ~** examining (*Brit*) *ou* committing (*US*) magistrate ♦ *nm/f* instructor.

instructif, ive [ɛ̃stRyktif, -iv] *a* instructive.

instruction [ɛ̃stRyksjɔ̃] *nf* (*enseignement, savoir*) education; (*JUR*) (preliminary) investigation and hearing; (*directive*) instruction; (*ADMIN*: *document*) directive; **~s** *nfpl* instructions; (*mode d'emploi*) directions, instructions; **~ civique** civics *sg*; **~ primaire/ publique** primary/public education; **~ religieuse** religious instruction; **~ professionnelle** vocational training.

instruire [ɛ̃stʀɥiʀ] *vt* (*élèves*) to teach; (*recrues*) to train; (*JUR*: *affaire*) to conduct the investigation for; **s'~** to educate o.s.; **s'~ auprès de qn de qch** (*s'informer*) to find sth out from sb; **~ qn de qch** (*informer*) to inform *ou* advise sb of sth; **~ contre qn** (*JUR*) to investigate sb.

instruit, e [ɛ̃stʀɥi, -it] *pp de* **instruire ♦** *a* educated.

instrument [ɛ̃stʀymɑ̃] *nm* instrument; **~ à cordes/vent** stringed/wind instrument; **~ de mesure** measuring instrument; **~ de musique** musical instrument; **~ de travail** (working) tool.

instrumental, e, aux [ɛ̃stʀymɑ̃tal, -o] *a* instrumental.

instrumentation [ɛ̃stʀymɑ̃tasjɔ̃] *nf* instrumentation.

instrumentiste [ɛ̃stʀymɑ̃tist(ə)] *nm/f* instrumentalist.

insu [ɛ̃sy] *nm*: **à l'~ de qn** without sb knowing.

insubmersible [ɛ̃sybmɛʀsibl(ə)] *a* unsinkable.

insubordination [ɛ̃sybɔʀdinasjɔ̃] *nf* rebelliousness; (*MIL*) insubordination.

insubordonné, e [ɛ̃sybɔʀdɔne] *a* insubordinate.

insuccès [ɛ̃syksɛ] *nm* failure.

insuffisamment [ɛ̃syfizamɑ̃] *ad* insufficiently.

insuffisance [ɛ̃syfizɑ̃s] *nf* insufficiency; inadequacy; **~s** *nfpl* (*lacunes*) inadequacies; **~ cardiaque** cardiac insufficiency *q*; **~ hépatique** liver deficiency.

insuffisant, e [ɛ̃syfizɑ̃, -ɑ̃t] *a* insufficient; (*élève, travail*) inadequate.

insuffler [ɛ̃syfle] *vt*: **~ qch dans** to blow sth into; **~ qch à qn** to inspire sb with sth.

insulaire [ɛ̃sylɛʀ] *a* island *cpd*; (*attitude*) insular.

insularité [ɛ̃sylaʀite] *nf* insularity.

insuline [ɛ̃sylin] *nf* insulin.

insultant, e [ɛ̃syltɑ̃, -ɑ̃t] *a* insulting.

insulte [ɛ̃sylt(ə)] *nf* insult.

insulter [ɛ̃sylte] *vt* to insult.

insupportable [ɛ̃sypɔʀtabl(ə)] *a* unbearable.

insurgé, e [ɛ̃syʀʒe] *a, nm/f* insurgent, rebel.

insurger [ɛ̃syʀʒe]: **s'~** *vi*: **s'~** (**contre**) to rise up *ou* rebel (against).

insurmontable [ɛ̃syʀmɔ̃tabl(ə)] *a* (*difficulté*) insuperable; (*aversion*) unconquerable.

insurpassable [ɛ̃syʀpasabl(ə)] *a* unsurpassable, unsurpassed.

insurrection [ɛ̃syʀɛksjɔ̃] *nf* insurrection, revolt.

insurrectionnel, le [ɛ̃syʀɛksjɔnɛl] *a* insurrectionary.

intact, e [ɛ̃takt] *a* intact.

intangible [ɛ̃tɑ̃ʒibl(ə)] *a* intangible; (*principe*) inviolable.

intarissable [ɛ̃taʀisabl(ə)] *a* inexhaustible.

intégral, e, aux [ɛ̃tegʀal, -o] *a* complete ♦ *nf* (*MATH*) integral; (*œuvres complètes*) complete works.

intégralement [ɛ̃tegʀalmɑ̃] *ad* in full, fully.

intégralité [ɛ̃tegʀalite] *nf* (*d'une somme, d'un revenu*) whole (*ou* full) amount; **dans son ~** in its entirety.

intégrant, e [ɛ̃tegʀɑ̃, -ɑ̃t] *a*: **faire partie ~e de** to be an integral part of, be part and parcel of.

intégration [ɛ̃tegʀasjɔ̃] *nf* integration.

intégrationniste [ɛ̃tegʀasjɔnist(ə)] *a, nm/f* integrationist.

intègre [ɛ̃tɛgʀ(ə)] *a* perfectly honest, upright.

intégré, e [ɛ̃tegʀe] *a*: **circuit ~** integrated circuit.

intégrer [ɛ̃tegʀe] *vt*: **~ qch à** *ou* **dans** to integrate sth into; **s'~ à** *ou* **dans** to become integrated into.

intégrisme [ɛ̃tegʀism(ə)] *nm* fundamentalism.

intégriste [ɛ̃tegʀist(ə)] *a, nm/f* fundamentalist.

intégrité [ɛ̃tegʀite] *nf* integrity.

intellect [ɛ̃telɛkt] *nm* intellect.

intellectualisme [ɛ̃telɛkyalism(ə)] *nm* intellectualism.

intellectuel, le [ɛ̃telɛktyɛl] *a, nm/f* intellectual; (*péj*) highbrow.

intellectuellement [ɛ̃telɛktyɛlmɑ̃] *ad* intellectually.

intelligemment [ɛ̃teliʒamɑ̃] *ad* intelligently.

intelligence [ɛ̃teliʒɑ̃s] *nf* intelligence; (*compréhension*): **l'~ de** the understanding of; (*complicité*): **regard d'~** glance of complicity, meaningful *ou* knowing look; (*accord*): **vivre en bonne ~ avec qn** to be on good terms with sb; **~s** *nfpl* (*MIL, fig*) secret contacts; **être d'~** to have an understanding; **~ artificielle** artificial intelligence (A.I.).

intelligent, e [ɛ̃teliʒɑ̃, -ɑ̃t] *a* intelligent; (*capable*): **~ en affaires** competent in business.

intelligentsia [ɛ̃telidʒɛnsja] *nf* intelligentsia.

intelligible [ɛ̃teliʒibl(ə)] *a* intelligible.

intello [ɛ̃telo] *a, nm/f* (*fam*) highbrow.

intempérance [ɛ̃tɑ̃peʀɑ̃s] *nf* overindulgence *q*; intemperance *q*.

intempérant, e [ɛ̃tɑ̃peʀɑ̃, -ɑ̃t] *a* overindulgent; (*moralement*) intemperate.

intempéries [ɛ̃tɑ̃peʀi] *nfpl* bad weather *sg*.

intempestif, ive [ɛ̃tɑ̃pɛstif, -iv] *a* untimely.

intenable [ɛ̃tnabl(ə)] *a* unbearable.

intendance [ɛ̃tɑ̃dɑ̃s] *nf* (*MIL*) supply corps; (: *bureau*) supplies office; (*SCOL*) bursar's office.

intendant, e [ɛ̃tɑ̃dɑ̃, -ɑ̃t] *nm/f* (*MIL*) quartermaster; (*SCOL*) bursar; (*d'une propriété*) steward.

intense [ɛ̃tɑ̃s] *a* intense.

intensément [ɛ̃tɑ̃semɑ̃] *ad* intensely.

intensif, ive [ɛ̃tɑ̃sif, -iv] *a* intensive; **cours ~** crash course; **~ en main- d'œuvre** labour-intensive; **~ en capital** capital-intensive.

intensifier [ɛ̃tɑ̃sifje] *vt*, **s'~** *vi* to intensify.

intensité [ɛ̃tɑ̃site] *nf* intensity.

intensivement [ɛ̃tɑ̃sivmɑ̃] *ad* intensively.

intenter [ɛ̃tɑ̃te] *vt*: **~ un procès contre** *ou* **à qn** to start proceedings against sb.

intention [ɛ̃tɑ̃sjɔ̃] *nf* intention; (*JUR*) intent; **avoir l'~ de faire** to intend to do, have the intention of doing; **dans l'~ de faire qch** with a view to doing sth; **à l'~ de** *prép* for; (*renseignement*) for the benefit *ou* information of; (*film, ouvrage*) aimed at; **à cette ~** with this aim in view; **sans** ~ unintentionally; **faire qch sans mauvaise** ~ to do sth without ill intent; **agir dans une bonne** ~ to act with good intentions.

intentionné, e [ɛ̃tɑ̃sjɔne] *a*: **bien** ~ well-meaning *ou* -intentioned; **mal** ~ ill-intentioned.

intentionnel, le [ɛ̃tɑ̃sjɔnɛl] *a* intentional, deliberate.

intentionnellement [ɛ̃tɑ̃sjɔnɛlmɑ̃] *ad* intentionally, deliberately.

inter [ɛ̃tɛʀ] *nm* (*TÉL*: = *interurbain*) long-distance call service; (*SPORT*): ~ **gauche/droit** inside-left/-right.

interactif, ive [ɛ̃tɛʀaktif, -iv] *a* (*aussi INFORM*) interactive.

interaction [ɛ̃tɛʀaksjɔ̃] *nf* interaction.

interarmées [ɛ̃tɛʀaʀme] *a inv* inter-army, combined.

interbancaire [ɛ̃tɛʀbɑ̃kɛʀ] *a* interbank.

intercalaire [ɛ̃tɛʀkalɛʀ] *a*, *nm*: **(feuillet)** ~ insert; **(fiche)** ~ divider.

intercaler [ɛ̃tɛʀkale] *vt* to insert; **s'**~ **entre** to come in between; to slip in between.

intercéder [ɛ̃tɛʀsede] *vi*: ~ **(pour qn)** to intercede (on behalf of sb).

intercepter [ɛ̃tɛʀsɛpte] *vt* to intercept; (*lumière, chaleur*) to cut off.

intercepteur [ɛ̃tɛʀsɛptœʀ] *nm* (*AVIAT*) interceptor.

interception [ɛ̃tɛʀsɛpsjɔ̃] *nf* interception; **avion d'**~ interceptor.

intercession [ɛ̃tɛʀsesjɔ̃] *nf* intercession.

interchangeable [ɛ̃tɛʀʃɑ̃ʒabl(ə)] *a* interchangeable.

interclasse [ɛ̃tɛʀklɑs] *nm* (*SCOL*) break (between classes).

interclubs [ɛ̃tɛʀklœb] *a inv* interclub.

intercommunal, e, aux [ɛ̃tɛʀkɔmynal, -o] *a* intervillage, intercommunity.

intercommunautaire [ɛ̃tɛʀkɔmynotɛʀ] *a* intercommunity.

interconnexion [ɛ̃tɛʀkɔnɛksjɔ̃] *nf* (*INFORM*) networking.

intercontinental, e, aux [ɛ̃tɛʀkɔ̃tinatal, -o] *a* intercontinental.

intercostal, e, aux [ɛ̃tɛʀkɔstal, -o] *a* intercostal, between the ribs.

interdépartemental, e, aux [ɛ̃tɛʀdepaʀtəmatal, -o] *a* interdepartmental.

interdépendance [ɛ̃tɛʀdepɑ̃dɑ̃s] *nf* interdependence.

interdépendant, e [ɛ̃tɛʀdepɑ̃dɑ̃, -ɑ̃t] *a* interdependent.

interdiction [ɛ̃tɛʀdiksjɔ̃] *nf* ban; ~ **de faire qch** ban on doing sth; ~ **de séjour** (*JUR*) order banning ex-prisoner from frequenting specified places.

interdire [ɛ̃tɛʀdiʀ] *vt* to forbid; (*ADMIN*: stationnement, meeting, passage) to ban, prohibit; (: *journal, livre*) to ban; ~ **qch à qn** to forbid sb sth; ~ **à qn de faire** to forbid sb to do, prohibit sb from doing; (*suj: empêchement*) to prevent *ou* preclude sb from doing; **s'**~ **qch** (*éviter*) to refrain *ou* abstain from sth; (*se refuser*) **il s'interdit d'y penser** he doesn't allow himself to think about it.

interdisciplinaire [ɛ̃tɛʀdisiplinɛʀ] *a* inter-disciplinary.

interdit, e [ɛ̃tɛʀdi, -it] *pp de* **interdire** ♦ *a* (*stupéfait*) taken aback; (*défendu*) forbidden, prohibited ♦ *nm* interdict, prohibition; **film** ~ **aux moins de 18/13 ans** ≈ 18-/PG-rated film; **sens** ~ one way; **stationnement** ~ no parking; ~ **de chéquier** having cheque book facilities suspended; ~ **de séjour** subject to an *interdiction de séjour*.

intéressant, e [ɛ̃teʀesɑ̃, -ɑ̃t] *a* interesting; **faire l'**~ to draw attention to o.s.

intéressé, e [ɛ̃teʀese] *a* (*parties*) involved, concerned; (*amitié, motifs*) self-interested ♦ *nm*: **l'**~ the interested party; **les** ~**s** those concerned *ou* involved.

intéressement [ɛ̃teʀesmɑ̃] *nm* (*COMM*) profit-sharing.

intéresser [ɛ̃teʀese] *vt* to interest; (*toucher*) to be of interest *ou* concern to; (*ADMIN*: concerner*) to affect, concern; (*COMM*: travailleur*) to give a share in the profits to; (: *partenaire*) to interest (in the business); **s'**~ **à** to take an interest in, be interested in; ~ **qn à qch** to get sb interested in sth.

intérêt [ɛ̃teʀɛ] *nm* (*aussi COMM*) interest; (*égoïsme*) self-interest; **porter de l'**~ **à qn** to take an interest in sb; **agir par** ~ to act out of self-interest; **avoir des** ~**s dans** (*COMM*) to have a financial interest *ou* a stake in; **avoir** ~ **à faire** to do well to do; **il y a** ~ **à** ... it would be a good thing to ...; ~ **composé** compound interest.

interface [ɛ̃tɛʀfas] *nf* (*INFORM*) interface.

interférence [ɛ̃tɛʀfeʀɑ̃s] *nf* interference.

interférer [ɛ̃tɛʀfeʀe] *vi*: ~ **(avec)** to interfere (with).

intergouvernemental, e, aux [ɛ̃tɛʀguvɛʀnəmatal, -o] *a* intergovernmental.

intérieur, e [ɛ̃teʀjœʀ] *a* (*mur, escalier, poche*) inside; (*commerce, politique*) domestic; (*cour, calme, vie*) inner; (*navigation*) inland ♦ *nm* (*d'une maison, d'un récipient etc*) inside; (*d'un pays, aussi: décor, mobilier*) interior; (*POL*): **l'l'**~ (the Department of) the Interior, ≈ the Home Office (*Brit*); **à l'**~ **(de)** inside; (*fig*) within; **de l'**~ (*fig*) from the inside; **en** ~ (*CINÉMA*) in the studio; **vêtement d'**~ indoor garment.

intérieurement [ɛ̃teʀjœʀmɑ̃] *ad* inwardly.

intérim [ɛ̃teʀim] *nm* interim period; **assurer l'**~ **(de)** to deputize (for); **par** ~ *a* interim ♦ *ad* in a temporary capacity.

intérimaire [ɛ̃teʀimɛʀ] *a* temporary, interim ♦ *nm/f* (*secrétaire etc*) temporary, temp (*Brit*); (*suppléant*) deputy.

intérioriser [ɛ̃teʀjɔʀize] *vt* to internalize.

interjection [ɛ̃tɛʀʒɛksjɔ̃] *nf* interjection.

interjeter [ɛ̃tɛʀʒəte] *vt* (*JUR*): ~ **appel** to lodge an appeal.

interligne [ɛ̃tɛʀliɲ] *nm* inter-line space ♦ *nf* (*TYPO*) lead, leading; **simple/double** ~ single/double spacing.

interlocuteur, trice [ɛ̃tɛʀlɔkytœʀ, -tʀis] *nm/f* speaker; (*POL*): ~ **valable** valid representative; **son** ~ the person he *ou* she was speaking to.

interlope [ɛ̃tɛʀlɔp] *a* illicit; (*milieu, bar*) shady.

interloquer [ɛ̃tɛʀlɔke] *vt* to take aback.

interlude [ɛ̃tɛʀlyd] *nm* interlude.
intermède [ɛ̃tɛʀmɛd] *nm* interlude.
intermédiaire [ɛ̃tɛʀmedjɛʀ] *a* intermediate; middle; half-way ♦ *nm/f* intermediary; (*COMM*) middleman; **sans** ~ directly; **par l'**~ **de** through.
interminable [ɛ̃tɛʀminabl(ə)] *a* never-ending.
interminablement [ɛ̃tɛʀminabləmɑ̃] *ad* interminably.
interministériel, le [ɛ̃tɛʀministeʀjɛl] *a*: **comité** ~ interdepartmental committee.
intermittence [ɛ̃tɛʀmitɑ̃s] *nf*: **par** ~ intermittently, sporadically.
intermittent, e [ɛ̃tɛʀmitɑ̃, -ɑ̃t] *a* intermittent, sporadic.
internat [ɛ̃tɛʀna] *nm* (*SCOL*) boarding school.
international, e, aux [ɛ̃tɛʀnasjɔnal, -o] *a, nm/f* international.
internationaliser [ɛ̃tɛʀnasjɔnalize] *vt* to internationalize.
internationalisme [ɛ̃tɛʀnasjɔnalism(ə)] *nm* internationalism.
interne [ɛ̃tɛʀn(ə)] *a* internal ♦ *nm/f* (*SCOL*) boarder; (*MÉD*) houseman (*Brit*), intern (*US*).
internement [ɛ̃tɛʀnəmɑ̃] *nm* (*POL*) internment; (*MÉD*) confinement.
interner [ɛ̃tɛʀne] *vt* (*POL*) to intern; (*MÉD*) to confine to a mental institution.
interparlementaire [ɛ̃tɛʀpaʀləmɑ̃tɛʀ] *a* interparliamentary.
interpellation [ɛ̃tɛʀpelasjɔ̃] *nf* interpellation; (*POL*) question.
interpeller [ɛ̃tɛʀpele] *vt* (*appeler*) to call out to; (*apostropher*) to shout at; (*POLICE*) to take in for questioning; (*POL*) to question; **s'**~ to exchange insults.
interphone [ɛ̃tɛʀfɔn] *nm* intercom.
interplanétaire [ɛ̃tɛʀplanetɛʀ] *a* interplanetary.
INTERPOL [ɛ̃tɛʀpɔl] *sigle m* Interpol.
interpoler [ɛ̃tɛʀpɔle] *vt* to interpolate.
interposer [ɛ̃tɛʀpoze] *vt* to interpose; **s'**~ *vi* to intervene; **par personnes interposées** through a third party.
interprétariat [ɛ̃tɛʀpʀetaʀja] *nm* interpreting.
interprétation [ɛ̃tɛʀpʀetɑsjɔ̃] *nf* interpretation.
interprète [ɛ̃tɛʀpʀɛt] *nm/f* interpreter; (*porte-parole*) spokesman.
interpréter [ɛ̃tɛʀpʀete] *vt* to interpret.
interprofessionnel, le [ɛ̃tɛʀpʀɔfesjɔnɛl] *a* interprofessional.
interrogateur, trice [ɛ̃tɛʀɔgatœʀ, -tʀis] *a* questioning, inquiring ♦ *nm/f* (*SCOL*) (oral) examiner.
interrogatif, ive [ɛ̃tɛʀɔgatif, -iv] *a* (*LING*) interrogative.
interrogation [ɛ̃tɛʀɔgasjɔ̃] *nf* question; (*SCOL*) (written *ou* oral) test.
interrogatoire [ɛ̃tɛʀɔgatwaʀ] *nm* (*POLICE*) questioning *q*; (*JUR*) cross-examination, interrogation.
interroger [ɛ̃tɛʀɔʒe] *vt* to question; (*INFORM*) to interrogate; (*SCOL*: *candidat*) to test; ~ **qn (sur qch)** to question sb (about sth); ~ **qn du regard** to look questioningly at sb, give sb a questioning look; **s'**~ **sur qch** to ask o.s. about sth, ponder (about) sth.

interrompre [ɛ̃tɛʀɔ̃pʀ(ə)] *vt* (*gén*) to interrupt; (*travail, voyage*) to break off, interrupt; **s'**~ to break off.
interrupteur [ɛ̃tɛʀyptœʀ] *nm* switch; ~ **à bascule** (*INFORM*) toggle switch.
interruption [ɛ̃tɛʀypsjɔ̃] *nf* interruption; **sans** ~ without a break; ~ **de grossesse** termination of pregnancy; ~ **volontaire de grossesse** voluntary termination of pregnancy, abortion.
interscolaire [ɛ̃tɛʀskɔlɛʀ] *a* interschool(s).
intersection [ɛ̃tɛʀsɛksjɔ̃] *nf* intersection.
intersidéral, e, aux [ɛ̃tɛʀsideʀal, -o] *a* intersidereal, interstellar.
interstice [ɛ̃tɛʀstis] *nm* crack, slit.
intersyndical, e, aux [ɛ̃tɛʀsɛ̃dikal, -o] *a* interunion.
interurbain [ɛ̃tɛʀyʀbɛ̃] (*TÉL*) *nm* long-distance call service ♦ *a* long-distance.
intervalle [ɛ̃tɛʀval] *nm* (*espace*) space; (*de temps*) interval; **dans l'**~ in the meantime; **à 2 mois d'**~ after a space of 2 months; **à** ~**s rapprochés** at close intervals; **par** ~**s** at intervals.
intervenant, e [ɛ̃tɛʀvənɑ̃, -ɑ̃t] *vb voir* **intervenir** ♦ *nm/f* speaker (*at conference*).
intervenir [ɛ̃tɛʀvəniʀ] *vi* (*gén*) to intervene; (*survenir*) to take place; (*faire une conférence*) to give a talk *ou* lecture; ~ **auprès de/en faveur de qn** to intervene with/on behalf of sb; **la police a dû** ~ police had to step in *ou* intervene; **les médecins ont dû** ~ the doctors had to operate.
intervention [ɛ̃tɛʀvɑ̃sjɔ̃] *nf* intervention; (*conférence*) talk, paper; ~ (**chirurgicale**) operation.
interventionnisme [ɛ̃tɛʀvɑ̃sjɔnism(ə)] *nm* interventionism.
intervenu, e [ɛ̃tɛʀv(ə)ny] *pp de* **intervenir**.
intervertible [ɛ̃tɛʀvɛʀtibl(ə)] *a* interchangeable.
intervertir [ɛ̃tɛʀvɛʀtiʀ] *vt* to invert (the order of), reverse.
interviendrai [ɛ̃tɛʀvjɛ̃dʀe], **interviens** [ɛ̃tɛʀvjɛ̃] *etc vb voir* **intervenir**.
interview [ɛ̃tɛʀvju] *nf* interview.
interviewer [ɛ̃tɛʀvjuve] *vt* to interview ♦ *nm* [ɛ̃tɛʀvjuvœʀ] (*journaliste*) interviewer.
intervins [ɛ̃tɛʀvɛ̃] *etc vb voir* **intervenir**.
intestat [ɛ̃tɛsta] *a* (*JUR*): **décéder** ~ to die intestate.
intestin, e [ɛ̃tɛstɛ̃, -in] *a* internal ♦ *nm* intestine; ~ **grêle** small intestine.
intestinal, e, aux [ɛ̃tɛstinal, -o] *a* intestinal.
intime [ɛ̃tim] *a* intimate; (*vie, journal*) private; (*convictions*) inmost; (*dîner, cérémonie*) held among friends, quiet ♦ *nm/f* close friend.
intimement [ɛ̃timmɑ̃] *ad* (*profondément*) deeply, firmly; (*étroitement*) intimately.
intimer [ɛ̃time] *vt* (*JUR*) to notify; ~ **à qn l'ordre de faire** to order sb to do.
intimider [ɛ̃timide] *vt* to intimidate.
intimité [ɛ̃timite] *nf* intimacy; (*vie privée*) privacy; private life; **dans l'**~ in private; (*sans formalités*) with only a few friends, quietly.
intitulé [ɛ̃tityle] *nm* title.
intituler [ɛ̃tityle] *vt*: **comment a-t-il intitulé**

son livre? what title did he give his book?; **s'~** to be entitled; *(personne)* to call o.s.

intolérable [ɛ̃tɔlerabl(ə)] *a* intolerable.

intolérant, e [ɛ̃tɔlerɑ̃, -ɑ̃t] *a* intolerant.

intonation [ɛ̃tɔnɑsjɔ̃] *nf* intonation.

intouchable [ɛ̃tuʃabl(ə)] *a (fig)* above the law, sacrosanct; *(REL)* untouchable.

intoxication [ɛ̃tɔksikɑsjɔ̃] *nf* poisoning *q*; *(toxicomanie)* drug addiction; *(fig)* brainwashing; **~ alimentaire** food poisoning.

intoxiqué, e [ɛ̃tɔksike] *nm/f* addict.

intoxiquer [ɛ̃tɔksike] *vt* to poison; *(fig)* to brainwash; **s'~** to poison o.s.

intraduisible [ɛ̃traduizibl(ə)] *a* untranslatable; *(fig)* inexpressible.

intraitable [ɛ̃trɛtabl(ə)] *a* inflexible, uncompromising.

intransigeance [ɛ̃trɑ̃ziʒɑ̃s] *nf* intransigence.

intransigeant, e [ɛ̃trɑ̃ziʒɑ̃, -ɑ̃t] *a* intransigent; *(morale, passion)* uncompromising.

intransitif, ive [ɛ̃trɑ̃zitif, -iv] *a (LING)* intransitive.

intransportable [ɛ̃trɑ̃spɔrtabl(ə)] *a (blessé)* unable to travel.

intraveineux, euse [ɛ̃travɛnø, -øz] *a* intravenous.

intrépide [ɛ̃trepid] *a* dauntless, intrepid.

intrigant, e [ɛ̃trigɑ̃, -ɑ̃t] *nm/f* schemer.

intrigue [ɛ̃trig] *nf* intrigue; *(scénario)* plot.

intriguer [ɛ̃trige] *vi* to scheme ♦ *vt* to puzzle, intrigue.

intrinsèque [ɛ̃trɛ̃sɛk] *a* intrinsic.

introductif, ive [ɛ̃trɔdyktif, -iv] *a* introductory.

introduction [ɛ̃trɔdyksjɔ̃] *nf* introduction; **paroles/chapitre d'~** introductory words/chapter; **lettre/mot d'~** letter/note of introduction.

introduire [ɛ̃trɔduir] *vt* to introduce; *(visiteur)* to show in; *(aiguille, clef)*: **~ qch dans** to insert *ou* introduce sth into; *(personne)*: **à qch** to introduce to sth; *(: présenter)*: **~ qn à qn/dans un club** to introduce sb to sb/to a club; *(INFORM)* to input, enter; **s'~** *(techniques, usages)* to be introduced; **s'~ dans** to gain entry into; to get o.s. accepted into; *(eau, fumée)* to get into; **~ au clavier** to key in.

introduit, e [ɛ̃trɔdui, -it] *pp de* **introduire** ♦ *a*: **bien ~** *(personne)* well-received.

introniser [ɛ̃trɔnize] *vt* to enthrone.

introspection [ɛ̃trɔspɛksjɔ̃] *nf* introspection.

introuvable [ɛ̃truvabl(ə)] *a* which cannot be found; *(COMM)* unobtainable.

introverti, e [ɛ̃trɔvɛrti] *nm/f* introvert.

intrus, e [ɛ̃try, -yz] *nm/f* intruder.

intrusion [ɛ̃tryzjɔ̃] *nf* intrusion; *(ingérence)* interference.

intuitif, ive [ɛ̃tuitif, -iv] *a* intuitive.

intuition [ɛ̃tuisjɔ̃] *nf* intuition; **avoir une ~** to have a feeling; **avoir l'~ de qch** to have an intuition of sth; **avoir de l'~** to have intuition.

intuitivement [ɛ̃tuitivmɑ̃] *ad* intuitively.

inusable [inyzabl(ə)] *a* hard-wearing.

inusité, e [inyzite] *a* rarely used.

inutile [inytil] *a* useless; *(superflu)* unnecessary.

inutilement [inytilmɑ̃] *ad* needlessly.

inutilisable [inytilizabl(ə)] *a* unusable.

inutilisé, e [inytilize] *a* unused.

inutilité [inytilite] *nf* uselessness.

invaincu, e [ɛ̃vɛ̃ky] *a* unbeaten; *(armée, peuple)* unconquered.

invalide [ɛ̃valid] *a* disabled ♦ *nm/f*: **~ de guerre** disabled ex-serviceman; **~ du travail** industrially disabled person.

invalider [ɛ̃valide] *vt* to invalidate.

invalidité [ɛ̃validite] *nf* disability.

invariable [ɛ̃varjabl(ə)] *a* invariable.

invariablement [ɛ̃varjabləmɑ̃] *ad* invariably.

invasion [ɛ̃vazjɔ̃] *nf* invasion.

invective [ɛ̃vɛktiv] *nf* invective.

invectiver [ɛ̃vɛktive] *vt* to hurl abuse at ♦ *vi*: **~ contre** to rail against.

invendable [ɛ̃vɑ̃dabl(ə)] *a* unsaleable, unmarketable.

invendu, e [ɛ̃vɑ̃dy] *a* unsold ♦ *nm* return; **~s** *nmpl* unsold goods.

inventaire [ɛ̃vɑ̃tɛr] *nm* inventory; *(COMM: liste)* stocklist; *(: opération)* stocktaking *q*; *(fig)* survey; **faire un ~** to make an inventory; *(COMM)* to take stock; **faire ou procéder à l'~** to take stock.

inventer [ɛ̃vɑ̃te] *vt* to invent; *(subterfuge)* to devise, invent; *(histoire, excuse)* to make up, invent; **~ de faire** to hit on the idea of doing.

inventeur, trice [ɛ̃vɑ̃tœr, -tris] *nm/f* inventor.

inventif, ive [ɛ̃vɑ̃tif, -iv] *a* inventive.

invention [ɛ̃vɑ̃sjɔ̃] *nf* invention; *(imagination, inspiration)* inventiveness.

inventivité [ɛ̃vɑ̃tivite] *nf* inventiveness.

inventorier [ɛ̃vɑ̃tɔrje] *vt* to make an inventory of.

invérifiable [ɛ̃verifjabl(ə)] *a* unverifiable.

inverse [ɛ̃vɛrs(ə)] *a (ordre)* reverse; *(sens)* opposite; *(rapport)* inverse ♦ *nm* reverse; inverse; **en proportion ~** in reverse proportion; **dans le sens ~ des aiguilles d'une montre** anti-clockwise; **en sens ~** in *(ou* from) the opposite direction; **à l'~** conversely.

inversement [ɛ̃vɛrsəmɑ̃] *ad* conversely.

inverser [ɛ̃vɛrse] *vt* to reverse, invert; *(ÉLEC)* to reverse.

inversion [ɛ̃vɛrsjɔ̃] *nf* reversal; inversion.

invertébré, e [ɛ̃vɛrtebre] *a, nm* invertebrate.

inverti, e [ɛ̃vɛrti] *nm/f* homosexual.

investigation [ɛ̃vɛstigɑsjɔ̃] *nf* investigation, inquiry.

investir [ɛ̃vɛstir] *vt* to invest; **s'~** *vi (PSYCH)* to involve o.s.; **~ qn de** to vest *ou* invest sb with.

investissement [ɛ̃vɛstismɑ̃] *nm* investment; *(PSYCH)* involvement.

investiture [ɛ̃vɛstityr] *nf* investiture; *(à une élection)* nomination.

invétéré, e [ɛ̃vetere] *a (habitude)* ingrained; *(bavard, buveur)* inveterate.

invincible [ɛ̃vɛ̃sibl(ə)] *a* invincible, unconquerable.

invinciblement [ɛ̃vɛ̃sibləmɑ̃] *ad (fig)* invincibly.

inviolabilité [ɛ̃vjɔlabilite] *nf*: **~ parlementaire** parliamentary immunity.

inviolable [ɛ̃vjɔlabl(ə)] *a* inviolable.

invisible [ɛ̃vizibl(ə)] *a* invisible; *(fig:*

personne) not available.

invitation [ɛ̃vitɑsjɔ̃] *nf* invitation; **à/sur l'~ de qn** at/on sb's invitation; **carte/lettre d'~** invitation card/letter.

invite [ɛ̃vit] *nf* invitation.

invité, e [ɛ̃vite] *nm/f* guest.

inviter [ɛ̃vite] *vt* to invite; **~ qn à faire qch** to invite sb to do sth; (*suj: chose*) to induce *ou* tempt sb to do sth.

invivable [ɛ̃vivabl(ə)] *a* unbearable, impossible.

involontaire [ɛ̃vɔlɔ̃tɛʀ] *a* (*mouvement*) involuntary; (*insulte*) unintentional; (*complice*) unwitting.

involontairement [ɛ̃vɔlɔ̃tɛʀmɑ̃] *ad* involuntarily.

invoquer [ɛ̃vɔke] *vt* (*Dieu, muse*) to call upon, invoke; (*prétexte*) to put forward (as an excuse); (*témoignage*) to call upon; (*loi, texte*) to refer to; **~ la clémence de qn** to beg sb *ou* appeal to sb for clemency.

invraisemblable [ɛ̃vʀɛsɑ̃blabl(ə)] *a* unlikely, improbable; (*bizarre*) incredible.

invraisemblance [ɛ̃vʀɛsɑ̃blɑ̃s] *nf* unlikelihood *q*, improbability.

invulnérable [ɛ̃vylneʀabl(ə)] *a* invulnerable.

iode [jɔd] *nm* iodine.

iodé, e [jɔde] *a* iodized.

ion [jɔ̃] *nm* ion.

ionique [jɔnik] *a* (*ARCHIT*) Ionic; (*SCIENCE*) ionic.

IPC *sigle m* (= *Indice des prix à la consommation*) CPI.

IR. *abr* = **infrarouge**.

IRA *sigle f* (= *Irish Republican Army*) IRA.

irai [iʀe] *etc vb voir* **aller**.

Irak [iʀɑk] *nm*: **l'~** Iraq *ou* Irak.

irakien, ne [iʀakjɛ̃, -ɛn] *a* Iraqi ♦ *nm* (*LING*) Iraqi ♦ *nm/f*: **l'~, ne** Iraqi.

Iran [iʀɑ̃] *nm*: **l'~** Iran.

iranien, ne [iʀanjɛ̃, -ɛn] *a* Iranian ♦ *nm* (*LING*) Iranian ♦ *nm/f*: **l'~, ne** Iranian.

Iraq [iʀɑk] = **Irak**.

iraquien, ne [iʀakjɛ̃, -ɛn] = **irakien, ne**.

irascible [iʀasibl(ə)] *a* short-tempered, irascible.

irions [iʀjɔ̃] *etc vb voir* **aller**.

iris [iʀis] *nm* iris.

irisé, e [iʀize] *a* iridescent.

irlandais, e [iʀlɑ̃dɛ, -ɛz] *a, nm* (*LING*) Irish ♦ *nm/f*: **l'~, e** Irishman/woman; **les l'~** the Irish.

Irlande [iʀlɑ̃d] *nf*: **l'~** (*pays*) Ireland; (*état*) the Irish Republic, the Republic of Ireland, Eire; **~ du Nord** Northern Ireland, Ulster; **~ du Sud** Southern Ireland, Irish Republic, Eire; **la mer d'~** the Irish Sea.

ironie [iʀɔni] *nf* irony.

ironique [iʀɔnik] *a* ironical.

ironiquement [iʀɔnikmɑ̃] *ad* ironically.

ironiser [iʀɔnize] *vi* to be ironical.

irons [iʀɔ̃] *etc vb voir* **aller**.

IRPP *sigle m* (= *impôt sur le revenu des personnes physiques*) income tax.

irradiation [iʀadjɑsjɔ̃] *nf* irradiation.

irradier [iʀadje] *vi* to radiate ♦ *vt* to irradiate.

irraisonné, e [iʀezɔne] *a* irrational, unreasoned.

irrationnel, le [iʀasjɔnɛl] *a* irrational.

irrattrapable [iʀatʀapabl(ə)] *a* (*retard*) that cannot be made up; (*bévue*) that cannot be made good.

irréalisable [iʀealizabl(ə)] *a* unrealizable; (*projet*) impracticable.

irréalisme [iʀealism(ə)] *nm* lack of realism.

irréaliste [iʀealist(ə)] *a* unrealistic.

irréalité [iʀealite] *nf* unreality.

irrecevable [iʀsəvabl(ə)] *a* unacceptable.

irréconciliable [iʀekɔ̃siljabl(ə)] *a* irreconcilable.

irrécouvrable [iʀekuvʀabl(ə)] *a* irrecoverable.

irrécupérable [iʀekypeʀabl(ə)] *a* unreclaimable, beyond repair; (*personne*) beyond redemption *ou* recall.

irrécusable [iʀekyzabl(ə)] *a* (*témoignage*) unimpeachable; (*preuve*) incontestable, indisputable.

irréductible [iʀedyktibl(ə)] *a* indomitable, implacable; (*MATH: fraction, équation*) irreducible.

irréductiblement [iʀedyktibləmɑ̃] *ad* implacably.

irréel, le [iʀeɛl] *a* unreal.

irréfléchi, e [iʀefleʃi] *a* thoughtless.

irréfutable [iʀefytabl(ə)] *a* irrefutable.

irréfutablement [iʀefytabləmɑ̃] *ad* irrefutably.

irrégularité [iʀegylaʀite] *nf* irregularity; unevenness *q*.

irrégulier, ière [iʀegylje, -jɛʀ] *a* irregular; (*surface, rythme, écriture*) uneven, irregular; (*élève, athlète*) erratic.

irrégulièrement [iʀegyljɛʀmɑ̃] *ad* irregularly.

irrémédiable [iʀemedjabl(ə)] *a* irreparable.

irrémédiablement [iʀemedjabləmɑ̃] *ad* irreparably.

irremplaçable [iʀɑ̃plasabl(ə)] *a* irreplaceable.

irréparable [iʀepaʀabl(ə)] *a* beyond repair, irreparable; (*fig*) irreparable.

irrépréhensible [iʀepʀeɑ̃sibl(ə)] *a* irreprehensible.

irrépressible [iʀepʀesibl(ə)] *a* irrepressible.

irréprochable [iʀepʀɔʃabl(ə)] *a* irreproachable, beyond reproach; (*tenue, toilette*) impeccable.

irrésistible [iʀezistibl(ə)] *a* irresistible; (*preuve, logique*) compelling.

irrésistiblement [iʀezistibləmɑ̃] *ad* irresistibly.

irrésolu, e [iʀezɔly] *a* irresolute.

irrésolution [iʀezɔlysjɔ̃] *nf* irresoluteness.

irrespectueux, euse [iʀespektɥø, -øz] *a* disrespectful.

irrespirable [iʀespiʀabl(ə)] *a* unbreathable; (*fig*) oppressive, stifling.

irresponsabilité [iʀespɔ̃sabilite] *nf* irresponsibility.

irresponsable [iʀespɔ̃sabl(ə)] *a* irresponsible.

irrévérencieux, euse [iʀeveʀɑ̃sjø, -øz] *a* irreverent.

irréversible [iʀevɛʀsibl(ə)] *a* irreversible.

irréversiblement [iʀevɛʀsibləmɑ̃] *ad* irreversibly.

irrévocable [iʀevɔkabl(ə)] *a* irrevocable.

irrévocablement [iʀevɔkabləmɑ̃] *ad* irrevocably.

irrigation [iʀigɑsjɔ̃] *nf* irrigation.

irriguer [iʀige] *vt* to irrigate.

irritabilité [iʀitabilite] *nf* irritability.

irritable [iʀitabl(ə)] *a* irritable.
irritant, e [iʀitɑ̃, -ɑ̃t] *a* irritating; (*MÉD*) irritant.
irritation [iʀitasjɔ̃] *nf* irritation.
irrité, e [iʀite] *a* irritated.
irriter [iʀite] *vt* (*agacer*) to irritate, annoy; (*MÉD*: *enflammer*) to irritate; **s'~ contre qn/de qch** to get annoyed *ou* irritated with sb/at sth.
irruption [iʀypsjɔ̃] *nf* irruption *q*; **faire ~ dans** to burst into.
ISBN *sigle m* (= *International Standard Book Number*) ISBN.
Islam [islam] *nm* Islam.
islamique [islamik] *a* Islamic.
islandais, e [islɑ̃dɛ, -ɛz] *a* Icelandic ♦ *nm* (*LING*) Icelandic ♦ *nm/f*: **I~, e** Icelander.
Islande [islɑ̃d] *nf*: **l'~** Iceland.
ISMH *sigle m* (= *Inventaire supplémentaire des monuments historiques*): **monument inscrit à l'~** ≈ listed building.
isocèle [izɔsɛl] *a* isoceles.
isolant, e [izɔlɑ̃, -ɑ̃t] *a* insulating; (*insonorisant*) soundproofing ♦ *nm* insulator.
isolateur [izɔlatœʀ] *nm* (*ÉLEC*) insulator.
isolation [izɔlasjɔ̃] *nf* insulation; **~ acoustique/thermique** sound/thermal insulation.
isolationnisme [izɔlasjɔnism(ə)] *nm* isolationism.
isolé, e [izɔle] *a* isolated; (*ÉLEC*) insulated.
isolement [izɔlmɑ̃] *nm* isolation; solitary confinement.
isolément [izɔlemɑ̃] *ad* in isolation.
isoler [izɔle] *vt* to isolate; (*prisonnier*) to put in solitary confinement; (*ville*) to cut off, isolate; (*ÉLEC*) to insulate.
isoloir [izɔlwaʀ] *nm* polling booth.
isorel [izɔʀɛl] *nm* ® hardboard.
isotherme [izɔtɛʀm(ə)] *a* (*camion*) refrigerated.
Israël [isʀaɛl] *nm*: **l'~** Israel.
israélien, ne [isʀaeljɛ̃, -ɛn] *a* Israeli ♦ *nm/f*: **I~, ne** Israeli.
israélite [isʀaelit] *a* Jewish; (*dans l'Ancien Testament*) Israelite ♦ *nm/f*: **I~** Jew/Jewess; Israelite.
issu, e [isy] *a*: **~ de** descended from; (*fig*) stemming from ♦ *nf* (*ouverture, sortie*) exit; (*solution*) way out, solution; (*dénouement*) outcome; **à l'~e de** at the conclusion *ou* close of; **rue sans ~e** dead end, no through road (*Brit*), no outlet (*US*); **~e de secours** emergency exit.
Istamboul *ou* **Istanbul** [istɑ̃bul] *n* Istanbul.
isthme [ism(ə)] *nm* isthmus.
Italie [itali] *nf*: **l'~** Italy.
italien, ne [italjɛ̃, -ɛn] *a* Italian ♦ *nm* (*LING*) Italian ♦ *nm/f*: **I~, ne** Italian.
italique [italik] *nm*: **en ~(s)** in italics.
item [itɛm] *nm* item; (*question*) question, test.
itinéraire [itineʀɛʀ] *nm* itinerary, route.
itinérant, e [itineʀɑ̃, -ɑ̃t] *a* itinerant, travelling.
ITP *sigle m* (= *ingénieur des travaux publics*) civil engineer.
IUT *sigle m* = **Institut universitaire de technologie.**
IVG *sigle f* (= *interruption volontaire de*

grossesse) abortion.
ivoire [ivwaʀ] *nm* ivory.
ivoirien, ne [ivwaʀjɛ̃, -ɛn] *a* of *ou* from the Ivory Coast.
ivraie [ivʀɛ] *nf*: **séparer l'~ du bon grain** (*fig*) to separate the wheat from the chaff.
ivre [ivʀ(ə)] *a* drunk; **~ de** (*colère*) wild with; (*bonheur*) drunk *ou* intoxicated with; **~ mort** dead drunk.
ivresse [ivʀɛs] *nf* drunkenness; (*euphorie*) intoxication.
ivrogne [ivʀɔɲ] *nm/f* drunkard.

J

J, j [ʒi] *nm inv* J, j ♦ *abr* (= *jour*): **jour ~ D-day**; (= *Joule*) J; **J comme Joseph** J for Jack (*Brit*) *ou* Jig (*US*).
j' [ʒ] *pronom voir* **je.**
jabot [ʒabo] *nm* (*ZOOL*) crop; (*de vêtement*) jabot.
JAC [ʒak] *sigle f* (= *Jeunesse agricole catholique*) youth organization.
jacasser [ʒakase] *vi* to chatter.
jachère [ʒaʃɛʀ] *nf*: **(être) en ~** (to lie) fallow.
jacinthe [ʒasɛ̃t] *nf* hyacinth; **~ des bois** bluebell.
jack [dʒak] *nm* jack plug.
jacquerie [ʒakʀi] *nf* riot.
jade [ʒad] *nm* jade.
jadis [ʒadis] *ad* in times past, formerly.
jaguar [ʒagwaʀ] *nm* (*ZOOL*) jaguar.
jaillir [ʒajiʀ] *vi* (*liquide*) to spurt out, gush out; (*lumière*) to flood out; (*fig*) to rear up; to burst out.
jaillissement [ʒajismɑ̃] *nm* spurt, gush.
jais [ʒɛ] *nm* jet; (**d'un noir) de ~** jet-black.
jalon [ʒalɔ̃] *nm* range pole; (*fig*) milestone; **poser des ~s** (*fig*) to pave the way.
jalonner [ʒalɔne] *vt* to mark out; (*fig*) to mark, punctuate.
jalousement [ʒaluzmɑ̃] *ad* jealously.
jalouser [ʒaluze] *vt* to be jealous of.
jalousie [ʒaluzi] *nf* jealousy; (*store*) (venetian) blind.
jaloux, ouse [ʒalu, -uz] *a* jealous; **être ~ de qn/qch** to be jealous of sb/sth.
jamaïquain, e [ʒamaikɛ̃, -ɛn] *a* Jamaican.
Jamaïque [ʒamaik] *nf*: **la ~** Jamaica.
jamais [ʒamɛ] *ad* never; (*sans négation*) ever; **ne ... ~** never; **~ de la vie!** never!; **si ~ ...** if ever ...; **à (tout) ~, pour ~** for ever, for ever and ever.
jambage [ʒɑ̃baʒ] *nm* (*de lettre*) downstroke; (*de porte*) jamb.
jambe [ʒɑ̃b] *nf* leg; **à toutes ~s** as fast as one's legs can carry one.
jambières [ʒɑ̃bjɛʀ] *nfpl* legwarmers; (*SPORT*) shin pads.
jambon [ʒɑ̃bɔ̃] *nm* ham.
jambonneau, x [ʒɑ̃bɔno] *nm* knuckle of ham.
jante [ʒɑ̃t] *nf* (wheel) rim.

janvier [ʒɑ̃vje] *nm* January; *voir aussi* **juillet**.
Japon [ʒapɔ̃] *nm*: **le ~** Japan.
japonais, e [ʒapɔnɛ, -ɛz] *a* Japanese ♦ *nm* (*LING*) Japanese ♦ *nm/f*: **J~, e** Japanese.
japonaiserie [ʒapɔnɛzʀi] *nf* (*bibelot*) Japanese curio.
jappement [ʒapmɑ̃] *nm* yap, yelp.
japper [ʒape] *vi* to yap, yelp.
jaquette [ʒakɛt] *nf* (*de cérémonie*) morning coat; (*de femme*) jacket; (*de livre*) dust cover, (dust) jacket.
jardin [ʒaʀdɛ̃] *nm* garden; **~ d'acclimatation** zoological gardens *pl*; **~ botanique** botanical gardens *pl*; **~ d'enfants** nursery school; **~ potager** vegetable garden; **~ public** (public) park, public gardens *pl*; **~s suspendus** hanging gardens.
jardinage [ʒaʀdinaʒ] *nm* gardening.
jardiner [ʒaʀdine] *vi* to garden, do some gardening.
jardinet [ʒaʀdinɛ] *nm* little garden.
jardinier, ière [ʒaʀdinje, -jɛʀ] *nm/f* gardener ♦ *nf* (*de fenêtre*) window box; **jardinière d'enfants** nursery school teacher; **jardinière (de légumes)** (*CULIN*) mixed vegetables.
jargon [ʒaʀgɔ̃] *nm* (*charabia*) gibberish; (*publicitaire, scientifique etc*) jargon.
jarre [ʒaʀ] *nf* (earthenware) jar.
jarret [ʒaʀɛ] *nm* back of knee; (*CULIN*) knuckle, shin.
jarretelle [ʒaʀtɛl] *nf* suspender (*Brit*), garter (*US*).
jarretière [ʒaʀtjɛʀ] *nf* garter.
jars [ʒaʀ] *nm* (*ZOOL*) gander.
jaser [ʒaze] *vi* to chatter, prattle; (*indiscrètement*) to gossip.
jasmin [ʒasmɛ̃] *nm* jasmin.
jaspe [ʒasp(ə)] *nm* jasper.
jaspé, e [ʒaspe] *a* marbled, mottled.
jatte [ʒat] *nf* basin, bowl.
jauge [ʒoʒ] *nf* (*capacité*) capacity, tonnage; (*instrument*) gauge; **~ (de niveau) d'huile** dipstick.
jauger [ʒoʒe] *vt* to gauge the capacity of; (*fig*) to size up; **~ 3000 tonneaux** to measure 3,000 tons.
jaunâtre [ʒonɑtʀ(ə)] *a* (*couleur, teint*) yellowish.
jaune [ʒon] *a, nm* yellow ♦ *nm/f* Asiatic; (*briseur de grève*) blackleg ♦ *ad* (*fam*): **rire ~** to laugh on the other side of one's face; **~ d'œuf** (egg) yolk.
jaunir [ʒoniʀ] *vi, vt* to turn yellow.
jaunisse [ʒonis] *nf* jaundice.
Java [ʒava] *nf* Java.
javanais, e [ʒavanɛ, -ɛz] *a* Javanese.
Javel [ʒavɛl] *nf voir* **eau**.
javelliser [ʒavelize] *vt* (*eau*) to chlorinate.
javelot [ʒavlo] *nm* javelin; (*SPORT*): **faire du ~** to throw the javelin.
jazz [dʒaz] *nm* jazz.
J.-C. *abr* = **Jésus-Christ**.
JCR *sigle f* (= *Jeunesse communiste révolutionnaire*) *communist youth movement*.
je, j' [ʒ(ə)] *pronom* I.
jean [dʒin] *nm* jeans *pl*.
jeannette [ʒanɛt] *nf* (*planchette*) sleeveboard; (*petite fille scout*) Brownie.
JEC [ʒɛk] *sigle f* (= *Jeunesse étudiante chrétienne*) *youth organization*.

jérémiades [ʒeʀemjad] *nfpl* moaning *sg*.
jerrycan [ʒeʀikan] *nm* jerrycan.
Jersey [ʒɛʀze] *nf* Jersey.
jersey [ʒɛʀzɛ] *nm* jersey; (*TRICOT*): **pointe de ~** stocking stitch.
jersiais, e [ʒɛʀzje, -ɛz] *a* Jersey *cpd*, of *ou* from Jersey.
Jérusalem [ʒeʀyzalɛm] *n* Jerusalem.
jésuite [ʒezɥit] *nm* Jesuit.
Jésus-Christ [ʒezykʀi(st)] *n* Jesus Christ; **600 avant/après ~** *ou* **J.-C.** 600 B.C./A.D.
jet [ʒɛ] *nm* (*lancer*) throwing *q*, throw; (*jaillissement*) jet; spurt; (*de tuyau*) nozzle; (*avion*) [dʒɛt] jet; (*fig*): **premier ~** (*ébauche*) rough outline; **arroser au ~** to hose; **d'un (seul) ~** (*d'un seul coup*) at (*ou* in) one go; **du premier ~** at the first attempt *or* shot; **~ d'eau** spray; (*fontaine*) fountain.
jetable [ʒətabl(ə)] *a* disposable.
jeté [ʒəte] *nm* (*TRICOT*): **un ~** make one; **~ de table** (table) runner; **~ de lit** bedspread.
jetée [ʒəte] *nf* jetty; pier.
jeter [ʒəte] *vt* (*gén*) to throw; (*se défaire de*) to throw away *ou* out; (*son, lueur etc*) to give out; **~ qch à qn** to throw sth to sb; (*de façon agressive*) to throw sth at sb; (*NAVIG*): **~ l'ancre** to cast anchor; **~ un coup d'œil (à)** to take a look (at); **~ les bras en avant/la tête en arrière** to throw one's arms forward/one's head back(ward); **~ l'effroi parmi** to spread fear among; **~ un sort à qn** to cast a spell on sb; **~ qn dans la misère** to reduce sb to poverty; **~ qn dehors/en prison** to throw sb out/into prison; **~ l'éponge** (*fig*) to throw in the towel; **~ des fleurs à qn** (*fig*) to say lovely things to sb; **~ la pierre à qn** (*accuser, blâmer*) to accuse sb; **se ~ sur** to throw o.s. onto; **se ~ dans** (*suj: fleuve*) to flow into; **se ~ par la fenêtre** to throw o.s. out of the window; **se ~ à l'eau** (*fig*) to take the plunge.
jeton [ʒətɔ̃] *nm* (*au jeu*) counter; (*de téléphone*) token; **~s de présence** (director's) fees.
jette [ʒɛt] *etc vb voir* **jeter**.
jeu, x [ʒø] *nm* (*divertissement, TECH: d'une pièce*) play; (*défini par des règles, TENNIS: partie, FOOTBALL etc: façon de jouer*) game; (*THÉÂTRE etc*) acting; (*au casino*): **le ~** gambling; (*fonctionnement*) working, interplay; (*série d'objets, jouet*) set; (*CARTES*) hand; **cacher son ~** (*fig*) to keep one's cards hidden, conceal one's hand; **c'est un ~ d'enfant!** (*fig*) it's child's play!; **en ~** at stake; at work; (*FOOTBALL*) in play; **remettre en ~** to throw in; **entrer/mettre en ~** to come/bring into play; **par ~** (*pour s'amuser*) for fun; **d'entrée de ~** (*tout de suite, dès le début*) from the outset; **entrer dans le ~/le ~ de qn** (*fig*) to play the game/sb's game; **jouer gros ~** to play for high stakes; **se piquer/se prendre au ~** to get excited over/get caught up in *ou* involved in the game; **~ de boules** game of bowls; (*endroit*) bowling pitch; (*boules*) set of bowls; **~ de cartes** card game; (*paquet*) pack of cards; **~ de construction** building set; **~ d'échecs** chess set; **~ d'écritures** (*COMM*) paper transac-

tion; ~ **de hasard** game of chance; ~ **de mots** pun; **le ~ de l'oie** snakes and ladders *sg*; ~ **d'orgue(s)** organ stop; ~ **de patience** puzzle; ~ **de physionomie** facial expressions *pl*; ~ **de société** parlour game; ~**x de lumière** lighting effects; **J~x olympiques (JO)** Olympic Games.

jeu-concours, *pl* **jeux-concours** [ʒøkɔ̃kuʀ] *nm* competition.

jeudi [ʒødi] *nm* Thursday; ~ **saint** Maundy Thursday; *voir aussi* **lundi**.

jeun [ʒœ̃]: **à ~** *ad* on an empty stomach.

jeune [ʒœn] *a* young ♦ *ad:* **faire/s'habiller ~** to look/dress young; **les ~s** young people, the young; ~ **fille** *nf* girl; ~ **homme** *nm* young man; ~ **loup** *nm* (*POL, ÉCON*) young go-getter; ~ **premier** leading man; ~**s gens** *nmpl* young people; ~**s mariés** *nmpl* newly weds.

jeûne [ʒøn] *nm* fast.

jeûner [ʒøne] *vi* to fast, go without food.

jeunesse [ʒœnɛs] *nf* youth; (*aspect*) youthfulness; (*jeunes*) young people *pl*, youth.

JF *sigle f* = **jeune fille**.

JH *sigle m* = **jeune homme**.

JI *sigle m* = **juge d'instruction**.

jiu-jitsu [ʒyʒitsy] *nm inv* (*SPORT*) jujitsu.

JMF *sigle f* (= *Jeunesses musicales de France*) association to promote music among the young.

JO *sigle m* = **Journal officiel** ♦ *sigle mpl* = **Jeux Olympiques**.

joaillerie [ʒɔajʀi] *nf* jewel trade; jewellery (*Brit*), jewelry (*US*).

joaillier, ière [ʒɔaje, -jɛʀ] *nm/f* jeweller (*Brit*), jeweler (*US*).

job [dʒɔb] *nm* job.

jobard [ʒɔbaʀ] *nm* (*péj*) sucker, mug.

JOC [ʒɔk] *sigle f* (= *Jeunesse ouvrière chrétienne*) *youth organization*.

jockey [ʒɔkɛ] *nm* jockey.

jodler [ʒɔdle] *vi* to yodel.

jogging [dʒɔgiŋ] *nm* tracksuit (*Brit*), sweatsuit (*US*); **faire du ~** to jog, go jogging.

joie [ʒwa] *nf* joy.

joignais [ʒwaɲɛ] *etc vb voir* **joindre**.

joindre [ʒwɛ̃dʀ(ə)] *vt* to join; (*à une lettre*): ~ **qch à** to enclose sth with; (*contacter*) to contact, get in touch with; ~ **les mains/talons** to put one's hands/heels together; ~ **les deux bouts** (*fig: du mois*) to make ends meet; **se ~** (*mains etc*) to come together; **se ~ à qn** to join sb; **se ~ à qch** to join in sth.

joint, e [ʒwɛ̃, -ɛ̃t] *pp de* **joindre** ♦ *a:* ~ **(à)** (*lettre, paquet*) attached (to), enclosed (with); **pièce ~e** enclosure ♦ *nm* joint; (*ligne*) join; (*de ciment etc*) pointing *q*; **chercher/trouver le ~** (*fig*) to look for/come up with the answer; ~ **de cardan** cardan joint; ~ **de culasse** cylinder head gasket; ~ **de robinet** washer; ~ **universel** universal joint.

jointure [ʒwɛ̃tyʀ] *nf* (*ANAT: articulation*) joint; (*TECH: assemblage*) joint; (*: ligne*) join.

joker [ʒɔkɛʀ] *nm* (*CARTES*) joker.

joli, e [ʒɔli] *a* pretty, attractive; **une ~e somme/situation** a nice little sum/situation; **un ~ gâchis** *etc* a nice mess *etc*; **c'est du ~!**

that's very nice!; **tout ça, c'est bien ~ mais** ... that's all very well but ....

joliment [ʒɔlimɑ̃] *ad* prettily, attractively; (*fam: très*) pretty.

jonc [ʒɔ̃] *nm* (*bul*)rush; (*bague, bracelet*) band.

joncher [ʒɔ̃ʃe] *vt* (*suj: choses*) to be strewed on; **jonché de** strewn with.

jonction [ʒɔ̃ksjɔ̃] *nf* joining; **(point de)** ~ (*de routes*) junction; (*de fleuves*) confluence; **opérer une ~** (*MIL etc*) to rendez-vous.

jongler [ʒɔ̃gle] *vi* to juggle; (*fig*): ~ **avec** to juggle with, play with.

jongleur, euse [ʒɔ̃glœʀ, -øz] *nm/f* juggler.

jonquille [ʒɔ̃kij] *nf* daffodil.

Jordanie [ʒɔʀdani] *nf:* **la ~** Jordan.

jordanien, ne [ʒɔʀdanjɛ̃, -ɛn] *a* Jordanian ♦ *nm/f:* **J~, ne** Jordanian.

jouable [ʒwabl(ə)] *a* playable.

joue [ʒu] *nf* cheek; **mettre en ~** to take aim at.

jouer [ʒwe] *vt* (*partie, carte, coup, MUS: morceau*) to play; (*somme d'argent, réputation*) to stake, wager; (*pièce, rôle*) to perform; (*film*) to show; (*simuler: sentiment*) to affect, feign ♦ *vi* to play; (*THÉÂTRE, CINÉMA*) to act, perform; (*bois, porte: se voiler*) to warp; (*clef, pièce: avoir du jeu*) to be loose; (*entrer ou être en jeu*) to come into play, come into it; ~ **sur** (*miser*) to gamble on; ~ **de** (*MUS*) to play; ~ **du couteau/des coudes** to use knives/one's elbows; ~ **à** (*jeu, sport, roulette*) to play; ~ **au héros** to act ou play the hero; ~ **avec** (*risquer*) to gamble with; **se ~ de** (*difficultés*) to make light of; **se ~ de qn** to deceive ou dupe sb; ~ **un tour à qn** to play a trick on sb; ~ **la comédie** (*fig*) to put on an act, put it on; ~ **aux courses** to back horses, bet on horses; ~ **à la baisse/hausse** (*BOURSE*) to play for a fall/rise; ~ **serré** to play a close game; ~ **de malchance** to be dogged with ill-luck; ~ **sur les mots** to play with words; **à toi/nous de ~** it's your/our go ou turn.

jouet [ʒwɛ] *nm* toy; **être le ~ de** (*illusion etc*) to be the victim of.

joueur, euse [ʒwœʀ, -øz] *nm/f* player ♦ *a* (*enfant, chat*) playful; **être beau/mauvais ~** to be a good/bad loser.

joufflu, e [ʒufly] *a* chubby(-cheeked).

joug [ʒu] *nm* yoke.

jouir [ʒwiʀ]: ~ **de** *vt* to enjoy.

jouissance [ʒwisɑ̃s] *nf* pleasure; (*JUR*) use.

jouisseur, euse [ʒwisœʀ, -øz] *nm/f* sensualist.

joujou [ʒuʒu] *nm* (*fam*) toy.

jour [ʒuʀ] *nm* day; (*opposé à la nuit*) day, daytime; (*clarté*) daylight; (*fig: aspect*): **sous un ~ favorable/nouveau** in a favourable/new light; (*ouverture*) opening; (*COUTURE*) openwork *q*; **au ~ le ~** from day to day; **de nos ~s** these days, nowadays; **tous les ~s** every day; **de ~ en ~** day by day; **d'un ~ à l'autre** from one day to the next; **du ~ au lendemain** overnight; **il fait ~** it's daylight; **en plein ~** in broad daylight; **au ~** in daylight; **au petit ~** at daybreak; **au grand ~** (*fig*) in the open; **mettre au ~** to uncover, disclose; **être à ~** to be up to date; **mettre à ~** to bring up to date, update; **mise**

à ~ updating; **donner le ~ à** to give birth to; **voir le ~** to be born; **se faire ~** (*fig*) to become clear; **~ férié** public holiday; **le ~ J** D-day.

Jourdain [ʒuʀdɛ̃] *nm*: **le ~** the (River) Jordan.

journal, aux [ʒuʀnal, -o] *nm* (news)paper; (*personnel*) journal, diary; **~ de bord** log; **~ de mode** fashion magazine; **le J~ officiel (de la République française) (JO)** *bulletin giving details of laws and official announcements*; **~ parlé/télévisé** radio/television news *sg*.

journalier, ière [ʒuʀnalje, -jɛʀ] *a* daily; (*banal*) everyday ♦ *nm* day labourer.

journalisme [ʒuʀnalism(ə)] *nm* journalism.

journaliste [ʒuʀnalist(ə)] *nm/f* journalist.

journalistique [ʒuʀnalistik] *a* journalistic.

journée [ʒuʀne] *nf* day; **la ~ continue** the 9 to 5 working day (*with short lunch break*).

journellement [ʒuʀnɛlmɑ̃] *ad* (*tous les jours*) daily; (*souvent*) every day.

joute [ʒut] *nf* (*tournoi*) duel; (*verbale*) duel, battle of words.

jouvence [ʒuvɑ̃s] *nf*: **bain de ~** rejuvenating experience.

jouxter [ʒukste] *vt* to adjoin.

jovial [ʒɔvjal] *a* jovial, jolly.

jovialité [ʒɔvjalite] *nf* joviality.

joyau, x [ʒwajo] *nm* gem, jewel.

joyeusement [ʒwajøzmɑ̃] *ad* joyfully, gladly.

joyeux, euse [ʒwajø, -øz] *a* joyful, merry; **Noël!** merry *ou* happy Christmas!; **~ anniversaire!** many happy returns!

JT *sigle m* = **journal télévisé.**

jubilation [ʒybilɑsjɔ̃] *nf* jubilation.

jubilé [ʒybile] *nm* jubilee.

jubiler [ʒybile] *vi* to be jubilant, exult.

jucher [ʒyʃe] *vt*: **~ qch sur** to perch sth (up)on ♦ *vi* (*oiseau*): **~ sur** to perch (up)on; **se ~ sur** to perch o.s. (up)on.

judaïque [ʒydaik] *a* (*loi*) Judaic; (*religion*) Jewish.

judaïsme [ʒydaism(ə)] *nm* Judaism.

judas [ʒyda] *nm* (*trou*) spy-hole.

Judée [ʒyde] *nf*: **la ~** Jud(a)ea.

judéo- [ʒydeɔ] *préfixe* Judeo-.

judéo-allemand, e [ʒydeɔalmɑ̃, -ɑ̃d] *a*, *nm* Yiddish.

judiciaire [ʒydisjɛʀ] *a* judicial.

judicieusement [ʒydisjøzmɑ̃] *ad* judiciously.

judicieux, euse [ʒydisjø, -øz] *a* judicious.

judo [ʒydo] *nm* judo.

judoka [ʒydɔka] *nm/f* judoka.

juge [ʒyʒ] *nm* judge; **~ des enfants** children's judge, ≈ juvenile magistrate; **~ d'instruction** examining (*Brit*) *ou* committing (*US*) magistrate; **~ de paix** justice of the peace; **~ de touche** linesman.

jugé [ʒyʒe]: **au ~** *ad* by guesswork.

jugement [ʒyʒmɑ̃] *nm* judgment; (*JUR: au pénal*) sentence; (: *au civil*) decision; **~ de valeur** value judgment.

jugeote [ʒyʒɔt] *nf* (*fam*) gumption.

juger [ʒyʒe] *vt* to judge ♦ *nm*: **au ~** by guesswork; **~ qn/qch satisfaisant** to consider sb/ sth (to be) satisfactory; **~ que** to think *ou* consider that; **~ bon de faire** to consider it a good idea to do, see fit to do; **~ de** *vt* to

judge; **jugez de ma surprise** imagine my surprise.

jugulaire [ʒygylɛʀ] *a* jugular ♦ *nf* (*MIL*) chinstrap.

juguler [ʒygyle] *vt* (*maladie*) to halt; (*révolte*) to suppress, put down; (*inflation etc*) to control, curb.

juif, ive [ʒɥif, -iv] *a* Jewish ♦ *nm/f*: **J~, ive** Jew/Jewess *ou* Jewish woman.

juillet [ʒɥijɛ] *nm* July; **le premier ~** the first of July (*Brit*), July first (*US*); **le deux/onze ~** the second/eleventh of July, July second/ eleventh; **il est venu le 5 ~** he came on 5th July *ou* July 5th; **en ~** in July; **début/fin ~** at the beginning/end of July.

juin [ʒɥɛ̃] *nm* June; *voir aussi* **juillet.**

juive [ʒɥiv] *voir* **juif.**

jumeau, elle, x [ʒymo, -ɛl] *a*, *nm/f* twin; **maisons jumelles** semidetached houses.

jumelage [ʒymlaʒ] *nm* twinning.

jumeler [ʒymle] *vt* to twin; **roues jumelées** double wheels; **billets de loterie jumelés** double series lottery tickets; **pari jumelé** double bet.

jumelle [ʒymɛl] *af*, *nf* voir **jumeau** ♦ *vb* voir **jumeler.**

jumelles [ʒymɛl] *nfpl* binoculars.

jument [ʒymɑ̃] *nf* mare.

jungle [ʒœ̃gl(ə)] *nf* jungle.

junior [ʒynjɔʀ] *a* junior.

junte [ʒœ̃t] *nf* junta.

jupe [ʒyp] *nf* skirt.

jupe-culotte, *pl* **jupes-culottes** [ʒypkylɔt] *nf* divided skirt, culotte(s).

jupette [ʒypɛt] *nf* short skirt.

jupon [ʒypɔ̃] *nm* waist slip *ou* petticoat.

Jura [ʒyʀa] *nm*: **le ~** the Jura (Mountains).

jurassien, ne [ʒyʀasjɛ̃, -ɛn] *a* of *ou* from the Jura Mountains.

juré, e [ʒyʀe] *nm/f* juror ♦ *a*: **ennemi ~** sworn *ou* avowed enemy.

jurer [ʒyʀe] *vt* (*obéissance etc*) to swear, vow ♦ *vi* (*dire des jurons*) to swear, curse; (*dissoner*): **~ (avec)** to clash (with); (*s'engager*): **~ de faire/que** to swear *ou* vow to do/that; (*affirmer*): **~ que** to swear *ou* vouch that; **~ de qch** (*s'en porter garant*) to swear to sth; **ils ne jurent que par lui** they swear by him; **je vous jure!** honestly!

juridiction [ʒyʀidiksjɔ̃] *nf* jurisdiction; (*tribunal, tribunaux*) court(s) of law.

juridique [ʒyʀidik] *a* legal.

juridiquement [ʒyʀidikmɑ̃] *ad* (*devant la justice*) juridically; (*du point de vue du droit*) legally.

jurisconsulte [ʒyʀikɔ̃sylt(ə)] *nm* jurisconsult.

jurisprudence [ʒyʀispʀydɑ̃s] *nf* (*JUR*) décisions; (*légal*) precedents; (*principes juridiques*) jurisprudence; **faire ~** (*faire autorité*) to set a precedent.

juriste [ʒyʀist(ə)] *nm/f* jurist; lawyer.

juron [ʒyʀɔ̃] *nm* curse, swearword.

jury [ʒyʀi] *nm* (*JUR*) jury; (*SCOL*) board (of examiners), jury.

jus [ʒy] *nm* juice; (*de viande*) gravy, (meat) juice; **~ de fruits** fruit juice; **~ de raisin/ tomates** grape/tomato juice.

jusant [ʒyzɑ̃] *nm* ebb (tide).

jusqu'au-boutiste [ʒyskobutist(ə)] *nm/f*

extremist, hardliner.

jusque [ʒysk(ə)]: **jusqu'à** *prép* (*endroit*) as far as, (up) to; (*moment*) until, till; (*limite*) up to; ~ **sur/dans** up to, as far as; (*y compris*) even on/in; **jusque vers** until about; **jusqu'à ce que** *cj* until; **jusque-là** (*temps*) until then; (*espace*) up to there; **jusqu'ici** (*temps*) until now; (*espace*) up to here; **jusqu'à présent** until now, so far.

justaucorps [ʒystokɔʀ] *nm inv* (*DANSE, SPORT*) leotard.

juste [ʒyst(ə)] *a* (*équitable*) just, fair; (*légitime*) just, justified; (*exact, vrai*) right; (*étroit, insuffisant*) tight ♦ *ad* right; tight; (*chanter*) in tune; (*seulement*) just; ~ **assez/au-dessus** just enough/above; **pouvoir tout** ~ **faire** to be only just able to do; **au** ~ exactly, actually; **comme de** ~ of course, naturally; **le** ~ **milieu** the happy medium; **à** ~ **titre** rightfully.

justement [ʒystəmɑ̃] *ad* rightly; justly; (*précisément*): **c'est** ~ **ce qu'il fallait faire** that's just *ou* precisely what needed doing.

justesse [ʒystɛs] *nf* (*précision*) accuracy; (*d'une remarque*) aptness; (*d'une opinion*) soundness; **de** ~ just, by a narrow margin.

justice [ʒystis] *nf* (*équité*) fairness, justice; (*ADMIN*) justice; **rendre la** ~ to dispense justice; **traduire en** ~ to bring before the courts; **obtenir** ~ to obtain justice; **rendre** ~ **à qn** to do sb justice; **se faire** ~ to take the law into one's own hands; (*se suicider*) to take one's life.

justiciable [ʒystisjabl(ə)] *a*: ~ **de** (*JUR*) answerable to.

justicier, ière [ʒystisje, -jɛʀ] *nm/f* judge, righter of wrongs.

justifiable [ʒystifjabl(ə)] *a* justifiable.

justificatif, ive [ʒystifikatif, -iv] *a* (*document etc*) supporting ♦ *nm* supporting proof.

justification [ʒystifikasjɔ̃] *nf* justification.

justifier [ʒystifje] *vt* to justify; ~ **de** *vt* to prove; **non justifié** unjustified; **justifié à droite/gauche** ranged right/left.

jute [ʒyt] *nm* jute.

juteux, euse [ʒytø, -øz] *a* juicy.

juvénile [ʒyvenil] *a* young, youthful.

juxtaposer [ʒykstapoze] *vt* to juxtapose.

juxtaposition [ʒykstapozisjɔ̃] *nf* juxtaposition.

K

K, k [ka] *nm inv* K, k ♦ *abr* (= *kilo*) kg; (= *kilooctet*) K; **K comme Kléber** K for King.

Kaboul, Kabul [kabul] *n* Kabul.

kabyle [kabil] *a* Kabyle ♦ *nm* (*LING*) Kabyle ♦ *nm/f*: **K~** Kabyle.

Kabylie [kabili] *nf*: **la** ~ Kabylia.

kaki [kaki] *a inv* khaki.

Kalahari [kalaaʀi] *n*: **désert de** ~ Kalahari Desert.

kaléidoscope [kaleidɔskɔp] *nm* kaleidoscope.

Kampala [kɑ̃pala] *n* Kampala.

Kampuchéa [kɑ̃putʃea] *nm*: **le** ~ (**démocratique**) (the People's Republic of) Kampuchea.

kangourou [kɑ̃guʀu] *nm* kangaroo.

kaolin [kaɔlɛ̃] *nm* kaolin.

kapok [kapɔk] *nm* kapok.

karaté [kaʀate] *nm* karate.

kart [kaʀt] *nm* go-cart.

karting [kaʀtiŋ] *nm* go-carting, karting.

kascher [kaʃɛʀ] *a inv* kosher.

kayac, kayak [kajak] *nm* kayak.

Kenya [kenja] *nm*: **le** ~ Kenya.

kenyan, e [kenjɑ̃, -an] *a* Kenyan ♦ *nm/f*: **K~**, **ne** Kenyan.

képi [kepi] *nm* kepi.

Kerguelen [kɛʀgelɛn]: **les (îles)** ~ Kerguelen.

kermesse [kɛʀmɛs] *nf* bazaar, (charity) fête; village fair.

kérosène [keʀozɛn] *nm* jet fuel; rocket fuel.

kg *abr* (= *kilogramme*) kg.

KGB *sigle m* KGB.

khmer, ère [kmɛʀ] *a* Khmer ♦ *nm* (*LING*) Khmer.

khôl [kol] *nm* khol.

kibboutz [kibuts] *nm* kibbutz.

kidnapper [kidnape] *vt* to kidnap.

kidnappeur, euse [kidnapœʀ, -øz] *nm/f* kidnapper.

Kilimandjaro [kilimɑ̃dʒaʀo] *nm*: **le** ~ Mount Kilimanjaro.

kilo [kilo] *nm* kilo.

kilogramme [kilɔgʀam] *nm* kilogramme (*Brit*), kilogram (*US*).

kilométrage [kilɔmetʀaʒ] *nm* number of kilometres travelled, ≈ mileage.

kilomètre [kilɔmetʀ(ə)] *nm* kilometre (*Brit*), kilometer (*US*); ~**s-heure** kilometres per hour.

kilométrique [kilɔmetʀik] *a* (*distance*) in kilometres; **compteur** ~ ≈ mileage indicator.

kilooctet [kilɔɔktɛ] *nm* kilobyte.

kilowatt [kilɔwat] *nm* kilowatt.

kinésithérapeute [kineziteʀapøt] *nm/f* physiotherapist.

kiosque [kjɔsk(ə)] *nm* kiosk, stall; (*TÉL etc*) telephone and/or videotext information service.

kirsch [kiʀʃ] *nm* kirsch.

kiwi [kiwi] *nm* (*ZOOL*) kiwi; (*BOT*) kiwi fruit.

klaxon [klaksɔn] *nm* horn.

klaxonner [klaksɔne] *vi, vt* to hoot (*Brit*), honk (one's horn) (*US*).

kleptomane [klɛptɔman] *nm/f* kleptomaniac.

km *abr* (= *kilomètre*) km.

km/h *abr* (= *kilomètres/heure*) km/h.

knock-out [nɔkawt] *nm* knock-out.

Ko *abr* (*INFORM*: = *kilooctet*) K.

K.-O. [kao] *a inv* (*knocked*) out, out for the count.

kolkhoze [kɔlkoz] *nm* kolkhoz.

Koweit *ou* **Kuweit** [kɔwɛt] *nm*: **le** ~ Kuwait, Koweit.

koweïtien, ne [kɔwɛtjɛ̃, -ɛn] *a* Kuwaiti ♦ *nm/f*: **K~**, **ne** Kuwaiti.

krach [kʀak] *nm* (*ÉCON*) crash.

kraft [kʀaft] *nm* brown *ou* kraft paper.

Kremlin [kʀɛmlɛ̃] *nm*: **le** ~ the Kremlin.

Kuala Lumpur [kwalalympuʀ] *n* Kuala

Lumpur.

kurde [kyʀd(ə)] *a* Kurdish ♦ *nm* (*LING*) Kurdish ♦ *nm/f*: **K~** Kurd.

Kurdistan [kyʀdistɑ̃] *nm*: **le ~** Kurdistan.

Kuweit [kɔwɛt] = **Koweit**.

kW *abr* (= *kilowatt*) kW.

kW/h *abr* (= *kilowatt/heure*) kW/h.

kyrielle [kiʀjɛl] *nf*: **une ~ de** a stream of.

kyste [kist(ə)] *nm* cyst.

L

L, l [ɛl] *nm inv* L, l ♦ *abr* (= *litre*) l; (*SCOL*): **L ès L** = Licence ès Lettres; **L en D** = Licence en Droit; **L comme Louis** L for Lucy (*Brit*) *ou* Love (*US*).

l' [l] *dét voir* **le**.

la [la] *dét, pronom voir* **le** ♦ *nm* (*MUS*) A; (*en chantant la gamme*) la.

là [la] *ad* (*voir aussi* **-ci, celui**) there; (*ici*) here; (*dans le temps*) then; **est-ce que Catherine est ~?** is Catherine there (*ou* here)?; **c'est ~ que** this is where; **~ où** where; **de ~** (*fig*) hence; **par ~** (*fig*) by that; **tout est ~** (*fig*) that's what it's all about.

là-bas [laba] *ad* there.

label [labɛl] *nm* stamp, seal.

labeur [labœʀ] *nm* toil *q*, toiling *q*.

labo [labo] *nm* (= *laboratoire*) lab.

laborantin, e [labɔʀɑ̃tɛ̃, -in] *nm/f* laboratory assistant.

laboratoire [labɔʀatwaʀ] *nm* laboratory; **~ de langues/d'analyses** language/(medical) analysis laboratory.

laborieux, euse [labɔʀjø, -øz] *a* (*tâche*) laborious; **classes ~euses** working classes.

labour [labuʀ] *nm* ploughing *q* (*Brit*), plowing *q* (*US*); **~s** *nmpl* (*champs*) ploughed fields; **cheval de ~** plough- *ou* cart-horse; **bœuf de ~** ox (*pl* oxen).

labourage [labuʀaʒ] *nm* ploughing (*Brit*), plowing (*US*).

labourer [labuʀe] *vt* to plough (*Brit*), plow (*US*); (*fig*) to make deep gashes *ou* furrows in.

laboureur [labuʀœʀ] *nm* ploughman (*Brit*), plowman (*US*).

labrador [labʀadɔʀ] *nm* (*chien*) labrador; (*GÉO*): **le L~** Labrador.

labyrinthe [labiʀɛ̃t] *nm* labyrinth, maze.

lac [lak] *nm* lake; **le ~ Léman** Lake Geneva; **les Grands L~s** the Great Lakes; *voir aussi* **lacs**.

lacer [lase] *vt* to lace *ou* do up.

lacérer [laseʀe] *vt* to tear to shreds.

lacet [lasɛ] *nm* (*de chaussure*) lace; (*de route*) sharp bend; (*piège*) snare; **chaussures à ~s** lace-up *ou* lacing shoes.

lâche [lɑʃ] *a* (*poltron*) cowardly; (*desserré*) loose, slack; (*morale, mœurs*) lax ♦ *nm/f* coward.

lâcher [lɑʃe] *nm* (*de ballons, oiseaux*) release

♦ *vt* to let go of; (*ce qui tombe, abandonner*) to drop; (*oiseau, animal: libérer*) to release, set free; (*fig: mot, remarque*) to let slip, come out with; (*SPORT: distancer*) to leave behind ♦ *vi* (*fil, amarres*) to break, give way; (*freins*) to fail; **~ les amarres** (*NAVIG*) to cast off (the moorings); **~ prise** to let go.

lâcheté [lɑʃte] *nf* cowardice; (*bassesse*) lowness.

lacis [lasi] *nm* (*de ruelles*) maze.

laconique [lakɔnik] *a* laconic.

lacrymal, e, aux [lakʀimal, -o] *a* (*canal, glande*) tear *cpd*.

lacrymogène [lakʀimɔʒɛn] *a*: **grenade/gaz ~** tear gas grenade/tear gas.

lacs [lɑ] *nm* (*piège*) snare.

lactation [laktɑsjɔ̃] *nf* lactation.

lacté, e [lakte] *a* milk *cpd*.

lactose [laktoz] *nm* lactose, milk sugar.

lacune [lakyn] *nf* gap.

lacustre [lakystʀ(ə)] *a* lake *cpd*, lakeside *cpd*.

lad [lad] *nm* stable-lad.

là-dedans [ladədɑ̃] *ad* inside (there), in it; (*fig*) in that.

là-dehors [ladəɔʀ] *ad* out there.

là-derrière [ladɛʀjɛʀ] *ad* behind there; (*fig*) behind that.

là-dessous [ladsu] *ad* underneath, under there; (*fig*) behind that.

là-dessus [ladsy] *ad* on there; (*fig*) at that point; (*: à ce sujet*) about that.

là-devant [ladvɑ̃] *ad* there (in front).

ladite [ladit] *dét voir* **ledit**.

ladre [lɑdʀ(ə)] *a* miserly.

lagon [lagɔ̃] *nm* lagoon.

Lagos [lagos] *n* Lagos.

lagune [lagyn] *nf* lagoon.

là-haut [lao] *ad* up there.

laïc [laik] *a, nm/f* = **laïque**.

laïcité [laisite] *nf* secularity, secularism.

laid, e [lɛ, lɛd] *a* ugly; (*fig: acte*) mean, cheap.

laideron [lɛdʀɔ̃] *nm* ugly girl.

laideur [lɛdœʀ] *nf* ugliness *q*; meanness *q*.

laie [lɛ] *nf* wild sow.

lainage [lɛnaʒ] *nm* woollen garment; (*étoffe*) woollen material.

laine [lɛn] *nf* wool; **~ peignée** worsted (wool); **~ à tricoter** knitting wool; **~ de verre** glass wool; **~ vierge** new wool.

laineux, euse [lɛnø, -øz] *a* woolly.

lainier, ière [lɛnje, -jɛʀ] *a* (*industrie etc*) woollen.

laïque [laik] *a* lay, civil; (*SCOL*) state *cpd* (*as opposed to private and Roman Catholic*) ♦ *nm/f* layman/woman.

laisse [lɛs] *nf* (*de chien*) lead, leash; **tenir en ~** to keep on a lead *ou* leash.

laissé-pour-compte, laissée-, laissés- [lesepuʀkɔ̃t] *a* (*COMM*) unsold; (*: refusé*) returned ♦ *nm/f* (*fig*) reject; **les laissés-pour-compte de la reprise économique** those who are left out of the economic upturn.

laisser [lese] *vt* to leave ♦ *vb auxiliaire*: **~ qn faire** to let sb do; **se ~ exploiter** to let o.s. be exploited; **se ~ aller** to let o.s. go; **~ qn tranquille** to let *ou* leave sb alone; **laisse-toi faire** let me (*ou* him) do it; **rien ne laisse penser que ...** there is no reason to think that

...; **cela ne laisse pas de surprendre** nonetheless it is surprising.

laisser-aller [leseale] *nm* carelessness, slovenliness.

laisser-faire [lesefɛʀ] *nm* laissez-faire.

laissez-passer [lesepase] *nm inv* pass.

lait [lɛ] *nm* milk; **frère/sœur de ~** foster brother/sister; **~ écrémé/concentré/ condensé** skimmed/condensed/evaporated milk; **~ en poudre** powdered milk, milk powder; **~ de chèvre/vache** goat's/cow's milk; **~ maternel** mother's milk; **~ démaquillant/de beauté** cleansing/beauty lotion.

laitage [lɛtaʒ] *nm* milk product.

laiterie [lɛtʀi] *nf* dairy.

laiteux, euse [lɛtø, -øz] *a* milky.

laitier, ière [lɛtje, -jɛʀ] *a* dairy ♦ *nm/f* milkman/dairywoman.

laiton [lɛtɔ̃] *nm* brass.

laitue [lety] *nf* lettuce.

laïus [lajys] *nm* (*péj*) spiel.

lama [lama] *nm* llama.

lambeau, x [lɑ̃bo] *nm* scrap; **en ~x** in tatters, tattered.

lambin, e [lɑ̃bɛ̃, -in] *a* (*péj*) slow.

lambiner [lɑ̃bine] *vi* (*péj*) to dawdle.

lambris [lɑ̃bʀi] *nm* panelling *q*.

lambrissé, e [lɑ̃bʀise] *a* panelled.

lame [lam] *nf* blade; (*vague*) wave; (*lamelle*) strip; **~ de fond** ground swell *q*; **~ de rasoir** razor blade.

lamé [lame] *nm* lamé.

lamelle [lamɛl] *nf* (*lame*) small blade; (*morceau*) sliver; (*de champignon*) gill; **couper en ~s** to slice thinly.

lamentable [lamɑ̃tabl(ə)] *a* (*déplorable*) appalling; (*pitoyable*) pitiful.

lamentation [lamɑ̃tasjɔ̃] *nf* wailing *q*, lamentation; moaning *q*.

lamenter [lamɑ̃te]: **se ~** *vi*: **se ~ (sur)** to moan (over).

laminage [laminaʒ] *nm* lamination.

laminer [lamine] *vt* to laminate; (*fig: écraser*) to wipe out.

laminoir [laminwaʀ] *nm* rolling mill; **passer au ~** (*fig*) to go (*ou* put) through the mill.

lampadaire [lɑ̃padɛʀ] *nm* (*de salon*) standard lamp; (*dans la rue*) street lamp.

lampe [lɑ̃p(ə)] *nf* lamp; (*TECH*) valve; **~ à alcool** spirit lamp; **~ à bronzer** sunlamp; **~ de poche** torch (*Brit*), flashlight (*US*); **~ à souder** blowlamp; **~ témoin** warning light.

lampée [lɑ̃pe] *nf* gulp, swig.

lampe-tempête, *pl* **lampes-tempête** [lɑ̃ptɑ̃pɛt] *nf* storm lantern.

lampion [lɑ̃pjɔ̃] *nm* Chinese lantern.

lampiste [lɑ̃pist(ə)] *nm* light (maintenance) man; (*fig*) underling.

lamproie [lɑ̃pʀwa] *nf* lamprey.

lance [lɑ̃s] *nf* spear; **~ d'arrosage** garden hose; **~ à eau** water hose; **~ d'incendie** fire hose.

lancée [lɑ̃se] *nf*: **être/continuer sur sa ~** to be under way/keep going.

lance-flammes [lɑ̃sflam] *nm inv* flame-thrower.

lance-fusées [lɑ̃sfyze] *nm inv* rocket launcher.

lance-grenades [lɑ̃sgʀənad] *nm inv* grenade

launcher.

lancement [lɑ̃smɑ̃] *nm* launching *q*, launch; **offre de ~** introductory offer.

lance-missiles [lɑ̃smisil] *nm inv* missile launcher.

lance-pierres [lɑ̃spjɛʀ] *nm inv* catapult.

lancer [lɑ̃se] *nm* (*SPORT*) throwing *q*, throw; (*PÊCHE*) rod and reel fishing ♦ *vt* to throw; (*émettre, projeter*) to throw out, send out; (*produit, fusée, bateau, artiste*) to launch; (*injure*) to hurl, fling; (*proclamation, mandat d'arrêt*) to issue; (*emprunt*) to float; (*moteur*) to send roaring away; **~ qch à qn** to throw sth to sb; (*de façon agressive*) to throw sth at sb; **~ un cri** *ou* **un appel** to shout *ou* call out; **se ~** *vi* (*prendre de l'élan*) to build up speed; (*se précipiter*): **se ~ sur** *ou* **contre** to rush at; **se ~ dans** (*discussion*) to launch into; (*aventure*) to embark on; (*les affaires, la politique*) to go into; **~ du poids** *nm* putting the shot.

lance-roquettes [lɑ̃sʀɔkɛt] *nm inv* rocket launcher.

lance-torpilles [lɑ̃stɔʀpij] *nm inv* torpedo tube.

lanceur, euse [lɑ̃sœʀ, -øz] *nm/f* bowler; (*BASEBALL*) pitcher ♦ *nm* (*ESPACE*) launcher.

lancinant, e [lɑ̃sinɑ̃, -ɑ̃t] *a* (*regrets etc*) haunting; (*douleur*) shooting.

lanciner [lɑ̃sine] *vi* to throb; (*fig*) to nag.

landais, e [lɑ̃dɛ, -ɛz] *a* of *ou* from the Landes.

landau [lɑ̃do] *nm* pram (*Brit*), baby carriage (*US*).

lande [lɑ̃d] *nf* moor.

Landes [lɑ̃d] *nfpl*: **les ~** the Landes.

langage [lɑ̃gaʒ] *nm* language; **~ d'assemblage** (*INFORM*) assembly language; **~ évolué/machine** (*INFORM*) high-level/machine language; **~ de programmation** (*INFORM*) programming language.

lange [lɑ̃ʒ] *nm* flannel blanket; **~s** *nmpl* swaddling clothes.

langer [lɑ̃ʒe] *vt* to change (the nappy (*Brit*) *ou* diaper (*US*) of); **table à ~** changing table.

langoureux, euse [lɑ̃guʀø, -øz] *a* languorous.

langouste [lɑ̃gust(ə)] *nf* crayfish *inv*.

langoustine [lɑ̃gustin] *nf* Dublin Bay prawn.

langue [lɑ̃g] *nf* (*ANAT, CULIN*) tongue; (*LING*) language; (*bande*): **~ de terre** spit of land; **tirer la ~ (à)** to stick out one's tongue (at); **donner sa ~ au chat** to give in, give in; **de ~ française** French-speaking; **~ de bois** officialese; **~ maternelle** native language, mother tongue; **~ verte** slang; **~ vivante** modern language.

langue-de-chat [lɑ̃gdəʃa] *nf* finger biscuit.

languedocien, ne [lɑ̃gdɔsjɛ̃, -ɛn] *a* of *ou* from the Languedoc.

languette [lɑ̃gɛt] *nf* tongue.

langueur [lɑ̃gœʀ] *nf* languidness.

languir [lɑ̃giʀ] *vi* to languish; (*conversation*) to flag; **se ~** *vi* to be languishing; **faire ~ qn** to keep sb waiting.

languissant, e [lɑ̃gisɑ̃, -ɑ̃t] *a* languid.

lanière [lanjɛʀ] *nf* (*de fouet*) lash; (*de valise, bretelle*) strap.

lanoline [lanɔlin] *nf* lanolin.

lanterne [lɑ̃tɛʀn(ə)] *nf* (*portable*) lantern; (*électrique*) light, lamp; (*de voiture*)

(side)light; ~ **rouge** (*fig*) tail-ender; ~
vénitienne Chinese lantern.
lanterneau, x [lɑ̃tɛʀno] *nm* skylight.
lanterner [lɑ̃tɛʀne] *vi*: **faire ~ qn** to keep sb
hanging around.
Laos [laɔs] *nm*: **le ~** Laos.
laotien, ne [laɔsjɛ̃, -ɛn] *a* Laotian.
lapalissade [lapalisad] *nf* statement of the
obvious.
La Paz [lapaz] *n* La Paz.
laper [lape] *vt* to lap up.
lapereau, x [lapʀo] *nm* young rabbit.
lapidaire [lapidɛʀ] *a* stone *cpd*; (*fig*) terse.
lapider [lapide] *vt* to stone.
lapin [lapɛ̃] *nm* rabbit; (*fourrure*) cony; **coup
du ~** rabbit punch; **poser un ~ à qn** to
stand sb up; **~ de garenne** wild rabbit.
lapon, e [lapɔ̃, -ɔn] *a* Lapp, Lappish ♦ *nm*
(*LING*) Lapp, Lappish ♦ *nm/f*: **L~, e** Lapp,
Laplander.
Laponie [lapɔni] *nf*: **la ~** Lapland.
laps [laps] *nm*: **~ de temps** space of time,
time *q*.
lapsus [lapsys] *nm* slip.
laquais [lakɛ] *nm* lackey.
laque [lak] *nf* lacquer; (*brute*) shellac; (*pour
cheveux*) hair spray ♦ *nm* lacquer; piece of
lacquer ware.
laqué, e [lake] *a* lacquered.
laquelle [lakɛl] *pronom voir* **lequel**.
larbin [laʀbɛ̃] *nm* (*péj*) flunkey.
larcin [laʀsɛ̃] *nm* theft.
lard [laʀ] *nm* (*graisse*) fat; (*bacon*) (streaky)
bacon.
larder [laʀde] *vt* (*CULIN*) to lard.
lardon [laʀdɔ̃] *nm* (*CULIN*) piece of chopped
bacon; (*fam: enfant*) kid.
large [laʀʒ(ə)] *a* wide; broad; (*fig*) generous ♦
ad: **calculer/voir ~** to allow extra/think big ♦
nm (*largeur*): **5 m de ~** 5 m wide *ou* in
width; (*mer*): **le ~** the open sea; **en ~** *ad*
sideways; **au ~ de** off; **~ d'esprit** broad-
minded; **ne pas en mener ~** to have one's
heart in one's boots.
largement [laʀʒəmɑ̃] *ad* widely; (*de loin*)
greatly; (*amplement, au minimum*) easily;
(*sans compter: donner etc*) generously.
largesse [laʀʒɛs] *nf* generosity; **~s** *nfpl*
liberalities.
largeur [laʀʒœʀ] *nf* (*qu'on mesure*) width;
(*impression visuelle*) wideness, width;
breadth; broadness.
larguer [laʀge] *vt* to drop; (*fam: se
débarrasser de*) to get rid of; **~ les amarres**
to cast off (the moorings).
larme [laʀm(ə)] *nf* tear; (*fig*): **une ~ de** a
drop of; **en ~s** in tears; **pleurer à chaudes
~s** to cry one's eyes out, cry bitterly.
larmoyant, e [laʀmwajɑ̃, -ɑ̃t] *a* tearful.
larmoyer [laʀmwaje] *vi* (*yeux*) to water; (*se
plaindre*) to whimper.
larron [laʀɔ̃] *nm* thief (*pl* thieves).
larve [laʀv(ə)] *nf* (*ZOOL*) larva (*pl* -ae); (*fig*)
worm.
larvé, e [laʀve] *a* (*fig*) latent.
laryngite [laʀɛ̃ʒit] *nf* laryngitis.
laryngologiste [laʀɛ̃gɔlɔʒist(ə)] *nm/f* throat
specialist.
larynx [laʀɛ̃ks] *nm* larynx.

las, lasse [lɑ, lɑs] *a* weary.
lasagne [lazaɲ] *nf* lasagne.
lascar [laskaʀ] *nm* character; (*malin*) rogue.
lascif, ive [lasif, -iv] *a* lascivious.
laser [lazɛʀ] *nm*: **(rayon) ~** laser (beam);
chaîne *ou* **platine ~** compact disc (player);
disque ~ compact disc.
lassant, e [lɑsɑ̃, -ɑ̃t] *a* tiresome, wearisome.
lasse [lɑs] *af voir* **las**.
lasser [lɑse] *vt* to weary, tire; **se ~ de** to
grow weary *ou* tired of.
lassitude [lɑsityd] *nf* lassitude, weariness.
lasso [laso] *nm* lasso; **prendre au ~** to lasso.
latent, e [latɑ̃, -ɑ̃t] *a* latent.
latéral, e, aux [lateʀal, -o] *a* side *cpd*, lateral.
latéralement [lateʀalmɑ̃] *ad* edgeways;
(*arriver, souffler*) from the side.
latex [latɛks] *nm inv* latex.
latin, e [latɛ̃, -in] *a* Latin ♦ *nm* (*LING*) Latin ♦
nm/f: **L~, e** Latin; **j'y perds mon ~** it's all
Greek to me.
latiniste [latinist(ə)] *nm/f* Latin scholar (*ou*
student).
latino-américain, e [latinɔameʀikɛ̃, -ɛn] *a*
Latin-American.
latitude [latityd] *nf* latitude; (*fig*): **avoir la ~
de faire** to be left free *ou* be at liberty to do;
à 48° de ~ Nord at latitude 48° North; **sous
toutes les ~s** (*fig*) world-wide, throughout
the world.
latrines [latʀin] *nfpl* latrines.
latte [lat] *nf* lath, slat; (*de plancher*) board.
lattis [lati] *nm* lathwork.
laudatif, ive [lodatif, -iv] *a* laudatory.
lauréat, e [lɔʀea, -at] *nm/f* winner.
laurier [lɔʀje] *nm* (*BOT*) laurel; (*CULIN*) bay
leaves *pl*; **~s** *nmpl* (*fig*) laurels.
laurier-rose, *pl* lauriers-rose [lɔʀjeʀoz] *nm*
oleander.
lavable [lavabl(ə)] *a* washable.
lavabo [lavabo] *nm* washbasin; **~s** *nmpl* toilet
sg.
lavage [lavaʒ] *nm* washing *q*, wash; **~
d'estomac/d'intestin** stomach/intestinal
wash; **~ de cerveau** brainwashing *q*.
lavande [lavɑ̃d] *nf* lavender.
lavandière [lavɑ̃djɛʀ] *nf* washerwoman.
lave [lav] *nf* lava *q*.
lave-glace [lavglas] *nm* (*AUTO*) windscreen
(*Brit*) *ou* windshield (*US*) washer.
lave-linge [lavlɛ̃ʒ] *nm inv* washing machine.
lavement [lavmɑ̃] *nm* (*MÉD*) enema.
laver [lave] *vt* to wash; (*tache*) to wash off;
(*fig: affront*) to avenge; **se ~** to have a
wash, wash; **se ~ les mains/dents** to wash
one's hands/clean one's teeth; **~ la vaisselle/
le linge** to wash the dishes/clothes; **~ qn de**
(*accusation*) to clear sb of.
laverie [lavʀi] *nf*: **~ (automatique)** launderette.
lavette [lavɛt] *nf* (*chiffon*) dish cloth; (*brosse*)
dish mop; (*fam: homme*) wimp, drip.
laveur, euse [lavœʀ, -øz] *nm/f* cleaner.
lave-vaisselle [lavvɛsɛl] *nm inv* dishwasher.
lavis [lavi] *nm* (*technique*) washing; (*dessin*)
wash drawing.
lavoir [lavwaʀ] *nm* wash house; (*bac*)
washtub.
laxatif, ive [laksatif, -iv] *a*, *nm* laxative.

laxisme [laksism(ə)] nm laxity.

laxiste [laksist(ə)] a lax.

layette [lɛjɛt] nf layette.

layon [lɛjɔ̃] nm trail.

lazaret [lazaʀɛ] nm quarantine area.

lazzi [ladzi] nm gibe.

LCR sigle f (= Ligue communiste révolutionnaire) political party.

le (l'), **la** (l'), **les** [l(ə), la, le] dét the ♦ pronom (personne: mâle) him; (: femelle) her; (animal, chose) it; (remplaçant une phrase) it ou non traduit; (indique la possession): **se casser la jambe** etc to break one's leg etc; voir note sous **il**; **les** them; **je ne le savais pas** I didn't know (about it); **il était riche et ne l'est plus** he was once rich but no longer is; **levez la main** put your hand up; **avoir les yeux gris/le nez rouge** to have grey eyes/a red nose; **le jeudi** etc ad (d'habitude) on Thursdays etc; (ce jeudi-là) on the Thursday etc; **le matin/soir** ad in the morning/evening; mornings/evenings; **nous venons le 3 décembre** (parlé) we're coming on the 3rd of December ou on December the 3rd; (écrit) we're coming (on) 3rd ou 3 December; **10 F le mètre/kilo** 10 F a ou per metre/kilo; **le tiers/quart de** a third/quarter of.

lé [le] nm (de tissu) width; (de papier peint) strip, length.

leader [lidœʀ] nm leader.

lèche-bottes [lɛʃbɔt] nm inv bootlicker.

lèchefrite [lɛʃfʀit] nf dripping pan ou tray.

lécher [leʃe] vt to lick; (laper: lait, eau) to lick ou lap up; (finir, polir) to over-refine; ~ **les vitrines** to go window-shopping; **se ~ les doigts/lèvres** to lick one's fingers/lips.

leçon [ləsɔ̃] nf lesson; **faire la ~** to teach; **faire la ~ à** (fig) to give a lecture to; **~s de conduite** driving lessons; **~s particulières** private lessons ou tuition sg (Brit).

lecteur, trice [lɛktœʀ, -tʀis] nm/f reader; (d'université) (foreign language) assistant (Brit), (foreign) teaching assistant (US) ♦ nm (TECH): ~ **de cassettes** cassette player; (INFORM): ~ **de disquette(s)** ou **de disque** disk drive; ~ **compact-disc** ou **CD** compact disc (player).

lectorat [lɛktɔʀa] nm (foreign language ou teaching) assistantship.

lecture [lɛktyʀ] nf reading.

LED [lɛd] sigle f (= light emitting diode) LED; **affichage** ~ LED display.

ledit [lədi], **ladite** [ladit], mpl **lesdits** [ledi], fpl **lesdites** [ledit] dét the aforesaid.

légal, e, aux [legal, -o] a legal.

légalement [legalmã] ad legally.

légaliser [legalize] vt to legalize.

légalité [legalite] nf legality, lawfulness; **être dans/sortir de la** ~ to be within/step outside the law.

légat [lega] nm (REL) legate.

légataire [legatɛʀ] nm legatee.

légendaire [leʒɑ̃dɛʀ] a legendary.

légende [leʒɑ̃d] nf (mythe) legend; (de carte, plan) key, legend; (de dessin) caption, legend.

léger, ère [leʒe, -ɛʀ] a light; (bruit, retard) slight; (boisson, parfum) weak; (couche, étoffe) thin; (superficiel) thoughtless; (vo-

lage) free and easy; flighty; (peu sérieux) lightweight; **blessé** ~ slightly injured person; **à la légère** ad (parler, agir) rashly, thoughtlessly.

légèrement [leʒɛʀmã] ad lightly; thoughtlessly, rashly; ~ **plus grand** slightly bigger.

légèreté [leʒɛʀte] nf lightness; thoughtlessness.

légiférer [leʒifeʀe] vi to legislate.

légion [leʒjɔ̃] nf legion; **la L~ étrangère** the Foreign Legion; **la L~ d'honneur** the Legion of Honour.

légionnaire [leʒjɔnɛʀ] nm (MIL) legionnaire; (de la Légion d'honneur) holder of the Legion of Honour.

législateur [leʒislatœʀ] nm legislator, lawmaker.

législatif, ive [leʒislatif, -iv] a legislative; **législatives** nfpl general election sg.

législation [leʒislasjɔ̃] nf legislation.

législature [leʒislatyʀ] nf legislature; (période) term (of office).

légiste [leʒist(ə)] nm jurist ♦ a: **médecin** ~ forensic scientist (Brit), medical examiner (US).

légitime [leʒitim] a (JUR) lawful, legitimate; (enfant) legitimate; (fig) rightful, legitimate; **en état de** ~ **défense** in self-defence.

légitimement [leʒitimmã] ad lawfully; legitimately; rightfully.

légitimer [leʒitime] vt (enfant) to legitimize; (justifier: conduite etc) to justify.

légitimité [leʒitimite] nf (JUR) legitimacy.

legs [lɛg] nm legacy.

léguer [lege] vt: ~ **qch à qn** (JUR) to bequeath sth to sb; (fig) to hand sth down ou pass sth on to sb.

légume [legym] nm vegetable; ~**s verts** green vegetables; ~**s secs** pulses.

légumier [legymje] nm vegetable dish.

Léman [lemã] nm voir **lac**.

lendemain [lɑ̃dmɛ̃] nm: **le** ~ the next ou following day; **le** ~ **matin/soir** the next ou following morning/evening; **le** ~ **de** the day after; **au** ~ **de** in the days following; in the wake of; **penser au** ~ to think of the future; **sans** ~ short-lived; **de beaux** ~**s** bright prospects; **des** ~**s qui chantent** a rosy future.

lénifiant, e [lenifjɑ̃, -ɑ̃t] a soothing.

léniniste [leninist(ə)] a, nm/f Leninist.

lent, e [lɑ̃, lɑ̃t] a slow.

lente [lɑ̃t] nf nit.

lentement [lɑ̃tmã] ad slowly.

lenteur [lɑ̃tœʀ] nf slowness q; ~**s** nfpl (actions, décisions lentes) slowness sg.

lentille [lɑ̃tij] nf (OPTIQUE) lens sg; (BOT) lentil; ~ **d'eau** duckweed; ~**s de contact** contact lenses.

léonin, e [leɔnɛ̃, -in] a (fig: contrat etc) one-sided.

léopard [leɔpaʀ] nm leopard.

LEP [lɛp] sigle m (= lycée d'enseignement professionnel) secondary school for vocational training, pre-1986.

lèpre [lɛpʀ(ə)] nf leprosy.

lépreux, euse [lepʀø, -øz] nm/f leper ♦ a (fig) flaking, peeling.

lequel [ləkɛl], **laquelle** [lakɛl], mpl **lesquels**,

fpl **lesquelles** [lɛkɛl] (*avec à, de*: **auquel, duquel** *etc*) *pronom* (*interrogatif*) which, which one; (*relatif: personne: sujet*) who; (: *objet, après préposition*) whom; (: *chose*) which ◆ *a*: **auquel cas** in which case.

les [le] *dét voir* **le**.

lesbienne [lɛsbjɛn] *nf* lesbian.

lesdits [ledi], **lesdites** [ledit] *dét voir* **ledit**.

léser [leze] *vt to wrong*; (*MÉD*) to injure.

lésiner [lezine] *vt*: ~ **(sur)** to skimp (on).

lésion [lezjɔ̃] *nf* lesion, damage *q*; ~**s cérébrales** brain damage.

Lesotho [lezoto] *nm*: **le** ~ Lesotho.

lesquels, lesquelles [lekɛl] *pronom voir* **lequel**.

lessivable [lesivabl(ə)] *a* washable.

lessive [lesiv] *nf* (*poudre*) washing powder; (*linge*) washing *q*, wash; (*opération*) washing *q*; **faire la** ~ to do the washing.

lessivé, e [lesive] *a* (*fam*) washed out.

lessiver [lesive] *vt* to wash.

lessiveuse [lesivøz] *nf* (*récipient*) (laundry) boiler.

lessiviel [lesivjɛl] *a* detergent.

lest [lɛst] *nm* ballast; **jeter** *ou* **lâcher du** ~ (*fig*) to make concessions.

leste [lɛst(ə)] *a* (*personne, mouvement*) sprightly, nimble; (*désinvolte: manières*) offhand; (*osé: plaisanterie*) risqué.

lestement [lɛstəmɑ̃] *ad* nimbly.

lester [lɛste] *vt* to ballast.

letchi [lɛtʃi] *nm* = **litchi**.

léthargie [letaʀʒi] *nf* lethargy.

léthargique [letaʀʒik] *a* lethargic.

letton, ne [lɛtɔ̃, -ɔn] *a* Latvian, Lett.

Lettonie [lɛtɔni] *nf*: **la** ~ Latvia.

lettre [lɛtʀ(ə)] *nf* letter; ~**s** *nfpl* (*étude, culture*) literature *sg*; (*SCOL*) arts (subjects); **à la** ~ (*au sens propre*) literally; (*ponctuellement*) to the letter; **en** ~**s majuscules** *ou* **capitales** in capital letters, in capitals; **en toutes** ~**s** in words, in full; ~ **de change** bill of exchange; ~ **piégée** letter bomb; ~ **de voiture (aérienne)** (air) waybill, (air) bill of lading; ~**s de noblesse** pedigree.

lettré, e [letʀe] *a* well-read, scholarly.

lettre-transfert, *pl* **lettres-transferts** [lɛtʀətʀɑ̃sfɛʀ] *nf* (pressure) transfer.

leu [lø] *voir* **queue**.

leucémie [løsemi] *nf* leukaemia.

leur [lœʀ] *dét* their ◆ *pronom* them; **le (la)** ~, **les** ~**s** theirs; **à** ~ **approche** as they came near; **à** ~ **vue** at the sight of them.

leurre [lœʀ] *nm* (*appât*) lure; (*fig*) delusion; (: *piège*) snare.

leurrer [lœʀe] *vt* to delude, deceive.

levain [ləvɛ̃] *nm* leaven; **sans** ~ unleavened.

levant, e [ləvɑ̃, -ɑ̃t] *a*: **soleil** ~ rising sun ◆ *nm*: **le L~** the Levant; **au soleil** ~ at sunrise.

levantin, e [ləvɑ̃tɛ̃, -in] *a* Levantine ◆ *nm/f*: **L~, e** Levantine.

levé, e [ləve] *a*: **être** ~ to be up ◆ *nm*: ~ **de terrain** land survey; **à mains** ~**es** (*vote*) by a show of hands; **au pied** ~ at a moment's notice.

levée [ləve] *nf* (*POSTES*) collection; (*CARTES*) trick; ~ **de boucliers** general outcry; ~ **du corps** *collection of the body from house of the*

deceased, before funeral; ~ **d'écrou** release from custody; ~ **de terre** levee; ~ **de troupes** levy.

lever [ləve] *vt* (*vitre, bras etc*) to raise; (*soulever de terre, supprimer: interdiction, siège*) to lift; (: *difficulté*) to remove; (*séance*) to close; (*impôts, armée*) to levy; (*CHASSE: lièvre*) to start; (: *perdrix*) to flush; (*fam: fille*) to pick up ◆ *vi* (*CULIN*) to rise ◆ *nm*: **au** ~ on getting up; **se** ~ *vi* to get up; (*soleil*) to rise; (*jour*) to break; (*brouillard*) to lift; **ça va se** ~ the weather will clear; ~ **du jour** daybreak; ~ **du rideau** (*THÉÂTRE*) curtain; ~ **de rideau** (*pièce*) curtain raiser; ~ **de soleil** sunrise.

lève-tard [lɛvtaʀ] *nm/f inv* late riser.

lève-tôt [lɛvto] *nm/f inv* early riser, early bird.

levier [ləvje] *nm* lever; **faire** ~ **sur** to lever up (*ou* off); ~ **de changement de vitesse** gear lever.

levraut [ləvʀo] *nm* (*ZOOL*) leveret.

lèvre [lɛvʀ(ə)] *nf* lip; ~**s** *nfpl* (*d'une plaie*) edges; **petites/grandes** ~**s** labia minora/majora; **du bout des** ~**s** half-heartedly.

lévrier [levʀije] *nm* greyhound.

levure [ləvyʀ] *nf* yeast; ~ **chimique** baking powder.

lexicographe [lɛksikɔgʀaf] *nm/f* lexicographer.

lexicographie [lɛksikɔgʀafi] *nf* lexicography, dictionary writing.

lexique [lɛksik] *nm* vocabulary, lexicon; (*glossaire*) vocabulary.

lézard [lezaʀ] *nm* lizard; (*peau*) lizardskin.

lézarde [lezaʀd(ə)] *nf* crack.

lézarder [lezaʀde]: **se** ~ *vi* to crack.

liaison [ljɛzɔ̃] *nf* (*rapport*) connection, link; (*RAIL, AVIAT etc*) link; (*relation: d'amitié*) friendship; (: *d'affaires*) relationship; (: *amoureuse*) affair; (*CULIN, PHONÉTIQUE*) liaison; **entrer/être en** ~ **avec** to get/be in contact with; ~ **radio** radio contact; ~ **(de transmission de données)** (*INFORM*) data link.

liane [ljan] *nf* creeper.

liant, e [ljɑ̃, -ɑ̃t] *a* sociable.

liasse [ljas] *nf* wad, bundle.

Liban [libɑ̃] *nm*: **le** ~ (the) Lebanon.

libanais [libanɛ, -ɛz] *a* Lebanese ◆ *nm/f*: **L~, e** Lebanese.

libations [libasjɔ̃] *nfpl* libations.

libelle [libɛl] *nm* lampoon.

libellé [libele] *nm* wording.

libeller [libele] *vt* (*chèque, mandat*): ~ **(au nom de)** to make out (to); (*lettre*) to word.

libellule [libelyl] *nf* dragonfly.

libéral, e, aux [libeʀal, -o] *a, nm/f* liberal; **les professions** ~**es** the professions.

libéralement [libeʀalmɑ̃] *ad* liberally.

libéralisation [libeʀalizasjɔ̃] *nf* liberalization; ~ **du commerce** easing of trade restrictions.

libéraliser [libeʀalize] *vt* to liberalize.

libéralisme [libeʀalism(ə)] *nm* liberalism.

libéralité [libeʀalite] *nf* liberality *q*, generosity *q*.

libérateur, trice [libeʀatœʀ, -tʀis] *a* liberating ◆ *nm/f* liberator.

libération [libeʀasjɔ̃] *nf* liberation, freeing; release; discharge; ~ **conditionnelle** release on parole.

libéré, e [libere] a liberated; ~ **de** freed from; **être ~ sous caution/sur parole** to be released on bail/on parole.

libérer [libere] vt (délivrer) to free, liberate; (: moralement, PSYCH) to liberate; (relâcher: prisonnier) to release; (: soldat) to discharge; (dégager: gaz, cran d'arrêt) to release; (ÉCON: échanges commerciaux) to ease restrictions on; **se ~** (de rendez-vous) to try and be free, get out of previous engagements; ~ **qn de** (liens, dette) to free sb from; (promesse) to release sb from.

Libéria [liberja] nm: **le ~** Liberia.

libérien, ne [liberjɛ̃, -ɛn] a Liberian ♦ nm/f: **L~, ne** Liberian.

libertaire [libertɛʀ] a libertarian.

liberté [libɛʀte] nf freedom; (loisir) free time; ~**s** nfpl (privautés) liberties; **mettre/être en ~** to set/be free; **en ~ provisoire/surveillée/ conditionnelle** on bail/probation/parole; ~ **d'association** right of association; ~ **de conscience** freedom of conscience; ~ **du culte** freedom of worship; ~ **d'esprit** independence of mind; ~ **d'opinion** freedom of thought; ~ **de la presse** freedom of the press; ~ **de réunion** right to hold meetings; ~ **syndicale** union rights pl; ~**s individuelles** personal freedom sg; ~**s publiques** civil rights.

libertin, e [libɛʀtɛ̃, -in] a libertine, licentious.

libertinage [libɛʀtinaʒ] nm licentiousness.

libidineux, euse [libidinø, -øz] a libidinous, lustful.

libido [libido] nf libido.

libraire [libʀɛʀ] nm/f bookseller.

libraire-éditeur, pl **libraires-éditeurs** [libʀɛʀeditœʀ] nm publisher and bookseller.

librairie [libʀɛʀi] nf bookshop.

librairie-papeterie, pl **librairies-papeteries** [libʀɛʀipapetʀi] bookseller's and stationer's.

libre [libʀ(ə)] a free; (route) clear; (place etc) vacant, free; (fig: propos, manières) open; (SCOL) private and Roman Catholic (as opposed to "laïque"); **de ~** (place) free; ~ **de qch/de faire** free from sth/to do; **vente ~** (COMM) unrestricted sale; ~ **arbitre** free will; ~ **concurrence** free-market economy; ~ **entreprise** free enterprise.

libre-échange [libʀeʃɑ̃ʒ] nm free trade.

librement [libʀəmɑ̃] ad freely.

libre-penseur, euse [libʀəpɑ̃sœʀ, -øz] nm/f free thinker.

libre-service [libʀəsɛʀvis] nm inv (magasin) self-service store; (restaurant) self-service restaurant.

librettiste [libʀetist(ə)] nm/f librettist.

Libye [libi] nf: **la ~** Libya.

libyen, ne [libjɛ̃, -ɛn] a Libyan ♦ nm/f: **L~, ne** Libyan.

lice [lis] nf: **entrer en ~** (fig) to enter the lists.

licence [lisɑ̃s] nf (permis) permit; (diplôme) (first) degree; (liberté) liberty; (poétique, orthographique) licence (Brit), license (US); (des mœurs) licentiousness; ~ **ès lettres/en droit** arts/law degree.

licencié, e [lisɑ̃sje] nm/f (SCOL): ~ **ès lettres/en droit** ≈ Bachelor of Arts/Law,

arts/law graduate; (SPORT) permit-holder.

licenciement [lisɑ̃simɑ̃] nm dismissal; redundancy; laying off q.

licencier [lisɑ̃sje] vt (renvoyer) to dismiss; (débaucher) to make redundant; to lay off.

licencieux, euse [lisɑ̃sjø, -øz] a licentious.

lichen [likɛn] nm lichen.

licite [lisit] a lawful.

licorne [likɔʀn(ə)] nf unicorn.

licou [liku] nm halter.

lie [li] nf dregs pl, sediment.

lié, e [lje] a: **très ~ avec** (fig) very friendly with ou close to; ~ **par** (serment, promesse) bound by; **avoir partie ~e (avec qn)** to be involved (with sb).

Liechtenstein [liʃtɛnʃtajn] nm: **le ~** Liechtenstein.

lie-de-vin [lidvɛ̃] a inv wine(-coloured).

liège [ljɛʒ] nm cork.

liégeois, e [ljeʒwa, -waz] a of ou from Liège ♦ nm/f: **L~, e** inhabitant ou native of Liège; **café/chocolat ~** coffee/chocolate ice cream topped with whipped cream.

lien [ljɛ̃] nm (corde, fig: affectif, culturel) bond; (rapport) link, connection; (analogie) link; ~ **de parenté** family tie.

lier [lje] vt (attacher) to tie up; (joindre) to link up; (fig: unir, engager) to bind; (CULIN) to thicken; ~ **qch à** (attacher) to tie sth to; (associer) to link sth to; ~ **amitié/ conversation (avec)** to strike up a friendship/ conversation (with); **se ~ avec** to make friends with.

lierre [ljɛʀ] nm ivy.

liesse [ljes] nf: **être en ~** to be jubilant.

lieu, x [ljø] nm place; ~**x** nmpl (locaux) premises; (endroit: d'un accident etc) scene sg; **en ~ sûr** in a safe place; **en haut ~** in high places; **vider ou quitter les ~x** to leave the premises; **arriver/être sur les ~x** to arrive/be on the scene; **en premier ~** in the first place; **en dernier ~** lastly; **avoir ~** to take place; **avoir ~ de faire** to have grounds ou good reason for doing; **tenir ~ de** to take the place of; (servir de) to serve as; **donner ~ à** to give rise to, give cause for; **au ~ de** instead of; **au ~ qu'il y aille** instead of him going; ~ **commun** commonplace; ~ **géométrique** locus; ~ **de naissance** place of birth; ~ **de rendez-vous** venue, meeting place.

lieu-dit, pl **lieux-dits** [ljødi] nm locality.

lieue [ljø] nf league.

lieutenant [ljøtnɑ̃] nm lieutenant; ~ **de vaisseau** (NAVIG) lieutenant.

lièvre [ljɛvʀ(ə)] nm hare; (coureur) pacemaker; **lever un ~** (fig) to bring up a prickly subject.

liftier, ière [liftje, -jɛʀ] nm/f lift (Brit) ou elevator (US) attendant.

lifting [liftiŋ] nm face lift.

ligament [ligamɑ̃] nm ligament.

ligature [ligatyʀ] nf ligature.

lige [liʒ] a: **homme ~** (péj) henchman.

ligne [liɲ] nf (gén) line; (TRANSPORTS: liaison) service; (: trajet) route; (silhouette) : **garder la ~** to keep one's figure; **en ~** (INFORM) on line; **en ~ droite** as the crow flies; **"à la ~"** "new paragraph"; **entrer en ~ de compte** to be taken into account; to come into it; ~ **de but/médiane** goal/halfway line; ~ **d'arrivée/de départ** finishing/starting line; ~ **de conduite** course of action; ~ **directrice** guiding line; ~ **d'horizon** skyline; ~ **de mire** line of sight; ~ **de touche** touchline.

ligné, e [liɲe] *a*: **papier** ~ ruled paper ♦ *nf* (*race, famille*) line, lineage; (*postérité*) descendants *pl*.

ligneux, euse [liɲø, -øz] *a* ligneous, woody.

lignite [liɲit] *nm* lignite.

ligoter [ligɔte] *vt* to tie up.

ligue [lig] *nf* league.

liguer [lige]: **se** ~ *vi* to form a league; **se** ~ **contre** (*fig*) to combine against.

lilas [lila] *nm* lilac.

lillois, e [lilwa, -waz] *a* of *ou* from Lille.

Lima [lima] *n* Lima.

limace [limas] *nf* slug.

limaille [limaj] *nf*: ~ **de fer** iron filings *pl*.

limande [limɑ̃d] *nf* dab.

limande-sole [limɑ̃dsɔl] *nf* lemon sole.

limbes [lɛ̃b] *nmpl* limbo *sg*; **être dans les** ~ (*fig: projet etc*) to be up in the air.

lime [lim] *nf* (*TECH*) file; (*BOT*) lime; ~ **à ongles** nail file.

limer [lime] *vt* (*bois, métal*) to file (down); (*ongles*) to file; (*fig: prix*) to pare down.

limier [limje] *nm* (*ZOOL*) bloodhound; (*détective*) sleuth.

liminaire [liminɛʀ] *a* (*propos*) introductory.

limitatif, ive [limitatif, -iv] *a* restrictive.

limitation [limitasjɔ̃] *nf* limitation, restriction; **sans** ~ **de temps** with no time limit; ~ **des naissances** birth control; ~ **de vitesse** speed limit.

limite [limit] *nf* (*de terrain*) boundary; (*partie ou point extrême*) limit; **dans la** ~ **de** within the limits of; **à la** ~ (*au pire*) if the worst comes (*ou* came) to the worst; **sans** ~**s** (*bêtise, richesse, pouvoir*) limitless, boundless; **vitesse/charge** ~ maximum speed/load; **cas** ~ borderline case; **date** ~ deadline; **date** ~ **de vente/consommation** sell-by/best-before date; **prix** ~ upper price limit; ~ **d'âge** maximum age, age limit.

limiter [limite] *vt* (*restreindre*) to limit, restrict; (*délimiter*) to border, form the boundary of; **se** ~ (**à qch/à faire**) (*personne*) to limit *ou* confine o.s. (to sth/to doing sth); **se** ~ **à** (*chose*) to be limited to.

limitrophe [limitʀɔf] *a* border *cpd*; ~ **de** bordering on.

limogeage [limɔʒaʒ] *nm* dismissal.

limoger [limɔʒe] *vt* to dismiss.

limon [limɔ̃] *nm* silt.

limonade [limɔnad] *nf* lemonade.

limonadier, ière [limɔnadje, -jɛʀ] *nm/f* (*commerçant*) café owner; (*fabricant de limonade*) soft drinks manufacturer.

limoneux, euse [limɔnø, -øz] *a* muddy.

limousin, e [limuzɛ̃, -in] *a* of *ou* from Limousin ♦ *nm* (*région*): **le L**~ the Limousin.

limpide [lɛ̃pid] *a* limpid.

lin [lɛ̃] *nm* (*BOT*) flax; (*tissu, toile*) linen.

linceul [lɛ̃sœl] *nm* shroud.

linéaire [lineɛʀ] *a* linear ♦ *nm*: ~ (**de vente**) shelves *pl*.

linéament [lineamɑ̃] *nm* outline.

linge [lɛ̃ʒ] *nm* (*serviettes etc*) linen; (*pièce de tissu*) cloth; (*aussi*: ~ **de corps**) underwear; (*aussi*: ~ **de toilette**) towel; (*lessive*) washing; ~ **sale** dirty linen.

lingerie [lɛ̃ʒʀi] *nf* lingerie, underwear.

lingot [lɛ̃go] *nm* ingot.

linguiste [lɛ̃gɥist(ə)] *nm/f* linguist.

linguistique [lɛ̃gɥistik] *a* linguistic ♦ *nf* linguistics *sg*.

lino(léum) [lino(leɔm)] *nm* lino(leum).

linotte [linɔt] *nf*: **tête de** ~ bird brain.

linteau, x [lɛ̃to] *nm* lintel.

lion, ne [ljɔ̃, ljɔn] *nm/f* lion/lioness; (*signe*): **le L**~ Leo, the Lion; **être du L**~ to be Leo; ~ **de mer** sealion.

lionceau, x [ljɔ̃so] *nm* lion cub.

lippu, e [lipy] *a* thick-lipped.

liquéfier [likefje] *vt* to liquefy; **se** ~ *vi* (*gaz etc*) to liquefy; (*fig: personne*) to succumb.

liqueur [likœʀ] *nf* liqueur.

liquidateur, trice [likidatœʀ, -tʀis] *nm/f* (*JUR*) receiver; ~ **judiciaire** official liquidator.

liquidation [likidasjɔ̃] *nf* liquidation; (*COMM*) clearance (sale); ~ **judiciaire** compulsory liquidation.

liquide [likid] *a* liquid ♦ *nm* liquid; (*COMM*): **en** ~ in ready money *ou* cash.

liquider [likide] *vt* (*société, biens, témoin gênant*) to liquidate; (*compte, problème*) to settle; (*COMM: articles*) to clear, sell off.

liquidités [likidite] *nfpl* (*COMM*) liquid assets.

liquoreux, euse [likɔʀø, -øz] *a* syrupy.

lire [liʀ] *nf* (*monnaie*) lira ♦ *vt, vi* to read; ~ **qch à qn** to read sth (out) to sb.

lis *vb* [li] *voir* **lire** ♦ *nm* [lis] = **lys**.

lisais [lize] *etc vb voir* **lire**.

Lisbonne [lizbɔn] *n* Lisbon.

lise [liz] *etc vb voir* **lire**.

liseré [lizʀe] *nm* border, edging.

liseron [lizʀɔ̃] *nm* bindweed.

liseuse [lizøz] *nf* book-cover; (*veste*) bedjacket.

lisible [lizibl(ə)] *a* legible; (*digne d'être lu*) readable.

lisiblement [lizibləmɑ̃] *ad* legibly.

lisière [lizjɛʀ] *nf* (*de forêt*) edge; (*de tissu*) selvage.

lisons [lizɔ̃] *vb voir* **lire**.

lisse [lis] *a* smooth.

lisser [lise] *vt* to smooth.

listage [listaʒ] *nm* (*INFORM*) listing.

liste [list(ə)] *nf* list; (*INFORM*) listing; **faire la** ~ **de** to list, make out a list of; ~ **d'attente** waiting list; ~ **civile** civil list; ~ **électorale** electoral roll; ~ **de mariage** wedding (present) list.

lister [liste] *vt* (*aussi INFORM*) to list; ~ **la mémoire** to dump.

listing [listiŋ] *nm* (*INFORM*) listing; **qualité** ~ draft quality.

lit [li] *nm* (*gén*) bed; **faire son** ~ to make one's bed; **aller/se mettre au** ~ to go to/get into bed; **prendre le** ~ to take to one's bed; **d'un premier** ~ (*JUR*) of a first marriage; ~ **de camp** campbed (*Brit*), cot (*US*); ~ **d'enfant** cot (*Brit*), crib (*US*).

litanie [litani] *nf* litany.

lit-cage, pl lits-cages [likaʒ] *nm* folding bed.

litchi [litʃi] *nm* lychee.

literie [litʀi] nf bedding; (linge) bedding, bedclothes pl.

litho [lito], **lithographie** [litɔgʀafi] nf litho(graphy); (épreuve) litho(graph).

litière [litjɛʀ] nf litter.

litige [litiʒ] nm dispute; **en ~** in contention.

litigieux, euse [litiʒjø, -øz] a litigious, contentious.

litote [litɔt] nf understatement.

litre [litʀ(ə)] nm litre; (récipient) litre measure.

littéraire [liteʀɛʀ] a literary.

littéral, e, aux [liteʀal, -o] a literal.

littérature [liteʀatyʀ] nf literature.

littoral, e, aux [litɔʀal, -o] a coastal ♦ nm coast.

Lituanie [lityani] nf: **la ~** Lithuania.

lituanien, ne [lityanjɛ̃, -ɛn] a Lithuanian.

liturgie [lityʀʒi] nf liturgy.

liturgique [lityʀʒik] a liturgical.

livide [livid] a livid, pallid.

living(-room) [liviŋ(ʀum)] nm living room.

livrable [livʀabl(ə)] a (COMM) that can be delivered.

livraison [livʀɛzɔ̃] nf delivery; **~ à domicile** home delivery (service).

livre [livʀ(ə)] nm book; (imprimerie etc): **le ~** the book industry ♦ nf (poids, monnaie) pound; **traduire qch à ~ ouvert** to translate sth off the cuff ou at sight; **~ blanc** official report (prepared by independent body, following war, natural disaster etc); **~ de bord** (NAVIG) logbook; **~ de comptes** account(s) book; **~ de cuisine** cookery book (Brit), cookbook; **~ de messe** mass ou prayer book; **~ d'or** visitors' book; **~ de poche** paperback (cheap and pocket size); **~ verte** green pound.

livré, e [livʀe] nf livery ♦ a: **~ à** (l'anarchie etc) given over to; **~ à soi-même** left to oneself ou one's own devices.

livrer [livʀe] vt (COMM) to deliver; (otage, coupable) to hand over; (secret, information) to give away; **se ~ à** (se confier) to confide in; (se rendre) to give o.s. up to; (s'abandonner à: débauche etc) to give o.s. up ou over to; (faire: pratiques, actes) to indulge in; (travail) to be engaged in, engage in; (: sport) to practise; (: enquête) to carry out; **~ bataille** to give battle.

livresque [livʀɛsk(ə)] a (péj) bookish.

livret [livʀɛ] nm booklet; (d'opéra) libretto (pl -s); **~ de caisse d'épargne** (savings) bankbook; **~ de famille** (official) family record book; **~ scolaire** (school) report book.

livreur, euse [livʀœʀ, -øz] nm/f delivery boy ou man/girl ou woman.

LO sigle f (= Lutte ouvrière) political party.

lobe [lɔb] nm: **~ de l'oreille** ear lobe.

lobé, e [lɔbe] a (ARCHIT) foiled.

lober [lɔbe] vt to lob.

local, e, aux [lɔkal, -o] a local ♦ nm (salle) premises pl ♦ nmpl premises.

localement [lɔkalmɑ̃] ad locally.

localisé, e [lɔkalize] a localized.

localiser [lɔkalize] vt (repérer) to locate, place; (limiter) to localize, confine.

localité [lɔkalite] nf locality.

locataire [lɔkatɛʀ] nm/f tenant; (de chambre) lodger.

locatif, ive [lɔkatif, -iv] a (charges, réparations) incumbent upon the tenant; (valeur) rental; (immeuble) with rented flats, used as a letting ou rental (US) concern.

location [lɔkasjɔ̃] nf (par le locataire) renting; (par l'usager: de voiture etc) hiring (Brit), renting (US); (par le propriétaire) renting out, letting; hiring out (Brit); (de billets, places) booking; (bureau) booking office; **"~ de voitures"** "car hire (Brit) ou rental (US)".

location-vente [lɔkasjɔ̃vɑ̃t] nf form of hire purchase (Brit) ou instalment plan (US).

lock-out [lɔkawt] nm inv lockout.

locomoteur, trice [lɔkɔmɔtœʀ, -tʀis] a, nf locomotive.

locomotion [lɔkɔmɔsjɔ̃] nf locomotion.

locomotive [lɔkɔmɔtiv] nf locomotive, engine; (fig) pacesetter, pacemaker.

locuteur, trice [lɔkytœʀ, -tʀis] nm/f (LING) speaker.

locution [lɔkysjɔ̃] nf phrase.

loden [lɔdɛn] nm loden.

lofer [lɔfe] vi (NAVIG) to luff.

logarithme [lɔgaʀitm(ə)] nm logarithm.

loge [lɔʒ] nf (THÉÂTRE: d'artiste) dressing room; (: de spectateurs) box; (de concierge, franc-maçon) lodge.

logeable [lɔʒabl(ə)] a habitable; (spacieux) roomy.

logement [lɔʒmɑ̃] nm flat (Brit), apartment (US); accommodation q (Brit), accommodations q (US); **le ~** housing; **chercher un ~** to look for a flat ou apartment, look for accommodation(s); **construire des ~s bon marché** to build cheap housing sg; **crise du ~** housing shortage; **~ de fonction** (ADMIN) company flat ou apartment, accommodation(s) provided with one's job.

loger [lɔʒe] vt to accommodate ♦ vi to live; **se ~: trouver à se ~** to find accommodation; **se ~ dans** (suj: balle, flèche) to lodge itself in.

logeur, euse [lɔʒœʀ, -øz] nm/f landlord/landlady.

loggia [lɔdʒja] nf loggia.

logiciel [lɔʒisjɛl] nm software.

logique [lɔʒik] a logical ♦ nf logic; **c'est ~** it stands to reason.

logiquement [lɔʒikmɑ̃] ad logically.

logis [lɔʒi] nm home; abode, dwelling.

logistique [lɔʒistik] nf logistics sg ♦ a logistic.

logo [lɔgo], **logotype** [lɔgɔtip] nm logo.

loi [lwa] nf law; **faire la ~** to lay down the law; **les ~s de la mode** (fig) the dictates of fashion; **proposition de ~** (private member's) bill; **projet de ~** (government) bill.

loin [lwɛ̃] ad far; (dans le temps: futur) a long way off; (: passé) a long time ago; **plus ~** further; **moins ~ (que)** not as far (as); **~ de** far from; **pas ~ de 1000 F** not far off 1000 F; **au ~** far off; **de ~** ad from a distance; (fig: de beaucoup) by far; **il vient de ~** he's come a long way; he comes from a long way away; **de ~ en ~** here and there; (de temps en temps) (every) now and then; **~ de là** (au contraire) far from it.

lointain, e [lwɛ̃tɛ̃, -ɛn] a faraway, distant;

(*dans le futur, passé*) distant, far-off; (*cause, parent*) remote, distant ♦ *nm*: **dans le ~** in the distance.

loi-programme, *pl* **lois-programmes** [lwapʀɔgʀam] *nf* (*POL*) *act providing framework for government programme*.

loir [lwaʀ] *nm* dormouse (*pl* -mice).

Loire [lwaʀ] *nf*: **la ~** the Loire.

loisible [lwazibl(ə)] *a*: **il vous est ~ de** ... you are free to ....

loisir [lwaziʀ] *nm*: **heures de ~** spare time; **~s** *nmpl* (*activités*) leisure activities; **avoir le ~ de faire** to have the time *ou* opportunity to do; **(tout) à ~** (*en prenant son temps*) at leisure; (*autant qu'on le désire*) at one's pleasure.

lombaire [lɔ̃bɛʀ] *a* lumbar.

lombalgie [lɔ̃balʒi] *nf* back pain.

lombard, e [lɔ̃baʀ, -aʀd(ə)] *a* Lombard.

Lombardie [lɔ̃baʀdi] *nf*: **la ~** Lombardy.

londonien, ne [lɔ̃dɔnjɛ̃, -ɛn] *a* London *cpd*, of London ♦ *nm/f*: **L~, ne** Londoner.

Londres [lɔ̃dʀ(ə)] *n* London.

long, longue [lɔ̃, lɔ̃g] *a* long ♦ *ad*: **en savoir ~** to know a great deal ♦ *nm*: **de 3 m de ~** 3 m long, 3 m in length ♦ *nf*: **à la longue** in the end; **faire ~ feu** to fizzle out; **ne pas faire ~ feu** not to last long; **au ~ cours** (*NAVIG*) ocean *cpd*, ocean-going; **de longue date** *a* long-standing; **longue durée** *a* long-term; **de longue haleine** *a* long-term; **être ~ à faire** to take a long time to do; **en ~** *ad* lengthwise, lengthways; **(tout) le ~ de** (all) along; **tout au ~ de** (*année, vie*) throughout; **de ~ en large** (*marcher*) to and fro, up and down; **en ~ et en large** (*fig*) in every detail.

longanimité [lɔ̃ganimite] *nf* forbearance.

long-courrier [lɔ̃kuʀje] *nm* (*AVIAT*) long-haul aircraft.

longe [lɔ̃ʒ] *nf* (*corde: pour attacher*) tether; (*pour mener*) lead; (*CULIN*) loin.

longer [lɔ̃ʒe] *vt* to go (*ou* walk *ou* drive) along(side); (*suj: mur, route*) to border.

longévité [lɔ̃ʒevite] *nf* longevity.

longiligne [lɔ̃ʒiliɲ] *a* long-limbed.

longitude [lɔ̃ʒityd] *nf* longitude; **à 45° de ~ ouest** at 45° longitude west.

longitudinal, e, aux [lɔ̃ʒitydinal, -o] *a* longitudinal, lengthways; (*entaille, vallée*) running lengthways.

longtemps [lɔ̃tɑ̃] *ad* (for) a long time, (for) long; **ça ne va pas durer ~** it won't last long; **avant ~** before long; **pour/pendant ~** for a long time; **je n'en ai pas pour ~** I shan't be long; **mettre ~ à faire** to take a long time to do; **il en a pour ~** he'll be a long time; **il y a ~ que je travaille** I have been working (for) a long time; **il n'y a pas ~ que je l'ai rencontré** it's not long since I met him.

longue [lɔ̃g] *af voir* **long**.

longuement [lɔ̃gmɑ̃] *ad* (*longtemps: parler, regarder*) for a long time; (*en détail: expliquer, raconter*) at length.

longueur [lɔ̃gœʀ] *nf* length; **~s** *nfpl* (*fig: d'un film etc*) tedious parts; **sur une ~ de 10 km** for *ou* over 10 km; **en ~** *ad* lengthwise, lengthways; **tirer en ~** to drag on; **à ~ de journée** all day long; **d'une ~** (*gagner*) by a

length; **~ d'onde** wavelength.

longue-vue [lɔ̃gvy] *nf* telescope.

looping [lupiŋ] *nm* (*AVIAT*): **faire des ~s** to loop the loop.

lopin [lɔpɛ̃] *nm*: **~ de terre** patch of land.

loquace [lɔkas] *a* talkative, loquacious.

loque [lɔk] *nf* (*personne*) wreck; **~s** *nfpl* (*habits*) rags; **être** *ou* **tomber en ~s** to be in rags.

loquet [lɔkɛ] *nm* latch.

lorgner [lɔʀɲe] *vt* to eye; (*convoiter*) to have one's eye on.

lorgnette [lɔʀɲɛt] *nf* opera glasses *pl*.

lorgnon [lɔʀɲɔ̃] *nm* (*face-à-main*) lorgnette; (*pince-nez*) pince-nez.

loriot [lɔʀjo] *nm* (golden) oriole.

lorrain, e [lɔʀɛ̃, -ɛn] *a* of *ou* from Lorraine; **quiche ~e** quiche lorraine.

lors [lɔʀ]: **~ de** *prép* (*au moment de*) at the time of; (*pendant*) during; **~ même que** even though.

lorsque [lɔʀsk(ə)] *cj* when, as.

losange [lɔzɑ̃ʒ] *nm* diamond; (*GÉOM*) lozenge; **en ~** diamond-shaped.

lot [lo] *nm* (*part*) share; (*de loterie*) prize; (*fig: destin*) fate, lot; (*COMM, INFORM*) batch; **~ de consolation** consolation prize.

loterie [lɔtʀi] *nf* lottery; (*tombola*) raffle; **L~ nationale** French national lottery.

loti, e [lɔti] *a*: **bien/mal ~** well-/badly off, lucky/unlucky.

lotion [losjɔ̃] *nf* lotion; **~ après rasage** after-shave (lotion); **~ capillaire** hair lotion.

lotir [lɔtiʀ] *vt* (*terrain: diviser*) to divide into plots; (*: vendre*) to sell by lots.

lotissement [lɔtismɑ̃] *nm* (*groupe de maisons, d'immeubles*) housing development; (*parcelle*) (building) plot, lot.

loto [lɔto] *nm* lotto.

lotte [lɔt] *nf* (*ZOOL: de rivière*) burbot; (*: de mer*) monkfish.

louable [lwabl(ə)] *a* (*appartement, garage*) rentable; (*action, personne*) praiseworthy, commendable.

louage [lwaʒ] *nm*: **voiture de ~** hired (*Brit*) *ou* rented (*US*) car; (*à louer*) hire (*Brit*) *ou* rental (*US*) car.

louange [lwɑ̃ʒ] *nf*: **à la ~ de** in praise of; **~s** *nfpl* praise *sg*.

loubar(d) [lubaʀ] *nm* (*fam*) lout.

louche [luʃ] *a* shady, fishy, dubious ♦ *nf* ladle.

loucher [luʃe] *vi* to squint; (*fig*): **~ sur** to have one's (beady) eye on.

louer [lwe] *vt* (*maison: suj: propriétaire*) to let, rent (out); (*: locataire*) to rent; (*voiture etc*) to hire out (*Brit*), rent (out); to hire (*Brit*), rent; (*réserver*) to book; (*faire l'éloge de*) to praise; **"à ~"** "to let" (*Brit*), "for rent" (*US*); **~ qn de** to praise sb for; **se ~ de** to congratulate o.s. on.

loufoque [lufɔk] *a* (*fam*) crazy, zany.

loukoum [lukum] *nm* Turkish delight.

loulou [lulu] *nm* (*chien*) spitz; **~ de Poméranie** Pomeranian (dog).

loup [lu] *nm* wolf (*pl* wolves); (*poisson*) bass; (*masque*) (eye) mask; **jeune ~** young go-getter; **~ de mer** (*marin*) old seadog.

loupe [lup] *nf* magnifying glass; **~ de noyer** burr walnut; **à la ~** (*fig*) in minute detail.

louper [lupe] *vt* (*fam*: *manquer*) to miss; (: *gâcher*) to mess up, bungle.

lourd, e [luʀ, luʀd(ə)] *a* heavy; (*chaleur*, *temps*) sultry; (*fig*: *personne*, *style*) heavy-handed ♦ *ad*: **peser** ~ to be heavy; ~ **de** (*menaces*) charged with; (*conséquences*) fraught with; **artillerie/industrie** ~**e** heavy artillery/industry.

lourdaud, e [luʀdo, -od] *a* oafish.

lourdement [luʀdəmɑ̃] *ad* heavily; **se tromper** ~ to make a big mistake.

lourdeur [luʀdœʀ] *nf* heaviness; ~ **d'estomac** indigestion *q*.

loustic [lustik] *nm* (*fam péj*) joker.

loutre [lutʀ(ə)] *nf* otter; (*fourrure*) otter skin.

louve [luv] *nf* she-wolf.

louveteau, x [luvto] *nm* (*ZOOL*) wolf-cub; (*scout*) cub (scout).

louvoyer [luvwaje] *vi* (*NAVIG*) to tack; (*fig*) to hedge, evade the issue.

lover [lɔve]: **se** ~ *vi* to coil up.

loyal, e, aux [lwajal, -o] *a* (*fidèle*) loyal, faithful; (*fair-play*) fair.

loyalement [lwajalmɑ̃] *ad* loyally, faithfully; fairly.

loyalisme [lwajalism(ə)] *nm* loyalty.

loyauté [lwajote] *nf* loyalty, faithfulness; fairness.

loyer [lwaje] *nm* rent; ~ **de l'argent** interest rate.

LP *sigle m* (= *lycée professionnel*) secondary school for vocational training.

LPO *sigle f* (= *Ligue pour la protection des oiseaux*) bird protection society.

LSD *sigle m* (= *Lyserg Säure Diäthylamid*) LSD.

lu, e [ly] *pp de* lire.

lubie [lybi] *nf* whim, craze.

lubricité [lybʀisite] *nf* lust.

lubrifiant [lybʀifjɑ̃] *nm* lubricant.

lubrifier [lybʀifje] *vt* to lubricate.

lubrique [lybʀik] *a* lecherous.

lucarne [lykaʀn(ə)] *nf* skylight.

lucide [lysid] *a* (*conscient*) lucid, conscious; (*perspicace*) clear-headed.

lucidité [lysidite] *nf* lucidity.

luciole [lysjɔl] *nf* firefly.

lucratif, ive [lykʀatif, -iv] *a* lucrative, profitable; **à but non** ~ non profit-making.

ludique [lydik] *a* play *cpd*, playing.

ludothèque [lydɔtɛk] *nf* toy library.

luette [lɥɛt] *nf* uvula.

lueur [lɥœʀ] *nf* (*chatoyante*) glimmer *q*; (*métallique*, *mouillée*) gleam *q*; (*rougeoyante*, *chaude*) glow *q*; (*pâle*) (faint) light; (*fig*) spark; (: *d'espérance*) glimmer, gleam.

luge [lyʒ] *nf* sledge (*Brit*), sled (*US*); **faire de la** ~ to sledge (*Brit*), sled (*US*), toboggan.

lugubre [lygybʀ(ə)] *a* gloomy; dismal.

lui [lɥi] *pp de* luire ♦ *pronom* (*chose*, *animal*) it; (*personne: mâle*) him; (: *en sujet*) he; (: *femelle*) her; *voir note sous* **il**; ~, **il** ... **HE** ... (*emphatic*); **je la connais mieux que** ~ (*que je ne le connais*) I know her better than (I know) him; (*qu'il ne la connaît*) I know her better than he does.

lui-même [lɥimɛm] *pronom* (*personne*) himself; (*chose*) itself.

luire [lɥiʀ] *vi* (*gén*) to shine, gleam; (*surface mouillée*) to glisten; (*reflets chauds*, *cuivrés*) to glow.

luisant, e [lɥizɑ̃, -ɑ̃t] *vb voir* luire ♦ *a* shining, gleaming.

lumbago [lɔ̃bago] *nm* lumbago.

lumière [lymjɛʀ] *nf* light; ~**s** *nfpl* (*d'une personne*) knowledge *sg*, wisdom *sg*; **à la** ~ **de** by the light of; (*fig*: *événements*) in the light of; **fais de la** ~ let's have some light, give us some light; **faire (toute) la** ~ **sur** (*fig*) to clarify (completely); **mettre en** ~ (*fig*) to highlight; ~ **du jour/soleil** day/sunlight.

luminaire [lyminɛʀ] *nm* lamp, light.

lumineux, euse [lyminø, -øz] *a* (*émettant de la lumière*) luminous; (*éclairé*) illuminated; (*ciel*, *journée*, *couleur*) bright; (*relatif à la lumière*: *rayon etc*) of light, light *cpd*; (*fig*: *regard*) radiant.

luminosité [lyminozite] *nf* (*TECH*) luminosity.

lump [lœp] *nm*: **œufs de** ~ lump-fish roe.

lunaire [lynɛʀ] *a* lunar, moon *cpd*.

lunatique [lynatik] *a* whimsical, temperamental.

lunch [lœntʃ] *nm* (*réception*) buffet lunch.

lundi [lœdi] *nm* Monday; **on est** ~ it's Monday; **le** ~ **20 août** Monday 20th August; **il est venu** ~ he came on Monday; **le(s)** ~**(s)** on Mondays; **à** ~! see you (on) Monday!; ~ **de Pâques** Easter Monday; ~ **de Pentecôte** Whit Monday (*Brit*).

lune [lyn] *nf* moon; **pleine/nouvelle** ~ full/new moon; **être dans la** ~ (*distrait*) to have one's head in the clouds; ~ **de miel** honeymoon.

luné, e [lyne] *a*: **bien/mal** ~ in a good/bad mood.

lunette [lynɛt] *nf*: ~**s** *nfpl* glasses, spectacles; (*protectrices*) goggles; ~ **d'approche** telescope; ~ **arrière** (*AUTO*) rear window; ~**s noires** dark glasses; ~**s de soleil** sunglasses.

lurent [lyʀ] *vb voir* lire.

lurette [lyʀɛt] *nf*: **il y a belle** ~ ages ago.

luron, ne [lyʀɔ̃, -ɔn] *nm/f* lad/lass; **joyeux** *ou* **gai** ~ gay dog.

lus [ly] *etc vb voir* lire.

lustre [lystʀ(ə)] *nm* (*de plafond*) chandelier; (*fig*: *éclat*) lustre.

lustrer [lystʀe] *vt*: ~ **qch** (*faire briller*) to make sth shine; (*user*) to make sth shiny.

lut [ly] *vb voir* lire.

luth [lyt] *nm* lute.

luthier [lytje] *nm* (stringed-)instrument maker.

lutin [lytɛ̃] *nm* imp, goblin.

lutrin [lytʀɛ̃] *nm* lectern.

lutte [lyt] *nf* (*conflit*) struggle; (*SPORT*): **la** ~ wrestling; **de haute** ~ after a hard-fought struggle; ~ **des classes** class struggle; ~ **libre** (*SPORT*) all-in wrestling.

lutter [lyte] *vi* to fight, struggle; (*SPORT*) to wrestle.

lutteur, euse [lytœʀ, -øz] *nm/f* (*SPORT*) wrestler; (*fig*) battler, fighter.

luxation [lyksasjɔ̃] *nf* dislocation.

luxe [lyks(ə)] *nm* luxury; **un** ~ **de** (*détails*, *précautions*) a wealth of; **de** ~ a luxury *cpd*.

Luxembourg [lyksɑ̃buʀ] *nm*: **le** ~ Luxembourg.

luxembourgeois, e [lyksɑ̃buʀʒwa, -waz] *a* of

ou from Luxembourg ♦ *nm/f:* **L~, e** inhabitant *ou* native of Luxembourg.
luxer [lykse] *vt:* **se ~ l'épaule** to dislocate one's shoulder.
luxueux, euse [lyksɥø, -øz] *a* luxurious.
luxure [lyksyʀ] *nf* lust.
luxuriant, e [lyksyʀjɑ̃, -ɑ̃t] *a* luxuriant, lush.
luzerne [lyzɛʀn(ə)] *nf* lucerne, alfalfa.
lycée [lise] *nm* (state) secondary (*Brit*) *ou* high (*US*) school; **~ technique** technical secondary *ou* high school.
lycéen, ne [liseɛ̃, -ɛn] *nm/f* secondary school pupil.
lymphatique [lɛ̃fatik] *a* (*fig*) lethargic, sluggish.
lymphe [lɛ̃f] *nf* lymph.
lyncher [lɛ̃ʃe] *vt* to lynch.
lynx [lɛ̃ks] *nm* lynx.
Lyon [ljɔ̃] *n* Lyons.
lyonnais, e [ljɔnɛ, -ɛz] *a* of *ou* from Lyons; (*CULIN*) Lyonnaise.
lyophilisé, e [ljɔfilize] *a* freeze-dried.
lyre [liʀ] *nf* lyre.
lyrique [liʀik] *a* lyrical; (*OPÉRA*) lyric; **artiste ~** opera singer; **comédie ~** comic opera; **théâtre ~** opera house (*for light opera*).
lyrisme [liʀism(ə)] *nm* lyricism.
lys [lis] *nm* lily.

M

M, m [ɛm] *nm inv* M, m ♦ *abr* = **majeur, masculin, mètre, Monsieur**; (= *million*) M; **M comme Marcel** M for Mike.
m′ [m] *pronom voir* **me**.
MA *sigle m* = **maître auxiliaire**.
ma [ma] *dét voir* **mon**.
maboul, e [mabul] *a* (*fam*) loony.
macabre [makɑbʀ(ə)] *a* macabre, gruesome.
macadam [makadam] *nm* tarmac (*Brit*), asphalt.
Macao [makao] *nf* Macao.
macaron [makaʀɔ̃] *nm* (*gâteau*) macaroon; (*insigne*) (round) badge.
macaroni(s) [makaʀɔni] *nm(pl)* macaroni *sg:* **~ au fromage** *ou* **au gratin** macaroni cheese (*Brit*), macaroni and cheese (*US*).
macédoine [masedwan] *nf:* **~ de fruits** fruit salad; **~ de légumes** mixed vegetables *pl.*
macérer [maseʀe] *vi, vt* to macerate; (*dans du vinaigre*) to pickle.
mâchefer [maʃfɛʀ] *nm* clinker, cinders *pl.*
mâcher [maʃe] *vt* to chew; **ne pas ~ ses mots** not to mince one's words; **~ le travail à qn** (*fig*) to spoonfeed sb, do half sb's work for him.
machiavélique [makjavelik] *a* Machiavellian.
machin [maʃɛ̃] *nm* (*fam*) thingamajig, thing; (*personne*): **M~** what's-his(*ou*-her)-name.
machinal, e, aux [maʃinal, -o] *a* mechanical, automatic.
machination [maʃinasjɔ̃] *nf* scheming, frame-up.

machine [maʃin] *nf* machine; (*locomotive; de navire etc*) engine; (*fig: rouages*) machinery; (*fam: personne*): **M~** what's-her-name; **faire ~ arrière** (*NAVIG*) to go astern; (*fig*) to back-pedal; **~ à laver/coudre/tricoter** washing/sewing/knitting machine; **~ à écrire** typewriter; **~ à sous** fruit machine; **~ à vapeur** steam engine.
machine-outil, *pl* **machines-outils** [maʃinuti] *nf* machine tool.
machinerie [maʃinʀi] *nf* machinery, plant; (*d'un navire*) engine room.
machinisme [maʃinism(ə)] *nm* mechanization.
machiniste [maʃinist(ə)] *nm* (*THÉÂTRE*) scene shifter; (*de bus, métro*) driver.
mâchoire [maʃwaʀ] *nf* jaw; **~ de frein** brake shoe.
mâchonner [maʃɔne] *vt* to chew (at).
mâcon [makɔ̃] *nm* Mâcon wine.
maçon [masɔ̃] *nm* bricklayer; (*constructeur*) builder.
maçonner [masɔne] *vt* (*revêtir*) to face, render (with cement); (*boucher*) to brick up.
maçonnerie [masɔnʀi] *nf* (*murs: de brique*) brickwork; (*: de pierre*) masonry, stonework; (*activité*) bricklaying; building; **~ de béton** concrete.
maçonnique [masɔnik] *a* masonic.
macramé [makʀame] *nm* macramé.
macrobiotique [makʀɔbjɔtik] *a* macrobiotic.
macro-économie [makʀɔekɔnɔmi] *nf* macroeconomics *sg.*
maculer [makyle] *vt* to stain; (*TYPO*) to mackle.
Madagascar [madagaskaʀ] *nf* Madagascar.
Madame [madam], *pl* **Mesdames** [medam] *nf:* **~ X** Mrs X [ˈmɪsɪz]; **occupez-vous de ~/ Monsieur/Mademoiselle** please serve this lady/gentleman/(young) lady; **bonjour ~/ Monsieur/Mademoiselle** good morning; (*ton déférent*) good morning Madam/Sir/Madam; (*le nom est connu*) good morning Mrs X/Mr X/Miss X; **~/Monsieur/Mademoiselle!** (*pour appeler*) excuse me!; (*ton déférent*) Madam/ Sir/Miss!; **~/Monsieur/Mademoiselle** (*sur lettre*) Dear Madam/Sir/Madam; **chère ~/ cher Monsieur/chère Mademoiselle** Dear Mrs X/Mr X/Miss X; **~ la Directrice** the director; the manageress; the headteacher; **Mesdames** Ladies.
Madeleine [madlɛn]: **îles de la ~** *nfpl* Magdalen Islands.
madeleine [madlɛn] *nf* madeleine, ≈ sponge finger cake.
Madelinot, e [madlino, -ɔt] *nm/f* inhabitant *ou* native of the Magdalen Islands.
Mademoiselle [madmwazɛl], *pl* **Mesdemoiselles** [medmwazɛl] *nf* Miss; *voir aussi* **Madame**.
Madère [madɛʀ] *nf* Madeira ♦ *nm:* **m~** Madeira (wine).
madone [madɔn] *nf* madonna.
madré, e [madʀe] *a* crafty, wily.
Madrid [madʀid] *n* Madrid.
madrier [madʀije] *nm* beam.
madrilène [madʀilɛn] *a* of *ou* from Madrid.
maestria [maɛstʀija] *nf* (masterly) skill.
maf(f)ia [mafja] *nf* Maf(f)ia.

magasin [magazẽ] *nm* (*boutique*) shop; (*entre-pôt*) warehouse; (*d'arme, appareil-photo*) magazine; **en ~** (*COMM*) in stock; **faire les ~s** to go (a)round the shops, do the shops; **~ d'alimentation** grocer's shop (*Brit*), grocery store (*US*).

magasinier [magazinje] *nm* warehouseman.

magazine [magazin] *nm* magazine.

mage [maʒ] *nm*: **les Rois M~s** the Magi, the (Three) Wise Men.

Maghreb [magrɛb] *nm*: **le ~** the Maghreb, North(-West) Africa.

maghrébin, e [magrebẽ, -in] *a* of *ou* from the Maghreb ♦ *nm/f*: **M~, e** North African, Maghrebi.

magicien, ne [maʒisjẽ, -ɛn] *nm/f* magician.

magie [maʒi] *nf* magic; **~ noire** black magic.

magique [maʒik] *a* (*occulte*) magic; (*fig*) magical.

magistral, e, aux [maʒistral, -o] *a* (*œuvre, addresse*) masterly; (*ton*) authoritative; (*gifle etc*) sound, resounding; (*ex cathedra*): **enseignement ~** lecturing, lectures *pl*; **cours ~** lecture.

magistrat [maʒistra] *nm* magistrate.

magistrature [maʒistratyr] *nf* magistracy, magistrature; **~ assise** judges *pl*, bench; **~ debout** state prosecutors *pl*.

magma [magma] *nm* (*GÉO*) magma; (*fig*) jumble.

magnanerie [maɲanri] *nf* silk farm.

magnanime [maɲanim] *a* magnanimous.

magnat [magna] *nm* tycoon, magnate; **~ de la presse** press baron.

magner [maɲe]: **se ~** *vi* (*fam*) to get a move on.

magnésie [maɲezi] *nf* magnesia.

magnésium [maɲezjɔm] *nm* magnesium.

magnétique [maɲetik] *a* magnetic.

magnétiser [maɲetize] *vt* to magnetize; (*fig*) to mesmerize, hypnotize.

magnétisme [maɲetism(ə)] *nm* magnetism.

magnéto [maɲeto] *nm* (= *magnétocassette*) cassette deck; (= *magnétophone*) tape recorder.

magnétocassette [maɲetokasɛt] *nm* cassette deck.

magnétophone [maɲetofon] *nm* tape recorder; **~ à cassettes** cassette recorder.

magnétoscope [maɲetoskɔp] *nm*: **~ (à cassette)** video (recorder).

magnificence [maɲifisɑ̃s] *nf* (*faste*) magnificence, splendour (*Brit*), splendor (*US*); (*générosité, prodigalité*) munificence, lavishness.

magnifier [maɲifje] *vt* (*glorifier*) to glorify; (*idéaliser*) to idealize.

magnifique [maɲifik] *a* magnificent.

magnolia [maɲɔlja] *nm* magnolia.

magnum [magnɔm] *nm* magnum.

magot [mago] *nm* (*argent*) pile (of money); (*économies*) nest egg.

magouille [maguj] *nf* (*fam*) scheming.

mahométan, e [maɔmetɑ̃, -an] *a* Mohammedan, Mahometan.

mai [mɛ] *nm* May; *voir aussi* **juillet**.

maigre [mɛgr(ə)] *a* (very) thin, skinny; (*viande*) lean; (*fromage*) low-fat; (*végéta-tion*) thin, sparse; (*fig*) poor, meagre, skimpy ♦ *ad*: **faire ~** not to eat meat; **jours ~s** days of abstinence, fish days.

maigrelet, te [mɛgrəlɛ, -ɛt] *a* skinny, scrawny.

maigreur [mɛgrœr] *nf* thinness.

maigrichon, ne [mɛgriʃɔ̃, -ɔn] *a* = **maigrelet, te**.

maigrir [mɛgrir] *vi* to get thinner, lose weight ♦ *vt*: **~ qn** (*suj: vêtement*) to make sb look slim(mer).

mailing [mɛliŋ] *nm* direct mail *q*; **un ~** a mailshot.

maille [maj] *nf* (*boucle*) stitch; (*ouverture*) hole (in the mesh); **avoir ~ à partir avec qn** to have a brush with sb; **~ à l'endroit/à l'envers** knit one/purl one; (*boucle*) plain/purl stitch.

maillechort [majʃɔr] *nm* nickel silver.

maillet [majɛ] *nm* mallet.

maillon [majɔ̃] *nm* link.

maillot [majo] *nm* (*aussi*: **~ de corps**) vest; (*de danseur*) leotard; (*de sportif*) jersey; **~ de bain** bathing costume (*Brit*), swimsuit; (*d'homme*) bathing trunks *pl*; **~ une pièce** one-piece swimsuit; **~ deux pièces** two-piece swimsuit, bikini.

main [mẽ] *nf* hand; **la ~ dans la ~** hand in hand; **à deux ~s** with both hands; **à une ~** with one hand; **à la ~** (*tenir, avoir*) in one's hand; (*faire, tricoter etc*) by hand; **se donner la ~** to hold hands; **donner** *ou* **tendre la ~ à qn** to hold out one's hand to sb; **se serrer la ~** to shake hands; **serrer la ~ à qn** to shake hands with sb; **sous la ~** to *ou* at hand; **haut les ~s!** hands up!; **à ~ levée** (*ART*) freehand; **à ~s levées** (*voter*) with a show of hands; **attaque à ~ armée** armed attack; **à ~ droite/gauche** to the right/left; **à remettre en ~s propres** to be delivered personally; **de première ~** (*renseignement*) first-hand; (*COMM: voiture etc*) with only one previous owner; **faire ~ basse sur** to help o.s. to; **mettre la dernière ~ à** to put the finishing touches to; **mettre la ~ à la pâte** (*fig*) to lend a hand; **prendre qch en ~** (*fig*) to take sth in hand; **avoir/passer la ~** (*CARTES*) to lead/hand over the lead; **s'en laver les ~s** (*fig*) to wash one's hands of it; **se faire/perdre la ~** to get one's hand in/lose one's touch; **avoir qch bien en ~** to have got the hang of sth; **en un tour de ~** (*fig*) in the twinkling of an eye; **~ courante** handrail.

mainate [mɛnat] *nm* myna(h) bird.

main-d'œuvre [mẽdœvr(ə)] *nf* manpower, labour (*Brit*), labor (*US*).

main-forte [mẽfɔrt(ə)] *nf*: **prêter ~ à qn** to come to sb's assistance.

mainmise [mẽmiz] *nf* seizure; (*fig*): **avoir la ~ sur** to have a complete hold on.

maint, e [mẽ, mẽt] *a* many a; **~s** many; **à ~es reprises** time and (time) again.

maintenance [mẽtnɑ̃s] *nf* maintenance.

maintenant [mẽtnɑ̃] *ad* now; (*actuellement*) nowadays.

maintenir [mẽtnir] *vt* (*retenir, soutenir*) to support; (*contenir: foule etc*) to keep in check, hold back; (*conserver*) to maintain, uphold; (*affirmer*) to maintain; **se ~** *vi* (*paix, temps*) to hold; (*préjugé*) to persist;

(*malade*) to remain stable.

maintien [mɛ̃tjɛ̃] *nm* maintaining, upholding; (*attitude*) bearing; ~ **de l'ordre** maintenance of law and order.

maintiendrai [mɛ̃tjɛ̃dʀe], **maintiens** [mɛ̃tjɛ̃] *etc vb voir* **maintenir**.

maire [mɛʀ] *nm* mayor.

mairie [meʀi] *nf* (*endroit*) town hall; (*administration*) town council.

mais [mɛ] *cj* but; ~ **non!** of course not!; ~ **enfin** but after all; (*indignation*) look here!; ~ **encore?** is that all?

maïs [mais] *nm* maize (*Brit*), corn (*US*).

maison [mɛzɔ̃] *nf* (*bâtiment*) house; (*chez-soi*) home; (*COMM*) firm; (*famille*): **ami de la** ~ friend of the family ♦ *a inv* (*CULIN*) homemade; (: *au restaurant*) made by the chef; (*COMM*) in-house, own; (*fam*) first-rate; **à la** ~ at home; (*direction*) home; ~ **d'arrêt** (short-stay) prison; ~ **de campagne** country cottage; ~ **centrale** prison; ~ **close** *ou* **de passe** brothel; ~ **de correction** ≈ remand home (*Brit*), ≈ reformatory (*US*); ~ **de la culture** ≈ arts centre; ~ **des jeunes** ≈ youth club; ~ **mère** parent company; ~ **de passe** = ~ **close**; ~ **de repos** convalescent home; ~ **de retraite** old people's home; ~ **de santé** mental home.

Maison-Blanche [mɛzɔ̃blɑ̃ʃ] *nf*: **la** ~ the White House.

maisonnée [mɛzɔne] *nf* household, family.

maisonnette [mɛzɔnɛt] *nf* small house, cottage.

maître, esse [mɛtʀ(ə), mɛtʀɛs] *nm/f* master/mistress; (*SCOL*) teacher, schoolmaster/mistress ♦ *nm* (*peintre etc*) master; (*titre*): **M~** (**M͏e**) Maître, *term of address for lawyers etc* ♦ *nf* (*amante*) mistress ♦ *a* (*principal, essentiel*) main; **maison de** ~ family seat; **être** ~ **de** (*soi-même, situation*) to be in control of; **se rendre** ~ **de** (*pays, ville*) to gain control of; (*situation, incendie*) to bring under control; **être passé** ~ **dans l'art de** to be a (past) master in the art of; **une maîtresse femme** a forceful woman; ~ **d'armes** fencing master; ~ **auxiliaire (MA)** (*SCOL*) temporary teacher; ~ **chanteur** blackmailer; ~ **de chapelle** choirmaster; ~ **de conférences** ≈ senior lecturer (*Brit*), ≈ assistant professor (*US*); ~/**maîtresse d'école** teacher, schoolmaster/mistress; ~ **d'hôtel** (*domestique*) butler; (*d'hôtel*) head waiter; ~ **de maison** host; ~ **nageur** lifeguard; ~ **d'œuvre** (*CONSTR*) project manager; ~ **d'ouvrage** (*CONSTR*) client; ~ **à penser** intellectual leader; ~ **queux** chef; **maîtresse de maison** hostess; (*ménagère*) housewife (*pl* -wives).

maître-assistant, e, *pl* **maîtres-assistants, es** [mɛtʀasistɑ̃, -ɑ̃t] *nm/f* ≈ lecturer.

maître-autel, *pl* **maîtres-autels** [mɛtʀotɛl] *nm* high altar.

maîtrise [mɛtʀiz] *nf* (*aussi*: ~ **de soi**) self-control, self-possession; (*habileté*) skill, mastery; (*suprématie*) mastery, command; (*diplôme*) ≈ master's degree; (*chefs d'équipe*) supervisory staff.

maîtriser [mɛtʀize] *vt* (*cheval, incendie*) to (bring under) control; (*sujet*) to master;

(*émotion*) to control; **se** ~ to control o.s.

majesté [maʒɛste] *nf* majesty.

majestueux, euse [maʒɛstɥø, -øz] *a* majestic.

majeur, e [maʒœʀ] *a* (*important*) major; (*JUR*) of age; (*fig*) adult ♦ *nm/f* (*JUR*) person who has come of age *ou* attained his (*ou* her) majority ♦ *nm* (*doigt*) middle finger; **en** ~**e partie** for the most part; **la** ~**e partie de** the major part of.

major [maʒɔʀ] *nm* adjutant; (*SCOL*): ~ **de la promotion** first in one's year.

majoration [maʒɔʀɑsjɔ̃] *nf* increase.

majorer [maʒɔʀe] *vt* to increase.

majorette [maʒɔʀɛt] *nf* majorette.

majoritaire [maʒɔʀitɛʀ] *a* majority *cpd*; **système/scrutin** ~ majority system/ballot.

majorité [maʒɔʀite] *nf* (*gén*) majority; (*parti*) party in power; **en** ~ (*composé etc*) mainly.

Majorque [maʒɔʀk(ə)] *nf* Majorca.

majorquin, e [maʒɔʀkɛ̃, -in] *a* Majorcan ♦ *nm/f*: **M~, e** Majorcan.

majuscule [maʒyskyl] *a, nf*: (**lettre**) ~ capital (letter).

MAL [mal] *sigle f* (= *Maison d'animation et des loisirs*) *cultural centre.*

mal, maux [mal, mo] *nm* (*opposé au bien*) evil; (*tort, dommage*) harm; (*douleur physique*) pain, ache; (*maladie*) illness, sickness *q*; (*difficulté, peine*) trouble; (*souffrance morale*) pain ♦ *ad* badly ♦ *a*: **c'est** ~ (**de faire**) it's bad *ou* wrong (to do); **être** ~ to be uncomfortable; **être** ~ **avec qn** to be on bad terms with sb; **être au plus** ~ (*malade*) to be very bad; (*brouillé*) to be at daggers drawn; **il comprend** ~ he has difficulty in understanding; **il a** ~ **compris** he misunderstood; ~ **tourner** to go wrong; **dire/penser du** ~ **de** to speak/think ill of; **ne vouloir de** ~ **à personne** to wish nobody any ill; **il n'a rien fait de** ~ he has done nothing wrong; **avoir du** ~ **à faire qch** to have trouble doing sth; **se donner du** ~ **pour faire qch** to go to a lot of trouble to do sth; **ne voir aucun** ~ **à** to see no harm in, see nothing wrong in; **craignant no faire** fearing he *etc* was doing the wrong thing; **sans penser** *ou* **songer à** ~ without meaning any harm; **faire du** ~ **à qn** to hurt sb; to harm sb; **se faire** ~ to hurt o.s.; **se faire** ~ **au pied** to hurt one's foot; **ça fait** ~ it hurts; **j'ai** ~ (**ici**) it hurts (here); **j'ai** ~ **au dos** my back aches, I've got a pain in my back; **avoir** ~ **à la tête/à la gorge/aux dents** to have a headache/a sore throat/ toothache; **avoir le** ~ **de l'air** to be airsick; **avoir le** ~ **du pays** to be homesick; ~ **de mer** seasickness; ~ **de la route** carsickness; ~ **en point** *a inv* in a bad state; **maux de ventre** stomach ache *sg*; *voir* **cœur.**

Malabar [malabaʀ] *nm*: **le** ~, **la côte de** ~ the Malabar (Coast).

malade [malad] *a* ill, sick; (*poitrine, jambe*) bad; (*plante*) diseased; (*fig: entreprise, monde*) ailing ♦ *nm/f* invalid, sick person; (*à l'hôpital etc*) patient; **tomber** ~ to fall ill; **être** ~ **du cœur** to have heart trouble *ou* a bad heart; **grand** ~ seriously ill person; ~ **mental** mentally sick *ou* ill person.

maladie [maladi] *nf* (*spécifique*) disease, illness; *(mauvaise santé)* illness, sickness; *(fig: manie)* mania; **être rongé par la** ~ to be wasting away (through illness); ~ **de peau** skin disease.

maladif, ive [maladif, -iv] *a* sickly; *(curiosité, besoin)* pathological.

maladresse [maladrɛs] *nf* clumsiness *q*; *(gaffe)* blunder.

maladroit, e [maladrwa, -wat] *a* clumsy.

maladroitement [maladrwatmã] *ad* clumsily.

malais, e [malɛ, -ɛz] *a* Malay, Malayan ♦ *nm (LING)* Malay ♦ *nm/f:* **M~, e** Malay, Malayan.

malaise [malɛz] *nm (MÉD)* feeling of faintness; feeling of discomfort; *(fig)* uneasiness, malaise; **avoir un** ~ to feel faint *ou* dizzy.

malaisé, e [maleze] *a* difficult.

Malaisie [malɛzi] *nf:* **la** ~ Malaya, West Malaysia; **la péninsule de** ~ the Malay Peninsula.

malappris, e [malapri, -iz] *nm/f* ill-mannered *ou* boorish person.

malaria [malarja] *nf* malaria.

malavisé, e [malavize] *a* ill-advised, unwise.

Malawi [malawi] *nm:* **le** ~ Malawi.

malaxer [malakse] *vt (pétrir)* to knead; *(mêler)* to mix.

Malaysia [malɛzja] *nf:* **la** ~ Malaysia.

malchance [malʃãs] *nf* misfortune, ill luck *q*; **par** ~ unfortunately; **quelle** ~! what bad luck!

malchanceux, euse [malʃãsø, -øz] *a* unlucky.

malcommode [malkɔmɔd] *a* impractical, inconvenient.

Maldives [maldiv] *nfpl:* **les** ~ the Maldive Islands.

maldonne [maldɔn] *nf (CARTES)* misdeal; **il y a** ~ *(fig)* there's been a misunderstanding.

mâle [mɑl] *a (aussi ÉLEC, TECH)* male; *(viril: voix, traits)* manly ♦ *nm* male.

malédiction [malediksjɔ̃] *nf* curse.

maléfice [malefis] *nm* evil spell.

maléfique [malefik] *a* evil, baleful.

malencontreux, euse [malãkɔ̃trø, -øz] *a* unfortunate, untoward.

malentendant, e [malãtãdã, -ãt] *nm/f:* **les** ~s the hard of hearing.

malentendu, e [malãtãdy] *nm* misunderstanding.

malfaçon [malfasɔ̃] *nf* fault.

malfaisant, e [malfəzã, -ãt] *a* evil, harmful.

malfaiteur [malfɛtœr] *nm* lawbreaker, criminal; *(voleur)* thief *(pl* thieves*)*.

malfamé, e [malfame] *a* disreputable, of ill repute.

malfrat [malfra] *nm* villain, crook.

malgache [malgaʃ] *a* Malagasy, Madagascan ♦ *nm (LING)* Malagasy ♦ *nm/f:* **M~** Malagasy, Madagascan.

malgré [malgre] *prép* in spite of, despite; ~ **tout** *ad* in spite of everything.

malhabile [malabil] *a* clumsy.

malheur [malœr] *nm (situation)* adversity, misfortune; *(événement)* misfortune; *(: plus fort)* disaster, tragedy; **par** ~ unfortunately; **quel** ~! what a shame *ou* pity!; **faire un** ~ *(fam: un éclat)* to do something desperate; *(: avoir du succès)* to be a smash hit.

malheureusement [malœrøzmã] *ad* un-

fortunately.

malheureux, euse [malœrø, -øz] *a (triste)* unhappy, miserable; *(infortuné, regrettable)* unfortunate; *(malchanceux)* unlucky; *(insignifiant)* wretched ♦ *nm/f (infortuné, misérable)* poor soul; *(indigent, miséreux)* unfortunate creature; **les** ~ the destitute; **avoir la main malheureuse** *(au jeu)* to be unlucky; *(tout casser)* to be ham-fisted.

malhonnête [malɔnɛt] *a* dishonest; *(impoli)* rude.

malhonnêteté [malɔnɛtte] *nf* dishonesty; rudeness *q*.

Mali [mali] *nm:* **le** ~ Mali.

malice [malis] *nf* mischievousness; *(méchanceté)*: **par** ~ out of malice *ou* spite; **sans** ~ guileless.

malicieux, euse [malisjø, -øz] *a* mischievous.

malien, ne [maljɛ̃, -ɛn] *a* Malian.

malignité [maliɲite] *nf (d'une tumeur, d'un mal)* malignancy.

malin, igne [malɛ̃, -iɲ] *a (futé: f gén:* **maline)** smart, shrewd; *(: sourire)* knowing; *(MÉD, influence)* malignant; **faire le** ~ to show off; **éprouver un** ~ **plaisir à** to take malicious pleasure in.

malingre [malɛ̃gr(ə)] *a* puny.

malintentionné, e [malɛ̃tãsjɔne] *a* ill-intentioned, malicious.

malle [mal] *nf* trunk; *(AUTO)*: ~ **(arrière)** boot *(Brit)*, trunk *(US)*.

malléable [maleabl(ə)] *a* malleable.

malle-poste, *pl* **malles-poste** [malpɔst(ə)] *nf* mail coach.

mallette [malɛt] *nf (valise)* (small) suitcase; *(aussi:* ~ **de voyage)** overnight case; *(pour documents)* attaché case.

malmener [malməne] *vt* to manhandle; *(fig)* to give a rough ride to.

malodorant, e [malɔdɔrã, -ãt] *a* foul- *ou* ill-smelling.

malotru [malɔtry] *nm* lout, boor.

malouin, e [malwɛ̃, -in] *a* of *ou* from Saint Malo.

Malouines [malwin] *nfpl:* **les** ~ the Falklands, the Falkland Islands.

malpoli, e [malpɔli] *nm/f* rude individual.

malpropre [malprɔpr(ə)] *a (personne, vêtement)* dirty; *(travail)* slovenly; *(histoire, plaisanterie)* unsavoury *(Brit)*, unsavory *(US)*, smutty; *(malhonnête)* dishonest.

malpropreté [malprɔprəte] *nf* dirtiness.

malsain, e [malsɛ̃, -ɛn] *a* unhealthy.

malséant, e [malseã, -ãt] *a* unseemly, unbecoming.

malsonnant, e [malsɔnã, -ãt] *a* offensive.

malt [malt] *nm* malt; **pur** ~ *(whisky)* malt *(whisky)*.

maltais, e [maltɛ, -ɛz] *a* Maltese.

Malte [malt(ə)] *nf* Malta.

malté, e [malte] *a (lait etc)* malted.

maltraiter [maltrete] *vt (brutaliser)* to manhandle, ill-treat; *(critiquer, éreinter)* to slate *(Brit)*, roast.

malus [malys] *nm (ASSURANCES)* car insurance weighting, penalty.

malveillance [malvɛjãs] *nf (animosité)* ill will; *(intention de nuire)* malevolence; *(JUR)* malicious intent *q*.

malveillant, e [malvɛjɑ̃, -ɑ̃t] *a* malevolent, malicious.

malvenu, e [malvəny] *a*: **être ~ de** *ou* **à faire qch** not to be in a position to do sth.

malversation [malvɛrsasjɔ̃] *nf* embezzlement, misappropriation (of funds).

maman [mamɑ̃] *nf* mum(my) (*Brit*), mom (*US*).

mamelle [mamɛl] *nf* teat.

mamelon [mamlɔ̃] *nm* (*ANAT*) nipple; (*colline*) knoll, hillock.

mamie [mami] *nf* (*fam*) granny.

mammifère [mamifɛr] *nm* mammal.

mammouth [mamut] *nm* mammoth.

manager [manadʒɛr] *nm* (*SPORT*) manager; (*COMM*): **~ commercial** commercial director.

manceau, elle, x [mɑ̃so, -ɛl] *a* of *ou* from Le Mans.

manche [mɑ̃ʃ] *nf* (*de vêtement*) sleeve; (*d'un jeu, tournoi*) round; (*GÉO*): **la M~** the (English) Channel ♦ *nm* (*d'outil, casserole*) handle; (*de pelle, pioche etc*) shaft; (*de violon, guitare*) neck; (*fam*) clumsy oaf; **faire la ~** to pass the hat; **~ à air** *nf* (*AVIAT*) wind-sock; **~ à balai** *nm* broomstick; (*AVIAT, INFORM*) joystick.

manchette [mɑ̃ʃɛt] *nf* (*de chemise*) cuff; (*coup*) forearm blow; (*titre*) headline.

manchon [mɑ̃ʃɔ̃] *nm* (*de fourrure*) muff; **~ à incandescence** incandescent (gas) mantle.

manchot [mɑ̃ʃo] *nm* one-armed man; armless man; (*ZOOL*) penguin.

mandarine [mɑ̃darin] *nf* mandarin (orange), tangerine.

mandat [mɑ̃da] *nm* (*postal*) postal *ou* money order; (*d'un député etc*) mandate; (*procuration*) power of attorney, proxy; (*POLICE*) warrant; **~ d'amener** summons *sg*; **~ d'arrêt** warrant for arrest; **~ de dépôt** committal order; **~ de perquisition** (*POLICE*) search warrant.

mandataire [mɑ̃datɛr] *nm/f* (*représentant, délégué*) representative; (*JUR*) proxy.

mandat-carte, *pl* **mandats-cartes** [mɑ̃dakart(ə)] *nm* money order (*in postcard form*).

mandater [mɑ̃date] *vt* (*personne*) to appoint; (*POL: député*) to elect.

mandat-lettre, *pl* **mandats-lettres** [mɑ̃dalɛtr(ə)] *nm* money order (*with space for correspondence*).

mandchou, e [mɑ̃tʃu] *a* Manchu, Manchurian ♦ *nm* (*LING*) Manchu; *nm/f*: **M~, e** Manchu. **Mandchourie** [mɑ̃tʃuri] *nf*: **la ~** Manchuria.

mander [mɑ̃de] *vt* to summon.

mandibule [mɑ̃dibyl] *nf* mandible.

mandoline [mɑ̃dɔlin] *nf* mandolin(e).

manège [manɛʒ] *nm* riding school; (*à la foire*) roundabout (*Brit*), merry-go-round; (*fig*) game, ploy; **faire un tour de ~** to go for a ride on a *ou* the roundabout *etc*; **~ (de chevaux de bois)** roundabout (*Brit*), merry-go-round.

manette [manɛt] *nf* lever, tap; **~ de jeu** (*INFORM*) joystick.

manganèse [mɑ̃ganɛz] *nm* manganese.

mangeable [mɑ̃ʒabl(ə)] *a* edible, eatable.

mangeaille [mɑ̃ʒaj] *nf* (*péj*) grub.

mangeoire [mɑ̃ʒwar] *nf* trough, manger.

manger [mɑ̃ʒe] *vt* to eat; (*ronger: suj: rouille etc*) to eat into *ou* away; (*utiliser, consommer*) to eat up ♦ *vi* to eat.

mange-tout [mɑ̃ʒtu] *nm inv* mange-tout.

mangeur, euse [mɑ̃ʒœr, -øz] *nm/f* eater.

mangouste [mɑ̃gust(ə)] *nf* mongoose.

mangue [mɑ̃g] *nf* mango.

maniable [manjabl(ə)] *a* (*outil*) handy; (*voiture, voilier*) easy to handle, manœuvrable (*Brit*), maneuvrable (*US*); (*fig: personne*) easily influenced, manipulable.

maniaque [manjak] *a* (*pointilleux, méticuleux*) finicky, fussy; (*atteint de manie*) suffering from a mania ♦ *nm/f* maniac.

manie [mani] *nf* mania; (*tic*) odd habit.

maniement [manimɑ̃] *nm* handling; **~ d'armes** arms drill.

manier [manje] *vt* to handle; **se ~** *vi* (*fam*) to get a move on.

manière [manjɛr] *nf* (*façon*) way, manner; (*genre, style*) style; **~s** *nfpl* (*attitude*) manners; (*chichis*) fuss *sg*; **de ~ à** so as to; **de telle ~ que** in such a way that; **de cette ~** in this way *ou* manner; **d'une ~ générale** generally speaking, as a general rule; **de toute ~** in any case; **d'une certaine ~** in a (certain) way; **faire des ~s** to put on airs; **employer la ~ forte** to use strong-arm tactics; **adverbe de ~** adverb of manner.

maniéré, e [manjere] *a* affected.

manif [manif] *nf* (= *manifestation*) demo (*pl -s*).

manifestant, e [manifestɑ̃, -ɑ̃t] *nm/f* demonstrator.

manifestation [manifestasjɔ̃] *nf* (*de joie, mécontentement*) expression, demonstration; (*symptôme*) outward sign; (*fête etc*) event; (*POL*) demonstration.

manifeste [manifest(ə)] *a* obvious, evident ♦ *nm* manifesto (*pl -s*).

manifester [manifeste] *vt* (*volonté, intentions*) to show, indicate; (*joie, peur*) to express, show ♦ *vi* (*POL*) to demonstrate; **se ~** *vi* (*émotion*) to show *ou* express itself; (*difficultés*) to arise; (*symptômes*) to appear; (*témoin etc*) to come forward.

manigance [manigɑ̃s] *nf* scheme.

manigancer [manigɑ̃se] *vt* to plot, devise.

Manille [manij] *n* Manila.

manioc [manjɔk] *nm* cassava, manioc.

manipulateur, trice [manipylatœr, -tris] *a* (*technicien*) technician, operator; (*prestidigitateur*) conjurer; (*péj*) manipulator.

manipulation [manipylasjɔ̃] *nf* handling; manipulation.

manipuler [manipyle] *vt* to handle; (*fig*) to manipulate.

manivelle [manivɛl] *nf* crank.

manne [man] *nf* (*REL*) manna; (*fig*) godsend.

mannequin [mankɛ̃] *nm* (*COUTURE*) dummy; (*MODE*) model.

manœuvrable [manœvrabl(ə)] *a* (*bateau, véhicule*) manœuvrable (*Brit*), maneuverable (*US*).

manœuvre [manœvr(ə)] *nf* (*gén*) manœuvre (*Brit*), maneuver (*US*) ♦ *nm* (*ouvrier*) labourer (*Brit*), laborer (*US*).

manœuvrer [manœvʀe] *vt* to manœuvre (*Brit*), maneuver (*US*); (*levier, machine*) to operate; (*personne*) to manipulate ♦ *vi* to manœuvre *ou* maneuver.

manoir [manwaʀ] *nm* manor *ou* country house.

manomètre [manɔmɛtʀ(ə)] *nm* gauge, manometer.

manquant, e [mɑ̃kɑ̃, -ɑ̃t] *a* missing.

manque [mɑ̃k] *nm* (*insuffisance*): ~ **de** lack of; (*vide*) emptiness, gap; (*MÉD*) withdrawal; ~**s** *nmpl* (*lacunes*) faults, defects; **par** ~ **de** for want of; ~ **à gagner** loss of profit *ou* earnings.

manqué, e [mɑ̃ke] *a* failed; **garçon** ~ tomboy.

manquement [mɑ̃kmɑ̃] *nm*: ~ **à** (*discipline, règle*) breach of.

manquer [mɑ̃ke] *vi* (*faire défaut*) to be lacking; (*être absent*) to be missing; (*échouer*) to fail ♦ *vt* to miss ♦ *vb impersonnel*: **il (nous) manque encore 100 F** we are still 100 F short; **il manque des pages (au livre)** there are some pages missing *ou* some pages are missing (from the book); **l'argent qui leur manque** the money they need *ou* are short of; **le pied/la voix lui manqua** he missed his footing/his voice failed him; ~ **à qn** (*absent etc*): **il/cela me manque** I miss him/that; ~ **à** *vt* (*règles etc*) to be in breach of, fail to observe; ~ **de** *vt* to lack; (*COMM*) to be out of (stock of); **ne pas** ~ **de faire: il n'a pas manqué de le dire** he certainly said it; ~ **(de) faire: il a manqué (de) se tuer** he very nearly got killed; **il ne manquerait plus qu'il fasse** all we need now is for him to do; **je n'y manquerai pas** leave it to me, I'll definitely do it.

mansarde [mɑ̃saʀd(ə)] *nf* attic.

mansardé, e [mɑ̃saʀde] *a* attic *cpd*.

mansuétude [mɑ̃sɥetyd] *nf* leniency.

mante [mɑ̃t] *nf*: ~ **religieuse** praying mantis.

manteau, x [mɑ̃to] *nm* coat; ~ **de cheminée** mantelpiece; **sous le** ~ (*fig*) under cover.

mantille [mɑ̃tij] *nf* mantilla.

Mantoue [mɑ̃tu] *n* Mantua.

manucure [manykyʀ] *nf* manicurist.

manuel, le [manɥɛl] *a* manual ♦ *nm/f* manually gifted pupil *etc* (*as opposed to intellectually gifted*) ♦ *nm* (*ouvrage*) manual, handbook.

manuellement [manɥɛlmɑ̃] *ad* manually.

manufacture [manyfaktyʀ] *nf* (*établissement*) factory; (*fabrication*) manufacture.

manufacturé, e [manyfaktyʀe] *a* manufactured.

manufacturier, ière [manyfaktyʀje, -jɛʀ] *nm/f* factory owner.

manuscrit, e [manyskʀi, -it] *a* handwritten ♦ *nm* manuscript.

manutention [manytɑ̃sjɔ̃] *nf* (*COMM*) handling; (*local*) storehouse.

manutentionnaire [manytɑ̃sjɔnɛʀ] *nm/f* warehouseman/woman, packer.

manutentionner [manytɑ̃sjɔne] *vt* to handle.

MAP *sigle f* (*PHOTO*: = *mise au point*) focusing.

mappemonde [mapmɔ̃d] *nf* (*plane*) map of the world; (*sphère*) globe.

maquereau, x [makʀo] *nm* mackerel *inv*;

(*fam: proxénète*) pimp.

maquerelle [makʀɛl] *nf* (*fam*) madam.

maquette [makɛt] *nf* (*d'un décor, bâtiment, véhicule*) (scale) model; (*TYPO*) mockup; (: *d'une page illustrée, affiche*) paste-up; (: *prêt à la réproduction*) artwork.

maquignon [makiɲɔ̃] *nm* horse-dealer.

maquillage [makijaʒ] *nm* making up; faking; (*produits*) make-up.

maquiller [makije] *vt* (*personne, visage*) to make up; (*truquer: passeport, statistique*) to fake; (: *voiture volée*) to do over (*respray etc*); **se** ~ to make o.s. up.

maquilleur, euse [makijœʀ, -øz] *nm/f* make-up artist.

maquis [maki] *nm* (*GÉO*) scrub; (*fig*) tangle; (*MIL*) maquis, underground fighting *q*.

maquisard, e [makizaʀ, -aʀd(ə)] *nm/f* maquis, member of the Resistance.

marabout [maʀabu] *nm* (*ZOOL*) marabou(t).

maraîcher, ère [maʀeʃe, maʀeʃɛʀ] *a*: **cultures maraîchères** market gardening *sg* ♦ *nm/f* market gardener.

marais [maʀɛ] *nm* marsh, swamp; ~ **salant** saltworks.

marasme [maʀasm(ə)] *nm* (*POL, ÉCON*) stagnation, sluggishness; (*accablement*) dejection, depression.

marathon [maʀatɔ̃] *nm* marathon.

marâtre [maʀɑtʀ(ə)] *nf* cruel mother.

maraude [maʀod] *nf* pilfering, thieving (*of poultry, crops*); (*dans un verger*) scrumping; (*vagabondage*) prowling; **en** ~ on the prowl; (*taxi*) cruising.

maraudeur, euse [maʀodœʀ, -øz] *nm/f* marauder; prowler.

marbre [maʀbʀ(ə)] *nm* (*pierre, statue*) marble; (*d'une table, commode*) marble top; (*TYPO*) stone, bed; **rester de** ~ to remain stonily indifferent.

marbrer [maʀbʀe] *vt* to mottle, blotch; (*TECH: papier*) to marble.

marbrier [maʀbʀije] *nm* monumental mason.

marbrière [maʀbʀijɛʀ] *nf* marble quarry.

marbrures [maʀbʀyʀ] *nfpl* blotches *pl*; (*TECH*) marbling *sg*.

marc [maʀ] *nm* (*de raisin, pommes*) marc; ~ **de café** coffee grounds *pl ou* dregs *pl*.

marcassin [maʀkasɛ̃] *nm* young wild boar.

marchand, e [maʀʃɑ̃, -ɑ̃d] *nm/f* shopkeeper, tradesman/woman; (*au marché*) stallholder; (*spécifique*): ~ **de cycles/tapis** bicycle/carpet dealer; ~ **de charbon/vins** coal/wine merchant ♦ *a*: **prix/valeur** ~**(e)** market price/value; **qualité** ~**e** standard quality; ~ **en gros/au détail** wholesaler/retailer; ~ **de biens** real estate agent; ~ **de canons** (*péj*) arms dealer; ~ **de couleurs** ironmonger (*Brit*), hardware dealer (*US*); ~**/e de fruits** fruiterer (*Brit*), fruit seller (*US*); ~**/e de journaux** newsagent; ~**/e de légumes** greengrocer (*Brit*), produce dealer (*US*); ~**/e de poisson** fishmonger (*Brit*), fish seller (*US*); ~**/e de(s) quatre-saisons** costermonger (*Brit*), street vendor (selling fresh fruit and vegetables); ~ **de sable** (*fig*) sandman; ~ **de tableaux** art dealer.

marchander [maʀʃɑ̃de] *vt* (*article*) to bargain *ou* haggle over; (*éloges*) to be sparing with ♦

vi to bargain, haggle.

marchandise [maʀʃãdiz] *nf* goods *pl*, merchandise *q*.

marche [maʀʃ(ə)] *nf* (*d'escalier*) step; (*activité*) walking; (*promenade, trajet, allure*) walk; (*démarche*) walk, gait; (*MIL etc, MUS*) march; (*fonctionnement*) running; (*progression*) progress; course; **à une heure de** ~ an hour's walk (away); **ouvrir/fermer la** ~ to lead the way/bring up the rear; **dans le sens de la** ~ (*RAIL*) facing the engine; **en** ~ (*monter etc*) while the vehicle is moving *ou* in motion; **mettre en** ~ to start; **remettre qch en** ~ to set *ou* start sth going again; **se mettre en** ~ (*personne*) to get moving; (*machine*) to start; ~ **arrière** (*AUTO*) reverse (gear); **faire** ~ **arrière** (*AUTO*) to reverse; (*fig*) to backtrack, back-pedal; ~ **à suivre** (correct) procedure; (*sur notice*) (step by step) instructions *pl*.

marché [maʀʃe] *nm* (*lieu, COMM, ÉCON*) market; (*ville*) trading centre; (*transaction*) bargain, deal; **par-dessus le** ~ into the bargain; **faire son** ~ to do one's shopping; **mettre le** ~ **en main à qn** to tell sb to take it or leave it; ~ **au comptant** (*BOURSE*) spot market; **M~ commun** Common Market; ~ **aux fleurs** flower market; ~ **noir** black market; **faire du** ~ **noir** to buy and sell on the black market; ~ **aux puces** flea market; ~ **à terme** (*BOURSE*) forward market; ~ **du travail** labour market.

marchepied [maʀʃəpje] *nm* (*RAIL*) step; (*AUTO*) running board; (*fig*) stepping stone.

marcher [maʀʃe] *vi* to walk; (*MIL*) to march; (*aller: voiture, train, affaires*) to go; (*prospérer*) to go well; (*fonctionner*) to work, run; (*fam*) to go along, agree; (*: croire naïvement*) to be taken in; ~ **sur** to walk on; (*mettre le pied sur*) to step on *ou* in; (*MIL*) to march upon; ~ **dans** (*herbe etc*) to walk in *ou* on; (*flaque*) to step in; **faire** ~ **qn** (*pour rire*) to pull sb's leg; (*pour tromper*) to lead sb up the garden path.

marcheur, euse [maʀʃœʀ, -øz] *nm/f* walker.

marcotter [maʀkɔte] *vt* to layer.

mardi [maʀdi] *nm* Tuesday; **M~ gras** Shrove Tuesday; *voir aussi* **lundi**.

mare [maʀ] *nf* pond; ~ **de sang** pool of blood.

marécage [maʀekaʒ] *nm* marsh, swamp.

marécageux, euse [maʀekaʒø, -øz] *a* marshy, swampy.

maréchal, aux [maʀeʃal, -o] *nm* marshal; ~ **des logis** (*MIL*) sergeant.

maréchal-ferrant, *pl* **maréchaux-ferrants** [maʀeʃalfɛʀã, maʀeʃo-] *nm* blacksmith, farrier (*Brit*).

maréchaussée [maʀeʃose] *nf* (*humoristique: gendarmes*) constabulary (*Brit*), police.

marée [maʀe] *nf* tide; (*poissons*) fresh (sea) fish; ~ **haute/basse** high/low tide; ~ **montante/descendante** rising/ebb tide; ~ **noire** oil slick.

marelle [maʀɛl] *nf*: (**jouer à**) **la** ~ (to play) hopscotch.

marémotrice [maʀemɔtʀis] *af* tidal.

mareyeur, euse [maʀejœʀ, -øz] *nm/f* wholesale (sea) fish merchant.

margarine [maʀɡaʀin] *nf* margarine.

marge [maʀʒ(ə)] *nf* margin; **en** ~ in the margin; **en** ~ **de** (*fig*) on the fringe of; (*en dehors de*) cut off from; (*qui se rapporte à*) connected with; ~ **bénéficiaire** profit margin, mark-up; ~ **de sécurité** safety margin.

margelle [maʀʒɛl] *nf* coping.

margeur [maʀʒœʀ] *nm* margin stop.

marginal, e, aux [maʀʒinal, -o] *a* marginal ♦ *nm/f* dropout.

marguerite [maʀɡəʀit] *nf* marguerite, (oxeye) daisy; (*INFORM*) daisy wheel.

marguillier [maʀɡije] *nm* churchwarden.

mari [maʀi] *nm* husband.

mariage [maʀjaʒ] *nm* (*union, état, fig*) marriage; (*noce*) wedding; ~ **civil/religieux** registry office (*Brit*) *ou* civil/church wedding; **un** ~ **de raison/d'amour** a marriage of convenience/a love match; ~ **blanc** unconsummated marriage; ~ **en blanc** white wedding.

marié, e [maʀje] *a* married ♦ *nm/f* (bride)groom/bride; **les** ~**s** the bride and groom; **les (jeunes)** ~**s** the newly-weds.

marier [maʀje] *vt* to marry; (*fig*) to blend; **se** ~ (**avec**) to marry, get married (to); (*fig*) to blend (with).

marijuana [maʀiʒwana] *nf* marijuana.

marin, e [maʀɛ̃, -in] *a* sea *cpd*, marine ♦ *nm* sailor ♦ *nf* navy; (*ART*) seascape; (*couleur*) navy (blue); **avoir le pied** ~ to be a good sailor; (*garder son équilibre*) to have one's sea legs; ~**e de guerre** navy; ~**e marchande** merchant navy; ~**e à voiles** sailing ships *pl*.

marinade [maʀinad] *nf* marinade.

marine [maʀin] *af, nf voir* **marin** ♦ *a inv* navy (blue) ♦ *nm* (*MIL*) marine.

mariner [maʀine] *vi, vt* to marinate, marinade.

marinier [maʀinje] *nm* bargee.

marinière [maʀinjɛʀ] *nf* (*blouse*) smock ♦ *a inv*: **moules** ~ (*CULIN*) mussels in white wine.

marionnette [maʀjɔnɛt] *nf* puppet.

marital, e, aux [maʀital, -o] *a*: **autorisation** ~**e** husband's permission.

maritalement [maʀitalmã] *ad*: **vivre** ~ to live together (as husband and wife).

maritime [maʀitim] *a* sea *cpd*, maritime; (*ville*) coastal, seaside; (*droit*) shipping, maritime.

marjolaine [maʀʒɔlɛn] *nf* marjoram.

mark [maʀk] *nm* (*monnaie*) mark.

marketing [maʀkɔtiŋ] *nm* (*COMM*) marketing.

marmaille [maʀmaj] *nf* (*péj*) (gang of) brats *pl*.

marmelade [maʀmələd] *nf* (*compote*) stewed fruit, compote; ~ **d'oranges** (orange) marmalade; **en** ~ (*fig*) crushed (to a pulp).

marmite [maʀmit] *nf* (cooking-)pot.

marmiton [maʀmitɔ̃] *nm* kitchen boy.

marmonner [maʀmɔne] *vt, vi* to mumble, mutter.

marmot [maʀmo] *nm* (*fam*) brat.

marmotte [maʀmɔt] *nf* marmot.

marmotter [maʀmɔte] *vt* (*prière*) to mumble, mutter.

marne [maʀn(ə)] *nf* (*GÉO*) marl.

Maroc [maʀɔk] *nm*: **le** ~ Morocco.

marocain, e [maʀɔkɛ̃, -ɛn] a Moroccan ♦ nm/
f: **M~, e** Moroccan.

maroquin [maʀɔkɛ̃] nm (peau) morocco
(leather); (fig) (minister's) portfolio.

maroquinerie [maʀɔkinʀi] nf (industrie)
leather craft; (commerce) leather shop;
(articles) fine leather goods pl.

marotte [maʀɔt] nf fad.

marquant, e [maʀkɑ̃, -ɑ̃t] a outstanding.

marque [maʀk(ə)] nf mark; (SPORT, JEU:
décompte des points) score; (COMM: de
produits) brand, make; (: de disques) label;
(insigne: d'une fonction) badge; (fig): ~
d'affection token of affection; ~ **de joie** sign
of joy; **à vos ~s!** (SPORT) on your marks!;
de ~ a (COMM) brand-name cpd:
proprietary; (fig) high-class; (: personnage,
hôte) distinguished; **produit de** ~ (COMM)
quality product; ~ **déposée** registered trademark; ~ **de fabrique** trademark.

marqué, e [maʀke] a marked.

marquer [maʀke] vt to mark; (inscrire) to
write down; (bétail) to brand; (SPORT: but
etc) to score; (: joueur) to mark;
(accentuer: taille etc) to emphasize;
(manifester: refus, intérêt) to show ♦ vi
(événement, personnalité) to stand out, be
outstanding; (SPORT) to score; ~ **qn de son
influence/empreinte** to have an influence/
leave its impression on sb; ~ **un temps
d'arrêt** to pause momentarily; ~ **le pas** (fig)
to mark time; **il a marqué ce jour-là d'une
pierre blanche** that was a red-letter day for
him; ~ **les points** (tenir la marque) to keep
the score.

marqueté, e [maʀkəte] a inlaid.

marqueterie [maʀkətʀi] nf inlaid work,
marquetry.

marqueur, euse [maʀkœʀ, -øz] nm/f (SPORT:
de but) scorer ♦ nm (crayon feutre) marker
pen.

marquis, e [maʀki, -iz] nm/f marquis ou
marquess/marchioness ♦ nf (auvent) glass
canopy ou awning.

Marquises [maʀkiz] nfpl: **les (îles)** ~ the
Marquesas Islands.

marraine [maʀɛn] nf godmother; (d'un navire,
d'une rose etc) namer.

Marrakech [maʀakɛʃ] n Marrakech ou
Marrakesh.

marrant, e [maʀɑ̃, -ɑ̃t] a (fam) funny.

marre [maʀ] ad (fam): **en avoir** ~ **de** to be
fed up with.

marrer [maʀe]: **se** ~ vi (fam) to have a
(good) laugh.

marron, ne [maʀɔ̃, -ɔn] nm (fruit) chestnut ♦
a inv brown ♦ a (péj) crooked; (: faux)
bogus; ~**s glacés** marrons glacés.

marronnier [maʀɔnje] nm chestnut (tree).

Mars [maʀs] nm ou nf Mars.

mars [maʀs] nm March; voir aussi **juillet**.

marseillais, e [maʀsɛjɛ, -ɛz] a of ou from
Marseilles ♦ nf: **la M~e** the French national
anthem.

Marseille [maʀsɛj] n Marseilles.

marsouin [maʀswɛ̃] nm porpoise.

marsupiaux [maʀsypjo] nmpl marsupials.

marteau, x [maʀto] nm hammer; (de porte)
knocker; ~ **pneumatique** pneumatic drill.

marteau-pilon, pl **marteaux-pilons**
[maʀtopilɔ̃] nm power hammer.

marteau-piqueur, pl **marteaux-piqueurs**
[maʀtopikœʀ] nm pneumatic drill.

martel [maʀtɛl] nm: **se mettre** ~ **en tête** to
worry o.s.

martèlement [maʀtɛlmɑ̃] nm hammering.

marteler [maʀtəle] vt to hammer; (mots,
phrases) to rap out.

martial, e, aux [maʀsjal, -o] a martial; **cour**
~**e** court-martial.

martien, ne [maʀsjɛ̃, -ɛn] a Martian, of ou
from Mars.

martinet [maʀtinɛ] nm (fouet) small whip;
(ZOOL) swift.

martingale [maʀtɛ̃gal] nf (COUTURE) half-
belt; (JEU) winning formula.

martiniquais, e [maʀtinikɛ, -ɛz] a of ou from
Martinique.

Martinique [maʀtinik] nf: **la** ~ Martinique.

martin-pêcheur, pl **martins-pêcheurs**
[maʀtɛ̃pɛʃœʀ] nm kingfisher.

martre [maʀtʀ(ə)] nf marten; ~ **zibeline**
sable.

martyr, e [maʀtiʀ] nm/f martyr ♦ a martyred;
enfants ~**s** battered children.

martyre [maʀtiʀ] nm martyrdom; (fig: sens
affaibli) agony, torture; **souffrir le** ~ to
suffer agonies.

martyriser [maʀtiʀize] vt (REL) to martyr;
(fig) to bully; (: enfant) to batter.

marxisme [maʀksism(ə)] nm Marxism.

marxiste [maʀksist(ə)] a, nm/f Marxist.

mas [mɑ(s)] nm traditional house or farm in
Provence.

mascarade [maskaʀad] nf masquerade.

mascotte [maskɔt] nf mascot.

masculin, e [maskylɛ̃, -in] a masculine; (sexe,
population) male; (équipe, vêtements)
men's; (viril) manly ♦ nm masculine.

masochisme [mazɔʃism(ə)] nm masochism.

masque [mask(ə)] nm mask; ~ **de beauté**
face pack; ~ **à gaz** gas mask; ~ **de plongée**
diving mask.

masqué, e [maske] a masked.

masquer [maske] vt (cacher: porte, goût) to
hide, conceal; (dissimuler: vérité, projet) to
mask, obscure.

massacrant, e [masakʀɑ̃, -ɑ̃t] a: **humeur** ~**e**
foul temper.

massacre [masakʀ(ə)] nm massacre, slaughter; **jeu de** ~ (fig) wholesale slaughter.

massacrer [masakʀe] vt to massacre,
slaughter; (fig: adversaire) to slaughter; (:
texte etc) to murder.

massage [masaʒ] nm massage.

masse [mas] nf mass; (péj): **la** ~ the masses
pl; (ÉLEC) earth; (maillet) sledgehammer;
~**s** nfpl masses; **une** ~ **de, des** ~**s de** (fam)
masses ou loads of; **en** ~ ad (en bloc) in
bulk; (en foule) en masse ♦ a (exécutions,
production) mass cpd; ~ **monétaire** (ÉCON)
money supply; ~ **salariale** (COMM) wage(s)
bill.

massepain [maspɛ̃] nm marzipan.

masser [mase] vt (assembler) to gather; (pétrir) to massage; **se** ~ vi to gather.

masseur, euse [masœʀ, -øz] nm/f (personne)
masseur/masseuse ♦ nm (appareil)

massager.

massicot [masiko] *nm* (*TYPO*) guillotine.

massif, ive [masif, -iv] *a* (*porte*) solid, massive; (*visage*) heavy, large; (*bois, or*) solid; (*dose*) massive; (*déportations etc*) mass *cpd* ♦ *nm* (*montagneux*) massif; (*de fleurs*) clump, bank.

massue [masy] *nf* club, bludgeon ♦ *a inv*: **argument** ~ sledgehammer argument.

mastic [mastik] *nm* (*pour vitres*) putty; (*pour fentes*) filler.

mastication [mastikasjɔ̃] *nf* chewing, mastication.

mastiquer [mastike] *vt* (*aliment*) to chew, masticate; (*fente*) to fill; (*vitre*) to putty.

mastoc [mastɔk] *a inv* hefty.

mastodonte [mastɔdɔ̃t] *nm* monster (*fig*).

masturbation [mastyʀbasjɔ̃] *nf* masturbation.

masturber [mastyʀbe] *vt*: **se** ~ to masturbate.

m'as-tu-vu [matyvy] *nm/f inv* show-off.

masure [mazyʀ] *nf* tumbledown cottage.

mat, e [mat] *a* (*couleur, métal*) mat(t); (*bruit, son*) dull ♦ *a inv* (*ÉCHECS*): **être** ~ to be checkmate.

mât [mɑ] *nm* (*NAVIG*) mast; (*poteau*) pole, post.

matamore [matamɔʀ] *nm* braggart, blusterer.

match [matʃ] *nm* match; ~ **nul** draw, tie (*US*); **faire** ~ **nul** to draw (*Brit*), tie (*US*); ~ **aller** first leg; ~ **retour** second leg, return match.

matelas [matla] *nm* mattress; ~ **pneumatique** air bed *ou* mattress; ~ **à ressorts** spring *ou* interior-sprung mattress.

matelasser [matlase] *vt* to pad.

matelot [matlo] *nm* sailor, seaman.

mater [mate] *vt* (*personne*) to bring to heel, subdue; (*révolte*) to put down; (*fam*) to watch, look at.

matérialiser [mateʀjalize]: **se** ~ *vi* to materialize.

matérialisme [mateʀjalism(ə)] *nm* materialism.

matérialiste [mateʀjalist(ə)] *a* materialistic ♦ *nm/f* materialist.

matériau, x [mateʀjo] *nm* material; ~**x** *nmpl* material(s); ~**x de construction** building materials.

matériel, le [mateʀjɛl] *a* material; (*organisation, aide, obstacle*) practical; (*fig: péj: personne*) materialistic ♦ *nm* equipment *q*; (*de camping etc*) gear *q*; **il n'a pas le temps** ~ **de le faire** he doesn't have the time (needed) to do it; ~ **d'exploitation** (*COMM*) plant; ~ **roulant** rolling stock.

maternel, le [mateʀnɛl] *a* (*amour, geste*) motherly, maternal; (*grand-père, oncle*) maternal ♦ *nf* (*aussi*: **école** ~**le**) (state) nursery school.

materner [mateʀne] *vt* (*personne*) to mother.

maternité [mateʀnite] *nf* (*établissement*) maternity hospital; (*état de mère*) motherhood, maternity; (*grossesse*) pregnancy.

math [mat] *nfpl* maths (*Brit*), math (*US*).

mathématicien, ne [matematisjɛ̃, -ɛn] *nm/f* mathematician.

mathématique [matematik] *a* mathematical.

mathématiques [matematik] *nfpl* mathematics *sg*.

matheux, euse [matø, -øz] *nm/f* (*fam*) maths (*Brit*) *ou* math (*US*) student; (*fort en math*) mathematical genius.

maths [mat] *nfpl* maths (*Brit*), math (*US*).

matière [matjɛʀ] *nf* (*PHYSIQUE*) matter; (*COMM, TECH*) material, matter *q*; (*fig: d'un livre etc*) subject matter; (*SCOL*) subject; **en** ~ **de** as regards; **donner** ~ **à** to give cause to; ~ **grise** grey matter; ~ **plastique** plastic; ~**s fécales** faeces; ~**s grasses** fat (content) *sg*; ~**s premières** raw materials.

MATIF [matif] *sigle m* (= *Marché à terme des instruments financiers*) body which regulates the activities of the French Stock Exchange.

Matignon [matiɲɔ̃] *n* French prime minister's offices.

matin [matɛ̃] *nm, ad* morning; **le** ~ (*pendant le* ~) in the morning; **demain** ~ tomorrow morning; **le lendemain** ~ (the) next morning; **du** ~ **au soir** from morning till night; **une heure du** ~ one o'clock in the morning; **de grand** *ou* **bon** ~ early in the morning.

matinal, e, aux [matinal, -o] *a* (*toilette, gymnastique*) morning *cpd*; (*de bonne heure*) early; **être** ~ (*personne*) to be up early; (: *habituellement*) to be an early riser.

mâtiné, e [matine] *a* crossbred, mixed race *cpd*.

matinée [matine] *nf* morning; (*spectacle*) matinée, afternoon performance.

matois, e [matwa, -waz] *a* wily.

matou [matu] *nm* tom(cat).

matraquage [matʀakaʒ] *nm* beating up; ~ **publicitaire** plug, plugging.

matraque [matʀak] *nf* (*de malfaiteur*) cosh (*Brit*), club; (*de policier*) truncheon (*Brit*), billy (*US*).

matraquer [matʀake] *vt* to beat up (with a truncheon *ou* billy); to cosh (*Brit*), club; (*fig: touristes etc*) to rip off; (: *disque*) to plug.

matriarcal, e, aux [matʀijaʀkal, -o] *a* matriarchal.

matrice [matʀis] *nf* (*ANAT*) womb; (*TECH*) mould; (*MATH etc*) matrix.

matricule [matʀikyl] *nf* (*aussi*: **registre** ~) roll, register ♦ *nm* (*aussi*: **numéro** ~: *MIL*) regimental number; (: *ADMIN*) reference number.

matrimonial, e, aux [matʀimɔnjal, -o] *a* marital, marriage *cpd*.

matrone [matʀɔn] *nf* matron.

mâture [mɑtyʀ] *nf* masts *pl*.

maturité [matyʀite] *nf* maturity; (*d'un fruit*) ripeness, maturity.

maudire [modiʀ] *vt* to curse.

maudit, e [modi, -it] *a* (*fam: satané*) blasted, confounded.

maugréer [mogʀee] *vi* to grumble.

mauresque [mɔʀɛsk(ə)] *a* Moorish.

Maurice [mɔʀis] *nf*: (**l'île**) ~ Mauritius.

mauricien, ne [mɔʀisjɛ̃, -ɛn] *a* Mauritian.

Mauritanie [mɔʀitani] *nf*: **la** ~ Mauritania.

mauritanien, ne [mɔʀitanjɛ̃, -ɛn] *a* Mauritanian.

mausolée [mozɔle] *nm* mausoleum.

maussade [mosad] *a* (*air, personne*) sullen; (*ciel, temps*) dismal.

mauvais, e [movɛ, -ɛz] *a* bad; (*faux*): **le** ~

numéro/moment the wrong number/
moment; (*méchant, malveillant*) malicious,
spiteful ♦ *nm*: **le ~** the bad side ♦ *ad*: **il fait
~** the weather is bad; **sentir ~** to have a
nasty smell, smell bad *ou* nasty; **la mer est
~e** the sea is rough; **~ coucheur** awkward
customer; **~ coup** (*fig*) criminal venture; **~
garçon** tough; **~ pas** tight spot; **~ plaisant**
hoaxer; **~ traitements** ill treatment *sg*; **~e
herbe** weed; **~e langue** gossip, scandal-
monger (*Brit*); **~e passe** difficult situation;
(*période*) bad patch; **~e tête** rebellious *ou*
headstrong customer.

mauve [mov] *a* (*couleur*) mauve ♦ *nf* (*BOT*)
mallow.

mauviette [movjɛt] *nf* (*péj*) weakling.

maux [mo] *nmpl voir* **mal**.

max. *abr* (= *maximum*) max.

maximal, e, aux [maksimal, -o] *a* maximal.

maxime [maksim] *nf* maxim.

maximum [maksimɔm] *a, nm* maximum;
atteindre un/son ~ to reach a/his peak; **au
~** *ad* (*le plus possible*) to the full; as much
as one can; (*tout au plus*) at the (very) most
ou maximum.

Mayence [majɑ̃s] *n* Mainz.

mayonnaise [majɔnɛz] *nf* mayonnaise.

Mayotte [majɔt] *nf* Mayotte.

mazout [mazut] *nm* (fuel) oil; **chaudière/
poêle à ~** oil-fired boiler/stove.

mazouté, e [mazute] *a* oil-polluted.

MDM *sigle mpl* (= *Médecins du Monde*)
*medical association for aid to Third World
countries*.

Mᵉ *abr* = **Maître**.

me, m' [m(ə)] *pronom* me; (*réfléchi*) myself.

méandres [meɑ̃dR(ə)] *nmpl* meanderings.

mec [mɛk] *nm* (*fam*) guy, bloke (*Brit*).

mécanicien, ne [mekanisjɛ̃, -ɛn] *nm/f* mechanic; (*RAIL*) (train *ou* engine) driver; **~
navigant** *ou* **de bord** (*AVIAT*) flight engineer.

mécanicien-dentiste [mekanisjɛ̃dɑ̃tist(ə)],
mécanicienne-dentiste [mekanisjɛn-] (*pl*
~s-~s) *nm/f* dental technician.

mécanique [mekanik] *a* mechanical ♦ *nf*
(*science*) mechanics *sg*; (*technologie*) mechanical engineering; (*mécanisme*) mechanism; engineering; works *pl*; **ennui ~** engine
trouble *q*; **s'y connaître en ~** to be me-
chanically minded; **~ hydraulique** hydraulics
sg; **~ ondulatoire** wave mechanics *sg*.

mécaniquement [mekanikmɑ̃] *ad* mechani-
cally.

mécanisation [mekanizɑsjɔ̃] *nf* mechanization.

mécaniser [mekanize] *vt* to mechanize.

mécanisme [mekanism(ə)] *nm* mechanism.

mécano [mekano] *nm* (*fam*) mechanic.

mécanographie [mekanɔgRafi] *nf* (mechanical) data processing.

mécène [mesɛn] *nm* patron.

méchamment [meʃamɑ̃] *ad* nastily, maliciously, spitefully; viciously.

méchanceté [meʃɑ̃ste] *nf* (*d'une personne,
d'une parole*) nastiness, maliciousness,
spitefulness; (*parole, action*) nasty *ou* spiteful
ou malicious remark (*ou* action).

méchant, e [meʃɑ̃, -ɑ̃t] *a* nasty, malicious,
spiteful; (*enfant: pas sage*) naughty;
(*animal*) vicious; (*avant le nom: valeur*

péjorative) nasty; miserable; (: *intensive*)
terrific.

mèche [mɛʃ] *nf* (*de lampe, bougie*) wick;
(*d'un explosif*) fuse; (*MÉD*) pack, dressing;
(*de vilebrequin, perceuse*) bit; (*de dentiste*)
drill; (*de fouet*) lash; (*de cheveux*) lock; **se
faire faire des ~s** (*chez le coiffeur*) to have
one's hair streaked, have highlights put in
one's hair; **vendre la ~** to give the game
away; **de ~ avec** in league with.

méchoui [meʃwi] *nm whole sheep barbecue*.

mécompte [mekɔ̃t] *nm* (*erreur*) miscalculation; (*déception*) disappointment.

méconnais [mekɔnɛ] *etc vb voir*
méconnaître.

méconnaissable [mekɔnɛsabl(ə)] *a* unrecognizable.

méconnaissais [mekɔnɛsɛ] *etc vb voir*
méconnaître.

méconnaissance [mekɔnɛsɑ̃s] *nf* ignorance.

méconnaître [mekɔnɛtR(ə)] *vt* (*ignorer*) to be
unaware of; (*mésestimer*) to misjudge.

méconnu, e [mekɔny] *pp de* **méconnaître** ♦ *a*
(*génie etc*) unrecognized.

mécontent, e [mekɔ̃tɑ̃, -ɑ̃t] *a*: **~ (de)** (*insatisfait*) discontented *ou* dissatisfied *ou* displeased (with); (*contrarié*) annoyed (at) ♦
nm/f malcontent, displeased person.

mécontentement [mekɔ̃tɑ̃tmɑ̃] *nm* dissatisfaction, discontent, displeasure;
annoyance.

mécontenter [mekɔ̃tɑ̃te] *vt* to displease.

Mecque [mɛk] *nf*: **la ~** Mecca.

mécréant, e [mekReɑ̃, -ɑ̃t] *a* (*peuple*) infidel;
(*personne*) atheistic.

méd. *abr* = **médecin**.

médaille [medaj] *nf* medal.

médaillé, e [medaje] *nm/f* (*SPORT*) medal-
holder.

médaillon [medajɔ̃] *nm* (*portrait*) medallion;
(*bijou*) locket; (*CULIN*) médaillon; **en ~** *a*
(*carte etc*) inset.

médecin [mɛdsɛ̃] *nm* doctor; **~ du bord**
(*NAVIG*) ship's doctor; **~ généraliste** general
practitioner, GP; **~ légiste** forensic scientist
(*Brit*), medical examiner (*US*); **~ traitant**
family doctor, GP.

médecine [mɛdsin] *nf* medicine; **~ générale**
general medicine; **~ infantile** paediatrics *sg*
(*Brit*), pediatrics *sg* (*US*); **~ légale** forensic
medicine; **~ préventive** preventive medicine;
~ du travail occupational *ou* industrial
medicine.

médian, e [medjɑ̃, -an] *a* median.

médias [medja] *nmpl*: **les ~** the media.

médiateur, trice [medjatœR, -tRis] *nm/f* (*voir
médiation*) mediator; arbitrator.

médiathèque [medjatɛk] *nf* media library.

médiation [medjɑsjɔ̃] *nf* mediation; (*dans
conflit social etc*) arbitration.

médiatique [medjatik] *a* media *cpd*.

médiator [medjatɔR] *nm* plectrum.

médical, e, aux [medikal, -o] *a* medical;
visiteur *ou* **délégué ~** medical rep *ou* representative.

médicament [medikamɑ̃] *nm* medicine, drug.

médicamenteux, euse [medikamɑ̃tø, -øz] *a*
medicinal.

médication [medikɑsjɔ̃] *nf* medication.

médicinal, e, aux [medisinal, -o] *a* medicinal.

médico-légal, e, aux [medikɔlegal, -o] *a* forensic.

médiéval, e, aux [medjeval, -o] *a* medieval.

médiocre [medjɔkʀ(ə)] *a* mediocre, poor.

médiocrité [medjɔkʀite] *nf* mediocrity.

médire [mediʀ] *vi*: ~ **de** to speak ill of.

médisance [medizɑ̃s] *nf* scandalmongering *q* (*Brit*), mud-slinging *q*; (*propos*) piece of scandal *ou* malicious gossip.

médisant, e [medizɑ̃, -ɑ̃t] *vb voir* **médire ♦** *a* slanderous, malicious.

médit, e [medi, -it] *pp de* **médire**.

méditatif, ive [meditatif, -iv] *a* thoughtful.

méditation [meditɑsjɔ̃] *nf* meditation.

méditer [medite] *vt* (*approfondir*) to meditate on, ponder (over); (*combiner*) to meditate ♦ *vi* to meditate; ~ **de faire** to contemplate doing, plan to do.

Méditerranée [mediteʀane] *nf*: **la (mer)** ~ the Mediterranean (Sea).

méditerranéen, ne [mediteʀaneɛ̃, -ɛn] *a* Mediterranean ♦ *nm/f*: **M~, ne** Mediterranean.

médium [medjɔm] *nm* medium (*spiritualist*).

médius [medjys] *nm* middle finger.

méduse [medyz] *nf* jellyfish.

méduser [medyze] *vt* to dumbfound.

meeting [mitiŋ] *nm* (*POL, SPORT*) rally, meeting; ~ **d'aviation** air show.

méfait [mefɛ] *nm* (*faute*) misdemeanour, wrongdoing; ~**s** *nmpl* (*ravages*) ravages.

méfiance [mefjɑ̃s] *nf* mistrust, distrust.

méfiant, e [mefjɑ̃, -ɑ̃t] *a* mistrustful, distrustful.

méfier [mefje]: **se** ~ *vi* to be wary; (*faire attention*) to be careful; **se** ~ **de** *vt* to mistrust, distrust, be wary of; to be careful about.

mégalomane [megalɔman] *a* megalomaniac.

mégalomanie [megalɔmani] *nf* megalomania.

méga-octet [megaɔktɛ] *nm* megabyte.

mégarde [megaʀd(ə)] *nf*: **par** ~ accidentally; (*par erreur*) by mistake.

mégatonne [megatɔn] *nf* megaton.

mégère [meʒɛʀ] *nf* (*péj: femme*) shrew.

mégot [mego] *nm* cigarette end *ou* butt.

mégoter [megote] *vi* to nitpick.

meilleur, e [mɛjœʀ] *a*, *ad* better; (*valeur superlative*) best ♦ *nm*: **le** ~ (*celui qui ...*) the best (one); (*ce qui ...*) the best ♦ *nf*: **la** ~**e** the best (one); **le** ~ **des deux** the better of the two; **de** ~**e heure** earlier; ~ **marché** cheaper.

méjuger [meʒyʒe] *vt* to misjudge.

mélancolie [melɑ̃kɔli] *nf* melancholy, gloom.

mélancolique [melɑ̃kɔlik] *a* melancholy, gloomy.

mélange [melɑ̃ʒ] *nm* (*opération*) mixing; blending; (*résultat*) mixture; blend; **sans** ~ unadulterated.

mélanger [melɑ̃ʒe] *vt* (*substances*) to mix; (*vins, couleurs*) to blend; (*mettre en désordre, confondre*) to mix up, muddle (up); **se** ~ (*liquides, couleurs*) to blend, mix.

mélanine [melanin] *nf* melanin.

mélasse [melas] *nf* treacle, molasses *sg*.

mêlée [mele] *nf* (*bataille, cohue*) mêlée, scramble; (*lutte, conflit*) tussle, scuffle;

(*RUGBY*) scrum(mage).

mêler [mele] *vt* (*substances, odeurs, races*) to mix; (*embrouiller*) to muddle (up), mix up; **se** ~ to mix; (*se joindre, s'allier*) to mingle; **se** ~ **à** (*suj: personne*) to join; to mix with; (*: odeurs etc*) to mingle with; **se** ~ **de** (*suj: personne*) to meddle with, interfere in; **mêle-toi de tes affaires!** mind your own business!; ~ **à** *ou* **avec** *ou* **de** to mix with; to mingle with; ~ **qn à** (*affaire*) to get sb mixed up *ou* involved in.

mélo [melo] *nm*, *a* = **mélodrame**, **mélodramatique**.

mélodie [melɔdi] *nf* melody.

mélodieux, euse [melɔdjø, -øz] *a* melodious, tuneful.

mélodique [melɔdik] *a* melodic.

mélodramatique [melɔdʀamatik] *a* melodramatic.

mélodrame [melɔdʀam] *nm* melodrama.

mélomane [melɔman] *nm/f* music lover.

melon [mɔlɔ̃] *nm* (*BOT*) (honeydew) melon; (*aussi*: **chapeau** ~) bowler (hat); ~ **d'eau** watermelon.

mélopée [melɔpe] *nf* monotonous chant.

membrane [mɑ̃bʀan] *nf* membrane.

membre [mɑ̃bʀ(ə)] *nm* (*ANAT*) limb; (*personne, pays, élément*) member ♦ *a* member; **être** ~ **de** to be a member of; ~ (**viril**) (male) organ.

mémé [meme] *nf* (*fam*) granny; (*: vieille femme*) old dear.

même [mɛm] *a* same ♦ *pronom*: **le (la)** ~ the same (one) ♦ *ad* even; **en** ~ **temps** at the same time; **ils ont les** ~ **goûts** they have the same tastes; **ce sont ses paroles/celles-là** ~**s** they are his very words/the very ones; **il est la loyauté** ~ he is loyalty itself, he is loyalty personified; **il n'a** ~ **pas pleuré** he didn't even cry; **ici** ~ at this very place; ~ **lui a ...** even he has ...; **à** ~ **la bouteille** straight from the bottle; **à** ~ **la peau** next to the skin; **être à** ~ **de faire** to be in a position *ou* be able to do; **mettre qn à** ~ **de faire** to enable sb to do; **faire de** ~ to do likewise; **lui de** ~ so does (*ou* did *ou* is) he; **de lui-**~ on his own initiative, off his own bat; **de** ~ **que** just as; **il en va/est allé de** ~ **pour** the same goes/happened for; ~ **si** even if.

mémento [memɛ̃to] *nm* (*agenda*) appointments diary; (*ouvrage*) summary.

mémoire [memwaʀ] *nf* memory ♦ *nm* (*ADMIN, JUR*) memorandum (*pl* -a); (*SCOL*) dissertation, paper; **avoir la** ~ **des visages/chiffres** to have a (good) memory for faces/figures; **n'avoir aucune** ~ to have a terrible memory; **avoir de la** ~ to have a good memory; **à la** ~ **de** to the *ou* in memory of; **pour** ~ *ad* for the record; **de** ~ *ad* from memory; **de** ~ **d'homme** in living memory; **mettre en** ~ (*INFORM*) to store; ~ **morte** ROM; ~ **rémanente** *ou* **non volatile** non-volatile memory; ~ **vive** RAM.

mémoires [memwaʀ] *nmpl* memoirs.

mémorable [memɔʀabl(ə)] *a* memorable.

mémorandum [memɔʀɑ̃dɔm] *nm* memorandum (*pl* -a); (*carnet*) notebook.

mémorial, aux [memɔʀjal, -o] *nm* memorial.

mémoriser [memɔʀize] *vt* to memorize;

(INFORM) to store.

menaçant, e [mənasɑ̃, -ɑ̃t] *a* threatening, menacing.

menace [mənas] *nf* threat; ~ **en l'air** empty threat.

menacer [mənase] *vt* to threaten; ~ **qn de qch/de faire qch** to threaten sb with sth/to do sth.

ménage [menaʒ] *nm (travail)* housekeeping, housework; *(couple)* (married) couple; *(famille, ADMIN)* household; **faire le** ~ to do the housework; **faire des** ~**s** to work as a cleaner *(in people's homes)*; **monter son** ~ to set up house; **se mettre en** ~ **(avec)** to set up house (with); **heureux en** ~ happily married; **faire bon** ~ **avec** to get on well with; ~ **de poupée** doll's kitchen set; ~ **à trois** love triangle.

ménagement [menaʒmɑ̃] *nm* care and attention; ~**s** *nmpl (égards)* consideration *sg*, attention *sg*.

ménager [menaʒe] *vt (traiter avec mesure)* to handle with tact; *(traiter considerately; (utiliser)* to use with care; *(: avec économie)* to use sparingly; *(prendre soin de)* to take (great) care of, look after; *(organiser)* to arrange; *(installer)* to put in; to make; **se** ~ to look after o.s.; ~ **qch à qn** *(réserver)* to have sth in store for sb.

ménager, ère [menaʒe, -ɛʀ] *a* household *cpd*, domestic ♦ *nf (femme)* housewife *(pl -*wives*)*; *(couverts)* canteen (of cutlery).

ménagerie [menaʒʀi] *nf* menagerie.

mendiant, e [mɑ̃djɑ̃, -ɑ̃t] *nm/f* beggar.

mendicité [mɑ̃disite] *nf* begging.

mendier [mɑ̃dje] *vi* to beg ♦ *vt* to beg (for); *(fig: éloges, compliments)* to fish for.

menées [məne] *nfpl* intrigues, manœuvres *(Brit)*, maneuvers *(US)*; *(COMM)* activities.

mener [məne] *vt* to lead; *(enquête)* to conduct; *(affaires)* to manage, conduct, run ♦ *vi*: ~ **(à la marque)** to lead, be in the lead; ~ **à/dans** *(emmener)* to take to/into; ~ **qch à bonne fin** *ou* **à terme** *ou* **à bien** to see sth through (to a successful conclusion), complete sth successfully.

meneur, euse [mənœʀ, -øz] *nm/f* leader; *(péj: agitateur)* ringleader; ~ **d'hommes** born leader; ~ **de jeu** host, quizmaster *(Brit)*.

menhir [meniʀ] *nm* standing stone.

méningite [menɛ̃ʒit] *nf* meningitis *q*.

ménopause [menopoz] *nf* menopause.

menotte [mənɔt] *nf (langage enfantin)* handie; ~**s** *nfpl* handcuffs; **passer les** ~**s à** to handcuff.

mens [mɑ̃] *vb voir* **mentir**.

mensonge [mɑ̃sɔ̃ʒ] *nm*: **le** ~ lying *q*; **un** ~ a lie.

mensonger, ère [mɑ̃sɔ̃ʒe, -ɛʀ] *a* false.

menstruation [mɑ̃stʀyasjɔ̃] *nf* menstruation.

menstruel, le [mɑ̃stʀyɛl] *a* menstrual.

mensualiser [mɑ̃syalize] *vt* to pay monthly.

mensualité [mɑ̃syalite] *nf (somme payée)* monthly payment; *(somme perçue)* monthly salary.

mensuel, le [mɑ̃syɛl] *a* monthly ♦ *nm/f (employé)* employee paid monthly ♦ *nm (PRESSE)* monthly.

mensuellement [mɑ̃syɛlmɑ̃] *ad* monthly.

mensurations [mɑ̃syʀasjɔ̃] *nfpl* measurements.

mentais [mɑ̃tɛ] *etc vb voir* **mentir**.

mental, e, aux [mɑ̃tal, -o] *a* mental.

mentalement [mɑ̃talmɑ̃] *ad* in one's head, mentally.

mentalité [mɑ̃talite] *nf* mentality.

menteur, euse [mɑ̃tœʀ, -øz] *nm/f* liar.

menthe [mɑ̃t] *nf* mint; ~ **(à l'eau)** peppermint cordial.

mentholé, e [mɑ̃tɔle] *a* menthol *cpd*, mentholated.

mention [mɑ̃sjɔ̃] *nf (note)* note, comment; *(SCOL)*: ~ **(très) bien/passable** *(very) good/satisfactory passmark*; **faire** ~ **de** to mention; **"rayer la** ~ **inutile"** "delete as appropriate".

mentionner [mɑ̃sjɔne] *vt* to mention.

mentir [mɑ̃tiʀ] *vi* to lie.

menton [mɑ̃tɔ̃] *nm* chin.

mentonnière [mɑ̃tɔnjɛʀ] *nf* chin strap.

menu, e [məny] *a (mince)* thin; *(petit)* tiny; *(frais, difficulté)* minor ♦ *ad (couper, hacher)* very fine ♦ *nm* menu; **par le** ~ *(raconter)* in minute detail; ~ **touristique** popular *ou* tourist menu; ~**e monnaie** small change.

menuet [mənyɛ] *nm* minuet.

menuiserie [mənyizʀi] *nf (travail)* joinery, carpentry; *(d'amateur)* woodwork; *(local)* joiner's workshop; *(ouvrages)* woodwork *q*.

menuisier [mənyizje] *nm* joiner, carpenter.

méprendre [mepʀɑ̃dʀ(ə)]: **se** ~ *vi*: **se** ~ **sur** to be mistaken about.

mépris, e [mepʀi, -iz] *pp de* **méprendre** ♦ *nm (dédain)* contempt, scorn; *(indifférence)*: **le** ~ **de** contempt *ou* disregard for; **au** ~ **de** regardless of, in defiance of.

méprisable [mepʀizabl(ə)] *a* contemptible, despicable.

méprisant, e [mepʀizɑ̃, -ɑ̃t] *a* contemptuous, scornful.

méprise [mepʀiz] *nf* mistake, error; *(malentendu)* misunderstanding.

mépriser [mepʀize] *vt* to scorn, despise; *(gloire, danger)* to scorn, spurn.

mer [mɛʀ] *nf* sea; *(marée)* tide; ~ **fermée** inland sea; **en** ~ at sea; **prendre la** ~ to put out to sea; **en haute** *ou* **pleine** ~ off shore, on the open sea; **la** ~ **du Nord/Rouge** the North/Red Sea.

mer [mɛʀ] *nf* sea; *(marée)* tide; ~ **fermée** inland sea; **en** ~ at sea; **prendre la** ~ to put out to sea; **en haute** *ou* **pleine** ~ off shore, on the open sea; **la** ~ **Adriatique** the Adriatic (Sea); **la** ~ **des Antilles** *ou* **des Caraïbes** the Caribbean (Sea); **la** ~ **Baltique** the Baltic (Sea); **la** ~ **Caspienne** the Caspian Sea; **la** ~ **de Corail** the Coral Sea; **la** ~ **Égée** the Aegean (Sea); **la** ~ **Ionienne** the Ionian Sea; **la** ~ **Morte** the Dead Sea; **la** ~ **Noire** the Black Sea; **la** ~ **du Nord** the North Sea; **la** ~ **Rouge** the Red Sea; **la** ~ **des Sargasses** the Sargasso Sea, the Sargasso Sea; **les** ~**s du Sud** the South Seas; **la** ~ **Tyrrhénienne** the Tyrrhenian Sea.

mercantile [mɛʀkɑ̃til] *a (péj)* mercenary.

mercenaire [mɛʀsənɛʀ] *nm* mercenary.

mercerie [mɛʀsəʀi] *nf (COUTURE)*

haberdashery (*Brit*), notions *pl* (*US*); (*boutique*) haberdasher's shop (*Brit*), notions store (*US*).

merci [mɛʀsi] *excl* thank you ♦ *nf*: **à la ~ de qn/qch** at sb's mercy/the mercy of sth; **~ beaucoup** thank you very much; **~ de** *ou* **pour** thank you for; **sans ~** *a* merciless ♦ *ad* mercilessly.

mercier, ière [mɛʀsje, -jɛʀ] *nm/f* haberdasher.

mercredi [mɛʀkʀədi] *nm* Wednesday; **~ des Cendres** Ash Wednesday; *voir aussi* **lundi**.

mercure [mɛʀkyʀ] *nm* mercury.

merde [mɛʀd(ə)] (*fam!*) *nf* shit (*!*) ♦ *excl* (bloody) hell (*!*).

merdeux, euse [mɛʀdø, -øz] *nm/f* (*fam!*) little bugger (*Brit!*), little devil.

mère [mɛʀ] *nf* mother ♦ *a inv* mother *cpd*; **~ célibataire** single parent, unmarried mother.

merguez [mɛʀgɛz] *nf* spicy North African sausage.

méridien [meʀidjɛ̃] *nm* meridian.

méridional, e, aux [meʀidjɔnal, -o] *a* southern; (*du midi de la France*) Southern (French) ♦ *nm/f* Southerner.

meringue [məʀɛ̃g] *nf* meringue.

mérinos [meʀinos] *nm* merino.

merisier [məʀizje] *nm* wild cherry (tree).

méritant, e [meʀitɑ̃, -ɑ̃t] *a* deserving.

mérite [meʀit] *nm* merit; **le ~ (de ceci) lui revient** the credit (for this) is his.

mériter [meʀite] *vt* to deserve; **~ de réussir** to deserve to succeed; **il mérite qu'on fasse ...** he deserves to do ....

méritocratie [meʀitɔkʀasi] *nf* meritocracy.

méritoire [meʀitwaʀ] *a* praiseworthy, commendable.

merlan [mɛʀlɑ̃] *nm* whiting.

merle [mɛʀl(ə)] *nm* blackbird.

mérou [meʀu] *nm* grouper (*fish*).

merveille [mɛʀvɛj] *nf* marvel, wonder; **faire ~** *ou* **des ~s** to work wonders; **à ~** perfectly, wonderfully.

merveilleux, euse [mɛʀvɛjø, -øz] *a* marvellous, wonderful.

mes [me] *dét voir* **mon**.

mésalliance [mezaljɑ̃s] *nf* misalliance, mismatch.

mésallier [mezalje]: **se ~** *vi* to marry beneath (*ou* above) o.s.

mésange [mezɑ̃ʒ] *nf* tit(mouse) (*pl* -mice); **~ bleue** bluetit.

mésaventure [mezavɑ̃tyʀ] *nf* misadventure, misfortune.

Mesdames [medam] *nfpl voir* **Madame**.

Mesdemoiselles [medmwazɛl] *nfpl voir* **Mademoiselle**.

mésentente [mezɑ̃tɑ̃t] *nf* dissension, disagreement.

mésestimer [mezɛstime] *vt* to underestimate, underrate.

Mésopotamie [mezɔpɔtami] *nf*: **la ~** Mesopotamia.

mésopotamien, ne [mezɔpɔtamjɛ̃, -ɛn] *a* Mesopotamian.

mesquin, e [mɛskɛ̃, -in] *a* a mean, petty.

mesquinerie [mɛskinʀi] *nf* meanness *q*, pettiness *q*.

mess [mɛs] *nm* mess.

message [mesaʒ] *nm* message; **~ d'erreur**

(*INFORM*) error message; **~ (de guidage)** (*INFORM*) prompt; **~ publicitaire** ad, advertisement; **~ téléphoné** telegram dictated by telephone.

messager, ère [mesaʒe, -ɛʀ] *nm/f* messenger.

messagerie [mesaʒʀi] *nf*: **~ (électronique)** (electronic) bulletin board; **~ rose** *lonely hearts and contact service on videotext*; **~s aériennes/ maritimes** air freight/shipping service *sg*; **~s de presse** press distribution service.

messe [mɛs] *nf* mass; **aller à la ~** to go to mass; **~ de minuit** midnight mass; **faire des ~s basses** (*fig, péj*) to mutter.

messie [mesi] *nm*: **le M~** the Messiah.

Messieurs [mesjø] *nmpl voir* **Monsieur**.

mesure [məzyʀ] *nf* (*évaluation, dimension*) measurement; (*étalon, récipient, contenu*) measure; (*MUS*: *cadence*) time, tempo; (*: division*) bar; (*retenue*) moderation; (*disposition*) measure, step; **unité/système de** ~ unit/system of measurement; **sur ~** (*costume*) made-to-measure; (*fig*) personally adapted; **à la ~ de** (*fig: personne*) worthy of; (*chambre etc*) on the same scale as; **dans la ~ où** insofar as, inasmuch as; **dans une certaine ~** to some *ou* a certain extent; **à ~ que** as; **en ~** (*MUS*) in time *ou* tempo; **être en ~ de** to be in a position to; **dépasser la ~** (*fig*) to overstep the mark.

mesuré, e [məzyʀe] *a* (*ton, effort*) measured; (*personne*) restrained.

mesurer [məzyʀe] *vt* to measure; (*juger*) to weigh up, assess; (*limiter*) to limit, ration; (*modérer*) to moderate; (*proportionner*): **~ qch à** to match sth to, gear sth to; **se ~ avec** to have a confrontation with; to tackle; **il mesure 1 m 80** he's 1 m 80 tall.

met [me] *vb voir* **mettre**.

métabolisme [metabɔlism(ə)] *nm* metabolism.

métairie [meteʀi] *nf* smallholding.

métal, aux [metal, -o] *nm* metal.

métalangage [metalɑ̃gaʒ] *nm* metalanguage.

métallique [metalik] *a* metallic.

métallisé, e [metalize] *a* metallic.

métallurgie [metalyʀʒi] *nf* metallurgy.

métallurgiste [metalyʀʒist(ə)] *nm/f* (*ouvrier*) steel *ou* metal worker; (*industriel*) metallurgist.

métamorphose [metamɔʀfoz] *nf* metamorphosis (*pl* -oses).

métaphore [metafɔʀ] *nf* metaphor.

métaphorique [metafɔʀik] *a* metaphorical, figurative.

métaphysique [metafizik] *nf* metaphysics *sg* ♦ *a* metaphysical.

métapsychique [metapsiʃik] *a* psychic, parapsychological.

métayer, ère [meteje, metɛjɛʀ] *nm/f* (*tenant*) farmer.

météo [meteo] *nf* (*bulletin*) (weather) forecast; (*service*) ≈ Met Office (*Brit*), ≈ National Weather Service (*US*).

météore [meteɔʀ] *nm* meteor.

météorite [meteɔʀit] *nf* meteorite.

météorologie [meteɔʀɔlɔʒi] *nf* (*étude*) meteorology; (*service*) ≈ Meteorological Office (*Brit*), ≈ National Weather Service (*US*).

météorologique [meteɔʀɔlɔʒik] *a* meteorological, weather *cpd*.

météorologue [meteɔʀɔlɔg] *nm/f*, **météorologiste** [meteɔʀɔlɔʒist(ə)] *nm/f* meteorologist, weather forecaster.

métèque [metɛk] *nm (péj)* wop.

méthane [metan] *nm* methane.

méthanier [metanje] *nm (bateau)* (liquefied) gas carrier *ou* tanker.

méthode [metɔd] *nf* method; *(livre, ouvrage)* manual, tutor.

méthodique [metɔdik] *a* methodical.

méthodiste [metɔdist(ə)] *a, nm/f (REL)* Methodist.

méthylène [metilɛn] *nm*: **bleu de ~** *nm* methylene blue.

méticuleux, euse [metikylø, -øz] *a* meticulous.

métier [metje] *nm (profession: gén)* job; *(: manuel)* trade; *(: artisanal)* craft; *(technique, expérience)* (acquired) skill *ou* technique; *(aussi: ~ à tisser)* (weaving) loom; **être du ~** to be in the trade *ou* profession.

métis, se [metis] *a, nm/f* half-caste, half-breed.

métisser [metise] *vt* to cross (breed).

métrage [metʀaʒ] *nm (de tissu)* length; *(CINÉMA)* footage, length; **long/moyen/court ~** feature *ou* full-length/medium-length/short film.

mètre [mɛtʀ(ə)] *nm* metre *(Brit)*, meter *(US)*; *(règle)* (metre *ou* meter) rule; *(ruban)* tape measure; **~ carré/cube** square/cubic metre *ou* meter.

métrer [metʀe] *vt (TECH)* to measure (in metres *ou* meters); *(CONSTR)* to survey.

métreur, euse [metʀœʀ, -øz] *nm/f*: **~ (vérificateur), métreuse (vérificatrice)** (quantity) surveyor.

métrique [metʀik] *a* metric ♦ *nf* metrics *sg*.

métro [metʀo] *nm* underground *(Brit)*, subway *(US)*.

métronome [metʀɔnɔm] *nm* metronome.

métropole [metʀɔpɔl] *nf (capitale)* metropolis; *(pays)* home country.

métropolitain, e [metʀɔpɔlitɛ̃, -ɛn] *a* metropolitan.

mets [mɛ] *nm* dish ♦ *vb voir* **mettre**.

mettable [metabl(ə)] *a* fit to be worn, decent.

metteur [metœʀ] *nm*: **~ en scène** *(THÉÂTRE)* producer; *(CINÉMA)* director; **~ en ondes** *(RADIO)* producer.

mettre [mɛtʀ(ə)] *vt (placer)* to put; *(vêtement: revêtir)* to put on; *(: porter)* to wear; *(installer: gaz, électricité)* to put in; *(faire fonctionner: chauffage, électricité)* to put on; *(: réveil)* to set; *(noter, écrire)* to say, put down; *(dépenser)* to lay out, give; *(supposer)*: **mettons que** let's suppose *ou* say that; **~ en bouteille/en sac** to bottle/put in bags *ou* sacks; **~ qn/qch en terre** to bury sb/plant sth; **~ à la poste** to post *(Brit)*, mail; **~ une note gaie/amusante** to inject a cheerful/an amusing note; **y ~ du sien** to pull one's weight; **~ du temps/2 heures à faire** to take time/2 hours to do; **~ qn debout** to stand sb up; **se ~: n'avoir rien à se ~** to have nothing to wear; **se ~ de l'encre sur les doigts** to get ink on one's fingers; **se ~ au lit** to get into bed; **se ~ au piano** *(s'asseoir)* to sit down at the piano; *(apprendre)* to start learning the piano; **se ~ à l'eau** to get into the water; **se ~ bien/mal avec qn** to get on sb's good/bad side; **se ~ qn à dos** to alienate sb, turn sb against one; **se ~ avec qn** *(prendre parti)* to side with *ou* go along with sb; *(en ménage)* to move in with sb; **se ~ à faire** to begin *ou* start doing *ou* to do; **se ~ au travail/à l'étude** to get down to work/one's studies.

meublant, e [mœblɑ̃, -ɑ̃t] *a (tissus etc)* effective (in the room).

meuble [mœbl(ə)] *nm (objet)* piece of furniture; *(ameublement)* furniture *q* ♦ *a (terre)* loose, friable; *(JUR)*: **biens ~s** movables.

meublé [mœble] *nm (pièce)* furnished room; *(appartement)* furnished flat *(Brit) ou* apartment *(US)*.

meubler [mœble] *vt* to furnish; *(fig)*: **~ qch (de)** to fill sth (with); **se ~** to furnish one's house.

meugler [møgle] *vi* to low, moo.

meule [møl] *nf (à broyer)* millstone; *(à aiguiser)* grindstone; *(à polir)* buffwheel; *(de foin, blé)* stack; *(de fromage)* round.

meunerie [mønʀi] *nf (industrie)* flour trade; *(métier)* milling.

meunier, ière [mønje, -jɛʀ] *nm* miller ♦ *nf* miller's wife ♦ *af (CULIN)* meunière.

meurs [mœʀ] *etc vb voir* **mourir**.

meurtre [mœʀtʀ(ə)] *nm* murder.

meurtrier, ière [mœʀtʀije, -jɛʀ] *a (arme, épidémie, combat)* deadly; *(accident)* fatal; *(carrefour, route)* lethal; *(fureur, instincts)* murderous ♦ *nm/f* murderer/murderess ♦ *nf (ouverture)* loophole.

meurtrir [mœʀtʀiʀ] *vt* to bruise; *(fig)* to wound.

meurtrissure [mœʀtʀisyʀ] *nf* bruise; *(fig)* scar.

meus [mœ] *etc vb voir* **mouvoir**.

Meuse [mœz] *nf*: **la ~** the Meuse.

meute [møt] *nf* pack.

meuve [mœv] *etc vb voir* **mouvoir**.

mévente [mevɑ̃t] *nf* slump (in sales).

mexicain, e [mɛksikɛ̃, -ɛn] *a* Mexican ♦ *nm/f*: **M~, e** Mexican.

Mexico [mɛksiko] *n* Mexico City.

Mexique [mɛksik] *nm*: **le ~** Mexico.

mezzanine [mɛdzanin] *nf* mezzanine (floor).

MF *sigle mpl = millions de francs* ♦ *sigle f (RADIO: = modulation de fréquence)* FM.

Mgr *abr =* **Monseigneur**.

mi [mi] *nm (MUS)* E; *(en chantant la gamme)* mi.

mi... [mi] *préfixe* half(-); mid-; **à la ~-janvier** in mid-January; **~-bureau, ~-chambre** half office, half bedroom; **à ~-jambes/-corps** (up *ou* down) to the knees/waist; **à ~-hauteur/-pente** halfway up (*ou* down)/up (*ou* down) the hill.

miaou [mjau] *nm* miaow.

miauler [mjole] *vi* to mew.

mi-bas [miba] *nm inv* knee-length sock.

mica [mika] *nm* mica.

mi-carême [mikaʀɛm] *nf*: **la ~** the third

Thursday in Lent.

miche [miʃ] *nf* round *ou* cob loaf.

mi-chemin [miʃmɛ̃]: **à ~** *ad* halfway, midway.

mi-clos, e [miklo, -kloz] *a* half-closed.

micmac [mikmak] *nm* (*péj*) carry-on.

mi-côte [mikot]: **à ~** *ad* halfway up (*ou* down) the hill.

mi-course [mikuRs]: **à ~** *ad* halfway through the race.

micro [mikRo] *nm* mike, microphone; (*INFORM*) micro; **~ cravate** lapel mike.

microbe [mikRɔb] *nm* germ, microbe.

microbiologie [mikRɔbjɔlɔʒi] *nf* microbiology.

microchirurgie [mikRɔʃiRyRʒi] *nf* microsurgery.

microcosme [mikRɔkɔsm(ə)] *nm* microcosm.

micro-édition [mikRɔedisjɔ̃] *nf* desk-top publishing.

micro-électronique [mikRɔelɛktRɔnik] *nf* microelectronics *sg*.

microfiche [mikRɔfiʃ] *nf* microfiche.

microfilm [mikRɔfilm] *nm* microfilm.

micro-onde [mikRɔɔ̃d] *nf*: **four à ~s** microwave oven.

micro-ordinateur [mikRɔɔRdinatœR] *nm* microcomputer.

microphone [mikRɔfɔn] *nm* microphone.

microplaquette [mikRɔplakɛt] *nf* microchip.

microprocesseur [mikRɔpRɔsɛsœR] *nm* microprocessor.

microscope [mikRɔskɔp] *nm* microscope; **au ~** under *ou* through the microscope.

microsillon [mikRɔsijɔ̃] *nm* long-playing record.

MIDEM [midɛm] *sigle m* (= *Marché international du disque et de l'édition musicale*) music industry trade fair.

midi [midi] *nm* (*milieu du jour*) midday, noon; (*moment du déjeuner*) lunchtime; (*sud*) south; (*: de la France*): **le M~** the South (of France), the Midi; **à ~** at 12 (o'clock) *ou* midday *ou* noon; **tous les ~s** every lunchtime; **le repas de ~** lunch; **en plein ~** (right) in the middle of the day; (*sud*) facing south.

midinette [midinɛt] *nf* silly young townie.

mie [mi] *nf* inside (of the loaf).

miel [mjɛl] *nm* honey; **être tout ~** (*fig*) to be all sweetness and light.

mielleux, euse [mjɛlø, -øz] *a* (*péj*) sugary, honeyed.

mien, ne [mjɛ̃, mjɛn] *a*, *pronom*: **le (la) ~(ne), les ~s** mine; **les ~s** (*ma famille*) my family.

miette [mjɛt] *nf* (*de pain, gâteau*) crumb; (*fig: de la conversation etc*) scrap; **en ~s** (*fig*) in pieces *ou* bits.

mieux [mjø] *ad* better ♦ *a* better; (*plus joli*) better-looking ♦ *nm* (*progrès*) improvement; **le ~** the best (thing); **le (la) ~, les ~** the best; **le ~ des deux** the better of the two; **les livres les ~ faits** the best made books; **de mon/ton ~** as best I/you can (*ou* could); **faire de son ~** to do one's best; **vous feriez ~ de faire ...** you would be better to do ...; **aimer ~** to prefer; **de ~ en ~** better and better; **pour le ~** for the best; **crier à qui ~ ~** to try to shout each other down *ou* outshout

each other; **du ~ qu'il peut** the best he can; **au ~** at best; **au ~ avec** on the best of terms with; **qui ~ est** even better, better still; **faute de ~** for lack of anything better.

mieux-être [mjøzɛtR(ə)] *nm* greater well-being; (*financier*) improved standard of living.

mièvre [mjɛvR(ə)] *a* sickly sentimental.

mignon, ne [miɲɔ̃, -ɔn] *a* sweet, cute.

migraine [migRɛn] *nf* headache; migraine.

migrant, e [migRɑ̃, -ɑ̃t] *a*, *nm/f* migrant.

migrateur, trice [migRatœR, -tRis] *a* migratory.

migration [migRasjɔ̃] *nf* migration.

mijaurée [miʒɔRe] *nf* pretentious (young) madam.

mijoter [miʒɔte] *vt* to simmer; (*préparer avec soin*) to cook lovingly; (*affaire, projet*) to plot, cook up ♦ *vi* to simmer.

mil [mil] *num* = **mille**.

Milan [milɑ̃] *n* Milan.

milanais, e [milanɛ, -ɛz] *a* Milanese.

mildiou [mildju] *nm* mildew.

milice [milis] *nf* militia.

milicien, ne [milisjɛ̃, -ɛn] *nm/f* militiaman/woman.

milieu, x [miljø] *nm* (*centre*) middle; (*fig*) middle course *ou* way; (*aussi*: **juste ~**) happy medium; (*BIO, GÉO*) environment; (*entourage social*) milieu; (*familial*) background; circle; (*pègre*): **le ~** the underworld; **au ~ de** in the middle of; **au beau ou en plein ~ (de)** right in the middle (of); **~ de terrain** (*FOOTBALL*: *joueur*) midfield player; (*: joueurs*) midfield.

militaire [militɛR] *a* military ♦ *nm* serviceman; **service ~** military service.

militant, e [militɑ̃, -ɑ̃t] *a*, *nm/f* militant.

militantisme [militɑ̃tism(ə)] *nm* militancy.

militariser [militaRize] *vt* to militarize.

militer [milite] *vi* to be a militant; **~ pour/contre** to militate in favour of/against.

mille [mil] *num* a *ou* one thousand ♦ *nm* (*mesure*): **~ (marin)** nautical mile; **mettre dans le ~** to hit the bull's-eye; (*fig*) to be bang on (target).

millefeuille [milfœj] *nm* cream *ou* vanilla slice.

millénaire [milenɛR] *nm* millennium ♦ *a* thousand-year-old; (*fig*) ancient.

mille-pattes [milpat] *nm inv* centipede.

millésime [milezim] *nm* year.

millésimé, e [milezime] *a* vintage *cpd*.

millet [mijɛ] *nm* millet.

milliard [miljaR] *nm* milliard, thousand million (*Brit*), billion (*US*).

milliardaire [miljaRdɛR] *nm/f* multimillionaire (*Brit*), billionaire (*US*).

millième [miljɛm] *num* thousandth.

millier [milje] *nm* thousand; **un ~ (de)** a thousand or so, about a thousand; **par ~s** in (their) thousands, by the thousand.

milligramme [miligRam] *nm* milligramme (*Brit*), milligram (*US*).

millimètre [milimɛtR(ə)] *nm* millimetre (*Brit*), millimeter (*US*).

millimétré, e [milimetRe] *a*: **papier ~** graph paper.

million [miljɔ̃] *nm* million; **deux ~s de** two

million; **riche à ~s** worth millions.
millionième [miljɔnjɛm] *num* millionth.
millionnaire [miljɔnɛʀ] *nm/f* millionaire.
mi-lourd [miluʀ] *am, nm* light heavyweight.
mime [mim] *nm/f* (*acteur*) mime(r); (*imitateur*) mimic ♦ *nm* (*art*) mime, miming.
mimer [mime] *vt* to mime; (*singer*) to mimic, take off.
mimétisme [mimetism(ə)] *nm* (*BIO*) mimicry.
mimique [mimik] *nf* (funny) face; (*signes*) gesticulations *pl*, sign language *q*.
mimosa [mimoza] *nm* mimosa.
mi-moyen [mimwajɛ̃] *am, nm* welterweight.
MIN *sigle m* (= *Marché d'intérêt national*) *wholesale market for fruit, vegetables and agricultural produce.*
min. *abr* (= *minimum*) min.
minable [minabl(ə)] *a* (*personne*) shabby(-looking); (*travail*) pathetic.
minaret [minaʀɛ] *nm* minaret.
minauder [minode] *vi* to mince, simper.
minauderies [minodʀi] *nfpl* simperings.
mince [mɛ̃s] *a* thin; (*personne, taille*) slim, slender; (*fig: profit, connaissances*) slight, small; (*: prétexte*) weak ♦ *excl:* **~ (alors)!** darn it!
minceur [mɛ̃sœʀ] *nf* thinness; slimness, slenderness.
mincir [mɛ̃siʀ] *vi* to get slimmer *ou* thinner.
mine [min] *nf* (*physionomie*) expression, look; (*extérieur*) exterior, appearance; (*de crayon*) lead; (*gisement, exploitation, explosif*) mine; **~s** *nfpl* (*péj*) simpering airs; **les M~s** (*ADMIN*) *the national mining and geological service; the government vehicle testing department;* **avoir bonne ~** (*personne*) to look well; (*ironique*) to look an utter idiot; **avoir mauvaise ~** to look unwell *ou* poorly; **faire ~ de faire** to make a pretence of doing; to make as if to do; **ne pas payer de ~** to be not much to look at; **~ de rien** *ad* with a casual air; although you wouldn't think so; **~ de charbon** coalmine; **~ à ciel ouvert** opencast (*Brit*) *ou* open-air (*US*) mine.
miner [mine] *vt* (*saper*) to undermine, erode; (*MIL*) to mine.
minerai [minʀɛ] *nm* ore.
minéral, e, aux [mineʀal, -o] *a* mineral; (*CHIMIE*) inorganic ♦ *nm* mineral.
minéralier [mineʀalje] *nm* (*bateau*) ore tanker.
minéralisé, e [mineʀalize] *a* mineralized.
minéralogie [mineʀalɔʒi] *nf* mineralogy.
minéralogique [mineʀalɔʒik] *a* mineralogical; **plaque ~** number (*Brit*) *ou* license (*US*) plate; **numéro ~** registration (*Brit*) *ou* license (*US*) number.
minet, te [minɛ, -ɛt] *nm/f* (*chat*) pussy-cat; (*péj*) young trendy.
mineur, e [minœʀ] *a* minor ♦ *nm/f* (*JUR*) minor ♦ *nm* (*travailleur*) miner; (*MIL*) sapper; **~ de fond** face worker.
miniature [minjatyʀ] *a, nf* miniature.
miniaturiser [minjatyʀize] *vt* to miniaturize.
minibus [minibys] *nm* minibus.
mini-cassette [minikasɛt] *nf* cassette (recorder).
minier, ière [minje, -jɛʀ] *a* mining.
mini-jupe [miniʒyp] *nf* mini-skirt.

minimal, e, aux [minimal, -o] *a* minimum.
minime [minim] *a* minor, minimal ♦ *nm/f* (*SPORT*) junior.
minimiser [minimize] *vt* to minimize; (*fig*) to play down.
minimum [minimɔm] *a, nm* minimum; **au ~** at the very least; **~ vital** (*salaire*) living wage; (*niveau de vie*) subsistence level.
mini-ordinateur [miniɔʀdinatœʀ] *nm* minicomputer.
ministère [ministɛʀ] *nm* (*cabinet*) government; (*département*) ministry (*Brit*), department; (*REL*) ministry; **~ public** (*JUR*) Prosecution, State Prosecutor.
ministériel, le [ministeʀjɛl] *a* government *cpd*; ministerial, departmental; (*partisan*) pro-government.
ministre [ministʀ(ə)] *nm* minister (*Brit*), secretary; (*REL*) minister; **~ d'État** senior minister *ou* secretary.
Minitel [minitɛl] *nm* ® *videotext terminal and service.*
minium [minjɔm] *nm* red lead paint.
minois [minwa] *nm* little face.
minorer [minɔʀe] *vt* to cut, reduce.
minoritaire [minɔʀitɛʀ] *a* minority *cpd*.
minorité [minɔʀite] *nf* minority; **être en ~** to be in the *ou* a minority; **mettre en ~** (*POL*) to defeat.
Minorque [minɔʀk] *nf* Minorca.
minorquin, e [minɔʀkɛ̃, -in] *a* Minorcan.
minoterie [minɔtʀi] *nf* flour-mill.
minuit [minɥi] *nm* midnight.
minuscule [minyskyl] *a* minute, tiny ♦ *nf:* **(lettre) ~** small letter.
minutage [minytaʒ] *nm* timing.
minute [minyt] *nf* minute; (*JUR: original*) minute, draft ♦ *excl* just a minute!, hang on!; **à la ~** (*présent*) (just) this instant; (*passé*) there and then; **entrecôte** *ou* **steak ~** minute steak.
minuter [minyte] *vt* to time.
minuterie [minytʀi] *nf* time switch.
minuteur [minytœʀ] *nm* timer.
minutie [minysi] *nf* meticulousness; minute detail; **avec ~** meticulously; in minute detail.
minutieux, euse [minysjø, -øz] *a* (*personne*) meticulous; (*inspection*) minutely detailed; (*travail*) requiring painstaking attention to detail.
mioche [mjɔʃ] *nm* (*fam*) nipper, brat.
mirabelle [miʀabɛl] *nf* (*fruit*) (cherry) plum; (*eau-de-vie*) plum brandy.
miracle [miʀakl(ə)] *nm* miracle.
miraculé, e [miʀakyle] *a* who has been miraculously cured (*ou* rescued).
miraculeux, euse [miʀakylø, -øz] *a* miraculous.
mirador [miʀadɔʀ] *nm* (*MIL*) watchtower.
mirage [miʀaʒ] *nm* mirage.
mire [miʀ] *nf* (*d'un fusil*) sight; (*TV*) test card; **point de ~** target; (*fig*) focal point; **ligne de ~** line of sight.
mirent [miʀ] *vb voir* **mettre**.
mirer [miʀe] *vt* (*œufs*) to candle; **se ~** *vi:* **se ~ dans** (*suj: personne*) to gaze at one's reflection in; (*: chose*) to be mirrored in.
mirifique [miʀifik] *a* wonderful.
mirobolant, e [miʀɔbɔlɑ̃, -ɑ̃t] *a* fantastic.

miroir [miʀwaʀ] *nm* mirror.

miroiter [miʀwate] *vi* to sparkle, shimmer; **faire ~ qch à qn** to paint sth in glowing colours for sb, dangle sth in front of sb's eyes.

miroiterie [miʀwatʀi] *nf* (*usine*) mirror factory; (*magasin*) mirror dealer's (shop).

mis, e [mi, miz] *pp de* **mettre ♦** *a* (*couvert, table*) set, laid; (*personne*): **bien ~** well dressed **♦** *nf* (*argent: au jeu*) stake; (*tenue*) clothing; attire; **être de ~e** to be acceptable *ou* in season; **~e en bouteilles** bottling; **~e à feu** blast-off; **~e de fonds** capital outlay; **~e à jour** updating; **~e à mort** kill; **~e à pied** (*d'un employé*) suspension; lay-off; **~e sur pied** (*d'une affaire, entreprise*) setting up; **~e en plis** set; **~e au point** (*PHOTO*) focusing; (*fig*) clarification; **~e à prix** reserve (*Brit*) *ou* upset price; **~e en scène** production.

misaine [mizɛn] *nf*: **mât de ~** foremast.

misanthrope [mizɑ̃tʀɔp] *nm/f* misanthropist.

Mis(e) *abr* = **marquis(e)**.

mise [miz] *af, nf voir* **mis**.

miser [mize] *vt* (*enjeu*) to stake, bet; **~ sur** *vt* (*cheval, numéro*) to bet on; (*fig*) to bank *ou* count on.

misérable [mizeʀabl(ə)] *a* (*lamentable, malheureux*) pitiful, wretched; (*pauvre*) poverty-stricken; (*insignifiant, mesquin*) miserable **♦** *nm/f* wretch; (*miséreux*) poor wretch.

misère [mizɛʀ] *nf* (*pauvreté*) (extreme) poverty, destitution; **~s** *nfpl* (*malheurs*) woes, miseries; (*ennuis*) little troubles; **être dans la ~** to be destitute *ou* poverty-stricken; **salaire de ~** starvation wage; **faire des ~s à qn** to torment sb; **~ noire** utter destitution, abject poverty.

miséreux, euse [mizeʀø, -øz] *a* poverty-stricken **♦** *nm/f* down-and-out.

miséricorde [mizeʀikɔʀd(ə)] *nf* mercy, forgiveness.

miséricordieux, euse [mizeʀikɔʀdjø, -øz] *a* merciful, forgiving.

misogyne [mizɔʒin] *a* misogynous **♦** *nm/f* misogynist.

missel [misɛl] *nm* missal.

missile [misil] *nm* missile.

mission [misjɔ̃] *nf* mission; **partir en ~** (*ADMIN, POL*) to go on an assignment.

missionnaire [misjɔnɛʀ] *nm/f* missionary.

missive [misiv] *nf* missive.

mistral [mistʀal] *nm* mistral (wind).

mit [mi] *vb voir* **mettre**.

mitaine [mitɛn] *nf* mitt(en).

mite [mit] *nf* clothes moth.

mité, e [mite] *a* moth-eaten.

mi-temps [mitɑ̃] *nf inv* (*SPORT: période*) half (*pl* halves); (*: pause*) half-time; **à ~** *a, ad* part-time.

miteux, euse [mitø, -øz] *a* seedy, shabby.

mitigé, e [mitiʒe] *a* (*conviction, ardeur*) lukewarm; (*sentiments*) mixed.

mitonner [mitɔne] *vt* (*préparer*) to cook with loving care; (*fig*) to cook up quietly.

mitoyen, ne [mitwajɛ̃, -ɛn] *a* common, party *cpd*; **maisons ~nes** semi-detached houses; (*plus de deux*) terraced (*Brit*) *ou* row (*US*) houses.

mitraille [mitʀaj] *nf* (*balles de fonte*) grapeshot; (*décharge d'obus*) shellfire.

mitrailler [mitʀaje] *vt* to machine-gun; (*fig: photographier*) to snap away at; **~ qn de** to pelt *ou* bombard sb with.

mitraillette [mitʀajɛt] *nf* submachine gun.

mitrailleur [mitʀajœʀ] *nm* machine gunner **♦** *am*: **fusil ~** machine gun.

mitrailleuse [mitʀajøz] *nf* machine gun.

mitre [mitʀ(ə)] *nf* mitre.

mitron [mitʀɔ̃] *nm* baker's boy.

mi-voix [mivwa]: **à ~** *ad* in a low *ou* hushed voice.

mixage [miksaʒ] *nm* (*CINÉMA*) (sound) mixing.

mixer, mixeur [miksœʀ] *nm* (*CULIN*) (food) mixer.

mixité [miksite] *nf* (*SCOL*) coeducation.

mixte [mikst(ə)] *a* (*gén*) mixed; (*SCOL*) mixed, coeducational; **à usage ~** dual-purpose; **cuisinière ~** combined gas and electric cooker; **équipe ~** combined team.

mixture [mikstyʀ] *nf* mixture; (*fig*) concoction.

MLF *sigle m* (= *Mouvement de libération de la femme*) Women's Movement.

Mlle, *pl* **Mlles** *abr* = **Mademoiselle**.

MM *abr* = **Messieurs;** *voir* **Monsieur**.

Mme, *pl* **Mmes** *abr* = **Madame**.

mn. *abr* (= *minute*) min.

mnémotechnique [mnemɔtɛknik] *a* mnemonic.

MNS *sigle m* (= *maître nageur sauveteur*) ≈ lifeguard.

MO *sigle f* (= *main-d'œuvre*) labour costs (*on invoices*).

Mo *abr* = **métro, méga-octet**.

mobile [mɔbil] *a* mobile; (*amovible*) loose, removable; (*pièce de machine*) moving; (*élément de meuble etc*) movable **♦** *nm* (*motif*) motive; (*œuvre d'art*) mobile; (*PHYSIQUE*) moving object *ou* body.

mobilier, ière [mɔbilje, -jɛʀ] *a* (*JUR*) personal **♦** *nm* (*meubles*) furniture; **valeurs mobilières** transferable securities; **vente mobilière** sale of personal property *ou* chattels.

mobilisation [mɔbilizasjɔ̃] *nf* mobilization.

mobiliser [mɔbilize] *vt* (*MIL, gén*) to mobilize.

mobilité [mɔbilite] *nf* mobility.

mobylette [mɔbilɛt] *nf* ® moped.

mocassin [mɔkasɛ̃] *nm* moccasin.

moche [mɔʃ] *a* (*fam: laid*) ugly; (*: mauvais, méprisable*) rotten.

modalité [mɔdalite] *nf* form, mode; **~s** *nfpl* (*d'un accord etc*) clauses, terms; **~s de paiement** methods of payment.

mode [mɔd] *nf* fashion; (*commerce*) fashion trade *ou* industry **♦** *nm* (*manière*) form, mode, method; (*LING*) mood; (*INFORM, MUS*) mode; **travailler dans la ~** to be in the fashion business; **à la ~** fashionable, in fashion; **~ dialogué** (*INFORM*) interactive *ou* conversational mode; **~ d'emploi** directions *pl* (for use); **~ de vie** way of life.

modelage [mɔdlaʒ] *nm* modelling.

modelé [mɔdle] *nm* (*GÉO*) relief; (*du corps etc*) contours *pl*.

modèle [mɔdɛl] *a* model **♦** *nm* model; (*qui*

pose: de peintre) sitter; *(type)* type; *(gabarit, patron)* pattern; ~ **courant** *ou* **de série** *(COMM)* production model; ~ **déposé** registered design; ~ **réduit** small-scale model.

modeler [mɔdle] *vt (ART)* to model, mould; *(suj: vêtement, érosion)* to mould, shape; ~ **qch sur/d'après** to model sth on.

modélisation [mɔdelizasjɔ̃] *nf (MATH)* modelling.

modéliste [mɔdelist(ə)] *nm/f (COUTURE)* designer; *(de modèles réduits)* model maker.

modem [mɔdɛm] *nm* modem.

Modène [mɔdɛn] *n* Modena.

modérateur, trice [mɔdeʀatœʀ, -tʀis] *a* moderating ♦ *nm/f* moderator.

modération [mɔdeʀasjɔ̃] *nf* moderation; ~ **de peine** reduction of sentence.

modéré, e [mɔdeʀe] *a, nm/f* moderate.

modérément [mɔdeʀemɑ̃] *ad* moderately, in moderation.

modérer [mɔdeʀe] *vt* to moderate; **se** ~ *vi* to restrain o.s.

moderne [mɔdɛʀn(ə)] *a* modern ♦ *nm (ART)* modern style; *(ameublement)* modern furniture.

moderniser [mɔdɛʀnize] *vt* to modernize.

modeste [mɔdɛst(ə)] *a* modest; *(origine)* humble, lowly.

modestie [mɔdɛsti] *nf* modesty; **fausse** ~ false modesty.

modicité [mɔdisite] *nf:* **la** ~ **des prix** *etc* the low prices *etc*.

modificatif, ive [mɔdifikatif, -iv] *a* modifying.

modification [mɔdifikasjɔ̃] *nf* modification.

modifier [mɔdifje] *vt* to modify, alter; *(LING)* to modify; **se** ~ *vi* to alter.

modique [mɔdik] *a (salaire, somme)* modest.

modiste [mɔdist(ə)] *nf* milliner.

modulaire [mɔdylɛʀ] *a* modular.

modulation [mɔdylasjɔ̃] *nf* modulation; ~ **de fréquence (FM** *ou* **MF)** frequency modulation (FM).

module [mɔdyl] *nm* module.

moduler [mɔdyle] *vt* to modulate; *(air)* to warble.

moelle [mwal] *nf* marrow; *(fig)* pith, core; ~ **épinière** spinal chord.

moelleux, euse [mwalø, -øz] *a* soft; *(au goût, à l'ouïe)* mellow; *(gracieux, souple)* smooth.

moellon [mwalɔ̃] *nm* rubble stone.

mœurs [mœʀ] *nfpl (conduite)* morals; *(manières)* manners; *(pratiques sociales)* habits; *(mode de vie)* life style *sg*; *(d'une espèce animale)* behaviour *sg (Brit)*, behavior *sg (US)*; **femme de mauvaises** ~ loose woman; **passer dans les** ~ to become the custom; **contraire aux bonnes** ~ contrary to proprieties.

mohair [mɔɛʀ] *nm* mohair.

moi [mwa] *pronom* me; *(emphatique)*: ~, **je** ... for my part, I ..., I myself ... ♦ *nm inv (PSYCH)* ego, self; **à** ~**!** *(à l'aide)* help (me)!

moignon [mwaɲɔ̃] *nm* stump.

moi-même [mwamɛm] *pronom* myself; *(emphatique)* I myself.

moindre [mwɛ̃dʀ(ə)] *a* lesser; lower; **le(la)** ~, **les** ~**s** the least; the slightest; **le(la)** ~ **de** the least of; **c'est la** ~ **des choses** it's noth-ing at all.

moindrement [mwɛ̃dʀəmɑ̃] *ad:* **pas le** ~ not in the least.

moine [mwan] *nm* monk, friar.

moineau, x [mwano] *nm* sparrow.

moins [mwɛ̃] *ad* less ♦ *cj:* ~ **2** minus 2 ♦ *prép:* **dix heures** ~ **cinq** five to ten ♦ *nm:* **(le signe)** ~ the minus sign; ~ **je travaille, mieux je me porte** the less I work, the better I feel; ~ **grand que** not as tall as, less tall than; **le (la)** ~ **doué(e)** the least gifted; **le** ~ the least; ~ **de** *(sable, eau)* less; *(livres, gens)* fewer; ~ **de 2 ans/100 F** less than 2 years/100 F; ~ **de midi** not yet midday; **100 F/3 jours de** ~ 100 F/3 days less; **3 livres en** ~ 3 books fewer; 3 books too few; **de l'argent en** ~ less money; **le soleil en** ~ but for the sun, minus the sun; **à** ~ **que** *cj* unless; **à** ~ **de faire** unless we do *(ou* he does*)*; **à** ~ **de** *(imprévu, accident)* barring any; **au** ~ at least; **il a 3 ans de** ~ **que moi** he is 3 years younger than me; **de** ~ **en** ~ less and less; **pour le** ~ at the very least; **du** ~ at least; **il fait** ~ **cinq** it's five below (freezing), it's minus five.

moins-value [mwɛ̃valy] *nf (ÉCON, COMM)* depreciation.

moire [mwaʀ] *nf* moiré.

moiré, e [mwaʀe] *a (tissu, papier)* moiré, watered; *(reflets)* shimmering.

mois [mwa] *nm* month; *(salaire, somme dû)* (monthly) pay *ou* salary; **treizième** ~, **double** ~ extra month's salary.

moïse [mɔiz] *nm* Moses basket.

moisi, e [mwazi] *a* mouldy *(Brit)*, moldy *(US)*, mildewed ♦ *nm* mould, mold, mildew; **odeur de** ~ musty smell.

moisir [mwaziʀ] *vi* to go mouldy *(Brit)* ou moldy *(US)*; *(fig)* to rot; *(personne)* to hang about ♦ *vt* to make mouldy *ou* moldy.

moisissure [mwazisyʀ] *nf* mould *q (Brit)*, mold *q (US)*.

moisson [mwasɔ̃] *nf* harvest; *(époque)* harvest (time); *(fig)*: **faire une** ~ **de** to gather a wealth of.

moissonner [mwasɔne] *vt* to harvest, reap; *(fig)* to collect.

moissonneur, euse [mwasɔnœʀ, -øz] *nm/f* harvester, reaper ♦ *nf (machine)* harvester.

moissonneuse-batteuse, *pl* **moissonneuses-batteuses** [mwasɔnɔzbatøz] *nf* combine harvester.

moite [mwat] *a (peau, mains)* sweaty, sticky; *(atmosphère)* muggy.

moitié [mwatje] *nf* half *(pl* halves*)*; *(épouse)*: **sa** ~ his better half; **la** ~ half; **la** ~ **de** half (of), half the amount *(ou* number*)* of; **la** ~ **du temps/des gens** half the time/the people; **à la** ~ **de** halfway through; ~ **moins grand** half as tall; ~ **plus long** half as long again, longer by half; **à** ~ half *(avant le verbe)*, half- *(avant l'adjectif)*; **à** ~ **prix** (at) half price, half-price; **de** ~ by half; ~ ~ half-and-half.

moka [mɔka] *nm (café)* mocha coffee; *(gâteau)* mocha cake.

mol [mɔl] *am voir* **mou**.

molaire [mɔlɛʀ] *nf* molar.

moldave [mɔldav] *a* Moldavian.

Moldavie [mɔldavi] *nf*: **la** ~ Moldavia.
môle [mol] *nm* jetty.
moléculaire [mɔlekylɛʀ] *a* molecular.
molécule [mɔlekyl] *nf* molecule.
moleskine [mɔleskin] *nf* imitation leather.
molester [mɔlɛste] *vt* to manhandle, maul (about).
molette [mɔlɛt] *nf* toothed *ou* cutting wheel.
mollasse [mɔlas] *a* (*péj*: *sans énergie*) sluggish; (: *flasque*) flabby.
molle [mɔl] *af voir* **mou**.
mollement [mɔlmɑ̃] *ad* softly; (*péj*) sluggishly; (*protester*) feebly.
mollesse [mɔlɛs] *nf* (*voir mou*) softness; flabbiness; limpness; sluggishness; feebleness.
mollet [mɔlɛ] *nm* calf (*pl* calves) ♦ *am*: **œuf** ~ soft-boiled egg.
molletière [mɔltjɛʀ] *af*: **bande** ~ puttee.
molleton [mɔltɔ̃] *nm* (*TEXTILES*) felt.
molletonné, e [mɔltɔne] *a* (*gants etc*) fleecelined.
mollir [mɔliʀ] *vi* (*jambes*) to give way; (*NAVIG*: *vent*) to drop, die down; (*fig*: *personne*) to relent; (: *courage*) to fail, flag.
mollusque [mɔlysk(ə)] *nm* (*ZOOL*) mollusc; (*fig*: *personne*) lazy lump.
molosse [mɔlɔs] *nm* big ferocious dog.
môme [mom] *nm/f* (*fam*: *enfant*) brat; (: *fille*) bird (*Brit*), chick.
moment [mɔmɑ̃] *nm* moment; (*occasion*): **profiter du** ~ to take (advantage of) the opportunity; **ce n'est pas le** ~ this is not the right time; **à un certain** ~ at some point; **à un** ~ **donné** at a certain point; **à quel** ~? when exactly?; **au même** ~ at the same time; (*instant*) at the same moment; **pour un bon** ~ for a good while; **pour le** ~ for the moment, for the time being; **au** ~ **de** at the time of; **au** ~ **où** as; at a time when; **à tout** ~ at any time *ou* moment; (*continuellement*) constantly, continually; **en ce** ~ at the moment; (*aujourd'hui*) at present; **sur le** ~ at the time; **par** ~**s** now and then, at times; **d'un** ~ **à l'autre** any time (now); **du** ~ **où** *ou* **que** seeing that, since; **n'avoir pas un** ~ **à soi** not to have a minute to oneself.
momentané, e [mɔmɑ̃tane] *a* temporary, momentary.
momie [mɔmi] *nf* mummy.
mon [mɔ̃], **ma** [ma], *pl* **mes** [me] *dét* my.
monacal, e, aux [mɔnakal, -o] *a* monastic.
Monaco [mɔnako] *nm*: **le** ~ Monaco.
monarchie [mɔnaʀʃi] *nf* monarchy.
monarchiste [mɔnaʀʃist(ə)] *a*, *nm/f* monarchist.
monarque [mɔnaʀk(ə)] *nm* monarch.
monastère [mɔnastɛʀ] *nm* monastery.
monastique [mɔnastik] *a* monastic.
monceau, x [mɔ̃so] *nm* heap.
mondain, e [mɔ̃dɛ̃, -ɛn] *a* (*soirée, vie*) society *cpd*; (*obligations*) social; (*peintre, écrivain*) fashionable; (*personne*) society *cpd* ♦ *nm/f* society man/woman, socialite ♦ *nf*: **la M**~**e**, **la police** ~**e** ≈ the vice squad.
mondanités [mɔ̃danite] *nfpl* (*vie mondaine*) society life *sg*; (*paroles*) (society) small talk *sg*; (*PRESSE*) (society) gossip column *sg*.
monde [mɔ̃d] *nm* world; (*personnes mon-*

daines): **le** ~ (high) society; (*milieu*): **être du même** ~ to move in the same circles; (*gens*): **il y a du** ~ (*beaucoup de gens*) there are a lot of people; (*quelques personnes*) there are some people; **y a-t-il du** ~ **dans le salon?** is there anybody in the lounge?; **beaucoup/peu de** ~ many/few people; **le meilleur** *etc* **du** ~ the best *etc* in the world *ou* on earth; **mettre au** ~ to bring into the world; **pas le moins du** ~ not in the least; **se faire un** ~ **de qch** to make a great deal of fuss about sth; **tour du** ~ round-the-world trip; **homme/femme du** ~ society man/woman.
mondial, e, aux [mɔ̃djal, -o] *a* (*population*) world *cpd*; (*influence*) world-wide.
mondialement [mɔ̃djalmɑ̃] *ad* throughout the world.
mondialisation [mɔ̃djalizɑsjɔ̃] *nf* (*d'une technique*) global application; (*d'un conflit*) global spread.
mondovision [mɔ̃dɔvizjɔ̃] *nf* (world coverage by) satellite television.
monégasque [mɔnegask(ə)] *a* Monegasque, of *ou* from Monaco ♦ *nm/f*: **M**~ Monegasque.
monétaire [mɔnetɛʀ] *a* monetary.
monétarisme [mɔnetaʀism(ə)] *nm* monetarism.
monétique [mɔnetik] *nf* electronic money.
mongol, e [mɔ̃gɔl] *a* Mongol, Mongolian ♦ *nm* (*LING*) Mongolian ♦ *nm/f*: **M**~, **e** (*MÉD*) Mongol, Mongoloid; (*de la Mongolie*) Mongolian.
Mongolie [mɔ̃gɔli] *nf*: **la** ~ Mongolia.
mongolien, ne [mɔ̃gɔljɛ̃, -ɛn] *a*, *nm/f* mongol.
mongolisme [mɔ̃gɔlism(ə)] *nm* mongolism, Down's syndrome.
moniteur, trice [mɔnitœʀ, -tʀis] *nm/f* (*SPORT*) instructor/instructress; (*de colonie de vacances*) supervisor ♦ *nm* (*écran*) monitor; ~ **cardiaque** cardiac monitor; ~ **d'auto-école** driving instructor.
monitorat [mɔnitɔʀa] *nm* (*formation*) instructor's training (course); (*fonction*) instructorship.
monnaie [mɔnɛ] *nf* (*pièce*) coin; (*ÉCON, gén*: *moyen d'échange*) currency; (*petites pièces*): **avoir de la** ~ to have (some) change; **faire de la** ~ to get (some) change; **avoir/faire la** ~ **de 20 F** to have change of/get change for 20 F; **faire** *ou* **donner à qn la** ~ **de 20 F** to give sb change for 20 F, change 20 F for sb; **rendre à qn la** ~ (**sur 20 F**) to give sb the change (from *ou* out of 20 F); **servir de** ~ **d'échange** (*fig*) to be used as a bargaining counter *ou* as bargaining counters; **payer en** ~ **de singe** to fob (sb) off with empty promises; **c'est** ~ **courante** it's a common occurrence; ~ **légale** legal tender.
monnayer [mɔneje] *vt* to convert into cash; (*talent*) to capitalize on.
monnayeur [mɔnejœʀ] *nm voir* **faux**.
mono [mɔno] *nf* (= *monophonie*) mono ♦ *nm* (= *monoski*) monoski.
monochrome [mɔnokʀom] *a* monochrome.
monocle [mɔnokl(ə)] *nm* monocle, eyeglass.
monocoque [mɔnokɔk] *a* (*voiture*) monocoque ♦ *nm* (*voilier*) monohull.
monocorde [mɔnokɔʀd(ə)] *a* monotonous.
monoculture [mɔnokyltyʀ] *nf* single-crop

farming, monoculture.

monogramme [mɔnɔgʀam] *nm* monogram.

monokini [mɔnɔkini] *nm* one-piece bikini, bikini pants *pl*.

monolingue [mɔnɔlɛ̃g] *a* monolingual.

monologue [mɔnɔlɔg] *nm* monologue, soliloquy; ~ **intérieur** stream of consciousness.

monologuer [mɔnɔlɔge] *vi* to soliloquize.

monôme [mɔnom] *nm* (*MATH*) monomial; (*d'étudiants*) students' rag procession.

monoparental, e, aux [mɔnɔpaʀɑ̃tal, -o] *a* one-parent *cpd*, single-parent *cpd*.

monophasé, e [mɔnɔfaze] *a* single-phase *cpd*.

monoplace [mɔnɔplas] *a, nm, nf* single-seater, one-seater.

monoplan [mɔnɔplɑ̃] *nm* monoplane.

monopole [mɔnɔpɔl] *nm* monopoly.

monopoliser [mɔnɔpɔlize] *vt* to monopolize.

monorail [mɔnɔʀaj] *nm* monorail; monorail train.

monoski [mɔnɔski] *nm* monoski.

monosyllabe [mɔnɔsilab] *nm* monosyllable, word of one syllable.

monotone [mɔnɔtɔn] *a* monotonous.

monotonie [mɔnɔtɔni] *nf* monotony.

monseigneur [mɔ̃sɛɲœʀ] *nm* (*archevêque, évêque*) Your (*ou* His) Grace; (*cardinal*) Your (*ou* His) Eminence; **Mgr Thomas** Bishop Thomas; Cardinal Thomas.

Monsieur [məsjø], *pl* **Messieurs** [mesjø] *titre* Mr ['mɪstə*] ♦ *nm* (*homme quelconque*): **un/le m~** a/the gentleman; *voir aussi* **Madame**.

monstre [mɔ̃stʀ(ə)] *nm* monster ♦ *a* (*fam: effet, publicité*) massive; **un travail** ~ a fantastic amount of work; an enormous job; ~ **sacré** superstar.

monstrueux, euse [mɔ̃stʀyø, -øz] *a* monstrous.

monstruosité [mɔ̃stʀyozite] *nf* monstrosity.

mont [mɔ̃] *nm*: **par** ~**s et par vaux** up hill and down dale; **le M~ Blanc** Mont Blanc; ~ **de Vénus** mons veneris.

montage [mɔ̃taʒ] *nm* putting up; (*d'un bijou*) mounting, setting; (*d'une machine etc*) assembly; (*PHOTO*) photomontage; (*CINÉMA*) editing; ~ **sonore** sound editing.

montagnard, e [mɔ̃taɲaʀ, -aʀd(ə)] *a* mountain *cpd* ♦ *nm/f* mountain-dweller.

montagne [mɔ̃taɲ] *nf* (*cime*) mountain; (*région*): **la** ~ the mountains *pl*; **la haute** ~ the high mountains; **les** ~**s Rocheuses** the Rocky Mountains, the Rockies; ~**s russes** big dipper *sg*, switchback *sg*.

montagneux, euse [mɔ̃taɲø, -øz] *a* mountainous; hilly.

montant, e [mɔ̃tɑ̃, -ɑ̃t] *a* (*mouvement, marée*) rising; (*chemin*) uphill; (*robe, corsage*) high-necked ♦ *nm* (*somme, total*) (sum) total, (total) amount; (*de fenêtre*) upright; (*de lit*) post.

mont-de-piété [mɔ̃dpjete] *pl* **monts-de-piété** *nm* pawnshop.

monte [mɔ̃t] *nf* (*accouplement*): **la** ~ stud; (*d'un jockey*) seat.

monté, e [mɔ̃te] *a*: **être** ~ **contre qn** to be angry with sb; (*fourni, équipé*): ~ **en** equipped with.

monte-charge [mɔ̃tʃaʀʒ(ə)] *nm inv* goods lift, hoist.

montée [mɔ̃te] *nf* rising, rise; (*escalade*) ascent, climb; (*chemin*) way up; (*côte*) hill; **au milieu de la** ~ halfway up; **le moteur chauffe dans les** ~**s** the engine overheats going uphill.

monte-plats [mɔ̃tpla] *nm inv* service lift.

monter [mɔ̃te] *vt* (*escalier, côte*) to go (*ou* come) up; (*valise, paquet*) to take (*ou* bring) up; (*cheval*) to mount; (*femelle*) to cover, serve; (*tente, échafaudage*) to put up; (*machine*) to assemble; (*bijou*) to mount, set; (*COUTURE*) to sew on; (: *manche*) to set in; (*CINÉMA*) to edit; (*THÉÂTRE*) to put on, stage; (*société, coup etc*) to set up; (*fournir, équiper*) to equip ♦ *vi* to go (*ou* come) up; (*avion, voiture*) to climb, go up; (*chemin, niveau, température, voix, prix*) to go up, rise; (*brouillard, bruit*) to rise, come up; (*passager*) to get on; (*à cheval*): ~ **bien/mal** to ride well/badly; ~ **à cheval/bicyclette** to get on *ou* mount a horse/bicycle; (*faire du cheval etc*) to ride (a horse); to (ride a) bicycle; ~ **à pied/en voiture** to walk/drive up, go up on foot/by car; ~ **dans le train/l'avion** to get into the train/plane, board the train/plane; ~ **sur** to climb up onto; ~ **sur** *ou* **à un arbre/une échelle** to climb (up) a tree/ladder; ~ **à bord** to (get on) board; ~ **à la tête de qn** to go to sb's head; ~ **sur les planches** to go on the stage; ~ **en grade** to be promoted; **se** ~ (*s'équiper*) to equip o.s., get kitted out (*Brit*); **se** ~ **à** (*frais etc*) to add up to, come to; ~ **qn contre qn** to set sb against sb; ~ **la tête à qn** to give sb ideas.

monteur, euse [mɔ̃tœʀ, -øz] *nm/f* (*TECH*) fitter; (*CINÉMA*) (film) editor.

monticule [mɔ̃tikyl] *nm* mound.

montmartrois, e [mɔ̃maʀtʀwa, -waz] *a* of *ou* from Montmartre.

montre [mɔ̃tʀ(ə)] *nf* watch; (*ostentation*): **pour la** ~ for show; ~ **en main** exactly, to the minute; **faire** ~ **de** to show, display; **contre la** ~ (*SPORT*) against the clock; ~ **de plongée** diver's watch.

Montréal [mɔ̃ʀeal] *n* Montreal.

montréalais, e [mɔ̃ʀeale, -ez] *a* of *ou* from Montreal ♦ *nm/f*: **M~, e** Montrealer.

montre-bracelet, *pl* **montres-bracelets** [mɔ̃tʀəbʀaslɛ] *nf* wrist watch.

montrer [mɔ̃tʀe] *vt* to show; **se** ~ to appear; ~ **qch à qn** to show sb sth; ~ **qch du doigt** to point to sth, point one's finger at sth; **se** ~ **intelligent** to prove (to be) intelligent.

montreur, euse [mɔ̃tʀœʀ, -øz] *nm/f*: ~ **de marionnettes** puppeteer.

monture [mɔ̃tyʀ] *nf* (*bête*) mount; (*d'une bague*) setting; (*de lunettes*) frame.

monument [mɔnymɑ̃] *nm* monument; ~ **aux morts** war memorial.

monumental, e, aux [mɔnymɑ̃tal, -o] *a* monumental.

moquer [mɔke]: **se** ~ **de** *vt* to make fun of, laugh at; (*fam: se désintéresser de*) not to care about; (*tromper*): **se** ~ **de qn** to take sb for a ride.

moquerie [mɔkʀi] *nf* mockery *q*.

moquette [mɔkɛt] *nf* fitted carpet, wall-to-wall carpeting *q*.

moquetter [mɔkete] *vt* to carpet.

moqueur, euse [mɔkœʀ, -øz] *a* mocking.

moral, e, aux [mɔʀal, -o] *a* moral ♦ *nm* morale ♦ *nf* (*conduite*) morals *pl*; (*règles*) moral code, ethic; (*valeurs*) moral standards *pl*, morality; (*science*) ethics *sg*, moral philosophy; (*conclusion: d'une fable etc*) moral; **au ~, sur le plan ~** morally; **avoir le ~ à zéro** to be really down; **faire la ~e à** to lecture, preach at.

moralement [mɔʀalmɑ̃] *ad* morally.

moralisateur, trice [mɔʀalizatœʀ, -tʀis] *a* moralizing, sanctimonious ♦ *nm/f* moralizer.

moraliser [mɔʀalize] *vt* (*sermonner*) to lecture, preach at.

moraliste [mɔʀalist(ə)] *nm/f* moralist ♦ *a* moralistic.

moralité [mɔʀalite] *nf* (*d'une action, attitude*) morality; (*conduite*) morals *pl*; (*conclusion, enseignement*) moral.

moratoire [mɔʀatwaʀ] *am:* **intérêts ~s** (*ÉCON*) interest on arrears.

morave [mɔʀav] *a* Moravian.

Moravie [mɔʀavi] *nf:* **la ~** Moravia.

morbide [mɔʀbid] *a* morbid.

morceau, x [mɔʀso] *nm* piece, bit; (*d'une œuvre*) passage, extract; (*MUS*) piece; (*CULIN: de viande*) cut; **mettre en ~x** to pull to pieces *ou* bits.

morceler [mɔʀsəle] *vt* to break up, divide up.

mordant, e [mɔʀdɑ̃, -ɑ̃t] *a* scathing, cutting; (*froid*) biting ♦ *nm* (*dynamisme, énergie*) spirit; (*fougue*) vitality, punch.

mordicus [mɔʀdikys] *ad* (*fam*) obstinately, stubbornly.

mordiller [mɔʀdije] *vt* to nibble at, chew at.

mordoré, e [mɔʀdɔʀe] *a* lustrous bronze.

mordre [mɔʀdʀ(ə)] *vt* to bite; (*suj: lime, vis*) to bite into ♦ *vi* (*poisson*) to bite; **~ dans** to bite into; **~ sur** (*fig*) to go over into, overlap into; **~ à qch** (*comprendre, aimer*) to take to; **~ à l'hameçon** to bite, rise to the bait.

mordu, e [mɔʀdy] *pp de* **mordre** ♦ *a* (*amoureux*) smitten ♦ *nm/f:* **un ~ du jazz/de la voile** a jazz/sailing fanatic *ou* buff.

morfondre [mɔʀfɔ̃dʀ(ə)]: **se ~** *vi* to mope.

morgue [mɔʀg(ə)] *nf* (*arrogance*) haughtiness; (*lieu: de la police*) morgue; (: *à l'hôpital*) mortuary.

moribond, e [mɔʀibɔ̃, -ɔ̃d] *a* dying, moribund.

morille [mɔʀij] *nf* morel (mushroom).

mormon, e [mɔʀmɔ̃, -ɔn] *a, nm/f* Mormon.

morne [mɔʀn(ə)] *a* (*personne, visage*) glum, gloomy; (*temps, vie*) dismal, dreary.

morose [mɔʀoz] *a* sullen, morose; (*marché*) sluggish.

morphine [mɔʀfin] *nf* morphine.

morphinomane [mɔʀfinɔman] *nm/f* morphine addict.

morphologie [mɔʀfɔlɔʒi] *nf* morphology.

mors [mɔʀ] *nm* bit.

morse [mɔʀs(ə)] *nm* (*ZOOL*) walrus; (*TÉL*) Morse (code).

morsure [mɔʀsyʀ] *nf* bite.

mort [mɔʀ] *nf* death; **se donner la ~** to take one's own life; **de ~** (*silence, pâleur*) deathly; **blessé à ~** fatally wounded *ou* injured; **à la vie, à la ~** for better, for worse; **~ clinique** brain death.

mort, e [mɔʀ, mɔʀt(ə)] *pp de* **mourir** ♦ *a* dead ♦ *nm/f* (*défunt*) dead man/woman; (*victime*): **il y a eu plusieurs ~s** several people were killed, there were several killed ♦ *nm* (*CARTES*) dummy; **~ ou vif** dead or alive; **~ de peur/fatigue** frightened to death/dead tired; **~s et blessés** casualties; **faire le ~** to play dead; (*fig*) to lie low.

mortadelle [mɔʀtadɛl] *nf* mortadella (*type of luncheon meat*).

mortalité [mɔʀtalite] *nf* mortality, death rate.

mort-aux-rats [mɔʀtoʀa] *nf inv* rat poison.

mortel, le [mɔʀtɛl] *a* (*poison etc*) deadly, lethal; (*accident, blessure*) fatal; (*REL, danger, frayeur*) mortal; (*fig: froid*) deadly; (: *ennui, soirée*) deadly (boring) ♦ *nm/f* mortal.

mortellement [mɔʀtɛlmɑ̃] *ad* (*blessé etc*) fatally, mortally; (*pâle etc*) deathly; (*fig: ennuyeux etc*) deadly.

morte-saison, *pl* **mortes-saisons** [mɔʀtəsezɔ̃] *nf* slack *ou* off season.

mortier [mɔʀtje] *nm* (*gén*) mortar.

mortifier [mɔʀtifje] *vt* to mortify.

mort-né, e [mɔʀne] *a* (*enfant*) stillborn; (*fig*) abortive.

mortuaire [mɔʀtɥɛʀ] *a* funeral *cpd*; **avis ~s** death announcements, intimations; **chapelle ~** mortuary chapel; **couronne ~** (funeral) wreath; **domicile ~** house of the deceased; **drap ~** pall.

morue [mɔʀy] *nf* (*ZOOL*) cod *inv*; (*CULIN: salée*) salt-cod.

morutier [mɔʀytje] *nm* (*pêcheur*) cod fisherman; (*bateau*) cod fishing boat.

morvandeau, elle, x [mɔʀvɑ̃do, -ɛl] *a* of *ou* from the Morvan region.

morveux, euse [mɔʀvø, -øz] *a* (*fam*) snottynosed.

mosaïque [mɔzaik] *nf* (*ART*) mosaic; (*fig*) patchwork.

Moscou [mɔsku] *n* Moscow.

moscovite [mɔskɔvit] *a* of *ou* from Moscow, Moscow *cpd* ♦ *nm/f:* **M~** Muscovite.

mosquée [mɔske] *nf* mosque.

mot [mo] *nm* word; (*message*) line, note; (*bon mot etc*) saying; **le ~ de la fin** the last word; **~ à ~** *a, ad* word for word; **~ pour ~** word for word, verbatim; **sur** *ou* **à ces ~s** with these words; **en un ~** in a word; **à ~s couverts** in veiled terms; **prendre qn au ~** to take sb at his word; **se donner le ~** to send the word round; **avoir son ~ à dire** to have a say; **~ d'ordre** watchword; **~ de passe** password; **~s croisés** crossword (puzzle) *sg*.

motard [mɔtaʀ] *nm* biker; (*policier*) motorcycle cop.

motel [mɔtɛl] *nm* motel.

moteur, trice [mɔtœʀ, -tʀis] *a* (*ANAT, PHYSIOL*) motor; (*TECH*) driving; (*AUTO*): **à 4 roues motrices** 4-wheel drive ♦ *nm* engine, motor; (*fig*) mover, mainspring; **à ~** power-driven, motor *cpd*; **~ à deux temps** two-stroke engine; **~ à explosion** internal combustion engine; **~ à réaction** jet engine; **~ thermique** heat engine.

motif [mɔtif] *nm* (*cause*) motive; (*décoratif*) design, pattern, motif; (*d'un tableau*) subject, motif; (MUS) figure, motif; ~s nmpl (JUR) grounds pl; sans ~ a groundless.

motion [mosjɔ̃] nf motion; ~ **de censure** motion of censure, vote of no confidence.

motivation [mɔtivasjɔ̃] nf motivation.

motivé, e [mɔtive] a (acte) justified; (personne) motivated.

motiver [mɔtive] vt (justifier) to justify, account for; (ADMIN, JUR, PSYCH) to motivate.

moto [mɔto] nf (motor)bike; ~ **verte** ou **de trial** trail (Brit) ou dirt (US) bike.

moto-cross [mɔtokrɔs] nm motocross.

motoculteur [mɔtokyltœr] nm (motorized) cultivator.

motocyclette [mɔtosiklɛt] nf motorbike, motorcycle.

motocyclisme [mɔtosiklism(ə)] nm motorcycle racing.

motocycliste [mɔtosiklist(ə)] nm/f motorcyclist.

motoneige [mɔtonɛʒ] nf snow bike.

motorisé, e [mɔtorize] a (troupe) motorized; (personne) having one's own transport.

motrice [mɔtris] af voir **moteur**.

motte [mɔt] nf: ~ **de terre** lump of earth, clod (of earth); ~ **de gazon** turf, sod; ~ **de beurre** lump of butter.

motus [mɔtys] excl: ~ **(et bouche cousue)!** mum's the word!

mou (mol), molle [mu, mɔl] a soft; (péj: visage, traits) flabby; (: geste) limp; (: personne) sluggish; (: résistance, protestations) feeble ♦ nm (homme mou) wimp; (abats) lights pl, lungs pl; (de la corde): **avoir du ~** to be slack; **donner du ~** to slacken, loosen; **avoir les jambes molles** to be weak at the knees.

mouchard, e [muʃar, -ard(ə)] nm/f (péj: SCOL) sneak; (: POLICE) stool pigeon, grass (Brit) ♦ nm (appareil) control device; (: de camion) tachograph.

mouche [muʃ] nf fly; (ESCRIME) button; (de taffetas) patch; **prendre la ~** to go into a huff; **faire ~** to score a bull's-eye.

moucher [muʃe] vt (enfant) to blow the nose of; (chandelle) to snuff (out); se ~ to blow one's nose.

moucheron [muʃrɔ̃] nm midge.

moucheté, e [muʃte] a (cheval) dappled; (laine) flecked; (ESCRIME) buttoned.

mouchoir [muʃwar] nm handkerchief, hanky; ~ **en papier** tissue, paper hanky.

moudre [mudr(ə)] vt to grind.

moue [mu] nf pout; **faire la ~** to pout; (fig) to pull a face.

mouette [mwɛt] nf (sea)gull.

mouf(f)ette [mufɛt] nf skunk.

moufle [mufl(ə)] nf (gant) mitt(en); (TECH) pulley block.

mouflon [muflɔ̃] nm mouf(f)lon.

mouillage [mujaʒ] nm (NAVIG: lieu) anchorage, moorings pl.

mouillé, e [muje] a wet.

mouiller [muje] vt (humecter) to wet, moisten; (tremper): ~ **qn/qch** to make sb/ sth wet; (CULIN: ragoût) to add stock ou wine to; (couper, diluer) to water down; (mine etc) to lay ♦ vi (NAVIG) to lie ou be at

anchor; **se** ~ to get wet; (fam) to commit o.s.; to get (o.s.) involved; ~ **l'ancre** to drop ou cast anchor.

mouillette [mujɛt] nf (bread) finger.

mouillure [mujyr] nf wet q; (tache) wet patch.

moulage [mulaʒ] nm moulding (Brit), molding (US); casting; (objet) cast.

moulais [mulɛ] etc vb voir **moudre**.

moulant, e [mulɑ̃, -ɑ̃t] a figure-hugging.

moule [mul] vb voir **moudre** ♦ nf (mollusque) mussel ♦ nm (creux, CULIN) mould (Brit), mold (US); (modèle plein) cast; ~ **à gâteau** nm cake tin (Brit) ou pan (US); ~ **à gaufre** nm waffle iron; ~ **à tarte** nm pie ou flan dish.

moulent [mul] vb voir **moudre, mouler**.

mouler [mule] vt (brique) to mould (Brit), mold (US); (statue) to cast; (visage, bas-relief) to make a cast of; (lettre) to shape with care; (suj: vêtement) to hug, fit closely round; ~ **qch sur** (fig) to model sth on.

moulin [mulɛ̃] nm mill; (fam) engine; ~ **à café** coffee mill; ~ **à eau** watermill; ~ **à légumes** (vegetable) shredder; ~ **à paroles** (fig) chatterbox; ~ **à poivre** pepper mill; ~ **à prières** prayer wheel; ~ **à vent** windmill.

mouliner [muline] vt to shred.

moulinet [mulinɛ] nm (de treuil) winch; (de canne à pêche) reel; (mouvement): **faire des** ~s **avec qch** to whirl sth around.

moulinette [mulinɛt] nf ® (vegetable) shredder.

moulons [mulɔ̃] etc vb voir **moudre**.

moulu, e [muly] pp de **moudre** ♦ a (café) ground.

moulure [mulyr] nf (ornement) moulding (Brit), molding (US).

mourant, e [murɑ̃, -ɑ̃t] vb voir **mourir** ♦ a dying ♦ nm/f dying man/woman.

mourir [murir] vi to die; (civilisation) to die out; ~ **assassiné** to be murdered; ~ **de froid/faim/vieillesse** to die of exposure/ hunger/old age; ~ **de faim/d'ennui** (fig) to be starving/be bored to death; ~ **d'envie de faire** to be dying to do; **s'ennuyer à** ~ to be bored to death.

mousquetaire [muskətɛr] nm musketeer.

mousqueton [muskətɔ̃] nm (fusil) carbine; (anneau) snap-link, karabiner.

moussant, e [musɑ̃, -ɑ̃t] a fɔ̃aming; **bain** ~ foam ou bubble bath, bath foam.

mousse [mus] nf (BOT) moss; (écume: sur eau, bière) froth, foam; (: shampooing) lather; (de champagne) bubbles pl; (CULIN) mousse; (en caoutchouc etc) foam ♦ nm (NAVIG) ship's boy; **bain de** ~ bubble bath; **bas** ~ stretch stockings; **balle** ~ rubber ball; ~ **carbonique** (fire-fighting) foam; ~ **de nylon** nylon foam; (tissu) stretch nylon; ~ **à raser** shaving foam.

mousseline [muslin] nf (TEXTILES) muslin; chiffon; **pommes** ~ (CULIN) creamed potatoes.

mousser [muse] vi to foam; to lather.

mousseux, euse [musø, -øz] a (chocolat) frothy; (eau) foamy, frothy; (vin) sparkling ♦ nm: (vin) ~ sparkling wine.

mousson [musɔ̃] nf monsoon.

moussu, e [musy] *a* mossy.

moustache [mustaʃ] *nf* moustache; **~s** *nfpl* (*d'animal*) whiskers *pl*.

moustachu, e [mustaʃy] *a* wearing a moustache.

moustiquaire [mustikɛR] *nf* (*rideau*) mosquito net; (*chassis*) mosquito screen.

moustique [mustik] *nm* mosquito.

moutarde [mutaRd(ə)] *nf* mustard ♦ *a inv* mustard(-coloured).

moutardier [mutaRdje] *nm* mustard jar.

mouton [mutɔ̃] *nm* (*ZOOL, péj*) sheep *inv*; (*peau*) sheepskin; (*CULIN*) mutton.

mouture [mutyR] *nf* grinding; (*péj*) rehash.

mouvant, e [muvã, -ãt] *a* unsettled; changing; shifting.

mouvement [muvmã] *nm* (*gén, aussi: mécanisme*) movement; (*ligne courbe*) contours *pl*; (*fig: tumulte, agitation*) activity, bustle; (*: impulsion*) impulse; reaction; (*geste*) gesture; (*MUS: rythme*) tempo (*pl* -s *ou* tempi); **en ~** in motion; on the move; **mettre qch en ~** to set sth in motion, set sth going; **~ d'humeur** fit *ou* burst of temper; **~ d'opinion** trend of (public) opinion; **le ~ perpétuel** perpetual motion.

mouvementé, e [muvmãte] *a* (*vie, poursuite*) eventful; (*réunion*) turbulent.

mouvoir [muvwaR] *vt* (*levier, membre*) to move; (*machine*) to drive; **se ~** to move.

moyen, ne [mwajɛ̃, -ɛn] *a* average; (*tailles, prix*) medium; (*de grandeur moyenne*) medium-sized ♦ *nm* (*façon*) means *sg*, way ♦ *nf* average; (*STATISTIQUE*) mean; (*SCOL: à l'examen*) pass mark; (*AUTO*) average speed; **~s** *nmpl* (*capacités*) means; **au ~ de** by means of; **y a-t-il ~ de ...?** is it possible to ...?, can one ...?; **par quel ~?** how?, which way?, by which means?; **par tous les ~s** by every possible means, every possible way; **avec les ~s du bord** (*fig*) with what's available *ou* what comes to hand; **employer les grands ~s** to resort to drastic measures; **par ses propres ~s** all by oneself; **en ~ne** on (an) average; **faire la ~ne** to work out the average; **~ de locomotion/d'expression** means of transport/expression; **~ âge** Middle Ages; **~ de transport** means of transport; **~ne d'âge** average age; **~ne entreprise** (*COMM*) medium-sized firm.

moyen-courrier [mwajɛ̃kuRje] *nm* (*AVIAT*) medium-haul aircraft.

moyennant [mwajɛnã] *prép* (*somme*) for; (*service, conditions*) in return for; (*travail, effort*) with.

moyennement [mwajɛnmã] *ad* fairly, moderately; (*faire qch*) fairly *ou* moderately well.

Moyen-Orient [mwajɛnɔRjã] *nm:* **le ~** the Middle East.

moyeu, x [mwajø] *nm* hub.

mozambicain, e [mɔzãbikɛ̃, -ɛn] *a* Mozambican.

Mozambique [mɔzãbik] *nm:* **le ~** Mozambique.

MRAP *sigle m* = *Mouvement contre le racisme, l'antisémitisme et pour la paix.*

MRG *sigle m* (= *Mouvement des radicaux de gauche*) political party.

MRP *sigle m* (= *Mouvement républicain*

populaire) political party.

ms *abr* (= *manuscrit*) MS., ms.

MST *sigle f* (= *maladie sexuellement transmissible*) STD (= *sexually transmitted disease*).

mû, mue [my] *pp de* **mouvoir.**

mucosité [mykozite] *nf* mucus *q*.

mucus [mykys] *nm* mucus *q*.

mue [my] *pp de* **mouvoir** ♦ *nf* moulting (*Brit*), molting (*US*); sloughing; breaking of the voice.

muer [mɥe] *vi* (*oiseau, mammifère*) to moult (*Brit*), molt (*US*); (*serpent*) to slough; (*jeune garçon*): **il mue** his voice is breaking; **se ~ en** to transform into.

muet, te [mɥɛ, -ɛt] *a* dumb; (*fig*): **~ d'admiration** *etc* speechless with admiration *etc*; (*joie, douleur, CINÉMA*) silent; (*LING: lettre*) silent, mute; (*carte*) blank ♦ *nm/f* mute ♦ *nm:* **le ~** (*CINÉMA*) the silent cinema *ou* movies (*esp US*).

mufle [myfl(ə)] *nm* muzzle; (*goujat*) boor ♦ *a* boorish.

mugir [myʒiR] *vi* (*bœuf*) to bellow; (*vache*) to low, moo; (*fig*) to howl.

mugissement [myʒismã] *nm* (*voir mugir*) bellowing; lowing, mooing; howling.

muguet [mygɛ] *nm* (*BOT*) lily of the valley; (*MÉD*) thrush.

mulâtre, tresse [mylɑtR(ə), -tRɛs] *nm/f* mulatto.

mule [myl] *nf* (*ZOOL*) (she-)mule.

mules [myl] *nfpl* (*pantoufles*) mules.

mulet [mylɛ] *nm* (*ZOOL*) (he-)mule; (*poisson*) mullet.

muletier, ière [myltje, -jɛR] *a:* **sentier** *ou* **chemin ~** mule track.

mulot [mylo] *nm* fieldmouse (*pl* -mice).

multicolore [myltikɔlɔR] *a* multicoloured (*Brit*), multicolored (*US*).

multicoque [myltikɔk] *nm* multihull.

multidisplinaire [myltidisiplinɛR] *a* multidisciplinary.

multiforme [myltifɔRm(ə)] *a* many-sided.

multilatéral, e, aux [myltilateRal, -o] *a* multilateral.

multimilliardaire [myltimiljaRdɛR], **multimillionnaire** [myltimiljɔnɛR] *a, nm/f* multimillionaire.

multinational, e, aux [myltinasjɔnal, -o] *a, nf* multinational.

multiple [myltipl(ə)] *a* multiple, numerous; (*varié*) many, manifold ♦ *nm* (*MATH*) multiple.

multiplicateur [myltiplikatœR] *nm* multiplier.

multiplication [myltiplikasjɔ̃] *nf* multiplication.

multiplicité [myltiplisite] *nf* multiplicity.

multiplier [myltiplije] *vt* to multiply; **se ~** *vi* to multiply; (*fig: personne*) to be everywhere at once.

multiprogrammation [myltipRɔgRamasjɔ̃] *nf* (*INFORM*) multiprogramming.

multipropriété [myltipRɔpRijete] *nf* timesharing *q*.

multitraitement [myltitRɛtmã] *nm* (*INFORM*) multiprocessing.

multitude [myltityd] *nf* multitude; mass; **une ~ de** a vast number of, a multitude of.

Munich [mynik] *n* Munich.

munichois, e [mynikwa, -waz] *a* of *ou* from Munich.

municipal, e, aux [mynisipal, -o] *a* municipal; town *cpd*.

municipalité [mynisipalite] *nf* (*corps municipal*) town council, corporation; (*commune*) town, municipality.

munir [myniʀ] *vt*: ~ **qn/qch de** to equip sb/sth with; **se** ~ **de** to provide o.s. with.

munitions [mynisjɔ̃] *nfpl* ammunition *sg*.

muqueuse [mykøz] *nf* mucous membrane.

mur [myʀ] *nm* wall; (*fig*) stone *ou* brick wall; **faire le** ~ (*interne, soldat*) to jump the wall; ~ **du son** sound barrier.

mûr, e [myʀ] *a* ripe; (*personne*) mature ♦ *nf* (*de la ronce*) blackberry; (*du mûrier*) mulberry.

muraille [myʀɑj] *nf* (high) wall.

mural, e, aux [myʀal, -o] *a* wall *cpd* ♦ *nm* (*ART*) mural.

mûre [myʀ] *nf voir* **mûr**.

mûrement [myʀmɑ̃] *ad*: **ayant** ~ **réfléchi** having given the matter much thought.

murène [myʀɛn] *nf* moray (eel).

murer [myʀe] *vt* (*enclos*) to wall (in); (*porte, issue*) to wall up; (*personne*) to wall up *ou* in.

muret [myʀɛ] *nm* low wall.

mûrier [myʀje] *nm* mulberry tree; (*ronce*) blackberry bush.

mûrir [myʀiʀ] *vi* (*fruit, blé*) to ripen; (*abcès, furoncle*) to come to a head; (*fig: idée, personne*) to mature; (*projet*) to develop ♦ *vt* (*fruit, blé*) to ripen; (*personne*) to (make) mature; (*pensée, projet*) to nurture.

murmure [myʀmyʀ] *nm* murmur; ~**s** *nmpl* (*plaintes*) murmurings, mutterings.

murmurer [myʀmyʀe] *vi* to murmur; (*se plaindre*) to mutter, grumble.

mus [my] *etc vb voir* **mouvoir**.

musaraigne [myzaʀɛɲ] *nf* shrew.

musarder [myzaʀde] *vi* to idle (about); (*en marchant*) to dawdle (along).

musc [mysk] *nm* musk.

muscade [myskad] *nf* (*aussi*: **noix** ~) nutmeg.

muscat [myska] *nm* (*raisin*) muscat grape; (*vin*) muscatel (wine).

muscle [myskl(ə)] *nm* muscle.

musclé, e [myskle] *a* (*personne, corps*) muscular; (*fig: politique, régime etc*) strong-arm *cpd*.

muscler [myskle] *vt* to develop the muscles of.

musculaire [myskylɛʀ] *a* muscular.

musculation [myskylɑsjɔ̃] *nf*: **exercices de** ~ muscle-developing exercises.

musculature [myskylatyʀ] *nf* muscle structure, muscles *pl*, musculature.

muse [myz] *nf* muse.

museau, x [myzo] *nm* muzzle.

musée [myze] *nm* museum; (*de peinture*) art gallery.

museler [myzle] *vt* to muzzle.

muselière [myzəljɛʀ] *nf* muzzle.

musette [myzɛt] *nf* (*sac*) lunchbag ♦ *a inv* (*orchestre etc*) accordion *cpd*.

muséum [myzeɔm] *nm* museum.

musical, e, aux [myzikal, -o] *a* musical.

music-hall [myzikol] *nm* variety theatre; (*genre*) variety.

musicien, ne [myzisjɛ̃, -ɛn] *a* musical ♦ *nm/f* musician.

musique [myzik] *nf* music; (*fanfare*) band; **faire de la** ~ to make music; (*jouer d'un instrument*) to play an instrument; ~ **de chambre** chamber music; ~ **de fond** background music.

musqué, e [myske] *a* musky.

must [mœst] *nm* must.

musulman, e [myzylmɑ̃, -an] *a*, *nm/f* Moslem, Muslim.

mutant, e [mytɑ̃, -ɑ̃t] *nm/f* mutant.

mutation [mytɑsjɔ̃] *nf* (*ADMIN*) transfer; (*BIO*) mutation.

muter [myte] *vt* (*ADMIN*) to transfer.

mutilation [mytilɑsjɔ̃] *nf* mutilation.

mutilé, e [mytile] *nm/f* disabled person (*through loss of limbs*); ~ **de guerre** disabled ex-serviceman; **grand** ~ severely disabled person.

mutiler [mytile] *vt* to mutilate, maim; (*fig*) to mutilate, deface.

mutin, e [mytɛ̃, -in] *a* (*enfant, air, ton*) mischievous, impish ♦ *nm/f* (*MIL, NAVIG*) mutineer.

mutiner [mytine]: **se** ~ *vi* to mutiny.

mutinerie [mytinʀi] *nf* mutiny.

mutisme [mytism(ə)] *nm* silence.

mutualité [mytɥalite] *nf* (*assurance*) mutual (benefit) insurance scheme.

mutuel, le [mytɥɛl] *a* mutual ♦ *nf* mutual benefit society.

myocarde [mjɔkaʀd(ə)] *nm voir* **infarctus**.

myope [mjɔp] *a* short-sighted.

myopie [mjɔpi] *nf* short-sightedness, myopia.

myosotis [mjɔzɔtis] *nm* forget-me-not.

myriade [miʀjad] *nf* myriad.

myrtille [miʀtij] *nf* bilberry (*Brit*), blueberry (*US*), whortleberry.

mystère [mistɛʀ] *nm* mystery.

mystérieusement [misteʀjøzmɑ̃] *ad* mysteriously.

mystérieux, euse [misteʀjø, -øz] *a* mysterious.

mysticisme [mistisism(ə)] *nm* mysticism.

mystificateur, trice [mistifikatœʀ, -tʀis] *nm/f* hoaxer, practical joker.

mystification [mistifikɑsjɔ̃] *nf* (*tromperie, mensonge*) hoax; (*mythe*) mystification.

mystifier [mistifje] *vt* to fool, take in; (*tromper*) to mystify.

mystique [mistik] *a* mystic, mystical ♦ *nm/f* mystic.

mythe [mit] *nm* myth.

mythifier [mitifje] *vt* to turn into a myth, mythologize.

mythique [mitik] *a* mythical.

mythologie [mitɔlɔʒi] *nf* mythology.

mythologique [mitɔlɔʒik] *a* mythological.

mythomane [mitɔman] *a*, *nm/f* mythomaniac.

N

N, n [ɛn] *nm inv* N, n ♦ *abr* (= *nord*) N; **N comme Nicolas** N for Nelly (*Brit*) *ou* Nan (*US*).

n' [n] *ad voir* **ne.**

nabot [nabo] *nm* dwarf.

nacelle [nasɛl] *nf* (*de ballon*) basket.

nacre [nakʀ(ə)] *nf* mother of pearl.

nacré, e [nakʀe] *a* pearly.

nage [naʒ] *nf* swimming; (*manière*) style of swimming, stroke; **traverser/s'éloigner à la ~** to swim across/away; **en ~** bathed in perspiration; **~ indienne** sidestroke; **~ libre** freestyle; **~ papillon** butterfly.

nageoire [naʒwaʀ] *nf* fin.

nager [naʒe] *vi* to swim; (*fig: ne rien comprendre*) to be all at sea; **~ dans** to be swimming in; (*vêtements*) to be lost in; **~ dans le bonheur** to be overjoyed.

nageur, euse [naʒœʀ, -øz] *nm/f* swimmer.

naguère [nagɛʀ] *ad* (*il y a peu de temps*) not long ago; (*autrefois*) formerly.

naïf, ïve [naif, naiv] *a* naïve.

nain, e [nɛ̃, nɛn] *a*, *nm/f* dwarf.

Nairobi [nairɔbi] *n* Nairobi.

nais [nɛ], **naissais** [nɛsɛ] *etc vb voir* **naître.**

naissance [nɛsɑ̃s] *nf* birth; **donner ~ à** to give birth to; (*fig*) to give rise to; **prendre ~** to originate; **aveugle de ~** born blind; **Français de ~** French by birth; **à la ~ des cheveux** at the roots of the hair; **lieu de ~** place of birth.

naissant, e [nɛsɑ̃, -ɑ̃t] *vb voir* **naître** ♦ *a* budding, incipient; (*jour*) dawning.

naît [nɛ] *vb voir* **naître.**

naître [nɛtʀ(ə)] *vi* to be born; (*conflit, complications*): **~ de** to arise from, be born out of; **~ à** (*amour, poésie*) to awaken to; **il est né en 1960** he was born in 1960; **il naît plus de filles que de garçons** there are more girls born than boys; **faire ~** (*fig*) to give rise to, arouse.

naïvement [naivmɑ̃] *ad* naïvely.

naïveté [naivte] *nf* naïvety.

Namibie [namibi] *nf*: **la ~** Namibia.

nana [nana] *nf* (*fam: fille*) bird (*Brit*), chick.

nancéien, ne [nɑ̃sejɛ̃, -ɛn] *a* of *ou* from Nancy.

nantais, e [nɑ̃tɛ, -ɛz] *a* of *ou* from Nantes.

nantir [nɑ̃tiʀ] *vt*: **~ qn de** to provide sb with; **les nantis** (*péj*) the well-to-do.

NAP *sigle a* (= *Neuilly Auteuil Passy*) ≈ preppy, ≈ Sloane Ranger *cpd* (*Brit*).

napalm [napalm] *nm* napalm.

naphtaline [naftalin] *nf*: **boules de ~** mothballs.

Naples [napl(ə)] *n* Naples.

napolitain, e [napɔlitɛ̃, -ɛn] *a* Neapolitan; **tranche ~e** Neapolitan ice cream.

nappe [nap] *nf* tablecloth; (*fig*) sheet; layer; **~ de mazout** oil slick; **~ (phréatique)** water table.

napper [nape] *vt*: **~ qch de** to coat sth with.

napperon [napʀɔ̃] *nm* table-mat; **~ individuel** place mat.

naquis [naki] *etc vb voir* **naître.**

narcisse [narsis] *nm* narcissus.

narcissique [narsisik] *a* narcissistic.

narcotique [narkɔtik] *a*, *nm* narcotic.

narguer [narge] *vt* to taunt.

narine [narin] *nf* nostril.

narquois, e [narkwa, -waz] *a* derisive, mocking.

narrateur, trice [naratœr, -tris] *nm/f* narrator.

narration [narasjɔ̃] *nf* narration, narrative; (*SCOL*) essay.

narrer [nare] *vt* to tell the story of, recount.

NASA [nasa] *sigle f* (= *National Aeronautics and Space Administration*) NASA.

nasal, e, aux [nazal, -o] *a* nasal.

naseau, x [nazo] *nm* nostril.

nasillard, e [nazijar, -ard(ə)] *a* nasal.

nasiller [nazije] *vi* to speak with a (nasal) twang.

Nassau [naso] *n* Nassau.

nasse [nas] *nf* fish-trap.

natal, e [natal] *a* native.

nataliste [natalist(ə)] *a* supporting a rising birth rate.

natalité [natalite] *nf* birth rate.

natation [natasjɔ̃] *nf* swimming; **faire de la ~** to go swimming (*regularly*).

natif, ive [natif, -iv] *a* native.

nation [nasjɔ̃] *nf* nation; **les N~s Unies (NU)** the United Nations (UN).

national, e, aux [nasjɔnal, -o] *a* national ♦ *nf*: **(route) ~e** ≈ A road (*Brit*), ≈ state highway (*US*); **obsèques ~es** state funeral.

nationalisation [nasjɔnalizasjɔ̃] *nf* nationalization.

nationaliser [nasjɔnalize] *vt* to nationalize.

nationalisme [nasjɔnalism(ə)] *nm* nationalism.

nationaliste [nasjɔnalist(ə)] *a*, *nm/f* nationalist.

nationalité [nasjɔnalite] *nf* nationality; **de ~ française** of French nationality.

natte [nat] *nf* (*tapis*) mat; (*cheveux*) plait.

natter [nate] *vt* (*cheveux*) to plait.

naturalisation [natyralizasjɔ̃] *nf* naturalization.

naturaliser [natyralize] *vt* to naturalize; (*empailler*) to stuff.

naturaliste [natyralist(ə)] *nm/f* naturalist; (*empailleur*) taxidermist.

nature [natyʀ] *nf* nature ♦ *a*, *ad* (*CULIN*) plain, without seasoning or sweetening; (*café, thé: sans lait*) black; (*: sans sucre*) without sugar; **payer en ~** to pay in kind; **peint d'après ~** painted from life; **être de ~ à** **faire qch** (*propre à*) to be the sort of thing (*ou* person) to do sth; **~ morte** still-life.

naturel, le [natyʀɛl] *a* (*gén, aussi: enfant*) natural ♦ *nm* naturalness; (*caractère*) disposition, nature; (*autochtone*) native; **au ~** (*CULIN*) in water; in its own juices.

naturellement [natyʀɛlmɑ̃] *ad* naturally; (*bien sûr*) of course.

naturisme [natyʀism(ə)] *nm* naturism.

naturiste [natyʀist(ə)] *nm/f* naturist.

naufrage [nofʀaʒ] *nm* (ship)wreck; *(fig)* wreck; **faire ~** to be shipwrecked.

naufragé, e [nofʀaʒe] *nm/f* shipwreck victim, castaway.

Nauru [noʀy] *nm* Nauru.

nauséabond, e [nozeabɔ̃, -ɔ̃d] *a* foul, nauseous.

nausée [noze] *nf* nausea; **avoir la ~** to feel sick; **avoir des ~s** to have waves of nausea, feel nauseous *ou* sick.

nautique [notik] *a* nautical, water *cpd*; **sports ~s** water sports.

nautisme [notism(ə)] *nm* water sports *pl*.

naval, e [naval] *a* naval.

navarrais, e [navaʀɛ, -ɛz] *a* Navarrian.

navet [navɛ] *nm* turnip; *(péj)* third-rate film.

navette [navɛt] *nf* shuttle; *(en car etc)* shuttle (service); **faire la ~ (entre)** to go to and fro (between), shuttle (between); **~ spatiale** space shuttle.

navigabilité [navigabilite] *nf* *(d'un navire)* seaworthiness; *(d'un avion)* airworthiness.

navigable [navigabl(ə)] *a* navigable.

navigant, e [navigɑ̃, -ɑ̃t] *a* *(AVIAT: personnel)* flying ♦ *nm/f*: **les ~s** the flying staff *ou* personnel.

navigateur [navigatœʀ] *nm* *(NAVIG)* seafarer, sailor; *(AVIAT)* navigator.

navigation [navigasjɔ̃] *nf* navigation, sailing; *(COMM)* shipping; **compagnie de ~** shipping company; **~ spatiale** space navigation.

naviguer [navige] *vi* to navigate, sail.

navire [naviʀ] *nm* ship; **~ de guerre** warship; **~ marchand** merchantman.

navire-citerne, *pl* **navires-citernes** [naviʀsitɛʀn(ə)] *nm* tanker.

navire-hôpital, *pl* **navires-hôpitaux** [naviʀɔpital, -to] *nm* hospital ship.

navrant, e [navʀɑ̃, -ɑ̃t] *a* *(affligeant)* upsetting; *(consternant)* annoying.

navrer [navʀe] *vt* to upset, distress; **je suis navré (de/de faire/que)** I'm so sorry (for/for doing/that).

nazaréen, ne [nazaʀeɛ̃, -ɛn] *a* Nazarene.

Nazareth [nazaʀɛt] *n* Nazareth.

NB *abr* (= *nota bene*) NB.

nbr. *abr* = **nombreux**.

nbses *abr* = **nombreuses**.

n.c. *abr* = *non communiqué, non coté*.

ND *sigle f* = *Notre Dame*.

n.d. *abr* = *non daté, non disponible*.

NDA *sigle f* = *note de l'auteur*.

NDE *sigle f* = *note de l'éditeur*.

NDLR *sigle f* = *note de la rédaction*.

ne, n' [n(ə)] *ad voir* **pas, plus, jamais** *etc*; *(explétif)* non traduit.

né, e [ne] *pp de* **naître**; **~ en 1960** born in 1960; **~e Scott** née Scott; **~(e) de ... et de ...** son/daughter of ... and of ...; **~ d'une mère française** having a French mother; **~ pour commander** born to lead ♦ *a*: **un comédien ~** a born comedian.

néanmoins [neɑ̃mwɛ̃] *ad* nevertheless, yet.

néant [neɑ̃] *nm* nothingness; **réduire à ~** to bring to nought; *(espoir)* to dash.

nébuleux, euse [nebylø, -øz] *a* *(ciel)* cloudy; *(fig)* nebulous.

nébuliser [nebylize] *vt* *(liquide)* to spray.

nébulosité [nebylozite] *nf* cloud cover; **~ variable** cloudy in places.

nécessaire [nesesɛʀ] *a* necessary ♦ *nm* necessary; *(sac)* kit; **faire le ~** to do the necessary; **n'emporter que le strict ~** to take only what is strictly necessary; **~ de couture** sewing kit; **~ de toilette** toilet bag; **~ de voyage** overnight bag.

nécessairement [nesesɛʀmɑ̃] *ad* necessarily.

nécessité [nesesite] *nf* necessity; **se trouver dans la ~ de faire qch** to find it necessary to do sth; **par ~** out of necessity.

nécessiter [nesesite] *vt* to require.

nécessiteux, euse [nesesitø, -øz] *a* needy.

nec plus ultra [nɛkplysyltʀa] *nm*: **le ~ de** the last word in.

nécrologie [nekʀɔlɔʒi] *nf* obituary.

nécrologique [nekʀɔlɔʒik] *a*: **article ~** obituary; **rubrique ~** obituary column.

nécromancie [nekʀɔmɑ̃si] *nf* necromancy.

nécromancien, ne [nekʀɔmɑ̃sjɛ̃, -ɛn] *nm/f* necromancer.

nécrose [nekʀoz] *nf* necrosis.

nectar [nektaʀ] *nm* nectar.

nectarine [nektaʀin] *nf* nectarine.

néerlandais, e [neɛʀlɑ̃dɛ, -ɛz] *a* Dutch, of the Netherlands ♦ *nm* *(LING)* Dutch ♦ *nm/f*: **N~, e** Dutchman/woman; **les N~** the Dutch.

nef [nɛf] *nf* *(d'église)* nave.

néfaste [nefast(ə)] *a* baneful; ill-fated.

négatif, ive [negatif, iv] *a* negative ♦ *nm* *(PHOTO)* negative.

négativement [negativmɑ̃] *ad*: **répondre ~** to give a negative response.

négligé, e [negliʒe] *a* *(en désordre)* slovenly ♦ *nm* *(tenue)* negligee.

négligeable [negliʒabl(ə)] *a* insignificant, negligible.

négligemment [negliʒamɑ̃] *ad* carelessly.

négligence [negliʒɑ̃s] *nf* carelessness *q*; *(faute)* careless omission.

négligent, e [negliʒɑ̃, -ɑ̃t] *a* careless; *(JUR etc)* negligent.

négliger [negliʒe] *vt* *(épouse, jardin)* to neglect; *(tenue)* to be careless about; *(avis, précautions)* to disregard, overlook; **~ de faire** to fail to do, not bother to do; **se ~** to neglect o.s.

négoce [negɔs] *nm* trade.

négociable [negɔsjabl(ə)] *a* negotiable.

négociant [negɔsjɑ̃] *nm* merchant.

négociateur [negɔsjatœʀ] *nm* negotiator.

négociation [negɔsjasjɔ̃] *nf* negotiation; **~s collectives** collective bargaining *sg*.

négocier [negɔsje] *vi, vt* to negotiate.

nègre [nɛgʀ(ə)] *nm* *(péj)* Negro; *(péj: écrivain)* ghost writer ♦ *a* a Negro.

négresse [negʀɛs] *nf* *(péj)* Negress.

négrier [negʀije] *nm* *(fig)* slave driver.

négroïde [negʀɔid] *a* negroid.

neige [nɛʒ] *nf* snow; **battre les œufs en ~** *(CULIN)* to whip *ou* beat the egg whites until stiff; **~ carbonique** dry ice; **~ fondue** *(par terre)* slush; *(qui tombe)* sleet; **~ poudreuse** powder snow.

neiger [nɛʒe] *vi* to snow.

neigeux, euse [nɛʒø, -øz] *a* snowy, snow-covered.

nénuphar [nenyfaʀ] *nm* water-lily.

néo-calédonien, ne [neɔkaledɔnjɛ̃, -ɛn] *a* New Caledonian ♦ *nm/f:* **N~, ne** native of New Caledonia.

néologisme [neɔlɔʒism(ə)] *nm* neologism.

néon [neɔ̃] *nm* neon.

néo-natal, e [neɔnatal] *a* neonatal.

néophyte [neɔfit] *nm/f* novice.

néo-zélandais, e [neɔzelɑ̃dɛ, -ɛz] *a* New Zealand *cpd* ♦ *nm/f:* **N~, e** New Zealander.

Népal [nepal] *nm:* **le ~** Nepal.

népalais, e [nepalɛ, -ɛz] *a* Nepalese, Nepali ♦ *nm* (*LING*) Nepalese, Nepali ♦ *nm/f:* **N~, e** Nepalese, Nepali.

néphrétique [nefretik] *a* (*MÉD:* *colique*) nephritic.

néphrite [nefrit] *nf* (*MÉD*) nephritis.

nerf [nɛʀ] *nm* nerve; (*fig*) spirit; (: *forces*) stamina; **~s** *nmpl* nerves; **être** *ou* **vivre sur les ~s** to live on one's nerves; **être à bout de ~s** to be at the end of one's tether; **passer ses ~s sur qn** to take it out on sb.

nerveusement [nɛʀvøzmɑ̃] *ad* nervously.

nerveux, euse [nɛʀvø, -øz] *a* nervous; (*cheval*) highly-strung; (*voiture*) nippy, responsive; (*tendineux*) sinewy.

nervosité [nɛʀvozite] *nf* nervousness; (*émotivité*) excitability.

nervure [nɛʀvyʀ] *nf* (*de feuille*) vein; (*ARCHIT, TECH*) rib.

n'est-ce pas [nɛspɑ] *ad* isn't it?, won't you? *etc*, *selon le verbe qui précède;* **c'est bon, ~?** it's good, isn't it?; **il a peur, ~?** he's afraid, isn't he?; **~ que c'est bon?** don't you think it's good?; **lui, ~, il peut se le permettre** he, of course, can afford to do that, can't he?

net, nette [nɛt] *a* (*sans équivoque, distinct*) clear; (*photo*) sharp; (*évident*) definite; (*propre*) neat, clean; (*COMM: prix, salaire, poids*) net ♦ *ad* (*refuser*) flatly ♦ *nm:* **mettre au ~** to copy out; **s'arrêter ~** to stop dead; **la lame a cassé ~** the blade snapped clean through; **faire place nette** to make a clean sweep; **~ d'impôt** tax free.

nettement [nɛtmɑ̃] *ad* (*distinctement*) clearly; (*évidemment*) definitely; (*avec comparatif, superlatif*): **~ mieux** definitely *ou* clearly better.

netteté [nɛtte] *nf* clearness.

nettoie [nɛtwa] *etc vb voir* **nettoyer.**

nettoiement [nɛtwamɑ̃] *nm* (*ADMIN*) cleaning; **service du ~** refuse collection.

nettoierai [nɛtwaʀe] *etc vb voir* **nettoyer.**

nettoyage [nɛtwajaʒ] *nm* cleaning; **~ à sec** dry cleaning.

nettoyant [nɛtwajɑ̃] *nm* (*produit*) cleaning agent.

nettoyer [nɛtwaje] *vt* to clean; (*fig*) to clean out.

neuf [nœf] *num* nine.

neuf, neuve [nœf, nœv] *a* new ♦ *nm:* **repeindre à ~** to redecorate; **remettre à ~** to do up (as good as new), refurbish; **n'acheter que du ~** to buy everything new; **quoi de ~?** what's new?

neurasthénique [nøʀastenik] *a* neurasthenic.

neurochirurgien [nøʀɔʃiʀyʀʒjɛ̃] *nm* neurosurgeon.

neuroleptique [nøʀɔleptik] *a* neuroleptic.

neurologique [nøʀɔlɔʒik] *a* neurological.

neurologue [nøʀɔlɔg] *nm/f* neurologist.

neuropsychiatre [nøʀɔpsikjatʀ(ə)] *nm/f* neuropsychiatrist.

neutralisation [nøtʀalizɑsjɔ̃] *nf* neutralization.

neutraliser [nøtʀalize] *vt* to neutralize.

neutraliste [nøtʀalist(ə)] (*a*) a neutralist.

neutralité [nøtʀalite] *nf* neutrality.

neutre [nøtʀ(ə)] *a, nm* (*aussi LING*) neutral.

neutron [nøtʀɔ̃] *nm* neutron.

neuve [nœv] *af voir* **neuf.**

neuvième [nœvjɛm] *num* ninth.

névé [neve] *nm* permanent snowpatch.

neveu, x [nəvø] *nm* nephew.

névralgie [nevralʒi] *nf* neuralgia.

névralgique [nevralʒik] *a* (*fig: sensible*) sensitive; **centre ~** nerve centre.

névrite [nevrit] *nf* neuritis.

névrose [nevroz] *nf* neurosis.

névrosé, e [nevroze] *a, nm/f* neurotic.

névrotique [nevrɔtik] *a* neurotic.

New York [njujɔʀk] *n* New York.

new yorkais, e [njujɔʀkɛ, -ɛz] *a* of *ou* from New York, New York *cpd* ♦ *nm/f:* **New Yorkais, e** New Yorker.

nez [ne] *nm* nose; **rire au ~ de qn** to laugh in sb's face; **avoir du ~** to have flair; **avoir le ~ fin** to have foresight; **~ à ~ avec** face to face with; **à vue de ~** roughly.

NF *sigle mpl* = *nouveaux francs* ♦ *sigle f* (*INDUSTRIE:* = *norme française*) industrial standard.

ni [ni] *cj:* **~ l'un ~ l'autre ne sont** *ou* **n'est** neither one nor the other is; **il n'a rien dit ~ fait** he hasn't said or done anything.

Niagara [njagaʀa] *nm:* **les chutes du ~** the Niagara Falls.

niais, e [njɛ, -ɛz] *a* silly, thick.

niaiserie [njɛzʀi] *nf* gullibility; (*action, propos, futilité*) silliness.

Nicaragua [nikaʀagwa] *nm:* **le ~** Nicaragua.

nicaraguayen, ne [nikaʀagwajɛ̃, -ɛn] *a* Nicaraguan ♦ *nm/f:* **N~, ne** Nicaraguan.

Nice [nis] *n* Nice.

niche [niʃ] *nf* (*du chien*) kennel; (*de mur*) recess, niche; (*farce*) trick.

nichée [niʃe] *nf* brood, nest.

nicher [niʃe] *vi* to nest; **se ~ dans** (*personne: se blottir*) to snuggle into; (: *se cacher*) to hide in; (*objet*) to lodge itself in.

nichon [niʃɔ̃] *nm* (*fam*) boob, tit.

nickel [nikɛl] *nm* nickel.

niçois, e [niswa, -waz] *a* of *ou* from Nice; (*CULIN*) Nicoise.

Nicosie [nikɔsi] *n* Nicosia.

nicotine [nikɔtin] *nf* nicotine.

nid [ni] *nm* nest; (*fig: repaire etc*) den, lair; **~ d'abeilles** (*COUTURE, TEXTILE*) honeycomb stitch; **~ de poule** pothole.

nièce [njɛs] *nf* niece.

nième [ɛnjɛm] *a:* **la ~ fois** the nth *ou* umpteenth time.

nier [nje] *vt* to deny.

nigaud, e [nigo, -od] *nm/f* booby, fool.

Niger [niʒɛʀ] *nm:* **le ~** Niger; (*fleuve*) the Niger.

Nigéria [niʒeʀja] *nm ou nf* Nigeria.

nigérian, e [niʒeʀjɑ̃, -an] *a* Nigerian ♦ *nm/f:* **N~, e** Nigerian.

nigérien, ne [niʒeʀjɛ̃, -ɛn] *a* of *ou* from Niger.

Nil [nil] *nm*: **le ~** the Nile.
n'importe [nɛ̃pɔʀt(ə)] *ad*: **~!** no matter!; **~ qui/quoi/où** anybody/anything/ anywhere; **~ quoi!** (*fam*: *désapprobation*) what rubbish!; **~ quand** any time; **~ quel/quelle** any; **~ lequel/laquelle** any (one); **~ comment** (*sans soin*) carelessly; **~ comment, il part ce soir** he's leaving tonight in any case.
nippes [nip] *nfpl* (*fam*) togs.
nippon, e *ou* **ne** [nipɔ̃, -ɔn] *a* Japanese.
nique [nik] *nf*: **faire la ~ à** to thumb one's nose at (*fig*).
nitouche [nituʃ] *nf* (*péj*): **c'est une sainte ~** she looks as if butter wouldn't melt in her mouth.
nitrate [nitʀat] *nm* nitrate.
nitrique [nitʀik] *a*: **acide ~** nitric acid.
nitroglycérine [nitʀɔgliseʀin] *nf* nitro-glycerin(e).
niveau, x [nivo] *nm* level; (*des élèves, études*) standard; **au ~ de** at the level of; (*personne*) on a level with; **de ~ (avec)** level (with); **le ~ de la mer** sea level; **~ (à bulle)** spirit level; **~ (d'eau)** water level; **~ de vie** standard of living.
niveler [nivle] *vt* to level.
niveleuse [nivløz] *nf* (*TECH*) grader.
nivellement [nivɛlmɑ̃] *nm* levelling.
nivernais, e [nivɛʀnɛ, -ɛz] *a* of *ou* from Nevers (and region) ♦ *nm/f*: **N~, e** inhabitant *ou* native of Nevers (and region).
NL *sigle f* = *nouvelle lune*.
NN *abr* (= *nouvelle norme*) revised standard of hotel classification.
n° *abr* (= *numéro*) no.
nobiliaire [nɔbiljɛʀ] *af voir* **particule.**
noble [nɔbl(ə)] *a* noble; (*de qualité: métal etc*) precious ♦ *nm/f* noble(man/woman).
noblesse [nɔblɛs] *nf* (*classe sociale*) nobility; (*d'une action etc*) nobleness.
noce [nɔs] *nf* wedding; (*gens*) wedding party (*ou* guests *pl*); **il l'a épousée en secondes ~s** she was his second wife; **faire la ~** (*fam*) to go on a binge; **~s d'or/d'argent/de diamant** golden/silver/diamond wedding.
nocif, ive [nɔsif, -iv] *a* harmful, noxious.
noctambule [nɔktɑ̃byl] *nm* night-bird.
nocturne [nɔktyʀn(ə)] *a* a nocturnal ♦ *nf* (*SPORT*) floodlit fixture; (*d'un magasin*) late opening.
Noël [nɔel] *nm* Christmas; **la (fête de) ~** Christmas time.
nœud [nø] *nm* (*de corde, du bois, NAVIG*) knot; (*ruban*) bow; (*fig: liens*) bond, tie; (*fig: d'une question*) crux; (*THÉÂTRE etc*): **le ~ de l'action** the web of events; **~ coulant** noose; **~ gordien** Gordian knot; **~ papillon** bow tie.
noie [nwa] *etc vb voir* **noyer.**
noir, e [nwaʀ] *a* black; (*obscur, sombre*) dark ♦ *nm/f* black man/woman, Negro/Negro woman ♦ *nm*: **dans le ~** in the dark ♦ *nf* (*MUS*) crotchet (*Brit*), quarter note (*US*); **il fait ~** it is dark; **au ~** *ad* (*acheter, vendre*) on the black market; **travail au ~** moonlighting.
noirâtre [nwaʀɑtʀ(ə)] *a* (*teinte*) blackish.
noirceur [nwaʀsœʀ] *nf* blackness; darkness.
noircir [nwaʀsiʀ] *vt, vi* to blacken.

noise [nwaz] *nf*: **chercher ~ à** to try and pick a quarrel with.
noisetier [nwaztje] *nm* hazel (tree).
noisette [nwazɛt] *nf* hazelnut; (*morceau: de beurre etc*) small knob ♦ *a* (*yeux*) hazel.
noix [nwa] *nf* walnut; (*fam*) twit; (*CULIN*): **une ~ de beurre** a knob of butter; **à la ~** (*fam*) worthless; **~ de cajou** cashew nut; **~ de coco** coconut; **~ muscade** nutmeg; **~ de veau** (*CULIN*) round fillet of veal.
nom [nɔ̃] *nm* name; (*LING*) noun; **connaître qn de ~** to know sb by name; **au ~ de** in the name of; **~ d'une pipe** *ou* **d'un chien!** (*fam*) for goodness' sake!; **~ de Dieu!** (*fam!*) bloody hell! (*Brit*), my God!; **~ commun/ propre** common/proper noun; **~ composé** (*LING*) compound noun; **~ déposé** trade name; **~ d'emprunt** assumed name; **~ de famille** surname; **~ de fichier** file name; **~ de jeune fille** maiden name.
nomade [nɔmad] *a* nomadic ♦ *nm/f* nomad.
nombre [nɔ̃bʀ(ə)] *nm* number; **venir en ~** to come in large numbers; **depuis ~ d'années** for many years; **ils sont au ~ de 3** there are 3 of them; **au ~ de mes amis** among my friends; **sans ~** countless; **(bon) ~ de** (*beaucoup, plusieurs*) a (large) number of; **~ premier/entier** prime/whole number.
nombreux, euse [nɔ̃bʀø, -øz] *a* many, numerous; (*avec nom sg: foule etc*) large; **peu ~** few; small; **de ~ cas** many cases.
nombril [nɔ̃bʀi] *nm* navel.
nomenclature [nɔmɑ̃klatyʀ] *nf* wordlist; list of items.
nominal, e, aux [nɔminal, -o] *a* nominal; (*appel, liste*) of names.
nominatif, ive [nɔminatif, -iv] *nm* (*LING*) nominative ♦ *a*: **liste ~ive** list of names; **carte ~ive** calling card; **titre ~** registered name.
nomination [nɔminasjɔ̃] *nf* nomination.
nommément [nɔmemɑ̃] *ad* (*désigner*) by name.
nommer [nɔme] *vt* (*baptiser*) to name, give a name to; (*qualifier*) to call; (*mentionner*) to name, give the name of; (*élire*) to appoint, nominate; **se ~**: **il se nomme Pascal** his name's Pascal, he's called Pascal.
non [nɔ̃] *ad* (*réponse*) no; (*suivi d'un adjectif, adverbe*) not; **Paul est venu, ~?** Paul came, didn't he?; **répondre** *ou* **dire que ~** to say no; **~ pas que** not that; **~ plus: moi ~ plus** neither do I, I don't either; **je préférerais que ~** I would prefer not; **il se trouve que ~** perhaps not; **je pense que ~** I don't think so; **~ mais!** well really!; **~ mais des fois!** you must be joking!; **~ alcoolisé** non-alcoholic; **~ loin/seulement** not far/only.
nonagénaire [nɔnaʒenɛʀ] *nm/f* nonagenarian.
non-agression [nɔnagʀesjɔ̃] *nf*: **pacte de ~** non-aggression pact.
non-aligné, e [nɔnaliɲe] *a* non-aligned.
nonante [nɔnɑ̃t] *num* (*Belgique, Suisse*) nine-ty.
nonce [nɔ̃s] *nm* (*REL*) nuncio.
nonchalance [nɔ̃ʃalɑ̃s] *nf* nonchalance, casual-ness.
nonchalant, e [nɔ̃ʃalɑ̃, -ɑ̃t] *a* nonchalant, casual.

non-conformiste [nɔ̃kɔ̃fɔrmist(ə)] *a*, *nm/f* non-conformist.

non-croyant, e [nɔ̃krwajɑ̃, -ɑ̃t] *nm/f* (*REL*) non-believer.

non(-)engagé, e [nɔnɑ̃gaʒe] *a* non-aligned.

non-fumeur [nɔ̃fymœr] *nm* non-smoker.

non-ingérence [nɔnɛ̃ʒerɑ̃s] *nf* non-interference.

non-inscrit, e [nɔnɛ̃skri, -it] *nm/f* (*POL*: *député*) independent.

non-intervention [nɔnɛ̃tervɑ̃sjɔ̃] *nf* non-intervention.

non-lieu [nɔ̃ljø] *nm*: **il y a eu ~** the case was dismissed.

nonne [nɔn] *nf* nun.

nonobstant [nɔnɔpstɑ̃] *prép* notwithstanding.

non-paiement [nɔ̃pemɑ̃] *nm* non-payment.

non-prolifération [nɔ̃proliferasjɔ̃] *nf* non-proliferation.

non-résident [nɔ̃rezidɑ̃] *nm* (*ÉCON*) non-resident.

non-retour [nɔ̃rətur] *nm*: **point de ~** point of no return.

non-sens [nɔ̃sɑ̃s] *nm* absurdity.

non-syndiqué, e [nɔ̃sɛ̃dike] *nm/f* non-union member.

non-violent, e [nɔ̃vjɔlɑ̃, -ɑ̃t] *a* non-violent.

nord [nɔr] *nm* North ♦ *a* northern; north; **au ~** (*situation*) in the north; (*direction*) to the north; **au ~ de** north of, to the north of; **perdre le ~** to lose the place (*fig*).

nord-africain, e [nɔrafrikɛ̃, -ɛn] *a* North-African ♦ *nm/f*: **Nord-Africain, e** North African.

nord-américain, e [nɔramerikɛ̃, -ɛn] *a* North American ♦ *nm/f*: **Nord-Américain, e** North American.

nord-coréen, ne [nɔrkɔreɛ̃, -ɛn] *a* North Korean ♦ *nm/f*: **Nord-Coréen, ne** North Korean.

nord-est [nɔrɛst] *nm* North-East.

nordique [nɔrdik] *a* (*pays, race*) Nordic; (*langues*) Scandinavian, Nordic ♦ *nm/f*: **N~** Scandinavian.

nord-ouest [nɔrwɛst] *nm* North-West.

nord-vietnamien, ne [nɔrvjɛtnamjɛ̃, -ɛn] *a* North Vietnamese ♦ *nm/f*: **Nord-Vietnamien, ne** North Vietnamese.

normal, e, aux [nɔrmal, -o] *a* normal ♦ *nf*: **la ~e** the norm, the average.

normalement [nɔrmalmɑ̃] *ad* (*en général*) normally; (*comme prévu*): **~, il le fera demain** he should be doing it tomorrow, he's supposed to do it tomorrow.

normalien, ne [nɔrmaljɛ̃, -ɛn] *nm/f* student of École normale supérieure.

normalisation [nɔrmalizasjɔ̃] *nf* standardization; normalization.

normaliser [nɔrmalize] *vt* (*COMM*, *TECH*) to standardize; (*POL*) to normalize.

normand, e [nɔrmɑ̃, -ɑ̃d] *a* (*de Normandie*) Norman ♦ *nm/f*: **N~, e** (*de Normandie*) Norman.

Normandie [nɔrmɑ̃di] *nf*: **la ~** Normandy.

norme [nɔrm(ə)] *nf* norm; (*TECH*) standard.

Norvège [nɔrvɛʒ] *nf*: **la ~** Norway.

norvégien, ne [nɔrveʒjɛ̃, -ɛn] *a* a Norwegian ♦ *nm* (*LING*) Norwegian ♦ *nm/f*: **N~, ne** Norwegian.

nos [no] *dét voir* **notre**.

nostalgie [nɔstalʒi] *nf* nostalgia.

nostalgique [nɔstalʒik] *a* nostalgic.

notabilité [nɔtabilite] *nf* notability.

notable [nɔtabl(ə)] *a* notable, noteworthy; (*marqué*) noticeable, marked ♦ *nm* prominent citizen.

notablement [nɔtabləmɑ̃] *ad* notably; (*sensiblement*) noticeably.

notaire [nɔtɛr] *nm* notary; solicitor.

notamment [nɔtamɑ̃] *ad* in particular, among others.

notariat [nɔtarja] *nm* profession of notary (*ou* solicitor).

notarié, e [nɔtarje] *a*: **acte ~** deed drawn up by a notary (*ou* solicitor).

notation [nɔtasjɔ̃] *nf* notation.

note [nɔt] *nf* (*écrite*, *MUS*) note; (*SCOL*) mark (*Brit*), grade; (*facture*) bill; **prendre des ~s** to take notes; **prendre ~ de** to note; (*par écrit*) to note, write down; **dans la ~** exactly right; **forcer la ~** to exaggerate; **une ~ de tristesse/de gaieté** a sad/happy note; **~ de service** memorandum.

noté, e [nɔte] *a*: **être bien/mal ~** (*employé etc*) to have a good/bad record.

noter [nɔte] *vt* (*écrire*) to write down, note; (*remarquer*) to note, notice; (*SCOL, ADMIN*: *donner une appréciation*) to mark, give a grade to; **notez bien que ...** (please) note that ....

notice [nɔtis] *nf* summary, short article; (*brochure*): **~ explicative** explanatory leaflet, instruction booklet.

notification [nɔtifikasjɔ̃] *nf* notification.

notifier [nɔtifje] *vt*: **~ qch à qn** to notify sb of sth, notify sth to sb.

notion [nosjɔ̃] *nf* notion, idea; **~s** *nfpl* (*rudiments*) rudiments.

notoire [nɔtwar] *a* widely known; (*en mal*) notorious; **le fait est ~** the fact is common knowledge.

notoriété [nɔtɔrjete] *nf*: **c'est de ~ publique** it's common knowledge.

notre, nos [nɔtr(ə), no] *dét* our.

nôtre [notr(ə)] *pronom*: **le/la ~** ours; **les ~s** ours; (*alliés etc*) our own people; **soyez des ~s** join us ♦ *a* ours.

nouer [nwe] *vt* to tie, knot; (*fig: alliance etc*) to strike up; **~ la conversation** to start a conversation; **se ~** *vi*: **c'est là où l'intrigue se noue** it's at that point that the strands of the plot come together; **ma gorge se noua** a lump came to my throat.

noueux, euse [nwø, -øz] *a* gnarled.

nougat [nuga] *nm* nougat.

nouille [nuj] *nf* (*pâtes*): **~s** noodles; pasta *sg*; (*fam*) noodle (*Brit*), fathead.

nounou [nunu] *nf* nanny.

nounours [nunurs] *nm* teddy (bear).

nourri, e [nuri] *a* (*feu etc*) sustained.

nourrice [nuris] *nf* ≈ baby-minder; (*autrefois*) wet-nurse.

nourrir [nurir] *vt* to feed; (*fig: espoir*) to harbour, nurse; **logé nourri** with board and lodging; **~ au sein** to breast-feed; **se ~ de légumes/rêves** to live on vegetables/dreams.

nourrissant, e [nurisɑ̃, -ɑ̃t] *a* nourishing, nutritious.

nourrisson [nurisɔ̃] *nm* (unweaned) infant.

nourriture [nuʀityʀ] *nf* food.

nous [nu] *pronom (sujet)* we; *(objet)* us.

nous-mêmes [numɛm] *pronom* ourselves.

nouveau (nouvel), elle, x [nuvo, -ɛl] *a* new; *(original)* novel ♦ *nm/f* new pupil *(ou* employee) ♦ *nm:* **il y a du ~** there's something new ♦ *nf* (piece of) news *sg; (LITTÉRATURE)* short story; **nouvelles** *nfpl (PRESSE, TV)* news; **de ~, à ~** again; **je suis sans nouvelles de lui** I haven't heard from him; **Nouvel An** New Year; **~ riche** nouveau riche; **~ venu, nouvelle venue** newcomer; **~x mariés** newly-weds; **nouvelle vague** new wave.

nouveau-né, e [nuvone] *nm/f* newborn (baby).

nouveauté [nuvote] *nf* novelty; *(chose nouvelle)* innovation, something new; *(COMM)* new film *(ou* book *ou* creation *etc).*

nouvel *am,* **nouvelle** *af, nf* [nuvɛl] *voir* **nouveau.**

Nouvelle-Angleterre [nuvɛlɑ̃glətɛʀ] *nf:* **la ~** New England.

Nouvelle-Calédonie [nuvɛlkaledɔni] *nf:* **la ~** New Caledonia.

Nouvelle-Écosse [nuvɛlekɔs] *nf:* **la ~** Nova Scotia.

Nouvelle-Galles du Sud [nuvɛlgaldysyd] *nf:* **la ~** New South Wales.

Nouvelle-Guinée [nuvɛlgine] *nf:* **la ~** New Guinea.

nouvellement [nuvɛlmɑ̃] *ad (arrivé etc)* recently, newly.

Nouvelle-Orléans [nuvɛlɔʀleɑ̃] *nf:* **la ~** New Orleans.

Nouvelles-Hébrides [nuvɛlsebʀid] *nfpl:* **les ~** the New Hebrides.

Nouvelle-Zélande [nuvɛlzelɑ̃d] *nf:* **la ~** New Zealand.

nouvelliste [nuvelist(ə)] *nm/f* editor *ou* writer of short stories.

novateur, trice [nɔvatœʀ, -tʀis] *a* innovative ♦ *nm/f* innovator.

novembre [nɔvɑ̃bʀ(ə)] *nm* November; *voir aussi* **juillet.**

novice [nɔvis] *a* inexperienced ♦ *nm/f* novice.

noviciat [nɔvisja] *nm (REL)* noviciate.

noyade [nwajad] *nf* drowning *q.*

noyau, x [nwajo] *nm (de fruit)* stone; *(BIO, PHYSIQUE)* nucleus; *(ÉLEC, GÉO, fig: centre)* core; *(fig: d'artistes etc)* group; (: *de résistants etc*) cell.

noyautage [nwajotaʒ] *nm (POL)* infiltration.

noyauter [nwajote] *vt (POL)* to infiltrate.

noyé, e [nwaje] *nm/f* drowning *(ou* drowned) man/woman ♦ *a (fig: dépassé)* out of one's depth.

noyer [nwaje] *nm* walnut (tree); *(bois)* walnut ♦ *vt* to drown; *(fig)* to flood; to submerge; *(AUTO: moteur)* to flood; **se ~** to be drowned, drown; *(suicide)* to drown o.s; **~ son chagrin** to drown one's sorrows; **~ le poisson** to duck the issue.

NSP *sigle m (REL) = Notre Saint Père; (dans les sondages: = ne sais pas)* don't know.

NT *sigle m (= Nouveau Testament)* NT.

NU *sigle fpl (= Nations Unies)* UN.

nu, e [ny] *a* naked; *(membres)* naked, bare; *(chambre, fil, plaine)* bare ♦ *nm (ART)* nude; **le ~ intégral** total nudity; **à mains ~es** with one's bare hands; **se mettre ~** to strip; **mettre à ~** to bare.

nuage [nɥaʒ] *nm* cloud; **être dans les ~s** *(distrait)* to have one's head in the clouds; **~ de lait** drop of milk.

nuageux, euse [nɥaʒø, -øz] *a* cloudy.

nuance [nɥɑ̃s] *nf (de couleur, sens)* shade; **il y a une ~ (entre)** there's a slight difference (between); **une ~ de tristesse** a tinge of sadness.

nuancé, e [nɥɑ̃se] *a (opinion)* finely-shaded, subtly differing; **être ~ dans ses opinions** to have finely-shaded opinions.

nuancer [nɥɑ̃se] *vt (pensée, opinion)* to qualify.

nubile [nybil] *a* nubile.

nucléaire [nykleɛʀ] *a* nuclear ♦ *nm* nuclear power.

nudisme [nydism(ə)] *nm* nudism.

nudiste [nydist(ə)] *a, nm/f* nudist.

nudité [nydite] *nf (voir nu)* nudity, nakedness; bareness.

nuée [nɥe] *nf:* **une ~ de** a cloud *ou* host *ou* swarm of.

nues [ny] *nfpl:* **tomber des ~** to be taken aback; **porter qn aux ~** to praise sb to the skies.

nui [nɥi] *pp de* **nuire.**

nuire [nɥiʀ] *vi* to be harmful; **~ à** to harm, do damage to.

nuisance [nɥizɑ̃s] *nf* nuisance; **~s** *nfpl* pollution *sg.*

nuisible [nɥizibl(ə)] *a* harmful; **(animal) ~** pest.

nuisis [nɥizi] *etc vb voir* **nuire.**

nuit [nɥi] *nf* night; **payer sa ~** to pay for one's overnight accommodation; **il fait ~** it's dark; **cette ~** *(hier)* last night; *(aujourd'hui)* tonight; **de ~** *(vol, service)* night *cpd;* **~ blanche** sleepless night; **~ de noces** wedding night; **~ de Noël** Christmas Eve.

nuitamment [nɥitamɑ̃] *ad* by night.

nuitées [nɥite] *nfpl* overnight stays, beds occupied *(in statistics).*

nul, nulle [nyl] *a (aucun)* no; *(minime)* nil, non-existent; *(non valable)* null; *(péj)* useless, hopeless ♦ *pronom* none, no one; **résultat ~, match ~** draw; **nulle part** *ad* nowhere.

nullement [nylmɑ̃] *ad* by no means.

nullité [nylite] *nf* nullity; *(péj)* hopelessness; (: *personne)* hopeless individual, nonentity.

numéraire [nymeʀɛʀ] *nm* cash; metal currency.

numéral, e, aux [nymeʀal, -o] *a* numeral.

numérateur [nymeʀatœʀ] *nm* numerator.

numération [nymeʀasjɔ̃] *nf:* **~ décimale/ binaire** decimal/binary notation.

numérique [nymeʀik] *a* numerical; *(INFORM)* digital.

numériquement [nymeʀikmɑ̃] *ad* numerically.

numériser [nymeʀize] *vt (INFORM)* to digitize.

numéro [nymeʀo] *nm* number; *(spectacle)* act, turn; **faire** *ou* **composer un ~** to dial a number; **~ d'identification personnel** personal identification number (PIN); **~ d'immatriculation** *ou* **minéralogique** *ou* **de police** registration *(Brit) ou* license *(US)* number; ~ **de téléphone** (tele)phone number; ~ **vert** ≈ Freefone ® number (*Brit*), ≈ toll-free number (*US*).

numérotage [nymeʀɔtaʒ] *nm* numbering.

numérotation [nymeʀɔtasjɔ̃] *nf* numeration.

numéroter [nymeʀɔte] *vt* to number.

numerus clausus [nymeʀysklozys] *nm inv* restriction *ou* limitation of numbers.

numismate [nymismat] *nm/f* numismatist, coin collector.

nu-pieds [nypje] *nm inv* sandal ♦ *a inv* barefoot.

nuptial, e, aux [nypsjal, -o] *a* nuptial; wedding *cpd*.

nuptialité [nypsjalite] *nf*: **taux de** ~ marriage rate.

nuque [nyk] *nf* nape of the neck.

nu-tête [nytɛt] *a inv* bareheaded.

nutritif, ive [nytʀitif, -iv] *a* nutritional; (*aliment*) nutritious, nourishing.

nutrition [nytʀisjɔ̃] *nf* nutrition.

nutritionnel, le [nytʀisjɔnɛl] *a* nutritional.

nutritionniste [nytʀisjɔnist(ə)] *nm/f* nutritionist.

nylon [nilɔ̃] *nm* nylon.

nymphomane [nɛ̃fɔman] *a*, *nf* nymphomaniac.

O

O, o [o] *nm inv* O, o ♦ *abr* (= *ouest*) W; **O comme Oscar** O for Oliver (*Brit*) *ou* Oboe (*US*).

OAS *sigle f* (= *Organisation de l'armée secrète*) *organization opposed to Algerian independence (1961-63)*.

oasis [ɔazis] *nf* oasis (*pl* oases).

obédience [ɔbedjɑ̃s] *nf* allegiance.

obéir [ɔbeiʀ] *vi* to obey; ~ **à** to obey; (*suj: moteur, véhicule*) to respond to.

obéissance [ɔbeisɑ̃s] *nf* obedience.

obéissant, e [ɔbeisɑ̃, -ɑ̃t] *a* obedient.

obélisque [ɔbelisk(ə)] *nm* obelisk.

obèse [ɔbɛz] *a* obese.

obésité [ɔbezite] *nf* obesity.

objecter [ɔbʒɛkte] *vt* (*prétexter*) to plead, put forward as an excuse; ~ **qch à** (*argument*) to put forward sth against; ~ **(à qn) que** to object (to sb) that.

objecteur [ɔbʒɛktœʀ] *nm*: ~ **de conscience** conscientious objector.

objectif, ive [ɔbʒɛktif, -iv] *a* objective ♦ *nm* (*OPTIQUE, PHOTO*) lens *sg*; (*MIL, fig*) objective; ~ **grand angulaire/à focale variable** wide-angle/zoom lens.

objection [ɔbʒɛksjɔ̃] *nf* objection; ~ **de conscience** conscientious objection.

objectivement [ɔbʒɛktivmã] *ad* objectively.

objectivité [ɔbʒɛktivite] *nf* objectivity.

objet [ɔbʒe] *nm* (*chose*) object; (*d'une discussion, recherche*) subject; **être** *ou* **faire l'**~ **de** (*discussion*) to be the subject of;

(*soins*) to be given *ou* shown; **sans** ~ *a* purposeless; (*sans fondement*) groundless; ~ **d'art** objet d'art; ~**s personnels** personal items; ~**s de toilette** toiletries; ~**s trouvés** lost property *sg* (*Brit*), lost-and-found *sg* (*US*).

objurgations [ɔbʒyʀgasjɔ̃] *nfpl* objurgations; (*prières*) entreaties.

obligataire [ɔbligatɛʀ] *a* bond *cpd* ♦ *nm/f* bondholder, debenture holder.

obligation [ɔbligasjɔ̃] *nf* obligation; (*gén pl: devoir*) duty; (*COMM*) bond, debenture; **sans** ~ **d'achat** with no obligation (to buy); **être dans l'**~ **de faire** to be obliged to do; **avoir l'**~ **de faire** to be under an obligation to do; ~**s familiales** family obligations *ou* responsibilities; ~**s militaires** military obligations *ou* duties.

obligatoire [ɔbligatwaʀ] *a* compulsory, obligatory.

obligatoirement [ɔbligatwaʀmã] *ad* compulsorily; (*fatalement*) necessarily.

obligé, e [ɔbliʒe] *a* (*redevable*): **être très** ~ **à qn** to be most obliged to sb; (*contraint*): **je suis (bien)** ~ **(de le faire)** I have to (do it); (*nécessaire: conséquence*) necessary; **c'est** ~**!** it's inevitable.

obligeamment [ɔbliʒamã] *ad* obligingly.

obligeance [ɔbliʒɑ̃s] *nf*: **avoir l'**~ **de** to be kind *ou* good enough to.

obligeant, e [ɔbliʒã, -ãt] *a* obliging; kind.

obliger [ɔbliʒe] *vt* (*contraindre*): ~ **qn à faire** to force *ou* oblige sb to do; (*JUR: engager*) to bind; (*rendre service à*) to oblige.

oblique [ɔblik] *a* oblique; **regard** ~ sidelong glance; **en** ~ *ad* diagonally.

obliquer [ɔblike] *vi*: ~ **vers** to turn off towards.

oblitération [ɔbliteʀasjɔ̃] *nf* cancelling *q*, cancellation; obstruction.

oblitérer [ɔbliteʀe] *vt* (*timbre-poste*) to cancel; (*MÉD: canal, vaisseau*) to obstruct.

oblong, oblongue [ɔblɔ̃, ɔblɔ̃g] *a* oblong.

obnubiler [ɔbnybile] *vt* to obsess.

obole [ɔbɔl] *nf* offering.

obscène [ɔpsɛn] *a* obscene.

obscénité [ɔpsenite] *nf* obscenity.

obscur, e [ɔpskyʀ] *a* (*sombre*) dark; (*fig: raisons*) obscure; (*: sentiment, malaise*) vague; (*: personne, vie*) humble, lowly.

obscurcir [ɔpskyʀsiʀ] *vt* to darken; (*fig*) to obscure; **s'**~ *vi* to grow dark.

obscurité [ɔpskyʀite] *nf* darkness; **dans l'**~ in the dark, in darkness; (*anonymat, médiocrité*) in obscurity.

obsédant, e [ɔpsedã, -ãt] *a* obsessive.

obsédé, e [ɔpsede] *nm/f* fanatic; ~**(e) sexuel(le)** sex maniac.

obséder [ɔpsede] *vt* to obsess, haunt.

obsèques [ɔpsɛk] *nfpl* funeral *sg*.

obséquieux, euse [ɔpsekjø, -øz] *a* obsequious.

observance [ɔpsɛʀvãs] *nf* observance.

observateur, trice [ɔpsɛʀvatœʀ, -tʀis] *a* observant, perceptive ♦ *nm/f* observer.

observation [ɔpsɛʀvasjɔ̃] *nf* observation; (*d'un règlement etc*) observance; (*commentaire*) observation, remark; (*reproche*) reproof; **en** ~ (*MÉD*) under observa-

tion.
observatoire [ɔpsɛRvatwaR] *nm* observatory;
(*lieu élevé*) observation post, vantage point.
observer [ɔpsɛRve] *vt* (*regarder*) to observe,
watch; (*examiner*) to examine;
(*scientifiquement, aussi: règlement, jeûne
etc*) to observe; (*surveiller*) to watch; (*remarquer*) to observe, notice; **faire ~ qch à
qn** (*dire*) to point out sth to sb; **s'~** (*se
surveiller*) to keep a check on o.s.
obsession [ɔpsesjɔ̃] *nf* obsession; **avoir l'~ de**
to have an obsession with.
obsessionnel, le [ɔpsesjɔnɛl] *a* obsessive.
obsolescent, e [ɔpsɔlesɑ̃, -ɑ̃t] *a* obsolescent.
obstacle [ɔpstakl(ə)] *nm* obstacle; (*ÉQUITA-
TION*) jump, hurdle; **faire ~ à** (*lumière*) to
block out; (*projet*) to hinder, put obstacles in
the path of; **~s antichars** tank defences.
obstétricien, ne [ɔpstetRisjɛ̃, -ɛn] *nm/f* obstetrician.
obstétrique [ɔpstetRik] *nf* obstetrics *sg*.
obstination [ɔpstinasjɔ̃] *nf* obstinacy.
obstiné, e [ɔpstine] *a* obstinate.
obstinément [ɔpstinemɑ̃] *ad* obstinately.
obstiner [ɔpstine]: **s'~** *vi* to insist, dig one's
heels in; **s'~ à faire** to persist (obstinately)
in doing; **s'~ sur qch** to keep working at sth,
labour away at sth.
obstruction [ɔpstRyksjɔ̃] *nf* obstruction, blockage; (*SPORT*) obstruction; **faire de l'~** (*fig*)
to be obstructive.
obstruer [ɔpstRye] *vt* to block, obstruct; **s'~** *vi*
to become blocked.
obtempérer [ɔptɑ̃peRe] *vi* to obey; **~ à** to
obey, comply with.
obtenir [ɔptəniR] *vt* to obtain, get; (*total*) to
arrive at, reach; (*résultat*) to achieve,
obtain; **~ de pouvoir faire** to obtain permission to do; **~ qch à qn** to obtain sth for sb;
~ de qn qu'il fasse to get sb to agree to
do(ing).
obtention [ɔptɑ̃sjɔ̃] *nf* obtaining.
obtenu, e [ɔpt(ə)ny] *pp de* **obtenir**.
obtiendrai [ɔptjɛ̃dRe], **obtiens** [ɔptjɛ̃], **obtint**
[ɔptɛ̃] *etc vb voir* **obtenir**.
obturateur [ɔptyRatœR] *nm* (*PHOTO*) shutter;
~ à rideau focal plane shutter.
obturation [ɔptyRasjɔ̃] *nf* closing (up); **~
(dentaire)** filling; **vitesse d'~** (*PHOTO*)
shutter speed.
obturer [ɔptyRe] *vt* to close (up); (*dent*) to fill.
obtus, e [ɔpty, -yz] *a* obtuse.
obus [ɔby] *nm* shell; **~ explosif** high-explosive
shell; **~ incendiaire** incendiary device, fire
bomb.
obvier [ɔbvje]: **~ à** *vt* to obviate.
OC *sigle fpl* (= *ondes courtes*) SW.
occasion [ɔkazjɔ̃] *nf* (*aubaine, possibilité*)
opportunity; (*circonstance*) occasion;
(*COMM: article non neuf*) secondhand buy; (:
acquisition avantageuse) bargain; **à plusieurs
~s** on several occasions; **à la première ~** at
the first *ou* earliest opportunity; **avoir l'~ de
faire** to have the opportunity to do; **être l'~
de** to occasion, give rise to; **à l'~** *ad* sometimes, on occasions; (*un jour*) some time; **à
l'~ de** on the occasion of; **d'~** *a*, *ad* secondhand.
occasionnel, le [ɔkazjɔnɛl] *a* (*fortuit*) chance

cpd; (*non régulier*) occasional; (: *travail*)
casual.
occasionner [ɔkazjɔne] *vt* to cause, bring
about; **~ qch à qn** to cause sb sth.
occident [ɔksidɑ̃] *nm*: **l'O~** the West.
occidental, e, aux [ɔksidɑ̃tal, -o] *a* western;
(*POL*) Western ♦ *nm/f* Westerner.
occidentaliser [ɔksidɑ̃talize] *vt* (*coutumes,
mœurs*) to westernize.
occiput [ɔksipyt] *nm* back of the head, occiput.
occire [ɔksiR] *vt* to slay.
occitan, e [ɔksitɑ̃, -an] *a* of the langue d'oc, of
Provençal French.
occlusion [ɔklyzjɔ̃] *nf*: **~ intestinale** obstruction of the bowel.
occulte [ɔkylt(ə)] *a* occult, supernatural.
occulter [ɔkylte] *vt* (*fig*) to overshadow.
occupant, e [ɔkypɑ̃, -ɑ̃t] *a* occupying ♦ *nm/f*
(*d'un appartement*) occupier, occupant; (*d'un
véhicule*) occupant ♦ *nm* (*MIL*) occupying forces *pl*; (*POL: d'usine etc*) occupier.
occupation [ɔkypasjɔ̃] *nf* occupation; **l'O~** the
Occupation (of France).
occupationnel, le [ɔkypasjɔnɛl] *a*: **thérapie
~le** occupational therapy.
occupé, e [ɔkype] *a* (*MIL, POL*) occupied;
(*personne: affairé, pris*) busy; (*esprit:
absorbé*) occupied; (*place, sièges*) taken;
(*toilettes, ligne*) engaged.
occuper [ɔkype] *vt* to occupy; (*poste, fonction*) to hold; (*main-d'œuvre*) to employ; **s'~
(à qch)** to occupy o.s. *ou* keep o.s. busy (with
sth); **s'~ de** (*être responsable de*) to be in
charge of; (*se charger de: affaire*) to take
charge of, deal with; (: *clients etc*) to attend
to; (*s'intéresser à, pratiquer: politique etc*)
to be involved in; **ça occupe trop de place** it
takes up too much room.
occurrence [ɔkyRɑ̃s] *nf*: **en l'~** in this case.
OCDE *sigle f* (= *Organisation de coopération
et de développement économique*) OECD.
océan [ɔseɑ̃] *nm* ocean; **l'~ Indien** the Indian
Ocean.
Océanie [ɔseani] *nf*: **l'~** Oceania, South Sea
Islands.
océanique [ɔseanik] *a* oceanic.
océanographe [ɔseanɔgraf] *nm/f* oceanog-
rapher.
océanographie [ɔseanɔgrafi] *nf* oceanog-
raphy.
océanologie [ɔseanɔlɔʒi] *nf* oceanology.
ocelot [ɔslo] *nm* (*ZOOL*) ocelot; (*fourrure*)
ocelot fur.
ocre [ɔkr(ə)] *a inv* ochre.
octane [ɔktan] *nm* octane.
octante [ɔktɑ̃t] *num* (*Belgique, Suisse*) eighty.
octave [ɔktav] *nf* octave.
octet [ɔktɛ] *nm* byte.
octobre [ɔktɔbr(ə)] *nm* October; *voir aussi*
juillet.
octogénaire [ɔktɔʒenɛR] *a, nm/f* octogenarian.
octogonal, e, aux [ɔktɔgɔnal, -o] *a* octagonal.
octogone [ɔktɔgɔn] *nm* octagon.
octroi [ɔktRwa] *nm* granting.
octroyer [ɔktRwaje] *vt*: **~ qch à qn** to grant
sth to sb, grant sb sth.
oculaire [ɔkylɛR] *a* ocular, eye *cpd* ♦ *nm* (*de
microscope*) eyepiece.
oculiste [ɔkylist(ə)] *nm/f* eye specialist, ocu-

list.

ode [ɔd] *nf* ode.

odeur [ɔdœʀ] *nf* smell.

odieusement [ɔdjøzmã] *ad* odiously.

odieux, euse [ɔdjø, -øz] *a* odious, hateful.

odontologie [ɔdɔ̃tɔlɔʒi] *nf* odontology.

odorant, e [ɔdɔʀã, -ãt] *a* sweet-smelling, fragrant.

odorat [ɔdɔʀa] *nm* (sense of) smell; **avoir l'~ fin** to have a keen sense of smell.

odoriférant, e [ɔdɔʀifeʀã, -ãt] *a* sweet-smelling, fragrant.

odyssée [ɔdise] *nf* odyssey.

OEA *sigle f* (= *Organisation des états américains*) OAS.

œcuménique [ekymenik] *a* ecumenical.

œdème [edɛm] *nm* oedema (*Brit*), edema (*US*).

œil [œj], *pl* **yeux** [jø] *nm* eye; **avoir un ~ poché** *ou* **au beurre noir** to have a black eye; **à l'~** (*fam*) for free; **à l'~ nu** with the naked eye; **tenir qn à l'~** to keep an eye *ou* a watch on sb; **avoir l'~ à** to keep an eye on; **faire de l'~ à qn** to make eyes at sb; **voir qch d'un bon/mauvais ~** to view sth in a favourable/an unfavourable light; **à l'~ vif** with a lively expression; **à mes/ses yeux** in my/his eyes; **de ses propres yeux** with his own eyes; **fermer les yeux (sur)** (*fig*) to turn a blind eye (to); **les yeux fermés** (*aussi fig*) with one's eyes shut; **fermer l'~** to get a moment's sleep; **~ pour ~, dent pour dent** an eye for an eye, a tooth for a tooth; **pour les beaux yeux de qn** (*fig*) for love of sb; **~ de verre** glass eye.

œil-de-bœuf, *pl* **œils-de-bœuf** [œjdəbœf] *nm* bull's-eye (window).

œillade [œjad] *nf:* **lancer une ~ à qn** to wink at sb, give sb a wink; **faire des ~s à** to make eyes at.

œillères [œjɛʀ] *nfpl* blinkers (*Brit*), blinders (*US*); **avoir des ~** (*fig*) to be blinkered, wear blinders.

œillet [œjɛ] *nm* (*BOT*) carnation; (*trou*) eyelet.

œnologue [enɔlɔg] *nm/f* wine expert.

œsophage [ezɔfaʒ] *nm* oesophagus (*Brit*), esophagus (*US*).

œstrogène [ɛstʀɔʒɛn] *a* oestrogen (*Brit*), estrogen (*US*).

œuf [œf, *pl* ø] *nm* egg; **étouffer dans l'~** to nip in the bud; **~ à la coque/dur/ mollet** boiled/hard-boiled/soft-boiled egg; **~ au plat/ poché** fried/poached egg; **~s brouillés** scrambled eggs; **~ de Pâques** Easter egg; **~ à repriser** darning egg.

œuvre [œvʀ(ə)] *nf* (*tâche*) task, undertaking; (*ouvrage achevé, livre, tableau etc*) work; (*ensemble de la production artistique*) works *pl*; (*organisation charitable*) charity ♦ *nm* (*d'un artiste*) works *pl*; (*CONSTR*): **le gros ~** the shell; **~s** *nfpl* (*actes*) deeds, works; **être/se mettre à l'~** to be at/get (down) to work; **mettre en ~** (*moyens*) to make use of; (*plan, loi, projet etc*) to implement; **~ d'art** work of art; **bonnes ~s** good works *ou* deeds; **~s de bienfaisance** charitable works.

OFCE *sigle m* (= *Observatoire français des conjonctures économiques*) economic research institute.

offensant, e [ɔfãsã, -ãt] *a* offensive, insulting.

offense [ɔfãs] *nf* (*affront*) insult; (*REL: péché*) transgression, trespass.

offenser [ɔfãse] *vt* to offend, hurt; (*principes, Dieu*) to offend against; **s'~ de** to take offence (*Brit*) *ou* offense (*US*) at.

offensif, ive [ɔfãsif, -iv] *a* (*armes, guerre*) offensive ♦ *nf* offensive; (*fig: du froid, de l'hiver*) onslaught; **passer à l'offensive** to go into the attack *ou* offensive.

offert, e [ɔfɛʀ, -ɛʀt] *pp de* **offrir**.

offertoire [ɔfɛʀtwaʀ] *nm* offertory.

office [ɔfis] *nm* (*charge*) office; (*agence*) bureau, agency; (*REL*) service ♦ *nm ou f* (*pièce*) pantry; **faire ~ de** to act as; to do duty as; **d'~** *ad* automatically; **bons ~s** (*POL*) good offices; **~ du tourisme** tourist bureau.

officialiser [ɔfisjalize] *vt* to make official.

officiel, le [ɔfisjɛl] *a, nm/f* official.

officiellement [ɔfisjɛlmã] *ad* officially.

officier [ɔfisje] *nm* officer ♦ *vi* (*REL*) to officiate; **~ de l'état-civil** registrar; **~ ministériel** member of the legal profession; **~ de police** ≈ police officer.

officieusement [ɔfisjøzmã] *ad* unofficially.

officieux, euse [ɔfisjø, -øz] *a* unofficial.

officinal, e, aux [ɔfisinal, -o] *a:* **plantes ~es** medicinal plants.

officine [ɔfisin] *nf* (*de pharmacie*) dispensary; (*ADMIN: pharmacie*) pharmacy; (*gén péj: bureau*) agency, office.

offrais [ɔfʀɛ] *etc vb voir* **offrir**.

offrande [ɔfʀãd] *nf* offering.

offrant [ɔfʀã] *nm:* **au plus ~** to the highest bidder.

offre [ɔfʀ(ə)] *vb voir* **offrir** ♦ *nf* offer; (*aux enchères: soumission*) tender; (*ÉCON*): **l'~** supply; **~ d'emploi** job advertised; **"~s d'emploi"** "situations vacant"; **~ publique d'achat (OPA)** takeover bid; **~s de service** offer of service.

offrir [ɔfʀiʀ] *vt:* **~ (à qn)** to offer (to sb); (*faire cadeau*) to give to (sb); **s'~** *vi* (*se présenter: occasion, paysage*) to present itself ♦ *vt* (*se payer: vacances, voiture*) to treat o.s. to; **~ (à qn) de faire qch** to offer to do sth (for sb); **~ à boire à qn** to offer sb a drink; **s'~ à faire qch** to offer *ou* volunteer to do sth; **s'~ comme guide/en otage** to offer one's services as (a) guide/offer o.s. as (a) hostage; **s'~ aux regards** (*suj: personne*) to expose o.s. to the public gaze.

offset [ɔfsɛt] *nm* offset (printing).

offusquer [ɔfyske] *vt* to offend; **s'~ de** to take offence (*Brit*) *ou* offense (*US*) at, be offended by.

ogive [ɔʒiv] *nf* (*ARCHIT*) diagonal rib; (*d'obus, de missile*) nose cone; **voûte en ~** rib vault; **arc en ~** lancet arch; **~ nucléaire** nuclear warhead.

ogre [ɔgʀ(ə)] *nm* ogre.

oh [o] *excl* oh!; **~ la la!** oh (dear)!; **pousser des ~! et des ah!** to gasp with admiration.

oie [wa] *nf* (*ZOOL*) goose (*pl* geese); **~ blanche** (*fig*) young innocent.

oignon [ɔɲɔ̃] *nm* (*CULIN*) onion; (*de tulipe etc: bulbe*) bulb; (*MÉD*) bunion; **ce ne sont**

pas tes ~s (*fam*) that's none of your business.

oindre [wɛ̃dʀ(ə)] *vt* to anoint.

oiseau, x [wazo] *nm* bird; **~ de proie** bird of prey.

oiseau-mouche, *pl* **oiseaux-mouches** [wazomuʃ] *nm* hummingbird.

oiseleur [wazlœʀ] *nm* bird-catcher.

oiselier, ière [wazəlje, -jɛʀ] *nm/f* bird-seller.

oisellerie [wazɛlʀi] *nf* bird shop.

oiseux, euse [wazø, -øz] *a* pointless, idle; (*sans valeur, importance*) trivial.

oisif, ive [wazif, -iv] *a* idle ♦ *nm/f* (*péj*) man/lady of leisure.

oisillon [wazijɔ̃] *nm* little ou baby bird.

oisiveté [wazivte] *nf* idleness.

OIT *sigle f* (= *Organisation internationale du travail*) ILO.

OK [okɛ] *excl* OK!, all right!

OL *sigle fpl* (= *ondes longues*) LW.

oléagineux, euse [ɔleaʒinø, -øz] *a* oleaginous, oil-producing.

oléiculture [ɔleikyltyʀ] *nm* olive growing.

oléoduc [ɔleɔdyk] *nm* (oil) pipeline.

olfactif, ive [ɔlfaktif, -iv] *a* olfactory.

olibrius [ɔlibʀijys] *nm* oddball.

oligarchie [ɔligaʀʃi] *nf* oligarchy.

oligo-élément [ɔligɔelemɑ̃] *nm* trace element.

oligopole [ɔligɔpɔl] *nm* oligopoly.

olivâtre [ɔlivɑtʀ(ə)] *a* olive-greenish; (*teint*) sallow.

olive [ɔliv] *nf* (*BOT*) olive ♦ *a inv* olive(-green).

oliveraie [ɔlivʀɛ] *nf* olive grove.

olivier [ɔlivje] *nm* olive (tree); (*bois*) olive (wood).

olographe [ɔlɔgʀaf] *a*: **testament ~** *will written, dated and signed by the testator.*

OLP *sigle f* (= *Organisation de libération de la Palestine*) PLO.

olympiade [ɔlɛ̃pjad] *nf* (*période*) Olympiad; **les ~s** (*jeux*) the Olympiad *sg*.

olympien, ne [ɔlɛ̃pjɛ̃, -ɛn] *a* Olympian, of Olympian aloofness.

olympique [ɔlɛ̃pik] *a* Olympic.

OM *sigle fpl* (= *ondes moyennes*) MW.

Oman [ɔman] *nm*: **l'~, le sultanat d'~** (the Sultanate of) Oman.

ombilical, e, aux [ɔ̃bilikal, -o] *a* umbilical.

ombrage [ɔ̃bʀaʒ] *nm* (*ombre*) (leafy) shade; (*fig*): **prendre ~ de** to take umbrage at; **faire** *ou* **porter ~ à qn** to offend sb.

ombragé, e [ɔ̃bʀaʒe] *a* shaded, shady.

ombrageux, euse [ɔ̃bʀaʒø, -øz] *a* (*cheval*) skittish, nervous; (*personne*) touchy, easily offended.

ombre [ɔ̃bʀ(ə)] *nf* (*espace non ensoleillé*) shade; (*ombre portée, tache*) shadow; **à l'~** in the shade; (*fam*: **en prison**) behind bars; **à l'~ de** in the shade of; (*tout près de, fig*) in the shadow of; **tu me fais de l'~** you're in my light; **ça nous donne de l'~** it gives us (some) shade; **il n'y a pas l'~ d'un doute** there's not the shadow of a doubt; **dans l'~** in the shade; **vivre dans l'~** (*fig*) to live in obscurity; **laisser dans l'~** (*fig*) to leave in the dark; **~ à paupières** eyeshadow; **~ portée** shadow; **~s chinoises** (*spectacle*) shadow show *sg*.

ombrelle [ɔ̃bʀɛl] *nf* parasol, sunshade.

ombrer [ɔ̃bʀe] *vt* to shade.

omelette [ɔmlɛt] *nf* omelette; **~ baveuse** runny omelette; **~ au fromage/au jambon** cheese/ham omelette; **~ aux herbes** omelette with herbs; **~ norvégienne** baked Alaska.

omettre [ɔmɛtʀ(ə)] *vt* to omit, leave out; **~ de faire** to fail *ou* omit to do.

omis, e [ɔmi, -iz] *pp de* **omettre**.

omission [ɔmisjɔ̃] *nf* omission.

omnibus [ɔmnibys] *nm* slow *ou* stopping train.

omnipotent, e [ɔmnipɔtɑ̃, -ɑ̃t] *a* omnipotent.

omnipraticien, ne [ɔmnipʀatisjɛ̃, -ɛn] *nm/f* (*MÉD*) general practitioner.

omniprésent, e [ɔmnipʀezɑ̃, -ɑ̃t] *a* omnipresent.

omniscient, e [ɔmnisjɑ̃, -ɑ̃t] *a* omniscient.

omnisports [ɔmnispɔʀ] *a inv* (*club*) general sports *cpd*; (*salle*) multi-purpose *cpd*; (*terrain*) all-purpose *cpd*.

omnium [ɔmnjɔm] *nm* (*COMM*) corporation; (*CYCLISME*) omnium; (*COURSES*) open handicap.

omnivore [ɔmnivɔʀ] *a* omnivorous.

omoplate [ɔmɔplat] *nf* shoulder blade.

OMS *sigle f* (= *Organisation mondiale de la santé*) WHO.

on [ɔ̃] *pronom* (*indéterminé*): **~ peut le faire ainsi** you *ou* one can do it like this, it can be done like this; (*quelqu'un*): **~ les a attaqués** they were attacked; (*nous*): **~ va y aller demain** we're going tomorrow; (*les gens*): **autrefois, ~ croyait aux fantômes** they used to believe in ghosts years ago; (*ironiquement, affectueusement*): **alors, ~ se promène?** off for a stroll then, are we?; **~ y va!** let's go!; **~ y va?** are we going?; **~ vous demande au téléphone** there's a phone call for you, there's somebody on the phone for you; **~ ne peut plus** *ad*: **~ ne peut plus stupide** as stupid as can be.

once [ɔ̃s] *nf*: **une ~ de** an ounce of.

oncle [ɔ̃kl(ə)] *nm* uncle.

onction [ɔ̃ksjɔ̃] *nf voir* **extrême-onction**.

onctueux, euse [ɔ̃ktɥø, -øz] *a* creamy, smooth; (*fig*) smooth, unctuous.

onde [ɔ̃d] *nf* (*PHYSIQUE*) wave; **sur l'~** on the waters; **sur les ~s** on the radio; **mettre en ~s** to produce for the radio; **~ de choc** shock wave; **~s courtes (OC)** short wave *sg*; **petites ~s (PO)**, **~s moyennes (OM)** medium wave *sg*; **grandes ~s (GO)**, **~s longues (OL)** long wave *sg*; **~s sonores** sound waves.

ondée [ɔ̃de] *nf* shower.

on-dit [ɔ̃di] *nm inv* rumour.

ondoyer [ɔ̃dwaje] *vi* to ripple, wave ♦ *vt* (*REL*) to baptize (*in an emergency*).

ondulant, e [ɔ̃dylɑ̃, -ɑ̃t] *a* (*démarche*) swaying; (*ligne*) undulating.

ondulation [ɔ̃dylɑsjɔ̃] *nf* undulation; wave.

ondulé, e [ɔ̃dyle] *a* undulating; wavy.

onduler [ɔ̃dyle] *vi* to undulate; (*cheveux*) to wave.

onéreux, euse [ɔneʀø, -øz] *a* costly; **à titre ~** in return for payment.

ONF *sigle m* (= *Office national des forêts*) ≈ Forestry Commission (*Brit*), ≈ National Forest Service (*US*).

ongle [ɔ̃gl(ə)] *nm* (*ANAT*) nail; **manger** *ou* **ronger ses** ~**s** to bite one's nails; **se faire les** ~**s** to do one's nails.

onglet [ɔ̃glɛ] *nm* (*rainure*) (thumbnail) groove; (*bande de papier*) tab.

onguent [ɔ̃gɑ̃] *nm* ointment.

onirique [ɔniʀik] *a* dreamlike, dream *cpd*.

onirisme [ɔniʀism(ə)] *nm* dreams *pl.*

onomatopée [ɔnɔmatɔpe] *nf* onomatopoeia.

ont [ɔ̃] *vb voir* **avoir**.

ontarien, ne [ɔ̃taʀjɛ̃, -ɛn] *a* Ontarian.

ONU [ɔny] *sigle f* (= *Organisation des Nations Unies*) UN(O).

onusien, ne [ɔnyzjɛ̃, -ɛn] *a* of the UN(O), of the United Nations (Organization).

onyx [ɔniks] *nm* onyx.

onze [ɔ̃z] *num* eleven.

onzième [ɔ̃zjɛm] *num* eleventh.

op [ɔp] *nf* (= *opération*): **salle d'**~ (operating) theatre.

OPA *sigle f* = **offre publique d'achat**.

opacité [ɔpasite] *nf* opaqueness.

opale [ɔpal] *nf* opal.

opalescent, e [ɔpalesɑ̃, -ɑ̃t] *a* opalescent.

opalin, e [ɔpalɛ̃, -in] *a*, *nf* opaline.

opaque [ɔpak] *a* (*vitre*, *verre*) opaque; (*brouillard*, *nuit*) impenetrable.

OPE *sigle f* (= *offre publique d'échange*) take-over bid where bidder offers shares in his company in exchange for shares in target company.

OPEP [ɔpɛp] *sigle f* (= *Organisation des pays exportateurs de pétrole*) OPEC.

opéra [ɔpeʀa] *nm* opera; (*édifice*) opera house.

opérable [ɔpeʀabl(ə)] *a* operable.

opéra-comique, *pl* **opéras-comiques** [ɔpeʀakɔmik] *nm* light opera, opéra comique.

opérant, e [ɔpeʀɑ̃, -ɑ̃t] *a* (*mesure*) effective.

opérateur, trice [ɔpeʀatœʀ, -tʀis] *nm/f* operator; ~ **(de prise de vues)** cameraman.

opération [ɔpeʀasjɔ̃] *nf* operation; (*COMM*) dealing; **salle/table d'**~ operating theatre/table; ~ **de sauvetage** rescue operation; ~ **à cœur ouvert** open-heart surgery *q*.

opérationel, le [ɔpeʀasjɔnɛl] *a* operational.

opératoire [ɔpeʀatwaʀ] *a* (*manœuvre*, *méthode*) operating; (*choc etc*) post-operative.

opéré, e [ɔpeʀe] *nm/f* post-operative patient.

opérer [ɔpeʀe] *vt* (*MÉD*) to operate on; (*faire*, *exécuter*) to carry out, make ♦ *vi* (*remède*: *faire effet*) to act, work; (*procéder*) to proceed; (*MÉD*) to operate; **s'**~ *vi* (*avoir lieu*) to occur, take place; **se faire** ~ to have an operation; **se faire** ~ **des amygdales/du cœur** to have one's tonsils out/have a heart operation.

opérette [ɔpeʀɛt] *nf* operetta, light opera.

ophtalmique [ɔftalmik] *a* ophthalmic.

ophtalmologie [ɔftalmɔlɔʒi] *nf* ophthalmology.

ophtalmologue [ɔftalmɔlɔg] *nm/f* ophthalmologist.

opiacé, e [ɔpjase] *a* opiate.

opiner [ɔpine] *vi*: ~ **de la tête** to nod assent ♦ *vt*: ~ **à** to consent to.

opiniâtre [ɔpinjatʀ(ə)] *a* stubborn.

opiniâtreté [ɔpinjatʀəte] *nf* stubbornness.

opinion [ɔpinjɔ̃] *nf* opinion; **l'**~ **(publique)** public opinion; **avoir bonne/mauvaise** ~ **de** to have a high/low opinion of.

opiomane [ɔpjɔman] *nm/f* opium addict.

opium [ɔpjɔm] *nm* opium.

OPJ *sigle m* (= *officier de police judiciaire*) ≈ DC (= *Detective Constable*).

opportun, e [ɔpɔʀtœ̃, -yn] *a* timely, opportune; **en temps** ~ at the appropriate time.

opportunément [ɔpɔʀtynemɑ̃] *ad* opportunely.

opportunisme [ɔpɔʀtynism(ə)] *nm* opportunism.

opportuniste [ɔpɔʀtynist(ə)] *a*, *nm/f* opportunist.

opportunité [ɔpɔʀtynite] *nf* timeliness, opportuneness.

opposant, e [ɔpozɑ̃, -ɑ̃t] *a* opposing ♦ *nm/f* opponent.

opposé, e [ɔpoze] *a* (*direction*, *rive*) opposite; (*faction*) opposing; (*couleurs*) contrasting; (*opinions*, *intérêts*) conflicting; (*contre*): ~ **à** opposed to, against ♦ *nm*: **l'**~ the other *ou* opposite side (*ou* direction); (*contraire*) the opposite; **être** ~ **à** to be opposed to; **à l'**~ (*fig*) on the other hand; **à l'**~ **de** on the other *ou* opposite side from; (*fig*) contrary to, unlike.

opposer [ɔpoze] *vt* (*meubles*, *objets*) to place opposite each other; (*personnes*, *armées*, *équipes*) to oppose; (*couleurs*, *termes*, *tons*) to contrast; (*comparer*: *livres*, *avantages*) to contrast; ~ **qch à** (*comme obstacle*, *défense*) to set sth against; (*comme objection*) to put sth forward against; (*en contraste*) to set sth opposite; to match sth with; **s'**~ (*sens réciproque*) to conflict; to clash; to face each other; to contrast; **s'**~ **à** (*interdire*, *empêcher*) to oppose; (*tenir tête à*) to rebel against; **sa religion s'y oppose** it's against his religion; **s'**~ **à ce que qn fasse** to be opposed to sb's doing.

opposition [ɔpozisjɔ̃] *nf* opposition; **par** ~ in contrast; **par** ~ **à** as opposed to, in contrast with; **entrer en** ~ **avec** to come into conflict with; **être en** ~ **avec** (*idées*, *conduite*) to be at variance with; **faire** ~ **à un chèque** to stop a cheque.

oppressant, e [ɔpʀesɑ̃, -ɑ̃t] *a* oppressive.

oppresser [ɔpʀese] *vt* to oppress; **se sentir oppressé** to feel breathless.

oppresseur [ɔpʀesœʀ] *nm* oppressor.

oppressif, ive [ɔpʀesif, -iv] *a* oppressive.

oppression [ɔpʀesjɔ̃] *nf* oppression; (*malaise*) feeling of suffocation.

opprimer [ɔpʀime] *vt* (*asservir*: *peuple*, *faibles*) to oppress; (*étouffer*: *liberté*, *opinion*) to suppress, stifle; (*suj*: *chaleur etc*) to suffocate, oppress.

opprobre [ɔpʀɔbʀ(ə)] *nm* disgrace.

opter [ɔpte] *vi*: ~ **pour** to opt for; ~ **entre** to choose between.

opticien, ne [ɔptisjɛ̃, -ɛn] *nm/f* optician.

optimal, e, aux [ɔptimal, -o] *a* optimal.

optimisation [ɔptimizasjɔ̃] *nf* optimization.

optimiser [ɔptimize] *vt* to optimize.

optimisme [ɔptimism(ə)] *nm* optimism.

optimiste [ɔptimist(ə)] *a* optimistic ♦ *nm/f*

optimist.

optimum [ɔptimɔm] *a, nm* optimum.

option [ɔpsjɔ̃] *nf* option; (*AUTO: supplément*) optional extra; **matière à** ~ (*SCOL*) optional subject (*Brit*), elective (*US*); **prendre une** ~ **sur** to take (out) an option on; ~ **par défaut** (*INFORM*) default (option).

optionnel, le [ɔpsjɔnɛl] *a* optional.

optique [ɔptik] *a* (*nerf*) optic; (*verres*) optical ♦ *nf* (*PHOTO: lentilles etc*) optics *pl*; (*science, industrie*) optics *sg*; (*fig: manière de voir*) perspective.

opulence [ɔpylɑ̃s] *nf* wealth, opulence.

opulent, e [ɔpylɑ̃, -ɑ̃t] *a* wealthy, opulent; (*formes, poitrine*) ample, generous.

or [ɔʀ] *nm* gold ♦ *cj* now, but; **d'**~ (*fig*) golden; **en** ~ gold *cpd*; (*occasion*) golden; **un mari/enfant en** ~ a treasure; **une affaire en** ~ (*achat*) a real bargain; (*commerce*) a gold mine; **plaqué** ~ gold-plated; ~ **noir** black gold.

oracle [ɔʀɑkl(ə)] *nm* oracle.

orage [ɔʀaʒ] *nm* (thunder)storm.

orageux, euse [ɔʀaʒø, -øz] *a* stormy.

oraison [ɔʀɛzɔ̃] *nf* orison, prayer; ~ **funèbre** funeral oration.

oral, e, aux [ɔʀal, -o] *a* (*déposition, promesse*) oral, verbal; (*MÉD*): **par voie** ~**e** by mouth, orally ♦ *nm* (*SCOL*) oral.

oralement [ɔʀalmɑ̃] *ad* orally.

orange [ɔʀɑ̃ʒ] *a inv, nf* orange; ~ **sanguine** blood orange; ~ **pressée** freshly-squeezed orange juice.

orangé, e [ɔʀɑ̃ʒe] *a* orangey, orange-coloured.

orangeade [ɔʀɑ̃ʒad] *nf* orangeade.

oranger [ɔʀɑ̃ʒe] *nm* orange tree.

orangeraie [ɔʀɑ̃ʒʀɛ] *nf* orange grove.

orangerie [ɔʀɑ̃ʒʀi] *nf* orangery.

orang-outan(g) [ɔʀɑ̃utɑ̃] *nm* orang-utan.

orateur [ɔʀatœʀ] *nm* speaker; orator.

oratoire [ɔʀatwaʀ] *nm* (*lieu, chapelle*) oratory; (*au bord du chemin*) wayside shrine ♦ *a* oratorical.

oratorio [ɔʀatɔʀjo] *nm* oratorio.

orbital, e, aux [ɔʀbital, -o] *a* orbital; **station** ~**e** space station.

orbite [ɔʀbit] *nf* (*ANAT*) (eye-)socket; (*PHYSIQUE*) orbit; **mettre sur** ~ to put into orbit; (*fig*) to launch; **dans l'**~ **de** (*fig*) within the sphere of influence of.

Orcades [ɔʀkad] *nfpl*: **les** ~ the Orkneys, the Orkney Islands.

orchestral, e, aux [ɔʀkɛstʀal, -o] *a* orchestral.

orchestrateur, trice [ɔʀkɛstʀatœʀ, -tʀis] *nm/f* orchestrator.

orchestration [ɔʀkɛstʀasjɔ̃] *nf* orchestration.

orchestre [ɔʀkɛstʀ(ə)] *nm* orchestra; (*de jazz, danse*) band; (*places*) stalls *pl* (*Brit*), orchestra (*US*).

orchestrer [ɔʀkɛstʀe] *vt* (*MUS*) to orchestrate; (*fig*) to mount, stage-manage.

orchidée [ɔʀkide] *nf* orchid.

ordinaire [ɔʀdinɛʀ] *a* ordinary; (*coutumier: maladresse etc*) usual; (*de tous les jours*) everyday; (*modèle, qualité*) standard ♦ *nm* ordinary; (*menus*) everyday fare ♦ *nf* (*essence*) ≈ two-star (petrol) (*Brit*), ≈ regular (gas) (*US*); **d'**~ usually, normally; **à l'**~

usually, ordinarily.

ordinairement [ɔʀdinɛʀmɑ̃] *ad* ordinarily, usually.

ordinal, e, aux [ɔʀdinal, -o] *a* ordinal.

ordinateur [ɔʀdinatœʀ] *nm* computer; **mettre sur** ~ to computerize, put on computer; ~ **domestique** home computer; ~ **individuel** *ou* **personnel** personal computer.

ordination [ɔʀdinasjɔ̃] *nf* ordination.

ordonnance [ɔʀdɔnɑ̃s] *nf* organization; (*groupement, disposition*) layout; (*MÉD*) prescription; (*JUR*) order; (*MIL*) orderly, batman (*Brit*); **d'**~ (*MIL*) regulation *cpd*; **officier d'**~ aide-de-camp.

ordonnateur, trice [ɔʀdɔnatœʀ, -tʀis] *nm/f* (*d'une cérémonie, fête*) organizer; ~ **des pompes funèbres** funeral director.

ordonné, e [ɔʀdɔne] *a* tidy, orderly; (*MATH*) ordered ♦ *nf* (*MATH*) Y-axis, ordinate.

ordonner [ɔʀdɔne] *vt* (*agencer*) to organize, arrange; (: *meubles, appartement*) to lay out, arrange; (*donner un ordre*): ~ **à qn de faire** to order sb to do; (*MATH*) to (arrange in) order; (*REL*) to ordain; (*MÉD*) to prescribe; (*JUR*) to order; **s'**~ (*faits*) to organize themselves.

ordre [ɔʀdʀ(ə)] *nm* (*gén*) order; (*propreté et soin*) orderliness, tidiness; (*association professionnelle, honorifique*) association; (*COMM*): **à l'**~ **de** payable to; (*nature*): **d'**~ **pratique** of a practical nature; ~**s** *nmpl* (*REL*) holy orders; **avoir de l'**~ to be tidy *ou* orderly; **mettre en** ~ to tidy (up), put in order; **mettre bon** ~ **à** to put things to rights, sort out; **procéder par** ~ to take things one at a time; **être aux** ~**s de qn/sous les** ~**s de qn** to be at sb's disposal/under sb's command; **rappeler qn à l'**~ to call sb to order; **jusqu'à nouvel** ~ until further notice; **dans le même** ~ **d'idées** in this connection; **par** ~ **d'entrée en scène** in order of appearance; **un** ~ **de grandeur** some idea of the size (*ou* amount); **de premier** ~ first-rate; ~ **de grève** strike call; ~ **du jour** (*d'une réunion*) agenda; (*MIL*) order of the day; **à l'**~ **du jour** on the agenda; (*fig*) topical; (*MIL*: *citer*) in dispatches; ~ **de mission** (*MIL*) orders *pl*; ~ **public** law and order; ~ **de route** marching orders *pl*.

ordure [ɔʀdyʀ] *nf* filth *q*; (*propos, écrit*) obscenity, (piece of) filth; ~**s** *nfpl* (*balayures, déchets*) rubbish *sg*, refuse *sg*; ~**s ménagères** household refuse.

ordurier, ière [ɔʀdyʀje, -jɛʀ] *a* lewd, filthy.

oreille [ɔʀɛj] *nf* (*ANAT*) ear; (*de marmite, tasse*) handle; (*TECH: d'un écrou*) wing; **avoir de l'**~ to have a good ear (for music); **avoir l'**~ **fine** to have good *ou* sharp ears; **l'**~ **basse** crestfallen, dejected; **se faire tirer l'**~ to take a lot of persuading; **dire qch à l'**~ **de qn** to have a word in sb's ear (about sth).

oreiller [ɔʀɛje] *nm* pillow.

oreillette [ɔʀɛjɛt] *nf* (*ANAT*) auricle.

oreillons [ɔʀɛjɔ̃] *nmpl* mumps *sg*.

ores [ɔʀ]: **d'**~ **et déjà** *ad* already.

orfèvre [ɔʀfɛvʀ(ə)] *nm* goldsmith; silversmith.

orfèvrerie [ɔʀfɛvʀəʀi] *nf* (*art, métier*) goldsmith's (*ou* silversmith's) trade; (*ouvrage*) (silver *ou* gold) plate.

orfraie [ɔRfRɛ] nm white-tailed eagle; **pousser des cris d'~** to yell at the top of one's voice.

organe [ɔRgan] nm organ; (véhicule, instrument) instrument; (voix) voice; (porte-parole) representative, mouthpiece; **~s de commande** (TECH) controls; **~s de transmission** (TECH) transmission system sg.

organigramme [ɔRganigRam] nm (hiérarchique, structurel) organization chart; (des opérations) flow chart.

organique [ɔRganik] a organic.

organisateur, trice [ɔRganizatœR, -tRis] nm/f organizer.

organisation [ɔRganizasjɔ̃] nf organization; **O~ des Nations Unies (ONU)** United Nations (Organization) (UN, UNO); **O~ mondiale de la santé (OMS)** World Health Organization (WHO); **O~ du traité de l'Atlantique Nord (OTAN)** North Atlantic Treaty Organization (NATO).

organisationnel, le [ɔRganizasjɔnɛl] a organizational.

organiser [ɔRganize] vt to organize; (mettre sur pied: service etc) to set up; **s'~** to get organized.

organisme [ɔRganism(ə)] nm (BIO) organism; (corps humain) body; (ADMIN, POL etc) body, organism.

organiste [ɔRganist(ə)] nm/f organist.

orgasme [ɔRgasm(ə)] nm orgasm, climax.

orge [ɔR(ʒ(ə)] nf barley.

orgeat [ɔRʒa] nm: **sirop d'~** barley water.

orgelet [ɔRʒəlɛ] nm sty(e).

orgie [ɔRʒi] nf orgy.

orgue [ɔRg(ə)] nm organ; **~s** nfpl organ sg; **~ de Barbarie** barrel ou street organ.

orgueil [ɔRgœj] nm pride.

orgueilleux, euse [ɔRgœjø, -øz] a proud.

Orient [ɔRjɑ̃] nm: **l'~** the East, the Orient.

orientable [ɔRjɑ̃tabl(ə)] a (phare, lampe etc) adjustable.

oriental, e, aux [ɔRjɑ̃tal, -o] a oriental, eastern; (frontière) eastern ♦ nm/f: **O~, e** O-riental.

orientation [ɔRjɑ̃tasjɔ̃] nf positioning; adjustment; orientation; direction; (d'une maison etc) aspect; (d'un journal) leanings pl; **avoir le sens de l'~** to have a (good) sense of direction; **course d'~** orienteering exercise; **~ professionnelle** careers advice ou guidance; (service) careers advisory service.

orienté, e [ɔRjɑ̃te] a (fig: article, journal) slanted; **bien/mal ~** (appartement) well/badly positioned; **~ au sud** facing south, with a southern aspect.

orienter [ɔRjɑ̃te] vt (situer) to position; (placer, disposer: pièce mobile) to adjust, position; (tourner) to direct, turn; (voyageur, touriste, recherches) to direct; (fig: élève) to orientate; **s'~** (se repérer) to find one's bearings; **s'~ vers** (fig) to turn towards.

orienteur, euse [ɔRjɑ̃tœR, -øz] nm/f (SCOL) careers adviser.

orifice [ɔRifis] nm opening, orifice.

oriflamme [ɔRiflam] nf banner, standard.

origan [ɔRigɑ̃] nm oregano.

originaire [ɔRiʒinɛR] a original; **être ~ de** (pays, lieu) to be a native of; (provenir de) to originate from; to be native to.

original, e, aux [ɔRiʒinal, -o] a original; (bizarre) eccentric ♦ nm/f (fam: excentrique) eccentric; (: fantaisiste) joker ♦ nm (document etc, ART) original; (dactylographie) top copy.

originalité [ɔRiʒinalite] nf (d'un nouveau modèle) originality q; (excentricité, bizarrerie) eccentricity.

origine [ɔRiʒin] nf origin; (d'un message, appel téléphonique) source; (d'une révolution, réussite) root; **~s** nfpl (d'une personne) origins; **d'~** of origin; (pneus etc) original; (bureau postal) dispatching; **d'~ française** of French origin; **dès l'~** at ou from the outset; **à l'~** originally; **avoir son ~ dans** to have its origins in, originate in.

originel, le [ɔRiʒinɛl] a original.

originellement [ɔRiʒinɛlmɑ̃] ad (à l'origine) originally; (dès l'origine) from the beginning.

oripeaux [ɔRipo] nmpl rags.

ORL sigle f (= oto-rhino-laryngologie) ENT ♦ sigle m/f (= oto-rhino-laryngologiste) ENT specialist; **être en ~** (malade) to be in the ENT hospital ou department.

orme [ɔRm(ə)] nm elm.

orné, e [ɔRne] a ornate; **~ de** adorned ou decorated with.

ornement [ɔRnəmɑ̃] nm ornament; (fig) embellishment, adornment; **~s sacerdotaux** vestments.

ornemental, e, aux [ɔRnəmɑ̃tal, -o] a ornamental.

ornementer [ɔRnəmɑ̃te] vt to ornament.

orner [ɔRne] vt to decorate, adorn; **~ qch de** to decorate sth with.

ornière [ɔRnjɛR] nf rut; (fig): **sortir de l'~** (routine) to get out of the rut; (impasse) to get out of a spot.

ornithologie [ɔRnitɔlɔʒi] nf ornithology.

ornithologue [ɔRnitɔlɔg] nm/f ornithologist; **~ amateur** birdwatcher.

orphelin, e [ɔRfəlɛ̃, -in] a orphan(ed) ♦ nm/f orphan; **~ de père/mère** fatherless/motherless.

orphelinat [ɔRfəlina] nm orphanage.

ORSEC [ɔRsɛk] sigle f (= Organisation des secours): **le plan ~** disaster contingency plan.

ORSECRAD [ɔRsɛkRad] sigle m = ORSEC en cas d'accident nucléaire.

orteil [ɔRtɛj] nm toe; **gros ~** big toe.

ORTF sigle m (= Office de radio-diffusion télévision française) (formerly) French broadcasting corporation.

orthodontiste [ɔRtɔdɔ̃tist(ə)] nm/f orthodontist.

orthodoxe [ɔRtɔdɔks(ə)] a orthodox.

orthodoxie [ɔRtɔdɔksi] nf orthodoxy.

orthogénie [ɔRtɔʒeni] nf family planning.

orthographe [ɔRtɔgRaf] nf spelling.

orthographier [ɔRtɔgRafje] vt to spell; **mal orthographié** misspelt.

orthopédie [ɔRtɔpedi] nf orthopaedics sg (Brit), orthopedics (US).

orthopédique [ɔRtɔpedik] a orthopaedic (Brit), orthopedic (US).

orthopédiste [ɔRtɔpedist(ə)] nm/f orthopaedic (Brit) ou orthopedic (US) specialist.

orthophonie [ɔRtɔfɔni] nf (MÉD) speech

therapy; (*LING*) correct pronunciation.

orthophoniste [ɔʀtɔfɔnist(ə)] *nm/f* speech therapist.

ortie [ɔʀti] *nf* (stinging) nettle; ~ **blanche** white dead-nettle.

OS *sigle m* = **ouvrier spécialisé**.

os [ɔs, *pl* o] *nm* bone; **sans** ~ (*BOUCHERIE*) off the bone, boned; ~ **à moelle** marrowbone.

oscillation [ɔsilasjɔ̃] *nf* oscillation; ~**s** *nfpl* (*fig*) fluctuations.

osciller [ɔsile] *vi* (*pendule*) to swing; (*au vent etc*) to rock; (*TECH*) to oscillate; (*fig*): ~ **entre** to waver *ou* fluctuate between.

osé, e [oze] *a* daring, bold.

oseille [ozɛj] *nf* sorrel.

oser [oze] *vi, vt* to dare; ~ **faire** to dare (to) do.

osier [ozje] *nm* (*BOT*) willow; **d'**~, **en** ~ wicker(work) *cpd*.

Oslo [ɔslo] *n* Oslo.

osmose [ɔsmoz] *nf* osmosis.

ossature [ɔsatyʀ] *nf* (*ANAT*: *squelette*) frame, skeletal structure; (: *du visage*) bone structure; (*fig*) framework.

osselet [ɔslɛ] *nm* (*ANAT*) ossicle; **jouer aux** ~**s** to play jacks.

ossements [ɔsmɑ̃] *nmpl* bones.

osseux, euse [ɔsø, -øz] *a* bony; (*tissu, maladie, greffe*) bone *cpd*.

ossifier [ɔsifje]: **s'**~ *vi* to ossify.

ossuaire [ɔsɥɛʀ] *nm* ossuary.

Ostende [ɔstɑ̃d] *n* Ostend.

ostensible [ɔstɑ̃sibl(ə)] *a* conspicuous.

ostensiblement [ɔstɑ̃sibləmɑ̃] *ad* conspicuously.

ostensoir [ɔstɑ̃swaʀ] *nm* monstrance.

ostentation [ɔstɑ̃tasjɔ̃] *nf* ostentation; **faire** ~ **de** to parade, make a display of.

ostentatoir [ɔstɑ̃tatwaʀ] *a* ostentatious.

ostracisme [ɔstʀasism(ə)] *nm* ostracism; **frapper d'**~ to ostracize.

ostréicole [ɔstʀeikɔl] *a* oyster *cpd*.

ostréiculture [ɔstʀeikyltyʀ] *nf* oyster-farming.

otage [ɔtaʒ] *nm* hostage; **prendre qn comme** ~ to take sb hostage.

OTAN [ɔtɑ̃] *sigle f* (= *Organisation du traité de l'Atlantique Nord*) NATO.

otarie [ɔtaʀi] *nf* sea-lion.

OTASE [ɔtaz] *sigle f* (= *Organisation du traité de l'Asie du Sud-Est*) SEATO (= *Southeast Asia Treaty Organization*).

ôter [ote] *vt* to remove; (*soustraire*) to take away; ~ **qch à qn** to take sth (away) from sb; ~ **qch de** to remove sth from; **6 ôté de 10 égale 4** 6 from 10 equals *ou* is 4.

otite [ɔtit] *nf* ear infection.

oto-rhino(-laryngologiste) [ɔtɔʀino(laʀɛ̃gɔlɔʒist(ə))] *nm/f* ear, nose and throat specialist.

ottomane [ɔtɔman] *nf* ottoman.

ou [u] *cj* or; ~ ... ~ either ... or; ~ **bien** or (else).

où [u] *ad, pronom* where; (*dans lequel*) in which, into which; from which, out of which; (*hors duquel, duquel*) from which; (*sur lequel*) on which; (*sens de 'que'*): **au train** ~ **ça va/prix** ~ **c'est** at the rate it's going/price it is; **le jour** ~ **il est parti** the day (that) he left; **par** ~ **passer?** which way should we

go?; **les villes par** ~ **il est passé** the towns he went through; **le village d'**~ **je viens** the village I come from; **la chambre** ~ **il était** the room he was in; **d'**~ **vient qu'il est parti?** how is it that he left?, how come he left?

OUA *sigle f* (= *Organisation de l'unité africaine*) OAU (= *Organization of African Unity*).

ouais [wɛ] *excl* yeah.

ouate [wat] *nf* cotton wool (*Brit*), cotton (*US*); (*bourre*) padding, wadding; ~ **(hydrophile)** cotton wool (*Brit*), (absorbent) cotton (*US*).

ouaté, e [wate] *a* cotton-wool; (*doublé*) padded; (*fig: atmosphère*) cocoon-like; (: *pas, bruit*) muffled.

oubli [ubli] *nm* (*acte*): **l'**~ **de** forgetting; (*étourderie*) forgetfulness *q*; (*négligence*) omission, oversight; (*absence de souvenirs*) oblivion; ~ **de soi** self-effacement, self-negation.

oublier [ublije] *vt* (*gén*) to forget; (*ne pas voir: erreurs etc*) to miss; (*ne pas mettre: virgule, nom*) to leave out, forget; (*laisser quelque part: chapeau etc*) to leave behind; **s'**~ to forget o.s; (*enfant, animal*) to have an accident (*euphemism*); ~ **l'heure** to forget (about) the time.

oubliettes [ublijɛt] *nfpl* dungeon *sg*; **(jeter) aux** ~ (*fig*) to put) completely out of mind.

oublieux, euse [ublijø, -øz] *a* forgetful.

oued [wɛd] *nm* wadi.

ouest [wɛst] *nm* west ♦ *a inv* west; (*région*) western; **à l'**~ in the west; (to the) west, westwards; **à l'**~ **de** (to the) west of; **vent d'**~ westerly wind.

ouest-allemand, e [wɛstalmɑ̃, -ɑ̃d] *a* West German.

ouf [uf] *excl* phew!

Ouganda [ugɑ̃da] *nm*: **l'**~ Uganda.

ougandais, e [ugɑ̃dɛ, -ɛz] *a* Ugandan.

oui [wi] *ad* yes; **répondre (par)** ~ to answer yes; **mais** ~, **bien sûr** ~, of course; **je pense que** ~ I think so; **pour un** ~ **ou pour un non** for no apparent reason.

ouï-dire [widiʀ]: **par** ~ *ad* by hearsay.

ouïe [wi] *nf* hearing; ~**s** *nfpl* (*de poisson*) gills; (*de violon*) sound-hole *sg*.

ouïr [wiʀ] *vt* to hear; **avoir ouï dire que** to have heard it said that.

ouistiti [wistiti] *nm* marmoset.

ouragan [uʀagɑ̃] *nm* hurricane; (*fig*) storm.

Oural [uʀal] *nm*: **l'**~ (*fleuve*) the Ural; (*aussi*: **les monts** ~) the Urals, the Ural Mountains.

ouralo-altaïque [uʀalɔaltaik] *a*, *nm* Ural-Altaic.

ourdir [uʀdiʀ] *vt* (*complot*) to hatch.

ourdou [uʀdu] *a inv* Urdu ♦ *nm* (*LING*) Urdu.

ourlé, e [uʀle] *a* hemmed; (*fig*) rimmed.

ourler [uʀle] *vt* to hem.

ourlet [uʀlɛ] *nm* hem; (*de l'oreille*) rim; **faire un** ~ **à** to hem.

ours [uʀs] *nm* bear; ~ **brun/blanc** brown/polar bear; ~ **marin** fur seal; ~ **mal léché** uncouth fellow; ~ **(en peluche)** teddy (bear).

ourse [uʀs(ə)] *nf* (*ZOOL*) she-bear; **la Grande/Petite O**~ the Great/Little Bear, Ursa Major/Minor.

oursin [uʀsɛ̃] *nm* sea urchin.

ourson [ursɔ̃] *nm* (bear-)cub.

ouste [ust(ə)] *excl* hop it!

outil [uti] *nm* tool.

outillage [utijaʒ] *nm* set of tools; (*d'atelier*) equipment *q*.

outiller [utije] *vt* (*ouvrier, usine*) to equip.

outrage [utraʒ] *nm* insult; **faire subir les derniers ~s à** (*femme*) to ravish; **~ aux bonnes mœurs** (*JUR*) outrage to public decency; **~ à magistrat** (*JUR*) contempt of court; **~ à la pudeur** (*JUR*) indecent behaviour *q*.

outragé, e [utraʒe] *a* offended; outraged.

outrageant, e [utraʒɑ̃, -ɑ̃t] *a* offensive.

outrager [utraʒe] *vt* to offend gravely; (*fig: contrevenir à*) to outrage, insult.

outrageusement [utraʒøzmɑ̃] *ad* outrageously.

outrance [utrɑ̃s] *nf* excessiveness *q*, excess; **à ~** *ad* excessively, to excess.

outrancier, ière [utrɑ̃sje, -jɛr] *a* extreme.

outre [utr(ə)] *nf* goatskin, water skin ♦ *prép* besides ♦ *ad*: **passer ~** to carry on regardless; **passer ~ à** to disregard, take no notice of; **en ~** besides, moreover; **~ que** apart from the fact that; **~ mesure** immoderately; unduly.

outré, e [utre] *a* (*flatterie, éloge*) excessive, exaggerated; (*indigné, scandalisé*) outraged.

outre-Atlantique [utratlɑ̃tik] *ad* across the Atlantic.

outrecuidance [utrəkɥidɑ̃s] *nf* presumptuousness *q*.

outre-Manche [utrəmɑ̃ʃ] *ad* across the Channel.

outremer [utrəmɛr] *a inv* ultramarine.

outre-mer [utrəmɛr] *ad* overseas; **d'~** overseas.

outrepasser [utrəpɑse] *vt* to go beyond, exceed.

outrer [utre] *vt* (*pensée, attitude*) to exaggerate; (*indigner: personne*) to outrage.

outre-Rhin [utrərɛ̃] *ad* across the Rhine, in Germany.

outsider [awtsajdœr] *nm* outsider.

ouvert, e [uvɛr, -ɛrt(ə)] *pp de* **ouvrir** ♦ *a* open; (*robinet, gaz etc*) on; **à bras ~s** with open arms.

ouvertement [uvɛrtəmɑ̃] *ad* openly.

ouverture [uvɛrtyr] *nf* opening; (*MUS*) overture; (*POL*): **l'~** the widening of the political spectrum; (*PHOTO*): **~ (du diaphragme)** aperture; **~s** *nfpl* (*propositions*) overtures; **~ d'esprit** open-mindedness; **heures d'~** (*COMM*) opening hours; **jours d'~** (*COMM*) days of opening.

ouvrable [uvrabl(ə)] *a*: **jour ~** working day, weekday; **heures ~s** business hours.

ouvrage [uvraʒ] *nm* (*tâche, de tricot etc, MIL*) work *q*; (*objet: COUTURE, ART*) (piece of) work; (*texte, livre*) work; **panier ou corbeille à ~** work basket; **~ d'art** (*GÉNIE CIVIL*) bridge or tunnel etc.

ouvragé, e [uvraʒe] *a* finely embroidered (*ou* worked *ou* carved).

ouvrant, e [uvrɑ̃, -ɑ̃t] *vb voir* **ouvrir** ♦ *a*: **toit ~** sunroof.

ouvré, e [uvre] *a* finely-worked; **jour ~** working day.

ouvre-boîte(s) [uvrəbwat] *nm inv* tin (*Brit*) *ou* can opener.

ouvre-bouteille(s) [uvrəbutɛj] *nm inv* bottle-opener.

ouvreuse [uvrøz] *nf* usherette.

ouvrier, ière [uvrije, -jɛr] *nm/f* worker ♦ *nf* (*ZOOL*) worker (bee) ♦ *a* working-class; (*problèmes, conflit*) industrial, labour *cpd* (*Brit*), labor *cpd* (*US*); (*revendications*) workers'; **classe ouvrière** working class; **~ agricole** farmworker; **~ qualifié** skilled worker; **~ spécialisé (OS)** semiskilled worker; **~ d'usine** factory worker.

ouvrir [uvrir] *vt* (*gén*) to open; (*brèche, passage*) to open up; (*commencer l'exploitation de, créer*) to open (up); (*eau, électricité, chauffage, robinet*) to turn on; (*MÉD: abcès*) to open up, cut open ♦ *vi* to open, to open up; (*CARTES*): **~ à trèfle** to open in clubs; **s'~** *vi* to open; **s'~ à** (*art etc*) to open one's mind to; **s'~ à qn (de qch)** to open one's heart to sb (about sth); **s'~ les veines** to slash *ou* cut one's wrists; **~ sur** to open onto; **~ l'appétit à qn** to whet sb's appetite; **~ des horizons** to open up new horizons; **~ l'esprit** to broaden one's horizons; **~ une session** (*INFORM*) to log in.

ouvroir [uvrwar] *nm* workroom, sewing room.

ovaire [ɔvɛr] *nm* ovary.

ovale [ɔval] *a* oval.

ovation [ɔvasjɔ̃] *nf* ovation.

ovationner [ɔvasjɔne] *vt*: **~ qn** to give sb an ovation.

ovin, e [ɔvɛ̃, -in] *a* ovine.

OVNI [ɔvni] *sigle m* (= *objet volant non identifié*) UFO.

ovoïde [ɔvɔid] *a* egg-shaped.

ovulation [ɔvylasjɔ̃] *nf* (*PHYSIOL*) ovulation.

ovule [ɔvyl] *nm* (*PHYSIOL*) ovum (*pl* ova); (*MÉD*) pessary.

oxfordien, ne [ɔksfɔrdjɛ̃, -ɛn] *a* Oxonian ♦ *nm/f*: **O~, ne** Oxonian.

oxydable [ɔksidabl(ə)] *a* liable to rust.

oxyde [ɔksid] *nm* oxide; **~ de carbone** carbon monoxide.

oxyder [ɔkside] **s'~** *vi* to become oxidized.

oxygène [ɔksiʒɛn] *nm* oxygen; (*fig*): **cure d'~** fresh air cure.

oxygéné, e [ɔksiʒene] *a*: **eau ~e** hydrogen peroxide; **cheveux ~s** bleached hair.

ozone [ozɔn] *nm* ozone.

P

P, p [pe] *nm inv* P, p ♦ *abr* (= *Père*) Fr; (= *page*) p; **P comme Pierre** P for Peter.

PA *sigle fpl* = **petites annonces**.

PAC *sigle f* (= *Politique agricole commune*) CAP.

pacage [pakaʒ] *nm* grazing, pasture.

pace-maker [pɛsmɛkœr] *nm* pacemaker.

pachyderme [paʃidɛrm(ə)] *nm* pachyderm;

elephant.

pacificateur, trice [pasifikatœʀ, -tʀis] *a* pacificatory.

pacifier [pasifje] *vt* to pacify.

pacifique [pasifik] *a* (*personne*) peaceable; (*intentions, coexistence*) peaceful ♦ *nm*: **le P~, l'océan P~** the Pacific (Ocean).

pacifiquement [pasifikmã] *ad* peaceably; peacefully.

pacifiste [pasifist(ə)] *nm/f* pacifist.

pack [pak] *nm* pack.

pacotille [pakɔtij] *nf* (*péj*) cheap goods *pl*; **de ~** cheap.

pacte [pakt(ə)] *nm* pact, treaty.

pactiser [paktize] *vi*: **~ avec** to come to terms with.

pactole [paktɔl] *nm* gold mine (*fig*).

paddock [padɔk] *nm* paddock.

Padoue [padu] *n* Padua.

PAF *sigle f* (= *Police de l'air et des frontières*) *police authority responsible for civil aviation, border control etc.*

pagaie [pagɛ] *nf* paddle.

pagaille [pagaj] *nf* mess, shambles *sg*; **il y en a en ~** there are loads *ou* heaps of them.

paganisme [paganism(ə)] *nm* paganism.

pagayer [pageje] *vi* to paddle.

page [paʒ] *nf* page; (*passage: d'un roman*) passage ♦ *nm* page (boy); **mettre en ~s** to make up (into pages); **mise en ~** layout; **à la ~** (*fig*) up-to-date; **~ blanche** blank page; **~ de garde** endpaper.

page-écran, *pl* **pages-écrans** [paʒekʀã] *nf* (*INFORM*) screen page.

pagination [paʒinasjɔ̃] *nf* pagination.

paginer [paʒine] *vt* to paginate.

pagne [paɲ] *nm* loincloth.

pagode [pagɔd] *nf* pagoda.

paie [pɛ] *nf* = **paye**.

paiement [pɛmã] *nm* = **payement**.

païen, ne [pajɛ̃, -ɛn] *a, nm/f* pagan, heathen.

paillard, e [pajaʀ, -aʀd(ə)] *a* bawdy.

paillasse [pajas] *nf* (*matelas*) straw mattress; (*d'un évier*) draining board.

paillasson [pajasɔ̃] *nm* doormat.

paille [pɑj] *nf* straw; (*défaut*) flaw; **être sur la ~** to be ruined; **~ de fer** steel wool.

paillé, e [paje] *a* with a straw seat.

pailleté, e [pajte] *a* sequined.

paillette [pajɛt] *nf* speck, flake; **~s** *nfpl* (*décoratives*) sequins, spangles; **lessive en ~s** soapflakes *pl*.

pain [pɛ̃] *nm* (*substance*) bread; (*unité*) loaf (*pl* loaves); (of bread); (*morceau*): **~ de cire** *etc* bar of wax *etc*; (*CULIN*): **~ de poisson/ légumes** fish/vegetable loaf; **petit ~** (bread) roll; **~ bis/complet** brown/wholemeal (*Brit*) *ou* wholewheat (*US*) bread; **~ de campagne** farmhouse bread; **~ d'épice** ≈ gingerbread; **~ grillé** toast; **~ de mie** sandwich loaf; **~ perdu** French toast; **~ de seigle** rye bread; **~ de sucre** sugar loaf.

pair, e [pɛʀ] *a* (*nombre*) even ♦ *nm* peer; **aller de ~ (avec)** to go hand in hand *ou* together (with); **au ~** (*FINANCE*) at par; **valeur au ~** par value; **jeune fille au ~** au pair.

paire [pɛʀ] *nf* pair; **une ~ de lunettes/ tenailles** a pair of glasses/pincers; **faire la ~:** **les deux font la ~** they are two of a kind.

pais [pɛ] *vb voir* **paître**.

paisible [pezibl(ə)] *a* peaceful, quiet.

paisiblement [pezibləmã] *ad* peacefully, quietly.

paître [pɛtʀ(ə)] *vi* to graze.

paix [pɛ] *nf* peace; (*fig*) peacefulness, peace; **faire la ~ avec** to make peace with; **avoir la ~** to have peace (and quiet).

Pakistan [pakistã] *nm*: **le ~** Pakistan.

pakistanais, e [pakistanɛ, -ɛz] *a* Pakistani.

PAL *sigle m* (= *Phase Alternation Line*) PAL.

palabrer [palabʀe] *vi* to argue endlessly.

palabres [palabʀ(ə)] *nfpl* endless discussions.

palace [palas] *nm* luxury hotel.

palais [palɛ] *nm* palace; (*ANAT*) palate; **le P~ Bourbon** *the seat of the French National Assembly*; **le P~ de l'Élysée** the Elysée Palace; **~ des expositions** exhibition centre; **le P~ de Justice** the Law Courts *pl*.

palan [palã] *nm* hoist.

Palatin [palatɛ̃]: **le (mont) ~** the Palatine (Hill).

pale [pal] *nf* (*d'hélice, de rame*) blade; (*de roue*) paddle.

pâle [pɑl] *a* pale; (*fig*): **une ~ imitation** a pale imitation; **bleu ~** pale blue; **~ de colère** white *ou* pale with anger.

palefrenier [palfʀənje] *nm* groom.

paléontologie [paleɔ̃tɔlɔʒi] *nf* paleontology.

Palerme [palɛʀm(ə)] *n* Palermo.

Palestine [palɛstin] *nf*: **la ~** Palestine.

palestinien, ne [palɛstinjɛ̃, -ɛn] *a* Palestinian ♦ *nm/f*: **P~, ne** Palestinian.

palet [palɛ] *nm* disc; (*HOCKEY*) puck.

paletot [palto] *nm* (short) coat.

palette [palɛt] *nf* palette; (*produits*) range.

palétuvier [paletyvje] *nm* mangrove.

pâleur [pɑlœʀ] *nf* paleness.

palier [palje] *nm* (*d'escalier*) landing; (*fig*) level, plateau; (*: phase stable*) levelling (*Brit*) *ou* leveling (*US*) off, new level; (*TECH*) bearing; **nos voisins de ~** our neighbo(u)rs across the landing (*Brit*) *ou* the hall (*US*); **en ~** *ad* level; **par ~s** in stages.

palière [paljɛʀ] *af* landing *cpd*.

pâlir [paliʀ] *vi* to turn *ou* go pale; (*couleur*) to fade; **faire ~ qn** (*de jalousie*) to make sb green (with envy).

palissade [palisad] *nf* fence.

palissandre [palisãdʀ(ə)] *nm* rosewood.

palliatif [paljatif] *nm* palliative; (*expédient*) stopgap measure.

pallier [palje] *vt*, **~ à** *vt* to offset, make up for.

palmarès [palmaʀɛs] *nm* record (of achievements); (*SCOL*) prize list; (*SPORT*) list of winners.

palme [palm(ə)] *nf* (*BOT*) palm leaf (*pl* leaves); (*symbole*) palm; (*de plongeur*) flipper; **~s (académiques)** *decoration for services to education*.

palmé, e [palme] *a* (*pattes*) webbed.

palmeraie [palməʀɛ] *nf* palm grove.

palmier [palmje] *nm* palm tree.

palmipède [palmiped] *nm* palmiped, webfooted bird.

palois, e [palwa, -waz] *a* of *ou* from Pau ♦ *nm/f*: **P~, e** inhabitant *ou* native of Pau.

palombe [palɔ̃b] *nf* woodpigeon, ringdove.

pâlot, te [palo, -ɔt] *a* pale, peaky.
palourde [palurd(ə)] *nf* clam.
palpable [palpabl(ə)] *a* tangible, palpable.
palper [palpe] *vt* to feel, finger.
palpitant, e [palpitɑ̃, -ɑ̃t] *a* thrilling, gripping.
palpitation [palpitasjɔ̃] *nf* palpitation.
palpiter [palpite] *vi* (*cœur, pouls*) to beat; (*: plus fort*) to pound, throb; (*narines, chair*) to quiver.
paludisme [palydism(ə)] *nm* malaria.
palustre [palystʀ(ə)] *a* (*coquillage etc*) marsh *cpd*; (*fièvre*) malarial.
pâmer [pame]: **se ~** *vi* to swoon; (*fig*): **se ~ devant** to go into raptures over.
pâmoison [pamwazɔ̃] *nf*: **tomber en ~** to swoon.
pampa [pɑ̃pa] *nf* pampas *pl*.
pamphlet [pɑ̃flɛ] *nm* lampoon, satirical tract.
pamphlétaire [pɑ̃fletɛʀ] *nm/f* lampoonist.
pamplemousse [pɑ̃pləmus] *nm* grapefruit.
pan [pɑ̃] *nm* section, piece; (*côté: d'un prisme, d'une tour*) side, face ♦ *excl* bang!; **~ de chemise** shirt tail; **~ de mur** section of wall.
panacée [panase] *nf* panacea.
panachage [panaʃaʒ] *nm* blend, mix; (*POL*) voting for candidates from different parties instead of for the set list of one party.
panache [panaʃ] *nm* plume; (*fig*) spirit, panache.
panaché, e [panaʃe] *a*: **œillet ~** variegated carnation; **glace ~e** mixed ice cream; **salade ~e** mixed salad; **bière ~e** shandy.
panais [panɛ] *nm* parsnip.
Panama [panama] *nm*: **le ~** Panama.
panaméen, ne [panameɛ̃, -ɛn] *a* Panamanian ♦ *nm/f*: **P~, ne** Panamanian.
panaris [panaʀi] *nm* whitlow.
pancarte [pɑ̃kaʀt(ə)] *nf* sign, notice; (*dans un défilé*) placard.
pancréas [pɑ̃kʀeas] *nm* pancreas.
panda [pɑ̃da] *nm* panda.
pané, e [pane] *a* fried in breadcrumbs.
panégyrique [paneʒiʀik] *nm*: **faire le ~ de qn** to extol sb's merits *ou* virtues.
panier [panje] *nm* basket; (*à diapositives*) magazine; **mettre au ~** to chuck away; **~ de crabes: c'est un ~ de crabes** (*fig*) they're constantly at one another's throats; **~ percé** (*fig*) spendthrift; **~ à provisions** shopping basket; **~ à salade** (*CULIN*) salad shaker; (*POLICE*) paddy wagon, police van.
panier-repas, *pl* **paniers-repas** [panjeʀ(ə)pa] *nm* packed lunch.
panification [panifikasjɔ̃] *nf* bread-making.
panique [panik] *a* panicky ♦ *nf* panic.
paniquer [panike] *vi* to panic.
panne [pan] *nf* (*d'un mécanisme, moteur*) breakdown; **être/tomber en ~** to have broken down/break down; **être en ~ d'essence** *ou* **en ~ sèche** to have run out of petrol (*Brit*) *ou* gas (*US*); **mettre en ~** (*NAVIG*) to bring to; **~ d'électricité** *ou* **de courant** power *ou* electrical failure.
panneau, x [pano] *nm* (*écriteau*) sign, notice; (*de boiserie, de tapisserie etc*) panel; **tomber dans le ~** (*fig*) to walk into the trap; **~ d'affichage** notice (*Brit*) *ou* bulletin (*US*) board; **~ électoral** board for election poster;

~ indicateur signpost; **~ publicitaire** hoarding (*Brit*), billboard (*US*); **~ de signalisation** roadsign.
panneau-réclame, *pl* **panneaux-réclame** [panoʀeklam] *nm* hoarding (*Brit*), billboard (*US*).
panonceau, x [panɔ̃so] *nm* (*de magasin etc*) sign; (*de médecin etc*) plaque.
panoplie [panɔpli] *nf* (*jouet*) outfit; (*d'armes*) display; (*fig*) array.
panorama [panɔʀama] *nm* (*vue*) all-round view, panorama; (*peinture*) panorama; (*fig: étude complète*) complete overview.
panoramique [panɔʀamik] *a* panoramic; (*carrosserie*) with panoramic windows ♦ *nm* (*CINÉMA, TV*) panoramic shot.
panse [pɑ̃s] *nf* paunch.
pansement [pɑ̃smɑ̃] *nm* dressing, bandage; **~ adhésif** sticking plaster (*Brit*), bandaid ® (*US*).
panser [pɑ̃se] *vt* (*plaie*) to dress, bandage; (*bras*) to put a dressing on, bandage; (*cheval*) to groom.
pantalon [pɑ̃talɔ̃] *nm* (*aussi:* **~s, paire de ~s**) trousers *pl* (*Brit*), pants *pl* (*US*), pair of trousers *ou* pants; **~ de ski** ski pants *pl*.
pantalonnade [pɑ̃talɔnad] *nf* slapstick (comedy).
pantelant, e [pɑ̃tlɑ̃, -ɑ̃t] *a* gasping for breath, panting.
panthère [pɑ̃tɛʀ] *nf* panther.
pantin [pɑ̃tɛ̃] *nm* (*jouet*) jumping jack; (*péj: personne*) puppet.
pantois [pɑ̃twa] *am*: **rester ~** to be flabbergasted.
pantomime [pɑ̃tɔmim] *nf* mime; (*pièce*) mime show; (*péj*) fuss, carry-on.
pantouflard, e [pɑ̃tuflaʀ, -aʀd(ə)] *a* (*péj*) stay-at-home.
pantoufle [pɑ̃tufl(ə)] *nf* slipper.
panure [panyʀ] *nf* breadcrumbs *pl*.
PAO *sigle f* (= *publication assistée par ordinateur*) desk-top publishing.
paon [pɑ̃] *nm* peacock.
papa [papa] *nm* dad(dy).
papauté [papote] *nf* papacy.
papaye [papaj] *nf* pawpaw.
pape [pap] *nm* pope.
paperasse [papʀas] *nf* (*péj*) bumf *q*, papers *pl*; forms *pl*.
paperasserie [papʀasʀi] *nf* (*péj*) red tape *q*; paperwork *q*.
papeterie [papetʀi] *nf* (*fabrication du papier*) paper-making (industry); (*usine*) paper mill; (*magasin*) stationer's (shop (*Brit*)); (*articles*) stationery.
papetier, ière [paptje, -jɛʀ] *nm/f* paper-maker; stationer.
papetier-libraire, *pl* **papetiers-libraires** [paptjelibʀɛʀ] *nm* bookseller and stationer.
papier [papje] *nm* paper; (*feuille*) sheet *ou* piece of paper; (*article*) article; (*écrit officiel*) document; **~s** *nmpl* (*aussi:* **~s d'identité**) (identity) papers; **sur le ~** (*théoriquement*) on paper; **noircir du ~** to write page after page; **~ couché/glacé** art/glazed paper; **~ (d')aluminium** aluminium (*Brit*) *ou* aluminum (*US*) foil, tinfoil; **~ d'Arménie** incense paper; **~ bible** India *ou*

bible paper; ~ **de brouillon** rough *ou* scrap paper; ~ **bulle** manil(l)a paper; ~ **buvard** blotting paper; ~ **calque** tracing paper; ~ **carbone** carbon paper; ~ **collant** Sellotape ® (*Brit*), Scotch ® (*US*) *ou* sticky tape; ~ **en continu** continuous stationery; ~ **à dessin** drawing paper; ~ **d'emballage** wrapping paper; ~ **gommé** gummed paper; ~ **hygiénique** toilet paper; ~ **journal** newsprint; (*pour emballer*) newspaper; ~ **à lettres** writing paper, notepaper; ~ **mâché** papier-mâché; ~ **machine** typing paper; ~ **peint** wallpaper; ~ **pelure** India paper; ~ **à pliage accordéon** fanfold paper; ~ **de soie** tissue paper; ~ **thermique** thermal paper; ~ **de tournesol** litmus paper; ~ **de verre** sandpaper.

papier-filtre, *pl* **papiers-filtres** [papjefiltʀ(ə)] *nm* filter paper.

papier-monnaie, *pl* **papiers-monnaies** [papjemɔnɛ] *nm* paper money.

papille [papij] *nf*: ~**s gustatives** taste buds.

papillon [papijɔ̃] *nm* butterfly; (*fam: contravention*) (parking) ticket; (*TECH*: *écrou*) wing *ou* butterfly nut; ~ **de nuit** moth.

papillonner [papijɔne] *vi* to flit from one thing (*ou* person) to another.

papillote [papijɔt] *nf* (*pour cheveux*) curlpaper; (*de gigot*) (paper) frill.

papilloter [papijɔte] *vi* (*yeux*) to blink; (*paupières*) to flutter; (*lumière*) to flicker.

papotage [papɔtaʒ] *nm* chitchat.

papoter [papɔte] *vi* to chatter.

papou, e [papu] *a* Papuan.

Papouasie-Nouvelle-Guinée [papwazinuvɛlgine] *nf*: **la** ~ Papua-New-Guinea.

paprika [paprika] *nm* paprika.

papyrus [papirys] *nm* papyrus.

Pâque [pɑk] *nf*: **la** ~ Passover; *voir aussi* **Pâques**.

paquebot [pakbo] *nm* liner.

pâquerette [pɑkʀɛt] *nf* daisy.

Pâques [pɑk] *nm*, *nfpl* Easter; **faire ses** ~ to do one's Easter duties; **l'île de** ~ Easter Island.

paquet [pakɛ] *nm* packet; (*colis*) parcel; (*ballot*) bundle; (*dans négociations*) package (deal); (*fig: tas*): ~ **de** pile *ou* heap of; ~**s** *nmpl* (*bagages*) bags; **mettre le** ~ (*fam*) to give one's all; ~ **de mer** big wave.

paquetage [paktaʒ] *nm* (*MIL*) kit, pack.

paquet-cadeau, *pl* **paquets-cadeaux** [pakɛkado] *nm* gift-wrapped parcel.

par [paʀ] *prép* by; **finir** *etc* ~ to end *etc* with; ~ **amour** out of love; **passer** ~ **Lyon/la côte** to go via *ou* through Lyons/along by the coast; ~ **la fenêtre** (*jeter, regarder*) out of the window; **3** ~ **jour/personne** 3 a *ou* per day/head; **2** ~ **2** two at a time; (*marcher etc*) in twos; ~ **où?** which way?; ~ **ici** this way; (*dans le coin*) round here; ~**-ci,** ~**-là** here and there.

para [paʀa] *nm* (= *parachutiste*) para.

parabole [paʀabɔl] *nf* (*REL*) parable; (*GÉOM*) parabola.

parabolique [paʀabɔlik] *a* parabolic.

parachever [paʀaʃve] *vt* to perfect.

parachute [paʀaʃyt] *nm* parachute.

parachuter [paʀaʃyte] *vt* (*soldat etc*) to para-

chute; (*fig*) to pitchfork.

parachutisme [paʀaʃytism(ə)] *nm* parachuting.

parachutiste [paʀaʃytist(ə)] *nm/f* parachutist; (*MIL*) paratrooper.

parade [paʀad] *nf* (*spectacle, défilé*) parade; (*ESCRIME, BOXE*) parry; (*ostentation*): **faire** ~ **de** to display, show off; (*défense, riposte*): **trouver la** ~ **à une attaque** to find the answer to an attack; **de** ~ *a* ceremonial; (*superficiel*) superficial, outward.

parader [paʀade] *vi* to swagger (around), show off.

paradis [paʀadi] *nm* heaven, paradise; **P**~ **terrestre** (*REL*) Garden of Eden; (*fig*) heaven on earth.

paradisiaque [paʀadizjak] *a* heavenly, divine.

paradoxal, e, aux [paʀadɔksal, -o] *a* paradoxical.

paradoxe [paʀadɔks(ə)] *nm* paradox.

parafe [paʀaf] *nm*, **parafer** [paʀafe] *vt* = **paraphe, parapher.**

paraffine [paʀafin] *nf* paraffin; paraffin wax.

paraffiné, e [paʀafine] *a*: **papier** ~ wax(ed) paper.

parafoudre [paʀafudʀ(ə)] *nm* (*ÉLEC*) lightning conductor.

parages [paʀaʒ] *nmpl* (*NAVIG*) waters; **dans les** ~ **(de)** in the area *ou* vicinity (of).

paragraphe [paʀagʀaf] *nm* paragraph.

Paraguay [paʀagwe] *nm*: **le** ~ Paraguay.

paraguayen, ne [paʀagwajɛ̃, -ɛn] *a* Paraguayan ♦ *nm/f*: **P**~, **ne** Paraguayan.

paraître [paʀɛtʀ(ə)] *vb avec attribut* to seem, look, appear ♦ *vi* to appear; (*être visible*) to show; (*PRESSE, ÉDITION*) to be published, come out, appear; (*briller*) to show off; **laisser** ~ **qch** to let (sth) show ♦ *vb impersonnel*: **il paraît que** it seems *ou* appears that; **il me paraît que** it seems to me that; **il paraît absurde de** it seems absurd to; **il ne paraît pas son âge** he doesn't look his age; ~ **en justice** to appear before the court(s); ~ **en scène/en public/à l'écran** to appear on stage/in public/on the screen.

parallèle [paʀalɛl] *a* parallel; (*police, marché*) unofficial; (*société, énergie*) alternative ♦ *nm* (*comparaison*): **faire un** ~ **entre** to draw a parallel between; (*GÉO*) parallel ♦ *nf* parallel (line); **en** ~ in parallel; **mettre en** ~ (*choses opposées*) to compare; (*choses semblables*) to parallel.

parallèlement [paʀalɛlmɑ̃] *ad* in parallel; (*fig: en même temps*) at the same time.

parallélisme [paʀalelism(ə)] *nm* parallelism; (*AUTO*) wheel alignment.

parallélogramme [paʀalelɔgʀam] *nm* parallelogram.

paralyser [paʀalize] *vt* to paralyze.

paralysie [paʀalizi] *nf* paralysis.

paralytique [paʀalitik] *a*, *nm/f* paralytic.

paramédical, e, aux [paʀamedikal, -o] *a* paramedical.

paramètre [paʀamɛtʀ(ə)] *nm* parameter.

paramilitaire [paʀamilitɛʀ] *a* paramilitary.

paranoïaque [paʀanɔjak] *nm/f* paranoiac.

paranormal, e, aux [paʀanɔʀmal, -o] *a* paranormal.

parapet [paʀapɛ] *nm* parapet.

paraphe [paʀaf] *nm* (*trait*) flourish; (*signature*) initials *pl*; signature.

parapher [paʀafe] *vt* to initial; to sign.

paraphrase [paʀafʀɑz] *nf* paraphrase.

paraphraser [paʀafʀɑze] *vt* to paraphrase.

paraplégique [paʀaplezik] *a*, *nm/f* paraplegic.

parapluie [paʀaplɥi] *nm* umbrella; ~ **atomique** *ou* **nucléaire** nuclear umbrella; ~ **pliant** telescopic umbrella.

parapsychique [paʀapsifik] *a* parapsychological.

parapsychologie [paʀapsikɔlɔʒi] *nf* parapsychology.

parapublic, ique [paʀapyblik] *a partly state-controlled*.

parascolaire [paʀaskɔlɛʀ] *a* extracurricular.

parasitaire [paʀazitɛʀ] *a* parasitic(al).

parasite [paʀazit] *nm* parasite ♦ *a* (*BOT*, *BIO*) parasitic(al); ~**s** *nmpl* (*TÉL*) interference *sg*.

parasol [paʀasɔl] *nm* parasol, sunshade.

paratonnerre [paʀatɔnɛʀ] *nm* lightning conductor.

paravent [paʀavɑ̃] *nm* folding screen; (*fig*) screen.

parc [paʀk] *nm* (*public*) park, gardens *pl*; (*de château etc*) grounds *pl*; (*pour le bétail*) pen, enclosure; (*d'enfant*) playpen; (*MIL*: *entrepôt*) depot; (*ensemble d'unités*) stock; (*de voitures etc*) fleet; ~ **d'attractions** amusement park; ~ **automobile** (*d'un pays*) number of cars on the roads; ~ **à huîtres** oyster bed; ~ **national** national park; ~ **naturel** nature reserve; ~ **de stationnement** car park; ~ **zoologique** zoological gardens *pl*.

parcelle [paʀsɛl] *nf* fragment, scrap; (*de terrain*) plot, parcel.

parcelliser [paʀselize] *vt* to divide *ou* split up.

parce que [paʀsk(ə)] *cj* because.

parchemin [paʀʃəmɛ̃] *nm* parchment.

parcheminé, e [paʀʃəmine] *a* wrinkled; (*papier*) with a parchment finish.

parcimonie [paʀsimɔni] *nf* parsimony, parsimoniousness.

parcimonieux, euse [paʀsimɔnjø, -øz] *a* parsimonious, miserly.

parc(o)mètre [paʀk(ɔ)mɛtʀ(ə)] *nm* parking meter.

parcotrain [paʀkɔtʀɛ̃] *nm* station car park (*Brit*) *ou* parking lot (*US*), park-and-ride car park (*Brit*).

parcourir [paʀkuʀiʀ] *vt* (*trajet, distance*) to cover; (*article, livre*) to skim *ou* glance through; (*lieu*) to go all over, travel up and down; (*suj: frisson, vibration*) to run through; ~ **des yeux** to run one's eye over.

parcours [paʀkuʀ] *vb voir* **parcourir** ♦ *nm* (*trajet*) journey; (*itinéraire*) route; (*SPORT*: *terrain*) course; (*: tour*) round; run; lap; ~ **du combattant** assault course.

parcouru, e [paʀkuʀy] *pp de* **parcourir**.

par-delà [paʀdəla] *prép* beyond.

par-dessous [paʀdəsu] *prép, ad* under(neath).

pardessus [paʀdəsy] *nm* overcoat.

par-dessus [paʀdəsy] *prép* over (the top of) ♦ *ad* over (the top); ~ **le marché** on top of it all.

par-devant [paʀdəvɑ̃] *prép* in the presence of,

before ♦ *ad* at the front; round the front.

pardon [paʀdɔ̃] *nm* forgiveness *q* ♦ *excl* (*excuses*) (I'm) sorry; (*pour interpeller etc*) excuse me; (*demander de répéter*) (I beg your) pardon? (*Brit*), pardon me? (*US*).

pardonnable [paʀdɔnabl(ə)] *a* forgivable, excusable.

pardonner [paʀdɔne] *vt* to forgive; ~ **qch à qn** to forgive sb for sth; **qui ne pardonne pas** (*maladie, erreur*) fatal.

paré, e [paʀe] *a* ready, prepared.

pare-balles [paʀbal] *a inv* bulletproof.

pare-boue [paʀbu] *nm inv* mudflap.

pare-brise [paʀbʀiz] *nm inv* windscreen (*Brit*), windshield (*US*).

pare-chocs [paʀʃɔk] *nm inv* bumper (*Brit*), fender (*US*).

pare-étincelles [paʀetɛ̃sɛl] *nm inv* fireguard.

pare-feu [paʀfø] *nm inv* firebreak ♦ *a inv*: **portes** ~ fire (resistant) doors.

pareil, le [paʀɛj] *a* (*identique*) the same, alike; (*similaire*) similar; (*tel*): **un courage/livre** ~ such courage/a book, courage/a book like this; **de** ~**s livres** such books ♦ *ad*: **habillés** ~ dressed the same (way), dressed alike; **faire** ~ to do the same (thing); **j'en veux un** ~ I'd like one just like it; **rien de** ~ no (*ou* any) such thing, nothing (*ou* anything) like it; **ses** ~**s** one's fellow men; one's peers; **ne pas avoir son (sa)** ~**(le)** to be second to none; ~ **à** the same as; similar to; **sans** ~ unparalleled, unequalled; **c'est du** ~ **au même** it comes to the same thing, it's six (of one) and half-a-dozen (of the other); **en** ~ **cas** in such a case; **rendre la** ~**le à qn** to pay sb back in his own coin.

pareillement [paʀɛjmɑ̃] *ad* the same, alike; in such a way; (*également*) likewise.

parement [paʀmɑ̃] *nm* (*CONSTR, revers d'un col, d'une manche*) facing; (*REL*): ~ **d'autel** antependium.

parent, e [paʀɑ̃, -ɑ̃t] *nm/f*: **un/une** ~**/e** a relative *ou* relation ♦ *a*: **être** ~ **de** to be related to; ~**s** *nmpl* (*père et mère*) parents; (*famille, proches*) relatives, relations; ~**s par alliance** relatives *ou* relations by marriage; ~**s en ligne directe** blood relations.

parental, e, aux [paʀɑ̃tal, -o] *a* parental.

parenté [paʀɑ̃te] *nf* (*lien*) relationship; (*personnes*) relatives *pl*, relations *pl*.

parenthèse [paʀɑ̃tɛz] *nf* (*ponctuation*) bracket, parenthesis; (*MATH*) bracket; (*digression*) parenthesis, digression; **ouvrir/fermer la** ~ to open/close the brackets; **entre** ~**s** in brackets; (*fig*) incidentally.

parer [paʀe] *vt* to adorn; (*CULIN*) to dress, trim; (*éviter*) to ward off; ~ **à** (*danger*) to ward off; (*inconvénient*) to deal with; **se** ~ **de** (*fig: qualité, titre*) to assume; ~ **à toute éventualité** to be ready for every eventuality; ~ **au plus pressé** to attend to what's most urgent.

pare-soleil [paʀsɔlɛj] *nm inv* sun visor.

paresse [paʀɛs] *nf* laziness.

paresser [paʀese] *vi* to laze around.

paresseusement [paʀesøzmɑ̃] *ad* lazily; sluggishly.

paresseux, euse [paʀesø, -øz] *a* lazy; (*fig*) slow, sluggish ♦ *nm* (*ZOOL*) sloth.

parfaire [paʀfɛʀ] *vt* to perfect, complete.
parfait, e [paʀfɛ, -ɛt] *pp de* **parfaire** ♦ *a*
perfect ♦ *nm* (*LING*) perfect (tense); (*CULIN*)
parfait ♦ *excl* fine, excellent.
parfaitement [paʀfɛtmɑ̃] *ad* perfectly ♦ *excl*
(most) certainly.
parfaites [paʀfɛt], **parfasse** [paʀfas], **parferai**
[paʀfʀe] *etc vb voir* **parfaire**.
parfois [paʀfwa] *ad* sometimes.
parfum [paʀfœ̃] *nm* (*produit*) perfume, scent;
(*odeur: de fleur*) scent, fragrance; (*: de
tabac, vin*) aroma; (*goût: de glace, milk-
shake*) flavour (*Brit*), flavor (*US*).
parfumé, e [paʀfyme] *a* (*fleur, fruit*) fragrant; (*papier à lettres etc*) scented;
(*femme*) wearing perfume *ou* scent,
perfumed; (*aromatisé*): ~ **au café** coffee-
flavoured (*Brit*) *ou* -flavored (*US*).
parfumer [paʀfyme] *vt* (*suj: odeur, bouquet*)
to perfume; (*mouchoir*) to put scent *ou*
perfume on; (*crème, gâteau*) to flavour
(*Brit*), flavor (*US*); **se** ~ to put on (some)
perfume *ou* scent; (*d'habitude*) to use
perfume *ou* scent.
parfumerie [paʀfymʀi] *nf* (*commerce*)
perfumery; (*produits*) perfumes *pl*;
(*boutique*) perfume shop (*Brit*) *ou* store
(*US*).
pari [paʀi] *nm* bet, wager; (*SPORT*) bet; ~
mutuel urbain (PMU) *system of betting on
horses.*
paria [paʀja] *nm* outcast.
parier [paʀje] *vt* to bet; **j'aurais parié que si/
non** I'd have said he (*ou* you *etc*) would/
wouldn't.
parieur [paʀjœʀ] *nm* (*turfiste etc*) punter.
Paris [paʀi] *n* Paris.
parisien, ne [paʀizjɛ̃, -ɛn] *a* Parisian; (*GÉO,
ADMIN*) Paris *cpd* ♦ *nm/f*: **P~, ne** Parisian.
paritaire [paʀitɛʀ] *a*: **commission** ~ joint
commission.
parité [paʀite] *nf* parity; ~ **de change** (*ÉCON*)
exchange parity.
parjure [paʀʒyʀ] *nm* (*faux serment*) false
oath, perjury; (*violation de serment*) breach
of oath, perjury ♦ *nm/f* perjurer.
parjurer [paʀʒyʀe]: **se** ~ *vi* to perjure o.s.
parka [paʀka] *nf* parka.
parking [paʀkiŋ] *nm* (*lieu*) car park (*Brit*),
parking lot (*US*).
parlant, e [paʀlɑ̃, -ɑ̃t] *a* (*fig*) graphic, vivid;
(*: comparaison, preuve*) eloquent; (*CINÉMA*)
talking ♦ *ad*: **généralement** ~ generally
speaking.
parlé, e [paʀle] *a*: **langue** ~**e** spoken
language.
parlement [paʀləmɑ̃] *nm* parliament.
parlementaire [paʀləmɑ̃tɛʀ] *a* parliamentary
♦ *nm/f* (*député*) ≈ Member of Parliament
(*Brit*) *ou* Congress (*US*); parliamentarian;
(*négociateur*) negotiator, mediator.
parlementarisme [paʀləmɑ̃taʀism(ə)] *nm*
parliamentary government.
parlementer [paʀləmɑ̃te] *vi* (*ennemis*) to
negotiate, parley; (*s'entretenir, discuter*) to
argue at length, have lengthy talks.
parler [paʀle] *nm* speech; dialect ♦ *vi* to
speak, talk; (*avouer*) to talk; ~ (**à qn**) **de** to
talk *ou* speak (to sb) about; ~ **pour qn**

(*intercéder*) to speak for sb; ~ **en l'air** to say
the first thing that comes into one's head; ~
le/en français to speak French/in French; ~
affaires to talk business; ~ **en dormant/du
nez** to talk in one's sleep/through one's nose;
sans ~ **de** (*fig*) not to mention, to say nothing of; **tu parles!** you must be joking!; **n'en
parlons plus!** let's forget it!
parleur [paʀlœʀ] *nm*: **beau** ~ fine talker.
parloir [paʀlwaʀ] *nm* (*d'une prison, d'un
hôpital*) visiting room; (*REL*) parlour (*Brit*),
parlor (*US*).
parlote [paʀlɔt] *nf* chitchat.
Parme [paʀm(ə)] *n* Parma.
parme [paʀm(ə)] *a* violet (blue).
parmesan [paʀməzɑ̃] *nm* Parmesan (cheese).
parmi [paʀmi] *prép* among(st).
parodie [paʀɔdi] *nf* parody.
parodier [paʀɔdje] *vt* (*œuvre, auteur*) to
parody.
paroi [paʀwa] *nf* wall; (*cloison*) partition; ~
rocheuse rock face.
paroisse [paʀwas] *nf* parish.
paroissial, e, aux [paʀwasjal, -o] *a* parish
cpd.
paroissien, ne [paʀwasjɛ̃, -ɛn] *nm/f* parishioner ♦ *nm* prayer book.
parole [paʀɔl] *nf* (*faculté*): **la** ~ speech; (*mot,
promesse*) word; (*REL*): **la bonne** ~ the
word of God; ~**s** *nfpl* (*MUS*) words, lyrics;
tenir ~ to keep one's word; **avoir la** ~ to
have the floor; **n'avoir qu'une** ~ to be true to
one's word; **donner la** ~ **à qn** to hand over
to sb; **prendre la** ~ to speak; **demander la** ~
to ask for permission to speak; **perdre la** ~
to lose the power of speech; (*fig*) to lose one's
tongue; **je le crois sur** ~ I'll take his word
for it, I'll take him at his word; **temps de** ~
(*TV, RADIO etc*) discussion time; **ma** ~**!** my
word!, good heavens!; ~ **d'honneur** word of
honour (*Brit*) *ou* honor (*US*).
parolier, ière [paʀɔlje, -jɛʀ] *nm/f* lyricist;
(*OPÉRA*) librettist.
paroxysme [paʀɔksism(ə)] *nm* height, paroxysm.
parpaing [paʀpɛ̃] *nm* bond-stone, parpen.
parquer [paʀke] *vt* (*voiture, matériel*) to
park; (*bestiaux*) to pen (in *ou* up);
(*prisonniers*) to pack in.
parquet [paʀke] *nm* (*parquet*) floor; (*JUR:
bureau*) public prosecutor's office; **le** ~
(*général*) (*magistrats*) ≈ the Bench.
parqueter [paʀkəte] *vt* to lay a parquet floor
in.
parrain [paʀɛ̃] *nm* godfather; (*d'un navire*)
namer; (*d'un nouvel adhérent*) sponsor,
proposer.
parrainage [paʀɛnaʒ] *nm* sponsorship.
parrainer [paʀɛne] *vt* (*nouvel adhérent*) to
sponsor, propose; (*entreprise*) to promote,
sponsor.
parricide [paʀisid] *nm, nf* parricide.
pars [paʀ] *vb voir* **partir**.
parsemer [paʀsəme] *vt* (*suj: feuilles, papiers*)
to be scattered over; ~ **qch de** to scatter sth
with.
parsi, e [paʀsi] *a* Parsee.
part [paʀ] *vb voir* **partir** ♦ *nf* (*qui revient à qn*)
share; (*fraction, partie*) part; (*de gâteau,*

fromage) portion; (_FINANCE_) (non-voting) share; **prendre ~ à** (_débat etc_) to take part in; (_soucis, douleur de qn_) to share in; **faire ~ de qch à qn** to announce sth to sb, inform sb of sth; **pour ma ~** as for me, as far as I'm concerned; **à ~ entière** _a_ full; **de la ~ de** (_au nom de_) on behalf of; (_donné par_) from; **c'est de la ~ de qui?** (_au téléphone_) who's calling _ou_ speaking (please)?; **de toute(s) ~(s)** from all sides _ou_ quarters; **de ~ et d'autre** on both sides, on either side; **de ~ en ~** right through; **d'une ~ ... d'autre ~** on the one hand ... on the other hand; **nulle/ autre/quelque ~** nowhere/elsewhere/ somewhere; **à ~** _ad_ separately; (_de côté_) aside ♦ _prép_ apart from, except for ♦ _a_ exceptional, special; **pour une large** _ou_ **bonne ~** to a great extent; **prendre qch en bonne/mauvaise ~** to take sth well/badly; **faire la ~ des choses** to make allowances; **faire la ~ du feu** (_fig_) to cut one's losses; **faire la ~ (trop) belle à qn** to give sb more than his (_ou_ her) share.

part. _abr_ = **particulier.**

partage [paʀtaʒ] _nm_ (_voir partager_) sharing (out) _q_, share-out; sharing; dividing up; (_POL: de suffrages_) share; **recevoir qch en ~** to receive sth as one's share (_ou_ lot); **sans ~** undivided.

partagé, e [paʀtaʒe] _a_ (_opinions etc_) divided; (_amour_) shared; **temps ~** (_INFORM_) time sharing; **être ~ entre** to be shared between; **être ~ sur** to be divided about.

partager [paʀtaʒe] _vt_ to share; (_distribuer, répartir_) to share (out); (_morceler, diviser_) to divide (up); **se ~** _vt_ (_héritage etc_) to share between themselves (_ou_ ourselves _etc_).

partance [paʀtɑ̃s]: **en ~** _ad_ outbound, due to leave; **en ~ pour** (bound) for.

partant, e [paʀtɑ̃, -ɑ̃t] _vb voir_ **partir** ♦ _a_: **être ~ pour qch** (_d'accord pour_) to be quite ready for sth ♦ _nm_ (_SPORT_) starter; (_HIPPISME_) runner.

partenaire [paʀtənɛʀ] _nm/f_ partner; **~s sociaux** management and workforce.

parterre [paʀtɛʀ] _nm_ (_de fleurs_) (flower) bed, border; (_THÉÂTRE_) stalls _pl_.

parti [paʀti] _nm_ (_POL_) party; (_décision_) course of action; (_personne à marier_) match; **tirer ~ de** to take advantage of, turn to good account; **prendre le ~ de faire** to make up one's mind to do, resolve to do; **prendre le ~ de qn** to stand up for sb, side with sb; **prendre ~ (pour/contre)** to take sides _ou_ a stand (for/against); **prendre son ~ de** to come to terms with; **~ pris** bias.

partial, e, aux [paʀsjal, -o] _a_ biased, partial.

partialement [paʀsjalmɑ̃] _ad_ in a biased way.

partialité [paʀsjalite] _nf_ bias, partiality.

participant, e [paʀtisipɑ̃, -ɑ̃t] _nm/f_ participant; (_à un concours_) entrant; (_d'une société_) member.

participation [paʀtisipasjɔ̃] _nf_ participation; sharing; (_COMM_) interest; **la ~ aux bénéfices** profit-sharing; **la ~ ouvrière** worker participation; **"avec la ~ de ..."** "featuring ...".

participe [paʀtisip] _nm_ participle; **~ passé/ présent** past/present participle.

participer [paʀtisipe]: **~ à** _vt_ (_course, réunion_) to take part in; (_profits etc_) to share in; (_frais etc_) to contribute to; (_entreprise: financièrement_) to cooperate in; (_chagrin, succès de qn_) to share (in); **~ de** _vt_ to partake of.

particulariser [paʀtikylaʀize] _vt_: **se ~** to mark o.s. (_ou_ itself) out.

particularisme [paʀtikylaʀism(ə)] _nm_ sense of identity.

particularité [paʀtikylaʀite] _nf_ particularity; (_distinctive_) characteristic, feature.

particule [paʀtikyl] _nf_ particle; **~ (nobiliaire)** nobiliary particle.

particulier, ière [paʀtikylje, -jɛʀ] _a_ (_personnel, privé_) private; (_spécial_) special, particular; (_caractéristique_) characteristic, distinctive; (_spécifique_) particular ♦ _nm_ (_individu: ADMIN_) private individual; **"~ vend ..."** (_COMM_) "for sale privately ...", "for sale by owner ..." (_US_); **~ à** peculiar to; **en ~** _ad_ (_surtout_) in particular, particularly; (_à part_) separately; (_en privé_) in private.

particulièrement [paʀtikyljɛʀmɑ̃] _ad_ particularly.

partie [paʀti] _nf_ (_gén_) part; (_profession, spécialité_) field, subject; (_JUR etc_: _protagonistes_) party; (_de cartes, tennis etc_) game; (_fig: lutte, combat_) struggle, fight; **une ~ de campagne/de pêche** an outing in the country/a fishing party _ou_ trip; **en ~** _ad_ partly, in part; **faire ~ de** to belong to; (_suj: chose_) to be part of; **prendre qn à ~** to take sb to task; (_malmener_) to set on sb; **en grande ~** largely, in the main; **ce n'est que ~ remise** it will be for another time _ou_ the next time; **avoir ~ liée avec qn** to be in league with sb; **~ civile** (_JUR_) party claiming damages in a criminal case.

partiel, le [paʀsjɛl] _a_ partial ♦ _nm_ (_SCOL_) class exam.

partiellement [paʀsjɛlmɑ̃] _ad_ partially, partly.

partir [paʀtiʀ] _vi_ (_gén_) to go; (_quitter_) to go, leave; (_s'éloigner_) to go (_ou_ drive _etc_) away _ou_ off; (_moteur_) to start; (_pétard_) to go off; (_bouchon_) to come out; (_bouton_) to come off; **~ de** (_lieu: quitter_) to leave; (: _commencer à_) to start from; (_date_) to run _ou_ start from; **~ pour/à** (_lieu, pays etc_) to leave for/go off to; **à ~ de** from.

partisan, e [paʀtizɑ̃, -an] _nm/f_ partisan; (_d'un parti, régime etc_) supporter ♦ _a_ (_lutte, querelle_) partisan, one-sided; **être ~ de qch/ faire** to be in favour (_Brit_) _ou_ favor (_US_) of sth/doing.

partitif, ive [paʀtitif, -iv] _a_: **article ~** partitive article.

partition [paʀtisjɔ̃] _nf_ (_MUS_) score.

partout [paʀtu] _ad_ everywhere; **~ où il allait** everywhere _ou_ wherever he went; **trente ~** (_TENNIS_) thirty all.

paru [paʀy] _pp de_ **paraître.**

parure [paʀyʀ] _nf_ (_bijoux etc_) finery _q_; jewellery _q_ (_Brit_), jewelry _q_ (_US_); (_assortiment_) set.

parus [paʀy] _etc vb voir_ **paraître.**

parution [paʀysjɔ̃] _nf_ publication, appearance.

parvenir [paʀvəniʀ]: **~ à** _vt_ (_atteindre_) to reach; (_obtenir, arriver à_) to attain; (_réus-_

sir): ~ **à faire** to manage to do, succeed in doing; **faire** ~ **qch à qn** to have sth sent to sb.

parvenu, e [parvəny] *pp de* **parvenir** ♦ *nm/f* (*péj*) parvenu, upstart.

parviendrai [parvjɛ̃dre], **parviens** [parvjɛ̃] *etc voir* **parvenir**.

parvis [parvi] *nm* square (*in front of a church*).

pas [pɑ] *nm voir le mot suivant* ♦ *ad* not; ~ **de** no; **ne ... ~**: **il ne le voit ~/ne l'a ~ vu/ ne le verra ~** he doesn't see it/hasn't seen it *ou* didn't see it/won't see it; **ils n'ont ~ de voiture/d'enfants** they haven't got a car/any children, they have no car/children; ~ **de sucre, merci** no sugar, thank you; **il m'a dit de ne ~ le faire** he told me not to do it; **il n'est ~ plus grand** he isn't bigger, he's no bigger; **... lui ~ ou ~ lui** he doesn't (*ou* isn't *etc*); **ceci est à vous ou ~?** is this yours or not?; **non ~ que** ... not that ...; **une pomme ~ mûre** an unripe apple, an apple which isn't ripe; ~ **du tout** not at all; ~ **encore** not yet; ~ **plus tard qu'hier** only yesterday; ~ **mal** a not bad, quite good (*ou* pretty *ou* nice) ♦ *ad* quite well; (*beaucoup*) quite a lot; ~ **mal de** quite a lot of.

pas [pɑ] *ad voir le mot précédent* ♦ *nm* (*allure, mesure*) pace; (*démarche*) tread; (*enjambée, DANSE, fig: étape*) step; (*bruit*) (foot)step; (*trace*) footprint; (*allure*) pace; (*d'un cheval*) walk; (*mesure*) pace; (*TECH: de vis, d'écrou*) thread; ~ **à** ~ step by step; **au** ~ at walking pace; **de ce** ~ (*à l'instant même*) straightaway, at once; **marcher à grands** ~ to stride along; **mettre qn au** ~ to bring sb to heel; **au** ~ **de gymnastique/de course** at a jog trot/at a run; **à** ~ **de loup** stealthily; **faire les cent** ~ to pace up and down; **faire les premiers** ~ to make the first move; **retourner** *ou* **revenir sur ses** ~ to retrace one's steps; **se tirer d'un mauvais** ~ to get o.s. out of a tight spot; **sur le** ~ **de la porte** on the doorstep; **le** ~ **de Calais** (*détroit*) the Straits *pl* of Dover; ~ **de porte** (*fig*) key money.

pascal, e, aux [paskal, -o] *a* Easter *cpd*.

passable [pɑsabl(ə)] *a* passable, tolerable.

passablement [pɑsabləmɑ̃] *ad* (*pas trop mal*) reasonably well; (*beaucoup*) quite a lot.

passade [pɑsad] *nf* passing fancy, whim.

passage [pɑsaʒ] *nm* (*fait de passer*) *voir* **passer**; (*lieu, prix de la traversée, extrait de livre etc*) passage; (*chemin*) way; (*itinéraire*): **sur le** ~ **du cortège** along the route of the procession; **"laissez/n'obstruez pas le ~"** "keep clear/do not obstruct"; **au** ~ (*en passant*) as I (*ou* he *etc*) went by; **de** ~ (*touristes*) passing through; (*amants etc*) casual; ~ **clouté** pedestrian crossing; **"~ interdit"** "no entry"; ~ **à niveau** level (*Brit*) *ou* grade (*US*) crossing; **"~ protégé"** *right of way over secondary road(s) on your right*; ~ **souterrain** subway (*Brit*), underpass; ~ **à tabac** beating-up; ~ **à vide** (*fig*) bad patch.

passager, ère [pɑsaʒe, -ɛr] *a* passing; (*hôte*) short-stay *cpd*; (*oiseau*) migratory ♦ *nm/f* passenger; ~ **clandestin** stowaway.

passagèrement [pɑsaʒɛrmɑ̃] *ad* temporarily, for a short time.

passant, e [pɑsɑ̃, -ɑ̃t] *a* (*rue, endroit*) busy ♦ *nm/f* passer-by ♦ *nm* (*pour ceinture etc*) loop; **en ~: remarquer qch en** ~ to notice sth in passing.

passation [pɑsɑsjɔ̃] *nf* (*JUR: d'un acte*) signing; ~ **des pouvoirs** transfer *ou* handover of power.

passe [pɑs] *nf* (*SPORT, magnétique*) pass; (*NAVIG*) channel ♦ *nm* (*passe-partout*) master *ou* skeleton key; **être en** ~ **de faire** to be on the way to doing; **être dans une bonne/mauvaise** ~ (*fig*) to be going through a good/bad patch; ~ **d'armes** (*fig*) heated exchange.

passé, e [pɑse] *a* (*événement, temps*) past; (*couleur, tapisserie*) faded; (*précédent*): **dimanche** ~ last Sunday ♦ *prép* after ♦ *nm* past; (*LING*) past (tense); **il est** ~ **midi** *ou* **midi** ~ it's gone (*Brit*) *ou* past twelve; ~ **de mode** out of fashion; ~ **composé** perfect (tense); ~ **simple** past historic.

passe-droit [pɑsdrwa] *nm* special privilege.

passéiste [pɑseist(ə)] *a* backward-looking.

passementerie [pɑsmɑ̃tri] *nf* trimmings *pl*.

passe-montagne [pɑsmɔ̃taɲ] *nm* balaclava.

passe-partout [pɑspartu] *nm inv* master *ou* skeleton key ♦ *a inv* all-purpose.

passe-passe [pɑspɑs] *nm*: **tour de** ~ trick, sleight of hand *q*.

passe-plat [pɑspla] *nm* serving hatch.

passeport [pɑspɔr] *nm* passport.

passer [pɑse] *vi* (*se rendre, aller*) to go; (*voiture, piétons: défiler*) to pass (by), go by; (*faire une halte rapide: facteur, laitier etc*) to come, call; (*: pour rendre visite*) to call *ou* drop in; (*courant, air, lumière, franchir un obstacle etc*) to get through; (*accusé, projet de loi*): ~ **devant** to come before; (*film, émission*) to be on; (*temps, jours*) to pass, go by; (*liquide, café*) to go through; (*être digéré, avalé*) to go down; (*couleur, papier*) to fade; (*mode*) to die out; (*douleur*) to pass, go away; (*CARTES*) to pass; (*SCOL*) to go up (to the next class); (*devenir*): ~ **président** to be appointed *ou* become president ♦ *vt* (*frontière, rivière etc*) to cross; (*douane*) to go through; (*examen*) to sit, take; (*visite médicale etc*) to have; (*journée, temps*) to spend; (*donner*): ~ **qch à qn** to pass sth to sb; to give sb sth; (*transmettre*): ~ **qch à qn** to pass sth on to sb; (*enfiler: vêtement*): to slip on; (*faire entrer, mettre*): **(faire)** ~ **qch dans/par** to get sth into/ through; (*café*) to pour the water on; (*thé, soupe*) to strain; (*film, pièce*) to show, put on; (*disque*) to play, put on; (*marché, accord*) to make; (*tolérer*): ~ **qch à qn** to let sb get away with sth; **se** ~ *vi* (*avoir lieu: scène, action*) to take place; (*se dérouler: entretien etc*) to go; (*arriver*): **que s'est-il passé?** what happened?; (*s'écouler: semaine etc*) to pass, go by; **se** ~ **de** *vt* to go *ou* do without; **se** ~ **les mains sous l'eau/de l'eau sur le visage** to put one's hands under the tap/run water over one's face; **en passant** in passing; ~ **par** to go through; **passez devant/par ici** go in front/this way; ~ **sur** *vt* *(faute, détail inutile)* to pass over; ~ **dans les mœurs/l'usage** to become the custom/ normal usage; ~ **avant qch/qn** *(fig)* to come before sth/sb; **laisser** ~ *(air, lumière, personne)* to let through; *(occasion)* to let slip, miss; *(erreur)* to overlook; **faire** ~ *(message)* to get over *ou* across; **faire** ~ **à qn le goût de qch** to cure sb of his *(ou* her) taste for sth; ~ **à la radio/ fouille** to be X-rayed/searched; ~ **à la radio/télévision** to be on the radio/on television; ~ **à table** to sit down to eat; ~ **au salon** to go into the sitting room; ~ **à l'opposition** to go over to the opposition; ~ **aux aveux** to confess, make a confession; ~ **à l'action** to go into action; ~ **pour riche** to be taken for a rich man; **il passait pour avoir** he was said to have; **faire** ~ **qn/qch pour** to make sb/sth out to be; **passe encore de le penser, mais de le dire!** it's one thing to think it, but to say it!; **passons!** let's say no more (about it); **et j'en passe!** and that's not all!; ~ **en seconde, la seconde** *(AUTO)* to change into second; ~ **qch en fraude** to smuggle sth in *(ou* out); ~ **la main par la portière** to stick one's hand out of the door; ~ **le balai/l'aspirateur** to sweep the floor/hoover; ~ **commande/la parole à qn** to hand over to sb; **je vous passe M X** *(je vous mets en communication avec lui)* I'm putting you through to Mr X; *(je lui passe l'appareil)* here is Mr X, I'll hand you over to Mr X; ~ **prendre** to (come and) collect.

passereau, x [pasʀo] *nm* sparrow.

passerelle [pasʀɛl] *nf* footbridge; *(de navire, avion)* gangway; *(NAVIG):* ~ **(de commandement)** bridge.

passe-temps [pastɑ̃] *nm inv* pastime.

passette [pasɛt] *nf* (tea-)strainer.

passeur, euse [pasœʀ, -øz] *nm/f* smuggler.

passible [pasibl(ə)] *a:* ~ **de** liable to.

passif, ive [pasif, -iv] *a* passive ♦ *nm* *(LING)* passive; *(COMM)* liabilities *pl.*

passion [pasjɔ̃] *nf* passion; **avoir la** ~ **de** to have a passion for; **fruit de la** ~ passion fruit.

passionnant, e [pasjɔnɑ̃, -ɑ̃t] *a* fascinating.

passionné, e [pasjɔne] *a (personne, tempérament)* passionate; *(description)* impassioned ♦ *nm/f:* **c'est un** ~ **d'échecs** he's a chess fanatic; **être** ~ **de** *ou* **pour qch** to have a passion for sth.

passionnel, le [pasjɔnɛl] *a* of passion.

passionnément [pasjɔnemɑ̃] *ad* passionately.

passionner [pasjɔne] *vt (personne)* to fascinate, grip; *(débat, discussion)* to in-flame; **se** ~ **pour** to take an avid interest in; to have a passion for.

passivement [pasivmɑ̃] *ad* passively.

passivité [pasivite] *nf* passivity, passiveness.

passoire [paswaʀ] *nf* sieve; *(à légumes)* colander; *(à thé)* strainer.

pastel [pastɛl] *nm, a inv (ART)* pastel.

pastèque [pastɛk] *nf* watermelon.

pasteur [pastœʀ] *nm (protestant)* minister, pastor.

pasteuriser [pastœʀize] *vt* to pasteurize.

pastiche [pastiʃ] *nm* pastiche.

pastille [pastij] *nf (à sucer)* lozenge, pastille;

(de papier etc) (small) disc; ~**s pour la toux** cough drops *ou* lozenges.

pastis [pastis] *nm* anise-flavoured alcoholic drink.

pastoral, e, aux [pastɔʀal, -o] *a* pastoral.

patagon, ne [patagɔ̃, -ɔn] *a* Patagonian.

Patagonie [patagɔni] *nf:* **la** ~ Patagonia.

patate [patat] *nf* spud; ~ **douce** sweet potato.

pataud, e [pato, -od] *a* lumbering.

patauger [patoʒe] *vi (pour s'amuser)* to splash about; *(avec effort)* to wade about; *(fig)* to flounder; ~ **dans** *(en marchant)* to wade through.

pâte [pat] *nf (à tarte)* pastry; *(à pain)* dough; *(à frire)* batter; *(substance molle)* paste; cream; ~**s** *nfpl (macaroni etc)* pasta *sg;* **fromage à** ~ **dure/molle** hard/soft cheese; ~ **d'amandes** almond paste; ~ **brisée** short-crust *(Brit)* ou pie crust *(US)* pastry; ~ **à choux/feuilletée** choux/puff *ou* flaky *(Brit)* pastry; ~ **de fruits** crystallized fruit *q;* ~ **à modeler** modelling clay, Plasticine ® *(Brit);* ~ **à papier** paper pulp.

pâté [pate] *nm (charcuterie: terrine)* pâté; *(tache)* ink blot; *(de sable)* sandpie; ~ **(en croûte)** ≈ meat pie; ~ **de foie** liver pâté; ~ **de maisons** block of houses.

pâtée [pate] *nf* mash, feed.

patelin [patlɛ̃] *nm* little place.

patente [patɑ̃t] *nf (COMM)* trading licence *(Brit)* ou license *(US).*

patenté, e [patɑ̃te] *a (COMM)* licensed; *(fig: attitré)* registered, (officially) recognized.

patère [patɛʀ] *nf* (coat-)peg.

paternaliste [patɛʀnalist(ə)] *a* paternalistic.

paternel, le [patɛʀnɛl] *a (amour, soins)* fatherly; *(ligne, autorité)* paternal.

paternité [patɛʀnite] *nf* paternity, fatherhood.

pâteux, euse [patø, -øz] *a* thick; pasty; **avoir la bouche** *ou* **langue pâteuse** to have a furred *(Brit)* ou coated tongue.

pathétique [patetik] *a* pathetic, moving.

pathologie [patɔlɔʒi] *nf* pathology.

pathologique [patɔlɔʒik] *a* pathological.

patibulaire [patibylɛʀ] *a* sinister.

patiemment [pasjamɑ̃] *ad* patiently.

patience [pasjɑ̃s] *nf* patience; **être à bout de** ~ to have run out of patience; **perdre/ prendre** ~ to lose (one's)/have patience.

patient, e [pasjɑ̃, -ɑ̃t] *a, nm/f* patient.

patienter [pasjɑ̃te] *vi* to wait.

patin [patɛ̃] *nm* skate; *(sport)* skating; *(de traineau, luge)* runner; *(pièce de tissu)* cloth pad *(used as slippers to protect polished floor);* ~ **(de frein)** brake block; ~**s (à glace)** (ice) skates; ~**s à roulettes** roller skates.

patinage [patinaʒ] *nm* skating; ~ **artistique/ de vitesse** figure/speed skating.

patine [patin] *nf* sheen.

patiner [patine] *vi* to skate; *(embrayage)* to slip; *(roue, voiture)* to spin; **se** ~ *vi (meu-ble, cuir)* to acquire a sheen, become polished.

patineur, euse [patinœʀ, -øz] *nm/f* skater.

patinoire [patinwaʀ] *nf* skating rink, (ice) rink.

patio [patjo] *nm* patio.

pâtir [patiʀ] ~ **de** *vt* to suffer because of.

pâtisserie [patisʀi] *nf (boutique)* cake shop;

(*métier*) confectionery; (*à la maison*) pastry-ou cake-making, baking; ~s *nfpl* (*gâteaux*) pastries, cakes.

pâtissier, ière [pɑtisje, -jɛʀ] *nm/f* pastrycook; confectioner.

patois [patwa] *nm* dialect, patois.

patriarche [patʀijaʀʃ(ə)] *nm* patriarch.

patrie [patʀi] *nf* homeland.

patrimoine [patʀimwan] *nm* inheritance, patrimony; (*culture*) heritage; ~ **génétique** *ou* **héréditaire** genetic inheritance.

patriote [patʀijɔt] *a* patriotic ♦ *nm/f* patriot.

patriotique [patʀijɔtik] *a* patriotic.

patron, ne [patʀɔ̃, -ɔn] *nm/f* (*chef*) boss, manager/eress; (*propriétaire*) owner, proprietor/tress; (*employeur*) employer; (*MÉD*) ≈ senior consultant; (*REL*) patron saint ♦ *nm* (*COUTURE*) pattern; ~ **de thèse** supervisor (*of postgraduate thesis*).

patronage [patʀɔnaʒ] *nm* patronage; (*organisation, club*) (parish) youth club; (parish) children's club.

patronal, e, aux [patʀɔnal, -o] *a* (*syndicat, intérêts*) employers'.

patronat [patʀɔna] *nm* employers *pl*.

patronner [patʀɔne] *vt* to sponsor, support.

patronnesse [patʀɔnɛs] *af*: **dame ~** patroness.

patronyme [patʀɔnim] *nm* name.

patronymique [patʀɔnimik] *a*: **nom ~** patronymic (name).

patrouille [patʀuj] *nf* patrol.

patrouiller [patʀuje] *vi* to patrol, be on patrol.

patrouilleur [patʀujœʀ] *nm* (*AVIAT*) scout (plane); (*NAVIG*) patrol boat.

patte [pat] *nf* (*jambe*) leg; (*pied: de chien, chat*) paw; (*: d'oiseau*) foot; (*languette*) strap; (*: de poche*) flap; (*favoris*): ~s (**de lapin**) (short) sideburns; **à ~s d'éléphant** *a* (*pantalon*) flared; ~s **de mouche** (*fig*) spidery scrawl *sg*; ~s **d'oie** (*fig*) crow's feet.

pattemouille [patmuj] *nf* damp cloth (*for ironing*).

pâturage [pɑtyʀaʒ] *nm* pasture.

pâture [pɑtyʀ] *nf* food.

paume [pom] *nf* palm.

paumé, e [pome] *nm/f* (*fam*) drop-out.

paumer [pome] *vt* (*fam*) to lose.

paupière [popjɛʀ] *nf* eyelid.

paupiette [popjɛt] *nf*: ~s **de veau** veal olives.

pause [poz] *nf* (*arrêt*) break; (*en parlant, MUS*) pause.

pause-café, *pl* **pauses-café** [pozkafe] *nf* coffee-break.

pauvre [povʀ(ə)] *a* poor ♦ *nm/f* poor man/woman; **les ~s** the poor; ~ **en calcium** low in calcium.

pauvrement [povʀəmɑ̃] *ad* poorly.

pauvreté [povʀəte] *nf* (*état*) poverty.

pavage [pavaʒ] *nm* paving; cobbles *pl*.

pavaner [pavane]: **se ~** *vi* to strut about.

pavé, e [pave] *a* (*cour*) paved; (*rue*) cobbled ♦ *nm* (*bloc*) paving stone; cobblestone; (*pavage*) paving; (*bifteck*) slab of steak; (*fam: livre*) hefty tome; **être sur le ~** (*sans domicile*) to be on the streets; (*sans emploi*) to be out of a job; ~ **numérique** (*INFORM*) keypad.

pavillon [pavijɔ̃] *nm* (*de banlieue*) small

(*detached*) house; (*kiosque*) lodge; pavilion; (*d'hôpital*) ward; (*MUS: de cor etc*) bell; (*ANAT: de l'oreille*) pavilion, pinna; (*NAVIG*) flag; ~ **de complaisance** flag of convenience.

pavoiser [pavwaze] *vt* to deck with flags ♦ *vi* to put out flags; (*fig*) to rejoice, exult.

pavot [pavo] *nm* poppy.

payable [pɛjabl(ə)] *a* payable.

payant, e [pɛjɑ̃, -ɑ̃t] *a* (*spectateurs etc*) paying; (*billet*) that you pay for, to be paid for; (*fig: entreprise*) profitable; **c'est ~** you have to pay, there is a charge.

paye [pɛj] *nf* pay, wages *pl*.

payement [pɛjmɑ̃] *nm* payment.

payer [pɛje] *vt* (*créancier, employé, loyer*) to pay; (*achat, réparations, fig: faute*) to pay for ♦ *vi* to pay; (*métier*) to pay, be well-paid; (*effort, tactique etc*) to pay off; **il me l'a fait ~ 10 F** he charged me 10 F for it; ~ **qn** (*ses efforts, peines*) to reward sb for; ~ **qch à qn** to buy sth for sb, buy sb sth; **ils nous ont payé le voyage** they paid for our trip; ~ **de sa personne** to give of oneself; ~ **d'audace** to act with great daring; ~ **cher qch** to pay dear(ly) for sth; **cela ne paie pas de mine** it doesn't look much; **se ~ qch** to buy o.s. sth; **se ~ des mots** to shoot one's mouth off; **se ~ la tête de qn** to take the mickey out of sb (*Brit*), make a fool of sb; (*duper*) to take sb for a ride.

payeur, euse [pɛjœʀ, -øz] *a* (*organisme, bureau*) payments *cpd* ♦ *nm/f* payer.

pays [pei] *nm* (*territoire, habitants*) country, land; (*région*) region; (*village*) village; **du ~** *a* local; **le ~ de Galles** Wales.

paysage [peizaʒ] *nm* landscape.

paysagiste [peizaʒist(ə)] *nm/f* (*de jardin*) landscape gardener; (*ART*) landscapist, landscape painter.

paysan, ne [peizɑ̃, -an] *nm/f* countryman/woman; farmer; (*péj*) peasant ♦ *a* country *cpd*, farming; farmers'.

paysannat [peizana] *nm* peasantry.

Pays-Bas [peiba] *nmpl*: **les ~** the Netherlands.

PC *sigle m* (*POL*) = **Parti communiste**; (*INFORM*: = *personal computer*) PC; (= *prêt conventionné*) *type of loan for house purchase*; (*CONSTR*) = **permis de construire**; (*MIL*) = **poste de commandement**.

pcc *abr* (= *pour copie conforme*) c.c.

Pce *abr* = **prince**.

Pcesse *abr* = **princesse**.

PCV *abr* (= *percevoir*) *voir* **communication**.

p de p *abr* = **pas de porte**.

PDG *sigle m* = **président directeur général**.

p.ê. *abr* = **peut-être**.

péage [peaʒ] *nm* toll; (*endroit*) tollgate; **pont à ~** toll bridge.

peau, x [po] *nf* skin; (*cuir*): **gants de ~** leather gloves; **être bien/mal dans sa ~** to be at ease/odds with oneself; **se mettre dans la ~ de qn** to put o.s. in sb's place *ou* shoes; **faire ~ neuve** (*se renouveler*) to change one's image; ~ **de chamois** (*chiffon*) chamois leather, shammy; ~ **d'orange** orange peel.

peaufiner [pofine] *vt* to polish (up).

Peau-Rouge [poʀuʒ] *nm/f* Red Indian, red-

skin.
peccadille [pekadij] *nf* trifle, peccadillo.
péché [peʃe] *nm* sin; ~ **mignon** weakness.
pêche [pεʃ] *nf* (*sport, activité*) fishing; (*poissons pêchés*) catch; (*fruit*) peach; **aller à la** ~ to go fishing; **avoir la** ~ (*fam*) to be on (top) form; ~ **à la ligne** (*en rivière*) angling; ~ **sous-marine** deep-sea fishing.
pêche-abricot, *pl* **pêches-abricots** [pεʃabriko] *nf* yellow peach.
pécher [peʃe] *vi* (*REL*) to sin; (*fig: personne*) to err; (: *chose*) to be flawed; ~ **contre la bienséance** to break the rules of good behaviour.
pêcher [peʃe] *nm* peach tree ♦ *vi* to go fishing; (*en rivière*) to go angling ♦ *vt* (*attraper*) to catch, land; (*chercher*) to fish for; ~ **au chalut** to trawl.
pécheur, eresse [peʃœr, peʃrεs] *nm/f* sinner.
pêcheur [peʃœr] *nm* (*voir pêcher*) fisherman; angler; ~ **de perles** pearl diver.
pectine [pεktin] *nf* pectin.
pectoral, e, aux [pεktɔral, -o] *a* (*ANAT*) pectoral; (*sirop*) throat *cpd*, cough *cpd* ♦ *nmpl* pectoral muscles.
pécule [pekyl] *nm* savings *pl*, nest egg; (*d'un détenu*) earnings *pl* (*paid on release*).
pécuniaire [pekynjεr] *a* financial.
pédagogie [pedagɔʒi] *nf* educational methods *pl*, pedagogy.
pédagogique [pedagɔʒik] *a* educational; **formation** ~ teacher training.
pédagogue [pedagɔg] *nm/f* teacher; education(al)ist.
pédale [pedal] *nf* pedal; **mettre la** ~ **douce** to soft-pedal.
pédaler [pedale] *vi* to pedal.
pédalier [pedalje] *nm* pedal and gear mechanism.
pédalo [pedalo] *nm* pedalo, pedal-boat.
pédant, e [pedɑ̃, -ɑ̃t] *a* (*péj*) pedantic ♦ *nm/f* pedant.
pédantisme [pedɑ̃tism(ə)] *nm* pedantry.
pédéraste [pederast(ə)] *nm* homosexual, pederast.
pédérastie [pederasti] *nf* homosexuality, pederasty.
pédestre [pedεstr(ə)] *a*: **tourisme** ~ hiking; **randonnée** ~ (*activité*) rambling; (*excursion*) ramble.
pédiatre [pedjatr(ə)] *nm/f* paediatrician (*Brit*), pediatrician *ou* pediatrist (*US*), child specialist.
pédiatrie [pedjatri] *nf* paediatrics *sg* (*Brit*), pediatrics *sg* (*US*).
pédicure [pedikyr] *nm/f* chiropodist.
pedigree [pedigre] *nm* pedigree.
peeling [piliŋ] *nm* exfoliation treatment.
PEEP *sigle f* = *Fédération des parents d'élèves de l'enseignement public*.
pègre [pεgr(ə)] *nf* underworld.
peigne [pεɲ] *vb voir* **peindre, peigner** ♦ *nm* comb.
peigné, e [peɲe] *a*: **laine** ~e wool worsted; combed wool.
peigner [peɲe] *vt* to comb (the hair of); **se** ~ to comb one's hair.
peignez [peɲe] *etc vb voir* **peindre**.
peignoir [peɲwar] *nm* dressing gown; ~ **de**

bain bathrobe; ~ **de plage** beach robe.
peignons [peɲɔ̃] *vb voir* **peindre**.
peinard, e [penar, -ard(ə)] *a* (*emploi*) cushy (*Brit*), easy; (*personne*): **on est** ~ **ici** we're left in peace here.
peindre [pε̃dr(ə)] *vt* to paint; (*fig*) to portray, depict.
peine [pεn] *nf* (*affliction*) sorrow, sadness *q*; (*mal, effort*) trouble *q*, effort; (*difficulté*) difficulty; (*punition, châtiment*) punishment; (*JUR*) sentence; **faire de la** ~ **à qn** to distress *ou* upset sb; **prendre la** ~ **de faire** to go to the trouble of doing; **se donner de la** ~ to make an effort; **ce n'est pas la** ~ **de faire** there's no point in doing, it's not worth doing; **ce n'est pas la** ~ **que vous fassiez** there's no point (in) you doing; **avoir de la** ~ **à faire** to have difficulty doing; **donnez-vous** *ou* **veuillez vous donner la** ~ **d'entrer** please do come in; **c'est** ~ **perdue** it's a waste of time (and effort); **à** ~ *ad* scarcely, hardly, barely; **à** ~ ... **que** hardly ... than; **c'est à** ~ **si** ... it's (*ou* it was) a job to ...; **sous** ~: **sous** ~ **d'être puni** for fear of being punished; **défense d'afficher sous** ~ **d'amende** bill-posters will be fined; ~ **capitale** capital punishment; ~ **de mort** death sentence *ou* penalty.
peiner [pene] *vi* to work hard; to struggle; (*moteur, voiture*) to labour (*Brit*), labor (*US*) ♦ *vt* to grieve, sadden.
peint, e [pε̃, pε̃t] *pp de* **peindre**.
peintre [pε̃tr(ə)] *nm* painter; ~ **en bâtiment** house painter, painter and decorator; ~ **d'enseignes** signwriter.
peinture [pε̃tyr] *nf* painting; (*couche de couleur, couleur*) paint; (*surfaces peintes: aussi*: ~**s**) paintwork; **je ne peux pas le voir en** ~ I can't stand the sight of him; ~ **mate/brillante** matt/gloss paint; "~ **fraîche**" "wet paint".
péjoratif, ive [peʒɔratif, -iv] *a* pejorative, derogatory.
Pékin [pekε̃] *n* Peking.
pékinois, e [pekinwa, -waz] *a* Pekin(g)ese ♦ *nm* (*chien*) peke, pekin(g)ese; (*LING*) Mandarin, Pekin(g)ese ♦ *nm/f*: **P**~, **e** Pekin(g)ese.
PEL *sigle m* (= *Plan d'épargne logement*) *savings scheme providing lower-interest mortgages*.
pelade [pəlad] *nf* alopecia.
pelage [pəlaʒ] *nm* coat, fur.
pelé, e [pəle] *a* (*chien*) hairless; (*vêtement*) threadbare; (*terrain*) bare.
pêle-mêle [pεlmεl] *ad* higgledy-piggledy.
peler [pəle] *vt, vi* to peel.
pèlerin [pεlrε̃] *nm* pilgrim.
pèlerinage [pεlrinaʒ] *nm* (*voyage*) pilgrimage; (*lieu*) place of pilgrimage, shrine.
pèlerine [pεlrin] *nf* cape.
pélican [pelikɑ̃] *nm* pelican.
pelle [pεl] *nf* shovel; (*d'enfant, de terrassier*) spade; ~ **à gâteau** cake slice; ~ **mécanique** mechanical digger.
pelletée [pεlte] *nf* shovelful; spadeful.
pelleter [pεlte] *vt* to shovel (up).
pelleteuse [pεltøz] *nf* mechanical digger, excavator.

pelletier [pɛltje] nm furrier.

pellicule [pelikyl] nf film; **~s** nfpl (MÉD) dandruff sg.

Péloponnèse [pelɔpɔnɛz] nm: **le ~** the Peloponnese.

pelote [pəlɔt] nf (de fil, laine) ball; (d'épingles) pin cushion; **~ basque** pelota.

peloter [pəlɔte] vt (fam) to feel (up); **se ~** to pet.

peloton [pəlɔtɔ̃] nm (groupe: personnes) group; (: pompiers, gendarmes) squad; (: SPORT) pack; (de laine) ball; **~ d'exécution** firing squad.

pelotonner [pəlɔtɔne]: **se ~** vi to curl (o.s.) up.

pelouse [pəluz] nf lawn; (HIPPISME) spectating area inside racetrack.

peluche [pəlyʃ] nf (bit of) fluff; **animal en ~** soft toy, fluffy animal.

pelucher [p(ə)lyʃe] vi to become fluffy, fluff up.

pelucheux, euse [p(ə)lyʃø, -øz] a fluffy.

pelure [pəlyʀ] nf peeling, peel q; **~ d'oignon** onion skin.

pénal, e, aux [penal, -o] a penal.

pénaliser [penalize] vt to penalize.

pénalité [penalite] nf penalty.

penalty, ies [penalti, -z] nm (SPORT) penalty (kick).

pénard, e [penaʀ, -aʀd(ə)] a = **peinard**.

pénates [penat] nmpl: **regagner ses ~** to return to the bosom of one's family.

penaud, e [pəno, -od] a sheepish, contrite.

penchant [pɑ̃ʃɑ̃] nm: **un ~ à faire/à qch** a tendency to do/to sth; **un ~ pour qch** a liking ou fondness for sth.

penché, e [pɑ̃ʃe] a slanting.

pencher [pɑ̃ʃe] vi to tilt, lean over ♦ vt to tilt; **se ~** vi to lean over; (se baisser) to bend down; **se ~ sur** to bend over; (fig: problème) to look into; **se ~ au dehors** to lean out; **~ pour** to be inclined to favour (Brit) ou favor (US).

pendable [pɑ̃dabl(ə)] a: **tour ~** rotten trick; **c'est un cas ~!** he (ou she) deserves to be shot!

pendaison [pɑ̃dɛzɔ̃] nf hanging.

pendant, e [pɑ̃dɑ̃, -ɑ̃t] a hanging (out); (ADMIN, JUR) pending ♦ nm counterpart; matching piece ♦ prép during; **faire ~ à** to match; **to be the counterpart of**; **~ que** while; **~s d'oreilles** drop ou pendant earrings.

pendeloque [pɑ̃dlɔk] nf pendant.

pendentif [pɑ̃dɑ̃tif] nm pendant.

penderie [pɑ̃dʀi] nf wardrobe; (placard) walk-in cupboard.

pendiller [pɑ̃dije] vi to flap (about).

pendre [pɑ̃dʀ(ə)] vt, vi to hang; **se ~ (à)** (se suicider) to hang o.s. (on); **se ~ à** (se suspendre) to hang from; **~ à** to hang (down) from; **~ qch à** (mur) to hang sth (up) on; (plafond) to hang sth (up) from.

pendu, e [pɑ̃dy] pp de **pendre** ♦ nm/f hanged man (ou woman).

pendulaire [pɑ̃dylɛʀ] a pendular, of a pendulum.

pendule [pɑ̃dyl] nf clock ♦ nm pendulum.

pendulette [pɑ̃dylɛt] nf small clock.

pêne [pɛn] nm bolt.

pénétrant, e [penetʀɑ̃, -ɑ̃t] a (air, froid) biting; (pluie) that soaks right through you; (fig: odeur) noticeable; (œil, regard) piercing; (clairvoyant, perspicace) perceptive ♦ nf (route) expressway.

pénétration [penetʀasjɔ̃] nf (fig: d'idées etc) penetration; (perspicacité) perception.

pénétré, e [penetʀe] a (air, ton) earnest; **être ~ de soi-même/son importance** to be full of oneself/one's own importance.

pénétrer [penetʀe] vi to come ou get in ♦ vt to penetrate; **~ dans** to enter; (suj: froid, projectile) to penetrate; (: air, eau) to come into, get into; (mystère, secret) to fathom; **se ~ de qch** to get sth firmly set in one's mind.

pénible [penibl(ə)] a (astreignant) hard; (affligeant) painful; (personne, caractère) tiresome; **il m'est ~ de ...** I'm sorry to ....

péniblement [penibləmɑ̃] ad with difficulty.

péniche [peniʃ] nf barge; **~ de débarquement** landing craft inv.

pénicilline [penisilin] nf penicillin.

péninsule [penɛ̃syl] nf peninsula.

pénis [penis] nm penis.

pénitence [penitɑ̃s] nf (repentir) penitence; (peine) penance; (punition, châtiment) punishment; **mettre un enfant en ~** ≈ to make a child stand in the corner; **faire ~** to do a penance.

pénitencier [penitɑ̃sje] nm prison, penitentiary (US).

pénitent, e [penitɑ̃, -ɑ̃t] a penitent.

pénitentiaire [penitɑ̃sjɛʀ] a prison cpd, penitentiary (US).

pénombre [penɔ̃bʀ(ə)] nf half-light.

pensable [pɑ̃sabl(ə)] a: **ce n'est pas ~** it's unthinkable.

pensant, e [pɑ̃sɑ̃, -ɑ̃t] a: **bien ~** right-thinking.

pense-bête [pɑ̃sbɛt] nm aide-mémoire, mnemonic device.

pensée [pɑ̃se] nf thought; (démarche, doctrine) thinking q; (BOT) pansy; **se représenter qch par la ~** to conjure up a mental picture of sth; **en ~** in one's mind.

penser [pɑ̃se] vi to think ♦ vt to think; (concevoir: problème, machine) to think out; **~ à** to think of; (songer à: ami, vacances) to think of ou about; (réfléchir à: problème, offre): **~ à qch** to think about sth, think sth over; **~ à faire qch** to think of doing sth; **~ faire qch** to be thinking of doing sth, intend to do sth; **faire ~ à** to remind one of; **n'y pensons plus** let's forget it; **vous n'y pensez pas!** don't let it bother you!; **sans ~ à mal** without meaning any harm; **je le pense aussi** I think so too; **je pense que oui/non** I think so/don't think so.

penseur [pɑ̃sœʀ] nm thinker; **libre ~** free-thinker.

pensif, ive [pɑ̃sif, -iv] a pensive, thoughtful.

pension [pɑ̃sjɔ̃] nf (allocation) pension; (prix du logement) board and lodging, bed and board; (maison particulière) boarding house; (hôtel) guesthouse, hotel; (école) boarding school; **prendre ~ chez** to take board and lodging at; **prendre qn en ~** to take sb (in) as a lodger; **mettre en** ~ to send to boarding school; ~ **alimentaire** (*d'étudiant*) living allowance; (*de divorcée*) maintenance allowance; *alimony*; ~ **complète** full board; ~ **de famille** boarding house, guesthouse; ~ **de guerre/d'invalidité** war/disablement pension.

pensionnaire [pãsjɔnɛʀ] *nm/f* boarder; guest.

pensionnat [pãsjɔna] *nm* boarding school.

pensionné, e [pãsjɔne] *nm/f* pensioner.

pensivement [pãsivmã] *ad* pensively, thoughtfully.

pensum [pɛ̃sɔm] *nm* (*SCOL*) punishment exercise; (*fig*) chore.

pentagone [pɛ̃tagɔn] *nm* pentagon; **le P**~ the Pentagon.

pentathlon [pɛ̃tatlɔ̃] *nm* pentathlon.

pente [pãt] *nf* slope; **en** ~ *a* sloping.

Pentecôte [pãtkot] *nf*: **la** ~ Whitsun (*Brit*), Pentecost; (*dimanche*) Whitsunday (*Brit*); **lundi de** ~ Whit Monday (*Brit*).

pénurie [penyʀi] *nf* shortage; ~ **de main-d'œuvre** undermanning.

pépé [pepe] *nm* (*fam*) grandad.

pépère [pepɛʀ] *a* (*fam*) cushy (*fam*), quiet ♦ *nm* (*fam*) grandad.

pépier [pepje] *vi* to chirp, tweet.

pépin [pepɛ̃] *nm* (*BOT: graine*) pip; (*fam: ennui*) snag, hitch; (*: parapluie*) brolly (*Brit*), umbrella.

pépinière [pepinjɛʀ] *nf* nursery; (*fig*) nest, breeding-ground.

pépiniériste [pepinjeʀist(ə)] *nm* nurseryman.

pépite [pepit] *nf* nugget.

PEPS *abr* (= *premier entré premier sorti*) first in first out.

PER [pɛʀ] *sigle m* (= *plan d'épargne retraite*) *type of personal pension plan.*

perçant, e [pɛʀsã, -ãt] *a* (*vue, regard, yeux*) sharp, keen; (*cri, voix*) piercing, shrill.

percée [pɛʀse] *nf* (*trouée*) opening; (*MIL, COMM, fig*) breakthrough; (*SPORT*) break.

perce-neige [pɛʀsɔnɛʒ] *nm ou f inv* snowdrop.

perce-oreille [pɛʀsɔʀɛj] *nm* earwig.

percepteur [pɛʀsɛptœʀ] *nm* tax collector.

perceptible [pɛʀsɛptibl(ə)] *a* (*son, différence*) perceptible; (*impôt*) payable, collectable.

perception [pɛʀsɛpsjɔ̃] *nf* perception; (*d'impôts etc*) collection; (*bureau*) tax (collector's) office.

percer [pɛʀse] *vt* to pierce; (*ouverture etc*) to make; (*mystère, énigme*) to penetrate ♦ *vi* to come through; (*réussir*) to break through; ~ **une dent** to cut a tooth.

perceuse [pɛʀsøz] *nf* drill; ~ **à percussion** hammer drill.

percevable [pɛʀsəvabl(ə)] *a* collectable, payable.

percevoir [pɛʀsəvwaʀ] *vt* (*distinguer*) to perceive, detect; (*taxe, impôt*) to collect; (*revenu, indemnité*) to receive.

perche [pɛʀʃ(ə)] *nf* (*ZOOL*) perch; (*bâton*) pole; ~ **à son** (*sound*) boom.

percher [pɛʀʃe] *vt*: ~ **qch sur** to perch sth on ♦ *vi*, **se** ~ *vi* (*oiseau*) to perch.

perchiste [pɛʀʃist(ə)] *nm/f* (*SPORT*) pole vaulter; (*TV etc*) boom operator.

perchoir [pɛʀʃwaʀ] *nm* perch; (*fig*) *presidency of the French National Assembly.*

perclus, e [pɛʀkly, -yz] *a*: ~ **de** (*rhumatismes*) crippled with.

perçois [pɛʀswa] *etc vb voir* **percevoir**.

percolateur [pɛʀkɔlatœʀ] *nm* percolator.

perçu, e [pɛʀsy] *pp de* **percevoir**.

percussion [pɛʀkysjɔ̃] *nf* percussion.

percussionniste [pɛʀkysjɔnist(ə)] *nm/f* percussionist.

percutant, e [pɛʀkytã, -ãt] *a* (*article etc*) resounding, forceful.

percuter [pɛʀkyte] *vt* to strike; (*suj: véhicule*) to crash into ♦ *vi*: ~ **contre** to crash into.

percuteur [pɛʀkytœʀ] *nm* firing pin, hammer.

perdant, e [pɛʀdã, -ãt] *nm/f* loser ♦ *a* losing.

perdition [pɛʀdisjɔ̃] *nf* (*morale*) ruin; **en** ~ (*NAVIG*) in distress; **lieu de** ~ den of vice.

perdre [pɛʀdʀ(ə)] *vt* to lose; (*gaspiller: temps, argent*) to waste; (*: occasion*) to waste, miss; (*personne: moralement etc*) to ruin ♦ *vi* to lose; (*sur une vente etc*) to lose out; (*récipient*) to leak; **se** ~ *vi* (*s'égarer*) to get lost, lose one's way; (*fig: se gâter*) to go to waste; (*disparaître*) to disappear, vanish; **il ne perd rien pour attendre** it can wait, it'll keep.

perdreau, x [pɛʀdro] *nm* (young) partridge.

perdrix [pɛʀdri] *nf* partridge.

perdu, e [pɛʀdy] *pp de* **perdre** ♦ *a* (*enfant, cause, objet*) lost; (*isolé*) out-of-the-way; (*COMM: emballage*) non-returnable; (*récolte etc*) ruined; (*malade*): **il est** ~ there's no hope left for him; **à vos moments** ~**s** in your spare time.

père [pɛʀ] *nm* father; ~**s** *nmpl* (*ancêtres*) forefathers; **de** ~ **en fils** from father to son; ~ **de famille** father; family man; **mon** ~ (*REL*) Father; **le** ~ **Noël** Father Christmas.

pérégrinations [peʀegʀinasjɔ̃] *nfpl* travels.

péremption [peʀãpsjɔ̃] *nf*: **date de** ~ expiry date.

péremptoire [peʀãptwaʀ] *a* peremptory.

pérennité [peʀenite] *nf* durability, lasting quality.

péréquation [peʀekwasjɔ̃] *nf* (*des salaires*) realignment; (*des prix, impôts*) equalization.

perfectible [pɛʀfɛktibl(ə)] *a* perfectible.

perfection [pɛʀfɛksjɔ̃] *nf* perfection; **à la** ~ *ad* to perfection.

perfectionné, e [pɛʀfɛksjɔne] *a* sophisticated.

perfectionnement [pɛʀfɛksjɔnmã] *nm* improvement.

perfectionner [pɛʀfɛksjɔne] *vt* to improve, perfect; **se** ~ **en anglais** to improve one's English.

perfectionniste [pɛʀfɛksjɔnist(ə)] *nm/f* perfectionist.

perfide [pɛʀfid] *a* perfidious, treacherous.

perfidie [pɛʀfidi] *nf* treachery.

perforant, e [pɛʀfɔrã, -ãt] *a* (*balle*) armour-piercing (*Brit*), armor-piercing (*US*).

perforateur, trice [pɛʀfɔratœʀ, -tʀis] *nm/f* punch-card operator ♦ *nm* (*perceuse*) borer; drill ♦ *nf* (*perceuse*) borer; drill; (*pour cartes*) card-punch; (*de bureau*) punch.

perforation [pɛʀfɔrasjɔ̃] *nf* perforation; punching; (*trou*) hole.

perforatrice [pɛʀfɔratʀis] *nf voir* **perforateur**.

perforé, e [pɛʀfɔre] *a*: **bande** ~ punched tape; **carte** ~ punch card.

perforer [pɛʀfɔʀe] vt to perforate, punch a hole (ou holes) in; (ticket, bande, carte) to punch.

perforeuse [pɛʀfɔʀøz] nf (machine) (card) punch; (personne) card punch operator.

performance [pɛʀfɔʀmɑ̃s] nf performance.

performant, e [pɛʀfɔʀmɑ̃, -ɑ̃t] a (ÉCON: produit, entreprise) high-return cpd; (TECH: appareil, machine) high-performance cpd.

perfusion [pɛʀfyzjɔ̃] nf perfusion; **faire une ~ à qn** to put sb on a drip.

péricliter [peʀiklite] vi to go downhill.

péridurale [peʀidyʀal] nf epidural.

périgourdin, e [peʀiguʀdɛ̃, -in] a of ou from the Perigord.

péril [peʀil] nm peril; **au ~ de sa vie** at the risk of his life; **à ses risques et ~s** at his (ou her) own risk.

périlleux, euse [peʀijø, -øz] a perilous.

périmé, e [peʀime] a (out)dated; (ADMIN) out-of-date, expired.

périmètre [peʀimɛtʀ(ə)] nm perimeter.

périnatal, e [peʀinatal] a perinatal.

période [peʀjɔd] nf period.

périodique [peʀjɔdik] a (phases) periodic; (publication) periodical; (MATH: fraction) recurring ♦ nm periodical; **garniture** ou **serviette ~** sanitary towel (Brit) ou napkin (US).

périodiquement [peʀjɔdikmɑ̃] ad periodically.

péripéties [peʀipesi] nfpl events, episodes.

périphérie [peʀifeʀi] nf periphery; (d'une ville) outskirts pl.

périphérique [peʀifeʀik] a (quartiers) outlying; (ANAT, TECH) peripheral; (station de radio) operating from a neighbouring country ♦ nm (INFORM) peripheral; (AUTO): **(boulevard) ~** ring road (Brit), circular route (US).

périphrase [peʀifʀɑz] nf circumlocution.

périple [peʀipl(ə)] nm journey.

périr [peʀiʀ] vi to die, perish.

périscolaire [peʀiskɔlɛʀ] a extracurricular.

périscope [peʀiskɔp] nm periscope.

périssable [peʀisabl(ə)] a perishable.

péritonite [peʀitɔnit] nf peritonitis.

perle [pɛʀl(ə)] nf pearl; (de plastique, métal, sueur) bead; (personne, chose) gem, treasure; (erreur) gem, howler.

perlé, e [pɛʀle] a (rire) rippling, tinkling; (travail) exquisite; (orge) pearl cpd; **grève ~e** go-slow, selective strike (action).

perler [pɛʀle] vi to form in droplets.

perlier, ière [pɛʀlje, -jɛʀ] a pearl cpd.

permanence [pɛʀmanɑ̃s] nf permanence; (local) (duty) office; strike headquarters; (service des urgences) emergency service; (SCOL) study room; **assurer une ~** (service public, bureaux) to operate ou maintain a basic service; **être de ~** to be on call ou duty; **en ~** ad (toujours) permanently; (continûment) continuously.

permanent, e [pɛʀmanɑ̃, -ɑ̃t] a permanent; (spectacle) continuous; (armée, comité) standing ♦ nf perm ♦ nm/f (d'un syndicat, parti) paid official.

perméable [pɛʀmeabl(ə)] a (terrain) permeable; **~ à** (fig) receptive ou open to.

permettre [pɛʀmɛtʀ(ə)] vt to allow, permit; **~ à qn de faire/qch** to allow sb to do/sth; **se ~ de faire qch** to take the liberty of doing sth; **permettez!** excuse me!

permis, e [pɛʀmi, -iz] pp de **permettre** ♦ nm permit, licence (Brit), license (US); **~ de chasse** hunting permit; **~ (de conduire)** (driving) licence (Brit), (driver's) license (US); **~ de construire** planning permission (Brit), building permit (US); **~ d'inhumer** burial certificate; **~ poids lourds** ≈ HGV (driving) licence (Brit), ≈ class E (driver's) license (US); **~ de séjour** residence permit; **~ de travail** work permit.

permissif, ive [pɛʀmisif, -iv] a permissive.

permission [pɛʀmisjɔ̃] nf permission; (MIL) leave; (: papier) pass; **en ~** on leave; **avoir la ~ de faire** to have permission to do, be allowed to do.

permissionnaire [pɛʀmisjɔnɛʀ] nm soldier on leave.

permutable [pɛʀmytabl(ə)] a which can be changed ou switched around.

permuter [pɛʀmyte] vt to change around, permutate ♦ vi to change, swap.

pernicieux, euse [pɛʀnisjø, -øz] a pernicious.

péroné [peʀɔne] nm fibula.

pérorer [peʀɔʀe] vi to hold forth.

Pérou [peʀu] nm: **le ~** Peru.

perpendiculaire [pɛʀpɑ̃dikylɛʀ] a, nf perpendicular.

perpète [pɛʀpɛt] nf (fam: loin): **à ~** miles away; (: longtemps) forever.

perpétrer [pɛʀpetʀe] vt to perpetrate.

perpétuel, le [pɛʀpetɥɛl] a perpetual; (ADMIN etc) permanent; for life.

perpétuellement [pɛʀpetɥɛlmɑ̃] ad perpetually, constantly.

perpétuer [pɛʀpetɥe] vt to perpetuate; **se ~** (usage, injustice) to be perpetuated; (espèces) to survive.

perpétuité [pɛʀpetɥite] nf: **à ~** a, ad for life; **être condamné à ~** to be sentenced to life imprisonment, receive a life sentence.

perplexe [pɛʀplɛks(ə)] a perplexed, puzzled.

perplexité [pɛʀplɛksite] nf perplexity.

perquisition [pɛʀkizisjɔ̃] nf (police) search.

perquisitionner [pɛʀkizisjɔne] vi to carry out a search.

perron [pɛʀɔ̃] nm steps pl (in front of mansion etc).

perroquet [pɛʀɔkɛ] nm parrot.

perruche [peʀyʃ] nf budgerigar (Brit), budgie (Brit), parakeet (US).

perruque [peʀyk] nf wig.

persan, e [pɛʀsɑ̃, -an] a Persian ♦ nm (LING) Persian.

perse [pɛʀs(ə)] a Persian ♦ nm (LING) Persian ♦ nm/f: **P~** Persian ♦ nf: **la P~** Persia.

persécuter [pɛʀsekyte] vt to persecute.

persécution [pɛʀsekysjɔ̃] nf persecution.

persévérance [pɛʀseveʀɑ̃s] nf perseverance.

persévérant, e [pɛʀseveʀɑ̃, -ɑ̃t] a persevering.

persévérer [pɛʀseveʀe] vi to persevere; **~ à croire que** to continue to believe that.

persiennes [pɛʀsjɛn] nfpl (slatted) shutters.

persiflage [pɛʀsiflaʒ] nm mockery q.

persifleur, euse [pɛʀsiflœʀ, -øz] a mocking.

persil [pɛʀsi] *nm* parsley.

persillé, e [pɛʀsije] *a* (sprinkled) with parsley; *(fromage)* veined; *(viande)* marbled, with fat running through.

Persique [pɛʀsik] *a*: **le golfe ~** the (Persian) Gulf.

persistance [pɛʀsistãs] *nf* persistence.

persistant, e [pɛʀsistã, -ãt] *a* persistent; *(feuilles)* evergreen; **à feuillage ~** evergreen.

persister [pɛʀsiste] *vi* to persist; **~ à faire qch** to persist in doing sth.

personnage [pɛʀsɔnaʒ] *nm* (*notable*) personality; figure; *(individu)* character, individual; *(THÉÂTRE)* character; *(PEINTURE)* figure.

personnaliser [pɛʀsɔnalize] *vt* to personalize; *(appartement)* to give a personal touch to.

personnalité [pɛʀsɔnalite] *nf* personality; *(personnage)* prominent figure.

personne [pɛʀsɔn] *nf* person ♦ *pronom* nobody, no one; *(quelqu'un)* anybody, anyone; **~s** *nfpl* people *pl*; **il n'y a ~** there's nobody in *ou* there, there isn't anybody in *ou* there; **10 F par ~** 10 F per person *ou* a head; **en ~** personally, in person; **~ âgée** elderly person; **~ à charge** *(JUR)* dependent; **~ morale** *ou* **civile** *(JUR)* legal entity.

personnel, le [pɛʀsɔnɛl] *a* personal; *(égoïste: personne)* selfish, self-centred; *(idée, opinion)*: **j'ai des idées ~les à ce sujet I** have my own ideas about that ♦ *nm* personnel, staff; **service du ~** personnel department.

personnellement [pɛʀsɔnɛlmã] *ad* personally.

personnifier [pɛʀsɔnifje] *vt* to personify; to typify; **c'est l'honnêteté personifiée** he *(ou* she *etc)* is honesty personified.

perspective [pɛʀspɛktiv] *nf* *(ART)* perspective; *(vue, coup d'œil)* view; *(point de vue)* viewpoint, angle; *(chose escomptée, envisagée)* prospect; **en ~** in prospect.

perspicace [pɛʀspikas] *a* clear-sighted, gifted with *(ou* showing) insight.

perspicacité [pɛʀspikasite] *nf* insight, perspicacity.

persuader [pɛʀsɥade] *vt*: **~ qn (de/de faire)** to persuade sb (of/to do); **j'en suis persuadé** I'm quite sure *ou* convinced (of it).

persuasif, ive [pɛʀsɥazif, -iv] *a* persuasive.

persuasion [pɛʀsɥazjɔ̃] *nf* persuasion.

perte [pɛʀt(ə)] *nf* loss; *(de temps)* waste; *(fig: morale)* ruin; **~s** *nfpl* losses; **à ~** *(COMM)* at a loss; **à ~ de vue** as far as the eye can see *(ou* could) see; *(fig)* interminably; **en pure ~** for absolutely nothing; **courir à sa ~** to be on the road to ruin; **être en ~ de vitesse** *(fig)* to be losing momentum; **avec ~ et fracas** forcibly; **~ de chaleur** heat loss; **~ sèche** dead loss; **~s blanches** (vaginal) discharge *sg*.

pertinemment [pɛʀtinamã] *ad* to the point; *(savoir)* perfectly well, full well.

pertinence [pɛʀtinãs] *nf* pertinence, relevance; discernment.

pertinent, e [pɛʀtinã, -ãt] *a* *(remarque)* apt, pertinent, relevant; *(analyse)* discerning, judicious.

perturbateur, trice [pɛʀtyʀbatœʀ, -tʀis] *a* disruptive.

perturbation [pɛʀtyʀbasjɔ̃] *nf* *(dans un* service *public)* disruption; *(agitation, trouble)* perturbation; **~ (atmosphérique)** atmospheric disturbance.

perturber [pɛʀtyʀbe] *vt* to disrupt; *(PSYCH)* to perturb, disturb.

péruvien, ne [peʀyvjɛ̃, -ɛn] *a* Peruvian ♦ *nm/f*: **P~, ne** Peruvian.

pervenche [pɛʀvãʃ] *nf* periwinkle; *(fam)* traffic warden *(Brit)*, meter maid *(US)*.

pervers, e [pɛʀvɛʀ, -ɛʀs(ə)] *a* perverted, depraved; *(malfaisant)* perverse.

perversion [pɛʀvɛʀsjɔ̃] *nf* perversion.

perversité [pɛʀvɛʀsite] *nf* depravity; perversity.

perverti, e [pɛʀvɛʀti] *nm/f* pervert.

pervertir [pɛʀvɛʀtiʀ] *vt* to pervert.

pesage [pəzaʒ] *nm* weighing; *(HIPPISME: action)* weigh-in; *(: salle)* weighing room; *(: enceinte)* enclosure.

pesamment [pəzamã] *ad* heavily.

pesant, e [pəzã, -ãt] *a* heavy; *(fig)* burdensome ♦ *nm*: **valoir son ~ de** to be worth one's weight in.

pesanteur [pəzãtœʀ] *nf* gravity.

pèse-bébé [pɛzbebe] *nm* (baby) scales *pl*.

pesée [pəze] *nf* weighing; *(BOXE)* weigh-in; *(pression)* pressure.

pèse-lettre [pɛzlɛtʀ(ə)] *nm* letter scales *pl*.

pèse-personne [pɛzpɛʀsɔn] *nm* (bathroom) scales *pl*.

peser [pəze] *vt*, *vb avec attribut* to weigh; *(considérer, comparer)* to weigh up ♦ *vi* to be heavy; *(fig)* to carry weight; **~ sur** *(levier, bouton)* to press, push; *(fig: accabler)* to lie heavy on; *(: influencer)* to influence; **~ à qn** to weigh heavy on sb.

pessaire [pɛsɛʀ] *nm* pessary.

pessimisme [pesimism(ə)] *nm* pessimism.

pessimiste [pesimist(ə)] *a* pessimistic ♦ *nm/f* pessimist.

peste [pɛst(ə)] *nf* plague; *(fig)* pest, nuisance.

pester [pɛste] *vi*: **~ contre** to curse.

pesticide [pɛstisid] *nm* pesticide.

pestiféré, e [pɛstifeʀe] *nm/f* plague victim.

pestilentiel, le [pɛstilãsjɛl] *a* foul.

pet [pɛ] *nm* *(fam!)* fart *(!)*.

pétale [petal] *nm* petal.

pétanque [petãk] *nf* type of bowls.

pétarader [petaʀade] *vi* to backfire.

pétard [petaʀ] *nm* *(feu d'artifice)* banger *(Brit)*, firecracker; *(de cotillon)* cracker; *(RAIL)* detonator.

pet-de-nonne, *pl* **pets-de-nonne** [pɛdnɔn] *nm* ≈ choux bun.

péter [pete] *vi* *(fam: casser, sauter)* to burst; to bust; *(fam!)* to fart *(!)*.

pète-sec [pɛtsɛk] *a inv* abrupt, sharp(-tongued).

pétillant, e [petijã, -ãt] *a* sparkling.

pétiller [petije] *vi* *(flamme, bois)* to crackle; *(mousse, champagne)* to bubble; *(pierre, métal)* to glisten; *(yeux)* to sparkle; *(fig)*: **~ d'esprit** to sparkle with wit.

petit, e [pəti, -it] *a* *(gén)* small; *(main, objet, colline, en âge: enfant)* small, little; *(mince, fin: personne, taille, pluie)* slight; *(voyage)* short, little; *(bruit etc)* faint, slight; *(mesquin)* mean; *(peu important)* minor ♦ *nm/f* *(petit enfant)* little one, child ♦ *nmpl* (*d'un animal*) young *pl*; **faire des** ~**s** to have kittens (*ou* puppies *etc*); **en** ~ in miniature; **mon** ~ son; little one; **ma** ~**e** dear; little one; **pauvre** ~ poor little thing; **la classe des** ~**s** the infant class; **pour** ~**s et grands** for children and adults; **les tout-**~**s** the little ones, the tiny tots; ~ **à** ~ bit by bit, gradually; ~**(e) ami/e** boyfriend/girlfriend; **les** ~**es annonces** the small ads; ~ **déjeuner** breakfast; ~ **doigt** little finger; **le** ~ **écran** the small screen; ~ **four** petit four; ~ **pain** (bread) roll; ~**e monnaie** small change; ~**e vérole** smallpox; ~**s pois** petit pois *pl*, garden peas; ~**es gens** people of modest means.

petit-beurre, *pl* **petits-beurre** [pɔtibœr] *nm* *sweet butter biscuit* (*Brit*) *ou cookie* (*US*).

petit(e)-bourgeois(e), *pl* **petit(e)s-bourgeois(es)** [pɔti(t)buɾʒwa(z)] *a* (*péj*) petit-bourgeois, middle-class.

petite-fille, *pl* **petites-filles** [pɔtitfij] *nf* granddaughter.

petitement [pɔtitmɑ̃] *ad* poorly; meanly; **être logé** ~ to be in cramped accommodation.

petitesse [pɔtitɛs] *nf* smallness; (*d'un salaire, de revenus*) modestness; (*mesquinerie*) meanness.

petit-fils, *pl* **petits-fils** [pɔtifis] *nm* grandson.

pétition [petisjɔ̃] *nf* petition; **faire signer une** ~ to get up a petition.

pétitionner [petisjɔne] *vt* to petition.

petit-lait, *pl* **petits-laits** [pɔtilɛ] *nm* whey *q*.

petit-nègre [pɔtinɛgɾ(ə)] *nm* (*péj*) pidgin French.

petits-enfants [pɔtizɑ̃fɑ̃] *nmpl* grandchildren.

petit-suisse, *pl* **petits-suisses** [pɔtisɥis] *nm* *small individual pot of cream cheese*.

pétoche [petɔʃ] *nf* (*fam*): **avoir la** ~ to be scared out of one's wits.

pétri, e [petɾi] *a*: ~ **d'orgueil** filled with pride.

pétrifier [petɾifje] *vt* to petrify; (*fig*) to paralyze, transfix.

pétrin [petɾɛ̃] *nm* kneading-trough; (*fig*): **dans le** ~ in a jam *ou* fix.

pétrir [petɾiɾ] *vt* to knead.

pétrochimie [petɾɔʃimi] *nf* petrochemistry.

pétrochimique [petɾɔʃimik] *a* petrochemical.

pétrodollar [petɾɔdɔlaɾ] *nm* petrodollar.

pétrole [petɾɔl] *nm* oil; (*aussi*: ~ **lampant**) paraffin (*Brit*), kerosene (*US*).

pétrolier, ière [petɾɔlje, -jɛɾ] *a* oil *cpd*; (*pays*) oil-producing ♦ *nm* (*navire*) oil tanker; (*financier*) oilman; (*technicien*) petroleum engineer.

pétrolifère [petɾɔlifɛɾ] *a* oil(-bearing).

P et T *sigle fpl* = *postes et télécommunications*.

pétulant, e [petylɑ̃, -ɑ̃t] *a* exuberant.

pétunia [petynja] *nm* petunia.

peu [pø] *ad* little, *tournure négative* + much; (*avec adjectif*) *tournure négative* + very; (*avec adverbe*) a little, slightly ♦ *pronom* few ♦ *nm* little; **le** ~ **de courage qui nous restait** what little courage we still had; ~ **avant/après** shortly before/afterwards; ~ **de** (*nombre*) few, *négation* + (very) many; (*quantité*) little, *négation* + (very) much; **pour** ~ **de temps** for (only) a short while; **le** ~ **de gens qui** the few people who; **le** ~ **de**

sable qui what little sand, the little sand which; **un (petit)** ~ a little (bit); **un** ~ **de** a little; **un** ~ **plus/moins de** slightly more/less (*ou* fewer); **pour** ~ **qu'il fasse** if he should do, if by any chance he does; **pour un** ~, **il** ... he very nearly ...; **de** ~ (only) just; ~ **à** ~ little by little; **à** ~ **près** *ad* just about, more or less; **à** ~ **près 10 kg/10 F** approximately 10 kg/10 F; **sous** *ou* **avant** ~ before long, shortly; **depuis** ~ for a short *ou* little while; **c'est** ~ **de chose** it's nothing; **c'est si** ~ **de chose** it's such a small thing; **essayez un** ~! have a go!, just try it!

peuplade [pœplad] *nf* (*horde, tribu*) tribe, people.

peuple [pœpl(ə)] *nm* people; (*masse indifférenciée*): **un** ~ **de vacanciers** a crowd of holiday-makers; **il y a du** ~ there are a lot of people.

peuplé, e [pœple] *a*: **très/peu** ~ densely/sparsely populated.

peupler [pœple] *vt* (*pays, région*) to populate; (*étang*) to stock; (*suj: hommes, poissons*) to inhabit; (*fig: imagination, rêves*) to fill; **se** ~ *vi* (*ville, région*) to become populated; (*fig: s'animer*) to fill (up), be filled.

peuplier [pøplije] *nm* poplar (tree).

peur [pœɾ] *nf* fear; **avoir** ~ (**de/de faire/que**) to be frightened *ou* afraid (of/of doing/that); **prendre** ~ to take fright; **faire** ~ **à** to frighten; **de** ~ **de/que** for fear of/that; **j'ai** ~ **qu'il ne soit trop tard** I'm afraid it might be too late; **j'ai** ~ **qu'il (ne) vienne (pas)** I'm afraid he may (not) come.

peureux, euse [pœɾø, -øz] *a* fearful, timorous.

peut [pø] *vb voir* **pouvoir**.

peut-être [pøtɛtɾ(ə)] *ad* perhaps, maybe; ~ **que** perhaps, maybe; ~ **bien qu'il fera/est** he may well do/be.

peuvent [pœv], **peux** [pø] *etc vb voir* **pouvoir**.

p. ex. *abr* (= *par exemple*) e.g.

phalange [falɑ̃ʒ] *nf* (*ANAT*) phalanx (*pl* phalanges); (*MIL, fig*) phalanx (*pl* -es).

phallique [falik] *a* phallic.

phallocrate [falɔkɾat] *nm* male chauvinist.

phallocratie [falɔkɾasi] *nf* male chauvinism.

phallus [falys] *nm* phallus.

pharaon [faɾaɔ̃] *nm* Pharaoh.

phare [faɾ] *nm* (*en mer*) lighthouse; (*d'aéroport*) beacon; (*de véhicule*) headlight, headlamp (*Brit*) ♦ *a*: **produit** ~ leading product; **se mettre en** ~**s**, **mettre ses** ~**s** to put on one's headlights; ~**s de recul** reversing (*Brit*) *ou* back-up (*US*) lights.

pharmaceutique [faɾmasøtik] *a* pharmaceutic(al).

pharmacie [faɾmasi] *nf* (*science*) pharmacology; (*magasin*) chemist's (*Brit*), pharmacy; (*officine*) dispensary; (*produits*) pharmaceuticals *pl*; (*armoire*) medicine chest *ou* cupboard, first-aid cupboard.

pharmacien, ne [faɾmasjɛ̃, -ɛn] *nm/f* pharmacist, chemist (*Brit*).

pharmacologie [faɾmakɔlɔʒi] *nf* pharmacology.

pharyngite [faɾɛ̃ʒit] *nf* pharyngitis *q*.

pharynx [faɾɛ̃ks] *nm* pharynx.

phase [fɑz] *nf* phase.
phénoménal, e, aux [fenɔmenal, -o] *a* phenomenal.
phénomène [fenɔmɛn] *nm* phenomenon (*pl* -a); (*monstre*) freak.
philanthrope [filɑ̃tʀɔp] *nm/f* philanthropist.
philanthropie [filɑ̃tʀɔpi] *nf* philanthropy.
philatélie [filateli] *nf* philately, stamp collecting.
philatéliste [filatelist(ə)] *nm/f* philatelist, stamp collector.
philharmonique [filaʀmɔnik] *a* philharmonic.
philippin, e [filipɛ̃, -in] *a* Filipino.
Philippines [filipin] *nfpl*: **les** ~ the Philippines.
philistin [filistɛ̃] *nm* philistine.
philo [filo] *nf* (*fam*: = *philosophie*) philosophy.
philosophe [filɔzɔf] *nm/f* philosopher ♦ *a* philosophical.
philosopher [filɔzɔfe] *vi* to philisophize.
philosophie [filɔzɔfi] *nf* philosophy.
philosophique [filɔzɔfik] *a* philosophical.
philtre [filtʀ(ə)] *nm* philtre, love potion.
phlébite [flebit] *nf* phlebitis.
phlébologue [flebɔlɔg] *nm/f* vein specialist.
phobie [fɔbi] *nf* phobia.
phonétique [fɔnetik] *a* phonetic ♦ *nf* phonetics *sg*.
phonographe [fɔnɔgʀaf] *nm* (wind-up) gramophone.
phoque [fɔk] *nm* seal; (*fourrure*) sealskin.
phosphate [fɔsfat] *nm* phosphate.
phosphaté, e [fɔsfate] *a* phosphate-enriched.
phosphore [fɔsfɔʀ] *nm* phosphorus.
phosphoré, e [fɔsfɔʀe] *a* phosphorous.
phosphorescent, e [fɔsfɔʀesɑ̃, -ɑ̃t] *a* luminous.
phosphorique [fɔsfɔʀik] *a*: **acide** ~ phosphoric acid.
photo [fɔto] *nf* (= *photographie*) photo ♦ *a*: **appareil/pellicule** ~ camera/film; **en** ~ in *ou* on a photo; **prendre en** ~ to take a photo of; **aimer la/faire de la** ~ to like taking/take photos; ~ **en couleurs** colour photo; ~ **d'identité** passport photo.
photo... [fɔtɔ] *préfixe* photo....
photocopie [fɔtɔkɔpi] *nf* (*procédé*) photocopying; (*document*) photocopy.
photocopier [fɔtɔkɔpje] *vt* to photocopy.
photocopieur [fɔtɔkɔpjœʀ] *nm*, **photocopieuse** [fɔtɔkɔpjøz] *nf* (photo)copier.
photo-électrique [fɔtɔelɛktʀik] *a* photo-electric.
photogénique [fɔtɔʒenik] *a* photogenic.
photographe [fɔtɔgʀaf] *nm/f* photographer.
photographie [fɔtɔgʀafi] *nf* (*procédé*, *technique*) photography; (*cliché*) photograph; **faire de la** ~ to have photography as a hobby; (*comme métier*) to be a photographer.
photographier [fɔtɔgʀafje] *vt* to photograph, take.
photographique [fɔtɔgʀafik] *a* photographic.
photogravure [fɔtɔgʀavyʀ] *nf* photoengraving.
photomaton [fɔtɔmatɔ̃] *nm* photo-booth, photomat.
photomontage [fɔtɔmɔ̃taʒ] *nm* photomontage.
photo-robot [fɔtɔʀɔbo] *nf* Identikit ® (picture).
photosensible [fɔtɔsɑ̃sibl(ə)] *a* photosensitive.
photostat [fɔtɔsta] *nm* photostat.
phrase [fʀɑz] *nf* (*LING*) sentence; (*propos*, *MUS*) phrase; ~**s** *nfpl* (*péj*) flowery language *sg*.
phraséologie [fʀazeɔlɔʒi] *nf* phraseology; (*rhétorique*) flowery language.
phraseur, euse [fʀazœʀ, -øz] *nm/f*: **c'est un** ~ he uses such flowery language.
phrygien, ne [fʀiʒjɛ̃, -ɛn] *a*: **bonnet** ~ Phrygian cap.
phtisie [ftizi] *nf* consumption.
phylloxéra [filɔkseʀa] *nm* phylloxera.
physicien, ne [fizisjɛ̃, -ɛn] *nm/f* physicist.
physiologie [fizjɔlɔʒi] *nf* physiology.
physiologique [fizjɔlɔʒik] *a* physiological.
physiologiquement [fizjɔlɔʒikmɑ̃] *ad* physiologically.
physionomie [fizjɔnɔmi] *nf* face; (*d'un paysage etc*) physiognomy.
physionomiste [fizjɔnɔmist(ə)] *nm/f* good judge of faces; person who has a good memory for faces.
physiothérapie [fizjɔteʀapi] *nf* natural medicine, alternative medicine.
physique [fizik] *a* physical ♦ *nm* physique ♦ *nf* physics *sg*; **au** ~ physically.
physiquement [fizikmɑ̃] *ad* physically.
phytothérapie [fitɔteʀapi] *nf* herbal medicine.
p.i. *abr* = **par intérim**; *voir* **intérim**.
piaffer [pjafe] *vi* to stamp.
piailler [pjaje] *vi* to squawk.
pianiste [pjanist(ə)] *nm/f* pianist.
piano [pjano] *nm* piano; ~ **à queue** grand piano.
pianoter [pjanɔte] *vi* to tinkle away (at the piano); (*tapoter*): ~ **sur** to drum one's fingers on.
piaule [pjol] *nf* (*fam*) pad.
piauler [pjole] *vi* (*enfant*) to whimper; (*oiseau*) to cheep.
PIB *sigle m* (= *produit intérieur brut*) GDP.
pic [pik] *nm* (*instrument*) pick(axe); (*montagne*) peak; (*ZOOL*) woodpecker; **à** ~ *ad* vertically; (*fig*) just at the right time; **couler à** ~ (*bateau*) to go straight down; ~ **à glace** ice pick.
picard, e [pikaʀ, -aʀd(ə)] *a* of *ou* from Picardy.
Picardie [pikaʀdi] *nf*: **la** ~ Picardy.
piccolo [pikɔlo] *nm* piccolo.
pichenette [piʃnɛt] *nf* flick.
pichet [piʃɛ] *nm* jug.
pickpocket [pikpɔkɛt] *nm* pickpocket.
pick-up [pikœp] *nm inv* record player.
picorer [pikɔʀe] *vt* to peck.
picot [piko] *nm* sprocket; **entraînement par roue à** ~**s** sprocket feed.
picotement [pikɔtmɑ̃] *nm* smarting *q*, prickling *q*.
picoter [pikɔte] *vt* (*suj*: *oiseau*) to peck ♦ *vi* (*irriter*) to smart, prickle.
pictural, e, aux [piktyʀal, -o] *a* pictorial.
pie [pi] *nf* magpie; (*fig*) chatterbox ♦ *a inv*: **cheval** ~ piebald; **vache** ~ black and white cow.
pièce [pjɛs] *nf* (*d'un logement*) room; (*THÉÂTRE*) play; (*de mécanisme, machine*)

part; (de monnaie) coin; (COUTURE) patch; (document) document; (de drap, fragment, d'une collection) piece; (de bétail) head; **mettre en ~s** to smash to pieces; **dix francs ~ ten** francs each; **vendre à la ~** to sell separately ou individually; **travailler/payer à la ~** to do piecework/pay piece rate; **de toutes ~s: c'est inventé de toutes ~s** it's a complete fabrication; **un maillot une ~** a one-piece swimsuit; **un deux-~s cuisine** a two-room(ed) flat (Brit) ou apartment (US) with kitchen; **tout d'une ~** (personne: franc) blunt; (: sans souplesse) inflexible; **~ à conviction** exhibit; **~ d'eau** ornamental lake ou pond; **~ d'identité: avez-vous une ~ d'identité?** have you got any (means of) identification?; **~ montée** tiered cake; **~ de rechange** spare (part); **~ de résistance** pièce de résistance; (plat) main dish; **~s détachées** spares, (spare) parts; **en ~s détachées** (à monter) in kit form; **~s justificatives** supporting documents.

pied [pje] nm foot (pl feet); (de verre) stem; (de table) leg; (de lampe) base; (plante) plant; **~s nus** barefoot; **à ~** on foot; **à ~ sec** without getting one's feet wet; **à ~ d'œuvre** ready to start (work); **au ~ de la lettre** literally; **au ~ levé** at a moment's notice; **de ~ en cap** from head to foot; **en ~** (portrait) full-length; **avoir ~** to be able to touch the bottom, not to be out of one's depth; **avoir le ~ marin** to be a good sailor; **perdre ~** to lose one's footing; (fig) to get out of one's depth; **sur ~** (AGR) on the stalk, uncut; (debout, rétabli) up and about; **mettre sur ~** (entreprise) to set up; **mettre à ~** to suspend; to lay off; **mettre qn au ~ du mur** to get sb with his (ou her) back to the wall; **sur le ~ de guerre** ready for action; **sur un ~ d'égalité** on an equal footing; **sur ~ d'intervention** on stand-by; **faire du ~ à qn** (prévenir) to give sb a (warning) kick; (galamment) to play footsy with sb; **mettre les ~s quelque part** to set foot somewhere; **faire des ~s et des mains** (fig) to move heaven and earth, pull out all the stops; **c'est le ~!** (fam) it's terrific!; **se lever du bon ~/du ~ gauche** to get out of bed on the right/wrong side; **~ de lit** footboard; **~ de nez: faire un ~ de nez à** to thumb one's nose at; **~ de vigne** vine.

pied-à-terre, pl **pied-à-terre** [pjetatɛʀ] nm inv pied-à-terre.

pied-bot, pl **pieds-bots** [pjebo] nm person with a club foot.

pied-de-biche, pl **pieds-de-biche** [pjedbiʃ] nm claw; (COUTURE) presser foot.

pied-de-poule [pjedpul] a inv hound's-tooth.

piédestal, aux [pjedestal, -o] nm pedestal.

pied-noir, pl pieds-noirs [pjenwaʀ] nm Algerian-born Frenchman.

piège [pjɛʒ] nm trap; **prendre au ~** to trap.

piéger [pjeʒe] vt (animal, fig) to trap; (avec une bombe) to booby-trap; **lettre/voiture piégée** letter-/car-bomb.

pierraille [pjɛʀɑj] nf loose stones pl.

pierre [pjɛʀ] nf stone; **première ~** (d'un édifice) foundation stone; **mur de ~s sèches** drystone wall; **faire d'une ~ deux coups** to kill two birds with one stone; **~ à briquet**

flint; **~ fine** semiprecious stone; **~ ponce** pumice stone; **~ de taille** freestone q; **~ tombale** tombstone, gravestone; **~ de touche** touchstone.

pierreries [pjɛʀʀi] nfpl gems, precious stones.

pierreux, euse [pjɛʀø, -øz] a stony.

piété [pjete] nf piety.

piétinement [pjetinmɑ̃] nm stamping q.

piétiner [pjetine] vi (trépigner) to stamp (one's foot); (marquer le pas) to stand about; (fig) to be at a standstill ♦ vt to trample on.

piéton, ne [pjetɔ̃, -ɔn] nm/f pedestrian ♦ a pedestrian cpd.

piétonnier, ière [pjetɔnje, -jɛʀ] a pedestrian cpd.

piètre [pjɛtʀ(ə)] a poor, mediocre.

pieu, x [pjø] nm (piquet) post; (pointu) stake; (fam: lit) bed.

pieusement [pjøzmɑ̃] ad piously.

pieuvre [pjœvʀ(ə)] nf octopus.

pieux, euse [pjø, -øz] a pious.

pif [pif] nm (fam) conk (Brit), beak; **au ~ = au pifomètre.**

piffer [pife] vt (fam): **je ne peux pas le ~** I can't stand him.

pifomètre [pifomɛtʀ(ə)] nm (fam): **choisir** etc **au ~** to follow one's nose when choosing etc.

pige [piʒ] nf piecework rate.

pigeon [piʒɔ̃] nm pigeon; **~ voyageur** homing pigeon.

pigeonnant, e [piʒɔnɑ̃, -ɑ̃t] a full, well-developed.

pigeonnier [piʒɔnje] nm pigeon house, dovecot(e).

piger [piʒe] vi (fam) to get it ♦ vt (fam) to get, understand.

pigiste [piʒist(ə)] nm/f (typographe) typesetter on piecework; (journaliste) freelance journalist (paid by the line).

pigment [pigmɑ̃] nm pigment.

pignon [piɲɔ̃] nm (de mur) gable; (d'engrenage) cog(wheel), gearwheel; (graine) pine kernel; **avoir ~ sur rue** (fig) to have a prosperous business.

pile [pil] nf (tas, pilier) pile; (ÉLEC) battery ♦ a: **le côté ~** tails ♦ ad (net, brusquement) dead; (à temps, à point nommé) just at the right time; **à deux heures ~** at two on the dot; **jouer à ~ ou face** to toss up (for it); **~ ou face?** heads or tails?

piler [pile] vt to crush, pound.

pileux, euse [pilø, -øz] a: **système ~** (body) hair.

pilier [pilje] nm (colonne, support) pillar; (personne) mainstay; (RUGBY) prop (forward).

pillage [pijaʒ] nm pillaging, plundering, looting.

pillard, e [pijaʀ, -aʀd(ə)] nm/f looter; plunderer.

piller [pije] vt to pillage, plunder, loot.

pilon [pilɔ̃] nm (instrument) pestle; (de volaille) drumstick; **mettre un livre au ~** to pulp a book.

pilonner [pilɔne] vt to pound.

pilori [pilɔʀi] nm: **mettre** ou **clouer au ~** to pillory.

pilotage [pilotaʒ] nm piloting; flying; **~**

automatique automatic piloting; ~ **sans visibilité** blind flying.

pilote [pilɔt] *nm* pilot; (*de char, voiture*) driver ♦ *a* pilot *cpd*; **usine/ferme** ~ experimental factory/farm; ~ **de chasse/d'essai/de ligne** fighter/test/airline pilot; ~ **de course** racing driver.

piloter [pilɔte] *vt* (*navire*) to pilot; (*avion*) to fly; (*automobile*) to drive; (*fig*): ~ **qn** to guide sb round; **piloté par menu** (*INFORM*) menu-driven.

pilotis [pilɔti] *nm* pile; stilt.

pilule [pilyl] *nf* pill; **prendre la** ~ to be on the pill.

pimbêche [pɛ̃bɛʃ] *nf* (*péj*) stuck-up girl.

piment [pimɑ̃] *nm* (*BOT*) pepper, capsicum; (*fig*) spice, piquancy; ~ **rouge** (*CULIN*) chilli.

pimenté, e [pimɑ̃te] *a* hot and spicy.

pimenter [pimɑ̃te] *vt* (*plat*) to season (with peppers *ou* chillis); (*fig*) to add *ou* give spice to.

pimpant, e [pɛ̃pɑ̃, -ɑ̃t] *a* spruce.

pin [pɛ̃] *nm* pine (tree); (*bois*) pine(wood).

pinacle [pinakl(ə)] *nm*: **porter qn au** ~ (*fig*) to praise sb to the skies.

pinard [pinaʀ] *nm* (*fam*) (cheap) wine, plonk (*Brit*).

pince [pɛ̃s] *nf* (*outil*) pliers *pl*; (*de homard, crabe*) pincer, claw; (*COUTURE*: *pli*) dart; ~ **à sucre/glace** sugar/ice tongs *pl*; ~ **à épiler** tweezers *pl*; ~ **à linge** clothes peg (*Brit*) *ou* pin (*US*); ~ **universelle** (universal) pliers *pl*; ~**s de cycliste** bicycle clips.

pincé, e [pɛ̃se] *a* (*air*) stiff; (*mince: bouche*) pinched ♦ *nf*: **une** ~**e de** a pinch of.

pinceau, x [pɛ̃so] *nm* (paint)brush.

pince-monseigneur, *pl* **pinces-monseigneur** [pɛ̃smɔ̃sɛɲœʀ] *nf* crowbar.

pince-nez [pɛ̃sne] *nm inv* pince-nez.

pincer [pɛ̃se] *vt* to pinch; (*MUS*: *cordes*) to pluck; (*COUTURE*) to dart, put darts in; (*fam*) to nab; **se** ~ **le doigt** to squeeze *ou* nip one's finger; **se** ~ **le nez** to hold one's nose.

pince-sans-rire [pɛ̃ssɑ̃ʀiʀ] *a inv* deadpan.

pincettes [pɛ̃sɛt] *nfpl* tweezers; (*pour le feu*) (fire) tongs.

pinçon [pɛ̃sɔ̃] *nm* pinch mark.

pinède [pinɛd] *nf* pinewood, pine forest.

pingouin [pɛ̃gwɛ̃] *nm* penguin.

ping-pong [piŋpɔ̃g] *nm* table tennis.

pingre [pɛ̃gʀ(ə)] *a* niggardly.

pinson [pɛ̃sɔ̃] *nm* chaffinch.

pintade [pɛ̃tad] *nf* guinea-fowl.

pin up [pinœp] *nf inv* pin-up (girl).

pioche [pjɔʃ] *nf* pickaxe.

piocher [pjɔʃe] *vt* to dig up (with a pickaxe); (*fam*) to swot (*Brit*) *ou* grind (*US*) at; ~ **dans** to dig into.

piolet [pjɔlɛ] *nm* ice axe.

pion, ne [pjɔ̃, pjɔn] *nm/f* (*SCOL*: *péj*) student paid to supervise schoolchildren ♦ *nm* (*ÉCHECS*) pawn; (*DAMES*) piece, draught (*Brit*), checker (*US*).

pionnier [pjɔnje] *nm* pioneer.

pipe [pip] *nf* pipe; **fumer la** *ou* **une** ~ to smoke a pipe; ~ **de bruyère** briar pipe.

pipeau, x [pipo] *nm* (reed-)pipe.

pipe-line [piplin] *nm* pipeline.

piper [pipe] *vt* (*dé*) to load; (*carte*) to mark; **sans** ~ **mot** (*fam*) without a squeak; **les dés sont pipés** (*fig*) the dice are loaded.

pipette [pipɛt] *nf* pipette.

pipi [pipi] *nm* (*fam*): **faire** ~ to have a wee.

piquant, e [pikɑ̃, -ɑ̃t] *a* (*barbe, rosier etc*) prickly; (*saveur, sauce*) hot, pungent; (*fig: description, style*) racy; (: *mordant, caustique*) biting ♦ *nm* (*épine*) thorn, prickle; (*de hérisson*) quill, spine; (*fig*) spiciness, spice.

pique [pik] *nf* (*arme*) pike; (*fig*): **envoyer** *ou* **lancer des** ~**s à qn** to make cutting remarks to sb ♦ *nm* (*CARTES: couleur*) spades *pl*; (: *carte*) spade.

piqué, e [pike] *a* (*COUTURE*) (machine-) stitched; quilted; (*livre, glace*) mildewed; (*vin*) sour; (*MUS: note*) staccato; (*fam: personne*) nuts ♦ *nm* (*AVIAT*) dive; (*TEXTILE*) piqué.

pique-assiette [pikasjɛt] *nm/f inv* (*péj*) scrounger, sponger.

pique-fleurs [pikflœʀ] *nm inv* flower holder.

pique-nique [piknik] *nm* picnic.

pique-niquer [piknike] *vi* to (have a) picnic.

pique-niqueur, euse [piknikœʀ, -øz] *nm/f* picnicker.

piquer [pike] *vt* (*percer*) to prick; (*planter*): ~ **qch dans** to stick sth into; (*fixer*): ~ **qch à** *ou* **sur** to pin sth onto; (*MÉD*) to give an injection to; (: *animal blessé etc*) to put to sleep; (*suj: insecte, fumée, ortie*) to sting; (: *poivre*) to burn; (: *froid*) to bite; (*COUTURE*) to machine (stitch); (*intérêt etc*) to arouse; (*fam: prendre*) to pick up; (: *voler*) to pinch; (: *arrêter*) to nab ♦ *vi* (*oiseau, avion*) to go into a dive; (*saveur*) to be pungent; to be sour; **se** ~ (*avec une aiguille*) to prick o.s.; (*se faire une piqûre*) to inject o.s.; (*se vexer*) to get annoyed; **se** ~ **de faire** to pride o.s. on doing; ~ **sur** to swoop down on; to head straight for; ~ **du nez** (*avion*) to go into a nose-dive; ~ **une tête** (*plonger*) to dive headfirst; ~ **un galop/un cent mètres** to break into a gallop/put on a sprint; ~ **une crise** to throw a fit; ~ **au vif** (*fig*) to sting.

piquet [pikɛ] *nm* (*pieu*) post, stake; (*de tente*) peg; **mettre un élève au** ~ to make a pupil stand in the corner; ~ **de grève** (strike-) picket; ~ **d'incendie** fire-fighting squad.

piqueté, e [pikte] *a*: ~ **de** dotted with.

piquette [pikɛt] *nf* (*fam*) cheap wine, plonk (*Brit*).

piqûre [pikyʀ] *nf* (*d'épingle*) prick; (*d'ortie*) sting; (*de moustique*) bite; (*MÉD*) injection, shot (*US*); (*COUTURE*) (straight) stitch; straight stitching; (*de ver*) hole; (*tache*) (spot of) mildew; **faire une** ~ **à qn** to give sb an injection.

piranha [piʀana] *nm* piranha.

piratage [piʀataʒ] *nm* piracy.

pirate [piʀat] *a* pirate *cpd* ♦ *nm* pirate; (*fig: escroc*) crook, shark; ~ **de l'air** hijacker.

pirater [piʀate] *vt* to pirate.

piraterie [piʀatʀi] *nf* (act of) piracy; ~ **aérienne** hijacking.

pire [piʀ] *a* (*comparatif*) worse; (*superlatif*): **le (la)** ~ ... the worst ... ♦ *nm*: **le** ~ **(de)** the worst (of).

Pirée [piʀe] *n* Piraeus.
pirogue [piʀɔg] *nf* dugout (canoe).
pirouette [piʀwɛt] *nf* pirouette; (*fig: volte-face*) about-turn.
pis [pi] *nm* (*de vache*) udder; (*pire*): **le ~** the worst ♦ *a, ad* worse; **qui ~ est** what is worse; **au ~ aller** if the worst comes to the worst, at worst.
pis-aller [pizale] *nm inv* stopgap.
pisciculture [pisikyltyʀ] *nf* fish farming.
piscine [pisin] *nf* (swimming) pool; **~ couverte** indoor (swimming) pool.
Pise [piz] *n* Pisa.
pissenlit [pisɑ̃li] *nm* dandelion.
pisser [pise] *vi* (*fam!*) to pee.
pissotière [pisɔtjɛʀ] *nf* (*fam*) public urinal.
pistache [pistaʃ] *nf* pistachio (nut).
pistard [pistaʀ] *nm* (*CYCLISME*) track cyclist.
piste [pist(ə)] *nf* (*d'un animal, sentier*) track, trail; (*indice*) lead; (*de stade, de magnéto-phone, INFORM*) track; (*de cirque*) ring; (*de danse*) floor; (*de patinage*) rink; (*de ski*) run; (*AVIAT*) runway; **~ cavalière** bridle path; **~ cyclable** cycle track, bikeway (*US*); **~ sonore** sound track.
pister [piste] *vt* to track, trail.
pisteur [pistœʀ] *nm* (*SKI*) member of the ski patrol.
pistil [pistil] *nm* pistil.
pistolet [pistɔlɛ] *nm* (*arme*) pistol, gun; (*à peinture*) spray gun; **~ à bouchon/air comprimé** popgun/airgun; **~ à eau** water pistol.
pistolet-mitrailleur, *pl* **pistolets-mitrailleurs** [pistɔlɛmitʀajœʀ] *nm* submachine gun.
piston [pistɔ̃] *nm* (*TECH*) piston; (*MUS*) valve; (*fig: appui*) string-pulling.
pistonner [pistɔne] *vt* (*candidat*) to pull strings for.
pitance [pitɑ̃s] *nf* (*péj*) (means of) sustenance.
piteux, euse [pitø, -øz] *a* pitiful, sorry (*avant le nom*); **en ~ état** in a sorry state.
pitié [pitje] *nf* pity; **sans ~** *a* pitiless, merciless; **faire ~** to inspire pity; **il me fait ~** I pity him, I feel sorry for him; **avoir ~ de** (*compassion*) to pity, feel sorry for; (*merci*) to have pity ou mercy on; **par ~!** for pity's sake!
piton [pitɔ̃] *nm* (*clou*) peg, bolt; **~ rocheux** rocky outcrop.
pitoyable [pitwajabl(ə)] *a* pitiful.
pitre [pitʀ(ə)] *nm* clown.
pitrerie [pitʀəʀi] *nf* tomfoolery *q.*
pittoresque [pitɔʀɛsk(ə)] *a* picturesque; (*expression, détail*) colourful (*Brit*), colorful (*US*).
pivert [pivɛʀ] *nm* green woodpecker.
pivoine [pivwan] *nf* peony.
pivot [pivo] *nm* pivot; (*d'une dent*) post.
pivoter [pivɔte] *vi* (*fauteuil*) to swivel; (*porte*) to revolve; **~ sur ses talons** to swing round.
pixel [piksɛl] *nm* pixel.
pizza [pidza] *nf* pizza.
PJ *sigle f* = **police judiciaire** ♦ *sigle fpl* (= **pièces jointes**) encl.
PL *sigle m* (*AUTO*) = **poids lourd**.
Pl. *abr* = **place**.
placage [plakaʒ] *nm* (*bois*) veneer.

placard [plakaʀ] *nm* (*armoire*) cupboard; (*affiche*) poster, notice; (*TYPO*) galley; **~ pu-blicitaire** display advertisement.
placarder [plakaʀde] *vt* (*affiche*) to put up; (*mur*) to stick posters on.
place [plas] *nf* (*emplacement, situation, classe-ment*) place; (*de ville, village*) square; (*ÉCON*): **~ financière/boursière** money/stock market; (*espace libre*) room, space; (*de parking*) space; (*siège: de train, cinéma, voiture*) seat; (*prix: au cinéma etc*) price; (*: dans un bus, taxi*) fare; (*emploi*) job; **en ~** (*mettre*) in its place; **de ~ en ~, par ~s** here and there, in places; **sur ~** on the spot; **faire ~ à** to give way to; **faire de la ~ à** to make room for; **ça prend de la ~** it takes up a lot of room ou space; **prendre ~** to take one's place; **remettre qn à sa ~** to put sb in his (*ou her*) place; **ne pas rester** ou **tenir en ~** to be always on the go; **à la ~ de** in place of, instead of; **une quatre ~s** (*AUTO*) a four-seater; **il y a 20 ~s assises/debout** there are 20 seats/there is standing room for 20; **~ forte** fortified town; **~ d'honneur** place (*ou* seat) of honour (*Brit*) ou honor (*US*).
placé, e [plase] *a* (*HIPPISME*) placed; **haut ~** (*fig*) high-ranking; **être bien/mal ~** to be well/badly placed; (*spectateur*) to have a good/bad seat; **être bien/mal ~ pour faire** to be in/not to be in a position to do.
placebo [plasebo] *nm* placebo.
placement [plasmɑ̃] *nm* placing; (*FINANCE*) investment; **agence** ou **bureau de ~** employment agency.
placenta [plasɑ̃ta] *nm* placenta.
placer [plase] *vt* to place, put; (*convive, spec-tateur*) to seat; (*capital, argent*) to place, invest; (*dans la conversation*) to put ou get in; **~ qn chez** to get sb a job at (*ou* with); **se ~ au premier rang** to go and stand (*ou* sit) in the first row.
placide [plasid] *a* placid.
placier, ière [plasje, -jɛʀ] *nm/f* commercial rep(resentative), salesman/woman.
plafond [plafɔ̃] *nm* ceiling.
plafonner [plafɔne] *vt* (*pièce*) to put a ceiling (up) in ♦ *vi* to reach one's (*ou* a) ceiling.
plafonnier [plafɔnje] *nm* ceiling light; (*AUTO*) interior light.
plage [plaʒ] *nf* beach; (*station*) (seaside) resort; (*fig*) band, bracket; (*de disque*) track, band; **~ arrière** (*AUTO*) parcel ou back shelf.
plagiaire [plaʒjɛʀ] *nm/f* plagiarist.
plagiat [plaʒja] *nm* plagiarism.
plagier [plaʒje] *vt* to plagiarize.
plagiste [plaʒist(ə)] *nm/f* beach attendant.
plaid [plɛd] *nm* (*tartan*) car rug, lap robe (*US*).
plaidant, e [plɛdɑ̃, -ɑ̃t] *a* litigant.
plaider [plede] *vi* (*avocat*) to plead; (*plaignant*) to go to court, litigate ♦ *vt* to plead; **~ pour** (*fig*) to speak for.
plaideur, euse [plɛdœʀ, -øz] *nm/f* litigant.
plaidoirie [plɛdwaʀi] *nf* (*JUR*) speech for the defence (*Brit*) ou defense (*US*).
plaidoyer [plɛdwaje] *nm* (*JUR*) speech for the defence (*Brit*) ou defense (*US*); (*fig*) plea.
plaie [plɛ] *nf* wound.
plaignant, e [plɛɲɑ̃, -ɑ̃t] *vb voir* **plaindre** ♦

nm/f plaintiff.

plaindre [plɛ̃dʀ(ə)] *vt* to pity, feel sorry for; **se ~** *vi* (*gémir*) to moan; (*protester, rouspéter*): **se ~ (à qn) (de)** to complain (to sb) (about); (*souffrir*): **se ~ de** to complain of.

plaine [plɛn] *nf* plain.

plain-pied [plɛ̃pje]: **de ~** *ad* at street-level; (*fig*) straight; **de ~ (avec)** on the same level (as).

plaint, e [plɛ̃, -ɛ̃t] *pp de* **plaindre** ♦ *nf* (*gémissement*) moan, groan; (*doléance*) complaint; **porter ~e** to lodge a complaint.

plaintif, ive [plɛ̃tif, -iv] *a* plaintive.

plaire [plɛʀ] *vi* to be a success, be successful; to please; **~ à**: **cela me plaît** I like it; **essayer de ~ à qn** (*en étant serviable etc*) to try and please sb; **elle plaît aux hommes** she's a success with men, men like her; **se ~ quelque part** to like being somewhere, like it somewhere; **se ~ à faire** to take pleasure in doing; **ce qu'il vous plaira** what(ever) you like *ou* wish; **s'il vous plaît** please.

plaisamment [plɛzamɑ̃] *ad* pleasantly.

plaisance [plɛzɑ̃s] *nf* (*aussi*: **navigation de ~**) (pleasure) sailing, yachting.

plaisancier [plɛzɑ̃sje] *nm* amateur sailor, yachting enthusiast.

plaisant, e [plɛzɑ̃, -ɑ̃t] *a* pleasant; (*histoire, anecdote*) amusing.

plaisanter [plɛzɑ̃te] *vi* to joke ♦ *vt* (*personne*) to tease, make fun of; **pour ~** for a joke; **on ne plaisante pas avec cela** that's no joking matter; **tu plaisantes!** you're joking *ou* kidding!

plaisanterie [plɛzɑ̃tʀi] *nf* joke; joking *q.*

plaisantin [plɛzɑ̃tɛ̃] *nm* joker; (*fumiste*) fly-by-night.

plaise [plɛz] *etc vb voir* **plaire**.

plaisir [plɛziʀ] *nm* pleasure; **faire ~ à qn** (*délibérément*) to be nice to sb, please sb; (*suj: cadeau, nouvelle etc*): **ceci me fait ~** I'm delighted *ou* very pleased with this; **prendre ~ à/à faire** to take pleasure in/in doing; **j'ai le ~ de ...** it is with great pleasure that I ...; **M. et Mme X ont le ~ de vous faire part de ...** M. and Mme X are pleased to announce ...; **se faire un ~ de faire qch** to be (only too) pleased to do sth; **faites-moi le ~ de ...** would you mind ..., would you be kind enough to ...; **à ~** freely; for the sake of it; **au ~ (de vous revoir)** (I hope to) see you again; **pour le** *ou* **pour son** *ou* **par ~** for pleasure.

plaît [plɛ] *vb voir* **plaire**.

plan, e [plɑ̃, -an] *a* flat ♦ *nm* plan; (*GÉOM*) plane; (*fig*) level, plane; (*CINÉMA*) shot; **au premier/second ~** in the foreground/middle distance; **à l'arrière ~** in the background; **mettre qch au premier ~** (*fig*) to consider sth to be of primary importance; **sur le ~ sexuel** sexually, as far as sex is concerned; **laisser/rester en ~** to abandon/be abandoned; **~ d'action** plan of action; **~ directeur** (*ÉCON*) master plan; **~ d'eau** lake; pond; **~ de travail** work-top, work surface; **~ de vol** (*AVIAT*) flight plan.

planche [plɑ̃ʃ] *nf* (*pièce de bois*) plank, (wooden) board; (*illustration*) plate; (*de salades, radis, poireaux*) bed; (*d'un plongeoir*) (diving) board; **les ~s** (*THÉÂTRE*) the boards; **en ~s** a wooden; **faire la ~** (*dans l'eau*) to float on one's back; **avoir du pain sur la ~** to have one's work cut out; **~ à découper** chopping board; **~ à dessin** drawing board; **~ à pain** breadboard; **~ à repasser** ironing board; **~ (à roulettes)** (*planche*) skateboard; (*sport*) skateboarding; **~ de salut** (*fig*) sheet anchor; **~ à voile** (*planche*) windsurfer, sailboard; (*sport*) windsurfing.

plancher [plɑ̃ʃe] *nm* floor; (*planches*) floorboards *pl*; (*fig*) minimum level ♦ *vi* to work hard.

planchiste [plɑ̃ʃist(ə)] *nm/f* windsurfer.

plancton [plɑ̃ktɔ̃] *nm* plankton.

planer [plane] *vi* (*oiseau, avion*) to glide; (*fumée, vapeur*) to float, hover; (*drogué*) to be (on a) high; **~ sur** (*fig*) to hang over; to hover above.

planétaire [planetɛʀ] *a* planetary.

planétarium [planetaʀjɔm] *nm* planetarium.

planète [planɛt] *nf* planet.

planeur [planœʀ] *nm* glider.

planification [planifikɑsjɔ̃] *nf* (economic) planning.

planifier [planifje] *vt* to plan.

planning [planiŋ] *nm* programme (*Brit*), program (*US*), schedule; **~ familial** family planning.

planque [plɑ̃k] *nf* (*fam: combine, filon*) cushy (*Brit*) *ou* easy number; (*: cachette*) hideout.

planquer [plɑ̃ke] *vt* (*fam*) to hide (away), stash away; **se ~** to hide.

plant [plɑ̃] *nm* seedling, young plant.

plantaire [plɑ̃tɛʀ] *a voir* **voûte**.

plantation [plɑ̃tɑsjɔ̃] *nf* planting; (*de fleurs, légumes*) bed; (*exploitation*) plantation.

plante [plɑ̃t] *nf* plant; **~ d'appartement** house *ou* pot plant; **~ du pied** sole (of the foot); **~ verte** house plant.

planter [plɑ̃te] *vt* (*plante*) to plant; (*enfoncer*) to hammer *ou* drive in; (*tente*) to put up, pitch; (*drapeau, échelle, décors*) to put up; (*fam: mettre*) to dump; (*: abandonner*): **~ là** to ditch; **se ~** *vi* (*fam: se tromper*) to get it wrong; **~ qch dans** to hammer *ou* drive sth into; to stick sth into; **se ~ dans** to sink into; to get stuck in; **se ~ devant** to plant o.s. in front of.

planteur [plɑ̃tœʀ] *nm* planter.

planton [plɑ̃tɔ̃] *nm* orderly.

plantureux, euse [plɑ̃tyʀø, -øz] *a* (*repas*) copious, lavish; (*femme*) buxom.

plaquage [plakaʒ] *nm* (*RUGBY*) tackle.

plaque [plak] *nf* plate; (*de verre*) sheet; (*de verglas, d'eczéma*) patch; (*dentaire*) plaque; (*avec inscription*) plaque; **~ (minéralogique** *ou* **de police** *ou* **d'immatriculation)** number (*Brit*) *ou* license (*US*) plate; **~ de beurre** slab of butter; **~ chauffante** hotplate; **~ de chocolat** bar of chocolate; **~ de cuisson** hob; **~ d'identité** identity disc; **~ tournante** (*fig*) centre (*Brit*), center (*US*).

plaqué, e [plake] *a*: **~ or/argent** gold-/silver-plated ♦ *nm*: **~ or/argent** gold/silver plate; **~ acajou** with a mahogany veneer.

plaquer [plake] *vt* (*bijou*) to plate; (*bois*) to

veneer; (*aplatir*): ~ **qch sur/contre** to make sth stick *ou* cling to; (*RUGBY*) to bring down; (*fam: laisser tomber*) to drop, ditch; **se ~ contre** to flatten o.s. against; ~ **qn contre** to pin sb to.

plaquette [plakɛt] *nf* tablet; (*de chocolat*) bar; (*de beurre*) slab, packet; (*livre*) small volume; (*MÉD: de pilules, gélules*) pack, packet; (*INFORM*) circuit board; ~ **de frein** (*AUTO*) brake pad.

plasma [plasma] *nm* plasma.

plastic [plastik] *nm* plastic explosive.

plastifié, e [plastifje] *a* plastic-coated.

plastiquage [plastikaʒ] *nm* bombing, bomb attack.

plastique [plastik] *a* plastic ♦ *nm* plastic ♦ *nf* plastic arts *pl*; (*d'une statue*) modelling.

plastiquer [plastike] *vt* to blow up.

plastiqueur [plastikœʀ] *nm* terrorist (*planting a plastic bomb*).

plastron [plastrɔ̃] *nm* shirt front.

plastronner [plastrɔne] *vi* to swagger.

plat, e [pla, -at] *a* flat; (*fade: vin*) flat-tasting, insipid; (*personne, livre*) dull ♦ *nm* (*récipient, CULIN*) dish; (*d'un repas*): **le premier ~** the first course; (*partie plate*): **le ~ de la main** the flat of the hand; (*: d'une route*) flat (part); **à ~ ventre** *ad* face down; (*tomber*) flat on one's face; **à ~ a** (*pneu, batterie*) flat; (*fam: fatigué*) dead beat, tired out; ~ **cuisiné** pre-cooked meal (*ou* dish); ~ **du jour** dish of the day; ~ **de résistance** main course; **~s préparés** convenience food(s).

platane [platan] *nm* plane tree.

plateau, x [plato] *nm* (*support*) tray; (*d'une table*) top; (*d'une balance*) pan; (*GÉO*) plateau; (*de tourne-disques*) turntable; (*CINÉMA*) set; (*TV*): **nous avons 2 journalistes sur le ~ ce soir** we have 2 journalists with us tonight; ~ **à fromages** cheeseboard.

plateau-repas, *pl* **plateaux-repas** [platoʀəpɑ] *nm* tray meal, TV dinner (*US*).

plate-bande, *pl* **plates-bandes** [platbɑ̃d] *nf* flower bed.

platée [plate] *nf* dish(ful).

plate-forme, *pl* **plates-formes** [platfɔʀm(ə)] *nf* platform; ~ **de forage/pétrolière** drilling/oil rig.

platine [platin] *nm* platinum ♦ *nf* (*d'un tourne-disque*) turntable; ~ **disque/cassette** record/cassette deck; ~ **laser** *ou* **compact-disc** compact disc (player).

platitude [platityd] *nf* platitude.

platonique [platɔnik] *a* platonic.

plâtras [plɑtʀa] *nm* rubble *q*.

plâtre [plɑtʀ(ə)] *nm* (*matériau*) plaster; (*statue*) plaster statue; (*MÉD*) (plaster) cast; **~s** *nmpl* plasterwork *sg*; **avoir un bras dans le ~** to have an arm in plaster.

plâtrer [plɑtʀe] *vt* to plaster; (*MÉD*) to set *ou* put in a (plaster) cast.

plâtrier [plɑtʀije] *nm* plasterer.

plausible [plozibl(ə)] *a* plausible.

play-back [plɛbak] *nm* miming.

plébiscite [plebisit] *nm* plebiscite.

plébisciter [plebisite] *vt* (*approuver*) to give overwhelming support to; (*élire*) to elect by an overwhelming majority.

plectre [plɛktʀ(ə)] *nm* plectrum.

plein, e [plɛ̃, -ɛn] *a* full; (*porte, roue*) solid; (*chienne, jument*) big (with young) ♦ *nm*: **faire le ~ (d'essence)** to fill up (with petrol (*Brit*) *ou* gas (*US*)) ♦ *prép*: **avoir de l'argent ~ les poches** to have loads of money; ~ **de** full of; **avoir les mains ~es** to have one's hands full; **à ~es mains** (*ramasser*) in handfuls; (*empoigner*) firmly; **à ~ régime** at maximum revs; (*fig*) at full speed; **à ~ temps** full-time; **en ~ air** in the open air; **jeux en ~ air** outdoor games; **en ~e mer** on the open sea; **en ~ soleil** in direct sunlight; **en ~e nuit/rue** in the middle of the night/street; **en ~ milieu** right in the middle; **en ~ jour** in broad daylight; **les ~s** the downstrokes (*in handwriting*); **faire le ~ des voix** to get the maximum number of votes possible; **en ~ sur** right on; **en avoir ~ le dos** (*fam*) to have had it up to here.

pleinement [plɛnmɑ̃] *ad* fully; to the full.

plein-emploi [plɛnɑ̃plwa] *nm* full employment.

plénière [plenjɛʀ] *af*: **assemblée ~** plenary assembly.

plénipotentiaire [plenipɔtɑ̃sjɛʀ] *nm* plenipotentiary.

plénitude [plenityd] *nf* fullness.

pléthore [pletɔʀ] *nf*: ~ **de** overabundance *ou* plethora of.

pleurer [plœʀe] *vi* to cry; (*yeux*) to water ♦ *vt* to mourn (for); ~ **sur** *vt* to lament (over), bemoan; ~ **de rire** to laugh till one cries.

pleurésie [plœʀezi] *nf* pleurisy.

pleureuse [plœʀøz] *nf* professional mourner.

pleurnicher [plœʀniʃe] *vi* to snivel, whine.

pleurs [plœʀ] *nmpl*: **en ~** in tears.

pleut [plø] *vb voir* **pleuvoir**.

pleutre [pløtʀ(ə)] *a* cowardly.

pleuvait [pløvɛ] *etc vb voir* **pleuvoir**.

pleuviner [pløvine] *vb impersonnel* to drizzle.

pleuvoir [pløvwaʀ] *vb impersonnel* to rain ♦ *vi* (*fig*): ~ **(sur)** to shower down (upon), be showered upon; **il pleut** it's raining; **il pleut des cordes** *ou* **à verse** *ou* **à torrents** it's pouring (down), it's raining cats and dogs.

pleuvra [pløvʀa] *etc vb voir* **pleuvoir**.

plexiglas [plɛksiglas] *nm* ® plexiglass ®.

pli [pli] *nm* fold; (*de jupe*) pleat; (*de pantalon*) crease; (*aussi: faux ~*) crease; (*enveloppe*) envelope; (*lettre*) letter; (*CARTES*) trick; **prendre le ~ de faire** to get into the habit of doing; **ça ne fait pas un ~!** don't you worry!; ~ **d'aisance** inverted pleat.

pliable [plijabl(ə)] *a* pliable, flexible.

pliage [plijaʒ] *nm* folding; (*ART*) origami.

pliant, e [plijɑ̃, -ɑ̃t] *a* folding ♦ *nm* folding stool, campstool.

plier [plije] *vt* to fold; (*pour ranger*) to fold up; (*table pliante*) to fold down; (*genou, bras*) to bend ♦ *vi* to bend; (*fig*) to yield; **se ~ à** to submit to; ~ **bagages** (*fig*) to pack up (and go).

plinthe [plɛ̃t] *nf* skirting board.

plissé, e [plise] *a* (*jupe, robe*) pleated; (*peau*) wrinkled; (*GÉO*) folded ♦ *nm* (*COUTURE*) pleats *pl*.

plissement [plismɑ̃] *nm* (*GÉO*) fold.

plisser [plise] *vt* (*chiffonner: papier, étoffe*) to

crease; (*rider: front*) to furrow, wrinkle; (*: bouche*) to pucker; (*jupe*) to put pleats in; **se ~ vi** (*vêtement, étoffe*) to crease.

pliure [plijyʀ] *nf* (*du bras, genou*) bend; (*d'un ourlet*) fold.

plomb [plɔ̃] *nm* (*métal*) lead; (*d'une cartouche*) (lead) shot; (*PÊCHE*) sinker; (*sceau*) (lead) seal; (*ÉLEC*) fuse; **de ~** (*soleil*) blazing; **sommeil de ~** heavy *ou* very deep sleep; **mettre à ~** to plumb.

plombage [plɔ̃baʒ] *nm* (*de dent*) filling.

plomber [plɔ̃be] *vt* (*canne, ligne*) to weight (with lead); (*colis, wagon*) to put a lead seal on; (*TECH: mur*) to plumb; (*dent*) to fill (*Brit*), stop (*US*); (*INFORM*) to protect.

plomberie [plɔ̃bʀi] *nf* plumbing.

plombier [plɔ̃bje] *nm* plumber.

plonge [plɔ̃ʒ] *nf:* **faire la ~** to be a washer-up (*Brit*) *ou* dishwasher (*person*).

plongeant, e [plɔ̃ʒɑ̃, -ɑ̃t] *a* (*vue*) from above; (*tir, décolleté*) plunging.

plongée [plɔ̃ʒe] *nf* (*SPORT*) diving *q*; (*: sans scaphandre*) skin diving; (*de sous-marin*) submersion, dive; **en ~** (*sous-marin*) submerged; (*prise de vue*) high angle.

plongeoir [plɔ̃ʒwaʀ] *nm* diving board.

plongeon [plɔ̃ʒɔ̃] *nm* dive.

plonger [plɔ̃ʒe] *vi* to dive ♦ *vt:* **~ qch dans** to plunge sth into; **~ dans un sommeil profond** to sink straight into a deep sleep; **~ qn dans l'embarras** to throw sb into a state of confusion.

plongeur, euse [plɔ̃ʒœʀ, -øz] *nm/f* diver; (*de café*) washer-up (*Brit*), dishwasher (*person*).

plot [plo] *nm* (*ÉLEC*) contact.

ploutocratie [plutɔkʀasi] *nf* plutocracy.

ployer [plwaje] *vt* to bend ♦ *vi* to bend; (*plancher*) to sag.

plu [ply] *pp de* **plaire, pleuvoir**.

pluie [plɥi] *nf* rain; (*averse, ondée*): **une ~ brève** a shower; (*fig*): **~ de** shower of; **une ~ fine** fine rain; **retomber en ~** to shower down; **sous la ~** in the rain.

plumage [plymaʒ] *nm* plumage *q*, feathers *pl*.

plume [plym] *nf* feather; (*pour écrire*) (pen) nib; (*fig*) pen; **dessin à la ~** pen and ink drawing.

plumeau, x [plymo] *nm* feather duster.

plumer [plyme] *vt* to pluck.

plumet [plymɛ] *nm* plume.

plumier [plymje] *nm* pencil box.

plupart [plypaʀ]: **la ~** *pronom* the majority, most (of them); **la ~ des** most, the majority of; **la ~ du temps/d'entre nous** most of the time/of us; **pour la ~** *ad* for the most part, mostly.

pluralisme [plyʀalism(ə)] *nm* pluralism.

pluralité [plyʀalite] *nf* plurality.

pluridisciplinaire [plyʀidisiplinɛʀ] *a* multidisciplinary.

pluriel [plyʀjɛl] *nm* plural; **au ~** in the plural.

plus *vb* [ply] *voir* **plaire** ♦ *ad* [ply, plyz + vowel] (*comparatif*) more, adjective *court* + ...er; (*davantage*) [plys] more; (*négatif*): **ne ... ~** no more, *tournure négative* + any more, no longer ♦ *cj* [plys]: **~ 2** plus 2; **~ que** more than; **~ grand que** bigger than; **~ de 10 personnes** more than 10 people, over 10 people; **~ de minuit** after *ou* past midnight;

~ de pain more bread; **~ il travaille, ~ il est heureux** the more he works, the happier he is; **le ~ intelligent/grand** the most intelligent/biggest; **3 heures/kilos de ~ que** 3 hours/kilos more than; **il a 3 ans de ~ que moi** he is 3 years older than me; **de ~** (*en outre*) what's more, moreover; **3 kilos en ~** 3 kilos more, 3 extra kilos; **en ~ de** in addition to; **de ~ en ~** more and more; **d'autant ~ que** all the more so since *ou* because; **(tout) au ~** at the (very) most; **sans ~** (but) no more than that, (but) that's all; **~ ou moins** more or less; **ni ~ ni moins** no more, no less; **qui ~ est** what is more.

plusieurs [plyzjœʀ] *dét, pronom* several; **ils sont ~** there are several of them.

plus-que-parfait [plyskəpaʀfɛ] *nm* pluperfect, past perfect.

plus-value [plyvaly] *nf* (*d'un bien*) appreciation; (*bénéfice*) capital gain; (*budgétaire*) surplus.

plut [ply] *vb voir* **plaire, pleuvoir**.

plutonium [plytɔnjɔm] *nm* plutonium.

plutôt [plyto] *ad* rather; **je ferais ~ ceci** I'd rather *ou* sooner do this; **fais ~ comme ça** try this way instead, you'd better try this way; **~ que (de) faire** rather than *ou* instead of doing.

pluvial, e, aux [plyvjal, -o] *a* (*eaux*) rain *cpd*.

pluvieux, euse [plyvjø, -øz] *a* rainy, wet.

pluviosité [plyvjozite] *nf* rainfall.

PM *sigle f* = **Police militaire**.

p.m. *abr* (= *pour mémoire*) for the record.

PME *sigle fpl* = *petites et moyennes entreprises*.

PMI *sigle fpl* = *petites et moyennes industries* ♦ *sigle f* = **protection maternelle et infantile**.

PMU *sigle m* (= *pari mutuel urbain*) system of betting on horses; (*café*) betting agency.

PNB *sigle m* (= *produit national brut*) GNP.

pneu [pnø] *nm* (*de roue*) tyre (*Brit*), tire (*US*); (*message*) letter sent by pneumatic tube.

pneumatique [pnømatik] *a* pneumatic; (*gonflable*) inflatable ♦ *nm* tyre (*Brit*), tire (*US*).

pneumonie [pnømɔni] *nf* pneumonia.

PO *sigle fpl* (= *petites ondes*) MW.

Pô [po] *nm:* **le ~** the Po.

po [po] *abr voir* **science**.

p.o. *abr* (= *par ordre*) p.p. (*on letters etc*).

poche [pɔʃ] *nf* (*de pantalon*) pocket; (*déformation*): **faire une/des ~(s)** to bag; (*sous les yeux*) bag, pouch; (*ZOOL*) pouch ♦ *nm* (= *livre de ~*) (pocket-size) paperback; **de ~** pocket *cpd*; **en être de sa ~** to be out of pocket; **c'est dans la ~** it's in the bag.

poché, e [pɔʃe] *a:* **œuf ~** poached egg; **œil ~** black eye.

pocher [pɔʃe] *vt* (*CULIN*) to poach; (*ART*) to sketch ♦ *vi* (*vêtement*) to bag.

poche-revolver *pl* **poches-revolver** [pɔʃʀəvɔlvɛʀ] *nf* hip pocket.

pochette [pɔʃɛt] *nf* (*de timbres*) wallet, envelope; (*d'aiguilles etc*) case; (*sac: de femme*) clutch bag, purse; (*: d'homme*) bag; (*sur veston*) breast pocket; (*mouchoir*) breast pocket handkerchief; **~ d'allumettes** book of matches; **~ de disque** record sleeve; **~ surprise** lucky bag.

pochoir [pɔʃwaʀ] *nm* (*ART*: *cache*) stencil; (*: tampon*) transfer.

podium [pɔdjɔm] *nm* podium (*pl* -ia).

poêle [pwal] *nm* stove ♦ *nf*: ~ **(à frire)** frying pan.

poêlon [pwalɔ̃] *nm* casserole.

poème [pɔɛm] *nm* poem.

poésie [pɔezi] *nf* (*poème*) poem; (*art*): **la ~** poetry.

poète [pɔɛt] *nm* poet; (*fig*) dreamer ♦ *a* poetic.

poétique [pɔetik] *a* poetic.

pognon [pɔɲɔ̃] *nm* (*fam*: *argent*) dough.

poids [pwa] *nm* weight; (*SPORT*) shot; **vendre au ~** to sell by weight; **de ~** *a* (*argument etc*) weighty; **prendre du ~** to put on weight; **faire le ~** (*fig*) to measure up; **~ plume/ mouche/coq/moyen** (*BOXE*) feather/fly/ bantam/ middleweight; **~ et haltères** *nmpl* weight lifting *sg*; **~ lourd** (*BOXE*) heavy- weight; (*camion*: *aussi*: **PL**) (big) lorry (*Brit*), truck (*US*); (*: ADMIN*) heavy goods vehicle (*Brit*), truck (*US*); **~ mort** dead weight; **~ utile** net weight.

poignant, e [pwaɲɑ̃, -ɑ̃t] *a* poignant, harrow- ing.

poignard [pwaɲaʀ] *nm* dagger.

poignarder [pwaɲaʀde] *vt* to stab, knife.

poigne [pwaɲ] *nf* grip; (*fig*) firm-handedness; **à ~** firm-handed.

poignée [pwaɲe] *nf* (*de sel etc*, *fig*) handful; (*de couvercle, porte*) handle; **~ de main** handshake.

poignet [pwaɲɛ] *nm* (*ANAT*) wrist; (*de chemise*) cuff.

poil [pwal] *nm* (*ANAT*) hair; (*de pinceau, brosse*) bristle; (*de tapis, tissu*) strand; (*pe- lage*) coat; (*ensemble des poils*): **avoir du ~ sur la poitrine** to have hair(s) on one's chest, have a hairy chest; **à ~** *a* (*fam*) starkers; **au ~** *a* (*fam*) hunky-dory; **de tout ~** of all kinds; **être de bon/mauvais ~** to be in a good/bad mood; **~ à gratter** itching powder.

poilu, e [pwaly] *a* hairy.

poinçon [pwɛ̃sɔ̃] *nm* awl, bodkin; (*marque*) hallmark.

poinçonner [pwɛ̃sɔne] *vt* (*marchandise*) to stamp; (*bijou etc*) to hallmark; (*billet, tick- et*) to clip, punch.

poinçonneuse [pwɛ̃sɔnøz] *nf* (*outil*) punch.

poindre [pwɛ̃dʀ(ə)] *vi* (*fleur*) to come up; (*aube*) to break; (*jour*) to dawn.

poing [pwɛ̃] *nm* fist; **dormir à ~s fermés** to sleep soundly.

point [pwɛ̃] *vb voir* **poindre** ♦ *nm* (*marque, signe*) dot; (*: de ponctuation*) full stop, period (*US*); (*moment, de score etc, fig*: *question*) point; (*endroit*) spot; (*COUTURE, TRICOT*) stitch ♦ *ad* = **pas**; **ne ... ~** not (at all); **faire le ~** (*NAVIG*) to take a bearing; (*fig*) to take stock (of the situation); **faire le ~ sur** to review; **en tout ~** in every respect; **sur le ~ de faire** (just) about to do; **au ~ que, à tel ~ que** so much so that; **mettre au ~** (*mécanisme, procédé*) to develop; (*appareil-photo*) to focus; (*affaire*) to settle; **à ~** (*CULIN*) just right; (*: viande*) medium; **à ~ (nommé)** just at the right time; **~ de croix/tige/chaînette** (*COUTURE*) cross/stem/

chain stitch; **~ mousse/jersey** (*TRICOT*) garter/stocking stitch; **~ de départ/ d'arrivée/d'arrêt** departure/arrival/stopping point; **~ chaud** (*MIL, POL*) hot spot; **~ de chute** landing place; (*fig*) stopping-off point; **~ (de côté)** stitch (*pain*); **~ culminant** summit; (*fig*) height, climax; **~ d'eau** spring; water point; **~ d'exclamation** exclamation mark; **~ faible** weak spot; **~ final** full stop, period (*US*); **~ d'interrogation** question mark; **~ mort** (*FINANCE*) break- even point; **au ~ mort** (*AUTO*) in neutral; (*affaire, entreprise*) at a standstill; **~ noir** (*sur le visage*) blackhead; (*AUTO*) accident black spot; **~ de non-retour** point of no re- turn; **~ de repère** landmark; (*dans le temps*) point of reference; **~ de vente** retail outlet; **~ de vue** viewpoint; (*fig: opinion*) point of view; **du ~ de vue de** from the point of view of; **~s cardinaux** points of the compass, cardinal points; **~s de suspension** suspension points.

pointage [pwɛ̃taʒ] *nm* ticking off; checking in.

pointe [pwɛ̃t] *nf* point; (*de la côte*) headland; (*allusion*) dig; sally; (*fig*): **une ~ d'ail/ d'accent** a touch *ou* hint of garlic/of an accent; **~s** *nfpl* (*DANSE*) points, point shoes; **être à la ~ de** (*fig*) to be in the forefront of; **faire** *ou* **pousser une ~ jusqu'à ...** to press on as far as ...; **sur la ~ des pieds** on tiptoe; **en ~** *ad* (*tailler*) into a point ♦ *a* pointed, tapered; **de ~** *a* (*technique etc*) leading; (*vitesse*) maximum, top; **heures/jours de ~** peak hours/days; **faire du 180 en ~** (*AUTO*) to have a top *ou* maximum speed of 180; **faire des ~s** (*DANSE*) to dance on points; **~ d'asperge** asparagus tip; **~ de courant** surge (of current); **~ de tension** (*INFORM*) spike; **~ de vitesse** burst of speed.

pointer [pwɛ̃te] *vt* (*cocher*) to tick off; (*em- ployés etc*) to check in; (*diriger: canon, longue-vue, doigt*): **~ vers qch** to point at sth; (*MUS: note*) to dot ♦ *vi* (*employé*) to clock in; (*pousses*) to come through; (*jour*) to break; **~ les oreilles** (*chien*) to prick up its ears.

pointeur, euse [pwɛ̃tœʀ, -øz] *nm/f* time- keeper ♦ *nf* timeclock.

pointillé [pwɛ̃tije] *nm* (*trait*) dotted line; (*ART*) stippling *q*.

pointilleux, euse [pwɛ̃tijø, -øz] *a* particular, pernickety.

pointu, e [pwɛ̃ty] *a* pointed; (*clou*) sharp; (*voix*) shrill; (*analyse*) precise.

pointure [pwɛ̃tyʀ] *nf* size.

point-virgule, *pl* **points-virgules** [pwɛ̃viʀgyl] *nm* semi-colon.

poire [pwaʀ] *nf* pear; (*fam: péj*) mug; **~ élec- trique** (*pear-shaped*) switch; **~ à injections** syringe.

poireau, x [pwaʀo] *nm* leek.

poireauter [pwaʀote] *vi* (*fam*) to hang about (waiting).

poirier [pwaʀje] *nm* pear tree; (*GYM*): **faire le ~** to do a headstand.

pois [pwa] *nm* (*BOT*) pea; (*sur une étoffe*) dot, spot; **à ~** (*cravate etc*) spotted, polka-dot *cpd*; **~ chiche** chickpea; **~ de senteur** sweet pea; **~ cassés** split peas.

poison [pwazɔ̃] *nm* poison.

poisse [pwas] *nf* rotten luck.

poisser [pwase] *vt* to make sticky.

poisseux, euse [pwasø, -øz] *a* sticky.

poisson [pwasɔ̃] *nm* fish *gén inv*; **les P~s** (*signe*) Pisces, the Fish; **être des P~s** to be Pisces; **pêcher** *ou* **prendre du** ~ *ou* **des ~s** to fish; ~ **d'avril** April fool; (*blague*) April fool's day trick; ~ **rouge** goldfish.

poisson-chat, *pl* **poissons-chats** [pwasɔ̃ʃa] *nm* catfish.

poissonnerie [pwasɔnʀi] *nf* fishmonger's (*Brit*), fish store (*US*).

poissonneux, euse [pwasɔnø, -øz] *a* abounding in fish.

poissonnier, ière [pwasɔnje, -jɛʀ] *nm/f* fishmonger (*Brit*), fish merchant (*US*) ♦ *nf* (*ustensile*) fish kettle.

poisson-scie, *pl* **poissons-scies** [pwasɔ̃si] *nm* sawfish.

poitevin, e [pwatvɛ̃, -in] *a* (*région*) of *ou* from Poitou; (*ville*) of *ou* from Poitiers.

poitrail [pwatʀaj] *nm* (*d'un cheval etc*) breast.

poitrine [pwatʀin] *nf* (*ANAT*) chest; (*seins*) bust, bosom; (*CULIN*) breast; ~ **de bœuf** brisket.

poivre [pwavʀ(ə)] *nm* pepper; ~ **en grains/moulu** whole/ground pepper; ~ **de cayenne** cayenne (pepper); ~ **et sel** *a* (*cheveux*) pepper-and-salt.

poivré, e [pwavʀe] *a* peppery.

poivrer [pwavʀe] *vt* to pepper.

poivrier [pwavʀije] *nm* (*BOT*) pepper plant.

poivrière [pwavʀijɛʀ] *nf* pepperpot, pepper shaker (*US*).

poivron [pwavʀɔ̃] *nm* pepper, capsicum; ~ **vert/rouge** green/red pepper.

poix [pwa] *nf* pitch (*tar*).

poker [pɔkɛʀ] *nm*: **le** ~ poker; **partie de** ~ (*fig*) gamble; ~ **d'as** four aces.

polaire [pɔlɛʀ] *a* polar.

polariser [pɔlaʀize] *vt* to polarize; (*fig: attirer*) to attract; (*: réunir, concentrer*) to focus; **être polarisé sur** (*personne*) to be completely bound up with *ou* absorbed by.

pôle [pol] *nm* (*GÉO, ÉLEC*) pole; **le** ~ **Nord/Sud** the North/South Pole; ~ **d'attraction** (*fig*) centre of attraction.

polémique [pɔlemik] *a* controversial, polemic(al) ♦ *nf* controversy.

polémiquer [pɔlemike] *vi* to be involved in controversy.

polémiste [pɔlemist(ə)] *nm/f* polemist, polemicist.

poli, e [pɔli] *a* polite; (*lisse*) smooth; polished.

police [pɔlis] *nf* police; (*discipline*): **assurer la** ~ **de** *ou* **dans** to keep order in; **peine de simple** ~ sentence given by a magistrates' or police court; ~ (**d'assurance**) (insurance) policy; ~ (**de caractères**) (*TYPO, INFORM*) typeface; ~ **judiciaire (PJ)** ≈ Criminal Investigation Department (CID) (*Brit*), ≈ Federal Bureau of Investigation (FBI) (*US*); ~ **des mœurs** ≈ vice squad; ~ **secours** ≈ emergency services *pl*.

polichinelle [pɔliʃinɛl] *nm* Punch; (*péj*) buffoon; **secret de** ~ open secret.

policier, ière [pɔlisje, -jɛʀ] *a* police *cpd* ♦ *nm* policeman; (*aussi*: **roman** ~) detective novel.

policlinique [pɔliklinik] *nf* ≈ outpatients (clinic).

poliment [pɔlimɑ̃] *ad* politely.

polio(myélite) [pɔljo(mjelit)] *nf* polio(myelitis).

polio(myélitique) [pɔljo(mjelitik)] *nm/f* polio patient *ou* case.

polir [pɔliʀ] *vt* to polish.

polisson, ne [pɔlisɔ̃, -ɔn] *a* naughty.

politesse [pɔlitɛs] *nf* politeness; ~**s** *nfpl* (exchange of) courtesies; **rendre une** ~ **à qn** to return sb's favour (*Brit*) *ou* favor (*US*).

politicard [pɔlitikaʀ] *nm* (*péj*) politico, political schemer.

politicien, ne [pɔlitisjɛ̃, -ɛn] *a* political ♦ *nm/f* politician.

politique [pɔlitik] *a* political ♦ *nf* (*science, activité*) politics *sg*; (*principes, tactique*) policy, policies *pl* ♦ *nm* (*politicien*) politician; ~ **étrangère/intérieure** foreign/domestic policy.

politique-fiction [pɔlitikfiksjɔ̃] *nf* political fiction.

politiquement [pɔlitikmɑ̃] *ad* politically.

politiser [pɔlitize] *vt* to politicize; ~ **qn** to make sb politically aware.

pollen [pɔlɛn] *nm* pollen.

polluant, e [pɔlɥɑ̃, -ɑ̃t] *a* polluting ♦ *nm* polluting agent, pollutant.

polluer [pɔlɥe] *vt* to pollute.

pollution [pɔlysjɔ̃] *nf* pollution.

polo [pɔlo] *nm* (*sport*) polo; (*tricot*) polo shirt.

Pologne [pɔlɔɲ] *nf*: **la** ~ Poland.

polonais, e [pɔlɔnɛ, -ɛz] *a* Polish ♦ *nm* (*LING*) Polish ♦ *nm/f*: **P~, e** Pole.

poltron, ne [pɔltʀɔ̃, -ɔn] *a* cowardly.

poly... [pɔli] *préfixe* poly....

polyamide [pɔliamid] *nf* polyamide.

polychrome [pɔlikʀom] *a* polychrome, polychromatic.

polyclinique [pɔliklinik] *nf* (private) clinic (*treating different illnesses*).

polycopié, e [pɔlikɔpje] *a* duplicated ♦ *nm* handout, duplicated notes *pl*.

polycopier [pɔlikɔpje] *vt* to duplicate.

polyculture [pɔlikyltyʀ] *nf* mixed farming.

polyester [pɔliɛstɛʀ] *nm* polyester.

polyéthylène [pɔlietilɛn] *nm* polyethylene.

polygame [pɔligam] *a* polygamous.

polygamie [pɔligami] *nf* polygamy.

polyglotte [pɔliglɔt] *a* polyglot.

polygone [pɔligɔn] *nm* polygon.

Polynésie [pɔlinezi] *nf*: **la** ~ Polynesia; **la** ~ **française** French Polynesia.

polynésien, ne [pɔlinezjɛ̃, -ɛn] *a* Polynesian.

polype [pɔlip] *nm* polyp.

polystyrène [pɔlistiʀɛn] *nm* polystyrene.

polytechnicien, ne [pɔliteknisjɛ̃, -ɛn] *nm/f* student or former student of the École Polytechnique.

polyvalent, e [pɔlivalɑ̃, -ɑ̃t] *a* (*vaccin*) polyvalent; (*personne*) versatile; (*salle*) multipurpose ♦ *nm* ≈ tax inspector.

pomélo [pɔmelo] *nm* pomelo, grapefruit.

Poméranie [pɔmeʀani] *nf*: **la** ~ Pomerania.

pomme [pɔm] *nf* (*BOT*) apple; (*boule décorative*) knob; (*pomme de terre*): **steak ~s**

(frites) steak and chips (*Brit*) *ou* (French) fries (*US*); **tomber dans les ~s** (*fam*) to pass out; **~ d'Adam** Adam's apple; **~s allumettes** French fries (*thin-cut*); **~ d'arrosoir** (sprinkler) rose; **~ de pin** pine *ou* fir cone; **~ de terre** potato; **~s vapeur** boiled potatoes.

pommé, e [pɔme] *a* (*chou etc*) firm, with a firm heart.

pommeau, x [pɔmo] *nm* (*boule*) knob; (*de selle*) pommel.

pommelé, e [pɔmle] *a*: **gris ~** dapple grey.

pommette [pɔmɛt] *nf* cheekbone.

pommier [pɔmje] *nm* apple tree.

pompe [pɔp] *nf* pump; (*faste*) pomp (and ceremony); **~ de bicyclette** bicycle pump; **~ à eau/essence** water/petrol pump; **~ à huile** oil pump; **~ à incendie** fire engine (*apparatus*); **~s funèbres** undertaker's *sg*, funeral parlour *sg* (*Brit*), mortician's *sg* (*US*).

Pompéi [pɔpei] *n* Pompeii.

pompéien, ne [pɔpejɛ̃, -ɛn] *a* Pompeiian.

pomper [pɔpe] *vt* to pump; (*évacuer*) to pump out; (*aspirer*) to pump up; (*absorber*) to soak up ♦ *vi* to pump.

pompeusement [pɔpøzmɑ̃] *ad* pompously.

pompeux, euse [pɔpø, -øz] *a* pompous.

pompier [pɔpje] *nm* fireman ♦ *am* (*style*) pretentious, pompous.

pompiste [pɔpist(ə)] *nm/f* petrol (*Brit*) *ou* gas (*US*) pump attendant.

pompon [pɔpɔ̃] *nm* pompom, bobble.

pomponner [pɔpɔne] *vt* to titivate (*Brit*), dress up.

ponce [pɔ̃s] *nf*: **pierre ~** pumice stone.

poncer [pɔ̃se] *vt* to sand (down).

ponceuse [pɔ̃søz] *nf* sander.

poncif [pɔ̃sif] *nm* cliché.

ponction [pɔ̃ksjɔ̃] *nf* (*d'argent etc*) withdrawal; **~ lombaire** lumbar puncture.

ponctualité [pɔ̃ktɥalite] *nf* punctuality.

ponctuation [pɔ̃ktɥasjɔ̃] *nf* punctuation.

ponctuel, le [pɔ̃ktɥɛl] *a* (*à l'heure, aussi TECH*) punctual; (*fig: opération etc*) one-off, single; (*scrupuleux*) punctilious, meticulous.

ponctuellement [pɔ̃ktɥɛlmɑ̃] *ad* punctually; punctiliously, meticulously.

ponctuer [pɔ̃ktɥe] *vt* to punctuate; (*MUS*) to phrase.

pondéré, e [pɔ̃deʀe] *a* level-headed, composed.

pondérer [pɔ̃deʀe] *vt* to balance.

pondeuse [pɔ̃døz] *nf* layer, laying hen.

pondre [pɔ̃dʀ(ə)] *vt* to lay; (*fig*) to produce ♦ *vi* to lay.

poney [pɔnɛ] *nm* pony.

pongiste [pɔ̃ʒist(ə)] *nm/f* table tennis player.

pont [pɔ̃] *nm* bridge; (*AUTO*): **~ arrière/avant** rear/front axle; (*NAVIG*) deck; **faire le ~** to take the extra day off; **faire un ~ d'or à qn** to offer sb a fortune to take a job; **~ aérien** airlift; **~ basculant** bascule bridge; **~ d'envol** flight deck; **~ élévateur** hydraulic ramp; **~ de graissage** ramp (*in garage*); **~ à péage** tollbridge; **~ roulant** travelling crane; **~ suspendu** suspension bridge; **~ tournant** swing bridge; **P~s et Chaussées** highways department.

ponte [pɔ̃t] *nf* laying; (*œufs pondus*) clutch ♦

nm (*fam*) big shot.

pontife [pɔ̃tif] *nm* pontiff.

pontifier [pɔ̃tifje] *vi* to pontificate.

pont-levis, *pl* **ponts-levis** [pɔ̃lvi] *nm* drawbridge.

ponton [pɔ̃tɔ̃] *nm* pontoon (*on water*).

pop [pɔp] *a inv* pop ♦ *nm*: **le ~** pop (music).

pop-corn [pɔpkɔʀn] *nm* popcorn.

popeline [pɔplin] *nf* poplin.

populace [pɔpylas] *nf* (*péj*) rabble.

populaire [pɔpylɛʀ] *a* popular; (*manifestation*) mass *cpd*, of the people; (*milieux, clientèle*) working-class; (*LING: mot etc*) used by the lower classes (of society).

populariser [pɔpylaʀize] *vt* to popularize.

popularité [pɔpylaʀite] *nf* popularity.

population [pɔpylasjɔ̃] *nf* population; **~ active/agricole** working/farming population.

populeux, euse [pɔpylø, -øz] *a* densely populated.

porc [pɔʀ] *nm* (*ZOOL*) pig; (*CULIN*) pork; (*peau*) pigskin.

porcelaine [pɔʀsəlɛn] *nf* (*substance*) porcelain, china; (*objet*) piece of china(ware).

porcelet [pɔʀsəlɛ] *nm* piglet.

porc-épic, *pl* **porcs-épics** [pɔʀkepik] *nm* porcupine.

porche [pɔʀʃ(ə)] *nm* porch.

porcher, ère [pɔʀʃe, -ɛʀ] *nm/f* pig-keeper.

porcherie [pɔʀʃəʀi] *nf* pigsty.

porcin, e [pɔʀsɛ̃, -in] *a* (*race*) porcine; (*élevage*) pig *cpd*; (*fig*) piglike.

pore [pɔʀ] *nm* pore.

poreux, euse [pɔʀø, -øz] *a* porous.

porno [pɔʀno] *a* porno ♦ *nm* porn.

pornographie [pɔʀnɔgʀafi] *nf* pornography.

pornographique [pɔʀnɔgʀafik] *a* pornographic.

port [pɔʀ] *nm* (*NAVIG*) harbour (*Brit*), harbor (*US*), port; (*ville, aussi INFORM*) port; (*de l'uniforme etc*) wearing; (*pour lettre*) postage; (*pour colis, aussi: posture*) carriage; **~ de commerce/de pêche** commercial/fishing port; **arriver à bon ~** to arrive safe and sound; **~ d'arme** (*JUR*) carrying of a firearm; **~ d'attache** (*NAVIG*) port of registry; (*fig*) home base; **~ d'escale** port of call; **~ franc** free port.

portable [pɔʀtabl(ə)] *a* (*vêtement*) wearable; (*portatif*) transportable.

portail [pɔʀtaj] *nm* gate; (*de cathédrale*) portal.

portant, e [pɔʀtɑ̃, -ɑ̃t] *a* (*murs*) structural, supporting; (*roues*) running; **bien/mal ~** in good/poor health.

portatif, ive [pɔʀtatif, -iv] *a* portable.

porte [pɔʀt(ə)] *nf* door; (*de ville, forteresse, SKI*) gate; **mettre à la ~** to throw out; **prendre la ~** to leave, go away; **à ma/sa ~** (*tout près*) on my/his (*ou* her) doorstep; **~ (d'embarquement)** (*AVIAT*) (departure) gate; **~ d'entrée** front door; **~ à ~** *nm* door-to-door selling; **~ de secours** emergency exit; **~ de service** service entrance.

porté, e [pɔʀte] *a*: **être ~ à faire qch** to be apt to do sth, tend to do sth; **être ~ sur qch** to be partial to sth.

porte-à-faux [pɔʀtafo] *nm*: **en ~**

cantilevered; (*fig*) in an awkward position.

porte-aiguilles [pɔʀteɡɥij] *nm inv* needle case.

porte-avions [pɔʀtavjɔ̃] *nm inv* aircraft carrier.

porte-bagages [pɔʀtbagaʒ] *nm inv* luggage rack (*ou* basket *etc*).

porte-bébé [pɔʀtbebe] *nm* baby sling *ou* carrier.

porte-bonheur [pɔʀtbɔnœʀ] *nm inv* lucky charm.

porte-bouteilles [pɔʀtbutɛj] *nm inv* bottle carrier; (*à casiers*) wine rack.

porte-cartes [pɔʀtəkaʀt(ə)] *nm inv* (*de cartes d'identité*) card holder; (*de cartes géographiques*) map wallet.

porte-cigarettes [pɔʀtsigaʀɛt] *nm inv* cigarette case.

porte-clefs [pɔʀtəkle] *nm inv* key ring.

porte-conteneurs [pɔʀtəkɔ̃tnœʀ] *nm inv* container ship.

porte-couteau, x [pɔʀtkuto] *nm* knife rest.

porte-crayon [pɔʀtkʀejɔ̃] *nm* pencil holder.

porte-documents [pɔʀtdɔkymɑ̃] *nm inv* attaché *ou* document case.

porte-drapeau, x [pɔʀtdʀapo] *nm* standard bearer.

portée [pɔʀte] *nf* (*d'une arme*) range; (*fig: importance*) impact, import; (*: capacités*) scope, capability; (*de chatte etc*) litter; (*MUS*) stave, staff (*pl* staves); **à/hors de ~ (de)** within/out of reach (of); **à ~ de (la) main** within (arm's) reach; **à ~ de voix** within earshot; **à la ~ de qn** (*fig*) at sb's level, within sb's capabilities; **à la ~ de toutes les bourses** to suit every pocket, within everyone's means.

portefaix [pɔʀtəfɛ] *nm inv* porter.

porte-fenêtre, *pl* **portes-fenêtres** [pɔʀtfənɛtʀ(ə)] *nf* French window.

portefeuille [pɔʀtəfœj] *nm* wallet; (*POL, BOURSE*) portfolio; **faire un lit en ~** to make an apple-pie bed.

porte-jarretelles [pɔʀtʒaʀtɛl] *nm inv* suspender belt.

porte-jupe [pɔʀtʒyp] *nm* skirt hanger.

portemanteau, x [pɔʀtmɑ̃to] *nm* coat rack.

porte-mine [pɔʀtəmin] *nm* propelling (*Brit*) *ou* mechanical (*US*) pencil.

porte-monnaie [pɔʀtmɔnɛ] *nm inv* purse.

porte-parapluies [pɔʀtpaʀaplyi] *nm inv* umbrella stand.

porte-parole [pɔʀtpaʀɔl] *nm inv* spokesperson.

porte-plume [pɔʀtəplym] *nm inv* penholder.

porter [pɔʀte] *vt* (*charge ou sac etc, aussi: fœtus*) to carry; (*sur soi: vêtement, barbe, bague*) to wear; (*fig: responsabilité etc*) to bear, carry; (*inscription, marque, titre, patronyme, suj: arbre: fruits, fleurs*) to bear; (*jugement*) to pass; (*apporter*): **~ qch quelque part/à qn** to take sth somewhere/to sb; (*inscrire*): **~ qch sur** to put sth down on; to enter sth in ♦ *vi* (*voix, regard, canon*) to carry; (*coup, argument*) to hit home; **se ~** *vi* (*se sentir*): **se ~ bien/mal** to be well/unwell; (*aller*): **se ~ vers** to go towards; **~ sur** (*peser*) to rest on; (*accent*) to fall on; (*conférence etc*) to concern; (*heurter*) to

strike; **être porté à faire** to be apt *ou* inclined to do; **elle portait le nom de Rosalie** she was called Rosalie; **~ qn au pouvoir** to bring sb to power; **~ bonheur à qn** to bring sb luck; **~ qn à croire** to lead sb to believe; **~ son âge** to look one's age; **~ un toast** to drink a toast; **~ de l'argent au crédit d'un compte** to credit an account with some money; **se ~ partie civile** *to associate in a court action with the public prosecutor*; **se ~ garant de qch** to guarantee sth, vouch for sth; **se ~ candidat à la députation** ≈ to stand for Parliament (*Brit*), ≈ run for Congress (*US*); **se faire ~ malade** to report sick; **~ la main à son chapeau** to raise one's hand to one's hat; **~ son effort sur** to direct one's efforts towards; **~ un fait à la connaissance de qn** to bring a fact to sb's attention *ou* notice.

porte-savon [pɔʀtsavɔ̃] *nm* soap dish.

porte-serviettes [pɔʀtsɛʀvjɛt] *nm inv* towel rail.

portes-ouvertes [pɔʀtuvɛʀt(ə)] *a inv*: **journée ~** open day.

porteur, euse [pɔʀtœʀ, -øz] *a* (*COMM*) strong, promising; (*nouvelle, chèque etc*): **être ~ de** to be the bearer of ♦ *nm/f* (*de messages*) bearer ♦ *nm* (*de bagages*) porter; (*COMM: de chèque*) bearer; (*: d'actions*) holder; (*avion*) **gros ~** wide-bodied aircraft, jumbo (jet).

porte-voix [pɔʀtəvwa] *nm inv* megaphone, loudhailer (*Brit*).

portier [pɔʀtje] *nm* doorman, commissionnaire (*Brit*).

portière [pɔʀtjɛʀ] *nf* door.

portillon [pɔʀtijɔ̃] *nm* gate.

portion [pɔʀsjɔ̃] *nf* (*part*) portion, share; (*partie*) portion, section.

portique [pɔʀtik] *nm* (*GYM*) crossbar; (*ARCHIT*) portico; (*RAIL*) gantry.

porto [pɔʀto] *nm* port (wine).

portoricain, e [pɔʀtɔʀikɛ̃, -ɛn] *a* Puerto Rican.

Porto Rico [pɔʀtɔʀiko] *nf* Puerto Rico.

portrait [pɔʀtʀɛ] *nm* portrait; (*photographie*) photograph; (*fig*): **elle est le ~ de sa mère** she's the image of her mother.

portraitiste [pɔʀtʀetist(ə)] *nm/f* portrait painter.

portrait-robot [pɔʀtʀɛʀɔbo] *nm* Identikit ® *ou* Photo-fit ® (*Brit*) picture.

portuaire [pɔʀtɥɛʀ] *a* port *cpd*, harbour *cpd* (*Brit*), harbor *cpd* (*US*).

portugais, e [pɔʀtygɛ, -ɛz] *a* Portuguese ♦ *nm* (*LING*) Portuguese ♦ *nm/f*: **P~, e** Portuguese.

Portugal [pɔʀtygal] *nm*: **le ~** Portugal.

pose [poz] *nf* (*de moquette*) laying; (*de rideaux, papier peint*) hanging; (*attitude, d'un modèle*) pose; (*PHOTO*) exposure.

posé, e [poze] *a* calm, unruffled.

posément [pozemɑ̃] *ad* calmly.

posemètre [pozmɛtʀ(ə)] *nm* exposure meter.

poser [poze] *vt* (*déposer*): **~ qch (sur)/qn à** to put sth down (on)/drop sb at; (*placer*): **~ qch sur/quelque part** to put sth on/ somewhere; (*installer: moquette, carrelage*) to lay; (*rideaux, papier peint*) to hang; (*MATH: chiffre*) to put (down); (*question*) to ask; (*principe, conditions*) to lay *ou* set down; (*problème*) to formulate; (*difficulté*) to

pose; (*personne: mettre en valeur*) to give
standing to ♦ *vi* (*modèle*) to pose; to sit; **se
~** (*oiseau, avion*) to land; (*question*) to a-
rise; **se ~ en** to pass o.s. off as, pose as; **~
son** *ou* **un regard sur qn/qch** to turn one's
gaze on sb/sth; **~ sa candidature** to apply;
(*POL*) to put o.s. up for election.

poseur, euse [pozœʀ, -øz] *nm/f* (*péj*) show-
off, poseur; **~ de parquets/ carrelages** floor/
tile layer.

positif, ive [pozitif, -iv] *a* positive.

position [pozisjɔ̃] *nf* position; **prendre ~** (*fig*)
to take a stand.

positionner [pozisjɔne] *vt* to position; (*compte
en banque*) to calculate the balance of.

positivement [pozitivmɑ̃] *ad* positively.

posologie [pozɔlɔʒi] *nf* directions *pl* for use,
dosage.

possédant, e [pɔsedɑ̃, -ɑ̃t] *a* (*classe*) wealthy
♦ *nm/f:* **les ~s** the haves, the wealthy.

possédé, e [pɔsede] *nm/f* person possessed.

posséder [pɔsede] *vt* to own, possess;
(*qualité, talent*) to have, possess; (*bien
connaître: métier, langue*) to have mastered,
have a thorough knowledge of; · (*sexuellement, aussi: suj: colère etc*) to possess;
(*fam: duper*) to take in.

possesseur [pɔsesœʀ] *nm* owner.

possessif, ive [pɔsesif, -iv] *a, nm* (*aussi
LING*) possessive.

possession [pɔsesjɔ̃] *nf* ownership *q*; possession; **être/entrer en ~ de qch** to be in/take
possession of sth.

possibilité [pɔsibilite] *nf* possibility; **~s** *nfpl*
(*moyens*) means; (*potentiel*) potential *sg*;
avoir la ~ de faire to be in a position to do;
to have the opportunity to do.

possible [pɔsibl(ə)] *a* possible; (*projet, entreprise*) feasible ♦ *nm:* **faire son ~** to do all
one can, do one's utmost; (**ce n'est) pas ~**!
impossible!; **le plus/moins de livres ~** as
many/few books as possible; **dès que ~** as
soon as possible; **gentil** *etc* **au ~** as nice *etc*
as it is possible to be.

postal, e, aux [pɔstal, -o] *a* postal, post office
cpd; **sac ~** mailbag, postbag.

postdater [pɔstdate] *vt* to postdate.

poste [pɔst(ə)] *nf* (*service*) post, postal
service; (*administration, bureau*) post office
♦ *nm* (*fonction, MIL*) post; (*TÉL*) extension;
(*de radio etc*) set; (*de budget*) item; **~s** *nfpl*
post office *sg*; **P~s télécommunications et
télédiffusion (PTT)** *postal and
telecommunications service;* **agent** *ou* **employé des ~s** post office worker; **mettre à la
~** to post; **~ de commandement (PC)** *nm*
(*MIL etc*) headquarters; **~ de contrôle** *nm*
checkpoint; **~ de douane** *nm* customs post;
~ émetteur *nm* transmitting set; **~
d'essence** *nm* filling station; **~ d'incendie**
nm fire point; **~ de péage** *nm* tollgate; **~ de
pilotage** *nm* cockpit; **~ (de police)** *nm* police
station; **~ de radio** *nm* radio set; **~ restante
(PR)** *nf* poste restante (*Brit*), general delivery
(*US*); **~ de secours** *nm* first-aid post; **~ de
télévision** *nm* television set; **~ de travail** *nm*
work station.

poster *vt* [pɔste] to post ♦ *nm* [pɔstɛʀ] poster;
se ~ to position o.s.

postérieur, e [pɔsteʀjœʀ] *a* (*date*) later;
(*partie*) back ♦ *nm* (*fam*) behind.

postérieurement [pɔsteʀjœʀmɑ̃] *ad* later,
subsequently; **~ à** after.

posteriori [pɔsteʀjɔʀi]: **a ~** *ad* with hindsight,
a posteriori.

postérité [pɔsteʀite] *nf* posterity.

postface [pɔstfas] *nf* appendix.

posthume [pɔstym] *a* posthumous.

postiche [pɔstiʃ] *a* false ♦ *nm* hairpiece.

postier, ière [pɔstje, -jɛʀ] *nm/f* post office
worker.

postillonner [pɔstijɔne] *vi* to spl(l)utter.

post-natal, e [pɔstnatal] *a* postnatal.

postopératoire [pɔstɔpeʀatwaʀ] *a* post-
operative.

postscolaire [pɔstskɔlɛʀ] *a* further, continuing.

post-scriptum [pɔstskʀiptɔm] *nm inv* postscript.

postsynchroniser [pɔstsɛ̃kʀɔnize] *vt* to dub.

postulant, e [pɔstylɑ̃, -ɑ̃t] *nm/f* (*candidat*)
applicant; (*REL*) postulant.

postulat [pɔstyla] *nm* postulate.

postuler [pɔstyle] *vt* (*emploi*) to apply for, put
in for.

posture [pɔstyʀ] *nf* posture, position; (*fig*)
position.

pot [po] *nm* jar, pot; (*en plastique, carton*)
carton; (*en métal*) tin; (*fam*): **avoir du ~** to
be lucky; **boire** *ou* **prendre un ~** (*fam*) to
have a drink; **découvrir le ~ aux roses** to
find out what's been going on; **~ (de chambre)** (chamber)pot; **~ d'échappement** exhaust pipe; **~ de fleurs** plant pot,
flowerpot; (*plante*) pot plant; **~ à tabac**
tobacco jar.

potable [pɔtabl(ə)] *a* (*fig: boisson*) drinkable;
(*: travail, devoir*) decent; **eau (non) ~** (not)
drinking water.

potache [pɔtaʃ] *nm* schoolboy.

potage [pɔtaʒ] *nm* soup.

potager, ère [pɔtaʒe, -ɛʀ] *a* (*plante*) edible,
vegetable *cpd*; (**jardin**) **~** kitchen *ou* vegetable garden.

potasse [pɔtas] *nf* potassium hydroxide; (*engrais*) potash.

potasser [pɔtase] *vt* (*fam*) to swot up (*Brit*),
cram.

potassium [pɔtasjɔm] *nm* potassium.

pot-au-feu [pɔtofø] *nm inv* (beef) stew;
(*viande*) stewing beef ♦ *a* (*fam: personne*)
stay-at-home.

pot-de-vin, *pl* **pots-de-vin** [podvɛ̃] *nm* bribe.

pote [pɔt] *nm* (*fam*) mate (*Brit*), pal.

poteau, x [pɔto] *nm* post; **~ de départ/
arrivée** starting/finishing post; **~
(d'exécution)** execution post, stake; **~
indicateur** signpost; **~ télégraphique** telegraph pole; **~x (de but)** goal-posts.

potée [pɔte] *nf* hotpot (*of pork and cabbage*).

potelé, e [pɔtle] *a* plump, chubby.

potence [pɔtɑ̃s] *nf* gallows *sg*; **en ~** T-shaped.

potentat [pɔtɑ̃ta] *nm* potentate; (*fig: péj*)
despot.

potentiel, le [pɔtɑ̃sjɛl] *a, nm* potential.

poterie [pɔtʀi] *nf* (*fabrication*) pottery; (*objet*)
piece of pottery.

potiche [pɔtiʃ] *nf* large vase.

potier [pɔtje] *nm* potter.

potins [pɔtɛ̃] *nmpl* gossip *sg*.

potion [posjɔ̃] *nf* potion.

potiron [pɔtiRɔ̃] *nm* pumpkin.

pot-pourri, *pl* **pots-pourris** [popuRi] *nm* (*MUS*) potpourri, medley.

pou, x [pu] *nm* louse (*pl* lice).

pouah [pwa] *excl* ugh!, yuk!

poubelle [pubɛl] *nf* (dust)bin.

pouce [pus] *nm* thumb; **se tourner** *ou* **se rouler les ~s** (*fig*) to twiddle one's thumbs; **manger sur le ~** to eat on the run, snatch something to eat.

poudre [pudR(ə)] *nf* powder; (*fard*) (face) powder; (*explosif*) gunpowder; **en ~: café en ~** instant coffee; **savon en ~** soap powder; **lait en ~** dried *ou* powdered milk; **~ à canon** gunpowder; **~ à éternuer** sneezing powder; **~ à récurer** scouring powder; **~ de riz** face powder.

poudrer [pudRe] *vt* to powder.

poudrerie [pudRəRi] *nf* gunpowder factory.

poudreux, euse [pudRø, -øz] *a* dusty; (*neige*) powdery, powder *cpd*.

poudrier [pudRije] *nm* (powder) compact.

poudrière [pudRijɛR] *nf* powder magazine; (*fig*) powder keg.

poudroyer [pudRwaje] *vi* to rise in clouds *ou* a flurry.

pouf [puf] *nm* pouffe.

pouffer [pufe] *vi:* **~ (de rire)** to snigger; to giggle.

pouffiasse [pufjas] *nf* (*fam*) fat cow; (*prostituée*) tart.

pouilleux, euse [pujø, -øz] *a* flea-ridden; (*fig*) seedy.

poulailler [pulaje] *nm* henhouse; (*THÉÂTRE*): **le ~** the gods *sg*.

poulain [pulɛ̃] *nm* foal; (*fig*) protégé.

poularde [pulaRd(ə)] *nf* fatted chicken.

poule [pul] *nf* (*ZOOL*) hen; (*CULIN*) (boiling) fowl; (*SPORT*) (round-robin) tournament; (*RUGBY*) group; (*fam*) bird (*Brit*), chick, broad (*US*); (*prostituée*) tart; **~ d'eau** moorhen; **~ mouillée** coward; **~ pondeuse** laying hen, layer; **~ au riz** chicken and rice.

poulet [pulɛ] *nm* chicken; (*fam*) cop.

poulette [pulɛt] *nf* (*jeune poule*) pullet.

pouliche [puliʃ] *nf* filly.

poulie [puli] *nf* pulley.

poulpe [pulp(ə)] *nm* octopus.

pouls [pu] *nm* pulse (*ANAT*); **prendre le ~ de qn** to feel sb's pulse.

poumon [pumɔ̃] *nm* lung; **~ d'acier** *ou* **artificiel** iron *ou* artificial lung.

poupe [pup] *nf* stern; **en ~** astern.

poupée [pupe] *nf* doll; **jouer à la ~** to play with one's doll (*ou* dolls); **de ~** (*très petit*): **jardin de ~** doll's garden, pocket-handkerchief-sized garden.

poupin, e [pupɛ̃, -in] *a* chubby.

poupon [pupɔ̃] *nm* babe-in-arms.

pouponner [pupɔne] *vi* to fuss (around).

pouponnière [pupɔnjɛR] *nf* crèche, day nursery.

pour [puR] *prép* for ♦ *nm:* **le ~ et le contre** the pros and cons; **~ faire** (so as) to do, in order to do; **~ avoir fait** for having done; **~ que** so that, in order that; **~ moi** (*à mon avis, pour ma part*) for my part, personally; **~ riche qu'il soit** rich though he may be; **~ 100 francs d'essence** 100 francs' worth of petrol; **~ cent** per cent; **~ ce qui est de** as for; **y être ~ quelque chose** to have something to do with it.

pourboire [puRbwaR] *nm* tip.

pourcentage [puRsɑ̃taʒ] *nm* percentage; **travailler au ~** to work on commission.

pourchasser [puRʃase] *vt* to pursue.

pourfendeur [puRfɑ̃dœR] *nm* sworn opponent.

pourfendre [puRfɑ̃dR(ə)] *vt* to assail.

pourlécher [puRleʃe]: **se ~** *vi* to lick one's lips.

pourparlers [puRpaRle] *nmpl* talks, negotiations; **être en ~ avec** to be having talks with.

pourpre [puRpR(ə)] *a* crimson.

pourquoi [puRkwa] *ad, cj* why ♦ *nm inv:* **le ~ (de)** the reason (for).

pourrai [puRe] *etc vb voir* **pouvoir.**

pourri, e [puRi] *a* rotten; (*roche, pierre*) crumbling; (*temps, climat*) filthy, foul ♦ *nm:* **sentir le ~** to smell rotten.

pourrir [puRiR] *vi* to rot; (*fruit*) to go rotten *ou* bad; (*fig: situation*) to deteriorate ♦ *vt* to rot; (*fig: corrompre: personne*) to corrupt; (*: gâter: enfant*) to spoil thoroughly.

pourrissement [puRismɑ̃] *nm* deterioration.

pourriture [puRityR] *nf* rot.

pourrons [puRɔ̃] *etc vb voir* **pouvoir.**

poursuis [puRsɥi] *etc vb voir* **poursuivre.**

poursuite [puRsɥit] *nf* pursuit, chase; **~s** *nfpl* (*JUR*) legal proceedings; (*course*) ~ track race; (*fig*) chase.

poursuivant, e [puRsɥivɑ̃, -ɑ̃t] *vb voir* **poursuivre** ♦ *nm/f* pursuer; (*JUR*) plaintiff.

poursuivre [puRsɥivR(ə)] *vt* to pursue, chase (after); (*relancer*) to hound, harry; (*obséder*) to haunt; (*JUR*) to bring proceedings against, prosecute; (*: au civil*) to sue; (*but*) to strive towards; (*voyage, études*) to carry on with, continue ♦ *vi* to carry on, go on; **se ~** *vi* to go on, continue.

pourtant [puRtɑ̃] *ad* and yet; **mais ~** but nevertheless, but even so; **c'est ~ facile** (and) yet it's easy.

pourtour [puRtuR] *nm* perimeter.

pourvoi [puRvwa] *nm* appeal.

pourvoir [puRvwaR] *nm* (*COMM*) supply ♦ *vt:* **~ qch/qn de** to equip sth/sb with ♦ *vi:* **~ à** to provide for; (*emploi*) to fill; **se ~** (*JUR*): **se ~ en cassation** to take one's case to the Court of Appeal.

pourvoyeur, euse [puRvwajœR, -øz] *nm/f* supplier.

pourvu, e [puRvy] *pp de* **pourvoir** ♦ *a:* **~ de** equipped with; **~ que** *cj* (*si*) provided that, so long as; (*espérons que*) let's hope (that).

pousse [pus] *nf* growth; (*bourgeon*) shoot.

poussé, e [puse] *a* sophisticated, advanced; (*moteur*) souped-up.

pousse-café [puskafe] *nm inv* (after-dinner) liqueur.

poussée [puse] *nf* thrust; (*coup*) push; (*MÉD*) eruption; (*fig*) upsurge.

pousse-pousse [puspus] *nm inv* rickshaw.

pousser [puse] *vt* to push; (*inciter*): **~ qn à** to urge *ou* press sb to + *infinitif*; (*acculer*):

~ **qn à** to drive sb to; (*moteur, voiture*) to drive hard; (*émettre: cri etc*) to give; (*stimuler*) to urge on; to drive hard; (*poursuivre*) to carry on ♦ *vi* to push; (*croître*) to grow; (*aller*): ~ **plus loin** to push on a bit further; **se** ~ *vi* to move over; **faire** ~ (*plante*) to grow; ~ **le dévouement** *etc* **jusqu'à** ... to take devotion *etc* as far as ....

poussette [pusɛt] *nf* (*voiture d'enfant*) pushchair (*Brit*), stroller (*US*).

poussette-canne, *pl* **poussettes-cannes** [pusɛtkan] *nf* baby buggy (*Brit*), (folding) stroller (*US*).

poussier [pusje] *nm* coaldust.

poussière [pusjɛR] *nf* dust; (*grain*) speck of dust; **et des** ~**s** (*fig*) and a bit; ~ **de charbon** coaldust.

poussiéreux, euse [pusjeRø, -øz] *a* dusty.

poussif, ive [pusif, -iv] *a* wheezy, wheezing.

poussin [pusɛ̃] *nm* chick.

poussoir [puswaR] *nm* button.

poutre [putR(ə)] *nf* beam; (*en fer, ciment armé*) girder; ~**s apparentes** exposed beams.

poutrelle [putRɛl] *nf* (*petite poutre*) small beam; (*barre d'acier*) girder.

pouvoir [puvwaR] *nm* power; (*POL: dirigeants*): **le** ~ those in power, the government ♦ *vb* + *infinitif* can; (*suj: personne*) can, to be able to; (*permission*) can, may; (*probabilité, hypothèse*) may; **il peut arriver que** it may happen that; **il pourrait pleuvoir** it might rain; **déçu de ne pas** ~ **le faire** disappointed not to be able to do it *ou* that he *etc* couldn't do it; **il aurait pu le dire!** he could *ou* might have said!; **il se peut que** it may be that; **je n'en peux plus** (*épuisé*) I'm exhausted; (*accablé*) I can't take any more; **tu ne peux pas savoir!** you have no idea!; **tu peux le dire!** you can say that again!; **on ne peut mieux** as well as it is possible to; **donner** ~ **de faire qch** (*JUR*) to give proxy to do sth; ~ **absolu** absolute power; ~ **d'achat** purchasing power; **les** ~**s publics** the authorities.

PP *sigle f* (= *préventive de la pellagre: vitamine*) niacin ♦ *abr* (= *pages*) pp.

p.p. *abr* (= *par procuration*) p.p.

p.p.c.m. *sigle m* (*MATH:* = *plus petit commun multiple*) LCM (= *lowest common multiple*).

PR *sigle m* = *Parti républicain* ♦ *sigle f* = **poste restante.**

pr *abr* = **pour.**

pragmatique [pRagmatik] *a* pragmatic.

Prague [pRag] *n* Prague.

prairie [pReRi] *nf* meadow.

praline [pRalin] *nf* (*bonbon*) sugared almond; (*au chocolat*) praline.

praliné, e [pRaline] *a* (*amande*) sugared; (*chocolat, glace*) praline *cpd*.

praticable [pRatikabl(ə)] *a* (*route etc*) passable, practicable; (*projet*) practicable.

praticien, ne [pRatisjɛ̃, -ɛn] *nm/f* practitioner.

pratiquant, e [pRatikɑ̃, -ɑ̃t] *a* practising (*Brit*), practicing (*US*).

pratique [pRatik] *nf* practice ♦ *a* practical; (*commode: horaire etc*) convenient; (*: outil*) handy, useful; **dans la** ~ in (actual) practice; **mettre en** ~ to put into practice.

pratiquement [pRatikmɑ̃] *ad* (*dans la pratique*) in practice; (*pour ainsi dire*) practically, virtually.

pratiquer [pRatike] *vt* to practise (*Brit*), practice (*US*); (*SPORT etc*) to go (in for), play; (*appliquer: méthode, théorie*) to apply; (*intervention, opération*) to carry out; (*ouverture, abri*) to make ♦ *vi* (*REL*) to be a churchgoer.

pré [pRe] *nm* meadow.

préalable [pRealabl(ə)] *a* preliminary; **condition** ~ (**de**) precondition (for), prerequisite (for); **sans avis** ~ without prior *ou* previous notice; **au** ~ first, beforehand.

préalablement [pRealabləmɑ̃] *ad* first, beforehand.

Préalpes [pRealp(ə)] *nfpl*: **les** ~ the Pre-Alps.

préalpin, e [pRealpɛ̃, -in] *a* of the Pre-Alps.

préambule [pReɑ̃byl] *nm* preamble; (*fig*) prelude; **sans** ~ straight away.

préau, x [pReo] *nm* (*d'une cour d'école*) covered playground; (*d'un monastère, d'une prison*) inner courtyard.

préavis [pReavi] *nm* notice; ~ **de congé** notice; **communication avec** ~ (*TÉL*) personal *ou* person-to-person call.

prébende [pRebɑ̃d] *nf* (*péj*) remuneration.

précaire [pRekɛR] *a* precarious.

précaution [pRekosjɔ̃] *nf* precaution; **avec** ~ cautiously; **prendre des** *ou* **ses** ~**s** to take precautions; **par** ~ as a precaution; **pour plus de** ~ to be on the safe side; ~**s oratoires** carefully phrased remarks.

précautionneux, euse [pRekosjɔnø, -øz] *a* cautious, careful.

précédemment [pResedamɑ̃] *ad* before, previously.

précédent, e [pResedɑ̃, -ɑ̃t] *a* previous ♦ *nm* precedent; **sans** ~ unprecedented; **le jour** ~ the day before, the previous day.

précéder [pResede] *vt* to precede; (*marcher ou rouler devant*) to be in front of; (*arriver avant*) to get ahead of.

précepte [pResɛpt(ə)] *nm* precept.

précepteur, trice [pResɛptœR, -tRis] *nm/f* (private) tutor.

préchauffer [pRefofe] *vt* to preheat.

prêcher [pRefe] *vt, vi* to preach.

prêcheur, euse [pRefœR, -øz] *a* moralizing ♦ *nm/f* (*REL*) preacher; (*fig*) moralizer.

précieusement [pResjøzmɑ̃] *ad* (*avec soin*) carefully; (*avec préciosité*) preciously.

précieux, euse [pResjø, -øz] *a* precious; (*collaborateur, conseils*) invaluable; (*style, écrivain*) précieux, precious.

préciosité [pResjozite] *nf* preciosity, preciousness.

précipice [pResipis] *nm* drop, chasm; (*fig*) abyss; **au bord du** ~ at the edge of the precipice.

précipitamment [pResipitamɑ̃] *ad* hurriedly, hastily.

précipitation [pResipitasjɔ̃] *nf* (*hâte*) haste; ~**s (atmosphériques)** *nfpl* precipitation *sg*.

précipité, e [pResipite] *a* (*respiration*) fast; (*pas*) hurried; (*départ*) hasty.

précipiter [pResipite] *vt* (*faire tomber*): ~ **qn/qch du haut de** to throw *ou* hurl sb/sth off *ou* from; (*hâter: marche*) to quicken; (*: départ*) to hasten; **se ~** *vi* (*événements*) to move faster; (*respiration*) to speed up; **se ~ sur/vers** to rush at/towards; **se ~ au-devant de qn** to throw o.s. before sb.

précis, e [pʀesi, -iz] *a* precise; (*tir, mesures*) accurate, precise ♦ *nm* handbook.

précisément [pʀesizemɑ̃] *ad* precisely; **ma vie n'est pas ~ distrayante** my life is not exactly entertaining.

préciser [pʀesize] *vt* (*expliquer*) to be more specific about, clarify; (*spécifier*) to state, specify; **se ~** *vi* to become clear(er).

précision [pʀesizjɔ̃] *nf* precision; accuracy; (*détail*) point *ou* detail (*made clear or to be clarified*); **~s** *nfpl* further details.

précoce [pʀekɔs] *a* early; (*enfant*) precocious; (*calvitie*) premature.

précocité [pʀekɔsite] *nf* earliness; precociousness.

préconçu, e [pʀekɔ̃sy] *a* preconceived.

préconiser [pʀekɔnize] *vt* to advocate.

précontraint, e [pʀekɔ̃tʀɛ̃, -ɛ̃t] *a*: **béton ~** prestressed concrete.

précuit, e [pʀekɥi, -it] *a* precooked.

précurseur [pʀekyʀsœʀ] *am* precursory ♦ *nm* forerunner, precursor.

prédateur [pʀedatœʀ] *nm* predator.

prédécesseur [pʀedesesœʀ] *nm* predecessor.

prédestiner [pʀedɛstine] *vt*: **~ qn à qch/à faire** to predestine sb for sth/to do.

prédicateur [pʀedikatœʀ] *nm* preacher.

prédiction [pʀediksjɔ̃] *nf* prediction.

prédilection [pʀedilɛksjɔ̃] *nf*: **avoir une ~ pour** to be partial to; **de ~** favourite (*Brit*), favorite (*US*).

prédire [pʀediʀ] *vt* to predict.

prédisposer [pʀedispoze] *vt*: **~ qn à qch/à faire** to predispose sb to sth/to do.

prédit, e [pʀedi, -it] *pp de* **prédire**.

prédominant, e [pʀedɔminɑ̃, -ɑ̃t] *a* predominant; prevailing.

prédominer [pʀedɔmine] *vi* to predominate; (*avis*) to prevail.

pré-électoral, e, aux [pʀeelɛktɔʀal, -o] *a* pre-election *cpd*.

pré-emballé, e [pʀeɑ̃bale] *a* pre-packed.

prééminent, e [pʀeeminɑ̃, -ɑ̃t] *a* pre-eminent.

préemption [pʀeɑ̃psjɔ̃] *nf*: **droit de ~** (*JUR*) pre-emptive right.

pré-encollé, e [pʀeɑ̃kɔle] *a* pre-pasted.

préétabli, e [pʀeetabli] *a* pre-established.

préexistant, e [pʀeɛgzistɑ̃, -ɑ̃t] *a* pre-existing.

préfabriqué, e [pʀefabʀike] *a* prefabricated; (*péj: sourire*) artificial ♦ *nm* prefabricated material.

préface [pʀefas] *nf* preface.

préfacer [pʀefase] *vt* to write a preface for.

préfectoral, e, aux [pʀefɛktɔʀal, -o] *a* prefectorial.

préfecture [pʀefɛktyʀ] *nf* prefecture; **~ de police** police headquarters.

préférable [pʀefeʀabl(ə)] *a* preferable.

préféré, e [pʀefeʀe] *a*, *nm/f* favourite (*Brit*), favorite (*US*).

préférence [pʀefeʀɑ̃s] *nf* preference; **de ~** preferably; **de** *ou* **par ~ à** in preference to, rather than; **donner la ~ à qn** to give preference to sb; **par ordre de ~** in order of pref-

erence; **obtenir la ~ sur** to have preference over.

préférentiel, le [pʀefeʀɑ̃sjɛl] *a* preferential.

préférer [pʀefeʀe] *vt*: **~ qn/qch (à)** to prefer sb/sth (to), like sb/sth better (than); **~ faire** to prefer to do; **je préférerais du thé** I would rather have tea, I'd prefer tea.

préfet [pʀefɛ] *nm* prefect; **~ de police** ≈ Chief Constable (*Brit*), ≈ Police Commissioner (*US*).

préfigurer [pʀefigyʀe] *vt* to prefigure.

préfixe [pʀefiks(ə)] *nm* prefix.

préhistoire [pʀeistwaʀ] *nf* prehistory.

préhistorique [pʀeistɔʀik] *a* prehistoric.

préjudice [pʀeʒydis] *nm* (*matériel*) loss; (*moral*) harm *q*; **porter ~ à** to harm, be detrimental to; **au ~ de** at the expense of.

préjudiciable [pʀeʒydisjabl(ə)] *a*: **~ à** prejudicial *ou* harmful to.

préjugé [pʀeʒyʒe] *nm* prejudice; **avoir un ~ contre** to be prejudiced *ou* biased against; **bénéficier d'un ~ favorable** to be viewed favourably.

préjuger [pʀeʒyʒe]: **~ de** *vt* to prejudge.

prélasser [pʀelase]: **se ~** *vi* to lounge.

prélat [pʀela] *nm* prelate.

prélavage [pʀelavaʒ] *nm* pre-wash.

prélèvement [pʀelɛvmɑ̃] *nm* deduction; withdrawal; **faire un ~ de sang** to take a blood sample.

prélever [pʀelve] *vt* (*échantillon*) to take; (*argent*): **~ (sur)** to deduct (from); (*: sur son compte*): **~ (sur)** to withdraw (from).

préliminaire [pʀeliminɛʀ] *a* preliminary; **~s** *nmpl* preliminaries; (*négociations*) preliminary talks.

prélude [pʀelyd] *nm* prelude; (*avant le concert*) warm-up.

prématuré, e [pʀematyʀe] *a* premature; (*retraite*) early ♦ *nm* premature baby.

prématurément [pʀematyʀemɑ̃] *ad* prematurely.

préméditation [pʀemeditasjɔ̃] *nf*: **avec ~** *a* premeditated ♦ *ad* with intent.

préméditer [pʀemedite] *vt* to premeditate, plan.

prémices [pʀemis] *nfpl* beginnings.

premier, ière [pʀəmje, -jɛʀ] *a* first; (*branche, marche, grade*) bottom; (*fig: fondamental*) basic; prime; (*en importance*) first, foremost ♦ *nm* (*~ étage*) first (*Brit*) *ou* second (*US*) floor ♦ *nf* (*AUTO*) first (gear); (*RAIL, AVIAT etc*) first class; (*SCOL: classe*) penultimate school year (*age 16-17*); (*THÉÂTRE*) first night; (*CINÉMA*) première; (*exploit*) first; **au ~ abord** at first sight; **au** *ou* **du ~ coup** at the first attempt *ou* go; **de ~ ordre** first-class, first-rate; **de première qualité, de ~ choix** best *ou* top quality; **de première importance** of the highest importance; **de première nécessité** absolutely essential; **le ~ venu** the first person to come along; **jeune ~** leading man; **le ~ de l'an** New Year's Day; **enfant du ~ lit** child of a first marriage; **en ~ lieu** in the first place; **~ âge** (*d'un enfant*) the first 3 months (of life); **P~ Ministre** Prime Minister.

premièrement [pʀəmjɛʀmɑ̃] *ad* firstly.

première-née, *pl* **premières-nées**

[prəmjɛrne] *nf* first-born.
premier-né, *pl* **premiers-nés** [prəmjene] *nm* first-born.
prémisse [premis] *nf* premise.
prémolaire [premɔlɛr] *nf* premolar.
prémonition [premɔnisjɔ̃] *nf* premonition.
prémonitoire [premɔnitwar] *a* premonitory.
prémunir [premynir]: **se ~** *vi*: **se ~ contre** to protect o.s. from, guard against.
prenant, e [prənɑ̃, -ɑ̃t] *vb voir* **prendre ♦** *a* absorbing, engrossing.
prénatal, e [prenatal] *a* (*MÉD*) antenatal; (*allocation*) maternity *cpd*.
prendre [prɑ̃dr(ə)] *vt* to take; (*ôter*): **~ qch à** to take sth from; (*aller chercher*) to get, fetch; (*se procurer*) to get; (*réserver: place*) to book; (*acquérir: du poids, de la valeur*) to put on, gain; (*malfaiteur, poisson*) to catch; (*passager*) to pick up; (*personnel, aussi: couleur, goût*) to take on; (*locataire*) to take in; (*traiter: enfant, problème*) to handle; (*voix, ton*) to put on; (*prélever: pourcentage, argent*) to take off; (*coincer*): **se ~ les doigts dans** to get one's fingers caught in ♦ *vi* (*liquide, ciment*) to set; (*greffe, vaccin*) to take; (*mensonge*) to be successful; (*feu: foyer*) to go; (: *incendie*) to start; (*allumette*) to light; (*se diriger*): **~ à gauche** to turn (to the) left; **~ son origine** *ou* **sa source** (*mot, rivière*) to have its source; **~ qn pour** to take sb for; **se ~ pour** to think one is; **~ sur soi de faire qch** to take it upon o.s. to do sth; **~ qn en sympathie/horreur** to get to like/loathe sb; **à tout ~** all things considered; **s'en ~ à** (*agresser*) to set about; (*passer sa colère sur*) to take it out on; (*critiquer*) to attack; (*remettre en question*) to challenge; **se ~ d'amitié/d'affection pour** to befriend/become fond of; **s'y ~** (*procéder*) to set about it; **s'y ~ à l'avance** to see to it in advance; **s'y ~ à deux fois** to try twice, make two attempts.
preneur [prənœr] *nm*: **être ~** to be willing to buy; **trouver ~** to find a buyer.
prénom [prenɔ̃] *nm* first name.
prénommer [prenɔme] *vt*: **elle se prénomme Claude** her (first) name is Claude.
prénuptial, e, aux [prenypsjal, -o] *a* premarital.
préoccupant, e [preɔkypɑ̃, -ɑ̃t] *a* worrying.
préoccupation [preɔkypasjɔ̃] *nf* (*souci*) concern; (*idée fixe*) preoccupation.
préoccupé, e [preɔkype] *a* concerned; preoccupied.
préoccuper [preɔkype] *vt* (*tourmenter, tracasser*) to concern; (*absorber, obséder*) to preoccupy; **se ~ de qch** to be concerned about sth; to show concern about sth.
préparateur, trice [preparatœr, -tris] *nm/f* assistant.
préparatifs [preparatif] *nmpl* preparations.
préparation [preparasjɔ̃] *nf* preparation; (*SCOL*) piece of homework.
préparatoire [preparatwar] *a* preparatory.
préparer [prepare] *vt* to prepare; (*café, repas*) to make; (*examen*) to prepare for; (*voyage, entreprise*) to plan; **se ~** *vi* (*orage, tragédie*) to brew, be in the air; **se ~ (à qch/à faire)** to prepare (o.s.) *ou* get ready

(for sth/to do); **~ qch à qn** (*surprise etc*) to have sth in store for sb; **~ qn à qch** (*nouvelle etc*) to prepare sb for sth.
prépondérant, e [prepɔ̃derɑ̃, -ɑ̃t] *a* major, dominating; **voix ~e** casting vote.
préposé, e [prepoze] *a*: **~ à** in charge of ♦ *nm/f* (*gén: employé*) employee; (*ADMIN: facteur*) postman/woman (*Brit*), mailman/woman (*US*); (*de la douane etc*) official; (*de vestiaire*) attendant.
préposer [prepoze] *vt*: **~ qn à qch** to appoint sb to sth.
préposition [prepozisjɔ̃] *nf* preposition.
préretraite [preʀətʀɛt] *nf* early retirement.
prérogative [preʀɔgativ] *nf* prerogative.
près [pre] *ad* near, close; **~ de** *prép* near (to), close to; (*environ*) nearly, almost; **de ~** *ad* closely; **à 5 kg ~** to within about 5 kg; **à cela ~ que** apart from the fact that; **je ne suis pas ~ de lui pardonner** I'm nowhere near ready to forgive him; **on n'est pas à un jour ~** one day (either way) won't make any difference, we're not going to quibble over the odd day.
présage [preza3] *nm* omen.
présager [preza3e] *vt* (*prévoir*) to foresee; (*annoncer*) to portend.
pré-salé, *pl* **prés-salés** [presale] *nm* (*CULIN*) salt-meadow lamb.
presbyte [presbit] *a* long-sighted (*Brit*), far-sighted (*US*).
presbytère [presbiter] *nm* presbytery.
presbytérien, ne [presbiterjɛ̃, -ɛn] *a, nm/f* Presbyterian.
presbytie [presbisi] *nf* long-sightedness (*Brit*), far-sightedness (*US*).
prescience [presjɑ̃s] *nf* prescience, foresight.
préscolaire [preskɔler] *a* preschool *cpd*.
prescription [preskripsjɔ̃] *nf* (*instruction*) order, instruction; (*MÉD, JUR*) prescription.
prescrire [preskrir] *vt* to prescribe; **se ~** *vi* (*JUR*) to lapse.
prescrit, e [preskri, -it] *pp de* **prescrire ♦** *a* (*date etc*) stipulated.
préséance [preseɑ̃s] *nf* precedence *q*.
présélectionner [preseleksjɔne] *vt* to preselect; (*dispositif*) to preset; (*candidats*) to make an initial selection from among, shortlist (*Brit*).
présence [prezɑ̃s] *nf* presence; (*au bureau etc*) attendance; **en ~** face to face; **en ~ de** in (the) presence of; (*fig*) in the face of; **faire acte de ~** to put in a token appearance; **~ d'esprit** presence of mind.
présent, e [prezɑ̃, -ɑ̃t] *a, nm* present; (*ADMIN, COMM*): **la ~e lettre/loi** this letter/law ♦ *nm/f*: **les ~s** (*personnes*) those present ♦ *nf* (*COMM: lettre*): **la ~e** this letter; **à ~** now, at present; **dès à ~** here and now; **jusqu'à ~** up till now, until now; **à ~ que** now that.
présentateur, trice [prezɑ̃tatœr, -tris] *nm/f* presenter.
présentation [prezɑ̃tasjɔ̃] *nf* presentation; introduction; (*allure*) appearance.
présenter [prezɑ̃te] *vt* to present; (*invité, candidat*) to introduce; (*félicitations, condoléances*) to offer; (*montrer: billet, pièce d'identité*) to show, produce; (*faire inscrire:*

candidat) to put forward; (soumettre) to submit ♦ vi: ~ **mal/bien** to have an unattractive/a pleasing appearance; **se ~ vi** (sur convocation) to report, come; (se faire connaître) to come forward; (à une élection) to stand; (occasion) to arise; **se ~ à un examen** to sit an exam; **se ~ bien/mal** to look good/not too good.

présentoir [pʀesɑ̃twaʀ] nm (étagère) display shelf (pl shelves); (vitrine) showcase; (étal) display stand.

préservatif [pʀezɛʀvatif] nm condom, sheath.

préservation [pʀezɛʀvasjɔ̃] nf protection, preservation.

préserver [pʀezɛʀve] vt: ~ **de** (protéger) to protect from; (sauver) to save from.

présidence [pʀezidɑ̃s] nf presidency; chairmanship.

président [pʀezidɑ̃] nm (POL) president; (d'une assemblée, COMM) chairman; ~ **directeur général (PDG)** chairman and managing director (Brit), chairman and president (US); ~ **du jury** (JUR) foreman of the jury; (d'examen) chief examiner.

présidente [pʀezidɑ̃t] nf president; (femme du président) president's wife; (d'une réunion) chairwoman.

présidentiable [pʀezidɑ̃sjabl(ə)] a, nm/f potential president.

présidentiel, le [pʀezidɑ̃sjɛl] a presidential; ~**les** nfpl presidential election(s).

présider [pʀeside] vt to preside over; (dîner) to be the guest of honour (Brit) ou honor (US) at; ~ **à** vt to direct; to govern.

présomption [pʀezɔ̃psjɔ̃] nf presumption.

présomptueux, euse [pʀezɔ̃ptɥø, -øz] a presumptuous.

presque [pʀɛsk(ə)] ad almost, nearly; ~ **rien** hardly anything; ~ **pas** hardly (at all); ~ **pas de** hardly any; **personne, ou ~** next to nobody, hardly anyone; **la ~ totalité (de)** almost ou nearly all.

presqu'île [pʀɛskil] nf peninsula.

pressant, e [pʀesɑ̃, -ɑ̃t] a urgent; (personne) insistent; **se faire ~** to become insistent.

presse [pʀɛs] nf press; (affluence): **heures de ~** busy times; **sous ~** gone to press; **mettre sous ~** to send to press; **avoir une bonne/mauvaise ~** to have a good/bad press; ~ **féminine** women's magazines pl; ~ **d'information** quality newspapers pl.

pressé, e [pʀese] a in a hurry; (air) hurried; (besogne) urgent ♦ nm: **aller au plus ~** to see to first things first; **être ~ de faire qch** to be in a hurry to do sth; **orange ~e** freshly squeezed orange juice.

presse-citron [pʀɛssitʀɔ̃] nm inv lemon squeezer.

pressentiment [pʀesɑ̃timɑ̃] nm foreboding, premonition.

pressentir [pʀesɑ̃tiʀ] vt to sense; (prendre contact avec) to approach.

presse-papiers [pʀɛspapje] nm inv paperweight.

presse-purée [pʀɛspyʀe] nm inv potato masher.

presser [pʀese] vt (fruit, éponge) to squeeze; (interrupteur, bouton) to press, push; (allure, affaire) to speed up; (débiteur etc) to press;

(inciter): ~ **qn de faire** to urge ou press sb to do ♦ vi to be urgent; **se ~** (se hâter) to hurry (up); (se grouper) to crowd; **rien ne presse** there's no hurry; **se ~ contre qn** to squeeze up against sb; ~ **le pas** to quicken one's step; ~ **qn entre ses bras** to squeeze sb tight.

pressing [pʀesiŋ] nm (repassage) steam-pressing; (magasin) dry-cleaner's.

pression [pʀesjɔ̃] nf pressure; (bouton) press stud (Brit), snap fastener; **faire ~ sur** to put pressure on; **sous ~** pressurized, under pressure; (fig) keyed up; ~ **artérielle** blood pressure.

pressoir [pʀeswaʀ] nm (wine ou oil etc) press.

pressurer [pʀesyʀe] vt (fig) to squeeze.

pressurisé, e [pʀesyʀize] a pressurized.

prestance [pʀɛstɑ̃s] nf presence, imposing bearing.

prestataire [pʀɛstatɛʀ] nm/f person receiving benefits; (COMM): ~ **de services** provider of services.

prestation [pʀɛstasjɔ̃] nf (allocation) benefit; (d'une assurance) cover q; (d'une entreprise) service provided; (d'un joueur, artiste) performance; ~ **de serment** taking the oath; ~ **de service** provision of a service; ~**s familiales** ≈ child benefit.

preste [pʀɛst(ə)] a nimble.

prestement [pʀɛstəmɑ̃] ad nimbly.

prestidigitateur, trice [pʀɛstidiʒitatœʀ, -tʀis] nm/f conjurer.

prestidigitation [pʀɛstidiʒitasjɔ̃] nf conjuring.

prestige [pʀɛstiʒ] nm prestige.

prestigieux, euse [pʀɛstiʒjø, -øz] a prestigious.

présumer [pʀezyme] vt: ~ **que** to presume ou assume that; ~ **de** to overrate; ~ **qn coupable** to presume sb guilty.

présupposé [pʀesypoze] nm presupposition.

présupposer [pʀesypoze] vt to presuppose.

présure [pʀezyʀ] nf rennet.

prêt, e [pʀɛ, pʀɛt] a ready ♦ nm lending q; (somme prêtée) loan; ~ **à faire** ready to do; ~ **à tout** ready for anything; ~ **sur gages** pawnbroking q.

prêt-à-porter, pl prêts-à-porter [pʀɛtapɔʀte] nm ready-to-wear ou off-the-peg (Brit) clothes pl.

prétendant [pʀetɑ̃dɑ̃] nm pretender; (d'une femme) suitor.

prétendre [pʀetɑ̃dʀ(ə)] vt (affirmer): ~ **que** to claim that; (avoir l'intention de): ~ **faire qch** to mean ou intend to do sth; ~ **à** vt (droit, titre) to lay claim to.

prétendu, e [pʀetɑ̃dy] a (supposé) so-called.

prétendument [pʀetɑ̃dymɑ̃] ad allegedly.

prête-nom [pʀɛtnɔ̃] nm (péj) figurehead; (COMM etc) dummy.

prétentieux, euse [pʀetɑ̃sjø, -øz] a pretentious.

prétention [pʀetɑ̃sjɔ̃] nf pretentiousness; (exigence, ambition) claim; **sans ~** unpretentious.

prêter [pʀete] vt (livres, argent): ~ **qch (à)** to lend sth (to); (supposer): ~ **à qn** (caractère, propos) to attribute to sb ♦ vi (aussi: **se ~**: tissu, cuir) to give; ~ **à** (commentaires etc) to be open to, give rise to; **se ~ à** to lend o.s.

(ou itself*)* to; *(manigances etc)* to go along with; **~ assistance à** to give help to; **~ attention** to pay attention; **~ serment** to take the oath; **~ l'oreille** to listen.

prêteur, euse [pʀɛtœʀ, -øz] *nm/f* money-lender; **~ sur gages** pawnbroker.

prétexte [pʀetɛkst(ə)] *nm* pretext, excuse; **sous aucun ~** on no account; **sous (le) ~ que/de** on the pretext that/of.

prétexter [pʀetɛkste] *vt* to give as a pretext *ou* an excuse.

prêtre [pʀɛtʀ(ə)] *nm* priest.

prêtre-ouvrier, *pl* **prêtres-ouvriers** [pʀɛtʀuvʀije] *nm* worker-priest.

prêtrise [pʀetʀiz] *nf* priesthood.

preuve [pʀœv] *nf* proof; *(indice)* proof, evidence *q*; **jusqu'à ~ du contraire** until proved otherwise; **faire ~ de** to show; **faire ses ~s** to prove o.s. *(ou* itself*)*; **~ matérielle** material evidence.

prévaloir [pʀevalwaʀ] *vi* to prevail; **se ~ de** *vt* to take advantage of; *(tirer vanité de)* to pride o.s. on.

prévarication [pʀevaʀikɑsjɔ̃] *nf* mal-administration.

prévaut [pʀevo] *etc vb voir* **prévaloir**.

prévenances [pʀevnɑ̃s] *nfpl* thoughtfulness *sg*, kindness *sg*.

prévenant, e [pʀevnɑ̃, -ɑ̃t] *a* thoughtful, kind.

prévenir [pʀevniʀ] *vt* *(avertir)*: **~ qn (de)** to warn sb (about); *(informer)*: **~ qn (de)** to tell *ou* inform sb (about); *(éviter)* to avoid, prevent; *(anticiper)* to anticipate; *(influencer)*: **~ qn contre** to prejudice sb against.

préventif, ive [pʀevɑ̃tif, -iv] *a* a preventive.

prévention [pʀevɑ̃sjɔ̃] *nf* prevention; *(préjugé)* prejudice; *(JUR)* custody, detention; **~ routière** road safety.

prévenu, e [pʀevny] *nm/f* *(JUR)* defendant, accused.

prévisible [pʀevizibl(ə)] *a* foreseeable.

prévision [pʀevizjɔ̃] *nf*: **~s** predictions; *(météorologiques, économiques)* forecast *sg*; **en ~ de** in anticipation of; **~s météorologiques** *ou* **du temps** weather forecast *sg*.

prévisionnel, le [pʀevizjɔnɛl] *a* concerned with future requirements.

prévit [pʀevi] *etc vb voir* **prévoir**.

prévoir [pʀevwaʀ] *vt* to foresee; *(deviner)* to foresee; *(s'attendre à)* to expect, reckon on; *(prévenir)* to anticipate; *(organiser)* to plan; *(préparer, réserver)* to allow; **prévu pour 4 personnes** designed for 4 people; **prévu pour 10h** scheduled for 10 o'clock.

prévoyance [pʀevwajɑ̃s] *nf* foresight; **société/caisse de ~** provident society/contingency fund.

prévoyant, e [pʀevwajɑ̃, -ɑ̃t] *vb voir* **prévoir** ♦ *a* gifted with *(ou* showing*)* foresight, far-sighted.

prévu, e [pʀevy] *pp de* **prévoir**.

prier [pʀije] *vi* to pray ♦ *vt* *(Dieu)* to pray to; *(implorer)* to beg; *(demander)*: **~ qn de faire** to ask sb to do; *(inviter)*: **~ qn à dîner** to invite sb to dinner; **se faire ~** to need coaxing *ou* persuading; **je vous en prie** *(allez-y)* please do; *(de rien)* don't mention

it; **je vous prie de faire** please (would you) do.

prière [pʀijɛʀ] *nf* prayer; *(demande instante)* plea, entreaty; **"~ de faire ..."** "please do ...".

primaire [pʀimɛʀ] *a* a primary; *(péj: personne)* simple-minded; *(: idées)* simplistic ♦ *nm* *(SCOL)* primary education.

primauté [pʀimote] *nf* *(fig)* primacy.

prime [pʀim] *nf* *(bonification)* bonus; *(subside)* allowance; *(COMM: cadeau)* free gift; *(ASSURANCES, BOURSE)* premium ♦ *a*: **de ~ abord** at first glance; **~ de risque** danger money *q*; **~ de transport** travel allowance.

primer [pʀime] *vt* *(l'emporter sur)* to prevail over; *(récompenser)* to award a prize to ♦ *vi* to dominate, prevail.

primesautier, ière [pʀimsotje, -jɛʀ] *a* impulsive.

primeur [pʀimœʀ] *nf*: **avoir la ~ de** to be the first to hear *(ou see etc)*; **~s** *nfpl* *(fruits, légumes)* early fruits and vegetables; **marchand de ~** greengrocer *(Brit)*, produce dealer *(US)*.

primevère [pʀimvɛʀ] *nf* primrose.

primitif, ive [pʀimitif, -iv] *a* primitive; *(originel)* original ♦ *nm/f* primitive.

primo [pʀimo] *ad* first (of all), firstly.

primordial, e, aux [pʀimɔʀdjal, -o] *a* essential, primordial.

prince [pʀɛ̃s] *nm* prince; **~ charmant** Prince Charming; **~ de Galles** *nm inv* *(tissu)* check cloth; **~ héritier** crown prince.

princesse [pʀɛ̃sɛs] *nf* princess.

princier, ière [pʀɛ̃sje, -jɛʀ] *a* princely.

principal, e, aux [pʀɛ̃sipal, -o] *a* principal, main ♦ *nm* *(SCOL)* head(teacher) *(Brit)*, principal *(US)*; *(essentiel)* main thing ♦ *nf* *(LING)*: **(proposition) ~e** main clause.

principalement [pʀɛ̃sipalmɑ̃] *ad* principally, mainly.

principauté [pʀɛ̃sipote] *nf* principality.

principe [pʀɛ̃sip] *nm* principle; **partir du ~ que** to work on the principle *ou* assumption that; **pour le ~** on principle, for the sake of it; **de ~** *a* *(hostilité)* automatic; *(accord)* in principle; **par ~** on principle; **en ~** *(habituellement)* as a rule; *(théoriquement)* in principle.

printanier, ière [pʀɛ̃tanje, -jɛʀ] *a* spring *cpd*; spring-like.

printemps [pʀɛ̃tɑ̃] *nm* spring; **au ~** in spring.

priori [pʀijɔʀi]: **a ~** *ad* at first glance; initially; a priori.

prioritaire [pʀijɔʀitɛʀ] *a* having priority; *(AUTO)* having right of way; *(INFORM)* foreground.

priorité [pʀijɔʀite] *nf* *(AUTO)*: **avoir la ~ (sur)** to have right of way (over); **~ à droite** right of way to vehicles coming from the right; **en ~** as a *(matter of)* priority.

pris, e [pʀi, pʀiz] *pp de* **prendre** ♦ *a* *(place)* taken; *(billets)* sold; *(journée, mains)* full; *(personne)* busy; *(crème, ciment)* set; *(MÉD: enflammé)*: **avoir le nez/la gorge ~(e)** to have a stuffy nose/a bad throat; *(saisi)*: **être ~ de peur/de fatigue** to be stricken with fear/overcome with fatigue.

prise [pʀiz] *nf* *(d'une ville)* capture; *(PÊCHE,*

CHASSE) catch; (de judo ou catch, point d'appui ou pour empoigner) hold; (ÉLEC: fiche) plug; (: femelle) socket; (: au mur) point; **en ~** (AUTO) in gear; **être aux ~s avec** to be grappling with; to be battling with; **lâcher ~** to let go; **donner ~ à** (fig) to give rise to; **avoir ~ sur qn** to have a hold over sb; **~ en charge** (taxe) pick-up charge; (par la sécurité sociale) undertaking to reimburse costs; **~ de contact** initial meeting, first contact; **~ de courant** power point; **~ d'eau** water (supply) point; tap; **~ multiple** adaptor; **~ d'otages** hostage-taking; **~ à partie** (JUR) action against a judge; **~ de sang** blood test; **~ de son** sound recording; **~ de tabac** pinch of snuff; **~ de terre** earth; **~ de vue** (photo) shot; (action): **~ de vue(s)** filming, shooting.

priser [pʀize] vt (tabac, héroïne) to take; (estimer) to prize, value ♦ vi to take snuff.

prisme [pʀism(ə)] nm prism.

prison [pʀizɔ̃] nf prison; **aller/être en ~** to go to/be in prison ou jail; **faire de la ~** to serve time; **être condamné à 5 ans de ~** to be sentenced to 5 years' imprisonment ou 5 years in prison.

prisonnier, ière [pʀizɔnje, -jɛʀ] nm/f prisoner ♦ a captive; **faire qn ~** to take sb prisoner.

prit [pʀi] vb voir prendre.

privatif, ive [pʀivatif, -iv] a (jardin etc) private; (peine) which deprives one of one's liberties.

privations [pʀivasjɔ̃] nfpl privations, hardships.

privatisation [pʀivatizasjɔ̃] nf privatization.

privatiser [pʀivatize] vt to privatize.

privautés [pʀivote] nfpl liberties.

privé, e [pʀive] a private; (dépourvu): **~ de** without, lacking; **en ~, dans le ~** in private.

priver [pʀive] vt: **~ qn de** to deprive sb of; **se ~ de** to go ou do without; **ne pas se ~ de faire** not to refrain from doing.

privilège [pʀivilɛʒ] nm privilege.

privilégié, e [pʀivileʒje] a privileged.

privilégier [pʀivileʒje] vt to favour (Brit), favor (US).

prix [pʀi] nm (valeur) price; (récompense, SCOL) prize; **mettre à ~** to set a reserve (Brit) ou upset (US) price on; **au ~ fort** at a very high price; **acheter qch à ~ d'or** to pay a (small) fortune for sth; **hors de ~** exorbitantly priced; **à aucun ~** not at any price; **à tout ~** at all costs; **grand ~** (SPORT) Grand Prix; **~ d'achat/de vente/de revient** purchasing/selling/cost price; **~ conseillé** manufacturer's recommended price (MRP).

pro [pʀo] nm (= professionnel) pro.

probabilité [pʀobabilite] nf probability; **selon toute ~** in all probability.

probable [pʀobabl(ə)] a likely, probable.

probablement [pʀobabləmã] ad probably.

probant, e [pʀobã, -ãt] a convincing.

probatoire [pʀobatwaʀ] a (examen, test) preliminary; (stage) probationary, trial cpd.

probité [pʀobite] nf integrity, probity.

problématique [pʀoblematik] a problematic(al) ♦ nf problematics sg; (problème) problem.

problème [pʀoblɛm] nm problem.

procédé [pʀosede] nm (méthode) process; (comportement) behaviour q (Brit), behavior q (US).

procéder [pʀosede] vi to proceed; to behave; **~ à** to carry out.

procédure [pʀosedyʀ] nf (ADMIN, JUR) procedure.

procès [pʀosɛ] nm (JUR) trial; (: poursuites) proceedings pl; **être en ~ avec** to be involved in a lawsuit with; **faire le ~ de qn/qch** (fig) to put sb/sth on trial; **sans autre forme de ~** without further ado.

processeur [pʀosesœʀ] nm processor.

procession [pʀosesjɔ̃] nf procession.

processus [pʀosesys] nm process.

procès-verbal, aux [pʀosɛvɛʀbal, -o] nm (constat) statement; (aussi: PV): **avoir un ~** to get a parking ticket; to be booked; (de réunion) minutes pl.

prochain, e [pʀoʃɛ̃, -ɛn] a next; (proche) impending; near ♦ nm fellow man; **la ~e fois/semaine ~e** next time/week; **à la ~e!** (fam) , **à la ~e fois** see you!, till the next time!; **un ~ jour** (some day) soon.

prochainement [pʀoʃɛnmã] ad soon, shortly.

proche [pʀoʃ] a nearby; (dans le temps) imminent; close at hand; (parent, ami) close; **~s** nmpl (parents) close relatives, next of kin; (amis): **l'un de ses ~s** one of those close to him (ou her); **être ~ (de)** to be near, be close (to); **de ~ en ~** gradually.

Proche-Orient [pʀoʃɔʀjã] nm: **le ~** the Near East.

proclamation [pʀoklamasjɔ̃] nf proclamation.

proclamer [pʀoklame] vt to proclaim; (résultat d'un examen) to announce.

procréer [pʀokʀee] vt to procreate.

procuration [pʀokyʀasjɔ̃] nf proxy; power of attorney; **voter par ~** to vote by proxy.

procurer [pʀokyʀe] vt (fournir): **~ qch à qn** to get ou obtain sth for sb; (causer: plaisir etc): **~ qch à qn** to bring ou give sb sth; **se ~ vt** to get.

procureur [pʀokyʀœʀ] nm public prosecutor; **~ général** public prosecutor (in appeal court).

prodigalité [pʀodigalite] nf (générosité) generosity; (extravagance) extravagance, wastefulness.

prodige [pʀodiʒ] nm (miracle, merveille) marvel, wonder; (personne) prodigy.

prodigieux, euse [pʀodiʒjø, -øz] a prodigious; phenomenal.

prodigue [pʀodig] a (généreux) generous; (dépensier) extravagant, wasteful; **fils ~** prodigal son.

prodiguer [pʀodige] vt (argent, biens) to be lavish with; (soins, attentions): **~ qch à qn** to lavish sth on sb.

producteur, trice [pʀodyktœʀ, -tʀis] a: **~ de blé** wheat-producing; (CINÉMA): **société productrice** film ou movie company ♦ nm/f producer.

productif, ive [pʀodyktif, -iv] a productive.

production [pʀodyksjɔ̃] nf (gén) production; (rendement) output; (produits) products pl, goods pl; (œuvres): **la ~ dramatique du XVIIe siècle** the plays of the 17th century.

productivité [pʀɔdyktivite] *nf* productivity.

produire [pʀɔdцiʀ] *vt*, *vi* to produce; **se ~** *vi* (*acteur*) to perform, appear; (*événement*) to happen, occur.

produit, e [pʀɔdцi, -it] *pp de* **produire** ♦ *nm* (*gén*) product; **~ d'entretien** cleaning product; **~ national brut (PNB)** gross national product (GNP); **~ net** net profit; **~ pour la vaisselle** washing-up (*Brit*) *ou* dishwashing (*US*) liquid; **~ des ventes** income from sales; **~s agricoles** farm produce *sg*; **~s alimentaires** foodstuffs; **~s de beauté** beauty products, cosmetics.

proéminent, e [pʀɔeminɑ̃, -ɑ̃t] *a* prominent.

prof [pʀɔf] *nm* (*fam*: = *professeur*) teacher; professor; lecturer.

prof. [pʀɔf] *abr* = **professeur, professionnel**.

profane [pʀɔfan] *a* (*REL*) secular; (*ignorant, non initié*) uninitiated ♦ *nm/f* layman.

profaner [pʀɔfane] *vt* to desecrate; (*fig: sentiment*) to defile; (: *talent*) to debase.

proférer [pʀɔfeʀe] *vt* to utter.

professer [pʀɔfese] *vt* to profess.

professeur [pʀɔfesœʀ] *nm* teacher; (*titulaire d'une chaire*) professor; **~ (de faculté)** (university) lecturer.

profession [pʀɔfesjɔ̃] *nf* (*libérale*) profession; (*gén*) occupation; **faire ~ de** (*opinion, religion*) to profess; **de ~** by profession; **"sans ~"** "unemployed"; (*femme mariée*) "housewife".

professionnel, le [pʀɔfesjɔnɛl] *a* professional ♦ *nm/f* professional; (*ouvrier qualifié*) skilled worker.

professoral, e, aux [pʀɔfesɔʀal, -o] *a* professorial; **le corps ~** the teaching profession.

professorat [pʀɔfesɔʀa] *nm*: **le ~** the teaching profession.

profil [pʀɔfil] *nm* profile; (*d'une voiture*) line, contour; **de ~** in profile.

profilé, e [pʀɔfile] *a* shaped; (*aile etc*) streamlined.

profiler [pʀɔfile] *vt* to streamline; **se ~** *vi* (*arbre, tour*) to stand out, be silhouetted.

profit [pʀɔfi] *nm* (*avantage*) benefit, advantage; (*COMM, FINANCE*) profit; **au ~ de** in aid of; **tirer ou retirer ~ de** to profit from; **mettre à ~** to take advantage of; to turn to good account; **~s et pertes** (*COMM*) profit and loss(es).

profitable [pʀɔfitabl(ə)] *a* beneficial; profitable.

profiter [pʀɔfite] *vi*: **~ de** to take advantage of; to make the most of; **~ de ce que ...** to take advantage of the fact that ...; **~ à** to be of benefit to, benefit; to be profitable to.

profiteur, euse [pʀɔfitœʀ, -øz] *nm/f* (*péj*) profiteer.

profond, e [pʀɔfɔ̃, -ɔ̃d] *a* deep; (*méditation, mépris*) profound; **au plus ~ de** in the depths of, at the very bottom of; **la France ~e** the heartlands of France.

profondément [pʀɔfɔ̃demɑ̃] *ad* deeply; profoundly.

profondeur [pʀɔfɔ̃dœʀ] *nf* depth.

profusément [pʀɔfyzemɑ̃] *ad* profusely.

profusion [pʀɔfyzjɔ̃] *nf* profusion; **à ~** in plenty.

progéniture [pʀɔʒenityʀ] *nf* offspring *inv*.

progiciel [pʀɔʒisjɛl] *nm* (*INFORM*) (software) package; **~ d'application** applications package, applications software *q*.

progouvernemental, e, aux [pʀɔguvɛʀnəmɑ̃tal, -o] *a* pro-government *cpd*.

programmable [pʀɔgʀamabl(ə)] *a* programmable.

programmateur, trice [pʀɔgʀamatœʀ, -tʀis] *nm/f* (*CINÉMA, TV*) programme (*Brit*) *ou* program (*US*) planner ♦ *nm* (*de machine à laver etc*) timer.

programmation [pʀɔgʀamɑsjɔ̃] *nf* programming.

programme [pʀɔgʀam] *nm* programme (*Brit*), program (*US*); (*TV, RADIO*) program(me)s *pl*; (*SCOL*) syllabus, curriculum; (*INFORM*) program; **au ~ de ce soir** (*TV*) among tonight's program(me)s.

programmé, e [pʀɔgʀame] *a*: **enseignement ~** programmed learning.

programmer [pʀɔgʀame] *vt* (*TV, RADIO*) to put on, show; (*organiser, prévoir*) to schedule; (*INFORM*) to program.

programmeur, euse [pʀɔgʀamœʀ, -øz] *nm/f* (computer) programmer.

progrès [pʀɔgʀɛ] *nm* progress *q*; **faire des/être en ~** to make/be making progress.

progresser [pʀɔgʀese] *vi* to progress; (*troupes etc*) to make headway *ou* progress.

progressif, ive [pʀɔgʀesif, -iv] *a* progressive.

progression [pʀɔgʀesjɔ̃] *nf* progression; (*d'une troupe etc*) advance, progress.

progressiste [pʀɔgʀesist(ə)] *a* progressive.

progressivement [pʀɔgʀesivmɑ̃] *ad* progressively.

prohiber [pʀɔibe] *vt* to prohibit, ban.

proie [pʀwa] *nf* prey *q*; **être la ~ de** to fall prey to; **être en ~ à** (*doutes, sentiment*) to be prey to; (*douleur, mal*) to be suffering.

projecteur [pʀɔʒɛktœʀ] *nm* projector; (*de théâtre, cirque*) spotlight.

projectile [pʀɔʒɛktil] *nm* missile; (*d'arme*) projectile, bullet (*ou* shell *etc*).

projection [pʀɔʒɛksjɔ̃] *nf* projection; showing; **conférence avec ~s** lecture with slides (*ou* a film).

projectionniste [pʀɔʒɛksjɔnist(ə)] *nm/f* (*CINÉMA*) projectionist.

projet [pʀɔʒɛ] *nm* plan; (*ébauche*) draft; **faire des ~s** to make plans; **~ de loi** bill.

projeter [pʀɔʒte] *vt* (*envisager*) to plan; (*film, photos*) to project; (*passer*) to show; (*ombre, lueur*) to throw, cast, project; (*jeter*) to throw up (*ou* off *ou* out); **~ de faire qch** to plan to do sth.

prolétaire [pʀɔletɛʀ] *a*, *nm/f* proletarian.

prolétariat [pʀɔletaʀja] *nm* proletariat.

proliférer [pʀɔlifeʀe] *vi* to proliferate.

prolifique [pʀɔlifik] *a* prolific.

prolixe [pʀɔliks(ə)] *a* verbose.

prolo [pʀɔlo] *nm/f* (*fam*: = *prolétaire*) prole (*péj*).

prologue [pʀɔlɔg] *nm* prologue.

prolongateur [pʀɔlɔ̃gatœʀ] *nm* (*ÉLEC*) extension cable.

prolongation [pʀɔlɔ̃gɑsjɔ̃] *nf* prolongation; extension; **~s** *nfpl* (*FOOTBALL*) extra time *sg*.

prolongement [prɔlɔ̃ʒmɑ̃] *nm* extension; **~s** *nmpl* (*fig*) repercussions, effects; **dans le ~ de** running on from.

prolonger [prɔlɔ̃ʒe] *vt* (*débat, séjour*) to prolong; (*délai, billet, rue*) to extend; (*suj: chose*) to be a continuation *ou* an extension of; **se ~** *vi* to go on.

promenade [prɔmnad] *nf* walk (*ou* drive *ou* ride); **faire une ~** to go for a walk; **une ~ (à pied)/en voiture/à vélo** a walk/drive/ (bicycle) ride.

promener [prɔmne] *vt* (*personne, chien*) to take out for a walk; (*fig*) to carry around; to trail round; (*doigts, regard*): **~ qch sur** to run sth over; **se ~** *vi* (*à pied*) to go for (*ou* be out for) a walk; (*en voiture*) to go for (*ou* be out for) a drive; (*fig*): **se ~ sur** to wander over.

promeneur, euse [prɔmnœr, -øz] *nm/f* walker, stroller.

promenoir [prɔmənwar] *nm* gallery, (covered) walkway.

promesse [prɔmɛs] *nf* promise; **~ d'achat** commitment to buy.

prometteur, euse [prɔmɛtœr, -øz] *a* promising.

promettre [prɔmɛtr(ə)] *vt* to promise ♦ *vi* (*récolte, arbre*) to look promising; (*enfant, musicien*) to be promising; **se ~ de faire** to resolve *ou* mean to do; **~ à qn de faire** to promise sb that one will do.

promeus [prɔmø] *etc vb voir* **promouvoir**.

promis, e [prɔmi, -iz] *pp de* **promettre** ♦ *a*: **être ~ à qch** (*destiné*) to be destined for sth.

promiscuité [prɔmiskɥite] *nf* crowding; lack of privacy.

promit [prɔmi] *vb voir* **promettre**.

promontoire [prɔmɔ̃twar] *nm* headland.

promoteur, trice [prɔmɔtœr, -tris] *nm/f* (*instigateur*) instigator, promoter; **(immobilier)** property developer (*Brit*), real estate promoter (*US*).

promotion [prɔmɔsjɔ̃] *nf* (*avancement*) promotion; (*SCOL*) year (*Brit*), class; **en ~** (*COMM*) on promotion, on (special) offer.

promotionnel, le [prɔmɔsjɔnɛl] *a* (*article*) on promotion, on (special) offer; (*vente*) promotional.

promouvoir [prɔmuvwar] *vt* to promote.

prompt, e [prɔ̃, prɔ̃t] *a* swift, rapid; (*intervention, changement*) sudden; **~ à faire qch** quick to do sth.

prompteur [prɔ̃tœr] *nm* ® teleprompter ®.

promptitude [prɔ̃tityd] *nf* swiftness, rapidity.

promu, e [prɔmy] *pp de* **promouvoir**.

promulguer [prɔmylge] *vt* to promulgate.

prôner [prone] *vt* (*louer*) to laud, extol; (*préconiser*) to advocate, commend.

pronom [prɔnɔ̃] *nm* pronoun.

pronominal, e, aux [prɔnɔminal, -o] *a* pronominal; (*verbe*) reflexive, pronominal.

prononcé, e [prɔnɔ̃se] *a* pronounced, marked.

prononcer [prɔnɔ̃se] *vt* (*son, mot, jugement*) to pronounce; (*dire*) to utter; (*allocution*) to deliver ♦ *vi* (*JUR*) to deliver *ou* give a verdict; **~ bien/mal** to have a good/poor pronunciation; **se ~** *vi* to reach a decision, give a verdict; **se ~ sur** to give an opinion on; **se ~ contre** to come down against; **ça se**

prononce comment? how do you pronounce this?

prononciation [prɔnɔ̃sjasjɔ̃] *nf* pronunciation.

pronostic [prɔnɔstik] *nm* (*MÉD*) prognosis (*pl* -oses); (*fig: aussi:* **~s**) forecast.

pronostiquer [prɔnɔstike] *vt* (*MÉD*) to prognosticate; (*annoncer, prévoir*) to forecast, foretell.

pronostiqueur, euse [prɔnɔstikœr, -øz] *nm/f* forecaster.

propagande [prɔpagɑ̃d] *nf* propaganda; **faire de la ~ pour qch** to plug *ou* push sth.

propager [prɔpaʒe] *vt* to spread; **se ~** *vi* to spread; (*PHYSIQUE*) to be propagated.

propane [prɔpan] *nm* propane.

propension [prɔpɑ̃sjɔ̃] *nf*: **~ à (faire) qch** propensity to (do) sth.

prophète [prɔfɛt], **prophétesse** [prɔfetɛs] *nm/f* prophet(ess).

prophétie [prɔfesi] *nf* prophecy.

prophétiser [prɔfetize] *vt* to prophesy.

prophylactique [prɔfilaktik] *a* prophylactic.

propice [prɔpis] *a* favourable (*Brit*), favorable (*US*).

proportion [prɔpɔrsjɔ̃] *nf* proportion; **il n'y a aucune ~ entre le prix demandé et le prix réel** the asking price bears no relation to the real price; **à ~ de** proportionally to, in proportion to; **en ~ (de)** in proportion (to); **hors de ~** out of proportion; **toute(s) ~(s) gardée(s)** making due allowance(s).

proportionné, e [prɔpɔrsjɔne] *a*: **bien ~** well-proportioned; **~ à** proportionate to.

proportionnel, le [prɔpɔrsjɔnɛl] *a* proportional; **~ à** proportional to.

proportionner [prɔpɔrsjɔne] *vt*: **~ qch à** to proportion *ou* adjust sth to.

propos [prɔpo] *nm* (*paroles*) talk *q*, remark; (*intention, but*) intention, aim; (*sujet*): **à quel ~?** what about?; **à ~ de** about, regarding; **à tout ~** for no reason at all; **à ce ~** on that subject, in this connection; **à ~ ad** by the way; (*opportunément*) (just) at the right moment; **hors de ~, mal à ~** *ad* at the wrong moment.

proposer [prɔpoze] *vt* (*suggérer*): **~ qch (à qn)/de faire** to suggest sth (to sb)/doing, propose sth (to sb)/to do; (*offrir*): **~ qch à qn/de faire** to offer sb sth/to do; (*candidat*) to nominate, put forward; (*loi, motion*) to propose; **se ~ (pour faire)** to offer one's services (to do); **se ~ de faire** to intend *ou* propose to do.

proposition [prɔpozisjɔ̃] *nf* suggestion; proposal; offer; (*LING*) clause; **sur la ~ de** at the suggestion of; **~ de loi** private bill.

propre [prɔpr(ə)] *a* clean; (*net*) neat, tidy; (*qui ne salit pas: chien, chat*) house-trained; (: *enfant*) toilet-trained; (*fig: honnête*) honest; (*possessif*) own; (*sens*) literal; (*particulier*): **~ à** peculiar to, characteristic of; (*approprié*): **~ à** suitable *ou* appropriate for; (*de nature à*): **~ à faire** likely to do, that will do ♦ *nm*: **recopier au ~** to make a fair copy of; (*particularité*): **le ~ de** the peculiarity of, the distinctive feature of; **au ~** (*LING*) literally; **appartenir à qn en ~** to belong to sb (exclusively); **~ à rien** *nm/f* (*péj*) good-for-nothing.

proprement [pʀɔpʀəmɑ̃] *ad* cleanly; neatly, tidily; **à ~ parler** strictly speaking; **le village ~ dit** the actual village, the village itself.

propret, te [pʀɔpʀɛ, -ɛt] *a* neat and tidy, spick-and-span.

propreté [pʀɔpʀəte] *nf* cleanliness, cleanness; neatness, tidiness.

propriétaire [pʀɔpʀijetɛʀ] *nm/f* owner; (*d'hôtel etc*) proprietor/tress, owner; (*pour le locataire*) landlord/lady; **~ (immobilier)** house-owner; householder; **~ récoltant** grower; **~ (terrien)** landowner.

propriété [pʀɔpʀijete] *nf* (*droit*) ownership; (*objet, immeuble etc*) property *gén q*; (*villa*) residence, property; (*terres*) property *gén q*, land *gén q*; (*qualité, CHIMIE, MATH*) property; (*correction*) appropriateness, suitability; **~ artistique et littéraire** artistic and literary copyright; **~ industrielle** patent rights *pl*.

propulser [pʀɔpylse] *vt* (*missile*) to propel; (*projeter*) to hurl, fling.

propulsion [pʀɔpylsjɔ̃] *nf* propulsion.

prorata [pʀɔʀata] *nm inv*: **au ~ de** in proportion to, on the basis of.

prorogation [pʀɔʀɔgasjɔ̃] *nf* deferment; extension; adjournment.

proroger [pʀɔʀɔʒe] *vt* to put back, defer; (*prolonger*) to extend; (*assemblée*) to adjourn, prorogue.

prosaïque [pʀɔzaik] *a* mundane, prosaic.

proscription [pʀɔskʀipsjɔ̃] *nf* banishment; (*interdiction*) banning; prohibition.

proscrire [pʀɔskʀiʀ] *vt* (*bannir*) to banish; (*interdire*) to ban, prohibit.

prose [pʀoz] *nf* prose (*style*).

prosélyte [pʀɔzelit] *nm/f* proselyte, convert.

prospecter [pʀɔspɛkte] *vt* to prospect; (*COMM*) to canvass.

prospecteur-placier, *pl* **prospecteurs-placiers** [pʀɔspɛktœʀplasje] *nm* placement officer.

prospectif, ive [pʀɔspɛktif, -iv] *a* prospective.

prospectus [pʀɔspɛktys] *nm* (*feuille*) leaflet; (*dépliant*) brochure, leaflet.

prospère [pʀɔspɛʀ] *a* prosperous; (*santé, entreprise*) thriving, flourishing.

prospérer [pʀɔspeʀe] *vi* to thrive.

prospérité [pʀɔspeʀite] *nf* prosperity.

prostate [pʀɔstat] *nf* prostate (gland).

prosterner [pʀɔstɛʀne]: **se ~** *vi* to bow low, prostrate o.s.

prostituée [pʀɔstitɥe] *nf* prostitute.

prostitution [pʀɔstitysjɔ̃] *nf* prostitution.

prostré, e [pʀɔstʀe] *a* prostrate.

protagoniste [pʀɔtagɔnist(ə)] *nm* protagonist.

protecteur, trice [pʀɔtɛktœʀ, -tʀis] *a* protective; (*air, ton: péj*) patronizing ♦ *nm/f* (*défenseur*) protector; (*des arts*) patron.

protection [pʀɔtɛksjɔ̃] *nf* protection; (*d'un personnage influent: aide*) patronage; **écran de ~** protective screen; **~ civile** state-financed civilian rescue service; **~ maternelle et infantile (PMI)** social service concerned with child welfare.

protectionniste [pʀɔtɛksjɔnist(ə)] *a* protectionist.

protégé, e [pʀɔteʒe] *nm/f* protégé/e.

protège-cahier [pʀɔtɛʒkaje] *nm* exercise-book cover.

protéger [pʀɔteʒe] *vt* to protect; (*aider, patronner: personne, arts*) to be a patron of; (: *carrière*) to further; **se ~ de/contre** to protect o.s. from.

protéine [pʀɔtein] *nf* protein.

protestant, e [pʀɔtɛstɑ̃, -ɑ̃t] *a, nm/f* Protestant.

protestantisme [pʀɔtɛstɑ̃tism(ə)] *nm* Protestantism.

protestataire [pʀɔtɛstatɛʀ] *nm/f* protestor.

protestation [pʀɔtɛstasjɔ̃] *nf* (*plainte*) protest; (*déclaration*) protestation, profession.

protester [pʀɔtɛste] *vi*: **~ (contre)** to protest (against *ou* about); **~ de** (*son innocence, sa loyauté*) to protest.

prothèse [pʀɔtɛz] *nf* artificial limb, prosthesis (*pl* -ses); **~ dentaire** (*appareil*) denture; (*science*) dental engineering.

protocolaire [pʀɔtɔkɔlɛʀ] *a* formal; (*questions, règles*) of protocol.

protocole [pʀɔtɔkɔl] *nm* protocol; (*fig*) etiquette; **~ d'accord** draft treaty; **~ opératoire** (*MÉD*) operating procedure.

prototype [pʀɔtɔtip] *nm* prototype.

protubérance [pʀɔtybeʀɑ̃s] *nf* bulge, protuberance.

protubérant, e [pʀɔtybeʀɑ̃, -ɑ̃t] *a* protruding, bulging, protuberant.

proue [pʀu] *nf* bow(s *pl*), prow.

prouesse [pʀuɛs] *nf* feat.

prouver [pʀuve] *vt* to prove.

provenance [pʀɔvnɑ̃s] *nf* origin; (*de mot, coutume*) source; **avion en ~ de** plane (arriving) from.

provençal, e, aux [pʀɔvɑ̃sal, -o] *a* Provençal ♦ *nm* (*LING*) Provençal.

Provence [pʀɔvɑ̃s] *nf*: **la ~** Provence.

provenir [pʀɔvniʀ]: **~ de** *vt* to come from; (*résulter de*) to be due to, be the result of.

proverbe [pʀɔvɛʀb(ə)] *nm* proverb.

proverbial, e, aux [pʀɔvɛʀbjal, -o] *a* proverbial.

providence [pʀɔvidɑ̃s] *nf*: **la ~** providence.

providentiel, le [pʀɔvidɑ̃sjɛl] *a* providential.

province [pʀɔvɛ̃s] *nf* province.

provincial, e, aux [pʀɔvɛ̃sjal, -o] *a, nm/f* provincial.

proviseur [pʀɔvizœʀ] *nm* ≈ head(teacher) (*Brit*), ≈ principal (*US*).

provision [pʀɔvizjɔ̃] *nf* (*réserve*) stock, supply; (*avance: à un avocat, avoué*) retainer, retaining fee; (*COMM*) funds *pl* (in account); reserve; **~s** *nfpl* (*vivres*) provisions, food *q*; **faire ~ de** to stock up with; **placard** *ou* **armoire à ~s** food cupboard.

provisoire [pʀɔvizwaʀ] *a* temporary; (*JUR*) provisional; **mise en liberté ~** release on bail.

provisoirement [pʀɔvizwaʀmɑ̃] *ad* temporarily, for the time being.

provocant, e [pʀɔvɔkɑ̃, -ɑ̃t] *a* provocative.

provocateur, trice [pʀɔvɔkatœʀ, -tʀis] *a* provocative ♦ *nm* (*meneur*) agitator.

provocation [pʀɔvɔkasjɔ̃] *nf* provocation.

provoquer [pʀɔvɔke] *vt* (*défier*) to provoke; (*causer*) to cause, bring about; (: *curiosité*) to arouse, give rise to; (: *aveux*) to prompt, elicit; (*inciter*): **~ qn à** to incite sb to.

prox. *abr* = **proximité**.

proxénète [pʀɔksɛnɛt] *nm* procurer.

proximité [pʀɔksimite] *nf* nearness, closeness, proximity; *(dans le temps)* imminence, closeness; **à ~** near *ou* close by; **à ~ de** near (to), close to.

prude [pʀyd] *a* prudish.

prudemment [pʀydamɑ̃] *ad* *(voir prudent)* carefully; cautiously; prudently; wisely, sensibly.

prudence [pʀydɑ̃s] *nf* carefulness; caution; prudence; **avec ~** carefully; cautiously; wisely; **par (mesure de) ~** as a precaution.

prudent, e [pʀydɑ̃, -ɑ̃t] *a* *(pas téméraire)* careful, cautious, prudent; *(: en général)* safety-conscious; *(sage, conseillé)* wise, sensible; *(réservé)* cautious; **ce n'est pas ~** it's risky; it's not sensible; **soyez ~** take care, be careful.

prune [pʀyn] *nf* plum.

pruneau, x [pʀyno] *nm* prune.

prunelle [pʀynɛl] *nf* pupil; *(œil)* eye; *(BOT)* sloe; *(eau de vie)* sloe gin.

prunier [pʀynje] *nm* plum tree.

PS *sigle m* = *Parti socialiste*; (= *postscriptum*) PS.

psalmodier [psalmɔdje] *vt* to chant; *(fig)* to drone out.

psaume [psom] *nm* psalm.

pseudonyme [psødɔnim] *nm* *(gén)* fictitious name; *(d'écrivain)* pseudonym, pen name; *(de comédien)* stage name.

PSIG *sigle m* (= *Peloton de surveillance et d'intervention de gendarmerie*) *type of police commando squad.*

PSU *sigle m* = *Parti socialiste unifié.*

psy [psi] *nm/f* *(fam, péj: = psychiatre, psychologue)* shrink.

psychanalyse [psikanaliz] *nf* psychoanalysis.

psychanalyser [psikanalize] *vt* to psychoanalyze; **se faire ~** to undergo (psycho)analysis.

psychanalyste [psikanalist(ə)] *nm/f* psychoanalyst.

psychédélique [psikedelik] *a* psychedelic.

psychiatre [psikjatʀ(ə)] *nm/f* psychiatrist.

psychiatrie [psikjatʀi] *nf* psychiatry.

psychiatrique [psikjatʀik] *a* psychiatric; *(hôpital)* mental, psychiatric.

psychique [psiʃik] *a* psychological.

psychisme [psiʃism(ə)] *nm* psyche.

psychologie [psikɔlɔʒi] *nf* psychology.

psychologique [psikɔlɔʒik] *a* psychological.

psychologue [psikɔlɔg] *nm/f* psychologist; **être ~** *(fig)* to be a good psychologist.

psychopathe [psikɔpat] *nm/f* psychopath.

psychopédagogie [psikɔpedagɔʒi] *nf* educational psychology.

psychose [psikoz] *nf* *(MÉD)* psychosis *(pl -ses)*; *(obsession, idée fixe)* obsessive fear.

psychosomatique [psikɔsɔmatik] *a* psychosomatic.

psychothérapie [psikɔteʀapi] *nf* psychotherapy.

psychotique [psikɔtik] *a* psychotic.

PTCA *sigle m* = *poids total en charge autorisé.*

Pte *abr* = **Porte**.

pte *abr* (= *pointe*) pt.

PTMA *sigle m* (= *poids total maximum autorisé*) maximum loaded weight.

PTT *sigle fpl voir* **poste**.

pu [py] *pp de* **pouvoir**.

puanteur [pɥɑ̃tœʀ] *nf* stink, stench.

pub [pyb] *nf* *(fam: = publicité)*: **la ~** advertising.

pubère [pybɛʀ] *a* pubescent.

puberté [pybɛʀte] *nf* puberty.

pubis [pybis] *nm* *(bas-ventre)* pubes *pl*; *(os)* pubis.

public, ique [pyblik] *a* public; *(école, instruction)* state *cpd*; *(scrutin)* open ♦ *nm* public; *(assistance)* audience; **en ~** in public; **le grand ~** the general public.

publication [pyblikɑsjɔ̃] *nf* publication.

publiciste [pyblisist(ə)] *nm/f* adman.

publicitaire [pyblisitɛʀ] *a* advertising *cpd*; *(film, voiture)* publicity *cpd*; *(vente)* promotional ♦ *nm* adman; **rédacteur ~** copywriter.

publicité [pyblisite] *nf* *(méthode, profession)* advertising; *(annonce)* advertisement; *(révélations)* publicity.

publier [pyblije] *vt* to publish; *(nouvelle)* to publicize, make public.

publique [pyblik] *af voir* **public**.

publiquement [pyblikmɑ̃] *ad* publicly.

puce [pys] *nf* flea; *(INFORM)* chip; **(marché aux) ~s** flea market *sg*; **mettre la ~ à l'oreille de qn** to give sb something to think about.

puceau, x [pyso] *am*: **être ~** to be a virgin.

pucelle [pysɛl] *af*: **être ~** to be a virgin.

puceron [pysʀɔ̃] *nm* aphid.

pudeur [pydœʀ] *nf* modesty.

pudibond, e [pydibɔ̃, -ɔ̃d] *a* prudish.

pudique [pydik] *a* *(chaste)* modest; *(discret)* discreet.

puer [pɥe] *(péj)* *vi* to stink ♦ *vt* to stink of, reek of.

puéricultrice [pɥeʀikyltʀis] *nf* ≈ nursery nurse.

puériculture [pɥeʀikyltyʀ] *nf* infant care.

puéril, e [pɥeʀil] *a* childish.

pugilat [pyʒila] *nm* *(fist)* fight.

puis [pɥi] *vb voir* **pouvoir** ♦ *ad* *(ensuite)* then; *(dans une énumération)* next; *(en outre)*: **et ~** and (then); **et ~ (après *ou* quoi)?** so (what)?

puisard [pɥizaʀ] *nm* *(égout)* cesspool.

puiser [pɥize] *vt*: **~ (dans)** to draw (from); **~ dans qch** to dip into sth.

puisque [pɥisk(ə)] *cj* since; *(valeur intensive)*: **~ je te le dis!** I'm telling you!

puissamment [pɥisamɑ̃] *ad* powerfully.

puissance [pɥisɑ̃s] *nf* power; **en ~** *a* potential; **2 (à la) ~ 5** 2 to the power (of) 5.

puissant, e [pɥisɑ̃, -ɑ̃t] *a* powerful.

puisse [pɥis] *etc vb voir* **pouvoir**.

puits [pɥi] *nm* well; **~ artésien** artesian well; **~ de mine** mine shaft; **~ de science** fount of knowledge.

pull(-over) [pyl(ɔvœʀ)] *nm* sweater, jumper *(Brit)*.

pulluler [pylyle] *vi* to swarm; *(fig: erreurs)* to abound, proliferate.

pulmonaire [pylmɔnɛʀ] *a* lung *cpd*; *(artère)* pulmonary.

pulpe [pylp(ə)] *nf* pulp.

pulsation [pylsɑsjɔ̃] *nf* (*MÉD*) beat.

pulsion [pylsjɔ̃] *nf* (*PSYCH*) drive, urge.

pulvérisateur [pylveʀizatœʀ] *nm* spray.

pulvérisation [pylveʀizasjɔ̃] *nf* spraying.

pulvériser [pylveʀize] *vt* (*solide*) to pulverize; (*liquide*) to spray; (*fig: anéantir: adversaire*) to pulverize; (*: record*) to smash, shatter; (*: argument*) to demolish.

puma [pyma] *nm* puma, cougar.

punaise [pynɛz] *nf* (*ZOOL*) bug; (*clou*) drawing pin (*Brit*), thumb tack (*US*).

punch [pɔ̃ʃ] *nm* (*boisson*) punch; [pœnʃ] (*BOXE*) punching ability; (*fig*) punch.

punching-ball [pœnʃiŋbol] *nm* punchball.

punir [pyniʀ] *vt* to punish; ~ **qn de qch** to punish sb for sth.

punitif, ive [pynitif, -iv] *a* punitive.

punition [pynisjɔ̃] *nf* punishment.

pupille [pypij] *nf* (*ANAT*) pupil ♦ *nm/f* (*enfant*) ward; ~ **de l'État** child in care; ~ **de la Nation** war orphan.

pupitre [pypitʀ(ə)] *nm* (*SCOL*) desk; (*REL*) lectern; (*de chef d'orchestre*) rostrum; (*INFORM*) console; ~ **de commande** control panel.

pupitreur, euse [pypitʀœʀ, -øz] *nm/f* (*INFORM*) (computer) operator, keyboarder.

pur, e [pyʀ] *a* pure; (*vin*) undiluted; (*whisky*) neat; (*intentions*) honourable (*Brit*), honorable (*US*) ♦ *nm* (*personne*) hard-liner; **en ~e perte** fruitlessly, to no avail.

purée [pyʀe] *nf*: ~ **(de pommes de terre)** ≈ mashed potatoes *pl*; ~ **de marrons** chestnut purée; ~ **de pois** (*fig*) peasoup(er).

purement [pyʀmɑ̃] *ad* purely.

pureté [pyʀte] *nf* purity.

purgatif [pyʀɡatif] *nm* purgative, purge.

purgatoire [pyʀɡatwaʀ] *nm* purgatory.

purge [pyʀʒ(ə)] *nf* (*POL*) purge; (*MÉD*) purging *q*; purge.

purger [pyʀʒe] *vt* (*radiateur*) to flush (out), drain; (*circuit hydraulique*) to bleed; (*MÉD, POL*) to purge; (*JUR: peine*) to serve.

purifier [pyʀifje] *vt* to purify; (*TECH: métal*) to refine.

purin [pyʀɛ̃] *nm* liquid manure.

puriste [pyʀist(ə)] *nm/f* purist.

puritain, e [pyʀitɛ̃, -ɛn] *a*, *nm/f* Puritan.

puritanisme [pyʀitanism(ə)] *nm* Puritanism.

pur-sang [pyʀsɑ̃] *nm inv* thoroughbred, pure-bred.

purulent, e [pyʀylɑ̃, -ɑ̃t] *a* purulent.

pus [py] *vb voir* **pouvoir** ♦ *nm* pus.

pusillanime [pyzilanim] *a* fainthearted.

putain [pytɛ̃] *nf* (*fam!*) whore (*!*); **ce/cette ~ de ...** this bloody (*Brit*) *ou* goddamn (*US*) ... (*!*).

putois [pytwa] *nm* polecat; **crier comme un ~** to yell one's head off.

putréfier [pytʀefje] *vt*, **se ~** *vi* to putrefy, rot.

putride [pytʀid] *a* putrid.

puzzle [pœzl(ə)] *nm* jigsaw (puzzle).

PV *sigle m* = **procès-verbal**.

PVC *sigle f* (= *polychlorure de vinyle*) PVC.

PVD *sigle mpl* (= *pays en voie de développement*) developing countries.

Px *abr* = **prix**.

pygmée [piɡme] *nm* pygmy.

pyjama [piʒama] *nm* pyjamas *pl*, pair of pyjamas.

pylône [pilon] *nm* pylon.

pyramide [piʀamid] *nf* pyramid.

pyrénéen, ne [piʀeneɛ̃, -ɛn] *a* Pyrenean.

Pyrénées [piʀene] *nfpl*: **les ~** the Pyrenees.

pyrex [piʀɛks] *nm* ® Pyrex ®.

pyrogravure [piʀoɡʀavyʀ] *nf* poker-work.

pyromane [piʀoman] *nm/f* arsonist.

python [pitɔ̃] *nm* python.

Q

Q, q [ky] *nm inv* Q, q ♦ *abr* (= *quintal*) q; **Q comme Quintal** Q for Queen.

Qatar [kataʀ] *nm*: **le ~** Qatar.

QCM *sigle fpl* (= *questions à choix multiples*) multiple choice *sg*.

QG *sigle m* (= *quartier général*) HQ.

QHS *sigle m* (= *quartier de haute sécurité*) high-security wing *ou* prison.

QI *sigle m* (= *quotient intellectuel*) IQ.

qqch. *abr* (= *quelque chose*) sth.

qqe(s) *abr* = **quelque(s)**.

qqn *abr* (= *quelqu'un*) sb., s.o.

quadragénaire [kadʀaʒenɛʀ] *nm/f* (*de quarante ans*) forty-year-old; (*de quarante à cinquante ans*) man/woman in his/her forties.

quadrangulaire [kwadʀɑ̃ɡylɛʀ] *a* quadrangular.

quadrature [kwadʀatyʀ] *nf*: **c'est la ~ du cercle** it's like trying to square the circle.

quadrichromie [kwadʀikʀɔmi] *nf* four-colour (*Brit*) *ou* -color (*US*) printing.

quadrilatère [k(w)adʀilatɛʀ] *nm* (*GÉOM, MIL*) quadrilateral; (*terrain*) four-sided area.

quadrillage [kadʀijaʒ] *nm* (*lignes etc*) square pattern, criss-cross pattern.

quadrillé, e [kadʀije] *a* (*papier*) squared.

quadriller [kadʀije] *vt* (*papier*) to mark out in squares; (*POLICE: ville, région etc*) to keep under tight control, be positioned throughout.

quadrimoteur [k(w)adʀimɔtœʀ] *nm* four-engined plane.

quadripartite [kwadʀipaʀtit] *a* (*entre pays*) four-power; (*entre partis*) four-party.

quadriphonie [kadʀifɔni] *nf* quadraphony.

quadriréacteur [k(w)adʀiʀeaktœʀ] *nm* four-engined jet.

quadrupède [k(w)adʀypɛd] *nm* quadruped.

quadruple [k(w)adʀypl(ə)] *nm*: **le ~ de** four times as much as.

quadrupler [k(w)adʀyple] *vt*, *vi* to quadruple, increase fourfold.

quadruplés, ées [k(w)adʀyple] *nm/fpl* quadruplets, quads.

quai [ke] *nm* (*de port*) quay; (*de gare*) platform; (*de cours d'eau, canal*) embankment; **être à ~** (*navire*) to be alongside; (*train*) to be in the station; **le Q~ d'Orsay** offices of the French Ministry for Foreign Affairs; **le Q~ des Orfèvres** central police headquarters.

qualifiable [kalifjabl(ə)] *a*: **ce n'est pas ~** it defies description.

qualificatif, ive [kalifikatif, -iv] *a* (*LING*) qualifying ♦ *nm* (*terme*) term; (*LING*) qualifier.

qualification [kalifikasjɔ̃] *nf* qualification.

qualifier [kalifje] *vt* to qualify; (*appeler*): **~ qch/qn de** to describe sth/sb as; **se ~** *vi* (*SPORT*) to qualify; **être qualifié pour** to be qualified for.

qualitatif, ive [kalitatif, -iv] *a* qualitative.

qualité [kalite] *nf* quality; (*titre, fonction*) position; **en ~ de** in one's capacity as; **ès ~s** in an official capacity; **avoir ~ pour** to have authority to; **de ~** *a* quality *cpd*; **rapport ~-prix** value (for money).

quand [kɑ̃] *cj, ad* when; **~ je serai riche** when I'm rich; **~ même** (*cependant, pourtant*) nevertheless; (*tout de même*) all the same; really; **~ bien même** even though.

quant [kɑ̃]: **~ à** *prép* (*pour ce qui est de*) as for, as to; (*au sujet de*) regarding.

quant-à-soi [kɑ̃taswa] *nm*: **rester sur son ~** to remain aloof.

quantième [kɑ̃tjɛm] *nm* date, day (of the month).

quantifiable [kɑ̃tifjabl(ə)] *a* quantifiable.

quantifier [kɑ̃tifje] *vt* to quantify.

quantitatif, ive [kɑ̃titatif, -iv] *a* quantitative.

quantitativement [kɑ̃titativmɑ̃] *ad* quantitatively.

quantité [kɑ̃tite] *nf* quantity, amount; (*SCIENCE*) quantity; (*grand nombre*): **une ou des ~(s) de** a great deal of; a lot of; **en grande ~** in large quantities; **en ~s industrielles** in vast quantities; **du travail en ~** a great deal of work; **~ de** many.

quarantaine [kaʀɑ̃tɛn] *nf* (*isolement*) quarantine; (*âge*): **avoir la ~** to be around forty; (*nombre*): **une ~ (de)** forty or so, about forty; **mettre en ~** to put into quarantine; (*fig*) to send to Coventry (*Brit*), ostracize.

quarante [kaʀɑ̃t] *num* forty.

quarantième [kaʀɑ̃tjɛm] *num* fortieth.

quart [kaʀ] *nm* (*fraction*) quarter; (*surveillance*) watch; (*partie*): **un ~ de poulet/fromage** a chicken quarter/a quarter of a cheese; **un ~ de beurre** a quarter kilo of butter, ≈ a half pound of butter; **un ~ de vin** a quarter litre of wine; **une livre un ~ ou et ~** one and a quarter pounds; **le ~ de** a quarter of; **~ d'heure** quarter of an hour; **2h et ou un ~** (a) quarter past two, (a) quarter after two (*US*); **il est le ~** it's (a) quarter past *ou* after (*US*); **1h moins le ~** (a) quarter to one, (a) quarter of one (*US*); **il est moins le ~** it's (a) quarter to; **être de/prendre le ~** to keep/take the watch; **~ de tour** quarter turn; **au ~ de tour** (*fig*) straight off; **~s de finale** (*SPORT*) quarter finals.

quarté [kaʀte] *nm* (*COURSES*) system of forecast betting giving first four horses.

quarteron [kaʀtəʀɔ̃] *nm* (*péj*) small bunch, handful.

quartette [kwaʀtɛt] *nm* quartet(te).

quartier [kaʀtje] *nm* (*de ville*) district, area; (*de bœuf, de la lune*) quarter; (*de fruit, fromage*) piece; **~s** *nmpl* (*MIL, BLASON*) quarters; **cinéma/salle de ~** local cinema/hall; **avoir ~ libre** to be free; (*MIL*) to have leave from barracks; **ne pas faire de ~** to spare no one, give no quarter; **~ commerçant/résidentiel** shopping/residential area; **~ général (QG)** headquarters (HQ).

quartier-maître [kaʀtjemɛtʀ(ə)] *nm* ≈ leading seaman.

quartz [kwaʀts] *nm* quartz.

quasi [kazi] *ad* almost, nearly ♦ *préfixe*: **~certitude** near certainty.

quasiment [kazimɑ̃] *ad* almost, very nearly.

quaternaire [kwatɛʀnɛʀ] *a* (*GÉO*) Quaternary.

quatorze [katɔʀz(ə)] *num* fourteen.

quatorzième [katɔʀzjɛm] *num* fourteenth.

quatrain [katʀɛ̃] *nm* quatrain.

quatre [katʀ(ə)] *num* four; **à ~ pattes** on all fours; **tiré à ~ épingles** dressed up to the nines; **faire les ~ cent coups** to be a bit wild; **se mettre en ~ pour qn** to go out of one's way for sb; **à ~** (*monter, descendre*) four at a time; **à ~ mains** (*jouer*) four-handed.

quatre-vingt-dix [katʀəvɛ̃dis] *num* ninety.

quatre-vingts [katʀəvɛ̃] *num* eighty.

quatrième [katʀijɛm] *num* fourth.

quatuor [kwatɥɔʀ] *nm* quartet(te).

que [kə] *cj* (*gén*) that; (*après comparatif*) than; as: *voir* **plus, aussi, autant** *etc*; (*seulement*): **ne ... ~** only; **il sait ~ tu es là** he knows (that) you're here; **je veux ~ tu acceptes** I want you to accept; **il a dit ~ oui** he said he would (*ou* it was *etc, suivant le contexte*); **si vous y allez ou ~ vous lui téléphoniez** if you go there or (if you) phone him; **quand il rentrera et qu'il aura mangé** when he gets back and (when he) has eaten; **qu'il le veuille ou non** whether he likes it or not; **tenez-le qu'il ne tombe pas** hold it so (that) it doesn't fall; **qu'il fasse ce qu'il voudra** let him do as he pleases; **il ne boit ~ de l'eau** he only drinks water; *voir* **avant, pour, tel, à peine** *etc* ♦ *ad*: **qu'il ou qu'est-ce qu'il est bête/court vite** he's so silly/he runs so fast; **~ de** what a lot of ♦ *pronom*: **l'homme ~ je vois** the man (whom) I see; **le livre ~ tu vois** the book (that *ou* which) you see; **un jour ~ j'étais** a day when I was; **c'est une erreur ~ de croire** it's a mistake to believe; **qu'est-ce que c'est?** (*ceci*) what is it?; (*cela*) what's that?; **~ fais-tu?, qu'est-ce tu fais?** what are you doing?; **~ préfères-tu, celui-ci ou celui-là?** which do you prefer, this one or that one?; **~ faire?** what can we do?

Québec [kebɛk] *n* (*ville*) Quebec ♦ *nm*: **le ~** Quebec (Province).

québécois, e [kebekwa, -waz] *a* Quebec *cpd* ♦ *nm* (*LING*) Quebec French ♦ *nm/f*: **Q~, e** Quebecois, Quebec(k)er.

quel, quelle [kɛl] *a*: **~ livre/homme?** what book/man?; (*parmi un certain choix*) which book/man?; **~ est cet homme?** who is this man?; **~ est ce livre?** what is this book?; **~ est le plus petit?** which is the smallest?; **~s acteurs préférez-vous?** which actors do you prefer?; **dans ~s pays êtes-vous allé?** which *ou* what countries did you go to?; **~le surprise!** what a surprise!; **~ que soit le**

coupable whoever is guilty; **~ que soit votre avis** whatever your opinion; whichever is your opinion.

quelconque [kɛlkɔ̃k] *a* (*médiocre*) indifferent, poor; (*sans attrait*) ordinary, plain; (*indéfini*): **un ami/prétexte ~** some friend/ pretext or other; **un livre ~ suffira** any book will do; **pour une raison ~** for some reason (or other).

quelque [kɛlk(ə)] *dét* some; a few, *tournure interrogative +* any ♦ *ad* (*environ*): **~ 100 mètres** some 100 metres; **~ espoir** some hope; **il a ~s amis** he has a few *ou* some friends; **a-t-il ~s amis?** has any friends?; **les ~s livres qui** the few books which; **~ livre qu'il choisisse** whatever (*ou* whichever) book he chooses; **20 kg et ~(s)** a bit over 20 kg; **~ chose** something, *tournure interrogative +* anything; **~ chose d'autre** something else; anything else; **~ part** somewhere; **~ peu** rather, somewhat; **en ~ sorte** as it were.

quelquefois [kɛlkəfwa] *ad* sometimes.

quelques-uns, -unes [kɛlkəzœ̃, -yn] *pronom* some, a few; **~ des lecteurs** some of the readers.

quelqu'un [kɛlkœ̃] *pronom* someone, somebody, *tournure interrogative ou négative +* anyone *ou* anybody; **~ d'autre** someone *ou* somebody else; anybody else.

quémander [kemɑ̃de] *vt* to beg for.

qu'en dira-t-on [kɑ̃diʀatɔ̃] *nm inv*: **le ~** gossip, what people say.

quenelle [kənɛl] *nf* quenelle.

quenouille [kənuj] *nf* distaff.

querelle [kəʀɛl] *nf* quarrel; **chercher ~ à qn** to pick a quarrel with sb.

quereller [kəʀele]: **se ~** *vi* to quarrel.

querelleur, euse [kəʀɛlœʀ, -øz] *a* quarrelsome.

qu'est-ce que (*ou* **qui**) [kɛskə(ki)] *voir* **que, qui.**

question [kɛstjɔ̃] *nf* (*gén*) question; (*fig*) matter; issue; **il a été ~ de** we (*ou* they) spoke about; **il est ~ de les emprisonner** there's talk of them being jailed; **c'est une ~ de temps** it's a matter *ou* question of time; **de quoi est-il ~?** what is it about?; **il n'en est pas ~** there's no question of it; **en ~** in question; **hors de ~** out of the question; **je ne me suis jamais posé la ~** I've never thought about it; **(re)mettre en ~** (*autorité, science*) to question; **poser la ~ de confiance** (*POL*) to ask for a vote of confidence; **~ piège** (*d'apparence facile*) trick question; (*pour nuire*) loaded question; **~ subsidiaire** tiebreaker.

questionnaire [kɛstjɔnɛʀ] *nm* questionnaire.

questionner [kɛstjɔne] *vt* to question.

quête [kɛt] *nf* (*collecte*) collection; (*recherche*) quest, search; **faire la ~** (*à l'église*) to take the collection; (*artiste*) to pass the hat round; **se mettre en ~ de qch** to go in search of sth.

quêter [kete] *vi* (*à l'église*) to take the collection; (*dans la rue*) to collect money (for charity) ♦ *vt* to seek.

quetsche [kwɛtʃ(ə)] *nf* damson.

queue [kø] *nf* tail; (*fig: du classement*)

bottom; (*: de poêle*) handle; (*: de fruit, feuille*) stalk; (*: de train, colonne, file*) rear; (*file: de personnes*) queue (*Brit*), line (*US*); **en ~ (de train)** at the rear (of the train); **faire la ~** to queue (up) (*Brit*), line up (*US*); **se mettre à la ~** to join the queue (*Brit*) ou line (*US*); **histoire sans ~ ni tête** cock and bull story; **à la ~ leu leu** in single file; (*fig*) one after the other; **~ de cheval** ponytail; **~ de poisson: faire une ~ de poisson à qn** (*AUTO*) to cut in front of sb; **finir en ~ de poisson** (*film*) to come to an abrupt end.

queue-de-pie, *pl* **queues-de-pie** [kødpi] *nf* (*habit*) tails *pl*, tail coat.

queux [kø] *am voir* **maître.**

qui [ki] *pronom* (*personne*) who, *prép +* whom; (*chose, animal*) which, that; (*interrogatif indirect: sujet*): **je me demande ~ est là?** I wonder who is there?; (*: objet*): **elle ne sait à ~ se plaindre** she doesn't know who to complain to *ou* to whom to complain; **qu'est-ce ~ est sur la table?** what is on the table?; **à ~ est ce sac?** whose bag is this?; **à ~ parlais-tu?** who were you talking to?, to whom were you talking?; **chez ~ allez-vous?** whose house are you going to?; **amenez ~ vous voulez** bring who(ever) you like; **~ est-ce ~ ...?** who?; **~ est-ce que ...?** who?; whom?; **~ que ce soit** whoever it may be.

quiche [kiʃ] *nf* quiche; **~ lorraine** quiche Lorraine.

quiconque [kikɔ̃k] *pronom* (*celui qui*) whoever, anyone who; (*n'importe qui, personne*) anyone, anybody.

quidam [kɥidam] *nm* (*hum*) fellow.

quiétude [kjetyd] *nf* (*d'un lieu*) quiet, tranquillity; (*d'une personne*) peace (of mind), serenity; **en toute ~** in complete peace; (*mentale*) with complete peace of mind.

quignon [kiɲɔ̃] *nm*: **~ de pain** (*croûton*) crust of bread; (*morceau*) hunk of bread.

quille [kij] *nf* ninepin, skittle (*Brit*); (*NAVIG: d'un bateau*) keel; **(jeu de) ~s** ninepins *sg*, skittles *sg* (*Brit*).

quincaillerie [kɛ̃kajʀi] *nf* (*ustensiles, métier*) hardware, ironmongery (*Brit*); (*magasin*) hardware shop *ou* store (*US*), ironmonger's (*Brit*).

quincaillier, ière [kɛ̃kaje, -jɛʀ] *nm/f* hardware dealer, ironmonger (*Brit*).

quinconce [kɛ̃kɔ̃s] *nm*: **en ~** in staggered rows.

quinine [kinin] *nf* quinine.

quinquagénaire [kɛ̃kaʒenɛʀ] *nm/f* (*de cinquante ans*) fifty-year old; (*de cinquante à soixante ans*) man/woman in his/her fifties.

quinquennal, e, aux [kɛ̃kenal, -o] *a* five-year, quinquennial.

quintal, aux [kɛ̃tal, -o] *nm* quintal (*100 kg*).

quinte [kɛ̃t] *nf*: **~ (de toux)** coughing fit.

quintessence [kɛ̃tesɑ̃s] *nf* quintessence, very essence.

quintette [kɛ̃tɛt] *nm* quintet(te).

quintuple [kɛ̃typl(ə)] *nm*: **le ~ de** five times as much as.

quintupler [kɛ̃typle] *vt, vi* to increase fivefold.

quintuplés, ées [kɛ̃typle] *nm/fpl* quintuplets, quins.

quinzaine [kɛ̃zɛn] *nf*: **une ~ (de)** about fifteen, fifteen or so; **une ~ (de jours)** (*deux semaines*) a fortnight (*Brit*), two weeks; **~ publicitaire** *ou* **commerciale** (two-week) sale.

quinze [kɛ̃z] *num* fifteen; **demain en ~** a fortnight (*Brit*) *ou* two weeks tomorrow; **dans ~ jours** in a fortnight('s time) (*Brit*), in two weeks(' time).

quinzième [kɛ̃zjɛm] *num* fifteenth.

quiproquo [kiprɔko] *nm* (*méprise sur une personne*) mistake; (*malentendu sur un sujet*) misunderstanding; (*THÉÂTRE*) (case of) mistaken identity.

Quito [kito] *n* Quito.

quittance [kitɑ̃s] *nf* (*reçu*) receipt; (*facture*) bill.

quitte [kit] *a*: **être ~ envers qn** to be no longer in sb's debt; (*fig*) to be quits with sb; **être ~ de** (*obligation*) to be clear of; **en être ~ à bon compte** to have got off lightly; **~ à faire** even if it means doing; **~ ou double** (*jeu*) double or quits; (*fig*): **c'est du ~ ou double** it's a big risk.

quitter [kite] *vt* to leave; (*espoir, illusion*) to give up; (*vêtement*) to take off; **se ~** (*couples, interlocuteurs*) to part; **ne quittez pas** (*au téléphone*) hold the line; **ne pas ~ qn d'une semelle** to stick to sb like glue.

quitus [kitys] *nm* final discharge; **donner ~ à** to discharge.

qui-vive [kiviv] *nm inv*: **être sur le ~** to be on the alert.

quoi [kwa] *pronom* (*interrogatif*) what; **~ de neuf** *ou* **de nouveau?** what's new *ou* the news?; **as-tu de ~ écrire?** have you anything to write with?; **il n'a pas de ~ se l'acheter** he can't afford it, he hasn't got the money to buy it; **il y a de ~ être fier** that's something to be proud of; **il n'y a pas de ~"** (please) don't mention it", "not at all"; **~ qu'il arrive** whatever happens; **~ qu'il en soit** be that as it may; **~ que ce soit** anything at all; **en ~ puis-je vous aider?** how can I help you?; **à ~ bon?** what's the use *ou* point?; **et puis ~ encore!** what(ever) next!; **~ faire?** what's to be done?; **sans ~** (*ou sinon*) otherwise.

quoique [kwak(ə)] *cj* (al)though.

quolibet [kɔlibɛ] *nm* gibe, jeer.

quorum [kɔrɔm] *nm* quorum.

quota [kwɔta] *nm* quota.

quote-part [kɔtpar] *nf* share.

quotidien, ne [kɔtidjɛ̃, -ɛn] *a* (*journalier*) daily; (*banal*) ordinary, everyday ♦ *nm* (*journal*) daily (paper); (*vie quotidienne*) daily life, day-to-day existence; **les grands ~s** the big (national) dailies.

quotidiennement [kɔtidjɛnmɑ̃] *ad* daily, every day.

quotient [kɔsjɑ̃] *nm* (*MATH*) quotient; **~ intellectuel (QI)** intelligence quotient (IQ).

quotité [kɔtite] *nf* (*FINANCE*) quota.

R

R, r [ɛr] *nm inv* R, r ♦ *abr* = **route, rue; R comme Raoul** R for Robert (*Brit*) *ou* Roger (*US*).

rab [rab] (*fam*), **rabiot** [rabjo] *nm* extra, more.

rabâcher [rabɑʃe] *vi* to harp on ♦ *vt* keep on repeating.

rabais [rabɛ] *nm* reduction, discount; **au ~** at a reduction *ou* discount.

rabaisser [rabese] *vt* (*rabattre*) to reduce; (*dénigrer*) to belittle.

rabane [raban] *nf* raffia (matting).

Rabat [raba(t)] *n* Rabat.

rabat [raba] *vb voir* **rabattre** ♦ *nm* flap.

rabat-joie [rabaʒwa] *nm/f inv* killjoy (*Brit*), spoilsport.

rabatteur, euse [rabatœr, -øz] *nm/f* (*de gibier*) beater; (*péj*) tout.

rabattre [rabatr(ə)] *vt* (*couvercle, siège*) to pull down; (*col*) to turn down; (*couture*) to stitch down; (*gibier*) to drive; (*somme d'un prix*) to deduct, take off; (*orgueil, prétentions*) to humble; (*TRICOT*) to decrease; **se ~** *vi* (*bords, couvercle*) to fall shut; (*véhicule, coureur*) to cut in; **se ~ sur** (*accepter*) to fall back on.

rabattu, e [rabaty] *pp de* **rabattre** ♦ *a* turned down.

rabbin [rabɛ̃] *nm* rabbi.

rabique [rabik] *a* rabies *cpd*.

râble [rɑbl(ə)] *nm* back; (*CULIN*) saddle.

râblé, e [rɑble] *a* broad-backed, stocky.

rabot [rabo] *nm* plane.

raboter [rabɔte] *vt* to plane (down).

raboteux, euse [rabɔtø, -øz] *a* uneven, rough.

rabougri, e [rabugri] *a* stunted.

rabrouer [rabrue] *vt* to snub, rebuff.

racaille [rakɑj] *nf* (*péj*) rabble, riffraff.

raccommodage [rakɔmɔdaʒ] *nm* mending *q*, repairing *q*; darning *q*.

raccommoder [rakɔmɔde] *vt* to mend, repair; (*chaussette etc*) to darn; (*fam: réconcilier: amis, ménage*) to bring together again; **se ~ (avec)** (*fam*) to patch it up (with).

raccompagner [rakɔ̃paɲe] *vt* to take *ou* see back.

raccord [rakɔr] *nm* link; **~ de maçonnerie** pointing *q*; **~ de peinture** join; touch-up.

raccordement [rakɔrdəmɑ̃] *nm* joining up; connection.

raccorder [rakɔrde] *vt* to join (up), link up; (*suj: pont etc*) to connect, link; **se ~ à** to join up with; (*fig: se rattacher à*) to tie in with; **~ au réseau du téléphone** to connect to the telephone service.

raccourci [rakursi] *nm* short cut; **en ~** in brief.

raccourcir [RakuRsiR] *vt* to shorten ♦ *vi* (*vêtement*) to shrink.

raccroc [RakRo]: **par ~** *ad* by chance.

raccrocher [RakRoʃe] *vt* (*tableau, vêtement*) to hang back up; (*récepteur*) to put down; (*fig: affaire*) to save ♦ *vi* (*TÉL*) to hang up, ring off; **se ~ à** *vt* to cling to, hang on to; **ne raccrochez pas** (*TÉL*) hold on, don't hang up.

race [Ras] *nf* race; (*d'animaux, fig: espèce*) breed; (*ascendance, origine*) stock, race; **de ~ a** purebred, pedigree.

racé, e [Rase] *a* thoroughbred.

rachat [Raʃa] *nm* buying; buying back; redemption; atonement.

racheter [Raʃte] *vt* (*article perdu*) to buy another; (*davantage*): **~ du lait/3 œufs** to buy more milk/another 3 eggs *ou* 3 more eggs; (*après avoir vendu*) to buy back; (*d'occasion*) to buy; (*COMM: part, firme*) to buy up; (*: pension, rente*) to redeem; (*REL: pécheur*) to redeem; (*: péché*) to atone for, expiate; (*mauvaise conduite, oubli, défaut*) to make up for; **se ~** (*REL*) to redeem o.s.; (*gén*) to make amends, make up for it.

rachidien, ne [Raʃidjɛ̃, -ɛn] *a* rachidian, of the spine.

rachitique [Raʃitik] *a* suffering from rickets; (*fig*) scraggy, scrawny.

rachitisme [Raʃitism(ə)] *nm* rickets *sg*.

racial, e, aux [Rasjal, -o] *a* racial.

racine [Rasin] *nf* root; (*fig: attache*) roots *pl*; **~ carrée/cubique** square/cube root; **prendre ~** (*fig*) to take root; to put down roots.

racisme [Rasism(ə)] *nm* racism, racialism.

raciste [Rasist(ə)] *a, nm/f* racist, racialist.

racket [Rakɛt] *nm* racketeering *q*.

racketteur [Raketœr] *nm* racketeer.

raclée [Rɑkle] *nf* (*fam*) hiding, thrashing.

raclement [Rɑkləmɑ̃] *nm* (*bruit*) scraping (noise).

racler [Rɑkle] *vt* (*os, plat*) to scrape; (*tache, boue*) to scrape off; (*fig: instrument*) to scrape on; (*suj: chose: frotter contre*) to scrape (against).

raclette [Rɑklɛt] *nf* (*CULIN*) raclette (*Swiss cheese dish*).

racloir [Rɑklwar] *nm* (*outil*) scraper.

racolage [Rakolaʒ] *nm* soliciting; touting.

racoler [Rakole] *vt* (*attirer: suj: prostituée*) to solicit; (*: parti, marchand*) to tout for; (*attraper*) to pick up.

racoleur, euse [Rakolœr, -øz] *a* (*péj: publicité*) cheap and alluring ♦ *nm* (*péj: de clients etc*) tout ♦ *nf* streetwalker.

racontars [Rakɔ̃tar] *nmpl* stories, gossip *sg*.

raconter [Rakɔ̃te] *vt*: **~ (à qn)** (*décrire*) to relate (to sb), tell (sb) about; (*dire*) to tell (sb).

racorni, e [Rakɔrni] *a* hard(ened).

racornir [Rakɔrnir] *vt* to harden.

radar [Radar] *nm* radar; **système ~** radar system; **écran ~** radar screen.

rade [Rad] *nf* (*natural*) harbour; **en ~ de Toulon** in Toulon harbour; **rester en ~** (*fig*) to be left stranded.

radeau, x [Rado] *nm* raft; **~ de sauvetage** life raft.

radial, e, aux [Radjal, -o] *a* radial; **pneu à carcasse ~e** radial tyre.

radiant, e [Radjɑ̃, -ɑ̃t] *a* radiant.

radiateur [Radjatœr] *nm* radiator, heater; (*AUTO*) radiator; **~ électrique/à gaz** electric/gas heater *ou* fire.

radiation [Radjasjɔ̃] *nf* (*voir radier*) striking off *q*; (*PHYSIQUE*) radiation.

radical, e, aux [Radikal, -o] *a* radical ♦ *nm* (*LING*) stem; (*MATH*) root sign; (*POL*) radical.

radicalement [Radikalmɑ̃] *ad* radically, completely.

radicaliser [Radikalize] *vt* (*durcir: opinions etc*) to harden; **se ~** *vi* (*mouvement etc*) to become more radical.

radicalisme [Radikalism(ə)] *nm* (*POL*) radicalism.

radier [Radje] *vt* to strike off.

radiesthésie [Radjɛstezi] *nf* divination (by radiation).

radiesthésiste [Radjɛstezist(ə)] *nm/f* diviner.

radieux, euse [Radjø, -øz] *a* (*visage, personne*) radiant; (*journée, soleil*) brilliant, glorious.

radin, e [Radɛ̃, -in] *a* (*fam*) stingy.

radio [Radjo] *nf* radio; (*MÉD*) X-ray ♦ *nm* (*personne*) radio operator; **à la ~** on the radio; **avoir la ~** to have a radio; **passer à la ~** to be on the radio; **se faire faire une ~/une ~ des poumons** to have an X-ray/a chest X-ray.

radio... [Radjo] *préfixe* radio....

radioactif, ive [Radjoaktif, -iv] *a* radioactive.

radioactivité [Radjoaktivite] *nf* radioactivity.

radioamateur [Radjoamatœr] *nm* (radio) ham.

radiobalise [Radjobaliz] *nf* radio beacon.

radiocassette [Radjokasɛt] *nf* cassette radio.

radiodiffuser [Radjodifyze] *vt* to broadcast.

radiodiffusion [Radjodifyzjɔ̃] *nf* (radio) broadcasting.

radioélectrique [Radjoelɛktrik] *a* radio *cpd*.

radiogoniomètre [Radjogonjomɛtr(ə)] *nm* direction finder, radiogoniometer.

radiographie [Radjografi] *nf* radiography; (*photo*) X-ray photograph, radiograph.

radiographier [Radjografje] *vt* to X-ray; **se faire ~** to have an X-ray.

radioguidage [Radjogidaʒ] *nm* (*NAVIG, AVIAT*) radio control; (*AUTO*) (broadcast of) traffic information.

radioguider [Radjogide] *vt* (*NAVIG, AVIAT*) to guide by radio, control by radio.

radiologie [Radjoloʒi] *nf* radiology.

radiologique [Radjoloʒik] *a* radiological.

radiologue [Radjolog] *nm/f* radiologist.

radionavigant [Radjonavigɑ̃] *nm* radio officer.

radiophare [Radjofar] *nm* radio beacon.

radiophonique [Radjofonik] *a*: **programme/ émission/jeu ~** radio programme/broadcast/ game.

radioreportage [Radjorəportaʒ] *nm* radio report.

radio(-)réveil [Radjorevɛj] *nm* clock radio.

radioscopie [Radjoskopi] *nf* radioscopy.

radio-taxi [Radjotaksi] *nm* radiotaxi.

radiotélégraphie [Radjotelegrafi] *nf* radiotelegraphy.

radiotéléphone [Radjotelefon] *nm* radiotelephone.

radiotélescope [Radjɔteleskɔp] *nm* radiotele-scope.

radiotélévisé, e [Radjɔtelevize] *a* broadcast on radio and television.

radiothérapie [RadjɔteRapi] *nf* radiotherapy.

radis [Radi] *nm* radish; ~ **noir** horseradish *q*.

radium [Radjɔm] *nm* radium.

radoter [Radɔte] *vi* to ramble on.

radoub [Radu] *nm*: **bassin** *ou* **cale de** ~ dry dock.

radouber [Radube] *vt* to repair, refit.

radoucir [Radusir]: **se** ~ *vi* (*se réchauffer*) to become milder; (*se calmer*) to calm down; to soften.

radoucissement [Radusismɑ̃] *nm* milder period, better weather.

rafale [Rafal] *nf* (*vent*) gust (of wind); (*de balles, d'applaudissements*) burst; ~ **de mi-trailleuse** burst of machine-gun fire.

raffermir [RafɛRmiR] *vt*, **se** ~ *vi* (*tissus, muscle*) to firm up; (*fig*) to strengthen.

raffermissement [RafɛRmismɑ̃] *nm* (*fig*) strengthening.

raffinage [Rafinaʒ] *nm* refining.

raffiné, e [Rafine] *a* refined.

raffinement [Rafinmɑ̃] *nm* refinement.

raffiner [Rafine] *vt* to refine.

raffinerie [RafinRi] *nf* refinery.

raffoler [Rafɔle]: ~ **de** *vt* to be very keen on.

raffut [Rafy] *nm* (*fam*) row, racket.

rafiot [Rafjo] *nm* tub.

rafistoler [Rafistɔle] *vt* (*fam*) to patch up.

rafle [Rafl(ə)] *nf* (*de police*) roundup, raid.

rafler [Rafle] *vt* (*fam*) to swipe, nick.

rafraîchir [RafReʃiR] *vt* (*atmosphère, température*) to cool (down); (*aussi*: **mettre à** ~) to chill; (*suj: air, eau*) to freshen up; (*: boisson*) to refresh; (*fig: rénover*) to brighten up ♦ *vi*: **mettre du vin/une boisson à** ~ to chill wine/a drink; **se** ~ to grow cooler; to freshen up (*personne: en buvant etc*) to re-fresh o.s.; ~ **la mémoire** *ou* **les idées à qn** to refresh sb's memory.

rafraîchissant, e [RafReʃisɑ̃, -ɑ̃t] *a* refreshing.

rafraîchissement [RafReʃismɑ̃] *nm* cooling; (*boisson*) cool drink; ~**s** *nmpl* (*boissons, fruits etc*) refreshments.

ragaillardir [RagajaRdiR] *vt* (*fam*) to perk *ou* buck up.

rage [Raʒ] *nf* (*MÉD*): **la** ~ rabies; (*fureur*) rage, fury; **faire** ~ to rage; ~ **de dents** (raging) toothache.

rager [Raʒe] *vi* to fume (with rage); **faire** ~ **qn** to enrage sb, get sb mad.

rageur, euse [RaʒœR, -øz] *a* snarling; ill-tempered.

raglan [Raglɑ̃] *a inv* raglan.

ragot [Rago] *nm* (*fam*) malicious gossip *q*.

ragoût [Ragu] *nm* (*plat*) stew.

ragoûtant, e [Ragutɑ̃, -ɑ̃t] *a*: **peu** ~ unpalat-able.

rai [Rɛ] *nm*: **un** ~ **de soleil/lumière** a shaft of sunshine/light.

raid [Rɛd] *nm* (*MIL*) raid; (*attaque aérienne*) air raid; (*SPORT*) long-distance trek.

raide [Rɛd] *a* (*tendu*) taut, tight; (*escarpé*) steep; (*droit: cheveux*) straight; (*ankylosé, dur, guindé*) stiff; (*fam: cher*) steep, stiff; (*: sans argent*) flat broke; (*osé, licencieux*) dar-ing ♦ *ad* (*en pente*) steeply; ~ **mort** stone dead.

raideur [RɛdœR] *nf* steepness; stiffness.

raidir [RɛdiR] *vt* (*muscles*) to stiffen; (*câble*) to pull taut, tighten; **se** ~ *vi* to stiffen; to become taut; (*personne: se crisper*) to tense up; (*: devenir intransigeant*) to harden.

raidissement [Rɛdismɑ̃] *nm* stiffening; tight-ening; hardening.

raie [Rɛ] *nf* (*ZOOL*) skate, ray; (*rayure*) stripe; (*des cheveux*) parting.

raifort [RɛfɔR] *nm* horseradish.

rail [Raj] *nm* (*barre d'acier*) rail; (*chemins de fer*) railways *pl* (*Brit*), railroads *pl* (*US*); **les** ~**s** (*la voie ferrée*) the rails, the track *sg*; **par** ~ by rail; ~ **conducteur** live *ou* con-ductor rail.

railler [Raje] *vt* to scoff at, jeer at.

raillerie [RajRi] *nf* mockery.

railleur, euse [RajœR, -øz] *a* mocking.

rail-route [Rajrut] *nm* road-rail.

rainurage [RenyRaʒ] *nm* (*AUTO*) uneven road surface.

rainure [RenyR] *nf* groove; slot.

rais [Rɛ] *nm inv* = **rai**.

raisin [Rɛzɛ̃] *nm* (*aussi*: ~**s**) grapes *pl*; (*va-riété*): ~ **blanc/noir** white (*ou* green)/black grape; ~ **muscat** muscat grape; ~**s secs** raisins.

raison [Rɛzɔ̃] *nf* reason; **avoir** ~ to be right; **donner** ~ **à qn** (*personne*) to agree with sb; (*fait*) to prove sb right; **avoir** ~ **de qn/qch** to get the better of sb/sth; **se faire une** ~ to learn to live with it; **perdre la** ~ to become insane; (*fig*) to take leave of one's senses; **recouvrer la** ~ to come to one's senses; **ramener qn à la** ~ to make sb see sense; **demander** ~ **à qn de** (*affront etc*) to demand satisfaction from sb for; **entendre** ~ to listen to reason, see reason; **plus que de** ~ too much, more than is reasonable; ~ **de plus** all the more reason; **à plus forte** ~ all the more so; **en** ~ **de** (*à cause de*) because of; (*à proportion de*) in proportion to; **à** ~ **de** at the rate of; ~ **d'État** reason of state; ~ **d'être** raison d'être; ~ **sociale** corporate name.

raisonnable [Rɛzɔnabl(ə)] *a* reasonable, sen-sible.

raisonnablement [Rɛzɔnabləmɑ̃] *ad* reason-ably.

raisonné, e [Rɛzɔne] *a* reasoned.

raisonnement [Rɛzɔnmɑ̃] *nm* reasoning; arguing; argument.

raisonner [Rɛzɔne] *vi* (*penser*) to reason; (*argumenter, discuter*) to argue ♦ *vt* (*personne*) to reason with; (*attitude: justifier*) to reason out; **se** ~ to reason with oneself.

raisonneur, euse [RɛzɔnœR, -øz] *a* (*péj*) quib-bling.

rajeunir [RaʒœniR] *vt* (*suj: coiffure, robe*): ~ **qn** to make sb look younger; (*suj: cure etc*) to rejuvenate; (*fig: rafraîchir*) to brighten up; (*: moderniser*) to give a new look to; (*: en recrutant*) to inject new blood into ♦ *vi* (*personne*) to become (*ou* look) younger; (*en-treprise, quartier*) to be modernized.

rajout [Raʒu] *nm* addition.

rajouter [ʀaʒute] vt (commentaire) to add; ~ du sel/un œuf to add some more salt/another egg; ~ que to add that; en ~ to lay it on thick.

rajustement [ʀaʒystəmɑ̃] nm adjustment.

rajuster [ʀaʒyste] vt (vêtement) to straighten, tidy; (salaires) to adjust; (machine) to readjust; **se ~** to tidy ou straighten o.s. up.

râle [ʀɑl] nm groan; ~ **d'agonie** death rattle.

ralenti [ʀalɑ̃ti] nm: **au ~** (AUTO): **tourner au ~** to tick over, idle; (CINÉMA) in slow motion; (fig) at a slower pace.

ralentir [ʀalɑ̃tiʀ] vt, vi, **se ~** vi to slow down.

ralentissement [ʀalɑ̃tismɑ̃] nm slowing down.

râler [ʀɑle] vi to groan; (fam) to grouse, moan (and groan).

ralliement [ʀalimɑ̃] nm (rassemblement) rallying; (adhésion: à une cause, une opinion) winning over; **point/signe de ~** rallying point/sign.

rallier [ʀalje] vt (rassembler) to rally; (rejoindre) to rejoin; (gagner à sa cause) to win over; **se ~ à** (avis) to come over ou round to.

rallonge [ʀalɔ̃ʒ] nf (de table) (extra) leaf (pl leaves); (argent etc) extra q; (ÉLEC) extension (cable ou flex); (fig: de crédit etc) extension.

rallonger [ʀalɔ̃ʒe] vt to lengthen.

rallumer [ʀalyme] vt to light up again, relight; (fig) to revive; **se ~** vi (lumière) to come on again.

rallye [ʀali] nm rally; (POL) march.

ramages [ʀamaʒ] nmpl (dessin) leaf pattern sg; (chants) songs.

ramassage [ʀamasaʒ] nm: ~ **scolaire** school bus service.

ramassé, e [ʀamase] a (trapu) squat, stocky; (concis: expression etc) compact.

ramasse-miettes [ʀamasmjɛt] nm inv tabletidy.

ramasse-monnaie [ʀamasmɔnɛ] nm inv change-tray.

ramasser [ʀamase] vt (objet tombé ou par terre, fam) to pick up; (recueillir) to collect; (récolter) to gather; (: pommes de terre) to lift; **se ~** vi (sur soi-même) to huddle up; to crouch.

ramasseur, euse [ʀamasœʀ, -øz] nm/f: ~ **de balles** ballboy/girl.

ramassis [ʀamasi] nm (péj: de gens) bunch; (: de choses) jumble.

rambarde [ʀɑ̃baʀd(ə)] nf guardrail.

rame [ʀam] nf (aviron) oar; (de métro) train; (de papier) ream; ~ **de haricots** bean support; **faire force de ~s** to row hard.

rameau, x [ʀamo] nm (small) branch; (fig) branch; **les R~x** (REL) Palm Sunday sg.

ramener [ʀamne] vt to bring back; (reconduire) to take back; (rabattre: couverture, visière): ~ **qch sur** to pull sth back over; ~ **qch à** (réduire à, aussi MATH) to reduce sth to; ~ **qn à la vie/raison** to bring sb back to life/bring sb to his (ou her) senses; **se ~** vi (fam) to roll ou turn up; **se ~ à** (se réduire à) to come ou boil down to.

ramequin [ʀamkɛ̃] nm ramekin.

ramer [ʀame] vi to row.

rameur, euse [ʀamœʀ, -øz] nm/f rower.

rameuter [ʀamøte] vt to gather together.

ramier [ʀamje] nm: **(pigeon) ~** woodpigeon.

ramification [ʀamifikasjɔ̃] nf ramification.

ramifier [ʀamifje]: **se ~** vi (tige, secte, réseau): **se ~ (en)** to branch out (into); (veines, nerfs) to ramify.

ramolli, e [ʀamɔli] a soft.

ramollir [ʀamɔliʀ] vt to soften; **se ~** vi (os, tissus) to get (ou go) soft; (beurre, asphalte) to soften.

ramonage [ʀamɔnaʒ] nm (chimney-)sweeping.

ramoner [ʀamɔne] vt (cheminée) to sweep; (pipe) to clean.

ramoneur [ʀamɔnœʀ] nm (chimney) sweep.

rampe [ʀɑ̃p] nf (d'escalier) banister(s pl); (dans un garage, d'un terrain) ramp; (THÉÂTRE): **la ~** the footlights pl; (lampes: lumineuse, de balisage) floodlights pl; **passer la ~** (toucher le public) to get across to the audience; ~ **de lancement** launching pad.

ramper [ʀɑ̃pe] vi (reptile, animal) to crawl; (plante) to creep.

rancard [ʀɑ̃kaʀ] nm (fam) date; tip.

rancart [ʀɑ̃kaʀ] nm: **mettre au ~** (article, projet) to scrap; (personne) to put on the scrapheap.

rance [ʀɑ̃s] a rancid.

rancir [ʀɑ̃siʀ] vi to go off, go rancid.

rancœur [ʀɑ̃kœʀ] nf rancour (Brit), rancor (US), resentment.

rançon [ʀɑ̃sɔ̃] nf ransom; (fig): **la ~ du succès** etc the price of success etc.

rançonner [ʀɑ̃sɔne] vt to hold to ransom.

rancune [ʀɑ̃kyn] nf grudge, rancour (Brit), rancor (US); **garder ~ à qn (de qch)** to bear sb a grudge (for sth); **sans ~!** no hard feelings!

rancunier, ière [ʀɑ̃kynje, -jɛʀ] a vindictive, spiteful.

randonnée [ʀɑ̃dɔne] nf ride; (à pied) walk, ramble; hike, hiking q.

randonneur, euse [ʀɑ̃dɔnœʀ, -øz] nm/f hiker.

rang [ʀɑ̃] nm (rangée) row; (de perles) row, string, rope; (grade, condition sociale, classement) rank; **~s** nmpl (MIL) ranks; **se mettre en ~s/sur un ~** to get into ou form rows/a line; **sur 3 ~s** (lined up) 3 deep; **se mettre en ~s par 4** to form fours ou rows of 4; **se mettre sur les ~s** (fig) to get into the running; **au premier ~** in the first row; (fig) ranking first; **rentrer dans le ~** to get into line; **au ~ de** (au nombre de) among (the ranks of); **avoir ~ de** to hold the rank of.

rangé, e [ʀɑ̃ʒe] a (sérieux) orderly, steady.

rangée [ʀɑ̃ʒe] nf row.

rangement [ʀɑ̃ʒmɑ̃] nm tidying-up, putting-away; **faire des ~s** to tidy up.

ranger [ʀɑ̃ʒe] vt (classer, grouper) to order, arrange; (mettre à sa place) to put away; (voiture dans la rue) to park; (mettre de l'ordre dans) to tidy up; (arranger, disposer: en cercle etc) to arrange; (fig: classer): ~ **qn/qch parmi** to rank sb/sth among; **se ~** vi (se placer, se disposer: autour d'une table etc) to take one's place, sit round; (véhicule, conducteur: s'écarter) to pull over; (: s'arrêter) to pull in; (piéton) to step aside; (s'assagir) to settle down; **se ~ à** (avis) to come round to, fall in with.

ranimer [ʀanime] vt (personne évanouie) to bring round; (revigorer: forces, courage) to restore; (réconforter: troupes etc) to kindle new life in; (douleur, souvenir) to revive; (feu) to rekindle.

rapace [ʀapas] nm bird of prey ♦ a (péj) rapacious, grasping; ~ **diurne/nocturne** diurnal/nocturnal bird of prey.

rapatrié, e [ʀapatʀije] nm/f repatriate (esp French North African settler).

rapatriement [ʀapatʀimã] nm repatriation.

rapatrier [ʀapatʀije] vt to repatriate; (capitaux) to bring (back) into the country.

râpe [ʀɑp] nf (CULIN) grater; (à bois) rasp.

râpé, e [ʀɑpe] a (tissu) threadbare; (CULIN) grated.

râper [ʀɑpe] vt (CULIN) to grate; (gratter, râcler) to rasp.

rapetasser [ʀaptase] vt (fam) to patch up.

rapetisser [ʀaptise] vt: ~ **qch** to shorten sth; to make sth look smaller ♦ vi, **se** ~ vi to shrink.

râpeux, euse [ʀɑpø, -øz] a rough.

raphia [ʀafja] nm raffia.

rapide [ʀapid] a fast; (prompt) quick; (intelligence) quick ♦ nm express (train); (de cours d'eau) rapid.

rapidement [ʀapidmã] ad fast; quickly.

rapidité [ʀapidite] nf speed; quickness.

rapiécer [ʀapjese] vt to patch.

rappel [ʀapɛl] nm (d'un ambassadeur, MIL) recall; (THÉÂTRE) curtain call; (MÉD: vaccination) booster; (ADMIN: de salaire) back pay q; (d'une aventure, d'un nom) reminder; (de limitation de vitesse: sur écriteau) speed limit sign (reminder); (TECH) return; (NAVIG) sitting out; (ALPINISME: aussi: ~ **de corde**) abseiling q, roping down q; abseil; ~ **à l'ordre** call to order.

rappeler [ʀaple] vt (pour faire revenir, retéléphoner) to call back; (ambassadeur, MIL, INFORM) to recall; (acteur) to call back (onto the stage); (faire se souvenir): ~ **qch à qn** to remind sb of sth; **se** ~ vt (se souvenir de) to remember, recall; ~ **qn à la vie** to bring sb back to life; ~ **qn à la décence** to recall sb to a sense of decency; **ça rappelle la Provence** it's reminiscent of Provence, it reminds you of Provence; **se** ~ **que...** to remember that....

rappelle [ʀapɛl] etc vb voir **rappeler**.

rappliquer [ʀaplike] vi (fam) to turn up.

rapport [ʀapɔʀ] nm (compte rendu) report; (profit) yield, return; revenue; (lien, analogie) relationship; (corrélation) connection; (proportion: MATH, TECH) ratio (pl -s); ~**s** nmpl (entre personnes, pays) relations; **avoir** ~ **à** to have something to do with, concern; **être en** ~ **avec** (idée de corrélation) to be related to; **être/se mettre en** ~ **avec qn** to be/get in touch with sb; **par** ~ **à** (comparé à) in relation to; (à propos de) with regard to; **sous le** ~ **de** from the point of view of; **sous tous (les)** ~**s** in all respects; ~**s (sexuels)** (sexual) intercourse sg; ~ **qualité-prix** value (for money).

rapporté, e [ʀapɔʀte] a: **pièce** ~**e** (COUTURE) patch.

rapporter [ʀapɔʀte] vt (rendre, ramener) to bring back; (apporter davantage) to bring more; (COUTURE) to sew on; (suj: investissement) to yield; (: activité) to bring in; (relater) to report; (JUR: annuler) to revoke ♦ vi (investissement) to give a good return ou yield; (activité) to be very profitable; (péj: moucharder) to tell; ~ **qch à** (fig: rattacher) to relate sth to; **se** ~ **à** (correspondre à) to relate to; **s'en** ~ **à** to rely on.

rapporteur, euse [ʀapɔʀtœʀ, -øz] nm/f (de procès, commission) reporter; (péj) telltale ♦ nm (GÉOM) protractor.

rapproché, e [ʀapʀɔʃe] a (proche) near, close at hand; ~**s** (l'un de l'autre) at close intervals.

rapprochement [ʀapʀɔʃmã] nm (réconciliation: de nations, familles) reconciliation; (analogie, rapport) parallel.

rapprocher [ʀapʀɔʃe] vt (chaise d'une table): ~ **qch (de)** to bring sth closer (to); (deux objets) to bring closer together; (réunir) to bring together; (comparer) to establish a parallel between; **se** ~ vi to draw closer ou nearer; (fig: familles, pays) to come together; to come closer together; **se** ~ **de** to come closer to; (présenter une analogie avec) to be close to.

rapt [ʀapt] nm abduction.

raquette [ʀakɛt] nf (de tennis) racket; (de ping-pong) bat; (à neige) snowshoe.

rare [ʀaʀ] a rare; (main-d'œuvre, denrées) scarce; (cheveux, herbe) sparse; **il est** ~ **que** it's rare that, it's unusual that; **se faire** ~ to become scarce; (fig: personne) to make oneself scarce.

raréfaction [ʀaʀefaksjɔ̃] nf scarcity; (de l'air) rarefaction.

raréfier [ʀaʀefje]: **se** ~ vi to grow scarce; (air) to rarefy.

rarement [ʀaʀmã] ad rarely, seldom.

rareté [ʀaʀte] nf (voir rare) rarity; scarcity.

rarissime [ʀaʀisim] a extremely rare.

RAS abr = **rien à signaler**.

ras, e [ʀɑ, ʀɑz] a (tête, cheveux) close-cropped; (poil, herbe) short; (mesure, cuillère) level ♦ ad short; **faire table** ~**e** to make a clean sweep; **en** ~**e campagne** in open country; **à** ~ **bords** to the brim; **au** ~ **de** level with; **en avoir** ~ **le bol** (fam) to be fed up; ~ **du cou** a (pull, robe) crew-neck.

rasade [ʀazad] nf glassful.

rascasse [ʀaskas] nf (ZOOL) scorpion fish.

rasé, e [ʀaze] a: ~ **de frais** freshly shaven; ~ **de près** close-shaven.

rase-mottes [ʀazmɔt] nm inv: **faire du** ~ to hedgehop; **vol en** ~ hedgehopping.

raser [ʀaze] vt (barbe, cheveux) to shave off; (menton, personne) to shave; (fam: ennuyer) to bore; (démolir) to raze (to the ground); (frôler) to graze, skim; **se** ~ to shave; (fam) to be bored (to tears).

rasoir [ʀazwaʀ] nm razor; ~ **électrique** electric shaver ou razor; ~ **mécanique** ou **de sûreté** safety razor.

rassasier [ʀasazje] vt to satisfy; **être rassasié** (dégoûté) to be sated; to have had more than enough.

rassemblement [ʀasɑ̃bləmã] nm (groupe)

gathering; (POL) union; association; (MIL):
le ~ parade.

rassembler [Rasãble] vt (réunir) to assemble,
gather; (regrouper, amasser) to gather
together, collect; **se** ~ vi to gather; ~ **ses
idées/ses esprits/son courage** to collect
one's thoughts/gather one's wits/screw up
one's courage.

rasseoir [RaswaR]: **se** ~ vi to sit down again.

rasséréner [RaseRene] vt: **se** ~ vi to recover
one's serenity.

rassir [RasiR] vi to go stale.

rassis, e [Rasi, -iz] a (pain) stale.

rassurant, e [Rasyrã, -ãt] a (nouvelles etc) reassuring.

rassuré, e [RasyRe] a: **ne pas être très** ~ to
be rather ill at ease.

rassurer [RasyRe] vt to reassure; **se** ~ to be
reassured; **rassure-toi** don't worry.

rat [Ra] nm rat; ~ **d'hôtel** hotel thief (pl
thieves); ~ **musqué** muskrat.

ratatiné, e [Ratatine] a shrivelled (up),
wrinkled.

ratatiner [Ratatine] vt to shrivel; (peau) to
wrinkle; **se** ~ vi to shrivel; to become
wrinkled.

ratatouille [Ratatuj] nf (CULIN) ratatouille.

rate [Rat] nf female rat; (ANAT) spleen.

raté, e [Rate] a (tentative) unsuccessful, failed
♦ nm/f failure ♦ nm misfiring q.

râteau, x [Rato] nm rake.

râtelier [Ratəlje] nm rack; (fam) false teeth
pl.

rater [Rate] vi (ne pas partir: coup de feu) to
fail to go off; (affaire, projet etc) to go
wrong, fail ♦ vt (cible, train, occasion) to
miss; (démonstration, plat) to spoil;
(examen) to fail; ~ **son coup** to fail, not to
bring it off.

raticide [Ratisid] nm rat poison.

ratification [Ratifikasjɔ̃] nf ratification.

ratifier [Ratifje] vt to ratify.

ratio [Rasjo] nm ratio (pl -s).

ration [Rasjɔ̃] nf ration; (fig) share; ~
alimentaire food intake.

rationalisation [Rasjɔnalizasjɔ̃] nf rationalization.

rationaliser [Rasjɔnalize] vt to rationalize.

rationnel, le [Rasjɔnɛl] a rational.

rationnellement [Rasjɔnɛlmã] ad rationally.

rationnement [Rasjɔnmã] nm rationing; **ticket de** ~ ration coupon.

rationner [Rasjɔne] vt to ration; (personne) to
put on rations; **se** ~ to ration o.s.

ratisser [Ratise] vt (allée) to rake; (feuilles) to
rake up; (suj: armée, police) to comb; ~
large to cast one's nets wide.

raton [Ratɔ̃] nm: ~ **laveur** raccoon.

RATP sigle f (= Régie autonome des
transports parisiens) Paris transport
authority.

rattacher [Ratafe] vt (animal, cheveux) to tie
up again; (incorporer: ADMIN etc): ~ **qch à**
to join sth to, unite sth with; (fig: relier): ~
qch à to link sth with, relate sth to; (: lier):
~ **qn à** to bind ou tie sb to; **se** ~ **à** (fig:
avoir un lien avec) to be linked (ou connected) with.

rattrapage [RatRapaʒ] nm (SCOL) remedial

classes pl; (ÉCON) catching up.

rattraper [RatRape] vt (fugitif) to recapture;
(retenir, empêcher de tomber) to catch (hold
of); (atteindre, rejoindre) to catch up with;
(réparer: imprudence, erreur) to make up
for; **se** ~ vi (regagner: du temps) to make
up for lost time; (: de l'argent etc) to make
good one's losses; (réparer une gaffe etc) to
make up for it; **se** ~ **(à)** (se raccrocher) to
stop o.s. falling (by catching hold of); ~ **son
retard/le temps perdu** to make up (for) lost
time.

rature [RatyR] nf deletion, erasure.

raturer [RatyRe] vt to cross out, delete, erase.

rauque [Rok] a raucous; hoarse.

ravagé, e [Ravaʒe] a (visage) harrowed.

ravager [Ravaʒe] vt to devastate, ravage.

ravages [Ravaʒ] nmpl ravages; **faire des** ~ to
wreak havoc; (fig: séducteur) to break
hearts.

ravalement [Ravalmã] nm restoration.

ravaler [Ravale] vt (mur, façade) to restore;
(déprécier) to lower; (avaler de nouveau) to
swallow again; ~ **sa colère/son dégoût** to
stifle one's anger/distaste.

ravaudage [Ravodaʒ] nm repairing, mending.

ravauder [Ravode] vt to repair, mend.

rave [Rav] nf (BOT) rape.

ravi, e [Ravi] a delighted; **être** ~ **de/que** to be
delighted with/that.

ravier [Ravje] nm hors d'œuvre dish.

ravigote [Ravigɔt] a: **sauce** ~ oil and vinegar
dressing with shallots.

ravigoter [Ravigɔte] vt (fam) to buck up.

ravin [Ravɛ̃] nm gully, ravine.

raviner [Ravine] vt to furrow, gully.

ravir [RaviR] vt (enchanter) to delight; (enlever): ~ **qch à qn** to rob sb of sth; **à** ~ ad
delightfully, beautifully; **être beau à** ~ to be
ravishingly beautiful.

raviser [Ravize]: **se** ~ vi to change one's mind.

ravissant, e [Ravisã, -ãt] a delightful.

ravissement [Ravismã] nm (enchantement,
délice) rapture.

ravisseur, euse [Ravisœr, -øz] nm/f abductor,
kidnapper.

ravitaillement [Ravitajmã] nm resupplying;
refuelling; (provisions) supplies pl; **aller au**
~ to go for fresh supplies; ~ **en vol** (AVIAT)
in-flight refuelling.

ravitailler [Ravitaje] vt to resupply; (véhicule)
to refuel; **se** ~ vi to get fresh supplies.

raviver [Ravive] vt (feu, douleur) to revive;
(couleurs) to brighten up.

ravoir [RavwaR] vt to get back.

rayé, e [Reje] a (à rayures) striped; (éraflé)
scratched.

rayer [Reje] vt (érafler) to scratch; (barrer) to
cross ou score out; (d'une liste: radier) to
cross ou strike off.

rayon [Rejɔ̃] nm (de soleil etc) ray; (GÉOM)
radius; (de roue) spoke; (étagère) shelf (pl
shelves); (de grand magasin) department; (de
ruche) (honey)comb; **dans un** ~ **de** within a
radius of; ~**s** nmpl (radiothérapie) radiation;
~ **d'action** range; ~ **de braquage** (AUTO)
turning circle; ~ **laser** laser beam; ~ **de
soleil** sunbeam, ray of sunshine; ~**s X** X-

rays.

rayonnage [ʀɛjɔnaʒ] *nm* set of shelves.

rayonnant, e [ʀɛjɔnɑ̃, -ɑ̃t] *a* radiant.

rayonne [ʀɛjɔn] *nf* rayon.

rayonnement [ʀɛjɔnmɑ̃] *nm* radiation; *(fig: éclat)* radiance; *(: influence)* influence.

rayonner [ʀɛjɔne] *vi (chaleur, énergie)* to radiate; *(fig: émotion)* to shine forth; *(: visage)* to be radiant; *(avenues, axes etc)* to radiate; *(touriste)* to go touring *(from one base)*.

rayure [ʀɛjyʀ] *nf (motif)* stripe; *(éraflure)* scratch; *(rainure, d'un fusil)* groove; **à ~s** striped.

raz-de-marée [ʀɑdmaʀe] *nm inv* tidal wave.

razzia [ʀazja] *nf* raid, foray.

RBE *sigle m (= revenu brut d'exploitation)* gross profit *(of a farm)*.

R-D *sigle f (= Recherche-Développement)* R & D.

RDA *sigle f (= République démocratique allemande)* GDR.

RDB *sigle m (STATISTIQUES: = revenu disponible brut)* total income *(of a family etc)*.

RdC. *abr* = **rez-de-chaussée.**

ré [ʀe] *nm (MUS)* D; *(en chantant la gamme)* re.

réabonnement [ʀeabɔnmɑ̃] *nm* renewal of subscription.

réabonner [ʀeabɔne] *vt*: **~ qn à** to renew sb's subscription to; **se ~ (à)** to renew one's subscription (to).

réac [ʀeak] *a, nm/f (fam: = réactionnaire)* reactionary.

réacteur [ʀeaktœʀ] *nm* jet engine; **~ nucléaire** nuclear reactor.

réactif [ʀeaktif] *nm* reagent.

réaction [ʀeaksjɔ̃] *nf* reaction; **par ~** jet-propelled; **avion/moteur à ~** jet (plane)/jet engine; **~ en chaîne** chain reaction.

réactionnaire [ʀeaksjɔnɛʀ] *a, nm/f* reactionary.

réadaptation [ʀeadaptasjɔ̃] *nf* readjustment, rehabilitation.

réadapter [ʀeadapte] *vt* to readjust; *(MÉD)* to rehabilitate; **se ~ (à)** to readjust (to).

réaffirmer [ʀeafiʀme] *vt* to reaffirm, reassert.

réagir [ʀeaʒiʀ] *vi* to react.

réajuster [ʀeaʒyste] *vt* = **rajuster.**

réalisable [ʀealizabl(ə)] *a (projet, plan)* feasible; *(COMM: valeur)* realizable.

réalisateur, trice [ʀealizatœʀ, -tʀis] *nm/f (TV, CINÉMA)* director.

réalisation [ʀealizasjɔ̃] *nf* carrying out; realization; fulfilment; achievement; production; *(œuvre)* production, work; *(création)* creation.

réaliser [ʀealize] *vt (projet, opération)* to carry out, realize; *(rêve, souhait)* to realize, fulfil; *(exploit)* to achieve; *(achat, vente)* to make; *(film)* to produce; *(se rendre compte de, COMM: bien, capital)* to realize; **se ~** *vi* to be realized.

réalisme [ʀealism(ə)] *nm* realism.

réaliste [ʀealist(ə)] *a* realistic; *(peintre, roman)* realist ♦ *nm/f* realist.

réalité [ʀealite] *nf* reality; **en ~** in (actual) fact; **dans la ~** in reality.

réanimation [ʀeanimasjɔ̃] *nf* resuscitation;

service de ~ intensive care unit.

réanimer [ʀeanime] *vt (MÉD)* to resuscitate.

réapparaître [ʀeapaʀɛtʀ(ə)] *vi* to reappear.

réapparition [ʀeapaʀisjɔ̃] *nf* reappearance.

réarmer [ʀeaʀme] *vt (arme)* to reload ♦ *vi (état)* to rearm.

réassortiment [ʀeasɔʀtimɑ̃] *nm (COMM)* restocking.

réassortir [ʀeasɔʀtiʀ] *vt* to match up.

réassurance [ʀeasyʀɑ̃s] *nf* reinsurance.

rébarbatif, ive [ʀebaʀbatif, -iv] *a* forbidding; *(style)* off-putting *(Brit)*, crabbed.

rebattre [ʀəbatʀ(ə)] *vt*: **~ les oreilles à qn de qch** to keep harping on to sb about sth.

rebattu, e [ʀəbaty] *pp de* **rebattre** ♦ *a* hackneyed.

rebelle [ʀəbɛl] *nm/f* rebel ♦ *a (troupes)* rebel; *(enfant)* rebellious; *(mèche etc)* unruly; **~ à qch** unamenable to sth; **~ à faire** unwilling to do.

rebeller [ʀəbele]: **se ~** *vi* to rebel.

rébellion [ʀebeljɔ̃] *nf* rebellion; *(rebelles)* rebel forces *pl*.

reboiser [ʀəbwaze] *vt* to replant with trees, reafforest.

rebond [ʀəbɔ̃] *nm (voir rebondir)* bounce; rebound.

rebondi, e [ʀəbɔ̃di] *a (ventre)* rounded; *(joues)* chubby, well-rounded.

rebondir [ʀəbɔ̃diʀ] *vi (ballon: au sol)* to bounce; *(: contre un mur)* to rebound; *(fig: procès, action, conversation)* to get moving again, be suddenly revived.

rebondissement [ʀəbɔ̃dismɑ̃] *nm* new development.

rebord [ʀəbɔʀ] *nm* edge.

reboucher [ʀəbuʃe] *vt (flacon)* to put the stopper *(ou* top) back on, recork; *(trou)* to stop up.

rebours [ʀəbuʀ]: **à ~** *ad* the wrong way.

rebouteux, euse [ʀəbutø, -øz] *nm/f (péj)* bonesetter.

reboutonner [ʀəbutɔne] *vt (vêtement)* to button up (again).

rebrousse-poil [ʀəbʀuspwal]: **à ~** *ad* the wrong way.

rebrousser [ʀəbʀuse] *vt (cheveux, poils)* to brush back, brush up; **~ chemin** to turn back.

rebuffade [ʀəbyfad] *nf* rebuff.

rébus [ʀebys] *nm inv (jeu d'esprit)* rebus; *(fig)* puzzle.

rebut [ʀəby] *nm*: **mettre au ~** to scrap, discard.

rebutant, e [ʀəbytɑ̃, -ɑ̃t] *a (travail, démarche)* off-putting, disagreeable.

rebuter [ʀəbyte] *vt* to put off.

récalcitrant, e [ʀekalsitʀɑ̃, -ɑ̃t] *a* refractory, recalcitrant.

recaler [ʀəkale] *vt (SCOL)* to fail.

récapitulatif, ive [ʀekapitylatif, -iv] *a (liste, tableau)* summary *cpd*, that sums up.

récapituler [ʀekapityle] *vt* to recapitulate; *(résumer)* to sum up.

recel [ʀəsɛl] *nm* receiving (stolen goods).

receler [ʀəsəle] *vt (produit d'un vol)* to receive; *(malfaiteur)* to harbour; *(fig)* to conceal.

receleur, euse [ʀəsəlœʀ, -øz] *nm/f* receiver.

récemment [ʀesamɑ̃] ad recently.

recensement [ʀəsɑ̃smɑ̃] nm census; inventory.

recenser [ʀəsɑ̃se] vt (population) to take a census of; (inventorier) to make an inventory of; (dénombrer) to list.

récent, e [ʀesɑ̃, -ɑ̃t] a recent.

recentrer [ʀəsɑ̃tʀe] vt (POL) to move towards the centre.

récépissé [ʀesepise] nm receipt.

récepteur, trice [ʀeseptœʀ, -tʀis] a receiving ♦ nm receiver; ~ **(de papier)** (INFORM) stacker; ~ **(de radio)** radio set ou receiver.

réceptif, ive [ʀeseptif, -iv] a: ~ **(à)** receptive (to).

réception [ʀesɛpsjɔ̃] nf receiving q; (d'une marchandise, commande) receipt; (accueil) reception, welcome; (bureau) reception (desk); (réunion mondaine) reception, party; (pièces) reception rooms pl; (SPORT: après un saut) landing; (du ballon) catching q; **jour/heures de** ~ day/hours for receiving visitors (ou students etc).

réceptionnaire [ʀesɛpsjɔnɛʀ] nm/f receiving clerk.

réceptionner [ʀesɛpsjɔne] vt (COMM) to take delivery of; (SPORT: ballon) to catch (and control).

réceptionniste [ʀesɛpsjɔnist(ə)] nm/f receptionist.

récession [ʀesesjɔ̃] nf recession.

recette [ʀəsɛt] nf (CULIN) recipe; (fig) formula, recipe; (COMM) takings pl; (bureau) tax ou revenue office; **~s** nfpl (COMM: rentrées) receipts; **faire** ~ (spectacle, exposition) to be a winner.

receveur, euse [ʀəsvœʀ, -øz] nm/f (des contributions) tax collector; (des postes) postmaster/mistress; (d'autobus) conductor/conductress; (MÉD: de sang, organe) recipient.

recevoir [ʀəsvwaʀ] vt to receive; (lettre, prime) to receive, get; (client, patient, représentant) to see; (jour, soleil: suj: pièce) to get; (SCOL: candidat) to pass ♦ vi to receive visitors; to give parties; to see patients etc; **se** ~ vi (athlète) to land; ~ **qn à dîner** to invite sb to dinner; **il reçoit de 8 à 10** he's at home from 8 to 10, he will see visitors from 8 to 10; (docteur, dentiste etc) he sees patients from 8 to 10; **être reçu** (à un examen) to pass; **être bien/mal reçu** to be well/badly received.

rechange [ʀəʃɑ̃ʒ]: **de** ~ a (pièces, roue) spare; (fig: solution) alternative; **des vêtements de** ~ a change of clothes.

rechaper [ʀəʃape] vt to remould (Brit), remold (US), retread.

réchapper [ʀeʃape]: ~ **de** ou **à** vt (accident, maladie) to come through; **va-t-il en** ~? is he going to get over it?, is he going to come through (it)?

recharge [ʀəʃaʀʒ(ə)] nf refill.

rechargeable [ʀəʃaʀʒabl(ə)] a refillable; rechargeable.

recharger [ʀəʃaʀʒe] vt (camion, fusil, appareil-photo) to reload; (briquet, stylo) to refill; (batterie) to recharge.

réchaud [ʀeʃo] nm (portable) stove; plate-warmer.

réchauffé [ʀeʃofe] nm (nourriture) reheated food; (fig) stale news (ou joke etc).

réchauffer [ʀeʃofe] vt (plat) to reheat; (mains, personne) to warm; **se** ~ vi to get warmer; **se** ~ **les doigts** to warm (up) one's fingers.

rêche [ʀɛʃ] a rough.

recherche [ʀəʃɛʀʃ(ə)] nf (action): **la** ~ **de** the search for; (raffinement) affectedness, studied elegance; (scientifique etc): **la** ~ research; **~s** nfpl (de la police) investigations; (scientifiques) research sg; **être/se mettre à la** ~ **de** to be/go in search of.

recherché, e [ʀəʃɛʀʃe] a (rare, demandé) much sought-after; (entouré: acteur, femme) in demand; (raffiné) studied, affected.

rechercher [ʀəʃɛʀʃe] vt (objet égaré, personne) to look for, search for; (témoins, coupable, main-d'œuvre) to look for; (causes d'un phénomène, nouveau procédé) to try to find; (bonheur etc, l'amitié de qn) to seek; **"~ et remplacer"** (INFORM) "search and replace".

rechigner [ʀəʃiɲe] vi: ~ **(à)** to balk (at).

rechute [ʀəʃyt] nf (MÉD) relapse; (dans le péché, le vice) lapse; **faire une** ~ to have a relapse.

rechuter [ʀəʃyte] vi (MÉD) to relapse.

récidive [ʀesidiv] nf (JUR) second (ou subsequent) offence; (fig) repetition; (MÉD) recurrence.

récidiver [ʀesidive] vi to commit a second (ou subsequent) offence; (fig) to do it again.

récidiviste [ʀesidivist(ə)] nm/f second (ou habitual) offender, recidivist.

récif [ʀesif] nm reef.

récipiendaire [ʀesipjɑ̃dɛʀ] nm recipient (of diploma etc); (d'une societé) newly elected member.

récipient [ʀesipjɑ̃] nm container.

réciproque [ʀesipʀɔk] a reciprocal ♦ nf: **la** ~ (l'inverse) the converse.

réciproquement [ʀesipʀɔkmɑ̃] ad reciprocally; **et** ~ and vice versa.

récit [ʀesi] nm (action de narrer) telling; (conte, histoire) story.

récital [ʀesital] nm recital.

récitant, e [ʀesitɑ̃, -ɑ̃t] nm/f narrator.

récitation [ʀesitasjɔ̃] nf recitation.

réciter [ʀesite] vt to recite.

réclamation [ʀeklamasjɔ̃] nf complaint; **~s** nfpl (bureau) complaints department sg.

réclame [ʀeklam] nf: **la** ~ advertising; **une** ~ an ad(vertisement), an advert (Brit); **faire de la** ~ **(pour qch/qn)** to advertise (sth/sb); **article en** ~ special offer.

réclamer [ʀeklame] vt (aide, nourriture etc) to ask for; (revendiquer: dû, part, indemnité) to claim, demand; (nécessiter) to demand, require ♦ vi to complain; **se** ~ **de** to give as one's authority; to claim filiation with.

reclassement [ʀəklasmɑ̃] nm reclassifying; regrading; rehabilitation.

reclasser [ʀəklase] vt (fiches, dossiers) to reclassify; (fig: fonctionnaire etc) to regrade; (: ouvrier licencié) to place, rehabilitate.

reclus, e [ʀəkly, -yz] nm/f recluse.

réclusion [ʀeklyzjɔ̃] nf imprisonment; ~ **à**

perpétuité life imprisonment.

recoiffer [Rəkwafe] vt: ~ **un enfant** to do a child's hair again; **se** ~ to do one's hair again.

recoin [Rəkwɛ̃] nm nook, corner; (fig) hidden recess.

reçois [Rəswa] etc vb voir **recevoir**.

reçoive [Rəswav] etc vb voir **recevoir**.

recoller [Rəkɔle] vt (enveloppe) to stick back down.

récolte [Rekɔlt(ə)] nf harvesting, gathering; (produits) harvest, crop; (fig) crop, collection; (: d'observations) findings.

récolter [Rekɔlte] vt to harvest, gather (in); (fig) to get.

recommandable [Rəkɔmɑ̃dabl(ə)] a commendable; **peu** ~ not very commendable.

recommandation [Rəkɔmɑ̃dasjɔ̃] nf recommendation.

recommandé [Rəkɔmɑ̃de] nm (méthode etc) recommended; (POSTES): **en** ~ by registered mail.

recommander [Rəkɔmɑ̃de] vt to recommend; (suj: qualités etc) to commend; (POSTES) to register; ~ **qch à qn** to recommend sth to sb; ~ **à qn de faire** to recommend sb to do; ~ **qn auprès de qn** ou **à qn** to recommend sb to sb; **il est recommandé de faire** ... it is recommended that one does ...; **se** ~ **à qn** to commend o.s. to sb; **se** ~ **de qn** to give sb's name as a reference.

recommencer [Rəkɔmɑ̃se] vt (reprendre: lutte, séance) to resume, start again; (refaire: travail, explications) to start afresh, start (over) again; (récidiver: erreur) to make again ♦ vi to start again; (récidiver) to do it again; ~ **à faire** to start doing again; **ne recommence pas!** don't do that again!

récompense [Rekɔ̃pɑ̃s] nf reward; (prix) award; **recevoir qch en** ~ to get sth as a reward, be rewarded with sth.

récompenser [Rekɔ̃pɑ̃se] vt: ~ **qn (de** ou **pour)** to reward sb (for).

réconciliation [Rekɔ̃siljasjɔ̃] nf reconciliation.

réconcilier [Rekɔ̃silje] vt to reconcile; ~ **qn avec qn** to reconcile sb with sb; ~ **qn avec qch** to reconcile sb to sth; **se** ~ **(avec)** to be reconciled (with).

reconductible [Rəkɔ̃dyktibl(ə)] a (JUR: contrat, bail) renewable.

reconduction [Rəkɔ̃dyksjɔ̃] nf renewal; (POL: d'une politique) continuation.

reconduire [Rəkɔ̃dɥiR] vt (raccompagner) to take ou see back; (: à la porte) to show out; (: à son domicile) to see home, take home; (JUR, POL: renouveler) to renew.

réconfort [Rekɔ̃fɔR] nm comfort.

réconfortant, e [Rekɔ̃fɔRtɑ̃, -ɑ̃t] a (idée, paroles) comforting; (boisson) fortifying.

réconforter [Rekɔ̃fɔRte] vt (consoler) to comfort; (revigorer) to fortify.

reconnais [Rək(ə)nɛ] etc vb voir **reconnaître**.

reconnaissable [Rəkɔnɛsabl(ə)] a recognizable.

reconnaissais [Rək(ə)nɛsɛ] etc vb voir **reconnaître**.

reconnaissance [Rəkɔnɛsɑ̃s] nf recognition; acknowledgement; (gratitude) gratitude,

gratefulness; (MIL) reconnaissance, recce; **en** ~ (MIL) on reconnaissance; ~ **de dette** acknowledgement of a debt, IOU.

reconnaissant, e [Rəkɔnɛsɑ̃, -ɑ̃t] vb voir **reconnaître** ♦ a grateful; **je vous serais** ~ **de bien vouloir** I should be most grateful if you would (kindly).

reconnaître [RəkɔnɛtR(ə)] vt to recognize; (MIL: lieu) to reconnoitre; (JUR: enfant, dette, droit) to acknowledge; ~ **que** to admit ou acknowledge that; ~ **qn/qch à** (l'identifier grâce à) to recognize sb/sth by; ~ **à qn: je lui reconnais certaines qualités** I recognize certain qualities in him; **se** ~ **quelque part** (s'y retrouver) to find one's way around (a place).

reconnu, e [R(ə)kɔny] pp de **reconnaître** ♦ a (indiscuté, connu) recognized.

reconquérir [Rəkɔ̃keRiR] vt (aussi fig) to reconquer, recapture; (sa dignité etc) to recover.

reconquête [Rəkɔ̃kɛt] nf recapture; recovery.

reconsidérer [Rəkɔ̃sidere] vt to reconsider.

reconstituant, e [Rəkɔ̃stitɥɑ̃, -ɑ̃t] a (régime) strength-building ♦ nm tonic, pick-me-up.

reconstituer [Rəkɔ̃stitɥe] vt (monument ancien) to recreate, build a replica of; (fresque, vase brisé) to piece together, reconstitute; (événement, accident) to reconstruct; (fortune, patrimoine) to rebuild; (BIO: tissus etc) to regenerate.

reconstitution [Rəkɔ̃stitysjɔ̃] nf (d'un accident etc) reconstruction.

reconstruction [Rəkɔ̃stRyksjɔ̃] nf rebuilding, reconstruction.

reconstruire [Rəkɔ̃stRɥiR] vt to rebuild, reconstruct.

reconversion [Rəkɔ̃vɛRsjɔ̃] nf (du personnel) redeployment.

reconvertir [Rəkɔ̃vɛRtiR] vt (usine) to reconvert; (personnel, troupes etc) to redeploy; **se** ~ **dans** (un métier, une branche) to move into, be redeployed into.

recopier [Rəkɔpje] vt (transcrire) to copy out again, write out again; (mettre au propre: devoir) to make a clean ou fair copy of.

record [RəkɔR] nm, a record; ~ **du monde** world record.

recoucher [Rəkuʃe] vt (enfant) to put back to bed.

recoudre [RəkudR(ə)] vt (bouton) to sew back on; (plaie, incision) to sew (back) up, stitch up.

recoupement [Rəkupmɑ̃] nm: **faire un** ~ ou **des** ~**s** to cross-check; **par** ~ by cross-checking.

recouper [Rəkupe] vt (tranche) to cut again; (vêtement) to recut ♦ vi (CARTES) to cut again; **se** ~ vi (témoignages) to tie ou match up.

recourais [RəkuRɛ] etc vb voir **recourir**.

recourbé, e [RəkuRbe] a curved; hooked; bent.

recourber [RəkuRbe] vt (branche, tige de métal) to bend.

recourir [RəkuRiR] vi (courir de nouveau) to run again; (refaire une course) to race again; ~ **à** vt (ami, agence) to turn ou appeal to; (force, ruse, emprunt) to resort to, have recourse to.

recours [ʀəkuʀ] *vb voir* **recourir** ♦ *nm* (*JUR*) appeal; **avoir ~ à** = **recourir à; en dernier ~** as a last resort; **sans ~** final; with no way out; **~ en grâce** plea for clemency (*ou* pardon).

recouru, e [ʀəkuʀy] *pp de* **recourir**.

recousu, e [ʀəkuzy] *pp de* **recoudre**.

recouvert, e [ʀəkuvɛʀ, -ɛʀt(ə)] *pp de* **recouvrir**.

recouvrable [ʀəkuvʀabl(ə)] *a* (*somme*) recoverable.

recouvrais [ʀəkuvʀɛ] *etc vb voir* **recouvrer**, **recouvrir**.

recouvrement [ʀəkuvʀəmɑ̃] *nm* recovery.

recouvrer [ʀəkuvʀe] *vt* (*vue, santé etc*) to recover, regain; (*impôts*) to collect; (*créance*) to recover.

recouvrir [ʀəkuvʀiʀ] *vt* (*couvrir à nouveau*) to re-cover; (*couvrir entièrement, aussi fig*) to cover; (*cacher, masquer*) to conceal, hide; **se ~** (*se superposer*) to overlap.

recracher [ʀəkʀaʃe] *vt* to spit out.

récréatif, ive [ʀekʀeatif, -iv] *a* of entertainment; recreational.

récréation [ʀekʀeɑsjɔ̃] *nf* recreation, entertainment; (*SCOL*) break.

recréer [ʀəkʀee] *vt* to recreate.

récrier [ʀekʀije]: **se ~** *vi* to exclaim.

récriminations [ʀekʀiminɑsjɔ̃] *nfpl* remonstrations, complaints.

récriminer [ʀekʀimine] *vi*: **~ contre qn/qch** to remonstrate against sb/sth.

recroqueviller [ʀəkʀɔkvije]: **se ~** *vi* (*feuilles*) to curl *ou* shrivel up; (*personne*) to huddle up.

recru, e [ʀəkʀy] *a*: **~ de fatigue** exhausted ♦ *nf* recruit.

recrudescence [ʀəkʀydesɑ̃s] *nf* fresh outbreak.

recrutement [ʀəkʀytmɑ̃] *nm* recruiting, recruitment.

recruter [ʀəkʀyte] *vt* to recruit.

rectal, e, aux [ʀɛktal, -o] *a*: **par voie ~e** rectally.

rectangle [ʀɛktɑ̃gl(ə)] *nm* rectangle; **~ blanc** (*TV*) "adults only" symbol.

rectangulaire [ʀɛktɑ̃gylɛʀ] *a* rectangular.

recteur [ʀɛktœʀ] *nm* ≈ (regional) director of education (*Brit*), ≈ state superintendent of education (*US*).

rectificatif, ive [ʀɛktifikatif, -iv] *a* corrected ♦ *nm* correction.

rectification [ʀɛktifikɑsjɔ̃] *nf* correction.

rectifier [ʀɛktifje] *vt* (*tracé, virage*) to straighten; (*calcul, adresse*) to correct; (*erreur, faute*) to rectify, put right.

rectiligne [ʀɛktiliɲ] *a* straight; (*GÉOM*) rectilinear.

rectitude [ʀɛktityd] *nf* rectitude, uprightness.

recto [ʀɛkto] *nm* front (*of a sheet of paper*).

reçu, e [ʀəsy] *pp de* **recevoir** ♦ *a* (*admis, consacré*) accepted ♦ *nm* (*COMM*) receipt.

recueil [ʀəkœj] *nm* collection.

recueillement [ʀəkœjmɑ̃] *nm* meditation, contemplation.

recueilli, e [ʀəkœji] *a* contemplative.

recueillir [ʀəkœjiʀ] *vt* to collect; (*voix, suffrages*) to win; (*accueillir: réfugiés, chat*) to

take in; **se ~** *vi* to gather one's thoughts; to meditate.

recuire [ʀəkɥiʀ] *vi*: **faire ~** to recook.

recul [ʀəkyl] *nm* retreat; recession; decline; (*d'arme à feu*) recoil, kick; **avoir un mouvement de ~** to recoil, start back; **prendre du ~** to stand back; **avec le ~** with the passing of time, in retrospect.

reculade [ʀəkylad] *nf* (*péj*) climb-down.

reculé, e [ʀəkyle] *a* remote.

reculer [ʀəkyle] *vi* to move back, back away; (*AUTO*) to reverse, back (up); (*fig: civilisation, épidémie*) to (be on the) decline; (: *se dérober*) to shrink back ♦ *vt* to move back; to reverse, back (up); (*fig: possibilités, limites*) to extend; (: *date, décision*) to postpone; **~ devant** (*danger, difficulté*) to shrink from; **~ pour mieux sauter** (*fig*) to postpone the evil day.

reculons [ʀəkylɔ̃]: **à ~** *ad* backwards.

récupérable [ʀekypeʀabl(ə)] *a* (*créance*) recoverable; (*heures*) which can be made up; (*ferraille*) salvageable.

récupération [ʀekypeʀɑsjɔ̃] *nf* (*de vieux métaux etc*) salvage, reprocessing; (*POL*) bringing into line.

récupérer [ʀekypeʀe] *vt* (*rentrer en possession de*) to recover, get back; (: *forces*) to recover; (*déchets etc*) to salvage (for reprocessing); (*remplacer: journée, heures de travail*) to make up; (*délinquant etc*) to rehabilitate; (*POL*) to bring into line ♦ *vi* to recover.

récurer [ʀekyʀe] *vt* to scour; **poudre à ~** scouring powder.

reçus [ʀəsy] *etc vb voir* **recevoir**.

récuser [ʀekyze] *vt* to challenge; **se ~** to decline to give an opinion.

recyclage [ʀəsiklaʒ] *nm* reorientation; retraining; recycling; **cours de ~** retraining course.

recycler [ʀəsikle] *vt* (*SCOL*) to reorientate; (*employés*) to retrain; (*matériau*) to recycle; **se ~** to retrain; to go on a retraining course.

rédacteur, trice [ʀedaktœʀ, -tʀis] *nm/f* (*journaliste*) writer; subeditor; (*d'ouvrage de référence*) editor, compiler; **~ en chef** chief editor; **~ publicitaire** copywriter.

rédaction [ʀedaksjɔ̃] *nf* writing; (*rédacteurs*) editorial staff; (*bureau*) editorial office(s); (*SCOL: devoir*) essay, composition.

reddition [ʀedisjɔ̃] *nf* surrender.

redéfinir [ʀədefiniʀ] *vt* to redefine.

redemander [ʀədmɑ̃de] *vt* (*renseignement*) to ask again for; (*nourriture*) to ask for more (*ou* another); (*objet prêté*): **~ qch** to ask for sth back.

redémarrer [ʀədemaʀe] *vi* (*véhicule*) to start again, get going again; (*fig: industrie etc*) to get going again.

rédemption [ʀedɑ̃psjɔ̃] *nf* redemption.

redéploiement [ʀədeplwamɑ̃] *nm* redeployment.

redescendre [ʀədesɑ̃dʀ(ə)] *vi* (*à nouveau*) to go back down; (*après la montée*) to go down (again) ♦ *vt* (*pente etc*) to go down.

redevable [ʀədvabl(ə)] *a*: **être ~ de qch à qn** (*somme*) to owe sb sth; (*fig*) to be indebted to sb for sth.

redevance [ʀədvɑ̃s] *nf* (*TÉL*) rental charge;

(*TV*) licence (*Brit*) *ou* license (*US*) fee.

redevenir [RədvəniR] *vi* to become again.

rediffuser [Rədifyze] *vt* (*RADIO*, *TV*) to repeat, broadcast again.

rediffusion [Rədifyzjɔ̃] *nf* repeat (programme).

rédiger [Rediʒe] *vt* to write; (*contrat*) to draw up.

redire [RədiR] *vt* to repeat; **trouver à ~ à** to find fault with.

redistribuer [RədistRibɥe] *vt* (*cartes etc*) to deal again; (*richesses, tâches, revenus*) to redistribute.

redite [Rədit] *nf* (needless) repetition.

redondance [Rədɔ̃dɑ̃s] *nf* redundancy.

redonner [Rədɔne] *vt* (*restituer*) to give back, return; (*du courage, des forces*) to restore.

redoublé, e [Rəduble] *a*: **à coups ~s** even harder, twice as hard.

redoubler [Rəduble] *vi* (*tempête, violence*) to intensify, get even stronger *ou* fiercer *etc*; (*SCOL*) to repeat a year ♦ *vt* (*SCOL*: *classe*) to repeat; (*LING*: *lettre*) to double; **~ de** *vt* to be twice as + *adjectif*; **le vent redouble de violence** the wind is blowing twice as hard.

redoutable [Rədutabl(ə)] *a* formidable, fearsome.

redouter [Rədute] *vt* to fear; (*appréhender*) to dread; **~ de faire** to dread doing.

redoux [Rədu] *nm* milder spell.

redressement [RədRɛsmɑ̃] *nm* (*de l'économie etc*) putting right; **maison de ~** reformatory; **~ fiscal** repayment of back taxes.

redresser [RədRese] *vt* (*arbre, mât*) to set upright, right; (*pièce tordue*) to straighten out; (*AVIAT*, *AUTO*) to straighten up; (*situation, économie*) to put right; **se ~** *vi* (*objet penché*) to right itself; to straighten up; (*personne*) to sit (*ou* stand) up; to sit (*ou* stand) up straight; (*fig: pays, situation*) to recover; **~ (les roues)** (*AUTO*) to straighten up.

redresseur [RədResœR] *nm*: **~ de torts** righter of wrongs.

réducteur, trice [RedyktœR, -tRis] *a* simplistic.

réduction [Redyksjɔ̃] *nf* reduction; **en ~** *ad* in miniature, scaled-down.

réduire [RedɥiR] *vt* (*gén, aussi CULIN, MATH*) to reduce; (*prix, dépenses*) to cut, reduce; (*carte*) to scale down, reduce; (*MÉD*: *fracture*) to set; **~ qn/qch à** to reduce sb/sth to; **se ~ à** (*revenir à*) to boil down to; **se ~ en** (*se transformer en*) to be reduced to; **en être réduit à** to be reduced to.

réduit, e [Redɥi, -it] *pp de* **réduire** ♦ *a* (*prix, tarif, échelle*) reduced; (*mécanisme*) scaled-down; (*vitesse*) reduced ♦ *nm* tiny room; recess.

rééchelonner [Reeʃlɔne] *vt* to reschedule.

rééditer [Reedite] *vt* to republish.

réédition [Reedisjɔ̃] *nf* new edition.

rééducation [Reedykasjɔ̃] *nf* (*d'un membre*) re-education; (*de délinquants, d'un blessé*) rehabilitation; **~ de la parole** speech therapy; **centre de ~** physiotherapy *ou* physical therapy (*US*) centre.

rééduquer [Reedyke] *vt* to reeducate; to re-

habilitate.

réel, le [Reɛl] *a* real ♦ *nm*: **le ~** reality.

réélection [Reelɛksjɔ̃] *nf* re-election.

réélire [ReeliR] *vt* to re-elect.

réellement [Reelmɑ̃] *ad* really.

réembaucher [Reɑ̃boʃe] *vt* to take on again.

réemploi [Reɑ̃plwa] *nm* = **remploi**.

réemployer [Reɑ̃plwaje] *vt* (*méthode, produit*) to re-use; (*argent*) to reinvest; (*personnel, employé*) to re-employ.

rééquilibrer [R‌ekilibRe] *vt* (*budget*) to balance (again).

réescompte [Reeskɔ̃t] *nm* rediscount.

réessayer [Reeseje] *vt* to try on again.

réévaluer [Reevalɥe] *vt* to revalue.

réexaminer [Reɛgzamine] *vt* to re-examine.

réexpédier [Reɛkspedje] *vt* (*à l'envoyeur*) to return, send back; (*au destinataire*) to send on, forward.

réexporter [RΥɛkspɔRte] *vt* to re-export.

réf. *abr* (= *référence(s)*): **V/~** Your ref.

refaire [RəfɛR] *vt* (*faire de nouveau, recommencer*) to do again; (*réparer, restaurer*) to do up; **se ~** *vi* (*en argent*) to make up one's losses; **se ~ une santé** to recuperate; **se ~ à qch** (*se réhabituer à*) to get used to sth again.

refasse [Rəfas] *etc vb voir* **refaire**.

réfection [Refɛksjɔ̃] *nf* repair; **en ~** under repair.

réfectoire [RefɛktwaR] *nm* refectory.

referai [R(ə)fRe] *etc vb voir* **refaire**.

référé [ReferΥ] *nm* (*JUR*) emergency interim proceedings *ou* ruling.

référence [ReferRɑ̃s] *nf* reference; **~s** *nfpl* (*recommandations*) reference *sg*; **faire ~ à** to refer to; **ouvrage de ~** reference work; **ce n'est pas une ~** (*fig*) that's no recommendation.

référendum [Referɑ̃dɔm] *nm* referendum.

référer [ReferΥ]: **se ~ à** *vt* to refer to; **en ~ à qn** to refer the matter to sb.

refermer [RəfɛRme] *vt* to close again, shut again.

refiler [Rəfile] *vt* (*fam*): **~ qch à qn** to palm (*Brit*) *ou* fob sth off on sb; to pass sth on to sb.

refit [Rəfi] *etc vb voir* **refaire**.

réfléchi, e [Refleʃi] *a* (*caractère*) thoughtful; (*action*) well-thought-out; (*LING*) reflexive.

réfléchir [RefleʃiR] *vt* to reflect ♦ *vi* to think; **~ à ou sur** to think about; **c'est tout réfléchi** my mind's made up.

réflecteur [ReflɛktœR] *nm* (*AUTO*) reflector.

reflet [Rəflɛ] *nm* reflection; (*sur l'eau etc*) sheen *q*, glint; **~s** *nmpl* gleam *sg*.

refléter [Rəflete] *vt* to reflect; **se ~** *vi* to be reflected.

réflex [Reflɛks] *a inv* (*PHOTO*) reflex.

réflexe [Reflɛks(ə)] *a*, *nm* reflex; **~ conditionné** conditioned reflex.

réflexion [Reflɛksjɔ̃] *nf* (*de la lumière etc, pensée*) reflection; (*fait de penser*) thought; (*remarque*) remark; **~s** *nfpl* (*méditations*) thought *sg*, reflection *sg*; **sans ~** without thinking; **~ faite, à la ~, après ~** on reflection; **délai de ~** cooling-off period; **groupe de ~** think tank.

refluer [Rəflɥe] *vi* to flow back; (*foule*) to

surge back.

reflux [Rəfly] *nm* (*de la mer*) ebb; (*fig*) backward surge.

refondre [Rəfɔ̃dʀ(ə)] *vt* (*texte*) to recast.

refont [R(ə)fɔ̃] *vb voir* **refaire**.

reformater [Rəfɔʀmate] *vt* to reformat.

réformateur, trice [Refɔʀmatœʀ, -tʀis] *nm/f* reformer ♦ *a* (*mesures*) reforming.

Réformation [Refɔʀmasjɔ̃] *nf*: **la ~** the Reformation.

réforme [Refɔʀm(ə)] *nf* reform; (*MIL*) declaration of unfitness for service; discharge (*on health grounds*); (*REL*): **la R~** the Reformation.

réformé, e [Refɔʀme] *a*, *nm/f* (*REL*) Protestant.

reformer [Rəfɔʀme] *vt*, **se ~** *vi* to reform; **~ les rangs** (*MIL*) to fall in again.

réformer [Refɔʀme] *vt* to reform; (*MIL*: *recrue*) to declare unfit for service; (: *soldat*) to discharge, invalid out; (*matériel*) to scrap.

réformisme [Refɔʀmism(ə)] *nm* reformism, policy of reform.

réformiste [Refɔʀmist(ə)] *a*, *nm/f* (*POL*) reformist.

refoulé, e [Rəfule] *a* (*PSYCH*) repressed.

refoulement [Rəfulmɑ̃] *nm* (*d'une armée*) driving back; (*PSYCH*) repression.

refouler [Rəfule] *vt* (*envahisseurs*) to drive back, repulse; (*liquide*) to force back; (*fig*) to suppress; (*PSYCH*) to repress.

réfractaire [Refʀaktɛʀ] *a* (*minerai*) refractory; (*brique*) fire *cpd*; (*maladie*) which is resistant to treatment; (*prêtre*) non-juring; **soldat ~** draft evader; **être ~ à** to resist.

réfracter [Refʀakte] *vt* to refract.

réfraction [Refʀaksjɔ̃] *nf* refraction.

refrain [Rəfʀɛ̃] *nm* (*MUS*) refrain, chorus; (*air, fig*) tune.

refréner, réfréner [Rəfʀene, Refʀene] *vt* to curb, check.

réfrigérant, e [Refʀiʒeʀɑ̃, -ɑ̃t] *a* a refrigerant, cooling.

réfrigérateur [Refʀiʒeʀatœʀ] *nm* refrigerator.

réfrigération [Refʀiʒeʀasjɔ̃] *nf* refrigeration.

réfrigérer [Refʀiʒeʀe] *vt* to refrigerate; (*fam*: *glacer, aussi fig*) to cool.

refroidir [Rəfʀwadiʀ] *vt* to cool; (*fig*) to have a cooling effect on ♦ *vi* to cool (down); **se ~** *vi* (*prendre froid*) to catch a chill; (*temps*) to get cooler *ou* colder; (*fig*) to cool (off).

refroidissement [Rəfʀwadismɑ̃] *nm* cooling; (*grippe etc*) chill.

refuge [Rəfyʒ] *nm* refuge; (*pour piétons*) (traffic) island; **demander ~ à qn** to ask sb for refuge.

réfugié, e [Refyʒje] *a*, *nm/f* refugee.

réfugier [Refyʒje]: **se ~** *vi* to take refuge.

refus [Rəfy] *nm* refusal; **ce n'est pas de ~** I won't say no, it's very welcome.

refuser [Rəfyze] *vt* to refuse; (*SCOL*: *candidat*) to fail ♦ *vi* to refuse; **~ qch à qn/de faire** to refuse sb sth/to do; **~ du monde** to have to turn people away; **se ~ à qch** *ou* **à faire qch** to refuse to do sth; **il ne se refuse rien** he doesn't stint himself; **se ~ à qn** to refuse sb.

réfuter [Refyte] *vt* to refute.

regagner [Rəgaɲe] *vt* (*argent, faveur*) to win back; (*lieu*) to get back to; **~ le temps**

perdu to make up (for) lost time; **~ du terrain** to regain ground.

regain [Rəgɛ̃] *nm* (*herbe*) second crop of hay; (*renouveau*): **un ~ de** renewed + *nom*.

régal [Regal] *nm* treat; **un ~ pour les yeux** a pleasure *ou* delight to look at.

régalade [Regalad] *ad*: **à la ~** from the bottle (held away from the lips).

régaler [Regale] *vt*: **~ qn** to treat sb to a delicious meal; **~ qn de** to treat sb to; **se ~** *vi* to have a delicious meal; (*fig*) to enjoy o.s.

regard [Rəgaʀ] *nm* (*coup d'œil*) look, glance; (*expression*) look (in one's eye); **parcourir/menacer du ~** to cast an eye over/look threateningly at; **au ~ de** (*loi, morale*) from the point of view of; **en ~** (*vis à vis*) opposite; **en ~ de** in comparison with.

regardant, e [Rəgaʀdɑ̃, -ɑ̃t] *a*: **très/peu ~ (sur)** quite fussy/very free (about); (*économe*) very tight-fisted/quite generous (with).

regarder [Rəgaʀde] *vt* (*examiner, observer, lire*) to look at; (*film, télévision, match*) to watch; (*envisager: situation, avenir*) to view; (*considérer: son intérêt etc*) to be concerned with; (*être orienté vers*): **~ (vers)** to face; (*concerner*) to concern ♦ *vi* to look; **~ à** *vt* (*dépense, qualité, détails*) to be fussy with *ou* over; **~ à faire** to hesitate to do; **dépenser sans ~** to spend freely; **~ qn/qch comme** to regard sb/sth as; **~ (qch) dans le dictionnaire/l'annuaire** to look (sth up) in the dictionary/directory; **~ par la fenêtre** to look out of the window; **cela me regarde** it concerns me, it's my business.

régate(s) [Regat] *nf(pl)* regatta.

régénérer [Reʒeneʀe] *vt* to regenerate; (*fig*) to revive.

régent [Reʒɑ̃] *nm* regent.

régenter [Reʒɑ̃te] *vt* to rule over; to dictate to.

régie [Reʒi] *nf* (*COMM, INDUSTRIE*) state-owned company; (*THÉÂTRE, CINÉMA*) production; (*RADIO, TV*) control room; **la ~ de l'État** state control.

regimber [Rəʒɛ̃be] *vi* to balk, jib.

régime [Reʒim] *nm* (*POL*) régime; (*ADMIN: carcéral, fiscal etc*) system; (*MÉD*) diet; (*GÉO*) régime; (*TECH*) (engine) speed; (*fig*) rate, pace; (*de bananes, dattes*) bunch; **se mettre au/suivre un ~** to go on/be on a diet; **~ sans sel** salt-free diet; **à bas/haut ~** (*AUTO*) at low/high revs; **à plein ~** flat out, at full speed; **~ matrimonial** marriage settlement.

régiment [Reʒimɑ̃] *nm* (*MIL*: unité) regiment; (*fig: fam*): **un ~ de** an army of; **un copain de ~** a pal from military service *ou* (one's) army days.

région [Reʒjɔ̃] *nf* region; **la ~ parisienne** the Paris area.

régional, e, aux [Reʒjɔnal, -o] *a* regional.

régionalisation [Reʒjɔnalizasjɔ̃] *nf* regionalization.

régionalisme [Reʒjɔnalism(ə)] *nm* regionalism.

régir [Reʒiʀ] *vt* to govern.

régisseur [Reʒisœʀ] *nm* (*d'un domaine*) steward; (*CINÉMA, TV*) assistant director;

(THÉÂTRE) stage manager.

registre [ʀɔʒistʀ(ə)] *nm (livre)* register; logbook; ledger; *(MUS, LING)* register; *(d'orgue)* stop; ~ **de comptabilité** ledger; ~ **de l'état civil** register of births, marriages and deaths.

réglable [ʀeglabl(ə)] *a (siège, flamme etc)* adjustable; *(achat)* payable.

réglage [ʀeglaʒ] *nm (d'une machine)* adjustment; *(d'un moteur)* tuning.

règle [ʀɛgl(ə)] *nf (instrument)* ruler; *(loi, prescription)* rule; ~**s** *nfpl (PHYSIOL)* period *sg*; **avoir pour ~ de** to make it a rule that *ou* to; **en ~** *(papiers d'identité)* in order; **être/ se mettre en ~** to be/put o.s. straight with the authorities; **en ~ générale** as a (general) rule; **être la ~** to be the rule; **être de ~** to be usual; ~ **à calcul** slide rule; ~ **de trois** *(MATH)* rule of three.

réglé, e [ʀegle] *a* a well-ordered; stable, steady; *(papier)* ruled; *(arrangé)* settled; *(femme)*: **bien ~e** whose periods are regular.

règlement [ʀegləmɑ̃] *nm* settling; *(paiement)* settlement; *(arrêté)* regulation; *(règles, statuts)* regulations *pl*, rules *pl*; ~ **à la commande** cash with order; ~ **de compte(s)** settling of scores; ~ **en espèces/par chèque** payment in cash/by cheque; ~ **intérieur** *(SCOL)* school rules *pl*; *(ADMIN)* by-laws *pl*; ~ **judiciaire** compulsory liquidation.

réglementaire [ʀegləmɑ̃tɛʀ] *a* conforming to the regulations; *(tenue, uniforme)* regulation *cpd*.

réglementation [ʀegləmɑ̃tɑsjɔ̃] *nf* regulation, control; *(règlements)* regulations *pl*.

réglementer [ʀegləmɑ̃te] *vt* to regulate, control.

régler [ʀegle] *vt (mécanisme, machine)* to regulate, adjust; *(moteur)* to tune; *(thermostat etc)* to set, adjust; *(emploi du temps etc)* to organize, plan; *(question, conflit, facture, dette)* to settle; *(fournisseur)* to settle up with, pay; *(papier)* to rule; ~ **qch sur** to model sth on; ~ **son compte à qn** to sort sb out, settle sb; ~ **un compte avec qn** to settle a score with sb.

réglisse [ʀeglis] *nf* liquorice; **bâton de ~** liquorice stick.

règne [ʀɛɲ] *nm (d'un roi etc, fig)* reign; *(BIO)*: **le ~ végétal/animal** the vegetable/ animal kingdom.

régner [ʀeɲe] *vi (roi)* to rule, reign; *(fig)* to reign.

regonfler [ʀ(ə)gɔ̃fle] *vt (ballon, pneu)* to re-inflate, blow up again.

regorger [ʀəgɔʀʒe] *vi* to overflow; ~ **de** to overflow with, be bursting with.

régresser [ʀegʀese] *vi (phénomène)* to decline; *(enfant, malade)* to regress.

régressif, ive [ʀegʀesif, -iv] *a* regressive.

régression [ʀegʀesjɔ̃] *nf* decline; regression; **être en ~** to be on the decline.

regret [ʀəgʀɛ] *nm* regret; **à ~** with regret; **avec ~** regretfully; **être au ~ de devoir/ne pas pouvoir faire** to regret to have to/that one is unable to do; **j'ai le ~ de vous informer que ...** I regret to inform you that ....

regrettable [ʀəgʀɛtabl(ə)] *a* regrettable.

regretter [ʀəgʀete] *vt* to regret; *(personne)* to miss; ~ **d'avoir fait** to regret doing; ~ **que** to regret that, be sorry that; **non, je regrette** no, I'm sorry.

regroupement [ʀ(ə)gʀupmɑ̃] *nm* grouping together; *(groupe)* group.

regrouper [ʀəgʀupe] *vt (grouper)* to group together; *(contenir)* to include, comprise; **se ~** *vi* to gather (together).

régulariser [ʀegylaʀize] *vt (fonctionnement, trafic)* to regulate; *(passeport, papiers)* to put in order; *(sa situation)* to straighten out, regularize.

régularité [ʀegylaʀite] *nf* regularity.

régulateur, trice [ʀegylatœʀ, -tʀis] *a* regulating ♦ *nm (TECH)*: ~ **de vitesse/de température** speed/temperature regulator.

régulation [ʀegylɑsjɔ̃] *nf (du trafic)* regulation; ~ **des naissances** birth control.

régulier, ière [ʀegylje, -jɛʀ] *a (gén)* regular; *(vitesse, qualité)* steady; *(répartition, pression, paysage)* even; *(TRANSPORTS: ligne, service)* scheduled, regular; *(légal, réglementaire)* lawful, in order; *(fam: correct)* straight, on the level.

régulièrement [ʀegyljɛʀmɑ̃] *ad* regularly; steadily; evenly; normally.

réhabiliter [ʀeabilite] *vt* to rehabilitate; *(fig)* to restore to favour *(Brit) ou* favor *(US)*.

réhabituer [ʀeabitɥe] *vt*: **se ~ à qch/à faire qch** to get used to sth again/to doing sth again.

rehausser [ʀəose] *vt* to heighten, raise; *(fig)* to set off, enhance.

réimporter [ʀeɛ̃pɔʀte] *vt* to reimport.

réimposer [ʀeɛ̃poze] *vt (FINANCE)* to re-impose; to tax again.

réimpression [ʀeɛ̃pʀesjɔ̃] *nf* reprinting; *(ouvrage)* reprint.

réimprimer [ʀeɛ̃pʀime] *vt* to reprint.

Reims [ʀis] *n* Rheims.

rein [ʀɛ̃] *nm* kidney; ~**s** *nmpl (dos)* back *sg*; **avoir mal aux ~s** to have backache; ~ **artificiel** kidney machine.

reine [ʀɛn] *nf* queen.

reine-claude [ʀɛnklod] *nf* greengage.

reinette [ʀɛnɛt] *nf* rennet, pippin.

réinitialisation [ʀeinisjalizɑsjɔ̃] *nf (INFORM)* reset.

réinsérer [ʀeɛ̃seʀe] *vt (délinquant, handicapé etc)* to rehabilitate.

réinsertion [ʀeɛ̃sɛʀsjɔ̃] *nf* rehabilitation.

réintégrer [ʀeɛ̃tegʀe] *vt (lieu)* to return to; *(fonctionnaire)* to reinstate.

réitérer [ʀeiteʀe] *vt* to repeat, reiterate.

rejaillir [ʀəʒajiʀ] *vi* to splash up; ~ **sur** to splash up onto; *(fig)* to rebound on; to fall upon.

rejet [ʀɔʒɛ] *nm (action, aussi MÉD)* rejection; *(POÉSIE)* enjambement, rejet; *(BOT)* shoot.

rejeter [ʀɔʒte] *vt (relancer)* to throw back; *(vomir)* to bring up *ou* throw up; *(écarter)* to reject; *(déverser)* to throw out, discharge; *(reporter)*: ~ **un mot à la fin d'une phrase** to transpose a word to the end of a sentence; **se ~ sur qch** *(accepter faute de mieux)* to fall back on sth; ~ **la tête/les épaules en arrière** to throw one's head/pull one's shoulders back; ~ **la responsabilité de qch sur qn** to lay the responsibility for sth at sb's door.

rejeton [ʀəʒtɔ̃] nm offspring.

rejette [ʀ(ə)ʒɛt] etc vb voir **rejeter**.

rejoignais [ʀ(ə)ʒwaɲɛ] etc vb voir **rejoindre**.

rejoindre [ʀɔʒwɛ̃dʀ(ə)] vt (famille, régiment) to rejoin, return to; (lieu) to get (back) to; (suj: route etc) to meet, join; (rattraper) to catch up (with); **se ~** vi to meet; **je te rejoins au café** I'll see ou meet you at the café.

réjoui, e [ʀeʒwi] a joyous.

réjouir [ʀeʒwiʀ] vt to delight; **se ~** vi to be delighted; **se ~ de qch/de faire** to be delighted about sth/to do; **se ~ que** to be delighted that.

réjouissances [ʀeʒwisɑ̃s] nfpl (joie) rejoicing sg; (fête) festivities, merry-making sg.

réjouissant, e [ʀeʒwisɑ̃, -ɑ̃t] a heartening, delightful.

relâche [ʀəlɑʃ]: **faire ~** vi (navire) to put into port; (CINÉMA) to be closed; **c'est le jour de ~** (CINÉMA) it's closed today; **sans ~** ad without respite ou a break.

relâché, e [ʀəlɑʃe] a loose, lax.

relâcher [ʀəlɑʃe] vt (ressort, prisonnier) to release; (étreinte, cordes) to loosen; (discipline) to relax ♦ vi (NAVIG) to put into port; **se ~** vi to loosen; (discipline) to become slack ou lax; (élève etc) to slacken off.

relais [ʀəlɛ] nm (SPORT): **(course de) ~** relay (race); (RADIO, TV) relay; (intermédiaire) go-between; **équipe de ~** shift team; (SPORT) relay team; **prendre le ~ (de)** to take over (from); **~ de poste** post house, coaching inn; **~ routier** ≈ transport café (Brit), ≈ truck stop (US).

relance [ʀəlɑ̃s] nf boosting, revival; (ÉCON) reflation.

relancer [ʀəlɑ̃se] vt (balle) to throw back (again); (moteur) to restart; (fig) to boost, revive; (personne): **~ qn** to pester sb; to get on to sb again.

relater [ʀəlate] vt to relate, recount.

relatif, ive [ʀəlatif, -iv] a relative.

relation [ʀəlasjɔ̃] nf (récit) account, report; (rapport) relation(ship); **~s** nfpl (rapports) relations; relationship; (connaissances) connections; **être/entrer en ~(s) avec** to be in contact ou be dealing/get in contact with; **mettre qn en ~(s) avec** to put sb in touch with; **~s internationales** international relations; **~s publiques (RP)** public relations (PR); **~s (sexuelles)** sexual relations, (sexual) intercourse sg.

relativement [ʀəlativmɑ̃] ad relatively; **~ à** in relation to.

relativiser [ʀəlativize] vt to see in relation to; to put into context.

relativité [ʀəlativite] nf relativity.

relax [ʀəlaks] a inv, **relaxe** [ʀəlaks(ə)] a relaxed, informal, casual; easy-going; **(fauteuil-)~** nm reclining chair.

relaxant, e [ʀəlaksɑ̃, -ɑ̃t] a (cure, médicament) relaxant; (ambiance) relaxing.

relaxation [ʀəlaksasjɔ̃] nf relaxation.

relaxer [ʀəlakse] vt to relax; (JUR) to discharge; **se ~** vi to relax.

relayer [ʀəleje] vt (collaborateur, coureur etc) to relieve, take over from; (RADIO, TV) to re-

lay; **se ~** (dans une activité) to take it in turns.

relecture [ʀ(ə)lɛktyʀ] nf rereading.

relégation [ʀəlegasjɔ̃] nf (SPORT) relegation.

reléguer [ʀəlege] vt to relegate; **~ au second plan** to push into the background.

relent(s) [ʀəlɑ̃] nm(pl) stench sg.

relevé, e [ʀəlve] a (bord de chapeau) turned-up; (manches) rolled-up; (fig: style) elevated; (: sauce) highly-seasoned ♦ nm (lecture) reading; (de cotes) plotting; (liste) statement; list; (facture) account; **~ de compte** bank statement; **~ d'identité bancaire (RIB)** (bank) account number.

relève [ʀəlɛv] nf relief; (équipe) relief team (ou troops pl); **prendre la ~** to take over.

relèvement [ʀəlɛvmɑ̃] nm (d'un taux, niveau) raising.

relever [ʀəlve] vt (statue, meuble) to stand up again; (personne tombée) to help up; (vitre, plafond, niveau de vie) to raise; (pays, économie, entreprise) to put back on its feet; (col) to turn up; (style, conversation) to elevate; (plat, sauce) to season; (sentinelle, équipe) to relieve; (souligner: fautes, points) to pick out; (constater: traces etc) to find, pick up; (répliquer à: remarque) to react to, reply to; (: défi) to accept, take up; (noter: adresse etc) to take down, note; (: plan) to sketch; (: cotes etc) to plot; (compteur) to read; (ramasser: cahiers, copies) to collect, take in ♦ vi (jupe, bord) to ride up; **~ de** vt (maladie) to be recovering from; (être du ressort de) to be a matter for; (ADMIN: dépendre de) to come under; (fig) to pertain to; **se ~** vi (se remettre debout) to get up; (fig): **se ~ (de)** to recover (from); **~ qn de** (vœux) to release sb from; (fonctions) to relieve sb of; **la tête** to look up; to hold up one's head.

relief [ʀəljɛf] nm relief; (de pneu) tread pattern; **~s** nmpl (restes) remains; **en ~** in relief; (photographie) three-dimensional; **mettre en ~** (fig) to bring out, highlight.

relier [ʀəlje] vt to link up; (livre) to bind; **~ qch à** to link sth to; **livre relié cuir** leather-bound book.

relieur, euse [ʀəljœʀ, -øz] nm/f (book)binder.

religieusement [ʀ(ə)liʒjøzmɑ̃] ad religiously; (enterré, mariés) in church; **vivre ~** to lead a religious life.

religieux, euse [ʀəliʒjø, -øz] a religious ♦ nm monk ♦ nf nun; (gâteau) cream bun.

religion [ʀəliʒjɔ̃] nf religion; (piété, dévotion) faith; **entrer en ~** to take one's vows.

reliquaire [ʀəlikɛʀ] nm reliquary.

reliquat [ʀəlika] nm (d'une somme) balance; (JUR: de succession) residue.

relique [ʀəlik] nf relic.

relire [ʀəliʀ] vt (à nouveau) to reread, read again; (vérifier) to read over; **se ~** to read through what one has written.

reliure [ʀəljyʀ] nf binding; (art, métier): **la ~** book-binding.

reloger [ʀ(ə)lɔʒe] vt (locataires, sinistrés) to rehouse.

relu, e [ʀəly] pp de **relire**.

reluire [ʀəlɥiʀ] vi to gleam.

reluisant, e [ʀəlɥizɑ̃, -ɑ̃t] vb voir **reluire** ♦ a

gleaming; **peu** ~ (*fig*) unattractive; unsavoury (*Brit*), unsavory (*US*).

reluquer [ʀ(ə)lyke] *vt* (*fam*) to eye (up), ogle.

remâcher [ʀəmɑʃe] *vt* to chew *ou* ruminate over.

remailler [ʀəmɑje] *vt* (*tricot*) to darn; (*filet*) to mend.

remaniement [ʀəmanimɑ̃] *nm*: ~ **ministériel** Cabinet reshuffle.

remanier [ʀəmanje] *vt* to reshape, recast; (*POL*) to reshuffle.

remarier [ʀ(ə)maʀje]: **se** ~ *vi* to remarry, get married again.

remarquable [ʀəmaʀkabl(ə)] *a* remarkable.

remarquablement [ʀ(ə)maʀkabləmɑ̃] *ad* remarkably.

remarque [ʀəmaʀk(ə)] *nf* remark; (*écrite*) note.

remarquer [ʀəmaʀke] *vt* (*voir*) to notice; (*dire*): ~ **que** to remark that; **se** ~ to be noticeable; **se faire** ~ to draw attention to o.s.; **faire** ~ **(à qn) que** to point out (to sb) that; **faire** ~ **qch (à qn)** to point sth out (to sb); **remarquez, ...** mark you, ..., mind you, ...

remballer [ʀɑ̃bale] *vt* to wrap up (again); (*dans un carton*) to pack up (again).

rembarrer [ʀɑ̃baʀe] *vt*: ~ **qn** (*repousser*) to rebuff sb; (*remettre à sa place*) to put sb in his (*ou* her) place.

remblai [ʀɑ̃ble] *nm* embankment.

remblayer [ʀɑ̃bleje] *vt* to bank up; (*fossé*) to fill in.

rembobiner [ʀɑ̃bɔbine] *vt* to rewind.

rembourrage [ʀɑ̃buʀaʒ] *nm* stuffing; padding.

rembourré, e [ʀɑ̃buʀe] *a* padded.

rembourrer [ʀɑ̃buʀe] *vt* to stuff; (*dossier, vêtement, souliers*) to pad.

remboursable [ʀɑ̃buʀsabl(ə)] *a* repayable.

remboursement [ʀɑ̃buʀsəmɑ̃] *nm* repayment; **envoi contre** ~ cash on delivery.

rembourser [ʀɑ̃buʀse] *vt* to pay back, repay.

rembrunir [ʀɑ̃bʀyniʀ]: **se** ~ *vi* to grow sombre (*Brit*) *ou* somber (*US*).

remède [ʀəmɛd] *nm* (*médicament*) medicine; (*traitement, fig*) remedy, cure; **trouver un** ~ **à** (*MÉD, fig*) to find a cure for.

remédier [ʀəmedje]: ~ **à** *vt* to remedy.

remembrement [ʀəmɑ̃bʀəmɑ̃] *nm* (*AGR*) regrouping of lands.

remémorer [ʀəmemɔʀe]: **se** ~ *vt* to recall, recollect.

remerciements [ʀəmɛʀsimɑ̃] *nmpl* thanks; **(avec) tous mes** ~ (with) grateful *ou* many thanks.

remercier [ʀəmɛʀsje] *vt* to thank; (*congédier*) to dismiss; ~ **qn de/d'avoir fait** to thank sb for/for having done; **non, je vous remercie** no thank you.

remettre [ʀəmɛtʀ(ə)] *vt* (*vêtement*): ~ **qch** to put sth back on, put sth on again; (*replacer*): ~ **qch quelque part** to put sth back somewhere; (*ajouter*): ~ **du sel/un sucre** to add more salt/another lump of sugar; (*rétablir: personne*): ~ **qn** to set sb back on his (*ou* her) feet; (*rendre, restituer*): ~ **qch à qn** to give sth back to sb, return sth to sb; (*donner, confier: paquet, argent*): ~ **qch à qn** to hand sth over to sb, deliver sth to sb; (*prix,*

décoration): ~ **qch à qn** to present sb with sth; (*ajourner*): ~ **qch (à)** to postpone sth *ou* put sth off (until); **se** ~ *vi* to get better, recover; **se** ~ **de** to recover from, get over; **s'en** ~ **à** to leave it (up) to; **se** ~ **à faire/qch** to start doing/sth again; ~ **une pendule à l'heure** to put a clock right; ~ **un moteur/une machine en marche** to get an engine/a machine going again; ~ **en état/en ordre** to repair/sort out; ~ **en cause/question** to challenge/question again; ~ **sa démission** to hand in one's notice; ~ **qch à neuf** to make sth as good as new; ~ **qn à sa place** (*fig*) to put sb in his (*ou* her) place.

remis, e [ʀəmi, -iz] *pp de* **remettre** ♦ *nf* delivery; presentation; (*rabais*) discount; (*local*) shed; ~ **en marche/en ordre** starting up again/sorting out; ~ **en cause/question** calling into question/challenging; ~ **de fonds** remittance; ~ **en jeu** (*FOOTBALL*) throw-in; ~ **à neuf** restoration; ~ **de peine** remission of sentence.

remiser [ʀəmize] *vt* to put away.

rémission [ʀemisjɔ̃]: **sans** ~ *a* irremediable ♦ *ad* unremittingly.

remodeler [ʀəmɔdle] *vt* to remodel; (*fig: restructurer*) to restructure.

rémois, e [ʀemwa, -waz] *a* of *ou* from Rheims ♦ *nm/f*: **R~, e** inhabitant *ou* native of Rheims.

remontant [ʀəmɔ̃tɑ̃] *nm* tonic, pick-me-up.

remontée [ʀəmɔ̃te] *nf* rising; ascent; ~**s mécaniques** (*SKI*) ski lifts, ski tows.

remonte-pente [ʀəmɔ̃tpɑ̃t] *nm* ski lift, (ski) tow.

remonter [ʀəmɔ̃te] *vi* (*à nouveau*) to go back up; (*sur un cheval*) to remount; (*après une descente*) to go up (again); (*dans une voiture*) to get back in; (*jupe*) to ride up ♦ *vt* (*pente*) to go up; (*fleuve*) to sail (*ou* swim *etc*) up; (*manches, pantalon*) to roll up; (*col*) to turn up; (*niveau, limite*) to raise; (*fig: personne*) to buck up; (*moteur, meuble*) to put back together, reassemble; (*garde-robe etc*) to renew, replenish; (*montre, mécanisme*) to wind up; ~ **le moral à qn** to raise sb's spirits; ~ **à** (*dater de*) to date *ou* go back to; ~ **en voiture** to get back into the car.

remontoir [ʀəmɔ̃twaʀ] *nm* winding mechanism, winder.

remontrance [ʀəmɔ̃tʀɑ̃s] *nf* reproof, reprimand.

remontrer [ʀəmɔ̃tʀe] *vt* (*montrer de nouveau*): ~ **qch (à qn)** to show sth again (to sb); (*fig*): **en** ~ **à** to prove one's superiority over.

remords [ʀəmɔʀ] *nm* remorse *q*; **avoir des** ~ to feel remorse, be conscience-stricken.

remorque [ʀəmɔʀk(ə)] *nf* trailer; **prendre/être en** ~ to tow/be on tow; **être à la** ~ (*fig*) to tag along (behind).

remorquer [ʀəmɔʀke] *vt* to tow.

remorqueur [ʀəmɔʀkœʀ] *nm* tug(boat).

rémoulade [ʀemulad] *nf* dressing with mustard and herbs.

rémouleur [ʀemulœʀ] *nm* (knife- *ou* scissor-) grinder.

remous [ʀəmu] *nm* (*d'un navire*) (back)wash

_q_; (_de rivière_) swirl, eddy ♦ _nmpl_ (_fig_) stir _sg_.

rempailler [Rɑ̃pɑje] _vt_ to reseat (_with straw_).

remparts [Rɑ̃paR] _nmpl_ walls, ramparts.

rempiler [Rɑ̃pile] _vt_ (_dossiers, livres etc_) to pile up again ♦ _vi_ (MIL: _fam_) to join up again.

remplaçant, e [Rɑ̃plasɑ̃, -ɑ̃t] _nm/f_ replacement, substitute, stand-in; (THÉÂTRE) understudy; (SCOL) supply (Brit) _ou_ substitute (US) teacher.

remplacement [Rɑ̃plasmɑ̃] _nm_ replacement; (_job_) replacement work _q_; (_suppléance_: SCOL) supply (Brit) _ou_ substitute (US) teacher; **assurer le ~ de qn** (_suj: remplaçant_) to stand in _ou_ substitute for sb; **faire des ~s** (_professeur_) to do supply _ou_ substitute teaching; (_médecin_) to do locum work.

remplacer [Rɑ̃plase] _vt_ to replace; (_prendre temporairement la place de_) to stand in for; (_tenir lieu de_) to take the place of, act as a substitute for; **~ qch/qn par** to replace sth/sb with.

rempli, e [Rɑ̃pli] _a_ (_emploi du temps_) full, busy; **~ de** full of, filled with.

remplir [Rɑ̃pliR] _vt_ to fill (up); (_questionnaire_) to fill out _ou_ up; (_obligations, fonction, condition_) to fulfill; **se ~** _vi_ to fill up; **~ qch de** to fill sth with.

remplissage [Rɑ̃plisaʒ] _nm_ (_fig: péj_) padding.

remploi [Rɑ̃plwa] _nm_ re-use.

rempocher [Rɑ̃pɔʃe] _vt_ to put back into one's pocket.

remporter [Rɑ̃pɔRte] _vt_ (_marchandise_) to take away; (_fig_) to win, achieve.

rempoter [Rɑ̃pɔte] _vt_ to repot.

remuant, e [Rəmɥɑ̃, -ɑ̃t] _a_ restless.

remue-ménage [Rəmymenaʒ] _nm inv_ commotion.

remuer [Rəmɥe] _vt_ to move; (_café, sauce_) to stir ♦ _vi_ to move; (_fig: opposants_) to show signs of unrest; **se ~** _vi_ to move; (_se démener_) to stir o.s.; (_fam_) to get a move on.

rémunérateur, trice [RemyneRatœR, -tRis] _a_ remunerative, lucrative.

rémunération [RemyneRɑsjɔ̃] _nf_ remuneration.

rémunérer [RemyneRe] _vt_ to remunerate, pay.

renâcler [Rənɑkle] _vi_ to snort; (_fig_) to grumble, balk.

renaissance [Rənɛsɑ̃s] _nf_ rebirth, revival; **la R~** the Renaissance.

renaître [RənɛtR(ə)] _vi_ to be revived; **~ à la vie** to take on a new lease of life; **~ à l'espoir** to find fresh hope.

rénal, e, aux [Renal, -o] _a_ renal, kidney _cpd_.

renard [RənaR] _nm_ fox.

renardeau [Rənardo] _nm_ fox cub.

rencard [Rɑ̃kaR] _nm_ = **rancard**.

rencart [Rɑ̃kaR] _nm_ = **rancart**.

renchérir [Rɑ̃ʃeRiR] _vi_ to become more expensive; (_fig_): **~ (sur)** to add something (to).

renchérissement [Rɑ̃ʃeRismɑ̃] _nm_ increase (in the cost _ou_ price of).

rencontre [Rɑ̃kɔ̃tR(ə)] _nf_ (_de cours d'eau_) confluence; (_véhicules_) collision; (_entrevue, congrès, match etc_) meeting; (_imprévue_) encounter; **faire la ~ de qn** to meet sb; **aller à**

la ~ de qn to go to and meet sb; **amours de ~** casual love affairs.

rencontrer [Rɑ̃kɔ̃tRe] _vt_ to meet; (_mot, expression_) to come across; (_difficultés_) to meet with; **se ~** to meet; (_véhicules_) to collide.

rendement [Rɑ̃dmɑ̃] _nm_ (_d'un travailleur, d'une machine_) output; (_d'une culture_) yield; (_d'un investissement_) return; **à plein ~** at full capacity.

rendez-vous [Rɑ̃devu] _nm_ (_rencontre_) appointment; (: _d'amoureux_) date; (_lieu_) meeting place; **donner ~ à qn** to arrange to meet sb; **recevoir sur ~** to have an appointment system; **fixer un ~ à qn** to give sb an appointment; **avoir/prendre ~ (avec)** to have/make an appointment (with); **prendre ~ chez le médecin** to make an appointment with the doctor; **~ spatial** _ou_ **orbital** docking (in space).

rendre [Rɑ̃dR(ə)] _vt_ (_livre, argent etc_) to give back, return; (_otages, visite, politesse_, JUR: _verdict_) to return; (_honneurs_) to pay; (_sang, aliments_) to bring up; (_sons: suj: instrument_) to produce, make; (_exprimer, traduire_) to render; (_jugement_) to pronounce, render; (_faire devenir_): **~ qn célèbre/qch possible** to make sb famous/sth possible; **se ~** _vi_ (_capituler_) to surrender, give o.s. up; (_aller_): **se ~ quelque part** to go somewhere; **se ~ à** (_arguments etc_) to bow to; (_ordres_) to comply with; **se ~ compte de qch** to realize sth; **~ la vue/la santé à qn** to restore sb's sight/health; **~ la liberté à qn** to set sb free; **~ la monnaie** to give change; **se ~ insupportable/malade** to become unbearable/make o.s. ill.

rendu, e [Rɑ̃dy] _pp de_ **rendre** ♦ _a_ (_fatigué_) exhausted.

renégat, e [Rənega, -at] _nm/f_ renegade.

renégocier [Rənegɔsje] _vt_ to renegociate.

rênes [Rɛn] _nfpl_ reins.

renfermé, e [Rɑ̃fɛRme] _a_ (_fig_) withdrawn ♦ _nm_: **sentir le ~** to smell stuffy.

renfermer [Rɑ̃fɛRme] _vt_ to contain; **se ~ (sur soi-même)** to withdraw into o.s.

renfiler [Rɑ̃file] _vt_ (_collier_) to rethread; (_pull_) to slip on.

renflé, e [Rɑ̃fle] _a_ bulging, bulbous.

renflement [Rɑ̃fləmɑ̃] _nm_ bulge.

renflouer [Rɑ̃flue] _vt_ to refloat; (_fig_) to set back on its ou his/her etc feet (again).

renfoncement [Rɑ̃fɔ̃smɑ̃] _nm_ recess.

renforcer [Rɑ̃fɔRse] _vt_ to reinforce; **~ qn dans ses opinions** to confirm sb's opinion.

renfort [Rɑ̃fɔR]: **~s** _nmpl_ reinforcements; **en ~** as a back-up; **à grand ~ de** with a great deal of.

renfrogné, e [Rɑ̃fRɔɲe] _a_ sullen, scowling.

renfrogner [Rɑ̃fRɔɲe]: **se ~** _vi_ to scowl.

rengager [Rɑ̃gaʒe] _vt_ (_personnel_) to take on again; **se ~** (MIL) to re-enlist.

rengaine [Rɑ̃gɛn] _nf_ (_péj_) old tune.

rengainer [Rɑ̃gɛne] _vt_ (_revolver_) to put back in its holster; (_épée_) to sheathe; (_fam: compliment, discours_) to save, withhold.

rengorger [Rɑ̃gɔRʒe]: **se ~** _vi_ (_fig_) to puff o.s. up.

renier [Rənje] _vt_ (_parents_) to disown, repudiate; (*engagements*) to go back on; (*foi*) to renounce.

renifler [ʀənifle] *vi* to sniff ♦ *vt* (*tabac*) to sniff up; (*odeur*) to sniff.

rennais, e [ʀɛnɛ, -ɛz] *a* of *ou* from Rennes ♦ *nm/f:* **R~, e** inhabitant *ou* native of Rennes.

renne [ʀɛn] *nm* reindeer *inv.*

renom [ʀənɔ̃] *nm* reputation; (*célébrité*) renown; **vin de grand ~** celebrated *ou* highly renowned wine.

renommé, e [ʀ(ə)nɔme] *a* celebrated, renowned ♦ *nf* fame.

renoncement [ʀənɔ̃smɑ̃] *nm* abnegation, renunciation.

renoncer [ʀənɔ̃se] *vi:* **~ à** *vt* to give up; **~ à faire** to give up the idea of doing; **j'y renonce!** I give up!

renouer [ʀənwe] *vt* (*cravate etc*) to retie; (*fig: conversation, liaison*) to renew, resume; **~ avec** (*tradition*) to revive; (*habitude*) to take up again; **~ avec qn** to take up with sb again.

renouveau, x [ʀənuvo] *nm* revival; **~ de succès** renewed success.

renouvelable [ʀ(ə)nuvlabl(ə)] *a* (*contrat, bail*) renewable; (*expérience*) which can be renewed.

renouveler [ʀənuvle] *vt* to renew; (*exploit, méfait*) to repeat; **se ~** *vi* (*incident*) to recur, happen again, be repeated; (*cellules etc*) to be renewed *ou* replaced; (*artiste, écrivain*) to try something new.

renouvellement [ʀ(ə)nuvɛlmɑ̃] *nm* renewal; recurrence.

rénovation [ʀenɔvasjɔ̃] *nf* renovation; restoration; reform(ing); redevelopment.

rénover [ʀenɔve] *vt* (*immeuble*) to renovate, do up; (*meuble*) to restore; (*enseignement*) to reform; (*quartier*) to redevelop.

renseignement [ʀɑ̃sɛɲmɑ̃] *nm* information *q*, piece of information; (*MIL*) intelligence *q*; **prendre des ~s sur** to make inquiries about, ask for information about; (**guichet des**) **~s** information desk; (**service des**) **~s** (*TÉL*) directory inquiries (*Brit*), information (*US*); **service/agent de ~s** (*MIL*) intelligence service/agent; **les ~s généraux** ≈ the secret police.

renseigner [ʀɑ̃seɲe] *vt:* **~ qn (sur)** to give information to sb (about); **se ~** *vi* to ask for information, make inquiries.

rentabiliser [ʀɑ̃tabilize] *vt* (*capitaux, production*) to make profitable.

rentabilité [ʀɑ̃tabilite] *nf* profitability; cost-effectiveness; (*d'un investissement*) return; **seuil de ~** break-even point.

rentable [ʀɑ̃tabl(ə)] *a* profitable; cost-effective.

rente [ʀɑ̃t] *nf* income; (*pension*) pension; (*titre*) government stock *ou* bond; **~ viagère** life annuity.

rentier, ière [ʀɑ̃tje, -jɛʀ] *nm/f* person of private *ou* independent means.

rentrée [ʀɑ̃tʀe] *nf:* **~ (d'argent)** cash *q* coming in; **la ~ (des classes)** the start of the new school year; **la ~ (parlementaire)** the reopening *ou* reassembly of parliament; **faire sa ~** (*artiste, acteur*) to make a comeback.

rentrer [ʀɑ̃tʀe] *vi* (*entrer de nouveau*) to go

(*ou* come) back in; (*entrer*) to go (*ou* come) in; (*revenir chez soi*) to go (*ou* come) (back) home; (*air, clou: pénétrer*) to go in; (*revenu, argent*) to come in ♦ *vt* (*foins*) to bring in; (*véhicule*) to put away; (*chemise dans pantalon etc*) to tuck in; (*griffes*) to draw in; (*train d'atterrissage*) to raise; (*fig: larmes, colère etc*) to hold back; **~ le ventre** to pull in one's stomach; **~ dans** to go (*ou* come) back into; to go (*ou* come) into; (*famille, patrie*) to go back *ou* return to; (*heurter*) to crash into; (*appartenir à*) to be included in; (*: catégorie etc*) to fall into; **~ dans l'ordre** to get back to normal; **~ dans ses frais** to recover one's expenses (*ou* initial outlay).

renverrai [ʀɑ̃vɛʀe] *etc vb voir* **renvoyer**.

renversant, e [ʀɑ̃vɛʀsɑ̃, -ɑ̃t] *a* amazing, astounding.

renverse [ʀɑ̃vɛʀs(ə)]: **à la ~** *ad* backwards.

renversé, e [ʀɑ̃vɛʀse] *a* (*écriture*) backhand; (*image*) reversed; (*stupéfait*) staggered.

renversement [ʀɑ̃vɛʀsəmɑ̃] *nm* (*d'un régime, des traditions*) overthrow; **~ de la situation** reversal of the situation.

renverser [ʀɑ̃vɛʀse] *vt* (*faire tomber: chaise, verre*) to knock over, overturn; (*piéton*) to knock down; (*liquide, contenu*) to spill, upset; (*retourner: verre, image*) to turn upside down, invert; (*: ordre des mots etc*) to reverse; (*fig: gouvernement etc*) to overthrow; (*stupéfier*) to bowl over, stagger; **se ~** *vi* to fall over; to overturn; to spill; **se ~ (en arrière)** to lean back; **~ la tête/le corps (en arrière)** to tip one's head back/throw oneself back; **~ la vapeur** (*fig*) to change course.

renvoi [ʀɑ̃vwa] *nm* dismissal; return; reflection; postponement; (*référence*) cross-reference; (*éructation*) belch.

renvoyer [ʀɑ̃vwaje] *vt* to send back; (*congédier*) to dismiss; (*TENNIS*) to return; (*lumière*) to reflect; (*son*) to echo; (*ajourner*): **~ qch (à)** to put sth off *ou* postpone sth (until); **~ qch à qn** (*rendre*) to return sth to sb; **~ qn à** (*fig*) to refer sb to.

réorganisation [ʀeɔʀganizasjɔ̃] *nf* reorganization.

réorganiser [ʀeɔʀganize] *vt* to reorganize.

réorienter [ʀeɔʀjɑ̃te] *vt* to reorient(ate), redirect.

réouverture [ʀeuvɛʀtyʀ] *nf* reopening.

repaire [ʀəpɛʀ] *nm* den.

repaître [ʀəpɛtʀ(ə)] *vt* to feast; to feed; **se ~ de** *vt* (*animal*) to feed on; (*fig*) to wallow *ou* revel in.

répandre [ʀepɑ̃dʀ(ə)] *vt* (*renverser*) to spill; (*étaler, diffuser*) to spread; (*lumière*) to shed; (*chaleur, odeur*) to give off; **se ~** *vi* to spill; to spread; **se ~ en** (*injures etc*) to pour out.

répandu, e [ʀepɑ̃dy] *pp de* **répandre** ♦ *a* (*opinion, usage*) widespread.

réparable [ʀeparabl(ə)] *a* (*montre etc*) repairable; (*perte etc*) which can be made up for.

reparaître [ʀəpaʀɛtʀ(ə)] *vi* to reappear.

réparateur, trice [ʀepaʀatœʀ, -tʀis] *nm/f* repairer.

réparation [ʀepaʀasjɔ̃] *nf* repairing *q*, repair; **en ~** (*machine etc*) under repair; **demander**

à qn ~ **de** (*offense etc*) to ask sb to make amends for.

réparer [ʀepaʀe] *vt* to repair; (*fig: offense*) to make up for, atone for; (*: oubli, erreur*) to put right.

reparler [ʀapaʀle] *vi:* ~ **de** qn/qch to talk about sb/sth again; ~ **à** qn to speak to sb again.

repars [ʀapaʀ] *etc vb voir* **repartir**.

repartie [ʀapaʀti] *nf* retort; **avoir de la** ~ to be quick at repartee.

repartir [ʀapaʀtiʀ] *vi* to set off again; to leave again; (*fig*) to get going again, pick up again; ~ **à zéro** to start from scratch (again).

répartir [ʀepaʀtiʀ] *vt* (*pour attribuer*) to share out; (*pour disperser, disposer*) to divide up; (*poids, chaleur*) to distribute; (*étaler: dans le temps*): ~ **sur** to spread over; (*classer, diviser*): ~ **en** to divide into, split up into; **se** ~ *vt* (*travail, rôles*) to share out between themselves.

répartition [ʀepaʀtisjɔ̃] *nf* sharing out; dividing up; distribution.

repas [ʀapɑ] *nm* meal; **à l'heure des** ~ at mealtimes.

repassage [ʀapɑsaʒ] *nm* ironing.

repasser [ʀapɑse] *vi* to come (*ou* go) back ♦ *vt* (*vêtement, tissu*) to iron; (*examen*) to retake, resit; (*film*) to show again; (*lame*) to sharpen; (*leçon, rôle: revoir*) to go over (again); (*plat, pain*): ~ qch à qn to pass sth back to sb.

repasseuse [ʀapɑsøz] *nf* (*machine*) ironing machine.

repayer [ʀapeje] *vt* to pay again.

repêchage [ʀapɛʃaʒ] *nm* (*SCOL*): **question de** ~ question to give candidates a second chance.

repêcher [ʀapeʃe] *vt* (*noyé*) to recover the body of, fish out; (*fam: candidat*) to pass (*by inflating marks*); to give a second chance to.

repeindre [ʀapɛ̃dʀ(ə)] *vt* to repaint.

repentir [ʀapɑ̃tiʀ] *nm* repentance; **se** ~ *vi:* **se** ~ (**de**) to repent (of).

répercussions [ʀepɛʀkysjɔ̃] *nfpl* repercussions.

répercuter [ʀepɛʀkyte] *vt* (*réfléchir, renvoyer: son, voix*) to reflect; (*faire transmettre: consignes, charges etc*) to pass on; **se** ~ *vi* (*bruit*) to reverberate; (*fig*): **se** ~ **sur** to have repercussions on.

repère [ʀapɛʀ] *nm* mark; (*monument etc*) landmark; (**point de**) ~ point of reference.

repérer [ʀapeʀe] *vt* (*erreur, connaissance*) to spot; (*abri, ennemi*) to locate; **se** ~ *vi* to get one's bearings; **se faire** ~ to be spotted.

répertoire [ʀepɛʀtwaʀ] *nm* (*liste*) (alphabetical) list; (*carnet*) index notebook; (*INFORM*) directory; (*de carnet*) thumb index; (*indicateur*) directory, index; (*d'un théâtre, artiste*) repertoire.

répertorier [ʀepɛʀtɔʀje] *vt* to itemize, list.

répéter [ʀepete] *vt* to repeat; (*préparer: leçon: aussi vi*) to learn, go over; (*THÉÂTRE*) to rehearse; **se** ~ (*redire*) to repeat o.s.; (*se reproduire*) to be repeated, recur.

répéteur [ʀepetœʀ] *nm* (*TÉL*) repeater.

répétitif, ive [ʀepetitif, -iv] *a* repetitive.

répétition [ʀepetisjɔ̃] *nf* repetition; (*THÉÂTRE*) rehearsal; ~**s** *nfpl* (*leçons*) private coaching *sg*; **armes à** ~ repeater weapons; ~ **générale** final dress rehearsal.

repeupler [ʀapœple] *vt* to repopulate; (*forêt, rivière*) to restock.

repiquage [ʀapikaʒ] *nm* pricking out, planting out; re-recording.

repiquer [ʀapike] *vt* (*plants*) to prick out, plant out; (*enregistrement*) to re-record.

répit [ʀepi] *nm* respite; **sans** ~ without letting up.

replacer [ʀaplase] *vt* to replace, put back.

replanter [ʀaplɑ̃te] *vt* to replant.

replat [ʀapla] *nm* ledge.

replâtrer [ʀaplɑtʀe] *vt* (*mur*) to replaster; (*fig*) to patch up.

replet, ète [ʀaplɛ, -ɛt] *a* chubby, fat.

repli [ʀapli] *nm* (*d'une étoffe*) fold; (*MIL, fig*) withdrawal.

replier [ʀaplije] *vt* (*rabattre*) to fold down *ou* over; **se** ~ *vi* (*troupes, armée*) to withdraw, fall back; **se** ~ **sur soi-même** to withdraw into oneself.

réplique [ʀeplik] *nf* (*repartie, fig*) reply; (*objection*) retort; (*THÉÂTRE*) line; (*copie*) replica; **donner la** ~ **à** to play opposite; **sans** ~ *a* no-nonsense; irrefutable.

répliquer [ʀeplike] *vi* to reply; (*avec impertinence*) to answer back; (*riposter*) to retaliate.

replonger [ʀaplɔ̃ʒe] *vt:* ~ qch **dans** to plunge sth back into; **se** ~ **dans** (*journal etc*) to immerse o.s. in again.

répondant, e [ʀepɔ̃dɑ̃, -ɑ̃t] *nm/f* (*garant*) guarantor, surety.

répondeur [ʀepɔ̃dœʀ] *nm:* ~ (**automatique**) (*TÉL*) (telephone) answering machine.

répondre [ʀepɔ̃dʀ(ə)] *vi* to answer, reply; (*freins, mécanisme*) to respond; ~ **à** *vt* to reply to, answer; (*avec impertinence*): ~ **à** qn to answer sb back; (*invitation, convocation*) to reply to; (*affection, salut*) to return; (*provocation, suj: mécanisme etc*) to respond to; (*correspondre à: besoin*) to answer; (*: conditions*) to meet; (*: description*) to match; ~ **que** to answer *ou* reply that; ~ **de** to answer for.

réponse [ʀepɔ̃s] *nf* answer, reply; **avec** ~ **payée** (*POSTES*) reply-paid, post-paid (*US*); **avoir** ~ **à tout** to have an answer for everything; **en** ~ **à** in reply to; **carte- /bulletin-**~ reply card/slip.

report [ʀapɔʀ] *nm* postponement; transfer; **d'incorporation** (*MIL*) deferment.

reportage [ʀapɔʀtaʒ] *nm* (*bref*) report; (*écrit: documentaire*) story; article; (*en direct*) commentary; (*genre, activité*): **le** ~ reporting.

reporter *nm* [ʀapɔʀtɛʀ] reporter ♦ *vt* [ʀapɔʀte] (*total*): ~ qch **sur** to carry sth forward *ou* over to; (*ajourner*): ~ qch (**à**) to postpone sth (until); (*transférer*): ~ qch **sur** to transfer sth to; **se** ~ **à** (*époque*) to think back to; (*document*) to refer to.

repos [ʀapo] *nm* rest; (*fig*) peace (and quiet); (*mental*) peace of mind; (*MIL*): ~**!** (stand) at ease!; **en** ~ at rest; **au** ~ at rest; (*soldat*) at ease; **de tout** ~ safe.

reposant, e [ʀ(ə)pozɑ̃, -ɑ̃t] *a* restful; (*sommeil*) refreshing.

repose [ʀəpoz] *nf* refitting.

reposé, e [ʀəpoze] *a* fresh, rested; **à tête ~e** in a leisurely way, taking time to think.

repose-pied [ʀəpozpje] *nm inv* footrest.

reposer [ʀəpoze] *vt* (*verre, livre*) to put down; (*rideaux, carreaux*) to put back; (*délasser*) to rest; (*problème*) to reformulate ♦ *vi* (*liquide, pâte*) to settle, rest; (*personne*): **ici repose ...** here lies ...; **~ sur** to be built on; (*fig*) to rest on; **se ~** *vi* to rest; **se ~ sur qn** to rely on sb.

repoussant, e [ʀəpusɑ̃, -ɑ̃t] *a* repulsive.

repoussé, e [ʀəpuse] *a* (*cuir*) embossed (by hand).

repousser [ʀəpuse] *vi* to grow again ♦ *vt* to repel, repulse; (*offre*) to turn down, reject; (*tiroir, personne*) to push back; (*différer*) to put back.

répréhensible [ʀepʀeɑ̃sibl(ə)] *a* reprehensible.

reprendre [ʀəpʀɑ̃dʀ(ə)] *vt* (*prisonnier, ville*) to recapture; (*objet prêté, donné*) to take back; (*chercher*): **je viendrai te ~ à 4h** I'll come and fetch you *ou* I'll come back for you at 4; (*se resservir de*): **~ du pain/un œuf** to take (*ou* eat) more bread/another egg; (*COMM*: *article usagé*) to take back; to take in part exchange; (*firme, entreprise*) to take over; (*travail, promenade*) to resume; (*emprunter: argument, idée*) to take up, use; (*refaire: article etc*) to go over again; (*jupe etc*) to alter; (*émission, pièce*) to put on again; (*réprimander*) to tell off; (*corriger*) to correct ♦ *vi* (*classes, pluie*) to start (up) again; (*activités, travaux, combats*) to resume, start (up) again; (*affaires, industrie*) to pick up; (*dire*): **reprit-il** he went on; **se ~** (*se ressaisir*) to recover, pull o.s. together; **s'y ~** to make another attempt; **~ des forces** to recover one's strength; **~ courage** to take new heart; **~ ses habitudes/sa liberté** to get back into one's old habits/regain one's freedom; **~ la route** to resume one's journey, set off again; **~ connaissance** to come to, regain consciousness; **~ haleine** *ou* **son souffle** to get one's breath back; **~ la parole** to speak again.

repreneur [ʀəpʀənœʀ] *nm* company fixer *ou* doctor.

reprenne [ʀəpʀɛn] *etc vb voir* **reprendre**.

représailles [ʀəpʀezaj] *nfpl* reprisals, retaliation *sg*.

représentant, e [ʀəpʀezɑ̃tɑ̃, -ɑ̃t] *nm/f* representative.

représentatif, ive [ʀəpʀezɑ̃tatif, -iv] *a* representative.

représentation [ʀəpʀezɑ̃tasjɔ̃] *nf* representation; performing; (*symbole, image*) representation; (*spectacle*) performance; (*COMM*): **la ~** commercial travelling; sales representation; **frais de ~** (*d'un diplomate*) entertainment allowance.

représenter [ʀəpʀezɑ̃te] *vt* to represent; (*donner: pièce, opéra*) to perform; **se ~** *vt* (*se figurer*) to imagine; to visualize ♦ *vi*: **se ~ à** (*POL*) to stand *ou* run again at; (*SCOL*) to resit.

répressif, ive [ʀepʀesif, -iv] *a* repressive.

répression [ʀepʀesjɔ̃] *nf* (*voir réprimer*) suppression; repression; (*POL*): **la ~** repression; **mesures de ~** repressive measures.

réprimande [ʀepʀimɑ̃d] *nf* reprimand, rebuke.

réprimander [ʀepʀimɑ̃de] *vt* to reprimand, rebuke.

réprimer [ʀepʀime] *vt* (*émotions*) to suppress; (*peuple etc*) repress.

repris, e [ʀəpʀi, -iz] *pp de* **reprendre** ♦ *nm*: **~ de justice** ex-prisoner, ex-convict.

reprise [ʀəpʀiz] *nf* (*recommencement*) resumption; (*économique*) recovery; (*TV*) repeat; (*CINÉMA*) rerun; (*BOXE etc*) round; (*AUTO*) acceleration *q*; (*COMM*) trade-in, part exchange; (*de location*) sum asked for any extras or improvements made to the property; (*raccommodage*) darn; mend; **la ~ des hostilités** the resumption of hostilities; **à plusieurs ~s** on several occasions, several times.

repriser [ʀəpʀize] *vt* to darn; to mend; **aiguille/coton à ~** darning needle/thread.

réprobateur, trice [ʀepʀɔbatœʀ, -tʀis] *a* reproving.

réprobation [ʀepʀɔbasjɔ̃] *nf* reprobation.

reproche [ʀəpʀɔʃ] *nm* (*remontrance*) reproach; **ton/air de ~** reproachful tone/look; **faire des ~s à qn** to reproach sb; **faire ~ à qn de qch** to reproach sb for sth; **sans ~(s)** beyond *ou* above reproach.

reprocher [ʀəpʀɔʃe] *vt*: **~ qch à qn** to reproach *ou* blame sb for sth; **~ qch à** (*machine, théorie*) to have sth against; **se ~ qch/d'avoir fait qch** to blame o.s. for sth/for doing sth.

reproducteur, trice [ʀəpʀɔdyktœʀ, -tʀis] *a* reproductive.

reproduction [ʀəpʀɔdyksjɔ̃] *nf* reproduction; **~ interdite** all rights (of reproduction) reserved.

reproduire [ʀəpʀɔdɥiʀ] *vt* to reproduce; **se ~** *vi* (*BIO*) to reproduce; (*recommencer*) to recur, re-occur.

réprouvé, e [ʀepʀuve] *nm/f* reprobate.

réprouver [ʀepʀuve] *vt* to reprove.

reptation [ʀɛptasjɔ̃] *nf* crawling.

reptile [ʀɛptil] *nm* reptile.

repu, e [ʀəpy] *pp de* **repaître** ♦ *a* satisfied, sated.

républicain, e [ʀepyblikɛ̃, -ɛn] *a*, *nm/f* republican.

république [ʀepyblik] *nf* republic; **R~ arabe du Yémen** Yemen Arab Republic; **R~ Centrafricaine** Central African Republic; **R~ de Corée** South Korea; **R~ démocratique allemande (RDA)** German Democratic Republic (GDR); **R~ dominicaine** Dominican Republic; **R~ fédérale d'Allemagne (RFA)** Federal Republic of Germany; **R~ d'Irlande** Irish Republic, Eire; **R~ populaire de Chine** People's Republic of China; **R~ populaire démocratique de Corée** Democratic People's Republic of Korea; **R~ populaire du Yémen** People's Democratic Republic of Yemen.

répudier [ʀepydje] *vt* (*femme*) to repudiate; (*doctrine*) to renounce.

répugnance [ʀepyɲɑ̃s] *nf* repugnance, loathing; **avoir** *ou* **éprouver de la ~ pour** (*médicament, comportement, travail etc*) to have an aversion to; **avoir** *ou* **éprouver de la ~ à faire qch** to be reluctant to do sth.

répugnant, e [Repyɲɑ̃, -ɑ̃t] *a* repulsive, loathsome.

répugner [Repyɲe]: **~ à** *vt*: **~ à qn** to repel *ou* disgust sb; **~ à faire** to be loath *ou* reluctant to do.

répulsion [Repylsjɔ̃] *nf* repulsion.

réputation [Repytɑsjɔ̃] *nf* reputation; **avoir la ~ d'être ...** to have a reputation for being ...; **connaître qn/qch de ~** to know sb/sth by repute; **de ~ mondiale** world-renowned.

réputé, e [Repyte] *a* renowned; **être ~ pour** to have a reputation for, be renowned for.

requérir [RəkeRiR] *vt* (*nécessiter*) to require, call for; (*au nom de la loi*) to call upon; (*JUR: peine*) to call for, demand.

requête [Rəkɛt] *nf* request, petition; (*JUR*) petition.

requiem [Rekɥijɛm] *nm* requiem.

requiers [RəkjɛR] *etc vb voir* **requérir**.

requin [Rəkɛ̃] *nm* shark.

requinquer [Rəkɛ̃ke] *vt* to set up, pep up.

requis, e [Rəki, -iz] *pp de* **requérir** ♦ *a* required.

réquisition [Rekizisjɔ̃] *nf* requisition.

réquisitionner [Rekizisjɔne] *vt* to requisition.

réquisitoire [RekizitwaR] *nm* (*JUR*) closing speech for the prosecution; (*fig*): **~ contre** indictment of.

RER *sigle m* (= *Réseau express régional*) Greater Paris high speed train service.

rescapé, e [Reskape] *nm/f* survivor.

rescousse [Reskus] *nf*: **aller à la ~ de qn** to go to sb's aid *ou* rescue; **appeler qn à la ~** to call on sb for help.

réseau, x [Rezo] *nm* network.

réséda [Rezeda] *nm* (*BOT*) reseda, mignonette.

réservation [RezeRvɑsjɔ̃] *nf* reservation; booking.

réserve [RezeRv(ə)] *nf* (*retenue*) reserve; (*entrepôt*) storeroom; (*restriction, aussi: d'Indiens*) reservation; (*de pêche, chasse*) preserve; (*restrictions*): **faire des ~s** to have reservations; **officier de ~** reserve officer; **sous toutes ~s** with all reserve; (*dire*) with reservations; **sous ~ de** subject to; **sans ~** *ad* unreservedly; **en ~** in reserve; **de ~** (*provisions etc*) in reserve.

réservé, e [RezeRve] *a* (*discret*) reserved; (*chasse, pêche*) private; **~ à** *ou* **pour** reserved for.

réserver [RezeRve] *vt* (*gén*) to reserve; (*chambre, billet etc*) to book, reserve; (*mettre de côté, garder*): **~ qch pour** *ou* **à** to keep *ou* save sth for; **~ qch à qn** to reserve (*ou* book) sth for sb; (*fig: destiner*) to have sth in store for sb; **se ~ le droit de faire** to reserve the right to do.

réserviste [RezeRvist(ə)] *nm* reservist.

réservoir [RezeRvwaR] *nm* tank.

résidence [Rezidɑ̃s] *nf* residence; **~ principale/secondaire** main/second home; **~ universitaire** hall of residence; **(en) ~ surveillée** (under) house arrest.

résident, e [Rezidɑ̃, -ɑ̃t] *nm/f* (*ressortissant*) foreign resident; (*d'un immeuble*) resident ♦ *a* (*INFORM*) resident.

résidentiel, le [Rezidɑ̃sjɛl] *a* residential.

résider [Rezide] *vi*: **~ à** *ou* **dans** *ou* **en** to reside in; **~ dans** (*fig*) to lie in.

résidu [Rezidy] *nm* residue *q*.

résiduel, le [Rezidɥɛl] *a* residual.

résignation [Reziɲɑsjɔ̃] *nf* resignation.

résigné, e [Reziɲe] *a* resigned.

résigner [Reziɲe] *vt* to relinquish, resign; **se ~** *vi*: **se ~ (à qch/à faire)** to resign o.s. (to sth/to doing).

résilier [Rezilje] *vt* to terminate.

résille [Rezij] *nf* (hair)net.

résine [Rezin] *nf* resin.

résiné, e [Rezine] *a*: **vin ~** retsina.

résineux, euse [Rezinø, -øz] *a* resinous ♦ *nm* coniferous tree.

résistance [Rezistɑ̃s] *nf* resistance; (*de réchaud, bouilloire: fil*) element.

résistant, e [Rezistɑ̃, -ɑ̃t] *a* (*personne*) robust, tough; (*matériau*) strong, hard-wearing ♦ *nm/f* (*patriote*) Resistance worker *ou* fighter.

résister [Reziste] *vi* to resist; **~ à** *vt* (*assaut, tentation*) to resist; (*effort, souffrance*) to withstand; (*suj: matériau, plante*) to stand up to, withstand; (*personne: désobéir à*) to stand up to, oppose.

résolu, e [Rezɔly] *pp de* **résoudre** ♦ *a* (*ferme*) resolute; **être ~ à qch/faire** to be set upon sth/doing.

résolution [Rezɔlysjɔ̃] *nf* solving; (*fermeté, décision, INFORM*) resolution; **prendre la ~ de** to make a resolution to.

résolvais [Rezɔlvɛ] *etc vb voir* **résoudre**.

résonance [Rezɔnɑ̃s] *nf* resonance.

résonner [Rezɔne] *vi* (*cloche, pas*) to reverberate, resound; (*salle*) to be resonant; **~ de** to resound with.

résorber [RezɔRbe]: **se ~** *vi* (*MÉD*) to be resorbed; (*fig*) to be absorbed.

résoudre [RezudR(ə)] *vt* to solve; **~ qn à faire qch** to get sb to make up his (*ou* her) mind to do sth; **~ de faire** to resolve to do; **se ~ à faire** to bring o.s. to do.

respect [Rɛspɛ] *nm* respect; **tenir en ~ to** keep at bay.

respectabilité [Rɛspɛktabilite] *nf* respectability.

respectable [Rɛspɛktabl(ə)] *a* respectable.

respecter [Rɛspɛkte] *vt* to respect; **faire ~ to** enforce; **le lexicographe qui se respecte** (*fig*) any self-respecting lexicographer.

respectif, ive [Rɛspɛktif, -iv] *a* respective.

respectivement [Rɛspɛktivmɑ̃] *ad* respectively.

respectueusement [Rɛspɛktɥøzmɑ̃] *ad* respectfully.

respectueux, euse [Rɛspɛktɥø, -øz] *a* respectful; **~ de** respectful of.

respirable [RɛspiRabl(ə)] *a*: **peu ~** unbreathable.

respiration [RɛspiRɑsjɔ̃] *nf* breathing *q*; **faire une ~ complète** to breathe in and out; **retenir sa ~** to hold one's breath; **~ artificielle** artificial respiration.

respiratoire [RɛspiRatwaR] *a* respiratory.

respirer [RɛspiRe] *vi* to breathe; (*fig: se reposer*) to get one's breath, have a break; (: *être soulagé*) to breathe again ♦ *vt* to breathe (in), inhale; (*manifester: santé, calme etc*) to exude.

resplendir [rɛsplɑ̃diʀ] *vi* to shine; *(fig)*: ~ **(de)** to be radiant (with).

resplendissant, e [rɛsplɑ̃disɑ̃, -ɑ̃t] *a* radiant.

responsabilité [rɛspɔ̃sabilite] *nf* responsibility; *(légale)* liability; **refuser la ~ de** to deny responsibility *(ou* liability) for; **prendre ses ~s** to assume responsibility for one's actions; ~ **civile** civil liability; ~ **pénale/ morale/collective** criminal/moral/collective responsibility.

responsable [rɛspɔ̃sabl(ə)] *a* responsible ♦ *nm/f (du ravitaillement etc)* person in charge; *(de parti, syndicat)* official; ~ **de** responsible for; *(légalement: de dégâts etc)* liable for; *(chargé de)* in charge of, responsible for.

resquiller [rɛskije] *vi (au cinéma, au stade)* to get in on the sly; *(dans le train)* to fiddle a free ride.

resquilleur, euse [rɛskijœʀ, -øz] *nm/f (qui n'est pas invité)* gatecrasher; *(qui ne paie pas)* fare dodger.

ressac [ʀəsak] *nm* backwash.

ressaisir [ʀəseziʀ]: **se** ~ *vi* to regain one's self-control; *(équipe sportive)* to rally.

ressasser [ʀəsase] *vt (remâcher)* to keep turning over; *(redire)* to keep trotting out.

ressemblance [ʀəsɑ̃blɑ̃s] *nf (visuelle)* resemblance, similarity, likeness; *(: ART)* likeness; *(analogie, trait commun)* similarity.

ressemblant, e [ʀəsɑ̃blɑ̃, -ɑ̃t] *a (portrait)* lifelike, true to life.

ressembler [ʀəsɑ̃ble]: ~ **à** *vt* to be like, resemble; *(visuellement)* to look like; **se** ~ to be *(ou* look) alike.

ressemeler [ʀəsəmle] *vt* to (re)sole.

ressens [ʀ(ə)sɑ̃] *etc vb voir* **ressentir.**

ressentiment [ʀəsɑ̃timɑ̃] *nm* resentment.

ressentir [ʀəsɑ̃tiʀ] *vt* to feel; **se** ~ **de** to feel *(ou* show) the effects of.

resserre [ʀəsɛʀ] *nf* shed.

resserrement [ʀ(ə)sɛʀmɑ̃] *nm* narrowing; strengthening; *(goulet)* narrow part.

resserrer [ʀəseʀe] *vt (pores)* to close; *(nœud, boulon)* to tighten (up); *(fig: liens)* to strengthen; **se** ~ *vi (route, vallée)* to narrow; *(liens)* to strengthen; **se** ~ **(autour de)** to draw closer (around); to close in (on).

ressers [ʀ(ə)sɛʀ] *etc vb voir* **resservir.**

resservir [ʀəseʀviʀ] *vi* to do *ou* serve again ♦ *vt*: ~ **qch (à qn)** to serve sth up again (to sb); ~ **de qch (à qn)** to give (sb) a second helping of sth; ~ **qn (d'un plat)** to give sb a second helping (of a dish); **se** ~ **de** *(plat)* to take a second helping of; *(outil etc)* to use again.

ressort [ʀəsɔʀ] *vb voir* **ressortir** ♦ *nm (pièce)* spring; *(force morale)* spirit; *(recours)*: **en dernier** ~ as a last resort; *(compétence)*: **être du** ~ **de** to fall within the competence of.

ressortir [ʀəsɔʀtiʀ] *vi* to go *(ou* come) out (again); *(contraster)* to stand out; ~ **de** *(résulter de)*: **il ressort de ceci que** it emerges from this that; ~ **à** *(JUR)* to come under the jurisdiction of; *(ADMIN)* to be the concern of; **faire** ~ *(fig: souligner)* to bring out.

ressortissant, e [ʀəsɔʀtisɑ̃, -ɑ̃t] *nm/f* national.

ressouder [ʀəsude] *vt* to solder together again.

ressource [ʀəsuʀs(ə)] *nf*: **avoir la** ~ **de** to have the possibility of; **~s** *nfpl* resources; *(fig)* possibilities; **leur seule** ~ **était de** the only course open to them was to; **~s d'énergie** energy resources.

ressusciter [ʀesysite] *vt* to resuscitate, restore to life; *(fig)* to revive, bring back ♦ *vi* to rise (from the dead); *(fig: pays)* to come back to life.

restant, e [ʀɛstɑ̃, -ɑ̃t] *a* remaining ♦ *nm*: **le** ~ **(de)** the remainder (of); **un** ~ **de** *(de trop)* some leftover; *(fig: vestige)* a remnant *ou* last trace of.

restaurant [ʀɛstɔʀɑ̃] *nm* restaurant; **manger au** ~ to eat out; ~ **d'entreprise** staff canteen *ou* cafeteria *(US)*; ~ **universitaire (RU)** university refectory *ou* cafeteria *(US)*.

restaurateur, trice [ʀɛstɔʀatœʀ, -tʀis] *nm/f* restaurant owner, restaurateur; *(de tableaux)* restorer.

restauration [ʀɛstɔʀɑsjɔ̃] *nf* restoration; *(hôtellerie)* catering; ~ **rapide** fast food.

restaurer [ʀɛstɔʀe] *vt* to restore; **se** ~ *vi* to have something to eat.

restauroute [ʀɛstɔʀut] *nm* = **restoroute**

reste [ʀɛst(ə)] *nm (restant)*: **le** ~ **(de)** the rest (of); *(de trop)*: **un** ~ **(de)** some leftover; *(vestige)*: **un** ~ **de** a remnant *ou* last trace of; *(MATH)* remainder; **~s** *nmpl* leftovers; *(d'une cité etc, dépouille mortelle)* remains; **avoir du temps de** ~ to have time to spare; **ne voulant pas être en** ~ not wishing to be outdone; **partir sans attendre** *ou* **demander son** ~ *(fig)* to leave without waiting to hear more; **du** ~, **au** ~ *ad* besides, moreover; **pour le reste, quant au** ~ *ad* as for the rest.

rester [ʀɛste] *vi (dans un lieu, un état, une position)* to stay, remain; *(subsister)* to remain, be left; *(durer)* to last, live on ♦ *vb impersonnel*: **il reste du pain/2 œufs** there's some bread/there are 2 eggs left (over); **il reste du temps/10 minutes** there's some time/there are 10 minutes left; **il me reste assez de temps** I have enough time left; **voilà tout ce qui (me) reste** that's all I've got left; **ce qui reste à faire** what remains to be done; **ce qui me reste à faire** what remains for me to do; **(il) reste à savoir/établir si** ... it remains to be seen/established if *ou* whether ...; **il n'en reste pas moins que** ... the fact remains that ..., it's nevertheless a fact that ...; **en** ~ **à** *(stade, menaces)* to go no further than, only go as far as; **restons-en là** let's leave it at that; ~ **sur une impression** to retain an impression; **y** ~: **il a failli y** ~ he nearly met his end.

restituer [ʀɛstitɥe] *vt (objet, somme)*: ~ **qch (à qn)** to return *ou* restore sth (to sb); *(énergie)* to release; *(son)* to reproduce.

restitution [ʀɛstitysjɔ̃] *nf* restoration.

restoroute [ʀɛstɔʀut] *nm* motorway *(Brit) ou* highway *(US)* restaurant.

restreindre [ʀɛstʀɛ̃dʀ(ə)] *vt* to restrict, limit; **se** ~ *(dans ses dépenses etc)* to cut down; *(champ de recherches)* to narrow.

restreint, e [ʀɛstʀɛ̃, -ɛ̃t] *pp de* **restreindre** ♦ *a* restricted, limited.

restrictif, ive [ʀɛstʀiktif, -iv] *a* restrictive, limiting.

restriction [ʀɛstʀiksjɔ̃] *nf* restriction; (*condition*) qualification; **~s** *nfpl* (*mentales*) reservations; **sans ~** *ad* unreservedly.

restructuration [ʀəstʀyktyʀɑsjɔ̃] *nf* restructuring.

restructurer [ʀəstʀyktyʀe] *vt* to restructure.

résultante [ʀezyltɑ̃t] *nf* (*conséquence*) result, consequence.

résultat [ʀezylta] *nm* result; (*conséquence*) outcome *q*, result; (*d'élection etc*) results *pl*; **~s** *nmpl* (*d'une enquête*) findings; **~s sportifs** sports results.

résulter [ʀezylte]: **~ de** *vt* to result from, be the result of; **il résulte de ceci que ...** the result of this is that ....

résumé [ʀezyme] *nm* summary, résumé; **faire le ~ de** to summarize; **en ~** *ad* in brief; (*pour conclure*) to sum up.

résumer [ʀezyme] *vt* (*texte*) to summarize; (*récapituler*) to sum up; (*fig*) to epitomize, typify; **se ~** *vi* (*personne*) to sum up (one's ideas); **se ~ à** to come down to.

resurgir [ʀəsyʀʒiʀ] *vi* to reappear, re-emerge.

résurrection [ʀezyʀɛksjɔ̃] *nf* resurrection; (*fig*) revival.

rétablir [ʀetabliʀ] *vt* to restore, re-establish; (*personne: suj: traitement*): **~ qn** to restore sb to health, help sb recover; (*ADMIN*): **~ qn dans son emploi/ses droits** to reinstate sb in his post/restore sb's rights; **se ~** *vi* (*guérir*) to recover; (*silence, calme*) to return, be restored; (*GYM etc*): **se ~ (sur)** to pull o.s. up (onto).

rétablissement [ʀetablismɑ̃] *nm* restoring; recovery; pull-up.

rétamer [ʀetame] *vt* to re-coat, re-tin.

rétameur [ʀetamœʀ] *nm* tinker.

retaper [ʀətape] *vt* (*maison, voiture etc*) to do up; (*fam: revigorer*) to buck up; (*redactylographier*) to retype.

retard [ʀətaʀ] *nm* (*d'une personne attendue*) lateness *q*; (*sur l'horaire, un programme, une échéance*) delay; (*fig: scolaire, mental etc*) backwardness; **être en ~** (*pays*) to be backward; (*dans paiement, travail*) to be behind; **en ~ de 2 heures** (2 hours) late; **avoir un ~ de 2 km** (*SPORT*) to be 2 km behind; **rattraper son ~** to catch up; **avoir du ~** to be late; (*sur un programme*) to be behind (schedule); **prendre du ~** (*train, avion*) to be delayed; (*montre*) to lose (time); **sans ~** *ad* without delay; **~ à l'allumage** (*AUTO*) retarded spark; **~ scolaire** backwardness at school.

retardataire [ʀətaʀdatɛʀ] *a* late; (*enfant, idées*) backward ♦ *nm/f* latecomer; backward child.

retardé, e [ʀətaʀde] *a* backward.

retardement [ʀətaʀdəmɑ̃]: **à ~** *a* delayed action *cpd*; **bombe à ~** time bomb.

retarder [ʀətaʀde] *vt* (*sur un horaire*): **~ qn (d'une heure)** to delay sb (an hour); (*sur un programme*): **~ qn (de 3 mois)** to set sb back (by three months); (*départ, date*): **~ qch (de 2 jours)** to put sth back (2 days), delay sth (for *ou* by 2 days); (*horloge*) to put back ♦ *vi* (*montre*) to be slow; (: *habituelle-*

ment) to lose (time); **je retarde (d'une heure)** I'm (an hour) slow.

retendre [ʀətɑ̃dʀ(ə)] *vt* (*câble etc*) to stretch again; (*MUS: cordes*) to retighten.

retenir [ʀətniʀ] *vt* (*garder, retarder*) to keep, detain; (*maintenir: objet qui glisse, fig: colère, larmes, rire*) to hold back; (: *objet suspendu*) to hold; (: *chaleur, odeur*) to retain; (*fig: empêcher d'agir*): **~ qn (de faire)** to hold sb back (from doing); (*se rappeler*) to retain; (*réserver*) to reserve; (*accepter*) to accept; (*prélever*): **~ qch (sur)** to deduct sth (from); **se ~** (*euphémisme*) to hold on; (*se raccrocher*): **se ~ à** to hold onto; (*se contenir*): **se ~ de faire** to restrain o.s. from doing; **~ son souffle** *ou* **haleine** to hold one's breath; **~ qn à dîner** to ask sb to stay for dinner; **je pose 3 et je retiens 2** put down 3 and carry 2.

rétention [ʀetɑ̃sjɔ̃] *nf*: **~ d'urine** urine retention.

retentir [ʀətɑ̃tiʀ] *vi* to ring out; (*salle*): **~ de** to ring *ou* resound with; **~ sur** *vt* (*fig*) to have an effect upon.

retentissant, e [ʀətɑ̃tisɑ̃, -ɑ̃t] *a* resounding; (*fig*) impact-making.

retentissement [ʀətɑ̃tismɑ̃] *nm* (*retombées*) repercussions *pl*; effect, impact.

retenu, e [ʀətny] *pp de* **retenir** ♦ *a* (*place*) reserved; (*personne: empêché*) held up; (*propos: contenu, discret*) restrained ♦ *nf* (*prélèvement*) deduction; (*MATH*) number to carry over; (*SCOL*) detention; (*modération*) (self-)restraint; (*réserve*) reserve, reticence; (*AUTO*) tailback.

réticence [ʀetisɑ̃s] *nf* reticence *q*, reluctance *q*; **sans ~** without hesitation.

réticent, e [ʀetisɑ̃, -ɑ̃t] *a* reticent, reluctant.

retiendrai [ʀətjɛ̃dʀe], **retiens** [ʀətjɛ̃] *etc vb voir* **retenir**.

rétif, ive [ʀetif, -iv] *a* restive.

rétine [ʀetin] *nf* retina.

retint [ʀətɛ̃] *etc vb voir* **retenir**.

retiré, e [ʀətiʀe] *a* (*solitaire*) secluded; (*éloigné*) remote.

retirer [ʀətiʀe] *vt* to withdraw; (*vêtement, lunettes*) to take off, remove; (*enlever*): **~ qch à qn** to take sth from sb; (*extraire*): **~ qn/qch de** to take sb away from/sth out of, remove sb/sth from; (*reprendre: bagages, billets*) to collect, pick up; **~ des avantages de** to derive advantages from; **se ~** *vi* (*partir, reculer*) to withdraw; (*prendre sa retraite*) to retire; **se ~ de** to withdraw from; to retire from.

retombées [ʀətɔ̃be] *nfpl* (*radioactives*) fallout *sg*; (*fig*) fallout; spin-offs.

retomber [ʀətɔ̃be] *vi* (*à nouveau*) to fall again; (*rechuter*): **~ malade/dans l'erreur** to fall ill again/fall back into error; (*atterrir: après un saut etc*) to land; (*tomber, redescendre*) to fall back; (*pendre*) to fall, hang (down); (*échoir*): **~ sur qn** to fall on sb.

retordre [ʀətɔʀdʀ(ə)] *vt*: **donner du fil à ~ à qn** to make life difficult for sb.

rétorquer [ʀetɔʀke] *vt*: **~ (à qn) que** to retort (to sb) that.

retors, e [ʀətɔʀ, -ɔʀs(ə)] *a* wily.

rétorsion [ʀetɔʀsjɔ̃] *nf*: **mesures de ~** reprisals.

retouche [ʀətuʃ] *nf* touching up *q*; alteration; **faire une ~** *ou* **des ~s à** to touch up.

retoucher [ʀətuʃe] *vt* (*photographie, tableau*) to touch up; (*texte, vêtement*) to alter.

retour [ʀətuʀ] *nm* return; **au ~** (*en arrivant*) when we (*ou they etc*) get (*ou got*) back; (*en route*) on the way back; **pendant le ~** on the way *ou* journey back; **à mon/ton ~** on my/ your return; **au ~ de** on the return of; **être de ~ (de)** to be back (from); **de ~ à .../chez moi** back at .../back home; **en ~** *ad* in return; **par ~ du courrier** by return of post; **par un juste ~ des choses** by a favourable twist of fate; **match ~** return match; **~ en arrière** (*CINÉMA*) flashback; (*mesure*) backward step; **~ de bâton** kickback; **~ de chariot** carriage return; **~ à l'envoyeur** (*POSTES*) return to sender; **~ de flamme** backfire; **~ (automatique) à la ligne** (*INFORM*) wordwrap; **~ de manivelle** (*fig*) backfire; **~ offensif** renewed attack; **~ aux sources** (*fig*) return to basics.

retournement [ʀətuʀnəmɑ̃] *nm* (*d'une personne: revirement*) turning (round); **~ de la situation** reversal of the situation.

retourner [ʀətuʀne] *vt* (*dans l'autre sens: matelas, crêpe*) to turn (over); (*: caisse*) to turn upside down; (*: sac, vêtement*) to turn inside out; (*fig: argument*) to turn back; (*en remuant: terre, sol, foin*) to turn over; (*émouvoir: personne*) to shake; (*renvoyer, restituer*) **~ qch à qn** to return sth to sb ♦ *vi* (*aller, revenir*): **~ quelque part/à** to go back *ou* return somewhere/to; **~ à** (*état, activité*) to return to, go back to; **se ~** *vi* to turn over; (*tourner la tête*) to turn round; **s'en ~** to go back; **se ~ contre** (*fig*) to turn against; **savoir de quoi il retourne** to know what it is all about; **~ sa veste** (*fig*) to turn one's coat; **~ en arrière** *ou* **sur ses pas** to turn back, retrace one's steps; **~ aux sources** to go back to basics.

retracer [ʀətʀase] *vt* to relate, recount.

rétracter [ʀetʀakte] *vt*, **se ~** *vi* to retract.

retraduire [ʀətʀaduiʀ] *vt* to translate again; (*dans la langue de départ*) to translate back.

retrait [ʀətʀɛ] *nm* (*voir retirer*) withdrawal; collection; (*voir se retirer*) withdrawal; (*rétrécissement*) shrinkage; **en ~** *a* set back; **écrire en ~** to indent; **~ du permis (de conduire)** disqualification from driving (*Brit*), revocation of driver's license (*US*).

retraite [ʀətʀɛt] *nf* (*d'une armée, REL, refuge*) retreat; (*d'un employé*) retirement; (*revenu*) (retirement) pension; **être/mettre à la ~** to be retired/pension off *ou* retire; **prendre sa ~** to retire; **~ anticipée** early retirement; **~ aux flambeaux** torchlight tattoo.

retraité, e [ʀətʀete] *a* retired ♦ *nm/f* (old age) pensioner.

retraitement [ʀətʀetmɑ̃] *nm* reprocessing.

retraiter [ʀətʀete] *vt* to reprocess.

retranchement [ʀətʀɑ̃ʃmɑ̃] *nm* entrenchment; **poursuivre qn dans ses derniers ~s** to drive sb into a corner.

retrancher [ʀətʀɑ̃ʃe] *vt* (*passage, détails*) to take out, remove; (*nombre, somme*): **~ qch**

de to take *ou* deduct sth from; (*couper*) to cut off; **se ~ derrière/dans** to entrench o.s. behind/in; (*fig*) to take refuge behind/in.

retranscrire [ʀətʀɑ̃skʀiʀ] *vt* to retranscribe.

retransmettre [ʀətʀɑ̃smɛtʀ(ə)] *vt* (*RADIO*) to broadcast, relay; (*TV*) to show.

retransmission [ʀətʀɑ̃smisjɔ̃] *nf* broadcast; showing.

retravailler [ʀətʀavaje] *vi* to start work again ♦ *vt* to work on again.

retraverser [ʀətʀavɛʀse] *vt* (*dans l'autre sens*) to cross back over.

rétréci, e [ʀetʀesi] *a* (*idées, esprit*) narrow.

rétrécir [ʀetʀesiʀ] *vt* (*vêtement*) to take in ♦ *vi* to shrink; **se ~** *vi* to narrow.

rétrécissement [ʀetʀesismɑ̃] *nm* narrowing.

retremper [ʀətʀɑ̃pe] *vt*: **se ~ dans** (*fig*) to re-immerse o.s. in.

rétribuer [ʀetʀibɥe] *vt* (*travail*) to pay for; (*personne*) to pay.

rétribution [ʀetʀibysjɔ̃] *nf* payment.

rétro [ʀetʀo] *a inv* old-style ♦ *nm* (= *rétroviseur*) (rear-view) mirror; **la mode ~** the nostalgia vogue.

rétroactif, ive [ʀetʀoaktif, -iv] *a* retroactive.

rétrocéder [ʀetʀosede] *vt* to retrocede.

rétrocession [ʀetʀosesjɔ̃] *nf* retrocession.

rétrofusée [ʀetʀofyze] *nf* retrorocket.

rétrograde [ʀetʀɔgʀad] *a* reactionary, backward-looking.

rétrograder [ʀetʀɔgʀade] *vi* (*élève*) to fall back; (*économie*) to regress; (*AUTO*) to change down.

rétroprojecteur [ʀetʀopʀɔʒɛktœʀ] *nm* overhead projector.

rétrospectif, ive [ʀetʀɔspɛktif, -iv] *a, nf* retrospective.

rétrospectivement [ʀetʀɔspɛktivmɑ̃] *ad* in retrospect.

retroussé, e [ʀətʀuse] *a*: **nez ~** turned-up nose.

retrousser [ʀətʀuse] *vt* to roll up; (*fig: nez*) to wrinkle; (*: lèvres*) to curl up.

retrouvailles [ʀətʀuvaj] *nfpl* reunion *sg*.

retrouver [ʀətʀuve] *vt* (*fugitif, objet perdu*) to find; (*occasion*) to find again; (*calme, santé*) to regain; (*reconnaître: expression, style*) to recognize; (*revoir*) to see again; (*rejoindre*) to meet (again), join; **se ~** *vi* to meet; (*s'orienter*) to find one's way; **se ~ quelque part** to find o.s. somewhere; to end up somewhere; **se ~ seul/sans argent** to find o.s. alone/with no money; **se ~ dans** (*calculs, dossiers, désordre*) to make sense of; **s'y ~** (*rentrer dans ses frais*) to break even.

rétroviseur [ʀetʀovizœʀ] *nm* (rear-view) mirror.

Réunion [ʀeynjɔ̃] *nf*: **la ~, l'île de la ~** Reunion.

réunion [ʀeynjɔ̃] *nf* bringing together; joining; (*séance*) meeting.

réunionnais, e [ʀeynjɔnɛ, -ɛz] *a* of *ou* from Reunion.

réunir [ʀeyniʀ] *vt* (*convoquer*) to call together; (*rassembler*) to gather together; (*cumuler*) to combine; (*rapprocher*) to bring together (again), reunite; (*rattacher*) to join (together); **se ~** *vi* (*se rencontrer*) to meet; (*s'allier*) to unite.

réussi, e [ʀeysi] *a* successful.

réussir [ʀeysiʀ] *vi* to succeed, be successful; (*à un examen*) to pass; (*plante, culture*) to thrive, do well ♦ *vt* to make a success of; to bring off; ~ **à faire** to succeed in doing; ~ **à qn** to go right for sb; (*aliment*) to agree with sb; **le travail/le mariage lui réussit** work/married life agrees with him.

réussite [ʀeysit] *nf* success; (*CARTES*) patience.

réutiliser [ʀeytilize] *vt* to re-use.

revaloir [ʀəvalwaʀ] *vt*: **je vous revaudrai cela** I'll repay you some day; (*en mal*) I'll pay you back for this.

revalorisation [ʀəvalɔʀizasjɔ̃] *nf* revaluation; raising.

revaloriser [ʀəvalɔʀize] *vt* (*monnaie*) to re-value; (*salaires, pensions*) to raise the level of; (*institution, tradition*) to reassert the value of.

revanche [ʀəvɑ̃ʃ] *nf* revenge; **prendre sa ~ (sur)** to take one's revenge (on); **en ~** (*par contre*) on the other hand; (*en compensation*) in return.

rêvasser [ʀɛvase] *vi* to daydream.

rêve [ʀɛv] *nm* dream; (*activité psychique*): **le ~** dreaming; **paysage/silence de ~** dream-like landscape/silence; ~ **éveillé** daydreaming *q*, daydream.

rêvé, e [ʀeve] *a* (*endroit, mari etc*) ideal.

revêche [ʀəvɛʃ] *a* surly, sour-tempered.

réveil [ʀevɛj] *nm* (*d'un dormeur*) waking up *q*; (*fig*) awakening; (*pendule*) alarm (clock); **au ~** when I (*ou* you *etc*) wake (*ou* woke) up, on waking (up); **sonner le ~** (*MIL*) to sound the reveille.

réveille-matin [ʀevɛjmatɛ̃] *nm inv* alarm clock.

réveiller [ʀeveje] *vt* (*personne*) to wake up; (*fig*) to awaken, revive; **se ~** *vi* to wake up; (*fig*) to be revived, reawaken.

réveillon [ʀevejɔ̃] *nm* Christmas Eve; (*de la Saint-Sylvestre*) New Year's Eve; Christmas Eve (*ou* New Year's Eve) party *ou* dinner.

réveillonner [ʀevejɔne] *vi* to celebrate Christmas Eve (*ou* New Year's Eve).

révélateur, trice [ʀevelatœʀ, -tʀis] *a*: ~ **(de qch)** revealing (sth) ♦ *nm* (*PHOTO*) developer.

révélation [ʀevelasjɔ̃] *nf* revelation.

révéler [ʀevele] *vt* (*gén*) to reveal; (*divulguer*) to disclose, reveal; (*dénoter*) to reveal, show; (*faire connaître au public*): ~ **qn/qch** to make sb/sth widely known, bring sb/sth to the public's notice; **se ~** *vi* to be revealed, reveal itself ♦ *vb avec attribut*: **se ~ facile/faux** to prove (to be) easy/false; **se ~ cruel/un allié sûr** to show o.s. to be cruel/a trustworthy ally.

revenant, e [ʀəvnɑ̃, -ɑ̃t] *nm/f* ghost.

revendeur, euse [ʀəvɑ̃dœʀ, -øz] *nm/f* (*détaillant*) retailer; (*d'occasions*) second-hand dealer.

revendicatif, ive [ʀəvɑ̃dikatif, -iv] *a* (*mouvement*) of protest.

revendication [ʀəvɑ̃dikasjɔ̃] *nf* claim, demand; **journée de ~** day of action (in support of one's claims).

revendiquer [ʀəvɑ̃dike] *vt* to claim, demand;

(*responsabilité*) to claim ♦ *vi* to agitate in favour of one's claims.

revendre [ʀəvɑ̃dʀ(ə)] *vt* (*d'occasion*) to resell; (*détailler*) to sell; (*vendre davantage de*): ~ **du sucre/un foulard/deux bagues** to sell more sugar/another scarf/another two rings; **à ~** *ad* (*en abondance*) to spare.

revenir [ʀəvniʀ] *vi* to come back; (*CULIN*): **faire ~** to brown; (*coûter*): ~ **cher/à 100 F (à qn)** to cost (sb) a lot/100 F; ~ **à** (*études, projet*) to return to, go back to; (*équivaloir à*) to amount to; ~ **à qn** (*rumeur, nouvelle*) to get back to sb, reach sb's ears; (*part, honneur*) to go to sb, be sb's; (*souvenir, nom*) to come back to sb; ~ **de** (*fig: maladie, étonnement*) to recover from; ~ **sur** (*question, sujet*) to go back over; (*engagement*) to go back on; ~ **à la charge** to return to the attack; ~ **à soi** to come round; **n'en pas ~**: **je n'en reviens pas** I can't get over it; ~ **sur ses pas** to retrace one's steps; **cela revient à dire que/au même** it amounts to saying that/to the same thing; ~ **de loin** (*fig*) to have been at death's door.

revente [ʀəvɑ̃t] *nf* resale.

revenu, e [ʀəvny] *pp de* **revenir** ♦ *nm* income; (*de l'État*) revenue; (*d'un capital*) yield; ~**s** *nmpl* income *sg*; ~ **national brut** gross national income.

revenu, e [ʀəvny] *pp de* **revenir**.

rêver [ʀeve] *vi, vt* to dream; (*rêvasser*) to (day)dream; ~ **de** (*voir en rêve*) to dream of *ou* about; ~ **de qch/de faire** to dream of sth/of doing; ~ **à** to dream of.

réverbération [ʀevɛʀbeʀasjɔ̃] *nf* reflection.

réverbère [ʀevɛʀbɛʀ] *nm* street lamp *ou* light.

réverbérer [ʀevɛʀbeʀe] *vt* to reflect.

reverdir [ʀəvɛʀdiʀ] *vi* (*arbre etc*) to turn green again.

révérence [ʀeveʀɑ̃s] *nf* (*vénération*) reverence; (*salut: d'homme*) bow; (: *de femme*) curtsey.

révérencieux, euse [ʀeveʀɑ̃sjø, -øz] *a* reverent.

révérend, e [ʀeveʀɑ̃, -ɑ̃d] *a*: **le ~ père Pascal** the Reverend Father Pascal.

révérer [ʀeveʀe] *vt* to revere.

rêverie [ʀɛvʀi] *nf* daydreaming *q*, daydream.

reverrai [ʀəveʀe] *etc vb voir* **revoir**.

revers [ʀəvɛʀ] *nm* (*de feuille, main*) back; (*d'étoffe*) wrong side; (*de pièce, médaille*) back, reverse; (*TENNIS, PING-PONG*) back-hand; (*de veston*) lapel; (*de pantalon*) turn-up; (*fig: échec*) setback; ~ **de fortune** reverse of fortune; **d'un ~ de main** with the back of one's hand; **le ~ de la médaille** (*fig*) the other side of the coin; **prendre à ~** (*MIL*) to take from the rear.

reverser [ʀəvɛʀse] *vt* (*reporter: somme etc*): ~ **sur** to put back into; (*liquide*): ~ **(dans)** to pour some more (into).

réversible [ʀevɛʀsibl(ə)] *a* reversible.

revêtement [ʀəvɛtmɑ̃] *nm* (*de paroi*) facing; (*des sols*) flooring; (*de chaussée*) surface; (*de tuyau etc: enduit*) coating.

revêtir [ʀəvetiʀ] *vt* (*habit*) to don, put on; (*fig*) to take on; ~ **qn de** to dress sb in; (*fig*) to endow *ou* invest sb with; ~ **qch de** to cover sth with; (*fig*) to cloak sth in; ~ **d'un visa** to append a visa to.

rêveur, euse [ʀɛvœʀ, -øz] *a* dreamy ♦ *nm/f* dreamer.

reviendrai [ʀəvjɛ̃dʀe] *etc vb voir* **revenir**.

revienne [ʀəvjɛn] *etc vb voir* **revenir**.

revient [ʀəvjɛ̃] *vb voir* **revenir** ♦ *nm*: prix de ~ cost price.

revigorer [ʀəvigɔʀe] *vt* to invigorate, revive, buck up.

revint [ʀəvɛ̃] *etc vb voir* **revenir**.

revirement [ʀəviʀmɑ̃] *nm* change of mind; (*d'une situation*) reversal.

revis [ʀəvi] *etc vb voir* **revoir**.

révisable [ʀevizabl(ə)] *a* (*procès, taux etc*) reviewable, subject to review.

réviser [ʀevize] *vt* (*texte, SCOL*: *matière*) to revise; (*comptes*) to audit; (*machine, installation, moteur*) to overhaul, service; (*JUR*: *procès*) to review.

révision [ʀevizjɔ̃] *nf* revision; auditing *q*; overhaul, servicing *q*; review; **conseil de ~** (*MIL*) recruiting board; **faire ses ~s** (*SCOL*) to do one's revision (*Brit*), revise (*Brit*), review (*US*); **la ~ des 10000 km** (*AUTO*) the 10,000 km service.

révisionnisme [ʀevizjɔnism(ə)] *nm* revisionism.

revisser [ʀəvise] *vt* to screw back again.

revit [ʀəvi] *vb voir* **revoir**.

revitaliser [ʀəvitalize] *vt* to revitalize.

revivifier [ʀəvivifje] *vt* to revitalize.

revivre [ʀəvivʀ(ə)] *vi* (*reprendre des forces*) to come alive again; (*traditions*) to be revived ♦ *vt* (*épreuve, moment*) to relive; **faire ~** (*mode, institution, usage*) to bring back to life.

révocable [ʀevɔkabl(ə)] *a* (*délégué*) dismissible; (*contrat*) revocable.

révocation [ʀevɔkasjɔ̃] *nf* dismissal; revocation.

revoir [ʀəvwaʀ] *vt* to see again; (*réviser*) to revise (*Brit*), review (*US*) ♦ *nm*: **au ~** goodbye; **dire au ~ à qn** to say goodbye to sb; **se ~** (*amis*) to meet (again), see each other again.

révoltant, e [ʀevɔltɑ̃, -ɑ̃t] *a* revolting.

révolte [ʀevɔlt(ə)] *nf* rebellion, revolt.

révolter [ʀevɔlte] *vt* to revolt, outrage; **se ~** *vi*: **se ~ (contre)** to rebel (against); **se ~ (à)** to be outraged (by).

révolu, e [ʀevɔly] *a* past; (*ADMIN*): **âgé de 18 ans ~s** over 18 years of age; **après 3 ans ~s** when 3 full years have passed.

révolution [ʀevɔlysjɔ̃] *nf* revolution; **être en ~** (*pays etc*) to be in revolt; **la ~ industrielle** the industrial revolution.

révolutionnaire [ʀevɔlysjɔnɛʀ] *a, nm/f* revolutionary.

révolutionner [ʀevɔlysjɔne] *vt* to revolutionize; (*fig*) to stir up.

revolver [ʀevɔlvɛʀ] *nm* gun; (*à barillet*) revolver.

révoquer [ʀevɔke] *vt* (*fonctionnaire*) to dismiss, remove from office; (*arrêt, contrat*) to revoke.

revoyais [ʀəvwaje] *etc vb voir* **revoir**.

revu, e [ʀəvy] *pp de* **revoir** ♦ *nf* (*inventaire, examen*) review; (*MIL*: *défilé*) review, march-past; (*: inspection*) inspection, review; (*périodique*) review, magazine; (*pièce*

satirique) revue; (*de music-hall*) variety show; **passer en ~** to review, inspect; (*fig*) to review; **~ de (la) presse** press review.

révulsé, e [ʀevylse] *a* (*yeux*) rolled upwards; (*visage*) contorted.

Reykjavik [ʀekjavik] *n* Reykjavik.

rez-de-chaussée [ʀedʃose] *nm inv* ground floor.

rez-de-jardin [ʀedʒaʀdɛ̃] *nm inv* garden level.

RF *sigle f = République française*.

RFA *sigle f* (*= République fédérale d'Allemagne*) FRG.

RFO *sigle f* (*= Radio-Télévision Française d'Outre-mer*) French overseas broadcasting service.

RG *sigle mpl* (*= renseignements généraux*) security section of the police force.

rhabiller [ʀabije] *vt*: **se ~** to get dressed again, put one's clothes on again.

rhapsodie [ʀapsɔdi] *nf* rhapsody.

rhénan, e [ʀenɑ̃, -an] *a* Rhine *cpd*, of the Rhine.

Rhénanie [ʀenani] *nf*: **la ~** the Rhineland.

rhésus [ʀezys] *a, nm* rhesus; **~ positif/ négatif** rhesus positive/negative.

rhétorique [ʀetɔʀik] *nf* rhetoric ♦ *a* rhetorical.

rhéto-roman, e [ʀetɔʀɔmɑ̃, -an] *a* Rhaeto-Romanic.

Rhin [ʀɛ̃] *nm*: **le ~** the Rhine.

rhinite [ʀinit] *nf* rhinitis.

rhinocéros [ʀinɔseʀɔs] *nm* rhinoceros.

rhinopharyngite [ʀinɔfaʀɛ̃ʒit] *nf* throat infection.

rhodanien, ne [ʀɔdanjɛ̃, -ɛn] *a* Rhône *cpd*, of the Rhône.

Rhodes [ʀɔd] *n*: **(l'île de) ~** (the island of) Rhodes.

Rhodésie [ʀɔdezi] *nf*: **la ~** Rhodesia.

rhodésien, ne [ʀɔdezjɛ̃, -ɛn] *a* Rhodesian.

rhododendron [ʀɔdɔdɛ̃dʀɔ̃] *nm* rhododendron.

Rhône [ʀon] *nm*: **le ~** the Rhone.

rhubarbe [ʀybaʀb(ə)] *nf* rhubarb.

rhum [ʀɔm] *nm* rum.

rhumatisant, e [ʀymatizɑ̃, -ɑ̃t] *a, nm/f* rheumatic.

rhumatismal, e, aux [ʀymatismal, -o] *a* rheumatic.

rhumatisme [ʀymatism(ə)] *nm* rheumatism *q*.

rhumatologue [ʀymatɔlɔg] *nm/f* rheumatologist.

rhume [ʀym] *nm* cold; **~ de cerveau** head cold; **le ~ des foins** hay fever.

rhumerie [ʀɔmʀi] *nf* (*distillerie*) rum distillery.

RI *sigle m* (*MIL*) = *régiment d'infanterie* ♦ *sigle mpl* (*= Républicains indépendants*) *political party*.

ri [ʀi] *pp de* **rire**.

riant, e [ʀjɑ̃, -ɑ̃t] *vb voir* **rire** ♦ *a* smiling, cheerful; (*campagne, paysage*) pleasant.

RIB *sigle m = relevé d'identité bancaire*.

ribambelle [ʀibɑ̃bɛl] *nf*: **une ~ de** a herd *ou* swarm of.

ricain, e [ʀikɛ̃, -ɛn] *a* (*fam*) Yank, Yankee.

ricanement [ʀikanmɑ̃] *nm* snigger; giggle.

ricaner [ʀikane] *vi* (*avec méchanceté*) to snigger; (*bêtement, avec gêne*) to giggle.

riche [ʀiʃ] *a* (*gén*) rich; (*personne, pays*) rich,

wealthy; **~ en** rich in; **~ de** full of; rich in.

richement [Riʃmã] *ad* richly.

richesse [Riʃɛs] *nf* wealth; *(fig)* richness; **~s** *nfpl* wealth *sg*; treasures; **~ en vitamines** high vitamin content.

richissime [Riʃisim] *a* extremely rich *ou* wealthy.

ricin [Risɛ̃] *nm*: **huile de ~** castor oil.

ricocher [Rikɔʃe] *vi*: **~ (sur)** to rebound (off); *(sur l'eau)* to bounce (on *ou* off); **faire ~** *(galet)* to skim.

ricochet [Rikɔʃe] *nm* rebound; bounce; **faire ~** to rebound, bounce; *(fig)* to rebound; **faire des ~s** to skip stones; **par ~** *ad* on the rebound; *(fig)* as an indirect result.

rictus [Riktys] *nm* grin; (snarling) grimace.

ride [Rid] *nf* wrinkle; *(fig)* ripple.

ridé, e [Ride] *a* wrinkled.

rideau, x [Rido] *nm* curtain; **tirer/ouvrir les ~x** to draw/open the curtains; **~ de fer** metal shutter; *(POL)*: **le ~ de fer** the Iron Curtain.

ridelle [Ridɛl] *nf* slatted side *(of truck)*.

rider [Ride] *vt* to wrinkle; *(fig)* to ripple, ruffle the surface of; **se ~** *vi* to become wrinkled.

ridicule [Ridikyl] *a* ridiculous ♦ *nm* ridiculousness *q*; **le ~** ridicule; *(travers: gén pl)* absurdities *pl*; **tourner en ~** to ridicule.

ridiculement [Ridikylmã] *ad* ridiculously.

ridiculiser [Ridikylize] *vt* to ridicule; **se ~** to make a fool of o.s.

ridule [Ridyl] *nf (euph: ride)* little wrinkle.

rie [Ri] *etc vb voir* **rire**.

rien [Rjɛ̃] *pronom* nothing; *(quelque chose)* anything; **ne ... ~** nothing, *tournure négative* + anything; **~ d'autre** nothing else; **~ du tout** nothing at all; **~ que** just, only; nothing but; **~ que cela/qu'à faire cela** just that/just doing that; **a-t-il jamais ~ fait pour nous?** has he ever done anything for us?; **il n'a ~** *(n'est pas blessé)* he's all right; **il n'a ~ d'un champion** he has nothing of the champion about him; **il n'y est pour ~** he's got nothing to do with it; **il n'en est ~!** nothing of the sort!; **ça ne fait ~** it doesn't matter; **~ à faire!** it's no good!; **il n'y ~ à faire ...** whatever I *(ou you etc)* do ...; **de ~!** *(formule)* not at all!, don't mention it!; **comme si de ~ n'était** as if nothing had happened; **un petit ~** *(cadeau)* a little something; **un ~ de ~** a hint of; **des ~s** trivia *pl*; **avoir peur d'un ~** to be frightened of every little thing.

rieur, euse [RjœR, -øz] *a* cheerful.

rigide [Riʒid] *a* stiff; *(fig)* rigid; *(moralement)* strict.

rigidité [Riʒidite] *nf* stiffness; **la ~ cadavérique** rigor mortis.

rigolade [Rigɔlad] *nf*: **la ~** fun; *(fig)*: **c'est de la ~** it's a big farce; *(c'est facile)* it's a cinch.

rigole [Rigɔl] *nf (conduit)* channel; *(filet d'eau)* rivulet.

rigoler [Rigɔle] *vi (rire)* to laugh; *(s'amuser)* to have (some) fun; *(plaisanter)* to be joking *ou* kidding.

rigolo, ote [Rigɔlo, -ɔt] *a (fam)* funny ♦ *nm/f* comic; *(péj)* fraud, phoney.

rigoureusement [RiguRøzmã] *ad* rigorously; **~ vrai/interdit** strictly true/forbidden.

rigoureux, euse [RiguRø, -øz] *a (morale)*

rigorous, strict; *(personne)* stern, strict; *(climat, châtiment)* rigorous, harsh, severe; *(interdiction, neutralité)* strict; *(preuves, analyse, méthode)* rigorous.

rigueur [RiguœR] *nf* rigour *(Brit)*, rigor *(US)*; strictness; harshness; **"tenue de soirée de ~"** "evening dress (to be worn)"; **être de ~** to be the usual thing, be the rule; **à la ~** at a pinch; possibly; **tenir ~ à qn de qch** to hold sth against sb.

riions [Rijɔ̃] *etc vb voir* **rire**.

rillettes [Rijɛt] *nfpl* ≈ potted meat *sg*.

rime [Rim] *nf* rhyme; **n'avoir ni ~ ni raison** to have neither rhyme nor reason.

rimer [Rime] *vi*: **~ (avec)** to rhyme (with); **ne ~ à rien** not to make sense.

Rimmel [Rimɛl] *nm* ® mascara.

rinçage [Rɛ̃saʒ] *nm* rinsing (out); *(opération)* rinse.

rince-doigts [Rɛ̃sdwa] *nm inv* finger-bowl.

rincer [Rɛ̃se] *vt* to rinse; *(récipient)* to rinse out; **se ~ la bouche** to rinse out one's mouth.

ring [Riŋ] *nm* (boxing) ring; **monter sur le ~** *(aussi fig)* to enter the ring; *(: faire carrière de boxeur)* to take up boxing.

ringard, e [Rɛ̃gaR, -aRd(ə)] *a (péj)* old-fashioned.

Rio de Janeiro [RiodʒaneR(o)] *n* Rio de Janeiro.

rions [Rjɔ̃] *vb voir* **rire**.

ripaille [Ripaj] *nf*: **faire ~** to feast.

riper [Ripe] *vi* to slip, slide.

ripoliné, e [Ripoline] *a* enamel-painted.

riposte [Ripost(ə)] *nf* retort, riposte; *(fig)* counter-attack, reprisal.

riposter [Riposte] *vi* to retaliate ♦ *vt*: **~ que** to retort that; **~ à** *vt* to counter; to reply to.

rire [RiR] *vi* to laugh; *(se divertir)* to have fun; *(plaisanter)* to joke ♦ *nm* laugh; **le ~** laughter; **~ de** *vt* to laugh at; **se ~ de** to make light of; **tu veux ~!** you must be joking!; **~ aux éclats/aux larmes** to roar with laughter/ laugh until one cries; **~ jaune** to force oneself to laugh; **~ sous cape** to laugh up one's sleeve; **~ au nez de qn** to laugh in sb's face; **pour ~** *(pas sérieusement)* for a joke *ou* a laugh.

ris [Ri] *vb voir* **rire** ♦ *nm*: **~ de veau** (calf) sweetbread.

risée [Rize] *nf*: **être la ~ de** to be the laughing stock of.

risette [Rizɛt] *nf*: **faire ~ (à)** to give a nice little smile (to).

risible [Rizibl(ə)] *a* laughable, ridiculous.

risque [Risk(ə)] *nm* risk; **l'attrait du ~** the lure of danger; **prendre des ~s** to take risks; **à ses ~s et périls** at his own risk; **au ~ de** at the risk of; **~ d'incendie** fire risk; **~ calculé** calculated risk.

risqué, e [Riske] *a* risky; *(plaisanterie)* risqué, daring.

risquer [Riske] *vt* to risk; *(allusion, question)* to venture, hazard; **tu risques qu'on te renvoie** you risk being dismissed; **ça ne risque rien** it's quite safe; **~ de: il risque de se tuer** he could *ou* risks getting himself killed; **il a risqué de se tuer** he almost got himself killed; **ce qui risque de se produire** what might *ou* could well happen; **il ne**

risque pas de recommencer there's no chance of him doing that again; **se ~ dans** (*s'aventurer*) to venture into; **se ~ à faire** (*tenter*) to venture *ou* dare to do; **~ le tout pour le tout** to risk the lot.

risque-tout [ʀiskətu] *nm/f inv* daredevil.

rissoler [ʀisɔle] *vi, vt*: **(faire) ~** to brown.

ristourne [ʀisturn(ə)] *nf* rebate; discount.

rit [ʀi] *etc vb voir* **rire.**

rite [ʀit] *nm* rite; (*fig*) ritual; **~s d'initiation** initiation rites.

ritournelle [ʀiturnɛl] *nf* (*fig*) tune; **c'est toujours la même ~** (*fam*) it's always the same old story.

rituel, le [ʀitɥɛl] *a, nm* ritual.

rituellement [ʀitɥɛlmɑ̃] *ad* religiously.

riv. *abr* (= *rivière*).

rivage [ʀivaʒ] *nm* shore.

rival, e, aux [ʀival, -o] *a, nm/f* rival; **sans ~** a unrivalled.

rivaliser [ʀivalize] *vi*: **~ avec** to rival, vie with; (*être comparable*) to hold its own against, compare with; **~ avec qn de** (*élégance etc*) to vie with *ou* rival sb in.

rivalité [ʀivalite] *nf* rivalry.

rive [ʀiv] *nf* shore; (*de fleuve*) bank.

river [ʀive] *vt* (*clou, pointe*) to clinch; (*plaques*) to rivet together; **être rivé sur/à** to be riveted on/to.

riverain, e [ʀivʀɛ̃, -ɛn] *a* riverside *cpd*; lakeside *cpd*; roadside *cpd* ♦ *nm/f* riverside (*ou* lakeside) resident; local *ou* roadside resident.

rivet [ʀivɛ] *nm* rivet.

riveter [ʀivte] *vt* to rivet (together).

Riviera [ʀivjeʀa] *nf*: **la ~ (italienne)** the Italian Riviera.

rivière [ʀivjɛʀ] *nf* river; **~ de diamants** diamond rivière.

rixe [ʀiks(ə)] *nf* brawl, scuffle.

Riyadh [ʀijad] *n* Riyadh.

riz [ʀi] *nm* rice; **~ au lait** ≈ rice pudding.

rizière [ʀizjɛʀ] *nf* paddy-field.

RMC *sigle f* = *Radio Monte Carlo*.

RN *sigle f* = **route nationale.**

robe [ʀɔb] *nf* dress; (*de juge, d'ecclésiastique*) robe; (*de professeur*) gown; (*pelage*) coat; **~ de soirée/de mariée** evening/wedding dress; **~ de baptême** christening robe; **~ de chambre** dressing gown; **~ de grossesse** maternity dress.

robinet [ʀɔbinɛ] *nm* tap, faucet (*US*); **~ du gaz** gas tap; **~ mélangeur** mixer tap.

robinetterie [ʀɔbinɛtʀi] *nf* taps *pl*, plumbing.

roboratif, ive [ʀɔbɔʀatif, -iv] *a* bracing, invigorating.

robot [ʀɔbo] *nm* robot; **~ de cuisine** food processor.

robotique [ʀɔbɔtik] *nf* robotics *sg*.

robotiser [ʀɔbɔtize] *vt* (*personne, travailleur*) to turn into a robot; (*monde, vie*) to automate.

robuste [ʀɔbyst(ə)] *a* robust, sturdy.

robustesse [ʀɔbystɛs] *nf* robustness, sturdiness.

roc [ʀɔk] *nm* rock.

rocade [ʀɔkad] *nf* (*AUTO*) bypass.

rocaille [ʀɔkaj] *nf* (*pierres*) loose stones *pl*; (*terrain*) rocky *ou* stony ground; (*jardin*) rockery, rock garden ♦ *a* (*style*) rocaille.

rocailleux, euse [ʀɔkajø, -øz] *a* rocky, stony; (*voix*) harsh.

rocambolesque [ʀɔkɑ̃bɔlɛsk(ə)] *a* fantastic, incredible.

roche [ʀɔʃ] *nf* rock.

rocher [ʀɔʃe] *nm* rock; (*ANAT*) petrosal bone.

rochet [ʀɔʃɛ] *nm*: **roue à ~** ratchet wheel.

rocheux, euse [ʀɔʃø, -øz] *a* rocky; **les (montagnes) Rocheuses** the Rockies, the Rocky Mountains.

rock (and roll) [ʀɔk(ɛnʀɔl)] *nm* (*musique*) rock(-'n'-roll); (*danse*) rock.

rocker [ʀɔkœʀ] *nm* (*chanteur*) rock musician; (*adepte*) rock fan.

rodage [ʀɔdaʒ] *nm* running in (*Brit*), breaking in (*US*); **en ~** (*AUTO*) running *ou* breaking in.

rodé, e [ʀɔde] *a* run in (*Brit*), broken in (*US*); (*personne*): **~ à qch** having got the hang of sth.

rodéo [ʀɔdeo] *nm* rodeo (*pl* -s).

roder [ʀɔde] *vt* (*moteur, voiture*) to run in (*Brit*), break in (*US*); **~ un spectacle/service** to iron out the initial problems of a show/service.

rôder [ʀɔde] *vi* to roam *ou* wander about; (*de façon suspecte*) to lurk (about *ou* around).

rôdeur, euse [ʀɔdœʀ, -øz] *nm/f* prowler.

rodomontades [ʀɔdɔmɔ̃tad] *nfpl* bragging *sg*; sabre rattling *sg*.

rogatoire [ʀɔgatwaʀ] *a*: **commission ~** letters rogatory.

rogne [ʀɔɲ] *nf*: **être en ~** to be mad *ou* in a temper; **se mettre en ~** to get mad *ou* in a temper.

rogner [ʀɔɲe] *vt* to trim; (*fig*) to whittle down; **~ sur** (*fig*) to cut down *ou* back on.

rognons [ʀɔɲɔ̃] *nmpl* kidneys.

rognures [ʀɔɲyʀ] *nfpl* trimmings.

rogue [ʀɔg] *a* arrogant.

roi [ʀwa] *nm* king; **les R~s mages** the Three Wise Men, the Magi; **le jour** *ou* **la fête des R~s, les R~s** Twelfth Night.

roitelet [ʀwatlɛ] *nm* wren; (*péj*) kinglet.

rôle [ʀol] *nm* role; (*contribution*) part.

rollmops [ʀɔlmɔps] *nm* rollmop.

romain, e [ʀɔmɛ̃, -ɛn] *a* Roman ♦ *nm/f*: **R~,** **e** Roman ♦ *nf* (*CULIN*) cos (lettuce).

roman, e [ʀɔmɑ̃, -an] *a* (*ARCHIT*) Romanesque; (*LING*) Romance *cpd*, Romanic ♦ *nm* novel; **~ policier** detective novel; **~ d'espionnage** spy novel *ou* story; **~ noir** thriller.

romance [ʀɔmɑ̃s] *nf* ballad.

romancer [ʀɔmɑ̃se] *vt* to romanticize.

romanche [ʀɔmɑ̃ʃ] *a, nm* Romansh.

romancier, ière [ʀɔmɑ̃sje, -jɛʀ] *nm/f* novelist.

romand, e [ʀɔmɑ̃, -ɑ̃d] *a* of *ou* from French-speaking Switzerland ♦ *nm/f*: **R~, e** French-speaking Swiss.

romanesque [ʀɔmanɛsk(ə)] *a* (*fantastique*) fantastic; storybook *cpd*; (*sentimental*) romantic; (*LITTÉRATURE*) novelistic.

roman-feuilleton, *pl* **romans-feuilletons** [ʀɔmɑ̃fœjtɔ̃] *nm* serialized novel.

roman-fleuve, *pl* **romans-fleuves** [ʀɔmɑ̃flœv] *nm* saga, roman-fleuve.

romanichel, le [ʀɔmaniʃɛl] *nm/f* gipsy.

roman-photo, *pl* **romans-photos** [ʀɔmɑ̃fɔto]

nm (romantic) picture story.
romantique [ʀɔmɑ̃tik] *a* romantic.
romantisme [ʀɔmɑ̃tism(ə)] *nm* romanticism.
romarin [ʀɔmaʀɛ̃] *nm* rosemary.
rombière [ʀɔ̃bjɛʀ] *nf* (*péj*) old bag.
Rome [ʀɔm] *n* Rome.
rompre [ʀɔ̃pʀ(ə)] *vt* to break; (*entretien, fiançailles*) to break off ♦ *vi* (*fiancés*) to break it off; **se ~** *vi* to break; (*MÉD*) to burst, rupture; **se ~ les os** *ou* **le cou** to break one's neck; **~ avec** to break with; **à tout ~** *ad* wildly; **applaudir à tout ~** to bring down the house, applaud wildly; **~ la glace** (*fig*) to break the ice; **rompez (les rangs)!** (*MIL*) dismiss!, fall out!
rompu, e [ʀɔ̃py] *pp de* **rompre** ♦ *a* (*fourbu*) exhausted, worn out; **~ à** with wide experience of; inured to.
romsteck [ʀɔ̃mstɛk] *nm* rump steak *q*.
ronce [ʀɔ̃s] *nf* (*BOT*) bramble branch; (*MENUISERIE*): **~ de noyer** burr walnut; **~s** *nfpl* brambles, thorns.
ronchonner [ʀɔ̃ʃɔne] *vi* (*fam*) to grouse, grouch.
rond, e [ʀɔ̃, ʀɔ̃d] *a* round; (*joues, mollets*) well-rounded; (*fam: ivre*) tight; (*sincère, décidé*): **être ~ en affaires** to be on the level in business, do an honest deal ♦ *nm* (*cercle*) ring; (*fam: sou*): **je n'ai plus un ~** I haven't a penny left ♦ *nf* (*gén: de surveillance*) rounds *pl*, patrol; (*danse*) round (dance); (*MUS*) semibreve (*Brit*), whole note (*US*) ♦ *ad*: **tourner ~** (*moteur*) to run smoothly; **ça ne tourne pas ~** (*fig*) there's something not quite right about it; **pour faire un compte ~** to make (it) a round figure, to round (it) off; **avoir le dos ~** to be round-shouldered; **en ~** (*s'asseoir, danser*) in a ring; **à la ~e** (*alentour*): **à 10 km à la ~e** for 10 km round; (*à chacun son tour*): **passer qch à la ~e** to pass sth (a)round; **faire des ~s de jambe** to bow and scrape; **~ de serviette** napkin ring.
rond-de-cuir, *pl* **ronds-de-cuir** [ʀɔ̃dkɥiʀ] *nm* (*péj*) penpusher.
rondelet, te [ʀɔ̃dlɛ, -ɛt] *a* plump; (*fig: somme*) tidy; (*: bourse*) well-lined, fat.
rondelle [ʀɔ̃dɛl] *nf* (*TECH*) washer; (*tranche*) slice, round.
rondement [ʀɔ̃dmɑ̃] *ad* (*avec décision*) briskly; (*loyalement*) frankly.
rondeur [ʀɔ̃dœʀ] *nf* (*d'un bras, des formes*) plumpness; (*bonhomie*) friendly straightforwardness; **~s** *nfpl* (*d'une femme*) curves.
rondin [ʀɔ̃dɛ̃] *nm* log.
rond-point, *pl* **ronds-points** [ʀɔ̃pwɛ̃] *nm* roundabout (*Brit*), traffic circle (*US*).
ronéotyper [ʀɔneɔtipe] *vt* to duplicate, roneo.
ronflant, e [ʀɔ̃flɑ̃, -ɑ̃t] *a* (*péj*) high-flown, grand.
ronflement [ʀɔ̃fləmɑ̃] *nm* snore, snoring *q*.
ronfler [ʀɔ̃fle] *vi* to snore; (*moteur, poêle*) to hum; (*: plus fort*) to roar.
ronger [ʀɔ̃ʒe] *vt* to gnaw (at); (*suj: vers, rouille*) to eat into; **~ son frein** to champ (at) the bit (*fig*); **se ~ de souci, se ~ les sangs** to worry o.s. sick, fret; **se ~ les ongles** to bite one's nails.

rongeur, euse [ʀɔ̃ʒœʀ, -øz] *nm/f* rodent.
ronronnement [ʀɔ̃ʀɔnmɑ̃] *nm* purring; (*bruit*) purr.
ronronner [ʀɔ̃ʀɔne] *vi* to purr.
roque [ʀɔk] *nm* (*ÉCHECS*) castling.
roquer [ʀɔke] *vi* to castle.
roquet [ʀɔkɛ] *nm* nasty little lap-dog.
roquette [ʀɔkɛt] *nf* rocket; **~ antichar** anti-tank rocket.
rosace [ʀozas] *nf* (*vitrail*) rose window, rosace; (*motif: de plafond etc*) rose.
rosaire [ʀozɛʀ] *nm* rosary.
rosbif [ʀɔsbif] *nm*: **du ~** roasting beef; (*cuit*) roast beef; **un ~** a joint of (roasting) beef.
rose [ʀoz] *nf* rose; (*vitrail*) rose window ♦ *a* pink; **~ bonbon** *a inv* candy pink; **~ des vents** compass card.
rosé, e [ʀoze] *a* pinkish; (*vin*) **~** rosé (wine).
roseau, x [ʀozo] *nm* reed.
rosée [ʀoze] *af voir* **rosé** ♦ *nf*: **goutte de ~** dewdrop.
roseraie [ʀozʀɛ] *nf* rose garden; (*plantation*) rose nursery.
rosette [ʀozɛt] *nf* rosette (*gen of the Légion d'honneur*).
rosier [ʀozje] *nm* rosebush, rose tree.
rosir [ʀoziʀ] *vi* to go pink.
rosse [ʀɔs] *nf* (*péj: cheval*) nag ♦ *a* nasty, vicious.
rosser [ʀɔse] *vt* (*fam*) to thrash.
rossignol [ʀɔsiɲɔl] *nm* (*ZOOL*) nightingale; (*crochet*) picklock.
rot [ʀo] *nm* belch; (*de bébé*) burp.
rotatif, ive [ʀɔtatif, -iv] *a* rotary ♦ *nf* rotary press.
rotation [ʀɔtɑsjɔ̃] *nf* rotation; (*fig*) rotation, swap-around; (*renouvellement*) turnover; **par ~** on a rota (*Brit*) *ou* rotation (*US*) basis; **~ des cultures** rotation of crops; **~ des stocks** stock turnover.
rotatoire [ʀɔtatwaʀ] *a*: **mouvement ~** rotary movement.
roter [ʀɔte] *vi* (*fam*) to burp, belch.
rôti [ʀoti] *nm*: **du ~** roasting meat; (*cuit*) roast meat; **un ~ de bœuf/porc** a joint of (roasting) beef/pork.
rotin [ʀɔtɛ̃] *nm* rattan (cane); **fauteuil en ~** cane (arm)chair.
rôtir [ʀotiʀ] *vt* (*aussi*: **faire ~**) to roast ♦ *vi* to roast; **se ~ au soleil** to bask in the sun.
rôtisserie [ʀotisʀi] *nf* (*restaurant*) steakhouse; (*comptoir, magasin*) roast meat counter (*ou* shop).
rôtissoire [ʀotiswaʀ] *nf* (roasting) spit.
rotonde [ʀɔtɔ̃d] *nf* (*ARCHIT*) rotunda; (*RAIL*) engine shed.
rotondité [ʀɔtɔ̃dite] *nf* roundness.
rotor [ʀɔtɔʀ] *nm* rotor.
Rotterdam [ʀɔtɛʀdam] *n* Rotterdam.
rotule [ʀɔtyl] *nf* kneecap, patella.
roturier, ière [ʀɔtyʀje, -jɛʀ] *nm/f* commoner.
rouage [ʀwaʒ] *nm* cog(wheel), gearwheel; (*de montre*) part; (*fig*) cog; **~s** *nmpl* (*fig*) internal structure *sg*.
Rouanda [ʀwɑ̃da] *nm*: **le ~** Rwanda.
roubaisien, ne [ʀubezjɛ̃, -ɛn] *a* of *ou* from Roubaix.
roublard, e [ʀublaʀ, -aʀd(ə)] *a* (*péj*) crafty, wily.

rouble [ʀubl(ə)] *nm* rouble.
roucouler [ʀukule] *vi* to coo; *(fig: péj)* to warble; (*: amoureux*) to bill and coo.
roue [ʀu] *nf* wheel; **faire la** ~ *(paon)* to spread *ou* fan its tail; *(GYM)* to do a cartwheel; **descendre en** ~ **libre** to freewheel *ou* coast down; **pousser à la** ~ to put one's shoulder to the wheel; **grande** ~ *(à la foire)* big wheel; ~ **à aubes** paddle wheel; ~ **dentée** cogwheel; ~ **de secours** spare wheel.
roué, e [ʀwe] *a* wily.
rouennais, e [ʀwanɛ, -ɛz] *a* of *ou* from Rouen.
rouer [ʀwe] *vt*: ~ **qn de coups** to give sb a thrashing.
rouet [ʀwɛ] *nm* spinning wheel.
rouge [ʀuʒ] *a*, *nm/f* red ♦ *nm* red; *(fard)* rouge; **(vin)** ~ red wine; **passer au** ~ *(signal)* to go red; *(automobiliste)* to go through a red light; **porter au** ~ *(métal)* to bring to red heat; **sur la liste** ~ *(TÉL)* ex-directory *(Brit)*, unlisted *(US)*; ~ **de honte/colère** red with shame/anger; **se fâcher tout/voir** ~ to blow one's top/see red; ~ **(à lèvres)** lipstick.
rougeâtre [ʀuʒɑtʀ(ə)] *a* reddish.
rougeaud, e [ʀuʒo, -od] *a* *(teint)* red; *(personne)* red-faced.
rouge-gorge [ʀuʒgɔʀʒ(ə)] *nm* robin (redbreast).
rougeoiement [ʀuʒwamɑ̃] *nm* reddish glow.
rougeole [ʀuʒɔl] *nf* measles *sg*.
rougeoyer [ʀuʒwaje] *vi* to glow red.
rouget [ʀuʒɛ] *nm* mullet.
rougeur [ʀuʒœʀ] *nf* redness; *(du visage)* red face; ~**s** *nfpl* *(MÉD)* red blotches.
rougir [ʀuʒiʀ] *vi* *(de honte, timidité)* to blush, flush; *(de plaisir, colère)* to flush; *(fraise, tomate)* to go *ou* turn red; *(ciel)* to redden.
rouille [ʀuj] *a inv* rust-coloured, rusty ♦ *nf* rust; *(CULIN)* spicy *(Provençal)* sauce served *with fish dishes.*
rouillé, e [ʀuje] *a* rusty.
rouiller [ʀuje] *vt* to rust ♦ *vi* to rust, go rusty; **se** ~ *vi* to rust; *(fig: mentalement)* to become rusty; (*: physiquement*) to grow stiff.
roulade [ʀulad] *nf* *(GYM)* roll; *(CULIN)* rolled meat *q*; *(MUS)* roulade, run.
roulant, e [ʀulɑ̃, -ɑ̃t] *a* *(meuble)* on wheels; *(surface, trottoir)* moving; **matériel** ~ *(RAIL)* rolling stock; **personnel** ~ *(RAIL)* train crews *pl.*
roulé, e [ʀule] *a*: **bien** ~**e** *(fam: femme)* shapely, curvy.
rouleau, x [ʀulo] *nm* *(de papier, tissu, pièces de monnaie, SPORT)* roll; *(de machine à écrire)* roller, platen; *(à mise en plis, à peinture, vague)* roller; **être au bout du** ~ *(fig)* to be at the end of the line; ~ **compresseur** steamroller; ~ **à pâtisserie** rolling pin; ~ **de pellicule** roll of film.
roulé-boulé, *pl* **roulés-boulés** [ʀulebule] *(SPORT)* roll.
roulement [ʀulmɑ̃] *nm* *(bruit)* rumbling *q*, rumble; *(rotation)* rotation; turnover; (*: de capitaux*) circulation; **par** ~ on a rota *(Brit)* *ou* rotation *(US)* basis; ~ **(à billes)** ball bearings *pl*; ~ **de tambour** drum roll; ~ **d'yeux** roll(ing) of the eyes.

rouler [ʀule] *vt* to roll; *(papier, tapis)* to roll up; *(CULIN: pâte)* to roll out; *(fam)* to do, con ♦ *vi* *(bille, boule)* to roll; *(voiture, train)* to go, run; *(automobiliste)* to drive; *(cycliste)* to ride; *(bateau)* to roll; *(tonnerre)* to rumble, roll; *(dégringoler)*: ~ **en bas de** to roll down; ~ **sur** *(suj: conversation)* to turn on; **se** ~ **dans** *(boue)* to roll in; *(couverture)* to roll o.s. (up) in; ~ **dans la farine** *(fam)* to con; ~ **les épaules/hanches** to sway one's shoulders/wiggle one's hips; ~ **les "r"** to roll one's r's; ~ **sur l'or** to be rolling in money, be rolling in it; ~ **(sa bosse)** to go places.
roulette [ʀulɛt] *nf* *(de table, fauteuil)* castor; *(de pâtissier)* pastry wheel; *(jeu)*: **la** ~ roulette; **à** ~**s** on castors; **la** ~ **russe** Russian roulette.
roulis [ʀuli] *nm* roll(ing).
roulotte [ʀulɔt] *nf* caravan.
roumain, e [ʀumɛ̃, -ɛn] *a* Rumanian, Romanian ♦ *nm* *(LING)* Rumanian, Romanian ♦ *nm/f*: **R~, e** Rumanian, Romanian.
Roumanie [ʀumani] *nf*: **la** ~ Rumania, Romania.
roupiller [ʀupije] *vi* *(fam)* to sleep.
roupillon, e [ʀukɛ̃, -in] *nm/f* *(péj)* redhead.
rouspéter [ʀuspete] *vi* *(fam)* to moan, grouse.
rousse [ʀus] *af voir* **roux**.
rousseur [ʀusœʀ] *nf*: **tache de** ~ freckle.
roussi [ʀusi] *nm*: **ça sent le** ~ there's a smell of burning; *(fig)* I can smell trouble.
roussir [ʀusiʀ] *vt* to scorch ♦ *vi* *(feuilles)* to go *ou* turn brown; *(CULIN)*: **faire** ~ to brown.
routage [ʀutaʒ] *nm* *(collective)* mailing.
routard, e [ʀutaʀ, -aʀd(ə)] *nm/f* traveller.
route [ʀut] *nf* road; *(fig: chemin)* way; *(itinéraire, parcours)* route; *(fig: voie)* road, path; **par (la)** ~ by road; **il y a 3h de** ~ it's a 3-hour ride *ou* journey; **en** ~ *ad* on the way; **en** ~**!** let's go!; **en cours de** ~ en route; **mettre en** ~ to start up; **se mettre en** ~ to set off; **faire** ~ **vers** to head towards; **faire fausse** ~ *(fig)* to be on the wrong track; ~ **nationale (RN)** ≈ A-road *(Brit)*, ≈ state highway *(US)*.
routier, ière [ʀutje, -jɛʀ] *a* road *cpd* ♦ *nm* *(camionneur)* (long-distance) lorry *(Brit)* *ou* truck driver; *(restaurant)* ≈ transport café *(Brit)*, ≈ truck stop *(US)*; *(scout)* ≈ rover; *(cycliste)* road racer ♦ *nf* *(voiture)* touring car; **vieux** ~ old stager; **carte routière** road map.
routine [ʀutin] *nf* routine; **visite/contrôle de** ~ routine visit/check.
routinier, ière [ʀutinje, -jɛʀ] *a* *(péj: travail)* humdrum, routine; (*: personne*) addicted to routine.
rouvert, e [ʀuvɛʀ, -ɛʀt(ə)] *pp de* **rouvrir**.
rouvrir [ʀuvʀiʀ] *vt, vi* to reopen, open again; **se** ~ *vi* *(blessure)* to open up again.
roux, rousse [ʀu, ʀus] *a* red; *(personne)* red-haired ♦ *nm/f* redhead ♦ *nm* *(CULIN)* roux.
royal, e, aux [ʀwajal, -o] *a* royal; *(fig)* fit for a king, princely; blissful; thorough.
royalement [ʀwajalmɑ̃] *ad* royally.
royaliste [ʀwajalist(ə)] *a, nm/f* royalist.
royaume [ʀwajom] *nm* kingdom; *(fig)* realm;

le ~ des cieux the kingdom of heaven.
Royaume-Uni [ʀwajomyni] *nm*: **le ~** the United Kingdom.
royauté [ʀwajote] *nf* (*dignité*) kingship; (*régime*) monarchy.
RP *sigle f* (= *recette principale*) ≈ main post office; = *région parisienne* ♦ *sigle fpl* (= *relations publiques*) PR.
RPR *sigle m* (= *Rassemblement pour la République*) political party.
R.S.V.P. *abr* (= *répondez s'il vous plaît*) R.S.V.P.
RTB *sigle f* = *Radio-Télévision belge*.
Rte *abr* = **route**.
RTL *sigle f* = *Radio-Télévision Luxembourg*.
RTVE *sigle f* = *Radio-Télévision espagnole*.
RU [ʀy] *sigle m* = **restaurant universitaire**.
ruade [ʀɥad] *nf* kick.
Ruanda [ʀwɑ̃da] *nm*: **le ~** Rwanda.
ruban [ʀybɑ̃] *nm* (*gén*) ribbon; (*pour ourlet, couture*) binding; (*de téléscripteur etc*) tape; (*d'acier*) strip; ~ **adhésif** adhesive tape; ~ **carbone** carbon ribbon.
rubéole [ʀybeɔl] *nf* German measles *sg*, rubella.
rubicond, e [ʀybikɔ̃, -ɔ̃d] *a* rubicund, ruddy.
rubis [ʀybi] *nm* ruby; (*HORLOGERIE*) jewel; **payer ~ sur l'ongle** to pay cash on the nail.
rubrique [ʀybʀik] *nf* (*titre, catégorie*) heading, rubric; (*PRESSE: article*) column.
ruche [ʀyʃ] *nf* hive.
rucher [ʀyʃe] *nm* apiary.
rude [ʀyd] *a* (*barbe, toile*) rough; (*métier, tâche*) hard, tough; (*climat*) severe, harsh; (*bourru*) harsh, rough; (*fruste*) rugged, tough; (*fam*) jolly good; **être mis à ~ épreuve** to be put through the mill.
rudement [ʀydmɑ̃] *ad* (*tomber, frapper*) hard; (*traiter, reprocher*) harshly; (*fam: très*) terribly; (*: beaucoup*) terribly hard.
rudesse [ʀydɛs] *nf* roughness; toughness; severity; harshness.
rudimentaire [ʀydimɑ̃tɛʀ] *a* rudimentary, basic.
rudiments [ʀydimɑ̃] *nmpl* rudiments; basic knowledge *sg*; basic principles.
rudoyer [ʀydwaje] *vt* to treat harshly.
rue [ʀy] *nf* street; **être/jeter qn à la ~** to be on the streets/throw sb out onto the street.
ruée [ʀɥe] *nf* rush; **la ~ vers l'or** the gold rush.
ruelle [ʀɥɛl] *nf* alley(-way).
ruer [ʀɥe] *vi* (*cheval*) to kick out; **se ~** *vi*: **se ~ sur** to pounce on; **se ~ vers/dans/hors de** to rush ou dash towards/into/out of; **~ dans les brancards** to become rebellious.
rugby [ʀygbi] *nm* Rugby (football); **~ à treize/quinze** Rugby League/Union.
rugir [ʀyʒiʀ] *vi* to roar.
rugissement [ʀyʒismɑ̃] *nm* roar, roaring *q*.
rugosité [ʀygozite] *nf* roughness; (*aspérité*) rough patch.
rugueux, euse [ʀygø, -øz] *a* rough.
ruine [ʀɥin] *nf* ruin; **~s** *nfpl* ruins; **tomber en ~** to fall into ruin(s).
ruiner [ʀɥine] *vt* to ruin.
ruineux, euse [ʀɥinø, -øz] *a* terribly expensive to buy (*ou* run), ruinous; extravagant.

ruisseau, x [ʀɥiso] *nm* stream, brook; (*caniveau*) gutter; (*fig*): **~x de larmes/sang** floods of tears/streams of blood.
ruisselant, e [ʀɥislɑ̃, -ɑ̃t] *a* streaming.
ruisseler [ʀɥisle] *vi* to stream; **~ (d'eau)** to be streaming (with water); **~ de lumière** to stream with light.
ruissellement [ʀɥisɛlmɑ̃] *nm* streaming; **~ de lumière** stream of light.
rumeur [ʀymœʀ] *nf* (*bruit confus*) rumbling; hubbub *q*; (*protestation*) murmur(ing); (*nouvelle*) rumour (*Brit*), rumor (*US*).
ruminer [ʀymine] *vt* (*herbe*) to ruminate; (*fig*) to ruminate on *ou* over, chew over ♦ *vi* (*vache*) to chew the cud, ruminate.
rumsteck [ʀɔ̃mstɛk] *nm* = **romsteck**.
rupestre [ʀypɛstʀ(ə)] *a* (*plante*) rock *cpd*; (*art*) wall *cpd*.
rupture [ʀyptyʀ] *nf* (*de câble, digue*) breaking; (*de tendon*) rupture, tearing; (*de négociations etc*) breakdown; (*de contrat*) breach; (*séparation, désunion*) break-up, split; **en ~ de ban** at odds with authority; **en ~ de stock** (*COMM*) out of stock.
rural, e, aux [ʀyʀal, -o] *a* rural, country *cpd* ♦ *nmpl*: **les ruraux** country people.
ruse [ʀyz] *nf*: **la ~** cunning, craftiness; trickery; **une ~** a trick, a ruse; **par ~** by trickery.
rusé, e [ʀyze] *a* cunning, crafty.
russe [ʀys] *a* Russian ♦ *nm* (*LING*) Russian ♦ *nm/f*: **R~** Russian.
Russie [ʀysi] *nf*: **la ~** Russia; **la ~ blanche** White Russia; **la ~ soviétique** Soviet Russia.
rustine [ʀystin] *nf* repair patch (*for bicycle inner tube*).
rustique [ʀystik] *a* rustic; (*plante*) hardy.
rustre [ʀystʀ(ə)] *nm* boor.
rut [ʀyt] *nm*: **être en ~** (*animal domestique*) to be in *ou* on heat; (*animal sauvage*) to be rutting.
rutabaga [ʀytabaga] *nm* swede.
rutilant, e [ʀytilɑ̃, -ɑ̃t] *a* gleaming.
RV *sigle m* = **rendez-vous**.
Rwanda [ʀwɑ̃da] *nm*: **le ~** Rwanda.
rythme [ʀitm(ə)] *nm* rhythm; (*vitesse*) rate; (*: de la vie*) pace, tempo; **au ~ de 10 par jour** at the rate of 10 a day.
rythmé, e [ʀitme] *a* rhythmic(al).
rythmer [ʀitme] *vt* to give rhythm to.
rythmique [ʀitmik] *a* rhythmic(al) ♦ *nf* rhythmics *sg*.

S

S, s [ɛs] *nm inv* S, s ♦ *abr* (= *sud*) S; **S comme Suzanne** S for Sugar.
s' [s] *pronom voir* **se**.
s/ *abr* = **sur**.
SA *sigle f* = **société anonyme**; (= *Son Altesse*) HH.
sa [sa] *dét voir* **son**.

sabbatique [sabatik] *a*: **année ~** sabbatical year.

sable [sabl(ə)] *nm* sand; **~s mouvants** quicksand(s).

sablé [sable] *a* (*allée*) sandy ♦ *nm* shortbread biscuit; **pâte ~e** (*CULIN*) shortbread dough.

sabler [sable] *vt* to sand; (*contre le verglas*) to grit; **~ le champagne** to drink champagne.

sableux, euse [sablø, -øz] *a* sandy.

sablier [sablije] *nm* hourglass; (*de cuisine*) egg timer.

sablière [sablijɛʀ] *nf* sand quarry.

sablonneux, euse [sablɔnø, -øz] *a* sandy.

saborder [sabɔʀde] *vt* (*navire*) to scuttle; (*fig*) to wind up, shut down.

sabot [sabo] *nm* clog; (*de cheval, bœuf*) hoof; **~ (de Denver)** (*wheel*) clamp; **~ de frein** brake shoe.

sabotage [sabɔtaʒ] *nm* sabotage.

saboter [sabɔte] *vt* (*travail, morceau de musique*) to botch, make a mess of; (*machine, installation, négociation etc*) to sabotage.

saboteur, euse [sabɔtœʀ, -øz] *nm/f* saboteur.

sabre [sabʀ(ə)] *nm* sabre; **le ~** (*fig*) the sword, the army.

sabrer [sabʀe] *vt* to cut down.

SAC [sak] *sigle m* (= *Service d'action civile*) *former Gaullist parapolice.*

sac [sak] *nm* bag; (*à charbon etc*) sack; (*pillage*) sack(ing); **mettre à ~** to sack; **~ à provisions/de voyage** shopping/travelling bag; **~ de couchage** sleeping bag; **~ à dos** rucksack; **~ à main** handbag; **~ de plage** beach bag.

saccade [sakad] *nf* jerk; **par ~s** jerkily; haltingly.

saccadé, e [sakade] *a* jerky.

saccage [sakaʒ] *nm* havoc.

saccager [sakaʒe] *vt* (*piller*) to sack, lay waste; (*dévaster*) to create havoc in, wreck.

saccharine [sakaʀin] *nf* saccharin(e).

SACEM [sasɛm] *sigle f* (= *Société des auteurs, compositeurs et éditeurs de musique*) *body responsible for collecting and distributing royalties.*

sacerdoce [sasɛʀdɔs] *nm* priesthood; (*fig*) calling, vocation.

sacerdotal, e, aux [sasɛʀdɔtal, -o] *a* priestly, sacerdotal.

sachant [saʃã] *etc vb voir* **savoir.**

sachet [saʃɛ] *nm* (small) bag; (*de lavande, poudre, shampooing*) sachet; **thé en ~s** tea bags; **~ de thé** tea bag.

sacoche [sakɔʃ] *nf* (*gén*) bag; (*de bicyclette*) saddlebag; (*du facteur*) (post-)bag; (*d'outils*) toolbag.

sacquer [sake] *vt* (*fam: candidat, employé*) to sack; (: *réprimander, mal noter*) to plough.

sacraliser [sakʀalize] *vt* to make sacred.

sacre [sakʀ(ə)] *nm* coronation; consecration.

sacré, e [sakʀe] *a* sacred; (*fam: satané*) blasted; (: *fameux*): **un ~ ...** a heck of a ...; (*ANAT*) sacral.

sacrement [sakʀəmã] *nm* sacrament; **les derniers ~s** the last rites.

sacrer [sakʀe] *vt* (*roi*) to crown; (*évêque*) to consecrate ♦ *vi* to curse, swear.

sacrifice [sakʀifis] *nm* sacrifice; **faire le ~ de** to sacrifice.

sacrificiel, le [sakʀifisjɛl] *a* sacrificial.

sacrifier [sakʀifje] *vt* to sacrifice; **~ à** *vt* to conform to; **se ~** to sacrifice o.s.; **articles sacrifiés** (*COMM*) items sold at rock-bottom *ou* give-away prices.

sacrilège [sakʀilɛʒ] *nm* sacrilege ♦ *a* sacrilegious.

sacristain [sakʀistɛ̃] *nm* sexton; sacristan.

sacristie [sakʀisti] *nf* sacristy; (*culte protestant*) vestry.

sacro-saint, e [sakʀosɛ̃, -ɛ̃t] *a* sacrosanct.

sadique [sadik] *a* sadistic ♦ *nm/f* sadist.

sadisme [sadism(ə)] *nm* sadism.

sadomasochiste [sadɔmazɔʃist(ə)] *nm/f* sadomasochist.

safari [safaʀi] *nm* safari; **faire un ~** to go on safari.

safari-photo [safaʀifɔto] *nm* photographic safari.

SAFER [safɛʀ] *sigle f* (= *société d'aménagement foncier et d'établissement rural*) *organization with the right to buy land in order to retain it for agricultural use.*

safran [safʀã] *nm* saffron.

sagace [sagas] *a* sagacious, shrewd.

sagacité [sagasite] *nf* sagacity, shrewdness.

sagaie [sage] *nf* assegai.

sage [saʒ] *a* wise; (*enfant*) good ♦ *nm* wise man; sage.

sage-femme [saʒfam] *nf* midwife (*pl* -wives).

sagement [saʒmã] *ad* (*raisonnablement*) wisely, sensibly; (*tranquillement*) quietly.

sagesse [saʒɛs] *nf* wisdom.

Sagittaire [saʒitɛʀ] *nm*: **le ~** Sagittarius, the Archer; **être du ~** to be Sagittarius.

Sahara [saaʀa] *nm*: **le ~** the Sahara (Desert); **le ~ occidental** (*pays*) Western Sahara.

saharien, ne [saaʀjɛ̃, -ɛn] *a* Saharan ♦ *nf* safari jacket.

sahélien, ne [saeljɛ̃, -ɛn] *a* Sahelian.

saignant, e [sɛɲã, -ãt] *a* (*viande*) rare; (*blessure, plaie*) bleeding.

saignée [sɛɲe] *nf* (*MÉD*) bleeding *q*, bloodletting *q*; (*ANAT*): **la ~ du bras** the bend of the arm; (*fig: MIL*) heavy losses *pl*; (: *prélèvement*) savage cut.

saignement [sɛɲmã] *nm* bleeding; **~ de nez** nosebleed.

saigner [sɛɲe] *vi* to bleed ♦ *vt* to bleed; (*animal*) to bleed to death; **~ qn à blanc** (*fig*) to bleed sb white; **~ du nez** to have a nosebleed.

Saigon [sajgɔ̃] *n* Saigon.

saillant, e [sajã, -ãt] *a* (*pommettes, menton*) prominent; (*corniche etc*) projecting; (*fig*) salient, outstanding.

saillie [saji] *nf* (*sur un mur etc*) projection; (*trait d'esprit*) witticism; (*accouplement*) covering, serving; **faire ~** to project, stick out; **en ~, formant ~** projecting, overhanging.

saillir [sajiʀ] *vi* to project, stick out; (*veine, muscle*) to bulge ♦ *vt* (*ÉLEVAGE*) to cover, serve.

sain, e [sɛ̃, sɛn] *a* healthy; (*dents, constitution*) healthy, sound; (*lectures*) wholesome; **~ et sauf** safe and sound, unharmed; **~ d'esprit** sound in mind, sane.

sacrifice [sakʀifis] *nm* sacrifice; **faire le ~ de** to sacrifice.

saindoux [sɛ̃du] nm lard.

sainement [sɛnmɑ̃] ad (vivre) healthily; (raisonner) soundly.

saint, e [sɛ̃, sɛ̃t] a holy; (fig) saintly ♦ nm/f saint; **le S~ Esprit** the Holy Spirit ou Ghost; **la S~e Vierge** the Blessed Virgin.

saint-bernard [sɛ̃bɛʀnaʀ] nm inv (chien) St Bernard.

Sainte-Hélène [sɛ̃telɛn] nf St Helena.

Sainte-Lucie [sɛ̃tlysi] nf Saint Lucia.

sainteté [sɛ̃tte] nf holiness; saintliness.

Saint-Laurent [sɛ̃lɔʀɑ̃] nm: **le ~** the St Lawrence.

Saint-Marin [sɛ̃maʀɛ̃] nm: **le ~** San Marino.

Saint-Père [sɛ̃pɛʀ] nm: **le ~** the Holy Father, the Pontiff.

Saint-Pierre [sɛ̃pjɛʀ] nm Saint Peter; (église) Saint Peter's.

Saint-Pierre-et-Miquelon [sɛ̃pjɛʀemiklɔ̃] nm Saint Pierre and Miquelon.

Saint-Siège [sɛ̃sjɛʒ] nm: **le ~** the Holy See.

Saint-Sylvestre [sɛ̃silvɛstʀ(ə)] nf: **la ~** New Year's Eve.

Saint-Thomas [sɛ̃tɔma] nf Saint Thomas.

Saint-Vincent et les Grenadines [sɛ̃vɛ̃sɑ̃elegʀənadin] nm St Vincent and the Grenadines.

sais [sɛ] etc vb voir **savoir**.

saisie [sezi] nf seizure; **à la ~** (texte) being keyed; **~ (de données)** (data) capture.

saisine [sezin] nf (JUR) submission of a case to the court.

saisir [seziʀ] vt to take hold of, grab; (fig: occasion) to seize; (comprendre) to grasp; (entendre) to get, catch; (suj: émotions) to take hold of, come over; (INFORM) to capture, keyboard; (CULIN) to fry quickly; (JUR: biens, publication) to seize; (: juridiction): **~ un tribunal d'une affaire** to submit ou refer a case to a court; **se ~ de** vt to seize; **être saisi** (frappé de) to be overcome.

saisissant, e [sezisɑ̃, -ɑ̃t] a startling, striking; (froid) biting.

saisissement [sezismɑ̃] nm: **muet/figé de ~** speechless/frozen with emotion.

saison [sɛzɔ̃] nf season; **la belle/mauvaise ~** the summer/winter months; **être de ~** to be in season; **en/hors ~** in/out of season; **haute/basse/morte ~** high/low/slack season; **la ~ des pluies/des amours** the rainy/mating season.

saisonnier, ière [sɛzɔnje, -jɛʀ] a seasonal ♦ nm (travailleur) seasonal worker; (vacancier) seasonal holidaymaker.

sait [sɛ] vb voir **savoir**.

salace [salas] a salacious.

salade [salad] nf (BOT) lettuce etc (generic term); (CULIN) (green) salad; (fam) tangle, muddle; **~s** nfpl (fam): **raconter des ~s** to tell tales (fam); **haricots en ~** bean salad; **~ de concombres** cucumber salad; **~ de fruits** fruit salad; **~ niçoise** salade niçoise; **~ russe** Russian salad.

saladier [saladje] nm (salad) bowl.

salaire [salɛʀ] nm (annuel, mensuel) salary; (hebdomadaire, journalier) pay, wages pl; (fig) reward; **~ de base** basic salary (ou wage); **~ de misère** starvation wage; **~ minimum interprofessionnel de croissance**

(SMIC) index-linked guaranteed minimum wage.

salaison [salɛzɔ̃] nf salting; **~s** nfpl salt meat sg.

salamandre [salamɑ̃dʀ(ə)] nf salamander.

salami [salami] nm salami q, salami sausage.

salant [salɑ̃] am: **marais ~** salt pan.

salarial, e, aux [salaʀjal, -o] a salary cpd, wage(s) cpd.

salariat [salaʀja] nm salaried staff.

salarié, e [salaʀje] a salaried; wage-earning ♦ nm/f salaried employee; wage-earner.

salaud [salo] nm (fam!) sod (!), bastard (!).

salé, e [sale] a (liquide, saveur) salty; (CULIN) salted, salt cpd; (fig) spicy, juicy; (: note, facture) steep, stiff ♦ nm (porc salé) salt pork; **petit ~** ≈ boiling bacon.

salement [salmɑ̃] ad (manger etc) dirtily, messily.

saler [sale] vt to salt.

saleté [salte] nf (état) dirtiness; (crasse) dirt, filth; (tache etc) dirt q, something dirty, dirty mark; (fig: tour) filthy trick; (: chose sans valeur) rubbish q; (: obscénité) filth q; (: microbe etc) bug; **vivre dans la ~** to live in squalor.

salière [saljɛʀ] nf saltcellar.

saligaud [saligo] nm (fam!) bastard (!), sod (!).

salin, e [salɛ̃, -in] a saline ♦ nf saltworks sg.

salinité [salinite] nf salinity, salt-content.

salir [saliʀ] vt to (make) dirty; (fig) to soil the reputation of; **se ~** to get dirty.

salissant, e [salisɑ̃, -ɑ̃t] a (tissu) which shows the dirt; (métier) dirty, messy.

salissure [salisyʀ] nf dirt q; (tache) dirty mark.

salive [saliv] nf saliva.

saliver [salive] vi to salivate.

salle [sal] nf room; (d'hôpital) ward; (de restaurant) dining room; (d'un cinéma) auditorium; (: public) audience; **faire ~ comble** to have a full house; **~ d'armes** (pour l'escrime) arms room; **~ d'attente** waiting room; **~ de bain(s)** bathroom; **~ de bal** ballroom; **~ de cinéma** cinema; **~ de classe** classroom; **~ commune** (d'hôpital) ward; **~ de concert** concert hall; **~ de consultation** consulting room (Brit), office (US); **~ de danse** dance hall; **~ de douches** shower-room; **~ d'eau** shower-room; **~ d'embarquement** (à l'aéroport) departure lounge; **~ d'exposition** showroom; **~ de jeux** games room; playroom; **~ des machines** engine room; **~ à manger** dining room; (mobilier) dining room suite; **~ obscure** cinema (Brit), movie theater (US); **~ d'opération** (d'hôpital) operating theatre; **~ de projection** film theatre; **~ de séjour** living room; **~ de spectacle** theatre; cinema; **~ des ventes** saleroom.

salmonellose [salmɔneloz] nf (MÉD) salmonella poisoning.

Salomon [salɔmɔ̃]: **les îles ~** the Solomon Islands.

salon [salɔ̃] nm lounge, sitting room; (mobilier) lounge suite; (exposition) exhibition, show; (mondain, littéraire) salon; **~ de**

coiffure hairdressing salon; ~ **de thé** tearoom.

salopard [salɔpaʀ] *nm* (*fam!*) bastard (*!*).

salope [salɔp] *nf* (*fam!*) bitch (*!*).

saloper [salɔpe] *vt* (*fam!*) to muck up, mess up.

saloperie [salɔpʀi] *nf* (*fam!*) filth *q*; dirty trick; rubbish *q*.

salopette [salɔpɛt] *nf* dungarees *pl*; (*d'ouvrier*) overall(s).

salpêtre [salpɛtʀ(ə)] *nm* saltpetre.

salsifis [salsifi] *nm* salsify, oyster-plant.

SALT [salt] *sigle* (= *Strategic Arms Limitation Talks*) SALT.

saltimbanque [saltɛ̃bɑ̃k] *nm/f* (travelling) acrobat.

salubre [salybʀ(ə)] *a* healthy, salubrious.

salubrité [salybʀite] *nf* healthiness, salubrity; ~ **publique** public health.

saluer [salɥe] *vt* (*pour dire bonjour, fig*) to greet; (*pour dire au revoir*) to take one's leave; (*MIL*) to salute.

salut [saly] *nm* (*sauvegarde*) safety; (*REL*) salvation; (*geste*) wave; (*parole*) greeting; (*MIL*) salute ♦ *excl* (*fam: pour dire bonjour*) hi (there); (: *pour dire au revoir*) see you!, 'bye!; (*style relevé*) (all) hail.

salutaire [salytɛʀ] *a* (*remède*) beneficial; (*conseils*) salutary.

salutations [salytasjɔ̃] *nfpl* greetings; **recevez mes ~ distinguées** *ou* **respectueuses** yours faithfully.

salutiste [salytist(ə)] *nm/f* Salvationist.

Salvador [salvadɔʀ] *nm*: **le ~** El Salvador.

salve [salv(ə)] *nf* salvo; volley of shots; ~ **d'applaudissements** burst of applause.

Samarie [samaʀi] *nf*: **la ~** Samaria.

samaritain [samaʀitɛ̃] *nm*: **le bon S~** the Good Samaritan.

samedi [samdi] *nm* Saturday; *voir aussi* **lundi**.

Samoa [samɔa] *nfpl*: **les (îles) ~** Samoa, the Samoa Islands.

SAMU [samy] *sigle m* (= *service d'assistance médicale d'urgence*) ≈ ambulance (service) (*Brit*), ≈ paramedics (*US*).

sanatorium [sanatɔʀjɔm] *nm* sanatorium (*pl* -a).

sanctifier [sɑ̃ktifje] *vt* to sanctify.

sanction [sɑ̃ksjɔ̃] *nf* sanction; (*fig*) penalty; **prendre des ~s contre** to impose sanctions on.

sanctionner [sɑ̃ksjɔne] *vt* (*loi, usage*) to sanction; (*punir*) to punish.

sanctuaire [sɑ̃ktɥɛʀ] *nm* sanctuary.

sandale [sɑ̃dal] *nf* sandal.

sandalette [sɑ̃dalɛt] *nf* sandal.

sandow [sɑ̃do] *nm* ® luggage elastic.

sandwich [sɑ̃dwitʃ] *nm* sandwich; **pris en ~** sandwiched.

sang [sɑ̃] *nm* blood; **en ~** covered in blood; **jusqu'au ~** (*mordre, pincer*) till the blood comes; **se faire du mauvais ~** to fret, get in a state.

sang-froid [sɑ̃fʀwa] *nm* calm, sangfroid; **garder/perdre/reprendre son ~** to keep/lose/regain one's cool; **de ~** in cold blood.

sanglant, e [sɑ̃glɑ̃, -ɑ̃t] *a* bloody, covered in blood; (*combat*) bloody; (*fig: reproche, affront*) cruel.

sangle [sɑ̃gl(ə)] *nf* strap; **~s** *nfpl* (*pour lit etc*) webbing *sg*.

sangler [sɑ̃gle] *vt* to strap up; (*animal*) to girth.

sanglier [sɑ̃glije] *nm* (wild) boar.

sanglot [sɑ̃glo] *nm* sob.

sangloter [sɑ̃glɔte] *vi* to sob.

sangsue [sɑ̃sy] *nf* leech.

sanguin, e [sɑ̃gɛ̃, -in] *a* blood *cpd*; (*fig*) fiery ♦ *nf* blood orange; (*ART*) red pencil drawing.

sanguinaire [sɑ̃ginɛʀ] *a* (*animal, personne*) bloodthirsty; (*lutte*) bloody.

sanguinolent, e [sɑ̃ginɔlɑ̃, -ɑ̃t] *a* streaked with blood.

sanisette [sanizɛt] *nf* (automatic) public toilet.

sanitaire [sanitɛʀ] *a* health *cpd*; ~**s** *nmpl* (*salle de bain et w.-c.*) bathroom *sg*; **installation/appareil ~** bathroom plumbing/appliance.

sans [sɑ̃] *prép* without; ~ **qu'il s'en aperçoive** without him *ou* his noticing; ~ **scrupules** unscrupulous; ~ **manches** sleeveless.

sans-abri [sɑ̃zabri] *nmpl* homeless.

sans-emploi [sɑ̃zɑ̃plwa] *nmpl* jobless.

sans-façon [sɑ̃fasɔ̃] *a inv* fuss-free; free and easy.

sans-gêne [sɑ̃ʒɛn] *a inv* inconsiderate ♦ *nm inv* (*attitude*) lack of consideration.

sans-logis [sɑ̃lɔʒi] *nmpl* homeless.

sans-souci [sɑ̃susi] *a inv* carefree.

sans-travail [sɑ̃tʀavaj] *nmpl* unemployed, jobless.

santal [sɑ̃tal] *nm* sandal(wood).

santé [sɑ̃te] *nf* health; **avoir une ~ de fer** to be bursting with health; **être en bonne ~** to be in good health, be healthy; **boire à la ~ de qn** to drink (to) sb's health; **"à la ~ de"** "here's to"; **à ta** *ou* **votre ~!** cheers!; **service de ~** (*dans un port etc*) quarantine service; **la ~ publique** public health.

Santiago (du Chili) [sɑ̃tjago(dyʃili)] *n* Santiago (de Chile).

santon [sɑ̃tɔ̃] *nm* ornamental figure at a Christmas crib.

saoudien, ne [saudjɛ̃, -ɛn] *a* Saudi (Arabian) ♦ *nm/f*: **S~, ne** Saudi (Arabian).

saoul, e [su, sul] *a* = **soûl, e**.

sape [sap] *nf*: **travail de ~** (*MIL*) sap; (*fig*) insidious undermining process *ou* work; ~**s** *nfpl* (*fam*) gear *sg*, togs.

saper [sape] *vt* to undermine, sap; **se ~** *vi* (*fam*) to dress.

sapeur [sapœʀ] *nm* sapper.

sapeur-pompier [sapœʀpɔ̃pje] *nm* fireman.

saphir [safiʀ] *nm* sapphire; (*d'électrophone*) needle, sapphire.

sapin [sapɛ̃] *nm* fir (tree); (*bois*) fir; ~ **de Noël** Christmas tree.

sapinière [sapinjɛʀ] *nf* fir plantation *ou* forest.

SAR *sigle f* (= *Son Altesse Royale*) HRH.

sarabande [saʀabɑ̃d] *nf* saraband; (*fig*) hullabaloo; whirl.

sarbacane [saʀbakan] *nf* blowpipe, blowgun; (*jouet*) peashooter.

sarcasme [saʀkasm(ə)] *nm* sarcasm *q*; (*propos*) piece of sarcasm.

sarcastique [saʀkastik] *a* sarcastic.

sarcastiquement [saʀkastikmɑ̃] *ad* sarcastically.

sarclage [saʀklaʒ] *nm* weeding.
sarcler [saʀkle] *vt* to weed.
sarcloir [saʀklwaʀ] *nm* (weeding) hoe, spud.
sarcophage [saʀkɔfaʒ] *nm* sarcophagus (*pl* -i).
Sardaigne [saʀdɛɲ] *nf*: **la ~** Sardinia.
sarde [saʀd(ə)] *a* Sardinian.
sardine [saʀdin] *nf* sardine; **~s à l'huile** sardines in oil.
sardinier, ière [saʀdinje, -jɛʀ] *a* (*pêche, industrie*) sardine *cpd* ♦ *nm* (*bateau*) sardine boat.
sardonique [saʀdɔnik] *a* sardonic.
sari [saʀi] *nm* sari.
SARL [saʀl] *sigle f* = **société à responsabilité limitée**.
sarment [saʀmɑ̃] *nm*: **~ (de vigne)** vine shoot.
sarrasin [saʀazɛ̃] *nm* buckwheat.
sarrau [saʀo] *nm* smock.
Sarre [saʀ] *nf*: **la ~** the Saar.
sarriette [saʀjɛt] *nf* savory.
sarrois, e [saʀwa, -waz] *a* Saar *cpd* ♦ *nm/f*: **S~, e** inhabitant *ou* native of the Saar.
sas [sas] *nm* (*de sous-marin, d'engin spatial*) airlock; (*d'écluse*) lock.
satané, e [satane] *a* confounded.
satanique [satanik] *a* satanic, fiendish.
satelliser [satelize] *vt* (*fusée*) to put into orbit; (*fig: pays*) to make into a satellite.
satellite [satelit] *nm* satellite; **pays ~** satellite country.
satellite-espion, *pl* **satellites-espions** [satelitɛspjɔ̃] *nm* spy satellite.
satellite-observatoire, *pl* **satellites-observatoires** [satelitɔpsɛʀvatwaʀ] *nm* observation satellite.
satellite-relais, *pl* **satellites-relais** [satelitʀəlɛ] *nm* (*TV*) relay satellite.
satiété [sasjete]: **à ~** *ad* to satiety *ou* satiation; (*répéter*) *ad* nauseam.
satin [satɛ̃] *nm* satin.
satiné, e [satine] *a* satiny; (*peau*) satin-smooth.
satinette [satinɛt] *nf* satinet, sateen.
satire [satiʀ] *nf* satire; **faire la ~** to satirize.
satirique [satiʀik] *a* satirical.
satiriser [satiʀize] *vt* to satirize.
satiriste [satiʀist(ə)] *nm/f* satirist.
satisfaction [satisfaksjɔ̃] *nf* satisfaction; **à ma grande ~** to my great satisfaction; **obtenir ~** to obtain *ou* get satisfaction; **donner ~ (à)** to give satisfaction (to).
satisfaire [satisfɛʀ] *vt* to satisfy; **se ~ de** to be satisfied *ou* content with; **~ à** (*engagement*) to fulfil; (*revendications, conditions*) to satisfy, meet.
satisfaisant, e [satisfəzɑ̃, -ɑ̃t] *vb voir* **satisfaire** ♦ *a* satisfactory; (*qui fait plaisir*) satisfying.
satisfait, e [satisfɛ, -ɛt] *pp de* **satisfaire** ♦ *a* satisfied; **~ de** happy *ou* satisfied with.
satisfasse [satisfas], **satisferai** [satisfʀe] *etc vb voir* **satisfaire**.
saturation [satyʀasjɔ̃] *nf* saturation; **arriver à ~** to reach saturation point.
saturer [satyʀe] *vt* to saturate; **~ qn/qch de** to saturate sb/sth with.
saturnisme [satyʀnism(ə)] *nm* (*MÉD*) lead poisoning.
satyre [satiʀ] *nm* satyr; (*péj*) lecher.
sauce [sos] *nf* sauce; (*avec un rôti*) gravy; **en ~** in a sauce; **~ blanche** white sauce; **~ chasseur** sauce chausseur; **~ tomate** tomato sauce.
saucer [sose] *vt* (*assiette*) to soak up the sauce from.
saucière [sosjɛʀ] *nf* sauceboat; gravy boat.
saucisse [sosis] *nf* sausage.
saucisson [sosisɔ̃] *nm* (slicing) sausage; **~ à l'ail** garlic sausage.
saucissonner [sosisɔne] *vt* to cut up, slice ♦ *vi* to picnic.
sauf [sof] *prép* except; **~ si** (*à moins que*) unless; **~ avis contraire** unless you hear to the contrary; **~ empêchement** barring (any) problems; **~ erreur** if I'm not mistaken; **~ imprévu** unless anything unforeseen arises, barring accidents.
sauf, sauve [sof, sov] *a* unharmed, unhurt; (*fig: honneur*) intact, saved; **laisser la vie sauve à qn** to spare sb's life.
sauf-conduit [sofkɔ̃dɥi] *nm* safe-conduct.
sauge [soʒ] *nf* sage.
saugrenu, e [sogʀəny] *a* preposterous, ludicrous.
saule [sol] *nm* willow (tree); **~ pleureur** weeping willow.
saumâtre [somɑtʀ(ə)] *a* briny; (*désagréable: plaisanterie*) unsavoury (*Brit*), unsavory (*US*).
saumon [somɔ̃] *nm* salmon *inv* ♦ *a inv* salmon (pink).
saumoné, e [somɔne] *a*: **truite saumonée** salmon trout.
saumure [somyʀ] *nf* brine.
sauna [sona] *nm* sauna.
saupoudrer [sopudʀe] *vt*: **~ qch de** to sprinkle sth with.
saupoudreuse [sopudʀøz] *nf* dredger.
saur [sɔʀ] *am*: **hareng ~** smoked *ou* red herring, kipper.
saurai [sɔʀe] *etc vb voir* **savoir**.
saut [so] *nm* jump; (*discipline sportive*) jumping; **faire un ~** to (make a) jump *ou* leap; **faire un ~ chez qn** to pop over to sb's (place); **au ~ du lit** on getting out of bed; **~ en hauteur/longueur** high/long jump; **~ à la corde** skipping; **~ de page** (*INFORM*) page break; **~ en parachute** parachuting *q*; **~ à la perche** pole vaulting; **~ périlleux** somersault.
saute [sot] *nf*: **~ de vent/température** sudden change of wind direction/in the temperature; **avoir des ~s d'humeur** to have sudden changes of mood.
sauté, e [sote] *a* (*CULIN*) sauté ♦ *nm*: **~ de veau** sauté of veal.
saute-mouton [sotmutɔ̃] *nm*: **jouer à ~** to play leapfrog.
sauter [sote] *vi* to jump, leap; (*exploser*) to blow up, explode; (*: fusibles*) to blow; (*se rompre*) to snap, burst; (*se détacher*) to pop out (*ou* off) ♦ *vt* to jump (over), leap (over); (*fig: omettre*) to skip, miss (out); **faire ~** to blow up; to burst open; (*CULIN*) to sauté; **~ à pieds joints/à cloche-pied** to make a standing jump/to hop; **~ en parachute** to make a

parachute jump; ~ **à la corde** to skip; ~ **de joie** to jump for joy; ~ **de colère** to be hopping with rage *ou* hopping mad; ~ **au cou de qn** to fly into sb's arms; ~ **aux yeux** to be quite obvious; ~ **au plafond** (*fig*) to hit the roof.

sauterelle [sotʀɛl] *nf* grasshopper.

sauterie [sotʀi] *nf* party, hop.

sauteur, euse [sotœʀ, -øz] *nm/f* (*athlète*) jumper ♦ *nf* (*casserole*) shallow pan, frying pan; ~ **à la perche** pole vaulter; ~ **à skis** skijumper.

sautiller [sotije] *vi* to hop; to skip.

sautoir [sotwaʀ] *nm* chain; (*SPORT: emplacement*) jumping pit; ~ **(de perles)** string of pearls.

sauvage [sovaʒ] *a* (*gén*) wild; (*peuplade*) savage; (*farouche*) unsociable; (*barbare*) wild, savage; (*non officiel*) unauthorized, unofficial ♦ *nm/f* savage; (*timide*) unsociable type, recluse.

sauvagement [sovaʒmɑ̃] *ad* savagely.

sauvageon, ne [sovaʒɔ̃, -ɔn] *nm/f* little savage.

sauvagerie [sovaʒʀi] *nf* wildness; savagery; unsociability.

sauve [sov] *af voir* **sauf**.

sauvegarde [sovgaʀd(ə)] *nf* safeguard; **sous la ~ de** under the protection of; **disquette/ fichier de ~** (*INFORM*) backup disk/file.

sauvegarder [sovgaʀde] *vt* to safeguard; (*INFORM: enregistrer*) to save; (: *copier*) to back up.

sauve-qui-peut [sovkipø] *nm inv* stampede, mad rush ♦ *excl* run for your life!

sauver [sove] *vt* to save; (*porter secours à*) to rescue; (*récupérer*) to salvage, rescue; **se ~** *vi* (*s'enfuir*) to run away; (*fam: partir*) to be off; ~ **qn de** to save sb from; ~ **la vie à qn** to save sb's life; ~ **les apparences** to keep up appearances.

sauvetage [sovtaʒ] *nm* rescue; ~ **en montagne** mountain rescue; **ceinture de ~** lifebelt (*Brit*), life preserver (*US*); **brassière** *ou* **gilet de ~** lifejacket (*Brit*), life preserver (*US*).

sauveteur [sovtœʀ] *nm* rescuer.

sauvette [sovɛt]: **à la ~** *ad* (*vendre*) without authorization; (*se marier etc*) hastily, hurriedly; **vente à la ~** (unauthorized) street trading, (street) peddling.

sauveur [sovœʀ] *nm* saviour (*Brit*), savior (*US*).

SAV *sigle m* = **service après vente**.

savais [save] *etc vb voir* **savoir**.

savamment [savamɑ̃] *ad* (*avec érudition*) learnedly; (*habilement*) skilfully, cleverly.

savane [savan] *nf* savannah.

savant, e [savɑ̃, -ɑ̃t] *a* scholarly, learned; (*calé*) clever ♦ *nm* scientist; **animal ~** performing animal.

savate [savat] *nf* worn-out shoe; (*SPORT*) (*type of*) boxing.

saveur [savœʀ] *nf* flavour (*Brit*), flavor (*US*); (*fig*) savour (*Brit*), savor (*US*).

Savoie [savwa] *nf*: **la ~** Savoy.

savoir [savwaʀ] *vt* to know; (*être capable de*): **il sait nager** he knows how to swim, he can swim ♦ *nm* knowledge; **se ~** (*être connu*) to be known; **se ~ malade/incurable** to know

that one is ill/incurably ill; **il est petit: tu ne peux pas ~!** you won't believe how small he is!; **vous n'êtes pas sans ~ que** you are not *ou* will not be unaware of the fact that; **je crois ~ que ...** I believe that ..., I think I know that ...; **je n'en sais rien** I (really) don't know; **à ~ (que)** that is, namely; **faire ~ qch à qn** to inform sb about sth, let sb know sth; **pas que je sache** not as far as I know; **sans le ~** *ad* unknowingly, unwittingly; **en ~ long** to know a lot.

savoir-faire [savwaʀfɛʀ] *nm inv* savoir-faire, know-how.

savoir-vivre [savwaʀvivʀ(ə)] *nm inv*: **le ~** savoir-faire, good manners *pl*.

savon [savɔ̃] *nm* (*produit*) soap; (*morceau*) bar *ou* tablet of soap; (*fam*): **passer un ~ à qn** to give sb a good dressing-down.

savonner [savɔne] *vt* to soap.

savonnerie [savɔnʀi] *nf* soap factory.

savonnette [savɔnɛt] *nf* bar *ou* tablet of soap.

savonneux, euse [savɔnø, -øz] *a* soapy.

savons [savɔ̃] *vb voir* **savoir**.

savourer [savuʀe] *vt* to savour (*Brit*), savor (*US*).

savoureux, euse [savuʀø, -øz] *a* tasty; (*fig*) spicy, juicy.

savoyard, e [savwajaʀ, -aʀd(ə)] *a* Savoyard.

sax [saks] *nm* sax.

Saxe [saks(ə)] *nf*: **la ~** Saxony.

saxo(phone) [saksɔ(fɔn)] *nm* sax(ophone).

saxophoniste [saksɔfɔnist(ə)] *nm/f* saxophonist, sax(ophone) player.

saynète [sɛnɛt] *nf* playlet.

SBB *sigle f* (= *Schweizerische Bundesbahn*) Swiss federal railways.

sbire [sbiʀ] *nm* (*péj*) henchman.

sc. *abr* = **scène**.

s/c *abr* (= *sous couvert de*) ≈ c/o.

scabreux, euse [skabʀø, -øz] *a* risky; (*indécent*) improper, shocking.

scalpel [skalpɛl] *nm* scalpel.

scalper [skalpe] *vt* to scalp.

scampi [skɑ̃pi] *nmpl* scampi.

scandale [skɑ̃dal] *nm* scandal; (*tapage*): **faire du ~** to make a scene, create a disturbance; **faire ~** to scandalize people; **au grand ~ de ...** to the great indignation of ....

scandaleusement [skɑ̃daløzmɑ̃] *ad* scandalously, outrageously.

scandaleux, euse [skɑ̃dalø, -øz] *a* scandalous, outrageous.

scandaliser [skɑ̃dalize] *vt* to scandalize; **se ~ (de)** to be scandalized (by).

scander [skɑ̃de] *vt* (*vers*) to scan; (*mots, syllabes*) to stress separately; (*slogans*) to chant.

scandinave [skɑ̃dinav] *a* Scandinavian ♦ *nm/f*: **S~** Scandinavian.

Scandinavie [skɑ̃dinavi] *nf*: **la ~** Scandinavia.

scanner [skanɛʀ] *nm* (*MÉD*) scanner.

scanographie [skanɔgʀafi] *nf* (*MÉD*) scanning; (*image*) scan.

scaphandre [skafɑ̃dʀ(ə)] *nm* (*de plongeur*) diving suit; (*de cosmonaute*) space-suit; ~ **autonome** aqualung.

scaphandrier [skafɑ̃dʀije] *nm* diver.

scarabée [skaʀabe] *nm* beetle.

scarlatine [skaʀlatin] *nf* scarlet fever.

scarole [skaʀɔl] *nf* endive.

scatologique [skatɔlɔʒik] *a* scatological, lavatorial.

sceau, x [so] *nm* seal; *(fig)* stamp, mark; **sous le ~ du secret** under the seal of secrecy.

scélérat, e [selɛʀa, -at] *nm/f* villain, blackguard ♦ *a* villainous, blackguardly.

sceller [sele] *vt* to seal.

scellés [sele] *nmpl* seals.

scénario [senaʀjo] *nm* (*CINÉMA*) screenplay, script; (: *idée, plan*) scenario; *(fig)* pattern; scenario.

scénariste [senaʀist(ə)] *nm/f* scriptwriter.

scène [sɛn] *nf* (*gén*) scene; (*estrade, fig: théâtre*) stage; **entrer en ~** to come on stage; **mettre en ~** (*THÉÂTRE*) to stage; (*CINÉMA*) to direct; *(fig)* to present, introduce; **sur le devant de la ~** (*en pleine actualité*) in the forefront; **porter à la ~** to adapt for the stage; **faire une ~ (à qn)** to make a scene (with sb); **~ de ménage** domestic fight *ou* scene.

scénique [senik] *a* (*effets*) theatrical; (*art*) scenic.

scepticisme [sɛptisism(ə)] *nm* scepticism.

sceptique [sɛptik] *a* sceptical ♦ *nm/f* sceptic.

sceptre [sɛptʀ(ə)] *nm* sceptre.

schéma [ʃema] *nm* (*diagramme*) diagram, sketch; *(fig)* outline.

schématique [ʃematik] *a* diagrammatic(al), schematic; *(fig)* oversimplified.

schématiquement [ʃematikmã] *ad* schematically, diagrammatically.

schématiser [ʃematize] *vt* to schematize; (*over*)simplify.

schismatique [ʃismatik] *a* schismatic.

schisme [ʃism(ə)] *nm* schism; rift, split.

schiste [ʃist(ə)] *nm* schist.

schizophrène [skizɔfʀɛn] *nm/f* schizophrenic.

schizophrénie [skizɔfʀeni] *nf* schizophrenia.

sciatique [sjatik] *a*: **nerf ~** sciatic nerve ♦ *nf* sciatica.

scie [si] *nf* saw; (*fam: rengaine*) catch-tune; (: *personne*) bore; **~ à bois** wood saw; **~ circulaire** circular saw; **~ à découper** fretsaw; **~ à métaux** hacksaw; **~ sauteuse** jigsaw.

sciemment [sjamã] *ad* knowingly, wittingly.

science [sjɑ̃s] *nf* science; (*savoir*) knowledge; (*savoir-faire*) art, skill; **~s humaines/sociales** social sciences; **~s naturelles** natural science *sg*, biology *sg*; **~s po** political studies.

science-fiction [sjɑ̃sfiksjɔ̃] *nf* science fiction.

scientifique [sjɑ̃tifik] *a* scientific ♦ *nm/f* (*savant*) scientist; (*étudiant*) science student.

scientifiquement [sjɑ̃tifikmã] *ad* scientifically.

scier [sje] *vt* to saw; (*retrancher*) to saw off.

scierie [siʀi] *nf* sawmill.

scieur [sjœʀ] *nm*: **~ de long** pit sawyer.

Scilly [sili]: **les îles ~** the Scilly Isles, the Scillies, the Isles of Scilly.

scinder [sɛ̃de] *vt*, **se ~** *vi* to split (up).

scintillant, e [sɛ̃tijɑ̃, -ɑ̃t] *a* sparkling.

scintillement [sɛ̃tijmã] *nm* sparkling *q*.

scintiller [sɛ̃tije] *vi* to sparkle.

scission [sisjɔ̃] *nf* split.

sciure [sjyʀ] *nf*: **~ (de bois)** sawdust.

sclérose [skleʀoz] *nf* sclerosis; *(fig)* ossification; **~ en plaques (SEP)** multiple sclerosis (MS).

sclérosé, e [skleʀoze] *a* sclerosed, sclerotic; ossified.

scléroser [skleʀoze]: **se ~** *vi* to become sclerosed; *(fig)* to become ossified.

scolaire [skɔlɛʀ] *a* school *cpd*; *(péj)* schoolish; **l'année ~** the school year; (*à l'université*) the academic year; **en âge ~** of school age.

scolariser [skɔlaʀize] *vt* to provide with schooling (*ou* schools).

scolarité [skɔlaʀite] *nf* schooling; **frais de ~** school fees (*Brit*), tuition (*US*).

scolastique [skɔlastik] *a* (*péj*) scholastic.

scoliose [skɔljoz] *nf* curvature of the spine, scoliosis.

scoop [skup] *nm* (*PRESSE*) scoop, exclusive.

scooter [skutœʀ] *nm* (motor) scooter.

scorbut [skɔʀbyt] *nm* scurvy.

score [skɔʀ] *nm* score; (*électoral etc*) result.

scories [skɔʀi] *nfpl* scoria *pl*.

scorpion [skɔʀpjɔ̃] *nm* (*signe*): **le S~** Scorpio, the Scorpion; **être du S~** to be Scorpio.

scotch [skɔtʃ] *nm* (*whisky*) scotch, whisky; (*adhésif*) Sellotape ® (*Brit*), Scotch tape ® (*US*).

scotcher [skɔtʃe] *vt* to sellotape ® (*Brit*), scotchtape ® (*US*).

scout, e [skut] *a, nm* scout.

scoutisme [skutism(ə)] *nm* (boy) scout movement; (*activités*) scouting.

scribe [skʀib] *nm* scribe; *(péj)* penpusher.

scribouillard [skʀibujaʀ] *nm* penpusher.

script [skʀipt] *nm* printing; (*CINÉMA*) (shooting) script.

script-girl [skʀiptgœʀl] *nf* continuity girl.

scriptural, e, aux [skʀiptyʀal, -o] *a*: **monnaie ~e** bank money.

scrupule [skʀypyl] *nm* scruple; **être sans ~s** to be unscrupulous; **se faire un ~ de qch** to have scruples *ou* qualms about doing sth.

scrupuleusement [skʀypyløzmã] *ad* scrupulously.

scrupuleux, euse [skʀypylø, -øz] *a* scrupulous.

scrutateur, trice [skʀytatœʀ, -tʀis] *a* searching ♦ *nm/f* scrutineer.

scruter [skʀyte] *vt* to search, scrutinize; (*l'obscurité*) to peer into; (*motifs, comportement*) to examine, scrutinize.

scrutin [skʀytɛ̃] *nm* (*vote*) ballot; (*ensemble des opérations*) poll; **~ proportionnel/majoritaire** election on a proportional/majority basis; **~ à deux tours** poll with two ballots *ou* rounds; **~ de liste** list system.

sculpter [skylte] *vt* to sculpt; (*suj: érosion*) to carve.

sculpteur [skyltœʀ] *nm* sculptor.

sculptural, e, aux [skyltyʀal, -o] *a* sculptural; *(fig)* statuesque.

sculpture [skyltyʀ] *nf* sculpture; **~ sur bois** wood carving.

sdb. *abr* = **salle de bain.**

SDN *sigle f* (= *Société des Nations*) League of Nations.

SE *sigle f* (= *Son Excellence*) HE.

se, s' [s(ə)] *pronom* (*emploi réfléchi*) oneself,

m himself, *f* herself, *sujet non humain* itself; *pl* themselves; (: *réciproque*) one another, each other; (: *passif*): **cela se répare facilement** it is easily repaired; (: *possessif*): ~ **casser la jambe/laver les mains** to break one's leg/wash one's hands; *autres emplois pronominaux: voir le verbe en question.*

séance [seɑ̃s] *nf* (*d'assemblée, récréative*) meeting, session; (*de tribunal*) sitting, session; (*musicale,* CINÉMA, THÉÂTRE) performance; **ouvrir/lever la** ~ to open/close the meeting; ~ **tenante** forthwith.

séant, e [seɑ̃, -ɑ̃t] *a* seemly, fitting ♦ *nm* posterior.

seau, x [so] *nm* bucket, pail; ~ **à glace** ice-bucket.

sébum [sebɔm] *nm* sebum.

sec, sèche [sɛk, sɛʃ] *a* dry; (*raisins, figues*) dried; (*cœur, personne: insensible*) hard, cold; (*maigre, décharné*) spare, lean; (*réponse, ton*) sharp, curt; (*démarrage*) sharp, sudden ♦ *nm*: **tenir au** ~ to keep in a dry place ♦ *ad* hard; (*démarrer*) sharply; **boire** ~ to be a heavy drinker; **je le bois** ~ I drink it straight *ou* neat; **à pied** ~ without getting one's feet wet; **à** ~ *a* dried up; (*à court d'argent*) broke.

SECAM [sekam] *sigle m* (= *procédé séquentiel à mémoire*) SECAM.

sécateur [sekatœʀ] *nm* secateurs *pl* (*Brit*), shears *pl*, pair of secateurs *ou* shears.

sécession [sesesjɔ̃] *nf*: **faire** ~ to secede; **la guerre de S~** the American Civil War.

séchage [seʃaʒ] *nm* drying; (*de bois*) seasoning.

sèche [sɛʃ] *af voir* **sec** ♦ *nf* (*fam*) cigarette, fag (*Brit*).

sèche-cheveux [sɛʃʃəvø] *nm inv* hair-drier.

sèche-linge [sɛʃlɛ̃ʒ] *nm inv* drying cabinet.

sèche-mains [sɛʃmɛ̃] *nm inv* hand drier.

sèchement [sɛʃmɑ̃] *ad* (*frapper etc*) sharply; (*répliquer etc*) drily, sharply.

sécher [seʃe] *vt* to dry; (*dessécher: peau, blé*) to dry (out); (: *étang*) to dry up; (*bois*) to season; (*fam: classe, cours*) to skip, miss ♦ *vi* to dry; to dry out; to dry up; (*fam: candidat*) to be stumped; **se** ~ (*après le bain*) to dry o.s.

sécheresse [seʃʀɛs] *nf* dryness; (*absence de pluie*) drought.

séchoir [seʃwaʀ] *nm* drier.

second, e [səgɔ̃, -ɔ̃d] *a* second ♦ *nm* (*assistant*) second in command; (*étage*) second floor (*Brit*), third floor (*US*); (NAVIG) first mate ♦ *nf* second; (SCOL: *degré*) ≈ fifth form (*Brit*), ≈ tenth grade (*US*); **en** ~ (*en second rang*) in second place; **voyager en** ~**e** to travel second-class; **doué de** ~**e vue** having (the gift of) second sight; **trouver son** ~ **souffle** (SPORT, *fig*) to get one's second wind; **être dans un état** ~ to be in a daze (*ou* trance); **de** ~**e main** second-hand.

secondaire [səgɔ̃dɛʀ] *a* secondary.

seconder [səgɔ̃de] *vt* to assist; (*favoriser*) to back.

secouer [səkwe] *vt* to shake; (*passagers*) to rock; (*traumatiser*) to shake (up); **se** ~ (*chien*) to shake itself; (*fam: se démener*) to

shake o.s. up; ~ **la poussière d'un tapis** to shake the dust off a carpet; ~ **la tête** to shake one's head.

secourable [səkuʀabl(ə)] *a* helpful.

secourir [səkuʀiʀ] *vt* (*aller sauver*) to (go and) rescue; (*prodiguer des soins à*) to help, assist; (*venir en aide à*) to assist, aid.

secourisme [səkuʀism(ə)] *nm* (*premiers soins*) first aid; (*sauvetage*) life saving.

secouriste [səkuʀist(ə)] *nm/f* first-aid worker.

secourons [səkuʀɔ̃] *etc vb voir* **secourir**.

secours [səkuʀ] *vb voir* **secourir** ♦ *nm* help, aid, assistance ♦ *nmpl* aid *sg*; **cela lui a été d'un grand** ~ this was a great help to him; **au** ~! help!; **appeler au** ~ to shout *ou* call for help; **appeler qn à son** ~ to call sb to one's assistance; **porter** ~ **à qn** to give sb assistance, help sb; **les premiers** ~ first aid *sg*; **le** ~ **en montagne** mountain rescue.

secouru, e [səkuʀy] *pp de* **secourir**.

secousse [səkus] *nf* jolt, bump; (*électrique*) shock; (*fig: psychologique*) jolt, shock; ~ **sismique** *ou* **tellurique** earth tremor.

secret, ète [səkʀɛ, -ɛt] *a* secret; (*fig: renfermé*) reticent, reserved ♦ *nm* secret; (*discrétion absolue*): **le** ~ secrecy; **en** ~ in secret, secretly; **au** ~ in solitary confinement; ~ **de fabrication** trade secret; ~ **professionnel** professional secrecy.

secrétaire [səkʀetɛʀ] *nm/f* secretary ♦ ~ *nm* (*meuble*) writing desk, secretaire; ~ **d'ambassade** embassy secretary; ~ **de direction** private *ou* personal secretary; ~ **d'État** ≈ junior minister; ~ **général** (SG) Secretary-General; (COMM) company secretary; ~ **de mairie** town clerk; ~ **médicale** medical secretary; ~ **de rédaction** sub-editor.

secrétariat [s(ə)kʀetaʀja] *nm* (*profession*) secretarial work; (*bureau: d'entreprise, d'école*) (secretary's) office; (: *d'organisation internationale*) secretariat; (POL *etc*: *fonction*) secretaryship, office of Secretary.

secrètement [səkʀɛtmɑ̃] *ad* secretly.

sécréter [sekʀete] *vt* to secrete.

sécrétion [sekʀesjɔ̃] *nf* secretion.

sectaire [sɛktɛʀ] *a* sectarian, bigoted.

sectarisme [sɛktaʀism(ə)] *nm* sectarianism.

secte [sɛkt(ə)] *nf* sect.

secteur [sɛktœʀ] *nm* sector; (ADMIN) district; (ÉLEC): **branché sur le** ~ plugged into the mains (supply); **fonctionne sur pile et** ~ battery or mains operated; **le** ~ **privé/public** (ÉCON) the private/public sector; **le** ~ **primaire/tertiaire** the primary/tertiary sector.

section [sɛksjɔ̃] *nf* section; (*de parcours d'autobus*) fare stage; (MIL: *unité*) platoon; ~ **rythmique** rhythm section.

sectionner [sɛksjɔne] *vt* to sever; **se** ~ *vi* to be severed.

sectionneur [sɛksjɔnœʀ] *nm* (ÉLEC) isolation switch.

sectoriel, le [sɛktɔʀjɛl] *a* sector-based.

sectoriser [sɛktɔʀize] *vt* to divide into sectors.

sécu [seky] *nf* (*fam*: = *sécurité sociale*) ≈ dole (*Brit*), ≈ Welfare (*US*).

séculaire [sekylɛʀ] *a* secular; (*très vieux*) age-old.

séculariser [sekylaʀize] *vt* to secularize.

séculier, ière [sekylje, -jɛʀ] *a* secular.

sécurisant, e [sekyʀizɑ̃, -ɑ̃t] *a* secure, giving a sense of security.

sécuriser [sekyʀize] *vt* to give a sense of security to.

sécurité [sekyʀite] *nf* security; (*absence de danger*) safety; **impression de** ~ sense of security; **la** ~ **internationale** international security; **système de** ~ security (*ou* safety) system; **être en** ~ to be safe; **la** ~ **de l'emploi** job security; **la** ~ **routière** road safety; **la** ~ **sociale** ≈ (the) Social Security (*Brit*), ≈ (the) Welfare (*US*).

sédatif, ive [sedatif, -iv] *a, nm* sedative.

sédentaire [sedɑ̃tɛʀ] *a* sedentary.

sédiment [sedimɑ̃] *nm* sediment; ~**s** *nmpl* (*alluvions*) sediment *sg*.

sédimentaire [sedimɑ̃tɛʀ] *a* sedimentary.

séditieux, euse [sedisjø, -øz] *a* insurgent; seditious.

sédition [sedisjɔ̃] *nf* insurrection; sedition.

séducteur, trice [sedyktœʀ, -tʀis] *a* seductive ♦ *nm/f* seducer/seductress.

séduction [sedyksjɔ̃] *nf* seduction; (*charme, attrait*) appeal, charm.

séduire [sedɥiʀ] *vt* to charm; (*femme: abuser de*) to seduce; (*suj: chose*) to appeal to.

séduisant, e [sedɥizɑ̃, -ɑ̃t] *vb voir* **séduire** ♦ *a* (*femme*) seductive; (*homme, offre*) very attractive.

séduit, e [sedɥi, -it] *pp de* **séduire**.

segment [sɛgmɑ̃] *nm* segment; (*AUTO*): ~ **(de piston)** piston ring; ~ **de frein** brake shoe.

segmenter [sɛgmɑ̃te] *vt,* **se** ~ *vi* to segment.

ségrégation [segʀegasjɔ̃] *nf* segregation.

ségrégationniste [segʀegasjɔnist(ə)] *a* segregationist.

seiche [sɛʃ] *nf* cuttlefish.

séide [seid] *nm* (*péj*) henchman.

seigle [sɛgl(ə)] *nm* rye.

seigneur [sɛɲœʀ] *nm* lord; **le S**~ the Lord.

seigneurial, e, aux [sɛɲœʀjal, -o] *a* lordly, stately.

sein [sɛ̃] *nm* breast; (*entrailles*) womb; **au** ~ **de** *prép* (*équipe, institution*) within; (*flots, bonheur*) in the midst of; **donner le** ~ **à** (*bébé*) to feed (at the breast); to breast-feed; **nourrir au** ~ to breast-feed.

Seine [sɛn] *nf*: **la** ~ the Seine.

séisme [seism(ə)] *nm* earthquake.

séismique *etc* [seismik] *voir* **sismique** *etc*.

SEITA [seita] *sigle f* = Société d'exploitation industrielle des tabacs et allumettes.

seize [sɛz] *num* sixteen.

seizième [sɛzjɛm] *num* sixteenth.

séjour [seʒuʀ] *nm* stay; (*pièce*) living room.

séjourner [seʒuʀne] *vi* to stay.

sel [sɛl] *nm* salt; (*fig*) wit; spice; ~ **de cuisine/de table** cooking/table salt; ~ **gemme** rock salt; ~**s de bain** bathsalts.

sélect, e [selɛkt] *a* select.

sélectif, ive [selɛktif, -iv] *a* selective.

sélection [selɛksjɔ̃] *nf* selection; **faire/opérer une** ~ **parmi** to make a selection from among; **épreuve de** ~ (*SPORT*) trial (for selection); ~ **naturelle** natural selection; ~ **professionnelle** professional recruitment.

sélectionné, e [selɛksjɔne] *a* (*joueur*)

selected; (*produit*) specially selected.

sélectionner [selɛksjɔne] *vt* to select.

sélectionneur, euse [selɛksjɔnœʀ, -øz] *nm/f* selector.

sélectivement [selɛktivmɑ̃] *ad* selectively.

sélénologie [selenɔlɔʒi] *nf* study of the moon, selenology.

self [sɛlf] *nm* (*fam*) self-service.

self-service [sɛlfsɛʀvis] *a* self-service ♦ *nm* self-service (*restaurant*); (*magasin*) self-service shop.

selle [sɛl] *nf* saddle; ~**s** *nfpl* (*MÉD*) stools; **aller à la** ~ (*MÉD*) to have a bowel movement; **se mettre en** ~ to mount, get into the saddle.

seller [sɛle] *vt* to saddle.

sellette [sɛlɛt] *nf*: **être sur la** ~ to be on the carpet (*fig*).

sellier [selje] *nm* saddler.

selon [səlɔ̃] *prép* according to; (*en se conformant à*) in accordance with; ~ **moi** as I see it; ~ **que** according to, depending on whether.

SEm *sigle f* (= Son Éminence) HE.

semailles [səmaj] *nfpl* sowing *sg*.

semaine [səmɛn] *nf* week; (*salaire*) week's wages *ou* pay, weekly wages *ou* pay; **en** ~ during the week, on weekdays; **à la petite** ~ from day to day; **la** ~ **sainte** Holy Week.

semainier [səmenje] *nm* (*bracelet*) bracelet made up of seven bands; (*calendrier*) desk diary; (*meuble*) chest of (seven) drawers.

sémantique [semɑ̃tik] *a* semantic ♦ *nf* semantics *sg*.

sémaphore [semafɔʀ] *nm* (*RAIL*) semaphore signal.

semblable [sɑ̃blabl(ə)] *a* similar; (*de ce genre*): **de** ~**s mésaventures** such mishaps ♦ *nm* fellow creature *ou* man; ~ **à** similar to, like.

semblant [sɑ̃blɑ̃] *nm*: **un** ~ **de vérité** a semblance of truth; **faire** ~ **(de faire)** to pretend (to do).

sembler [sɑ̃ble] *vb avec attribut* to seem ♦ *vb impersonnel*: **il semble (bien) que/inutile de** it (really) seems *ou* appears that/useless to; **il me semble (bien) que** it (really) seems to me that, I (really) think (that); **il me semble le connaître** I think *ou* I've a feeling I know him; ~ **être** to seem to be; **comme bon lui semble** as he sees fit; **me semble- t-il, à ce qu'il me semble** it seems to me, to my mind.

semelle [səmɛl] *nf* sole; (*intérieure*) insole, inner sole; **battre la** ~ to stamp one's feet (to keep them warm); (*fig*) to hang around (waiting); ~**s compensées** platform soles.

semence [səmɑ̃s] *nf* (*graine*) seed; (*clou*) tack.

semer [səme] *vt* to sow; (*fig: éparpiller*) to scatter; (*confusion*) to spread; (: *poursuivants*) to lose, shake off; ~ **la discorde/terreur parmi** to sow discord/terror among; **semé de** (*difficultés*) riddled with.

semestre [səmɛstʀ(ə)] *nm* half-year; (*SCOL*) semester.

semestriel, le [səmɛstʀijɛl] *a* half-yearly; semestral.

semeur, euse [səmœʀ, -øz] *nm/f* sower.

semi-automatique [səmiɔtɔmatik] *a* semiautomatic.

semiconducteur [səmikɔ̃dyktœʀ] *nm* (*INFORM*) semiconductor.

sémillant, e [semijɑ̃, -ɑ̃t] *a* vivacious; dashing.

séminaire [seminɛʀ] *nm* seminar; (*REL*) seminary.

séminariste [seminaʀist(ə)] *nm* seminarist.

sémiologie [semjɔlɔʒi] *nf* semiology.

semi-public, ique [səmipyblik] *a* (*JUR*) semi-public.

semi-remorque [səmiʀəmɔʀk(ə)] *nf* trailer ♦ *nm* articulated lorry (*Brit*), semi(trailer) (*US*).

semis [səmi] *nm* (*terrain*) seedbed, seed plot; (*plante*) seedling.

sémite [semit] *a* Semitic.

sémitique [semitik] *a* Semitic.

semoir [səmwaʀ] *nm* seed-bag; seeder.

semonce [səmɔ̃s] *nf*: **un coup de** ~ a shot across the bows.

semoule [səmul] *nf* semolina; ~ **de riz** ground rice.

sempiternel, le [sɛpitɛʀnɛl] *a* eternal, never-ending.

sénat [sena] *nm* senate.

sénateur [senatœʀ] *nm* senator.

Sénégal [senegal] *nm*: **le** ~ Senegal.

sénégalais, e [senegalɛ, -ɛz] *a* Senegalese.

sénevé [sɛnve] *nm* (*BOT*) mustard; (*graine*) mustard seed.

sénile [senil] *a* senile.

sénilité [senilite] *nf* senility.

senior [senjɔʀ] *nm/f* (*SPORT*) senior.

sens [sɑ̃] *vb voir* **sentir** ♦ *nm* [sɑ̃s] (*PHYSIOL, instinct*) sense; (*signification*) meaning, sense; (*direction*) direction, way ♦ *nmpl* (*sensualité*) senses; **reprendre ses** ~ to regain consciousness; **avoir le** ~ **des affaires/de la mesure** to have business sense/a sense of moderation; **ça n'a pas de** ~ that doesn't make (any) sense; **en dépit du bon** ~ contrary to all good sense; **tomber sous le** ~ to stand to reason, be perfectly obvious; **en un** ~, **dans un** ~ in a way; **en ce** ~ **que** in the sense that; **à mon** ~ to my mind; **dans le** ~ **des aiguilles d'une montre** clockwise; **dans le** ~ **de la longueur/largeur** lengthways/widthways; **dans le mauvais** ~ the wrong way; in the wrong direction; **bon** ~ good sense; ~ **commun** common sense; ~ **dessus dessous** upside down; ~ **interdit**, ~ **unique** one-way street.

sensass [sɑ̃sas] *a* (*fam*) fantastic.

sensation [sɑ̃sasjɔ̃] *nf* sensation; **faire** ~ to cause a sensation, create a stir; **à** ~ (*péj*) sensational.

sensationnel, le [sɑ̃sasjɔnɛl] *a* sensational.

sensé, e [sɑ̃se] *a* sensible.

sensibiliser [sɑ̃sibilize] *vt* to sensitize; ~ **qn (à)** to make sb sensitive (to).

sensibilité [sɑ̃sibilite] *nf* sensitivity; (*affectivité, émotivité*) sensitivity, sensibility.

sensible [sɑ̃sibl(ə)] *a* sensitive; (*aux sens*) perceptible; (*appréciable: différence, progrès*) appreciable, noticeable; ~ **à** sensitive to.

sensiblement [sɑ̃sibləmɑ̃] *ad* (*notablement*) appreciably, noticeably; (*à peu près*): **ils ont**

~ **le même poids** they weigh approximately the same.

sensiblerie [sɑ̃sibləʀi] *nf* sentimentality; squeamishness.

sensitif, ive [sɑ̃sitif, -iv] *a* (*nerf*) sensory; (*personne*) oversensitive.

sensoriel, le [sɑ̃sɔʀjɛl] *a* sensory, sensorial.

sensualité [sɑ̃sɥalite] *nf* sensuality, sensuousness.

sensuel, le [sɑ̃sɥɛl] *a* sensual; sensuous.

sent [sɑ̃] *vb voir* **sentir**.

sente [sɑ̃t] *nf* path.

sentence [sɑ̃tɑ̃s] *nf* (*jugement*) sentence; (*adage*) maxim.

sentencieux, euse [sɑ̃tɑ̃sjø, -øz] *a* sententious.

senteur [sɑ̃tœʀ] *nf* scent, perfume.

senti, e [sɑ̃ti] *a*: **bien** ~ (*mots etc*) well-chosen.

sentier [sɑ̃tje] *nm* path.

sentiment [sɑ̃timɑ̃] *nm* feeling; (*conscience, impression*): **avoir le** ~ **de/que** to be aware of/have the feeling that; **recevez mes** ~**s respectueux** yours faithfully; **faire du** ~ (*péj*) to be sentimental; **si vous me prenez par les** ~**s** if you appeal to my feelings.

sentimental, e, aux [sɑ̃timɑ̃tal, -o] *a* sentimental; (*vie, aventure*) love *cpd*.

sentimentalisme [sɑ̃timɑ̃talism(ə)] *nm* sentimentalism.

sentimentalité [sɑ̃timɑ̃talite] *nf* sentimentality.

sentinelle [sɑ̃tinɛl] *nf* sentry; **en** ~ standing guard; (*soldat: en faction*) on sentry duty.

sentir [sɑ̃tiʀ] *vt* (*par l'odorat*) to smell; (*par le goût*) to taste; (*au toucher, fig*) to feel; (*répandre une odeur de*) to smell of; (: *ressemblance*) to smell like; (*avoir la saveur de*) to taste of; to taste like; (*fig: dénoter, annoncer*) to be indicative of; to smack of; to foreshadow ♦ *vi* to smell; ~ **mauvais** to smell bad; **se** ~ **bien** to feel good; **se** ~ **mal** (*être indisposé*) to feel unwell *ou* ill; **se** ~ **le courage/la force de** to feel brave/strong enough to do; **ne plus se** ~ **de joie** to be beside o.s. with joy; **il ne peut pas le** ~ (*fam*) he can't stand him.

seoir [swaʀ] ~ **à** *vt* to become, befit; **comme il (leur) sied** as it is fitting (to them).

Seoul [seul] *n* Seoul.

SEP *sigle f* (= *sclérose en plaques*) MS.

séparation [sepaʀasjɔ̃] *nf* separation; (*cloison*) division, partition; ~ **de biens** division of property (*in marriage settlement*); ~ **de corps** legal separation.

séparatiste [sepaʀatist(ə)] *a*, *nm/f* (*POL*) separatist.

séparé, e [sepaʀe] *a* (*appartements, pouvoirs*) separate; (*époux*) separated; ~ **de** separate from; separated from.

séparément [sepaʀemɑ̃] *ad* separately.

séparer [sepaʀe] *vt* (*gén*) to separate; (*suj: divergences etc*) to divide; to drive apart; (: *différences, obstacles*) to stand between; (*détacher*): ~ **qch** to pull sth (off) from; (*dissocier*) to distinguish between; (*diviser*): ~ **qch par** to divide sth (up) with; ~ **une pièce en deux** to divide a room into two; **se** ~ (*époux*) to separate, part; (*prendre congé:*

amis etc) to part, leave each other; (*adversaires*) to separate; (*se diviser: route, tige etc*) to divide; (*se détacher*): **se ~ (de)** to split off (from); to come off; **se ~ de** (*époux*) to separate *ou* part from; (*employé, objet personnel*) to part with.

sépia [sepja] *nf* sepia.

sept [sɛt] *num* seven.

septante [sɛptɑ̃t] *num* (*Belgique, Suisse*) seventy.

septembre [sɛptɑ̃bʀ(ə)] *nm* September; *voir aussi* **juillet**.

septennal, e, aux [sɛptenal, -o] *a* seven-year; (*festival*) seven-year, septennial.

septennat [sɛptena] *nm* seven-year term (of office); seven-year reign.

septentrional, e, aux [sɛptɑ̃tʀijɔnal, -o] *a* northern.

septicémie [sɛptisemi] *nf* blood poisoning, septicaemia.

septième [sɛtjɛm] *num* seventh; **être au ~ ciel** to be on cloud nine.

septique [sɛptik] *a*: **fosse ~** septic tank.

septuagénaire [sɛptɥaʒenɛʀ] *a, nmf* septuagenarian.

sépulcral, e, aux [sepylkʀal, -o] *a* (*voix*) sepulchral.

sépulcre [sepylkʀ(ə)] *nm* sepulchre.

sépulture [sepyltyʀ] *nf* burial; (*tombeau*) burial place, grave.

séquelles [sekɛl] *nfpl* after-effects; (*fig*) aftermath *sg*; consequences.

séquence [sekɑ̃s] *nf* sequence.

séquentiel, le [sekɑ̃sjɛl] *a* sequential.

séquestration [sekɛstʀasjɔ̃] *nf* illegal confinement; impounding.

séquestre [sekɛstʀ(ə)] *nm* impoundment; **mettre sous ~** to impound.

séquestrer [sekɛstʀe] *vt* (*personne*) to confine illegally; (*biens*) to impound.

serai [səʀe] *etc vb voir* **être**.

sérail [seʀaj] *nm* seraglio; harem; **rentrer au ~** to return to the fold.

serbe [sɛʀb(ə)] *a* Serbian ♦ *nm* (*LING*) Serbian ♦ *nm/f*: **S~** Serb.

Serbie [sɛʀbi] *nf*: **la ~** Serbia.

serbo-croate [sɛʀbɔkʀɔat] *a* Serbo-Croat, Serbo-Croatian ♦ *nm* (*LING*) Serbo-Croat.

serein, e [səʀɛ̃, -ɛn] *a* serene; (*jugement*) dispassionate.

sereinement [səʀɛnmɑ̃] *ad* serenely.

sérénade [seʀenad] *nf* serenade; (*fam*) hullabaloo.

sérénité [seʀenite] *nf* serenity.

serez [səʀe] *vb voir* **être**.

serf, serve [sɛʀ, sɛʀv(ə)] *nm/f* serf.

serfouette [sɛʀfwɛt] *nf* weeding hoe.

serge [sɛʀʒ(ə)] *nf* serge.

sergent [sɛʀʒɑ̃] *nm* sergeant.

sergent-chef [sɛʀʒɑ̃ʃɛf] *nm* staff sergeant.

sergent-major [sɛʀʒɑ̃maʒɔʀ] *nm* ≈ quartermaster sergeant.

sériciculture [seʀisikyltyʀ] *nf* silkworm breeding, sericulture.

série [seʀi] *nf* (*de questions, d'accidents, TV*) series *inv*; (*de clés, casseroles, outils*) set; (*catégorie: SPORT*) rank; class; **en ~** in quick succession; (*COMM*) mass *cpd*; **de ~** *a* standard; **hors ~** (*COMM*) custom-built; (*fig*)

outstanding; **imprimante ~** (*INFORM*) serial printer; **soldes de fin de ~s** end of line special offers; **~ noire** *nm* (*crime*) thriller ♦ *nf* (*suite de malheurs*) run of bad luck.

sérier [seʀje] *vt* to classify, sort out.

sérieusement [seʀjøzmɑ̃] *ad* seriously; reliably; responsibly; **il parle ~** he's serious, he means it; **~?** are you serious?, do you mean it?

sérieux, euse [seʀjø, -øz] *a* serious; (*élève, employé*) reliable, responsible; (*client, maison*) reliable, dependable; (*offre, proposition*) genuine, serious; (*grave, sévère*) serious, solemn; (*maladie, situation*) serious, grave; (*important*) considerable ♦ *nm* seriousness; reliability; **ce n'est pas ~** (*raisonnable*) that's not on; **garder son ~** to keep a straight face; **manquer de ~** not to be very responsible (*ou* reliable); **prendre qch/qn au ~** to take sth/sb seriously.

sérigraphie [seʀigʀafi] *nf* silk screen printing.

serin [səʀɛ̃] *nm* canary.

seriner [səʀine] *vt*: **~ qch à qn** to drum sth into sb.

seringue [səʀɛ̃g] *nf* syringe.

serions [səʀjɔ̃] *etc vb voir* **être**.

serment [sɛʀmɑ̃] *nm* (*juré*) oath; (*promesse*) pledge, vow; **prêter ~** to take the *ou* an oath; **faire le ~ de** to take a vow to, swear to; **sous ~** on *ou* under oath.

sermon [sɛʀmɔ̃] *nm* sermon; (*péj*) sermon, lecture.

sermonner [sɛʀmɔne] *vt* to lecture.

SERNAM [sɛʀnam] *sigle m* (= *Service national de messageries*) rail delivery service.

sérologie [seʀɔlɔʒi] *nf* serology.

serpe [sɛʀp(ə)] *nf* billhook.

serpent [sɛʀpɑ̃] *nm* snake; **~ à sonnettes** rattlesnake; **~ monétaire (européen)** (European) monetary snake.

serpenter [sɛʀpɑ̃te] *vi* to wind.

serpentin [sɛʀpɑ̃tɛ̃] *nm* (*tube*) coil; (*ruban*) streamer.

serpillière [sɛʀpijɛʀ] *nf* floorcloth.

serrage [seʀaʒ] *nm* tightening; **collier de ~** clamp.

serre [sɛʀ] *nf* (*AGR*) greenhouse; **~ chaude** hothouse; **~ froide** unheated greenhouse.

serré, e [seʀe] *a* (*tissu*) closely woven; (*réseau*) dense; (*écriture*) close; (*habits*) tight; (*fig: lutte, match*) tight, close-fought; (*passagers etc*) (tightly) packed; (*café*) strong ♦ *ad*: **jouer ~** to play it close, play a close game; **écrire ~** to write a cramped hand; **avoir la gorge ~e** to have a lump in one's throat.

serre-livres [sɛʀlivʀ(ə)] *nm inv* book ends *pl*.

serrement [sɛʀmɑ̃] *nm*: **~ de main** handshake; **~ de cœur** pang of anguish.

serrer [seʀe] *vt* (*tenir*) to grip *ou* hold tight; (*comprimer, coincer*) to squeeze; (*poings, mâchoires*) to clench; (*suj: vêtement*) to be too tight for; to fit tightly; (*rapprocher*) to close up, move closer together; (*ceinture, nœud, frein, vis*) to tighten ♦ *vi*: **~ à droite** to keep to the right; to move into the right-hand lane; **se ~** (*se rapprocher*) to squeeze up; **se ~ contre qn** to huddle up to sb; **se ~**

les coudes to stick together, back one another up; **se ~ la ceinture** to tighten one's belt; **~ la main à qn** to shake sb's hand; **~ qn dans ses bras** to hug sb, clasp sb in one's arms; **~ la gorge à qn** (*suj: chagrin*) to bring a lump to sb's throat; **~ les dents** to clench *ou* grit one's teeth; **~ qn de près** to follow close behind sb; **~ le trottoir** to hug the kerb; **~ sa droite** to keep well to the right; **~ la vis à qn** to crack down harder on sb; **~ les rangs** to close ranks.

serres [sɛʀ] *nfpl* (*griffes*) claws, talons.

serre-tête [sɛʀtɛt] *nm inv* (*bandeau*) headband; (*bonnet*) skullcap.

serrure [sɛʀyʀ] *nf* lock.

serrurerie [sɛʀyʀʀi] *nf* (*métier*) locksmith's trade; (*ferronnerie*) ironwork; **~ d'art** ornamental ironwork.

serrurier [sɛʀyʀje] *nm* locksmith.

sers, sert [sɛʀ] *vb voir* **servir**.

sertir [sɛʀtiʀ] *vt* (*pierre*) to set; (*pièces métalliques*) to crimp.

sérum [seʀɔm] *nm* serum; **~ antivenimeux** snakebite serum; **~ sanguin** (blood) serum; **~ de vérité** truth drug.

servage [sɛʀvaʒ] *nm* serfdom.

servant [sɛʀvɑ̃] *nm* server.

servante [sɛʀvɑ̃t] *nf* (maid)servant.

serve [sɛʀv] *nf voir* **serf ♦** *vb voir* **servir**.

serveur, euse [sɛʀvœʀ, -øz] *nm/f* waiter/ waitress ♦ *a*: **centre ~** (*INFORM*) service centre.

servi, e [sɛʀvi] *a*: **être bien ~** to get a large helping (*ou* helpings); **vous êtes ~?** are you being served?

serviable [sɛʀvjabl(ə)] *a* obliging, willing to help.

service [sɛʀvis] *nm* (*gén*) service; (*série de repas*): **premier ~** first sitting; (*pourboire*) service (charge); (*assortiment de vaisselle*) set, service; (*linge de table*) set; (*bureau: de la vente etc*) department, section; (*travail*): **pendant le ~** on duty; **~s** *nmpl* (*travail, ÉCON*) services, inclusive/exclusive of service; **faire le ~** to serve; **être en ~ chez qn** (*domestique*) to be in sb's service; **être au ~ de** (*patron, patrie*) to be in the service of; **être au ~ de qn** (*collaborateur, voiture*) to be at sb's service; **porte de ~** tradesman's entrance; **rendre ~ à** to help; **il aime rendre ~** he likes to help; **rendre un ~ à qn** to do sb a favour; **heures de ~** hours of duty; **être de ~** to be on duty; **reprendre du ~** to get back into action; **avoir 25 ans de ~** to have completed 25 years' service; **être/ mettre en ~** to be in/put into service *ou* operation; **hors ~** not in use; out of order; **~ à thé/café** tea/coffee set *ou* service; **~ après vente (SAV)** after-sales service; **en ~ commandé** on an official assignment; **~ funèbre** funeral service; **~ militaire** military service; **~ d'ordre** police (*ou* stewards) in charge of maintaining order; **~s publics** public services, (public) utilities; **~s secrets** secret service *sg*; **~s sociaux** social services.

serviette [sɛʀvjɛt] *nf* (*de table*) (table) napkin, serviette; (*de toilette*) towel; (*porte-documents*) briefcase; **~ éponge** terry towel; **~ hygiénique** sanitary towel.

servile [sɛʀvil] *a* servile.

servir [sɛʀviʀ] *vt* (*gén*) to serve; (*dîneur: au restaurant*) to wait on; (*client: au magasin*) to serve, attend to; (*fig: aider*): **~ qn** to aid sb; to serve sb's interests; to stand sb in good stead; (*COMM: rente*) to pay ♦ *vi* (*TENNIS*) to serve; (*CARTES*) to deal; (*être militaire*) to serve; **~ qch à qn** to serve sb with sth, help sb to sth; **qu'est-ce que je vous sers?** what can I get you?; **~ à** (*prendre d'un plat*) to help o.s.; (*s'approvisionner*): **se ~ chez** to shop at; **se ~ de** (*plat*) to help o.s. to; (*voiture, outil, relations*) to use; **~ à qn** (*diplôme, livre*) to be of use to sb; **ça m'a servi pour faire** it was useful to me when I did; I used it to do; **~ à qch/à faire** (*outil etc*) to be used for sth/for doing; **ça peut ~** it may come in handy; **ça peut encore ~** it can still be used (*ou* of use); **à quoi cela sert-il (de faire)?** what's the use (of doing)?; **cela ne sert à rien** it's no use; **~ (à qn) de** to serve as (for sb); **~ à dîner (à qn)** to serve dinner (to sb).

serviteur [sɛʀvitœʀ] *nm* servant.

servitude [sɛʀvityd] *nf* servitude; (*fig*) constraint; (*JUR*) easement.

servofrein [sɛʀvɔfʀɛ̃] *nm* servo(-assisted) brake.

servomécanisme [sɛʀvɔmekanism(ə)] *nm* servo system.

ses [se] *dét voir* **son**.

sésame [sezam] *nm* (*BOT*) sesame; (*graine*) sesame seed.

session [sesjɔ̃] *nf* session.

set [sɛt] *nm* set; (*napperon*) placemat; **~ de table** set of placemats.

seuil [sœj] *nm* doorstep; (*fig*) threshold; **sur le ~ de sa maison** in the doorway of his house, on his doorstep; **au ~ de** (*fig*) on the threshold *ou* brink *ou* edge of; **~ de rentabilité** (*COMM*) breakeven point.

seul, e [sœl] *a* (*sans compagnie*) alone; (*avec nuance affective: isolé*) lonely; (*unique*): **un ~ livre** only one book, a single book; **le ~ livre** the only book; **~ ce livre, ce livre ~** this book alone, only this book; **d'un ~ coup** (*soudainement*) all at once; (*à la fois*) at one blow ♦ *ad* (*vivre*) alone, on one's own; **parler tout ~** to talk to oneself; **faire qch (tout) ~** to do sth (all) on one's own *ou* (all) by oneself ♦ *nm, nf*: **il en reste un(e) ~(e)** there's only one left; **pas un(e) ~(e)** not a single; **à lui (tout) ~** single-handed, on his own; **~ à ~** in private.

seulement [sœlmɑ̃] *ad* (*pas davantage*): **~ 5, 5 ~** only 5; (*exclusivement*): **~ eux** only them, them alone; (*pas avant*): **~ hier/à 10h** only yesterday/at 10 o'clock; (*mais, toutefois*): **il consent, ~ il demande des garanties** he agrees, only he wants guarantees; **non ~ ... mais aussi** *ou* **encore** not only ... but also.

sève [sɛv] *nf* sap.

sévère [seveʀ] *a* severe.

sévèrement [seveʀmɑ̃] *ad* severely.

sévérité [seveʀite] *nf* severity.

sévices [sevis] *nmpl* (physical) cruelty *sg*, ill treatment *sg*.

Séville [sevil] *n* Seville.

sévir [seviʀ] *vi* (*punir*) to use harsh measures, crack down; (*suj: fléau*) to rage, be rampant; ~ **contre** (*abus*) to deal ruthlessly with, crack down on.

sevrage [səvʀaʒ] *nm* weaning; deprivation; (*d'un toxicomane*) withdrawal.

sevrer [səvʀe] *vt* to wean; (*fig*): ~ **qn de** to deprive sb of.

sexagénaire [sɛgzaʒenɛʀ] *a*, *nm/f* sexagenarian.

SExc *sigle f* (= *Son Excellence*) HE.

sexe [sɛks(ə)] *nm* sex; (*organe mâle*) member.

sexisme [sɛksism(ə)] *nm* sexism.

sexiste [sɛksist(ə)] *a*, *nm* sexist.

sexologue [sɛksɔlɔg] *nm/f* sexologist, sex specialist.

sextant [sɛkstɑ̃] *nm* sextant.

sexualité [sɛksɥalite] *nf* sexuality.

sexué, e [sɛksɥe] *a* sexual.

sexuel, le [sɛksɥɛl] *a* sexual; **acte** ~ sex act.

sexuellement [sɛksɥɛlmɑ̃] *ad* sexually.

seyant, e [sɛjɑ̃, -ɑ̃t] *vb voir* **seoir** ♦ *a* becoming.

Seychelles [seʃɛl] *nfpl*: **les** ~ the Seychelles.

SFIO *sigle f* (= *Section française de l'internationale ouvrière*) *former name of French Socialist Party*.

SG *sigle m* = **secrétaire général**.

SGEN *sigle m* (= *Syndicat général de l'éducation nationale*) *trades union*.

shaker [ʃɛkœʀ] *nm* (cocktail) shaker.

shampooiner [ʃɑ̃pwine] *vt* to shampoo.

shampooineur, euse [ʃɑ̃pwinœʀ, -øz] *nm/f* (*personne*) junior (*who does the shampooing*).

shampooing [ʃɑ̃pwɛ̃] *nm* shampoo; **se faire un** ~ to shampoo one's hair; ~ **colorant** (colour) rinse; ~ **traitant** medicated shampoo.

Shetland [ʃɛtlɑ̃d] *n*: **les îles** ~ the Shetland Islands, Shetland.

shooter [ʃute] *vi* (*FOOTBALL*) to shoot; **se** ~ (*drogué*) to mainline.

short [ʃɔʀt] *nm* (pair of) shorts *pl*.

SI *sigle m* = **syndicat d'initiative**.

si [si] *nm* (*MUS*) B; (*en chantant la gamme*) ti, te ♦ *ad* (*oui*) yes; (*tellement*) so ♦ *cj* if; (*d'opposition*): **s'il est amiable, eux par contre** ... whereas he's nice, they on the other hand ...; **Paul n'est pas venu,** ~? Paul didn't come, did he?; **je vous assure que** ~ I can assure you that it is (*ou* he did *etc*); ~ **seulement** if only; (*tant et*) ~ **bien que** so much so that; ~ **rapide qu'il soit** however fast he may be, fast though he is; **je me demande** ~ I wonder if *ou* whether.

siamois, e [sjamwa, -waz] *a* Siamese; **frères/sœurs** ~**(es)** Siamese twins.

Sibérie [sibeʀi] *nf*: **la** ~ Siberia.

sibérien, ne [sibeʀjɛ̃, -ɛn] *a* Siberian ♦ *nm/f*: **S**~, **ne** Siberian.

sibyllin, e [sibilɛ̃, -in] *a* sibylline.

SICAV [sikav] *sigle f* (= *société d'investissement à capital variable*) open-ended investment trust; share in such a trust.

Sicile [sisil] *nf*: **la** ~ Sicily.

sicilien, ne [sisiljɛ̃, -ɛn] *a* Sicilian.

SIDA, sida [sida] *nm* (= *syndrome immuno-déficitaire acquis*) AIDS *sg*.

sidéral, e, aux [sideʀal, -o] *a* sideral.

sidéré, e [sideʀe] *a* staggered.

sidérurgie [sideʀyʀʒi] *nf* steel industry.

sidérurgique [sideʀyʀʒik] *a* steel *cpd*.

sidérurgiste [sideʀyʀʒist(ə)] *nm/f* steel worker.

siècle [sjɛkl(ə)] *nm* century; (*époque*): **le** ~ **des lumières/de l'atome** the age of enlightenment/atomic age; (*REL*): **le** ~ the world.

sied [sje] *vb voir* **seoir**.

siège [sjɛʒ] *nm* seat; (*d'entreprise*) head office; (*d'organisation*) headquarters *pl*; (*MIL*) siege; **lever le** ~ to raise the siege; **mettre le** ~ **devant** to besiege; **présentation par le** ~ (*MÉD*) breech presentation; ~ **avant/arrière** (*AUTO*) front/back seat; ~ **baquet** bucket seat; ~ **social** registered office.

siéger [sjeʒe] *vi* (*assemblée, tribunal*) to sit; (*résider, se trouver*) to lie, be located.

sien, ne [sjɛ̃, sjɛn] *pronom*: **le(la)** ~**(ne)**, **les** ~**s(**~**nes)** *m* his; *f* hers; *non humain* its; **y mettre du** ~ to pull one's weight; **faire des** ~**nes** (*fam*) to be up to one's (usual) tricks; **les** ~**s** (*sa famille*) one's family.

siérait [sjeʀɛ] *etc vb voir* **seoir**.

Sierra Leone [sjeʀaleɔne] *nf*: **la** ~ Sierra Leone.

sieste [sjɛst(ə)] *nf* (afternoon) snooze *ou* nap, siesta; **faire la** ~ to have a snooze *ou* nap.

sieur [sjœʀ] *nm*: **le** ~ **Thomas** Mr Thomas; (*en plaisantant*) Master Thomas.

sifflant, e [siflɑ̃, -ɑ̃t] *a* (*bruit*) whistling; (*toux*) wheezing; (**consonne**) ~**e** sibilant.

sifflement [sifləmɑ̃] *nm* whistle, whistling *q*; wheezing *q*; hissing *q*.

siffler [sifle] *vi* (*gén*) to whistle; (*avec un sifflet*) to blow (on) one's whistle; (*en respirant*) to wheeze; (*serpent, vapeur*) to hiss ♦ *vt* (*chanson*) to whistle; (*chien etc*) to whistle for; (*fille*) to whistle at; (*pièce, orateur*) to hiss, boo; (*faute*) to blow one's whistle at; (*fin du match, départ*) to blow one's whistle for; (*fam: verre, bouteille*) to guzzle, knock back (*Brit*).

sifflet [sifle] *nm* whistle; ~**s** *nmpl* (*de mécontentement*) whistles, boos; **coup de** ~ whistle.

siffloter [siflɔte] *vi*, *vt* to whistle.

sigle [sigl(ə)] *nm* acronym, (set of) initials *pl*.

signal, aux [siɲal, -o] *nm* (*signe convenu, appareil*) signal; (*indice, écriteau*) sign; **donner le** ~ **de** to give the signal for; ~ **d'alarme** alarm signal; ~ **d'alerte/de détresse** warning/distress signal; ~ **horaire** time signal; ~ **optique/sonore** warning light/sound; visual/acoustic signal; **signaux (lumineux)** (*AUTO*) traffic signals; **signaux routiers** road signs; (*lumineux*) traffic lights.

signalement [siɲalmɑ̃] *nm* description, particulars *pl*.

signaler [siɲale] *vt* to indicate; to announce; to report; (*être l'indice de*) to indicate; (*faire remarquer*): ~ **qch à qn/à qn que** to point out sth to sb/to sb that; (*appeler l'attention sur*): ~ **qn à la police** to bring sb to the notice of the police; **se** ~ **par** to distinguish o.s. by; **se** ~ **à l'attention de qn** to attract sb's attention.

signalétique [siɲaletik] *a*: **fiche ~** identification sheet.

signalisation [siɲalizasjɔ̃] *nf* signalling, signposting; signals *pl*; roadsigns *pl*; **panneau de ~** roadsign.

signaliser [siɲalize] *vt* to put up roadsigns on; to put signals on.

signataire [siɲatɛʀ] *nm/f* signatory.

signature [siɲatyʀ] *nf* signature; *(action)* signing.

signe [siɲ] *nm* sign; *(TYPO)* mark; **ne pas donner ~ de vie** to give no sign of life; **c'est bon ~** it's a good sign; **c'est ~ que** it's a sign that; **faire un ~ de la main/tête** to give a sign with one's hand/shake one's head; **faire ~ à qn** *(fig)* to get in touch with sb; **faire ~ à qn d'entrer** to motion (to) sb to come in; **en ~ de** as a sign *ou* mark of; **le ~ de la croix** the sign of the Cross; **~ de ponctuation** punctuation mark; **~ du zodiaque** sign of the zodiac; **~s particuliers** distinguishing marks.

signer [siɲe] *vt* to sign; **se ~** *vi* to cross o.s.

signet [siɲɛ] *nm* bookmark.

significatif, ive [siɲifikatif, -iv] *a* significant.

signification [siɲifikasjɔ̃] *nf* meaning.

signifier [siɲifje] *vt* *(vouloir dire)* to mean, signify; *(faire connaître)*: **~ qch (à qn)** to make sth known (to sb); *(JUR)*: **~ qch à qn** to serve notice of sth on sb.

silence [silɑ̃s] *nm* silence; *(MUS)* rest; **garder le ~ (sur qch)** to keep silent (about sth), say nothing (about sth); **passer sous ~** to pass over (in silence); **réduire au ~** to silence.

silencieusement [silɑ̃sjøzmɑ̃] *ad* silently.

silencieux, euse [silɑ̃sjø, -øz] *a* quiet, silent ♦ *nm* silencer *(Brit)*, muffler *(US)*.

silex [silɛks] *nm* flint.

silhouette [silwɛt] *nf* outline, silhouette; *(lignes, contour)* outline; *(figure)* figure.

silice [silis] *nf* silica.

siliceux, euse [silisø, -øz] *a* *(terrain)* chalky.

silicium [silisjɔm] *nm* silicon; **plaquette de ~** silicon chip.

silicone [silikon] *nf* silicone.

silicose [silikoz] *nf* silicosis, dust disease.

sillage [sijaʒ] *nm* wake; *(fig)* trail; **dans le ~ de** *(fig)* in the wake of.

sillon [sijɔ̃] *nm* *(d'un champ)* furrow; *(de disque)* groove.

sillonner [sijɔne] *vt* *(creuser)* to furrow; *(traverser)* to cross, criss-cross.

silo [silo] *nm* silo.

simagrées [simagʀe] *nfpl* fuss *sg*; airs and graces.

simiesque [simjɛsk(ə)] *a* monkey-like, apelike.

similaire [similɛʀ] *a* similar.

similarité [similaʀite] *nf* similarity.

simili [simili] *nm* imitation; *(TYPO)* half-tone ♦ *nf* half-tone engraving.

simili... [simili] *préfixe* imitation *cpd*, artificial.

similicuir [similikɥiʀ] *nm* imitation leather.

similigravure [similigʀavyʀ] *nf* half-tone engraving.

similitude [similityd] *nf* similarity.

simple [sɛ̃pl(ə)] *a* *(gén)* simple; *(non multiple)* single; **~s** *nmpl* *(MÉD)* medicinal plants; **~ messieurs** *nm* *(TENNIS)* men's singles *sg*; **un ~ particulier** an ordinary citizen; **une ~ formalité** a mere formality; **cela varie du ~ au double** it can double, it can double the price *etc*; **dans le plus ~ appareil** in one's birthday suit; **~ course** *a* single; **~ d'esprit** *nm/f* simpleton; **~ soldat** private.

simplement [sɛ̃pləmɑ̃] *ad* simply.

simplet, te [sɛ̃plɛ, -ɛt] *a* *(personne)* simple-minded.

simplicité [sɛ̃plisite] *nf* simplicity; **en toute ~** quite simply.

simplification [sɛ̃plifikasjɔ̃] *nf* simplification.

simplifier [sɛ̃plifje] *vt* to simplify.

simpliste [sɛ̃plist(ə)] *a* simplistic.

simulacre [simylakʀ(ə)] *nm* enactment; *(péj)*: **un ~ de** a pretence of, a sham.

simulateur, trice [simylatœʀ, -tʀis] *nm/f* shammer, pretender; *(qui se prétend malade)* malingerer ♦ *nm*: **~ de vol** flight simulator.

simulation [simylasjɔ̃] *nf* shamming, simulation; malingering.

simuler [simyle] *vt* to sham, simulate.

simultané, e [simyltane] *a* simultaneous.

simultanéité [simyltaneite] *nf* simultaneity.

simultanément [simyltanemɑ̃] *ad* simultaneously.

Sinaï [sinai] *nm*: **le ~** Sinai.

sinapisme [sinapism(ə)] *nm* *(MÉD)* mustard poultice.

sincère [sɛ̃sɛʀ] *a* sincere; genuine; heartfelt; **mes ~s condoléances** my deepest sympathy.

sincèrement [sɛ̃sɛʀmɑ̃] *ad* sincerely; genuinely.

sincérité [sɛ̃seʀite] *nf* sincerity; **en toute ~** in all sincerity.

sinécure [sinekyʀ] *nf* sinecure.

sine die [sinedje] *ad* sine die, indefinitely.

sine qua non [sinekwanɔn] *a*: **condition ~** indispensable condition.

Singapour [sɛ̃gapuʀ] *nm*: **le ~** Singapore.

singe [sɛ̃ʒ] *nm* monkey; *(de grande taille)* ape.

singer [sɛ̃ʒe] *vt* to ape, mimic.

singeries [sɛ̃ʒʀi] *nfpl* antics; *(simagrées)* airs and graces.

singulariser [sɛ̃gylaʀize] *vt* to mark out; **se ~** to call attention to o.s.

singularité [sɛ̃gylaʀite] *nf* peculiarity.

singulier, ière [sɛ̃gylje, -jɛʀ] *a* remarkable, singular; *(LING)* singular ♦ *nm* singular.

singulièrement [sɛ̃gyljɛʀmɑ̃] *ad* singularly, remarkably.

sinistre [sinistʀ(ə)] *a* sinister; *(intensif)*: **un ~ imbécile** an incredible idiot ♦ *nm* *(incendie)* blaze; *(catastrophe)* disaster; *(ASSURANCES)* damage *(giving rise to a claim)*.

sinistré, e [sinistʀe] *a* disaster-stricken ♦ *nm/f* disaster victim.

sinistrose [sinistʀoz] *nf* pessimism.

sino... [sino] *préfixe*: **~-indien** Sino-Indian, Chinese-Indian.

sinon [sinɔ̃] *cj* *(autrement, sans quoi)* otherwise, or else; *(sauf)* except, other than; *(si ce n'est)* if not.

sinueux, euse [sinɥø, -øz] *a* winding; *(fig)* tortuous.

sinuosités [sinɥozite] *nfpl* winding *sg*, curves.
sinus [sinys] *nm* (*ANAT*) sinus; (*GÉOM*) sine.
sinusite [sinyzit] *nf* sinusitis, sinus infection.
sionisme [sjɔnism(ə)] *nm* Zionism.
sioniste [sjɔnist(ə)] *a*, *nm/f* Zionist.
siphon [sifɔ̃] *nm* (*tube, d'eau gazeuse*) siphon;
(*d'évier etc*) U-bend.
siphonner [sifɔne] *vt* to siphon.
sire [siʀ] *nm* (*titre*): **S~** Sire; **un triste ~** an
unsavoury individual.
sirène [siʀɛn] *nf* siren; **~ d'alarme** fire alarm;
(*pendant la guerre*) air-raid siren.
sirop [siʀo] *nm* (*à diluer: de fruit etc*) syrup,
cordial (*Brit*); (*boisson*) fruit drink;
(*pharmaceutique*) syrup, mixture; **~ de
menthe** mint syrup *ou* cordial; **~ contre la
toux** cough syrup *ou* mixture.
siroter [siʀɔte] *vt* to sip.
sirupeux, euse [siʀypø, -øz] *a* syrupy.
sis, e [si, siz] *a*: **~ rue de la Paix** located in
the rue de la Paix.
sisal [sizal] *nm* (*BOT*) sisal.
sismique [sismik] *a* seismic.
sismographe [sismɔgʀaf] *nm* seismograph.
sismologie [sismɔlɔʒi] *nf* seismology.
site [sit] *nm* (*paysage, environnement*) setting;
(*d'une ville etc: emplacement*) site; **~
(pittoresque)** beauty spot; **~s touristiques**
places of interest; **~s naturels/historiques**
natural/historic sites.
sitôt [sito] *ad*: **~ parti** as soon as he *etc* had
left; **~ après** straight after; **pas de ~** not for
a long time; **~ (après) que** as soon as.
situation [sitɥasjɔ̃] *nf* (*gén*) situation; (*d'un
édifice, d'une ville*) situation, position;
(*emplacement*) location; **être en ~ de faire
qch** to be in a position to do sth; **~ de
famille** marital status.
situé, e [sitɥe] *a*: **bien ~** well situated, in a
good location; **~ à/près de** situated at/near.
situer [sitɥe] *vt* to site, situate; (*en pensée*) to
set, place; **se ~** *vi*: **se ~ à/près de** to be
situated at/near.
SIVOM [sivɔm] *sigle m* (= *syndicat
intercommunal à vocation multiple*)
association of "*communes*".
six [sis] *num* six.
sixième [sizjɛm] *num* sixth.
skate (board) [sket(bɔʀd)] *nm* (*SPORT*)
skateboarding; (*planche*) skateboard.
sketch [skɛtʃ] *nm* (variety) sketch.
ski [ski] *nm* (*objet*) ski; (*sport*) skiing; **faire
du ~** to ski; **~ alpin** Alpine skiing; **~ courts**
short skis; **~ évolutif** short ski method; **~ de
fond** cross-country skiing; **~ nautique**
water-skiing; **~ de piste** downhill skiing; **~
de randonnée** cross-country skiing.
ski-bob [skibɔb] *nm* skibob.
skier [skje] *vi* to ski.
skieur, euse [skjœʀ, -øz] *nm/f* skier.
skif(f) [skif] *nm* skiff.
slalom [slalɔm] *nm* slalom; **faire du ~ entre**
to slalom between; **~ géant/spécial** giant/
special slalom.
slave [slav] *a* Slav(onic), Slavic ♦ *nm* (*LING*)
Slavonic ♦ *nm/f*: **S~** Slav.
slip [slip] *nm* (*sous-vêtement*) underpants *pl*,
pants *pl* (*Brit*), briefs *pl*; (*de bain:
d'homme*) (bathing *ou* swimming) trunks *pl*;

(*: du bikini*) (bikini) briefs *pl ou* bottoms *pl*.
slogan [slɔgɑ̃] *nm* slogan.
slovaque [slɔvak] *a* Slovak ♦ *nm* (*LING*)
Slovak ♦ *nm/f*: **S~** Slovak.
Slovaquie [slɔvaki] *nf*: **la ~** Slovakia.
slovène [slɔvɛn] *a* Slovene.
Slovénie [slɔveni] *nf*: **la ~** Slovenia.
SM *sigle f* (= *Sa Majesté*) HM.
SMAG [smag] *sigle m* = *salaire minimum
agricole garanti*.
smasher [smaʃe] *vi* to smash the ball ♦ *vt*
(*balle*) to smash.
SME *sigle m* (= *Système monétaire européen*)
EMS.
SMIC [smik] *sigle m* = **salaire minimum
interprofessionnel de croissance**.
smicard, e [smikaʀ, -aʀd(ə)] *nm/f* minimum
wage earner.
smocks [smɔk] *nmpl* (*COUTURE*) smocking *q*.
smoking [smɔkiŋ] *nm* dinner *ou* evening suit.
SMUR [smyʀ] *sigle m* (= *service médical
d'urgence et de réanimation*) specialist
mobile emergency unit.
snack [snak] *nm* snack bar.
SNC *abr* = *service non compris*.
SNCB *sigle f* (= *Société nationale des chemins
de fer belges*) Belgian railways.
SNCF *sigle f* (= *Société nationale des chemins
de fer français*) French railways.
SNES [snɛs] *sigle m* (= *Syndicat national de
l'enseignement secondaire*) secondary teachers' union.
SNE-sup [ɛsɛnəsyp] *sigle m* (= *Syndicat
national de l'enseignement supérieur*)
university teachers' union.
SNI *sigle m* (= *Syndicat national des instituteurs*) primary teachers' union.
SNJ *sigle m* (= *Syndicat national des
journalistes*) journalists' union.
snob [snɔb] *a* snobbish ♦ *nm/f* snob.
snober [snɔbe] *vt*: **~ qn** to give sb the cold
shoulder, treat sb with disdain.
snobinard, e [snɔbinaʀ, -aʀd(ə)] *nm/f* snooty
ou stuck-up person.
snobisme [snɔbism] *nm* snobbery.
SNSM *sigle f* (= *Société nationale de
sauvetage en mer*) national sea-rescue
association.
s.o. *abr* (= *sans objet*) no longer applicable.
sobre [sɔbʀ(ə)] *a* temperate, abstemious;
(*élégance, style*) restrained, sober; **~ de**
(*gestes, compliments*) sparing of.
sobrement [sɔbʀəmɑ̃] *ad* in moderation, ab-
stemiously; soberly.
sobriété [sɔbʀijete] *nf* temperance, ab-
stemiousness; sobriety.
sobriquet [sɔbʀikɛ] *nm* nickname.
soc [sɔk] *nm* ploughshare.
sociable [sɔsjabl(ə)] *a* sociable.
social, e, aux [sɔsjal, -o] *a* social.
socialement [sɔsjalmɑ̃] *ad* socially.
socialisant, e [sɔsjalizɑ̃, -ɑ̃t] *a* with socialist
tendencies.
socialisation [sɔsjalizasjɔ̃] *nf* socialisation.
socialiser [sɔsjalize] *vt* to socialize.
socialisme [sɔsjalism(ə)] *nm* socialism.
socialiste [sɔsjalist(ə)] *a*, *nm/f* socialist.
sociétaire [sɔsjetɛʀ] *nm/f* member.
société [sɔsjete] *nf* society; (*d'abeilles, de*

fourmis) colony; (*sportive*) club; (*COMM*) company; **la bonne** ~ polite society; **se plaire dans la** ~ **de** to enjoy the society of; **l'archipel de la S~** the Society Islands; **la** ~ **d'abondance/de consommation** the affluent/ consumer society; ~ **par actions** joint stock company; ~ **anonyme (SA)** ≈ limited company (Ltd) (*Brit*), ≈ incorporated company (Inc.) (*US*); ~ **d'investissement à capital variable (SICAV)** ≈ investment trust (*Brit*), ≈ mutual fund (*US*); ~ **à responsabilité limitée (SARL)** *type of limited liability company (with non-negotiable shares)*; ~ **savante** learned society; ~ **de services** service company.

socio-économique [sɔsjɔekɔnɔmik] *a* socioeconomic.

sociolinguistique [sɔsjɔlɛ̃gy̆istik] *a* sociolinguistic.

sociologie [sɔsjɔlɔʒi] *nf* sociology.

sociologique [sɔsjɔlɔʒik] *a* sociological.

sociologue [sɔsjɔlɔg] *nm/f* sociologist.

socio-professionnel, le [sɔsjɔpRɔfesjɔnel] *a* socioprofessional.

socle [sɔkl(ə)] *nm* (*de colonne, statue*) plinth, pedestal; (*de lampe*) base.

socquette [sɔkɛt] *nf* ankle sock.

soda [sɔda] *nm* (*boisson*) fizzy drink, soda (*US*).

sodium [sɔdjɔm] *nm* sodium.

sodomie [sɔdɔmi] *nf* sodomy.

sœur [sœʀ] *nf* sister; (*religieuse*) nun, sister; ~ **Élisabeth** (*REL*) Sister Elizabeth; ~ **de lait** foster sister.

sofa [sɔfa] *nm* sofa.

Sofia [sɔfja] *n* Sofia.

SOFRES [sɔfRES] *sigle f* (= *Société française d'enquête par sondage*) *company which conducts opinion polls*.

soi [swa] *pronom* oneself; **cela va de** ~ that *ou* it goes without saying, it stands to reason.

soi-disant [swadizɑ̃] *a inv* so-called ♦ *ad* supposedly.

soie [swa] *nf* silk; (*de porc, sanglier: poil*) bristle.

soient [swa] *vb voir* **être**.

soierie [swaRi] *nf* (*industrie*) silk trade; (*tissu*) silk.

soif [swaf] *nf* thirst; (*fig*): ~ **de** thirst *ou* craving for; **avoir** ~ to be thirsty; **donner** ~ **à qn** to make sb thirsty.

soigné, e [swaɲe] *a* (*tenue*) well-groomed, neat; (*travail*) careful, meticulous; (*fam*) whopping; stiff.

soigner [swaɲe] *vt* (*malade, maladie: suj: docteur*) to treat; (*: suj: infirmière, mère*) to nurse, look after; (*blessé*) to tend; (*travail, détails*) to take care over; (*jardin, chevelure, invités*) to look after.

soigneur [swaɲœR] *nm* (*CYCLISME, FOOTBALL*) trainer; (*BOXE*) second.

soigneusement [swaɲøzmɑ̃] *ad* carefully.

soigneux, euse [swaɲø, -øz] *a* (*propre*) tidy, neat; (*méticuleux*) painstaking, careful; ~ **de** careful with.

soi-même [swamɛm] *pronom* oneself.

soin [swɛ̃] *nm* (*application*) care; (*propreté, ordre*) tidiness, neatness; (*responsabilité*): **le** ~ **de qch** the care of sth; ~**s** *nmpl* (*à un*

malade, blessé) treatment *sg*, medical attention *sg*; (*attentions, prévenance*) care and attention *sg*; (*hygiène*) care *sg*; ~**s de la chevelure/de beauté** hair/beauty care; ~**s du corps/ménage** care of one's body/the home; **avoir** *ou* **prendre** ~ **de** to take care of, look after; **avoir** *ou* **prendre** ~ **de faire** to take care to do; **sans** ~ *a* careless; untidy; **les premiers** ~**s** first aid *sg*; **aux bons** ~**s de** c/o, care of; **être aux petits** ~**s pour qn** to wait on sb hand and foot, see to sb's every need; **confier qn aux** ~**s de qn** to hand sb over to sb's care.

soir [swaR] *nm, ad* evening; **le** ~ in the evening(s); **ce** ~ this evening, tonight; **à ce** ~**!** see you this evening (*ou* tonight)!; **la veille au** ~ the previous evening; **sept/dix heures du** ~ seven in the evening/ten at night; **le repas/journal du** ~ the evening meal/ newspaper: **dimanche** ~ Sunday evening; **hier** ~ yesterday evening; **demain** ~ tomorrow evening, tomorrow night.

soirée [swaRe] *nf* evening; (*réception*) party; **donner en** ~ (*film, pièce*) to give an evening performance of.

soit [swa] *vb voir* **être**; ~ **un triangle ABC** let ABC be a triangle ♦ *cj* (*à savoir*) namely, to wit; (*ou*): ~ ... ~ ... either ... or ♦ *ad* so be it, very well; ~ **que** ... ~ **que** *ou* **ou que** whether ... or whether.

soixantaine [swasɑ̃tɛn] *nf*: **une** ~ (**de**) sixty or so, about sixty; **avoir la** ~ to be around sixty.

soixante [swasɑ̃t] *num* sixty.

soixante-dix [swasɑ̃tdis] *num* seventy.

soixante-dixième [swasɑ̃tdizjɛm] *num* seventieth.

soixante-huitard, e [swazɑ̃ty̆itaR, -aRd(ə)] *a* relating to the demonstrations of May 1968 ♦ *nm/f* participant in the demonstrations of May 1968.

soixantième [swasɑ̃tjɛm] *num* sixtieth.

soja [sɔʒa] *nm* soya; (*graines*) soya beans *pl*; **germes de** ~ beansprouts.

sol [sɔl] *nm* ground; (*de logement*) floor; (*revêtement*) flooring *q*; (*territoire, AGR, GÉO*) soil; (*MUS*) G; (*: en chantant la gamme*) so(h).

solaire [sɔlɛR] *a* solar, sun *cpd*.

solarium [sɔlaRjɔm] *nm* solarium.

soldat [sɔlda] *nm* soldier; **S~ inconnu** Unknown Warrior *ou* Soldier; ~ **de plomb** tin *ou* toy soldier.

solde [sɔld(ə)] *nf* pay ♦ *nm* (*COMM*) balance; ~**s** *nmpl ou nfpl* (*COMM*) sales; (*articles*) sale goods; **à la** ~ **de qn** (*péj*) in sb's pay; ~ **créditeur/débiteur** credit/debit balance; ~ **à payer** balance outstanding; **en** ~ at sale price; **aux** ~**s** at the sales.

solder [sɔlde] *vt* (*compte*) to settle; (*marchandise*) to sell at sale price, sell off; **se** ~ **par** (*fig*) to end in; **article soldé (à) 10 F** item reduced to 10 F.

soldeur, euse [sɔldœR, -øz] *nm/f* (*COMM*) discounter.

sole [sɔl] *nf* sole *inv* (*fish*).

soleil [sɔlej] *nm* sun; (*lumière*) sun(light); (*temps ensoleillé*) sun(shine); (*feu d'artifice*) Catherine wheel; (*ACROBATIE*) grand circle;

(*BOT*) sunflower; **il y a** *ou* **il fait du** ~ it's sunny; **au** ~ in the sun; **en plein** ~ in full sun; **le** ~ **levant/couchant** the rising/setting sun; **le** ~ **de minuit** the midnight sun.

solennel, le [sɔlanɛl] *a* solemn; ceremonial.

solennellement [sɔlanɛlmɑ̃] *ad* solemnly.

solenniser [sɔlanize] *vt* to solemnize.

solennité [sɔlanite] *nf* (*d'une fête*) solemnity; ~**s** *nfpl* (*formalités*) formalities.

solénoïde [sɔlenɔid] *nm* (*ÉLEC*) solenoid.

solfège [sɔlfɛʒ] *nm* rudiments *pl* of music; (*exercices*) ear training *q*.

solfier [sɔlfje] *vt*: ~ **un morceau** to sing a piece using the sol-fa.

soli [sɔli] *pl de* **solo**.

solidaire [sɔlidɛʀ] *a* (*personnes*) who stand together, who show solidarity; (*pièces mécaniques*) interdependent; (*JUR*: *engagement*) binding on all parties; (: *débiteurs*) jointly liable; **être** ~ **de** (*collègues*) to stand by; (*mécanisme*) to be bound up with, be dependent on.

solidairement [sɔlidɛʀmɑ̃] *ad* jointly.

solidariser [sɔlidaʀize]: **se** ~ **avec** *vt* to show solidarity with.

solidarité [sɔlidaʀite] *nf* (*entre personnes*) solidarity; (*de mécanisme, phénomènes*) interdependence; **par** ~ (**avec**) (*cesser le travail etc*) in sympathy (with).

solide [sɔlid] *a* solid; (*mur, maison, meuble*) solid, sturdy; (*connaissances, argument*) sound; (*personne*) robust, sturdy; (*estomac*) strong ♦ *nm* solid; **avoir les reins** ~**s** (*fig*) to be in a good financial position; to have sound financial backing.

solidement [sɔlidmɑ̃] *ad* solidly; (*fermement*) firmly.

solidifier [sɔlidifje] *vt*, **se** ~ *vi* to solidify.

solidité [sɔlidite] *nf* solidity; sturdiness.

soliloque [sɔlilɔk] *nm* soliloquy.

soliste [sɔlist(ə)] *nm/f* soloist.

solitaire [sɔlitɛʀ] *a* (*sans compagnie*) solitary, lonely; (*isolé*) solitary, isolated, lone; (*lieu*) lonely ♦ *nm/f* recluse; loner ♦ *nm* (*diamant, jeu*) solitaire.

solitude [sɔlityd] *nf* loneliness; (*paix*) solitude.

solive [sɔliv] *nf* joist.

sollicitations [sɔlisitasjɔ̃] *nfpl* (*requêtes*) entreaties, appeals; (*attractions*) enticements; (*TECH*) stress *sg*.

solliciter [sɔlisite] *vt* (*personne*) to appeal to; (*emploi, faveur*) to seek; (*moteur*) to prompt; (*suj: occupations, attractions etc*): ~ **qn** to appeal to sb's curiosity *etc*; to entice sb; to make demands on sb's time; ~ **qn de faire** to appeal to sb *ou* request sb to do.

sollicitude [sɔlisityd] *nf* concern.

solo [sɔlo] *nm*, *pl* **soli** [sɔli] (*MUS*) solo (*pl* -s *ou* soli).

solstice [sɔlstis] *nm* solstice; ~ **d'hiver/d'été** winter/summer solstice.

solubilisé, e [sɔlybilize] *a* soluble.

soluble [sɔlybl(ə)] *a* (*sucre, cachet*) soluble; (*problème etc*) soluble, solvable.

soluté [sɔlyte] *nm* solution.

solution [sɔlysjɔ̃] *nf* solution; ~ **de continuité** gap, break; ~ **de facilité** easy way out.

solutionner [sɔlysjɔne] *vt* to solve, find a solution for.

solvabilité [sɔlvabilite] *nf* solvency.

solvable [sɔlvabl(ə)] *a* solvent.

solvant [sɔlvɑ̃] *nm* solvent.

Somalie [sɔmali] *nf*: **la** ~ Somalia.

somalien, ne [sɔmaljɛ̃, -ɛn] *a* Somalian.

sombre [sɔ̃bʀ(ə)] *a* dark; (*fig*) sombre, gloomy; (*sinistre*) awful, dreadful.

sombrer [sɔ̃bʀe] *vi* (*bateau*) to sink, go down; ~ **corps et biens** to go down with all hands; ~ **dans** (*misère, désespoir*) to sink into.

sommaire [sɔmɛʀ] *a* (*simple*) basic; (*expéditif*) summary ♦ *nm* summary; **faire le** ~ **de** to make a summary of, summarize; **exécution** ~ summary execution.

sommairement [sɔmɛʀmɑ̃] *ad* basically; summarily.

sommation [sɔmasjɔ̃] *nf* (*JUR*) summons *sg*; (*avant de faire feu*) warning.

somme [sɔm] *nf* (*MATH*) sum; (*fig*) amount; (*argent*) sum, amount ♦ *nm*: **faire un** ~ to have a (short) nap; **faire la** ~ **de** to add up; **en** ~, ~ **toute** *ad* all in all.

sommeil [sɔmɛj] *nm* sleep; **avoir** ~ to be sleepy; **avoir le** ~ **léger** to be a light sleeper; **en** ~ (*fig*) dormant.

sommeiller [sɔmeje] *vi* to doze; (*fig*) to lie dormant.

sommelier [sɔmalje] *nm* wine waiter.

sommer [sɔme] *vt*: ~ **qn de faire** to command *ou* order sb to do; (*JUR*) to summon sb to do.

sommes [sɔm] *vb voir* **être**; *voir aussi* **somme**.

sommet [sɔmɛ] *nm* top; (*d'une montagne*) summit, top; (*fig: de la perfection, gloire*) height; (*GÉOM: d'angle*) vertex (*pl* vertices); (*conférence*) summit (conference).

sommier [sɔmje] *nm* bed base, bedspring (*US*); (*ADMIN: registre*) register; ~ **à ressorts** (interior sprung) divan base (*Brit*), box spring (*US*); ~ **à lattes** slatted bed base.

sommité [sɔmite] *nf* prominent person, leading light.

somnambule [sɔmnɑ̃byl] *nm/f* sleepwalker.

somnambulisme [sɔmnɑ̃bylism(ə)] *nm* sleepwalking.

somnifère [sɔmnifɛʀ] *nm* sleeping drug; (*comprimé*) sleeping pill *ou* tablet.

somnolence [sɔmnɔlɑ̃s] *nf* drowsiness.

somnolent, e [sɔmnɔlɑ̃, -ɑ̃t] *a* sleepy, drowsy.

somnoler [sɔmnɔle] *vi* to doze.

somptuaire [sɔ̃ptɥɛʀ] *a*: **lois** ~**s** sumptuary laws; **dépenses** ~**s** extravagant expenditure *sg*.

somptueusement [sɔ̃ptɥøzmɑ̃] *ad* sumptuously.

somptueux, euse [sɔ̃ptɥø, -øz] *a* sumptuous; (*cadeau*) lavish.

son [sɔ̃], **sa** [sa], *pl* **ses** [se] *dét* (*antécédent humain mâle*) his; (: *femelle*) her; (: *valeur indéfinie*) one's, his/her; (: *non humain*) its; *voir note sous* **il**.

son [sɔ̃] *nm* sound; (*de blé etc*) bran; ~ **et lumière** *a inv* son et lumière.

sonar [sɔnaʀ] *nm* (*NAVIG*) sonar.

sonate [sɔnat] *nf* sonata.

sondage [sɔ̃daʒ] *nm* (*de terrain*) boring, drilling; (*mer, atmosphère*) sounding; probe; (*enquête*) survey, sounding out of opinion; ~

(d'opinion) (opinion) poll.

sonde [sɔ̃d] *nf* (*NAVIG*) lead *ou* sounding line; (*MÉTÉOROLOGIE*) sonde; (*MÉD*) probe; catheter; (*d'alimentation*) feeding tube; (*TECH*) borer, driller; (*de forage, sondage*) drill; (*pour fouiller etc*) probe; ~ **à avalanche** pole (*for probing snow and locating victims*); ~ **spatiale** probe.

sonder [sɔ̃de] *vt* (*NAVIG*) to sound; (*atmosphère, plaie, bagages etc*) to probe; (*TECH*) to bore, drill; (*fig: personne*) to sound out; (: *opinion*) to probe; ~ **le terrain** (*fig*) to see how the land lies.

songe [sɔ̃ʒ] *nm* dream.

songer [sɔ̃ʒe] *vi* to dream; ~ **à** (*rêver à*) to muse over, think over; (*penser à*) to think of; (*envisager*) to contemplate, think of, consider; ~ **que** to consider that; to think that.

songerie [sɔ̃ʒri] *nf* reverie.

songeur, euse [sɔ̃ʒœR, -øz] *a* pensive; **ça me laisse** ~ that makes me wonder.

sonnailles [sɔnaj] *nfpl* jingle of bells.

sonnant, e [sɔnɑ̃, -ɑ̃t] *a*: **en espèces** ~**es et trébuchantes** in coin of the realm; **à 8 heures** ~**es** on the stroke of 8.

sonné, e [sɔne] *a* (*fam*) cracked; (*passé*): **il est midi** ~ it's gone twelve; **il a quarante ans bien** ~**s** he's well into his forties.

sonner [sɔne] *vi* (*retentir*) to ring; (*donner une impression*) to sound ♦ *vt* (*cloche*) to ring; (*glas, tocsin*) to sound; (*portier, infirmière*) to ring for; (*messe*) to ring the bell for; (*fam: suj: choc, coup*) to knock out; ~ **du clairon** to sound the bugle; ~ **bien/mal/creux** to sound good/bad/hollow; ~ **faux** (*instrument*) to sound out of tune; (*rire*) to ring false; ~ **les heures** to strike the hours; **minuit vient de** ~ midnight has just struck; ~ **chez qn** to ring sb's doorbell, ring at sb's door.

sonnerie [sɔnri] *nf* (*son*) ringing; (*sonnette*) bell; (*mécanisme d'horloge*) striking mechanism; ~ **d'alarme** alarm bell; ~ **de clairon** bugle call.

sonnet [sɔnɛ] *nm* sonnet.

sonnette [sɔnɛt] *nf* bell; ~ **d'alarme** alarm bell; ~ **de nuit** night-bell.

sono [sɔno] *nf* (= *sonorisation*) PA (system).

sonore [sɔnɔR] *a* (*voix*) sonorous, ringing; (*salle, métal*) resonant; (*ondes, film, signal*) sound *cpd*; (*LING*) voiced; **effets** ~**s** sound effects.

sonorisation [sɔnɔRizasjɔ̃] *nf* (*installations*) public address system.

sonoriser [sɔnɔRize] *vt* (*film, spectacle*) to add the sound track to; (*salle*) to fit with a public address system.

sonorité [sɔnɔRite] *nf* (*de piano, violon*) tone; (*de voix, mot*) sonority; (*d'une salle*) resonance; acoustics *pl*.

sonothèque [sɔnɔtɛk] *nf* sound library.

sont [sɔ̃] *vb voir* **être**.

sophistication [sɔfistikasjɔ̃] *nf* sophistication.

sophistiqué, e [sɔfistike] *a* sophisticated.

soporifique [sɔpɔRifik] *a* soporific.

soprano [sɔpRano] *nm/f* soprano (*pl* -s).

sorbet [sɔRbɛ] *nm* water ice, sorbet.

sorbetière [sɔRbətjɛR] *nf* ice-cream maker.

sorbier [sɔRbje] *nm* service tree.

sorcellerie [sɔRsɛlRi] *nf* witchcraft *q*, sorcery *q*.

sorcier, ière [sɔRsje, -jɛR] *nm/f* sorcerer/witch *ou* sorceress ♦ *a*: **ce n'est pas** ~ (*fam*) it's as easy as pie.

sordide [sɔRdid] *a* sordid; squalid.

Sorlingues [sɔRlɛ̃g] *nfpl*: **les (îles)** ~ the Scilly Isles, the Isles of Scilly, the Scillies.

sornettes [sɔRnɛt] *nfpl* twaddle *sg*.

sort [sɔR] *vb voir* **sortir** ♦ *nm* (*fortune, destinée*) fate; (*condition, situation*) lot; (*magique*): **jeter un** ~ to cast a spell; **un coup du** ~ a blow dealt by fate; **le** ~ **en est jeté** the die is cast; **tirer au** ~ to draw lots; **tirer qch au** ~ to draw lots for sth.

sortable [sɔRtabl(ə)] *a*: **il n'est pas** ~ he doesn't know how to behave.

sortant, e [sɔRtɑ̃, -ɑ̃t] *vb voir* **sortir** ♦ *a* (*numéro*) which comes up (*in a draw etc*); (*député, président*) outgoing.

sorte [sɔRt(ə)] *vb voir* **sortir** ♦ *nf* sort, kind; **de la** ~ *ad* in that way; **en quelque** ~ in a way; **de** ~ **à** so as to, in order to; **de (telle)** ~ **que, en** ~ **que** (*de manière que*) so that; (*si bien que*) so much so that; **faire en** ~ **que** to see to it that.

sortie [sɔRti] *nf* (*issue*) way out, exit; (*MIL*) sortie; (*fig: verbale*) outburst; sally; (: *parole incongrue*) odd remark; (*d'un gaz, de l'eau*) outlet; (*promenade*) outing; (*le soir: au restaurant etc*) night out; (*de produits*) export; (*de capitaux*) outflow; (*COMM: somme*): ~**s** items of expenditure; outgoings *sans sg*; (*INFORM*) output; (*d'imprimante*) printout; **à sa** ~ as he went out *ou* left; **à la** ~ **de l'école/l'usine** (*moment*) after school/work; when school/the factory comes out; (*lieu*) at the school/factory gates; **à la** ~ **de ce nouveau modèle** when this new model comes (*ou* came) out, when they bring (*ou* brought) out this new model; ~ **de bain** (*vêtement*) bathrobe; **"~ de camions"** "vehicle exit"; ~ **papier** hard copy; ~ **de secours** emergency exit.

sortilège [sɔRtilɛʒ] *nm* (magic) spell.

sortir [sɔRtiR] *vi* (*gén*) to come out; (*partir, se promener, aller au spectacle etc*) to go out; (*bourgeon, plante, numéro gagnant*) to come up ♦ *vt* (*gén*) to take out; (*produit, ouvrage, modèle*) to bring out; (*boniments, incongruités*) to come out with; (*INFORM*) to output; (: *sur papier*) to print out; (*fam: expulser*) to throw out ♦ *nm*: **au** ~ **de l'hiver/l'enfance** as winter/childhood nears its end; ~ **qch de** to take sth out of; ~ **qn d'embarras** to get sb out of trouble; ~ **de** (*gén*) to leave; (*endroit*) to go (*ou* come) out of, leave; (*rainure etc*) to come out of; (*maladie*) to get over; (*époque*) to get through; (*cadre, compétence*) to be outside; (*provenir de: famille etc*) to come from; ~ **de table** to leave the table; ~ **du système** (*INFORM*) to log out; ~ **de ses gonds** (*fig*) to fly off the handle; **se** ~ **de** (*affaire, situation*) to get out of; **s'en** ~ (*malade*) to pull through; (*d'une difficulté etc*) to come through all right; to get through, be able to manage.

SOS *sigle m* mayday, SOS.

sosie [sɔzi] *nm* double.

sot, sotte [so, sɔt] *a* silly, foolish ♦ *nm/f* fool.
sottement [sɔtmɑ̃] *ad* foolishly.
sottise [sɔtiz] *nf* silliness *q*, foolishness *q*; (*propos, acte*) silly *ou* foolish thing (to do *ou* say).
sou [su] *nm*: **près de ses ~s** tight-fisted; **sans le ~** penniless; **~ à ~** penny by penny; **pas un ~ de bon sens** not a scrap *ou* an ounce of good sense; **de quatre ~s** worthless.
souahéli, e [swaeli] *a* Swahili ♦ *nm* (*LING*) Swahili.
soubassement [subɑsmɑ̃] *nm* base.
soubresaut [subʀəso] *nm* (*de peur etc*) start; (*cahot: d'un véhicule*) jolt.
soubrette [subʀɛt] *nf* soubrette, maidservant.
souche [suʃ] *nf* (*d'arbre*) stump; (*de carnet*) counterfoil (*Brit*), stub; **dormir comme une ~** to sleep like a log; **de vieille ~** of old stock.
souci [susi] *nm* (*inquiétude*) worry; (*préoccupation*) concern; (*BOT*) marigold; **se faire du ~** to worry; **avoir (le) ~ de** to have concern for; **par ~ de** for the sake of, out of concern for.
soucier [susje]: **se ~ de** *vt* to care about.
soucieux, euse [susjø, -øz] *a* concerned, worried; **~ de** concerned about; **peu ~ de/ que** caring little about/whether.
soucoupe [sukup] *nf* saucer; **~ volante** flying saucer.
soudain, e [sudɛ̃, -ɛn] *a* (*douleur, mort*) sudden ♦ *ad* suddenly, all of a sudden.
soudainement [sudɛnmɑ̃] *ad* suddenly.
soudaineté [sudɛnte] *nf* suddenness.
Soudan [sudɑ̃] *nm*: **le ~** the Sudan.
soudanais, e [sudanɛ, -ɛz] *a* Sudanese.
soude [sud] *nf* soda.
soudé, e [sude] *a* (*fig: pétales, organes*) joined (together).
souder [sude] *vt* (*avec fil à souder*) to solder; (*par soudure autogène*) to weld; (*fig*) to bind *ou* knit together; to fuse (together); **se ~** *vi* (*os*) to knit (together).
soudeur, euse [sudœʀ, -øz] *nm/f* (*ouvrier*) welder.
soudoyer [sudwaje] *vt* (*péj*) to bribe, buy over.
soudure [sudyʀ] *nf* soldering; welding; (*joint*) soldered joint; weld; **faire la ~** (*COMM*) to fill a gap; (*fig: assurer une transition*) to bridge the gap.
souffert, e [sufɛʀ, -ɛʀt(ə)] *pp de* **souffrir**.
soufflage [suflaʒ] *nm* (*du verre*) glass-blowing.
souffle [sufl(ə)] *nm* (*en expirant*) breath; (*en soufflant*) puff, blow; (*respiration*) breathing; (*d'explosion, de ventilateur*) blast; (*du vent*) blowing; (*fig*) inspiration; **retenir son ~** to hold one's breath; **avoir du/manquer de ~** to have a lot of puff/be short of breath; **être à bout de ~** to be out of breath; **avoir le ~ court** to be short-winded; **un ~ d'air** *ou* **de vent** a breath of air, a puff of wind; **~ au cœur** (*MÉD*) heart murmur.
soufflé, e [sufle] *a* (*CULIN*) soufflé; (*fam: ahuri, stupéfié*) staggered ♦ *nm* (*CULIN*) soufflé.
souffler [sufle] *vi* (*gén*) to blow; (*haleter*) to puff (and blow) ♦ *vt* (*feu, bougie*) to blow

out; (*chasser: poussière etc*) to blow away; (*TECH: verre*) to blow; (*suj: explosion*) to destroy (with its blast); (*dire*): **~ qch à qn** to whisper sth to sb; (*fam: voler*): **~ qch à qn** to pinch sth from sb; **~ son rôle à qn** to prompt sb; **ne pas ~ mot** not to breathe a word; **laisser ~ qn** (*fig*) to give sb a breather.
soufflet [suflɛ] *nm* (*instrument*) bellows *pl*; (*entre wagons*) vestibule; (*COUTURE*) gusset; (*gifle*) slap (in the face).
souffleur, euse [suflœʀ, -øz] *nm/f* (*THÉÂTRE*) prompter; (*TECH*) glass-blower.
souffrance [sufʀɑ̃s] *nf* suffering; **en ~** (*marchandise*) awaiting delivery; (*affaire*) pending.
souffrant, e [sufʀɑ̃, -ɑ̃t] *a* unwell.
souffre-douleur [sufʀədulœʀ] *nm inv* whipping boy (*Brit*), butt, underdog.
souffreteux, euse [sufʀətø, -øz] *a* sickly.
souffrir [sufʀiʀ] *vi* to suffer; (*éprouver des douleurs*) to be in pain ♦ *vt* to suffer, endure; (*supporter*) to bear, stand; (*admettre: exception etc*) to allow *ou* admit of; **~ de** (*maladie, froid*) to suffer from; **~ des dents** to have trouble with one's teeth; **ne pas pouvoir ~ qch/que ...** not to be able to endure *ou* bear sth/that ...; **faire ~ qn** (*suj: personne*) to make sb suffer; (*: dents, blessure etc*) to hurt sb.
soufre [sufʀ(ə)] *nm* sulphur (*Brit*), sulfur (*US*).
soufrer [sufʀe] *vt* (*vignes*) to treat with sulphur *ou* sulfur.
souhait [swɛ] *nm* wish; **tous nos ~s de** good wishes *ou* our best wishes for; **riche etc à ~** as rich *etc* as one could wish; **à vos ~s!** bless you!
souhaitable [swɛtabl(ə)] *a* desirable.
souhaiter [swɛte] *vt* to wish for; **~ le bonjour à qn** to bid sb good day; **~ la bonne année à qn** to wish sb a happy New Year; **il est à ~ que** it is to be hoped that.
souiller [suje] *vt* to dirty, soil; (*fig*) to sully, tarnish.
souillure [sujyʀ] *nf* stain.
soûl, e [su, sul] *a* drunk; (*fig*): **~ de musique/plaisirs** drunk with music/pleasure ♦ *nm*: **tout son ~** to one's heart's content.
soulagement [sulaʒmɑ̃] *nm* relief.
soulager [sulaʒe] *vt* to relieve; **~ qn de** to relieve sb of.
soûler [sule] *vt*: **~ qn** to get sb drunk; (*suj: boisson*) to make sb drunk; (*fig*) to make sb's head spin *ou* reel; **se ~** to get drunk; **se ~ de** (*fig*) to intoxicate o.s. with.
soûlerie [sulʀi] *nf* (*péj*) drunken binge.
soulèvement [sulɛvmɑ̃] *nm* uprising; (*GÉO*) upthrust.
soulever [sulve] *vt* to lift; (*vagues, poussière*) to send up; (*peuple*) to stir up (to revolt); (*enthousiasme*) to arouse; (*question, débat, protestations, difficultés*) to raise; **se ~** *vi* (*peuple*) to rise up; (*personne couchée*) to lift o.s. up; (*couvercle etc*) to lift; **cela me soulève le cœur** it makes me feel sick.
soulier [sulje] *nm* shoe; **~s bas** low-heeled shoes; **~s plats/à talons** flat/heeled shoes.
souligner [suliɲe] *vt* to underline; (*fig*) to

emphasize, stress.

soumettre [sumɛtʀ] *vt* (*pays*) to subject, subjugate; (*rebelles*) to put down, subdue; ~ **qn/qch à** to subject sb/sth to; ~ **qch à qn** (*projet etc*) to submit sth to sb; **se ~ (à)** (*se rendre, obéir*) to submit (to); **se ~ à** (*formalités etc*) to submit to; (*régime etc*) to submit o.s. to.

soumis, e [sumi, -iz] *pp de* **soumettre ♦** *a* submissive; **revenus ~ à l'impôt** taxable income.

soumission [sumisjɔ̃] *nf* (*voir se soumettre*) submission; (*docilité*) submissiveness; (*COMM*) tender.

soumissionner [sumisjɔne] *vt* (*COMM*: *travaux*) to bid for, tender for.

soupape [supap] *nf* valve; ~ **de sûreté** safety valve.

soupçon [supsɔ̃] *nm* suspicion; (*petite quantité*): **un ~ de** a hint *ou* touch of; **avoir ~ de** to suspect; **au dessus de tout ~** above (all) suspicion.

soupçonner [supsɔne] *vt* to suspect; ~ **qn de qch/d'être** to suspect sb of sth/of being.

soupçonneux, euse [supsɔnø, -øz] *a* suspicious.

soupe [sup] *nf* soup; ~ **au lait** *a inv* quick-tempered; ~ **à l'oignon/de poisson** onion/fish soup; ~ **populaire** soup kitchen.

soupente [supɑ̃t] *nf* (*mansarde*) attic; (*placard*) cupboard (*Brit*) *ou* closet (*US*) under the stairs.

souper [supe] *vi* to have supper ♦ *nm* supper; **avoir soupé de** (*fam*) to be sick and tired of.

soupeser [supəze] *vt* to weigh in one's hand(s), feel the weight of; (*fig*) to weigh up.

soupière [supjɛʀ] *nf* (soup) tureen.

soupir [supiʀ] *nm* sigh; (*MUS*) crotchet rest (*Brit*), quarter note rest (*US*); **rendre le dernier ~** to breathe one's last.

soupirail, aux [supiʀaj, -o] *nm* (small) basement window.

soupirant [supiʀɑ̃] *nm* (*péj*) suitor, wooer.

soupirer [supiʀe] *vi* to sigh; ~ **après qch** to yearn for sth.

souple [supl(ə)] *a* supple; (*col*) soft; (*fig*: *règlement, caractère*) flexible; (: *démarche, taille*) lithe, supple; **disque(tte)** ~ (*INFORM*) floppy disk, diskette.

souplesse [suplɛs] *nf* suppleness; flexibility.

source [suʀs(ə)] *nf* (*point d'eau*) spring; (*d'un cours d'eau, fig*) source; **prendre sa ~ à/ dans** (*suj: cours d'eau*) to have its source at/ in; **tenir qch de bonne ~/de ~ sûre** to have sth on good authority/from a reliable source; ~ **thermale/d'eau minérale** hot *ou* thermal/ mineral spring.

sourcier, ière [suʀsje, -jɛʀ] *nm* water diviner.

sourcil [suʀsij] *nm* (eye)brow.

sourcilière [suʀsiljɛʀ] *af voir* **arcade**.

sourciller [suʀsije] *vi*: **sans ~** without turning a hair *ou* batting an eyelid.

sourcilleux, euse [suʀsijø, -øz] *a* (*hautain, sévère*) haughty, supercilious; (*pointilleux*) finicky, pernickety.

sourd, e [suʀ, suʀd(ə)] *a* deaf; (*bruit, voix*) muffled; (*couleur*) muted; (*douleur*) dull; (*lutte*) silent, hidden; (*LING*) voiceless ♦ *nm/f* deaf person; **être ~ à** to be deaf to.

sourdement [suʀdəmɑ̃] *ad* (*avec un bruit sourd*) dully; (*secrètement*) silently.

sourdine [suʀdin] *nf* (*MUS*) mute; **en ~** *ad* softly, quietly; **mettre une ~ à** (*fig*) to tone down.

sourd-muet, sourde-muette [suʀmyɛ, suʀdmyɛt] *a* deaf-and-dumb ♦ *nm/f* deaf-mute.

sourdre [suʀdʀ(ə)] *vi* (*eau*) to spring up; (*fig*) to rise.

souriant, e [suʀjɑ̃, -ɑ̃t] *vb voir* **sourire ♦** *a* cheerful.

souricière [suʀisjɛʀ] *nf* mousetrap; (*fig*) trap.

sourie [suʀi] *etc vb voir* **sourire**.

sourire [suʀiʀ] *nm* smile ♦ *vi* to smile; ~ **à qn** to smile at sb; (*fig*) to appeal to sb; (: *chance*) to smile on sb; **faire un ~ à qn** to give sb a smile; **garder le ~** to keep smiling.

souris [suʀi] *nf* mouse (*pl* mice); (*INFORM*) mouse.

sournois, e [suʀnwa, -waz] *a* deceitful, underhand.

sournoisement [suʀnwazmɑ̃] *ad* deceitfully.

sous [su] *prép* (*gén*) under; ~ **la pluie/ le soleil** in the rain/sunshine; ~ **mes yeux** before my eyes; ~ **terre** *a, ad* underground; ~ **vide** *a, ad* vacuum-packed; ~ **l'influence/ l'action de** under the influence of/by the action of; ~ **antibiotiques/perfusion** on antibiotics/a drip; ~ **cet angle/ce rapport** from this angle/in this respect; ~ **peu** *ad* shortly, before long.

sous... [su, suz + *vowel*] *préfixe* sub-; under....

sous-alimenté, e [suzalimɑ̃te] *a* undernourished.

sous-bois [subwa] *nm inv* undergrowth.

sous-catégorie [sukategɔʀi] *nf* sub-category.

sous-chef [suʃɛf] *nm* deputy chief, second in command; ~ **de bureau** deputy head clerk.

sous-comité [sukɔmite] *nm* subcommittee.

sous-commission [sukɔmisjɔ̃] *nf* sub-committee.

sous-continent [sukɔ̃tinɑ̃] *nm* subcontinent.

sous-couche [sukuʃ] *nf* (*de peinture*) undercoat.

souscripteur, trice [suskʀiptœʀ, -tʀis] *nm/f* subscriber.

souscription [suskʀipsjɔ̃] *nf* subscription; **offert en ~** available on subscription.

souscrire [suskʀiʀ]: ~ **à** *vt* to subscribe to.

sous-cutané, e [sukytane] *a* subcutaneous.

sous-développé, e [sudevlɔpe] *a* underdeveloped.

sous-directeur, trice [sudiʀɛktœʀ, -tʀis] *nm/f* assistant manager/manageress, sub-manager/manageress.

sous-emploi [suzɑ̃plwa] *nm* underemployment.

sous-employé, e [suzɑ̃plwaje] *a* underemployed.

sous-ensemble [suzɑ̃sɑ̃bl(ə)] *nm* subset.

sous-entendre [suzɑ̃tɑ̃dʀ(ə)] *vt* to imply, infer.

sous-entendu, e [suzɑ̃tɑ̃dy] *a* implied; (*LING*) understood ♦ *nm* innuendo, insinuation.

sous-equipé, e [suzekipe] *a* underequipped.

sous-estimer [suzɛstime] *vt* to under-estimate.

sous-exploiter [suzɛksplwate] *vt* to under-exploit.

sous-exposer [suzɛkspoze] *vt* to underexpose.
sous-fifre [sufifʀ(ə)] *nm* (*péj*) underling.
sous-groupe [sugʀup] *nm* subgroup.
sous-homme [suzɔm] *nm* sub-human.
sous-jacent, e [suʒasɑ̃, -ɑ̃t] *a* underlying.
sous-lieutenant [suljøtnɑ̃] *nm* sub-lieutenant.
sous-locataire [sulɔkatɛʀ] *nm/f* subtenant.
sous-location [sulɔkasjɔ̃] *nf* subletting.
sous-louer [sulwe] *vt* to sublet.
sous-main [sumɛ̃] *nm inv* desk blotter; **en ~ ad** secretly.
sous-marin, e [sumaʀɛ̃, -in] *a* (*flore, volcan*) submarine; (*navigation, pêche, explosif*) underwater ♦ *nm* submarine.
sous-médicalisé, e [sumedikalize] *a* lacking adequate medical care.
sous-nappe [sunap] *nf* undercloth.
sous-officier [suzɔfisje] *nm* ≈ noncommissioned officer (NCO).
sous-ordre [suzɔʀdʀ(ə)] *nm* subordinate; **créancier en ~** creditor's creditor.
sous-payé, e [supeje] *a* underpaid.
sous-préfecture [supʀefɛktyʀ] *nf* subprefecture.
sous-préfet [supʀefɛ] *nm* sub-prefect.
sous-production [supʀɔdyksjɔ̃] *nf* underproduction.
sous-produit [supʀɔdɥi] *nm* by-product; (*fig: péj*) pale imitation.
sous-programme [supʀɔgʀam] *nm* (*INFORM*) subroutine.
sous-pull [supul] *nm* thin poloneck sweater.
sous-secrétaire [susəkʀetɛʀ] *nm*: **~ d'État** Under-Secretary of State.
soussigné, e [susiɲe] *a*: **je ~** I the undersigned.
sous-sol [susɔl] *nm* basement; (*GÉO*) subsoil.
sous-tasse [sutas] *nf* saucer.
sous-tendre [sutɑ̃dʀ(ə)] *vt* to underlie.
sous-titre [sutitʀ(ə)] *nm* subtitle.
sous-titré, e [sutitʀe] *a* with subtitles.
soustraction [sustʀaksjɔ̃] *nf* subtraction.
soustraire [sustʀɛʀ] *vt* to subtract, take away; (*dérober*): **~ qch à qn** to remove sth from sb; **~ qn à** (*danger*) to shield sb from; **se ~ à** (*autorité, obligation, devoir*) to elude, escape from.
sous-traitance [sutʀɛtɑ̃s(ə)] *nf* subcontracting.
sous-traitant [sutʀɛtɑ̃] *nm* subcontractor.
sous-traiter [sutʀɛte] *vt, vi* to subcontract.
soustrayais [sustʀɛjɛ] *etc vb voir* **soustraire**.
sous-verre [suvɛʀ] *nm inv* glass mount.
sous-vêtement [suvɛtmɑ̃] *nm* undergarment, item of underwear; **~s** *nmpl* underwear *sg*.
soutane [sutan] *nf* cassock, soutane.
soute [sut] *nf* hold; **~ à bagages** baggage hold.
soutenable [sutnabl(ə)] *a* (*opinion*) tenable, defensible.
soutenance [sutnɑ̃s] *nf*: **~ de thèse** ≈ viva (*voce*).
soutènement [sutɛnmɑ̃] *nm*: **mur de ~** retaining wall.
souteneur [sutnœʀ] *nm* procurer.
soutenir [sutniʀ] *vt* to support; (*assaut, choc, regard*) to stand up to, withstand; (*intérêt, effort*) to keep up; (*assurer*): **~ que** to maintain that; **se ~** (*dans l'eau etc*) to hold o.s.

up; (*être soutenable: point de vue*) to be tenable; (*s'aider mutuellement*) to stand by each other; **~ la comparaison avec** to bear *ou* stand comparison with; **~ le regard de qn** to be able to look sb in the face.
soutenu, e [sutny] *pp de* **soutenir** ♦ *a* (*efforts*) sustained, unflagging; (*style*) elevated; (*couleur*) strong.
souterrain, e [sutɛʀɛ̃, -ɛn] *a* underground; (*fig*) subterranean ♦ *nm* underground passage.
soutien [sutjɛ̃] *nm* support; **apporter son ~ à** to lend one's support to; **~ de famille** breadwinner.
soutiendrai [sutjɛ̃dʀe] *etc vb voir* **soutenir**.
soutien-gorge, *pl* **soutiens-gorge** [sutjɛ̃gɔʀʒ(ə)] *nm* bra; (*de maillot de bain*) top.
soutiens [sutjɛ̃], **soutint** [sutɛ̃] *etc vb voir* **soutenir**.
soutirer [sutiʀe] *vt*: **~ qch à qn** to squeeze *ou* get sth out of sb.
souvenance [suvnɑ̃s] *nf*: **avoir ~ de** to recollect.
souvenir [suvniʀ] *nm* (*réminiscence*) memory; (*cadeau*) souvenir, keepsake; (*de voyage*) souvenir ♦ *vb*: **se ~ de** *vt* to remember; **se ~ que** to remember that; **garder le ~ de** to retain the memory of; **en ~ de** in memory *ou* remembrance of; **avec mes affectueux/meilleurs ~s**, ... with love from, .../regards, ...
souvent [suvɑ̃] *ad* often; **peu ~** seldom, infrequently; **le plus ~** more often than not, most often.
souvenu, e [suvəny] *pp de* **se souvenir**.
souverain, e [suvʀɛ̃, -ɛn] *a* sovereign; (*fig: mépris*) supreme ♦ *nm/f* sovereign, monarch.
souverainement [suvʀɛnmɑ̃] *ad* (*sans appel*) with sovereign power; (*extrêmement*) supremely, intensely.
souveraineté [suvʀɛnte] *nf* sovereignty.
souviendrai [suvjɛ̃dʀe], **souviens** [suvjɛ̃], **souvint** [suvɛ̃] *etc vb voir* **se souvenir**.
soviétique [sɔvjetik] *a* Soviet ♦ *nm/f*: **S~** Soviet citizen.
soviétiser [sɔvjetize] *vt* to sovietize.
soviétologue [sɔvjetɔlɔg] *nm/f* Kremlinologist.
soyeux, euse [swajø, -øz] *a* silky.
soyez [swaje] *etc vb voir* **être**.
SPA *sigle f* (= *Société protectrice des animaux*) ≈ RSPCA (*Brit*), ≈ SPCA (*US*).
spacieux, euse [spasjø, -øz] *a* spacious; roomy.
spaciosité [spasjɔzite] *nf* spaciousness.
spaghettis [spageti] *nmpl* spaghetti *sg*.
sparadrap [spaʀadʀa] *nm* adhesive *ou* sticking (*Brit*) plaster, bandaid ® (*US*).
Sparte [spaʀt(ə)] *nf* Sparta.
spartiate [spaʀsjat] *a* Spartan; **~s** *nfpl* (*sandales*) Roman sandals.
spasme [spazm(ə)] *nm* spasm.
spasmodique [spazmɔdik] *a* spasmodic.
spatial, e, aux [spasjal, -o] *a* (*AVIAT*) space *cpd*; (*PSYCH*) spatial.
spatule [spatyl] *nf* (*ustensile*) slice; spatula; (*bout*) tip.
speaker, ine [spikœʀ, -kʀin] *nm/f* announcer.
spécial, e, aux [spesjal, -o] *a* special;

(*bizarre*) peculiar.

spécialement [spesjalmã] *ad* especially, particularly; (*tout exprès*) specially; **pas ~** not particularly.

spécialisation [spesjalizɑsjɔ̃] *nf* specialization.

spécialisé, e [spesjalize] *a* specialised; **ordinateur ~** dedicated computer.

spécialiser [spesjalize]: **se ~** *vi* to specialize.

spécialiste [spesjalist(ə)] *nm/f* specialist.

spécialité [spesjalite] *nf* speciality; (*SCOL*) special field; **~ pharmaceutique** patent medicine.

spécieux, euse [spesjø, -øz] *a* specious.

spécification [spesifikɑsjɔ̃] *nf* specification.

spécifier [spesifje] *vt* to specify, state.

spécifique [spesifik] *a* specific.

spécifiquement [spesifikmã] *ad* (*typiquement*) typically; (*tout exprès*) specifically.

spécimen [spesimen] *nm* specimen; (*revue etc*) specimen *ou* sample copy.

spectacle [spektakl(ə)] *nm* (*tableau, scène*) sight; (*représentation*) show; (*industrie*) show business, entertainment; **se donner en ~** (*péj*) to make a spectacle *ou* an exhibition of o.s; **pièce/revue à grand ~** spectacular (play/revue); **au ~ de ...** at the sight of ....

spectaculaire [spektakylɛʀ] *a* spectacular.

spectateur, trice [spektatœʀ, -tʀis] *nm/f* (*CINÉMA etc*) member of the audience; (*SPORT*) spectator; (*d'un événement*) onlooker, witness.

spectre [spɛktʀ(ə)] *nm* (*fantôme, fig*) spectre; (*PHYSIQUE*) spectrum (*pl* -a); **~ solaire** solar spectrum.

spéculateur, trice [spekylatœʀ, -tʀis] *nm/f* speculator.

spéculatif, ive [spekylatif, -iv] *a* speculative.

spéculation [spekylɑsjɔ̃] *nf* speculation.

spéculer [spekyle] *vi* to speculate; **~ sur** (*COMM*) to speculate in; (*réfléchir*) to speculate on; (*tabler sur*) to bank ou rely on.

spéléologie [speleɔlɔʒi] *nf* (*étude*) speleology; (*activité*) potholing.

spéléologue [speleɔlɔg] *nm/f* speleologist; potholer.

spermatozoïde [spɛʀmatozɔid] *nm* sperm, spermatozoon (*pl* -zoa).

sperme [spɛʀm(ə)] *nm* semen, sperm.

spermicide [spɛʀmisid] *a, nm* spermicide.

sphère [sfɛʀ] *nf* sphere.

sphérique [sfeʀik] *a* spherical.

sphincter [sfɛ̃ktɛʀ] *nm* sphincter.

sphinx [sfɛ̃ks] *nm inv* sphinx; (*ZOOL*) hawkmoth.

spiral, aux [spiʀal, -o] *nm* hairspring.

spirale [spiʀal] *nf* spiral; **en ~** in a spiral.

spire [spiʀ] *nf* (*d'une spirale*) turn; (*d'une coquille*) whorl.

spiritisme [spiʀitism(ə)] *nm* spiritualism, spiritism.

spirituel, le [spiʀitɥɛl] *a* spiritual; (*fin, piquant*) witty; **musique ~le** sacred music; **concert ~** concert of sacred music.

spirituellement [spiʀitɥɛlmã] *ad* spiritually; wittily.

spiritueux [spiʀitɥø] *nm* spirit.

splendeur [splɑ̃dœʀ] *nf* splendour (*Brit*), splendor (*US*).

splendide [splɑ̃did] *a* splendid, magnificent.

spolier [spɔlje] *vt*: **~ qn (de)** to despoil sb (of).

spongieux, euse [spɔ̃ʒjø, -øz] *a* spongy.

sponsor [spɔ̃sɔʀ] *nm* sponsor.

sponsoriser [spɔ̃sɔʀize] *vt* to sponsor.

spontané, e [spɔ̃tane] *a* spontaneous.

spontanément [spɔ̃tanemã] *ad* spontaneously.

sporadique [spɔʀadik] *a* sporadic.

sport [spɔʀ] *nm* sport ♦ *a inv* (*vêtement*) casual; (*fair-play*) sporting; **faire du ~** to do sport; **~ individuel/d'équipe** individual/team sport; **~ de combat** combative sport; **~s d'hiver** winter sports.

sportif, ive [spɔʀtif, -iv] *a* (*journal, association, épreuve*) sports *cpd*; (*allure, démarche*) athletic; (*attitude, esprit*) sporting; **les résultats ~s** the sports results.

sportivement [spɔʀtivmã] *ad* sportingly.

sportivité [spɔʀtivite] *nf* sportsmanship.

spot [spɔt] *nm* (*lampe*) spot(light); (*annonce*): **~ (publicitaire)** commercial (break).

spray [spʀɛ] *nm* spray, aerosol.

sprint [spʀint] *nm* sprint; **piquer un ~** to put on a (final) spurt.

squale [skwal] *nm* (*type of*) shark.

square [skwaʀ] *nm* public garden(s).

squash [skwaʃ] *nm* squash.

squatter *nm* [skwatœʀ] squatter ♦ *vt* [skwate] to squat.

squelette [skəlɛt] *nm* skeleton.

squelettique [skəletik] *a* scrawny; (*fig*) skimpy.

Sri Lanka [sʀilɑ̃ka] *nm* Sri Lanka.

sri-lankais, e [sʀilɑ̃kɛ, -ɛz] *a* Sri-Lankan.

SS *sigle f* = **sécurité sociale**; (= *Sa Sainteté*) HH.

ss *abr* = **sous**.

S/S *sigle m* (= *steamship*) SS.

SSR *sigle f* (= *Société suisse romande*) the Swiss French-language broadcasting company.

stabilisateur, trice [stabilizatœʀ, -tʀis] *a* stabilizing ♦ *nm* stabilizer; (*véhicule*) anti-roll device; (*avion*) tailplane.

stabiliser [stabilize] *vt* to stabilize; (*terrain*) to consolidate.

stabilité [stabilite] *nf* stability.

stable [stabl(ə)] *a* stable, steady.

stade [stad] *nm* (*SPORT*) stadium; (*phase, niveau*) stage.

stage [staʒ] *nm* training period; training course; (*d'avocat stagiaire*) articles *pl*.

stagiaire [staʒjɛʀ] *nm/f, a* trainee (*cpd*).

stagnant, e [stagnã, -ãt] *a* stagnant.

stagner [stagne] *vi* to stagnate.

stalactite [stalaktit] *nf* stalactite.

stalagmite [stalagmit] *nf* stalagmite.

stalle [stal] *nf* stall, box.

stand [stɑ̃d] *nm* (*d'exposition*) stand; (*de foire*) stall; **~ de tir** (*à la foire, SPORT*) shooting range; **~ de ravitaillement** pit.

standard [stɑ̃daʀ] *a inv* standard ♦ *nm* (*type, norme*) standard; (*téléphonique*) switchboard.

standardiser [stɑ̃daʀdize] *vt* to standardize.

standardiste [stɑ̃daʀdist(ə)] *nm/f* switchboard operator.

standing [stɑ̃diŋ] *nm* standing; **immeuble de**

grand ~ block of luxury flats (*Brit*), condo(minium) (*US*).

star [staʀ] *nf* star.

starlette [staʀlɛt] *nf* starlet.

starter [staʀtɛʀ] *nm* (*AUTO*) choke; (*SPORT*: *personne*) starter; **mettre le** ~ to pull out the choke.

station [stɑsjɔ̃] *nf* station; (*de bus*) stop; (*de villégiature*) resort; (*posture*): **la** ~ **debout** standing, an upright posture; ~ **balnéaire** seaside resort; ~ **de graissage** lubrication bay; ~ **de lavage** carwash; ~ **de ski** ski resort; ~ **de sports d'hiver** winter sports resort; ~ **de taxis** taxi rank (*Brit*) *ou* stand (*US*); ~ **thermale** thermal spa.

stationnaire [stɑsjɔnɛʀ] *a* stationary.

stationnement [stɑsjɔnmɑ̃] *nm* parking; **zone de** ~ **interdit** no parking area; ~ **alterné** parking on alternate sides.

stationner [stɑsjɔne] *vi* to park.

station-service [stɑsjɔ̃sɛʀvis] *nf* service station.

statique [statik] *a* static.

statisticien, ne [statistisjɛ̃, -ɛn] *nm/f* statistician.

statistique [statistik] *nf* (*science*) statistics *sg*; (*rapport, étude*) statistic ♦ *a* statistical; ~**s** *nfpl* (*données*) statistics *pl*.

statistiquement [statistikmɑ̃] *ad* statistically.

statue [staty] *nf* statue.

statuer [statɥe] *vi*: ~ **sur** to rule on, give a ruling on.

statuette [statɥɛt] *nf* statuette.

statu quo [statykwo] *nm* status quo.

stature [statyʀ] *nf* stature; **de haute** ~ of great stature.

statut [staty] *nm* status; ~**s** *nmpl* (*JUR*, *ADMIN*) statutes.

statutaire [statytɛʀ] *a* statutory.

Sté *abr* (= *société*) soc.

St(e) *abr* (= *Saint(e)*) St.

steak [stɛk] *nm* steak.

stèle [stɛl] *nf* stela, stele.

stellaire [stelɛʀ] *a* stellar.

stencil [stɛnsil] *nm* stencil.

sténodactylo [stenɔdaktilo] *nf* shorthand typist (*Brit*), stenographer (*US*).

sténodactylographie [stenɔdaktilɔgʀafi] *nf* shorthand typing (*Brit*), stenography (*US*).

sténo(graphie) [stenɔ(gʀafi)] *nf* shorthand; **prendre en** ~ to take down in shorthand.

sténographier [stenɔgʀafje] *vt* to take down in shorthand.

sténographique [stenɔgʀafik] *a* shorthand *cpd*.

stentor [stɑ̃tɔʀ] *nm*: **voix de** ~ stentorian voice.

stéphanois, e [stefanwa, -waz] *a* of *ou* from Saint-Étienne.

steppe [stɛp] *nf* steppe.

stère [stɛʀ] *nm* stere.

stéréo(phonie) [steʀeɔ(fɔni)] *nf* stereo(phony); **émission en** ~ stereo broadcast.

stéréo(phonique) [steʀeɔ(fɔnik)] *a* stereo(phonic).

stéréoscope [steʀeɔskɔp] *nm* stereoscope.

stéréoscopique [steʀeɔskɔpik] *a* stereoscopic.

stéréotype [steʀeɔtip] *nm* stereotype.

stéréotypé, e [steʀeɔtipe] *a* stereotyped.

stérile [steʀil] *a* sterile; (*terre*) barren; (*fig*) fruitless, futile.

stérilement [steʀilmɑ̃] *ad* fruitlessly.

stérilet [steʀilɛ] *nm* coil, loop.

stérilisateur [steʀilizatœʀ] *nm* sterilizer.

stérilisation [steʀilizɑsjɔ̃] *nf* sterilization.

stériliser [steʀilize] *vt* to sterilize.

stérilité [steʀilite] *nf* sterility.

sternum [stɛʀnɔm] *nm* breastbone, sternum.

stéthoscope [stetɔskɔp] *nm* stethoscope.

stick [stik] *nm* stick.

stigmates [stigmat] *nmpl* scars, marks; (*REL*) stigmata *pl*.

stigmatiser [stigmatize] *vt* to denounce, stigmatize.

stimulant, e [stimylɑ̃, -ɑ̃t] *a* stimulating ♦ *nm* (*MÉD*) stimulant; (*fig*) stimulus (*pl* -i), incentive.

stimulateur [stimylatœʀ] *nm*: ~ **cardiaque** pacemaker.

stimulation [stimylɑsjɔ̃] *nf* stimulation.

stimuler [stimyle] *vt* to stimulate.

stimulus, i [stimylys, -i] *nm* stimulus (*pl* -i).

stipulation [stipylɑsjɔ̃] *nf* stipulation.

stipuler [stipyle] *vt* to stipulate, specify.

stock [stɔk] *nm* stock; **en** ~ in stock.

stockage [stɔkaʒ] *nm* stocking; storage.

stocker [stɔke] *vt* to stock; (*déchets*) to store.

Stockholm [stɔkɔlm] *n* Stockholm.

stockiste [stɔkist(ə)] *nm* stockist.

stoïcisme [stɔisism(ə)] *nm* stoicism.

stoïque [stɔik] *a* stoic, stoical.

stomacal, e, aux [stɔmakal, -o] *a* gastric, stomach *cpd*.

stomatologie [stɔmatɔlɔʒi] *nf* stomatology.

stop [stɔp] *nm* (*AUTO*: *écriteau*) stop sign; (: *signal*) brake-light; (*dans un télégramme*) stop ♦ *excl* stop!

stoppage [stɔpaʒ] *nm* invisible mending.

stopper [stɔpe] *vt* to stop, halt; (*COUTURE*) to mend ♦ *vi* to stop, halt.

store [stɔʀ] *nm* blind; (*de magasin*) shade, awning.

strabisme [stʀabism(ə)] *nm* squint(ing).

strangulation [stʀɑ̃gylɑsjɔ̃] *nf* strangulation.

strapontin [stʀapɔ̃tɛ̃] *nm* jump *ou* foldaway seat.

Strasbourg [stʀazbuʀ] *n* Strasbourg.

strass [stʀas] *nm* paste, strass.

stratagème [stʀataʒɛm] *nm* stratagem.

strate [stʀat] *nf* (*GÉO*) stratum, layer.

stratège [stʀatɛʒ] *nm* strategist.

stratégie [stʀateʒi] *nf* strategy.

stratégique [stʀateʒik] *a* strategic.

stratégiquement [stʀateʒikmɑ̃] *ad* strategically.

stratifié, e [stʀatifje] *a* (*GÉO*) stratified; (*TECH*) laminated.

stratosphère [stʀatɔsfɛʀ] *nf* stratosphere.

stress [stʀɛs] *nm inv* stress.

stressant, e [stʀɛsɑ̃, -ɑ̃t] *a* stressful.

stresser [stʀɛse] *vt* to stress, cause stress in.

strict, e [stʀikt(ə)] *a* strict; (*tenue, décor*) severe, plain; **son droit le plus** ~ his most basic right; **dans la plus** ~**e intimité** strictly in private; **le** ~ **nécessaire/minimum** the bare essentials/minimum.

strictement [stʀiktəmɑ̃] *ad* strictly; plainly.

strident, e [stʀidɑ̃, -ɑ̃t] a shrill, strident.
stridulations [stʀidylɑsjɔ̃] nfpl stridulations, chirrings.
strie [stʀi] nf streak; (ANAT, GÉO) stria (pl -ae).
strier [stʀije] vt to streak; to striate.
strip-tease [stʀiptiz] nm striptease.
strip-teaseuse [stʀiptizøz] nf stripper, striptease artist.
striures [stʀijyʀ] nfpl streaking sg.
strophe [stʀɔf] nf verse, stanza.
structure [stʀyktyʀ] nf structure; **~s d'accueil/touristiques** reception/tourist facilities.
structurer [stʀyktyʀe] vt to structure.
strychnine [stʀiknin] nf strychnine.
stuc [styk] nm stucco.
studieusement [stydjøzmɑ̃] ad studiously.
studieux, euse [stydjø, -øz] a (élève) studious; (vacances) study cpd.
studio [stydjo] nm (logement) studio flat (Brit) ou apartment (US); (d'artiste, TV etc) studio (pl -s).
stupéfaction [stypefaksjɔ̃] nf stupefaction, astonishment.
stupéfait, e [stypefɛ, -ɛt] a astonished.
stupéfiant, e [stypefjɑ̃, -ɑ̃t] a stunning, astonishing ♦ nm (MÉD) drug, narcotic.
stupéfier [stypefje] vt to stupefy; (étonner) to stun, astonish.
stupeur [stypœʀ] nf (inertie, insensibilité) stupor; (étonnement) astonishment, amazement.
stupide [stypid] a stupid; (hébété) stunned.
stupidement [stypidmɑ̃] ad stupidly.
stupidité [stypidite] nf stupidity q; (propos, action) stupid thing (to say ou do).
stups [styp] nmpl (= stupéfiants): **brigade des ~** narcotics bureau ou squad.
style [stil] nm style; **meuble/robe de ~** piece of period furniture/period dress; **~ de vie** lifestyle.
stylé, e [stile] a well-trained.
stylet [stilɛ] nm (poignard) stiletto; (CHIRURGIE) stylet.
stylisé, e [stilize] a stylized.
styliste [stilist(ə)] nm/f designer; stylist.
stylistique [stilistik] nf stylistics sg ♦ a stylistic.
stylo [stilo] nm: **~ (à encre)** (fountain) pen; **~ (à) bille** ballpoint pen.
stylo-feutre [stiloføtʀ(ə)] nm felt-tip pen.
su, e [sy] pp de **savoir** ♦ nm: **au ~ de** with the knowledge of.
suaire [sɥɛʀ] nm shroud.
suant, e [sɥɑ̃, -ɑ̃t] a sweaty.
suave [sɥav] a (odeur) sweet; (voix) suave, smooth; (coloris) soft, mellow.
subalterne [sybaltɛʀn(ə)] a (employé, officier) junior; (rôle) subordinate, subsidiary ♦ nm/f subordinate, inferior.
subconscient [sypkɔ̃sjɑ̃] nm subconscious.
subdiviser [sybdivize] vt to subdivide.
subdivision [sybdivizjɔ̃] nf subdivision.
subir [sybiʀ] vt (affront, dégâts, mauvais traitements) to suffer; (influence, charme) to be under, be subjected to; (traitement, opération, châtiment) to undergo; (personne) to suffer, be subjected to.

subit, e [sybi, -it] a sudden.
subitement [sybitmɑ̃] ad suddenly, all of a sudden.
subjectif, ive [syb3ɛktif, -iv] a subjective.
subjectivement [syb3ɛktivmɑ̃] ad subjectively.
subjonctif [syb3ɔ̃ktif] nm subjunctive.
subjuguer [syb3yge] vt to subjugate.
sublime [syblim] a sublime.
sublimer [syblime] vt to sublimate.
submergé, e [sybmɛʀ3e] a submerged; (fig): **~ de** snowed under with; overwhelmed with.
submerger [sybmɛʀ3e] vt to submerge; (suj: foule) to engulf; (fig) to overwhelm.
submersible [sybmɛʀsibl(ə)] nm submarine.
subordination [sybɔʀdinasjɔ̃] nf subordination.
subordonné, e [sybɔʀdɔne] a, nm/f subordinate; **~ à** (personne) subordinate to; (résultats etc) subject to, depending on.
subordonner [sybɔʀdɔne] vt: **~ qn/qch à** to subordinate sb/sth to.
subornation [sybɔʀnasjɔ̃] nf bribing.
suborner [sybɔʀne] vt to bribe.
subrepticement [sybʀɛptismɑ̃] ad surreptitiously.
subroger [sybʀɔ3e] vt (JUR) to subrogate.
subside [sypsid] nm grant.
subsidiaire [sypsidjɛʀ] a subsidiary; **question ~** deciding question.
subsistance [sybzistɑ̃s] nf subsistence; **pourvoir à la ~ de qn** to keep sb, provide for sb's subsistence ou keep.
subsister [sybziste] vi (rester) to remain, subsist; (vivre) to live; (survivre) to live on.
substance [sypstɑ̃s] nf substance; **en ~** in substance.
substantiel, le [sypstɑ̃sjɛl] a substantial.
substantif [sypstɑ̃tif] nm noun, substantive.
substantiver [sypstɑ̃tive] vt to nominalize.
substituer [sypstitɥe] vt: **~ qn/qch à** to substitute sb/sth for; **se ~ à qn** (représenter) to substitute for sb; (évincer) to substitute o.s. for sb.
substitut [sypstity] nm (JUR) deputy public prosecutor; (succédané) substitute.
substitution [sypstitysjɔ̃] nf substitution.
subterfuge [syptɛʀfy3] nm subterfuge.
subtil, e [syptil] a subtle.
subtilement [syptilmɑ̃] ad subtly.
subtiliser [syptilize] vt: **~ qch (à qn)** to spirit sth away (from sb).
subtilité [syptilite] nf subtlety.
suburbain, e [sybyʀbɛ̃, -ɛn] a suburban.
subvenir [sybvəniʀ]: **~ à** vt to meet.
subvention [sybvɑ̃sjɔ̃] nf subsidy, grant.
subventionner [sybvɑ̃sjɔne] vt to subsidize.
subversif, ive [sybvɛʀsif, -iv] a subversive.
subversion [sybvɛʀsjɔ̃] nf subversion.
suc [syk] nm (BOT) sap; (de viande, fruit) juice; **~s gastriques** gastric juices.
succédané [syksedane] nm substitute.
succéder [syksede]: **~ à** vt (directeur, roi etc) to succeed; (venir après: dans une série) to follow, succeed; **se ~** vi (accidents, années) to follow one another.
succès [syksɛ] nm success; **avec ~** successfully; **sans ~** unsuccessfully; **avoir du ~** to be a success, be successful; **à ~** successful;

livre à ~ bestseller; ~ **de librairie** bestseller; ~ **(féminins)** conquests.

successeur [syksesœʀ] *nm* successor.

successif, ive [syksesif, -iv] *a* successive.

succession [syksesjɔ̃] *nf* (*série*, POL) succession; (*JUR: patrimoine*) estate, inheritance; **prendre la ~ de** (*directeur*) to succeed, take over from; (*entreprise*) to take over.

successivement [syksesivmɑ̃] *ad* successively.

succinct, e [syksɛ̃, -ɛ̃t] *a* succinct.

succinctement [syksɛ̃tmɑ̃] *ad* succinctly.

succion [syksjɔ̃] *nf*: **bruit de ~** sucking noise.

succomber [sykɔ̃be] *vi* to die, succumb; (*fig*) ~ **à** to give way to, succumb to.

succulent, e [sykylɑ̃, -ɑ̃t] *a* succulent.

succursale [sykyʀsal] *nf* branch; **magasin à ~s multiples** chain *ou* multiple store.

sucer [syse] *vt* to suck.

sucette [sysɛt] *nf* (*bonbon*) lollipop; (*de bébé*) dummy (*Brit*), pacifier (*US*), comforter (*US*).

suçoter [sysɔte] *vt* to suck.

sucre [sykʀ(ə)] *nm* (*substance*) sugar; (*morceau*) lump of sugar, sugar lump *ou* cube; ~ **de canne/betterave** cane/beet sugar; ~ **en morceaux/cristallisé/en poudre** lump *ou* cube/granulated/caster sugar; ~ **glace** icing sugar; ~ **d'orge** barley sugar.

sucré, e [sykʀe] *a* (*produit alimentaire*) sweetened; (*au goût*) sweet; (*péj*) sugary, honeyed.

sucrer [sykʀe] *vt* (*thé, café*) to sweeten, put sugar in; ~ **qn** to put sugar in sb's tea (*ou* coffee *etc*); **se ~** to help o.s. to sugar, have some sugar; (*fam*) to line one's pocket(s).

sucrerie [sykʀəʀi] *nf* (*usine*) sugar refinery; **~s** *nfpl* (*bonbons*) sweets, sweet things.

sucrier, ière [sykʀije, -jɛʀ] *a* (*industrie*) sugar *cpd*; (*région*) sugar-producing ♦ *nm* (*fabricant*) sugar producer; (*récipient*) sugar bowl *ou* basin.

sud [syd] *nm*: **le ~** the south ♦ *a inv* south; (*côte*) south, southern; **au ~** (*situation*) in the south; (*direction*) to the south; **au ~ de** (to the) south of.

sud-africain, e [sydafʀikɛ̃, -ɛn] *a* South African ♦ *nm/f*: **Sud-Africain, e** South African.

sud-américain, e [sydameʀikɛ̃, -ɛn] *a* South American ♦ *nm/f*: **Sud-Américain, e** South American.

sudation [sydasjɔ̃] *nf* sweating, sudation.

sud-coréen, ne [sydkɔʀeɛ̃, -ɛn] *a* South Korean ♦ *nm/f*: **Sud-Coréen, ne** South Korean.

sud-est [sydɛst] *nm, a inv* south-east.

sud-ouest [sydwɛst] *nm, a inv* south-west.

sud-vietnamien, ne [sydvjɛtnamjɛ̃, -ɛn] *a* South Vietnamese ♦ *nm/f*: **Sud-Vietnamien, ne** South Vietnamese.

Suède [sɥɛd] *nf*: **la ~** Sweden.

suédois, e [sɥedwa, -waz] *a* Swedish ♦ *nm* (*LING*) Swedish ♦ *nm/f*: **S~, e** Swede.

suer [sɥe] *vi* to sweat; (*suinter*) to ooze ♦ *vt* (*fig*) to exude; ~ **à grosses gouttes** to sweat profusely.

sueur [sɥœʀ] *nf* sweat; **en ~** sweating, in a sweat; **avoir des ~s froides** to be in a cold sweat.

suffire [syfiʀ] *vi* (*être assez*): ~ (**à qn/pour qch/pour faire**) to be enough *ou* sufficient

(for sb/for sth/to do); (*satisfaire*): **cela lui suffit** he's content with this, this is enough for him; **se ~** *vi* to be self-sufficient; **cela suffit pour les irriter/qu'ils se fâchent** it's enough to annoy them/for them to get angry; **il suffit d'une négligence/qu'on oublie pour que ...** it only takes one act of carelessness/one only needs to forget for ...; **ça suffit!** that's enough!, that'll do!

suffisamment [syfizamɑ̃] *ad* sufficiently, enough; ~ **de** sufficient, enough.

suffisance [syfizɑ̃s] *nf* (*vanité*) self-importance, bumptiousness; (*quantité*): **en ~** in plenty.

suffisant, e [syfizɑ̃, -ɑ̃t] *a* (*temps, ressources*) sufficient; (*résultats*) satisfactory; (*vaniteux*) self-important, bumptious.

suffisons [syfizɔ̃] *etc vb voir* **suffire**.

suffixe [syfiks(ə)] *nm* suffix.

suffocant, e [syfɔkɑ̃, -ɑ̃t] *a* (*étouffant*) suffocating; (*stupéfiant*) staggering.

suffocation [syfɔkasjɔ̃] *nf* suffocation.

suffoquer [syfɔke] *vt* to choke, suffocate; (*stupéfier*) to stagger, astound ♦ *vi* to choke, suffocate; ~ **de colère/d'indignation** to choke with anger/indignation.

suffrage [syfʀaʒ] *nm* (POL: *voix*) vote; (: *méthode*): ~ **universel/direct/indirect** universal/direct/indirect suffrage; (*du public etc*) approval *q*; **~s exprimés** valid votes.

suggérer [sygʒeʀe] *vt* to suggest; ~ **que/de faire** to suggest that/doing.

suggestif, ive [sygʒɛstif, -iv] *a* suggestive.

suggestion [sygʒɛstjɔ̃] *nf* suggestion.

suicidaire [sɥisidɛʀ] *a* suicidal.

suicide [sɥisid] *nm* suicide ♦ *a*: **opération ~** suicide mission.

suicidé, e [sɥiside] *nm/f* suicide.

suicider [sɥiside]: **se ~** *vi* to commit suicide.

suie [sɥi] *nf* soot.

suif [sɥif] *nm* tallow.

suinter [sɥɛ̃te] *vi* to ooze.

suis [sɥi] *vb voir* **être, suivre**.

suisse [sɥis] *a* Swiss ♦ *nm* (*bedeau*) ≈ verger ♦ *nm/f*: **S~** Swiss *pl inv* ♦ *nf*: **la S~** Switzerland; **la S~ romande/allemande** French-speaking/German-speaking Switzerland; ~ **romand** Swiss French.

suisse-allemand, e [sɥisalmɑ̃, -ɑ̃d] *a, nm/f* Swiss German.

Suissesse [sɥisɛs] *nf* Swiss (woman *ou* girl).

suit [sɥi] *vb voir* **suivre**.

suite [sɥit] *nf* (*continuation: d'énumération etc*) rest, remainder; (: *de feuilleton*) continuation; (: *second film etc sur le même thème*) sequel; (*série: de maisons, succès*): **une ~ de** a series *ou* succession of; (*MATH*) series *sg*; (*conséquence*) result; (*ordre, liaison logique*) coherence; (*appartement, MUS*) suite; (*escorte*) retinue, suite; **~s** *nfpl* (*d'une maladie etc*) effects; **prendre la ~ de** (*directeur etc*) to succeed, take over from; **donner ~ à** (*requête, projet*) to follow up; **faire ~ à** to follow; (**faisant**) ~ **à votre lettre du** further to your letter of the; **sans ~** *a* incoherent, disjointed ♦ *ad* incoherently, disjointedly; **de ~** *ad* (*d'affilée*) in succession; (*immédiatement*) at once; **par la ~** afterwards, subsequently; **à la ~** *ad* one after the other; **à la ~ de** (*derrière*) behind; (*en conséquence de*) following; **par ~ de** owing to, as a result of; **avoir de la ~ dans les idées** to show great singleness of purpose; **attendre la ~ des événements** to (wait and see) what happens.

suivant, e [sɥivã, -ãt] *vb voir* **suivre ♦** *a* next, following; (*ci-après*): **l'exercice ~** the following exercise **♦** *prép* (*selon*) according to; **~ que** according to whether; **au ~!** next!

suive [sɥiv] *etc vb voir* **suivre**.

suiveur [sɥivœʀ] *nm* (*CYCLISME*) (official) follower; (*péj*) (camp) follower.

suivi, e [sɥivi] *pp de* **suivre ♦** *a* (*régulier*) regular; (*COMM: article*) in general production; (*cohérent*) consistent; coherent **♦** *nm* follow-up; **très/peu ~** (*cours*) well-/poorly-attended; (*mode*) widely/not widely adopted; (*feuilleton etc*) widely/not widely followed.

suivre [sɥivʀ(ə)] *vt* (*gén*) to follow; (*SCOL: cours*) to attend; (: *leçon*) to follow, attend to; (: *programme*) to keep up with; (*COMM: article*) to continue to stock **♦** *vi* to follow; (*élève: écouter*) to attend, pay attention; (: *assimiler le programme*) to keep up, follow; **se ~** (*accidents, personnes, voitures etc*) to follow one after the other; (*raisonnement*) to be coherent; **des yeux** to follow with one's eyes; **faire ~** (*lettre*) to forward; **~ son cours** (*suj: enquête etc*) to run *ou* take its course; **"à ~"** "to be continued".

sujet, te [syʒɛ, -ɛt] *a*: **être ~ à** (*accidents*) to be prone to; (*vertige etc*) to be liable *ou* subject to **♦** *nm/f* (*d'un souverain*) subject **♦** *nm* subject; **un ~ de dispute/discorde/mécontentement** a cause for argument/dissension/dissatisfaction; **c'est à quel ~?** what is it about?; **avoir ~ de se plaindre** to have cause for complaint; **au ~ de** *prép* about; **~ à caution** *a* questionable; **~ de conversation** topic *ou* subject of conversation; **~ d'examen** (*SCOL*) examination question; examination paper; **~ d'expérience** (*BIO etc*) experimental subject.

sujétion [syʒesjɔ̃] *nf* subjection; (*fig*) constraint.

sulfater [sylfate] *vt* to spray with copper sulphate.

sulfureux, euse [sylfyʀø, -øz] *a* sulphurous (*Brit*), sulfurous (*US*).

sulfurique [sylfyʀik] *a*: **acide ~** sulphuric (*Brit*) *ou* sulfuric (*US*) acid.

sulfurisé, e [sylfyʀize] *a*: **papier ~** greaseproof (*Brit*) *ou* wax (*US*) paper.

Sumatra [symatʀa] *nf* Sumatra.

summum [sɔmɔm] *nm*: **le ~ de** the height of.

super [sypɛʀ] *a inv* great, fantastic **♦** *nm* (= *supercarburant*) ≈ 4-star (*Brit*), ≈ premium (*US*).

superbe [sypɛʀb(ə)] *a* magnificent, superb **♦** *nf* arrogance.

superbement [sypɛʀbəmã] *ad* superbly.

supercarburant [sypɛʀkaʀbyʀã] *nm* ≈ 4-star petrol (*Brit*), ≈ premium gas (*US*).

supercherie [sypɛʀʃəʀi] *nf* trick, trickery *q*; (*fraude*) fraud.

supérette [sypeʀɛt] *nf* minimarket.

superfétatoire [sypɛʀfetatwaʀ] *a* superfluous.

superficie [sypɛʀfisi] *nf* (surface) area; (*fig*)

surface.

superficiel, le [sypɛʀfisjɛl] *a* superficial.

superficiellement [sypɛʀfisjɛlmã] *ad* superficially.

superflu, e [sypɛʀfly] *a* superfluous **♦** *nm*: **le ~** the superfluous.

superforme [sypɛʀfɔʀm(ə)] *nf* (*fam*) top form, excellent shape.

super-grand [sypɛʀgʀã] *nm* superpower.

super-huit [sypɛʀɥit] *a*: **camera/film ~** super-eight camera/film.

supérieur, e [sypeʀjœʀ] *a* (*lèvre, étages, classes*) upper; (*plus élevé: température, niveau*): **~ (à)** higher (than); (*meilleur: qualité, produit*): **~ (à)** superior (to); (*excellent, hautain*) superior **♦** *nm, nf* superior; **Mère ~e** Mother Superior; **à l'étage ~** on the next floor up; **~ en nombre** superior in number.

supérieurement [sypeʀjœʀmã] *ad* exceptionally well, exceptionally + *adj*.

supériorité [sypeʀjɔʀite] *nf* superiority.

superlatif [sypɛʀlatif] *nm* superlative.

supermarché [sypɛʀmaʀʃe] *nm* supermarket.

superposable [sypɛʀpozabl(ə)] *a* (*figures*) that may be superimposed; (*lits*) stackable.

superposer [sypɛʀpoze] *vt* to superpose; (*meubles, caisses*) to stack; (*faire chevaucher*) to superimpose; **se ~** (*images, souvenirs*) to be superimposed; **lits superposés** bunk beds.

superposition [sypɛʀpozisjɔ̃] *nf* superposition; superimposition.

superpréfet [sypɛʀpʀefɛ] *nm* prefect in charge of a region.

superproduction [sypɛʀpʀɔdyksjɔ̃] *nf* (*film*) spectacular.

superpuissance [sypɛʀpɥisãs] *nf* super-power.

supersonique [sypɛʀsɔnik] *a* supersonic.

superstitieux, euse [sypɛʀstisjø, -øz] *a* superstitious.

superstition [sypɛʀstisjɔ̃] *nf* superstition.

superstructure [sypɛʀstʀyktyʀ] *nf* superstructure.

supertanker [sypɛʀtãkœʀ] *nm* supertanker.

superviser [sypɛʀvize] *vt* to supervise.

supervision [sypɛʀvizjɔ̃] *nf* supervision.

supplanter [syplãte] *vt* to supplant.

suppléance [sypleãs] *nf* (*poste*) supply post (*Brit*), substitute teacher's post (*US*).

suppléant, e [sypleã, -ãt] *a* (*juge, fonctionnaire*) deputy *cpd*; (*professeur*) supply *cpd* (*Brit*), substitute *cpd* (*US*) **♦** *nm/f* deputy; supply *ou* substitute teacher; **médecin ~** locum.

suppléer [syplee] *vt* (*ajouter: mot manquant etc*) to supply, provide; (*compenser: lacune*) to fill in; (: *défaut*) to make up for; (*remplacer: professeur*) to stand in for; (: *juge*) to deputize for; **~ à** *vt* to make up for; to substitute for.

supplément [syplemã] *nm* supplement; **un ~ de travail** extra *ou* additional work; **un ~ de frites** *cpd* an extra portion of chips *etc*; **un ~ de 100 F** a supplement of 100 F, an extra *ou* additional 100 F; **ceci est en ~** (*au menu etc*) this is extra, there is an extra charge for this; **~ d'information** additional information.

supplémentaire [syplemãtɛʀ] *a* additional,

further; (*train, bus*) relief *cpd*, extra.

supplétif, ive [sypletif, -iv] *a* (*MIL*) auxiliary.

suppliant, e [syplijɑ̃, -ɑ̃t] *a* imploring.

supplication [syplikasjɔ̃] *nf* (*REL*) supplication; **~s** *nfpl* (*adjurations*) pleas, entreaties.

supplice [syplis] *nm* (*peine corporelle*) torture *q*; form of torture; (*douleur physique, morale*) torture, agony; **être au ~** to be in agony.

supplier [syplije] *vt* to implore, beseech.

supplique [syplik] *nf* petition.

support [sypɔʀ] *nm* support; (*pour livre, outils*) stand; **~ audio-visuel** audio-visual aid; **~ publicitaire** advertising medium.

supportable [sypɔʀtabl(ə)] *a* (*douleur, température*) bearable; (*procédé, conduite*) tolerable.

supporter *nm* [sypɔʀtɛʀ] supporter, fan ♦ *vt* [sypɔʀte] (*poids, poussée, SPORT*: concurrent, *équipe*) to support; (*conséquences, épreuve*) to bear, endure; (*défauts, personne*) to tolerate, put up with; (*suj: chose: chaleur etc*) to withstand; (*suj: personne: chaleur, vin*) to take.

supposé, e [sypoze] *a* (*nombre*) estimated; (*auteur*) supposed.

supposer [sypoze] *vt* to suppose; (*impliquer*) to presuppose; **en supposant** *ou* **à ~ que** supposing (that).

supposition [sypozisjɔ̃] *nf* supposition.

suppositoire [sypozitwaʀ] *nm* suppository.

suppôt [sypo] *nm* (*péj*) henchman.

suppression [sypʀesjɔ̃] *nf* (*voir supprimer*) removal; deletion; cancellation; suppression.

supprimer [sypʀime] *vt* (*cloison, cause, anxiété*) to remove; (*clause, mot*) to delete; (*congés, service d'autobus etc*) to cancel; (*publication, article*) to suppress; (*emplois, privilèges, témoin gênant*) to do away with; **~ qch à qn** to deprive sb of sth.

suppurer [sypyʀe] *vi* to suppurate.

supputations [sypytasjɔ̃] *nfpl* calculations, reckonings.

supputer [sypyte] *vt* to calculate, reckon.

supranational, e, aux [sypʀanasjɔnal, -o] *a* supranational.

suprématie [sypʀemasi] *nf* supremacy.

suprême [sypʀɛm] *a* supreme.

suprêmement [sypʀɛmmɑ̃] *ad* supremely.

sur [syʀ] *prép* (*gén*) on; (*par-dessus*) over; (*au-dessus*) above; (*direction*) towards; (*à propos de*) about, on; **un ~ 10** one out of 10, one in 10; (*SCOL*) one out of 10; **4m ~ 2** 4m by 2; **~ sa recommandation/leur invitation** on his (*ou* her) recommendation/their invitation; **avoir accident ~ accident** to have accident after accident; **je n'ai pas d'argent ~ moi** I haven't got any money with *ou* on me; **~ ce** *ad* hereupon.

sur, e [syʀ] *a* sour.

sûr, e [syʀ] *a* sure, certain; (*digne de confiance*) reliable; (*sans danger*) safe; **peu ~** unreliable; **~ de qch** sure *ou* certain of sth; **être ~ de qn** to be sure of sb; **~ et certain** absolutely certain; **~ de soi** self-assured, self-confident; **le plus ~ est de** the safest thing is to.

surabondant, e [syʀabɔ̃dɑ̃, -ɑ̃t] *a* overabundant.

surabonder [syʀabɔ̃de] *vi* to be overabundant; **~ de** to abound with, have an overabundance of.

suractivité [syʀaktivite] *nf* hyperactivity.

suraigu, ë [syʀegy] *a* very shrill.

surajouter [syʀaʒute] *vt*: **~ qch à** to add sth to.

suralimenté, e [syʀalimɑ̃te] *a* (*personne*) overfed; (*moteur*) turbocharged.

suranné, e [syʀane] *a* outdated, outmoded.

surarmement [syʀaʀməmɑ̃] *nm* (excess) stockpiling of arms (*ou* weapons).

surbaissé, e [syʀbese] *a* lowered, low.

surcharge [syʀʃaʀʒ(ə)] *nf* (*de passagers, marchandises*) excess load; (*de détails, d'ornements*) overabundance, excess; (*correction*) alteration; (*POSTES*) surcharge; **prendre des passagers en ~** to take on excess *ou* extra passengers; **~ de bagages** excess luggage; **~ de travail** extra work.

surchargé, e [syʀʃaʀʒe] *a* (*décoration, style*) over-elaborate, overfussy; (*voiture, emploi du temps*) overloaded.

surcharger [syʀʃaʀʒe] *vt* to overload; (*timbre-poste*) to surcharge; (*décoration*) to overdo.

surchauffe [syʀʃof] *nf* overheating.

surchauffé, e [syʀʃofe] *a* overheated; (*fig: imagination*) overactive.

surchoix [syʀʃwa] *a inv* top-quality.

surclasser [syʀklase] *vt* to outclass.

surconsommation [syʀkɔ̃sɔmasjɔ̃] *nf* (*ÉCON*) overconsumption.

surcoté, e [syʀkote] *a* overpriced.

surcouper [syʀkupe] *vt* to overtrump.

surcroît [syʀkʀwa] *nm*: **un ~ de** additional + *nom*; **par** *ou* **de ~** moreover; **en ~** in addition.

surdi-mutité [syʀdimytite] *nf*: **atteint de ~** deaf and dumb.

surdité [syʀdite] *nf* deafness; **atteint de ~ totale** profoundly deaf.

surdoué, e [syʀdwe] *a* gifted.

sureau, x [syʀo] *nm* elder (tree).

sureffectif [syʀefektif] *nm* overmanning.

surélever [syʀelve] *vt* to raise, heighten.

sûrement [syʀmɑ̃] *ad* reliably; safely, securely; (*certainement*) certainly; **~ pas** certainly not.

suremploi [syʀɑ̃plwa] *nm* (*ÉCON*) overemployment.

surenchère [syʀɑ̃ʃɛʀ] *nf* (*aux enchères*) higher bid; (*sur prix fixe*) overbid; (*fig*) overstatement; outbidding tactics *pl*; **~ de violence** build-up of violence; **~ électorale** political (*ou* electoral) one-upmanship.

surenchérir [syʀɑ̃ʃeʀiʀ] *vi* to bid higher; to raise one's bid; (*fig*) to try and outbid each other.

surent [syʀ] *vb voir* **savoir**.

suréquipé, e [syʀekipe] *a* overequipped.

surestimer [syʀestime] *vt* (*tableau*) to overvalue; (*possibilité, personne*) to overestimate.

sûreté [syʀte] *nf* (*voir sûr*) reliability; safety; (*JUR*) guaranty; surety; **mettre en ~** to put in a safe place; **pour plus de ~** as an extra precaution; **to be on the safe side; la ~** de l'État State security; **la S~ (nationale)** division of the Ministère de l'Intérieur *heading all police forces except the gendarmerie and the Paris préfecture de police.*

surexcité, e [syʀɛksite] *a* overexcited.

surexploiter [syʀɛksplwate] *vt* to overexploit.

surexposer [syʀɛkspoze] *vt* to overexpose.

surf [sœʀf] *nm* surfing; **faire du ~** to go surfing.

surface [syʀfas] *nf* surface; (*superficie*) surface area; **faire ~** to surface; **en ~** *ad* near the surface; (*fig*) superficially; **la pièce fait 100m² de ~** the room has a surface area of 100m²; **~ de réparation** (*SPORT*) penalty area; **~ porteuse** *ou* **de sustentation** (*AVIAT*) aerofoil.

surfait, e [syʀfɛ, -ɛt] *a* overrated.

surfiler [syʀfile] *vt* (*COUTURE*) to oversew.

surfin, e [syʀfɛ̃, -in] *a* superfine.

surgélateur [syʀʒelatœʀ] *nm* deep freeze.

surgelé, e [syʀʒəle] *a* (deep-)frozen.

surgeler [syʀʒəle] *vt* to (deep-)freeze.

surgir [syʀʒiʀ] *vi* (*personne, véhicule*) to appear suddenly; (*jaillir*) to shoot up; (*montagne etc*) to rise up, loom up; (*fig: problème, conflit*) to arise.

surhomme [syʀɔm] *nm* superman.

surhumain, e [syʀymɛ̃, -ɛn] *a* superhuman.

surimposer [syʀɛ̃poze] *vt* to overtax.

surimpression [syʀɛ̃pʀesjɔ̃] *nf* (*PHOTO*) double exposure; **en ~** superimposed.

surimprimer [syʀɛ̃pʀime] *vt* to overstrike, overprint.

Surinam [syʀinam] *nm*: **le ~** Surinam.

surinfection [syʀɛ̃fɛksjɔ̃] *nf* (*MÉD*) secondary infection.

surjet [syʀʒɛ] *nm* (*COUTURE*) overcast seam.

sur-le-champ [syʀləʃɑ̃] *ad* immediately.

surlendemain [syʀlɑ̃dmɛ̃] *nm*: **le ~ (soir)** two days later (in the evening); **le ~ de** two days after.

surligneur [syʀliɲœʀ] *nm* (*feutre*) highlighter (pen).

surmenage [syʀmənaʒ] *nm* overwork; **le ~ intellectuel** mental fatigue.

surmené, e [syʀməne] *a* overworked.

surmener [syʀməne] *vt*, **se ~** *vi* to overwork.

surmonter [syʀmɔ̃te] *vt* (*suj: coupole etc*) to surmount, top; (*vaincre*) to overcome, surmount.

surmultiplié, e [syʀmyltiplije] *a, nf*: **(vitesse) ~e** overdrive.

surnager [syʀnaʒe] *vi* to float.

surnaturel, le [syʀnatyʀɛl] *a, nm* supernatural.

surnom [syʀnɔ̃] *nm* nickname.

surnombre [syʀnɔ̃bʀ(ə)] *nm*: **être en ~** to be too many (*ou* one too many).

surnommer [syʀnɔme] *vt* to nickname.

surnuméraire [syʀnymeʀɛʀ] *nm/f* supernumerary.

suroît [syʀwa] *nm* sou'wester.

surpasser [syʀpase] *vt* to surpass; **se ~** to surpass o.s., excel o.s.

surpayer [syʀpeje] *vt* (*personne*) to overpay; (*article etc*) to pay too much for.

surpeuplé, e [syʀpœple] *a* overpopulated.

surpeuplement [syʀpœpləmɑ̃] *nm* overpopulation.

surpiquer [syʀpike] *vt* (*COUTURE*) to over-

stitch.

surpiqûre [syʀpikyʀ] *nf* (*COUTURE*) overstitching.

surplace [syʀplas] *nm*: **faire du ~** to mark time.

surplis [syʀpli] *nm* surplice.

surplomb [syʀplɔ̃] *nm* overhang; **en ~** overhanging.

surplomber [syʀplɔ̃be] *vi* to be overhanging ♦ *vt* to overhang; (*dominer*) to tower above.

surplus [syʀply] *nm* (*COMM*) surplus; (*reste*): **~ de bois** wood left over; **au ~** moreover; **~ américains** American army surplus *sg*.

surpopulation [syʀpɔpylasjɔ̃] *nf* overpopulation.

surprenant, e [syʀpʀənɑ̃, -ɑ̃t] *vb voir* **surprendre** ♦ *a* amazing.

surprendre [syʀpʀɑ̃dʀ(ə)] *vt* (*étonner, prendre à l'improviste*) to amaze, surprise; (*secret*) to discover; (*tomber sur: intrus etc*) to catch; (*fig*) to detect; to chance *ou* happen upon; (*clin d'œil*) to intercept; (*conversation*) to overhear; (*suj: orage, nuit etc*) to catch out, take by surprise; **~ la vigilance/bonne foi de qn** to catch sb out/betray sb's good faith; **se ~ à faire** to catch *ou* find o.s. doing.

surprime [syʀpʀim] *nf* additional premium.

surpris, e [syʀpʀi, -iz] *pp de* **surprendre** ♦ *a*: **~ (de/que)** amazed *ou* surprised (at/that).

surprise [syʀpʀiz] *nf* surprise; **faire une ~ à qn** to give sb a surprise; **voyage sans ~s** uneventful journey; **par ~** *ad* by surprise.

surprise-partie [syʀpʀizpaʀti] *nf* party.

surprit [syʀpʀi] *vb voir* **surprendre**.

surproduction [syʀpʀɔdyksjɔ̃] *nf* overproduction.

surréaliste [syʀʀealist(ə)] *a, nm/f* surrealist.

sursaut [syʀso] *nm* start, jump; **~ de** (*énergie, indignation*) sudden fit *ou* burst of; **en ~** *ad* with a start.

sursauter [syʀsote] *vi* to (give a) start, jump.

surseoir [syʀswaʀ] *vi*: **~ à** *vt* to defer; (*JUR*) to stay.

sursis [syʀsi] *nm* (*JUR: gén*) suspended sentence; (*à l'exécution capitale, aussi fig*) reprieve; (*MIL*): **~ (d'appel** *ou* **d'incorporation)** deferment; **condamné à 5 mois (de prison) avec ~** given a 5-month suspended (prison) sentence.

sursitaire [syʀsitɛʀ] *nm* (*MIL*) deferred conscript.

sursois [syʀswa], **sursoyais** [syʀswaje] *etc vb voir* **surseoir**.

surtaxe [syʀtaks(ə)] *nf* surcharge.

surtout [syʀtu] *ad* (*avant tout, d'abord*) above all; (*spécialement, particulièrement*) especially; **il aime le sport, ~ le football** he likes sport, especially football; **cet été, il a ~ fait de la pêche** this summer he went fishing more than anything (else); **~ pas d'histoires!** no fuss now!; **~, ne dites rien!** whatever you do - don't say anything!; **~ pas!** certainly *ou* definitely not!; **~ que ...** especially as ....

survécu, e [syʀveky] *pp de* **survivre**.

surveillance [syʀvɛjɑ̃s] *nf* watch; (*POLICE, MIL*) surveillance; **sous ~ médicale** under medical supervision; **la ~ du territoire** internal security; *voir aussi* **DST**.

surveillant, e [syʀvɛjã, -ãt] *nm/f (de prison)* warder; *(SCOL)* monitor; *(de travaux)* supervisor, overseer.

surveiller [syʀveje] *vt (enfant, élèves, bagages)* to watch, keep an eye on; *(malade)* to watch over; *(prisonnier, suspect)* to keep (a) watch on; *(territoire, bâtiment)* to (keep) watch over; *(travaux, cuisson)* to supervise; *(SCOL: examen)* to invigilate; **se ~** to keep a check *ou* watch on o.s.; **~ son langage/sa ligne** to watch one's language/figure.

survenir [syʀvəniʀ] *vi (incident, retards)* to occur, arise; *(événement)* to take place; *(personne)* to appear, arrive.

survenu, e [syʀv(ə)ny] *pp de* **survenir**.

survêt(ement) [syʀvɛt(mã)] *nm* tracksuit *(Brit)*, sweat suit *(US)*.

survie [syʀvi] *nf* survival; *(REL)* afterlife; **équipement de ~** survival equipment; **une ~ de quelques mois** a few more months of life.

surviens [syʀvjɛ̃], **survint** [syʀvɛ̃] *etc vb voir* **survenir**.

survit [syʀvi] *etc vb voir* **survivre**.

survitrage [syʀvitʀaʒ] *nm* double-glazing.

survivance [syʀvivãs] *nf* relic.

survivant, e [syʀvivã, -ãt] *vb voir* **survivre ♦** *nm/f* survivor.

survivre [syʀvivʀ(ə)] *vi* to survive; **~ à** *vt (accident etc)* to survive; *(personne)* to outlive; **la victime a peu de chance de ~** the victim has little hope of survival.

survol [syʀvɔl] *nm* flying over.

survoler [syʀvɔle] *vt* to fly over; *(fig: livre)* to skim through; *(: question, problèmes)* to skim over.

survolté, e [syʀvɔlte] *a (ÉLEC)* stepped up, boosted; *(fig)* worked up.

sus [sy(s)]: **en ~ de** *prép* in addition to, over and above; **en ~** *ad* in addition; **~ à** *excl*: **~ au tyran!** at the tyrant! **♦** *vb* [sy] *voir* **savoir**.

susceptibilité [syseptibilite] *nf* sensitivity *q*.

susceptible [syseptibl(ə)] *a* touchy, sensitive; **~ d'amélioration** *ou* **d'être amélioré** that can be improved, open to improvement; **~ de faire** *(capacité)* able to do; *(probabilité)* liable to do.

susciter [sysite] *vt (admiration)* to arouse; *(obstacles, ennuis)*: **~ (à qn)** to create (for sb).

susdit, e [sysdi, -dit] *a* foresaid.

susmentionné, e [sysmãsjɔne] *a* abovementioned.

susnommé, e [sysnɔme] *a* above-named.

suspect, e [syspɛ(kt), -ɛkt(ə)] *a* suspicious; *(témoignage, opinions, vin etc)* suspect **♦** *nm/f* suspect; **peu ~ de** most unlikely to be suspected of.

suspecter [syspɛkte] *vt* to suspect; *(honnêteté de qn)* to question, have one's suspicions about; **~ qn d'être/d'avoir fait qch** to suspect sb of being/having done sth.

suspendre [syspãdʀ(ə)] *vt (accrocher: vêtement)*: **~ qch (à)** to hang sth up (on); *(fixer: lustre etc)*: **~ qch à** to hang sth from; *(interrompre, démettre)* to suspend; *(remettre)* to defer; **se ~ à** to hang from.

suspendu, e [syspãdy] *pp de* **suspendre ♦** *a (accroché)*: **~ à** hanging on *(ou* from);

(perché): **~ au-dessus de** suspended over; *(AUTO)*: **bien/mal ~** with good/poor suspension; **être ~ aux lèvres de qn** to hang upon sb's every word.

suspens [syspã]: **en ~** *ad (affaire)* in abeyance; **tenir en ~** to keep in suspense.

suspense [syspãs] *nm* suspense.

suspension [syspãsjɔ̃] *nf* suspension; deferment; *(AUTO)* suspension; *(lustre)* pendant light fitting; **en ~** in suspension, suspended; **~ d'audience** adjournment.

suspicieux, euse [syspisjø, -øz] *a* suspicious.

suspicion [syspisjɔ̃] *nf* suspicion.

sustenter [systãte]: **se ~** *vi* to take sustenance.

susurrer [sysyʀe] *vt* to whisper.

sut [sy] *vb voir* **savoir**.

suture [sytyʀ] *nf*: **point de ~** stitch.

suturer [sytyʀe] *vt* to stitch up, suture.

suzeraineté [syzʀɛnte] *nf* suzerainty.

svelte [svɛlt(ə)] *a* slender, svelte.

SVP *sigle (= s'il vous plaît)* please.

Swaziland [swazilãd] *nm*: **le ~** Swaziland.

syllabe [silab] *nf* syllable.

syllaber [silabe] *vi* to pronounce syllable by syllable.

sylvestre [silvɛstʀ(ə)] *a*: **pin ~** Scots pine, Scotch fir.

sylvicole [silvikɔl] *a* forestry *cpd*.

sylviculteur [silvikyltœʀ] *nm* forester.

sylviculture [silvikyltyʀ] *nf* forestry, sylviculture.

symbole [sɛ̃bɔl] *nm* symbol; **~ graphique** *(INFORM)* icon.

symbolique [sɛ̃bɔlik] *a* symbolic; *(geste, offrande)* token *cpd*; *(salaire, dommages-intérêts)* nominal.

symboliquement [sɛ̃bɔlikmã] *ad* symbolically.

symboliser [sɛ̃bɔlize] *vt* to symbolize.

symétrie [simetʀi] *nf* symmetry.

symétrique [simetʀik] *a* symmetrical.

symétriquement [simetʀikmã] *ad* symmetrically.

sympa [sɛ̃pa] *a inv (= sympathique)* nice; friendly; good.

sympathie [sɛ̃pati] *nf (inclination)* liking; *(affinité)* fellow feeling; *(condoléances)* sympathy; **accueillir avec ~** *(projet)* to receive favourably; **avoir de la ~ pour qn** to like sb, have a liking for sb; **témoignages de ~** expressions of sympathy; **croyez à toute ma ~** you have my deepest sympathy.

sympathique [sɛ̃patik] *a (personne, figure)* nice, friendly, likeable; *(geste)* friendly; *(livre)* good; *(déjeuner)* nice; *(réunion, endroit)* pleasant, nice.

sympathisant, e [sɛ̃patizã, -ãt] *nm/f* sympathizer.

sympathiser [sɛ̃patize] *vi (voisins etc: s'entendre)* to get on *(Brit) ou* along *(US)* (well); *(: se fréquenter)* to socialize, see each other; **~ avec** to get on *ou* along (well) with; to see, socialize with.

symphonie [sɛ̃fɔni] *nf* symphony.

symphonique [sɛ̃fɔnik] *a (orchestre, concert)* symphony *cpd*; *(musique)* symphonic.

symposium [sɛ̃pozjɔm] *nm* symposium.

symptomatique [sɛ̃ptɔmatik] *a* symptomatic.

symptôme [sɛ̃ptom] *nm* symptom.
synagogue [sinagɔg] *nf* synagogue.
synchrone [sɛ̃kʀɔn] *a* synchronous.
synchronique [sɛ̃kʀɔnik] *a:* **tableau** ~ synchronic table of events.
synchronisation [sɛ̃kʀɔnizasjɔ̃] *nf* synchronization.
synchronisé, e [sɛ̃kʀɔnize] *a* synchronized.
synchroniser [sɛ̃kʀɔnize] *vt* to synchronize.
syncope [sɛ̃kɔp] *nf* (*MÉD*) blackout; (*MUS*) syncopation; **tomber en** ~ to faint, pass out.
syncopé, e [sɛ̃kɔpe] *a* syncopated.
syndic [sɛ̃dik] *nm* managing agent.
syndical, e, aux [sɛ̃dikal, -o] *a* (trade-)union *cpd*; **centrale** ~**e** group of affiliated trade unions.
syndicalisme [sɛ̃dikalism(ə)] *nm* (*mouvement*) trade unionism; (*activités*) union(ist) activities *pl*.
syndicaliste [sɛ̃dikalist(ə)] *nm/f* trade unionist.
syndicat [sɛ̃dika] *nm* (*d'ouvriers, employés*) (trade(s)) union; (*autre association d'intérêts*) union, association; ~ **d'initiative** (SI) tourist office *ou* bureau; ~ **patronal** employers' syndicate, federation of employers; ~ **de propriétaires** association of property owners.
syndiqué, e [sɛ̃dike] *a* belonging to a (trade) union; **non** ~ non-union.
syndiquer [sɛ̃dike]: **se** ~ *vi* to form a trade union; (*adhérer*) to join a trade union.
syndrome [sɛ̃dʀom] *nm* syndrome; ~ **prémenstruel** premenstrual syndrome (PMS).
synergie [sinɛʀʒi] *nf* synergy.
synode [sinɔd] *nm* synod.
synonyme [sinɔnim] *a* synonymous ♦ *nm* synonym; ~ **de** synonymous with.
synopsis [sinɔpsis] *nm ou nf* synopsis.
synoptique [sinɔptik] *a:* **tableau** ~ synoptic table.
synovie [sinɔvi] *nf* synovia; **épanchement de** ~ water on the knee.
syntaxe [sɛ̃taks(ə)] *nf* syntax.
synthèse [sɛ̃tɛz] *nf* synthesis (*pl* -es); **faire la** ~ **de** to synthesize.
synthétique [sɛ̃tetik] *a* synthetic.
synthétiser [sɛ̃tetize] *vt* to synthesize.
synthétiseur [sɛ̃tetizœʀ] *nm* (*MUS*) synthesizer.
syphilis [sifilis] *nf* syphilis.
Syrie [siʀi] *nf:* **la** ~ Syria.
syrien, ne [siʀjɛ̃, -ɛn] *a* Syrian ♦ *nm/f:* **S**~, **ne** Syrian.
systématique [sistematik] *a* systematic.
systématiquement [sistematikmɑ̃] *ad* systematically.
systématiser [sistematize] *vt* to systematize.
système [sistɛm] *nm* system; **le** ~ **D** resourcefulness; ~ **décimal** decimal system; ~ **expert** expert system; ~ **d'exploitation à disques** (*INFORM*) disk operating system; ~ **métrique** metric system; ~ **solaire** solar system.

T

T, t [te] *nm inv* T, t ♦ *abr* (= *tonne*) t; **T comme Thérèse** T for Tommy.
t' [t(ə)] *pronom voir* **te**.
ta [ta] *dét voir* **ton**.
tabac [taba] *nm* tobacco; (*aussi:* **débit** *ou* **bureau de** ~) tobacconist's (shop) ♦ *a inv:* (**couleur**) ~ buff, tobacco *cpd*; **passer qn à** ~ to beat sb up; **faire un** ~ (*fam*) to be a big hit; ~ **blond/brun** light/dark tobacco; ~ **gris** shag; ~ **à priser** snuff.
tabagie [tabaʒi] *nf* smoke den.
tabagisme [tabaʒism(ə)] *nm* nicotine addiction.
tabasser [tabase] *vt* to beat up.
tabatière [tabatjɛʀ] *nf* snuffbox.
tabernacle [tabɛʀnakl(ə)] *nm* tabernacle.
table [tabl(ə)] *nf* table; **avoir une bonne** ~ to keep a good table; **à** ~! dinner *etc* is ready!; **se mettre à** ~ to sit down to eat; (*fig: fam*) to come clean; **mettre** *ou* **dresser/desservir la** ~ to lay *ou* set/clear the table; **faire** ~ **rase de** to make a clean sweep of; ~ **basse** coffee table; ~ **de cuisson** (*à l'électricité*) hotplate; (*au gas*) gas ring; ~ **d'écoute** wire-tapping set; ~ **d'harmonie** sounding board; ~ **d'hôte** set menu; ~ **de lecture** turntable; ~ **des matières** (table of) contents *pl*; ~ **de multiplication** multiplication table; ~ **de nuit** *ou* **de chevet** bedside table; ~ **ronde** (*débat*) round table; ~ **roulante** (tea) trolley; ~ **de toilette** washstand; ~ **traçante** (*INFORM*) plotter.
tableau, x [tablo] *nm* (*ART*) painting; (*reproduction, fig*) picture; (*panneau*) board; (*schéma*) table, chart; ~ **d'affichage** notice board; ~ **de bord** dashboard; (*AVIAT*) instrument panel; ~ **de chasse** tally; ~ **de contrôle** console, control panel; ~ **de maître** masterpiece; ~ **noir** blackboard.
tablée [table] *nf* (*personnes*) table.
tabler [table] *vi:* ~ **sur** to count *ou* bank on.
tablette [tablɛt] *nf* (*planche*) shelf (*pl* shelves); ~ **de chocolat** bar of chocolate.
tableur [tablœʀ] *nm* (*INFORM*) spreadsheet.
tablier [tablije] *nm* apron; (*de pont*) roadway; (*de cheminée*) (flue-)shutter.
tabou, e [tabu] *a, nm* taboo.
tabouret [tabuʀɛ] *nm* stool.
tabulateur [tabylatœʀ] *nm* (*TECH*) tabulator.
TAC *sigle m* (= *train-auto-couchettes*) carsleeper train, ≈ Motorail ® (*Brit*).
tac [tak] *nm:* **du** ~ **au** ~ tit for tat.
tache [taʃ] *nf* (*saleté*) stain, mark; (*ART, de couleur, lumière*) spot; splash, patch; **faire** ~ **d'huile** to spread, gain ground; ~ **de rousseur** *ou* **de son** freckle; ~ **de vin** (*sur la peau*) strawberry mark.
tâche [taʃ] *nf* task; **travailler à la** ~ to do piecework.

tacher [taʃe] *vt* to stain, mark; (*fig*) to sully, stain; **se ~** *vi* (*fruits*) to become marked.

tâcher [taʃe] *vi*: **~ de faire** to try to do, endeavour (*Brit*) *ou* endeavor (*US*) to do.

tâcheron [taʃʀɔ̃] *nm* (*fig*) drudge.

tacheté, e [taʃte] *a*: **~ de** speckled *ou* spotted with.

tachisme [taʃism(ə)] *nm* (*PEINTURE*) tachisme.

tachygraphe [takigʀaf] *nm* tachograph.

tachymètre [takimɛtʀ(ə)] *nm* tachometer.

tacite [tasit] *a* tacit.

tacitement [tasitmɑ̃] *ad* tacitly.

taciturne [tasityʀn(ə)] *a* taciturn.

tacot [tako] *nm* (*péj: voiture*) banger (*Brit*), clunker (*US*).

tact [takt] *nm* tact; **avoir du ~** to be tactful, have tact.

tacticien, ne [taktisjɛ̃, -ɛn] *nm/f* tactician.

tactile [taktil] *a* tactile.

tactique [taktik] *a* tactical ♦ *nf* (*technique*) tactics *sg*; (*plan*) tactic.

taffetas [tafta] *nm* taffeta.

Tage [taʒ] *nm*: **le ~** the (river) Tagus.

Tahiti [taiti] *nf* Tahiti.

tahitien, ne [taisjɛ̃, -ɛn] *a* Tahitian.

taie [tɛ] *nf*: **~ (d'oreiller)** pillowslip, pillowcase.

taillader [tajade] *vt* to gash.

taille [taj] *nf* cutting; pruning; (*milieu du corps*) waist; (*hauteur*) height; (*grandeur*) size; **de ~ à faire** capable of doing; **de ~ a** sizeable; **quelle ~ faites- vous?** what size are you?

taillé, e [taje] *a* (*moustache, ongles, arbre*) trimmed; **~ pour** (*fait pour, apte à*) cut out for; tailor-made for; **~ en pointe** sharpened to a point.

taille-crayon(s) [tajkʀɛjɔ̃] *nm inv* pencil sharpener.

tailler [taje] *vt* (*pierre, diamant*) to cut; (*arbre, plante*) to prune; (*vêtement*) to cut out; (*crayon*) to sharpen; **se ~** *vt* (*ongles, barbe*) to trim, cut; (*fig: réputation*) to gain, win ♦ *vi* (*fam: s'enfuir*) to beat it; **~ dans** (*chair, bois*) to cut into; **~ grand/petit** to be on the large/small side.

tailleur [tajœʀ] *nm* (*couturier*) tailor; (*vêtement*) suit, costume; **en ~** (*assis*) cross-legged; **~ de diamants** diamond-cutter.

tailleur-pantalon [tajœʀpɑ̃talɔ̃] *nm* trouser (*Brit*) *ou* pant(s) suit.

taillis [taji] *nm* copse.

tain [tɛ̃] *nm* silvering; **glace sans ~** two-way mirror.

taire [tɛʀ] *vt* to keep to o.s., conceal ♦ *vi*: **faire ~ qn** to make sb be quiet; (*fig*) to silence sb; **se ~** *vi* (*s'arrêter de parler*) to fall silent, stop talking; (*ne pas parler*) to be silent *ou* quiet; (*s'abstenir de s'exprimer*) to keep quiet; (*bruit, voix*) to disappear; **tais-toi!**, **taisez-vous!** be quiet!

Taiwan [tajwan] *nf* Taiwan.

talc [talk] *nm* talc, talcum powder.

talé, e [tale] *a* (*fruit*) bruised.

talent [talɑ̃] *nm* talent; **avoir du ~** to be talented, have talent.

talentueux, euse [talɑ̃tɥø, -øz] *a* talented.

talion [taljɔ̃] *nm*: **la loi du ~** an eye for an eye.

talisman [talismɑ̃] *nm* talisman.

talkie-walkie [tɔkiwɔki] *nm* walkie-talkie.

taloche [talɔʃ] *nf* (*fam: claque*) slap; (*TECH*) plaster float.

talon [talɔ̃] *nm* heel; (*de chèque, billet*) stub, counterfoil (*Brit*); **~s plats/aiguilles** flat/stiletto heels; **être sur les ~s de qn** to be on sb's heels; **tourner les ~s** to turn on one's heel; **montrer les ~s** (*fig*) to show a clean pair of heels.

talonner [talɔne] *vt* to follow hard behind; (*fig*) to hound; (*RUGBY*) to heel.

talonnette [talɔnɛt] *nf* (*de chaussure*) heel-piece; (*de pantalon*) stirrup.

talquer [talke] *vt* to put talc(um powder) on.

talus [taly] *nm* embankment; **~ de remblai/déblai** embankment/excavation slope.

tamarin [tamaʀɛ̃] *nm* (*BOT*) tamarind.

tambour [tɑ̃buʀ] *nm* (*MUS, aussi TECH*) drum; (*musicien*) drummer; (*porte*) revolving door(s *pl*); **sans ~ ni trompette** unobtrusively.

tambourin [tɑ̃buʀɛ̃] *nm* tambourine.

tambouriner [tɑ̃buʀine] *vi*: **~ contre** to drum against *ou* on.

tambour-major, *pl* **tambours-majors** [tɑ̃buʀmaʒɔʀ] *nm* drum major.

tamis [tami] *nm* sieve.

Tamise [tamiz] *nf*: **la ~** the Thames.

tamisé, e [tamize] *a* (*fig*) subdued, soft.

tamiser [tamize] *vt* to sieve, sift.

tampon [tɑ̃pɔ̃] *nm* (*de coton, d'ouate*) pad; (*aussi*: **~ hygiénique** *ou* **périodique**) tampon; (*amortisseur, INFORM: aussi*: **mémoire ~**) buffer; (*bouchon*) plug, stopper; (*cachet, timbre*) stamp; (*CHIMIE*) buffer; **~ buvard** blotter; **~ encreur** inking pad; **~ (à récurer)** scouring pad.

tamponné, e [tɑ̃pɔne] *a*: **solution ~e** buffer solution.

tamponner [tɑ̃pɔne] *vt* (*timbres*) to stamp; (*heurter*) to crash *ou* ram into; (*essuyer*) to mop up; **se ~** (*voitures*) to crash (into each other).

tamponneuse [tɑ̃pɔnøz] *af*: **autos ~s** dodgems, bumper cars.

tam-tam [tamtam] *nm* tomtom.

tancer [tɑ̃se] *vt* to scold.

tanche [tɑ̃ʃ] *nf* tench.

tandem [tɑ̃dɛm] *nm* tandem; (*fig*) duo, pair.

tandis [tɑ̃di]: **~ que** *cj* while.

tangage [tɑ̃gaʒ] *nm* pitching (and tossing).

tangent, e [tɑ̃ʒɑ̃, -ɑ̃t] *a* (*MATH*): **~ à** tangential to; (*fam: de justesse*) close ♦ *nf* (*MATH*) tangent.

Tanger [tɑ̃ʒe] *n* Tangier.

tangible [tɑ̃ʒibl(ə)] *a* tangible, concrete.

tango [tɑ̃go] *nm* (*MUS*) tango ♦ *a inv* (*couleur*) bright orange.

tanguer [tɑ̃ge] *vi* to pitch (and toss).

tanière [tanjɛʀ] *nf* lair, den.

tanin [tanɛ̃] *nm* tannin.

tank [tɑ̃k] *nm* tank.

tanker [tɑ̃kɛʀ] *nm* tanker.

tanné, e [tane] *a* weather-beaten.

tanner [tane] *vt* to tan.

tannerie [tanʀi] *nf* tannery.

tanneur [tanœʀ] *nm* tanner.

tant [tɑ̃] *ad* so much; ~ **de** (*sable, eau*) so much; (*gens, livres*) so many; ~ **que** *cj* as long as; ~ **que** (*comparatif*) as much as; ~ **mieux** that's great; so much the better; ~ **mieux pour lui** good for him; ~ **pis** too bad; **un** ~ **soit peu** (*un peu*) a little bit; (*même un peu*) (even) remotely; ~ **bien que mal** as well as can be expected; ~ **s'en faut** far from it, not by a long way.

tante [tɑ̃t] *nf* aunt.

tantinet [tɑ̃tinɛ]: **un** ~ *ad* a tiny bit.

tantôt [tɑ̃to] *ad* (*parfois*): ~ ... ~ now ... now; (*cet après-midi*) this afternoon.

Tanzanie [tɑ̃zani] *nf*: **la** ~ Tanzania.

tanzanien, ne [tɑ̃zanjɛ̃, -ɛn] *a* Tanzanian.

TAO *sigle f* (= *traduction assistée par ordinateur*) MAT (= *machine-aided translation*).

taon [tɑ̃] *nm* horsefly, gadfly.

tapage [tapaʒ] *nm* uproar, din; (*fig*) fuss, row; ~ **nocturne** (*JUR*) disturbance of the peace (*at night*).

tapageur, euse [tapaʒœʀ, -øz] *a* (*bruyant*: *enfants etc*) noisy; (*toilette*) loud, flashy; (*publicité*) obtrusive.

tape [tap] *nf* slap.

tape-à-l'œil [tapalœj] *a inv* flashy, showy.

taper [tape] *vt* (*personne*) to clout; (*porte*) to bang, slam; (*dactylographier*) to type (out); (*INFORM*) to key(board); (*fam*: *emprunter*): ~ **qn de 10 F** to touch sb for 10 F, cadge 10 F off sb ♦ *vi* (*soleil*) to beat down; **se** ~ *vt* (*fam*: *travail*) to get landed with; (: *boire, manger*) to down; ~ **sur qn** to thump sb; (*fig*) to run sb down; ~ **sur qch** (*clou etc*) to hit sth; (*table etc*) to bang on sth; ~ **à** (*porte etc*) to knock on; ~ **dans** (*se servir*) to dig into; ~ **des mains/pieds** to clap one's hands/ stamp one's feet; ~ **(à la machine)** to type.

tapi, e [tapi] *a*: ~ **dans/derrière** (*blotti*) crouching *ou* cowering in/behind; (*caché*) hidden away in/behind.

tapinois [tapinwa]: **en** ~ *ad* stealthily.

tapioca [tapjɔka] *nm* tapioca.

tapir [tapiʀ]: **se** ~ *vi* to hide away.

tapis [tapi] *nm* carpet; (*de table*) cloth; **mettre sur le** ~ (*fig*) to bring up for discussion; **aller au** ~ (*BOXE*) to go down; **envoyer au** ~ (*BOXE*) to floor; ~ **roulant** conveyor belt; ~ **de sol** (*de tente*) groundsheet.

tapis-brosse [tapibʀɔs] *nm* doormat.

tapisser [tapise] *vt* (*avec du papier peint*) to paper; (*recouvrir*): ~ **qch (de)** to cover sth (with).

tapisserie [tapisʀi] *nf* (*tenture, broderie*) tapestry; (: *travail*) tapestry-making; (: *ouvrage*) tapestry work; (*papier peint*) wallpaper; (*fig*): **faire** ~ to sit out, be a wallflower.

tapissier, ière [tapisje, -jɛʀ] *nm/f*: ~**(-décorateur)** upholsterer (and decorator).

tapoter [tapɔte] *vt* to pat, tap.

taquet [takɛ] *nm* (*cale*) wedge; (*cheville*) peg.

taquin, e [takɛ̃, -in] *a* teasing.

taquiner [takine] *vt* to tease.

taquinerie [takinʀi] *nf* teasing *q*.

tarabiscoté, e [taʀabiskɔte] *a* over-ornate, fussy.

tarabuster [taʀabyste] *vt* to bother, worry.

tarama [taʀama] *nm* (*CULIN*) taramasalata.

tarauder [taʀode] *vt* (*TECH*) to tap; to thread; (*fig*) to pierce.

tard [taʀ] *ad* late; **au plus** ~ at the latest; **plus** ~ later (on) ♦ *nm*: **sur le** ~ (*à une heure avancée*) late in the day; (*vers la fin de la vie*) late in life.

tarder [taʀde] *vi* (*chose*) to be a long time coming; (*personne*): ~ **à faire** to delay doing; **il me tarde d'être** I am longing to be; **sans (plus)** ~ without (further) delay.

tardif, ive [taʀdif, -iv] *a* (*heure, repas, fruit*) late; (*talent, goût*) late in developing.

tardivement [taʀdivmɑ̃] *ad* late.

tare [taʀ] *nf* (*COMM*) tare; (*fig*) defect; taint, blemish.

targette [taʀʒɛt] *nf* (*verrou*) bolt.

targuer [taʀge]: **se** ~ **de** *vt* to boast about.

tarif [taʀif] *nm* (*liste*) price list, tariff (*Brit*); (*barème*) rate, rates *pl*, tariff (*Brit*); (: *de taxis etc*) fares *pl*; **voyager à plein** ~/**à** ~ **réduit** to travel at full/reduced fare.

tarifaire [taʀifɛʀ] *a* (*voir tarif*) relating to price lists *etc*.

tarifé, e [taʀife] *a*: ~ **10 F** priced at 10 F.

tarifer [taʀife] *vt* to fix the price *ou* rate for.

tarir [taʀiʀ] *vi* to dry up, run dry ♦ *vt* to dry up.

tarot(s) [taʀo] *nm(pl)* tarot cards.

tartare [taʀtaʀ] *a* (*CULIN*) tartar(e).

tarte [taʀt(ə)] *nf* tart; ~ **aux pommes/à la crème** apple/custard tart.

tartelette [taʀtəlɛt] *nf* tartlet.

tartine [taʀtin] *nf* slice of bread (and butter (*ou* jam)); ~ **de miel** slice of bread and honey; ~ **beurrée** slice of bread and butter.

tartiner [taʀtine] *vt* to spread; **fromage à** ~ cheese spread.

tartre [taʀtʀ(ə)] *nm* (*des dents*) tartar; (*de chaudière*) fur, scale.

tas [tɑ] *nm* heap, pile; (*fig*): **un** ~ **de** heaps of, lots of; **en** ~ in a heap *ou* pile; **dans le** ~ (*fig*) in the crowd; among them; **formé sur le** ~ trained on the job.

Tasmanie [tasmani] *nf*: **la** ~ Tasmania.

tasmanien, ne [tasmanjɛ̃, -ɛn] *a* Tasmanian.

tasse [tɑs] *nf* cup; **boire la** ~ (*en se baignant*) to swallow a mouthful; ~ **à café/thé** coffee/ teacup.

tassé, e [tɑse] *a*: **bien** ~ (*café etc*) strong.

tasseau, x [tɑso] *nm* length of wood.

tassement [tɑsmɑ̃] *nm* (*de vertèbres*) compression; (*ÉCON, POL*): *ralentissement*) fall-off, slowdown; (*BOURSE*) dullness.

tasser [tɑse] *vt* (*terre, neige*) to pack down; (*entasser*): ~ **qch dans** to cram sth into; (*INFORM*) to pack; **se** ~ *vi* (*terrain*) to settle; (*personne: avec l'âge*) to shrink; (*fig*) to sort itself out, settle down.

tâter [tɑte] *vt* to feel; (*fig*) to sound out; ~ **de** (*prison etc*) to have a taste of; **se** ~ (*hésiter*) to be in two minds; ~ **le terrain** (*fig*) to test the ground.

tatillon, ne [tatijɔ̃, -ɔn] *a* pernickety.

tâtonnement [tɑtɔnmɑ̃] *nm*: **par** ~**s** (*fig*) by trial and error.

tâtonner [tɑtɔne] *vi* to grope one's way along; (*fig*) to grope around (in the dark).

tâtons [tɑtɔ̃]: **à** ~ *ad*: **chercher/avancer à** ~

to grope around for/grope one's way forward.
tatouage [tatwaʒ] *nm* tattooing; *(dessin)* tattoo.
tatouer [tatwe] *vt* to tattoo.
taudis [todi] *nm* hovel, slum.
taule [tol] *nf (fam)* nick *(Brit)*, jail.
taupe [top] *nf* mole; *(peau)* moleskin.
taupinière [topinjɛʀ] *nf* molehill.
taureau, x [tɔʀo] *nm* bull; *(signe):* **le T~** Taurus, the Bull; **être du T~** to be Taurus.
taurillon [tɔʀijɔ̃] *nm* bull-calf.
tauromachie [tɔʀɔmaʃi] *nf* bullfighting.
taux [to] *nm* rate; *(d'alcool)* level; **~ d'escompte** discount rate; **~ d'intérêt** interest rate; **~ de mortalité** mortality rate.
tavelé, e [tavle] *a* marked.
taverne [tavɛʀn(ə)] *nf* inn, tavern.
taxable [taksabl(ə)] *a* taxable.
taxation [taksasjɔ̃] *nf* taxation; *(TÉL)* charges *pl.*
taxe [taks(ə)] *nf* tax; *(douanière)* duty; **toutes ~s comprises (TTC)** inclusive of tax; **~ de base** *(TÉL)* unit charge; **~ de séjour** tourist tax; **~ à** *ou* **sur la valeur ajoutée (TVA)** value added tax (VAT).
taxer [takse] *vt (personne)* to tax; *(produit)* to put a tax on, tax; *(fig):* **~ qn de** *(qualifier de)* to call sb + *attribut; (accuser de)* to accuse sb of, tax sb with.
taxi [taksi] *nm* taxi.
taxidermie [taksidɛʀmi] *nf* taxidermy.
taximètre [taksimɛtʀ(ə)] *nm* (taxi)meter.
taxiphone [taksifɔn] *nm* pay phone.
tb *abr (= très bien; = très bon)* VG.
tbe *abr (= très bon état)* VGC, vgc.
TCA *sigle f (= taxe sur le chiffre d'affaires)* tax on turnover.
TCF *sigle m (= Touring Club de France)* ≈ AA *ou* RAC *(Brit)*, ≈ AAA *(US)*.
Tchad [tʃad] *nm:* **le ~** Chad.
tchadien, ne [tʃadjɛ̃, -ɛn] *a* Chad(ian), of *ou* from Chad.
tchao [tʃao] *excl (fam)* bye(-bye)!
tchécoslovaque [tʃekɔslɔvak] *a* Czechoslovak(ian) ♦ *nm/f:* **T~** Czechoslovak(ian).
Tchécoslovaquie [tʃekɔslɔvaki] *nf:* **la ~** Czechoslovakia.
tchèque [tʃɛk] *a* Czech ♦ *nm (LING)* Czech ♦ *nm/f:* **T~** Czech.
TCS *sigle m (= Touring Club de Suisse)* ≈ AA *ou* RAC *(Brit)*, ≈ AAA *(US)*.
TD *sigle mpl* = **travaux dirigés.**
TDF *sigle f (= Télévision de France)* French broadcasting authority.
te, t' [t(ə)] *pronom* you; *(réfléchi)* yourself.
té [te] *nm* T-square.
technicien, ne [tɛknisjɛ̃, -ɛn] *nm/f* technician.
technicité [tɛknisite] *nf* technical nature.
technique [tɛknik] *a* technical ♦ *nf* technique.
techniquement [tɛknikmã] *ad* technically.
technocrate [tɛknɔkʀat] *nm/f* technocrat.
technocratie [tɛknɔkʀasi] *nf* technocracy.
technologie [tɛknɔlɔʒi] *nf* technology.
technologique [tɛknɔlɔʒik] *a* technological.
technologue [tɛknɔlɔg] *nm f* technologist.
teck [tɛk] *nm* teak.
teckel [tekɛl] *nm* dachshund.
TEE *sigle m* = *Trans-Europ-Express.*
tee-shirt [tiʃœʀt] *nm* T-shirt, tee-shirt.

Téhéran [teeʀã] *n* Teheran.
teigne [tɛɲ] *vb voir* **teindre** ♦ *nf (ZOOL)* moth; *(MÉD)* ringworm.
teigneux, euse [tɛɲø, -øz] *a (péj)* nasty, scabby.
teindre [tɛ̃dʀ(ə)] *vt* to dye; **se ~ (les cheveux)** to dye one's hair.
teint, e [tɛ̃, tɛ̃t] *pp de* **teindre** ♦ *a* dyed ♦ *nm (du visage: permanent)* complexion, colouring *(Brit)*, coloring *(US); (momentané)* colour *(Brit)*, color *(US)* ♦ *nf* shade, colour, color; *(fig: petite dose):* **une ~e de** a hint of; **grand ~** *a inv* colourfast; **bon ~** *a inv (couleur)* fast; *(tissu)* colourfast; *(personne)* staunch, firm.
teinté, e [tɛ̃te] *a (verres)* tinted; *(bois)* stained; **~ acajou** mahogany-stained; **~ de** *(fig)* tinged with.
teinter [tɛ̃te] *vt* to tint; *(bois)* to stain; *(fig: d'ironie etc)* to tinge.
teinture [tɛ̃tyʀ] *nf* dyeing; *(substance)* dye; *(MÉD):* **~ d'iode** tincture of iodine.
teinturerie [tɛ̃tyʀʀi] *nf* dry cleaner's.
teinturier, ière [tɛ̃tyʀje, -jɛʀ] *nm/f* dry cleaner.
tel, telle [tɛl] *a (pareil)* such; *(comme):* **~ un/des ...** like a/like ...; *(indéfini)* such-and-such a, a given; *(intensif):* **un ~/de ~s ...** such (a)/such ...; **rien de ~** nothing like it, no such thing; **~ que** *cj* like, such as; **~ quel** as it is *ou* stands *(ou* was *etc)*.
tél. *abr* = **téléphone.**
Tel Aviv [tɛlaviv] *n* Tel Aviv.
télé [tele] *nf (= télévision)* TV, telly *(Brit)*; **à la ~** on TV *ou* telly.
télébenne [teleben] *nm, nf* telecabine, gondola.
télécabine [telekabin] *nm, nf* telecabine, gondola.
télécarte [telekaʀt(ə)] *nf* phonecard.
télécharger [teleʃaʀʒe] *vt (INFORM)* to download.
télécommande [telekɔmãd] *nf* remote control.
télécommander [telekɔmãde] *vt* to operate by remote control, radio-control.
télécommunications [telekɔmynikasjɔ̃] *nfpl* telecommunications.
télécopie [telekɔpi] *nf* fax, telefax.
télécopieur [telekɔpjœʀ] *nm* fax (machine).
télédétection [teledetɛksjɔ̃] *nf* remote sensing.
télédiffuser [teledifyze] *vt* to broadcast (on television).
télédiffusion [teledifyzjɔ̃] *nf* television broadcasting.
télédistribution [teledistʀibysjɔ̃] *nf* cable TV.
téléenseignement [teleãsɛɲmã] *nm* distance teaching *(ou* learning).
téléférique [teleferik] *nm* = **téléphérique.**
téléfilm [telefilm] *nm* film made for TV, TV film.
télégramme [telegʀam] *nm* telegram.
télégraphe [telegʀaf] *nm* telegraph.
télégraphie [telegʀafi] *nf* telegraphy.
télégraphier [telegʀafje] *vt* to telegraph, cable.
télégraphique [telegʀafik] *a* telegraph *cpd*, telegraphic; *(fig)* telegraphic.
télégraphiste [telegʀafist(ə)] *nm/f* telegraph-

ist.

téléguider [telegide] *vt* to operate by remote control, radio-control.

téléinformatique [teleɛ̃fɔʀmatik] *nf* remote access computing.

téléjournal, aux [teleʒuʀnal, -o] *nm* television news magazine programme.

télématique [telematik] *nf* telematics *sg* ♦ *a* telematic.

téléobjectif [teleɔbʒɛktif] *nm* telephoto lens *sg*.

télépathie [telepati] *nf* telepathy.

téléphérique [teleferik] *nm* cable-car.

téléphone [telefɔn] *nm* telephone; **avoir le ~** to be on the (tele)phone; **au ~** on the phone; **les T~s** the (tele)phone service *sg*; **~ arabe** bush telegraph; **~ manuel** manually-operated telephone system; **~ rouge** hotline.

téléphoner [telefɔne] *vt* to telephone ♦ *vi* to telephone; to make a phone call; **~ à** to phone up, ring up, call up.

téléphonique [telefɔnik] *a* telephone *cpd*, phone *cpd*; **cabine ~** call box (*Brit*), (tele)phone box (*Brit*) *ou* booth; **conversation/appel ~** (tele)phone conversation/call.

téléphoniste [telefɔnist(ə)] *nm/f* telephonist, telephone operator; (*d'entreprise*) switchboard operator.

téléport [telepɔʀ] *nm* teleport.

téléprospection [teleprɔspɛksjɔ̃] *nf* telephone selling.

télescope [telɛskɔp] *nm* telescope.

télescoper [telɛskɔpe] *vt* to smash up; **se ~** (*véhicules*) to concertina.

télescopique [telɛskɔpik] *a* telescopic.

téléscripteur [teleskriptœʀ] *nm* teleprinter.

télésiège [telesjɛʒ] *nm* chairlift.

téléski [teleski] *nm* ski-tow; **~ à archets** T-bar tow; **~ à perche** button lift.

téléspectateur, trice [telespɛktatœʀ, -tʀis] *nm/f* (television) viewer.

télétraitement [teletʀɛtmɑ̃] *nm* remote processing.

télétransmission [teletʀɑ̃smisjɔ̃] *nf* remote transmission.

télétype [teletip] *nm* teleprinter.

téléviser [televize] *vt* to televise.

téléviseur [televizœʀ] *nm* television set.

télévision [televizjɔ̃] *nf* television; **(poste de) ~** television (set); **avoir la ~** to have a television; **à la ~** on television; **~ par câble** cable television.

télex [telɛks] *nm* telex.

télexer [telɛkse] *vt* to telex.

télexiste [telɛksist(ə)] *nm/f* telex operator.

telle [tɛl] *af voir* **tel**.

tellement [tɛlmɑ̃] *ad* (*tant*) so much; (*si*) so; **~ plus grand (que)** so much bigger (than); **~ de** (*sable, eau*) so much; (*gens, livres*) so many; **il s'est endormi ~** il était fatigué he was so tired (that) he fell asleep; **pas ~** not really; **pas ~ fort/lentement** not (all) that strong/slowly; **il ne mange pas ~** he doesn't eat (all that) much.

tellurique [telyʀik] *a*: **secousse ~** earth tremor.

téméraire [temeʀɛʀ] *a* reckless, rash.

témérité [temeʀite] *nf* recklessness, rashness.

témoignage [temwaɲaʒ] *nm* (*JUR*: *déclaration*) testimony *q*, evidence *q*; (: *faits*) evidence *q*; (*gén*: *rapport, récit*) account; (*fig*: *d'affection etc*) token, mark; expression.

témoigner [temwaɲe] *vt* (*manifester*: *intérêt, gratitude*) to show ♦ *vi* (*JUR*) to testify, give evidence; **~ que** to testify that; (*fig*: *démontrer*) to reveal that, testify to the fact that; **~ de** *vt* (*confirmer*) to bear witness to, testify to.

témoin [temwɛ̃] *nm* witness; (*fig*) testimony; (*SPORT*) baton; (*CONSTR*) telltale ♦ *a* control *cpd*, test *cpd* ♦ *ad*: **~ le fait que ...** (as) witness the fact that ...; **appartement~** show flat (*Brit*), model apartment (*US*); **être ~ de** (*voir*) to witness; **prendre à ~** to call to witness; **~ à charge** witness for the prosecution; **T~ de Jehovah** Jehovah's Witness; **~ de moralité** character reference; **~ oculaire** eyewitness.

tempe [tɑ̃p] *nf* (*ANAT*) temple.

tempérament [tɑ̃peʀamɑ̃] *nm* temperament, disposition; (*santé*) constitution; **à ~** (*vente*) on deferred (payment) terms; (*achat*) by instalments, hire purchase *cpd*; **avoir du ~** to be hot-blooded.

tempérance [tɑ̃peʀɑ̃s] *nf* temperance; **société de ~** temperance society.

tempérant, e [tɑ̃peʀɑ̃, -ɑ̃t] *a* temperate.

température [tɑ̃peʀatyʀ] *nf* temperature; **prendre la ~ de** to take the temperature of; (*fig*) to gauge the feeling of; **avoir** *ou* **faire de la ~** to be running *ou* have a temperature.

tempéré, e [tɑ̃peʀe] *a* temperate.

tempérer [tɑ̃peʀe] *vt* to temper.

tempête [tɑ̃pɛt] *nf* storm; **~ de sable/neige** sand/snowstorm; **vent de ~** gale.

tempêter [tɑ̃pɛte] *vi* to rant and rave.

temple [tɑ̃pl(ə)] *nm* temple; (*protestant*) church.

tempo [tɛmpo] *nm* tempo (*pl* -s).

temporaire [tɑ̃pɔʀɛʀ] *a* temporary.

temporairement [tɑ̃pɔʀɛʀmɑ̃] *ad* temporarily.

temporel, le [tɑ̃pɔʀɛl] *a* temporal.

temporisateur, trice [tɑ̃pɔʀizatœʀ, -tʀis] *a* temporizing, delaying.

temporiser [tɑ̃pɔʀize] *vi* to temporize, play for time.

temps [tɑ̃] *nm* (*atmosphérique*) weather; (*durée*) time; (*époque*) time, times *pl*; (*LING*) tense; (*MUS*) beat; (*TECH*) stroke; **les ~ changent/sont durs** times are changing/hard; **il fait beau/mauvais ~** the weather is fine/bad; **avoir le ~/tout le ~/juste le ~** to have time/plenty of time/just enough time; **avoir fait son ~** (*fig*) to have had its (*ou* his *etc*) day; **en ~ de paix/guerre** in peacetime/wartime; **en ~ utile** *ou* **voulu** in due time *ou* course; **de ~ en ~, de ~ à autre** from time to time, now and again; **en même ~** at the same time; **à ~** (*partir, arriver*) in time; **à plein/mi-~** *ad, a* full-/part-time; **à ~ partiel** *ad, a* part-time; **dans le ~** at one time; **de tout ~** always; **du ~ que** at the time when, in the days when; **dans le** *ou* **du** *ou* **au ~ où** at the time when; **pendant ce ~** in the meantime; **~ d'accès** (*INFORM*) access time; **~ d'arrêt** pause, halt; **~ mort** (*SPORT*) stoppage (time); (*COMM*) slack period; ~ **partagé** (*INFORM*) time-sharing; ~ **réel** (*INFORM*) real time.

tenable [tənabl(ə)] *a* bearable.

tenace [tənas] *a* tenacious, persistent.

ténacité [tenasite] *nf* tenacity, persistence.

tenailler [tənaje] *vt* (*fig*) to torment, torture.

tenailles [tənaj] *nfpl* pincers.

tenais [t(ə)nɛ] *etc vb voir* **tenir**.

tenancier, ière [tənãsje, -jɛʀ] *nm/f* (*d'hôtel, de bistro*) manager/manageress.

tenant, e [tənã, -ãt] *af voir* **séance** ♦ *nm/f* (*SPORT*): ~ **du titre** title-holder ♦ *nm*: **d'un seul** ~ in one piece; **les** ~**s et les aboutissants** (*fig*) the ins and outs.

tendance [tãdãs] *nf* (*opinions*) leanings *pl*, sympathies *pl*; (*inclination*) tendency; (*évolution*) trend; ~ **à la hausse/baisse** upward/downward trend; **avoir** ~ **à** to have a tendency to, tend to.

tendancieux, euse [tãdãsjø, -øz] *a* tendentious.

tendeur [tãdœʀ] *nm* (*de vélo*) chain-adjuster; (*de câble*) wire-strainer; (*de tente*) runner; (*attache*) elastic strap.

tendon [tãdɔ̃] *nm* tendon, sinew; ~ **d'Achille** Achilles' tendon.

tendre [tãdʀ(ə)] *a* (*viande, légumes*) tender; (*bois, roche, couleur*) soft; (*affectueux*) tender, loving ♦ *vt* (*élastique, peau*) to stretch, draw tight; (*muscle*) to tense; (*donner*): ~ **qch à qn** to hold sth out to sb; to offer sb sth; (*fig: piège*) to set, lay; (*tapisserie*): **tendu de soie** hung with silk, with silk hangings; **se** ~ *vi* (*corde*) to tighten; (*relations*) to become strained; ~ **à qch/à faire** to tend towards sth/to do; ~ **l'oreille** to prick up one's ears; ~ **la main/le bras** to hold out one's hand/stretch out one's arm; ~ **la perche à qn** (*fig*) to throw sb a line.

tendrement [tãdʀəmã] *ad* tenderly, lovingly.

tendresse [tãdʀɛs] *nf* tenderness; ~**s** *nfpl* (*caresses etc*) tenderness *q*, caresses.

tendu, e [tãdy] *pp de* **tendre** ♦ *a* tight; tensed, strained.

ténèbres [tenɛbʀ(ə)] *nfpl* darkness *sg*.

ténébreux, euse [tenebʀø, -øz] *a* obscure, mysterious; (*personne*) saturnine.

Ténérife [tenerif] *nf* Tenerife.

teneur [tənœʀ] *nf* content, substance; (*d'une lettre*) terms *pl*, content; ~ **en cuivre** copper content.

ténia [tenja] *nm* tapeworm.

tenir [təniʀ] *vt* to hold; (*magasin, hôtel*) to run; (*promesse*) to keep ♦ *vi* to hold; (*neige, gel*) to last; (*survivre*) to survive; **se** ~ *vi* (*avoir lieu*) to be held, take place; (*être: personne*) to stand; **se** ~ **droit** to stand up (*ou* sit up) straight; **bien se** ~ to behave well; **se** ~ **à qch** to hold on to sth; **s'en** ~ **à qch** to confine o.s. to sth; to stick to sth; ~ **à** *vt* to be attached to, care about (*ou* for); (*avoir pour cause*) to be due to, stem from; ~ **à faire** to want to do, be keen to do; ~ **à ce que qn fasse qch** to be anxious that sb should do sth; ~ **de** *vt* to partake of; (*ressembler à*) to take after; **ça ne tient qu'à lui** it's entirely up to him; ~ **qn pour** to take sb for; ~ **qch de qn** (*histoire*) to

have heard *ou* learnt sth from sb; (*qualité, défaut*) to have inherited *ou* got sth from sb; ~ **les comptes** to keep the books; ~ **un rôle** to play a part; ~ **de la place** to take up space *ou* room; ~ **l'alcool** to be able to hold a drink; ~ **le coup** to hold out; ~ **bon** to stand *ou* hold fast; ~ **3 jours/2 mois** (*résister*) to hold out *ou* last 3 days/2 months; ~ **au chaud/à l'abri** to keep hot/under shelter *ou* cover; ~ **prêt** to have ready; ~ **sa langue** (*fig*) to hold one's tongue; **tiens** (*ou* **tenez**), **voilà le stylo** there's the pen!; **tiens, Alain!** look, here's Alain!; **tiens?** (*surprise*) really?; **tiens-toi bien!** (*pour informer*) brace yourself!, take a deep breath!

tennis [tenis] *nm* tennis; (*aussi:* **court de** ~) tennis court ♦ *nmpl ou fpl* (*aussi:* **chaussures de** ~) tennis *ou* gym shoes; ~ **de table** table tennis.

tennisman [tenisman] *nm* tennis player.

ténor [tenɔʀ] *nm* tenor.

tension [tãsjɔ̃] *nf* tension; (*fig: des relations, de la situation*) tension; (: *concentration, effort*) strain; (*MÉD*) blood pressure; **faire** *ou* **avoir de la** ~ to have high blood pressure; ~ **nerveuse/raciale** nervous/racial tension.

tentaculaire [tãtakylɛʀ] *a* (*fig*) sprawling.

tentacule [tãtakyl] *nm* tentacle.

tentant, e [tãtã, -ãt] *a* tempting.

tentateur, trice [tãtatœʀ, -tʀis] *a* tempting ♦ *nm* (*REL*) tempter.

tentation [tãtasjɔ̃] *nf* temptation.

tentative [tãtativ] *nf* attempt, bid; ~ **d'évasion** escape bid; ~ **de suicide** suicide attempt.

tente [tãt] *nf* tent; ~ **à oxygène** oxygen tent.

tenter [tãte] *vt* (*éprouver, attirer*) to tempt; (*essayer*): ~ **qch/de faire** to attempt *ou* try sth/to do; **être tenté de** to be tempted to; ~ **sa chance** to try one's luck.

tenture [tãtyʀ] *nf* hanging.

tenu, e [təny] *pp de* **tenir** ♦ *a* (*maison, comptes*): **bien** ~ well-kept; (*obligé*): ~ **de faire** under an obligation to do ♦ *nf* (*action de tenir*) running; keeping; holding; (*vêtements*) clothes *pl*, gear; (*allure*) dress *q*, appearance; (*comportement*) manners *pl*, behaviour (*Brit*), behavior (*US*); **être en** ~**e** to be dressed (up); **se mettre en** ~**e** to dress (up); **en grande** ~**e** in full dress; **en petite** ~**e** scantily dressed *ou* clad; **avoir de la** ~**e** to have good manners; (*journal*) to have a high standard; ~**e de combat** combat gear *ou* dress; ~**e de pompier** fireman's uniform; ~**e de route** (*AUTO*) road-holding; ~**e de soirée** evening dress; ~**e de sport/voyage** sports/travelling clothes *pl ou* gear *q*.

ténu, e [teny] *a* (*indice, nuance*) tenuous, subtle; (*fil, objet*) fine; (*voix*) thin.

TEP *sigle m* = *Théâtre de l'Est parisien*.

ter [tɛʀ] *a*: **16** ~ 16b *ou* B.

térébenthine [teʀebãtin] *nf*: (**essence de**) ~ (oil of) turpentine.

tergal [tɛʀgal] *nm* ® Terylene ®.

tergiversations [tɛʀʒivɛʀsasjɔ̃] *nfpl* shilly-shallying *q*.

tergiverser [tɛʀʒivɛʀse] *vi* to shilly-shally.

terme [tɛʀm(ə)] *nm* term; (*fin*) end; **être en bons/mauvais** ~**s avec qn** to be on good/bad terms with sb; **vente/achat à ~** (*COMM*) forward sale/purchase; **au ~ de** at the end of; **en d'autres ~s** in other words; **moyen ~** (*solution intermédiaire*) middle course; **à court/long ~** *a* short-/long-term *ou* -range ♦ *ad* in the short/long term; **à ~ a** (*MÉD*) fullterm ♦ *ad* sooner or later, eventually; (*MÉD*) at term; **avant ~** (*MÉD*) a premature ♦ *ad* prematurely; **mettre un ~ à** to put an end *ou* a stop to; **toucher à son ~** to be nearing its end.

terminaison [tɛʀminɛzɔ̃] *nf* (*LING*) ending.

terminal, e, aux [tɛʀminal, -o] *a* (*partie, phase*) final; (*MÉD*) terminal ♦ *nm* terminal ♦ *nf* (*SCOL*) ≈ sixth form *ou* year (*Brit*), ≈ twelfth grade (*US*).

terminer [tɛʀmine] *vt* to end; (*travail, repas*) to finish; **se ~** *vi* to end; **se ~ par** to end with.

terminologie [tɛʀminɔlɔʒi] *nf* terminology.

terminus [tɛʀminys] *nm* terminus (*pl* -i); **~!** all change!

termite [tɛʀmit] *nm* termite, white ant.

termitière [tɛʀmitjɛʀ] *nf* ant-hill.

ternaire [tɛʀnɛʀ] *a* compound.

terne [tɛʀn(ə)] *a* dull.

ternir [tɛʀniʀ] *vt* to dull; (*fig*) to sully, tarnish; **se ~** *vi* to become dull.

terrain [tɛʀɛ̃] *nm* (*sol, fig*) ground; (*COMM*) land *q*, plot (of land); (*: à bâtir*) site; **sur le ~** (*fig*) on the field; **~ de football/rugby** football/rugby pitch (*Brit*) *ou* field (*US*); **~ d'atterrissage** landing strip; **~ d'aviation** airfield; **~ de camping** campsite; **un ~ d'entente** an area of agreement; **~ de golf** golf course; **~ de jeu** playground; (*SPORT*) games field; **~ de sport** sports ground; **~ vague** waste ground *q*.

terrasse [tɛʀas] *nf* terrace; (*de café*) pavement area, terrasse; **à la ~** (*café*) outside.

terrassement [tɛʀasmɑ̃] *nm* earth-moving, earthworks *pl*; embankment.

terrasser [tɛʀase] *vt* (*adversaire*) to floor, bring down; (*suj: maladie etc*) to lay low.

terrassier [tɛʀasje] *nm* navvy, roadworker.

terre [tɛʀ] *nf* (*gén, aussi ÉLEC*) earth; (*substance*) soil, earth; (*opposé à mer*) land *q*; (*contrée*) land; **~s** *nfpl* (*terrains*) lands, land *sg*; **travail de la ~** work on the land; **en ~** (*pipe, poterie*) clay *cpd*; **mettre en ~** (*plante etc*) to plant; (*personne: enterrer*) to bury; **à ou par ~** (*mettre, être*) on the ground (*ou* floor); (*jeter, tomber*) to the ground, down; **~ à ~** *a inv* down-to-earth, matter-of-fact; **la T~ Adélie** Adélie Coast *ou* Land; **~ de bruyère** (heath-)peat; **~ cuite** earthenware; terracotta; **la ~ ferme** dry land, terra firma; **la T~ de feu** Tierra del Fuego; **~ glaise** clay; **la T~ promise** the Promised Land; **la T~ Sainte** the Holy Land.

terreau [tɛʀo] *nm* compost.

Terre-Neuve [tɛʀnœv] *nf*: **la ~** (*aussi*: **l'île de ~**) Newfoundland.

terre-plein [tɛʀplɛ̃] *nm* platform.

terrer [tɛʀe]: **se ~** *vi* to hide away; to go to ground.

terrestre [tɛʀɛstʀ(ə)] *a* (*surface*) earth's, of the earth; (*BOT, ZOOL, MIL*) land *cpd*; (*REL*) earthly, worldly.

terreur [tɛʀœʀ] *nf* terror *q*, fear.

terreux, euse [tɛʀø, -øz] *a* muddy; (*goût*) earthy.

terrible [tɛʀibl(ə)] *a* terrible, dreadful; (*fam: fantastique*) terrific.

terriblement [tɛʀibləmɑ̃] *ad* (*très*) terribly, awfully.

terrien, ne [tɛʀjɛ̃, -ɛn] *a*: **propriétaire ~** landowner ♦ *nm/f* countryman/woman, man/woman of the soil; (*non martien etc*) earthling; (*non marin*) landsman.

terrier [tɛʀje] *nm* burrow, hole; (*chien*) terrier.

terrifiant, e [tɛʀifjɑ̃, -ɑ̃t] *a* (*effrayant*) terrifying; (*extraordinaire*) terrible, awful.

terrifier [tɛʀifje] *vt* to terrify.

terril [tɛʀil] *nm* slag heap.

terrine [tɛʀin] *nf* (*récipient*) terrine; (*CULIN*) pâté.

territoire [tɛʀitwaʀ] *nm* territory; **T~ des Afars et des Issas** French Territory of Afars and Issas.

territorial, e, aux [tɛʀitɔʀjal, -o] *a* territorial; **eaux ~es** territorial waters; **armée ~e** regional defence force, ≈ Territorial Army (*Brit*); **collectivités ~es** local and regional authorities.

terroir [tɛʀwaʀ] *nm* (*AGR*) soil; (*région*) region; **accent du ~** country *ou* rural accent.

terroriser [tɛʀɔʀize] *vt* to terrorize.

terrorisme [tɛʀɔʀism(ə)] *nm* terrorism.

terroriste [tɛʀɔʀist(ə)] *nm/f* terrorist.

tertiaire [tɛʀsjɛʀ] *a* tertiary ♦ *nm* (*ÉCON*) tertiary sector, service industries *pl*.

tertre [tɛʀtʀ(ə)] *nm* hillock, mound.

tes [te] *dét voir* **ton**.

tesson [tesɔ̃] *nm*: **~ de bouteille** piece of broken bottle.

test [tɛst] *nm* test.

testament [tɛstamɑ̃] *nm* (*JUR*) will; (*fig*) legacy; (*REL*): **T~** Testament; **faire son ~** to make one's will.

testamentaire [tɛstamɑ̃tɛʀ] *a* of a will.

tester [tɛste] *vt* to test.

testicule [tɛstikyl] *nm* testicle.

tétanos [tetanɔs] *nm* tetanus.

têtard [tɛtaʀ] *nm* tadpole.

tête [tɛt] *nf* head; (*cheveux*) hair *q*; (*visage*) face; (*longueur*) **gagner d'une (courte) ~** to win by a (short) head; (*FOOTBALL*) header; **de ~** *a* (*wagon etc*) front *cpd*; (*concurrent*) leading ♦ *ad* (*calculer*) in one's head, mentally; **par ~** (*par personne*) per head; **se mettre en ~ que** to get it into one's head that; **se mettre en ~ de** to take it into one's head to do; **prendre la ~ de qch** to take the lead in sth; **perdre la ~** (*fig: s'affoler*) to lose one's head; (*: devenir fou*) to go off one's head; **ça ne va pas, la ~?** (*fam*) are you crazy?; **tenir ~ à qn** to stand up to *ou* defy sb; **la ~ en bas** with one's head down; **la ~ la première** (*tomber*) headfirst; **la ~ basse** hanging one's head; **avoir la ~ dure** (*fig*) to be thickheaded; **faire une ~** (*FOOTBALL*) to head the ball; **faire la ~** (*fig*) to sulk; **en ~** (*SPORT*) in the lead; at the front *ou* head; **de la ~ aux pieds** from head to toe; **~ d'affiche** (*THÉÂTRE etc*) top of the bill; **~ de bétail** head *inv* of cattle; **~**

brulée desperado; ~ **chercheuse** homing device; ~ **d'enregistrement** recording head; ~ **d'impression** printhead; ~ **de lecture** (playback) head; ~ **de ligne** (*TRANSPORTS*) start of the line; ~ **de liste** (*POL*) chief candidate; ~ **de mort** skull and crossbones; ~ **de pont** (*MIL*) bridge- *ou* beachhead; ~ **de série** (*TENNIS*) seeded player, seed; ~ **de Turc** (*fig*) whipping boy (*Brit*), butt; ~ **de veau** (*CULIN*) calf's head.

tête-à-queue [tɛtakø] *nm inv:* **faire un** ~ to spin round.

tête-à-tête [tɛtatɛt] *nm inv* tête-à-tête; (*service*) breakfast set for two; **en** ~ in private, alone together.

tête-bêche [tɛtbɛʃ] *ad* head to tail.

tétée [tete] *nf* (*action*) sucking; (*repas*) feed.

téter [tete] *vt:* ~ **(sa mère)** to suck at one's mother's breast, feed.

tétine [tetin] *nf* teat; (*sucette*) dummy (*Brit*), pacifier (*US*).

téton [tetɔ̃] *nm* breast.

têtu, e [tety] *a* stubborn, pigheaded.

texte [tɛkst(ə)] *nm* text; (*SCOL: d'un devoir*) subject, topic; **apprendre son** ~ (*THÉÂTRE*) to learn one's lines; **un** ~ **de loi** the wording of a law.

textile [tɛkstil] *a* textile *cpd* ♦ *nm* textile; (*industrie*) textile industry.

textuel, le [tɛkstɥɛl] *a* literal, word for word.

textuellement [tɛkstɥɛlmɑ̃] *ad* literally.

texture [tɛkstyʀ] *nf* texture; (*fig: d'un texte, livre*) feel.

TF1 *sigle f* (= *Télévision française 1*) *TV channel.*

TG *sigle f* = **Trésorerie générale.**

TGI *sigle m* = **tribunal de grande instance.**

TGV *sigle m* = **train à grande vitesse.**

thaï, e [taj] *a* Thai ♦ *nm* (*LING*) Thai.

thaïlandais, e [tailɑ̃dɛ, -ɛz] *a* Thai.

Thaïlande [tailɑ̃d] *nf:* **la** ~ Thailand.

thalassothérapie [talasoteʀapi] *nf* sea-water therapy.

thé [te] *nm* tea; (*réunion*) tea party; **prendre le** ~ to have tea; ~ **au lait/citron** tea with milk/lemon.

théâtral, e, aux [teɑtʀal, -o] *a* theatrical.

théâtre [teɑtʀ(ə)] *nm* theatre; (*techniques, genre*) drama, theatre; (*activité*) stage, theatre; (*œuvres*) plays *pl*, dramatic works *pl*; (*fig: lieu*): **le** ~ **de** the scene of; (*péj*) histrionics *pl*, playacting; **faire du** ~ (*en professionnel*) to be on the stage; (*en amateur*) to do some acting; ~ **filmé** filmed stage productions *pl*.

thébain, e [tebɛ̃, -ɛn] *a* Theban.

Thèbes [tɛb] *n* Thebes.

théière [tejɛʀ] *nf* teapot.

théine [tein] *nf* theine.

théisme [teism(ə)] *nm* theism.

thématique [tematik] *a* thematic.

thème [tɛm] *nm* theme; (*SCOL: traduction*) prose (composition); ~ **astral** birth chart.

théocratie [teɔkʀasi] *nf* theocracy.

théologie [teɔlɔʒi] *nf* theology.

théologien, ne [teɔlɔʒjɛ̃, -ɛn] *nm* theologian.

théologique [teɔlɔʒik] *a* theological.

théorème [teɔʀɛm] *nm* theorem.

théoricien, ne [teɔʀisjɛ̃, -ɛn] *nm/f*

theoretician, theorist.

théorie [teɔʀi] *nf* theory; **en** ~ in theory.

théorique [teɔʀik] *a* theoretical.

théoriser [teɔʀize] *vi* to theorize.

thérapeutique [teʀapøtik] *a* therapeutic ♦ *nf* (*MÉD: branche*) therapeutics *sg*; (*: traitement*) therapy.

thérapie [teʀapi] *nf* therapy.

thermal, e, aux [tɛʀmal, -o] *a* thermal; **station** ~**e** spa; **cure** ~**e** water cure.

thermes [tɛʀm(ə)] *nmpl* thermal baths; (*romains*) thermae *pl*.

thermique [tɛʀmik] *a* (*énergie*) thermic; (*unité*) thermal.

thermodynamique [tɛʀmodinamik] *nf* thermodynamics *sg*.

thermomètre [tɛʀmɔmɛtʀ(ə)] *nm* thermometer.

thermonucléaire [tɛʀmonykleɛʀ] *a* thermonuclear.

thermos [tɛʀmos] *nm ou nf* ®: **(bouteille)** ~ vacuum *ou* Thermos ® flask (*Brit*) *ou* bottle (*US*).

thermostat [tɛʀmosta] *nm* thermostat.

thésauriser [tezoʀize] *vi* to hoard money.

thèse [tɛz] *nf* thesis (*pl* theses).

Thessalie [tesali] *nf:* **la** ~ Thessaly.

thessalien, ne [tesaljɛ̃, -ɛn] *a* Thessalian.

thibaude [tibod] *nf* carpet underlay.

thon [tɔ̃] *nm* tuna (fish).

thoracique [tɔʀasik] *a* thoracic.

thorax [tɔʀaks] *nm* thorax.

thrombose [tʀɔ̃boz] *nf* thrombosis.

thym [tɛ̃] *nm* thyme.

thyroïde [tiʀɔid] *nf* thyroid (gland).

TI *sigle m* = **tribunal d'instance.**

tiare [tjaʀ] *nf* tiara.

Tibet [tibɛ] *nm:* **le** ~ Tibet.

tibétain, e [tibetɛ̃, -ɛn] *a* Tibetan.

tibia [tibja] *nm* shin; (*os*) shinbone, tibia.

Tibre [tibʀ(ə)] *nm:* **le** ~ the Tiber.

tic [tik] *nm* tic, (nervous) twitch; (*de langage etc*) mannerism.

ticket [tikɛ] *nm* ticket; ~ **de caisse** till receipt; ~ **modérateur** *patient's contribution towards medical costs*; ~ **de quai** platform ticket; ~ **repas** luncheon voucher.

tic-tac [tiktak] *nm inv* tick-tock.

tictaquer [tiktake] *vi* to tick (away).

tiède [tjɛd] *a* (*bière etc*) lukewarm; (*thé, café etc*) tepid; (*bain, accueil, sentiment*) lukewarm; (*vent, air*) mild, warm ♦ *ad:* **boire** ~ to drink things lukewarm.

tièdement [tjɛdmɑ̃] *ad* coolly, half-heartedly.

tiédir [tjediʀ] *vi* (*se réchauffer*) to grow warmer; (*refroidir*) to cool.

tien, tienne [tjɛ̃, tjɛn] *pronom:* **le** ~ **(la tienne)**, **les** ~**s (tiennes)** yours; **à la tienne!** cheers!

tiendrai [tjɛ̃dʀe] *etc vb voir* **tenir.**

tienne [tjɛn] *vb, excl voir* **tenir.**

tiens [tjɛ̃] *vb, excl voir* **tenir.**

tierce [tjɛʀs(ə)] *af, nf voir* **tiers.**

tiercé [tjɛʀse] *nm* system of forecast betting giving first 3 horses.

tiers, tierce [tjɛʀ, tjɛʀs(ə)] *a* third ♦ *nm* (*JUR*) third party; (*fraction*) third ♦ *nm* (*MUS*) third; (*CARTES*) tierce; **une tierce personne** a third party; **assurance au** ~ third-party insurance;

le ~ **monde** the third world; ~ **payant** *direct payment by insurers of medical expenses*; ~ **provisionnel** *interim payment of tax*.

tiersmondisme [tjɛrmɔ̃dism(ə)] *nm* support for the Third World.

TIG *sigle m* = **travail d'intérêt général**.

tige [tiʒ] *nf* stem; (*baguette*) rod.

tignasse [tiɲas] *nf* (*péj*) shock *ou* mop of hair.

Tigre [tigʀ(ə)] *nm*: **le** ~ the Tigris.

tigre [tigʀ(ə)] *nm* tiger.

tigré, e [tigʀe] *a* (*rayé*) striped; (*tacheté*) spotted.

tigresse [tigʀɛs] *nf* tigress.

tilleul [tijœl] *nm* lime (tree), linden (tree); (*boisson*) lime(-blossom) tea.

tilt [tilt(ə)] *nm*: **faire** ~ (*fig: échouer*) to miss the target; (*: inspirer*) to ring a bell.

timbale [tɛ̃bal] *nf* (metal) tumbler; ~**s** *nfpl* (*MUS*) timpani, kettledrums.

timbrage [tɛ̃bʀaʒ] *nm*: **dispensé de** ~ post(age) paid.

timbre [tɛ̃bʀ(ə)] *nm* (*tampon*) stamp; (*aussi*: ~**-poste**) (postage) stamp; (*cachet de la poste*) postmark; (*sonnette*) bell; (*MUS: de voix, instrument*) timbre, tone; ~ **dateur** date stamp.

timbré, e [tɛ̃bʀe] *a* (*enveloppe*) stamped; (*voix*) resonant; (*fam: fou*) cracked, nuts.

timbrer [tɛ̃bʀe] *vt* to stamp.

timide [timid] *a* (*emprunté*) shy, timid; (*timoré*) timid, timorous.

timidement [timidmɑ̃] *ad* shyly; timidly.

timidité [timidite] *nf* shyness; timidity.

timonerie [timonʀi] *nf* wheelhouse.

timonier [timɔnje] *nm* helmsman.

timoré, e [timɔʀe] *a* timorous.

tint [tɛ̃] *etc vb voir* **tenir**.

tintamarre [tɛ̃tamar] *nm* din, uproar.

tintement [tɛ̃tmɑ̃] *nm* ringing, chiming; ~**s d'oreilles** ringing in the ears.

tinter [tɛ̃te] *vi* to ring, chime; (*argent, clefs*) to jingle.

Tipp-Ex [tipɛks] *nm* ® Tipp-Ex ®.

tique [tik] *nf* tick (*insect*).

tiquer [tike] *vi* (*personne*) to make a face.

TIR *sigle mpl* (= *Transports internationaux routiers*) TIR.

tir [tiʀ] *nm* (*sport*) shooting; (*fait ou manière de tirer*) firing *q*; (*FOOTBALL*) shot; (*stand*) shooting gallery; ~ **d'obus/de mitraillette** shell/machine gun fire; ~ **à l'arc** archery; ~ **de barrage** barrage fire; ~ **au fusil** (rifle) shooting; ~ **au pigeon** (*d'argile*) clay pigeon shooting.

tirade [tiʀad] *nf* tirade.

tirage [tiʀaʒ] *nm* (*action*) printing; (*PHOTO*) print; (*INFORM*) printout; (*de journal*) circulation; (*de livre*) (print-)run; edition; (*de cheminée*) draught (*Brit*), draft (*US*); (*de loterie*) draw; (*fig: désaccord*) friction; ~ **au sort** drawing lots.

tiraillement [tiʀajmɑ̃] *nm* (*douleur*) sharp pain; (*fig: doutes*) agony *q* of indecision; (*conflits*) friction *q*.

tirailler [tiʀaje] *vt* to pull at, tug at; (*fig*) to gnaw at ♦ *vi* to fire at random.

tirailleur [tiʀajœʀ] *nm* skirmisher.

tirant [tiʀɑ̃] *nm*: ~ **d'eau** draught (*Brit*), draft (*US*).

tire [tiʀ] *nf*: **vol à la** ~ pickpocketing.

tiré [tiʀe] *a* (*visage, traits*) drawn ♦ *nm* (*COMM*) drawee; ~ **par les cheveux** far-fetched; ~ **à part** off-print.

tire-au-flanc [tiʀoflɑ̃] *nm inv* (*péj*) skiver.

tire-bouchon [tiʀbuʃɔ̃] *nm* corkscrew.

tire-bouchonner [tiʀbuʃɔne] *vt* to twirl.

tire-d'aile [tiʀdɛl]: **à** ~ *ad* swiftly.

tire-fesses [tiʀfɛs] *nm inv* ski-tow.

tire-lait [tiʀlɛ] *nm inv* breast-pump.

tire-larigot [tiʀlaʀigo]: **à** ~ *ad* as much as one likes, to one's heart's content.

tirelire [tiʀliʀ] *nf* moneybox.

tirer [tiʀe] *vt* (*gén*) to pull; (*extraire*): ~ **qch de** to take *ou* pull sth out of; to get sth out of; to extract sth from; (*tracer: ligne, trait*) to draw, trace; (*fermer: volet, porte, trappe*) to pull to, close; (*: rideau*) to draw; (*choisir: carte, conclusion, aussi COMM: chèque*) to draw; (*en faisant feu: balle, coup*) to fire; (*: animal*) to shoot; (*journal, livre, photo*) to print; (*FOOTBALL: corner etc*) to take ♦ *vi* (*faire feu*) to fire; (*faire du tir, FOOTBALL*) to shoot; (*cheminée*) to draw; **se** ~ *vi* (*fam*) to push off; **s'en** ~ to pull through; ~ **sur** (*corde, poignée*) to pull on *ou* at; (*faire feu sur*) to shoot *ou* fire at; (*pipe*) to draw on; (*fig: avoisiner*) to verge *ou* border on; ~ **6 mètres** (*NAVIG*) to draw 6 metres of water; ~ **son nom de** to take *ou* get its name from; ~ **la langue** to stick out one's tongue; ~ **qn de** (*embarras etc*) to help *ou* get sb out of; ~ **à l'arc/la carabine** to shoot with a bow and arrow/with a rifle; ~ **en longueur** to drag on; ~ **à sa fin** to be drawing to an end; ~ **les cartes** to read *ou* tell the cards.

tiret [tiʀɛ] *nm* dash; (*en fin de ligne*) hyphen.

tireur, euse [tiʀœʀ, -øz] *nm/f* gunman; (*COMM*) drawer; **bon** ~ good shot; ~ **d'élite** marksman; ~ **de cartes** fortuneteller.

tiroir [tiʀwaʀ] *nm* drawer.

tiroir-caisse [tiʀwaʀkɛs] *nm* till.

tisane [tizan] *nf* herb tea.

tison [tizɔ̃] *nm* brand.

tisonner [tizɔne] *vt* to poke.

tisonnier [tizɔnje] *nm* poker.

tissage [tisaʒ] *nm* weaving *q*.

tisser [tise] *vt* to weave.

tisserand, e [tisʀɑ̃, -ɑ̃d] *nm/f* weaver.

tissu [tisy] *nm* fabric, material, cloth *q*; (*fig*) fabric; (*ANAT, BIO*) tissue; ~ **de mensonges** web of lies.

tissu, e [tisy] *a*: ~ **de** woven through with.

tissu-éponge [tisyepɔ̃ʒ] *nm* (terry) towelling *q*.

titane [titan] *nm* titanium.

titanesque [titanɛsk(ə)] *a* titanic.

titiller [titile] *vt* to titillate.

titre [titʀ(ə)] *nm* (*gén*) title; (*de journal*) headline; (*diplôme*) qualification; (*COMM*) security; (*CHIMIE*) titre; **en** ~ (*champion, responsable*) official, recognized; **à juste** ~ with just cause, rightly; **à quel** ~**?** on what grounds?; **à aucun** ~ on no account; **au même** ~ (**que**) in the same way (as); **au** ~ **de la coopération** *etc* in the name of co-operation *etc*; **à** ~ **d'exemple** as an *ou* by way of an example; **à** ~ **exceptionnel** exceptionally; **à** ~ **d'information** for (your) information; **à ~ gracieux** free of charge; **à ~ d'essai** on a trial basis; **à ~ privé** in a private capacity; **~ courant** running head; **~ de propriété** title deed; **~ de transport** ticket.

titré, e [titʀe] *a* (*livre, film*) entitled; (*personne*) titled.

titrer [titʀe] *vt* (*CHIMIE*) to titrate; to assay; (*PRESSE*) to run as a headline; (*suj: vin*): **~ 10°** to be 10° proof.

titubant, e [titybɑ̃, -ɑ̃t] *a* staggering, reeling.

tituber [titybe] *vi* to stagger *ou* reel (along).

titulaire [titylɛʀ] *a* (*ADMIN*) appointed, with tenure ♦ *nm* (*ADMIN*) incumbent; **être ~ de** to hold.

titulariser [titylaʀize] *vt* to give tenure to.

TNP *sigle m = Théâtre national populaire*.

TNT *sigle m* (= *Trinitrotoluène*) TNT.

toast [tost] *nm* slice *ou* piece of toast; (*de bienvenue*) (welcoming) toast; **porter un ~ à** qn to propose *ou* drink a toast to sb.

toboggan [tɔbɔgɑ̃] *nm* toboggan; (*jeu*) slide; (*AUTO*) flyover (*Brit*), overpass (*US*); **~ de secours** (*AVIAT*) escape chute.

toc [tɔk] *nm*: **en ~** imitation *cpd*.

tocsin [tɔksɛ̃] *nm* alarm (bell).

toge [tɔʒ] *nf* toga; (*de juge*) gown.

Togo [tɔgo] *nm*: **le ~** Togo.

togolais, e [tɔgɔlɛ, -ɛz] *a* Togolese.

tohu-bohu [tɔybɔy] *nm* (*désordre*) confusion; (*tumulte*) commotion.

toi [twa] *pronom* you; **~, tu l'as fait?** did YOU do it?

toile [twal] *nf* (*matériau*) cloth *q*; (*bâche*) piece of canvas; (*tableau*) canvas; **grosse ~** canvas; **tisser sa ~** (*araignée*) to spin its web; **~ d'araignée** spider's web; (*au plafond etc: à enlever*) cobweb; **~ cirée** oilcloth; **~ émeri** emery cloth; **~ de fond** (*fig*) backdrop; **~ de jute** hessian; **~ de lin** linen; **~ de tente** canvas.

toilettage [twalɛtaʒ] *nm* grooming *q*; (*d'un texte*) tidying up.

toilette [twalɛt] *nf* wash; (*s'habiller et se préparer*) getting ready, washing and dressing; (*habits*) outfit; dress *q*; **~s** *nfpl* toilet *sg*; **les ~s des dames/messieurs** the ladies'/gents' (toilets) (*Brit*), the ladies'/mens' (rest)room (*US*); **faire sa ~** to have a wash, get washed; **faire la ~ de** (*animal*) to groom; (*voiture etc*) to clean, wash; (*texte*) to tidy up; **articles de ~** toiletries; **~ intime** personal hygiene.

toi-même [twamɛm] *pronom* yourself.

toise [twaz] *nf*: **passer à la ~** to have one's height measured.

toiser [twaze] *vt* to eye up and down.

toison [twazɔ̃] *nf* (*de mouton*) fleece; (*cheveux*) mane.

toit [twa] *nm* roof; **~ ouvrant** sun roof.

toiture [twatyʀ] *nf* roof.

Tokyo [tɔkjo] *n* Tokyo.

tôle [tol] *nf* sheet metal *q*; (*plaque*) steel (*ou* iron) sheet; **~s** *nfpl* (*carrosserie*) bodywork *sg* (*Brit*), body *sg*; panels; **~ d'acier** sheet steel *q*; **~ ondulée** corrugated iron.

Tolède [tɔlɛd] *n* Toledo.

tolérable [tɔleʀabl(ə)] *a* tolerable, bearable.

tolérance [tɔleʀɑ̃s] *nf* tolerance; (*hors taxe*) allowance.

tolérant, e [tɔleʀɑ̃, -ɑ̃t] *a* tolerant.

tolérer [tɔleʀe] *vt* to tolerate; (*ADMIN*: *hors taxe etc*) to allow.

tôlerie [tolʀi] *nf* sheet metal manufacture; (*atelier*) sheet metal workshop; (*ensemble des tôles*) panels *pl*.

tollé [tɔle] *nm*: **un ~ (de protestations)** a general outcry.

TOM [*parfois*: tɔm] *sigle m(pl)* = *territoire(s) d'outre-mer*.

tomate [tɔmat] *nf* tomato.

tombal, e [tɔ̃bal] *a*: **pierre ~e** tombstone, gravestone.

tombant, e [tɔ̃bɑ̃, -ɑ̃t] *a* (*fig*) drooping, sloping.

tombe [tɔ̃b] *nf* (*sépulture*) grave; (*avec monument*) tomb.

tombeau, x [tɔ̃bo] *nm* tomb; **à ~ ouvert** at breakneck speed.

tombée [tɔ̃be] *nf*: **à la ~ du jour** *ou* **de la nuit** at the close of day, at nightfall.

tomber [tɔ̃be] *vi* to fall ♦ *vt*: **~ la veste** to slip off one's jacket; **laisser ~** to drop; **~ sur** *vt* (*rencontrer*) to come across; (*attaquer*) to set about; **~ de fatigue/sommeil** to drop from exhaustion/be falling asleep on one's feet; **~ à l'eau** (*fig*: *projet etc*) to fall through; **~ en panne** to break down; **~ juste** (*opération, calcul*) to come out right; **~ en ruine** to fall into ruins; **ça tombe bien/mal** (*fig*) that's come at the right/wrong time; **il est bien/mal tombé** (*fig*) he's been lucky/unlucky.

tombereau, x [tɔ̃bʀo] *nm* tipcart.

tombeur [tɔ̃bœʀ] *nm* (*péj*) Casanova.

tombola [tɔ̃bɔla] *nf* tombola.

Tombouctou [tɔ̃buktu] *n* Timbuktu.

tome [tɔm] *nm* volume.

tommette [tɔmɛt] *nf* hexagonal floor tile.

ton, ta, *pl* **tes** [tɔ̃, ta, te] *dét* your.

ton [tɔ̃] *nm* (*gén*) tone; (*MUS*) key; (*couleur*) shade, tone; (*de la voix: hauteur*) pitch; **donner le ~** to set the tone; **élever** *ou* **hausser le ~** to raise one's voice; **de bon ~** in good taste; **si vous le prenez sur ce ~** if you're going to take it like that; **~ sur ~** in matching shades.

tonal, e [tɔnal] *a* tonal.

tonalité [tɔnalite] *nf* (*au téléphone*) dialling tone; (*MUS*) tonality; (: *ton*) key; (*fig*) tone.

tondeuse [tɔ̃døz] *nf* (*à gazon*) (lawn)mower; (*du coiffeur*) clippers *pl*; (*pour la tonte*) shears *pl*.

tondre [tɔ̃dʀ(ə)] *vt* (*pelouse, herbe*) to mow; (*haie*) to cut, clip; (*mouton, toison*) to shear; (*cheveux*) to crop.

tondu, e [tɔ̃dy] *pp de* **tondre** ♦ *a* (*cheveux*) cropped; (*mouton, crâne*) shorn.

Tonga [tɔ̃ga]: **les îles ~** Tonga.

tonicité [tɔnisite] *nf* (*MÉD*: *des tissus*) tone; (*fig*: *de l'air, la mer*) bracing effect.

tonifiant, e [tɔnifjɑ̃, -ɑ̃t] *a* invigorating, revivifying.

tonifier [tɔnifje] *vt* (*air, eau*) to invigorate; (*peau, organisme*) to tone up.

tonique [tɔnik] *a* fortifying; (*personne*) dynamic ♦ *nm, nf* tonic.

tonitruant, e [tɔnitʀyɑ̃, -ɑ̃t] *a*: **voix ~e**

thundering voice.

Tonkin [tɔ̃kɛ̃] *nm*: **le ~** Tonkin, Tongking.

tonkinois, e [tɔ̃kinwa, -waz] *a* Tonkinese.

tonnage [tɔnaʒ] *nm* tonnage.

tonnant, e [tɔnɑ̃, -ɑ̃t] *a* thunderous.

tonne [tɔn] *nf* metric ton, tonne.

tonneau, x [tɔno] *nm* (*à vin, cidre*) barrel; (*NAVIG*) ton; **faire des ~x** (*voiture, avion*) to roll over.

tonnelet [tɔnlɛ] *nm* keg.

tonnelier [tɔnəlje] *nm* cooper.

tonnelle [tɔnɛl] *nf* bower, arbour (*Brit*), arbor (*US*).

tonner [tɔne] *vi* to thunder; (*parler avec véhémence*): **~ contre qn/qch** to inveigh against sb/sth; **il tonne** it is thundering, there's some thunder.

tonnerre [tɔnɛʀ] *nm* thunder; **coup de ~** (*fig*) thunderbolt, bolt from the blue; **un ~ d'applaudissements** thunderous applause; **du ~** *a* (*fam*) terrific.

tonsure [tɔ̃syʀ] *nf* bald patch; (*de moine*) tonsure.

tonte [tɔ̃t] *nf* shearing.

tonus [tɔnys] *nm* (*des muscles*) tone; (*d'une personne*) dynamism.

top [tɔp] *nm*: **au 3ème ~** at the 3rd stroke ♦ *a*: **~ secret** top secret ♦ *excl* go!

topaze [tɔpaz] *nf* topaz.

toper [tɔpe] *vi*: **tope-/topez-là** it's a deal!, you're on!

topinambour [tɔpinɑ̃buʀ] *nm* Jerusalem artichoke.

topo [tɔpo] *nm* (*discours, exposé*) talk; (*fam*) spiel.

topographie [tɔpɔgʀafi] *nf* topography.

topographique [tɔpɔgʀafik] *a* topographical.

toponymie [tɔpɔnimi] *nf* study of place-names, toponymy.

toquade [tɔkad] *nf* fad, craze.

toque [tɔk] *nf* (*de fourrure*) fur hat; **~ de jockey/juge** jockey's/judge's cap; **~ de cuisinier** chef's hat.

toqué, e [tɔke] *a* (*fam*) touched, cracked.

torche [tɔʀʃ(ə)] *nf* torch; **se mettre en ~** (*parachute*) to candle.

torcher [tɔʀʃe] *vt* (*fam*) to wipe.

torchère [tɔʀʃɛʀ] *nf* flare.

torchon [tɔʀʃɔ̃] *nm* cloth, duster; (*à vaisselle*) tea towel *ou* cloth.

tordre [tɔʀdʀ(ə)] *vt* (*chiffon*) to wring; (*barre, fig: visage*) to twist; **se ~** *vi* (*barre*) to bend; (*roue*) to twist, buckle; (*ver, serpent*) to writhe; **se ~ le pied/bras** to twist one's foot/arm; **se ~ de douleur/rire** to writhe in pain/be doubled up with laughter.

tordu, e [tɔʀdy] *pp de* **tordre** ♦ *a* (*fig*) warped, twisted.

torero [tɔʀeʀo] *nm* bullfighter.

tornade [tɔʀnad] *nf* tornado.

toron [tɔʀɔ̃] *nm* strand (of rope).

Toronto [tɔʀɔ̃to] *n* Toronto.

torontois, e [tɔʀɔ̃twa, -waz] *a* Torontonian ♦ *nm/f*: **T~, e** Torontonian.

torpeur [tɔʀpœʀ] *nf* torpor, drowsiness.

torpille [tɔʀpij] *nf* torpedo.

torpiller [tɔʀpije] *vt* to torpedo.

torpilleur [tɔʀpijœʀ] *nm* torpedo boat.

torréfaction [tɔʀefaksjɔ̃] *nf* roasting.

torréfier [tɔʀefje] *vt* to roast.

torrent [tɔʀɑ̃] *nm* torrent, mountain stream; (*fig*): **un ~ de** a torrent *ou* flood of; **il pleut à ~s** the rain is lashing down.

torrentiel, le [tɔʀɑ̃sjɛl] *a* torrential.

torride [tɔʀid] *a* torrid.

tors, torse *ou* **torte** [tɔʀ, tɔʀs(ə) *ou* tɔʀt(ə)] *a* twisted.

torsade [tɔʀsad] *nf* twist; (*ARCHIT*) cable moulding (*Brit*) *ou* molding (*US*).

torsader [tɔʀsade] *vt* to twist.

torse [tɔʀs(ə)] *nm* torso; (*poitrine*) chest.

torsion [tɔʀsjɔ̃] *nf* (*action*) twisting; (*TECH, PHYSIQUE*) torsion.

tort [tɔʀ] *nm* (*défaut*) fault; (*préjudice*) wrong *q*; **~s** *nmpl* (*JUR*) fault *sg*; **avoir ~** to be wrong; **être dans son ~** to be in the wrong; **donner ~ à qn** to lay the blame on sb; (*fig*) to prove sb wrong; **causer du ~ à** to harm; to be harmful *ou* detrimental to; **en ~** in the wrong, at fault; **à ~** wrongly; **à ~ ou à raison** rightly or wrongly; **à ~ et à travers** wildly.

torte [tɔʀt(ə)] *af voir* **tors**.

torticolis [tɔʀtikɔli] *nm* stiff neck.

tortiller [tɔʀtije] *vt* (*corde, mouchoir*) to twist; (*doigts*) to twiddle; **se ~** *vi* to wriggle, squirm.

tortionnaire [tɔʀsjɔnɛʀ] *nm* torturer.

tortue [tɔʀty] *nf* tortoise; (*fig*) slowcoach (*Brit*), slowpoke (*US*).

tortueux, euse [tɔʀtɥø, -øz] *a* (*rue*) twisting; (*fig*) tortuous.

torture [tɔʀtyʀ] *nf* torture.

torturer [tɔʀtyʀe] *vt* to torture; (*fig*) to torment.

torve [tɔʀv(ə)] *a*: **regard ~** menacing *ou* grim look.

toscan, e [tɔskɑ̃, -an] *a* Tuscan.

Toscane [tɔskan] *nf*: **la ~** Tuscany.

tôt [to] *ad* early; **~ ou tard** sooner or later; **si ~** so early; (*déjà*) so soon; **au plus ~** at the earliest, as soon as possible; **plus ~** earlier; **il eut ~ fait de faire ...** he soon did ....

total, e, aux [tɔtal, -o] *a, nm* total; **au ~** in total *ou* all; (*fig*) all in all; **faire le ~** to work out the total.

totalement [tɔtalmɑ̃] *ad* totally, completely.

totalisateur [tɔtalizatœʀ] *nm* adding machine.

totaliser [tɔtalize] *vt* to total (up).

totalitaire [tɔtalitɛʀ] *a* totalitarian.

totalitarisme [tɔtalitaʀism(ə)] *nm* totalitarianism.

totalité [tɔtalite] *nf*: **la ~ de**: **la ~ des élèves** all (of) the pupils; **la ~ de la population/classe** the whole population/class; **en ~** entirely.

totem [tɔtɛm] *nm* totem.

toubib [tubib] *nm* (*fam*) doctor.

touchant, e [tuʃɑ̃, -ɑ̃t] *a* touching.

touche [tuʃ] *nf* (*de piano, de machine à écrire*) key; (*de violon*) fingerboard; (*de télécommande etc*) key, button; (*PEINTURE etc*) stroke, touch; (*fig: de couleur, nostalgie*) touch, hint; (*RUGBY*) line-out; (*FOOTBALL: aussi:* **remise en ~**) throw-in; (*aussi:* **ligne de ~**) touch-line; (*ESCRIME*) hit; **en ~** in (*ou* into) touch; **avoir une drôle de ~** to look a sight; **~ de commande/de fonction/de**

retour (*INFORM*) control/function/return key; **~ à effleurement** *ou* **sensitive** touch-sensitive control *ou* key.

touche-à-tout [tuʃatu] *nm inv* (*péj: gén: enfant*) meddler; (*: fig: inventeur etc*) dabbler.

toucher [tuʃe] *nm* touch ♦ *vt* to touch; (*palper*) to feel; (*atteindre: d'un coup de feu etc*) to hit; (*affecter*) to touch, affect; (*concerner*) to concern, affect; (*contacter*) to reach, contact; (*recevoir: récompense*) to receive, get; (*: salaire*) to draw, get; (*chèque*) to cash; (*aborder: problème, sujet*) to touch on; **au ~** to the touch; by the feel; **se ~** (*être en contact*) to touch; **~ à** to touch; (*modifier*) to touch, tamper *ou* meddle with; (*traiter de, concerner*) to have to do with, concern; **je vais lui en ~ un mot** I'll have a word with him about it; **~ au but** (*fig*) to near one's goal; **~ à sa fin** to be drawing to a close.

touffe [tuf] *nf* tuft.

touffu, e [tufy] *a* thick, dense; (*fig*) complex, involved.

toujours [tuʒuR] *ad* always; (*encore*) still; (*constamment*) forever; **depuis ~** always; **essaie ~** (you can) try anyway; **pour ~** forever; **~ est-il que** the fact remains that; **~ plus** more and more.

toulonnais, e [tulɔnɛ, -ɛz] *a* of *ou* from Toulon.

toulousain, e [tuluzɛ̃, -ɛn] *a* of *ou* from Toulouse.

toupet [tupɛ] *nm* quiff (*Brit*), tuft; (*fam*) nerve, cheek (*Brit*).

toupie [tupi] *nf* (spinning) top.

tour [tuR] *nf* tower; (*immeuble*) high-rise block (*Brit*) *ou* building (*US*), tower block (*Brit*); (*ÉCHECS*) castle, rook ♦ *nm* (*excursion: à pied*) stroll, walk; (*: en voiture etc*) run, ride; (*: plus long*) trip; (*SPORT: aussi: ~ de piste*) lap; (*d'être servi ou de jouer etc, tournure, de vis ou clef*) turn; (*de roue etc*) revolution; (*circonférence*): **de 3 m de ~** 3 m round, with a circumference *ou* girth of 3 m; (*POL: aussi: ~ de scrutin*) ballot; (*ruse, de prestidigitation, de cartes*) trick; (*de potier*) wheel; (*à bois, métaux*) lathe; **faire le ~ de** to go (a)round; (*à pied*) to walk (a)round; (*fig*) to review; **faire le ~ de l'Europe** to tour Europe; **faire un ~** to go for a walk; (*en voiture etc*) to go for a ride; **faire 2 ~s** to go (a)round twice; (*hélice etc*) to turn *ou* revolve twice; **fermer à double ~** *vi* to double-lock the door; **c'est au ~ de Renée** it's Renée's turn; **à ~ de rôle, ~ à ~** in turn; **à ~ de bras** with all one's strength; (*fig*) non-stop, relentlessly; **~ de taille/tête** waist/head measurement; **~ de chant** song recital; **~ de contrôle** *nf* control tower; **~ de garde** spell of duty; **~ d'horizon** (*fig*) general survey; **~ de lit** valance; **~ de main** dexterity, knack; **en un ~ de main** (as) quick as a flash; **~ de passe-passe** trick, sleight of hand; **~ de reins** sprained back.

tourangeau, elle, x [tuRɑ̃ʒo, -el] *a* (*de la région*) of *ou* from Touraine; (*de la ville*) of *ou* from Tours.

tourbe [tuRb(ə)] *nf* peat.

tourbière [tuRbjɛR] *nf* peat-bog.

tourbillon [tuRbijɔ̃] *nm* whirlwind; (*d'eau*) whirlpool; (*fig*) whirl, swirl.

tourbillonner [tuRbijɔne] *vi* to whirl, swirl; (*objet, personne*) to whirl *ou* twirl round.

tourelle [tuRɛl] *nf* turret.

tourisme [tuRism(ə)] *nm* tourism; **agence de ~** tourist agency; **avion/voiture de ~** private plane/car; **faire du ~** to do some sightseeing, go touring.

touriste [tuRist(ə)] *nm/f* tourist.

touristique [tuRistik] *a* tourist *cpd*; (*région*) touristic (*péj*), with tourist appeal.

tourment [tuRmɑ̃] *nm* torment.

tourmente [tuRmɑ̃t] *nf* storm.

tourmenté, e [tuRmɑ̃te] *a* tormented, tortured; (*mer, période*) turbulent, tempestuous.

tourmenter [tuRmɑ̃te] *vt* to torment; **se ~** *vi* to fret, worry o.s.

tournage [tuRnaʒ] *nm* (*d'un film*) shooting.

tournant, e [tuRnɑ̃, -ɑ̃t] *a* (*feu, scène*) revolving; (*chemin*) winding; (*escalier*) spiral *cpd*; (*mouvement*) circling; voir **plaque**, **grève** ♦ *nm* (*de route*) bend (*Brit*), curve (*US*); (*fig*) turning point.

tourné, e [tuRne] *a* (*lait, vin*) sour, off; (*MENUISERIE: bois*) turned; (*fig: compliment*) well-phrased; **bien ~** (*personne*) shapely; **mal ~** (*lettre*) badly expressed; **avoir l'esprit mal ~** to have a dirty mind.

tournebroche [tuRnəbRɔʃ] *nm* roasting spit.

tourne-disque [tuRnədisk(ə)] *nm* record player.

tournedos [tuRnədo] *nm* tournedos.

tournée [tuRne] *nf* (*du facteur etc*) round; (*d'artiste, politicien*) tour; (*au café*) round (of drinks); **~ électorale/musicale** election/concert tour; **faire la ~ de** to go (a)round.

tournemain [tuRnəmɛ̃]: **en un ~** *ad* in a flash.

tourner [tuRne] *vt* to turn; (*sauce, mélange*) to stir; (*contourner*) to get (a)round; (*CINÉMA*) to shoot; to make ♦ *vi* to turn; (*moteur*) to run; (*compteur*) to tick away; (*lait etc*) to turn (sour); (*fig: chance, vie*) to turn out; **se ~** *vi* to turn (a)round; **se ~ vers** to turn to; to turn towards; **bien ~** to turn out well; **~ autour de** to go (a)round; (*planète*) to revolve (a)round; (*péj*) to hang (a)round; **~ autour du pot** (*fig*) to go (a)round in circles; **~ à/en** to turn into; **~ à la pluie/au rouge** to turn rainy/red; **~ en ridicule** to ridicule; **~ le dos à** (*mouvement*) to turn one's back on; (*position*) to have one's back to; **~ court** to come to a sudden end; **se ~ les pouces** to twiddle one's thumbs; **~ la tête** to look away; **~ la tête à qn** (*fig*) to go to sb's head; **~ de l'œil** to pass out; **~ la page** (*fig*) to turn the page.

tournesol [tuRnəsɔl] *nm* sunflower.

tourneur [tuRnœR] *nm* turner; lathe-operator.

tournevis [tuRnəvis] *nm* screwdriver.

tourniquer [tuRnike] *vi* to go (a)round in circles.

tourniquet [tuRnikɛ] *nm* (*pour arroser*) sprinkler; (*portillon*) turnstile; (*présentoir*) revolving stand, spinner; (*CHIRURGIE*) tourniquet.

tournis [tuRni] *nm*: **avoir/donner le ~** to feel/make dizzy.

tournoi [tuʀnwa] *nm* tournament.

tournoyer [tuʀnwaje] *vi* (*oiseau*) to wheel (a)round; (*fumée*) to swirl (a)round.

tournure [tuʀnyʀ] *nf* (*LING*: *syntaxe*) turn of phrase; form; (: *d'une phrase*) phrasing; (*évolution*): **la ~ de qch** the way sth is developing; (*aspect*): **la ~ de** the look of; **la ~ des événements** the turn of events; **prendre ~** to take shape; **~ d'esprit** turn *ou* cast of mind.

tour-opérateur [tuʀɔpeʀatœʀ] *nm* tour operator.

tourte [tuʀt(ə)] *nf* pie.

tourteau, x [tuʀto] *nm* (*AGR*) oilcake, cattlecake; (*ZOOL*) edible crab.

tourtereaux [tuʀtəʀo] *nmpl* lovebirds.

tourterelle [tuʀtəʀɛl] *nf* turtledove.

tourtière [tuʀtjɛʀ] *nf* pie dish *ou* plate.

tous *dét* [tu] , *pronom* [tus] *voir* **tout**.

Toussaint [tusɛ̃] *nf*: **la ~** All Saints' Day.

tousser [tuse] *vi* to cough.

toussoter [tusɔte] *vi* to have a slight cough; to cough a little; (*pour avertir*) to give a slight cough.

tout, e, *pl* **tous, toutes** [tu, tus, tut] *dét* all; **~ le lait** all the milk, the whole of the milk; **~e la nuit** all night, the whole night; **~ le livre** the whole book; **~ un pain** a whole loaf; **tous les livres** all the books; **toutes les nuits** every night; **à ~ âge** at any age; **toutes les fois** every time; **toutes les 3/2 semaines** every third/other *ou* second week; **tous les 2** both *ou* each of us (*ou* them); **toutes les 3** all 3 of us (*ou* them); **~ le temps** *ad* all the time; (*sans cesse*) the whole time; **c'est ~ le contraire** it's quite the opposite; **il avait pour ~e nourriture** his only food was ♦ *pronom* everything, all; **tous, toutes** all (of them); **je les vois tous** I can see them all *ou* all of them; **nous y sommes tous allés** all of us went, we all went; **en ~** in all; **en ~ et pour ~ all** in all ♦ *ad* (*assez*) quite; (*très*) very; **~ en haut** right at the top; **le ~ premier** the very first; **le livre ~ entier** the whole book; **~ court** quite simply; **~ seul** all alone; **~ droit** straight ahead; **~ en travaillant/mangeant** while working/eating, as *ou* while he *etc* works/eats ♦ *nm* whole; **le ~ all of it** (*ou* them), the whole lot; **le ~ est de** the main thing is to; **du ~ au ~** (*complètement*) utterly; **avoir ~ de: elle a ~ d'une mère** she's a real mother; **~ ce que ...** all that ...; **~ ce qu'il y a de plus aimable** the nicest possible, as nice as possible; **~ ou rien** all or nothing; **~ d'abord** first of all; **~ à coup** suddenly; **~ à fait** absolutely; **~ à l'heure** (*passé*) a short while ago; (*futur*) in a short while, shortly; **à ~ à l'heure!** see you later!; **~ de même** all the same; **~ le monde** everybody, everyone; **~ de suite** immediately, straightaway; **~ terrain** *ou* **tous terrains** *a inv* all-terrain.

tout-à-l'égout [tutalegu] *nm inv* mains drainage.

toutefois [tutfwa] *ad* however.

toutou [tutu] *nm* (*fam*) doggie.

tout-petit [tup(ə)ti] *nm* toddler.

tout-puissant, toute-puissante [tupɥisɑ̃, tutpɥisɑ̃t] *a* all-powerful, omnipotent.

tout-venant [tuvnɑ̃] *nm*: **le ~** everyday stuff.

toux [tu] *nf* cough.

toxémie [tɔksemi] *nf* toxaemia (*Brit*), toxemia (*US*).

toxicité [tɔksisite] *nf* toxicity.

toxicomane [tɔksikɔman] *nm/f* drug addict.

toxicomanie [tɔksikɔmani] *nf* drug addiction.

toxine [tɔksin] *nf* toxin.

toxique [tɔksik] *a* toxic, poisonous.

TP *sigle mpl* = **travaux pratiques, travaux publics** ♦ *sigle m* = **trésor public**.

TPG *sigle m* = **Trésorier-payeur général**.

tps *abr* = **temps**.

trac [tʀak] *nm* nerves *pl*; (*THÉÂTRE*) stage fright; **avoir le ~** to get an attack of nerves; to have stage fright; **tout à ~** all of a sudden.

traçant, e [tʀasɑ̃, -ɑ̃t] *a*: **table ~e** (*INFORM*) (graph) plotter.

tracas [tʀaka] *nm* bother *q*, worry *q*.

tracasser [tʀakase] *vt* to worry, bother; (*harceler*) to harass; **se ~** *vi* to worry o.s., fret.

tracasserie [tʀakasʀi] *nf* annoyance *q*; harassment *q*.

tracassier, ière [tʀakasje, -jɛʀ] *a* irksome.

trace [tʀas] *nf* (*empreintes*) tracks *pl*; (*marques, aussi fig*) mark; (*restes, vestige*) trace; (*indice*) sign; **suivre à la ~** to track; **~s de pas** footprints.

tracé [tʀase] *nm* (*contour*) line; (*plan*) layout.

tracer [tʀase] *vt* to draw; (*mot*) to trace; (*piste*) to open up; (*fig: chemin*) to show.

traceur [tʀasœʀ] *nm* (*INFORM*) plotter.

trachée(-artère) [tʀaʃe(aʀtɛʀ)] *nf* windpipe, trachea.

trachéite [tʀakeit] *nf* tracheitis.

tract [tʀakt] *nm* tract, pamphlet; (*publicitaire*) handout.

tractations [tʀaktɑsjɔ̃] *nfpl* dealings, bargaining *sg*.

tracter [tʀakte] *vt* to tow.

tracteur [tʀaktœʀ] *nm* tractor.

traction [tʀaksjɔ̃] *nf* traction; (*GYM*) pull-up; **~ avant/arrière** front-wheel/rear-wheel drive; **~ électrique** electric(al) traction *ou* haulage.

tradition [tʀadisjɔ̃] *nf* tradition.

traditionaliste [tʀadisjɔnalist(ə)] *a*, *nm/f* traditionalist.

traditionnel, le [tʀadisjɔnɛl] *a* traditional.

traditionnellement [tʀadisjɔnɛlmɑ̃] *ad* traditionally.

traducteur, trice [tʀadyktœʀ, -tʀis] *nm/f* translator.

traduction [tʀadyksjɔ̃] *nf* translation.

traduire [tʀadɥiʀ] *vt* to translate; (*exprimer*) to render, convey; **se ~ par** to find expression in; **~ en français** to translate into French; **~ en justice** to bring before the courts.

traduis [tʀadɥi] *etc vb voir* **traduire**.

traduisible [tʀadɥizibl(ə)] *a* translatable.

traduit, e [tʀadɥi, -it] *pp de* **traduire**.

trafic [tʀafik] *nm* traffic; **~ d'armes** arms dealing; **~ de drogue** drug peddling.

trafiquant, e [tʀafikɑ̃, -ɑ̃t] *nm/f* trafficker; dealer.

trafiquer [tʀafike] *vt* (*péj*) to doctor, tamper with ♦ *vi* to traffic, be engaged in trafficking.

tragédie [tʀaʒedi] *nf* tragedy.

tragédien, ne [tʀaʒedjɛ̃, -ɛn] *nm/f* tragedian/ tragedienne.

tragi-comique [tʀaʒikɔmik] *a* tragi-comic.

tragique [tʀaʒik] *a* tragic ♦ *nm*: **prendre qch au** ~ to make a tragedy out of sth.

tragiquement [tʀaʒikmɑ̃] *ad* tragically.

trahir [tʀaiʀ] *vt* to betray; *(fig)* to give away, reveal; **se** ~ to betray o.s., give o.s. away.

trahison [tʀaizɔ̃] *nf* betrayal; *(JUR)* treason.

traie [tʀɛ] *etc vb voir* **traire**.

train [tʀɛ̃] *nm* (*RAIL*) train; *(allure)* pace; *(fig: ensemble)* set; **être en** ~ **de faire qch** to be doing sth; **mettre qch en** ~ to get sth under way; **mettre qn en** ~ to put sb in good spirits; **se mettre en** ~ *(commencer)* to get started; *(faire de la gymnastique)* to warm up; **se sentir en** ~ to feel in good form; **aller bon** ~ to make good progress; ~ **avant/ arrière** front-wheel/rear-wheel axle unit; ~ **à grande vitesse (TGV)** high-speed train; ~ **d'atterrissage** undercarriage; ~**-autos- couchettes** car-sleeper train; ~ **électrique** *(jouet)* (electric) train set; ~ **de pneus** set of tyres *ou* tires; ~ **de vie** style of living.

traînailler [tʀɛnɑje] *vi* = **traînasser**.

traînant, e [tʀɛnɑ̃, -ɑ̃t] *a* *(voix, ton)* drawling.

traînard, e [tʀɛnaʀ, -aʀd(ə)] *nm/f* *(péj)* slowcoach *(Brit)*, slowpoke *(US)*.

traînasser [tʀɛnase] *vi* to dawdle.

traîne [tʀɛn] *nf* *(de robe)* train; **être à la** ~ to be in tow; *(en arrière)* to lag behind; *(en désordre)* to be lying around.

traîneau, x [tʀɛno] *nm* sleigh, sledge.

traînée [tʀɛne] *nf* streak, trail; *(péj)* slut.

traîner [tʀɛne] *vt* *(remorque)* to pull; *(enfant, chien)* to drag *ou* trail along; *(maladie)*: **il traîne un rhume depuis l'hiver** he has a cold which has been dragging on since winter ♦ *vi* *(être en désordre)* to lie around; *(marcher lentement)* to dawdle (along); *(vagabonder)* to hang about; *(agir lentement)* to idle about; *(durer)* to drag on; **se** ~ *vi* *(ramper)* to crawl along; *(marcher avec difficulté)* to drag o.s. along; *(durer)* to drag on; **se** ~ **par terre** to crawl (on the ground); ~ **qn au cinéma** to drag sb to the cinema; ~ **les pieds** to drag one's feet; ~ **par terre** to trail on the ground; ~ **en longueur** to drag out.

training [tʀɛniŋ] *nm* *(pull)* tracksuit top; *(chaussure)* trainer *(Brit)*, sneaker *(US)*.

train-train [tʀɛ̃tʀɛ̃] *nm* humdrum routine.

traire [tʀɛʀ] *vt* to milk.

trait, e [tʀɛ, -ɛt] *pp de* **traire** ♦ *nm* *(ligne)* line; *(de dessin)* stroke; *(caractéristique)* feature, trait; *(flèche)* dart, arrow; shaft; ~**s** *nmpl* *(du visage)* features; **d'un** ~ *(boire)* in one gulp; **de** ~ *a* *(animal)* draught *(Brit)*, draft *(US)*; **avoir** ~ **à** to concern; ~ **pour** ~ line for line; ~ **de caractère** characteristic, trait; ~ **d'esprit** flash of wit; ~ **de génie** brainwave; ~ **d'union** hyphen; *(fig)* link.

traitable [tʀɛtabl(ə)] *a* *(personne)* accommodating; *(sujet)* manageable.

traitant, e [tʀɛtɑ̃, -ɑ̃t] *a*: **votre médecin** ~ your usual *ou* family doctor; **shampooing** ~ medicated shampoo; **crème** ~**e** conditioning cream, conditioner.

traite [tʀɛt] *nf* *(COMM)* draft; *(AGR)* milking; *(trajet)* stretch; **d'une (seule)** ~ without stopping (once); **la** ~ **des noirs** the slave trade; **la** ~ **des blanches** the white slave trade.

traité [tʀɛte] *nm* treaty.

traitement [tʀɛtmɑ̃] *nm* treatment; process- ing; *(salaire)* salary; **suivre un** ~ to undergo treatment; **mauvais** ~ ill-treatment; ~ **de données** *ou* **de l'information** *(INFORM)* data processing; ~ **par lots** *(INFORM)* batch processing; ~ **de texte** *(INFORM)* word processing.

traiter [tʀɛte] *vt* *(gén)* to treat; *(TECH: maté- riaux)* to process, treat; *(INFORM)* to pro- cess; *(affaire)* to deal with, handle; *(quali- fier)*: ~ **qn d'idiot** to call sb a fool ♦ *vi* to deal; ~ **de** *vt* to deal with; **bien/mal** ~ to treat well/ill-treat.

traiteur [tʀɛtœʀ] *nm* caterer.

traître, esse [tʀɛtʀ(ə), -tʀɛs] *a* *(dangereux)* treacherous ♦ *nm* traitor; **prendre qn en** ~ to make an insidious attack on sb.

traîtrise [tʀɛtʀiz] *nf* treachery.

trajectoire [tʀaʒɛktwaʀ] *nf* trajectory, path.

trajet [tʀaʒɛ] *nm* journey; *(itinéraire)* route; *(fig)* path, course.

tralala [tʀalala] *nm* *(péj)* fuss.

tram [tʀam] *nm* tram *(Brit)*, streetcar *(US)*.

trame [tʀam] *nf* *(de tissu)* weft; *(fig)* frame- work; texture; *(TYPO)* screen.

tramer [tʀame] *vt* to plot, hatch.

trampoline [tʀɑ̃pɔlin], **trampolino** [tʀɑ̃pɔlino] *nm* trampoline; *(SPORT)* trampolining.

tramway [tʀamwɛ] *nm* tram(way); *(voiture)* tram(car) *(Brit)*, streetcar *(US)*.

tranchant, e [tʀɑ̃ʃɑ̃, -ɑ̃t] *a* sharp; *(fig: personne)* peremptory; *(: couleurs)* striking ♦ *nm* *(d'un couteau)* cutting edge; *(de la main)* edge; **à double** ~ *(argument, procédé)* double-edged.

tranche [tʀɑ̃ʃ] *nf* *(morceau)* slice; *(arête)* edge; *(partie)* section; *(série)* block; *(d'impôts, revenus etc)* bracket; *(loterie)* issue; ~ **d'âge** age bracket; ~ **(de silicium)** wafer.

tranché, e [tʀɑ̃ʃe] *a* *(couleurs)* distinct, sharply contrasted; *(opinions)* clear-cut, definite ♦ *nf* trench.

trancher [tʀɑ̃ʃe] *vt* to cut, sever; *(fig: ré- soudre)* to settle ♦ *vi* to be decisive; *(entre deux choses)* to settle the argument; ~ **avec** to contrast sharply with.

tranchet [tʀɑ̃ʃɛ] *nm* knife.

tranchoir [tʀɑ̃ʃwaʀ] *nm* chopper.

tranquille [tʀɑ̃kil] *a* calm, quiet; *(enfant, élève)* quiet; *(rassuré)* easy in one's mind, with one's mind at rest; **se tenir** ~ *(enfant)* to be quiet; **avoir la conscience** ~ to have an easy conscience; **laisse-moi/laisse-ça** ~ leave me/it alone.

tranquillement [tʀɑ̃kilmɑ̃] *ad* calmly.

tranquillisant, e [tʀɑ̃kiliza, -ɑ̃t] *a* *(nouvelle)* reassuring ♦ *nm* tranquillizer.

tranquilliser [tʀɑ̃kilize] *vt* to reassure; **se** ~ to calm (o.s.) down.

tranquillité [tʀɑ̃kilite] *nf* quietness; peace (and quiet); **en toute** ~ with complete peace of mind; ~ **d'esprit** peace of mind.

transaction [tʀɑ̃zaksjɔ̃] *nf* *(COMM)* transaction, deal.

transafricain, e [tʀɑ̃safʀikɛ̃, -ɛn] *a* transafrican.

transalpin, e [tʀɑ̃zalpɛ̃, -in] *a* transalpine.

transaméricain, e [tʀɑ̃zameʀikɛ̃, -ɛn] *a* transamerican.

transat [tʀɑ̃zat] *nm* deckchair ♦ *nf* = *course transatlantique.*

transatlantique [tʀɑ̃zatlɑ̃tik] *a* transatlantic ♦ *nm* transatlantic liner.

transborder [tʀɑ̃sbɔʀde] *vt* to tran(s)ship.

transcendant, e [tʀɑ̃sɑ̃dɑ̃, -ɑ̃t] *a* (*PHILOSOPHIE*, *MATH*) transcendental; (*supérieur*) transcendent.

transcodeur [tʀɑ̃skɔdœʀ] *nm* compiler.

transcription [tʀɑ̃skʀipsjɔ̃] *nf* transcription.

transcrire [tʀɑ̃skʀiʀ] *vt* to transcribe.

transe [tʀɑ̃s] *nf*: **entrer en ~** to go into a trance; **~s** *nfpl* agony *sg*.

transfèrement [tʀɑ̃sfɛʀmɑ̃] *nm* transfer.

transférer [tʀɑ̃sfeʀe] *vt* to transfer.

transfert [tʀɑ̃sfɛʀ] *nm* transfer.

transfigurer [tʀɑ̃sfigyʀe] *vt* to transform.

transfo [tʀɑ̃sfo] *nm* (= *transformateur*) transformer.

transformable [tʀɑ̃sfɔʀmabl(ə)] *a* convertible.

transformateur [tʀɑ̃sfɔʀmatœʀ] *nm* transformer.

transformation [tʀɑ̃sfɔʀmasjɔ̃] *nf* transformation; (*RUGBY*) conversion; **industries de ~** processing industries.

transformer [tʀɑ̃sfɔʀme] *vt* to transform, alter (*'alter' implique un changement moins radical*); (*matière première, appartement, RUGBY*) to convert; **~ en** to transform into; to turn into; to convert into; **se ~** *vi* to be transformed; to alter.

transfuge [tʀɑ̃sfyʒ] *nm* renegade.

transfuser [tʀɑ̃sfyze] *vt* to transfuse.

transfusion [tʀɑ̃sfyzjɔ̃] *nf*: **~ sanguine** blood transfusion.

transgresser [tʀɑ̃sgʀese] *vt* to contravene, disobey.

transhumance [tʀɑ̃zymɑ̃s] *nf* transhumance, seasonal move to new pastures.

transi, e [tʀɑ̃zi] *a* numb (with cold), chilled to the bone.

transiger [tʀɑ̃ziʒe] *vi* to compromise, come to an agreement; **~ sur** *ou* **avec qch** to compromise on sth.

transistor [tʀɑ̃zistɔʀ] *nm* transistor.

transistorisé, e [tʀɑ̃zistɔʀize] *a* transistorized.

transit [tʀɑ̃zit] *nm* transit; **de ~** transit *cpd*; **en ~** in transit.

transitaire [tʀɑ̃zitɛʀ] *nm/f* forwarding agent.

transiter [tʀɑ̃zite] *vi* to pass in transit.

transitif, ive [tʀɑ̃zitif, -iv] *a* transitive.

transition [tʀɑ̃zisjɔ̃] *nf* transition; **de ~** transitional.

transitoire [tʀɑ̃zitwaʀ] *a* (*mesure, gouvernement*) transitional, provisional; (*fugitif*) transient.

translucide [tʀɑ̃slysid] *a* translucent.

transmet [tʀɑ̃smɛ] *etc vb voir* **transmettre**.

transmettais [tʀɑ̃smɛtɛ] *etc vb voir* **transmettre**.

transmetteur [tʀɑ̃smɛtœʀ] *nm* transmitter.

transmettre [tʀɑ̃smɛtʀ(ə)] *vt* (*passer*): **~ qch à qn** to pass sth on to sb; (*TECH, TÉL, MÉD*) to transmit; (*TV, RADIO: retransmettre*) to broadcast.

transmis, e [tʀɑ̃smi, -iz] *pp de* **transmettre**.

transmissible [tʀɑ̃smisibl(ə)] *a* transmissible.

transmission [tʀɑ̃smisjɔ̃] *nf* transmission, passing on; (*AUTO*) transmission; **~s** *nfpl* (*MIL*) ≈ signals corps; **~ de données** (*INFORM*) data transmission; **~ de pensée** thought transmission.

transocéanien, ne [tʀɑ̃zɔseanjɛ̃, -ɛn] *a*, **transocéanique** [tʀɑ̃zɔseanik] *a* transoceanic.

transparaître [tʀɑ̃spaʀɛtʀ(ə)] *vi* to show (through).

transparence [tʀɑ̃spaʀɑ̃s] *nf* transparence; **par ~** (*regarder*) against the light; (*voir*) showing through.

transparent, e [tʀɑ̃spaʀɑ̃, -ɑ̃t] *a* transparent.

transpercer [tʀɑ̃spɛʀse] *vt* to go through, pierce.

transpiration [tʀɑ̃spiʀasjɔ̃] *nf* perspiration.

transpirer [tʀɑ̃spiʀe] *vi* to perspire; (*information, nouvelle*) to come to light.

transplant [tʀɑ̃splɑ̃] *nm* transplant.

transplantation [tʀɑ̃splɑ̃tasjɔ̃] *nf* transplant.

transplanter [tʀɑ̃splɑ̃te] *vt* (*MÉD, BOT*) to transplant; (*personne*) to uproot, move.

transport [tʀɑ̃spɔʀ] *nm* transport; (*émotions*): **~ de colère** fit of rage; **~ de joie** transport of delight; **~ de voyageurs/marchandises** passenger/goods transportation; **~s en commun** public transport *sg*; **~s routiers** haulage (*Brit*), trucking (*US*).

transportable [tʀɑ̃spɔʀtabl(ə)] *a* (*marchandises*) transportable; (*malade*) fit (enough) to be moved.

transporter [tʀɑ̃spɔʀte] *vt* to carry, move; (*COMM*) to transport, convey; (*fig*): **~ qn (de joie)** to send sb into raptures; **se ~ quelque part** (*fig*) to let one's imagination carry one away (somewhere); **~ qn à l'hôpital** to take sb to hospital.

transporteur [tʀɑ̃spɔʀtœʀ] *nm* haulage contractor (*Brit*), trucker (*US*).

transposer [tʀɑ̃spoze] *vt* to transpose.

transposition [tʀɑ̃spozisjɔ̃] *nf* transposition.

transrhénan, e [tʀɑ̃sʀenɑ̃, -an] *a* transrhenane.

transsaharien, ne [tʀɑ̃ssaaʀjɛ̃, -ɛn] *a* trans-Saharan.

transsexuel, le [tʀɑ̃ssɛksɥɛl] *a*, *nm/f* transsexual.

transsibérien, ne [tʀɑ̃ssibeʀjɛ̃, -ɛn] *a* trans-Siberian.

transvaser [tʀɑ̃svaze] *vt* to decant.

transversal, e, aux [tʀɑ̃svɛʀsal, -o] *a* transverse, cross(-); (*route etc*) cross-country; (*mur, chemin, rue*) running at right angles; (*AUTO*): **axe ~** main cross-country road (*Brit*) *ou* highway (*US*).

transversalement [tʀɑ̃svɛʀsalmɑ̃] *ad* crosswise.

trapèze [tʀapɛz] *nm* (*GÉOM*) trapezium; (*au cirque*) trapeze.

trapéziste [tʀapezist(ə)] *nm/f* trapeze artist.

trappe [tʀap] *nf* (*de cave, grenier*) trap door; (*piège*) trap.

trappeur [tʀapœʀ] *nm* trapper, fur trader.

trapu, e [tʀapy] *a* squat, stocky.

traquenard [tʀaknaʀ] *nm* trap.

traquer [tʀake] *vt* to track down; (*harceler*) to hound.

traumatisant, e [tʀomatizɑ̃, -ɑ̃t] traumatic.

traumatiser [tʀomatize] *vt* to traumatize.

traumatisme [tʀomatism(ə)] *nm* traumatism; ~ **crânien** cranial traumatism.

traumatologie [tʀomatɔlɔʒi] *nf branch of medicine concerned with accidents.*

travail, aux [tʀavaj, -o] *nm* (*gén*) work; (*tâche, métier*) work *q*, job; (*ÉCON, MÉD*) labour (*Brit*), labor (*US*); (*INFORM*) job ♦ *nmpl* (*de réparation, agricoles etc*) work *sg*; (*sur route*) roadworks; (*de construction*) building (work) *sg*; **être/entrer en** ~ (*MÉD*) to be in/start labour; **être sans** ~ (*employé*) to be out of work, be unemployed; ~ **d'intérêt général (TIG)** ≈ community service; ~ (**au**) **noir** moonlighting; ~ **posté** shift-work; **travaux des champs** farmwork *sg*; **travaux dirigés (TD)** (*SCOL*) supervised practical work *sg*; **travaux forcés** hard labour *sg*; **travaux manuels** (*SCOL*) handi-crafts; **travaux ménagers** housework *sg*; **travaux pratiques (TP)** (*gén*) practical work; (*en laboratoire*) lab work (*Brit*), lab (*US*); **travaux publics (TP)** ≈ public works *sg*.

travaillé, e [tʀavaje] *a* (*style*) polished.

travailler [tʀavaje] *vi* to work; (*bois*) to warp ♦ *vt* (*bois, métal*) to work; (*pâte*) to knead; (*objet d'art, discipline, fig: influencer*) to work on; **cela le travaille** it is on his mind; ~ **la terre** to work the land; ~ **son piano** to do one's piano practice; ~ **à** to work on; (*fig: contribuer à*) to work towards; ~ **à faire** to endeavour (*Brit*) *ou* endeavor (*US*) to do.

travailleur, euse [tʀavajœʀ, -øz] *a* hard-working ♦ *nm/f* worker; ~ **de force** labourer (*Brit*), laborer (*US*); ~ **intellectuel** non-manual worker; ~ **social** social worker; **travailleuse familiale** home help.

travailliste [tʀavajist(ə)] *a* ≈ Labour *cpd* ♦ *nm/f* member of the Labour party.

travée [tʀave] *nf* row; (*ARCHIT*) bay; span.

travelling [tʀavliŋ] *nm* (*chariot*) dolly; (*technique*) tracking; ~ **optique** zoom shots *pl*.

travelo [tʀavlo] *nm* (*fam*) (drag) queen.

travers [tʀavɛʀ] *nm* fault, failing; **en** ~ (**de**) across; **au** ~ (**de**) through; **de** ~ *a* askew ♦ *ad* sideways; (*fig*) the wrong way; **à** ~ through; **regarder de** ~ (*fig*) to look askance at.

traverse [tʀavɛʀs(ə)] *nf* (*de voie ferrée*) sleeper; **chemin de** ~ shortcut.

traversée [tʀavɛʀse] *nf* crossing.

traverser [tʀavɛʀse] *vt* (*gén*) to cross; (*ville, tunnel, aussi: percer, fig*) to go through; (*suj: ligne, trait*) to run across.

traversin [tʀavɛʀsɛ̃] *nm* bolster.

travesti [tʀavɛsti] *nm* (*costume*) fancy dress; (*artiste de cabaret*) female impersonator, drag artist; (*pervers*) transvestite.

travestir [tʀavɛstiʀ] *vt* (*vérité*) to mis-represent; **se** ~ (*se costumer*) to dress up; (*artiste*) to put on drag; (*PSYCH*) to dress as a woman.

trayais [tʀɛjɛ] *etc vb voir* **traire.**

trayeuse [tʀɛjøz] *nf* milking machine.

trébucher [tʀebyʃe] *vi*: ~ (**sur**) to stumble (over), trip (over).

trèfle [tʀɛfl(ə)] *nm* (*BOT*) clover; (*CARTES: couleur*) clubs *pl*; (*: carte*) club; ~ **à quatre feuilles** four-leaf clover.

treillage [tʀɛjaʒ] *nm* lattice work.

treille [tʀɛj] *nf* (*tonnelle*) vine arbour (*Brit*) *ou* arbor (*US*); (*vigne*) climbing vine.

treillis [tʀɛji] *nm* (*métallique*) wire-mesh; (*toile*) canvas; (*uniforme*) battle-dress.

treize [tʀɛz] *num* thirteen.

treizième [tʀɛzjɛm] *num* thirteenth.

tréma [tʀema] *nm* diaeresis.

tremblant, e [tʀɑ̃blɑ̃, -ɑ̃t] *a* trembling, shak-ing.

tremble [tʀɑ̃bl(ə)] *nm* (*BOT*) aspen.

tremblé, e [tʀɑ̃ble] *a* shaky.

tremblement [tʀɑ̃bləmɑ̃] *nm* trembling *q*, shaking *q*, shivering *q*; ~ **de terre** earth-quake.

trembler [tʀɑ̃ble] *vi* to tremble, shake; ~ **de** (*froid, fièvre*) to shiver *ou* tremble with; (*peur*) to shake *ou* tremble with; ~ **pour qn** to fear for sb.

trembloter [tʀɑ̃blɔte] *vi* to tremble *ou* shake slightly.

trémolo [tʀemɔlo] *nm* (*d'un instrument*) tremolo; (*de la voix*) quaver.

trémousser [tʀemuse]: **se** ~ *vi* to jig about, wriggle about.

trempe [tʀɑ̃p] *nf* (*fig*): **de cette/sa** ~ of this/his calibre (*Brit*) *ou* caliber (*US*).

trempé, e [tʀɑ̃pe] *a* soaking (wet), drenched; (*TECH*): **acier** ~ tempered steel.

tremper [tʀɑ̃pe] *vt* to soak, drench; (*aussi:* **faire** ~, **mettre à** ~) to soak; (*plonger*): ~ **qch dans** to dip sth in(to) ♦ *vi* to soak; (*fig*): ~ **dans** to be involved *ou* have a hand in; **se** ~ *vi* to have a quick dip; **se faire** ~ to get soaked *ou* drenched.

trempette [tʀɑ̃pɛt] *nf*: **faire** ~ to go paddling.

tremplin [tʀɑ̃plɛ̃] *nm* springboard; (*SKI*) ski-jump.

trentaine [tʀɑ̃tɛn] *nf* (*âge*): **avoir la** ~ to be around thirty; **une** ~ (**de**) thirty or so, about thirty.

trente [tʀɑ̃t] *num* thirty; **voir** ~-**six chandelles** (*fig*) to see stars; **être/se mettre sur son** ~ **et un** to be/get dressed to kill; ~-**trois tours** *nm* long-playing record, LP.

trentième [tʀɑ̃tjɛm] *num* thirtieth.

trépaner [tʀepane] *vt* to trepan, trephine.

trépasser [tʀepase] *vi* to pass away.

trépidant, e [tʀepidɑ̃, -ɑ̃t] *a* (*fig: rythme*) pulsating; (*: vie*) hectic.

trépidation [tʀepidasjɔ̃] *nf* (*d'une machine, d'un moteur*) vibration; (*fig: de la vie*) whirl.

trépider [tʀepide] *vi* to vibrate.

trépied [tʀepje] *nm* (*d'appareil*) tripod; (*meuble*) trivet.

trépigner [tʀepiɲe] *vi* to stamp (one's feet).

très [tʀɛ] *ad* very; much + *pp*, highly + *pp*; ~ **beau/bien** very beautiful/well; ~ **critiqué** much criticized; ~ **industrialisé** highly in-dustrialized; **j'ai** ~ **faim** I'm very hungry.

trésor [tʀezɔʀ] *nm* treasure; (*ADMIN*) finances *pl*; (*d'un organisation*) funds *pl*; ~ (**public**) **(TP)** public revenue; (*service*) public revenue office.

trésorerie [tʀezɔʀʀi] *nf* (*fonds*) funds *pl*;

(gestion) accounts *pl*; *(bureaux)* accounts department; *(poste)* treasurership; **difficultés de** ~ cash problems, shortage of cash *ou* funds; ~ **générale (TG)** *local government finance office.*
trésorier, ière [tʀezɔʀje, -jɛʀ] *nm/f* treasurer.
trésorier-payeur [tʀezɔʀjepɛjœʀ] *nm*: ~ **général (TPG)** paymaster.
tressaillement [tʀesajmɑ̃] *nm* shiver, shudder; quiver.
tressaillir [tʀesajiʀ] *vi (de peur etc)* to shiver, shudder; *(de joie)* to quiver.
tressauter [tʀesote] *vi* to start, jump.
tresse [tʀɛs] *nf (de cheveux)* braid, plait; *(cordon, galon)* braid.
tresser [tʀese] *vt (cheveux)* to braid, plait; *(fil, jonc)* to plait; *(corbeille)* to weave; *(corde)* to twist.
tréteau, x [tʀeto] *nm* trestle; **les ~x** *(fig: THÉÂTRE)* the boards.
treuil [tʀœj] *nm* winch.
trêve [tʀɛv] *nf (MIL, POL)* truce; *(fig)* respite; **sans** ~ unremittingly; ~ **de ...** enough of this ...; **les États de la T~** the Trucial States.
tri [tʀi] *nm (voir trier)* sorting (out) *q*; selection; screening; *(INFORM)* sort; *(POSTES: action)* sorting; *(: bureau)* sorting office.
triage [tʀijaʒ] *nm (RAIL)* shunting; *(gare)* marshalling yard.
triangle [tʀijɑ̃gl(ə)] *nm* triangle; **isocèle/ équilatéral** isosceles/equilateral triangle; ~ **rectangle** right-angled triangle.
triangulaire [tʀijɑ̃gylɛʀ] *a* triangular.
tribal, e, aux [tʀibal, -o] *a* tribal.
tribord [tʀibɔʀ] *nm*: **à** ~ to starboard, on the starboard side.
tribu [tʀiby] *nf* tribe.
tribulations [tʀibylɑsjɔ̃] *nfpl* tribulations, trials.
tribunal, aux [tʀibynal, -o] *nm (JUR)* court; *(MIL)* tribunal; ~ **de police/pour enfants** police/juvenile court; ~ **d'instance (TI)** ≈ magistrates' court *(Brit)*, ≈ district court *(US)*; ~ **de grande instance (TGI)** ≈ High Court *(Brit)*, ≈ Supreme Court *(US)*.
tribune [tʀibyn] *nf (estrade)* platform, rostrum; *(débat)* forum; *(d'église, de tribunal)* gallery; *(de stade)* stand; ~ **libre** *(PRESSE)* opinion column.
tribut [tʀiby] *nm* tribute.
tributaire [tʀibytɛʀ] *a*: **être** ~ **de** to be dependent on; *(GÉO)* to be a tributary of.
tricentenaire [tʀisɑ̃tnɛʀ] *nm* tercentenary, tricentennial.
tricher [tʀiʃe] *vi* to cheat.
tricherie [tʀiʃʀi] *nf* cheating *q*.
tricheur, euse [tʀiʃœʀ, -øz] *nm/f* cheat.
trichromie [tʀikʀɔmi] *nf* three-colour *(Brit) ou* -color *(US)* printing.
tricolore [tʀikɔlɔʀ] *a* three-coloured *(Brit)*, three-colored *(US)*; *(français: drapeau)* red, white and blue; *(: équipe etc)* French.
tricot [tʀiko] *nm (technique, ouvrage)* knitting *q*; *(tissu)* knitted fabric; *(vêtement)* jersey, sweater; ~ **de corps** vest *(Brit)*, undershirt *(US)*.
tricoter [tʀikɔte] *vt* to knit; **machine/aiguille à** ~ knitting machine/needle *(Brit) ou* pin *(US)*.
trictrac [tʀiktʀak] *nm* backgammon.

tricycle [tʀisikl(ə)] *nm* tricycle.
triennal, e, aux [tʀiɛnal, -o] *a (prix, foire, élection)* three-yearly; *(charge, mandat, plan)* three-year.
trier [tʀije] *vt (classer)* to sort (out); *(choisir)* to select; *(visiteurs)* to screen; *(POSTES, INFORM)* to sort.
trieur, euse [tʀijœʀ, -øz] *nm/f* sorter.
trigonométrie [tʀigɔnɔmetʀi] *nf* trigonometry.
trilingue [tʀilɛ̃g] *a* trilingual.
trilogie [tʀilɔʒi] *nf* trilogy.
trimbaler [tʀɛ̃bale] *vt* to cart around, trail along.
trimer [tʀime] *vi* to slave away.
trimestre [tʀimɛstʀ(ə)] *nm (SCOL)* term; *(COMM)* quarter.
trimestriel, le [tʀimɛstʀijɛl] *a* quarterly; *(SCOL)* end-of-term.
tringle [tʀɛ̃gl(ə)] *nf* rod.
Trinité [tʀinite] *nf* Trinity.
Trinité et Tobago [tʀiniteetɔbago] *nf* Trinidad and Tobago.
trinquer [tʀɛ̃ke] *vi* to clink glasses; *(fam)* to cop it; ~ **à qch/la santé de qn** to drink to sth/sb.
trio [tʀijo] *nm* trio.
triolet [tʀijɔle] *nm (MUS)* triplet.
triomphal, e, aux [tʀijɔ̃fal, -o] *a* triumphant, triumphal.
triomphant, e [tʀijɔ̃fɑ̃, -ɑ̃t] *a* triumphant.
triomphateur, trice [tʀijɔ̃fatœʀ, -tʀis] *nm/f (triumphant)* victor.
triomphe [tʀijɔ̃f] *nm* triumph; **être reçu/porté en** ~ to be given a triumphant welcome/be carried shoulder-high in triumph.
triompher [tʀijɔ̃fe] *vi* to triumph; ~ **de** to triumph over, overcome.
triparti, e [tʀipaʀti] *a (aussi: **tripartite**: réunion, assemblée)* tripartite, three-party.
triperie [tʀipʀi] *nf* tripe shop.
tripes [tʀip] *nfpl (CULIN)* tripe *sg*; *(fam)* guts.
triplace [tʀiplas] *a* three-seater *cpd*.
triple [tʀipl(ə)] *a (à trois éléments)* triple; *(trois fois plus grand)* treble ♦ *nm*: **le** ~ **(de)** *(comparaison)* three times as much (as); **en** ~ **exemplaire** in triplicate.
triplé [tʀiple] *nm* hat-trick *(Brit)*, triple success.
triplement [tʀipləmɑ̃] *ad (à un degré triple)* three times over; *(de trois façons)* in three ways; *(pour trois raisons)* on three counts ♦ *nm* trebling, threefold increase.
tripler [tʀiple] *vi, vt* to triple, treble, increase threefold.
triplés, es [tʀiple] *nm/fpl* triplets.
Tripoli [tʀipɔli] *n* Tripoli.
tripot [tʀipo] *nm (péj)* dive.
tripotage [tʀipɔtaʒ] *nm (péj)* jiggery-pokery.
tripoter [tʀipɔte] *vt* to fiddle with, finger ♦ *vi (fam)* to rummage about.
trique [tʀik] *nf* cudgel.
trisannuel, le [tʀizanɥɛl] *a* triennial.
triste [tʀist(ə)] *a* sad; *(péj)*: ~ **personnage/ affaire** sorry individual/affair; **c'est pas** ~! *(fam)* it's something else!
tristement [tʀistəmɑ̃] *ad* sadly.
tristesse [tʀistɛs] *nf* sadness.
triton [tʀitɔ̃] *nm* triton.
triturer [tʀityʀe] *vt (pâte)* to knead; *(objets)*

to manipulate.

trivial, e, aux [tʀivjal, -o] *a* coarse, crude; (*commun*) mundane.

trivialité [tʀivjalite] *nf* coarseness, crudeness; mundaneness.

troc [tʀɔk] *nm* (*ÉCON*) barter; (*transaction*) exchange, swap.

troène [tʀɔɛn] *nm* privet.

troglodyte [tʀɔglɔdit] *nm/f* cave dweller, troglodyte.

trognon [tʀɔɲɔ̃] *nm* (*de fruit*) core; (*de légume*) stalk.

trois [tʀwa] *num* three.

trois-huit [tʀwaɥit] *nm inv*: **faire les ~ to** work eight-hour shifts (round the clock).

troisième [tʀwazjɛm] *num* third; **le ~ âge** the years of retirement.

troisièmement [tʀwazjɛmmɑ̃] *ad* thirdly.

trois-quarts [tʀwakaʀ] *nmpl*: **les ~ de** three-quarters of.

trolleybus [tʀɔlɛbys] *nm* trolley bus.

trombe [tʀɔ̃b] *nf* waterspout; **des ~s d'eau** a downpour; **en ~** (*arriver, passer*) like a whirlwind.

trombone [tʀɔ̃bɔn] *nm* (*MUS*) trombone; (*de bureau*) paper clip; **~ à coulisse** slide trombone.

tromboniste [tʀɔ̃bɔnist(ə)] *nm/f* trombonist.

trompe [tʀɔ̃p] *nf* (*d'éléphant*) trunk; (*MUS*) trumpet, horn; **~ d'Eustache** Eustachian tube; **~s utérines** Fallopian tubes.

trompe-l'œil [tʀɔ̃plœj] *nm*: **en ~** in trompe-l'œil style.

tromper [tʀɔ̃pe] *vt* to deceive; (*fig: espoir, attente*) to disappoint; (*vigilance, poursuivants*) to elude; **se ~** *vi* to make a mistake, be mistaken; **se ~ de voiture/jour** to take the wrong car/get the day wrong; **se ~ de 3 cm/20 F** to be out by 3 cm/20 F.

tromperie [tʀɔ̃pʀi] *nf* deception, trickery *q*.

trompette [tʀɔ̃pɛt] *nf* trumpet; **en ~** (*nez*) turned-up.

trompettiste [tʀɔ̃petist(ə)] *nm/f* trumpet player.

trompeur, euse [tʀɔ̃pœʀ, -øz] *a* deceptive, misleading.

tronc [tʀɔ̃] *nm* (*BOT, ANAT*) trunk; (*d'église*) collection box; **~ d'arbre** tree trunk; **~ commun** (*SCOL*) common-core syllabus; **~ de cône** truncated cone.

tronche [tʀɔ̃ʃ] *nf* (*fam*) mug, face.

tronçon [tʀɔ̃sɔ̃] *nm* section.

tronçonner [tʀɔ̃sɔne] *vt* (*arbre*) to saw up; (*pierre*) to cut up.

tronçonneuse [tʀɔ̃sɔnøz] *nf* chain saw.

trône [tʀon] *nm* throne; **monter sur le ~ to** ascend the throne.

trôner [tʀone] *vi* (*fig*) to have (*ou* take) pride of place (*Brit*), have the place of honour (*Brit*) *ou* honor (*US*).

tronquer [tʀɔ̃ke] *vt* to truncate; (*fig*) to curtail.

trop [tʀo] *ad vb* + too much, too + *adjectif, adverbe*; **~ (nombreux)** too many; **~ peu (nombreux)** too few; **~ (souvent)** too often; **~ (longtemps)** (for) too long; **~ de** (*nombre*) too many; (*quantité*) too much; **de ~, en ~**: **des livres en ~** a few books too many, a few extra books; **du lait en ~** too

much milk; **3 livres/5 F de ~** 3 books too many/5 F too much.

trophée [tʀɔfe] *nm* trophy.

tropical, e, aux [tʀɔpikal, -o] *a* tropical.

tropique [tʀɔpik] *nm* tropic; **~s** *nmpl* tropics; **~ du Cancer/Capricorne** Tropic of Cancer/Capricorn.

trop-plein [tʀɔplɛ̃] *nm* (*tuyau*) overflow *ou* outlet (pipe); (*liquide*) overflow.

troquer [tʀɔke] *vt*: **~ qch contre** to barter *ou* trade sth for; (*fig*) to swap sth for.

trot [tʀo] *nm* trot; **aller au ~** to trot along; **partir au ~** to set off at a trot.

trotter [tʀɔte] *vi* to trot; (*fig*) to scamper along (*ou* about).

trotteuse [tʀɔtøz] *nf* (*de montre*) second hand.

trottiner [tʀɔtine] *vi* (*fig*) to scamper along (*ou* about).

trottinette [tʀɔtinɛt] *nf* (child's) scooter.

trottoir [tʀɔtwaʀ] *nm* pavement (*Brit*), sidewalk (*US*); **faire le ~** (*péj*) to walk the streets; **~ roulant** moving pavement (*Brit*) *ou* walkway.

trou [tʀu] *nm* hole; (*fig*) gap; (*COMM*) deficit; **~ d'aération** (air) vent; **~ d'air** air pocket; **~ de mémoire** blank, lapse of memory; **~ noir** black hole; **~ de la serrure** keyhole.

troublant, e [tʀublɑ̃, -ɑ̃t] *a* disturbing.

trouble [tʀubl(ə)] *a* (*liquide*) cloudy; (*image, mémoire*) indistinct, hazy; (*affaire*) shady, murky ♦ *ad* indistinctly ♦ *nm* (*désarroi*) distress, agitation; (*émoi sensuel*) turmoil, agitation; (*embarras*) confusion; (*zizanie*) unrest, discord; **~s** *nmpl* (*POL*) disturbances, troubles, unrest *sg*; (*MÉD*) trouble *sg*, disorders; **~s de la personnalité** personality problems; **~s de la vision** eye trouble.

trouble-fête [tʀubləfɛt] *nm/f inv* spoilsport.

troubler [tʀuble] *vt* (*embarrasser*) to confuse, disconcert; (*émouvoir*) to agitate; to disturb; to perturb; (*perturber: ordre etc*) to disrupt, disturb; (*liquide*) to make cloudy; **se ~** *vi* (*personne*) to become flustered *ou* confused; **~ l'ordre public** to cause a breach of the peace.

troué, e [tʀue] *a* with a hole (*ou* holes) in it ♦ *nf* gap; (*MIL*) breach.

trouer [tʀue] *vt* to make a hole (*ou* holes) in; (*fig*) to pierce.

trouille [tʀuj] *nf* (*fam*): **avoir la ~** to be scared stiff, be scared out of one's wits.

troupe [tʀup] *nf* (*MIL*) troop; (*groupe*) troop, group; **la ~** (*MIL: l'armée*) the army; (: *les simples soldats*) the troops *pl*; **~ (de théâtre)** (theatrical) company; **~s de choc** shock troops.

troupeau, x [tʀupo] *nm* (*de moutons*) flock; (*de vaches*) herd.

trousse [tʀus] *nf* case, kit; (*d'écolier*) pencil case; (*de docteur*) instrument case; **aux ~s de** (*fig*) on the heels *ou* tail of; **~ à outils** toolkit; **~ de toilette** toilet *ou* sponge (*Brit*) bag.

trousseau, x [tʀuso] *nm* (*de mariée*) trousseau; **~ de clefs** bunch of keys.

trouvaille [tʀuvaj] *nf* find; (*fig: idée, expression etc*) brainwave.

trouvé, e [tʀuve] *a*: **tout ~** ready-made.

trouver [tʀuve] vt to find; (rendre visite):
aller/venir ~ qn to go/come and see sb; **je
trouve que** I find ou think that; **~ à boire/
critiquer** to find something to drink/criticize;
~ asile/refuge to find refuge/shelter; **se ~** vi
(être) to be; (être soudain) to find o.s.; **se ~
être/avoir** to be/have; **il se trouve
que** it happens that, it turns out that; **se ~
bien** to feel well; **se ~ mal** to pass out.

truand [tʀyɑ̃] nm villain, crook.

truander [tʀyɑ̃de] vi (fam) to cheat, do.

trublion [tʀyblijɔ̃] nm troublemaker.

truc [tʀyk] nm (astuce) way, device; (de
cinéma, prestidigitateur) trick effect; (chose)
thing; (machin) thingumajig, whatsit (Brit);
avoir le ~ to have the knack; **c'est pas son
(ou mon etc) ~** (fam) it's not really his (ou
my etc) thing.

truchement [tʀyʃmɑ̃] nm: **par le ~ de qn**
through (the intervention of) sb.

trucider [tʀyside] vt (fam) to do in, bump off.

truculent, e [tʀykylɑ̃, -ɑ̃t] a colourful (Brit),
colorful (US).

truelle [tʀyɛl] nf trowel.

truffe [tʀyf] nf truffle; (nez) nose.

truffer [tʀyfe] vt (CULIN) to garnish with
truffles; **truffé de** (fig: citations) peppered
with; (: pièges) bristling with.

truie [tʀɥi] nf sow.

truite [tʀɥit] nf trout inv.

truquage [tʀyka3] nm fixing; (CINÉMA)
special effects pl.

truquer [tʀyke] vt (élections, serrure, dés) to
fix; (CINÉMA) to use special effects in.

trust [tʀœst] nm (COMM) trust.

truster [tʀœste] vt (COMM) to monopolize.

ts abr = **tous**.

tsar [dzaʀ] nm tsar.

tsé-tsé [tsetse] nf: **mouche ~** tsetse fly.

TSF sigle f (= télégraphie sans fil) wireless.

tsigane [tsigan] a, nm/f = **tzigane**.

TSVP abr (= tournez s'il vous plaît) PTO.

tt abr = **tout**.

TT(A) sigle m (= transit temporaire (autorisé)) vehicle registration for cars etc bought
in France for export tax-free by non-
residents.

TTC abr = **toutes taxes comprises**.

ttes abr = **toutes**.

TU sigle m = temps universel.

tu [ty] pronom you ♦ nm: **employer le ~** to
use the "tu" form.

tu, e [ty] pp de **taire**.

tuant, e [tɥɑ̃, -ɑ̃t] a (épuisant) killing; (énervant) infuriating.

tuba [tyba] nm (MUS) tuba; (SPORT) snorkel.

tube [tyb] nm tube; (de canalisation,
métallique etc) pipe; (chanson, disque) hit
song ou record; **~ digestif** alimentary canal,
digestive tract; **~ à essai** test tube.

tuberculeux, euse [tybɛʀkylø, -øz] a
tubercular ♦ nm/f tuberculosis ou TB patient.

tuberculose [tybɛʀkyloz] nf tuberculosis, TB.

tubulaire [tybylɛʀ] a tubular.

tubulure [tybylyʀ] nf pipe; piping q; (AUTO):
~ d'échappement/d'admission exhaust/inlet
manifold.

TUC [tyk] sigle m (= travail d'utilité collective) community work scheme for the young

unemployed.

tuciste [tysist(ə)] nm/f young person on a
community work scheme.

tué, e [tɥe] nm/f: **5 ~s** 5 killed ou dead.

tue-mouche [tymuʃ] a: **papier ~(s)** flypaper.

tuer [tɥe] vt to kill; **se ~** (se suicider) to kill
o.s.; (dans un accident) to be killed; **se ~ au
travail** (fig) to work o.s. to death.

tuerie [tyʀi] nf slaughter q, massacre.

tue-tête [tytɛt]: **à ~** ad at the top of one's
voice.

tueur [tɥœʀ] nm killer; **~ à gages** hired killer.

tuile [tɥil] nf tile; (fam) spot of bad luck,
blow.

tulipe [tylip] nf tulip.

tuméfié, e [tymefje] a puffy, swollen.

tumeur [tymœʀ] nf growth, tumour (Brit),
tumor (US).

tumulte [tymylt(ə)] nm commotion, hubbub.

tumultueux, euse [tymyltɥø, -øz] a stormy,
turbulent.

tuner [tynɛʀ] nm tuner.

tungstène [tœkstɛn] nm tungsten.

tunique [tynik] nf tunic; (de femme) smock,
tunic.

Tunis [tynis] n Tunis.

Tunisie [tynizi] nf: **la ~** Tunisia.

tunisien, ne [tynizjɛ̃, -ɛn] a Tunisian ♦ nm/f:
T~, ne Tunisian.

tunisois, e [tynizwa, -waz] a of ou from Tunis.

tunnel [tynɛl] nm tunnel.

TUP sigle m (= titre universel de paiement) ≈
payment slip.

turban [tyʀbɑ̃] nm turban.

turbin [tyʀbɛ̃] nm (fam) work q.

turbine [tyʀbin] nf turbine.

turbomoteur [tyʀbomotœʀ] nm turbo(-
boosted) engine.

turbopropulseur [tyʀbopʀopylsœʀ] nm
turboprop.

turboréacteur [tyʀboʀeaktœʀ] nm turbojet.

turbot [tyʀbo] nm turbot.

turbotrain [tyʀbotʀɛ̃] nm turbotrain.

turbulences [tyʀbylɑ̃s] nfpl (AVIAT)
turbulence sg.

turbulent, e [tyʀbylɑ̃, -ɑ̃t] a boisterous, unruly.

turc, turque [tyʀk(ə)] a Turkish; (w.-c.) seat-
less ♦ nm (LING) Turkish ♦ nm/f: **T~,
Turque** Turk/Turkish woman; **à la turque** ad
(assis) cross-legged.

turf [tyʀf] nm racing.

turfiste [tyʀfist(ə)] nm/f racegoer.

Turks et Caïques ou **Caicos** [tyʀkekaik(ɔs)]
nfpl Turks and Caicos Islands.

turpitude [tyʀpityd] nf base act, baseness q.

turque [tyʀk(ə)] af, nf voir **turc**.

Turquie [tyʀki] nf: **la ~** Turkey.

turquoise [tyʀkwaz] nf, a inv turquoise.

tut [ty] etc vb voir **taire**.

tutelle [tytɛl] nf (JUR) guardianship; (POL)
trusteeship; **sous la ~ de** (fig) under the
supervision of.

tuteur, trice [tytœʀ, -tʀis] nm/f (JUR)
guardian; (de plante) stake, support.

tutoiement [tytwamɑ̃] nm use of familiar "tu"
form.

tutoyer [tytwaje] vt: **~ qn** to address sb as

"tu".

tutti quanti [tutikwãti] *nmpl:* **et ~** and all the rest (of them).

tutu [tyty] *nm* (*DANSE*) tutu.

Tuvalu [tyvaly] *nm:* **le ~** Tuvalu.

tuyau, x [tɥijo] *nm* pipe; (*flexible*) tube; (*fam: conseil*) tip; (: *mise au courant*) gen *q;* **~ d'arrosage** hosepipe; **~ d'échappement** exhaust pipe; **~ d'incendie** fire hose.

tuyauté, e [tɥijote] *a* fluted.

tuyauterie [tɥijotʀi] *nf* piping *q.*

tuyère [tɥijɛʀ] *nf* nozzle.

TV [teve] *nf* TV, telly (*Brit*).

TVA *sigle f* = **taxe à** *ou* **sur la valeur ajoutée.**

tweed [twid] *nm* tweed.

tympan [tɛ̃pã] *nm* (*ANAT*) eardrum.

type [tip] *nm* type; (*personne, chose: représentant*) classic example, epitome; (*fam*) chap, guy ♦ *a* typical, standard; **avoir le ~ nordique** to be Nordic-looking.

typé, e [tipe] *a* ethnic (*euph*).

typhoïde [tifɔid] *nf* typhoid (fever).

typhon [tifɔ̃] *nm* typhoon.

typhus [tifys] *nm* typhus (fever).

typique [tipik] *a* typical.

typiquement [tipikmã] *ad* typically.

typographe [tipɔgʀaf] *nm/f* typographer.

typographie [tipɔgʀafi] *nf* typography; (*procédé*) letterpress (printing).

typographique [tipɔgʀafik] *a* typographical; letterpress *cpd.*

typologie [tipɔlɔʒi] *nf* typology.

tyran [tiʀã] *nm* tyrant.

tyrannie [tiʀani] *nf* tyranny.

tyrannique [tiʀanik] *a* tyrannical.

tyranniser [tiʀanize] *vt* to tyrannize.

Tyrol [tiʀɔl] *nm:* **le ~** the Tyrol.

tyrolien, ne [tiʀɔljɛ̃, -ɛn] *a* Tyrolean.

tzar [dzaʀ] *nm* = **tsar.**

tzigane [dzigan] *a* gipsy, tzigane ♦ *nm/f* (Hungarian) gipsy, Tzigane.

U

U, u [y] *nm inv* U, u ♦ *abr* (= *unité*) *10,000 francs;* **maison à vendre 50 U** house for sale: 500,000 francs; **U comme Ursule** U for Uncle.

ubiquité [ybikɥite] *nf:* **avoir le don d'~** to be everywhere at once, be ubiquitous.

UDF *sigle f* (= *Union pour la démocratie française*) *political party.*

UEFA *sigle f* (= *Union of European Football Associations*) UEFA.

UER *sigle f* (= *unité d'enseignement et de recherche*) *old title of* UFR; (= *Union européenne de radiodiffusion*) EBU (= *European Broadcasting Union*).

UFC *sigle f* (= *Union fédérale des consommateurs*) *national consumer group.*

UFR *sigle f* (= *unité de formation et de re-*

cherche) ≈ university department.

UHF *sigle f* (= *ultra-haute fréquence*) UHF.

UHT *sigle* (= *ultra-haute température*) UHT.

UIT *sigle f* (= *Union internationale des télécommunications*) ITU (= *International Telecommunications Union*).

UJP *sigle f* (= *Union des jeunes pour le progrès*) *political party.*

Ukraine [ykʀɛn] *nf:* **l'~** the Ukraine.

ukrainien, ne [ykʀɛnjɛ̃, -ɛn] *a* Ukrainian.

ulcère [ylsɛʀ] *nm* ulcer; **~ à l'estomac** stomach ulcer.

ulcérer [ylseʀe] *vt* (*MÉD*) to ulcerate; (*fig*) to sicken, appal.

ulcéreux, euse [ylseʀø, -øz] *a* (*plaie, lésion*) ulcerous; (*membre*) ulcerated.

ULM *sigle m* (= *ultra léger motorisé*) microlight.

ultérieur, e [ylteʀjœʀ] *a* later, subsequent; **remis à une date ~e** postponed to a later date.

ultérieurement [ylteʀjœʀmã] *ad* later.

ultimatum [yltimatɔm] *nm* ultimatum.

ultime [yltim] *a* final.

ultra... [yltʀa] *préfixe* ultra....

ultramoderne [yltʀamɔdɛʀn(ə)] *a* ultramodern.

ultra-rapide [yltʀaʀapid] *a* ultra-fast.

ultra-sensible [yltʀasãsibl(ə)] *a* (*PHOTO*) high-speed.

ultra-sons [yltʀasɔ̃] *nmpl* ultrasonics *sg.*

ultra-violet, te [yltʀavjɔlɛ, -ɛt] *a* ultraviolet.

ululer [ylyle] *vi* = **hululer.**

un, une [œ̃, yn] *dét* a, an + *voyelle* ♦ *pronom, num, a* one; **l'~ l'autre, les ~s les autres** each other, one another; **l'~ ..., l'autre** (the) one ..., the other; **les ~s ..., les autres** some ..., others; **l'~ et l'autre** both (of them); **l'~ ou l'autre** either (of them); **l'~ des meilleurs** one of the best; **la une** (*PRESSE*) the front page.

unanime [ynanim] *a* unanimous; **ils sont ~s (à penser que)** they are unanimous (in thinking that).

unanimement [ynanimmã] *ad* (*par tous*) unanimously; (*d'un commun accord*) with one accord.

unanimité [ynanimite] *nf* unanimity; **à l'~** unanimously; **faire l'~** to be approved unanimously.

UNEF [ynɛf] *sigle f* = *Union nationale des étudiants de France.*

UNESCO [ynɛsko] *sigle f* (= *United Nations Educational, Scientific and Cultural Organization*) UNESCO.

unetelle [yntɛl] *nf voir* **untel.**

UNI *sigle f* = *Union nationale interuniversitaire.*

uni, e [yni] *a* (*ton, tissu*) plain; (*surface*) smooth, even; (*famille*) close(-knit); (*pays*) united.

UNICEF [ynisɛf] *sigle m* (= *United Nations International Children's Emergency Fund*) UNICEF.

unième [ynjɛm] *num:* **vingt/trente et ~** twenty-/thirty-first; **cent ~** (one) hundred and first.

unificateur, trice [ynifikatœʀ, -tʀis] *a* unifying.

unification [ynifikasjɔ̃] *nf* uniting; unification;

standardization.
unifier [ynifje] *vt* to unite, unify; (*systèmes*) to standardize, unify; **s'~** to become united.
uniforme [ynifɔʀm(ə)] *a* (*mouvement*) regular, uniform; (*surface, ton*) even; (*objets, maisons*) uniform; (*fig: vie, conduite*) unchanging ♦ *nm* uniform; **être sous l'~** (*MIL*) to be serving.
uniformément [ynifɔʀmemɑ̃] *ad* uniformly.
uniformiser [ynifɔʀmize] *vt* to make uniform; (*systèmes*) to standardize.
uniformité [ynifɔʀmite] *nf* regularity; uniformity; evenness.
unijambiste [yniʒɑ̃bist(ə)] *nm/f* one-legged man/woman.
unilatéral, e, aux [ynilateʀal, -o] *a* unilateral; **stationnement ~** parking on one side only.
unilatéralement [ynilateʀalmɑ̃] *ad* unilaterally.
uninominal, e, aux [yninɔminal, -o] *a* uncontested.
union [ynjɔ̃] *nf* union; **~ conjugale** union of marriage; **~ de consommateurs** consumers' association; **~ libre** free love; **l'U~ des Républiques socialistes soviétiques (URSS)** the Union of Soviet Socialist Republics (USSR); **l'U~ soviétique** the Soviet Union.
unique [ynik] *a* (*seul*) only; (*le même*): **un prix/système ~** a single price/system; (*exceptionnel*) unique; **ménage à salaire ~** one-salary family; **route à voie ~** single-lane road; **fils/fille ~** only son/daughter, only child; **~ en France** the only one of its kind in France.
uniquement [ynikmɑ̃] *ad* only, solely; (*juste*) only, merely.
unir [yniʀ] *vt* (*nations*) to unite; (*éléments, couleurs*) to combine; (*en mariage*) to unite, join together; **~ qch à** to unite sth with; to combine sth with; **s'~** to unite; (*en mariage*) to be joined together; **s'~ à** *ou* **avec** to unite with.
unisexe [yniseks] *a* unisex.
unisson [ynisɔ̃]: **à l'~** *ad* in unison.
unitaire [yniteʀ] *a* unitary; (*POL*) unitarian; **prix ~** unit price.
unité [ynite] *nf* (*harmonie, cohésion*) unity; (*COMM, MIL, de mesure, MATH*) unit; **~ centrale (de traitement)** central processing unit (CPU); **~ de valeur (UV)** (university) course, credit.
univers [yniveʀ] *nm* universe.
universaliser [yniveʀsalize] *vt* to universalize.
universel, le [yniveʀsel] *a* universal; (*esprit*) all-embracing.
universellement [yniveʀselmɑ̃] *ad* universally.
universitaire [yniveʀsiteʀ] *a* university *cpd*; (*diplôme, études*) academic, university *cpd* ♦ *nm/f* academic.
université [yniveʀsite] *nf* university.
univoque [ynivɔk] *a* unambiguous; (*MATH*) one-to-one.
UNR *sigle f* (= *Union pour la nouvelle république*) *former political party*.
UNSS *sigle f* = *Union nationale de sport scolaire*.
untel, unetelle [œ̃tel, yntel] *nm/f* so-and-so.
uranium [yʀanjɔm] *nm* uranium.

urbain, e [yʀbɛ̃, -ɛn] *a* urban, city *cpd*, town *cpd*; (*poli*) urbane.
urbanisation [yʀbanizasjɔ̃] *nf* urbanization.
urbaniser [yʀbanize] *vt* to urbanize.
urbanisme [yʀbanism(ə)] *nm* town planning.
urbaniste [yʀbanist(ə)] *nm/f* town planner.
urbanité [yʀbanite] *nf* urbanity.
urée [yʀe] *nf* urea.
urémie [yʀemi] *nf* uraemia (*Brit*), uremia (*US*).
urgence [yʀʒɑ̃s] *nf* urgency; (*MÉD etc*) emergency; **d'~** *a* emergency *cpd* ♦ *ad* as a matter of urgency; **en cas d'~** in case of emergency; **service des ~s** emergency service.
urgent, e [yʀʒɑ̃, -ɑ̃t] *a* urgent.
urinaire [yʀineʀ] *a* urinary.
urinal, aux [yʀinal, -o] *nm* (bed) urinal.
urine [yʀin] *nf* urine.
uriner [yʀine] *vi* to urinate.
urinoir [yʀinwaʀ] *nm* (public) urinal.
urne [yʀn(ə)] *nf* (*électorale*) ballot box; (*vase*) urn; **aller aux ~s** (*voter*) to go to the polls.
urologie [yʀɔlɔʒi] *nf* urology.
URSS [*parfois:* yʀs] *sigle f* (= *Union des Républiques Socialistes Soviétiques*) USSR.
URSSAF [yʀsaf] *sigle f* (= *Union pour le recouvrement de la sécurité sociale et des allocations familiales*) *administrative body responsible for social security funds and payments*.
urticaire [yʀtikeʀ] *nf* nettle rash, urticaria.
Uruguay [yʀygwe] *nm*: **l'~** Uruguay.
uruguayen, ne [yʀygwajɛ̃, -ɛn] *a* Uruguayan ♦ *nm/f*: **U~, ne** Uruguayan.
us [ys] *nmpl*: **~ et coutumes** (habits and) customs.
US(A) *sigle mpl* (= *United States (of America)*) US(A).
usage [yzaʒ] *nm* (*emploi, utilisation*) use; (*coutume*) custom; (*éducation*) (good) manners *pl*, (good) breeding; (*LING*): **l'~** usage; **faire ~ de** (*pouvoir, droit*) to exercise; **avoir l'~ de** to have the use of; **à l'~** *ad* with use; **à l'~ de** (*pour*) for (use of); **en ~** in use; **hors d'~** out of service; **à ~ interne** to be taken; **à ~ externe** for external use only.
usagé, e [yzaʒe] *a* (*usé*) worn; (*d'occasion*) used.
usager, ère [yzaʒe, -eʀ] *nm/f* user.
usé, e [yze] *a* worn (down *ou* out *ou* away); ruined; (*banal*) hackneyed.
user [yze] *vt* (*outil*) to wear down; (*vêtement*) to wear out; (*matière*) to wear away; (*consommer: charbon etc*) to use; (*fig: santé*) to ruin; (: *personne*) to wear out; **s'~** *vi* to wear; to wear out; (*fig*) to decline; **s'~ à la tâche** to wear o.s. out with work; **~ de** *vt* (*moyen, procédé*) to use, employ; (*droit*) to exercise.
usine [yzin] *nf* factory; **~ atomique** nuclear power plant; **~ à gaz** gasworks *sg*; **~ marémotrice** tidal power station.
usiner [yzine] *vt* (*TECH*) to machine; (*fabriquer*) to manufacture.
usité, e [yzite] *a* in common use, common; **peu ~** rarely used.
ustensile [ystɑ̃sil] *nm* implement; **~ de**

cuisine kitchen utensil.

usuel, le [yzɥɛl] a everyday, common.

usufruit [yzyfʀɥi] nm usufruct.

usuraire [yzyʀɛʀ] a usurious.

usure [yzyʀ] nf wear; worn state; (de l'usurier) usury; **avoir qn à l'~** to wear sb down; **~ normale** fair wear and tear.

usurier, ière [yzyʀje, -jɛʀ] nm/f usurer.

usurpateur, trice [yzyʀpatœʀ, -tʀis] nm/f usurper.

usurper [yzyʀpe] vt to usurp.

ut [yt] nm (MUS) C.

UTA sigle f = Union des transporteurs aériens.

utérin, e [yteʀɛ̃, -in] a uterine.

utérus [yteʀys] nm uterus, womb.

utile [ytil] a useful; **~ à qn/qch** of use to sb/sth.

utilement [ytilmã] ad usefully.

utilisable [ytilizabl(ə)] a usable.

utilisateur, trice [ytilizatœʀ, -tʀis] nm/f user.

utilisation [ytilizasjɔ̃] nf use.

utiliser [ytilize] vt to use.

utilitaire [ytilitɛʀ] a utilitarian; (objets) practical ♦ nm (INFORM) utility.

utilité [ytilite] nf usefulness q; **jouer les ~s** (THÉÂTRE) to play bit parts; **reconnu d'~ publique** state-approved; **c'est d'une grande ~** it's extremely useful; **il n'y a aucune ~ à ...** there's no use in ....

utopie [ytɔpi] nf (idée, conception) utopian idea ou view; (société etc idéale) utopia.

utopiste [ytɔpist(ə)] nm/f utopian.

UV sigle f (SCOL) = unité de valeur.

uvule [yvyl] nf uvula.

V

V, v [ve] nm inv V, v ♦ abr (= voir, verset) v.; (= vers: de poésie) l.; (: en direction de) toward(s); **V comme Victor** V for Victor; **en ~ V**-shaped; **encolure en ~** V-neck; **décolleté en ~** plunging neckline.

va [va] vb voir **aller.**

vacance [vakãs] nf (ADMIN) vacancy; **~s** nfpl holiday(s pl) (Brit), vacation sg (US); **les grandes ~s** the summer holidays ou vacation; **prendre des/ses ~s** to take a holiday ou vacation/one's holiday(s) ou vacation; **aller en ~s** to go on holiday ou vacation.

vacancier, ière [vakãsje, -jɛʀ] nm/f holiday-maker (Brit), vacationer (US).

vacant, e [vakã, -ãt] a vacant.

vacarme [vakaʀm(ə)] nm row, din.

vacataire [vakatɛʀ] nm/f temporary (employee); (enseignement) supply (Brit) ou substitute (US) teacher; (UNIVERSITÉ) part-time temporary lecturer.

vaccin [vaksɛ̃] nm vaccine; (opération) vaccination.

vaccination [vaksinasjɔ̃] nf vaccination.

vacciner [vaksine] vt to vaccinate; (fig) to make immune; **être vacciné** (fig) to be immune.

vache [vaʃ] nf (ZOOL) cow; (cuir) cowhide ♦ a (fam) rotten, mean; **~ à eau** (canvas) water bag; **(manger de la) ~ enragée** (to go through) hard times; **~ à lait** (péj) mug, sucker; **~ laitière** dairy cow; **période des ~s maigres** lean times pl, lean period.

vachement [vaʃmã] ad (fam) damned, fantastically.

vacher, ère [vaʃe, -ɛʀ] nm/f cowherd.

vacherie [vaʃʀi] nf (fam) meanness q; (action) dirty trick; (propos) nasty remark.

vacherin [vaʃʀɛ̃] nm (fromage) vacherin cheese; (gâteau): **~ glacé** vacherin (type of cream gâteau).

vachette [vaʃɛt] nf calfskin.

vacillant, e [vasijã, -ãt] a wobbly; flickering; failing, faltering.

vaciller [vasije] vi to sway, wobble; (bougie, lumière) to flicker; (fig) to be failing, falter; **~ dans ses réponses** to falter in one's replies; **~ dans ses résolutions** to waver in one's resolutions.

vacuité [vakɥite] nf emptiness, vacuity.

vade-mecum [vademekɔm] nm inv pocketbook.

vadrouille [vadʀuj] nf: **être/partir en ~** to be on/go for a wander.

vadrouiller [vadʀuje] vi to wander around ou about.

va-et-vient [vaevjɛ̃] nm inv (de pièce mobile) to and fro (ou up and down) movement; (de personnes, véhicules) comings and goings pl, to-ings and fro-ings pl; (ÉLEC) two-way switch.

vagabond, e [vagabɔ̃, -ɔ̃d] a wandering; (imagination) roaming, roving ♦ nm (rôdeur) tramp, vagrant; (voyageur) wanderer.

vagabondage [vagabɔ̃daʒ] nm roaming, wandering; (JUR) vagrancy.

vagabonder [vagabɔ̃de] vi to roam, wander.

vagin [vaʒɛ̃] nm vagina.

vaginal, e, aux [vaʒinal, -o] a vaginal.

vagissement [vaʒismã] nm cry (of newborn baby).

vague [vag] nf wave ♦ a vague; (regard) far-away; (manteau, robe) loose(-fitting); (quelconque): **un ~ bureau/cousin** some office/cousin or other ♦ nm: **être dans le ~** to be rather in the dark; **rester dans le ~** to keep things rather vague; **regarder dans le ~** to gaze into space; **~ à l'âme** nm vague melancholy; **~ d'assaut** nf (MIL) wave of assault; **~ de chaleur** nf heatwave; **~ de fond** nf ground swell; **~ de froid** nf cold spell.

vaguelette [vaglɛt] nf ripple.

vaguement [vagmã] ad vaguely.

vaillamment [vajamã] ad bravely, gallantly.

vaillant, e [vajã, -ãt] a (courageux) brave, gallant; (robuste) vigorous, hale and hearty; **n'avoir plus un sou ~** to be penniless.

vaille [vaj] vb voir **valoir.**

vain, e [vɛ̃, vɛn] a vain; **en ~** ad in vain.

vaincre [vɛ̃kʀ(ə)] vt to defeat; (fig) to conquer, overcome.

vaincu, e [vɛ̃ky] pp de **vaincre** ♦ nm/f defeated party.

vainement [vɛnmã] ad vainly.

vainquais [vɛ̃kɛ] *etc vb voir* **vaincre**.

vainqueur [vɛ̃kœʀ] *nm* victor; (*SPORT*) winner ♦ *am* victorious.

vais [vɛ] *vb voir* **aller**.

vaisseau, x [vɛso] *nm* (*ANAT*) vessel; (*NAVIG*) ship, vessel; ~ **spatial** spaceship.

vaisselier [vɛsəlje] *nm* dresser.

vaisselle [vɛsɛl] *nf* (*service*) crockery; (*plats etc à laver*) (dirty) dishes *pl*; **faire la** ~ to do the washing-up (*Brit*) *ou* the dishes.

val, vaux *ou* **vals** [val, vo] *nm* valley.

valable [valabl(ə)] *a* valid; (*acceptable*) decent, worthwhile.

valablement [valabləmɑ̃] *ad* legitimately; (*de façon satisfaisante*) satisfactorily.

Valence [valɑ̃s] *n* (*en Espagne*) Valencia; (*en France*) Valence.

valent [val] *etc vb voir* **valoir**.

valet [valɛ] *nm* valet; (*péj*) lackey; (*CARTES*) jack, knave (*Brit*); ~ **de chambre** manservant, valet; ~ **de ferme** farmhand; ~ **de pied** footman.

valeur [valœʀ] *nf* (*gén*) value; (*mérite*) worth, merit; (*COMM: titre*) security; **mettre en** ~ (*bien*) to exploit; (*terrain, région*) to develop; (*fig*) to highlight; to show off to advantage; **avoir de la** ~ to be valuable; **prendre de la** ~ to go up *ou* gain in value; **sans** ~ worthless; ~ **absolue** absolute value; ~ **d'échange** exchange value; ~ **nominale** face value; ~**s mobilières** transferable securities.

valeureux, euse [valœʀø, -øz] *a* valorous.

valide [valid] *a* (*en bonne santé*) fit, well; (*indemne*) able-bodied, fit; (*valable*) valid.

valider [valide] *vt* to validate.

validité [validite] *nf* validity.

valions [valjɔ̃] *etc vb voir* **valoir**.

valise [valiz] *nf* (suit)case; **faire sa** ~ to pack one's (suit)case; **la** ~ (**diplomatique**) the diplomatic bag.

vallée [vale] *nf* valley.

vallon [valɔ̃] *nm* small valley.

vallonné, e [valɔne] *a* undulating.

valoir [valwaʀ] *vi* (*être valable*) to hold, apply ♦ *vt* (*prix, valeur, effort*) to be worth; (*causer*): ~ **qch à qn** to earn sb sth; **se** ~ to be of equal merit; (*péj*) to be two of a kind; **faire** ~ (*droits, prérogatives*) to assert; (*domaine, capitaux*) to exploit; **faire** ~ **que** to point out that; **se faire** ~ to make the most of o.s.; **à** ~ on account; **à** ~ **sur** to be deducted from; **vaille que vaille** somehow or other; **cela ne me dit rien qui vaille** I don't like the look of it at all; **ce climat ne me vaut rien** this climate doesn't suit me; ~ **la peine** to be worth the trouble, be worth it; ~ **mieux: il vaut mieux se taire** it's better to say nothing; **il vaut mieux que je fasse/ comme ceci** it's better if I do/like this; **ça ne vaut rien** it's worthless; **que vaut ce candidat?** how good is this applicant?

valorisation [valɔʀizasjɔ̃] *nf* (economic) development; increased standing.

valoriser [valɔʀize] *vt* (*ÉCON*) to develop (the economy of); (*produit*) to increase the value of; (*PSYCH*) to increase the standing of; (*fig*) to highlight, bring out.

valse [vals(ə)] *nf* waltz; **c'est la** ~ **des étiquettes** the prices don't stay the same from one moment to the next.

valser [valse] *vi* to waltz; (*fig*): **aller** ~ to go flying.

valu, e [valy] *pp de* **valoir**.

valve [valv(ə)] *nf* valve.

vamp [vɑ̃p] *nf* vamp.

vampire [vɑ̃piʀ] *nm* vampire.

van [vɑ̃] *nm* horse box (*Brit*) *ou* trailer (*US*).

vandale [vɑ̃dal] *nm/f* vandal.

vandalisme [vɑ̃dalism(ə)] *nm* vandalism.

vanille [vanij] *nf* vanilla; **glace à la** ~ vanilla ice cream.

vanillé, e [vanije] *a* vanilla *cpd*.

vanité [vanite] *nf* vanity.

vaniteux, euse [vanitø, -øz] *a* vain, conceited.

vanne [van] *nf* gate; (*fam: remarque*) dig, (nasty) crack; **lancer une** ~ **à qn** to have a go at sb (*Brit*), knock sb.

vanneau, x [vano] *nm* lapwing.

vanner [vane] *vt* to winnow.

vannerie [vanʀi] *nf* basketwork.

vantail, aux [vɑ̃taj, -o] *nm* door, leaf (*pl* leaves).

vantard, e [vɑ̃taʀ, -aʀd(ə)] *a* boastful.

vantardise [vɑ̃taʀdiz] *nf* boastfulness *q*; boast.

vanter [vɑ̃te] *vt* to speak highly of, vaunt; **se** ~ *vi* to boast, brag; **se** ~ **de** to pride o.s. on; (*péj*) to boast of.

Vanuatu [vanwatu] *nm*: **le** ~ Vanuatu.

va-nu-pieds [vanypje] *nm/f inv* tramp, beggar.

vapeur [vapœʀ] *nf* steam; (*émanation*) vapour (*Brit*), vapor (*US*), fumes *pl*; (*brouillard, buée*) haze; ~**s** *nfpl* (*bouffées*) vapours, vapors; **à** ~ steam-powered, steam *cpd*; **à toute** ~ full steam ahead; (*fig*) at full tilt; **renverser la** ~ to reverse engines; (*fig*) to backtrack, backpedal; **cuit à la** ~ steamed.

vapocuiseur [vapokyizœʀ] *nm* pressure cooker.

vaporeux, euse [vapoʀø, -øz] *a* (*flou*) hazy, misty; (*léger*) filmy, gossamer *cpd*.

vaporisateur [vapoʀizatœʀ] *nm* spray.

vaporiser [vapoʀize] *vt* (*CHIMIE*) to vaporize; (*parfum etc*) to spray.

vaquer [vake] *vi* (*ADMIN*) to be on vacation; ~ **à ses occupations** to attend to one's affairs, go about one's business.

varappe [vaʀap] *nf* rock climbing.

varappeur, euse [vaʀapœʀ, -øz] *nm/f* (rock) climber.

varech [vaʀɛk] *nm* wrack, varec.

vareuse [vaʀøz] *nf* (*blouson*) pea jacket; (*d'uniforme*) tunic.

variable [vaʀjabl(ə)] *a* variable; (*temps, humeur*) changeable; (*TECH*: *à plusieurs positions etc*) adaptable; (*LING*) inflectional; (*divers: résultats*) varied, various ♦ *nf* (*INFORM, MATH*) variable.

variante [vaʀjɑ̃t] *nf* variant.

variation [vaʀjasjɔ̃] *nf* variation; changing *q*, change; (*MUS*) variation.

varice [vaʀis] *nf* varicose vein.

varicelle [vaʀisɛl] *nf* chickenpox.

varié, e [vaʀje] *a* varied; (*divers*) various; **hors-d'œuvre** ~**s** selection of hors d'œuvres.

varier [vaʀje] *vi* to vary; (*temps, humeur*) to change ♦ *vt* to vary.

variété [vaʀjete] *nf* variety; **spectacle de** ~**s**

variety show.
variole [varjɔl] *nf* smallpox.
variqueux, euse [varikø, -øz] *a* varicose.
Varsovie [varsɔvi] *n* Warsaw.
vas [va] *vb voir* **aller**; ∼**-y!** [vazi] go on!
vasculaire [vaskylɛr] *a* vascular.
vase [vɑz] *nm* vase ♦ *nf* silt, mud; **en** ∼ **clos** in isolation; ∼ **de nuit** chamberpot; ∼**s communicants** communicating vessels.
vasectomie [vazɛktɔmi] *nf* vasectomy.
vaseline [vazlin] *nf* Vaseline ®.
vaseux, euse [vɑzø, -øz] *a* silty, muddy; (*fig: confus*) woolly, hazy; (*: fatigué*) peaky; (*: étourdi*) woozy.
vasistas [vazistɑs] *nm* fanlight.
vasque [vask(ə)] *nf* (*bassin*) basin; (*coupe*) bowl.
vaste [vast(ə)] *a* vast, immense.
Vatican [vatikɑ̃] *nm*: **le** ∼ the Vatican.
vaticiner [vatisine] *vi* (*péj*) to make pompous predictions.
va-tout [vatu] *nm*: **jouer son** ∼ to stake one's all.
vaudeville [vodvil] *nm* vaudeville, light comedy.
vaudrai [vodʀe] *etc vb voir* **valoir**.
vau-l'eau [volo]: **à** ∼ *ad* with the current; **s'en aller à** ∼ (*fig: projets*) to be adrift.
vaurien, ne [voʀjɛ̃, -ɛn] *nm/f* good-for-nothing, guttersnipe.
vaut [vo] *vb voir* **valoir**.
vautour [votuʀ] *nm* vulture.
vautrer [votʀe]: **se** ∼ *vi*: **se** ∼ **dans** to wallow in; **se** ∼ **sur** to sprawl on.
vaux [vo] *pl de* **val** ♦ *vb voir* **valoir**.
va-vite [vavit]: **à la** ∼ *ad* in a rush.
vd *abr* = **vend**.
VDQS *abr* (= *vin délimité de qualité supérieure*) label guaranteeing quality of wine.
vds *abr* = **vends**.
veau, x [vo] *nm* (*ZOOL*) calf (*pl* calves); (*CULIN*) veal; (*peau*) calfskin; **tuer le** ∼ **gras** to kill the fatted calf.
vecteur [vɛktœʀ] *nm* vector; (*MIL*, *BIO*) carrier.
vécu, e [veky] *pp de* **vivre** ♦ *a* (*aventure*) real (-life).
vedettariat [vədɛtaʀja] *nm* stardom; (*attitude*) acting like a star.
vedette [vədɛt] *nf* (*artiste etc*) star; (*canot*) patrol boat; launch; **avoir la** ∼ to top the bill, get star billing; **mettre qn en** ∼ (*CINÉMA etc*) to give sb the starring role; (*fig*) to push sb into the limelight.
végétal, e, aux [veʒetal, -o] *a* vegetable ♦ *nm* vegetable, plant.
végétalien, ne [veʒetaljɛ̃, -ɛn] *a, nm/f* vegan.
végétarien, ne [veʒetaʀjɛ̃, -ɛn] *a, nm/f* vegetarian.
végétarisme [veʒetaʀism(ə)] *nm* vegetarianism.
végétatif, ive [veʒetatif, -iv] *a*: **une vie** ∼**ive** a vegetable existence.
végétation [veʒetasjɔ̃] *nf* vegetation; ∼**s** *nfpl* (*MÉD*) adenoids.
végéter [veʒete] *vi* (*fig*) to vegetate; to stagnate.
véhémence [veemɑ̃s] *nf* vehemence.
véhément, e [veemɑ̃, -ɑ̃t] *a* vehement.

véhicule [veikyl] *nm* vehicle; ∼ **utilitaire** commercial vehicle.
véhiculer [veikyle] *vt* (*personnes, marchandises*) to transport, convey; (*fig: idées, substances*) to convey, serve as a vehicle for.
veille [vɛj] *nf* (*garde*) watch; (*PSYCH*) wakefulness; (*jour*): **la** ∼ the day before, the previous day; **la** ∼ **au soir** the previous evening; **la** ∼ **de** the day before; **à la** ∼ **de** on the eve of; **l'état de** ∼ the waking state.
veillée [veje] *nf* (*soirée*) evening; (*réunion*) evening gathering; ∼ **d'armes** night before combat; (*fig*) vigil; ∼ (**mortuaire**) watch.
veiller [veje] *vi* (*rester debout*) to stay ou sit up; (*ne pas dormir*) to be awake; (*être de garde*) to be on watch; (*être vigilant*) to be watchful ♦ *vt* (*malade, mort*) to watch over, sit up with; ∼ **à** *vt* to attend to, see to; ∼ **à ce que** to make sure that, see to it that; ∼ **sur** *vt* to keep a watch ou an eye on.
veilleur [vɛjœʀ] *nm*: ∼ **de nuit** night watchman.
veilleuse [vɛjøz] *nf* (*lampe*) night light; (*AUTO*) sidelight; (*flamme*) pilot light; **en** ∼ *a* (*lampe*) dimmed; (*fig: affaire*) shelved, set aside.
veinard, e [vɛnaʀ, -aʀd(ə)] *nm/f* (*fam*) lucky devil.
veine [vɛn] *nf* (*ANAT, du bois etc*) vein; (*filon*) vein, seam; (*fam: chance*): **avoir de la** ∼ to be lucky; (*inspiration*) inspiration.
veiné, e [vene] *a* veined; (*bois*) grained.
veineux, euse [venø, -øz] *a* venous.
vêler [vele] *vi* to calve.
vélin [velɛ̃] *nm*: (**papier**) ∼ vellum (paper).
véliplanchiste [veliplɑ̃ʃist(ə)] *nm/f* windsurfer.
velléitaire [veleitɛʀ] *a* irresolute, indecisive.
velléités [veleite] *nfpl* vague impulses.
vélo [velo] *nm* bike, cycle; **faire du** ∼ to go cycling.
véloce [velɔs] *a* swift.
vélocité [velɔsite] *nf* (*MUS*) nimbleness, swiftness; (*vitesse*) velocity.
vélodrome [velɔdʀɔm] *nm* velodrome.
vélomoteur [velɔmɔtœʀ] *nm* moped.
velours [vəluʀ] *nm* velvet; ∼ **côtelé** corduroy.
velouté, e [vəlute] *a* (*au toucher*) velvety; (*à la vue*) soft, mellow; (*au goût*) smooth, mellow ♦ *nm*: ∼ **d'asperges/de tomates** cream of asparagus/tomato soup.
velu, e [vəly] *a* hairy.
venaison [vənɛzɔ̃] *nf* venison.
vénal, e, aux [venal, -o] *a* venal.
vénalité [venalite] *nf* venality.
venant [vənɑ̃]: **à tout** ∼ *ad* to all and sundry.
vendable [vɑ̃dabl(ə)] *a* saleable, marketable.
vendange [vɑ̃dɑ̃ʒ] *nf* (*opération, période: aussi*: ∼**s**) grape harvest; (*raisins*) grape crop, grapes *pl*.
vendanger [vɑ̃dɑ̃ʒe] *vi* to harvest the grapes.
vendangeur, euse [vɑ̃dɑ̃ʒœʀ, -øz] *nm/f* grape-picker.
vendéen, ne [vɑ̃deɛ̃, -ɛn] *a* of ou from the Vendée.
vendeur, euse [vɑ̃dœʀ, -øz] *nm/f* (*de magasin*) shop ou sales assistant (*Brit*), sales clerk (*US*); (*COMM*) salesman/woman ♦ *nm* (*JUR*) vendor, seller; ∼ **de journaux** news-

paper seller.

vendre [vɑ̃dʀ(ə)] vt to sell; ~ **qch à qn** to sell sb sth; **cela se vend à la douzaine** these are sold by the dozen; **cela se vend bien** it's selling well; **"à ~"** "for sale".

vendredi [vɑ̃dʀədi] nm Friday; **V~ saint** Good Friday; voir aussi **lundi**.

vendu, e [vɑ̃dy] pp de **vendre** ♦ a (péj) corrupt.

venelle [vənɛl] nf alley.

vénéneux, euse [venenø, -øz] a poisonous.

vénérable [venerabl(ə)] a venerable.

vénération [venerasjɔ̃] nf veneration.

vénérer [venere] vt to venerate.

vénerie [vɛnʀi] nf hunting.

vénérien, ne [venerjɛ̃, -ɛn] a venereal.

Venezuela [venezɥela] nm: **le ~** Venezuela.

vénézuélien, ne [venezɥeljɛ̃, -ɛn] a Venezuelan ♦ nm/f: **V~, ne** Venezuelan.

vengeance [vɑ̃ʒɑ̃s] nf vengeance q, revenge q; (acte) act of vengeance ou revenge.

venger [vɑ̃ʒe] vt to avenge; **se ~** vi to avenge o.s.; (par rancune) to take revenge; **se ~ de qch** to avenge o.s. for sth; to take one's revenge for sth; **se ~ de qn** to take revenge on sb; **se ~ sur** to wreak vengeance upon; to take revenge on ou through; to take it out on.

vengeur, eresse [vɑ̃ʒœʀ, -ʒʀɛs] a vengeful ♦ nm/f avenger.

véniel, le [venjɛl] a venial.

venimeux, euse [vənimø, -øz] a poisonous, venomous; (fig: haineux) venomous, vicious.

venin [vənɛ̃] nm venom, poison; (fig) venom.

venir [vəniʀ] vi to come; ~ **de** to come from; ~ **de faire: je viens d'y aller/de le voir** I've just been there/seen him; **s'il vient à pleuvoir** if it should rain, if it happens to rain; **en ~ à faire: j'en viens à croire que** I am coming to believe that; **où veux-tu en ~?** what are you getting at?; **il en est venu à mendier** he has been reduced to begging; **en ~ aux mains** to come to blows; **les années/générations à ~** the years/generations to come; **il me vient une idée** an idea has just occurred to me; **il me vient des soupçons** I'm beginning to be suspicious; **je te vois ~** I know what you're after; **faire ~** (docteur, plombier) to call (out); **d'où vient que ...?** how is it that ...?; ~ **au monde** to come into the world.

Venise [vəniz] n Venice.

vénitien, ne [venisjɛ̃, -ɛn] a Venetian.

vent [vɑ̃] nm wind; **il y a du ~** it's windy; **c'est du ~** it's all hot air; **au ~** to windward; **sous le ~** to leeward; **avoir le ~ debout/arrière** to head into the wind/have the wind astern; **dans le ~** (fam) trendy; **prendre le ~** (fig) to see which way the wind blows; **avoir ~ de** to get wind of; **contre ~s et marées** come hell or high water.

vente [vɑ̃t] nf sale; **la ~** (activité) selling; (secteur) sales pl; **mettre en ~** to put on sale; (objets personnels) to put up for sale; ~ **de charité** jumble (Brit) ou rummage (US) sale; ~ **par correspondance (VPC)** mail-order selling; ~ **aux enchères** auction sale.

venté, e [vɑ̃te] a windswept, windy.

venter [vɑ̃te] vb impersonnel: **il vente** the wind is blowing.

venteux, euse [vɑ̃tø, -øz] a windswept, windy.

ventilateur [vɑ̃tilatœʀ] nm fan.

ventilation [vɑ̃tilasjɔ̃] nf ventilation.

ventiler [vɑ̃tile] vt to ventilate; (total, statistiques) to break down.

ventouse [vɑ̃tuz] nf (ampoule) cupping glass; (de caoutchouc) suction pad; (ZOOL) sucker.

ventre [vɑ̃tʀ(ə)] nm (ANAT) stomach; (fig) belly; **prendre du ~** to be getting a paunch; **avoir mal au ~** to have (a) stomach ache.

ventricule [vɑ̃tʀikyl] nm ventricle.

ventriloque [vɑ̃tʀilɔk] nm/f ventriloquist.

ventripotent, e [vɑ̃tʀipɔtɑ̃, -ɑ̃t] a potbellied.

ventru, e [vɑ̃tʀy] a potbellied.

venu, e [vəny] pp de **venir** ♦ a: **être mal ~ à ou de faire** to have no grounds for doing, be in no position to do; **mal ~** ill-timed, unwelcome; **bien ~** timely, welcome ♦ nf coming.

vêpres [vepʀ(ə)] nfpl vespers.

ver [vɛʀ] nm voir aussi **vers**; worm; (des fruits etc) maggot; (du bois) woodworm q; ~ **blanc** May beetle grub; ~ **luisant** glowworm; ~ **à soie** silkworm; ~ **solitaire** tapeworm; ~ **de terre** earthworm.

véracité [verasite] nf veracity.

véranda [verɑ̃da] nf veranda(h).

verbal, e, aux [vɛʀbal, -o] a verbal.

verbalement [vɛʀbalmɑ̃] ad verbally.

verbaliser [vɛʀbalize] vi (POLICE) to book ou report an offender; (PSYCH) to verbalize.

verbe [vɛʀb(ə)] nm (LING) verb; (voix): **avoir le ~ sonore** to have a sonorous tone (of voice); (expression): **la magie du ~** the magic of language ou the word; (REL): **le V~** the Word.

verbeux, euse [vɛʀbø, -øz] a verbose, wordy.

verbiage [vɛʀbjaʒ] nm verbiage.

verdâtre [vɛʀdɑtʀ(ə)] a greenish.

verdeur [vɛʀdœʀ] nf (vigueur) vigour (Brit), vigor (US), vitality; (crudité) forthrightness; (défaut de maturité) tartness, sharpness.

verdict [vɛʀdik(t)] nm verdict.

verdir [vɛʀdiʀ] vi, vt to turn green.

verdoyant, e [vɛʀdwajɑ̃, -ɑ̃t] a green, verdant.

verdure [vɛʀdyʀ] nf (arbres, feuillages) greenery; (légumes verts) green vegetables pl, greens pl.

véreux, euse [verø, -øz] a worm-eaten; (malhonnête) shady, corrupt.

verge [vɛʀʒ(ə)] nf (ANAT) penis; (baguette) stick, cane.

verger [vɛʀʒe] nm orchard.

vergeture [vɛʀʒətyʀ] nf gén pl stretch mark.

verglacé, e [vɛʀglase] a icy, iced-over.

verglas [vɛʀgla] nm (black) ice.

vergogne [vɛʀgɔɲ]: **sans ~** ad shamelessly.

véridique [veʀidik] a truthful.

verificateur, trice [veʀifikatœʀ, -tʀis] nm/f controller, checker ♦ nf (machine) verifier; ~ **des comptes** (FINANCE) auditor.

vérification [veʀifikasjɔ̃] nf checking q, check; ~ **d'identité** identity check.

vérifier [veʀifje] vt to check; (corroborer) to confirm, bear out; (INFORM) to verify; **se ~** vi to be confirmed ou verified.

vérin [veʀɛ̃] nm jack.

véritable [veʀitabl(ə)] a real; (ami, amour)

true; **un ~ désastre** an absolute disaster; **que le ~ X sorte du rang!** ≈ will the real X (please) stand up!

véritablement [veʀitabləmɑ̃] *ad* (*effectivement*) really; (*absolument*) absolutely.

vérité [veʀite] *nf* truth; (*d'un portrait*) lifelikeness; (*sincérité*) truthfulness, sincerity; **en ~, à la ~** to tell the truth.

vermeil, le [veʀmɛj] *a* bright red, ruby red ♦ *nm* (*substance*) vermeil.

vermicelles [veʀmisɛl] *nmpl* vermicelli *sg*.

vermifuge [veʀmifyʒ] *nm*: **poudre ~** worm powder.

vermillon [veʀmijɔ̃] *a inv* vermilion, scarlet.

vermine [veʀmin] *nf* vermin *pl*.

vermoulu, e [veʀmuly] *a* worm-eaten, with woodworm.

vermout(h) [veʀmut] *nm* vermouth.

verni, e [veʀni] *a* varnished; glazed; (*fam*) lucky; **cuir ~** patent leather; **souliers ~s** patent (leather) shoes.

vernir [veʀniʀ] *vt* (*bois, tableau, ongles*) to varnish; (*poterie*) to glaze.

vernis [veʀni] *nm* (*enduit*) varnish; glaze; (*fig*) veneer; **~ à ongles** nail varnish (*Brit*) *ou* polish.

vernissage [veʀnisaʒ] *nm* varnishing; glazing; (*d'une exposition*) preview.

vernisser [veʀnise] *vt* to glaze.

vérole [veʀɔl] *nf* (*variole*) smallpox; (*fam*: *syphilis*) pox.

Vérone [veʀɔn] *n* Verona.

verrai [veʀe] *etc vb voir* **voir**.

verre [veʀ] *nm* glass; (*de lunettes*) lens *sg*; **~s** *nmpl* (*lunettes*) glasses; **boire** *ou* **prendre un ~** to have a drink; **~ à vin/à liqueur** wine/liqueur glass; **~ à dents** tooth mug; **~ dépoli** frosted glass; **~ de lampe** lamp glass *ou* chimney; **~ de montre** watch glass; **~ à pied** stemmed glass; **~s de contact** contact lenses; **~s fumés** tinted lenses.

verrerie [veʀʀi] *nf* (*fabrique*) glassworks *sg*; (*activité*) glass-making, glass-working; (*objets*) glassware.

verrier [veʀje] *nm* glass-blower.

verrière [veʀjɛʀ] *nf* (*grand vitrage*) window; (*toit vitré*) glass roof.

verrons [veʀɔ̃] *etc vb voir* **voir**.

verroterie [veʀɔtʀi] *nf* glass beads *pl*, glass jewellery (*Brit*) *ou* jewelry (*US*).

verrou [veʀu] *nm* (*targette*) bolt; (*fig*) constriction; **mettre le ~** to bolt the door; **mettre qn sous les ~s** to put sb behind bars.

verrouillage [veʀujaʒ] *nm* (*dispositif*) locking mechanism; (*AUTO*): **~ central** central locking.

verrouiller [veʀuje] *vt* to bolt; to lock; (*MIL*: *brèche*) to close.

verrue [veʀy] *nf* wart; (*plantaire*) verruca; (*fig*) eyesore.

vers [veʀ] *nm* line ♦ *nmpl* (*poésie*) verse *sg* ♦ *prép* (*en direction de*) toward(s); (*près de*) around (about); (*temporel*) about, around.

versant [veʀsɑ̃] *nm* slopes *pl*, side.

versatile [veʀsatil] *a* fickle, changeable.

verse [veʀs(ə)]: **à ~** *ad*: **il pleut à ~** it's pouring (with rain).

versé, e [veʀse] *a*: **être ~ dans** (*science*) to be (well-)versed in.

Verseau [veʀso] *nm*: **le ~** Aquarius, the water-carrier; **être du ~** to be Aquarius.

versement [veʀsəmɑ̃] *nm* payment; (*sur un compte*) deposit, remittance; **en 3 ~s** in 3 instalments.

verser [veʀse] *vt* (*liquide, grains*) to pour; (*larmes, sang*) to shed; (*argent*) to pay; (*soldat: affecter*): **~ qn dans** to assign sb to ♦ *vi* (*véhicule*) to overturn; (*fig*): **~ dans** to lapse into; **~ à un compte** to pay into an account.

verset [veʀsɛ] *nm* verse; versicle.

verseur [veʀsœʀ] *am voir* **bec, bouchon**.

versifier [veʀsifje] *vt* to put into verse ♦ *vi* to versify, write verse.

version [veʀsjɔ̃] *nf* version; (*SCOL*) translation (*into the mother tongue*); **film en ~ originale** film in the original language.

verso [veʀso] *nm* back; **voir au ~** see over (leaf).

vert, e [veʀ, veʀt(ə)] *a* green; (*vin*) young; (*vigoureux*) sprightly; (*cru*) forthright ♦ *nm* green; **dire des ~es (et des pas mûres)** to say some pretty spicy things; **il en a vu des ~es** he's seen a thing or two; **~ bouteille** *a inv* bottle-green; **~ d'eau** *a inv* sea-green; **~ pomme** *a inv* apple-green.

vert-de-gris [veʀdəgʀi] *nm* verdigris ♦ *a inv* grey(ish)-green.

vertébral, e, aux [veʀtebʀal, -o] *a* back *cpd*; *voir* **colonne**.

vertèbre [veʀtɛbʀ(ə)] *nf* vertebra (*pl* -ae).

vertébré, e [veʀtebʀe] *a, nm* vertebrate.

vertement [veʀtəmɑ̃] *ad* (*réprimander*) sharply.

vertical, e, aux [veʀtikal, -o] *a, nf* vertical; **à la ~e** *ad* vertically.

verticalement [veʀtikalmɑ̃] *ad* vertically.

verticalité [veʀtikalite] *nf* verticalness, verticality.

vertige [veʀtiʒ] *nm* (*peur du vide*) vertigo; (*étourdissement*) dizzy spell; (*fig*) fever; **ça me donne le ~** it makes me dizzy; (*fig*) it makes my head spin *ou* reel.

vertigineux, euse [veʀtiʒinø, -øz] *a* (*hausse, vitesse*) breathtaking; (*altitude, gorge*) breathtakingly high (*ou* deep).

vertu [veʀty] *nf* virtue; **une ~** a saint, a paragon of virtue; **avoir la ~ de faire** to have the virtue of doing; **en ~ de** *prép* in accordance with.

vertueusement [veʀtɥøzmɑ̃] *ad* virtuously.

vertueux, euse [veʀtɥø, -øz] *a* virtuous.

verve [veʀv(ə)] *nf* witty eloquence; **être en ~** to be in brilliant form.

verveine [veʀvɛn] *nf* (*BOT*) verbena, vervain; (*infusion*) verbena tea.

vésicule [vezikyl] *nf* vesicle; **~ biliaire** gallbladder.

vespasienne [vɛspazjɛn] *nf* urinal.

vespéral, e, aux [vɛspeʀal, -o] *a* vespertine, evening *cpd*.

vessie [vesi] *nf* bladder.

veste [vɛst(ə)] *nf* jacket; **~ droite/croisée** single-/double-breasted jacket; **retourner sa ~** (*fig*) to change one's colours.

vestiaire [vɛstjɛʀ] *nm* (*au théâtre etc*) cloakroom; (*de stade etc*) changing-room (*Brit*), locker-room (*US*); (*métallique*): **(armoire) ~**

locker.

vestibule [vɛstibyl] *nm* hall.

vestige [vɛstiʒ] *nm* (*objet*) relic; (*fragment*) trace; (*fig*) remnant, vestige; **~s** *nmpl* (*d'une ville*) remains; (*d'une civilisation, du passé*) remnants, relics.

vestimentaire [vɛstimᾶtɛʀ] *a* (*dépenses*) clothing; (*détail*) of dress; (*élégance*) sartorial.

veston [vɛstɔ̃] *nm* jacket.

Vésuve [vezyv] *nm*: **le ~** Vesuvius.

vêtais [vɛtɛ] *etc vb voir* **vêtir**.

vêtement [vɛtmᾶ] *nm* garment, item of clothing; (*COMM*): **le ~** the clothing industry; **~s** *nmpl* clothes; **~s de sport** sportswear *sg*, sports clothes.

vétéran [veteʀᾶ] *nm* veteran.

vétérinaire [veteʀinɛʀ] *a* veterinary ♦ *nm/f* vet, veterinary surgeon (*Brit*), veterinarian (*US*).

vétille [vetij] *nf* trifle, triviality.

vétilleux, euse [vetijø, -øz] *a* punctilious.

vêtir [vetiʀ] *vt* to clothe, dress; **se ~** to dress (o.s.).

vêtit [veti] *etc vb voir* **vêtir**.

veto [veto] *nm* veto; **opposer un ~ à** to veto.

vêtu, e [vety] *pp de* **vêtir** ♦ *a*: **~ de** dressed in, wearing; **chaudement ~** warmly dressed.

vétuste [vetyst(ə)] *a* ancient, timeworn.

vétusté [vetyste] *nf* age, delapidation.

veuf, veuve [vœf, vœv] *a* widowed ♦ *nm* widower ♦ *nf* widow.

veuille [vœj], **veuillez** [vœje] *etc vb voir* **vouloir**.

veule [vøl] *a* spineless.

veulent [vœl] *etc vb voir* **vouloir**.

veulerie [vølʀi] *nf* spinelessness.

veut [vø] *vb voir* **vouloir**.

veuvage [vœvaʒ] *nm* widowhood.

veuve [vœv] *af, nf voir* **veuf**.

veux [vø] *vb voir* **vouloir**.

vexant, e [vɛksᾶ, -ᾶt] *a* (*contrariant*) annoying; (*blessant*) upsetting.

vexations [vɛksɑsjɔ̃] *nfpl* humiliations.

vexatoire [vɛksatwaʀ] *a*: **mesures ~s** harassment *sg*.

vexer [vɛkse] *vt* to hurt, upset; **se ~** *vi* to be hurt, get upset.

VF *sigle f* (*CINÉMA*) = **version française**.

VHF *sigle f* (= *Very High Frequency*) VHF.

via [vja] *prép* via.

viabiliser [vjabilize] *vt* to provide with services (*water etc*).

viabilité [vjabilite] *nf* viability; (*d'un chemin*) practicability.

viable [vjabl(ə)] *a* viable.

viaduc [vjadyk] *nm* viaduct.

viager, ère [vjaʒe, -ɛʀ] *a*: **rente ~ère** life annuity ♦ *nm*: **mettre en ~** to sell in return for a life annuity.

viande [vjᾶd] *nf* meat.

viatique [vjatik] *nm* (*REL*) viaticum; (*fig*) provisions *pl ou* money for the journey.

vibrant, e [vibʀᾶ, -ᾶt] *a* (*vibrating*) vibrating; (*voix*) vibrant; (*émouvant*) emotive.

vibraphone [vibʀafɔn] *nm* vibraphone, vibes *pl*.

vibration [vibʀasjɔ̃] *nf* vibration.

vibratoire [vibʀatwaʀ] *a* vibratory.

vibrer [vibʀe] *vi* to vibrate; (*son, voix*) to be vibrant; (*fig*) to be stirred; **faire ~** to (cause to) vibrate; to stir, thrill.

vibromasseur [vibʀɔmasœʀ] *nm* vibrator.

vicaire [vikɛʀ] *nm* curate.

vice... [vis] *préfixe* vice-.

vice [vis] *nm* vice; (*défaut*) fault; **~ caché** (*COMM*) latent *ou* inherent defect; **~ de forme** legal flaw *ou* irregularity.

vice-consul [viskɔ̃syl] *nm* vice-consul.

vice-président, e [vispʀezidᾶ, -ᾶt] *nm/f* vice-president; vice-chairman.

vice-roi [visʀwa] *nm* viceroy.

vice versa [visevɛʀsa] *ad* vice versa.

vichy [viʃi] *nm* (*toile*) gingham; (*eau*) Vichy water; **carottes V~** boiled carrots.

vichyssois, e [viʃiswa, -waz] *a* of *ou* from Vichy, Vichy *cpd* ♦ *nf* (*soupe*) vichyssoise (soup), cream of leek and potato soup ♦ *nm/f*: **V~, e** native *ou* inhabitant of Vichy.

vicié, e [visje] *a* (*air*) polluted, tainted; (*JUR*) invalidated.

vicier [visje] *vt* (*JUR*) to invalidate.

vicieux, euse [visjø, -øz] *a* (*pervers*) dirty(-minded); (*méchant*) nasty; (*fautif*) incorrect, wrong.

vicinal, e, aux [visinal, -o] *a*: **chemin ~** by-road, byway.

vicissitudes [visisityd] *nfpl* (trials and) tribulations.

vicomte [vikɔ̃t] *nm* viscount.

vicomtesse [vikɔ̃tɛs] *nf* viscountess.

victime [viktim] *nf* victim; (*d'accident*) casualty; **être (la) ~ de** to be the victim of; **être ~ d'une attaque/d'un accident** to suffer a stroke/be involved in an accident.

victoire [viktwaʀ] *nf* victory.

victorieux, euse [viktɔʀjø, -øz] *a* victorious; (*sourire, attitude*) triumphant.

victuailles [viktɥaj] *nfpl* provisions.

vidange [vidᾶʒ] *nf* (*d'un fossé, réservoir*) emptying; (*AUTO*) oil change; (*de lavabo: bonde*) waste outlet; **~s** *nfpl* (*matières*) sewage *sg*; **faire la ~** (*AUTO*) to change the oil, do an oil change; **tuyau de ~** drainage pipe.

vidanger [vidᾶʒe] *vt* to empty; **faire ~ la voiture** to have the oil changed in one's car.

vide [vid] *a* empty ♦ *nm* (*PHYSIQUE*) vacuum; (*espace*) (empty) space, gap; (*sous soi: dans une falaise etc*) drop; (*futilité, néant*) void; **~ de** empty of; (*de sens etc*) devoid of; **sous ~** in a vacuum; **emballé sous ~** vacuum packed; **regarder dans le ~** to stare into space; **avoir peur du ~** to be afraid of heights; **parler dans le ~** to waste one's breath; **faire le ~** (*dans son esprit*) to make one's mind go blank; **faire le ~ autour de qn** to isolate sb; **à ~** *ad* (*sans occupants*) empty; (*sans charge*) unladen; (*TECH*) without gripping *ou* being in gear.

vidé, e [vide] *a* (*épuisé*) done in, all in.

vidéo [video] *nf, a inv* video; **~ inverse** reverse video.

vidéocassette [videokasɛt] *nf* video cassette.

vidéoclub [videoklœb] *nm* video club.

vidéodisque [videodisk] *nm* videodisc.

vide-ordures [vidɔʀdyʀ] *nm inv* (rubbish) chute.

vidéotex [videotɛks] *nm* ® teletext.

vide-poches [vidpɔʃ] *nm inv* tidy; *(AUTO)* glove compartment.

vide-pomme [vidpɔm] *nm inv* apple-corer.

vider [vide] *vt* to empty; *(CULIN: volaille, poisson)* to gut, clean out; *(régler: querelle)* to settle; *(fatiguer)* to wear out; *(fam: expulser)* to throw out, chuck out; **se ~** *vi* to empty; **~ les lieux** to quit *ou* vacate the premises.

videur [vidœʀ] *nm (de boîte de nuit)* bouncer.

vie [vi] *nf* life *(pl* lives); **être en ~** to be alive; **sans ~** lifeless; **à ~** for life; **membre à ~** life member; **dans la ~ courante** in everyday life; **avoir la ~ dure** to have nine lives; to die hard; **mener la ~ dure à qn** to make life a misery for sb.

vieil [vjɛj] *am voir* **vieux**.

vieillard [vjɛjaʀ] *nm* old man; **les ~s** old people, the elderly.

vieille [vjɛj] *af, nf voir* **vieux**.

vieilleries [vjɛjʀi] *nfpl* old things *ou* stuff *sg*.

vieillesse [vjɛjɛs] *nf* old age; *(vieillards):* **la ~** the old *pl,* the elderly *pl.*

vieilli, e [vjeji] *a (marqué par l'âge)* aged; *(suranné)* dated.

vieillir [vjejiʀ] *vi (prendre de l'âge)* to grow old; *(population, vin)* to age; *(doctrine, auteur)* to become dated ♦ *vt* to age; **il a beaucoup vieilli** he has aged a lot; **se ~** to make o.s. older.

vieillissement [vjejismɑ̃] *nm* growing old; ageing.

vieillot, te [vjɛjo, -ɔt] *a* antiquated, quaint.

vielle [vjɛl] *nf* hurdy-gurdy.

viendrai [vjɛ̃dʀe] *etc vb voir* **venir**.

Vienne [vjɛn] *n (en Autriche)* Vienna.

vienne [vjɛn], **viens** [vjɛ̃] *etc vb voir* **venir**.

viennois, e [vjɛnwa, -waz] *a* Viennese.

vierge [vjɛʀʒ(ə)] *a* virgin; *(film)* blank; *(page)* clean, blank; *(jeune fille):* **être ~** to be a virgin ♦ *nf* virgin; *(signe):* **la V~** Virgo, the Virgin; **être de la V~** to be Virgo; **~ de** *(sans)* free from, unsullied by.

Viet-Nam, Vietnam [vjɛtnam] *nm:* **le ~** Vietnam; **le ~ du Nord/du Sud** North/South Vietnam.

vietnamien, ne [vjɛtnamjɛ̃, -ɛn] *a* Vietnamese ♦ *nm (LING)* Vietnamese ♦ *nm/f:* **V~, ne** Vietnamese; **V~, ne du Nord/Sud** North/South Vietnamese.

vieux (vieil), vieille [vjø, vjɛj] *a* old ♦ *nm/f* old man/woman ♦ *nmpl:* **les ~** the old, old people; *(fam: parents)* the old folk *ou* ones; **un petit ~** a little old man; **mon ~/ma vieille** *(fam)* old man/girl; **pauvre ~** poor old soul; **prendre un coup de ~** to put years on; **se faire ~** to make o.s. look older; **un ~ de la vieille** one of the old brigade; **~ garçon** *nm* bachelor; **~ jeu** *a inv* old-fashioned; **~ rose** *a inv* old rose; **vieil or** *a inv* old gold; **vieille fille** *nf* spinster.

vif, vive [vif, viv] *a (animé)* lively; *(alerte)* sharp, quick; *(brusque)* sharp, brusque; *(aigu)* sharp; *(lumière, couleur)* brilliant; *(air)* crisp; *(vent, émotion)* keen; *(froid)* bitter; *(fort: regret, déception)* great, deep; *(vivant):* **brûlé ~** burnt alive; **eau vive** running water; **de vive voix** personally; **piquer qn au ~** to cut sb to the quick; **tailler**

dans le **~** to cut into the living flesh; **à ~** *(plaie)* open; **avoir les nerfs à ~** to be on edge; **sur le ~** *(ART)* from life; **entrer dans le ~ du sujet** to get to the very heart of the matter.

vif-argent [vifaʀʒɑ̃] *nm inv* quicksilver.

vigie [viʒi] *nf (matelot)* look-out; *(poste)* look-out post, crow's nest.

vigilance [viʒilɑ̃s] *nf* vigilance.

vigilant, e [viʒilɑ̃, -ɑ̃t] *a* vigilant.

vigile [viʒil] *nm (veilleur de nuit)* (night) watchman; *(police privée)* vigilante.

vigne [viɲ] *nf (plante)* vine; *(plantation)* vineyard; **~ vierge** Virginia creeper.

vigneron [viɲʀɔ̃] *nm* wine grower.

vignette [viɲɛt] *nf (motif)* vignette; *(de marque)* manufacturer's label *ou* seal; *(petite illustration)* (small) illustration; *(ADMIN)* ≈ (road) tax disc *(Brit)*, ≈ license plate sticker *(US)*; (: *sur médicament)* price label *(on medicines for reimbursement by Social Security)*.

vignoble [viɲɔbl(ə)] *nm (plantation)* vineyard; *(vignes d'une région)* vineyards *pl.*

vigoureusement [viguʀøzmɑ̃] *ad* vigorously.

vigoureux, euse [viguʀø, -øz] *a* vigorous, robust.

vigueur [vigœʀ] *nf* vigour *(Brit)*, vigor *(US)*; **être/entrer en ~** to be in/come into force; **en ~ current.**

vil, e [vil] *a* vile, base; **à ~ prix** at a very low price.

vilain, e [vilɛ̃, -ɛn] *a (laid)* ugly; *(affaire, blessure)* nasty; *(pas sage: enfant)* naughty ♦ *nm (paysan)* villein, villain; **ça va tourner au ~** things are going to turn nasty; **~ mot** bad word.

vilebrequin [vilbʀəkɛ̃] *nm (outil)* (bit-)brace; *(AUTO)* crankshaft.

vilenie [vilni] *nf* vileness *q*, baseness *q.*

vilipender [vilipɑ̃de] *vt* to revile, vilify.

villa [vila] *nf (detached)* house.

village [vilaʒ] *nm* village; **~ de toile** tent village; **~ de vacances** holiday village.

villageois, e [vilaʒwa, -waz] *a* village *cpd* ♦ *nm/f* villager.

ville [vil] *nf* town; *(importante)* city; *(administration):* **la ~** ≈ the Corporation; ≈ the (town) council; **aller en ~** to go to town; **habiter en ~** to live in town; **~ nouvelle** new town.

ville-champignon, *pl* **villes-champignons** [vilʃɑ̃piɲɔ̃] *nf* boom town.

ville-dortoir, *pl* **villes-dortoirs** [vildɔʀtwaʀ] *nf* dormitory town.

villégiature [vileʒjatyʀ] *nf (séjour)* holiday; *(lieu)* (holiday) resort.

vin [vɛ̃] *nm* wine; **avoir le ~ gai/triste** to get happy/miserable after a few drinks; **~ blanc/rosé/rouge** white/rosé/red wine; **~ d'honneur** reception *(with wine and snacks)*; **~ de messe** altar wine; **~ ordinaire** *ou* **de table** table wine; **~ de pays** local wine.

vinaigre [vinɛgʀ(ə)] *nm* vinegar; **tourner au ~** *(fig)* to turn sour; **~ de vin/d'alcool** wine/spirit vinegar.

vinaigrette [vinɛgʀɛt] *nf* vinaigrette, French dressing.

vinaigrier [vinɛgʀije] *nm (fabricant)* vinegarmaker; (*flacon*) vinegar cruet *ou* bottle.

vinasse [vinas] *nf* (*péj*) cheap wine, plonk (*Brit*).

vindicatif, ive [vɛ̃dikatif, -iv] *a* vindictive.

vindicte [vɛ̃dikt(ə)] *nf*: **désigner qn à la ~ publique** to expose sb to public condemnation.

vineux, euse [vinø, -øz] *a* win(e)y.

vingt [vɛ̃, vɛ̃t + *vowel and in 22, 23 etc*] *num* twenty; **~-quatre heures sur ~-quatre** twenty-four hours a day, round the clock.

vingtaine [vɛ̃tɛn] *nf*: **une ~ (de)** around twenty, twenty or so.

vingtième [vɛ̃tjɛm] *num* twentieth.

vinicole [vinikɔl] *a* (*production*) wine *cpd*; (*région*) wine-growing.

vinification [vinifikasjɔ̃] *nf* wine-making, wine production; (*des sucres*) vinification.

vinyle [vinil] *nm* vinyl.

viol [vjɔl] *nm* (*d'une femme*) rape; (*d'un lieu sacré*) violation.

violacé, e [vjɔlase] *a* purplish, mauvish.

violation [vjɔlasjɔ̃] *nf* desecration; violation; (*d'un droit*) breach.

violemment [vjɔlamɑ̃] *ad* violently.

violence [vjɔlɑ̃s] *nf* violence; **~s** *nfpl* acts of violence; **faire ~ à qn** to do violence to sb; **se faire ~** to force o.s.

violent, e [vjɔlɑ̃, -ɑ̃t] *a* violent; (*remède*) drastic; (*besoin, désir*) intense, urgent.

violenter [vjɔlɑ̃te] *vt* to assault (sexually).

violer [vjɔle] *vt* (*femme*) to rape; (*sépulture*) to desecrate, violate; (*loi, traité*) to violate.

violet, te [vjɔlɛ, -ɛt] *a, nm* purple, mauve ♦ *nf* (*fleur*) violet.

violeur [vjɔlœr] *nm* rapist.

violon [vjɔlɔ̃] *nm* violin; (*dans la musique folklorique etc*) fiddle; (*fam: prison*) lock-up; **premier ~** first violin; **~ d'Ingres** (*artistic*) hobby.

violoncelle [vjɔlɔ̃sɛl] *nm* cello.

violoncelliste [vjɔlɔ̃selist(ə)] *nm/f* cellist.

violoniste [vjɔlɔnist(ə)] *nm/f* violinist, violin-player; (*folklorique etc*) fiddler.

VIP *sigle m* (= *Very Important Person*) VIP.

vipère [vipɛr] *nf* viper, adder.

virage [viraʒ] *nm* (*d'un véhicule*) turn; (*d'une route, piste*) bend; (*CHIMIE*) change in colour (*Brit*) *ou* color (*US*); (*de cuti-réaction*) positive reaction; (*PHOTO*) toning; (*fig: POL*) about-turn; **prendre un ~** to go into a bend, take a bend; **~ sans visibilité** blind bend.

viral, e, aux [viral, -o] *a* viral.

virée [vire] *nf* (*courte*) run; (: *à pied*) walk; (*longue*) trip; hike, walking tour.

virement [virmɑ̃] *nm* (*COMM*) transfer; **~ bancaire** (bank) credit transfer, ≈ (bank) giro transfer (*Brit*); **~ postal** Post office credit transfer, ≈ Girobank ® transfer (*Brit*).

virent [vir] *vb voir* **voir**.

virer [vire] *vt* (*COMM*): **~ qch (sur)** to transfer sth (into); (*PHOTO*) to tone; (*fam: renvoyer*) to sack, boot out ♦ *vi* to turn; (*CHIMIE*) to change colour (*Brit*) *ou* color (*US*); (*cuti-réaction*) to come up positive; (*PHOTO*) to tone; **~ au bleu** to turn blue; **~ de bord** to tack; (*fig*) to change tack; **~ sur l'aile** to bank.

virevolte [virvɔlt(ə)] *nf* twirl; (*d'avis, d'opinion*) about-turn.

virevolter [virvɔlte] *vi* to twirl around.

virginal, e, aux [virʒinal, -o] *a* virginal.

virginité [virʒinite] *nf* virginity; (*fig*) purity.

virgule [virgyl] *nf* comma; (*MATH*) point; **4 ~ 2** 4 point 2; **~ flottante** floating decimal.

viril, e [viril] *a* (*propre à l'homme*) masculine; (*énergique, courageux*) manly, virile.

viriliser [virilize] *vt* to make (more) manly *ou* masculine.

virilité [virilite] *nf* (*attributs masculins*) masculinity; (*fermeté, courage*) manliness; (*sexuelle*) virility.

virologie [virɔlɔʒi] *nf* virology.

virtualité [virtɥalite] *nf* virtuality; potentiality.

virtuel, le [virtɥɛl] *a* potential; (*théorique*) virtual.

virtuellement [virtɥɛlmɑ̃] *a* potentially; (*presque*) virtually.

virtuose [virtɥoz] *nm/f* (*MUS*) virtuoso; (*gén*) master.

virtuosité [virtɥozite] *nf* virtuosity; masterliness, masterful skills *pl*.

virulence [virylɑ̃s] *nf* virulence.

virulent, e [virylɑ̃, -ɑ̃t] *a* virulent.

virus [virys] *nm* virus.

vis *vb* [vi] *voir* **voir, vivre** ♦ *nf* [vis] screw; **~ à tête plate/ronde** flat-headed/round-headed screw; **~ platinées** (*AUTO*) (contact) points; **~ sans fin** worm, endless screw.

visa [viza] *nm* (*sceau*) stamp; (*validation de passeport*) visa; **~ de censure** (censor's) certificate.

visage [vizaʒ] *nm* face; **à ~ découvert** (*franchement*) openly.

visagiste [vizaʒist(ə)] *nm/f* beautician.

vis-à-vis [vizavi] *ad* face to face ♦ *nm* person opposite; house *etc* opposite; **~ de** *prép* opposite; (*fig*) towards, vis-à-vis; **en ~** facing *ou* opposite each other; **sans ~** (*immeuble*) with an open outlook.

viscéral, e, aux [viseral, -o] *a* (*fig*) deep-seated, deep-rooted.

viscères [visɛr] *nmpl* intestines, entrails.

viscose [viskoz] *nf* viscose.

viscosité [viskozite] *nf* viscosity.

visée [vize] *nf* (*avec une arme*) aiming; (*ARPENTAGE*) sighting; **~s** *nfpl* (*intentions*) designs; **avoir des ~s sur qn/qch** to have designs on sb/sth.

viser [vize] *vi* to aim ♦ *vt* to aim at; (*concerner*) to be aimed *ou* directed at; (*apposer un visa sur*) to stamp, visa; **~ à qch/faire** to aim at sth/at doing *ou* to do.

viseur [vizœr] *nm* (*d'arme*) sights *pl*; (*PHOTO*) viewfinder.

visibilité [vizibilite] *nf* visibility; **sans ~** (*pilotage, virage*) blind *cpd*.

visible [vizibl(ə)] *a* visible; (*disponible*): **est-il ~?** can he see me?, will he see visitors?

visiblement [vizibləmɑ̃] *ad* visibly, obviously.

visière [vizjɛr] *nf* (*de casquette*) peak; (*qui s'attache*) eyeshade.

vision [vizjɔ̃] *nf* vision; (*sens*) (eye)sight, vision; (*fait de voir*): **la ~ de** the sight of; **première ~** (*CINÉMA*) first showing.

visionnaire [vizjɔnɛr] *a, nm/f* visionary.

visionner [vizjɔne] *vt* to view.

visionneuse [vizjɔnøz] *nf* viewer.

visite [vizit] *nf* visit; *(visiteur)* visitor; *(touristique: d'un musée etc)* tour; *(COMM: de représentant)* call; *(expertise, d'inspection)* inspection; *(médicale, à domicile)* visit, call; **la ~** *(MÉD)* medical examination; *(MIL: d'entrée)* medicals *pl*; *(: quotidienne)* sick parade; **faire une ~ à qn** to call on sb, pay sb a visit; **rendre ~ à qn** to visit sb, pay sb a visit; **être en ~ (chez qn)** to be visiting (sb); **heures de ~** *(hôpital, prison)* visiting hours; **le droit de ~** *(JUR: aux enfants)* right of access, access; **~ de douane** customs inspection *ou* examination.

visiter [vizite] *vt* to visit; *(musée, ville)* to visit, go round.

visiteur, euse [vizitœr, -øz] *nm/f* visitor; **~ des douanes** customs inspector; **~ médical** medical rep(resentative); **~ de prison** prison visitor.

vison [vizɔ̃] *nm* mink.

visqueux, euse [viskø, -øz] *a* viscous; *(péj)* gooey; *(: manières)* slimy.

visser [vise] *vt*: **~ qch** *(fixer, serrer)* to screw sth on.

visu [vizy]: **de ~** *ad* with one's own eyes.

visualisation [vizɥalizasjɔ̃] *nf (INFORM)* display; **écran de ~** visual display unit (VDU).

visualiser [vizɥalize] *vt* to visualize; *(INFORM)* to display, bring up on screen.

visuel, le [vizɥɛl] *a* visual ♦ *nm* (visual) display; *(INFORM)* visual display unit (VDU).

visuellement [vizɥɛlmɑ̃] *ad* visually.

vit [vi] *vb voir* **voir, vivre**.

vital, e, aux [vital, -o] *a* vital.

vitalité [vitalite] *nf* vitality.

vitamine [vitamin] *nf* vitamin.

vitaminé, e *a* [vitamine] with (added) vitamins.

vitaminique [vitaminik] *a* vitamin *cpd*.

vite [vit] *ad (rapidement)* quickly, fast; *(sans délai)* quickly; soon; **faire ~** *(agir rapidement)* to act fast; *(se dépêcher)* to be quick; **ce sera ~ fini** this will soon be finished; **viens ~** come quick(ly).

vitesse [vitɛs] *nf* speed; *(AUTO: dispositif)* gear; **faire de la ~** to drive fast *ou* at speed; **prendre qn de ~** to outstrip sb, get ahead of sb; **prendre de la ~** to pick up *ou* gather speed; **à toute ~** at full *ou* top speed; **en perte de ~** *(avion)* losing lift; *(fig)* losing momentum; **changer de ~** *(AUTO)* to change gear; **~ acquise** momentum; **~ de croisière** cruising speed; **~ de pointe** top speed; **~ du son** speed of sound.

viticole [vitikɔl] *a (industrie)* wine *cpd*; *(région)* wine-growing.

viticulteur [vitikyltœr] *nm* wine grower.

viticulture [vitikyltyr] *nf* wine growing.

vitrage [vitraʒ] *nm (cloison)* glass partition; *(toit)* glass roof; *(rideau)* net curtain.

vitrail, aux [vitraj, -o] *nm* stained-glass window.

vitre [vitr(ə)] *nf* (window) pane; *(de portière, voiture)* window.

vitré, e [vitre] *a* glass *cpd*.

vitrer [vitre] *vt* to glaze.

vitreux, euse [vitrø, -øz] *a* vitreous; *(terne)* glassy.

vitrier [vitrije] *nm* glazier.

vitrifier [vitrifje] *vt* to vitrify; *(parquet)* to glaze.

vitrine [vitrin] *nf (devanture)* (shop) window; *(étalage)* display; *(petite armoire)* display cabinet; **en ~** in the window, on display; **~ publicitaire** display case, showcase.

vitriol [vitrijɔl] *nm* vitriol; **au ~** *(fig)* vitriolic.

vitupérations [vityperasjɔ̃] *nfpl* invective *sg*.

vitupérer [vitypere] *vi* to rant and rave; **~ contre** to rail against.

vivable *a* [vivabl(ə)] *a (personne)* livable-with; *(endroit)* fit to live in.

vivace *a* [vivas] *(arbre, plante)* hardy; *(fig)* enduring ♦ *ad* [vivatʃe] *(MUS)* vivace.

vivacité [vivasite] *nf (voir vif)* liveliness, vivacity; sharpness; brilliance.

vivant, e [vivɑ̃, -ɑ̃t] *vb voir* **vivre** ♦ *a (qui vit)* living, alive; *(animé)* lively; *(preuve, exemple)* living; *(langue)* modern ♦ *nm*: **du ~ de qn** in sb's lifetime; **les ~s et les morts** the living and the dead.

vivarium [vivarjɔm] *nm* vivarium.

vivats [viva] *nmpl* cheers.

vive [viv] *af voir* **vif** ♦ *vb voir* **vivre** ♦ *excl*: **~ le roi!** long live the king!; **~ les vacances!** hurrah for the holidays!

vivement [vivmɑ̃] *ad* vivaciously; sharply ♦ *excl*: **~ les vacances!** I can't wait for the holidays!, roll on the holidays!

viveur [vivœr] *nm (péj)* high liver, pleasure-seeker.

vivier [vivje] *nm (au restaurant etc)* fish tank; *(étang)* fishpond.

vivifiant, e [vivifjɑ̃, -ɑ̃t] *a* invigorating.

vivifier [vivifje] *vt* to invigorate; *(fig: souvenirs, sentiments)* to liven up, enliven.

vivisection [vivisɛksjɔ̃] *nf* vivisection.

vivoter [vivɔte] *vi (personne)* to scrape a living, get by; *(fig: affaire etc)* to struggle along.

vivre [vivr(ə)] *vi, vt* to live ♦ *nm*: **le ~ et le logement** board and lodging ♦ **~s** *nmpl* provisions, food supplies; **il vit encore** he is still alive; **se laisser ~** to take life as it comes; **ne plus ~** *(être anxieux)* to live on one's nerves; **il a vécu** *(eu une vie aventureuse)* he has seen life; **ce régime a vécu** this regime has had its day; **être facile à ~** to be easy to get on with; **faire ~ qn** *(pourvoir à sa subsistance)* to provide (a living) for sb; **~ mal** *(chichement)* to have a meagre existence; **~ de** *(salaire etc)* to live on.

vivrier, ière [vivrije, -jɛr] *a* food-producing *cpd*.

vlan [vlɑ̃] *excl* wham!, bang!

VO *sigle f (CINÉMA: = version originale)*: **voir un film en ~** to see a film in its original language.

v° *abr =* **verso**.

vocable [vɔkabl(ə)] *nm* term.

vocabulaire [vɔkabylɛr] *nm* vocabulary.

vocal, e, aux [vɔkal, -o] *a* vocal.

vocalique [vɔkalik] *a* a vocalic, vowel *cpd*.

vocalise [vɔkaliz] *nf* singing exercise.

vocaliser [vɔkalize] *vi (LING)* to vocalize; *(MUS)* to do one's singing exercises.

vocation [vɔkasjɔ̃] *nf* vocation, calling; **avoir la ~** to have a vocation.

vociférations [vɔsiferasjɔ̃] *nfpl* cries of rage, screams.

vociférer [vɔsifeʀe] *vi, vt* to scream.

vodka [vɔdka] *nf* vodka.

vœu, x [vø] *nm* wish; (*à Dieu*) vow; **faire ~ de** to take a vow of; **avec tous nos ~x** with every good wish *ou* our best wishes; **~x de bonheur** best wishes for your future happiness; **~x de bonne année** best wishes for the New Year.

vogue [vɔg] *nf* fashion, vogue; **en ~** in fashion, in vogue.

voguer [vɔge] *vi* to sail.

voici [vwasi] *prép* (*pour introduire, désigner*) here is + *sg*, here are + *pl*; **et ~ que ...** and now it (*ou* he) ...; **il est parti ~ 3 ans** he left 3 years ago; **~ une semaine que je l'ai vue** it's a week since I've seen her; **me ~** here I am; *voir aussi* **voilà**.

voie [vwa] *vb voir* **voir** ♦ *nf* way; (*RAIL*) track, line; (*AUTO*) lane; **par ~ buccale** *ou* **orale** orally; **par ~ rectale** rectally; **suivre la ~ hiérarchique** to go through official channels; **ouvrir/montrer la ~** to open up/show the way; **être en bonne ~** to be shaping *ou* going well; **mettre qn sur la ~** to put sb on the right track; **être en ~ d'achèvement/de rénovation** to be nearing completion/in the process of renovation; **à ~ étroite** narrow-gauge; **à ~ unique** single-track; **route à 2/3 ~s** 2-/3-lane road; **par la ~ aérienne/ maritime** by air/sea; **~ d'eau** (*NAVIG*) leak; **~ express** expressway; **~ de fait** (*JUR*) assault (and battery); **~ ferrée** track; rail-way line (*Brit*), railroad (*US*); **par ~ ferrée** by rail, by railroad; **~ de garage** (*RAIL*) siding; **la ~ lactée** the Milky Way; **~ naviga-ble** waterway; **~ prioritaire** (*AUTO*) road with right of way; **~ privée** private road; **la ~ publique** the public highway.

voilà [vwala] *prép* (*en désignant*) there is + *sg*, there are + *pl*; **les ~** *ou* **voici here** *ou* there they are; **en ~** *ou* **voici un** here's one, there's one; **~** *ou* **voici deux ans** two years ago; **~** *ou* **voici deux ans que** it's two years since; **et ~!** there we are!; **~ tout** that's all; **"~** *ou* **voici"** (*en offrant etc*) "there *ou* here you are".

voilage [vwalaʒ] *nm* (*rideau*) net curtain; (*tissu*) net.

voile [vwal] *nm* veil; (*tissu léger*) net ♦ *nf* sail; (*sport*) sailing; **prendre le ~** to take the veil; **mettre à la ~** to make way under sail; **~ du palais** *nm* soft palate, velum; **~ au poumon** *nm* shadow on the lung.

voiler [vwale] *vt* to veil; (*PHOTO*) to fog; (*fausser: roue*) to buckle; (: *bois*) to warp; **se ~** *vi* (*lune, regard*) to mist over; (*ciel*) to grow hazy; (*voix*) to become husky; (*roue, disque*) to buckle; (*planche*) to warp; **se ~ la face** to hide one's face.

voilette [vwalɛt] *nf* (hat) veil.

voilier [vwalje] *nm* sailing ship; (*de plaisance*) sailing boat.

voilure [vwalyʀ] *nf* (*de voilier*) sails *pl*; (*d'avion*) aerofoils *pl* (*Brit*), airfoils *pl* (*US*); (*de parachute*) canopy.

voir [vwaʀ] *vi, vt* to see; **se ~: se ~ critiquer/transformer** to be criticized/ transformed; **cela se voit** (*cela arrive*) it happens; (*c'est visible*) that's obvious, it shows; **~ à faire qch** to see to it that sth is done; **~ loin** (*fig*) to be far-sighted; **~ venir** (*fig*) to wait and see; **faire ~ qch à qn** to show sb sth; **en faire ~ à qn** (*fig*) to give sb a hard time; **ne pas pouvoir ~ qn** (*fig*) not to be able to stand sb; **regardez ~** just look; **montrez ~** show (me); **dites ~** tell me; **voyons!** let's see now; (*indignation etc*) come (along) now!; **c'est à ~!** we'll see!; **c'est ce qu'on va ~** we'll see about that!; **avoir quelque chose à ~ avec** to have something to do with; **ça n'a rien à ~ avec lui** that has nothing to do with him.

voire [vwaʀ] *ad* indeed; nay; or even.

voirie [vwaʀi] *nf* highway maintenance; (*administration*) highways department; (*enlèvement des ordures*) refuse (*Brit*) *ou* garbage (*US*) collection.

vois [vwa] *vb voir* **voir**.

voisin, e [vwazɛ̃, -in] *a* (*proche*) neighbouring (*Brit*), neighboring (*US*); (*contigu*) next; (*ressemblant*) connected ♦ *nm/f* neighbo(u)r; (*de table, de dortoir etc*) person next to me (*ou* him *etc*); **~ de palier** neighbo(u)r across the landing (*Brit*) *ou* hall (*US*).

voisinage [vwazinaʒ] *nm* (*proximité*) prox-imity; (*environs*) vicinity; (*quartier, voisins*) neighbourhood (*Brit*), neighborhood (*US*); **relations de bon ~** neighbo(u)rly terms.

voisiner [vwazine] *vi*: **~ avec** to be side by side with.

voit [vwa] *vb voir* **voir**.

voiture [vwatyʀ] *nf* car; (*wagon*) coach, car-riage; **en ~!** all aboard!; **~ à bras** handcart; **~ d'enfant** pram (*Brit*), baby carriage (*US*); **~ d'infirme** invalid carriage; **~ de sport** sports car.

voiture-lit, *pl* **voitures-lits** [vwatyʀli] *nf* sleeper.

voiture-restaurant, *pl* **voitures-restaurants** [vwatyʀʀɛstɔʀɑ̃] *nf* dining car.

voix [vwa] *nf* voice; (*POL*) vote; **la ~ de la conscience/raison** the voice of conscience/ reason; **à haute ~** aloud; **à ~ basse** in a low voice; **faire la grosse ~** to speak gruffly; **avoir de la ~** to have a good voice; **rester sans ~** to be speechless; **~ de basse/ténor** *etc* bass/tenor *etc* voice; **à 2/4 ~** (*MUS*) in 2/4 parts; **avoir ~ au chapitre** to have a say in the matter; **mettre aux ~** to put to the vote.

vol [vɔl] *nm* (*mode de locomotion*) flying; (*trajet, voyage, groupe d'oiseaux*) flight; (*mode d'appropriation*) theft, stealing; (*larcin*) theft; **à ~ d'oiseau** as the crow flies; **au ~: attraper qch au ~** to catch sth as it flies past; **saisir une remarque au ~** to pick up a passing remark; **prendre son ~** to take flight; **de haut ~** (*fig*) of the highest order; **en ~** in flight; **~ avec effraction** breaking and entering *q*, break-in; **~ à l'étalage** shop-lifting *q*; **~ libre** hang-gliding; **~ à main armée** armed robbery; **~ de nuit** night flight; **~ plané** (*AVIAT*) glide, gliding *q*; **~ à la tire** pickpocketing *q*; **~ à voile** gliding.

vol. *abr* (= *volume*) vol.

volage [vɔlaʒ] *a* fickle.

volaille [vɔlaj] *nf* (*oiseaux*) poultry *pl*;

(viande) poultry *q*; *(oiseau)* fowl.
volailler [vɔlɑje] *nm* poulterer.
volant, e [vɔlɑ̃, -ɑ̃t] *a voir* **feuille** *etc* ♦ *nm*
(d'automobile) (steering) wheel; *(de
commande)* wheel; *(objet lancé)* shuttlecock;
(jeu) battledore and shuttlecock; *(bande de
tissu)* flounce; *(feuillet détachable)* tear-off
portion; **le personnel ~, les ~s** *(AVIAT)* the
flight staff; **~ de sécurité** *(fig)* reserve,
margin, safeguard.
volatil, e [vɔlatil] *a* volatile.
volatile [vɔlatil] *nm* *(volaille)* bird; *(tout
oiseau)* winged creature.
volatiliser [vɔlatilize]: **se ~** *vi* *(CHIMIE)* to
volatilize; *(fig)* to vanish into thin air.
vol-au-vent [vɔlovɑ̃] *nm inv* vol-au-vent.
volcan [vɔlkɑ̃] *nm* volcano; *(fig: personne)*
hothead.
volcanique [vɔlkanik] *a* volcanic; *(fig:
tempérament)* volatile.
volcanologue [vɔlkanɔlɔg] *nm/f* vulcanologist.
volée [vɔle] *nf* *(groupe d'oiseaux)* flight, flock;
(TENNIS) volley; **~ de coups/de flèches**
volley of blows/arrows; **à la ~: rattraper à la
~** to catch in midair; **lancer à la ~** to fling
about; **semer à la ~** to (sow) broadcast; **à
toute ~** *(sonner les cloches)* vigorously;
(lancer un projectile) with full force; **de
haute ~** *(fig)* of the highest order.
voler [vɔle] *vi* *(avion, oiseau, fig)* to fly;
(voleur) to steal ♦ *vt* *(objet)* to steal;
(personne) to rob; **~ en éclats** to smash to
smithereens; **~ de ses propres ailes** *(fig)* to
stand on one's own two feet; **~ au vent** to fly
in the wind; **~ qch à qn** to steal sth from sb.
volet [vɔlɛ] *nm* *(de fenêtre)* shutter; *(AVIAT)*
flap; *(de feuillet, document)* section; *(fig:
d'un plan)* facet; **trié sur le ~** hand-picked.
voleter [vɔlte] *vi* to flutter (about).
voleur, euse [vɔlœʀ, -øz] *nm/f* thief *(pl
thieves)* ♦ *a* thieving.
volière [vɔljɛʀ] *nf* aviary.
volley(-ball) [vɔlɛ(bol)] *nm* volleyball.
volleyeur, euse [vɔlɛjœʀ, -øz] *nm/f* volleyball
player.
volontaire [vɔlɔ̃tɛʀ] *a* *(acte, activité)*
voluntary; *(délibéré)* deliberate; *(caractère,
personne: décidé)* self-willed ♦ *nm/f*
volunteer.
volontairement [vɔlɔ̃tɛʀmɑ̃] *ad* voluntarily;
deliberately.
volontariat [vɔlɔ̃taʀja] *nm* voluntary service.
volontariste [vɔlɔ̃taʀist(ə)] *a, nm/f* voluntarist.
volonté [vɔlɔ̃te] *nf* *(faculté de vouloir)* will;
(énergie, fermeté) will(power); *(souhait,
désir)* wish; **se servir/boire à ~** to take/drink
as much as one likes; **bonne ~** goodwill,
willingness; **mauvaise ~** lack of goodwill, un-
willingness.
volontiers [vɔlɔ̃tje] *ad* *(de bonne grâce)* willingly; *(avec plaisir)* willingly, gladly;
(habituellement, souvent) readily, willingly;
"~" "with pleasure", "I'd be glad to".
volt [vɔlt] *nm* volt.
voltage [vɔltaʒ] *nm* voltage.
volte-face [vɔltəfas] *nf inv* about-turn; *(fig)*
about-turn, U-turn; **faire ~** to do an about-
turn; to do a U-turn.
voltige [vɔltiʒ] *nf* *(ÉQUITATION)* trick riding;

(au cirque) acrobatics *sg*; *(AVIAT)* (aerial)
acrobatics *sg*; **numéro de haute ~** acrobatic
act.
voltiger [vɔltiʒe] *vi* to flutter (about).
voltigeur [vɔltiʒœʀ] *nm* *(au cirque)* acrobat;
(MIL) light infantryman.
voltmètre [vɔltmɛtʀ(ə)] *nm* voltmeter.
volubile [vɔlybil] *a* voluble.
volubilis [vɔlybilis] *nm* convolvulus.
volume [vɔlym] *nm* volume; *(GÉOM: solide)*
solid.
volumineux, euse [vɔyminø, -øz] *a*
voluminous, bulky.
volupté [vɔlypte] *nf* sensual delight *ou*
pleasure.
voluptueusement [vɔlyptɥøzmɑ̃] *ad* volup-
tuously.
voluptueux, euse [vɔlyptɥø, -øz] *a* voluptuous.
volute [vɔlyt] *nf* *(ARCHIT)* volute; **~ de fumée**
curl of smoke.
vomi [vɔmi] *nm* vomit.
vomir [vɔmiʀ] *vi* to vomit, be sick ♦ *vt* to
vomit, bring up; *(fig)* to belch out, spew out;
(exécrer) to loathe, abhor.
vomissement [vɔmismɑ̃] *nm* *(action)* vomiting *q*; **des ~s** vomit.
vomissure [vɔmisyʀ] *nf* vomit *q*.
vomitif [vɔmitif] *nm* emetic.
vont [vɔ̃] *vb voir* **aller**.
vorace [vɔʀas] *a* voracious.
voracement [vɔʀasmɑ̃] *ad* voraciously.
vos [vo] *dét voir* **votre**.
Vosges [voʒ] *nfpl*: **les ~** the Vosges.
vosgien, ne [voʒjɛ̃, -ɛn] *a* of *ou* from the
Vosges ♦ *nm/f* inhabitant *ou* native of the
Vosges.
VOST *sigle f* *(CINÉMA: = version originale
sous-titrée)* sub-titled version.
votant, e [vɔtɑ̃, -ɑ̃t] *nm/f* voter.
vote [vɔt] *nm* vote; **~ par correspondance/
procuration** postal/proxy vote; **~ à main
levée** vote by show of hands; **~ secret, ~ à
bulletins secrets** secret ballot.
voter [vɔte] *vi* to vote ♦ *vt* *(loi, décision)* to
vote for.
votre [vɔtʀ(ə)], *pl* **vos** [vo] *dét* your.
vôtre [votʀ(ə)] *pronom*: **le ~, la ~, les ~s**
yours; **les ~s** *(fig)* your family *ou* folks; **à la
~** *(toast)* your (good) health!
voudrai [vudʀe] *etc vb voir* **vouloir**.
voué, e [vwe] *a*: **~ à** doomed to, destined for.
vouer [vwe] *vt*: **~ qch à** *(Dieu/un saint)* to
dedicate sth to; **~ sa vie/son temps à**
(étude, cause etc) to devote one's life/time to;
~ une haine/amitié éternelle à qn to vow
undying hatred/friendship to sb.
vouloir [vulwaʀ] *vi* to show will, have willpower ♦ *vt* to want ♦ *nm*: **le bon ~ de qn**
sb's goodwill; sb's pleasure; **~ que qn fasse**
to want sb to do; **~ faire** to want to do; **je
voudrais ceci** I would like this; **il voudrait
que l'on vienne** he would like us to come; **le
hasard a voulu que** fate decreed that; **la
tradition veut que** tradition requires that; ...
qui se veut moderne ... which purports to be
modern; **veuillez attendre** please wait; **je
veux bien** *(bonne volonté)* I'll be happy to;
(concession) fair enough, that's fine; **si on**

veut, comme vous voudrez as you wish; *(en quelque sorte)* if you like; **que me veut-il?** what does he want with me?; ~ **dire (que)** *(signifier)* to mean (that); **sans le** ~ *(involontairement)* without meaning to, unintentionally; ~ **qch à qn** to wish sth for sb; **en** ~ **à qn** to bear sb a grudge; **en** ~ **à qch** *(avoir des visées sur)* to be after sth; **s'en** ~ **de** to be annoyed with o.s. for; ~ **de qch/qn** *(accepter)* to want sth/sb.

voulu, e [vuly] *pp de* **vouloir ♦** *a (requis)* required, requisite; *(délibéré)* deliberate, intentional.

voulus [vuly] *etc vb voir* **vouloir**.

vous [vu] *pronom* you; *(objet indirect)* (to) you; *(réfléchi)* yourself *(pl* yourselves); *(réciproque)* each other **♦** *nm:* **employer le** ~ *(vouvoyer)* to use the "vous" form; ~**-même** yourself; ~**-mêmes** yourselves.

voûte [vut] *nf* vault; **la** ~ **céleste** the vault of heaven; ~ **du palais** *(ANAT)* roof of the mouth; ~ **plantaire** arch (of the foot).

voûté, e [vute] *a* vaulted, arched; *(dos, personne)* bent, stooped.

voûter [vute] *vt (ARCHIT)* to arch, vault; **se** ~ *vi (dos, personne)* to become stooped.

vouvoiement [vuvwamã] *nm* use of formal "vous" form.

vouvoyer [vuvwaje] *vt:* ~ **qn** to address sb as "vous".

voyage [vwajaʒ] *nm* journey, trip; *(fait de voyager)*: **le** ~ travel(ling); **partir/être en** ~ to go off/be away on a journey *ou* trip; **faire un** ~ to go on *ou* make a trip *ou* journey; **faire bon** ~ to have a good journey; **les gens du** ~ travelling people; ~ **d'agrément/ d'affaires** pleasure/business trip; ~ **de noces** honeymoon; ~ **organisé** package tour.

voyager [vwajaʒe] *vi* to travel.

voyageur, euse [vwajaʒœR, -øz] *nm/f* traveller; *(passager)* passenger **♦** *a (tempérament)* nomadic, wayfaring; ~ **(de commerce)** commercial traveller.

voyagiste [vwajaʒist(ə)] *nm* tour operator.

voyais [vwajɛ] *etc vb voir* **voir**.

voyance [vwajãs] *nf* clairvoyance.

voyant, e [vwajã, -ãt] *a (couleur)* loud, gaudy **♦** *nm/f (personne qui voit)* sighted person **♦** *nm (signal)* (warning) light **♦** *nf* clairvoyant.

voyelle [vwajɛl] *nf* vowel.

voyeur, euse [vwajœR, -øz] *nm/f* voyeur; peeping Tom.

voyons [vwajɔ̃] *etc vb voir* **voir**.

voyou [vwaju] *nm* lout, hoodlum; *(enfant)* guttersnipe.

VPC *sigle f (= vente par correspondance)* mail order selling.

vrac [vRak]: **en** ~ *ad* higgledy-piggledy; *(COMM)* in bulk.

vrai, e [vRɛ] *a (véridique: récit, faits)* true; *(non factice, authentique)* real **♦** *nm:* **le** ~ the truth; **à** ~ **dire** to tell the truth; **il est** ~ **que** it is true that; **être dans le** ~ to be right.

vraiment [vRɛmã] *ad* really.

vraisemblable [vRɛsãblabl(ə)] *a (plausible)* likely, plausible; *(probable)* likely, probable.

vraisemblablement [vRɛsãblabləmã] *ad* in all likelihood, very likely.

vraisemblance [vRɛsãblãs] *nf* likelihood, plausibility; *(romanesque)* verisimilitude; **selon toute** ~ in all likelihood.

vraquier [vRakje] *nm* freighter.

vrille [vRij] *nf (de plante)* tendril; *(outil)* gimlet; *(spirale)* spiral; *(AVIAT)* spin.

vriller [vRije] *vt* to bore into, pierce.

vrombir [vRɔ̃biR] *vi* to hum.

vrombissant, e [vRɔ̃bisã, -ãt] *a* humming.

vrombissement [vRɔ̃bismã] *nm* hum(ming).

VRP *sigle m (= voyageur, représentant, placier)* (sales) rep.

vu [vy] *prép (en raison de)* in view of; ~ **que** in view of the fact that.

vu, e [vy] *pp de* **voir ♦** *a:* **bien/mal** ~ *(personne)* well/poorly thought of; *(conduite)* good/bad form **♦** *nm:* **au** ~ **et au su de tous** openly and publicly; **ni** ~ **ni connu** what the eye doesn't see ...!, no one will be any the wiser; **c'est tout** ~ it's a foregone conclusion.

vue [vy] *nf (fait de voir)*: **la** ~ **de** the sight of; *(sens, faculté)* (eye)sight; *(panorama, image, photo)* view; *(spectacle)* sight; ~**s** *nfpl (idées)* views; *(dessein)* designs; **perdre la** ~ to lose one's (eye)sight; **perdre de** ~ to lose sight of; **à la** ~ **de tous** in full view of everybody; **hors de** ~ out of sight; **à première** ~ at first sight; **connaître de** ~ to know by sight; **à** ~ *(COMM)* at sight; **tirer à** ~ to shoot on sight; **à** ~ **d'œil** *ad* visibly; *(à première vue)* at a quick glance; **avoir** ~ **sur** to have a view of; **en** ~ *(visible)* in sight; *(COMM)* in the public eye; **avoir qch en** ~ *(intentions)* to have one's sights on sth; **en** ~ **de faire** with the intention of doing, with a view to doing; ~ **d'ensemble** overall view; ~ **de l'esprit** theoretical view.

vulcaniser [vylkanize] *vt* to vulcanize.

vulcanologue [vylkanɔlɔg] *nm/f* = **volcanologue**.

vulgaire [vylgɛR] *a (grossier)* vulgar, coarse; *(trivial)* commonplace, mundane; *(péj: quelconque)*: **de** ~**s touristes/chaises de cuisine** common tourists/kitchen chairs; *(BOT, ZOOL: non latin)* common.

vulgairement [vylgɛRmã] *ad* vulgarly, coarsely; *(communément)* commonly.

vulgarisation [vylgaRizasjɔ̃] *nf:* **ouvrage de** ~ popularizing work, popularization.

vulgariser [vylgaRize] *vt* to popularize.

vulgarité [vylgaRite] *nf* vulgarity, coarseness.

vulnérable [vylneRabl(ə)] *a* vulnerable.

vulve [vylv(ə)] *nf* vulva.

Vve *abr* = **veuve**.

VVF *sigle m (= village vacances famille)* state-subsidized holiday village.

vx *abr* = **vieux**.

W

W, w [dubləve] *nm inv* W, w ♦ *abr* (= *watt*) W; **W comme William** W for William.
wagon [vagɔ̃] *nm* (*de voyageurs*) carriage; (*de marchandises*) truck, wagon.
wagon-citerne, *pl* **wagons-citernes** [vagɔ̃sitɛrn(ə)] *nm* tanker.
wagon-lit, *pl* **wagons-lits** [vagɔ̃li] *nm* sleeper, sleeping car.
wagonnet [vagɔnɛ] *nm* small truck.
wagon-poste, *pl* **wagons-postes** [vagɔ̃pɔst(ə)] *nm* mail van.
wagon-restaurant, *pl* **wagons-restaurants** [vagɔ̃rɛstɔrɑ̃] *nm* restaurant *ou* dining car.
walkman [wɔkman] *nm* ® walkman ®, personal stereo.
Wallis et Futuna [walisefytyna]: **les îles ~** the Wallis and Futuna Islands.
wallon, ne [walɔ̃, -ɔn] *a* Walloon ♦ *nm* (*LING*) Walloon ♦ *nm/f:* **W~, ne** Walloon.
waters [watɛr] *nmpl* toilet *sg*, loo *sg* (*Brit*).
watt [wat] *nm* watt.
w.-c. [vese] *nmpl* toilet *sg*, lavatory *sg*.
week-end [wikɛnd] *nm* weekend.
western [wɛstɛrn] *nm* western.
Westphalie [vɛsfali] *nf:* **la ~** Westphalia.
whisky, *pl* **whiskies** [wiski] *nm* whisky.
Winchester [wintʃɛstɛr]: **disque ~** Winchester disk.

X

X, x [iks] *nm inv* X, x ♦ *sigle m* = École Polytechnique; **plainte contre X** (*JUR*) action against person or persons unknown; **X comme Xavier** X for Xmas.
xénophobe [ksenɔfɔb] *a* xenophobic ♦ *nm/f* xenophobe.
xérès [gzerɛs] *nm* sherry.
xylographie [ksilɔgrafi] *nf* xylography; (*image*) xylograph.
xylophone [ksilɔfɔn] *nm* xylophone.

Y

Y, y [igrɛk] *nm inv* Y, y; **Y comme Yvonne** Y for Yellow (*Brit*) *ou* Yoke (*US*).
y [i] *ad* (*à cet endroit*) there; (*dessus*) on it (*ou* them); (*dedans*) in it (*ou* them) ♦ *pronom* (about *ou* on *ou* of) it : *vérifier la syntaxe du verbe employé;* **j'~ pense** I'm thinking about it; *voir aussi* **aller, avoir.**
yacht [jɔt] *nm* yacht.
yaourt [jaurt] *nm* yoghurt.
yaourtière [jaurtjɛr] *nf* yoghurt-maker.
Yémen [jemɛn] *nm:* **le ~** Yemen.
yéménite [jemenit] *a* Yemini.
yeux [jø] *pl de* **œil.**
yoga [jɔga] *nm* yoga.
yoghourt [jɔgurt] *nm* = **yaourt.**
yole [jɔl] *nf* skiff.
yougoslave [jugɔslav] *a* Yugoslav(ian) ♦ *nm/f:* **Y~** Yugoslav(ian).
Yougoslavie [jugɔslavi] *nf:* **la ~** Yugoslavia.
youyou [juju] *nm* dinghy.
yo-yo [jojo] *nm inv* yo-yo.
yucca [juka] *nm* yucca (tree *ou* plant).

Z

Z, z [zɛd] *nm inv* Z, z; **Z comme Zoé** Z for Zebra.
ZAC [zak] *sigle f* (= *zone d'aménagement concerté*) urban development zone.
ZAD [zad] *sigle f* (= *zone d'aménagement différé*) future development zone.
Zaïre [zair] *nm:* **le ~** Zaïre.
zaïrois, e [zairwa, -waz] *a* Zairese.
Zambèze [zɑ̃bez] *nm:* **le ~** the Zambezi.
Zambie [zɑ̃bi] *nf:* **la ~** Zambia.
zambien, ne [zɑ̃bjɛ̃, -ɛn] *a* Zambian.
zèbre [zɛbr(ə)] *nm* (*ZOOL*) zebra.
zébré, e [zebre] *a* striped, streaked.
zébrure [zebryr] *nf* stripe, streak.
zélateur, trice [zelatœr, -tris] *nm/f* partisan, zealot.
zèle [zɛl] *nm* diligence, assiduousness; **faire du ~** (*péj*) to be over-zealous.
zélé, e [zele] *a* zealous.
zénith [zenit] *nm* zenith.
ZEP [zep] *sigle f* (= *zone d'éducation prioritaire*) area targeted for special help in education.
zéro [zero] *nm* zero, nought (*Brit*); **au-dessous de ~** below zero (Centigrade), below freezing; **partir de ~** to start from scratch; **réduire à ~** to reduce to nothing;

trois (buts) à ~ 3 (goals to) nil.
zeste [zɛst(ə)] *nm* peel, zest; **un ~ de citron** a piece of lemon peel.
zézaiement [zezɛmɑ̃] *nm* lisp.
zézayer [zezeje] *vi* to have a lisp.
ZI *sigle f* = **zone industrielle**.
zibeline [ziblin] *nf* sable.
ZIF [zif] *sigle f* (= *zone d'intervention foncière*) intervention zone.
zigouiller [ziguje] *vt* (*fam*) to do in.
zigzag [zigzag] *nm* zigzag.
zigzaguer [zigzage] *vi* to zigzag (along).
Zimbabwe [zimbabwe] *nm*: **le ~** Zimbabwe.
zimbabwéen, ne [zimbabweɛ̃, -ɛn] *a* Zimbabwean.
zinc [zɛ̃g] *nm* (*CHIMIE*) zinc; (*comptoir*) bar, counter.
zinguer [zɛ̃ge] *vt* to cover with zinc.
zircon [ziRkɔ̃] *nm* zircon.
zizanie [zizani] *nf*: **semer la ~** to stir up ill-feeling.
zizi [zizi] *nm* (*fam*) willy (*Brit*), peter.
zodiaque [zɔdjak] *nm* zodiac.

zona [zona] *nm* shingles *sg*.
zonage [zonaʒ] *nm* (*ADMIN*) zoning.
zonard, e [zonaR, -aRd] *nm/f* (*fam*) (young) hooligan *ou* thug.
zone [zon] *nf* zone, area; (*INFORM*) field; (*quartiers*): **la ~** the slum belt; **de seconde ~** (*fig*) second-rate; **~ d'action** (*MIL*) sphere of activity; **~ bleue** ≈ restricted parking area; **~ d'extension** *ou* **d'urbanisation** urban development area; **~ franche** free zone; **~ industrielle (ZI)** industrial estate; **~ résidentielle** residential area.
zoner [zone] *vi* (*fam*) to hang around.
zoo [zoo] *nm* zoo.
zoologie [zɔɔlɔʒi] *nf* zoology.
zoologique [zɔɔlɔʒik] *a* zoological.
zoologiste [zɔɔlɔʒist(ə)] *nm/f* zoologist.
zoom [zum] *nm* (*PHOTO*) zoom (lens).
ZUP [zyp] *sigle f* (= *zone à urbaniser en priorité*) = **ZAC**.
Zurich [zyRik] *n* Zurich.
zut [zyt] *excl* dash (it)! (*Brit*), nuts! (*US*).

ENGLISH-FRENCH
ANGLAIS-FRANÇAIS

A

A, a [eɪ] *n* (*letter*) A, a *m*; (*SCOL*: *mark*) A; (*MUS*): **A for Andrew**, (*US*) **A for Able** A comme Anatole; **A road** *n* (*Brit AUT*) route nationale; **A shares** *npl* (*Brit STOCK EXCHANGE*) actions *fpl* prioritaires.

a, an [eɪ, ə, æn, ən, n] *indefinite article* un(e); **an apple** une pomme; **I haven't got ~ car** je n'ai pas de voiture; **he's ~ doctor** il est médecin; **3 ~ day/week** 3 par jour/semaine; **10 km an hour** 10 km à l'heure.

a. *abbr* = **acre**.

AA *n abbr* (*Brit*: = *Automobile Association*) ≈ ACF *m*; (*US*: = *Associate in/of Arts*) diplôme universitaire; (= *Alcoholics Anonymous*) AA; (= *anti-aircraft*) AA.

AAA *n abbr* (= *American Automobile Association*) ≈ ACF *m*; (*Brit*) = *Amateur Athletics Association*.

AAUP *n abbr* (= *American Association of University Professors*) syndicat universitaire.

AB *abbr* (*Brit*) = **able-bodied seaman**; (*Canada*) = *Alberta*.

aback [ə'bæk] *ad*: **to be taken ~** être décontenancé(e).

abacus, *pl* abaci ['æbəkəs, -saɪ] *n* boulier *m*.

abandon [ə'bændən] *vt* abandonner ♦ *n* abandon *m*; **to ~ ship** évacuer le navire.

abandoned [ə'bændənd] *a* (*child, house etc*) abandonné(e); (*unrestrained*) sans retenue.

abase [ə'beɪs] *vt*: **to ~ o.s. (so far as to do)** s'abaisser (à faire).

abashed [ə'bæʃt] *a* confus(e), embarrassé(e).

abate [ə'beɪt] *vi* s'apaiser, se calmer.

abatement [ə'beɪtmənt] *n*: **noise ~** lutte *f* contre le bruit.

abattoir ['æbətwɑ:*] *n* (*Brit*) abattoir *m*.

abbey ['æbɪ] *n* abbaye *f*.

abbot ['æbət] *n* père supérieur.

abbreviate [ə'bri:vɪeɪt] *vt* abréger.

abbreviation [əbri:vɪ'eɪʃən] *n* abréviation *f*.

ABC *n abbr* (= *American Broadcasting Company*) chaîne de télévision.

abdicate ['æbdɪkeɪt] *vt, vi* abdiquer.

abdication [æbdɪ'keɪʃən] *n* abdication *f*.

abdomen ['æbdəmɛn] *n* abdomen *m*.

abdominal [æb'dɔmɪnl] *a* abdominal(e).

abduct [æb'dʌkt] *vt* enlever.

abduction [æb'dʌkʃən] *n* enlèvement *m*.

Aberdonian [æbə'dəunɪən] *a* d'Aberdeen ♦ *n* habitant/e d'Aberdeen; natif/ive d'Aberdeen.

aberration [æbə'reɪʃən] *n* anomalie *f*; **in a moment of mental ~** dans un moment d'égarement.

abet [ə'bɛt] *vt see* **aid.**

abeyance [ə'beɪəns] *n*: **in ~** (*law*) en désuétude; (*matter*) en suspens.

abhor [əb'hɔ:*] *vt* abhorrer, exécrer.

abhorrent [əb'hɔrənt] *a* odieux(euse), exécrable.

abide [ə'baɪd] *vt* souffrir, supporter.

abide by *vt fus* observer, respecter.

ability [ə'bɪlɪtɪ] *n* compétence *f*; capacité *f*; (*skill*) talent *m*; **to the best of my ~** de mon mieux.

abject ['æbdʒɛkt] *a* (*poverty*) sordide; (*coward*) méprisable; **an ~ apology** les excuses les plus plates.

ablaze [ə'bleɪz] *a* en feu, en flammes; **~ with light** resplendissant de lumière.

able ['eɪbl] *a* compétent(e); **to be ~ to do sth** pouvoir faire qch, être capable de faire qch.

able-bodied ['eɪbl'bɔdɪd] *a* robuste; **~ seaman** (*Brit*) matelot breveté.

ably ['eɪblɪ] *ad* avec compétence *or* talent, habilement.

ABM *n abbr* = *anti-ballistic missile*.

abnormal [æb'nɔ:məl] *a* anormal(e).

abnormality [æbnɔ:'mælɪtɪ] *n* (*condition*) caractère anormal; (*instance*) anomalie *f*.

aboard [ə'bɔ:d] *ad* à bord ♦ *prep* à bord de; (*train*) dans.

abode [ə'bəud] *n* (*old*) demeure *f*; (*LAW*): **of no fixed ~** sans domicile fixe.

abolish [ə'bɔlɪʃ] *vt* abolir.

abolition [æbə'lɪʃən] *n* abolition *f*.

abominable [ə'bɔmɪnəbl] *a* abominable.

aborigine [æbə'rɪdʒɪnɪ] *n* aborigène *m/f*.

abort [ə'bɔ:t] *vt* (*MED, fig*) faire avorter; (*COMPUT*) abandonner.

abortion [ə'bɔ:ʃən] *n* avortement *m*; **to have an ~** se faire avorter.

abortive [ə'bɔ:tɪv] *a* manqué(e).

abound [ə'baund] *vi* abonder; **to ~ in** abonder en, regorger de.

about [ə'baut] *prep* au sujet de, à propos de ♦ *ad* environ; (*here and there*) de côté et d'autre, çà et là; **do something ~ it!** faites quelque chose!; **it takes ~ 10 hours** ça prend environ *or* à peu près 10 heures, ça prend une dizaine d'heures; **at ~ 2 o'clock** vers 2 heures; **it's just ~ finished** c'est presque fini; **is Paul ~?** (*Brit*) est-ce que Paul est là?; **it's the other way ~** (*Brit*) c'est l'inverse; **it's ~ here** c'est par ici, c'est dans les parages; **to walk ~ the town** se promener dans *or* à travers la ville; **to run ~** (*Brit*) courir çà et là; **they left all their things lying ~** ils ont laissé traîner toutes leurs affaires; **to be ~ to**: **he was ~ to cry** il allait pleurer, il était sur le point de pleurer; **I'm not ~ to do all that for nothing** (*col*) je ne vais quand même pas faire tout ça pour rien; **what *or* how ~ doing this?** et si on faisait ça?

about face, about turn *n* (*MIL*) demi-tour *m*; (*fig*) volte-face *f*.

above [ə'bʌv] *ad* au-dessus ♦ *prep* au-dessus de; **mentioned** ~ mentionné ci-dessus; **costing** ~ **£10** coûtant plus de 10 livres; ~ **all** par-dessus tout, surtout.

aboveboard [ə'bʌv'bɔːd] *a* franc(franche), loyal(e); honnête.

abrasion [ə'breɪʒən] *n* frottement *m*; (*on skin*) écorchure *f*.

abrasive [ə'breɪzɪv] *a* abrasif(ive); (*fig*) caustique, agressif(ive).

abreast [ə'brest] *ad* de front; **to keep** ~ **of** se tenir au courant de.

abridge [ə'brɪdʒ] *vt* abréger.

abroad [ə'brɔːd] *ad* à l'étranger; **there is a rumour** ~ **that...** (*fig*) le bruit court que....

abrupt [ə'brʌpt] *a* (*steep, blunt*) abrupt(e); (*sudden, gruff*) brusque.

abscess ['æbsɪs] *n* abcès *m*.

abscond [əb'skɔnd] *vi* disparaître, s'enfuir.

absence ['æbsəns] *n* absence *f*; **in the** ~ **of** (*person*) en l'absence de; (*thing*) faute de.

absent ['æbsənt] *a* absent(e); ~ **without leave (AWOL)** (*MIL*) en absence irrégulière.

absentee [æbsən'tiː] *n* absent/e.

absenteeism [æbsən'tiːɪzəm] *n* absentéisme *m*.

absent-minded ['æbsənt'maɪndɪd] *a* distrait(e).

absent-mindedness ['æbsənt'maɪndɪdnɪs] *n* distraction *f*.

absolute ['æbsəluːt] *a* absolu(e).

absolutely [æbsə'luːtlɪ] *ad* absolument.

absolve [əb'zɔlv] *vt*: **to** ~ **sb (from)** (*sin etc*) absoudre qn (de); **to** ~ **sb from** (*oath*) délier qn de.

absorb [əb'zɔːb] *vt* absorber; **to be** ~**ed in a book** être plongé(e) dans un livre.

absorbent [əb'zɔːbənt] *a* absorbant(e).

absorbent cotton *n* (*US*) coton *m* hydrophile.

absorbing [əb'zɔːbɪŋ] *a* absorbant(e); (*book, film etc*) captivant(e).

absorption [əb'sɔːpʃən] *n* absorption *f*.

abstain [əb'steɪn] *vi*: **to** ~ **(from)** s'abstenir (de).

abstemious [əb'stiːmɪəs] *a* sobre, frugal(e).

abstention [əb'stenʃən] *n* abstention *f*.

abstinence ['æbstɪnəns] *n* abstinence *f*.

abstract *a, n* ['æbstrækt] *a* abstrait(e) ♦ *n* (*summary*) résumé *m* ♦ *vt* [æb'strækt] extraire.

absurd [əb'sɜːd] *a* absurde.

absurdity [əb'sɜːdɪtɪ] *n* absurdité *f*.

ABTA ['æbtə] *n abbr* = *Association of British Travel Agents*.

Abu Dhabi ['æbuː'dɑːbɪ] *n* Ab(o)u Dhabi *m*.

abundance [ə'bʌndəns] *n* abondance *f*.

abundant [ə'bʌndənt] *a* abondant(e).

abuse *n* [ə'bjuːs] insultes *fpl*, injures *fpl*; (*of power etc*) abus *m* ♦ *vt* [ə'bjuːz] abuser de; **to be open to** ~ se prêter à des abus.

abusive [ə'bjuːsɪv] *a* grossier(ière), injurieux(euse).

abysmal [ə'bɪzməl] *a* exécrable; (*ignorance etc*) sans bornes.

abyss [ə'bɪs] *n* abîme *m*, gouffre *m*.

AC *n abbr* (*US*) = *athletic club*.

a/c *abbr* (*BANKING etc*) = *account, account current*.

academic [ækə'demɪk] *a* universitaire; (*pej: issue*) oiseux(euse), purement théorique ♦ *n* universitaire *m/f*; ~ **freedom** liberté *f* académique.

academic year *n* année *f* universitaire.

academy [ə'kædəmɪ] *n* (*learned body*) académie *f*; (*school*) collège *m*; **military/ naval** ~ école militaire/navale; ~ **of music** conservatoire *m*.

ACAS ['eɪkæs] *n abbr* (*Brit*: = *Advisory, Conciliation and Arbitration Service*) organisme de conciliation et d'arbitrage des conflits du travail.

accede [æk'siːd] *vi*: **to** ~ **to** (*request, throne*) accéder à.

accelerate [æk'seləreɪt] *vt, vi* accélérer.

acceleration [ækselə'reɪʃən] *n* accélération *f*.

accelerator [æk'seləreɪtə*] *n* accélérateur *m*.

accent ['æksent] *n* accent *m*.

accentuate [æk'sentjueɪt] *vt* (*syllable*) accentuer; (*need, difference etc*) souligner.

accept [ək'sept] *vt* accepter.

acceptable [ək'septəbl] *a* acceptable.

acceptance [ək'septəns] *n* acceptation *f*; **to meet with general** ~ être favorablement accueilli par tous.

access ['ækses] *n* accès *m* ♦ *vt* (*COMPUT*) accéder à; **to have** ~ **to** (*information, library etc*) avoir accès à, pouvoir utiliser *or* consulter; (*person*) avoir accès auprès de; **the burglars gained** ~ **through a window** les cambrioleurs sont entrés par une fenêtre.

accessible [æk'sesəbl] *a* accessible.

accession [æk'seʃən] *n* accession *f*; (*of king*) avènement *m*; (*to library*) acquisition *f*.

accessory [æk'sesərɪ] *n* accessoire *m*; **toilet accessories** (*Brit*) articles *mpl* de toilette.

access road *n* voie *f* d'accès; (*to motorway*) bretelle *f* de raccordement.

access time *n* (*COMPUT*) temps *m* d'accès.

accident ['æksɪdənt] *n* accident *m*; (*chance*) hasard *m*; **to meet with** *or* **to have an** ~ avoir un accident; ~**s at work** accidents du travail; **by** ~ par hasard; (*not deliberately*) accidentellement.

accidental [æksɪ'dentl] *a* accidentel(le).

accidentally [æksɪ'dentəlɪ] *ad* accidentellement.

accident insurance *n* assurance *f* accident.

accident-prone ['æksɪdənt'prəun] *a* sujet(te) aux accidents.

acclaim [ə'kleɪm] *vt* acclamer ♦ *n* acclamation *f*.

acclamation [æklə'meɪʃən] *n* (*approval*) acclamation *f*; (*applause*) ovation *f*.

acclimatize [ə'klaɪmətaɪz], (*US*) **acclimate** [ə'klaɪmət] *vt*: **to become** ~**d** s'acclimater.

accolade ['ækəleɪd] *n* accolade *f*; (*fig*) marque *f* d'honneur.

accommodate [ə'kɔmədeɪt] *vt* loger, recevoir; (*oblige, help*) obliger; (*adapt*): **to** ~ **one's plans to** adapter ses projets à; **this car** ~**s 4 people comfortably** on tient confortablement à 4 dans cette voiture.

accommodating [ə'kɔmədeɪtɪŋ] *a* obligeant(e), arrangeant(e).

accommodation [əkɔmə'deɪʃən(z)] *n(pl)* logement *m*; **he's found** ~ il a trouvé à se loger; **"~ to let"**, (*US*) **accommodations**

(*Brit*) "appartement (*or* studio *etc*) à louer"; **they have ~ for 500** ils peuvent recevoir 500 personnes, il y a de la place pour 500 personnes; **the hall has seating ~ for 600** (*Brit*) la salle contient 600 places assises.

accompaniment [ə'kʌmpənɪmənt] *n* accompagnement *m*.

accompanist [ə'kʌmpənɪst] *n* accompagnateur/trice.

accompany [ə'kʌmpənɪ] *vt* accompagner.

accomplice [ə'kʌmplɪs] *n* complice *m/f*.

accomplish [ə'kʌmplɪʃ] *vt* accomplir.

accomplished [ə'kʌmplɪʃt] *a* accompli(e).

accomplishment [ə'kʌmplɪʃmənt] *n* accomplissement *m*; (*achievement*) réussite *f*; **~s** *npl* (*skills*) talents *mpl*.

accord [ə'kɔ:d] *n* accord *m* ♦ *vt* accorder; **of his own ~** de son plein gré; **with one ~** d'un commun accord.

accordance [ə'kɔ:dəns] *n*: **in ~ with** conformément à.

according [ə'kɔ:dɪŋ]: **~ to** *prep* selon; **~ to plan** comme prévu.

accordingly [ə'kɔ:dɪŋlɪ] *ad* en conséquence.

accordion [ə'kɔ:dɪən] *n* accordéon *m*.

accost [ə'kɔst] *vt* accoster, aborder.

account [ə'kaunt] *n* (*COMM*) compte *m*; (*report*) compte rendu, récit *m*; **~s** *npl* (*BOOK-KEEPING*) comptabilité *f*, comptes; **"~ payee only"** (*Brit*) "chèque non endossable"; **to keep an ~ of** noter; **to bring sb to ~ for sth/for having done sth** amener qn à rendre compte de qch/d'avoir fait qch; **by all ~s** au dire de tous; **of little ~** de peu d'importance; **to pay £5 on ~** verser un acompte de 5 livres; **to buy sth on ~** acheter qch à crédit; **on no ~** en aucun cas; **on ~ of** à cause de; **to take into ~, take ~ of** tenir compte de.

account for *vt fus* expliquer, rendre compte de; **all the children were ~ed for** aucun enfant ne manquait; **4 people are still not ~ed for** on n'a toujours pas retrouvé 4 personnes.

accountability [ə'kauntə'bɪlɪtɪ] *n* responsabilité *f*; (*financial, political*) transparence *f*.

accountable [ə'kauntəbl] *a* responsable.

accountancy [ə'kauntənsɪ] *n* comptabilité *f*.

accountant [ə'kauntənt] *n* comptable *m/f*.

accounting [ə'kauntɪŋ] *n* comptabilité *f*.

accounting period *n* exercice financier, période *f* comptable.

account number *n* numéro *m* de compte.

account payable *n* compte *m* fournisseurs.

account receivable *n* compte *m* clients.

accredited [ə'kredɪtɪd] *a* (*person*) accrédité(e).

accretion [ə'kri:ʃən] *n* accroissement *m*.

accrue [ə'kru:] *vi* s'accroître; (*mount up*) s'accumuler; **to ~ to** s'ajouter à; **~d interest** intérêt couru.

accumulate [ə'kju:mjuleɪt] *vt* accumuler, amasser ♦ *vi* s'accumuler, s'amasser.

accumulation [əkju:mju'leɪʃən] *n* accumulation *f*.

accuracy ['ækjurəsɪ] *n* exactitude *f*, précision *f*.

accurate ['ækjurɪt] *a* exact(e), précis(e).

accurately ['ækjurɪtlɪ] *ad* avec précision.

accusation [ækju'zeɪʃən] *n* accusation *f*.

accusative [ə'kju:zətɪv] *n* (*LING*) accusatif *m*.

accuse [ə'kju:z] *vt* accuser.

accused [ə'kju:zd] *n* accusé/e.

accustom [ə'kʌstəm] *vt* accoutumer, habituer; **to ~ o.s. to sth** s'habituer à qch.

accustomed [ə'kʌstəmd] *a* (*usual*) habituel(le); **~ to** habitué(e) *or* accoutumé(e) à.

AC/DC *abbr* = **alternating current/direct current**.

ACE [eɪs] *n abbr* = *American Council on Education*.

ace [eɪs] *n* as *m*; **within an ~ of** (*Brit*) à deux doigts *or* un cheveu de.

acerbic [ə'sə:bɪk] *a* (*also fig*) acerbe.

acetate ['æsɪteɪt] *n* acétate *m*.

ache [eɪk] *n* mal *m*, douleur *f* ♦ *vi* (*be sore*) faire mal, être douloureux(euse); (*yearn*): **to ~ to do sth** mourir d'envie de faire qch; **I've got stomach ~** *or* (*US*) **a stomach ~** j'ai mal à l'estomac; **my head ~s** j'ai mal à la tête; **I'm aching all over** j'ai mal partout.

achieve [ə'tʃi:v] *vt* (*aim*) atteindre; (*victory, success*) remporter, obtenir; (*task*) accomplir.

achievement [ə'tʃi:vmənt] *n* exploit *m*, réussite *f*; (*of aims*) réalisation *f*.

acid ['æsɪd] *a*, *n* acide (*m*).

acidity [ə'sɪdɪtɪ] *n* acidité *f*.

acid rain *n* pluie(s) *f(pl)* acide(s).

acknowledge [ək'nɔlɪdʒ] *vt* (*also*: **~ receipt of**) accuser réception de; (*fact*) reconnaître.

acknowledgement [ək'nɔlɪdʒmənt] *n* accusé *m* de réception; **~s** (*in book*) remerciements *mpl*.

ACLU *n abbr* (= *American Civil Liberties Union*) ligue des droits de l'homme.

acme ['ækmɪ] *n* point culminant.

acne ['æknɪ] *n* acné *m*.

acorn ['eɪkɔ:n] *n* gland *m*.

acoustic [ə'ku:stɪk] *a* acoustique.

acoustic coupler *n* (*COMPUT*) coupleur *m* acoustique.

acoustics [ə'ku:stɪks] *n*, *npl* acoustique *f*.

acoustic screen *n* panneau *m* d'isolation phonique.

acquaint [ə'kweɪnt] *vt*: **to ~ sb with sth** mettre qn au courant de qch; **to be ~ed with** (*person*) connaître; (*fact*) savoir.

acquaintance [ə'kweɪntəns] *n* connaissance *f*; **to make sb's ~** faire la connaissance de qn.

acquiesce [ækwɪ'ɛs] *vi* (*agree*): **to ~ (in)** acquiescer (à).

acquire [ə'kwaɪə*] *vt* acquérir.

acquired [ə'kwaɪəd] *a* acquis(e); **an ~ taste** un goût acquis.

acquisition [ækwɪ'zɪʃən] *n* acquisition *f*.

acquisitive [ə'kwɪzɪtɪv] *a* qui a l'instinct de possession *or* le goût de la propriété.

acquit [ə'kwɪt] *vt* acquitter; **to ~ o.s. well** s'en tirer très honorablement.

acquittal [ə'kwɪtl] *n* acquittement *m*.

acre ['eɪkə*] *n* acre *f* (= 4047 *m²*).

acreage ['eɪkərɪdʒ] *n* superficie *f*.

acrid ['ækrɪd] *a* (*smell*) âcre; (*fig*) mordant(e).

acrimonious [ækrɪ'məunɪəs] *a* acrimonieux(euse), aigre.

acrobat ['ækrəbæt] *n* acrobate *m/f*.

acrobatic [ækrə'bætɪk] *a* acrobatique.

acrobatics [ækrə'bætıks] *n, npl* acrobatie *f*.
Acropolis [ə'krɔpəlıs] *n*: **the ~** l'Acropole *f*.
across [ə'krɔs] *prep (on the other side)* de l'autre côté de; *(crosswise)* en travers de ♦ *ad* de l'autre côté; en travers; **to walk ~ (the road)** traverser (la route); **to take sb ~ the road** faire traverser la route à qn; **a road ~ the wood** une route qui traverse le bois; **the lake is 12 km ~** le lac fait 12 km de large; **~ from** en face de; **to get sth ~ (to sb)** faire comprendre qch (à qn).
acrylic [ə'krılık] *a, n* acrylique *(m)*.
ACT *n abbr* (= *American College Test*) *examen de fin d'études secondaires.*
act [ækt] *n* acte *m,* action *f*; *(THEATRE: part of play)* acte; (: *of performer)* numéro *m*; *(LAW)* loi *f* ♦ *vi* agir; *(THEATRE)* jouer; *(pretend)* jouer la comédie ♦ *vt (rôle)* jouer, tenir; **~ of God** *(LAW)* catastrophe naturelle; **to catch sb in the ~** prendre qn sur le fait; **it's only an ~** c'est du cinéma; **to ~ Hamlet** *(Brit)* tenir *or* jouer le rôle d'Hamlet; **to ~ the fool** *(Brit)* faire l'idiot; **to ~ as** servir de; **it ~s as a deterrent** cela a un effet dissuasif; **~ing in my capacity as chairman, I ...** en ma qualité de président, je ....
act on *vt*: **to ~ on sth** agir sur la base de qch.
act out *vt (event)* raconter en mimant; *(fantasies)* réaliser.
acting ['æktıŋ] *a* suppléant(e), par intérim ♦ *n (of actor)* jeu *m*; *(activity)*: **to do some ~** faire du théâtre *(or* du cinéma); **he is the ~ manager** il remplace (provisoirement) le directeur.
action ['ækʃən] *n* action *f*; *(MIL)* combat(s) *m(pl)*; *(LAW)* procès *m*, action en justice; **to bring an ~ against sb** *(LAW)* poursuivre qn en justice, intenter un procès contre qn; **killed in ~** *(MIL)* tué au champ d'honneur; **out of ~** hors de combat; *(machine etc)* hors d'usage; **to take ~** agir, prendre des mesures; **to put a plan into ~** mettre un projet à exécution.
action replay *n (Brit TV)* retour *m* sur une séquence.
activate ['æktıveıt] *vt (mechanism)* actionner, faire fonctionner; *(CHEM, PHYSICS)* activer.
active ['æktıv] *a* actif(ive); *(volcano)* en activité; **to play an ~ part in** jouer un rôle actif dans.
active duty (AD) *n (US MIL)* campagne *f*.
actively ['æktıvlı] *ad* activement.
active partner *n (COMM)* associé/e.
active service *n (Brit MIL)* campagne *f*.
activist ['æktıvıst] *n* activiste *m/f*.
activity [æk'tıvıtı] *n* activité *f*.
actor ['æktə*] *n* acteur *m*.
actress ['æktrıs] *n* actrice *f*.
ACTT *n abbr (Brit:* = *Association of Cinematographic, Television and Allied Technicians)* syndicat des techniciens du cinéma et de l'audiovisuel.
actual ['æktjuəl] *a* réel(le), véritable.
actually ['æktjuəlı] *ad* réellement, véritablement; *(in fact)* en fait.
actuary ['æktjuərı] *n* actuaire *m*.
actuate ['æktjueıt] *vt* déclencher, actionner.

acuity [ə'kju:ıtı] *n* acuité *f*.
acumen ['ækjumən] *n* perspicacité *f*; **business ~** sens *m* des affaires.
acupuncture ['ækjupʌŋktʃə*] *n* acuponcture *f*.
acute [ə'kju:t] *a* aigu(ë); *(mind, observer)* pénétrant(e).
AD *ad abbr* (= *Anno Domini)* ap. J.-C. ♦ *n abbr (US MIL)* = **active duty**.
ad [æd] *n abbr* = **advertisement**.
adamant ['ædəmənt] *a* inflexible.
Adam's apple ['ædənız-] *n* pomme *f* d'Adam.
adapt [ə'dæpt] *vt* adapter ♦ *vi*: **to ~ (to)** s'adapter (à).
adaptability [ədæptə'bılıtı] *n* faculté *f* d'adaptation.
adaptable [ə'dæptəbl] *a (device)* adaptable; *(person)* qui s'adapte facilement.
adaptation [ædæp'teıʃən] *n* adaptation *f*.
adapter [ə'dæptə*] *n (ELEC)* adaptateur *m*.
ADC *n abbr (MIL)* = aide-de-camp; *(US:* = *Aid to Dependent Children)* aide pour enfants assistés.
add [æd] *vt* ajouter; *(figures)* additionner ♦ *vi*: **to ~ to** *(increase)* ajouter à, accroître.
add on *vt* ajouter.
add up *vt (figures)* additionner ♦ *vi (fig)*: **it doesn't ~ up** cela ne rime à rien; **it doesn't ~ up to much** ça n'est pas grand'chose.
adder ['ædə*] *n* vipère *f*.
addict ['ædıkt] *n* toxicomane *m/f*; *(fig)* fanatique *m/f*; **heroin ~** héroïnomane *m/f*; **drug ~** drogué/e *m/f*.
addicted [ə'dıktıd] *a*: **to be ~ to** *(drink etc)* être adonné(e) à; *(fig:* football *etc)* être un(e) fanatique de.
addiction [ə'dıkʃən] *n (MED)* dépendance *f*.
adding machine ['ædıŋ-] *n* machine *f* à calculer.
Addis Ababa ['ædıs'æbəbə] *n* Addis Abeba, Addis Ababa.
addition [ə'dıʃən] *n* addition *f*; **in ~** de plus, de surcroît; **in ~ to** en plus de.
additional [ə'dıʃənl] *a* supplémentaire.
additive ['ædıtıv] *n* additif *m*.
addled ['ædld] *a (Brit: egg)* pourri(e).
address [ə'dres] *n* adresse *f*; *(talk)* discours *m*, allocution *f* ♦ *vt* adresser; *(speak to)* s'adresser à; **form of ~** titre *m*; **what form of ~ do you use for...?** comment s'adresse-t-on à...?; **to ~ (o.s. to)** *(problem, issue)* aborder qch; **absolute/relative ~** *(COMPUT)* adresse absolue/relative.
Aden ['eıdən] *n*: **Gulf of ~** Golfe *m* d'Aden.
adenoids ['ædınɔıdz] *npl* végétations *fpl*.
adept ['ædept] *a*: **~ at** expert(e) à *or* en.
adequate ['ædıkwıt] *a (enough)* suffisant(e); **to feel ~ to the task** se sentir à la hauteur de la tâche.
adequately ['ædıkwıtlı] *ad* de façon adéquate.
adhere [əd'hıə*] *vi*: **to ~ to** adhérer à; *(fig: rule, decision)* se tenir à.
adhesion [əd'hi:ʒən] *n* adhésion *f*.
adhesive [əd'hi:zıv] *a* adhésif(ive) ♦ *n* adhésif *m*; **~ tape** *(Brit)* ruban adhésif; *(US)* spara-drap *m*.
ad hoc [æd'hɔk] *a (decision)* de circonstance; *(committee)* ad hoc.
ad infinitum ['ædınfı'naıtəm] *ad* à l'infini.
adjacent [ə'dʒeısənt] *a* adjacent(e),

contigu(ë); ~ **to** adjacent à.
adjective ['ædʒɛktɪv] *n* adjectif *m*.
adjoin [ə'dʒɔɪn] *vt* jouxter.
adjoining [ə'dʒɔɪnɪŋ] *a* voisin(e), adjacent(e), attenant(e) ♦ *prep* voisin de, adjacent à.
adjourn [ə'dʒəːn] *vt* ajourner ♦ *vi* suspendre la séance; lever la séance; clore la session; (*go*) se retirer; **to ~ a meeting till the following week** reporter une réunion à la semaine suivante; **they ~ed to the pub** (*Brit col*) ils ont filé au pub.
adjournment [ə'dʒəːnmənt] *n* (*period*) ajournement *m*.
Adjt *abbr* (*MIL*: = *adjutant*) Adj.
adjudicate [ə'dʒuːdɪkeɪt] *vt* (*contest*) juger; (*claim*) statuer (sur) ♦ *vi* se prononcer.
adjudication [ədʒuːdɪ'keɪʃən] *n* (*LAW*) jugement *m*.
adjust [ə'dʒʌst] *vt* ajuster, régler; rajuster ♦ *vi*: **to ~ (to)** s'adapter (à).
adjustable [ə'dʒʌstəbl] *a* réglable.
adjuster [ə'dʒʌstə*] *n see* **loss**.
adjustment [ə'dʒʌstmənt] *n* ajustage *m*, réglage *m*; (*of prices, wages*) rajustement *m*; (*of person*) adaptation *f*.
adjutant ['ædʒətənt] *n* adjudant *m*.
ad-lib [æd'lɪb] *vt, vi* improviser ♦ *n* improvisation *f* ♦ *ad*: **ad lib** à volonté, à discrétion.
adman ['ædmæn] *n* (*col*) publicitaire *m*.
admin ['ædmɪn] *n abbr* (*col*) = **administration**.
administer [əd'mɪnɪstə*] *vt* administrer; (*justice*) rendre.
administration [ədmɪnɪs'treɪʃən] *n* administration *f*; **the A~** (*US*) le gouvernement.
administrative [əd'mɪnɪstrətɪv] *a* administratif(ive).
administrator [əd'mɪnɪstreɪtə*] *n* administrateur/trice.
admirable ['ædmərəbl] *a* admirable.
admiral ['ædmərəl] *n* amiral *m*.
Admiralty ['ædmərəltɪ] *n* (*Brit*: *also*: ~ **Board**) ministère *m* de la Marine.
admiration [ædmə'reɪʃən] *n* admiration *f*.
admire [əd'maɪə*] *vt* admirer.
admirer [əd'maɪərə*] *n* admirateur/trice.
admission [əd'mɪʃən] *n* admission *f*; (*to exhibition, night club etc*) entrée *f*; (*confession*) aveu *m*; "~ **free**", "**free ~**" "entrée libre"; **by his own ~** de son propre aveu.
admit [əd'mɪt] *vt* laisser entrer; admettre; (*agree*) reconnaître, admettre; "**children not ~ted**" "entrée interdite aux enfants"; **this ticket ~s two** ce billet est valable pour deux personnes; **I must ~ that...** je dois admettre *or* reconnaître que....
admit of *vt fus* admettre, permettre.
admit to *vt fus* reconnaître, avouer.
admittance [əd'mɪtəns] *n* admission *f*, (droit *m* d')entrée *f*; "**no ~**" "défense d'entrer".
admittedly [əd'mɪtɪdlɪ] *ad* il faut en convenir.
admonish [əd'mɔnɪʃ] *vt* donner un avertissement à; réprimander.
ad nauseam [æd'nɔːsɪæm] *ad* à satiété.
ado [ə'duː] *n*: **without (any) more ~** sans plus de cérémonies.
adolescence [ædəu'lɛsns] *n* adolescence *f*.

adolescent [ædəu'lɛsnt] *a, n* adolescent(e).
adopt [ə'dɔpt] *vt* adopter.
adopted [ə'dɔptɪd] *a* adoptif(ive), adopté(e).
adoption [ə'dɔpʃən] *n* adoption *f*.
adore [ə'dɔː*] *vt* adorer.
adoringly [ə'dɔːrɪŋlɪ] *ad* avec adoration.
adorn [ə'dɔːn] *vt* orner.
adornment [ə'dɔːnmənt] *n* ornement *m*.
ADP *n abbr* = **automatic data processing**.
adrenalin [ə'drɛnəlɪn] *n* adrénaline *f*; **to get the ~ going** faire monter le taux d'adrénaline.
Adriatic (Sea) [eɪdrɪ'ætɪk-] *n* Adriatique *f*.
adrift [ə'drɪft] *ad* à la dérive; **to come ~** (*boat*) aller à la dérive; (*wire, rope, fastening etc*) se défaire.
adroit [ə'drɔɪt] *a* adroit(e), habile.
ADT *abbr* (*US*: = *Atlantic Daylight Time*) heure d'été de New York.
adult ['ædʌlt] *n* adulte *m/f*.
adult education *n* éducation *f* des adultes.
adulterate [ə'dʌltəreɪt] *vt* frelater, falsifier.
adultery [ə'dʌltərɪ] *n* adultère *m*.
adulthood ['ædʌlthud] *n* âge *m* adulte.
advance [əd'vɑːns] *n* avance *f* ♦ *vt* avancer ♦ *vi* s'avancer; **in ~** en avance, d'avance; **to make ~s to sb** (*gen*) faire des propositions à qn; (*amorously*) faire des avances à qn.
advanced [əd'vɑːnst] *a* avancé(e); (*SCOL*: *studies*) supérieur(e); **~ in years** d'un âge avancé.
advancement [əd'vɑːnsmənt] *n* avancement *m*.
advance notice *n* préavis *m*.
advantage [əd'vɑːntɪdʒ] *n* (*also TENNIS*) avantage *m*; **to take ~ of** profiter de; **it's to our ~** c'est notre intérêt; **it's to our ~ to ...** nous avons intérêt à ....
advantageous [ædvən'teɪdʒəs] *a* avantageux(euse).
advent ['ædvənt] *n* avènement *m*, venue *f*; **A~** (*REL*) Avent *m*.
Advent calendar *n* calendrier *m* de l'avent.
adventure [əd'vɛntʃə*] *n* aventure *f*.
adventurous [əd'vɛntʃərəs] *a* aventureux(euse).
adverb ['ædvəːb] *n* adverbe *m*.
adversary ['ædvəsərɪ] *n* adversaire *m/f*.
adverse ['ædvəːs] *a* contraire, adverse; **~ to** hostile à; **in ~ circumstances** dans l'adversité.
adversity [əd'vəːsɪtɪ] *n* adversité *f*.
advert ['ædvəːt] *n abbr* (*Brit*) = **advertisement**.
advertise ['ædvətaɪz] *vi* (*vt*) faire de la publicité *or* de la réclame (pour); (*in classified ads etc*) mettre une annonce (pour vendre); **to ~ for** (*staff*) recruter par (voie d')annonce.
advertisement [əd'vəːtɪsmənt] *n* (*COMM*) réclame *f*, publicité *f*; (*in classified ads etc*) annonce *f*.
advertiser ['ædvətaɪzə*] *n* annonceur *m*.
advertising ['ædvətaɪzɪŋ] *n* publicité *f*.
advertising agency *n* agence *f* de publicité.
advertising campaign *n* campagne *f* de publicité.
advice [əd'vaɪs] *n* conseils *mpl*; (*notification*) avis *m*; **piece of ~** conseil *m*; **to ask (sb) for ~**

demander conseil (à qn); **to take legal ~** consulter un avocat.

advice note *n* (*Brit*) avis *m* d'expédition.

advisable [əd'vaızəbl] *a* recommandable, indiqué(e).

advise [əd'vaız] *vt* conseiller; **to ~ sb of sth** aviser *or* informer qn de qch; **to ~ sb against sth** déconseiller qch à qn; **to ~ sb against doing sth** conseiller à qn de ne pas faire qch; **you would be well/ill ~d to go** vous feriez mieux d'y aller/de ne pas y aller, vous auriez intérêt à y aller/à ne pas y aller.

advisedly [əd'vaızıdlı] *ad* (*deliberately*) délibérément.

adviser [əd'vaızə*] *n* conseiller/ère.

advisory [əd'vaızərı] *a* consultatif(ive); **in an ~ capacity** à titre consultatif.

advocate *n* ['ædvəkıt] (*upholder*) défenseur *m*, avocat/e ♦ *vt* ['ædvəkeıt] recommander, prôner; **to be an ~ of** être partisan/e de.

advt. *abbr* = **advertisement**.

AEA *n abbr* (*Brit*: = *Atomic Energy Authority*) ≈ AEN *f* (= *Agence pour l'énergie nucléaire*).

AEC *n abbr* (*US*: = *Atomic Energy Commission*) ≈ AEN *f* (= *Agence pour l'énergie nucléaire*).

Aegean (Sea) [i:'dʒi:ən-] *n* mer *f* Égée.

aegis ['i:dʒıs] *n*: **under the ~ of** sous l'égide de.

aeon ['i:ən] *n* éternité *f*.

aerial ['ɛərıəl] *n* antenne *f* ♦ *a* aérien(ne).

aerobatics ['ɛərəu'bætıks] *npl* acrobaties aériennes.

aerobics [ɛə'rəubıks] *n* aérobic *m*.

aerodrome ['ɛərədrəum] *n* (*Brit*) aérodrome *m*.

aerodynamic ['ɛərəudaı'næmık] *a* aérodynamique.

aeronautics [ɛərə'nɔ:tıks] *n* aéronautique *f*.

aeroplane ['ɛərəpleın] *n* (*Brit*) avion *m*.

aerosol ['ɛərəsɔl] *n* aérosol *m*.

aerospace industry ['ɛərəuspeıs-] *n* (industrie) aérospatiale.

aesthetic [ıs'θɛtık] *a* esthétique.

AEU *n abbr* (*Brit*: = *Amalgamated Engineering Union*) *syndicat de techniciens*.

afar [ə'fɑ:*] *ad*: **from ~** de loin.

AFB *n abbr* (*US*) = *Air Force Base*.

AFDC *n abbr* (*US*: = *Aid to Families with Dependent Children*) *aide pour enfants assistés*.

affable ['æfəbl] *a* affable.

affair [ə'fɛə*] *n* affaire *f*; (*also:* **love ~**) liaison *f*; aventure *f*; **~s** (*business*) affaires *f*.

affect [ə'fɛkt] *vt* affecter.

affectation [æfɛk'teıʃən] *n* affectation *f*.

affected [ə'fɛktıd] *a* affecté(e).

affection [ə'fɛkʃən] *n* affection *f*.

affectionate [ə'fɛkʃənıt] *a* affectueux(euse).

affectionately [ə'fɛkʃənıtlı] *ad* affectueusement.

affidavit [æfı'deıvıt] *n* (*LAW*) déclaration écrite sous serment.

affiliated [ə'fılıeıtıd] *a* affilié(e); **~ company** filiale *f*.

affinity [ə'fınıtı] *n* affinité *f*.

affirm [ə'fə:m] *vt* affirmer.

affirmation [æfə'meıʃən] *n* affirmation *f*,

assertion *f*.

affirmative [ə'fə:mətıv] *a* affirmatif(ive) ♦ *n*: **in the ~** dans *or* par l'affirmative.

affix [ə'fıks] *vt* apposer, ajouter.

afflict [ə'flıkt] *vt* affliger.

affliction [ə'flıkʃən] *n* affliction *f*.

affluence ['æfluəns] *n* aisance *f*, opulence *f*.

affluent ['æfluənt] *a* opulent(e); (*person*) dans l'aisance, riche; **the ~ society** la société d'abondance.

afford [ə'fɔ:d] *vt* (*goods etc*) avoir les moyens d'acheter *or* d'entretenir; (*behaviour*) se permettre; (*provide*) fournir, procurer; **can we ~ a car?** avons-nous de quoi acheter *or* les moyens d'acheter une voiture?; **I can't ~ the time** je n'ai vraiment pas le temps.

affray [ə'freı] *n* (*Brit LAW*) échauffourée *f*, rixe *f*.

affront [ə'frʌnt] *n* affront *m*.

affronted [ə'frʌntıd] *a* insulté(e).

Afghan ['æfgæn] *n* a afghan(e) ♦ *n* Afghan/e.

Afghanistan [æf'gænıstæn] *n* Afghanistan *m*.

afield [ə'fi:ld] *ad*: **far ~** loin.

AFL-CIO *n abbr* (= *American Federation of Labor and Congress of Industrial Organizations*) *confédération syndicale*.

afloat [ə'fləut] *a* à flot ♦ *ad*: **to stay ~** surnager; **to keep/get a business ~** maintenir à flot/lancer une affaire.

afoot [ə'fut] *ad*: **there is something ~** il se prépare quelque chose.

aforementioned [ə'fɔ:mɛnʃənd] *a*, **aforesaid** [ə'fɔ:sɛd] *a* susdit(e), susmentionné(e).

afraid [ə'freıd] *a* effrayé(e); **to be ~ of** *or* **to** avoir peur de; **I am ~ that** je crains que + *sub*; **I'm ~ so/not** oui/non, malheureusement.

afresh [ə'frɛʃ] *ad* de nouveau.

Africa ['æfrıkə] *n* Afrique *f*.

African ['æfrıkən] *a* africain(e) ♦ *n* Africain/e.

Afrikaans [æfrı'kɑ:ns] *n* afrikaans *m*.

Afrikaner [æfrı'kɑ:nə*] *n* Afrikaner *or* Afrikander *m/f*.

Afro-American ['æfrəuə'mɛrıkən] *a* afro-américain(e).

AFT *n abbr* (= *American Federation of Teachers*) *syndicat enseignant*.

aft [ɑ:ft] *ad* à l'arrière, vers l'arrière.

after ['ɑ:ftə*] *prep*, *ad* après ♦ *cj* après que, après avoir *or* être + *pp*; **~ dinner** après (le) dîner; **the day ~ tomorrow** après demain; **quarter ~ two** (*US*) deux heures et quart; **what/who are you ~?** que/qui cherchez-vous?; **the police are ~ him** la police est à ses trousses; **~ you!** après vous!; **~ all** après tout.

aftercare ['ɑ:ftəkɛə*] *n* (*Brit MED*) post-cure *f*.

after-effects ['ɑ:ftərıfɛkts] *npl* répercussions *fpl*; (*of illness*) séquelles *fpl*, suites *fpl*.

afterlife ['ɑ:ftəlaıf] *n* vie future.

aftermath ['ɑ:ftəmɑ:θ] *n* conséquences *fpl*; **in the ~ of** dans les mois *or* années *etc* qui suivirent, au lendemain de.

afternoon ['ɑ:ftə'nu:n] *n* après-midi *m* *or* *f*; **good ~!** bonjour!; (*goodbye*) au revoir!

afters ['ɑ:ftəz] *n* (*Brit col*: *dessert*) dessert *m*.

after-sales service [ɑ:ftə'seılz-] *n* service *m* après-vente, SAV *m*.

after-shave (lotion) ['ɑ:ftəʃeıv-] *n* lotion *f* après-rasage.

aftershock ['ɑ:ftəʃɔk] *n* réplique *f* (sismique).

afterthought ['ɑ:ftəθɔ:t] *n*: **I had an** ~ il m'est venu une idée après coup.

afterwards ['ɑ:ftəwədz] *ad* après.

again [ə'gɛn] *ad* de nouveau, encore une fois; **to begin/see** ~ recommencer/revoir; **not** ... ~ ne ... plus; ~ **and** ~ à plusieurs reprises; **he's opened it** ~ il l'a rouvert, il l'a de nouveau *or* l'a encore ouvert; **now and** ~ de temps à autre.

against [ə'gɛnst] *prep* contre; ~ **a blue background** sur un fond bleu; **(as)** ~ **(Brit)** contre.

age [eɪdʒ] *n* âge *m* ♦ *vt, vi* vieillir; **what** ~ **is he?** quel âge a-t-il?; **he is 20 years of** ~ il a 20 ans; **under** ~ mineur(e); **to come of** ~ atteindre sa majorité; **it's been** ~**s since** ça fait une éternité que ... ne.

aged ['eɪdʒd] *a* âgé(e); ~ **10** âgé de 10 ans; **the** ~ ['eɪdʒɪd] *npl* les personnes âgées.

age group *n* tranche *f* d'âge; **the 40 to 50** ~ la tranche d'âge des 40 à 50 ans.

ageless ['eɪdʒlɪs] *a* sans âge.

age limit *n* limite *f* d'âge.

agency ['eɪdʒənsɪ] *n* agence *f*; **through** *or* **by the** ~ **of** par l'entremise *or* l'action de.

agenda [ə'dʒɛndə] *n* ordre *m* du jour; **on the** ~ à l'ordre du jour.

agent ['eɪdʒənt] *n* agent *m*.

aggravate ['ægrəveɪt] *vt* aggraver; *(annoy)* exaspérer, agacer.

aggravation [ægrə'veɪʃən] *n* agacements *mpl*.

aggregate ['ægrɪgɪt] *n* ensemble *m*, total *m*; **on** ~ *(SPORT)* au total des points.

aggression [ə'grɛʃən] *n* agression *f*.

aggressive [ə'grɛsɪv] *a* agressif(ive).

aggressiveness [ə'grɛsɪvnɪs] *n* agressivité *f*.

aggrieved [ə'gri:vd] *a* chagriné(e), affligé(e).

aghast [ə'gɑ:st] *a* consterné(e), atterré(e).

agile ['ædʒaɪl] *a* agile.

agitate ['ædʒɪteɪt] *vt* rendre inquiet(ète) *or* agité(e) ♦ *vi* faire de l'agitation (politique); **to** ~ **for** faire campagne pour.

agitator ['ædʒɪteɪtə*] *n* agitateur/trice (politique).

AGM *n abbr* = **annual general meeting**.

ago [ə'gəu] *ad*: **2 days** ~ il y a 2 jours; **not long** ~ il n'y a pas longtemps; **as long** ~ **as 1960** déjà en 1960; **how long** ~**?** il y a combien de temps (de cela)?

agog [ə'gɔg] *a*: **(all)** ~ en émoi.

agonize ['ægənaɪz] *vi*: **he** ~**d over the problem** ce problème lui a causé bien du tourment.

agonizing ['ægənaɪzɪŋ] *a* angoissant(e); *(cry)* déchirant(e).

agony ['ægənɪ] *n* grande souffrance *or* angoisse; **to be in** ~ souffrir le martyre.

agony column *n* courrier *m* du cœur.

agree [ə'gri:] *vt (price)* convenir de ♦ *vi*: **to** ~ **(with)** *(person)* être d'accord (avec); *(statements etc)* concorder (avec); *(LING)* s'accorder (avec); **to** ~ **to do** accepter de *or* consentir à faire; **to** ~ **to sth** consentir à qch; **to** ~ **that** *(admit)* convenir *or* reconnaître que; **it was** ~**d that...** il a été convenu que...; **they** ~ **on this** ils sont d'accord sur ce point; **they** ~**d on going/a price** ils se mirent d'accord pour y aller/sur un prix;

garlic doesn't ~ **with me** je ne supporte pas l'ail.

agreeable [ə'gri:əbl] *a (pleasant)* agréable; *(willing)* consentant(e), d'accord; **are you** ~ **to this?** est-ce que vous êtes d'accord?

agreed [ə'gri:d] *a (time, place)* convenu(e); **to be** ~ être d'accord.

agreement [ə'gri:mənt] *n* accord *m*; **in** ~ d'accord; **by mutual** ~ d'un commun accord.

agricultural [ægrɪ'kʌltʃərəl] *a* agricole.

agriculture ['ægrɪkʌltʃə*] *n* agriculture *f*.

aground [ə'graund] *ad*: **to run** ~ s'échouer.

ahead [ə'hɛd] *ad* en avant; devant; **go right** *or* **straight** ~ allez tout droit; **go** ~**!** *(fig)* allez-y!; ~ **of** devant; *(fig: schedule etc)* en avance sur; ~ **of time** en avance; **they were (right)** ~ **of us** ils nous précédaient (de peu), ils étaient (juste) devant nous.

AI *n abbr* = *Amnesty International*; *(COMPUT)* = **artificial intelligence**.

AIB *n abbr (Brit:* = *Accident Investigation Bureau)* commission d'enquête sur les accidents.

AID *n abbr* = *artificial insemination by donor)* IAD *f*; *(US:* = *Agency for International Development)* agence pour le développement international.

aid [eɪd] *n* aide *f* ♦ *vt* aider; **with the** ~ **of** avec l'aide de; **in** ~ **of** en faveur de; **to** ~ **and abet** *(LAW)* se faire le complice de.

aide [eɪd] *n (person)* assistant/e.

AIDS [eɪdz] *n abbr (= acquired immune deficiency syndrome)* SIDA *m*.

AIH *n abbr* = *artificial insemination by husband)* IAC *f*.

ailment ['eɪlmənt] *n* affection *f*.

aim [eɪm] *n* but *m* ♦ *vt*: **to** ~ **sth at** *(gun, camera)* braquer *or* pointer qch sur, diriger qch contre; *(missile)* pointer qch vers *or* sur; *(remark, blow)* destiner *or* adresser qch à ♦ *vi (also:* **to take** ~*)* viser; **to** ~ **at** viser; *(fig)* viser (à); avoir pour but *or* ambition; **to** ~ **to do** avoir l'intention de faire.

aimless ['eɪmlɪs] *a* sans but.

aimlessly ['eɪmlɪslɪ] *ad* sans but.

ain't [eɪnt] *(col)* = **am not, aren't, isn't.**

air [ɛə*] *n* air *m* ♦ *vt* aérer; *(idea, grievance, views)* mettre sur le tapis; *(knowledge)* faire étalage de ♦ *cpd (currents, attack etc)* aérien(ne); **by** ~ par avion; **to be on the** ~ *(RADIO, TV: programme)* être diffusé(e); *(: station)* émettre.

air base *n* base aérienne.

airbed ['ɛəbɛd] *n (Brit)* matelas *m* pneumatique.

airborne ['ɛəbɔ:n] *a (plane)* en vol; *(troops)* aéroporté(e); *(particles)* dans l'air; **as soon as the plane was** ~ dès que l'avion eut décollé.

air cargo *n* fret aérien.

air-conditioned ['ɛəkən'dɪʃənd] *a* climatisé(e), à air conditionné.

air conditioning *n* climatisation *f*.

air-cooled ['ɛəku:ld] *a* à refroidissement à air.

aircraft ['ɛəkrɑ:ft] *n (pl inv)* avion *m*.

aircraft carrier *n* porte-avions *m inv*.

air cushion *n* coussin *m* d'air.

airfield ['ɛəfi:ld] *n* terrain *m* d'aviation.

Air Force *n* Armée *f* de l'air.

air freight n fret aérien.
airgun ['ɛɔgʌn] n fusil m à air comprimé.
air hostess n (Brit) hôtesse f de l'air.
airily ['ɛərɪlɪ] ad d'un air dégagé.
airing ['ɛərɪŋ] n: **to give an ~ to** aérer; (fig: ideas, views etc) mettre sur le tapis.
air letter n (Brit) aérogramme m.
airlift ['ɛəlɪft] n pont aérien.
airline ['ɛəlaɪn] n ligne aérienne, compagnie aérienne.
airliner ['ɛəlaɪnə*] n avion m de ligne.
airlock ['ɛəlɔk] n sas m.
airmail ['ɛəmeɪl] n: **by ~** par avion.
air mattress n matelas m pneumatique.
airplane ['ɛəpleɪn] n (US) avion m.
airport ['ɛəpɔːt] n aéroport m.
air raid n attaque aérienne.
airsick ['ɛəsɪk] a: **to be ~** avoir le mal de l'air.
airstrip ['ɛəstrɪp] n terrain m d'atterrissage.
air terminal n aérogare f.
airtight ['ɛətaɪt] a hermétique.
air traffic control n contrôle m de la navigation aérienne.
air traffic controller n aiguilleur m du ciel.
air waybill n lettre f de transport aérien.
airy ['ɛərɪ] a bien aéré(e); (manners) dégagé(e).
aisle [aɪl] n (of church) allée centrale; nef latérale; (in theatre) allée f; (on plane) couloir m.
ajar [ə'dʒɑː*] a entrouvert(e).
AK abbr (US POST) = Alaska.
aka abbr (= also known as) alias.
akin [ə'kɪn] a: **~ to** semblable à, du même ordre que.
AL abbr (US POST) = Alabama.
ALA n abbr = American Library Association.
alacrity [ə'lækrɪtɪ] n: **with ~** avec empressement, promptement.
alarm [ə'lɑːm] n alarme f ♦ vt alarmer.
alarm clock n réveille-matin m, réveil m.
alarming [ə'lɑːmɪŋ] a alarmant(e).
alarmist [ə'lɑːmɪst] n alarmiste m/f.
alas [ə'læs] excl hélas.
Alaska [ə'læskə] n Alaska m.
Albania [æl'beɪnɪə] n Albanie f.
Albanian [æl'beɪnɪən] a albanais(e) ♦ n Albanais/e; (LING) albanais m.
albeit [ɔːl'biːɪt] cj bien que + sub, encore que + sub.
album ['ælbəm] n album m.
albumen ['ælbjumɪn] n albumine f; (of egg) albumen m.
alchemy ['ælkɪmɪ] n alchimie f.
alcohol ['ælkəhɔl] n alcool m.
alcoholic [ælkə'hɔlɪk] a, n alcoolique (m/f).
alcoholism ['ælkəhɔlɪzəm] n alcoolisme m.
alcove ['ælkəuv] n alcôve f.
Ald. abbr = alderman.
alderman ['ɔːldəmən] n conseiller municipal (en Angleterre).
ale [eɪl] n bière f.
alert [ə'lɜːt] a alerte, vif(vive); (watchful) vigilant(e) ♦ n alerte f ♦ vt: **to ~ sb (to sth)** attirer l'attention de qn (sur qch); **to ~ sb to the dangers of sth** avertir qn des dangers de qch; **on the ~** sur le qui-vive; (MIL) en état d'alerte.

Aleutian Islands [ə'luːʃən-] npl îles Aléoutiennes.
Alexandria [ælɪg'zɑːndrɪə] n Alexandrie f.
alfresco [æl'frɛskəu] a, ad en plein air.
algebra ['ældʒɪbrə] n algèbre m.
Algeria [æl'dʒɪərɪə] n Algérie f.
Algerian [æl'dʒɪərɪən] a algérien(ne) ♦ n Algérien/ne.
Algiers [æl'dʒɪəz] n Alger.
algorithm ['ælgərɪðəm] n algorithme m.
alias ['eɪlɪəs] ad alias ♦ n faux nom, nom d'emprunt.
alibi ['ælɪbaɪ] n alibi m.
alien ['eɪlɪən] n étranger/ère ♦ a: **~ (to)** étranger(ère) (à).
alienate ['eɪlɪəneɪt] vt aliéner; (subj: person) s'aliéner.
alienation [eɪlɪə'neɪʃən] n aliénation f.
alight [ə'laɪt] a, ad en feu ♦ vi mettre pied à terre; (passenger) descendre; (bird) se poser.
align [ə'laɪn] vt aligner.
alignment [ə'laɪnmənt] n alignement m; **it's out of ~ (with)** ce n'est pas aligné (avec).
alike [ə'laɪk] a semblable, pareil(le) ♦ ad de même; **to look ~** se ressembler.
alimony ['ælɪmənɪ] n (payment) pension f alimentaire.
alive [ə'laɪv] a vivant(e); (active) plein(e) de vie; **~ with** grouillant(e) de; **~ to** sensible à.
alkali ['ælkəlaɪ] n alcali m.
all [ɔːl] a tout(e), tous(toutes) pl ♦ pronoun tout m; (pl) tous(toutes) ♦ ad tout; **~ wrong/alone** tout faux/seul; **~ the time/his life** tout le temps/toute sa vie; **~ five (of them)** tous les cinq; **~ five girls** les cinq filles; **~ of them** tous, toutes; **~ of it** tout; **~ of us went** nous y sommes tous allés; **~ day** toute la journée; **is that ~?** c'est tout?; (in shop) ce sera tout?; **for ~ their efforts** malgré tous leurs efforts; **not as hard** etc **as ~ that** pas si dur etc que ça; **at ~: not at ~** (in answer to question) pas du tout; (in answer to thanks) je vous en prie!; **I'm not at ~ tired** je ne suis pas du tout fatigué; **anything at ~ will do** n'importe quoi fera l'affaire; **~ but** presque, pratiquement; **to be ~ in** (Brit col) être complètement à plat; **~ in ~** en somme, somme toute, finalement; **~ out** ad à fond.
allay [ə'leɪ] vt (fears) apaiser, calmer.
all clear n (also fig) fin f d'alerte.
allegation [ælɪ'geɪʃən] n allégation f.
allege [ə'lɛdʒ] vt alléguer, prétendre; **he is ~d to have said** il aurait dit.
alleged [ə'lɛdʒd] a prétendu(e).
allegedly [ə'lɛdʒɪdlɪ] ad à ce que l'on prétend, paraît-il.
allegiance [ə'liːdʒəns] n fidélité f, obéissance f.
allegory ['ælɪgərɪ] n allégorie f.
ali-embracing ['ɔːlɪm'breɪsɪŋ] a universel(le).
allergic [ə'lɜːdʒɪk] a: **~ to** allergique à.
allergy ['ælədʒɪ] n allergie f.
alleviate [ə'liːvɪeɪt] vt soulager, adoucir.
alley ['ælɪ] n ruelle f; (in garden) allée f.
alliance [ə'laɪəns] n alliance f.
allied ['ælaɪd] a allié(e).
alligator ['ælɪgeɪtə*] n alligator m.

all-important ['ɔːlɪm'pɔːtənt] *a* capital(e), crucial(e).

all-in ['ɔːlɪn] *a* (*Brit: also ad: charge*) tout compris.

all-in wrestling *n* (*Brit*) catch *m*.

alliteration [əlɪtə'reɪʃən] *n* allitération *f*.

all-night ['ɔːl'naɪt] *a* ouvert(e) *or* qui dure toute la nuit.

allocate ['æləkeɪt] *vt* (*share out*) répartir, distribuer; (*duties*): **to ~ sth to** assigner *or* attribuer qch à; (*sum, time*): **to ~ sth to** allouer qch à; **to ~ sth for** affecter qch à.

allocation [æləu'keɪʃən] *n* (*see vb*) répartition *f*; attribution *f*; allocation *f*; affectation *f*; (*money*) crédit(s) *m(pl)*, somme(s) allouée(s).

allot [ə'lɒt] *vt* (*share out*) répartir, distribuer; (*time*): **to ~ sth to** allouer qch à; (*duties*): **to ~ sth to** assigner qch à; **in the ~ted time** dans le temps imparti.

allotment [ə'lɒtmənt] *n* (*share*) part *f*; (*garden*) lopin *m* de terre (*loué à la municipalité*).

all-out [ɔːl'aut] *a* (*effort etc*) total(e).

allow [ə'lau] *vt* (*practice, behaviour*) permettre, autoriser; (*sum to spend etc*) accorder, allouer; (*sum, time estimated*) compter, prévoir; (*concede*): **to ~ that** convenir que; **to ~ sb to do** permettre à qn de faire, autoriser qn à faire; **he is ~ed to ...** on lui permet de ...; **smoking is not ~ed** il est interdit de fumer; **we must ~ 3 days for the journey** il faut compter 3 jours pour le voyage.

allow for *vt fus* tenir compte de.

allowance [ə'lauəns] *n* (*money received*) allocation *f*; (*: from parent etc*) subside *m*; (*: for expenses*) indemnité *f*; (*TAX*) somme *f* déductible du revenu imposable, abattement *m*; **to make ~s for** tenir compte de.

alloy ['ælɔɪ] *n* alliage *m*.

all right *ad* (*feel, work*) bien; (*as answer*) d'accord.

all-round ['ɔːl'raund] *a* compétent(e) dans tous les domaines; (*athlete etc*) complet(ète).

all-rounder [ɔːl'raundə*] *n* (*Brit*): **to be a good ~** être doué(e) en tout.

allspice ['ɔːlspaɪs] *n* poivre *m* de la Jamaïque.

all-time ['ɔːl'taɪm] *a* (*record*) sans précédent, absolu(e).

allude [ə'luːd] *vi*: **to ~ to** faire allusion à.

alluring [ə'ljuərɪŋ] *a* séduisant(e), alléchant(e).

allusion [ə'luːʒən] *n* allusion *f*.

alluvium [ə'luːvɪəm] *n* alluvions *fpl*.

ally *n* ['ælaɪ] allié *m* ♦ *vt* [ə'laɪ]: **to ~ o.s. with** s'allier avec.

almighty [ɔːl'maɪtɪ] *a* tout-puissant.

almond ['ɑːmənd] *n* amande *f*.

almost ['ɔːlməust] *ad* presque; **he ~ fell** il a failli tomber.

alms [ɑːmz] *n* aumône(s) *f(pl)*.

aloft [ə'lɒft] *ad* en haut, en l'air; (*NAUT*) dans la mâture.

alone [ə'ləun] *a, ad* seul(e); **to leave sb ~** laisser qn tranquille; **to leave sth ~** ne pas toucher à qch; **let ~ ...** sans parler de ...; encore moins ....

along [ə'lɒŋ] *prep* le long de ♦ *ad*: **is he com-**

ing ~? vient-il avec nous?; **he was hopping/limping ~** il venait *or* avançait en sautillant/boitant; **~ with** avec, en plus de; (*person*) en compagnie de.

alongside [ə'lɒŋ'saɪd] *prep* le long de; au côté de ♦ *ad* bord à bord; côte à côte; **we brought our boat ~** (*of a pier, shore etc*) nous avons accosté.

aloof [ə'luːf] *a, ad* à distance, à l'écart; **to stand ~** se tenir à l'écart *or* à distance.

aloofness [ə'luːfnɪs] *n* réserve (hautaine), attitude distante.

aloud [ə'laud] *ad* à haute voix.

alphabet ['ælfəbɛt] *n* alphabet *m*.

alphabetical [ælfə'bɛtɪkl] *a* alphabétique; **in ~ order** par ordre alphabétique.

alphanumeric ['ælfənjuː'mɛrɪk] *a* alphanumérique.

alpine ['ælpaɪn] *a* alpin(e), alpestre; **~ hut** cabane *f* or refuge *m* de montagne; **~ pasture** pâturage *m* (de montagne); **~ skiing** ski alpin.

Alps [ælps] *npl*: **the ~** les Alpes *fpl*.

already [ɔːl'rɛdɪ] *ad* déjà.

alright ['ɔːl'raɪt] *ad* (*Brit*) = **all right**.

Alsace ['ælsæs] *n* Alsace *f*.

Alsatian [æl'seɪʃən] *a* alsacien(ne), d'Alsace ♦ *n* Alsacien/ne; (*Brit: dog*) berger allemand.

also ['ɔːlsəu] *ad* aussi.

altar ['ɔːltə*] *n* autel *m*.

alter ['ɔːltə*] *vt, vi* changer, modifier.

alteration [ɔːltə'reɪʃən] *n* changement *m*, modification *f*; **~s** (*SEWING*) retouches *fpl*; (*ARCHIT*) modifications *fpl*; **timetable subject to ~** horaires sujets à modifications.

alternate *a* [ɔːl'tɜːnɪt] alterné(e), alternant(e), alternatif(ive) ♦ *vi* ['ɔːltə:neɪt] alterner; **on ~ days** un jour sur deux, tous les deux jours.

alternately [ɔːl'tɜːnɪtlɪ] *ad* alternativement, en alternant.

alternating ['ɔːltə:neɪtɪŋ] *a* (*current*) alternatif(ive).

alternative [ɔːl'tɜːnətɪv] *a* (*solutions*) interchangeable, possible; (*solution*) autre, de remplacement; (*energy*) doux(douce); (*society*) parallèle ♦ *n* (*choice*) alternative *f*; (*other possibility*) autre possibilité *f*.

alternatively [ɔːl'tɜːnətɪvlɪ] *ad*: **~ one could** une autre *or* l'autre solution serait de.

alternator ['ɔːltə:neɪtə*] *n* (*AUT*) alternateur *m*.

although [ɔːl'ðəu] *cj* bien que + *sub*.

altitude ['æltɪtjuːd] *n* altitude *f*.

alto ['æltəu] *n* (*female*) contralto *m*; (*male*) haute-contre *f*.

altogether [ɔːltə'gɛðə*] *ad* entièrement, tout à fait; (*on the whole*) tout compte fait; (*in all*) en tout; **how much is that ~?** ça fait combien en tout?

altruistic [æltru'ɪstɪk] *a* altruiste.

aluminium [ælju'mɪnɪəm], (*US*) **aluminum** [ə'luːmɪnəm] *n* aluminium *m*.

always ['ɔːlweɪz] *ad* toujours.

AM *abbr* = *amplitude modulation*.

am [æm] *vb see* **be**.

a.m. *ad abbr* (= *ante meridiem*) du matin.

AMA *n abbr* = *American Medical Association*.

amalgam [ə'mælgəm] *n* amalgame *m*.

amalgamate [ə'mælgəmeɪt] *vt, vi* fusionner.

amalgamation [əmælgə'meɪʃən] *n* fusion *f*; (*COMM*) fusionnement *m*.

amass [ə'mæs] *vt* amasser.

amateur ['æmətə*] *n* amateur *m* ♦ *a* (*SPORT*) amateur *inv*; ~ **dramatics** le théâtre amateur.

amateurish ['æmətərɪʃ] *a* (*pej*) d'amateur, un peu amateur.

amaze [ə'meɪz] *vt* surprendre, étonner; **to be ~d (at)** être surpris *or* étonné (de).

amazement [ə'meɪzmənt] *n* surprise *f*, étonnement *m*.

amazing [ə'meɪzɪŋ] *a* étonnant(e), incroyable; (*bargain, offer*) exceptionnel(le).

amazingly [ə'meɪzɪŋlɪ] *ad* incroyablement.

Amazon ['æməzən] *n* (*GEO, MYTHOLOGY*) Amazone *f* ♦ *cpd* amazonien(ne), de l'Amazone; **the ~ basin** le bassin de l'Amazone; **the ~ jungle** la forêt amazonienne.

Amazonian [æmə'zəʊnɪən] *a* amazonien(ne).

ambassador [æm'bæsədə*] *n* ambassadeur *m*.

amber ['æmbə*] *n* ambre *m*; **at ~** (*Brit AUT*) à l'orange.

ambidextrous [æmbɪ'dɛkstrəs] *a* ambidextre.

ambience ['æmbɪəns] *n* ambiance *f*.

ambiguity [æmbɪ'gjuɪtɪ] *n* ambiguïté *f*.

ambiguous [æm'bɪgjuəs] *a* ambigu(ë).

ambition [æm'bɪʃən] *n* ambition *f*.

ambitious [æm'bɪʃəs] *a* ambitieux(euse).

ambivalent [æm'bɪvələnt] *a* (*attitude*) ambivalent(e).

amble ['æmbl] *vi* (*also*: **to ~ along**) aller d'un pas tranquille.

ambulance ['æmbjuləns] *n* ambulance *f*.

ambush ['æmbuʃ] *n* embuscade *f* ♦ *vt* tendre une embuscade à.

ameba [ə'mi:bə] *n* (*US*) = **amoeba**.

ameliorate [ə'mi:lɪəreɪt] *vt* améliorer.

amen ['ɑ:'mɛn] *excl* amen.

amenable [ə'mi:nəbl] *a*: ~ **to** (*advice etc*) disposé(e) à écouter *or* suivre; ~ **to the law** responsable devant la loi.

amend [ə'mɛnd] *vt* (*law*) amender; (*text*) corriger; (*habits*) réformer ♦ *vi* s'amender, se corriger; **to make ~s** réparer ses torts, faire amende honorable.

amendment [ə'mɛndmənt] *n* (*to law*) amendement *m*; (*to text*) correction *f*.

amenities [ə'mi:nɪtɪz] *npl* aménagements *mpl*, équipements *mpl*.

amenity [ə'mi:nɪtɪ] *n* charme *m*, agrément *m*.

America [ə'mɛrɪkə] *n* Amérique *f*.

American [ə'mɛrɪkən] *a* américain(e) ♦ *n* Américain/e.

americanize [ə'mɛrɪkənaɪz] *vt* américaniser.

amethyst ['æmɪθɪst] *n* améthyste *f*.

Amex ['æmɛks] *n abbr* = *American Stock Exchange*.

amiable ['eɪmɪəbl] *a* aimable, affable.

amicable ['æmɪkəbl] *a* amical(e).

amid(st) [ə'mɪd(st)] *prep* parmi, au milieu de.

amiss [ə'mɪs] *a, ad*: **there's something ~** il y a quelque chose qui ne va pas *or* qui cloche; **to take sth ~** prendre qch mal *or* de travers.

ammo ['æməʊ] *n abbr* (*col*) = **ammunition**.

ammonia [ə'məʊnɪə] *n* (*gas*) ammoniac *m*; (*liquid*) ammoniaque *f*.

ammunition [æmju'nɪʃən] *n* munitions *fpl*;

(*fig*) arguments *mpl*.

ammunition dump *n* dépôt *m* de munitions.

amnesia [æm'ni:zɪə] *n* amnésie *f*.

amnesty ['æmnɪstɪ] *n* amnistie *f*; **to grant an ~ to** accorder une amnistie à.

amoeba, (US) ameba [ə'mi:bə] *n* amibe *f*.

amok [ə'mɔk] *ad*: **to run ~** être pris(e) d'un accès de folie furieuse.

among(st) [ə'mʌŋ(st)] *prep* parmi, entre.

amoral [æ'mɔrəl] *a* amoral(e).

amorous ['æmərəs] *a* amoureux(euse).

amorphous [ə'mɔ:fəs] *a* amorphe.

amortization [əmɔ:taɪ'zeɪʃən] *n* (*COMM*) amortissement *m*.

amount [ə'maunt] *n* (*sum of money*) somme *f*; (*total*) montant *m*; (*quantity*) quantité *f*; nombre *m* ♦ *vi*: **to ~ to** (*total*) s'élever à; (*be same as*) équivaloir à, revenir à; **this ~s to a refusal** cela équivaut à un refus; **the total ~** (*of money*) le montant total.

amp(ère) ['æmp(ɛə*)] *n* ampère *m*; **a 13 amp plug** une fiche de 13 A.

ampersand ['æmpəsænd] *n* signe &, "et" commercial.

amphibian [æm'fɪbɪən] *n* batracien *m*.

amphibious [æm'fɪbɪəs] *a* amphibie.

amphitheatre, (US) amphitheater ['æmfɪθɪətə*] *n* amphithéâtre *m*.

ample ['æmpl] *a* ample; spacieux(euse); (*enough*): **this is ~** c'est largement suffisant; **to have ~ time/room** avoir bien assez de temps/place, avoir largement le temps/la place.

amplifier ['æmplɪfaɪə*] *n* amplificateur *m*.

amplify ['æmplɪfaɪ] *vt* amplifier.

amply ['æmplɪ] *ad* amplement, largement.

ampoule, (US) ampule ['æmpu:l] *n* (*MED*) ampoule *f*.

amputate ['æmpjuteɪt] *vt* amputer.

Amsterdam ['æmstədæm] *n* Amsterdam.

amt *abbr* = **amount**.

amuck [ə'mʌk] *ad* = **amok**.

amuse [ə'mju:z] *vt* amuser; **to ~ o.s. with sth/by doing sth** se divertir avec qch/à faire qch; **to be ~d at** être amusé par; **he was not ~d** il n'a pas apprécié.

amusement [ə'mju:zmənt] *n* amusement *m*.

amusement arcade *n* salle *f* de jeu.

amusing [ə'mju:zɪŋ] *a* amusant(e), divertissant(e).

an [æn, ən, n] *indefinite article see* **a**.

ANA *n abbr* = *American Newspaper Association, American Nurses Association*.

anachronism [ə'nækrənɪzəm] *n* anachronisme *m*.

anaemia [ə'ni:mɪə] *n* anémie *f*.

anaemic [ə'ni:mɪk] *a* anémique.

anaesthetic [ænɪs'θɛtɪk] *a, n* anesthésique (*m*); **under the ~** sous anesthésie; **local/ general ~** anesthésie locale/générale.

anaesthetist [æ'ni:sθɪtɪst] *n* anesthésiste *m/f*.

anagram ['ænəgræm] *n* anagramme *m*.

analgesic [ænæl'dʒi:sɪk] *a, n* analgésique (*m*).

analog(ue) ['ænəlɔg] *a* (*watch, computer*) analogique.

analogy [ə'nælədʒɪ] *n* analogie *f*; **to draw an ~ between** établir une analogie entre.

analyse ['ænəlaɪz] *vt* (*Brit*) analyser.

analysis, *pl* **analyses** [ə'næləsɪs, -si:z] *n*

analyse *f*; **in the last** ~ en dernière analyse.
analyst ['ænəlɪst] *n* (*political* ~ *etc*) analyste *m/f*; (*US*) psychanalyste *m/f*.
analytic(al) [ænə'lɪtɪk(əl)] *a* analytique.
analyze ['ænəlaɪz] *vt* (*US*) = **analyse**.
anarchist ['ænəkɪst] *a, n* anarchiste *(m/f)*.
anarchy ['ænəkɪ] *n* anarchie *f*.
anathema [ə'næθɪmə] *n*: **it is** ~ **to him** il a cela en abomination.
anatomical [ænə'tɔmɪkəl] *a* anatomique.
anatomy [ə'nætəmɪ] *n* anatomie *f*.
ANC *n* *abbr* (= *African National Congress*) ANC *m*.
ancestor ['ænsɪstə*] *n* ancêtre *m*, aïeul *m*.
ancestral [æn'sɛstrəl] *a* ancestral(e).
ancestry ['ænsɪstrɪ] *n* ancêtres *mpl*; ascendance *f*.
anchor ['æŋkə*] *n* ancre *f* ♦ *vi* (*also*: **to drop** ~) jeter l'ancre, mouiller ♦ *vt* mettre à l'ancre.
anchorage ['æŋkərɪdʒ] *n* mouillage *m*, ancrage *m*.
anchovy ['æntʃəvɪ] *n* anchois *m*.
ancient ['eɪnʃənt] *a* ancien(ne), antique; (*fig*) d'un âge vénérable, antique; ~ **monument** monument *m* historique.
ancillary [æn'sɪlərɪ] *a* auxiliaire.
and [ænd] *cj* et; ~ **so on** et ainsi de suite; **try** ~ **come** tâchez de venir; **come** ~ **sit here** venez vous asseoir ici; **better** ~ **better** de mieux en mieux; **more** ~ **more** de plus en plus.
Andes ['ændi:z] *npl*: **the** ~ les Andes *fpl*.
anecdote ['ænɪkdəʊt] *n* anecdote *f*.
anemia [ə'ni:mɪə] *n* = **anaemia**.
anemic [ə'ni:mɪk] *a* = **anaemic**.
anemone [ə'nɛmənɪ] *n* (*BOT*) anémone *f*; **sea** ~ anémone de mer.
anesthetic [ænɪs'θɛtɪk] *a, n* = **anaesthetic**.
anesthetist [æ'ni:sθɪtɪst] *n* = **anaesthetist**.
anew [ə'nju:] *ad* à nouveau.
angel ['eɪndʒəl] *n* ange *m*.
anger ['æŋgə*] *n* colère *f* ♦ *vt* mettre en colère, irriter.
angina [æn'dʒaɪnə] *n* angine *f* de poitrine.
angle ['æŋgl] *n* angle *m* ♦ *vi*: **to** ~ **for** (*trout*) pêcher; (*compliments*) chercher, quêter; **from their** ~ de leur point de vue.
angler ['æŋglə*] *n* pêcheur/euse à la ligne.
Anglican ['æŋglɪkən] *a, n* anglican(e).
anglicize ['æŋglɪsaɪz] *vt* angliciser.
angling ['æŋglɪŋ] *n* pêche *f* à la ligne.
Anglo- ['æŋgləʊ] *prefix* anglo(-).
Anglo-French ['æŋgləʊ'frɛntʃ] *a* anglo-français(e).
Anglo-Saxon ['æŋgləʊ'sæksən] *a, n* anglo-saxon(ne).
Angola [æŋ'gəʊlə] *n* Angola *m*.
Angolan [æŋ'gəʊlən] *a* angolais(e) ♦ *n* Angolais/e.
angrily ['æŋgrɪlɪ] *ad* avec colère.
angry ['æŋgrɪ] *a* en colère, furieux(euse); **to be** ~ **with sb/at sth** être furieux contre qn/ de qch; **to get** ~ se fâcher, se mettre en colère; **to make sb** ~ mettre qn en colère.
anguish ['æŋgwɪʃ] *n* angoisse *f*.
angular ['æŋgjulə*] *a* anguleux(euse).
animal ['ænɪməl] *n* animal *m* ♦ *a* animal(e).
animal spirits *npl* entrain *m*, vivacité *f*.

animate *vt* ['ænɪmeɪt] animer ♦ *a* ['ænɪmɪt] animé(e), vivant(e).
animated ['ænɪmeɪtɪd] *a* animé(e).
animosity [ænɪ'mɔsɪtɪ] *n* animosité *f*.
aniseed ['ænɪsi:d] *n* anis *m*.
Ankara ['æŋkərə] *n* Ankara.
ankle ['æŋkl] *n* cheville *f*.
ankle socks *npl* socquettes *fpl*.
annex *n* ['ænɛks] (*also*: *Brit*: **annexe**) annexe *f* ♦ *vt* [ə'nɛks] annexer.
annexation [ænɛks'eɪʃən] *n* annexion *f*.
annihilate [ə'naɪəleɪt] *vt* annihiler, anéantir.
anniversary [ænɪ'vɜːsərɪ] *n* anniversaire *m*.
anniversary dinner *n* dîner commémoratif *or* anniversaire.
annotate ['ænəuteɪt] *vt* annoter.
announce [ə'nauns] *vt* annoncer; (*birth, death*) faire part de; **he** ~**d that he wasn't going** il a déclaré qu'il n'irait pas.
announcement [ə'naunsmənt] *n* annonce *f*; (*for births etc: in newspaper*) avis *m* de faire-part; (*: letter, card*) faire-part *m*; **I'd like to make an** ~ j'ai une communication à faire.
announcer [ə'naunsə*] *n* (*RADIO, TV: between programmes*) speaker/ine; (*: in a programme*) présentateur/trice.
annoy [ə'nɔɪ] *vt* agacer, ennuyer, contrarier; **to be** ~**ed (at sth/with sb)** être en colère *or* irrité (contre qch/qn); **don't get** ~**ed!** ne vous fâchez pas!
annoyance [ə'nɔɪəns] *n* mécontentement *m*, contrariété *f*.
annoying [ə'nɔɪɪŋ] *a* ennuyeux(euse), agaçant(e), contrariant(e).
annual ['ænjuəl] *a* annuel(le) ♦ *n* (*BOT*) plante annuelle; (*book*) album *m*.
annual general meeting (AGM) *n* (*Brit*) assemblée générale annuelle (AGA).
annually ['ænjuəlɪ] *ad* annuellement.
annual report *n* rapport annuel.
annuity [ə'nju:ɪtɪ] *n* rente *f*; **life** ~ rente viagère.
annul [ə'nʌl] *vt* annuler; (*law*) abroger.
annulment [ə'nʌlmənt] *n* (*see vb*) annulation *f*; abrogation *f*.
annum ['ænəm] *n* *see* **per annum**.
Annunciation [ənʌnsɪ'eɪʃən] *n* Annonciation *f*.
anode ['ænəud] *n* anode *f*.
anoint [ə'nɔɪnt] *vt* oindre.
anomalous [ə'nɔmələs] *a* anormal(e).
anomaly [ə'nɔmlɪ] *n* anomalie *f*.
anon. [ə'nɔn] *abbr* = **anonymous**.
anonymity [ænə'nɪmɪtɪ] *n* anonymat *m*.
anonymous [ə'nɔnɪməs] *a* anonyme; **to re-main** ~ garder l'anonymat.
anorak ['ænəræk] *n* anorak *m*.
anorexia [ænə'rɛksɪə] *n* (*also*: ~ **nervosa**) anorexie *f*.
another [ə'nʌðə*] *a*: ~ **book** (*one more*) un autre livre, encore un livre, un livre de plus; (*a different one*) un autre livre; ~ **drink?** encore un verre?; **in** ~ **5 years** dans 5 ans ♦ *pronoun* un(e) autre, encore un(e), un(e) de plus; *see also* **one**.
ANSI *n* *abbr* (= *American National Standards Institute*) association de normalisation.
answer ['ɑ:nsə*] *n* réponse *f*; (*to problem*) solution *f* ♦ *vi* répondre ♦ *vt* (*reply to*) répon-

dre à; (*problem*) résoudre; (*prayer*) exaucer; **to ~ the phone** répondre (au téléphone); **in ~ to your letter** suite à *or* en réponse à votre lettre; **to ~ the bell** *or* **the door** aller *or* venir ouvrir (la porte).

answer back *vi* répondre, répliquer.

answer for *vt fus* répondre de, se porter garant de; (*crime, one's actions*) répondre de.

answer to *vt fus* (*description*) répondre *or* correspondre à.

answerable ['ɑ:nsərəbl] *a:* ~ **(to sb/for sth)** responsable (devant qn/de qch); **I am ~ to no-one** je n'ai de comptes à rendre à personne.

answering machine ['ɑ:nsərɪŋ-] *n* répondeur *m*.

ant [ænt] *n* fourmi *f*.

ANTA *n abbr = American National Theatre and Academy.*

antagonism [æn'tægənɪzəm] *n* antagonisme *m*.

antagonist [æn'tægənɪst] *n* antagoniste *m/f*, adversaire *m/f*.

antagonistic [æntægə'nɪstɪk] *a* (*attitude, feelings*) hostile.

antagonize [æn'tægənaɪz] *vt* éveiller l'hostilité de, contrarier.

Antarctic [ænt'ɑ:ktɪk] *a* antarctique, austral(e) ♦ *n:* **the ~** l'Antarctique *m*.

Antarctica [ænt'ɑ:ktɪkə] *n* Antarctique *m*, Terres Australes.

Antarctic Circle *n* cercle *m* Antarctique.

Antarctic Ocean *n* océan *m* Antarctique *or* Austral.

ante ['æntɪ] *n:* **to up the ~** faire monter les enjeux.

ante... ['æntɪ] *prefix* anté..., anti..., pré....

anteater ['ænti:tə*] *n* fourmilier *m*, tamanoir *m*.

antecedent [æntɪ'si:dənt] *n* antécédent *m*.

antechamber ['æntɪtʃeɪmbə*] *n* antichambre *f*.

antelope ['æntɪləʊp] *n* antilope *f*.

antenatal ['æntɪ'neɪtl] *a* prénatal(e).

antenatal clinic *n* service *m* de consultation prénatale.

antenna, *pl* ~**e** [æn'tɛnə, -ni:] *n* antenne *f*.

anthem ['ænθəm] *n* motet *m*; **national ~** hymne national.

ant-hill ['ænthɪl] *n* fourmilière *f*.

anthology [æn'θɒlədʒɪ] *n* anthologie *f*.

anthropologist [ænθrə'pɒlədʒɪst] *n* anthropologue *m/f*.

anthropology [ænθrə'pɒlədʒɪ] *n* anthropologie *f*.

anti- ['æntɪ] *prefix* anti-.

anti-aircraft ['æntɪ'ɛəkrɑ:ft] *a* antiaérien(ne).

anti-aircraft defence *n* défense *f* contre avions, DCA *f*.

antiballistic ['æntɪbə'lɪstɪk] *a* antibalistique.

antibiotic ['æntɪbaɪ'ɒtɪk] *a, n* antibiotique *(m)*.

antibody ['æntɪbɒdɪ] *n* anticorps *m*.

anticipate [æn'tɪsɪpeɪt] *vt* s'attendre à, prévoir; (*wishes, request*) aller au devant de, devancer; **this is worse than I ~d** c'est pire que je ne pensais; **as ~d** comme prévu.

anticipation [æntɪsɪ'peɪʃən] *n* attente *f*; **thanking you in ~** en vous remerciant d'avance, avec mes remerciements anticipés.

anticlimax ['æntɪ'klaɪmæks] *n* réalisation décevante d'un événement que l'on escomptait important, intéressant etc.

anticlockwise ['æntɪ'klɒkwaɪz] *a* dans le sens inverse des aiguilles d'une montre.

antics ['æntɪks] *npl* singeries *fpl*.

anticyclone ['æntɪ'saɪkləʊn] *n* anticyclone *m*.

antidote ['æntɪdəʊt] *n* antidote *m*, contrepoison *m*.

antifreeze ['æntɪfri:z] *n* antigel *m*.

antihistamine ['æntɪ'hɪstəmɪn] *n* antihistaminique *m*.

Antilles [æn'tɪli:z] *npl:* **the ~** les Antilles *fpl*.

antipathy [æn'tɪpəθɪ] *n* antipathie *f*.

Antipodean [æntɪpə'di:ən] *a* australien(ne) et néozélandais(e), d'Australie et de Nouvelle-Zélande.

Antipodes [æn'tɪpədi:z] *npl:* **the ~** l'Australie *f* et la Nouvelle-Zélande.

antiquarian [æntɪ'kwɛərɪən] *a:* ~ **bookshop** librairie *f* d'ouvrages anciens ♦ *n* expert *m* en objets *or* livres anciens; amateur *m* d'antiquités.

antiquated ['æntɪkweɪtɪd] *a* vieilli(e), suranné(e), vieillot(te).

antique [æn'ti:k] *n* objet *m* d'art ancien, meuble ancien *or* d'époque, antiquité *f* ♦ *a* ancien(ne); (*pre-mediaeval*) antique.

antique dealer *n* antiquaire *m/f*.

antique shop *n* magasin *m* d'antiquités.

antiquity [æn'tɪkwɪtɪ] *n* antiquité *f*.

anti-Semitic ['æntɪsɪ'mɪtɪk] *a* antisémite.

anti-Semitism ['æntɪ'sɛmɪtɪzəm] *n* antisémitisme *m*.

antiseptic [æntɪ'sɛptɪk] *a, n* antiseptique *(m)*.

antisocial ['æntɪ'səʊʃəl] *a* peu liant(e), sauvage, insociable; (*against society*) antisocial(e).

antitank ['æntɪ'tæŋk] *a* antichar.

antithesis, *pl* **antitheses** [æn'tɪθɪsɪs, -si:z] *n* antithèse *f*.

antitrust ['æntɪ'trʌst] *a:* ~ **legislation** loi *f* anti-trust.

antlers ['æntləz] *npl* bois *mpl*, ramure *f*.

Antwerp ['æntwə:p] *n* Anvers.

anus ['eɪnəs] *n* anus *m*.

anvil ['ænvɪl] *n* enclume *f*.

anxiety [æŋ'zaɪətɪ] *n* anxiété *f*; (*keenness*): ~ **to do** grand désir *or* impatience *f* de faire.

anxious ['æŋkʃəs] *a* anxieux(euse), (très) inquiet(ète); (*keen*): ~ **to do/that** qui tient beaucoup à faire/à ce que; impatient(e) de faire/que; **I'm very ~ about you** je me fais beaucoup de souci pour toi.

anxiously ['æŋkʃəslɪ] *ad* anxieusement.

any ['ɛnɪ] *a* (*in negative and interrogative sentences = some*) de, d'; du, de l', de la, des; (*no matter which*) n'importe quel(le), quelconque; (*each and every*) tout(e), chaque; **I haven't ~ money/books** je n'ai pas d'argent/de livres; **have you ~ butter/children?** avez-vous du beurre/des enfants?; **without ~ difficulty** sans la moindre difficulté; **come (at) ~ time** venez à n'importe quelle heure; **at ~ moment** à tout moment, d'un instant à l'autre; ~ **day now** d'un jour à l'autre; **in ~ case** de toute façon; (*at least*) en tout cas; **at ~ rate** de toute façon ♦ *pronoun* n'importe lequel(laquelle);

(anybody) n'importe qui; *(in negative and interrogative sentences)*: **I haven't ~** je n'en ai pas, je n'en ai aucun; **have you got ~?** en avez-vous?; **can ~ of you sing?** est-ce que l'un d'entre vous *or* quelqu'un parmi vous sait chanter? ♦ *ad (in negative sentences)* nullement, aucunement; *(in interrogative and conditional constructions)* un peu; tant soit peu; **I can't hear him ~ more** je ne l'entends plus; **are you feeling ~ better?** vous sentez-vous un peu mieux?; **do you want ~ more soup?** voulez-vous encore un peu de soupe?

anybody ['ɛnɪbɔdɪ] *pronoun* n'importe qui; *(in interrogative sentences)* quelqu'un; *(in negative sentences)*: **I don't see ~** je ne vois personne.

anyhow ['ɛnɪhau] *ad* quoi qu'il en soit; *(haphazardly)* n'importe comment; **I shall go ~** j'irai de toute façon.

anyone ['ɛnɪwʌn] = **anybody**.

anyplace ['ɛnɪpleɪs] *ad (US)* = **anywhere**.

anything ['ɛnɪθɪŋ] *pronoun* n'importe quoi; *(in interrogative sentences)* quelque chose; *(in negative sentences)*: **I don't want ~** je ne veux rien; **~ else?** *(in shop)* et avec ça?; **it can cost ~ between £15 and £20** *(Brit)* ça peut coûter dans les 15 à 20 livres.

anytime ['ɛnɪtaɪm] *ad* n'importe quand.

anyway ['ɛnɪweɪ] *ad* de toute façon.

anywhere ['ɛnɪwɛə*] *ad* n'importe où; *(in interrogative sentences)* quelque part; *(in negative sentences)*: **I don't see him ~** je ne le vois nulle part; **~ in the world** n'importe où dans le monde.

Anzac ['ænzæk] *n abbr (= Australia-New Zealand Army Corps) soldat du corps ANZAC.*

apart [ə'pɑːt] *ad (to one side)* à part; de côté; à l'écart; *(separately)* séparément; **10 miles/a long way ~** à 10 milles/très éloignés l'un de l'autre; **they are living ~** ils sont séparés; **~ from** *prep* à part, excepté.

apartheid [ə'pɑːteɪt] *n* apartheid *m*.

apartment [ə'pɑːtmənt] *n (US)* appartement *m*, logement *m*.

apartment building *n (US)* immeuble *m*; maison divisée en appartements.

apathetic [æpə'θɛtɪk] *a* apathique, indifférent(e).

apathy ['æpəθɪ] *n* apathie *f*, indifférence *f*.

APB *n abbr (US: = all points bulletin) expression de la police signifiant 'découvrir et appréhender le suspect'.*

ape [eɪp] *n* (grand) singe ♦ *vt* singer.

Apennines ['æpənaɪnz] *npl*: **the ~** les Apennins *mpl*.

aperitif [ə'pɛrɪtɪf] *n* apéritif *m*.

aperture ['æpətʃjuə*] *n* orifice *m*, ouverture *f*; *(PHOT)* ouverture (du diaphragme).

APEX ['eɪpɛks] *n abbr (Brit: = Association of Professional, Executive, Clerical and Computer Staff) syndicat des professions libérales, cadres, administratifs et informaticiens; (AVIAT: = advance passenger excursion) APEX m.*

apex ['eɪpɛks] *n* sommet *m*.

aphid ['æfɪd] *n* puceron *m*.

aphrodisiac [æfrəu'dɪzɪæk] *a, n* aphrodisiaque *(m)*.

API *n abbr = American Press Institute.*

apiece [ə'piːs] *ad (for each person)* chacun(e), par tête; *(for each item)* chacun(e), (la) pièce.

aplomb [ə'plɒm] *n* sang-froid *m*, assurance *f*.

APO *n abbr (US: = Army Post Office) service postal de l'armée.*

apocalypse [ə'pɒkəlɪps] *n* apocalypse *f*.

apolitical [eɪpə'lɪtɪkl] *a* apolitique.

apologetic [əpɒlə'dʒɛtɪk] *a (tone, letter)* d'excuse; **to be very ~ about** s'excuser vivement de.

apologetically [əpɒlə'dʒɛtɪkəlɪ] *ad (say)* en s'excusant.

apologize [ə'pɒlədʒaɪz] *vi*: **to ~ (for sth to sb)** s'excuser (de qch auprès de qn), présenter des excuses (à qn pour qch).

apology [ə'pɒlədʒɪ] *n* excuses *fpl*; **to send one's apologies** envoyer une lettre *or* un mot d'excuse, s'excuser (de ne pas pouvoir venir); **please accept my apologies** vous voudrez bien m'excuser.

apoplectic [æpə'plɛktɪk] *a (MED)* apoplectique; *(col)*: **~ with rage** fou(folle) de rage.

apoplexy ['æpəplɛksɪ] *n* apoplexie *f*.

apostle [ə'pɒsl] *n* apôtre *m*.

apostrophe [ə'pɒstrəfɪ] *n* apostrophe *f*.

appal [ə'pɔːl] *vt* consterner, atterrer; horrifier.

Appalachian Mountains [æpə'leɪʃən-] *npl*: **the ~** les (monts *mpl*) Appalaches.

appalling [ə'pɔːlɪŋ] *a* épouvantable; *(stupidity)* consternant(e); **she's an ~ cook** c'est une très mauvaise cuisinière.

apparatus [æpə'reɪtəs] *n* appareil *m*, dispositif *m*; *(in gymnasium)* agrès *mpl*.

apparel [ə'pærl] *n (US)* habillement *m*, confection *f*.

apparent [ə'pærənt] *a* apparent(e); **it is ~ that** il est évident que.

apparently [ə'pærəntlɪ] *ad* apparemment.

apparition [æpə'rɪʃən] *n* apparition *f*.

appeal [ə'piːl] *vi (LAW)* faire *or* interjeter appel ♦ *n (LAW)* appel *m*; *(request)* appel; prière *f*; *(charm)* attrait *m*, charme *m*; **to ~ for** demander (instamment); implorer; **to ~ to** *(subj: person)* faire appel à; *(subj: thing)* plaire à; **to ~ to sb for mercy** implorer la pitié de qn, prier *or* adjurer qn d'avoir pitié; **it doesn't ~ to me** cela ne m'attire pas; **right of ~** droit *m* de recours.

appealing [ə'piːlɪŋ] *a (nice)* attrayant(e); *(touching)* attendrissant(e).

appear [ə'pɪə*] *vi* apparaître, se montrer; *(LAW)* comparaître; *(publication)* paraître, sortir, être publié(e); *(seem)* paraître, sembler; **it would ~ that** il semble que; **to ~ in Hamlet** jouer dans Hamlet; **to ~ on TV** passer à la télé.

appearance [ə'pɪərəns] *n* apparition *f*; parution *f*; *(look, aspect)* apparence *f*, aspect *m*; **to put in** *or* **make an ~** faire acte de présence; *(THEATRE)*: **by order of ~** par ordre d'entrée en scène; **to keep up ~s** sauver les apparences; **to all ~s** selon toute apparence.

appease [ə'piːz] *vt* apaiser, calmer.

appeasement [ə'piːzmənt] *n (POL)* apaisement *m*.

append [ə'pɛnd] vt (COMPUT) ajouter (à la fin d'un fichier).

appendage [ə'pɛndɪdʒ] n appendice m.

appendicitis [əpɛndɪ'saɪtɪs] n appendicite f.

appendix, pl **appendices** [ə'pɛndɪks, -siːz] n appendice m; **to have one's ~ out** se faire opérer de l'appendicite.

appetite ['æpɪtaɪt] n appétit m; **that walk has given me an ~** cette promenade m'a ouvert l'appétit.

appetizer ['æpɪtaɪzə*] n (food) amuse-gueule m; (drink) apéritif m.

appetizing ['æpɪtaɪzɪŋ] a appétissant(e).

applaud [ə'plɔːd] vt, vi applaudir.

applause [ə'plɔːz] n applaudissements mpl.

apple ['æpl] n pomme f; (also: ~ **tree**) pommier m; **it's the ~ of my eye** j'y tiens comme à la prunelle de mes yeux.

apple turnover n chausson m aux pommes.

appliance [ə'plaɪəns] n appareil m; **electrical ~s** l'électroménager.

applicable [ə'plɪkəbl] a applicable; **the law is ~ from January** la loi entre en vigueur au mois de janvier; **to be ~ to** valoir pour.

applicant ['æplɪkənt] n: ~ **(for)** (ADMIN: for benefit etc) demandeur/euse (de); (for post) candidat/e (à).

application [æplɪ'keɪʃən] n application f; (for a job, a grant etc) demande f; candidature f; **on ~** sur demande.

application form n formulaire m de demande.

application program n (COMPUT) programme m d'application.

applications package n (COMPUT) progiciel m d'application.

applied [ə'plaɪd] a appliqué(e); ~ **arts** npl arts décoratifs.

apply [ə'plaɪ] vt: **to ~ (to)** (paint, ointment) appliquer (sur); (theory, technique) appliquer (à) ♦ vi: **to ~ to** (ask) s'adresser à; (be suitable for, relevant to) s'appliquer à, être valable pour; **to ~ (for)** (permit, grant) faire une demande (en vue d'obtenir); (job) poser sa candidature (pour), faire une demande d'emploi (concernant); **to ~ the brakes** actionner les freins, freiner; **to ~ o.s. to** s'appliquer à.

appoint [ə'pɔɪnt] vt nommer, engager; (date, place) fixer, désigner.

appointee [əpɔɪn'tiː] n personne nommée; candidat retenu.

appointment [ə'pɔɪntmənt] n (to post) nomination f; (arrangement to meet) rendez-vous m; **to make an ~ (with)** prendre rendez-vous (avec); **"~s (vacant)"** (PRESS) "offres d'emploi"; **by ~** sur rendez-vous.

apportion [ə'pɔːʃən] vt (share out) répartir, distribuer; **to ~ sth to sb** attribuer or assigner or allouer qch à qn.

appraisal [ə'preɪzl] n évaluation f.

appraise [ə'preɪz] vt (value) estimer; (situation etc) évaluer.

appreciable [ə'priːʃəbl] a appréciable.

appreciate [ə'priːʃɪeɪt] vt (like) apprécier, faire cas de; (be grateful for) être reconnaissant(e) de; (assess) évaluer; (be aware of) comprendre, se rendre compte de ♦ vi (FINANCE) prendre de la valeur; **I ~ your**

help je vous remercie pour votre aide.

appreciation [əpriːʃɪ'eɪʃən] n appréciation f; (gratitude) reconnaissance f; (FINANCE) hausse f, valorisation f.

appreciative [ə'priːʃɪətɪv] a (person) sensible; (comment) élogieux(euse).

apprehend [æprɪ'hɛnd] vt appréhender, arrêter; (understand) comprendre.

apprehension [æprɪ'hɛnʃən] n appréhension f, inquiétude f.

apprehensive [æprɪ'hɛnsɪv] a inquiet(ète), appréhensif(ive).

apprentice [ə'prɛntɪs] n apprenti m ♦ vt: **to be ~d to** être en apprentissage chez.

apprenticeship [ə'prɛntɪsʃɪp] n apprentissage m; **to serve one's ~** faire son apprentissage.

appro. ['æprəu] abbr (Brit COMM: col) = **approval**.

approach [ə'prəutʃ] vi approcher ♦ vt (come near) approcher de; (ask, apply to) s'adresser à; (subject, passer-by) aborder ♦ n approche f; accès m, abord m; démarche f (auprès de qn); démarche (intellectuelle); **to ~ sb about sth** aller or venir voir qn pour qch.

approachable [ə'prəutʃəbl] a accessible.

approach road n voie f d'accès.

approbation [æprə'beɪʃən] n approbation f.

appropriate vt [ə'prəuprɪeɪt] (take) s'approprier; (allot): **to ~ sth for** affecter qch à ♦ a [ə'prəuprɪɪt] qui convient, approprié(e); (timely) opportun(e); **~ for** or **to** approprié à; **it would not be ~ for me to comment** il ne me serait pas approprié de commenter.

appropriately [ə'prəuprɪɪtlɪ] ad pertinemment, avec à-propos.

appropriation [əprəuprɪ'eɪʃən] n dotation f, affectation f.

approval [ə'pruːvəl] n approbation f; **to meet with sb's** (proposal etc) recueillir l'assentiment de qn; **on ~** (COMM) à l'examen.

approve [ə'pruːv] vt approuver.

approve of vt fus approuver.

approved school n (Brit) centre m d'éducation surveillée.

approvingly [ə'pruːvɪŋlɪ] ad d'un air approbateur.

approx. abbr (= approximately) env.

approximate a [ə'prɔksɪmɪt] approximatif(ive) ♦ vt [ə'prɔksɪmeɪt] se rapprocher de; être proche de.

approximation [ə'prɔksɪ'meɪʃən] n approximation f.

Apr. abbr = **April**.

apr n abbr (= annual percentage rate) taux (d'intérêt) annuel.

apricot ['eɪprɪkɔt] n abricot m.

April ['eɪprəl] n avril m; ~ **fool!** poisson d'avril!; for phrases see also **July**.

April Fool's Day n le premier avril.

apron ['eɪprən] n tablier m; (AVIAT) aire f de stationnement.

apse [æps] n (ARCHIT) abside f.

APT n abbr (Brit: = advanced passenger train) ≈ TGV m.

Apt. abbr (= apartment) appt.

apt [æpt] a (suitable) approprié(e); (able): ~ **(at)** doué(e) (pour); apte (à); (likely): ~ **to**

do susceptible de faire; ayant tendance à faire.

aptitude ['æptɪtjuːd] *n* aptitude *f*.

aptitude test *n* test *m* d'aptitude.

aptly ['æptlɪ] *ad* (fort) à propos.

aqualung ['ækwəlʌŋ] *n* scaphandre *m* autonome.

aquarium [ə'kwɛərɪəm] *n* aquarium *m*.

Aquarius [ə'kwɛərɪəs] *n* le Verseau; **to be ~** être du Verseau.

aquatic [ə'kwætɪk] *a* aquatique; (*sport*) nautique.

aqueduct ['ækwɪdʌkt] *n* aqueduc *m*.

AR *abbr* (*US POST*) = *Arkansas*.

ARA *n abbr* (*Brit*) = *Associate of the Royal Academy*.

Arab ['ærəb] *n* Arabe *m/f* ♦ *a* arabe.

Arabia [ə'reɪbɪə] *n* Arabie *f*.

Arabian [ə'reɪbɪən] *a* arabe.

Arabian Desert *n* désert *m* d'Arabie.

Arabian Sea *n* mer *f* d'Arabie.

Arabic ['ærəbɪk] *a, n* arabe *(m)*.

Arabic numerals *npl* chiffres *mpl* arabes.

arable ['ærəbl] *a* arable.

ARAM *n abbr* (*Brit*) = *Associate of the Royal Academy of Music*.

arbiter ['ɑːbɪtə*] *n* arbitre *m*.

arbitrary ['ɑːbɪtrərɪ] *a* arbitraire.

arbitrate ['ɑːbɪtreɪt] *vi* arbitrer; trancher.

arbitration [ɑːbɪ'treɪʃən] *n* arbitrage *m*; **the dispute went to ~** le litige a été soumis à arbitrage.

arbitrator ['ɑːbɪtreɪtə*] *n* arbitre *m*, médiateur/trice.

ARC *n abbr* = *American Red Cross*.

arc [ɑːk] *n* arc *m*.

arcade [ɑː'keɪd] *n* arcade *f*; (*passage with shops*) passage *m*, galerie *f*.

arch [ɑːtʃ] *n* arche *f*; (*of foot*) cambrure *f*, voûte *f* plantaire ♦ *vt* arquer, cambrer ♦ *a* malicieux(euse) ♦ *prefix*: **~(-)** achevé(e); par excellence; **pointed ~** ogive *f*.

archaeological [ɑːkɪə'lɒdʒɪkl] *a* archéologique.

archaeologist [ɑːkɪ'ɒlədʒɪst] *n* archéologue *m/f*.

archaeology [ɑːkɪ'ɒlədʒɪ] *n* archéologie *f*.

archaic [ɑː'keɪɪk] *a* archaïque.

archangel ['ɑːkeɪndʒəl] *n* archange *m*.

archbishop [ɑːtʃ'bɪʃəp] *n* archevêque *m*.

arch-enemy ['ɑːtʃ'ɛnəmɪ] *n* ennemi *m* de toujours *or* par excellence.

archeology *etc* [ɑːkɪ'ɒlədʒɪ] (*US*) = **archaeology** *etc*.

archer ['ɑːtʃə*] *n* archer *m*.

archery ['ɑːtʃərɪ] *n* tir *m* à l'arc.

archetypal ['ɑːkɪtaɪpəl] *a* archétype.

archetype ['ɑːkɪtaɪp] *n* prototype *m*, archétype *m*.

archipelago [ɑːkɪ'pɛlɪgəu] *n* archipel *m*.

architect ['ɑːkɪtɛkt] *n* architecte *m*.

architectural [ɑːkɪ'tɛktʃərəl] *a* architectural(e).

architecture ['ɑːkɪtɛktʃə*] *n* architecture *f*.

archive file *n* (*COMPUT*) fichier *m* d'archives.

archives ['ɑːkaɪvz] *npl* archives *fpl*.

archivist ['ɑːkɪvɪst] *n* archiviste *m/f*.

archway ['ɑːtʃweɪ] *n* voûte *f*, porche voûté *or* cintré.

ARCM *n abbr* (*Brit*) = *Associate of the Royal College of Music*.

Arctic ['ɑːktɪk] *a* arctique ♦ *n*: **the ~** l'Arctique *m*.

Arctic Circle *n* cercle *m* Arctique.

Arctic Ocean *n* océan *m* Arctique.

ARD *n abbr* (*US MED*) = *acute respiratory disease*.

ardent ['ɑːdənt] *a* fervent(e).

ardour, (*US*) **ardor** ['ɑːdə*] *n* ardeur *f*.

arduous ['ɑːdjuəs] *a* ardu(e).

are [ɑː*] *vb see* **be**.

area ['ɛərɪə] *n* (*GEOM*) superficie *f*; (*zone*) région *f*; (*: smaller*) secteur *m*; **dining ~** coin *m* salle à manger; **the London ~** la région Londonienne.

area code *n* (*TEL*) indicatif *m* de zone.

arena [ə'riːnə] *n* arène *f*.

aren't [ɑːnt] = **are not**.

Argentina [ɑːdʒən'tiːnə] *n* Argentine *f*.

Argentinian [ɑːdʒən'tɪnɪən] *a* argentin(e) ♦ *n* Argentin/e.

arguable ['ɑːgjuəbl] *a* discutable, contestable; **it is ~ whether** on peut se demander si.

arguably ['ɑːgjuəblɪ] *ad*: **it is ~...** on peut soutenir que c'est....

argue ['ɑːgjuː] *vi* (*quarrel*) se disputer; (*reason*) argumenter ♦ *vt* (*debate: case, matter*) débattre; **to ~ about sth (with sb)** se disputer (avec qn) au sujet de qch; **to ~ that** objecter *or* alléguer que, donner comme argument que.

argument ['ɑːgjumənt] *n* (*reasons*) argument *m*; (*quarrel*) dispute *f*, discussion *f*; (*debate*) discussion, controverse *f*; **~ for/against** argument pour/contre.

argumentative [ɑːgju'mɛntətɪv] *a* ergoteur(euse), raisonneur(euse).

aria ['ɑːrɪə] *n* aria *f*.

ARIBA *n abbr* (*Brit*) = *Associate of the Royal Institute of British Architects*.

arid ['ærɪd] *a* aride.

aridity [ə'rɪdɪtɪ] *n* aridité *f*.

Aries ['ɛərɪz] *n* le Bélier; **to be ~** être du Bélier.

arise, *pt* **arose,** *pp* **arisen** [ə'raɪz, ə'rəuz, ə'rɪzn] *vi* survenir, se présenter; **to ~ from** résulter de; **should the need ~** en cas de besoin.

aristocracy [ærɪs'tɒkrəsɪ] *n* aristocratie *f*.

aristocrat ['ærɪstəkræt] *n* aristocrate *m/f*.

aristocratic [ærɪstə'krætɪk] *a* aristocratique.

arithmetic [ə'rɪθmətɪk] *n* arithmétique *f*.

arithmetical [ærɪθ'mɛtɪkl] *a* arithmétique.

ark [ɑːk] *n*: **Noah's A~** l'Arche *f* de Noé.

arm [ɑːm] *n* bras *m* ♦ *vt* armer; **~ in ~** bras dessus bras dessous.

armaments ['ɑːməmənts] *npl* (*weapons*) armement *m*.

armband ['ɑːmbænd] *n* brassard *m*.

armchair ['ɑːmtʃɛə*] *n* fauteuil *m*.

armed [ɑːmd] *a* armé(e); **the ~ forces** les forces armées.

armed robbery *n* vol *m* à main armée.

Armenia [ɑː'miːnɪə] *n* Arménie *f*.

Armenian [ɑː'miːnɪən] *a* arménien(ne) ♦ *n* Arménien/ne; (*LING*) arménien *m*.

armful ['ɑːmful] *n* brassée *f*.

armistice ['ɑːmɪstɪs] *n* armistice *m*.

armour, (US) **armor** ['ɑːmə*] n armure f; (also: ~-plating) blindage m; (MIL: tanks) blindés mpl.

armo(u)red car n véhicule blindé.

armo(u)ry ['ɑːmərɪ] n arsenal m.

armpit ['ɑːmpɪt] n aisselle f.

armrest ['ɑːmrɛst] n accoudoir m.

arms [ɑːmz] npl (weapons, HERALDRY) armes fpl.

arms control n contrôle m des armements.

arms race n course f aux armements.

army ['ɑːmɪ] n armée f.

aroma [ə'rəumə] n arôme m.

aromatic [ærə'mætɪk] a aromatique.

arose [ə'rəuz] pt of **arise**.

around [ə'raund] ad (tout) autour; (nearby) dans les parages ♦ prep autour de; (fig: about) environ; vers; **is he** ~? est-il dans les parages or là?

arouse [ə'rauz] vt (sleeper) éveiller; (curiosity, passions) éveiller, susciter; exciter.

arpeggio [ɑː'pɛdʒɪəu] n arpège m.

arrange [ə'reɪndʒ] vt arranger; (programme) arrêter, convenir de ♦ vi: **we have** ~**d for a car to pick you up** nous avons prévu qu'une voiture vienne vous prendre; **it was** ~**d that**... il a été convenu que..., il a été décidé que...; **to** ~ **to do sth** prévoir de faire qch.

arrangement [ə'reɪndʒmənt] n arrangement m; (plans etc): ~**s** dispositions fpl; **to come to an** ~ **(with sb)** se mettre d'accord (avec qn); **home deliveries by** ~ livraison à domicile sur demande; **I'll make** ~**s for you to be met** je vous enverrai chercher.

array [ə'reɪ] n (of objects) déploiement m, étalage m; (MATH, COMPUT) tableau m.

arrears [ə'rɪəz] npl arriéré m; **to be in** ~ **with one's rent** devoir un arriéré de loyer, être en retard pour le paiement de son loyer.

arrest [ə'rɛst] vt arrêter; (sb's attention) retenir, attirer ♦ n arrestation f; **under** ~ en état d'arrestation.

arresting [ə'rɛstɪŋ] a (fig: beauty) saisissante(e); (: charm, candour) désarmant(e).

arrival [ə'raɪvl] n arrivée f; (COMM) arrivage m; (person) arrivant/e; **new** ~ nouveau venu/nouvelle venue.

arrive [ə'raɪv] vi arriver.

arrive at vt fus (fig) parvenir à.

arrogance ['ærəgəns] n arrogance f.

arrogant ['ærəgənt] a arrogant(e).

arrow ['ærəu] n flèche f.

arse [ɑːs] n (Brit col!) cul m (!).

arsenal ['ɑːsɪnl] n arsenal m.

arsenic ['ɑːsnɪk] n arsenic m.

arson ['ɑːsn] n incendie criminel.

art [ɑːt] n art m; (craft) métier m; **work of** ~ œuvre f d'art.

artefact ['ɑːtɪfækt] n objet fabriqué.

arterial [ɑː'tɪərɪəl] a (ANAT) artériel(le); (road etc) à grande circulation.

artery ['ɑːtərɪ] n artère f.

artful ['ɑːtful] a rusé(e).

art gallery n musée m d'art; (small and private) galerie f de peinture.

arthritis [ɑː'θraɪtɪs] n arthrite f.

artichoke ['ɑːtɪtʃəuk] n artichaut m; **Jerusalem** ~ topinambour m.

article ['ɑːtɪkl] n article m; (Brit LAW: training): ~**s** npl ≈ stage m; ~**s of clothing** vêtements mpl.

articles of association npl (COMM) statuts mpl d'une société.

articulate a [ɑː'tɪkjulɪt] (person) qui s'exprime clairement et aisément; (speech) bien articulé(e), prononcé(e) clairement ♦ vi [ɑː'tɪkjuleɪt] articuler, parler distinctement.

articulated lorry n (Brit) (camion m) semi-remorque m.

artifice ['ɑːtɪfɪs] n ruse f.

artificial [ɑːtɪ'fɪʃəl] a artificiel(le).

artificial insemination [-ɪnsɛmɪ'neɪʃən] n insémination artificielle.

artificial intelligence (A.I.) n intelligence artificielle (IA).

artificial respiration n respiration artificielle.

artillery [ɑː'tɪlərɪ] n artillerie f.

artisan ['ɑːtɪzæn] n artisan/e.

artist ['ɑːtɪst] n artiste m/f.

artistic [ɑː'tɪstɪk] a artistique.

artistry ['ɑːtɪstrɪ] n art m, talent m.

artless ['ɑːtlɪs] a naïf(naïve), simple, ingénu(e).

arts [ɑːts] npl (SCOL) lettres fpl.

art school n ≈ école f des beaux-arts.

ARV n abbr (= American Revised Version) traduction américaine de la Bible.

AS n abbr (US SCOL: = Associate in/of Science) diplôme universitaire ♦ abbr (US POST) = American Samoa.

as [æz, əz] cj (cause) comme, puisque; (time: moment) alors que, comme; (: duration) tandis que; (manner) comme ♦ prep (in the capacity of) en tant que, en qualité de; ~ **big** ~ aussi grand que; **twice** ~ **big** = deux fois plus grand que; **big** ~ **it is** si grand que ce soit; **much** ~ **I like them**, I ... je les aime bien, mais je ...; ~ **the years went by** à mesure que les années passaient; ~ **she said** comme elle l'avait dit; **he gave it to me** ~ **a present** il m'en a fait cadeau; ~ **if** or **though** comme si; ~ **for** or **to** en ce qui concerne, quant à; ~ or **so long** ~ cj à condition que; si; ~ **much/many (~)** autant (que); ~ **soon** ~ cj aussitôt que, dès que; ~ **soon** ~ **possible** aussitôt or dès que possible; ~ **such** ad en tant que tel(le); ~ **well** ad aussi; ~ **well** ~ cj en plus de, en même temps que; see also **so**, **such**.

ASA n abbr (= American Standards Association) association de normalisation.

a.s.a.p. abbr = **as soon as possible**.

asbestos [æz'bɛstəs] n asbeste m, amiante m.

ascend [ə'sɛnd] vt gravir.

ascendancy [ə'sɛndənsɪ] n ascendant m.

ascendant [ə'sɛndənt] n: **to be in the** ~ monter.

ascension [ə'sɛnʃən] n: **the A**~ (REL) l'Ascension f.

Ascension Island n île f de l'Ascension.

ascent [ə'sɛnt] n ascension f.

ascertain [æsə'teɪn] vt s'assurer de, vérifier; établir.

ascetic [ə'sɛtɪk] a ascétique.

asceticism [ə'sɛtɪsɪzəm] n ascétisme m.

ASCII ['æskiː] n abbr (= American Standard

Code for Information Interchange) ASCII.
ascribe [ə'skraɪb] *vt*: **to ~ sth to** attribuer qch à; (*blame*) imputer qch à.
ASCU *n abbr* (*US*) = *Association of State Colleges and Universities.*
ASE *n abbr* = *American Stock Exchange.*
ASH [æʃ] *n abbr* (*Brit*: = *Action on Smoking and Health*) ligue anti-tabac.
ash [æʃ] *n* (*dust*) cendre *f*; (*also*: ~ **tree**) frêne *m*.
ashamed [ə'ʃeɪmd] *a* honteux(euse), confus(e); **to be ~ of** avoir honte de; **to be ~ (of o.s.) for having done** avoir honte d'avoir fait.
ashen ['æʃən] *a* (*pale*) cendreux(euse), blême.
ashore [ə'ʃɔ:*] *ad* à terre; **to go ~** aller à terre, débarquer.
ashtray ['æʃtreɪ] *n* cendrier *m*.
Ash Wednesday *n* mercredi *m* des Cendres.
Asia ['eɪʃə] *n* Asie *f*.
Asia Minor *n* Asie Mineure.
Asian ['eɪʃən] *n* Asiatique *m/f* ♦ *a* asiatique.
Asiatic [eɪsɪ'ætɪk] *a* asiatique.
aside [ə'saɪd] *ad* de côté; à l'écart ♦ *n* aparté *m*; ~ **from** *prep* à part, excepté.
ask [ɑ:sk] *vt* demander; (*invite*) inviter; **to ~ sb sth/to do sth** demander à qn qch/de faire qch; **to ~ sb the time** demander l'heure à qn; **to ~ sb about sth** questionner qn au sujet de qch; se renseigner auprès de qn au sujet de qch; **to ~ about the price** s'informer du prix, se renseigner au sujet du prix; **to ~ (sb) a question** poser une question (à qn); **to ~ sb out to dinner** inviter qn au restaurant.
ask after *vt fus* demander des nouvelles de.
ask for *vt fus* demander; **it's just ~ing for trouble** *or* **for it** ce serait chercher des ennuis.
askance [ə'skɑ:ns] *ad*: **to look ~ at sb** regarder qn de travers *or* d'un œil désapprobateur.
askew [ə'skju:] *ad* de travers, de guinguois.
asking price ['ɑ:skɪŋ-] *n* prix demandé.
asleep [ə'sli:p] *a* endormi(e); **to be ~** dormir, être endormi; **to fall ~** s'endormir.
ASLEF ['æzlɛf] *n abbr* (*Brit*: = *Associated Society of Locomotive Engineers and Firemen*) syndicat des conducteurs de locomotives et des pompiers.
asp [æsp] *n* aspic *m*.
asparagus [əs'pærəgəs] *n* asperges *fpl*.
asparagus tips *npl* pointes *fpl* d'asperges.
ASPCA *n abbr* (= *American Society for the Prevention of Cruelty to Animals*) ≈ SPA *f*.
aspect ['æspɛkt] *n* aspect *m*; (*direction in which a building etc faces*) orientation *f*, exposition *f*.
aspersions [əs'pɔ:ʃənz] *npl*: **to cast ~ on** dénigrer.
asphalt ['æsfælt] *n* asphalte *m*.
asphyxiate [æs'fɪksɪeɪt] *vt* asphyxier.
asphyxiation [æsfɪksɪ'eɪʃən] *n* asphyxie *f*.
aspirate *vt* ['æspəreɪt] aspirer ♦ *a* ['æspərɪt] aspiré(e).
aspiration [æspə'reɪʃən] *n* aspiration *f*.
aspire [əs'paɪə*] *vi*: **to ~ to** aspirer à.
aspirin ['æsprɪn] *n* aspirine *f*.
ass [æs] *n* âne *m*; (*col*) imbécile *m/f*; (*US*

col!) cul *m* (*!*).
assail [ə'seɪl] *vt* assaillir.
assailant [ə'seɪlənt] *n* agresseur *m*; assaillant *m*.
assassin [ə'sæsɪn] *n* assassin *m*.
assassinate [ə'sæsɪneɪt] *vt* assassiner.
assassination [əsæsɪ'neɪʃən] *n* assassinat *m*.
assault [ə'sɔ:lt] *n* (*MIL*) assaut *m*; (*gen: attack*) agression *f*; (*LAW*): ~ **(and battery)** voies *fpl* de fait, coups *mpl* et blessures *fpl* ♦ *vt* attaquer; (*sexually*) violenter.
assemble [ə'sɛmbl] *vt* assembler ♦ *vi* s'assembler, se rassembler.
assembly [ə'sɛmblɪ] *n* (*meeting*) rassemblement *m*; (*construction*) assemblage *m*.
assembly language *n* (*COMPUT*) langage *m* d'assemblage.
assembly line *n* chaîne *f* de montage.
assent [ə'sɛnt] *n* assentiment *m*, consentement *m* ♦ *vi*: **to ~ (to sth)** donner son assentiment (à qch), consentir (à qch).
assert [ə'sɔ:t] *vt* affirmer, déclarer; établir; ~ **o.s.** s'imposer.
assertion [ə'sɔ:ʃən] *n* assertion *f*, affirmation *f*.
assertive [ə'sɔ:tɪv] *a* assuré(e); péremptoire.
assess [ə'sɛs] *vt* évaluer, estimer; (*tax, damages*) établir *or* fixer le montant de; (*property etc: for tax*) calculer la valeur imposable de.
assessment [ə'sɛsmənt] *n* évaluation *f*, estimation *f*; (*judgment*): ~ **(of)** jugement *m* *or* opinion *f* (sur).
assessor [ə'sɛsə*] *n* expert *m* (en matière d'impôt et d'assurance).
asset ['æsɛt] *n* avantage *m*, atout *m*; (*person*) atout; ~**s** *npl* (*COMM*) capital *m*; avoir(s) *m(pl)*; actif *m*.
asset-stripping ['æsɛt'strɪpɪŋ] *n* (*COMM*) récupération *f* (et démantèlement *m*) d'une entreprise en difficulté.
assiduous [ə'sɪdjuəs] *a* assidu(e).
assign [ə'saɪn] *vt* (*date*) fixer, arrêter; (*task*): **to ~ sth to** assigner qch à; (*resources*): **to ~ sth to** affecter qch à; (*cause, meaning*): **to ~ sth to** attribuer qch à.
assignment [ə'saɪnmənt] *n* tâche *f*, mission *f*.
assimilate [ə'sɪmɪleɪt] *vt* assimiler.
assimilation [əsɪmɪ'leɪʃən] *n* assimilation *f*.
assist [ə'sɪst] *vt* aider, assister; (*injured person etc*) secourir.
assistance [ə'sɪstəns] *n* aide *f*, assistance *f*; secours *mpl*.
assistant [ə'sɪstənt] *n* assistant/e, adjoint/e; (*Brit: also*: **shop ~**) vendeur/euse.
assistant manager *n* sous-directeur *m*.
assizes [ə'saɪzɪz] *npl* assises *fpl*.
associate *a*, *n* [ə'səʊʃɪɪt] associé(e) ♦ *vb* [ə'səʊʃɪeɪt] *vt* associer ♦ *vi*: **to ~ with sb** fréquenter qn; ~ **director** directeur adjoint; ~**d company** société affiliée.
association [əsəʊsɪ'eɪʃən] *n* association *f*; **in ~ with** en collaboration avec.
association football *n* (*Brit*) football *m*.
assorted [ə'sɔ:tɪd] *a* assorti(e); **in ~ sizes** en plusieurs tailles.
assortment [ə'sɔ:tmənt] *n* assortiment *m*.
Asst. *abbr* = **assistant**.
assuage [ə'sweɪdʒ] *vt* (*grief, pain*) soulager;

(thirst, appetite) assouvir.

assume [ə'sju:m] vt supposer; (responsibilities etc) assumer; (attitude, name) prendre, adopter.

assumed name n nom m d'emprunt.

assumption [ə'sʌmpʃən] n supposition f, hypothèse f; **on the ~ that** dans l'hypothèse où; (on condition that) à condition que.

assurance [ə'ʃuərəns] n assurance f; **I can give you no ~s** je ne peux rien vous garantir.

assure [ə'ʃuə*] vt assurer.

AST abbr (US: = Atlantic Standard Time) heure d'hiver de New York.

asterisk ['æstərisk] n astérisque m.

astern [ə'stə:n] ad à l'arrière.

asteroid ['æstərɔid] n astéroïde m.

asthma ['æsmə] n asthme m.

asthmatic [æs'mætik] a, n asthmatique (m/f).

astigmatism [ə'stigmətizəm] n astigmatisme m.

astir [ə'stə:*] ad en émoi.

ASTMS ['æstəmz] n abbr (Brit: = Association of Scientific, Technical and Managerial Staffs) syndicat des personnels scientifiques, techniques et administratifs.

astonish [ə'stɔniʃ] vt étonner, stupéfier.

astonishing [ə'stɔniʃiŋ] a étonnant(e), stupéfiant(e); **I find it ~ that...** je trouve incroyable que....

astonishingly [ə'stɔniʃiŋli] ad incroyablement.

astonishment [ə'stɔniʃmənt] n (grand) étonnement, stupéfaction f.

astound [ə'staund] vt stupéfier, sidérer.

astray [ə'strei] ad: **to go ~** s'égarer; (fig) quitter le droit chemin; **to go ~ in one's calculations** faire fausse route dans ses calculs.

astride [ə'straid] ad à cheval ♦ prep à cheval sur.

astringent [əs'trindʒənt] a astringent(e) ♦ n astringent m.

astrologer [əs'trɔlədʒə*] n astrologue m.

astrology [əs'trɔlədʒi] n astrologie f.

astronaut ['æstrənɔ:t] n astronaute m/f.

astronomer [əs'trɔnəmə*] n astronome m.

astronomical [æstrə'nɔmikl] a astronomique.

astronomy [əs'trɔnəmi] n astronomie f.

astrophysics ['æstrəu'fiziks] n astrophysique f.

astute [əs'tju:t] a astucieux(euse), malin(igne).

asunder [ə'sʌndə*] ad: **to tear ~** déchirer.

ASV n abbr (= American Standard Version) traduction de la Bible.

asylum [ə'sailəm] n asile m; **to seek political ~** demander l'asile politique.

asymmetric(al) [eisi'metrik(l)] a asymétrique.

at [æt] prep à; (because of: following surprised, annoyed etc) de; par; **~ the top** au sommet; **~ Pierre's** chez Pierre; **~ the baker's** chez le boulanger, à la boulangerie; **~ times** parfois; **~ 4 o'clock** à 4 heures; **~ night** la nuit; (in the evening) le soir; **~ £1 a kilo** une livre le kilo; **two ~ a time** deux à la fois; **~ full speed** à toute vitesse.

ate [eit] pt of **eat**.

atheism ['eiθiizəm] n athéisme m.

atheist ['eiθiist] n athée m/f.

Athenian [ə'θi:niən] a athénien(ne) ♦ n Athénien/ne.

Athens ['æθinz] n Athènes.

athlete ['æθli:t] n athlète m/f.

athletic [æθ'letik] a athlétique.

athletics [æθ'letiks] n athlétisme m.

Atlantic [ət'læntik] a atlantique ♦ n: **the ~ (Ocean)** l'Atlantique m, l'océan m Atlantique.

atlas ['ætləs] n atlas m.

Atlas Mountains npl: **the ~** les monts mpl de l'Atlas, l'Atlas m.

A.T.M. abbr (= Automatic Telling Machine) guichet m automatique.

atmosphere ['ætməsfiə*] n atmosphère f; (air) air m.

atmospheric [ætməs'ferik] a atmosphérique.

atmospherics [ætməs'feriks] n (RADIO) parasites mpl.

atoll ['ætɔl] n atoll m.

atom ['ætəm] n atome m.

atomic [ə'tɔmik] a atomique.

atom(ic) bomb n bombe f atomique.

atomizer ['ætəmaizə*] n atomiseur m.

atone [ə'təun] vi: **to ~ for** expier, racheter.

atonement [ə'təunmənt] n expiation f.

ATP n abbr (= Association of Tennis Professionals) ATP f (= Association des tennismen professionnels).

atrocious [ə'trəuʃəs] a (very bad) atroce, exécrable.

atrocity [ə'trɔsiti] n atrocité f.

atrophy ['ætrəfi] n atrophie f ♦ vt atrophier ♦ vi s'atrophier.

attach [ə'tætʃ] vt (gen) attacher; (document, letter) joindre; (employee, troops) affecter; **to be ~ed to sb/sth** (to like) être attaché à qn/qch; **the ~ed letter** la lettre ci-jointe.

attaché [ə'tæʃei] n attaché m.

attaché case n mallette f, attaché-case m.

attachment [ə'tætʃmənt] n (tool) accessoire m; (love): **~ (to)** affection f (pour), attachement m (à).

attack [ə'tæk] vt attaquer; (task etc) s'attaquer à ♦ n attaque f; (also: **heart ~**) crise f cardiaque.

attacker [ə'tækə*] n attaquant m; agresseur m.

attain [ə'tein] vt (also: **to ~ to**) parvenir à, atteindre; acquérir.

attainments [ə'teinmənts] npl connaissances fpl, résultats mpl.

attempt [ə'tempt] n tentative f ♦ vt essayer, tenter; **~ed theft** etc (LAW) tentative de vol etc; **to make an ~ on sb's life** attenter à la vie de qn; **he made no ~ to help** il n'a rien fait pour m'aider (or l'aider etc).

attend [ə'tend] vt (course) suivre; (meeting, talk) assister à; (school, church) aller à, fréquenter; (patient) soigner, s'occuper de; **to ~ (up)on** servir; être au service de.

attend to vt fus (needs, affairs etc) s'occuper de; (customer) s'occuper de, servir.

attendance [ə'tendəns] n (being present) présence f; (people present) assistance f.

attendant [ə'tendənt] n employé/e; gardien/ne ♦ a concomitant(e), qui accompagne or s'ensuit.

attention [ə'tenʃən] n attention f; **~s**

attentions *fpl*, prévenances *fpl*; ~! (*MIL*) garde-à-vous!; **at ~** (*MIL*) au garde-à-vous; **for the ~ of** (*ADMIN*) à l'attention de; **it has come to my ~ that...** je constate que....

attentive [ə'tɛntɪv] *a* attentif(ive); (*kind*) prévenant(e).

attentively [ə'tɛntɪvlɪ] *ad* attentivement, avec attention.

attenuate [ə'tɛnjueɪt] *vt* atténuer ♦ *vi* s'atténuer.

attest [ə'tɛst] *vi:* **to ~ to** témoigner de, attester (de).

attic ['ætɪk] *n* grenier *m*, combles *mpl*.

attire [ə'taɪə*] *n* habit *m*, atours *mpl*.

attitude ['ætɪtjuːd] *n* (*behaviour*) attitude *f*, manière *f*; (*posture*) pose *f*, attitude; (*view*): **~ (to)** attitude (envers).

attorney [ə'tɜːnɪ] *n* (*US: lawyer*) avocat *m*; (*having proxy*) mandataire *m*; **power of ~** procuration *f*.

Attorney General *n* (*Brit*) ≈ procureur général; (*US*) ≈ garde *m* des Sceaux, ministre *m* de la Justice.

attract [ə'trækt] *vt* attirer.

attraction [ə'trækʃən] *n* (*gen pl: pleasant things*) attraction *f*, attrait *m*; (*PHYSICS*) attraction; (*fig: towards sth*) attirance *f*.

attractive [ə'træktɪv] *a* séduisant(e), attrayant(e).

attribute *n* ['ætrɪbjuːt] attribut *m* ♦ *vt* [ə'trɪbjuːt]: **to ~ sth to** attribuer qch à.

attrition [ə'trɪʃən] *n:* **war of ~** guerre *f* d'usure.

Atty. Gen. *abbr* = **Attorney General**.

ATV *n abbr* (*Brit: = Associated Television*) chaîne de télévision commerciale; (*= all terrain vehicle*) véhicule *m* tout-terrain.

aubergine ['əubəʒiːn] *n* aubergine *f*.

auburn ['ɔːbən] *a* auburn *inv*, châtain roux *inv*.

auction ['ɔːkʃən] *n* (*also:* **sale by ~**) vente *f* aux enchères ♦ *vt* (*also:* **to sell by ~**) vendre aux enchères; (*also:* **to put up for ~**) mettre aux enchères.

auctioneer [ɔːkʃə'nɪə*] *n* commissaire-priseur *m*.

auction room *n* salle *f* des ventes.

audacious [ɔː'deɪʃəs] *a* impudent(e); audacieux(euse), intrépide.

audacity [ɔː'dæsɪtɪ] *n* impudence *f*; audace *f*.

audible ['ɔːdɪbl] *a* audible.

audience ['ɔːdɪəns] *n* (*people*) assistance *f*, auditoire *m*; auditeurs *mpl*; spectateurs *mpl*; (*interview*) audience *f*.

audio typist ['ɔːdɪəu'taɪpɪst] *n* audiotypiste *m/f*.

audiovisual ['ɔːdɪəu'vɪzjuəl] *a* audio-visuel(le); **~ aids** supports *or* moyens audiovisuels.

audit ['ɔːdɪt] *n* vérification *f* des comptes, apurement *m* ♦ *vt* vérifier, apurer.

audition [ɔː'dɪʃən] *n* audition *f* ♦ *vi* auditionner.

auditor ['ɔːdɪtə*] *n* vérificateur *m* des comptes.

auditorium [ɔːdɪ'tɔːrɪəm] *n* auditorium *m*, salle *f* de concert *or* de spectacle.

AUEW *n abbr* (*Brit: = Amalgamated Union of Engineering Workers*) syndicat des industries mécaniques.

Aug. *abbr* = **August**.

augment [ɔːg'mɛnt] *vt*, *vi* augmenter.

augur ['ɔːgə*] *vt* (*be a sign of*) présager, annoncer ♦ *vi:* **it ~s well** c'est bon signe *or* de bon augure, cela s'annonce bien.

August ['ɔːgəst] *n* août *m*; *for phrases see also* **July**.

august [ɔː'gʌst] *a* majestueux(euse), imposant(e).

aunt [ɑːnt] *n* tante *f*.

auntie, aunty ['ɑːntɪ] *n diminutive of* **aunt**.

au pair ['əu'pɛə*] *n* (*also:* **~ girl**) jeune fille *f* au pair.

aura ['ɔːrə] *n* atmosphère *f*.

auspices ['ɔːspɪsɪz] *npl:* **under the ~ of** sous les auspices de.

auspicious [ɔːs'pɪʃəs] *a* de bon augure, propice.

austere [ɔs'tɪə*] *a* austère.

austerity [ɔs'tɛrɪtɪ] *n* austérité *f*.

Australasia [ɔːstrə'leɪzɪə] *n* Australasie *f*.

Australia [ɔs'treɪlɪə] *n* Australie *f*.

Australian [ɔs'treɪlɪən] *a* australien(ne) ♦ *n* Australien/ne.

Austria ['ɔstrɪə] *n* Autriche *f*.

Austrian ['ɔstrɪən] *a* autrichien(ne) ♦ *n* Autrichien/ne.

AUT *n abbr* (*Brit: = Association of University Teachers*) syndicat universitaire.

authentic [ɔː'θɛntɪk] *a* authentique.

authenticate [ɔː'θɛntɪkeɪt] *vt* établir l'authenticité de.

authenticity [ɔːθɛn'tɪsɪtɪ] *n* authenticité *f*.

author ['ɔːθə*] *n* auteur *m*.

authoritarian [ɔːθɔrɪ'tɛərɪən] *a* autoritaire.

authoritative [ɔː'θɔrɪtətɪv] *a* (*account*) digne de foi; (*study, treatise*) qui fait autorité; (*manner*) autoritaire.

authority [ɔː'θɔrɪtɪ] *n* autorité *f*; (*permission*) autorisation (formelle); **the authorities** les autorités, l'administration *f*; **to have ~ to do sth** être habilité à faire qch.

authorization [ɔːθəraɪ'zeɪʃən] *n* autorisation *f*.

authorize ['ɔːθəraɪz] *vt* autoriser.

authorized capital *n* (*COMM*) capital social.

authorship ['ɔːθəʃɪp] *n* paternité *f* (*littéraire etc*).

autistic [ɔː'tɪstɪk] *a* autistique.

auto ['ɔːtəu] *n* (*US*) auto *f*, voiture *f*.

autobiography [ɔːtəbaɪ'ɔgrəfɪ] *n* autobiographie *f*.

autocratic [ɔːtə'krætɪk] *a* autocratique.

autograph ['ɔːtəgrɑːf] *n* autographe *m* ♦ *vt* signer, dédicacer.

automat ['ɔːtəmæt] *n* (*vending machine*) distributeur *m* (automatique); (*US: place*) cafétéria *f* avec distributeurs automatiques.

automated ['ɔːtəmeɪtɪd] *a* automatisé(e).

automatic [ɔːtə'mætɪk] *a* automatique ♦ *n* (*gun*) automatique *m*; (*washing machine*) lave-linge *m* automatique; (*Brit AUT*) voiture *f* à transmission automatique.

automatically [ɔːtə'mætɪklɪ] *ad* automatiquement.

automatic data processing (ADP) *n* traitement *m* automatique des données.

automation [ɔːtə'meɪʃən] *n* automatisation *f*.

automaton, *pl* automata [ɔː'tɔmətən, -tə] *n* automate *m*.

automobile [ˈɔːtəməbiːl] *n* (*US*) automobile *f*.
autonomous [ɔːˈtɔnəməs] *a* autonome.
autonomy [ɔːˈtɔnəmɪ] *n* autonomie *f*.
autopsy [ˈɔːtɔpsɪ] *n* autopsie *f*.
autumn [ˈɔːtəm] *n* automne *m*.
auxiliary [ɔːgˈzɪlɪərɪ] *a*, *n* auxiliaire (*m/f*).
AV *n abbr* (= *Authorized Version*) *traduction anglaise de la Bible* ♦ *abbr* = **audiovisual**.
Av. *abbr* (= *avenue*) Av.
avail [əˈveɪl] *vt*: **to ~ o.s. of** user de; profiter de ♦ *n*: **to no ~** sans résultat, en vain, en pure perte.
availability [əveɪləˈbɪlɪtɪ] *n* disponibilité *f*.
available [əˈveɪləbl] *a* disponible; **every ~ means** tous les moyens possibles *or* à sa (*or* notre *etc*) disposition; **is the manager ~?** est-ce que le directeur peut (me) recevoir?; (*on phone*) pourrais-je parler au directeur?; **to make sth ~ to sb** mettre qch à la disposition de qn.
avalanche [ˈævəlɑːnʃ] *n* avalanche *f*.
avant-garde [ˈævãˈgɑːd] *a* d'avant-garde.
avaricious [ævəˈrɪʃəs] *a* âpre au gain.
avdp. *abbr* = *avoirdupoids*.
Ave. *abbr* (= *avenue*) Av.
avenge [əˈvendʒ] *vt* venger.
avenue [ˈævənjuː] *n* avenue *f*.
average [ˈævərɪdʒ] *n* moyenne *f* ♦ *a* moyen(ne) ♦ *vt* (*a certain figure*) atteindre *or* faire *etc* en moyenne; **on ~** en moyenne; **above/below (the) ~** au-dessus/en-dessous de la moyenne.
average out *vi*: **to ~ out at** représenter en moyenne, donner une moyenne de.
averse [əˈvəːs] *a*: **to be ~ to sth/doing** éprouver une forte répugnance envers qch/à faire; **I wouldn't be ~ to a drink** un petit verre ne serait pas de refus, je ne dirais pas non à un petit verre.
aversion [əˈvəːʃən] *n* aversion *f*, répugnance *f*.
avert [əˈvəːt] *vt* prévenir, écarter; (*one's eyes*) détourner.
aviary [ˈeɪvɪərɪ] *n* volière *f*.
aviation [eɪvɪˈeɪʃən] *n* aviation *f*.
avid [ˈævɪd] *a* avide.
avidly [ˈævɪdlɪ] *ad* avidement, avec avidité.
avocado [ævəˈkɑːdəu] *n* (*also: Brit: ~* **pear**) avocat *m*.
avoid [əˈvɔɪd] *vt* éviter.
avoidable [əˈvɔɪdəbl] *a* évitable.
avoidance [əˈvɔɪdəns] *n* le fait d'éviter.
avowed [əˈvaud] *a* déclaré(e).
AVP *n abbr* (*US*) = *assistant vice-president*.
AWACS [ˈeɪwæks] *n abbr* (= *airborne warning and control system*) AWACS (*système aéroporté d'alerte et de contrôle*).
await [əˈweɪt] *vt* attendre; **~ing attention/delivery** (*COMM*) en souffrance; **long ~ed** tant attendu(e).
awake [əˈweɪk] *a* éveillé(e); (*fig*) en éveil ♦ *vb* (*pt* **awoke** [əˈwəuk], *pp* **awoken** [əˈwəukən], **awaked**) *vt* éveiller ♦ *vi* s'éveiller; **~ to** conscient de; **he was still ~** il ne dormait pas encore.
awakening [əˈweɪknɪŋ] *n* réveil *m*.
award [əˈwɔːd] *n* récompense *f*, prix *m* ♦ *vt* (*prize*) décerner; (*LAW: damages*) accorder.
aware [əˈwɛə*] *a*: **~ of** (*conscious*) conscient(e) de; (*informed*) au courant de;

to become ~ of avoir conscience de, prendre conscience de; se rendre compte de; **politically/socially ~** sensibilisé(e) aux *or* ayant pris conscience des problèmes politiques/sociaux; **I am fully ~ that** je me rends parfaitement compte que.
awareness [əˈwɛənɪs] *n* conscience *f*, connaissance *f*; **to develop people's ~ (of)** sensibiliser le public (à).
awash [əˈwɔʃ] *a* recouvert(e) (d'eau); **~ with** inondé(e) de.
away [əˈweɪ] *a*, *ad* (au) loin; absent(e); **two kilometres ~** à (une distance de) deux kilomètres, à deux kilomètres de distance; **two hours ~ by car** à deux heures de voiture *or* de route; **the holiday was two weeks ~** il restait deux semaines jusqu'aux vacances; **~ from** loin de; **he's ~ for a week** il est parti (pour) une semaine; **he's ~ in Milan** il est (parti) à Milan; **to take ~** *vt* emporter; **to pedal/work/laugh** *etc* **~** *la particule indique la constance et l'énergie de l'action*: il pédalait *etc* tant qu'il pouvait; **to fade/wither** *etc* **~** *la particule renforce l'idée de la disparition, l'éloignement*.
away game *n* (*SPORT*) match *m* à l'extérieur.
awe [ɔː] *n* respect mêlé de crainte, effroi mêlé d'admiration.
awe-inspiring [ˈɔːɪnspaɪərɪŋ], **awesome** [ˈɔːsəm] *a* impressionnant(e).
awestruck [ˈɔːstrʌk] *a* frappé(e) d'effroi.
awful [ˈɔːfəl] *a* affreux(euse); **an ~ lot of** énormément de.
awfully [ˈɔːfəlɪ] *ad* (*very*) terriblement, vraiment.
awhile [əˈwaɪl] *ad* un moment, quelque temps.
awkward [ˈɔːkwəd] *a* (*clumsy*) gauche, maladroit(e); (*inconvenient*) malaisé(e), d'emploi malaisé, peu pratique; (*embarrassing*) gênant(e), délicat(e); (*difficult: problem, task*) délicat, difficile.
awkwardness [ˈɔːkwədnɪs] *n* (*embarrassment*) gêne *f*.
awl [ɔːl] *n* alêne *f*.
awning [ˈɔːnɪŋ] *n* (*of tent*) auvent *m*; (*of shop*) store *m*; (*of hotel etc*) marquise *f* (de toile).
awoke [əˈwəuk] *pt of* **awake**.
awoken [əˈwəukən] *pp of* **awake**.
AWOL [ˈeɪwɔl] *abbr* (*MIL*) = **absent without leave**.
awry [əˈraɪ] *ad*, *a* de travers; **to go ~** mal tourner.
axe, (*US*) **ax** [æks] *n* hache *f* ♦ *vt* (*employee*) renvoyer; (*project etc*) abandonner; (*jobs*) supprimer; **to have an ~ to grind** (*fig*) prêcher pour son saint.
axes [ˈæksiːz] *npl of* **axis**.
axiom [ˈæksɪəm] *n* axiome *m*.
axiomatic [æksɪəˈmætɪk] *a* axiomatique.
axis, *pl* **axes** [ˈæksɪs, -siːz] *n* axe *m*.
axle [ˈæksl] *n* (*also:* **~-tree**) essieu *m*.
ay(e) [aɪ] *excl* (*yes*) oui ♦ *n*: **the ~s** les oui.
AYH *n abbr* = *American Youth Hostels*.
AZ *abbr* (*US POST*) = *Arizona*.
azalea [əˈzeɪlɪə] *n* azalée *f*.
Azores [əˈzɔːz] *npl*: **the ~** les Açores *fpl*.
Aztec [ˈæztɛk] *a* aztèque ♦ *n* Aztèque *m/f*.

azure ['eɪʒə*] a azuré(e).

B

B, b [bi:] n (letter) B, b m; (SCOL: mark) B; (MUS): **B** si m; **B for Benjamin**, (US) **B for Baker** B comme Berthe; **B road** n (Brit AUT) route départementale.
b. abbr = **born**.
BA n abbr = British Academy; (SCOL) = **Bachelor of Arts**.
babble ['bæbl] vi babiller ♦ n babillage m.
baboon [bə'bu:n] n babouin m.
baby ['beɪbɪ] n bébé m.
baby carriage n (US) voiture f d'enfant.
baby grand n (also: ~ **piano**) (piano m) demi-queue m.
babyhood ['beɪbɪhud] n petite enfance.
babyish ['beɪbɪʃ] a enfantin(e), de bébé.
baby-minder ['beɪbɪ'maɪndə*] n (Brit) gardienne f (d'enfants).
baby-sit ['beɪbɪsɪt] vi garder les enfants.
baby-sitter ['beɪbɪsɪtə*] n baby-sitter m/f.
bachelor ['bætʃələ*] n célibataire m; **B~ of Arts/Science (BA/BSc)** ≈ licencié/e ès or en lettres/sciences; **B~ of Arts/Science degree (BA/BSc)** n ≈ licence f ès or en lettres/ sciences.
bachelorhood ['bætʃələhud] n célibat m.
bachelor party n (US) enterrement m de vie de garçon.
back [bæk] n (of person, horse) dos m; (of hand) dos, revers m; (of house) derrière m; (of car, train) arrière m; (of chair) dossier m; (of page) verso m; (FOOTBALL) arrière m; **to have one's ~ to the wall** être au pied du mur; **to break the ~ of a job** (Brit) faire le gros d'un travail; **~ to front** à l'envers ♦ vt (financially) soutenir (financièrement); (candidate: also: ~ **up**) soutenir, appuyer; (horse: at races) parier or miser sur; (car) (faire) reculer ♦ vi reculer; (car etc) faire marche arrière ♦ a (in compounds) de derrière, à l'arrière; **~ seats/wheels** (AUT) sièges mpl/roues fpl arrière; **~ payments/rent** arriéré m de paiements/loyer; **to take a ~ seat** (fig) se contenter d'un second rôle, être relégué(e) au second plan ♦ ad (not forward) en arrière; (returned): **he's ~** il est rentré, il est de retour; **when will you be ~?** quand seras-tu de retour?; **he ran ~** il est revenu en courant; (restitution): **throw the ball ~** renvoie la balle; **can I have it ~?** puis-je le ravoir?, peux-tu me le rendre?; (again): **he called ~** il a rappelé.
back down vi rabattre de ses prétentions.
back on to vt fus: **the house ~s on to the golf course** la maison donne derrière sur le terrain de golf.
back out vi (of promise) se dédire.

back up vt (COMPUT) faire une copie de sauvegarde de.
backache ['bækeɪk] n maux mpl de reins.
backbencher ['bæk'bentʃə*] n (Brit) membre du parlement sans portefeuille.
backbiting ['bækbaɪtɪŋ] n médisance(s) f(pl).
backbone ['bækbəun] n colonne vertébrale, épine dorsale; **he's the ~ of the organization** c'est sur lui que repose l'organisation.
backchat ['bæktʃæt] n (Brit col) impertinences fpl.
back-cloth ['bækklɔθ] n (Brit) toile f de fond.
backcomb ['bækkəum] vt (Brit) crêper.
backdate [bæk'deɪt] vt (letter) antidater; **~d pay rise** augmentation f avec effet rétroactif.
backdrop ['bækdrɔp] n = **backcloth**.
backer ['bækə*] n partisan m; (COMM) commanditaire m.
backfire [bæk'faɪə*] vi (AUT) pétarader; (plans) mal tourner.
backgammon ['bækgæmən] n trictrac m.
background ['bækgraund] n arrière-plan m; (of events) situation f, conjoncture f; (basic knowledge) éléments mpl de base; (experience) formation f ♦ cpd (noise, music) de fond; **~ reading** lecture(s) générale(s) (sur un sujet); **family ~** milieu familial.
backhand ['bækhænd] n (TENNIS: also: **~hand stroke**) revers m.
backhanded ['bæk'hændɪd] a (fig) déloyal(e); équivoque.
backhander ['bæk'hændə*] n (Brit: bribe) pot-de-vin m.
backing ['bækɪŋ] n (fig) soutien m, appui m; (COMM) soutien (financier); (MUS) accompagnement m.
backlash ['bæklæʃ] n contre-coup m, répercussion f.
backlog ['bæklɔg] n: **~ of work** travail m en retard.
back number n (of magazine etc) vieux numéro.
backpack ['bækpæk] n sac m à dos.
backpacker ['bækpækə*] n randonneur/euse.
back pay n rappel m de salaire.
backpedal ['bækpedl] vi (fig) faire marche arrière.
backside ['bæksaɪd] n (col) derrière m, postérieur m.
backslash ['bækslæʃ] n barre oblique inversée.
backslide ['bækslaɪd] vi retomber dans l'erreur.
backspace ['bækspeɪs] vi (in typing) appuyer sur la touche retour.
backstage [bæk'steɪdʒ] ad dans les coulisses.
back-street ['bækstri:t] a (abortion) clandestin(e); **~ abortionist** avorteur/euse (clandestin).
backstroke ['bækstrəuk] n dos crawlé.
backtrack ['bæktræk] vi (fig) = **backpedal**.
backup ['bækʌp] a (train, plane) supplémentaire, de réserve; (COMPUT) de sauvegarde ♦ n (support) appui m, soutien m; (COMPUT: also: ~ **file**) sauvegarde f.
backward ['bækwəd] a (movement) en arrière; (measure) rétrograde; (person, country) arriéré(e); attardé(e); (shy) hésitant(e); **~ and forward movement** mouvement de va-et-vient.

backwards ['bækwədz] *ad* (*move, go*) en arrière; (*read a list*) à l'envers, à rebours; (*fall*) à la renverse; (*walk*) à reculons; (*in time*) en arrière, vers le passé; **to know sth ~ or** (*US*) **~ and forwards** (*col*) connaître qch sur le bout des doigts.

backwater ['bækwɔːtə*] *n* (*fig*) coin reculé; bled perdu.

backyard [bæk'jɑːd] *n* arrière-cour *f*.

bacon ['beɪkən] *n* bacon *m*, lard *m*.

bacteria [bæk'tɪərɪə] *npl* bactéries *fpl*.

bacteriology [bæktɪərɪ'ɔlədʒɪ] *n* bactériologie *f*.

bad [bæd] *a* mauvais(e); (*child*) vilain(e); (*meat, food*) gâté(e), avarié(e); **his ~ leg** sa jambe malade; **to go ~** (*meat, food*) se gâter; (*milk*) tourner; **to have a ~ time of it** traverser une mauvaise passe; **I feel ~ about it** (*guilty*) j'ai un peu mauvaise conscience; **~ debt** créance douteuse; **in ~ faith** de mauvaise foi.

bade [bæd] *pt of* **bid**.

badge [bædʒ] *n* insigne *m*; (*of policeman*) plaque *f*; (*stick-on, sew-on*) badge *m*.

badger ['bædʒə*] *n* blaireau *m* ♦ *vt* harceler.

badly ['bædlɪ] *ad* (*work, dress etc*) mal; **~ wounded** grièvement blessé; **he needs it ~** il en a un absolument besoin; **things are going ~** les choses vont mal; **~ off** *a*, *ad* dans la gêne.

bad-mannered ['bæd'mænəd] *a* mal élevé(e).

badminton ['bædmɪntən] *n* badminton *m*.

bad-tempered ['bæd'tempəd] *a* (*by nature*) ayant mauvais caractère; (*on one occasion*) de mauvaise humeur.

baffle ['bæfl] *vt* (*puzzle*) déconcerter.

baffling ['bæflɪŋ] *a* déroutant(e), déconcertant(e).

bag [bæg] *n* sac *m*; (*of hunter*) gibecière *f*, chasse *f* ♦ *vt* (*col: take*) empocher; s'approprier; (*TECH*) mettre en sacs; **~s of** (*col: lots of*) des masses de; **to pack one's ~s** faire ses valises *or* bagages; **~s under the eyes** poches *fpl* sous les yeux.

bagful ['bægful] *n* plein sac.

baggage ['bægɪdʒ] *n* bagages *mpl*.

baggage claim *n* (*at airport*) livraison *f* des bagages.

baggy ['bægɪ] *a* avachi(e), qui fait des poches.

Baghdad [bæg'dæd] *n* Baghdâd, Bagdad.

bagpipes ['bægpaɪps] *npl* cornemuse *f*.

bag-snatcher ['bægsnætʃə*] *n* (*Brit*) voleur *m* à l'arraché.

bag-snatching ['bægsnætʃɪŋ] *n* (*Brit*) vol *m* à l'arraché.

Bahamas [bə'hɑːməz] *npl*: **the ~** les Bahamas *fpl*.

Bahrain [bɑː'reɪn] *n* Bahreïn *m*.

bail [beɪl] *n* caution *f* ♦ *vt* (*prisoner: also:* **grant ~ to**) mettre en liberté sous caution; (*boat: also:* **~ out**) écoper; **to be released on ~** être libéré(e) sous caution; *see* **bale**.

bail out *vt* (*prisoner*) payer la caution de.

bailiff ['beɪlɪf] *n* huissier *m*.

bait [beɪt] *n* appât *m* ♦ *vt* appâter; (*fig*) tourmenter.

bake [beɪk] *vt* (*faire*) cuire au four ♦ *vi* (*bread etc*) cuire (au four); (*make cakes etc*) faire de la pâtisserie.

baked beans *npl* haricots blancs à la sauce tomate.

baker ['beɪkə*] *n* boulanger *m*.

bakery ['beɪkərɪ] *n* boulangerie *f*; boulangerie industrielle.

baking ['beɪkɪŋ] *n* cuisson *f*.

baking powder *n* levure *f* (chimique).

baking tin *n* (*for cake*) moule *m* à gâteaux; (*for meat*) plat *m* pour le four.

baking tray *n* plaque *f* à gâteaux.

balaclava [bælə'klɑːvə] *n* (*also:* **~ helmet**) passe-montagne *m*.

balance ['bæləns] *n* équilibre *m*; (*COMM: sum*) solde *m*; (*scales*) balance *f* ♦ *vt* mettre *or* faire tenir en équilibre; (*pros and cons*) peser; (*budget*) équilibrer; (*account*) balancer; (*compensate*) compenser, contrebalancer; **~ of trade/payments** balance commerciale/des comptes *or* paiements; **~ carried forward** solde *m* à reporter; **~ brought forward** solde reporté; **to ~ the books** arrêter les comptes, dresser le bilan.

balanced ['bælənst] *a* (*personality, diet*) équilibré(e).

balance sheet *n* bilan *m*.

balance wheel *n* balancier *m*.

balcony ['bælkənɪ] *n* balcon *m*.

bald [bɔːld] *a* chauve; (*tyre*) lisse.

baldness ['bɔːldnɪs] *n* calvitie *f*.

bale [beɪl] *n* balle *f*, ballot *m*.

bale out *vi* (*of a plane*) sauter en parachute ♦ *vt* (*NAUT: water, boat*) écoper.

Balearic Islands [bælɪ'ærɪk-] *npl*: **the ~** les (îles *fpl*) Baléares.

baleful ['beɪlful] *a* funeste, maléfique.

balk [bɔːk] *vi*: **to ~ (at)** (*person*) regimber (contre); (*horse*) se dérober (devant).

Balkan ['bɔːlkən] *a* balkanique ♦ *n*: **the ~s** les Balkans *mpl*.

ball [bɔːl] *n* boule *f*; (*football*) ballon *m*; (*for tennis, golf*) balle *f*; (*dance*) bal *m*; **to play ~ (with sb)** jouer au ballon (*or* à la balle) (avec qn); (*fig*) coopérer (avec qn); **to be on the ~** (*fig: competent*) être à la hauteur; (*: alert*) être éveillé(e), être vif(vive); **to start the ~ rolling** (*fig*) commencer; **the ~ is in their court** (*fig*) la balle est dans leur camp.

ballad ['bæləd] *n* ballade *f*.

ballast ['bæləst] *n* lest *m*.

ball bearing *n* roulement *m* à billes.

ball cock *n* robinet *m* à flotteur.

ballerina [bælə'riːnə] *n* ballerine *f*.

ballet ['bæleɪ] *n* ballet *m*; (*art*) danse *f* (classique).

ballet dancer *n* danseur/euse de ballet.

ballistic [bə'lɪstɪk] *a* balistique.

ballistics [bə'lɪstɪks] *n* balistique *f*.

balloon [bə'luːn] *n* ballon *m*; (*in comic strip*) bulle *f* ♦ *vi* gonfler.

balloonist [bə'luːnɪst] *n* aéronaute *m/f*.

ballot ['bælət] *n* scrutin *m*.

ballot box *n* urne *f* (électorale).

ballot paper *n* bulletin *m* de vote.

ballpark ['bɔːlpɑːk] *n* (*US*) stade *m* de base-ball.

ballpark figure *n* (*col*) chiffre approximatif.

ball-point pen ['bɔːlpɔɪnt-] *n* stylo *m* à bille.

ballroom ['bɔ:lrum] n salle f de bal.
balls [bɔ:lz] npl (col!) couilles fpl (!).
balm [ba:m] n baume m.
balmy ['ba:mɪ] a (breeze, air) doux(douce); (Brit col) = **barmy**.
BALPA ['bælpə] n abbr (= British Airline Pilots' Association) syndicat des pilotes de ligne.
balsam ['bɔ:lsəm] n baume m.
balsa (wood) ['bɔ:lsə-] n balsa m.
Baltic [bɔ:ltɪk] a, n: **the ~ (Sea)** la (mer) Baltique.
balustrade [bæləs'treɪd] n balustrade f.
bamboo [bæm'bu:] n bambou m.
bamboozle [bæm'bu:zl] vt (col) embobiner.
ban [bæn] n interdiction f ♦ vt interdire; **he was ~ned from driving** (Brit) on lui a retiré le permis (de conduire).
banal [bə'na:l] a banal(e).
banana [bə'na:nə] n banane f.
band [bænd] n bande f; (at a dance) orchestre m; (MIL) musique f, fanfare f.
band together vi se liguer.
bandage ['bændɪdʒ] n bandage m, pansement m ♦ vt (wound, leg) mettre un pansement or un bandage sur; (person) mettre un pansement or un bandage à.
bandaid ['bændeɪd] n (US) pansement adhésif.
bandit ['bændɪt] n bandit m.
bandstand ['bændstænd] n kiosque m (à musique).
bandwagon ['bændwægən] n: **to jump on the ~** (fig) monter dans or prendre le train en marche.
bandy ['bændɪ] vt (jokes, insults) échanger.
bandy about vt employer à tout bout de champ or à tort et à travers.
bandy-legged ['bændɪ'lɛgɪd] a aux jambes arquées.
bane [beɪn] n: **it (or he etc) is the ~ of my life** c'est (or il est etc) le drame de ma vie.
bang [bæŋ] n détonation f; (of door) claquement m; (blow) coup (violent) ♦ vt frapper (violemment); (door) claquer ♦ vi détoner; claquer ♦ ad: **to be ~ on time** (Brit col) être à l'heure pile; **to ~ at the door** cogner à la porte; **to ~ into sth** se cogner contre qch.
banger ['bæŋə*] n (Brit: car: also: **old ~**) (vieux) tacot; (Brit col: sausage) saucisse f; (firework) pétard m.
Bangkok [bæŋ'kɔk] n Bangkok.
Bangladesh [bæŋglə'dɛʃ] n Bangladesh m.
bangle ['bæŋgl] n bracelet m.
bangs [bæŋz] npl (US: fringe) frange f.
banish ['bænɪʃ] vt bannir.
banister(s) ['bænɪstə(z)] n(pl) rampe f (d'escalier).
banjo, **~es** or **~s** ['bændʒəu] n banjo m.
bank [bæŋk] n banque f; (of river, lake) bord m, rive f; (of earth) talus m, remblai m ♦ vi (AVIAT) virer sur l'aile; (COMM): **they ~ with Pitt's** leur banque or banquier est Pitt's.
bank on vt fus miser or tabler sur.
bank account n compte m en banque.
bank card n = **banker's card.**
bank charges npl (Brit) frais mpl de banque.
bank draft n traite f bancaire.
banker ['bæŋkə*] n banquier m; **~'s card**

(Brit) carte f d'identité bancaire; **~'s order** (Brit) ordre m de virement.
bank giro n paiement m par virement.
Bank holiday n (Brit) jour férié (où les banques sont fermées).
banking ['bæŋkɪŋ] n opérations fpl bancaires; profession f de banquier.
banking hours npl heures fpl d'ouverture des banques.
bank loan n prêt m bancaire.
bank manager n directeur m d'agence (bancaire).
banknote ['bæŋknəut] n billet m de banque.
bank rate n taux m de l'escompte.
bankrupt ['bæŋkrʌpt] n failli/e ♦ a en faillite; **to go ~** faire faillite.
bankruptcy ['bæŋkrʌptsɪ] n faillite f.
bank statement n relevé m de compte.
banner ['bænə*] n bannière f.
bannister(s) ['bænɪstə(z)] n(pl) = **banister(s).**
banns [bænz] npl bans mpl (de mariage).
banquet ['bæŋkwɪt] n banquet m, festin m.
bantam-weight ['bæntəmweɪt] n poids m coq inv.
banter ['bæntə*] n badinage m.
BAOR n abbr (= British Army of the Rhine) forces britanniques en Allemagne.
baptism ['bæptɪzəm] n baptême m.
Baptist ['bæptɪst] n baptiste m/f.
baptize [bæp'taɪz] vt baptiser.
bar [ba:*] n barre f; (of window etc) barreau m; (of chocolate) tablette f, plaque f; (fig) obstacle m; mesure f d'exclusion; (pub) bar m; (counter: in pub) comptoir m, bar; (MUS) mesure f ♦ vt (road) barrer; (window) munir de barreaux; (person) exclure; (activity) interdire; **~ of soap** savonnette f; **behind ~s** (prisoner) derrière les barreaux; **the B~** (LAW) le barreau; **~ none** sans exception.
Barbados [ba:'beɪdɔs] n Barbade f.
barbaric [ba:'bærɪk] a barbare.
barbarous ['ba:bərəs] a barbare, cruel(le).
barbecue ['ba:bɪkju:] n barbecue m.
barbed wire ['ba:bd-] n fil m de fer barbelé.
barber ['ba:bə*] n coiffeur m (pour hommes).
barbiturate [ba:'bɪtjurɪt] n barbiturique m.
Barcelona [ba:sə'ləunə] n Barcelone.
bar chart n diagramme m en bâtons.
bar code n code m à barres.
bare [bɛə*] a nu(e) ♦ vt mettre à nu, dénuder; (teeth) montrer; **the ~ essentials** le strict nécessaire.
bareback ['bɛəbæk] ad à cru, sans selle.
barefaced ['bɛəfeɪst] a impudent(e), effronté(e).
barefoot ['bɛəfut] a, ad nu-pieds, (les) pieds nus.
bareheaded [bɛə'hɛdɪd] a, ad nu-tête, (la) tête nue.
barely ['bɛəlɪ] ad à peine.
Barents Sea ['bærənts-] n: **the ~** la mer de Barents.
bargain ['ba:gɪn] n (transaction) marché m; (good buy) affaire f, occasion f ♦ vi (haggle) marchander; (trade) négocier, traiter; **into the ~** par-dessus le marché.
bargain for (col): **he got more than he ~ed for!** il en a eu pour son argent!
bargaining ['ba:gənɪŋ] n marchandage m;

négociations *fpl*.
barge [bɑ:dʒ] *n* péniche *f*.
  barge in *vi* (*walk in*) faire irruption; (*interrupt talk*) intervenir mal à propos.
  barge into *vt fus* rentrer dans.
baritone ['bærɪtəun] *n* baryton *m*.
barium meal ['bɛərɪəm-] *n* (bouillie *f* de) sulfate *m* de baryum.
bark [bɑ:k] *n* (*of tree*) écorce *f*; (*of dog*) aboiement *m* ♦ *vi* aboyer.
barley ['bɑ:lɪ] *n* orge *f*.
barley sugar *n* sucre *m* d'orge.
barmaid ['bɑ:meɪd] *n* serveuse *f* (*de bar*), barmaid *f*.
barman ['bɑ:mən] *n* serveur *m* (*de bar*), barman *m*.
barmy ['bɑ:mɪ] *a* (*Brit col*) timbré(e), cinglé(e).
barn [bɑ:n] *n* grange *f*.
barnacle ['bɑ:nəkl] *n* anatife *m*, bernache *f*.
barometer [bə'rɒmɪtə*] *n* baromètre *m*.
baron ['bærən] *n* baron *m*; **the press/oil ~s** les magnats *mpl or* barons *mpl* de la presse/ du pétrole.
baroness ['bærənɪs] *n* baronne *f*.
barracks ['bærəks] *npl* caserne *f*.
barrage ['bærɑ:ʒ] *n* (*MIL*) tir *m* de barrage; (*dam*) barrage *m*; **a ~ of questions** un feu roulant de questions.
barrel ['bærəl] *n* tonneau *m*; (*of gun*) canon *m*.
barrel organ *n* orgue *m* de Barbarie.
barren ['bærən] *a* stérile; (*hills*) aride.
barricade [bærɪ'keɪd] *n* barricade *f* ♦ *vt* barricader.
barrier ['bærɪə*] *n* barrière *f*; (*Brit: also:* **crash ~**) rail *m* de sécurité.
barrier cream *n* (*Brit*) crème protectrice.
barring ['bɑ:rɪŋ] *prep* sauf.
barrister ['bærɪstə*] *n* (*Brit*) avocat (plaidant).
barrow ['bærəu] *n* (*cart*) charrette *f* à bras.
barstool ['bɑ:stu:l] *n* tabouret *m* de bar.
Bart. *abbr* (*Brit*) = **baronet**.
bartender ['bɑ:tɛndə*] *n* (*US*) serveur *m* (de bar), barman *m*.
barter ['bɑ:tə*] *n* échange *m*, troc *m* ♦ *vt*: **to ~ sth for** échanger qch contre.
base [beɪs] *n* base *f* ♦ *vt* (*troops*): **to be ~d at** être basé(e) à; (*opinion, belief*): **to ~ sth on** baser *or* fonder qch sur ♦ *a* vil(e), bas(se); **coffee-~d** à base de café; **a Paris-~d firm** une maison opérant de Paris *or* dont le siège est à Paris; **I'm ~d in London** je suis basé(e) à Londres.
baseball ['beɪsbɔ:l] *n* base-ball *m*.
baseboard ['beɪsbɔ:d] *n* (*US*) plinthe *f*.
base camp *n* camp *m* de base.
Basel [bɑ:l] *n* = **Basle**.
basement ['beɪsmənt] *n* sous-sol *m*.
base rate *n* taux *m* de base.
bases ['beɪsi:z] *npl of* **basis**; ['beɪsɪz] *npl of* **base**.
bash [bæʃ] *vt* (*col*) frapper, cogner ♦ *n*: **I'll have a ~ (at it)** (*Brit col*) je vais essayer un coup; **~ed in** *a* enfoncé(e), défoncé(e).
  bash up *vt* (*col: car*) bousiller; (*: Brit: person*) tabasser.
bashful ['bæʃful] *a* timide; modeste.
bashing ['bæʃɪŋ] *n* (*col*) raclée *f*; **Paki- ~** ≈ ratonnade *f*; **queer-~** chasse *f* aux pédés.

BASIC ['beɪsɪk] *n* (*COMPUT*) BASIC *m*.
basic ['beɪsɪk] *a* (*precautions, rules*) élémentaire; (*principles, research*) fondamental(e); (*vocabulary, salary*) de base; réduit(e) au minimum, rudimentaire.
basically ['beɪsɪklɪ] *ad* (*really*) en fait; (*essentially*) fondamentalement.
basic rate *n* (*of tax*) première tranche d'imposition.
basil ['bæzl] *n* basilic *m*.
basin ['beɪsn] *n* (*vessel, also GEO*) cuvette *f*, bassin *m*; (*Brit: for food*) bol *m*; (*: bigger*) saladier *m*; (*also:* **wash~**) lavabo *m*.
basis, *pl* **bases** ['beɪsɪs, -si:z] *n* base *f*; **on the ~ of what you've said** d'après *or* compte tenu de ce que vous dites.
bask [bɑ:sk] *vi*: **to ~ in the sun** se chauffer au soleil.
basket ['bɑ:skɪt] *n* corbeille *f*; (*with handle*) panier *m*.
basketball ['bɑ:skɪtbɔ:l] *n* basket-ball *m*.
basketball player *n* basketteur/euse.
Basle [bɑ:l] *n* Bâle.
Basque [bæsk] *a* basque ♦ *n* Basque *m/f*.
bass [beɪs] *n* (*MUS*) basse *f*.
bass clef *n* clé *f* de fa.
bassoon [bə'su:n] *n* basson *m*.
bastard ['bɑ:stəd] *n* enfant naturel(le), bâtard/e; (*col!*) salaud *m* (!).
baste [beɪst] *vt* (*CULIN*) arroser; (*SEWING*) bâtir, faufiler.
bastion ['bæstɪən] *n* bastion *m*.
BASW *n abbr* (= *British Association of Social Workers*) syndicat *des travailleurs sociaux*.
bat [bæt] *n* chauve-souris *f*; (*for baseball etc*) batte *f*; (*Brit: for table tennis*) raquette *f* ♦ *vt*: **he didn't ~ an eyelid** il n'a pas sourcillé *or* bronché; **off one's own ~** de sa propre initiative.
batch [bætʃ] *n* (*of bread*) fournée *f*; (*of papers*) liasse *f*; (*of applicants, letters*) paquet *m*; (*of work*) monceau *m*; (*of goods*) lot *m*.
batch processing *n* (*COMPUT*) traitement *m* par lot.
bated ['beɪtɪd] *a*: **with ~ breath** en retenant son souffle.
bath [bɑ:θ, *pl* bɑ:ðz] *n* bain *m*; (*bathtub*) baignoire *f* ♦ *vt* baigner, donner un bain à; **to have a ~** prendre un bain; *see also* **baths**.
bathchair ['bɑ:θtʃɛə*] *n* (*Brit*) fauteuil roulant.
bathe [beɪð] *vi* se baigner ♦ *vt* baigner; (*wound etc*) laver.
bather ['beɪðə*] *n* baigneur/euse.
bathing ['beɪðɪŋ] *n* baignade *f*.
bathing cap *n* bonnet *m* de bain.
bathing costume, (*US*) **bathing suit** *n* maillot *m* (de bain).
bathmat ['bɑ:θmæt] *n* tapis *m* de bain.
bathrobe ['bɑ:θrəub] *n* peignoir *m* de bain.
bathroom ['bɑ:θrum] *n* salle *f* de bains.
baths [bɑ:ðz] *npl* établissement *m* de bains(-douches).
bath towel *n* serviette *f* de bain.
bathtub ['bɑ:θtʌb] *n* baignoire *f*.
batman ['bætmən] *n* (*Brit MIL*) ordonnance *f*.
baton ['bætən] *n* bâton *m*; (*MUS*) baguette *f*; (*club*) matraque *f*.

battalion [bə'tælɪən] n bataillon m.
batten ['bætn] n (CARPENTRY) latte f; (NAUT: on sail) latte de voile.
  batten down vt (NAUT): **to ~ down the hatches** fermer les écoutilles.
batter ['bætə*] vt battre ♦ n pâte f à frire.
battered ['bætəd] a (hat, pan) cabossé(e); **~ wife/child** épouse/enfant maltraité(e) or martyr(e).
battering ram ['bætərɪŋ-] n bélier m (fig).
battery ['bætərɪ] n batterie f; (of torch) pile f.
battery charger n chargeur m.
battery farming n élevage m en batterie.
battle ['bætl] n bataille f, combat m ♦ vi se battre, lutter; **that's half the ~** (fig) c'est déjà bien; **it's a** or **we're fighting a losing ~** (fig) c'est perdu d'avance, c'est peine perdue.
battle dress n tenue f de campagne or d'assaut.
battlefield ['bætlfiːld] n champ m de bataille.
battlements ['bætlmənts] npl remparts mpl.
battleship ['bætlʃɪp] n cuirassé m.
bauble ['bɔːbl] n babiole f.
baud [bɔːd] n (COMPUT) baud m.
baud rate n (COMPUT) vitesse f de transmission.
baulk [bɔːlk] vi = **balk**.
bauxite ['bɔːksaɪt] n bauxite f.
Bavaria [bə'vɛərɪə] n Bavière f.
Bavarian [bə'vɛərɪən] a bavarois(e) ♦ n Bavarois/e.
bawdy ['bɔːdɪ] a paillard(e).
bawl [bɔːl] vi hurler, brailler.
bay [beɪ] n (of sea) baie f; (Brit: for parking) place f de stationnement; (: for loading) aire f de chargement; (horse) bai(e m/f; **to hold sb at ~** tenir qn à distance or en échec.
bay leaf n laurier m.
bayonet ['beɪənɪt] n baïonnette f.
bay tree n laurier m.
bay window n baie vitrée.
bazaar [bə'zaː*] n bazar m; vente f de charité.
bazooka [bə'zuːkə] n bazooka m.
BB n abbr (Brit: = Boys' Brigade) mouvement de garçons.
B & B n abbr = **bed and breakfast**.
BBB n abbr (US: = Better Business Bureau) organisme de défense du consommateur.
BBC n abbr (= British Broadcasting Corporation) office de la radiodiffusion et télévision britannique.
BBE n abbr (US: = Benevolent and Protective Order of Elks) association charitable.
BC ad abbr (= before Christ) av. J.-C. ♦ abbr (Canada) = British Columbia.
BCG n abbr (= Bacillus Calmette-Guérin) BCG m.
BD n abbr (= Bachelor of Divinity) diplôme universitaire.
B/D abbr = **bank draft**.
BDS n abbr (= Bachelor of Dental Surgery) diplôme universitaire.
be, pt **was, were,** pp **been** [biː, wɔz, wəː*, biːn] vi être; **how are you?** comment allez-vous?; **I am warm** j'ai chaud; **it is cold** il fait froid; **how much is it?** combien ça coûte?; **what are you doing?** que faites-vous?; **he is four (years old)** il a quatre ans; **it's 8 o'clock** il est 8 heures; **2 and 2 are 4** 2

et 2 font 4; **where have you been?** où êtes-vous allé(s)?; où étiez-vous?; **I've been waiting for her for two hours** cela fait deux heures que je l'attends, je l'attends depuis deux heures; **to ~ killed** être tué, se faire tuer; **he is nowhere to ~ found** on ne sait pas où il se trouve; **the car is to ~ sold** la voiture est à vendre; **he was to have come yesterday** il devait venir hier; **if I were you,** I ... à votre place, je ..., si j'étais vous, je ...; **am I to understand that ...?** dois-je comprendre que ...?
B/E abbr = **bill of exchange**.
beach [biːtʃ] n plage f ♦ vt échouer.
beachcomber ['biːtʃkəumə*] n ramasseur m d'épaves; (fig) glandeur m.
beachwear ['biːtʃwɛə*] n tenues fpl de plage.
beacon ['biːkən] n (lighthouse) fanal m; (marker) balise f; (also: **radio ~**) radiophare m.
bead [biːd] n perle f; (of dew, sweat) goutte f; **~s** (necklace) collier m.
beady ['biːdɪ] a: **~ eyes** yeux mpl de fouine.
beagle [biːgl] n beagle m.
beak [biːk] n bec m.
beaker ['biːkə*] n gobelet m.
beam [biːm] n poutre f; (of light) rayon m; (RADIO) faisceau m radio ♦ vi rayonner; **to drive on full** or **main** or (US) **high ~** rouler en pleins phares.
beaming ['biːmɪŋ] a (sun, smile) radieux(euse).
bean [biːn] n haricot m; (of coffee) grain m.
beanshoots [biːnʃuːts], **beansprouts** ['biːnsprauts] npl pousses fpl (de soja).
bear [bɛə*] n ours m; (STOCK EXCHANGE) baissier m ♦ vb (pt **bore,** pp **borne** [bɔː*, bɔːn]) vt porter; (endure) supporter; (traces, signs) porter; (COMM: interest) rapporter ♦ vi: **to ~ right/left** obliquer à droite/gauche, se diriger vers la droite/gauche; **to ~ the responsibility of** assumer la responsabilité de; **to ~ comparison with** soutenir la comparaison avec; **I can't ~ him** je ne peux pas le supporter or souffrir; **to bring pressure to ~ on sb** faire pression sur qn.
bear out vt (theory, suspicion) confirmer.
bear up vi supporter, tenir le coup; **he bore up well** il a tenu le coup.
bear with vt fus (sb's moods, temper) supporter; **~ with me a minute** un moment, s'il vous plaît.
bearable ['bɛərəbl] a supportable.
beard [bɪəd] n barbe f.
bearded ['bɪədɪd] a barbu(e).
bearer ['bɛərə*] n porteur m; (of passport etc) titulaire m/f.
bearing ['bɛərɪŋ] n maintien m, allure f; (connection) rapport m; (TECH): **(ball) ~s** npl roulement m (à billes); **to take a ~** faire le point; **to find one's ~s** s'orienter.
beast [biːst] n bête f; (col): **he's a ~** c'est une brute.
beastly ['biːstlɪ] a infect(e).
beat [biːt] n battement m; (MUS) temps m, mesure f; (of policeman) ronde f ♦ vt (pt **beat,** pp **beaten**) battre; **off the ~en track** hors des chemins or sentiers battus; **to ~ about the bush** tourner autour du pot; **to ~**

time battre la mesure; **that ~s everything!** c'est le comble!

beat down vt (door) enfoncer; (price) faire baisser; (seller) faire descendre ♦ vi (rain) tambouriner; (sun) taper.

beat off vt repousser.

beat up vt (eggs) battre; (col: person) tabasser.

beater ['bi:tə*] n (for eggs, cream) fouet m, batteur m.

beating ['bi:tɪŋ] n raclée f.

beat-up ['bi:t'ʌp] a (col) déglingué(e).

beautician [bju:'tɪʃən] n esthéticien/ne.

beautiful ['bju:tɪful] a beau(belle).

beautifully ['bju:tɪflɪ] ad admirablement.

beautify ['bju:tɪfaɪ] vt embellir.

beauty ['bju:tɪ] n beauté f; **the ~ of it is that** ... le plus beau, c'est que ....

beauty contest n concours m de beauté.

beauty queen n reine f de beauté.

beauty salon n institut m de beauté.

beauty spot n grain m de beauté; (Brit TOURISM) site naturel (d'une grande beauté).

beaver ['bi:və*] n castor m.

becalmed [bɪ'kɑ:md] a immobilisé(e) par le calme plat.

became [bɪ'keɪm] pt of **become.**

because [bɪ'kɔz] cj parce que; **~ of** prep à cause de.

beck [bɛk] n: **to be at sb's ~ and call** être à l'entière disposition de qn.

beckon ['bɛkən] vt (also: **~ to**) faire signe (de venir) à.

become [bɪ'kʌm] vt (irg: like **come**) devenir; **to ~ fat/thin** grossir/maigrir; **to ~ angry** se mettre en colère; **it became known that** on apprit que; **what has ~ of him?** qu'est-il devenu?

becoming [bɪ'kʌmɪŋ] a (behaviour) convenable, bienséant(e); (clothes) seyant(e).

BEd n abbr (= Bachelor of Education) diplôme d'aptitude à l'enseignement.

bed [bɛd] n lit m; (of flowers) parterre m; (of coal, clay) couche f; (of sea, lake) fond m; **to go to ~** aller se coucher.

bed down vi se coucher.

bed and breakfast (B & B) n (terms) chambre et petit déjeuner; (place) ≈ chambre f d'hôte.

bedbug ['bɛdbʌg] n punaise f.

bedclothes ['bɛdkləuðz] npl couvertures fpl et draps mpl.

bedcover ['bɛdkʌvə*] n couvre-lit m, dessus-de-lit m.

bedding ['bɛdɪŋ] n literie f.

bedevil [bɪ'dɛvl] vt (harass) harceler; **to be ~led by** être victime de.

bedfellow ['bɛdfɛləu] n: **they are strange ~s** (fig) ça fait un drôle de mélange.

bedlam ['bɛdləm] n chahut m, cirque m.

bedpan ['bɛdpæn] n bassin m (hygiénique).

bedpost ['bɛdpəust] n colonne f de lit.

bedraggled [bɪ'drægld] a dépenaillé(e), les vêtements en désordre.

bedridden ['bɛdrɪdn] a cloué(e) au lit.

bedrock ['bɛdrɔk] n (fig) principes essentiels or de base, essentiel m; (GEO) roche f en place, socle m.

bedroom ['bɛdrum] n chambre f (à coucher).

Beds abbr (Brit) = Bedfordshire.

bedside ['bɛdsaɪd] n: **at sb's ~** au chevet de qn ♦ cpd (book, lamp) de chevet.

bedsit(ter) ['bɛdsɪt(ə*)] n (Brit) chambre meublée, studio m.

bedspread ['bɛdsprɛd] n couvre-lit m, dessus-de-lit m.

bedtime ['bɛdtaɪm] n: **it's ~** c'est l'heure de se coucher.

bee [bi:] n abeille f; **to have a ~ in one's bonnet (about sth)** être obnubilé(e) (par qch).

beech [bi:tʃ] n hêtre m.

beef [bi:f] n bœuf m.

beef up vt (col: support) renforcer; (: essay) étoffer.

beefburger ['bi:fbə:gə*] n hamburger m.

beefeater ['bi:fi:tə*] n hallebardier m (de la tour de Londres).

beehive ['bi:haɪv] n ruche f.

beeline ['bi:laɪn] n: **to make a ~ for** se diriger tout droit vers.

been [bi:n] pp of **be.**

beer [bɪə*] n bière f.

beer can n canette f de bière.

beetle ['bi:tl] n scarabée m, coléoptère m.

beetroot ['bi:tru:t] n (Brit) betterave f.

befall [bɪ'fɔ:l] vi(vt) (irg: like **fall**) advenir (à).

befit [bɪ'fɪt] vt seoir à.

before [bɪ'fɔ:*] prep (of time) avant; (of space) devant ♦ cj avant que + sub; avant de ♦ ad avant; **~ going** avant de partir; **~ she goes** avant qu'elle (ne) parte; **the week ~** la semaine précédente or d'avant; **I've seen it ~** je l'ai déjà vu; **I've never seen it ~** c'est la première fois que je le vois.

beforehand [bɪ'fɔ:hænd] ad au préalable, à l'avance.

befriend [bɪ'frɛnd] vt venir en aide à; traiter en ami.

befuddled [bɪ'fʌdld] a: **to be ~** avoir les idées brouillées.

beg [bɛg] vi mendier ♦ vt mendier; (favour) quémander, solliciter; (entreat) supplier; **I ~ your pardon** (apologising) excusez-moi; (: not hearing) pardon?; **that ~s the question of** ..., cela soulève la question de ..., cela suppose réglée la question de ....

began [bɪ'gæn] pt of **begin.**

beggar ['bɛgə*] n (also: **~man, ~woman**) mendiant/e.

begin [bɪ'gɪn] vt, vi (pt **began**, pp **begun** [bɪ'gɪn, -'gæn, -'gʌn]) commencer; **to ~ doing** or **to do sth** commencer à faire qch; **~ning (from) Monday** à partir de lundi; **I can't ~ to thank you** je ne saurais vous remercier; **to ~ with** d'abord, pour commencer.

beginner [bɪ'gɪnə*] n débutant/e.

beginning [bɪ'gɪnɪŋ] n commencement m, début m; **right from the ~** dès le début.

begrudge [bɪ'grʌdʒ] vt: **to ~ sb sth** envier qch à qn; donner qch à contrecœur or regret à qn.

beguile [bɪ'gaɪl] vt (enchant) enjôler.

beguiling [bɪ'gaɪlɪŋ] a (charming) séduisant(e), enchanteur(eresse).

begun [bɪ'gʌn] pp of **begin.**

behalf [bɪ'hɑ:f] n: **on ~ of**, (US) **in ~ of** de la part de; au nom de; pour le compte de.

behave [bɪ'heɪv] *vi* se conduire, se comporter; (*well: also:* ~ **o.s.**) se conduire bien *or* comme il faut.

behaviour, *(US)* **behavior** [bɪ'heɪvjə*] *n* comportement *m*, conduite *f*.

behead [bɪ'hɛd] *vt* décapiter.

beheld [bɪ'hɛld] *pt, pp of* **behold**.

behind [bɪ'haɪnd] *prep* derrière; (*time*) en retard sur ♦ *ad* derrière; en retard ♦ *n* derrière *m*; ~ **the scenes** dans les coulisses; **to leave sth** ~ (*forget*) oublier de prendre qch; **to be** ~ **(schedule) with sth** être en retard dans qch.

behold [bɪ'həʊld] *vt* (*irg: like* **hold**) apercevoir, voir.

beige [beɪʒ] *a* beige.

being ['biːɪŋ] *n* être *m*; **to come into** ~ prendre naissance.

Beirut [beɪ'ruːt] *n* Beyrouth.

belated [bɪ'leɪtɪd] *a* tardif(ive).

belch [bɛltʃ] *vi* avoir un renvoi, roter ♦ *vt* (*also:* ~ **out:** *smoke etc*) vomir, cracher.

beleaguered [bɪ'liːgɪd] *a* (*city*) assiégé(e); (*army*) cerné(e); (*fig*) sollicité(e) de toutes parts.

Belfast ['bɛlfɑːst] *n* Belfast.

belfry ['bɛlfrɪ] *n* beffroi *m*.

Belgian ['bɛldʒən] *a* belge, de Belgique ♦ *n* Belge *m/f*.

Belgium ['bɛldʒəm] *n* Belgique *f*.

Belgrade [bɛl'greɪd] *n* Belgrade.

belie [bɪ'laɪ] *vt* démentir; (*give false impression of*) occulter.

belief [bɪ'liːf] *n* (*opinion*) conviction *f*; (*trust, faith*) foi *f*; (*acceptance as true*) croyance *f*; **it's beyond** ~ c'est incroyable; **in the** ~ **that** dans l'idée que.

believable [bɪ'liːvəbl] *a* croyable.

believe [bɪ'liːv] *vt, vi* croire, estimer; **to** ~ **in** (*God*) croire en; (*ghosts, method*) croire à; **I don't** ~ **in corporal punishment** je ne suis pas partisan des châtiments corporels; **he is** ~**d to be abroad** il serait à l'étranger.

believer [bɪ'liːvə*] *n* (*in idea, activity*): ~ **in** partisan/e de; (*REL*) croyant/e.

belittle [bɪ'lɪtl] *vt* déprécier, rabaisser.

Belize [bɛ'liːz] *n* Bélize *m*.

bell [bɛl] *n* cloche *f*; (*small*) clochette *f*, grelot *m*; (*on door*) sonnette *f*; (*electric*) sonnerie *f*; **that rings a** ~ (*fig*) cela me rappelle qch.

bell-bottoms ['bɛlbɒtəmz] *npl* pantalon *m* à pattes d'éléphant.

bellboy ['bɛlbɔɪ], *(US)* **bellhop** ['bɛlhɒp] *n* groom *m*, chasseur *m*.

belligerent [bɪ'lɪdʒərənt] *a* (*at war*) belligérant(e); (*fig*) agressif(ive).

bellow ['bɛləʊ] *vi* mugir; beugler ♦ *vt* (*orders*) hurler.

bellows ['bɛləʊz] *npl* soufflet *m*.

bell push [Brit] bouton *m* de sonnette.

belly ['bɛlɪ] *n* ventre *m*.

bellyache ['bɛleɪk] *n* (*col*) colique *f* ♦ *vi* ronchonner.

bellybutton ['bɛlɪbʌtn] *n* nombril *m*.

belong [bɪ'lɒŋ] *vi*: **to** ~ **to** appartenir à; (*club etc*) faire partie de; **this book** ~**s here** ce livre va ici, la place de ce livre est ici.

belongings [bɪ'lɒŋɪŋz] *npl* affaires *fpl*, possessions *fpl*; **personal** ~ effets personnels.

beloved [bɪ'lʌvɪd] *a* (bien-)aimé(e), chéri(e) ♦ *n* bien-aimé/e.

below [bɪ'ləʊ] *prep* sous, au-dessous de ♦ *ad* en dessous; en contre-bas; **see** ~ voir plus bas *or* plus loin *or* ci-dessous; **temperatures** ~ **normal** températures inférieures à la normale.

belt [bɛlt] *n* ceinture *f*; (*TECH*) courroie *f* ♦ *vt* (*thrash*) donner une raclée à ♦ *vi* (Brit col) filer (à toutes jambes); **industrial** ~ zone industrielle.

belt out *vt* (*song*) chanter à tue-tête *or* à pleins poumons.

belt up *vi* (Brit col) la boucler.

beltway ['bɛltweɪ] *n* (US AUT) route *f* de ceinture; (: *motorway*) périphérique *m*.

bemoan [bɪ'məʊn] *vt* se lamenter sur.

bemused [bɪ'mjuːzd] *a* médusé(e).

bench [bɛntʃ] *n* banc *m*; (*in workshop*) établi *m*; **the B**~ (LAW) la magistrature, la Cour.

bench mark *n* repère *m*.

bend [bɛnd] *vb* (*pt, pp* **bent** [bɛnt]) *vt* courber; (*leg, arm*) plier ♦ *vi* se courber ♦ *n* (Brit: *in road*) virage *m*, tournant *m*; (*in pipe, river*) coude *m*.

bend down *vi* se baisser.

bend over *vi* se pencher.

bends [bɛndz] *npl* (MED) maladie *f* des caissons.

beneath [bɪ'niːθ] *prep* sous, au-dessous de; (*unworthy of*) indigne de ♦ *ad* dessous, au-dessous, en bas.

benefactor ['bɛnɪfæktə*] *n* bienfaiteur *m*.

benefactress ['bɛnɪfæktrɪs] *n* bienfaitrice *f*.

beneficial [bɛnɪ'fɪʃəl] *a*: ~ (**to**) salutaire (pour), bénéfique (à).

beneficiary [bɛnɪ'fɪʃərɪ] *n* (LAW) bénéficiaire *m/f*.

benefit ['bɛnɪfɪt] *n* avantage *m*, profit *m*; (*allowance of money*) allocation *f* ♦ *vt* faire du bien à, profiter à ♦ *vi*: **he'll** ~ **from it** cela lui fera du bien, il y gagnera *or* s'en trouvera bien.

benefit performance *n* représentation *f* or gala *m* de bienfaisance.

Benelux ['bɛnɪlʌks] *n* Bénélux *m*.

benevolent [bɪ'nɛvələnt] *a* bienveillant(e).

BEng *n abbr* (= *Bachelor of Engineering*) diplôme universitaire.

benign [bɪ'naɪn] *a* (*person, smile*) bienveillant(e), affable; (MED) bénin(igne).

bent [bɛnt] *pt, pp of* **bend** ♦ *n* inclination *f*, penchant *m* ♦ *a* (*wire, pipe*) coudé(e); (*col: dishonest*) véreux(euse); **to be** ~ **on** être résolu(e) à.

bequeath [bɪ'kwiːð] *vt* léguer.

bequest [bɪ'kwɛst] *n* legs *m*.

bereaved [bɪ'riːvd] *n*: **the** ~ la famille du disparu ♦ *a* endeuillé(e).

bereavement [bɪ'riːvmənt] *n* deuil *m*.

beret ['bɛreɪ] *n* béret *m*.

Bering Sea ['beɪrɪŋ-] *n*: **the** ~ la mer de Béring.

Berks *abbr* (Brit) = Berkshire.

Berlin [bəː'lɪn] *n* Berlin; **East/West** ~ Berlin Est/Ouest.

berm [bəːm] *n* (US AUT) accotement *m*.

Bermuda [bəː'mjuːdə] *n* Bermudes *fpl*.

Bermuda shorts *npl* bermuda *m*.

Bern [bɔːn] *n* Berne.

berry ['bɛrɪ] *n* baie *f*.

berserk [bə'sɔːk] *a*: **to go** ~ être pris(e) d'une rage incontrôlable; se déchaîner.

berth [bɔːθ] *n* (*bed*) couchette *f*; (*for ship*) poste *m* d'amarrage, mouillage *m* ♦ *vi* (*in harbour*) venir à quai; (*at anchor*) mouiller; **to give sb a wide** ~ (*fig*) éviter qn.

beseech, *pt*, *pp* **besought** [bɪ'siːtʃ, -'sɔːt] *vt* implorer, supplier.

beset, *pt*, *pp* **beset** [bɪ'sɛt] *vt* assaillir ♦ *a*: ~ **with** semé(e) de.

besetting [bɪ'sɛtɪŋ] *a*: **his** ~ **sin** son vice, son gros défaut.

beside [bɪ'saɪd] *prep* à côté de; (*compared with*) par rapport à; **that's** ~ **the point** ça n'a rien à voir; **to be** ~ **o.s.** (**with anger**) être hors de soi.

besides [bɪ'saɪdz] *ad* en outre, de plus ♦ *prep* en plus de; (*except*) excepté.

besiege [bɪ'siːdʒ] *vt* (*town*) assiéger; (*fig*) assaillir.

besotted [bɪ'sɔtɪd] *a* (*Brit*): ~ **with** enti-ché(e) de.

besought [bɪ'sɔːt] *pt*, *pp of* **beseech**.

bespectacled [bɪ'spɛktɪkld] *a* à lunettes.

bespoke [bɪ'spəuk] *a* (*Brit*: *garment*) fait(e) sur mesure; ~ **tailor** tailleur *m* à façon.

best [bɛst] *a* meilleur(e) ♦ *ad* le mieux; **the** ~ **part of** (*quantity*) le plus clair de, la plus grande partie de; **at** ~ au mieux; **to make the** ~ **of sth** s'accommoder de qch (du mieux que l'on peut); **to do one's** ~ faire de son mieux; **to the** ~ **of my knowledge** pour autant que je sache; **to the** ~ **of my ability** du mieux que je pourrai; **he's not exactly patient at the** ~ **of times** il n'est jamais spécialement patient; **the** ~ **thing to do is** ... le mieux, c'est de ....

best man *n* garçon *m* d'honneur.

bestow [bɪ'stəu] *vt* accorder; (*title*) conférer.

bestseller ['bɛst'sɛlə*] *n* bestseller *m*, succès *m* de librairie.

bet [bɛt] *n* pari *m* ♦ *vt*, *vi* (*pt*, *pp* **bet** *or* **betted**) parier; **it's a safe** ~ (*fig*) il y a de fortes chances.

Bethlehem ['bɛθlɪhɛm] *n* Bethléem.

betray [bɪ'treɪ] *vt* trahir.

betrayal [bɪ'treɪəl] *n* trahison *f*.

better ['bɛtə*] *a* meilleur(e) ♦ *ad* mieux ♦ *vt* améliorer ♦ *n*: **to get the** ~ **of** triompher de, l'emporter sur; **a change for the** ~ une amélioration; **I had** ~ **go** il faut que je m'en aille; **you had** ~ **do it** vous feriez mieux de le faire; **he thought** ~ **of it** il s'est ravisé; **to get** ~ aller mieux; s'améliorer; **that's** ~! c'est mieux!; ~ **off** *a* plus à l'aise financièrement; (*fig*): **you'd be** ~ **off this way** vous vous en trouveriez mieux ainsi, ce serait mieux *or* plus pratique ainsi.

betting ['bɛtɪŋ] *n* paris *mpl*.

betting shop *n* (*Brit*) bureau *m* de paris.

between [bɪ'twiːn] *prep* entre ♦ *ad* au milieu, dans l'intervalle; **the road** ~ **here and London** la route d'ici à Londres; **we only had 5** ~ **us** nous n'en avions que 5 en tout.

bevel ['bɛvəl] *n* (*also*: ~ **edge**) biseau *m*.

beverage ['bɛvərɪdʒ] *n* boisson *f* (*gén sans alcool*).

bevy ['bɛvɪ] *n*: **a** ~ **of** un essaim *or* une volée de.

bewail [bɪ'weɪl] *vt* se lamenter sur.

beware [bɪ'wɛə*] *vt*, *vi*: **to** ~ (**of**) prendre garde (à).

bewildered [bɪ'wɪldəd] *a* dérouté(e), ahuri(e).

bewildering [bɪ'wɪldrɪŋ] *a* déroutant(e), ahurissant(e).

bewitching [bɪ'wɪtʃɪŋ] *a* enchanteur(teresse).

beyond [bɪ'jɔnd] *prep* (*in space*) au-delà de; (*exceeding*) au-dessus de ♦ *ad* au-delà; ~ **doubt** hors de doute; ~ **repair** irréparable.

b/f *abbr* = **brought forward**.

BFPO *n abbr* (= *British Forces Post Office*) service postal de l'armée.

bhp *n abbr* (*AUT*: = *brake horsepower*) puissance *f* aux freins.

bi... [baɪ] *prefix* bi....

biannual [baɪ'ænjuəl] *a* semestriel(le).

bias ['baɪəs] *n* (*prejudice*) préjugé *m*, parti pris; (*preference*) prévention *f*.

bias(s)ed ['baɪəst] *a* partial(e), montrant un parti pris; **to be** ~ **against** avoir un préjugé contre.

bib [bɪb] *n* bavoir *m*, bavette *f*.

Bible ['baɪbl] *n* Bible *f*.

bibliography [bɪblɪ'ɔgrəfɪ] *n* bibliographie *f*.

bicarbonate of soda [baɪ'kɑːbənɪt-] *n* bicarbonate *m* de soude.

bicentenary [baɪsɛn'tiːnərɪ] *n*, **bicentennial** [baɪsɛn'tɛnɪəl] *n* bicentenaire *m*.

biceps ['baɪsɛps] *n* biceps *m*.

bicker ['bɪkə*] *vi* se chamailler.

bicycle ['baɪsɪkl] *n* bicyclette *f*.

bicycle path *n*, **bicycle track** *n* piste *f* cycla-ble.

bicycle pump *n* pompe *f* à vélo.

bid [bɪd] *n* offre *f*; (*at auction*) enchère *f*; (*attempt*) tentative *f* ♦ *vb* (*pt* **bid** *or* **bade** [bæd], *pp* **bid** *or* **bidden** ['bɪdn]) *vi* faire une enchère *or* offre ♦ *vt* faire une enchère *or* of-fre de; **to** ~ **sb good day** souhaiter le bonjour à qn.

bidder ['bɪdə*] *n*: **the highest** ~ le plus of-frant.

bidding ['bɪdɪŋ] *n* enchères *fpl*.

bide [baɪd] *vt*: **to** ~ **one's time** attendre son heure.

bidet ['biːdeɪ] *n* bidet *m*.

bidirectional ['baɪdɪ'rɛkʃənl] *a* bidirec-tionnel(le).

biennial [baɪ'ɛnɪəl] *a* biennal(e), bisannuel(le) ♦ *n* biennale *f*; (*plant*) plante bisannuelle.

bier [bɪə*] *n* bière *f* (*cercueil*).

bifocals [baɪ'fəuklz] *npl* lunettes *fpl* à double foyer.

big [bɪg] *a* grand(e), gros(se); **to do things in a** ~ **way** faire les choses en grand.

bigamy ['bɪgəmɪ] *n* bigamie *f*.

big dipper [-'dɪpə*] *n* montagnes *fpl* russes.

big end *n* (*Aut*) tête *f* de bielle.

bigheaded ['bɪg'hɛdɪd] *a* prétentieux(euse).

big-hearted ['bɪg'hɑːtɪd] *a* au grand cœur.

bigot ['bɪgət] *n* fanatique *m/f*, sectaire *m/f*.

bigoted ['bɪgətɪd] *a* fanatique, sectaire.

bigotry ['bɪgətrɪ] *n* fanatisme *m*, sectarisme *m*.

big toe *n* gros orteil.

big top *n* grand chapiteau.

big wheel n (at fair) grande roue.
bigwig ['bɪgwɪg] n (col) grosse légume, huile f.
bike [baɪk] n vélo m, bécane f.
bikini [bɪ'ki:nɪ] n bikini m.
bilateral [baɪ'lætərl] a bilatéral(e).
bile [baɪl] n bile f.
bilingual [baɪ'lɪŋgwəl] a bilingue.
bilious ['bɪlɪəs] a bilieux(euse); (fig) maussade, irritable.
bill [bɪl] n note f, facture f; (POL) projet m de loi; (US: banknote) billet m (de banque); (in restaurant) addition f, note f; (notice) affiche f; (THEATRE): **on the ~** à l'affiche; (of bird) bec m ♦ vt (item) facturer; (customer) remettre la facture à; **may I have the ~ please?** (est-ce que je peux avoir) l'addition, s'il vous plaît?; "**stick** or **post no ~s**" "défense d'afficher"; **to fit** or **fill the ~** (fig) faire l'affaire; **~ of exchange** lettre f de change; **~ of lading** connaissement m; **~ of sale** contrat m de vente.
billboard ['bɪlbɔ:d] n panneau m d'affichage.
billet ['bɪlɪt] n cantonnement m (chez l'habitant) ♦ vt (troops) cantonner.
billfold ['bɪlfəuld] n (US) portefeuille m.
billiards ['bɪljədz] n (jeu m de) billard m.
billion ['bɪljən] n (Brit) billion m (million de millions); (US) milliard m.
billow ['bɪləu] n nuage m ♦ vi (smoke) s'élever en nuage; (sail) se gonfler.
billy goat ['bɪlɪgəut] n bouc m.
bin [bɪn] n boîte f; (Brit: also: **dust~, litter~**) poubelle f; (for coal) coffre m.
binary ['baɪnərɪ] a binaire.
bind, pt, pp **bound** [baɪnd, baund] vt attacher; (book) relier; (oblige) obliger, contraindre.
bind over vt (LAW) mettre en liberté conditionnelle.
bind up vt (wound) panser; **to be bound up in** (work, research etc) être complètement absorbé par, être accroché par; **to be bound up with** (person) être accroché à.
binder ['baɪndə*] n (file) classeur m.
binding ['baɪndɪŋ] n (of book) reliure f ♦ a (contract) qui constitue une obligation.
binge [bɪndʒ] n (col): **to go on a ~** faire la bringue.
bingo ['bɪŋgəu] n sorte de jeu de loto pratiqué dans des établissements publics.
binoculars [bɪ'nɔkjuləz] npl jumelles fpl.
biochemistry [baɪə'kemɪstrɪ] n biochimie f.
biodegradable ['baɪəudɪ'greɪdəbl] a biodégradable.
biographer [baɪ'ɔgrəfə*] n biographe m/f.
biographic(al) [baɪə'græfɪk(l)] a biographique.
biography [baɪ'ɔgrəfɪ] n biographie f.
biological [baɪə'lɔdʒɪkl] a biologique.
biologist [baɪ'ɔlədʒɪst] n biologiste m/f.
biology [baɪ'ɔlədʒɪ] n biologie f.
biophysics ['baɪəu'fɪzɪks] n biophysique f.
biopsy ['baɪɔpsɪ] n biopsie f.
biotechnology ['baɪəutek'nɔlədʒɪ] n biotechnologie f.
birch [bə:tʃ] n bouleau m.
bird [bə:d] n oiseau m; (Brit col: girl) nana f.
bird's-eye view ['bə:dzaɪ-] n vue f à vol d'oiseau; (fig) vue d'ensemble or générale.

bird watcher n ornithologue m/f amateur.
Biro ['baɪərəu] n ® stylo m à bille.
birth [bə:θ] n naissance f; **to give ~ to** donner naissance à, mettre au monde; (animal) mettre bas.
birth certificate n acte m de naissance.
birth control n limitation f des naissances; méthode(s) contraceptive(s).
birthday ['bə:θdeɪ] n anniversaire m.
birthmark ['bə:θmɑ:k] n envie f, tache f de vin.
birthplace ['bə:θpleɪs] n lieu m de naissance.
birth rate ['bə:θreɪt] n (taux m de) natalité f.
Biscay ['bɪskeɪ] n: **the Bay of ~** le golfe de Gascogne.
biscuit ['bɪskɪt] n (Brit) biscuit m; (US) petit pain au lait.
bisect [baɪ'sekt] vt couper or diviser en deux.
bishop ['bɪʃəp] n évêque m; (CHESS) fou m.
bit [bɪt] pt of **bite** ♦ n morceau m; (of tool) mèche f; (of horse) mors m; (COMPUT) bit m, élément m binaire; **a ~ of** un peu de; **a ~ mad/dangerous** un peu fou/risqué; **~ by ~** petit à petit; **to come to ~s** (break) tomber en morceaux, se déglinguer; **bring all your ~s and pieces** apporte toutes tes affaires; **to do one's ~** y mettre du sien.
bitch [bɪtʃ] n (dog) chienne f; (col!) salope f (!), garce f.
bite [baɪt] vt, vi (pt bit [bɪt], pp bitten ['bɪtn]) mordre ♦ n morsure f; (insect ~) piqûre f; (mouthful) bouchée f; **let's have a ~ (to eat)** mangeons un morceau; **to ~ one's nails** se ronger les ongles.
biting ['baɪtɪŋ] a mordant(e).
bit part n (THEATRE) petit rôle.
bitten ['bɪtn] pp of **bite**.
bitter ['bɪtə*] a amer(ère); (criticism) cinglant(e); (icy: weather, wind) glacial(e) ♦ n (Brit: beer) bière f (à forte teneur en houblon); **to the ~ end** jusqu'au bout.
bitterly ['bɪtəlɪ] ad (complain, weep) amèrement; (oppose, criticise) durement, âprement; (jealous, disappointed) horriblement; **it's ~ cold** il fait un froid de loup.
bitterness ['bɪtənɪs] n amertume f; goût amer.
bittersweet ['bɪtəswi:t] a aigre-doux(douce).
bitty ['bɪtɪ] a (Brit col) décousu(e).
bitumen ['bɪtjumɪn] n bitume m.
bivouac ['bɪvuæk] n bivouac m.
bizarre [bɪ'zɑ:*] a bizarre.
bk abbr = **bank, book**.
BL n abbr (= Bachelor of Law(s), Bachelor of Letters) diplôme universitaire; (US: = Bachelor of Literature) diplôme universitaire.
bl abbr = **bill of lading**.
blab [blæb] vi jaser, trop parler ♦ vt (also: ~ out) laisser échapper, aller raconter.
black [blæk] a noir(e) ♦ n (colour) noir m; (person): **B~** noir/e ♦ vt (shoes) cirer; (Brit INDUSTRY) boycotter; **to give sb a ~ eye** pocher l'œil à qn, faire un œil au beurre noir à qn; **~ coffee** café noir; **there it is in ~ and white** (fig) c'est écrit noir sur blanc; **to be in the ~** (in credit) avoir un compte créditeur; **~ and blue** a couvert(e) de bleus.
black out vi (faint) s'évanouir.
black belt n (US) région à forte population

noire.

blackberry ['blækbərɪ] *n* mûre *f.*

blackbird ['blækbə:d] *n* merle *m.*

blackboard ['blækbɔ:d] *n* tableau noir.

black box *n* (AVIAT) boîte noire.

Black Country *n* (Brit): **the** ~ le Pays Noir (*dans les Midlands*).

blackcurrant ['blæk'kʌrənt] *n* cassis *m.*

black economy *n* (Brit) travail *m* au noir.

blacken ['blækn] *vt* noircir.

Black Forest *n*: **the** ~ la Forêt Noire.

blackhead ['blækhed] *n* point noir.

black ice *n* verglas *m.*

blackjack ['blækdʒæk] *n* (CARDS) vingt-et-un *m*; (US: *truncheon*) matraque *f.*

blackleg ['blækleg] *n* (Brit) briseur *m* de grève, jaune *m.*

blacklist ['blæklɪst] *n* liste noire ♦ *vt* mettre sur la liste noire.

blackmail ['blækmeɪl] *n* chantage *m* ♦ *vt* faire chanter, soumettre au chantage.

blackmailer ['blækmeɪlə*] *n* maître-chanteur *m.*

black market *n* marché noir.

blackout ['blækaut] *n* panne *f* d'électricité; (in *wartime*) black-out *m*; (TV) interruption *f* d'émission; (*fainting*) syncope *f.*

Black Sea *n*: **the** ~ la mer Noire.

black sheep *n* brebis galeuse.

blacksmith ['blæksmɪθ] *n* forgeron *m.*

black spot *n* (AUT) point noir.

bladder ['blædə*] *n* vessie *f.*

blade [bleɪd] *n* lame *f*; (of *oar*) plat *m*; ~ **of grass** brin *m* d'herbe.

blame [bleɪm] *n* faute *f*, blâme *m* ♦ *vt*: **to** ~ **sb/sth for sth** attribuer à qn/qch la responsabilité de qch; reprocher qch à qn/qch; **who's to** ~? qui est le fautif *or* coupable *or* responsable?; **I'm not to** ~ ce n'est pas ma faute.

blameless ['bleɪmlɪs] *a* irréprochable.

blanch [blɑ:ntʃ] *vi* (*person, face*) blêmir ♦ *vt* (CULIN) blanchir.

bland [blænd] *a* affable; (*taste*) doux(douce), fade.

blank [blæŋk] *a* blanc(blanche); (*look*) sans expression, dénué(e) d'expression ♦ *n* espace *m* vide, blanc *m*; (*cartridge*) cartouche *f* à blanc; **we drew a** ~ (fig) nous n'avons abouti à rien.

blank cheque, (US) **blank check** *n* chèque *m* en blanc; **to give sb a** ~ **to do** ... (fig) donner carte blanche à qn pour faire ....

blanket ['blæŋkɪt] *n* couverture *f* ♦ *a* (*statement, agreement*) global(e), de portée générale; **to give** ~ **cover** (*subj: insurance policy*) couvrir tous les risques.

blare [blɛə*] *vi* (*brass band, horns, radio*) beugler.

blarney ['blɑ:nɪ] *n* boniment *m.*

blasé ['blɑ:zeɪ] *a* blasé(e).

blasphemous ['blæsfɪməs] *a* (*words*) blasphématoire; (*person*) blasphémateur(trice).

blasphemy ['blæsfɪmɪ] *n* blasphème *m.*

blast [blɑ:st] *n* explosion *f*; (*shock wave*) souffle *m*; (of *air, steam*) bouffée *f* ♦ *vt* faire sauter *or* exploser ♦ *excl* (Brit col) zut!; (**at**) **full** ~ (*play music etc*) à plein volume.

blast off *vi* (SPACE) décoller.

blast-off ['blɑ:stɔf] *n* (SPACE) lancement *m.*

blatant ['bleɪtənt] *a* flagrant(e), criant(e).

blatantly ['bleɪtəntlɪ] *ad* (*lie*) ouvertement; **it's** ~ **obvious** c'est l'évidence même.

blaze [bleɪz] *n* (*fire*) incendie *m*; (*flames: of fire, sun etc*) embrasement *m*; (: *in hearth*) flamme *f*, flambée *f*; (fig) flamboiement *m* ♦ *vi* (*fire*) flamber; (fig) flamboyer, resplendir ♦ *vt*: **to** ~ **a trail** (fig) montrer la voie; **in a** ~ **of publicity** à grand renfort de publicité.

blazer ['bleɪzə*] *n* blazer *m.*

bleach [bli:tʃ] *n* (*also*: **household** ~) eau *f* de Javel ♦ *vt* (*linen*) blanchir.

bleached [bli:tʃt] *a* (*hair*) oxygéné(e), décoloré(e).

bleachers ['bli:tʃəz] *npl* (US SPORT) gradins *mpl* (*en plein soleil*).

bleak [bli:k] *a* morne, désolé(e); (*weather*) triste, maussade; (*smile*) lugubre; (*prospect, future*) morose.

bleary-eyed ['blɪərɪ'aɪd] *a* aux yeux pleins de sommeil.

bleat [bli:t] *n* bêlement *m* ♦ *vi* bêler.

bleed, *pt, pp* **bled** [bli:d, bled] *vt* saigner; (*brakes, radiator*) purger ♦ *vi* saigner; **my nose is** ~**ing** je saigne du nez.

bleeper ['bli:pə*] *n* (of *doctor etc*) bip *m.*

blemish ['blemɪʃ] *n* défaut *m*; (on *reputation*) tache *f.*

blend [blend] *n* mélange *m* ♦ *vt* mélanger ♦ *vi* (*colours etc*) se mélanger, se fondre, s'allier.

blender ['blendə*] *n* (CULIN) mixeur *m.*

bless, *pt, pp* **blessed** *or* **blest** [bles, blest] *vt* bénir; **to be** ~**ed with** avoir le bonheur de jouir de *or* d'avoir.

blessed ['blesɪd] *a* (REL: *holy*) béni(e); (*happy*) bienheureux(euse); **it rains every** ~ **day** il ne se passe pas de jour sans qu'il ne pleuve.

blessing ['blesɪŋ] *n* bénédiction *f*; bienfait *m*; **to count one's** ~**s** s'estimer heureux; **it was a** ~ **in disguise** c'est un bien pour un mal.

blew [blu:] *pt of* **blow.**

blight [blaɪt] *n* (of *plants*) rouille *f* ♦ *vt* (*hopes etc*) anéantir, briser.

blimey ['blaɪmɪ] *excl* (Brit col) mince alors!

blind [blaɪnd] *a* aveugle ♦ *n* (for *window*) store *m* ♦ *vt* aveugler; **to turn a** ~ **eye (on** *or* **to)** fermer les yeux (sur).

blind alley *n* impasse *f.*

blind corner *n* (Brit) virage *m* sans visibilité.

blindfold ['blaɪndfəuld] *n* bandeau *m* ♦ *a, ad* les yeux bandés ♦ *vt* bander les yeux à.

blindly ['blaɪndlɪ] *ad* aveuglément.

blindness ['blaɪndnɪs] *n* cécité *f*; (fig) aveuglement *m.*

blind spot *n* (AUT *etc*) angle *m* aveugle; (fig) angle mort.

blink [blɪŋk] *vi* cligner des yeux; (*light*) clignoter ♦ *n*: **the TV's on the** ~ (col) la télé ne va pas tarder à nous lâcher.

blinkers ['blɪŋkəz] *npl* œillères *fpl.*

blinking ['blɪŋkɪŋ] *a* (Brit col): **this** ~ ... ce fichu *or* sacré ....

bliss [blɪs] *n* félicité *f*, bonheur *m* sans mélange.

blissful ['blɪsful] *a* (*event, day*) merveilleux(euse); (*smile*) de bonheur; **a** ~ **sigh** un soupir d'aise; **in** ~ **ignorance** dans une ignorance béate.

blissfully ['blɪsfʊlɪ] *ad* (*smile*) béatement; (*happy*) merveilleusement.

blister ['blɪstə*] *n* (*on skin*) ampoule *f*, cloque *f*; (*on paintwork*) boursouflure *f* ♦ *vi* (*paint*) se boursoufler, se cloquer.

blithely ['blaɪðlɪ] *ad* (*unconcernedly*) tranquillement; (*joyfully*) gaiement.

blithering ['blɪðərɪŋ] *a* (*col*): this ~ idiot cet espèce d'idiot.

BLit(t) *n abbr* (= *Bachelor of Literature*) diplôme universitaire.

blitz [blɪts] *n* bombardement (aérien); **to have a ~ on sth** (*fig*) s'attaquer à qch.

blizzard ['blɪzəd] *n* blizzard *m*, tempête *f* de neige.

BLM *n abbr* (*US*: = *Bureau of Land Management*) ≈ les domaines.

bloated ['bləʊtɪd] *a* (*face*) bouffi(e); (*stomach*) gonflé(e).

blob [blɒb] *n* (*drop*) goutte *f*; (*stain*, *spot*) tache *f*.

bloc [blɒk] *n* (*POL*) bloc *m*.

block [blɒk] *n* bloc *m*; (*in pipes*) obstruction *f*; (*toy*) cube *m*; (*of buildings*) pâté *m* (de maisons) ♦ *vt* bloquer; (*COMPUT*) grouper; ~ **of flats** (*Brit*) immeuble (locatif); **3 ~s from here** à trois rues d'ici; **mental ~** blocage *m*; **~ and tackle** (*TECH*) palan *m*.

block up *vt* boucher.

blockade [blɒ'keɪd] *n* blocus *m* ♦ *vt* faire le blocus de.

blockage ['blɒkɪdʒ] *n* obstruction *f*.

block booking *n* réservation *f* en bloc.

blockbuster ['blɒkbʌstə*] *n* (*film*, *book*) grand succès.

block capitals *npl* majuscules *fpl* d'imprimerie.

blockhead ['blɒkhɛd] *n* imbécile *m/f*.

block letters *npl* majuscules *fpl*.

block release *n* (*Brit*) congé *m* de formation.

block vote *n* (*Brit*) vote *m* de délégation.

bloke [bləʊk] *n* (*Brit col*) type *m*.

blonde [blɒnd] *a*, *n* blond(e).

blood [blʌd] *n* sang *m*.

bloodcurdling ['blʌdkə:dlɪŋ] *a* à vous glacer le sang.

blood donor *n* donneur/euse de sang.

blood group *n* groupe sanguin.

bloodhound ['blʌdhaʊnd] *n* limier *m*.

bloodless ['blʌdlɪs] *a* (*victory*) sans effusion de sang; (*pale*) anémié(e).

bloodletting ['blʌdlɛtɪŋ] *n* (*MED*) saignée *f*; (*fig*) effusion *f* de sang, représailles *fpl*.

blood poisoning *n* empoisonnement *m* du sang.

blood pressure *n* tension (artérielle); **to have high/low ~** faire de l'hypertension/ l'hypotension.

bloodshed ['blʌdʃɛd] *n* effusion *f* de sang, carnage *m*.

bloodshot ['blʌdʃɒt] *a*: ~ **eyes** yeux injectés de sang.

bloodstained ['blʌdsteɪnd] *a* taché(e) de sang.

bloodstream ['blʌdstri:m] *n* sang *m*, système sanguin.

blood test *n* analyse *f* de sang.

bloodthirsty ['blʌdθə:stɪ] *a* sanguinaire.

blood transfusion *n* transfusion *f* de sang.

blood vessel *n* vaisseau sanguin.

bloody ['blʌdɪ] *a* sanglant(e); (*Brit col!*): this ~ ... ce foutu ..., ce putain de ... (!); ~ **strong/good** (*col!*) vachement *or* sacrément fort/bon.

bloody-minded ['blʌdɪ'maɪndɪd] *a* (*Brit col*) contrariant(e), obstiné(e).

bloom [blu:m] *n* fleur *f*; (*fig*) épanouissement *m* ♦ *vi* être en fleur; (*fig*) s'épanouir; être florissant(e).

blooming ['blu:mɪŋ] *a* (*col*): this ~ ... ce fichu *or* sacré ....

blossom ['blɒsəm] *n* fleur(s) *f(pl)* ♦ *vi* être en fleurs; (*fig*) s'épanouir; **to ~ into** (*fig*) devenir.

blot [blɒt] *n* tache *f* ♦ *vt* tacher; (*ink*) sécher; **to be a ~ on the landscape** gâcher le paysage; **to ~ one's copy book** (*fig*) faire un impair.

blot out *vt* (*memories*) effacer; (*view*) cacher, masquer; (*nation*, *city*) annihiler.

blotchy ['blɒtʃɪ] *a* (*complexion*) couvert(e) de marbrures.

blotter ['blɒtə*] *n*, **blotting paper** ['blɒtɪŋ-] *n* buvard *m*.

blouse [blaʊz] *n* (*feminine garment*) chemisier *m*, corsage *m*.

blow [bləʊ] *n* coup *m* ♦ *vb* (*pt* **blew**, *pp* **blown** [blu:, bləʊn]) *vi* souffler ♦ *vt* (*glass*) souffler; (*fuse*) faire sauter; **to ~ one's nose** se moucher; **to ~ a whistle** siffler; **to come to ~s** en venir aux coups.

blow away *vi* s'envoler ♦ *vt* chasser, faire s'envoler.

blow down *vt* faire tomber, renverser.

blow off *vi* s'envoler ♦ *vt* (*hat*) emporter; (*ship*): **to ~ off course** faire dévier.

blow out *vi* (*tyre*) éclater; (*fuse*) sauter.

blow over *vi* s'apaiser.

blow up *vi* exploser, sauter ♦ *vt* faire sauter; (*tyre*) gonfler; (*PHOT*) agrandir.

blow-dry ['bləʊdraɪ] *n* (*hairstyle*) brushing *m* ♦ *vt* faire un brushing à.

blowlamp ['bləʊlæmp] *n* (*Brit*) chalumeau *m*.

blow-out ['bləʊaʊt] *n* (*of tyre*) éclatement *m*; (*col*: *big meal*) gueuleton *m*.

blowtorch ['bləʊtɔ:tʃ] *n* chalumeau *m*.

blowzy ['blaʊzɪ] *a* (*Brit*) peu soigné(e).

BLS *n abbr* (*US*) = *Bureau of Labor Statistics*.

blubber ['blʌbə*] *n* blanc *m* de baleine ♦ *vi* (*pej*) pleurer comme un veau.

bludgeon ['blʌdʒən] *n* gourdin *m*, trique *f*.

blue [blu:] *a* bleu(e); ~ **film/joke** film *m*/ histoire *f* pornographique; (**only**) **once in a ~ moon** tous les trente-six du mois; **out of the ~** (*fig*) à l'improviste, sans qu'on si attende.

blue baby *n* enfant bleu(e).

bluebell ['blu:bɛl] *n* jacinthe *f* des bois.

bluebottle ['blu:bɒtl] *n* mouche *f* à viande.

blue cheese *n* (fromage) bleu *m*.

blue-chip ['blu:tʃɪp] *a*: ~ **investment** investissement *m* de premier ordre.

blue-collar worker ['blu:kɒlə*-] *n* ouvrier/ ère, col bleu.

blue jeans *npl* blue-jeans *mpl*.

blueprint ['blu:prɪnt] *n* bleu *m*; (*fig*) projet *m*, plan directeur.

blues [blu:z] *npl*: **the ~** (*MUS*) le blues; **to**

have the ~ (col: feeling) avoir le cafard.
bluff [blʌf] vi bluffer ♦ n bluff m; (cliff) promontoire m, falaise f ♦ a (person) bourru(e), brusque; **to call sb's** ~ mettre qn au défi d'exécuter ses menaces.
blunder ['blʌndə*] n gaffe f, bévue f ♦ vi faire une gaffe or une bévue; **to** ~ **into** sb/sth buter contre qn/qch.
blunt [blʌnt] a émoussé(e), peu tranchant(e); (pencil) mal taillé(e); (person) brusque, ne mâchant pas ses mots ♦ vt émousser; ~ **instrument** (LAW) instrument contondant.
bluntly ['blʌntlɪ] ad carrément, sans prendre de gants.
bluntness ['blʌntnɪs] n (of person) brusquerie f, franchise brutale.
blur [bləː*] n tache or masse floue or confuse ♦ vt brouiller, rendre flou(e).
blurb [bləːb] n (for book) texte m de présentation; (pej) baratin m.
blurred [bləːd] a flou(e).
blurt [bləːt]: **to** ~ **out** vt (reveal) lâcher; (say) balbutier, dire d'une voix entrecoupée.
blush [blʌʃ] vi rougir ♦ n rougeur f.
blusher ['blʌʃə*] n rouge m à joues.
bluster ['blʌstə*] n paroles fpl en l'air; (boasting) fanfaronnades fpl; (threats) menaces fpl en l'air ♦ vi parler en l'air; fanfaronner.
blustering ['blʌstərɪŋ] a fanfaron(ne).
blustery ['blʌstərɪ] a (weather) à bourrasques.
Blvd abbr (= boulevard) Bd.
BM n abbr = British Museum; (SCOL: = Bachelor of Medicine) diplôme universitaire.
BMA n abbr = British Medical Association.
BMJ n abbr = British Medical Journal.
BMus n abbr (= Bachelor of Music) diplôme universitaire.
BO n abbr (col: = body odour) odeurs corporelles; (US) = **box office**.
boar [bɔː*] n sanglier m.
board [bɔːd] n planche f; (on wall) panneau m; (for chess etc) plateau m; (committee) conseil m, comité m; (in firm) conseil d'administration; (NAUT, AVIAT): **on** ~ à bord ♦ vt (ship) monter à bord de; (train) monter dans; **full** ~ (Brit) pension complète; **half** ~ (Brit) demi-pension f; ~ **and lodging** n chambre f avec pension; **with** ~ **and lodging** logé nourri; **above** ~ (fig) régulier(ère); **across the** ~ (fig: ad) systématiquement; (: a) de portée générale; **to go by the** ~ être abandonné(e); (be unimportant) compter pour rien, n'avoir aucune importance.
board up vt (door) condamner (au moyen de planches, de tôle).
boarder ['bɔːdə*] n pensionnaire m/f; (SCOL) interne m/f, pensionnaire.
board game n jeu m de société.
boarding card ['bɔːdɪŋ-] n (AVIAT, NAUT) carte f d'embarquement.
boarding house ['bɔːdɪŋ-] n pension f.
boarding pass ['bɔːdɪŋ-] n (Brit) = **boarding card**.
boarding school ['bɔːdɪŋ-] n internat m, pensionnat m.
board meeting n réunion f du conseil d'administration.

board room n salle f du conseil d'administration.
boardwalk ['bɔːdwɔːk] n (US) cheminement m en planches.
boast [bəust] vi: **to** ~ **(about** or **of)** se vanter (de) ♦ vt s'enorgueillir de ♦ n vantardise f; sujet m d'orgueil or de fierté.
boastful ['bəustful] a vantard(e).
boastfulness ['bəustfulnɪs] n vantardise f.
boat [bəut] n bateau m; (small) canot m; barque f; **to go by** ~ aller en bateau; **to be in the same** ~ (fig) être logé à la même enseigne.
boater ['bəutə*] n (hat) canotier m.
boating ['bəutɪŋ] n canotage m.
boatswain ['bəusn] n maître m d'équipage.
bob [bɔb] vi (boat, cork on water: also: ~ **up and down**) danser, se balancer ♦ n (Brit col) = **shilling**.
bob up vi surgir or apparaître brusquement.
bobbin ['bɔbɪn] n bobine f; (of sewing machine) navette f.
bobby ['bɔbɪ] n (Brit col) ≈ agent m (de police).
bobsleigh ['bɔbsleɪ] n bob m.
bode [bəud] vi: **to** ~ **well/ill (for)** être de bon/mauvais augure (pour).
bodice ['bɔdɪs] n corsage m.
bodily ['bɔdɪlɪ] a corporel(le); (pain, comfort) physique; (needs) matériel(le) ♦ ad (carry, lift) dans ses bras.
body ['bɔdɪ] n corps m; (of car) carrosserie f; (of plane) fuselage m; (fig: society) organe m, organisme m; (: quantity) ensemble m, masse f; (of wine) corps m; **ruling** ~ organe directeur; **in a** ~ en masse, ensemble; (speak) comme un seul et même homme.
body-building ['bɔdɪ'bɪldɪŋ] n body-building m, culturisme m.
bodyguard ['bɔdɪgɑːd] n garde m du corps.
body repairs npl travaux mpl de carrosserie.
bodywork ['bɔdɪwɜːk] n carrosserie f.
boffin ['bɔfɪn] n (Brit) savant m.
bog [bɔg] n tourbière f ♦ vt: **to get** ~**ged down (in)** (fig) s'enliser (dans).
boggle ['bɔgl] vi: **the mind** ~**s** c'est incroyable, on en reste sidéré.
bogie ['bəugɪ] n bogie m.
Bogotá [bəugə'tɑː] n Bogotá.
bogus ['bəugəs] a bidon inv; fantôme.
Bohemia [bəu'hiːmɪə] n Bohême f.
Bohemian [bəu'hiːmɪən] a bohémien(ne) ♦ n Bohémien(ne); (gipsy: also: **b**~) bohémien(ne).
boil [bɔɪl] vt (faire) bouillir ♦ vi bouillir ♦ n (MED) furoncle m; **to come to the** or (US) **a** ~ bouillir; **to bring to the** or (US) **a** ~ porter à ébullition; ~**ed egg** œuf m à la coque; ~**ed potatoes** pommes fpl à l'anglaise or à l'eau.
boil down vi (fig): **to** ~ **down to** se réduire or ramener à.
boil over vi déborder.
boiler ['bɔɪlə*] n chaudière f.
boiler suit n (Brit) bleu m de travail, combinaison f.
boiling ['bɔɪlɪŋ] a: **I'm** ~ **(hot)** (col) je crève de chaud.
boiling point n point m d'ébullition.

boisterous ['bɔɪstərəs] *a* bruyant(e), tapageur(euse).

bold [bəuld] *a* hardi(e), audacieux(euse); (*pej*) effronté(e); (*outline, colour*) franc(franche), tranché(e), marqué(e).

boldness ['bəuldnıs] *n* hardiesse *f*, audace *f*; aplomb *m*, effronterie *f*.

bold type *n* (*TYP*) caractères *mpl* gras.

Bolivia [bə'lıvıə] *n* Bolivie *f*.

Bolivian [bə'lıvıən] *a* bolivien(ne) ♦ *n* Bolivien/ne.

bollard ['bɔləd] *n* (*NAUT*) bitte *f* d'amarrage; (*Brit AUT*) borne lumineuse *or* de signalisation.

bolster ['bəulstə*] *n* traversin *m*.

bolster up *vt* soutenir.

bolt [bəult] *n* verrou *m*; (*with nut*) boulon *m* ♦ *ad*: ~ **upright** droit(e) comme un piquet ♦ *vt* verrouiller; (*food*) engloutir ♦ *vi* se sauver, filer (comme une flèche); **a ~ from the blue** (*fig*) un coup de tonnerre dans un ciel bleu.

bomb [bɔm] *n* bombe *f* ♦ *vt* bombarder.

bombard [bɔm'bɑ:d] *vt* bombarder.

bombardment [bɔm'bɑ:dmənt] *n* bombardement *m*.

bombastic [bɔm'bæstɪk] *a* grandiloquent(e), pompeux(euse).

bomb disposal *n*: ~ **unit** section *f* de déminage; ~ **expert** artificier *m*.

bomber ['bɔmə*] *n* caporal *m* d'artillerie; (*AVIAT*) bombardier *m*; (*terrorist*) poseur *m* de bombes.

bombing ['bɔmıŋ] *n* bombardement *m*.

bombshell ['bɔmʃel] *n* obus *m*; (*fig*) bombe *f*.

bomb site *n* zone *f* de bombardement.

bona fide ['bəunə'faɪdɪ] *a* de bonne foi; (*offer*) sérieux(euse).

bonanza [bə'nænzə] *n* filon *m*.

bond [bɔnd] *n* lien *m*; (*binding promise*) engagement *m*, obligation *f*; (*FINANCE*) obligation *f*; **in** ~ (*of goods*) en entrepôt.

bondage ['bɔndɪdʒ] *n* esclavage *m*.

bonded warehouse ['bɔndıd-] *n* entrepôt *m* sous douanes.

bone [bəun] *n* os *m*; (*of fish*) arête *f* ♦ *vt* désosser; ôter les arêtes de.

bone china *n* porcelaine *f* tendre.

bone-dry ['bəun'draɪ] *a* absolument sec(sèche).

bone idle *a* fainéant(e).

boner ['bəunə*] *n* (*US*) gaffe *f*, bourde *f*.

bonfire ['bɔnfaɪə*] *n* feu *m* (de joie); (*for rubbish*) feu.

Bonn [bɔn] *n* Bonn.

bonnet ['bɔnıt] *n* bonnet *m*; (*Brit: of car*) capot *m*.

bonny [bɔnı] *a* (*Scottish*) joli(e).

bonus ['bəunəs] *n* prime *f*, gratification *f*; (*on wages*) prime.

bony ['bəunı] *a* (*arm, face*, *MED*: *tissue*) osseux(euse); (*thin: person*) squelettique; (*meat*) plein(e) d'os; (*fish*) plein d'arêtes.

boo [bu:] *excl* hou!, peuh! ♦ *vt* huer ♦ *n* huée *f*.

boob [bu:b] *n* (*col: breast*) nichon *m*; (: *Brit: mistake*) gaffe *f*.

booby prize ['bu:bɪ-] *n* timbale *f* (*ironique*).

booby trap ['bu:bɪ-] *n* guet-apens *m*.

booby-trapped ['bu:bɪtræpt] *a* piégé(e).

book [buk] *n* livre *m*; (*of stamps etc*) carnet *m*; (*COMM*): ~**s** comptes *mpl*, comptabilité *f* ♦ *vt* (*ticket*) prendre; (*seat, room*) réserver; (*driver*) dresser un procès-verbal à; (*football player*) prendre le nom de, donner un carton à; **to keep the** ~**s** tenir la comptabilité; **by the** ~ à la lettre, selon les règles; **to throw the** ~ **at sb** passer un savon à qn.

book in *vi* (*Brit: at hotel*) prendre sa chambre.

book up *vt* réserver; **all seats are** ~**ed up** tout est pris, c'est complet; **the hotel is** ~**ed up** l'hôtel est complet.

bookable ['bukəbl] *a*: **seats are** ~ on peut réserver ses places.

bookcase ['bukkeɪs] *n* bibliothèque *f* (*meuble*).

book ends *npl* serre-livres *m inv*.

booking ['bukıŋ] *n* (*Brit*) réservation *f*.

booking office *n* (*Brit*) bureau *m* de location.

book-keeping ['buk'ki:pıŋ] *n* comptabilité *f*.

booklet ['buklıt] *n* brochure *f*.

bookmaker ['bukmeɪkə*] *n* bookmaker *m*.

bookseller ['buksɛlə*] *n* libraire *m/f*.

bookshop ['bukʃɔp] *n* librairie *f*.

bookstall ['bukstɔ:l] *n* kiosque *m* à journaux.

bookstore ['bukstɔ:*] *n* = **bookshop**.

book token *n* bon-cadeau *m* (pour un livre).

book value *n* valeur *f* comptable.

boom [bu:m] *n* (*noise*) grondement *m*; (*busy period*) boom *m*, vague *f* de prospérité ♦ *vi* gronder; prospérer.

boomerang ['bu:məræŋ] *n* boomerang *m*.

boom town *n* ville *f* en plein essor.

boon [bu:n] *n* bénédiction *f*, grand avantage.

boorish ['buərıʃ] *a* grossier(ère), rustre.

boost [bu:st] *n* stimulant *m*, remontant *m* ♦ *vt* stimuler; **to give a** ~ **to sb's spirits** *or* **to sb** remonter le moral à qn.

booster ['bu:stə*] *n* (*TV*) amplificateur *m* (de signal); (*ELEC*) survolteur *m*; (*also*: ~ **rocket**) booster *m*; (*MED: vaccine*) rappel *m*.

booster seat *n* (*AUT: for children*) siège *m* rehausseur.

boot [bu:t] *n* botte *f*; (*for hiking*) chaussure *f* (de marche); (*for football etc*) soulier *m*; (*ankle* ~) bottine *f*; (*Brit: of car*) coffre *m* ♦ *vt* (*COMPUT*) lancer, mettre en route; **to** ~ (*in addition*) par-dessus le marché, en plus; **to give sb the** ~ (*col*) flanquer qn dehors, virer qn.

booth [bu:ð] *n* (*at fair*) baraque (foraine); (*of cinema, telephone etc*) cabine *f*; (*also*: **voting** ~) isoloir *m*.

bootleg ['bu:tleg] *a* de contrebande; ~ **record** enregistrement *m* pirate.

booty ['bu:tı] *n* butin *m*.

booze [bu:z] (*col*) *n* boissons *fpl* alcooliques, alcool *m* ♦ *vi* boire, picoler.

boozer ['bu:zə*] *n* (*col: person*): **he's a** ~ il picole pas mal; (*Brit col: pub*) pub *m*.

border ['bɔ:də*] *n* bordure *f*; bord *m*; (*of a country*) frontière *f*; **the B~** *la frontière entre l'Ecosse et l'Angleterre*; **the B~s** *la région frontière entre l'Ecosse et l'Angleterre*.

border on *vt fus* être voisin(e) de, toucher à.

borderline ['bɔ:dəlaın] *n* (*fig*) ligne *f* de

démarcation ♦ *a*: ~ **case** cas *m* limite.

bore [bɔ:*] *pt of* **bear** ♦ *vt* (*hole*) percer; (*person*) ennuyer, raser ♦ *n* (*person*) raseur/euse; (*of gun*) calibre *m*; **he's ~d to tears** *or* **~d to death** *or* **~d stiff** il s'ennuie à mourir.

boredom ['bɔ:dəm] *n* ennui *m*.

boring ['bɔ:rɪŋ] *a* ennuyeux(euse).

born [bɔ:n] *a*: **to be ~** naître; **I was ~ in 1960** je suis né en 1960; **~ blind** aveugle de naissance; **a ~ comedian** un comédien-né.

borne [bɔ:n] *pp of* **bear**.

Borneo ['bɔ:nɪəu] *n* Bornéo *f*.

borough ['bʌrə] *n* municipalité *f*.

borrow ['bɔrəu] *vt*: **to ~ sth (from sb)** emprunter qch (à qn); **may I ~ your car?** est-ce que je peux vous emprunter votre voiture?

borrower ['bɔrəuə*] *n* emprunteur/euse.

borrowing ['bɔrəuɪŋ] *n* emprunt(s) *m(pl)*.

borstal ['bɔ:stl] *n* (*Brit*) ≈ maison *f* de correction.

bosom ['buzəm] *n* poitrine *f*; (*fig*) sein *m*.

bosom friend *n* ami/e intime.

boss [bɔs] *n* patron/ne ♦ *vt* (*also*: ~ **about**, ~ **around**) mener à la baguette.

bossy ['bɔsɪ] *a* autoritaire.

bosun ['bəusn] *n* maître *m* d'équipage.

botanical [bə'tænɪkl] *a* botanique.

botanist ['bɔtənɪst] *n* botaniste *m/f*.

botany ['bɔtənɪ] *n* botanique *f*.

botch [bɔtʃ] *vt* (*also*: ~ **up**) saboter, bâcler.

both [bəuθ] *a* les deux, l'un(e) et l'autre ♦ *pronoun*: ~ **(of them)** les deux, tous(toutes) (les) deux, l'un(e) et l'autre; ~ **of us went, we ~ went** nous y sommes allés tous les deux ♦ *ad*: **they sell ~ the fabric and the finished curtains** ils vendent (et) le tissu et les rideaux (finis), ils vendent à la fois le tissu et les rideaux (finis).

bother ['bɔðə*] *vt* (*worry*) tracasser; (*needle, bait*) importuner, ennuyer; (*disturb*) déranger ♦ *vi* (*also*: ~ **o.s.**) se tracasser, se faire du souci ♦ *n*: **it is a ~ to have to do** c'est vraiment ennuyeux d'avoir à faire ♦ *excl* zut!; **to ~ doing** prendre la peine de faire; **I'm sorry to ~ you** excusez-moi de vous déranger; **please don't ~** ne vous dérangez pas; **don't ~** ce n'est pas la peine; **it's no ~** aucun problème.

Botswana [bɔt'swɑ:nə] *n* Botswana *m*.

bottle ['bɔtl] *n* bouteille *f*; (*baby's*) biberon *m*; (*of perfume, medicine*) flacon *m* ♦ *vt* mettre en bouteille(s); ~ **of wine/milk** bouteille de vin/lait; **wine/milk ~** bouteille à vin/lait.

bottle up *vt* refouler, contenir.

bottleneck ['bɔtlnɛk] *n* étranglement *m*.

bottle-opener ['bɔtləupnə*] *n* ouvre-bouteille *m*.

bottom ['bɔtəm] *n* (*of container, sea etc*) fond *m*; (*buttocks*) derrière *m*; (*of page, list*) bas *m*; (*of chair*) siège *m*; (*of mountain, tree, hill*) pied *m* ♦ *a* du fond; du bas; **to get to the ~ of sth** (*fig*) découvrir le fin fond de qch.

bottomless ['bɔtəmlɪs] *a* sans fond, insondable.

bough [bau] *n* branche *f*, rameau *m*.

bought [bɔ:t] *pt, pp of* **buy**.

boulder ['bəuldə*] *n* gros rocher (*gén lisse,*

arrondi).

bounce [bauns] *vi* (*ball*) rebondir; (*cheque*) être refusé (*étant sans provision*); (*also*: **to ~ forward/out etc**) bondir, s'élancer ♦ *vt* faire rebondir ♦ *n* (*rebound*) rebond *m*; **he's got plenty of ~** (*fig*) il est plein d'entrain *or* d'allant.

bouncer ['baunsə*] *n* (*col*) videur *m*.

bound [baund] *pt, pp of* **bind** ♦ *n* (*gen pl*) limite *f*; (*leap*) bond *m* ♦ *vt* (*leap*) bondir; (*limit*) borner ♦ *a*: **to be ~ to do sth** (*obliged*) être obligé(e) *or* avoir obligation de faire qch; **he's ~ to fail** (*likely*) il est sûr d'échouer, son échec est inévitable *or* assuré; ~ **for** à destination de; **out of ~s** dont l'accès est interdit.

boundary ['baundrɪ] *n* frontière *f*.

boundless ['baundlɪs] *a* illimité(e), sans bornes.

bountiful ['bauntɪful] *a* (*person*) généreux(euse); (*God*) bienfaiteur(trice); (*supply*) ample.

bounty ['bauntɪ] *n* (*generosity*) générosité *f*.

bouquet ['bukeɪ] *n* bouquet *m*.

bourbon ['buəbən] *n* (*US*: *also*: ~ **whiskey**) bourbon *m*.

bourgeois ['buəʒwɑ:] *a, n* bourgeois(e).

bout [baut] *n* période *f*; (*of malaria etc*) accès *m*, crise *f*, attaque *f*; (*BOXING etc*) combat *m*, match *m*.

boutique [bu:'ti:k] *n* boutique *f*.

bow *n* [bəu] nœud *m*; (*weapon*) arc *m*; (*MUS*) archet *m*; [bau] (*with body*) révérence *f*, inclination *f* (*du buste or corps*); (*NAUT*: *also*: ~**s**) proue *f* ♦ *vi* [bau] faire une révérence, s'incliner; (*yield*): **to ~ to** *or* **before** s'incliner devant, se soumettre à; **to ~ to the inevitable** accepter l'inévitable *or* l'inéluctable.

bowels [bauəlz] *npl* intestins *mpl*; (*fig*) entrailles *fpl*.

bowl [bəul] *n* (*for eating*) bol *m*; (*for washing*) cuvette *f*; (*ball*) boule *f*; (*of pipe*) fourneau *m* ♦ *vi* (*CRICKET*) lancer (la balle).

bowl over *vt* (*fig*) renverser.

bow-legged ['bəu'lɛgɪd] *a* aux jambes arquées.

bowler ['bəulə*] *n* joueur *m* de boules; (*CRICKET*) lanceur *m* (de la balle); (*Brit*: *also*: ~ **hat**) (chapeau *m*) melon *m*.

bowling ['bəulɪŋ] *n* (*game*) jeu *m* de boules; jeu de quilles.

bowling alley *n* bowling *m*.

bowling green *n* terrain *m* de boules (*gazonné et carré*).

bowls [bəulz] *n* (jeu *m* de) boules *fpl*.

bow tie [bəu-] *n* nœud *m* papillon.

box [bɔks] *n* (*also*: **cardboard ~**) carton *m*; (*crate*) caisse *f*; (*THEATRE*) loge *f*; (*Brit AUT*) intersection *f* (*matérialisée par des marques au sol*) ♦ *vt* mettre en boîte; (*SPORT*) boxer avec ♦ *vi* boxer, faire de la boxe.

boxer ['bɔksə*] *n* (*person*) boxeur *m*; (*dog*) boxer *m*.

boxing ['bɔksɪŋ] *n* (*sport*) boxe *f*.

Boxing Day *n* (*Brit*) le lendemain de Noël.

boxing gloves *npl* gants *mpl* de boxe.

boxing ring *n* ring *m*.

box number n (for advertisements) numéro m d'annonce.
box office n bureau m de location.
box room n débarras m; chambrette f.
boy [bɔɪ] n garçon m.
boycott ['bɔɪkɔt] n boycottage m ♦ vt boycotter.
boyfriend ['bɔɪfrɛnd] n (petit) ami.
boyish ['bɔɪɪʃ] a d'enfant, de garçon.
Bp abbr = **bishop**.
BR abbr = **British Rail**.
bra [brɑ:] n soutien-gorge m.
brace [breɪs] n attache f, agrafe f; (on teeth) appareil m (dentaire); (tool) vilbrequin m; (TYP: also: ~ **bracket**) accolade f ♦ vt consolider, soutenir; **to** ~ **o.s.** (fig) se préparer mentalement.
bracelet ['breɪslɪt] n bracelet m.
braces ['breɪsɪz] npl (Brit) bretelles fpl.
bracing ['breɪsɪŋ] a tonifiant(e), tonique.
bracken ['brækən] n fougère f.
bracket ['brækɪt] n (TECH) tasseau m, support m; (group) classe f, tranche f; (also: **brace** ~) accolade f; (also: **round** ~) parenthèse f; (also: **square** ~) crochet m ♦ vt mettre entre parenthèses; (fig: also: ~ **together**) regrouper; **income** ~ tranche f des revenus; **in** ~**s** entre parenthèses (or crochets).
brackish ['brækɪʃ] a (water) saumâtre.
brag [bræg] vi se vanter.
braid [breɪd] n (trimming) galon m; (of hair) tresse f, natte f.
Braille [breɪl] n braille m.
brain [breɪn] n cerveau m; ~**s** npl cervelle f; **he's got** ~**s** il est intelligent.
brainchild ['breɪntʃaɪld] n trouvaille (personnelle), invention f.
brainless ['breɪnlɪs] a sans cervelle, stupide.
brainstorm ['breɪnstɔ:m] n (fig) moment m d'égarement; (US: brainwave) idée f de génie.
brainwash ['breɪnwɔʃ] vt faire subir un lavage de cerveau à.
brainwave ['breɪnweɪv] n idée f de génie.
brainy ['breɪnɪ] a intelligent(e), doué(e).
braise [breɪz] vt braiser.
brake [breɪk] n (on vehicle) frein m ♦ vt, vi freiner.
brake light n feu m de stop.
brake pedal n pédale f de frein.
bramble ['bræmbl] n ronces fpl; (fruit) mûre f.
bran [bræn] n son m.
branch [brɑ:ntʃ] n branche f; (COMM) succursale f; (: bank) agence f; (of association) section locale ♦ vi bifurquer.
branch out vi diversifier ses activités; **to** ~ **out into** étendre ses activités à.
branch line n (RAIL) bifurcation f, embranchement m.
branch manager n directeur/trice de succursale (or d'agence).
brand [brænd] n marque (commerciale) ♦ vt (cattle) marquer (au fer rouge); (fig: pej): **to** ~ **sb a communist** etc traiter or qualifier qn de communiste etc.
brandish ['brændɪʃ] vt brandir.
brand name n nom m de marque.
brand-new ['brænd'nju:] a tout(e)

neuf(neuve), flambant neuf(neuve).
brandy ['brændɪ] n cognac m, fine f.
brash [bræʃ] a effronté(e).
Brasilia [brə'zɪlɪə] n Brasilia.
brass [brɑ:s] n cuivre m (jaune), laiton m; **the** ~ (MUS) les cuivres.
brass band n fanfare f.
brassière ['bræsɪə*] n soutien-gorge m.
brass tacks npl: **to get down to** ~ en venir au fait.
brat [bræt] n (pej) mioche m/f, môme m/f.
bravado [brə'vɑ:dəu] n bravade f.
brave [breɪv] a courageux(euse), brave ♦ n guerrier indien ♦ vt braver, affronter.
bravery ['breɪvərɪ] n bravoure f, courage m.
bravo [brɑ:'vəu] excl bravo!
brawl [brɔ:l] n rixe f, bagarre f ♦ vi se bagarrer.
brawn [brɔ:n] n muscle m; (meat) fromage m de tête.
brawny ['brɔ:nɪ] a musclé(e), costaud(e).
bray [breɪ] n braiement m ♦ vi braire.
brazen ['breɪzn] a impudent(e), effronté(e) ♦ vt: **to** ~ **it out** payer d'effronterie, crâner.
brazier ['breɪzɪə*] n brasero m.
Brazil [brə'zɪl] n Brésil m.
Brazilian [brə'zɪljən] a brésilien(ne) ♦ n Brésilien/ne.
Brazil nut n noix f du Brésil.
breach [bri:tʃ] vt ouvrir une brèche dans ♦ n (gap) brèche f; (estrangement) brouille f; (breaking): ~ **of contract** rupture f de contrat; ~ **of the peace** attentat m à l'ordre public; ~ **of trust** abus m de confiance.
bread [brɛd] n pain m; (col: money) fric m; ~ **and butter** n tartines (beurrées); (fig) subsistance f; **to earn one's daily** ~ gagner son pain; **to know which side one's** ~ **is buttered (on)** savoir où est son avantage or intérêt.
breadbin ['brɛdbɪn] n (Brit) boîte f or huche f à pain.
breadboard ['brɛdbɔ:d] n planche f à pain; (COMPUT) montage expérimental.
breadbox ['brɛdbɔks] n (US) boîte f or huche f à pain.
breadcrumbs ['brɛdkrʌmz] npl miettes fpl de pain; (CULIN) chapelure f, panure f.
breadline ['brɛdlaɪn] n: **to be on the** ~ être sans le sou or dans l'indigence.
breadth [brɛtθ] n largeur f.
breadwinner ['brɛdwɪnə*] n soutien m de famille.
break [breɪk] vb (pt **broke** [brəuk], pp **broken** ['brəukən]) vt casser, briser; (promise) rompre; (law) violer ♦ vi (se) casser, se briser; (weather) tourner ♦ n (gap) brèche f; (fracture) cassure f; (rest) interruption f, arrêt m; (: short) pause f; (: at school) récréation f; (chance) chance f, occasion f favorable; **to** ~ **one's leg** etc se casser la jambe etc; **to** ~ **a record** battre un record; **to** ~ **the news to sb** annoncer la nouvelle à qn; **to** ~ **with sb** rompre avec qn; **to even** vi rentrer dans ses frais; **to** ~ **free** or **loose** vi se dégager, s'échapper; **to take a** ~ (few minutes) faire une pause, s'arrêter cinq minutes; (holiday) prendre un peu de repos; **without a** ~ sans interruption, sans arrêt.

break down vt (door etc) enfoncer; (resistance) venir à bout de; (figures, data) décomposer, analyser ♦ vi s'effondrer; (MED) faire une dépression (nerveuse); (AUT) tomber en panne.

break in vt (horse etc) dresser ♦ vi (burglar) entrer par effraction.

break into vt fus (house) s'introduire or pénétrer par effraction dans.

break off vi (speaker) s'interrompre; (branch) se rompre ♦ vt (talks, engagement) rompre.

break open vt (door etc) forcer, fracturer.

break out vi éclater, se déclarer; **to ~ out in spots** se couvrir de boutons.

break through vi: **the sun broke through** le soleil a fait son apparition ♦ vt fus (defences, barrier) franchir; (crowd) se frayer un passage à travers.

break up vi (partnership) cesser, prendre fin; (marriage) se briser; (friends) se séparer ♦ vt fracasser, casser; (fight etc) interrompre, faire cesser; (marriage) désunir.

breakable ['breɪkəbl] a cassable, fragile ♦ n: **~s** objets mpl fragiles.

breakage ['breɪkɪdʒ] n casse f; **to pay for ~s** payer la casse.

breakaway ['breɪkəweɪ] a (group etc) dissident(e).

breakdown ['breɪkdaun] n (AUT) panne f; (in communications) rupture f; (MED: also: **nervous ~**) dépression (nerveuse); (of figures) ventilation f, répartition f.

breakdown service n (Brit) service m de dépannage.

breakdown van n (Brit) dépanneuse f.

breaker ['breɪkə*] n brisant m.

breakeven ['breɪk'i:vn] cpd: **~ chart** n graphique m de rentabilité; **~ point** n seuil m de rentabilité.

breakfast ['brɛkfəst] n petit déjeuner m.

breakfast cereal n céréales fpl.

break-in ['breɪkɪn] n cambriolage m.

breaking point ['breɪkɪŋ-] n limites fpl.

breakthrough ['breɪkθru:] n percée f.

break-up ['breɪkʌp] n (of partnership, marriage) rupture f.

break-up value n (COMM) valeur f de liquidation.

breakwater ['breɪkwɔ:tə*] n brise-lames m inv, digue f.

breast [brɛst] n (of woman) sein m; (chest) poitrine f.

breast-feed ['brɛstfi:d] vt, vi (irg: like **feed**) allaiter.

breast pocket n poche f (de) poitrine.

breaststroke ['brɛststrəuk] n brasse f.

breath [brɛθ] n haleine f, souffle m; **to go out for a ~ of air** sortir prendre l'air; **out of ~** à bout de souffle, essoufflé(e).

Breathalyser ['brɛθəlaɪzə*] n ® alcootest m.

breathe [bri:ð] vt, vi respirer; **I won't ~ a word about it** je n'en soufflerai pas un mot, je n'en dirai rien à personne.

breathe in vi inspirer ♦ vt aspirer.

breathe out vi, vt expirer.

breather ['bri:ðə*] n moment m de repos or de répit.

breathing ['bri:ðɪŋ] n respiration f.

breathing space n (fig) (moment m de) répit m.

breathless ['brɛθlɪs] a essoufflé(e), haletant(e); oppressé(e); **~ with excitement** le souffle coupé par l'émotion.

breath-taking ['brɛθteɪkɪŋ] a stupéfiant(e), à vous couper le souffle.

-bred [brɛd] suffix: **well/ill~** bien/mal élevé(e).

breed [bri:d] vb (pt, pp **bred** [brɛd]) vt élever, faire l'élevage de; (fig: hate, suspicion) engendrer ♦ vi se reproduire ♦ n race f, variété f.

breeder ['bri:də*] n (person) éleveur m; (PHYSICS: also: **~ reactor**) (réacteur m) surrégénérateur m.

breeding ['bri:dɪŋ] n reproduction f; élevage m; (upbringing) éducation f.

breeze [bri:z] n brise f.

breezeblock ['bri:zblɔk] n (Brit) parpaing m.

breezy ['bri:zɪ] a frais(fraîche); aéré(e); désinvolte, jovial(e).

Breton ['brɛtən] a breton(ne) ♦ n Breton/ne; (LING) breton m.

brevity ['brɛvɪtɪ] n brièveté f.

brew [bru:] vt (tea) faire infuser; (beer) brasser; (plot) tramer, préparer ♦ vi (tea) infuser; (beer) fermenter; (fig) se préparer, couver.

brewer ['bru:ə*] n brasseur m.

brewery ['bru:ərɪ] n brasserie f (fabrique).

briar ['braɪə*] n (thorny bush) ronces fpl; (wild rose) églantine f.

bribe [braɪb] n pot-de-vin m ♦ vt acheter; soudoyer; **to ~ sb to do sth** soudoyer qn pour qu'il fasse qch.

bribery ['braɪbərɪ] n corruption f.

bric-a-brac ['brɪkəbræk] n bric-à-brac m.

brick [brɪk] n brique f.

bricklayer ['brɪkleɪə*] n maçon m.

brickwork ['brɪkwə:k] n briquetage m, maçonnerie f.

brickworks ['brɪkwə:ks] n briqueterie f.

bridal ['braɪdl] a nuptial(e); **~ party** noce f.

bride [braɪd] n mariée f, épouse f.

bridegroom ['braɪdgru:m] n marié m, époux m.

bridesmaid ['braɪdzmeɪd] n demoiselle f d'honneur.

bridge [brɪdʒ] n pont m; (NAUT) passerelle f (de commandement); (of nose) arête f; (CARDS, DENTISTRY) bridge m ♦ vt (river) construire un pont sur; (gap) combler.

bridging loan ['brɪdʒɪŋ-] n (Brit) prêt m relais.

bridle ['braɪdl] n bride f ♦ vt refréner, mettre la bride à; (horse) brider.

bridle path n piste or allée cavalière.

brief [bri:f] a bref(brève) ♦ n (LAW) dossier m, cause f ♦ vt (MIL etc) donner des instructions à; **in ~ ...** (en) bref ...; **to ~ sb (about sth)** mettre qn au courant (de qch).

briefcase ['bri:fkeɪs] n serviette f; porte-documents m inv.

briefing ['bri:fɪŋ] n instructions fpl.

briefly ['bri:flɪ] ad brièvement; (visit) en coup de vent; **to glimpse ~** entrevoir.

briefness ['bri:fnɪs] n brièveté f.

briefs [bri:fs] npl slip m.

Brig. abbr = **brigadier.**

brigade [brɪˈgeɪd] n (MIL) brigade f.

brigadier [brɪgəˈdɪə*] n brigadier général.

bright [braɪt] a brillant(e); (room, weather) clair(e); (person) intelligent(e), doué(e); (colour) vif(vive); **to look on the ~ side** regarder le bon côté des choses.

brighten [ˈbraɪtn] (also: ~ **up**) vt (room) éclaircir; égayer ♦ vi s'éclaircir; (person) retrouver un peu de sa gaieté.

brightly [ˈbraɪtlɪ] ad brillamment.

brilliance [ˈbrɪljəns] n éclat m; (fig: of person) brio m.

brilliant [ˈbrɪljənt] a brillant(e).

brim [brɪm] n bord m.

brimful [ˈbrɪmˈful] a plein(e) à ras bord; (fig) débordant(e).

brine [braɪn] n eau salée; (CULIN) saumure f.

bring, pt, pp **brought** [brɪŋ, brɔːt] vt (thing) apporter; (person) amener; **to ~ sth to an end** mettre fin à qch; **I can't ~ myself to fire him** je ne peux me résoudre à le mettre à la porte.

bring about vt provoquer, entraîner.

bring back vt rapporter; (person) ramener.

bring down vt (lower) abaisser; (shoot down) abattre; (government) faire s'effondrer.

bring forward vt avancer; (BOOK-KEEPING) reporter.

bring in vt (person) faire entrer; (object) rentrer; (POL: legislation) introduire; (LAW: verdict) rendre; (produce: income) rapporter.

bring off vt (task, plan) réussir, mener à bien; (deal) mener à bien.

bring out vt (meaning) faire ressortir, mettre en relief; (new product, book) sortir.

bring round , **bring to** vt (unconscious person) ranimer.

bring up vt élever; (question) soulever; (food: vomit) vomir, rendre.

brink [brɪŋk] n bord m; **on the ~ of doing** sur le point de faire, à deux doigts de faire; **she was on the ~ of tears** elle était au bord des larmes.

brisk [brɪsk] a vif(vive); (abrupt) brusque; (trade etc) actif(ive); **to go for a ~ walk** se promener d'un bon pas; **business is ~** les affaires marchent (bien).

bristle [ˈbrɪsl] n poil m ♦ vi se hérisser; **bristling with** hérissé(e) de.

bristly [ˈbrɪslɪ] a (beard, hair) hérissé(e); **your chin's all ~** ton menton gratte.

Brit [brɪt] n abbr (col: = British person) Britannique m/f.

Britain [ˈbrɪtən] n (also: **Great ~**) la Grande-Bretagne; **in ~** en Grande-Bretagne.

British [ˈbrɪtɪʃ] a britannique; **the ~** npl les Britanniques mpl; **the ~ Isles** les îles fpl Britanniques.

British Rail (BR) n compagnie ferroviaire britannique, ≈ SNCF f.

Briton [ˈbrɪtən] n Britannique m/f.

Brittany [ˈbrɪtənɪ] n Bretagne f.

brittle [ˈbrɪtl] a cassant(e), fragile.

Br(o). abbr (REL) = **brother.**

broach [brəutʃ] vt (subject) aborder.

broad [brɔːd] a large; (distinction) général(e); (accent) prononcé(e) ♦ n (US col) nana f; **~ hint** allusion transparente; **in ~ daylight** en plein jour; **the ~ outlines** les grandes lignes.

broad bean n fève f.

broadcast [ˈbrɔːdkɑːst] n émission f ♦ vb (pt, pp **broadcast**) vt radiodiffuser; téléviser ♦ vi émettre.

broadcasting [ˈbrɔːdkɑːstɪŋ] n radiodiffusion f; télévision f.

broadcasting station n station f de radio (or de télévision).

broaden [ˈbrɔːdn] vt élargir ♦ vi s'élargir.

broadly [ˈbrɔːdlɪ] ad en gros, généralement.

broad-minded [ˈbrɔːdˈmaɪndɪd] a large d'esprit.

broccoli [ˈbrɔkəlɪ] n brocoli m.

brochure [ˈbrəuʃjuə*] n prospectus m, dépliant m.

brogue [brəug] n (accent) accent régional; (shoe) (sorte de) chaussure basse de cuir épais.

broil [brɔɪl] vt rôtir.

broiler [ˈbrɔɪlə*] n (fowl) poulet m (à rôtir).

broke [brəuk] pt of **break** ♦ a (col) fauché(e); **to go ~** (business) faire faillite.

broken [ˈbrəukn] pp of **break** ♦ a (stick, leg etc) cassé(e); (promise, vow) rompu(e); **a ~ marriage** un couple dissocié; **a ~ home** un foyer désuni; **in ~ French/English** dans un français/anglais approximatif or hésitant.

broken-down [ˈbrəuknˈdaun] a (car) en panne; (machine) fichu(e); (house) en ruines.

broken-hearted [ˈbrəuknˈhɑːtɪd] a (ayant) le cœur brisé.

broker [ˈbrəukə*] n courtier m.

brokerage [ˈbrəukrɪdʒ] n courtage m.

brolly [ˈbrɔlɪ] n (Brit col) pépin m, parapluie m.

bronchitis [brɔŋˈkaɪtɪs] n bronchite f.

bronze [brɔnz] n bronze m.

bronzed [brɔnzd] a bronzé(e), hâlé(e).

brooch [brəutʃ] n broche f.

brood [bruːd] n couvée f ♦ vi (hen, storm) couver; (person) méditer (sombrement), ruminer.

broody [ˈbruːdɪ] a (fig) taciturne, mélancolique.

brook [bruk] n ruisseau m.

broom [brum] n balai m.

broomstick [ˈbrumstɪk] n manche m à balai.

Bros. abbr (COMM: = brothers) Frères.

broth [brɔθ] n bouillon m de viande et de légumes.

brothel [ˈbrɔθl] n maison close, bordel m.

brother [ˈbrʌðə*] n frère m.

brotherhood [ˈbrʌðəhud] n fraternité f.

brother-in-law [ˈbrʌðərɪnˈlɔː*] n beau-frère m.

brotherly [ˈbrʌðəlɪ] a fraternel(le).

brought [brɔːt] pt, pp of **bring.**

brow [brau] n front m; (rare: gen: **eye~**) sourcil m; (of hill) sommet m.

browbeat [ˈbraubiːt] vt intimider, brusquer.

brown [braun] a brun(e), marron inv; (hair) châtain inv; (rice, bread, flour) complet(ète) ♦ n (colour) brun m, marron m ♦ vt brunir;

(*CULIN*) faire dorer, faire roussir; **to go ~** (*person*) bronzer; (*leaves*) jaunir.

brownie ['braunɪ] n jeannette f, éclaireuse (cadette).

brown paper n papier m d'emballage, papier kraft.

brown sugar n cassonade f.

browse [brauz] vi (*among books*) bouquiner, feuilleter les livres; (*animal*) paître; **to ~ through a book** feuilleter un livre.

bruise [bru:z] n bleu m, ecchymose f, contusion f ♦ vt contusionner, meurtrir ♦ vi (*fruit*) se taler, se meurtrir; **to ~ one's arm** se faire un bleu au bras.

Brum [brʌm] n abbr, **Brummagem** ['brʌmədʒəm] n (*col*) = Birmingham.

Brummie ['brʌmɪ] n (*col*) habitant/e de Birmingham; natif/ive de Birmingham.

brunch [brʌntʃ] n brunch m.

brunette [bru:'net] n (*femme*) brune.

brunt [brʌnt] n: **the ~ of** (*attack, criticism etc*) le plus gros de.

brush [brʌʃ] n brosse f; (*quarrel*) accrochage m, prise f de bec ♦ vt brosser; (*also*: **~ past, ~ against**) effleurer, frôler; **to have a ~ with sb** s'accrocher avec qn; **to have a ~ with the police** avoir maille à partir avec la police.

brush aside vt écarter, balayer.

brush up vt (*knowledge*) rafraîchir, réviser.

brushed [brʌʃt] a (*TECH*: *steel, chrome etc*) brossé(e); (*nylon, denim etc*) gratté(e).

brush-off ['brʌʃɔf] n (*col*): **to give sb the ~** envoyer qn promener.

brushwood ['brʌʃwud] n broussailles fpl, taillis m.

brusque [bru:sk] a (*person, manner*) brusque, cassant(e); (*tone*) sec(sèche), cassant(e).

Brussels ['brʌslz] n Bruxelles.

Brussels sprout n chou m de Bruxelles.

brutal ['bru:tl] a brutal(e).

brutality [bru:'tælɪtɪ] n brutalité f.

brute [bru:t] n brute f ♦ a: **by ~ force** par la force.

brutish ['bru:tɪʃ] a grossier(ère), brutal(e).

BS n abbr (*US*: = *Bachelor of Science*) diplôme universitaire.

bs abbr = **bill of sale**.

BSA n abbr = *Boy Scouts of America*.

BSc n abbr = **Bachelor of Science**.

BSI n abbr (= *British Standards Institution*) association de normalisation.

BST abbr (= *British Summer Time*) heure f d'été.

Bt. abbr (*Brit*) = baronet.

btu n abbr (= *British thermal unit*) btu (= 1054,2 joules).

bubble ['bʌbl] n bulle f ♦ vi bouillonner, faire des bulles; (*sparkle, fig*) pétiller.

bubble bath n bain moussant.

Bucharest [bu:kə'rest] n Bucarest.

buck [bʌk] n mâle m (*d'un lapin, lièvre, daim etc*); (*US col*) dollar m ♦ vi ruer, lancer une ruade; **to pass the ~ (to sb)** se décharger de la responsabilité (sur qn).

buck up vi (*cheer up*) reprendre du poil de la bête, se remonter ♦ vt: **to ~ one's ideas up** se reprendre.

bucket ['bʌkɪt] n seau m ♦ vi (*Brit col*): **the rain is ~ing (down)** il pleut à verse.

buckle ['bʌkl] n boucle f ♦ vt boucler, attacher; (*warp*) tordre, gauchir; (: *wheel*) voiler.

buckle down vi s'y mettre.

Bucks [bʌks] abbr (*Brit*) = *Buckinghamshire*.

bud [bʌd] n bourgeon m; (*of flower*) bouton m ♦ vi bourgeonner; (*flower*) éclore.

Budapest [bju:də'pest] n Budapest.

Buddha ['budə] n Bouddha m.

Buddhism ['budɪzəm] n bouddhisme m.

Buddhist ['budɪst] a bouddhiste ♦ n Bouddhiste m/f.

budding ['bʌdɪŋ] a (*flower*) en bouton; (*poet etc*) en herbe; (*passion etc*) naissant(e).

buddy ['bʌdɪ] n (*US*) copain m.

budge [bʌdʒ] vt faire bouger ♦ vi bouger.

budgerigar ['bʌdʒərɪgɑ:*] n perruche f.

budget ['bʌdʒɪt] n budget m ♦ vi: **to ~ for sth** inscrire qch au budget; **I'm on a tight ~** je dois faire attention à mon budget.

budgie ['bʌdʒɪ] n = **budgerigar**.

Buenos Aires ['bweɪnɒs'aɪrɪz] n Buenos Aires.

buff [bʌf] a (*couleur f*) chamois m ♦ n (*enthusiast*) mordu/e.

buffalo, pl ~ or ~es ['bʌfələu] n buffle m; (*US*) bison m.

buffer ['bʌfə*] n tampon m; (*COMPUT*) mémoire f tampon.

buffering ['bʌfərɪŋ] n (*COMPUT*) mise f en mémoire tampon.

buffer state n état m tampon.

buffet n ['bufeɪ] (*food, Brit: bar*) buffet m ♦ vt ['bʌfɪt] gifler, frapper; secouer, ébranler.

buffet car n (*Brit RAIL*) voiture-bar f.

buffet lunch n lunch m.

buffoon [bə'fu:n] n buffon m, pitre m.

bug [bʌg] n (*insect*) punaise f; (: *gen*) insecte m, bestiole f; (*fig: germ*) virus m, microbe m; (*spy device*) dispositif m d'écoute (électronique), micro clandestin; (*COMPUT: of program*) erreur f; (: *of equipment*) défaut m ♦ vt (*room*) poser des micros dans; (*col: annoy*) embêter; **I've got the travel ~** (*fig*) j'ai le virus du voyage.

bugbear ['bʌgbeə*] n cauchemar m, bête noire.

bugger ['bʌgə*] (*col!*) n salaud m (!); connard m (!) ♦ vb: **~ off!** tire-toi! (!); **~ (it)!** merde! (!).

bugle ['bju:gl] n clairon m.

build [bɪld] n (*of person*) carrure f, charpente f ♦ vt (pt, pp **built** [bɪlt]) construire, bâtir.

build on vt fus (*fig*) tirer parti de, partir de.

build up vt accumuler, amasser; (*business*) développer; (*reputation*) bâtir; (*increase: production*) développer, accroître.

builder ['bɪldə*] n entrepreneur m.

building ['bɪldɪŋ] n construction f; (*structure*) bâtiment m, construction; (: *residential, offices*) immeuble m.

building contractor n entrepreneur m (en bâtiment).

building industry n (industrie f du) bâtiment m.

building site n chantier m (de construction).

building society n (*Brit*) société f de crédit

immobilier.

building trade n = **building industry**.

build-up ['bɪldʌp] n (of gas etc) accumulation f; (publicity): **to give sb/sth a good ~** faire de la pub pour qn/qch.

built [bɪlt] pt, pp of **build**.

built-in ['bɪlt'ɪn] a (cupboard) encastré(e); (device) incorporé(e); intégré(e).

built-up area ['bɪltʌp-] n agglomération (urbaine); zone urbanisée.

bulb [bʌlb] n (BOT) bulbe m, oignon m; (ELEC) ampoule f.

bulbous ['bʌlbəs] a bulbeux(euse).

Bulgaria [bʌl'gɛərɪə] n Bulgarie f.

Bulgarian [bʌl'gɛərɪən] a bulgare ♦ n Bulgare m/f; (LING) bulgare m.

bulge [bʌldʒ] n renflement m, gonflement m; (in birth rate, sales) brusque augmentation f ♦ vi faire saillie; présenter un renflement; **to be bulging with** être plein(e) à craquer de.

bulk [bʌlk] n masse f, volume m; **in ~** (COMM) en gros, en vrac; **the ~ of** la plus grande or grosse partie de.

bulk buying n achat m en gros.

bulkhead ['bʌlkhɛd] n cloison f (étanche).

bulky ['bʌlkɪ] a volumineux(euse), encombrant(e).

bull [bul] n taureau m; (STOCK EXCHANGE) haussier m; (REL) bulle f.

bulldog ['buldɔg] n bouledogue m.

bulldoze ['buldəuz] vt passer or raser au bulldozer; **I was ~d into doing it** (fig: col) on m'a forcé la main.

bulldozer ['buldəuzə*] n bulldozer m.

bullet ['bulɪt] n balle f (de fusil etc).

bulletin ['bulɪtɪn] n bulletin m, communiqué m.

bulletin board n (COMPUT) messagerie f (électronique).

bulletproof ['bulɪtpruːf] a à l'épreuve des balles; **~ vest** gilet m pare-balles.

bullfight ['bulfaɪt] n corrida f, course f de taureaux.

bullfighter ['bulfaɪtə*] n torero m.

bullfighting ['bulfaɪtɪŋ] n tauromachie f.

bullion ['buljən] n or m or argent m en lingots.

bullock ['bulək] n bœuf m.

bullring ['bulrɪŋ] n arène f.

bull's-eye ['bulzaɪ] n centre m (de la cible).

bully ['bulɪ] n brute f, tyran m ♦ vt tyranniser, rudoyer; (frighten) intimider.

bullying ['bulɪɪŋ] n brimades fpl.

bum [bʌm] n (col: backside) derrière m; (: tramp) vagabond/e, traîne-savates m/f inv; (: idler) glandeur m.

bum around vi (col) vagabonder.

bumblebee ['bʌmblbiː] n bourdon m.

bumf [bʌmf] n (col: forms etc) paperasses fpl.

bump [bʌmp] n (blow) coup m, choc m; (jolt) cahot m; (on road etc, on head) bosse f ♦ vt heurter, cogner; (car) emboutir.

bump along vi avancer en cahotant.

bump into vt fus rentrer dans, tamponner; (col: meet) tomber sur.

bumper ['bʌmpə*] n pare-chocs m inv ♦ a: **~ crop/harvest** récolte/moisson exceptionnelle.

bumper cars npl (US) autos tamponneuses.

bumph [bʌmf] n = **bumf**.

bumptious ['bʌmpʃəs] a suffisant(e), pré-

tentieux(euse).

bumpy ['bʌmpɪ] a cahoteux(euse); **it was a ~ flight/ride** on a été secoués dans l'avion/la voiture.

bun [bʌn] n petit pain au lait; (of hair) chignon m.

bunch [bʌntʃ] n (of flowers) bouquet m; (of keys) trousseau m; (of bananas) régime m; (of people) groupe m; **~ of grapes** grappe f de raisin.

bundle ['bʌndl] n paquet m ♦ vt (also: ~ up) faire un paquet de; (put): **to ~ sth/sb into** fourrer or enfourner qch/qn dans.

bundle off vt (person) faire sortir (en toute hâte); expédier.

bundle out vt éjecter, sortir (sans ménagements).

bun fight n (Brit col) réception f; (tea party) thé m.

bung [bʌŋ] n bonde f, bouchon m ♦ vt (Brit: throw: also: ~ into) flanquer; (also: ~ up: pipe, hole) boucher; **my nose is ~ed up** j'ai le nez bouché.

bungalow ['bʌŋgələu] n bungalow m.

bungle ['bʌŋgl] vt bâcler, gâcher.

bunion ['bʌnjən] n oignon m (au pied).

bunk [bʌŋk] n couchette f.

bunk beds npl lits superposés.

bunker ['bʌŋkə*] n (coal store) soute f à charbon; (MIL, GOLF) bunker m.

bunny ['bʌnɪ] n (also: ~ rabbit) Jeannot m lapin.

bunny girl n (Brit) hôtesse de cabaret.

bunny hill n (US SKI) piste f pour débutants.

bunting ['bʌntɪŋ] n pavoisement m, drapeaux mpl.

buoy [bɔɪ] n bouée f.

buoy up vt faire flotter; (fig) soutenir, épauler.

buoyancy ['bɔɪənsɪ] n (of ship) flottabilité f.

buoyant ['bɔɪənt] a (ship) flottable; (carefree) gai(e), plein(e) d'entrain; (COMM: market) actif(ive); (: prices, currency) soutenu(e).

burden ['bəːdn] n fardeau m, charge f ♦ vt charger; (oppress) accabler, surcharger; **to be a ~ to sb** être un fardeau pour qn.

bureau, pl **~x** ['bjuərəu, -z] n (Brit: writing desk) bureau m, secrétaire m; (US: chest of drawers) commode f; (office) bureau, office m.

bureaucracy [bjuə'rɔkrəsɪ] n bureaucratie f.

bureaucrat ['bjuərəkræt] n bureaucrate m/f, rond-de-cuir m.

bureaucratic [bjuərə'krætɪk] a bureaucratique.

burgeon ['bəːdʒən] vi (fig) être en expansion rapide.

burglar ['bəːglə*] n cambrioleur m.

burglar alarm n sonnerie f d'alarme.

burglarize ['bəːgləraɪz] vt (US) cambrioler.

burglary ['bəːglərɪ] n cambriolage m.

burgle ['bəːgl] vt cambrioler.

Burgundy ['bəːgəndɪ] n Bourgogne f.

burial ['bɛrɪəl] n enterrement m.

burial ground n cimetière m.

burlesque [bəː'lɛsk] n caricature f, parodie f.

burly ['bəːlɪ] a de forte carrure, costaud(e).

Burma ['bəːmə] n Birmanie f.

Burmese [bəː'miːz] a birman(e), de Birmanie ♦ n (pl inv) Birman/e; (LING) birman m.

burn [bəːn] *vt, vi* (*pt, pp* **burned** *or* **burnt** [bəːnt]) brûler ♦ *n* brûlure *f*; **the cigarette ~t a hole in her dress** la cigarette a fait un trou dans sa robe; **I've ~t myself!** je me suis brûlé(e)!
burn down *vt* incendier, détruire par le feu.
burn out *vt* (*subj: writer etc*): **to ~ o.s. out** s'user (à force de travailler).
burner ['bəːnə*] *n* brûleur *m*.
burning ['bəːnɪŋ] *a* (*building, forest*) en flammes; (*issue, question*) brûlant(e).
burnish ['bəːnɪʃ] *vt* polir.
burnt [bəːnt] *pt, pp* of **burn**.
burnt sugar *n* (*Brit*) caramel *m*.
burp [bəːp] (*col*) *n* rot *m* ♦ *vi* roter.
burrow ['bʌrəu] *n* terrier *m* ♦ *vt* creuser.
bursar ['bəːsə*] *n* économe *m/f*; (*Brit: student*) boursier/ère.
bursary ['bəːsərɪ] *n* (*Brit*) bourse *f* (d'études).
burst [bəːst] *vb* (*pt, pp* **burst**) *vt* faire éclater ♦ *vi* éclater ♦ *n* explosion *f*; (*also: ~ pipe*) fuite *f* (*due à une rupture*); **~ of energy** déploiement soudain d'énergie, activité soudaine; **~ of laughter** éclat *m* de rire; **a ~ of applause** une salve d'applaudissement; **a ~ of speed** une pointe de vitesse; **~ blood vessel** rupture *f* de vaisseau sanguin; **the river has ~ its banks** le cours d'eau est sorti de son lit; **to ~ into flames** s'enflammer soudainement; **to ~ out laughing** éclater de rire; **to ~ into tears** fondre en larmes; **to ~ open** *vi* s'ouvrir violemment *or* soudainement; **to be ~ing with** être plein(e) (à craquer) de; regorger de.
burst into *vt fus* (*room etc*) faire irruption dans.
burst out of *vt fus* sortir précipitamment de.
bury ['bɛrɪ] *vt* enterrer; **to ~ one's face in one's hands** se couvrir le visage de ses mains; **to ~ one's head in the sand** (*fig*) pratiquer la politique de l'autruche; **to ~ the hatchet** (*fig*) enterrer la hache de guerre.
bus, ~es [bʌs, 'bʌsɪz] *n* autobus *m*.
bush [buʃ] *n* buisson *m*; (*scrub land*) brousse *f*.
bushel ['buʃl] *n* boisseau *m*.
bushy ['buʃɪ] *a* broussailleux(euse), touffu(e).
busily ['bɪzɪlɪ] *ad*: **to be ~ doing sth** s'affairer à faire qch.
business ['bɪznɪs] *n* (*matter, firm*) affaire *f*; (*trading*) affaires *fpl*; (*job, duty*) travail *m*; **to be away on ~** être en déplacement d'affaires; **I'm here on ~** je suis là pour affaires; **he's in the insurance/transport ~** il est dans les assurances/les transports; **to do ~ with sb** traiter avec qn; **it's none of my ~** cela ne me regarde pas, ce ne sont pas mes affaires; **he means ~** il ne plaisante pas, il est sérieux.
business address *n* adresse professionnelle *or* au bureau.
business card *n* carte *f* de visite (professionnelle).
businesslike ['bɪznɪslaɪk] *a* sérieux(euse); efficace.
businessman ['bɪznɪsmən] *n* homme *m* d'affaires.

business trip *n* voyage *m* d'affaires.
businesswoman ['bɪznɪswumən] *n* femme *f* d'affaires.
busker ['bʌskə*] *n* (*Brit*) artiste ambulant(e).
bus lane *n* (*Brit*) voie réservée aux autobus.
bus shelter *n* abribus *m*.
bus station *n* gare routière.
bus stop *n* arrêt *m* d'autobus.
bust [bʌst] *n* buste *m* ♦ *a* (*col: broken*) fichu(e), fini(e) ♦ *vt* (*col: POLICE: arrest*) pincer; **to go ~** faire faillite.
bustle ['bʌsl] *n* remue-ménage *m*, affairement *m* ♦ *vi* s'affairer, se démener.
bustling ['bʌslɪŋ] *a* (*person*) affairé(e); (*town*) très animé(e).
bust-up ['bʌstʌp] *n* (*Brit col*) engueulade *f*.
busy ['bɪzɪ] *a* occupé(e); (*shop, street*) très fréquenté(e); (*US: telephone, line*) occupé ♦ *vt*: **to ~ o.s.** s'occuper; **he's a ~ man** (*normally*) c'est un homme très pris; (*temporarily*) il est très pris.
busybody ['bɪzɪbɒdɪ] *n* mouche *f* du coche, âme *f* charitable.
busy signal *n* (*US*) tonalité *f* occupé.
but [bʌt] *cj* mais ♦ *prep* excepté, sauf; **nothing ~** rien d'autre que; **~ for** sans, si ce n'était pour; **no one ~ him** lui seul; **the last ~ one** (*Brit*) l'avant-dernier(ère); **all ~ finished** pratiquement fini; **anything ~ finished** tout sauf fini, très loin d'être fini.
butane ['bjuːteɪn] *n* (*also: ~ gas*) butane *m*.
butcher ['butʃə*] *n* boucher *m* ♦ *vt* massacrer; (*cattle etc for meat*) tuer; **~'s (shop)** boucherie *f*.
butler ['bʌtlə*] *n* maître *m* d'hôtel.
butt [bʌt] *n* (*cask*) gros tonneau *m*; (*thick end*) (gros) bout; (*of gun*) crosse *f*; (*of cigarette*) mégot *m*; (*Brit fig: target*) cible *f* ♦ *vt* donner un coup de tête à.
butt in *vi* (*interrupt*) interrompre.
butter ['bʌtə*] *n* beurre *m* ♦ *vt* beurrer.
buttercup ['bʌtəkʌp] *n* bouton *m* d'or.
butter dish *n* beurrier *m*.
butterfingers ['bʌtəfɪŋɡəz] *n* (*col*) maladroit/e.
butterfly ['bʌtəflaɪ] *n* papillon *m*; (*SWIMMING: also: ~ stroke*) brasse *f* papillon.
buttocks ['bʌtəks] *npl* fesses *fpl*.
button ['bʌtn] *n* bouton *m* ♦ *vt* (*also: ~ up*) boutonner ♦ *vi* se boutonner.
buttonhole ['bʌtnhəul] *n* boutonnière *f* ♦ *vt* accrocher, arrêter, retenir.
buttress ['bʌtrɪs] *n* contrefort *m*.
buxom ['bʌksəm] *a* aux formes avantageuses *or* épanouies, bien galbé(e).
buy [baɪ] *vb* (*pt, pp* **bought** [bɔːt]) *vt* acheter; (*COMM: company*) (r)acheter ♦ *n*: **that was a good/bad ~** c'était un bon/mauvais achat; **to ~ sb sth/sth from sb** acheter qch à qn; **to ~ sb a drink** offrir un verre *or* à boire à qn.
buy back *vt* racheter.
buy in *vt* (*Brit: goods*) acheter, faire venir.
buy into *vt fus* (*Brit COMM*) acheter des actions de.
buy off *vt* (*bribe*) acheter.
buy out *vt* (*partner*) désintéresser; (*business*) racheter.
buy up *vt* acheter en bloc, rafler.

buyer ['baɪə*] *n* acheteur/euse; **~'s market** marché *m* favorable aux acheteurs.

buzz [bʌz] *n* bourdonnement *m*; (*col: phone call*) coup *m* de fil ♦ *vi* bourdonner ♦ *vt* (*call on intercom*) appeler; (*with buzzer*) sonner; (*AVIAT: plane, building*) raser; **my head is ~ing** j'ai la tête qui bourdonne.
  buzz off *vi* (*col*) s'en aller, ficher le camp.

buzzard ['bʌzəd] *n* buse *f*.

buzzer ['bʌzə*] *n* timbre *m* électrique.

buzz word *n* (*col*) mot *m* à la mode *or* dans le vent.

by [baɪ] *prep* par; (*beside*) à côté de; au bord de; (*before*): **~ 4 o'clock** avant 4 heures, d'ici 4 heures; **~ this time tomorrow** demain à la même heure ♦ *ad see* **pass, go** *etc*; **I picture ~ Picasso** un tableau de Picasso; **surrounded ~ enemies** entouré d'ennemis; **~ bus/car** en autobus/voiture; **paid ~ the hour** payé à l'heure; **to increase** *etc* **~ the hour** augmenter d'heure en heure; **~ the kilo/metre** au kilo/mètre; **to pay ~ cheque** payer par chèque; **a room 3 metres ~ 4** une pièce de 3 mètres sur 4; **the bullet missed him ~ inches** la balle est passée à quelques centimètres de lui; **~ saving hard, he ...** à force d'économiser, il ...; (**all**) **~ oneself** tout(e) seul(e); **~ the way** à propos; **~ and large** dans l'ensemble; **~ and ~** bientôt.

bye(-bye) ['baɪ('baɪ)] *excl* au revoir!, salut!

by(e)-law ['baɪlɔ:] *n* arrêté municipal.

by-election ['baɪɪlekʃən] *n* (*Brit*) élection (législative) partielle.

bygone ['baɪgɔn] *a* passé(e) ♦ *n*: **let ~s be ~s** passons l'éponge, oublions le passé.

bypass ['baɪpɑ:s] *n* (*route f de*) contournement *m*; (*MED*) pontage *m* ♦ *vt* éviter.

by-product ['baɪprɔdʌkt] *n* sous-produit *m*, dérivé *m*; (*fig*) conséquence *f* secondaire, retombée *f*.

byre ['baɪə*] *n* (*Brit*) étable *f* (à vaches).

bystander ['baɪstændə*] *n* spectateur/trice, badaud/e.

byte [baɪt] *n* (*COMPUT*) octet *m*.

byway ['baɪweɪ] *n* chemin détourné.

byword ['baɪwə:d] *n*: **to be a ~ for** être synonyme de (*fig*).

by-your-leave ['baɪjɔ:'li:v] *n*: **without so much as a ~** sans même demander la permission.

C

C, c [si:] *n* (*letter*) C, c *m*; (*SCOL: mark*) C; (*MUS*): **C** do *m*; **C for Charlie** C comme Célestin.

C *abbr* (= *Celsius, centigrade*) C.

c *abbr* (= *century*) s.; (= *circa*) v.; (*US etc*) = **cent(s)**.

CA *n abbr* = **Central America**; (*Brit*) = **chartered accountant** ♦ *abbr* (*US POST*) = *California*.

ca. *abbr* (= *circa*) v.

c/a *abbr* = **capital account, credit account, current account.**

CAA *n abbr* (*Brit*: = *Civil Aviation Authority*, *US*: = *Civil Aeronautics Authority*) direction de l'aviation civile.

CAB *n abbr* (*Brit*: = *Citizens' Advice Bureau*) service d'information du consommateur.

cab [kæb] *n* taxi *m*; (*of train, truck*) cabine *f*; (*horse-drawn*) fiacre *m*.

cabaret ['kæbəreɪ] *n* attractions *fpl*, spectacle *m* de cabaret.

cabbage ['kæbɪdʒ] *n* chou *m*.

cabin ['kæbɪn] *n* cabane *f*, hutte *f*; (*on ship*) cabine *f*.

cabin cruiser *n* yacht *m* (à moteur).

cabinet ['kæbɪnɪt] *n* (*POL*) cabinet *m*; (*furniture*) petit meuble à tiroirs et rayons; (*also*: **display ~**) vitrine *f*, petite armoire vitrée.

cabinet-maker ['kæbɪnɪt'meɪkə*] *n* ébéniste *m*.

cabinet minister *n* ministre *m* (*membre du cabinet*).

cable ['keɪbl] *n* câble *m* ♦ *vt* câbler, télégraphier.

cable-car ['keɪblkɑ:*] *n* téléphérique *m*.

cablegram ['keɪblgræm] *n* câblogramme *m*.

cable railway *n* (*Brit*) funiculaire *m*.

cable television *n* télévision *f* par câble.

cache [kæʃ] *n* cachette *f*; **a ~ of food** *etc* un dépôt secret de provisions *etc*, une cachette contenant des provisions *etc*.

cackle ['kækl] *vi* caqueter.

cactus, pl cacti ['kæktəs, -taɪ] *n* cactus *m*.

CAD *n abbr* (= *computer-aided design*) CAO *f*.

caddie ['kædɪ] *n* caddie *m*.

caddy ['kædɪ] *n* caddie *m*.

cadet [kə'det] *n* (*MIL*) élève *m* officier; **police ~** élève agent de police.

cadge [kædʒ] *vt* (*col*) se faire donner; **to ~ a meal (off sb)** se faire inviter à manger (par qn).

cadger ['kædʒə*] *n* pique-assiette *m/f inv*, tapeur/euse.

cadre ['kædrɪ] *n* cadre *m*.

Caesarean, (*US*) **Cesarean** [si:'zɛərɪən] *a*: **~ (section)** césarienne *f*.

CAF *abbr* (*Brit*: = *cost and freight*) C et F.

café ['kæfeɪ] *n* ≈ café(-restaurant) *m* (*sans alcool*).

cafeteria [kæfɪ'tɪərɪə] *n* cafeteria *f*.

caffein(e) ['kæfi:n] *n* caféine *f*.

cage [keɪdʒ] *n* cage *f* ♦ *vt* mettre en cage.

cagey ['keɪdʒɪ] *a* (*col*) réticent(e); méfiant(e).

cagoule [kə'gu:l] *n* K-way *m* ®.

CAI *n abbr* (= *computer-aided instruction*) EAO *m*.

Cairo ['kaɪərəu] *n* le Caire.

cajole [kə'dʒəul] *vt* couvrir de flatteries *or* de gentillesses.

cake [keɪk] *n* gâteau *m*; **~ of soap** savonnette *f*; **it's a piece of ~** (*col*) c'est un jeu d'enfant; **he wants to have his ~ and eat it (too)** (*fig*) il veut tout avoir.

caked [keɪkt] *a*: **~ with** raidi(e) par, couvert(e) d'une croûte de.

cake shop *n* pâtisserie *f*.

calamitous [kə'læmɪtəs] *a* catastrophique, désastreux(euse).

calamity [kə'læmɪtɪ] n calamité f, désastre m.
calcium ['kælsɪəm] n calcium m.
calculate ['kælkjuleɪt] vt calculer; (estimate: chances, effect) évaluer.
   calculate on vt fus: **to ~ on** sth/on doing sth compter sur qch/faire qch.
calculated ['kælkjuleɪtɪd] a (insult, action) délibéré(e); **a ~ risk** un risque pris en toute connaissance de cause.
calculating ['kælkjuleɪtɪŋ] a calculateur(trice).
calculation [kælkju'leɪʃən] n calcul m.
calculator ['kælkjuleɪtə*] n machine f à calculer, calculatrice f.
calculus ['kælkjuləs] n analyse f (mathématique), calcul infinitésimal; **integral/differential ~** calcul intégral/différentiel.
calendar ['kæləndə*] n calendrier m.
calendar month n mois m (de calendrier).
calendar year n année civile.
calf, pl **calves** [kɑ:f, kɑ:vz] n (of cow) veau m; (of other animals) petit m; (also: ~skin) veau m, vachette f; (ANAT) mollet m.
caliber ['kælɪbə*] n (US) = **calibre**.
calibrate ['kælɪbreɪt] vt (gun etc) calibrer; (scale of measuring instrument) étalonner.
calibre, (US) **caliber** ['kælɪbə*] n calibre m.
calico ['kælɪkəu] n (Brit) calicot m; (US) indienne f.
California [kælɪ'fɔ:nɪə] n Californie f.
calipers ['kælɪpəz] npl (US) = **callipers**.
call [kɔ:l] vt (gen, also TEL) appeler; (announce: flight) annoncer; (meeting) convoquer; (strike) lancer ♦ vi appeler; (visit: also: **~ in, ~ round**): **to ~ (for)** passer (prendre) ♦ n (shout) appel m, cri m; (summons: for flight etc, fig: lure) appel; (visit) visite f; (also: **telephone ~**) coup m de téléphone; communication f; **to be on ~** être de permanence; **she's ~ed Suzanne** elle s'appelle Suzanne; **who is ~ing?** (TEL) qui est à l'appareil?; **London ~ing** (RADIO) ici Londres; **please give me a ~ at 7** appelez-moi à 7 heures; **to make a ~** téléphoner, passer un coup de fil; **to pay a ~ on sb** rendre visite à qn, passer voir qn; **there's not much ~ for these items** ces articles ne sont pas très demandés.
   call at vt fus (subj: ship) faire escale à; (: train) s'arrêter à.
   call back vi (return) repasser; (TEL) rappeler ♦ vt (TEL) rappeler.
   call for vt fus demander.
   call in vt (doctor, expert, police) appeler, faire venir.
   call off vt annuler; **the strike was ~ed off** l'ordre de grève a été rapporté.
   call on vt fus (visit) rendre visite à, passer voir; (request): **to ~ on sb to do** inviter qn à faire.
   call out vi pousser un cri or des cris ♦ vt (doctor, police, troops) appeler.
   call up vt (MIL) appeler, mobiliser.
callbox ['kɔ:lbɔks] n (Brit) cabine f téléphonique.
caller ['kɔ:lə*] n personne f qui appelle, visiteur m; **hold the line, ~!** (TEL) ne quittez pas, Monsieur (or Madame)!
call girl n call-girl f.
call-in ['kɔ:lɪn] n (US RADIO, TV) programme

m à ligne ouverte.
calling ['kɔ:lɪŋ] n vocation f; (trade, occupation) état m.
calling card n (US) carte f de visite.
callipers, (US) **calipers** ['kælɪpəz] npl (MATH) compas m; (MED) appareil m orthopédique; gouttière f; étrier m.
callous ['kæləs] a dur(e), insensible.
callousness ['kæləsnɪs] n dureté f, manque m de cœur, insensibilité f.
callow ['kæləu] a sans expérience (de la vie).
calm [kɑ:m] a calme ♦ n calme m ♦ vt calmer, apaiser.
   calm down vi se calmer, s'apaiser ♦ vt calmer, apaiser.
calmly ['kɑ:mlɪ] ad calmement, avec calme.
calmness ['kɑ:mnɪs] n calme m.
Calor gas ['kælə*-] n ® (Brit) butane m, butagaz m ®.
calorie ['kælərɪ] n calorie f; **low ~ product** produit m pauvre en calories.
calve [kɑ:v] vi vêler, mettre bas.
calves [kɑ:vz] npl of **calf**.
CAM n abbr (= computer-aided manufacturing) FAO f.
camber ['kæmbə*] n (of road) bombement m.
Cambodia [kæm'bəudjə] n Cambodge m.
Cambodian [kæm'bəudɪən] a cambodgien(ne) ♦ n Cambodgien/ne.
Cambs abbr (Brit) = Cambridgeshire.
came [keɪm] pt of **come**.
camel ['kæməl] n chameau m.
cameo ['kæmɪəu] n camée m.
camera ['kæmərə] n appareil-photo m; (CINEMA, TV) caméra f; **35mm ~** appareil 24 x 36 or petit format; **in ~** à huis clos, en privé.
cameraman ['kæmərəmæn] n caméraman m.
Cameroon, Cameroun [kæmə'ru:n] n Cameroun m.
camouflage ['kæməflɑ:ʒ] n camouflage m ♦ vt camoufler.
camp [kæmp] n camp m ♦ vi camper; **to go ~ing** faire du camping.
campaign [kæm'peɪn] n (MIL, POL etc) campagne f ♦ vi (also fig) faire campagne; **to ~ for/against** militer pour/contre.
campaigner [kæm'peɪnə*] n: **~ for** partisan/e de; **~ against** opposant/e à.
campbed ['kæmp'bed] n (Brit) lit m de camp.
camper ['kæmpə*] n campeur/euse.
camping ['kæmpɪŋ] n camping m.
camp(ing) site n (terrain m de) camping m.
campus ['kæmpəs] n campus m.
camshaft ['kæmʃɑ:ft] n arbre m à came.
can [kæn] auxiliary vb see next headword ♦ n (of milk, oil, water) bidon m; (tin) boîte f (de conserve) ♦ vt mettre en conserve; **a ~ of beer** une canette de bière; **he had to carry the ~** (Brit col) on lui a fait porter le chapeau.
can [kæn] n, vt see previous headword ♦ auxiliary vb (gen) pouvoir; (know how to) savoir; **I ~ swim** etc je sais nager etc; **I ~ speak French** je parle français; **I ~'t see you** je ne vous vois pas; **could I have a word with you?** est-ce que je pourrais vous parler un instant?; **he could be in the library** il est peut-être dans la bibliothèque; **they could**

have forgotten ils ont pu oublier.
Canada ['kænədə] n Canada m.
Canadian [kə'neɪdɪən] a canadien(ne) ♦ n Canadien/ne.
canal [kə'næl] n canal m.
canary [kə'nɛərɪ] n canari m, serin m.
Canary Islands, Canaries [kə'nɛərɪz] npl: **the ~** les (îles fpl) Canaries fpl.
Canberra ['kænbərə] n Canberra.
cancel ['kænsəl] vt annuler; (train) supprimer; (party, appointment) décommander; (cross out) barrer, rayer; (stamp) oblitérer; (cheque) faire opposition à.
cancel out vt annuler; **they ~ each other out** ils s'annulent.
cancellation [kænsə'leɪʃən] n annulation f; suppression f; oblitération f; (TOURISM) réservation annulée, client etc qui s'est décommandé.
cancer ['kænsə*] n cancer m; **C~** (sign) le Cancer; **to be C~** être du Cancer.
cancerous ['kænsrəs] a cancéreux(euse).
cancer patient n cancéreux/euse.
cancer research n recherche f contre le cancer.
C and F abbr (Brit: = cost and freight) C et F.
candid ['kændɪd] a (très) franc(franche), sincère.
candidacy ['kændɪdəsɪ] n candidature f.
candidate ['kændɪdeɪt] n candidat/e.
candidature ['kændɪdətʃə*] n (Brit) = **candidacy**.
candied ['kændɪd] a confit(e); **~ apple** (US) pomme caramélisée.
candle ['kændl] n bougie f; (of tallow) chandelle f; (in church) cierge m.
candlelight ['kændllaɪt] n: **by ~** à la lumière d'une bougie; (dinner) aux chandelles.
candlestick n (also: **candle holder**) bougeoir m; (bigger, ornate) chandelier m.
candour, (US) candor ['kændə*] a (grande) franchise or sincérité.
candy ['kændɪ] n sucre candi; (US) bonbon m.
candy-floss ['kændɪflɒs] n (Brit) barbe f à papa.
candy store n (US) confiserie f.
cane [keɪn] n canne f; (for baskets, chairs etc) rotin m ♦ vt (Brit SCOL) administrer des coups de bâton à.
canine ['keɪnaɪn] a canin(e).
canister ['kænɪstə*] n boîte f (gén en métal).
cannabis ['kænəbɪs] n (drug) cannabis m; (also: **~ plant**) chanvre indien.
canned ['kænd] a (food) en boîte, en conserve; (col: music) enregistré(e); (Brit col: drunk) bourré(e); (US col: worker) mis(e) à la porte.
cannibal ['kænɪbəl] n cannibale m/f, anthropophage m/f.
cannibalism ['kænɪbəlɪzəm] n cannibalisme m, anthropophagie f.
cannon, pl ~ or ~s ['kænən] n (gun) canon m.
cannonball ['kænənbɔ:l] n boulet m de canon.
cannon fodder n chair f à canon.
cannot ['kænɒt] = **can not**.
canny ['kænɪ] a madré(e), finaud(e).
canoe [kə'nu:] n pirogue f; (SPORT) canoë m.

canoeing [kə'nu:ɪŋ] n (sport) canoë m.
canoeist [kə'nu:ɪst] n canoéiste m/f.
canon ['kænən] n (clergyman) chanoine m; (standard) canon m.
canonize ['kænənaɪz] vt canoniser.
can opener [-'əupnə*] n ouvre-boîte m.
canopy ['kænəpɪ] n baldaquin m; dais m.
cant [kænt] n jargon m ♦ vt, vi pencher.
can't [kænt] = **can not**.
Cantab. abbr (Brit: = cantabrigiensis) = of Cambridge.
cantankerous [kæn'tæŋkərəs] a querelleur(euse), acariâtre.
canteen [kæn'ti:n] n cantine f; (Brit: of cutlery) ménagère f.
canter ['kæntə*] n petit galop ♦ vi aller au petit galop.
cantilever ['kæntɪli:və*] n porte-à-faux m inv.
canvas ['kænvəs] n (gen) toile f; **under ~** (camping) sous la tente; (NAUT) toutes voiles dehors.
canvass ['kænvəs] vt (POL: district) faire la tournée électorale dans; (: person) solliciter le suffrage de; (COMM: district) prospecter; (citizens, opinions) sonder.
canvasser ['kænvəsə*] n (POL) agent électoral; (COMM) démarcheur m.
canvassing ['kænvəsɪŋ] n (POL) prospection électorale, démarchage électoral; (COMM) démarchage, prospection.
canyon ['kænjən] n cañon m, gorge f (profonde).
CAP n abbr (= Common Agricultural Policy) PAC f.
cap [kæp] n casquette f; (for swimming) bonnet m de bain; (of pen) capuchon m; (of bottle) capsule f; (Brit: contraceptive: also: **Dutch ~**) diaphragme m; (: FOOTBALL) sélection f pour l'équipe nationale ♦ vt capsuler; (outdo) surpasser; **~ped with** coiffé(e) de; **and to ~ it all, he ...** (Brit) pour couronner le tout, il ....
capability [keɪpə'bɪlɪtɪ] n aptitude f, capacité f.
capable ['keɪpəbl] a capable; **~ of** (interpretation etc) susceptible de.
capacious [kə'peɪʃəs] a vaste.
capacity [kə'pæsɪtɪ] n (of container) capacité f, contenance f; (ability) aptitude f; **filled to ~** plein(e); **in his ~ as** en sa qualité de; **this work is beyond my ~** ce travail dépasse mes capacités; **in an advisory ~** à titre consultatif; **to work at full ~** travailler à plein rendement.
cape [keɪp] n (garment) cape f; (GEO) cap m.
Cape of Good Hope n cap m de Bonne Espérance.
caper ['keɪpə*] n (CULIN: also: **~s**) câpre f.
Cape Town n Le Cap.
capita ['kæpɪtə] see **per capita**.
capital ['kæpɪtl] n (also: **~ city**) capitale f; (money) capital m; (also: **~ letter**) majuscule f.
capital account n balance f des capitaux; (of country) compte capital.
capital allowance n provision f pour amortissement.
capital assets npl immobilisations fpl.
capital expenditure n dépenses fpl

d'équipement.
capital gains tax n impôt m sur les plus-values.
capital goods n biens mpl d'équipement.
capital-intensive ['kæpɪtlɪn'tɛnsɪv] a à forte proportion de capitaux.
capitalism ['kæpɪtəlɪzəm] n capitalisme m.
capitalist ['kæpɪtəlɪst] a, n capitaliste (m/f).
capitalize ['kæpɪtəlaɪz] vt (provide with capital) financer.
  capitalize on vt fus (fig) profiter de.
capital punishment n peine capitale.
capital transfer tax n (Brit) impôt m sur le transfert de propriété.
capitulate [kə'pɪtjuleɪt] vi capituler.
capitulation [kəpɪtju'leɪʃən] n capitulation f.
capricious [kə'prɪʃəs] a capricieux(euse), fantasque.
Capricorn ['kæprɪkɔːn] n le Capricorne; **to be ~** être du Capricorne.
caps [kæps] abbr = **capital letters.**
capsize [kæp'saɪz] vt faire chavirer ♦ vi chavirer.
capstan ['kæpstən] n cabestan m.
capsule ['kæpsjuːl] n capsule f.
Capt. abbr (= captain) Cne.
captain ['kæptɪn] n capitaine m ♦ vt commander, être le capitaine de.
caption ['kæpʃən] n légende f.
captivate ['kæptɪveɪt] vt captiver, fasciner.
captive ['kæptɪv] a, n captif(ive).
captivity [kæp'tɪvɪtɪ] n captivité f.
captor ['kæptə*] n (unlawful) ravisseur m; (lawful): **his ~s** les gens (or ceux etc) qui l'ont arrêté.
capture ['kæptʃə*] vt capturer, prendre; (attention) capter ♦ n capture f.
car [kɑː*] n voiture f, auto f; (US RAIL) wagon m, voiture; **by ~** en voiture.
Caracas [kə'rækəs] n Caracas.
carafe [kə'ræf] n carafe f.
carafe wine n (in restaurant) ≈ vin ouvert.
caramel ['kærəməl] n caramel m.
carat ['kærət] n carat m; **18 ~ gold** or m à 18 carats.
caravan ['kærəvæn] n caravane f.
caravan site n (Brit) camping m pour caravanes.
caraway ['kærəweɪ] n: **~ seed** graine f de cumin, cumin m.
carbohydrates [kɑːbəu'haɪdreɪts] npl (foods) aliments mpl riches en hydrate de carbone.
carbolic acid [kɑː'bɔlɪk-] n phénol m.
carbon ['kɑːbən] n carbone m.
carbonated ['kɑːbəneɪtɪd] a (drink) gazeux(euse).
carbon copy n carbone m.
carbon dioxyde n gas m carbonique, dioxyde m de carbone.
carbon paper n papier m carbone.
carbon ribbon n ruban m carbone.
carburettor, (US) carburetor [kɑːbju'rɛtə*] n carburateur m.
carcass ['kɑːkəs] n carcasse f.
carcinogenic [kɑːsɪnə'dʒɛnɪk] a cancérigène.
card [kɑːd] n carte f; (membership ~) carte d'adhérent; **to play ~s** jouer aux cartes.
cardamom ['kɑːdəməm] n cardamome f.
cardboard ['kɑːdbɔːd] n carton m.

cardboard box n (boîte f en) carton m.
card-carrying member ['kɑː'd'kærɪŋ-] n membre actif.
card game n jeu m de cartes.
cardiac ['kɑːdɪæk] a cardiaque.
cardigan ['kɑːdɪgən] n cardigan m.
cardinal ['kɑːdɪnl] a cardinal(e) ♦ n cardinal m.
card index n fichier m (alphabétique).
Cards abbr (Brit) = Cardiganshire.
cardsharp ['kɑːdʃɑːp] n tricheur/euse professionnel(le).
card vote n (Brit) vote m de délégués.
CARE [kɛə*] n abbr (= Cooperative for American Relief Everywhere) association charitable.
care [kɛə*] n soin m, attention f; (worry) souci m ♦ vi: **to ~ about** se soucier de, s'intéresser à; **would you ~ to/for ...?** voulez-vous ...?; **I wouldn't ~ to do it** je n'aimerais pas le faire; **in sb's ~** à la garde de qn, confié à qn; **~ of (c/o)** (on letter) aux bons soins de; **"with ~"** "fragile"; **to take ~ (to do)** faire attention (à faire); **to take ~ of** vt s'occuper de, prendre soin de; (details, arrangements) s'occuper de; **the child has been taken into ~** l'enfant a été placé en institution; **I don't ~** ça m'est bien égal, peu m'importe; **I couldn't ~ less** cela m'est complètement égal, je m'en fiche complètement.
  care for vt fus s'occuper de; (like) aimer.
careen [kə'riːn] vi (ship) donner de la bande ♦ vt caréner, mettre en carène.
career [kə'rɪə*] n carrière f ♦ vi (also: **~ along**) aller à toute allure.
career girl n jeune fille f (or femme f) qui veut faire carrière.
careers officer n conseiller/ère d'orientation (professionnelle).
carefree ['kɛəfriː] a sans souci, insouciant(e).
careful ['kɛəful] a soigneux(euse); (cautious) prudent(e); **(be) ~!** (fais) attention!; **to be ~ with one's money** regarder à la dépense.
carefully ['kɛəfəlɪ] ad avec soin, soigneusement; prudemment.
careless ['kɛəlɪs] a négligent(e); (heedless) insouciant(e).
carelessly ['kɛəlɪslɪ] ad négligemment; avec insouciance.
carelessness ['kɛəlɪsnɪs] n manque m de soin, négligence f; insouciance f.
caress [kə'rɛs] n caresse f ♦ vt caresser.
caretaker ['kɛəteɪkə*] n gardien/ne, concierge m/f.
caretaker government n (Brit) gouvernement m intérimaire.
car-ferry ['kɑːfɛrɪ] n (on sea) ferry(-boat) m; (on river) bac m.
cargo, pl ~es ['kɑːgəu] n cargaison f, chargement m.
cargo boat n cargo m.
cargo plane n avion-cargo m.
car hire n (Brit) location f de voitures.
Caribbean [kærɪ'biːən] a des Caraïbes; **the ~ (Sea)** la mer des Antilles or des Caraïbes.
caricature ['kærɪkətjuə*] n caricature f.
caring ['kɛərɪŋ] a (person) bienveillant(e); (society, organization) humanitaire.

carnage ['kɑːnɪdʒ] *n* carnage *m*.
carnal ['kɑːnl] *a* charnel(le).
carnation [kɑːˈneɪʃən] *n* œillet *m*.
carnival ['kɑːnɪvl] *n* (*public celebration*) carnaval *m*; (*US: funfair*) fête foraine.
carnivorous [kɑːˈnɪvərəs] *a* carnivore, carnassier(ière).
carol ['kærəl] *n*: (**Christmas**) ~ chant *m* de Noël.
carouse [kəˈrauz] *vi* faire la bringue.
carousel [kærəˈsɛl] *n* (*US*) manège *m*.
carp [kɑːp] *n* (*fish*) carpe *f*.
carp at *vt fus* critiquer.
car park *n* parking *m*, parc *m* de stationnement.
carpenter ['kɑːpɪntə*] *n* charpentier *m*.
carpentry ['kɑːpɪntrɪ] *n* charpenterie *f*, métier *m* de charpentier; (*woodwork: at school etc*) menuiserie *f*.
carpet ['kɑːpɪt] *n* tapis *m* ♦ *vt* recouvrir (d'un tapis); **fitted** ~ (*Brit*) moquette *f*.
carpet slippers *npl* pantoufles *fpl*.
carpet sweeper [-ˈswiːpə*] *n* balai *m* mécanique.
car rental *n* (*US*) location *f* de voitures.
carriage ['kærɪdʒ] *n* voiture *f*; (*of goods*) transport *m*; (*: cost*) port *m*; (*of typewriter*) chariot *m*; (*bearing*) maintien *m*, port *m*; ~ **forward** port dû; ~ **free** franco de port; ~ **paid** (en) port payé.
carriage return *n* retour *m* à la ligne.
carriageway ['kærɪdʒweɪ] *n* (*Brit: part of road*) chaussée *f*.
carrier ['kærɪə*] *n* transporteur *m*, camionneur *m*; (*MED*) porteur/euse; (*NAUT*) porte-avions *m inv*.
carrier bag *n* (*Brit*) sac *m* en papier *or* en plastique.
carrier pigeon *n* pigeon voyageur.
carrion ['kærɪən] *n* charogne *f*.
carrot ['kærət] *n* carotte *f*.
carry ['kærɪ] *vt* (*subj: person*) porter; (*: vehicle*) transporter; (*a motion, bill*) voter, adopter; (*MATH: figure*) retenir; (*COMM: interest*) rapporter; (*involve: responsibilities etc*) comporter, impliquer ♦ *vi* (*sound*) porter; **to be carried away** (*fig*) s'emballer, s'enthousiasmer; **this loan carries 10% interest** ce prêt est à 10% (d'intérêt).
carry forward *vt* (*gen, BOOK-KEEPING*) reporter.
carry on *vi* (*continue*): **to** ~ **on with sth/doing** continuer qch/à faire; (*col: make a fuss*) faire des histoires ♦ *vt* entretenir, poursuivre.
carry out *vt* (*orders*) exécuter; (*investigation*) effectuer; (*idea, threat*) mettre à exécution.
carrycot ['kærɪkɔt] *n* (*Brit*) porte-bébé *m*.
carry-on ['kærɪ'ɔn] *n* (*col: fuss*) histoires *fpl*; (*: annoying behaviour*) cirque *m*, cinéma *m*.
cart [kɑːt] *n* charrette *f* ♦ *vt* transporter.
carte blanche ['kɑːt'blɔnʃ] *n*: **to give sb** ~ donner carte blanche à qn.
cartel [kɑːˈtɛl] *n* (*COMM*) cartel *m*.
cartilage ['kɑːtɪlɪdʒ] *n* cartilage *m*.
cartographer [kɑːˈtɔgrəfə*] *n* cartographe *m/f*.
cartography [kɑːˈtɔgrəfɪ] *n* cartographie *f*.

carton ['kɑːtən] *n* (*box*) carton *m*; (*of yogurt*) pot *m* (en carton); (*of cigarettes*) cartouche *f*.
cartoon [kɑːˈtuːn] *n* (*PRESS*) dessin *m* (humoristique); (*satirical*) caricature *f*; (*comic strip*) bande dessinée; (*CINEMA*) dessin animé.
cartoonist [kɑːˈtuːnɪst] *n* dessinateur/trice humoristique; caricaturiste *m/f*; auteur *m* de dessins animés; auteur de bandes dessinées.
cartridge ['kɑːtrɪdʒ] *n* (*for gun, pen*) cartouche *f*; (*for camera*) chargeur *m*; (*music tape*) cassette *f*; (*of record player*) cellule *f*.
cartwheel ['kɑːtwiːl] *n* roue *f*; **to turn a** ~ faire la roue.
carve [kɑːv] *vt* (*meat: also*: ~ **up**) découper; (*wood, stone*) tailler, sculpter.
carving ['kɑːvɪŋ] *n* (*in wood etc*) sculpture *f*.
carving knife *n* couteau *m* à découper.
car wash *n* station *f* de lavage (de voitures).
Casablanca [kæsəˈblæŋkə] *n* Casablanca.
cascade [kæsˈkeɪd] *n* cascade *f* ♦ *vi* tomber en cascade.
case [keɪs] *n* cas *m*; (*LAW*) affaire *f*, procès *m*; (*box*) caisse *f*, boîte *f*, étui *m*; (*Brit: also*: **suit**~) valise *f*; (*TYP*): **lower/upper** ~ minuscule *f*/majuscule *f*; **to have a good** ~ avoir de bons arguments; **there's a strong** ~ **for reform** il y aurait lieu d'engager une réforme; **in** ~ **of** en cas de; **in** ~ **he** au cas où il; **just in** ~ à tout hasard.
case-hardened ['keɪshɑːdnd] *a* endurci(e).
case history *n* (*MED*) dossier médical, antécédents médicaux.
case study *n* étude *f* de cas.
cash [kæʃ] *n* argent *m*; (*COMM*) argent liquide, numéraire *m*; liquidités *fpl*; (*: in payment*) argent comptant, espèces *fpl* ♦ *vt* encaisser; **to pay (in)** ~ payer (en argent) comptant *or* en espèces; ~ **with order/on delivery** (*COMM*) payable *or* paiement à la commande/livraison; **to be short of** ~ être à court d'argent.
cash account *n* compte *m* caisse.
cashbook ['kæʃbuk] *n* livre *m* de caisse.
cash box *n* caisse *f*.
cash card *n* carte *f* de retrait *or* accréditive.
cash desk *n* (*Brit*) caisse *f*.
cash discount *n* escompte *m* de caisse (pour paiement au comptant), remise *f* au comptant.
cash dispenser *n* distributeur *m* automatique de billets.
cashew [kæˈʃuː] *n* (*also*: ~ **nut**) noix *f* de cajou.
cash flow *n* cash-flow *m*, marge brute d'autofinancement.
cashier [kæˈʃɪə*] *n* caissier/ère ♦ *vt* (*MIL*) destituer, casser.
cashmere ['kæʃmɪə*] *n* cachemire *m*.
cash payment *n* paiement comptant, versement *m* en espèces.
cash price *n* prix comptant.
cash register *n* caisse enregistreuse.
cash sale *n* vente *f* au comptant.
casing ['keɪsɪŋ] *n* revêtement (protecteur), enveloppe (protectrice).

casino [kə'siːnəu] *n* casino *m*.
cask [kɑːsk] *n* tonneau *m*.
casket ['kɑːskɪt] *n* coffret *m*; (*US: coffin*) cercueil *m*.
Caspian Sea ['kæspɪən-] *n*: **the ~** la mer Caspienne.
casserole ['kæsərəul] *n* cocotte *f*; (*food*) ragoût *m* (en cocotte).
cassette [kæ'sɛt] *n* cassette *f*, musicassette *f*.
cassette deck *n* platine *f* cassette.
cassette player *n* lecteur *m* de cassettes.
cassette recorder *n* magnétophone *m* à cassettes.
cast [kɑːst] *vb* (*pt, pp* **cast**) *vt* (*throw*) jeter; (*shed*) perdre; se dépouiller de; (*metal*) couler, fondre; (*THEATRE*): **to ~ sb as Hamlet** attribuer à qn le rôle d'Hamlet ♦ *n* (*THEATRE*) distribution *f*; (*mould*) moule *m*; (*also:* **plaster ~**) plâtre *m*; **to ~ one's vote** voter, exprimer son suffrage.
cast aside *vt* (*reject*) rejeter.
cast off *vi* (*NAUT*) larguer les amarres; (*KNITTING*) arrêter les mailles ♦ *vt* (*KNITTING*) arrêter.
cast on (*KNITTING*) *vt* monter ♦ *vi* monter les mailles.
castanets [kæstə'nɛts] *npl* castagnettes *fpl*.
castaway ['kɑːstəweɪ] *n* naufragé/e.
caste [kɑːst] *n* caste *f*, classe sociale.
caster sugar *n* (*Brit*) sucre *m* semoule.
casting vote ['kɑːstɪŋ-] *n* (*Brit*) voix prépondérante (*pour départager*).
cast iron *n* fonte *f* ♦ *a*: **cast-iron** (*fig: will*) de fer; (*: alibi*) en béton.
castle ['kɑːsl] *n* château-fort *m*; (*manor*) château *m*.
castor ['kɑːstə*] *n* (*wheel*) roulette *f*.
castor oil *n* huile *f* de ricin.
castrate [kæs'treɪt] *vt* châtrer.
casual ['kæʒjul] *a* (*by chance*) de hasard, fait(e) au hasard, fortuit(e); (*irregular: work etc*) temporaire; (*unconcerned*) désinvolte; **~ wear** vêtements *mpl* sport *inv*.
casual labour *n* main-d'œuvre *f* temporaire.
casually ['kæʒjulɪ] *ad* avec désinvolture, négligemment; (*by chance*) fortuitement.
casualty ['kæʒjultɪ] *n* accidenté/e, blessé/e; (*dead*) victime *f*, mort/e; **heavy casualties** lourdes pertes.
casualty ward *n* (*Brit*) service *m* des urgences.
cat [kæt] *n* chat *m*.
catacombs ['kætəkuːmz] *npl* catacombes *fpl*.
catalogue, (*US*) **catalog** ['kætəlɔg] *n* catalogue *m* ♦ *vt* cataloguer.
catalyst ['kætəlɪst] *n* catalyseur *m*.
catapult ['kætəpʌlt] *n* lance-pierres *m inv*, fronde *m*; (*HISTORY*) catapulte *f*.
cataract ['kætərækt] *n* (*also MED*) cataracte *f*.
catarrh [kə'tɑː*] *n* rhume *m* chronique, catarrhe *f*.
catastrophe [kə'tæstrəfɪ] *n* catastrophe *f*.
catastrophic [kætə'strɔfɪk] *a* catastrophique.
catcall ['kætkɔːl] *n* (*at meeting etc*) sifflet *m*.
catch [kætʃ] *vb* (*pt, pp* **caught** [kɔːt]) *vt* (*ball, train, thief, cold*) attraper; (*person: by surprise*) prendre, surprendre; (*understand*) saisir; (*get entangled*) accrocher ♦ *vi* (*fire*) prendre; (*get entangled*) s'accrocher ♦ *n* (*fish*

etc caught) prise *f*; (*thief etc caught*) capture *f*; (*trick*) attrape *f*; (*TECH*) loquet *m*; cliquet *m*; **to ~ sb's attention** *or* **eye** attirer l'attention de qn; **to ~ fire** prendre feu; **to ~ sight of** apercevoir.
catch on *vi* (*become popular*) prendre; (*understand*): **to ~ on (to sth)** saisir (qch).
catch out *vt* (*Brit fig: with trick question*) prendre en défaut.
catch up *vi* se rattraper, combler son retard ♦ *vt* (*also:* **~ up with**) rattraper.
catching ['kætʃɪŋ] *a* (*MED*) contagieux(euse).
catchment area ['kætʃmənt-] *n* (*Brit SCOL*) aire *f* de recrutement; (*GEO*) bassin *m* hydrographique.
catch phrase *n* slogan *m*; expression toute faite.
catch-22 ['kætʃtwentɪ'tuː] *n*: **it's a ~ situation** c'est (une situation) sans issue.
catchy ['kætʃɪ] *a* (*tune*) facile à retenir.
catechism ['kætɪkɪzəm] *n* catéchisme *m*.
categoric(al) [kætɪ'gɔrɪk(l)] *a* catégorique.
categorize ['kætɪgəraɪz] *vt* classer par catégories.
category ['kætɪgərɪ] *n* catégorie *f*.
cater ['keɪtə*] *vi* (*provide food*): **to ~ (for)** préparer des repas (pour), se charger de la restauration (pour).
cater for *vt fus* (*Brit: needs*) satisfaire, pourvoir à; (*: readers, consumers*) s'adresser à, pourvoir aux besoins de.
caterer ['keɪtərə*] *n* traiteur *m*; fournisseur *m*.
catering ['keɪtərɪŋ] *n* restauration *f*; approvisionnement *m*, ravitaillement *m*.
caterpillar ['kætəpɪlə*] *n* chenille *f* ♦ *cpd* (*vehicle*) à chenille; **~ track** chenille *f*.
cathedral [kə'θiːdrəl] *n* cathédrale *f*.
cathode ['kæθəud] *n* cathode *f*.
cathode ray tube *n* tube *m* cathodique.
catholic ['kæθəlɪk] *a* éclectique; universel(le); libéral(e); **C~** *a, n* (*REL*) catholique (*m/f*).
cat's-eye ['kæts'aɪ] *n* (*Brit AUT*) (clou *m* à) catadioptre *m*.
catsup ['kætsəp] *n* (*US*) ketchup *m*.
cattle ['kætl] *npl* bétail *m*, bestiaux *mpl*.
catty ['kætɪ] *a* méchant(e).
Caucasian *a, n* caucasien(ne).
Caucasus ['kɔːkəsəs] *n* Caucase *m*.
caucus ['kɔːkəs] *n* (*US POL*) comité électoral (pour désigner des candidats); (*Brit POL: group*) comité local (*d'un parti politique*).
caught [kɔːt] *pt, pp of* **catch**.
cauliflower ['kɔlɪflauə*] *n* chou-fleur *m*.
cause [kɔːz] *n* cause *f* ♦ *vt* causer; **there is no ~ for concern** il n'y a pas lieu de s'inquiéter; **to ~ sth to be done** faire faire qch; **to ~ sb to do sth** faire faire qch à qn.
causeway ['kɔːzweɪ] *n* chaussée (surélevée).
caustic ['kɔːstɪk] *a* caustique.
caution ['kɔːʃən] *n* prudence *f*; (*warning*) avertissement *m* ♦ *vt* avertir, donner un avertissement à.
cautious ['kɔːʃəs] *a* prudent(e).
cautiously ['kɔːʃəslɪ] *ad* prudemment, avec prudence.
cautiousness ['kɔːʃəsnɪs] *n* prudence *f*.
cavalier [kævə'lɪə*] *a* cavalier(ère), désinvolte ♦ *n* (*knight*) cavalier *m*.

cavalry ['kævəlrɪ] *n* cavalerie *f.*
cave [keɪv] *n* caverne *f*, grotte *f* ♦ *vi:* **to go caving** faire de la spéléo(logie).
cave in *vi* (*roof etc*) s'effondrer.
caveman ['keɪvmæn] *n* homme *m* des cavernes.
cavern ['kævən] *n* caverne *f.*
caviar(e) ['kævɪɑː*] *n* caviar *m.*
cavity ['kævɪtɪ] *n* cavité *f.*
cavity wall insulation *n* isolation *f* des murs creux.
cavort [kə'vɔːt] *vi* cabrioler, faire des cabrioles.
cayenne [keɪ'ɛn] *n* (*also:* ~ **pepper**) poivre *m* de cayenne.
CB *n abbr* (= *Citizens' Band (Radio)*) CB *f*; (*Brit:* = *Companion of (the Order of) the Bath*) *titre honorifique.*
CBC *n abbr* (= *Canadian Broadcasting Corporation*) *organisme de radiodiffusion.*
CBE *n abbr* (= *Companion of (the Order of) the British Empire*) *titre honorifique.*
CBI *n abbr* (= *Confederation of British Industry*) ≈ CNPF *m* (= *Conseil national du patronat français*).
CBS *n abbr* (*US:* = *Columbia Broadcasting System*) *chaîne de télévision.*
CC *abbr* (*Brit*) = *county council.*
cc *abbr* (= *cubic centimetre*) cm³; (*on letter etc*) = **carbon copy.**
CCA *n abbr* (*US:* = *Circuit Court of Appeals*) cour d'appel itinérante.
CCU *n abbr* (*US:* = *coronary care unit*) unité *f* de soins cardiologiques.
CD *n abbr* (= *compact disc*) CD *m*; (*MIL*) = *Civil Defence (Corps)* (*Brit*), *Civil Defense (US)* ♦ *abbr* (*Brit:* = *Corps Diplomatique*) CD.
CDC *n abbr* (*US*) = *center for disease control.*
Cdr. *abbr* (= *commander*) Cdt.
CDT *abbr* (*US:* = *Central Daylight Time*) *heure d'été du centre.*
CDW *n abbr* = **collision damage waiver.**
cease [siːs] *vt, vi* cesser.
ceasefire ['siːsfaɪə*] *n* cessez-le-feu *m.*
ceaseless ['siːslɪs] *a* incessant(e), continuel(le).
CED *n abbr* (*US*) = *Committee for Economic Development.*
cedar ['siːdə*] *n* cèdre *m.*
cede [siːd] *vt* céder.
cedilla [sɪ'dɪlə] *n* cédille *f.*
CEEB *n abbr* (*US:* = *College Entry Examination Board*) *commission d'admission dans l'enseignement supérieur.*
ceiling ['siːlɪŋ] *n* (*also fig*) plafond *m.*
celebrate ['sɛlɪbreɪt] *vt, vi* célébrer.
celebrated ['sɛlɪbreɪtɪd] *a* célèbre.
celebration [sɛlɪ'breɪʃən] *n* célébration *f.*
celebrity [sɪ'lɛbrɪtɪ] *n* célébrité *f.*
celeriac [sə'lɛrɪæk] *n* céleri(-rave) *m.*
celery ['sɛlərɪ] *n* céleri *m* (en branches).
celestial [sɪ'lɛstɪəl] *a* céleste.
celibacy ['sɛlɪbəsɪ] *n* célibat *m.*
cell [sɛl] *n* (*gen*) cellule *f*; (*ELEC*) élément *m* (de pile).
cellar ['sɛlə*] *n* cave *f.*
'cellist ['tʃɛlɪst] *n* violoncelliste *m/f.*
'cello ['tʃɛləu] *n* violoncelle *m.*

cellophane ['sɛləfeɪn] *n* ® cellophane *f* ®.
cellular ['sɛljulə*] *a* cellulaire.
Celluloid ['sɛljulɔɪd] *n* ® celluloïd *m* ®.
cellulose ['sɛljuləus] *n* cellulose *f.*
Celsius ['sɛlsɪəs] *a* Celsius *inv.*
Celt [kɛlt, sɛlt] *n* Celte *m/f.*
Celtic ['kɛltɪk, 'sɛltɪk] *a* celte, celtique ♦ *n* (*LING*) celtique *m.*
cement [sə'mɛnt] *n* ciment *m* ♦ *vt* cimenter.
cement mixer *n* bétonnière *f.*
cemetery ['sɛmɪtrɪ] *n* cimetière *m.*
cenotaph ['sɛnətɑːf] *n* cénotaphe *m.*
censor ['sɛnsə*] *n* censeur *m* ♦ *vt* censurer.
censorship ['sɛnsəʃɪp] *n* censure *f.*
censure ['sɛnʃə*] *vt* blâmer, critiquer.
census ['sɛnsəs] *n* recensement *m.*
cent [sɛnt] *n* (*US: coin*) cent *m* (= *1:100 du dollar*); *see also* **per.**
centenary [sɛn'tiːnərɪ], **centennial** [sɛn'tɛnɪəl] *n* centenaire *m.*
center ['sɛntə*] *n, vt* (*US*) = **centre.**
centigrade ['sɛntɪgreɪd] *a* centigrade.
centilitre, (*US*) **centiliter** ['sɛntɪliːtə*] *n* centilitre *m.*
centimetre, (*US*) **centimeter** ['sɛntɪmiːtə*] *n* centimètre *m.*
centipede ['sɛntɪpiːd] *n* mille-pattes *m inv.*
central ['sɛntrəl] *a* central(e).
Central African Republic *n* République Centrafricaine.
central heating *n* chauffage central.
centralize ['sɛntrəlaɪz] *vt* centraliser.
central processing unit (CPU) *n* (*COMPUT*) unité centrale (de traitement).
central reservation *n* (*Brit AUT*) terre-plein central.
centre, (*US*) **center** ['sɛntə*] *n* centre *m* ♦ *vt* centrer; (*PHOT*) cadrer; (*concentrate*): **to ~ (on)** centrer (sur).
centrefold, (*US*) **centerfold** ['sɛntəfəuld] *n* (*PRESS*) pages centrales détachables (*avec photo de pin up*).
centre-forward ['sɛntə'fɔːwəd] *n* (*SPORT*) avant-centre *m.*
centre-half ['sɛntə'hɑːf] *n* (*SPORT*) demi-centre *m.*
centrepiece, (*US*) **centerpiece** ['sɛntəpiːs] *n* milieu *m* de table; (*fig*) pièce maîtresse.
centre spread *n* (*Brit*) publicité *f* en double page.
centrifugal [sɛn'trɪfjugl] *a* centrifuge.
centrifuge ['sɛntrɪfjuːʒ] *n* centrifugeuse *f.*
century ['sɛntjurɪ] *n* siècle *m*; **in the twentieth ~** au vingtième siècle.
CEO *n abbr* (*US*) = **chief executive officer.**
ceramic [sɪ'ræmɪk] *a* céramique.
cereal ['siːrɪəl] *n* céréale *f.*
cerebral ['sɛrɪbrəl] *a* cérébral(e).
ceremonial [sɛrɪ'məunɪəl] *n* cérémonial *m*; (*rite*) rituel *m.*
ceremony ['sɛrɪmənɪ] *n* cérémonie *f*; **to stand on ~** faire des façons.
cert [sɜːt] *n* (*Brit col*): **it's a dead ~** ça ne fait pas un pli.
certain ['sɜːtən] *a* certain(e); **to make ~ of** s'assurer de; **for ~** certainement, sûrement.
certainly ['sɜːtənlɪ] *ad* certainement.
certainty ['sɜːtəntɪ] *n* certitude *f.*
certificate [sə'tɪfɪkɪt] *n* certificat *m.*

certified letter ['sə:tɪfaɪd-] *n* (*US*) lettre recommandée.

certified public accountant (**CPA**) ['sə:tɪfaɪd-] *n* (*US*) expert-comptable *m*.

certify ['sə:tɪfaɪ] *vt* certifier ♦ *vi*: **to ~ to** attester.

cervical ['sə:vɪkl] *a*: **~ cancer** cancer *m* du col de l'utérus; **~ smear** frottis vaginal.

cervix ['sə:vɪks] *n* col *m* de l'utérus.

Cesarean [si:'zɛərɪən] *a*, *n* (*US*) = **Caesarean**.

cessation [sə'seɪʃən] *n* cessation *f*, arrêt *m*.

cesspit ['sɛspɪt] *n* fosse *f* d'aisance.

CET *abbr* (= *Central European Time*) heure d'Europe centrale.

Ceylon [sɪ'lɔn] *n* Ceylan *m*.

cf. *abbr* (= *compare*) cf., voir.

c/f *abbr* (*COMM*) = *carried forward*.

CG *n abbr* (*US*) = **coastguard**.

cg *abbr* (= *centigram*) cg.

CH *n abbr* (*Brit*: = *Companion of Honour*) titre honorifique.

ch *abbr* (*Brit*: = *central heating*) c.c.

ch. *abbr* (= *chapter*) chap.

Chad [tʃæd] *n* Tchad *m*.

chafe [tʃeɪf] *vt* irriter, frotter contre ♦ *vi* (*fig*): **to ~ against** se rebiffer contre, regimber contre.

chaffinch ['tʃæfɪntʃ] *n* pinson *m*.

chagrin ['ʃægrɪn] *n* contrariété *f*, déception *f*.

chain [tʃeɪn] *n* (*gen*) chaîne *f* ♦ *vt* (*also*: **~ up**) enchaîner, attacher (avec une chaîne).

chain reaction *n* réaction *f* en chaîne.

chain-smoke ['tʃeɪnsməuk] *vi* fumer cigarette sur cigarette.

chain store *n* magasin *m* à succursales multiples.

chair [tʃɛə*] *n* chaise *f*; (*armchair*) fauteuil *m*; (*of university*) chaire *f* ♦ *vt* (*meeting*) présider; **the ~** (*US*: *electric* **~**) la chaise électrique.

chairlift ['tʃɛəlɪft] *n* télésiège *m*.

chairman ['tʃɛəmən] *n* président *m*.

chairperson ['tʃɛəpə:sn] *n* président/e.

chairwoman ['tʃɛəwumən] *n* présidente *f*.

chalet ['ʃæleɪ] *n* chalet *m*.

chalice ['tʃælɪs] *n* calice *m*.

chalk [tʃɔ:k] *n* craie *f*.

chalk up *vt* écrire à la craie; (*fig: success etc*) remporter.

challenge ['tʃælɪndʒ] *n* défi *m* ♦ *vt* défier; (*statement*, *right*) mettre en question, contester; **to ~ sb to a fight/game** inviter qn à se battre/à jouer (*sous forme d'un défi*); **to ~ sb to do** mettre qn au défi de faire.

challenger ['tʃælɪndʒə*] *n* (*SPORT*) challenger *m*.

challenging ['tʃælɪndʒɪŋ] *a* de défi, provocateur(trice).

chamber ['tʃeɪmbə*] *n* chambre *f*; **~ of commerce** chambre de commerce.

chambermaid ['tʃeɪmbəmeɪd] *n* femme *f* de chambre.

chamber music *n* musique *f* de chambre.

chamberpot ['tʃeɪmbəpɔt] *n* pot *m* de chambre.

chameleon [kə'mi:lɪən] *n* caméléon *m*.

chamois ['ʃæmwɑ:] *n* chamois *m*.

chamois leather ['ʃæmɪ-] *n* peau *f* de chamois.

champagne [ʃæm'peɪn] *n* champagne *m*.

champion ['tʃæmpɪən] *n* (*also of cause*) champion/ne ♦ *vt* défendre.

championship ['tʃæmpɪənʃɪp] *n* championnat *m*.

chance [tʃɑ:ns] *n* hasard *m*; (*opportunity*) occasion *f*, possibilité *f*; (*hope*, *likelihood*) chance *f* ♦ *vt* (*risk*): **to ~ it** risquer (le coup), essayer; (*happen*): **to ~ to do** faire par hasard ♦ *a* fortuit(e), de hasard; **there is little ~ of his coming** il est peu probable *or* il y a peu de chances qu'il vienne; **to take a ~** prendre un risque; **it's the ~ of a lifetime** c'est une occasion unique; **by ~** par hasard.

chance (up)on *vt fus* (*person*) tomber sur, rencontrer par hasard; (*thing*) trouver par hasard.

chancel ['tʃɑ:nsəl] *n* chœur *m*.

chancellor ['tʃɑ:nsələ*] *n* chancelier *m*; **C~ of the Exchequer** (*Brit*) chancelier de l'Échiquier.

chandelier [ʃændə'lɪə*] *n* lustre *m*.

change [tʃeɪndʒ] *vt* (*alter, replace*, *COMM*: *money*) changer; (*switch, substitute: gear, hands, trains, clothes, one's name etc*) changer de; (*transform*): **to ~ sb into** changer *or* transformer qn en ♦ *vi* (*gen*) changer; (*change clothes*) se changer; (*be transformed*): **to ~ into** se changer *or* transformer en ♦ *n* changement *m*; (*money*) monnaie *f*; **to ~ one's mind** changer d'avis; **she ~d into an old skirt** elle (s'est changée et) a enfilé une vieille jupe; **a ~ of clothes** des vêtements de rechange; **for a ~** pour changer; **small ~** petite monnaie; **to give sb ~ for** *or* **of £10** faire à qn la monnaie de 10 livres.

changeable ['tʃeɪndʒəbl] *a* (*weather*) variable; (*person*) d'humeur changeante.

change machine *n* distributeur *m* de monnaie.

changeover ['tʃeɪndʒəuvə*] *n* (*to new system*) changement *m*, passage *m*.

changing ['tʃeɪndʒɪŋ] *a* changeant(e).

changing room *n* (*Brit*: *in shop*) salon *m* d'essayage; (: *SPORT*) vestiaire *m*.

channel ['tʃænl] *n* (*TV*) chaîne *f*; (*waveband, groove, fig: medium*) canal *m*; (*of river, sea*) chenal *m* ♦ *vt* canaliser; (*fig: interest, energies*): **to ~ into** diriger vers; **through the usual ~s** en suivant la filière habituelle; **green/red ~** (*CUSTOMS*) couloir *m or* sortie *f* 'rien à déclarer'/'marchandises à déclarer'; **the (English) C~** la Manche.

Channel Islands *npl*: **the ~** les îles de la Manche, les îles anglo-normandes.

chant [tʃɑ:nt] *n* chant *m*; mélopée *f*; psalmodie *f* ♦ *vt* chanter, scander; psalmodier.

chaos ['keɪɔs] *n* chaos *m*.

chaotic [keɪ'ɔtɪk] *a* chaotique.

chap [tʃæp] *n* (*Brit col: man*) type *m*; (*term of address*): **old ~** mon vieux ♦ *vt* (*skin*) gercer, crevasser.

chapel ['tʃæpl] *n* chapelle *f*.

chaperon ['ʃæpərəun] *n* chaperon *m* ♦ *vt* chaperonner.

chaplain ['tʃæplɪn] *n* aumônier *m*.

chapter ['tʃæptə*] *n* chapitre *m*.

char [tʃɑ:] vt (burn) carboniser ♦ vi (Brit: cleaner) faire des ménages ♦ n (Brit) = **charlady.**

character ['kærɪktə*] n caractère m; (in novel, film) personnage m; (eccentric) numéro m, phénomène m; **a person of good ~** une personne bien.

character code n (COMPUT) code m de caractère.

characteristic ['kærɪktə'rɪstɪk] a, n caractéristique (f).

characterize ['kærɪktəraɪz] vt caractériser; **to ~ (as)** définir (comme).

charade [ʃə'rɑ:d] n charade f.

charcoal ['tʃɑ:kəul] n charbon m de bois.

charge [tʃɑ:dʒ] n accusation f; (LAW) inculpation f; (cost) prix (demandé); (of gun, battery, MIL: attack) charge f ♦ vt (LAW): **to ~ sb (with)** inculper qn (de); (gun, battery, MIL: enemy) charger; (customer, sum) faire payer ♦ vi (gen with: up, along etc) foncer; **~s** npl: **bank/labour ~s** frais mpl de banque/main-d'œuvre; **to ~ in/out** entrer/sortir en trombe; **to ~ down/up** dévaler/grimper à toute allure; **is there a ~?** doit-on payer?; **there's no ~** c'est gratuit, on ne fait pas payer; **extra ~** supplément m; **to take ~ of** se charger de; **to be in ~ of** être responsable de, s'occuper de; **to have ~ of sb** avoir la charge de qn; **they ~d us £10 for the meal** ils nous ont fait payer le repas 10 livres, ils nous ont compté 10 livres pour le repas; **how much do you ~ for this repair?** combien demandez-vous pour cette réparation?; **to ~ an expense (up) to sb** mettre une dépense sur le compte de qn; **~ it to my account** facturez-le sur mon compte.

charge account n compte m client.

charge card n carte f de client (émise par un grand magasin).

chargehand ['tʃɑ:dʒhænd] n (Brit) chef m d'équipe.

charger ['tʃɑ:dʒə*] n (also: **battery ~**) chargeur m; (old: warhorse) cheval m de bataille.

charitable ['tʃærɪtəbl] a charitable.

charity ['tʃærɪtɪ] n charité f; (organization) institution f charitable or de bienfaisance, œuvre f (de charité).

charlady ['tʃɑ:leɪdɪ] n (Brit) femme f de ménage.

charm [tʃɑ:m] n charme m ♦ vt charmer, enchanter.

charm bracelet n bracelet m à breloques.

charming ['tʃɑ:mɪŋ] a charmant(e).

chart [tʃɑ:t] n tableau m, diagramme m; graphique m; (map) carte marine; (weather ~) carte f du temps ♦ vt dresser or établir la carte de; (sales, progress) établir la courbe de; **to be in the ~s** (record, pop group) figurer au hit-parade.

charter ['tʃɑ:tə*] vt (plane) affréter ♦ n (document) charte f; **on ~** (plane) affrété(e).

chartered accountant (CA) n (Brit) expert-comptable m.

charter flight n charter m.

charwoman ['tʃɑ:wumən] n = **charlady.**

chase [tʃeɪs] vt poursuivre, pourchasser ♦ n poursuite f, chasse f.

chase down vt (US) = **chase up.**

chase up vt (Brit: person) relancer; (: information) rechercher.

chasm ['kæzəm] n gouffre m, abîme m.

chassis ['ʃæsɪ] n châssis m.

chastened ['tʃeɪsnd] a assagi(e), rappelé(e) à la raison.

chastening ['tʃeɪsnɪŋ] a qui fait réfléchir.

chastise [tʃæs'taɪz] vt punir, châtier; corriger.

chastity ['tʃæstɪtɪ] n chasteté f.

chat [tʃæt] vi (also: **have a ~**) bavarder, causer ♦ n conversation f.

chat up vt (Brit col: girl) baratiner.

chat show n (Brit) entretien télévisé.

chattel ['tʃætl] see **goods.**

chatter ['tʃætə*] vi (person) bavarder, papoter ♦ n bavardage m, papotage m; **my teeth are ~ing** je claque des dents.

chatterbox ['tʃætəbɒks] n moulin m à paroles, babillard/e.

chatty ['tʃætɪ] a (style) familier(ière); (person) enclin(e) à bavarder or au papotage.

chauffeur ['ʃəufə*] n chauffeur m (de maître).

chauvinism ['ʃəuvɪnɪzəm] n (also: **male ~**) phallocratie f, machisme m; (nationalism) chauvinisme m.

chauvinist ['ʃəuvɪnɪst] n (also: **male ~**) phallocrate m, macho m; (nationalist) chauvin/e.

ChE abbr = chemical engineer.

cheap [tʃi:p] a à bon marché inv, pas cher(chère); (reduced: ticket) à prix réduit; (: fare) réduit(e); (joke) facile, d'un goût douteux; (poor quality) à bon marché, de qualité médiocre ♦ ad à bon marché, pour pas cher; **~er** a moins cher(chère).

cheapen ['tʃi:pn] vt rabaisser, déprécier.

cheaply ['tʃi:plɪ] ad à bon marché, à bon compte.

cheat [tʃi:t] vi tricher; (in exam) copier ♦ vt tromper, duper; (rob) escroquer ♦ n tricheur/euse; escroc m; (trick) duperie f, tromperie f; **to ~ on sb** (col: husband, wife etc) tromper qn.

cheating ['tʃi:tɪŋ] n tricherie f.

check [tʃɛk] vt vérifier; (passport, ticket) contrôler; (halt) enrayer; (restrain) maîtriser ♦ vi (official etc) se renseigner ♦ n vérification f; contrôle m; (curb) frein m; (bill) addition f; (pattern: gen pl) carreaux mpl; (US) = **cheque** ♦ a (also: **~ed**: pattern, cloth) à carreaux; **to ~ with sb** demander à qn; **to keep a ~ on sb/sth** surveiller qn/qch.

check in vi (in hotel) remplir sa fiche (d'hôtel); (at airport) se présenter à l'enregistrement ♦ vt (luggage) (faire) enregistrer.

check off vt cocher.

check out vi (in hotel) régler sa note ♦ vt (luggage) retirer; (investigate: story) vérifier; (person) prendre des renseignements sur.

check up vi: **to ~ up (on sth)** vérifier (qch); **to ~ up on sb** se renseigner sur le compte de qn.

checkered ['tʃɛkəd] a (US) = **chequered.**

checkers ['tʃɛkəz] n (US) jeu m de dames.

check guarantee card n (US) carte f (d'identité) bancaire.

check-in ['tʃɛkɪn] n (also: ~ **desk**: at airport) enregistrement m.

checking account ['tʃɛkɪŋ-] n (US) compte courant.

checklist ['tʃɛklɪst] n liste f de contrôle.

checkmate ['tʃɛkmeɪt] n échec et mat m.

checkout ['tʃɛkaut] n (in supermarket) caisse f.

checkpoint ['tʃɛkpɔɪnt] n contrôle m.

checkup ['tʃɛkʌp] n (MED) examen médical, check-up m.

cheek [tʃiːk] n joue f; (impudence) toupet m, culot m.

cheekbone ['tʃiːkbəun] n pommette f.

cheeky ['tʃiːkɪ] a effronté(e), culotté(e).

cheep [tʃiːp] n (of bird) piaulement m ♦ vi piauler.

cheer [tʃɪə*] vt acclamer, applaudir; (gladden) réjouir, réconforter ♦ vi applaudir ♦ n (gen pl) acclamations fpl, applaudissements mpl; bravos mpl, hourras mpl; ~s! (à votre) santé!

cheer on vt encourager (par des cris etc).

cheer up vi se dérider, reprendre courage ♦ vt remonter le moral à or de, dérider, égayer.

cheerful ['tʃɪəful] a gai(e), joyeux(euse).

cheerfulness ['tʃɪəfulnɪs] n gaieté f, bonne humeur.

cheerio [tʃɪərɪ'əu] excl (Brit) salut!, au revoir!

cheerless ['tʃɪəlɪs] a sombre, triste.

cheese [tʃiːz] n fromage m.

cheeseboard ['tʃiːzbɔːd] n plateau m à fromages; (with cheese on it) plateau m de fromages.

cheesecake ['tʃiːzkeɪk] n tarte f au fromage.

cheetah ['tʃiːtə] n guépard m.

chef [ʃɛf] n chef (cuisinier).

chemical ['kɛmɪkl] a chimique ♦ n produit m chimique.

chemist ['kɛmɪst] n (Brit: pharmacist) pharmacien/ne; (scientist) chimiste m/f; ~'s (shop) n (Brit) pharmacie f.

chemistry ['kɛmɪstrɪ] n chimie f.

cheque, (US) **check** [tʃɛk] n chèque m; to **pay by** ~ payer par chèque.

chequebook, (US) **checkbook** ['tʃɛkbuk] n chéquier m, carnet m de chèques.

cheque card n (Brit) carte f (d'identité) bancaire.

chequered, (US) **checkered** ['tʃɛkəd] a (fig) varié(e).

cherish ['tʃɛrɪʃ] vt chérir; (hope etc) entretenir.

cheroot [ʃə'ruːt] n cigare m de Manille.

cherry ['tʃɛrɪ] n cerise f.

Ches abbr (Brit) = Cheshire.

chess [tʃɛs] n échecs mpl.

chessboard ['tʃɛsbɔːd] n échiquier m.

chessman ['tʃɛsmən] n pièce f (de jeu d'échecs).

chessplayer ['tʃɛspleɪə*] n joueur/euse d'échecs.

chest [tʃɛst] n poitrine f; (box) coffre m, caisse f; to **get sth off one's** ~ (col) vider son sac; ~ **of drawers** n commode f.

chest measurement n tour m de poitrine.

chestnut ['tʃɛsnʌt] n châtaigne f; (also: ~ **tree**) châtaignier m; (colour) châtain m ♦ a (hair) châtain inv; (horse) alezan.

chew [tʃuː] vt mâcher.

chewing gum ['tʃuːɪŋ-] n chewing-gum m.

chic [ʃiːk] a chic inv, élégant(e).

chick [tʃɪk] n poussin m; (US col) pépée f.

chicken ['tʃɪkɪn] n poulet m; (col: coward) poule mouillée.

chicken out vi (col) se dégonfler.

chicken feed n (fig) broutilles fpl, bagatelle f.

chickenpox ['tʃɪkɪnpɔks] n varicelle f.

chick pea ['tʃɪkpiː] n pois m chiche.

chicory ['tʃɪkərɪ] n (for coffee) chicorée f; (salad) endive f.

chide [tʃaɪd] vt réprimander, gronder.

chief [tʃiːf] n chef m ♦ a principal(e); **C~ of Staff** (MIL) chef d'État-major.

chief constable n (Brit) ≈ préfet m de police.

chief executive, (US) **chief executive officer** n directeur général.

chiefly ['tʃiːflɪ] ad principalement, surtout.

chiffon ['ʃɪfɔn] n mousseline f de soie.

chilblain ['tʃɪlbleɪn] n engelure f.

child, pl ~ren [tʃaɪld, 'tʃɪldrən] n enfant m/f.

childbirth ['tʃaɪldbəːθ] n accouchement m.

childhood ['tʃaɪldhud] n enfance f.

childish ['tʃaɪldɪʃ] a puéril(e), enfantin(e).

childless ['tʃaɪldlɪs] a sans enfants.

childlike ['tʃaɪldlaɪk] a innocent(e), pur(e).

child minder n (Brit) garde f d'enfants.

Chile ['tʃɪlɪ] n Chili m.

Chilean ['tʃɪlɪən] a chilien(ne) ♦ n Chilien/ne.

chill [tʃɪl] n froid m; (MED) refroidissement m, coup m de froid ♦ a froid(e), glacial(e) ♦ vt faire frissonner; refroidir; (CULIN) mettre au frais, rafraîchir; **"serve ~ed"** "à servir frais".

chilli, (US) **chili** ['tʃɪlɪ] n piment m (rouge).

chilly ['tʃɪlɪ] a froid(e), glacé(e); (sensitive to cold) frileux(euse); to **feel** ~ avoir froid.

chime [tʃaɪm] n carillon m ♦ vi carillonner, sonner.

chimney ['tʃɪmnɪ] n cheminée f.

chimney sweep n ramonneur m.

chimpanzee [tʃɪmpæn'ziː] n chimpanzé m.

chin [tʃɪn] n menton m.

China ['tʃaɪnə] n Chine f.

china ['tʃaɪnə] n porcelaine f; (vaisselle f en) porcelaine.

Chinese [tʃaɪ'niːz] a chinois(e) ♦ n (pl inv) Chinois/e; (LING) chinois m.

chink [tʃɪŋk] n (opening) fente f, fissure f; (noise) tintement m.

chip [tʃɪp] n (gen pl: CULIN) frite f; (: US: also: **potato** ~) chip m; (of wood) copeau m; (of glass, stone) éclat m; (also: **micro~**) puce f; (in gambling) fiche f ♦ vt (cup, plate) ébrécher; **when the** ~**s are down** (fig) au moment critique.

chip in vi (col) mettre son grain de sel.

chipboard ['tʃɪpbɔːd] n aggloméré m, panneau m de particules.

chipmunk ['tʃɪpmʌŋk] n suisse m (animal).

chippings ['tʃɪpɪŋz] npl: **loose** ~ gravillons mpl.

chiropodist [kɪ'rɔpədɪst] *n* (*Brit*) pédicure *m/f*.

chiropody [kɪ'rɔpədɪ] *n* (*Brit*) pédicurie *f*.

chirp [tʃɜːp] *n* pépiement *m*, gazouillis *m*; (*of crickets*) stridulation *f* ♦ *vi* pépier, gazouiller; chanter, striduler.

chirpy ['tʃɜːpɪ] *a* (*col*) plein(e) d'entrain, tout guilleret(te).

chisel ['tʃɪzl] *n* ciseau *m*.

chit [tʃɪt] *n* mot *m*, note *f*.

chitchat ['tʃɪttʃæt] *n* bavardage *m*, papotage *m*.

chivalrous ['ʃɪvəlrəs] *a* chevaleresque.

chivalry ['ʃɪvəlrɪ] *n* chevalerie *f*; esprit *m* chevaleresque.

chives [tʃaɪvz] *npl* ciboulette *f*, civette *f*.

chloride ['klɔːraɪd] *n* chlorure *m*.

chlorinate ['klɔrɪneɪt] *vt* chlorer.

chlorine ['klɔːriːn] *n* chlore *m*.

chock [tʃɔk] *n* cale *f*.

chock-a-block ['tʃɔkə'blɔk], **chock-full** [tʃɔk'ful] *a* plein(e) à craquer.

chocolate ['tʃɔklɪt] *n* chocolat *m*.

choice [tʃɔɪs] *n* choix *m* ♦ *a* de choix; **by** or **from** ~ par choix; **a wide** ~ un grand choix.

choir ['kwaɪə*] *n* chœur *m*, chorale *f*.

choirboy ['kwaɪəbɔɪ] *n* jeune choriste *m*, petit chanteur.

choke [tʃəuk] *vi* étouffer ♦ *vt* étrangler; étouffer; (*block*) boucher, obstruer ♦ *n* (*AUT*) starter *m*.

cholera ['kɔlərə] *n* choléra *m*.

cholesterol [kə'lɛstərɔl] *n* cholestérol *m*.

choose, *pt* **chose**, *pp* **chosen** [tʃuːz, tʃəuz, 'tʃəuzn] *vt* choisir ♦ *vi*: **to** ~ **between** choisir entre; **to** ~ **from** choisir parmi; **to** ~ **to do** décider de faire, juger bon de faire.

choosy ['tʃuːzɪ] *a*: (**to be**) ~ (faire le) difficile.

chop [tʃɔp] *vt* (*wood*) couper (à la hache); (*CULIN: also*: ~ **up**) couper (fin), émincer, hacher (en morceaux) ♦ *n* coup *m* (*de hache, du tranchant de la main*); (*CULIN*) côtelette *f*; **to get the** ~ (*Brit col: project*) tomber à l'eau; (*: person: be sacked*) se faire renvoyer.

  chop down *vt* (*tree*) abattre.

chopper ['tʃɔpə*] *n* (*helicopter*) hélicoptère *m*, hélico *m*.

choppy ['tʃɔpɪ] *a* (*sea*) un peu agité(e).

chops [tʃɔps] *npl* (*jaws*) mâchoires *fpl*; babines *fpl*.

chopsticks ['tʃɔpstɪks] *npl* baguettes *fpl*.

choral ['kɔːrəl] *a* choral(e), chanté(e) en chœur.

chord [kɔːd] *n* (*MUS*) accord *m*.

chore [tʃɔː*] *n* travail *m* de routine; **household** ~s travaux *mpl* du ménage.

choreographer [kɔrɪ'ɔgrəfə*] *n* chorégraphe *m/f*.

chorister ['kɔrɪstə*] *n* choriste *m/f*.

chortle ['tʃɔːtl] *vi* glousser.

chorus ['kɔːrəs] *n* chœur *m*; (*repeated part of song, also fig*) refrain *m*.

chose [tʃəuz] *pt of* **choose**.

chosen ['tʃəuzn] *pp of* **choose**.

chow [tʃau] *n* (*dog*) chow-chow *m*.

chowder ['tʃaudə*] *n* soupe *f* de poisson.

Christ [kraɪst] *n* Christ *m*.

christen ['krɪsn] *vt* baptiser.

christening ['krɪsnɪŋ] *n* baptême *m*.

Christian ['krɪstɪən] *a*, *n* chrétien(ne).

Christianity [krɪstɪ'ænɪtɪ] *n* christianisme *m*.

Christian name *n* prénom *m*.

Christmas ['krɪsməs] *n* Noël *m* or *f*; **happy** or **merry** ~! joyeux Noël!

Christmas card *n* carte *f* de Noël.

Christmas Day *n* le jour de Noël.

Christmas Eve *n* la veille de Noël; la nuit de Noël.

Christmas Island *n* île *f* Christmas.

Christmas tree *n* arbre *m* de Noël.

chrome [krəum] *n* = **chromium**.

chromium ['krəumɪəm] *n* chrome *m*; (*also*: ~ **plating**) chromage *m*.

chromosome ['krəuməsəum] *n* chromosome *m*.

chronic ['krɔnɪk] *a* chronique; (*fig: liar, smoker*) invétéré(e).

chronicle ['krɔnɪkl] *n* chronique *f*.

chronological [krɔnə'lɔdʒɪkl] *a* chronologique.

chrysanthemum [krɪ'sænθəməm] *n* chrysanthème *m*.

chubby ['tʃʌbɪ] *a* potelé(e), rondelet(te).

chuck [tʃʌk] *vt* lancer, jeter; **to** ~ (**up** or **in**) *vt* (*Brit: job*) lâcher; (*: person*) plaquer.

  chuck out *vt* flanquer dehors or à la porte.

chuckle ['tʃʌkl] *vi* glousser.

chug [tʃʌg] *vi* faire teuf-teuf; souffler.

chum [tʃʌm] *n* copain/copine.

chump ['tʃʌmp] *n* (*col*) imbécile *m/f*, crétin/e.

chunk [tʃʌŋk] *n* gros morceau; (*of bread*) quignon *m*.

chunky ['tʃʌŋkɪ] *a* (*furniture etc*) massif(ive); (*person*) trapu(e); (*knitwear*) en grosse laine.

church [tʃɜːtʃ] *n* église *f*; **the C**~ **of England** l'Église anglicane.

churchyard ['tʃɜːtʃjɑːd] *n* cimetière *m*.

churlish ['tʃɜːlɪʃ] *a* grossier(ère); hargneux(euse).

churn [tʃɜːn] *n* (*for butter*) baratte *f*; (*for transport: also*: **milk** ~) (grand) bidon à lait.

  churn out *vt* débiter.

chute [ʃuːt] *n* glissoire *f*; (*also*: **rubbish** ~) vide-ordures *m inv*; (*Brit: children's slide*) toboggan *m*.

chutney ['tʃʌtnɪ] *n* chutney *m*.

CIA *n abbr* (*US*: = *Central Intelligence Agency*) CIA *f*.

CID *n abbr* (*Brit*: = *Criminal Investigation Department*) ≈ P.J. *f* (= *police judiciaire*).

cider ['saɪdə*] *n* cidre *m*.

CIF *abbr* (= *cost, insurance and freight*) CAF.

cigar [sɪ'gɑː*] *n* cigare *m*.

cigarette [sɪgə'rɛt] *n* cigarette *f*.

cigarette case *n* étui *m* à cigarettes.

cigarette end *n* mégot *m*.

cigarette holder *n* fume-cigarettes *m inv*.

C-in-C *abbr* = **commander-in-chief**.

cinch [sɪntʃ] *n* (*col*): **it's a** ~ c'est du gâteau, c'est l'enfance de l'art.

cinder ['sɪndə*] *n* cendre *f*.

Cinderella [sɪndə'rɛlə] *n* Cendrillon.

cine-camera ['sɪnɪ'kæmərə] *n* (*Brit*) caméra *f*.

cine-film ['sɪnɪfɪlm] *n* (*Brit*) film *m*.

cinema ['sɪnəmə] *n* cinéma *m*.

cine-projector ['sɪnɪprə'dʒɛktə*] *n* (*Brit*) projecteur *m* de cinéma.

cinnamon ['sɪnəmən] *n* cannelle *f*.

cipher ['saɪfə*] *n* code secret; (*fig: faceless employee etc*) numéro *m*; **in ~** codé(e).

circa ['sɜːkə] *prep* circa, environ.

circle ['sɜːkl] *n* cercle *m*; (*in cinema*) balcon *m* ♦ *vi* faire *or* décrire des cercles ♦ *vt* (*surround*) entourer, encercler; (*move round*) faire le tour de, tourner autour de.

circuit ['sɜːkɪt] *n* circuit *m*.

circuit board *n* plaquette *f*.

circuitous [sɜː'kjuːɪtəs] *a* indirect(e), qui fait un détour.

circular ['sɜːkjulə*] *a* circulaire ♦ *n* circulaire *f*; (*as advertisement*) prospectus *m*.

circulate ['sɜːkjuleɪt] *vi* circuler ♦ *vt* faire circuler.

circulation [sɜːkju'leɪʃən] *n* circulation *f*; (*of newspaper*) tirage *m*.

circumcise ['sɜːkəmsaɪz] *vt* circoncire.

circumference [sə'kʌmfərəns] *n* circonférence *f*.

circumflex ['sɜːkəmflɛks] *n* (*also:* **~ accent**) accent *m* circonflexe.

circumscribe ['sɜːkəmskraɪb] *vt* circonscrire.

circumspect ['sɜːkəmspɛkt] *a* circonspect(e).

circumstances ['sɜːkəmstənsɪz] *npl* circonstances *fpl*; (*financial condition*) moyens *mpl*, situation financière; **in the ~** dans ces conditions; **under no ~** en aucun cas, sous aucun prétexte.

circumstantial [sɜːkəm'stænʃl] *a* (*report, statement*) circonstancié(e); **~ evidence** preuve indirecte.

circumvent [sɜːkəm'vɛnt] *vt* (*rule etc*) tourner.

circus ['sɜːkəs] *n* cirque *m*; (*also:* **C~**: *in place names*) place *f*.

cistern ['sɪstən] *n* réservoir *m* (d'eau); (*in toilet*) réservoir de la chasse d'eau.

citation [saɪ'teɪʃən] *n* citation *f*; (*US*) P.-V. *m*.

cite [saɪt] *vt* citer.

citizen ['sɪtɪzn] *n* (*POL*) citoyen/ne; (*resident*): **the ~s of this town** les habitants de cette ville.

citizenship ['sɪtɪznʃɪp] *n* citoyenneté *f*.

citric ['sɪtrɪk] *a*: **~ acid** acide *m* citrique.

citrus fruit ['sɪtrəs-] *n* agrume *m*.

city ['sɪtɪ] *n* ville *f*, cité *f*; **the C~** la Cité de Londres (*centre des affaires*).

city centre *n* centre ville *m*.

civic ['sɪvɪk] *a* civique.

civic centre *n* (*Brit*) centre administratif (municipal).

civil ['sɪvɪl] *a* civil(e); (*polite*) poli(e), civil.

civil disobedience *n* désobéissance civile.

civil engineer *n* ingénieur civil.

civil engineering *n* génie civil, travaux publics.

civilian [sɪ'vɪlɪən] *a, n* civil(e).

civilization [sɪvɪlaɪ'zeɪʃən] *n* civilisation *f*.

civilized ['sɪvɪlaɪzd] *a* civilisé(e); (*fig*) où règnent les bonnes manières, empreint(e) d'une courtoisie de bon ton.

civil law *n* code civil; (*study*) droit civil.

civil rights *npl* droits *mpl* civiques.

civil servant *n* fonctionnaire *m/f*.

Civil Service *n* fonction publique, adminis-

tration *f*.

civil war *n* guerre civile.

cl *abbr* (= *centilitre*) cl.

clad [klæd] *a*: **~ (in)** habillé(e) de, vêtu(e) de.

claim [kleɪm] *vt* (*rights etc*) revendiquer; (*compensation*) réclamer; **to ~ that/to be** prétendre que/être ♦ *vi* (*for insurance*) faire une déclaration de sinistre ♦ *n* revendication *f*; prétention *f*; (*right*) droit *m*; (*for expenses*) note *f* de frais; (*insurance*) **~** demande *f* d'indemnisation, déclaration *f* de sinistre; **to put in a ~ for** (*pay rise etc*) demander.

claimant ['kleɪmənt] *n* (*ADMIN, LAW*) requérant/e.

claim form *n* (*gen*) formulaire *m* de demande.

clairvoyant [klɛə'vɔɪənt] *n* voyant/e, extralucide *m/f*.

clam [klæm] *n* palourde *f*.

clam up *vi* (*col*) la boucler.

clamber ['klæmbə*] *vi* grimper, se hisser.

clammy ['klæmɪ] *a* humide et froid(e) (au toucher), moite.

clamour, (*US*) **clamor** ['klæmə*] *n* (*noise*) clameurs *fpl*; (*protest*) protestations bruyantes ♦ *vi*: **to ~ for sth** réclamer qch à grands cris.

clamp [klæmp] *n* étau *m* à main; agrafe *f*, crampon *m* ♦ *vt* serrer; cramponner.

clamp down on *vt fus* sévir contre, prendre des mesures draconiennes à l'égard de.

clan [klæn] *n* clan *m*.

clandestine [klæn'dɛstɪn] *a* clandestin(e).

clang [klæŋ] *n* bruit *m or* fracas *m* métallique ♦ *vi* émettre un bruit *or* fracas métallique.

clansman ['klænzmən] *n* membre *m* d'un clan (écossais).

clap [klæp] *vi* applaudir ♦ *vt*: **to ~ (one's hands)** battre des mains ♦ *n* claquement *m*; tape *f*; **a ~ of thunder** un coup de tonnerre.

clapping ['klæpɪŋ] *n* applaudissements *mpl*.

claret ['klærət] *n* (vin *m* de) bordeaux *m* (rouge).

clarification [klærɪfɪ'keɪʃən] *n* (*fig*) clarification *f*, éclaircissement *m*.

clarify ['klærɪfaɪ] *vt* clarifier.

clarinet [klærɪ'nɛt] *n* clarinette *f*.

clarity ['klærɪtɪ] *n* clarté *f*.

clash [klæʃ] *n* (*sound*) choc *m*, fracas *m*; (*with police*) affrontement *m*; (*fig*) conflit *m* ♦ *vi* se heurter; être *or* entrer en conflit; (*dates, events*) tomber en même temps.

clasp [klɑːsp] *n* fermoir *m* ♦ *vt* serrer, étreindre.

class [klɑːs] *n* (*gen*) classe *f*; (*group, category*) catégorie *f* ♦ *vt* classer, classifier.

class-conscious ['klɑːs'kɔnʃəs] *a* conscient(e) de son appartenance sociale.

class consciousness *n* conscience *f* de classe.

classic ['klæsɪk] *a* classique ♦ *n* (*author*) classique *m*; (*race etc*) classique *f*.

classical ['klæsɪkl] *a* classique.

classics ['klæsɪks] *npl* (*SCOL*) lettres *fpl* classiques.

classification [klæsɪfɪ'keɪʃən] *n* classification *f*.

classified ['klæsɪfaɪd] *a* (*information*) secret(ète); **~ ads** petites annonces.

classify ['klæsɪfaɪ] vt classifier, classer.

classmate ['klɑːsmeɪt] n camarade m/f de classe.

classroom ['klɑːsrum] n (salle f de) classe f.

clatter ['klætə*] n cliquetis m ♦ vi cliqueter.

clause [klɔːz] n clause f; (LING) proposition f.

claustrophobia [klɔːstrə'fəubɪə] n claustrophobie f.

claw [klɔː] n griffe f; (of bird of prey) serre f; (of lobster) pince f ♦ vt griffer; déchirer.

clay [kleɪ] n argile f.

clean [kliːn] a propre; (clear, smooth) net(te) ♦ vt nettoyer ♦ ad: **he ~ forgot** il a complètement oublié; **to come ~** (col: admit guilt) se mettre à table; **to ~ one's teeth** (Brit) se laver les dents; **~ driving licence** or (US) **record** permis où n'est portée aucune indication de contravention.

clean off vt enlever.

clean out vt nettoyer (à fond).

clean up vt nettoyer; (fig) remettre de l'ordre dans ♦ vi (fig: make profit): **to ~ up on** faire son beurre avec.

clean-cut ['kliːn'kʌt] a (man) soigné; (situation etc) bien délimité(e), net(te), clair(e).

cleaner ['kliːnə*] n (person) nettoyeur/euse, femme f de ménage; (also: **dry ~er**) teinturier/ière; (product) détachant m.

cleaning ['kliːnɪŋ] n nettoyage m.

cleaning lady n femme f de ménage.

cleanliness ['klɛnlɪnɪs] n propreté f.

cleanly ['kliːnlɪ] ad proprement; nettement.

cleanse [klɛnz] vt nettoyer; purifier.

cleanser ['klɛnzə*] n détergent m; (for face) démaquillant m.

clean-shaven ['kliːn'ʃeɪvn] a rasé(e) de près.

cleansing department ['klɛnzɪŋ-] n (Brit) service m de voirie.

clean-up ['kliːnʌp] n nettoyage m.

clear [klɪə*] a clair(e); (road, way) libre, dégagé(e); (profit, majority) net(te) ♦ vt dégager, déblayer, débarrasser; (room etc: of people) faire évacuer; (woodland) défricher; (cheque) compenser; (COMM: goods) liquider; (LAW: suspect) innocenter; (obstacle) franchir or sauter sans heurter ♦ vi (weather) s'éclaircir; (fog) se dissiper ♦ ad: **~ of** à distance de, à l'écart de ♦ n: **to be in the ~** (out of debt) être dégagé(e) de toute dette; (out of suspicion) être lavé(e) de tout soupçon; (out of danger) être hors de danger; **to ~ the table** débarrasser la table, desservir; **to ~ one's throat** s'éclaircir la gorge; **to ~ a profit** faire un bénéfice net; **to make o.s. ~** se faire bien comprendre; **to make it ~ to sb that ...** bien faire comprendre à qn que ...; **I have a ~ day tomorrow** (Brit) je n'ai rien de prévu demain; **to keep ~ of sb/sth** éviter qn/qch.

clear off vi (col: leave) dégager.

clear up vi s'éclaircir, se dissiper ♦ vt ranger, mettre en ordre; (mystery) éclaircir, résoudre.

clearance ['klɪərəns] n (removal) déblayage m; (free space) dégagement m; (permission) autorisation f.

clearance sale n (COMM) liquidation f.

clear-cut ['klɪə'kʌt] a précise(e), nettement défini(e).

clearing ['klɪərɪŋ] n (in forest) clairière f; (Brit BANKING) compensation f, clearing m.

clearing bank n (Brit) banque f qui appartient à une chambre de compensation.

clearly ['klɪəlɪ] ad clairement; (obviously) de toute évidence.

clearway ['klɪəweɪ] n (Brit) route f à stationnement interdit.

cleavage ['kliːvɪdʒ] n (of dress) décolleté m.

cleaver ['kliːvə*] n fendoir m, couperet m.

clef [klɛf] n (MUS) clé f.

cleft [klɛft] n (in rock) crevasse f, fissure f.

clemency ['klɛmənsɪ] n clémence f.

clement ['klɛmənt] a (weather) clément(e).

clench [klɛntʃ] vt serrer.

clergy ['klɜːdʒɪ] n clergé m.

clergyman ['klɜːdʒɪmən] n ecclésiastique m.

clerical ['klɛrɪkl] a de bureau, d'employé de bureau; (REL) clérical(e), du clergé.

clerk [klɑːk, (US) klɜːrk] n employé/e de bureau; (US: salesman/woman) vendeur/euse; **C~ of Court** (LAW) greffier m (du tribunal).

clever ['klɛvə*] a (mentally) intelligent(e); (deft, crafty) habile, adroit(e); (device, arrangement) ingénieux(euse), astucieux(euse).

clew [kluː] n (US) = **clue.**

cliché ['kliːʃeɪ] n cliché m.

click [klɪk] vi faire un bruit sec or un déclic ♦ vt: **to ~ one's tongue** faire claquer sa langue; **to ~ one's heels** claquer des talons.

client ['klaɪənt] n client/e.

clientele [kliːɑ̃ːn'tɛl] n clientèle f.

cliff [klɪf] n falaise f.

cliffhanger ['klɪfhæŋə*] n (TV, fig) histoire pleine de suspense.

climactic [klaɪ'mæktɪk] a à son point culminant, culminant(e).

climate ['klaɪmɪt] n climat m.

climax ['klaɪmæks] n apogée m, point culminant; (sexual) orgasme m.

climb [klaɪm] vi grimper, monter; (plane) prendre de l'altitude ♦ vt gravir, escalader, monter sur ♦ n montée f, escalade f; **to ~ over a wall** passer par dessus un mur.

climb down vi (re)descendre; (Brit fig) rabattre de ses prétentions.

climbdown ['klaɪmdaun] n (Brit) reculade f.

climber ['klaɪmə*] n (also: **rock ~**) grimpeur/euse, varappeur/euse.

climbing ['klaɪmɪŋ] n (also: **rock ~**) escalade f, varappe f.

clinch [klɪntʃ] vt (deal) conclure, sceller.

cling, pt, pp **clung** [klɪŋ, klʌŋ] vi: **to ~ (to)** se cramponner (à), s'accrocher (à); (of clothes) coller (à).

clinic ['klɪnɪk] n clinique f; centre médical; (session: MED) consultation(s) f(pl), séance(s) f(pl); (: SPORT) séance(s) de perfectionnement.

clinical ['klɪnɪkl] a clinique; (fig) froid(e).

clink [klɪŋk] vi tinter, cliqueter.

clip [klɪp] n (for hair) barrette f; (also: **paper ~**) trombone m; (Brit: also: **bulldog ~**) pince f de bureau; (holding hose etc) collier m or bague f (métallique de serrage ♦ vt (also: **~ together**: papers) attacher; (hair, nails) couper; (hedge) tailler.

clippers ['klɪpəz] npl tondeuse f; (also: **nail** ~) coupe-ongles m inv.

clipping ['klɪpɪŋ] n (from newspaper) coupure f de journal.

clique [kli:k] n clique f, coterie f.

cloak [kləuk] n grande cape.

cloakroom ['kləukrum] n (for coats etc) vestiaire m; (Brit: W.C.) toilettes fpl.

clock [klɔk] n (large) horloge f; (small) pendule f; **round the** ~ (work etc) vingt-quatre heures sur vingt-quatre; **to sleep round the** ~ or the ~ **round** faire le tour du cadran; **30,000 on the** ~ (Brit AUT) 30 000 km au compteur; **to work against the** ~ faire la course contre la montre.

clock in , **clock on** vi (Brit) pointer (en arrivant).

clock off , **clock out** vi (Brit) pointer (en partant).

clock up vt (miles, hours etc) faire.

clockwise ['klɔkwaɪz] ad dans le sens des aiguilles d'une montre.

clockwork ['klɔkwə:k] n mouvement m (d'horlogerie); rouages mpl, mécanisme m ♦ a (toy, train) mécanique.

clog [klɔg] n sabot m ♦ vt boucher, encrasser ♦ vi se boucher, s'encrasser.

cloister ['klɔɪstə*] n cloître m.

clone [kləun] n clone m.

close a, ad and derivatives [kləus] a (near): ~ **(to)** près (de), proche (de); (writing, texture) serré(e); (watch) étroit(e), strict(e); (examination) attentif(ive), minutieux(euse); (weather) lourd(e), étouffant(e); (room) mal aéré(e) ♦ ad près, à proximité; ~ **to** prep près de; ~ **by**, ~ **at hand** a, ad tout(e) près; **how** ~ **is Edinburgh to Glasgow?** combien de kilomètres y-a-t-il entre Edimbourg et Glasgow?; **a** ~ **friend** un ami intime; **to have a** ~ **shave** (fig) l'échapper belle; **at** ~ **quarters** tout près, à côté ♦ vb and derivatives [kləuz] vt fermer; (bargain, deal) conclure ♦ vi (shop etc) fermer; (lid, door etc) se fermer; (end) se terminer, conclure ♦ n (end) conclusion f; **to bring sth to a** ~ mettre fin à qch.

close down vt, vi fermer (définitivement).

close in vi (hunters) approcher; (night, fog) tomber; **the days are closing in** les jours raccourcissent; **to** ~ **in on sb** cerner qn.

close off vt (area) boucler.

closed [kləuzd] a (shop etc) fermé(e); (road) fermé à la circulation.

closed-circuit ['kləuzd'sə:kɪt] a: ~ **television** télévision f en circuit fermé.

closed shop n organisation f qui n'admet que des travailleurs syndiqués.

close-knit ['kləus'nɪt] a (family, community) très uni(e).

closely ['kləuslɪ] ad (examine, watch) de près; **we are** ~ **related** nous sommes proches parents; **a** ~ **guarded secret** un secret bien gardé.

closet ['klɔzɪt] n (cupboard) placard m, réduit m.

close-up ['kləusʌp] n gros plan.

closing ['kləuzɪŋ] a (stages, remarks) final(e); ~ **price** (STOCK EXCHANGE) cours m de clôture.

closure ['kləuʒə*] n fermeture f.

clot [klɔt] n (gen: **blood** ~) caillot m; (col: person) ballot m ♦ vi (blood) former des caillots; (: external bleeding) se coaguler.

cloth [klɔθ] n (material) tissu m, étoffe f; (Brit: also: **tea**~) torchon m; lavette f; (also: **table**~) nappe f.

clothe [kləuð] vt habiller, vêtir.

clothes [kləuðz] npl vêtements mpl, habits mpl; **to put one's** ~ **on** s'habiller; **to take one's** ~ **off** enlever ses vêtements.

clothes brush n brosse f à habits.

clothes line n corde f (à linge).

clothes peg, (US) **clothes pin** n pince f à linge.

clothing ['kləuðɪŋ] n = **clothes**.

clotted cream ['klɔtɪd-] n (Brit) crème caillée.

cloud [klaud] n nuage m ♦ vt (liquid) troubler; **to** ~ **the issue** brouiller les cartes; **every** ~ **has a silver lining** (proverb) à quelque chose malheur est bon (proverbe).

cloud over vi se couvrir; (fig) s'assombrir.

cloudburst ['klaudbə:st] n violente averse.

cloud-cuckoo-land ['klaud'kuku:'lænd] n (Brit) monde m imaginaire.

cloudy ['klaudɪ] a nuageux(euse), couvert(e); (liquid) trouble.

clout [klaut] n (blow) taloche f; (fig) pouvoir m ♦ vt flanquer une taloche à.

clove [kləuv] n clou m de girofle; ~ **of garlic** gousse f d'ail.

clover ['kləuvə*] n trèfle m.

cloverleaf ['kləuvəli:f] n feuille f de trèfle; (AUT) croisement m en trèfle.

clown [klaun] n clown m ♦ vi (also: ~ **about**, ~ **around**) faire le clown.

cloying ['klɔɪŋ] a (taste, smell) écœurant(e).

club [klʌb] n (society) club m; (weapon) massue f, matraque f; (also: **golf** ~) club ♦ vt matraquer ♦ vi: **to** ~ **together** s'associer; ~**s** npl (CARDS) trèfle m.

club car n (US RAIL) wagon-restaurant m.

clubhouse ['klʌbhaus] n pavillon m.

cluck [klʌk] vi glousser.

clue [klu:] n indice m; (in crosswords) définition f; **I haven't a** ~ je n'en ai pas la moindre idée.

clued up, (US) **clued in** [klu:d-] a (col) (vachement) calé(e).

clump [klʌmp] n: ~ **of trees** bouquet m d'arbres.

clumsy ['klʌmzɪ] a (person) gauche, maladroit(e); (object) malcommode, peu maniable.

clung [klʌŋ] pt, pp of **cling**.

cluster ['klʌstə*] n (petit) groupe ♦ vi se rassembler.

clutch [klʌtʃ] n (grip, grasp) étreinte f, prise f; (AUT) embrayage m ♦ vt agripper, serrer fort; **to** ~ **at** se cramponner à.

clutter ['klʌtə*] vt (also: ~ **up**) encombrer ♦ n désordre m, fouillis m.

CM abbr (US POST) = North Marianna Islands.

cm abbr (= centimetre) cm.

CNAA n abbr (Brit: = Council for National Academic Awards) organisme non universitaire délivrant des diplômes.

CND *n abbr* = *Campaign for Nuclear Disarmament.*

CO *n abbr* (= *commanding officer*) Cdt; (*Brit*) = *Commonwealth Office* ♦ *abbr* (*US POST*) = *Colorado.*

Co. *abbr* = **company, county.**

c/o *abbr* (= *care of*) c/o, aux bons soins de.

coach [kəutʃ] *n* (*bus*) autocar *m*; (*horse-drawn*) diligence *f*; (*of train*) voiture *f*, wagon *m*; (*SPORT: trainer*) entraîneur/euse; (*school: tutor*) répétiteur/trice ♦ *vt* entraîner; donner des leçons particulières à.

coach trip *n* excursion *f* en car.

coagulate [kəu'ægjuleɪt] *vt* coaguler ♦ *vi* se coaguler.

coal [kəul] *n* charbon *m*.

coal face *n* front *m* de taille.

coalfield ['kəulfiːld] *n* bassin houiller.

coalition [kəuə'lɪʃən] *n* coalition *f*.

coalman, coal merchant ['kəulmən, 'kəulmɜːtʃənt] *n* charbonnier *m*, marchand *m* de charbon.

coal mine *n* mine *f* de charbon.

coal miner *n* mineur *m*.

coal mining *n* extraction *f* du charbon.

coarse [kɔːs] *a* grossier(ère), rude; (*vulgar*) vulgaire.

coast [kəust] *n* côte *f* ♦ *vi* (*with cycle etc*) descendre en roue libre.

coastal ['kəustl] *a* côtier(ère).

coaster ['kəustə*] *n* (*NAUT*) caboteur *m*; (*for glass*) dessous *m* de verre.

coastguard ['kəustgaːd] *n* garde-côte *m*.

coastline ['kəustlaɪn] *n* côte *f*, littoral *m*.

coat [kəut] *n* manteau *m*; (*of animal*) pelage *m*, poil *m*; (*of paint*) couche *f* ♦ *vt* couvrir, enduire; ~ **of arms** *n* blason *m*, armoiries *fpl*.

coat hanger *n* cintre *m*.

coating ['kəutɪŋ] *n* couche *f*, enduit *m*.

co-author ['kəu'ɔːθə*] *n* co-auteur *m*.

coax [kəuks] *vt* persuader par des cajoleries.

cob [kɒb] *n see* **corn.**

cobbler ['kɒblə*] *n* cordonnier *m*.

cobbles, cobblestones ['kɒblz, 'kɒblstəunz] *npl* pavés (ronds).

COBOL ['kəubɒl] *n* COBOL *m*.

cobra ['kəubrə] *n* cobra *m*.

cobweb ['kɒbweb] *n* toile *f* d'araignée.

cocaine [kə'keɪn] *n* cocaïne *f*.

cock [kɒk] *n* (*rooster*) coq *m*; (*male bird*) mâle *m* ♦ *vt* (*gun*) armer; **to** ~ **one's ears** (*fig*) dresser l'oreille.

cock-a-hoop [kɒkə'huːp] *a* jubilant(e).

cockerel ['kɒkərl] *n* jeune coq *m*.

cock-eyed ['kɒkaɪd] *a* (*fig*) de travers; qui louche; qui ne tient pas debout (*fig*).

cockle ['kɒkl] *n* coque *f*.

cockney ['kɒknɪ] *n* cockney *m/f* (*habitant des quartiers populaires de l'East End de Londres*), ≈ faubourien/ne.

cockpit ['kɒkpɪt] *n* (*in aircraft*) poste *m* de pilotage, cockpit *m*.

cockroach ['kɒkrəutʃ] *n* cafard *m*, cancrelat *m*.

cocktail ['kɒkteɪl] *n* cocktail *m*; **prawn** ~, (*US*) **shrimp** ~ cocktail de crevettes.

cocktail cabinet *n* (meuble-)bar *m*.

cocktail party *n* cocktail *m*.

cocktail shaker [-'ʃeɪkə*] *n* shaker *m*.

cocoa ['kəukəu] *n* cacao *m*.

coconut ['kəukənʌt] *n* noix *f* de coco.

cocoon [kə'kuːn] *n* cocon *m*.

COD *abbr* = **cash on delivery, collect on delivery** (*US*).

cod [kɒd] *n* morue (fraîche), cabillaud *m*.

code [kəud] *n* code *m*; ~ **of behaviour** règles *fpl* de conduite; ~ **of practice** déontologie *f*.

codeine ['kəudiːn] *n* codéine *f*.

codicil ['kɒdɪsɪl] *n* codicille *m*.

codify ['kəudɪfaɪ] *vt* codifier.

cod-liver oil *n* huile *f* de foie de morue.

co-driver ['kəu'draɪvə*] *n* (*in race*) copilote *m*; (*of lorry*) deuxième chauffeur *m*.

co-ed ['kəu'ed] *a abbr* = **coeducational** ♦ *n abbr* (*US: female student*) étudiante d'une université mixte; (*Brit: school*) école *f* mixte.

coeducational ['kəuedju'keɪʃənl] *a* mixte.

coerce [kəu'ɜːs] *vt* contraindre.

coercion [kəu'ɜːʃən] *n* contrainte *f*.

coexistence ['kəuɪg'zɪstəns] *n* coexistence *f*.

C. of C. *n abbr* = **chamber of commerce.**

C of E *abbr* = **Church of England.**

coffee ['kɒfɪ] *n* café *m*; **white** ~, (*US*) ~ **with cream** (café-)crème *m*.

coffee bar *n* (*Brit*) café *m*.

coffee bean *n* grain *m* de café.

coffee break *n* pause-café *f*.

coffeecake ['kɒfɪkeɪk] *n* (*US*) ≈ petit pain aux raisins.

coffee cup *n* tasse *f* à café.

coffeepot ['kɒfɪpɒt] *n* cafetière *f*.

coffee table *n* (petite) table basse.

coffin ['kɒfɪn] *n* cercueil *m*.

C of I *abbr* = *Church of Ireland.*

C of S *abbr* = *Church of Scotland.*

cog [kɒg] *n* dent *f* (d'engrenage).

cogent ['kəudʒənt] *a* puissant(e), convaincant(e).

cognac ['kɒnjæk] *n* cognac *m*.

cogwheel ['kɒgwiːl] *n* roue dentée.

cohabit [kəu'hæbɪt] *vi* (*formal*): **to** ~ (**with sb**) cohabiter (avec qn).

coherent [kəu'hɪərənt] *a* cohérent(e).

cohesion [kəu'hiːʒən] *n* cohésion *f*.

cohesive [kə'hiːsɪv] *a* (*fig*) cohésif(ive).

COHSE ['kəuzɪ] *n abbr* (*Brit*: = *Confederation of Health Service Employees*) *syndicat des employés des services de santé.*

COI *n abbr* (*Brit*: = *Central Office of Information*) *service d'information gouvernemental.*

coil [kɒɪl] *n* rouleau *m*, bobine *f*; (*one loop*) anneau *m*, spire *f*; (*of smoke*) volute *f*; (*contraceptive*) stérilet *m* ♦ *vt* enrouler.

coin [kɒɪn] *n* pièce *f* de monnaie ♦ *vt* (*word*) inventer.

coinage ['kɒɪnɪdʒ] *n* monnaie *f*, système *m* monétaire.

coin-box ['kɒɪnbɒks] *n* (*Brit*) cabine *f* téléphonique.

coincide [kəuɪn'saɪd] *vi* coïncider.

coincidence [kəu'ɪnsɪdəns] *n* coïncidence *f*.

coin-operated ['kɒɪn'ɒpəreɪtɪd] *a* (*machine, launderette*) automatique.

coke [kəuk] *n* coke *m*; (®: *Coca-Cola*) coca *m*.

Col. *abbr* (= *colonel*) Col.

COLA *n abbr* (*US*: = *cost-of-living adjustment*) *réajustement (des salaires, indemnités etc) en fonction du coût de la vie.*

colander ['kɔləndə*] *n* passoire *f* (à légumes).

cold [kəuld] *a* froid(e) ♦ *n* froid *m*; (*MED*) rhume *m*; **it's ~** il fait froid; **to be ~** avoir froid; **to catch ~** prendre *or* attraper froid; **to catch a ~** s'enrhumer, attraper un rhume; **in ~ blood** de sang-froid; **to have ~ feet** avoir froid aux pieds; (*fig*) avoir la frousse *or* la trouille; **to give sb the ~ shoulder** battre froid à qn.

cold-blooded ['kəuld'blʌdɪd] *a* (*ZOOL*) à sang froid.

cold cream *n* crème *f* de soins.

coldly ['kəuldlɪ] *ad* froidement.

cold sore *n* bouton *m* de fièvre.

coleslaw ['kəulslɔ:] *n* sorte de salade de chou cru.

colic ['kɔlɪk] *n* colique(s) *f(pl)*.

collaborate [kə'læbəreɪt] *vi* collaborer.

collaboration [kəlæbə'reɪʃən] *n* collaboration *f*.

collaborator [kə'læbəreɪtə*] *n* collaborateur/trice.

collage [kɔ'lɑ:ʒ] *n* (*ART*) collage *m*.

collagen ['kɔlədʒən] *n* collagène *m*.

collapse [kə'læps] *vi* s'effondrer, s'écrouler ♦ *n* effondrement *m*, écroulement *m*; (*of government*) chute *f*.

collapsible [kə'læpsəbl] *a* pliant(e); télescopique.

collar ['kɔlə*] *n* (*of coat, shirt*) col *m*; (*for dog*) collier *m*; (*TECH*) collier, bague *f* ♦ *vt* (*col: person*) pincer.

collarbone ['kɔləbəun] *n* clavicule *f*.

collate [kɔ'leɪt] *vt* collationner.

collateral [kɔ'lætərl] *n* nantissement *m*.

collation [kə'leɪʃən] *n* collation *f*.

colleague ['kɔli:g] *n* collègue *m/f*.

collect [kə'lɛkt] *vt* rassembler; (*pick up*) ramasser; (*as a hobby*) collectionner; (*Brit: call for*) (passer) prendre; (*mail*) faire la levée de, ramasser; (*money owed*) encaisser; (*donations, subscriptions*) recueillir ♦ *vi* (*people*) se rassembler; (*dust, dirt*) s'amasser; **to ~ one's thoughts** réfléchir, réunir ses idées; **~ on delivery (COD)** (*US COMM*) payable *or* paiement à la livraison; **to call ~** (*US TEL*) téléphoner en PCV.

collected [kə'lɛktɪd] *a*: **~ works** œuvres complètes.

collection [kə'lɛkʃən] *n* collection *f*; (*of mail*) levée *f*; (*for money*) collecte *f*, quête *f*.

collective [kə'lɛktɪv] *a* collectif(ive) ♦ *n* collectif *m*.

collective bargaining *n* convention collective.

collector [kə'lɛktə*] *n* collectionneur *m*; (*of taxes*) percepteur *m*; (*of rent, cash*) encaisseur *m*; **~'s item** *or* **piece** pièce *f* de collection.

college ['kɔlɪdʒ] *n* collège *m*; (*of technology, agriculture etc*) institut *m*; **to go to ~** faire des études supérieures; **~ of education** ≈ école normale.

collide [kə'laɪd] *vi*: **to ~ (with)** entrer en collision (avec).

collie ['kɔlɪ] *n* (*dog*) colley *m*.

colliery ['kɔlɪərɪ] *n* (*Brit*) mine *f* de charbon, houillère *f*.

collision [kə'lɪʒən] *n* collision *f*, heurt *m*; **to be on a ~ course** aller droit à la collision; (*fig*) aller vers l'affrontement.

collision damage waiver *n* (*INSURANCE*) rachat *m* de franchise.

colloquial [kə'ləukwɪəl] *a* familier(ère).

collusion [kə'lu:ʒən] *n* collusion *f*; **in ~ with** en complicité avec.

cologne [kə'ləun] *n* (*also*: **eau de ~**) eau *f* de cologne.

Colombia [kə'lɔmbɪə] *n* Colombie *f*.

Colombian [kə'lɔmbɪən] *a* colombien(ne) ♦ *n* Colombien/ne.

colon ['kəulən] *n* (*sign*) deux-points *mpl*; (*MED*) côlon *m*.

colonel ['kɔ:nl] *n* colonel *m*.

colonial [kə'ləunɪəl] *a* colonial(e).

colonize ['kɔlənaɪz] *vt* coloniser.

colony ['kɔlənɪ] *n* colonie *f*.

color *etc* ['kʌlə*] (*US*) = **colour** *etc*.

Colorado beetle [kɔlə'rɑ:dəu-] *n* doryphore *m*.

colossal [kə'lɔsl] *a* colossal(e).

colour, (*US*) **color** ['kʌlə*] *n* couleur *f* ♦ *vt* colorer; peindre; (*with crayons*) colorier; (*news*) fausser, exagérer ♦ *vi* rougir ♦ *cpd* (*film, photograph, television*) en couleur; **~s** *npl* (*of party, club*) couleurs *fpl*.

colo(u)r bar *n* discrimination raciale (*dans un établissement etc*).

colo(u)r-blind [kʌləblaɪnd] *a* daltonien(ne).

colo(u)red ['kʌləd] *a* coloré(e); (*photo*) en couleur ♦ *n*: **~s** personnes *fpl* de couleur.

colo(u)rful ['kʌləful] *a* coloré(e), vif(vive); (*personality*) pittoresque, haut(e) en couleurs.

colo(u)ring ['kʌlərɪŋ] *n* colorant *m*; (*complexion*) teint *m*.

colo(u)r scheme *n* combinaison *f* de(s) couleur(s).

colour supplement *n* (*Brit PRESS*) supplément *m* magazine.

colt [kəult] *n* poulain *m*.

column ['kɔləm] *n* colonne *f*; (*fashion ~, sports ~ etc*) rubrique *f*; **the editorial ~** l'éditorial *m*.

columnist ['kɔləmnɪst] *n* rédacteur/trice d'une rubrique.

coma ['kəumə] *n* coma *m*.

comb [kəum] *n* peigne *m* ♦ *vt* (*hair*) peigner; (*area*) ratisser, passer au peigne fin.

combat ['kɔmbæt] *n* combat *m* ♦ *vt* combattre, lutter contre.

combination [kɔmbɪ'neɪʃən] *n* (*gen*) combinaison *f*.

combination lock *n* serrure *f* à combinaison.

combine *vb* [kəm'baɪn] *vt* combiner; (*one quality with another*): **to ~ sth with sth** joindre qch à qch, allier qch à qch ♦ *vi* s'associer; (*CHEM*) se combiner ♦ *n* ['kɔmbaɪn] association *f*; (*ECON*) trust *m*; **a ~d effort** un effort conjugué.

combine (harvester) *n* moissonneuse-batteuse(-lieuse) *f*.

combo ['kɔmbəu] *n* (*JAZZ etc*) groupe *m* de musiciens.

combustible [kəm'bʌstɪbl] *a* combustible.

combustion [kəm'bʌstʃən] n combustion f.
come, pt **came**, pp **come** [kʌm, keɪm] vi
venir; (col: sexually) jouir; ~ **with me**
suivez-moi; **we've just** ~ **from Paris** nous
arrivons de Paris; ... **what might** ~ **of it** ...
ce qui pourrait en résulter, ... ce qui pourrait
advenir or se produire; **to** ~ **into sight** or
view apparaître; **to** ~ **to** (decision etc)
parvenir or arriver à; **to** ~ **undone/loose** se
défaire/desserrer; **coming!** j'arrive!; **if it** ~**s**
to it s'il le faut, dans le pire des cas.
come about vi se produire, arriver.
come across vt fus rencontrer par hasard,
tomber sur ♦ vi: **to** ~ **across well/badly**
faire une bonne/mauvaise impression.
come along vi (pupil, work) faire des progrès, avancer; ~ **along!** viens!; allons!,
allez!
come apart vi s'en aller en morceaux; se
détacher.
come away vi partir, s'en aller; (become
detached) se détacher.
come back vi revenir; (reply): **can I** ~
back to you on that one? est-ce qu'on peut
revenir là-dessus plus tard?
come by vt fus (acquire) obtenir, se
procurer.
come down vi descendre; (prices) baisser;
(buildings) s'écrouler; (: be demolished) être
démoli(e).
come forward vi s'avancer; (make o.s.
known) se présenter, s'annoncer.
come from vt fus venir de; (place) venir
de, être originaire de.
come in vi entrer.
come in for vt fus (criticism etc) être
l'objet de.
come into vt fus (money) hériter de.
come off vi (button) se détacher; (stain)
s'enlever; (attempt) réussir.
come on vi (lights, electricity) s'allumer;
(central heating) se mettre en marche;
(pupil, work, project) faire des progrès,
avancer; ~ **on!** viens!; allons!, allez!
come out vi sortir; (book) paraître;
(strike) cesser le travail, se mettre en grève.
come over vt fus: **I don't know what's** ~
over him! je ne sais pas ce qui lui a pris!
come round vi (after faint, operation)
revenir à soi, reprendre connaissance.
come through vi (survive) s'en sortir;
(telephone call): **the call came through**
l'appel est bien parvenu.
come to vi revenir à soi; (add up to:
amount): **how much does it** ~ **to?** ça fait
combien?
come under vt fus (heading) se trouver
sous; (influence) subir.
come up vi monter.
come up against vt fus (resistance,
difficulties) rencontrer.
come up to vt fus arriver à; **the film
didn't** ~ **up to our expectations** le film nous
a déçu.
come up with vt fus: **he came up with an
idea** il a eu une idée, il a proposé quelque
chose.
come upon vt fus tomber sur.
comeback ['kʌmbæk] n (reaction) réaction f;

(response) réponse f; (THEATRE etc) rentrée
f.
Comecon ['kɔmɪkɔn] n abbr (= Council for
Mutual Economic Aid) COMECON m.
comedian [kə'miːdɪən] n (in music hall etc)
comique m; (THEATRE) comédien m.
comedienne [kəmiːdɪ'ɛn] n comique f.
comedown ['kʌmdaun] n déchéance f.
comedy ['kɔmɪdɪ] n comédie f.
comet ['kɔmɪt] n comète f.
comeuppance [kʌm'ʌpəns] n: **to get one's** ~
recevoir ce qu'on mérite.
comfort ['kʌmfət] n confort m, bien-être m;
(solace) consolation f, réconfort m ♦ vt
consoler, réconforter.
comfortable ['kʌmfətəbl] a confortable; **I
don't feel very** ~ **about it** cela m'inquiète un
peu.
comfortably ['kʌmfətəblɪ] ad (sit) confortablement; (live) à l'aise.
comforter ['kʌmfətə*] n (US) édredon m.
comforts ['kʌmfəts] npl aises fpl.
comfort station n (US) toilettes fpl.
comic ['kɔmɪk] a comique ♦ n comique m;
(magazine) illustré m.
comical ['kɔmɪkl] a amusant(e).
comic strip n bande dessinée.
coming ['kʌmɪŋ] n arrivée f ♦ a (next) pro-
chain(e); (future) à venir; **in the** ~ **weeks**
dans les prochaines semaines.
coming(s) and going(s) n(pl) va-et-vient m
inv.
Comintern ['kɔmɪntəːn] n Comintern m.
comma ['kɔmə] n virgule f.
command [kə'mɑːnd] n ordre m,
commandement m; (MIL: authority)
commandement; (mastery) maîtrise f;
(COMPUT) commande f ♦ vt (troops)
commander; (be able to get) (pouvoir)
disposer de, avoir à sa disposition; (deserve)
avoir droit à; **to** ~ **sb to do** donner l'ordre
or commander à qn de faire; **to have/take** ~
of avoir/prendre le commandement de; **to
have at one's** ~ (money, resources etc)
disposer de.
commandeer [kɔmən'dɪə*] vt réquisitionner
(par la force).
commander [kə'mɑːndə*] n chef m; (MIL)
commandant m.
commander-in-chief [kə'mɑːndərɪn'tʃiːf] n
(MIL) commandant m en chef.
commanding [kə'mɑːndɪŋ] a (appearance)
imposant(e); (voice, tone) autoritaire; (lead,
position) dominant(e).
commanding officer n commandant m.
commandment [kə'mɑːndmənt] n (REL)
commandement m.
command module n (SPACE) module m de
commande.
commando [kə'mɑːndəu] n commando m;
membre m d'un commando.
commemorate [kə'mɛməreɪt] vt commémorer.
commemoration [kəmɛmə'reɪʃən] n commémoration f.
commemorative [kə'mɛmərətɪv] a commé-
moratif(ive).
commence [kə'mɛns] vt, vi commencer.
commend [kə'mɛnd] vt louer; recommander.

commendable [kə'mɛndəbl] *a* louable.
commendation [kɔmɛn'deɪʃən] *n* éloge *m*; recommandation *f*.
commensurate [kə'mɛnʃərɪt] *a*: ~ **with/to** en rapport avec/selon.
comment ['kɔmɛnt] *n* commentaire *m* ♦ *vi* faire des remarques ou commentaires; **to** ~ **on** faire des remarques sur; **to** ~ **that** faire remarquer que; *"no* ~*"* "je n'ai rien à déclarer".
commentary ['kɔməntərɪ] *n* commentaire *m*; *(SPORT)* reportage *m* (en direct).
commentator ['kɔmənteɪtə*] *n* commentateur *m*; *(SPORT)* reporter *m*.
commerce ['kɔmə:s] *n* commerce *m*.
commercial [kə'mə:ʃəl] *a* commercial(e) ♦ *n* *(TV: also:* ~ **break**) annonce *f* publicitaire, spot *m* (publicitaire).
commercial bank *n* banque *f* d'affaires.
commercial college *n* école *f* de commerce.
commercialism [kə'mə:ʃəlɪzəm] *n* mercantilisme *m*.
commercialize [kə'mə:ʃəlaɪz] *vt* commercialiser.
commercial television *n* publicité *f* à la télévision; chaînes indépendantes (financées par la publicité).
commercial traveller *n* voyageur *m* de commerce.
commercial vehicle *n* véhicule *m* utilitaire.
commiserate [kə'mɪzəreɪt] *vi*: **to** ~ **with sb** témoigner de la sympathie pour qn.
commission [kə'mɪʃən] *n* *(committee; fee: also for salesman)* commission *f*; *(order for work of art etc)* commande *f* ♦ *vt* *(MIL)* nommer (à un commandement); *(work of art)* commander, charger un artiste de l'exécution de; **out of** ~ *(NAUT)* hors de service; *(machine)* hors service; **I get 10%** ~ je reçois une commission de 10%; ~ **of inquiry** *(Brit)* commission d'enquête.
commissionaire [kəmɪʃə'nɛə*] *n* *(Brit: at shop, cinema etc)* portier *m* (en uniforme).
commissioner [kə'mɪʃənə*] *n* membre *m* d'une commission; *(POLICE)* préfet *m* (de police).
commit [kə'mɪt] *vt* *(act)* commettre; *(to sb's care)* confier (à); **to** ~ **o.s. (to do)** s'engager (à faire); **to** ~ **suicide** se suicider; **to** ~ **to writing** coucher par écrit; **to** ~ **sb for trial** traduire qn en justice.
commitment [kə'mɪtmənt] *n* engagement *m*; *(obligation)* responsabilité(s) *f(pl)*.
committed [kə'mɪtɪd] *a* *(writer, politician etc)* engagé(e).
committee [kə'mɪtɪ] *n* comité *m*; commission *f*; **to be on a** ~ siéger dans un comité *(or* une commission).
committee meeting *n* réunion *f* de comité *or* commission.
commodity [kə'mɔdɪtɪ] *n* produit *m*, marchandise *f*, article *m*; *(food)* denrée *f*.
commodity exchange *n* bourse *f* de marchandises.
common ['kɔmən] *a* *(gen, also pej)* commun(e); *(usual)* courant(e) ♦ *n* terrain communal; **in** ~ en commun; **in** ~ **use** d'un usage courant; **it's** ~ **knowledge that** il est bien connu *or* notoire que; **to the** ~ **good**

pour le bien de tous, dans l'intérêt général.
commoner ['kɔmənə*] *n* roturier/ière.
common ground *n* *(fig)* terrain *m* d'entente.
common law *n* droit coutumier.
common-law ['kɔmənlɔ:] *a*: ~ **wife** épouse *f* de facto.
commonly ['kɔmənlɪ] *ad* communément, généralement; couramment.
Common Market *n* Marché commun.
commonplace ['kɔmənpleɪs] *a* banal(e), ordinaire.
commonroom ['kɔmənrum] *n* salle commune; *(SCOL)* salle des professeurs.
Commons ['kɔmənz] *npl* (*Brit POL*): **the (House of)** ~ la chambre des Communes.
common sense *n* bon sens.
Commonwealth ['kɔmənwɛlθ] *n*: **the** ~ le Commonwealth.
commotion [kə'məuʃən] *n* désordre *m*, tumulte *m*.
communal ['kɔmju:nl] *a* *(life)* communautaire; *(for common use)* commun(e).
commune *n* ['kɔmju:n] *(group)* communauté *f* ♦ *vi* [kə'mju:n]: **to** ~ **with** converser intimement avec; communier avec.
communicate [kə'mju:nɪkeɪt] *vt* communiquer, transmettre ♦ *vi*: **to** ~ **(with)** communiquer (avec).
communication [kəmju:nɪ'keɪʃən] *n* communication *f*.
communication cord *n* *(Brit)* sonnette *f* d'alarme.
communications network *n* réseau *m* de communications.
communications satellite *n* satellite *m* de télécommunications.
communicative [kə'mju:nɪkətɪv] *a* communicatif(ive).
communion [kə'mju:nɪən] *n* *(also:* **Holy C~**) communion *f*.
communiqué [kə'mju:nɪkeɪ] *n* communiqué *m*.
communism ['kɔmjunɪzəm] *n* communisme *m*.
communist ['kɔmjunɪst] *a, n* communiste *(m/f)*.
community [kə'mju:nɪtɪ] *n* communauté *f*.
community centre *n* foyer socio-éducatif, centre *m* de loisirs.
community chest *n* *(US)* fonds commun.
community health centre *n* centre médico-social.
community service *n* ≈ travail *m* d'intérêt général, TIG *m*.
community spirit *n* solidarité *f*.
commutation ticket [kɔmju'teɪʃən-] *n* *(US)* carte *f* d'abonnement.
commute [kə'mju:t] *vi* faire le trajet journalier (de son domicile à un lieu de travail assez éloigné) ♦ *vt* *(LAW)* commuer; *(MATH: terms etc)* opérer la commutation de.
commuter [kə'mju:tə*] *n* banlieusard/e (qui ... *see vi*).
compact *a* [kəm'pækt] compact(e) ♦ *n* ['kɔmpækt] contrat *m*, entente *f*; *(also:* **powder** ~) poudrier *m*.
compact disk *n* disque compact.

companion [kəm'pænjən] n compagnon/ compagne.
companionship [kəm'pænjənʃɪp] n cama- raderie f.
companionway [kəm'pænjənweɪ] n (NAUT) escalier m des cabines.
company ['kʌmpənɪ] n (also COMM, MIL, THEATRE) compagnie f; **he's good** ~ il est d'une compagnie agréable; **we have** ~ nous avons de la visite; **to keep sb** ~ tenir compagnie à qn; **to part** ~ **with** se séparer de; **Smith and C**~ Smith et Compagnie.
company car n voiture f de fonction.
company director n administrateur/trice.
company secretary n (Brit COMM) se- crétaire général (d'une société).
comparable ['kɒmpərəbl] a comparable.
comparative [kəm'pærətɪv] a comparatif(ive); (relative) relatif(ive).
comparatively [kəm'pærətɪvlɪ] ad (relatively) relativement.
compare [kəm'pɛə*] vt: **to** ~ **sth/sb with/to** comparer qch/qn avec or et/à ♦ vi: **to** ~ **(with)** se comparer (à); être comparable (à); **how do the prices** ~? comment sont les prix?, est-ce que les prix sont comparables?; ~**d with** or **to** par rapport à.
comparison [kəm'pærɪsn] n comparaison f; **in** ~ **(with)** en comparaison (de).
compartment [kəm'pɑ:tmənt] n (also RAIL) compartiment m.
compass ['kʌmpəs] n boussole f; **within the** ~ **of** dans les limites de.
compasses ['kʌmpəsɪz] npl compas m.
compassion [kəm'pæʃən] n compassion f, humanité f.
compassionate [kəm'pæʃənɪt] a accessible à la compassion, au cœur charitable et bienveillant; **on** ~ **grounds** pour raisons personnelles or de famille.
compatibility [kəmpætɪ'bɪlɪtɪ] n compatibilité f.
compatible [kəm'pætɪbl] a compatible.
compel [kəm'pɛl] vt contraindre, obliger.
compelling [kəm'pɛlɪŋ] a (fig: argument) irrésistible.
compendium [kəm'pɛndɪəm] n (summary) abrégé m.
compensate ['kɒmpənseɪt] vt indemniser, dédommager ♦ vi: **to** ~ **for** compenser.
compensation [kɒmpən'seɪʃən] n compensation f; (money) dédommagement m, indemnité f.
compère ['kɒmpɛə*] n présentateur/trice, animateur/trice.
compete [kəm'pi:t] vi (take part) concourir; (vie): **to** ~ **(with)** rivaliser (avec), faire concurrence (à).
competence ['kɒmpɪtəns] n compétence f, aptitude f.
competent ['kɒmpɪtənt] a compétent(e), capable.
competition [kɒmpɪ'tɪʃən] n compétition f, concours m; (ECON) concurrence f; **in** ~ **with** en concurrence avec.
competitive [kəm'pɛtɪtɪv] a (ECON) concurrentiel(le); (sports) de compétition.
competitive examination n concours m.
competitor [kəm'pɛtɪtə*] n concurrent/e.

compile [kəm'paɪl] vt compiler.
complacency [kəm'pleɪsnsɪ] n contentement m de soi, autosatisfaction f.
complacent [kəm'pleɪsnt] a (trop) content(e) de soi.
complain [kəm'pleɪn] vi: **to** ~ **(about)** se plaindre (de); (in shop etc) réclamer (au sujet de).
complain of vt fus (MED) se plaindre de.
complaint [kəm'pleɪnt] n plainte f; (in shop etc) réclamation f; (MED) affection f.
complement ['kɒmplɪmənt] n complément m; (esp of ship's crew etc) effectif complet ♦ vt compléter.
complementary [kɒmplɪ'mɛntərɪ] a complémentaire.
complete [kəm'pli:t] a complet(ète) ♦ vt achever, parachever; (a form) remplir.
completely [kəm'pli:tlɪ] ad complètement.
completion [kəm'pli:ʃən] n achèvement m; **to be nearing** ~ être presque terminé; **on** ~ **of contract** dès signature du contrat.
complex ['kɒmplɛks] a complexe ♦ n (PSYCH, buildings etc) complexe m.
complexion [kəm'plɛkʃən] n (of face) teint m; (of event etc) aspect m, caractère m.
complexity [kəm'plɛksɪtɪ] n complexité f.
compliance [kəm'plaɪəns] n (submission) docilité f; (agreement): ~ **with** le fait de se conformer à; **in** ~ **with** en conformité avec, conformément à.
compliant [kəm'plaɪənt] a docile, très accommodant(e).
complicate ['kɒmplɪkeɪt] vt compliquer.
complicated ['kɒmplɪkeɪtɪd] a compliqué(e).
complication [kɒmplɪ'keɪʃən] n complication f.
complicity [kəm'plɪsɪtɪ] n complicité f.
compliment n ['kɒmplɪmənt] compliment m ♦ vt ['kɒmplɪmənt] complimenter; ~**s** npl compliments mpl, hommages mpl; vœux mpl; **to pay sb a** ~ faire or adresser un compliment à qn; **to** ~ **sb (on sth/on doing sth)** féliciter qn (pour qch/de faire qch).
complimentary [kɒmplɪ'mɛntərɪ] a flatteur(euse); (free) à titre gracieux.
complimentary ticket n billet m de faveur.
compliments slip n fiche f de transmission.
comply [kəm'plaɪ] vi: **to** ~ **with** se soumettre à, se conformer à.
component [kəm'pəunənt] a composant(e), constituant(e) ♦ n composant m, élément m.
compose [kəm'pəuz] vt composer; **to** ~ **o.s.** se calmer, se maîtriser; prendre une contenance.
composed [kəm'pəuzd] a calme, posé(e).
composer [kəm'pəuzə*] n (MUS) compositeur m.
composite ['kɒmpəzɪt] a composite; (BOT, MATH) composé(e).
composition [kɒmpə'zɪʃən] n composition f.
compost ['kɒmpɒst] n compost m.
composure [kəm'pəuʒə*] n calme m, maîtrise f de soi.
compound ['kɒmpaund] n (CHEM, LING) composé m; (enclosure) enclos m, enceinte f ♦ a composé(e) ♦ vt [kəm'paund] (fig: problem etc) aggraver.
compound fracture n fracture compliquée.

compound interest n intérêt composé.
comprehend [kɔmprɪ'hɛnd] vt comprendre.
comprehension [kɔmprɪ'hɛnʃən] n compréhension f.
comprehensive [kɔmprɪ'hɛnsɪv] a (très) complet(ète).
comprehensive insurance policy n assurance f tous risques.
comprehensive (school) n (Brit) école secondaire non sélective avec libre circulation d'une section à l'autre, ≈ CES m.
compress vt [kəm'prɛs] comprimer ♦ n ['kɔmprɛs] (MED) compresse f.
compression [kəm'prɛʃən] n compression f.
comprise [kəm'praɪz] vt (also: be ~d of) comprendre.
compromise ['kɔmprəmaɪz] n compromis m ♦ vt compromettre ♦ vi transiger, accepter un compromis ♦ cpd (decision, solution) de compromis.
compulsion [kəm'pʌlʃən] n contrainte f, force f; **under ~** sous la contrainte.
compulsive [kəm'pʌlsɪv] a (PSYCH) compulsif(ive); **he's a ~ smoker** c'est un fumeur invétéré.
compulsory [kəm'pʌlsərɪ] a obligatoire.
compulsory purchase n expropriation f.
compunction [kəm'pʌŋkʃən] n scrupule m; **to have no ~ about doing sth** n'avoir aucun scrupule à faire qch.
computer [kəm'pju:tə*] n ordinateur m; (mechanical) calculatrice f.
computerize [kəm'pju:təraɪz] vt traiter or automatiser par ordinateur.
computer language n langage m machine or informatique.
computer peripheral n périphérique m.
computer program n programme m informatique.
computer programmer n programmeur/euse.
computer programming n programmation f.
computer science n informatique f.
computer scientist n informaticien/ne.
computing [kəm'pju:tɪŋ] n informatique f.
comrade ['kɔmrɪd] n camarade m/f.
comradeship ['kɔmrɪdʃɪp] n camaraderie f.
comsat ['kɔmsæt] n abbr = **communications satellite**.
con [kɔn] vt duper; escroquer ♦ n escroquerie f; **to ~ sb into doing sth** tromper qn pour lui faire faire qch.
concave ['kɔn'keɪv] a concave.
conceal [kən'si:l] vt cacher, dissimuler.
concede [kən'si:d] vt concéder ♦ vi céder.
conceit [kən'si:t] n vanité f, suffisance f, prétention f.
conceited [kən'si:tɪd] a vaniteux(euse), suffisant(e).
conceivable [kən'si:vəbl] a concevable, imaginable; **it is ~ that** il est concevable que.
conceivably [kən'si:vəblɪ] ad: **he may ~ be right** il n'est pas impossible qu'il ait raison.
conceive [kən'si:v] vt concevoir ♦ vi: **to ~ of sth/of doing sth** imaginer qch/de faire qch.
concentrate ['kɔnsəntreɪt] vi se concentrer ♦ vt concentrer.

concentration [kɔnsən'treɪʃən] n concentration f.
concentration camp n camp m de concentration.
concentric [kən'sɛntrɪk] a concentrique.
concept ['kɔnsɛpt] n concept m.
conception [kən'sɛpʃən] n conception f; (idea) idée f.
concern [kən'sə:n] n affaire f; (COMM) entreprise f, firme f; (anxiety) inquiétude f, souci m ♦ vt concerner; **to be ~ed (about)** s'inquiéter (de), être inquiet(ète) (au sujet de); **"to whom it may ~"** "à qui de droit"; **as far as I am ~ed** en ce qui me concerne; **to be ~ed with** (person: involved with) s'occuper de; **the department ~ed** (under discussion) le service en question; (involved) le service concerné.
concerning [kən'sə:nɪŋ] prep en ce qui concerne, à propos de.
concert ['kɔnsət] n concert m; **in ~** à l'unisson, en chœur; ensemble.
concerted [kən'sə:tɪd] a concerté(e).
concert hall n salle f de concert.
concertina [kɔnsə'ti:nə] n concertina m ♦ vi se télescoper, se caramboler.
concerto [kən'tʃə:təu] n concerto m.
concession [kən'sɛʃən] n concession f.
concessionaire [kənsɛʃə'nɛə*] n concessionnaire m/f.
concessionary [kən'sɛʃənrɪ] a (ticket, fare) à tarif réduit.
conciliation [kənsɪlɪ'eɪʃən] n conciliation f, apaisement m.
conciliatory [kən'sɪlɪətrɪ] a conciliateur(trice); conciliant(e).
concise [kən'saɪs] a concis(e).
conclave ['kɔnkleɪv] n assemblée secrète; (REL) conclave m.
conclude [kən'klu:d] vt conclure ♦ vi (speaker) conclure; (events): **to ~ (with)** se terminer (par).
conclusion [kən'klu:ʒən] n conclusion f; **to come to the ~ that** (en) conclure que.
conclusive [kən'klu:sɪv] a concluant(e), définitif(ive).
concoct [kən'kɔkt] vt confectionner, composer.
concoction [kən'kɔkʃən] n (food, drink) mélange m.
concord ['kɔŋkɔ:d] n (harmony) harmonie f; (treaty) accord m.
concourse ['kɔŋkɔ:s] n (hall) hall m, salle f des pas perdus; (crowd) affluence f; multitude f.
concrete ['kɔŋkri:t] n béton m ♦ a concret(ète); (CONSTR) en béton.
concrete mixer n bétonnière f.
concur [kən'kə:*] vi être d'accord.
concurrently [kən'kʌrntlɪ] ad simultanément.
concussion [kən'kʌʃən] n (MED) commotion (cérébrale).
condemn [kən'dɛm] vt condamner.
condemnation [kɔndɛm'neɪʃən] n condamnation f.
condensation [kɔndɛn'seɪʃən] n condensation f.
condense [kən'dɛns] vi se condenser ♦ vt condenser.
condensed milk n lait concentré (sucré).

condescend [kɔndɪ'sɛnd] *vi* condescendre, s'abaisser; **to ~ to do sth** daigner faire qch.

condescending ' [kɔndɪ'sɛndɪŋ] *a* condescendant(e).

condition [kən'dɪʃən] *n* condition *f*; (*disease*) maladie *f* ♦ *vt* déterminer, conditionner; **in good/poor ~** en bon/mauvais état; **a heart ~** une maladie cardiaque; **weather ~s** conditions *fpl* météorologiques; **on ~ that** à condition que + *sub*, à condition de.

conditional [kən'dɪʃənl] *a* conditionnel(le); **to be ~ upon** dépendre de.

conditioner [kən'dɪʃənə*] *n* (*for hair*) baume démêlant.

condo ['kɔndəu] *n abbr* (*US col*) = **condominium.**

condolences [kən'dəulənsɪz] *npl* condoléances *fpl.*

condom ['kɔndəm] *n* préservatif *m.*

condominium [kɔndə'mɪnɪəm] *n* (*US: building*) immeuble *m* (en copropriété); (: *rooms*) appartement *m* (dans un immeuble en copropriété).

condone [kən'dəun] *vt* fermer les yeux sur, approuver (tacitement).

conducive [kən'dju:sɪv] *a*: ~ **to** favorable à, qui contribue à.

conduct *n* ['kɔndʌkt] conduite *f* ♦ *vt* [kən'dʌkt] conduire; (*manage*) mener, diriger; (*MUS*) diriger; **to ~ o.s.** se conduire, se comporter.

conducted tour *n* voyage organisé; (*of building*) visite guidée.

conductor [kən'dʌktə*] *n* (*of orchestra*) chef *m* d'orchestre; (*on bus*) receveur *m*; (*US: on train*) chef *m* de train; (*ELEC*) conducteur *m.*

conductress [kən'dʌktrɪs] *n* (*on bus*) receveuse *f.*

conduit ['kɔndɪt] *n* conduit *m*, tuyau *m*; tube *m.*

cone [kəun] *n* cône *m*; (*for ice-cream*) cornet *m*; (*BOT*) pomme *f* de pin, cône.

confectioner [kən'fɛkʃənə*] *n* (*of cakes*) pâtissier/ière; (*of sweets*) confiseur/euse; **~'s (shop)** confiserie(-pâtisserie) *f.*

confectionery [kən'fɛkʃənrɪ] *n* (*cakes*) pâtisserie *f*; (*sweets*) confiserie *f.*

confederate [kən'fɛdrɪt] *a* confédéré(e) ♦ *n* (*pej*) acolyte *m*; (*US HISTORY*) confédéré/e.

confederation [kənfɛdə'reɪʃən] *n* confédération *f.*

confer [kən'fə:*] *vt*: **to ~ sth on** conférer qch à ♦ *vi* conférer, s'entretenir; **to ~ (with sb about sth)** s'entretenir (de qch avec qn).

conference ['kɔnfərns] *n* conférence *f*; **to be in ~** être en réunion ou en conférence.

conference room *n* salle *f* de conférence.

confess [kən'fɛs] *vt* confesser, avouer ♦ *vi* se confesser.

confession [kən'fɛʃən] *n* confession *f.*

confessional [kən'fɛʃənl] *n* confessional *m.*

confessor [kən'fɛsə*] *n* confesseur *m.*

confetti [kən'fɛtɪ] *n* confettis *mpl.*

confide [kən'faɪd] *vi*: **to ~ in** s'ouvrir à, se confier à.

confidence ['kɔnfɪdns] *n* confiance *f*; (*also:* **self-~**) assurance *f*, confiance en soi; (*secret*) confidence *f*; **to have (every) ~ that** être certain que; **motion of no ~** motion *f* de censure; **to tell sb sth in strict ~** dire qch à qn en toute confidence.

confidence trick *n* escroquerie *f.*

confident ['kɔnfɪdənt] *a* sûr(e), assuré(e).

confidential [kɔnfɪ'dɛnʃəl] *a* confidentiel(le); (*secretary*) particulier(ère).

confidentiality ['kɔnfɪdɛnʃɪ'ælɪtɪ] *n* confidentialité *f.*

configuration [kən'fɪgju'reɪʃən] *n* (*also COMPUT*) configuration *f.*

confine [kən'faɪn] *vt* limiter, borner; (*shut up*) confiner, enfermer; **to ~ o.s. to doing sth/ to sth** se contenter de faire qch/se limiter à qch.

confined [kən'faɪnd] *a* (*space*) restreint(e), réduit(e).

confinement [kən'faɪnmənt] *n* emprisonnement *m*, détention *f*; (*MIL*) consigne *f* (au quartier); (*MED*) accouchement *m.*

confines ['kɔnfaɪnz] *npl* confins *mpl*, bornes *fpl.*

confirm [kən'fə:m] *vt* (*report, REL*) confirmer; (*appointment*) ratifier.

confirmation [kɔnfə'meɪʃən] *n* confirmation *f*; ratification *f.*

confirmed [kən'fə:md] *a* invétéré(e), incorrigible.

confiscate ['kɔnfɪskeɪt] *vt* confisquer.

confiscation [kɔnfɪs'keɪʃən] *n* confiscation *f.*

conflagration [kɔnflə'greɪʃən] *n* incendie *m*; (*fig*) conflagration *f.*

conflict *n* ['kɔnflɪkt] conflit *m*, lutte *f* ♦ *vi* [kən'flɪkt] être or entrer en conflit; (*opinions*) s'opposer, se heurter.

conflicting [kən'flɪktɪŋ] *a* contradictoire.

conform [kən'fɔ:m] *vi*: **to ~ (to)** se conformer (à).

conformist [kən'fɔ:mɪst] *n* conformiste *m/f.*

confound [kən'faund] *vt* confondre; (*amaze*) rendre perplexe.

confounded [kən'faundɪd] *a* maudit(e), sacré(e).

confront [kən'frʌnt] *vt* confronter, mettre en présence; (*enemy, danger*) affronter, faire face à.

confrontation [kɔnfrən'teɪʃən] *n* confrontation *f.*

confuse [kən'fju:z] *vt* embrouiller; (*one thing with another*) confondre.

confused [kən'fju:zd] *a* (*person*) dérouté(e), désorienté(e); (*situation*) embrouillé(e).

confusing [kən'fju:zɪŋ] *a* peu clair(e), déroutant(e).

confusion [kən'fju:ʒən] *n* confusion *f.*

congeal [kən'dʒi:l] *vi* (*oil*) se figer; (*blood*) se coaguler.

congenial [kən'dʒi:nɪəl] *a* sympathique, agréable.

congenital [kən'dʒɛnɪtl] *a* congénital(e).

conger eel ['kɔngər-] *n* congre *m.*

congested [kən'dʒɛstɪd] *a* (*MED*) congestionné(e); (*fig*) surpeuplé(e); congestionné; bloqué(e); (*telephone lines*) encombré(e).

congestion [kən'dʒɛstʃən] *n* congestion *f*; (*fig*) encombrement *m.*

conglomerate [kən'glɔmərɪt] *n* (*COMM*) conglomérat *m.*

conglomeration [kənglɔmə'reɪʃən] *n* groupement *m*; agglomération *f.*

Congo ['kɔŋgəu] *n* (*state*) (république *f* du) Congo.

congratulate [kən'grætjuleɪt] *vt*: **to ~ sb (on)** féliciter qn (de).

congratulations [kəngrætju'leɪʃənz] *npl*: **~ (on)** félicitations *fpl* (pour) ♦ *excl*: **~!** (toutes mes) félicitations!

congregate ['kɔŋgrɪgeɪt] *vi* se rassembler, se réunir.

congregation [kɔŋgrɪ'geɪʃən] *n* assemblée *f* (des fidèles).

congress ['kɔŋgrɛs] *n* congrès *m*.

congressman ['kɔŋgrɛsmən], **congress-woman** ['kɔŋgrɛswumən] *n* (*US*) membre *m* du Congrès.

conical ['kɔnɪkl] *a* (de forme) conique.

conifer ['kɔnɪfə*] *n* conifère *m*.

coniferous [kə'nɪfərəs] *a* (*forest*) de conifères.

conjecture [kən'dʒɛktʃə*] *n* conjecture *f* ♦ *vt*, *vi* conjecturer.

conjugal ['kɔndʒugl] *a* conjugal(e).

conjugate ['kɔndʒugeɪt] *vt* conjuguer.

conjugation [kɔndʒə'geɪʃən] *n* conjugaison *f*.

conjunction [kən'dʒʌŋkʃən] *n* conjonction *f*; **in ~ with** (conjointement) avec.

conjunctivitis [kəndʒʌŋktɪ'vaɪtɪs] *n* conjonctivite *f*.

conjure ['kʌndʒə*] *vt* faire apparaître (par la prestidigitation); [kən'dʒuə*] conjurer, supplier ♦ *vi* faire des tours de passe-passe.

conjure up *vt* (*ghost, spirit*) faire apparaître; (*memories*) évoquer.

conjurer ['kʌndʒərə*] *n* prestidigitateur *m*, illusionniste *m/f*.

conjuring trick ['kʌndʒərɪŋ-] *n* tour *m* de prestidigitation.

conker ['kɔŋkə*] *n* (*Brit*) marron *m* (d'Inde).

conk out [kɔŋk-] *vi* (*col*) tomber *or* rester en panne.

conman ['kɔnmæn] *n* escroc *m*.

connect [kə'nɛkt] *vt* joindre, relier; (*ELEC*) connecter; (*fig*) établir un rapport entre, faire un rapprochement entre ♦ *vi* (*train*): **to ~ with** assurer la correspondance avec; **to be ~ed with** avoir un rapport avec; (*have dealings with*) avoir des rapports avec, être en relation avec; **I am trying to ~ you** (*TEL*) j'essaie d'obtenir votre communication.

connection [kə'nɛkʃən] *n* relation *f*, lien *m*; (*ELEC*) connexion *f*; (*TEL*) communication *f*; (*train etc*) correspondance *f*; **in ~ with** à propos de; **what is the ~ between them?** quel est le lien entre eux?; **business ~s** relations d'affaires; **to miss/get one's ~** (*train etc*) rater/avoir sa correspondance.

connexion [kə'nɛkʃən] *n* (*Brit*) = **connection**.

conning tower ['kɔnɪŋ-] *n* kiosque *m* (de *sous-marin*).

connive [kə'naɪv] *vi*: **to ~ at** se faire le complice de.

connoisseur [kɔnɪ'sə:*] *n* connaisseur *m*.

connotation [kɔnə'teɪʃən] *n* connotation *f*, implication *f*.

connubial [kə'nju:bɪəl] *a* conjugal(e).

conquer ['kɔŋkə*] *vt* conquérir; (*feelings*) vaincre, surmonter.

conqueror ['kɔŋkərə*] *n* conquérant *m*, vainqueur *m*.

conquest ['kɔŋkwɛst] *n* conquête *f*.

cons [kɔnz] *npl see* **pro, convenience**.

conscience ['kɔnʃəns] *n* conscience *f*; **in all ~** en conscience.

conscientious [kɔnʃɪ'ɛnʃəs] *a* consciencieux(euse); (*scruple, objection*) de conscience.

conscientious objector *n* objecteur *m* de conscience.

conscious ['kɔnʃəs] *a* conscient(e); (*deliberate: insult, error*) délibéré(e); **to become ~ of sth/that** prendre conscience de qch/que.

consciousness ['kɔnʃəsnɪs] *n* conscience *f*; (*MED*) connaissance *f*; **to lose/regain ~** perdre/reprendre connaissance.

conscript ['kɔnskrɪpt] *n* conscrit *m*.

conscription [kən'skrɪpʃən] *n* conscription *f*.

consecrate ['kɔnsɪkreɪt] *vt* consacrer.

consecutive [kən'sɛkjutɪv] *a* consécutif(ive); **on three ~ occasions** trois fois de suite.

consensus [kən'sɛnsəs] *n* consensus *m*; **the ~ (of opinion)** le consensus (d'opinion).

consent [kən'sɛnt] *n* consentement *m* ♦ *vi*: **to ~ (to)** consentir (à); **age of ~** âge nubile (*légal*); **by common ~** d'un commun accord.

consequence ['kɔnsɪkwəns] *n* suites *fpl*, conséquence *f*; importance *f*; **in ~** en conséquence, par conséquent.

consequently ['kɔnsɪkwəntlɪ] *ad* par conséquent, donc.

conservation [kɔnsə'veɪʃən] *n* préservation *f*, protection *f*; (*also*: **nature ~**) défense *f* de l'environnement; **energy ~** économies *fpl* d'énergie.

conservationist [kɔnsə'veɪʃnɪst] *n* protecteur/trice de la nature.

conservative [kən'sə:vətɪv] *a* conservateur(trice); (*cautious*) prudent(e); **C~ *a, n*** (*Brit POL*) conservateur(trice).

conservatory [kən'sə:vətrɪ] *n* (*greenhouse*) serre *f*.

conserve [kən'sə:v] *vt* conserver, préserver; (*supplies, energy*) économiser ♦ *n* confiture *f*, conserve *f* (de fruits).

consider [kən'sɪdə*] *vt* considérer, réfléchir à; (*take into account*) penser à, prendre en considération; (*regard, judge*) considérer, estimer; **to ~ doing sth** envisager de faire qch; **~ yourself lucky** estimez-vous heureux; **all things ~ed** (toute) réflexion faite.

considerable [kən'sɪdərəbl] *a* considérable.

considerably [kən'sɪdərəblɪ] *ad* nettement.

considerate [kən'sɪdərɪt] *a* prévenant(e), plein(e) d'égards.

consideration [kənsɪdə'reɪʃən] *n* considération *f*; (*reward*) rétribution *f*, rémunération *f*; **out of ~ for** par égard pour; **under ~** à l'étude; **my first ~ is my family** ma famille passe avant tout le reste.

considering [kən'sɪdərɪŋ] *prep*: **~ (that)** étant donné (que).

consign [kən'saɪn] *vt* expédier, livrer.

consignee [kɔnsaɪ'ni:] *n* destinataire *m/f*.

consignment [kən'saɪnmənt] *n* arrivage *m*, envoi *m*.

consignment note *n* (*COMM*) bordereau *m* d'expédition.

consignor [kən'saɪnə*] *n* expéditeur/trice.

consist [kən'sɪst] *vi*: **to ~ of** consister en, se

composer de.

consistency [kən'sıstənsı] *n* consistance *f*; (*fig*) cohérence *f*.

consistent [kən'sıstənt] *a* logique, cohérent(e); ~ **with** compatible avec, en accord avec.

consolation [kɔnsə'leıʃən] *n* consolation *f*.

console *vt* [kən'səul] consoler ♦ *n* ['kɔnsəul] console *f*.

consolidate [kən'sɔlıdeıt] *vt* consolider.

consols ['kɔnsɔlz] *npl* (*Brit STOCK EXCHANGE*) rente *f* d'Etat.

consommé [kən'sɔmeı] *n* consommé *m*.

consonant ['kɔnsənənt] *n* consonne *f*.

consort *n* ['kɔnsɔ:t] époux/épouse; **prince** ~ prince *m* consort ♦ *vi* [kən'sɔ:t] (*often pej*): **to** ~ **with sb** frayer avec qn.

consortium [kən'sɔ:tıəm] *n* consortium *m*, comptoir *m*.

conspicuous [kən'spıkjuəs] *a* voyant(e), qui attire la vue *or* l'attention; **to make o.s.** ~ se faire remarquer.

conspiracy [kən'spırəsı] *n* conspiration *f*, complot *m*.

conspiratorial [kənspırə'tɔ:rıəl] *a* (*behaviour*) de conspirateur; (*glance*) conspirateur(trice).

conspire [kən'spaıə*] *vi* conspirer, comploter.

constable ['kʌnstəbl] *n* (*Brit*) ≈ agent *m* de police, gendarme *m*.

constabulary [kən'stæbjulərı] *n* ≈ police *f*, gendarmerie *f*.

constant ['kɔnstənt] *a* constant(e); incessant(e).

constantly ['kɔnstəntlı] *ad* constamment, sans cesse.

constellation [kɔnstə'leıʃən] *n* constellation *f*.

consternation [kɔnstə'neıʃən] *n* consternation *f*.

constipated ['kɔnstıpeıtıd] *a* constipé(e).

constipation [kɔnstı'peıʃən] *n* constipation *f*.

constituency [kən'stıtjuənsı] *n* circonscription électorale; (*people*) électorat *m*.

constituency party *n* section locale (d'un parti).

constituent [kən'stıtjuənt] *n* électeur/trice; (*part*) élément constitutif, composant *m*.

constitute ['kɔnstıtju:t] *vt* constituer.

constitution [kɔnstı'tju:ʃən] *n* constitution *f*.

constitutional [kɔnstı'tju:ʃənl] *a* constitutionnel(le).

constrain [kən'streın] *vt* contraindre, forcer.

constrained [kən'streınd] *a* contraint(e), gêné(e).

constraint [kən'streınt] *n* contrainte *f*; (*embarrassment*) gêne *f*.

constrict [kən'strıkt] *vt* rétrécir, resserrer; gêner, limiter.

construct [kən'strʌkt] *vt* construire.

construction [kən'strʌkʃən] *n* construction *f*; (*fig: interpretation*) interprétation *f*; **under** ~ (*building etc*) en construction.

construction industry *n* (industrie *f* du) bâtiment.

constructive [kən'strʌktıv] *a* constructif(ive).

construe [kən'stru:] *vt* analyser, expliquer.

consul ['kɔnsl] *n* consul *m*.

consulate ['kɔnsjulıt] *n* consulat *m*.

consult [kən'sʌlt] *vt* consulter; **to** ~ **sb (about sth)** consulter qn (à propos de qch).

consultancy [kən'sʌltənsı] *n* service *m* de conseils.

consultancy fee *n* honoraires *mpl* d'expert.

consultant [kən'sʌltənt] *n* (*MED*) médecin consultant; (*other specialist*) consultant *m*, (expert-)conseil *m* ♦ *cpd*: ~ **engineer** *n* ingénieur-conseil *m*; ~ **paediatrician** *n* pédiatre *m*; **legal/management** ~ conseiller *m* juridique/en gestion.

consultation [kɔnsəl'teıʃən] *n* consultation *f*; **in** ~ **with** en consultation avec.

consulting room *n* (*Brit*) cabinet *m* de consultation.

consume [kən'sju:m] *vt* consommer.

consumer [kən'sju:mə*] *n* consommateur/trice; (*of electricity, gas etc*) usager *m*.

consumer credit *n* crédit *m* aux consommateurs.

consumer durables *npl* biens *mpl* de consommation durables.

consumer goods *npl* biens *mpl* de consommation.

consumerism [kən'sju:mərızəm] *n* (*consumer protection*) défense *f* du consommateur; (*ECON*) consumérisme *m*.

consumer society *n* société *f* de consommation.

consummate ['kɔnsʌmeıt] *vt* consommer.

consumption [kən'sʌmpʃən] *n* consommation *f*; (*MED*) consomption *f* (pulmonaire); **not fit for human** ~ non comestible.

cont. *abbr* = **continued**.

contact ['kɔntækt] *n* contact *m*; (*person*) connaissance *f*, relation *f* ♦ *vt* se mettre en contact *or* en rapport avec; **to be in** ~ **with sb/sth** être en contact avec qn/qch; **business** ~**s** relations *fpl* d'affaires, contacts *mpl*.

contact lenses *npl* verres *mpl* de contact.

contagious [kən'teıdʒəs] *a* contagieux(euse).

contain [kən'teın] *vt* contenir; **to** ~ **o.s.** se contenir, se maîtriser.

container [kən'teınə*] *n* récipient *m*; (*for shipping etc*) conteneur *m*.

containerize [kən'teınəraız] *vt* conteneuriser.

contaminate [kən'tæmıneıt] *vt* contaminer.

contamination [kəntæmı'neıʃən] *n* contamination *f*.

cont'd *abbr* = **continued**.

contemplate ['kɔntəmpleıt] *vt* contempler; (*consider*) envisager.

contemplation [kɔntəm'pleıʃən] *n* contemplation *f*.

contemporary [kən'tɛmpərərı] *a* contemporain(e); (*design, wallpaper*) moderne ♦ *n* contemporain/e.

contempt [kən'tɛmpt] *n* mépris *m*, dédain *m*; ~ **of court** (*LAW*) outrage *m* à l'autorité de la justice.

contemptible [kən'tɛmptəbl] *a* méprisable, vil(e).

contemptuous [kən'tɛmptjuəs] *a* dédaigneux(euse), méprisant(e).

contend [kən'tɛnd] *vt*: **to** ~ **that** soutenir *or* prétendre que ♦ *vi*: **to** ~ **with** (*compete*) lutter avec; **to have to** ~ **with** (*be faced with*) avoir affaire à, être aux prises avec.

contender *n* prétendant/e; candidat/e.

content [kən'tɛnt] *a* content(e), satisfait(e) ♦ *vt* contenter, satisfaire ♦ *n* ['kɔntɛnt] contenu _m_; teneur _f_; **~s** _npl_ contenu _m_; **(table of)** **~s** table _f_ des matières; **to be ~ with** se contenter de; **to ~ o.s. with sth/with doing sth** se contenter de qch/de faire qch.

contented [kən'tɛntɪd] _a_ content(e), satisfait(e).

contentedly [kən'tɛntɪdlɪ] _ad_ avec un sentiment de (profonde) satisfaction.

contention [kən'tɛnʃən] _n_ dispute _f_, contestation _f_; _(argument)_ assertion _f_, affirmation _f_; **bone of ~** sujet _m_ de discorde.

contentious [kən'tɛnʃəs] _a_ querelleur(euse); litigieux(euse).

contentment [kən'tɛntmənt] _n_ contentement _m_, satisfaction _f_.

contest _n_ ['kɔntɛst] combat _m_, lutte _f_; _(competition)_ concours _m_ ♦ _vt_ [kən'tɛst] contester, discuter; _(compete for)_ disputer; _(LAW)_ attaquer.

contestant [kən'tɛstənt] _n_ concurrent/e; _(in fight)_ adversaire _m/f_.

context ['kɔntɛkst] _n_ contexte _m_; **in/out of ~** dans le/hors contexte.

continent ['kɔntɪnənt] _n_ continent _m_; **the C~** _(Brit)_ l'Europe continentale; **on the C~** en Europe (continentale).

continental [kɔntɪ'nɛntl] _a_ continental(e) ♦ _n_ _(Brit)_ Européen/ne (continental(e)).

continental breakfast _n_ café _(or_ thé) complet.

continental quilt _n_ _(Brit)_ couette _f_.

contingency [kən'tɪndʒənsɪ] _n_ éventualité _f_, événement imprévu.

contingency plan _n_ plan _m_ d'urgence.

contingent [kən'tɪndʒənt] _a_ contingent(e) ♦ _n_ contingent _m_; **to be ~ upon** dépendre de.

continual [kən'tɪnjuəl] _a_ continuel(le).

continually [kən'tɪnjuəlɪ] _ad_ continuellement, sans cesse.

continuation [kəntɪnju'eɪʃən] _n_ continuation _f_; _(after interruption)_ reprise _f_; _(of story)_ suite _f_.

continue [kən'tɪnju:] _vi_ continuer ♦ _vt_ continuer; _(start again)_ reprendre; **to be ~d** _(story)_ à suivre; **~d on page 10** suite page 10.

continuity [kɔntɪ'nju:ɪtɪ] _n_ continuité _f_; _(CINEMA)_ script _m_.

continuity girl _n_ _(CINEMA)_ script-girl _f_.

continuous [kən'tɪnjuəs] _a_ continu(e), permanent(e); **~ performance** _(CINEMA)_ séance permanente; **~ stationery** _(COMPUT)_ papier _m_ en continu.

continuously [kən'tɪnjuəslɪ] _ad_ _(repeatedly)_ continuellement; _(uninterruptedly)_ sans interruption.

contort [kən'tɔ:t] _vt_ tordre, crisper.

contortion [kən'tɔ:ʃən] _n_ crispation _f_, torsion _f_; _(of acrobat)_ contorsion _f_.

contortionist [kən'tɔ:ʃənɪst] _n_ contorsionniste _m/f_.

contour ['kɔntuə*] _n_ contour _m_, profil _m_; _(also:_ **~ line)** courbe _f_ de niveau.

contraband ['kɔntrəbænd] _n_ contrebande _f_ ♦ _a_ de contrebande.

contraception [kɔntrə'sɛpʃən] _n_ contraception _f_.

contraceptive [kɔntrə'sɛptɪv] _a_ contra-ceptif(ive), anticonceptionnel(le) ♦ _n_ contra-

ceptif _m_.

contract _n_ ['kɔntrækt] contrat _m_ ♦ _cpd_ ['kɔntrækt] _(price, date)_ contractuel(le); _(work)_ à forfait ♦ _vb_ [kən'trækt] _vi_ _(become smaller)_ se contracter, se resserrer; _(COMM)_: **to ~ to do sth** s'engager (par contrat) à faire qch ♦ _vt_ contracter; **~ of employment/service** contrat de travail/de service.

contract in _vi_ s'engager (par contrat); _(Brit ADMIN)_ s'affilier au régime de retraite complémentaire.

contract out _vi_ se dégager; _(Brit ADMIN)_ opter pour la non-affiliation au régime de re-traite complémentaire.

contraction [kən'trækʃən] _n_ contraction _f_; _(LING)_ forme contractée.

contractor [kən'træktə*] _n_ entrepreneur _m_.

contractual [kən'træktʃuəl] _a_ contractuel(le).

contradict [kɔntrə'dɪkt] _vt_ contredire; _(be con-trary to)_ démentir, être en contradiction avec.

contradiction [kɔntrə'dɪkʃən] _n_ contradiction _f_; **to be in ~ with** contredire, être en contradiction avec.

contradictory [kɔntrə'dɪktərɪ] _a_ contra-dictoire.

contralto [kən'træltəu] _n_ contralto _m_.

contraption [kən'træpʃən] _n_ _(pej)_ machin _m_, truc _m_.

contrary ['kɔntrərɪ] _a_ contraire, opposé(e); [kən'trɛərɪ] _(perverse)_ contrariant(e), entêté(e) ♦ _n_ contraire _m_; **on the ~** au contraire; **unless you hear to the ~** sauf avis contraire; **~ to what we thought** contrairement à ce que nous pensions.

contrast _n_ ['kɔntrɑ:st] contraste _m_ ♦ _vt_ [kən'trɑ:st] mettre en contraste, contraster; **in ~ to** _or_ **with** contrairement à, par opposition à.

contrasting [kən'trɑ:stɪŋ] _a_ opposé(e), contrasté(e).

contravene [kɔntrə'vi:n] _vt_ enfreindre, violer, contrevenir à.

contravention [kɔntrə'vɛnʃən] _n_: **~ (of)** in-fraction _f_ (à).

contribute [kən'trɪbju:t] _vi_ contribuer ♦ _vt_: **to ~ £10/an article to** donner 10 livres/un arti-cle à; **to ~ to** _(gen)_ contribuer à; _(newspaper)_ collaborer à; _(discussion)_ pren-dre part à.

contribution [kɔntrɪ'bju:ʃən] _n_ contribution _f_.

contributor [kən'trɪbjutə*] _n_ _(to newspaper)_ collaborateur/trice.

contributory [kən'trɪbjutərɪ] _a_ _(cause)_ annexe; **it was a ~ factor in ...** ce facteur a contribué à ....

contributory pension scheme _n_ _(Brit)_ régime _m_ de retraite salariale.

contrite ['kɔntraɪt] _a_ contrit(e).

contrivance [kən'traɪvəns] _n_ _(scheme)_ ma-chination _f_, combinaison _f_; _(device)_ appareil _m_, dispositif _m_.

contrive [kən'traɪv] _vt_ combiner, inventer ♦ _vi_: **to ~ to do** s'arranger pour faire, trouver le moyen de faire.

control [kən'trəul] _vt_ maîtriser; _(check)_ contrôler ♦ _n_ maîtrise _f_; **~s** _npl_ commandes _fpl_; **to take ~ of** se rendre maître de;

(*COMM*) acquérir une participation majoritaire dans; **to be in** ~ **of** être maître de, maîtriser; (*in charge of*) être responsable de; **to** ~ **o.s.** se contrôler; **everything is under** ~ j'ai (*or* il a *etc*) la situation en main; **the car went out of** ~ j'ai (*or* il a *etc*) perdu le contrôle du véhicule; **beyond our** ~ indépendant(e) de notre volonté.

control key *n* (*COMPUT*) touche *f* de commande.

controller [kən'trəʊlə*] *n* contrôleur *m*.

controlling interest *n* (*COMM*) participation *f* majoritaire.

control panel *n* (*on aircraft, ship, TV etc*) tableau *m* de commandes.

control point *n* (poste *m* de) contrôle *m*.

control room *n* (*NAUT, MIL*) salle *f* des commandes; (*RADIO, TV*) régie *f*.

control tower *n* (*AVIAT*) tour *f* de contrôle.

control unit *n* (*COMPUT*) unité *f* de contrôle.

controversial [kɔntrə'vɜːʃl] *a* discutable, controversé(e).

controversy ['kɔntrəvɜːsɪ] *n* controverse *f*, polémique *f*.

conurbation [kɔnə'beɪʃən] *n* conurbation *f*.

convalesce [kɔnvə'les] *vi* relever de maladie, se remettre (d'une maladie).

convalescence [kɔnvə'lesns] *n* convalescence *f*.

convalescent [kɔnvə'lesnt] *a, n* convalescent(e).

convector [kən'vektə*] *n* radiateur *m* à convection, appareil *m* de chauffage par convection.

convene [kən'viːn] *vt* convoquer, assembler ♦ *vi* se réunir, s'assembler.

convener [kən'viːnə*] *n* organisateur *m*.

convenience [kən'viːnɪəns] *n* commodité *f*; **at your** ~ quand *or* comme cela vous convient; **at your earliest** ~ (*COMM*) dans les meilleurs délais, le plus tôt possible; **all modern** ~**s**, (*Brit*) **all mod cons** avec tout le confort moderne, tout confort.

convenience foods *npl* plats cuisinés.

convenient [kən'viːnɪənt] *a* commode; **if it is** ~ **to you** si cela vous convient, si cela ne vous dérange pas.

conveniently [kən'viːnɪəntlɪ] *ad* (*happen*) à pic; (*situated*) commodément.

convent ['kɔnvənt] *n* couvent *m*.

convention [kən'venʃən] *n* convention *f*.

conventional [kən'venʃənl] *a* conventionnel(le).

convent school *n* couvent *m*.

converge [kən'vɜːdʒ] *vi* converger.

conversant [kən'vɜːsnt] *a*: **to be** ~ **with** s'y connaître en; être au courant de.

conversation [kɔnvə'seɪʃən] *n* conversation *f*.

conversational [kɔnvə'seɪʃənl] *a* de la conversation; (*COMPUT*) conversationnel(le).

conversationalist [kɔnvə'seɪʃnəlɪst] *n* brillant(e) causeur/euse.

converse *n* ['kɔnvɜːs] contraire *m*, inverse *m* ♦ *vi* [kən'vɜːs]: **to** ~ **(with sb about sth)** s'entretenir (avec qn de qch).

conversely [kɔn'vɜːslɪ] *ad* inversement, réciproquement.

conversion [kən'vɜːʃən] *n* conversion *f*; (*Brit: of house*) transformation *f*, aménagement *m*.

conversion table *n* table *f* de conversion.

convert *vt* [kən'vɜːt] (*REL, COMM*) convertir; (*alter*) transformer, aménager; (*RUGBY*) transformer ♦ *n* ['kɔnvɜːt] converti/e.

convertible [kən'vɜːtəbl] *a* convertible ♦ *n* (voiture *f*) décapotable *f*.

convex ['kɔn'veks] *a* convexe.

convey [kən'veɪ] *vt* transporter; (*thanks*) transmettre; (*idea*) communiquer.

conveyance [kən'veɪəns] *n* (*of goods*) transport *m* de marchandises; (*vehicle*) moyen *m* de transport.

conveyancing [kən'veɪənsɪŋ] *n* (*LAW*) rédaction *f* des actes de cession de propriété.

conveyor belt *n* convoyeur *m*, tapis roulant.

convict *vt* [kən'vɪkt] déclarer (*or* reconnaître) coupable ♦ *n* ['kɔnvɪkt] forçat *m*, convict *m*.

conviction [kən'vɪkʃən] *n* condamnation *f*; (*belief*) conviction *f*.

convince [kən'vɪns] *vt* convaincre, persuader; **to** ~ **sb (of sth/that)** persuader qn (de qch/ que).

convincing [kən'vɪnsɪŋ] *a* persuasif(ive), convaincant(e).

convincingly [kən'vɪnsɪŋlɪ] *ad* de façon convaincante.

convivial [kən'vɪvɪəl] *a* joyeux(euse), plein(e) d'entrain.

convoluted ['kɔnvəlutɪd] *a* (*shape*) tarabiscoté(e); (*argument*) compliqué(e).

convoy ['kɔnvɔɪ] *n* convoi *m*.

convulse [kən'vʌls] *vt* ébranler; **to be** ~**d with laughter** se tordre de rire.

convulsion [kən'vʌlʃən] *n* convulsion *f*.

coo [kuː] *vi* roucouler.

cook [kuk] *vt* (faire) cuire ♦ *vi* cuire; (*person*) faire la cuisine ♦ *n* cuisinier/ière.

cook up *vt* (*col: excuse, story*) inventer.

cookbook ['kukbuk]22 *n* livre *m* de cuisine.

cooker ['kukə*] *n* cuisinière *f*.

cookery ['kukərɪ] *n* cuisine *f*.

cookery book *n* (*Brit*) = **cookbook**.

cookie ['kukɪ] *n* (*US*) biscuit *m*, petit gâteau sec.

cooking ['kukɪŋ] *n* cuisine *f* ♦ *cpd* (*apples, chocolate*) à cuire; (*utensils, salt*) de cuisine.

cookout ['kukaut] *n* (*US*) barbecue *m*.

cool [kuːl] *a* frais(fraîche); (*not afraid*) calme; (*unfriendly*) froid(e); (*impertinent*) effronté(e) ♦ *vt, vi* rafraîchir, refroidir; **it's** ~ (*weather*) il fait frais; **to keep sth** ~ *or* **in a** ~ **place** garder *or* conserver qch au frais.

cool down *vi* refroidir; (*fig: person, situation*) se calmer.

cool box, (*US*) **cooler** ['kuːlə*] *n* boîte *f* isotherme.

cooling tower ['kuːlɪŋ-] *n* refroidisseur *m*.

coolly ['kuːlɪ] *ad* (*calmly*) calmement; (*audaciously*) sans se gêner; (*unenthusiastically*) froidement.

coolness ['kuːlnɪs] *n* fraîcheur *f*; sang-froid *m*, calme *m*; froideur *f*.

coop [kuːp] *n* poulailler *m* ♦ *vt*: **to** ~ **up** (*fig*) cloîtrer, enfermer.

co-op ['kəuɔp] *n* *abbr* (= *cooperative (society)*) coop *f*.

cooperate [kəu'ɔpəreɪt] *vi* coopérer, collaborer.

cooperation [kəuɔpə'reɪʃən] *n* coopération *f*,

collaboration f.

cooperative [kəu'ɔpərətɪv] a coopératif(ive) ♦ n coopérative f.

coopt [kəu'ɔpt] vt: **to ~ sb onto a committee** coopter qn pour faire partie d'un comité.

coordinate vt [kəu'ɔ:dɪneɪt] coordonner ♦ [kəu'ɔdɪnət] (MATH) coordonnée f; **~s** npl (clothes) ensemble m, coordonnés mpl.

coordination [kəuɔ:dɪ'neɪʃən] n coordination f.

coot [ku:t] n foulque f.

co-ownership ['kəu'əunəʃɪp] n copropriété f.

cop [kɔp] n (col) flic m.

cope [kəup] vi s'en sortir, tenir le coup; **to ~ with** faire face à; (take care of) s'occuper de.

Copenhagen ['kəupn'heɪgən] n Copenhague.

copier ['kɔpɪə*] n (also: **photo~**) copieur m.

co-pilot ['kəu'paɪlət] n copilote m.

copious ['kəupɪəs] a copieux(euse), abondant(e).

copper ['kɔpə*] n cuivre m; (col: policeman) flic m; **~s** npl petite monnaie.

coppice ['kɔpɪs], **copse** [kɔps] n taillis m.

copulate ['kɔpjuleɪt] vi copuler.

copy ['kɔpɪ] n copie f; (book etc) exemplaire m; (material: for printing) copie ♦ vt copier; (imitate) imiter; **rough ~** (gen) premier jet; (SCOL) brouillon m; **fair ~** version définitive; propre m; **to make good ~** (PRESS) faire un bon sujet d'article.
copy out vt copier.

copycat ['kɔpɪkæt] n (pej) copieur/euse.

copyright ['kɔpɪraɪt] n droit m d'auteur, copyright m; **~ reserved** tous droits (de reproduction) réservés.

copy typist n dactylo m/f.

copywriter ['kɔpɪraɪtə*] n rédacteur/trice publicitaire.

coral ['kɔrəl] n corail m.

coral reef n récif m de corail.

Coral Sea n: **the ~** la mer de Corail.

cord [kɔ:d] n corde f; (fabric) velours côtelé; whipcord m; corde f; (ELEC) cordon m (d'alimentation), fil m (électrique); **~s** npl (trousers) pantalon m de velours côtelé.

cordial ['kɔ:dɪəl] a cordial(e), chaleureux(euse) ♦ n sirop m; cordial m.

cordless ['kɔ:dlɪs] a sans fil.

cordon ['kɔ:dn] n cordon m.
cordon off vt (area) interdire l'accès à; (crowd) tenir à l'écart.

corduroy ['kɔ:dərɔɪ] n velours côtelé.

CORE [kɔ:*] n abbr (US) = Congress of Racial Equality.

core [kɔ:*] n (of fruit) trognon m, cœur m; (TECH: also of earth) noyau m; (of nuclear reactor, fig: of problem etc) cœur ♦ vt enlever le trognon or le cœur de; **rotten to the ~** complètement pourri.

Corfu [kɔ:'fu:] n Corfou.

coriander [kɔrɪ'ændə*] n coriandre f.

cork [kɔ:k] n liège m; (of bottle) bouchon m.

corkage ['kɔ:kɪdʒ] n droit payé par le client qui apporte sa propre bouteille de vin.

corked [kɔ:kt], (US) **corky** ['kɔ:kɪ] a (wine) qui sent le bouchon.

corkscrew ['kɔ:kskru:] n tire-bouchon m.

corm [kɔ:m] n bulbe m.

cormorant ['kɔ:mərnt] n cormoran m.

Corn abbr (Brit) = **Cornwall**.

corn [kɔ:n] n (Brit: wheat) blé m; (US: maize) maïs m; (on foot) cor m; **~ on the cob** (CULIN) épi m de maïs au naturel.

cornea ['kɔ:nɪə] n cornée f.

corned beef ['kɔ:nd-] n corned-beef m.

corner ['kɔ:nə*] n coin m; (AUT) tournant m, virage m; (FOOTBALL) ~ **kick**) corner m ♦ vt acculer, mettre au pied du mur; coincer; (COMM: market) accaparer ♦ vi prendre un virage; **to cut ~s** (fig) prendre des raccourcis.

corner flag n (FOOTBALL) piquet m de coin.

corner kick n (FOOTBALL) corner m.

cornerstone ['kɔ:nəstəun] n pierre f angulaire.

cornet ['kɔ:nɪt] n (MUS) cornet m à pistons; (Brit: of ice-cream) cornet (de glace).

cornflakes ['kɔ:nfleɪks] npl cornflakes mpl.

cornflour ['kɔ:nflauə*] n (Brit) farine f de maïs, maïzena f ®.

cornice ['kɔ:nɪs] n corniche f.

Cornish ['kɔ:nɪʃ] a de Cornouailles, cornouaillais(e).

corn oil n huile f de maïs.

cornstarch ['kɔ:nstɑ:tʃ] n (US) farine f de maïs, maïzena f ®.

cornucopia [kɔ:nju'kəupɪə] n corne f d'abondance.

Cornwall ['kɔ:nwɔl] n Cornouailles f.

corny ['kɔ:nɪ] a (col) rebattu(e), galvaudé(e).

corollary [kə'rɔlərɪ] n corollaire m.

coronary ['kɔrənərɪ] n: ~ **(thrombosis)** infarctus m (du myocarde), thrombose f coronaire.

coronation [kɔrə'neɪʃən] n couronnement m.

coroner ['kɔrənə*] n coroner m.

coronet ['kɔrənɪt] n couronne f.

Corp. abbr = **corporation**.

corporal ['kɔ:pərl] n caporal m, brigadier m ♦ a: ~ **punishment** châtiment corporel.

corporate ['kɔ:pərɪt] a en commun; (COMM) constitué(e) (en corporation).

corporate identity, corporate image n (of organization) image f de l'entreprise.

corporation [kɔ:pə'reɪʃən] n (of town) municipalité f, conseil municipal; (COMM) société f.

corporation tax n ≈ impôt m sur les bénéfices.

corps [kɔ:*], pl **corps** [kɔ:z] n corps m; **the press ~** la presse.

corpse [kɔ:ps] n cadavre m.

corpuscle ['kɔ:pʌsl] n corpuscule m.

corral [kə'rɑ:l] n corral m.

correct [kə'rekt] a (accurate) correct(e), exact(e); (proper) correct, convenable ♦ vt corriger; **you are ~** vous avez raison.

correction [kə'rekʃən] n correction f.

correlate ['kɔrɪleɪt] vt mettre en corrélation ♦ vi: **to ~ with** correspondre à.

correlation [kɔrɪ'leɪʃən] n corrélation f.

correspond [kɔrɪs'pɔnd] vi correspondre.

correspondence [kɔrɪs'pɔndəns] n correspondance f.

correspondence column n (PRESS) courrier m des lecteurs.

correspondence course n cours m par

correspondance.

correspondent [kɔrɪs'pɔndənt] *n* correspondant/e.

corridor ['kɔrɪdɔ:*] *n* couloir *m*, corridor *m*.

corroborate [kə'rɔbəreɪt] *vt* corroborer, confirmer.

corrode [kə'rəud] *vt* corroder, ronger ♦ *vi* se corroder.

corrosion [kə'rəuʒən] *n* corrosion *f*.

corrosive [kə'rəuzɪv] *a* corrosif(ive).

corrugated ['kɔrəgeɪtɪd] *a* plissé(e); ondulé(e).

corrugated iron *n* tôle ondulée.

corrupt [kə'rʌpt] *a* corrompu(e) ♦ *vt* corrompre; (*data*) altérer; **~ practices** (*dishonesty, bribery*) malversation *f*.

corruption [kə'rʌpʃən] *n* corruption *f*; altération *f* (de données).

corset ['kɔ:sɪt] *n* corset *m*.

Corsica ['kɔ:sɪkə] *n* Corse *f*.

Corsican ['kɔ:sɪkən] *a* corse ♦ *n* Corse *m/f*.

cortège [kɔ:'teɪʒ] *n* cortège *m* (*gén funèbre*).

cortisone ['kɔ:tɪzəun] *n* cortisone *f*.

coruscating ['kɔrəskeɪtɪŋ] *a* scintillant(e).

c.o.s. *abbr* (= *cash on shipment*) paiement *m* à l'expédition.

cosh [kɔʃ] *n* (*Brit*) matraque *f*.

cosignatory ['kəu'sɪgnətərɪ] *n* cosignataire *m/f*.

cosiness ['kəuzɪnɪs] *n* atmosphère douillette, confort *m*.

cos lettuce ['kɔs'letɪs] *n* (laitue *f*) romaine *f*.

cosmetic [kɔz'metɪk] *n* produit *m* de beauté, cosmétique *m* ♦ *a* (*preparation*) cosmétique; (*surgery*) esthétique; (*fig: reforms*) symbolique, superficiel(le).

cosmic ['kɔzmɪk] *a* cosmique.

cosmonaut ['kɔzmənɔ:t] *n* cosmonaute *m/f*.

cosmopolitan [kɔzmə'pɔlɪtn] *a* cosmopolite.

cosmos ['kɔzmɔs] *n* cosmos *m*.

cosset ['kɔsɪt] *vt* choyer, dorloter.

cost [kɔst] *n* coût *m* ♦ *vb* (*pt, pp* cost) *vi* coûter ♦ *vt* établir or calculer le prix de revient de; **~s** *npl* (*LAW*) dépens *mpl*; **how much does it ~?** combien ça coûte?; **it ~s £5/too much** cela coûte 5 livres/trop cher; **what will it ~ to have it repaired?** combien cela coûtera de le faire réparer?; **it ~ him his life/job** ça lui a coûté la vie/son emploi; **the ~ of living** le coût de la vie; **at all ~s** coûte que coûte, à tout prix.

cost accountant *n* analyste *m/f* de coûts.

co-star ['kəustɑ:*] *n* partenaire *m/f*.

Costa Rica ['kɔstə'ri:kə] *n* Costa Rica *m*.

cost centre *n* centre *m* de coût.

cost control *n* contrôle *m* des coûts.

cost-effective ['kɔstɪ'fektɪv] *a* rentable.

cost-effectiveness ['kɔstɪ'fektɪvnɪs] *n* rentabilité *f*.

costing ['kɔstɪŋ] *n* calcul *m* du prix de revient.

costly ['kɔstlɪ] *a* coûteux(euse).

cost-of-living ['kɔstəv'lɪvɪŋ] *a*: **~ allowance** indemnité *f* de vie chère; **~ index** indice *m* du coût de la vie.

cost price *n* (*Brit*) prix coûtant or de revient.

costume ['kɔstju:m] *n* costume *m*; (*lady's suit*) tailleur *m*; (*Brit: also:* **swimming ~**) maillot *m* (de bain).

costume jewellery *n* bijoux *mpl* de fantaisie.

cosy, (*US*) **cozy** ['kəuzɪ] *a* (*bed*) douillet(te); (*scarf, gloves*) bien chaud(e); (*atmosphere*) chaleureux(euse); (*room*) mignon(ne).

cot [kɔt] *n* (*Brit: child's*) lit *m* d'enfant, petit lit; (*US: campbed*) lit de camp.

Cotswolds ['kɔtswəuldz] *npl*: **the ~** région de collines du Gloucestershire.

cottage ['kɔtɪdʒ] *n* petite maison (à la campagne), cottage *m*.

cottage cheese *n* fromage blanc (*maigre*).

cottage industry *n* industrie familiale or artisanale.

cottage pie *n* ≈ hachis *m* Parmentier.

cotton ['kɔtn] *n* coton *m*; **~ dress** *etc* robe *etc* en or de coton.

cotton on *vi* (*col*): **to ~ on (to sth)** piger (qch).

cotton wool *n* (*Brit*) ouate *f*, coton *m* hydrophile.

couch [kautʃ] *n* canapé *m*; divan *m*; (*doctor's*) table *f* d'examen; (*psychiatrist's*) divan ♦ *vt* formuler, exprimer.

couchette [ku:'ʃet] *n* couchette *f*.

cough [kɔf] *vi* tousser ♦ *n* toux *f*.

cough drop *n* pastille *f* pour or contre la toux.

cough mixture, cough syrup *n* sirop *m* pour la toux.

could [kud] *pt of* **can**.

couldn't ['kudnt] = **could not**.

council ['kaunsl] *n* conseil *m*; **city** or **town ~** conseil municipal; **C~ of Europe** Conseil de l'Europe.

council estate *n* (*Brit*) (quartier *m* or zone *f* de) logements loués à/par la municipalité.

council house *n* (*Brit*) maison *f* (à loyer modéré) louée par la municipalité.

councillor ['kaunslə*] *n* conseiller/ère.

counsel ['kaunsl] *n* consultation *f*, délibération *f*; (*person*) avocat/e ♦ *vt*: **to ~ sth/sb to do sth** conseiller qch/à qn de faire qch; **~ for the defence/the prosecution** (avocat de la) défense/avocat du ministère public.

counsellor, (*US*) **counselor** ['kaunslə*] *n* conseiller/ère; (*US LAW*) avocat *m*.

count [kaunt] *vt, vi* compter ♦ *n* compte *m*; (*nobleman*) comte *m*; **to ~ (up) to 10** compter jusqu'à 10; **to keep ~ of sth** tenir le compte de qch; **not ~ing the children** sans compter les enfants; **10 ~ing him** 10 avec lui, 10 en le comptant; **to ~ the cost of** établir le coût de; **it ~s for very little** cela n'a pas beaucoup d'importance; **~ yourself lucky** estimez-vous heureux.

count on *vt fus* compter sur; **to ~ on doing sth** compter faire qch.

count up *vt* compter, additionner.

countdown ['kauntdaun] *n* compte *m* à rebours.

countenance ['kauntɪnəns] *n* expression *f* ♦ *vt* approuver.

counter ['kauntə*] *n* comptoir *m*; (*in post office, bank*) guichet *m*; (*in game*) jeton *m* ♦ *vt* aller à l'encontre de, opposer; (*blow*) parer ♦ *ad*: **~ to** à l'encontre de; contrairement à; **to buy under the ~** (*fig*) acheter sous le manteau or en sous-main; **to ~ sth with sth/by doing sth** contrer or riposter à qch par qch/en faisant qch.

counteract ['kauntər'ækt] *vt* neutraliser, contrebalancer.

counterattack ['kauntərə'tæk] *n* contre-attaque *f* ♦ *vi* contre-attaquer.

counterbalance ['kauntə'bæləns] *vt* contrebalancer, faire contrepoids à.

counter-clockwise ['kauntə'klɔkwaɪz] *ad* en sens inverse des aiguilles d'une montre.

counter-espionage ['kauntər'ɛspɪənɑːʒ] *n* contre-espionnage *m*.

counterfeit ['kauntəfɪt] *n* faux *m*, contrefaçon *f* ♦ *vt* contrefaire ♦ *a* faux (fausse).

counterfoil ['kauntəfɔɪl] *n* talon *m*, souche *f*.

counterintelligence ['kauntərɪn'tɛlɪdʒəns] *n* contre-espionnage *m*.

countermand ['kauntəmɑːnd] *vt* annuler.

countermeasure ['kauntəmɛʒə*] *n* contre-mesure *f*.

counteroffensive ['kauntərə'fɛnsɪv] *n* contre-offensive *f*.

counterpane ['kauntəpeɪn] *n* dessus-de-lit *m*.

counterpart ['kauntəpɑːt] *n* (*of document etc*) double *m*; (*of person*) homologue *m/f*.

counterproductive ['kauntəprə'dʌktɪv] *a* contre-productif (ive).

counterproposal ['kauntəprə'pəuzl] *n* contre-proposition *f*.

countersign ['kauntəsaɪn] *vt* contresigner.

countersink ['kauntəsɪŋk] *vt* (*hole*) fraiser.

countess ['kauntɪs] *n* comtesse *f*.

countless ['kauntlɪs] *a* innombrable.

countrified ['kʌntrɪfaɪd] *a* rustique, à l'air campagnard.

country ['kʌntrɪ] *n* pays *m*; (*native land*) patrie *f*; (*as opposed to town*) campagne *f*; (*region*) région *f*, pays; **in the ~** à la campagne; **mountainous ~** pays de montagne, région montagneuse.

country and western (music) *n* musique *f* country.

country dancing *n* (*Brit*) danse *f* folklorique.

country house *n* manoir *m*, (petit) château.

countryman ['kʌntrɪmən] *n* (*national*) compatriote *m*; (*rural*) habitant *m* de la campagne, campagnard *m*.

countryside ['kʌntrɪsaɪd] *n* campagne *f*.

country-wide ['kʌntrɪ'waɪd] *a* s'étendant à l'ensemble du pays; (*problem*) à l'échelle du pays entier ♦ *ad* à travers *or* dans tout le pays.

county ['kauntɪ] *n* comté *m*.

county town *n* (*Brit*) chef-lieu *m*.

coup, **~s** [kuː, -z] *n* beau coup; (*also*: ~ **d'état**) coup d'État.

coupé [kuː'peɪ] *n* (*AUT*) coupé *m*.

couple ['kʌpl] *n* couple *m* ♦ *vt* (*carriages*) atteler; (*TECH*) coupler; (*ideas, names*) associer; **a ~ of** deux; (*a few*) deux ou trois.

couplet ['kʌplɪt] *n* distique *m*.

coupling ['kʌplɪŋ] *n* (*RAIL*) attelage *m*.

coupon ['kuːpɔn] *n* (*voucher*) bon-prime *m*, bon-réclame *m*; (*detachable form*) coupon *m* détachable, coupon-réponse *m*; (*FINANCE*) coupon.

courage ['kʌrɪdʒ] *n* courage *m*.

courageous [kə'reɪdʒəs] *a* courageux (euse).

courgette [kuə'ʒɛt] *n* (*Brit*) courgette *f*.

courier ['kurɪə*] *n* messager *m*, courrier *m*;

(*for tourists*) accompagnateur/trice.

course [kɔːs] *n* cours *m*; (*of ship*) route *f*; (*for golf*) terrain *m*; (*part of meal*) plat *m*; **first ~** entrée *f*; **of ~** *ad* bien sûr; **(no) of ~ not!** bien sûr que non!, évidemment que non!; **in the ~ of the next few days** au cours des prochains jours; **in due ~** en temps utile *or* voulu; **~ (of action)** parti *m*, ligne *f* de conduite; **the best ~ would be to ...** le mieux serait de ...; **we have no other ~ but to ...** nous n'avons pas d'autre solution que de ...; **~ of lectures** série *f* de conférences; **~ of treatment** (*MED*) traitement *m*.

court [kɔːt] *n* cour *f*; (*LAW*) cour, tribunal *m*; (*TENNIS*) court *m* ♦ *vt* (*woman*) courtiser, faire la cour à; (*fig*: *favour, popularity*) rechercher; (*: death, disaster*) courir après, flirter avec; **out of ~** (*LAW*: *settle*) à l'amiable; **to take to ~** actionner *or* poursuivre en justice; **~ of appeal** cour d'appel.

courteous ['kɜːtɪəs] *a* courtois (e), poli (e).

courtesan [kɔːtɪ'zæn] *n* courtisane *f*.

courtesy ['kɜːtəsɪ] *n* courtoisie *f*, politesse *f*; **by ~ of** avec l'aimable autorisation de.

courtesy coach *n* navette gratuite.

courtesy light *n* (*AUT*) plafonnier *m*.

court-house ['kɔːthaus] *n* (*US*) palais *m* de justice.

courtier ['kɔːtɪə*] *n* courtisan *m*, dame *f* de cour.

courtmartial, *pl* **courtsmartial** ['kɔːt'mɑːʃəl] *n* cour martiale, conseil *m* de guerre.

courtroom ['kɔːtrum] *n* salle *f* de tribunal.

court shoe *n* escarpin *m*.

courtyard ['kɔːtjɑːd] *n* cour *f*.

cousin ['kʌzn] *n* cousin/e.

cove [kəuv] *n* petite baie, anse *f*.

covenant ['kʌvənənt] *n* contrat *m*, engagement *m* ♦ *vt*: **to ~ £200 per year to a charity** s'engager à verser 200 livres par an à une œuvre de bienfaisance.

Coventry ['kɔvəntrɪ] *n*: **to send sb to ~** (*fig*) mettre qn en quarantaine.

cover ['kʌvə*] *vt* couvrir; (*PRESS*: *report on*) faire un reportage sur ♦ *n* (*for bed, of book*, *COMM*) couverture *f*; (*of pan*) couvercle *m*; (*over furniture*) housse *f*; (*shelter*) abri *m*; **to take ~** se mettre à l'abri; **under ~** à l'abri; **under ~ of darkness** à la faveur de la nuit; **under separate ~** (*COMM*) sous pli séparé; **£10 will ~ everything** 10 livres suffiront (pour tout payer).

cover up *vt* (*person, object*): **to ~ up (with)** couvrir (de); (*fig*: *truth, facts*) occulter; **to ~ up for sb** (*fig*) couvrir qn.

coverage ['kʌvərɪdʒ] *n* (*in media*) reportage *m*; (*INSURANCE*) couverture *f*.

cover charge *n* couvert *m* (*supplément à payer*).

covering ['kʌvərɪŋ] *n* couverture *f*, enveloppe *f*.

covering letter, (*US*) **cover letter** *n* lettre explicative.

cover note *n* (*INSURANCE*) police *f* provisoire.

cover price *n* prix *m* de l'exemplaire.

covert ['kʌvət] *a* (*threat*) voilé (e), caché (e); (*attack*) indirect (e); (*glance*) furtif (ive).

cover-up ['kʌvərʌp] *n* tentative *f* pour étouffer

une affaire.

covet ['kʌvɪt] vt convoiter.

cow [kau] n vache f ♦ cpd femelle ♦ vt effrayer, intimider.

coward ['kauəd] n lâche m/f.

cowardice ['kauədɪs] n lâcheté f.

cowardly ['kauədlɪ] a lâche.

cowboy ['kaubɔɪ] n cow-boy m.

cower ['kauə*] vi se recroqueviller; trembler.

cowshed ['kauʃed] n étable f.

cowslip ['kauslɪp] n (BOT) (fleur f de) coucou m.

coxswain ['kɔksn] n (abbr: cox) barreur m; (of ship) patron m.

coy [kɔɪ] a faussement effarouché(e) or timide.

coyote [kɔɪ'əutɪ] n coyote m.

cozy ['kəuzɪ] a (US) = cosy.

CP n abbr (= Communist Party) PC m.

cp. abbr (= compare) cf.

c/p abbr (Brit) = **carriage paid**.

CPA n abbr (US) = **certified public accountant**.

CPI n abbr (= Consumer Price Index) IPC m.

Cpl. abbr (= corporal) C/C.

CP/M n abbr (= Central Program for Microprocessors) CP/M m.

c.p.s. abbr (= characters per second) caractères/seconde.

CPSA n abbr (Brit: = Civil and Public Services Association) syndicat de la fonction publique.

CPU n abbr = **central processing unit**.

cr. abbr = **credit, creditor**.

crab [kræb] n crabe m.

crab apple n pomme f sauvage.

crack [kræk] n fente f, fissure f; (in bone, dish, glass) fêlure f; (in wall) lézarde f; (noise) craquement m, coup (sec); (joke) plaisanterie f; (col: attempt): **to have a ~ (at sth)** essayer (qch); (DRUGS) crack m ♦ vt fendre, fissurer; fêler; lézarder; (whip) faire claquer; (nut) casser; (solve) résoudre, trouver la clef de; déchiffrer ♦ cpd (athlete) de première classe, d'élite; **to ~ jokes** (col) raconter des blagues; **to get ~ing** (col) s'y mettre, se magner.

crack down on vt fus (crime) sévir contre, réprimer; (spending) mettre un frein à.

crack up vi être au bout de son rouleau, flancher.

crackdown ['krækdaun] n: **~ (on)** (on crime) répression f (de); (on spending) restrictions fpl (de).

cracked [krækt] a (col) toqué(e), timbré(e).

cracker ['krækə*] n pétard m; (biscuit) biscuit (salé), craquelin m; **a ~ of a ...** (Brit col) un(e) ... formidable; **he's ~s** (Brit col) il est cinglé.

crackle ['krækl] vi crépiter, grésiller.

crackling ['kræklɪŋ] n crépitement m, grésillement m; (on radio, telephone) grésillement, friture f; (of pork) couenne f.

cradle ['kreɪdl] n berceau m ♦ vt (child) bercer; (object) tenir dans ses bras.

craft [krɑ:ft] n métier (artisanal); (cunning) ruse f, astuce f; (boat) embarcation f, barque f.

craftsman ['krɑ:ftsmən] n artisan m, ouvrier (qualifié).

craftsmanship ['krɑ:ftsmənʃɪp] n métier m, habileté f.

crafty ['krɑ:ftɪ] a rusé(e), malin(igne), astucieux(euse).

crag [kræg] n rocher escarpé.

craggy ['krægɪ] a escarpé(e), rocheux(euse).

cram [kræm] vt (fill): **to ~ sth with** bourrer qch de; (put): **to ~ sth into** fourrer qch dans.

cramming ['kræmɪŋ] n (for exams) bachotage m.

cramp [kræmp] n crampe f ♦ vt gêner, entraver.

cramped [kræmpt] a à l'étroit, très serré(e).

crampon ['kræmpən] n crampon m.

cranberry ['krænbərɪ] n canneberge f.

crane [kreɪn] n grue f ♦ vt, vi: **to ~ forward**, **to ~ one's neck** allonger le cou.

cranium, pl crania ['kreɪnɪəm, 'kreɪnɪə] n boîte crânienne.

crank [kræŋk] n manivelle f; (person) excentrique m/f.

crankshaft ['kræŋkʃɑ:ft] n vilebrequin m.

cranky ['kræŋkɪ] a excentrique, loufoque; (bad-tempered) grincheux(euse), revêche.

cranny ['krænɪ] n see **nook**.

crap [kræp] n (col!) conneries fpl (!); **to have a ~** chier (!).

crash [kræʃ] n fracas m; (of car, plane) collision f; (of business) faillite f; (STOCK EXCHANGE) krach m ♦ vt (plane) écraser ♦ vi (plane) s'écraser; (two cars) se percuter, s'emboutir; (fig) s'effondrer; **to ~ into** se jeter or se fracasser contre; **he ~ed the car into a wall** il s'est écrasé contre un mur avec sa voiture.

crash barrier n (Brit AUT) rail m de sécurité.

crash course n cours intensif.

crash helmet n casque (protecteur).

crash landing n atterrissage forcé or en catastrophe.

crass [kræs] a grossier(ière), crasse.

crate [kreɪt] n cageot m.

crater ['kreɪtə*] n cratère m.

cravat(e) [krə'væt] n foulard (noué autour du cou).

crave [kreɪv] vt, vi: **to ~ for** désirer violemment, avoir un besoin physiologique de, avoir une envie irrésistible de.

craving ['kreɪvɪŋ] n: **~ (for)** (for food, cigarettes etc) envie f irrésistible (de).

crawl [krɔ:l] vi ramper; (vehicle) avancer au pas ♦ n (SWIMMING) crawl m; **to ~ to sb** (col) faire de la lèche à qn.

crayfish ['kreɪfɪʃ] n (pl inv) (freshwater) écrevisse f; (saltwater) langoustine f.

crayon ['kreɪən] n crayon m (de couleur).

craze [kreɪz] n engouement m.

crazed [kreɪzd] a (look, person) affolé(e); (pottery, glaze) craquelé(e).

crazy ['kreɪzɪ] a fou(folle); **to go ~** devenir fou; **to be ~ about sb** (col) aimer qn à la folie; **he's ~ about skiing** (col) c'est un fana(tique) de ski.

crazy paving n (Brit) dallage irrégulier (en pierres plates).

creak [kri:k] vi (hinge) grincer; (floor, shoes)

craquer.
cream [kri:m] *n* crème *f* ♦ *a* (*colour*) crème *inv*; **whipped** ~ crème fouettée.
cream off *vt* (*fig*) prélever.
cream cake *n* (petit) gâteau à la crème.
cream cheese *n* fromage *m* à la crème, fromage blanc.
creamery ['kri:məri] *n* (*shop*) crémerie *f*; (*factory*) laiterie *f*.
creamy ['kri:mi] *a* crémeux(euse).
crease [kri:s] *n* pli *m* ♦ *vt* froisser, chiffonner ♦ *vi* se froisser, se chiffonner.
crease-resistant ['kri:srizistənt] *a* infroissable.
create [kri:'eit] *vt* créer; (*impression, fuss*) faire.
creation [kri:'eiʃən] *n* création *f*.
creative [kri:'eitiv] *a* créateur(trice).
creativity [kri:ei'tiviti] *n* créativité *f*.
creator [kri:'eitə*] *n* créateur/trice.
creature ['kri:tʃə*] *n* créature *f*.
crèche, creche [krɛʃ] *n* garderie *f*, crèche *f*.
credence ['kri:dns] *n* croyance *f*, foi *f*.
credentials [kri'denʃlz] *npl* (*papers*) références *fpl*; (*letters of reference*) pièces justificatives.
credibility [kredi'biliti] *n* crédibilité *f*.
credible ['kredibl] *a* digne de foi, crédible.
credit ['kredit] *n* crédit *m*; (*SCOL*) unité *f* de valeur ♦ *vt* (*COMM*) créditer; (*believe: also*: **give** ~ **to**) ajouter foi à, croire; **to** ~ **sb with** (*fig*) prêter or attribuer à qn; **to** ~ **£5 to sb** créditer (le compte de) qn de 5 livres; **to be in** ~ (*person, bank account*) être créditeur(trice); **on** ~ à crédit; **to one's** ~ à son honneur; à son actif; **to take the** ~ **for** s'attribuer le mérite de; **it does him** ~ cela lui fait honneur.
creditable ['kreditəbl] *a* honorable, estimable.
credit account *n* compte *m* client.
credit agency *n* (*Brit*) agence *f* de renseignements commerciaux.
credit balance *n* solde créditeur.
credit bureau *n* (*US*) agence *f* de renseignements commerciaux.
credit card *n* carte *f* de crédit.
credit control *n* suivi *m* des factures.
credit facilities *npl* facilités *fpl* de paiement.
credit limit *n* limite *f* de crédit.
credit note *n* (*Brit*) avoir *m*.
creditor ['kreditə*] *n* créancier/ière.
credits ['kredits] *npl* (*CINEMA*) générique *m*.
credit transfer *n* virement *m*.
creditworthy ['kredit'wə:ði] *a* solvable.
credulity [kri'dju:liti] *n* crédulité *f*.
creed [kri:d] *n* croyance *f*; credo *m*, principes *mpl*.
creek [kri:k] *n* crique *f*, anse *f*; (*US*) ruisseau *m*, petit cours d'eau.
creel ['kri:l] *n* panier *m* de pêche; (*also*: **lobster** ~) panier à homards.
creep, *pt, pp* **crept** [kri:p, krept] *vi* ramper; (*fig*) se faufiler, se glisser; (*plant*) grimper ♦ *n* (*col*) saligaud *m*; **he's a** ~ c'est un type puant; **it gives me the** ~**s** cela me fait froid dans le dos; **to** ~ **up on sb** s'approcher furtivement de qn.
creeper ['kri:pə*] *n* plante grimpante.
creepers ['kri:pəz] *npl* (*US: for baby*)

barboteuse *f*.
creepy ['kri:pi] *a* (*frightening*) qui fait frissonner, qui donne la chair de poule.
creepy-crawly ['kri:pi'krɔ:li] *n* (*col*) bestiole *f*.
cremate [kri'meit] *vt* incinérer.
cremation [kri'meiʃən] *n* incinération *f*.
crematorium, *pl* **crematoria** [kremə'tɔ:riəm, -'tɔ:riə] *n* four *m* crématoire.
creosote ['kriəsəut] *n* créosote *f*.
crêpe [kreip] *n* crêpe *m*.
crêpe bandage *n* (*Brit*) bande *f* Velpeau ®.
crêpe paper *n* papier *m* crépon.
crêpe sole *n* semelle *f* de crêpe.
crept [krept] *pt, pp of* **creep.**
crescendo [kri'ʃendəu] *n* crescendo *m*.
crescent ['kresnt] *n* croissant *m*; (*street*) rue *f* (*en arc de cercle*).
cress [kres] *n* cresson *m*.
crest [krest] *n* crête *f*; (*of helmet*) cimier *m*; (*of coat of arms*) timbre *m*.
crestfallen ['krestfɔ:lən] *a* déconfit(e), découragé(e).
Crete ['kri:t] *n* Crète *f*.
crevasse [kri'væs] *n* crevasse *f*.
crevice ['krevis] *n* fissure *f*, lézarde *f*, fente *f*.
crew [kru:] *n* équipage *m*; (*CINEMA*) équipe *f* (de tournage); (*gang*) bande *f*.
crew-cut ['kru:kʌt] *n*: **to have a** ~ avoir les cheveux en brosse.
crew-neck ['kru:nek] *n* col ras.
crib [krib] *n* lit *m* d'enfant ♦ *vt* (*col*) copier.
cribbage ['kribidʒ] *n* sorte de jeu de cartes.
crick [krik] *n* crampe *f*; ~ **in the neck** torticolis *m*.
cricket ['krikit] *n* (*insect*) grillon *m*, cri-cri *m inv*; (*game*) cricket *m*.
cricketer ['krikitə*] *n* joueur *m* de cricket.
crime [kraim] *n* crime *m*; **minor** ~ délit *m or* infraction *f* mineur(e).
crime wave *n* poussée *f* de la criminalité.
criminal ['kriminl] *a, n* criminel(le).
crimp [krimp] *vt* friser, frisotter.
crimson ['krimzn] *a* cramoisi(e).
cringe [krindʒ] *vi* avoir un mouvement de recul; (*fig*) s'humilier, ramper.
crinkle ['krinkl] *vt* froisser, chiffonner.
cripple ['kripl] *n* boiteux/euse, infirme *m/f* ♦ *vt* estropier, paralyser; (*ship, plane*) immobiliser; (*production, exports*) paralyser; ~**d with rheumatism** perclus(e) de rhumatismes.
crippling ['kriplin] *a* (*disease*) handicapant(e); (*taxation, debts*) écrasant(e).
crisis, *pl* **crises** ['kraisis, -si:z] *n* crise *f*.
crisp [krisp] *a* croquant(e); (*fig*) vif(vive); brusque.
crisps [krisps] *npl* (*Brit*) (pommes) chips *fpl*.
criss-cross ['kriskrɔs] *a* entrecroisé(e), en croisillons ♦ *vt* sillonner; ~ **pattern** croisillons *mpl*.
criterion, *pl* **criteria** [krai'tiəriən, -'tiəriə] *n* critère *m*.
critic ['kritik] *n* critique *m/f*.
critical ['kritikl] *a* critique; **to be** ~ **of sb/sth** critiquer qn/qch.
critically ['kritikli] *ad* (*examine*) d'un œil critique; (*speak*) sévèrement; ~ **ill** gravement malade.

criticism ['krɪtɪsɪzəm] n critique f.
criticize ['krɪtɪsaɪz] vt critiquer.
croak [krəuk] vi (frog) coasser; (raven) croasser.
crochet ['krəuʃeɪ] n travail m au crochet.
crock [krɒk] n cruche f; (col: also: **old ~**) épave f.
crockery ['krɒkərɪ] n vaisselle f.
crocodile ['krɒkədaɪl] n crocodile m.
crocus ['krəukəs] n crocus m.
croft [krɒft] n (Brit) petite ferme.
crofter ['krɒftə*] n (Brit) fermier m.
crone [krəun] n vieille bique, (vieille) sorcière.
crony ['krəunɪ] n copain/copine.
crook [kruk] n escroc m; (of shepherd) houlette f.
crooked ['krukɪd] a courbé(e), tordu(e); (action) malhonnête.
crop [krɒp] n (produce) culture f; (amount produced) récolte f; (riding ~) cravache f; (of bird) jabot m ♦ vt (hair) tondre; (subj: animals: grass) brouter.
   crop up vi surgir, se présenter, survenir.
cropper ['krɒpə*] n: **to come a ~** (col) faire la culbute, s'étaler.
crop spraying n pulvérisation f des cultures.
croquet ['krəukeɪ] n croquet m.
croquette [krə'kɛt] n croquette f.
cross [krɒs] n croix f; (BIOL) croisement m ♦ vt (street etc) traverser; (arms, legs, BIOL) croiser; (cheque) barrer; (thwart: person, plan) contrarier ♦ vi: **the boat ~es from ... to ...** le bateau fait la traversée de ... à ... ♦ a en colère, fâché(e); **to ~ o.s.** se signer, faire le signe de (la) croix; **we have a ~ed line** (Brit: on telephone) il y a des interférences; **they've got their lines ~ed** (fig) il y a un malentendu entre eux; **to be/ get ~ with sb (about sth)** être en colère/se fâcher contre qn (à propos de qch).
   cross out vt barrer, biffer.
   cross over vi traverser.
crossbar ['krɒsbɑ:*] n barre transversale.
crossbreed ['krɒsbri:d] n hybride m, métis/se.
cross-Channel ferry ['krɒs'tʃænl-] n ferry m qui fait la traversée de la manche.
cross-check ['krɒstʃɛk] n recoupement m ♦ vi vérifier par recoupement.
cross-country (race) ['krɒs'kʌntrɪ-] n cross(-country) m.
cross-examination ['krɒsɪgzæmɪ'neɪʃən] n (LAW) examen m contradictoire (d'un témoin).
cross-examine ['krɒsɪg'zæmɪn] vt (LAW) faire subir un examen contradictoire à.
cross-eyed ['krɒsaɪd] a qui louche.
crossfire ['krɒsfaɪə*] n feux croisés.
crossing ['krɒsɪŋ] n croisement m, carrefour m; (sea passage) traversée f; (also: **pedestrian ~**) passage clouté.
cross-purposes ['krɒs'pə:pəsɪz] npl: **to be at ~ with sb** comprendre qn de travers; **we're (talking) at ~** on ne parle pas de la même chose.
cross-reference ['krɒs'rɛfrəns] n renvoi m, référence f.
crossroads ['krɒsrəudz] n carrefour m.
cross section n (BIOL) coupe transversale; (in population) échantillon m.

crosswalk ['krɒswɔ:k] n (US) passage clouté.
crosswind ['krɒswɪnd] n vent m de travers.
crosswise ['krɒswaɪz] ad en travers.
crossword ['krɒswɔ:d] n mots croisés mpl.
crotch [krɒtʃ] n (of garment) entre-jambes m inv.
crotchet ['krɒtʃɪt] n (MUS) noire f.
crotchety ['krɒtʃɪtɪ] a (person) grognon(ne), grincheux(euse).
crouch [krautʃ] vi s'accroupir; se tapir; se ramasser.
croup [kru:p] n (MED) croup m.
crouton ['kru:tɒn] n croûton m.
crow [krəu] n (bird) corneille f; (of cock) chant m du coq, cocorico m ♦ vi (cock) chanter; (fig) pavoiser, chanter victoire.
crowbar ['krəubɑ:*] n levier m.
crowd [kraud] n foule f ♦ vt bourrer, remplir ♦ vi affluer, s'attrouper, s'entasser; **~s of people** une foule de gens.
crowded ['kraudɪd] a bondé(e), plein(e); **~ with** plein de.
crowd scene n (CINEMA, THEATRE) scène f de foule.
crown [kraun] n couronne f; (of head) sommet m de la tête, calotte crânienne; (of hat) fond m; (of hill) sommet m ♦ vt (also tooth) couronner.
crown court n (Brit) ≈ Cour f d'assises.
crowning ['kraunɪŋ] a (achievement, glory) suprême.
crown jewels npl joyaux mpl de la Couronne.
crown prince n prince héritier.
crow's-feet ['krəuzfi:t] npl pattes fpl d'oie (fig).
crow's-nest ['krəuznest] n (on sailing-ship) nid m de pie.
crucial ['kru:ʃl] a crucial(e), décisif(ive); **~ to** essentiel(le) à.
crucifix ['kru:sɪfɪks] n crucifix m.
crucifixion [kru:sɪ'fɪkʃən] n crucifiement m, crucifixion f.
crucify ['kru:sɪfaɪ] vt crucifier, mettre en croix; (fig) crucifier.
crude [kru:d] a (materials) brut(e); non raffiné(e); (basic) rudimentaire, sommaire; (vulgar) cru(e), grossier(ière).
crude (oil) n (pétrole) brut m.
cruel ['kruəl] a cruel(le).
cruelty ['kruəltɪ] n cruauté f.
cruet ['kru:ɪt] n huilier m; vinaigrier m.
cruise [kru:z] n croisière f ♦ vi (ship) croiser; (car) rouler; (aircraft) voler; (taxi) être en maraude.
cruise missile n missile m de croisière.
cruiser ['kru:zə*] n croiseur m.
cruising speed n vitesse f de croisière.
crumb [krʌm] n miette f.
crumble ['krʌmbl] vt émietter ♦ vi s'émietter; (plaster etc) s'effriter; (land, earth) s'ébouler; (building) s'écrouler, crouler; (fig) s'effondrer.
crumbly ['krʌmblɪ] a friable.
crummy ['krʌmɪ] a (col) minable; (: unwell) mal fichu(e), patraque.
crumpet ['krʌmpɪt] n petite crêpe (épaisse).
crumple ['krʌmpl] vt froisser, friper.
crunch [krʌntʃ] vt croquer; (underfoot) faire

craquer, écraser; faire crisser ♦ *n* (*fig*) instant *m or* moment *m* critique, moment de vérité.

crunchy ['krʌntʃɪ] *a* croquant(e), croustillant(e).

crusade [kruː'seɪd] *n* croisade *f* ♦ *vi* (*fig*): to ~ **for/against** partir en croisade pour/contre.

crusader [kruː'seɪdə*] *n* croisé *m*; (*fig*): ~ **(for)** champion *m* (de).

crush [krʌʃ] *n* foule *f*, cohue *f*; (*love*): **to have a ~ on sb** avoir le béguin pour qn; (*drink*): **lemon ~** citron pressé ♦ *vt* écraser; (*crumple*) froisser; (*grind, break up: garlic, ice*) piler; (*: grapes*) presser.

crush barrier *n* (*Brit*) barrière *f* de sécurité.

crushing ['krʌʃɪŋ] *a* écrasant(e).

crust [krʌst] *n* croûte *f*.

crustacean [krʌs'teɪʃən] *n* crustacé *m*.

crusty ['krʌstɪ] *a* (*loaf*) croustillant(e).

crutch [krʌtʃ] *n* béquille *f*; (*TECH*) support *m*; (*also*: **crotch**) entrejambe *m*.

crux [krʌks] *n* point crucial.

cry [kraɪ] *vi* pleurer; (*shout: also*: ~ **out**) crier ♦ *n* cri *m*; **what are you ~ing about?** pourquoi pleures-tu?; **to ~ for help** appeler à l'aide; **she had a good ~** elle a pleuré un bon coup; **it's a far ~ from** ... (*fig*) on est loin de ....
cry off *vi* se dédire; se décommander.

crying ['kraɪɪŋ] *a* (*fig*) criant(e), flagrant(e).

crypt [krɪpt] *n* crypte *f*.

cryptic ['krɪptɪk] *a* énigmatique.

crystal ['krɪstl] *n* cristal *m*.

crystal-clear ['krɪstl'klɪə*] *a* clair(e) comme de l'eau de roche.

crystallize ['krɪstəlaɪz] *vt* cristalliser ♦ *vi* (se) cristalliser; **~d fruits** (*Brit*) fruits confits.

CSA *n abbr* = *Confederate States of America.*

CSC *n abbr* (= *Civil Service Commission*) commission de recrutement des fonctionnaires.

CSE *n abbr* (*Brit*: = *Certificate of Secondary Education*) ≈ BEPC *m*.

CSEU *n abbr* (*Brit*: = *Confederation of Shipbuilding and Engineering Unions*) confédération des syndicats de la construction navale et de la mécanique.

CS gas *n* (*Brit*) gaz *m* C.S.

CST *abbr* (*US*: = *Central Standard Time*) fuseau horaire.

CSU *n abbr* (*Brit*: = *Civil Service Union*) syndicat de la fonction publique.

CT *abbr* (*US POST*) = *Connecticut.*

ct *abbr* = **carat.**

cu. *abbr* = **cubic.**

cub [kʌb] *n* petit *m* (*d'un animal*); (*also*: ~ **scout**) louveteau *m*.

Cuba ['kjuːbə] *n* Cuba *m*.

Cuban ['kjuːbən] *a* cubain(e) ♦ *n* Cubain/e.

cubbyhole ['kʌbɪhəul] *n* cagibi *m*.

cube [kjuːb] *n* cube *m* ♦ *vt* (*MATH*) élever au cube.

cube root *n* racine *f* cubique.

cubic ['kjuːbɪk] *a* cubique; ~ **metre** *etc* mètre *m etc* cube; ~ **capacity** (*AUT*) cylindrée *f*.

cubicle ['kjuːbɪkl] *n* box *m*, cabine *f*.

cuckoo ['kuːkuː] *n* coucou *m*.

cuckoo clock *n* (pendule *f* à) coucou *m*.

cucumber ['kjuːkʌmbə*] *n* concombre *m*.

cud [kʌd] *n*: **to chew the ~** ruminer.

cuddle ['kʌdl] *vt* câliner, caresser ♦ *vi* se blottir l'un contre l'autre.

cuddly ['kʌdlɪ] *a* câlin(e).

cudgel ['kʌdʒl] *n* gourdin *m* ♦ *vt*: **to ~ one's brains** se creuser la tête.

cue [kjuː] *n* queue *f* de billard; (*THEATRE etc*) signal *m*.

cuff [kʌf] *n* (*of shirt, coat etc*) poignet *m*, manchette *f*; (*US: on trousers*) revers *m*; (*blow*) gifle *f* ♦ *vt* gifler; **off the ~** *ad* de chic, à l'improviste.

cufflink ['kʌflɪŋk] *n* bouton *m* de manchette.

cu. in. *abbr* = *cubic inches.*

cuisine [kwɪ'ziːn] *n* cuisine *f*, art *m* culinaire.

cul-de-sac ['kʌldəsæk] *n* cul-de-sac *m*, impasse *f*.

culinary ['kʌlɪnərɪ] *a* culinaire.

cull [kʌl] *vt* sélectionner; (*kill selectively*) pratiquer l'abattage sélectif de.

culminate ['kʌlmɪneɪt] *vi*: **to ~ in** finir *or* se terminer par; (*lead to*) mener à.

culmination [kʌlmɪ'neɪʃən] *n* point culminant.

culottes [kjuː'lɔts] *npl* jupe-culotte *f*.

culpable ['kʌlpəbl] *a* coupable.

culprit ['kʌlprɪt] *n* coupable *m/f*.

cult [kʌlt] *n* culte *m*.

cult figure *n* idole *f*.

cultivate ['kʌltɪveɪt] *vt* (*also fig*) cultiver.

cultivation [kʌltɪ'veɪʃən] *n* culture *f*.

cultural ['kʌltʃərəl] *a* culturel(le).

culture ['kʌltʃə*] *n* (*also fig*) culture *f*.

cultured ['kʌltʃəd] *a* cultivé(e) (*fig*).

cumbersome ['kʌmbəsəm] *a* encombrant(e), embarrassant(e).

cumin ['kʌmɪn] *n* (*spice*) cumin *m*.

cumulative ['kjuːmjulətɪv] *a* cumulatif(ive).

cunning ['kʌnɪŋ] *n* ruse *f*, astuce *f* ♦ *a* rusé(e), malin(igne); (*clever: device, idea*) astucieux(euse).

cup [kʌp] *n* tasse *f*; (*prize, event*) coupe *f*; (*of bra*) bonnet *m*; **a ~ of tea** une tasse de thé.

cupboard ['kʌbəd] *n* placard *m*.

cup final *n* (*Brit FOOTBALL*) finale *f* de la coupe.

Cupid ['kjuːpɪd] *n* Cupidon *m*; (*figurine*) amour *m*.

cupidity [kjuː'pɪdɪtɪ] *n* cupidité *f*.

cupola ['kjuːpələ] *n* coupole *f*.

cup-tie ['kʌptaɪ] *n* (*Brit FOOTBALL*) match *m* de coupe.

curable ['kjuərəbl] *a* guérissable, curable.

curate ['kjuərɪt] *n* vicaire *m*.

curator [kjuə'reɪtə*] *n* conservateur *m* (*d'un musée etc*).

curb [kəːb] *vt* refréner, mettre un frein à; (*expenditure*) limiter, juguler ♦ *n* frein *m* (*fig*); (*US*) = **kerb.**

curd cheese *n* ≈ fromage blanc.

curdle ['kəːdl] *vi* (se) cailler.

curds [kəːdz] *npl* lait caillé.

cure [kjuə*] *vt* guérir; (*CULIN*) saler; fumer; sécher ♦ *n* remède *m*; **to be ~d of sth** être guéri de qch.

cure-all ['kjuərɔːl] *n* (*also fig*) panacée *f*.

curfew ['kəːfjuː] *n* couvre-feu *m*.

curio ['kjuərɪəu] *n* bibelot *m*, curiosité *f*.

curiosity [kjuərɪ'ɔsɪtɪ] *n* curiosité *f*.

curious ['kjuərɪəs] *a* curieux(euse); **I'm ~**

about him il m'intrigue.

curiously *ad* curieusement; *(inquisitively)* avec curiosité; **~ enough,** ... bizarrement ....

curl [kə:l] *n* boucle *f* (de cheveux); *(of smoke etc)* volute *f* ♦ *vt, vi* boucler; *(tightly)* friser. **curl up** *vi* s'enrouler; se pelotonner.

curler ['kə:lə*] *n* bigoudi *m*, rouleau *m*; *(SPORT)* joueur/euse de curling.

curlew ['kə:lu:] *n* courlis *m*.

curling ['kə:lɪŋ] *n* *(sport)* curling *m*.

curling tongs, *(US)* **curling irons** *npl* fer *m* à friser.

curly ['kə:lɪ] *a* bouclé(e); *(tightly curled)* frisé(e).

currant ['kʌrnt] *n* raisin *m* de Corinthe, raisin sec.

currency ['kʌrnsɪ] *n* monnaie *f*; **foreign ~** devises étrangères, monnaie étrangère; **to gain ~** *(fig)* s'accréditer.

current ['kʌrnt] *n* courant *m* ♦ *a* courant(e); *(tendency, price, event)* actuel(le); **direct/ alternating ~** *(ELEC)* courant continu/ alternatif; **the ~ issue of a magazine** le dernier numéro d'un magazine; **in ~ use** d'usage courant.

current account *n* *(Brit)* compte courant. *f*.

current affairs *npl* (questions *fpl* d')actualité *f*.

current assets *npl* *(COMM)* actif *m* disponible.

current liabilities *npl* *(COMM)* passif *m* exigible.

currently ['kʌrntlɪ] *ad* actuellement.

curriculum, *pl* **~s** or **curricula** [kə'rɪkjuləm, -lə] *n* programme *m* d'études.

curriculum vitae (CV) *n* curriculum vitae (CV) *m*.

curry ['kʌrɪ] *n* curry *m* ♦ *vt:* **to ~ favour with** chercher à gagner la faveur *or* à s'attirer les bonnes grâces de; **chicken ~** curry de poulet, poulet *m* au curry.

curry powder *n* poudre *f* de curry.

curse [kə:s] *vi* jurer, blasphémer ♦ *vt* maudire ♦ *n* malédiction *f*; fléau *m*; *(swearword)* juron *m*.

cursor ['kə:sə*] *n* *(COMPUT)* curseur *m*.

cursory ['kə:sərɪ] *a* superficiel(le), hâtif(ive).

curt [kə:t] *a* brusque, sec(sèche).

curtail [kə:'teɪl] *vt* *(visit etc)* écourter; *(expenses etc)* réduire.

curtain ['kə:tn] *n* rideau *m*; **to draw the ~s** *(together)* fermer *or* tirer les rideaux; *(apart)* ouvrir les rideaux.

curtain call *n* *(THEATRE)* rappel *m*.

curts(e)y ['kə:tsɪ] *n* révérence *f* ♦ *vi* faire une révérence.

curvature ['kə:vətʃə*] *n* courbure *f*.

curve [kə:v] *n* courbe *f*; *(in the road)* tournant *m*, virage *m* ♦ *vt* courber ♦ *vi* se courber; *(road)* faire une courbe.

curved [kə:vd] *a* courbe.

cushion ['kuʃən] *n* coussin *m* ♦ *vt* *(seat)* rembourrer; *(shock)* amortir.

cushy ['kuʃɪ] *a* *(col):* **a ~ job** un boulot de tout repos; **to have a ~ time** se la couler douce.

custard ['kʌstəd] *n* *(for pouring)* crème anglaise.

custard powder *n* *(Brit)* ≈ crème pâtissière

instantanée.

custodian [kʌs'təudɪən] *n* gardien/ne; *(of collection etc)* conservateur/trice.

custody ['kʌstədɪ] *n* *(of child)* garde *f*; *(for offenders)* détention préventive; **to take sb into ~** placer qn en détention préventive; **in the ~ of** sous la garde de.

custom ['kʌstəm] *n* coutume *f*, usage *m*; *(LAW)* droit coutumier, coutume; *(COMM)* clientèle *f*.

customary ['kʌstəmərɪ] *a* habituel(le); **it is ~ to do it** l'usage veut qu'on le fasse.

custom-built ['kʌstəm'bɪlt] *a* see **custommade.**

customer ['kʌstəmə*] *n* client/e; **he's an awkward ~** *(col)* ce n'est pas quelqu'un de facile.

customer profile *n* profil *m* du client.

customized ['kʌstəmaɪzd] *a* personnalisé(e).

custom-made ['kʌstəm'meɪd] *a* *(clothes)* fait(e) sur mesure; *(other goods: also:* **custom-built)** hors série, fait(e) sur commande.

customs ['kʌstəmz] *npl* douane *f*; **to go through (the) ~** passer la douane.

Customs and Excise *n* *(Brit)* administration *f* des douanes.

customs duty *n* droits *mpl* de douane.

customs officer *n* douanier *m*.

cut [kʌt] *vb* *(pt, pp* **cut)** *vt* couper; *(meat)* découper; *(shape, make)* tailler; couper; creuser; graver; *(reduce)* réduire; *(col: lecture, appointment)* manquer ♦ *vi* couper; *(intersect)* se couper ♦ *n* *(gen)* coupure *f*; *(of clothes)* coupe *f*; *(of jewel)* taille *f*; *(in salary etc)* réduction *f*; *(of meat)* morceau *m*; **cold ~s** *npl* *(US)* viandes froides; **to ~ teeth** *(baby)* faire ses dents; **to ~ a tooth** percer une dent; **to ~ one's finger** se couper le doigt; **to get one's hair ~** se faire couper les cheveux; **to ~ sth short** couper court à qch; **to ~ sb dead** ignorer (complètement) qn.

cut back *vt* *(plants)* tailler; *(production, expenditure)* réduire.

cut down *vt* *(tree)* abattre; *(reduce)* réduire; **to ~ sb down to size** *(fig)* remettre qn à sa place.

cut down on *vt fus* réduire.

cut in *vi* *(interrupt: conversation):* **to ~ in (on)** couper la parole (à); *(AUT)* faire une queue de poisson.

cut off *vt* couper; *(fig)* isoler; **we've been ~ off** *(TEL)* nous avons été coupés.

cut out *vt* *(picture etc)* découper; *(remove)* ôter; supprimer.

cut up *vt* découper.

cut-and-dried ['kʌtən'draɪd] *a* *(also:* **cut-and-dry)** tout(e) fait(e), tout(e) décidé(e).

cutaway ['kʌtəweɪ] *a, n:* **~ (drawing)** écorché *m*.

cutback ['kʌtbæk] *n* réduction *f*.

cute [kju:t] *a* mignon(ne), adorable; *(clever)* rusé(e), astucieux(euse).

cut glass *n* cristal taillé.

cuticle ['kju:tɪkl] *n* *(on nail):* **~ remover** repousse-peaux *m inv.*

cutlery ['kʌtlərɪ] *n* couverts *mpl*; *(trade)* coutellerie *f.*

cutlet ['kʌtlɪt] n côtelette f.
cutoff ['kʌtɔf] n (also: ~ **point**) seuil-limite m.
cutoff switch n interrupteur m.
cutout ['kʌtaut] n coupe-circuit m inv; (paper figure) découpage m.
cut-price ['kʌt'praɪs], (US) **cut-rate** ['kʌt'reɪt] a au rabais, à prix réduit.
cutthroat ['kʌtθrəut] n assassin m ♦ a: ~ **competition** concurrence f sauvage.
cutting ['kʌtɪŋ] a tranchant(e), coupant(e); (fig) cinglant(e), mordant(e) ♦ n (Brit: from newspaper) coupure f (de journal); (: RAIL) tranchée f; (CINEMA) montage m.
cuttlefish ['kʌtlfɪʃ] n seiche f.
cut-up ['kʌtʌp] a affecté(e), démoralisé(e).
CV n abbr = **curriculum vitae.**
C & W n abbr = **country and western** (music).
cwo abbr (COMM) = **cash with order.**
cwt. abbr = **hundredweight.**
cyanide ['saɪənaɪd] n cyanure m.
cybernetics [saɪbə'nɛtɪks] n cybernétique f.
cyclamen ['sɪkləmən] n cyclamen m.
cycle ['saɪkl] n cycle m ♦ vi faire de la bicyclette.
cycle race n course f cycliste.
cycle rack n râtelier m à bicyclette.
cycling ['saɪklɪŋ] n cyclisme m; **to go on a ~ holiday** (Brit) faire du cyclotourisme.
cyclist ['saɪklɪst] n cycliste m/f.
cyclone ['saɪkləun] n cyclone m.
cygnet ['sɪgnɪt] n jeune cygne m.
cylinder ['sɪlɪndə*] n cylindre m.
cylinder block n bloc-cylindres m.
cylinder capacity n cylindrée f.
cylinder head n culasse f.
cylinder-head gasket n joint m de culasse.
cymbals ['sɪmblz] npl cymbales fpl.
cynic ['sɪnɪk] n cynique m/f.
cynical ['sɪnɪkl] a cynique.
cynicism ['sɪnɪsɪzəm] n cynisme m.
CYO n abbr (US: = Catholic Youth Organization) ≈ JC f.
cypress ['saɪprɪs] n cyprès m.
Cypriot ['sɪprɪət] a cypriote, chypriote ♦ n Cypriote m/f, Chypriote m/f.
Cyprus ['saɪprəs] n Chypre f.
cyst [sɪst] n kyste m.
cystitis [sɪs'taɪtɪs] n cystite f.
CZ n abbr (US: = Central Zone) zone du canal de Panama.
czar [zɑː*] n tsar m.
Czech [tʃɛk] a tchèque ♦ n Tchèque m/f; (LING) tchèque m.
Czechoslovak [tʃɛkə'sləuvæk] a, n = **Czechoslovakian.**
Czechoslovakia [tʃɛkəslə'vækɪə] n Tchécoslovaquie f.
Czechoslovakian [tʃɛkəslə'vækɪən] a tchécoslovaque ♦ n Tchécoslovaque m/f.

D

D, d [diː] n (letter) D, d m; (MUS): **D** ré m; **D for David**, (US) **D for Dog** D comme Désirée.
D abbr (US POL) = **democrat(ic).**
d abbr (Brit: old) = **penny.**
d. abbr = died.
DA n abbr (US) = **district attorney.**
dab [dæb] vt (eyes, wound) tamponner; (paint, cream) appliquer (par petites touches or rapidement); **a ~ of paint** un petit coup de peinture.
dabble ['dæbl] vi: **to ~ in** faire or se mêler or s'occuper un peu de.
Dacca ['dækə] n Dacca.
dachshund ['dækshund] n teckel m.
dad, daddy [dæd, 'dædɪ] n papa m.
daddy-long-legs [dædɪ'lɔŋlɛgz] n tipule f; faucheux m.
daffodil ['dæfədɪl] n jonquille f.
daft [dɑːft] a (col) idiot(e), stupide; **to be ~ about** être toqué(e) or mordu(e) de.
dagger ['dægə*] n poignard m; **to be at ~s drawn with sb** être à couteaux tirés avec qn; **to look ~s at sb** foudroyer qn du regard.
dahlia ['deɪljə] n dahlia m.
daily ['deɪlɪ] a quotidien(ne), journalier(ière) ♦ n quotidien m; (Brit: servant) femme f de ménage (à la journée) ♦ ad tous les jours; **twice ~** deux fois par jour.
dainty ['deɪntɪ] a délicat(e), mignon(ne).
dairy ['dɛərɪ] n (shop) crémerie f, laiterie f; (on farm) laiterie ♦ a laitier(ière).
dairy cow n vache laitière.
dairy farm n exploitation f pratiquant l'élevage laitier.
dairy produce n produits laitiers.
dais ['deɪɪs] n estrade f.
daisy ['deɪzɪ] n pâquerette f.
daisy wheel n (on printer) marguerite f.
daisy-wheel printer n imprimante f à marguerite.
Dakar ['dækə] n Dakar.
dale [deɪl] n vallon m.
dally ['dælɪ] vi musarder, flâner.
dalmatian [dæl'meɪʃən] n (dog) dalmatien/ne.
dam [dæm] n barrage m; (reservoir) réservoir m, lac m de retenue ♦ vt endiguer.
damage ['dæmɪdʒ] n dégâts mpl, dommages mpl; (fig) tort m ♦ vt endommager, abîmer; (fig) faire du tort à; **~ to property** dégâts matériels.
damages ['dæmɪdʒɪz] npl (LAW) dommages-intérêts mpl; **to pay £5000 in ~** payer 5000 livres de dommages-intérêts.
damaging ['dæmɪdʒɪŋ] a: **~ (to)** préjudiciable (à), nuisible (à).
Damascus [də'mɑːskəs] n Damas.
dame n (title) titre porté par une femme décorée de l'ordre de l'Empire Britannique ou d'un ordre de chevalerie; titre porté par la

femme ou la veuve d'un chevalier ou baronnet; (*US col*) nana *f*; (*THEATRE*) vieille dame (*rôle comique joué par un homme*).

damn [dæm] *vt* condamner; (*curse*) maudire ♦ *n* (*col*): **I don't give a ~** je m'en fous ♦ *a* (*col*): **this ~** ... ce sacré *or* foutu ...; **~ (it)!** zut!

damnable ['dæmnəbl] *a* (*col: behaviour*) odieux(euse), détestable; (*: weather*) épouvantable, abominable.

damnation [dæm'neɪʃən] *n* (*REL*) damnation *f* ♦ *excl* (*col*) malédiction!, merde!

damning ['dæmɪŋ] *a* (*evidence*) accablant(e).

damp [dæmp] *a* humide ♦ *n* humidité *f* ♦ *vt* (*also*: **~en**: *cloth, rag*) humecter; (*: enthusiasm etc*) refroidir.

dampcourse ['dæmpkɔːs] *n* couche isolante (contre l'humidité).

damper ['dæmpə*] *n* (*MUS*) étouffoir *m*; (*of fire*) registre *m*; **to put a ~ on** (*fig: atmosphere, enthusiasm*) refroidir.

dampness ['dæmpnɪs] *n* humidité *f*.

damson ['dæmzən] *n* prune *f* de Damas.

dance [dɑːns] *n* danse *f*; (*ball*) bal *m* ♦ *vi* danser; **to ~ about** sautiller, gambader.

dance hall *n* salle *f* de bal, dancing *m*.

dancer ['dɑːnsə*] *n* danseur/euse.

dancing ['dɑːnsɪŋ] *n* danse *f*.

D and C *n* abbr (*MED*: = dilation and curettage) curetage *m*.

dandelion ['dændɪlaɪən] *n* pissenlit *m*.

dandruff ['dændrəf] *n* pellicules *fpl*.

dandy ['dændɪ] *n* dandy *m*, élégant *m* ♦ *a* (*US col*) fantastique, super.

Dane [deɪn] *n* Danois/e.

danger ['deɪndʒə*] *n* danger *m*; **there is a ~ of fire** il y a (un) risque d'incendie; **in ~** en danger; **he was in ~ of falling** il risquait de tomber; **out of ~** hors de danger.

danger list *n* (*MED*): **on the ~** dans un état critique.

dangerous ['deɪndʒrəs] *a* dangereux(euse).

dangerously ['deɪndʒrəslɪ] *ad* dangereusement; **~ ill** très gravement malade, en danger de mort.

danger zone *n* zone dangereuse.

dangle ['dæŋgl] *vt* balancer; (*fig*) faire miroiter ♦ *vi* pendre, se balancer.

Danish ['deɪnɪʃ] *a* danois(e) ♦ *n* (*LING*) danois *m*.

Danish pastry *n* feuilleté *m* (*recouvert d'un glaçage et fourré aux fruits etc*).

dank [dæŋk] *a* froid(e) et humide.

Danube ['dænjuːb] *n*: **the ~** le Danube.

dapper ['dæpə*] *a* pimpant(e).

Dardanelles [dɑːdə'nɛlz] *npl* Dardanelles *fpl*.

dare [dɛə*] *vt*: **to ~ sb to do** défier qn *or* mettre qn au défi de faire ♦ *vi*: **to ~ (to) do sth** oser faire qch; **I ~n't tell him** (*Brit*) je n'ose pas le lui dire; **I ~ say he'll turn up** il est probable qu'il viendra.

daredevil ['dɛədɛvl] *n* casse-cou *m inv*.

Dar-es-Salaam [dɑːrɛssə'lɑːm] *n* Dar-es-Salaam, Dar-es-Salam.

daring ['dɛərɪŋ] *a* hardi(e), audacieux(euse) ♦ *n* audace *f*, hardiesse *f*.

dark [dɑːk] *a* (*night, room*) obscur(e), sombre; (*colour, complexion*) foncé(e), sombre; (*fig*) sombre ♦ *n*: **in the ~** dans le noir; **in the ~**

about (*fig*) ignorant tout de; **after ~** après la tombée de la nuit; **it is/is getting ~** il fait nuit/commence à faire nuit.

darken [dɑːkn] *vt* obscurcir, assombrir ♦ *vi* s'obscurcir, s'assombrir.

dark glasses *npl* lunettes noires.

darkly ['dɑːklɪ] *ad* (*gloomily*) mélancoliquement; (*in a sinister way*) lugubrement.

darkness ['dɑːknɪs] *n* obscurité *f*.

dark room *n* chambre noire.

darling ['dɑːlɪŋ] *a*, *n* chéri(e).

darn [dɑːn] *vt* repriser.

dart [dɑːt] *n* fléchette *f* ♦ *vi*: **to ~ towards** (*also*: **make a ~ towards**) se précipiter *or* s'élancer vers; **to ~ away/along** partir/ passer comme une flèche.

dartboard ['dɑːtbɔːd] *n* cible *f* (*de jeu de fléchettes*).

darts [dɑːts] *n* jeu *m* de fléchettes.

dash [dæʃ] *n* (*sign*) tiret *m*; (*small quantity*) goutte *f*, larme *f* ♦ *vt* (*missile*) jeter *or* lancer violemment; (*hopes*) anéantir ♦ *vi*: **to ~ towards** (*also*: **make a ~ towards**) se précipiter *or* se ruer vers; **a ~ of soda** un peu d'eau gazeuse.

dash away *vi* partir à toute allure.

dashboard ['dæʃbɔːd] *n* (*AUT*) tableau *m* de bord.

dashing ['dæʃɪŋ] *a* fringant(e).

dastardly ['dæstədlɪ] *a* lâche.

data ['deɪtə] *npl* données *fpl*.

database ['deɪtəbeɪs] *n* base *f* de données.

data capture *n* saisie *f* de données.

data processing *n* traitement *m* (électronique) de l'information.

data transmission *n* transmission *f* de données.

date [deɪt] *n* date *f*; (*appointment*) rendez-vous *m*; (*fruit*) datte *f* ♦ *vt* dater; (*col: girl etc*) sortir avec; **what's the ~ today?** quelle date sommes-nous aujourd'hui?; **~ of birth** date de naissance; **closing ~** date de clôture; **to ~** *ad* à ce jour; **out of ~** périmé(e); **up to ~** à la page; moderne; **to bring up to ~** (*correspondence, information*) mettre à jour; (*method*) moderniser; (*person*) mettre au courant; **letter ~d 5th July** *or* (*US*) **July 5th** lettre (datée) du 5 juillet.

dated ['deɪtɪd] *a* démodé(e).

dateline ['deɪtlaɪn] *n* ligne *f* de changement de date.

date stamp *n* timbre-dateur *m*.

daub [dɔːb] *vt* barbouiller.

daughter ['dɔːtə*] *n* fille *f*.

daughter-in-law ['dɔːtərɪnlɔː] *n* belle-fille *f*, bru *f*.

daunt [dɔːnt] *vt* intimider, décourager.

daunting ['dɔːntɪŋ] *a* décourageant(e), intimidant(e).

dauntless ['dɔːntlɪs] *a* intrépide.

dawdle ['dɔːdl] *vi* traîner, lambiner; **to ~ over one's work** traînasser *or* lambiner sur son travail.

dawn [dɔːn] *n* aube *f*, aurore *f* ♦ *vi* (*day*) se lever, poindre; (*fig*) naître, se faire jour; **at ~** à l'aube; **from ~ to dusk** du matin au soir; **it ~ed on him that** ... il lui vint à l'esprit que ....

dawn chorus n (Brit) chant m des oiseaux à l'aube.

day [deɪ] n jour m; (as duration) journée f; (period of time, age) époque f, temps m; **the ~ before** la veille, le jour précédent; **the ~ after, the following ~** le lendemain, le jour suivant; **the ~ before yesterday** avant-hier; **the ~ after tomorrow** après-demain; **(on) the ~ that ...** le jour où ...; **~ by ~** jour après jour; **by ~** de jour; **paid by the ~** payé(e) à la journée; **these ~s, in the present ~** de nos jours, à l'heure actuelle.

daybook ['deɪbuk] n (Brit) main courante, brouillard m, journal m.

day boy n (SCOL) externe m.

daybreak ['deɪbreɪk] n point m du jour.

daydream ['deɪdri:m] n rêverie f ♦ vi rêver (tout éveillé).

day girl n (SCOL) externe f.

daylight ['deɪlaɪt] n (lumière f du) jour m.

Daylight Saving Time n (US) heure f d'été.

day release n: **to be on ~** avoir une journée de congé pour formation professionnelle.

day return (ticket) n (Brit) billet m d'aller-retour (valable pour la journée).

day shift n équipe f de jour.

daytime ['deɪtaɪm] n jour m, journée f.

day-to-day ['deɪtə'deɪ] a (routine, expenses) journalier(ière); **on a ~ basis** au jour le jour.

day trip n excursion f (d'une journée).

day tripper n excursionniste m/f.

daze [deɪz] vt (subj: drug) hébéter; (: blow) étourdir ♦ n: **in a ~** hébété(e); étourdi(e).

dazzle ['dæzl] vt éblouir, aveugler.

dazzling ['dæzlɪŋ] a (light) aveuglant(e), éblouissant(e); (fig) éblouissant(e).

DC abbr (ELEC) = **direct current**; (US POST) = District of Columbia.

DD n abbr (= Doctor of Divinity) titre universitaire.

dd. abbr (COMM) = **delivered**.

D/D abbr = **direct debit**.

D-day ['di:deɪ] n le jour J.

DDS n abbr (US: = Doctor of Dental Science , Doctor of Dental Surgery) titres universitaires.

DDT n abbr (= dichlorodiphenyl trichloro-ethane) DDT m.

DE abbr (US POST) = Delaware.

DEA n abbr (US: = Drug Enforcement Administration) ≈ brigade f des stupéfiants.

deacon ['di:kən] n diacre m.

dead [dɛd] a mort(e); (numb) engourdi(e), insensible ♦ ad absolument, complètement; **the ~** npl les morts; **he was shot ~** il a été tué d'un coup de revolver; **~ on time** à l'heure pile; **~ tired** éreinté(e), complètement fourbu(e); **to stop ~** s'arrêter pile or net; **the line has gone ~** (TEL) on n'entend plus rien.

deaden [dɛdn] vt (blow, sound) amortir; (make numb) endormir, rendre insensible.

dead end n impasse f.

dead-end ['dɛdend] a: **a ~ job** un emploi or poste sans avenir.

dead heat n (SPORT): **to finish in a ~** terminer ex-aequo.

dead-letter office [dɛd'lɛtə-] n ≈ centre m de recherche du courrier.

deadline ['dɛdlaɪn] n date f or heure f limite; **to work to a ~** avoir des délais stricts à respecter.

deadlock ['dɛdlɔk] n impasse f (fig).

dead loss n (col): **to be a ~** (person) n'être bon(bonne) à rien; (thing) ne rien valoir.

deadly ['dɛdlɪ] a (weapon) meurtrier(ière); **~ dull** ennuyeux(euse) à mourir, mortellement ennuyeux.

deadpan ['dɛdpæn] a impassible; (humour) pince-sans-rire inv.

Dead Sea n: **the ~** la mer Morte.

dead season n (TOURISM) morte saison.

deaf [dɛf] a sourd(e); **to turn a ~ ear to sth** faire la sourde oreille à qch.

deaf-aid ['dɛfeɪd] n (Brit) appareil auditif.

deaf-and-dumb ['dɛfən'dʌm] a sourd(e)-muet(te); **~ alphabet** alphabet m des sourds-muets.

deafen ['dɛfn] vt rendre sourd(e); (fig) assourdir.

deafening ['dɛfnɪŋ] a assourdissant(e).

deaf-mute ['dɛfmju:t] n sourd/e-muet/te.

deafness ['dɛfnɪs] n surdité f.

deal [di:l] n affaire f, marché m ♦ vt (pt, pp dealt [dɛlt]) (blow) porter; (cards) donner, distribuer; **to strike a ~ with sb** faire or conclure un marché avec qn; **it's a ~!** (col) marché conclu!, tope-là!, topez-là!; **he got a bad ~ from them** ils ont mal agi envers lui; **he got a fair ~ from them** ils ont agi loyalement envers lui; **a good ~** (a lot) beaucoup; **a good ~ of, a great ~ of** beaucoup de, énormément de.

deal in vt fus (COMM) faire le commerce de, être dans le commerce de.

deal with vt fus (COMM) traiter avec; (handle) s'occuper or se charger de; (be about: book etc) traiter de.

dealer ['di:lə*] n marchand m.

dealership ['di:ləʃɪp] n concession f.

dealings ['di:lɪŋz] npl (in goods, shares) opérations fpl, transactions fpl; (relations) relations fpl, rapports mpl.

dean [di:n] n (REL, Brit SCOL) doyen m; (US SCOL) conseiller/ère (principal(e)) d'éducation.

dear [dɪə*] a cher(chère); (expensive) cher, coûteux(euse) ♦ n: **my ~** mon cher/ma chère; **~ me!** mon Dieu!; **D~ Sir/Madam** (in letter) Monsieur/Madame; **D~ Mr/Mrs X** Cher Monsieur/Chère Madame X.

dearly ['dɪəlɪ] ad (love) tendrement; (pay) cher.

dearth [də:θ] n disette f, pénurie f.

death [dɛθ] n mort f; (ADMIN) décès m.

deathbed ['dɛθbɛd] n lit m de mort.

death certificate n acte m de décès.

death duties npl (Brit) droits mpl de succession.

deathly ['dɛθlɪ] a de mort ♦ ad comme la mort.

death penalty n peine f de mort.

death rate n taux m de mortalité.

death sentence n condamnation f à mort.

deathtrap ['dɛθtræp] n endroit (or véhicule etc) dangereux.

deb [dɛb] *n abbr* (*col*) = **debutante**.

debar [dɪˈbɑː*] *vt*: **to ~ sb from a club** *etc* exclure qn d'un club *etc*; **to ~ sb from doing** interdire à qn de faire.

debase [dɪˈbeɪs] *vt* (*currency*) déprécier, dévaloriser; (*person*) abaisser, avilir.

debatable [dɪˈbeɪtəbl] *a* discutable, contestable; **it is ~ whether** ... il est douteux que ....

debate [dɪˈbeɪt] *n* discussion *f*, débat *m* ♦ *vt* discuter, débattre ♦ *vi* (*consider*): **to ~ whether** se demander si.

debauchery [dɪˈbɔːtʃərɪ] *n* débauche *f*.

debenture [dɪˈbɛntʃə*] *n* (*COMM*) obligation *f*.

debilitate [dɪˈbɪlɪteɪt] *vt* débiliter.

debit [ˈdebɪt] *n* débit *m* ♦ *vt*: **to ~ a sum to sb** *or* **to sb's account** porter une somme au débit de qn, débiter qn d'une somme.

debit balance *n* solde débiteur.

debit note *n* note *f* de débit.

debrief [diːˈbriːf] *vt* demander un compte rendu de fin de mission à.

debriefing [diːˈbriːfɪŋ] *n* compte rendu *m*.

debris [ˈdebriː] *n* débris *mpl*, décombres *mpl*.

debt [dɛt] *n* dette *f*; **to be in ~** avoir des dettes, être endetté(e); **bad ~** créance *f* irrécouvrable.

debt collector *n* agent *m* de recouvrements.

debtor [ˈdetə*] *n* débiteur/trice.

debug [ˈdiːˈbʌɡ] *vt* (*COMPUT*) déverminer.

debunk [diːˈbʌŋk] *vt* (*theory, claim*) montrer le ridicule de.

debut [ˈdeɪbjuː] *n* début(s) *m(pl)*.

debutante [ˈdebjutænt] *n* débutante *f*.

Dec. *abbr* (= *december*) déc.

decade [ˈdekeɪd] *n* décennie *f*, décade *f*.

decadence [ˈdekədəns] *n* décadence *f*.

decadent [ˈdekədənt] *a* décadent(e).

decaffeinated [dɪˈkæfɪneɪtɪd] *a* décaféiné(e).

decamp [dɪˈkæmp] *vi* (*col*) décamper, filer.

decant [dɪˈkænt] *vt* (*wine*) décanter.

decanter [dɪˈkæntə*] *n* carafe *f*.

decarbonize [diːˈkɑːbənaɪz] *vt* (*AUT*) décalaminer.

decay [dɪˈkeɪ] *n* décomposition *f*, pourrissement *m*; (*fig*) déclin *m*, délabrement *m*; (*also*: **tooth ~**) carie *f* (dentaire) ♦ *vi* (*rot*) se décomposer, pourrir; (*fig*) se délabrer; décliner; se détériorer.

decease [dɪˈsiːs] *n* décès *m*.

deceased [dɪˈsiːst] *n*: **the ~** le/la défunt/e.

deceit [dɪˈsiːt] *n* tromperie *f*, supercherie *f*.

deceitful [dɪˈsiːtful] *a* trompeur(euse).

deceive [dɪˈsiːv] *vt* tromper; **to ~ o.s.** s'abuser.

decelerate [diːˈseləreɪt] *vt, vi* ralentir.

December [dɪˈsembə*] *n* décembre *m*; *for phrases see also* **July**.

decency [ˈdiːsənsɪ] *n* décence *f*.

decent [ˈdiːsənt] *a* décent(e), convenable; **they were very ~ about it** ils se sont montrés très chics.

decently [ˈdiːsəntlɪ] *ad* (*respectably*) décemment, convenablement; (*kindly*) décemment.

decentralization [ˈdiːsentrəlaɪˈzeɪʃən] *n* décentralisation *f*.

decentralize [diːˈsentrəlaɪz] *vt* décentraliser.

deception [dɪˈsepʃən] *n* tromperie *f*.

deceptive [dɪˈseptɪv] *a* trompeur(euse).

decibel [ˈdesɪbel] *n* décibel *m*.

decide [dɪˈsaɪd] *vt* (*person*) décider; (*question, argument*) trancher, régler ♦ *vi* se décider, décider; **to ~ to do/that** décider de faire/ que; **to ~ on** décider, se décider pour; **to ~ on doing** décider de faire; **to ~ against doing** décider de ne pas faire.

decided [dɪˈsaɪdɪd] *a* (*resolute*) résolu(e), décidé(e); (*clear, definite*) net(te), marqué(e).

decidedly [dɪˈsaɪdɪdlɪ] *ad* résolument; incontestablement, nettement.

deciding [dɪˈsaɪdɪŋ] *a* décisif(ive).

deciduous [dɪˈsɪdjuəs] *a* à feuilles caduques.

decimal [ˈdesɪməl] *a* décimal(e) ♦ *n* décimale *f*; **to 3 ~ places** (jusqu')à la troisième décimale.

decimalize [ˈdesɪməlaɪz] *vt* (*Brit*) décimaliser.

decimal point *n* ≈ virgule *f*.

decimate [ˈdesɪmeɪt] *vt* décimer.

decipher [dɪˈsaɪfə*] *vt* déchiffrer.

decision [dɪˈsɪʒən] *n* décision *f*; **to make a ~** prendre une décision.

decisive [dɪˈsaɪsɪv] *a* décisif(ive); (*influence*) décisif, déterminant(e); (*manner, person*) décidé(e), catégorique; (*reply*) ferme, catégorique.

deck [dɛk] *n* (*NAUT*) pont *m*; (*of bus*): **top ~** impériale *f*; (*of cards*) jeu *m*; **to go up on ~** monter sur le pont; **below ~** dans l'entrepont; **record/cassette ~** platine-disques/-cassettes *f*.

deckchair [ˈdektʃeə*] *n* chaise longue.

deck hand *n* matelot *m*.

declaration [dekləˈreɪʃən] *n* déclaration *f*.

declare [dɪˈkleə*] *vt* déclarer.

declassify [diːˈklæsɪfaɪ] *vt* rendre accessible au public *or* à tous.

decline [dɪˈklaɪn] *n* (*decay*) déclin *m*; (*lessening*) baisse *f* ♦ *vt* refuser, décliner ♦ *vi* décliner; être en baisse, baisser; **~ in living standards** baisse du niveau de vie; **to ~ to do sth** refuser (poliment) de faire qch.

declutch [ˈdiːˈklʌtʃ] *vi* (*Brit*) débrayer.

decode [ˈdiːˈkəud] *vt* décoder.

decoder [diːˈkəudə*] *n* décodeur *m*.

decompose [diːkəmˈpəuz] *vi* se décomposer.

decomposition [diːkɔmpəˈzɪʃən] *n* décomposition *f*.

decompression [diːkəmˈpreʃən] *n* décompression *f*.

decompression chamber *n* caisson *m* de décompression.

decongestant [diːkənˈdʒestənt] *n* décongestif *m*.

decontaminate [diːkənˈtæmɪneɪt] *vt* décontaminer.

decontrol [diːkənˈtrəul] *vt* (*prices etc*) libérer.

décor [ˈdeɪkɔː*] *n* décor *m*.

decorate [ˈdekəreɪt] *vt* (*adorn, give a medal to*) décorer; (*paint and paper*) peindre et tapisser.

decoration [dekəˈreɪʃən] *n* (*medal etc, adornment*) décoration *f*.

decorative [ˈdekərətɪv] *a* décoratif(ive).

decorator [ˈdekəreɪtə*] *n* peintre *m* en bâtiment.

decorum [dɪˈkɔːrəm] *n* décorum *m*, bienséance *f*.

decoy ['di:kɔɪ] *n* piège *m*; **they used him as a** ~ **for the enemy** ils se sont servis de lui pour attirer l'ennemi.

decrease *n* ['di:kri:s] diminution *f* ♦ *vt, vi* [di:'kri:s] diminuer; **to be on the** ~ diminuer, être en diminution.

decreasing [di:'kri:sɪŋ] *a* en voie de diminution.

decree [dɪ'kri:] *n* (POL, REL) décret *m*; (LAW) arrêt *m*, jugement *m* ♦ *vt*: **to** ~ **(that)** décréter (que), ordonner (que); ~ **absolute** jugement définitif (de divorce); ~ **nisi** jugement provisoire de divorce.

decrepit [dɪ'krɛpɪt] *a* (*person*) décrépit(e); (*building*) délabré(e).

decry [dɪ'kraɪ] *vt* condamner ouvertement, déplorer; (*disparage*) dénigrer, décrier.

dedicate ['dɛdɪkeɪt] *vt* consacrer; (*book etc*) dédier.

dedicated ['dɛdɪkeɪtɪd] *a* (*person*) dévoué(e); (COMPUT) spécialisé(e), dédié(e); ~ **word processor** station *f* de traitement de texte.

dedication [dɛdɪ'keɪʃən] *n* (*devotion*) dévouement *m*; (*in book*) dédicace *f*.

deduce [dɪ'dju:s] *vt* déduire, conclure.

deduct [dɪ'dʌkt] *vt*: **to** ~ **sth (from)** déduire qch (de), retrancher qch (de); (*from wage etc*) prélever qch (sur), retenir qch (sur).

deduction [dɪ'dʌkʃən] *n* (*deducting*) déduction *f*; (*from wage etc*) prélèvement *m*, retenue *f*; (*deducing*) déduction, conclusion *f*.

deed [di:d] *n* action *f*, acte *m*; (LAW) acte notarié, contrat *m*; ~ **of covenant** (acte *m* de) donation *f*.

deem [di:m] *vt* (*formal*) juger, estimer; **to** ~ **it wise to do** juger bon de faire.

deep [di:p] *a* (*water, sigh, sorrow, thoughts*) profond(e); (*voice*) grave ♦ *ad*: ~ **in snow** recouvert(e) d'une épaisse couche de neige; **spectators stood 20** ~ il y avait 20 rangs de spectateurs; **knee-**~ **in water** dans l'eau jusqu'aux genoux; **4 metres** ~ de 4 mètres de profondeur; **he took a** ~ **breath** il inspira profondément, il prit son souffle.

deepen [di:pn] *vt* (*hole*) approfondir ♦ *vi* s'approfondir; (*darkness*) s'épaissir.

deep-freeze ['di:p'fri:z] *n* congélateur *m* ♦ *vt* surgeler.

deep-fry ['di:p'fraɪ] *vt* faire frire (dans une friteuse).

deeply ['di:plɪ] *ad* profondément; (*dig*) en profondeur; (*regret, interest*) vivement.

deep-rooted ['di:p'ru:tɪd] *a* (*prejudice*) profondément enraciné(e); (*affection*) profond(e); (*habit*) invétéré(e).

deep-sea ['di:p'si:] *a*: ~ **diver** plongeur sous-marin; ~ **diving** *n* plongée sous-marine.

deep-sea fishing *n* pêche hauturière.

deep-seated ['di:p'si:tɪd] *a* (*beliefs*) profondément enraciné(e).

deep-set ['di:pset] *a* (*eyes*) enfoncé(e).

deer [dɪə*] *n* (*pl inv*): **the** ~ les cervidés *mpl* (ZOOL); (**red**) ~ cerf *m*; (**fallow**) ~ daim *m*; (**roe**) ~ chevreuil *m*.

deerskin [di:skɪn] *n* peau *f* de daim.

deerstalker ['dɪəstɔ:kə*] *n* (*person*) chasseur *m* de cerf; (*hat*) casquette *f* à la Sherlock Holmes.

deface [dɪ'feɪs] *vt* dégrader; barbouiller; rendre illisible.

defamation [dɛfə'meɪʃən] *n* diffamation *f*.

defamatory [dɪ'fæmətrɪ] *a* diffamatoire, diffamant(e).

default [dɪ'fɔ:lt] *vi* (LAW) faire défaut; (*gen*) manquer à ses engagements ♦ *n* (COMPUT: *also*: ~ **value**) valeur *f* par défaut; **by** ~ (LAW) par défaut, par contumace; (SPORT) par forfait; **to** ~ **on a debt** ne pas s'acquitter d'une dette.

defaulter [dɪ'fɔ:ltə*] *n* (*on debt*) débiteur défaillant.

default option *n* (COMPUT) option *f* par défaut.

defeat [dɪ'fi:t] *n* défaite *f* ♦ *vt* (*team, opponents*) battre; (*fig: plans, efforts*) faire échouer.

defeatism [dɪ'fi:tɪzəm] *n* défaitisme *m*.

defeatist [dɪ'fi:tɪst] *a, n* défaitiste (*m/f*).

defect *n* ['di:fɛkt] défaut *m* ♦ *vi* [dɪ'fɛkt]: **to** ~ **to the enemy/the West** passer à l'ennemi/l'Ouest; **physical** ~ malformation *f*, vice *m* de conformation; **mental** ~ anomalie *or* déficience mentale.

defective [dɪ'fɛktɪv] *a* défectueux(euse).

defector [dɪ'fɛktə*] *n* transfuge *m/f*.

defence, (US) defense [dɪ'fɛns] *n* défense *f*; **in** ~ **of** pour défendre; **witness for the** ~ témoin *m* à décharge; **the Ministry of D**~, (US) **the Department of Defense** le ministère de la Défense nationale.

defenceless [dɪ'fɛnslɪs] *a* sans défense.

defend [dɪ'fɛnd] *vt* défendre; (*decision, action, opinion*) justifier, défendre.

defendant [dɪ'fɛndənt] *n* défendeur/deresse; (*in criminal case*) accusé/e, prévenu/e.

defender [dɪ'fɛndə*] *n* défenseur *m*.

defending champion [dɪ'fɛndɪŋ-] *n* (SPORT) champion/ne en titre.

defending counsel [dɪ'fɛndɪŋ-] *n* (LAW) avocat *m* de la défense.

defense [dɪ'fɛns] *n* (US) = **defence**.

defensive [dɪ'fɛnsɪv] *a* défensif(ive) ♦ *n* défensive *f*; **on the** ~ sur la défensive.

defer [dɪ'fə:*] *vt* (*postpone*) différer, ajourner ♦ *vi* (*submit*): **to** ~ **to sb/sth** déférer à qn/qch, en remettre à qn/qch.

deference ['dɛfərəns] *n* déférence *f*, égards *mpl*; **out of** *or* **in** ~ **to** par déférence *or* égards pour.

defiance [dɪ'faɪəns] *n* défi *m*; **in** ~ **of** au mépris de.

defiant [dɪ'faɪənt] *a* provocant(e), de défi.

defiantly [dɪ'faɪəntlɪ] *ad* d'un air (*or* d'un ton) de défi.

deficiency [dɪ'fɪʃənsɪ] *n* insuffisance *f*, déficience *f*; carence *f*; (COMM) déficit *m*, découvert *m*.

deficiency disease *n* maladie *f* de carence.

deficient [dɪ'fɪʃənt] *a* insuffisant(e); défectueux(euse); déficient(e); **to be** ~ **in** manquer de.

deficit ['dɛfɪsɪt] *n* déficit *m*.

defile [dɪ'faɪl] *vt* souiller ♦ *vi* défiler ♦ *n* ['di:faɪl] défilé *m*.

define [dɪ'faɪn] *vt* définir.

definite ['dɛfɪnɪt] *a* (*fixed*) défini(e), (*bien*) déterminé(e); (*clear, obvious*) net(te), manifeste; (LING) défini(e); **he was** ~ **about**

it il a été catégorique; il était sûr de son fait.

definitely ['dɛfɪnɪtlɪ] *ad* sans aucun doute.

definition [dɛfɪ'nɪʃən] *n* définition *f*.

definitive [dɪ'fɪnɪtɪv] *a* définitif(ive).

deflate [di:'fleɪt] *vt* dégonfler; (*pompous person*) rabattre le caquet à; (*ECON*) provoquer la déflation de; (*: prices*) faire tomber *or* baisser.

deflation [di:'fleɪʃən] *n* (*ECON*) déflation *f*.

deflationary [di:'fleɪʃənrɪ] *a* (*ECON*) déflationniste.

deflect [dɪ'flɛkt] *vt* détourner, faire dévier.

defog ['di:'fɔg] *vt* (*US AUT*) désembuer.

defogger ['di:'fɔgə*] *n* (*US AUT*) dispositif *m* anti-buée *inv*.

deform [dɪ'fɔːm] *vt* déformer.

deformed [dɪ'fɔːmd] *a* difforme.

deformity [dɪ'fɔːmɪtɪ] *n* difformité *f*.

defraud [dɪ'frɔːd] *vt* frauder; **to ~ sb of sth** soutirer qch malhonnêtement à qn; escroquer qch à qn; frustrer qn de qch.

defray [dɪ'freɪ] *vt*: **to ~ sb's expenses** défrayer qn (de ses frais), rembourser *or* payer à qn ses frais.

defrost [di:'frɔst] *vt* (*fridge*) dégivrer; (*frozen food*) décongeler.

deft [dɛft] *a* adroit(e), preste.

defunct [dɪ'fʌŋkt] *a* défunt(e).

defuse [di:'fjuːz] *vt* désamorcer.

defy [dɪ'faɪ] *vt* défier; (*efforts etc*) résister à.

degenerate *vi* [dɪ'dʒɛnəreɪt] dégénérer ♦ *a* [dɪ'dʒɛnərɪt] dégénéré(e).

degradation [dɛgrə'deɪʃən] *n* dégradation *f*.

degrade [dɪ'greɪd] *vt* dégrader.

degrading [dɪ'greɪdɪŋ] *a* dégradant(e).

degree [dɪ'griː] *n* degré *m*; (*SCOL*) diplôme *m* (universitaire); **10 ~s below (zero)** 10 degrés au-dessous de zéro; **a (first) ~ in maths** (*Brit*) une licence en maths; **a considerable ~ of risk** un considérable facteur *or* élément de risque; **by ~s** (*gradually*) par degrés; **to some ~, to a certain ~** jusqu'à un certain point, dans une certaine mesure.

dehydrated [di:haɪ'dreɪtɪd] *a* déshydraté(e); (*milk, eggs*) en poudre.

dehydration [di:haɪ'dreɪʃən] *n* déshydratation *f*.

de-ice ['di:'aɪs] *vt* (*windscreen*) dégivrer.

de-icer ['di:'aɪsə*] *n* dégivreur *m*.

deign [deɪn] *vi*: **to ~ to do** daigner faire.

deity ['di:ɪtɪ] *n* divinité *f*; dieu *m*, déesse *f*.

dejected [dɪ'dʒɛktɪd] *a* abattu(e), déprimé(e).

dejection [dɪ'dʒɛkʃən] *n* abattement *m*, découragement *m*.

del. *abbr* = **delete.**

delay [dɪ'leɪ] *vt* (*journey, operation*) retarder, différer; (*travellers, trains*) retarder; (*payment*) différer ♦ *vi* s'attarder ♦ *n* délai *m*, retard *m*; **without ~** sans délai, sans tarder.

delayed-action [dɪ'leɪd'ækʃən] *a* à retardement.

delectable [dɪ'lɛktəbl] *a* délicieux(euse).

delegate *n* ['dɛlɪgɪt] délégué/e ♦ *vt* ['dɛlɪgeɪt] déléguer; **to ~ sth to sb/sb to do sth** déléguer qch à qn/qn pour faire qch.

delegation [dɛlɪ'geɪʃən] *n* délégation *f*.

delete [dɪ'liːt] *vt* rayer, supprimer; (*COMPUT*) effacer.

Delhi ['dɛlɪ] *n* Delhi.

deliberate *a* [dɪ'lɪbərɪt] (*intentional*) délibéré(e); (*slow*) mesuré(e) ♦ *vi* [dɪ'lɪbəreɪt] délibérer, réfléchir.

deliberately [dɪ'lɪbərɪtlɪ] *ad* (*on purpose*) exprès, délibérément.

deliberation [dɪlɪbə'reɪʃən] *n* délibération *f*, réflexion *f*; (*gen pl: discussion*) délibérations, débats *mpl*.

delicacy ['dɛlɪkəsɪ] *n* délicatesse *f*; (*choice food*) mets fin *or* délicat, friandise *f*.

delicate ['dɛlɪkɪt] *a* délicat(e).

delicately ['dɛlɪkɪtlɪ] *ad* délicatement; (*act, express*) avec délicatesse, avec tact.

delicatessen [dɛlɪkə'tɛsn] *n* épicerie fine.

delicious [dɪ'lɪʃəs] *a* délicieux(euse), exquis(e).

delight [dɪ'laɪt] *n* (grande) joie, grand plaisir ♦ *vt* enchanter; **a ~ to the eyes** un régal *or* plaisir pour les yeux; **to take ~ in** prendre grand plaisir à; **to be the ~ of** faire les délices *or* la joie de.

delighted [dɪ'laɪtɪd] *a*: **~ (at *or* with sth)** ravi(e) (de qch); **to be ~ to do sth/that** être enchanté(e) *or* ravi(e) de faire qch/que; **I'd be ~** j'en serais enchanté *or* ravi.

delightful [dɪ'laɪtful] *a* (*person, child*) absolument charmant(e), adorable; (*evening, view*) merveilleux(euse); (*meal*) délicieux(euse).

delimit [di:'lɪmɪt] *vt* délimiter.

delineate [dɪ'lɪnɪeɪt] *vt* tracer, esquisser; (*fig*) dépeindre, décrire.

delinquency [dɪ'lɪŋkwənsɪ] *n* délinquance *f*.

delinquent [dɪ'lɪŋkwənt] *a, n* délinquant(e).

delirious [dɪ'lɪrɪəs] *a* (*MED, fig*) délirant(e); **to be ~** délirer.

delirium [dɪ'lɪrɪəm] *n* délire *m*.

deliver [dɪ'lɪvə*] *vt* (*mail*) distribuer; (*goods*) livrer; (*message*) remettre; (*speech*) prononcer; (*warning, ultimatum*) lancer; (*free*) délivrer; (*MED*) accoucher; **to ~ the goods** (*fig*) tenir ses promesses.

deliverance [dɪ'lɪvrəns] *n* délivrance *f*, libération *f*.

delivery [dɪ'lɪvərɪ] *n* (*of mail*) distribution *f*; (*of goods*) livraison *f*; (*of speaker*) élocution *f*; (*MED*) accouchement *m*; **to take ~ of** prendre livraison de.

delivery note *n* bon *m* de livraison.

delivery van, (*US*) **delivery truck** *n* fourgonnette *f or* camionnette *f* de livraison.

delouse ['di:'laus] *vt* épouiller, débarrasser de sa (*or* leur *etc*) vermine.

delta ['dɛltə] *n* delta *m*.

delude [dɪ'luːd] *vt* tromper, leurrer; **to ~ o.s.** se leurrer, se faire des illusions.

deluge ['dɛljuːdʒ] *n* déluge *m* ♦ *vt* (*fig*): **to ~ (with)** inonder (de).

delusion [dɪ'luːʒən] *n* illusion *f*; **to have ~s of grandeur** être un peu mégalomane.

de luxe [də'lʌks] *a* de luxe.

delve [dɛlv] *vi*: **to ~ into** fouiller dans.

Dem. *abbr* (*US POL*) = **democrat(ic).**

demagogue ['dɛməgɔg] *n* démagogue *m/f*.

demand [dɪ'mɑːnd] *vt* réclamer, exiger; (*need*) exiger, requérir ♦ *n* exigence *f*; (*claim*) revendication *f*; (*ECON*) demande *f*; **to ~ sth (from *or* of sb)** exiger qch (de qn),

réclamer qch (à qn); **in** ~ demandé(e), re-
cherché(e); **on** ~ sur demande.

demanding [dɪ'mɑːndɪŋ] *a* (*person*)
exigeant(e); (*work*) astreignant(e).

demarcation [diːmɑː'keɪʃən] *n* démarcation *f*.

demarcation dispute *n* (*INDUSTRY*) conflit
m d'attributions.

demean [dɪ'miːn] *vt*: **to** ~ **o.s.** s'abaisser.

demeanour, (*US*) **demeanor** [dɪ'miːnə*] *n*
comportement *m*; maintien *m*.

demented [dɪ'mɛntɪd] *a* dément(e), fou(folle).

demilitarized zone [diː'mɪlɪtəraɪzd-] *n* zone
démilitarisée.

demise [dɪ'maɪz] *n* décès *m*.

demist [diː'mɪst] *vt* (*Brit AUT*) désembuer.

demister [diː'mɪstə*] *n* (*Brit AUT*) dispositif *m*
anti-buée *inv*.

demo ['dɛməʊ] *n abbr* (*col*: = *demonstration*)
manif *f*.

demobilize [diː'məʊbɪlaɪz] *vt* démobiliser.

democracy [dɪ'mɒkrəsɪ] *n* démocratie *f*.

democrat ['dɛməkræt] *n* démocrate *m/f*.

democratic [dɛmə'krætɪk] *a* démocratique.

demography [dɪ'mɒgrəfɪ] *n* démographie *f*.

demolish [dɪ'mɒlɪʃ] *vt* démolir.

demolition [dɛmə'lɪʃən] *n* démolition *f*.

demon ['diːmən] *n* démon *m* ♦ *cpd*: **a** ~
squash player un crack en squash; **a** ~
driver un fou du volant.

demonstrate ['dɛmənstreɪt] *vt* démontrer,
prouver ♦ *vi*: **to** ~ **(for/against)** manifester
(en faveur de/contre).

demonstration [dɛmən'streɪʃən] *n* démonstration *f*; (*POL etc*) manifestation *f*; **to hold
a** ~ (*POL etc*) organiser une manifestation,
manifester.

demonstrative [dɪ'mɒnstrətɪv] *a* démons-
tratif(ive).

demonstrator ['dɛmənstreɪtə*] *n* (*POL etc*)
manifestant/e; (*COMM*: *sales person*)
vendeur/euse; (: *car, computer etc*) modèle
m de démonstration.

demoralize [dɪ'mɒrəlaɪz] *vt* démoraliser.

demote [dɪ'məʊt] *vt* rétrograder.

demotion [dɪ'məʊʃən] *n* rétrogradation *f*.

demur [dɪ'mɜː*] *vi*: **to** ~ **(at sth)** hésiter
(devant qch); (*object*) élever des objections
(contre qch) ♦ *n*: **without** ~ sans hésiter;
sans faire de difficultés.

demure [dɪ'mjʊə*] *a* sage, réservé(e); d'une
modestie affectée.

demurrage [dɪ'mʌrɪdʒ] *n* droits *mpl* de
magasinage; surestarie *f*.

den [dɛn] *n* tanière *f*, antre *m*.

denationalization ['diːnæ∫nəlaɪ'zeɪʃən] *n*
dénationalisation *f*.

denationalize [diː'næ∫nəlaɪz] *vt*
dénationaliser.

denial [dɪ'naɪəl] *n* (*of accusation*) démenti *m*;
(*of rights, guilt, truth*) dénégation *f*.

denier ['dɛnɪə*] *n* denier *m*; **15** ~ **stockings**
bas de 15 deniers.

denigrate ['dɛnɪgreɪt] *vt* dénigrer.

denim ['dɛnɪm] *n* coton émerisé.

denim jacket *n* veste *f* en jean.

denims ['dɛnɪmz] *npl* (blue-)jeans *mpl*.

denizen ['dɛnɪzn] *n* (*inhabitant*) habitant/e;
(*foreigner*) étranger/ère.

Denmark ['dɛnmɑːk] *n* Danemark *m*.

denomination [dɪnɒmɪ'neɪʃən] *n* (*money*)
valeur *f*; (*REL*) confession *f*; culte *m*.

denominator [dɪ'nɒmɪneɪtə*] *n* dénominateur
m.

denote [dɪ'nəʊt] *vt* dénoter.

denounce [dɪ'naʊns] *vt* dénoncer.

dense [dɛns] *a* dense; (*col: stupid*) obtus(e),
dur(e) *or* lent(e) à la comprenette.

densely ['dɛnslɪ] *ad*: ~ **wooded** couvert(e)
d'épaisses forêts; ~ **populated** à forte
densité (de population), très peuplé(e).

density ['dɛnsɪtɪ] *n* densité *f*; **single/double** ~
disk (*COMPUT*) disquette *f* (à) simple/double
densité.

dent [dɛnt] *n* bosse *f* ♦ *vt* (*also*: **make a** ~ **in**)
cabosser; **to make a** ~ **in** (*fig*) entamer.

dental ['dɛntl] *a* dentaire.

dental surgeon *n* (chirurgien/ne) dentiste.

dentifrice ['dɛntɪfrɪs] *n* dentifrice *m*.

dentist ['dɛntɪst] *n* dentiste *m/f*; ~'s **surgery**
(*Brit*) cabinet *m* de dentiste.

dentistry ['dɛntɪstrɪ] *n* art *m* dentaire.

denture(s) ['dɛnt∫ə(z)] *n(pl)* dentier *m*.

denunciation [dɪnʌnsɪ'eɪʃən] *n* dénonciation *f*.

deny [dɪ'naɪ] *vt* nier; (*refuse*) refuser;
(*disown*) renier; **he denies having said it** il
nie l'avoir dit.

deodorant [diː'əʊdərənt] *n* désodorisant *m*,
déodorant *m*.

depart [dɪ'pɑːt] *vi* partir; **to** ~ **from** (*leave*)
quitter, partir de; (*fig: differ from*) s'écarter
de.

department [dɪ'pɑːtmənt] *n* (*COMM*) rayon
m; (*SCOL*) section *f*; (*POL*) ministère *m*,
département *m*; **that's not my** ~ (*fig*) ce
n'est pas mon domaine *or* ma compétence, ce
n'est pas mon rayon; **D**~ **of State** (*US*)
Département d'État.

departmental [diːpɑːt'mɛntl] *a* d'une *or* de la
section; d'un *or* du ministère, d'un *or* du
département; ~ **manager** chef *m* de service;
(*in shop*) chef de rayon.

department store *n* grand magasin.

departure [dɪ'pɑːt∫ə*] *n* départ *m*; (*fig*): ~
from écart *m* par rapport à; **a new** ~ une
nouvelle voie.

departure lounge *n* salle *f* de départ.

depend [dɪ'pɛnd] *vi*: **to** ~ **(up)on** dépendre
de; (*rely on*) compter sur; (*financially*)
dépendre (financièrement) de, être à la
charge de; **it** ~s cela dépend; ~**ing on the
result** ... selon le résultat ...

dependable [dɪ'pɛndəbl] *a* sûr(e), digne de
confiance.

dependant [dɪ'pɛndənt] *n* personne *f* à
charge.

dependence [dɪ'pɛndəns] *n* dépendance *f*.

dependent [dɪ'pɛndənt] *a*: **to be** ~ **(on)**
dépendre (de) ♦ *n* = **dependant**.

depict [dɪ'pɪkt] *vt* (*in picture*) représenter; (*in
words*) (dé)peindre, décrire.

depilatory [dɪ'pɪlətrɪ] *n* (*also*: ~ **cream**)
dépilatoire *m*, crème *f* à épiler.

depleted [dɪ'pliːtɪd] *a* (considérablement)
réduit(e) *or* diminué(e).

deplorable [dɪ'plɔːrəbl] *a* déplorable, lamentable.

deplore [dɪ'plɔː*] *vt* déplorer.

deploy [dɪ'plɔɪ] *vt* déployer.

depopulate |di:'pɔpjuleɪt| vt dépeupler.
depopulation |'di:pɔpju'leɪʃən| n dépopulation f, dépeuplement m.
deport |dɪ'pɔːt| vt déporter, expulser.
deportation |di:pɔː'teɪʃən| n déportation f, expulsion f.
deportation order n arrêté m d'expulsion.
deportment |dɪ'pɔːtmənt| n maintien m, tenue f.
depose |dɪ'pəuz| vt déposer.
deposit |dɪ'pɔzɪt| n (CHEM, COMM, GEO) dépôt m; (of ore, oil) gisement m; (part payment) arrhes fpl, acompte m; (on bottle etc) consigne f; (for hired goods etc) cautionnement m, garantie f ♦ vt déposer; (valuables) mettre or laisser en dépôt; **to put down a ~ of £50** verser 50 livres d'arrhes or d'acompte; laisser 50 livres en garantie.
deposit account n compte m de dépôt.
depositor |dɪ'pɔzɪtə*| n déposant/e.
depository |dɪ'pɔzɪtərɪ| n (person) dépositaire m/f; (place) dépôt m.
depot |'dɛpəu| n dépôt m.
depraved |dɪ'preɪvd| a dépravé(e), perverti(e).
depravity |dɪ'prævɪtɪ| n dépravation f.
deprecate |'dɛprɪkeɪt| vt désapprouver.
deprecating |'dɛprɪkeɪtɪŋ| a (disapproving) désapprobateur(trice); (apologetic): **a ~ smile** un sourire d'excuse.
depreciate |dɪ'priːʃɪeɪt| vt déprécier ♦ vi se déprécier, se dévaloriser.
depreciation |dɪpriːʃɪ'eɪʃən| n dépréciation f.
depress |dɪ'prɛs| vt déprimer; (press down) appuyer sur, abaisser.
depressant |dɪ'prɛsnt| n (MED) dépresseur m.
depressed |dɪ'prɛst| a (person) déprimé(e), abattu(e); (area) en déclin, touché(e) par le sous-emploi; (COMM: market, trade) maussade; **to get ~** se démoraliser, se laisser abattre.
depressing |dɪ'prɛsɪŋ| a déprimant(e).
depression |dɪ'prɛʃən| n (also ECON) dépression f.
deprivation |dɛprɪ'veɪʃən| n privation f; (loss) perte f.
deprive |dɪ'praɪv| vt: **to ~ sb of** priver qn de; enlever à qn.
deprived |dɪ'praɪvd| a déshérité(e).
dept. abbr (= department) dép., dépt.
depth |dɛpθ| n profondeur f; **in the ~s of** au fond de; au cœur de; au plus profond de; **at a ~ of 3 metres** à 3 mètres de profondeur; **to be out of one's ~** (Brit: swimmer) ne plus avoir pied; (fig) être dépassé(e), nager; **to study sth in ~** étudier qch en profondeur.
depth charge n grenade sous-marine.
deputation |dɛpju'teɪʃən| n députation f, délégation f.
deputize |'dɛpjutaɪz| vi: **to ~ for** assurer l'intérim de.
deputy |'dɛpjutɪ| a: **~ chairman** vice-président m; **~ head** (SCOL) directeur/trice adjoint(e), sous-directeur/trice; **~ leader** (Brit POL) vice-président/e, secrétaire adjoint(e) ♦ n (replacement) suppléant/e, intérimaire m/f; (second in command) adjoint/e.
derail |dɪ'reɪl| vt faire dérailler; **to be ~ed**

dérailler.
derailment |dɪ'reɪlmənt| n déraillement m.
deranged |dɪ'reɪndʒd| a: **to be (mentally) ~** avoir le cerveau dérangé.
derby |'dɜːbɪ| n (US) (chapeau m) melon m.
Derbys abbr (Brit) = **Derbyshire**.
deregulate |dɪ'rɛgjuleɪt| vt libérer, dérégler.
deregulation |dɪ'rɛgju'leɪʃən| n libération f, dérèglement m.
derelict |'dɛrɪlɪkt| a abandonné(e), à l'abandon.
deride |dɪ'raɪd| vt railler.
derision |dɪ'rɪʒən| n dérision f.
derisive |dɪ'raɪsɪv| a moqueur(euse), railleur(euse).
derisory |dɪ'raɪsərɪ| a (sum) dérisoire; (smile, person) moqueur(euse), railleur(euse).
derivation |dɛrɪ'veɪʃən| n dérivation f.
derivative |dɪ'rɪvətɪv| n dérivé m ♦ a dérivé(e).
derive |dɪ'raɪv| vt: **to ~ sth from** tirer qch de; trouver qch dans ♦ vi: **to ~ from** provenir de, dériver de.
dermatitis |dɜːmə'taɪtɪs| n dermatite f.
dermatology |dɜːmə'tɔlədʒɪ| n dermatologie f.
derogatory |dɪ'rɔgətərɪ| a désobligeant(e); péjoratif(ive).
derrick |'dɛrɪk| n mât m de charge; derrick m.
derv |dɜːv| n (Brit) gas-oil m, diesel m.
DES n abbr (Brit: = Department of Education and Science) ministère de l'éducation nationale et des sciences.
desalination |diːsælɪ'neɪʃən| n dessalement m, dessalage m.
descend |dɪ'sɛnd| vt, vi descendre; **to ~ from** descendre de, être issu(e) de; **in ~ing order of importance** par ordre d'importance décroissante.
descend on vt fus (subj: enemy, angry person) tomber or sauter sur; (: misfortune) s'abattre sur; (: gloom, silence) envahir; **visitors ~ed (up)on us** des gens sont arrivés chez nous à l'improviste.
descendant |dɪ'sɛndənt| n descendant/e.
descent |dɪ'sɛnt| n descente f; (origin) origine f.
describe |dɪs'kraɪb| vt décrire.
description |dɪs'krɪpʃən| n description f; (sort) sorte f, espèce f; **of every ~** de toutes sortes.
descriptive |dɪs'krɪptɪv| a descriptif(ive).
desecrate |'dɛsɪkreɪt| vt profaner.
desert n |'dɛzət| désert m ♦ vb |dɪ'zɜːt| vt déserter, abandonner ♦ vi (MIL) déserter.
deserter |dɪ'zɜːtə*| n déserteur m.
desertion |dɪ'zɜːʃən| n désertion f.
desert island n île déserte.
deserts |dɪ'zɜːts| npl: **to get one's just ~** n'avoir que ce qu'on mérite.
deserve |dɪ'zɜːv| vt mériter.
deservedly |dɪ'zɜːvɪdlɪ| ad à juste titre, à bon droit.
deserving |dɪ'zɜːvɪŋ| a (person) méritant(e); (action, cause) méritoire.
desiccated |'dɛsɪkeɪtɪd| a séché(e).
design |dɪ'zaɪn| n (sketch) plan m, dessin m; (layout, shape) conception f, ligne f; (pattern) dessin m, motif(s) m(pl); (of dress,

car) modèle *m*; (*art*) design *m*, stylisme *m*; (*intention*) dessein *m* ♦ *vt* dessiner; (*plan*) concevoir; **to have ~s on** avoir des visées sur; **well-~ed** *a* bien conçu(e); **industrial ~** esthétique industrielle.

designate *vt* ['dɛzɪgneɪt] désigner ♦ *a* ['dɛzɪgnɪt] désigné(e).

designation [dɛzɪg'neɪʃən] *n* désignation *f*.

designer [dɪ'zaɪnə*] *n* (*ARCHIT, ART*) dessinateur/trice; (*INDUSTRY*) concepteur *m*, designer *m*; (*FASHION*) modéliste *m/f*.

desirability [dɪzaɪərə'bɪlɪtɪ] *n* avantage *m*; attrait *m*.

desirable [dɪ'zaɪərəbl] *a* désirable; **it is ~ that** il est souhaitable que.

desire [dɪ'zaɪə*] *n* désir *m* ♦ *vt* désirer, vouloir; **to ~ to do sth/that** désirer faire qch/que.

desirous [dɪ'zaɪərəs] *a:* **~ of** désireux(euse) de.

desk [dɛsk] *n* (*in office*) bureau *m*; (*for pupil*) pupitre *m*; (*Brit: in shop, restaurant*) caisse *f*; (*in hotel, at airport*) réception *f*.

desk-top publishing ['dɛsktɒp-] *n* publication assistée par ordinateur, PAO *f*.

desolate ['dɛsəlɪt] *a* désolé(e).

desolation [dɛsə'leɪʃən] *n* désolation *f*.

despair [dɪs'pɛə*] *n* désespoir *m* ♦ *vi*: **to ~ of** désespérer de; **to be in ~** être au désespoir.

despatch [dɪs'pætʃ] *n*, *vt* = **dispatch**.

desperate ['dɛspərɪt] *a* désespéré(e); (*fugitive*) prêt(e) à tout; (*measures*) désespéré, extrême; **we are getting ~** nous commençons à désespérer.

desperately ['dɛspərɪtlɪ] *ad* désespérément; (*very*) terriblement, extrêmement; **~ ill** très gravement malade.

desperation [dɛspə'reɪʃən] *n* désespoir *m*; **in ~** en désespoir de cause.

despicable [dɪs'pɪkəbl] *a* méprisable.

despise [dɪs'paɪz] *vt* mépriser, dédaigner.

despite [dɪs'paɪt] *prep* malgré, en dépit de.

despondent [dɪs'pɒndənt] *a* découragé(e), abattu(e).

despot ['dɛspɒt] *n* despote *m/f*.

dessert [dɪ'zɜ:t] *n* dessert *m*.

dessertspoon [dɪ'zɜ:tspu:n] *n* cuiller *f* à dessert.

destabilize [di:'steɪbɪlaɪz] *vt* déstabiliser.

destination [dɛstɪ'neɪʃən] *n* destination *f*.

destine ['dɛstɪn] *vt* destiner.

destined ['dɛstɪnd] *a:* **to be ~ to do sth** être destiné(e) à faire qch; **~ for London** à destination de Londres.

destiny ['dɛstɪnɪ] *n* destinée *f*, destin *m*.

destitute ['dɛstɪtju:t] *a* indigent(e), dans le dénuement; **~ of** dépourvu(e) *or* dénué(e) de.

destroy [dɪs'trɔɪ] *vt* détruire.

destroyer [dɪs'trɔɪə*] *n* (*NAUT*) contre-torpilleur *m*.

destruction [dɪs'trʌkʃən] *n* destruction *f*.

destructive [dɪs'trʌktɪv] *a* destructeur(trice).

desultory ['dɛsəltərɪ] *a* (*reading, conversation*) décousu(e); (*contact*) irrégulier(ière).

detach [dɪ'tætʃ] *vt* détacher.

detachable [dɪ'tætʃəbl] *a* amovible, détachable.

detached [dɪ'tætʃt] *a* (*attitude*) détaché(e).

detached house *n* pavillon *m*, maison(nette) (individuelle).

detachment [dɪ'tætʃmənt] *n* (*MIL*) détachement *m*; (*fig*) détachement, indifférence *f*.

detail ['di:teɪl] *n* détail *m*; (*MIL*) détachement *m* ♦ *vt* raconter en détail, énumérer; (*MIL*): **to ~ sb (for)** affecter qn (à), détacher qn (pour); **in ~** en détail; **to go into ~(s)** entrer dans les détails.

detailed ['di:teɪld] *a* détaillé(e).

detain [dɪ'teɪn] *vt* retenir; (*in captivity*) détenir; (*in hospital*) hospitaliser.

detainee [di:teɪ'ni:] *n* détenu/e.

detect [dɪ'tɛkt] *vt* déceler, percevoir; (*MED, POLICE*) dépister; (*MIL, RADAR, TECH*) détecter.

detection [dɪ'tɛkʃən] *n* découverte *f*; (*MED, POLICE*) dépistage *m*; (*MIL, RADAR, TECH*) détection *f*; **to escape ~** échapper aux recherches, éviter d'être découvert(e); (*mistake*) passer inaperçu(e); **crime ~** le dépistage des criminels.

detective [dɪ'tɛktɪv] *n* agent *m* de la sûreté, policier *m*; **private ~** détective privé.

detective story *n* roman policier.

detector [dɪ'tɛktə*] *n* détecteur *m*.

détente [deɪ'tɑ:nt] *n* détente *f*.

detention [dɪ'tɛnʃən] *n* détention *f*; (*SCOL*) retenue *f*, consigne *f*.

deter [dɪ'tɜ:*] *vt* dissuader.

detergent [dɪ'tɜ:dʒənt] *n* détersif *m*, détergent *m*.

deteriorate [dɪ'tɪərɪəreɪt] *vi* se détériorer, se dégrader.

deterioration [dɪtɪərɪə'reɪʃən] *n* détérioration *f*.

determination [dɪtə:mɪ'neɪʃən] *n* détermination *f*.

determine [dɪ'tə:mɪn] *vt* déterminer; **to ~ to do** résoudre de faire, se déterminer à faire.

determined [dɪ'tə:mɪnd] *a* (*person*) déterminé(e), décidé(e); (*quantity*) déterminé, établi(e); (*effort*) très gros(se).

deterrence [dɪ'tɛrns] *n* dissuasion *f*.

deterrent [dɪ'tɛrnt] *n* effet *m* de dissuasion; force *f* de dissuasion; **to act as a ~** avoir un effet dissuasif.

detest [dɪ'tɛst] *vt* détester, avoir horreur de.

detestable [dɪ'tɛstəbl] *a* détestable, odieux(euse).

detonate ['dɛtəneɪt] *vi* exploser ♦ *vt* faire exploser *or* détoner.

detonator ['dɛtəneɪtə*] *n* détonateur *m*.

detour ['di:tuə*] *n* détour *m*; (*US AUT: diversion*) déviation *f*.

detract [dɪ'trækt] *vt:* **to ~ from** (*quality, pleasure*) diminuer; (*reputation*) porter atteinte à.

detractor [dɪ'træktə*] *n* détracteur/trice.

detriment ['dɛtrɪmənt] *n:* **to the ~ of** au détriment de, au préjudice de; **without ~ to** sans porter atteinte *or* préjudice à, sans conséquences fâcheuses pour.

detrimental [dɛtrɪ'mɛntl] *a:* **~ to** préjudiciable *or* nuisible à.

deuce [dju:s] *n* (*TENNIS*) égalité *f*.

devaluation [dɪvælju'eɪʃən] *n* dévaluation *f*.

devalue ['di:'vælju:] *vt* dévaluer.

devastate ['dɛvəsteɪt] *vt* dévaster; **he was ~d by the news** cette nouvelle lui a porté un coup terrible.

devastating ['dɛvəsteɪtɪŋ] *a* dévastateur(trice).

devastation [dɛvəs'teɪʃən] *n* dévastation *f*.

develop [dɪ'vɛləp] *vt* (*gen*) développer; (*habit*) contracter; (*resources*) mettre en valeur, exploiter; (*land*) aménager ♦ *vi* se développer; (*situation, disease: evolve*) évoluer; (*facts, symptoms: appear*) se manifester, se produire; **to ~ a taste for sth** prendre goût à qch; **to ~ into** devenir.

developer [dɪ'vɛləpə*] *n* (*PHOT*) révélateur *m*; (*of land*) promoteur *m*; (*also:* **property ~**) promoteur immobilier.

developing country *n* pays *m* en voie de développement.

development [dɪ'vɛləpmənt] *n* développement *m*; (*of affair, case*) rebondissement *m*, fait(s) nouveau(x).

development area *n* zone *f* à urbaniser.

deviate ['di:vɪeɪt] *vi:* **to ~ (from)** dévier (de).

deviation [di:vɪ'eɪʃən] *n* déviation *f*.

device [dɪ'vaɪs] *n* (*scheme*) moyen *m*, expédient *m*; (*apparatus*) engin *m*, dispositif *m*; **explosive ~** engin explosif.

devil ['dɛvl] *n* diable *m*; démon *m*.

devilish ['dɛvlɪʃ] *a* diabolique.

devil-may-care ['dɛvlmeɪ'kɛə*] *a* je-m'en-foutiste.

devious ['di:vɪəs] *a* (*means*) détourné(e); (*person*) sournois(e), dissimulé(e).

devise [dɪ'vaɪz] *vt* imaginer, concevoir.

devoid [dɪ'vɔɪd] *a:* **~ of** dépourvu(e) de, dénué(e) de.

devolution [di:və'lu:ʃən] *n* (*POL*) décentralisation *f*.

devolve [dɪ'vɔlv] *vi:* **to ~ (up)on** retomber sur.

devote [dɪ'vəut] *vt:* **to ~ sth to** consacrer qch à.

devoted [dɪ'vəutɪd] *a* dévoué(e); **to be ~ to** être dévoué(e) *or* très attaché(e) à; (*subj: book etc*) être consacré(e) à.

devotee [dɛvəu'ti:] *n* (*REL*) adepte *m/f*; (*MUS, SPORT*) fervent/e.

devotion [dɪ'vəuʃən] *n* dévouement *m*, attachement *m*; (*REL*) dévotion *f*, piété *f*.

devour [dɪ'vauə*] *vt* dévorer.

devout [dɪ'vaut] *a* pieux(euse), dévot(e).

dew [dju:] *n* rosée *f*.

dexterity [dɛks'tɛrɪtɪ] *n* dextérité *f*, adresse *f*.

dext(e)rous ['dɛkstrəs] *a* adroit(e).

dg *abbr* (= *decigram*) dg.

DHSS *n abbr* (*Brit*) = **Department of Health and Social Security.**

diabetes [daɪə'bi:ti:z] *n* diabète *m*.

diabetic [daɪə'bɛtɪk] *n* diabétique *m/f* ♦ *a* (*person*) diabétique; (*chocolate, jam*) pour diabétiques.

diabolical [daɪə'bɔlɪkl] *a* diabolique; (*col: dreadful*) infernal(e), atroce.

diaeresis [daɪ'ɛrɪsɪs] *n* tréma *m*.

diagnose [daɪəg'nəuz] *vt* diagnostiquer.

diagnosis, *pl* **diagnoses** [daɪəg'nəusɪs, -si:z] *n* diagnostic *m*.

diagonal [daɪ'ægənl] *a* diagonal(e) ♦ *n* diagonale *f*.

diagram ['daɪəgræm] *n* diagramme *m*, schéma *m*.

dial ['daɪəl] *n* cadran *m* ♦ *vt* (*number*) faire, composer; **to ~ a wrong number** faire un faux numéro; **can I ~ London direct?** puis-je *or* est-ce-que je peux avoir Londres par l'automatique?

dial. *abbr* = **dialect.**

dialect ['daɪəlɛkt] *n* dialecte *m*.

dialling code ['daɪəlɪŋ-], (*US*) **dial code** *n* indicatif *m* (téléphonique).

dialling tone ['daɪəlɪŋ-], (*US*) **dial tone** *n* tonalité *f*.

dialogue ['daɪəlɔg] *n* dialogue *m*.

dialysis [daɪ'ælɪsɪs] *n* dialyse *f*.

diameter [daɪ'æmɪtə*] *n* diamètre *m*.

diametrically [daɪə'mɛtrɪklɪ] *ad:* **~ opposed (to)** diamétralement opposé(e) (à).

diamond ['daɪəmənd] *n* diamant *m*; (*shape*) losange *m*; **~s** *npl* (*CARDS*) carreau *m*.

diamond ring *n* bague *f* de diamant(s).

diaper ['daɪəpə*] *n* (*US*) couche *f*.

diaphragm ['daɪəfræm] *n* diaphragme *m*.

diarrhoea, (*US*) **diarrhea** [daɪə'ri:ə] *n* diarrhée *f*.

diary ['daɪərɪ] *n* (*daily account*) journal *m*; (*book*) agenda *m*; **to keep a ~** tenir un journal.

diatribe ['daɪətraɪb] *n* diatribe *f*.

dice [daɪs] *n* (*pl inv*) dé *m* ♦ *vt* (*CULIN*) couper en dés *or* en cubes.

dicey ['daɪsɪ] *a* (*col*): **it's a bit ~** c'est un peu risqué.

dichotomy [daɪ'kɔtəmɪ] *n* dichotomie *f*.

Dictaphone ['dɪktəfəun] *n* ® Dictaphone *m* ®.

dictate *vt* [dɪk'teɪt] dicter ♦ *vi:* **to ~ to** (*person*) imposer sa volonté à, régenter; **I won't be ~d to** je n'ai d'ordres à recevoir de personne ♦ *n* ['dɪkteɪt] injonction *f*.

dictation [dɪk'teɪʃən] *n* dictée *f*; **at ~ speed** à une vitesse de dictée.

dictator [dɪk'teɪtə*] *n* dictateur *m*.

dictatorship [dɪk'teɪtəʃɪp] *n* dictature *f*.

diction ['dɪkʃən] *n* diction *f*, élocution *f*.

dictionary ['dɪkʃənrɪ] *n* dictionnaire *m*.

did [dɪd] *pt of* **do.**

didactic [daɪ'dæktɪk] *a* didactique.

die [daɪ] *n* (*pl:* **dice**) dé *m*; (*pl:* **dies**) coin *m*; matrice *f*; étampe *f* ♦ *vi:* **to ~ (of** *or* **from)** mourir (de); **to be dying** être mourant(e); **to be dying for sth** avoir une envie folle de qch; **to be dying to do sth** mourir d'envie de faire qch.

die away *vi* s'éteindre.

die down *vi* se calmer, s'apaiser.

die out *vi* disparaître, s'éteindre.

diehard ['daɪhɑ:d] *n* réactionnaire *m/f*, jusqu'au-boutiste *m/f*.

diesel ['di:zl] *n* diesel *m*.

diesel engine *n* moteur *m* diesel.

diesel fuel, diesel oil *n* carburant *m* diesel.

diet ['daɪət] *n* alimentation *f*; (*restricted food*) régime *m* ♦ *vi* (*also:* **be on a ~**) suivre un régime; **to live on a ~ of** se nourrir de.

dietician [daɪə'tɪʃən] *n* diététicien/ne.

differ ['dɪfə*] *vi:* **to ~ from sth** être différent(e) de; différer de; **to ~ from sb over sth** ne pas être d'accord avec qn au sujet de qch.

difference ['dıfrəns] n différence f; (quarrel) différend m, désaccord m; **it makes no ~ to me** cela m'est égal, cela m'est indifférent; **to settle one's ~s** résoudre la situation.

different ['dıfrənt] a différent(e).

differential [dıfə'rɛnʃəl] n (AUT, wages) différentiel m.

differentiate [dıfə'rɛnʃıeıt] vt différencier ♦ vi se différencier; **to ~ between** faire une différence entre.

differently ['dıfrəntlı] ad différemment.

difficult ['dıfıkəlt] a difficile; **~ to understand** difficile à comprendre.

difficulty ['dıfıkəltı] n difficulté f; **to have difficulties with** avoir des ennuis or problèmes avec; **to be in ~** avoir des difficultés, avoir des problèmes.

diffidence ['dıfıdəns] n manque m de confiance en soi, manque d'assurance.

diffident ['dıfıdənt] a qui manque de confiance or d'assurance, peu sûr(e) de soi.

diffuse a [dı'fju:s] diffus(e) ♦ vt [dı'fju:z] diffuser, répandre.

dig [dıg] vt (pt, pp **dug** [dʌg]) (hole) creuser; (garden) bêcher ♦ n (prod) coup m de coude; (fig) coup de griffe or de patte; (ARCHAEOLOGY) fouille f; **to ~ into** (snow, soil) creuser; **to ~ into one's pockets for sth** fouiller dans ses poches pour chercher or prendre qch; **to ~ one's nails into** enfoncer ses ongles dans.

dig in vi (also: ~ o.s. in: MIL) se retrancher; (: fig) tenir bon, se braquer; (col: eat) attaquer (un repas or un plat etc) ♦ vt (compost) bien mélanger à la bêche; (knife, claw) enfoncer; **to ~ in one's heels** (fig) se braquer, se buter.

dig out vt (survivors, car from snow) sortir or dégager (à coups de pelles or pioches).

dig up vt déterrer.

digest vt [daı'dʒɛst] digérer ♦ n ['daıdʒɛst] sommaire m, résumé m.

digestible [dı'dʒɛstəbl] a digestible.

digestion [dı'dʒɛstʃən] n digestion f.

digestive [dı'dʒɛstıv] a digestif(ive).

digit ['dıdʒıt] n chiffre m (de 0 à 9); (finger) doigt m.

digital ['dıdʒıtl] a digital(e); (watch) à affichage numérique or digital.

dignified ['dıgnıfaıd] a digne.

dignitary ['dıgnıtərı] n dignitaire m.

dignity ['dıgnıtı] n dignité f.

digress [daı'grɛs] vi: **to ~ from** s'écarter de, s'éloigner de.

digression [daı'grɛʃən] n digression f.

digs [dıgz] npl (Brit col) piaule f, chambre meublée.

dilapidated [dı'læpıdeıtıd] a délabré(e).

dilate [daı'leıt] vt dilater ♦ vi se dilater.

dilatory ['dılətərı] a dilatoire.

dilemma [daı'lɛmə] n dilemme m; **to be in a ~** être pris dans un dilemme.

diligent ['dılıdʒənt] a appliqué(e), assidu(e).

dill [dıl] n aneth m.

dilly-dally ['dılı'dælı] vi hésiter, tergiverser; traînasser, lambiner.

dilute [daı'lu:t] vt diluer ♦ a dilué(e).

dim [dım] a (light, eyesight) faible; (memory, outline) vague, indécis(e); (stupid) borné(e),

obtus(e) ♦ vt (light) réduire, baisser; (US AUT) mettre en code, baisser; **to take a ~ view of sth** voir qch d'un mauvais œil.

dime [daım] n (US) = 10 cents.

dimension [daı'mɛnʃən] n dimension f.

-dimensional [dı'mɛnʃənl] a suffix: **two~** à deux dimensions.

diminish [dı'mınıʃ] vt, vi diminuer.

diminished [dı'mınıʃt] a: **~ responsibility** (LAW) responsabilité atténuée.

diminutive [dı'mınjutıv] a minuscule, tout(e) petit(e) ♦ n (LING) diminutif m.

dimly ['dımlı] ad faiblement; vaguement.

dimmers ['dıməz] npl (US AUT) phares mpl code inv; (: parking lights) feux mpl de position.

dimple ['dımpl] n fossette f.

dim-witted ['dım'wıtıd] a (col) stupide, borné(e).

din [dın] n vacarme m ♦ vt: **to ~ sth into sb** (col) enfoncer qch dans la tête or la caboche de qn.

dine [daın] vi dîner.

diner ['daınə*] n (person) dîneur/euse; (RAIL) = **dining car**; (US: eating place) petit restaurant.

dinghy ['dıŋgı] n youyou m; (inflatable) canot m pneumatique; (also: **sailing ~**) voilier m, dériveur m.

dingy ['dındʒı] a miteux(euse), minable.

dining car ['daınıŋ-] n voiture-restaurant f, wagon-restaurant m.

dining room ['daınıŋ-] n salle f à manger.

dinner ['dınə*] n dîner m; (public) banquet m; **~'s ready!** à table!

dinner jacket n smoking m.

dinner party n dîner m.

dinner time n heure f du dîner.

dinosaur ['daınəsɔ:*] n dinosaure m.

dint [dınt] n: **by ~ of (doing) sth** à force de (faire) qch.

diocese ['daıəsıs] n diocèse m.

dioxide [daı'ɔksaıd] n dioxyde m.

Dip. abbr (Brit) = **diploma**.

dip [dıp] n déclivité f; (in sea) baignade f, bain m ♦ vt tremper, plonger; (Brit AUT: lights) mettre en code, baisser ♦ vi plonger.

diphtheria [dıf'θıərıə] n diphtérie f.

diphthong ['dıfθɔŋ] n diphtongue f.

diploma [dı'pləumə] n diplôme m.

diplomacy [dı'pləuməsı] n diplomatie f.

diplomat ['dıpləmæt] n diplomate m.

diplomatic [dıplə'mætık] a diplomatique; **to break off ~ relations (with)** rompre les relations diplomatiques (avec).

diplomatic corps n corps m diplomatique.

dipstick ['dıpstık] n (AUT) jauge f de niveau d'huile.

dipswitch ['dıpswıtʃ] n (Brit AUT) commutateur m de code.

dire [daıə*] a extrême, affreux(euse).

direct [daı'rɛkt] a direct(e); (manner, person) direct, franc(franche) ♦ vt diriger, orienter; **can you ~ me to ...?** pouvez-vous m'indiquer le chemin de ...?; **to ~ sb to do sth** ordonner à qn de faire qch.

direct cost n (COMM) coût m variable.

direct current n (ELEC) courant continu.

direct debit n (BANKING) prélèvement m

automatique.
direct dialling n (TEL) automatique m.
direct hit n (MIL) coup m au but, touché m.
direction [dɪ'rɛkʃən] n direction f; (THEATRE)
mise f en scène; (CINEMA, TV) réalisation f;
~**s** npl (instructions: to a place) indications
fpl; ~**s for use** mode m d'emploi; **to ask for**
~**s** demander sa route or son chemin; **sense
of** ~ sens m de l'orientation; **in the** ~ **of**
dans la direction de, vers.
directive [dɪ'rɛktɪv] n directive f; **a government** ~ une directive du gouvernement.
direct labour n main-d'œuvre directe; employés municipaux.
directly [dɪ'rɛktlɪ] ad (in straight line)
directement, tout droit; (at once) tout de
suite, immédiatement.
direct mail n vente f par publicité directe.
direct mailshot n (Brit) publicité postale.
directness [daɪ'rɛktnɪs] n (of person, speech)
franchise f.
director [dɪ'rɛktə*] n directeur m; (board
member) administrateur m; (THEATRE)
metteur m en scène; (CINEMA, TV)
réalisateur/trice; **D**~ **of Public Prosecutions**
(Brit) ≈ procureur général.
directory [dɪ'rɛktərɪ] n annuaire m; (also:
street ~) indicateur m de rues; (also: **trade**
~) annuaire du commerce; (COMPUT)
répertoire m.
directory enquiries, (US) **directory
assistance** n (TEL: service) renseignements
mpl.
dirt [də:t] n saleté f; (mud) boue f; **to treat sb
like** ~ traiter qn comme un chien.
dirt-cheap ['də:t'ʃi:p] a (ne) coûtant presque
rien.
dirt road n chemin non macadamisé or non
revêtu.
dirty ['də:tɪ] a sale ♦ vt salir; ~ **story** histoire
cochonne; ~ **trick** coup tordu.
disability [dɪsə'bɪlɪtɪ] n invalidité f, infirmité f.
disability allowance n allocation f
d'invalidité or d'infirmité.
disable [dɪs'eɪbl] vt (subj: illness, accident)
rendre or laisser infirme; (tank, gun) mettre
hors d'action.
disabled [dɪs'eɪbld] a infirme, invalide;
(maimed) mutilé(e); (through illness, old
age) impotent(e).
disadvantage [dɪsəd'vɑ:ntɪdʒ] n désavantage
m, inconvénient m.
disadvantaged [dɪsəd'vɑ:ntɪdʒd] a (person)
désavantagé(e).
disadvantageous [dɪsædvɑ:n'teɪdʒəs] a dés-
avantageux(euse).
disaffected [dɪsə'fɛktɪd] a: ~ **(to or towards)**
mécontent(e) (de).
disaffection [dɪsə'fɛkʃən] n désaffection f,
mécontentement m.
disagree [dɪsə'gri:] vi (differ) ne pas
concorder; (be against, think otherwise): **to**
~ **(with)** ne pas être d'accord (avec); **garlic**
~**s with me** l'ail ne me convient pas, je ne
supporte pas l'ail.
disagreeable [dɪsə'gri:əbl] a désagréable.
disagreement [dɪsə'gri:mənt] n désaccord m,
différend m.
disallow ['dɪsə'lau] vt rejeter, désavouer;

(Brit FOOTBALL: goal) refuser.
disappear [dɪsə'pɪə*] vi disparaître.
disappearance [dɪsə'pɪərəns] n disparition f.
disappoint [dɪsə'pɔɪnt] vt décevoir.
disappointed [dɪsə'pɔɪntɪd] a déçu(e).
disappointing [dɪsə'pɔɪntɪŋ] a décevant(e).
disappointment [dɪsə'pɔɪntmənt] n déception
f.
disapproval [dɪsə'pru:vəl] n désapprobation f.
disapprove [dɪsə'pru:v] vi: **to** ~ **of** désapprouver.
disapproving [dɪsə'pru:vɪŋ] a désap-
probateur(trice), de désapprobation.
disarm [dɪs'ɑ:m] vt désarmer.
disarmament [dɪs'ɑ:məmənt] n désarmement
m.
disarming [dɪs'ɑ:mɪŋ] a (smile) désarmant(e).
disarray [dɪsə'reɪ] n désordre m, confusion f;
in ~ (troops) en déroute; (thoughts) em-
brouillé(e); (clothes) en désordre; **to throw
into** ~ semer la confusion or le désordre
dans (or parmi).
disaster [dɪ'zɑ:stə*] n catastrophe f, désastre
m.
disastrous [dɪ'zɑ:strəs] a désastreux(euse).
disband [dɪs'bænd] vt démobiliser; disperser ♦
vi se séparer; se disperser.
disbelief [dɪsbə'li:f] n incrédulité f; **in** ~ avec
incrédulité.
disbelieve ['dɪsbə'li:v] vt (person) ne pas
croire; (story) mettre en doute; **I don't** ~
you je veux bien vous croire.
disc [dɪsk] n disque m.
disc. abbr (COMM) = **discount**.
discard [dɪs'kɑ:d] vt (old things) se défaire de,
mettre au rencart or au rebut; (fig) écarter,
renoncer à.
disc brake n frein m à disque.
discern [dɪ'sə:n] vt discerner, distinguer.
discernible [dɪ'sə:nəbl] a discernable,
perceptible; (object) visible.
discerning [dɪ'sə:nɪŋ] a judicieux(euse),
perspicace.
discharge vt [dɪs'tʃɑ:dʒ] (duties) s'acquitter
de; (settle: debt) s'acquitter de, régler;
(waste etc) déverser; décharger; (ELEC,
MED) émettre; (patient) renvoyer (chez lui);
(employee, soldier) congédier, licencier;
(defendant) relaxer, élargir ♦ n ['dɪstʃɑ:dʒ]
(ELEC, MED etc) émission f; (also: **vaginal**
~) pertes blanches; (dismissal) renvoi m;
licenciement m; élargissement m; **to** ~
one's gun faire feu; ~**d bankrupt** failli/e
réhabilité(e).
disciple [dɪ'saɪpl] n disciple m.
disciplinary ['dɪsɪplɪnərɪ] a disciplinaire; **to
take** ~ **action against sb** prendre des
mesures disciplinaires à l'encontre de qn.
discipline ['dɪsɪplɪn] n discipline f ♦ vt discipliner; (punish) punir; **to** ~ **o.s. to do sth**
s'imposer or s'astreindre à une discipline
pour faire qch.
disc jockey (DJ) n disque-jockey m (DJ).
disclaim [dɪs'kleɪm] vt désavouer, dénier.
disclaimer [dɪs'kleɪmə*] n démenti m,
dénégation f; **to issue a** ~ publier un
démenti.
disclose [dɪs'kləuz] vt révéler, divulguer.
disclosure [dɪs'kləuʒə*] n révélation f,

divulgation *f*.
disco ['dıskəu] *n abbr* = **discothèque**.
discolour, (*US*) **discolor** [dıs'kʌlə*] *vt* décolorer; (*sth white*) jaunir ♦ *vi* se décolorer; jaunir.
discolo(u)ration [dıskʌlə'reıʃən] *n* décoloration *f*; jaunissement *m*.
discolo(u)red [dıs'kʌləd] *a* décoloré(e); jauni(e).
discomfort [dıs'kʌmfət] *n* malaise *m*, gêne *f*; (*lack of comfort*) manque *m* de confort.
disconcert [dıskən'sə:t] *vt* déconcerter, décontenancer.
disconnect [dıskə'nɛkt] *vt* détacher; (*ELEC, RADIO*) débrancher; (*gas, water*) couper.
disconnected [dıskə'nɛktıd] *a* (*speech, thoughts*) décousu(e), peu cohérent(e).
disconsolate [dıs'kɔnsəlıt] *a* inconsolable.
discontent [dıskən'tɛnt] *n* mécontentement *m*.
discontented [dıskən'tɛntıd] *a* mécontent(e).
discontinue [dıskən'tınju:] *vt* cesser, interrompre; "**~d**" (*COMM*) "fin de série".
discord ['dıskɔ:d] *n* discorde *f*, dissension *f*; (*MUS*) dissonance *f*.
discordant [dıs'kɔ:dənt] *a* discordant(e), dissonant(e).
discothèque ['dıskəutɛk] *n* discothèque *f*.
discount *n* ['dıskaunt] remise *f*, rabais *m* ♦ *vt* [dıs'kaunt] (*report etc*) ne pas tenir compte de; **to give sb a ~ on sth** faire une remise *or* un rabais à qn sur qch; **~ for cash** escompte *f* au comptant; **at a ~** avec une remise *or* réduction, au rabais.
discount house *n* (*FINANCE*) banque *f* d'escompte; (*COMM: also:* **discount store**) magasin *m* de discount.
discount rate *n* taux *m* de remise.
discourage [dıs'kʌrıdʒ] *vt* décourager; (*dissuade, deter*) dissuader, décourager.
discouragement [dıs'kʌrıdʒmənt] *n* (*depression*) découragement *m*; **to act as a ~ to sb** dissuader qn.
discouraging [dıs'kʌrıdʒıŋ] *a* décourageant(e).
discourteous [dıs'kə:tıəs] *a* incivil(e), discourtois(e).
discover [dıs'kʌvə*] *vt* découvrir.
discovery [dıs'kʌvərı] *n* découverte *f*.
discredit [dıs'krɛdıt] *vt* mettre en doute; discréditer ♦ *n* discrédit *m*.
discreet [dı'skri:t] *a* discret(ète).
discreetly [dı'skri:tlı] *ad* discrètement.
discrepancy [dı'skrɛpənsı] *n* divergence *f*, contradiction *f*.
discretion [dı'skrɛʃən] *n* discrétion *f*; **use your own ~** à vous de juger.
discretionary [dı'skrɛʃənrı] *a* (*powers*) discrétionnaire.
discriminate [dı'skrımıneıt] *vi*: **to ~ between** établir une distinction entre, faire la différence entre; **to ~ against** pratiquer une discrimination contre.
discriminating [dı'skrımıneıtıŋ] *a* qui a du discernement.
discrimination [dıskrımı'neıʃən] *n* discrimination *f*; (*judgment*) discernement *m*; **racial/sexual ~** discrimination raciale/sexuelle.
discus ['dıskəs] *n* disque *m*.

discuss [dı'skʌs] *vt* discuter de; (*debate*) discuter.
discussion [dı'skʌʃən] *n* discussion *f*; **under ~** en discussion.
disdain [dıs'deın] *n* dédain *m*.
disease [dı'zi:z] *n* maladie *f*.
diseased [dı'zi:zd] *a* malade.
disembark [dısım'bɑ:k] *vt, vi* débarquer.
disembarkation [dısɛmbɑ:'keıʃən] *n* débarquement *m*.
disembodied ['dısım'bɔdıd] *a* désincarné(e).
disembowel ['dısım'bauəl] *vt* éviscérer, étriper.
disenchanted ['dısın'tʃɑ:ntıd] *a*: **~ (with)** désenchanté(e) (de), désabusé(e) (de).
disenfranchise ['dısın'fræntʃaız] *vt* priver du droit de vote; (*COMM*) retirer la franchise à.
disengage [dısın'geıdʒ] *vt* dégager; (*TECH*) déclencher; **to ~ the clutch** (*AUT*) débrayer.
disengagement [dısın'geıdʒmənt] *n* (*POL*) désengagement *m*.
disentangle [dısın'tæŋgl] *vt* démêler.
disfavour, (*US*) **disfavor** [dıs'feıvə*] *n* défaveur *f*; disgrâce *f*.
disfigure [dıs'fıgə*] *vt* défigurer.
disgorge [dıs'gɔ:dʒ] *vt* déverser.
disgrace [dıs'greıs] *n* honte *f*; (*disfavour*) disgrâce *f* ♦ *vt* déshonorer, couvrir de honte.
disgraceful [dıs'greısful] *a* scandaleux(euse), honteux(euse).
disgruntled [dıs'grʌntld] *a* mécontent(e).
disguise [dıs'gaız] *n* déguisement *m* ♦ *vt* déguiser; (*voice*) déguiser, contrefaire; (*feelings etc*) masquer, dissimuler; **in ~** déguisé(e); **to ~ o.s. as** se déguiser en; **there's no disguising the fact that ...** on ne peut pas se dissimuler que ....
disgust [dıs'gʌst] *n* dégoût *m*, aversion *f* ♦ *vt* dégoûter, écœurer.
disgusting [dıs'gʌstıŋ] *a* dégoûtant(e), révoltant(e).
dish [dıʃ] *n* plat *m*; **to do** *or* **wash the ~es** faire la vaisselle.
dish out *vt* distribuer.
dish up *vt* servir; (*facts, statistics*) sortir, débiter.
dishcloth ['dıʃklɔθ] *n* (*for drying*) torchon *m*; (*for washing*) lavette *f*.
dishearten [dıs'hɑ:tn] *vt* décourager.
dishevelled, (*US*) **disheveled** [dı'ʃɛvəld] *a* ébouriffé(e); décoiffé(e); débraillé(e).
dishonest [dıs'ɔnıst] *a* malhonnête.
dishonesty [dıs'ɔnıstı] *n* malhonnêteté *f*.
dishonour, (*US*) **dishonor** [dıs'ɔnə*] *n* déshonneur *m*.
dishono(u)rable [dıs'ɔnərəbl] *a* déshonorant(e).
dish soap *n* (*US*) produit *m* pour la vaisselle.
dishtowel ['dıʃtauəl] *n* torchon *m* (à vaisselle).
dishwasher ['dıʃwɔʃə*] *n* lave-vaisselle *m*; (*person*) plongeur/euse.
disillusion [dısı'lu:ʒən] *vt* désabuser, désenchanter ♦ *n* désenchantement *m*; **to become ~ed (with)** perdre ses illusions (en ce qui concerne).
disillusionment [dısı'lu:ʒənmənt] *n* désillusionnement *m*, désillusion *f*.
disincentive [dısın'sɛntıv] *n*: **it's a ~** c'est

démotivant; **to be a ~ to sb** démotiver qn.
disinclined [ˈdɪsɪnˈklaɪnd] *a*: **to be ~ to do sth** être peu disposé(e) *or* peu enclin(e) à faire qch.
disinfect [dɪsɪnˈfɛkt] *vt* désinfecter.
disinfectant [dɪsɪnˈfɛktənt] *n* désinfectant *m*.
disinflation [dɪsɪnˈfleɪʃən] *n* désinflation *f*.
disinherit [dɪsɪnˈhɛrɪt] *vt* déshériter.
disintegrate [dɪsˈɪntɪɡreɪt] *vi* se désintégrer.
disinterested [dɪsˈɪntrəstɪd] *a* désintéressé(e).
disjointed [dɪsˈdʒɔɪntɪd] *a* décousu(e), incohérent(e).
disk [dɪsk] *n* (COMPUT) disquette *f*; **single-/double-sided ~** disquette une face/double face.
disk drive *n* lecteur *m* de disquette.
diskette [dɪsˈkɛt] *n* (COMPUT) disquette *f*.
disk operating system (DOS) *n* système *m* d'exploitation à disques (DOS).
dislike [dɪsˈlaɪk] *n* aversion *f*, antipathie *f* ♦ *vt* ne pas aimer; **to take a ~ to sb/sth** prendre qn/qch en grippe; **I ~ the idea** l'idée me déplaît.
dislocate [ˈdɪsləkeɪt] *vt* disloquer, déboîter; (*services etc*) désorganiser; **he has ~d his shoulder** il s'est disloqué l'épaule.
dislodge [dɪsˈlɔdʒ] *vt* déplacer, faire bouger; (*enemy*) déloger.
disloyal [dɪsˈlɔɪəl] *a* déloyal(e).
dismal [ˈdɪzml] *a* lugubre, maussade.
dismantle [dɪsˈmæntl] *vt* démonter; (*fort, warship*) démanteler.
dismast [dɪsˈmɑːst] *vt* démâter.
dismay [dɪsˈmeɪ] *n* consternation *f* ♦ *vt* consterner; **much to my ~** à ma grande consternation, à ma grande inquiétude.
dismiss [dɪsˈmɪs] *vt* congédier, renvoyer; (*idea*) écarter; (*LAW*) rejeter ♦ *vi* (*MIL*) rompre les rangs.
dismissal [dɪsˈmɪsl] *n* renvoi *m*.
dismount [dɪsˈmaʊnt] *vi* mettre pied à terre.
disobedience [dɪsəˈbiːdɪəns] *n* désobéissance *f*.
disobedient [dɪsəˈbiːdɪənt] *a* désobéissant(e), indiscipliné(e).
disobey [dɪsəˈbeɪ] *vt* désobéir à; (*rule*) transgresser, enfreindre.
disorder [dɪsˈɔːdə*] *n* désordre *m*; (*rioting*) désordres *mpl*; (*MED*) troubles *mpl*.
disorderly [dɪsˈɔːdəlɪ] *a* (*room*) en désordre; (*behaviour, retreat, crowd*) désordonné(e).
disorderly conduct *n* (*LAW*) conduite *f* contraire aux bonnes mœurs.
disorganized [dɪsˈɔːɡənaɪzd] *a* désorganisé(e).
disorientated [dɪsˈɔːrɪenteɪtɪd] *a* désorienté(e).
disown [dɪsˈəʊn] *vt* renier.
disparaging [dɪsˈpærɪdʒɪŋ] *a* désobligeant(e); **to be ~ about sb/sth** faire des remarques désobligeantes sur qn/qch.
disparate [ˈdɪspərɪt] *a* disparate.
disparity [dɪsˈpærɪtɪ] *n* disparité *f*.
dispassionate [dɪsˈpæʃənət] *a* calme, froid(e); impartial(e), objectif(ive).
dispatch [dɪsˈpætʃ] *vt* expédier, envoyer; (*deal with: business*) régler, en finir avec ♦ *n* envoi *m*, expédition *f*; (*MIL, PRESS*) dépêche *f*.
dispatch department *n* service *m* des expéditions.

dispatch rider *n* (*MIL*) estafette *f*.
dispel [dɪsˈpɛl] *vt* dissiper, chasser.
dispensary [dɪsˈpɛnsərɪ] *n* pharmacie *f*; (*in chemist's*) officine *f*.
dispense [dɪsˈpɛns] *vt* distribuer, administrer; (*medicine*) préparer (et vendre); **to ~ sb from** dispenser qn de.
dispense with *vt fus* se passer de; (*make unnecessary*) rendre superflu(e).
dispenser [dɪsˈpɛnsə*] *n* (*device*) distributeur *m*.
dispensing chemist *n* (*Brit*) pharmacie *f*.
dispersal [dɪsˈpɔːsl] *n* dispersion *f*; (*ADMIN*) déconcentration *f*.
disperse [dɪsˈpɔːs] *vt* disperser; (*knowledge*) disséminer ♦ *vi* se disperser.
dispirited [dɪsˈpɪrɪtɪd] *a* découragé(e), déprimé(e).
displace [dɪsˈpleɪs] *vt* déplacer.
displaced person *n* (*POL*) personne déplacée.
displacement [dɪsˈpleɪsmənt] *n* déplacement *m*.
display [dɪsˈpleɪ] *n* (*of goods*) étalage *m*; affichage *m*; (*computer ~:* visualisation *f*; (*: device*) visuel *m*; (*of feeling*) manifestation *f*; (*pej*) ostentation *f*; (*show, spectacle*) spectacle *m*; (*military ~*) parade *f* militaire ♦ *vt* montrer; (*goods*) mettre à l'étalage, exposer; (*results, departure times*) afficher; (*pej*) faire étalage de; **on ~** (*exhibits*) exposé(e), exhibé(e); (*goods*) à l'étalage.
display advertising *n* publicité rédactionnelle.
displease [dɪsˈpliːz] *vt* mécontenter, contrarier; **~d with** mécontent(e) de.
displeasure [dɪsˈplɛʒə*] *n* mécontentement *m*.
disposable [dɪsˈpəʊzəbl] *a* (*pack etc*) jetable; (*income*) disponible; **~ nappy** (*Brit*) couche *f* à jeter, couche-culotte *f*.
disposal [dɪsˈpəʊzl] *n* (*availability, arrangement*) disposition *f*; (*of property etc: by selling*) vente *f*; (*: by giving away*) cession *f*; (*of rubbish*) évacuation *f*, destruction *f*; **at one's ~** à sa disposition; **to put sth at sb's ~** mettre qch à la disposition de qn.
dispose [dɪsˈpəʊz] *vt* disposer.
dispose of *vt fus* (*time, money*) disposer de; (*unwanted goods*) se débarrasser de, se défaire de; (*COMM: stock*) écouler, vendre; (*problem*) expédier.
disposed [dɪsˈpəʊzd] *a*: **~ to do** disposé(e) à faire.
disposition [dɪspəˈzɪʃən] *n* disposition *f*; (*temperament*) naturel *m*.
dispossess [ˈdɪspəˈzɛs] *vt*: **to ~ sb (of)** déposséder qn (de).
disproportion [dɪsprəˈpɔːʃən] *n* disproportion *f*.
disproportionate [dɪsprəˈpɔːʃənət] *a* disproportionné(e).
disprove [dɪsˈpruːv] *vt* réfuter.
dispute [dɪsˈpjuːt] *n* discussion *f*; (*also:* **industrial ~**) conflit *m* ♦ *vt* contester; (*matter*) discuter; (*victory*) disputer; **to be in** *or* **under ~** (*matter*) être en discussion; (*territory*) être contesté(e).

disqualification [dıskwɔlıfı'keıʃən] n disqualification f; ~ **(from driving)** (Brit) retrait m du permis (de conduire).

disqualify [dıs'kwɔlıfaı] vt (SPORT) disqualifier; **to ~ sb for sth/from doing** (status, situation) rendre qn inapte à qch/à faire; (authority) signifier à qn l'interdiction de faire; **to ~ sb (from driving)** (Brit) retirer à qn son permis (de conduire).

disquiet [dıs'kwaıət] n inquiétude f, trouble m.

disquieting [dıs'kwaıətıŋ] a inquiétant(e), alarmant(e).

disregard [dısrı'gɑːd] vt ne pas tenir compte de ♦ n (indifference): ~ **(for)** (feelings) indifférence f (pour), insensibilité f (à); (danger, money) mépris m (pour).

disrepair ['dısrı'pεə*] n mauvais état; **to fall into** ~ (building) tomber en ruine; (street) se dégrader.

disreputable [dıs'rεpjutəbl] a (person) de mauvaise réputation, peu recommandable; (behaviour) déshonorant(e); (area) mal famé(e), louche.

disrepute ['dısrı'pjuːt] n déshonneur m, discrédit m; **to bring into** ~ faire tomber dans le discrédit.

disrespectful [dısrı'spεktful] a irrespectueux(euse).

disrupt [dıs'rʌpt] vt (plans, meeting, lesson) perturber, déranger.

disruption [dıs'rʌpʃən] n perturbation f, dérangement m.

disruptive [dıs'rʌptıv] a perturbateur(trice).

dissatisfaction [dıssætıs'fækʃən] n mécontentement m, insatisfaction f.

dissatisfied [dıs'sætısfaıd] a: ~ **(with)** mécontent(e) or insatisfait(e) (de).

dissect [dı'sεkt] vt disséquer; (fig) disséquer, éplucher.

disseminate [dı'sεmıneıt] vt disséminer.

dissent [dı'sεnt] n dissentiment m, différence f d'opinion.

dissenter [dı'sεntə*] n (REL, POL etc) dissident/e.

dissertation [dısə'teıʃən] n (SCOL) mémoire m.

disservice [dıs'səːvıs] n: **to do sb a** ~ rendre un mauvais service à qn; desservir qn.

dissident ['dısıdnt] a, n dissident(e).

dissimilar [dı'sımılə*] a: ~ **(to)** dissemblable (à), différent(e) (de).

dissipate ['dısıpeıt] vt dissiper; (energy, efforts) disperser.

dissipated ['dısıpeıtıd] a dissolu(e); débauché(e).

dissociate [dı'səuʃıeıt] vt dissocier; **to ~ o.s. from** se désolidariser de.

dissolute ['dısəluːt] a débauché(e), dissolu(e).

dissolution [dısə'luːʃən] n dissolution f.

dissolve [dı'zɔlv] vt dissoudre ♦ vi se dissoudre, fondre; (fig) disparaître.

dissuade [dı'sweıd] vt: **to ~ sb (from)** dissuader qn (de).

distaff ['dıstɑːf] n: ~ **side** côté maternel.

distance ['dıstns] n distance f; **what's the ~ to London?** à quelle distance se trouve Londres?; **it's within walking** ~ on peut y aller à pied; **in the** ~ au loin.

distant ['dıstnt] a lointain(e), éloigné(e); (manner) distant(e), froid(e).

distaste [dıs'teıst] n dégoût m.

distasteful [dıs'teıstful] a déplaisant(e), désagréable.

Dist. Atty. abbr (US) = **district attorney.**

distemper [dıs'tεmpə*] n (paint) détrempe f, badigeon m; (of dogs) maladie f de Carré.

distended [dıs'tεndıd] a (stomach) dilaté(e).

distil [dıs'tıl] vt distiller.

distillery [dıs'tılərı] n distillerie f.

distinct [dıs'tıŋkt] a distinct(e); (preference, progress) marqué(e); **as ~ from** par opposition à, en contraste avec.

distinction [dıs'tıŋkʃən] n distinction f; (in exam) mention f très bien; **to draw a ~ between** faire une distinction entre; **a writer of** ~ un écrivain réputé.

distinctive [dıs'tıŋktıv] a distinctif(ive).

distinctly [dıs'tıŋktlı] ad distinctement; (specify) expressément.

distinguish [dıs'tıŋgwıʃ] vt distinguer; **to ~ between** (concepts) distinguer entre, faire une distinction entre; **to ~ o.s.** se distinguer.

distinguished [dıs'tıŋgwıʃt] a (eminent, refined) distingué(e); (career) remarquable, brillant(e).

distinguishing [dıs'tıŋgwıʃıŋ] a (feature) distinctif(ive), caractéristique.

distort [dıs'tɔːt] vt déformer.

distortion [dıs'tɔːʃən] n déformation f.

distract [dıs'trækt] vt distraire, déranger.

distracted [dıs'træktıd] a (look etc) éperdu(e), égaré(e).

distraction [dıs'trækʃən] n distraction f, dérangement m; **to drive sb to** ~ rendre qn fou(folle).

distraught [dıs'trɔːt] a éperdu(e).

distress [dıs'trεs] n détresse f; (pain) douleur f ♦ vt affliger; **in** ~ (ship) en perdition; (plane) en détresse; **~ed area** (Brit) zone sinistrée.

distressing [dıs'trεsıŋ] a douloureux(euse), pénible, affligeant(e).

distress signal n signal m de détresse.

distribute [dıs'trıbjuːt] vt distribuer.

distribution [dıstrı'bjuːʃən] n distribution f.

distribution cost n coût m de distribution.

distributor [dıs'trıbjutə*] n (gen, TECH) distributeur m; (COMM) concessionnaire m/f.

district ['dıstrıkt] n (of country) région f; (of town) quartier m; (ADMIN) district m.

district attorney n (US) ≈ procureur m de la République.

district council n (Brit) ≈ conseil municipal.

district nurse n (Brit) infirmière visiteuse.

distrust [dıs'trʌst] n méfiance f, doute m ♦ vt se méfier de.

distrustful [dıs'trʌstful] a méfiant(e).

disturb [dıs'təːb] vt troubler; (inconvenience) déranger; **sorry to ~ you** excusez-moi de vous déranger.

disturbance [dıs'təːbəns] n dérangement m; (political etc) troubles mpl; (by drunks etc) tapage m; **to cause a ~** troubler l'ordre public; **~ of the peace** (LAW) tapage injurieux or nocturne.

disturbed [dıs'təːbd] a agité(e), troublé(e); **to be mentally/emotionally ~** avoir des problèmes psychologiques/affectifs.

disturbing [dɪs'tə:bɪŋ] *a* troublant(e), inquiétant(e).
disuse [dɪs'ju:s] *n*: **to fall into** ~ tomber en désuétude.
disused [dɪs'ju:zd] *a* désaffecté(e).
ditch [dɪtʃ] *n* fossé *m* ♦ *vt* (*col*) abandonner.
dither ['dɪðə*] *vi* hésiter.
ditto ['dɪtəu] *ad* idem.
divan [dɪ'væn] *n* divan *m*.
divan bed *n* divan-lit *m*.
dive [daɪv] *n* plongeon *m*; (*of submarine*) plongée *f*; (*AVIAT*) piqué *m*; (*pej: café, bar etc*) bouge *m* ♦ *vi* plonger.
diver ['daɪvə*] *n* plongeur *m*.
diverge [daɪ'və:dʒ] *vi* diverger.
divergent [daɪ'və:dʒənt] *a* divergent(e).
diverse [daɪ'və:s] *a* divers(e).
diversification [daɪvə:sɪfɪ'keɪʃən] *n* diversification *f*.
diversify [daɪ'və:sɪfaɪ] *vt* diversifier.
diversion [daɪ'və:ʃən] *n* (*Brit AUT*) déviation *f*; (*distraction, MIL*) diversion *f*.
diversity [daɪ'və:sɪtɪ] *n* diversité *f*, variété *f*.
divert [daɪ'və:t] *vt* (*Brit: traffic*) dévier; (*plane*) dérouter; (*train, river*) détourner; (*amuse*) divertir.
divest [daɪ'vɛst] *vt*: **to** ~ **sb of** dépouiller qn de.
divide [dɪ'vaɪd] *vt* diviser; (*separate*) séparer ♦ *vi* se diviser; **to** ~ **(between** *or* **among)** répartir *or* diviser (entre); **40** ~**d by 5** 40 divisé par 5.
divide out *vt*: **to** ~ **out (between** *or* **among)** distribuer *or* répartir (entre).
divided [dɪ'vaɪdɪd] *a* (*fig: country, couple*) désuni(e); (*opinions*) partagé(e).
divided skirt *n* jupe-culotte *f*.
dividend ['dɪvɪdɛnd] *n* dividende *m*.
dividend cover *n* rapport *m* dividendes-résultat.
dividers [dɪ'vaɪdəz] *npl* compas *m* à pointes sèches; (*between pages*) feuillets *mpl* intercalaires.
divine [dɪ'vaɪn] *a* divin(e) ♦ *vt* (*future*) prédire; (*truth*) deviner, entrevoir; (*water, metal*) détecter la présence de (*par l'intermédiaire de la radiesthésie*).
diving ['daɪvɪŋ] *n* plongée (sous-marine).
diving board *n* plongeoir *m*.
diving suit *n* scaphandre *m*.
divinity [dɪ'vɪnɪtɪ] *n* divinité *f*; (*as study*) théologie *f*.
division [dɪ'vɪʒən] *n* (*also Brit FOOTBALL*) division *f*; (*separation*) séparation *f*; (*Brit POL*) vote *m*; ~ **of labour** division du travail.
divisive [dɪ'vaɪsɪv] *a* qui entraîne la division, qui crée des dissensions.
divorce [dɪ'vɔ:s] *n* divorce *m* ♦ *vt* divorcer d'avec.
divorced [dɪ'vɔ:st] *a* divorcé(e).
divorcee [dɪvɔ:'si:] *n* divorcé/e.
divulge [daɪ'vʌldʒ] *vt* divulguer, révéler.
DIY *a, n abbr* (*Brit*) = **do-it-yourself**.
dizziness ['dɪzɪnɪs] *n* vertige *m*, étourdissement *m*.
dizzy ['dɪzɪ] *a* (*height*) vertigineux(euse); **to make sb** ~ donner le vertige à qn; **I feel** ~ la tête me tourne, j'ai la tête qui tourne.
DJ *n abbr* = **disc jockey**.

Djakarta [dʒə'kɑ:tə] *n* Djakarta.
DJIA *n abbr* (*US STOCK EXCHANGE*) = *Dow-Jones Industrial Average*.
dl *abbr* (= *decilitre*) dl.
DLit(t) *n abbr* (= *Doctor of Literature, Doctor of Letters*) titre universitaire.
DLO *n abbr* = **dead-letter office**.
dm *abbr* (= *decimetre*) dm.
DMus *n abbr* (= *Doctor of Music*) titre universitaire.
DMZ *n abbr* = **demilitarized zone**.
DNA *n abbr* (= *deoxyribonucleic acid*) ADN *m*.
do *abbr* (= *ditto*) dᵒ.
do [du:] *vt, vi* (*pt* **did** [dɪd], *pp* **done** [dʌn]) faire; (*visit: city, museum*) faire, visiter ♦ *n* (*col: party*) fête *f*, soirée *f*; (*: formal gathering*) réception *f*; **he didn't laugh** il n'a pas ri; ~ **you want any?** en voulez-vous?, est-ce que vous en voulez?; **she swims better than I** ~ elle nage mieux que moi; **he laughed, didn't he?** il a ri, n'est-ce pas?; ~ **they?** ah oui?, vraiment?; **who broke it? - I did** qui l'a cassé? - (c'est) moi; ~ **you agree?** - oui; **you speak better than I** ~ tu parles mieux que moi; **so does he** lui aussi; **DO come!** je t'en prie, viens, il faut absolument que tu viennes; **I DO wish I could go** j'aimerais tant y aller; **but I DO like it!** mais si, je l'aime!; **to** ~ **one's nails/teeth** se faire les ongles/brosser les dents; **to** ~ **one's hair** se coiffer; **will it** ~? est-ce que ça ira?; **that'll** ~! (*in annoyance*) ça suffit!, c'en est assez!; **to make** ~ **(with)** se contenter (de); **to** ~ **without sth** se passer de qch; **what did he** ~ **with the cat?** qu'a-t-il fait du chat?; **what has that got to** ~ **with it?** quel rapport y-a-t-il?, qu'est-ce que cela vient faire là-dedans?
do away with *vt fus* supprimer, abolir; (*kill*) supprimer.
do for *vt fus* (*Brit col: clean for*) faire le ménage chez.
do up *vt* remettre à neuf; **to** ~ **o.s. up** se faire beau(belle).
do with *vt fus*: **I could** ~ **with a drink** je prendrais bien un verre; **I could** ~ **with some help** j'aurais bien besoin d'un petit coup de main; **it could** ~ **with a wash** ça ne lui ferait pas de mal d'être lavé.
DOA *abbr* (= *dead on arrival*) décédé(e) à l'admission.
d.o.b. *abbr* = **date of birth**.
docile ['dəusaɪl] *a* docile.
dock [dɔk] *n* dock *m*; (*wharf*) quai *m*; (*LAW*) banc *m* des accusés ♦ *vi* se mettre à quai ♦ *vt*: **they** ~**ed a third of his wages** ils lui ont retenu *or* décompté un tiers de son salaire.
dock dues *npl* droits *mpl* de bassin.
docker ['dɔkə*] *n* docker *m*.
docket ['dɔkɪt] *n* bordereau *m*; (*on parcel etc*) étiquette *f or* fiche *f* (*décrivant le contenu d'un paquet etc*).
dockyard ['dɔkjɑ:d] *n* chantier *m* de construction navale.
doctor ['dɔktə*] *n* médecin *m*, docteur *m*; (*PhD etc*) docteur ♦ *vt* (*cat*) couper; (*interfere with: food*) altérer; (*: drink*) frelater; (*: text, document*) arranger; ~**'s office** (*US*)

cabinet m de consultation; **D~ of Philosophy (PhD)** doctorat m; titulaire m/f d'un doctorat.

doctorate ['dɔktərɪt] n doctorat m.

doctrine ['dɔktrɪn] n doctrine f.

document n ['dɔkjumənt] document m ♦ vt ['dɔkjument] documenter.

documentary [dɔkju'mentərɪ] a, n documentaire (m).

documentation [dɔkjumən'teɪʃən] n documentation f.

DOD n abbr (US) = **Department of Defense**.

doddering ['dɔdərɪŋ] a (senile) gâteux(euse).

Dodecanese (Islands) [dəudɪkə'niːz-] n(pl) Dodécanèse m.

dodge [dɔdʒ] n truc m; combine f ♦ vt esquiver, éviter ♦ vi faire un saut de côté; (SPORT) faire une esquive; **to ~ out of the way** s'esquiver; **to ~ through the traffic** se faufiler or faire de savantes manœuvres entre les voitures.

dodgems ['dɔdʒəmz] npl (Brit) autos tamponneuses.

DOE n abbr (Brit) = **Department of the Environment**; (US) = **Department of Energy**.

doe [dəu] n (deer) biche f; (rabbit) lapine f.

does [dʌz] see **do**.

doesn't ['dʌznt] = **does not**.

dog [dɔg] n chien/ne ♦ vt (follow closely) suivre de près, ne pas lâcher d'une semelle; (fig: memory etc) poursuivre, harceler; **to go to the ~s** (nation etc) aller à vau-l'eau.

dog biscuits npl biscuits mpl pour chien.

dog collar n collier m de chien; (fig) faux-col m d'ecclésiastique.

dog-eared ['dɔgɪəd] a corné(e).

dog food n nourriture f pour les chiens or le chien.

dogged ['dɔgɪd] a obstiné(e), opiniâtre.

dogma ['dɔgmə] n dogme m.

dogmatic [dɔg'mætɪk] a dogmatique.

do-gooder [du:'gudə*] n (pej) faiseur/euse de bonnes œuvres.

dogsbody ['dɔgzbɔdɪ] n (Brit) bonne f à tout faire, tâcheron m.

doing ['duɪŋ] n: **this is your ~** c'est votre travail, c'est vous qui avez fait ça.

doings ['duɪŋz] npl activités fpl.

do-it-yourself ['du:ɪtjɔː'self] n bricolage m.

doldrums ['dɔldrəmz] npl: **to be in the ~** avoir le cafard; être dans le marasme.

dole [dəul] n (Brit: payment) allocation f de chômage; **on the ~** au chômage.

dole out vt donner au compte-goutte.

doleful ['dəulful] a triste, lugubre.

doll [dɔl] n poupée f.

doll up vt: **to ~ o.s. up** se faire beau(belle).

dollar ['dɔlə*] n dollar m.

dollar area n zone f dollar.

dolphin ['dɔlfɪn] n dauphin m.

domain [də'meɪn] n (also fig) domaine m.

dome [dəum] n dôme m.

domestic [də'mestɪk] a (duty, happiness) familial(e); (policy, affairs, flights) intérieur(e); (news) national(e); (animal) domestique.

domesticated [də'mestɪkeɪtɪd] a

domestiqué(e); (pej) d'intérieur; **he's very ~** il participe volontiers aux tâches ménagères; question ménage, il est très organisé.

domesticity [dəumes'tɪsɪtɪ] n vie f de famille.

domestic servant n domestique m/f.

domicile ['dɔmɪsaɪl] n domicile m.

dominant ['dɔmɪnənt] a dominant(e).

dominate ['dɔmɪneɪt] vt dominer.

domination [dɔmɪ'neɪʃən] n domination f.

domineering [dɔmɪ'nɪərɪŋ] a dominateur(trice), autoritaire.

Dominican Republic [də'mɪnɪkən-] n République Dominicaine.

dominion [də'mɪnɪən] n domination f; territoire m; dominion m.

domino, ~es ['dɔmɪnəu] n domino m; **~es** n (game) dominos mpl.

don [dɔn] n (Brit) professeur m d'université ♦ vt revêtir.

donate [də'neɪt] vt faire don de, donner.

donation [də'neɪʃən] n donation f, don m.

done [dʌn] pp of **do**.

donkey ['dɔŋkɪ] n âne m.

donkey-work ['dɔŋkɪwəːk] n (Brit col) le gros du travail, le plus dur (du travail).

donor ['dəunə*] n (of blood etc) donneur/euse; (to charity) donateur/trice.

don't [dəunt] = **do not**.

doodle ['du:dl] n griffonnage m, gribouillage m ♦ vi griffonner, gribouiller.

doom [du:m] n (fate) destin m; (ruin) ruine f ♦ vt: **to be ~ed (to failure)** être voué(e) à l'échec.

doomsday ['du:mzdeɪ] n le Jugement dernier.

door [dɔː*] n porte f; (of vehicle) portière f, porte; **to go from ~ to ~** aller de porte en porte.

doorbell ['dɔːbel] n sonnette f.

door handle n poignée f de porte.

doorman ['dɔːmən] n (in hotel) portier m; (in block of flats) concierge m.

doormat ['dɔːmæt] n paillasson m.

doorpost ['dɔːpəust] n montant m de porte.

doorstep ['dɔːstep] n pas m de (la) porte, seuil m.

door-to-door ['dɔːtə'dɔː*] a: **~ selling** vente f à domicile.

doorway ['dɔːweɪ] n (embrasure f de) porte f.

dope [dəup] n (col) drogue f; (: information) tuyaux mpl, rancards mpl ♦ vt (horse etc) doper.

dopey ['dəupɪ] a (col) à moitié endormi(e).

dormant ['dɔːmənt] a assoupi(e), en veilleuse; (rule, law) inappliqué(e).

dormer ['dɔːmə*] n (also: ~ **window**) lucarne f.

dormice ['dɔːmaɪs] npl of **dormouse**.

dormitory ['dɔːmɪtrɪ] n dortoir m; (US: hall of residence) foyer m d'étudiants.

dormouse, pl dormice ['dɔːmaus, -maɪs] n loir m.

Dors abbr (Brit) = **Dorset**.

DOS [dɔs] n abbr = **disk operating system**.

dosage ['dəusɪdʒ] n dose f; dosage m; (on label) posologie f.

dose [dəus] n dose f; (Brit: bout) attaque f ♦ vt: **to ~ o.s.** se bourrer de médicaments; **a ~ of flu** une belle or bonne grippe.

doss house ['dɔs-] n (Brit) asile m de nuit.

dossier ['dɔsɪeɪ] n dossier m.
DOT n abbr (US) = **Department of Transportation**.
dot [dɔt] n point m ♦ vt: **~ted with** parsemé(e) de; **on the ~** à l'heure tapante.
dot command n (COMPUT) commande précédée d'un point.
dote [dəut]: **to ~ on** vt fus être fou(folle) de.
dot-matrix printer [dɔt'meɪtrɪks-] n imprimante matricielle.
dotted line ['dɔtɪd-] n ligne pointillée; (AUT) ligne discontinue; **to sign on the ~** signer à l'endroit indiqué or sur la ligne pointillée; (fig) donner son consentement.
dotty ['dɔtɪ] a (col) loufoque, farfelu(e).
double ['dʌbl] a double ♦ ad (fold) en deux; (twice): **to cost ~ (sth)** coûter le double (de qch) or deux fois plus (que qch) ♦ n double m; (CINEMA) doublure f ♦ vt doubler; (fold) plier en deux ♦ vi doubler; (have two uses): **to ~ as** servir aussi de; **~ five two six (5526)** (Brit TEL) cinquante-cinq - vingt-six; **it's spelt with a ~ "l"** ça s'écrit avec deux "l"; **on the ~**, (Brit) **at the ~** au pas de course.
 double back vi (person) revenir sur ses pas.
 double up vi (bend over) se courber, se plier; (share room) partager la chambre.
double bass n contrebasse f.
double bed n grand lit.
double bend n (Brit) virage m en S.
double-breasted ['dʌbl'brestɪd] a croisé(e).
double-check ['dʌbl'tʃɛk] vt, vi revérifier.
double-clutch ['dʌbl'klʌtʃ] vi (US) faire un double débrayage.
double cream n (Brit) crème fraîche épaisse.
doublecross ['dʌbl'krɔs] vt doubler, trahir.
doubledecker ['dʌbl'dɛkə*] n autobus m à impériale.
double declutch vi (Brit) faire un double débrayage.
double exposure n (PHOT) surimpression f.
double glazing n (Brit) double vitrage m.
double-page ['dʌbl'peɪdʒ] a: **~ spread** publicité f en double page.
double parking n stationnement m en double file.
double room n chambre f pour deux.
doubles ['dʌblz] n (TENNIS) double m.
doubly ['dʌblɪ] ad doublement, deux fois plus.
doubt [daut] n doute m ♦ vt douter de; **without (a) ~** sans aucun doute; **beyond ~** ad indubitablement ♦ a indubitable; **to ~ that** douter que; **I ~ it very much** j'en doute fort.
doubtful ['dautful] a douteux(euse); (person) incertain(e); **to be ~ about sth** avoir des doutes sur qch, ne pas être convaincu de qch; **I'm a bit ~** je n'en suis pas certain or sûr.
doubtless ['dautlɪs] ad sans doute, sûrement.
dough [dəu] n pâte f; (col: money) fric m, pognon m.
doughnut ['dəunʌt] n beignet m.
dour [duə*] a austère.
douse [dauz] vt (with water) tremper, inonder; (flames) éteindre.
dove [dʌv] n colombe f.
Dover ['dəuvə*] n Douvres.

dovetail ['dʌvteɪl] n: **~ joint** assemblage m à queue d'aronde ♦ vi (fig) concorder.
dowager ['dauədʒə*] n douairière f.
dowdy ['daudɪ] a démodé(e); mal fagoté(e).
Dow-Jones average ['dau'dʒəunz-] n (US) indice boursier Dow-Jones.
down [daun] n (fluff) duvet m; (hill) colline (dénudée) ♦ ad en bas ♦ prep en bas de ♦ vt (enemy) abattre; (col: drink) siffler; **~ there** là-bas (en bas), là au fond; **~ here** ici en bas; **the price of meat is ~** le prix de la viande a baissé; **I've got it ~ in my diary** c'est inscrit dans mon agenda; **to pay £2 ~** verser 2 livres d'arrhes or en acompte; **England is two goals ~** l'Angleterre a deux buts de retard; **to ~ tools** (Brit) cesser le travail; **~ with X!** à bas X!
down-and-out ['daunəndaut] n (tramp) clochard/e.
down-at-heel ['daunət'hi:l] a (fig) miteux(euse).
downbeat ['daunbi:t] n (MUS) temps frappé ♦ a sombre, négatif(ive).
downcast ['daunka:st] a démoralisé(e).
downer ['daunə*] n (col: drug) tranquillisant m; **to be on a ~** (depressed) flipper.
downfall ['daunfɔ:l] n chute f; ruine f.
downgrade ['daungreɪd] vt déclasser.
downhearted ['daun'ha:tɪd] a découragé(e).
downhill ['daun'hɪl] ad (face, look) en aval, vers l'aval; (roll, go) vers le bas, en bas ♦ n (SKI: also: **~ race**) descente f; **to go ~** descendre; (business) péricliter, aller à vau-l'eau.
Downing Street ['daunɪŋ-] n (Brit): **10 ~** résidence du Premier ministre.
download ['daunləud] vt télécharger.
down-market ['daun'ma:kɪt] a (product) bas de gamme inv.
down payment n acompte m.
downplay ['daunpleɪ] vt (US) minimiser (l'importance de).
downpour ['daunpɔ:*] n pluie torrentielle, déluge m.
downright ['daunraɪt] a franc(franche); (refusal) catégorique.
Downs [daunz] npl (Brit): **the ~** collines crayeuses du sud-est de l'Angleterre.
downstairs ['daun'stɛəz] ad (on or to ground floor) au rez-de-chaussée; (on or to floor below) à l'étage inférieur; **to come ~, to go ~** descendre (l'escalier).
downstream ['daunstri:m] ad en aval.
downtime ['dauntaɪm] n (of machine etc) temps mort; (of person) temps d'arrêt.
down-to-earth ['dauntu'ə:θ] a terre à terre inv.
downtown ['daun'taun] ad en ville ♦ a (US): **~ Chicago** le centre commerçant de Chicago.
downtrodden ['dauntrɔdn] a opprimé(e).
down under ad en Australie (or Nouvelle Zélande).
downward ['daunwəd] a vers le bas; **a ~ trend** une tendance à la baisse, une diminution progressive.
downward(s) ['daunwəd(z)] ad vers le bas.
dowry ['daurɪ] n dot f.
doz. abbr (= dozen) douz.
doze [dəuz] vi sommeiller.

doze off *vi* s'assoupir.

dozen ['dʌzn] *n* douzaine *f*; **a ~ books** une douzaine de livres; **80p a ~** 80p la douzaine; **~s of times** des centaines de fois.

DPh, DPhil *n abbr* (= *Doctor of Philosophy*) titre universitaire.

DPP *n abbr* (*Brit*) = **Director of Public Prosecutions.**

DPT *n abbr* (*MED*: = *diphtheria, pertussis, tetanus*) DCT *m*.

DPW *n abbr* (*US*) = *Department of Public Works.*

Dr, Dr. *abbr* (= *doctor*) Dr.

Dr. *abbr* (*in street names*) = **drive.**

dr *abbr* (*COMM*) = **debtor.**

drab [dræb] *a* terne, morne.

draft [drɑ:ft] *n* brouillon *m*; (*of contract, document*) version *f* préliminaire; (*COMM*) traite *f*; (*US MIL*) contingent *m*; (: *call-up*) conscription *f* ♦ *vt* faire le brouillon de; (*document, report*) rédiger une version préliminaire de; *see also* **draught.**

drag [dræg] *vt* traîner; (*river*) draguer ♦ *vi* traîner ♦ *n* (*AVIAT, NAUT*) résistance *f*, (*col: person*) raseur/euse; (: *task etc*) corvée *f*; (*women's clothing*): **in ~** (en) travesti.

drag away *vt*: **to ~ away (from)** arracher *or* emmener de force (de).

drag on *vi* s'éterniser.

dragnet ['drægnet] *n* drège *f*; (*fig*) piège *m*, filets *mpl*.

dragon ['drægn] *n* dragon *m*.

dragonfly ['drægənflaɪ] *n* libellule *f*.

dragoon [drə'gu:n] *n* (*cavalryman*) dragon *m* ♦ *vt*: **to ~ sb into doing sth** (*Brit*) forcer qn à faire qch.

drain [dreɪn] *n* égout *m*; (*on resources*) saignée *f* ♦ *vt* (*land, marshes*) drainer, assécher; (*vegetables*) égoutter; (*reservoir etc*) vider ♦ *vi* (*water*) s'écouler; **to feel ~ed (of energy or emotion)** être miné(e).

drainage ['dreɪnɪdʒ] *n* système *m* d'égouts.

draining board ['dreɪnɪŋ-], (*US*) **drainboard** ['dreɪnbɔ:d] *n* égouttoir *m*.

drainpipe ['dreɪnpaɪp] *n* tuyau *m* d'écoulement.

drake [dreɪk] *n* canard *m* (mâle).

dram [dræm] *n* petit verre.

drama ['drɑ:mə] *n* (*art*) théâtre *m*, art *m* dramatique; (*play*) pièce *f*; (*event*) drame *m*.

dramatic [drə'mætɪk] *a* (*THEATRE*) dramatique; (*impressive*) spectaculaire.

dramatically [drə'mætɪklɪ] *ad* de façon spectaculaire.

dramatist ['dræmətɪst] *n* auteur *m* dramatique.

dramatize ['dræmətaɪz] *vt* (*events etc*) dramatiser; (*adapt*) adapter pour la télévision (*or pour l'écran*).

drank [dræŋk] *pt of* **drink.**

drape [dreɪp] *vt* draper.

draper ['dreɪpə*] *n* (*Brit*) marchand/e de nouveautés.

drapes [dreɪps] *npl* (*US*) rideaux *mpl*.

drastic ['dræstɪk] *a* (*measures*) d'urgence, énergique; (*change*) radical(e).

drastically ['dræstɪklɪ] *ad* radicalement.

draught, (*US*) **draft** [drɑ:ft] *n* courant *m*

d'air; (*of chimney*) tirage *m*; (*NAUT*) tirant *m* d'eau; **on ~** (*beer*) à la pression.

draughtboard ['drɑ:ftbɔ:d] *n* (*Brit*) damier *m*.

draughts [drɑ:fts] *n* (*Brit*) (jeu *m* de) dames *fpl*.

draughtsman, (*US*) **draftsman** ['drɑ:ftsmən] *n* dessinateur/trice (industriel(le)).

draughtsmanship, (*US*) **draftsmanship** ['drɑ:ftsmənʃɪp] *n* (*technique*) dessin industriel; (*art*) graphisme *m*.

draw [drɔ:] *vb* (*pt* **drew** [dru:, drɔ:n] *pp* **drawn** [dru:, drɔ:n]) *vt* tirer; (*attract*) attirer; (*picture*) dessiner; (*line, circle*) tracer; (*money*) retirer; (*comparison, distinction*): **to ~ (between)** faire (entre) ♦ *vi* (*SPORT*) faire match nul ♦ *n* match nul; (*lottery*) loterie *f*; (: *picking of ticket*) tirage *m* au sort; **to ~ to a close** toucher à *or* tirer à sa fin; **to ~ near** *vi* s'approcher; approcher.

draw back *vi* (*move back*): **to ~ back (from)** reculer (de).

draw in *vi* (*Brit: car*) s'arrêter le long du trottoir; (: *train*) entrer en gare *or* dans la station.

draw on *vt* (*resources*) faire appel à; (*imagination, person*) avoir recours à, faire appel à.

draw out *vi* (*lengthen*) s'allonger ♦ *vt* (*money*) retirer.

draw up *vi* (*stop*) s'arrêter ♦ *vt* (*document*) établir, dresser; (*plans*) formuler, dessiner.

drawback ['drɔ:bæk] *n* inconvénient *m*, désavantage *m*.

drawbridge ['drɔ:brɪdʒ] *n* pont-levis *m*.

drawee [drɔ:'i:] *n* tiré *m*.

drawer [drɔ:*] *n* tiroir *m*; ['drɔ:ə*] (*of cheque*) tireur *m*.

drawing ['drɔ:ɪŋ] *n* dessin *m*.

drawing board *n* planche *f* à dessin.

drawing pin *n* (*Brit*) punaise *f*.

drawing room *n* salon *m*.

drawl [drɔ:l] *n* accent traînant.

drawn [drɔ:n] *pp of* **draw** ♦ *a* (*haggard*) tiré(e), crispé(e).

drawstring ['drɔ:strɪŋ] *n* cordon *m*.

dread [dred] *n* épouvante *f*, effroi *m* ♦ *vt* redouter, appréhender.

dreadful ['dredful] *a* épouvantable, affreux(euse).

dream [dri:m] *n* rêve *m* ♦ *vt, vi* (*pt, pp* **dreamed** *or* **dreamt** [dremt]) rêver; **to have a ~ about sb/sth** rêver à qn/qch; **sweet ~s!** faites de beaux rêves!

dream up *vt* inventer.

dreamer ['dri:mə*] *n* rêveur/euse.

dream world *n* monde *m* imaginaire.

dreamy ['dri:mɪ] *a* (*absent-minded*) rêveur(euse).

dreary ['drɪərɪ] *a* triste; monotone.

dredge [dredʒ] *vt* draguer.

dredge up *vt* draguer; (*fig: unpleasant facts*) (faire) ressortir.

dredger ['dredʒə*] *n* (*ship*) dragueur *m*; (*machine*) drague *f*; (*Brit: also:* **sugar ~**) saupoudreuse *f*.

dregs [dregz] *npl* lie *f*.

drench [drentʃ] *vt* tremper; **~ed to the skin** trempé(e) jusqu'aux os.

dress [drɛs] n robe f; (clothing) habillement m, tenue f ♦ vt habiller; (wound) panser; (food) préparer ♦ vi: she ~es very well elle s'habille très bien; to ~ o.s., to get ~ed s'habiller; to ~ a shop window faire l'étalage or la vitrine.

dress up vi s'habiller; (in fancy dress) se déguiser.

dress circle n premier balcon.

dress designer n modéliste m/f, dessinateur/trice de mode.

dresser ['drɛsə*] n (THEATRE) habilleur/euse; (also: **window** ~) étalagiste m/f; (furniture) vaisselier m.

dressing ['drɛsɪŋ] n (MED) pansement m; (CULIN) sauce f, assaisonnement m.

dressing gown n (Brit) robe f de chambre.

dressing room n (THEATRE) loge f; (SPORT) vestiaire m.

dressing table n coiffeuse f.

dressmaker ['drɛsmeɪkə*] n couturière f.

dressmaking ['drɛsmeɪkɪŋ] n couture f; travaux mpl de couture.

dress rehearsal n (répétition f) générale.

dress shirt n chemise f à plastron.

dressy ['drɛsɪ] a (col: clothes) (qui fait) habillé(e).

drew [dru:] pt of draw.

dribble ['drɪbl] vi tomber goutte à goutte; (baby) baver ♦ vt (ball) dribbler.

dried [draɪd] a (fruit, beans) sec(sèche); (eggs, milk) en poudre.

drier ['draɪə*] n = dryer.

drift [drɪft] n (of current etc) force f; direction f; (of sand etc) amoncellement m; (of snow) rafale f; coulée f; (: on ground) congère f; (general meaning) sens général f ♦ vi (boat) aller à la dérive, dériver; (sand, snow) s'amonceler, s'entasser; **to let things ~ apart** (friends, lovers) s'éloigner l'un de l'autre; **I get** or **catch your** ~ je vois en gros ce que vous voulez dire.

drifter ['drɪftə*] n personne f sans but dans la vie.

driftwood ['drɪftwʊd] n bois flotté.

drill [drɪl] n perceuse f; (bit) foret m; (of dentist) roulette f, fraise f; (MIL) exercice m ♦ vt percer; (soldiers) faire faire l'exercice à; (pupils: in grammar) faire faire des exercices à ♦ vi (for oil) faire un or des forage(s).

drilling ['drɪlɪŋ] n (for oil) forage m.

drilling rig n (on land) tour f (de forage), derrick m; (at sea) plate-forme f de forage.

drily ['draɪlɪ] ad = dryly.

drink [drɪŋk] n boisson f ♦ vt, vi (pt drank, pp drunk [dræŋk, drʌŋk]) boire; **to have a ~** boire quelque chose, boire un verre; **a ~ of water** un verre d'eau; **would you like something to ~?** aimeriez-vous boire quelque chose?; **we had ~s before lunch** on a pris l'apéritif.

drink in vt (fresh air) inspirer profondément; (story) avaler, ne pas perdre une miette de; (sight) se remplir la vue de.

drinkable ['drɪŋkəbl] a (not dangerous) potable; (palatable) buvable.

drinker ['drɪŋkə*] n buveur/euse.

drinking ['drɪŋkɪŋ] n (drunkenness) boisson f, alcoolisme m.

drinking fountain n (in park etc) fontaine publique; (in building) jet m d'eau potable.

drinking water n eau f potable.

drip [drɪp] n goutte f; (sound: of water etc) bruit m de l'eau qui tombe goutte à goutte; (MED) goutte-à-goutte m inv, perfusion f; (col: person) lavette f, nouille f ♦ vi tomber goutte à goutte; (washing) s'égoutter; (wall) suinter.

drip-dry ['drɪp'draɪ] a (shirt) sans repassage.

drip-feed ['drɪpfi:d] vt alimenter au goutte-à-goutte or par perfusion.

dripping ['drɪpɪŋ] n graisse f de rôti ♦ a: ~ **wet** trempé(e).

drive [draɪv] n promenade f or trajet m en voiture; (also: ~way) allée f; (energy) dynamisme m, énergie f; (PSYCH) besoin m; pulsion f; (push) effort (concerté); campagne f; (SPORT) drive m; (TECH) entraînement m; traction f; transmission f ♦ vb (pt drove, pp driven [drəuv, 'drɪvn]) vt conduire; (nail) enfoncer; (push) chasser, pousser; (TECH: motor) actionner; entraîner; (COMPUT: also: disk ~) lecteur m de disquette ♦ vi (be at the wheel) conduire; (travel by car) aller en voiture; **to go for a ~** aller faire une promenade en voiture; **it's 3 hours' ~ from London** Londres est à 3 heures de route; **left/right-hand** ~ (AUT) conduite f à gauche/droite; **front-/rear-wheel** ~ (AUT) traction f avant/arrière; **to ~ sb to (do) sth** pousser or conduire qn à (faire) qch; **to ~ sb mad** rendre qn fou(folle).

drive at vt fus (fig: intend, mean) vouloir dire, en venir à.

drive on vi poursuivre sa route, continuer; (after stopping) reprendre sa route, repartir ♦ vt (incite, encourage) inciter.

drive-in ['draɪvɪn] a, n (esp US) drive-in (m).

drive-in window n (US) guichet-auto m.

drivel ['drɪvl] n (col) idioties fpl, imbécillités fpl.

driven ['drɪvn] pp of drive.

driver ['draɪvə*] n conducteur/trice; (of taxi, bus) chauffeur m.

driver's license n (US) permis m de conduire.

driveway ['draɪvweɪ] n allée f.

driving ['draɪvɪŋ] a: ~ **rain** n pluie battante ♦ n conduite f.

driving belt n courroie f de transmission.

driving force n locomotive f, élément m dynamique.

driving instructor n moniteur m d'auto-école.

driving lesson n leçon f de conduite.

driving licence n (Brit) permis m de conduire.

driving mirror n (Brit) rétroviseur m.

driving school n auto-école f.

driving test n examen m du permis de conduire.

drizzle ['drɪzl] n bruine f, crachin m ♦ vi bruiner.

droll [drəul] a drôle.

dromedary ['drɒmədərɪ] n dromadaire m.

drone [drəun] vi (bee) bourdonner; (engine

etc) ronronner; (*also*: ~ **on**) parler d'une voix monocorde ♦ *n* bourdonnement *m*; ronronnement *m*; (*male bee*) faux-bourdon *m*.

drool [dru:l] *vi* baver; **to ~ over sb/sth** (*fig*) baver d'admiration *or* être en extase devant qn/qch.

droop [dru:p] *vi* s'affaisser; tomber.

drop [drɔp] *n* goutte *f*; (*fall: also in price*) baisse *f*; (: *in salary*) réduction *f*; (*also*: **parachute ~**) saut *m*; (*of cliff*) dénivellation *f*; à-pic *m* ♦ *vt* laisser tomber; (*voice, eyes, price*) baisser; (*set down from car*) déposer ♦ *vi* (*wind, temperature, price, voice*) tomber; (*numbers, attendance*) diminuer; **~s** *npl* (*MED*) gouttes; **cough ~s** pastilles *fpl* pour la toux; **a ~ of 10%** une baisse (*or* réduction) de 10%; **to ~ anchor** jeter l'ancre; **to ~ sb a line** mettre un mot à qn.

drop in *vi* (*col: visit*): **to ~ in (on)** faire un saut (chez), passer (chez).

drop off *vi* (*sleep*) s'assoupir ♦ *vt*: **to ~ sb off** déposer qn.

drop out *vi* (*withdraw*) se retirer; (*student etc*) abandonner, décrocher.

droplet ['drɔplɪt] *n* gouttelette *f*.

dropout ['drɔpaʊt] *n* (*from society*) marginal/e; (*from university*) drop-out *m/f*, dropé/e.

dropper ['drɔpə*] *n* (*MED etc*) compte-gouttes *m inv*.

droppings ['drɔpɪŋz] *npl* crottes *fpl*.

dross [drɔs] *n* déchets *mpl*; rebut *m*.

drought [draʊt] *n* sécheresse *f*.

drove [drəʊv] *pt of* **drive** ♦ *n*: **~s of people** une foule de gens.

drown [draʊn] *vt* noyer; (*also*: ~ **out**: *sound*) couvrir, étouffer ♦ *vi* se noyer.

drowse [draʊz] *vi* somnoler.

drowsy ['draʊzɪ] *a* somnolent(e).

drudge [drʌdʒ] *n* bête *f* de somme (*fig*).

drudgery ['drʌdʒərɪ] *n* corvée *f*.

drug [drʌg] *n* médicament *m*; (*narcotic*) drogue *f* ♦ *vt* droguer; **he's on ~s** il se drogue; (*MED*) il est sous médication.

drug addict *n* toxicomane *m/f*.

druggist ['drʌgɪst] *n* (*US*) pharmacien/ne-droguiste.

drug peddler *n* revendeur/euse de drogue.

drugstore ['drʌgstɔ:*] *n* (*US*) pharmacie-droguerie *f*, drugstore *m*.

drum [drʌm] *n* tambour *m*; (*for oil, petrol*) bidon *m* ♦ *vt*: **to ~ one's fingers on the table** pianoter *or* tambouriner sur la table; **~s** *npl* (*MUS*) batterie *f*.

drum up *vt* (*enthusiasm, support*) susciter, rallier.

drummer ['drʌmə*] *n* (joueur *m* de) tambour *m*.

drum roll *n* roulement *m* de tambour.

drumstick ['drʌmstɪk] *n* (*MUS*) baguette *f* de tambour; (*of chicken*) pilon *m*.

drunk [drʌŋk] *pp of* **drink** ♦ *a* ivre, soûl(e) ♦ *n* soûlard/e; homme/femme soûl(e); **to get ~** s'enivrer, se soûler.

drunkard ['drʌŋkəd] *n* ivrogne *m/f*.

drunken ['drʌŋkən] *a* ivre, soûl(e); (*habitual*) ivrogne, d'ivrogne; **~ driving** conduite *f* en état d'ivresse.

drunkenness ['drʌŋkənnɪs] *n* ivresse *f*; ivro-

gnerie *f*.

dry [draɪ] *a* sec(sèche); (*day*) sans pluie; (*humour*) pince-sans-rire; (*uninteresting*) aride, rébarbatif(ive) ♦ *vt* sécher; (*clothes*) faire sécher ♦ *vi* sécher; **on ~ land** sur la terre ferme; **to ~ one's hands/hair/eyes** se sécher les mains/les cheveux/les yeux.

dry up *vi* (*also fig: source of supply, imagination*) se tarir; (: *speaker*) sécher, rester sec.

dry-clean ['draɪ'kli:n] *vt* nettoyer à sec.

dry-cleaner ['draɪ'kli:nə*] *n* teinturier *m*.

dry-cleaner's ['draɪ'kli:nəz] *n* teinturerie *f*.

dry-cleaning ['draɪ'kli:nɪŋ] *n* nettoyage *m* à sec.

dry dock *n* (*NAUT*) cale sèche, bassin *m* de radoub.

dryer ['draɪə*] *n* séchoir *m*; (*US*: *spin-~*) essoreuse *f*.

dry goods *npl* (*COMM*) textiles *mpl*, mercerie *f*.

dry goods store *n* (*US*) magasin *m* de nouveautés.

dry ice *n* neige *f* carbonique.

dryness ['draɪnɪs] *n* sécheresse *f*.

dry rot *n* pourriture sèche (*du bois*).

dry run *n* (*fig*) essai *m*.

dry ski slope *n* piste (de ski) artificielle.

DSc *n abbr* (= *Doctor of Science*) titre universitaire.

DST *abbr* (*US*: = *Daylight Saving Time*) heure d'été.

DT *n abbr* (*COMPUT*) = **data transmission**.

DTI *n abbr* (*Brit*) = **Department of Trade and Industry**.

DT's *n abbr* (*col*: = *delirium tremens*) delirium tremens *m*.

dual ['djuəl] *a* double.

dual carriageway *n* (*Brit*) route *f* à quatre voies.

dual-control ['djuəlkən'trəʊl] *a* à doubles commandes.

dual nationality *n* double nationalité *f*.

dual-purpose ['djuəl'pə:pəs] *a* à double emploi.

dubbed [dʌbd] *a* (*CINEMA*) doublé(e); (*nicknamed*) surnommé(e).

dubious ['dju:bɪəs] *a* hésitant(e), incertain(e); (*reputation, company*) douteux(euse); **I'm very ~ about it** j'ai des doutes sur la question, je n'en suis pas sûr du tout.

Dublin ['dʌblɪn] *n* Dublin.

Dubliner ['dʌblɪnə*] *n* habitant/e de Dublin; originaire *m/f* de Dublin.

duchess ['dʌtʃɪs] *n* duchesse *f*.

duck [dʌk] *n* canard *m* ♦ *vi* se baisser vivement, baisser subitement la tête ♦ *vt* plonger dans l'eau.

duckling ['dʌklɪŋ] *n* caneton *m*.

duct [dʌkt] *n* conduite *f*, canalisation *f*; (*ANAT*) conduit *m*.

dud [dʌd] *n* (*shell*) obus non éclaté; (*object, tool*): **it's a ~** c'est de la camelote, ça ne marche pas ♦ *a* (*Brit*: *cheque*) sans provision; (: *note, coin*) faux(fausse).

due [dju:] *a* dû(due); (*expected*) attendu(e); (*fitting*) qui convient ♦ *n* dû *m* ♦ *ad*: ~ **north** droit vers le nord; **~s** *npl* (*for club, union*) cotisation *f*; (*in harbour*) droits *mpl* (de

port); **in ~ course** en temps utile *or* voulu; (*in the end*) finalement; **~ to** dû à; causé par; **the rent is ~ on the 30th** il faut payer le loyer le 30; **the train is ~ at 8** le train est attendu à 8h; **she is ~ back tomorrow** elle doit rentrer demain; **I am ~ 6 days' leave** j'ai droit à 6 jours de congé.
due date *n* date *f* d'échéance.
duel ['djuəl] *n* duel *m*.
duet [dju:'ɛt] *n* duo *m*.
duff [dʌf] *a* (*Brit col*) nullard(e), nul(le).
duffelbag, duffle bag ['dʌflbæg] *n* sac marin.
duffelcoat, duffle coat ['dʌflkəut] *n* duffelcoat *m*.
duffer ['dʌfə*] *n* (*col*) nullard/e.
dug [dʌg] *pt, pp of* dig.
duke [dju:k] *n* duc *m*.
dull [dʌl] *a* (*boring*) ennuyeux(euse); (*slow*) borné(e); (*lacklustre*) morne, terne; (*sound, pain*) sourd(e); (*weather, day*) gris(e), maussade; (*blade*) émoussé(e) ♦ *vt* (*pain, grief*) atténuer; (*mind, senses*) engourdir.
duly ['dju:lɪ] *ad* (*on time*) en temps voulu; (*as expected*) comme il se doit.
dumb [dʌm] *a* muet(te); (*stupid*) bête; **to be struck ~** (*fig*) rester abasourdi(e), être sidéré(e).
dumbbell ['dʌmbɛl] *n* (*SPORT*) haltère *m*.
dumbfounded [dʌm'faundɪd] *a* sidéré(e).
dummy ['dʌmɪ] *n* (*tailor's model*) mannequin *m*; (*SPORT*) feinte *f*; (*Brit: for baby*) tétine *f* ♦ *a* faux(fausse), factice.
dummy run *n* essai *m*.
dump [dʌmp] *n* tas *m* d'ordures; (*place*) décharge (publique); (*MIL*) dépôt *m*; (*COMPUT*) listage *m* (de la mémoire) ♦ *vt* (*put down*) déposer; déverser; (*get rid of*) se débarrasser de; (*COMPUT*) lister; (*COMM: goods*) vendre à perte (*sur le marché extérieur*); **to be (down) in the ~s** (*col*) avoir le cafard, broyer du noir.
dumping ['dʌmpɪŋ] *n* (*ECON*) dumping *m*; (*of rubbish*): **"no ~"** "décharge interdite".
dumpling ['dʌmplɪŋ] *n* boulette *f* (de pâte).
dumpy ['dʌmpɪ] *a* courtaud(e), boulot(te).
dunce [dʌns] *n* âne *m*, cancre *m*.
dune [dju:n] *n* dune *f*.
dung [dʌŋ] *n* fumier *m*.
dungarees [dʌŋgə'ri:z] *npl* bleu(s) *m(pl)*; (*for child, woman*) salopette *f*.
dungeon ['dʌndʒən] *n* cachot *m*.
dunk [dʌŋk] *vt* tremper.
Dunkirk [dʌn'kə:k] *n* Dunkerque.
duo ['dju:əu] *n* (*gen, MUS*) duo *m*.
duodenal [dju:əu'di:nl] *a* duodénal(e); **~ ulcer** ulcère *m* du duodénum.
dupe [dju:p] *n* dupe *f* ♦ *vt* duper, tromper.
duplex ['dju:plɛks] *n* (*US: also:* **~ apartment**) duplex *m*.
duplicate *n* ['dju:plɪkət] double *m*, copie exacte; (*copy of letter etc*) duplicata *m* ♦ *a* (*copy*) en double ♦ *vt* ['dju:plɪkeɪt] faire un double de; (*on machine*) polycopier; **in ~** en deux exemplaires, en double; **~ key** double *m* de la (*or* d'une) clé.
duplicating machine ['dju:plɪkeɪtɪŋ-], **duplicator** ['dju:plɪkeɪtə*] *n* duplicateur *m*.
duplicity [dju:'plɪsɪtɪ] *n* duplicité *f*, fausseté *f*.

Dur *abbr* (*Brit*) = Durham.
durability [djuərə'bɪlɪtɪ] *n* solidité *f*; durabilité *f*.
durable ['djuərəbl] *a* durable; (*clothes, metal*) résistant(e), solide.
duration [djuə'reɪʃən] *n* durée *f*.
duress [djuə'rɛs] *n*: **under ~** sous la contrainte.
Durex ['djuərɛks] *n* ® (*Brit*) préservatif (masculin).
during ['djuərɪŋ] *prep* pendant, au cours de.
dusk [dʌsk] *n* crépuscule *m*.
dusky ['dʌskɪ] *a* sombre.
dust [dʌst] *n* poussière *f* ♦ *vt* (*furniture*) essuyer, épousseter; (*cake etc*): **to ~ with** saupoudrer de.
dust off *vt* (*also fig*) dépoussiérer.
dustbin ['dʌstbɪn] *n* (*Brit*) poubelle *f*.
duster ['dʌstə*] *n* chiffon *m*.
dust jacket *n* jaquette *f*.
dustman ['dʌstmən] *n* (*Brit*) boueux *m*, éboueur *m*.
dustpan ['dʌstpæn] *n* pelle *f* à poussière.
dusty ['dʌstɪ] *a* poussiéreux(euse).
Dutch [dʌtʃ] *a* hollandais(e), néerlandais(e) ♦ *n* (*LING*) hollandais *m*, néerlandais *m* ♦ *ad*: **to go ~** *or* **d~** partager les frais; **the ~** *npl* les Hollandais, les Néerlandais.
Dutch auction *n* enchères *fpl* à la baisse.
Dutchman ['dʌtʃmən], **Dutchwoman** ['dʌtʃwumən] *n* Hollandais/e.
dutiable ['dju:tɪəbl] *a* taxable; soumis(e) à des droits de douane.
dutiful ['dju:tɪful] *a* (*child*) respectueux(euse); (*husband, wife*) plein(e) d'égards, prévenant(e); (*employee*) consciencieux(euse).
duty ['dju:tɪ] *n* devoir *m*; (*tax*) droit *m*, taxe *f*; **duties** *npl* fonctions *fpl*; **to make it one's ~ to do sth** se faire un devoir de faire qch; **to pay ~ on sth** payer un droit *or* une taxe sur qch; **on ~** de service; (*at night etc*) de garde; **off ~** libre, pas de service *or* de garde.
duty-free ['dju:tɪ'fri:] *a* exempté(e) de douane, hors-taxe; **~ shop** boutique *f* hors-taxe.
duty officer *n* (*MIL etc*) officier *m* de permanence.
duvet ['du:veɪ] *n* (*Brit*) couette *f*.
DV *abbr* (= *Deo volente*) si Dieu le veut.
DVLC *n abbr* (*Brit*: = *Driver and Vehicle Licensing Office*) service des immatriculations et des permis de conduire.
DVM *n abbr* (*US*: = *Doctor of Veterinary Medicine*) titre universitaire.
dwarf [dwɔ:f] *n* nain/e ♦ *vt* écraser.
dwell, *pt, pp* **dwelt** [dwɛl, dwɛlt] *vi* demeurer.
dwell on *vt fus* s'étendre sur.
dweller ['dwɛlə*] *n* habitant/e.
dwelling ['dwɛlɪŋ] *n* habitation *f*, demeure *f*.
dwindle ['dwɪndl] *vi* diminuer, décroître.
dwindling ['dwɪndlɪŋ] *a* décroissant(e), en diminution.
dye [daɪ] *n* teinture *f* ♦ *vt* teindre; **hair ~** teinture pour les cheveux.
dyestuffs ['daɪstʌfs] *npl* colorants *mpl*.
dying ['daɪɪŋ] *a* mourant(e), agonisant(e).
dyke [daɪk] *n* (*embankment*) digue *f*.
dynamic [daɪ'næmɪk] *a* dynamique.

dynamics [daɪ'næmɪks] n or npl dynamique f.
dynamite ['daɪnəmaɪt] n dynamite f ♦ vt dynamiter, faire sauter à la dynamite.
dynamo ['daɪnəməu] n dynamo f.
dynasty ['dɪnəstɪ] n dynastie f.
dysentery ['dɪsntrɪ] n dysenterie f.
dyslexia [dɪs'lɛksɪə] n dyslexie f.
dyslexic [dɪs'lɛksɪk] a, n dyslexique m/f.
dyspepsia [dɪs'pɛpsɪə] n dyspepsie f.
dystrophy ['dɪstrəfɪ] n dystrophie f; **muscular** ~ dystrophie musculaire.

E

E, e [i:] n (letter) E, e m; (MUS): **E** mi m; **E for Edward**, (US) **E for Easy** E comme Eugène.
E abbr (= east) E.
E111 n abbr (also: **form** ~) formulaire m E111.
ea. abbr = **each**.
E.A. n abbr (US: = educational age) niveau scolaire.
each [i:tʃ] a chaque ♦ pronoun chacun(e); ~ **one** chacun(e); ~ **other** se (or nous etc); **they hate** ~ **other** ils se détestent (mutuellement); **you are jealous of** ~ **other** vous êtes jaloux l'un de l'autre; ~ **day** chaque jour, tous les jours; **they have 2 books** ~ ils ont 2 livres chacun; **they cost £5** ~ ils coûtent 5 livres (la) pièce; ~ **of us** chacun(e) de nous.
eager ['i:gə*] a impatient(e); avide; ardent(e), passionné(e); (keen: pupil) plein(e) d'enthousiasme, qui se passionne pour les études; **to be** ~ **to do sth** être impatient de faire qch, brûler de faire qch; désirer vivement faire qch; **to be** ~ **for** désirer vivement, être avide de.
eagle ['i:gl] n aigle m.
E and OE abbr = **errors and omissions excepted**.
ear [ɪə*] n oreille f; (of corn) épi m; **up to one's** ~**s in debt** endetté(e) jusqu'au cou.
earache ['ɪəreɪk] n douleurs fpl aux oreilles.
eardrum ['ɪədrʌm] n tympan m.
earl [ə:l] n comte m.
earlier ['ə:lɪə*] a (date etc) plus rapproché(e); (edition etc) plus ancien(ne), antérieur(e) ♦ ad plus tôt.
early ['ə:lɪ] ad tôt, de bonne heure; (ahead of time) en avance ♦ a précoce; qui se manifeste (or se fait) tôt or de bonne heure; (Christians, settlers) premier(ière); **have an** ~ **night/start** couchez-vous/partez tôt or de bonne heure; **take the** ~ **train** prenez le premier train; **in the** ~ or ~ **in the spring/ 19th century** au début or commencement du printemps/19ème siècle; **you're** ~! tu es en avance!; ~ **in the morning** tôt le matin; **she's in her** ~ **forties** elle a un peu plus de quarante ans or de la quarantaine; **at your**

earliest convenience (COMM) dans les meilleurs délais.
early retirement n retraite anticipée.
early warning system n système m de première alerte.
earmark ['ɪəmɑ:k] vt: **to** ~ **sth for** réserver or destiner qch à.
earn [ə:n] vt gagner; (COMM: yield) rapporter; **to** ~ **one's living** gagner sa vie; **this** ~**ed him much praise, he** ~**ed much praise for this** ceci lui a valu de nombreux éloges; **he's** ~**ed his rest/reward** il mérite or a bien mérité or a bien gagné son repos/sa récompense.
earned income n revenu m du travail.
earnest ['ə:nɪst] a sérieux(euse) ♦ n (also: ~ **money**) acompte m, arrhes fpl; **in** ~ ad sérieusement, pour de bon.
earnings ['ə:nɪŋz] npl salaire m; gains mpl; (of company etc) profits mpl, bénéfices mpl.
ear nose and throat specialist n oto-rhino-laryngologiste m/f.
earphones ['ɪəfəunz] npl écouteurs mpl.
earplugs ['ɪəplʌgz] npl boules fpl Quiès ®; (to keep out water) protège-tympans mpl.
earring ['ɪərɪŋ] n boucle f d'oreille.
earshot ['ɪəʃɔt] n: **out of/within** ~ hors de portée/à portée de la voix.
earth [ə:θ] n (gen, also Brit ELEC) terre f; (of fox etc) terrier m ♦ vt (Brit ELEC) relier à la terre.
earthenware ['ə:θnwɛə*] n poterie f; faïence f ♦ a de or en faïence.
earthly ['ə:θlɪ] a terrestre; ~ **paradise** paradis m terrestre; **there is no** ~ **reason to think** ... il n'y a absolument aucune raison or pas la moindre raison de penser ....
earthquake ['ə:θkweɪk] n tremblement m de terre, séisme m.
earth tremor n secousse f sismique.
earthworks ['ə:θwə:ks] npl travaux mpl de terrassement.
earthworm ['ə:θwə:m] n ver m de terre.
earthy ['ə:θɪ] a (fig) terre à terre inv; truculent(e).
earwax ['ɪəwæks] n cérumen m.
earwig ['ɪəwɪg] n perce-oreille m.
ease [i:z] n facilité f, aisance f ♦ vt (soothe) calmer; (loosen) relâcher, détendre; (help pass): **to** ~ **sth in/out** faire pénétrer/sortir qch délicatement or avec douceur; faciliter la pénétration/la sortie de qch ♦ vi (situation) se détendre; **with** ~ sans difficulté, aisément; **life of** ~ vie oisive; **at** ~ à l'aise; (MIL) au repos.
ease off, ease up vi diminuer; (slow down) ralentir; (relax) se détendre.
easel ['i:zl] n chevalet m.
easily ['i:zɪlɪ] ad facilement.
easiness ['i:sɪnɪs] n facilité f; (of manner) aisance f; nonchalance f.
east [i:st] n est m ♦ a d'est ♦ ad à l'est, vers l'est; **the E~** l'Orient m; (POL) les pays mpl de l'Est.
Easter ['i:stə*] n Pâques fpl ♦ a (holidays) de Pâques, pascal(e).
Easter egg n œuf m de Pâques.
Easter Island n île f de Pâques.
easterly ['i:stəlɪ] a d'est.

Easter Monday *n* le lundi de Pâques.
eastern ['iːstən] *a* de l'est, oriental(e); **E~ Europe** l'Europe de l'Est; **the E~ bloc** (*POL*) les pays *mpl* de l'est.
Easter Sunday *n* le dimanche de Pâques.
East Germany *n* Allemagne *f* de l'Est.
eastward(s) ['iːstwəd(z)] *ad* vers l'est, à l'est.
easy ['iːzɪ] *a* facile; (*manner*) aisé(e) ♦ *ad*: **to take it** *or* **things ~** ne pas se fatiguer; (*not worry*) ne pas (trop) s'en faire; **payment on ~ terms** (*COMM*) facilités *fpl* de paiement; **that's easier said than done** c'est plus facile à dire qu'à faire, c'est vite dit; **I'm ~** (*col*) ça m'est égal.
easy chair *n* fauteuil *m*.
easy-going ['iːzɪ'gəuɪŋ] *a* accommodant(e), facile à vivre.
eat, *pt* **ate**, *pp* **eaten** [iːt, eɪt, 'iːtn] *vt*, *vi* manger.
　eat away *vt* (*subj: sea*) saper, éroder; (*: acid*) ronger, corroder.
　eat away at , **eat into** *vt fus* ronger, attaquer.
　eat out *vi* manger au restaurant.
　eat up *vt* (*food*) finir (de manger); **it ~s up electricity** ça bouffe du courant, ça consomme beaucoup d'électricité.
eatable ['iːtəbl] *a* mangeable; (*safe to eat*) comestible.
eau de Cologne ['əudəkə'ləun] *n* eau *f* de Cologne.
eaves [iːvz] *npl* avant-toit *m*.
eavesdrop ['iːvzdrɔp] *vi*: **to ~ (on)** écouter de façon indiscrète.
ebb [eb] *n* reflux *m* ♦ *vi* refluer; (*fig: also:* ~ **away**) décliner; **the ~ and flow** le flux et le reflux; **to be at a low ~** (*fig*) être bien bas(se), ne pas aller bien fort.
ebb tide *n* marée descendante, reflux *m*.
ebony ['ebənɪ] *n* ébène *f*.
ebullient [ɪ'bʌlɪənt] *a* exubérant(e).
EC *n abbr* (= *European Community*) CE *f* (= *Communauté européenne*).
eccentric [ɪk'sɛntrɪk] *a*, *n* excentrique (*m/f*).
ecclesiastic(al) [ɪkliːzɪ'æstɪk(l)] *a* ecclésiastique.
ECG *n abbr* = **electrocardiogram**.
ECGD *n abbr* (= *Export Credits Guarantee Department*) service de garantie financière à l'exportation.
echo, **~es** ['ɛkəu] *n* écho *m* ♦ *vt* répéter; faire chorus avec ♦ *vi* résonner; faire écho.
éclair ['eɪkleə*] *n* éclair *m* (*CULIN*).
eclipse [ɪ'klɪps] *n* éclipse *f* ♦ *vt* éclipser.
ECM *n abbr* (*US*) = *European Common Market*.
ecologist [ɪ'kɔlədʒɪst] *n* écologiste *m/f*.
ecology [ɪ'kɔlədʒɪ] *n* écologie *f*.
economic [iːkə'nɔmɪk] *a* économique; (*profitable*) rentable.
economical [iːkə'nɔmɪkl] *a* économique; (*person*) économe.
economically [iːkə'nɔmɪklɪ] *ad* économiquement.
economics [iːkə'nɔmɪks] *n* économie *f* politique ♦ *npl* côté *m* or aspect *m* économique.
economist [ɪ'kɔnəmɪst] *n* économiste *m/f*.
economize [ɪ'kɔnəmaɪz] *vi* économiser, faire

des économies.
economy [ɪ'kɔnəmɪ] *n* économie *f*; **economies of scale** économies d'échelle.
economy class *n* (*AVIAT etc*) classe *f* touriste.
economy size *n* taille *f* économique.
ECSC *n abbr* (= *European Coal & Steel Community*) CECA *f* (= *Communauté européenne du charbon et de l'acier*).
ecstasy ['ɛkstəsɪ] *n* extase *f*; **to go into ecstasies over** s'extasier sur.
ecstatic [ɛks'tætɪk] *a* extatique, en extase.
ECT *n abbr* = **electroconvulsive therapy**.
ECU *n abbr* (= *European Currency Unit*) ECU *m*.
Ecuador ['ɛkwədɔ:*] *n* Équateur *m*.
ecumenical [iːkju'mɛnɪkl] *a* œcuménique.
eczema ['ɛksɪmə] *n* eczéma *m*.
eddy ['ɛdɪ] *n* tourbillon *m*.
edge [ɛdʒ] *n* bord *m*; (*of knife etc*) tranchant *m*, fil *m* ♦ *vt* border ♦ *vi*: **to ~ forward** avancer petit à petit; **to ~ away from** s'éloigner furtivement de; **on ~** (*fig*) = **edgy**; **to have the ~ on** (*fig*) l'emporter (de justesse) sur, être légèrement meilleur que.
edgeways ['ɛdʒweɪz] *ad* latéralement; **he couldn't get a word in ~** il ne pouvait pas placer un mot.
edging ['ɛdʒɪŋ] *n* bordure *f*.
edgy ['ɛdʒɪ] *a* crispé(e), tendu(e).
edible ['ɛdɪbl] *a* comestible; (*meal*) mangeable.
edict ['iːdɪkt] *n* décret *m*.
edifice ['ɛdɪfɪs] *n* édifice *m*.
edifying ['ɛdɪfaɪɪŋ] *a* édifiant(e).
Edinburgh ['ɛdɪnbərə] *n* Edimbourg.
edit ['ɛdɪt] *vt* éditer; (*magazine*) diriger; (*newspaper*) être le rédacteur *or* la rédactrice en chef de.
edition [ɪ'dɪʃən] *n* édition *f*.
editor ['ɛdɪtə*] *n* (*in newspaper*) rédacteur/trice; rédacteur/trice en chef; (*of sb's work*) éditeur/trice; (*also:* **film ~**) monteur/euse.
editorial [ɛdɪ'tɔːrɪəl] *a* de la rédaction, éditorial(e) ♦ *n* éditorial *m*; **the ~ staff** la rédaction.
EDP *n abbr* = **electronic data processing**.
EDT *n abbr* (*US*: = *Eastern Daylight Time*) heure d'été de New York.
educate ['ɛdjukeɪt] *vt* instruire; éduquer; **~d at ...** qui a fait ses études à ....
education [ɛdju'keɪʃən] *n* éducation *f*; (*schooling*) enseignement *m*, instruction *f*; (*at university: subject etc*) pédagogie *f*; **primary** *or* (*US*) **elementary/secondary ~** instruction *f* primaire/secondaire.
educational [ɛdju'keɪʃənl] *a* pédagogique; scolaire; (*useful*) instructif(ive); (*games, toys*) éducatif(ive); **~ technology** technologie *f* de l'enseignement.
Edwardian [ɛd'wɔːdɪən] *a* de l'époque du roi Édouard VII, des années 1900.
EE *abbr* = **electrical engineer**.
EEC *n abbr* (= *European Economic Community*) C.E.E. *f* (= *Communauté économique européenne*).
EEG *n abbr* = **electroencephalogram**.
eel [iːl] *n* anguille *f*.
EENT *n abbr* (*US MED*) = *eye, ear, nose and*

throat.

EEOC *n abbr* (*US*) = **Equal Employment Opportunity Commission**.

eerie ['ɪərɪ] *a* inquiétant(e), spectral(e), surnaturel(le).

EET *abbr* (= *Eastern European Time*) HEO (= *heure d'Europe orientale*).

effect [ɪ'fɛkt] *n* effet *m* ♦ *vt* effectuer; **to take ~** (*LAW*) entrer en vigueur, prendre effet; (*drug*) agir, faire son effet; **to put into ~** (*plan*) mettre en application *or* à exécution; **to have an ~ on sb/sth** avoir *or* produire un effet sur qn/qch; **in ~** en fait; **his letter is to the ~ that** ... sa lettre nous apprend que ....

effective [ɪ'fɛktɪv] *a* efficace; (*striking: display, outfit*) frappant(e), qui produit *or* fait de l'effet; **to become ~** (*LAW*) entrer en vigueur, prendre effet; **~ date** date *f* d'effet *or* d'entrée en vigueur.

effectively [ɪ'fɛktɪvlɪ] *ad* efficacement; (*strikingly*) d'une manière frappante, avec beaucoup d'effet; (*in reality*) effectivement, en fait.

effectiveness [ɪ'fɛktɪvnɪs] *n* efficacité *f*.

effects [ɪ'fɛkts] *npl* (*THEATRE*) effets *mpl*; (*property*) effets, affaires *fpl*.

effeminate [ɪ'fɛmɪnɪt] *a* efféminé(e).

effervescent [ɛfə'vɛsnt] *a* effervescent(e).

efficacy ['ɛfɪkəsɪ] *n* efficacité *f*.

efficiency [ɪ'fɪʃənsɪ] *n* efficacité *f*; rendement *m*.

efficiency apartment *n* (*US*) studio *m* avec coin cuisine.

efficient [ɪ'fɪʃənt] *a* efficace; (*machine, car*) d'un bon rendement.

efficiently [ɪ'fɪʃəntlɪ] *ad* efficacement.

effigy ['ɛfɪdʒɪ] *n* effigie *f*.

effluent ['ɛfluənt] *n* effluent *m*.

effort ['ɛfət] *n* effort *m*; **to make an ~ to do sth** faire *or* fournir un effort pour faire qch.

effortless ['ɛfətlɪs] *a* sans effort, aisé(e).

effrontery [ɪ'frʌntərɪ] *n* effronterie *f*.

effusive [ɪ'fju:sɪv] *a* (*person*) expansif(ive); (*welcome*) chaleureux(euse).

EFL *n abbr* (*SCOL*) = *English as a foreign language*.

EFTA ['ɛftə] *n abbr* (= *European Free Trade Association*) AELE *f* (= *Association européenne de libre échange*).

e.g. *ad abbr* (= *exempli gratia*) par exemple, p. ex.

egalitarian [ɪgælɪ'tɛərɪən] *a* égalitaire.

egg [ɛg] *n* œuf *m*.

   egg on *vt* pousser.

eggcup ['ɛgkʌp] *n* coquetier *m*.

eggplant ['ɛgplɑ:nt] *n* aubergine *f*.

eggshell ['ɛgʃɛl] *n* coquille *f* d'œuf ♦ *a* (*colour*) blanc cassé *inv*.

egg white *n* blanc *m* d'œuf.

egg yolk *n* jaune *m* d'œuf.

ego ['i:gəu] *n* moi *m*.

egoism ['ɛgəuɪzəm] *n* égoïsme *m*.

egoist ['ɛgəuɪst] *n* égoïste *m/f*.

egotism ['ɛgəutɪzəm] *n* égotisme *m*.

egotist ['ɛgəutɪst] *n* égocentrique *m/f*.

Egypt ['i:dʒɪpt] *n* Egypte *f*.

Egyptian [ɪ'dʒɪpʃən] *a* égyptien(ne) ♦ *n* Egyptien/ne.

eiderdown ['aɪdədaun] *n* édredon *m*.

eight [eɪt] *num* huit.

eighteen [eɪ'ti:n] *num* dix-huit.

eighth [eɪtθ] *num* huitième.

eighty ['eɪtɪ] *num* quatre-vingt(s).

Eire ['ɛərə] *n* République *f* d'Irlande.

EIS *n abbr* (= *Educational Institute of Scotland*) syndicat enseignant.

either ['aɪðə*] *a* l'un ou l'autre; (*both, each*) chaque; **on ~ side** de chaque côté ♦ *pronoun*: **~ (of them)** l'un ou l'autre; **I don't like ~** je n'aime ni l'un ni l'autre ♦ *ad* non plus; **no, I don't ~** moi non plus ♦ *cj*: **~ good or bad** ou bon ou mauvais, soit bon soit mauvais; **I haven't seen ~ one or the other** je n'ai vu ni l'un ni l'autre.

ejaculation [ɪdʒækju'leɪʃən] *n* (*PHYSIOL*) éjaculation *f*.

eject [ɪ'dʒɛkt] *vt* expulser; éjecter ♦ *vi* (*pilot*) s'éjecter.

ejector seat [ɪ'dʒɛktə-] *n* siège *m* éjectable.

eke [i:k]: **to ~ out** *vt* faire durer; augmenter.

EKG *n abbr* (*US*) = **electrocardiogram**.

el [ɛl] *n abbr* (*US col*) = **elevated railroad**.

elaborate *a* [ɪ'læbərɪt] compliqué(e), recherché(e), minutieux(euse) ♦ *vb* [ɪ'læbəreɪt] *vt* élaborer ♦ *vi* entrer dans les détails.

elapse [ɪ'læps] *vi* s'écouler, passer.

elastic [ɪ'læstɪk] *a, n* élastique (*m*).

elastic band *n* (*Brit*) élastique *m*.

elasticity [ɪlæs'tɪsɪtɪ] *n* élasticité *f*.

elated [ɪ'leɪtɪd] *a* transporté(e) de joie.

elation [ɪ'leɪʃən] *n* (grande) joie, allégresse *f*.

elbow ['ɛlbəu] *n* coude *m* ♦ *vt*: **to ~ one's way through the crowd** se frayer un passage à travers la foule (en jouant des coudes).

elder ['ɛldə*] *a* aîné(e) ♦ *n* (*tree*) sureau *m*; **one's ~s** ses aînés.

elderly ['ɛldəlɪ] *a* âgé(e) ♦ *npl*: **the ~** les personnes âgées.

eldest ['ɛldɪst] *a, n*: **the ~ (child)** l'aîné(e) (des enfants).

elect [ɪ'lɛkt] *vt* élire; (*choose*): **to ~ to do** choisir de faire ♦ *a*: **the president ~** le président désigné.

election [ɪ'lɛkʃən] *n* élection *f*; **to hold an ~** procéder à une élection.

election campaign *n* campagne électorale.

electioneering [ɪlɛkʃə'nɪərɪŋ] *n* propagande électorale, manœuvres électorales.

elector [ɪ'lɛktə*] *n* électeur/trice.

electoral [ɪ'lɛktərəl] *a* électoral(e).

electoral college *n* collège électoral.

electoral roll *n* (*Brit*) liste électorale.

electorate [ɪ'lɛktərɪt] *n* électorat *m*.

electric [ɪ'lɛktrɪk] *a* électrique.

electrical [ɪ'lɛktrɪkl] *a* électrique.

electrical engineer *n* ingénieur électricien.

electrical failure *n* panne d'électricité *or* de courant.

electric blanket *n* couverture chauffante.

electric chair *n* chaise *f* électrique.

electric cooker *n* cuisinière *f* électrique.

electric current *n* courant *m* électrique.

electric fire *n* (*Brit*) radiateur *m* électrique.

electrician [ɪlɛk'trɪʃən] *n* électricien *m*.

electricity [ɪlɛk'trɪsɪtɪ] *n* électricité *f*; **to switch on/off the ~** rétablir/couper le courant.

electricity board n (Brit) ≈ agence régionale de l'E.D.F.

electric light n lumière f électrique.

electric shock n choc m or décharge f électrique.

electrify [ɪ'lɛktrɪfaɪ] vt (RAIL) électrifier; (audience) électriser.

electro... [ɪ'lɛktrəu] prefix électro....

electrocardiogram (ECG) [ɪ'lɛktrə'kɑːdɪəgræm] n électrocardiogramme m (ECG).

electro-convulsive therapy [ɪ'lɛktrəkən'vʌlsɪv-] n électrochocs mpl.

electrocute [ɪ'lɛktrəkjuːt] vt électrocuter.

electrode [ɪ'lɛktrəud] n électrode f.

electroencephalogram (EEG) [ɪ'lɛktrəuɛn'sɛfələgræm] n électroencéphalogramme m (EEG).

electrolysis [ɪlɛk'trɒlɪsɪs] n électrolyse f.

electromagnetic [ɪ'lɛktrəmæg'nɛtɪk] a électromagnétique.

electron [ɪ'lɛktrɒn] n électron m.

electronic [ɪlɛk'trɒnɪk] a électronique.

electronic data processing (EDP) n traitement m électronique des données.

electronic mail n courrier m électronique.

electronics [ɪlɛk'trɒnɪks] n électronique f.

electron microscope n microscope m électronique.

electroplated [ɪ'lɛktrə'pleɪtɪd] a plaqué(e) or doré(e) or argenté(e) par galvanoplastie.

electrotherapy [ɪ'lɛktrə'θɛrəpɪ] n électrothérapie f.

elegance ['ɛlɪgəns] n élégance f.

elegant ['ɛlɪgənt] a élégant(e).

element ['ɛlɪmənt] n (gen) élément m; (of heater, kettle etc) résistance f.

elementary [ɛlɪ'mɛntərɪ] a élémentaire; (school, education) primaire.

elephant ['ɛlɪfənt] n éléphant m.

elevate ['ɛlɪveɪt] vt élever.

elevated railroad n (US) métro aérien.

elevation [ɛlɪ'veɪʃən] n élévation f; (height) altitude f.

elevator ['ɛlɪveɪtə*] n élévateur m, montecharge m inv; (US: lift) ascenseur m.

eleven [ɪ'lɛvn] num onze.

elevenses [ɪ'lɛvnzɪz] npl (Brit) ≈ pause-café f.

eleventh [ɪ'lɛvnθ] a onzième; **at the ~ hour** (fig) à la dernière minute.

elf, pl **elves** [ɛlf, ɛlvz] n lutin m.

elicit [ɪ'lɪsɪt] vt: **to ~ (from)** obtenir (de); tirer (de).

eligible ['ɛlɪdʒəbl] a éligible; (for membership) admissible; **~ for a pension** ayant droit à la retraite.

eliminate [ɪ'lɪmɪneɪt] vt éliminer.

elimination [ɪlɪmɪ'neɪʃən] n élimination f; **by process of ~** par élimination.

élite [eɪ'liːt] n élite f.

élitist [eɪ'liːtɪst] a (pej) élitiste.

elixir [ɪ'lɪksə*] n élixir m.

Elizabethan [ɪlɪzə'biːθən] a élisabéthain(e).

ellipse ['ɪlɪps] n ellipse f.

elliptical [ɪ'lɪptɪkl] a elliptique.

elm [ɛlm] n orme m.

elocution [ɛlə'kjuːʃən] n élocution f.

elongated ['iːlɒŋgeɪtɪd] a étiré(e), allongé(e).

elope [ɪ'ləup] vi (lovers) s'enfuir (ensemble).

elopement [ɪ'ləupmənt] n fugue amoureuse.

eloquence ['ɛləkwəns] n éloquence f.

eloquent ['ɛləkwənt] a éloquent(e).

else [ɛls] ad d'autre; **something ~** quelque chose d'autre, autre chose; **somewhere ~** ailleurs, autre part; **everywhere ~** partout ailleurs; **everyone ~** tous les autres; **nothing ~** rien d'autre; **is there anything ~ I can do?** est-ce que je peux faire quelque chose d'autre?; **where ~?** à quel autre endroit?; **little ~** pas grand-chose d'autre.

elsewhere [ɛls'wɛə*] ad ailleurs, autre part.

ELT n abbr (SCOL) = English Language Teaching.

elucidate [ɪ'luːsɪdeɪt] vt élucider.

elude [ɪ'luːd] vt échapper à; (question) éluder.

elusive [ɪ'luːsɪv] a insaisissable; (answer) évasif(ive).

elves [ɛlvz] npl of **elf**.

emaciated [ɪ'meɪsɪeɪtɪd] a émacié(e), décharné(e).

emanate ['ɛməneɪt] vi: **to ~ from** émaner de.

emancipate [ɪ'mænsɪpeɪt] vt émanciper.

emancipation [ɪmænsɪ'peɪʃən] n émancipation f.

emasculate [ɪ'mæskjuleɪt] vt émasculer.

embalm [ɪm'bɑːm] vt embaumer.

embankment [ɪm'bæŋkmənt] n (of road, railway) remblai m, talus m; (riverside) berge f, quai m; (dyke) digue f.

embargo, ~es [ɪm'bɑːgəu] n (COMM, NAUT) embargo m ♦ vt frapper d'embargo, mettre l'embargo sur; **to put an ~ on sth** mettre l'embargo sur qch.

embark [ɪm'bɑːk] vi: **to ~ (on)** (s')embarquer (à bord de or sur) ♦ vt embarquer; **to ~ on** (journey etc) commencer, entreprendre; (fig) se lancer or s'embarquer dans.

embarkation [ɛmbɑː'keɪʃən] n embarquement m.

embarkation card n carte f d'embarquement.

embarrass [ɪm'bærəs] vt embarrasser, gêner; **to be ~ed** être gêné(e).

embarrassing [ɪm'bærəsɪŋ] a gênant(e), embarrassant(e).

embarrassment [ɪm'bærəsmənt] n embarras m, gêne f.

embassy ['ɛmbəsɪ] n ambassade f; **the French E~** l'ambassade de France.

embed [ɪm'bɛd] vt enfoncer; sceller.

embellish [ɪm'bɛlɪʃ] vt embellir; enjoliver.

embers ['ɛmbəz] npl braise f.

embezzle [ɪm'bɛzl] vt détourner.

embezzlement [ɪm'bɛzlmənt] n détournement m (de fonds).

embezzler [ɪm'bɛzlə*] n escroc m.

embitter [ɪm'bɪtə*] vt aigrir; envenimer.

emblem ['ɛmbləm] n emblème m.

embodiment [ɪm'bɒdɪmənt] n personification f, incarnation f.

embody [ɪm'bɒdɪ] vt (features) réunir, comprendre; (ideas) formuler, exprimer.

embolden [ɪm'bəuldn] vt enhardir.

embolism ['ɛmbəlɪzəm] n embolie f.

embossed [ɪm'bɒst] a repoussé(e); gaufré(e); **~ with** où figure(nt) en relief.

embrace [ɪm'breɪs] vt embrasser, étreindre; (include) embrasser, couvrir, comprendre ♦

vi s'embrasser, s'étreindre ♦ *n* étreinte *f*.

embroider [ɪmˈbrɔɪdə*] *vt* broder; (*fig: story*) enjoliver.

embroidery [ɪmˈbrɔɪdərɪ] *n* broderie *f*.

embroil [ɪmˈbrɔɪl] *vt*: **to become ~ed (in sth)** se retrouver mêlé(e) (à qch), se laisser entraîner (dans qch).

embryo [ˈɛmbrɪəu] *n* (*also fig*) embryon *m*.

emend [ɪˈmɛnd] *vt* (*text*) corriger.

emerald [ˈɛmərəld] *n* émeraude *f*.

emerge [ɪˈmɜːdʒ] *vi* apparaître, surgir; **it ~s that** (*Brit*) il ressort que.

emergence [ɪˈmɜːdʒəns] *n* apparition *f*; (*of nation*) naissance *f*.

emergency [ɪˈmɜːdʒənsɪ] *n* urgence *f*; **in an ~** en cas d'urgence; **state of ~** état *m* d'urgence.

emergency exit *n* sortie *f* de secours.

emergency landing *n* atterrissage forcé.

emergency lane *n* (*US AUT*) accotement stabilisé.

emergency road service *n* (*US*) service *m* de dépannage.

emergency service *n* service *m* d'urgence.

emergency stop *n* (*Brit AUT*) arrêt *m* d'urgence.

emergent [ɪˈmɜːdʒənt] *a*: **~ nation** pays *m* en voie de développement.

emery board [ˈɛmərɪ-] *n* lime *f* à ongles (*en carton émerisé*).

emery paper [ˈɛmərɪ-] *n* papier *m* (d')émeri.

emetic [ɪˈmɛtɪk] *n* vomitif *m*, émétique *m*.

emigrant [ˈɛmɪgrənt] *n* émigrant/e.

emigrate [ˈɛmɪgreɪt] *vi* émigrer.

emigration [ɛmɪˈgreɪʃən] *n* émigration *f*.

émigré [ˈɛmɪgreɪ] *n* émigré/e.

eminence [ˈɛmɪnəns] *n* éminence *f*.

eminent [ˈɛmɪnənt] *a* éminent(e).

eminently [ˈɛmɪnəntlɪ] *ad* éminemment, admirablement.

emirate [ˈɛmɪrɪt] *n* émirat *m*.

emission [ɪˈmɪʃən] *n* émission *f*.

emit [ɪˈmɪt] *vt* émettre.

emolument [ɪˈmɔljumənt] *n* (*often pl: formal*) émoluments *mpl*; (*fee*) honoraires *mpl*; (*salary*) traitement *m*.

emotion [ɪˈməuʃən] *n* sentiment *m*; (*as opposed to reason*) émotion *f*, sentiments.

emotional [ɪˈməuʃənl] *a* (*person*) émotif(ive), très sensible; (*scene*) émouvant(e); (*tone, speech*) qui fait appel aux sentiments.

emotionally [ɪˈməuʃnəlɪ] *ad* (*behave*) émotivement; (*be involved*) affectivement; (*speak*) avec émotion; **~ disturbed** qui souffre de troubles de l'affectivité.

emotive [ɪˈməutɪv] *a* émotif(ive); **~ power** capacité *f* d'émouvoir or de toucher.

empathy [ˈɛmpəθɪ] *n* communion *f* d'idées or de sentiments; empathie *f*; **to feel ~ with sb** se mettre à la place de qn.

emperor [ˈɛmpərə*] *n* empereur *m*.

emphasis, *pl* **-ases** [ˈɛmfəsɪs, -siːz] *n* accent *m*; force *f*, insistance *f*; **to lay** or **place ~ on sth** (*fig*) mettre l'accent sur, insister sur; **the ~ is on reading** la lecture tient une place primordiale, on accorde une importance particulière à la lecture.

emphasize [ˈɛmfəsaɪz] *vt* (*syllable, word, point*) appuyer or insister sur; (*feature*) souligner, accentuer.

emphatic [ɛmˈfætɪk] *a* (*strong*) énergique, vigoureux(euse); (*unambiguous, clear*) catégorique.

emphatically [ɛmˈfætɪklɪ] *ad* avec vigueur or énergie; catégoriquement.

empire [ˈɛmpaɪə*] *n* empire *m*.

empirical [ɛmˈpɪrɪkl] *a* empirique.

employ [ɪmˈplɔɪ] *vt* employer; **he's ~ed in a bank** il est employé de banque, il travaille dans une banque.

employee [ɪmplɔɪˈiː] *n* employé/e.

employer [ɪmˈplɔɪə*] *n* employeur/euse.

employment [ɪmˈplɔɪmənt] *n* emploi *m*; **to find ~** trouver un emploi or du travail; **without ~** au chômage, sans emploi; **place of ~** lieu *m* de travail.

employment agency *n* agence *f* or bureau *m* de placement.

employment exchange *n* (*Brit*) agence *f* pour l'emploi.

empower [ɪmˈpauə*] *vt*: **to ~ sb to do** autoriser or habiliter qn à faire.

empress [ˈɛmprɪs] *n* impératrice *f*.

emptiness [ˈɛmptɪnɪs] *n* vide *m*.

empty [ˈɛmptɪ] *a* vide; (*street, area*) désert(e); (*threat, promise*) en l'air, vain(e) ♦ *n* (*bottle*) bouteille *f* vide ♦ *vt* vider ♦ *vi* se vider; (*liquid*) s'écouler; **on an ~ stomach** à jeun; **to ~ into** (*river*) se jeter dans, se déverser dans.

empty-handed [ˈɛmptɪˈhændɪd] *a* les mains vides.

empty-headed [ˈɛmptɪˈhɛdɪd] *a* écervelé(e), qui n'a rien dans la tête.

EMS *n abbr* (= *European Monetary System*) SME *m*.

EMT *n abbr* = *emergency medical technician*.

emulate [ˈɛmjuleɪt] *vt* rivaliser avec, imiter.

emulsion [ɪˈmʌlʃən] *n* émulsion *f*; (*also:* **~ paint**) peinture mate.

enable [ɪˈneɪbl] *vt*: **to ~ sb to do** permettre à qn de faire, donner à qn la possibilité de faire.

enact [ɪˈnækt] *vt* (*LAW*) promulguer; (*play, scene*) jouer, représenter.

enamel [ɪˈnæməl] *n* émail *m*.

enamel paint *n* peinture émaillée.

enamoured [ɪˈnæməd] *a*: **~ of** amoureux(euse) de; (*idea*) enchanté(e) par.

encampment [ɪnˈkæmpmənt] *n* campement *m*.

encased [ɪnˈkeɪst] *a*: **~ in** enfermé(e) dans, recouvert(e) de.

encash [ɪnˈkæʃ] *vt* (*Brit*) toucher, encaisser.

enchant [ɪnˈtʃɑːnt] *vt* enchanter.

enchanting [ɪnˈtʃɑːntɪŋ] *a* ravissant(e), enchanteur(eresse).

encircle [ɪnˈsɜːkl] *vt* entourer, encercler.

encl. *abbr* (*on letters etc* = *enclosed, enclosure*) PJ.

enclose [ɪnˈkləuz] *vt* (*land*) clôturer; (*letter etc*): **to ~ (with)** joindre (à); **please find ~d** veuillez trouver ci-joint.

enclosure [ɪnˈkləuʒə*] *n* enceinte *f*; (*in letter etc*) annexe *f*.

encoder [ɪnˈkəudə*] *n* (*COMPUT*) encodeur *m*.

encompass [ɪnˈkʌmpəs] *vt* encercler, entourer; (*include*) contenir, inclure.

encore [ɔŋ'kɔ:*] *excl*, *n* bis *(m)*.

encounter [ɪn'kauntə*] *n* rencontre *f* ♦ *vt* rencontrer.

encourage [ɪn'kʌrɪdʒ] *vt* encourager; *(industry, growth)* favoriser; **to ~ sb to do sth** encourager qn à faire qch.

encouragement [ɪn'kʌrɪdʒmənt] *n* encouragement *m*.

encouraging [ɪn'kʌrɪdʒɪŋ] *a* encourageant(e).

encroach [ɪn'krəutʃ] *vi*: **to ~ (up)on** empiéter sur.

encrusted [ɪn'krʌstɪd] *a*: **~ (with)** incrusté(e) (de).

encumber [ɪn'kʌmbə*] *vt*: **to be ~ed with** *(luggage)* être encombré(e) de; *(debts)* être grevé(e) de.

encyclop(a)edia [ɛnsaɪkləu'pi:dɪə] *n* encyclopédie *f*.

end [ɛnd] *n (gen, also: aim)* fin *f*; *(of table, street, line, rope etc)* bout *m*, extrémité *f*; *(of pointed object)* pointe *f*; *(of town)* bout ♦ *vt* terminer; *(also:* **bring to an ~, put an ~ to)** mettre fin à ♦ *vi* se terminer, finir; **from ~ to ~** d'un bout à l'autre; **to come to an ~** prendre fin; **to be at an ~** être fini(e), être terminé(e); **in the ~** finalement; **on ~** *(object)* debout, dressé(e); **to stand on ~** *(hair)* se dresser sur la tête; **for 5 hours on ~** durant 5 heures d'affilée *or* de suite; **for hours on ~** pendant des heures (et des heures); **at the ~ of the day** *(Brit fig)* en fin de compte; **to this ~, with this ~** **in view** à cette fin, dans ce but.

end up *vi*: **to ~ up in** finir *or* se terminer par; *(place)* finir *or* aboutir à.

endanger [ɪn'deɪndʒə*] *vt* mettre en danger; **an ~ed species** une espèce en voie de disparition.

endear [ɪn'dɪə*] *vt*: **to ~ o.s. to sb** se faire aimer de qn.

endearing [ɪn'dɪərɪŋ] *a* attachant(e).

endearment [ɪn'dɪəmənt] *n*: **to whisper ~s** murmurer des mots *or* choses tendres; **term of ~** terme *m* d'affection.

endeavour, *(US)* **endeavor** [ɪn'dɛvə*] *n* tentative *f*, effort *m* ♦ *vi*: **to ~ to do** tenter *or* s'efforcer de faire.

endemic [ɛn'dɛmɪk] *a* endémique.

ending [ˈɛndɪŋ] *n* dénouement *m*, conclusion *f*; *(LING)* terminaison *f*.

endive [ˈɛndaɪv] *n (curly)* chicorée *f*; *(smooth, flat)* endive *f*.

endless [ˈɛndlɪs] *a* sans fin, interminable; *(patience, resources)* inépuisable, sans limites; *(possibilities)* illimité(e).

endorse [ɪn'dɔ:s] *vt (cheque)* endosser; *(approve)* appuyer, approuver, sanctionner.

endorsee [ɪndɔ:'si:] *n* bénéficiaire *m/f*, endossataire *m/f*.

endorsement [ɪn'dɔ:smənt] *n (approval)* caution *f*, aval *m*; *(signature)* endossement *m*; *(Brit: on driving licence)* contravention *f (portée au permis de conduire)*.

endorser [ɪn'dɔ:sə*] *n* avaliste *m*, endosseur *m*.

endow [ɪn'dau] *vt (provide with money)* faire une donation à, doter; *(equip)*: **to ~ with** gratifier de, doter de.

endowment [ɪn'daumənt] *n* dotation *f*.

endowment assurance *n* assurance *f* mixte.

end product *n (INDUSTRY)* produit fini; *(fig)* résultat *m*, aboutissement *m*.

end result *n* résultat final.

endurable [ɪn'djuərəbl] *a* supportable.

endurance [ɪn'djuərəns] *n* endurance *f*, résistance *f*; patience *f*.

endurance test *n* test *m* d'endurance.

endure [ɪn'djuə*] *vt* supporter, endurer ♦ *vi* durer.

end user *n (COMPUT)* utilisateur final.

enema [ˈɛnɪmə] *n (MED)* lavement *m*.

enemy [ˈɛnəmɪ] *a, n* ennemi(e); **to make an ~ of sb** se faire un(e) ennemi(e) de qn, se mettre qn à dos.

energetic [ɛnə'dʒɛtɪk] *a* énergique; *(activity)* très actif(ive), qui fait se dépenser (physiquement).

energy [ˈɛnədʒɪ] *n* énergie *f*; **Department of E~** ministère *m* de l'Énergie.

energy crisis *n* crise *f* de l'énergie.

energy-saving [ˈɛnədʒɪ'seɪvɪŋ] *a (policy)* d'économie d'énergie; *(device)* qui permet de réaliser des économies d'énergie.

enervating [ˈɛnəveɪtɪŋ] *a* débilitant(e), affaiblissant(e)..

enforce [ɪn'fɔ:s] *vt (LAW)* appliquer, faire respecter.

enforced [ɪn'fɔ:st] *a* forcé(e).

enfranchise [ɪn'fræntʃaɪz] *vt* accorder le droit de vote à; *(set free)* affranchir.

engage [ɪn'geɪdʒ] *vt* engager; *(MIL)* engager le combat avec; *(lawyer)* prendre ♦ *vi (TECH)* s'enclencher, s'engrener; **to ~ in** se lancer dans; **to ~ sb in conversation** engager la conversation avec qn.

engaged [ɪn'geɪdʒd] *a (Brit: busy, in use)* occupé(e); *(betrothed)* fiancé(e); **to get ~** se fiancer; **he is ~ in research/a survey** il fait de la recherche/une enquête.

engaged tone *n (Brit TEL)* tonalité *f* occupé.

engagement [ɪn'geɪdʒmənt] *n* obligation *f*, engagement *m*; *(appointment)* rendez-vous *m inv*; *(to marry)* fiançailles *fpl*; *(MIL)* combat *m*; **I have a previous ~** j'ai déjà un rendez-vous, je suis déjà pris(e).

engagement ring *n* bague *f* de fiançailles.

engaging [ɪn'geɪdʒɪŋ] *a* engageant(e), attirant(e).

engender [ɪn'dʒɛndə*] *vt* produire, causer.

engine [ˈɛndʒɪn] *n (AUT)* moteur *m*; *(RAIL)* locomotive *f*.

engine driver *n (Brit: of train)* mécanicien *m*.

engineer [ɛndʒɪ'nɪə*] *n* ingénieur *m*; *(Brit: for domestic appliances)* réparateur *m*; *(US RAIL)* mécanicien *m*; **civil/mechanical ~** ingénieur des Travaux Publics *or* des Ponts et Chaussées/mécanicien.

engineering [ɛndʒɪ'nɪərɪŋ] *n* engineering *m*, ingénierie *f*; *(of bridges, ships)* génie *m*; *(of machine)* mécanique *f* ♦ *cpd*: **~ works** *or* **factory** atelier *m* de construction mécanique.

engine failure *n* panne *f*.

engine trouble *n* ennuis *mpl* mécaniques.

England [ˈɪŋglənd] *n* Angleterre *f*.

English [ˈɪŋglɪʃ] *a* anglais(e) ♦ *n (LING)* anglais *m*; **the ~** *npl* les Anglais; **an ~**

speaker un anglophone.
English Channel *n*: **the ~** la Manche.
Englishman [ˈɪŋglɪʃmən], **Englishwoman** [ˈɪŋglɪʃwumən] *n* Anglais/e.
English-speaking [ˈɪŋglɪʃ'spiːkɪŋ] *a* qui parle anglais; anglophone.
engrave [ɪn'greɪv] *vt* graver.
engraving [ɪn'greɪvɪŋ] *n* gravure *f*.
engrossed [ɪn'grəust] *a*: **~ in** absorbé(e) par, plongé(e) dans.
engulf [ɪn'gʌlf] *vt* engloutir.
enhance [ɪn'hɑːns] *vt* rehausser, mettre en valeur; *(position)* améliorer; *(reputation)* accroître.
enigma [ɪ'nɪgmə] *n* énigme *f*.
enigmatic [ɛnɪg'mætɪk] *a* énigmatique.
enjoy [ɪn'dʒɔɪ] *vt* aimer, prendre plaisir à; *(have benefit of: health, fortune)* jouir de; *(: success)* connaître; **to ~ o.s.** s'amuser.
enjoyable [ɪn'dʒɔɪəbl] *a* agréable.
enjoyment [ɪn'dʒɔɪmənt] *n* plaisir *m*.
enlarge [ɪn'lɑːdʒ] *vt* accroître; *(PHOT)* agrandir ♦ *vi*: **to ~ on** *(subject)* s'étendre sur.
enlarged [ɪn'lɑːdʒd] *a* *(edition)* augmenté(e); *(MED: organ, gland)* anormalement gros(se), hypertrophié(e).
enlargement [ɪn'lɑːdʒmənt] *n* *(PHOT)* agrandissement *m*.
enlighten [ɪn'laɪtn] *vt* éclairer.
enlightened [ɪn'laɪtnd] *a* éclairé(e).
enlightening [ɪn'laɪtnɪŋ] *a* instructif(ive), révélateur(trice).
enlightenment [ɪn'laɪtnmənt] *n* édification *f*; éclaircissements *mpl*; *(HISTORY)*: **the E~** le Siècle des lumières.
enlist [ɪn'lɪst] *vt* recruter; *(support)* s'assurer ♦ *vi* s'engager; **~ed man** *(US MIL)* simple soldat *m*.
enliven [ɪn'laɪvn] *vt* animer, égayer.
enmity [ˈɛnmɪtɪ] *n* inimitié *f*.
ennoble [ɪ'nəubl] *vt* *(with title)* anoblir.
enormity [ɪ'nɔːmɪtɪ] *n* énormité *f*.
enormous [ɪ'nɔːməs] *a* énorme.
enormously [ɪ'nɔːməslɪ] *ad* *(increase)* dans des proportions énormes; *(rich)* extrêmement.
enough [ɪ'nʌf] *a, n*: **~ time/books** assez *or* suffisamment de temps/livres; **have you got ~?** (en) avez-vous assez?; **will 5 be ~?** est-ce que 5 suffiront?, est-ce qu'il y en aura assez avec 5?; **that's ~!** ça suffit!, assez!; **that's ~, thanks** cela suffit *or* c'est assez, merci; **I've had ~!** je n'en peux plus! ♦ *ad*: **big ~** assez *or* suffisamment grand; **he has not worked ~** il n'a pas assez *or* suffisamment travaillé, il n'a pas travaillé assez *or* suffisamment; **~! assez!, ça suffit!;** **it's hot ~ (as it is)!** il fait assez chaud comme ça!; **he was kind ~ to lend me the money** il a eu la gentillesse de me prêter l'argent; **... which, funnily ~ ...** qui, chose curieuse.
enquire [ɪn'kwaɪə*] *vt, vi* = **inquire**.
enrage [ɪn'reɪdʒ] *vt* mettre en fureur *or* en rage, rendre furieux(euse).
enrich [ɪn'rɪtʃ] *vt* enrichir.
enrol, *(US)* **enroll** [ɪn'rəul] *vt* inscrire ♦ *vi* s'inscrire.

enrol(l)ment [ɪn'rəulmənt] *n* inscription *f*.
en route [ɔn'ruːt] *ad* en route, en chemin; **~ for** *or* **to** en route vers, à destination de.
ensconced [ɪn'skɔnst] *a*: **~ in** bien calé(e) dans.
enshrine [ɪn'ʃraɪn] *vt* *(fig)* préserver.
ensign *n* *(NAUT)* [ˈɛnsən] enseigne *f*, pavillon *m*; *(MIL)* [ˈɛnsaɪn] porte-étendard *m*.
enslave [ɪn'sleɪv] *vt* asservir.
ensue [ɪn'sjuː] *vi* s'ensuivre, résulter.
ensure [ɪn'ʃuə*] *vt* assurer, garantir; **to ~ that** s'assurer que.
ENT *n abbr* (= *Ear, Nose & Throat*) ORL *f*.
entail [ɪn'teɪl] *vt* entraîner, nécessiter.
entangle [ɪn'tæŋgl] *vt* emmêler, embrouiller; **to become ~d in sth** *(fig)* se laisser entraîner *or* empêtrer dans qch.
enter [ˈɛntə*] *vt* *(room)* entrer dans, pénétrer dans; *(club, army)* entrer à; *(profession)* embrasser; *(competition)* s'inscrire à *or* pour; *(sb for a competition)* (faire) inscrire; *(write down)* inscrire, noter; *(COMPUT)* entrer, introduire ♦ *vi* entrer.
enter for *vt fus* s'inscrire à, se présenter pour *or* à.
enter into *vt fus* *(explanation)* se lancer dans; *(negotiations)* entamer; *(debate)* prendre part à; *(agreement)* conclure.
enter up *vt* inscrire.
enter (up)on *vt fus* commencer.
enteritis [ɛntə'raɪtɪs] *n* entérite *f*.
enterprise [ˈɛntəpraɪz] *n* *(company, undertaking)* entreprise *f*; *(initiative)* (esprit *m* d')initiative *f*.
enterprising [ˈɛntəpraɪzɪŋ] *a* entreprenant(e), dynamique.
entertain [ɛntə'teɪn] *vt* amuser, distraire; *(invite)* recevoir (à dîner); *(idea, plan)* envisager.
entertainer [ɛntə'teɪnə*] *n* artiste *m/f* de variétés.
entertaining [ɛntə'teɪnɪŋ] *a* amusant(e), distrayant(e) ♦ *n*: **to do a lot of ~** beaucoup recevoir.
entertainment [ɛntə'teɪnmənt] *n* *(amusement)* distraction *f*, divertissement *m*, amusement *m*; *(show)* spectacle *m*.
entertainment allowance *n* frais *mpl* de représentation.
enthralling [ɪn'θrɔːlɪŋ] *a* captivant(e); enchanteur(eresse).
enthuse [ɪn'θuːz] *vi*: **to ~ about** *or* **over** parler avec enthousiasme de.
enthusiasm [ɪn'θuːzɪæzəm] *n* enthousiasme *m*.
enthusiast [ɪn'θuːzɪæst] *n* enthousiaste *m/f*; **a jazz** *etc* **~** un fervent *or* passionné du jazz *etc*.
enthusiastic [ɪnθuːzɪ'æstɪk] *a* enthousiaste; **to be ~ about** être enthousiasmé(e) par.
entice [ɪn'taɪs] *vt* attirer, séduire.
enticing [ɪn'taɪsɪŋ] *a* *(person, offer)* séduisant(e); *(food)* alléchant(e).
entire [ɪn'taɪə*] *a* (tout) entier(ère).
entirely [ɪn'taɪəlɪ] *ad* entièrement, complètement.
entirety [ɪn'taɪərətɪ] *n*: **in its ~** dans sa totalité.
entitle [ɪn'taɪtl] *vt* *(allow)*: **to ~ sb to do** donner (le) droit à qn de faire; **to ~ sb to**

sth donner droit à qch à qn.
entitled [ɪn'taɪtld] a (book) intitulé(e); **to be ~ to sth/to do sth** avoir droit à qch/le droit de faire qch.
entity ['entɪtɪ] n entité f.
entrails ['entreɪlz] npl entrailles fpl.
entrance n ['entrns] entrée f ♦ vt [ɪn'trɑːns] enchanter, ravir; **to gain ~ to** (university etc) être admis à.
entrance examination n examen m d'entrée or d'admission.
entrance fee n droit m d'inscription; (to museum etc) prix m d'entrée.
entrance ramp n (US AUT) bretelle f d'accès.
entrancing [ɪn'trɑːnsɪŋ] a enchanteur(teresse), ravissant(e).
entrant ['entrnt] n (in race etc) participant/e, concurrent/e; (Brit: in exam) candidat/e.
entreat [ɛn'triːt] vt supplier.
entreaty [ɛn'triːtɪ] n supplication f, prière f.
entrée ['ɔntreɪ] n (CULIN) entrée f.
entrenched [ɛn'trɛntʃt] a retranché(e).
entrepreneur ['ɔntrəprə'nɜ:*] n entrepreneur m.
entrepreneurial ['ɔntrəprə'nɜ:rɪəl] a animé(e) d'un esprit d'entreprise.
entrust [ɪn'trʌst] vt: **to ~ sth to** confier qch à.
entry ['entrɪ] n entrée f; (in register, diary) inscription f; (in ledger) écriture f; **"no ~"** "défense d'entrer", "entrée interdite"; (AUT) "sens interdit"; **single/double ~ bookkeeping** comptabilité f en partie simple/double.
entry form n feuille f d'inscription.
entry phone n (Brit) interphone m (à l'entrée d'un immeuble).
entwine [ɪn'twaɪn] vt entrelacer.
enumerate [ɪ'njuːməreɪt] vt énumérer.
enunciate [ɪ'nʌnsɪeɪt] vt énoncer; prononcer.
envelop [ɪn'vɛləp] vt envelopper.
envelope ['envələup] n enveloppe f.
enviable ['envɪəbl] a enviable.
envious ['envɪəs] a envieux(euse).
environment [ɪn'vaɪərnmənt] n milieu m; environnement m; **Department of the E~** (Brit) ministère de l'équipement et de l'aménagement du territoire.
environmental [ɪnvaɪərn'mɛntl] a écologique, relatif(ive) à l'environnement; **~ studies** (in school etc) environnement m.
environmentalist [ɪnvaɪərn'mɛntlɪst] n écologiste m/f.
Environmental Protection Agency (EPA) n (US) ≈ ministère m de l'Environnement.
envisage [ɪn'vɪzɪdʒ] vt envisager; prévoir.
envision [ɪn'vɪʒən] vt envisager, concevoir.
envoy ['envɔɪ] n envoyé/e.
envy ['envɪ] n envie f ♦ vt envier; **to ~ sb sth** envier qch à qn.
enzyme ['enzaɪm] n enzyme m.
EPA n abbr (US) = **Environmental Protection Agency.**
ephemeral [ɪ'femərl] a éphémère.
epic ['epɪk] n épopée f ♦ a épique.
epicentre, (US) **epicenter** ['epɪsentə*] n épicentre m.
epidemic [epɪ'demɪk] n épidémie f.
epilepsy ['epɪlepsɪ] n épilepsie f.

epileptic [epɪ'leptɪk] a, n épileptique (m/f).
epilogue ['epɪlɔg] n épilogue m.
episcopal [ɪ'pɪskəpl] a épiscopal(e).
episode ['epɪsəud] n épisode m.
epistle [ɪ'pɪsl] n épître f.
epitaph ['epɪtɑ:f] n épitaphe f.
epithet ['epɪθet] n épithète f.
epitome [ɪ'pɪtəmɪ] n (fig) quintessence f, type m.
epitomize [ɪ'pɪtəmaɪz] vt (fig) illustrer, incarner.
epoch ['iːpɔk] n époque f, ère f.
epoch-making ['iːpɔkmeɪkɪŋ] a qui fait époque.
eponymous [ɪ'pɔnɪməs] a de ce or du même nom, éponyme.
equable ['ekwəbl] a égal(e); de tempérament égal.
equal ['iːkwl] a égal(e) ♦ n égal/e ♦ vt égaler; **~ to** (task) à la hauteur de; **~ to doing** de taille à or capable de faire.
equality [iː'kwɔlɪtɪ] n égalité f.
equalize ['iːkwəlaɪz] vt, vi égaliser.
equalizer ['iːkwəlaɪzə*] n but égalisateur.
equally ['iːkwəlɪ] ad également; (just as) tout aussi; **they are ~ clever** ils sont tous aussi intelligents.
Equal Opportunities Commission, (US) **Equal Employment Opportunity Commission** n commission pour la non discrimination dans l'emploi.
equal(s) sign n signe m d'égalité.
equanimity [ekwə'nɪmɪtɪ] n égalité f d'humeur.
equate [ɪ'kweɪt] vt: **to ~ sth with** comparer qch à; assimiler qch à; **to ~ sth to** mettre qch en équation avec; égaler qch à.
equation [ɪ'kweɪʃən] n (MATH) équation f.
equator [ɪ'kweɪtə*] n équateur m.
equatorial [ekwə'tɔ:rɪəl] a équatorial(e).
Equatorial Guinea n Guinée équatoriale.
equestrian [ɪ'kwestrɪən] a équestre ♦ n écuyer/ère, cavalier/ère.
equilibrium [iːkwɪ'lɪbrɪəm] n équilibre m.
equinox ['iːkwɪnɔks] n équinoxe m.
equip [ɪ'kwɪp] vt équiper; **to ~ sb/sth with** équiper or munir qn/qch de; **he is well ~ped for the job** il a les compétences or les qualités requises pour ce travail.
equipment [ɪ'kwɪpmənt] n équipement m; (electrical etc) appareillage m, installation f.
equitable ['ekwɪtəbl] a équitable.
equities ['ekwɪtɪz] npl (Brit COMM) actions cotées en Bourse.
equity ['ekwɪtɪ] n équité f.
equity capital n capitaux mpl propres.
equivalent [ɪ'kwɪvəlnt] a équivalent(e) ♦ n équivalent m; **to be ~ to** équivaloir à, être équivalent(e) à.
equivocal [ɪ'kwɪvəkl] a équivoque; (open to suspicion) douteux(euse).
equivocate [ɪ'kwɪvəkeɪt] vi user de faux-fuyants; éviter de répondre.
equivocation [ɪkwɪvə'keɪʃən] n équivoque f.
ER abbr (Brit: = Elizabeth Regina) la reine Élisabeth.
ERA n abbr (US POL: = Equal Rights Amendment) amendement sur l'égalité des droits des femmes.

era ['ɪərə] n ère f, époque f.
eradicate [ɪ'rædɪkeɪt] vt éliminer.
erase [ɪ'reɪz] vt effacer.
eraser [ɪ'reɪzə*] n gomme f.
erect [ɪ'rɛkt] a droit(e) ♦ vt construire; (monument) ériger, élever; (tent etc) dresser.
erection [ɪ'rɛkʃən] n (PHYSIOL) érection f; (of building) construction f; (of machinery etc) installation f.
ergonomics [ə:gə'nɔmɪks] n ergonomie f.
ERISA n abbr (US: = Employee Retirement Income Security Act) loi sur les pensions de retraite.
ermine ['ə:mɪn] n hermine f.
ERNIE [ə:nɪ] n abbr (Brit: = Electronic Random Number Indicator Equipment) ordinateur servant au tirage des bons à lots gagnants.
erode [ɪ'rəud] vt éroder; (metal) ronger.
erosion [ɪ'rəuʒən] n érosion f.
erotic [ɪ'rɔtɪk] a érotique.
eroticism [ɪ'rɔtɪsɪzəm] n érotisme m.
err [ə:*] vi se tromper; (REL) pécher.
errand ['ɛrnd] n course f, commission f; to run ~s faire des courses; ~ of mercy mission f de charité, acte m charitable.
errand boy n garçon m de courses.
erratic [ɪ'rætɪk] a irrégulier(ière); inconstant(e).
erroneous [ɪ'rəunɪəs] a erroné(e).
error ['ɛrə*] n erreur f; typing/spelling ~ faute f de frappe/d'orthographe; in ~ par erreur, par méprise; ~s and omissions excepted sauf erreur ou omission.
error message n (COMPUT) message m d'erreur.
erstwhile ['ə:stwaɪl] a précédent(e), d'autrefois.
erudite ['ɛrjudaɪt] a savant(e).
erupt [ɪ'rʌpt] vi entrer en éruption; (fig) éclater, exploser.
eruption [ɪ'rʌpʃən] n éruption f; (of anger, violence) explosion f.
ESA n abbr (= European Space Agency) ASE f (= Agence spatiale européenne).
escalate ['ɛskəleɪt] vi s'intensifier; (costs) monter en flèche.
escalation [ɛskə'leɪʃən] n escalade f.
escalation clause n clause f d'indexation.
escalator ['ɛskəleɪtə*] n escalier roulant.
escapade [ɛskə'peɪd] n fredaine f; équipée f.
escape [ɪ'skeɪp] n évasion f, fuite f; (of gas etc) fuite; (TECH) échappement m ♦ vi s'échapper, fuir; (from jail) s'évader; (fig) s'en tirer, en réchapper; (leak) fuir; s'échapper ♦ vt échapper à; to ~ from (person) échapper à; (place) s'échapper de; (fig) fuir; to ~ to (another place) fuir à, s'enfuir à; to ~ to safety se réfugier dans or gagner un endroit sûr; to ~ notice passer inaperçu(e).
escape artist n virtuose m/f de l'évasion.
escape clause n clause f dérogatoire.
escape key n (COMPUT) touche f d'échappement.
escape route n (from fire) issue f de secours; (of prisoners etc) voie empruntée pour s'échapper.

escapism [ɪ'skeɪpɪzəm] n évasion f (fig).
escapist [ɪ'skeɪpɪst] a (literature) d'évasion ♦ n personne f qui se réfugie hors de la réalité.
escapologist [ɛskə'pɔlədʒɪst] n (Brit) = escape artist.
escarpment [ɪs'ka:pmənt] n escarpement m.
eschew [ɪs'tʃu:] vt éviter.
escort vt [ɪ'skɔ:t] escorter ♦ n ['ɛskɔ:t] escorte f; (to dance etc): her ~ son compagnon or cavalier; his ~ sa compagne.
escort agency n bureau m d'hôtesses.
Eskimo ['ɛskɪməu] a esquimau(de), eskimo ♦ n Esquimau/de; (LING) esquimau m.
ESL n abbr (SCOL) = English as a Second Language.
esophagus [i:'sɔfəgəs] n (US) = oesophagus.
esoteric [ɛsə'tɛrɪk] a ésotérique.
ESP n abbr = extrasensory perception.
esp. abbr = especially.
especially [ɪ'spɛʃlɪ] ad (specifically) spécialement, exprès; (more than usually) particulièrement; (above all) particulièrement, surtout.
espionage ['ɛspɪəna:ʒ] n espionnage m.
esplanade [ɛsplə'neɪd] n esplanade f.
espouse [ɪ'spauz] vt épouser, embrasser.
Esquire [ɪ'skwaɪə*] n (Brit: abbr Esq.): J. Brown, ~ Monsieur J. Brown.
essay ['ɛseɪ] n (SCOL) dissertation f; (LITERATURE) essai m; (attempt) tentative f.
essence ['ɛsns] n essence f; in ~ en substance; speed is of the ~ l'essentiel, c'est la rapidité.
essential [ɪ'sɛnʃl] a essentiel(le); (basic) fondamental(e) ♦ n élément essentiel; it is ~ that il est essentiel or primordial que.
essentially [ɪ'sɛnʃlɪ] ad essentiellement.
EST abbr (US: = Eastern Standard Time) heure d'hiver de New York.
est. abbr = established, estimate(d).
establish [ɪ'stæblɪʃ] vt établir; (business) fonder, créer; (one's power etc) asseoir, affermir.
establishment [ɪ'stæblɪʃmənt] n établissement m; création f; (institution) établissement m; the E~ les pouvoirs établis; l'ordre établi.
estate [ɪ'steɪt] n (land) domaine m, propriété f; (LAW) biens mpl, succession f; (Brit: also: housing ~) lotissement m.
estate agency n (Brit) agence immobilière.
estate agent n (Brit) agent immobilier.
estate car n (Brit) break m.
esteem [ɪ'sti:m] n estime f ♦ vt estimer; apprécier; to hold sb in high ~ tenir qn en haute estime.
esthetic [ɪs'θɛtɪk] a (US) = aesthetic.
estimate n ['ɛstɪmət] estimation f; (COMM) devis m ♦ vt ['ɛstɪmeɪt] estimer ♦ vi (Brit COMM): to ~ for estimer, faire une estimation de; (bid for) faire un devis pour; to give sb an ~ of faire or donner un devis à qn pour; at a rough ~ approximativement.
estimation [ɛstɪ'meɪʃən] n opinion f; estime f; in my ~ à mon avis, selon moi.
estimator ['ɛstɪmeɪtə*] n personne f qui évalue.
Estonia [ɛ'stəunɪə] n Estonie f.
estranged [ɪs'treɪndʒd] a (couple) séparé(e);

(husband, wife) dont on s'est séparé(e).
estrangement [ɪs'treɪndʒmənt] *n (from wife, family)* séparation *f*.
estrogen ['i:strəudʒən] *n (US)* = **oestrogen**.
estuary ['ɛstjuərɪ] *n* estuaire *m*.
ET *abbr (US: = Eastern Time) heure de New York*.
ETA *n abbr (= estimated time of arrival)* HPA *f (= heure probable d'arrivée)*.
et al. *abbr (= et alii: and others)* et coll.
etc. *abbr (= et cetera)* etc.
etch [ɛtʃ] *vt* graver à l'eau forte.
etching ['ɛtʃɪŋ] *n* eau-forte *f*.
ETD *n abbr (= estimated time of departure)* HPA *f (= heure probable de départ)*.
eternal [ɪ'tə:nl] *a* éternel(le).
eternity [ɪ'tə:nɪtɪ] *n* éternité *f*.
ether ['i:θə*] *n* éther *m*.
ethereal [ɪ'θɪərɪəl] *a* éthéré(e).
ethical ['ɛθɪkl] *a* moral(e).
ethics ['ɛθɪks] *n* éthique *f* ♦ *npl* moralité *f*.
Ethiopia [i:θɪ'əupɪə] *n* Éthiopie *f*.
Ethiopian [i:θɪ'əupɪən] *a* éthiopien(ne) ♦ *n* Éthiopien/ne.
ethnic ['ɛθnɪk] *a* ethnique; *(clothes, food)* folklorique, *exotique: propre aux minorités ethniques non-occidentales*.
ethnology [ɛθ'nɔlədʒɪ] *n* ethnologie *f*.
ethos ['i:θɔs] *n* (système *m* de) valeurs *fpl*.
etiquette ['ɛtɪkɛt] *n* convenances *fpl*, étiquette *f*.
ETU *n abbr (Brit: = Electrical Trades Union)* syndicat des électriciens.
ETV *n abbr (US: = Educational Television)* télévision scolaire.
etymology [ɛtɪ'mɔlədʒɪ] *n* étymologie *f*.
eucalyptus [ju:kə'lɪptəs] *n* eucalyptus *m*.
eulogy ['ju:lədʒɪ] *n* éloge *m*.
euphemism ['ju:fəmɪzəm] *n* euphémisme *m*.
euphemistic [ju:fə'mɪstɪk] *a* euphémique.
euphoria [ju:'fɔ:rɪə] *n* euphorie *f*.
Eurasia [juə'reɪʃə] *n* Eurasie *f*.
Eurasian [juə'reɪʃən] *a* eurasien(ne); *(continent)* eurasiatique ♦ *n* Eurasien/ne.
Euratom [juə'rætəm] *n abbr (= European Atomic Energy Community)* EURATOM *f*.
Eurocheque ['juərəutʃɛk] *n* eurochèque *m*.
Eurocrat ['juərəukræt] *n* eurocrate *m/f*.
Eurodollar ['juərəudɔlə*] *n* eurodollar *m*.
Europe ['juərəp] *n* Europe *f*.
European [juərə'pi:ən] *a* européen(ne) ♦ *n* Européen/ne.
European Court of Justice *n* Cour *f* de Justice de la CEE.
euthanasia [ju:θə'neɪzɪə] *n* euthanasie *f*.
evacuate [ɪ'vækjueɪt] *vt* évacuer.
evacuation [ɪvækju'eɪʃən] *n* évacuation *f*.
evade [ɪ'veɪd] *vt* échapper à; *(question etc)* éluder; *(duties)* se dérober à.
evaluate [ɪ'væljueɪt] *vt* évaluer.
evangelist [ɪ'vændʒəlɪst] *n* évangéliste *m*.
evangelize [ɪ'vændʒəlaɪz] *vt* évangéliser, prêcher l'Évangile à.
evaporate [ɪ'væpəreɪt] *vi* s'évaporer ♦ *vt* faire évaporer.
evaporated milk *n* lait condensé (non sucré).
evaporation [ɪvæpə'reɪʃən] *n* évaporation *f*.
evasion [ɪ'veɪʒən] *n* dérobade *f*; *(excuse)* faux-fuyant *m*.

evasive [ɪ'veɪsɪv] *a* évasif(ive).
eve [i:v] *n*: **on the ~ of** à la veille de.
even ['i:vn] *a* régulier(ière), égal(e); *(number)* pair(e) ♦ *ad* même; ~ **if** même si + *indicative*; ~ **though** quand (bien) même + *conditional*, alors même que + *conditional*; ~ **more** encore plus; ~ **faster** encore plus vite; ~ **so** quand même; **not** ~ pas même; **to break** ~ s'y retrouver, équilibrer ses comptes; **to get** ~ **with sb** prendre sa revanche sur qn.
even out *vi* s'égaliser.
evening ['i:vnɪŋ] *n* soir *m*; *(as duration, event)* soirée *f*; **in the** ~ le soir; **this** ~ ce soir; **tomorrow/yesterday** ~ demain/hier soir.
evening class *n* cours *m* du soir.
evening dress *n (man's)* habit *m* de soirée, smoking *m*; *(woman's)* robe *f* de soirée.
evenly ['i:vnlɪ] *ad* uniformément, également; *(space)* régulièrement.
evensong ['i:vnsɔŋ] *n* office *m* du soir.
event [ɪ'vɛnt] *n* événement *m*; *(SPORT)* épreuve *f*; **in the course of** ~s par la suite; **in the** ~ **of** en cas de; **in the** ~ en réalité, en fait; **at all** ~s *(Brit)*, **in any** ~ en tout cas, de toute manière.
eventful [ɪ'vɛntful] *a* mouvementé(e).
eventing [ɪ'vɛntɪŋ] *n (HORSERIDING)* concours complet *(équitation)*.
eventual [ɪ'vɛntʃuəl] *a* final(e).
eventuality [ɪvɛntʃu'ælɪtɪ] *n* possibilité *f*, éventualité *f*.
eventually [ɪ'vɛntʃuəlɪ] *ad* finalement.
ever ['ɛvə*] *ad* jamais; *(at all times)* toujours; **the best** ~ le meilleur qu'on ait jamais vu; **did you** ~ **meet him?** est-ce qu'il vous est arrivé de le rencontrer?; **have you** ~ **been there?** y êtes-vous déjà allé?; **for** ~ pour toujours; **hardly** ~ ne ... presque jamais; ~ **since** *ad* depuis ♦ *cj* depuis que; ~ **so pretty** si joli; **thank you** ~ **so much** merci mille fois; **yours** ~ *(Brit: in letters)* cordialement vôtre.
Everest ['ɛvərɪst] *n (also:* **Mount** ~*)* le mont Everest, l'Everest *m*.
evergreen ['ɛvəgri:n] *n* arbre *m* à feuilles persistantes.
everlasting [ɛvə'lɑ:stɪŋ] *a* éternel(le).
every ['ɛvrɪ] *a* chaque; ~ **day** tous les jours, chaque jour; ~ **other/third day** tous les deux/trois jours; ~ **other car** une voiture sur deux; ~ **now and then** de temps en temps; **I have** ~ **confidence in him** j'ai entièrement *or* pleinement confiance en lui.
everybody ['ɛvrɪbɔdɪ] *pronoun* tout le monde, tous *pl*; ~ **knows about it** tout le monde le sait; ~ **else** tous les autres.
everyday ['ɛvrɪdeɪ] *a (expression)* courant(e), d'usage courant; *(use)* courant; *(occurrence, experience)* de tous les jours, ordinaire.
everyone ['ɛvrɪwʌn] = **everybody**.
everything ['ɛvrɪθɪŋ] *pronoun* tout; ~ **is ready** tout est prêt; **he did** ~ **possible** il a fait tout son possible.
everywhere ['ɛvrɪwɛə*] *ad* partout; ~ **you go you meet** ... où qu'on aille, on rencontre ....
evict [ɪ'vɪkt] *vt* expulser.
eviction [ɪ'vɪkʃən] *n* expulsion *f*.

eviction notice *n* préavis *m* d'expulsion.

evidence ['ɛvɪdns] *n* (*proof*) preuve(s) *f(pl)*; (*of witness*) témoignage *m*; (*sign*): **to show** ~ **of** donner des signes de; **to give** ~ témoigner, déposer; **in** ~ (*obvious*) en évidence; en vue.

evident ['ɛvɪdnt] *a* évident(e).

evidently ['ɛvɪdntlɪ] *ad* de toute évidence.

evil ['iːvl] *a* mauvais(e) ♦ *n* mal *m*.

evince [ɪ'vɪns] *vt* manifester.

evocative [ɪ'vɔkətɪv] *a* évocateur(trice).

evoke [ɪ'vəuk] *vt* évoquer; (*admiration*) susciter.

evolution [iːvə'luːʃən] *n* évolution *f*.

evolve [ɪ'vɔlv] *vt* élaborer ♦ *vi* évoluer, se transformer.

ewe [juː] *n* brebis *f*.

ewer ['juːə*] *n* broc *m*.

ex- [ɛks] *prefix* (*former: husband, president etc*) ex-; (*out of*): **the price** ~ **works** le prix départ usine.

exacerbate [ɛks'æsəbeɪt] *vt* (*pain*) exacerber, accentuer; (*fig*) aggraver.

exact [ɪg'zækt] *a* exact(e) ♦ *vt*: **to** ~ **sth (from)** extorquer qch (à); exiger qch (de).

exacting [ɪg'zæktɪŋ] *a* exigeant(e); (*work*) fatigant(e).

exactitude [ɪg'zæktɪtjuːd] *n* exactitude *f*, précision *f*.

exactly [ɪg'zæktlɪ] *ad* exactement; ~! parfaitement!, précisément!

exaggerate [ɪg'zædʒəreɪt] *vt, vi* exagérer.

exaggeration [ɪgzædʒə'reɪʃən] *n* exagération *f*.

exalted [ɪg'zɔːltɪd] *a* (*rank*) élevé(e); (*person*) haut placé(e); (*elated*) exalté(e).

exam [ɪg'zæm] *n abbr* (*SCOL*) = **examination**.

examination [ɪgzæmɪ'neɪʃən] *n* (*SCOL, MED*) examen *m*; **to take** *or* (*Brit*) **sit an** ~ passer un examen; **the matter is under** ~ la question est à l'examen.

examine [ɪg'zæmɪn] *vt* (*gen*) examiner; (*SCOL, LAW: person*) interroger; (*inspect: machine, premises*) inspecter; (*passport*) contrôler; (*luggage*) fouiller.

examiner [ɪg'zæmɪnə*] *n* examinateur/trice.

example [ɪg'zɑːmpl] *n* exemple *m*; **for** ~ par exemple; **to set a good/bad** ~ donner le bon/mauvais exemple.

exasperate [ɪg'zɑːspəreɪt] *vt* exaspérer, agacer.

exasperation [ɪgzɑːspə'reɪʃən] *n* exaspération *f*, irritation *f*.

excavate ['ɛkskəveɪt] *vt* excaver; (*object*) mettre au jour.

excavation [ɛkskə'veɪʃən] *n* excavation *f*.

excavator ['ɛkskəveɪtə*] *n* excavateur *m*, excavatrice *f*.

exceed [ɪk'siːd] *vt* dépasser; (*one's powers*) outrepasser.

exceedingly [ɪk'siːdɪŋlɪ] *ad* excessivement.

excel [ɪk'sɛl] *vi* exceller ♦ *vt* surpasser; **to** ~ **o.s.** (*Brit*) se surpasser.

excellence ['ɛksələns] *n* excellence *f*.

Excellency ['ɛksələnsɪ] *n*: **His** ~ son Excellence *f*.

excellent ['ɛksələnt] *a* excellent(e).

except [ɪk'sɛpt] *prep* (*also*: ~ **for,** ~**ing**) sauf, excepté, à l'exception de ♦ *vt* excepter; ~ **if/**

when sauf si/quand; ~ **that** excepté que, si ce n'est que.

exception [ɪk'sɛpʃən] *n* exception *f*; **to take** ~ **to** s'offusquer de; **with the** ~ **of** à l'exception de.

exceptional [ɪk'sɛpʃənl] *a* exceptionnel(le).

excerpt ['ɛksəːpt] *n* extrait *m*.

excess [ɪk'sɛs] *n* excès *m*; **in** ~ **of** plus de.

excess baggage *n* excédent *m* de bagages.

excess fare *n* supplément *m*.

excessive [ɪk'sɛsɪv] *a* excessif(ive).

excess supply *n* suroffre *f*, offre *f* excédentaire.

exchange [ɪks'tʃeɪndʒ] *n* échange *m*; (*also*: **telephone** ~) central *m* ♦ *vt*: **to** ~ **(for)** échanger (contre); **in** ~ **for** en échange de; **foreign** ~ (*COMM*) change *m*.

exchange control *n* contrôle *m* des changes.

exchange market *n* marché *m* des changes.

exchange rate *n* taux *m* de change.

exchequer [ɪks'tʃɛkə*] *n* (*Brit*) Echiquier *m*, ≈ ministère *m* des Finances.

excisable [ɪk'saɪzəbl] *a* taxable.

excise *n* ['ɛksaɪz] taxe *f* ♦ *vt* [ɛk'saɪz] exciser.

excise duties *npl* impôts indirects.

excitable [ɪk'saɪtəbl] *a* excitable, nerveux(euse).

excite [ɪk'saɪt] *vt* exciter; **to get** ~**d** s'exciter.

excitement [ɪk'saɪtmənt] *n* excitation *f*.

exciting [ɪk'saɪtɪŋ] *a* passionnant(e).

excl. *abbr* = **excluding, exclusive (of)**.

exclaim [ɪk'skleɪm] *vi* s'exclamer.

exclamation [ɛksklə'meɪʃən] *n* exclamation *f*.

exclamation mark *n* point *m* d'exclamation.

exclude [ɪk'skluːd] *vt* exclure.

excluding [ɪk'skluːdɪŋ] *prep*: ~ **VAT** la TVA non comprise.

exclusion [ɪk'skluːʒən] *n* exclusion *f*; **to the** ~ **of** à l'exclusion de.

exclusion clause *n* clause *f* d'exclusion.

exclusive [ɪk'skluːsɪv] *a* exclusif(ive); (*club, district*) sélect(e); (*item of news*) en exclusivité ♦ *ad* (*COMM*) exclusivement, non inclus; ~ **of VAT** TVA non comprise; ~ **of postage** (les) frais de poste non compris; **from 1st to 15th March** ~ du 1er au 15 mars exclusivement *or* exclu; ~ **rights** (*COMM*) exclusivité *f*.

exclusively [ɪk'skluːsɪvlɪ] *ad* exclusivement.

excommunicate [ɛkskə'mjuːnɪkeɪt] *vt* excommunier.

excrement ['ɛkskrəmənt] *n* excrément *m*.

excruciating [ɪk'skruːʃɪeɪtɪŋ] *a* atroce, déchirant(e).

excursion [ɪk'skəːʃən] *n* excursion *f*.

excursion ticket *n* billet *m* tarif excursion.

excusable [ɪk'skjuːzəbl] *a* excusable.

excuse *n* [ɪk'skjuːs] excuse *f* ♦ *vt* [ɪk'skjuːz] excuser; (*justify*) excuser, justifier; **to** ~ **sb from** (*activity*) dispenser qn de; ~ **me!** excusez-moi!, pardon!; **now if you will** ~ **me, ...** maintenant, si vous (le) permettez ...; **to make** ~**s for sb** trouver des excuses à qn; **to** ~ **o.s. for sth/for doing sth** s'excuser de/d'avoir fait qch.

ex-directory ['ɛksdɪ'rɛktərɪ] *a* (*Brit*): ~ **(phone) number** numéro *m* (de téléphone) sur la liste rouge.

execute ['ɛksɪkjuːt] *vt* exécuter.

execution [ɛksɪ'kju:ʃən] *n* exécution *f*.
executioner [ɛksɪ'kju:ʃnə*] *n* bourreau *m*.
executive [ɪg'zɛkjutɪv] *n* (*COMM*) cadre *m*; (*POL*) exécutif *m* ♦ *a* exécutif(ive); (*position, job*) de cadre; (*secretary*) de direction; (*offices*) de la direction; (*car, plane*) de fonction.
executive director *n* administrateur/trice.
executor [ɪg'zɛkjutə*] *n* exécuteur/trice testamentaire.
exemplary [ɪg'zɛmplərɪ] *a* exemplaire.
exemplify [ɪg'zɛmplɪfaɪ] *vt* illustrer.
exempt [ɪg'zɛmpt] *a*: ~ **from** exempté(e) *or* dispensé(e) de ♦ *vt*: **to** ~ **sb from** exempter *or* dispenser qn de.
exemption [ɪg'zɛmpʃən] *n* exemption *f*, dispense *f*.
exercise ['ɛksəsaɪz] *n* exercice *m* ♦ *vt* exercer; (*patience etc*) faire preuve de; (*dog*) promener ♦ *vi* (*also*: **to take** ~) prendre de l'exercice.
exercise book *n* cahier *m*.
exert [ɪg'zə:t] *vt* exercer, employer; (*strength, force*) employer; **to** ~ **o.s.** se dépenser.
exertion [ɪg'zə:ʃən] *n* effort *m*.
ex gratia ['ɛks'greɪʃə] *a*: ~ **payment** gratification *f*.
exhale [ɛks'heɪl] *vt* expirer; exhaler ♦ *vi* expirer.
exhaust [ɪg'zɔ:st] *n* (*also*: ~ **fumes**) gaz *mpl* d'échappement; (*also*: ~ **pipe**) tuyau *m* d'échappement ♦ *vt* épuiser; **to** ~ **o.s.** s'épuiser.
exhausted [ɪg'zɔ:stɪd] *a* épuisé(e).
exhausting [ɪg'zɔ:stɪŋ] *a* épuisant(e).
exhaustion [ɪg'zɔ:stʃən] *n* épuisement *m*; **nervous** ~ fatigue nerveuse.
exhaustive [ɪg'zɔ:stɪv] *a* très complet(ète).
exhibit [ɪg'zɪbɪt] *n* (*ART*) pièce *f* *or* objet *m* exposé(e); (*LAW*) pièce à conviction ♦ *vt* exposer; (*courage, skill*) faire preuve de.
exhibition [ɛksɪ'bɪʃən] *n* exposition *f*; ~ **of temper** manifestation *f* de colère.
exhibitionist [ɛksɪ'bɪʃənɪst] *n* exhibitionniste *m/f*.
exhibitor [ɪg'zɪbɪtə*] *n* exposant/e.
exhilarating [ɪg'zɪləreɪtɪŋ] *a* grisant(e); stimulant(e).
exhilaration [ɪgzɪlə'reɪʃən] *n* euphorie *f*, ivresse *f*.
exhort [ɪg'zɔ:t] *vt* exhorter.
exile ['ɛksaɪl] *n* exil *m*; (*person*) exilé/e ♦ *vt* exiler; **in** ~ en exil.
exist [ɪg'zɪst] *vi* exister.
existence [ɪg'zɪstəns] *n* existence *f*; **to be in** ~ exister.
existentialism [ɛgzɪs'tɛnʃlɪzəm] *n* existentialisme *m*.
existing [ɪg'zɪstɪŋ] *a* (*laws*) existant(e); (*system, regime*) actuel(le).
exit ['ɛksɪt] *n* sortie *f* ♦ *vi* (*COMPUT, THEATRE*) sortir.
exit ramp *n* (*US AUT*) bretelle *f* d'accès.
exit visa *n* visa *m* de sortie.
exodus ['ɛksədəs] *n* exode *m*.
ex officio ['ɛksə'fɪʃɪəu] *a, ad* d'office, de droit.
exonerate [ɪg'zɔnəreɪt] *vt*: **to** ~ **from** disculper de.
exorbitant [ɪg'zɔ:bɪtnt] *a* (*price*)

exorbitant(e), excessif(ive); (*demands*) exorbitant, démesuré(e).
exorcize ['ɛksɔ:saɪz] *vt* exorciser.
exotic [ɪg'zɔtɪk] *a* exotique.
expand [ɪk'spænd] *vt* (*area*) agrandir; (*quantity*) accroître; (*influence etc*) étendre ♦ *vi* (*population, production*) s'accroître; (*trade, influence etc*) se développer, s'étendre; (*gas, metal*) se dilater; **to** ~ **on** (*notes, story etc*) développer.
expanse [ɪk'spæns] *n* étendue *f*.
expansion [ɪk'spænʃən] *n* (*see expand*) développement *m*; accroissement *m*; extension *f*; dilatation *f*.
expansionism [ɪk'spænʃənɪzəm] *n* expansionnisme *m*.
expansionist [ɪk'spænʃənɪst] *a* expansionniste.
expatriate *n* [ɛks'pætrɪət] expatrié/e ♦ *vt* [ɛks'pætrɪeɪt] expatrier, exiler.
expect [ɪk'spɛkt] *vt* (*anticipate*) s'attendre à, s'attendre à ce que + *sub*; (*count on*) compter sur, escompter; (*hope for*) espérer; (*require*) demander, exiger; (*suppose*) supposer; (*await, also baby*) attendre ♦ *vi*: **to be** ~**ing** être enceinte; **to** ~ **sb to do** (*anticipate*) s'attendre à ce que qn fasse; (*demand*) attendre de qn qu'il fasse; **to** ~ **to do sth** penser *or* compter faire qch, s'attendre à faire qch; **as** ~**ed** comme prévu; **I** ~ **so** je crois que oui, je crois bien.
expectancy [ɪks'pɛktənsɪ] *n* attente *f*; **life** ~ espérance *f* de vie.
expectant [ɪk'spɛktənt] *a* qui attend (quelque chose); ~ **mother** future maman.
expectantly [ɪk'spɛktəntlɪ] *ad* (*look, listen*) avec l'air d'attendre quelque chose.
expectation [ɛkspɛk'teɪʃən] *n* attente *f*, prévisions *fpl*; espérance(s) *f(pl)*; **in** ~ **of** dans l'attente de, en prévision de; **against** *or* **contrary to all** ~(**s**) contre toute attente, contrairement à ce qu'on attendait; **to come** *or* **live up to sb's** ~**s** répondre à l'attente *or* aux espérances de qn.
expedience, expediency [ɪk'spi:dɪəns, ɪk'spi:dɪənsɪ] *n* opportunité *f*; convenance *f* (du moment); **for the sake of** ~ parce que c'est (*or* c'était) plus simple *or* plus commode.
expedient [ɪk'spi:dɪənt] *a* indiqué(e), opportun(e); commode ♦ *n* expédient *m*.
expedite ['ɛkspədaɪt] *vt* hâter; expédier.
expedition [ɛkspə'dɪʃən] *n* expédition *f*.
expeditionary force [ɛkspə'dɪʃənrɪ-] *n* corps *m* expéditionnaire.
expeditious [ɛkspə'dɪʃəs] *a* expéditif(ive), prompt(e).
expel [ɪk'spɛl] *vt* chasser, expulser; (*SCOL*) renvoyer, exclure.
expend [ɪk'spɛnd] *vt* consacrer; (*use up*) dépenser.
expendable [ɪk'spɛndəbl] *a* remplaçable.
expenditure [ɪk'spɛndɪtʃə*] *n* dépense *f*; dépenses *fpl*.
expense [ɪk'spɛns] *n* (*cost*) coût *m*; (*spending*) dépense *f*, frais *mpl*; ~**s** *npl* frais *mpl*; dépenses; **to go to the** ~ **of** faire la dépense de; **at great/little** ~ à grands/peu de frais; **at the** ~ **of** aux frais de; (*fig*) aux dépens de.

expense account n (note f de) frais mpl.

expensive [ɪk'spɛnsɪv] a cher(chère), coûteux(euse); **to be ~** coûter cher; **~ tastes** goûts mpl de luxe.

experience [ɪk'spɪərɪəns] n expérience f ♦ vt connaître; éprouver; **to know by ~** savoir par expérience.

experienced [ɪk'spɪərɪənst] a expérimenté(e).

experiment [ɪk'spɛrɪmənt] n expérience f ♦ vi faire une expérience; **to ~ with** expérimenter; **to perform** or **carry out an ~** faire une expérience; **as an ~** à titre d'expérience.

experimental [ɪkspɛrɪ'mɛntl] a expérimental(e).

expert ['ɛkspə:t] a expert(e) ♦ n expert m; **in** or **at doing sth** spécialiste de qch; **an ~ on sth** un spécialiste de qch; **~ witness** (LAW) expert m.

expertise [ɛkspə:'ti:z] n (grande) compétence.

expire [ɪk'spaɪə*] vi expirer.

expiry [ɪk'spaɪərɪ] n expiration f.

explain [ɪk'spleɪn] vt expliquer.

explain away vt justifier, excuser.

explanation [ɛksplə'neɪʃən] n explication f; **to find an ~ for sth** trouver une explication à qch.

explanatory [ɪk'splænətrɪ] a explicatif(ive).

explicit [ɪk'splɪsɪt] a explicite; (definite) formel(le).

explode [ɪk'spləud] vi exploser ♦ vt faire exploser; (fig: theory) démolir; **to ~ a myth** détruire un mythe.

exploit n ['ɛksplɔɪt] exploit m ♦ vt [ɪk'splɔɪt] exploiter.

exploitation [ɛksplɔɪ'teɪʃən] n exploitation f.

exploration [ɛksplə'reɪʃən] n exploration f.

exploratory [ɪk'splɔrətrɪ] a (fig: talks) préliminaire; **~ operation** (MED) intervention f (à visée) exploratrice.

explore [ɪk'splɔ:*] vt explorer; (possibilities) étudier, examiner.

explorer [ɪk'splɔ:rə*] n explorateur/trice.

explosion [ɪk'spləuʒən] n explosion f.

explosive [ɪk'spləusɪv] a explosif(ive) ♦ n explosif m.

exponent [ɪk'spəunənt] n (of school of thought etc) interprète m, représentant m; (MATH) exposant m.

export vt [ɛk'spɔ:t] exporter ♦ n ['ɛkspɔ:t] exportation f ♦ cpd d'exportation.

exportation [ɛkspɔ:'teɪʃən] n exportation f.

exporter [ɛk'spɔ:tə*] n exportateur m.

export licence n licence f d'exportation.

expose [ɪk'spəuz] vt exposer; (unmask) démasquer, dévoiler; **to ~ o.s.** (LAW) commettre un outrage à la pudeur.

exposed [ɪk'spəuzd] a (land, house) exposé(e); (ELEC: wire) à nu; (pipe, beam) apparent(e).

exposition [ɛkspə'zɪʃən] n exposition f.

exposure [ɪk'spəuʒə*] n exposition f; (PHOT) (temps m de) pose f; (: shot) pose; **suffering from ~** (MED) souffrant des effets du froid et de l'épuisement; **to die of ~** (MED) mourir de froid.

exposure meter n posemètre m.

expound [ɪk'spaund] vt exposer, expliquer.

express [ɪk'sprɛs] a (definite) formel(le), exprès(esse); (Brit: letter etc) exprès inv ♦ n (train) rapide m ♦ ad (send) exprès ♦ vt exprimer; **to ~ o.s.** s'exprimer; **to send sth ~** envoyer qch exprès.

expression [ɪk'sprɛʃən] n expression f.

expressionism [ɪk'sprɛʃənɪzəm] n expressionnisme m.

expressive [ɪk'sprɛsɪv] a expressif(ive).

expressly [ɪk'sprɛslɪ] ad expressément, formellement.

expressway [ɪk'sprɛsweɪ] n (US) voie f express (à plusieurs files).

expropriate [ɛks'prəuprɪeɪt] vt exproprier.

expulsion [ɪk'spʌlʃən] n expulsion f; renvoi m.

exquisite [ɛk'skwɪzɪt] a exquis(e).

ex-serviceman ['ɛks'sə:vɪsmən] n ancien combattant.

ext. abbr (TEL) = **extension**.

extemporize [ɪk'stɛmpəraɪz] vi improviser.

extend [ɪk'stɛnd] vt (visit, street) prolonger; (deadline) reporter, remettre; (building) agrandir; (offer) présenter, offrir; (COMM: credit) accorder ♦ vi (land) s'étendre.

extension [ɪk'stɛnʃən] n (see extend) prolongation f; agrandissement m; (building) annexe f; (to wire, table) rallonge f; (telephone: in offices) poste m; (: in private house) téléphone m supplémentaire; **~ 3718** (TEL) poste 3718.

extension cable n (ELEC) rallonge f.

extensive [ɪk'stɛnsɪv] a étendu(e), vaste; (damage, alterations) considérable; (inquiries) approfondi(e); (use) largement répandu(e).

extensively [ɪk'stɛnsɪvlɪ] ad (altered, damaged etc) considérablement; **he's travelled ~** il a beaucoup voyagé.

extent [ɪk'stɛnt] n étendue f; (degree: of damage, loss) importance f; **to some ~** dans une certaine mesure; **to a certain ~** dans une certaine mesure, jusqu'à un certain point; **to a large ~** en grande partie; **to what ~?** dans quelle mesure?, jusqu'à quel point?; **to such an ~ that ...** à tel point que ....

extenuating [ɪk'stɛnjueɪtɪŋ] a: **~ circumstances** circonstances atténuantes.

exterior [ɛk'stɪərɪə*] a extérieur(e), du dehors ♦ n extérieur m; dehors m.

exterminate [ɪk'stə:mɪneɪt] vt exterminer.

extermination [ɪkstə:mɪ'neɪʃən] n extermination f.

external [ɛk'stə:nl] a externe ♦ n: **the ~s** les apparences fpl; **for ~ use only** (MED) à usage externe.

externally [ɛk'stə:nəlɪ] ad extérieurement.

extinct [ɪk'stɪŋkt] a éteint(e).

extinction [ɪk'stɪŋkʃən] n extinction f.

extinguish [ɪk'stɪŋgwɪʃ] vt éteindre.

extinguisher [ɪk'stɪŋgwɪʃə*] n extincteur m.

extol, (US) **extoll** [ɪk'stəul] vt (merits) chanter, prôner; (person) chanter les louanges de.

extort [ɪk'stɔ:t] vt: **to ~ sth (from)** extorquer qch (à).

extortion [ɪk'stɔ:ʃən] n extorsion f.

extortionate [ɪk'stɔ:ʃnɪt] a exorbitant(e).

extra ['ɛkstrə] a supplémentaire, de plus ♦ ad (in addition) en plus ♦ n supplément m; (THEATRE) figurant/e; **wine will cost ~** le vin sera en supplément; ~ **large sizes** très grandes tailles.

extra... ['ekstrə] *prefix* extra....

extract *vt* [ɪk'strækt] extraire; *(tooth)* arracher; *(money, promise)* soutirer ♦ *n* ['ekstrækt] extrait *m*.

extraction [ɪk'strækʃən] *n (also descent)* extraction *f*.

extracurricular ['ekstrəkə'rɪkjulə*] *a (SCOL)* parascolaire.

extradite ['ekstrədaɪt] *vt* extrader.

extradition [ekstrə'dɪʃən] *n* extradition *f*.

extramarital ['ekstrə'mærɪtl] *a* extra-conjugal(e).

extramural ['ekstrə'mjuərl] *a* hors-faculté *inv*.

extraneous [ek'streɪnɪəs] *a*: ~ **to** étranger(ère) à.

extraordinary [ɪk'strɔ:dnrɪ] *a* extraordinaire; **the ~ thing is that ...** le plus étrange *or* étonnant c'est que ....

extraordinary general meeting *n* assemblée générale extraordinaire.

extrapolation [ekstræpə'leɪʃən] *n* extrapolation *f*.

extrasensory perception (ESP) ['ekstrə'sensərɪ-] *n* perception extrasensorielle.

extra time *n (FOOTBALL)* prolongations *fpl*.

extravagance [ɪk'strævəgəns] *n (excessive spending)* prodigalités *fpl*; *(thing bought)* folie *f*, dépense excessive *or* exagérée.

extravagant [ɪk'strævəgənt] *a* extravagant(e); *(in spending: person)* prodigue, dépensier(ière); *(: tastes)* dispendieux(euse).

extreme [ɪk'stri:m] *a*, *n* extrême *(m)*; **the ~ left/right** *(POL)* l'extrême gauche *f*/droite *f*; **~s of temperature** différences *fpl* extrêmes de température.

extremely [ɪk'stri:mlɪ] *ad* extrêmement.

extremist [ɪk'stri:mɪst] *a*, *n* extrémiste *(m/f)*.

extremity [ɪk'stremɪtɪ] *n* extrémité *f*.

extricate ['ekstrɪkeɪt] *vt*: **to ~ sth (from)** dégager qch (de).

extrovert ['ekstrəvɔ:t] *n* extraverti/e.

exuberance [ɪg'zju:bərns] *n* exubérance *f*.

exuberant [ɪg'zju:bərnt] *a* exubérant(e).

exude [ɪg'zju:d] *vt* exsuder; *(fig)* respirer; **the charm** *etc* **he ~s** le charme *etc* qui émane de lui.

exult [ɪg'zʌlt] *vi* exulter, jubiler.

exultant [ɪg'zʌltənt] *a (shout, expression)* de triomphe; **to be ~** jubiler, triompher.

exultation [egzʌl'teɪʃən] *n* exultation *f*, jubilation *f*.

eye [aɪ] *n* œil *m (pl* yeux); *(of needle)* trou *m*, chas *m* ♦ *vt* examiner; **as far as the ~ can see** à perte de vue; **to keep an ~ on** surveiller; **to have an ~ for sth** avoir l'œil pour qch; **in the public ~** en vue; **with an ~ to doing sth** *(Brit)* en vue de faire qch; **there's more to this than meets the ~** ce n'est pas aussi simple que cela paraît.

eyeball ['aɪbɔ:l] *n* globe *m* oculaire.

eyebath ['aɪbɑ:θ] *n (Brit)* œillère *f (pour bains d'œil)*.

eyebrow ['aɪbrau] *n* sourcil *m*.

eyebrow pencil *n* crayon *m* à sourcils.

eye-catching ['aɪkætʃɪŋ] *a* voyant(e), accrocheur(euse).

eye cup *n (US)* = **eyebath**.

eyedrops ['aɪdrɔps] *npl* gouttes *fpl* pour les yeux.

eyeglass ['aɪglɑ:s] *n* monocle *m*.

eyelash ['aɪlæʃ] *n* cil *m*.

eyelet ['aɪlɪt] *n* œillet *m*.

eye-level ['aɪlevl] *a* en hauteur.

eyelid ['aɪlɪd] *n* paupière *f*.

eyeliner ['aɪlaɪnə*] *n* eye-liner *m*.

eye-opener ['aɪəupnə*] *n* révélation *f*.

eyeshadow ['aɪʃædəu] *n* ombre *f* à paupières.

eyesight ['aɪsaɪt] *n* vue *f*.

eyesore ['aɪsɔ:*] *n* horreur *f*, chose *f* qui dépare *or* enlaidit.

eyestrain ['aɪstreɪn] *a*: **to get ~** se fatiguer la vue *or* les yeux.

eyetooth, *pl* **-teeth** ['aɪtu:θ, -ti:θ] *n* canine supérieure; **to give one's eyeteeth for sth/to do sth** *(fig)* donner n'importe quoi pour qch/pour faire qch.

eyewash ['aɪwɔʃ] *n* bain *m* d'œil; *(fig)* frime *f*.

eye witness *n* témoin *m* oculaire.

eyrie ['ɪərɪ] *n* aire *f*.

F

F, f [ef] *n (letter)* F, f *m*; *(MUS)*: **F** fa *m*; **F for Frederick**, *(US)* **F for Fox** F comme François.

F *abbr (= Fahrenheit)* F.

FA *n abbr (Brit: = Football Association)* fédération de football.

FAA *n abbr (US) = Federal Aviation Administration*.

fable ['feɪbl] *n* fable *f*.

fabric ['fæbrɪk] *n* tissu *m* ♦ *cpd*: **~ ribbon** *n (for typewriter)* ruban *m* (en) tissu.

fabricate ['fæbrɪkeɪt] *vt* fabriquer, inventer.

fabrication [fæbrɪ'keɪʃən] *n* fabrication *f*, invention *f*.

fabulous ['fæbjuləs] *a* fabuleux(euse); *(col: super)* formidable, sensationnel(le).

façade [fə'sɑ:d] *n* façade *f*.

face [feɪs] *n* visage *m*, figure *f*; expression *f*; grimace *f*; *(of clock)* cadran *m*; *(of building)* façade *f*; *(side, surface)* face *f* ♦ *vt* faire face à; *(facts etc)* accepter; **~ down** *(person)* à plat ventre; *(card)* face en dessous; **to lose/save ~** perdre/sauver la face; **to pull a ~** faire une grimace; **in the ~ of** *(difficulties etc)* face à, devant; **on the ~ of it** à première vue.

face up to *vt fus* faire face à, affronter.

face cloth *n (Brit)* gant *m* de toilette.

face cream *n* crème *f* pour le visage.

face lift *n* lifting *m*; *(of façade etc)* ravalement *m*, retapage *m*.

face powder *n* poudre *f* (pour le visage).

face-saving ['feɪs'seɪvɪŋ] *a* qui sauve la face.

facet ['fæsɪt] *n* facette *f*.

facetious [fə'si:ʃəs] *a* facétieux(euse).

face-to-face ['feɪstə'feɪs] *ad* face à face.
face value ['feɪs'vælju:] *n* (*of coin*) valeur nominale; **to take sth at** ~ (*fig*) prendre qch pour argent comptant.
facia ['feɪʃə] *n* = **fascia.**
facial ['feɪʃl] *a* facial(e) ♦ *n* soin complet du visage.
facile ['fæsaɪl] *a* facile.
facilitate [fə'sɪlɪteɪt] *vt* faciliter.
facility [fə'sɪlɪtɪ] *n* facilité *f*; **facilities** *npl* installations *fpl*, équipement *m*; **credit facilities** facilités de paiement.
facing ['feɪsɪŋ] *prep* face à, en face de ♦ *n* (*of wall etc*) revêtement *m*; (*SEWING*) revers *m*.
facsimile [fæk'sɪmɪlɪ] *n* (*exact replica*) facsimilé *m*; (*also*: ~ **machine**) télécopieur *m*; (*transmitted document*) télécopie *f*.
fact [fækt] *n* fait *m*; **in** ~ en fait; **to know for a** ~ **that** ... savoir pertinemment que ....
fact-finding ['fæktfaɪndɪŋ] *a*: **a** ~ **tour** *or* **mission** une mission d'enquête.
faction ['fækʃən] *n* faction *f*.
factor ['fæktə*] *n* facteur *m*; (*COMM*) factor *m*, société *f* d'affacturage; (: *agent*) dépositaire *m/f* ♦ *vi* faire du factoring; **safety** ~ facteur de sécurité.
factory ['fæktərɪ] *n* usine *f*, fabrique *f*.
factory farming *n* (*Brit*) élevage industriel.
factory ship *n* navire-usine *m*.
factual ['fæktjʊəl] *a* basé(e) sur les faits.
faculty ['fækəltɪ] *n* faculté *f*; (*US: teaching staff*) corps enseignant.
fad [fæd] *n* (*col*) manie *f*; engouement *m*.
fade [feɪd] *vi* se décolorer, passer; (*light, sound, hope*) s'affaiblir, disparaître; (*flower*) se faner.
fade in *vt* (*picture*) ouvrir en fondu; (*sound*) monter progressivement.
fade out *vt* (*picture*) fermer en fondu; (*sound*) baisser progressivement.
faeces, (*US*) **feces** ['fi:si:z] *npl* fèces *fpl*.
fag [fæg] *n* (*Brit col: cigarette*) sèche *f*; (: *chore*): **what a** ~! quelle corvée!; (*US col: homosexual*) pédé *m*.
fag end *n* (*Brit col*) mégot *m*.
fagged out *a* (*Brit col*) crevé(e).
fail [feɪl] *vt* (*exam*) échouer à; (*candidate*) recaler; (*subj: courage, memory*) faire défaut à ♦ *vi* échouer; (*supplies*) manquer; (*eyesight, health, light: also*: **be** ~**ing**) baisser, s'affaiblir; (*brakes*) lâcher; **to** ~ **to do sth** (*neglect*) négliger de *or* ne pas faire qch; (*be unable*) ne pas arriver *or* parvenir à faire qch; **without** ~ à coup sûr; sans faute.
failing ['feɪlɪŋ] *n* défaut *m* ♦ *prep* faute de; ~ **that** à défaut, sinon.
failsafe ['feɪlseɪf] *a* (*device etc*) à sûreté intégrée.
failure ['feɪljə*] *n* échec *m*; (*person*) raté/e; (*mechanical etc*) défaillance *f*; **his** ~ **to turn up** le fait de n'être pas venu *or* qu'il ne soit pas venu.
faint [feɪnt] *a* faible; (*recollection*) vague; (*mark*) à peine visible; (*smell, breeze, trace*) léger(ère) ♦ *n* évanouissement *m* ♦ *vi* s'évanouir; **to feel** ~ défaillir.
faint-hearted ['feɪnt'hɑ:tɪd] *a* pusillanime.
faintly ['feɪntlɪ] *ad* faiblement; vaguement.
faintness ['feɪntnɪs] *n* faiblesse *f*.

fair [fɛə*] *a* équitable, juste; (*reasonable*) correct(e), honnête; (*hair*) blond(e); (*skin, complexion*) pâle, blanc, blanc(blanche); (*weather*) beau(belle); (*good enough*) assez bon(ne) ♦ *ad*: **to play** ~ jouer franc jeu ♦ *n* foire *f*; (*Brit: funfair*) fête (foraine); (*also*: **trade** ~) foire(-exposition) commerciale; **it's not** ~! ce n'est pas juste!; **a** ~ **amount of** une quantité considérable de.
fair copy *n* copie *f* au propre; corrigé *m*.
fair-haired [fɛə'hɛəd] *a* (*person*) aux cheveux clairs, blond(e).
fairly ['fɛəlɪ] *ad* équitablement; (*quite*) assez; **I'm** ~ **sure** j'en suis quasiment *or* presque sûr.
fairness ['fɛənɪs] *n* (*of trial etc*) justice *f*, équité *f*; (*of person*) sens *m* de la justice; **in all** ~ en toute justice.
fair play *n* fair play *m*.
fairy ['fɛərɪ] *n* fée *f*.
fairy godmother *n* bonne fée.
fairy lights *npl* (*Brit*) guirlande *f* électrique.
fairy tale *n* conte *m* de fées.
faith [feɪθ] *n* foi *f*; (*trust*) confiance *f*; (*sect*) culte *m*, religion *f*; **to have** ~ **in sb/sth** avoir confiance en qn/qch.
faithful ['feɪθfʊl] *a* fidèle.
faithfully ['feɪθfəlɪ] *ad* fidèlement; **yours** ~ (*Brit: in letters*) veuillez agréer l'expression de mes salutations les plus distinguées.
faith healer *n* guérisseur/euse.
fake [feɪk] *n* (*painting etc*) faux *m*; (*photo*) trucage *m*; (*person*) imposteur *m* ♦ *a* faux(fausse) ♦ *vt* (*emotions*) simuler; (*photo*) truquer; (*story*) fabriquer; **his illness is a** ~ sa maladie est une comédie *or* de la simulation.
falcon ['fɔ:lkən] *n* faucon *m*.
Falkland Islands ['fɔ:lklənd-] *npl*: **the** ~ les Malouines *fpl*, les îles *fpl* Falkland.
fall [fɔ:l] *n* chute *f*; (*decrease*) baisse *f*; (*US: autumn*) automne *m* ♦ *vi* (*pt* **fell**, *pp* **fallen**) [fɛl, 'fɔ:lən]) tomber; ~**s** *npl* (*waterfall*) chute *f* d'eau, cascade *f*; **to** ~ **flat** *vi* (*on one's face*) tomber de tout son long, s'étaler; (*joke*) tomber à plat; (*plan*) échouer; **to** ~ **short of** (*sb's expectations*) ne pas répondre à; **a** ~ **of snow** (*Brit*) une chute de neige.
fall apart *vi* tomber en morceaux; (*col: emotionally*) craquer.
fall back *vi* reculer, se retirer.
fall back on *vt fus* se rabattre sur; **to have something to** ~ **back on** (*money etc*) avoir quelque chose en réserve; (*job etc*) avoir une solution de rechange.
fall behind *vi* prendre du retard.
fall down *vi* (*person*) tomber; (*building, hopes*) s'effondrer, s'écrouler.
fall for *vt fus* (*trick*) se laisser prendre à; (*person*) tomber amoureux(euse) de.
fall in *vi* s'effondrer; (*MIL*) se mettre en rangs.
fall in with *vt fus* (*sb's plans etc*) accepter.
fall off *vi* tomber; (*diminish*) baisser, diminuer.
fall out *vi* (*friends etc*) se brouiller.
fall over *vi* tomber (par terre).
fall through *vi* (*plan, project*) tomber à l'eau.

fallacy ['fæləsı] *n* erreur *f*, illusion *f*.
fallback ['fɔ:lbæk] *a*: ~ **position** position *f* de repli.
fallen ['fɔ:lən] *pp of* **fall**.
fallible ['fæləbl] *a* faillible.
fallopian tube [fə'ləupıən-] *n* (*ANAT*) trompe *f* de Fallope.
fallout ['fɔ:laut] *n* retombées (radioactives).
fallout shelter *n* abri *m* anti-atomique.
fallow ['fæləu] *a* en jachère; en friche.
false [fɔ:ls] *a* faux(fausse); **under ~ pretences** sous un faux prétexte.
false alarm *n* fausse alerte.
falsehood ['fɔ:lshud] *n* mensonge *m*.
falsely ['fɔ:lslı] *ad* (*accuse*) à tort.
false teeth *npl* (*Brit*) fausses dents.
falsify ['fɔ:lsıfaı] *vt* falsifier; (*accounts*) maquiller.
falter ['fɔ:ltə*] *vi* chanceler, vaciller.
fame [feım] *n* renommée *f*, renom *m*.
familiar [fə'mılıə*] *a* familier(ière); **to be ~ with sth** connaître qch; **to make o.s. ~ with sth** se familiariser avec qch; **to be on ~ terms with sb** bien connaître qn.
familiarity [fəmılı'ærıtı] *n* familiarité *f*.
familiarize [fə'mılıəraız] *vt* familiariser.
family ['fæmılı] *n* famille *f*.
family allowance *n* (*Brit*) allocations familiales.
family business *n* entreprise familiale.
family doctor *n* médecin *m* de famille.
family life *n* vie *f* de famille.
family planning clinic *n* centre *m* de planning familial.
family tree *n* arbre *m* généalogique.
famine ['fæmın] *n* famine *f*.
famished ['fæmıʃt] *a* affamé(e); **I'm ~!** (*col*) je meurs de faim!
famous ['feıməs] *a* célèbre.
famously ['feıməslı] *ad* (*get on*) fameusement, à merveille.
fan [fæn] *n* (*folding*) éventail *m*; (*ELEC*) ventilateur *m*; (*person*) fan *m*, admirateur/trice; (: *SPORT*) supporter *m/f* ♦ *vt* éventer; (*fire, quarrel*) attiser.
fan out *vi* se déployer (en éventail).
fanatic [fə'nætık] *n* fanatique *m/f*.
fanatical [fə'nætıkl] *a* fanatique.
fan belt *n* courroie *f* de ventilateur.
fancied ['fænsıd] *a* imaginaire.
fanciful ['fænsıful] *a* fantaisiste.
fancy ['fænsı] *n* fantaisie *f*, envie *f*; imagination *f* ♦ *cpd* (de) fantaisie *inv* ♦ *vt* (*feel like, want*) avoir envie de; (*imagine*) imaginer; **to take a ~ to** se prendre d'affection pour; s'enticher de; **it took or caught my ~** ça m'a plu;. **when the ~ takes him** quand ça lui prend; **to ~ that ...** se figurer *or* s'imaginer que ...; **he fancies her** elle lui plaît.
fancy dress *n* déguisement *m*, travesti *m*.
fancy-dress ball *n* bal masqué *or* costumé.
fancy goods *npl* articles *mpl* (de) fantaisie.
fanfare ['fænfeə] *n* fanfare *f* (*musique*).
fanfold paper ['fænfəuld-] *n* papier *m* à pliage accordéon.
fang [fæŋ] *n* croc *m*; (*of snake*) crochet *m*.
fan heater *n* (*Brit*) radiateur soufflant.
fanlight ['fænlaıt] *n* imposte *f*.

fantasize ['fæntəsaız] *vi* fantasmer.
fantastic [fæn'tæstık] *a* fantastique.
fantasy ['fæntəsı] *n* imagination *f*, fantaisie *f*; fantasme *m*.
FAO *n abbr* (= *Food and Agriculture Organization*) FAO *f*.
FAQ *abbr* (= *free alongside quay*) FLQ.
far [fɑ:*] *a*: **the ~ side/end** l'autre côté/bout; **the ~ left/right** (*POL*) l'extrême gauche *f*/droite *f* ♦ *ad* loin; **is it ~ to London?** est-ce qu'on est loin de Londres?; **it's not ~ (from here)** ce n'est pas loin (d'ici); **~ away, ~ off** au loin, dans le lointain; **~ better** beaucoup mieux; **~ from** loin de; **by ~** de loin, de beaucoup; **as ~ back as the 13th century** dès le 13e siècle; **go as ~ as the farm** allez jusqu'à la ferme; **as ~ as I know** pour autant que je sache; **as ~ as possible** dans la mesure du possible; **how ~ have you got with your work?** où en êtes-vous dans votre travail?
faraway ['fɑ:rəweı] *a* lointain(e); (*look*) absent(e).
farce [fɑ:s] *n* farce *f*.
farcical ['fɑ:sıkl] *a* grotesque.
fare [fcə*] *n* (*on trains, buses*) prix *m* du billet; (*in taxi*).prix de la course; (*passenger in taxi*) client *m*; (*food*) table *f*, chère *f* ♦ *vi* se débrouiller.
Far East *n*: **the ~** l'Extrême-Orient *m*.
farewell [fcə'wel] *excl, n* adieu (*m*) ♦ *cpd* (*party etc*) d'adieux.
far-fetched ['fɑ:'fetʃt] *a* exagéré(e), poussé(e).
farm [fɑ:m] *n* ferme *f* ♦ *vt* cultiver.
farm out *vt* (*work etc*) distribuer.
farmer ['fɑ:mə*] *n* fermier/ière; cultivateur/trice.
farmhand ['fɑ:mhænd] *n* ouvrier/ière agricole.
farmhouse ['fɑ:mhaus] *n* (maison *f* de) ferme *f*.
farming ['fɑ:mıŋ] *n* agriculture *f*; **intensive ~** culture intensive; **sheep ~** élevage *m* du mouton.
farm labourer *n* = **farmhand**.
farmland ['fɑ:mlænd] *n* terres cultivées *or* arables.
farm produce *n* produits *mpl* agricoles.
farm worker *n* = **farmhand**.
farmyard ['fɑ:mjɑ:d] *n* cour *f* de ferme.
Faroe Islands ['fcərəu-] *npl*, **Faroes** ['fcərəuz] *npl*: **the ~** les îles *fpl* Féroé *or* Faeroe.
far-reaching ['fɑ:'ri:tʃıŋ] *a* d'une grande portée.
far-sighted ['fɑ:'saıtıd] *a* presbyte; (*fig*) prévoyant(e), qui voit loin.
fart [fɑ:t] (*col!*) *n* pet *m* ♦ *vi* péter.
farther ['fɑ:ðə*] *ad* plus loin ♦ *a* plus eloigné(e), plus lointain(e).
farthest ['fɑ:ðıst] *superlative of* **far**.
FAS *abbr* (*Brit*: = *free alongside ship*) FLB.
fascia ['feıʃə] *n* (*AUT*) (garniture *f* du) tableau *m* de bord.
fascinate ['fæsıneıt] *vt* fasciner, captiver.
fascinating ['fæsıneıtıŋ] *a* fascinant(e).
fascination [fæsı'neıʃən] *n* fascination *f*.
fascism ['fæʃızəm] *n* fascisme *m*.
fascist ['fæʃıst] *a*, *n* fasciste (*m/f*).
fashion ['fæʃən] *n* mode *f*; (*manner*) façon *f*,

manière f ♦ vt façonner; **in** ~ à la mode; **out of** ~ démodé(e); **in the Greek** ~ à la grecque; **after a** ~ (finish, manage etc) tant bien que mal.

fashionable ['fæʃnəbl] a à la mode.

fashion designer n (grand(e)) couturier/ière.

fashion show n défilé m de mannequins or de mode.

fast [fɑ:st] a rapide; (clock): **to be** ~ avancer; (dye, colour) grand or bon teint inv ♦ ad vite, rapidement; (stuck, held) solidement ♦ n jeûne m ♦ vi jeûner; **my watch is 5 minutes** ~ ma montre avance de 5 minutes; ~ **asleep** profondément endormi; **as** ~ **as I can** aussi vite que je peux; **to make a boat** ~ (Brit) amarrer un bateau.

fasten ['fɑ:sn] vt attacher, fixer; (coat) attacher, fermer ♦ vi se fermer, s'attacher.
   fasten (up)on vt fus (idea) se cramponner à.

fastener ['fɑ:snə*], **fastening** ['fɑ:snɪŋ] n fermeture f, attache f; (Brit: zip ~) fermeture éclair inv ® or à glissière.

fast food n fast food m, restauration f rapide.

fastidious [fæs'tɪdɪəs] a exigeant(e), difficile.

fast lane n (AUT: in Britain) voie f de droite.

fat [fæt] a gros(se) ♦ n graisse f; (on meat) gras m; **to live off the** ~ **of the land** vivre grassement.

fatal ['feɪtl] a fatal(e); (leading to death) mortel(le).

fatalism ['feɪtlɪzəm] n fatalisme m.

fatality [fə'tælɪtɪ] n (road death etc) victime f, décès m.

fatally ['feɪtəlɪ] ad fatalement; mortellement.

fate [feɪt] n destin m; (of person) sort m; **to meet one's** ~ trouver la mort.

fated ['feɪtɪd] a (person) condamné(e); (project) voué(e) à l'échec.

fateful ['feɪtful] a fatidique.

father ['fɑ:ðə*] n père m.

Father Christmas n le Père Noël.

fatherhood ['fɑ:ðəhud] n paternité f.

father-in-law ['fɑ:ðərənlɔ:] n beau-père m.

fatherland ['fɑ:ðəlænd] n (mère f) patrie f.

fatherly ['fɑ:ðəlɪ] a paternel(le).

fathom ['fæðəm] n brasse f (= 1828 mm) ♦ vt (mystery) sonder, pénétrer.

fatigue [fə'ti:g] n fatigue f; (MIL) corvée f; **metal** ~ fatigue du métal.

fatness ['fætnɪs] n corpulence f, grosseur f.

fatten ['fætn] vt, vi engraisser; **chocolate is** ~**ing** le chocolat fait grossir.

fatty ['fætɪ] a (food) gras(se) ♦ n (col) gros/grosse.

fatuous ['fætjuəs] a stupide.

faucet ['fɔ:sɪt] n (US) robinet m.

fault [fɔ:lt] n faute f; (defect) défaut m; (GEO) faille f ♦ vt trouver des défauts à, prendre en défaut; **it's my** ~ c'est de ma faute; **to find** ~ **with** trouver à redire or à critiquer à; **at** ~ fautif(ive), coupable; **to a** ~ à l'excès.

faultless ['fɔ:ltlɪs] a impeccable; irréprochable.

faulty ['fɔ:ltɪ] a défectueux(euse).

fauna ['fɔ:nə] n faune f.

faux pas ['fəu'pɑ:] n impair m, bévue f, gaffe f.

favour, (US) **favor** ['feɪvə*] n faveur f; (help) service m ♦ vt (proposition) être en faveur de; (pupil etc) favoriser; (team, horse) donner gagnant; **to do sb a** ~ rendre un service à qn; **in** ~ **of** en faveur de; **to be in** ~ **of sth/of doing sth** être partisan de qch/de faire qch; **to find** ~ **with sb** trouver grâce aux yeux de qn.

favo(u)rable ['feɪvrəbl] a favorable; (price) avantageux(euse).

favo(u)rably ['feɪvrəblɪ] ad favorablement.

favo(u)rite ['feɪvrɪt] a, n favori(te).

favo(u)ritism ['feɪvrɪtɪzəm] n favoritisme m.

fawn [fɔ:n] n faon m ♦ a (also: ~-**coloured**) fauve ♦ vi: **to** ~ (**up)on** flatter servilement.

fax [fæks] n (document) télécopie f; (machine) télécopieur m ♦ vt envoyer par télécopie.

FBI n abbr (US: = Federal Bureau of Investigation) FBI m.

FCC n abbr (US) = Federal Communications Commission.

FCO n abbr (Brit: = Foreign and Commonwealth Office) ministère des Affaires étrangères et du Commonwealth.

FD n abbr (US) = **fire department**.

FDA n abbr (US: = Food and Drug Administration) office de contrôle des produits pharmaceutiques et alimentaires.

fear [fɪə*] n crainte f, peur f ♦ vt craindre ♦ vi: **to** ~ **for** craindre pour; **to** ~ **that** craindre que; ~ **of heights** vertige m; **for** ~ **of** de peur que + sub or de + infinitive.

fearful ['fɪəful] a craintif(ive); (sight, noise) affreux(euse), épouvantable; **to be** ~ **of** avoir peur de, craindre.

fearfully ['fɪəfəlɪ] ad (timidly) craintivement; (col: very) affreusement.

fearless ['fɪəlɪs] a intrépide, sans peur.

fearsome ['fɪəsəm] a (opponent) redoutable; (sight) épouvantable.

feasibility [fi:zə'bɪlɪtɪ] n (of plan) possibilité f de réalisation, faisabilité f.

feasibility study n étude f de faisabilité.

feasible ['fi:zəbl] a faisable, réalisable.

feast [fi:st] n festin m, banquet m; (REL: also: ~ **day**) fête f ♦ vi festoyer; **to** ~ **on** se régaler de.

feat [fi:t] n exploit m, prouesse f.

feather ['feðə*] n plume f ♦ vt: **to** ~ **one's nest** (fig) faire sa pelote ♦ cpd (bed etc) de plumes.

feather-weight ['feðəweɪt] n poids m plume inv.

feature ['fi:tʃə*] n caractéristique f; (article) chronique f, rubrique f ♦ vt (subj: film) avoir pour vedette(s) ♦ vi figurer (en bonne place); ~**s** npl (of face) traits mpl; **a (special)** ~ **on sth/sb** un reportage sur qch/qn; **it** ~**d prominently in** ... cela a figuré en bonne place sur or dans ....

feature film n long métrage m.

featureless ['fi:tʃəlɪs] a anonyme, sans traits distinctifs.

Feb. abbr (= February) fév.

February ['fɛbruərɪ] n février m; for phrases see also **July**.

feces ['fi:si:z] npl (US) = **faeces**.

feckless ['fɛklɪs] a inepte.

Fed abbr (US) = **federal, federation**.

fed [fɛd] pt, pp of **feed**; **to be ~ up** en avoir marre or plein le dos.

Fed. [fɛd] n abbr (US col) = **Federal Reserve Board**.

federal ['fɛdərəl] a fédéral(e).

Federal Reserve Board n (US) organe de contrôle de la banque centrale américaine.

Federal Trade Commission (FTC) n (US) organisme de protection contre les pratiques commerciales abusives.

federation [fɛdə'reɪʃən] n fédération f.

fee [fiː] n rémunération f; (of doctor, lawyer) honoraires mpl; (of school, college etc) frais mpl de scolarité; (for examination) droits mpl; **entrance/membership ~** droit d'entrée/d'inscription; **for a small ~** pour une somme modique.

feeble ['fiːbl] a faible.

feeble-minded ['fiːbl'maɪndɪd] a faible d'esprit.

feed [fiːd] n (of baby) tétée f; (of animal) fourrage m; pâture f; (on printer) mécanisme m d'alimentation ♦ vt (pt, pp **fed** [fɛd]) nourrir; (horse etc) donner à manger à; (machine) alimenter; (data etc): **to ~ sth into** fournir qch à, introduire qch dans.

feed back vt (results) donner en retour.

feed on vt fus se nourrir de.

feedback ['fiːdbæk] n feed-back m; (from person) réactions fpl.

feeder ['fiːdə*] n (bib) bavette f.

feeding bottle n (Brit) biberon m.

feel [fiːl] n sensation f ♦ vt (pt, pp **felt** [fɛlt]) (touch) toucher; tâter, palper; (cold, pain) sentir; (grief, anger) ressentir, éprouver; (think, believe): **to ~ (that)** trouver que; **I ~ that you ought to do it** il me semble que vous devriez le faire; **to ~ hungry/cold** avoir faim/froid; **to ~ lonely/better** se sentir seul/mieux; **I don't ~ well** je ne me sens pas bien; **to ~ sorry for** avoir pitié de; **it ~s soft** c'est doux au toucher; **it ~s colder here** je trouve qu'il fait plus froid ici; **it ~s like velvet** on dirait du velours, ça ressemble au velours; **to ~ like** (want) avoir envie de; **~ about** or **around** fouiller, tâtonner; **to get the ~ of sth** (fig) s'habituer à qch.

feeler ['fiːlə*] n (of insect) antenne f; (fig): **to put out a ~** or **~s** tâter le terrain.

feeling ['fiːlɪŋ] n sensation f, sentiment m; (impression) sentiment; **to hurt sb's ~s** froisser qn; **~s ran high about it** cela a déchaîné les passions; **what are your ~s about the matter?** quel est votre sentiment sur cette question?; **my ~ is that ...** j'estime que ...; **I have a ~ that ...** j'ai l'impression que ....

feet [fiːt] npl of **foot**.

feign [feɪn] vt feindre, simuler.

felicitous [fɪ'lɪsɪtəs] a heureux(euse).

fell [fɛl] pt of **fall** ♦ vt (tree) abattre ♦ n (Brit: mountain) montagne f; (: moorland): **the ~s** la lande ♦ a: **with one ~ blow** d'un seul coup.

fellow ['fɛləu] n type m; (comrade) compagnon m; (of learned society) membre m; (of university) universitaire m/f (membre du conseil) ♦ cpd: **their ~ prisoners/students**

leurs camarades prisonniers/étudiants; **his ~ workers** ses collègues mpl (de travail).

fellow citizen n concitoyen/ne.

fellow countryman n compatriote m.

fellow feeling n sympathie f.

fellow men npl semblables mpl.

fellowship ['fɛləuʃɪp] n (society) association f; (comradeship) amitié f, camaraderie f; (SCOL) sorte de bourse universitaire.

fellow traveller n compagnon/compagne de route; (POL) communisant/e.

fell-walking ['fɛlwɔːkɪŋ] n (Brit) randonnée f en montagne.

felon ['fɛlən] n (LAW) criminel/le.

felony ['fɛlənɪ] n (LAW) crime m, forfait m.

felt [fɛlt] pt, pp of **feel** ♦ n feutre m.

felt-tip pen ['fɛlttɪp-] n stylo-feutre m.

female ['fiːmeɪl] n (ZOOL) femelle f; (pej: woman) bonne femme ♦ a (BIOL, ELEC) femelle; (sex, character) féminin(e); (vote etc) des femmes; (child etc) du sexe féminin; **male and ~ students** étudiants et étudiantes.

female impersonator n (THEATRE) travesti m.

feminine ['fɛmɪnɪn] a féminin(e) ♦ n féminin m.

femininity [fɛmɪ'nɪnɪtɪ] n féminité f.

feminism ['fɛmɪnɪzəm] n féminisme m.

feminist ['fɛmɪnɪst] n féministe m/f.

fen [fɛn] n (Brit): **the F~s** les plaines fpl du Norfolk (anciennement marécageuses).

fence [fɛns] n barrière f; (SPORT) obstacle m; (col: person) receleur/euse ♦ vt (also: **~ in**) clôturer ♦ vi faire de l'escrime; **to sit on the ~** (fig) ne pas se mouiller.

fencing ['fɛnsɪŋ] n (sport) escrime m.

fend [fɛnd] vi: **to ~ for o.s.** se débrouiller (tout seul).

fend off vt (attack etc) parer.

fender ['fɛndə*] n (of fireplace) garde-feu m inv; (on boat) défense f; (US: of car) aile f.

fennel ['fɛnl] n fenouil m.

ferment vi [fə'mɛnt] fermenter ♦ n ['fəːmɛnt] agitation f, effervescence f.

fermentation [fəːmɛn'teɪʃən] n fermentation f.

fern [fəːn] n fougère f.

ferocious [fə'rəuʃəs] a féroce.

ferocity [fə'rɔsɪtɪ] n férocité f.

ferret ['fɛrɪt] n furet m.

ferret about, ferret around vi fureter.

ferret out vt dénicher.

ferry ['fɛrɪ] n (small) bac m; (large: also: **~boat**) ferry(-boat) m ♦ vt transporter; **to ~ sth/sb across** or **over** faire traverser qch/qn.

ferryman ['fɛrɪmən] n passeur m.

fertile ['fəːtaɪl] a fertile; (BIOL) fécond(e); **~ period** période f de fécondité.

fertility [fə'tɪlɪtɪ] n fertilité f; fécondité f.

fertility drug n médicament m contre la stérilité.

fertilize ['fəːtɪlaɪz] vt fertiliser; féconder.

fertilizer ['fəːtɪlaɪzə*] n engrais m.

fervent ['fəːvənt] a fervent(e), ardent(e).

fervour, (US) fervor ['fəːvə*] n ferveur f.

fester ['fɛstə*] vi suppurer.

festival ['fɛstɪvəl] n (REL) fête f; (ART, MUS) festival m.

festive ['fɛstɪv] a de fête; **the ~ season** (Brit:

Christmas) la période des fêtes.
festivities [fes'tɪvɪtɪz] *npl* réjouissances *fpl*.
festoon [fes'tu:n] *vt*: **to ~ with** orner de.
fetch [fetʃ] *vt* aller chercher; (*Brit: sell for*) se vendre; **how much did it ~?** ça a atteint quel prix?
   fetch up *vi* (*Brit*) se retrouver.
fetching ['fetʃɪŋ] *a* charmant(e).
fête [feɪt] *n* fête *f*, kermesse *f*.
fetid ['fetɪd] *a* fétide.
fetish ['fetɪʃ] *n* fétiche *m*.
fetter ['fetə*] *vt* entraver.
fetters ['fetəz] *npl* chaînes *fpl*.
fettle ['fetl] *n* (*Brit*): **in fine ~** en bonne forme.
fetus ['fi:təs] *n* (*US*) = **foetus**.
feud [fju:d] *n* dispute *f*, dissension *f* ♦ *vi* se disputer, se quereller; **a family ~** une querelle de famille.
feudal ['fju:dl] *a* féodal(e).
feudalism ['fju:dlɪzəm] *n* féodalité *f*.
fever ['fi:və*] *n* fièvre *f*; **he has a ~** il a de la fièvre.
feverish ['fi:vərɪʃ] *a* fiévreux(euse), fébrile.
few [fju:] *a* peu de ♦ *pronoun*: **~ succeed** il y en a peu qui réussissent, (bien) peu réussissent; **they were ~** ils étaient peu (nombreux), il y en avait peu; **a ~ ...** quelques ...; **I know a ~** j'en connais quelques-uns; **quite a ~ ...** un certain nombre de ..., pas mal de ...; **in the next ~ days** dans les jours qui viennent; **in the past ~ days** ces derniers jours; **every ~ days/ months** tous les deux ou trois jours/mois; **a ~ more ...** encore quelques ..., quelques ... de plus.
fewer ['fju:ə*] *a* moins de ♦ *pronoun* moins; **they are ~ now** il y en a moins maintenant, ils sont moins (nombreux) maintenant.
fewest ['fju:ɪst] *a* le moins nombreux.
FFA *n abbr* = *Future Farmers of America*.
FH *abbr* (*Brit*) = **fire hydrant**.
FHA *n abbr* (*US*: = *Federal Housing Administration*) *office fédéral du logement*.
fiancé [fɪ'ã:ŋseɪ] *n* fiancé *m*.
fiancée [fɪ'ã:ŋseɪ] *n* fiancée *f*.
fiasco [fɪ'æskəu] *n* fiasco *m*.
fib [fɪb] *n* bobard *m*.
fibre, (*US*) **fiber** ['faɪbə*] *n* fibre *f*.
fibreboard, (*US*) **fiberboard** ['faɪbɔ:d] *n* panneau *m* de fibres.
fibre-glass, (*US*) **fiber-glass** ['faɪbəglɑ:s] *n* fibre de verre.
fibrositis [faɪbrə'saɪtɪs] *n* aponévrosite *f*.
FICA *n abbr* (*US*) = *Federal Insurance Contributions Act*.
fickle ['fɪkl] *a* inconstant(e), volage, capricieux(euse).
fiction ['fɪkʃən] *n* romans *mpl*, littérature *f* romanesque; (*invention*) fiction *f*.
fictional ['fɪkʃənl] *a* fictif(ive).
fictionalize ['fɪkʃnəlaɪz] *vt* romancer.
fictitious [fɪk'tɪʃəs] *a* fictif(ive), imaginaire.
fiddle ['fɪdl] *n* (*MUS*) violon *m*; (*cheating*) combine *f*; escroquerie *f* ♦ *vt* (*Brit: accounts*) falsifier, maquiller; **tax ~** fraude fiscale, combine *f* pour échapper au fisc; **to work a ~** traficoter.
   fiddle with *vt fus* tripoter.

fiddler ['fɪdlə*] *n* violoniste *m/f*.
fiddly ['fɪdlɪ] *a* (*task*) minutieux(euse).
fidelity [fɪ'delɪtɪ] *n* fidélité *f*.
fidget ['fɪdʒɪt] *vi* se trémousser, remuer.
fidgety ['fɪdʒɪtɪ] *a* agité(e), qui a la bougeotte.
fiduciary [fɪ'dju:ʃɪərɪ] *n* agent *m* fiduciaire.
field [fi:ld] *n* champ *m*; (*fig*) domaine *m*, champ; (*SPORT*: *ground*) terrain *m*; (*COMPUT*) champ, zone *f*; **to lead the ~** (*SPORT, COMM*) dominer; **the children had a ~ day** (*fig*) c'était un grand jour pour les enfants.
field glasses *npl* jumelles *fpl*.
field marshal *n* maréchal *m*.
fieldwork ['fi:ldwə:k] *n* travaux *mpl* pratiques (*or* recherches *fpl*) sur le terrain.
fiend [fi:nd] *n* démon *m*.
fiendish ['fi:ndɪʃ] *a* diabolique.
fierce [fɪəs] *a* (*look*) féroce, sauvage; (*wind, attack*) (très) violent(e); (*fighting, enemy*) acharné(e).
fiery ['faɪərɪ] *a* ardent(e), brûlant(e); fougueux(euse).
FIFA ['fi:fə] *n abbr* (= *Fédération Internationale de Football Association*) FIFA *f*.
fifteen [fɪf'ti:n] *num* quinze.
fifth [fɪfθ] *num* cinquième.
fiftieth ['fɪftɪɪθ] *num* cinquantième.
fifty ['fɪftɪ] *num* cinquante.
fifty-fifty ['fɪftɪ'fɪftɪ] *ad*: **to share ~ with sb** partager moitié-moitié avec qn ♦ *a*: **to have a ~ chance (of success)** avoir une chance sur deux (de réussir).
fig [fɪg] *n* figue *f*.
fight [faɪt] *n* bagarre *f*; (*MIL*) combat *m*; (*against cancer etc*) lutte *f* ♦ *vb* (*pt, pp* **fought** [fɔ:t]) *vt* se battre contre; (*cancer, alcoholism*) combattre, lutter contre; (*LAW: case*) défendre ♦ *vi* se battre; (*fig*): **to ~ (for/against)** lutter (pour/contre).
fighter ['faɪtə*] *n* lutteur *m* (*fig*); (*plane*) chasseur *m*.
fighter pilot *n* pilote *m* de chasse.
fighting ['faɪtɪŋ] *n* combats *mpl*; (*brawls*) bagarres *fpl*.
figment ['fɪgmənt] *n*: **a ~ of the imagination** une invention.
figurative ['fɪgjurətɪv] *a* figuré(e).
figure ['fɪgə*] *n* (*DRAWING, GEOM*) figure *f*; (*number, cipher*) chiffre *m*; (*body, outline*) silhouette *f*, ligne *f*, formes *fpl*; (*person*) personnage *m* ♦ *vt* (*US*) supposer ♦ *vi* (*appear*) figurer; (*US: make sense*) s'expliquer; **public ~** personnalité *f*; **~ of speech** figure *f* de rhétorique.
   figure on *vt fus* (*US*): **to ~ on doing** compter faire.
   figure out *vt* arriver à comprendre; calculer.
figurehead ['fɪgəhed] *n* (*NAUT*) figure *f* de proue; (*pej*) prête-nom *m*.
figure skating *n* figures imposées (*en patinage*); patinage *m* artistique.
Fiji (Islands) ['fi:dʒi:-] *n(pl)* (îles *fpl*) Fi(d)ji *fpl*.
filament ['fɪləmənt] *n* filament *m*.
filch [fɪltʃ] *vt* (*col: steal*) voler, chiper.
file [faɪl] *n* (*tool*) lime *f*; (*dossier*) dossier *m*; (*folder*) dossier, chemise *f*; (: *binder*)

classeur m; (COMPUT) fichier m; (row) file f
♦ vt (nails, wood) limer; (papers) classer;
(LAW: claim) faire enregistrer; déposer ♦ vi:
to ~ in/out entrer/sortir l'un derrière l'autre; to ~ past défiler devant; to ~ a suit
against sb (LAW) intenter un procès à qn.
file name n (COMPUT) nom m de fichier.
filibuster ['fɪlɪbʌstə*] (esp US POL) n (also:
~er) obstructionniste m/f ♦ vi faire de l'obs-
tructionnisme.
filing ['faɪlɪŋ] n (travaux mpl de) classement
m; ~s npl limaille f.
filing cabinet n classeur m (meuble).
filing clerk n documentaliste m/f.
Filipino [fɪlɪ'piːnəu] n (person) Philippin/e;
(LING) tagalog m.
fill [fɪl] vt remplir; (vacancy) pourvoir à ♦ n:
to eat one's ~ manger à sa faim.
fill in vt (hole) boucher; (form) remplir;
(details, report) compléter.
fill out vt (form, receipt) remplir.
fill up vt remplir ♦ vi (AUT) faire le plein;
~ it up, please (AUT) le plein, s'il vous plaît.
fillet ['fɪlɪt] n filet m ♦ vt préparer en filets.
fillet steak n filet m de bœuf, tournedos m.
filling ['fɪlɪŋ] n (CULIN) garniture f, farce f;
(for tooth) plombage m.
filling station n station f d'essence.
fillip ['fɪlɪp] n coup m de fouet (fig).
filly ['fɪlɪ] n pouliche f.
film [fɪlm] n film m; (PHOT) pellicule f, film ♦
vt (scene) filmer.
film star n vedette f de cinéma.
filmstrip ['fɪlmstrɪp] n (film m pour) projection
f fixe.
film studio n studio m (de cinéma).
filter ['fɪltə*] n filtre m ♦ vt filtrer.
filter coffee n café m filtre.
filter lane n (Brit AUT) voie f de sortie.
filter tip n bout m filtre.
filth [fɪlθ] n saleté f.
filthy ['fɪlθɪ] a sale, dégoûtant(e); (language)
ordurier(ière), grossier(ière).
fin [fɪn] n (of fish) nageoire f.
final ['faɪnl] a final(e), dernier(ière); (decision,
answer) définitif(ive) ♦ n (SPORT) finale f;
~s npl (SCOL) examens mpl de dernière
année; ~ demand (on invoice etc) dernier
rappel.
finale [fɪ'nɑːlɪ] n finale m.
finalist ['faɪnəlɪst] n (SPORT) finaliste m/f.
finalize ['faɪnəlaɪz] vt mettre au point.
finally ['faɪnəlɪ] ad (lastly) en dernier lieu;
(eventually) enfin, finalement; (irrevocably)
définitivement.
finance [faɪ'næns] n finance f ♦ vt financer; ~s
npl finances fpl.
financial [faɪ'nænʃəl] a financier(ière); ~
statement bilan m, exercice financier.
financially [faɪ'nænʃəlɪ] ad financièrement.
financial year n année f budgétaire.
financier [faɪ'nænsɪə*] n financier m.
find [faɪnd] vt (pt, pp found [faund]) trouver;
(lost object) retrouver ♦ n trouvaille f,
découverte f; to ~ sb guilty (LAW) déclarer
qn coupable; to ~ (some) difficulty in doing
sth avoir du mal à faire qch.
find out vt se renseigner sur; (truth, secret) découvrir; (person) démasquer ♦ vi: to

~ out about se renseigner sur; (by chance)
apprendre.
findings ['faɪndɪŋz] npl (LAW) conclusions fpl,
verdict m; (of report) constatations fpl.
fine [faɪn] a beau(belle); excellent(e); (subtle,
not coarse) fin(e) ♦ ad (well) très bien;
(small) fin, finement ♦ n (LAW) amende f;
contravention f ♦ vt (LAW) condamner à une
amende; donner une contravention à; he's ~
il va bien; the weather is ~ il fait beau;
you're doing ~ c'est bien, vous vous dé-
brouillez bien; to cut it ~ calculer un peu
juste.
fine arts npl beaux-arts mpl.
finery ['faɪnərɪ] n parure f.
finesse [fɪ'nɛs] n finesse f, élégance f.
fine-tooth comb ['faɪntuːθ-] n: to go
through sth with a ~ (fig) passer qch au
peigne fin or au crible.
finger ['fɪŋgə*] n doigt m ♦ vt palper, toucher.
fingernail ['fɪŋgəneɪl] n ongle m (de la main).
fingerprint ['fɪŋgəprɪnt] n empreinte digitale ♦
vt (person) prendre les empreintes digitales
de.
fingerstall ['fɪŋgəstɔːl] n doigtier m.
fingertip ['fɪŋgətɪp] n bout m du doigt; (fig):
to have sth at one's ~s avoir qch à sa
disposition; (knowledge) savoir qch sur le
bout du doigt.
finicky ['fɪnɪkɪ] a tatillon(ne), méticu-
leux(euse); minutieux(euse).
finish ['fɪnɪʃ] n fin f; (SPORT) arrivée f; (polish etc) finition f ♦ vt finir, terminer ♦ vi
finir, se terminer; (session) s'achever; to ~
doing sth finir de faire qch; to ~ third
arriver or terminer troisième.
finish off vt finir, terminer; (kill) achever.
finish up vi, vt finir.
finished product ['fɪnɪʃt-] n produit fini.
finishing line ['fɪnɪʃɪŋ-] n ligne f d'arrivée.
finishing school ['fɪnɪʃɪŋ-] n institution privée
(pour jeunes filles).
finite ['faɪnaɪt] a fini(e); (verb) conjugué(e).
Finland ['fɪnlənd] n Finlande f.
Finn [fɪn] n Finnois/e; Finlandais/e.
Finnish ['fɪnɪʃ] a finnois(e); finlandais(e) ♦ n
(LING) finnois m.
fiord [fjɔːd] n fjord m.
fir [fəː*] n sapin m.
fire ['faɪə*] n feu m; incendie m ♦ vt (discharge): to ~ a gun tirer un coup de feu;
(fig) enflammer, animer; (dismiss) mettre à
la porte, renvoyer ♦ vi tirer, faire feu ♦ cpd:
~ hazard, ~ risk: that's a ~ hazard or risk
cela présente un risque d'incendie; on ~ en
feu; to set ~ to sth, set sth on ~ mettre le
feu à qch; insured against ~ assuré contre
l'incendie.
fire alarm n avertisseur m d'incendie.
firearm ['faɪərɑːm] n arme f à feu.
fire brigade n (Brit) (régiment m de
sapeurs-)pompiers mpl.
fire chief n (US) = fire master.
fire department n (US) = fire brigade.
fire engine n pompe f à incendie.
fire escape n escalier m de secours.
fire extinguisher n extincteur m.
fireguard ['faɪəgɑːd] n (Brit) garde-feu m inv.
fire insurance n assurance f incendie.

fireman ['faɪəmən] n pompier m.
fire master n (Brit) capitaine m des pompiers.
fireplace ['faɪəpleɪs] n cheminée f.
fireproof ['faɪəpruːf] a ignifuge.
fire regulations npl consignes fpl en cas d'incendie.
fire screen n (decorative) écran m de cheminée; (for protection) garde-feu m inv.
fireside ['faɪəsaɪd] n foyer m, coin m du feu.
fire station n caserne f de pompiers.
firewood ['faɪəwud] n bois m de chauffage.
firework ['faɪəwɜːk] n feu m d'artifice; ~s npl (display) feu(x) d'artifice.
firing ['faɪərɪŋ] n (MIL) feu m, tir m.
firing squad n peloton m d'exécution.
firm [fɜːm] a ferme ♦ n compagnie f, firme f.
firmly ['fɜːmlɪ] ad fermement.
firmness ['fɜːmnɪs] n fermeté f.
first [fɜːst] a premier(ière) ♦ ad (before others) le premier, la première; (before other things) en premier, d'abord; (when listing reasons etc) en premier lieu, premièrement ♦ n (person: in race) premier/ière; (Brit SCOL) mention f très bien; (AUT) première f; **the ~ of January** le premier janvier; **at ~** au commencement, au début; **~ of all** tout d'abord, pour commencer; **in the ~ instance** en premier lieu; **I'll do it ~ thing tomorrow** je le ferai tout de suite demain matin.
first aid n premiers secours or soins.
first-aid kit n trousse f à pharmacie.
first-class ['fɜːst'klɑːs] a de première classe.
first-class mail n courrier m rapide.
first-hand ['fɜːst'hænd] a de première main.
first lady n (US) femme f du président.
firstly ['fɜːstlɪ] ad premièrement, en premier lieu.
first name n prénom m.
first night n (THEATRE) première f.
first-rate ['fɜːst'reɪt] a excellent(e).
fir tree n sapin m.
FIS n abbr (Brit: = Family Income Supplement) complément familial.
fiscal ['fɪskl] a fiscal(e); **~ year** exercice financier.
fish [fɪʃ] n (pl inv) poisson m; poissons mpl ♦ vt, vi pêcher; **to ~ a river** pêcher dans une rivière; **to go ~ing** aller à la pêche.
fisherman ['fɪʃəmən] n pêcheur m.
fishery ['fɪʃərɪ] n pêcherie f.
fish factory n (Brit) conserverie f de poissons.
fish farm n établissement m piscicole.
fish fingers npl (Brit) bâtonnets de poisson (congelés).
fish hook n hameçon m.
fishing boat n barque f de pêche.
fishing industry n industrie f de la pêche.
fishing line n ligne f (de pêche).
fishing rod n canne f à pêche.
fishing tackle n attirail m de pêche.
fish market n marché m au poisson.
fishmonger ['fɪʃmʌŋgə*] n marchand m de poisson; **~'s (shop)** poissonnerie f.
fish slice n (Brit) pelle f à poisson.
fish sticks npl (US) = **fish fingers**.
fishy ['fɪʃɪ] a (fig) suspect(e), louche.

fission ['fɪʃən] n fission f; **atomic** or **nuclear ~** fission nucléaire.
fissure ['fɪʃə*] n fissure f.
fist [fɪst] n poing m.
fistfight ['fɪstfaɪt] n pugilat m, bagarre f (à coups de poing).
fit [fɪt] a (MED, SPORT) en (bonne) forme; (proper) convenable; approprié(e) ♦ vt (subj: clothes) aller à; (adjust) ajuster; (put in, attach) installer, poser; adapter; (equip) équiper, garnir, munir ♦ vi (clothes) aller; (parts) s'adapter; (in space, gap) entrer, s'adapter ♦ n (MED) accès m, crise f; (of coughing) quinte f; **~ to** en état de; **~ for** digne de; apte à; **to keep ~** se maintenir en forme; **this dress is a tight/good ~** cette robe est un peu juste/(me) va très bien; **a ~ of anger** un accès de colère; **to have a ~** (MED) faire or avoir une crise; (col) piquer une crise; **by ~s and starts** par à-coups.
fit in vi s'accorder; (person) s'adapter.
fit out vt (Brit: also: **fit up**) équiper.
fitful ['fɪtful] a intermittent(e).
fitment ['fɪtmənt] n meuble encastré, élément m.
fitness ['fɪtnɪs] n (MED) forme f physique; (of remark) à-propos m, justesse f.
fitted kitchen ['fɪtɪd-] n (Brit) cuisine équipée.
fitter ['fɪtə*] n monteur m; (DRESSMAKING) essayeur/euse.
fitting ['fɪtɪŋ] a approprié(e) ♦ n (of dress) essayage m; (of piece of equipment) pose f, installation f.
fitting room n (in shop) cabine f d'essayage.
fittings ['fɪtɪŋz] npl installations fpl.
five [faɪv] num cinq.
five-day week ['faɪvdeɪ'wiːk] n semaine f de cinq jours.
fiver ['faɪvə*] n (col: Brit) billet m de cinq livres; (: US) billet de cinq dollars.
fix [fɪks] vt fixer; (sort out) arranger; (mend) réparer; (make ready: meal, drink) préparer; (col: game etc) truquer ♦ n: **to be in a ~** être dans le pétrin.
fix up vt (meeting) arranger; **to ~ sb up with sth** faire avoir qch à qn.
fixation [fɪk'seɪʃən] n (PSYCH) fixation f; (fig) obsession f.
fixed [fɪkst] a (prices etc) fixe; **there's a ~ charge** il y a un prix forfaitaire; **how are you ~ for money?** (col) question fric, ça va?
fixed assets npl immobilisations fpl.
fixture ['fɪkstʃə*] n installation f (fixe); (SPORT) rencontre f (au programme).
fizz [fɪz] vi pétiller.
fizzle ['fɪzl] vi pétiller.
fizzle out vi rater.
fizzy ['fɪzɪ] a pétillant(e); gazeux(euse).
fjord [fjɔːd] n = **fiord**.
FL abbr (US POST) = Florida.
flabbergasted ['flæbəgɑːstɪd] a sidéré(e), ahuri(e).
flabby ['flæbɪ] a mou(molle).
flag [flæg] n drapeau m; (also: **~stone**) dalle f ♦ vi faiblir; fléchir; **~ of convenience** pavillon m de complaisance.
flag down vt héler, faire signe (de s'arrêter) à.

flagon ['flægən] n bonbonne f.

flagpole ['flægpəul] n mât m.

flagrant ['fleɪgrənt] a flagrant(e).

flag stop n (US: for bus) arrêt facultatif.

flair [flɛə*] n flair m.

flak [flæk] n (MIL) tir antiaérien; (col: criticism) critiques fpl.

flake [fleɪk] n (of rust, paint) écaille f; (of snow, soap powder) flocon m ♦ vi (also: ~ off) s'écailler.

flaky ['fleɪkɪ] a (paintwork) écaillé(e); (skin) desquamé(e); (pastry) feuilleté(e).

flamboyant [flæm'bɔɪənt] a flamboyant(e), éclatant(e); (person) haut(e) en couleur.

flame [fleɪm] n flamme f.

flamingo [flə'mɪŋgəu] n flamant m (rose).

flammable ['flæməbl] a inflammable.

flan [flæn] n (Brit) tarte f.

Flanders ['flɑːndəz] n Flandre(s) f(pl).

flange [flændʒ] n boudin m; collerette f.

flank [flæŋk] n flanc m ♦ vt flanquer.

flannel ['flænl] n (Brit: also: face ~) gant m de toilette; (fabric) flanelle f; (Brit col) baratin m; ~s npl pantalon m de flanelle.

flap [flæp] n (of pocket, envelope) rabat m ♦ vt (wings) battre (de) ♦ vi (sail, flag) claquer; (col: also: **be in a** ~) paniquer.

flapjack ['flæpdʒæk] n (US: pancake) ≈ crêpe f; (Brit: biscuit) galette f.

flare [flɛə*] n fusée éclairante; (in skirt etc) évasement m.

flare up vi s'embraser; (fig: person) se mettre en colère, s'emporter; (: revolt) éclater.

flared ['flɛəd] a (trousers) à jambes évasées; (skirt) évasé(e).

flash [flæʃ] n éclair m; (also: **news** ~) flash m (d'information); (PHOT) flash ♦ vt (switch on) allumer (brièvement); (direct): **to** ~ **sth at** braquer qch sur; (flaunt) étaler, exhiber; (send: message) câbler ♦ vi briller; jeter des éclairs; (light on ambulance etc) clignoter; **in a** ~ en un clin d'œil; **to** ~ **one's headlights** faire un appel de phares; **he** ~**ed by** or **past** il passa (devant nous) comme un éclair.

flashback ['flæʃbæk] n flashback m, retour m en arrière.

flashbulb ['flæʃbʌlb] n ampoule f de flash.

flash card n (SCOL) carte f (support visuel).

flashcube ['flæʃkjuːb] n cube-flash m.

flasher ['flæʃə*] n (AUT) clignotant m.

flashlight ['flæʃlaɪt] n lampe f de poche.

flashpoint ['flæʃpɔɪnt] n point m d'ignition; (fig): **to be at** ~ être sur le point d'exploser.

flashy ['flæʃɪ] a (pej) tape-à-l'œil inv, tapageur(euse).

flask [flɑːsk] n flacon m, bouteille f; (CHEM) ballon m; (also: **vacuum** ~) bouteille f thermos ®.

flat [flæt] a plat(e); (tyre) dégonflé(e), à plat; (denial) catégorique; (MUS) bémolisé(e); (: voice) faux(fausse) ♦ n (Brit: rooms) appartement m; (AUT) crevaison f, pneu crevé; (MUS) bémol m; ~ **out** (work) sans relâche; (race) à fond; ~ **rate of pay** (COMM) (salaire m) fixe.

flat-footed ['flæt'futɪd] a: **to be** ~ avoir les pieds plats.

flatly ['flætlɪ] ad catégoriquement.

flatmate ['flætmeɪt] n (Brit): **he's my** ~ il partage l'appartement avec moi.

flatness ['flætnɪs] n (of land) absence f de relief, aspect plat.

flatten ['flætn] vt (also: ~**ten out**) aplatir; (house, city) raser.

flatter ['flætə*] vt flatter.

flatterer ['flætərə*] n flatteur m.

flattering ['flætərɪŋ] a flatteur(euse); (clothes etc) seyant(e).

flattery ['flætərɪ] n flatterie f.

flatulence ['flætjuləns] n flatulence f.

flaunt [flɔːnt] vt faire étalage de.

flavour, (US) **flavor** ['fleɪvə*] n goût m, saveur f; (of ice cream etc) parfum m ♦ vt parfumer, aromatiser; **vanilla-~ed** à l'arôme de vanille, vanillé(e); **to give** or **add** ~ **to** donner du goût à, relever.

flavo(u)ring ['fleɪvərɪŋ] n arôme m (synthétique).

flaw [flɔː] n défaut m.

flawless ['flɔːlɪs] a sans défaut.

flax [flæks] n lin m.

flaxen ['flæksn] a blond(e).

flea [fliː] n puce f.

flea market n marché m aux puces.

fleck [flek] n (of dust) particule f; (of mud, paint, colour) tacheture f, moucheture f ♦ vt tacher, éclabousser; **brown ~ed with white** brun moucheté de blanc.

fledg(e)ling ['fledʒlɪŋ] n oisillon m.

flee, pt, pp **fled** [fliː, fled] vt fuir, s'enfuir de ♦ vi fuir, s'enfuir.

fleece [fliːs] n toison f ♦ vt (col) voler, filouter.

fleecy ['fliːsɪ] a (blanket) moelleux(euse); (cloud) floconneux(euse).

fleet [fliːt] n flotte f; (of lorries, cars etc) parc m; convoi m.

fleeting ['fliːtɪŋ] a fugace, fugitif(ive); (visit) très bref(brève).

Flemish ['flemɪʃ] a flamand(e) ♦ n (LING) flamand m; **the** ~ npl les Flamands.

flesh [fleʃ] n chair f.

flesh wound n blessure superficielle.

flew [fluː] pt of **fly**.

flex [fleks] n fil m or câble m électrique (souple) ♦ vt fléchir; (muscles) tendre.

flexibility [fleksɪ'bɪlɪtɪ] n flexibilité f.

flexible ['fleksəbl] a flexible; (person, schedule) souple.

flick [flɪk] n petite tape; chiquenaude f; sursaut m.

flick through vt fus feuilleter.

flicker ['flɪkə*] vi vaciller ♦ n vacillement m; **a** ~ **of light** une brève lueur.

flick knife n (Brit) couteau m à cran d'arrêt.

flicks [flɪks] npl (col) ciné m.

flier ['flaɪə*] n aviateur m.

flight [flaɪt] n vol m; (escape) fuite f; (also: ~ **of steps**) escalier m; **to take** ~ prendre la fuite; **to put to** ~ mettre en fuite.

flight attendant n (US) steward m, hôtesse f de l'air.

flight crew n équipage m.

flight deck n (AVIAT) poste m de pilotage; (NAUT) pont m d'envol.

flight recorder n enregistreur m de vol.

flimsy ['flɪmzɪ] a (partition, fabric) peu solide,

mince; (*excuse*) pauvre, mince.
flinch [flɪntʃ] *vi* tressaillir; **to ~ from** se
dérober à, reculer devant.
fling [flɪŋ] *vt* (*pt, pp* **flung** [flʌŋ]) jeter, lancer
♦ *n* (*love affair*) brève liaison, passade *f*.
flint [flɪnt] *n* silex *m*; (*in lighter*) pierre *f* (à
briquet).
flip [flɪp] *n* chiquenaude *f* ♦ *vt* donner une
chiquenaude à; (*US: pancake*) faire sauter ♦
vi: **to ~ for sth** (*US*) jouer qch à pile ou
face.
flip through *vt fus* feuilleter.
flippant ['flɪpənt] *a* désinvolte,
irrévérencieux(euse).
flipper ['flɪpə*] *n* (*of animal*) nageoire *f*; (*for
swimmer*) palme *f*.
flip side *n* (*of record*) deuxième face *f*.
flirt [flə:t] *vi* flirter ♦ *n* flirteuse *f*.
flirtation [flə:'teɪʃən] *n* flirt *m*.
flit [flɪt] *vi* voleter.
float [fləut] *n* flotteur *m*; (*in procession*) char
m; (*sum of money*) réserve *f* ♦ *vi* flotter;
(*bather*) flotter, faire la planche ♦ *vt* faire
flotter; (*loan, business, idea*) lancer.
floating ['fləutɪŋ] *a* flottant(e); **~ vote** voix
flottante; **~ voter** électeur indécis.
flock [flɔk] *n* troupeau *m*; (*of birds*) vol *m*; (*of
people*) foule *f*.
floe [fləu] *n* (*also:* **ice ~**) iceberg *m*.
flog [flɔg] *vt* fouetter.
flood [flʌd] *n* inondation *f*; (*of words, tears
etc*) flot *m*, torrent *m* ♦ *vt* inonder; (*AUT:
carburettor*) noyer; **to ~ the market**
(*COMM*) inonder le marché; **in ~** en crue.
flooding ['flʌdɪŋ] *n* inondation *f*.
floodlight ['flʌdlaɪt] *n* projecteur *m* ♦ *vt*
éclairer aux projecteurs, illuminer.
floodlit ['flʌdlɪt] *pt, pp* of **floodlight** ♦ *a*
illuminé(e).
flood tide *n* marée montante.
floor [flɔ:*] *n* sol *m*; (*storey*) étage *m*; (*of sea,
valley*) fond *m*; (*fig: at meeting*): **the ~**
l'assemblée *f*, les membres *mpl* de l'assemblée ♦ *vt* terrasser; (*baffle*) désorienter; **on
the ~** par terre; **ground ~**, (*US*) **first ~**
rez-de-chaussée *m*; **first ~**, (*US*) **second ~**
premier étage; **top ~** dernier étage; **to have
the ~** (*speaker*) avoir la parole.
floorboard ['flɔ:bɔ:d] *n* planche *f* (*du plancher*).
flooring ['flɔ:rɪŋ] *n* sol *m*; (*wooden*) plancher
m; (*material to make floor*) matériau(x)
m(pl) pour planchers; (*covering*) revêtement
m de sol.
floor lamp *n* (*US*) lampadaire *m*.
floor show *n* spectacle *m* de variétés.
floorwalker ['flɔ:wɔ:kə*] *n* (*esp US*)
surveillant *m* (de grand magasin).
flop [flɔp] *n* fiasco *m* ♦ *vi* (*fail*) faire fiasco.
floppy ['flɔpɪ] *a* lâche, flottant(e); **~ hat**
chapeau *m* à bords flottants.
floppy disk *n* disquette *f*, disque *m* souple.
flora ['flɔ:rə] *n* flore *f*.
floral ['flɔ:rl] *a* floral(e).
Florence ['flɔrəns] *n* Florence *f*.
florid ['flɔrɪd] *a* (*complexion*) fleuri(e); (*style*)
plein(e) de fioritures.
florist ['flɔrɪst] *n* fleuriste *m/f*; **~'s (shop)**
magasin *m* or boutique *f* de fleuriste.

flotation [fləu'teɪʃən] *n* (*of shares*) émission *f*;
(*of company*) lancement *m* (en Bourse).
flounce [flauns] *n* volant *m*.
flounce out *vi* sortir dans un mouvement
d'humeur.
flounder ['flaundə*] *n* (*ZOOL*) flet *m* ♦ *vi*
patauger.
flour ['flauə*] *n* farine *f*.
flourish ['flʌrɪʃ] *vi* prospérer ♦ *vt* brandir ♦ *n*
fioriture *f*; (*of trumpets*) fanfare *f*.
flourishing ['flʌrɪʃɪŋ] *a* prospère, florissant(e).
flout [flaut] *vt* se moquer de, faire fi de.
flow [fləu] *n* (*of water, traffic etc*) écoulement
m; (*tide, influx*) flux *m*; (*of orders, letters
etc*) flot *m*; (*of blood, ELEC*) circulation *f*; (*of
river*) courant *m* ♦ *vi* couler; (*traffic*)
s'écouler; (*robes, hair*) flotter.
flow chart, flow diagram *n* organigramme
m.
flower ['flauə*] *n* fleur *f* ♦ *vi* fleurir; **in ~** en
fleur.
flower bed *n* plate-bande *f*.
flowerpot ['flauəpɔt] *n* pot *m* (à fleurs).
flowery ['flauərɪ] *a* fleuri(e).
flown [fləun] *pp* of **fly**.
flu [flu:] *n* grippe *f*.
fluctuate ['flʌktjueɪt] *vi* varier, fluctuer.
fluctuation [flʌktju'eɪʃən] *n* fluctuation *f*,
variation *f*.
flue [flu:] *n* conduit *m*.
fluency ['flu:ənsɪ] *n* facilité *f*, aisance *f*.
fluent ['flu:ənt] *a* (*speech, style*) coulant(e),
aisé(e); **he's a ~ speaker/reader** il
s'exprime/lit avec aisance or facilité; **he
speaks ~ French, he's ~ in French** il parle
le français couramment.
fluently ['flu:əntlɪ] *ad* couramment; avec
aisance or facilité.
fluff [flʌf] *n* duvet *m*; peluche *f*.
fluffy ['flʌfɪ] *a* duveteux(euse); pelu-
cheux(euse); **~ toy** jouet *m* en peluche.
fluid ['flu:ɪd] *n* fluide *m*; (*in diet*) liquide *m* ♦ *a*
fluide.
fluid ounce *n* (*Brit*) = 0.028 *l*; 0.05 pints.
fluke [flu:k] *n* (*col*) coup *m* de veine.
flummox ['flʌməks] *vt* dérouter, déconcerter.
flung [flʌŋ] *pt, pp* of **fling**.
flunky ['flʌŋkɪ] *n* larbin *m*.
fluorescent [fluə'rɛsnt] *a* fluorescent(e).
fluoride ['fluəraɪd] *n* fluor *m*.
fluorine ['fluəri:n] *n* fluor *m*.
flurry ['flʌrɪ] *n* (*of snow*) rafale *f*, bourrasque
f; **~ of activity/excitement** affairement *m*/
excitation *f* soudain(e).
flush [flʌʃ] *n* rougeur *f*; (*fig*) éclat *m*; afflux *m*
♦ *vt* nettoyer à grande eau; (*also:* **~ out**)
débusquer ♦ *vi* rougir ♦ *a* (*col*) en fonds;
(*level*): **~ with** au ras de, de niveau avec; **to
~ the toilet** tirer la chasse (d'eau); **hot ~es**
(*MED*) bouffées *fpl* de chaleur.
flushed [flʌʃt] *a* (tout(e)) rouge.
fluster ['flʌstə*] *n* agitation *f*, trouble *m*.
flustered ['flʌstəd] *a* énervé(e).
flute [flu:t] *n* flûte *f*.
fluted ['flu:tɪd] *a* cannelé(e).
flutter ['flʌtə*] *n* agitation *f*; (*of wings*)
battement *m* ♦ *vi* battre des ailes, voleter;
(*person*) aller et venir dans une grande
agitation.

flux [flʌks] *n*: **in a state of** ~ fluctuant sans cesse.

fly [flaɪ] *n* (*insect*) mouche *f*; (*on trousers: also:* **flies**) braguette *f* ♦ *vb* (*pt* **flew**, *pp* **flown** [flu:, fləun]) *vt* (*plane*) piloter; (*passengers, cargo*) transporter (par avion); (*distances*) parcourir ♦ *vi* voler; (*passengers*) aller en avion; (*escape*) s'enfuir, fuir; (*flag*) se déployer; **to** ~ **open** s'ouvrir brusquement; **to** ~ **off the handle** s'énerver, s'emporter.
fly away *vi* s'envoler.
fly in *vi* (*plane*) atterrir; (*person*): **he flew in yesterday** il est arrivé hier (par avion).
fly off *vi* s'envoler.
fly out *vi* (*see fly in*) s'envoler; partir (par avion).

fly-fishing ['flaɪfɪʃɪŋ] *n* pêche *f* à la mouche.
flying ['flaɪɪŋ] *n* (*activity*) aviation *f* ♦ *a*: ~ **visit** visite *f* éclair *inv*; **with** ~ **colours** haut la main; **he doesn't like** ~ il n'aime pas voyager en avion.
flying buttress *n* arc-boutant *m*.
flying saucer *n* soucoupe volante.
flying start *n*: **to get off to a** ~ faire un excellent départ.
flyleaf ['flaɪli:f] *n* page *f* de garde.
flyover ['flaɪəuvə*] *n* (*Brit: overpass*) saut-de-mouton *m*, pont autoroutier.
flypast ['flaɪpɑ:st] *n* défilé aérien.
flysheet ['flaɪʃi:t] *n* (*for tent*) double toit *m*.
flywheel ['flaɪwi:l] *n* volant *m* (de commande).
FM *abbr* (*Brit MIL*) = **field marshal**; (*RADIO*) = **frequency modulation**.
FMB *n abbr* (*US*) = *Federal Maritime Board*.
FMCS *n abbr* (*US:* = *Federal Mediation and Conciliation Services*) *organisme de conciliation en cas de conflits du travail.*
FO *n abbr* (*Brit*) = **Foreign Office**.
foal [fəul] *n* poulain *m*.
foam [fəum] *n* écume *f*; (*on beer*) mousse *f*; (*also:* **plastic** ~) mousse cellulaire *or* de plastique ♦ *vi* écumer; (*soapy water*) mousser.
foam rubber *n* caoutchouc *m* mousse.
FOB *abbr* (= *free on board*) fob.
fob [fɔb] *n* (*also:* **watch** ~) chaîne *f*, ruban *m* ♦ *vt*: **to** ~ **sb off with** refiler à qn; se débarrasser de qn avec.
foc *abbr* (*Brit*) = **free of charge**.
focal ['fəukl] *a* (*also fig*) focal(e).
focal point *n* foyer *m*; (*fig*) centre *m* de l'attention, point focal.
focus ['fəukəs] *n* (*pl:* ~**es**) foyer *m*; (*of interest*) centre *m* ♦ *vt* (*field glasses etc*) mettre au point; (*light rays*) faire converger ♦ *vi*: **to** ~ (**on**) (*with camera*) régler la mise au point (sur); (*person*) fixer son regard (sur); **in** ~ au point; **out of** ~ pas au point.
fodder ['fɔdə*] *n* fourrage *m*.
FOE *n abbr* (= *Friends of the Earth*) AT mpl (= *Amis de la Terre*); (*US:* = *Fraternal Order of Eagles*) *organisation charitable.*
foe [fəu] *n* ennemi *m*.
foetus, (*US*) **fetus** ['fi:təs] *n* fœtus *m*.
fog [fɔg] *n* brouillard *m*.
fogbound *a* bloqué(e) par le brouillard.
foggy ['fɔgɪ] *a*: **it's** ~ il y a du brouillard.
fog lamp, (*US*) **fog light** *n* (*AUT*) phare *m*

anti-brouillard.
foible ['fɔɪbl] *n* faiblesse *f*.
foil [fɔɪl] *vt* déjouer, contrecarrer ♦ *n* feuille *f* de métal; (*kitchen* ~) papier *m* d'alu(minium); (*FENCING*) fleuret *m*; **to act as a** ~ **to** (*fig*) servir de repoussoir *or* de faire valoir à.
foist [fɔɪst] *vt*: **to** ~ **sth on sb** imposer qch à qn.
fold [fəuld] *n* (*bend, crease*) pli *m*; (*AGR*) parc *m* à moutons; (*fig*) bercail *m* ♦ *vt* plier; **to** ~ **one's arms** croiser les bras.
fold up *vi* (*map etc*) se plier, se replier; (*business*) fermer boutique ♦ *vt* (*map etc*) plier, replier.
folder ['fəuldə*] *n* (*for papers*) chemise *f*; (*: binder*) classeur *m*; (*brochure*) dépliant *m*.
folding ['fəuldɪŋ] *a* (*chair, bed*) pliant(e).
foliage ['fəulɪdʒ] *n* feuillage *m*.
folk [fəuk] *npl* gens *mpl* ♦ *cpd* folklorique; ~**s** *npl* famille *f*, parents *mpl*.
folklore ['fəuklɔ:*] *n* folklore *m*.
folksong ['fəuksɔŋ] *n* chanson *f* folklorique; (*contemporary*) chanson folk *inv*.
follow ['fɔləu] *vt* suivre ♦ *vi* suivre; (*result*) s'ensuivre; **to** ~ **sb's advice** suivre les conseils de qn; **I don't quite** ~ **you** je ne vous suis plus; **to** ~ **in sb's footsteps** emboîter le pas à qn; (*fig*) suivre les traces de qn; **it** ~**s that** ... de ce fait, il s'ensuit que ...; **he** ~**ed suit** il fit de même.
follow out *vt* (*idea, plan*) poursuivre, mener à terme.
follow through *vt* = **follow out**.
follow up *vt* (*victory*) tirer parti de; (*letter, offer*) donner suite à; (*case*) suivre.
follower ['fɔləuə*] *n* disciple *m/f*, partisan/e.
following ['fɔləuɪŋ] *a* suivant(e) ♦ *n* partisans *mpl*, disciples *mpl*.
follow-up ['fɔləuʌp] *n* suite *f*; suivi *m*.
folly ['fɔlɪ] *n* inconscience *f*; sottise *f*; (*building*) folie *f*.
fond [fɔnd] *a* (*memory, look*) tendre, affectueux(euse); **to be** ~ **of** aimer beaucoup.
fondle ['fɔndl] *vt* caresser.
fondly ['fɔndlɪ] *ad* (*lovingly*) tendrement; (*naïvely*) naïvement.
fondness ['fɔndnɪs] *n* (*for things*) attachement *m*; (*for people*) sentiments affectueux; **a special** ~ **for** une prédilection pour.
font [fɔnt] *n* (*REL*) fonts baptismaux; (*TYP*) police *f* de caractères.
food [fu:d] *n* nourriture *f*.
food mixer *n* mixeur *m*.
food poisoning *n* intoxication *f* alimentaire.
food processor *n* robot *m* de cuisine.
foodstuffs ['fu:dstʌfs] *npl* denrées *fpl* alimentaires.
fool [fu:l] *n* idiot/e; (*HISTORY: of king*) bouffon *m*, fou *m*; (*CULIN*) purée *f* de fruits à la crème ♦ *vt* berner, duper ♦ *vi* (*also:* ~ **around**) faire l'idiot *or* l'imbécile; **to make a** ~ **of sb** (*ridicule*) ridiculiser qn; (*trick*) avoir *or* duper qn; **to make a** ~ **of o.s.** se couvrir de ridicule; **you can't** ~ **me** vous (ne) me la ferez pas, on (ne) me la fait pas.
fool about, fool around *vi* (*pej: waste time*) traînailler, glandouiller; (*: behave*

foolishly) faire l'imbécile.

foolhardy ['fu:lhɑ:dɪ] *a* téméraire, imprudent(e).

foolish ['fu:lɪʃ] *a* idiot(e), stupide; (*rash*) imprudent(e).

foolishly ['fu:lɪʃlɪ] *ad* stupidement.

foolishness ['fu:lɪʃnɪs] *n* idiotie *f*, stupidité *f*.

foolproof ['fu:lpru:f] *a* (*plan etc*) infaillible.

foolscap ['fu:lskæp] *n* ≈ papier *m* ministre.

foot [fut] *n* (*pl*: **feet** [fi:t]) pied *m*; (*measure*) pied (= 304 *mm*; 12 *inches*); (*of animal*) patte *f* ♦ *vt* (*bill*) casquer, payer; **on ~** à pied; **to find one's feet** (*fig*) s'acclimater; **to put one's ~ down** (*AUT*) appuyer sur le champignon; (*say no*) s'imposer.

footage ['futɪdʒ] *n* (*CINEMA: length*) ≈ métrage *m*; (*: material*) séquences *fpl*.

foot and mouth (disease) *n* fièvre aphteuse.

football ['futbɔ:l] *n* ballon *m* (de football); (*sport: Brit*) football *m*; (*: US*) football américain.

footballer ['futbɔ:lə*] *n* (*Brit*) = **football player**.

football ground *n* terrain *m* de football.

football match *n* (*Brit*) match *m* de foot(ball).

football player *n* footballeur *m*, joueur *m* de football.

footbrake ['futbreɪk] *n* frein *m* à pied.

footbridge ['futbrɪdʒ] *n* passerelle *f*.

foothills ['futhɪlz] *npl* contreforts *mpl*.

foothold ['futhəuld] *n* prise *f* (de pied).

footing ['futɪŋ] *n* (*fig*) position *f*; **to lose one's ~** perdre pied; **on an equal ~** sur un pied d'égalité.

footlights ['futlaɪts] *npl* rampe *f*.

footman ['futmən] *n* laquais *m*.

footnote ['futnəut] *n* note *f* (en bas de page).

footpath ['futpɑ:θ] *n* sentier *m*; (*in street*) trottoir *m*.

footprint ['futprɪnt] *n* trace *f* (de pied).

footrest ['futrɛst] *n* marchepied *m*.

footsore ['futsɔ:*] *a* aux pieds endoloris.

footstep ['futstep] *n* pas *m*.

footwear ['futweə*] *n* chaussure(s) *f(pl)* (*terme générique en anglais*).

FOR *abbr* (= *free on rail*) franco wagon.

for [fɔ:*] *prep* pour; (*during*) pendant; (*in spite of*) malgré ♦ *cj* car; **I haven't seen him ~ a week** je ne l'ai pas vu depuis une semaine, cela fait une semaine que je ne l'ai pas vu; **I'll be away ~ 3 weeks** je serai absent pendant 3 semaines; **he went down ~ the paper** il est descendu chercher le journal; **I sold it for £5** je l'ai vendu 5 livres; **~ sale** à vendre; **the train ~ London** le train pour Londres; **it's time ~ lunch** c'est l'heure de déjeuner; **what ~?** (*why*) pourquoi?; (*to what end*) pourquoi faire?, à quoi bon?; **what's this button ~?** à quoi sert ce bouton?; **~ all that** malgré cela, néanmoins; **there's nothing ~ it but to jump** (*Brit*) il n'y a plus qu'à sauter.

forage ['fɔrɪdʒ] *n* fourrage *m* ♦ *vi* fourrager, fouiller.

forage cap *n* calot *m*.

foray ['fɔreɪ] *n* incursion *f*.

forbad(e) [fə'bæd] *pt of* **forbid**.

forbearing [fɔ:'bɛərɪŋ] *a* patient(e), tolérant(e).

forbid, *pt* **forbad(e),** *pp* **forbidden** [fə'bɪd, -'bæd, -'bɪdn] *vt* défendre, interdire; **to ~ sb to do** défendre *or* interdire à qn de faire.

forbidden [fə'bɪdn] *a* défendu(e).

forbidding [fə'bɪdɪŋ] *a* d'aspect *or* d'allure sévère *or* sombre.

force [fɔ:s] *n* force *f* ♦ *vt* forcer; **the F~s** *npl* (*Brit*) l'armée *f*; **to ~ sb to do sth** forcer qn à faire qch; **in ~** en force; **to come into ~** entrer en vigueur; **a ~ 5 wind** un vent de force 5; **the sales** *~* (*COMM*) la force de vente; **to join ~s** unir ses forces.

force back *vt* (*crowd, enemy*) repousser; (*tears*) refouler.

force down *vt* (*food*) se forcer à manger.

forced [fɔ:st] *a* forcé(e).

force-feed ['fɔ:sfi:d] *vt* nourrir de force.

forceful ['fɔ:sful] *a* énergique, volontaire.

forcemeat ['fɔ:smi:t] *n* (*Brit CULIN*) farce *f*.

forceps ['fɔ:seps] *npl* forceps *m*.

forcibly ['fɔ:səblɪ] *ad* par la force, de force; (*vigorously*) énergiquement.

ford [fɔ:d] *n* gué *m* ♦ *vt* passer à gué.

fore [fɔ:*] *n*: **to the ~** en évidence.

forearm ['fɔ:rɑ:m] *n* avant-bras *m inv*.

forebear ['fɔ:bɛə*] *n* ancêtre *m*.

foreboding [fɔ:'bəudɪŋ] *n* pressentiment *m* (néfaste).

forecast ['fɔ:kɑ:st] *n* prévision *f*; (*also:* **weather** *~*) prévisions météorologiques, météo *f* ♦ *vt* (*irg: like* **cast**) prévoir.

foreclose [fɔ:'kləuz] *vt* (*LAW: also:* **~ on**) saisir.

foreclosure [fɔ:'kləuʒə*] *n* saisie *f* du bien hypothéqué.

forecourt ['fɔ:kɔ:t] *n* (*of garage*) devant *m*.

forefathers ['fɔ:fɑ:ðəz] *npl* ancêtres *mpl*.

forefinger ['fɔ:fɪŋgə*] *n* index *m*.

forefront ['fɔ:frʌnt] *n*: **in the ~ of** au premier rang *or* plan de.

forego, *pt* **forewent,** *pp* **foregone** [fɔ:'gəu, -'wɛnt, -'gɔn] *vt* = **forgo**.

foregoing ['fɔ:gəuɪŋ] *a* susmentionné(e) ♦ *n*: **the ~** ce qui précède.

foregone ['fɔ:gɔn] *a*: **it's a ~ conclusion** c'est à prévoir, c'est couru d'avance.

foreground ['fɔ:graund] *n* premier plan ♦ *cpd* (*COMPUT*) prioritaire.

forehand ['fɔ:hænd] *n* (*TENNIS*) coup droit.

forehead ['fɔrɪd] *n* front *m*.

foreign ['fɔrɪn] *a* étranger(ère); (*trade*) extérieur(e).

foreign body *n* corps étranger.

foreign currency *n* devises étrangères.

foreigner ['fɔrɪnə*] *n* étranger/ère.

foreign exchange *n* (*system*) change *m*; (*money*) devises *fpl*.

foreign exchange market *n* marché *m* des devises.

foreign exchange rate *n* cours *m* des devises.

foreign investment *n* investissement *m* à l'étranger.

Foreign Office *n* (*Brit*) ministère *m* des Affaires étrangères.

foreign secretary *n* (*Brit*) ministre *m* des Affaires étrangères.

foreleg ['fɔːlɛg] n patte f de devant; jambe antérieure.

foreman ['fɔːmən] n contremaître m; (LAW: of jury) président m (du jury).

foremost ['fɔːməust] a le(la) plus en vue; premier(ière) ♦ ad: **first and ~** avant tout, tout d'abord.

forename ['fɔːneɪm] n prénom m.

forensic [fə'rɛnsɪk] a: **~ medicine** médecine légale; **~ expert** expert m de la police, expert légiste.

forerunner ['fɔːrʌnə*] n précurseur m.

foresee, pt **foresaw**, pp **foreseen** [fɔː'siː, -'sɔː, -'siːn] vt prévoir.

foreseeable [fɔː'siːəbl] a prévisible.

foreshadow [fɔː'ʃædəu] vt présager, annoncer, laisser prévoir.

foreshorten [fɔː'ʃɔːtn] vt (figure, scene) réduire, faire en raccourci.

foresight ['fɔːsaɪt] n prévoyance f.

foreskin ['fɔːskɪn] n (ANAT) prépuce m.

forest ['fɔrɪst] n forêt f.

forestall [fɔː'stɔːl] vt devancer.

forestry ['fɔrɪstrɪ] n sylviculture f.

foretaste ['fɔːteɪst] n avant-goût m.

foretell, pt, pp **foretold** [fɔː'tɛl, -'təuld] vt prédire.

forethought ['fɔːθɔːt] n prévoyance f.

forever [fə'rɛvə*] ad pour toujours; (fig) continuellement.

forewarn [fɔː'wɔːn] vt avertir.

forewent [fɔː'wɛnt] pt of **forego**.

foreword ['fɔːwəːd] n avant-propos m inv.

forfeit ['fɔːfɪt] n prix m, rançon f ♦ vt perdre; (one's life, health) payer de.

forgave [fə'geɪv] pt of **forgive**.

forge [fɔːdʒ] n forge f ♦ vt (signature) contrefaire; (wrought iron) forger; **to ~ documents/a will** fabriquer de faux papiers/ un faux testament; **to ~ money** (Brit) fabriquer de la fausse monnaie.

forge ahead vi pousser de l'avant, prendre de l'avance.

forger ['fɔːdʒə*] n faussaire m.

forgery ['fɔːdʒərɪ] n faux m, contrefaçon f.

forget, pt **forgot**, pp **forgotten** [fə'gɛt, -'gɔt, -'gɔtn] vt, vi oublier.

forgetful [fə'gɛtful] a distrait(e), étourdi(e); **~ of** oublieux(euse) de.

forgetfulness [fə'gɛtfulnɪs] n tendance f aux oublis; (oblivion) oubli m.

forget-me-not [fə'gɛtmɪnɔt] n myosotis m.

forgive, pt **forgave**, pp **forgiven** [fə'gɪv, -'geɪv, -'gɪvn] vt pardonner; **to ~ sb for sth/ for doing sth** pardonner qch à qn/à qn de faire qch.

forgiveness [fə'gɪvnɪs] n pardon m.

forgiving [fə'gɪvɪŋ] a indulgent(e).

forgo, pt **forwent**, pp **forgone** [fɔː'gəu, -'wɛnt, -'gɔn] vt renoncer à.

forgot [fə'gɔt] pt of **forget**.

forgotten [fə'gɔtn] pp of **forget**.

fork [fɔːk] n (for eating) fourchette f; (for gardening) fourche f; (of roads) bifurcation f; (of railways) embranchement m ♦ vi (road) bifurquer.

fork out (col: pay) vt allonger, se fendre de ♦ vi casquer.

forked [fɔːkt] a (lightning) en zigzags,

ramifié(e).

fork-lift truck ['fɔːklɪft-] n chariot élévateur.

forlorn [fə'lɔːn] a abandonné(e), délaissé(e); (hope, attempt) désespéré(e).

form [fɔːm] n forme f; (SCOL) classe f; (questionnaire) formulaire m ♦ vt former; **in the ~ of** sous forme de; **to ~ part of sth** faire partie de qch; **to be in good ~** (SPORT, fig) être en forme; **in top ~** en pleine forme.

formal ['fɔːməl] a (offer, receipt) en bonne et due forme; (person) cérémonieux(euse), à cheval sur les convenances; (occasion, dinner) officiel(le); (ART, PHILOSOPHY) formel(le); **~ dress** tenue f de cérémonie; (evening dress) tenue de soirée.

formality [fɔː'mælɪtɪ] n formalité f, cérémonie(s) f(pl).

formalize ['fɔːməlaɪz] vt officialiser.

formally ['fɔːməlɪ] ad officiellement; formellement; cérémonieusement.

format ['fɔːmæt] n format m ♦ vt (COMPUT) formater.

formation [fɔː'meɪʃən] n formation f.

formative ['fɔːmətɪv] a: **~ years** années fpl d'apprentissage (fig) or de formation (d'un enfant, d'un adolescent).

former ['fɔːmə*] a ancien(ne) (before n), précédent(e); **the ~ ... the latter** le premier ... le second, celui-là ... celui-ci; **the ~ president** l'ex-président.

formerly ['fɔːməlɪ] ad autrefois.

form feed n (on printer) alimentation f en feuilles.

formidable ['fɔːmɪdəbl] a redoutable.

formula ['fɔːmjulə] n formule f; **F~ One** (AUT) Formule un.

formulate ['fɔːmjuleɪt] vt formuler.

fornicate ['fɔːnɪkeɪt] vi forniquer.

forsake, pt **forsook**, pp **forsaken** [fə'seɪk, -'suk, -'seɪkən] vt abandonner.

fort [fɔːt] n fort m; **to hold the ~** (fig) assurer la permanence.

forte ['fɔːtɪ] n (point) fort m.

forth [fɔːθ] ad en avant; **to go back and ~** aller et venir; **and so ~** et ainsi de suite.

forthcoming [fɔːθ'kʌmɪŋ] a qui va paraître or avoir lieu prochainement; (character) ouvert(e), communicatif(ive).

forthright ['fɔːθraɪt] a franc(franche), direct(e).

forthwith ['fɔːθ'wɪθ] ad sur le champ.

fortieth ['fɔːtɪɪθ] num quarantième.

fortification [fɔːtɪfɪ'keɪʃən] n fortification f.

fortified wine n vin liquoreux or de liqueur.

fortify ['fɔːtɪfaɪ] vt fortifier.

fortitude ['fɔːtɪtjuːd] n courage m, force f d'âme.

fortnight ['fɔːtnaɪt] n (Brit) quinzaine f, quinze jours mpl; **it's a ~ since ...** il y a quinze jours que ...

fortnightly ['fɔːtnaɪtlɪ] a bimensuel(le) ♦ ad tous les quinze jours.

FORTRAN ['fɔːtræn] n FORTRAN m.

fortress ['fɔːtrɪs] n forteresse f.

fortuitous [fɔː'tjuːɪtəs] a fortuit(e).

fortunate ['fɔːtʃənɪt] a: **to be ~** avoir de la chance; **it is ~ that** c'est une chance que, il est heureux que.

fortunately ['fɔːtʃənɪtlɪ] ad heureusement, par

bonheur.

fortune ['fɔːtʃən] n chance f; (wealth) fortune f; **to make a ~** faire fortune.

fortuneteller ['fɔːtʃəntelə*] n diseuse f de bonne aventure.

forty ['fɔːtɪ] num quarante.

forum ['fɔːrəm] n forum m, tribune f.

forward ['fɔːwəd] a (movement, position) en avant, vers l'avant; (not shy) effronté(e); (COMM: delivery, sales, exchange) à terme ♦ ad en avant ♦ n (SPORT) avant m ♦ vt (letter) faire suivre; (parcel, goods) expédier; (fig) promouvoir, contribuer au développement or à l'avancement de; **to move ~** avancer; **"please ~"** "prière de faire suivre"; **~ planning** planification f à long terme.

forward(s) ['fɔːwəd(z)] ad en avant.

forwent [fɔː'went] pt of **forgo**.

fossil ['fɔsl] a, n fossile (m); **~ fuel** combustible m fossile.

foster ['fɔstə*] vt encourager, favoriser.

foster brother n frère adoptif; frère de lait.

foster child n enfant adopté.

foster mother n mère adoptive; mère nourricière.

fought [fɔːt] pt, pp of **fight**.

foul [faul] a (weather, smell, food) infect(e); (language) ordurier(ière); (deed) infâme ♦ n (FOOTBALL) faute f ♦ vt salir, encrasser; (football player) commettre une faute sur; (entangle: anchor, propeller) emmêler.

foul play n (SPORT) jeu déloyal; **~ is not suspected** la mort (or l'incendie etc) n'a pas de causes suspectes, on écarte l'hypothèse d'un meurtre (or d'un acte criminel).

found [faund] pt, pp of **find** ♦ vt (establish) fonder.

foundation [faun'deɪʃən] n (act) fondation f; (base) fondement m; (also: **~ cream**) fond m de teint; **~s** npl (of building) fondations fpl; **to lay the ~s** (fig) poser les fondements.

foundation stone n première pierre.

founder ['faundə*] n fondateur m ♦ vi couler, sombrer.

founding ['faundɪŋ] a: **~ fathers** (esp US) pères mpl fondateurs; **~ member** membre m fondateur.

foundry ['faundrɪ] n fonderie f.

fount [faunt] n source f; (TYP) fonte f.

fountain ['fauntɪn] n fontaine f.

fountain pen n stylo m (à encre).

four [fɔː*] num quatre; **on all ~s** à quatre pattes.

four-poster ['fɔː'pəustə*] n (also: **~ bed**) lit m à baldaquin.

foursome ['fɔːsəm] n partie f à quatre; sortie f à quatre.

fourteen ['fɔː'tiːn] num quatorze.

fourth ['fɔːθ] num quatrième ♦ n (AUT: also: **~ gear**) quatrième f.

four-wheel drive ['fɔːwiːl-] n (AUT): **with ~** à quatre roues motrices.

fowl [faul] n volaille f.

fox [fɔks] n renard m ♦ vt mystifier.

fox fur n renard m.

foxglove ['fɔksglʌv] n (BOT) digitale f.

fox-hunting ['fɔkshʌntɪŋ] n chasse f au renard.

foyer ['fɔɪeɪ] n vestibule m; (THEATRE) foyer m.

FP n abbr (Brit) = former pupil; (US) = **fireplug**.

FPA n abbr (Brit) = Family Planning Association.

Fr. abbr (= father: REL) P; (= friar) F.

fr. abbr (= franc) F.

fracas ['frækɑː] n bagarre f.

fraction ['frækʃən] n fraction f.

fractionally ['frækʃnəlɪ] ad: **~ smaller** etc un poil plus petit etc.

fractious ['frækʃəs] a grincheux(euse).

fracture ['fræktʃə*] n fracture f ♦ vt fracturer.

fragile ['frædʒaɪl] a fragile.

fragment ['frægmənt] n fragment m.

fragmentary ['frægməntərɪ] a fragmentaire.

fragrance ['freɪgrəns] n parfum m.

fragrant ['freɪgrənt] a parfumé(e), odorant(e).

frail [freɪl] a fragile, délicat(e).

frame [freɪm] n (of building) charpente f; (of human, animal) charpente, ossature f; (of picture) cadre m; (of door, window) encadrement m, chambranle m; (of spectacles: also: **~s**) monture f ♦ vt encadrer; (theory, plan) construire, élaborer; **to ~ sb** (col) monter un coup contre qn; **~ of mind** disposition f d'esprit.

framework ['freɪmwɔːk] n structure f.

France [frɑːns] n la France; **in ~** en France.

franchise ['fræntʃaɪz] n (POL) droit m de vote; (COMM) franchise f.

franchisee [fræntʃaɪ'ziː] n franchisé m.

franchiser ['fræntʃaɪzə*] n franchiseur m.

frank [fræŋk] n franc(franche) ♦ vt (letter) affranchir.

Frankfurt ['fræŋkfɔːt] n Francfort.

franking machine ['fræŋkɪŋ-] n machine f à affranchir.

frankly ['fræŋklɪ] ad franchement.

frankness ['fræŋknɪs] n franchise f.

frantic ['fræntɪk] a frénétique; (desperate: need, desire) effréné(e); (person) hors de soi.

frantically ['fræntɪklɪ] ad frénétiquement.

fraternal [frə'tɔːnl] a fraternel(le).

fraternity [frə'tɔːnɪtɪ] n (club) communauté f, confrérie f; (spirit) fraternité f.

fraternize ['frætənaɪz] vi fraterniser.

fraud [frɔːd] n supercherie f, fraude f, tromperie f; (person) imposteur m.

fraudulent ['frɔːdjulənt] a frauduleux(euse).

fraught [frɔːt] a (tense: person) très tendu(e); (: situation) pénible; **~ with** (difficulties etc) chargé(e) de, plein(e) de.

fray [freɪ] n bagarre f; (MIL) combat m ♦ vt effilocher ♦ vi s'effilocher; **tempers were ~ed** les gens commençaient à s'énerver; **her nerves were ~ed** elle était à bout de nerfs.

FRB n abbr (US) = Federal Reserve Board.

FRCM n abbr (Brit) = Fellow of the Royal College of Music.

FRCO n abbr (Brit) = Fellow of the Royal College of Organists.

FRCP n abbr (Brit) = Fellow of the Royal College of Physicians.

FRCS n abbr (Brit) = Fellow of the Royal College of Surgeons.

freak [friːk] n (also cpd) phénomène m,

créature ou événement exceptionnel par sa rareté, son caractère d'anomalie; (pej: fanatic): **health** ~ fana *m/f or* obsédé/e de l'alimentation saine *(or* de la forme physique).
freak out *vi (col: drop out)* se marginaliser; *(: on drugs)* se défoncer.
freakish ['fri:kɪʃ] *a* insolite; anormal(e).
freckle ['frɛkl] *n* tache *f* de rousseur.
free [fri:] *a* libre; *(gratis)* gratuit(e); *(liberal)* généreux(euse), large ♦ *vt (prisoner etc)* libérer; *(jammed object or person)* dégager; to give sb a ~ hand donner carte blanche à qn; ~ **and easy** sans façon, décontracté(e); **admission** ~ entrée libre; ~ **(of charge)** *ad* gratuitement.
freebie ['fri:bɪ] *n (col)*: **it's a** ~ c'est gratuit.
freedom ['fri:dəm] *n* liberté *f*.
freedom fighter *n* combattant *m* de la liberté.
free enterprise *n* libre entreprise *f*.
free-for-all ['fri:fərɔ:l] *n* mêlée générale.
free gift *n* prime *f*.
freehold ['fri:həuld] *n* propriété foncière libre.
free kick *n (SPORT)* coup franc.
freelance ['fri:lɑ:ns] *a (journalist etc)* indépendant(e); *(work)* à la pige, à la tâche.
freeloader ['fri:ləudə*] *n (pej)* parasite *m*.
freely ['fri:lɪ] *ad* librement; *(liberally)* libéralement.
freemason ['fri:meɪsn] *n* franc-maçon *m*.
freemasonry ['fri:meɪsnrɪ] *n* franc-maçonnerie *f*.
freepost ['fri:pəust] *n* franchise postale.
free-range ['fri:'reɪndʒ] *a (eggs)* de ferme.
free sample *n* échantillon gratuit.
free speech *n* liberté *f* d'expression.
free trade *n* libre-échange *m*.
freeway ['fri:weɪ] *n (US)* autoroute *f*.
freewheel [fri:'wi:l] *vi* descendre en roue libre.
freewheeling [fri:'wi:lɪŋ] *a* indépendant(e), libre.
free will *n* libre arbitre *m*; **of one's own** ~ de son plein gré.
freeze [fri:z] *vb (pt* froze, *pp* frozen [frəuz, 'frəuzn]) *vi* geler ♦ *vt* geler; *(food)* congeler; *(prices, salaries)* bloquer, geler ♦ *n* gel *m*; blocage *m*.
freeze over *vi (river)* geler; *(windscreen)* se couvrir de givre *or* de glace.
freeze up *vi* geler.
freeze-dried ['fri:zdraɪd] *a* lyophilisé(e).
freezer ['fri:zə*] *n* congélateur *m*.
freezing ['fri:zɪŋ] *a*: ~ **(cold)** *(room etc)* glacial(e); *(person, hands)* gelé(e), glacé(e) ♦ *n*: **3 degrees below** ~ 3 degrés au-dessous de zéro.
freezing point *n* point *m* de congélation.
freight [freɪt] *n (goods)* fret *m*, cargaison *f*; *(money charged)* fret, prix *m* du transport; ~ **forward** port dû; ~ **inward** port payé par le destinataire.
freighter ['freɪtə*] *n (NAUT)* cargo *m*.
freight forwarder *n* transitaire *m*.
freight train *n (US)* train *m* de marchandises.
French [frɛntʃ] *a* français(e) ♦ *n (LING)* français *m*; **the** ~ *npl* les Français.

French bean *n (Brit)* haricot vert.
French Canadian *a* canadien(ne) français(e) ♦ *n* Canadien/ne français(e); *(LING)* français canadien.
French dressing *n (CULIN)* vinaigrette *f*.
French fried potatoes, *(US)* **French fries** *npl* (pommes de terre *fpl*) frites.
French Guiana [-gaɪ'ænə] *n* Guyane française.
Frenchman ['frɛntʃmən] *n* Français *m*.
French Riviera *n*: **the** ~ la Côte d'Azur.
French window *n* porte-fenêtre *f*.
Frenchwoman ['frɛntʃwumən] *n* Française *f*.
frenetic [frə'nɛtɪk] *a* frénétique.
frenzy ['frɛnzɪ] *n* frénésie *f*.
frequency ['fri:kwənsɪ] *n* fréquence *f*.
frequency modulation (FM) *n* modulation *f* de fréquence (FM, MF).
frequent *a* ['fri:kwənt] fréquent(e) ♦ *vt* [frɪ'kwɛnt] fréquenter.
frequently ['fri:kwəntlɪ] *ad* fréquemment.
fresco ['frɛskəu] *n* fresque *f*.
fresh [frɛʃ] *a* frais(fraîche); *(new)* nouveau(nouvelle); *(cheeky)* familier(ière), culotté(e); **to make a** ~ **start** prendre un nouveau départ.
freshen ['frɛʃən] *vi (wind, air)* fraîchir.
freshen up *vi* faire un brin de toilette.
freshener ['frɛʃnə*] *n*: **skin** ~ astringent *m*; **air** ~ désodorisant *m*.
fresher ['frɛʃə*] *n (Brit SCOL: col)* = **freshman.**
freshly ['frɛʃlɪ] *ad* nouvellement, récemment.
freshman ['frɛʃmən] *n (SCOL)* bizuth *m*, étudiant/e de première année.
freshness ['frɛʃnɪs] *n* fraîcheur *f*.
freshwater ['frɛʃwɔ:tə*] *a (fish)* d'eau douce.
fret [frɛt] *vi* s'agiter, se tracasser.
fretful ['frɛtful] *a (child)* grincheux(euse).
Freudian ['frɔɪdɪən] *a* freudien(ne); ~ **slip** lapsus *m*.
FRG *n abbr (= Federal Republic of Germany)* RFA *f*.
Fri. *abbr (= Friday)* ve.
friar ['fraɪə*] *n* moine *m*, frère *m*.
friction ['frɪkʃən] *n* friction *f*, frottement *m*.
friction feed *n (on printer)* entraînement *m* par friction.
Friday ['fraɪdɪ] *n* vendredi *m*; *for phrases see also* **Tuesday.**
fridge [frɪdʒ] *n (Brit)* frigo *m*, frigidaire *m* ®.
fried [fraɪd] *pt, pp of* **fry** ♦ *a* frit(e); ~ **egg** œuf *m* sur le plat.
friend [frɛnd] *n* ami/e; **to make** ~s **with** se lier (d'amitié) avec.
friendliness ['frɛndlɪnɪs] *n* attitude amicale.
friendly ['frɛndlɪ] *a* amical(e); *(kind)* sympathique, gentil(le); *(POL: country, government)* ami(e) ♦ *n (also:* ~ **match)** match amical; **to be** ~ **with** être ami(e) avec; **to be** ~ **to** être bien disposé(e) à l'égard de.
friendly society *n* société *f* mutualiste.
friendship ['frɛndʃɪp] *n* amitié *f*.
frieze [fri:z] *n* frise *f*, bordure *f*.
frigate ['frɪgɪt] *n (NAUT: modern)* frégate *f*.
fright [fraɪt] *n* peur *f*, effroi *m*; **to take** ~ prendre peur, s'effrayer; **she looks a** ~ elle a l'air d'un épouvantail.

frighten ['fraɪtn] vt effrayer, faire peur à.
  frighten away, **frighten off** vt (birds, children etc) faire fuir, effaroucher.
frightened ['fraɪtnd] a: **to be ~ (of)** avoir peur (de).
frightening ['fraɪtnɪŋ] a effrayant(e).
frightful ['fraɪtful] a affreux(euse).
frightfully ['fraɪtfəlɪ] ad affreusement.
frigid ['frɪdʒɪd] a (woman) frigide.
frigidity [frɪ'dʒɪdɪtɪ] n frigidité f.
frill [frɪl] n (of dress) volant m; (of shirt) jabot m; **without ~s** (fig) sans manières.
fringe [frɪndʒ] n frange f; (edge: of forest etc) bordure f; (fig): **on the ~** en marge.
fringe benefits npl avantages sociaux or en nature.
fringe theatre n théâtre m d'avant-garde.
frisk [frɪsk] vt fouiller.
frisky ['frɪskɪ] a vif(vive), sémillant(e).
fritter ['frɪtə*] n beignet m.
  fritter away vt gaspiller.
frivolity [frɪ'vɔlɪtɪ] n frivolité f.
frivolous ['frɪvələs] a frivole.
frizzy ['frɪzɪ] a crépu(e).
fro [frəu] see **to**.
frock [frɔk] n robe f.
frog [frɔg] n grenouille f; **to have a ~ in one's throat** avoir un chat dans la gorge.
frogman ['frɔgmən] n homme-grenouille m.
frogmarch ['frɔgmɑːtʃ] vt (Brit): **to ~ sb in/ out** faire entrer/sortir qn de force.
frolic ['frɔlɪk] n ébats mpl ♦ vi folâtrer, batifoler.
from [frɔm] prep de; **where is he ~?** d'où est-il?; **where has he come ~?** d'où arrive-t-il?; **(as) ~ Friday** à partir de vendredi; **a telephone call ~ Mr. Smith** un appel de M. Smith; **prices range ~ £10 to £50** les prix vont de 10 livres à 50 livres; **~ what he says** d'après ce qu'il dit.
frond [frɔnd] n fronde f.
front [frʌnt] n (of house, dress) devant m; (of coach, train) avant m; (of book) couverture f; (promenade: also: **sea ~**) bord m de mer; (MIL, POL, METEOROLOGY) front m; (fig: appearances) contenance f, façade f ♦ a de devant; premier(ière) ♦ vi: **to ~ onto sth** donner sur qch; **in ~ (of)** devant.
frontage ['frʌntɪdʒ] n façade f; (of shop) devanture f.
frontal ['frʌntl] a frontal(e).
front bench n (Brit POL) les dirigeants du parti au pouvoir ou de l'opposition.
front desk n (US: in hotel, at doctor's) réception f.
front door n porte f d'entrée; (of car) portière f avant.
frontier ['frʌntɪə*] n frontière f.
frontispiece ['frʌntɪspiːs] n frontispice m.
front page n première page.
front room n (Brit) pièce f de devant, salon m.
front runner n (fig) favori/te.
front-wheel drive ['frʌntwiːl-] n traction f avant.
frost [frɔst] n gel m, gelée f; (also: **hoar~**) givre m.
frostbite ['frɔstbaɪt] n gelures fpl.
frosted ['frɔstɪd] a (glass) dépoli(e); (esp US:

cake) glacé(e).
frosting ['frɔstɪŋ] n (esp US: on cake) glaçage m.
frosty ['frɔstɪ] a (window) couvert(e) de givre; (welcome) glacial(e).
froth ['frɔθ] n mousse f; écume f.
frown [fraun] n froncement m de sourcils ♦ vi froncer les sourcils.
  frown on vt (fig) désapprouver.
froze [frəuz] pt of **freeze**.
frozen ['frəuzn] pp of **freeze** ♦ a (food) congelé(e); (COMM: assets) gelé(e).
FRS n abbr (Brit: = Fellow of the Royal Society) association d'encouragement à la recherche scientifique; (US: = Federal Reserve System) banque centrale américaine.
frugal ['fruːgl] a frugal(e).
fruit [fruːt] n (pl inv) fruit m.
fruiterer ['fruːtərə*] n fruitier m, marchand/e de fruits; **~'s (shop)** fruiterie f.
fruitful ['fruːtful] a fructueux(euse); (plant, soil) fécond(e).
fruition [fruː'ɪʃən] n: **to come to ~** se réaliser.
fruit juice n jus m de fruit.
fruitless ['fruːtlɪs] a (fig) vain(e), infructueux(euse).
fruit machine n (Brit) machine f à sous.
fruit salad n salade f de fruits.
frump [frʌmp] n mocheté f.
frustrate [frʌs'treɪt] vt frustrer; (plot, plans) faire échouer.
frustrated [frʌs'treɪtɪd] a frustré(e).
frustrating [frʌs'treɪtɪŋ] a (job) frustrant(e); (day) démoralisant(e).
frustration [frʌs'treɪʃən] n frustration f.
fry, pt, pp **fried** [fraɪ, -d] vt (faire) frire; **the small ~** le menu fretin.
frying pan ['fraɪɪŋ-] n poêle f (à frire).
FT n abbr (Brit: = Financial Times) journal financier; **the ~ index** l'indice boursier du Financial Times.
ft. abbr = **foot, feet**.
FTC n abbr (US) = **Federal Trade Commission**.
fuchsia ['fjuːʃə] n fuchsia m.
fuck [fʌk] vt, vi (col!) baiser (!); **~ off!** fous le camp! (!).
fuddled ['fʌdld] a (muddled) embrouillé(e), confus(e).
fuddy-duddy ['fʌdɪdʌdɪ] a (pej) vieux jeu inv, ringard(e).
fudge [fʌdʒ] n (CULIN) sorte de confiserie à base de sucre, de beurre et de lait ♦ vt (issue, problem) esquiver.
fuel [fjuəl] n (for heating) combustible m; (for propelling) carburant m.
fuel oil n mazout m.
fuel pump n (AUT) pompe f d'alimentation.
fuel tank n cuve f à mazout, citerne f; (in vehicle) réservoir m de or à carburant.
fug [fʌg] n (Brit) puanteur f, odeur f de renfermé.
fugitive ['fjuːdʒɪtɪv] n fugitif/ive.
fulfil, (US) **fulfill** [ful'fɪl] vt (function) remplir; (order) exécuter; (wish, desire) satisfaire, réaliser.
fulfilled [ful'fɪld] a (person) comblé(e), épanoui(e).

fulfil(l)ment [ful'fɪlmənt] *n* (*of wishes*) réalisation *f*.

full [ful] *a* plein(e); (*details, information*) complet(ète); (*price*) fort(e), normal(e); (*skirt*) ample, large ♦ *ad*: **to know ~ well that** savoir fort bien que; **~ (up)** (*hotel etc*) complet(ète); **I'm ~ (up)** j'ai bien mangé; **~ employment/fare** plein emploi/tarif; **a ~ two hours** deux bonnes heures; **at ~ speed** à toute vitesse; **in ~** (*reproduce, quote, pay*) intégralement; (*write name etc*) en toutes lettres.

fullback ['fulbæk] *n* (*RUGBY, FOOTBALL*) arrière *m*.

full-blooded ['ful'blʌdɪd] *a* (*vigorous*) vigoureux(euse).

full-cream ['ful'kri:m] *a*: **~ milk** (*Brit*) lait entier.

full-grown ['ful'grəun] *a* arrivé(e) à maturité, adulte.

full-length ['ful'lɛŋθ] *a* (*portrait*) en pied; **~ film** long métrage.

full moon *n* pleine lune.

full-scale ['fulskeɪl] *a* (*model*) grandeur nature *inv*; (*search, retreat*) complet(ète), total(e).

full-sized ['ful'saɪzd] *a* (*portrait etc*) grandeur nature *inv*.

full stop *n* point *m*.

full-time ['ful'taɪm] *a* (*work*) à plein temps ♦ *n* (*SPORT*) fin *f* du match.

fully ['fulɪ] *ad* entièrement, complètement; (*at least*): **~ as big** au moins aussi grand.

fully-fledged ['ful'flɛdʒd] *a* (*teacher, barrister*) diplômé(e); (*citizen, member*) à part entière.

fulsome ['fulsəm] *a* (*pej: praise*) excessif(ive); (*: manner*) exagéré(e).

fumble ['fʌmbl] *vi* fouiller, tâtonner ♦ *vt* (*ball*) mal réceptionner, cafouiller.

fumble with *vt fus* tripoter.

fume [fju:m] *vi* rager; **~s** *npl* vapeurs *fpl*, émanations *fpl*, gaz *mpl*.

fumigate ['fju:mɪgeɪt] *vt* désinfecter (par fumigation).

fun [fʌn] *n* amusement *m*, divertissement *m*; **to have ~** s'amuser; **for ~** pour rire; **it's not much ~** ce n'est pas très drôle *or* amusant; **to make ~ of** se moquer de.

function ['fʌŋkʃən] *n* fonction *f*; (*reception, dinner*) cérémonie *f*, soirée officielle ♦ *vi* fonctionner; **to ~ as** faire office de.

functional ['fʌŋkʃnl] *a* fonctionnel(le).

function key *n* (*COMPUT*) touche *f* de fonction.

fund [fʌnd] *n* caisse *f*, fonds *m*; (*source, store*) source *f*, mine *f*; **~s** *npl* fonds *mpl*.

fundamental [fʌndə'mɛntl] *a* fondamental(e); **~s** *npl* principes *mpl* de base.

fundamentalist [fʌndə'mɛntəlɪst] intégriste *m/f*.

fundamentally [fʌndə'mɛntəlɪ] *ad* fondamentalement.

fund-raising ['fʌndreɪzɪŋ] *n* collecte *f* de fonds.

funeral ['fju:nərəl] *n* enterrement *m*, obsèques *fpl* (*more formal occasion*).

funeral director *n* entrepreneur *m* des pompes funèbres.

funeral parlour *n* dépôt *m* mortuaire.

funeral service *n* service *m* funèbre.

funereal [fju:'nɪərɪəl] *a* lugubre, funèbre.

fun fair *n* (*Brit*) fête (foraine).

fungus, *pl* **fungi** ['fʌŋgəs, -gaɪ] *n* champignon *m*; (*mould*) moisissure *f*.

funicular [fju:'nɪkjulə*] *n* (*also*: **~ railway**) funiculaire *m*.

funnel ['fʌnl] *n* entonnoir *m*; (*of ship*) cheminée *f*.

funnily ['fʌnɪlɪ] *ad* (*see funny*) drôlement; curieusement.

funny ['fʌnɪ] *a* amusant(e), drôle; (*strange*) curieux(euse), bizarre.

funny bone *n* endroit sensible du coude.

fur [fə:*] *n* fourrure *f*; (*Brit: in kettle etc*) (dépôt *m* de) tartre *m*.

fur coat *n* manteau *m* de fourrure.

furious ['fjuərɪəs] *a* furieux(euse); (*effort*) acharné(e); **to be ~ with sb** être dans une fureur noire contre qn.

furiously ['fjuərɪəslɪ] *ad* furieusement; avec acharnement.

furl [fə:l] *vt* rouler; (*NAUT*) ferler.

furlong ['fə:lɔŋ] *n* = 201.17 *m* (*terme d'hippisme*).

furlough ['fə:ləu] *n* permission *f*, congé *m*.

furnace ['fə:nɪs] *n* fourneau *m*.

furnish ['fə:nɪʃ] *vt* meubler; (*supply*) fournir; **~ed flat** *or* (*US*) **apartment** meublé *m*.

furnishings ['fə:nɪʃɪŋz] *npl* mobilier *m*, articles *mpl* d'ameublement.

furniture ['fə:nɪtʃə*] *n* meubles *mpl*, mobilier *m*; **piece of ~** meuble *m*.

furniture polish *n* encaustique *f*.

furore [fjuə'rɔ:rɪ] *n* (*protests*) protestations *fpl*.

furrier ['fʌrɪə*] *n* fourreur *m*.

furrow ['fʌrəu] *n* sillon *m*.

furry ['fə:rɪ] *a* (*animal*) à fourrure; (*toy*) en peluche.

further ['fə:ðə*] *a* supplémentaire, autre; nouveau(nouvelle) ♦ *ad* plus loin; (*more*) davantage; (*moreover*) de plus ♦ *vt* faire avancer *or* progresser, promouvoir; **how much ~ is it?** quelle distance *or* combien reste-t-il à parcourir?; **until ~ notice** jusqu'à nouvel ordre *or* avis; **~ to your letter of ...** (*COMM*) suite à votre lettre du ....

further education *n* enseignement *m* post-scolaire (*recyclage, formation professionnelle*).

furthermore [fə:ðə'mɔ:*] *ad* de plus, en outre.

furthermost ['fə:ðəməust] *a* le(la) plus éloigné(e).

furthest ['fə:ðɪst] *superlative of* **far**.

furtive ['fə:tɪv] *a* furtif(ive).

furtively ['fə:tɪvlɪ] *ad* furtivement.

fury ['fjuərɪ] *n* fureur *f*.

fuse, (*US*) **fuze** [fju:z] *n* fusible *m*; (*for bomb etc*) amorce *f*, détonateur *m* ♦ *vt, vi* (*metal*) fondre; (*fig*) fusionner; (*ELEC*): **to ~ the lights** faire sauter les fusibles *or* les plombs; **a ~ has blown** un fusible a sauté.

fuse box *n* boîte *f* à fusibles.

fuselage ['fju:zəlɑ:ʒ] *n* fuselage *m*.

fuse wire *n* fusible *m*.

fusillade [fju:zɪ'leɪd] *n* fusillade *f*; (*fig*) feu roulant.

fusion ['fju:ʒən] *n* fusion *f*.

fuss [fʌs] *n* (*anxiety, excitement*) chichis *mpl*,

façons *fpl*; (*commotion*) tapage *m*; (*complaining, trouble*) histoire(s) *f(pl)* ♦ *vt* faire des histoires ♦ *vt* (*person*) embêter; **to make a ~** faire des façons (*or* des histoires); **to make a ~ of sb** dorloter qn.
fuss over *vt fus* (*person*) dorloter.
fussy ['fʌsɪ] *a* (*person*) tatillon(ne), difficile; chichiteux(euse); (*dress,* *style*) tarabiscoté(e); **I'm not ~** (*col*) ça m'est égal.
futile ['fjuːtaɪl] *a* futile.
futility [fjuː'tɪlɪtɪ] *n* futilité *f*.
future ['fjuːtʃə*] *a* futur(e) ♦ *n* avenir *m*; (*LING*) futur *m*; **in (the) ~** à l'avenir; **in the near/immediate ~** dans un avenir proche/immédiat.
futures ['fjuːtʃəz] *npl* (*COMM*) opérations *fpl* à terme.
futuristic [fjuːtʃə'rɪstɪk] *a* futuriste.
fuze [fjuːz] *n*, *vt*, *vi* (*US*) = **fuse**.
fuzzy ['fʌzɪ] *a* (*PHOT*) flou(e); (*hair*) crépu(e).
fwd. *abbr* = **forward**.
fwy *abbr* (*US*) = **freeway**.
FY *abbr* = **fiscal year**.
FYI *abbr* = **for your information**.

G

G, g [dʒiː] *n* (*letter*) G, g *m*; (*MUS*): **G** sol *m*; **G for George** G comme Gaston.
G *n abbr* (*Brit SCOL*: = *good*) b (= *bien*); (*US CINEMA*: = *general (audience)*) ≈ tous publics.
g *abbr* (= *gram, gravity*) g.
GA *abbr* (*US POST*) = *Georgia*.
gab [gæb] *n* (*col*): **to have the gift of the ~** avoir la langue bien pendue.
gabble ['gæbl] *vi* bredouiller; jacasser.
gaberdine [gæbə'diːn] *n* gabardine *f*.
gable ['geɪbl] *n* pignon *m*.
Gabon [gə'bɔn] *n* Gabon *m*.
gad about ['gædə'baut] *vi* (*col*) se balader.
gadget ['gædʒɪt] *n* gadget *m*.
Gaelic ['geɪlɪk] *a*, *n* gaélique (*m*).
gaffe [gæf] *n* gaffe *f*.
gag [gæg] *n* bâillon *m*; (*joke*) gag *m* ♦ *vt* bâillonner.
gaga ['gaːgaː] *a*: **to go ~** devenir gaga *or* gâteux(euse).
gaiety ['geɪtɪ] *n* gaieté *f*.
gaily ['geɪlɪ] *ad* gaiement.
gain [geɪn] *n* gain *m*, profit *m* ♦ *vt* gagner ♦ *vi* (*watch*) avancer; **to ~ in/by** gagner en/à; **to ~ 3lbs (in weight)** prendre 3 livres; **to ~ ground** gagner du terrain.
gain (up)on *vt fus* rattraper.
gainful ['geɪnful] *a* profitable, lucratif(ive).
gainsay [geɪn'seɪ] *vt irg* (*like* **say**) contredire; nier.
gait [geɪt] *n* démarche *f*.
gal. *abbr* = **gallon**.
gala ['gaːlə] *n* gala *m*; **swimming ~** grand concours de natation.
Galapagos (Islands) [gə'læpəgəs-] *npl*: **the ~** les (îles *fpl*) Galapagos *fpl*.
galaxy ['gæləksɪ] *n* galaxie *f*.
gale [geɪl] *n* coup *m* de vent; **~ force 10** vent *m* de force 10.
gall [gɔːl] *n* (*ANAT*) bile *f*; (*fig*) effronterie *f* ♦ *vt* ulcérer, irriter.
gall. *abbr* = **gallon**.
gallant ['gælənt] *a* vaillant(e), brave; (*towards ladies*) empressé(e), galant(e).
gallantry ['gæləntrɪ] *n* bravoure *f*, vaillance *f*; empressement *m*, galanterie *f*.
gall-bladder ['gɔːlblædə*] *n* vésicule *f* biliaire.
galleon ['gælɪən] *n* galion *m*.
gallery ['gælərɪ] *n* galerie *f*; (*for spectators*) tribune *f*; (: *in theatre*) dernier balcon; (*also*: **art ~**) musée *m*; (: *private*) galerie.
galley ['gælɪ] *n* (*ship's kitchen*) cambuse *f*; (*ship*) galère *f*; (*also*: **~ proof**) placard *m*, galée *f*.
Gallic ['gælɪk] *a* (*of Gaul*) gaulois(e); (*French*) français(e).
galling ['gɔːlɪŋ] *a* irritant(e).
gallon ['gæln] *n* gallon *m* (= *8 pints; Brit* = *4.543 l; US* = *3.785 l*).
gallop ['gæləp] *n* galop *m* ♦ *vi* galoper; **~ing inflation** inflation galopante.
gallows ['gæləuz] *n* potence *f*.
gallstone ['gɔːlstəun] *n* calcul *m* (biliaire).
galore [gə'lɔː*] *ad* en abondance, à gogo.
galvanize ['gælvənaɪz] *vt* galvaniser; (*fig*): **to ~ sb into action** galvaniser qn.
Gambia ['gæmbɪə] *n* Gambie *f*.
gambit ['gæmbɪt] *n* (*fig*): **(opening) ~** manœuvre *f* stratégique.
gamble ['gæmbl] *n* pari *m*, risque calculé ♦ *vt*, *vi* jouer; **to ~ on the Stock Exchange** jouer en *or* à la Bourse; **to ~ on** (*fig*) miser sur.
gambler ['gæmblə*] *n* joueur *m*.
gambling ['gæmblɪŋ] *n* jeu *m*.
gambol ['gæmbl] *vi* gambader.
game [geɪm] *n* jeu *m*; (*event*) match *m*; (*HUNTING*) gibier *m* ♦ *a* brave; (*ready*): **to be ~ (for sth/to do)** être prêt(e) (à qch/à faire), se sentir de taille (à faire); **a ~ of football/tennis** une partie de football/tennis; **~s** (*SCOL*) sport *m*; **big ~** gros gibier.
game bird *n* gibier *m* à plume.
gamekeeper ['geɪmkiːpə*] *n* garde-chasse *m*.
gamely ['geɪmlɪ] *ad* vaillamment.
game reserve *n* réserve animalière.
gamesmanship ['geɪmzmənʃɪp] *n* roublardise *f*.
gammon ['gæmən] *n* (*bacon*) quartier *m* de lard fumé; (*ham*) jambon fumé.
gamut ['gæmət] *n* gamme *f*.
gang [gæŋ] *n* bande *f*, groupe *m* ♦ *vi*: **to ~ up on sb** se liguer contre qn.
Ganges ['gændʒiːz] *n*: **the ~** le Gange.
gangling ['gæŋglɪŋ] *a* dégingandé(e).
gangplank ['gæŋplæŋk] *n* passerelle *f*.
gangrene ['gæŋgriːn] *n* gangrène *f*.
gangster ['gæŋstə*] *n* gangster *m*, bandit *m*.
gangway ['gæŋweɪ] *n* passerelle *f*; (*Brit: of bus*) couloir central.
gantry ['gæntrɪ] *n* portique *m*; (*for rocket*) tour *f* de lancement.
GAO *n abbr* (*US*: = *General Accounting*

Office) ≈ Cour *f* des comptes.
gaol [dʒeɪl] *n, vt (Brit)* = **jail.**
gap [gæp] *n* trou *m*; *(in time)* intervalle *m*; *(fig)* lacune *f*; vide *m*.
gape [geɪp] *vi* être *or* rester bouche bée.
gaping ['geɪpɪŋ] *a (hole)* béant(e).
garage ['gærɑ:ʒ] *n* garage *m*.
garb [gɑ:b] *n* tenue *f*, costume *m*.
garbage ['gɑ:bɪdʒ] *n* ordures *fpl*, détritus *mpl*; *(fig: col)* conneries *fpl*.
garbage can *n (US)* poubelle *f*, boîte *f* à ordures.
garbage disposal (unit) *n* broyeur *m* d'ordures.
garbled ['gɑ:bld] *a* déformé(e); faussé(e).
garden ['gɑ:dn] *n* jardin *m* ♦ *vi* jardiner; **~s** *npl (public)* jardin public; *(private)* parc *m*.
garden centre *n* garden-centre *m*, pépinière *f*.
gardener ['gɑ:dnə*] *n* jardinier *m*.
gardening ['gɑ:dnɪŋ] *n* jardinage *m*.
gargle ['gɑ:gl] *vi* se gargariser ♦ *n* gargarisme *m*.
gargoyle ['gɑ:gɔɪl] *n* gargouille *f*.
garish ['gεərɪʃ] *a* criard(e), voyant(e).
garland ['gɑ:lənd] *n* guirlande *f*; couronne *f*.
garlic ['gɑ:lɪk] *n* ail *m*.
garment ['gɑ:mənt] *n* vêtement *m*.
garner ['gɑ:nə*] *vt* engranger, amasser.
garnish ['gɑ:nɪʃ] *vt* garnir.
garret ['gærɪt] *n* mansarde *f*.
garrison ['gærɪsn] *n* garnison *f* ♦ *vt* mettre en garnison, stationner.
garrulous ['gærjuləs] *a* volubile, loquace.
garter ['gɑ:tə*] *n* jarretière *f*; *(US: suspender)* jarretelle *f*.
garter belt *n (US)* porte-jarretelles *m inv.*
gas [gæs] *n* gaz *m*; *(used as anaesthetic)*: **to be given ~** se faire endormir; *(US: gasoline)* essence *f* ♦ *vt* asphyxier; *(MIL)* gazer.
Gascony ['gæskənɪ] *n* Gascogne *f*.
gas cooker *n (Brit)* cuisinière *f* à gaz.
gas cylinder *n* bouteille *f* de gaz.
gaseous ['gæsɪəs] *a* gazeux(euse).
gas fire *n (Brit)* radiateur *m* à gaz.
gash [gæʃ] *n* entaille *f*; *(on face)* balafre *f* ♦ *vt* taillader; balafrer.
gasket ['gæskɪt] *n (AUT)* joint *m* de culasse.
gas mask *n* masque *m* à gaz.
gas meter *n* compteur *m* à gaz.
gasoline ['gæsəli:n] *n (US)* essence *f*.
gasp [gɑ:sp] *vi* haleter; *(fig)* avoir le souffle coupé.
gasp out *vt (say)* dire dans un souffle *or* d'une voix entrecoupée.
gas ring *n* brûleur *m*.
gas station *n (US)* station-service *f*.
gas stove *n* réchaud *m* à gaz; *(cooker)* cuisinière *f* à gaz.
gassy ['gæsɪ] *a* gazeux(euse).
gas tank *n (US AUT)* réservoir *m* d'essence.
gas tap *n* bouton *m* (de cuisinière à gaz); *(on pipe)* robinet *m* à gaz.
gastric ['gæstrɪk] *a* gastrique.
gastric ulcer *n* ulcère *m* de l'estomac.
gastroenteritis ['gæstrəuεntə'raɪtɪs] *n* gastroentérite *f*.
gastronomy [gæs'trɒnəmɪ] *n* gastronomie *f*.
gasworks ['gæswə:ks] *n, npl* usine *f* à gaz.

gate [geɪt] *n (of garden)* portail *m*; *(of farm, at level crossing)* barrière *f*; *(of building, town, at airport)* porte *f*; *(of lock)* vanne *f*.
gateau, *pl* **~x** ['gætəu, -z] *n* gros gâteau à la crème.
gatecrash ['geɪtkræʃ] *vt* s'introduire sans invitation dans.
gatecrasher ['geɪtkræʃə*] *n* intrus/e.
gateway ['geɪtweɪ] *n* porte *f*.
gather ['gæðə*] *vt (flowers, fruit)* cueillir; *(pick up)* ramasser; *(assemble)* rassembler, réunir; recueillir; *(understand)* comprendre ♦ *vi (assemble)* se rassembler; *(dust)* s'amasser; *(clouds)* s'amonceler; **to ~ (from/that)** conclure *or* déduire (de/que); **as far as I can ~** d'après ce que je comprends; **to ~ speed** prendre de la vitesse.
gathering ['gæðərɪŋ] *n* rassemblement *m*.
GATT [gæt] *n abbr (= General Agreement on Tariffs and Trade)* GATT *m*.
gauche [gəuʃ] *a* gauche, maladroit(e).
gaudy ['gɔ:dɪ] *a* voyant(e).
gauge [geɪdʒ] *n (standard measure)* calibre *m*; *(RAIL)* écartement *m*; *(instrument)* jauge *f* ♦ *vt* jauger; *(fig: sb's capabilities, character)* juger de; **to ~ the right moment** calculer le moment propice; **petrol ~**, *(US)* **gas ~** jauge d'essence.
Gaul [gɔ:l] *n (country)* Gaule *f*; *(person)* Gaulois/e.
gaunt [gɔ:nt] *a* décharné(e); *(grim, desolate)* désolé(e).
gauntlet ['gɔ:ntlɪt] *n (fig)*: **to throw down the ~** jeter le gant; **to run the ~ through an angry crowd** se frayer un passage à travers une foule hostile *or* entre deux haies de manifestants *etc* hostiles.
gauze [gɔ:z] *n* gaze *f*.
gave [geɪv] *pt of* **give**.
gavel ['gævl] *n* marteau *m*.
gawky ['gɔ:kɪ] *a* dégingandé(e), godiche.
gawp [gɔ:p] *vi*: **to ~ at** regarder bouche bée.
gay [geɪ] *a (homosexual)* homosexuel(le); *(slightly old-fashioned: cheerful)* gai(e); réjoui(e); *(colour)* gai, vif(vive).
gaze [geɪz] *n* regard *m* fixe ♦ *vi*: **to ~ at** *vt* fixer du regard.
gazelle [gə'zεl] *n* gazelle *f*.
gazette [gə'zεt] *n (newspaper)* gazette *f*; *(official publication)* journal officiel.
gazetteer [gæzə'tɪə*] *n* dictionnaire *m* géographique.
gazumping [gə'zʌmpɪŋ] *n* le fait de revenir sur une promesse de vente pour accepter un prix plus élevé.
GB *abbr* = **Great Britain**.
GBH *n abbr (Brit LAW: col)* = **grievous bodily harm**.
GC *n abbr (Brit: = George Cross)* distinction honorifique.
GCE *n abbr (Brit)* = General Certificate of Education.
GCHQ *n abbr (Brit: = Government Communications Headquarters)* centre d'interception des télécommunications étrangères.
GCSE *n abbr (Brit)* = General Certificate of Secondary Education.
Gdns. *abbr* = gardens.

GDP n abbr = **gross domestic product**.
GDR n abbr (= German Democratic Republic)
  RDA f.
gear [gɪə*] n matériel m, équipement m;
  (TECH) engrenage m; (AUT) vitesse f ♦ vt
  (fig: adapt) adapter; **top** or (US) **high/low/
  bottom** ~ quatrième (or cinquième)/
  deuxième/première vitesse; **in** ~ en prise;
  out of ~ au point mort; **our service is ~ed
  to meet the needs of the disabled** notre
  service répond de façon spécifique aux
  besoins des handicapés.
  gear up vi: **to** ~ **up (to do)** se préparer (à
  faire).
gear box n boîte f de vitesse.
gear lever, (US) **gear shift** n levier m de
  vitesse.
GED n abbr (US SCOL) = general educational
  development.
geese [giːs] npl of **goose**.
Geiger counter ['gaɪgə-] n compteur m
  Geiger.
gel [dʒɛl] n gelée f; (CHEMISTRY) colloïde m.
gelatin(e) ['dʒɛləti:n] n gélatine f.
gelignite ['dʒɛlɪgnaɪt] n plastic m.
gem [dʒɛm] n pierre précieuse.
Gemini ['dʒɛmɪnaɪ] n les Gémeaux mpl; **to be**
  ~ être des Gémeaux.
gen [dʒɛn] n (Brit col): **to give sb the** ~ **on**
  sth mettre qn au courant de qch.
Gen. abbr (MIL: = general) Gal.
gen. abbr (= general, generally) gén.
gender ['dʒɛndə*] n genre m.
gene [dʒi:n] n (BIOL) gène m.
genealogy [dʒi:nɪ'ælədʒɪ] n généalogie f.
general ['dʒɛnərl] n général m ♦ a général(e);
  in ~ en général; **the** ~ **public** le grand public; ~ **audit** (COMM) vérification annuelle.
general anaesthetic n anesthésie générale.
general election n élection(s) législative(s).
generalization   ['dʒɛnrəlaɪ'zeɪʃən]   n
  généralisation f.
generalize ['dʒɛnrəlaɪz] vi généraliser.
generally ['dʒɛnrəlɪ] ad généralement.
general manager n directeur général.
general practitioner (GP) n généraliste m/
  f; **who's your GP?** qui est votre médecin
  traitant?
general strike n grève générale.
generate ['dʒɛnəreɪt] vt engendrer; (electricity) produire.
generation [dʒɛnə'reɪʃən] n génération f; (of
  electricity etc) production f.
generator ['dʒɛnəreɪtə*] n générateur m.
generic [dʒɪ'nɛrɪk] a générique.
generosity [dʒɛnə'rɔsɪtɪ] n générosité f.
generous ['dʒɛnərəs] a généreux(euse);
  (copious) copieux(euse).
genesis ['dʒɛnɪsɪs] n genèse f.
genetic [dʒɪ'nɛtɪk] a génétique; ~ **engineering**
  génie m génétique.
genetics [dʒɪ'nɛtɪks] n génétique f.
Geneva [dʒɪ'ni:və] n Genève; **Lake** ~ le lac
  Léman.
genial   ['dʒi:nɪəl]   a   cordial(e),
  chaleureux(euse); (climate) clément(e).
genitals ['dʒɛnɪtlz] npl organes génitaux.
genitive ['dʒɛnɪtɪv] n génitif m.
genius ['dʒi:nɪəs] n génie m.

Genoa ['dʒɛnəuə] n Gênes.
genocide ['dʒɛnəusaɪd] n génocide m.
gent [dʒɛnt] n abbr (Brit col) = **gentleman**.
genteel [dʒɛn'ti:l] a de bon ton, distingué(e).
gentle ['dʒɛntl] a doux(douce).
gentleman ['dʒɛntlmən] n monsieur m; (well-
  bred man) gentleman m; ~'s **agreement**
  gentleman's agreement m.
gentlemanly ['dʒɛntlmənlɪ] a bien élevé(e).
gentleness ['dʒɛntlnɪs] n douceur f.
gently ['dʒɛntlɪ] ad doucement.
gentry ['dʒɛntrɪ] n petite noblesse.
gents [dʒɛnts] n W.-C. mpl (pour hommes).
genuine ['dʒɛnjuɪn] a véritable, authentique;
  (person, emotion) sincère.
genuinely   ['dʒɛnjuɪnlɪ]   ad   sincèrement,
  vraiment.
geographer [dʒɪ'ɔgrəfə*] n géographe m/f.
geographic(al)   [dʒɪə'græfɪk(l)]   a   géographique.
geography [dʒɪ'ɔgrəfɪ] n géographie f.
geological [dʒɪə'lɔdʒɪkl] a géologique.
geologist [dʒɪ'ɔlədʒɪst] n géologue m/f.
geology [dʒɪ'ɔlədʒɪ] n géologie f.
geometric(al) [dʒɪə'mɛtrɪk(l)] a géométrique.
geometry [dʒɪ'ɔmətrɪ] n géométrie f.
Geordie ['dʒɔ:dɪ] n (col) habitant/e de
  Tyneside; originaire m/f de Tyneside.
geranium [dʒɪ'reɪnɪəm] n géranium m.
geriatric [dʒɛrɪ'ætrɪk] a gériatrique.
germ [dʒə:m] n (MED) microbe m; (BIO, fig)
  germe m.
German ['dʒə:mən]   a   allemand(e) ♦ n
  Allemand/e; (LING) allemand m.
German measles n rubéole f.
Germany ['dʒə:mənɪ] n Allemagne f.
germination [dʒə:mɪ'neɪʃən] n germination f.
germ warfare n guerre f bactériologique.
gerrymandering ['dʒɛrɪmændərɪŋ] n tripotage
  m du découpage électoral.
gestation [dʒɛs'teɪʃən] n gestation f.
gesticulate [dʒɛs'tɪkjuleɪt] vi gesticuler.
gesture ['dʒɛstjə*] n geste m; **as a** ~ **of
  friendship** en témoignage d'amitié.
get, pt, pp **got**, (US) pp **gotten** [gɛt, gɔt,
  'gɔtn] vt (obtain) avoir, obtenir; (receive)
  recevoir; (find) trouver, acheter; (catch) attraper; (fetch) aller chercher; (take, move)
  emmener; (understand) comprendre, saisir;
  (have): **to have got** avoir; (become): **to** ~
  rich/old s'enrichir/vieillir; (col: annoy): **he
  really** ~s **me!** il me porte sur les nerfs! ♦ vi
  (go): **to** ~ **to** (place) aller à; arriver à;
  parvenir à; (modal auxiliary vb): **you've got
  to do it** il faut que vous le fassiez; **he got
  across the bridge/under the fence** il a
  traversé le pont/est passé par-dessous la
  barrière; **to** ~ **sth for sb** obtenir qch pour
  qn, procurer qch à qn; (fetch) aller chercher
  qch (pour qn); ~ **me Mr Jones, please**
  (TEL) appelez-moi Mr Jones (au téléphone),
  s'il vous plaît; **can I** ~ **you a drink?** puis-je
  vous offrir quelque chose à boire?; **to** ~
  ready/washed/shaved etc se préparer/laver/
  raser etc; **to** ~ **sth done** (do) faire qch;
  arriver à faire qch; (have done) faire faire
  qch; **to** ~ **sth/sb ready** préparer qch/qn; **to**
  ~ **one's hair cut** se faire couper les cheveux;
  to ~ **sb to do sth** faire faire qch à qn; **to** ~

sth through/out of faire passer qch par/sortir qch de; **let's ~ going** or **started!** allons-y!

get about vi se déplacer; (news) se répandre.

get across vt: **to ~ across (to)** (message, meaning) faire passer (à) ♦ vi: **to ~ across to** (subj: speaker) se faire comprendre (par).

get along vi (agree) s'entendre; (depart) s'en aller; (manage) = **to get by.**

get at vt fus (attack) s'en prendre à; (reach) attraper, atteindre; **what are you ~ting at?** à quoi voulez-vous en venir?

get away vi partir, s'en aller; (escape) s'échapper.

get away with vt fus en être quitte pour; se faire passer or pardonner.

get back vi (return) rentrer ♦ vt récupérer, recouvrer; **to ~ back to** (start again) retourner or revenir à; (contact again) recontacter.

get back at vt fus (col): **to ~ back at sb** rendre la monnaie de sa pièce à qn.

get by vi (pass) passer; (manage) se débrouiller; **I can ~ by in Dutch** je me débrouille en hollandais.

get down vi, vt fus descendre ♦ vt descendre; (depress) déprimer.

get down to vt fus (work) se mettre à (faire); **to ~ down to business** passer aux choses sérieuses.

get in vi arriver; (train) arriver; (arrive home) rentrer ♦ vt (bring in: harvest) rentrer; (: coal) faire rentrer; (: supplies) faire des provisions de.

get into vt fus entrer dans; (vehicle) monter dans; (clothes) mettre, enfiler; **to ~ into bed/a rage** se mettre au lit/en colère.

get off vi (from train etc) descendre; (depart: person, car) s'en aller; (escape) s'en tirer ♦ vt (remove: clothes, stain) enlever; (send off) expédier; (have as leave: day, time): **we got 2 days off** nous avons eu 2 jours de congé ♦ vt fus (train, bus) descendre de; **to ~ off to a good start** (fig) prendre un bon départ.

get on vi (at exam etc) se débrouiller; (agree): **to ~ on (with)** s'entendre (avec) ♦ vt fus monter dans; (horse) monter sur; **how are you ~ting on?** comment ça va?

get on to vt fus (Brit: deal with: problem) s'occuper de; (: contact: person) contacter.

get out vi sortir; (of vehicle) descendre; (news etc) s'ébruiter ♦ vt sortir.

get out of vt fus sortir de; (duty etc) échapper à, se soustraire à.

get over vt fus (illness) se remettre de ♦ vt (communicate: idea etc) communiquer; (finish): **let's ~ it over (with)** finissons-en.

get round vi: **to ~ round to doing sth** se mettre (finalement) à faire qch ♦ vt fus contourner; (fig: person) entortiller.

get through vi (TEL) avoir la communication ♦ vt fus (finish: work, book) finir, terminer.

get through to vt fus (TEL) atteindre.

get together vi se réunir ♦ vt rassembler.

get up vi (rise) se lever ♦ vt fus monter.

get up to vt fus (reach) arriver à; (Brit: prank etc) faire.

getaway ['gɛtəweɪ] n fuite f.

getaway car n voiture prévue pour prendre la fuite.

get-together ['gɛttəgɛðə*] n petite réunion, petite fête.

get-up ['gɛtʌp] n (col: outfit) accoutrement m.

get-well card [gɛt'wɛl-] n carte f de vœux de bon rétablissement.

geyser ['giːzə*] n chauffe-eau m inv; (GEO) geyser m.

Ghana ['gɑːnə] n Ghana m.

Ghanaian [gɑː'neɪən] a ghanéen(ne) ♦ n Ghanéen/ne.

ghastly ['gɑːstlɪ] a atroce, horrible; (pale) livide, blême.

gherkin ['gɜːkɪn] n cornichon m.

ghetto ['gɛtəʊ] n ghetto m.

ghost [gəʊst] n fantôme m, revenant m ♦ vt (sb else's book) écrire.

ghostly ['gəʊstlɪ] a fantomatique.

ghostwriter ['gəʊstraɪtə*] n nègre m (fig).

ghoul [guːl] n (ghost) vampire m.

ghoulish ['guːlɪʃ] a (tastes etc) morbide.

GHQ n abbr (MIL: = general headquarters) GQG m.

GI n abbr (US col: = government issue) soldat de l'armée américaine, GI m.

giant ['dʒaɪənt] n géant/e ♦ a géant(e), énorme; **~ (size) packet** paquet géant.

gibber ['dʒɪbə*] vi émettre des sons inintelligibles.

gibberish ['dʒɪbərɪʃ] n charabia m.

gibe [dʒaɪb] n sarcasme m ♦ vi: **to ~ at** railler.

giblets ['dʒɪblɪts] npl abats mpl.

Gibraltar [dʒɪ'brɔːltə*] n Gibraltar m.

giddiness ['gɪdɪnɪs] n vertige m.

giddy ['gɪdɪ] a (dizzy): **to be** (or **feel**) **~** avoir le vertige; (height) vertigineux(euse); (thoughtless) sot(te), étourdi(e).

gift [gɪft] n cadeau m, présent m; (donation) don m; (COMM: also: **free ~**) cadeau(-réclame) m; (talent): **to have a ~ for sth** avoir des dons pour or le don de qch.

gifted ['gɪftɪd] a doué(e).

gift token, gift voucher n bon m d'achat.

gig [gɪg] n (col: of musician) gig f.

gigantic [dʒaɪ'gæntɪk] a gigantesque.

giggle ['gɪgl] vi pouffer, ricaner sottement ♦ n petit rire sot, ricanement m.

GIGO ['gaɪgəʊ] abbr (COMPUT: col: = garbage in, garbage out) qualité d'entrée = qualité de sortie.

gild [gɪld] vt dorer.

gill [dʒɪl] n (measure) = 0.25 pints (Brit = 0.148 l; US = 0.118 l).

gills [gɪlz] npl (of fish) ouïes fpl, branchies fpl.

gilt [gɪlt] n dorure f ♦ a doré(e).

gilt-edged ['gɪltedʒd] a (stocks, securities) de premier ordre.

gimlet ['gɪmlɪt] n vrille f.

gimmick ['gɪmɪk] n truc m; **sales ~** offre promotionnelle.

gin [dʒɪn] n gin m.

ginger ['dʒɪndʒə*] n gingembre m.

ginger up vt secouer; animer.

ginger ale, ginger beer n boisson gazeuse au

gingembre.

gingerbread ['dʒɪndʒəbrɛd] n pain m d'épices.

ginger group n (Brit) groupe m de pression.

ginger-haired ['dʒɪndʒə'hɛəd] a roux(rousse).

gingerly ['dʒɪndʒəlɪ] ad avec précaution.

gingham ['gɪŋəm] n vichy m.

gipsy ['dʒɪpsɪ] n gitan/e, bohémien/ne ♦ cpd: ~ **caravan** n roulotte f.

giraffe [dʒɪ'rɑːf] n girafe f.

girder ['gəːdəʳ] n poutrelle f.

girdle ['gəːdl] n (corset) gaine f ♦ vt ceindre.

girl [gəːl] n fille f, fillette f; (young unmarried woman) jeune fille; (daughter) fille; **an English** ~ une jeune Anglaise; **a little English** ~ une petite Anglaise.

girlfriend ['gəːlfrɛnd] n (of girl) amie f; (of boy) petite amie.

girlish ['gəːlɪʃ] a de jeune fille.

Girl Scout n (US) guide f.

Giro ['dʒaɪrəu] n: **the National** ~ (Brit) ≈ les comptes chèques postaux.

giro ['dʒaɪrəu] n (bank ~) virement m bancaire; (post office ~) mandat m.

girth [gəːθ] n circonférence f; (of horse) sangle f.

gist [dʒɪst] n essentiel m.

give [gɪv] n (of fabric) élasticité f ♦ vb (pt **gave**, pp **given** [geɪv, 'gɪvn]) vt donner ♦ vi (break) céder; (stretch: fabric) se prêter; **to** ~ **sb sth**, ~ **sth to sb** donner qch à qn; **to** ~ **a cry/sigh** pousser un cri/un soupir; **how much did you** ~ **for it?** combien (l')avez-vous payé?; **12 o'clock,** ~ **or take a few minutes** midi, à quelques minutes près; **to give way** vi céder; (Brit AUT) donner la priorité.

give away vt donner; (give free) faire cadeau de; (betray) donner, trahir; (disclose) révéler; (bride) conduire à l'autel.

give back vt rendre.

give in vi céder ♦ vt donner.

give off vt dégager.

give out vt (food etc) distribuer; (news) annoncer ♦ vi (be exhausted: supplies) s'épuiser; (fail) lâcher.

give up vi renoncer ♦ vt renoncer à; **to** ~ **up smoking** arrêter de fumer; **to** ~ **o.s. up** se rendre.

give-and-take ['gɪvənd'teɪk] n concessions mutuelles.

giveaway ['gɪvəweɪ] n (col): **her expression was a** ~ son expression la trahissait; **the exam was a** ~! cet examen, c'était du gâteau! ♦ cpd: ~ **prices** prix sacrifiés.

given ['gɪvn] pp of **give** ♦ a (fixed: time, amount) donné(e), déterminé(e) ♦ cj: ~ **the circumstances** ... étant donné les circonstances ..., vu les circonstances ...; ~ **that** ... étant donné que ....

glacial ['gleɪsɪəl] a (GEO) glaciaire; (wind, weather) glacial(e).

glacier ['glæsɪəʳ] n glacier m.

glad [glæd] a content(e); **to be** ~ **about sth/ that** être heureux(euse) or bien content de qch/que; **I was** ~ **of his help** j'étais bien content de (pouvoir compter sur) son aide or qu'il m'aide.

gladden ['glædn] vt réjouir.

glade [gleɪd] n clairière f.

gladioli [glædɪ'əulaɪ] npl glaïeuls mpl.

gladly ['glædlɪ] ad volontiers.

glamorous ['glæmərəs] a séduisant(e).

glamour ['glæməʳ] n éclat m, prestige m.

glance [glɑːns] n coup m d'œil ♦ vi: **to** ~ **at** jeter un coup d'œil à.

glance off vt fus (bullet) ricocher sur.

glancing ['glɑːnsɪŋ] a (blow) oblique.

gland [glænd] n glande f.

glandular ['glændjuləʳ] a: ~ **fever** (Brit) mononucléose infectieuse.

glare [glɛəʳ] n lumière éblouissante ♦ vi briller d'un éclat aveuglant; **to** ~ **at** lancer un or des regard(s) furieux à.

glaring ['glɛərɪŋ] a (mistake) criant(e), qui saute aux yeux.

glass [glɑːs] n verre m; (also: **looking** ~) miroir m.

glass-blowing ['glɑːsbləuɪŋ] n soufflage m (du verre).

glasses ['glɑːsəs] npl lunettes fpl.

glass fibre n fibre f de verre.

glasshouse ['glɑːshaus] n serre f.

glassware ['glɑːswɛəʳ] n verrerie f.

glassy ['glɑːsɪ] a (eyes) vitreux(euse).

Glaswegian [glæs'wiːdʒən] a de Glasgow ♦ n habitant/e de Glasgow; natif/ive de Glasgow.

glaze [gleɪz] vt (door) vitrer; (pottery) vernir; (CULIN) glacer ♦ n vernis m; (CULIN) glaçage m.

glazed ['gleɪzd] a (eye) vitreux(euse); (pottery) verni(e); (tiles) vitrifié(e).

glazier ['gleɪzɪəʳ] n vitrier m.

GLC n abbr (Brit: old: = Greater London Council) communauté urbaine londonienne.

gleam [gliːm] n lueur f ♦ vi luire, briller; **a** ~ **of hope** une lueur d'espoir.

gleaming ['gliːmɪŋ] a luisant(e).

glean [gliːn] vt (information) recueillir.

glee [gliː] n joie f.

gleeful ['gliːful] a joyeux(euse).

glen [glɛn] n vallée f.

glib [glɪb] a qui a du bagou; facile.

glide [glaɪd] vi glisser; (AVIAT, bird) planer ♦ n glissement m; vol plané.

glider ['glaɪdəʳ] n (AVIAT) planeur m.

gliding ['glaɪdɪŋ] n (AVIAT) vol m à voile.

glimmer ['glɪməʳ] vi luire ♦ n lueur f.

glimpse [glɪmps] n vision passagère, aperçu m ♦ vt entrevoir, apercevoir; **to catch a** ~ **of** entrevoir.

glint [glɪnt] n éclair m ♦ vi étinceler.

glisten ['glɪsn] vi briller, luire.

glitter ['glɪtəʳ] vi scintiller, briller ♦ n scintillement m.

glitz [glɪts] n (col) clinquant m.

gloat [gləut] vi: **to** ~ **(over)** jubiler (à propos de).

global ['gləubl] a (world-wide) mondial(e); (overall) global(e).

globe [gləub] n globe m.

globe-trotter ['gləubtrɔtəʳ] n globe-trotter m.

globule ['glɔbjuːl] n (ANAT) globule m; (of water etc) gouttelette f.

gloom [gluːm] n obscurité f; (sadness) tristesse f, mélancolie f.

gloomy ['gluːmɪ] a sombre, triste, mélancolique; **to feel** ~ avoir or se faire des idées noires.

glorification [glɔ:rɪfɪˈkeɪʃən] n glorification f.

glorify [ˈglɔ:rɪfaɪ] vt glorifier.

glorious [ˈglɔ:rɪəs] a glorieux(euse); (*beautiful*) splendide.

glory [ˈglɔ:rɪ] n gloire f; splendeur f ♦ vi: **to ~ in** se glorifier de.

glory hole n (col) capharnaüm m.

Glos abbr (*Brit*) = *Gloucestershire*.

gloss [glɒs] n (*shine*) brillant m, vernis m; (*also*: **~ paint**) peinture brillante or laquée.

gloss over vt fus glisser sur.

glossary [ˈglɒsərɪ] n glossaire m, lexique m.

glossy [ˈglɒsɪ] a brillant(e), luisant(e) ♦ n (*also*: **~ magazine**) revue f de luxe.

glove [glʌv] n gant m.

glove compartment n (AUT) boîte f à gants, vide-poches m inv.

glow [gləu] vi rougeoyer; (*face*) rayonner ♦ n rougeoiement m.

glower [ˈglauə*] vi lancer des regards mauvais.

glowing [ˈgləuɪŋ] a (*fire*) rougeoyant(e); (*complexion*) éclatant(e); (*report, description etc*) dithyrambique.

glow-worm [ˈgləuwə:m] n ver luisant.

glucose [ˈglu:kəus] n glucose m.

glue [glu:] n colle f ♦ vt coller.

glue-sniffing [ˈglu:snɪfɪŋ] n inhalation f de colle.

glum [glʌm] a maussade, morose.

glut [glʌt] n surabondance f ♦ vt rassasier; (*market*) encombrer.

glutinous [ˈglu:tɪnəs] a visqueux(euse).

glutton [ˈglʌtn] n glouton/ne; **a ~ for work** un bourreau de travail.

gluttonous [ˈglʌtənəs] a glouton(ne).

gluttony [ˈglʌtənɪ] n gloutonnerie f; (*sin*) gourmandise f.

glycerin(e) [ˈglɪsəri:n] n glycérine f.

gm abbr (= gram) g.

GMAT n abbr (US: = *Graduate Management Admissions Test*) examen d'admission dans le 2e cycle de l'enseignement supérieur.

GMT abbr (= *Greenwich Mean Time*) GMT.

GMWU n abbr (*Brit*: = *General and Municipal Workers' Union*) syndicat des employés municipaux.

gnarled [nɑ:ld] a noueux(euse).

gnash [næʃ] vt: **to ~ one's teeth** grincer des dents.

gnat [næt] n moucheron m.

gnaw [nɔ:] vt ronger.

gnome [nəum] n gnome m, lutin m.

GNP n abbr = **gross national product**.

go [gəu] vb (pt **went**, pp **gone** [wɛnt, gɔn]) vi aller; (*depart*) partir, s'en aller; (*work*) marcher; (*be sold*): **to ~ for £10** se vendre 10 livres; (*fit, suit*): **to ~ with** aller avec; (*become*): **to ~ pale/mouldy** pâlir/moisir; (*break etc*) céder ♦ n (pl: **~es**): **to have a ~ (at)** essayer (de faire); **to be on the ~** être en mouvement; **whose ~ is it?** à qui est-ce de jouer?; **to ~ by car/on foot** aller en voiture/à pied; **he's going to do it** il va faire, il est sur le point de faire; **to ~ for a walk** aller se promener; **to ~ dancing/shopping** aller danser/faire les courses; **to ~ looking for sb/sth** aller or partir à la recherche de qn/qch; **to ~ to sleep** s'endormir; **to ~ and**

see sb, to ~ to see sb aller voir qn; **how is it ~ing?** comment ça marche?; **how did it ~?** comment est-ce que ça s'est passé?; **to ~ round the back/by the shop** passer par derrière/devant le magasin; **my voice has gone** j'ai une extinction de voix; **the cake is all gone** il n'y a plus de gâteau; **I'll take whatever is ~ing** (*Brit*) je prendrai ce qu'il y a (or ce que vous avez); **... to ~** (US: *food*) ... à emporter.

go about vi (*also*: **~ around**) aller çà et là; (: *rumour*) se répandre ♦ vt fus: **how do I ~ about this?** comment dois-je m'y prendre (pour faire ceci)?; **to ~ about one's business** s'occuper de ses affaires.

go after vt fus (*pursue*) poursuivre, courir après; (*job, record etc*) essayer d'obtenir.

go against vt fus (*be unfavourable to*) être défavorable à; (*be contrary to*) être contraire à.

go ahead vi (*make progress*) avancer; (*get going*) y aller.

go along vi aller, avancer ♦ vt fus longer, parcourir; **as you ~ along (with your work)** au fur et à mesure (de votre travail); **to ~ along with** (*accompany*) accompagner; (*agree with:*. *idea*) être d'accord sur; (: *person*) suivre.

go away vi partir, s'en aller.

go back vi rentrer; revenir; (*go again*) retourner.

go back on vt fus (*promise*) revenir sur.

go by vi (*years, time*) passer, s'écouler ♦ vt fus s'en tenir à; (*believe*) en croire.

go down vi descendre; (*ship*) couler; (*sun*) se coucher ♦ vt fus descendre; **that should ~ down well with him** (*fig*) ça devrait lui plaire.

go for vt fus (*fetch*) aller chercher; (*like*) aimer; (*attack*) s'en prendre à; attaquer.

go in vi entrer.

go in for vt fus (*competition*) se présenter à; (*like*) aimer.

go into vt fus entrer dans; (*investigate*) étudier, examiner; (*embark on*) se lancer dans.

go off vi partir, s'en aller; (*food*) se gâter; (*bomb*) sauter; (*lights etc*) s'éteindre; (*event*) se dérouler ♦ vt fus ne plus aimer, ne plus avoir envie de; **the gun went off** le coup est parti; **to ~ off to sleep** s'endormir; **the party went off well** la fête s'est bien passée or était très réussie.

go on vi continuer; (*happen*) se passer; (*lights*) s'allumer ♦ vt fus (*be guided by*: *evidence etc*) se fonder sur; **to ~ on doing** continuer à faire; **what's ~ing on here?** qu'est-ce qui se passe ici?

go on at vt fus (*nag*) tomber sur le dos de.

go on with vt fus poursuivre, continuer.

go out vi sortir; (*fire, light*) s'éteindre; (*tide*) descendre; **to ~ out with sb** sortir avec qn.

go over vi (*ship*) chavirer ♦ vt fus (*check*) revoir, vérifier; **to ~ over sth in one's mind** repasser qch dans son esprit.

go round vi (*circulate*: *news, rumour*) circuler; (*revolve*) tourner; (*visit*): **to ~ round to sb's** passer chez qn; aller chez qn;

(*make a detour*): **to ~ round (by)** faire un détour (par); (*suffice*) suffire (pour tout le monde).

go through *vt fus* (*town etc*) traverser; (*search through*) fouiller; (*examine: list, book*) lire *or* regarder en détail, éplucher; (*perform: lesson*) réciter; (*: formalities*) remplir; (*: programme*) exécuter.

go through with *vt fus* (*plan, crime*) aller jusqu'au bout de.

go under *vi* (*sink: also fig*) couler; (*: person*) succomber.

go up *vi* monter; (*price*) augmenter ♦ *vt fus* gravir; **to ~ up in flames** flamber, s'enflammer brusquement.

go without *vt fus* se passer de.

goad [gəud] *vt* aiguillonner.

go-ahead ['gəuəhɛd] *a* dynamique, entreprenant(e) ♦ *n* feu vert.

goal [gəul] *n* but *m*.

goalkeeper ['gəulki:pə*] *n* gardien *m* de but.

goal post *n* poteau *m* de but.

goat [gəut] *n* chèvre *f*.

gobble ['gɔbl] *vt* (*also:* **~ down, ~ up**) engloutir.

go-between ['gəubɪtwi:n] *n* médiateur *m*.

Gobi Desert ['gəubɪ-] *n* désert *m* de Gobi.

goblet ['gɔblɪt] *n* goblet *m*.

goblin ['gɔblɪn] *n* lutin *m*.

go-cart ['gəukɑ:t] *n* kart *m* ♦ *cpd:* **~ racing** *n* karting *m*.

god [gɔd] *n* dieu *m*; **G~** Dieu.

godchild ['gɔdtʃaɪld] *n* filleul/e.

goddaughter ['gɔddɔ:tə*] *n* filleule *f*.

goddess ['gɔdɪs] *n* déesse *f*.

godfather ['gɔdfɑːðə*] *n* parrain *m*.

god-forsaken ['gɔdfəseɪkən] *a* maudit(e).

godmother ['gɔdmʌðə*] *n* marraine *f*.

godparents ['gɔdpɛərənts] *npl:* **the ~** le parrain et la marraine.

godsend ['gɔdsɛnd] *n* aubaine *f*.

godson ['gɔdsʌn] *n* filleul *m*.

goes [gəuz] *vb see* **go**.

go-getter ['gəugɛtə*] *n* arriviste *m/f*.

goggle ['gɔgl] *vi:* **to ~ at** regarder avec des yeux ronds.

goggles ['gɔglz] *npl* lunettes *fpl* (protectrices) (*de motocycliste etc*).

going ['gəuɪŋ] *n* (*conditions*) état *m* du terrain ♦ *a:* **the ~ rate** le tarif (en vigueur); **a ~ concern** une affaire prospère; **it was slow ~** les progrès étaient lents, ça n'avançait pas vite.

goings-on ['gəuɪŋz'ɔn] *npl* (*col*) manigances *fpl*.

go-kart ['gəukɑ:t] *n* = **go-cart**.

gold [gəuld] *n or m* or; (*reserves*) d'or.

golden ['gəuldən] *a* (*made of gold*) en or; (*gold in colour*) doré(e).

golden age *n* âge *m* d'or.

golden handshake *n* (*Brit*) prime *f* de départ.

golden rule *n* règle *f* d'or.

goldfish ['gəuldfɪʃ] *n* poisson *m* rouge.

gold leaf *n* or *m* en feuille.

gold medal *n* (*SPORT*) médaille *f* d'or.

goldmine ['gəuldmaɪn] *n* mine *f* d'or.

gold-plated ['gəuld'pleɪtɪd] *a* plaqué(e) or *inv*.

goldsmith ['gəuldsmɪθ] *n* orfèvre *m*.

gold standard *n* étalon-or *m*.

golf [gɔlf] *n* golf *m*.

golf ball *n* balle *f* de golf; (*on typewriter*) boule *f*.

golf club *n* club *m* de golf; (*stick*) club *m*, crosse *f* de golf.

golf course *n* terrain *m* de golf.

golfer ['gɔlfə*] *n* joueur/euse de golf.

gondola ['gɔndələ] *n* gondole *f*.

gondolier [gɔndə'lɪə*] *n* gondolier *m*.

gone [gɔn] *pp of* **go** ♦ *a* parti(e).

gong [gɔŋ] *n* gong *m*.

good [gud] *a* bon(ne); (*kind*) gentil(le); (*child*) sage ♦ *n* bien *m*; **~!** bon!, très bien!; **to be ~ at** être bon en; **it's ~ for you** c'est bon pour vous; **it's a ~ thing you were there** heureusement que vous étiez là; **she is ~ with children/her hands** elle sait bien s'occuper des enfants/sait se servir de ses mains; **to feel ~** se sentir bien; **it's ~ to see you** ça me fait plaisir de vous voir, je suis content de vous voir; **he's up to no ~** il prépare quelque mauvais coup; **it's no ~ complaining** cela ne sert à rien de se plaindre; **for the common ~** dans l'intérêt commun; **for ~** (*for ever*) pour de bon, une fois pour toutes; **would you be ~ enough to ...?** auriez-vous la bonté *or* l'amabilité de ...?; **that's very ~ of you** c'est très gentil de votre part; **is this any ~?** (*will it do?*) est-ce que ceci fera l'affaire?; est-ce que cela peut vous rendre service?; (*what's it like?*) qu'est-ce que ça vaut?; **a ~ deal (of)** beaucoup (de); **a ~ many** beaucoup (de); **~ morning/afternoon!** bonjour!; **~ evening!** bonsoir!; **~ night!** bonsoir!; (*on going to bed*) bonne nuit!

goodbye [gud'baɪ] *excl* au revoir!; **to say ~ to** dire au revoir à.

good faith *n* bonne foi.

good-for-nothing ['gudfənʌθɪŋ] *a* bon(ne) *or* propre à rien.

Good Friday *n* Vendredi saint.

good-humoured ['gud'hju:məd] *a* (*person*) jovial(e); (*remark, joke*) sans malice.

good-looking ['gud'lukɪŋ] *a* bien *inv*.

good-natured ['gud'neɪtʃəd] *a* (*person*) qui a un bon naturel; (*discussion*) enjoué(e).

goodness ['gudnɪs] *n* (*of person*) bonté *f*; **for ~ sake!** je vous en prie!; **~ gracious!** mon Dieu!

goods ['gudz] *npl* marchandise *f*, articles *mpl*; (*COMM etc*) marchandises; **~ and chattels** biens *mpl* et effets *mpl*.

goods train *n* (*Brit*) train *m* de marchandises.

goodwill [gud'wɪl] *n* bonne volonté; (*COMM*) réputation *f* (auprès de la clientèle).

goody-goody ['gudɪgudɪ] *n* (*pej*) petit saint, sainte nitouche.

goose, pl geese [gu:s, gi:s] *n* oie *f*.

gooseberry ['guzbərɪ] *n* groseille *f* à maquereau; **to play ~** (*Brit*) tenir la chandelle.

gooseflesh ['gu:sfleʃ] *n*, **goosepimples** ['gu:spɪmplz] *npl* chair *f* de poule.

goose step *n* (*MIL*) pas *m* de l'oie.

GOP *n abbr* (*US POL: col:* = *Grand Old Party*) parti républicain.

gore [gɔ:*] vt encorner ♦ n sang m.
gorge [gɔ:dʒ] n gorge f ♦ vt: **to ~ o.s. (on)** se gorger (de).
gorgeous [ˈgɔːdʒəs] a splendide, superbe.
gorilla [gəˈrɪlə] n gorille m.
gormless [ˈgɔːmlɪs] a (Brit col) lourdaud(e).
gorse [gɔːs] n ajoncs mpl.
gory [ˈgɔːrɪ] a sanglant(e).
go-slow [ˈgəuˈsləu] n (Brit) grève perlée.
gospel [ˈgɔspl] n évangile m.
gossamer [ˈgɔsəmə*] n (cobweb) fils mpl de la vierge; (light fabric) étoffe très légère.
gossip [ˈgɔsɪp] n bavardages mpl; (malicious) commérage m, cancans mpl; (person) commère f ♦ vi bavarder; cancaner, faire des commérages; **a piece of ~** un ragot, un racontar.
gossip column n (PRESS) échos mpl.
got [gɔt] pt, pp of **get**.
Gothic [ˈgɔθɪk] a gothique.
gotten [ˈgɔtn] (US) pp of **get**.
gouge [gaudʒ] vt (also: ~ **out**: hole etc) évider; (: initials) tailler; **to ~ sb's eyes out** crever les yeux à qn.
gourd [guəd] n calebasse f, gourde f.
gourmet [ˈguəmeɪ] n gourmet m, gastronome m/f.
gout [gaut] n goutte f.
govern [ˈgʌvən] vt (gen, LING) gouverner.
governess [ˈgʌvənɪs] n gouvernante f.
governing [ˈgʌvənɪŋ] a (POL) au pouvoir, au gouvernement; ~ **body** conseil m d'administration.
government [ˈgʌvnmənt] n gouvernement m; (Brit: ministers) ministère m ♦ cpd de l'État; **local ~** administration locale.
governmental [gʌvnˈmentl] a gouvernemental(e).
government housing n (US) logements sociaux.
government stock n titres mpl d'État.
governor [ˈgʌvənə*] n (of colony, state, bank) gouverneur m; (of school, hospital etc) administrateur/trice; (Brit: of prison) directeur/trice.
Govt abbr (= government) gvt.
gown [gaun] n robe f; (of teacher; Brit: of judge) toge f.
GP n abbr (MED) = **general practitioner**.
GPO n abbr (Brit: old) = General Post Office; (US) = Government Printing Office.
gr. abbr (COMM) = **gross**.
grab [græb] vt saisir, empoigner; (property, power) se saisir de ♦ vi: **to ~ at** essayer de saisir.
grace [greɪs] n grâce f ♦ vt honorer; **5 days' ~** répit m de 5 jours; **to say ~** dire le bénédicité; (after meal) dire les grâces; **with a good/bad ~** de bonne/mauvaise grâce; **his sense of humour is his saving ~** il se rachète par son sens de l'humour.
graceful [ˈgreɪsful] a gracieux(euse), élégant(e).
gracious [ˈgreɪʃəs] a (kind) charmant(e), bienveillant(e); (elegant) plein(e) d'élégance, d'une grande élégance; (formal: pardon etc) miséricordieux(euse) ♦ excl: **(good) ~!** mon Dieu!
gradation [grəˈdeɪʃən] n gradation f.

grade [greɪd] n (COMM) qualité f; calibre m; catégorie f; (in hierarchy) grade m, échelon m; (US: SCOL) note f; classe f; (: gradient) pente f ♦ vt classer; calibrer; graduer; **to make the ~** (fig) réussir.
grade crossing n (US) passage m à niveau.
grade school n (US) école f primaire.
gradient [ˈgreɪdɪənt] n inclinaison f, pente f; (GEOM) gradient m.
gradual [ˈgrædjuəl] a graduel(le), progressif(ive).
gradually [ˈgrædjuəlɪ] ad peu à peu, graduellement.
graduate n [ˈgrædjuɪt] diplômé/e d'université; (US) diplômé/e de fin d'études ♦ vi [ˈgrædjueɪt] obtenir un diplôme d'université (or de fin d'études).
graduated pension [ˈgrædjueɪtɪd-] n retraite calculée en fonction des derniers salaires.
graduation [grædjuˈeɪʃən] n cérémonie f de remise des diplômes.
graffiti [grəˈfiːtɪ] npl graffiti mpl.
graft [grɑːft] n (AGR, MED) greffe f; (bribery) corruption f ♦ vt greffer; **hard ~** n (col) boulot acharné.
grain [greɪn] n grain m; (no pl: cereals) céréales fpl; (US: corn) blé m; **it goes against the ~** cela va à l'encontre de sa (or ma etc) nature.
gram [græm] n gramme m.
grammar [ˈgræmə*] n grammaire f.
grammar school n (Brit) ≈ lycée m.
grammatical [grəˈmætɪkl] a grammatical(e).
gramme [græm] n = **gram**.
gramophone [ˈgræməfəun] n (Brit) gramophone m.
granary [ˈgrænərɪ] n grenier m.
grand [grænd] a splendide, imposant(e); (terrific) magnifique, formidable; (also humorous: gesture etc) noble ♦ n (col: thousand) mille livres fpl (or dollars mpl).
grandchildren [ˈgræntʃɪldrən] npl petits-enfants mpl.
granddad [ˈgrændæd] n grand-papa m.
granddaughter [ˈgrændɔːtə*] n petite-fille f.
grandeur [ˈgrændjə*] n magnificence f, splendeur f; (of position etc) éminence f.
grandfather [ˈgrændfɑːðə*] n grand-père m.
grandiose [ˈgrændɪəus] a grandiose; (pej) pompeux(euse).
grand jury n (US) jury m d'accusation (formé de 12 à 23 jurés).
grandma [ˈgrænmɑː] n grand-maman f.
grandmother [ˈgrænmʌðə*] n grand-mère f.
grandpa [ˈgrænpɑː] n = **granddad**.
grandparent [ˈgrændpeərənt] n grand-père/grand-mère.
grand piano n piano m à queue.
Grand Prix [ˈgrɑ̃ːˈpriː] n (AUT) grand prix automobile.
grandson [ˈgrænsʌn] n petit-fils m.
grandstand [ˈgrændstænd] n (SPORT) tribune f.
grand total n total général.
granite [ˈgrænɪt] n granit m.
granny [ˈgrænɪ] n grand-maman f.
grant [grɑːnt] vt accorder; (a request) accéder à; (admit) concéder ♦ n (SCOL) bourse f; (ADMIN) subside m, subvention f; **to take sth**

for ~ed considérer qch comme acquis; **to ~ that** admettre que.

granulated ['grænjuleɪtɪd] *a*: ~ **sugar** sucre *m* en poudre.

granule ['grænju:l] *n* granule *m*.

grape [greɪp] *n* raisin *m*; **a bunch of** ~**s** une grappe de raisin.

grapefruit ['greɪpfru:t] *n* pamplemousse *m*.

grapevine ['greɪpvaɪn] *n* vigne *f*; **I heard it on the** ~ (*fig*) je l'ai appris par le téléphone arabe.

graph [grɑ:f] *n* graphique *m*, courbe *f*.

graphic ['græfɪk] *a* graphique; (*vivid*) vivant(e).

graphic designer *n* graphiste *m/f*.

graphics ['græfɪks] *n* (*art*) arts *mpl* graphiques; (*process*) graphisme *m*; (*pl: drawings*) illustrations *fpl*.

graphite ['græfaɪt] *n* graphite *m*.

graph paper *n* papier millimétré.

grapple ['græpl] *vi*: **to** ~ **with** être aux prises avec.

grappling iron ['græplɪŋ'aɪən] *n* (*NAUT*) grappin *m*.

grasp [grɑ:sp] *vt* saisir, empoigner; (*understand*) saisir, comprendre ♦ *n* (*grip*) prise *f*; (*fig*) compréhension *f*, connaissance *f*; **to have sth within one's** ~ avoir qch à sa portée; **to have a good** ~ **of sth** (*fig*) bien comprendre qch.

grasp at *vt fus* (*rope etc*) essayer de saisir; (*fig: opportunity*) sauter sur.

grasping ['grɑ:spɪŋ] *a* avide.

grass [grɑ:s] *n* herbe *f*; (*Brit col: informer*) mouchard/e; (: *ex-terrorist*) balanceur/euse.

grasshopper ['grɑ:shɔpə*] *n* sauterelle *f*.

grassland ['grɑ:slænd] *n* prairie *f*.

grass roots *npl* (*fig*) base *f*.

grass snake *n* couleuvre *f*.

grassy ['grɑ:sɪ] *a* herbeux(euse).

grate [greɪt] *n* grille *f* de cheminée ♦ *vi* grincer ♦ *vt* (*CULIN*) râper.

grateful ['greɪtful] *a* reconnaissant(e).

gratefully ['greɪtfəlɪ] *ad* avec reconnaissance.

grater ['greɪtə*] *n* râpe *f*.

gratification [grætɪfɪ'keɪʃən] *n* satisfaction *f*.

gratify ['grætɪfaɪ] *vt* faire plaisir à; (*whim*) satisfaire.

gratifying ['grætɪfaɪɪŋ] *a* agréable; satisfaisant(e).

grating ['greɪtɪŋ] *n* (*iron bars*) grille *f* ♦ *a* (*noise*) grinçant(e).

gratitude ['grætɪtju:d] *n* gratitude *f*.

gratuitous [grə'tju:ɪtəs] *a* gratuit(e).

gratuity [grə'tju:ɪtɪ] *n* pourboire *m*.

grave [greɪv] *n* tombe *f* ♦ *a* grave, sérieux(euse).

gravedigger ['greɪvdɪgə*] *n* fossoyeur *m*.

gravel ['grævl] *n* gravier *m*.

gravely ['greɪvlɪ] *ad* gravement, sérieusement; ~ **ill** gravement malade.

gravestone ['greɪvstəun] *n* pierre tombale.

graveyard ['greɪvjɑ:d] *n* cimetière *m*.

gravitate ['grævɪteɪt] *vi* graviter.

gravity ['grævɪtɪ] *n* (*PHYSICS*) gravité *f*; pesanteur *f*; (*seriousness*) gravité, sérieux *m*.

gravy ['greɪvɪ] *n* jus *m* (de viande); sauce *f* (au jus de viande).

gravy boat *n* saucière *f*.

gravy train *n* (*col*): **to ride the** ~ avoir une bonne planque.

gray [greɪ] *a* = **grey**.

graze [greɪz] *vi* paître, brouter ♦ *vt* (*touch lightly*) frôler, effleurer; (*scrape*) écorcher ♦ *n* écorchure *f*.

grazing ['greɪzɪŋ] *n* (*pasture*) pâturage *m*.

grease [gri:s] *n* (*fat*) graisse *f*; (*lubricant*) lubrifiant *m* ♦ *vt* graisser; lubrifier; **to** ~ **the skids** (*US*: *fig*) huiler les rouages.

grease gun *n* graisseur *m*.

greasepaint ['gri:speɪnt] *n* produits *mpl* de maquillage.

greaseproof paper ['gri:spru:f-] *n* (*Brit*) papier sulfurisé.

greasy ['gri:sɪ] *a* gras(se), graisseux(euse); (*hands, clothes*) graisseux; (*Brit: road, surface*) glissant(e).

great [greɪt] *a* grand(e); (*heat, pain etc*) très fort(e), intense; (*col*) formidable; **they're** ~ **friends** ils sont très amis, ce sont de grands amis; **we had a** ~ **time** nous nous sommes bien amusés; **it was** ~! c'était fantastique *or* super!; **the** ~ **thing is that** ... ce qu'il y a de vraiment bien c'est que ....

Great Barrier Reef *n*: **the** ~ la Grande Barrière.

Great Britain *n* Grande-Bretagne *f*.

great-grandchild,   *pl*   **-children** [greɪt'græntʃaɪld, -tʃɪldrən] *n* arrière-petit(e)-enfant.

great-grandfather [greɪt'grænfɑ:ðə*] *n* arrière-grand-père *m*.

great-grandmother [greɪt'grænmʌðə*] *n* arrière-grand-mère *f*.

Great Lakes *npl*: **the** ~ les Grands Lacs.

greatly ['greɪtlɪ] *ad* très, grandement; (*with verbs*) beaucoup.

greatness ['greɪtnɪs] *n* grandeur *f*.

Grecian ['gri:ʃən] *a* grec(grecque).

Greece [gri:s] *n* Grèce *f*.

greed [gri:d] *n* (*also*: ~**iness**) avidité *f*; (*for food*) gourmandise *f*.

greedily ['gri:dɪlɪ] *ad* avidement; avec gourmandise.

greedy ['gri:dɪ] *a* avide; gourmand(e).

Greek [gri:k] *a* grec(grecque) ♦ *n* Grec/ Grecque; (*LING*) grec *m*; **ancient/modern** ~ grec classique/moderne.

green [gri:n] *a* vert(e); (*inexperienced*) (bien) jeune, naïf(ïve) ♦ *n* (*colour, of golf course*) vert *m*; (*stretch of grass*) pelouse *f*; (*also*: **village** ~) ≈ place *f* du village; ~**s** *npl* légumes verts; **to have** ~ **fingers** *or* (*US*) **a** ~ **thumb** (*fig*) avoir le pouce vert.

green belt *n* (*round town*) ceinture verte.

green card *n* (*AUT*) carte verte.

greenery ['gri:nərɪ] *n* verdure *f*.

greenfly ['gri:nflaɪ] *n* (*Brit*) puceron *m*.

greengage ['gri:ngeɪdʒ] *n* reine-claude *f*.

greengrocer ['gri:ngrəusə*] *n* (*Brit*) marchand *m* de fruits et légumes.

greenhouse ['gri:nhaus] *n* serre *f*.

greenish ['gri:nɪʃ] *a* verdâtre.

Greenland ['gri:nlənd] *n* Groenland *m*.

Greenlander ['gri:nləndə*] *n* Groenlandais/e.

green pepper *n* poivron (vert).

greet [gri:t] *vt* accueillir.

greeting ['gri:tɪŋ] *n* salutation *f*; **Christmas/**

birthday ~s souhaits *mpl* de Noël/de bon anniversaire.

greeting(s) card *n* carte *f* de vœux.

gregarious [grə'gɛərɪəs] *a* grégaire; sociable.

grenade [grə'neɪd] *n* (*also*: **hand** ~) grenade *f*.

grew [gru:] *pt of* **grow**.

grey [greɪ] *a* gris(e); (*dismal*) sombre; **to go** ~ (commencer à) grisonner.

grey-haired [greɪ'hɛəd] *a* aux cheveux gris.

greyhound ['greɪhaund] *n* lévrier *m*.

grid [grɪd] *n* grille *f*; (*ELEC*) réseau *m*; (*US AUT*) intersection *f* (*matérialisée par des marques au sol*).

griddle [grɪdl] *n* (*on cooker*) plaque chauffante.

gridiron ['grɪdaɪən] *n* gril *m*.

grief [gri:f] *n* chagrin *m*, douleur *f*; **to come to** ~ (*plan*) échouer; (*person*) avoir un malheur.

grievance ['gri:vəns] *n* doléance *f*, grief *m*; (*cause for complaint*) grief.

grieve [gri:v] *vi* avoir du chagrin; se désoler ♦ *vt* faire de la peine à, affliger; **to** ~ **at** se désoler de; pleurer.

grievous ['gri:vəs] *a* grave; cruel(le); ~ **bodily harm** (*LAW*) coups *mpl* et blessures *fpl*.

grill [grɪl] *n* (*on cooker*) gril *m* ♦ *vt* (*Brit*) griller; (*question*) interroger longuement, cuisiner.

grille [grɪl] *n* grillage *m*; (*AUT*) calandre *f*.

grill(room) ['grɪl(rum)] *n* rôtisserie *f*.

grim [grɪm] *a* sinistre, lugubre.

grimace [grɪ'meɪs] *n* grimace *f* ♦ *vi* grimacer, faire une grimace.

grime [graɪm] *n* crasse *f*.

grimy ['graɪmɪ] *a* crasseux(euse).

grin [grɪn] *n* large sourire *m* ♦ *vi* sourire; **to** ~ **(at)** faire un grand sourire (à).

grind [graɪnd] *vb* (*pt, pp* **ground** [graund]) *vt* écraser; (*coffee, pepper etc*) moudre; (*US: meat*) hacher; (*make sharp*) aiguiser; (*polish: gem, lens*) polir ♦ *vi* (*car gears*) grincer ♦ *n* (*work*) corvée *f*; **to** ~ **one's teeth** grincer des dents; **to** ~ **to a halt** (*vehicle*) s'arrêter dans un grincement de freins; (*fig*) s'arrêter, s'immobiliser; **the daily** ~ (*col*) le train-train quotidien.

grinder ['graɪndə*] *n* (*machine: for coffee*) moulin *m* (à café); (*: for waste disposal etc*) broyeur *m*.

grindstone ['graɪndstəun] *n*: **to keep one's nose to the** ~ travailler sans relâche.

grip [grɪp] *n* (*control, grasp*) étreinte *f*; (*hold*) prise *f*; (*handle*) poignée *f*; (*holdall*) sac *m* de voyage ♦ *vt* saisir, empoigner; étreindre; **to come to** ~**s with** se colleter avec, en venir aux prises avec; **to** ~ **the road** (*AUT*) adhérer à la route; **to lose one's** ~ lâcher prise; (*fig*) perdre les pédales, être dépassé(e).

gripe [graɪp] *n* (*MED*) coliques *fpl*; (*col: complaint*) ronchonnement *m*, rouspétance *f* ♦ *vi* (*col*) râler.

gripping ['grɪpɪŋ] *a* prenant(e), palpitant(e).

grisly ['grɪzlɪ] *a* sinistre, macabre.

grist [grɪst] *n* (*fig*): **it's (all)** ~ **to his mill** ça l'arrange, ça apporte de l'eau à son moulin.

gristle ['grɪsl] *n* cartilage *m* (*de poulet etc*).

grit [grɪt] *n* gravillon *m*; (*courage*) cran *m* ♦ *vt* (*road*) sabler; **to** ~ **one's teeth** serrer les dents; **to have a piece of** ~ **in one's eye** avoir une poussière *or* saleté dans l'œil.

grits [grɪts] *npl* (*US*) gruau *m* de maïs.

grizzle ['grɪzl] *vi* (*Brit*) pleurnicher.

grizzly ['grɪzlɪ] *n* (*also*: ~ **bear**) grizzli *m*, ours gris.

groan [grəun] *n* gémissement *m*; grognement *m* ♦ *vi* gémir; grogner.

grocer ['grəusə*] *n* épicier *m*; **at the** ~**'s** à l'épicerie, chez l'épicier.

groceries ['grəusərɪz] *npl* provisions *fpl*.

grocery ['grəusərɪ] *n* (*shop*) épicerie *f*.

grog [grɔg] *n* grog *m*.

groggy ['grɔgɪ] *a* groggy *inv*.

groin [grɔɪn] *n* aine *f*.

groom [gru:m] *n* palefrenier *m*; (*also*: **bride~**) marié *m* ♦ *vt* (*horse*) panser; (*fig*): **to** ~ **sb for** former qn pour.

groove [gru:v] *n* sillon *m*, rainure *f*.

grope [grəup] *vi* tâtonner; **to** ~ **for** *vt fus* chercher à tâtons.

grosgrain ['grəugreɪn] *n* gros-grain *m*.

gross [grəus] *a* grossier(ière); (*COMM*) brut(e) ♦ *n* (*pl inv*) (*twelve dozen*) grosse *f* ♦ *vt* (*COMM*): **to** ~ **£500,000** gagner 500.000 livres avant impôt.

gross domestic product (GDP) *n* produit brut intérieur (PIB).

grossly ['grəuslɪ] *ad* (*greatly*) très, grandement.

gross national product (GNP) *n* produit national brut (PNB).

grotesque [grə'tɛsk] *a* grotesque.

grotto ['grɔtəu] *n* grotte *f*.

grotty ['grɔtɪ] *a* (*Brit col*) minable.

grouch [grautʃ] (*col*) *vi* rouspéter ♦ *n* (*person*) rouspéteur/euse.

ground [graund] *pt, pp of* **grind** ♦ *n* sol *m*, terre *f*; (*land*) terrain *m*, terres *fpl*; (*SPORT*) terrain; (*reason: gen pl*) raison *f*; (*US: also*: ~ **wire**) terre *f* ♦ *vt* (*plane*) empêcher de décoller, retenir au sol; (*US ELEC*) équiper d'une prise de terre, mettre à la terre ♦ *vi* (*ship*) s'échouer ♦ *a* (*coffee etc*) moulu(e); (*US: meat*) haché(e); ~**s** *npl* (*gardens etc*) parc *m*, domaine *m*; (*of coffee*) marc *m*; **on the** ~, **to the** ~ par terre; **below** ~ sous terre; **to gain/lose** ~ gagner/perdre du terrain; **common** ~ terrain d'entente; **he covered a lot of** ~ **in his lecture** sa conférence a traité un grand nombre de questions *or* la question en profondeur.

ground cloth *n* (*US*) = **groundsheet**.

ground control *n* (*AVIAT, SPACE*) centre *m* de contrôle (au sol).

ground floor *n* rez-de-chaussée *m*.

grounding ['graundɪŋ] *n* (*in education*) connaissances *fpl* de base.

groundless ['graundlɪs] *a* sans fondement.

groundnut ['graundnʌt] *n* arachide *f*.

ground rent *n* (*Brit*) fermage *m*.

groundsheet ['graundʃi:t] *n* (*Brit*) tapis *m* de sol.

groundsman ['graundzmən], (*US*) **grounds-keeper** ['graundzki:pə*] *n* (*SPORT*) gardien *m* de stade.

ground staff *n* équipage *m* au sol.

groundswell ['graundswɛl] *n* lame *f* or vague *f* de fond.

ground-to-ground ['grauntə'graund] *a*: ~ **missile** missile *m* sol-sol.

groundwork ['graundwə:k] *n* préparation *f*.

group [gru:p] *n* groupe *m* ♦ *vt* (*also*: ~ **together**) grouper ♦ *vi* (*also*: ~ **together**) se grouper.

grouse [graus] *n* (*pl inv*) (*bird*) grouse *f* (*sorte de coq de bruyère*) ♦ *vi* (*complain*) rouspéter, râler.

grove [grəuv] *n* bosquet *m*.

grovel ['grɒvl] *vi* (*fig*): **to** ~ **(before)** ramper (devant).

grow, *pt* **grew**, *pp* **grown** [grəu, gru:, grəun] *vi* (*plant*) pousser, croître; (*person*) grandir; (*increase*) augmenter, se développer; (*become*): **to** ~ **rich/weak** s'enrichir/ s'affaiblir ♦ *vt* cultiver, faire pousser.
   grow apart *vi* (*fig*) se détacher (l'un de l'autre).
   grow away from *vt fus* (*fig*) s'éloigner de.
   grow on *vt fus*: **that painting is** ~**ing on me** je finirai par aimer ce tableau.
   grow out of *vt fus* (*clothes*) devenir trop grand pour; (*habit*) perdre (avec le temps); **he'll** ~ **out of it** ça lui passera.
   grow up *vi* grandir.

grower ['grəuə*] *n* producteur *m*; (*AGR*) cultivateur/trice.

growing ['grəuɪŋ] *a* (*fear*, *amount*) croissant(e), grandissant(e); ~ **pains** (*MED*) fièvre *f* de croissance; (*fig*) difficultés *fpl* de croissance.

growl [graul] *vi* grogner.

grown [grəun] *pp* of **grow** ♦ *a* adulte.

grown-up [grəun'ʌp] *n* adulte *m/f*, grande personne.

growth [grəuθ] *n* croissance *f*, développement *m*; (*what has grown*) pousse *f*; poussée *f*; (*MED*) grosseur *f*, tumeur *f*.

growth rate *n* taux *m* de croissance.

GRSM *n abbr* (*Brit*) = *Graduate of the Royal Schools of Music*.

grub [grʌb] *n* larve *f*; (*col*: *food*) bouffe *f*.

grubby ['grʌbɪ] *a* crasseux(euse).

grudge [grʌdʒ] *n* rancune *f* ♦ *vt*: **to** ~ **sb sth** donner qch à qn à contre-cœur; reprocher qch à qn; **to bear sb a** ~ **(for)** garder rancune *or* en vouloir à qn (de); **he** ~**s spending** il rechigne à dépenser.

grudgingly ['grʌdʒɪŋlɪ] *ad* à contre-cœur, de mauvaise grâce.

gruelling ['gruəlɪŋ] *a* exténuant(e).

gruesome ['gru:səm] *a* horrible.

gruff [grʌf] *a* bourru(e).

grumble ['grʌmbl] *vi* rouspéter, ronchonner.

grumpy ['grʌmpɪ] *a* grincheux(euse).

grunt [grʌnt] *vi* grogner ♦ *n* grognement *m*.

G-string ['dʒi:strɪŋ] *n* (*garment*) cache-sexe *m inv*.

GSUSA *n abbr* = *Girl Scouts of the United States of America*.

GU *abbr* (*US POST*) = *Guam*.

guarantee [gærən'ti:] *n* garantie *f* ♦ *vt* garantir; **he can't** ~ **(that)** he'll come il n'est pas absolument certain de pouvoir venir.

guarantor [gærən'tɔ:*] *n* garant/e.

guard [gɑ:d] *n* garde *f*, surveillance *f*; (*squad*, *BOXING*, *FENCING*) garde *f*; (*one man*) garde *m*; (*Brit RAIL*) chef *m* de train; (*safety device*: *on machine*) dispositif *m* de sûreté; (*also*: **fire**~) garde-feu *m inv* ♦ *vt* garder, surveiller; (*protect*): **to** ~ **(against** or **from)** protéger (contre); **to be on one's** ~ (*fig*) être sur ses gardes.

guard against *vi*: **to** ~ **against doing sth** se garder de faire qch.

guard dog *n* chien *m* de garde.

guarded ['gɑ:dɪd] *a* (*fig*) prudent(e).

guardian ['gɑ:dɪən] *n* gardien/ne; (*of minor*) tuteur/trice.

guard's van *n* (*Brit RAIL*) fourgon *m*.

Guatemala [gwɑ:tɪ'mɑ:lə] *n* Guatémala *m*.

Guernsey ['gə:nzɪ] *n* Guernesey *m* or *f*.

guerrilla [gə'rɪlə] *n* guérillero *m*.

guerrilla warfare *n* guérilla *f*.

guess [gɛs] *vi* deviner ♦ *vt* deviner; (*US*) croire, penser ♦ *n* supposition *f*, hypothèse *f*; **to take** *or* **have a** ~ essayer de deviner; **to keep sb** ~**ing** laisser qn dans le doute *or* l'incertitude, tenir qn en haleine.

guesstimate ['gɛstɪmɪt] *n* (*col*) estimation *f*.

guesswork ['gɛswə:k] *n* hypothèse *f*; **I got the answer by** ~ j'ai deviné la réponse.

guest [gɛst] *n* invité/e; (*in hotel*) client/e; **be my** ~ faites comme chez vous.

guest-house ['gɛsthaus] *n* pension *f*.

guest room *n* chambre *f* d'amis.

guffaw [gʌ'fɔ:] *n* gros rire ♦ *vi* pouffer de rire.

guidance ['gaɪdəns] *n* conseils *mpl*; **under the** ~ **of** conseillé(e) *or* encadré(e) par, sous la conduite de; **vocational** ~ orientation professionnelle; **marriage** ~ conseils conjugaux.

guide [gaɪd] *n* (*person*, *book etc*) guide *m*; (*also*: **girl** ~) guide *f* ♦ *vt* guider; **to be** ~**d by sb/sth** se laisser guider par qn/qch.

guidebook ['gaɪdbuk] *n* guide *m*.

guided missile *n* missile téléguidé.

guide dog *n* chien *m* d'aveugle.

guide lines *npl* (*fig*) instructions générales, conseils *mpl*.

guild [gɪld] *n* corporation *f*; cercle *m*, association *f*.

guildhall ['gɪldhɔ:l] *n* (*Brit*) hôtel *m* de ville.

guile [gaɪl] *n* astuce *f*.

guileless ['gaɪllɪs] *a* candide.

guillotine ['gɪləti:n] *n* guillotine *f*; (*for paper*) massicot *m*.

guilt [gɪlt] *n* culpabilité *f*.

guilty ['gɪltɪ] *a* coupable; **to plead** ~/**not** ~ plaider coupable/non coupable; **to feel** ~ **about doing sth** avoir mauvaise conscience à faire qch.

Guinea ['gɪnɪ] *n*: **Republic of** ~ (République *f* de) Guinée *f*.

guinea ['gɪnɪ] *n* (*Brit*) guinée *f* (= *21 shillings*: *cette monnaie de compte ne s'emploie plus*).

guinea pig *n* cobaye *m*.

guise [gaɪz] *n* aspect *m*, apparence *f*.

guitar [gɪ'tɑ:*] *n* guitare *f*.

guitarist [gɪ'tɑ:rɪst] *n* guitariste *m/f*.

gulch [gʌltʃ] *n* (*US*) ravin *m*.

gulf [gʌlf] *n* golfe *m*; (*abyss*) gouffre *m*; **the (Persian) G**~ le golfe Persique.

Gulf States *npl*: **the ~** (*in Middle East*) les pays *mpl* du Golfe.
Gulf Stream *n*: **the ~** le Gulf Stream.
gull [gʌl] *n* mouette *f*.
gullet ['gʌlɪt] *n* gosier *m*.
gullibility [gʌlɪ'bɪlɪtɪ] *n* crédulité *f*.
gullible ['gʌlɪbl] *a* crédule.
gully ['gʌlɪ] *n* ravin *m*; ravine *f*; couloir *m*.
gulp [gʌlp] *vi* avaler sa salive; (*from emotion*) avoir la gorge serrée, s'étrangler ♦ *vt* (*also:* **~ down**) avaler ♦ *n* (*of drink*) gorgée *f*; **at one ~** d'un seul coup.
gum [gʌm] *n* (*ANAT*) gencive *f*; (*glue*) colle *f*; (*sweet*) boule *f* de gomme; (*also:* **chewing-~**) chewing-gum *m* ♦ *vt* coller.
gum up *vt*: **to ~ up the works** (*col*) bousiller tout.
gumboil ['gʌmbɔɪl] *n* abcès *m* dentaire.
gumboots ['gʌmbuːts] *npl* (*Brit*) bottes *fpl* en caoutchouc.
gumption ['gʌmpʃən] *n* bon sens, jugeote *f*.
gun [gʌn] *n* (*small*) revolver *m*, pistolet *m*; (*rifle*) fusil *m*, carabine *f*; (*cannon*) canon *m* ♦ *vt* (*also:* **~ down**) abattre; **to stick to one's ~s** (*fig*) ne pas en démordre.
gunboat ['gʌnbəut] *n* canonnière *f*.
gun dog *n* chien *m* de chasse.
gunfire ['gʌnfaɪə*] *n* fusillade *f*.
gunk [gʌŋk] *n* (*col*) saleté *f*.
gunman ['gʌnmən] *n* bandit armé.
gunner ['gʌnə*] *n* artilleur *m*.
gunpoint ['gʌnpɔɪnt] *n*: **at ~** sous la menace du pistolet (*or* fusil).
gunpowder ['gʌnpaudə*] *n* poudre *f* à canon.
gunrunner ['gʌnrʌnə*] *n* trafiquant *m* d'armes.
gunrunning ['gʌnrʌnɪŋ] *n* trafic *m* d'armes.
gunshot ['gʌnʃɔt] *n* coup *m* de feu; **within ~** à portée de fusil.
gunsmith ['gʌnsmɪθ] *n* armurier *m*.
gurgle ['gəːgl] *n* gargouillis *m* ♦ *vi* gargouiller.
guru ['guruː] *n* gourou *m*.
gush [gʌʃ] *n* jaillissement *m*, jet *m* ♦ *vi* jaillir; (*fig*) se répandre en effusions.
gusset ['gʌsɪt] *n* gousset *m*, soufflet *m*; (*in tights, pants*) entre-jambes *m*.
gust [gʌst] *n* (*of wind*) rafale *f*; (*of smoke*) bouffée *f*.
gusto ['gʌstəu] *n* enthousiasme *m*.
gut [gʌt] *n* intestin *m*, boyau *m*; (*MUS etc*) boyau ♦ *vt* (*poultry, fish*) vider; (*building*) ne laisser que les murs de; **~s** *npl* boyaux *mpl*; (*col: courage*) cran *m*; **to hate sb's ~s** ne pas pouvoir voir qn en peinture *or* sentir qn.
gut reaction *n* réaction instinctive.
gutter ['gʌtə*] *n* (*of roof*) gouttière *f*; (*in street*) caniveau *m*; (*fig*) ruisseau *m*.
guttural ['gʌtərl] *a* guttural(e).
guy [gaɪ] *n* (*also:* **~rope**) corde *f*; (*col: man*) type *m*; (*figure*) effigie de Guy Fawkes.
Guyana [gaɪ'ænə] *n* Guyane *f*.
guzzle ['gʌzl] *vi* s'empiffrer ♦ *vt* avaler gloutonnement.
gym [dʒɪm] *n* (*also:* **gymnasium**) gymnase *m*; (*also:* **gymnastics**) gym *f*.
gymkhana [dʒɪm'kɑːnə] *n* gymkhana *m*.
gymnasium [dʒɪm'neɪzɪəm] *n* gymnase *m*.
gymnast ['dʒɪmnæst] *n* gymnaste *m/f*.
gymnastics [dʒɪm'næstɪks] *n*, *npl* gymnastique *f*.
gym shoes *npl* chaussures *fpl* de gym(nastique).
gym slip *n* (*Brit*) tunique *f* (d'écolière).
gynaecologist, (*US*) **gynecologist** [gaɪnɪ'kɔlədʒɪst] *n* gynécologue *m/f*.
gynaecology, (*US*) **gynecology** [gaɪnə'kɔlədʒɪ] *n* gynécologie *f*.
gypsy ['dʒɪpsɪ] *n* = **gipsy**.
gyrate [dʒaɪ'reɪt] *vi* tournoyer.
gyroscope ['dʒaɪərəskəup] *n* gyroscope *m*.

H

H, h [eɪtʃ] *n* (*letter*) H, h *m*; **H for Harry,** (*US*) **H for How** H comme Henri.
habeas corpus ['heɪbɪəs'kɔːpəs] *n* (*LAW*) habeas corpus *m*.
haberdashery [hæbə'dæʃərɪ] *n* (*Brit*) mercerie *f*.
habit ['hæbɪt] *n* habitude *f*; (*costume*) habit *m*, tenue *f*; **to get out of/into the ~ of doing sth** perdre/prendre l'habitude de faire qch.
habitable ['hæbɪtəbl] *a* habitable.
habitat ['hæbɪtæt] *n* habitat *m*.
habitation [hæbɪ'teɪʃən] *n* habitation *f*.
habitual [hə'bɪtjuəl] *a* habituel(le); (*drinker, liar*) invétéré(e).
habitually [hə'bɪtjuəlɪ] *ad* habituellement, d'habitude.
hack [hæk] *vt* hacher, tailler ♦ *n* (*cut*) entaille *f*; (*blow*) coup *m*; (*pej: writer*) nègre *m*; (*old horse*) canasson *m*.
hackles ['hæklz] *npl*: **to make sb's ~ rise** (*fig*) mettre qn hors de soi.
hackney cab ['hæknɪ-] *n* fiacre *m*.
hackneyed ['hæknɪd] *a* usé(e), rebattu(e).
had [hæd] *pt*, *pp* of **have**.
haddock, *pl* **~** *or* **~s** ['hædək] *n* églefin *m*; **smoked ~** haddock *m*.
hadn't ['hædnt] = **had not**.
haematology, (*US*) **hematology** ['hiːmə'tɔlədʒɪ] *n* hématologie *f*.
haemoglobin, (*US*) **hemoglobin** ['hiːmə'gləubɪn] *n* hémoglobine *f*.
haemophilia, (*US*) **hemophilia** [hiːmə'fɪlɪə] *n* hémophilie *f*.
haemorrhage, (*US*) **hemorrhage** ['hɛmərɪdʒ] *n* hémorragie *f*.
haemorrhoids, (*US*) **hemorrhoids** ['hɛmərɔɪdz] *npl* hémorroïdes *fpl*.
hag [hæg] *n* (*ugly*) vieille sorcière; (*nasty*) chameau *m*, harpie *f*; (*witch*) sorcière.
haggard ['hægəd] *a* hagard(e), égaré(e).
haggis ['hægɪs] *n* haggis *m*.
haggle ['hægl] *vi* marchander; **to ~ over** chicaner sur.
haggling ['hæglɪŋ] *n* marchandage *m*.
Hague [heɪg] *n*: **The ~** La Haye.
hail [heɪl] *n* grêle *f* ♦ *vt* (*call*) héler; (*greet*) acclamer ♦ *vi* grêler; (*originate*): **he ~s from Scotland** il est originaire d'Écosse.

hailstone ['heɪlstəun] *n* grêlon *m*.
hailstorm ['heɪlstɔːm] *n* averse *f* de grêle.
hair [hɛə*] *n* cheveux *mpl*; (*on body*) poils *mpl*, pilosité *f*; (*single hair: on head*) cheveu *m*; (*: on body*) poil *m*; **to do one's ~** se coiffer.
hairbrush ['hɛəbrʌʃ] *n* brosse *f* à cheveux.
haircut ['hɛəkʌt] *n* coupe *f* (de cheveux).
hairdo ['hɛəduː] *n* coiffure *f*.
hairdresser ['hɛədrɛsə*] *n* coiffeur/euse.
hair-dryer ['hɛədraɪə*] *n* sèche-cheveux *m*.
-haired [hɛəd] *suffix*: **fair/long~** aux cheveux blonds/longs.
hairgrip ['hɛəgrɪp] *n* pince *f* à cheveux.
hairline ['hɛəlaɪn] *n* naissance *f* des cheveux.
hairline fracture *n* fêlure *f*.
hairnet ['hɛənɛt] *n* résille *f*.
hair oil *n* huile *f* capillaire.
hairpiece ['hɛəpiːs] *n* postiche *m*.
hairpin ['hɛəpɪn] *n* épingle *f* à cheveux.
hairpin bend, (*US*) **hairpin curve** *n* virage *m* en épingle à cheveux.
hairraising ['hɛəreɪzɪŋ] *a* à (vous) faire dresser les cheveux sur la tête.
hair remover *n* dépilateur *m*.
hair spray *n* laque *f* (pour les cheveux).
hairstyle ['hɛəstaɪl] *n* coiffure *f*.
hairy ['hɛərɪ] *a* poilu(e); chevelu(e); (*fig*) effrayant(e).
Haiti ['heɪtɪ] *n* Haïti *m*.
hake [heɪk] *n* colin *m*, merlu *m*.
halcyon ['hælsɪən] *a* merveilleux(euse).
hale [heɪl] *a*: **~ and hearty** robuste, en pleine santé.
half [hɑːf] *n* (*pl* **halves** [hɑːvz]) moitié *f*; (*SPORT: of match*) mi-temps *f*; (*: of ground*) moitié (du terrain) ♦ *a* demi(e) ♦ *ad* (à) moitié, à demi; **~-an-hour** une demi-heure; **~ a dozen** une demi-douzaine; **~ a pound** une demi-livre, ≈ 250 g; **two and a ~** deux et demi; **a week and a ~** une semaine et demie; **~ (of it)** la moitié; **~ (of)** la moitié de; **~ the amount of** la moitié de; **to cut sth in ~** couper qch en deux; **~ past three** trois heures et demie; **~ empty/closed** à moitié vide/fermé; **to go halves (with sb)** se mettre de moitié avec qn.
half-back ['hɑːfbæk] *n* (*SPORT*) demi *m*.
half-baked ['hɑːf'beɪkt] *a* (*col: idea, scheme*) qui ne tient pas debout.
half-breed ['hɑːfbriːd] *n* = **halfcaste**.
half-brother ['hɑːfbrʌðə*] *n* demi-frère *m*.
half-caste ['hɑːfkɑːst] *n* métis/se.
half-hearted ['hɑːf'hɑːtɪd] *a* tiède, sans enthousiasme.
half-hour [hɑːf'auə*] *n* demi-heure *f*.
half-mast ['hɑːf'mɑːst] *n*: **at ~** (*flag*) en berne, à mi-mât.
halfpenny ['heɪpnɪ] *n* demi-penny *m*.
half-price ['hɑːf'praɪs] *a* à moitié prix ♦ *ad* (*also*: **at ~**) à moitié prix.
half term *n* (*Brit SCOL*) congé *m* de demi-trimestre.
half-time [hɑːf'taɪm] *n* mi-temps *f*.
halfway ['hɑːf'weɪ] *ad* à mi-chemin; **to meet sb ~** (*fig*) parvenir à un compromis avec qn.
half-yearly [hɑːf'jɪəlɪ] *ad* deux fois par an ♦ *a* semestriel(le).
halibut ['hælɪbət] *n* (*pl inv*) flétan *m*.

halitosis [hælɪ'təusɪs] *n* mauvaise haleine.
hall [hɔːl] *n* salle *f*; (*entrance way*) hall *m*, entrée *f*; (*corridor*) couloir *m*; (*mansion*) château *m*, manoir *m*; **~ of residence** *n* (*Brit*) pavillon *m or* résidence *f* universitaire.
hallmark ['hɔːlmɑːk] *n* poinçon *m*; (*fig*) marque *f*.
hallo [hə'ləu] *excl* = **hello**.
Hallowe'en ['hæləu'iːn] *n* veille *f* de la Toussaint.
hallucination [həluːsɪ'neɪʃən] *n* hallucination *f*.
hallway ['hɔːlweɪ] *n* vestibule *m*; couloir *m*.
halo ['heɪləu] *n* (*of saint etc*) auréole *f*; (*of sun*) halo *m*.
halt [hɔːlt] *n* halte *f*, arrêt *m* ♦ *vt* faire arrêter ♦ *vi* faire halte, s'arrêter; **to call a ~ to sth** (*fig*) mettre fin à qch.
halter ['hɔːltə*] *n* (*for horse*) licou *m*.
halterneck ['hɔːltənɛk] *a* (*dress*) (avec) dos nu *inv*.
halve [hɑːv] *vt* (*apple etc*) partager *or* diviser en deux; (*reduce by half*) réduire de moitié.
halves [hɑːvz] *npl of* **half**.
ham [hæm] *n* jambon *m*; (*col: also*: **radio ~**) radio-amateur *m*; (*: also*: **~ actor**) cabotin/e.
Hamburg ['hæmbəːg] *n* Hambourg.
hamburger ['hæmbəːgə*] *n* hamburger *m*.
ham-fisted ['hæm'fɪstɪd], (*US*) **ham-handed** ['hæm'hændɪd] *a* maladroit(e).
hamlet ['hæmlɪt] *n* hameau *m*.
hammer ['hæmə*] *n* marteau *m* ♦ *vt* (*fig*) éreinter, démolir ♦ *vi* (*at door*) frapper à coups redoublés; **to ~ a point home to sb** faire rentrer qch dans la tête de qn.
hammer out *vt* (*metal*) étendre au marteau; (*fig: solution*) élaborer.
hammock ['hæmək] *n* hamac *m*.
hamper ['hæmpə*] *vt* gêner ♦ *n* panier *m* (d'osier).
hamster ['hæmstə*] *n* hamster *m*.
hamstring ['hæmstrɪŋ] *n* (*ANAT*) tendon *m* du jarret.
hand [hænd] *n* main *f*; (*of clock*) aiguille *f*; (*handwriting*) écriture *f*; (*at cards*) jeu *m*; (*measurement: of horse*) paume *f*; (*worker*) ouvrier/ière ♦ *vt* passer, donner; **to give sb a ~** donner un coup de main à qn; **at ~** à portée de la main; **in ~** en main; (*work*) en cours; **we have the situation in ~** nous avons la situation bien en main; **to be on ~** (*person*) être disponible; (*emergency services*) se tenir prêt(e) (à intervenir); **to ~** (*information etc*) sous la main, à portée de la main; **to force sb's ~** forcer la main à qn; **to have a free ~** avoir carte blanche; **to have sth in one's ~** tenir qch à la main; **on the one ~ ...**, **on the other ~** d'une part ..., d'autre part.
hand down *vt* passer; (*tradition, heirloom*) transmettre; (*US*: *sentence, verdict*) prononcer.
hand in *vt* remettre.
hand out *vt* distribuer.
hand over *vt* remettre; (*powers etc*) transmettre.
hand round *vt* (*Brit*: *information*) faire circuler; (*: chocolates etc*) faire passer.
handbag ['hændbæg] *n* sac *m* à main.

handball ['hændbɔːl] *n* handball *m*.
handbasin ['hændbeɪsn] *n* lavabo *m*.
handbook ['hændbʊk] *n* manuel *m*.
handbrake ['hændbreɪk] *n* frein *m* à main.
hand cream *n* crème *f* pour les mains.
handcuffs ['hændkʌfs] *npl* menottes *fpl*.
handful ['hændfʊl] *n* poignée *f*.
handicap ['hændɪkæp] *n* handicap *m* ♦ *vt* handicaper; **mentally/physically** ~**ped** handicapé(e) mentalement/physiquement.
handicraft ['hændɪkrɑːft] *n* travail *m* d'artisanat, technique artisanale.
handiwork ['hændɪwɜːk] *n* ouvrage *m*; **this looks like his** ~ (*pej*) ça a tout l'air d'être son œuvre.
handkerchief ['hæŋkətʃɪf] *n* mouchoir *m*.
handle ['hændl] *n* (*of door etc*) poignée *f*; (*of cup etc*) anse *f*; (*of knife etc*) manche *m*; (*of saucepan*) queue *f*; (*for winding*) manivelle *f* ♦ *vt* toucher, manier; (*deal with*) s'occuper de; (*treat: people*) prendre; "~ **with care**" "fragile".
handlebar(s) ['hændlbɑː(z)] *n (pl)* guidon *m*.
handling charges *npl* frais *mpl* de manutention; (*BANKING*) agios *mpl*.
hand-luggage ['hændlʌgɪdʒ] *n* bagages *mpl* à main.
handmade ['hænd'meɪd] *a* fait(e) à la main.
handout ['hændaʊt] *n* documentation *f*, prospectus *m*; (*press* ~) communiqué *m* de presse.
hand-picked ['hænd'pɪkt] *a* (*produce*) cueilli(e) à la main; (*staff etc*) trié(e) sur le volet.
handrail ['hændreɪl] *n* (*on staircase etc*) rampe *f*, main courante.
handshake ['hændʃeɪk] *n* poignée *f* de main; (*COMPUT*) établissement *m* de la liaison.
handsome ['hænsəm] *a* beau(belle); (*gift*) généreux(euse); (*profit*) considérable.
handstand ['hændstænd] *n*: **to do a** ~ faire l'arbre droit.
hand-to-mouth ['hændtə'maʊθ] *a* (*existence*) au jour le jour.
handwriting ['hændraɪtɪŋ] *n* écriture *f*.
handwritten ['hændrɪtn] *a* manuscrit(e), écrit(e) à la main.
handy ['hændɪ] *a* (*person*) adroit(e); (*close at hand*) sous la main; (*convenient*) pratique; **to come in** ~ être (*or* s'avérer) utile.
handyman ['hændɪmæn] *n* bricoleur *m*; (*servant*) homme *m* à tout faire.
hang, *pt*, *pp* **hung** [hæŋ, hʌŋ] *vt* accrocher; (*criminal: pt, pp* **hanged**) pendre ♦ *vi* pendre; (*hair, drapery*) tomber; **to get the** ~ **of (doing) sth** (*col*) attraper le coup pour faire qch.
hang about *vi* flâner, traîner.
hang back *vi* (*hesitate*): **to** ~ **back (from doing)** être réticent(e) (pour faire).
hang on *vi* (*wait*) attendre ♦ *vt fus* (*depend on*) dépendre de; **to** ~ **on to** (*keep hold of*) ne pas lâcher; (*keep*) garder.
hang out *vt* (*washing*) étendre (dehors) ♦ *vi* pendre; (*col: live*) habiter, percher.
hang together *vi* (*argument etc*) se tenir, être cohérent(e).
hang up *vi* (*TEL*) raccrocher ♦ *vt* accrocher, suspendre; **to** ~ **up on sb** (*TEL*) rac-

crocher au nez de qn.
hangar ['hæŋə*] *n* hangar *m*.
hangdog ['hæŋdɔg] *a* (*look, expression*) de chien battu.
hanger ['hæŋə*] *n* cintre *m*, portemanteau *m*.
hanger-on [hæŋər'ɔn] *n* parasite *m*.
hang-gliding ['hæŋglaɪdɪŋ] *n* vol *m* libre *or* sur aile delta.
hanging ['hæŋɪŋ] *n* (*execution*) pendaison *f*.
hangman ['hæŋmən] *n* bourreau *m*.
hangover ['hæŋəʊvə*] *n* (*after drinking*) gueule *f* de bois.
hang-up ['hæŋʌp] *n* complexe *m*.
hank [hæŋk] *n* écheveau *m*.
hanker ['hæŋkə*] *vi*: **to** ~ **after** avoir envie de.
hankie, hanky ['hæŋkɪ] *n abbr* = **handkerchief**.
Hants *abbr* (*Brit*) = Hampshire.
haphazard [hæp'hæzəd] *a* fait(e) au hasard, fait(e) au petit bonheur.
hapless ['hæplɪs] *a* malheureux(euse).
happen ['hæpən] *vi* arriver, se passer, se produire; **what's** ~**ing?** que se passe-t-il?; **she** ~**ed to be free** il s'est trouvé (*or* se trouvait) qu'elle était libre; **if anything** ~**ed to him** s'il lui arrivait quoi que ce soit; **as it** ~**s** justement.
happen (up)on *vt fus* tomber sur.
happening ['hæpnɪŋ] *n* événement *m*.
happily ['hæpɪlɪ] *ad* heureusement.
happiness ['hæpɪnɪs] *n* bonheur *m*.
happy ['hæpɪ] *a* heureux(euse); ~ **with** (*arrangements etc*) satisfait(e) de; **yes, I'd be** ~ **to** oui, avec plaisir *or* (bien) volontiers; ~ **birthday!** bon anniversaire!; ~ **Christmas/New Year!** joyeux Noël/bonne année!
happy-go-lucky ['hæpɪgəʊ'lʌkɪ] *a* insouciant(e).
harangue [hə'ræŋ] *vt* haranguer.
harass ['hærəs] *vt* accabler, tourmenter.
harassed ['hærəst] *a* tracassé(e).
harassment ['hærəsmənt] *n* tracasseries *fpl*.
harbour, (*US*) **harbor** ['hɑːbə*] *n* port *m* ♦ *vt* héberger, abriter; (*hopes, suspicions*) entretenir; **to** ~ **a grudge against sb** en vouloir à qn.
harbo(u)r dues *npl* droits *mpl* de port.
harbo(u)r master *n* capitaine *m* du port.
hard [hɑːd] *a* dur(e) ♦ *ad* (*work*) dur; (*think, try*) sérieusement; **to look** ~ **at** regarder fixement; regarder de près; **to drink** ~ boire sec; ~ **luck!** pas de veine!; **no** ~ **feelings!** sans rancune!; **to be** ~ **of hearing** être dur(e) d'oreille; **to be** ~ **done by** être traité(e) injustement; **to be** ~ **on sb** être dur(e) avec qn; **I find it** ~ **to believe that** ... je n'arrive pas à croire que ....
hard-and-fast ['hɑːdən'fɑːst] *a* strict(e), absolu(e).
hardback ['hɑːdbæk] *n* livre relié.
hardboard ['hɑːdbɔːd] *n* Isorel *m* ®.
hard-boiled egg ['hɑːd'bɔɪld-] *n* œuf dur.
hard cash *n* espèces *fpl*.
hard copy *n* (*COMPUT*) sortie *f or* copie *f* papier.
hard-core ['hɑːd'kɔː*] *a* (*pornography*) (dit(e)) dur(e); (*supporters*) incondi-

tionnel(le).

hard court n (TENNIS) court m en dur.

hard disk n (COMPUT) disque dur.

harden ['ha:dn] vt durcir; (steel) tremper; (fig) endurcir ♦ vi (substance) durcir.

hardened ['ha:dnd] a (criminal) endurci(e); **to be ~ to sth** s'être endurci(e) à qch, être (devenu(e)) insensible à qch.

hardening ['ha:dniŋ] n durcissement m.

hard-headed ['ha:d'hɛdid] a réaliste; décidé(e).

hard-hearted ['ha:d'ha:tid] a dur(e), impitoyable.

hard labour n travaux forcés.

hardliner [ha:d'lainə*] n intransigeant/e, dur/e.

hardly ['ha:dli] ad (scarcely) à peine; (harshly) durement; **it's ~ the case** ce n'est guère le cas; **~ anywhere/ever** presque nulle part/jamais; **I can ~ believe it** j'ai du mal à le croire.

hardness ['ha:dnis] n dureté f.

hard sell n vente agressive.

hardship ['ha:dʃip] n épreuves fpl; privations fpl.

hard shoulder n (Brit AUT) accotement stabilisé.

hard-up [ha:d'ʌp] a (col) fauché(e).

hardware ['ha:dwɛə*] n quincaillerie f; (COMPUT) matériel m.

hardware shop n quincaillerie f.

hard-wearing [ha:d'wɛəriŋ] a solide.

hard-working [ha:d'wə:kiŋ] a travailleur(euse), consciencieux(euse).

hardy ['ha:di] a robuste; (plant) résistant(e) au gel.

hare [hɛə*] n lièvre m.

hare-brained ['hɛəbreind] a farfelu(e); écervelé(e).

harelip ['hɛəlip] n (MED) bec-de-lièvre m.

harem [ha:'ri:m] n harem m.

hark back [ha:k-] vi: **to ~ back to** (en) revenir toujours à.

harm [ha:m] n mal m; (wrong) tort m ♦ vt (person) faire du mal or du tort à; (thing) endommager; **to mean no ~** ne pas avoir de mauvaises intentions; **there's no ~ in trying** on peut toujours essayer; **out of ~'s way** à l'abri du danger, en lieu sûr.

harmful ['ha:mful] a nuisible.

harmless [ha:mlis] a inoffensif(ive); sans méchanceté.

harmonic [ha:'mɔnik] a harmonique.

harmonica [ha:'mɔnikə] n harmonica m.

harmonics [ha:'mɔniks] npl harmoniques mpl or fpl.

harmonious [ha:'məuniəs] a harmonieux(euse).

harmonium [ha:'məuniəm] n harmonium m.

harmonize ['ha:mənaiz] vt harmoniser ♦ vi s'harmoniser.

harmony ['ha:məni] n harmonie f.

harness ['ha:nis] n harnais m ♦ vt (horse) harnacher; (resources) exploiter.

harp [ha:p] n harpe f ♦ vi: **to ~ on about** parler tout le temps de.

harpist ['ha:pist] n harpiste m/f.

harpoon [ha:'pu:n] n harpon m.

harpsichord ['ha:psikɔ:d] n clavecin m.

harrow ['hærəu] n (AGR) herse f.

harrowing ['hærəuiŋ] a déchirant(e).

harry ['hæri] vt (MIL, fig) harceler.

harsh [ha:ʃ] a (hard) dur(e), sévère; (rough: surface) rugueux(euse); (: sound) discordant(e); (: taste) âpre.

harshly ['ha:ʃli] ad durement, sévèrement.

harshness ['ha:ʃnis] n dureté f, sévérité f.

harvest ['ha:vist] n (of corn) moisson f; (of fruit) récolte f; (of grapes) vendange f ♦ vi, vt moissonner; récolter; vendanger.

harvester ['ha:vistə*] n (machine) moissonneuse f; (also: **combine ~**) moissonneuse-batteuse(-lieuse) f; (person) moissonneur/euse.

has [hæz] vb see **have**.

has-been ['hæzbi:n] n (col: person): **he/she's a ~** il/elle a fait son temps or est fini(e).

hash [hæʃ] n (CULIN) hachis m; (fig: mess) gâchis m ♦ n abbr (col) = **hashish**.

hashish ['hæʃiʃ] n haschisch m.

hasn't ['hæznt] = **has not**.

hassle ['hæsl] n (col: fuss) histoire(s) f(pl).

haste [heist] n hâte f, précipitation f; **in ~** à la hâte, précipitemment.

hasten ['heisn] vt hâter, accélérer ♦ vi se hâter, s'empresser; **I ~ to add that ...** je m'empresse d'ajouter que ....

hastily ['heistili] ad à la hâte, précipitamment.

hasty ['heisti] a hâtif(ive), précipité(e).

hat [hæt] n chapeau m.

hatbox ['hætbɔks] n carton m à chapeau.

hatch [hætʃ] n (NAUT: also: **~way**) écoutille f; (Brit: also: **service ~**) passe-plats m inv ♦ vi éclore ♦ vt faire éclore; (fig: scheme) tramer, ourdir.

hatchback ['hætʃbæk] n (AUT) modèle m avec hayon arrière.

hatchet ['hætʃit] n hachette f.

hate [heit] vt haïr, détester ♦ n haine f; **to ~ to do** or **doing** détester faire; **I ~ to trouble you, but ...** désolé de vous déranger, mais ....

hateful ['heitful] a odieux(euse), détestable.

hatred ['heitrid] n haine f.

hat trick n (Brit SPORT, also fig): **to get a ~** réussir trois coups (or gagner trois matchs etc) consécutifs.

haughty ['hɔ:ti] a hautain(e), arrogant(e).

haul [hɔ:l] vt traîner, tirer; (by lorry) camionner; (NAUT) haler ♦ n (of fish) prise f; (of stolen goods etc) butin m.

haulage ['hɔ:lidʒ] n transport routier.

haulage contractor n (Brit: firm) entreprise f de transport (routier); (: person) transporteur routier.

haulier ['hɔ:liə*], (US) **hauler** ['hɔ:lə*] n transporteur (routier), camionneur m.

haunch [hɔ:ntʃ] n hanche f; **~ of venison** cuissot m de chevreuil.

haunt [hɔ:nt] vt (subj: ghost, fear) hanter; (: person) fréquenter ♦ n repaire m.

haunted ['hɔ:ntid] a (castle etc) hanté(e); (look) égaré(e), hagard(e).

haunting ['hɔ:ntiŋ] a (sight, music) obsédant(e).

Havana [hə'vænə] n La Havane f.

have [hæv], pt, pp **had** [hæv, hæd] vt avoir; (meal, shower) prendre ♦ auxiliary vb: **to ~ eaten** avoir mangé; **to ~ arrived** être arrivé(e); **to ~ breakfast** prendre son petit déjeuner; **to ~**

lunch déjeuner; **to ~ dinner** dîner; **I'll ~ a coffee** je prendrai un café; **to ~ an operation** se faire opérer; **to ~ a party** donner une réception *or* une soirée; **to ~ sth done** faire faire qch; **he had a suit made** il s'est fait faire un costume; **let me ~ a try** laissez-moi essayer; **she has to do it** il faut qu'elle le fasse, elle doit le faire; **I had better leave** je ferais mieux de partir; **I won't ~ it** cela ne se passera pas ainsi; **he's been had** *(col)* il s'est fait avoir *or* rouler.

have in *vt:* **to ~ it in for sb** *(col)* avoir une dent contre qn.

have on *vt:* **~ you anything on tomorrow?** *(Brit)* est-ce que vous êtes pris demain?; **I don't ~ any money on me** je n'ai pas d'argent sur moi; **to ~ sb on** *(Brit col)* faire marcher qn.

have out *vt:* **to ~ it out with sb** s'expliquer (franchement) avec qn.

haven ['heɪvn] *n* port *m*; *(fig)* havre *m*.

haversack ['hævəsæk] *n* sac *m* à dos.

haves [hævz] *npl* *(col)*: **the ~ and have-nots** les riches et les pauvres.

havoc ['hævək] *n* ravages *mpl*; **to play ~ with** *(fig)* désorganiser; détraquer.

Hawaii [hə'waɪi:] *n* (îles *fpl*) Hawaii *m*.

Hawaiian [hə'waɪjən] *a* hawaïen(ne) ♦ *n* Hawaïen/ne; *(LING)* hawaïen *m*.

hawk [hɔːk] *n* faucon *m* ♦ *vt (goods for sale)* colporter.

hawker ['hɔːkə*] *n* colporteur *m*.

hawthorn ['hɔːθɔːn] *n* aubépine *f*.

hay [heɪ] *n* foin *m*.

hay fever *n* rhume *m* des foins.

haystack ['heɪstæk] *n* meule *f* de foin.

haywire ['heɪwaɪə*] *a* *(col)*: **to go ~** perdre la tête; mal tourner.

hazard ['hæzəd] *n* *(chance)* hasard *m*, chance *f*; *(risk)* danger *m*, risque *m* ♦ *vt* risquer, hasarder; **to be a health/fire ~** présenter un risque d'incendie/pour la santé; **to ~ a guess** émettre *or* hasarder une hypothèse.

hazardous ['hæzədəs] *a* hasardeux(euse), risqué(e).

hazard pay *n* *(US)* prime *f* de risque.

hazard warning lights *npl* *(AUT)* feux *mpl* de détresse.

haze [heɪz] *n* brume *f*.

hazel [heɪzl] *n* *(tree)* noisetier *m* ♦ *a* *(eyes)* noisette *inv*.

hazelnut ['heɪzlnʌt] *n* noisette *f*.

hazy ['heɪzɪ] *a* brumeux(euse); *(idea)* vague; *(photograph)* flou(e).

H-bomb ['eɪtʃbɔm] *n* bombe *f* H.

h & c *abbr* *(Brit)* = **hot and cold** *(water)*.

HE *abbr* = **high explosive**; *(REL, DIPLOMACY)* = **His (or Her) Excellency**.

he [hiː] *pronoun* il; **it is ~ who** ... c'est lui qui ...; **here ~ is** le voici; **~-bear** *etc* ours *etc* mâle.

head [hed] *n* tête *f*; *(leader)* chef *m* ♦ *vt* *(list)* être en tête de; *(group)* être à la tête de; **~s** *(on coin)* (le côté) face; **~s or tails** pile ou face; **~ first** la tête la première; **~ over heels in love** follement *or* éperdument amoureux(euse); **to ~ the ball** faire une tête; **10 francs a** *or* **per ~** 10F par personne; **to sit at the ~ of the table** présider la ta-

blée; **to have a ~ for business** avoir des dispositions pour les affaires; **to have no ~ for heights** être sujet(te) au vertige; **to come to a ~** *(fig: situation etc)* devenir critique.

head for *vt fus* se diriger vers.

head off *vt* *(threat, danger)* détourner.

headache ['hedeɪk] *n* mal *m* de tête; **to have a ~** avoir mal à la tête.

head cold *n* rhume *m* de cerveau.

headdress ['heddres] *n* coiffure *f*.

header ['hedə*] *n* *(Brit col: FOOTBALL)* (coup *m* de) tête *f*; *(: fall)* chute *f* (or plongeon *m*) la tête la première.

headhunter ['hedhʌntə*] *n* chasseur *m* de têtes.

heading ['hedɪŋ] *n* titre *m*; *(subject title)* rubrique *f*.

headlamp ['hedlæmp] *n* *(Brit)* = **headlight**.

headland ['hedlənd] *n* promontoire *m*, cap *m*.

headlight ['hedlaɪt] *n* phare *m*.

headline ['hedlaɪn] *n* titre *m*.

headlong ['hedlɔŋ] *ad* *(fall)* la tête la première; *(rush)* tête baissée.

headmaster [hed'maːstə*] *n* directeur *m*, proviseur *m*.

headmistress [hed'mɪstrɪs] *n* directrice *f*.

head office *n* siège *m*, direction *f* (générale).

head-on [hed'ɔn] *a* *(collision)* de plein fouet.

headphones ['hedfəʊnz] *npl* casque *m* (à écouteurs).

headquarters (HQ) ['hedkwɔːtəz] *npl* *(of business)* siège *m*, direction *f* (générale); *(MIL)* quartier général.

head-rest ['hedrest] *n* appui-tête *m*.

headroom ['hedrum] *n* *(in car)* hauteur *f* de plafond; *(under bridge)* hauteur limite; dégagement *m*.

headscarf ['hedskaːf] *n* foulard *m*.

headset ['hedset] *n* = **headphones**.

headstone ['hedstəʊn] *n* *(on grave)* pierre tombale.

headstrong ['hedstrɔŋ] *a* têtu(e), entêté(e).

head waiter *n* maître *m* d'hôtel.

headway ['hedweɪ] *n:* **to make ~** avancer, faire des progrès.

headwind ['hedwɪnd] *n* vent *m* contraire.

heady ['hedɪ] *a* capiteux(euse); enivrant(e).

heal [hiːl] *vt, vi* guérir.

health [helθ] *n* santé *f*; **Department of H~** *(US)* ≈ ministère *m* de la Santé; **Department of H~ and Social Security (DHSS)** *(Brit)* ≈ ministère de la Santé et de la Sécurité Sociale.

health centre *n* *(Brit)* centre *m* de santé.

health food(s) *n(pl)* aliment(s) naturel(s).

health food shop *n* magasin *m* diététique.

health hazard *n* risque *m* pour la santé.

Health Service *n:* **the ~** *(Brit)* ≈ la Sécurité Sociale.

healthy ['helθɪ] *a* *(person)* en bonne santé; *(climate, food, attitude etc)* sain(e).

heap [hiːp] *n* tas *m*, monceau *m* ♦ *vt* entasser, amonceler; **~s (of)** *(col: lots)* des tas (de); **to ~ favours/praise/gifts** *etc* **on sb** combler qn de faveurs/d'éloges/de cadeaux *etc*.

hear, *pt, pp* **heard** [hɪə*, hɜːd] *vt* entendre; *(news)* apprendre; *(lecture)* assister à, écouter ♦ *vi* entendre; **to ~ about** entendre

parler de; (have news of) avoir des nouvelles de; **did you ~ about the move?** tu es au courant du déménagement?; **to ~ from sb** recevoir des nouvelles de qn; **I've never heard of that book** je n'ai jamais entendu parler de ce livre.
hear out vt écouter jusqu'au bout.
hearing ['hɪərɪŋ] n (sense) ouïe f; (of witnesses) audition f; (of a case) audience f; (of committee) séance f; **to give sb a ~** (Brit) écouter ce que qn a à dire.
hearing aid n appareil m acoustique.
hearsay ['hɪəseɪ] n on-dit mpl, rumeurs fpl; **by ~** ad par ouï-dire.
hearse [hɜːs] n corbillard m.
heart [hɑːt] n cœur m; **~s** npl (CARDS) cœur; **at ~** au fond; **by ~** (learn, know) par cœur; **to have a weak ~** avoir le cœur malade, avoir des problèmes de cœur; **to lose ~** perdre courage, se décourager; **to take ~** prendre courage; **to set one's ~ on sth/on doing sth** vouloir absolument qch/faire qch; **the ~ of the matter** le fond du problème.
heart attack n crise f cardiaque.
heartbeat ['hɑːtbiːt] n battement m de cœur.
heartbreak ['hɑːtbreɪk] n immense chagrin m.
heartbreaking ['hɑːtbreɪkɪŋ] a navrant(e), déchirant(e).
heartbroken ['hɑːtbrəukən] a: **to be ~** avoir beaucoup de chagrin.
heartburn ['hɑːtbɜːn] n brûlures fpl d'estomac.
-hearted ['hɑːtɪd] suffix: **kind~** généreux(euse), qui a bon cœur.
heartening ['hɑːtnɪŋ] a encourageant(e), réconfortant(e).
heart failure n (MED) arrêt m du cœur.
heartfelt ['hɑːtfɛlt] a sincère.
hearth [hɑːθ] n foyer m, cheminée f.
heartily ['hɑːtɪlɪ] ad chaleureusement; (laugh) de bon cœur; (eat) de bon appétit; **to agree ~** être entièrement d'accord; **to be ~ sick of** (Brit) en avoir ras le bol de.
heartland ['hɑːtlænd] n centre m, cœur m; **France's ~s** la France profonde.
heartless ['hɑːtlɪs] a sans cœur, insensible; cruel(le).
heart-to-heart ['hɑːt'tə'hɑːt] a, ad à cœur ouvert.
heart transplant n greffe f du cœur.
heartwarming ['hɑːtwɔːmɪŋ] a réconfortant(e).
hearty ['hɑːtɪ] a chaleureux(euse); robuste; vigoureux(euse).
heat [hiːt] n chaleur f; (fig) ardeur f; feu m; (SPORT: also: **qualifying ~**) éliminatoire f; (ZOOL): **in** or (Brit) **on ~** en chaleur ♦ vt chauffer.
heat up vi (liquids) chauffer; (room) se réchauffer ♦ vt réchauffer.
heated ['hiːtɪd] a chauffé(e); (fig) passionné(e); échauffé(e), excité(e).
heater ['hiːtə*] n appareil m de chauffage; radiateur m.
heath [hiːθ] n (Brit) lande f.
heathen ['hiːðn] a, n païen(ne).
heather ['hɛðə*] n bruyère f.
heating ['hiːtɪŋ] n chauffage m.
heat-resistant ['hiːtrɪzɪstənt] a résistant(e) à la chaleur.
heatstroke ['hiːtstrəuk] n coup m de chaleur.
heatwave ['hiːtweɪv] n vague f de chaleur.
heave [hiːv] vt soulever (avec effort) ♦ vi se soulever; (retch) avoir des haut-le-cœur ♦ n (push) poussée f; **to ~ a sigh** pousser un gros soupir.
heaven ['hɛvn] n ciel m, paradis m; **~ forbid!** surtout pas!; **thank ~!** Dieu merci!; **for ~'s sake!** (pleading) je vous en prie!; (protesting) mince alors!
heavenly ['hɛvnlɪ] a céleste, divin(e).
heavily ['hɛvɪlɪ] ad lourdement; (drink, smoke) beaucoup; (sleep, sigh) profondément.
heavy ['hɛvɪ] a lourd(e); (work, rain, user, eater) gros(se); (drinker, smoker) grand(e); **it's ~ going** ça ne va pas tout seul, c'est pénible.
heavy cream n (US) crème fraîche épaisse.
heavy-duty ['hɛvɪ'djuːtɪ] a à usage intensif.
heavy goods vehicle (HGV) n (Brit) poids lourd m (P.L.).
heavy-handed ['hɛvɪ'hændɪd] a (fig) maladroit(e), qui manque de tact.
heavyweight ['hɛvɪweɪt] n (SPORT) poids lourd.
Hebrew ['hiːbruː] a hébraïque ♦ n (LING) hébreu m.
Hebrides ['hɛbrɪdiːz] n: **the ~** les Hébrides fpl.
heckle ['hɛkl] vt interpeller (un orateur).
heckler ['hɛklə*] n interrupteur m; élément m perturbateur.
hectare ['hɛktɑː*] n (Brit) hectare m.
hectic ['hɛktɪk] a agité(e), trépidant(e); (busy) trépidant.
hector ['hɛktə*] vt rudoyer, houspiller.
he'd [hiːd] = **he would, he had**.
hedge [hɛdʒ] n haie f ♦ vi se défiler; **to ~ one's bets** (fig) se couvrir; **as a ~ against** inflation pour se prémunir contre l'inflation.
hedge in vt entourer d'une haie.
hedgehog ['hɛdʒhɒg] n hérisson m.
hedgerow ['hɛdʒrəu] n haie(s) f(pl).
hedonism ['hiːdənɪzəm] n hédonisme m.
heed [hiːd] vt (also: **take ~ of**) tenir compte de, prendre garde à.
heedless ['hiːdlɪs] a insouciant(e).
heel [hiːl] n talon m ♦ vt (shoe) retalonner; **to bring to ~** (dog) faire venir à ses pieds; (fig: person) rappeler à l'ordre; **to take to one's ~s** prendre ses jambes à son cou.
hefty ['hɛftɪ] a (person) costaud(e); (parcel) lourd(e); (piece, price) gros(se).
heifer ['hɛfə*] n génisse f.
height [haɪt] n (of person) taille f, grandeur f; (of object) hauteur f; (of plane, mountain) altitude f; (high ground) hauteur, éminence f; (fig: of glory) sommet m; (: of stupidity) comble m; **what ~ are you?** combien mesurez-vous?, quelle est votre taille?; **of average ~** de taille moyenne; **to be afraid of ~s** être sujet(te) au vertige; **it's the ~ of fashion** c'est le dernier cri.
heighten ['haɪtn] vt hausser, surélever; (fig) augmenter.
heinous ['heɪnəs] a odieux(euse), atroce.
heir [ɛə*] n héritier m.

heir apparent n héritier présomptif.
heiress ['ɛərɛs] n héritière f.
heirloom ['ɛəluːm] n meuble m (or bijou m or tableau m) de famille.
heist [haɪst] n (US col: hold-up) casse m.
held [held] pt, pp of **hold**.
helicopter ['helɪkɔptə*] n hélicoptère m.
heliport ['helɪpɔːt] n (AVIAT) héliport m.
helium ['hiːlɪəm] n hélium m.
hell [hel] n enfer m; **a ~ of a** ... (col) un(e) sacré(e) ...; **oh ~!** (col) merde!
he'll [hiːl] = **he will**, **he shall**.
hellish ['helɪʃ] a infernal(e).
hello [hə'ləu] excl bonjour!; salut! (to sb one addresses as 'tu'); (surprise) tiens!
helm [helm] n (NAUT) barre f.
helmet ['helmɪt] n casque m.
helmsman ['helmzmən] n timonier m.
help [help] n aide f; (charwoman) femme f de ménage; (assistant etc) employé/e ♦ vt aider; **~!** au secours!; **~ yourself (to bread)** servez-vous (de pain); **can I ~ you?** (in shop) vous désirez?; **with the ~ of** (person) avec l'aide de; (tool etc) à l'aide de; **to be of ~ to sb** être utile à qn; **to ~ sb (to) do sth** aider qn à faire qch; **I can't ~ saying** je ne peux pas m'empêcher de dire; **he can't ~ it** il n'y peut rien.
helper ['helpə*] n aide m/f, assistant/e.
helpful ['helpful] a serviable, obligeant(e); (useful) utile.
helping ['helpɪŋ] n portion f.
helpless ['helplɪs] a impuissant(e); (baby) sans défense.
helplessly ['helplɪslɪ] ad (watch) sans pouvoir rien faire.
Helsinki ['helsɪŋkɪ] n Helsinki.
helter-skelter ['heltə'skeltə*] n (Brit: at amusement park) toboggan m.
hem [hem] n ourlet m ♦ vt ourler.
hem in vt cerner; **to feel ~med in** (fig) avoir l'impression d'étouffer, se sentir oppressé(e) or écrasé(e).
he-man ['hiːmæn] n (col) macho m.
hematology ['hiːmə'tɔlədʒɪ] n (US) = **haematology**.
hemisphere ['hemɪsfɪə*] n hémisphère m.
hemlock ['hemlɔk] n ciguë f.
hemoglobin ['hiːmə'gləubɪn] n (US) = **haemoglobin**.
hemophilia ['hiːmə'fɪlɪə] n (US) = **haemophilia**.
hemorrhage ['hemərɪdʒ] n (US) = **haemorrhage**.
hemorrhoids ['hemərɔɪdz] npl (US) = **haemorrhoids**.
hemp [hemp] n chanvre m.
hen [hen] n poule f; (female bird) femelle f.
hence [hens] ad (therefore) d'où, de là; **2 years ~** d'ici 2 ans.
henceforth [hens'fɔːθ] ad dorénavant.
henchman ['hentʃmən] n (pej) acolyte m, séide m.
henna ['henə] n henné m.
hen party n (col) réunion f or fête f entre femmes.
henpecked ['henpekt] a dominé par sa femme.
hepatitis [hepə'taɪtɪs] n hépatite f.

her [həː*] pronoun (direct) la, l' + vowel or h mute; (indirect) lui; (stressed, after prep) elle; see note at **she** ♦ a son(sa), ses pl; **I see ~** je la vois; **give ~ a book** donne-lui un livre; **after ~** après elle.
herald ['herəld] n héraut m ♦ vt annoncer.
heraldic [he'rældɪk] a héraldique.
heraldry ['herəldrɪ] n héraldique f; (coat of arms) blason m.
herb [həːb] n herbe f; **~s** npl (CULIN) fines herbes.
herbaceous [həː'beɪʃəs] a herbacé(e).
herbal ['həːbl] a à base de plantes; **~ tea** tisane f.
herbicide ['həːbɪsaɪd] n herbicide m.
herd [həːd] n troupeau m; (of wild animals, swine) troupeau m, troupe f ♦ vt (drive: animals, people) mener, conduire; (gather) rassembler; **~ed together** parqués (comme du bétail).
here [hɪə*] ad ici ♦ excl tiens!, tenez!; **~!** présent!; **~ is, ~ are** voici; **~'s my sister** voici ma sœur; **~ he/she is** le/la voici; **~ she comes** la voici qui vient; **come ~!** viens ici!; **~ and there** ici et là.
hereabouts ['hɪərə'bauts] ad par ici, dans les parages.
hereafter [hɪər'aːftə*] ad après, plus tard; ci-après ♦ n: **the ~** l'au-delà m.
hereby [hɪə'baɪ] ad (in letter) par la présente.
hereditary [hɪ'redɪtrɪ] a héréditaire.
heredity [hɪ'redɪtɪ] n hérédité f.
heresy ['herəsɪ] n hérésie f.
heretic ['herətɪk] n hérétique m/f.
heretical [hɪ'retɪkl] a hérétique.
herewith [hɪə'wɪð] ad avec ceci, ci-joint.
heritage ['herɪtɪdʒ] n héritage m, patrimoine m; **our national ~** notre patrimoine national.
hermetically [həː'metɪklɪ] ad hermétiquement; **~ sealed** hermétiquement fermé or clos.
hermit ['həːmɪt] n ermite m.
hernia ['həːnɪə] n hernie f.
hero, pl **~es** ['hɪərəu] n héros m.
heroic [hɪ'rəuɪk] a héroïque.
heroin ['herəuɪn] n héroïne f.
heroin addict n héroïnomane m/f.
heroine ['herəuɪn] n héroïne f (femme).
heroism ['herəuɪzəm] n héroïsme m.
heron ['herən] n héron m.
hero worship n culte m (du héros).
herring ['herɪŋ] n hareng m.
hers [həːz] pronoun le(la) sien(ne), les siens(siennes); **a friend of ~** un(e) ami(e) à elle, un(e) de ses ami(e)s; **this is ~** c'est à elle, c'est le sien.
herself [həː'self] pronoun (reflexive) se; (emphatic) elle-même; (after prep) elle.
Herts abbr (Brit) = **Hertfordshire**.
he's [hiːz] = **he is**, **he has**.
hesitant ['hezɪtənt] a hésitant(e), indécis(e); **to be ~ about doing sth** hésiter à faire qch.
hesitate ['hezɪteɪt] vi: **to ~ (about/to do)** hésiter (sur/à faire).
hesitation [hezɪ'teɪʃən] n hésitation f; **I have no ~ in saying (that)** ... je n'hésiterai pas à dire (que) ...
hessian ['hesɪən] n (toile f de) jute m.
heterogeneous ['hetərə'dʒiːnɪəs] a

hétérogène.

heterosexual ['hɛtərəu'sɛksjuəl] *a*, *n* hétérosexuel(le).

het up [hɛt'ʌp] *a* (*col*) agité(e), excité(e).

HEW *n abbr* (*US*: = *Department of Health, Education and Welfare*) ministère de la santé publique, de l'enseignement et du bien-être.

hew [hju:] *vt* tailler (*à la hache*).

hex [hɛks] (*US*) *n* sort *m* ♦ *vt* jeter un sort sur.

hexagon ['hɛksəgən] *n* hexagone *m*.

hexagonal [hɛk'sægənl] *a* hexagonal(e).

hey [heɪ] *excl* hé!

heyday ['heɪdeɪ] *n*: **the ~ of** l'âge *m* d'or de, les beaux jours de.

HF *n abbr* (= *high frequency*) HF *f*.

HGV *n abbr* = **heavy goods vehicle**.

HI *abbr* (*US POST*) = *Hawaii*.

hi [haɪ] *excl* salut!

hiatus [haɪ'eɪtəs] *n* trou *m*, lacune *f*; (*LING*) hiatus *m*.

hibernate ['haɪbəneɪt] *vi* hiberner.

hibernation [haɪbə'neɪʃən] *n* hibernation *f*.

hiccough, hiccup ['hɪkʌp] *vi* hoqueter ♦ *n* hoquet *m*; **to have (the) ~s** avoir le hoquet.

hid [hɪd] *pt of* **hide**.

hidden ['hɪdn] *pp of* **hide** ♦ *a*: **there are no ~ extras** absolument tout est compris dans le prix.

hide [haɪd] *n* (*skin*) peau *f* ♦ *vb* (*pt* **hid**, *pp* **hidden** [hɪd, 'hɪdn]) *vt*: **to ~ sth (from sb)** cacher qch (à qn); (*feelings, truth*) dissimuler qch (à qn) ♦ *vi*: **to ~ (from sb)** se cacher de qn.

hide-and-seek ['haɪdən'si:k] *n* cache-cache *m*.

hideaway ['haɪdəweɪ] *n* cachette *f*.

hideous ['hɪdɪəs] *a* hideux(euse); atroce.

hide-out ['haɪdaut] *n* cachette *f*.

hiding ['haɪdɪŋ] *n* (*beating*) correction *f*, volée *f* de coups; **to be in ~** (*concealed*) se tenir caché(e).

hiding place *n* cachette *f*.

hierarchy ['haɪərɑ:kɪ] *n* hiérarchie *f*.

hieroglyphic [haɪərə'glɪfɪk] *a* hiéroglyphique; **~s** *npl* hiéroglyphes *mpl*.

hi-fi ['haɪfaɪ] *a*, *n abbr* (= *high fidelity*) hi-fi (*f*) *inv*.

higgledy-piggledy ['hɪgldɪ'pɪgldɪ] *ad* pêle-mêle, dans le plus grand désordre.

high [haɪ] *a* haut(e); (*speed, respect, number*) grand(e); (*price*) élevé(e); (*wind*) fort(e), violent(e); (*voice*) aigu(aiguë); (*col: person: on drugs*) défoncé(e), fait(e); (*: on drink*) soûl(e), bourré(e); (*Brit CULIN: meat, game*) faisandé(e); (*: spoilt*) avarié(e) ♦ *ad* haut, en haut ♦ *n*: **exports have reached a new ~** les exportations ont atteint un nouveau record; **20 m ~** haut(e) de 20 m; **to pay a ~ price for sth** payer cher pour qch.

highball ['haɪbɔ:l] *n* (*US*) whisky *m* à l'eau avec des glaçons.

highboy ['haɪbɔɪ] *n* (*US*) grande commode.

highbrow ['haɪbrau] *a*, *n* intellectuel(le).

highchair ['haɪtʃɛə*] *n* chaise haute (*pour enfant*).

high-class ['haɪ'klɑ:s] *a* (*neighbourhood, hotel*) chic *inv*, de grand standing; (*performance etc*) de haut niveau.

high court *n* (*LAW*) cour *f* suprême.

higher ['haɪə*] *a* (*form of life, study etc*) supérieur(e) ♦ *ad* plus haut.

higher education *n* études supérieures.

high finance *n* la haute finance.

high-flier [haɪ'flaɪə*] *n* étudiant/e (*or* employé/e) particulièrement doué(e) et ambitieux(euse).

high-flying [haɪ'flaɪɪŋ] *a* (*fig*) ambitieux(euse), de haut niveau.

high-handed [haɪ'hændɪd] *a* très autoritaire; très cavalier(ière).

high-heeled [haɪ'hi:ld] *a* à hauts talons.

highjack ['haɪdʒæk] *n*, *vt* = **hijack**.

high jump *n* (*SPORT*) saut *m* en hauteur.

highlands ['haɪləndz] *npl* région montagneuse; **the H~** (*in Scotland*) les Highlands *mpl*.

high-level ['haɪlɛvl] *a* (*talks etc*) à un haut niveau; **~ language** (*COMPUT*) langage évolué.

highlight ['haɪlaɪt] *n* (*fig: of event*) point culminant ♦ *vt* faire ressortir, souligner; **~s** *npl* (*hairstyle*) reflets *mpl*.

highlighter ['haɪlaɪtə*] *n* (*pen*) surligneur (lumineux).

highly ['haɪlɪ] *ad* très, fort, hautement; **~ paid** très bien payé(e); **to speak ~ of** dire beaucoup de bien de.

highly-strung ['haɪlɪ'strʌŋ] *a* nerveux(euse), toujours tendu(e).

High Mass *n* grand-messe *f*.

highness ['haɪnɪs] *n* hauteur *f*; **Her H~** son Altesse *f*.

high-pitched [haɪ'pɪtʃt] *a* aigu(ë).

high-powered [haɪ'pauəd] *a* (*engine*) performant(e); (*fig: person*) dynamique; (*: job, businessman*) très important(e).

high-pressure ['haɪprɛʃə*] *a* à haute pression.

high-rise block ['haɪraɪz'blɔk] *n* tour *f* (d'habitation).

high school *n* lycée *m*; (*US*) établissement *m* d'enseignement supérieur.

high season *n* (*Brit*) haute saison.

high spirits *npl* pétulance *f*; **to be in ~** être plein(e) d'entrain.

high street *n* (*Brit*) grand-rue *f*.

highway ['haɪweɪ] *n* grand'route *f*, route nationale.

Highway Code *n* (*Brit*) code *m* de la route.

highwayman ['haɪweɪmən] *n* voleur *m* de grand chemin.

hijack ['haɪdʒæk] *vt* détourner (*par la force*) ♦ *n* (*also*: **~ing**) détournement *m* (d'avion).

hijacker ['haɪdʒækə*] *n* auteur *m* d'un détournement d'avion, pirate *m* de l'air.

hike [haɪk] *vi* aller à pied ♦ *n* excursion *f* à pied, randonnée *f*; (*col: in prices etc*) augmentation *f* ♦ *vt* (*col*) augmenter.

hiker ['haɪkə*] *n* promeneur/euse, excursionniste *m/f*.

hiking ['haɪkɪŋ] *n* excursions *fpl* à pied, randonnée *f*.

hilarious [hɪ'lɛərɪəs] *a* (*behaviour, event*) désopilant(e).

hilarity [hɪ'lærɪtɪ] *n* hilarité *f*.

hill [hɪl] *n* colline *f*; (*fairly high*) montagne *f*; (*on road*) côte *f*.

hillbilly ['hɪlbɪlɪ] *n* (*US*) montagnard/e du sud des USA; (*pej*) péquenaud *m*.

hillock ['hɪlək] *n* petite colline, butte *f*.

hillside ['hɪlsaɪd] n (flanc m de) coteau m.

hill start n (AUT) démarrage m en côte.

hilly ['hɪlɪ] a vallonné(e); montagneux(euse); (road) à fortes côtes.

hilt [hɪlt] n (of sword) garde f; **to the ~** (fig: support) à fond.

him [hɪm] pronoun (direct) le, l' + vowel or h mute; (stressed, indirect, after prep) lui; **I see ~** je le vois; **give ~ a book** donne-lui un livre; **after ~** après lui.

Himalayas [hɪmə'leɪəz] npl: **the ~** l'Himalaya m.

himself [hɪm'sɛlf] pronoun (reflexive) se; (emphatic) lui-même; (after prep) lui.

hind [haɪnd] a de derrière ♦ n biche f.

hinder ['hɪndə*] vt gêner; (delay) retarder; (prevent): **to ~ sb from doing** empêcher qn de faire.

hindquarters ['haɪnd'kwɔ:təz] npl (ZOOL) arrière-train m.

hindrance ['hɪndrəns] n gêne f, obstacle m.

hindsight ['haɪndsaɪt] n bon sens après coup; **with the benefit of ~** avec du recul, rétrospectivement.

Hindu ['hɪndu:] n Hindou/e.

hinge [hɪndʒ] n charnière f ♦ vi (fig): **to ~ on** dépendre de.

hint [hɪnt] n allusion f; (advice) conseil m ♦ vt: **to ~ that** insinuer que ♦ vi: **to ~ at** faire une allusion à; **to drop a ~** faire une allusion or insinuation; **give me a ~** (clue) mettez-moi sur la voie, donnez-moi une indication.

hip [hɪp] n hanche f; (BOT) fruit m de l'églantier or du rosier.

hip flask n flacon m (pour la poche).

hippie, hippy ['hɪpɪ] n hippie m/f.

hip pocket n poche-revolver f.

hippopotamus, pl ~es or **hippopotami** [hɪpə'pɔtəməs, -'pɔtəmaɪ] n hippopotame m.

hippy ['hɪpɪ] n = **hippie**.

hire ['haɪə*] vt (Brit: car, equipment) louer; (worker) embaucher, engager ♦ n location f; **for ~** à louer; (taxi) libre; **on ~** en location.

hire out vt louer.

hire(d) car n (Brit) voiture louée.

hire purchase (H.P.) n (Brit) achat m (or vente f) à tempérament or crédit; **to buy sth on ~** acheter qch en location-vente.

his [hɪz] pronoun le(la) sien(ne), les siens(siennes) ♦ a son(sa), ses pl; **this is ~** c'est à lui, c'est le sien.

hiss [hɪs] vi siffler ♦ n sifflement m.

histogram ['hɪstəgræm] n histogramme m.

historian [hɪ'stɔ:rɪən] n historien/ne.

historic(al) [hɪ'stɔrɪk(l)] a historique.

history ['hɪstərɪ] n histoire f; **medical ~** (of patient) passé médical.

histrionics [hɪstrɪ'ɔnɪks] n gestes mpl dramatiques, cinéma m (fig).

hit [hɪt] vt (pt, pp **hit**) frapper; (knock against) cogner; (reach: target) atteindre, toucher; (collide with: car) entrer en collision avec, heurter; (fig: affect) toucher; (find) tomber sur ♦ n coup m; (success) coup réussi; succès m; (song) chanson f à succès, tube m; **to ~ it off** with sb bien s'entendre avec qn; **to ~ the headlines** être à la une des journaux; **to ~ the road** (col) se mettre en route.

hit back vi: **to ~ back at sb** prendre sa revanche sur qn.

hit out at vt fus envoyer un coup à; (fig) attaquer.

hit (up)on vt fus (answer) trouver (par hasard); (solution) tomber sur (par hasard).

hit-and-run driver ['hɪtænd'rʌn-] n chauffard m.

hitch [hɪtʃ] vt (fasten) accrocher, attacher; (also: ~ **up**) remonter d'une saccade ♦ n (knot) nœud m; (difficulty) anicroche f, contretemps m; **to ~ a lift** faire du stop; **technical ~** incident m technique.

hitch up vt (horse, cart) atteler; see also **hitch**.

hitch-hike ['hɪtʃhaɪk] vi faire de l'auto-stop.

hitch-hiker ['hɪtʃhaɪkə*] n auto-stoppeur/euse.

hi-tech ['haɪ'tɛk] a à la pointe de la technologie, technologiquement avancé(e) ♦ n high-tech m.

hitherto [hɪðə'tu:] ad jusqu'ici, jusqu'à présent.

hitman ['hɪtmæn] n tueur m.

hit-or-miss ['hɪtə'mɪs] a fait(e) au petit bonheur; **it's ~ whether...** il est loin d'être certain que... + sub.

hit parade n hit parade m.

hive [haɪv] n ruche f; **the shop was a ~ of activity** (fig) le magasin était une véritable ruche.

hive off vt (col) mettre à part, séparer.

hl abbr (= hectolitre) hl.

HM abbr (= His (or Her) Majesty) SM.

HMG abbr (Brit) = His (or Her) Majesty's Government.

HMI n abbr (Brit SCOL) = His (or Her) Majesty's Inspector.

HMO n abbr (US: = health maintenance organization) organisme médical assurant un forfait entretien de santé.

HMS abbr (Brit) = His (or Her) Majesty's Ship.

HMSO n abbr (= His (or Her) Majesty's Stationery Office) ≈ Imprimerie nationale.

HNC n abbr (Brit: = Higher National Certificate) ≈ DUT m.

HND n abbr (Brit: = Higher National Diploma) ≈ licence f de sciences et techniques.

hoard [hɔ:d] n (of food) provisions fpl; réserves fpl; (of money) trésor m ♦ vt amasser.

hoarding ['hɔ:dɪŋ] n (Brit) panneau m d'affichage or publicitaire.

hoarfrost ['hɔ:frɔst] n givre m.

hoarse [hɔ:s] a enroué(e).

hoax [həuks] n canular m.

hob [hɔb] n plaque chauffante.

hobble ['hɔbl] vi boitiller.

hobby ['hɔbɪ] n passe-temps favori.

hobby-horse ['hɔbɪhɔ:s] n cheval m à bascule; (fig) dada m.

hobnob ['hɔbnɔb] vi: **to ~ with** frayer avec, fréquenter.

hobo ['həubəu] n (US) vagabond m.

hock [hɔk] n (Brit: wine) vin m du Rhin; (of animal, CULIN) jarret m; (col): **to be in ~** (person) avoir des dettes; (object) être en gage or au clou.

hockey ['hɔkɪ] n hockey m.

hocus-pocus ['həukəs'pəukəs] *n* (*trickery*) supercherie *f*; (*words: of magician*) formules *fpl* magiques; (*: jargon*) galimatias *m*.

hodgepodge ['hɔdʒpɔdʒ] *n* = **hotchpotch**.

hoe [həu] *n* houe *f*, binette *f* ♦ *vt* (*ground*) biner; (*plants etc*) sarcler.

hog [hɔg] *n* sanglier *m* ♦ *vt* (*fig*) accaparer; **to go the whole ~** aller jusqu'au bout.

hoist [hɔist] *n* palan *m* ♦ *vt* hisser.

hold [həuld] *vb* (*pt, pp* **held** [hɛld]) *vt* tenir; (*contain*) contenir; (*keep back*) retenir; (*believe*) maintenir; considérer; (*possess*) avoir; détenir ♦ *vi* (*withstand pressure*) tenir (bon); (*be valid*) valoir ♦ *n* prise *f*; (*fig*) influence *f*; (*NAUT*) cale *f*; **to catch** *or* **get (a) ~ of** saisir; **to get ~ of** (*fig*) trouver; **to get ~ of o.s.** se contrôler; **~ the line!** (*TEL*) ne quittez pas!; **to ~ one's own** (*fig*) (bien) se défendre; **to ~ office** (*POL*) avoir un portefeuille; **to ~ firm** *or* **fast** tenir bon; **he ~s the view that ...** il pense *or* estime que ..., d'après lui ...; **to ~ sb responsible for sth** tenir qn pour responsable de qch.

hold back *vt* retenir; (*secret*) cacher; **to ~ sb back from doing sth** empêcher qn de faire qch.

hold down *vt* (*person*) maintenir à terre; (*job*) occuper.

hold forth *vi* pérorer.

hold off *vt* tenir à distance ♦ *vi* (*rain*): **if the rain ~s off** s'il ne pleut pas, s'il ne se met pas à pleuvoir.

hold on *vi* tenir bon; (*wait*) attendre; **~ on!** (*TEL*) ne quittez-pas!

hold on to *vt fus* se cramponner à; (*keep*) conserver, garder.

hold out *vt* offrir ♦ *vi* (*resist*): **to ~ out (against)** résister (devant), tenir bon (devant).

hold over *vt* (*meeting etc*) ajourner, reporter.

hold up *vt* (*raise*) lever; (*support*) soutenir; (*delay*) retarder; (*: traffic*) ralentir; (*rob*) braquer.

holdall ['həuldɔ:l] *n* (*Brit*) fourre-tout *m inv*.

holder ['həuldə*] *n* (*of ticket, record*) détenteur/trice; (*of office, title, passport etc*) titulaire *m/f*.

holding ['həuldiŋ] *n* (*share*) intérêts *mpl*; (*farm*) ferme *f*.

holding company *n* holding *m*.

holdup ['həuldʌp] *n* (*robbery*) hold-up *m*; (*delay*) retard *m*; (*Brit: in traffic*) embouteillage *m*.

hole [həul] *n* trou *m* ♦ *vt* trouer, faire un trou dans; **~ in the heart** (*MED*) communication *f* interventriculaire; **to pick ~s (in)** (*fig*) chercher des poux (dans).

hole up *vi* se terrer.

holiday ['hɔlədi] *n* (*Brit: vacation*) vacances *fpl*; (*day off*) jour *m* de congé; (*public*) jour férié; **to be on ~** être en congé; **tomorrow is a ~** demain c'est fête, on a congé demain.

holiday camp *n* (*Brit: for children*) colonie *f* de vacances; (*: also:* **holiday centre**) camp *m* de vacances.

holidaymaker ['hɔlədimeikə*] *n* (*Brit*) vacancier/ière.

holiday pay *n* paie *f* des vacances.

holiday resort *n* centre *m* de villégiature *or* de vacances.

holiday season *n* période *f* des vacances.

holiness ['həulinis] *n* sainteté *f*.

Holland ['hɔlənd] *n* Hollande *f*.

hollow ['hɔləu] *a* creux(euse); (*fig*) faux(fausse) ♦ *n* creux *m*; (*in land*) dépression *f* (de terrain), cuvette *f* ♦ *vt*: **to ~ out** creuser, évider.

holly ['hɔli] *n* houx *m*.

hollyhock ['hɔlihɔk] *n* rose trémière.

holocaust ['hɔləkɔ:st] *n* holocauste *m*.

holster ['həulstə*] *n* étui *m* de revolver.

holy ['həuli] *a* saint(e); (*bread, water*) bénit(e); (*ground*) sacré(e).

Holy Communion *n* la (sainte) communion.

Holy Ghost, Holy Spirit *n* Saint-Esprit *m*.

Holy Land *n*: **the ~** la Terre Sainte.

holy orders *npl* ordres (majeurs).

homage ['hɔmidʒ] *n* hommage *m*; **to pay ~ to** rendre hommage à.

home [həum] *n* foyer *m*, maison *f*; (*country*) pays natal, patrie *f*; (*institution*) maison ♦ *a* de famille; (*ECON, POL*) national(e), intérieur(e); (*SPORT: team*) qui reçoit; (*: match, win*) sur leur (*or* notre) terrain ♦ *ad* chez soi, à la maison; au pays natal; (*right in: nail etc*) à fond; **at ~** chez soi, à la maison; **to go** (*or* **come**) **~** rentrer (chez soi), rentrer à la maison (*or* au pays); **make yourself at ~** faites comme chez vous; **near my ~** près de chez moi.

home in on *vt fus* (*missiles*) se diriger automatiquement vers *or* sur.

home address *n* domicile permanent.

home-brew [həum'bru:] *n* vin *m* (*or* bière *f*) maison.

homecoming ['həumkʌmiŋ] *n* retour *m* (au bercail).

home computer *n* ordinateur *m* domestique.

Home Counties *npl* les comtés autour de Londres.

home economics *n* économie *f* domestique.

home-grown ['həumgrəun] *a* (*not foreign*) du pays; (*from garden*) du jardin.

homeland ['həumlænd] *n* patrie *f*.

homeless ['həumlis] *a* sans foyer, sans abri; **the ~** *npl* les sans-abri *mpl*.

home loan *n* prêt *m* sur hypothèque.

homely ['həumli] *a* simple, sans prétention; accueillant(e).

home-made [həum'meid] *a* fait(e) à la maison.

Home Office *n* (*Brit*) ministère *m* de l'Intérieur.

homeopathy *etc* [həumi'ɔpəθi] (*US*) = **homoeopathy** *etc*.

home rule *n* autonomie *f*.

Home Secretary *n* (*Brit*) ministre *m* de l'Intérieur.

homesick ['həumsik] *a*: **to be ~** avoir le mal du pays; (*missing one's family*) s'ennuyer de sa famille.

homestead ['həumstɛd] *n* propriété *f*; (*farm*) ferme *f*.

home town *n* ville natale.

homeward ['həumwəd] *a* (*journey*) du retour.

homeward(s) ['həumwəd(z)] *ad* vers la maison.

homework ['həumwə:k] *n* devoirs *mpl*.
homicidal [hɔmɪ'saɪdl] *a* homicide.
homicide ['hɔmɪsaɪd] *n* (*US*) homicide *m*.
homily ['hɔmɪlɪ] *n* homélie *f*.
homing ['həumɪŋ] *a* (*device, missile*) à tête chercheuse; ~ **pigeon** pigeon voyageur.
homoeopath, (*US*) **homeopath** ['həumɪəupæθ] *n* homéopathe *m/f*.
homoeopathy, (*US*) **homeopathy** [həumɪ'ɔpəθɪ] *n* homéopathie *f*.
homogeneous [hɔməu'dʒi:nɪəs] *a* homogène.
homogenize [hə'mɔdʒənaɪz] *vt* homogénéiser.
homosexual [hɔməu'sɛksjuəl] *a*, *n* homosexuel(le).
Hon. *abbr* (= *honourable, honorary*) *dans un titre*.
Honduras [hɔn'djuərəs] *n* Honduras *m*.
hone [həun] *n* pierre *f* à aiguiser ♦ *vt* affûter, aiguiser.
honest ['ɔnɪst] *a* honnête; (*sincere*) franc(franche); **to be quite** ~ **with you** ... à dire vrai ....
honestly ['ɔnɪstlɪ] *ad* honnêtement; franchement.
honesty ['ɔnɪstɪ] *n* honnêteté *f*.
honey ['hʌnɪ] *n* miel *m*; (*US col: darling*) chéri/e.
honeycomb ['hʌnɪkəum] *n* rayon *m* de miel; (*pattern*) nid *m* d'abeilles, motif alvéolé ♦ *vt* (*fig*): **to** ~ **with** cribler de.
honeymoon ['hʌnɪmu:n] *n* lune *f* de miel, voyage *m* de noces.
honeysuckle ['hʌnɪsʌkl] *n* chèvrefeuille *m*.
Hong Kong ['hɔŋ'kɔŋ] *n* Hong Kong.
honk [hɔŋk] *n* (*AUT*) coup *m* de klaxon ♦ *vi* klaxonner.
Honolulu [hɔnə'lu:lu:] *n* Honolulu.
honorary ['ɔnərərɪ] *a* honoraire; (*duty, title*) honorifique.
honour, (*US*) **honor** ['ɔnə*] *vt* honorer ♦ *n* honneur *m*; **in** ~ **of** en l'honneur de.
hono(u)rable ['ɔnərəbl] *a* honorable.
hono(u)r-bound ['ɔnə'baund] *a*: **to be** ~ **to do** se devoir de faire.
hono(u)rs degree *n* (*SCOL*) licence avec mention.
Hons. *abbr* (*SCOL*) = **hono(u)rs degree**.
hood [hud] *n* capuchon *m*; (*Brit AUT*) capote *f*; (*US AUT*) capot *m*; (*col*) truand *m*.
hoodlum ['hu:dləm] *n* truand *m*.
hoodwink ['hudwɪŋk] *vt* tromper.
hoof, *pl* ~**s** *or* **hooves** [hu:f, hu:vz] *n* sabot *m*.
hook [huk] *n* crochet *m*; (*on dress*) agrafe *f*; (*for fishing*) hameçon *m* ♦ *vt* accrocher; (*dress*) agrafer; ~ **and eye** agrafe; **by** ~ **or by crook** de gré ou de force, coûte que coûte; **to be** ~**ed (on)** (*col*) être accroché(e) (par); (*person*) être dingue (de).
hook up *vt* (*RADIO, TV etc*) faire un duplex entre.
hooligan ['hu:lɪgən] *n* voyou *m*.
hoop [hu:p] *n* cerceau *m*; (*of barrel*) cercle *m*.
hoot [hu:t] *vi* (*AUT*) klaxonner; (*siren*) mugir; (*owl*) hululer ♦ *vt* (*jeer at*) huer ♦ *n* huée *f*; coup *m* de klaxon; mugissement *m*; hululement *m*; **to** ~ **with laughter** rire aux éclats.

hooter ['hu:tə*] *n* (*Brit AUT*) klaxon *m*; (*NAUT, factory*) sirène *f*.
hoover ® ['hu:və*] (*Brit*) *n* aspirateur *m* ♦ *vt* (*room*) passer l'aspirateur dans; (*carpet*) passer l'aspirateur sur.
hooves [hu:vz] *npl of* **hoof**.
hop [hɔp] *vi* sauter; (*on one foot*) sauter à cloche-pied ♦ *n* saut *m*.
hope [həup] *vt, vi* espérer ♦ *n* espoir *m*; **I** ~ **so** je l'espère; **I** ~ **not** j'espère que non.
hopeful ['həupful] *a* (*person*) plein(e) d'espoir; (*situation*) prometteur(euse), encourageant(e); **I'm** ~ **that she'll manage to come** j'ai bon espoir qu'elle pourra venir.
hopefully ['həupfulɪ] *ad* avec espoir, avec optimisme; ~, **they'll come back** espérons bien qu'ils reviendront.
hopeless ['həuplɪs] *a* désespéré(e), sans espoir; (*useless*) nul(le).
hopelessly ['həuplɪslɪ] *ad* (*live etc*) sans espoir; ~ **confused** *etc* complètement désorienté *etc*.
hopper ['hɔpə*] *n* (*chute*) trémie *f*.
hops [hɔps] *npl* houblon *m*.
horde [hɔ:d] *n* horde *f*.
horizon [hə'raɪzn] *n* horizon *m*.
horizontal [hɔrɪ'zɔntl] *a* horizontal(e).
hormone ['hɔ:məun] *n* hormone *f*.
horn [hɔ:n] *n* corne *f*; (*MUS*) cor *m*; (*AUT*) klaxon *m*.
horned [hɔ:nd] *a* (*animal*) à cornes.
hornet ['hɔ:nɪt] *n* frelon *m*.
horny ['hɔ:nɪ] *a* corné(e); (*hands*) calleux(euse); (*col: aroused*) excité(e).
horoscope ['hɔrəskəup] *n* horoscope *m*.
horrendous [hə'rɛndəs] *a* horrible, affreux(euse).
horrible ['hɔrɪbl] *a* horrible, affreux(euse).
horrid ['hɔrɪd] *a* méchant(e), désagréable.
horrific [hɔ'rɪfɪk] *a* horrible.
horrify ['hɔrɪfaɪ] *vt* horrifier.
horrifying ['hɔrɪfaɪɪŋ] *a* horrifiant(e).
horror ['hɔrə*] *n* horreur *f*.
horror film *n* film *m* d'épouvante.
horror-struck ['hɔrəstrʌk], **horror-stricken** ['hɔrəstrɪkn] *a* horrifié(e).
hors d'œuvre [ɔ:'də:vrə] *n* hors d'œuvre *m*.
horse [hɔ:s] *n* cheval *m*.
horseback ['hɔ:sbæk]: **on** ~ *a, ad* à cheval.
horsebox ['hɔ:sbɔks] *n* van *m*.
horse chestnut *n* marron *m* (d'Inde).
horse-drawn ['hɔ:sdrɔ:n] *a* tiré(e) par des chevaux.
horsefly ['hɔ:sflaɪ] *n* taon *m*.
horseman ['hɔ:smən] *n* cavalier *m*.
horsemanship ['hɔ:smənʃɪp] *n* talents *mpl* de cavalier.
horseplay ['hɔ:spleɪ] *n* chahut *m* (*blagues etc*).
horsepower (hp) ['hɔ:spauə*] *n* puissance *f* (en chevaux); cheval-vapeur *m* (CV).
horse-racing ['hɔ:sreɪsɪŋ] *n* courses *fpl* de chevaux.
horseradish ['hɔ:srædɪʃ] *n* raifort *m*.
horseshoe ['hɔ:sʃu:] *n* fer *m* à cheval.
horse show *n* concours *m* hippique.
horse-trading ['hɔ:streɪdɪŋ] *n* maquignonage *m*.
horse trials *npl* = **horse show**.

horsewhip ['hɔ:swip] *vt* cravacher.

horsewoman ['hɔ:swumən] *n* cavalière *f*.

horsey ['hɔ:sɪ] *a* féru(e) d'équitation *or* de cheval; *(appearance)* chevalin(e).

horticulture ['hɔ:tɪkʌltʃə*] *n* horticulture *f*.

hose [həuz] *n (also:* **~pipe)** tuyau *m; (also:* **garden ~)** tuyau d'arrosage.

hose down *vt* laver au jet.

hosiery ['həuzɪərɪ] *n (in shop)* (rayon *m* des) bas *mpl*.

hospice ['hɔspɪs] *n* hospice *m*.

hospitable ['hɔspɪtəbl] *a* hospitalier(ière).

hospital ['hɔspɪtl] *n* hôpital *m;* **in ~,** *(US)* **in the ~** à l'hôpital.

hospitality [hɔspɪ'tælɪtɪ] *n* hospitalité *f*.

hospitalize ['hɔspɪtəlaɪz] *vt* hospitaliser.

host [həust] *n* hôte *m; (in hotel etc)* patron *m; (TV, RADIO)* présentateur/trice, animateur/trice; *(large number):* **a ~ of** une foule de; *(REL)* hostie *f ♦ vt (TV programme)* présenter, animer.

hostage ['hɔstɪdʒ] *n* otage *m*.

host country *n* pays *m* d'accueil, pays-hôte *m*.

hostel ['hɔstl] *n* foyer *m; (also:* **youth ~)** auberge *f* de jeunesse.

hostelling ['hɔstlɪŋ] *n:* **to go (youth) ~** faire une virée *or* randonnée en séjournant dans des auberges de jeunesse.

hostess ['həustɪs] *n* hôtesse *f; (AVIAT)* hôtesse de l'air; *(in nightclub)* entraîneuse *f*.

hostile ['hɔstaɪl] *a* hostile.

hostility [hɔ'stɪlɪtɪ] *n* hostilité *f*.

hot [hɔt] *a* chaud(e); *(as opposed to only warm)* très chaud; *(spicy)* fort(e); *(fig)* acharné(e); brûlant(e); violent(e), passionné(e); **to be ~** *(person)* avoir chaud; *(thing)* être (très) chaud; *(weather)* faire chaud.

hot up *(Brit col) vi (situation)* devenir tendu(e); *(party)* s'animer ♦ *vt (pace)* accélérer, forcer; *(engine)* gonfler.

hot-air balloon [hɔt'ɛə-] *n* montgolfière *f*, ballon *m*.

hotbed ['hɔtbed] *n (fig)* foyer *m*, pépinière *f*.

hotchpotch ['hɔtʃpɔtʃ] *n (Brit)* mélange *m* hétéroclite.

hot dog *n* hot-dog *m*.

hotel [həu'tɛl] *n* hôtel *m*.

hotelier [həu'tɛlɪə*] *n* hôtelier/ière.

hotel industry *n* industrie hôtelière.

hotel room *n* chambre *f* d'hôtel.

hotfoot ['hɔtfut] *ad* à toute vitesse.

hotheaded [hɔt'hɛdɪd] *a* impétueux(euse).

hothouse ['hɔthaus] *n* serre chaude.

hot line *n (POL)* téléphone *m* rouge, ligne directe.

hotly ['hɔtlɪ] *ad* passionnément, violemment.

hotplate ['hɔtpleɪt] *n (on cooker)* plaque chauffante.

hotpot ['hɔtpɔt] *n (Brit CULIN)* ragoût *m*.

hot seat *n (fig)* poste chaud.

hot spot *n* point chaud.

hot spring *n* source thermale.

hot-tempered [hɔt'tɛmpəd] *a* emporté(e).

hot-water bottle [hɔt'wɔ:tə-] *n* bouillotte *f*.

hound [haund] *vt* poursuivre avec acharnement ♦ *n* chien courant; **the ~s** la meute.

hour ['auə*] *n* heure *f;* **at 30 miles an ~** ≈ à 50 km à l'heure; **lunch ~** heure du déjeuner; **to pay sb by the ~** payer qn à l'heure.

hourly ['auəlɪ] *a* toutes les heures; *(rate)* horaire; **~ paid** *a* payé(e) à l'heure.

house *n* [haus] *(pl:* **~s** ['hauzɪz] *)* maison *f; (POL)* chambre *f; (THEATRE)* salle *f;* auditoire *m ♦ vt* [hauz] *(person)* loger, héberger; **at** *(or* **to) my ~** chez moi; **the H~ (of Commons)** *(Brit)* la Chambre des communes; **the H~ (of Representatives)** *(US)* la Chambre des représentants; **on the ~** *(fig)* aux frais de la maison.

house arrest *n* assignation *f* à domicile.

houseboat ['hausbəut] *n* bateau (aménagé en habitation).

housebound ['hausbaund] *a* confiné(e) chez soi.

housebreaking ['hausbreɪkɪŋ] *n* cambriolage *m* (avec effraction).

house-broken ['hausbrəukn] *a (US)* = **house-trained**

housecoat ['hauskəut] *n* peignoir *m*.

household ['haushəuld] *n* ménage *m; (people)* famille *f*, maisonnée *f;* **~ name** nom connu de tout le monde.

householder ['haushəuldə*] *n* propriétaire *m/f; (head of house)* chef *m* de ménage *or* de famille.

househunting ['haushʌntɪŋ] *n:* **to go ~** se mettre en quête d'une maison *(or* d'un appartement).

housekeeper ['hauski:pə*] *n* gouvernante *f*.

housekeeping ['hauski:pɪŋ] *n (work)* ménage *m; (also:* **~ money)** argent *m* du ménage; *(COMPUT)* gestion *f* (des disques).

houseman ['hausmən] *n (Brit MED)* ≈ interne *m*.

house-proud ['hauspraud] *a* qui tient à avoir une maison impeccable.

house-to-house ['haustə'haus] *a (enquiries etc)* chez tous les habitants (du quartier *etc*).

house-trained ['haustreɪnd] *a (Brit: animal)* propre.

house-warming ['hauswɔ:mɪŋ] *n (also:* **~ party)** pendaison *f* de crémaillère.

housewife ['hauswaɪf] *n* ménagère *f;* femme *f* du foyer.

housework ['hauswə:k] *n* (travaux *mpl* du) ménage *m*.

housing ['hauzɪŋ] *n* logement *m ♦ cpd (problem, shortage)* de *or* du logement.

housing association *n* fondation *f* charitable fournissant des logements.

housing conditions *npl* conditions *fpl* de logement.

housing development, *(Brit)* **housing estate** *n* cité *f;* lotissement *m*.

hovel ['hɔvl] *n* taudis *m*.

hover ['hɔvə*] *vi* planer; **to ~ round sb** rôder *or* tourner autour de qn.

hovercraft ['hɔvəkrɑ:ft] *n* aéroglisseur *m*.

hoverport ['hɔvəpɔ:t] *n* hoverport *m*.

how [hau] *ad* comment; **~ are you?** comment allez-vous?; **~ do you do?** bonjour; *(on being introduced)* enchanté(e); **~ far is it to ...?** combien y a-t-il jusqu'à ...?; **~ long have you been here?** depuis combien de temps êtes-vous là?; **~ lovely!** que *or* comme c'est joli!; ~ **many/much?** combien?; ~ **many people/much** milk combien de gens/lait; ~ **old are you?** quel âge avez-vous?; ~**'s life?** (col) comment ça va?; ~ **about a drink?** si on buvait quelque chose?; ~ **is it that ...?** comment se fait-il que ... + sub?

however [hauˈɛvə*] cj pourtant, cependant ♦ ad de quelque façon or manière que + sub; (+ adjective) quelque or si ... que + sub; (in questions) comment.

howitzer [ˈhauɪtsə*] n (MIL) obusier m.

howl [ˈhaul] n hurlement m ♦ vi hurler.

howler [ˈhaulə*] n gaffe f, bourde f.

HP n abbr (Brit) = **hire purchase.**

hp abbr (AUT) = **horsepower.**

HQ n abbr (= headquarters) QG m.

HR n abbr (US) = **House of Representatives.**

HRH abbr (= His (or Her) Royal Highness) SAR.

hr(s) abbr (= hour(s)) h.

HS abbr (US) = **high school.**

HST abbr (US: = Hawaiian Standard Time) heure de Hawaii.

hub [hʌb] n (of wheel) moyeu m; (fig) centre m, foyer m.

hubbub [ˈhʌbʌb] n brouhaha m.

hub cap n (AUT) enjoliveur m.

HUD n abbr (US: = Department of Housing and Urban Development) ministère de l'urbanisme et du logement.

huddle [ˈhʌdl] vi: **to ~ together** se blottir les uns contre les autres.

hue [hju:] n teinte f, nuance f; ~ **and cry** n tollé (général), clameur f.

huff [hʌf] n: **in a ~** fâché(e); **to take the ~** prendre la mouche.

hug [hʌg] vt serrer dans ses bras; (shore, kerb) serrer ♦ n étreinte f; **to give sb a ~** serrer qn dans ses bras.

huge [hju:dʒ] a énorme, immense.

hulk [hʌlk] n (ship) vieux rafiot; (car, building) carcasse f; (person) mastodonte m, malabar m.

hulking [ˈhʌlkɪŋ] a balourd(e).

hull [hʌl] n (of ship, nuts) coque f; (of peas) cosse f.

hullabaloo [ˈhʌləbəˈlu:] n (col: noise) tapage m, raffut m.

hullo [həˈləu] excl = **hello.**

hum [hʌm] vt (tune) fredonner ♦ vi fredonner; (insect) bourdonner; (plane, tool) vrombir ♦ n fredonnement m; bourdonnement m; vrombissement m.

human [ˈhju:mən] a humain(e) ♦ n (also: ~ being) être humain.

humane [hju:ˈmeɪn] a humain(e), humanitaire.

humanism [ˈhju:mənɪzəm] n humanisme m.

humanitarian [hju:mænɪˈtɛərɪən] a humanitaire.

humanity [hju:ˈmænɪtɪ] n humanité f.

humanly [ˈhju:mənlɪ] ad humainement.

humanoid [ˈhju:mənɔɪd] a, n humanoïde (m/f).

humble [ˈhʌmbl] a humble, modeste ♦ vt humilier.

humbly [ˈhʌmblɪ] ad humblement, modestement.

humbug [ˈhʌmbʌg] n fumisterie f; (Brit: sweet) bonbon m à la menthe.

humdrum [ˈhʌmdrʌm] a monotone, routinier(ière).

humid [ˈhju:mɪd] a humide.

humidifier [hju:ˈmɪdɪfaɪə*] n humidificateur m.

humidity [hju:ˈmɪdɪtɪ] n humidité f.

humiliate [hju:ˈmɪlɪeɪt] vt humilier.

humiliation [hju:mɪlɪˈeɪʃən] n humiliation f.

humility [hju:ˈmɪlɪtɪ] n humilité f.

humorist [ˈhju:mərɪst] n humoriste m/f.

humorous [ˈhju:mərəs] a humoristique; (person) plein(e) d'humour.

humour, (US) **humor** [ˈhju:mə*] n humour m; (mood) humeur f ♦ vt (person) faire plaisir à; se prêter aux caprices de; **sense of ~** sens m de l'humour; **to be in a good/bad ~** être de bonne/mauvaise humeur.

humo(u)rless [ˈhu:məlɪs] a dépourvu(e) d'humour.

hump [hʌmp] n bosse f.

humpback [ˈhʌmpbæk] n bossu/e; (Brit: also: ~ **bridge**) dos-d'âne m.

humus [ˈhju:məs] n humus m.

hunch [hʌntʃ] n bosse f; (premonition) intuition f; **I have a ~ that** j'ai (comme une vague) idée que.

hunchback [ˈhʌntʃbæk] n bossu/e.

hunched [hʌntʃt] a arrondi(e), voûté(e).

hundred [ˈhʌndrəd] num cent; **about a ~ people** une centaine de personnes; ~**s of people** des centaines de gens; **I'm a ~ per cent sure** j'en suis absolument certain.

hundredweight [ˈhʌndrɪdweɪt] n (Brit) = 50.8 kg; 112 lb; (US) = 45.3 kg; 100 lb.

hung [hʌŋ] pt, pp of **hang.**

Hungarian [hʌŋˈgɛərɪən] a hongrois(e) ♦ n Hongrois/e; (LING) hongrois m.

Hungary [ˈhʌŋgərɪ] n Hongrie f.

hunger [ˈhʌŋgə*] n faim f ♦ vi: **to ~ for** avoir faim de, désirer ardemment.

hunger strike n grève f de la faim.

hungrily [ˈhʌŋgrəlɪ] ad voracement; (fig) avidement.

hungry [ˈhʌŋgrɪ] a affamé(e); **to be ~** avoir faim; ~ **for** (fig) avide de.

hung up a (col) complexé(e), bourré(e) de complexes.

hunk [hʌŋk] n gros morceau; (col: man) beau mec.

hunt [hʌnt] vt (seek) chercher; (SPORT) chasser ♦ vi chasser ♦ n chasse f.

hunt down vt pourchasser.

hunter [ˈhʌntə*] n chasseur m; (Brit: horse) cheval m de chasse.

hunting [ˈhʌntɪŋ] n chasse f.

hurdle [ˈhə:dl] n (for fences) claie f; (SPORT) haie f; (fig) obstacle m.

hurl [hə:l] vt lancer (avec violence).

hurrah, hurray [huˈrɑ:, huˈreɪ] n hourra m.

hurricane [ˈhʌrɪkən] n ouragan m.

hurried [ˈhʌrɪd] a pressé(e), précipité(e); (work) fait(e) à la hâte.

hurriedly [ˈhʌrɪdlɪ] ad précipitamment, à la hâte.

hurry [ˈhʌrɪ] n hâte f, précipitation f ♦ vi se presser, se dépêcher ♦ vt (person) faire presser, faire se dépêcher; (work) presser; **to be in a ~** être pressé(e); **to do sth in a**

~ faire qch en vitesse; **to ~ in/out** entrer/
sortir précipitamment; **to ~ home** se dépêcher de rentrer.

hurry along *vi* marcher d'un pas pressé.

hurry away, hurry off *vi* partir
précipitamment.

hurry up *vi* se dépêcher.

hurt [hɜːt] *vb* (*pt, pp* **hurt**) *vt* (*cause pain to*)
faire mal à; (*injure, fig*) blesser; (*damage:
business, etc*) nuire à, faire du tort
à ♦ *vi* faire mal ♦ *a* blessé(e); **I ~ my arm** je
me suis fait mal au bras; **where does it ~?**
où avez-vous mal?, où est-ce que ça vous fait
mal?

hurtful ['hɜːtful] *a* (*remark*) blessant(e).

hurtle ['hɜːtl] *vt* lancer (de toutes ses forces) ♦
vi: **to ~ past** passer en trombe; **to ~ down**
dégringoler.

husband ['hʌzbənd] *n* mari *m*.

hush [hʌʃ] *n* calme *m*, silence *m* ♦ *vt* faire
taire; **~!** chut!

hush up *vt* (*fact*) étouffer.

hush-hush [hʌʃ'hʌʃ] *a* (*col*) ultra-secret(ète).

husk [hʌsk] *n* (*of wheat*) balle *f*; (*of rice,
maize*) enveloppe *f*; (*of peas*) cosse *f*.

husky ['hʌskɪ] *a* rauque; (*burly*) costaud(e) ♦
n chien *m* esquimau *or* de traîneau.

hustings ['hʌstɪŋz] *npl* (*Brit POL*) plate-forme
électorale.

hustle ['hʌsl] *vt* pousser, bousculer ♦ *n*
bousculade *f*; **~ and bustle** *n* tourbillon *m*
(d'activité).

hut [hʌt] *n* hutte *f*; (*shed*) cabane *f*.

hutch [hʌtʃ] *n* clapier *m*.

hyacinth ['haɪəsɪnθ] *n* jacinthe *f*.

hybrid ['haɪbrɪd] *a, n* hybride *(m)*.

hydrant ['haɪdrənt] *n* prise *f* d'eau; (*also:* **fire
~**) bouche *f* d'incendie.

hydraulic [haɪ'drɔːlɪk] *a* hydraulique.

hydraulics [haɪ'drɔːlɪks] *n* hydraulique *f*.

hydrochloric ['haɪdrəu'klɔrɪk] *a:* **~ acid** acide
m chlorhydrique.

hydroelectric ['haɪdrəuɪ'lɛktrɪk] *a* hydro-
électrique.

hydrofoil ['haɪdrəfɔɪl] *n* hydrofoil *m*.

hydrogen ['haɪdrədʒən] *n* hydrogène *m*.

hydrogen bomb *n* bombe *f* à hydrogène.

hydrophobia ['haɪdrə'fəubɪə] *n* hydrophobie *f*.

hydroplane ['haɪdrəpleɪn] *n* (*seaplane*) hydravion *m*; (*jetfoil*) hydroglisseur *m*.

hyena [haɪ'iːnə] *n* hyène *f*.

hygiene ['haɪdʒiːn] *n* hygiène *f*.

hygienic [haɪ'dʒiːnɪk] *a* hygiénique.

hymn [hɪm] *n* hymne *m*; cantique *m*.

hype [haɪp] *n* (*col*) matraquage *m* publicitaire
or médiatique.

hyperactive ['haɪpər'æktɪv] *a* hyperactif(ive).

hypermarket ['haɪpəmɑːkɪt] *n* (*Brit*)
hypermarché *m*.

hypertension ['haɪpə'tɛnʃən] *n* (*MED*)
hypertension *f*.

hyphen ['haɪfn] *n* trait *m* d'union.

hypnosis [hɪp'nəusɪs] *n* hypnose *f*.

hypnotic [hɪp'nɔtɪk] *a* hypnotique.

hypnotism ['hɪpnətɪzəm] *n* hypnotisme *m*.

hypnotist ['hɪpnətɪst] *n* hypnotiseur/euse.

hypnotize ['hɪpnətaɪz] *vt* hypnotiser.

hypoallergenic ['haɪpəuæləˈdʒɛnɪk] *a*
hypoallergique.

hypochondriac [haɪpə'kɔndrɪæk] *n*
hypocondriaque *m/f*.

hypocrisy [hɪ'pɔkrɪsɪ] *n* hypocrisie *f*.

hypocrite ['hɪpəkrɪt] *n* hypocrite *m/f*.

hypocritical [hɪpə'krɪtɪkl] *a* hypocrite.

hypodermic [haɪpə'dəːmɪk] *a* hypodermique ♦
n (*syringe*) seringue *f* hypodermique.

hypothermia [haɪpə'θəːmɪə] *n* hypothermie *f*.

hypothesis, *pl* **hypotheses** [haɪ'pɔθɪsɪs, -siːz]
n hypothèse *f*.

hypothetic(al) [haɪpə'θɛtɪk(l)] *a* hypothétique.

hysterectomy [hɪstə'rɛktəmɪ] *n* hystérectomie
f.

hysteria [hɪ'stɪərɪə] *n* hystérie *f*.

hysterical [hɪ'stɛrɪkl] *a* hystérique; **to become
~** avoir une crise de nerfs.

hysterics [hɪ'stɛrɪks] *npl* (*violente*) crise de
nerfs; (*laughter*) crise de rire; **to have ~**
avoir une crise de nerfs; attraper un fou rire.

Hz *abbr* (= *hertz*) Hz.

I

I, i [aɪ] *n* (*letter*) I, i *m*; **I for Isaac,** (*US*) **I for
Item** I comme Irma.

I [aɪ] *pronoun* je; (*before vowel*) j'; (*stressed*)
moi ♦ *abbr* (= *island, isle*) I.

IA *abbr* (*US POST*) = Iowa.

IAEA *n abbr* = **International Atomic Energy
Agency.**

IBA *n abbr* (*Brit:* = *Independent Broadcasting
Authority*) ≈ CNCL *f* (= *Commission
nationale de la communication audio-
visuelle*).

Iberian [aɪ'bɪərɪən] *a* ibérique, ibérien(ne).

Iberian Peninsula *n:* **the ~** la péninsule
Ibérique.

IBEW *n abbr* (*US:* = *International Brotherhood of Electrical Workers*) syndicat international des électriciens.

i/c *abbr* (*Brit*) = **in charge.**

ICC *n abbr* (= *International Chamber of
Commerce*) CCI *f*; (*US*) = *Interstate
Commerce Commission.*

ice [aɪs] *n* glace *f*; (*on road*) verglas *m* ♦ *vt*
(*cake*) glacer; (*drink*) faire rafraîchir ♦ *vi*
(*also:* **~ over**) geler; (*also:* **~ up**) se givrer;
to put sth on ~ (*fig*) mettre qch en attente.

Ice Age *n* ère *f* glaciaire.

ice axe *n* piolet *m*.

iceberg ['aɪsbəːg] *n* iceberg *m*; **the tip of the
~** (*also fig*) la partie émergée de l'iceberg.

icebox ['aɪsbɔks] *n* (*US*) réfrigérateur *m*;
(*Brit*) compartiment *m* à glace; (*insulated
box*) glacière *f*.

icebreaker ['aɪsbreɪkə*] *n* brise-glace *m*.

ice bucket *n* seau *m* à glace.

ice-cold [aɪs'kəuld] *a* glacé(e).

ice cream *n* glace *f*.

ice cube *n* glaçon *m*.

iced [aɪst] *a* (*drink*) frappé(e); (*coffee, tea,*

also cake) glacé(e).
ice hockey *n* hockey *m* sur glace.
Iceland ['aislənd] *n* Islande *f.*
Icelander ['aisləndə•] *n* Islandais/e.
Icelandic [ais'lændik] *a* islandais(e) ♦ *n* (*LING*) islandais *m.*
ice lolly *n* (*Brit*) esquimau *m.*
ice pick *n* pic *m* à glace.
ice rink *n* patinoire *f.*
ice-skate ['aisskeit] *n* patin *m* à glace ♦ *vi* faire du patin à glace.
ice-skating ['aisskeitiŋ] *n* patinage *m* (sur glace).
icicle ['aisikl] *n* glaçon *m* (*naturel*).
icing ['aisiŋ] *n* (*AVIAT etc*) givrage *m*; (*CULIN*) glaçage *m.*
icing sugar *n* (*Brit*) sucre *m* glace.
ICJ *n abbr* = **International Court of Justice.**
icon ['aikɔn] *n* icône *f.*
ICR *n abbr* (*US*) = *Institute for Cancer Research.*
ICU *n abbr* = **intensive care unit.**
icy ['aisi] *a* glacé(e); (*road*) verglacé(e); (*weather, temperature*) glacial(e).
ID *abbr* (*US POST*) = *Idaho.*
I'd [aid] = **I would, I had.**
ID card *n* = **identity card.**
IDD *n abbr* (*Brit TEL*: = *international direct dialling*) *automatique international.*
idea [ai'diə] *n* idée *f*; **good** ~! bonne idée!; **to have an** ~ **that ...** avoir idée que ...; **I haven't the least** ~ je n'ai pas la moindre idée.
ideal [ai'diəl] *n* idéal *m* ♦ *a* idéal(e).
idealist [ai'diəlist] *n* idéaliste *m/f.*
ideally [ai'diəli] *ad* idéalement, dans l'idéal; ~ **the book should have ...** l'idéal serait que le livre ait ....
identical [ai'dentikl] *a* identique.
identification [aidentifi'keiʃən] *n* identification *f*; **means of** ~ pièce *f* d'identité.
identify [ai'dentifai] *vt* identifier ♦ *vi*: **to** ~ **with** s'identifier à.
Identikit [ai'dentikit] *n* ®: ~ **(picture)** portrait-robot *m.*
identity [ai'denti] *n* identité *f.*
identity card *n* carte *f* d'identité.
identity parade *n* (*Brit*) parade *f* d'identification.
ideological [aidiə'lɔdʒikl] *a* idéologique.
ideology [aidi'ɔlədʒi] *n* idéologie *f.*
idiocy ['idiəsi] *n* idiotie *f*, stupidité *f.*
idiom ['idiəm] *n* langue *f*, idiome *m*; (*phrase*) expression *f* idiomatique.
idiomatic [idiə'mætik] *a* idiomatique.
idiosyncrasy [idiəu'siŋkrəsi] *n* particularité *f*, caractéristique *f.*
idiot ['idiət] *n* idiot/e, imbécile *m/f.*
idiotic [idi'ɔtik] *a* idiot(e), bête, stupide.
idle ['aidl] *a* sans occupation, désœuvré(e); (*lazy*) oisif(ive), paresseux(euse); (*unemployed*) au chômage; (*machinery*) au repos; (*question, pleasures*) vain(e), futile ♦ *vi* (*engine*) tourner au ralenti; **to lie** ~ être arrêté, ne pas fonctionner.
idle away *vt*: **to** ~ **away one's time** passer son temps à ne rien faire.
idleness ['aidlnis] *n* désœuvrement *m*; oisiveté *f.*

idler ['aidlə•] *n* désœuvré/e; oisif/ive.
idle time *n* (*COMM*) temps mort.
idol ['aidl] *n* idole *f.*
idolize ['aidəlaiz] *vt* idolâtrer, adorer.
idyllic [i'dilik] *a* idyllique.
i.e. *abbr* (= *id est: that is*) c. à d., c'est-à-dire.
if [if] *cj* si ♦ *n*: **there are a lot of** ~**s and buts** il y a beaucoup de si *mpl* et de mais *mpl*; **I'd be pleased** ~ **you could do it** je serais très heureux si vous pouviez le faire; ~ **necessary** si nécessaire, le cas échéant; ~ **only he were here** si seulement il était là; ~ **only to show him my gratitude** ne serait-ce que pour lui témoigner ma gratitude.
igloo ['iglu:] *n* igloo *m.*
ignite [ig'nait] *vt* mettre le feu à, enflammer ♦ *vi* s'enflammer.
ignition [ig'niʃən] *n* (*AUT*) allumage *m*; **to switch on/off the** ~ mettre/couper le contact.
ignition key *n* (*AUT*) clé *f* de contact.
ignoble [ig'nəubl] *a* ignoble, indigne.
ignominious [ignə'miniəs] *a* honteux(euse), ignominieux(euse).
ignoramus [ignə'reiməs] *n* personne *f* ignare.
ignorance ['ignərəns] *n* ignorance *f*; **to keep sb in** ~ **of sth** tenir qn dans l'ignorance de qch.
ignorant ['ignərənt] *a* ignorant(e); **to be** ~ **of** (*subject*) ne rien connaître en; (*events*) ne pas être au courant de.
ignore [ig'nɔ:•] *vt* ne tenir aucun compte de, ne pas relever; (*person*) faire semblant de ne pas reconnaître, ignorer; (*fact*) méconnaître.
ikon ['aikɔn] *n* = **icon.**
IL *abbr* (*US POST*) = *Illinois.*
ILA *n abbr* (*US*: = *International Longshoremen's Association*) *syndicat international des dockers.*
ILEA ['iliə] *n abbr* (*Brit*: = *Inner London Education Authority*) *services londoniens de l'enseignement.*
ILGWU *n abbr* (*US*: = *International Ladies' Garment Workers Union*) *syndicat employés de l'habillement féminin.*
ill [il] *a* (*sick*) malade; (*bad*) mauvais(e) ♦ *n* mal *m* ♦ *ad*: **to speak/think** ~ **of sb** dire/penser du mal de qn; **to take** *or* **be taken** ~ tomber malade.
I'll [ail] = **I will, I shall.**
ill-advised [iləd'vaizd] *a* (*decision*) peu judicieux(euse); (*person*) malavisé(e).
ill-at-ease [ilət'i:z] *a* mal à l'aise.
ill-considered [ilkən'sidəd] *a* (*plan*) inconsidéré(e), irréfléchi(e).
ill-disposed [ildis'pəuzd] *a*: **to be** ~ **towards sb/sth** être mal disposé(e) envers qn/qch.
illegal [i'li:gl] *a* illégal(e).
illegally [i'li:gəli] *ad* illégalement.
illegible [i'ledʒibl] *a* illisible.
illegitimate [ili'dʒitimət] *a* illégitime.
ill-fated [il'feitid] *a* malheureux(euse); (*day*) néfaste.
ill-favoured, (*US*) ill-favored [il'feivəd] *a* déplaisant(e).
ill feeling *n* ressentiment *m*, rancune *f.*
ill-gotten ['ilgɔtn] *a* (*gains etc*) mal acquis(e).
illicit [i'lisit] *a* illicite.
ill-informed [ilin'fɔ:md] *a* (*judgment*)

erroné(e); (*person*) mal renseigné(e).
illiterate [ɪ'lɪtərət] *a* illettré(e); (*letter*) plein(e) de fautes.
ill-mannered [ɪl'mænəd] *a* impoli(e), grossier(ière).
illness ['ɪlnɪs] *n* maladie *f*.
illogical [ɪ'lɒdʒɪkl] *a* illogique.
ill-suited [ɪl'su:tɪd] *a* (*couple*) mal assorti(e); **he is ~ to the job** il n'est pas vraiment fait pour ce travail.
ill-timed [ɪl'taɪmd] *a* inopportun(e).
ill-treat [ɪl'tri:t] *vt* maltraiter.
ill-treatment [ɪl'tri:tmənt] *n* mauvais traitement.
illuminate [ɪ'lu:mɪneɪt] *vt* (*room, street*) éclairer; (*building*) illuminer; **~d sign** *n* enseigne lumineuse.
illuminating [ɪ'lu:mɪneɪtɪŋ] *a* éclairant(e).
illumination [ɪlu:mɪ'neɪʃən] *n* éclairage *m*; illumination *f*.
illusion [ɪ'lu:ʒən] *n* illusion *f*; **to be under the ~ that** avoir l'illusion que.
illusive, illusory [ɪ'lu:sɪv, ɪ'lu:sərɪ] *a* illusoire.
illustrate ['ɪləstreɪt] *vt* illustrer.
illustration [ɪlə'streɪʃən] *n* illustration *f*.
illustrator ['ɪləstreɪtə*] *n* illustrateur/trice.
illustrious [ɪ'lʌstrɪəs] *a* illustre.
ill will *n* malveillance *f*.
ILO *n abbr* (= *International Labour Organization*) OIT *f*.
ILWU *n abbr* (*US*: = *International Longshoremen's and Warehousemen's Union*) syndicat international des dockers et des magaziniers.
I'm [aɪm] = **I am**.
image ['ɪmɪdʒ] *n* image *f*; (*public face*) image de marque.
imagery ['ɪmɪdʒərɪ] *n* images *fpl*.
imaginable [ɪ'mædʒɪnəbl] *a* imaginable.
imaginary [ɪ'mædʒɪnərɪ] *a* imaginaire.
imagination [ɪmædʒɪ'neɪʃən] *n* imagination *f*.
imaginative [ɪ'mædʒɪnətɪv] *a* imaginatif(ive), plein(e) d'imagination.
◆ imagine [ɪ'mædʒɪn] *vt* s'imaginer; (*suppose*) imaginer, supposer.
imbalance [ɪm'bæləns] *n* déséquilibre *m*.
imbecile ['ɪmbəsi:l] *n* imbécile *m/f*.
imbue [ɪm'bju:] *vt*: **to ~ sth with** imprégner qch de.
IMF *n abbr* = **International Monetary Fund**.
imitate ['ɪmɪteɪt] *vt* imiter.
imitation [ɪmɪ'teɪʃən] *n* imitation *f*.
imitator ['ɪmɪteɪtə*] *n* imitateur/trice.
immaculate [ɪ'mækjʊlət] *a* impeccable; (*REL*) immaculé(e).
immaterial [ɪmə'tɪərɪəl] *a* sans importance, insignifiant(e).
immature [ɪmə'tjʊə*] *a* (*fruit*) qui n'est pas mûr(e); (*person*) qui manque de maturité.
immaturity [ɪmə'tjʊərɪtɪ] *n* immaturité *f*.
immeasurable [ɪ'meʒrəbl] *a* incommensurable.
immediacy [ɪ'mi:dɪəsɪ] *n* (*of events etc*) caractère *or* rapport immédiat; (*of needs*) urgence *f*.
immediate [ɪ'mi:dɪət] *a* immédiat(e).
immediately [ɪ'mi:dɪətlɪ] *ad* (*at once*) immédiatement; **~ next to** juste à côté de.
immense [ɪ'mens] *a* immense; énorme.
immensity [ɪ'mensɪtɪ] *n* immensité *f*.

immerse [ɪ'mə:s] *vt* immerger, plonger; **to ~ sth in** plonger qch dans.
immersion heater [ɪ'mə:ʃən-] *n* (*Brit*) chauffe-eau *m* électrique.
immigrant ['ɪmɪgrənt] *n* immigrant/e; (*already established*) immigré/e.
immigration [ɪmɪ'greɪʃən] *n* immigration *f*.
immigration authorities *npl* service *m* de l'immigration.
immigration laws *npl* lois *fpl* sur l'immigration.
imminent ['ɪmɪnənt] *a* imminent(e).
immobile [ɪ'məʊbaɪl] *a* immobile.
immobilize [ɪ'məʊbɪlaɪz] *vt* immobiliser.
immoderate [ɪ'mɒdərət] *a* immodéré(e), démesuré(e).
immodest [ɪ'mɒdɪst] *a* (*indecent*) indécent(e); (*boasting*) pas modeste, présomptueux(euse).
immoral [ɪ'mɒrl] *a* immoral(e).
immorality [ɪmə'rælɪtɪ] *n* immoralité *f*.
immortal [ɪ'mɔ:tl] *a, n* immortel(le).
immortalize [ɪ'mɔ:tlaɪz] *vt* immortaliser.
immovable [ɪ'mu:vəbl] *a* (*object*) fixe; immobilier(ière); (*person*) inflexible; (*opinion*) immuable.
immune [ɪ'mju:n] *a*: **~ (to)** immunisé(e) (contre).
immunity [ɪ'mju:nɪtɪ] *n* immunité *f*; **diplomatic ~** immunité diplomatique.
immunization [ɪmjʊnaɪ'zeɪʃən] *n* immunisation *f*.
immunize ['ɪmjʊnaɪz] *vt* immuniser.
imp [ɪmp] *n* (*small devil*) lutin *m*; (*child*) petit diable.
impact ['ɪmpækt] *n* choc *m*, impact *m*; (*fig*) impact.
impair [ɪm'peə*] *vt* détériorer, diminuer.
impale [ɪm'peɪl] *vt* empaler.
impart [ɪm'pɑ:t] *vt* (*make known*) communiquer, transmettre; (*bestow*) confier, donner.
impartial [ɪm'pɑ:ʃl] *a* impartial(e).
impartiality [ɪmpɑ:ʃɪ'ælɪtɪ] *n* impartialité *f*.
impassable [ɪm'pɑ:səbl] *a* infranchissable; (*road*) impraticable.
impasse [æm'pɑ:s] *n* (*fig*) impasse *f*.
impassioned [ɪm'pæʃənd] *a* passionné(e).
impassive [ɪm'pæsɪv] *a* impassible.
impatience [ɪm'peɪʃəns] *n* impatience *f*.
impatient [ɪm'peɪʃənt] *a* impatient(e); **to get** *or* **grow ~** s'impatienter.
impeach [ɪm'pi:tʃ] *vt* accuser, attaquer; (*public official*) mettre en accusation.
impeachment [ɪm'pi:tʃmənt] *n* (*LAW*) (mise *f* en) accusation *f*.
impeccable [ɪm'pekəbl] *a* impeccable, parfait(e).
impecunious [ɪmpɪ'kju:nɪəs] *a* sans ressources.
impede [ɪm'pi:d] *vt* gêner.
impediment [ɪm'pedɪmənt] *n* obstacle *m*; (*also*: **speech ~**) défaut *m* d'élocution.
impel [ɪm'pel] *vt* (*force*): **to ~ sb (to do sth)** forcer qn (à faire qch).
impending [ɪm'pendɪŋ] *a* imminent(e).
impenetrable [ɪm'penɪtrəbl] *a* impénétrable.
imperative [ɪm'perətɪv] *a* nécessaire; urgent(e), pressant(e); (*tone*) impérieux(euse) ◆ *n* (*LING*) impératif *m*.

imperceptible [ɪmpə'sɛptɪbl] a imperceptible.

imperfect [ɪm'pɔ:fɪkt] a imparfait(e); (goods etc) défectueux(euse) ♦ n (LING: also: ~ **tense**) imparfait m.

imperfection [ɪmpɔ:'fɛkʃən] n imperfection f; défectuosité f.

imperial [ɪm'pɪərɪəl] a impérial(e); (Brit: measure) légal(e).

imperialism [ɪm'pɪərɪəlɪzəm] n impérialisme m.

imperil [ɪm'pɛrɪl] vt mettre en péril.

imperious [ɪm'pɪərɪəs] a impérieux(euse).

impersonal [ɪm'pɔ:sənl] a impersonnel(le).

impersonate [ɪm'pɔ:səneɪt] vt se faire passer pour; (THEATRE) imiter.

impersonation [ɪmpɔ:sə'neɪʃən] n (LAW) usurpation f d'identité; (THEATRE) imitation f.

impersonator [ɪm'pɔ:səneɪtə*] n imposteur m; (THEATRE) imitateur/trice.

impertinence [ɪm'pɔ:tɪnəns] n impertinence f, insolence f.

impertinent [ɪm'pɔ:tɪnənt] a impertinent(e), insolent(e).

imperturbable [ɪmpə'tɔ:bəbl] a imperturbable.

impervious [ɪm'pɔ:vɪəs] a imperméable; (fig): ~ **to** insensible à; inaccessible à.

impetuous [ɪm'pɛtjuəs] a impétueux(euse), fougueux(euse).

impetus ['ɪmpətəs] n impulsion f; (of runner) élan m.

impinge [ɪm'pɪndʒ]: **to ~ on** vt fus (person) affecter, toucher; (rights) empiéter sur.

impish ['ɪmpɪʃ] a espiègle.

implacable [ɪm'plækəbl] a implacable.

implant [ɪm'plɑ:nt] vt (MED) implanter; (fig) inculquer.

implausible [ɪm'plɔ:zɪbl] a peu plausible.

implement n ['ɪmplɪmənt] outil m, instrument m; (for cooking) ustensile m ♦ vt ['ɪmplɪmɛnt] exécuter, mettre à effet.

implicate ['ɪmplɪkeɪt] vt impliquer, compromettre.

implication [ɪmplɪ'keɪʃən] n implication f; **by ~** indirectement.

implicit [ɪm'plɪsɪt] a implicite; (complete) absolu(e), sans réserve.

implicitly [ɪm'plɪsɪtlɪ] ad implicitement; absolument, sans réserve.

implore [ɪm'plɔ:*] vt implorer, supplier.

imply [ɪm'plaɪ] vt (hint) suggérer, laisser entendre; (mean) indiquer, supposer.

impolite [ɪmpə'laɪt] a impoli(e).

imponderable [ɪm'pɔndərəbl] a impondérable.

import vt [ɪm'pɔ:t] importer ♦ n ['ɪmpɔ:t] (COMM) importation f; (meaning) portée f, signification f ♦ cpd (duty, licence etc) d'importation.

importance [ɪm'pɔ:tns] n importance f; **to be of great/little ~** avoir beaucoup/peu d'importance.

important [ɪm'pɔ:tnt] a important(e); **it is ~ that** il importe que, il est important que; **it's not ~** c'est sans importance, ce n'est pas important.

importantly [ɪm'pɔ:tntlɪ] ad (with an air of importance) d'un air important; (essentially): **but, more ~** ... mais, (ce qui est) plus important encore ....

importation [ɪmpɔ:'teɪʃən] n importation f.

imported [ɪm'pɔ:tɪd] a importé(e), d'importation.

importer [ɪm'pɔ:tə*] n importateur/trice.

impose [ɪm'pəuz] vt imposer ♦ vi: **to ~ on sb** abuser de la gentillesse de qn.

imposing [ɪm'pəuzɪŋ] a imposant(e), impressionnant(e).

imposition [ɪmpə'zɪʃən] n (of tax etc) imposition f; **to be an ~ on** (person) abuser de la gentillesse or la bonté de.

impossibility [ɪmpɔsə'bɪlɪtɪ] n impossibilité f.

impossible [ɪm'pɔsɪbl] a impossible; **it is ~ for me to leave** il m'est impossible de partir.

impostor [ɪm'pɔstə*] n imposteur m.

impotence ['ɪmpətns] n impuissance f.

impotent ['ɪmpətnt] a impuissant(e).

impound [ɪm'paund] vt confisquer, saisir.

impoverished [ɪm'pɔvərɪʃt] a pauvre, appauvri(e).

impracticable [ɪm'præktɪkəbl] a impraticable.

impractical [ɪm'præktɪkl] a pas pratique; (person) qui manque d'esprit pratique.

imprecise [ɪmprɪ'saɪs] a imprécis(e).

impregnable [ɪm'prɛgnəbl] a (fortress) imprenable; (fig) inattaquable; irréfutable.

impregnate ['ɪmprɛgneɪt] vt imprégner; (fertilize) féconder.

impresario [ɪmprɪ'sɑ:rɪəu] n impresario m.

impress [ɪm'prɛs] vt impressionner, faire impression sur; (mark) imprimer, marquer; **to ~ sth on sb** faire bien comprendre qch à qn.

impression [ɪm'prɛʃən] n impression f; (of stamp, seal) empreinte f; **to make a good/bad ~ on sb** faire bonne/mauvaise impression sur qn; **to be under the ~ that** avoir l'impression que.

impressionable [ɪm'prɛʃnəbl] a impressionnable, sensible.

impressionist [ɪm'prɛʃnɪst] n impressionniste m/f.

impressive [ɪm'prɛsɪv] a impressionnant(e).

imprint ['ɪmprɪnt] n empreinte f; (PUBLISHING) notice f; (: label) nom m (de collection or d'éditeur).

imprinted [ɪm'prɪntɪd] a: ~ **on** imprimé(e) sur; (fig) imprimé(e) or gravé(e) dans.

imprison [ɪm'prɪzn] vt emprisonner, mettre en prison.

imprisonment [ɪm'prɪznmənt] n emprisonnement m.

improbable [ɪm'prɔbəbl] a improbable; (excuse) peu plausible.

impromptu [ɪm'prɔmptju:] a impromptu(e) ♦ ad impromptu.

improper [ɪm'prɔpə*] a (wrong) incorrect(e); (unsuitable) déplacé(e), de mauvais goût; indécent(e).

impropriety [ɪmprə'praɪətɪ] n inconvenance f; (of expression) impropriété f.

improve [ɪm'pru:v] vt améliorer ♦ vi s'améliorer; (pupil etc) faire des progrès.

improve (up)on vt fus (offer) enchérir sur.

improvement [ɪm'pru:vmənt] n amélioration f; (of pupil etc) progrès m; **to make ~s to** apporter des améliorations à.

improvisation [ɪmprəvaɪ'zeɪʃən] n improvisation f.

improvise ['ɪmprəvaɪz] *vt, vi* improviser.
imprudence [ɪm'pruːdns] *n* imprudence *f*.
imprudent [ɪm'pruːdnt] *a* imprudent(e).
impudent ['ɪmpjudnt] *a* impudent(e).
impugn [ɪm'pjuːn] *vt* contester, attaquer.
impulse ['ɪmpʌls] *n* impulsion *f*; **on ~** impulsivement, sur un coup de tête.
impulse buy *n* achat *m* d'impulsion.
impulsive [ɪm'pʌlsɪv] *a* impulsif(ive).
impunity [ɪm'pjuːnɪtɪ] *n*: **with ~** impunément.
impure [ɪm'pjuə*] *a* impur(e).
impurity [ɪm'pjuərɪtɪ] *n* impureté *f*.
IN *abbr* (*US POST*) = Indiana.
in [ɪn] *prep* dans; (*with time: during, within*): **~ May/2 days** en mai/2 jours; (*: after*): **~ 2 weeks** dans 2 semaines; (*with substance*) en; (*with town*) à; (*with country*): **it's ~ France/Portugal** c'est en France/au Portugal ♦ *ad* dedans, à l'intérieur; (*fashionable*) à la mode; **is he ~?** est-il là?; **~ the United States** aux États-Unis; **~ 1986** en 1986; **~ spring/autumn** au printemps/en automne; **~ the morning** le matin; dans la matinée; **~ the country** à la campagne; **~ town** en ville; **~ here/there** ici/là(-dedans); **~ the sun** au soleil; **~ the rain** sous la pluie; **~ French** en français; **~ writing** par écrit; **~ pencil** au crayon; **to pay ~ dollars** payer en dollars; **a man ~ 10** un homme sur 10; **once ~ a hundred years** une fois tous les cent ans; **~ hundreds** par centaines; **the best pupil ~ the class** le meilleur élève de la classe; **to be ~ teaching/publishing** être dans l'enseignement/l'édition; **~ saying this** en disant ceci; **their party is ~** leur parti est au pouvoir; **to ask sb ~** inviter qn à entrer; **to run/limp** *etc* **~** entrer en courant/boitant *etc*; **the ~s and outs of** les tenants et aboutissants de.
in., ins *abbr* = **inch**(es).
inability [ɪnə'bɪlɪtɪ] *n* incapacité *f*; **~ to pay** incapacité de payer.
inaccessible [ɪnək'sɛsɪbl] *a* inaccessible.
inaccuracy [ɪn'ækjurəsɪ] *n* inexactitude *f*; manque *m* de précision.
inaccurate [ɪn'ækjurət] *a* inexact(e); (*person*) qui manque de précision.
inaction [ɪn'ækʃən] *n* inaction *f*, inactivité *f*.
inactivity [ɪnæk'tɪvɪtɪ] *n* inactivité *f*.
inadequacy [ɪn'ædɪkwəsɪ] *n* insuffisance *f*.
inadequate [ɪn'ædɪkwət] *a* insuffisant(e), inadéquat(e).
inadmissible [ɪnəd'mɪsəbl] *a* (*behaviour*) inadmissible; (*LAW: evidence*) irrecevable.
inadvertent [ɪnəd'vɜːtnt] *a* (*mistake*) commis(e) par inadvertance.
inadvertently [ɪnəd'vɜːtntlɪ] *ad* par mégarde.
inadvisable [ɪnəd'vaɪzəbl] *a* à déconseiller; **it is ~ to** il est déconseillé de.
inane [ɪ'neɪn] *a* inepte, stupide.
inanimate [ɪn'ænɪmət] *a* inanimé(e).
inapplicable [ɪn'æplɪkəbl] *a* inapplicable.
inappropriate [ɪnə'prəuprɪət] *a* inopportun(e), mal à propos; (*word, expression*) impropre.
inapt [ɪn'æpt] *a* inapte; peu approprié(e).
inaptitude [ɪn'æptɪtjuːd] *n* inaptitude *f*.
inarticulate [ɪnɑː'tɪkjulət] *a* (*person*) qui s'exprime mal; (*speech*) indistinct(e).
inasmuch as [ɪnəz'mʌtʃæz] *ad* dans la mesure

où; (*seeing that*) attendu que.
inattention [ɪnə'tɛnʃən] *n* manque *m* d'attention.
inattentive [ɪnə'tɛntɪv] *a* inattentif(ive), distrait(e); négligent(e).
inaudible [ɪn'ɔːdɪbl] *a* inaudible.
inaugural [ɪ'nɔːgjurəl] *a* inaugural(e).
inaugurate [ɪ'nɔːgjureɪt] *vt* inaugurer; (*president, official*) investir de ses fonctions.
inauguration [ɪnɔːgju'reɪʃən] *n* inauguration *f*; investiture *f*.
inauspicious [ɪnɔːs'pɪʃəs] *a* peu propice.
in-between [ɪnbɪ'twiːn] *a* entre les deux.
inborn [ɪn'bɔːn] *a* (*feeling*) inné(e); (*defect*) congénital(e).
inbred [ɪn'brɛd] *a* inné(e), naturel(le); (*family*) consanguin(e).
inbreeding [ɪn'briːdɪŋ] *n* croisement *m* d'animaux de même souche; unions consanguines.
Inc. *abbr* = **incorporated**.
Inca ['ɪŋkə] *a* (*also*: **~n**) inca *inv* ♦ *n* Inca *m/f*.
incalculable [ɪn'kælkjuləbl] *a* incalculable.
incapability [ɪnkeɪpə'bɪlɪtɪ] *n* incapacité *f*.
incapable [ɪn'keɪpəbl] *a*: **~ (of)** incapable (de).
incapacitate [ɪnkə'pæsɪteɪt] *vt*: **to ~ sb from doing** rendre qn incapable de faire.
incapacitated [ɪnkə'pæsɪteɪtɪd] *a* (*LAW*) frappé(e) d'incapacité.
incapacity [ɪnkə'pæsɪtɪ] *n* incapacité *f*.
incarcerate [ɪn'kɑːsəreɪt] *vt* incarcérer.
incarnate *a* [ɪn'kɑːnɪt] incarné(e) ♦ *vt* ['ɪnkɑːneɪt] incarner.
incarnation [ɪnkɑː'neɪʃən] *n* incarnation *f*.
incendiary [ɪn'sɛndɪərɪ] *a* incendiaire ♦ *n* (*bomb*) bombe *f* incendiaire.
incense *n* ['ɪnsɛns] encens *m* ♦ *vt* [ɪn'sɛns] (*anger*) mettre en colère.
incense burner *n* encensoir *m*.
incentive [ɪn'sɛntɪv] *n* encouragement *m*, raison *f* de se donner de la peine.
incentive scheme *n* système *m* de primes d'encouragement.
inception [ɪn'sɛpʃən] *n* commencement *m*, début *m*.
incessant [ɪn'sɛsnt] *a* incessant(e).
incessantly [ɪn'sɛsntlɪ] *ad* sans cesse, constamment.
incest ['ɪnsɛst] *n* inceste *m*.
inch [ɪntʃ] *n* pouce *m* (= 25 mm; 12 in a foot); **within an ~ of** à deux doigts de; **he wouldn't give an ~** (*fig*) il n'a pas voulu céder d'un pouce *or* faire la plus petite concession.
inch forward *vi* avancer petit à petit.
inch tape *n* (*Brit*) centimètre *m* (de couturière).
incidence ['ɪnsɪdns] *n* (*of crime, disease*) fréquence *f*.
incident ['ɪnsɪdnt] *n* incident *m*; (*in book*) péripétie *f*.
incidental [ɪnsɪ'dɛntl] *a* accessoire; (*unplanned*) accidentel(le); **~ to** qui accompagne; **~ expenses** faux frais *mpl*.
incidentally [ɪnsɪ'dɛntəlɪ] *ad* (*by the way*) à propos.
incidental music *n* musique *f* de fond.
incinerate [ɪn'sɪnəreɪt] *vt* incinérer.

incinerator [ɪn'sɪnəreɪtə*] n incinérateur m.
incipient [ɪn'sɪpɪənt] a naissant(e).
incision [ɪn'sɪʒən] n incision f.
incisive [ɪn'saɪsɪv] a incisif(ive); mordant(e).
incisor [ɪn'saɪzə*] n incisive f.
incite [ɪn'saɪt] vt inciter, pousser.
incl. abbr = **including, inclusive (of)**.
inclement [ɪn'klɛmənt] a inclément(e), rigoureux(euse).
inclination [ɪnklɪ'neɪʃən] n inclination f.
incline n ['ɪnklaɪn] pente f, plan incliné ♦ vb [ɪn'klaɪn] vt incliner ♦ vi: **to ~ to** avoir tendance à; **to be ~d to do** être enclin(e) à faire; (have a tendency to do) avoir tendance à faire; **to be well ~d towards sb** être bien disposé(e) à l'égard de qn.
include [ɪn'klu:d] vt inclure, comprendre; **the tip is/is not ~d** le service est compris/n'est pas compris.
including [ɪn'klu:dɪŋ] prep y compris; **~ tip** service compris.
inclusion [ɪn'klu:ʒən] n inclusion f.
inclusive [ɪn'klu:sɪv] a inclus(e), compris(e); **£50 ~ of all surcharges** 50 livres tous frais compris.
inclusive terms npl (Brit) prix tout compris.
incognito [ɪnkɒg'ni:təu] ad incognito.
incoherent [ɪnkəu'hɪərənt] a incohérent(e).
income ['ɪnkʌm] n revenu m; **gross/net ~** revenu brut/net; **~ and expenditure account** compte m de recettes et de dépenses.
income tax n impôt m sur le revenu.
income tax inspector n inspecteur m des contributions directes.
income tax return n déclaration f des revenus.
incoming ['ɪnkʌmɪŋ] a (passengers, mail) à l'arrivée; (government, tenant) nouveau(nouvelle); **~ tide** marée montante.
incommunicado ['ɪnkəmjunɪ'ka:dəu] a: **to hold sb ~** tenir qn au secret.
incomparable [ɪn'kɒmpərəbl] a incomparable.
incompatible [ɪnkəm'pætɪbl] a incompatible.
incompetence [ɪn'kɒmpɪtns] n incompétence f, incapacité f.
incompetent [ɪn'kɒmpɪtnt] a incompétent(e), incapable.
incomplete [ɪnkəm'pli:t] a incomplet(ète).
incomprehensible [ɪnkɒmprɪ'hɛnsɪbl] a incompréhensible.
inconceivable [ɪnkən'si:vəbl] a inconcevable.
inconclusive [ɪnkən'klu:sɪv] a peu concluant(e); (argument) peu convaincant(e).
incongruous [ɪn'kɒŋgruəs] a peu approprié(e); (remark, act) incongru(e), déplacé(e).
inconsequential [ɪnkɒnsɪ'kwɛnʃl] a sans importance.
inconsiderable [ɪnkən'sɪdərəbl] a: **not ~** non négligeable.
inconsiderate [ɪnkən'sɪdərət] a (action) inconsidéré(e); (person) qui manque d'égards.
inconsistency [ɪnkən'sɪstənsɪ] n (of actions etc) inconséquence f; (of work) irrégularité f; (of statement etc) incohérence f.
inconsistent [ɪnkən'sɪstnt] a inconséquent(e); irrégulier(ière); peu cohérent(e); **~ with** en

contradiction avec.
inconsolable [ɪnkən'səuləbl] a inconsolable.
inconspicuous [ɪnkən'spɪkjuəs] a qui passe inaperçu(e); (colour, dress) discret(ète); **to make o.s. ~** ne pas se faire remarquer.
inconstant [ɪn'kɒnstnt] a inconstant(e); variable.
incontinence [ɪn'kɒntɪnəns] n incontinence f.
incontinent [ɪn'kɒntɪnənt] a incontinent(e).
incontrovertible [ɪnkɒntrə'və:təbl] a irréfutable.
inconvenience [ɪnkən'vi:njəns] n inconvénient m; (trouble) dérangement m ♦ vt déranger; **don't ~ yourself** ne vous dérangez pas.
inconvenient [ɪnkən'vi:njənt] a malcommode; (time, place) mal choisi(e), qui ne convient pas; **that time is very ~ for me** c'est un moment qui ne me convient pas du tout.
incorporate [ɪn'kɔ:pəreɪt] vt incorporer; (contain) contenir ♦ vi fusionner; (two firms) se constituer en société.
incorporated [ɪn'kɔ:pəreɪtɪd] a: **~ company** (US: abbr **Inc.**) ≈ société f anonyme (S.A.).
incorrect [ɪnkə'rɛkt] a incorrect(e); (opinion, statement) inexact(e).
incorrigible [ɪn'kɒrɪdʒɪbl] a incorrigible.
incorruptible [ɪnkə'rʌptɪbl] a incorruptible.
increase n ['ɪnkri:s] augmentation f ♦ vi, vt [ɪn'kri:s] augmenter; **an ~ of 5%** une augmentation de 5%; **to be on the ~** être en augmentation.
increasing [ɪn'kri:sɪŋ] a croissant(e).
increasingly [ɪn'kri:sɪŋlɪ] ad de plus en plus.
incredible [ɪn'krɛdɪbl] a incroyable.
incredulous [ɪn'krɛdjuləs] a incrédule.
increment ['ɪnkrɪmənt] n augmentation f.
incriminate [ɪn'krɪmɪneɪt] vt incriminer, compromettre.
incriminating [ɪn'krɪmɪneɪtɪŋ] a compromettant(e).
incrust [ɪn'krʌst] vt = **encrust**.
incubate ['ɪnkjubeɪt] vt (egg) couver, incuber ♦ vi (eggs) couver; (disease) couver.
incubation [ɪnkju'beɪʃən] n incubation f.
incubation period n période f d'incubation.
incubator ['ɪnkjubeɪtə*] n incubateur m; (for babies) couveuse f.
inculcate ['ɪnkʌlkeɪt] vt: **to ~ sth in sb** inculquer qch à qn.
incumbent [ɪn'kʌmbənt] a: **it is ~ on him to ...** il lui incombe or appartient de ... ♦ n titulaire m/f.
incur [ɪn'kə:*] vt (expenses) encourir; (anger, risk) s'exposer à; (debt) contracter; (loss) subir.
incurable [ɪn'kjuərəbl] a incurable.
incursion [ɪn'kə:ʃən] n incursion f.
indebted [ɪn'dɛtɪd] a: **to be ~ to sb (for)** être redevable à qn (de).
indecency [ɪn'di:snsɪ] n indécence f.
indecent [ɪn'di:snt] a indécent(e), inconvenant(e).
indecent assault n (Brit) attentat m à la pudeur.
indecent exposure n outrage m public à la pudeur.
indecipherable [ɪndɪ'saɪfərəbl] a indéchiffrable.
indecision [ɪndɪ'sɪʒən] n indécision f.

indecisive [ˌɪndɪˈsaɪsɪv] a indécis(e); (discussion) peu concluant(e).

indeed [ɪnˈdiːd] ad en effet, effectivement; (furthermore) d'ailleurs; **yes ~!** certainement!

indefatigable [ˌɪndɪˈfætɪgəbl] a infatigable.

indefensible [ˌɪndɪˈfensɪbl] a (conduct) indéfendable.

indefinable [ˌɪndɪˈfaɪnəbl] a indéfinissable.

indefinite [ɪnˈdefɪnɪt] a indéfini(e); (answer) vague; (period, number) indéterminé(e).

indefinitely [ɪnˈdefɪnɪtlɪ] ad (wait) indéfiniment; (speak) vaguement, avec imprécision.

indelible [ɪnˈdelɪbl] a indélébile.

indelicate [ɪnˈdelɪkɪt] a (tactless) indélicat(e), grossier(ière); (not polite) inconvenant(e), malséant(e).

indemnify [ɪnˈdemnɪfaɪ] vt indemniser, dédommager.

indemnity [ɪnˈdemnɪtɪ] n (insurance) assurance f, garantie f; (compensation) indemnité f.

indent [ɪnˈdent] vt (text) commencer en retrait.

indentation [ˌɪndenˈteɪʃən] n découpure f; (TYP) alinéa m; (on metal) bosse f.

indenture [ɪnˈdentʃə*] n contrat m d'emploi-formation.

independence [ˌɪndɪˈpendns] n indépendance f.

independent [ˌɪndɪˈpendnt] a indépendant(e); **to become ~** s'affranchir.

independently [ˌɪndɪˈpendntlɪ] ad de façon indépendante; **~ of** indépendamment de.

indescribable [ˌɪndɪˈskraɪbəbl] a indescriptible.

indeterminate [ˌɪndɪˈtəːmɪnɪt] a indéterminé(e).

index [ˈɪndeks] n (pl: ~es: in book) index m; (: in library etc) catalogue m; (pl: indices [ˈɪndɪsiːz]) (ratio, sign) indice m.

index card n fiche f.

index finger n index m.

index-linked [ˈɪndeksˈlɪŋkt], (US) **indexed** [ˈɪndekst] a indexé(e) (sur le coût de la vie etc).

India [ˈɪndɪə] n Inde f.

Indian [ˈɪndɪən] a indien(ne) ♦ n Indien/ne.

Indian ink n encre f de Chine.

Indian Ocean n: **the ~** l'océan Indien.

Indian summer n (fig) été indien, beaux jours en automne.

India paper n papier m bible.

India rubber n gomme f.

indicate [ˈɪndɪkeɪt] vt indiquer ♦ vi (Brit AUT): **to ~ left/right** mettre son clignotant à gauche/à droite.

indication [ˌɪndɪˈkeɪʃən] n indication f, signe m.

indicative [ɪnˈdɪkətɪv] a indicatif(ive) ♦ n (LING) indicatif m; **to be ~ of sth** être symptomatique de qch.

indicator [ˈɪndɪkeɪtə*] n (sign) indicateur m; (AUT) clignotant m.

indices [ˈɪndɪsiːz] npl of **index**.

indict [ɪnˈdaɪt] vt accuser.

indictable [ɪnˈdaɪtəbl] a (person) passible de poursuites; **~ offence** délit m tombant sous le coup de la loi.

indictment [ɪnˈdaɪtmənt] n accusation f.

indifference [ɪnˈdɪfrəns] n indifférence f.

indifferent [ɪnˈdɪfrənt] a indifférent(e); (poor) médiocre, quelconque.

indigenous [ɪnˈdɪdʒɪnəs] a indigène.

indigestible [ˌɪndɪˈdʒestɪbl] a indigeste.

indigestion [ˌɪndɪˈdʒestʃən] n indigestion f, mauvaise digestion.

indignant [ɪnˈdɪgnənt] a: **~ (at sth/with sb)** indigné(e) (de qch/contre qn).

indignation [ˌɪndɪgˈneɪʃən] n indignation f.

indignity [ɪnˈdɪgnɪtɪ] n indignité f, affront m.

indigo [ˈɪndɪgəu] a indigo inv ♦ n indigo m.

indirect [ˌɪndɪˈrekt] a indirect(e).

indirectly [ˌɪndɪˈrektlɪ] ad indirectement.

indiscreet [ˌɪndɪˈskriːt] a indiscret(ète); (rash) imprudent(e).

indiscretion [ˌɪndɪˈskreʃən] n (see indiscreet) indiscrétion f; imprudence f.

indiscriminate [ˌɪndɪˈskrɪmɪnət] a (person) qui manque de discernement; (admiration) aveugle; (killings) commis(e) au hasard.

indispensable [ˌɪndɪˈspensəbl] a indispensable.

indisposed [ˌɪndɪˈspəuzd] a (unwell) indisposé(e), souffrant(e).

indisposition [ˌɪndɪspəˈzɪʃən] n (illness) indisposition f, malaise m.

indisputable [ˌɪndɪˈspjuːtəbl] a incontestable, indiscutable.

indistinct [ˌɪndɪˈstɪŋkt] a indistinct(e); (memory, noise) vague.

indistinguishable [ˌɪndɪˈstɪŋgwɪʃəbl] a impossible à distinguer.

individual [ˌɪndɪˈvɪdjuəl] n individu m ♦ a individuel(le); (characteristic) particulier(ière), original(e).

individualist [ˌɪndɪˈvɪdjuəlɪst] n individualiste m/f.

individuality [ˌɪndɪvɪdjuˈælɪtɪ] n individualité f.

individually [ˌɪndɪˈvɪdjuəlɪ] ad individuellement.

indivisible [ˌɪndɪˈvɪzɪbl] a indivisible; (MATH) insécable.

Indo-China [ˈɪndəuˈtʃaɪnə] n Indochine f.

indoctrinate [ɪnˈdɔktrɪneɪt] vt endoctriner.

indoctrination [ɪndɔktrɪˈneɪʃən] n endoctrinement m.

indolent [ˈɪndələnt] a indolent(e), nonchalant(e).

Indonesia [ˌɪndəˈniːzɪə] n Indonésie f.

Indonesian [ˌɪndəˈniːzɪən] a indonésien(ne) ♦ n Indonésien/ne.

indoor [ˈɪndɔː*] a d'intérieur; (plant) d'appartement; (swimming pool) couvert(e); (sport, games) pratiqué(e) en salle.

indoors [ɪnˈdɔːz] ad à l'intérieur; (at home) à la maison.

indubitable [ɪnˈdjuːbɪtəbl] a indubitable, incontestable.

induce [ɪnˈdjuːs] vt persuader; (bring about) provoquer; **to ~ sb to do sth** inciter or pousser qn à faire qch.

inducement [ɪnˈdjuːsmənt] n incitation f; (incentive) but m; (pej: bribe) pot-de-vin m.

induct [ɪnˈdʌkt] vt établir dans ses fonctions; (fig) initier.

induction [ɪnˈdʌkʃən] n (MED: of birth) accouchement provoqué.

induction course n (Brit) stage m de mise au courant.

indulge [ɪn'dʌldʒ] vt (whim) céder à, satisfaire; (child) gâter ♦ vi: **to ~ in sth** s'offrir qch, se permettre qch; se livrer à qch.

indulgence [ɪn'dʌldʒəns] n fantaisie f (que l'on s'offre); (leniency) indulgence f.

indulgent [ɪn'dʌldʒənt] a indulgent(e).

industrial [ɪn'dʌstrɪəl] a industriel(le); (injury) du travail; (dispute) ouvrier(ière).

industrial action n action revendicative.

industrial estate n (Brit) zone industrielle.

industrialist [ɪn'dʌstrɪəlɪst] n industriel m.

industrialize [ɪn'dʌstrɪəlaɪz] vt industrialiser.

industrial park n (US) zone industrielle.

industrial relations npl relations fpl dans l'entreprise.

industrial tribunal n (Brit) ≈ conseil m de prud'hommes.

industrial unrest n (Brit) agitation sociale, conflits sociaux.

industrious [ɪn'dʌstrɪəs] a travailleur(euse).

industry ['ɪndəstrɪ] n industrie f; (diligence) zèle m, application f.

inebriated [ɪ'niːbrɪeɪtɪd] a ivre.

inedible [ɪn'edɪbl] a immangeable; (plant etc) non comestible.

ineffective [ɪnɪ'fektɪv], **ineffectual** [ɪnɪ'fektʃuəl] a inefficace; incompétent(e).

inefficiency [ɪnɪ'fɪʃənsɪ] n inefficacité f.

inefficient [ɪnɪ'fɪʃənt] a inefficace.

inelegant [ɪn'elɪgənt] a peu élégant(e), inélégant(e).

ineligible [ɪn'elɪdʒɪbl] a (candidate) inéligible; **to be ~ for sth** ne pas avoir droit à qch.

inept [ɪ'nept] a inepte.

ineptitude [ɪ'neptɪtjuːd] n ineptie f.

inequality [ɪnɪ'kwɒlɪtɪ] n inégalité f.

inequitable [ɪn'ekwɪtəbl] a inéquitable, inique.

ineradicable [ɪnɪ'rædɪkəbl] a indéracinable, tenace.

inert [ɪ'nɜːt] a inerte.

inertia [ɪ'nɜːʃə] n inertie f.

inertia-reel seat belt [ɪ'nɜːʃə'riːl-] n ceinture f de sécurité à enrouleur.

inescapable [ɪnɪ'skeɪpəbl] a inéluctable, inévitable.

inessential [ɪnɪ'senʃl] a superflu(e).

inestimable [ɪn'estɪməbl] a inestimable, incalculable.

inevitable [ɪn'evɪtəbl] a inévitable.

inevitably [ɪn'evɪtəblɪ] ad inévitablement, fatalement.

inexact [ɪnɪg'zækt] a inexact(e).

inexcusable [ɪnɪks'kjuːzəbl] a inexcusable.

inexhaustible [ɪnɪg'zɔːstɪbl] a inépuisable.

inexorable [ɪn'eksərəbl] a inexorable.

inexpensive [ɪnɪk'spensɪv] a bon marché inv.

inexperience [ɪnɪk'spɪərɪəns] n inexpérience f, manque m d'expérience.

inexperienced [ɪnɪk'spɪərɪənst] a inexpérimenté(e); **to be ~ in sth** manquer d'expérience dans qch.

inexplicable [ɪnɪk'splɪkəbl] a inexplicable.

inexpressible [ɪnɪk'spresɪbl] a inexprimable; indicible.

inextricable [ɪnɪk'strɪkəbl] a inextricable.

infallibility [ɪnfælə'bɪlɪtɪ] n infaillibilité f.

infallible [ɪn'fælɪbl] a infaillible.

infamous ['ɪnfəməs] a infâme, abominable.

infamy ['ɪnfəmɪ] n infamie f.

infancy ['ɪnfənsɪ] n petite enfance, bas âge; (fig) enfance, débuts mpl.

infant ['ɪnfənt] n (baby) nourrisson m; (young child) petit(e) enfant.

infantile ['ɪnfəntaɪl] a infantile.

infant mortality n mortalité f infantile.

infantry ['ɪnfəntrɪ] n infanterie f.

infantryman ['ɪnfəntrɪmən] n fantassin m.

infant school n (Brit) classes fpl préparatoires (entre 5 et 7 ans).

infatuated [ɪn'fætjueɪtɪd] a: **~ with** entiché(e) de; **to become ~ (with sb)** s'enticher (de qn).

infatuation [ɪnfætju'eɪʃən] n toquade f; engouement m.

infect [ɪn'fekt] vt infecter, contaminer; (fig: pej) corrompre; **~ed with** (illness) atteint(e) de; **to become ~ed** (wound) s'infecter.

infection [ɪn'fekʃən] n infection f; contagion f.

infectious [ɪn'fekʃəs] a infectieux(euse); (also fig) contagieux(euse).

infer [ɪn'fɜː*] vt: **to ~ (from)** conclure (de), déduire (de).

inference ['ɪnfərəns] n conclusion f, déduction f.

inferior [ɪn'fɪərɪə*] a inférieur(e); (goods) de qualité inférieure ♦ n inférieur/e; (in rank) subalterne m/f; **to feel ~** avoir un sentiment d'infériorité.

inferiority [ɪnfɪərɪ'ɒrətɪ] n infériorité f.

inferiority complex n complexe m d'infériorité.

infernal [ɪn'fɜːnl] a infernal(e).

infernally [ɪn'fɜːnəlɪ] ad abominablement.

inferno [ɪn'fɜːnəu] n enfer m; brasier m.

infertile [ɪn'fɜːtaɪl] a stérile.

infertility [ɪnfɜː'tɪlɪtɪ] n infertilité f, stérilité f.

infested [ɪn'festɪd] a: **~ (with)** infesté(e) (de).

infidelity [ɪnfɪ'delɪtɪ] n infidélité f.

in-fighting ['ɪnfaɪtɪŋ] n querelles fpl internes.

infiltrate ['ɪnfɪltreɪt] vt (troops etc) faire s'infiltrer; (enemy line etc) s'infiltrer dans ♦ vi s'infiltrer.

infinite ['ɪnfɪnɪt] a infini(e); (time, money) illimité(e).

infinitely ['ɪnfɪnɪtlɪ] ad infiniment.

infinitesimal [ɪnfɪnɪ'tesɪməl] a infinitésimal(e).

infinitive [ɪn'fɪnɪtɪv] n infinitif m.

infinity [ɪn'fɪnɪtɪ] n infinité f; (also MATH) infini m.

infirm [ɪn'fɜːm] a infirme.

infirmary [ɪn'fɜːmərɪ] n hôpital m; (in school, factory) infirmerie f.

infirmity [ɪn'fɜːmɪtɪ] n infirmité f.

inflamed [ɪn'fleɪmd] a enflammé(e).

inflammable [ɪn'flæməbl] a (Brit) inflammable.

inflammation [ɪnflə'meɪʃən] n inflammation f.

inflammatory [ɪn'flæmətərɪ] a (speech) incendiaire.

inflatable [ɪn'fleɪtəbl] a gonflable.

inflate [ɪn'fleɪt] vt (tyre, balloon) gonfler; (fig) grossir; gonfler; faire monter.

inflated [ɪn'fleɪtɪd] a (style) enflé(e); (value) exagéré(e).

inflation [ɪn'fleɪʃən] n (ECON) inflation f.

inflationary [ɪn'fleɪʃənərɪ] a inflationniste.

inflexible [ɪn'fleksɪbl] a inflexible, rigide.

inflict [ɪn'flɪkt] *vt*: **to ~ on** infliger à.
infliction [ɪn'flɪkʃən] *n* infliction *f*; affliction *f*.
in-flight ['ɪnflaɪt] *a* (*refuelling*) en vol; (*service etc*) à bord.
inflow ['ɪnfləu] *n* afflux *m*.
influence ['ɪnfluəns] *n* influence *f* ♦ *vt* influencer; **under the ~ of** sous l'effet de; **under the ~ of drink** en état d'ébriété.
influential [ɪnflu'enʃl] *a* influent(e).
influenza [ɪnflu'enzə] *n* grippe *f*.
influx ['ɪnflʌks] *n* afflux *m*.
inform [ɪn'fɔ:m] *vt*: **to ~ sb (of)** informer *or* avertir qn (de) / **vi**: **to ~ on sb** dénoncer qn, informer contre qn; **to ~ sb about** renseigner qn sur, mettre qn au courant de.
informal [ɪn'fɔ:ml] *a* (*person, manner*) simple, sans cérémonie; (*announcement, visit*) non officiel(le); "**dress ~**" "tenue de ville".
informality [ɪnfɔ'mælɪtɪ] *n* simplicité *f*, absence *f* de cérémonie; caractère non officiel.
informal language *n* langage *m* de la conversation.
informally [ɪn'fɔ:məlɪ] *ad* sans cérémonie, en toute simplicité; non officiellement.
informant [ɪn'fɔ:mənt] *n* informateur/trice.
information [ɪnfə'meɪʃən] *n* information(s) *f(pl)*; renseignements *mpl*; (*knowledge*) connaissances *fpl*; **to get ~ on** se renseigner sur; **a piece of ~** un renseignement; **for your ~** à titre d'information.
information bureau *n* bureau *m* de renseignements.
information processing *n* traitement *m* de l'information.
information retrieval *n* recherche *f* (informatique) de renseignements.
information technology *n* informatique *f*.
informative [ɪn'fɔ:mətɪv] *a* instructif(ive).
informed [ɪn'fɔ:md] *a* (bien) informé(e); **an ~ guess** une hypothèse fondée sur la connaissance des faits.
informer [ɪn'fɔ:mə*] *n* dénonciateur/trice; (*also*: **police ~**) indicateur/trice.
infra dig ['ɪnfrə'dɪg] *a abbr* (*col*: = *infra dignitatem*) au-dessous de ma (*or* sa *etc*) dignité.
infra-red [ɪnfrə'red] *a* infrarouge.
infrastructure ['ɪnfrəstrʌktʃə*] *n* infrastructure *f*.
infrequent [ɪn'fri:kwənt] *a* peu fréquent(e), rare.
infringe [ɪn'frɪndʒ] *vt* enfreindre ♦ *vi*: **to ~ on** empiéter sur.
infringement [ɪn'frɪndʒmənt] *n*: **~ (of)** infraction *f* (à).
infuriate [ɪn'fjuərɪeɪt] *vt* mettre en fureur.
infuriating [ɪn'fjuərɪeɪtɪŋ] *a* exaspérant(e).
infuse [ɪn'fju:z] *vt*: **to ~ sb with sth** (*fig*) insuffler qch à qn.
infusion [ɪn'fju:ʒən] *n* (*tea etc*) infusion *f*.
ingenious [ɪn'dʒi:njəs] *a* ingénieux(euse).
ingenuity [ɪndʒɪ'nju:ɪtɪ] *n* ingéniosité *f*.
ingenuous [ɪn'dʒɛnjuəs] *a* franc(franche), ouvert(e).
ingot ['ɪŋgət] *n* lingot *m*.
ingrained [ɪn'greɪnd] *a* enraciné(e).
ingratiate [ɪn'greɪʃɪeɪt] *vt*: **to ~ o.s. with** s'insinuer dans les bonnes grâces de, se faire bien voir de.
ingratiating [ɪn'greɪʃɪeɪtɪŋ] *a* (*smile, speech*) insinuant(e); (*person*) patelin(e).
ingratitude [ɪn'grætɪtju:d] *n* ingratitude *f*.
ingredient [ɪn'gri:dɪənt] *n* ingrédient *m*; élément *m*.
ingrowing ['ɪngrəuɪŋ], **ingrown** ['ɪngrəun] *a*: **~ toenail** ongle incarné.
inhabit [ɪn'hæbɪt] *vt* habiter.
inhabitable [ɪn'hæbɪtəbl] *a* habitable.
inhabitant [ɪn'hæbɪtnt] *n* habitant/e.
inhale [ɪn'heɪl] *vt* inhaler; (*perfume*) respirer ♦ *vi* (*in smoking*) avaler la fumée.
inherent [ɪn'hɪərənt] *a*: **~ (in** or **to)** inhérent(e) (à).
inherently [ɪn'hɪərəntlɪ] *ad* (*easy, difficult*) en soi; (*lazy*) fondamentalement.
inherit [ɪn'herɪt] *vt* hériter (de).
inheritance [ɪn'herɪtəns] *n* héritage *m*; **law of ~** droit *m* de la succession.
inhibit [ɪn'hɪbɪt] *vt* (*PSYCH*) inhiber; **to ~ sb from doing** empêcher *or* retenir qn de faire.
inhibited [ɪn'hɪbɪtɪd] *a* (*person*) inhibé(e).
inhibiting [ɪn'hɪbɪtɪŋ] *a* gênant(e).
inhibition [ɪnhɪ'bɪʃən] *n* inhibition *f*.
inhospitable [ɪnhɔs'pɪtəbl] *a* inhospitalier(ière).
inhuman [ɪn'hju:mən] *a* inhumain(e).
inhumane [ɪnhju:'meɪn] *a* inhumain(e).
inimitable [ɪ'nɪmɪtəbl] *a* inimitable.
iniquity [ɪ'nɪkwɪtɪ] *n* iniquité *f*.
initial [ɪ'nɪʃl] *a* initial(e) ♦ *n* initiale *f* ♦ *vt* parafer; **~s** *npl* initiales *fpl*; (*as signature*) parafe *m*.
initialize [ɪ'nɪʃəlaɪz] *vt* (*COMPUT*) initialiser.
initially [ɪ'nɪʃəlɪ] *ad* initialement, au début.
initiate [ɪ'nɪʃɪeɪt] *vt* (*start*) entreprendre; amorcer; lancer; (*person*) initier; **to ~ sb into a secret** initier qn à un secret; **to ~ proceedings against sb** (*LAW*) intenter une action à qn, engager des poursuites contre qn.
initiation [ɪnɪʃɪ'eɪʃən] *n* (*into secret etc*) initiation *f*.
initiative [ɪ'nɪʃətɪv] *n* initiative *f*; **to take the ~** prendre l'initiative.
inject [ɪn'dʒɛkt] *vt* (*liquid, fig: money*) injecter; (*person*) faire une piqûre à.
injection [ɪn'dʒɛkʃən] *n* injection *f*, piqûre *f*; **to have an ~** se faire faire une piqûre.
injudicious [ɪndʒu'dɪʃəs] *a* peu judicieux(euse).
injunction [ɪn'dʒʌŋkʃən] *n* (*LAW*) injonction *f*, ordre *m*.
injure [ɪn'dʒə*] *vt* blesser; (*wrong*) faire du tort à; (*damage: reputation etc*) compromettre; (*feelings*) heurter; **to ~ o.s.** se blesser.
injured [ɪn'dʒəd] *a* (*person, leg etc*) blessé(e); (*tone, feelings*) offensé(e); **~ party** (*LAW*) partie lésée.
injurious [ɪn'dʒuərɪəs] *a*: **~ (to)** préjudiciable (à).
injury ['ɪndʒərɪ] *n* blessure *f*; (*wrong*) tort *m*; **to escape without ~** s'en sortir sain et sauf.
injury time *n* (*SPORT*) arrêts *mpl* de jeu.
injustice [ɪn'dʒʌstɪs] *n* injustice *f*; **you do me an ~** vous êtes injuste envers moi.
ink [ɪŋk] *n* encre *f*.
ink-jet printer ['ɪŋkdʒɛt-] *n* imprimante *f* à

jet d'encre.

inkling ['ɪŋklɪŋ] *n* soupçon *m*, vague idée *f*.

inkpad ['ɪŋkpæd] *n* tampon *m* encreur.

inky ['ɪŋkɪ] *a* taché(e) d'encre.

inlaid ['ɪnleɪd] *a* incrusté(e); (*table etc*) marqueté(e).

inland *a* ['ɪnlənd] intérieur(e) ♦ *ad* [ɪn'lænd] à l'intérieur, dans les terres; ~ **waterways** canaux *mpl* et rivières *fpl*.

Inland Revenue *n* (*Brit*) fisc *m*.

in-laws ['ɪnlɔːz] *npl* beaux-parents *mpl*; belle famille.

inlet ['ɪnlet] *n* (*GEO*) crique *f*.

inlet pipe *n* (*TECH*) tuyau *m* d'arrivée.

inmate ['ɪnmeɪt] *n* (*in prison*) détenu/e; (*in asylum*) interné/e.

inmost ['ɪnməust] *a* le(la) plus profond(e).

inn [ɪn] *n* auberge *f*.

innards ['ɪnədz] *npl* (*col*) entrailles *fpl*.

innate [ɪ'neɪt] *a* inné(e).

inner ['ɪnə*] *a* intérieur(e).

inner city *n* (vieux quartiers du) centre urbain (*souffrant souvent de délabrement, d'embouteillages etc*).

innermost ['ɪnəməust] *a* le(la) plus profond(e).

inner tube *n* (*of tyre*) chambre *f* à air.

innings ['ɪnɪŋz] *n* (*CRICKET*) tour *m* de batte; (*Brit fig*): **he has had a good** ~ il (en) a bien profité.

innocence ['ɪnəsns] *n* innocence *f*.

innocent ['ɪnəsnt] *a* innocent(e).

innocuous [ɪ'nɔkjuəs] *a* inoffensif(ive).

innovation [ɪnəu'veɪʃən] *n* innovation *f*.

innuendo, ~**es** [ɪnju'ɛndəu] *n* insinuation *f*, allusion (malveillante).

innumerable [ɪ'njuːmrəbl] *a* innombrable.

inoculate [ɪ'nɔkjuleɪt] *vt*: **to** ~ **sb with sth** inoculer qch à qn; **to** ~ **sb against sth** vacciner qn contre qch.

inoculation [ɪnɔkju'leɪʃən] *n* inoculation *f*.

inoffensive [ɪnə'fɛnsɪv] *a* inoffensif(ive).

inopportune [ɪn'ɔpətjuːn] *a* inopportun(e).

inordinate [ɪ'nɔːdɪnət] *a* démesuré(e).

inordinately [ɪ'nɔːdɪnətlɪ] *ad* démesurément.

inorganic [ɪnɔː'gænɪk] *a* inorganique.

in-patient ['ɪnpeɪʃənt] *n* malade hospitalisé(e).

input ['ɪnput] *n* (*ELEC*) énergie *f*, puissance *f*; (*of machine*) consommation *f*; (*of computer*) information fournie ♦ *vt* (*COMPUT*) introduire, entrer.

inquest ['ɪnkwɛst] *n* enquête (criminelle).

inquire [ɪn'kwaɪə*] *vi* demander ♦ *vt* demander, s'informer de; **to** ~ **about** s'informer de, se renseigner sur; **to** ~ **when/where/whether** demander quand/où/si.

inquire after *vt fus* demander des nouvelles de.

inquire into *vt fus* faire une enquête sur.

inquiring [ɪn'kwaɪərɪŋ] *a* (*mind*) curieux(euse), investigateur(trice).

inquiry [ɪn'kwaɪərɪ] *n* demande *f* de renseignements; (*LAW*) enquête *f*, investigation *f*; **to hold an** ~ **into sth** enquêter sur qch.

inquiry desk *n* (*Brit*) guichet *m* de renseignements.

inquiry office *n* (*Brit*) bureau *m* de renseignements.

inquisition [ɪnkwɪ'zɪʃən] *n* enquête *f*,

investigation *f*; (*REL*): **the** I~ l'Inquisition.

inquisitive [ɪn'kwɪzɪtɪv] *a* curieux(euse).

inroads ['ɪnrəudz] *npl*: **to make** ~ **into** (*savings, supplies*) entamer.

insane [ɪn'seɪn] *a* fou(folle); (*MED*) aliéné(e).

insanitary [ɪn'sænɪtərɪ] *a* insalubre.

insanity [ɪn'sænɪtɪ] *n* folie *f*; (*MED*) aliénation (mentale).

insatiable [ɪn'seɪʃəbl] *a* insatiable.

inscribe [ɪn'skraɪb] *vt* inscrire; (*book etc*): **to** ~ **(to sb)** dédicacer (à qn).

inscription [ɪn'skrɪpʃən] *n* inscription *f*; (*in book*) dédicace *f*.

inscrutable [ɪn'skruːtəbl] *a* impénétrable.

inseam ['ɪnsiːm] *n* (*US*): ~ **measurement** hauteur *f* d'entre-jambe.

insect ['ɪnsɛkt] *n* insecte *m*.

insect bite *n* piqûre *f* d'insecte.

insecticide [ɪn'sɛktɪsaɪd] *n* insecticide *m*.

insect repellent *n* crème *f* anti-insectes.

insecure [ɪnsɪ'kjuə*] *a* peu solide; peu sûr(e); (*person*) anxieux(euse).

insecurity [ɪnsɪ'kjuərɪtɪ] *n* insécurité *f*.

insensible [ɪn'sɛnsɪbl] *a* insensible; (*unconscious*) sans connaissance.

insensitive [ɪn'sɛnsɪtɪv] *a* insensible.

insensitivity [ɪnsɛnsɪ'tɪvɪtɪ] *n* insensibilité *f*.

inseparable [ɪn'sɛprəbl] *a* inséparable.

insert *vt* [ɪn'səːt] insérer ♦ *n* ['ɪnsəːt] insertion *f*.

insertion [ɪn'səːʃən] *n* insertion *f*.

in-service ['ɪn'səːvɪs] *a* (*training*) continu(e); (*course*) d'initiation; de perfectionnement; de recyclage.

inshore [ɪn'ʃɔː*] *a* côtier(ière) ♦ *ad* près de la côte; vers la côte.

inside ['ɪn'saɪd] *n* intérieur *m*; (*of road: Brit*) côté *m* gauche (*de la route*); (: *US, Europe etc*) côté droit (*de la route*) ♦ *a* intérieur(e) ♦ *ad* à l'intérieur, dedans ♦ *prep* à l'intérieur de; (*of time*): ~ **10 minutes** en moins de 10 minutes; ~**s** *npl* (*col*) intestins *mpl*; ~ **out** *ad* à l'envers; **to turn sth** ~ **out** retourner qch; **to know sth** ~ **out** connaître qch à fond *or* comme sa poche; ~ **information** renseignements *mpl* à la source; ~ **story** histoire racontée par un témoin.

inside forward *n* (*SPORT*) intérieur *m*.

inside lane *n* (*AUT*: *in Britain*) voie *f* de gauche; (: *in US, Europe*) voie *f* de droite.

inside leg measurement *n* (*Brit*) hauteur *f* d'entre-jambe.

insider [ɪn'saɪdə*] *n* initié/e.

insider dealing *n* (*STOCK EXCHANGE*) délit *m* d'initié(s).

insidious [ɪn'sɪdɪəs] *a* insidieux(euse).

insight ['ɪnsaɪt] *n* perspicacité *f*; (*glimpse, idea*) aperçu *m*; **to gain (an)** ~ **into** parvenir à comprendre.

insignia [ɪn'sɪgnɪə] *npl* insignes *mpl*.

insignificant [ɪnsɪg'nɪfɪknt] *a* insignifiant(e).

insincere [ɪnsɪn'sɪə*] *a* hypocrite.

insincerity [ɪnsɪn'sɛrɪtɪ] *n* manque *m* de sincérité, hypocrisie *f*.

insinuate [ɪn'sɪnjueɪt] *vt* insinuer.

insinuation [ɪnsɪnju'eɪʃən] *n* insinuation *f*.

insipid [ɪn'sɪpɪd] *a* insipide, fade.

insist [ɪn'sɪst] *vi* insister; **to** ~ **on doing** insister pour faire; **to** ~ **that** insister pour que; (*claim*) maintenir *or* soutenir *f*.

insistence [ɪn'sɪstəns] *n* insistance *f*.

insistent [ɪn'sɪstənt] *a* insistant(e), pressant(e).

insole ['ɪnsəul] *n* semelle intérieure; (*fixed part of shoe*) première *f*.

insolence ['ɪnsələns] *n* insolence *f*.

insolent ['ɪnsələnt] *a* insolent(e).

insoluble [ɪn'sɔljubl] *a* insoluble.

insolvency [ɪn'sɔlvənsɪ] *n* insolvabilité *f*; faillite *f*.

insolvent [ɪn'sɔlvənt] *a* insolvable; (*bankrupt*) en faillite.

insomnia [ɪn'sɔmnɪə] *n* insomnie *f*.

insomniac [ɪn'sɔmnɪæk] *n* insomniaque *m/f*.

inspect [ɪn'spɛkt] *vt* inspecter; (*Brit: ticket*) contrôler.

inspection [ɪn'spɛkʃən] *n* inspection *f*; contrôle *m*.

inspector [ɪn'spɛktə*] *n* inspecteur/trice; contrôleur/euse.

inspiration [ɪnspə'reɪʃən] *n* inspiration *f*.

inspire [ɪn'spaɪə*] *vt* inspirer.

inspired [ɪn'spaɪəd] *a* (*writer, book etc*) inspiré(e); **in an ~ moment** dans un moment d'inspiration.

inspiring [ɪn'spaɪərɪŋ] *a* inspirant(e).

inst. *abbr* (*Brit COMM: = instant*): **of the 16th ~** du 16 courant.

instability [ɪnstə'bɪlɪtɪ] *n* instabilité *f*.

install [ɪn'stɔ:l] *vt* installer.

installation [ɪnstə'leɪʃən] *n* installation *f*.

installment plan *n* (*US*) achat *m* (*or* vente *f*) à tempérament *or* crédit.

instalment, (*US*) **installment** [ɪn'stɔ:lmənt] *n* acompte *m*, versement partiel; (*of TV serial etc*) épisode *m*; **in ~s** (*pay*) à tempérament; (*receive*) en plusieurs fois.

instance ['ɪnstəns] *n* exemple *m*; **for ~** par exemple; **in many ~s** dans bien des cas; **in that ~** dans ce cas; **in the first ~** tout d'abord, en premier lieu.

instant ['ɪnstənt] *n* instant *m* ♦ *a* immédiat(e); urgent(e); (*coffee, food*) instantané(e), en poudre; **the 10th ~** le 10 courant.

instantaneous [ɪnstən'teɪnɪəs] *a* instantané(e).

instantly ['ɪnstəntlɪ] *ad* immédiatement, tout de suite.

instant replay *n* (*US TV*) retour *m* sur une séquence.

instead [ɪn'stɛd] *ad* au lieu de cela; **~ of** au lieu de; **~ of sb** à la place de qn.

instep ['ɪnstɛp] *n* cou-de-pied *m*; (*of shoe*) cambrure *f*.

instigate ['ɪnstɪgeɪt] *vt* (*rebellion, strike, crime*) inciter à; (*new ideas etc*) susciter.

instigation [ɪnstɪ'geɪʃən] *n* instigation *f*; **at sb's ~** à l'instigation de qn.

instil [ɪn'stɪl] *vt*: **to ~ (into)** inculquer (à); (*courage*) insuffler (à).

instinct ['ɪnstɪŋkt] *n* instinct *m*.

instinctive [ɪn'stɪŋktɪv] *a* instinctif(ive).

instinctively [ɪn'stɪŋktɪvlɪ] *ad* instinctivement.

institute ['ɪnstɪtju:t] *n* institut *m* ♦ *vt* instituer, établir; (*inquiry*) ouvrir; (*proceedings*) entamer.

institution [ɪnstɪ'tju:ʃən] *n* institution *f*; (*school*) établissement *m* (scolaire); (*for*

care) établissement (psychiatrique *etc*).

institutional [ɪnstɪ'tju:ʃənl] *a* institutionnel(le); **~ care** soins *mpl* fournis par un établissement médico-social.

instruct [ɪn'strʌkt] *vt* instruire, former; **to ~ sb in sth** enseigner qch à qn; **to ~ sb to do** charger qn *or* ordonner à qn de faire.

instruction [ɪn'strʌkʃən] *n* instruction *f*; **~s** *npl* directives *fpl*; **~s for use** mode *m* d'emploi.

instruction book *n* manuel *m* d'instructions.

instructive [ɪn'strʌktɪv] *a* instructif(ive).

instructor [ɪn'strʌktə*] *n* professeur *m*; (*for skiing, driving*) moniteur *m*.

instrument ['ɪnstrumənt] *n* instrument *m*.

instrumental [ɪnstru'mɛntl] *a* (*MUS*) instrumental(e); **to be ~ in sth/in doing sth** contribuer à qch/à faire qch.

instrumentalist [ɪnstru'mɛntəlɪst] *n* instrumentiste *m/f*.

instrument panel *n* tableau *m* de bord.

insubordinate [ɪnsə'bɔ:dənɪt] *a* insubordonné(e).

insubordination [ɪnsəbɔ:də'neɪʃən] *n* insubordination *f*.

insufferable [ɪn'sʌfrəbl] *a* insupportable.

insufficient [ɪnsə'fɪʃənt] *a* insuffisant(e).

insufficiently [ɪnsə'fɪʃəntlɪ] *ad* insuffisamment.

insular ['ɪnsjulə*] *a* insulaire; (*outlook*) étroit(e); (*person*) aux vues étroites.

insulate ['ɪnsjuleɪt] *vt* isoler; (*against sound*) insonoriser.

insulating tape ['ɪnsjuleɪtɪŋ-] *n* ruban isolant.

insulation [ɪnsju'leɪʃən] *n* isolation *f*; insonorisation *f*.

insulin ['ɪnsjulɪn] *n* insuline *f*.

insult *n* ['ɪnsʌlt] insulte *f*, affront *m* ♦ *vt* [ɪn'sʌlt] insulter, faire un affront à.

insulting [ɪn'sʌltɪŋ] *a* insultant(e), injurieux(euse).

insuperable [ɪn'sju:prəbl] *a* insurmontable.

insurance [ɪn'ʃuərəns] *n* assurance *f*; **fire/life ~** assurance-incendie/-vie; **to take out ~ (against)** s'assurer (contre).

insurance agent *n* agent *m* d'assurances.

insurance broker *n* courtier *m* en assurances.

insurance policy *n* police *f* d'assurance.

insurance premium *n* prime *f* d'assurance.

insure [ɪn'ʃuə*] *vt* assurer; **to ~ sb/sb's life** assurer qn/la vie de qn; **to be ~d for £5000** être assuré(e) pour 5000 livres.

insured [ɪn'ʃuəd] *n*: **the ~** l'assuré/e.

insurer [ɪn'ʃuərə*] *n* assureur *m*.

insurgent [ɪn'sɜ:dʒənt] *a*, *n* insurgé(e).

insurmountable [ɪnsə'mauntəbl] *a* insurmontable.

insurrection [ɪnsə'rɛkʃən] *n* insurrection *f*.

intact [ɪn'tækt] *a* intact(e).

intake ['ɪnteɪk] *n* (*TECH*) admission *f*; adduction *f*; (*of food*) consommation *f*; (*Brit SCOL*): **an ~ of 200 a year** 200 admissions par an.

intangible [ɪn'tændʒɪbl] *a* intangible; (*assets*) immatériel(le).

integral ['ɪntɪgrəl] *a* intégral(e); (*part*) intégrant(e).

integrate ['ɪntɪgreɪt] *vt* intégrer ♦ *vi* s'intégrer.

integrated circuit n (COMPUT) circuit intégré.

integration [ɪntɪ'greɪʃən] n intégration f; **racial** ~ intégration raciale.

integrity [ɪn'tɛgrɪtɪ] n intégrité f.

intellect ['ɪntəlɛkt] n intelligence f.

intellectual [ɪntə'lɛktjuəl] a, n intellectuel(le).

intelligence [ɪn'tɛlɪdʒəns] n intelligence f; (MIL etc) informations fpl, renseignements mpl.

intelligence quotient (IQ) n quotient intellectuel (QI).

Intelligence Service n services mpl de renseignements.

intelligence test n test m d'intelligence.

intelligent [ɪn'tɛlɪdʒənt] a intelligent(e).

intelligently [ɪn'tɛlɪdʒəntlɪ] ad intelligemment.

intelligible [ɪn'tɛlɪdʒɪbl] a intelligible.

intemperate [ɪn'tɛmpərət] a immodéré(e); (drinking too much) adonné(e) à la boisson.

intend [ɪn'tɛnd] vt (gift etc): **to ~ sth for** destiner qch à; **to ~ to do** avoir l'intention de faire.

intended [ɪn'tɛndɪd] a (insult) intentionnel(le); (journey) projeté(e); (effect) voulu(e).

intense [ɪn'tɛns] a intense; (person) véhément(e).

intensely [ɪn'tɛnslɪ] ad intensément; (moving) profondément.

intensify [ɪn'tɛnsɪfaɪ] vt intensifier.

intensity [ɪn'tɛnsɪtɪ] n intensité f.

intensive [ɪn'tɛnsɪv] a intensif(ive).

intensive care n: **to be in ~** être en réanimation; **~ unit** n service m de réanimation.

intent [ɪn'tɛnt] n intention f ♦ a attentif(ive), absorbé(e); **to all ~s and purposes** en fait, pratiquement; **to be ~ on doing sth** être (bien) décidé à faire qch.

intention [ɪn'tɛnʃən] n intention f.

intentional [ɪn'tɛnʃənl] a intentionnel(le), délibéré(e).

intently [ɪn'tɛntlɪ] ad attentivement.

inter [ɪn'tə:*] vt enterrer.

interact [ɪntər'ækt] vi avoir une action réciproque.

interaction [ɪntər'ækʃən] n interaction f.

interactive [ɪntər'æktɪv] a interactif(ive).

intercede [ɪntə'si:d] vi: **to ~ with sb/on behalf of sb** intercéder auprès de qn/en faveur de qn.

intercept [ɪntə'sɛpt] vt intercepter; (person) arrêter au passage.

interception [ɪntə'sɛpʃən] n interception f.

interchange n ['ɪntətʃeɪndʒ] (exchange) échange m; (on motorway) échangeur m ♦ vt [ɪntə'tʃeɪndʒ] échanger; mettre à la place l'un(e) de l'autre.

interchangeable [ɪntə'tʃeɪndʒəbl] a interchangeable.

intercity [ɪntə'sɪtɪ] a: ~ **(train)** train m rapide.

intercom ['ɪntəkɔm] n interphone m.

interconnect [ɪntəkə'nɛkt] vi (rooms) communiquer.

intercontinental ['ɪntəkɔntɪ'nɛntl] a intercontinental(e).

intercourse ['ɪntəkɔ:s] n rapports mpl; **sexual ~** rapports sexuels.

interdependent [ɪntədɪ'pɛndənt] a interdépendant(e).

interest ['ɪntrɪst] n intérêt m; (COMM: stake, share) participation f, intérêts mpl ♦ vt intéresser; **compound/simple ~** intérêt composé/simple; **British ~s in the Middle East** les intérêts britanniques au Moyen-Orient; **his main ~ is ...** ce qui l'intéresse le plus est ....

interested ['ɪntrɪstɪd] a intéressé(e); **to be ~ in** s'intéresser à.

interest-free ['ɪntrɪst'fri:] a sans intérêt.

interesting ['ɪntrɪstɪŋ] a intéressant(e).

interest rate n taux m d'intérêt.

interface ['ɪntəfeɪs] n (COMPUT) interface f.

interfere [ɪntə'fɪə*] vi: **to ~ in** (quarrel, other people's business) se mêler à; **to ~ with** (object) tripoter, toucher à; (plans) contrecarrer; (duty) être en conflit avec; **don't ~** mêlez-vous de vos affaires.

interference [ɪntə'fɪərəns] n (gen) intrusion f; (PHYSICS) interférence f; (RADIO, TV) parasites mpl.

interfering [ɪntə'fɪərɪŋ] a importun(e).

interim ['ɪntərɪm] a provisoire; (post) intérimaire ♦ n: **in the ~** dans l'intérim.

interior [ɪn'tɪərɪə*] n intérieur m ♦ a intérieur(e).

interior decorator, interior designer n décorateur/trice d'intérieur.

interjection [ɪntə'dʒɛkʃən] n interjection f.

interlock [ɪntə'lɔk] vi s'enclencher ♦ enclencher.

interloper ['ɪntələupə*] n intrus/e.

interlude ['ɪntəlu:d] n intervalle m; (THEATRE) intermède m.

intermarry [ɪntə'mærɪ] vi former des alliances entre familles (or tribus); former des unions consanguines.

intermediary [ɪntə'mi:dɪərɪ] n intermédiaire m/f.

intermediate [ɪntə'mi:dɪət] a intermédiaire; (SCOL: course, level) moyen(ne).

interminable [ɪn'tə:mɪnəbl] a sans fin, interminable.

intermission [ɪntə'mɪʃən] n pause f; (THEATRE, CINEMA) entracte m.

intermittent [ɪntə'mɪtnt] a intermittent(e).

intermittently [ɪntə'mɪtntlɪ] ad par intermittence, par intervalles.

intern vt [ɪn'tə:n] interner ♦ n ['ɪntə:n] (US) interne m/f.

internal [ɪn'tə:nl] a interne; (dispute, reform etc) intérieur(e); **~ injuries** lésions fpl internes.

internally [ɪn'tə:nəlɪ] ad intérieurement; "not to be taken ~" "pour usage externe".

Internal Revenue (Service) (IRS) n (US) fisc m.

international [ɪntə'næʃənl] a international(e) ♦ n (Brit SPORT) international m.

International Atomic Energy Agency (IAEA) n Agence Internationale de l'Energie Atomique (AIEA).

International Court of Justice (ICJ) n Cour internationale de justice (CIJ).

international date line n ligne f de changement de date.

internationally [ɪntə'næʃnəlɪ] ad dans le

monde entier.

International Monetary Fund (IMF) n Fond monétaire international (FMI).

internecine [ɪntə'niːsaɪn] a mutuellement destructeur(trice).

internee [ɪntəː'niː] n interné/e.

internment [ɪn'təːnmənt] n internement m.

interplay ['ɪntəpleɪ] n effet m réciproque, jeu m.

Interpol ['ɪntəpɒl] n Interpol m.

interpret [ɪn'təːprɪt] vt interpréter ♦ vi servir d'interprète.

interpretation [ɪntəːprɪ'teɪʃən] n interprétation f.

interpreter [ɪn'təːprɪtə*] n interprète m/f.

interpreting [ɪn'təːprɪtɪŋ] n (profession) interprétariat m.

interrelated [ɪntərɪ'leɪtɪd] a en corrélation, en rapport étroit.

interrogate [ɪn'tɛrəʊgeɪt] vt interroger; (suspect etc) soumettre à un interrogatoire.

interrogation [ɪntɛrəʊ'geɪʃən] n interrogation f; interrogatoire m.

interrogative [ɪntə'rɒgətɪv] a interrogateur(trice) ♦ n (LING) interrogatif m.

interrogator [ɪn'tɛrəgeɪtə*] n interrogateur/trice.

interrupt [ɪntə'rʌpt] vt interrompre.

interruption [ɪntə'rʌpʃən] n interruption f.

intersect [ɪntə'sɛkt] vt couper, croiser; (MATH) intersecter ♦ vi se croiser, se couper; s'intersecter.

intersection [ɪntə'sɛkʃən] n intersection f; (of roads) croisement m.

intersperse [ɪntə'spəːs] vt: **to ~ with** parsemer de.

intertwine [ɪntə'twaɪn] vt entrelacer ♦ vi s'entrelacer.

interval ['ɪntəvl] n intervalle m; (Brit: SCOL) récréation f; (: THEATRE) entracte m; (: SPORT) mi-temps f; **bright ~s** (in weather) éclaircies fpl; **at ~s** par intervalles.

intervene [ɪntə'viːn] vi (time) s'écouler (entre-temps); (event) survenir; (person) intervenir.

intervention [ɪntə'vɛnʃən] n intervention f.

interview ['ɪntəvjuː] n (RADIO, TV etc) interview f; (for job) entrevue f ♦ vt interviewer; avoir une entrevue avec.

interviewer ['ɪntəvjuə*] n interviewer m.

intestate [ɪn'tɛsteɪt] a intestat.

intestinal [ɪn'tɛstɪnl] a intestinal(e).

intestine [ɪn'tɛstɪn] n intestin m; **large ~** gros intestin; **small ~** intestin grêle.

intimacy ['ɪntɪməsɪ] n intimité f.

intimate a ['ɪntɪmət] intime; (knowledge) approfondi(e) ♦ vt ['ɪntɪmeɪt] suggérer, laisser entendre; (announce) faire savoir.

intimately ['ɪntɪmətlɪ] ad intimement.

intimation [ɪntɪ'meɪʃən] n annonce f.

intimidate [ɪn'tɪmɪdeɪt] vt intimider.

intimidation [ɪntɪmɪ'deɪʃən] n intimidation f.

into ['ɪntu] prep dans; **~ pieces/French** en morceaux/français; **to change pounds ~ dollars** changer des livres en dollars.

intolerable [ɪn'tɒlərəbl] a intolérable.

intolerance [ɪn'tɒlərns] n intolérance f.

intolerant [ɪn'tɒlərnt] a: **~ (of)** intolérant(e)

(de); (MED) intolérant (à).

intonation [ɪntəʊ'neɪʃən] n intonation f.

intoxicate [ɪn'tɒksɪkeɪt] vt enivrer.

intoxicated [ɪn'tɒksɪkeɪtɪd] a ivre.

intoxication [ɪntɒksɪ'keɪʃən] n ivresse f.

intractable [ɪn'træktəbl] a (child, temper) indocile, insoumis(e); (problem) insoluble; (illness) incurable.

intransigent [ɪn'trænsɪdʒənt] a intransigeant(e).

intransitive [ɪn'trænsɪtɪv] a intransitif(ive).

intra-uterine device (IUD) ['ɪntrə'juːtəraɪn-] n dispositif intra-utérin (DIU), stérilet m.

intravenous [ɪntrə'viːnəs] a intraveineux(euse).

in-tray ['ɪntreɪ] n courrier m 'arrivée'.

intrepid [ɪn'trepɪd] a intrépide.

intricacy ['ɪntrɪkəsɪ] n complexité f.

intricate ['ɪntrɪkət] a complexe, compliqué(e).

intrigue [ɪn'triːg] n intrigue f ♦ vt intriguer ♦ vi intriguer, comploter.

intriguing [ɪn'triːgɪŋ] a fascinant(e).

intrinsic [ɪn'trɪnsɪk] a intrinsèque.

introduce [ɪntrə'djuːs] vt introduire; **to ~ sb (to sb)** présenter qn (à qn); **to ~ sb to** (pastime, technique) initier qn à; **may I ~ ...?** je vous présente ....

introduction [ɪntrə'dʌkʃən] n introduction f; (of person) présentation f; **a letter of ~** une lettre de recommendation.

introductory [ɪntrə'dʌktərɪ] a préliminaire, introductif(ive); **~ remarks** remarques fpl liminaires; **an ~ offer** une offre de lancement.

introspection [ɪntrəʊ'spekʃən] n introspection f.

introspective [ɪntrəʊ'spektɪv] a introspectif(ive).

introvert ['ɪntrəʊvəːt] a, n introverti(e).

intrude [ɪn'truːd] vi (person) être importun(e); **to ~ on** or **into** (conversation etc) s'immiscer dans; **am I intruding?** est-ce que je vous dérange?

intruder [ɪn'truːdə*] n intrus/e.

intrusion [ɪn'truːʒən] n intrusion f.

intrusive [ɪn'truːsɪv] a importun(e), gênant(e).

intuition [ɪntjuː'ɪʃən] n intuition f.

intuitive [ɪn'tjuːɪtɪv] a intuitif(ive).

inundate ['ɪnʌndeɪt] vt: **to ~ with** inonder de.

inure [ɪn'jʊə*] vt: **to ~ (to)** habituer (à).

invade [ɪn'veɪd] vt envahir.

invader [ɪn'veɪdə*] n envahisseur m.

invalid n ['ɪnvəlɪd] malade m/f; (with disability) invalide m/f ♦ a [ɪn'vælɪd] (not valid) invalide, non valide.

invalidate [ɪn'vælɪdeɪt] vt invalider, annuler.

invalid chair n (Brit) fauteuil m d'infirme.

invaluable [ɪn'væljuəbl] a inestimable, inappréciable.

invariable [ɪn'vɛərɪəbl] a invariable; (fig) immanquable.

invariably [ɪn'vɛərɪəblɪ] ad invariablement; **she is ~ late** elle est toujours en retard.

invasion [ɪn'veɪʒən] n invasion f.

invective [ɪn'vɛktɪv] n invective f.

inveigle [ɪn'viːgl] vt: **to ~ sb into (doing) sth** amener qn à (faire) qch (par la ruse or la flatterie).

invent [ɪn'vɛnt] vt inventer.

invention [ɪn'vɛnʃən] n invention f.
inventive [ɪn'vɛntɪv] a inventif(ive).
inventiveness [ɪn'vɛntɪvnɪs] n esprit inventif or d'invention.
inventor [ɪn'vɛntə*] n inventeur/trice.
inventory ['ɪnvəntrɪ] n inventaire m.
inventory control n (COMM) contrôle m des stocks.
inverse [ɪn'və:s] a inverse ♦ n inverse m, contraire m; **in ~ proportion (to)** inversement proportionel(le) (à).
inversely [ɪn'və:slɪ] ad inversement.
invert [ɪn'və:t] vt intervertir; (cup, object) retourner.
invertebrate [ɪn'və:tɪbrət] n invertébré m.
inverted commas [ɪn'və:tɪd-] npl (Brit) guillemets mpl.
invest [ɪn'vɛst] vt investir; (endow): **to ~ sb with sth** conférer qch à qn ♦ vi faire un investissement, investir; **to ~ in** placer de l'argent or investir dans; (acquire) s'offrir, faire l'acquisition de.
investigate [ɪn'vɛstɪgeɪt] vt étudier, examiner; (crime) faire une enquête sur.
investigation [ɪnvɛstɪ'geɪʃən] n examen m; (of crime) enquête f, investigation f.
investigative [ɪn'vɛstɪgeɪtɪv] a: **~ journalism** journalisme m d'enquête.
investigator [ɪn'vɛstɪgeɪtə*] n investigateur/trice; **private ~** détective privé.
investiture [ɪn'vɛstɪtʃə*] n investiture f.
investment [ɪn'vɛstmənt] n investissement m, placement m.
investment income n revenu m de placement.
investment trust n société f d'investissements.
investor [ɪn'vɛstə*] n épargnant/e; (shareholder) actionnaire m/f.
inveterate [ɪn'vɛtərət] a invétéré(e).
invidious [ɪn'vɪdɪəs] a injuste; (task) déplaisant(e).
invigilate [ɪn'vɪdʒɪleɪt] (Brit) vt surveiller ♦ vi être de surveillance.
invigilator [ɪn'vɪdʒɪleɪtə*] n (Brit) surveillant m (d'examen).
invigorating [ɪn'vɪgəreɪtɪŋ] a vivifiant(e); stimulant(e).
invincible [ɪn'vɪnsɪbl] a invincible.
inviolate [ɪn'vaɪələt] a inviolé(e).
invisible [ɪn'vɪzɪbl] a invisible.
invisible assets npl (Brit) actif incorporel.
invisible ink n encre f sympathique.
invisible mending n stoppage m.
invitation [ɪnvɪ'teɪʃən] n invitation f; **by ~ only** sur invitation; **at sb's ~** à la demande de qn.
invite [ɪn'vaɪt] vt inviter; (opinions etc) demander; (trouble) chercher; **to ~ sb (to do)** inviter qn (à faire); **to ~ sb to dinner** inviter qn à dîner.
invite out vt inviter (à sortir).
invite over vt inviter (chez soi).
inviting [ɪn'vaɪtɪŋ] a engageant(e), attrayant(e); (gesture) encourageant(e).
invoice ['ɪnvɔɪs] n facture f ♦ vt facturer; **to ~ sb for goods** facturer des marchandises à qn.
invoke [ɪn'vəʊk] vt invoquer.

involuntary [ɪn'vɒləntrɪ] a involontaire.
involve [ɪn'vɒlv] vt (entail) impliquer; (concern) concerner; (require) nécessiter; **to ~ sb in** (theft etc) impliquer qn dans; (activity, meeting) faire participer qn à.
involved [ɪn'vɒlvd] a complexe; **to feel ~** se sentir concerné(e); **to become ~ (in love etc)** s'engager.
involvement [ɪn'vɒlvmənt] n (personal role) participation f; (of resources, funds) mise f en jeu.
invulnerable [ɪn'vʌlnərəbl] a invulnérable.
inward [ɪn'wəd] a (movement) vers l'intérieur; (thought, feeling) profond(e), intime.
inwardly ['ɪnwədlɪ] ad (feel, think etc) secrètement, en son for intérieur.
inward(s) ['ɪnwəd(z)] ad vers l'intérieur.
I/O abbr (COMPUT: = input/output) E/S.
IOC n abbr (= International Olympic Committee) CIO m (= Comité international olympique).
iodine ['aɪəʊdi:n] n iode m.
ion ['aɪən] n ion m.
Ionian Sea [aɪ'əʊnɪən-] n: **the ~** la mer Ionienne.
iota [aɪ'əʊtə] n (fig) brin m, grain m.
IOU n abbr (= I owe you) reconnaissance f de dette.
IOW abbr (Brit) = Isle of Wight.
IPA n abbr (= International Phonetic Alphabet) A.P.I. m.
IQ n abbr = **intelligence quotient**.
IRA n abbr (= Irish Republican Army) IRA f; (US) = individual retirement account.
Iran [ɪ'rɑ:n] n Iran m.
Iranian [ɪ'reɪnɪən] a iranien(ne) ♦ n Iranien/ne; (LING) iranien m.
Iraq [ɪ'rɑ:k] n Irak m.
Iraqi [ɪ'rɑ:kɪ] a irakien(ne) ♦ n Irakien/ne; (LING) irakien m.
irascible [ɪ'ræsɪbl] a irascible.
irate [aɪ'reɪt] a courroucé(e).
Ireland ['aɪələnd] n Irlande f; **Republic of ~** République f d'Irlande.
iris, ~es ['aɪrɪs, -ɪz] n iris m.
Irish ['aɪrɪʃ] a irlandais(e) ♦ n (LING) irlandais m; **the ~** npl les Irlandais.
Irishman ['aɪrɪʃmən] n Irlandais m.
Irish Sea n: **the ~** la mer d'Irlande.
Irishwoman ['aɪrɪʃwʊmən] n Irlandaise f.
irk [ə:k] vt ennuyer.
irksome ['ə:ksəm] a ennuyeux(euse).
IRN n abbr (= Independent Radio News) agence de presse radiophonique.
IRO n abbr (US) = International Refugee Organization.
iron ['aɪən] n fer m; (for clothes) fer m à repasser ♦ a de or en fer ♦ vt (clothes) repasser; **~s** npl (chains) fers mpl, chaînes fpl.
iron out vt (crease) faire disparaître au fer; (fig) aplanir; faire disparaître.
Iron Curtain n: **the ~** le rideau de fer.
iron foundry n fonderie f de fonte.
ironic(al) [aɪ'rɒnɪk(l)] a ironique.
ironically [aɪ'rɒnɪklɪ] ad ironiquement.
ironing ['aɪənɪŋ] n repassage m.
ironing board n planche f à repasser.

ironmonger ['aɪənmʌŋgə*] n (Brit) quincailler m; **~'s (shop)** quincaillerie f.
iron ore ['aɪən'ɔ:*] n minerai m de fer.
ironworks ['aɪənwɔ:ks] n usine f sidérurgique.
irony ['aɪrənɪ] n ironie f.
irrational [ɪ'ræʃənl] a irrationnel(le); déraisonnable; qui manque de logique.
irreconcilable [ɪrekən'saɪləbl] a irréconciliable; (opinion): **~ with** inconciliable avec.
irredeemable [ɪrɪ'di:məbl] a (COMM) non remboursable.
irrefutable [ɪrɪ'fju:təbl] a irréfutable.
irregular [ɪ'regjulə*] a irrégulier(ière).
irregularity [ɪregju'lærɪtɪ] n irrégularité f.
irrelevance [ɪ'reləvəns] n manque m de rapport or d'à-propos.
irrelevant [ɪ'reləvənt] a sans rapport, hors de propos.
irreligious [ɪrɪ'lɪdʒəs] a irréligieux(euse).
irreparable [ɪ'repərəbl] a irréparable.
irreplaceable [ɪrɪ'pleɪsəbl] a irremplaçable.
irrepressible [ɪrɪ'presəbl] a irrépressible.
irreproachable [ɪrɪ'prəutʃəbl] a irréprochable.
irresistible [ɪrɪ'zɪstɪbl] a irrésistible.
irresolute [ɪ'rezəlu:t] a irrésolu(e), indécis(e).
irrespective [ɪrɪ'spektɪv]: **~ of** prep sans tenir compte de.
irresponsible [ɪrɪ'spɔnsɪbl] a (act) irréfléchi(e); (person) qui n'a pas le sens des responsabilités.
irretrievable [ɪrɪ'tri:vəbl] a irréparable, irrémédiable; (object) introuvable.
irreverent [ɪ'revərnt] a irrévérencieux(euse).
irrevocable [ɪ'revəkəbl] a irrévocable.
irrigate ['ɪrɪgeɪt] vt irriguer.
irrigation [ɪrɪ'geɪʃən] n irrigation f.
irritable ['ɪrɪtəbl] a irritable.
irritate ['ɪrɪteɪt] vt irriter.
irritation [ɪrɪ'teɪʃən] n irritation f.
IRS n abbr (US) = **Internal Revenue Service**.
is [ɪz] vb see **be**.
ISBN n abbr (= International Standard Book Number) ISBN m.
Islam ['ɪzlɑ:m] n Islam m.
island ['aɪlənd] n île f; (also: **traffic ~**) refuge m (pour piétons).
islander ['aɪləndə*] n habitant/e d'une île, insulaire m/f.
isle [aɪl] n île f.
isn't ['ɪznt] = **is not**.
isolate ['aɪsəleɪt] vt isoler.
isolated ['aɪsəleɪtɪd] a isolé(e).
isolation [aɪsə'leɪʃən] n isolement m.
isolationism [aɪsə'leɪʃənɪzəm] n isolationnisme m.
isotope ['aɪsəutəup] n isotope m.
Israel ['ɪzreɪl] n Israël m.
Israeli [ɪz'reɪlɪ] a israélien(ne) ♦ n Israélien/ne.
issue ['ɪʃu:] n question f, problème m; (outcome) résultat m, issue f; (of banknotes etc) émission f; (of newspaper etc) numéro m; (offspring) descendance f ♦ vt (rations, equipment) distribuer; (orders) donner; (book) faire paraître, publier; (banknotes, cheques, stamps) émettre, mettre en circulation ♦ vi: **to ~ from** provenir de; **at ~** en jeu, en cause; **to avoid the ~** éluder le problème; **to take ~ with sb (over sth)** ex-

primer son désaccord avec qn (sur qch); **to make an ~ of sth** faire de qch un problème; **to confuse** or **obscure the ~** embrouiller la question.
Istanbul [ɪstæn'bu:l] n Istamboul, Istanbul.
isthmus ['ɪsməs] n isthme m.
IT n abbr = **information technology**.
it [ɪt] pronoun (subject) il(elle); (direct object) le(la), l'; (indirect object) lui; (impersonal) il; ce, cela, ça; **of ~**, **from ~**, **about ~**, **out of ~** etc en; **in ~**, **to ~**, **at ~** etc y; **above ~**, **over ~** (au-)dessus; **below ~**, **under ~** (en-) dessous; **in front of/behind ~** devant/ derrière; **who is ~?** qui est-ce?; **~'s me** c'est moi; **what is ~?** qu'est-ce que c'est?; **where is ~?** où est-ce?, où est-ce que c'est?; **~'s Friday tomorrow** demain, c'est vendredi; **~'s raining** il pleut; **~'s 6 o'clock** il est 6 heures; **~'s 2 hours by train** c'est à 2 heures de train; **I've come from ~** j'en viens; **it's on ~** c'est dessus; **he's proud of ~** il en est fier; **he agreed to ~** il y a consenti.
ITA n abbr (Brit: = initial teaching alphabet) alphabet en partie phonétique utilisé pour l'enseignement de la lecture.
Italian [ɪ'tæljən] a italien(ne) ♦ n Italien/ne; (LING) italien m.
italic [ɪ'tælɪk] a italique; **~s** npl italique m.
Italy ['ɪtəlɪ] n Italie f.
itch [ɪtʃ] n démangeaison f ♦ vi (person) éprouver des démangeaisons; (part of body) démanger; **I'm ~ing to do** l'envie me démange de faire.
itching ['ɪtʃɪŋ] n démangeaison f.
itchy ['ɪtʃɪ] a qui démange; **my back is ~** j'ai le dos qui me démange.
it'd ['ɪtd] = **it would**, **it had**.
item ['aɪtəm] n (gen) article m; (on agenda) question f, point m; (in programme) numéro m; (also: **news ~**) nouvelle f; **~s of clothing** articles vestimentaires.
itemize ['aɪtəmaɪz] vt détailler, spécifier.
itinerant [ɪ'tɪnərənt] a itinérant(e); (musician) ambulant(e).
itinerary [aɪ'tɪnərərɪ] n itinéraire m.
it'll ['ɪtl] = **it will**, **it shall**.
ITN n abbr (Brit: = Independent Television News) chaîne de télévision commerciale.
its [ɪts] a son(sa), ses pl ♦ pronoun le(la) sien(ne), les siens(siennes).
it's [ɪts] = **it is**, **it has**.
itself [ɪt'self] pronoun (emphatic) lui-même(elle-même); (reflexive) se.
ITV n abbr (Brit: = Independent Television) chaîne de télévision commerciale.
IUD n abbr = **intra-uterine device**.
I've [aɪv] = **I have**.
ivory ['aɪvərɪ] n ivoire m.
Ivory Coast n Côte f d'Ivoire.
ivory tower n (fig) tour f d'ivoire.
ivy ['aɪvɪ] n lierre m.
Ivy League n (US) les grandes universités du nord-est des Etats Unis (Harvard, Yale, Princeton etc).

J

J, j [dʒeɪ] *n* (*letter*) J, j *m*; **J for Jack**, (*US*) **J for Jig** J comme Joseph.
JA *n abbr* = **judge advocate**.
J/A *abbr* = **joint account**.
jab [dʒæb] *vt*: **to ~ sth into** enfoncer *or* planter qch dans ♦ *n* coup *m*; (*MED*: *col*) piqûre *f*.
jabber ['dʒæbə*] *vt*, *vi* bredouiller, baragouiner.
jack [dʒæk] *n* (*AUT*) cric *m*; (*BOWLS*) cochonnet *m*; (*CARDS*) valet *m*.
jack in *vt* (*col*) laisser tomber.
jack up *vt* soulever (au cric).
jackal ['dʒækl] *n* chacal *m*.
jackass ['dʒækæs] *n* (*also fig*) âne *m*.
jackdaw ['dʒækdɔ:] *n* choucas *m*.
jacket ['dʒækɪt] *n* veste *f*, veston *m*; (*of boiler etc*) enveloppe *f*; (*of book*) couverture *f*, jaquette *f*; **potatoes in their ~s** (*Brit*) pommes de terre en robe des champs.
jack-in-the-box ['dʒækɪnðəbɔks] *n* diable *m* à ressort.
jack-knife ['dʒæknaɪf] *n* couteau *m* de poche ♦ *vi*: **the lorry ~d** la remorque (du camion) s'est mise en travers.
jack-of-all-trades ['dʒækəv'ɔ:ltreɪdz] *n* bricoleur *m*.
jack plug *n* (*Brit*) jack *m*.
jackpot ['dʒækpɔt] *n* gros lot.
jacuzzi [dʒə'ku:zɪ] *n* ⓡ jacuzzi *m* ⓡ.
jade [dʒeɪd] *n* (*stone*) jade *m*.
jaded ['dʒeɪdɪd] *a* éreinté(e), fatigué(e).
JAG *n abbr* = **Judge Advocate General**.
jagged ['dʒægɪd] *a* dentelé(e).
jaguar ['dʒægjuə*] *n* jaguar *m*.
jail [dʒeɪl] *n* prison *f* ♦ *vt* emprisonner, mettre en prison.
jailbird ['dʒeɪlbə:d] *n* récidiviste *m/f*.
jailbreak ['dʒeɪlbreɪk] *n* évasion *f*.
jailer ['dʒeɪlə*] *n* geôlier/ière.
jalopy [dʒə'lɔpɪ] *n* (*col*) vieux clou.
jam [dʒæm] *n* confiture *f*; (*of shoppers etc*) cohue *f*; (*also*: **traffic ~**) embouteillage *m* ♦ *vt* (*passage etc*) encombrer, obstruer; (*mechanism, drawer etc*) bloquer, coincer; (*RADIO*) brouiller ♦ *vi* (*mechanism, sliding part*) se coincer, se bloquer; (*gun*) s'enrayer; **to get sb out of a ~** (*col*) sortir qn du pétrin; **to ~ sth into** entasser *or* comprimer qch dans; enfoncer qch dans; **the telephone lines are ~med** les lignes (téléphoniques) sont encombrées.
Jamaica [dʒə'meɪkə] *n* Jamaïque *f*.
Jamaican [dʒə'meɪkən] *a* jamaïquain(e) ♦ *n* Jamaïquain/e.
jamb [dʒæm] *n* jambage *m*.
jam-packed [dʒæm'pækt] *a*: **~ (with)** bourré(e) (de).
jam session *n* jam session *f*.

Jan. *abbr* (= *January*) janv.
jangle ['dʒæŋgl] *vi* cliqueter.
janitor ['dʒænɪtə*] *n* (*caretaker*) huissier *m*; concierge *m*.
January ['dʒænjuərɪ] *n* janvier *m*; *for phrases see also* **July**.
Japan [dʒə'pæn] *n* Japon *m*.
Japanese [dʒæpə'ni:z] *a* japonais(e) ♦ *n* (*pl inv*) Japonais/e; (*LING*) japonais *m*.
jar [dʒa:*] *n* (*container*) pot *m*, bocal *m* ♦ *vi* (*sound*) produire un son grinçant *or* discordant; (*colours etc*) détonner, jurer ♦ *vt* (*shake*) ébranler, secouer.
jargon ['dʒa:gən] *n* jargon *m*.
jarring ['dʒa:rɪŋ] *a* (*sound*, *colour*) discordant(e).
Jas. *abbr* = *James*.
jasmin(e) ['dʒæzmɪn] *n* jasmin *m*.
jaundice ['dʒɔ:ndɪs] *n* jaunisse *f*.
jaundiced ['dʒɔ:ndɪst] *a* (*fig*) envieux(euse), désapprobateur(trice).
jaunt [dʒɔ:nt] *n* balade *f*.
jaunty ['dʒɔ:ntɪ] *a* enjoué(e); désinvolte.
Java ['dʒa:və] *n* Java *f*.
javelin ['dʒævlɪn] *n* javelot *m*.
jaw [dʒɔ:] *n* mâchoire *f*.
jawbone ['dʒɔ:bəun] *n* maxillaire *m*.
jay [dʒeɪ] *n* geai *m*.
jaywalker ['dʒeɪwɔ:kə*] *n* piéton indiscipliné.
jazz [dʒæz] *n* jazz *m*.
jazz up *vt* animer, égayer.
jazz band *n* orchestre *m or* groupe *m* de jazz.
jazzy ['dʒæzɪ] *a* bariolé(e), tapageur(euse).
JCS *n abbr* (*US*) = *Joint Chiefs of Staff*.
JD *n abbr* (*US*: = *Doctor of Laws*) titre universitaire; (: = *Justice Department*) ministère de la Justice.
jealous ['dʒɛləs] *a* jaloux(ouse).
jealously ['dʒɛləslɪ] *ad* jalousement.
jealousy ['dʒɛləsɪ] *n* jalousie *f*.
jeans [dʒi:nz] *npl* (blue-)jean *m*.
Jeep [dʒi:p] *n* ⓡ jeep *f*.
jeer [dʒɪə*] *vi*: **to ~ (at)** huer; se moquer cruellement (de), railler.
jeering ['dʒɪərɪŋ] *a* railleur(euse), moqueur(euse) ♦ *n* huées *fpl*.
jeers ['dʒɪəz] *npl* huées *fpl*; sarcasmes *mpl*.
jelly ['dʒɛlɪ] *n* gelée *f*.
jellyfish ['dʒɛlɪfɪʃ] *n* méduse *f*.
jeopardize ['dʒɛpədaɪz] *vt* mettre en danger *or* péril.
jeopardy ['dʒɛpədɪ] *n*: **in ~** en danger *or* péril.
jerk [dʒə:k] *n* secousse *f*; saccade *f*; sursaut *m*, spasme *m*; (*col*) pauvre type *m* ♦ *vt* donner une secousse à ♦ *vi* (*vehicles*) cahoter.
jerkin ['dʒə:kɪn] *n* blouson *m*.
jerky ['dʒə:kɪ] *a* saccadé(e); cahotant(e).
jerry-built ['dʒɛrɪbɪlt] *a* de mauvaise qualité.
jerry can ['dʒɛrɪ-] *n* bidon *m*.
Jersey ['dʒə:zɪ] *n* Jersey *f*.
jersey ['dʒə:zɪ] *n* tricot *m*; (*fabric*) jersey *m*.
Jerusalem [dʒə'ru:sləm] *n* Jérusalem.
jest [dʒɛst] *n* plaisanterie *f*; **in ~** en plaisantant.
jester ['dʒɛstə*] *n* (*HISTORY*) plaisantin *m*.
Jesus ['dʒi:zəs] *n* Jésus; **~ Christ** Jésus-Christ.

jet [dʒɛt] *n* (*of gas, liquid*) jet *m*; (*AUT*) gicleur *m*; (*AVIAT*) avion *m* à réaction, jet *m*.
jet-black ['dʒɛt'blæk] *a* (d'un noir) de jais.
jet engine *n* moteur *m* à réaction.
jet lag *n* décalage *m* horaire.
jetsam ['dʒɛtsəm] *n* objets jetés à la mer (et rejetés sur la côte).
jettison ['dʒɛtɪsn] *vt* jeter par-dessus bord.
jetty ['dʒɛtɪ] *n* jetée *f*, digue *f*.
Jew [dʒuː] *n* Juif *m*.
jewel ['dʒuːəl] *n* bijou *m*, joyau *m*.
jeweller ['dʒuːələ*] *n* bijoutier/ière, joaillier *m*; ~'s (shop) *n* bijouterie *f*, joaillerie *f*.
jewellery ['dʒuːəlrɪ] *n* bijoux *mpl*.
Jewess ['dʒuːɪs] *n* Juive *f*.
Jewish ['dʒuːɪʃ] *a* juif(juive).
JFK *n abbr* (*US*) = *John Fitzgerald Kennedy International Airport*.
jib [dʒɪb] *n* (*NAUT*) foc *m*; (*of crane*) flèche *f* ♦ *vi* (*horse*) regimber; to ~ at doing sth rechigner à faire qch.
jibe [dʒaɪb] *n* sarcasme *m*.
jiffy ['dʒɪfɪ] *n* (*col*): in a ~ en un clin d'œil.
jig [dʒɪg] *n* (*dance, tune*) gigue *m*.
jigsaw ['dʒɪgsɔː] *n* (*also*: ~ puzzle) puzzle *m*; (*tool*) scie sauteuse.
jilt [dʒɪlt] *vt* laisser tomber, plaquer.
jingle ['dʒɪŋgl] *n* (*advertising* ~) couplet *m* publicitaire ♦ *vi* cliqueter, tinter.
jingoism ['dʒɪŋgəʊɪzəm] *n* chauvinisme *m*.
jinx [dʒɪŋks] *n* (*col*) (mauvais) sort.
jitters ['dʒɪtəz] *npl* (*col*): to get the ~ avoir la trouille *or* la frousse.
jittery ['dʒɪtərɪ] *a* (*col*) froussard(e).
jiujitsu [dʒuː'dʒɪtsuː] *n* jiu-jitsu *m*.
job [dʒɔb] *n* travail *m*; (*employment*) emploi *m*, poste *m*, place *f*; a part- time/full-time ~ un emploi à temps partiel/à plein temps; he's only doing his ~ il fait son boulot; it's a good ~ that ... c'est heureux *or* c'est une chance que ...; just the ~! (c'est) juste *or* exactement ce qu'il faut!
jobber ['dʒɔbə*] *n* (*Brit STOCK EXCHANGE*) négociant *m* en titres.
jobbing ['dʒɔbɪŋ] *a* (*Brit: workman*) à la tâche, à la journée.
Jobcentre ['dʒɔbsentə*] *n* agence *f* pour l'emploi.
job creation scheme *n* plan *m* pour la création d'emplois.
job description *n* description *f* du poste.
jobless ['dʒɔblɪs] *a* sans travail, au chômage.
job lot *n* lot *m* (d'articles divers).
job satisfaction *n* satisfaction professionnelle.
job security *n* sécurité *f* de l'emploi.
job specification *n* caractéristiques *fpl* du poste.
jockey ['dʒɔkɪ] *n* jockey *m* ♦ *vi*: to ~ for position manœuvrer pour être bien placé.
jockey box *n* (*US AUT*) boîte *f* à gants, videpoches *m inv*.
jocular ['dʒɔkjulə*] *a* jovial(e), enjoué(e); facétieux(euse).
jog [dʒɔg] *vt* secouer ♦ *vi* (*SPORT*) faire du jogging; to ~ along cahoter; trotter; to ~ sb's memory rafraîchir la mémoire de qn.
jogger ['dʒɔgə*] *n* jogger *m/f*.
jogging ['dʒɔgɪŋ] *n* jogging *m*.

join [dʒɔɪn] *vt* unir, assembler; (*become member of*) s'inscrire à; (*meet*) rejoindre, retrouver; se joindre à ♦ *vi* (*roads, rivers*) se rejoindre, se rencontrer ♦ *n* raccord *m*; will you ~ us for dinner? vous dînerez bien avec nous?; I'll ~ you later je vous rejoindrai plus tard; to ~ forces (with) s'associer (à).
join in *vi* se mettre de la partie ♦ *vt* se mêler à.
join up *vi* s'engager.
joiner ['dʒɔɪnə*] *n* menuisier *m*.
joinery ['dʒɔɪnərɪ] *n* menuiserie *f*.
joint [dʒɔɪnt] *n* (*TECH*) jointure *f*; joint *m*; (*ANAT*) articulation *f*, jointure; (*Brit: CULIN*) rôti *m*; (*col: place*) boîte *f* ♦ *a* commun(e); (*committee*) mixte, paritaire; ~ responsibility coresponsabilité *f*.
joint account *n* compte joint.
jointly ['dʒɔɪntlɪ] *ad* ensemble, en commun.
joint ownership *n* copropriété *f*.
joint-stock company ['dʒɔɪntstɔk-] *n* société *f* par actions.
joint venture *n* entreprise commune.
joist [dʒɔɪst] *n* solive *f*.
joke [dʒəuk] *n* plaisanterie *f*; (*also*: practical ~) farce *f* ♦ *vi* plaisanter; to play a ~ on jouer un tour à, faire une farce à.
joker ['dʒəukə*] *n* plaisantin *m*, blagueur/euse; (*CARDS*) joker *m*.
joking ['dʒəukɪŋ] *n* plaisanterie *f*.
jollity ['dʒɔlɪtɪ] *n* réjouissances *fpl*, gaieté *f*.
jolly ['dʒɔlɪ] *a* gai(e), enjoué(e) ♦ *ad* (*Brit col*) rudement, drôlement ♦ *vt* (*Brit*): to ~ sb along amadouer qn, convaincre *or* entraîner qn à force d'encouragements; ~ good! (*Brit*) formidable!
jolt [dʒəult] *n* cahot *m*, secousse *f* ♦ *vt* cahoter, secouer.
Jordan [dʒɔːdən] *n* (*country*) Jordanie *f*; (*river*) Jourdain *m*.
Jordanian [dʒɔː'deɪnɪən] *a* jordanien(ne) ♦ *n* Jordanien/ne.
joss stick ['dʒɔsstɪk] *n* bâton *m* d'encens.
jostle ['dʒɔsl] *vt* bousculer, pousser ♦ *vi* jouer des coudes.
jot [dʒɔt] *n*: not one ~ pas un brin.
jot down *vt* inscrire rapidement, noter.
jotter ['dʒɔtə*] *n* (*Brit*) cahier *m* (de brouillon); bloc-notes *m*.
journal ['dʒɔːnl] *n* journal *m*.
journalese [dʒɔː'nəliːz] *n* (*pej*) style *m* journalistique.
journalism ['dʒɔːnəlɪzəm] *n* journalisme *m*.
journalist ['dʒɔːnəlɪst] *n* journaliste *m/f*.
journey ['dʒɔːnɪ] *n* voyage *m*; (*distance covered*) trajet *m*; a 5-hour ~ un voyage de 5 heures ♦ *vi* voyager.
jovial ['dʒəuvɪəl] *a* jovial(e).
jowl [dʒaul] *n* mâchoire *f* (*inférieure*); bajoue *f*.
joy [dʒɔɪ] *n* joie *f*.
joyful ['dʒɔɪful], **joyous** ['dʒɔɪəs] *a* joyeux(euse).
joy ride *n* virée *f* (*gén avec une voiture volée*).
joystick ['dʒɔɪstɪk] *n* (*AVIAT*) manche *m* à balai; (*COMPUT*) manche à balai, manette *f* (de jeu).
JP *n abbr* = **Justice of the Peace**.

Jr. *abbr* = **junior**.

JTPA *n abbr* (*US*: = *Job Training Partnership Act*) programme gouvernemental de formation.

jubilant ['dʒuːbɪlnt] *a* triomphant(e); réjoui(e).

jubilation [dʒuːbɪ'leɪʃən] *n* jubilation *f*.

jubilee ['dʒuːbɪliː] *n* jubilé *m*; **silver** ~ (jubilé du) vingt-cinquième anniversaire.

judge [dʒʌdʒ] *n* juge *m* ♦ *vt* juger; (*estimate: weight, size etc*) apprécier; (*consider*) estimer ♦ *vi*: **judging** *or* **to** ~ **by his expression** d'après son expression; **as far as I can** ~ autant que je puisse en juger; **I** ~**d it necessary to inform him** j'ai jugé nécessaire de l'informer.

judge advocate (JA) *n* (*MIL*) magistrat *m* militaire.

Judge Advocate General (JAG) *n* (*MIL*) magistrat *m* militaire en chef.

judg(e)ment ['dʒʌdʒmənt] *n* jugement *m*; (*punishment*) châtiment *m*; **in my** ~ à mon avis; **to pass** ~ **on** (*LAW*) prononcer un jugement (sur).

judicial [dʒuː'dɪʃl] *a* judiciaire; (*fair*) impartial(e).

judiciary [dʒuː'dɪʃɪərɪ] *n* (pouvoir *m*) judiciaire *m*.

judicious [dʒuː'dɪʃəs] *a* judicieux(euse).

judo ['dʒuːdəu] *n* judo *m*.

jug [dʒʌg] *n* pot *m*, cruche *f*.

jugged hare ['dʒʌgd'hɛə*] *n* (*Brit*) civet *m* de lièvre.

juggernaut ['dʒʌgənɔːt] *n* (*Brit*: *huge truck*) mastodonte *m*.

juggle ['dʒʌgl] *vi* jongler.

juggler ['dʒʌglə*] *n* jongleur *m*.

Jugoslav ['juːgəu'slɑːv] *a, n* = **Yugoslav**.

jugular ['dʒʌgjulə*] *a*: ~ **(vein)** veine *f* jugulaire.

juice [dʒuːs] *n* jus *m*; (*col: petrol*): **we've run out of** ~ c'est la panne sèche.

juicy ['dʒuːsɪ] *a* juteux(euse).

jukebox ['dʒuːkbɒks] *n* juke-box *m*.

Jul. *abbr* (= *July*) juil.

July [dʒuː'laɪ] *n* juillet *m*; **the first of** ~ le premier juillet; **(on) the eleventh of** ~ le onze juillet; **in the month of** ~ au mois de juillet; **at the beginning/end of** ~ au début/à la fin (du mois) de juillet, début/fin juillet; **in the middle of** ~ au milieu (du mois) de juillet, à la mi-juillet; **during** ~ pendant le mois de juillet; **in** ~ **of next year** en juillet de l'année prochaine; **each** *or* **every** ~ tous les ans *or* chaque année en juillet; ~ **was wet this year** il a beaucoup plu cette année en juillet.

jumble ['dʒʌmbl] *n* fouillis *m* ♦ *vt* (*also*: ~ **up**, ~ **together**) mélanger, brouiller.

jumble sale *n* (*Brit*) vente *f* de charité.

jumbo ['dʒʌmbəu] *a*: ~ **jet** (avion) gros porteur (à réaction); ~ **size** format maxi *or* extra-grand.

jump [dʒʌmp] *vi* sauter, bondir; (*start*) sursauter; (*increase*) monter en flèche ♦ *vt* sauter, franchir ♦ *n* saut *m*, bond *m*; sursaut *m*; (*fence*) obstacle *m*; **to** ~ **the queue** (*Brit*) passer avant son tour.

jump about *vi* sautiller.

jump at *vt fus* (*fig*) sauter sur; **he** ~**ed at the offer** il s'est empressé d'accepter la proposition.

jump down *vi* sauter (pour descendre).

jump up *vi* se lever (d'un bond).

jumped-up ['dʒʌmptʌp] *a* (*Brit pej*) parvenu(e).

jumper ['dʒʌmpə*] *n* (*Brit*: *pullover*) pull-over *m*; (*US*: *pinafore dress*) robe-chasuble *f*; (*SPORT*) sauteur/euse.

jump leads, (*US*) **jumper cables** *npl* câbles *mpl* de démarrage.

jumpy ['dʒʌmpɪ] *a* nerveux(euse), agité(e).

Jun. *abbr* = **June**.

Jun., Junr *abbr* = **junior**.

junction ['dʒʌnkʃən] *n* (*Brit*: *of roads*) carrefour *m*; (*of rails*) embranchement *m*.

juncture ['dʒʌnktʃə*] *n*: **at this** ~ à ce moment-là, sur ces entrefaites.

June [dʒuːn] *n* juin *m*; *for phrases see also* July.

jungle ['dʒʌngl] *n* jungle *f*.

junior ['dʒuːnɪə*] *a, n*: **he's** ~ **to me (by 2 years)**, **he's my** ~ **(by 2 years)** il est mon cadet (de 2 ans), il est plus jeune que moi (de 2 ans); **he's** ~ **to me** (*seniority*) il est en dessous de moi (dans la hiérarchie), j'ai plus d'ancienneté que lui.

junior executive *n* cadre moyen.

junior high school *n* (*US*) ≈ collège *m* d'enseignement secondaire.

junior minister *n* (*Brit*) ministre *m* sous tutelle.

junior partner *n* associé(-adjoint) *m*.

junior school *n* (*Brit*) école *f* primaire, cours moyen.

junior sizes *npl* (*COMM*) tailles *fpl* fillettes/garçonnets.

juniper ['dʒuːnɪpə*] *n*: ~ **berry** baie *f* de genièvre.

junk [dʒʌnk] *n* (*rubbish*) bric-à-brac *m inv*; (*ship*) jonque *f* ♦ *vt* (*col*) abandonner, mettre au rancart.

junk dealer *n* brocanteur/euse.

junket ['dʒʌnkɪt] *n* (*CULIN*) lait caillé; (*Brit col*): **to go on a** ~, **go** ~**ing** voyager aux frais de la princesse.

junk foods *npl* snacks *mpl* (vite prêts).

junkie ['dʒʌnkɪ] *n* (*col*) junkie *m*, drogué/e.

junk room *n* (*US*) débarras *m*.

junk shop *n* (boutique *f* de) brocanteur *m*.

junta ['dʒʌntə] *n* junte *f*.

Jupiter ['dʒuːpɪtə*] *n* (*planet*) Jupiter *f*.

jurisdiction [dʒuərɪs'dɪkʃən] *n* juridiction *f*; **it falls** *or* **comes within/outside our** ~ cela est/n'est pas de notre compétence *or* ressort.

jurisprudence [dʒuərɪs'pruːdəns] *n* jurisprudence *f*.

juror ['dʒuərə*] *n* juré *m*.

jury ['dʒuərɪ] *n* jury *m*.

jury box *n* banc *m* des jurés.

juryman ['dʒuərɪmən] *n* = **juror**.

just [dʒʌst] *a* juste ♦ *ad*: **he's** ~ **done it/left** il vient de le faire/partir; ~ **as I expected** exactement *or* précisément comme je m'y attendais; ~ **right/two o'clock** exactement *or* juste ce qu'il faut/deux heures; **we were** ~ **going** nous partions; **I was** ~ **about to phone** j'allais téléphoner; **as he was leav-**

ing au moment *or* à l'instant précis où il partait; ~ **before/enough/here** juste avant/ assez/là; **it's ~ me/a mistake** ce n'est que moi/(rien) qu'une erreur; ~ **missed/caught** manqué/attrapé de justesse; ~ **listen to this!** écoutez un peu ça!; ~ **ask someone the way** vous n'avez qu'à demander votre chemin à quelqu'un; **it's ~ as good** c'est (vraiment) aussi bon; **it's ~ as well that you ...** heureusement que vous ...; **not ~ now** pas tout de suite; ~ **a minute!**, ~ **one moment!** un instant (s'il vous plaît)!

justice ['dʒʌstɪs] *n* justice *f*; **Lord Chief J~** (*Brit*) premier président de la cour d'appel; **this photo doesn't do you** ~ cette photo ne vous avantage pas.

Justice of the Peace (JP) *n* juge *m* de paix.

justifiable [dʒʌstɪ'faɪəbl] *a* justifiable.

justifiably [dʒʌstɪ'faɪəblɪ] *ad* légitimement, à juste titre.

justification [dʒʌstɪfɪ'keɪʃən] *n* justification *f*.

justify ['dʒʌstɪfaɪ] *vt* justifier; **to be justified in doing sth** être en droit de faire qch.

justly ['dʒʌstlɪ] *ad* avec raison, justement.

justness ['dʒʌstnɪs] *n* justesse *f*.

jut [dʒʌt] *vi* (*also*: ~ **out**) dépasser, faire saillie.

jute [dʒuːt] *n* jute *m*.

juvenile ['dʒuːvənaɪl] *a* juvénile; (*court, books*) pour enfants ♦ *n* adolescent/e.

juvenile delinquency *n* délinquance *f* juvénile.

juxtapose ['dʒʌkstəpəuz] *vt* juxtaposer.

juxtaposition ['dʒʌkstəpə'zɪʃən] *n* juxtaposition *f*.

K

K, k [keɪ] *n* (*letter*) K, k *m*; **K for King** K comme Kléber.

K *abbr* (= *kilobyte*) Ko; (*Brit*: = *Knight*) titre honorifique ♦ *n abbr* (= *one thousand*) K.

kaftan ['kæftæn] *n* cafetan *m*.

Kalahari Desert [kælə'hɑːrɪ-] *n* désert *m* de Kalahari.

kale [keɪl] *n* chou frisé.

kaleidoscope [kə'laɪdəskəup] *n* kaléidoscope *m*.

Kampala [kæm'pɑːlə] *n* Kampala.

Kampuchea [kæmpu'tʃɪə] *n* Kampuchéa *m*.

kangaroo [kæŋgə'ruː] *n* kangourou *m*.

kaput [kə'put] *a* (*col*) kapout, capout.

karate [kə'rɑːtɪ] *n* karaté *m*.

Kashmir [kæʃ'mɪə*] *n* Cachemire *m*.

KC *n abbr* (*Brit LAW*: = *King's Counsel*) titre donné à certains avocats.

kd *abbr* (*US*: = *knocked down*) en pièces détachées.

kebab [kə'bæb] *n* kébab *m*.

keel [kiːl] *n* quille *f*; **on an even** ~ (*fig*) à flot.

keel over *vi* (*NAUT*) chavirer, dessaler; (*person*) tomber dans les pommes.

keen [kiːn] *a* (*interest, desire, competition*) vif(vive); (*eye, intelligence*) pénétrant(e); (*edge*) effilé(e); (*eager*) plein(e) d'enthousiasme; **to be ~ to do** *or* **on doing sth** désirer vivement faire qch, tenir beaucoup à faire qch; **to be ~ on sth/sb** aimer beaucoup qch/qn; **I'm not ~ on going** je ne suis pas chaud pour aller, je n'ai pas très envie d'y aller.

keenly ['kiːnlɪ] *ad* (*enthusiastically*) avec enthousiasme; (*feel*) vivement, profondément; (*look*) intensément.

keenness ['kiːnnɪs] *n* (*eagerness*) enthousiasme *m*; ~ **to do** vif désir de faire.

keep [kiːp] *vb* (*pt, pp* **kept** [kept]) *vt* (*retain, preserve*) garder; (*hold back*) retenir; (*a shop, the books, a diary*) tenir; (*feed: one's family etc*) entretenir, assurer la subsistance de; (*a promise*) tenir; (*chickens, bees, pigs etc*) élever ♦ *vi* (*food*) se conserver; (*remain: in a certain state or place*) rester ♦ *n* (*of castle*) donjon *m*; (*food etc*): **enough for his** ~ assez pour (assurer) sa subsistance; **to** ~ **doing sth** continuer à faire qch; faire qch continuellement; **to** ~ **sb from doing/sth from happening** empêcher qn de faire *or* que qch (ne) fasse/que qch (n')arrive; **to** ~ **sb happy/a place tidy** faire que qn soit content/ qu'un endroit reste propre; **to** ~ **sb waiting** faire attendre qn; **to** ~ **an appointment** ne pas manquer un rendez-vous; **to** ~ **a record of sth** prendre note de qch; **to** ~ **sth to o.s.** garder qch pour soi, tenir qch secret; **to** ~ **sth (back) from sb** cacher qch à qn; **to** ~ **time** (*clock*) être à l'heure, ne pas retarder.

keep away *vt*: **to** ~ **sth/sb away from sb** tenir qch/qn éloigné de qn ♦ *vi*: **to** ~ **away (from)** ne pas s'approcher (de).

keep back *vt* (*crowds, tears, money*) retenir ♦ *vi* rester en arrière.

keep down *vt* (*control: prices, spending*) empêcher d'augmenter, limiter; (*retain: food*) garder ♦ *vi* (*person*) rester assis(e); rester par terre.

keep in *vt* (*invalid, child*) garder à la maison; (*SCOL*) consigner ♦ *vi* (*col*): **to** ~ **in with sb** rester en bons termes avec qn.

keep off *vi* ne pas s'approcher; "~ **off the grass**" "pelouse interdite".

keep on *vi* continuer; **to** ~ **on doing** continuer à faire.

keep out *vt* empêcher d'entrer ♦ *vi* rester en dehors; "~ **out**" "défense d'entrer".

keep up *vi* se maintenir; (*fig: in comprehension*) suivre ♦ *vt* continuer, maintenir; **to** ~ **up with sb** se maintenir au niveau de; **to** ~ **up with sb** (*in race etc*) aller aussi vite que qn, être du même niveau que qn.

keeper ['kiːpə*] *n* gardien/ne.

keep-fit [kiːp'fɪt] *n* gymnastique *f* de maintien.

keeping ['kiːpɪŋ] *n* (*care*) garde *f*; **in** ~ **with** à l'avenant de; en accord avec.

keeps [kiːps] *n*: **for** ~**s** (*col*) pour de bon, pour toujours.

keepsake ['kiːpseɪk] *n* souvenir *m*.

keg [keg] *n* barrique *f*, tonnelet *m*.

kennel ['kenl] *n* niche *f*; ~**s** *npl* chenil *m*.

Kenya ['kenjə] *n* Kenya *m*.

Kenyan ['kɛnjən] a Kenyen(ne) ♦ n Kenyen/ne.
kept [kɛpt] pt, pp of **keep**.
kerb [kəːb] n (Brit) bordure f du trottoir.
kernel ['kəːnl] n amande f; (fig) noyau m.
kerosene ['kɛrəsiːn] n kérosène m.
ketchup ['kɛtʃəp] n ketchup m.
kettle ['kɛtl] n bouilloire f.
kettle drums npl timbales fpl.
key [kiː] n (gen, MUS) clé f; (of piano, typewriter) touche f; (on map) légende f ♦ cpd (-)clé.
　key in vt (text) introduire au clavier.
keyboard ['kiːbɔːd] n clavier m ♦ vt (text) saisir.
keyed up [kiːd'ʌp] a: **to be (all)** ~ être surexcité(e).
keyhole ['kiːhəul] n trou m de la serrure.
keynote ['kiːnəut] n (MUS) tonique f; (fig) note dominante.
keypad ['kiːpæd] n pavé m numérique.
key ring n porte-clés m.
keystroke ['kiːstrəuk] n frappe f.
kg abbr (= kilogram) K.
KGB n abbr KGB m.
khaki ['kɑːki] a, n kaki (m).
kibbutz [kɪ'buts] n kibboutz m.
kick [kɪk] vt donner un coup de pied à ♦ vi (horse) ruer ♦ n coup m de pied; (of rifle) recul m; (col: thrill): **he does it for** ~**s** il le fait parce que ça l'excite, il le fait pour le plaisir.
　kick around vi (col) traîner.
　kick off vi (SPORT) donner le coup d'envoi.
kick-off ['kɪkɔf] n (SPORT) coup m d'envoi.
kick-start ['kɪkstɑːt] n (also: ~er) lanceur m au pied.
kid [kɪd] n (col: child) gamin/e, gosse m/f; (animal, leather) chevreau m ♦ vi (col) plaisanter, blaguer.
kidnap ['kɪdnæp] vt enlever, kidnapper.
kidnapper ['kɪdnæpə*] n ravisseur/euse.
kidnapping ['kɪdnæpɪŋ] n enlèvement m.
kidney ['kɪdnɪ] n (ANAT) rein m; (CULIN) rognon m.
kidney bean n haricot m rouge.
kidney machine n (MED) rein artificiel.
Kilimanjaro [kɪlɪmən'dʒɑːrəu] n: **Mount** ~ Kilimandjaro m.
kill [kɪl] vt tuer; (fig) faire échouer; détruire; supprimer ♦ n mise f à mort; **to** ~ **time** tuer le temps.
　kill off vt exterminer; (fig) éliminer.
killer ['kɪlə*] n tueur/euse; meurtrier/ière.
killing ['kɪlɪŋ] n meurtre m; tuerie f, massacre m; (col): **to make a** ~ se remplir les poches, réussir un beau coup ♦ a (col) tordant(e).
kill-joy ['kɪldʒɔɪ] n rabat-joie m inv.
kiln [kɪln] n four m.
kilo ['kiːləu] n abbr (= kilogram) kilo m.
kilobyte ['kiːləubaɪt] n kilo-octet m.
kilogram(me) ['kɪləugræm] n kilogramme m.
kilometre, (US) **kilometer** ['kɪləmiːtə*] n kilomètre m.
kilowatt ['kɪləuwɔt] n kilowatt m.
kilt [kɪlt] n kilt m.
kilter ['kɪltə*] n: **out of** ~ déréglé(e), détraqué(e).
kimono [kɪ'məunəu] n kimono m.

kin [kɪn] n see **next**, **kith**.
kind [kaɪnd] a gentil(le), aimable ♦ n sorte f, espèce f; (species) genre m; **to be two of a** ~ se ressembler; **would you be** ~ **enough to ...?**, **would you be so** ~ **as to ...?** auriez-vous la gentillesse or l'obligeance de ...?; **it's very** ~ **of you (to do)** c'est très aimable à vous (de faire); **in** ~ (COMM) en nature; (fig): **to repay sb in** ~ rendre la pareille à qn.
kindergarten ['kɪndəgɑːtn] n jardin m d'enfants.
kind-hearted [kaɪnd'hɑːtɪd] a bon(bonne).
kindle ['kɪndl] vt allumer, enflammer.
kindling ['kɪndlɪŋ] n petit bois.
kindly ['kaɪndlɪ] a bienveillant(e), plein(e) de gentillesse ♦ ad avec bonté; **will you** ~ ... auriez-vous la bonté or l'obligeance de ...; **he didn't take it** ~ il l'a mal pris.
kindness ['kaɪndnɪs] n bonté f, gentillesse f.
kindred ['kɪndrɪd] a apparenté(e); ~ **spirit** âme f sœur.
kinetic [kɪ'nɛtɪk] a cinétique.
king [kɪŋ] n roi m.
kingdom ['kɪŋdəm] n royaume m.
kingfisher ['kɪŋfɪʃə*] n martin-pêcheur m.
kingpin ['kɪŋpɪn] n (TECH) pivot m; (fig) cheville ouvrière.
king-size(d) ['kɪŋsaɪz(d)] a (cigarette) (format) extra-long(longue).
kink [kɪŋk] n (of rope) entortillement m; (in hair) ondulation f; (col: fig) aberration f.
kinky ['kɪŋkɪ] a (fig) excentrique; (pej) aux goûts spéciaux.
kinship ['kɪnʃɪp] n parenté f.
kinsman ['kɪnzmən] n parent m.
kinswoman ['kɪnzwumən] n parente f.
kiosk ['kiːɔsk] n kiosque m; (Brit: also: **telephone** ~) cabine f (téléphonique); (: also: **newspaper** ~) kiosque à journaux.
kipper ['kɪpə*] n hareng fumé et salé.
kiss [kɪs] n baiser m ♦ vt embrasser; **to** ~ **(each other)** s'embrasser; **to** ~ **sb goodbye** dire au revoir à qn en l'embrassant; ~ **of life** n (Brit) bouche à bouche m.
kit [kɪt] n équipement m, matériel m; (set of tools etc) trousse f; (for assembly) kit m; **tool** ~ nécessaire m à outils.
　kit out vt (Brit) équiper.
kitbag ['kɪtbæg] n sac m de voyage or de marin.
kitchen ['kɪtʃɪn] n cuisine f.
kitchen garden n jardin m potager.
kitchen sink n évier m.
kitchen unit n (Brit) élément m de cuisine.
kitchenware ['kɪtʃɪnwɛə*] n vaisselle f; ustensiles mpl de cuisine.
kite [kaɪt] n (toy) cerf-volant m; (ZOOL) milan m.
kith [kɪθ] n: ~ **and kin** parents et amis mpl.
kitten ['kɪtn] n petit chat, chaton m.
kitty ['kɪtɪ] n (money) cagnotte f.
KKK n abbr (US) = Ku Klux Klan.
Kleenex ['kliːnɛks] n ® Kleenex m ®.
kleptomaniac [klɛptəu'meɪnɪæk] n kleptomane m/f.
km abbr (= kilometre) km.
km/h abbr (= kilometres per hour) km/h.
knack [næk] n: **to have the** ~ **(of doing)** avoir

le coup (pour faire); **there's a** ~ il y a un coup à prendre *or* une combine.

knapsack ['næpsæk] *n* musette *f*.

knave [neɪv] *n* (*CARDS*) valet *m*.

knead [niːd] *vt* pétrir.

knee [niː] *n* genou *m*.

kneecap ['niːkæp] *n* rotule *f*.

knee-deep ['niː'diːp] *a*: **the water was** ~ l'eau arrivait aux genoux.

kneel, *pt*, *pp* **knelt** [niːl, nɛlt] *vi* (*also:* ~ **down**) s'agenouiller.

kneepad ['niːpæd] *n* genouillère *f*.

knell [nɛl] *n* glas *m*.

knelt [nɛlt] *pt*, *pp of* **kneel**.

knew [njuː] *pt of* **know**.

knickers ['nɪkəz] *npl* (*Brit*) culotte *f* (de femme).

knick-knack ['nɪknæk] *n* colifichet *m*.

knife [naɪf] *n* (*pl* **knives**) couteau *m* ♦ *vt* poignarder, frapper d'un coup de couteau; ~, **fork and spoon** couvert *m*.

knight [naɪt] *n* chevalier *m*; (*CHESS*) cavalier *m*.

knighthood ['naɪthud] *n* chevalerie *f*; (*title*): **to get a** ~ être fait chevalier.

knit [nɪt] *vt* tricoter; (*fig*): **to** ~ **together** unir ♦ *vi* (*broken bones*) se ressouder.

knitted ['nɪtɪd] *a* en tricot.

knitting ['nɪtɪŋ] *n* tricot *m*.

knitting machine *n* machine *f* à tricoter.

knitting needle *n* aiguille *f* à tricoter.

knitting pattern *n* modèle *m* (pour tricot).

knitwear ['nɪtwɛə*] *n* tricots *mpl*, lainages *mpl*.

knives [naɪvz] *npl of* **knife**.

knob [nɔb] *n* bouton *m*; (*Brit*): **a** ~ **of butter** une noix de beurre.

knobbly ['nɔblɪ], (*US*) **knobby** ['nɔbɪ] *a* (*wood*, *surface*) noueux(euse); (*knees*) noueux.

knock [nɔk] *vt* frapper; (*make: hole etc*): **to** ~ **a hole in** faire un trou dans, trouer; (*force: nail etc*): **to** ~ **a nail into** enfoncer un clou dans; (*fig: col*) dénigrer ♦ *vi* (*engine*) cogner; (*at door etc*): **to** ~ **at/on** frapper à/ sur ♦ *n* coup *m*; **he** ~**ed at the door** il frappa à la porte.

knock down *vt* renverser; (*price*) réduire.

knock off *vi* (*col: finish*) s'arrêter (de travailler); ♦ *vt* (*vase*, *object*) faire tomber; (*fig: from price etc*): **to** ~ **off £10** faire une remise de 10 livres; (*col: steal*) piquer.

knock out *vt* assommer; (*BOXING*) mettre k.-o.

knock over *vt* (*object*) faire tomber; (*pedestrian*) renverser.

knockdown ['nɔkdaun] *a* (*price*) sacrifié(e).

knocker ['nɔkə*] *n* (*on door*) heurtoir *m*.

knock-for-knock ['nɔkfə'nɔk] *a* (*Brit*): ~ **agreement** convention entre compagnies d'assurances par laquelle chacune s'engage à dédommager son propre client.

knocking ['nɔkɪŋ] *n* coups *mpl*.

knock-kneed [nɔk'niːd] *a* aux genoux cagneux.

knockout ['nɔkaut] *n* (*BOXING*) knock-out *m*, K.-O. *m*.

knockout competition *n* (*Brit*) compétition *f* avec épreuves éliminatoires.

knock-up ['nɔkʌp] *n* (*TENNIS*): **to have a** ~ faire des balles.

knot [nɔt] *n* (*gen*) nœud *m* ♦ *vt* nouer; **to tie a** ~ faire un nœud.

knotty ['nɔtɪ] *a* (*fig*) épineux(euse).

know [nəu] *vt* (*pt* **knew**, *pp* **known** [nju:, nəun]) savoir; (*person*, *place*) connaître; **to** ~ **that** savoir que; **to** ~ **how to do** savoir faire; **to** ~ **about/of sth** être au courant de/ connaître qch; **to get to** ~ **sth** (*fact*) apprendre qch; (*place*) apprendre à connaître qch; **I don't** ~ **him** je ne le connais pas; **to** ~ **right from wrong** savoir distinguer le bon du mauvais; **as far as I** ~ ... à ma connaissance ..., autant que je sache ....

know-all ['nəuɔːl] *n* (*Brit pej*) je-sais-tout *m/f*.

know-how ['nəuhau] *n* savoir-faire *m*, technique *f*, compétence *f*.

knowing ['nəuɪŋ] *a* (*look etc*) entendu(e).

knowingly ['nəuɪŋlɪ] *ad* sciemment; d'un air entendu.

know-it-all ['nəuitɔːl] *n* (*US*) = **know-all**.

knowledge ['nɔlɪdʒ] *n* connaissance *f*; (*learning*) connaissances, savoir *m*; **to have no** ~ **of** ignorer; **not to my** ~ pas à ma connaissance; **without my** ~ à mon insu; **to have a working** ~ **of French** se débrouiller en français; **it is common** ~ **that** ... chacun sait que ...; **it has come to my** ~ **that** ... j'ai appris que ....

knowledgeable ['nɔlɪdʒəbl] *a* bien informé(e).

known [nəun] *pp of* **know** ♦ *a* (*thief*, *facts*) notoire; (*expert*) célèbre.

knuckle ['nʌkl] *n* articulation *f* (des phalanges), jointure *f*.

knuckle under *vi* (*col*) céder.

knuckleduster ['nʌkldʌstə*] *n* coup-de-poing américain.

KO *abbr* (= *knock out*) *n* K.-O. *m* ♦ *vt* mettre K.-O.

koala [kəu'ɑːlə] *n* (*also:* ~ **bear**) koala *m*.

kook [kuːk] *n* (*US col*) loufoque *m/f*.

Koran [kɔ'rɑːn] *n* Coran *m*.

Korea [kə'rɪə] *n* Corée *f*; **North/South** ~ Corée du Nord/Sud.

Korean [kə'rɪən] *a* coréen(ne) ♦ *n* Coréen/ne.

kosher ['kəuʃə*] *a* kascher *inv*.

kowtow ['kau'tau] *vi*: **to** ~ **to sb** s'aplatir devant qn.

Kremlin ['krɛmlɪn] *n*: **the** ~ le Kremlin.

KS *abbr* (*US POST*) = *Kansas*.

Kt *abbr* (*Brit*: = *Knight*) *titre honorifique*.

Kuala Lumpur ['kwɑːlə'lumpuə*] *n* Kuala Lumpur.

kudos ['kjuːdɔs] *n* gloire *f*, lauriers *mpl*.

Kuwait [ku'weɪt] *n* Koweït *f*, Kuwait *f*.

Kuwaiti [ku'weɪtɪ] *a* koweïtien(ne) ♦ *n* Koweïtien/ne.

kW *abbr* (= *kilowatt*) kW.

KY *abbr* (*US POST*) = *Kentucky*.

L

L, l [ɛl] n (letter) L, l m; **L for Lucy,** (US) L **for Love** L comme Louis.
L abbr (= lake, large) L; (= left) g; (Brit AUT: = learner) signale un conducteur débutant.
l abbr (= litre) l.
LA n abbr (US) = Los Angeles ♦ abbr (US POST) = Louisiana.
lab [læb] n abbr (= laboratory) labo m.
label ['leɪbl] n étiquette f; (brand: of record) marque f ♦ vt étiqueter; **to ~ sb a ...** qualifier qn de ....
labor etc ['leɪbə*] (US) = **labour** etc.
laboratory [lə'bɔrətərɪ] n laboratoire m.
Labor Day n (US) fête f du travail.
laborious [lə'bɔːrɪəs] a laborieux(euse).
labor union n (US) syndicat m.
Labour ['leɪbə*] n (Brit POL: also: **the ~ Party**) le parti travailliste, les travaillistes mpl.
labour, (US) **labor** ['leɪbə*] n (task) travail m; (workmen) main-d'œuvre f; (MED) travail, accouchement m ♦ vi: **to ~ (at)** travailler dur (à), peiner (sur); **in ~** (MED) en travail.
labo(u)r camp n camp m de travaux forcés.
labo(u)r cost n coût m de la main-d'œuvre; coût de la façon.
labo(u)red ['leɪbəd] a lourd(e), laborieux(euse); (breathing) difficile, pénible; (style) lourd, embarrassé(e).
labo(u)rer ['leɪbərə*] n manœuvre m; (on farm) ouvrier m agricole.
labo(u)r force n main-d'œuvre f.
labo(u)r-intensive [leɪbərɪn'tɛnsɪv] a intensif(ive) en main-d'œuvre.
labo(u)r market n marché m du travail.
labo(u)r pains npl douleurs fpl de l'accouchement.
labo(u)r relations npl relations fpl dans l'entreprise.
labo(u)r-saving ['leɪbəseɪvɪŋ] a qui simplifie le travail.
labo(u)r unrest n agitation sociale.
labyrinth ['læbɪrɪnθ] n labyrinthe m, dédale m.
lace [leɪs] n dentelle f; (of shoe etc) lacet m ♦ vt (shoe) lacer; (drink) arroser, corser.
lacemaking ['leɪsmeɪkɪŋ] n fabrication f de dentelle.
laceration [læsə'reɪʃən] n lacération f.
lace-up ['leɪsʌp] a (shoes etc) à lacets.
lack [læk] n manque m ♦ vt manquer de; **through** or **for ~ of** faute de, par manque de; **to be ~ing** manquer, faire défaut; **to be ~ing in** manquer de.
lackadaisical [lækə'deɪzɪkl] a nonchalant(e), indolent(e).
lackey ['lækɪ] n (also fig) laquais m.
lacklustre ['læklʌstə*] a terne.

laconic [lə'kɔnɪk] a laconique.
lacquer ['lækə*] n laque f.
lacy ['leɪsɪ] a comme de la dentelle, qui ressemble à de la dentelle.
lad [læd] n garçon m, gars m; (Brit: in stable etc) lad m.
ladder ['lædə*] n échelle f; (Brit: in tights) maille filée ♦ vt, vi (Brit: tights) filer.
laden ['leɪdn] a: **~ (with)** chargé(e) (de); **fully ~** (truck, ship) en pleine charge.
ladle ['leɪdl] n louche f.
lady ['leɪdɪ] n dame f; **L~ Smith** lady Smith; **the ladies' (room)** les toilettes fpl des dames; **a ~ doctor** une doctoresse, une femme médecin.
ladybird ['leɪdɪbɔːd], (US) **ladybug** ['leɪdɪbʌg] n coccinelle f.
lady-in-waiting ['leɪdɪɪn'weɪtɪŋ] n dame f d'honneur.
ladykiller ['leɪdɪkɪlə*] n don Juan m.
ladylike ['leɪdɪlaɪk] a distingué(e).
ladyship ['leɪdɪʃɪp] n: **your L~** Madame la comtesse (or la baronne etc).
lag [læg] n = **time ~** ♦ vi (also: **~ behind**) rester en arrière, traîner ♦ vt (pipes) calorifuger.
lager ['lɑːgə*] n bière blonde.
lagging ['lægɪŋ] n enveloppe isolante, calorifuge m.
lagoon [lə'guːn] n lagune f.
Lagos ['leɪgɔs] n Lagos.
laid [leɪd] pt, pp of **lay**.
laid-back [leɪd'bæk] a (col) relaxe, décontracté(e).
lain [leɪn] pp of **lie**.
lair [lɛə*] n tanière f, gîte m.
laissez-faire [lɛseɪ'fɛə*] n libéralisme m.
laity ['leɪətɪ] n laïques mpl.
lake [leɪk] n lac m.
Lake District n: **the ~** (Brit) la région des lacs.
lamb [læm] n agneau m.
lamb chop n côtelette f d'agneau.
lambskin ['læmskɪn] n (peau f d')agneau m.
lambswool ['læmzwul] n laine f d'agneau.
lame [leɪm] a boiteux(euse); **~ duck** (fig) canard boiteux.
lamely ['leɪmlɪ] ad (fig) sans conviction.
lament [lə'mɛnt] n lamentation f ♦ vt pleurer, se lamenter sur.
lamentable ['læməntəbl] a déplorable, lamentable.
laminated ['læmɪneɪtɪd] a laminé(e); (windscreen) (en verre) feuilleté.
lamp [læmp] n lampe f.
lamplight ['læmplaɪt] n: **by ~** à la lumière de la (or d'une) lampe.
lampoon [læm'puːn] n pamphlet m.
lamppost ['læmppəust] n (Brit) réverbère m.
lampshade ['læmpʃeɪd] n abat-jour m inv.
lance [lɑːns] n lance f ♦ vt (MED) inciser.
lance corporal n (Brit) (soldat m de) première classe m.
lancet ['lɑːnsɪt] n (MED) bistouri m.
Lancs [læŋks] abbr (Brit) = Lancashire.
land [lænd] n (as opposed to sea) terre f (ferme); (country) pays m; (soil) terre; terrain m; (estate) terre(s), domaine(s) m(pl) ♦ vi (from ship) débarquer; (AVIAT)

atterrir; (fig: fall) (re)tomber ♦ vt (passengers, goods) débarquer; (obtain) décrocher; **to go/travel by** ~ se déplacer par voie de terre; **to own** ~ être propriétaire foncier; **to** ~ **on one's feet** (also fig) retomber sur ses pieds.
land up vi atterrir, (finir par) se retrouver.

landed gentry ['lændɪd-] n (Brit) propriétaires terriens or fonciers.

landing ['lændɪŋ] n (from ship) débarquement m; (AVIAT) atterrissage m; (of staircase) palier m.

landing card n carte f de débarquement.

landing craft n péniche f de débarquement.

landing gear n train m d'atterrissage.

landing stage n (Brit) débarcadère m, embarcadère m.

landing strip n piste f d'atterrissage.

landlady ['lændleɪdɪ] n propriétaire f, logeuse f.

landlocked ['lændlɔkt] a entouré(e) de terre(s), sans accès à la mer.

landlord ['lændlɔːd] n propriétaire m, logeur m; (of pub etc) patron m.

landlubber ['lændlʌbə*] n terrien/ne.

landmark ['lændmaːk] n (point m de) repère m; **to be a** ~ (fig) faire date or époque.

landowner ['lændəunə*] n propriétaire foncier or terrien.

landscape ['lænskeɪp] n paysage m.

landscape architect, landscape gardener n paysagiste m/f.

landscape painting n (ART) paysage m.

landslide ['lændslaɪd] n (GEO) glissement m (de terrain); (fig: POL) raz-de-marée (électoral).

lane [leɪn] n (in country) chemin m; (in town) ruelle f; (AUT) voie f; file f; (in race) couloir m; **shipping** ~ route f maritime or de navigation.

language ['læŋgwɪdʒ] n langue f; (way one speaks) langage m; **bad** ~ grossièretés fpl, langage grossier.

language laboratory n laboratoire m de langues.

languid ['læŋgwɪd] a languissant(e); langoureux(euse).

languish ['læŋgwɪʃ] vi languir.

lank [læŋk] a (hair) raide et terne.

lanky ['læŋkɪ] a grand(e) et maigre, efflanqué(e).

lanolin(e) ['lænəlɪn] n lanoline f.

lantern ['læntn] n lanterne f.

Laos [laus] n Laos m.

lap [læp] n (of track) tour m (de piste); (of body): **in** or **on one's** ~ sur les genoux ♦ vt (also: ~ **up**) laper ♦ vi (waves) clapoter.
lap up vt (fig) boire comme du petit-lait, se gargariser de; (: lies etc) gober.

La Paz [læ'pæz] n La Paz.

lapdog ['læpdɔg] n chien m d'appartement.

lapel [lə'pɛl] n revers m.

Lapland ['læplænd] n Laponie f.

lapse [læps] n défaillance f; (in behaviour) écart m (de conduite) ♦ vi (LAW) cesser d'être en vigueur; se périmer; **to** ~ **into bad habits** prendre de mauvaises habitudes; ~ **of time** laps m de temps, intervalle m; **a** ~ **of memory** un trou de mémoire.

larceny ['laːsənɪ] n vol m.

lard [laːd] n saindoux m.

larder ['laːdə*] n garde-manger m inv.

large [laːdʒ] a grand(e); (person, animal) gros(grosse); **to make** ~r agrandir; **a** ~ **number of people** beaucoup de gens; **by and** ~ en général; **on a** ~ **scale** sur une grande échelle; **at** ~ (free) en liberté; (generally) en général; pour la plupart.

largely ['laːdʒlɪ] ad en grande partie.

large-scale ['laːdʒ'skeɪl] a (map, drawing etc) à grande échelle; (fig) important(e).

lark [laːk] n (bird) alouette f; (joke) blague f, farce f.
lark about vi faire l'idiot, rigoler.

larva, pl **larvae** ['laːvə, -iː] n larve f.

laryngitis [lærɪn'dʒaɪtɪs] n laryngite f.

larynx ['lærɪŋks] n larynx m.

lascivious [lə'sɪvɪəs] a lascif(ive).

laser ['leɪzə*] n laser m.

laser beam n rayon m laser.

laser printer n imprimante f laser.

lash [læʃ] n coup m de fouet; (also: **eyelash**) cil m ♦ vt fouetter; (tie) attacher.
lash down vt attacher; amarrer; arrimer ♦ vi (rain) tomber avec violence.
lash out vi: **to** ~ **out** (at or against sb/sth) attaquer violemment (qn/qch); **to** ~ **out** (on sth) (col: spend) se fendre (de qch).

lashing ['læʃɪŋ] n: ~**s of** (Brit col: cream etc) des masses de.

lass [læs] n (jeune) fille f.

lasso [læ'suː] n lasso m ♦ vt prendre au lasso.

last [laːst] a dernier(ière) ♦ ad en dernier ♦ vi durer; ~ **week** la semaine dernière; ~ **night** hier soir; la nuit dernière; **at** ~ enfin; **to** ~ **but one** avant-dernier(ière); **the** ~ **time** la dernière fois; **it** ~**s (for) 2 hours** ça dure 2 heures.

last-ditch ['laːst'dɪtʃ] a ultime, désespéré(e).

lasting ['laːstɪŋ] a durable.

lastly ['laːstlɪ] ad en dernier lieu, pour finir.

last-minute ['laːstmɪnɪt] a de dernière minute.

latch [lætʃ] n loquet m.
latch on to vt (cling to: person) s'accrocher à; (: idea) trouver bon(ne).

latchkey ['lætʃkiː] n clé f (de la porte d'entrée).

late [leɪt] a (not on time) en retard; (far on in day etc) dernier(ière); tardif(ive); (recent) récent(e), dernier; (former) ancien(ne); (dead) défunt(e) ♦ ad tard; (behind time, schedule) en retard; **to be** ~ avoir du retard; **to be 10 minutes** ~ avoir 10 minutes de retard; **to work** ~ travailler tard; ~ **in life** sur le tard, à un âge avancé; **of** ~ dernièrement; **in** ~ **May** vers la fin (du mois) de mai, fin mai; **the** ~ **Mr X** feu M. X.

latecomer ['leɪtkʌmə*] n retardataire m/f.

lately ['leɪtlɪ] ad récemment.

lateness ['leɪtnɪs] n (of person) retard m; (of event) heure tardive.

latent ['leɪtnt] a latent(e); ~ **defect** vice caché.

later ['leɪtə*] a (date etc) ultérieur(e); (version etc) plus récent(e) ♦ ad plus tard; ~ **on today** plus tard dans la journée.

lateral ['lætərl] a latéral(e).

latest ['leɪtɪst] a tout(e) dernier(ière); **the** ~

news les dernières nouvelles; **at the ~** au plus tard.
latex ['leɪteks] *n* latex *m*.
lath, **~s** [læθ, læðz] *n* latte *f*.
lathe [leɪð] *n* tour *m*.
lather ['lɑ:ðə*] *n* mousse *f* (de savon) ♦ *vt* savonner ♦ *vi* mousser.
Latin ['lætɪn] *n* latin *m* ♦ *a* latin(e).
Latin America *n* Amérique latine.
Latin American *a* latino-américain(e), d'Amérique latine ♦ *n* Latino-Américain/e.
latitude ['lætɪtju:d] *n* (*also fig*) latitude *f*.
latrine [lə'tri:n] *n* latrines *fpl*.
latter ['lætə*] *a* deuxième, dernier(ière) ♦ *n*: **the ~** ce dernier, celui-ci.
latterly ['lætəlɪ] *ad* dernièrement, récemment.
lattice ['lætɪs] *n* treillis *m*; treillage *m*.
lattice window *n* fenêtre treillissée, fenêtre à croisillons.
Latvia ['lætvɪə] *n* Lettonie *f*.
laudable ['lɔ:dəbl] *a* louable.
laudatory ['lɔ:dətrɪ] *a* élogieux(euse).
laugh [lɑ:f] *n* rire *m* ♦ *vi* rire.
  laugh at *vt fus* se moquer de; (*joke*) rire de.
  laugh off *vt* écarter *or* rejeter par une plaisanterie *or* par une boutade.
laughable ['lɑ:fəbl] *a* risible, ridicule.
laughing ['lɑ:fɪŋ] *a* rieur(euse); **this is no ~ matter** il n'y a pas de quoi rire, ça n'a rien d'amusant.
laughing gas *n* gaz hilarant.
laughing stock *n*: **the ~ of** la risée de.
laughter ['lɑ:ftə*] *n* rire *m*; (*people laughing*) rires *mpl*.
launch [lɔ:ntʃ] *n* lancement *m*; (*boat*) chaloupe *f*; (*also*: **motor ~**) vedette *f* ♦ *vt* (*ship, rocket, plan*) lancer.
  launch out *vi*: **to ~ out (into)** se lancer (dans).
launching ['lɔ:ntʃɪŋ] *n* lancement *m*.
launch(ing) pad *n* rampe *f* de lancement.
launder ['lɔ:ndə*] *vt* blanchir.
launderette [lɔ:n'drɛt], (*US*) **laundromat** ['lɔ:ndrəmæt] *n* laverie *f* (automatique).
laundry ['lɔ:ndrɪ] *n* blanchisserie *f*; (*clothes*) linge *m*; **to do the ~** faire la lessive.
laureate ['lɔ:rɪət] *a see* **poet laureate**.
laurel ['lɔrl] *n* laurier *m*; **to rest on one's ~s** se reposer sur ses lauriers.
lava ['lɑ:və] *n* lave *f*.
lavatory ['lævətərɪ] *n* toilettes *fpl*.
lavatory paper *n* (*Brit*) papier *m* hygiénique.
lavender ['lævəndə*] *n* lavande *f*.
lavish ['lævɪʃ] *a* copieux(euse); somptueux(euse); (*giving freely*): **~ with** prodigue de ♦ *vt*: **to ~ sth on sb** prodiguer qch à qn.
lavishly ['lævɪʃlɪ] *ad* (*give, spend*) sans compter; (*furnished*) luxueusement.
law [lɔ:] *n* loi *f*; (*science*) droit *m*; **against the ~** contraire à la loi; **to study ~** faire du droit; **to go to ~** (*Brit*) avoir recours à la justice; **~ and order** *n* l'ordre public.
law-abiding ['lɔ:əbaɪdɪŋ] *a* respectueux(euse) des lois.
lawbreaker ['lɔ:breɪkə*] *n* personne *f* qui transgresse la loi.
law court *n* tribunal *m*, cour *f* de justice.

lawful ['lɔ:ful] *a* légal(e); permis(e).
lawfully ['lɔ:fəlɪ] *ad* légalement.
lawless ['lɔ:lɪs] *a* sans loi.
lawmaker ['lɔ:meɪkə*] *n* législateur/trice.
lawn [lɔ:n] *n* pelouse *f*.
lawnmower ['lɔ:nməuə*] *n* tondeuse *f* à gazon.
lawn tennis *n* tennis *m*.
law school *n* faculté *f* de droit.
law student *n* étudiant/e en droit.
lawsuit ['lɔ:su:t] *n* procès *m*; **to bring a ~ against** engager des poursuites contre.
lawyer ['lɔ:jə*] *n* (*consultant, with company*) juriste *m*; (*for sales, wills etc*) ≈ notaire *m*; (*partner, in court*) ≈ avocat *m*.
lax [læks] *a* relâché(e).
laxative ['læksətɪv] *n* laxatif *m*.
laxity ['læksɪtɪ] *n* relâchement *m*.
lay [leɪ] *pt of* **lie** ♦ *a* laïque; profane ♦ *vt* (*pt, pp* **laid** [leɪd]) poser, mettre; (*eggs*) pondre; (*trap*) tendre; (*plans*) élaborer; **to ~ the table** mettre la table; **to ~ the facts/one's proposals before sb** présenter les faits/ses propositions à qn; **to get laid** (*col!*) baiser (*!*); se faire baiser (*!*).
  lay aside , **lay by** *vt* mettre de côté.
  lay down *vt* poser; **to ~ down the law** (*fig*) faire la loi.
  lay in *vt* accumuler, s'approvisionner en.
  lay into *vi* (*col: attack*) tomber sur; (*: scold*) passer une engueulade à.
  lay off *vt* (*workers*) licencier.
  lay on *vt* (*water, gas*) mettre, installer; (*provide: meal etc*) fournir; (*paint*) étaler.
  lay out *vt* (*design*) dessiner, concevoir; (*display*) disposer; (*spend*) dépenser.
  lay up *vt* (*to store*) amasser; (*car*) remiser; (*ship*) désarmer; (*subj: illness*) forcer à s'aliter.
layabout ['leɪəbaut] *n* fainéant/e.
lay-by ['leɪbaɪ] *n* (*Brit*) aire *f* de stationnement (sur le bas-côté).
lay days *npl* (*NAUT*) estarie *f*.
layer ['leɪə*] *n* couche *f*.
layette [leɪ'ɛt] *n* layette *f*.
layman ['leɪmən] *n* laïque *m*; profane *m*.
lay-off ['leɪɔf] *n* licenciement *m*.
layout ['leɪaut] *n* disposition *f*, plan *m*, agencement *m*; (*PRESS*) mise *f* en page.
laze [leɪz] *vi* paresser.
laziness ['leɪzɪnɪs] *n* paresse *f*.
lazy ['leɪzɪ] *a* paresseux(euse).
LB *abbr* (*Canada*) = *Labrador*.
lb. *abbr* (= *libra: pound*) unité de poids.
lbw *abbr* (*CRICKET*: = *leg before wicket*) faute dans laquelle le joueur a la jambe devant le guichet.
LC *n abbr* (*US*) = *Library of Congress*.
lc *abbr* (*TYP*: = *lower case*) b.d.c.
L/C *abbr* = **letter of credit**.
LCD *n abbr* = **liquid crystal display**.
Ld *abbr* (*Brit*: = *lord*) titre honorifique.
LDS *n abbr* (= *Licentiate in Dental Surgery*) diplôme universitaire; (= *Latter-day Saints*) Église de Jésus-Christ des Saints du dernier jour.
LEA *n abbr* (*Brit*: = *local education authority*) services locaux de l'enseignement.
lead [li:d] *n* (*front position*) tête *f*; (*distance,*

time ahead) avance *f*; (*clue*) piste *f*; (*to battery*) raccord *m*; (*ELEC*) fil *m*; (*for dog*) laisse *f*; (*THEATRE*) rôle principal; [led] (*chemical*) plomb *m*; (*in pencil*) mine *f* ♦ *vb* (*pt, pp* **led** [led]) *vt* mener, conduire; (*induce*) amener; (*be leader of*) être à la tête de; (*SPORT*) être en tête de; (*orchestra: Brit*) être le premier violon de; (: *US*) diriger ♦ *vi* mener, être en tête; **to ~ to** mener à; (*result in*) conduire à; aboutir à; **to ~ sb astray** détourner qn du droit chemin; **to be in the ~** (*SPORT: in race*) mener, être en tête; (: *match*) mener (à la marque); **to take the ~** (*SPORT*) passer en tête, prendre la tête; mener; (*fig*) prendre l'initiative; **to ~ sb to believe that ...** amener qn à croire que ...; **to ~ sb to do sth** amener qn à faire qch.
lead away *vt* emmener.
lead back *vt* ramener.
lead off *vi* (*in game etc*) commencer.
lead on *vt* (*tease*) faire marcher; **to ~ sb on to** (*induce*) amener qn à.
lead up to *vt* conduire à.
leaded ['lɛdɪd] *a* (*windows*) à petits carreaux.
leaden ['lɛdn] *a* de *or* en plomb.
leader ['liːdə*] *n* (*of team*) chef *m*; (*of party etc*) dirigeant/e, leader *m*; (*in newspaper*) éditorial *m*; **they are ~s in their field** (*fig*) ils sont à la pointe du progrès dans leur domaine; **the L~ of the House** (*Brit*) le chef de la majorité ministérielle.
leadership ['liːdəʃɪp] *n* direction *f*; **under the ~ of ...** sous la direction de ...; **qualities of ~** qualités *fpl* de chef *or* de meneur.
lead-free ['lɛdfriː] *a* sans plomb.
leading ['liːdɪŋ] *a* de premier plan; (*main*) principal(e); **a ~ question** une question tendancieuse; **~ role** rôle prépondérant *or* de premier plan.
leading lady *n* (*THEATRE*) vedette (féminine).
leading light *n* (*person*) sommité *f*, personnalité *f* de premier plan.
leading man *n* (*THEATRE*) vedette (masculine).
lead pencil *n* crayon noir *or* à papier.
lead poisoning *n* saturnisme *m*.
lead time *n* (*COMM*) délai *m* de livraison.
lead weight *n* plomb *m*.
leaf, *pl* **leaves** [liːf, liːvz] *n* feuille *f*; (*of table*) rallonge *f*; **to turn over a new ~** (*fig*) changer de conduite *or* d'existence; **to take a ~ out of sb's book** (*fig*) prendre exemple sur qn.
leaf through *vt* (*book*) feuilleter.
leaflet ['liːflɪt] *n* prospectus *m*, brochure *f*; (*POL, REL*) tract *m*.
leafy ['liːfɪ] *a* feuillu(e).
league [liːg] *n* ligue *f*; (*FOOTBALL*) championnat *m*; (*measure*) lieue *f*; **to be in ~ with** avoir partie liée avec, être de mèche avec.
leak [liːk] *n* (*out, also fig*) fuite *f*; (*in*) infiltration *f* ♦ *vi* (*pipe, liquid etc*) fuir; (*shoes*) prendre l'eau ♦ *vt* (*liquid*) répandre; (*information*) divulguer.
leak out *vi* fuir; (*information*) être divulgué(e).

leakage ['liːkɪdʒ] *n* (*also fig*) fuite *f*.
leaky ['liːkɪ] *a* (*pipe, bucket*) qui fuit, percé(e); (*roof*) qui coule; (*shoe*) qui prend l'eau; (*boat*) qui fait eau.
lean [liːn] *a* maigre ♦ *n* (*of meat*) maigre *m* ♦ *vb* (*pt, pp* **leaned** *or* **leant** [lɛnt]) *vt*: **to ~ sth on** appuyer qch sur ♦ *vi* (*slope*) pencher; (*rest*): **to ~ against** s'appuyer contre; être appuyé(e) contre; **to ~ on** s'appuyer sur.
lean back *vi* se pencher en arrière.
lean forward *vi* se pencher en avant.
lean out *vi*: **to ~ out (of)** se pencher au dehors (de).
lean over *vi* se pencher.
leaning ['liːnɪŋ] *a* penché(e) ♦ *n*: **~ (towards)** penchant *m* (pour); **the ~ Tower of Pisa** la tour penchée de Pise.
leant [lɛnt] *pt, pp of* **lean.**
lean-to ['liːntuː] *n* appentis *m*.
leap [liːp] *n* bond *m*, saut *m* ♦ *vi* (*pt, pp* **leaped** *or* **leapt** [lɛpt]) bondir, sauter; **to ~ at an offer** saisir une offre.
leap up *vi* (*person*) faire un bond; se lever d'un bond.
leapfrog ['liːpfrɔg] *n* jeu *m* de saute-mouton.
leapt [lɛpt] *pt, pp of* **leap.**
leap year *n* année *f* bissextile.
learn, *pt, pp* **learned** *or* **learnt** [lɜːn, -t] *vt, vi* apprendre; **to ~ how to do sth** apprendre à faire qch; **we were sorry to ~ that ...** nous apprenons avec regret que ...; **to ~ about sth** (*SCOL*) étudier qch; (*hear*) apprendre qch.
learned ['lɜːnɪd] *a* érudit(e), savant(e).
learner ['lɜːnə*] *n* débutant/e; (*Brit: also: ~ driver*) (conducteur/trice) débutant(e).
learning ['lɜːnɪŋ] *n* savoir *m*.
lease [liːs] *n* bail *m* ♦ *vt* louer à bail; **on ~** en location.
lease back *vt* vendre en cession-bail.
leaseback ['liːsbæk] *n* cession-bail *f*.
leasehold ['liːshəuld] *n* (*contract*) bail *m* ♦ *a* loué(e) à bail.
leash [liːʃ] *n* laisse *f*.
least [liːst] *a*: **the ~ +** *noun* le(la) plus petit(e), le(la) moindre; (*smallest amount of*) le moins de; **the ~ +** *adjective* le(la) moins; **the ~ money** le moins d'argent; **the ~ expensive** le moins cher; **at ~** au moins; **not in the ~** pas le moins du monde.
leather ['lɛðə*] *n* cuir *m* ♦ *cpd* en *or* de cuir; **~ goods** maroquinerie *f*.
leave [liːv] *vb* (*pt, pp* **left** [lɛft]) *vt* laisser; (*go away from*) quitter ♦ *vi* partir, s'en aller ♦ *n* (*time off*) congé *m*; (*MIL, also: consent*) permission *f*; **to be left** rester; **there's some milk left over** il reste du lait; **to ~ school** quitter l'école, terminer sa scolarité; **~ it to me!** laissez-moi faire!, je m'en occupe!; **on ~** en permission; **to take one's ~ of** prendre congé de; **~ of absence** *n* congé exceptionnel; (*MIL*) permission spéciale.
leave behind *vt* (*also fig*) laisser; (*opponent in race*) distancer; (*forget*) laisser, oublier.
leave off *vt* (*cover, lid, heating*) ne pas (re)mettre; (*light*) ne pas (r)allumer, laisser éteint(e); (*Brit col: stop*): **to ~ off (doing sth)** s'arrêter (de faire qch).

leave on vt (coat etc) garder, ne pas enlever; (lid) laisser dessus; (light, fire, cooker) laisser allumé(e).

leave out vt oublier, omettre.

leaves [li:vz] npl of **leaf**.

leavetaking ['li:vteɪkɪŋ] n adieux mpl.

Lebanese [lɛbə'ni:z] a libanais(e) ♦ n (pl inv) Libanais/e.

Lebanon ['lɛbənən] n Liban m.

lecherous ['lɛtʃərəs] a lubrique.

lectern ['lɛktə:n] n lutrin m, pupitre m.

lecture ['lɛktʃə*] n conférence f; (SCOL) cours (magistral) ♦ vi donner des cours; enseigner ♦ vt (reprove) sermonner, réprimander; **to ~ on** faire un cours (or son cours) sur; **to give a ~ (on)** faire une conférence (sur); faire un cours (sur).

lecture hall n amphithéâtre m.

lecturer ['lɛktʃərə*] n (speaker) conférencier/ière; (Brit: at university) professeur m (d'université), ≈ maître assistant, maître de conférences; **assistant ~** (Brit) ≈ assistant/e; **senior ~** (Brit) ≈ chargé/e d'enseignement.

lecture theatre n = **lecture hall**.

LED n abbr (= light-emitting diode) LED f, diode électroluminescente.

led [lɛd] pt, pp of **lead**.

ledge [lɛdʒ] n (of window, on wall) rebord m; (of mountain) saillie f, corniche f.

ledger ['lɛdʒə*] n registre m, grand livre.

lee [li:] n côté m sous le vent; **in the ~ of** à l'abri de.

leech [li:tʃ] n sangsue f.

leek [li:k] n poireau m.

leer [lɪə*] vi: **to ~ at sb** regarder qn d'un air mauvais or concupiscent, lorgner qn.

leeward ['li:wəd] a, ad sous le vent ♦ n côté m sous le vent; **to ~** sous le vent.

leeway ['li:weɪ] n (fig): **to make up ~** rattraper son retard; **to have some ~** avoir une certaine liberté d'action.

left [lɛft] pt, pp of **leave** ♦ a gauche ♦ ad à gauche ♦ n gauche f; **on the ~, to the ~** à gauche; **the L~** (POL) la gauche.

left-hand drive ['lɛfthænd-] n (Brit) conduite f à gauche.

left-handed [lɛft'hændɪd] a gaucher(ère); (scissors etc) pour gauchers.

left-hand side ['lɛfthænd-] n gauche f, côté m gauche.

leftist ['lɛftɪst] a (POL) gauchiste, de gauche.

left-luggage (office) [lɛft'lʌgɪdʒ(-)] n (Brit) consigne f.

left-overs ['lɛftəuvəz] npl restes mpl.

left wing n (MIL, SPORT) aile f gauche; (POL) gauche f ♦ a: **left-wing** (POL) de gauche.

left-winger ['lɛft'wɪŋgə*] n (POL) membre m de la gauche; (SPORT) ailier m gauche.

leg [lɛg] n jambe f; (of animal) patte f; (of furniture) pied m; (CULIN: of chicken) cuisse f; **1st/2nd ~** (SPORT) match m aller/retour; (of journey) 1ère/2ème étape; **~ of lamb** (CULIN) gigot m d'agneau; **to stretch one's ~s** se dégourdir les jambes.

legacy ['lɛgəsɪ] n (also fig) héritage m, legs m.

legal ['li:gl] a légal(e); **to take ~ action or proceedings against sb** poursuivre qn en justice.

legal adviser n conseiller/ère juridique.

legality [lɪ'gælɪtɪ] n légalité f.

legalize ['li:gəlaɪz] vt légaliser.

legally ['li:gəlɪ] ad légalement; **~ binding** juridiquement contraignant(e).

legal tender n monnaie légale.

legation [lɪ'geɪʃən] n légation f.

legend ['lɛdʒənd] n légende f.

legendary ['lɛdʒəndərɪ] a légendaire.

-legged ['lɛgɪd] suffix: **two~** à deux pattes (or jambes or pieds).

leggings ['lɛgɪŋz] npl jambières fpl, guêtres fpl.

legibility [lɛdʒɪ'bɪlɪtɪ] n lisibilité f.

legible ['lɛdʒəbl] a lisible.

legibly ['lɛdʒəblɪ] ad lisiblement.

legion ['li:dʒən] n légion f.

legionnaire [li:dʒə'nɛə*] n légionnaire m; **~'s disease** maladie f du légionnaire.

legislate ['lɛdʒɪsleɪt] vi légiférer.

legislation [lɛdʒɪs'leɪʃən] n législation f; **a piece of ~** un texte de loi.

legislative ['lɛdʒɪslətɪv] a législatif(ive).

legislator ['lɛdʒɪsleɪtə*] n législateur/trice.

legislature ['lɛdʒɪslətʃə*] n corps législatif.

legitimacy [lɪ'dʒɪtɪməsɪ] n légitimité f.

legitimate [lɪ'dʒɪtɪmət] a légitime.

legitimize [lɪ'dʒɪtɪmaɪz] vt légitimer.

leg-room ['lɛgru:m] n place f pour les jambes.

Leics abbr (Brit) = Leicestershire.

leisure ['lɛʒə*] n (time) loisir m, temps m; (free time) temps libre, loisirs mpl; **at ~** (tout) à loisir; à tête reposée.

leisure centre n centre m de loisirs.

leisurely ['lɛʒəlɪ] a tranquille; fait(e) sans se presser.

leisure suit n (Brit) survêtement m (mode).

lemon ['lɛmən] n citron m.

lemonade [lɛmə'neɪd] n limonade f.

lemon cheese n, **lemon curd** n crème f de citron.

lemon juice n jus m de citron.

lemon squeezer n presse-citron m inv.

lemon tea n thé m au citron.

lend, pt, pp **lent** [lɛnd, lɛnt] vt: **to ~ sth (to sb)** prêter qch (à qn); **to ~ a hand** donner un coup de main.

lender ['lɛndə*] n prêteur/euse.

lending library ['lɛndɪŋ-] n bibliothèque f de prêt.

length [lɛŋθ] n longueur f; (section: of road, pipe etc) morceau m, bout m; **~ of time** durée f; **what ~ is it?** quelle longueur fait-il?; **it is 2 metres in ~** cela fait 2 mètres de long; **to fall full ~** tomber de tout son long; **at ~** (at last) enfin, à la fin; (lengthily) longuement; **to go to any ~(s) to do sth** faire n'importe quoi pour faire qch, ne reculer devant rien pour faire qch.

lengthen ['lɛŋθn] vt allonger, prolonger ♦ vi s'allonger.

lengthways ['lɛŋθweɪz] ad dans le sens de la longueur, en long.

lengthy ['lɛŋθɪ] a (très) long(longue).

leniency ['li:nɪənsɪ] n indulgence f, clémence f.

lenient ['li:nɪənt] a indulgent(e), clément(e).

leniently ['li:nɪəntlɪ] ad avec indulgence or clémence.

lens [lɛnz] n lentille f; (of spectacles) verre

m; (*of camera*) objectif *m*.
Lent [lɛnt] *n* Carême *m*.
lent [lɛnt] *pt, pp of* **lend**.
lentil ['lɛntl] *n* lentille *f*.
Leo ['li:əu] *n* le Lion; **to be ~** être du Lion.
leopard ['lɛpəd] *n* léopard *m*.
leotard ['li:əta:d] *n* maillot *m* (*de danseur etc*).
leper ['lɛpə*] *n* lépreux/euse.
leper colony *n* léproserie *f*.
leprosy ['lɛprəsɪ] *n* lèpre *f*.
lesbian ['lɛzbɪən] *n* lesbienne *f* ♦ *a* lesbien(ne).
lesion ['li:ʒən] *n* (*MED*) lésion *f*.
Lesotho [lɪ'su:tu:] *n* Lesotho *m*.
less [lɛs] *a* moins de ♦ *pronoun, ad* moins; **~ than that/you** moins que cela/vous; **~ than half** moins de la moitié; **~ than 1/a kilo/3 metres** moins de un/d'un kilo /de 3 mètres; **~ and ~** de moins en moins; **the ~ he works ...** moins il travaille ....
lessee [lɛ'si:] *n* locataire *m/f* (à bail), preneur/euse du bail.
lessen ['lɛsn] *vi* diminuer, s'amoindrir, s'atténuer ♦ *vt* diminuer, réduire, atténuer.
lesser ['lɛsə*] *a* moindre; **to a ~ extent** *or* **degree** à un degré moindre.
lesson ['lɛsn] *n* leçon *f*; **a maths ~** une leçon *or* un cours de maths; **to give ~s in** donner des cours de; **it taught him a ~** (*fig*) cela lui a servi de leçon.
lessor ['lɛsə*] *n* bailleur/eresse.
lest [lɛst] *cj* de peur de + *infinitive*, de peur que + *sub*.
let, *pt, pp* **let** [lɛt] *vt* laisser; (*Brit: lease*) louer; **to ~ sb do sth** laisser qn faire qch; **to ~ sb know sth** faire savoir qch à qn, prévenir qn de qch; **he ~ me go** il m'a laissé partir; **~ the water boil and ...** faites bouillir l'eau et ...; **~'s go** allons-y; **~ him come** qu'il vienne; **"to ~"** "à louer".
let down *vt* (*lower*) baisser; (*dress*) rallonger; (*hair*) défaire; (*Brit: tyre*) dégonfler; (*disappoint*) décevoir.
let go *vi* lâcher prise ♦ *vt* lâcher.
let in *vt* laisser entrer; (*visitor etc*) faire entrer; **what have you ~ yourself in for?** à quoi t'es-tu engagé?
let off *vt* (*allow to leave*) laisser partir; (*not punish*) ne pas punir; (*subj: taxi driver, bus driver*) déposer; (*firework etc*) faire partir; (*smell etc*) dégager; **to ~ off steam** (*fig: col*) se défouler, décharger sa rate *or* bile.
let on *vi* (*col*): **to ~ on that ...** révéler que ..., dire que ....
let out *vt* laisser sortir; (*dress*) élargir; (*scream*) laisser échapper; (*rent out*) louer.
let up *vi* diminuer, s'arrêter.
let-down ['lɛtdaun] *n* (*disappointment*) déception *f*.
lethal ['li:θl] *a* mortel(le), fatal(e).
lethargic [lɛ'θɑ:dʒɪk] *a* léthargique.
lethargy ['lɛθədʒɪ] *n* léthargie *f*.
letter ['lɛtə*] *n* lettre *f*; **~s** *npl* (*LITERATURE*) lettres; **small/capital ~** minuscule *f*/ majuscule *f*; **~ of credit** lettre *f* de crédit.
letter bomb *n* lettre piégée.
letterbox ['lɛtəbɒks] *n* (*Brit*) boîte *f* aux *or* à lettres.

letterhead ['lɛtəhɛd] *n* en-tête *m*.
lettering ['lɛtərɪŋ] *n* lettres *fpl*; caractères *mpl*.
letter opener *n* coupe-papier *m*.
letterpress ['lɛtəprɛs] *n* (*method*) typographie *f*.
letter quality *n* qualité *f* "courrier".
letters patent *npl* brevet *m* d'invention.
lettuce ['lɛtɪs] *n* laitue *f*, salade *f*.
let-up ['lɛtʌp] *n* répit *m*, détente *f*.
leukaemia, (*US*) **leukemia** [lu:'ki:mɪə] *n* leucémie *f*.
level ['lɛvl] *a* plat(e), plan(e), uni(e); horizontal(e) ♦ *n* niveau *m*; (*flat place*) terrain plat; (*also: spirit ~*) niveau à bulle ♦ *vt* niveler, aplanir; (*gun*) pointer, braquer; (*accusation*): **to ~ (against)** lancer *or* porter (contre) ♦ *vi* (*col*): **to ~ with sb** être franc(franche) avec qn; **"A" ~s** *npl* (*Brit*) ≈ baccalauréat *m*; **"O" ~s** *npl* (*Brit*) ≈ B.E.P.C; **a ~ spoonful** (*CULIN*) une cuillerée à raser; **to be ~ with** être au même niveau que; **to draw ~ with** (*team*) arriver à égalité de points avec, égaliser avec; arriver au même classement que; (*runner, car*) arriver à la hauteur de, rattraper; **on the ~** à l'horizontale; (*fig: honest*) régulier(ière).
level off, **level out** (*prices etc*) se stabiliser ♦ *vt* (*ground*) aplanir, niveler.
level crossing *n* (*Brit*) passage *m* à niveau.
level-headed [lɛvl'hɛdɪd] *a* équilibré(e).
levelling, (*US*) **leveling** ['lɛvlɪŋ] *a* (*process, effect*) de nivellement.
lever ['li:və*] *n* levier *m* ♦ *vt*: **to ~ up/out** soulever/extraire au moyen d'un levier.
leverage ['li:vərɪdʒ] *n*: **~ (on** *or* **with)** prise *f* (sur).
levity ['lɛvɪtɪ] *n* manque *m* de sérieux, légèreté *f*.
levy ['lɛvɪ] *n* taxe *f*, impôt *m* ♦ *vt* prélever, imposer; percevoir.
lewd [lu:d] *a* obscène, lubrique.
LI *abbr* (*US*) = *Long Island*.
liabilities [laɪə'bɪlɪtɪz] *npl* (*COMM*) obligations *fpl*, engagements *mpl*; (*on balance sheet*) passif *m*.
liability [laɪə'bɪlɪtɪ] *n* responsabilité *f*; (*handicap*) handicap *m*.
liable ['laɪəbl] *a* (*subject*): **~ to** sujet(te) à; passible de; (*responsible*): **~ (for)** responsable (de); (*likely*): **~ to do** susceptible de faire; **to be ~ to a fine** être passible d'une amende.
liaise [li:'eɪz] *vi*: **to ~ with** rester en liaison avec.
liaison [li:'eɪzɒn] *n* liaison *f*.
liar ['laɪə*] *n* menteur/euse.
libel ['laɪbl] *n* écrit *m* diffamatoire; diffamation *f* ♦ *vt* diffamer.
libellous ['laɪbləs] *a* diffamatoire.
liberal ['lɪbərl] *a* libéral(e); (*generous*): **~ with** prodigue de, généreux(euse) avec ♦ *n*: **L~** (*POL*) libéral/e.
liberality [lɪbə'rælɪtɪ] *n* (*generosity*) générosité *f*, libéralité *f*.
liberalize ['lɪbərəlaɪz] *vt* libéraliser.
liberal-minded ['lɪbərl'maɪndɪd] *a* libéral(e), tolérant(e).
liberate ['lɪbəreɪt] *vt* libérer.

liberation [lɪbə'reɪʃən] n libération f.
Liberia [laɪ'bɪərɪə] n Libéria m, Liberia m.
Liberian [laɪ'bɪərɪən] a libérien(ne) ♦ n Libérien/ne.
liberty ['lɪbətɪ] n liberté f; **at ~ to do** libre de faire; **to take the ~ of** prendre la liberté de, se permettre de.
libido [lɪ'biːdəu] n libido f.
Libra ['liːbrə] n la Balance; **to be ~** être de la Balance.
librarian [laɪ'brɛərɪən] n bibliothécaire m/f.
library ['laɪbrərɪ] n bibliothèque f.
library book n livre m de bibliothèque.
libretto [lɪ'brɛtəu] n livret m.
Libya ['lɪbɪə] n Libye f.
Libyan ['lɪbɪən] a libyen(ne), de Libye ♦ n Libyen/ne.
lice [laɪs] npl of **louse**.
licence, (US) **license** ['laɪsns] n autorisation f, permis m; (COMM) licence f; (RADIO, TV) redevance f; (also: **driving ~**, (US) **driver's ~**) permis m (de conduire); (excessive freedom) licence; **import ~** licence d'importation; **produced under ~** fabriqué(e) sous licence.
licence number n (Brit AUT) numéro m d'immatriculation.
license ['laɪsns] n (US) = **licence** ♦ vt donner une licence à; (car) acheter la vignette de; délivrer la vignette de.
licensed ['laɪsnst] a (for alcohol) patenté(e) pour la vente des spiritueux, qui a une patente de débit de boissons.
licensee [laɪsən'siː] n (Brit: of pub) patron/ne, gérant/e.
license plate n (esp US AUT) plaque f minéralogique.
licentious [laɪ'sɛnʃəs] a licentieux(euse).
lichen ['laɪkən] n lichen m.
lick [lɪk] vt lécher; (col: defeat) écraser, flanquer une piquette or raclée à ♦ n coup m de langue; **a ~ of paint** un petit coup de peinture.
licorice ['lɪkərɪs] n = **liquorice**.
lid [lɪd] n couvercle m; **to take the ~ off sth** (fig) exposer or étaler qch au grand jour.
lido ['laɪdəu] n piscine f en plein air; complexe m balnéaire.
lie [laɪ] n mensonge m ♦ vi mentir; (pt **lay**, pp **lain** [leɪ, leɪn]) (rest) être étendu(e) or allongé(e) or couché(e); (in grave) être enterré(e), reposer; (of object: be situated) se trouver, être; **to ~ low** (fig) se cacher, rester caché(e); **to tell ~s** mentir.
lie about, lie around vi (things) traîner; (person) traînasser, flemmarder.
lie back vi se renverser en arrière.
lie down vi se coucher, s'étendre.
lie up vi (hide) se cacher.
Liechtenstein ['lɪktənstaɪn] n Liechtenstein m.
lie detector n détecteur m de mensonges.
lie-down ['laɪdaun] n (Brit): **to have a ~** s'allonger, se reposer.
lie-in ['laɪɪn] n (Brit): **to have a ~** faire la grasse matinée.
lieu [luː]: **in ~ of** prep au lieu de, à la place de.
Lieut. abbr (= lieutenant) Lt.
lieutenant [lɛf'tɛnənt, (US) luː'tɛnənt] n lieutenant m.
lieutenant-colonel [lɛf'tɛnənt'kəːnl, (US) luː'tɛnənt'kəːnl] n lieutenant-colonel m.
life, pl **lives** [laɪf, laɪvz] n vie f ♦ cpd de vie; de la vie; **à vie**; **true to ~** réaliste, fidèle à la réalité; **to paint from ~** peindre d'après nature; **to be sent to prison for ~** être condamné(e) (à la réclusion criminelle) à perpétuité; **country/city ~** la vie à la campagne/à la ville.
life annuity n pension f, rente viagère.
life assurance n (Brit) = **life insurance**.
lifebelt ['laɪfbɛlt] n (Brit) bouée f de sauvetage.
lifeblood ['laɪfblʌd] n (fig) élément moteur.
lifeboat ['laɪfbəut] n canot m or chaloupe f de sauvetage.
lifebuoy ['laɪfbɔɪ] n bouée f de sauvetage.
life expectancy n espérance f de vie.
lifeguard ['laɪfgaːd] n surveillant m de baignade.
life imprisonment n prison f à vie; (LAW) réclusion f à perpétuité.
life insurance n assurance-vie f.
life jacket n gilet m or ceinture f de sauvetage.
lifeless ['laɪflɪs] a sans vie, inanimé(e); (dull) qui manque de vie or de vigueur.
lifelike ['laɪflaɪk] a qui semble vrai(e) or vivant(e); ressemblant(e).
lifeline ['laɪflaɪn] n corde f de sauvetage.
lifelong ['laɪflɔŋ] a de toute une vie, de toujours.
life preserver n (US) gilet m or ceinture f de sauvetage.
life-raft ['laɪfraːft] n radeau m de sauvetage.
life-saver ['laɪfseɪvə*] n surveillant m de baignade.
life sentence n condamnation f à vie or à perpétuité.
life-sized ['laɪfsaɪzd] a grandeur nature inv.
life span n (durée f de) vie f.
life style n style m de vie.
life support system n (MED) respirateur artificiel.
lifetime ['laɪftaɪm] n: **in his ~** de son vivant; **the chance of a ~** la chance de ma (or sa etc) vie, une occasion unique.
lift [lɪft] vt soulever, lever; (steal) prendre, voler ♦ vi (fog) se lever ♦ n (Brit: elevator) ascenseur m; **to give sb a ~** (Brit) emmener or prendre qn en voiture.
lift off vi (rocket, helicopter) décoller.
lift out vt sortir; (troops, evacuees etc) évacuer par avion or hélicoptère.
lift up vt soulever.
lift-off ['lɪftɔf] n décollage m.
ligament ['lɪgəmənt] n ligament m.
light [laɪt] n lumière f; (daylight) lumière, jour m; (lamp) lampe f; (AUT: traffic ~, rear ~) feu m; (: headlamp) phare m; (for cigarette etc): **have you got a ~?** avez-vous du feu? ♦ vt (pt, pp **lighted** or **lit** [lɪt]) (candle, cigarette, fire) allumer; (room) éclairer ♦ a (room, colour) clair(e); (not heavy, also fig) léger(ère) ♦ ad (travel) avec peu de bagages; **to turn the ~ on/off** allumer/éteindre; **to cast** or **shed** or **throw ~ on** éclaircir; **to come to ~** être dévoilé(e) or

découvert(e); **in the ~ of** à la lumière de; étant donné; **to make ~ of sth** (fig) prendre qch à la légère, faire peu de cas de qch.

light up vi s'allumer; (face) s'éclairer ♦ vt (illuminate) éclairer, illuminer.

light bulb n ampoule f.

lighten ['laɪtn] vi s'éclairer ♦ vt (give light to) éclairer; (make lighter) éclaircir; (make less heavy) alléger.

lighter ['laɪtə*] n (also: **cigarette ~**) briquet m; (: in car) allume-cigare m inv; (boat) péniche f.

light-fingered [laɪt'fɪŋgəd] a chapardeur(euse).

light-headed [laɪt'hɛdɪd] a étourdi(e), écervelé(e).

light-hearted [laɪt'hɑːtɪd] a gai(e), joyeux(euse), enjoué(e).

lighthouse ['laɪthaus] n phare m.

lighting ['laɪtɪŋ] n (on road) éclairage m; (in theatre) éclairages.

lighting-up time [laɪtɪŋ'ʌp-] n (Brit) heure officielle de la tombée du jour.

lightly ['laɪtlɪ] ad légèrement; **to get off ~** s'en tirer à bon compte.

light meter n (PHOT) photomètre m, cellule f.

lightness ['laɪtnɪs] n clarté f; (in weight) légèreté f.

lightning ['laɪtnɪŋ] n éclair m, foudre f.

lightning conductor, (US) **lightning rod** n paratonnerre m.

lightning strike n (Brit) grève f surprise.

light pen n crayon m optique.

lightship ['laɪtʃɪp] n bateau-phare m.

lightweight ['laɪtweɪt] a (suit) léger(ère); (boxer) poids léger inv.

light year ['laɪtjɪə*] n année-lumière f.

like [laɪk] vt aimer (bien) ♦ prep comme ♦ a semblable, pareil(le) ♦ n: **the ~** un(e) pareil(le) or semblable; le(la) pareil(le); (pej) (d')autres du même genre or acabit; **his ~s and dislikes** ses goûts mpl or préférences fpl; **I would ~, I'd ~** je voudrais, j'aimerais; **would you ~ a coffee?** voulez-vous du café?; **to be/look ~ sb/sth** ressembler à qn/qch; **what's he ~?** comment est-il?; **what's the weather ~?** quel temps fait-il?; **that's just ~ him** c'est bien de lui, ça lui ressemble; **something ~ that** quelque chose comme ça; **I feel ~ a drink** je boirais bien quelque chose; **if you ~** si vous voulez; **there's nothing ~ ...** il n'y a rien de tel que ....

likeable ['laɪkəbl] a sympathique, agréable.

likelihood ['laɪklɪhud] n probabilité f; **in all ~** selon toute vraisemblance.

likely ['laɪklɪ] a (result, outcome) probable; (excuse) plausible; **he's ~ to leave** il va sûrement partir, il risque fort de partir; **not ~!** (col) pas de danger!

like-minded ['laɪk'maɪndɪd] a de même opinion.

liken ['laɪkən] vt: **to ~ sth to** comparer qch à.

likeness ['laɪknɪs] n ressemblance f.

likewise ['laɪkwaɪz] ad de même, pareillement.

liking ['laɪkɪŋ] n affection f, penchant m; goût m; **to take a ~ to sb** se prendre d'amitié pour qn; **to be to sb's ~** être au goût de qn,

plaire à qn.

lilac ['laɪlək] n lilas m ♦ a lilas inv.

lilt [lɪlt] n rythme m, cadence f.

lilting ['lɪltɪŋ] a aux cadences mélodieuses; chantant(e).

lily ['lɪlɪ] n lis m; **~ of the valley** muguet m.

Lima ['liːmə] n Lima.

limb [lɪm] n membre m; **to be out on a ~** (fig) être isolé(e).

limber ['lɪmbə*]: **to ~ up** vi se dégourdir, se mettre en train.

limbo ['lɪmbəu] n: **to be in ~** (fig) être tombé(e) dans l'oubli.

lime [laɪm] n (tree) tilleul m; (fruit) citron vert, lime f; (GEO) chaux f.

lime juice n jus m de citron vert.

limelight ['laɪmlaɪt] n: **in the ~** (fig) en vedette, au premier plan.

limerick ['lɪmərɪk] n petit poème humoristique.

limestone ['laɪmstəun] n pierre f à chaux; (GEO) calcaire m.

limit ['lɪmɪt] n limite f ♦ vt limiter; **weight/speed ~** limite de poids/de vitesse.

limitation [lɪmɪ'teɪʃən] n limitation f, restriction f.

limited ['lɪmɪtɪd] a limité(e), restreint(e); **~ edition** édition f à tirage limité.

limited (liability) company (Ltd) n (Brit) ≈ société f anonyme (SA).

limitless ['lɪmɪtlɪs] a illimité(e).

limousine ['lɪməziːn] n limousine f.

limp [lɪmp] n: **to have a ~** boiter ♦ vi boiter ♦ a mou(molle).

limpet ['lɪmpɪt] n patelle f; **like a ~** (fig) comme une ventouse.

limpid ['lɪmpɪd] a limpide.

linchpin ['lɪntʃpɪn] n esse f; (fig) pivot m.

Lincs [lɪŋks] abbr (Brit) = Lincolnshire.

line [laɪn] n (gen) ligne f; (rope) corde f; (wire) fil m; (of poem) vers m; (row, series) rangée f; file f, queue f; (COMM: series of goods) article(s) m(pl), ligne de produits ♦ vt (clothes): **to ~ (with)** doubler (de); (box): **to ~ (with)** garnir or tapisser (de); (subj: trees, crowd) border; **to cut in ~** (US) passer avant son tour; **in his ~ of business** dans sa partie, dans son rayon; **on the right ~s** sur la bonne voie; **a new ~ in cosmetics** une nouvelle ligne de produits de beauté; **hold the ~ please** (Brit TEL) ne quittez pas; **to be in ~ for sth** (fig) être en lice pour qch; **in ~ with** en accord avec, en conformité avec; **to bring sth into ~ with sth** aligner qch sur qch; **to draw the ~ at (doing) sth** (fig) se refuser à (faire) qch, ne pas tolérer or admettre (qu'on fasse) qch; **to take the ~ that ...** être d'avis or de l'opinion que ....

line up vi s'aligner, se mettre en rang(s) ♦ vt aligner; (set up, have ready) prévoir; trouver; **to have sb/sth ~d up** avoir qn/qch en vue or de prévu(e).

linear ['lɪnɪə*] a linéaire.

lined ['laɪnd] a (paper) réglé(e); (face) marqué(e), ridé(e); (clothes) doublé(e).

line feed n (COMPUT) interligne m.

linen ['lɪnɪn] n linge m (de corps or de maison); (cloth) lin m.

line printer n imprimante f (ligne par) ligne.

liner ['laɪnə*] n paquebot m de ligne.

linesman ['laɪnzmən] n (TENNIS) juge m de ligne; (FOOTBALL) juge de touche.

line-up ['laɪnʌp] n file f; (also: **police** ~) parade f d'identification; (SPORT) (composition f de l')équipe f.

linger ['lɪŋgə*] vi s'attarder; traîner; (smell, tradition) persister.

lingerie ['lænʒəri:] n lingerie f.

lingering ['lɪŋgərɪŋ] a persistant(e); qui subsiste; (death) lent(e).

lingo, ~es ['lɪŋgəu] n (pej) jargon m.

linguist ['lɪŋgwɪst] n linguiste m/f; personne douée pour les langues.

linguistic [lɪŋ'gwɪstɪk] a linguistique.

linguistics [lɪŋ'gwɪstɪks] n linguistique f.

lining ['laɪnɪŋ] n doublure f; (TECH) revêtement m; (: of brakes) garniture f.

link [lɪŋk] n (of a chain) maillon m; (connection) lien m, rapport m ♦ vt relier, lier, unir; **rail** ~ liaison f ferroviaire.
link up vt relier ♦ vi se rejoindre; s'associer.

links [lɪŋks] npl (terrain m de) golf m.

link-up ['lɪŋkʌp] n lien m, rapport m; (of roads) jonction f, raccordement m; (of spaceships) arrimage m; (RADIO, TV) liaison f; (: programme) duplex m.

linoleum [lɪ'nəuliəm] n linoléum m.

linseed oil ['lɪnsi:d-] n huile f de lin.

lint [lɪnt] n tissu ouaté (pour pansements).

lintel ['lɪntl] n linteau m.

lion ['laɪən] n lion m.

lion cub n lionceau m.

lioness ['laɪənɪs] n lionne f.

lip [lɪp] n lèvre f; (of cup etc) rebord m; (insolence) insolences fpl.

lipread ['lɪpri:d] vi lire sur les lèvres.

lip salve n pommade f pour les lèvres, pommade rosat.

lip service n: **to pay** ~ **to sth** ne reconnaître le mérite de qch que pour la forme or qu'en paroles.

lipstick ['lɪpstɪk] n rouge m à lèvres.

liquefy ['lɪkwɪfaɪ] vt liquéfier ♦ vi se liquéfier.

liqueur [lɪ'kjuə*] n liqueur f.

liquid ['lɪkwɪd] n liquide m ♦ a liquide.

liquid assets npl liquidités fpl, disponibilités fpl.

liquidate ['lɪkwɪdeɪt] vt liquider.

liquidation [lɪkwɪ'deɪʃən] n liquidation f; **to go into** ~ déposer son bilan.

liquidator ['lɪkwɪdeɪtə*] n liquidateur m.

liquid crystal display (LCD) n affichage m à cristaux liquides.

liquidize ['lɪkwɪdaɪz] vt (Brit CULIN) passer au mixer.

liquidizer ['lɪkwɪdaɪzə*] n (Brit CULIN) mixer m.

liquor ['lɪkə*] n spiritueux m, alcool m.

liquorice ['lɪkərɪs] n (Brit) réglisse m.

Lisbon ['lɪzbən] n Lisbonne.

lisp [lɪsp] n zézaiement m.

lissom ['lɪsəm] a souple, agile.

list [lɪst] n liste f; (of ship) inclinaison f ♦ vt (write down) inscrire; faire la liste de; (enumerate) énumérer; (COMPUT) lister ♦ vi (ship) gîter, donner de la bande; **shopping** ~ liste des courses.

listed building n (ARCHIT) monument classé.

listed company n société cotée en bourse.

listen ['lɪsn] vi écouter; **to** ~ **to** écouter.

listener ['lɪsnə*] n auditeur/trice.

listing [lɪstɪŋ] n (COMPUT) listage m; (: résultat) liste f, listing m.

listless ['lɪstlɪs] a indolent(e), apathique.

listlessly ['lɪstlɪslɪ] ad avec indolence or apathie.

list price n prix m de catalogue.

lit [lɪt] pt, pp of **light**.

litany ['lɪtənɪ] n litanie f.

liter ['li:tə*] n (US) = **litre**.

literacy ['lɪtərəsɪ] n degré m d'alphabétisation, fait m de savoir lire et écrire.

literal ['lɪtərl] a littéral(e).

literally ['lɪtrəlɪ] ad littéralement.

literary ['lɪtərərɪ] a littéraire.

literate ['lɪtərət] a qui sait lire et écrire, instruit(e).

literature ['lɪtrɪtʃə*] n littérature f; (brochures etc) copie f publicitaire, prospectus mpl.

lithe [laɪð] a agile, souple.

lithography [lɪ'θɔgrəfɪ] n lithographie f.

Lithuania [lɪθju'eɪnɪə] n Lituanie f.

litigate ['lɪtɪgeɪt] vt mettre en litige ♦ vi plaider.

litigation [lɪtɪ'geɪʃən] n litige m; contentieux m.

litmus ['lɪtməs] n: ~ **paper** papier m de tournesol.

litre, (US) liter ['li:tə*] n litre m.

litter ['lɪtə*] n (rubbish) détritus mpl, ordures fpl; (young animals) portée f ♦ vt éparpiller; laisser des détritus dans; ~**ed with** jonché(e) de, couvert(e) de.

litter bin n (Brit) boîte f à ordures, poubelle f.

litter lout, (US) litterbug ['lɪtəbʌg] n personne qui jette des détritus par terre.

little ['lɪtl] a (small) petit(e); (not much): **it's** ~ c'est peu; ~ **milk** peu de lait ♦ ad peu; **a** ~ un peu (de); **a** ~ **milk** un peu de lait; **for a** ~ **while** pendant un petit moment; **with** ~ **difficulty** sans trop de difficulté; **as** ~ **as possible** le moins possible; ~ **by** ~ petit à petit, peu à peu; **to make** ~ **of** faire peu de cas de.

liturgy ['lɪtədʒɪ] n liturgie f.

live vi [lɪv] vivre; (reside) vivre, habiter ♦ a [laɪv] (animal) vivant(e), en vie; (wire) sous tension; (broadcast) transmis(e) en direct; (issue) d'actualité, brûlant(e); (unexploded) non explosé(e); **to** ~ **in London** habiter (à) Londres; **to** ~ **together** vivre ensemble, cohabiter; ~ **ammunition** munitions fpl de combat.
live down vt faire oublier (avec le temps).

live in vi être logé(e) et nourri(e); être interne.

live off vt (land, fish etc) vivre de; (pej: parents etc) vivre aux crochets de.

live on vt fus (food) vivre de ♦ vi survivre; **to** ~ **on £50 a week** vivre avec 50 livres par semaine.

live out vi (Brit: students) être externe ♦ vt: **to** ~ **out one's days** or **life** passer sa vie.

live up vt: **to** ~ **it up** (col) faire la fête; mener la grande vie.

live up to vt fus se montrer à la hauteur

de.

livelihood ['laɪvlɪhud] *n* moyens *mpl* d'existence.

liveliness ['laɪvlɪnəs] *n* vivacité *f*, entrain *m*.

lively ['laɪvlɪ] *a* vif(vive), plein(e) d'entrain.

liven up ['laɪvn-] *vt* (*room etc*) égayer; (*discussion, evening*) animer.

liver ['lɪvə*] *n* foie *m*.

liverish ['lɪvərɪʃ] *a* qui a mal au foie; (*fig*) grincheux(euse).

Liverpudlian [lɪvə'pʌdlɪən] *a* de Liverpool ♦ *n* habitant/e de Liverpool; natif/ive de Liverpool.

livery ['lɪvərɪ] *n* livrée *f*.

lives [laɪvz] *npl of* **life**.

livestock ['laɪvstɔk] *n* cheptel *m*, bétail *m*.

livid ['lɪvɪd] *a* livide, blafard(e); (*furious*) furieux(euse), furibond(e).

living ['lɪvɪŋ] *a* vivant(e), en vie ♦ *n*: **to earn** *or* **make a ~** gagner sa vie; **cost of ~** coût *m* de la vie; **within ~ memory** de mémoire d'homme.

living conditions *npl* conditions *fpl* de vie.

living expenses *npl* dépenses courantes.

living room *n* salle *f* de séjour.

living wage *n* salaire *m* permettant de vivre (décemment).

lizard ['lɪzəd] *n* lézard *m*.

llama ['lɑːmə] *n* lama *m*.

LLB *n abbr* (= *Bachelor of Laws*) *titre universitaire*.

LLD *n abbr* (= *Doctor of Laws*) *titre universitaire*.

LMT *abbr* (*US*: = *Local Mean Time*) *heure locale*.

load [ləud] *n* (*weight*) poids *m*; (*thing carried*) chargement *m*, charge *f*; (*ELEC, TECH*) charge ♦ *vt* (*lorry, ship*): **to ~ (with)** charger (de); (*gun, camera*): **to ~ (with)** charger (avec); (*COMPUT*) charger; **a ~ of**, **~s of** (*fig*) un *or* des tas de, des masses de.

loaded ['ləudɪd] *a* (*dice*) pipé(e); (*question*) insidieux(euse); (*col: rich*) bourré(e) de fric; (: *drunk*) bourré.

loading bay ['ləudɪŋ-] *n* aire *f* de chargement.

loaf, loaves [ləuf, ləuvz] *n* pain *m*, miche *f* ♦ *vi* (*also: ~ **about**, ~ **around**) fainéanter, traîner.

loam [ləum] *n* terreau *m*.

loan [ləun] *n* prêt *m* ♦ *vt* prêter; **on ~** prêté(e), en prêt; **public ~** emprunt public.

loan account *n* compte *m* de prêt.

loan capital *n* capital-obligations *m*.

loath [ləuθ] *a*: **to be ~ to do** répugner à faire.

loathe [ləuð] *vt* détester, avoir en horreur.

loathing ['ləuðɪŋ] *n* dégoût *m*, répugnance *f*.

loathsome ['ləuðsəm] *a* répugnant(e), détestable.

loaves [ləuvz] *npl of* **loaf**.

lob [lɔb] *vt* (*ball*) lober.

lobby ['lɔbɪ] *n* hall *m*, entrée *f*; (*POL*) groupe *m* de pression, lobby *m* ♦ *vt* faire pression sur.

lobbyist ['lɔbɪɪst] *n* membre *m/f* d'un groupe de pression.

lobe [ləub] *n* lobe *m*.

lobster ['lɔbstə*] *n* homard *m*.

lobster pot *n* casier *m* à homards.

local ['ləukl] *a* local(e) ♦ *n* (*pub*) pub *m* *or* café *m* du coin; **the ~s** *npl* les gens *mpl* du pays *or* du coin.

local anaesthetic *n* anesthésie locale.

local authority *n* collectivité locale, municipalité *f*.

local call *n* (*TEL*) communication urbaine.

local government *n* administration locale *or* municipale.

locality [ləu'kælɪtɪ] *n* région *f*, environs *mpl*; (*position*) lieu *m*.

localize ['ləukəlaɪz] *vt* localiser.

locally ['ləukəlɪ] *ad* localement; dans les environs *or* la région.

locate [ləu'keɪt] *vt* (*find*) trouver, repérer; (*situate*) situer.

location [ləu'keɪʃən] *n* emplacement *m*; **on ~** (*CINEMA*) en extérieur.

loch [lɔx] *n* lac *m*, loch *m*.

lock [lɔk] *n* (*of door, box*) serrure *f*; (*of canal*) écluse *f*; (*of hair*) mèche *f*, boucle *f* ♦ *vt* (*with key*) fermer à clé; (*immobilize*) bloquer ♦ *vi* (*door etc*) fermer à clé; (*wheels*) se bloquer; **~ stock and barrel** (*fig*) en bloc; **on full ~** (*Brit AUT*) le volant tourné à fond.

lock away *vt* (*valuables*) mettre sous clé; (*criminal*) mettre sous les verrous, enfermer.

lock out *vt* enfermer dehors; (*on purpose*) mettre à la porte; (: *workers*) lock-outer.

lock up *vi* tout fermer (à clé).

locker ['lɔkə*] *n* casier *m*.

locket ['lɔkɪt] *n* médaillon *m*.

lockjaw ['lɔkdʒɔː] *n* tétanos *m*.

lockout ['lɔkaut] *n* (*INDUSTRY*) lock-out *m*, grève patronale.

locksmith ['lɔksmɪθ] *n* serrurier *m*.

lock-up ['lɔkʌp] *n* (*prison*) prison *f*; (*cell*) cellule *f* provisoire; (*also: ~ **garage**) box *m*.

locomotive [ləukə'məutɪv] *n* locomotive *f*.

locum ['ləukəm] *n* (*MED*) suppléant/e (de médecin).

locust ['ləukəst] *n* locuste *f*, sauterelle *f*.

lodge [lɔdʒ] *n* pavillon *m* (de gardien); (*FREEMASONRY*) loge *f* ♦ *vi* (*person*): **to ~ with** être logé(e) chez, être en pension chez ♦ *vt* (*appeal etc*) présenter; déposer; **to ~ a complaint** porter plainte; **to ~ (itself) in/ between** se loger dans/entre.

lodger ['lɔdʒə*] *n* locataire *m/f*; (*with room and meals*) pensionnaire *m/f*.

lodging ['lɔdʒɪŋ] *n* logement *m*; *see also* **board**.

lodging house ['lɔdʒɪŋ-] *n* (*Brit*) pension *f* de famille.

lodgings ['lɔdʒɪŋz] *n* chambre *f*, meublé *m*.

loft [lɔft] *n* grenier *m*; (*US*) grenier aménagé (en appartement) (*gén dans ancien entrepôt ou fabrique*).

lofty ['lɔftɪ] *a* élevé(e); (*haughty*) hautain(e); (*sentiments, aims*) noble.

log [lɔg] *n* (*of wood*) bûche *f*; (*book*) = **logbook** ♦ *n abbr* (= *logarithm*) log *m* ♦ *vt* enregistrer.

log in, log on *vi* (*COMPUT*) ouvrir une session, entrer dans le système.

log off, log out *vi* (*COMPUT*) clore une session, sortir du système.

logarithm ['lɔgərɪðm] *n* logarithme *m*.

logbook ['lɔgbuk] n (NAUT) livre m or journal m de bord; (AVIAT) carnet m de vol; (of lorry-driver) carnet de route; (of events, movement of goods etc) registre m; (of car) ≈ carte grise.

log cabin n cabane f en rondins.

log fire n feu m de bois.

loggerheads ['lɔgəhɛdz] npl: **at ~ (with)** à couteaux tirés (avec).

logic ['lɔdʒɪk] n logique f.

logical ['lɔdʒɪkl] a logique.

logically ['lɔdʒɪkəlɪ] ad logiquement.

logistics [lɔ'dʒɪstɪks] n logistique f.

logo ['laugəu] n logo m.

loin [lɔɪn] n (CULIN) filet m, longe f; **~s** npl reins mpl.

loin cloth n pagne m.

loiter ['lɔɪtə*] vi s'attarder; **to ~ (about)** traîner, musarder; (pej) rôder.

loll [lɔl] vi (also: **~ about**) se prélasser, fainéanter.

lollipop ['lɔlɪpɔp] n sucette f.

lollipop man n, **lollipop lady** n (Brit) contractuel/le qui fait traverser la rue aux enfants.

lollop ['lɔləp] vi (Brit) avancer (or courir) maladroitement.

Lombardy ['lɔmbədɪ] n Lombardie f.

London ['lʌndən] n Londres.

Londoner ['lʌndənə*] n Londonien/ne.

lone [ləun] a solitaire.

loneliness ['ləunlɪnɪs] n solitude f, isolement m.

lonely ['ləunlɪ] a seul(e); (childhood etc) solitaire; (place) solitaire, isolé(e); **to feel ~** se sentir seul.

loner ['ləunə*] n solitaire m/f.

lonesome ['ləunsəm] a seul(e); solitaire.

long [lɔŋ] a long(longue) ♦ ad longtemps ♦ n: **the ~ and the short of it is that ...** (fig) le fin mot de l'histoire c'est que ... ♦ vi: **to ~ for sth/to do** avoir très envie de qch/de faire; attendre qch avec impatience/impatience de faire; **he had ~ understood that ...** il avait compris depuis longtemps que ...; **how ~ is this river/course?** quelle est la longueur de ce fleuve/la durée de ce cours?; **6 metres ~** (long) de 6 mètres; **6 months ~** qui dure 6 mois, de 6 mois; **all night ~** toute la nuit; **he no ~er comes** il ne vient plus; **~ before** longtemps avant; **before ~** (+ future) avant peu, dans peu de temps; (+ past) peu de temps après; **~ ago** il y a longtemps; **don't be ~!** fais vite!, dépêche-toi!; **I shan't be ~** je n'en ai pas pour longtemps; **at ~ last** enfin; **in the ~ run** à la longue; finalement; **so** or **as ~ as** pourvu que.

long-distance [lɔŋ'dɪstəns] a (race) de fond; (call) interurbain(e).

long-haired ['lɔŋ'hɛəd] a (person) aux cheveux longs; (animal) aux longs poils.

longhand ['lɔŋhænd] n écriture normale or courante.

longing ['lɔŋɪŋ] n désir m, envie f, nostalgie f ♦ a plein(e) d'envie or de nostalgie.

longingly ['lɔŋɪŋlɪ] ad avec désir or nostalgie.

longitude ['lɔŋgɪtjuːd] n longitude f.

long johns [-dʒɔnz] npl caleçons longs.

long jump n saut m en longueur.

long-lost ['lɔŋlɔst] a perdu(e) depuis longtemps.

long-playing ['lɔŋpleɪɪŋ] a: **~ record (LP)** (disque m) 33 tours m inv.

long-range ['lɔŋ'reɪndʒ] a à longue portée; (weather forecast) à long terme.

longshoreman ['lɔŋʃɔːmən] n (US) docker m, débardeur m.

long-sighted ['lɔŋ'saɪtɪd] a (Brit) presbyte; (fig) prévoyant(e).

long-standing ['lɔŋ'stændɪŋ] a de longue date.

long-suffering [lɔŋ'sʌfərɪŋ] a empreint(e) d'une patience résignée; extrêmement patient(e).

long-term ['lɔŋtəːm] a à long terme.

long wave n (RADIO) grandes ondes, ondes longues.

long-winded [lɔŋ'wɪndɪd] a intarissable, interminable.

loo [luː] n (Brit col) w.-c. mpl, petit coin.

loofah ['luːfə] n sorte d'éponge végétale.

look [luk] vi regarder; (seem) sembler, paraître, avoir l'air; (building etc): **to ~ south/ on to the sea** donner au sud/sur la mer ♦ n regard m; (appearance) air m, allure f, aspect m; **~s** npl physique m, beauté f; **to ~ like** ressembler à; **it ~s like him** on dirait que c'est lui; **it ~s like 4 metres long** je dirais que ça fait 4 mètres de long, à vue de nez, ça fait 4 mètres de long; **it ~s all right to me** ça me paraît bien; **to have a ~ at sth** jeter un coup d'œil à qch; **to have a ~ for sth** chercher qch; **to ~ ahead** regarder devant soi; (fig) envisager l'avenir.

look after vt fus s'occuper de, prendre soin de; (luggage etc: watch over) garder, surveiller.

look around vi regarder autour de soi.

look at vt fus regarder.

look back vi: **to ~ back at sth/sb** se retourner pour regarder qch/qn; **to look back on** (event, period) évoquer, repenser à.

look down on vt fus (fig) regarder de haut, dédaigner.

look for vt fus chercher.

look forward to vt fus attendre avec impatience; **I'm not ~ing forward to it** cette perspective ne me réjouit guère; **~ing forward to hearing from you** (in letter) dans l'attente de vous lire.

look in vi: **to ~ in on sb** passer voir qn.

look into vt fus (matter, possibility) examiner, étudier.

look on vi regarder (en spectateur).

look out vi (beware): **to ~ out (for)** prendre garde (à), faire attention (à).

look out for vt fus être à la recherche de; guetter.

look over vt (essay) jeter un coup d'œil à; (town, building) visiter (rapidement); (person) jeter un coup d'œil à; examiner de la tête aux pieds.

look round vi (turn) regarder derrière soi, se retourner; **to ~ round for sth** chercher qch.

look through vt fus (papers, book) examiner; (: briefly) parcourir; (telescope) regarder à travers.

look to vt fus veiller à; (rely on) compter

sur.
look up *vi* lever les yeux; (*improve*) s'améliorer ♦ *vt* (*word*) chercher; (*friend*) passer voir.
look up to *vt fus* avoir du respect pour.
look-out ['lukaut] *n* poste *m* de guet; guetteur *m*; **to be on the ~ (for)** guetter.
look-up table ['lukʌp-] *n* (COMPUT) table *f* à consulter.
LOOM *n abbr* (US: = *Loyal Order of Moose*) *association charitable*.
loom [lu:m] *n* métier *m* à tisser ♦ *vi* surgir; (*fig*) menacer, paraître imminent(e).
loony ['lu:nɪ] *a*, *n* (*col*) timbré(e), cinglé(e) (*m/f*).
loop [lu:p] *n* boucle *f*; (*contraceptive*) stérilet *m*.
loophole ['lu:phəul] *n* porte *f* de sortie (*fig*); échappatoire *f*.
loose [lu:s] *a* (*knot, screw*) desserré(e); (*stone*) branlant(e); (*clothes*) vague, ample, lâche; (*animal*) en liberté, échappé(e); (*life*) dissolu(e); (*morals, discipline*) relâché(e); (*thinking*) peu rigoureux(euse), vague; (*translation*) approximatif(ive) ♦ *vt* (*free: animal*) lâcher; (: *prisoner*) relâcher, libérer; (*slacken*) détendre, relâcher; desserrer; défaire; donner du mou a; donner du ballant à; (*Brit: arrow*) tirer; **~ connection** (ELEC) mauvais contact; **to be at a ~ end** *or* (US) **at ~ ends** (*fig*) ne pas trop savoir quoi faire; **to tie up ~ ends** (*fig*) mettre au point *or* régler les derniers détails.
loose change *n* petite monnaie.
loose-fitting ['lu:sfɪtɪŋ] *a* (*clothes*) ample.
loose-leaf ['lu:sli:f] *a*: **~ binder** *or* **folder** classeur *m* à feuilles *or* feuillets mobiles.
loose-limbed [lu:s'lɪmd] *a* agile, souple.
loosely ['lu:slɪ] *ad* sans serrer; approximativement.
loosen ['lu:sn] *vt* desserrer, relâcher, défaire.
loosen up *vi* (*before game*) s'échauffer; (*col: relax*) se détendre, se laisser aller.
loot [lu:t] *n* butin *m* ♦ *vt* piller.
looter ['lu:tə*] *n* pillard *m*, casseur *m*.
looting ['lu:tɪŋ] *n* pillage *m*.
lop [lɔp]: **to ~ off** *vt* couper, trancher.
lop-sided ['lɔp'saɪdɪd] *a* de travers, asymétrique.
lord [lɔ:d] *n* seigneur *m*; **L~ Smith** lord Smith; **the L~** (REL) le Seigneur; **the (House of) L~s** (*Brit*) la Chambre des Lords.
lordly ['lɔ:dlɪ] *a* noble, majestueux(euse); (*arrogant*) hautain(e).
lordship ['lɔ:dʃɪp] *n* (*Brit*): **your L~** Monsieur le comte (*or* le baron *or* le Juge).
lore [lɔ:*] *n* tradition(s) *f(pl)*.
lorry ['lɔrɪ] *n* (*Brit*) camion *m*.
lorry driver *n* (*Brit*) camionneur *m*, routier *m*.
lose, *pt*, *pp* **lost** [lu:z, lɔst] *vt* perdre; (*opportunity*) manquer, perdre; (*pursuers*) distancer, semer ♦ *vi* perdre; **to ~ (time)** (*clock*) retarder; **to ~ no time (in doing sth)** ne pas perdre de temps (à faire qch); **to get lost** *vi* (*person*) se perdre; **my watch has got lost** ma montre est perdue.
loser ['lu:zə*] *n* perdant/e; **to be a good/bad ~** être beau/mauvais joueur.

loss [lɔs] *n* perte *f*; **to cut one's ~es** limiter les dégâts; **to make a ~** enregistrer une perte; **to sell sth at a ~** vendre qch à perte; **to be at a ~** être perplexe *or* embarrassé(e); **to be at a ~ to do** se trouver incapable de faire.
loss adjuster *n* (INSURANCE) responsable *m/f* de l'évaluation des dommages.
loss leader *n* (COMM) article sacrifié.
lost [lɔst] *pt*, *pp of* **lose** ♦ *a* perdu(e); **~ in thought** perdu dans ses pensées; **~ and found property** *n* (US) objets trouvés; **~ and found** *n* (US) (bureau *m* des) objets trouvés.
lost property *n* (*Brit*) objets trouvés; **~ office** *or* **department** (bureau *m* des) objets trouvés.
lot [lɔt] *n* (*at auctions*) lot *m*; (*destiny*) sort *m*, destinée *f*; **the ~** le tout; tous *mpl*, toutes *fpl*; **a ~** beaucoup; **a ~ of** beaucoup de; **~s of** des tas de; **to draw ~s (for sth)** tirer (qch) au sort.
lotion ['ləuʃən] *n* lotion *f*.
lottery ['lɔtərɪ] *n* loterie *f*.
loud [laud] *a* bruyant(e), sonore, fort(e); (*gaudy*) voyant(e), tapageur(euse) ♦ *ad* (*speak etc*) fort; **out ~** tout haut.
loudhailer [laud'heɪlə*] *n* (*Brit*) porte-voix *m inv*.
loudly ['laudlɪ] *ad* fort, bruyamment.
loudspeaker [laud'spi:kə*] *n* haut-parleur *m*.
lounge [laundʒ] *n* salon *m*; (*of airport*) salle *f* ♦ *vi* se prélasser, paresser.
lounge bar *n* (salle *f* de) bar *m*.
lounge suit *n* (*Brit*) complet *m*; (: *on invitation*) "tenue de ville".
louse, *pl* **lice** [laus, laɪs] *n* pou *m*.
louse up *vt* (*col*) gâcher.
lousy ['lauzɪ] *a* (*fig*) infect(e), moche.
lout [laut] *n* rustre *m*, butor *m*.
louvre, (US) **louver** ['lu:və*] *a* (*door, window*) à claire-voie.
lovable ['lʌvəbl] *a* très sympathique; adorable.
love [lʌv] *n* amour *m* ♦ *vt* aimer; aimer beaucoup; **to ~ to do** aimer beaucoup *or* adorer faire; **I'd ~ to come** cela me ferait très plaisir (de venir); **"15 ~"** (TENNIS) "15 à rien *or* zéro"; **to be/fall in ~ with** être/tomber amoureux(euse) de; **to make ~** faire l'amour; **~ at first sight** le coup de foudre; **to send one's ~ to sb** adresser ses amitiés à qn; **~ from Anne, ~, Anne** affectueusement, Anne.
love affair *n* liaison (amoureuse).
love letter *n* lettre *f* d'amour.
love life *n* vie sentimentale.
lovely ['lʌvlɪ] *a* (*house, garden*) ravissant(e); (*friend, wife*) charmant(e); (*holiday, surprise*) très agréable, merveilleux(euse); **we had a ~ time** c'était vraiment très bien, nous avons eu beaucoup de plaisir.
lover ['lʌvə*] *n* amant *m*; (*amateur*): **a ~ of** un(e) ami(e) de, un(e) amoureux(euse) de.
lovesick ['lʌvsɪk] *a* qui se languit d'amour.
lovesong ['lʌvsɔŋ] *n* chanson *f* d'amour.
loving ['lʌvɪŋ] *a* affectueux(euse), tendre, aimant(e).
low [ləu] *a* bas(basse) ♦ *ad* bas ♦ *n* (METEOROLOGY) dépression *f* ♦ *vi* (*cow*) mugir; **to feel ~** se sentir déprimé(e); **he's**

very ~ (*ill*) il est bien bas *or* très affaibli; **to turn (down) ~** *vt* baisser; **to reach a new** *or* **an all-time ~** tomber au niveau le plus bas.

lowbrow ['ləubrau] *a* sans prétentions intellectuelles.

low-calorie ['ləu'kælərı] *a* hypocalorique.

low-cut ['ləukʌt] *a* (*dress*) décolleté(e).

low-down ['ləudaun] *n* (*col*): **he gave me the ~ (on it)** il m'a mis au courant ♦ *a* (*mean*) méprisable.

lower ['ləuə*] *a, ad* comparative of **low** ♦ *vt* baisser; (*resistance*) diminuer ♦ *vi* ['lauə*] (*person*): **to ~ at sb** jeter un regard mauvais *or* noir à qn; (*sky, clouds*) être menaçant.

low-fat ['ləu'fæt] *a* maigre.

low-key ['ləu'ki:] *a* modéré(e); discret(ète).

lowland ['ləulənd] *n* plaine *f*.

low-level ['ləulɛvl] *a* bas(basse); (*flying*) à basse altitude.

low-loader ['ləuləudə*] *n* semi-remorque *f* à plate-forme surbaissée.

lowly ['ləulı] *a* humble, modeste.

low-lying [ləu'laıŋ] *a* à faible altitude.

low-paid [ləu'peıd] *a* mal payé(e), aux salaires bas.

loyal ['lɔıəl] *a* loyal(e), fidèle.

loyalist ['lɔıəlıst] *n* loyaliste *m/f*.

loyalty ['lɔıəltı] *n* loyauté *f*, fidélité *f*.

lozenge ['lɔzındʒ] *n* (*MED*) pastille *f*; (*GEOM*) losange *m*.

LP *n abbr* = **long-playing record**.

L-plates ['ɛlpleıts] *npl* (*Brit*) plaques *fpl* (obligatoires) d'apprenti conducteur.

LPN *n abbr* (*US*) = *Licensed Practical Nurse* infirmier/ière diplômé(e).

LRAM *n abbr* (*Brit*) = *Licentiate of the Royal Academy of Music*.

LSAT *n abbr* (*US*) = *Law School Admissions Test*.

LSD *n abbr* (= *lysergic acid diethylamide*) LSD *m*; (*Brit*: = *pounds, shillings and pence*) système monétaire en usage en GB jusqu'en 1971.

LSE *n abbr* = *London School of Economics*.

LT *abbr* (*ELEC*: = *low tension*) BT.

Lt. *abbr* (= *lieutenant*) Lt.

Ltd *abbr* (*COMM*) = **limited**.

lubricant ['lu:brıkənt] *n* lubrifiant *m*.

lubricate ['lu:brıkeıt] *vt* lubrifier, graisser.

lucid ['lu:sıd] *a* lucide.

lucidity [lu:'sıdıtı] *n* lucidité *f*.

luck [lʌk] *n* chance *f*; **bad ~** malchance *f*, malheur *m*; **to be in ~** avoir de la chance; **to be out of ~** ne pas avoir de chance; **good ~!** bonne chance!

luckily ['lʌkılı] *ad* heureusement, par bonheur.

lucky ['lʌkı] *a* (*person*) qui a de la chance; (*coincidence*) heureux(euse); (*number etc*) qui porte bonheur.

lucrative ['lu:krətıv] *a* lucratif(ive), rentable, qui rapporte.

ludicrous ['lu:dıkrəs] *a* ridicule, absurde.

ludo ['lu:dəu] *n* jeu *m* des petits chevaux.

lug [lʌg] *vt* traîner, tirer.

luggage ['lʌgıdʒ] *n* bagages *mpl*.

luggage rack *n* (*in train*) porte-bagages *m inv*; (: *made of string*) filet *m* à bagages; (*on car*) galerie *f*.

luggage van, (*US*) **luggage car** *n* (*RAIL*) fourgon *m* (à bagages).

lugubrious [lu'gu:brıəs] *a* lugubre.

lukewarm ['lu:kwɔ:m] *a* tiède.

lull [lʌl] *n* accalmie *f* ♦ *vt* (*child*) bercer; (*person, fear*) apaiser, calmer.

lullaby ['lʌləbaı] *n* berceuse *f*.

lumbago [lʌm'beıgəu] *n* lumbago *m*.

lumber ['lʌmbə*] *n* bric-à-brac *m inv* ♦ *vt* (*Brit col*): **to ~ sb with sth/sb** coller *or* refiler qch/qn à qn ♦ *vi* (*also*: **~ about, ~ along**) marcher pesamment.

lumberjack ['lʌmbədʒæk] *n* bûcheron *m*.

lumber room *n* (*Brit*) débarras *m*.

lumber yard *n* entrepôt *m* de bois.

luminous ['lu:mınəs] *a* lumineux(euse).

lump [lʌmp] *n* morceau *m*; (*in sauce*) grumeau *m*; (*swelling*) grosseur *f* ♦ *vt* (*also*: **~ together**) réunir, mettre en tas.

lump sum *n* somme globale *or* forfaitaire.

lumpy ['lʌmpı] *a* (*sauce*) qui a des grumeaux.

lunacy ['lu:nəsı] *n* démence *f*, folie *f*.

lunar ['lu:nə*] *a* lunaire.

lunatic ['lu:nətık] *n* fou/folle, dément/e ♦ *a* fou(folle), dément(e).

lunatic asylum *n* asile *m* d'aliénés.

lunch [lʌntʃ] *n* déjeuner *m* ♦ *vi* déjeuner; **it is his ~ hour** c'est l'heure où il déjeune; **to invite sb to** *or* **for ~** inviter qn à déjeuner.

luncheon ['lʌntʃən] *n* déjeuner *m*.

luncheon meat *n* sorte de saucisson.

luncheon voucher *n* chèque-repas *m*, ticket-repas *m*.

lunchtime ['lʌntʃtaım] *n* l'heure *f* du déjeuner.

lung [lʌŋ] *n* poumon *m*.

lung cancer *n* cancer *m* du poumon.

lunge [lʌndʒ] *vi* (*also*: **~ forward**) faire un mouvement brusque en avant; **to ~ at sb** envoyer *or* assener un coup à qn.

lupin ['lu:pın] *n* lupin *m*.

lurch [lə:tʃ] *vi* vaciller, tituber ♦ *n* écart *m* brusque, embardée *f*; **to leave sb in the ~** laisser qn se débrouiller *or* se dépêtrer tout(e) seul(e).

lure [luə*] *n* appât *m*, leurre *m* ♦ *vt* attirer *or* persuader par la ruse.

lurid ['luərıd] *a* affreux(euse), atroce.

lurk [lə:k] *vi* se tapir, se cacher.

luscious ['lʌʃəs] *a* succulent(e); appétissant(e).

lush [lʌʃ] *a* luxuriant(e).

lust [lʌst] *n* luxure *f*; lubricité *f*; désir *m*; (*fig*): **~ for** soif *f* de.

lust after *vt fus* convoiter, désirer.

luster ['lʌstə*] *n* (*US*) = **lustre**.

lustful ['lʌstful] *a* lascif(ive).

lustre, (*US*) **luster** ['lʌstə*] *n* lustre *m*, brillant *m*.

lusty ['lʌstı] *a* vigoureux(euse), robuste.

lute [lu:t] *n* luth *m*.

Luxembourg ['lʌksəmbə:g] *n* Luxembourg *m*.

luxuriant [lʌg'zjuərıənt] *a* luxuriant(e).

luxurious [lʌg'zjuərıəs] *a* luxueux(euse).

luxury ['lʌkʃərı] *n* luxe *m* ♦ *cpd* de luxe.

LV *n abbr* (*Brit*) = **luncheon voucher**.

LW *abbr* (*RADIO*: = *long wave*) GO.

lying ['laııŋ] *n* mensonge(s) *m(pl)* ♦ *a* (*statement, story*) mensonger(ère), faux(fausse); (*person*) menteur(euse).

lynch [lɪntʃ] vt luncher.
lynx [lɪŋks] n lynx m inv.
Lyons ['laɪənz] n Lyon.
lyre ['laɪə*] n lyre f.
lyric ['lɪrɪk] a lyrique; ~s npl (of song) paroles fpl.
lyrical ['lɪrɪkl] a lyrique.
lyricism ['lɪrɪsɪzəm] n lyrisme m.

M

M, m [ɛm] n (letter) M, m m; **M for Mary**, (US) **M for Mike** M comme Marcel.
M n abbr (Brit: = motorway): **the M8** ≈ l'A8 ♦ abbr (= medium) M.
m abbr (= metre) m; (= million) M; (= mile) mi.
MA n abbr (SCOL) = **Master of Arts**; (US) = **military academy**; (US POST) = **Massachusetts**.
mac [mæk] n (Brit) imper(méable) m.
macabre [mə'kɑ:brə] a macabre.
macaroni [mækə'rəʊnɪ] n macaronis mpl.
macaroon [mækə'ru:n] n macaron m.
mace [meɪs] n masse f; (spice) macis m.
machinations [mækɪ'neɪʃənz] npl machinations fpl, intrigues fpl.
machine [mə'ʃi:n] n machine f ♦ vt (dress etc) coudre à la machine; (TECH) usiner.
machine code n (COMPUT) code m machine.
machine gun n mitrailleuse f.
machine language n (COMPUT) langage m machine.
machine-readable [mə'ʃi:nri:dəbl] a (COMPUT) exploitable par une machine.
machinery [mə'ʃi:nərɪ] n machinerie f, machines fpl; (fig) mécanisme(s) m(pl).
machine shop n atelier m d'usinage.
machine tool n machine-outil f.
machine washable a (garment) lavable en machine.
machinist [mə'ʃi:nɪst] n machiniste m/f.
macho ['mætʃəʊ] a macho inv.
mackerel ['mækrl] n (pl inv) maquereau m.
mackintosh ['mækɪntɒʃ] n (Brit) imperméable m.
macro... ['mækrəʊ] prefix macro....
macro-economics ['mækrəʊi:kə'nɒmɪks] n macro-économie f.
mad [mæd] a fou(folle); (foolish) insensé(e); (angry) furieux(euse); **to go ~** devenir fou; **to be ~ (keen) about** or **on sth** (col) être follement passionné de qch, être fou de qch.
madam ['mædəm] n madame f; **yes ~** oui Madame; **M~ Chairman** Madame la Présidente.
madden ['mædn] vt exaspérer.
maddening ['mædnɪŋ] a exaspérant(e).
made [meɪd] pt, pp of **make**.
Madeira [mə'dɪərə] n (GEO) Madère f; (wine) madère m.
made-to-measure ['meɪdtə'mɛʒə*] a (Brit)

fait(e) sur mesure.
madly ['mædlɪ] ad follement.
madman ['mædmən] n fou m, aliéné m.
madness ['mædnɪs] n folie f.
Madrid [mə'drɪd] n Madrid.
Mafia ['mæfɪə] n maf(f)ia f.
mag. [mæg] n abbr (Brit col) = **magazine** (PRESS).
magazine [mægə'zi:n] n (PRESS) magazine m, revue f; (MIL: store) dépôt m, arsenal m; (of firearm) magasin m.
maggot ['mægət] n ver m, asticot m.
magic ['mædʒɪk] n magie f ♦ a magique.
magical ['mædʒɪkl] a magique.
magician [mə'dʒɪʃən] n magicien/ne.
magistrate ['mædʒɪstreɪt] n magistrat m; juge m.
magnanimous [mæg'nænɪməs] a magnanime.
magnate ['mægneɪt] n magnat m.
magnesium [mæg'ni:zɪəm] n magnésium m.
magnet ['mægnɪt] n aimant m.
magnetic [mæg'nɛtɪk] a magnétique.
magnetic disk n (COMPUT) disque m magnétique.
magnetic tape n bande f magnétique.
magnetism ['mægnɪtɪzəm] n magnétisme m.
magnification [mægnɪfɪ'keɪʃən] n grossissement m.
magnificence [mæg'nɪfɪsns] n magnificence f.
magnificent [mæg'nɪfɪsnt] a superbe, magnifique.
magnify ['mægnɪfaɪ] vt grossir; (sound) amplifier.
magnifying glass ['mægnɪfaɪɪŋ-] n loupe f.
magnitude ['mægnɪtju:d] n ampleur f.
magnolia [mæg'nəʊlɪə] n magnolia m.
magpie ['mægpaɪ] n pie f.
mahogany [mə'hɒgənɪ] n acajou m ♦ cpd en (bois d')acajou.
maid [meɪd] n bonne f; **old ~** (pej) vieille fille.
maiden ['meɪdn] n jeune fille f ♦ a (aunt etc) non mariée; (speech, voyage) inaugural(e).
maiden name n nom m de jeune fille.
mail [meɪl] n poste f; (letters) courrier m ♦ vt envoyer (par la poste); **by ~** par la poste.
mailbox ['meɪlbɒks] n (US: for letters etc; COMPUT) boîte f aux lettres.
mailing list ['meɪlɪŋ-] n liste f d'adresses.
mailman ['meɪlmæn] n (US) facteur m.
mail-order ['meɪlɔ:də*] n vente f or achat m par correspondance ♦ cpd: **~ firm** or **house** maison f de vente par correspondance.
mailshot ['meɪlʃɒt] n (Brit) mailing m.
mail train n train postal.
mail truck n (US AUT) = **mail van**.
mail van n (Brit: AUT) voiture f or fourgonnette f des postes; (: RAIL) wagon-poste m.
maim [meɪm] vt mutiler.
main [meɪn] a principal(e) ♦ n (pipe) conduite principale, canalisation f; **the ~s** (ELEC) le secteur; **in the ~** dans l'ensemble.
main course n (CULIN) plat m de résistance.
mainframe ['meɪnfreɪm] n (also: ~ computer) (gros) ordinateur, unité centrale.
mainland ['meɪnlənd] n continent m.
mainline ['meɪnlaɪn] a (RAIL) de grande ligne ♦ vb (drugs slang) vt se shooter à ♦ vi se

shooter.

main line n (RAIL) grande ligne.

mainly ['meɪnlɪ] ad principalement, surtout.

main road n grand axe, route nationale.

mainstay ['meɪnsteɪ] n (fig) pilier m.

mainstream ['meɪnstriːm] n (fig) courant principal.

maintain [meɪn'teɪn] vt entretenir; (continue) maintenir, préserver; (affirm) soutenir; **to ~ that** ... soutenir que ....

maintenance ['meɪntənəns] n entretien m; (LAW: alimony) pension f alimentaire.

maintenance contract n contrat m d'entretien.

maintenance order n (LAW) obligation f alimentaire.

maisonette [meɪzə'nɛt] n (Brit) appartement m en duplex.

maize [meɪz] n maïs m.

Maj. abbr (MIL) = **major**.

majestic [mə'dʒɛstɪk] a majestueux(euse).

majesty ['mædʒɪstɪ] n majesté f.

major ['meɪdʒə*] n (MIL) commandant m ♦ a important(e), principal(e); (MUS) majeur(e) ♦ vi (US SCOL): **to ~ (in)** se spécialiser (en); **a ~ operation** (MED) une grosse opération.

Majorca [mə'jɔːkə] n Majorque f.

major general n (MIL) général m de division.

majority [mə'dʒɔrɪtɪ] n majorité f ♦ cpd (verdict, holding) majoritaire.

make [meɪk] vt (pt, pp **made** [meɪd]) faire; (manufacture) faire, fabriquer; (cause to be): **to ~ sb sad** etc rendre qn triste etc; (force): **to ~ sb do sth** obliger qn à faire qch, faire faire qch à qn; (equal): **2 and 2 ~ 4** 2 et 2 font 4 ♦ n fabrication f; (brand) marque f; **to ~ it** (in time etc) y arriver; (succeed) réussir; **what time do you ~ it?** quelle heure avez-vous?; **to ~ good** vi (succeed) faire son chemin, réussir ♦ vt (deficit) combler; (losses) compenser; **to ~ do with** se contenter de; se débrouiller avec.

make for vi fus (place) se diriger vers.

make off vi filer.

make out vt (write out) écrire; (understand) comprendre; (see) distinguer; (claim, imply) prétendre, vouloir faire croire; **to ~ out a case for sth** présenter des arguments solides en faveur de qch.

make over vt (assign): **to ~ over (to)** céder (à), transférer (au nom de).

make up vt (invent) inventer, imaginer; (parcel) faire ♦ vi se réconcilier; (with cosmetics) se maquiller, se farder; **to be made up of** se composer de.

make up for vt fus compenser; racheter.

make-believe ['meɪkbɪliːv] n: **a world of ~** un monde de chimères or d'illusions; **it's just ~** c'est de la fantaisie; c'est une illusion.

maker ['meɪkə*] n fabricant m.

makeshift ['meɪkʃɪft] a provisoire, improvisé(e).

make-up ['meɪkʌp] n maquillage m.

make-up bag n trousse f de maquillage.

make-up remover n démaquillant m.

making ['meɪkɪŋ] n (fig): **in the ~** en formation or gestation; **he has the ~s of an actor** il a l'étoffe d'un acteur.

maladjusted [mælə'dʒʌstɪd] a inadapté(e).

malaise [mæ'leɪz] n malaise m.

malaria [mə'lɛərɪə] n malaria f, paludisme m.

Malawi [mə'lɑːwɪ] n Malawi m.

Malay [mə'leɪ] a malais(e) ♦ n (person) Malais/e; (language) malais m.

Malaya [mə'leɪə] n Malaisie f.

Malayan [mə'leɪən] a, n = **Malay**.

Malaysia [mə'leɪzɪə] n Malaisie f.

Malaysian [mə'leɪzɪən] a malaisien(ne) ♦ n Malaisien/ne.

Maldives ['mɔːldaɪvz] npl: **the ~** les Maldives fpl.

male [meɪl] n (BIOL, ELEC) mâle m ♦ a (sex, attitude) masculin(e); mâle; (child etc) du sexe masculin; **~ and female students** étudiants et étudiantes.

male chauvinist n phallocrate m.

male nurse n infirmier m.

malevolence [mə'lɛvələns] n malveillance f.

malevolent [mə'lɛvələnt] a malveillant(e).

malfunction [mæl'fʌŋkʃən] n fonctionnement défectueux.

malice ['mælɪs] n méchanceté f, malveillance f.

malicious [mə'lɪʃəs] a méchant(e), malveillant(e); (LAW) avec intention criminelle.

malign [mə'laɪn] vt diffamer, calomnier.

malignant [mə'lɪgnənt] a (MED) malin(igne).

malingerer [mə'lɪŋgərə*] n simulateur/trice.

mall [mɔːl] n (also: **shopping ~**) centre commercial.

malleable ['mælɪəbl] a malléable.

mallet ['mælɪt] n maillet m.

malnutrition [mælnjuː'trɪʃən] n malnutrition f.

malpractice [mæl'præktɪs] n faute professionnelle; négligence f.

malt [mɔːlt] n malt m ♦ cpd (whisky) pur malt.

Malta ['mɔːltə] n Malte f.

Maltese [mɔːl'tiːz] a maltais(e) ♦ n (pl inv) Maltais/e; (LING) maltais m.

maltreat [mæl'triːt] vt maltraiter.

mammal ['mæml] n mammifère m.

mammoth ['mæməθ] n mammouth m ♦ a géant(e), monstre.

man, pl men [mæn, mɛn] n homme m; (CHESS) pièce f; (DRAUGHTS) pion m ♦ vt garnir d'hommes; servir, assurer le fonctionnement de; être de service à; **an old ~** un vieillard; **~ and wife** mari et femme.

manacles ['mænəklz] npl menottes fpl.

manage ['mænɪdʒ] vi se débrouiller; y arriver, réussir ♦ vt (business) gérer; (team, operation) diriger; (device, things to do, carry etc) arriver à se débrouiller avec, s'en tirer avec; **to ~ to do** se débrouiller pour faire; (succeed) réussir à faire.

manageable ['mænɪdʒəbl] a maniable; (task etc) faisable.

management ['mænɪdʒmənt] n administration f, direction f; (persons: of business, firm) dirigeants mpl, cadres mpl; (: of hotel, shop, theatre) direction; **"under new ~"** "changement de gérant", "changement de propriétaire".

management accounting n comptabilité f de gestion.

management consultant n conseiller/ère de

direction.

manager ['mænɪdʒə*] n (of business) directeur m; (of institution etc) administrateur m; (of department, unit) responsable m/f, chef m; (of hotel etc) gérant m; (of artist) impresario m; **sales ~** responsable or chef des ventes.

manageress [mænɪdʒə'rɛs] n directrice f; (of hotel etc) gérante f.

managerial [mænɪ'dʒɪərɪəl] a directorial(e); **~ staff** cadres mpl.

managing director ['mænɪdʒɪŋ-] n directeur général.

Mancunian [mæŋ'kjuːnɪən] a de Manchester ♦ n habitant/e de Manchester; natif/ive de Manchester.

mandarin ['mændərɪn] n (also: **~ orange**) mandarine f; (person) mandarin m.

mandate ['mændeɪt] n mandat m.

mandatory ['mændətərɪ] a obligatoire; (powers etc) mandataire.

mandolin(e) ['mændəlɪn] n mandoline f.

mane [meɪn] n crinière f.

maneuver etc [mə'nuːvə*] (US) = **manoeuvre** etc.

manfully ['mænfəlɪ] ad vaillamment.

manganese [mæŋgə'niːz] n manganèse m.

mangle ['mæŋgl] vt déchiqueter; mutiler ♦ n essoreuse f; calandre f.

mango, ~es ['mæŋgəu] n mangue f.

mangrove ['mæŋgrəuv] n palétuvier m.

mangy ['meɪndʒɪ] a galeux(euse).

manhandle ['mænhændl] vt (mistreat) maltraiter, malmener; (move by hand) manutentionner.

manhole ['mænhəul] n trou m d'homme.

manhood ['mænhud] n âge m d'homme; virilité f.

man-hour ['mænauə*] n heure-homme f, heure f de main-d'œuvre.

manhunt ['mænhʌnt] n chasse f à l'homme.

mania ['meɪnɪə] n manie f.

maniac ['meɪnɪæk] n maniaque m/f.

manic ['mænɪk] a maniaque.

manic-depressive ['mænɪkdɪ'prɛsɪv] a, n (PSYCH) maniaco-dépressif(ive).

manicure ['mænɪkjuə*] n manucure f ♦ vt (person) faire les mains à.

manicure set n trousse f à ongles.

manifest ['mænɪfɛst] vt manifester ♦ a manifeste, évident(e) ♦ n (AVIAT, NAUT) manifeste m.

manifestation [mænɪfɛs'teɪʃən] n manifestation f.

manifesto [mænɪ'fɛstəu] n manifeste m (POL).

manifold ['mænɪfəuld] a multiple, varié(e) ♦ n (AUT etc): **exhaust ~** collecteur m d'échappement.

Manila [mə'nɪlə] n Manille, Manila.

manila [mə'nɪlə] a: **~ paper** papier m bulle.

manipulate [mə'nɪpjuleɪt] vt manipuler.

manipulation [mənɪpju'leɪʃən] n manipulation f.

mankind [mæn'kaɪnd] n humanité f, genre humain.

manliness ['mænlɪnɪs] n virilité f.

manly ['mænlɪ] a viril(e); courageux(euse).

man-made ['mæn'meɪd] a artificiel(le).

manna ['mænə] n manne f.

mannequin ['mænɪkɪn] n mannequin m.

manner ['mænə*] n manière f, façon f; **(good) ~s** (bonnes) manières; **bad ~s** mauvaises manières; **all ~ of** toutes sortes de.

mannerism ['mænərɪzəm] n particularité f de langage (or de comportement), tic m.

mannerly ['mænəlɪ] a poli(e), courtois(e).

manoeuvrable, (US) **maneuverable** [mə'nuːvrəbl] a facile à manœuvrer.

manoeuvre, (US) **maneuver** [mə'nuːvə*] vt, vi manœuvrer ♦ n manœuvre f; **to ~ sb into doing sth** manipuler qn pour lui faire faire qch.

manor ['mænə*] n (also: **~ house**) manoir m.

manpower ['mænpauə*] n main-d'œuvre f.

Manpower Services Commission (MSC) n agence nationale pour l'emploi.

manservant, pl **menservants** ['mænsə:vənt, 'mɛn-] n domestique m.

mansion ['mænʃən] n château m, manoir m.

manslaughter ['mænslɔːtə*] n homicide m involontaire.

mantelpiece ['mæntlpiːs] n cheminée f.

mantle ['mæntl] n cape f; (fig) manteau m.

man-to-man ['mæntə'mæn] a, ad d'homme à homme.

manual ['mænjuəl] a manuel(le) ♦ n manuel m.

manual worker n travailleur manuel.

manufacture [mænju'fæktʃə*] vt fabriquer ♦ n fabrication f.

manufactured goods npl produits manufacturés.

manufacturer [mænju'fæktʃərə*] n fabricant m.

manufacturing industries [mænju'fæktʃərɪŋ-] npl industries fpl de transformation.

manure [mə'njuə*] n fumier m; (artificial) engrais m.

manuscript ['mænjuskrɪpt] n manuscrit m.

many ['mɛnɪ] a beaucoup de, de nombreux(euses) ♦ pronoun beaucoup, un grand nombre; **how ~?** combien?; **a great ~** un grand nombre (de); **too ~ difficulties** trop de difficultés; **twice as ~** deux fois plus; **~ a ...** bien des ..., plus d'un(e) ....

map [mæp] n carte f ♦ vt dresser la carte de.

map out vt tracer; (fig: career, holiday) organiser, préparer (à l'avance); (: essay) faire le plan de.

maple ['meɪpl] n érable m.

Mar. abbr = **March.**

mar [mɑː*] vt gâcher, gâter.

marathon ['mærəθən] n marathon m ♦ a: **a ~ session** une séance-marathon.

marathon runner n coureur/euse de marathon, marathonien/ne.

marauder [mə'rɔːdə*] n maraudeur/euse.

marble ['mɑːbl] n marbre m; (toy) bille f; **~s** n (game) billes f.

March [mɑːtʃ] n mars m; for phrases see also **July.**

march [mɑːtʃ] vi marcher au pas; (demonstrators) défiler ♦ n marche f; (demonstration) rallye m; **to ~ out of/into** etc sortir de/entrer dans etc (de manière décidée ou impulsive).

marcher ['mɑːtʃə*] n (demonstrator)

manifestant/e, marcheur/euse.

marching ['maːtʃɪŋ] n: **to give sb his ~ orders** (fig) renvoyer qn; envoyer promener qn.

march-past ['maːtʃpaːst] n défilé m.

mare [mɛə*] n jument f.

marg. [maːdʒ] n abbr (col) = **margarine**.

margarine [maːdʒə'riːn] n margarine f.

margin ['maːdʒɪn] n marge f.

marginal ['maːdʒɪnl] a marginal(e); **~ seat** (POL) siège disputé.

marginally ['maːdʒɪnəlɪ] ad très légèrement, sensiblement.

marigold ['mærɪɡəuld] n souci m.

marijuana [mærɪ'waːnə] n marijuana f.

marina [mə'riːnə] n marina f.

marinade n [mærɪ'neɪd] marinade f ♦ vt ['mærɪneɪd] = **marinate**.

marinate ['mærɪneɪt] vt (faire) mariner.

marine [mə'riːn] a marin(e) ♦ n fusilier marin; (US) marine m.

marine insurance n assurance f maritime.

marital ['mærɪtl] a matrimonial(e); **~ status** situation f de famille.

maritime ['mærɪtaɪm] a maritime.

maritime law n droit m maritime.

marjoram ['maːdʒərəm] n marjolaine f.

mark [maːk] n marque f; (of skid etc) trace f; (Brit SCOL) note f; (SPORT) cible f; (currency) mark m; (Brit TECH): **M~ 2/3** 2ème/3ème série f or version f ♦ vt (also SPORT: player) marquer; (stain) tacher; (Brit SCOL) noter; corriger; **punctuation ~s** signes mpl de ponctuation; **to ~ time** marquer le pas; **to be quick off the ~ (in doing)** (fig) ne pas perdre de temps (pour faire); **up to the ~** (in efficiency) à la hauteur.

mark down vt (prices, goods) démarquer, réduire le prix de.

mark off vt (tick off) cocher, pointer.

mark out vt désigner.

mark up vt (price) majorer.

marked [maːkt] a marqué(e), net(te).

markedly ['maːkɪdlɪ] ad visiblement, manifestement.

marker ['maːkə*] n (sign) jalon m; (bookmark) signet m.

market ['maːkɪt] n marché m ♦ vt (COMM) commercialiser; **to be on the ~** être sur le marché; **on the open ~** en vente libre; **to play the ~** jouer à la or spéculer en Bourse.

marketable ['maːkɪtəbl] a commercialisable.

market analysis n analyse f de marché.

market day n jour m de marché.

market demand n besoins mpl du marché.

market forces npl tendances fpl du marché.

market garden n (Brit) jardin maraîcher.

marketing ['maːkɪtɪŋ] n marketing m.

marketplace ['maːkɪtpleɪs] n place f du marché; (COMM) marché m.

market price n prix marchand.

market research n étude f de marché.

market value n valeur marchande; valeur du marché.

marking ['maːkɪŋ] n (on animal) marque f, tache f; (on road) signalisation f.

marksman ['maːksmən] n tireur m d'élite.

marksmanship ['maːksmənʃɪp] n adresse f au

tir.

mark-up ['maːkʌp] n (COMM: margin) marge f (bénéficiaire); (: increase) majoration f.

marmalade ['maːməleɪd] n confiture f d'oranges.

maroon [mə'ruːn] vt (fig): **to be ~ed (in or at)** être bloqué(e) (à) ♦ a bordeaux inv.

marquee [maː'kiː] n chapiteau m.

marquess, marquis ['maːkwɪs] n marquis m.

Marrakech, Marrakesh [mærə'keʃ] n Marrakech.

marriage ['mærɪdʒ] n mariage m.

marriage bureau n agence matrimoniale.

marriage certificate n extrait m d'acte de mariage.

marriage guidance, (US) **marriage counselling** n conseils conjugaux.

married ['mærɪd] a marié(e); (life, love) conjugal(e).

marrow ['mærəu] n moelle f; (vegetable) courge f.

marry ['mærɪ] vt épouser, se marier avec; (subj: father, priest etc) marier ♦ vi (also: **get married**) se marier.

Mars [maːz] n (planet) Mars f.

Marseilles [maː'seɪlz] n Marseille.

marsh [maːʃ] n marais m, marécage m.

marshal ['maːʃl] n maréchal m; (US: fire, police) ≈ capitaine m; (for demonstration, meeting) membre m du service d'ordre ♦ vt rassembler.

marshalling yard ['maːʃlɪŋ-] n (RAIL) gare f de triage.

marshmallow [maː'ʃmæləu] n (BOT) guimauve f; (sweet) (pâte f de) guimauve.

marshy ['maːʃɪ] a marécageux(euse).

marsupial [maː'suːpɪəl] a marsupial(e) ♦ n marsupial m.

martial ['maːʃl] a martial(e).

martial law n loi martiale.

Martian ['maːʃən] n Martien/ne.

martin ['maːtɪn] n (also: **house ~**) martinet m.

martyr ['maːtə*] n martyr/e ♦ vt martyriser.

martyrdom ['maːtədəm] n martyre m.

marvel ['maːvl] n merveille f ♦ vi: **to ~ (at)** s'émerveiller (de).

marvellous, (US) **marvelous** ['maːvləs] a merveilleux(euse).

Marxism ['maːksɪzəm] n marxisme m.

Marxist ['maːksɪst] a, n marxiste (m/f).

marzipan ['maːzɪpæn] n pâte f d'amandes.

mascara [mæs'kaːrə] n mascara m.

mascot ['mæskət] n mascotte f.

masculine ['mæskjulɪn] a masculin(e) ♦ n masculin m.

masculinity [mæskju'lɪnɪtɪ] n masculinité f.

MASH [mæʃ] n abbr (US MIL) = mobile army surgical hospital.

mash [mæʃ] n (CULIN) faire une purée de.

mashed [mæʃt] a: **~ potatoes** purée f de pommes de terre.

mask [maːsk] n masque m ♦ vt masquer.

masochism ['mæsəukɪzəm] n masochisme m.

masochist ['mæsəukɪst] n masochiste m/f.

mason ['meɪsn] n (also: **stone~**) maçon m; (also: **free~**) franc-maçon m.

masonic [mə'sɒnɪk] a maçonnique.

masonry ['meɪsnrɪ] n maçonnerie f.

masquerade [mæskə'reɪd] *n* bal masqué; (*fig*) mascarade *f* ♦ *vi*: **to ~ as** se faire passer pour.

mass [mæs] *n* multitude *f*, masse *f*; (*PHYSICS*) masse; (*REL*) messe *f* ♦ *vi* se masser; **the ~es** les masses; **to go to ~** aller à la messe.

massacre ['mæskə*] *n* massacre *m* ♦ *vt* massacrer.

massage ['mæsɑ:ʒ] *n* massage *m* ♦ *vt* masser.

masseur [mæ'sə:*] *n* masseur *m*.

masseuse [mæ'sə:z] *n* masseuse *f*.

massive ['mæsɪv] *a* énorme, massif(ive).

mass market *n* marché *m* grand public.

mass media *npl* mass-media *mpl*.

mass meeting *n* rassemblement *m* de masse.

mass-produce ['mæsprə'dju:s] *vt* fabriquer en série.

mass production *n* fabrication *f* en série.

mast [mɑ:st] *n* mât *m*; (*RADIO*, *TV*) pylône *m*.

master ['mɑ:stə*] *n* maître *m*; (*in secondary school*) professeur *m*; (*title for boys*): **M~ X** Monsieur X ♦ *vt* maîtriser; (*learn*) apprendre à fond; (*understand*) posséder parfaitement *or* à fond; **~ of ceremonies (MC)** *n* maître des cérémonies; **M~ of Arts/Science (MA/ MSc)** *n* ≈ titulaire *m/f* d'une maîtrise (en lettres/science); **M~ of Arts/Science degree (MA/MSc)** *n* ≈ maîtrise *f*; **M~'s degree** *n* ≈ maîtrise.

master disk *n* (*COMPUT*) disque original.

masterful ['mɑ:stəful] *a* autoritaire, impérieux(euse).

master key *n* passe-partout *m* inv.

masterly ['mɑ:stəlɪ] *a* magistral(e).

mastermind ['mɑ:stəmaɪnd] *n* esprit supérieur ♦ *vt* diriger, être le cerveau de.

masterpiece ['mɑ:stəpi:s] *n* chef-d'œuvre *m*.

master plan *n* stratégie *f* d'ensemble.

master stroke *n* coup *m* de maître.

mastery ['mɑ:stərɪ] *n* maîtrise *f*; connaissance parfaite.

mastiff ['mæstɪf] *n* mastiff *m*.

masturbate ['mæstəbeɪt] *vi* se masturber.

masturbation [mæstə'beɪʃən] *n* masturbation *f*.

mat [mæt] *n* petit tapis; (*also*: **door~**) paillasson *m* ♦ *a* = **matt**.

match [mætʃ] *n* allumette *f*; (*game*) match *m*, partie *f*; (*fig*) égal/e; mariage *m*; parti *m* ♦ *vt* assortir; (*go well with*) aller bien avec, s'assortir à; (*equal*) égaler, valoir ♦ *vi* être assorti(e); **to be a good ~** être bien assorti(e).

match up *vt* assortir.

matchbox ['mætʃbɒks] *n* boîte *f* d'allumettes.

matching ['mætʃɪŋ] *a* assorti(e).

matchless ['mætʃlɪs] *a* sans égal.

mate [meɪt] *n* camarade *m/f* de travail; (*col*) copain/copine; (*animal*) partenaire *m/f*, mâle/femelle; (*in merchant navy*) second *m* ♦ *vi* s'accoupler ♦ *vt* accoupler.

material [mə'tɪərɪəl] *n* (*substance*) matière *f*, matériau *m*; (*cloth*) tissu *m*, étoffe *f* ♦ *a* matériel(le); (*important*) essentiel(le); **~s** *npl* matériaux *mpl*; **reading ~** de quoi lire, de la lecture.

materialistic [mətɪərɪə'lɪstɪk] *a* matérialiste.

materialize [mə'tɪərɪəlaɪz] *vi* se matérialiser,

se réaliser.

materially [mə'tɪərɪəlɪ] *ad* matériellement; essentiellement.

maternal [mə'tə:nl] *a* maternel(le).

maternity [mə'tə:nɪtɪ] *n* maternité *f* ♦ *cpd* de maternité, de grossesse.

maternity benefit *n* prestation *f* de maternité.

maternity hospital *n* maternité *f*.

matey ['meɪtɪ] *a* (*Brit col*) copain-copain inv.

math. [mæθ] *n* abbr (*US*: = *mathematics*) maths *fpl*.

mathematical [mæθə'mætɪkl] *a* mathématique.

mathematician [mæθəmə'tɪʃən] *n* mathématicien/ne.

mathematics [mæθə'mætɪks] *n* mathématiques *fpl*.

maths [mæθs] *n* abbr (*Brit*: = *mathematics*) maths *fpl*.

matinée ['mætɪneɪ] *n* matinée *f*.

mating ['meɪtɪŋ] *n* accouplement *m*.

mating call *n* appel *m* du mâle.

mating season *n* saison *f* des amours.

matriarchal [meɪtrɪ'ɑ:kl] *a* matriarcal(e).

matrices ['meɪtrɪsi:z] *npl of* **matrix**.

matriculation [mətrɪkju'leɪʃən] *n* inscription *f*.

matrimonial [mætrɪ'məʊnɪəl] *a* matrimonial(e), conjugal(e).

matrimony ['mætrɪmənɪ] *n* mariage *m*.

matrix, *pl* **matrices** ['meɪtrɪks, 'meɪtrɪsi:z] *n* matrice *f*.

matron ['meɪtrən] *n* (*in hospital*) infirmière-chef *f*; (*in school*) infirmière.

matronly ['meɪtrənlɪ] *a* de matrone; imposant(e).

matt [mæt] *a* mat(e).

matted ['mætɪd] *a* emmêlé(e).

matter ['mætə*] *n* question *f*; (*PHYSICS*) matière *f*, substance *f*; (*content*) contenu *m*, fond *m*; (*MED*: *pus*) pus *m* ♦ *vi* importer; **it doesn't ~** cela n'a pas d'importance; (*I don't mind*) cela ne fait rien; **what's the ~?** qu'est-ce qu'il y a?, qu'est-ce qui ne va pas? **no ~ what** quoiqu'il arrive; **that's another ~** c'est une autre affaire; **as a ~ of course** tout naturellement; **as a ~ of fact** en fait; **it's a ~ of habit** c'est une question d'habitude; **printed ~** imprimés *mpl*; **reading ~** (*Brit*) de quoi lire, de la lecture.

matter-of-fact ['mætərəv'fækt] *a* terre à terre, neutre.

matting ['mætɪŋ] *n* natte *f*.

mattress ['mætrɪs] *n* matelas *m*.

mature [mə'tjuə*] *a* mûr(e); (*cheese*) fait(e) ♦ *vi* mûrir; se faire.

maturity [mə'tjuərɪtɪ] *n* maturité *f*.

maudlin ['mɔ:dlɪn] *a* larmoyant(e).

maul [mɔ:l] *vt* lacérer.

Mauritania [mɔ:rɪ'teɪnɪə] *n* Mauritanie *f*.

Mauritius [mə'rɪʃəs] *n* l'île *f* Maurice.

mausoleum [mɔ:sə'lɪəm] *n* mausolée *m*.

mauve [məʊv] *a* mauve.

maverick ['mævrɪk] *n* (*fig*) franc-tireur *m*, non-conformiste *m/f*.

mawkish ['mɔ:kɪʃ] *a* mièvre; fade.

max. abbr = **maximum**.

maxim ['mæksɪm] *n* maxime *f*.

maxima ['mæksɪmə] *npl of* **maximum**.

maximize ['mæksımaız] *vt* (*profits etc, chances*) maximiser.

maximum ['mæksıməm] *a* maximum ♦ *n* (*pl* **maxima** ['mæksımə]) maximum *m*.

May [meı] *n* mai *m*; *for phrases see also* **July**.

may [meı] *vi* (*conditional*: **might**) (*indicating possibility*): **he ~ come** il se peut qu'il vienne; (*be allowed to*): **~ I smoke?** puis-je fumer?; (*wishes*): **~ God bless you!** (que) Dieu vous bénisse!; **~ I sit here?** vous permettez que je m'assoie ici?; **he might be there** il pourrait bien y être, il se pourrait qu'il y soit; **I might as well go** je ferais aussi bien d'y aller, autant y aller; **you might like to try** vous pourriez (peut-être) essayer.

maybe ['meıbi:] *ad* peut-être; **~ he'll ...** peut-être qu'il ...; **~ not** peut-être pas.

May Day *n* le Premier mai.

mayday ['meıdeı] *n* S.O.S. *m*.

mayhem ['meıhem] *n* grabuge *m*.

mayonnaise [meıə'neız] *n* mayonnaise *f*.

mayor [mɛə*] *n* maire *m*.

mayoress ['mɛərɛs] *n* maire *m*; épouse *f* du maire.

maypole ['meıpəul] *n* mât enrubanné (*autour duquel on danse*).

maze [meız] *n* labyrinthe *m*, dédale *m*.

MB *abbr* (*COMPUT*) = **megabyte**; (*Canada*) = Manitoba.

MBA *n abbr* (= *Master of Business Administration*) *titre universitaire*.

MBBS, MBChB *n abbr* (*Brit*: = *Bachelor of Medicine and Surgery*) *titre universitaire*.

MBE *n abbr* (*Brit*: = *Member of the Order of the British Empire*) *titre honorifique*.

MC *n abbr* = **master of ceremonies**.

MCAT *n abbr* (*US*) = *Medical College Admissions Test*.

MCP *n abbr* (*Brit col*: = *male chauvinist pig*) phallocrate *m*.

MD *n abbr* (= *Doctor of Medicine*) *titre universitaire*; (*COMM*) = **managing director** ♦ *abbr* (*US POST*) = Maryland.

MDT *abbr* (*US*: = *Mountain Daylight Time*) heure d'été des Montagnes Rocheuses.

ME *abbr* (*US POST*) = Maine ♦ *n abbr* (*US MED*) = *medical examiner*.

me [mi:] *pronoun* me, m' + *vowel*; (*stressed, after prep*) moi; **it's ~** c'est moi; **it's for ~** c'est pour moi.

meadow ['mɛdəu] *n* prairie *f*, pré *m*.

meagre, (*US*) **meager** ['mi:gə*] *a* maigre.

meal [mi:l] *n* repas *m*; (*flour*) farine *f*; **to go out for a ~** sortir manger.

mealtime ['mi:ltaım] *n* heure *f* du repas.

mealy-mouthed ['mi:lımauðd] *a* mielleux(euse).

mean [mi:n] *a* (*with money*) avare, radin(e); (*unkind*) mesquin(e), méchant(e); (*US col*: *animal*) méchant, vicieux(euse); (*: person*) vache; (*average*) moyen(ne) ♦ *vt* (*pt, pp* **meant** [mɛnt]) (*signify*) signifier, vouloir dire; (*intend*): **to ~ to do** avoir l'intention de faire ♦ *n* moyenne *f*; **to be meant for** être destiné(e) à; **do you ~ it?** vous êtes sérieux?; **what do you ~?** que voulez-vous dire?

meander [mı'ændə*] *vi* faire des méandres;

(*fig*) flâner.

meaning ['mi:nıŋ] *n* signification *f*, sens *m*.

meaningful ['mi:nıŋful] *a* significatif(ive); (*relationship*) valable.

meaningless ['mi:nıŋlıs] *a* dénué(e) de sens.

meanness ['mi:nnıs] *n* avarice *f*; mesquinerie *f*.

means [mi:nz] *npl* moyens *mpl*; **by ~ of** par l'intermédiaire de; au moyen de; **by all ~** je vous en prie.

means test *n* (*ADMIN*) contrôle *m* des conditions de ressources.

meant [mɛnt] *pt, pp of* **mean**.

meantime ['mi:ntaım] *ad*, **meanwhile** ['mi:nwaıl] *ad* (*also*: **in the ~**) pendant ce temps.

measles ['mi:zlz] *n* rougeole *f*.

measly ['mi:zlı] *a* (*col*) minable.

measurable ['mɛʒərəbl] *a* mesurable.

measure ['mɛʒə*] *vt, vi* mesurer ♦ *n* mesure *f*; (*ruler*) règle (graduée); **a litre ~** un litre; **some ~ of success** un certain succès; **to take ~s to do sth** prendre des mesures pour faire qch.

measure up *vi*: **to ~ up (to)** être à la hauteur (de).

measured ['mɛʒəd] *a* mesuré(e).

measurement ['mɛʒəmənt] *n*: **chest/hip ~** tour *m* de poitrine/hanches; **~s** *npl* mesures *fpl*; **to take sb's ~s** prendre les mesures de qn.

meat [mi:t] *n* viande *f*; **cold ~s** (*Brit*) viandes froides; **crab ~** crabe *f*.

meatball ['mi:tbɔ:l] *n* boulette *f* de viande.

meat pie *n* pâté *m* en croûte.

meaty ['mi:tı] *a* avec beaucoup de viande, plein(e) de viande; (*fig*) substantiel(le).

Mecca ['mɛkə] *n* la Mecque; (*fig*): **a ~ (for)** la Mecque *f*.

mechanic [mı'kænık] *n* mécanicien *m*.

mechanical [mı'kænıkl] *a* mécanique.

mechanical engineering *n* (*science*) mécanique *f*; (*industry*) construction *f* mécanique.

mechanics [mə'kænıks] *n* mécanique *f* ♦ *npl* mécanisme *m*.

mechanism ['mɛkənızəm] *n* mécanisme *m*.

mechanization [mɛkənaı'zeıʃən] *n* mécanisation *f*.

MEd *n abbr* (= *Master of Education*) *titre universitaire*.

medal ['mɛdl] *n* médaille *f*.

medallion [mı'dælıən] *n* médaillon *m*.

medallist, (*US*) **medalist** ['mɛdlıst] *n* (*SPORT*) médaillé/e.

meddle ['mɛdl] *vi*: **to ~ in** se mêler de, s'occuper de; **to ~ with** toucher à.

meddlesome ['mɛdlsəm], **meddling** ['mɛdlıŋ] *a* indiscret(ète), qui se mêle de ce qui ne le (*or* la) regarde pas; touche-à-tout *inv*.

media ['mi:dıə] *npl* media *mpl*.

mediaeval [mɛdı'i:vl] *a* = **medieval**.

median ['mi:dıən] *n* (*US: also:* **~ strip**) bande médiane.

media research *n* étude *f* de l'audience.

mediate ['mi:dıeıt] *vi* s'interposer; servir d'intermédiaire.

mediation [mi:dı'eıʃən] *n* médiation *f*.

mediator ['mi:dıeıtə*] *n* médiateur/trice.

medical ['mɛdɪkl] a médical(e) ♦ n (also: ~ **examination**) visite médicale; examen médical.

medical certificate n certificat médical.

medical student n étudiant/e en médecine.

Medicare ['mɛdɪkɛə*] n (US) régime d'assurance maladie.

medicated ['mɛdɪkeɪtɪd] a traitant(e), médicamenteux(euse).

medication [mɛdɪ'keɪʃən] n (drugs etc) médication f.

medicinal [mɛ'dɪsɪnl] a médicinal(e).

medicine ['mɛdsɪn] n médecine f; (drug) médicament m.

medicine chest n pharmacie f (murale ou portative).

medicine man n sorcier m.

medieval [mɛdɪ'i:vl] a médiéval(e).

mediocre [mi:dɪ'əukə*] a médiocre.

mediocrity [mi:dɪ'ɔkrɪtɪ] n médiocrité f.

meditate ['mɛdɪteɪt] vi: to ~ (on) méditer (sur).

meditation [mɛdɪ'teɪʃən] n méditation f.

Mediterranean [mɛdɪtə'reɪnɪən] a méditerranéen(ne); the ~ (Sea) la (mer) Méditerranée.

medium ['mi:dɪəm] a moyen(ne) ♦ n (pl media) (means) moyen m; (pl mediums) (person) médium m; the happy ~ le juste milieu.

medium-sized ['mi:dɪəm'saɪzd] a de taille moyenne.

medium wave n (RADIO) ondes moyennes, petites ondes.

medley ['mɛdlɪ] n mélange m.

meek [mi:k] a doux(douce), humble.

meet, pt, pp **met** [mi:t, mɛt] vt rencontrer; (by arrangement) retrouver, rejoindre; (for the first time) faire la connaissance de; (go and fetch): **I'll ~ you at the station** j'irai te chercher à la gare; (problem) faire face à; (requirements) satisfaire à, répondre à; (bill, expenses) régler, honorer ♦ vi se rencontrer; se retrouver; (in session) se réunir; (join: objects) se joindre ♦ n (Brit: HUNTING) rendez-vous m de chasse; (US SPORT) rencontre f, meeting m; **pleased to ~ you!** enchanté!

meet up vi: to ~ up with sb rencontrer qn.

meet with vt fus rencontrer.

meeting ['mi:tɪŋ] n rencontre f; (session: of club etc) réunion f; (formal) assemblée f; (SPORT: rally) rencontre, meeting m; (interview) entrevue f; **she's at a ~** (COMM) elle est en conférence; **to call a ~** convoquer une réunion.

meeting place n lieu m de (la) réunion; (for appointment) lieu de rendez-vous.

megabyte ['mɛgəbaɪt] n (COMPUT) méga-octet m.

megalomaniac [mɛgələ'meɪnɪæk] n mégalomane m/f.

megaphone ['mɛgəfəun] n porte-voix m inv.

melancholy ['mɛlənkəlɪ] n mélancolie f ♦ a mélancolique.

mellow ['mɛləu] a velouté(e); doux(douce); (colour) riche et profond(e); (fruit) mûr(e) ♦ vi (person) s'adoucir.

melodious [mɪ'ləudɪəs] a mélodieux(euse).

melodrama ['mɛləudrɑ:mə] n mélodrame m.

melodramatic [mɛlədrə'mætɪk] a mélodramatique.

melody ['mɛlədɪ] n mélodie f.

melon ['mɛlən] n melon m.

melt [mɛlt] vi fondre; (become soft) s'amollir; (fig) s'attendrir ♦ vt faire fondre; (person) attendrir.

melt away vi fondre complètement.

melt down vt fondre.

meltdown ['mɛltdaun] n fusion f (du cœur d'un réacteur nucléaire).

melting point ['mɛltɪŋ-] n point m de fusion.

melting pot ['mɛltɪŋ-] n (fig) creuset m; **to be in the ~** être encore en discussion.

member ['mɛmbə*] n membre m; (of club, political party) membre, adhérent/e ♦ cpd: ~ **country/state** n pays m/état m membre; **M~ of Parliament (MP)** n (Brit) député m; **M~ of the European Parliament (MEP)** n Eurodéputé m; **M~ of the House of Representatives (MHR)** n (US) membre de la Chambre des représentants.

membership ['mɛmbəʃɪp] n (becoming a member) adhésion f; admission f; (being a member) qualité f de membre, fait m d'être membre; (the members) membres mpl, adhérents mpl; (number of members) nombre m des membres or adhérents.

membership card n carte f de membre.

membrane ['mɛmbreɪn] n membrane f.

memento [mə'mɛntəu] n souvenir m.

memo ['mɛməu] n note f (de service).

memoir ['mɛmwɑ:*] n mémoire m, étude f; ~s npl mémoires.

memo pad n bloc-notes m.

memorable ['mɛmərəbl] a mémorable.

memorandum, pl **memoranda** [mɛmə'rændəm, -də] n note f (de service); (DIPLOMACY) mémorandum m.

memorial [mɪ'mɔ:rɪəl] n mémorial m ♦ a commémoratif(ive).

memorize ['mɛməraɪz] vt apprendre or retenir par cœur.

memory ['mɛmərɪ] n mémoire f; (recollection) souvenir m; **to have a good/ bad ~** avoir une bonne/mauvaise mémoire; **loss of ~** perte f de mémoire; **in ~ of** à la mémoire de.

men [mɛn] npl of **man**.

menace ['mɛnɪs] n menace f; (col: nuisance) peste f, plaie f ♦ vt menacer; **a public ~** un danger public.

menacing ['mɛnɪsɪŋ] a menaçant(e).

menagerie [mɪ'nædʒərɪ] n ménagerie f.

mend [mɛnd] vt réparer; (darn) raccommoder, repriser ♦ n reprise f; **on the ~** en voie de guérison.

mending ['mɛndɪŋ] n raccommodages mpl.

menial ['mi:nɪəl] a de domestique, inférieur(e); subalterne.

meningitis [mɛnɪn'dʒaɪtɪs] n méningite f.

menopause ['mɛnəupɔ:z] n ménopause f.

menservants ['mɛnsə:vənts] npl of **manservant**.

menstruate ['mɛnstrueɪt] vi avoir ses règles.

menstruation [mɛnstru'eɪʃən] n menstruation f.

mental ['mɛntl] *a* mental(e); ~ **illness** maladie mentale.

mentality [mɛn'tælɪtɪ] *n* mentalité *f*.

mentally ['mɛntlɪ] *ad*: **to be ~ handicapped** être handicapé/e mental(e).

menthol ['mɛnθɔl] *n* menthol *m*.

mention ['mɛnʃən] *n* mention *f* ♦ *vt* mentionner, faire mention de; **don't ~ it!** je vous en prie, il n'y a pas de quoi!; **I need hardly ~ that** ... est-il besoin de rappeler que ...?; **not to ~** ..., **without ~ing** ... sans parler de ..., sans compter ....

mentor ['mɛntɔ:*] *n* mentor *m*.

menu ['mɛnju:] *n* (*in restaurant*, COMPUT) menu *m*; (*printed*) carte *f*.

menu-driven ['mɛnju:drɪvn] *a* (COMPUT) piloté(e) par menu.

MEP *n abbr* = **Member of the European Parliament.**

mercantile ['mə:kəntaɪl] *a* marchand(e); (*law*) commercial(e).

mercenary ['mə:sɪnərɪ] *a* mercantile ♦ *n* mercenaire *m*.

merchandise ['mə:tʃəndaɪz] *n* marchandises *fpl* ♦ *vt* commercialiser.

merchandiser ['mə:tʃəndaɪzə*] *n* marchandiseur *m*.

merchant ['mə:tʃənt] *n* négociant *m*, marchand *m*; **timber/wine ~** négociant en bois/vins, marchand de bois/vins.

merchant bank *n* (*Brit*) banque *f* d'affaires.

merchantman ['mə:tʃəntmən] *n* navire marchand.

merchant navy, (*US*) **merchant marine** *n* marine marchande.

merciful ['mə:sɪful] *a* miséricordieux(euse), clément(e).

mercifully ['mə:sɪflɪ] *ad* avec clémence; (*fortunately*) par bonheur, Dieu merci.

merciless ['mə:sɪlɪs] *a* impitoyable, sans pitié.

mercurial [mə:'kjuərɪəl] *a* changeant(e); (*lively*) vif(vive).

mercury ['mə:kjurɪ] *n* mercure *m*.

mercy ['mə:sɪ] *n* pitié *f*, merci *f*; (REL) miséricorde *f*; **to have ~ on sb** avoir pitié de qn; **at the ~ of** à la merci de.

mercy killing *n* euthanasie *f*.

mere [mɪə*] *a* simple.

merely ['mɪəlɪ] *ad* simplement, purement.

merge [mə:dʒ] *vt* unir; (COMPUT) fusionner, interclasser ♦ *vi* se fondre; (COMM) fusionner.

merger ['mə:dʒə*] *n* (COMM) fusion *f*.

meridian [mə'rɪdɪən] *n* méridien *m*.

meringue [mə'ræŋ] *n* meringue *f*.

merit ['mɛrɪt] *n* mérite *m*, valeur *f* ♦ *vt* mériter.

meritocracy [mɛrɪ'tɔkrəsɪ] *n* méritocratie *f*.

mermaid ['mə:meɪd] *n* sirène *f*.

merrily ['mɛrɪlɪ] *ad* joyeusement, gaiement.

merriment ['mɛrɪmənt] *n* gaieté *f*.

merry ['mɛrɪ] *a* gai(e); **M~ Christmas!** joyeux Noël!

merry-go-round ['mɛrɪɡəuraund] *n* manège *m*.

mesh [mɛʃ] *n* maille *f*; filet *m* ♦ *vi* (*gears*) s'engrener; **wire ~** grillage *m* (métallique), treillis *m* (métallique).

mesmerize ['mɛzməraɪz] *vt* hypnotiser;

fasciner.

mess [mɛs] *n* désordre *m*, fouillis *m*, pagaille *f*; (MIL) mess *m*, cantine *f*; **to be (in) a ~** être en désordre; **to be/get o.s. in a ~** (*fig*) être/se mettre dans le pétrin.

mess about, **mess around** *vi* (*col*) perdre son temps.

mess about *or* **around with** *vt fus* (*col*) chambarder, tripoter.

mess up *vt* salir; chambarder; gâcher.

message ['mɛsɪdʒ] *n* message *m*; **to get the ~** (*fig*: *col*) saisir, piger.

message switching *n* (COMPUT) commutation *f* de messages.

messenger ['mɛsɪndʒə*] *n* messager *m*.

Messiah [mɪ'saɪə] *n* Messie *m*.

Messrs, Messrs. ['mɛsəz] *abbr* (*on letters*: = *messieurs*) MM.

messy ['mɛsɪ] *a* sale; en désordre.

Met [mɛt] *n abbr* (US) = Metropolitan Opera.

met [mɛt] *pt, pp of* meet ♦ *a abbr* (= *meteorological*) météo *inv*.

metabolism [mɛ'tæbəlɪzəm] *n* métabolisme *m*.

metal ['mɛtl] *n* métal *m* ♦ *vt* empierrer.

metallic [mɛ'tælɪk] *a* métallique.

metallurgy [mɛ'tælədʒɪ] *n* métallurgie *f*.

metalwork ['mɛtlwə:k] *n* (*craft*) ferronnerie *f*.

metamorphosis, *pl* **-phoses** [mɛtə'mɔ:fəsɪs, -i:z] *n* métamorphose *f*.

metaphor ['mɛtəfə*] *n* métaphore *f*.

metaphysics [mɛtə'fɪzɪks] *n* métaphysique *f*.

mete [mi:t]: **to ~ out** *vt fus* infliger.

meteor ['mi:tɪə*] *n* météore *m*.

meteoric [mi:tɪ'ɔrɪk] *a* (*fig*) fulgurant(e).

meteorite ['mi:tɪəraɪt] *n* météorite *m or f*.

meteorological [mi:tɪərə'lɔdʒɪkl] *a* météorologique.

meteorology [mi:tɪə'rɔlədʒɪ] *n* météorologie *f*.

meter ['mi:tə*] *n* (*instrument*) compteur *m*; (*also*: **parking ~**) parc(o)mètre *m*; (US) = metre.

methane ['mi:θeɪn] *n* méthane *m*.

method ['mɛθəd] *n* méthode *f*; ~ **of payment** mode *m or* modalité *f* de paiement.

methodical [mɪ'θɔdɪkl] *a* méthodique.

Methodist ['mɛθədɪst] *a*, *n* méthodiste (*m/f*).

methylated spirit ['mɛθɪleɪtɪd-] *n* (*Brit*: *also*: **meths**) alcool *m* à brûler.

meticulous [mɛ'tɪkjuləs] *a* méticuleux(euse).

metre, (US) **meter** ['mi:tə*] *n* mètre *m*.

metric ['mɛtrɪk] *a* métrique; **to go ~** adopter le système métrique.

metrical ['mɛtrɪkl] *a* métrique.

metrication [mɛtrɪ'keɪʃən] *n* conversion *f* au système métrique.

metric system *n* système *m* métrique.

metric ton *n* tonne *f*.

metronome ['mɛtrənəum] *n* métronome *m*.

metropolis [mɪ'trɔpəlɪs] *n* métropole *f*.

metropolitan [mɛtrə'pɔlɪtən] *a* métropolitain(e).

Metropolitan Police *n* (*Brit*): **the ~** la police londonienne.

mettle ['mɛtl] *n* courage *m*.

mew [mju:] *vi* (*cat*) miauler.

mews [mju:z] *n* (*Brit*): ~ **cottage** maisonnette aménagée dans une ancienne écurie ou remise.

Mexican ['mɛksɪkən] *a* mexicain(e) ♦ *n*

Mexicain/e.
Mexico ['mɛksɪkəu] n Mexique m.
Mexico City n Mexico.
mezzanine ['mɛtsəni:n] n mezzanine f; (of shops, offices) entresol m.
MFA n abbr (US: = Master of Fine Arts) titre universitaire.
mfr abbr = **manufacture, manufacturer**.
mg abbr (= milligram) mg.
Mgr abbr (= Monseigneur, Monsignor) Mgr; (= manager) dir.
MHR n abbr (US) = **Member of the House of Representatives**.
MHz abbr (= megahertz) MHz.
MI abbr (US POST) = Michigan.
MI5 n abbr (Brit: = Military Intelligence 5) ≈ DST f.
MI6 n abbr (Brit: = Military Intelligence 6) ≈ DGSE f.
MIA abbr (= missing in action) disparu au combat.
miaow [mi:'au] vi miauler.
mice [maɪs] npl of **mouse**.
microbe ['maɪkrəub] n microbe m.
microbiology [maɪkrəbaɪ'ɔlədʒɪ] n microbiologie f.
microchip ['maɪkrəutʃɪp] n (ELEC) puce f.
micro(computer) ['maɪkrəu(kəm'pju:tə*)] n micro(-ordinateur) m.
microcosm ['maɪkrəukɔzəm] n microcosme m.
microeconomics ['maɪkrəui:kə'nɔmɪks] n micro-économie f.
microfiche ['maɪkrəufi:ʃ] n microfiche f.
microfilm ['maɪkrəufɪlm] n microfilm m ♦ vt microfilmer.
micrometer [maɪ'krɔmɪtə*] n palmer m, micromètre m.
microphone ['maɪkrəfəun] n microphone m.
microprocessor ['maɪkrəu'prəusesə*] n microprocesseur m.
microscope ['maɪkrəskəup] n microscope m; **under the ~** au microscope.
microscopic [maɪkrə'skɔpɪk] a microscopique.
microwave ['maɪkrəuweɪv] n (also: ~ **oven**) four m à micro-ondes.
mid [mɪd] a: ~ **May** la mi-mai; ~ **afternoon** le milieu de l'après-midi; **in** ~ **air** en plein ciel; **he's in his** ~ **thirties** il a dans les trente-cinq ans.
midday [mɪd'deɪ] n midi m.
middle ['mɪdl] n milieu m; (waist) ceinture f, taille f ♦ a du milieu; **in the** ~ **of the night** au milieu de la nuit; **I'm in the** ~ **of reading it** je suis (justement) en train de le lire.
middle age n tranche d'âge aux limites floues, entre la quarantaine et le début du troisième âge.
middle-aged [mɪdl'eɪdʒd] a (people) see middle age; d'un certain âge, ni vieux ni jeune; (pej: values, outlook) conventionnel(le), rassis(e).
Middle Ages npl: **the** ~ le moyen âge.
middle class n: **the** ~**(es)** ≈ les classes moyennes ♦ a (also: **middle-class**) ≈ (petit(e)-)bourgeois(e).
Middle East n: **the** ~ le Proche-Orient, le Moyen-Orient.
middleman ['mɪdlmæn] n intermédiaire m.
middle management n cadres moyens.

middle name n second prénom.
middle-of-the-road ['mɪdləvðə'rəud] a (policy) modéré(e), du juste milieu; (music etc) plutôt classique, assez traditionnel(le).
middleweight ['mɪdlweɪt] n (BOXING) poids moyen.
middling ['mɪdlɪŋ] a moyen(ne).
Middx abbr (Brit) = Middlesex.
midge [mɪdʒ] n moucheron m.
midget ['mɪdʒɪt] n nain/e ♦ a minuscule.
Midlands ['mɪdləndz] npl comtés du centre de l'Angleterre.
midnight ['mɪdnaɪt] n minuit m; **at** ~ à minuit.
midriff ['mɪdrɪf] n estomac m, taille f.
midst [mɪdst] n: **in the** ~ **of** au milieu de.
midsummer [mɪd'sʌmə*] n milieu m de l'été.
midway [mɪd'weɪ] a, ad: ~ **(between)** à mi-chemin (entre).
midweek [mɪd'wi:k] n milieu m de la semaine ♦ ad au milieu de la semaine, en pleine semaine.
midwife, midwives ['mɪdwaɪf, -vz] n sage-femme f.
midwifery ['mɪdwɪfərɪ] n obstétrique f.
midwinter [mɪd'wɪntə*] n milieu m de l'hiver.
might [maɪt] vb see **may** ♦ n puissance f, force f.
mighty ['maɪtɪ] a puissant(e) ♦ ad (col) rudement.
migraine ['mi:greɪn] n migraine f.
migrant ['maɪgrənt] n (bird, animal) migrateur m; (person) migrant/e; nomade m/f ♦ a migrateur(trice); migrant(e); nomade; (worker) saisonnier(ière).
migrate [maɪ'greɪt] vi émigrer.
migration [maɪ'greɪʃən] n migration f.
mike [maɪk] n abbr (= microphone) micro m.
Milan [mɪ'læn] n Milan.
mild [maɪld] a doux(douce); (reproach) léger(ère); (illness) bénin(igne) ♦ n bière légère.
mildew ['mɪldju:] n mildiou m.
mildly ['maɪldlɪ] ad doucement; légèrement; **to put it** ~ (col) c'est le moins qu'on puisse dire.
mildness ['maɪldnɪs] n douceur f.
mile [maɪl] n mil(l)e m (= 1609 m); **to do 30** ~**s per gallon** ≈ faire 9,4 litres aux cent.
mileage ['maɪlɪdʒ] n distance f en milles, ≈ kilométrage m.
mileage allowance n ≈ indemnité f kilométrique.
mileometer [maɪ'lɔmɪtə*] n (Brit) = milometer.
milestone ['maɪlstəun] n borne f; (fig) jalon m.
milieu ['mi:ljə:] n milieu m.
militant ['mɪlɪtnt] a, n militant(e).
militarism ['mɪlɪtərɪzəm] n militarisme m.
militaristic [mɪlɪtə'rɪstɪk] a militariste.
military ['mɪlɪtərɪ] a militaire ♦ n: **the** ~ l'armée f, les militaires mpl.
militate ['mɪlɪteɪt] vi: **to** ~ **against** militer contre.
militia [mɪ'lɪʃə] n milice f.
milk [mɪlk] n lait m ♦ vt (cow) traire; (fig) dépouiller, plumer.
milk chocolate n chocolat m au lait.

milk float *n* (*Brit*) voiture *f or* camionnette *f* du *or* de laitier.

milking ['mɪlkɪŋ] *n* traite *f*.

milkman ['mɪlkmən] *n* laitier *m*.

milk shake *n* milk-shake *m*.

milk tooth *n* dent *f* de lait.

milk truck *n* (*US*) = **milk float**.

milky ['mɪlkɪ] *a* lacté(e); (*colour*) laiteux(euse).

Milky Way *n* Voie lactée.

mill [mɪl] *n* moulin *m*; (*factory*) usine *f*, fabrique *f*; (*spinning* ~) filature *f*; (*flour* ~) minoterie *f* ♦ *vt* moudre, broyer ♦ *vi* (*also*: ~ **about**) grouiller.

millennium, *pl* ~**s** *or* **millennia** [mɪ'lɛnɪəm, -'lɛnɪə] *n* millénaire *m*.

miller ['mɪlə*] *n* meunier *m*.

millet ['mɪlɪt] *n* millet *m*.

milli... ['mɪlɪ] *prefix* milli....

milligram(me) ['mɪlɪgræm] *n* milligramme *m*.

millilitre, (*US*) **milliliter** ['mɪlɪliːtə*] *n* millilitre *m*.

millimetre, (*US*) **millimeter** ['mɪlɪmiːtə*] *n* millimètre *m*.

milliner ['mɪlɪnə*] *n* modiste *f*.

millinery ['mɪlɪnərɪ] *n* modes *fpl*.

million ['mɪljən] *n* million *m*.

millionaire [mɪljə'nɛə*] *n* millionnaire *m*.

millipede ['mɪlɪpiːd] *n* mille-pattes *m inv*.

millstone ['mɪlstəun] *n* meule *f*.

millwheel ['mɪlwiːl] *n* roue *f* de moulin.

milometer [maɪ'lɒmɪtə*] *n* (*Brit*) ≈ compteur *m* kilométrique.

mime [maɪm] *n* mime *m* ♦ *vt, vi* mimer.

mimic ['mɪmɪk] *n* imitateur/trice ♦ *vt, vi* imiter, contrefaire.

mimicry ['mɪmɪkrɪ] *n* imitation *f*; (*ZOOL*) mimétisme *m*.

Min. *abbr* (*Brit POL*) = **ministry**.

min. *abbr* (= *minute*) mn.; (= *minimum*) min.

minaret [mɪnə'rɛt] *n* minaret *m*.

mince [mɪns] *vt* hacher ♦ *vi* (*in walking*) marcher à petits pas maniérés ♦ *n* (*Brit CULIN*) viande hachée, hachis *m*; **he does not** ~ **(his) words** il ne mâche pas ses mots.

mincemeat ['mɪnsmiːt] *n* hachis de fruits secs utilisés en pâtisserie.

mince pie *n* sorte de tarte aux fruits secs.

mincer ['mɪnsə*] *n* hachoir *m*.

mincing ['mɪnsɪŋ] *a* affecté(e).

mind [maɪnd] *n* esprit *m* ♦ *vt* (*attend to, look after*) s'occuper de; (*be careful*) faire attention à; (*object to*): **I don't** ~ **the noise** je ne crains pas le bruit, le bruit ne me dérange pas; **do you** ~ **if ...?** est-ce que cela vous gêne si ...?; **I don't** ~ cela ne me dérange pas; ~ **you,** ... remarquez, ...; **never** ~ peu importe, ça ne fait rien; **it is on my** ~ cela me préoccupe; **to change one's** ~ changer d'avis; **to be in two** ~**s about sth** (*Brit*) être indécis(e) *or* irrésolu(e) en ce qui concerne qch; **to my** ~ à mon avis, selon moi; **to be out of one's** ~ ne plus avoir toute sa raison; **to keep sth in** ~ ne pas oublier qch; **to bear sth in** ~ tenir compte de qch; **to have sb/sth in** ~ avoir qn/qch en tête; **to have in** ~ **to do** avoir l'intention de faire; **it went right out of my** ~ ça m'est

complètement sorti de la tête; **to bring** *or* **call sth to** ~ se rappeler qch; **to make up one's** ~ se décider; "~ **the step**" "attention à la marche".

-minded ['maɪndɪd] *a*: **fair**~ impartial(e); **an industrially**~ **nation** une nation orientée vers l'industrie.

minder ['maɪndə*] *n* (*child* ~) gardienne *f*; (*bodyguard*) ange gardien (*fig*).

mindful ['maɪndful] *a*: ~ **of** attentif(ive) à, soucieux(euse) de.

mindless ['maɪndlɪs] *a* irréfléchi(e); (*violence, crime*) insensé(e).

mine [maɪn] *pronoun* le(la) mien(ne), les miens(miennes); **this book is** ~ ce livre est à moi ♦ *n* mine *f* ♦ *vt* (*coal*) extraire; (*ship, beach*) miner.

mine detector *n* détecteur *m* de mines.

minefield ['maɪnfiːld] *n* champ *m* de mines.

miner ['maɪnə*] *n* mineur *m*.

mineral ['mɪnərəl] *a* minéral(e) ♦ *n* minéral *m*; ~**s** *npl* (*Brit*: *soft drinks*) boissons gazeuses (sucrées).

mineralogy [mɪnə'rælədʒɪ] *n* minéralogie *f*.

mineral water *n* eau minérale.

minesweeper ['maɪnswiːpə*] *n* dragueur *m* de mines.

mingle ['mɪŋgl] *vt* mêler, mélanger ♦ *vi*: **to** ~ **with** se mêler à.

mingy ['mɪndʒɪ] *a* (*col*) radin(e).

miniature ['mɪnətʃə*] *a* (en) miniature ♦ *n* miniature *f*.

minibus ['mɪnɪbʌs] *n* minibus *m*.

minicab ['mɪnɪkæb] *n* (*Brit*) minitaxi *m*.

minicomputer ['mɪnɪkəm'pjuːtə*] *n* mini-ordinateur *m*.

minim ['mɪnɪm] *n* (*MUS*) blanche *f*.

minima ['mɪnɪmə] *npl of* **minimum**.

minimal ['mɪnɪml] *a* minimale(e).

minimize ['mɪnɪmaɪz] *vt* minimiser.

minimum ['mɪnɪməm] *n* (*pl*: **minima** ['mɪnɪmə]) minimum *m* ♦ *a* minimum; **to reduce to a** ~ réduire au minimum.

minimum lending rate (MLR) *n* (*ECON*) taux *m* de crédit minimum.

mining ['maɪnɪŋ] *n* exploitation minière ♦ *a* minier(ière); de mineurs.

minion ['mɪnjən] *n* (*pej*) laquais *m*; favori/te.

miniskirt ['mɪnɪskəːt] *n* mini-jupe *f*.

minister ['mɪnɪstə*] *n* (*Brit POL*) ministre *m*; (*REL*) pasteur *m* ♦ *vi*: **to** ~ **to sb** donner ses soins à qn; **to** ~ **to sb's needs** pourvoir aux besoins de qn.

ministerial [mɪnɪs'tɪərɪəl] *a* (*Brit POL*) ministériel(le).

ministry ['mɪnɪstrɪ] *n* (*Brit POL*) ministère *m*; (*REL*): **to go into the** ~ devenir pasteur.

mink [mɪŋk] *n* vison *m*.

mink coat *n* manteau *m* de vison.

minnow ['mɪnəu] *n* vairon *m*.

minor ['maɪnə*] *a* petit(e), de peu d'importance; (*MUS*) mineur(e) ♦ *n* (*LAW*) mineur/e.

Minorca [mɪ'nɔːkə] *n* Minorque *f*.

minority [maɪ'nɔrɪtɪ] *n* minorité *f*; **to be in a** ~ être en minorité.

minster ['mɪnstə*] *n* église abbatiale.

minstrel ['mɪnstrəl] *n* trouvère *m*, ménestrel *m*.

mint [mɪnt] n (plant) menthe f; (sweet) bonbon m à la menthe ♦ vt (coins) battre; **the (Royal) M~**, (US) **the (US) M~** ≈ l'hôtel m de la Monnaie; **in ~ condition** à l'état de neuf.

mint sauce n sauce f à la menthe.

minuet [mɪnju:'et] n menuet m.

minus ['maɪnəs] n (also: ~ **sign**) signe m moins ♦ prep moins.

minute a [maɪ'nju:t] minuscule; (detailed) minutieux(euse) ♦ n ['mɪnɪt] minute f; (official record) procès-verbal m, compte rendu; **~s** npl procès-verbal; **it is 5 ~s past 3** il est 3 heures 5; **wait a ~!** (attendez) un instant!; **at the last ~** à la dernière minute; **up to the ~** (fashion) dernier cri; (news) de dernière minute; (machine, technology) de pointe; **in ~ detail** par le menu.

minute book n registre m des procès-verbaux.

minute hand n aiguille f des minutes.

minutely [maɪ'nju:tlɪ] ad (by a small amount) de peu, de manière infime; (in detail) minutieusement, dans les moindres détails.

miracle ['mɪrəkl] n miracle m.

miraculous [mɪ'rækjuləs] a miraculeux(euse).

mirage ['mɪrɑ:ʒ] n mirage m.

mire ['maɪə*] n bourbe f, boue f.

mirror ['mɪrə*] n miroir m, glace f ♦ vt refléter.

mirror image n image inversée.

mirth [mə:θ] n gaieté f.

misadventure [mɪsəd'ventʃə*] n mésaventure f; **death by ~** (Brit) décès accidentel.

misanthropist [mɪ'zænθrəpɪst] n misanthrope m/f.

misapply [mɪsə'plaɪ] vt mal employer.

misapprehension ['mɪsæprɪ'henʃən] n malentendu m, méprise f.

misappropriate [mɪsə'prəuprɪeɪt] vt détourner.

misappropriation ['mɪsəprəuprɪ'eɪʃən] n escroquerie f, détournement m.

misbehave [mɪsbɪ'heɪv] vi se conduire mal.

misbehaviour, (US) **misbehavior** [mɪsbɪ'heɪvjə*] n mauvaise conduite.

misc. abbr = **miscellaneous**.

miscalculate [mɪs'kælkjuleɪt] vt mal calculer.

miscalculation ['mɪskælkju'leɪʃən] n erreur f de calcul.

miscarriage ['mɪskærɪdʒ] n (MED) fausse couche; **~ of justice** erreur f judiciaire.

miscarry [mɪs'kærɪ] vi (MED) faire une fausse couche; (fail: plans) échouer, mal tourner.

miscellaneous [mɪsɪ'leɪnɪəs] a (items, expenses) divers(es); (selection) varié(e).

miscellany [mɪ'selənɪ] n recueil m.

mischance [mɪs'tʃɑ:ns] n malchance f; **by (some) ~** par malheur.

mischief ['mɪstʃɪf] n (naughtiness) sottises fpl; (harm) mal m, dommage m; (maliciousness) méchanceté f.

mischievous ['mɪstʃɪvəs] a (naughty) coquin(e), espiègle; (harmful) méchant(e).

misconception ['mɪskən'sepʃən] n idée fausse.

misconduct [mɪs'kɒndʌkt] n inconduite f; **professional ~** faute professionnelle.

misconstrue [mɪskən'stru:] vt mal interpréter.

miscount [mɪs'kaunt] vt, vi mal compter.

misdeed ['mɪs'di:d] n méfait m.

misdemeanour, (US) **misdemeanor** [mɪsdɪ'mi:nə*] n écart m de conduite; infraction f.

misdirect [mɪsdɪ'rekt] vt (person) mal renseigner; (letter) mal adresser.

miser ['maɪzə*] n avare m/f.

miserable ['mɪzərəbl] a malheureux(euse); (wretched) misérable; **to feel ~** avoir le cafard.

miserably ['mɪzərəblɪ] ad (smile, answer) tristement; (live, pay) misérablement; (fail) lamentablement.

miserly ['maɪzəlɪ] a avare.

misery ['mɪzərɪ] n (unhappiness) tristesse f; (pain) souffrances fpl; (wretchedness) misère f.

misfire [mɪs'faɪə*] vi rater; (car engine) avoir des ratés.

misfit ['mɪsfɪt] n (person) inadapté/e.

misfortune [mɪs'fɔ:tʃən] n malchance f, malheur m.

misgiving(s) [mɪs'gɪvɪŋ(z)] n(pl) craintes fpl, soupçons mpl; **to have ~s about sth** avoir des doutes quant à qch.

misguided [mɪs'gaɪdɪd] a malavisé(e).

mishandle [mɪs'hændl] vt (treat roughly) malmener; (mismanage) mal s'y prendre pour faire or résoudre etc.

mishap ['mɪshæp] n mésaventure f.

mishear [mɪs'hɪə*] vt, vi irg mal entendre.

mishmash ['mɪʃmæʃ] n (col) fatras m, méli-mélo m.

misinform [mɪsɪn'fɔ:m] vt mal renseigner.

misinterpret [mɪsɪn'tə:prɪt] vt mal interpréter.

misinterpretation ['mɪsɪntə:prɪ'teɪʃən] n interprétation erronée, contresens m.

misjudge [mɪs'dʒʌdʒ] vt méjuger, se méprendre sur le compte de.

mislay [mɪs'leɪ] vt irg égarer.

mislead [mɪs'li:d] vt irg induire en erreur.

misleading [mɪs'li:dɪŋ] a trompeur(euse).

misled [mɪs'led] pt, pp of **mislead**.

mismanage [mɪs'mænɪdʒ] vt mal gérer; mal s'y prendre pour faire or résoudre etc.

mismanagement [mɪs'mænɪdʒmənt] n mauvaise gestion.

misnomer [mɪs'nəumə*] n terme or qualificatif trompeur or peu approprié.

misogynist [mɪ'sɔdʒɪnɪst] n misogyne m/f.

misplace [mɪs'pleɪs] vt égarer; **to be ~d** (trust etc) être mal placé(e).

misprint ['mɪsprɪnt] n faute f d'impression.

mispronounce [mɪsprə'nauns] vt mal prononcer.

misquote ['mɪs'kwəut] vt citer erronément or inexactement.

misread [mɪs'ri:d] vt irg mal lire.

misrepresent [mɪsreprɪ'zent] vt présenter sous un faux jour.

Miss [mɪs] n Mademoiselle; **Dear ~ Smith** Chère Mademoiselle Smith

miss [mɪs] vt (fail to get) manquer, rater; (appointment, class) manquer; (escape, avoid) échapper à, éviter; (notice loss of: money etc) s'apercevoir de l'absence de; (regret the absence of): **I ~ him/it** il/cela me manque ♦ vi manquer ♦ n (shot) coup manqué; **the bus just ~ed the wall** le bus a

évité le mur de justesse; **you're** ~**ing the point** vous êtes à côté de la question.
miss out vt (Brit) oublier.
miss out on vt fus (fun, party) rater, manquer; (chance, bargain) laisser passer.
missal ['mɪsl] n missel m.
misshapen [mɪs'ʃeɪpən] a difforme.
missile ['mɪsaɪl] n (AVIAT) missile m; (object thrown) projectile m.
missile base n base f de missiles.
missile launcher n lance-missiles m.
missing ['mɪsɪŋ] a manquant(e); (after escape, disaster: person) disparu(e); **to go** ~ disparaître; ~ **person** personne disparue, disparu/e.
mission ['mɪʃən] n mission f; **on a** ~ **to sb** en mission auprès de qn.
missionary ['mɪʃənrɪ] n missionnaire m/f.
missive ['mɪsɪv] n missive f.
misspell ['mɪs'spɛl] vt (irg: like **spell**) mal orthographier.
misspent ['mɪs'spɛnt] a: **his** ~ **youth** sa folle jeunesse.
mist [mɪst] n brume f, brouillard m ♦ vi (also: ~ **over**, ~ **up**) devenir brumeux(euse); (Brit: windows) s'embuer.
mistake [mɪs'teɪk] n erreur f, faute f ♦ vt (irg: like **take**) (meaning) mal comprendre; (intentions) se méprendre sur; **to** ~ **for** prendre pour; **by** ~ par erreur, par inadvertance; **to make a** ~ (in writing) faire une faute; (in calculating etc) faire une erreur; **to make a** ~ **about sb/sth** se tromper sur le compte de qn/sur qch.
mistaken [mɪs'teɪkən] pp of **mistake** ♦ a (idea etc) erroné(e); **to be** ~ faire erreur, se tromper.
mistaken identity n erreur f d'identité.
mistakenly [mɪs'teɪkənlɪ] ad par erreur, par mégarde.
mister ['mɪstə*] n (col) Monsieur m; see **Mr.**
mistletoe ['mɪsltəʊ] n gui m.
mistook [mɪs'tʊk] pt of **mistake.**
mistranslation [mɪstrænz'leɪʃən] n erreur f de traduction, contresens m.
mistreat [mɪs'tri:t] vt maltraiter.
mistress ['mɪstrɪs] n maîtresse f; (Brit: in primary school) institutrice f; see **Mrs.**
mistrust [mɪs'trʌst] vt se méfier de ♦ n: ~ (**of**) méfiance f (à l'égard de).
mistrustful [mɪs'trʌstfʊl] a: ~ (**of**) méfiant(e) (à l'égard de).
misty ['mɪstɪ] a brumeux(euse).
misty-eyed ['mɪstɪ'aɪd] a les yeux embués de larmes; (fig) sentimental(e).
misunderstand [mɪsʌndə'stænd] vt, vi irg mal comprendre.
misunderstanding ['mɪsʌndə'stændɪŋ] n méprise f, malentendu m.
misunderstood [mɪsʌndə'stʊd] pt, pp of **misunderstand.**
misuse n [mɪs'ju:s] mauvais emploi; (of power) abus m ♦ vt [mɪs'ju:z] mal employer; abuser de.
MIT n abbr (US) = Massachusetts Institute of Technology.
mite [maɪt] n (small quantity) grain m, miette f; (Brit: small child) petit/e.
mitigate ['mɪtɪɡeɪt] vt atténuer; **mitigating**

circumstances circonstances atténuantes.
mitigation [mɪtɪ'ɡeɪʃən] n atténuation f.
mitre, (US) **miter** ['maɪtə*] n mitre f; (CARPENTRY) onglet m.
mitt(en) ['mɪt(n)] n mitaine f; moufle f.
mix [mɪks] vt mélanger ♦ vi se mélanger ♦ n mélange m; dosage m; **to** ~ **sth with sth** mélanger qch à qch; **to** ~ **business with pleasure** unir l'utile à l'agréable; **cake** ~ préparation f pour gâteau.
mix in vt incorporer, mélanger.
mix up vt mélanger; (confuse) confondre; **to be** ~**ed up in sth** être mêlé(e) à qch or impliqué(e) dans qch.
mixed [mɪkst] a (assorted) assortis(ies); (school etc) mixte.
mixed doubles npl (SPORT) double m mixte.
mixed economy n économie f mixte.
mixed grill n (Brit) assortiment m de grillades.
mixed-up [mɪkst'ʌp] a (person) désorienté(e) (fig).
mixer ['mɪksə*] n (for food) batteur m, mixeur m; (person): **he is a good** ~ il est très sociable.
mixture ['mɪkstʃə*] n assortiment m, mélange m; (MED) préparation f.
mix-up ['mɪksʌp] n confusion f.
MK abbr (Brit TECH) = **mark.**
mk abbr = **mark** (currency).
mkt abbr = **market.**
MLitt n abbr (= Master of Literature, Master of Letters) titre universitaire.
MLR n abbr (Brit) = **minimum lending rate.**
mm abbr (= millimetre) mm.
MN abbr (Brit) = **Merchant Navy;** (US POST) = Minnesota.
MO n abbr (MED) = medical officer; (US col: = modus operandi) méthode f ♦ abbr (US POST) = Missouri.
m.o. abbr = **money order.**
moan [məʊn] n gémissement m ♦ vi gémir; (col: complain): **to** ~ (**about**) se plaindre (de).
moaning ['məʊnɪŋ] n gémissements mpl.
moat [məʊt] n fossé m, douves fpl.
mob [mɒb] n foule f; (disorderly) cohue f; (pej): **the** ~ la populace ♦ vt assaillir.
mobile ['məʊbaɪl] a mobile ♦ n (ART) mobile m; **applicants must be** ~ (Brit) les candidats devront être prêts à accepter tout déplacement.
mobile home n caravane f.
mobile shop n (Brit) camion m magasin.
mobility [məʊ'bɪlɪtɪ] n mobilité f.
mobilize ['məʊbɪlaɪz] vt, vi mobiliser.
moccasin ['mɒkəsɪn] n mocassin m.
mock [mɒk] vt ridiculiser, se moquer de ♦ a faux(fausse).
mockery ['mɒkərɪ] n moquerie f, raillerie f; **to make a** ~ **of** ridiculiser, tourner en dérision.
mocking ['mɒkɪŋ] a moqueur(euse).
mockingbird ['mɒkɪŋbə:d] n moqueur m.
mock-up ['mɒkʌp] n maquette f.
MOD n abbr (Brit) = **Ministry of Defence.**
mod cons ['mɒd'kɒnz] npl abbr (Brit) = **modern conveniences.**
mode [məʊd] n mode m; (of transport) moyen

m.

model ['mɔdl] *n* modèle *m*; (*person: for fashion*) mannequin *m*; (: *for artist*) modèle ♦ *vt* modeler ♦ *vi* travailler comme mannequin ♦ *a* (*railway: toy*) modèle réduit *inv*; (*child, factory*) modèle; **to ~ clothes** présenter des vêtements; **to ~ sb/sth on** modeler qn/qch sur.

modeller, (*US*) **modeler** ['mɔdlə*] *n* modeleur *m*; (*model maker*) maquettiste *m/f*; fabricant *m* de modèles réduits.

modem ['məudɛm] *n* modem *m*.

moderate *a, n* ['mɔdərət] *a* modéré(e) ♦ *n* (*POL*) modéré/e ♦ *vb* ['mɔdəreɪt] *vi* se modérer, se calmer ♦ *vt* modérer.

moderately ['mɔdərətlɪ] *ad* (*act*) avec modération *or* mesure; (*expensive, difficult*) moyennement; (*pleased, happy*) raisonnablement, assez; **~ priced** à un prix raisonnable.

moderation [mɔdə'reɪʃən] *n* modération *f*, mesure *f*; **in ~** à dose raisonnable, pris(e) *or* pratiqué(e) modérément.

modern ['mɔdən] *a* moderne; **~ languages** langues vivantes.

modernization [mɔdənaɪ'zeɪʃən] *n* modernisation *f*.

modernize ['mɔdənaɪz] *vt* moderniser.

modest ['mɔdɪst] *a* modeste.

modesty ['mɔdɪstɪ] *n* modestie *f*.

modicum ['mɔdɪkəm] *n*: **a ~ of** un minimum de.

modification [mɔdɪfɪ'keɪʃən] *n* modification *f*; **to make ~s** faire *or* apporter des modifications.

modify ['mɔdɪfaɪ] *vt* modifier.

Mods [mɔdz] *n abbr* (*Brit*: = (*Honour*) *Moderations*) *premier examen universitaire* (*à Oxford*).

modular ['mɔdjulə*] *a* (*filing, unit*) modulaire.

modulate ['mɔdjuleɪt] *vt* moduler.

modulation [mɔdju'leɪʃən] *n* modulation *f*.

module ['mɔdjuːl] *n* module *m*.

mogul ['məugl] *n* (*fig*) nabab *m*; (*SKI*) bosse *f*.

MOH *n abbr* (*Brit*) = *Medical Officer of Health*.

mohair ['məuhɛə*] *n* mohair *m*.

Mohammed [mə'hæmed] *n* Mahomet *m*.

moist [mɔɪst] *a* humide, moite.

moisten ['mɔɪsn] *vt* humecter, mouiller légèrement.

moisture ['mɔɪstʃə*] *n* humidité *f*; (*on glass*) buée *f*.

moisturize ['mɔɪstʃəraɪz] *vt* (*skin*) hydrater.

moisturizer ['mɔɪstʃəraɪzə*] *n* produit hydratant.

molar ['məulə*] *n* molaire *f*.

molasses [mə'læsɪz] *n* mélasse *f*.

mold [məuld] *n, vt* (*US*) = **mould**.

mole [məul] *n* (*animal*) taupe *f*; (*spot*) grain *m* de beauté.

molecule ['mɔlɪkjuːl] *n* molécule *f*.

molehill ['məulhɪl] *n* taupinière *f*.

molest [məu'lɛst] *vt* tracasser; molester.

mollusc ['mɔləsk] *n* mollusque *m*.

mollycoddle ['mɔlɪkɔdl] *vt* chouchouter, couver.

molt [məult] *vi* (*US*) = **moult**.

molten ['məultən] *a* fondu(e).

mom [mɔm] *n* (*US*) = **mum**.

moment ['məumənt] *n* moment *m*, instant *m*; (*importance*) importance *f*; **at the ~** en ce moment; **for the ~** pour l'instant; **in a ~** dans un instant; **"one ~ please"** (*TEL*) "ne quittez pas".

momentarily ['məuməntrɪlɪ] *ad* momentanément; (*US: soon*) bientôt.

momentary ['məuməntərɪ] *a* momentané(e), passager(ère).

momentous [məu'mɛntəs] *a* important(e), capital(e).

momentum [məu'mɛntəm] *n* élan *m*, vitesse acquise; **to gather ~** prendre de la vitesse.

mommy ['mɔmɪ] *n* (*US*) = **mummy**.

Mon. *abbr* (= *Monday*) l.

Monaco ['mɔnəkəu] *n* Monaco *f*.

monarch ['mɔnək] *n* monarque *m*.

monarchist ['mɔnəkɪst] *n* monarchiste *m/f*.

monarchy ['mɔnəkɪ] *n* monarchie *f*.

monastery ['mɔnəstərɪ] *n* monastère *m*.

monastic [mə'næstɪk] *a* monastique.

Monday ['mʌndɪ] *n* lundi *m*; *for phrases see also* **Tuesday.**

monetarist ['mʌnɪtərɪst] *n* monétariste *m/f*.

monetary ['mʌnɪtərɪ] *a* monétaire.

money ['mʌnɪ] *n* argent *m*; **to make ~** (*person*) gagner de l'argent; (*business*) rapporter; **danger ~** (*Brit*) prime *f* de risque; **I've got no ~ left** je n'ai plus d'argent, je n'ai plus un sou.

moneyed ['mʌnɪd] *a* riche.

moneylender ['mʌnɪlɛndə*] *n* prêteur/euse.

moneymaking ['mʌnɪmeɪkɪŋ] *a* lucratif(ive), qui rapporte (de l'argent).

money market *n* marché financier.

money order *n* mandat *m*.

money-spinner ['mʌnɪspɪnə*] *n* (*col*) mine *f* d'or (*fig*).

money supply *n* masse *f* monétaire.

Mongol ['mɔngəl] *n* Mongol/e; (*LING*) mongol *m*.

mongol ['mɔngəl] *a, n* (*MED*) mongolien(ne).

Mongolia [mɔn'gəulɪə] *n* Mongolie *f*.

Mongolian [mɔn'gəulɪən] *a* mongol(e) ♦ *n* Mongol/e; (*LING*) mongol *m*.

mongoose ['mɔnguːs] *n* mangouste *f*.

mongrel ['mʌngrəl] *n* (*dog*) bâtard *m*.

monitor ['mɔnɪtə*] *n* (*Brit SCOL*) chef *m* de classe; (*US SCOL*) surveillant *m* (d'examen); (*TV, COMPUT*) écran *m*, moniteur *m* ♦ *vt* contrôler; (*foreign station*) être à l'écoute de.

monk [mʌŋk] *n* moine *m*.

monkey ['mʌŋkɪ] *n* singe *m*.

monkey nut *n* (*Brit*) cacahuète *f*.

monkey wrench *n* clé *f* à molette.

mono ['mɔnəu] *a* mono *inv*.

mono... ['mɔnəu] *prefix* mono....

monochrome ['mɔnəkrəum] *a* monochrome.

monocle ['mɔnəkl] *n* monocle *m*.

monogram ['mɔnəgræm] *n* monogramme *m*.

monolith ['mɔnəlɪθ] *n* monolithe *m*.

monologue ['mɔnəlɔg] *n* monologue *m*.

monoplane ['mɔnəpleɪn] *n* monoplan *m*.

monopolize [mə'nɔpəlaɪz] *vt* monopoliser.

monopoly [mə'nɔpəlɪ] *n* monopole *m*; **Monopolies and Mergers Commission** (*Brit*) *Commission britannique d'enquête sur les monopoles.*

monorail ['mɔnəʊreɪl] n monorail m.
monosodium glutamate [mɔnə'səʊdɪəm-'glu:təmeɪt] n glutamate m de sodium.
monosyllabic [mɔnəsɪ'læbɪk] a monosyllabique; (person) laconique.
monosyllable ['mɔnəsɪləbl] n monosyllabe m.
monotone ['mɔnətəʊn] n ton m (or voix f) monocorde; **to speak in a** ~ parler sur un ton monocorde.
monotonous [mə'nɔtənəs] a monotone.
monotony [mə'nɔtənɪ] n monotonie f.
monoxide [mə'nɔksaɪd] n: **carbon** ~ oxyde m de carbone.
monsoon [mɔn'su:n] n mousson f.
monster ['mɔnstə*] n monstre m.
monstrosity [mɔns'trɔsɪtɪ] n monstruosité f, atrocité f.
monstrous ['mɔnstrəs] a (huge) gigantesque; (atrocious) monstrueux(euse), atroce.
montage [mɔn'tɑ:ʒ] n montage m.
Mont Blanc [mɔ̃blɑ̃] n Mont Blanc m.
month [mʌnθ] n mois m; **every** ~ tous les mois; **300 dollars a** ~ 300 dollars par mois.
monthly ['mʌnθlɪ] a mensuel(le) ♦ ad mensuellement ♦ n (magazine) mensuel m, publication mensuelle; **twice** ~ deux fois par mois.
Montreal [mɔntrɪ'ɔ:l] n Montréal.
monument ['mɔnjumənt] n monument m.
monumental [mɔnju'mɛntl] a monumental(e).
monumental mason n marbrier m.
moo [mu:] vi meugler, beugler.
mood [mu:d] n humeur f, disposition f; **to be in a good/bad** ~ être de bonne/mauvaise humeur; **to be in the** ~ **for** être d'humeur à, avoir envie de.
moody ['mu:dɪ] a (variable) d'humeur changeante, lunatique; (sullen) morose, maussade.
moon [mu:n] n lune f.
moonbeam ['mu:nbi:m] n rayon m de lune.
moon landing n alunissage m.
moonlight ['mu:nlaɪt] n clair m de lune ♦ vi travailler au noir.
moonlighting ['mu:nlaɪtɪŋ] n travail m au noir.
moonlit ['mu:nlɪt] a éclairé(e) par la lune; **a** ~ **night** une nuit de lune.
moonshot ['mu:nʃɔt] n (SPACE) tir m lunaire.
moonstruck ['mu:nstrʌk] a fou(folle), dérangé(e).
Moor [mʊə*] n Maure/Mauresque.
moor [mʊə*] n lande f ♦ vt (ship) amarrer ♦ vi mouiller.
moorings ['mʊərɪŋz] npl (chains) amarres fpl; (place) mouillage m.
Moorish ['mʊərɪʃ] a maure(mauresque).
moorland ['mʊələnd] n lande f.
moose [mu:s] n (pl inv) élan m.
moot [mu:t] vt soulever ♦ a: ~ **point** point m discutable.
mop [mɔp] n balai m à laver ♦ vt éponger, essuyer; ~ **of hair** tignasse f.
mop up vt éponger.
mope [məʊp] vi avoir le cafard, se morfondre.
mope about, mope around vi broyer du noir, se morfondre.
moped ['məʊpɛd] n cyclomoteur m.
moquette [mɔ'kɛt] n moquette f.

moral ['mɔrl] a moral(e) ♦ n morale f; ~**s** npl moralité f.
morale [mɔ'rɑ:l] n moral m.
morality [mə'rælɪtɪ] n moralité f.
moralize ['mɔrəlaɪz] vi: **to** ~ **(about)** moraliser (sur).
morally ['mɔrəlɪ] ad moralement.
morass [mə'ræs] n marais m, marécage m.
moratorium [mɔrə'tɔ:rɪəm] n moratoire m.
morbid ['mɔ:bɪd] a morbide.
more [mɔ:*] a plus de, davantage de ♦ ad plus; ~ **people** plus de gens; **I want** ~ j'en veux plus or davantage; **is there any** ~? est-ce qu'il en reste?; **many/much** ~ beaucoup plus; ~ **and** ~ de plus en plus; **once** ~ encore une fois, une fois de plus; **no** ~, **not any** ~ ne ... plus; **and what's** ~ ... et de plus ..., et qui plus est ...; ~ **dangerous than** plus dangereux que; ~ **or less** plus ou moins; ~ **than ever** plus que jamais.
moreover [mɔ:'rəʊvə*] ad de plus.
morgue [mɔ:g] n morgue f.
MORI ['mɔ:rɪ] n abbr (Brit: = Market & Opinion Research Institute) institut de sondage.
moribund ['mɔrɪbʌnd] a moribond(e).
morning ['mɔ:nɪŋ] n matin m; (as duration) matinée f; **in the** ~ le matin; **7 o'clock in the** ~ 7 heures du matin; **this** ~ ce matin.
morning sickness n nausées matinales.
Moroccan [mə'rɔkən] a marocain(e) ♦ n Marocain/e.
Morocco [mə'rɔkəʊ] n Maroc m.
moron ['mɔ:rɔn] n idiot/e, minus m/f.
moronic [mə'rɔnɪk] a idiot(e), imbécile.
morose [mə'rəʊs] a morose, maussade.
morphine ['mɔ:fi:n] n morphine f.
Morse [mɔ:s] n (also: ~ **code**) morse m.
morsel ['mɔ:sl] n bouchée f.
mortal ['mɔ:tl] a, n mortel(le).
mortality [mɔ:'tælɪtɪ] n mortalité f.
mortality rate n (taux m de) mortalité f.
mortar ['mɔ:tə*] n mortier m.
mortgage ['mɔ:gɪdʒ] n hypothèque f; (loan) prêt m (or crédit m) hypothécaire ♦ vt hypothéquer; **to take out a** ~ prendre une hypothèque, faire un emprunt.
mortgage company n (US) société f de crédit immobilier.
mortgagee [mɔ:gə'dʒi:] n prêteur/euse (sur hypothèque).
mortgagor ['mɔ:gədʒə*] n emprunteur/euse (sur hypothèque).
mortician [mɔ:'tɪʃən] n (US) entrepreneur m de pompes funèbres.
mortified ['mɔ:tɪfaɪd] a mortifié(e).
mortise lock ['mɔ:tɪs-] n serrure encastrée.
mortuary ['mɔ:tjʊərɪ] n morgue f.
mosaic [məʊ'zeɪɪk] n mosaïque f.
Moscow ['mɔskəʊ] n Moscou.
Moslem ['mɔzləm] a, n = **Muslim**.
mosque [mɔsk] n mosquée f.
mosquito, ~es [mɔs'ki:təʊ] n moustique m.
mosquito net n moustiquaire f.
moss [mɔs] n mousse f.
mossy ['mɔsɪ] a moussu(e).
most [məʊst] a la plupart de; le plus de ♦ pronoun la plupart ♦ ad le plus; (very) très, extrêmement; **the** ~ (also: + adjective) le

plus; ~ **fish** la plupart des poissons; ~ **of** la plus grande partie de; ~ **of them** la plupart d'entre eux; **I saw** ~ j'en ai vu la plupart; c'est moi qui en ai vu le plus; **at the (very)** ~ au plus; **to make the** ~ **of** profiter au maximum de.

mostly ['məustlɪ] *ad* surtout, principalement.

MOT *n abbr* (*Brit*: = *Ministry of Transport*): **the** ~ **(test)** *visite technique (annuelle) obligatoire des véhicules à moteur.*

motel [məu'tɛl] *n* motel *m*.

moth [mɔθ] *n* papillon *m* de nuit; mite *f*.

mothball ['mɔθbɔːl] *n* boule *f* de naphtaline.

moth-eaten ['mɔθiːtn] *a* mité(e).

mother ['mʌðə*] *n* mère *f* ♦ *vt* (*care for*) dorloter.

mother board *n* (*COMPUT*) carte-mère *f*.

motherhood ['mʌðəhud] *n* maternité *f*.

mother-in-law ['mʌðərɪnlɔː] *n* belle-mère *f*.

motherly ['mʌðəlɪ] *a* maternel(le).

mother-of-pearl ['mʌðərəv'pɜːl] *n* nacre *f*.

mother's help *n* aide *f or* auxiliaire *f* familiale.

mother-to-be ['mʌðətə'biː] *n* future maman.

mother tongue *n* langue maternelle.

mothproof ['mɔθpruːf] *a* traité(e) à l'antimite.

motif [məu'tiːf] *n* motif *m*.

motion ['məuʃən] *n* mouvement *m*; (*gesture*) geste *m*; (*at meeting*) motion *f*; (*Brit*: *also*: **bowel** ~) selles *fpl* ♦ *vt, vi*: **to** ~ **(to) sb to do** faire signe à qn de faire; **to be in** ~ (*vehicle*) être en marche; **to set in** ~ mettre en marche; **to go through the** ~s **of doing sth** (*fig*) faire qch machinalement *or* sans conviction.

motionless ['məuʃənlɪs] *a* immobile, sans mouvement.

motion picture *n* film *m*.

motivate ['məutɪveɪt] *vt* motiver.

motivated ['məutɪveɪtɪd] *a* motivé(e).

motivation [məutɪ'veɪʃən] *n* motivation *f*.

motive ['məutɪv] *n* motif *m*, mobile *m* ♦ *a* moteur(trice); **from the best (of)** ~s avec les meilleures intentions (du monde).

motley ['mɔtlɪ] *a* hétéroclite; bigarré(e), bariolé(e).

motor ['məutə*] *n* moteur *m*; (*Brit col*: *vehicle*) auto *f* ♦ *a* à moteur(trice).

motorbike ['məutəbaɪk] *n* moto *f*.

motorboat ['məutəbəut] *n* bateau *m* à moteur.

motorcar ['məutəkɑː] *n* (*Brit*) automobile *f*.

motorcoach ['məutəkəutʃ] *n* (*Brit*) car *m*.

motorcycle ['məutəsaɪkl] *n* vélomoteur *m*.

motorcyclist ['məutəsaɪklɪst] *n* motocycliste *m/f*.

motoring ['məutərɪŋ] (*Brit*) *n* tourisme *m* automobile ♦ *a* (*accident*) de voiture, de la route; ~ **holiday** vacances *fpl* en voiture; ~ **offence** infraction *f* au code de la route.

motorist ['məutərɪst] *n* automobiliste *m/f*.

motorize ['məutəraɪz] *vt* motoriser.

motor oil *n* huile *f* de graissage.

motor racing *n* (*Brit*) course *f* automobile.

motor scooter *n* scooter *m*.

motor vehicle *n* véhicule *m* automobile.

motorway ['məutəweɪ] *n* (*Brit*) autoroute *f*.

mottled ['mɔtld] *a* tacheté(e), marbré(e).

motto, ~es ['mɔtəu] *n* devise *f*.

mould, (*US*) **mold** [məuld] *n* moule *m*; (*mildew*) moisissure *f* ♦ *vt* mouler, modeler; (*fig*) façonner.

mo(u)lder ['məuldə*] *vi* (*decay*) moisir.

mo(u)lding ['məuldɪŋ] *n* (*ARCHIT*) moulure *f*.

mo(u)ldy ['məuldɪ] *a* moisi(e).

moult, (*US*) **molt** [məult] *vi* muer.

mound [maund] *n* monticule *m*, tertre *m*.

mount [maunt] *n* mont *m*, montagne *f*; (*horse*) monture *f*; (*for jewel etc*) monture ♦ *vt* monter; (*exhibition*) organiser, monter; (*picture*) monter sur carton; (*stamp*) coller dans un album ♦ *vi* (*also*: ~ **up**) s'élever, monter.

mountain ['mauntɪn] *n* montagne *f* ♦ *cpd* de (la) montagne; **to make a** ~ **out of a mole-hill** (*fig*) se faire une montagne d'un rien.

mountaineer [mauntɪ'nɪə*] *n* alpiniste *m/f*.

mountaineering [mauntɪ'nɪərɪŋ] *n* alpinisme *m*; **to go** ~ faire de l'alpinisme.

mountainous ['mauntɪnəs] *a* montagneux(euse).

mountain rescue team *n* colonne *f* de secours.

mountainside ['mauntɪnsaɪd] *n* flanc *m or* versant *m* de la montagne.

mounted ['mauntɪd] *a* monté(e).

Mount Everest *n* le mont Everest.

mourn [mɔːn] *vt* pleurer ♦ *vi*: **to** ~ **(for)** se lamenter (sur).

mourner ['mɔːnə*] *n* parent/e *or* ami/e du défunt; personne *f* en deuil *or* venue rendre hommage au défunt.

mournful ['mɔːnful] *a* triste, lugubre.

mourning ['mɔːnɪŋ] *n* deuil *m* ♦ *cpd* (*dress*) de deuil; **in** ~ en deuil.

mouse, *pl* **mice** [maus, maɪs] *n* (*also COMPUT*) souris *f*.

mousetrap ['maustræp] *n* souricière *f*.

mousse [muːs] *n* mousse *f*.

moustache [məs'tɑːʃ] *n* moustache(s) *f(pl)*.

mousy ['mausɪ] *a* (*person*) effacé(e); (*hair*) d'un châtain terne.

mouth [mauθ, ~s [mauθ, -ðz] *n* bouche *f*; (*of dog, cat*) gueule *f*; (*of river*) embouchure *f*; (*of bottle*) goulot *m*; (*opening*) orifice *m*.

mouthful ['mauθful] *n* bouchée *f*.

mouth organ *n* harmonica *m*.

mouthpiece ['mauθpiːs] *n* (*of musical instrument*) bec *m*, embouchure *f*; (*spokesman*) porte-parole *m inv*.

mouth-to-mouth ['mauθtə'mauθ] *a*: ~ **resuscitation** bouche à bouche *m*.

mouthwash ['mauθwɔʃ] *n* eau *f* dentifrice.

mouth-watering ['mauθwɔːtərɪŋ] *a* qui met l'eau à la bouche.

movable ['muːvəbl] *a* mobile.

move [muːv] *n* (*movement*) mouvement *m*; (*in game*) coup *m*; (*: turn to play*) tour *m*; (*change of house*) déménagement *m* ♦ *vt* déplacer, bouger; (*emotionally*) émouvoir; (*POL*: *resolution etc*) proposer ♦ *vi* (*gen*) bouger, remuer; (*traffic*) circuler; (*also*: ~ **house**) déménager; **to** ~ **towards** se diriger vers; **to** ~ **sb to do sth** pousser *or* inciter qn à faire qch; **to get a** ~ **on** se dépêcher, se remuer.

move about, **move around** *vi* (*fidget*) remuer; (*travel*) voyager, se déplacer.

move along vi se pousser.
move away vi s'en aller, s'éloigner.
move back vi revenir, retourner.
move forward vi avancer ♦ vt avancer;
(people) faire avancer.
move in vi (to a house) emménager.
move off vi s'éloigner, s'en aller.
move on vi se remettre en route ♦ vt
(onlookers) faire circuler.
move out vi (of house) déménager.
move over vi se pousser, se déplacer.
move up vi avancer; (employee) avoir de
l'avancement.
movement ['mu:vmənt] n mouvement m; ~
(of the bowels) (MED) selles fpl.
mover ['mu:və*] n auteur m d'une proposition.
movie ['mu:vɪ] n film m; **the** ~**s** le cinéma.
movie camera n caméra f.
moviegoer ['mu:vɪgəuə*] n (US) cinéphile m/
f.
moving ['mu:vɪŋ] a en mouvement; (touching)
émouvant(e) ♦ n (US) déménagement m.
mow, pt **mowed**, pp **mowed** or **mown**
[məu, -n] vt faucher; (lawn) tondre.
mow down vt faucher.
mower ['məuə*] n (also: **lawn**~) tondeuse f à
gazon.
Mozambique [məuzæm'bi:k] n Mozambique
m.
MP n abbr (= Military Police) PM; (Brit) =
Member of Parliament; (Canada) = Mounted
Police.
mpg n abbr = miles per gallon (30 mpg = 9,4
l. aux 100 km).
mph abbr = miles per hour (60 mph = 96 km/
h).
MPhil n abbr (US: = Master of Philosophy)
titre universitaire.
MPS n abbr (Brit) = Member of the
Pharmaceutical Society.
Mr, Mr. ['mɪstə*] n: ~ **X** Monsieur X, M. X.
MRC n abbr (Brit: = Medical Research
Council) conseil de la recherche médicale.
MRCP n abbr (Brit) = Member of the Royal
College of Physicians.
MRCS n abbr (Brit) = Member of the Royal
College of Surgeons.
MRCVS n abbr (Brit) = Member of the Royal
College of Veterinary Surgeons.
Mrs, Mrs. ['mɪsɪz] n: ~ **X** Madame X, Mme
X.
MS n abbr (= manuscript) ms; (= multiple
sclerosis) SEP f; (US: = Master of Science)
titre universitaire ♦ abbr (US POST) =
Mississippi.
Ms, Ms. [mɪz] n (= Miss or Mrs): ~ **X**
Madame X, Mme X.
MSA n abbr (US: = Master of Science in
Agriculture) titre universitaire.
MSC n abbr = **Manpower Services
Commission**.
MSc n abbr = **Master of Science**.
MSG n abbr = **monosodium glutamate**.
MST abbr (US: = Mountain Standard Time)
heure d'hiver des Montagnes Rocheuses.
MSW n abbr (US: = Master of Social Work)
titre universitaire.
MT n abbr (= machine translation) TM ♦ abbr
(US POST) = Montana.

Mt abbr (GEO: = mount) Mt.
much [mʌtʃ] a beaucoup de ♦ ad, n or pronoun
beaucoup; ~ **milk** beaucoup de lait; **how** ~
is it? combien est-ce que ça coûte?; **it's not**
~ ce n'est pas beaucoup; **too** ~ trop (de);
so ~ tant (de); **I like it very/so** ~ j'aime
beaucoup/tellement ça; **thank you very** ~
merci beaucoup; ~ **to my amazement** ... à
mon grand étonnement ....
muck [mʌk] n (mud) boue f; (dirt) ordures
fpl.
muck about vi (col) faire l'imbécile; (:
waste time) traînasser; (: tinker) bricoler;
tripoter.
muck in vi (Brit col) donner un coup de
main.
muck out vt (stable) nettoyer.
muck up vt (col: ruin) gâcher, esquinter;
(: dirty) salir.
muckraking ['mʌkreɪkɪŋ] n (fig: col)
déterrement m d'ordures.
mucky ['mʌkɪ] a (dirty) boueux(euse), sale.
mucus ['mju:kəs] n mucus m.
mud [mʌd] n boue f.
muddle ['mʌdl] n pagaille f; désordre m,
fouillis m ♦ vt (also: ~ up) brouiller, embrouiller; **to be in a** ~ (person) ne plus
savoir ou l'on en est; **to get in a** ~ (while
explaining etc) s'embrouiller.
muddle along vi aller son chemin tant bien
que mal.
muddle through vi se débrouiller.
muddle-headed [mʌdl'hɛdɪd] a (person) à
l'esprit embrouillé or confus, dans le
brouillard.
muddy ['mʌdɪ] a boueux(euse).
mud flats npl plage f de vase.
mudguard ['mʌdgɑ:d] n garde-boue m inv.
mudpack ['mʌdpæk] n masque m de beauté.
mud-slinging ['mʌdslɪŋɪŋ] n médisance f,
dénigrement m.
muff [mʌf] n manchon m ♦ vt (col: shot, catch
etc) rater, louper; **to** ~ **it** rater or louper son
coup.
muffin ['mʌfɪn] n petit pain rond et plat.
muffle ['mʌfl] vt (sound) assourdir, étouffer;
(against cold) emmitoufler.
muffled ['mʌfld] a étouffé(e), voilé(e).
muffler ['mʌflə*] n (scarf) cache-nez m inv;
(US AUT) silencieux m.
mufti ['mʌftɪ] n: **in** ~ en civil.
mug [mʌg] n (cup) tasse f (sans soucoupe); (:
for beer) chope f; (col: face) bouille f; (:
fool) poire f ♦ vt (assault) agresser; **it's a**
~**'s game** (Brit) c'est bon pour les imbéciles.
mug up vt (Brit col: also: ~ **up on**)
bosser, bûcher.
mugger ['mʌgə*] n agresseur m.
mugging ['mʌgɪŋ] n agression f.
muggy ['mʌgɪ] a lourd(e), moite.
mulatto, ~**es** [mju:'lætəu] n mulâtre/esse.
mulberry ['mʌlbrɪ] n (fruit) mûre f; (tree)
mûrier m.
mule [mju:l] n mule f.
mull [mʌl]: **to** ~ **over** vt réfléchir à, ruminer.
mulled [mʌld] a: ~ **wine** vin chaud.
multi... ['mʌltɪ] prefix multi....
multi-access ['mʌltɪ'æksɛs] a (COMPUT) à
accès multiple.

multicoloured, (US) **multicolored** ['mʌltɪkʌləd] a multicolore.
multifarious [mʌltɪ'fɛərɪəs] a divers(es); varié(e).
multilateral [mʌltɪ'lætərl] a (POL) multilatéral(e).
multi-level ['mʌltɪlɛvl] a (US) = **multistorey**.
multimillionaire [mʌltɪmɪljə'nɛə*] n milliardaire m/f.
multinational [mʌltɪ'næʃənl] n multinationale f ♦ a multinational(e).
multiple ['mʌltɪpl] a multiple ♦ n multiple m; (Brit: also: ~ **store**) magasin m à succursales (multiples).
multiple choice a à choix multiple.
multiple crash n carambolage m.
multiple sclerosis n sclérose f en plaques.
multiplication [mʌltɪplɪ'keɪʃən] n multiplication f.
multiplication table n table f de multiplication.
multiplicity [mʌltɪ'plɪsɪtɪ] n multiplicité f.
multiply ['mʌltɪplaɪ] vt multiplier ♦ vi se multiplier.
multiracial [mʌltɪ'reɪʃl] a multiracial(e).
multistorey ['mʌltɪ'stɔːrɪ] a (Brit: building) à étages; (: car park) à étages or niveaux multiples.
multitude ['mʌltɪtjuːd] n multitude f.
mum [mʌm] n (Brit) maman f ♦ a: to keep ~ ne pas souffler mot; ~'s the word! motus et bouche cousue!
mumble ['mʌmbl] vt, vi marmotter, marmonner.
mummify ['mʌmɪfaɪ] vt momifier.
mummy ['mʌmɪ] n (Brit: mother) maman f; (embalmed) momie f.
mumps [mʌmps] n oreillons mpl.
munch [mʌntʃ] vt, vi mâcher.
mundane [mʌn'deɪn] a banal(e), terre à terre inv.
municipal [mjuː'nɪsɪpl] a municipal(e).
municipality [mjuːnɪsɪ'pælɪtɪ] n municipalité f.
munitions [mjuː'nɪʃənz] npl munitions fpl.
mural ['mjuərl] n peinture murale.
murder ['mɜːdə*] n meurtre m, assassinat m ♦ vt assassiner; to commit ~ commettre un meurtre.
murderer ['mɜːdərə*] n meurtrier m, assassin m.
murderess ['mɜːdərɪs] n meurtrière f.
murderous ['mɜːdərəs] a meurtrier(ière).
murk [mɜːk] n obscurité f.
murky ['mɜːkɪ] a sombre, ténébreux(euse).
murmur ['mɜːmə*] n murmure m ♦ vt, vi murmurer; **heart** ~ (MED) souffle m au cœur.
MusB(ac) n abbr (= Bachelor of Music) titre universitaire.
muscle ['mʌsl] n muscle m.
muscle in vi s'imposer, s'immiscer.
muscular ['mʌskjulə*] a musculaire; (person, arm) musclé(e).
MusD(oc) n abbr (= Doctor of Music) titre universitaire.
muse [mjuːz] vi méditer, songer ♦ n muse f.
museum [mjuː'zɪəm] n musée m.
mush [mʌʃ] n bouillie f; (pej) sentimentalité f à l'eau de rose.

mushroom ['mʌʃrum] n champignon m ♦ vi (fig) pousser comme un (or des) champignon(s).
mushy ['mʌʃɪ] a en bouillie; (pej) à l'eau de rose.
music ['mjuːzɪk] n musique f.
musical ['mjuːzɪkl] a musical(e); (person) musicien(ne) ♦ n (show) comédie musicale.
music(al) box n boîte f à musique.
musical instrument n instrument m de musique.
music hall n music-hall m.
musician [mjuː'zɪʃən] n musicien/ne.
music stand n pupitre m à musique.
musk [mʌsk] n musc m.
musket ['mʌskɪt] n mousquet m.
muskrat ['mʌskræt] n rat musqué.
musk rose n (BOT) rose f muscade.
Muslim ['mʌzlɪm] a, n musulman(e).
muslin ['mʌzlɪn] n mousseline f.
musquash ['mʌskwɔʃ] n loutre f; (fur) rat m d'Amérique, ondatra m.
mussel ['mʌsl] n moule f.
must [mʌst] auxiliary vb (obligation): I ~ **do** it je dois le faire, il faut que je le fasse; (probability): he ~ **be there by now** il doit y être maintenant, il y est probablement maintenant; I ~ **have made a mistake** j'ai dû me tromper ♦ n nécessité f, impératif m; it's a ~ c'est indispensable.
mustache ['mʌstæʃ] n (US) = **moustache**.
mustard ['mʌstəd] n moutarde f.
mustard gas n ypérite f, gaz m moutarde.
muster ['mʌstə*] vt rassembler; (also: ~ **up**: strength, courage) rassembler.
mustiness ['mʌstɪnɪs] n goût m de moisi; odeur f de moisi or de renfermé.
mustn't ['mʌsnt] = **must not**.
musty ['mʌstɪ] a qui sent le moisi or le renfermé.
mutant ['mjuːtənt] a mutant(e) ♦ n mutant m.
mutate [mjuː'teɪt] vi subir une mutation.
mutation [mjuː'teɪʃən] n mutation f.
mute [mjuːt] a, n muet(te).
muted ['mjuːtɪd] a (noise) sourd(e), assourdi(e); (criticism) voilé(e); (MUS) en sourdine; (: trumpet) bouché(e).
mutilate ['mjuːtɪleɪt] vt mutiler.
mutilation [mjuːtɪ'leɪʃən] n mutilation f.
mutinous ['mjuːtɪnəs] a (troops) mutiné(e); (attitude) rebelle.
mutiny ['mjuːtɪnɪ] n mutinerie f ♦ vi se mutiner.
mutter ['mʌtə*] vt, vi marmonner, marmotter.
mutton ['mʌtn] n mouton m.
mutual ['mjuːtʃuəl] a mutuel(le), réciproque.
mutually ['mjuːtʃuəlɪ] ad mutuellement, réciproquement.
muzzle ['mʌzl] n museau m; (protective device) muselière f; (of gun) gueule f ♦ vt museler.
MVP n abbr (US SPORT) = most valuable player.
MW abbr (= medium wave) PO.
my [maɪ] a mon(ma), mes pl.
myopic [maɪ'ɔpɪk] a myope.
myriad ['mɪrɪəd] n myriade f.
myself [maɪ'sɛlf] pronoun (reflexive) me; (emphatic) moi-même; (after prep) moi.

mysterious [mɪs'tɪərɪəs] *a* mystérieux(euse).
mystery ['mɪstərɪ] *n* mystère *m*.
mystery story *n* roman *m* à suspense.
mystic ['mɪstɪk] *n* mystique *m/f* ♦ *a* (*mysterious*) ésotérique.
mystical ['mɪstɪkl] *a* mystique.
mystify ['mɪstɪfaɪ] *vt* mystifier; (*puzzle*) ébahir.
mystique [mɪs'ti:k] *n* mystique *f*.
myth [mɪθ] *n* mythe *m*.
mythical ['mɪθɪkl] *a* mythique.
mythological [mɪθə'lɔdʒɪkl] *a* mythologique.
mythology [mɪ'θɔlədʒɪ] *n* mythologie *f*.

N

N, n [ɛn] *n* (*letter*) N, n *m*; **N for Nellie**, (*US*) **N for Nan** N comme Nicolas.
N *abbr* (= *north*) N.
NA *n abbr* (*US*: = *Narcotics Anonymous*) association d'aide aux drogués; (*US*) = *National Academy*.
n/a *abbr* (= *not applicable*) n.a.; (*COMM etc*) = *no account*.
NAACP *n abbr* (*US*) = *National Association for the Advancement of Colored People*.
NAAFI ['næfɪ] *n abbr* (*Brit*: = *Navy, Army & Air Force Institute*) *organisme responsable des magasins et cantines de l'armée*.
nab [næb] *vt* (*col*) pincer, attraper.
NACU *n abbr* (*US*) = *National Association of Colleges and Universities*.
nadir ['neɪdɪə*] *n* (*ASTRONOMY*) nadir *m*; (*fig*) fond *m*, point *m* extrême.
nag [næg] *vt* (*person*) être toujours après, reprendre sans arrêt ♦ *n* (*pej: horse*) canasson *m*; (*person*): **she's an awful ~** elle est constamment après lui (*or* eux *etc*), elle est terriblement casse-pieds.
nagging ['nægɪŋ] *a* (*doubt, pain*) persistant(e) ♦ *n* remarques continuelles.
nail [neɪl] *n* (*human*) ongle *m*; (*metal*) clou *m* ♦ *vt* clouer; **to ~ sb down to a date/price** contraindre qn à accepter *or* donner une date/un prix; **to pay cash on the ~** (*Brit*) payer rubis sur l'ongle.
nailbrush ['neɪlbrʌʃ] *n* brosse *f* à ongles.
nailfile ['neɪlfaɪl] *n* lime *f* à ongles.
nail polish *n* vernis *m* à ongles.
nail polish remover *n* dissolvant *m*.
nail scissors *npl* ciseaux *mpl* à ongles.
nail varnish *n* (*Brit*) = **nail polish**.
Nairobi [naɪ'rəubɪ] *n* Nairobi.
naïve [naɪ'i:v] *a* naïf(ïve).
naïveté [naɪ'i:vteɪ], **naïvety** [naɪ'i:vɪtɪ] *n* naïveté *f*.
naked ['neɪkɪd] *a* nu(e); **with the ~ eye** à l'œil nu.
nakedness *n* nudité *f*.
NALGO ['nælgəu] *n abbr* (*Brit*: = *National and Local Government Officers' Association*) *syndicat des agents de la fonction publique*.

NAM *n abbr* (*US*) = *National Association of Manufacturers*.
name [neɪm] *n* nom *m*; (*reputation*) réputation *f* ♦ *vt* nommer; citer; (*price, date*) fixer, donner; **by ~** par son nom; de nom; **in the ~ of** au nom de; **what's your ~?** quel est votre nom?; **my ~ is Peter** je m'appelle Peter; **to take sb's ~ and address** relever l'identité de qn *or* les nom et adresse de qn; **to make a ~ for o.s.** se faire un nom; **to get (o.s.) a bad ~** se faire une mauvaise réputation; **to call sb ~s** traiter qn de tous les noms.
name dropping *n* mention *f* (pour se faire valoir) du nom de personnalités qu'on connaît (ou prétend connaître).
nameless ['neɪmlɪs] *a* sans nom; (*witness, contributor*) anonyme.
namely ['neɪmlɪ] *ad* à savoir.
nameplate ['neɪmpleɪt] *n* (*on door etc*) plaque *f*.
namesake ['neɪmseɪk] *n* homonyme *m*.
nanny ['nænɪ] *n* bonne *f* d'enfants.
nanny goat *n* chèvre *f*.
nap [næp] *n* (*sleep*) (petit) somme ♦ *vi*: **to be caught ~ping** être pris(e) à l'improviste *or* en défaut.
NAPA *n abbr* (*US*: = *National Association of Performing Artists*) *syndicat des gens du spectacle*.
napalm ['neɪpɑ:m] *n* napalm *m*.
nape [neɪp] *n*: **~ of the neck** nuque *f*.
napkin ['næpkɪn] *n* serviette *f* (de table).
Naples ['neɪplz] *n* Naples.
Napoleonic [nəpəulɪ'ɔnɪk] *a* napoléonien(ne).
nappy ['næpɪ] *n* (*Brit*) couche *f* (*gen pl*).
nappy liner *n* (*Brit*) protège-couche *m*.
narcissistic [nɑ:sɪ'sɪstɪk] *a* narcissique.
narcissus, *pl* **narcissi** [nɑ:'sɪsəs, -saɪ] *n* narcisse *m*.
narcotic [nɑ:'kɔtɪk] *n* (*MED*) narcotique *m*; **~s** *npl* (*drugs*) stupéfiants *mpl*.
nark [nɑ:k] *vt* (*Brit col*) mettre en rogne.
narrate [nə'reɪt] *vt* raconter, narrer.
narration [nə'reɪʃən] *n* narration *f*.
narrative ['nærətɪv] *n* récit *m* ♦ *a* narratif(ive).
narrator [nə'reɪtə*] *n* narrateur/trice.
narrow ['nærəu] *a* étroit(e); (*fig*) restreint(e), limité(e) ♦ *vi* devenir plus étroit, se rétrécir; **to have a ~ escape** l'échapper belle; **to ~ sth down to** réduire qch à.
narrow gauge *a* (*RAIL*) à voie étroite.
narrowly ['nærəulɪ] *ad*: **he ~ missed injury/the tree** il a failli se blesser/rentrer dans l'arbre; **he only ~ missed the target** il a manqué la cible de peu *or* de justesse.
narrow-minded [nærəu'maɪndɪd] *a* à l'esprit étroit, borné(e).
NAS *n abbr* (*US*) = *National Academy of Sciences*.
NASA ['næsə] *n abbr* (*US*: = *National Aeronautics and Space Administration*) NASA *f*.
nasal ['neɪzl] *a* nasal(e).
Nassau ['næsɔ:] *n* (*in Bahamas*) Nassau.
nastily ['nɑ:stɪlɪ] *ad* (*say, act*) méchamment.
nastiness ['nɑ:stɪnɪs] *n* (*of person, remark*) méchanceté *f*.
nasturtium [nəs'tə:ʃəm] *n* capucine *f*.
nasty ['nɑ:stɪ] *a* (*person*) méchant(e); très

désagréable; (*smell*) dégoûtant(e); (*wound*, *situation*) mauvais(e), vilain(e); (*weather*) affreux(euse); **to turn** ~ (*situation*) mal tourner; (*weather*) se gâter; (*person*) devenir méchant; **it's a ~ business** c'est une sale affaire.

NAS/UWT *n abbr* (*Brit*: = *National Association of Schoolmasters/Union of Women Teachers*) *syndicat enseignant*.

nation ['neɪʃən] *n* nation *f*.

national ['næʃənl] *a* national(e) ♦ *n* (*abroad*) ressortissant/e; (*when home*) national/e.

national anthem *n* hymne national.

national debt *n* dette publique.

national dress *n* costume national.

National Guard *n* (*US*) milice *f* (*de volontaires dans chaque État*).

National Health Service (NHS) *n* (*Brit*) service national de santé, ≈ Sécurité Sociale.

National Insurance *n* (*Brit*) ≈ Sécurité Sociale.

nationalism ['næʃnəlɪzəm] *n* nationalisme *m*.

nationalist ['næʃnəlɪst] *a*, *n* nationaliste (*m/f*).

nationality [næʃə'nælɪtɪ] *n* nationalité *f*.

nationalization [næʃnəlaɪ'zeɪʃən] *n* nationalisation *f*.

nationalize ['næʃnəlaɪ] *vt* nationaliser.

nationally ['næʃnəlɪ] *ad* du point de vue national; dans le pays entier.

national park *n* parc national.

national press *n* presse nationale.

National Security Council *n* (*US*) conseil national de sécurité.

national service *n* (*MIL*) service *m* militaire.

nation-wide ['neɪʃənwaɪd] *a* s'étendant à l'ensemble du pays; (*problem*) à l'échelle du pays entier ♦ *ad* à travers *or* dans tout le pays.

native ['neɪtɪv] *n* habitant/e du pays, autochtone *m/f*; (*in colonies*) indigène *m/f* ♦ *a* du pays, indigène; (*country*) natal(e); (*language*) maternel(le); (*ability*) inné(e); **a ~ of Russia** une personne originaire de Russie; **a ~ speaker of French** une personne de langue maternelle française.

Nativity [nə'tɪvɪtɪ] *n* (*REL*): **the ~** la Nativité.

NATO ['neɪtəu] *n abbr* (= *North Atlantic Treaty Organization*) OTAN *f*.

NATSOPA [næt'səupə] *n abbr* (*Brit*: = *National Society of Operative Printers, Graphical and Media Personnel*) *syndicat de la presse et des industries graphiques*.

natter ['nætə*] *vi* (*Brit*) bavarder.

NATTKE *n abbr* (*Brit*: = *National Association of Television, Theatrical and Kinematographic Employees*) *syndicat des employés de la télévision, du théâtre et du cinéma*.

natural ['nætʃrəl] *a* naturel(le); **to die of ~ causes** mourir d'une mort naturelle.

natural childbirth *n* accouchement *m* sans douleur.

natural gas *n* gaz naturel.

naturalist ['nætʃrəlɪst] *n* naturaliste *m/f*.

naturalization ['nætʃrəlaɪ'zeɪʃən] *n* naturalisation *f*; acclimatation *f*.

naturalize ['nætʃrəlaɪz] *vt* naturaliser; (*plant*) acclimater; **to become ~d** (*person*) se faire naturaliser.

naturally ['nætʃrəlɪ] *ad* naturellement.

naturalness ['nætʃrəlnɪs] *n* naturel *m*.

natural resources *npl* ressources naturelles.

natural wastage *n* (*INDUSTRY*) départs naturels et volontaires.

nature ['neɪtʃə*] *n* nature *f*; **by ~** par tempérament, de nature; **documents of a confidential ~** documents à caractère confidentiel.

-natured ['neɪtʃəd] *suffix*: **ill~** qui a mauvais caractère.

nature reserve *n* (*Brit*) réserve naturelle.

nature trail *n* sentier de découverte de la nature.

naturist ['neɪtʃərɪst] *n* naturiste *m/f*.

naught [nɔ:t] *n* = **nought**.

naughtiness ['nɔ:tɪnɪs] *n* (*of child*) désobéissance *f*; (*of story etc*) grivoiserie *f*.

naughty ['nɔ:tɪ] *a* (*child*) vilain(e), pas sage; (*story*, *film*) grivois(e).

nausea ['nɔ:sɪə] *n* nausée *f*.

nauseate ['nɔ:sɪeɪt] *vt* écœurer, donner la nausée à.

nauseating ['nɔ:sɪeɪtɪŋ] *a* écœurant(e), dégoûtant(e).

nauseous ['nɔ:sɪəs] *a* nauséabond(e), écœurant(e); (*feeling sick*): **to be ~** avoir des nausées.

nautical ['nɔ:tɪkl] *a* nautique.

nautical mile *n* mille marin (= 1853 m).

naval ['neɪvl] *a* naval(e).

naval officer *n* officier *m* de marine.

nave [neɪv] *n* nef *f*.

navel ['neɪvl] *n* nombril *m*.

navigable ['nævɪgəbl] *a* navigable.

navigate ['nævɪgeɪt] *vt* diriger, piloter ♦ *vi* naviguer; (*AUT*) indiquer la route à suivre.

navigation [nævɪ'geɪʃən] *n* navigation *f*.

navigator ['nævɪgeɪtə*] *n* navigateur *m*.

navvy ['nævɪ] *n* (*Brit*) terrassier *m*.

navy ['neɪvɪ] *n* marine *f*; **Department of the N~** (*US*) ministère *m* de la Marine.

navy(-blue) ['neɪvɪ('blu:)] *a* bleu marine *inv*.

Nazareth ['næzərɪθ] *n* Nazareth.

Nazi ['nɑ:tsɪ] *a* nazi(e) ♦ *n* Nazi/e.

NB *abbr* (= *nota bene*) NB; (*Canada*) = *New Brunswick*.

NBA *n abbr* (*US*) = *National Basketball Association, National Boxing Association*.

NBC *n abbr* (*US*: = *National Broadcasting Company*) *chaîne de télévision*.

NBS *n abbr* (*US*: = *National Bureau of Standards*) *office de normalisation*.

NC *abbr* (*COMM etc*) = *no charge*; (*US POST*) = *North Carolina*.

NCB *n abbr* (*Brit*: old: = *National Coal Board*) *charbonnages britanniques*.

NCC *n abbr* (*Brit*: = *Nature Conservancy Council*) *organisme de protection de la nature*; (*US*) = *National Council of Churches*.

NCCL *n abbr* (*Brit*: = *National Council for Civil Liberties*) *association de défense des libertés publiques*.

NCO *n abbr* = **non-commissioned officer**.

ND *abbr* (*US POST*) = *North Dakota*.

NE *abbr* (*US POST*) = *Nebraska, New England*.

NEA *n abbr* (*US*) = *National Education Association*.

neap [ni:p] *n* (*also*: **~tide**) mortes-eaux *fpl*.

Neapolitan [nɪəˈpɒlɪtən] a napolitain(e) ♦ n
Napolitain/e.

near [nɪə*] a proche ♦ ad près ♦ prep (also: ~
to) près de ♦ vt approcher de; ~ here/there
près d'ici/non loin de là; **£25,000 or ~est
offer** (Brit) 25 000 livres à débattre; **in the ~
future** dans un proche avenir; **the building is
~ing completion** le bâtiment est presque
terminé; **to come ~** vi s'approcher.

nearby [nɪəˈbaɪ] a proche ♦ ad tout près, à
proximité.

Near East n: **the ~** le Proche-Orient.

nearer [ˈnɪərə*] a plus proche ♦ ad plus près.

nearly [ˈnɪəlɪ] ad presque; **I ~ fell** j'ai failli
tomber; **it's not ~ big enough** ce n'est
vraiment pas assez grand, c'est loin d'être
assez grand.

near miss n collision évitée de justesse;
(when aiming) coup manqué de peu or de
justesse.

nearness [ˈnɪənɪs] n proximité f.

nearside [ˈnɪəsaɪd] (AUT) n (right-hand drive)
côté m gauche; (left-hand drive) côté droit ♦
a de gauche; de droite.

near-sighted [nɪəˈsaɪtɪd] a myope.

neat [niːt] a (person, work) soigné(e); (room
etc) bien tenu(e) or rangé(e); (solution,
plan) habile; (spirits) pur(e); **I drink it ~** je
le bois sec or sans eau.

neatly [ˈniːtlɪ] ad avec soin or ordre;
habilement.

neatness [ˈniːtnɪs] n (tidiness) netteté f;
(skilfulness) habileté f.

nebulous [ˈnɛbjuləs] a nébuleux(euse).

necessarily [ˈnɛsɪsrɪlɪ] ad nécessairement; **not
~ pas nécessairement or forcément.

necessary [ˈnɛsɪsrɪ] a nécessaire; **if ~** si
besoin est, le cas échéant.

necessitate [nɪˈsɛsɪteɪt] vt nécessiter.

necessity [nɪˈsɛsɪtɪ] n nécessité f; chose
nécessaire or essentielle; **in case of ~** en cas
d'urgence.

neck [nɛk] n cou m; (of horse, garment)
encolure f; (of bottle) goulot m ♦ vi (col) se
peloter; **~ and ~** à égalité; **to stick one's ~
out** (col) se mouiller.

necklace [ˈnɛklɪs] n collier m.

neckline [ˈnɛklaɪn] n encolure f.

necktie [ˈnɛktaɪ] n (esp US) cravate f.

nectar [ˈnɛktə*] n nectar m.

nectarine [ˈnɛktərɪn] n brugnon m, nectarine
f.

NEDC n abbr (Brit: = National Economic
Development Council) conseil national pour le
développement économique.

Neddy [ˈnɛdɪ] n abbr (Brit col) = **NEDC**.

née [neɪ] a: **~ Scott** née Scott.

need [niːd] n besoin m ♦ vt avoir besoin de; **to
~ to do** devoir faire; avoir besoin de faire;
you don't ~ to go vous n'avez pas besoin or
vous n'êtes pas obligé de partir; **a signature
is ~ed** il faut une signature; **to be in ~ of** or
have ~ of avoir besoin de; **£10 will meet my
immediate ~s** 10 livres suffiront pour mes
besoins immédiats; **in case of ~** en cas de
besoin, au besoin; **there's no ~ to do ...** il
n'y a pas lieu de faire ..., il n'est pas
nécessaire de faire ...; **there's no ~ for that**
ce n'est pas la peine, cela n'est pas

nécessaire.

needle [ˈniːdl] n aiguille f; (on record player)
saphir m ♦ vt (col) asticoter, tourmenter.

needlecord [ˈniːdlkɔːd] n (Brit) velours m
milleraies.

needless [ˈniːdlɪs] a inutile; **~ to say, ...**
inutile de dire que ...

needlessly [ˈniːdlɪslɪ] ad inutilement.

needlework [ˈniːdlwəːk] n (activity) travaux
mpl d'aiguille; (object) ouvrage m.

needn't [ˈniːdnt] = **need not**.

needy [ˈniːdɪ] a nécessiteux(euse).

negation [nɪˈgeɪʃən] n négation f.

negative [ˈnɛgətɪv] n (PHOT, ELEC) négatif m;
(LING) terme m de négation ♦ a négatif(ive);
to answer in the ~ répondre par la négative.

neglect [nɪˈglɛkt] vt négliger ♦ n (of person,
duty, garden) le fait de négliger; (state of) ~
abandon m; **to ~ to do sth** négliger or omettre de faire qch.

neglected [nɪˈglɛktɪd] a négligé(e), à
l'abandon.

neglectful [nɪˈglɛktful] a (gen) négligent(e);
to be ~ of sb/sth négliger qn/qch.

negligee [ˈnɛglɪʒeɪ] n déshabillé m.

negligence [ˈnɛglɪdʒəns] n négligence f.

negligent [ˈnɛglɪdʒənt] a négligent(e).

negligently [ˈnɛglɪdʒəntlɪ] ad par négligence;
(offhandedly) négligemment.

negligible [ˈnɛglɪdʒɪbl] a négligeable.

negotiable [nɪˈgəuʃɪəbl] a négociable; **not ~**
(cheque) non négociable.

negotiate [nɪˈgəuʃɪeɪt] vi négocier ♦ vt
(COMM); (obstacle) franchir,
négocier; (bend in road) négocier; **to ~ with
sb for sth** négocier avec qn en vue d'obtenir
qch.

negotiation [nɪgəuʃɪˈeɪʃən] n négociation f,
pourparlers mpl; **to enter into ~s with sb**
engager des négociations avec qn.

negotiator [nɪˈgəuʃɪeɪtə*] n négociateur/trice.

Negress [ˈniːgrɪs] n négresse f.

Negro [ˈniːgrəu] a (gen) noir(e); (music, arts)
nègre, noir ♦ n (pl: ~es) Noir/e.

neigh [neɪ] vi hennir.

neighbour, (US) **neighbor** [ˈneɪbə*] n voisin/
e.

neighbo(u)rhood [ˈneɪbəhud] n quartier m;
voisinage m.

neighbo(u)ring [ˈneɪbərɪŋ] a voisin(e),
avoisinant(e).

neighbo(u)rly [ˈneɪbəlɪ] a obligeant(e);
(relations) de bon voisinage.

neither [ˈnaɪðə*] a, pronoun aucun(e) (des
deux), ni l'un(e) ni l'autre ♦ cj: **I didn't
move and ~ did Claude** je n'ai pas bougé,
(et) Claude non plus; ..., **~ did I refuse** ...,
(et or mais) je n'ai pas non plus refusé ♦ ad:
~ good nor bad ni bon ni mauvais.

neo... [ˈniːəu] prefix néo-.

neolithic [niːəuˈlɪθɪk] a néolithique.

neologism [nɪˈɒlədʒɪzəm] n néologisme m.

neon [ˈniːɒn] n néon m.

neon light n lampe f au néon.

neon sign n enseigne (lumineuse) au néon.

Nepal [nɪˈpɔːl] n Népal m.

nephew [ˈnɛvjuː] n neveu m.

nepotism [ˈnɛpətɪzəm] n népotisme m.

nerve [nəːv] n nerf m; (bravery) sang-froid m,

courage *m*; (*cheek*) aplomb *m*, toupet *m*; **he gets on my ~s** il m'énerve; **to have a fit of ~s** avoir le trac; **to lose one's ~** (*self-confidence*) perdre son sang-froid.

nerve centre *n* (*ANAT*) centre nerveux; (*fig*) centre névralgique.

nerve gas *n* gaz *m* neuroplégique.

nerve-racking ['nə:vrækɪŋ] *a* angoissant(e).

nervous ['nə:vəs] *a* nerveux(euse); (*apprehensive*) inquiet(ète), plein(e) d'appréhension.

nervous breakdown *n* dépression nerveuse.

nervously ['nə:vəslɪ] *ad* nerveusement.

nervousness ['nə:vəsnɪs] *n* nervosité *f*; inquiétude *f*, appréhension *f*.

nest [nɛst] *n* nid *m* ♦ *vi* (se) nicher, faire son nid; **~ of tables** table *f* gigogne.

nest egg *n* (*fig*) bas *m* de laine, magot *m*.

nestle ['nɛsl] *vi* se blottir.

nestling ['nɛstlɪŋ] *n* oisillon *m*.

net [nɛt] *n* (*also fabric*) filet *m* ♦ *a* net(te) ♦ *vt* (*fish etc*) prendre au filet; (*money: subj: person*) toucher; (: *deal, sale*) rapporter; **~ of tax** net d'impôt; **he earns £10,000 ~ per year** il gagne 10 000 livres net par an.

netball ['nɛtbɔ:l] *n* netball *m*.

net curtains *npl* voilages *mpl*.

Netherlands ['nɛðələndz] *npl*: **the ~** les Pays-Bas *mpl*.

net profit *n* bénéfice net.

nett [nɛt] *a* = **net**.

netting ['nɛtɪŋ] *n* (*for fence etc*) treillis *m*, grillage *m*; (*fabric*) voile *m*.

nettle ['nɛtl] *n* ortie *f*.

network ['nɛtwə:k] *n* réseau *m* ♦ *vt* (*RADIO*, *TV*) diffuser sur l'ensemble du réseau; (*computers*) interconnecter.

neuralgia [njuə'rældʒə] *n* névralgie *f*.

neurosis, *pl* **neuroses** [njuə'rəusıs, -si:z] *n* névrose *f*.

neurotic [njuə'rɔtık] *a*, *n* névrosé(e).

neuter ['nju:tə*] *a*, *n* neutre (*m*) ♦ *vt* (*cat etc*) châtrer, couper.

neutral ['nju:trəl] *a* neutre ♦ *n* (*AUT*) point mort.

neutrality [nju:'trælıtı] *n* neutralité *f*.

neutralize ['nju:trəlaız] *vt* neutraliser.

neutron bomb ['nju:trɔn-] *n* bombe *f* à neutrons.

never ['nɛvə*] *ad* (ne ...) jamais; **~ again** plus jamais; **~ in my life** jamais de ma vie; *see also* **mind**.

never-ending [nɛvər'ɛndıŋ] *a* interminable.

nevertheless [nɛvəðə'lɛs] *ad* néanmoins, malgré tout.

new [nju:] *a* nouveau(nouvelle); (*brand new*) neuf(neuve); **as good as ~** comme neuf.

newborn ['nju:bɔ:n] *a* nouveau-né(e).

newcomer ['nju:kʌmə*] *n* nouveau venu/nouvelle venue.

new-fangled ['nju:fæŋgld] *a* (*pej*) ultramoderne (et farfelu(e)).

new-found ['nju:faund] *a* de fraîche date; (*friend*) nouveau/nouvelle.

Newfoundland ['nju:fənlənd] *n* Terre-Neuve *f*.

New Guinea *n* Nouvelle-Guinée *f*.

newly ['nju:lı] *ad* nouvellement, récemment.

newly-weds ['nju:lıwɛdz] *npl* jeunes mariés *mpl*.

new moon *n* nouvelle lune.

newness ['nju:nıs] *n* nouveauté *f*; (*of fabric, clothes etc*) état neuf.

New Orleans [-'ɔ:li:ənz] *n* la Nouvelle-Orléans.

news [nju:z] *n* nouvelle(s) *f(pl)*; (*RADIO*, *TV*) informations *fpl*; **a piece of ~** une nouvelle; **good/bad ~** bonne/mauvaise nouvelle; **financial ~** (*PRESS*, *RADIO*, *TV*) page financière.

news agency *n* agence *f* de presse.

newsagent ['nju:zeɪdʒənt] *n* (*Brit*) marchand *m* de journaux.

news bulletin *n* (*RADIO*, *TV*) bulletin *m* d'informations.

newscaster ['nju:zkɑ:stə*] *n* (*RADIO*, *TV*) présentateur/trice.

newsdealer ['nju:zdi:lə*] *n* (*US*) = **newsagent**.

news flash *n* flash *m* d'information.

newsletter ['nju:zlɛtə*] *n* bulletin *m*.

newspaper ['nju:zpeɪpə*] *n* journal *m*; **daily ~** quotidien *m*; **weekly ~** hebdomadaire *m*.

newsprint ['nju:zprɪnt] *n* papier *m* (de) journal.

newsreader ['nju:zri:də*] *n* = **newscaster**.

newsreel ['nju:zri:l] *n* actualités (filmées).

newsroom ['nju:zru:m] *n* (*PRESS*) salle *f* de rédaction; (*RADIO*, *TV*) studio *m*.

news stand *n* kiosque *m* à journaux.

newt [nju:t] *n* triton *m*.

New Year *n* Nouvel An; **Happy ~!** Bonne Année!; **to wish sb a happy ~** souhaiter la Bonne Année à qn.

New Year's Day *n* le jour de l'An.

New Year's Eve *n* la Saint-Sylvestre.

New York [-'jɔ:k] *n* New York; (*also*: **~ State**) New York *m*.

New Zealand [-'zi:lənd] *n* Nouvelle-Zélande *f* ♦ *a* néo-zélandais(e).

New Zealander [-'zi:ləndə*] *n* Néo-Zélandais/e.

next [nɛkst] *a* (*seat, room*) voisin(e), d'à côté; (*meeting, bus stop*) suivant(e); prochain(e) ♦ *ad* la fois suivante; la prochaine fois; (*afterwards*) ensuite; **~ to** *prep* à côté de; **~ to nothing** presque rien; **~ time** *ad* la prochaine fois; **the ~ day** le lendemain, le jour suivant *or* d'après; **~ week** la semaine prochaine; **the ~ week** la semaine suivante; **~ year** l'année prochaine; **"turn to the ~ page"** "voir page suivante"; **who's ~?** c'est à qui?; **the week after ~** dans deux semaines; **when do we meet ~?** quand nous revoyons-nous?

next door *ad* à côté.

next-of-kin ['nɛkstəv'kɪn] *n* parent *m* le plus proche.

NF *n abbr* (*Brit POL*: = *National Front*) ≈ FN ♦ *abbr* (*Canada*) = *Newfoundland*.

NFL *n abbr* (*US*) = *National Football League*.

NFU *n abbr* (*Brit*: = *National Farmers' Union*) syndicat des exploitants agricoles.

NG *abbr* (*US*) = **National Guard**.

NGA *n abbr* (*Brit*: = *National Graphical Association*) *syndicat des industries graphiques*.

NGO *n abbr* (*US*: = *non-governmental*

mpl.

organization) ONG *f*.

NH *abbr* (*US POST*) = New Hampshire.

NHL *n abbr* (*US*) = National Hockey League.

NHS *n abbr* (*Brit*) = **National Health Service**.

NI *abbr* = Northern Ireland; (*Brit*) = **National Insurance**.

Niagara Falls [naɪˈægərə-] *npl*: **the ~** les chutes *fpl* du Niagara.

nib [nɪb] *n* (*of pen*) (bec *m* de) plume *f*.

nibble [ˈnɪbl] *vt* grignoter.

Nicaragua [nɪkəˈrægjuə] *n* Nicaragua *m*.

Nicaraguan [nɪkəˈrægjuən] *a* nicaraguayen(ne) ♦ *n* Nicaraguayen/ne.

nice [naɪs] *a* (*holiday, trip, taste*) agréable; (*flat, picture*) joli(e); (*person*) gentil(le); (*distinction, point*) subtil(e).

nice-looking [ˈnaɪslukɪŋ] *a* joli(e).

nicely [ˈnaɪslɪ] *ad* agréablement; joliment; gentiment; subtilement; **that will do ~** ce sera parfait.

niceties [ˈnaɪsɪtɪz] *npl* subtilités *fpl*.

niche [niːʃ] *n* (*ARCHIT*) niche *f*.

nick [nɪk] *n* encoche *f*; (*Brit col*): **in good ~** en bon état ♦ *vt* (*cut*): **to ~ o.s.** se couper; (*col: steal*) faucher, piquer; (*: Brit: arrest*) choper, pincer; **in the ~ of time** juste à temps.

nickel [ˈnɪkl] *n* nickel *m*; (*US*) pièce *f* de 5 cents.

nickname [ˈnɪkneɪm] *n* surnom *m* ♦ *vt* surnommer.

Nicosia [nɪkəˈsiːə] *n* Nicosie.

nicotine [ˈnɪkətiːn] *n* nicotine *f*.

niece [niːs] *n* nièce *f*.

nifty [ˈnɪftɪ] *a* (*col: car, jacket*) qui a du chic *or* de la classe; (*: gadget, tool*) astucieux(euse).

Niger [ˈnaɪdʒə*] *n* (*country, river*) Niger *m*.

Nigeria [naɪˈdʒɪərɪə] *n* Nigéria *m or f*.

Nigerian [naɪˈdʒɪərɪən] *a* nigérien(ne) ♦ *n* Nigérien/ne.

niggardly [ˈnɪgədlɪ] *a* (*person*) parcimonieux(euse), pingre; (*allowance, amount*) misérable.

nigger [ˈnɪgə*] *n* (*col!: highly offensive*) nègre/négresse.

niggle [ˈnɪgl] *vt* tracasser ♦ *vi* (*find fault*) trouver toujours à redire; (*fuss*) n'être jamais content(e).

niggling [ˈnɪglɪŋ] *a* tatillon(ne); (*detail*) insignifiant(e); (*doubt, pain*) persistant(e).

night [naɪt] *n* nuit *f*; (*evening*) soir *m*; **at ~** la nuit; **by ~** de nuit; **in the ~, during the ~** pendant la nuit; **the ~ before last** avant-hier soir.

night-bird [ˈnaɪtbəːd] *n* oiseau *m* nocturne; (*fig*) couche-tard *m inv*, noctambule *m/f*.

nightcap [ˈnaɪtkæp] *n boisson prise avant le coucher*.

night club *n* boîte *f* de nuit.

nightdress [ˈnaɪtdrɛs] *n* chemise *f* de nuit.

nightfall [ˈnaɪtfɔːl] *n* tombée *f* de la nuit.

nightie [ˈnaɪtɪ] *n* chemise *f* de nuit.

nightingale [ˈnaɪtɪŋgeɪl] *n* rossignol *m*.

night life *n* vie *f* nocturne.

nightly [ˈnaɪtlɪ] *a* de chaque nuit *or* soir; (*by night*) nocturne ♦ *ad* chaque nuit *or* soir; nuitamment.

nightmare [ˈnaɪtmɛə*] *n* cauchemar *m*.

night porter *n* gardien *m* de nuit, concierge *m* de service la nuit.

night safe *n* coffre *m* de nuit.

night school *n* cours *mpl* du soir.

nightshade [ˈnaɪtʃeɪd] *n*: **deadly ~** (*BOT*) belladone *f*.

nightshift [ˈnaɪtʃɪft] *n* équipe *f* de nuit.

night-time [ˈnaɪttaɪm] *n* nuit *f*.

night watchman *n* veilleur *m* de nuit; poste *m* de nuit.

nihilism [ˈnaɪɪlɪzəm] *n* nihilisme *m*.

nil [nɪl] *n* rien *m*; (*Brit SPORT*) zéro *m*.

Nile [naɪl] *n*: **the ~** le Nil.

nimble [ˈnɪmbl] *a* agile.

nine [naɪn] *num* neuf.

nineteen [ˈnaɪnˈtiːn] *num* dix-neuf.

ninety [ˈnaɪntɪ] *num* quatre-vingt-dix.

ninth [naɪnθ] *num* neuvième.

nip [nɪp] *vt* pincer ♦ *vi* (*Brit col*): **to ~ out/down/up** sortir/descendre/monter en vitesse ♦ *n* pincement *m*; (*drink*) petit verre; **to ~ into a shop** faire un saut dans un magasin.

nipple [ˈnɪpl] *n* (*ANAT*) mamelon *m*, bout *m* du sein.

nippy [ˈnɪpɪ] *a* (*Brit: person*) alerte, leste; (*: car*) nerveux(euse).

nit [nɪt] *n* (*in hair*) lente *f*; (*col: idiot*) imbécile *m/f*, crétin/e.

nit-pick [ˈnɪtpɪk] *vi* (*col*) être tatillon(ne).

nitrogen [ˈnaɪtrədʒən] *n* azote *m*.

nitroglycerin(e) [ˈnaɪtrəuˈglɪsəriːn] *n* nitroglycérine *f*.

nitty-gritty [ˈnɪtɪˈgrɪtɪ] *n* (*fam*): **to get down to the ~** en venir au fond du problème.

nitwit [ˈnɪtwɪt] *n* (*col*) nigaud/e.

NJ *abbr* (*US POST*) = New Jersey.

NLF *n abbr* (= National Liberation Front) FLN *m*.

NLQ *abbr* (= near letter quality) qualité *f* courrier.

NLRB *n abbr* (*US*: = National Labor Relations Board*) organisme de protection des travailleurs.

NM *abbr* (*US POST*) = New Mexico.

no [nəu] *a* pas de, aucun(e) + *sg* ♦ *ad*, *n* non (*m*); **I have ~ more wine** je n'ai plus de vin; **"~ entry"** "défense d'entrer", "entrée interdite"; **"~ dogs"** "les chiens ne sont pas admis"; **I won't take ~ for an answer** il n'est pas question de refuser.

no. *abbr* (= *number*) nᵒ.

nobble [ˈnɔbl] *vt* (*Brit col: bribe: person*) soudoyer, acheter; (*: person: to speak to*) mettre le grappin sur; (*RACING: horse, dog*) droguer (*pour l'empêcher de gagner*).

Nobel prize [nəuˈbɛl-] *n* prix *m* Nobel.

nobility [nəuˈbɪlɪtɪ] *n* noblesse *f*.

noble [ˈnəubl] *a* noble.

nobleman [ˈnəublmən] *n* noble *m*.

nobly [ˈnəublɪ] *ad* noblement.

nobody [ˈnəubədɪ] *pronoun* personne (*with negative*).

no-claims bonus [ˈnəukleɪmz-] *n* bonus *m*.

nocturnal [nɔkˈtəːnl] *a* nocturne.

nod [nɔd] *vi* faire un signe de (la) tête (*affirmatif ou amical*); (*sleep*) somnoler ♦ *vt*: **to ~ one's head** faire un signe de (la) tête; (*in agreement*) faire signe que oui ♦ *n*

signe *m* de (la) tête; **they ~ded their agreement** ils ont acquiescé d'un signe de la tête.
  nod off *vi* s'assoupir.
noise [nɔɪz] *n* bruit *m*.
noiseless ['nɔɪzlɪs] *a* silencieux(euse).
noisily ['nɔɪzɪlɪ] *ad* bruyamment.
noisy ['nɔɪzɪ] *a* bruyant(e).
nomad ['nəumæd] *n* nomade *m/f*.
nomadic [nəu'mædɪk] *a* nomade.
no man's land *n* no man's land *m*.
nominal ['nɔmɪnl] *a* (*rent, fee*) symbolique;
  (*value*) nominal(e).
nominate ['nɔmɪneɪt] *vt* (*propose*) proposer;
  (*elect*) nommer.
nomination [nɔmɪ'neɪʃən] *n* nomination *f*.
nominee [nɔmɪ'niː] *n* candidat agréé;
  personne nommée.
non- [nɔn] *prefix* non-.
non-alcoholic [nɔnælkə'hɔlɪk] *a* non-
  alcoolisé(e).
non-breakable [nɔn'breɪkəbl] *a* incassable.
nonce word ['nɔns-] *n* mot créé pour
  l'occasion.
nonchalant ['nɔnʃələnt] *a* nonchalant(e).
non-commissioned [nɔnkə'mɪʃənd] *a*: ~
  officer sous-officier *m*.
non-committal [nɔnkə'mɪtl] *a* évasif(ive).
nonconformist [nɔnkən'fɔːmɪst] *n* non-
  conformiste *m/f* ♦ *a* non-conformiste,
  dissident(e).
non-contributory [nɔnkən'trɪbjutərɪ] *a*: ~
  pension scheme *or* (US) **plan** *régime de retraite payée par l'employeur.*
non-cooperation ['nɔnkəuɔpə'reɪʃən] *n* refus
  m de coopérer, non-coopération *f*.
nondescript ['nɔndɪskrɪpt] *a* quelconque,
  indéfinissable.
none [nʌn] *pronoun* aucun/e; ~ **of you** aucun
  d'entre vous, personne parmi vous; **I have ~**
  je n'en ai pas; **I have ~ left** je n'en ai plus;
  ~ **at all** (*not one*) aucun(e); **how much
  milk? - ~ at all** combien de lait? - pas du
  tout; **he's ~ the worse for it** il ne s'en porte
  pas plus mal.
nonentity [nɔ'nentɪtɪ] *n* personne insignifiante.
non-essential [nɔnɪ'senʃl] *a* accessoire,
  superflu(e) ♦ *n*: ~**s** le superflu.
nonetheless ['nʌnðə'les] *ad* néanmoins.
non-executive [nɔnɪg'zekjutɪv] *a*: ~ **director**
  administrateur/trice, conseiller/ère de
  direction.
non-existent [nɔnɪg'zɪstənt] *a* inexistant(e).
non-fiction [nɔn'fɪkʃən] *n* littérature *f* non-
  romanesque.
non-flammable [nɔn'flæməbl] *a* ininflammable.
non-intervention ['nɔnɪntə'venʃən] *n* non-
  intervention *f*.
non obst. *abbr* (= *non obstante*:
  notwithstanding) nonobstant.
non-payment [nɔn'peɪmənt] *n* non-paiement
  m.
nonplussed [nɔn'plʌst] *a* perplexe.
non-profit-making [nɔn'prɔfɪtmeɪkɪŋ] *a* à but
  non lucratif.
nonsense ['nɔnsəns] *n* absurdités *fpl*, idioties
  fpl; ~**!** ne dites pas d'idioties!; **it is ~ to say
  that ...** il est absurde de dire que ....
non-shrink [nɔn'ʃrɪŋk] *a* (*Brit*) irrétrécissa-

ble.
non-skid [nɔn'skɪd] *a* antidérapant(e).
non-smoker ['nɔn'sməukə*] *n* non-fumeur *m*.
non-stick ['nɔn'stɪk] *a* qui n'attache pas.
non-stop ['nɔn'stɔp] *a* direct(e), sans arrêt
  (*or* escale) ♦ *ad* sans arrêt.
non-taxable [nɔn'tæksəbl] *a*: ~ **income**
  revenu *m* non imposable.
non-U ['nɔnju:] *a* *abbr* (*Brit col*: = *non-upper
  class*) qui ne se dit (*or* se fait) pas.
non-volatile [nɔn'vɔlətaɪl] *a*: ~ **memory**
  (*COMPUT*) mémoire rémanente *or* non
  volatile.
non-voting [nɔn'vəutɪŋ] *a*: ~ **shares** actions
  fpl sans droit de vote.
non-white ['nɔn'waɪt] *a* de couleur ♦ *n*
  personne *f* de couleur.
noodles ['nu:dlz] *npl* nouilles *fpl*.
nook [nuk] *n*: ~**s and crannies** recoins *mpl*.
noon [nu:n] *n* midi *m*.
no one ['nəuwʌn] *pronoun* = **nobody**.
noose [nu:s] *n* nœud coulant; (*hangman's*)
  corde *f*.
nor [nɔː*] *cj* = **neither** ♦ *ad see* **neither.**
Norf *abbr* (*Brit*) = *Norfolk.*
norm [nɔːm] *n* norme *f*.
normal ['nɔːml] *a* normal(e) ♦ *n*: **to return to
  ~** redevenir normal(e).
normality [nɔː'mælɪtɪ] *n* normalité *f*.
normally ['nɔːməlɪ] *ad* normalement.
Normandy ['nɔːməndɪ] *n* Normandie *f*.
north [nɔːθ] *n* nord *m* ♦ *a* du nord, nord *inv* ♦
  ad au *or* vers le nord.
North Africa *n* Afrique *f* du Nord.
North African *a* nord-africain(e), d'Afrique
  du Nord ♦ *n* Nord-Africain/e.
North America *n* Amérique *f* du Nord.
North American *n* Nord-Américain/e ♦ *a*
  nord-américain(e), d'Amérique du Nord.
Northants [nɔː'θænts] *abbr* (*Brit*) = *North-
  amptonshire.*
northbound ['nɔːθbaund] *a* (*traffic*) en
  direction du nord; (*carriageway*) nord *inv.*
Northd *abbr* (*Brit*) = *Northumberland.*
north-east [nɔːθ'iːst] *n* nord-est *m*.
northerly ['nɔːðəlɪ] *a* (*wind, direction*) du
  nord.
northern ['nɔːðən] *a* du nord, septentrional(e).
Northern Ireland *n* Irlande *f* du Nord.
North Pole *n*: **the ~** le pôle Nord.
North Sea *n*: **the ~** la mer du Nord.
North Sea oil *n* pétrole *m* de la mer du
  Nord.
northward(s) ['nɔːθwəd(z)] *ad* vers le nord.
north-west [nɔːθ'west] *n* nord-ouest *m*.
Norway ['nɔːweɪ] *n* Norvège *f*.
Norwegian [nɔː'wiːdʒən] *a* norvégien(ne) ♦ *n*
  Norvégien/ne; (*LING*) norvégien *m*.
nos. *abbr* (= *numbers*) nᵒ.
nose [nəuz] *n* nez *m*; (*fig*) flair *m* ♦ *vi* (*also:*
  ~ **one's way**) avancer précautionneusement;
  to pay through the ~ (for sth) (*col*) payer
  un prix excessif (pour qch).
nose about, nose around *vi* fouiner *or*
  fureter (partout).
nosebleed ['nəuzbliːd] *n* saignement *m* de nez.
nose-dive ['nəuzdaɪv] *n* (descente *f* en) piqué
  m.
nose drops *npl* gouttes *fpl* pour le nez.

nosey ['nəuzı] *a* curieux(euse).
nostalgia [nɔs'tældʒıə] *n* nostalgie *f*.
nostalgic [nɔs'tældʒık] *a* nostalgique.
nostril ['nɔstrıl] *n* narine *f*; (*of horse*) naseau *m*.
nosy ['nəuzı] *a* = **nosey**.
not [nɔt] *ad* (ne ...) pas; **I hope ~** j'espère que non; **~ at all** pas du tout; (*after thanks*) de rien; **you must ~** *or* **mustn't do this** tu ne dois pas faire ça; **he isn't ...** il n'est pas ....
notable ['nəutəbl] *a* notable.
notably ['nəutəblı] *ad* en particulier.
notary ['nəutərı] *n* (*also*: **~ public**) notaire *m*.
notation [nəu'teıʃən] *n* notation *f*.
notch [nɔtʃ] *n* encoche *f*.
notch up *vt* (*score*) marquer; (*victory*) remporter.
note [nəut] *n* note *f*; (*letter*) mot *m*; (*banknote*) billet *m* ♦ *vt* (*also*: **~ down**) noter; (*notice*) constater; **just a quick ~ to let you know ...** juste un mot pour vous dire ...; **to take ~s** prendre des notes; **to compare ~s** (*fig*) échanger des (*or* leurs *etc*) impressions; **to take ~ of** prendre note de; **a person of ~** une personne éminente.
notebook ['nəutbuk] *n* carnet *m*; (*for short-hand etc*) bloc-notes *m*.
note-case ['nəutkeıs] *n* (*Brit*) porte-feuille *m*.
noted ['nəutıd] *a* réputé(e).
notepad ['nəutpæd] *n* bloc-notes *m*.
notepaper ['nəutpeıpə*] *n* papier *m* à lettres.
noteworthy ['nəutwə:ðı] *a* remarquable.
nothing ['nʌθıŋ] *n* rien *m*; **he does ~** il ne fait rien; **~ new** rien de nouveau; **for ~** (*free*) pour rien, gratuitement; **~ at all** rien du tout.
notice ['nəutıs] *n* avis *m*; (*of leaving*) congé *m*; (*Brit*: *review: of play etc*) critique *f*, compte-rendu *m* ♦ *vt* remarquer, s'apercevoir de; **without ~** sans préavis; **advance ~** préavis *m*; **to give sb ~ of sth** notifier qn de qch; **at short ~** dans un délai très court; **until further ~** jusqu'à nouvel ordre; **to give ~, hand in one's ~** (*subj: employee*) donner sa démission, démissionner; **to take ~ of** prêter attention à; **to bring sth to sb's ~** porter qch à la connaissance de qn; **it has come to my ~ that ...** on m'a signalé que ...; **to escape** *or* **avoid ~** (essayer de) passer inaperçu *or* ne pas se faire remarquer.
noticeable ['nəutısəbl] *a* visible.
notice board *n* (*Brit*) panneau *m* d'affichage.
notification [nəutıfı'keıʃən] *n* notification *f*.
notify ['nəutıfaı] *vt*: **to ~ sth to sb** notifier qch à qn; **to ~ sb of sth** avertir qn de qch.
notion ['nəuʃən] *n* idée *f*; (*concept*) notion *f*.
notions ['nəuʃənz] *npl* (*US: haberdashery*) mercerie *f*.
notoriety [nəutə'raıətı] *n* notoriété *f*.
notorious [nəu'tɔ:rıəs] *a* notoire (*souvent en mal*).
notoriously [nəu'tɔ:rıəslı] *a* notoirement.
Notts [nɔts] *abbr* (*Brit*) = *Nottinghamshire*.
notwithstanding [nɔtwıθ'stændıŋ] *ad* néanmoins ♦ *prep* en dépit de.
nougat ['nu:ga:] *n* nougat *m*.
nought [nɔ:t] *n* zéro *m*.
noun [naun] *n* nom *m*.

nourish ['nʌrıʃ] *vt* nourrir.
nourishing ['nʌrıʃıŋ] *a* nourrissant(e).
nourishment ['nʌrıʃmənt] *n* nourriture *f*.
Nov. *abbr* (= *November*) nov.
Nova Scotia ['nəuvə'skəuʃə] *n* Nouvelle-Écosse *f*.
novel ['nɔvl] *n* roman *m* ♦ *a* nouveau(nouvelle), original(e).
novelist ['nɔvəlıst] *n* romancier *m*.
novelty ['nɔvəltı] *n* nouveauté *f*.
November [nəu'vɛmbə*] *n* novembre *m*; *for phrases see also* **July**.
novice ['nɔvıs] *n* novice *m/f*.
NOW [nau] *n abbr* (*US*) = *National Organization for Women*.
now [nau] *ad* maintenant ♦ *cj*: **~ (that)** maintenant (que); **right ~** tout de suite; **by ~** à l'heure qu'il est; **just ~: that's the fashion just ~** c'est la mode en ce moment *or* maintenant; **I saw her just ~** je viens de la voir, je l'ai vue à l'instant; **I'll read it just ~** je vais le lire à l'instant *or* dès maintenant; **~ and then, ~ and again** de temps en temps; **from ~ on** dorénavant; **in 3 days from ~** dans *or* d'ici trois jours; **between ~ and Monday** d'ici (à) lundi; **that's all for ~** c'est tout pour l'instant.
nowadays ['nauədeız] *ad* de nos jours.
nowhere ['nəuwɛə*] *ad* nulle part; **~ else** nulle part ailleurs.
noxious ['nɔkʃəs] *a* toxique.
nozzle ['nɔzl] *n* (*of hose*) jet *m*, lance *f*.
NP *n abbr* = **notary public**.
NS *abbr* (*Canada*) = *Nova Scotia*.
NSC *n abbr* (*US*) = **National Security Council**.
NSF *n abbr* (*US*) = *National Science Foundation*.
NSPCC *n abbr* (*Brit*) = *National Society for the Prevention of Cruelty to Children*.
NSW *abbr* (*Australia*) = *New South Wales*.
NT *n abbr* (= *New Testament*) NT *m*.
nth [ɛnθ] *a*: **for the ~ time** (*col*) pour la énième fois.
NUAAW *n abbr* (*Brit*: = *National Union of Agricultural and Allied Workers*) syndicat agricole.
nuance ['nju:ɑ:ns] *n* nuance *f*.
NUBE *n abbr* (*Brit*: = *National Union of Bank Employees*) syndicat des employés de banque.
nubile ['nju:baıl] *a* nubile; (*attractive*) jeune et désirable.
nuclear ['nju:klıə*] *a* nucléaire.
nuclear disarmament *n* désarmement *m* nucléaire.
nucleus, pl nuclei ['nju:klıəs, 'nju:klıaı] *n* noyau *m*.
nude [nju:d] *a* nu(e) ♦ *n* (*ART*) nu *m*; **in the ~** (tout(e)) nu(e).
nudge [nʌdʒ] *vt* donner un (petit) coup de coude à.
nudist ['nju:dıst] *n* nudiste *m/f*.
nudist colony *n* colonie *f* de nudistes.
nudity ['nju:dıtı] *n* nudité *f*.
nugget ['nʌgıt] *n* pépite *f*.
nuisance ['nju:sns] *n*: **it's a ~** c'est (très) ennuyeux *or* gênant; **he's a ~** il est assommant *or* casse-pieds; **what a ~!** quelle

barbe!

NUJ *n abbr* (*Brit*: = *National Union of Journalists*) *syndicat des journalistes*.

nuke [nju:k] *n* (*col*) bombe *f* atomique.

null [nʌl] *a*: ~ **and void** nul(le) et non avenu(e).

nullify ['nʌlɪfaɪ] *vt* invalider.

NUM *n abbr* (*Brit*: = *National Union of Mineworkers*) *syndicat des mineurs*.

numb [nʌm] *a* engourdi(e) ♦ *vt* engourdir; ~ **with cold** engourdi(e) par le froid, transi(e) (de froid); ~ **with fear** transi de peur, paralysé(e) par la peur.

number ['nʌmbə*] *n* nombre *m*; (*numeral*) chiffre *m*; (*of house, car, telephone, newspaper*) numéro *m* ♦ *vt* numéroter; (*include*) compter; ~ **of** un certain nombre de; **to be ~ed among** compter parmi; **the staff ~s 20** le nombre d'employés s'élève à *or* est de 20; **wrong** ~ (*TEL*) mauvais numéro.

numbered account *n* (*in bank*) compte numéroté.

number plate *n* (*Brit AUT*) plaque *f* minéralogique *or* d'immatriculation.

Number Ten *n* (*Brit*: = *10 Downing Street*) *résidence du Premier ministre*.

numbness ['nʌmnɪs] *n* torpeur *f*; (*due to cold*) engourdissement *m*.

numeral ['nju:mərəl] *n* chiffre *m*.

numerate ['nju:mərɪt] *a* (*Brit*): **to be** ~ avoir des notions d'arithmétique.

numerical [nju:'mɛrɪkl] *a* numérique.

numerous ['nju:mərəs] *a* nombreux(euse).

nun [nʌn] *n* religieuse *f*, sœur *f*.

NUPE ['nju:pɪ] *n abbr* (*Brit*: = *National Union of Public Employees*) *syndicat des employés de la fonction publique*.

nuptial ['nʌpʃəl] *a* nuptial(e).

NUR *n abbr* (*Brit*: = *National Union of Railwaymen*) *syndicat des cheminots*.

nurse [nə:s] *n* infirmière *f*; (*also*: **nursemaid**) bonne *f* d'enfants ♦ *vt* (*patient, cold*) soigner; (*baby: Brit*) bercer (dans ses bras); (*: US*) allaiter, nourrir; (*hope*) nourrir *f*.

nursery ['nə:sərɪ] *n* (*room*) nursery *f*; (*institution*) pouponnière *f*; (*for plants*) pépinière *f*.

nursery rhyme *n* comptine *f*, chansonnette *f* pour enfants.

nursery school *n* école maternelle.

nursery slope *n* (*Brit SKI*) piste *f* pour débutants.

nursing ['nə:sɪŋ] *n* (*profession*) profession *f* d'infirmière ♦ *a* (*mother*) qui allaite.

nursing home *n* clinique *f*; maison *f* de convalescence.

nurture ['nə:tʃə*] *vt* élever.

NUS *n abbr* (*Brit*: = *National Union of Seamen*) *syndicat des gens de mer*; (*: = National Union of Students*) *syndicat des étudiants*.

NUT *n abbr* (*Brit*: = *National Union of Teachers*) *syndicat enseignant*.

nut [nʌt] *n* (*of metal*) écrou *m*; (*fruit*) noix *f*, noisette *f*, cacahuète *f* (*terme générique en anglais*) ♦ *a* (*chocolate etc*) aux noisettes; **he's ~s** (*col*) il est dingue.

nutcase ['nʌtkeɪs] *n* (*col*) dingue *m/f*.

nutcrackers ['nʌtkrækəz] *npl* casse-noix *m inv*, casse-noisette(s) *m*.

nutmeg ['nʌtmɛg] *n* (noix *f*) muscade *f*.

nutrient ['nju:trɪənt] *a* nutritif(ive) ♦ *n* substance nutritive.

nutrition [nju:'trɪʃən] *n* nutrition *f*, alimentation *f*.

nutritionist [nju:'trɪʃənɪst] *n* nutritionniste *m/f*.

nutritious [nju:'trɪʃəs] *a* nutritif(ive), nourrissant(e).

nutshell ['nʌtʃɛl] *n* coquille *f* de noix; **in a** ~ en un mot.

nuzzle ['nʌzl] *vi*: **to** ~ **up to** fourrer son nez contre.

NV *abbr* (*US POST*) = *Nevada*.

NWT *abbr* (*Canada*) = *Northwest Territories*.

NY *abbr* (*US POST*) = *New York*.

NYC *abbr* (*US POST*) = *New York City*.

nylon ['naɪlɔn] *n* nylon *m* ♦ *a* de *or* en nylon; ~**s** *npl* bas *mpl* nylon.

nymph [nɪmf] *n* nymphe *f*.

nymphomaniac ['nɪmfəu'meɪnɪæk] *a*, *n* nymphomane (*f*).

NYSE *n abbr* (*US*) = *New York Stock Exchange*.

NZ *abbr* = **New Zealand**.

O

O, o [əu] *n* (*letter*) O, o *m*; (*US SCOL*: = *outstanding*) tb ← (= *très bien*), (*US*) **O for Oboe** O comme Oscar.

oaf [əuf] *n* balourd *m*.

oak [əuk] *n* chêne *m* ♦ *cpd* de *or* en (bois de) chêne.

OAP *n abbr* (*Brit*) = **old-age pensioner**.

oar [ɔ:*] *n* aviron *m*, rame *f*; **to put** *or* **shove one's** ~ **in** (*fig: col*) mettre son grain de sel.

oarsman ['ɔ:zmən], **oarswoman** ['ɔ:zwumən] *n* rameur/euse.

OAS *n abbr* (= *Organization of American States*) OEA *f* (= *Organisation des états américains*).

oasis, *pl* oases [əu'eɪsɪs, əu'eɪsi:z] *n* oasis *f*.

oath [əuθ] *n* serment *m*; (*swear word*) juron *m*; **to take the** ~ prêter serment; **on** (*Brit*) *or* **under** ~ sous serment; assermenté(e).

oatmeal ['əutmi:l] *n* flocons *mpl* d'avoine.

oats [əuts] *n* avoine *f*.

OAU *n abbr* (= *Organization of African Unity*) OUA *f* (= *Organisation de l'unité africaine*).

obdurate ['ɔbdjurɪt] *a* obstiné(e), impénitent(e); intraitable.

OBE *n abbr* (*Brit*: = *Order of the British Empire*) *distinction honorifique*.

obedience [ə'bi:dɪəns] *n* obéissance *f*; **in** ~ **to** conformément à.

obedient [ə'bi:dɪənt] *a* obéissant(e); **to be** ~ **to sb/sth** obéir à qn/qch.

obelisk ['ɔbɪlɪsk] *n* obélisque *m*.

obesity [əu'bi:sɪtɪ] *n* obésité *f*.

obey [ə'beɪ] *vt* obéir à; (*instructions,*

regulations) se conformer à ♦ *vi* obéir.
obituary [ə'bɪtjuərɪ] *n* nécrologie *f*.
object *n* ['ɔbdʒɪkt] objet *m*; (*purpose*) but *m*, objet; (*LING*) complément *m* d'objet ♦ *vi* [əb'dʒɛkt]: **to ~ to** (*attitude*) désapprouver; (*proposal*) protester contre, élever une objection contre; **I ~!** je proteste!; **he ~ed that ...** il a fait valoir *or* a objecté que ...; **do you ~ to my smoking?** est-ce que cela vous gêne si je fume?; **what's the ~ of doing that?** quel est l'intérêt de faire cela?; **money is no ~** l'argent n'est pas un problème.
objection [əb'dʒɛkʃən] *n* objection *f*; (*drawback*) inconvénient *m*; **if you have no ~** si vous n'y voyez pas d'inconvénient; **to make** *or* **raise an ~** élever une objection.
objectionable [əb'dʒɛkʃənəbl] *a* très désagréable; choquant(e).
objective [əb'dʒɛktɪv] *n* objectif *m* ♦ *a* objectif(ive).
objectivity [ɔbdʒɪk'tɪvɪtɪ] *n* objectivité *f*.
object lesson *n* (*fig*) (bonne) illustration.
objector [əb'dʒɛktə*] *n* opposant/e.
obligation [ɔblɪ'geɪʃən] *n* obligation *f*, devoir *m*; (*debt*) dette *f* (de reconnaissance); **"without ~"** "sans engagement".
obligatory [ə'blɪgətərɪ] *a* obligatoire.
oblige [ə'blaɪdʒ] *vt* (*force*): **to ~ sb to do** obliger *or* forcer qn à faire; (*do a favour*) rendre service à, obliger; **to be ~d to sb for sth** être obligé(e) à qn de qch; **anything to ~!** (*col*) (toujours prêt à rendre) service!
obliging [ə'blaɪdʒɪŋ] *a* obligeant(e), serviable.
oblique [ə'bliːk] *a* oblique; (*allusion*) indirect(e) ♦ *n* (*Brit TYP*): **~ (stroke)** barre *f* oblique.
obliterate [ə'blɪtəreɪt] *vt* effacer.
oblivion [ə'blɪvɪən] *n* oubli *m*.
oblivious [ə'blɪvɪəs] *a*: **~ of** oublieux(euse) de.
oblong ['ɔblɔŋ] *a* oblong(ue) ♦ *n* rectangle *m*.
obnoxious [əb'nɔkʃəs] *a* odieux(euse); (*smell*) nauséabond(e).
o.b.o. *abbr* (*US*: = *or best offer*: *in classified ads*) ≈ à discuter.
oboe ['əubəu] *n* hautbois *m*.
obscene [əb'siːn] *a* obscène.
obscenity [əb'sɛnɪtɪ] *n* obscénité *f*.
obscure [əb'skjuə*] *a* obscur(e) ♦ *vt* obscurcir; (*hide*: *sun*) cacher.
obscurity [əb'skjuərɪtɪ] *n* obscurité *f*.
obsequious [əb'siːkwɪəs] *a* obséquieux(euse).
observable [əb'zə:vəbl] *a* observable; (*appreciable*) notable.
observance [əb'zə:vns] *n* observance *f*, observation *f*; **religious ~s** observances religieuses.
observant [əb'zə:vnt] *a* observateur(trice).
observation [ɔbzə'veɪʃən] *n* observation *f*; (*by police etc*) surveillance *f*.
observation post *n* (*MIL*) poste *m* d'observation.
observatory [əb'zə:vətrɪ] *n* observatoire *m*.
observe [əb'zə:v] *vt* observer; (*remark*) faire observer *or* remarquer.
observer [əb'zə:və*] *n* observateur/trice.
obsess [əb'sɛs] *vt* obséder; **to be ~ed by** *or* **with sb/sth** être obsédé(e) par qn/qch.
obsession [əb'sɛʃən] *n* obsession *f*.

obsessive [əb'sɛsɪv] *a* obsédant(e).
obsolescence [ɔbsə'lɛsns] *n* vieillissement *m*; obsolescence *f*; **built-in** *or* **planned ~** (*COMM*) désuétude calculée.
obsolescent [ɔbsə'lɛsnt] *a* obsolescent(e), en voie d'être périmé(e).
obsolete ['ɔbsəliːt] *a* dépassé(e), périmé(e).
obstacle ['ɔbstəkl] *n* obstacle *m*.
obstacle race *n* course *f* d'obstacles.
obstetrics [ɔb'stɛtrɪks] *n* obstétrique *f*.
obstinacy ['ɔbstɪnəsɪ] *n* obstination *f*.
obstinate ['ɔbstɪnɪt] *a* obstiné(e); (*pain, cold*) persistant(e).
obstreperous [əb'strɛpərəs] *a* turbulent(e).
obstruct [əb'strʌkt] *vt* (*block*) boucher, obstruer; (*halt*) arrêter; (*hinder*) entraver.
obstruction [əb'strʌkʃən] *n* obstruction *f*; obstacle *m*.
obstructive [əb'strʌktɪv] *a* obstructionniste.
obtain [əb'teɪn] *vt* obtenir ♦ *vi* avoir cours.
obtainable [əb'teɪnəbl] *a* qu'on peut obtenir.
obtrusive [əb'truːsɪv] *a* (*person*) importun(e); (*smell*) pénétrant(e); (*building etc*) trop en évidence.
obtuse [əb'tjuːs] *a* obtus(e).
obverse ['ɔbvə:s] *n* (*of medal, coin*) côté *m* face; (*fig*) contrepartie *f*.
obviate ['ɔbvɪeɪt] *vt* parer à, obvier à.
obvious ['ɔbvɪəs] *a* évident(e), manifeste.
obviously ['ɔbvɪəslɪ] *ad* manifestement; (*of course*): **~, he ...** *or* **he ~ ...** il est bien évident qu'il ...; **~!** bien sûr!; **~ not!** évidemment pas!, bien sûr que non!
OCAS *n abbr* (= *Organization of Central American States*) ODEAC *f* (= *Organisation des États d'Amérique Centrale*).
occasion [ə'keɪʒən] *n* occasion *f*; (*event*) événement *m* ♦ *vt* occasionner, causer; **on that ~** à cette occasion; **to rise to the ~** se montrer à la hauteur de la situation.
occasional [ə'keɪʒənl] *a* pris(e) (*or* fait(e) *etc*) de temps en temps; occasionnel(le).
occasionally [ə'keɪʒənəlɪ] *ad* de temps en temps; **very ~** (assez) rarement.
occasional table *n* table décorative.
occult [ɔ'kʌlt] *a* occulte ♦ *n*: **the ~** le surnaturel.
occupancy ['ɔkjupənsɪ] *n* occupation *f*.
occupant ['ɔkjupənt] *n* occupant *m*.
occupation [ɔkju'peɪʃən] *n* occupation *f*; (*job*) métier *m*, profession *f*; **unfit for ~** (*house*) impropre à l'habitation.
occupational [ɔkju'peɪʃənl] *a* (*accident, disease*) du travail; (*hazard*) du métier.
occupational guidance *n* (*Brit*) orientation professionnelle.
occupational pension *n* retraite professionnelle.
occupational therapy *n* ergothérapie *f*.
occupier ['ɔkjupaɪə*] *n* occupant/e.
occupy ['ɔkjupaɪ] *vt* occuper; **to ~ o.s. with** *or* **by doing** s'occuper à faire; **to be occupied with sth** être occupé avec qch.
occur [ə'kə:*] *vi* se produire; (*difficulty, opportunity*) se présenter; (*phenomenon, error*) se rencontrer; **to ~ to sb** venir à l'esprit de qn.
occurrence [ə'kʌrəns] *n* présence *f*, existence *f*; cas *m*, fait *m*.

ocean ['əuʃən] n océan m; **~s of** (col) des masses de.

ocean bed n fond (sous-)marin.

ocean-going ['əuʃəngəuɪŋ] a de haute mer.

Oceania [əuʃɪ'eɪnɪə] n Océanie f.

ocean liner n paquebot m.

ochre ['əukə*] a ocre.

o'clock [ə'klɔk] ad: **it is 5 ~** il est 5 heures.

OCR n abbr = **optical character reader**, **optical character recognition**.

Oct. abbr (= October) oct.

octagonal [ɔk'tægənl] a octogonal(e).

octane ['ɔkteɪn] n octane m; **high-~ petrol** or (US) **gas** essence f à indice d'octane élevé.

octave ['ɔktɪv] n octave f.

October [ɔk'təubə*] n octobre m; for phrases see also **July**.

octogenarian ['ɔktəudʒɪ'nɛərɪən] n octogénaire m/f.

octopus ['ɔktəpəs] n pieuvre f.

odd [ɔd] a (strange) bizarre, curieux(euse); (number) impair(e); (left over) qui reste, en plus; (not of a set) dépareillé(e); **60-~** 60 et quelques; **at ~ times** de temps en temps; **the ~ one out** l'exception f.

oddball ['ɔdbɔːl] n (col) excentrique m/f.

oddity ['ɔdɪtɪ] n bizarrerie f; (person) excentrique m/f.

odd-job man [ɔd'dʒɔb-] n homme m à tout faire.

odd jobs npl petits travaux divers.

oddly ['ɔdlɪ] ad bizarrement, curieusement.

oddments ['ɔdmənts] npl (Brit COMM) fins fpl de série.

odds [ɔdz] npl (in betting) cote f; **the ~ are against his coming** il y a peu de chances qu'il vienne; **it makes no ~** cela n'a pas d'importance; **to succeed against all the ~** réussir contre toute attente; **~ and ends** de petites choses; **at ~** en désaccord.

ode [əud] n ode f.

odious ['əudɪəs] a odieux(euse), détestable.

odometer [ɔ'dɔmɪtə*] n odomètre m.

odour, (US) **odor** ['əudə*] n odeur f.

odo(u)rless ['əudəlɪs] a inodore.

OECD n abbr (= Organization for Economic Cooperation and Development) OCDE f (= Organisation de coopération et de développement économique).

oesophagus, (US) **esophagus** [iː'sɔfəgəs] n œsophage m.

oestrogen, (US) **estrogen** ['iːstrəudʒən] n œstrogène m.

of [ɔv, əv] prep de; **a friend ~ ours** un de nos amis; **3 ~ them** went 3 d'entre eux y sont allés; **the 5th ~ July** le 5 juillet; **a boy ~ 10** un garçon de 10 ans; **made ~ wood** (fait) en bois; **a kilo ~ flour** un kilo de farine; **that was very kind ~ you** c'était très gentil de votre part; **a quarter ~ 4** (US) 4 heures moins le quart.

off [ɔf] a, ad (engine) coupé(e); (tap) fermé(e); (Brit: food) mauvais(e), avancé(e); (: milk) tourné(e); (absent) absent(e); (cancelled) annulé(e); (removed): **the lid was ~** le couvercle était retiré or n'était pas mis ♦ prep de; sur; **to be ~** (to leave) partir, s'en aller; **I must be ~** il faut que je file; **to be ~ sick** être absent pour

cause de maladie; **a day ~** un jour de congé; **to have an ~ day** n'être pas en forme; **he had his coat ~** il avait enlevé son manteau; **the hook is ~** le crochet s'est détaché; le crochet n'est pas mis; **10% ~** (COMM) 10% de rabais; **5 km ~ (the road)** à 5 km (de la route); **~ the coast** au large de la côte; **a house ~ the main road** une maison à l'écart de la grand-route; **it's a long way ~** c'est loin (d'ici); **I'm ~ meat** je ne mange plus de viande; je n'aime plus la viande; **on the ~ chance** à tout hasard; **to be well/badly ~** être bien/mal loti; (financially) être aisé/dans la gêne; **~ and on, on and ~** de temps à autre; **I'm afraid the chicken is ~** (Brit: not available) je regrette, il n'y a plus de poulet; **that's a bit ~** (fig: col) c'est un peu fort.

offal ['ɔfl] n (CULIN) abats mpl.

offbeat ['ɔfbiːt] a excentrique.

off-centre [ɔf'sɛntə*] a décentré(e), excentré(e).

off-colour ['ɔf'kʌlə*] a (Brit: ill) malade, mal fichu(e); **to feel ~** être mal fichu.

offence, (US) **offense** [ə'fɛns] n (crime) délit m, infraction f; **to give ~ to** blesser, offenser; **to take ~ at** se vexer de, s'offenser de; **to commit an ~** commettre une infraction.

offend [ə'fɛnd] vt (person) offenser, blesser ♦ vi: **to ~ against** (law, rule) contrevenir à, enfreindre.

offender [ə'fɛndə*] n délinquant/e; (against regulations) contrevenant/e.

offense [ə'fɛns] n (US) = **offence**.

offensive [ə'fɛnsɪv] a offensant(e), choquant(e); (smell etc) très déplaisant(e); (weapon) offensif(ive) ♦ n (MIL) offensive f.

offer ['ɔfə*] n offre f, proposition f ♦ vt offrir, proposer; **to make an ~ for sth** faire une offre pour qch; **to ~ to do sth** proposer de faire qch; **"on ~"** (COMM) "en promotion".

offering ['ɔfərɪŋ] n offrande f.

offhand [ɔf'hænd] a désinvolte ♦ ad spontanément; **I can't tell you ~** je ne peux pas vous le dire comme ça.

office ['ɔfɪs] n (place) bureau m; (position) charge f, fonction f; **doctor's ~** (US) cabinet (médical); **to take ~** entrer en fonctions; **through his good ~s** (fig) grâce à ses bons offices; **O~ of Fair Trading** (Brit) organisme de protection contre les pratiques commerciales abusives.

office automation n bureautique f.

office bearer n (of club etc) membre m du bureau.

office block, (US) **office building** n immeuble m de bureaux.

office boy n garçon m de bureau.

office hours npl heures fpl de bureau; (US MED) heures de consultation.

office manager n responsable administratif(ive).

officer ['ɔfɪsə*] n (MIL etc) officier m; (of organization) membre m du bureau directeur; (also: **police ~**) agent m (de police).

office work n travail m de bureau.

office worker n employé/e de bureau.

official [ə'fɪʃl] *a* (*authorized*) officiel(le) ♦ *n* officiel *m*; (*civil servant*) fonctionnaire *m/f*; employé/e.

officialdom [ə'fɪʃldəm] *n* bureaucratie *f*.

officially [ə'fɪʃəlɪ] *ad* officiellement.

official receiver *n* administrateur *m* judiciaire, syndic *m* de faillite.

officiate [ə'fɪʃɪeɪt] *vi* (*REL*) officier; **to ~ as Mayor** exercer les fonctions de maire; **to ~ at a marriage** célébrer un mariage.

officious [ə'fɪʃəs] *a* trop empressé(e).

offing ['ɔfɪŋ] *n*: **in the ~** (*fig*) en perspective.

off-key [ɔf'kiː] *a* faux(fausse) ♦ *ad* faux.

off-licence ['ɔflaɪsns] *n* (*Brit*: *shop*) débit *m* de vins et de spiritueux.

off-limits [ɔf'lɪmɪts] *a* (*esp US*) dont l'accès est interdit.

off line *a* (*COMPUT*) (en mode) autonome; (: *switched off*) non connecté(e).

off-load ['ɔfləud] *vt*: **to ~ sth (onto)** (*goods*) décharger qch (sur); (*job*) se décharger de qch (sur).

off-peak ['ɔf'piːk] *a* aux heures creuses.

off-putting ['ɔfputɪŋ] *a* (*Brit*) rébarbatif(ive); rebutant(e), peu engageant(e).

off-season ['ɔf'siːzn] *a*, *ad* hors-saison (*inv*).

offset ['ɔfsɛt] *vt irg* (*counteract*) contrebalancer, compenser ♦ *n* (*also*: **~ printing**) offset *m*.

offshoot ['ɔfʃuːt] *n* (*fig*) ramification *f*, antenne *f*; (: *of discussion etc*) conséquence *f*.

offshore [ɔf'ʃɔː*] *a* (*breeze*) de terre; (*island*) proche du littoral; (*fishing*) côtier(ière); **~ oilfield** gisement *m* pétrolifère en mer.

offside ['ɔf'saɪd] *n* (*AUT*: *with right-hand drive*) côté droit; (: *with left-hand drive*) côté gauche ♦ *a* (*AUT*) de droite; de gauche; (*SPORT*) hors jeu.

offspring ['ɔfsprɪŋ] *n* progéniture *f*.

offstage [ɔf'steɪdʒ] *ad* dans les coulisses.

off-the-cuff [ɔfðə'kʌf] *ad* au pied levé; de chic.

off-the-job ['ɔfðə'dʒɔb] *a*: **~ training** formation professionnelle extérieure.

off-the-peg ['ɔfðə'pɛg], (*US*) **off-the-rack** ['ɔfðə'ræk] *ad* en prêt-à-porter.

off-white ['ɔfwaɪt] *a* blanc cassé *inv*.

often ['ɔfn] *ad* souvent; **how ~ do you go?** vous y allez tous les combien?; **how ~ have you gone there?** vous y êtes allé combien de fois?; **as ~ as not** la plupart du temps.

ogle ['əugl] *vt* lorgner.

ogre ['əugə*] *n* ogre *m*.

OH *abbr* (*US POST*) = Ohio.

oh [əu] *excl* ô!, oh!, ah!

OHMS *abbr* (*Brit*) = On His (or Her) Majesty's Service.

oil [ɔɪl] *n* huile *f*; (*petroleum*) pétrole *m*; (*for central heating*) mazout *m* ♦ *vt* (*machine*) graisser.

oilcan ['ɔɪlkæn] *n* burette *f* de graissage; (*for storing*) bidon *m* à huile.

oil change *n* vidange *f*.

oilfield ['ɔɪfiːld] *n* gisement *m* de pétrole.

oil filter *n* (*AUT*) filtre *m* à huile.

oil-fired ['ɔɪfaɪəd] *a* au mazout.

oil gauge *n* jauge *f* de niveau d'huile.

oil industry *n* industrie pétrolière.

oil level *n* niveau *m* d'huile.

oil painting *n* peinture *f* à l'huile.

oil refinery *n* raffinerie *f* de pétrole.

oil rig *n* derrick *m*; (*at sea*) plate-forme pétrolière.

oilskins ['ɔɪlskɪnz] *npl* ciré *m*.

oil slick *n* nappe *f* de mazout.

oil tanker *n* pétrolier *m*.

oil well *n* puits *m* de pétrole.

oily ['ɔɪlɪ] *a* huileux(euse); (*food*) gras(se).

ointment ['ɔɪntmənt] *n* onguent *m*.

OK *abbr* (*US POST*) = Oklahoma.

O.K., okay ['əu'keɪ] *excl* d'accord! ♦ *vt* approuver, donner son accord à ♦ *n*: **to give sth one's ~** donner son accord à qch ♦ *a* en règle; en bon état; sain et sauf; acceptable; **is it ~?, are you ~?** ça va?; **are you ~ for money?** ça va *or* ira question argent?; **it's ~ with** *or* **by me** ça me va, c'est d'accord en ce qui me concerne.

old [əuld] *a* vieux(vieille); (*person*) vieux, âgé(e); (*former*) ancien(ne), vieux; **how ~ are you?** quel âge avez-vous?; **he's 10 years ~** il a 10 ans, il est âgé de 10 ans; **~er brother/sister** frère/sœur aîné(e); **any ~ thing will do** n'importe quoi fera l'affaire.

old age *n* vieillesse *f*.

old-age pensioner (OAP) ['əuldeɪdʒ-] *n* (*Brit*) retraité/e.

old-fashioned ['əuld'fæʃnd] *a* démodé(e); (*person*) vieux jeu *inv*.

old maid *n* vieille fille.

old people's home *n* maison *f* de retraite.

old-time ['əuld'taɪm] *a* du temps jadis, d'autrefois.

old-timer [əuld'taɪmə*] *n* ancien *m*.

old wives' tale *n* conte *m* de bonne femme.

olive ['ɔlɪv] *n* (*fruit*) olive *f*; (*tree*) olivier *m* ♦ *a* (*also*: **~-green**) (vert) olive *inv*.

olive oil *n* huile *f* d'olive.

Olympic [əu'lɪmpɪk] *a* olympique; **the ~ Games, the ~s** les Jeux *mpl* olympiques.

OM *n abbr* (*Brit*: = Order of Merit) titre honorifique.

O&M *n abbr* = organization and method.

Oman [əu'mɑːn] *n* Oman *m*.

OMB *n abbr* (*US*: = Office of Management and Budget) service conseillant le président en matière budgétaire.

omelet(te) ['ɔmlɪt] *n* omelette *f*; **ham/cheese ~** omelette au jambon/fromage.

omen ['əumən] *n* présage *m*.

ominous ['ɔmɪnəs] *a* menaçant(e), inquiétant(e); (*event*) de mauvais augure.

omission [əu'mɪʃən] *n* omission *f*.

omit [əu'mɪt] *vt* omettre; **to ~ to do sth** négliger de faire qch.

omnivorous [ɔm'nɪvrəs] *a* omnivore.

ON *abbr* (*Canada*) = Ontario.

on [ɔn] *prep* sur ♦ *ad* (*machine*) en marche; (*light, radio*) allumé(e); (*tap*) ouvert(e); **is the meeting still ~?** est-ce que la réunion a bien lieu?; **la réunion dure-t-elle encore?**; **when is this film ~?** quand passe *or* passe-t-on ce film?; **~ the train** dans le train; **~ the wall** sur le *or* au mur; **~ television** à la télévision; **~ the Continent** sur le continent; **a book ~ physics** un livre de physique; **~ learning this** en apprenant cela; **~ arrival** à l'arrivée; ~ **the left** à gauche; ~ **Friday** vendredi; ~ **Fridays** le vendredi; **a week** ~ **Friday** vendredi en huit; ~ **holiday,** (US) ~ **vacation** en vacances; **I haven't any money** ~ **me** je n'ai pas d'argent sur moi; **this round's** ~ **me** c'est ma tournée; **to have one's coat** ~ avoir (mis) son manteau; **to walk** etc ~ continuer à marcher etc; **from that day** ~ depuis ce jour; **it was well** ~ **in the evening** c'était tard dans la soirée; **that's not** ~! (not acceptable) cela ne se fait pas!; (not possible) pas question!; ~ **and off** de temps à autre.

ONC n abbr (Brit: = Ordinary National Certificate) ≈ BT m.

once [wʌns] ad une fois; (formerly) autrefois ♦ cj une fois que; ~ **he had left/it was done** une fois qu'il fut parti/que ce fut terminé; **at** ~ **tout** de suite, immédiatement; (simultaneously) à la fois; **all at** ~ ad tout d'un coup; ~ **a week** une fois par semaine; ~ **more** encore une fois; **I knew him** ~ je l'ai connu autrefois; ~ **and for all** une fois pour toutes; ~ **upon a time** il y avait une fois, il était une fois.

oncoming ['ɒnkʌmɪŋ] a (traffic) venant en sens inverse.

OND n abbr (Brit: = Ordinary National Diploma) ≈ BTS m.

one [wʌn] a, num un(e) ♦ pronoun un(e); (impersonal) on; **this** ~ celui-ci/celle-ci; **that** ~ celui-là/celle-là; **the** ~ **book which** ... l'unique livre que ...; ~ **by** ~ un(e) par un(e); ~ **never knows** on ne sait jamais; ~ **another** l'un(e) l'autre; **it's** ~ **(o'clock)** il est une heure; **which** ~ **do you want?** lequel voulez-vous?; **to be** ~ **up on sb** avoir l'avantage sur qn; **to be at** ~ **(with sb)** être d'accord (avec qn).

one-armed bandit ['wʌnɑːmd-] n machine f à sous.

one-day excursion ['wʌndeɪ-] n (US) billet m d'aller-retour (valable pour la journée).

one-man ['wʌnmæn] a (business) dirigé(e) etc par un seul homme.

one-man band n homme-orchestre m.

one-off [wʌn'ɒf] (Brit col) n exemplaire m unique ♦ a unique.

one-piece ['wʌnpiːs] a: ~ **bathing suit** maillot m une pièce.

onerous ['ɒnərəs] a (task, duty) pénible; (responsibility) lourd(e).

oneself [wʌn'sɛlf] pronoun se; (after prep, also emphatic) soi-même; **by** ~ tout seul.

one-sided [wʌn'saɪdɪd] a (decision) unilatéral(e); (judgment, account) partial(e); (contest) inégal(e).

one-time ['wʌntaɪm] a d'autrefois.

one-to-one ['wʌntəwʌn] a (relationship) univoque.

one-upmanship [wʌn'ʌpmənʃɪp] n: **the art of** ~ l'art de faire mieux que les autres.

one-way ['wʌnweɪ] a (street, traffic) à sens unique.

ongoing ['ɒngəʊɪŋ] a en cours; suivi(e).

onion ['ʌnjən] n oignon m.

on line a (COMPUT) en ligne; (: switched on) connecté(e).

onlooker ['ɒnlʊkə*] n spectateur/trice.

only ['əʊnlɪ] ad seulement ♦ a seul(e), unique ♦ cj seulement, mais; **an** ~ **child** un enfant unique; **not** ~ non seulement; **I** ~ **took one** j'en ai seulement pris un, je n'en ai pris qu'un; **I saw her** ~ **yesterday** je l'ai vue hier encore; **I'd be** ~ **too pleased to help** je ne serais que trop content de vous aider; **I would come,** ~ **I'm very busy** je viendrais bien mais j'ai beaucoup à faire.

ono abbr (= or nearest offer: in classified ads) ≈ à discuter.

onset ['ɒnsɛt] n début m; (of winter, old age) approche f.

onshore ['ɒnʃɔː*] a (wind) du large.

onslaught ['ɒnslɔːt] n attaque f, assaut m.

on-the-job ['ɒnðə'dʒɒb] a: ~ **training** formation f sur place.

onto ['ɒntu] prep = **on to.**

onus ['əʊnəs] n responsabilité f; **the** ~ **is upon him to prove it** c'est à lui de le prouver.

onward(s) ['ɒnwəd(z)] ad (move) en avant.

onyx ['ɒnɪks] n onyx m.

ooze [uːz] vi suinter.

opacity [əʊ'pæsɪtɪ] n opacité f.

opal ['əʊpl] n opale f.

opaque [əʊ'peɪk] a opaque.

OPEC ['əʊpɛk] n abbr (= Organization of Petroleum-Exporting Countries) OPEP f (= Organisation des pays exportateurs de pétrole).

open ['əʊpn] a ouvert(e); (car) découvert(e); (road, view) dégagé(e); (meeting) public(ique); (admiration) manifeste; (question) non résolu(e); (enemy) déclaré(e) ♦ vt ouvrir ♦ vi (flower, eyes, door, debate) s'ouvrir; (shop, bank, museum) ouvrir; (book etc: commence) commencer, débuter; **in the** ~ **(air)** en plein air; **the** ~ **sea** le large; ~ **ground** (among trees) clairière f; (waste ground) terrain m vague; **to have an** ~ **mind (on sth)** avoir l'esprit ouvert (sur qch).

open on to vt fus (subj: room, door) donner sur.

open out vt ouvrir ♦ vi s'ouvrir.

open up vt ouvrir; (blocked road) dégager ♦ vi s'ouvrir.

open-air [əʊpn'ɛə*] a en plein air.

open-and-shut ['əʊpnən'ʃʌt] a: ~ **case** cas m limpide.

open day n journée f portes ouvertes.

open-ended [əʊpn'ɛndɪd] a (fig) non limité(e).

opener ['əʊpnə*] n (also: **can** ~, **tin** ~) ouvre-boîtes m.

open-heart surgery [əʊpn'hɑːt-] n chirurgie f à cœur ouvert.

opening ['əʊpnɪŋ] n ouverture f; (opportunity) occasion f; débouché m; (job) poste vacant.

opening night n (THEATRE) première f.

openly ['əʊpnlɪ] ad ouvertement.

open-minded [əʊpn'maɪndɪd] a à l'esprit ouvert.

open-necked ['əʊpnnɛkt] a à col ouvert.

openness ['əʊpnnɪs] n (frankness) franchise f.

open-plan ['əʊpn'plæn] a sans cloisons.

open sandwich n canapé m.

open shop n entreprise qui admet les travailleurs non syndiqués.

Open University *n* (*Brit*) cours universitaires par correspondance.

opera ['ɔpərə] *n* opéra *m*.

opera glasses *npl* jumelles *fpl* de théâtre.

opera house *n* opéra *m*.

opera singer *n* chanteur/euse d'opéra.

operate ['ɔpəreɪt] *vt* (*machine*) faire marcher, faire fonctionner; (*system*) pratiquer ♦ *vi* fonctionner; (*drug*) faire effet; **to ~ on sb (for)** (*MED*) opérer qn (de).

operatic [ɔpə'rætɪk] *a* d'opéra.

operating ['ɔpəreɪtɪŋ] *a* (*COMM: costs, profit*) d'exploitation; (*MED*): **~ table/theatre** table *f*/salle *f* d'opération.

operating system *n* (*COMPUT*) système *m* d'exploitation.

operation [ɔpə'reɪʃən] *n* opération *f*; (*of machine*) fonctionnement *m*; **to have an ~ (for)** se faire opérer (de); **to be in ~** (*machine*) être en service; (*system*) être en vigueur.

operational [ɔpə'reɪʃənl] *a* opérationnel(le); (*ready for use or action*) en état de marche; **when the service is fully ~** lorsque le service fonctionnera pleinement.

operative ['ɔpərətɪv] *a* (*measure*) en vigueur ♦ *n* (*in factory*) ouvrier/ière; **the ~ word** le mot clef.

operator ['ɔpəreɪtə*] *n* (*of machine*) opérateur/trice; (*TEL*) téléphoniste *m/f*.

operetta [ɔpə'rɛtə] *n* opérette *f*.

ophthalmologist [ɔfθæl'mɔlədʒɪst] *n* ophtalmologiste *m/f*, ophtalmologue *m/f*.

opinion [ə'pɪnjən] *n* opinion *f*, avis *m*; **in my ~** à mon avis; **to seek a second ~** demander un deuxième avis.

opinionated [ə'pɪnjəneɪtɪd] *a* aux idées bien arrêtées.

opinion poll *n* sondage *m* d'opinion.

opium ['əupɪəm] *n* opium *m*.

opponent [ə'pəunənt] *n* adversaire *m/f*.

opportune ['ɔpətjuːn] *a* opportun(e).

opportunist [ɔpə'tjuːnɪst] *n* opportuniste *m/f*.

opportunity [ɔpə'tjuːnɪtɪ] *n* occasion *f*; **to take the ~ to do** *or* **of doing** profiter de l'occasion pour faire.

oppose [ə'pəuz] *vt* s'opposer à; **~d to** *a* opposé(e) à; **as ~d to** par opposition à.

opposing [ə'pəuzɪŋ] *a* (*side*) opposé(e).

opposite ['ɔpəzɪt] *a* opposé(e); (*house etc*) d'en face ♦ *ad* en face ♦ *prep* en face de ♦ *n* opposé *m*, contraire *m*; (*of word*) contraire; **"see ~ page"** "voir ci-contre".

opposite number *n* (*Brit*) homologue *m/f*.

opposite sex *n*: **the ~** l'autre sexe.

opposition [ɔpə'zɪʃən] *n* opposition *f*.

oppress [ə'prɛs] *vt* opprimer.

oppression [ə'prɛʃən] *n* oppression *f*.

oppressive [ə'prɛsɪv] *a* oppressif(ive).

opprobrium [ə'prəubrɪəm] *n* (*formal*) opprobre *m*.

opt [ɔpt] *vi*: **to ~ for** opter pour; **to ~ to do** choisir de faire; **to ~ out of** choisir de quitter.

optical ['ɔptɪkl] *a* optique; (*instrument*) d'optique.

optical character reader/recognition (OCR) *n* lecteur *m*/lecture *f* optique.

optical fibre *n* fibre *f* optique.

optician [ɔp'tɪʃən] *n* opticien/ne.

optics ['ɔptɪks] *n* optique *f*.

optimism ['ɔptɪmɪzəm] *n* optimisme *m*.

optimist ['ɔptɪmɪst] *n* optimiste *m/f*.

optimistic [ɔptɪ'mɪstɪk] *a* optimiste.

optimum ['ɔptɪməm] *a* optimum.

option ['ɔpʃən] *n* choix *m*, option *f*; (*SCOL*) matière *f* à option; (*COMM*) option; **to keep one's ~s open** ne pas s'engager; **I have no ~** je n'ai pas le choix.

optional ['ɔpʃənl] *a* facultatif(ive); (*COMM*) en option; **~ extras** accessoires *mpl* en option, options *fpl*.

opulence ['ɔpjuləns] *n* opulence *f*; abondance *f*.

opulent ['ɔpjulənt] *a* opulent(e); abondant(e).

OR *abbr* (*US POST*) = Oregon.

or [ɔː*] *cj* ou; (*with negative*): **he hasn't seen ~ heard anything** il n'a rien vu ni entendu; **~ else** sinon; ou bien, ou alors.

oracle ['ɔrəkl] *n* oracle *m*.

oral ['ɔːrəl] *a* oral(e) ♦ *n* oral *m*.

orange ['ɔrɪndʒ] *n* (*fruit*) orange *f* ♦ *a* orange *inv*.

orangeade [ɔrɪndʒ'eɪd] *n* orangeade *f*.

oration [ɔː'reɪʃən] *n* discours solennel.

orator ['ɔrətə*] *n* orateur/trice.

oratorio [ɔrə'tɔːrɪəu] *n* oratorio *m*.

orb [ɔːb] *n* orbe *m*.

orbit ['ɔːbɪt] *n* orbite *f* ♦ *vt* décrire une *or* des orbite(s) autour de; **to be in/go into ~ (round)** être/entrer en orbite (autour de).

orchard ['ɔːtʃəd] *n* verger *m*; **apple ~** verger de pommiers.

orchestra ['ɔːkɪstrə] *n* orchestre *m*; (*US: seating*) (fauteuils *mpl* d')orchestre.

orchestral [ɔː'kɛstrəl] *a* orchestral(e); (*concert*) symphonique.

orchestrate ['ɔːkɪstreɪt] *vt* (*MUS*, *fig*) orchestrer.

orchid ['ɔːkɪd] *n* orchidée *f*.

ordain [ɔː'deɪn] *vt* (*REL*) ordonner; (*decide*) décréter.

ordeal [ɔː'diːl] *n* épreuve *f*.

order ['ɔːdə*] *n* ordre *m*; (*COMM*) commande *f* ♦ *vt* ordonner; (*COMM*) commander; **in ~** en ordre; (*of document*) en règle; **out of ~** hors service; (*telephone*) en dérangement; **a machine in working ~** une machine en état de marche; **in ~ of size** par ordre de grandeur; **in ~ to do/that** pour faire/que + *sub*; **to ~ sb to do** ordonner à qn de faire; **to place an ~ for sth with sb** commander qch auprès de qn, passer commande de qch à qn; **to be on ~** être en commande; **made to ~** fait sur commande; **to be under ~s to do sth** avoir ordre de faire qch; **a point of ~** un point de procédure; **to the ~ of** (*BANKING*) à l'ordre de.

order book *n* carnet *m* de commandes.

order form *n* bon *m* de commande.

orderly ['ɔːdəlɪ] *n* (*MIL*) ordonnance *f* ♦ *a* (*room*) en ordre; (*mind*) méthodique; (*person*) qui a de l'ordre.

order number *n* numéro *m* de commande.

ordinal ['ɔːdɪnl] *a* (*number*) ordinal(e).

ordinary ['ɔːdnrɪ] *a* ordinaire, normal(e); (*pej*) ordinaire, quelconque; **out of the ~** exceptionnel(le).

ordinary seaman (OS) *n* (*Brit*) matelot *m*.

ordinary shares *npl* actions *fpl* ordinaires.

ordination [ɔːdɪ'neɪʃən] *n* ordination *f*.

ordnance ['ɔːdnəns] *n* (*MIL: unit*) service *m* du matériel.

Ordnance Survey map *n* (*Brit*) ≈ carte *f* d'État-major.

ore [ɔː*] *n* minerai *m*.

organ ['ɔːgən] *n* organe *m*; (*MUS*) orgue *m*, orgues *fpl*.

organic [ɔː'gænɪk] *a* organique; (*crops etc*) biologique, naturel(le).

organism ['ɔːgənɪzəm] *n* organisme *m*.

organist ['ɔːgənɪst] *n* organiste *m/f*.

organization [ɔːgənaɪ'zeɪʃən] *n* organisation *f*.

organization chart *n* organigramme *m*.

organize ['ɔːgənaɪz] *vt* organiser; **to get ~d** s'organiser.

organized labour *n* main-d'œuvre syndiquée.

organizer ['ɔːgənaɪzə*] *n* organisateur/trice.

orgasm ['ɔːgæzəm] *n* orgasme *m*.

orgy ['ɔːdʒɪ] *n* orgie *f*.

Orient ['ɔːrɪənt] *n*: **the ~** l'Orient *m*.

oriental [ɔːrɪ'entl] *a* oriental(e) ♦ *n* Oriental/e.

orientate ['ɔːrɪənteɪt] *vt* orienter.

orifice ['ɔrɪfɪs] *n* orifice *m*.

origin ['ɔrɪdʒɪn] *n* origine *f*; **country of ~** pays *m* d'origine.

original [ə'rɪdʒɪnl] *a* original(e); (*earliest*) originel(le) ♦ *n* original *m*.

originality [ərɪdʒɪ'nælɪtɪ] *n* originalité *f*.

originally [ə'rɪdʒɪnəlɪ] *ad* (*at first*) à l'origine.

originate [ə'rɪdʒɪneɪt] *vi*: **to ~ from** être originaire de; (*suggestion*) provenir de; **to ~ in** prendre naissance dans; avoir son origine dans.

originator [ə'rɪdʒɪneɪtə*] *n* auteur *m*.

Orkneys ['ɔːknɪz] *npl*: **the ~** (*also*: **the Orkney Islands**) les Orcades *fpl*.

ornament ['ɔːnəmənt] *n* ornement *m*; (*trinket*) bibelot *m*.

ornamental [ɔːnə'mentl] *a* décoratif(ive); (*garden*) d'agrément.

ornamentation [ɔːnəmen'teɪʃən] *n* ornementation *f*.

ornate [ɔː'neɪt] *a* très orné(e).

ornithologist [ɔːnɪ'θɔlədʒɪst] *n* ornithologue *m/f*.

ornithology [ɔːnɪ'θɔlədʒɪ] *n* ornithologie *f*.

orphan ['ɔːfn] *n* orphelin/e ♦ *vt*: **to be ~ed** devenir orphelin.

orphanage ['ɔːfənɪdʒ] *n* orphelinat *m*.

orthodox ['ɔːθədɔks] *a* orthodoxe.

orthopaedic, (*US*) **orthopedic** [ɔːθə'piːdɪk] *a* orthopédique.

OS *abbr* (*Brit*: = *Ordnance Survey*) ≈ IGN *m* (= *Institut géographique national*); (: *NAUT*) = **ordinary seaman**; (: *DRESS*) = **outsize**.

O/S *abbr* = **out of stock**.

oscillate ['ɔsɪleɪt] *vi* osciller.

OSHA *n abbr* (*US*: = *Occupational Safety and Health Administration*) office de l'hygiène et de la sécurité au travail.

Oslo ['ɔzləu] *n* Oslo.

ostensible [ɔs'tensɪbl] *a* prétendu(e); apparent(e).

ostensibly [ɔs'tensɪblɪ] *ad* en apparence.

ostentation [ɔsten'teɪʃən] *n* ostentation *f*.

ostentatious [ɔsten'teɪʃəs] *a* prétentieux(euse); ostentatoire.

osteopath ['ɔstɪəpæθ] *n* ostéopathe *m/f*.

ostracize ['ɔstrəsaɪz] *vt* frapper d'ostracisme.

ostrich ['ɔstrɪtʃ] *n* autruche *f*.

OT *n abbr* (= *Old Testament*) AT *m*.

OTB *n abbr* (*US*: = *off-track betting*) *paris pris en dehors du champ de course.*

O.T.E. *abbr* (= *on-target earnings*) primes sur objectifs inclus.

other ['ʌðə*] *a* autre ♦ *pronoun*: **the ~ (one)** l'autre; **~s** (~ *people*) d'autres; **some ~ people have still to arrive** on attend encore quelques personnes; **the ~ day** l'autre jour; **~ than** autrement que; à part; **some actor or ~** un certain acteur, je ne sais quel acteur; **somebody or ~** quelqu'un; **the car was none ~ than John's** la voiture n'était autre que celle de John.

otherwise ['ʌðəwaɪz] *ad, cj* autrement; **an ~ good piece of work** par ailleurs, un beau travail.

OTT *abbr* (*col*) = **over the top**; *see* **top.**

otter ['ɔtə*] *n* loutre *f*.

OU *n abbr* (*Brit*) = **Open University**.

ouch [autʃ] *excl* aïe!

ought, *pt* **ought** [ɔːt] *auxiliary vb*: **I ~ to do it** je devrais le faire, il faudrait que je le fasse; **this ~ to have been corrected** cela aurait dû être corrigé; **he ~ to win** il devrait gagner; **you ~ to go and see it** vous devriez aller le voir.

ounce [auns] *n* once *f* (= *28.35g; 16 in a pound*).

our ['auə*] *a* notre, nos *pl*.

ours [auəz] *pronoun* le(la) nôtre, les nôtres.

ourselves [auə'selvz] *pronoun pl* (*reflexive, after preposition*) nous; (*emphatic*) nous-mêmes; **we did it (all) by ~** nous avons fait ça tout seuls.

oust [aust] *vt* évincer.

out [aut] *ad* dehors; (*published, not at home etc*) sorti(e); (*light, fire*) éteint(e); (*on strike*) en grève; **~ here** ici; **~ there** là-bas; **he's ~** (*absent*) il est sorti; (*unconscious*) il est sans connaissance; **to be ~ in one's calculations** s'être trompé dans ses calculs; **to run/back etc ~** sortir en courant/en reculant *etc*; **to be ~ and about** *or* (*US*) **around again** être de nouveau sur pied; **before the week was ~** avant la fin de la semaine; **the journey ~** l'aller *m*; **the boat was 10 km ~** le bateau était à 10 km du rivage; **~ loud** *ad* à haute voix; **~ of** *prep* (*outside*) en dehors de; (*because of: anger etc*) par; (*from among*): **~ of 10** sur 10; (*without*): **~ of petrol** sans essence, à court d'essence; **made ~ of wood** en *or* de bois; **~ of order** (*machine*) en panne; (*TEL: line*) en dérangement; **~ of stock** (*COMM: article*) épuisé(e); (: *shop*) en rupture de stock.

outage ['autɪdʒ] *n* (*esp US: power failure*) panne *f or* coupure *f* de courant.

out-and-out ['autəndaut] *a* véritable.

outback ['autbæk] *n* campagne isolée; (*in Australia*) intérieur *m*.

outbid [aut'bɪd] *vt* surenchérir.

outboard ['autbɔːd] *n*: **~ (motor)** (moteur *m*) hors-bord *m*.

outbreak ['autbreɪk] *n* éruption *f*, explosion *f*; (*start*) déclenchement *m*.

outbuilding ['autbɪldɪŋ] n dépendance f.
outburst ['autbə:st] n explosion f, accès m.
outcast ['autkɑ:st] n exilé/e; (socially) paria m.
outclass [aut'klɑ:s] vt surclasser.
outcome ['autkʌm] n issue f, résultat m.
outcrop ['autkrop] n affleurement m.
outcry ['autkraɪ] n tollé (général).
outdated [aut'deɪtɪd] a démodé(e).
outdistance [aut'dɪstəns] vt distancer.
outdo [aut'du:] vt irg surpasser.
outdoor [aut'dɔ:*] a de or en plein air.
outdoors [aut'dɔ:z] ad dehors; au grand air.
outer ['autə*] a extérieur(e); ~ **suburbs** grande banlieue.
outer space n espace m cosmique.
outfit ['autfɪt] n équipement m; (clothes) tenue f; (col: COMM) organisation f, boîte f.
outfitter ['autfɪtə*] n (Brit): "(gent's) ~'s" "confection pour hommes".
outgoing ['autgəuɪŋ] a (president, tenant) sortant(e); (character) ouvert(e), extraverti(e).
outgoings ['autgəuɪŋz] npl (Brit: expenses) dépenses fpl.
outgrow [aut'grəu] vt irg (clothes) devenir trop grand(e) pour.
outhouse ['authaus] n appentis m, remise f.
outing ['autɪŋ] n sortie f; excursion f.
outlandish [aut'lændɪʃ] a étrange.
outlast [aut'lɑ:st] vt survivre à.
outlaw ['autlɔ:] n hors-la-loi m inv ♦ vt (person) mettre hors la loi; (practice) proscrire.
outlay ['autleɪ] n dépenses fpl; (investment) mise f de fonds.
outlet ['autlɛt] n (for liquid etc) issue f, sortie f; (for emotion) exutoire m; (for goods) débouché m; (also: retail ~) point m de vente; (US: ELEC) prise f de courant.
outline ['autlaɪn] n (shape) contour m; (summary) esquisse f, grandes lignes.
outlive [aut'lɪv] vt survivre à.
outlook ['autluk] n perspective f.
outlying ['autlaɪɪŋ] a écarté(e).
outmanoeuvre [autmə'nu:və*] vt (rival etc) avoir au tournant.
outmoded [aut'məudɪd] a démodé(e); dépassé(e).
outnumber [aut'nʌmbə*] vt surpasser en nombre.
out-of-date [autəv'deɪt] a (passport, ticket) périmé(e); (theory, idea) dépassé(e); (custom) désuet(ète); (clothes) démodé(e).
out-of-the-way ['autəvðə'weɪ] a loin de tout; (fig) insolite.
outpatient ['autpeɪʃənt] n malade m/f en consultation externe.
outpost ['autpəust] n avant-poste m.
output ['autput] n rendement m, production f ♦ vt (COMPUT).
outrage ['autreɪdʒ] n atrocité f, acte m de violence; scandale m ♦ vt outrager.
outrageous [aut'reɪdʒəs] a atroce; scandaleux(euse).
outrider ['autraɪdə*] n (on motorcycle) motard m.
outright ad [aut'raɪt] complètement; catégoriquement; carrément; sur le coup ♦ a

['autraɪt] complet(ète); catégorique.
outrun [aut'rʌn] vt irg dépasser.
outset ['autsɛt] n début m.
outshine [aut'ʃaɪn] vt irg (fig) éclipser.
outside [aut'saɪd] n extérieur m ♦ a extérieur(e); (remote, unlikely): **an ~ chance** une (très) faible chance ♦ ad (au) dehors, à l'extérieur ♦ prep hors de, à l'extérieur de; **at the ~** (fig) au plus or maximum; ~ **left/right** n (FOOTBALL) ailier gauche/droit.
outside broadcast n (RADIO, TV) reportage m.
outside lane n (AUT: in Britain) voie f de droite; (: in US, Europe) voie de gauche.
outside line n (TEL) ligne extérieure.
outsider [aut'saɪdə*] n (in race etc) outsider m; (stranger) étranger/ère.
outsize ['autsaɪz] a énorme; (clothes) grande taille inv.
outskirts ['autskə:ts] npl faubourgs mpl.
outsmart [aut'smɑ:t] vt se montrer plus malin(igne) or futé(e) que.
outspoken [aut'spəukən] a très franc(franche).
outspread [aut'sprɛd] a (wings) déployé(e).
outstanding [aut'stændɪŋ] a remarquable, exceptionnel(le); (unfinished) en suspens; en souffrance; non réglé(e); **your account is still ~** vous n'avez pas encore tout remboursé.
outstay [aut'steɪ] vt: **to ~ one's welcome** abuser de l'hospitalité de son hôte.
outstretched [aut'strɛtʃt] a (hand) tendu(e); (body) étendu(e).
outstrip [aut'strɪp] vt (also fig) dépasser.
out-tray ['auttreɪ] n courrier m 'départ'.
outvote [aut'vəut] vt: **to ~ sb (by)** mettre qn en minorité (par); **to ~ sth (by)** rejeter qch (par).
outward ['autwəd] a (sign, appearances) extérieur(e); (journey) (d')aller.
outwardly ['autwədlɪ] ad extérieurement; en apparence.
outweigh [aut'weɪ] vt l'emporter sur.
outwit [aut'wɪt] vt se montrer plus malin que.
oval ['əuvl] a, n ovale (m).
ovary ['əuvərɪ] n ovaire m.
ovation [əu'veɪʃən] n ovation f.
oven ['ʌvn] n four m.
ovenproof ['ʌvnpru:f] a allant au four.
oven-ready ['ʌvnrɛdɪ] a prêt(e) à cuire.
ovenware ['ʌvnwɛə*] n plats mpl allant au four.
over ['əuvə*] ad (par-)dessus; (excessively) trop ♦ a (or ad) (finished) fini(e), terminé(e); (too much) en plus ♦ prep sur; par-dessus; (above) au-dessus de; (on the other side of) de l'autre côté de; (more than) plus de; (during) pendant; (about, concerning): **they fell out ~ money/her** ils se sont brouillés pour des questions d'argent/à cause d'elle; **~ here** ici; **~ there** là-bas; **all ~** (everywhere) partout; (finished) fini(e); **~ and ~ (again)** à plusieurs reprises; **~ and above** en plus de; **to ask sb ~** inviter qn (à passer); **to go ~ to sb's** passer chez qn; **now ~ to our Paris correspondent** nous passons l'antenne à notre correspondant à

Paris; **the world** ~ dans le monde entier; **she's not** ~ **intelligent** (*Brit*) elle n'est pas particulièrement intelligente.

over... ['əuvə*] *prefix*: **~abundant** surabondant(e).

overact [əuvər'ækt] *vi* (*THEATRE*) outrer son rôle.

overall *a, n* ['əuvərɔ:l] *a* (*length*) total(e); (*study*) d'ensemble ♦ *n* (*Brit*) blouse *f* ♦ *ad* [əuvər'ɔ:l] dans l'ensemble, en général; **~s** *npl* bleus *mpl* (de travail).

overanxious [əuvər'æŋkʃəs] *a* trop anxieux(euse).

overawe [əuvər'ɔ:] *vt* impressionner.

overbalance [əuvə'bæləns] *vi* basculer.

overbearing [əuvə'bɛərɪŋ] *a* impérieux(euse), autoritaire.

overboard ['əuvəbɔ:d] *ad* (*NAUT*) par-dessus bord; **to go** ~ **for sth** (*fig*) s'emballer (pour qch).

overbook [əuvə'buk] *vi* faire du surbooking.

overcapitalize [əuvə'kæpɪtəlaɪz] *vt* surcapitaliser.

overcast ['əuvəkɑ:st] *a* couvert(e).

overcharge [əuvə'tʃɑ:dʒ] *vt*: **to** ~ **sb for sth** faire payer qch trop cher à qn.

overcoat ['əuvəkəut] *n* pardessus *m*.

overcome [əuvə'kʌm] *vt irg* triompher de; surmonter ♦ *a* (*emotionally*) bouleversé(e); ~ **with grief** accablé(e) de douleur.

overconfident [əuvə'kɔnfɪdənt] *a* trop sûr(e) de soi.

overcrowded [əuvə'kraudɪd] *a* bondé(e).

overcrowding [əuvə'kraudɪŋ] *n* surpeuplement *m*; (*in bus*) encombrement *m*.

overdo [əuvə'du:] *vt irg* exagérer; (*overcook*) trop cuire; **to** ~ **it, to** ~ **things** (*work too hard*) en faire trop, se surmener.

overdose ['əuvədəus] *n* dose excessive.

overdraft ['əuvədrɑ:ft] *n* découvert *m*.

overdrawn [əuvə'drɔ:n] *a* (*account*) à découvert.

overdrive ['əuvədraɪv] *n* (*AUT*) (vitesse) surmultipliée *f*.

overdue [əuvə'dju:] *a* en retard; (*bill*) impayé(e); (*recognition*) tardif(ive); **that change was long** ~ ce changement n'avait que trop tardé.

overestimate [əuvər'ɛstɪmeɪt] *vt* surestimer.

overexcited [əuvərɪk'saɪtɪd] *a* surexcité(e).

overexertion [əuvərɪg'zə:ʃən] *n* surmenage *m* (physique).

overexpose [əuvərɪk'spəuz] *vt* (*PHOT*) surexposer.

overflow *vi* [əuvə'fləu] déborder ♦ *n* ['əuvəfləu] trop-plein *m*; (*also*: ~ **pipe**) tuyau *m* d'écoulement, trop-plein *m*.

overfly [əuvə'flaɪ] *vt irg* survoler.

overgenerous [əuvə'dʒɛnərəs] *a* (*person*) prodigue; (*offer*) excessif(ive).

overgrown [əuvə'grəun] *a* (*garden*) envahi(e) par la végétation; **he's just an** ~ **schoolboy** (*fig*) c'est un écolier attardé.

overhang ['əuvə'hæŋ] *vt irg* surplomber ♦ *vi* faire saillie.

overhaul *vt* [əuvə'hɔ:l] réviser ♦ *n* ['əuvəhɔ:l] révision *f*.

overhead *ad* [əuvə'hɛd] au-dessus ♦ *a, n* ['əuvəhɛd] *a* aérien(ne); (*lighting*) vertical(e)

♦ *n* (*US*) = **overheads**.

overheads ['əuvəhɛdz] *npl* (*Brit*) frais généraux.

overhear [əuvə'hɪə*] *vt irg* entendre (par hasard).

overheat [əuvə'hi:t] *vi* devenir surchauffé(e); (*engine*) chauffer.

overjoyed [əuvə'dʒɔɪd] *a* ravi(e), enchanté(e).

overkill ['əuvəkɪl] *n* (*fig*): **it would be** ~ ce serait de trop.

overland ['əuvəlænd] *a, ad* par voie de terre.

overlap *vi* [əuvə'læp] se chevaucher ♦ *n* ['əuvəlæp] chevauchement *m*.

overleaf [əuvə'li:f] *ad* au verso.

overload [əuvə'ləud] *vt* surcharger.

overlook [əuvə'luk] *vt* (*have view of*) donner sur; (*miss*) oublier, négliger; (*forgive*) fermer les yeux sur.

overlord ['əuvəlɔ:d] *n* chef *m* suprême.

overmanning [əuvə'mænɪŋ] *n* sureffectif *m*, main-d'œuvre *f* pléthorique.

overnight *ad* [əuvə'naɪt] (*happen*) durant la nuit; (*fig*) soudain ♦ *a* ['əuvənaɪt] d'une (*or* de) nuit; soudain(e); **he stayed there** ~ il y a passé la nuit; **if you travel** ~ ... si tu fais le voyage de nuit ...; **he'll be away** ~ il ne rentrera pas ce soir.

overpass ['əuvəpɑ:s] *n* pont autoroutier; (*US*) passerelle *f*, pont *m*.

overpay [əuvə'peɪ] *vt*: **to** ~ **sb by £50** donner à qn 50 livres de trop.

overpower [əuvə'pauə*] *vt* vaincre; (*fig*) accabler.

overpowering [əuvə'pauərɪŋ] *a* irrésistible; (*heat, stench*) suffocant(e).

overproduction ['əuvəprə'dʌkʃən] *n* surproduction *f*.

overrate [əuvə'reɪt] *vt* surestimer.

overreact [əuvəri:'ækt] *vi* réagir de façon excessive.

override [əuvə'raɪd] *vt* (*irg*: *like* **ride**) (*order, objection*) passer outre à; (*decision*) annuler.

overriding [əuvə'raɪdɪŋ] *a* prépondérant(e).

overrule [əuvə'ru:l] *vt* (*decision*) annuler; (*claim*) rejeter.

overrun [əuvə'rʌn] *vt irg* (*MIL*: *country etc*) occuper; (*time limit etc*) dépasser ♦ *vi irg* dépasser le temps imparti; **the town is** ~ **with tourists** la ville est envahie de touristes.

overseas [əuvə'si:z] *ad* outre-mer; (*abroad*) à l'étranger ♦ *a* (*trade*) extérieur(e); (*visitor*) étranger(ère).

overseer ['əuvəsɪə*] *n* (*in factory*) contremaître *m*.

overshadow [əuvə'ʃædəu] *vt* (*fig*) éclipser.

overshoot [əuvə'ʃu:t] *vt irg* dépasser.

oversight ['əuvəsaɪt] *n* omission *f*, oubli *m*; **due to an** ~ par suite d'une inadvertance.

oversimplify [əuvə'sɪmplɪfaɪ] *vt* simplifier à l'excès.

oversleep [əuvə'sli:p] *vi irg* se réveiller (trop) tard.

overspend [əuvə'spɛnd] *vi irg* dépenser de trop; **we have overspent by 5,000 dollars** nous avons dépassé notre budget de 5.000 dollars, nous avons dépensé 5.000 dollars de trop.

overspill ['əuvəspɪl] *n* excédent *m* de population.

overstaffed [əuvə'stɑ:ft] a: **to be ~** avoir trop de personnel, être en surnombre.

overstate [əuvə'steit] vt exagérer.

overstatement [əuvə'steitmənt] n exagération f.

overstep [əuvə'step] vt: **to ~ the mark** dépasser la mesure.

overstock [əuvə'stɔk] vt stocker en surabondance.

overstrike n ['əuvəstraik] (on printer) superposition f, double frappe f ♦ vt irg [əuvə'straik] surimprimer.

overt [əu'və:t] a non dissimulé(e).

overtake [əuvə'teik] vt irg dépasser; (AUT) dépasser, doubler.

overtaking [əuvə'teikiŋ] n (AUT) dépassement m.

overtax [əuvə'tæks] vt (ECON) surimposer; (fig: strength, patience) abuser de; **to ~ o.s.** se surmener.

overthrow [əuvə'θrəu] vt irg (government) renverser.

overtime ['əuvətaim] n heures fpl supplémentaires; **to do** or **work ~** faire des heures supplémentaires.

overtime ban n refus m de faire des heures supplémentaires.

overtone ['əuvətəun] n (also: **~s**) note f, sous-entendus mpl.

overture ['əuvətʃuə*] n (MUS, fig) ouverture f.

overturn [əuvə'tə:n] vt renverser ♦ vi se retourner.

overweight [əuvə'weit] a (person) trop gros(se); (luggage) trop lourd(e).

overwhelm [əuvə'welm] vt accabler; submerger; écraser.

overwhelming [əuvə'welmiŋ] a (victory, defeat) écrasant(e); (desire) irrésistible; **one's ~ impression is of** heat on a une impression dominante de chaleur.

overwhelmingly [əuvə'welmiŋli] ad (vote) en masse; (win) d'une manière écrasante.

overwork [əuvə'wə:k] n surmenage m ♦ vt surmener ♦ vi se surmener.

overwrite [əuvə'rait] vt (COMPUT) écraser.

overwrought [əuvə'rɔ:t] a excédé(e).

ovulation [ɔvju'leiʃən] n ovulation f.

owe [əu] vt devoir; **to ~ sb sth, to ~ sth to sb** devoir qch à qn.

owing to ['əuiŋtu:] prep à cause de, en raison de.

owl [aul] n hibou m.

own [əun] vt posséder ♦ vi (Brit): **to ~ to sth** reconnaître or avouer qch; **to ~ to having done sth** avouer avoir fait qch ♦ a propre; **a room of my ~** une chambre à moi, ma propre chambre; **can I have it for my (very) ~?** puis-je l'avoir pour moi (tout) seul?; **to get one's ~ back** prendre sa revanche; **on one's ~** tout(e) seul(e); **to come into one's ~** trouver sa voie; trouver sa justification.
own up vi avouer.

own brand n (COMM) marque f de distributeur.

owner ['əunə*] n propriétaire m/f.

owner-occupier ['əunər'ɔkjupaiə*] n propriétaire occupant.

ownership ['əunəʃip] n possession f; **it's under new ~** (shop etc) il y a eu un changement de propriétaire.

ox, pl **oxen** [ɔks, 'ɔksn] n bœuf m.

Oxfam ['ɔksfæm] n abbr (Brit: = Oxford Committee for Famine Relief) association humanitaire.

oxide ['ɔksaid] n oxyde m.

Oxon. ['ɔksn] abbr (Brit: = Oxoniensis) = of Oxford.

oxtail ['ɔksteil] n: **~ soup** soupe f à la queue de bœuf.

oxyacetylene ['ɔksiə'setili:n] a oxyacétylénique; **~ burner, ~ lamp** chalumeau m oxyacétylénique.

oxygen ['ɔksidʒən] n oxygène m.

oxygen mask n masque m à oxygène.

oxygen tent n tente f à oxygène.

oyster ['ɔistə*] n huître f.

oz. abbr = ounce.

ozone ['əuzəun] n ozone m.

P

P, p [pi:] n (letter) P, p m; **P for Peter** P comme Pierre.

P abbr = **president, prince.**

p abbr (= page) p; (Brit) = **penny, pence.**

PA n abbr = **personal assistant, public address system** ♦ abbr (US POST) = Pennsylvania.

pa [pɑ:] n (col) papa m.

p.a. abbr = **per annum.**

PAC n abbr (US) = political action committee.

pace [peis] n pas m; (speed) allure f; vitesse f ♦ vi: **to ~ up and down** faire les cent pas; **to keep ~ with** aller à la même vitesse que; (events) se tenir au courant de; **to set the ~** (running) donner l'allure; (fig) donner le ton; **to put sb through his ~s** (fig) mettre qn à l'épreuve.

pacemaker ['peismeikə*] n (MED) stimulateur m cardiaque.

pacific [pə'sifik] a pacifique ♦ n: **the P~ (Ocean)** le Pacifique, l'océan m Pacifique.

pacification [pæsifi'keiʃən] n pacification f.

pacifier ['pæsifaiə*] n (US: dummy) tétine f.

pacifist ['pæsifist] n pacifiste m/f.

pacify ['pæsifai] vt (COMPUT) écraser; (soothe) calmer.

pack [pæk] n paquet m; ballot m; (of hounds) meute f; (of thieves, wolves etc) bande f; (of cards) jeu m ♦ vt (goods) empaqueter, emballer; (in suitcase etc) emballer; (box) remplir; (cram) entasser; (press down) tasser; damer; (COMPUT) grouper, tasser ♦ vi: **to ~ (one's bags)** faire ses bagages; **to ~ into** (room, stadium) s'entasser dans; **to send sb ~ing** (col) envoyer promener qn.
pack in (Brit col) vi (machine) tomber en panne ♦ vt (boyfriend) plaquer; **~ it in!** laisse tomber!
pack off vt (person) envoyer (promener), expédier.
pack up vi (Brit col: machine) tomber en

panne; (: *person*) se tirer ♦ *vt* (*belongings*) ranger; (*goods, presents*) empaqueter, emballer.

package ['pækɪdʒ] *n* paquet *m*; (*of goods*) emballage *m*, conditionnement *m*; (*also*: ~ **deal**) marché global; forfait *m*; (*COMPUT*) progiciel *m* ♦ *vt* (*goods*) conditionner.

package holiday *n* (*Brit*) vacances organisées.

package tour *n* voyage organisé.

packaging ['pækɪdʒɪŋ] *n* conditionnement *m*.

packed [pækt] *a* (*crowded*) bondé(e); ~ **lunch** (*Brit*) repas froid.

packer ['pækə*] *n* (*person*) emballeur/euse; conditionneur/euse.

packet ['pækɪt] *n* paquet *m*.

packet switching *n* (*COMPUT*) commutation *f* de paquets.

pack ice ['pækaɪs] *n* banquise *f*.

packing ['pækɪŋ] *n* emballage *m*.

packing case *n* caisse *f* (d'emballage).

pact [pækt] *n* pacte *m*, traité *m*.

pad [pæd] *n* bloc(-notes) *m*; (*for inking*) tampon encreur; (*col: flat*) piaule *f* ♦ *vt* rembourrer ♦ *vi*: **to ~ in/about** *etc* entrer/aller et venir *etc* à pas feutrés.

padding ['pædɪŋ] *n* rembourrage *m*; (*fig*) délayage *m*.

paddle ['pædl] *n* (*oar*) pagaie *f* ♦ *vi* barboter, faire trempette ♦ *vt*: **to ~ a canoe** *etc* pagayer.

paddle steamer *n* bateau *m* à aubes.

paddling pool *n* petit bassin.

paddock ['pædək] *n* enclos *m*; paddock *m*.

paddy ['pædɪ] *n* (*also*: ~ **field**) rizière *f*.

padlock ['pædlɔk] *n* cadenas *m* ♦ *vt* cadenasser.

padre ['pɑːdrɪ] *n* aumônier *m*.

paediatrics, (*US*) **pediatrics** [piːdɪ'ætrɪks] *n* pédiatrie *f*.

pagan ['peɪgən] *a, n* païen(ne).

page [peɪdʒ] *n* (*of book*) page *f*; (*also*: ~ **boy**) groom *m*, chasseur *m*; (*at wedding*) garçon *m* d'honneur ♦ *vt* (*in hotel etc*) (faire) appeler.

pageant ['pædʒənt] *n* spectacle *m* historique; grande cérémonie.

pageantry ['pædʒəntrɪ] *n* apparat *m*, pompe *f*.

page break *n* fin *f* or saut *m* de page.

pager ['peɪdʒə*] *n* système *m* de téléappel.

paginate ['pædʒɪneɪt] *vt* paginer.

pagination [pædʒɪ'neɪʃən] *n* pagination *f*.

pagoda [pə'gəudə] *n* pagode *f*.

paid [peɪd] *pt, pp of* **pay** ♦ *a* (*work, official*) rémunéré(e); **to put ~ to** (*Brit*) mettre fin à, mettre par terre.

paid-up ['peɪdʌp], (*US*) **paid-in** ['peɪdɪn] *a* (*member*) à jour de sa cotisation; (*shares*) libéré(e); ~ **capital** capital versé.

pail [peɪl] *n* seau *m*.

pain [peɪn] *n* douleur *f*; **to be in** ~ souffrir, avoir mal; **to have a** ~ **in** avoir mal à *or* une douleur à *or* dans; **to take** ~**s to do se** donner du mal pour faire; **on** ~**s of death** sous peine de mort.

pained [peɪnd] *a* peiné(e), chagrin(e).

painful ['peɪnful] *a* douloureux(euse); (*difficult*) difficile, pénible.

painfully ['peɪnfəlɪ] *ad* (*fig: very*) terri-

blement.

painkiller ['peɪnkɪlə*] *n* calmant *m*.

painless ['peɪnlɪs] *a* indolore.

painstaking ['peɪnzteɪkɪŋ] *a* (*person*) soigneux(euse); (*work*) soigné(e).

paint [peɪnt] *n* peinture *f* ♦ *vt* peindre; (*fig*) dépeindre; **to ~ the door blue** peindre la porte en bleu; **to ~ in oils** faire de la peinture à l'huile.

paintbox ['peɪntbɔks] *n* boîte *f* de couleurs.

paintbrush ['peɪntbrʌʃ] *n* pinceau *m*.

painter ['peɪntə*] *n* peintre *m*.

painting ['peɪntɪŋ] *n* peinture *f*; (*picture*) tableau *m*.

paint-stripper ['peɪntstrɪpə*] *n* décapant *m*.

paintwork ['peɪntwəːk] *n* (*Brit*) peintures *fpl*; (: *of car*) peinture *f*.

pair [pɛə*] *n* (*of shoes, gloves etc*) paire *f*; (*couple*) couple *m*; (*twosome*) duo *m*; ~ **of scissors** (paire de) ciseaux *mpl*; ~ **of trousers** pantalon *m*.

pair off *vi* se mettre par deux.

pajamas [pə'dʒɑːməz] *npl* (*US*) pyjama(s) *m(pl)*.

Pakistan [pɑːkɪ'stɑːn] *n* Pakistan *m*.

Pakistani [pɑːkɪ'stɑːnɪ] *a* pakistanais(e) ♦ *n* Pakistanais/e.

PAL [pæl] *n abbr* (*TV: phase alternation line*) PAL *m*.

pal [pæl] *n* (*col*) copain/copine.

palace ['pæləs] *n* palais *m*.

palatable ['pælɪtəbl] *a* bon(bonne), agréable au goût.

palate ['pælɪt] *n* palais *m* (*ANAT*).

palatial [pə'leɪʃəl] *a* grandiose, magnifique.

palaver [pə'lɑːvə*] *n* palabres *fpl or mpl*; histoire(s) *f(pl)*.

pale [peɪl] *a* pâle ♦ *vi* pâlir ♦ *n*: **to be beyond the** ~ être au ban de la société; **to grow** *or* **turn** ~ (*person*) pâlir; ~ **blue** *a* bleu pâle *inv*; **to ~ into insignificance (beside)** perdre beaucoup d'importance (par rapport à).

paleness ['peɪlnɪs] *n* pâleur *f*.

Palestine ['pælɪstaɪn] *n* Palestine *f*.

Palestinian [pælɪs'tɪnɪən] *a* palestinien(ne) ♦ *n* Palestinien/ne.

palette ['pælɪt] *n* palette *f*.

paling ['peɪlɪŋ] *n* (*stake*) palis *m*; (*fence*) palissade *f*.

palisade [pælɪ'seɪd] *n* palissade *f*.

pall [pɔːl] *n* (*of smoke*) voile *m* ♦ *vi*: **to ~ (on)** devenir lassant (pour).

pallet ['pælɪt] *n* (*for goods*) palette *f*.

pallid ['pælɪd] *a* blême.

pallor ['pælə*] *n* pâleur *f*.

pally ['pælɪ] *a* (*col*) copain(copine).

palm [pɑːm] *n* (*ANAT*) paume *f*; (*also*: ~ **tree**) palmier *m*; (*leaf, symbol*) palme *f* ♦ *vt*: **to ~ sth off on sb** (*col*) refiler qch à qn.

palmist ['pɑːmɪst] *n* chiromancien/ne.

Palm Sunday *n* le dimanche des Rameaux.

palpable ['pælpəbl] *a* évident(e), manifeste.

palpitation [pælpɪ'teɪʃən] *n* palpitation *f*.

paltry ['pɔːltrɪ] *a* dérisoire; piètre.

pamper ['pæmpə*] *vt* gâter, dorloter.

pamphlet ['pæmflət] *n* brochure *f*; (*political etc*) tract *m*.

pan [pæn] *n* (*also*: **sauce**~) casserole *f*; (*also*: **frying** ~) poêle *f*; (*of lavatory*) cuvette *f* ♦ *vi*

(*CINEMA*) faire un panoramique ♦ *vt* (*col*: *book, film*) éreinter; **to** ~ **for gold** laver du sable aurifère.

panacea [pænə'sɪə] *n* panacée *f*.

Panama ['pænəmɑ:] *n* Panama *m*.

Panama canal *n* canal *m* de Panama.

pancake ['pænkeɪk] *n* crêpe *f*.

Pancake Day *n* (*Brit*) mardi gras.

pancreas ['pæŋkrɪəs] *n* pancréas *m*.

panda ['pændə] *n* panda *m*.

panda car *n* (*Brit*) ≈ voiture *f* pie *inv*.

pandemonium [pændɪ'məʊnɪəm] *n* tohu-bohu *m*.

pander ['pændə*] *vi*: **to** ~ **to** flatter bassement; obéir servilement à.

pane [peɪn] *n* carreau *m* (de fenêtre).

panel ['pænl] *n* (*of wood, cloth etc*) panneau *m*; (*RADIO, TV*) panel *m*, invités *mpl*; (*of experts*) table ronde, comité *m*.

panel game *n* (*Brit*) jeu *m* (radiophonique/télévisé).

panelling, (*US*) **paneling** ['pænəlɪŋ] *n* boiseries *fpl*.

panellist, (*US*) **panelist** ['pænəlɪst] *n* invité/e (*d'un panel*), membre d'un panel.

pang [pæŋ] *n*: ~**s of remorse** pincements *mpl* de remords; ~**s of hunger/conscience** tiraillements *mpl* d'estomac/de la conscience.

panic ['pænɪk] *n* panique *f*, affolement *m* ♦ *vi* s'affoler, paniquer.

panicky ['pænɪkɪ] *a* (*person*) qui panique *or* s'affole facilement.

panic-stricken ['pænɪkstrɪkən] *a* affolé(e).

pannier ['pænɪə*] *n* (*on animal*) bât *m*; (*on bicycle*) sacoche *f*.

panorama [pænə'rɑ:mə] *n* panorama *m*.

panoramic [pænə'ræmɪk] *a* panoramique.

pansy ['pænzɪ] *n* (*BOT*) pensée *f*; (*col*) tapette *f*, pédé *m*.

pant [pænt] *vi* haleter.

pantechnicon [pæn'teknɪkən] *n* (*Brit*) (grand) camion de déménagement.

panther ['pænθə*] *n* panthère *f*.

panties ['pæntɪz] *npl* slip *m*, culotte *f*.

pantihose ['pæntɪhəʊz] *n* (*US*) collant *m*.

pantomime ['pæntəmaɪm] *n* (*Brit*) spectacle *m* de Noël.

pantry ['pæntrɪ] *n* garde-manger *m inv*; (*room*) office *f or m*.

pants [pænts] *n* (*Brit: woman's*) culotte *f*, slip *m*; (: *man's*) slip *m*, caleçon *m*; (*US: trousers*) pantalon *m*.

pantsuit ['pæntsu:t] *n* (*US*) tailleur-pantalon *m*.

papacy ['peɪpəsɪ] *n* papauté *f*.

papal ['peɪpəl] *a* papal(e), pontifical(e).

paper ['peɪpə*] *n* papier *m*; (*also:* **wall**~) papier peint; (*also:* **news**~) journal *m*; (*study, article*) article *m*; (*exam*) épreuve écrite ♦ *a* en *or* de papier ♦ *vt* tapisser (de papier peint); **a piece of** ~ (*odd bit*) un bout de papier; (*sheet*) une feuille de papier; **to put sth down on** ~ mettre qch par écrit.

paper advance *n* (*on printer*) avance *f* (du) papier.

paperback ['peɪpəbæk] *n* livre *m* de poche; livre broché *or* non relié ♦ *a*: ~ **edition** édition brochée.

paper bag *n* sac *m* en papier.

paperboy ['peɪpəbɔɪ] *n* (*selling*) vendeur *m* de journaux; (*delivering*) livreur *m* de journaux.

paper clip *n* trombone *m*.

paper handkerchief *n* mouchoir *m* en papier.

paper mill *n* papeterie *f*.

paper money *n* papier-monnaie *m*.

paper profit *n* profit *m* théorique.

papers ['peɪpəz] *npl* (*also:* **identity** ~) papiers *mpl* (d'identité).

paperweight ['peɪpəweɪt] *n* presse-papiers *m inv*.

paperwork ['peɪpəwɜ:k] *n* paperasserie *f*.

papier-mâché ['pæpɪeɪ'mæʃeɪ] *n* papier mâché.

paprika ['pæprɪkə] *n* paprika *m*.

Pap test, Pap smear ['pæp-] *n* (*MED*) frottis *m*.

par [pɑ:*] *n* pair *m*; (*GOLF*) normale *f* du parcours; **on a** ~ **with** à égalité avec, au même niveau que; **at** ~ au pair; **above/below** ~ au-dessus/au-dessous du pair; **to feel below** *or* **under** *or* **not up to** ~ ne pas se sentir en forme.

parable ['pærəbl] *n* parabole *f* (*REL*).

parabola [pə'ræbələ] *n* parabole *f* (*MATH*).

parachute ['pærəʃu:t] *n* parachute *m* ♦ *vi* sauter en parachute.

parachute jump *n* saut *m* en parachute.

parachutist ['pærəʃu:tɪst] *n* parachutiste *m/f*.

parade [pə'reɪd] *n* défilé *m*; (*inspection*) revue *f*; (*street*) boulevard *m* ♦ *vt* (*fig*) faire étalage de ♦ *vi* défiler; **a fashion** ~ (*Brit*) un défilé de mode.

parade ground *n* terrain *m* de manœuvre.

paradise ['pærədaɪs] *n* paradis *m*.

paradox ['pærədɔks] *n* paradoxe *m*.

paradoxical [pærə'dɔksɪkl] *a* paradoxal(e).

paradoxically [pærə'dɔksɪklɪ] *ad* paradoxalement.

paraffin ['pærəfɪn] *n* (*Brit*): ~ (**oil**) pétrole (lampant); **liquid** ~ huile *f* de paraffine.

paraffin heater *n* (*Brit*) poêle *m* à mazout.

paraffin lamp *n* (*Brit*) lampe *f* à pétrole.

paragon ['pærəgən] *n* parangon *m*.

paragraph ['pærəgrɑ:f] *n* paragraphe *m*; **to begin a new** ~ aller à la ligne.

Paraguay ['pærəgwaɪ] *n* Paraguay *m*.

Paraguayan [pærə'gwaɪən] *a* paraguayen(ne) ♦ *n* Paraguayen(ne).

parallel ['pærəlel] *a*: ~ (**with** *or* **to**) parallèle (à); (*fig*) analogue (à) ♦ *n* (*line*) parallèle *f*; (*fig*, *GEO*) parallèle *m*.

paralysis, pl paralyses [pə'rælɪsɪs, -si:z] *n* paralysie *f*.

paralytic [pærə'lɪtɪk] *a* paralytique; (*Brit col*: *drunk*) ivre mort(e).

paralyze ['pærəlaɪz] *vt* paralyser.

parameter [pə'ræmɪtə*] *n* paramètre *m*.

paramilitary [pærə'mɪlɪtərɪ] *a* paramilitaire.

paramount ['pærəmaunt] *a*: **of** ~ **importance** de la plus haute *or* grande importance.

paranoia [pærə'nɔɪə] *n* paranoïa *f*.

paranoid ['pærənɔɪd] *a* (*PSYCH*) paranoïaque; (*neurotic*) paranoïde.

paranormal [pærə'nɔ:ml] *a* paranormal(e).

paraphernalia [pærəfə'neɪlɪə] *n* attirail *m*, affaires *fpl*.

paraphrase ['pærəfreɪz] *vt* paraphraser.

paraplegic [pærə'pli:dʒɪk] n paraplégique m/f.
parapsychology [pærəsaɪ'kɔlədʒɪ] n parapsychologie f.
parasite ['pærəsaɪt] n parasite m.
parasol ['pærəsɔl] n ombrelle f; (at café etc) parasol m.
paratrooper ['pærətru:pə*] n parachutiste m (soldat).
parcel ['pɑ:sl] n paquet m, colis m ♦ vt (also: ~ up) empaqueter.
  parcel out vt répartir.
parcel bomb n (Brit) colis piégé.
parcel post n service m de colis postaux.
parch [pɑ:tʃ] vt dessécher.
parched [pɑ:tʃt] a (person) assoiffé(e).
parchment ['pɑ:tʃmənt] n parchemin m.
pardon ['pɑ:dn] n pardon m; grâce f ♦ vt pardonner à; (LAW) gracier; ~! pardon!; ~ me! excusez-moi!; I beg your ~! pardon!, je suis désolé!; (I beg your) ~?, (US) ~ me? pardon?
pare [pɛə*] vt (Brit: nails) couper; (fruit etc) peler; (fig: costs etc) réduire.
parent ['pɛərənt] n père m or mère f; ~s npl parents mpl.
parentage ['pɛərəntɪdʒ] n naissance f; of unknown ~ de parents inconnus.
parental [pə'rɛntl] a parental(e), des parents.
parent company n société f mère.
parenthesis, pl **parentheses** [pə'rɛnθɪsɪs, -si:z] n parenthèse f; in parentheses entre parenthèses.
parenthood ['pɛərənthud] n paternité f or maternité f.
parenting ['pɛərəntɪŋ] n le métier de parent, le travail d'un parent.
Paris ['pærɪs] n Paris.
parish ['pærɪʃ] n paroisse f; (civil) ≈ commune f ♦ a paroissial(e).
parish council n (Brit) ≈ conseil municipal.
parishioner [pə'rɪʃənə*] n paroissien/ne.
Parisian [pə'rɪzɪən] a parisien(ne) ♦ n Parisien/ne.
parity ['pærɪtɪ] n parité f.
park [pɑ:k] n parc m, jardin public ♦ vt garer ♦ vi se garer.
parka ['pɑ:kə] n parka m.
parking ['pɑ:kɪŋ] n stationnement m; "no ~" "stationnement interdit".
parking lights npl feux mpl de stationnement.
parking lot n (US) parking m, parc m de stationnement.
parking meter n parcomètre m.
parking offence, (US) **parking violation** n infraction f au stationnement.
parking place n place f de stationnement.
parking ticket n P.-V. m.
parkway ['pɑ:kweɪ] n (US) route f express (en site vert ou aménagé).
parlance ['pɑ:ləns] n: in common/modern ~ dans le langage courant/actuel.
parliament ['pɑ:ləmənt] n parlement m.
parliamentary [pɑ:lə'mɛntərɪ] a parlementaire.
parlour, (US) **parlor** ['pɑ:lə*] n salon m.
parlous ['pɑ:ləs] a (formal) précaire.
Parmesan [pɑ:mɪ'zæn] n (also: ~ cheese) Parmesan m.

parochial [pə'rəukɪəl] a paroissial(e); (pej) à l'esprit de clocher.
parody ['pærədɪ] n parodie f.
parole [pə'rəul] n: on ~ en liberté conditionnelle.
paroxysm ['pærəksɪzəm] n (MED, of grief) paroxysme m; (of anger) accès m.
parquet ['pɑ:keɪ] n: ~ floor(ing) parquet m.
parrot ['pærət] n perroquet m.
parrot fashion ad comme un perroquet.
parry ['pærɪ] vt esquiver, parer à.
parsimonious [pɑ:sɪ'məunɪəs] a parcimonieux(euse).
parsley ['pɑ:slɪ] n persil m.
parsnip ['pɑ:snɪp] n panais m.
parson ['pɑ:sn] n ecclésiastique m; (Church of England) pasteur m.
parsonage ['pɑ:snɪdʒ] n presbytère m.
part [pɑ:t] n partie f; (of machine) pièce f; (THEATRE etc) rôle m; (MUS) voix f; partie ♦ a partiel(le) ♦ ad = **partly** ♦ vt séparer ♦ vi (people) se séparer; (roads) se diviser; to take ~ in participer à, prendre part à; to take sb's ~ prendre le parti de qn, prendre parti pour qn; on his ~ de sa part; for my ~ en ce qui me concerne; for the most ~ en grande partie; dans la plupart des cas; for the better ~ of the day pendant la plus grande partie de la journée; to be ~ and parcel of faire partie de; to take sth in good/bad ~ prendre qch du bon/mauvais côté; ~ of speech (LING) partie f du discours.
  part with vt fus se séparer de; se défaire de.
partake [pɑ:'teɪk] vi irg (formal): to ~ of sth prendre part à qch, partager qch.
part exchange n (Brit): in ~ en reprise.
partial ['pɑ:ʃl] a partiel(le); (unjust) partial(e); to be ~ to aimer, avoir un faible pour.
partially ['pɑ:ʃəlɪ] ad en partie, partiellement; partialement.
participant [pɑ:'tɪsɪpənt] n: ~ (in) participant/e (à).
participate [pɑ:'tɪsɪpeɪt] vi: to ~ (in) participer (à), prendre part (à).
participation [pɑ:tɪsɪ'peɪʃən] n participation f.
participle ['pɑ:tɪsɪpl] n participe m.
particle ['pɑ:tɪkl] n particule f.
particular [pə'tɪkjulə*] a (specific) particulier(ière); (special) particulier, spécial(e); (fussy) difficile, exigeant(e); méticuleux(euse); ~s npl détails mpl; (information) renseignements mpl; in ~ surtout, en particulier.
particularly [pə'tɪkjuləlɪ] ad particulièrement; (in particular) en particulier.
parting ['pɑ:tɪŋ] n séparation f; (Brit: in hair) raie f ♦ a d'adieu; his ~ shot was ... il lança en partant ....
partisan [pɑ:tɪ'zæn] n partisan/e ♦ a partisan(e); de parti.
partition [pɑ:'tɪʃən] n (POL) partition f, division f; (wall) cloison f.
partly ['pɑ:tlɪ] ad en partie, partiellement.
partner ['pɑ:tnə*] n (COMM) associé/e; (SPORT) partenaire m/f; (at dance) cavalier/ière ♦ vt être l'associé or le partenaire or le

cavalier de.

partnership ['pɑ:tnəʃip] n association f; **to go into ~ (with), form a ~ (with)** s'associer (avec).

part payment n acompte m.

partridge ['pɑ:trɪdʒ] n perdrix f.

part-time ['pɑ:t'taɪm] a, ad à mi-temps, à temps partiel.

part-timer [pɑ:t'taɪmə*] n (also: **part- time worker**) travailleur/euse à temps partiel.

party ['pɑ:tɪ] n (POL) parti m; (team) équipe f; groupe m; (LAW) partie f; (celebration) réception f; soirée f; réunion f, fête f; **dinner ~ dîner** m; **to give** or **throw a ~** donner une réception; **we're having a ~ next Saturday** nous organisons une soirée or réunion entre amis samedi prochain; **it's for our son's birthday ~** c'est pour la fête (or le goûter) d'anniversaire de notre garçon; **to be a ~ to a crime** être impliqué(e) dans un crime.

party line n (POL) ligne f politique; (TEL) ligne partagée.

par value n (of share, bond) valeur nominale.

pass [pɑ:s] vt (time, object) passer; (place) passer devant; (car, friend) croiser; (exam) être reçu(e) à, réussir; (candidate) admettre; (overtake, surpass) dépasser; (approve) approuver, accepter; (law) promulguer ♦ vi passer; (SCOL) être reçu(e) or admis(e), réussir ♦ n (permit) laissez-passer m inv; carte f d'accès or d'abonnement; (in mountains) col m; (SPORT) passe f; (SCOL: also: ~ **mark**): **to get a ~** être reçu(e) (sans mention); **she could ~ for 25** on lui donnerait 25 ans; **to ~ sth through a ring etc** (faire) passer qch dans un anneau etc; **could you ~ the vegetables round?** pourriez-vous faire passer les légumes?; **things have come to a pretty ~** (Brit) voilà où on en est!; **to make a ~ at sb** (col) faire des avances à qn.

pass away vi mourir.

pass by vi passer ♦ vt négliger.

pass down vt (customs, inheritance) transmettre.

pass on vi (die) s'éteindre, décéder ♦ vt (hand on): **to ~ on (to)** transmettre (à); (: illness) passer (à); (: price rises) répercuter (sur).

pass out vi s'évanouir; (Brit MIL) sortir (d'une école militaire).

pass over vt (ignore) passer sous silence.

pass up vt (opportunity) laisser passer.

passable ['pɑ:səbl] a (road) praticable; (work) acceptable.

passage ['pæsɪdʒ] n (also: ~**way**) couloir m; (gen, in book) passage m; (by boat) traversée f.

passbook ['pɑ:sbuk] n livret m.

passenger ['pæsɪndʒə*] n passager/ère.

passer-by [pɑ:sə'baɪ] n passant/e.

passing ['pɑ:sɪŋ] a (fig) passager(ère); **in ~** en passant.

passing place n (AUT) aire f de croisement.

passion ['pæʃən] n passion f; **to have a ~ for sth** avoir la passion de qch.

passionate ['pæʃənɪt] a passionné(e).

passive ['pæsɪv] a (also LING) passif(ive).

passkey ['pɑ:ski:] n passe m.

Passover ['pɑ:səuvə*] n Pâque juive.

passport ['pɑ:spɔ:t] n passeport m.

passport control n contrôle m des passeports.

password ['pɑ:swə:d] n mot m de passe.

past [pɑ:st] prep (further than) au delà de, plus loin que; (later than) après ♦ a passé(e); (president etc) ancien(ne) ♦ n passé m; **quarter/half ~ four** quatre heures et quart/demie; **ten/twenty ~ four** quatre heures dix/vingt; **he's ~ forty** il a dépassé la quarantaine, il a plus de or passé quarante ans; **it's ~ midnight** il est plus de minuit, il est passé minuit; **for the ~ few/3 days** depuis quelques/3 jours; **ces derniers/3** derniers jours; **to run ~** passer en courant; **he ran ~ me** il m'a dépassé en courant; il a passé devant moi en courant; **in the ~** (gen) dans le temps, autrefois; (LING) au passé; **I'm ~ caring** je ne m'en fais plus; **to be ~ it** (Brit col: person) avoir passé l'âge.

pasta ['pæstə] n pâtes fpl.

paste [peɪst] n (glue) colle f (de pâte); (jewellery) strass m; (CULIN) pâté m (à tartiner); pâte f ♦ vt coller; **tomato ~** concentré m de tomate, purée f de tomate.

pastel ['pæstl] a pastel inv.

pasteurized ['pæstəraɪzd] a pasteurisé(e).

pastille ['pæstl] n pastille f.

pastime ['pɑ:staɪm] n passe-temps m inv, distraction f.

past master n (Brit): **to be a ~ at** être expert en.

pastor ['pɑ:stə*] n pasteur m.

pastoral ['pɑ:stərl] a pastoral(e).

pastry ['peɪstrɪ] n pâte f; (cake) pâtisserie f.

pasture ['pɑ:stʃə*] n pâturage m.

pasty n ['pæstɪ] petit pâté (en croûte) ♦ a ['peɪstɪ] pâteux(euse); (complexion) terreux (euse).

pat [pæt] vt donner une petite tape à ♦ n: **a ~ of butter** une noisette de beurre; **to give sb/ o.s. a ~ on the back** (fig) congratuler qn/se congratuler; **he knows it (off) ~, (US) he has it down ~** il sait cela sur le bout des doigts.

patch [pætʃ] n (of material) pièce f; (spot) tache f; (of land) parcelle f ♦ vt (clothes) rapiécer; **a bad ~** (Brit) une période difficile.

patch up vt réparer.

patchwork ['pætʃwə:k] n patchwork m.

patchy ['pætʃɪ] a inégal(e).

pate [peɪt] n: **a bald ~** un crâne chauve or dégarni.

pâté ['pæteɪ] n pâté m, terrine f.

patent ['peɪtnt] n brevet m (d'invention) ♦ vt faire breveter ♦ a patent(e), manifeste.

patent leather n cuir verni.

patently ['peɪtntlɪ] ad manifestement.

patent medicine n spécialité f pharmaceutique.

patent office n bureau m des brevets.

paternal [pə'tə:nl] a paternel(le).

paternity [pə'tə:nɪtɪ] n paternité f.

paternity suit n (LAW) action f en recherche de paternité.

path [pɑ:θ] n chemin m, sentier m; allée f; (of planet) course f; (of missile) trajectoire f.

pathetic [pə'θetık] a (pitiful) pitoyable; (very bad) lamentable, minable; (moving) pathétique.

pathological [pæθə'lɔdʒıkl] a pathologique.

pathologist [pə'θɔlədʒıst] n pathologiste m/f.

pathology [pə'θɔlədʒı] n pathologie f.

pathos ['peıθɔs] n pathétique m.

pathway ['pɑ:θweı] n chemin m, sentier m.

patience ['peıʃns] n patience f; (Brit: CARDS) réussite f; **to lose (one's)** ~ perdre patience.

patient ['peıʃnt] n patient/e; (in hospital) malade m/f ♦ a patient(e).

patiently ['peıʃntlı] ad patiemment.

patio ['pætıəu] n patio m.

patriot ['peıtrıət] n patriote m/f.

patriotic [pætrı'ɔtık] a patriotique; (person) patriote.

patriotism ['pætrıətızəm] n patriotisme m.

patrol [pə'trəul] n patrouille f ♦ vt patrouiller dans; **to be on** ~ être de patrouille.

patrol boat n patrouilleur m.

patrol car n voiture f de police.

patrolman [pə'trəulmən] n (US) agent m de police.

patron ['peıtrən] n (in shop) client/e; (of charity) patron/ne; ~ **of the arts** mécène m.

patronage ['pætrənıdʒ] n patronage m, appui m.

patronize ['pætrənaız] vt être (un) client or un habitué de; (fig) traiter avec condescendance.

patronizing ['pætrənaızıŋ] a condescendant(e).

patron saint n saint(e) patron/ne.

patter ['pætə*] n crépitement m, tapotement m; (sales talk) boniment m ♦ vi crépiter, tapoter.

pattern ['pætən] n modèle m; (SEWING) patron m; (design) motif m; (sample) échantillon m; **behaviour** ~ mode m de comportement.

patterned ['pætənd] a à motifs.

paucity ['pɔ:sıtı] n pénurie f, carence f.

paunch [pɔ:ntʃ] n gros ventre, bedaine f.

pauper ['pɔ:pə*] n indigent/e; ~'s **grave** n fosse commune.

pause [pɔ:z] n pause f, arrêt m; (MUS) silence m ♦ vi faire une pause, s'arrêter; **to** ~ **for breath** reprendre son souffle; (fig) faire une pause.

pave [peıv] vt paver, daller; **to** ~ **the way for** ouvrir la voie à.

pavement ['peıvmənt] n (Brit) trottoir m; (US) chaussée f.

pavilion [pə'vılıən] n pavillon m; tente f; (SPORT) stand m.

paving ['peıvıŋ] n pavage m, dallage m.

paving stone n pavé m.

paw [pɔ:] n patte f ♦ vt donner un coup de patte à; (subj: person: pej) tripoter.

pawn [pɔ:n] n gage m; (CHESS, also fig) pion m ♦ vt mettre en gage.

pawnbroker ['pɔ:nbrəukə*] n prêteur m sur gages.

pawnshop ['pɔ:nʃɔp] n mont-de-piété m.

pay [peı] n salaire m; (of manual worker) paie f ♦ vb (pt, pp **paid** [peıd]) vt payer; (be profitable to: also fig) rapporter à ♦ vi payer; (be profitable) être rentable; **how much did**

you ~ **for it?** combien l'avez-vous payé?, vous l'avez payé combien?; **I paid £5 for that record** j'ai payé ce disque 5 livres; **to** ~ **one's way** payer sa part; (company) couvrir ses frais; **to** ~ **dividends** (fig) porter ses fruits, s'avérer rentable; **it won't** ~ **you to do that** vous ne gagnerez rien à faire cela; **to** ~ **attention (to)** prêter attention (à).

pay back vt rembourser.

pay in vt verser.

pay off vt (debts) régler, acquitter; (creditor, mortgage) rembourser; (workers) licencier ♦ vi (plan, patience) se révéler payant(e); **to** ~ **sth off in instalments** payer qch à tempérament.

pay out vt (money) payer, sortir de sa poche; (rope) laisser filer.

pay up vt (debts) régler; (amount) payer.

payable ['peıəbl] a payable; **to make a cheque** ~ **to sb** établir un chèque à l'ordre de qn.

pay day n jour m de paie.

PAYE n abbr (Brit: = pay as you earn) système de retenue des impôts à la source.

payee [peı'i:] n bénéficiaire m/f.

pay envelope n (US) (enveloppe f de) paie f.

paying ['peııŋ] a payant(e); ~ **guest** hôte payant.

payload ['peıləud] n charge f utile.

payment ['peımənt] n paiement m; (of bill) règlement m; (of deposit, cheque) versement m; **advance** ~ (part sum) acompte m; (total sum) paiement anticipé; **deferred** ~, ~ **by instalments** paiement par versements échelonnés; **monthly** ~ mensualité f; **in** ~ **for, in** ~ **of** en règlement de; **on** ~ **of £5** pour 5 livres.

pay packet n (Brit) paie f.

payphone ['peıfəun] n cabine f téléphonique, téléphone public.

payroll ['peırəul] n registre m du personnel; **to be on a firm's** ~ être employé par une entreprise.

pay slip n (Brit) bulletin m de paie, feuille f de paie.

pay station n (US) cabine f téléphonique.

PBS n abbr (US: = Public Broadcasting Service) groupement d'aide à la réalisation d'émissions pour la TV publique.

PC n abbr = **personal computer**; (Brit) = **police constable** ♦ abbr (Brit) = **Privy Councillor**.

pc abbr = **per cent, postcard**.

p/c abbr = **petty cash**.

PCB n abbr = **printed circuit board**.

PD n abbr (US) = **police department**.

pd abbr = **paid**.

PDSA n abbr (Brit) = People's Dispensary for Sick Animals.

PDT abbr (US: = Pacific Daylight Time) heure d'été du Pacifique.

PE n abbr (= physical education) EPS f ♦ abbr (Canada) = Prince Edward Island.

pea [pi:] n (petit) pois.

peace [pi:s] n paix f; (calm) calme m, tranquillité f; **to be at** ~ **with sb/sth** être en paix avec qn/qch; **to keep the** ~ (subj: policeman) assurer le maintien de l'ordre; (: citizen) ne pas troubler l'ordre.

peaceable ['pi:səbl] a paisible, pacifique.
peaceful ['pi:sful] a paisible, calme.
peace-keeping ['pi:ski:pɪŋ] n maintien m de la paix.
peace offering n gage m de réconciliation; (humorous) gage de paix.
peach [pi:tʃ] n pêche f.
peacock ['pi:kɔk] n paon m.
peak [pi:k] n (mountain) pic m, cime f; (fig: highest level) maximum m; (: of career, fame) apogée m.
peak-hour ['pi:kauə*] a (traffic etc) de pointe.
peak hours npl heures fpl d'affluence.
peak period n période f de pointe.
peaky ['pi:kɪ] a (Brit col) fatigué(e).
peal [pi:l] n (of bells) carillon m; ~s of laughter éclats mpl de rire.
peanut ['pi:nʌt] n arachide f, cacahuète f.
peanut butter n beurre m de cacahuète.
pear [pɛə*] n poire f.
pearl [pə:l] n perle f.
peasant ['pɛznt] n paysan/ne.
peat [pi:t] n tourbe f.
pebble ['pɛbl] n galet m, caillou m.
peck [pɛk] vt (also: ~ at) donner un coup de bec à; (food) picorer ♦ n coup m de bec; (kiss) bécot m.
pecking order ['pɛkɪŋ-] n ordre m hiérarchique.
peckish ['pɛkɪʃ] a (Brit col): I feel ~ je mangerais bien quelque chose, j'ai la dent.
peculiar [pɪ'kju:lɪə*] a (odd) étrange, bizarre, curieux(euse); (particular) particulier(ière); ~ to particulier à.
peculiarity [pɪkju:lɪ'ærɪtɪ] n bizarrerie f, particularité f.
pecuniary [pɪ'kju:nɪərɪ] a pécuniaire.
pedal ['pɛdl] n pédale f ♦ vi pédaler.
pedal bin n (Brit) poubelle f à pédale.
pedantic [pɪ'dæntɪk] a pédant(e).
peddle ['pɛdl] vt colporter; (drugs) faire le trafic de.
peddler ['pɛdlə*] n colporteur m; camelot m.
pedestal ['pɛdəstl] n piédestal m.
pedestrian [pɪ'dɛstrɪən] n piéton m ♦ a piétonnier(ière); (fig) prosaïque, terre à terre inv.
pedestrian crossing n (Brit) passage clouté.
pedestrian precinct n (Brit) zone piétonne.
pediatrics [pi:dɪ'ætrɪks] n (US) = **paediatrics**.
pedigree ['pɛdɪgri:] n ascendance f; (of animal) pedigree m ♦ cpd (animal) de race.
pedlar ['pɛdlə*] n = **peddler**.
pee [pi:] vi (col) faire pipi, pisser.
peek [pi:k] vi jeter un coup d'œil (furtif).
peel [pi:l] n pelure f, épluchure f; (of orange, lemon) écorce f ♦ vt peler, éplucher ♦ vi (paint etc) s'écailler; (wallpaper) se décoller.
peel back vt décoller.
peeler ['pi:lə*] n (potato etc ~) éplucheur m.
peelings ['pi:lɪŋz] npl pelures fpl, épluchures fpl.
peep [pi:p] n (Brit: look) coup d'œil furtif; (sound) pépiement m ♦ vi (Brit) jeter un coup d'œil (furtif).
peep out vi (Brit) se montrer (furtivement).
peephole ['pi:phəul] n judas m.
peer [pɪə*] vi: to ~ at regarder

attentivement, scruter ♦ n (noble) pair m; (equal) pair, égal/e.
peerage ['pɪərɪdʒ] n pairie f.
peerless ['pɪəlɪs] a incomparable, sans égal.
peeved [pi:vd] a irrité(e), ennuyé(e).
peevish ['pi:vɪʃ] a grincheux(euse), maussade.
peg [pɛg] n cheville f; (for coat etc) patère f; (Brit: also: clothes ~) pince f à linge ♦ vt (clothes) accrocher; (Brit: groundsheet) fixer (avec des piquets); (fig: prices, wages) contrôler, stabiliser.
pejorative [pɪ'dʒɔrətɪv] a péjoratif(ive).
Pekin [pi:'kɪn] n, **Peking** [pi:'kɪŋ] n Pékin.
pekingese [pi:kɪ'ni:z] n pékinois m.
pelican ['pɛlɪkən] n pélican m.
pelican crossing n (Brit AUT) feu m à commande manuelle.
pellet ['pɛlɪt] n boulette f; (of lead) plomb m.
pell-mell ['pɛl'mɛl] ad pêle-mêle.
pelmet ['pɛlmɪt] n cantonnière f; lambrequin m.
pelt [pɛlt] vt: to ~ sb (with) bombarder qn (de) ♦ vi (rain) tomber à seaux ♦ n peau f.
pelvis ['pɛlvɪs] n bassin m.
pen [pɛn] n (for writing) stylo m; (for sheep) parc m; (US col: prison) taule f; to put ~ to paper prendre la plume.
penal ['pi:nl] a pénal(e).
penalize ['pi:nəlaɪz] vt pénaliser; (fig) désavantager.
penal servitude [-'sə:vɪtju:d] n travaux forcés.
penalty ['pɛnltɪ] n pénalité f; sanction f; (fine) amende f; (SPORT) pénalisation f; (FOOTBALL: also: ~ kick) penalty m.
penalty area n (Brit SPORT) surface f de réparation.
penalty clause n clause pénale.
penalty kick n (FOOTBALL) penalty m.
penance ['pɛnəns] n pénitence f.
pence [pɛns] npl (Brit) = **penny**.
penchant ['pɑ̃:ʃɑ̃:ŋ] n penchant m.
pencil ['pɛnsl] n crayon m ♦ vt: to ~ sth in noter qch provisoirement.
pencil case n trousse f (d'écolier).
pencil sharpener n taille-crayon(s) m inv.
pendant ['pɛndnt] n pendentif m.
pending ['pɛndɪŋ] prep en attendant ♦ a en suspens.
pendulum ['pɛndjuləm] n pendule m; (of clock) balancier m.
penetrate ['pɛnɪtreɪt] vt pénétrer dans; pénétrer.
penetrating ['pɛnɪtreɪtɪŋ] a pénétrant(e).
penetration [pɛnɪ'treɪʃən] n pénétration f.
penfriend ['pɛnfrɛnd] n (Brit) correspondant/e.
penguin ['pɛŋgwɪn] n pingouin m.
penicillin [pɛnɪ'sɪlɪn] n pénicilline f.
peninsula [pə'nɪnsjulə] n péninsule f.
penis ['pi:nɪs] n pénis m, verge f.
penitence ['pɛnɪtns] n repentir m.
penitent ['pɛnɪtnt] a repentant(e).
penitentiary [pɛnɪ'tɛnʃərɪ] n (US) prison f.
penknife ['pɛnnaɪf] n canif m.
pen name n nom m de plume, pseudonyme m.
pennant ['pɛnənt] n flamme f, banderole f.
penniless ['pɛnɪlɪs] a sans le sou.

Pennines ['pɛnaɪnz] npl Pennines fpl.

penny, pl **pennies** or **pence** ['pɛnɪ, 'pɛnɪz, pɛns] n penny m (pl pennies) (new: 100 in a pound; old: 12 in a shilling; on tend à employer 'pennies' ou 'two-pence piece' etc pour les pièces, 'pence' pour la valeur); (US) = **cent**.

penpal ['pɛnpæl] n correspondant/e.

pension ['pɛnʃən] n retraite f; (MIL) pension f.

   pension off vt mettre à la retraite.

pensionable ['pɛnʃnəbl] a qui a droit à une retraite.

pensioner ['pɛnʃənə*] n (Brit) retraité/e.

pension fund n caisse f de retraite.

pensive ['pɛnsɪv] a pensif(ive).

pentagon ['pɛntəgən] n pentagone m.

Pentecost ['pɛntɪkɔst] n Pentecôte f.

penthouse ['pɛnthaus] n appartement m (de luxe) en attique.

pent-up ['pɛntʌp] a (feelings) refoulé(e).

penultimate [pɛ'nʌltɪmət] a pénultième, avant-dernier(ière).

penury ['pɛnjurɪ] n misère f.

people ['pi:pl] npl gens mpl; personnes fpl; (citizens) peuple m ♦ n (nation, race) peuple m ♦ vt peupler; **several ~ came** plusieurs personnes sont venues; **I know ~ who ...** je connais des gens qui ...; **the room was full of ~** la salle était pleine de monde or de gens; **~ say that ...** on dit or les gens disent que ...; **old ~** les personnes âgées; **young ~** les jeunes; **a man of the ~** un homme du peuple.

pep [pɛp] n (col) entrain m, dynamisme m.

   pep up vt (col) remonter.

pepper ['pɛpə*] n poivre m; (vegetable) poivron m ♦ vt poivrer.

peppermint ['pɛpəmɪnt] n (plant) menthe poivrée; (sweet) pastille f de menthe.

pepperpot ['pɛpəpɔt] n poivrière f.

peptalk ['pɛptɔ:k] n (col) (petit) discours d'encouragement.

per [pə:*] prep par; **~ hour** (miles etc) à l'heure; (fee) (de) l'heure; **~ kilo** etc le kilo etc; **~ day/person** par jour/personne; **as ~ your instructions** conformément à vos instructions.

per annum ad par an.

per capita a, ad par habitant, par personne.

perceive [pə'si:v] vt percevoir; (notice) remarquer, s'apercevoir de.

per cent ad pour cent; **a 20 ~ discount** une réduction de 20 pour cent.

percentage [pə'sɛntɪdʒ] n pourcentage m; **on a ~ basis** au pourcentage.

perceptible [pə'sɛptɪbl] a perceptible.

perception [pə'sɛpʃən] n perception f; (insight) sensibilité f.

perceptive [pə'sɛptɪv] a (remark, person) perspicace.

perch [pə:tʃ] n (fish) perche f; (for bird) perchoir m ♦ vi (se) percher.

percolate ['pə:kəleɪt] vt, vi passer.

percolator ['pə:kəleɪtə*] n percolateur m; cafetière f électrique.

percussion [pə'kʌʃən] n percussion f.

peremptory [pə'rɛmptərɪ] a péremptoire.

perennial [pə'rɛnɪəl] a perpétuel(le); (BOT)

vivace ♦ n plante f vivace.

perfect a, n ['pə:fɪkt] a parfait(e) ♦ n (also: ~ **tense**) parfait m ♦ vt [pə'fɛkt] parfaire; mettre au point; **he's a ~ stranger to me** il m'est totalement inconnu.

perfection [pə'fɛkʃən] n perfection f.

perfectionist [pə'fɛkʃənɪst] n perfectionniste m/f.

perfectly ['pə:fɪktlɪ] ad parfaitement: **I'm ~ happy with the situation** cette situation me convient parfaitement; **you know ~ well** vous le savez très bien.

perforate ['pə:fəreɪt] vt perforer, percer.

perforated ulcer n (MED) ulcère perforé.

perforation [pə:fə'reɪʃən] n perforation f; (line of holes) pointillé m.

perform [pə'fɔ:m] vt (carry out) exécuter, remplir; (concert etc) jouer, donner ♦ vi jouer.

performance [pə'fɔ:məns] n représentation f, spectacle m; (of an artist) interprétation f; (of player etc) prestation f; (of car, engine) performance f; **the team put up a good ~** l'équipe a bien joué.

performer [pə'fɔ:mə*] n artiste m/f.

performing [pə'fɔ:mɪŋ] a (animal) savant(e).

perfume ['pə:fju:m] n parfum m ♦ vt parfumer.

perfunctory [pə'fʌŋktərɪ] a négligent(e), pour la forme.

perhaps [pə'hæps] ad peut-être; **~ he'll ...** peut-être qu'il ...; **~ so/not** peut-être que oui/que non.

peril ['pɛrɪl] n péril m.

perilous ['pɛrɪləs] a périlleux(euse).

perilously ['pɛrɪləslɪ] ad: **they came ~ close to being caught** ils ont été à deux doigts de se faire prendre.

perimeter [pə'rɪmɪtə*] n périmètre m.

perimeter wall n mur m d'enceinte.

period ['pɪərɪəd] n période f; (HISTORY) époque f; (SCOL) cours m; (full stop) point m; (MED) règles fpl ♦ a (costume, furniture) d'époque; **for a ~ of three weeks** pour (une période de) trois semaines; **the holiday ~** (Brit) la période des vacances.

periodic [pɪərɪ'ɔdɪk] a périodique.

periodical [pɪərɪ'ɔdɪkl] a périodique ♦ n périodique m.

periodically [pɪərɪ'ɔdɪklɪ] ad périodiquement.

period pains npl (Brit) douleurs menstruelles.

peripatetic [pɛrɪpə'tɛtɪk] a (salesman) ambulant; (Brit: teacher) qui travaille dans plusieurs établissements.

peripheral [pə'rɪfərəl] a périphérique ♦ n (COMPUT) périphérique m.

periphery [pə'rɪfərɪ] n périphérie f.

periscope ['pɛrɪskəup] n périscope m.

perish ['pɛrɪʃ] vi périr, mourir; (decay) se détériorer.

perishable ['pɛrɪʃəbl] a périssable.

perishables ['pɛrɪʃəblz] npl denrées fpl périssables.

perishing ['pɛrɪʃɪŋ] a (Brit col: cold) glacial(e).

peritonitis [pɛrɪtə'naɪtɪs] n péritonite f.

perjure ['pə:dʒə*] vt: **to ~ o.s.** se parjurer.

perjury ['pə:dʒərɪ] n (LAW: in court) faux

témoignage; (*breach of oath*) parjure *m*.

perk [pə:k] *n* (*col*) avantage *m*, à-côté *m*.

perk up *vi* (*col: cheer up*) se ragaillardir.

perky ['pə:kı] *a* (*cheerful*) guilleret(te), gai(e).

perm [pə:m] *n* (*for hair*) permanente *f* ♦ *vt*: **to have one's hair** ~**ed** se faire faire une permanente.

permanence ['pə:mənəns] *n* permanence *f*.

permanent ['pə:mənənt] *a* permanent(e); (*job, position*) permanent, fixe; (*dye, ink*) indélébile; **I'm not** ~ **here** je ne suis pas ici à titre définitif; ~ **address** adresse habituelle.

permanently ['pə:mənəntlı] *ad* de façon permanente.

permeable ['pə:mıəbl] *a* perméable.

permeate ['pə:mıeıt] *vi* s'infiltrer ♦ *vt* s'infiltrer dans; pénétrer.

permissible [pə'mısıbl] *a* permis(e), acceptable.

permission [pə'mıʃən] *n* permission *f*, autorisation *f*; **to give sb** ~ **to do sth** donner à qn la permission de faire qch.

permissive [pə'mısıv] *a* tolérant(e); **the** ~ **society** la société de tolérance.

permit *n* ['pə:mıt] permis *m*; (*entrance pass*) autorisation *f*, laisser-passer *m*; (*for goods*) licence *f* ♦ *vt* [pə'mıt] permettre; **to** ~ **sb to do** autoriser qn à faire, permettre à qn de faire; **weather** ~**ting** si le temps le permet.

permutation [pə:mju'teıʃən] *n* permutation *f*.

pernicious [pə:'nıʃəs] *a* pernicieux(euse), nocif(ive).

pernickety [pə'nıkıtı] *a* (*col*) pointilleux(euse), tatillon(ne); (*task*) minutieux(euse).

perpendicular [pə:pən'dıkjulə*] *a*, *n* perpendiculaire (*f*).

perpetrate ['pə:pıtreıt] *vt* perpétrer, commettre.

perpetual [pə'pɛtjuəl] *a* perpétuel(le).

perpetuate [pə'pɛtjueıt] *vt* perpétuer.

perpetuity [pə:pı'tju:ıtı] *n*: **in** ~ à perpétuité.

perplex [pə'plɛks] *vt* rendre perplexe; (*complicate*) embrouiller.

perplexing [pə:'plɛksıŋ] *a* embarrassant(e).

perquisites ['pə:kwızıts] *npl* (*also*: **perks**) avantages *mpl* annexes.

persecute ['pə:sıkju:t] *vt* persécuter.

persecution [pə:sı'kju:ʃən] *n* persécution *f*.

perseverance [pə:sı'vıərns] *n* persévérance *f*, ténacité *f*.

persevere [pə:sı'vıə*] *vi* persévérer.

Persia ['pə:ʃə] *n* Perse *f*.

Persian ['pə:ʃən] *a* persan(e) ♦ *n* (*LING*) persan *m*; **the** (~) **Gulf** le golfe Persique.

persist [pə'sıst] *vi*: **to** ~ (**in doing**) persister (à faire), s'obstiner (à faire).

persistence [pə'sıstəns] *n* persistance *f*, obstination *f*; opiniâtreté *f*.

persistent [pə'sıstənt] *a* persistant(e), tenace; (*lateness, rain*) persistant; ~ **offender** (*LAW*) multirécidiviste *m/f*.

persnickety [pə'snıkıtı] *a* (*US col*) = **pernickety**.

person ['pə:sn] *n* personne *f*; **in** ~ en personne; **on** *or* **about one's** ~ sur soi; ~ **to** ~ **call** (*TEL*) appel *m* avec préavis.

personable ['pə:snəbl] *a* de belle prestance, au physique attrayant.

personal ['pə:snl] *a* personnel(le); ~ **belongings**, ~ **effects** effets personnels; ~ **hygiene** hygiène *f* intime; **a** ~ **interview** un entretien.

personal allowance *n* (*TAX*) part *f* du revenu non imposable.

personal assistant (PA) *n* secrétaire personnel(le).

personal call *n* (*TEL*) communication *f* avec préavis.

personal column *n* annonces personnelles.

personal computer (PC) *n* ordinateur individuel, PC *m*.

personal details *npl* (*on form etc*) coordonnées *fpl*.

personal identification number (PIN) *n* (*COMPUT*, *BANKING*) numéro *m* d'identification personnel.

personality [pə:sə'nælıtı] *n* personnalité *f*.

personally ['pə:snlı] *ad* personnellement.

personal property *n* biens personnels.

personify [pə:'sonıfaı] *vt* personnifier.

personnel [pə:sə'nɛl] *n* personnel *m*.

personnel department *n* service *m* du personnel.

personnel manager *n* chef *m* du personnel.

perspective [pə'spɛktıv] *n* perspective *f*; **to get sth into** ~ ramener qch à sa juste mesure.

perspex ['pə:spɛks] *n* ® (*Brit*) Plexiglas *m* ®.

perspicacity [pə:spı'kæsıtı] *n* perspicacité *f*.

perspiration [pə:spı'reıʃən] *n* transpiration *f*.

perspire [pə'spaıə*] *vi* transpirer.

persuade [pə'sweıd] *vt*: **to** ~ **sb to do sth** persuader qn de faire qch, amener *or* décider qn à faire qch; **to** ~ **sb of sth/that** persuader qn de qch/que.

persuasion [pə'sweıʒən] *n* persuasion *f*; (*creed*) conviction *f*.

persuasive [pə'sweısıv] *a* persuasif(ive).

pert [pə:t] *a* coquin(e), mutin(e).

pertaining [pə:'teınıŋ]: ~ **to** *prep* relatif(ive) à.

pertinent ['pə:tınənt] *a* pertinent(e).

perturb [pə'tə:b] *vt* troubler, inquiéter.

perturbing [pə'tə:bıŋ] *a* troublant(e).

Peru [pə'ru:] *n* Pérou *m*.

perusal [pə'ru:zl] *n* lecture (attentive).

Peruvian [pə'ru:vjən] *a* péruvien(ne) ♦ *n* Péruvien/ne.

pervade [pə'veıd] *vt* se répandre dans, envahir.

pervasive [pə'veızıv] *a* (*smell*) pénétrant(e); (*influence*) insidieux(euse); (*gloom, ideas*) diffus(e).

perverse [pə'və:s] *a* pervers(e); (*stubborn*) entêté(e), contrariant(e).

perversion [pə'və:ʃən] *n* perversion *f*.

perversity [pə'və:sıtı] *n* perversité *f*.

pervert *n* ['pə:və:t] perverti/e ♦ *vt* [pə'və:t] pervertir.

pessimism ['pɛsımızəm] *n* pessimisme *m*.

pessimist ['pɛsımıst] *n* pessimiste *m/f*.

pessimistic [pɛsı'mıstık] *a* pessimiste.

pest [pɛst] *n* animal *m* (*or* insecte *m*) nuisible; (*fig*) fléau *m*.

pest control *n* lutte *f* contre les nuisibles.

pester ['pɛstə*] vt importuner, harceler.
pesticide ['pɛstɪsaɪd] n pesticide m.
pestilent ['pɛstɪlənt], **pestilential** [pɛstɪ'lɛnʃəl] a (col: exasperating) empoisonnant(e).
pestle ['pɛsl] n pilon m.
pet [pɛt] n animal familier; (favourite) chouchou m ♦ vt choyer ♦ vi (col) se peloter; ~ **lion** etc lion etc apprivoisé.
petal ['pɛtl] n pétale m.
peter ['pi:tə*]: **to ~ out** vi s'épuiser; s'affaiblir.
petite [pə'ti:t] a menu(e).
petition [pə'tɪʃən] n pétition f ♦ vt adresser une pétition à ♦ vi: **to ~ for divorce** demander le divorce.
pet name n (Brit) petit nom.
petrified ['pɛtrɪfaɪd] a (fig) mort(e) de peur.
petrify ['pɛtrɪfaɪ] vt pétrifier.
petrochemical [pɛtrə'kɛmɪkl] a pétrochimique.
petrodollars ['pɛtrəudɔləz] npl pétrodollars mpl.
petrol ['pɛtrəl] n (Brit) essence f.
petrol can n (Brit) bidon m à essence.
petrol engine n (Brit) moteur m à essence.
petroleum [pə'trəuliəm] n pétrole m.
petroleum jelly n vaseline f.
petrol pump n (Brit: in car, at garage) pompe f à essence.
petrol station n (Brit) station-service f.
petrol tank n (Brit) réservoir m d'essence.
petticoat ['pɛtɪkəut] n jupon m.
pettifogging ['pɛtɪfɔgɪŋ] a chicanier(ière).
pettiness ['pɛtɪnɪs] n mesquinerie f.
petty ['pɛtɪ] a (mean) mesquin(e); (unimportant) insignifiant(e), sans importance.
petty cash n caisse f des dépenses courantes, petite caisse.
petty officer n second-maître m.
petulant ['pɛtjulənt] a irritable.
pew [pju:] n banc m (d'église).
pewter ['pju:tə*] n étain m.
Pfc abbr (US MIL) = private first class.
PG n abbr (CINEMA: = parental guidance) avis des parents recommandé.
PGA n abbr = Professional Golfers Association.
PH n abbr (US MIL: = Purple Heart) décoration accordée aux blessés de guerre.
p&h abbr (US: = postage and handling) frais mpl de port.
PHA n abbr (US: = Public Housing Administration) organisme d'aide à la construction.
phallic ['fælɪk] a phallique.
phantom ['fæntəm] n fantôme m; (vision) fantasme m.
Pharaoh ['fɛərəu] n pharaon m.
pharmaceutical [fɑːmə'sju:tɪkl] a pharmaceutique ♦ n: ~s produits mpl pharmaceutiques.
pharmacist ['fɑːməsɪst] n pharmacien/ne.
pharmacy ['fɑːməsɪ] n pharmacie f.
phase [feɪz] n phase f, période f ♦ vt: **to ~ sth in/out** introduire/supprimer qch progressivement.
PhD abbr (= Doctor of Philosophy) title ≈ Docteur m en Droit or Lettres etc ♦ n ≈ doctorat m; titulaire m d'un doctorat.

pheasant ['fɛznt] n faisan m.
phenomenon, pl phenomena [fə'nɔmɪnən, -nə] n phénomène m.
phew [fju:] excl ouf!
phial ['faɪəl] n fiole f.
philanderer [fɪ'lændərə*] n don Juan m.
philanthropic [fɪlən'θrɔpɪk] a philanthropique.
philanthropist [fɪ'lænθrəpɪst] n philanthrope m/f.
philatelist [fɪ'lætəlɪst] n philatéliste m/f.
philately [fɪ'lætəlɪ] n philatélie f.
Philippines ['fɪlɪpi:nz] npl (also: **Philippine Islands**): **the ~** les Philippines fpl.
philosopher [fɪ'lɔsəfə*] n philosophe m.
philosophical [fɪlə'sɔfɪkl] a philosophique.
philosophy [fɪ'lɔsəfɪ] n philosophie f.
phlegm [flɛm] n flegme m.
phlegmatic [flɛg'mætɪk] a flegmatique.
phobia ['fəubjə] n phobie f.
phone [fəun] n téléphone m ♦ vt téléphoner à ♦ vi téléphoner; **to be on the ~** avoir le téléphone; (be calling) être au téléphone.
phone back vt, vi rappeler.
phone book n annuaire m.
phone box, phone booth n cabine f téléphonique.
phone call n coup m de fil or de téléphone.
phone-in ['fəunɪn] n (Brit RADIO, TV) programme m à ligne ouverte.
phonetics [fə'nɛtɪks] n phonétique f.
phoney ['fəunɪ] a faux(fausse), factice ♦ n (person) charlatan m; fumiste m/f.
phonograph ['fəunəgrɑːf] n (US) électrophone m.
phony ['fəunɪ] a, n = **phoney**.
phosphate ['fɔsfeɪt] n phosphate m.
phosphorus ['fɔsfərəs] n phosphore m.
photo ['fəutəu] n photo f.
photo... ['fəutəu] prefix photo...
photocopier ['fəutəukɔpɪə*] n copieur m.
photocopy ['fəutəukɔpɪ] n photocopie f ♦ vt photocopier.
photoelectric [fəutəuɪ'lɛktrɪk] a photoélectrique; ~ **cell** cellule f photoélectrique.
photogenic [fəutəu'dʒɛnɪk] a photogénique.
photograph ['fəutəgrɑːf] n photographie f ♦ vt photographier; **to take a ~ of sb** prendre qn en photo.
photographer [fə'tɔgrəfə*] n photographe m/f.
photographic [fəutə'græfɪk] a photographique.
photography [fə'tɔgrəfɪ] n photographie f.
photostat ['fəutəustæt] n photocopie f, photostat m.
photosynthesis [fəutəu'sɪnθəsɪs] n photosynthèse f.
phrase [freɪz] n expression f; (LING) locution f ♦ vt exprimer; (letter) rédiger.
phrasebook ['freɪzbuk] n recueil m d'expressions (pour touristes).
physical ['fɪzɪkl] a physique; ~ **examination** examen médical; ~ **education** éducation physique; ~ **exercises** gymnastique f.
physically ['fɪzɪklɪ] ad physiquement.
physician [fɪ'zɪʃən] n médecin m.
physicist ['fɪzɪsɪst] n physicien/ne.
physics ['fɪzɪks] n physique f.
physiological ['fɪzɪə'lɔdʒɪkl] a physiologique.
physiology [fɪzɪ'ɔlədʒɪ] n physiologie f.
physiotherapist [fɪzɪəu'θɛrəpɪst] n kinési-

thérapeute *m/f*.

physiotherapy |fɪzɪəu'θɛrəpɪ| *n* kinésithérapie *f*.

physique |fɪ'zi:k| *n* (*appearance*) physique *m*; (*health etc*) constitution *f*.

pianist |'pi:ənɪst| *n* pianiste *m/f*.

piano |pɪ'ænəu| *n* piano *m*.

piano accordion *n* (*Brit*) accordéon *m* à touches.

Picardy |'pɪkədɪ| *n* Picardie *f*.

piccolo |'pɪkələu| *n* piccolo *m*.

pick |pɪk| *n* (*tool: also:* ~-**axe**) pic *m*, pioche *f*
♦ *vt* choisir; (*gather*) cueillir; (*scab, spot*)
gratter, écorcher; **take your** ~ faites votre
choix; **the** ~ **of** le(la) meilleur(e) de; **to** ~ **a**
bone ronger un os; **to** ~ **one's nose** se mettre le doigt dans le nez; **to** ~ **one's teeth** se
curer les dents; **to** ~ **sb's brains** faire appel
aux lumières de qn; **to** ~ **pockets** pratiquer
le vol à la tire; **to** ~ **a quarrel/fight with sb**
chercher querelle à/la bagarre avec qn.

pick off *vt* (*kill*) (viser soigneusement et)
abattre.

pick on *vt fus* (*person*) harceler.

pick out *vt* choisir; (*distinguish*) distinguer.

pick up *vi* (*improve*) remonter, s'améliorer
♦ *vt* ramasser; (*telephone*) décrocher;
(*collect*) passer prendre; (*AUT: give lift to*)
prendre; (*learn*) apprendre; (*RADIO, TV,
TEL*) capter; **to** ~ **up speed** prendre de la
vitesse; **to** ~ **o.s. up** se relever; **to** ~ **up**
where one left off reprendre là où l'on s'est
arrêté.

pickaxe, (*US*) **pickax** |'pɪkæks| *n* pioche *f*.

picket |'pɪkɪt| *n* (*in strike*) gréviste *m/f*
participant à un piquet de grève; piquet *m* de
grève ♦ *vt* mettre un piquet de grève devant.

picket line *n* piquet *m* de grève.

pickings |'pɪkɪŋz| *npl*: **there are rich** ~ **to be**
had in ... il y a gros à gagner dans ....

pickle |'pɪkl| *n* (*also:* ~**s**: *as condiment*)
pickles *mpl*; (*fig*): **in a** ~ dans le pétrin ♦ *vt*
conserver dans du vinaigre ou dans de la
saumure.

pick-me-up |'pɪkmɪʌp| *n* remontant *m*.

pickpocket |'pɪkpɔkɪt| *n* pickpocket *m*.

pickup |'pɪkʌp| *n* (*Brit: on record player*)
bras *m* pick-up; (*small truck: also:* ~ **truck**,
~ **van**) camionnette *f*.

picnic |'pɪknɪk| *n* pique-nique *m* ♦ *vi* pique-
niquer.

picnicker |'pɪknɪkə*| *n* pique-niqueur/euse.

pictorial |pɪk'tɔ:rɪəl| *a* illustré(e).

picture |'pɪktʃə*| *n* (*also TV*) image *f*;
(*painting*) peinture *f*, tableau *m*; (*photograph*) photo(graphie) *f*; (*drawing*) dessin
m; (*film*) film *m* ♦ *vt* se représenter; (*describe*) dépeindre, représenter; **the** ~**s** (*Brit*)
le cinéma; **to take a** ~ **of sb/sth** prendre
qn/qch en photo; **the overall** ~ le tableau
d'ensemble; **to put sb in the** ~ mettre qn au
courant.

picture book *n* livre *m* d'images.

picturesque |pɪktʃə'rɛsk| *a* pittoresque.

picture window *n* baie vitrée, fenêtre *f*
panoramique.

piddling |'pɪdlɪŋ| *a* (*col*) insignifiant(e).

pidgin |'pɪdʒɪn| *a*: ~ **English** pidgin *m*.

pie |paɪ| *n* tourte *f*; (*of meat*) pâté *m* en

croûte.

piebald |'paɪbɔ:ld| *a* pie *inv*.

piece |pi:s| *n* morceau *m*; (*of land*) parcelle *f*;
(*item*): **a** ~ **of furniture/advice** un meuble/
conseil; (*DRAUGHTS etc*) pion *m* ♦ *vt*: **to** ~
together rassembler; **in** ~**s** (*broken*) en
morceaux, en miettes; (*not yet assembled*)
en pièces détachées; **to take to** ~**s**
démonter; **in one** ~ (*object*) intact(e); **to**
get back all in one ~ (*person*) rentrer sain
et sauf; **a 10p** ~ (*Brit*) une pièce de 10p; ~
by ~ morceau par morceau; **a six-**~ **band**
un orchestre de six musiciens; **to say one's**
~ réciter son morceau.

piecemeal |'pi:smi:l| *ad* par bouts.

piece rate *n* taux *m* or tarif *m* à la pièce.

piecework |'pi:swə:k| *n* travail *m* aux pièces
or à la pièce.

pie chart *n* graphique *m* à secteurs,
camembert *m*.

Piedmont |'pi:dmɔnt| *n* Piémont *m*.

pier |pɪə*| *n* jetée *f*; (*of bridge etc*) pile *f*.

pierce |pɪəs| *vt* percer, transpercer; **to have**
one's ears ~**d** se faire percer les oreilles.

piercing |'pɪəsɪŋ| *a* (*cry*) perçant(e).

piety |'paɪətɪ| *n* piété *f*.

piffling |'pɪflɪŋ| *a* insignifiant(e).

pig |pɪg| *n* cochon *m*, porc *m*.

pigeon |'pɪdʒən| *n* pigeon *m*.

pigeonhole |'pɪdʒənhəul| *n* casier *m*.

pigeon-toed |'pɪdʒəntəud| *a* marchant les
pieds en dedans.

piggy bank |'pɪgɪ-| *n* tirelire *f*.

pigheaded |'pɪg'hɛdɪd| *a* entêté(e), têtu(e).

piglet |'pɪglɪt| *n* petit cochon, porcelet *m*.

pigment |'pɪgmənt| *n* pigment *m*.

pigmentation |pɪgmən'teɪʃən| *n* pigmentation
f.

pigmy |'pɪgmɪ| *n* = **pygmy**.

pigskin |'pɪgskɪn| *n* (*peau f de*) porc *m*.

pigsty |'pɪgstaɪ| *n* porcherie *f*.

pigtail |'pɪgteɪl| *n* natte *f*, tresse *f*.

pike |paɪk| *n* (*spear*) pique *f*; (*fish*) brochet *m*.

pilchard |'pɪltʃəd| *n* pilchard *m* (*sorte de
sardine*).

pile |paɪl| *n* (*pillar, of books*) pile *f*; (*heap*) tas
m; (*of carpet*) épaisseur *f* ♦ *vb* (*also:* ~ **up**)
vt empiler, entasser ♦ *vi* s'entasser; **in a** ~
en tas.

pile on *vt*: **to** ~ **it on** (*col*) exagérer.

piles |paɪlz| *npl* hémorroïdes *fpl*.

pileup |'paɪlʌp| *n* (*AUT*) télescopage *m*,
collision *f* en série.

pilfer |'pɪlfə*| *vt* chaparder ♦ *vi* commettre des
larcins.

pilfering |'pɪlfərɪŋ| *n* chapardage *m*.

pilgrim |'pɪlgrɪm| *n* pèlerin *m*.

pilgrimage |'pɪlgrɪmɪdʒ| *n* pèlerinage *m*.

pill |pɪl| *n* pilule *f*; **the** ~ la pilule; **to be on**
the ~ prendre la pilule.

pillage |'pɪlɪdʒ| *vt* piller.

pillar |'pɪlə*| *n* pilier *m*.

pillar box *n* (*Brit*) boîte *f* aux lettres.

pillion |'pɪljən| *n* (*of motor cycle*) siège *m*
arrière; **to ride** ~ être derrière; (*on horse*)
être en croupe.

pillory |'pɪlərɪ| *n* pilori *m* ♦ *vt* mettre au pilori.

pillow |'pɪləu| *n* oreiller *m*.

pillowcase |'pɪləukeɪs|, **pillowslip** |'pɪləuslɪp|

n taie *f* d'oreiller.

pilot ['paɪlət] *n* pilote *m* ♦ *cpd* (*scheme etc*) pilote, expérimental(e) ♦ *vt* piloter.

pilot boat *n* bateau-pilote *m*.

pilot light *n* veilleuse *f*.

pimento [pɪ'mɛntəʊ] *n* piment *m*.

pimp [pɪmp] *n* souteneur *m*, maquereau *m*.

pimple ['pɪmpl] *n* bouton *m*.

pimply ['pɪmplɪ] *a* boutonneux(euse).

PIN *n abbr* = **personal identification number**.

pin [pɪn] *n* épingle *f*; (*TECH*) cheville *f*; (*Brit: drawing* ~) punaise *f*; (*in grenade*) goupille *f*; (*Brit ELEC: of plug*) broche *f* ♦ *vt* épingler; ~**s and needles** fourmis *fpl*; **to** ~ **sb against/to** clouer qn contre/à; **to** ~ **sth on sb** (*fig*) mettre qch sur le dos de qn.

pin down *vt* (*fig*): **to** ~ **sb down** obliger qn à répondre; **there's something strange here but I can't quite** ~ **it down** il y a quelque chose d'étrange ici, mais je n'arrive pas exactement à savoir quoi.

pinafore ['pɪnəfɔ:*] *n* tablier *m*.

pinafore dress *n* robe-chasuble *f*.

pinball ['pɪnbɔ:l] *n* flipper *m*.

pincers ['pɪnsəz] *npl* tenailles *fpl*.

pinch [pɪntʃ] *n* pincement *m*; (*of salt etc*) pincée *f* ♦ *vt* pincer; (*col: steal*) chiper ♦ *vi* (*shoe*) serrer; **at a** ~ à la rigueur; **to feel the** ~ (*fig*) se ressentir des restrictions (*or* de la récession *etc*).

pinched [pɪntʃt] *a* (*drawn*) tiré(e); ~ **with cold** transi(e) de froid; ~ **for** (*short of*): ~ **for money** à court d'argent; ~ **for space** à l'étroit.

pincushion ['pɪnkuʃən] *n* pelote *f* à épingles.

pine [paɪn] *n* (*also:* ~ **tree**) pin *m* ♦ *vi*: **to** ~ **for** aspirer à, désirer ardemment.

pine away *vi* dépérir.

pineapple ['paɪnæpl] *n* ananas *m*.

pine nut, (*Brit*) **pine kernel** *n* pignon *m*.

ping [pɪŋ] *n* (*noise*) tintement *m*.

ping-pong ['pɪŋpɒŋ] *n* ® ping-pong *m* ®.

pink [pɪŋk] *a* rose ♦ *n* (*colour*) rose *m*; (*BOT*) œillet *m*, mignardise *f*.

pinking shears, pinking scissors ['pɪŋkɪŋ-] *npl* ciseaux *mpl* à denteler.

pin money *n* (*Brit*) argent *m* de poche.

pinnacle ['pɪnəkl] *n* pinacle *m*.

pinpoint ['pɪnpɔɪnt] *vt* indiquer (avec précision).

pinstripe ['pɪnstraɪp] *n* rayure très fine.

pint [paɪnt] *n* pinte *f* (*Brit* = 0.57 *l*; *US* = 0.47 *l*); (*Brit col*) ≈ demi *m*, ≈ pot *m*.

pinup ['pɪnʌp] *n* pin-up *f inv*.

pioneer [paɪə'nɪə*] *n* explorateur/trice; (*early settler*) pionnier *m*; (*fig*) pionnier, précurseur *m* ♦ *vt* être un pionnier de.

pious ['paɪəs] *a* pieux(euse).

pip [pɪp] *n* (*seed*) pépin *m*; (*Brit: time signal on radio*) top *m*.

pipe [paɪp] *n* tuyau *m*, conduite *f*; (*for smoking*) pipe *f*; (*MUS*) pipeau *m* ♦ *vt* amener par tuyau; ~**s** *npl* (*also:* **bag**~**s**) cornemuse *f*.

pipe down *vi* (*col*) se taire.

pipe cleaner *n* cure-pipe *m*.

piped music *n* musique *f* de fond.

pipe dream *n* chimère *f*, utopie *f*.

pipeline ['paɪplaɪn] *n* (*for gas*) gazoduc *m*, pipeline *m*; (*for oil*) oléoduc *m*, pipeline; **it is in the** ~ (*fig*) c'est en route, ça va se faire.

piper ['paɪpə*] *n* joueur/euse de pipeau (*or* de cornemuse).

pipe tobacco *n* tabac *m* pour la pipe.

piping ['paɪpɪŋ] *ad*: ~ **hot** très chaud(e).

piquant ['pi:kənt] *a* piquant(e).

pique ['pi:k] *n* dépit *m*.

piracy ['paɪərəsɪ] *n* piraterie *f*.

pirate ['paɪərət] *n* pirate *m* ♦ *vt* (*record, video, book*) pirater.

pirate radio *n* (*Brit*) radio *f* pirate.

pirouette [pɪru'ɛt] *n* pirouette *f* ♦ *vi* faire une *or* des pirouette(s).

Pisces ['paɪsi:z] *n* les Poissons *mpl*; **to be** ~ être des Poissons.

piss [pɪs] *vi* (*col!*) pisser (*!*); ~ **off!** tire-toi! (*!*).

pissed [pɪst] *a* (*Brit col: drunk*) bourré(e).

pistol ['pɪstl] *n* pistolet *m*.

piston ['pɪstən] *n* piston *m*.

pit [pɪt] *n* trou *m*, fosse *f*; (*also: coal* ~) puits *m* de mine; (*also: orchestra* ~) fosse d'orchestre ♦ *vt*: **to** ~ **sb against sb** opposer qn à qn; **to** ~ **o.s. against** se mesurer à; ~**s** *npl* (*in motor racing*) aire *f* de service.

pitapat ['pɪtə'pæt] *ad* (*Brit*): **to go** ~ (*heart*) battre la chamade; (*rain*) tambouriner.

pitch [pɪtʃ] *n* (*throw*) lancement *m*; (*MUS*) ton *m*; (*of voice*) hauteur *f*; (*fig: degree*) degré *m*; (*also: sales* ~) baratin *m*, boniment *m*; (*Brit SPORT*) terrain *m*; (*NAUT*) tangage *m*; (*tar*) poix *f* ♦ *vt* (*throw*) lancer; (*tent*) dresser; (*set: price, message*) adapter, positionner ♦ *vi* (*NAUT*) tanguer; (*fall*): **to into/off** tomber dans/de; **to be** ~**ed forward** être projeté(e) en avant; **at this** ~ à ce rythme.

pitch-black ['pɪtʃ'blæk] *a* noir(e) comme poix.

pitched battle *n* bataille rangée.

pitcher ['pɪtʃə*] *n* cruche *f*.

pitchfork ['pɪtʃfɔ:k] *n* fourche *f*.

piteous ['pɪtɪəs] *a* pitoyable.

pitfall ['pɪtfɔ:l] *n* trappe *f*, piège *m*.

pith [pɪθ] *n* (*of plant*) moelle *f*; (*of orange*) intérieur *m* de l'écorce; (*fig*) essence *f*; vigueur *f*.

pithead ['pɪthɛd] *n* (*Brit*) bouche *f* de puits.

pithy ['pɪθɪ] *a* piquant(e); vigoureux(euse).

pitiable ['pɪtɪəbl] *a* pitoyable.

pitiful ['pɪtɪful] *a* (*touching*) pitoyable; (*contemptible*) lamentable.

pitifully ['pɪtɪfəlɪ] *ad* pitoyablement; lamentablement.

pitiless ['pɪtɪlɪs] *a* impitoyable.

pittance ['pɪtns] *n* salaire *m* de misère.

pitted ['pɪtɪd] *a*: ~ **with** (*chickenpox*) grêlé(e) par; (*rust*) piqué(e) de.

pity ['pɪtɪ] *n* pitié *f* ♦ *vt* plaindre; **what a** ~! quel dommage!; **it is a** ~ **that you can't come** c'est dommage que vous ne puissiez venir; **to have** *or* **take** ~ **on sb** avoir pitié de qn.

pitying ['pɪtɪɪŋ] *a* compatissant(e).

pivot ['pɪvət] *n* pivot *m* ♦ *vi* pivoter.

pixel ['pɪksl] *n* (*COMPUT*) pixel *m*.

pixie ['pɪksɪ] *n* lutin *m*.

pizza ['pi:tsə] *n* pizza *f*.

P&L *abbr* = **profit and loss**.

placard ['plækɑ:d] *n* affiche *f*.

placate [plə'keɪt] *vt* apaiser, calmer.

placatory [plə'keɪtərɪ] *a* d'apaisement, lénifiant(e).

place [pleɪs] *n* endroit *m*, lieu *m*; (*proper position*, *rank*, *seat*) place *f*; (*house*) maison *f*, logement *m*; (*in street names*): **Laurel ~** ≈ rue des Lauriers; (*home*): **at/to his ~** chez lui ♦ *vt* (*position*) placer, mettre; (*identify*) situer; reconnaître; **to take ~** avoir lieu; (*occur*) se produire; **from ~ to ~** d'un endroit à l'autre; **all over the ~** partout; **out of ~** (*not suitable*) déplacé(e), inopportun(e); **I feel out of ~ here** je ne me sens pas à ma place ici; **in the first ~** d'abord, en premier; **to put sb in his ~** (*fig*) remettre qn à sa place; **he's going ~s** (*fig*: *col*) il fait son chemin; **it is not my ~ to do it** ce n'est pas à moi de le faire; **to ~ an order with sb (for)** (*COMM*) passer commande à qn (de); **to be ~d** (*in race, exam*) se placer; **how are you ~d next week?** comment ça se présente pour la semaine prochaine?

placebo [plə'si:bəʊ] *n* placebo *m*.

place mat *n* set *m* de table; (*in linen etc*) napperon *m*.

placement ['pleɪsmənt] *n* placement *m*; poste *m*.

place name *n* nom *m* de lieu.

placenta [plə'sɛntə] *n* placenta *m*.

placid ['plæsɪd] *a* placide.

placidity [plə'sɪdɪtɪ] *n* placidité *f*.

plagiarism ['pleɪdʒjərɪzəm] *n* plagiat *m*.

plagiarist ['pleɪdʒjərɪst] *n* plagiaire *m/f*.

plagiarize ['pleɪdʒjəraɪz] *vt* plagier.

plague [pleɪg] *n* fléau *m*; (*MED*) peste *f* ♦ *vt* (*fig*) tourmenter; **to ~ sb with questions** harceler qn de questions.

plaice [pleɪs] *n* (*pl inv*) carrelet *m*.

plaid [plæd] *n* tissu écossais.

plain [pleɪn] *a* (*clear*) clair(e), évident(e); (*simple*) simple, ordinaire; (*frank*) franc(franche); (*not handsome*) quelconque, ordinaire; (*cigarette*) sans filtre; (*without seasoning etc*) nature *inv*; (*in one colour*) uni(e) ♦ *ad* franchement, carrément ♦ *n* plaine *f*; **in ~ clothes** (*police*) en civil; **to make sth ~ to sb** faire clairement comprendre qch à qn.

plain chocolate *n* chocolat *m* à croquer.

plainly ['pleɪnlɪ] *ad* clairement; (*frankly*) carrément, sans détours.

plainness ['pleɪnnɪs] *n* simplicité *f*.

plaintiff ['pleɪntɪf] *n* plaignant/e.

plaintive ['pleɪntɪv] *a* plaintif(ive).

plait [plæt] *n* tresse *f*, natte *f* ♦ *vt* tresser, natter.

plan [plæn] *n* plan *m*; (*scheme*) projet *m* ♦ *vt* (*think in advance*) projeter; (*prepare*) organiser ♦ *vi* faire des projets; **to ~ to do** projeter de faire; **how long do you ~ to stay?** combien de temps comptez-vous rester?

plane [pleɪn] *n* (*AVIAT*) avion *m*; (*tree*) platane *m*; (*tool*) rabot *m*; (*ART, MATH etc*) plan *m* ♦ *a* plan(e), plat(e) ♦ *vt* (*with tool*) raboter.

planet ['plænɪt] *n* planète *f*.

planetarium [plænɪ'tɛərɪəm] *n* planétarium *m*.

plank [plæŋk] *n* planche *f*; (*POL*) point *m* d'un programme.

plankton ['plæŋktən] *n* plancton *m*.

planner ['plænə*] *n* planificateur/trice; (*chart*) planning *m*; **town** *or* (*US*) **city ~** urbaniste *m/f*.

planning ['plænɪŋ] *n* planification *f*; **family ~** planning familial.

planning permission *n* (*Brit*) permis *m* de construire.

plant [plɑ:nt] *n* plante *f*; (*machinery*) matériel *m*; (*factory*) usine *f* ♦ *vt* planter; (*bomb*) déposer, poser.

plantation [plæn'teɪʃən] *n* plantation *f*.

plant pot *n* (*Brit*) pot *m* de fleurs.

plaque [plæk] *n* plaque *f*.

plasma ['plæzmə] *n* plasma *m*.

plaster ['plɑ:stə*] *n* plâtre *m*; (*Brit: also:* **sticking ~**) pansement adhésif ♦ *vt* plâtrer; (*cover*): **to ~ with** couvrir de; **in ~** (*Brit: leg etc*) dans le plâtre; **~ of Paris** plâtre à mouler.

plaster cast *n* (*MED*) plâtre *m*; (*model, statue*) moule *m*.

plastered ['plɑ:stəd] *a* (*col*) soûl(e).

plasterer ['plɑ:stərə*] *n* plâtrier *m*.

plastic ['plæstɪk] *n* plastique *m* ♦ *a* (*made of plastic*) en plastique; (*flexible*) plastique, malléable; (*art*) plastique.

plastic bag *n* sac *m* en plastique.

plasticine ['plæstɪsi:n] *n* ® pâte *f* à modeler.

plastic surgery *n* chirurgie *f* esthétique.

plate [pleɪt] *n* (*dish*) assiette *f*; (*sheet of metal, on door, PHOT*) plaque *f*; (*TYP*) cliché *m*; (*in book*) gravure *f*; (*AUT: number ~*) plaque minéralogique; **gold/silver ~** (*dishes*) vaisselle *f* d'or/d'argent.

plateau ['plætəʊ], **~s** *or* **~x** ['plætəʊ, -z] *n* plateau *m*.

plateful ['pleɪtful] *n* assiette *f*, assiettée *f*.

plate glass *n* verre *m* à vitre, vitre *f*.

platelayer ['pleɪtleɪə*] *n* (*Brit RAIL*) poseur *m* de rails.

platen ['plætən] *n* (*on typewriter, printer*) rouleau *m*.

plate rack *n* égouttoir *m*.

platform ['plætfɔ:m] *n* (*at meeting*) tribune *f*; (*Brit: of bus*) plate-forme *f*; (*stage*) estrade *f*; (*RAIL*) quai *m*; **the train leaves from ~ 7** le train part de la voie 7.

platform ticket *n* (*Brit*) billet *m* de quai.

platinum ['plætɪnəm] *n* platine *m*.

platitude ['plætɪtju:d] *n* platitude *f*, lieu commun.

platoon [plə'tu:n] *n* peloton *m*.

platter ['plætə*] *n* plat *m*.

plaudits ['plɔ:dɪts] *npl* applaudissements *mpl*.

plausible ['plɔ:zɪbl] *a* plausible; (*person*) convaincant(e).

play [pleɪ] *n* jeu *m*; (*THEATRE*) pièce *f* (de théâtre) ♦ *vt* (*game*) jouer à; (*team, opponent*) jouer contre; (*instrument*) jouer de; (*play, part, piece of music, note*) jouer ♦ *vi* jouer; **to bring** *or* **call into ~** faire entrer en jeu; **~ on words** jeu de mots; **to ~ a trick on sb** jouer un tour à qn; **they're ~ing at soldiers** ils jouent aux soldats; **to ~ for time** (*fig*) chercher à gagner du temps; **to ~**

into sb's hands (*fig*) faire le jeu de qn.
play about , **play around** *vi* (*person*) s'amuser.
play along *vi* (*fig*): **to ~ along with** (*person*) entrer dans le jeu de ♦ *vt* (*fig*): **to ~ sb along** faire marcher qn.
play back *vt* repasser, réécouter.
play down *vt* minimiser.
play on *vt fus* (*sb's feelings, credulity*) jouer sur; **to ~ on sb's nerves** porter sur les nerfs de qn.
play up *vi* (*cause trouble*) faire des siennes.
playact ['pleıækt] *vi* jouer la comédie.
playboy ['pleıbɔı] *n* playboy *m*.
played-out ['pleıd'aut] *a* épuisé(e).
player ['pleıə*] *n* joueur/euse; (*THEATRE*) acteur/trice; (*MUS*) musicien/ne.
playful ['pleıful] *a* enjoué(e).
playgoer ['pleıgəuə*] *n* amateur/trice de théâtre, habitué/e des théâtres.
playground ['pleıgraund] *n* cour *f* de récréation.
playgroup ['pleıgru:p] *n* garderie *f*.
playing card *n* carte *f* à jouer.
playing field *n* terrain *m* de sport.
playmate ['pleımeıt] *n* camarade *m/f*, copain/copine.
play-off ['pleıɔf] *n* (*SPORT*) belle *f*.
playpen ['pleıpen] *n* parc *m* (pour bébé).
playroom ['pleıru:m] *n* salle *f* de jeux.
plaything ['pleıθıŋ] *n* jouet *m*.
playtime ['pleıtaım] *n* (*SCOL*) récréation *f*.
playwright ['pleıraıt] *n* dramaturge *m*.
plc *abbr* (*Brit*) = **public limited company**.
plea [pli:] *n* (*request*) appel *m*; (*excuse*) excuse *f*; (*LAW*) défense *f*.
plead [pli:d] *vt* plaider; (*give as excuse*) invoquer ♦ *vi* (*LAW*) plaider; (*beg*): **to ~ with sb (for sth)** implorer qn (d'accorder qch); **to ~ for sth** implorer qch; **to ~ guilty/not guilty** plaider coupable/non coupable.
pleasant ['pleznt] *a* agréable.
pleasantly ['plezntlı] *ad* agréablement.
pleasantness ['plezntnıs] *n* (*of person*) amabilité *f*; (*of place*) agrément *m*.
pleasantry ['plezntrı] *n* (*joke*) plaisanterie *f*; **pleasantries** *npl* (*polite remarks*) civilités *fpl*.
please [pli:z] *vt* plaire à ♦ *vi* (*think fit*): **do as you ~** faites comme il vous plaira; **~!** s'il te (*or* vous) plaît; **my bill, ~** l'addition, s'il vous plaît; **~ don't cry!** je t'en prie, ne pleure pas!; **~ yourself!** (faites) comme vous voulez!
pleased [pli:zd] *a*: **~ (with)** content(e) (de); **~ to meet you** enchanté (de faire votre connaissance); **we are ~ to inform you that** ... nous sommes heureux de vous annoncer que ....
pleasing ['pli:zıŋ] *a* plaisant(e), qui fait plaisir.
pleasurable ['pleʒərəbl] *a* très agréable.
pleasure ['pleʒə*] *n* plaisir *m*; **"it's a ~"** "je vous en prie"; **with ~** avec plaisir; **is this trip for business or ~?** est-ce un voyage d'affaires ou d'agrément?
pleasure steamer *n* vapeur *m* de plaisance.
pleat [pli:t] *n* pli *m*.
plebiscite ['plebısıt] *n* plébiscite *m*.

plebs [plebz] *npl* (*pej*) bas peuple.
plectrum ['plektrəm] *n* plectre *m*.
pledge [pledʒ] *n* gage *m*; (*promise*) promesse *f* ♦ *vt* engager; promettre; **to ~ support for sb** s'engager à soutenir qn; **to ~ sb to secrecy** faire promettre à qn de garder le secret.
plenary ['pli:nərı] *a*: **in ~ session** en séance plénière.
plentiful ['plentıful] *a* abondant(e), copieux(euse).
plenty ['plentı] *n* abondance *f*; **~ of** beaucoup de; (*sufficient*) (bien) assez de; **we've got ~ of time** nous avons largement le temps.
pleurisy ['pluərısı] *n* pleurésie *f*.
Plexiglas ['pleksıgla:s] *n* ® (*US*) Plexiglas *m* ®.
pliable ['plaıəbl] *a* flexible; (*person*) malléable.
pliers ['plaıəz] *npl* pinces *fpl*.
plight [plaıt] *n* situation *f* critique.
plimsolls ['plımsəlz] *npl* (*Brit*) (chaussures *fpl*) tennis *fpl*.
plinth [plınθ] *n* socle *m*.
PLO *n abbr* (= *Palestine Liberation Organization*) OLP *f*.
plod [plɔd] *vi* avancer péniblement; (*fig*) peiner.
plodder ['plɔdə*] *n* bûcheur/euse.
plodding ['plɔdıŋ] *a* pesant(e).
plonk [plɔŋk] (*col*) *n* (*Brit: wine*) pinard *m*, piquette *f* ♦ *vt*: **to ~ sth down** poser brusquement qch.
plot [plɔt] *n* complot *m*, conspiration *f*; (*of story, play*) intrigue *f*; (*of land*) lot *m* de terrain, lopin *m* ♦ *vt* (*mark out*) pointer; relever; (*conspire*) comploter ♦ *vi* comploter; **a vegetable ~** (*Brit*) un carré de légumes.
plotter ['plɔtə*] *n* conspirateur/trice; (*COMPUT*) traceur *m*.
plough, (*US*) **plow** [plau] *n* charrue *f* ♦ *vt* (*earth*) labourer.
plough back *vt* (*COMM*) réinvestir.
plough through *vt fus* (*snow etc*) avancer péniblement dans.
ploughing, (*US*) **plowing** ['plauıŋ] *n* labourage *m*.
ploughman, (*US*) **plowman** ['plaumən] *n* laboureur *m*; **~'s lunch** (*Brit*) repas sommaire de pain et de fromage.
ploy [plɔı] *n* stratagème *m*.
pluck [plʌk] *vt* (*fruit*) cueillir; (*musical instrument*) pincer; (*bird*) plumer ♦ *n* courage *m*, cran *m*; **to ~ one's eyebrows** s'épiler les sourcils; **to ~ up courage** prendre son courage à deux mains.
plucky ['plʌkı] *a* courageux(euse).
plug [plʌg] *n* bouchon *m*, bonde *f*; (*ELEC*) prise *f* de courant; (*AUT: also:* **spark(ing) ~**) bougie *f* ♦ *vt* (*hole*) boucher; (*col: advertise*) faire du battage pour, matraquer; **to give sb/sth a ~** (*col*) faire de la pub pour qn/qch.
plug in (*ELEC*) *vt* brancher ♦ *vi* se brancher.
plughole ['plʌghəul] *n* (*Brit*) trou *m* (d'écoulement).
plum [plʌm] *n* (*fruit*) prune *f* ♦ *a*: **~ job** (*col*) travail *m* en or.
plumage ['plu:mıdʒ] *n* plumage *m*.

plumb [plʌm] a vertical(e) ♦ n plomb m ♦ ad (exactly) en plein ♦ vt sonder.
  plumb in vt (washing machine) faire le raccordement de.
plumber ['plʌmə*] n plombier m.
plumbing ['plʌmɪŋ] n (trade) plomberie f; (piping) tuyauterie f.
plumbline ['plʌmlaɪn] n fil m à plomb.
plume [plu:m] n plume f, plumet m.
plummet ['plʌmɪt] vi plonger, dégringoler.
plump [plʌmp] a rondelet(te), dodu(e), bien en chair ♦ vt: **to ~ sth (down) on** laisser tomber qch lourdement sur.
  plump for vt fus (col: choose) se décider pour.
  plump up vt (cushion) battre (pour lui redonner forme).
plunder ['plʌndə*] n pillage m ♦ vt piller.
plunge [plʌndʒ] n plongeon m ♦ vt plonger ♦ vi (fall) tomber, dégringoler; **to take the ~** se jeter à l'eau; **to ~ a room into darkness** plonger une pièce dans l'obscurité.
plunger ['plʌndʒə*] n piston m; (for blocked sink) (débouchoir m à) ventouse f.
plunging ['plʌndʒɪŋ] a (neckline) plongeant(e).
pluperfect [plu:'pə:fɪkt] n plus-que-parfait m.
plural ['pluərl] a pluriel(le) ♦ n pluriel m.
plus [plʌs] n (also: **~ sign**) signe m plus ♦ prep plus; **ten/twenty ~** plus de dix/vingt; **it's a ~** c'est un plus.
plus fours npl pantalon m (de) golf.
plush [plʌʃ] a somptueux(euse) ♦ n peluche f.
plutonium [plu:'təuniəm] n plutonium m.
ply [plaɪ] n (of wool) fil m; (of wood) feuille f, épaisseur f ♦ vt (tool) manier; (a trade) exercer ♦ vi (ship) faire la navette; **three ~ (wool)** n laine f trois fils; **to ~ sb with drink** donner continuellement à boire à qn.
plywood ['plaɪwud] n contre-plaqué m.
PM n abbr (Brit) = **prime minister**.
p.m. ad abbr (= post meridiem) de l'après-midi.
pneumatic [nju:'mætɪk] a pneumatique; **~ drill** marteau-piqueur m.
pneumonia [nju:'məuniə] n pneumonie f.
PO n abbr (= Post Office) PTT fpl; (MIL) = **petty officer**.
po abbr = **postal order**.
POA n abbr (Brit) = **Prison Officers' Association**.
poach [pəutʃ] vt (cook) pocher; (steal) pêcher (or chasser) sans permis ♦ vi braconner.
poached [pəutʃt] a (egg) poché(e).
poacher ['pəutʃə*] n braconnier m.
poaching ['pəutʃɪŋ] n braconnage m.
PO Box n abbr = **Post Office Box**.
pocket ['pɔkɪt] n poche f ♦ vt empocher; **to be (£5) out of ~** (Brit) en être de sa poche (pour 5 livres).
pocketbook ['pɔkɪtbuk] n (wallet) portefeuille m; (notebook) carnet m; (US: handbag) sac m à main.
pocket knife n canif m.
pocket money n argent m de poche.
pockmarked ['pɔkmɑ:kt] a (face) grêlé(e).
pod [pɔd] n cosse f ♦ vt écosser.
podgy ['pɔdʒɪ] a rondelet(te).
podiatrist [pɔ'di:ətrɪst] n (US) pédicure m/f.

podiatry [pɔ'di:ətrɪ] n (US) pédicurie f.
podium ['pəudiəm] n podium m.
POE n abbr = **port of embarkation**, **port of entry**.
poem ['pəuɪm] n poème m.
poet ['pəuɪt] n poète m.
poetic [pəu'etɪk] a poétique.
poet laureate n poète lauréat (nommé et appointé par la Cour royale).
poetry ['pəuɪtrɪ] n poésie f.
POEU n abbr (Brit: = Post Office Engineering Union) syndicat des agents techniques des postes.
poignant ['pɔɪnjənt] a poignant(e); (sharp) vif(vive).
point [pɔɪnt] n (tip) pointe f; (in time) moment m; (in space) endroit m; (GEOM, SCOL, SPORT, on scale) point m; (subject, idea) point, sujet m; (also: **decimal ~**): **2 ~ 3 (2.3)** 2 virgule 3 (2,3); (Brit ELEC: also: **power ~**) prise f (de courant) ♦ vt (show) indiquer; (wall, window) jointoyer; (gun etc): **to ~ sth at** braquer or diriger qch sur ♦ vi montrer du doigt; **to ~ to** montrer du doigt; (fig) signaler; **~s** npl (AUT) vis platinées; (RAIL) aiguillage m; **good ~s** qualités fpl; **the train stops at Carlisle and all ~s south** le train dessert Carlisle et toutes les gares vers le sud; **to make a ~** faire une remarque; **to make a ~ of doing sth** ne pas manquer de faire qch; **to make one's ~** se faire comprendre; **to get the ~** comprendre, saisir; **to come to the ~** en venir au fait; **when it comes to the ~** le moment venu; **there's no ~ (in doing)** cela ne sert à rien (de faire); **to be on the ~ of doing sth** être sur le point de faire qch; **that's the whole ~!** précisément!; **to be beside the ~** être à côté de la question; **you've got a ~ there!** (c'est) juste!; **in ~ of fact** en fait, en réalité; **~ of departure** (also fig) point de départ; **~ of order** point de procédure; **~ of sale** (COMM) point de vente; **~ of view** point de vue.
point out vt faire remarquer, souligner.
point-blank ['pɔɪnt'blæŋk] ad (also: **at ~ range**) à bout portant ♦ a (fig) catégorique.
point duty n (Brit): **to be on ~** diriger la circulation.
pointed ['pɔɪntɪd] a (shape) pointu(e); (remark) plein(e) de sous-entendus.
pointedly ['pɔɪntɪdlɪ] ad d'une manière significative.
pointer ['pɔɪntə*] n (stick) baguette f; (needle) aiguille f; (dog) chien m d'arrêt; (clue) indication f; (advice) tuyau m.
pointless ['pɔɪntlɪs] a inutile, vain(e).
poise [pɔɪz] n (balance) équilibre m; (of head, body) port m; (calmness) calme m ♦ vt placer en équilibre; **to be ~d for** (fig) être prêt à.
poison ['pɔɪzn] n poison m ♦ vt empoisonner.
poisoning ['pɔɪznɪŋ] n empoisonnement m.
poisonous ['pɔɪznəs] a (snake) venimeux(euse); (substance etc) vénéneux(euse); (fumes) toxique; (fig) pernicieux(euse).
poke [pəuk] vt (fire) tisonner; (jab with finger, stick etc) piquer; pousser du doigt;

(put): **to ~ sth into** fourrer *or* enfoncer qch dans ♦ *n (jab)* (petit) coup; *(to fire)* coup *m* de tisonnier; **to ~ one's head out of the window** passer la tête par la fenêtre; **to ~ fun at sb** se moquer de qn.
poke about *vi* fureter.
poker ['pəukə*] *n* tisonnier *m*; *(CARDS)* poker *m*.
poker-faced ['pəukə'feist] *a* au visage impassible.
poky ['pəuki] *a* exigu(ë).
Poland ['pəulənd] *n* Pologne *f*.
polar ['pəulə*] *a* polaire.
polar bear *n* ours blanc.
polarize ['pəuləraiz] *vt* polariser.
Pole [pəul] *n* Polonais/e.
pole [pəul] *n (of wood)* mât *m*, perche *f*; *(ELEC)* poteau *m*; *(GEO)* pôle *m*.
pole bean *n (US)* haricot *m* (à rames).
polecat ['pəulkæt] *n* putois *m*.
Pol. Econ. ['pɔlikɔn] *n abbr = political economy*.
polemic [pɔ'lɛmik] *n* polémique *f*.
pole star ['pəulstɑ:*] *n* étoile *f* polaire.
pole vault ['pəulvɔ:lt] *n* saut *m* à la perche.
police [pə'li:s] *npl* police *f* ♦ *vt* maintenir l'ordre dans; **a large number of ~ were hurt** de nombreux policiers ont été blessés.
police car *n* voiture *f* de police.
police constable *n (Brit)* agent *m* de police.
police department *n (US)* services *mpl* de police.
police force *n* police *f*, forces *fpl* de l'ordre.
policeman [pə'li:smən] *n* agent *m* de police, policier *m*.
police officer *n* agent *m* de police.
police record *n* casier *m* judiciaire.
police state *n* état policier.
police station *n* commissariat *m* de police.
policewoman [pə'li:swumən] *n* femme-agent *f*.
policy ['pɔlisi] *n* politique *f*; *(also:* **insurance ~)** police *f* (d'assurance); *(of newspaper, company)* politique générale; **to take out a ~** *(INSURANCE)* souscrire une police d'assurance.
policy holder *n* assuré/e.
polio ['pəuliəu] *n* polio *f*.
Polish ['pəuliʃ] *a* polonais(e) ♦ *n (LING)* polonais *m*.
polish ['pɔliʃ] *n (for shoes)* cirage *m*; *(for floor)* cire *f*, encaustique *f*; *(for nails)* vernis *m*; *(shine)* éclat *m*, poli *m*; *(fig: refinement)* raffinement *m* ♦ *vt (put polish on : shoes, wood)* cirer; *(make shiny)* astiquer, faire briller; *(fig: improve)* perfectionner.
polish off *vt (work)* expédier; *(food)* liquider.
polished ['pɔliʃt] *a (fig)* raffiné(e).
polite [pə'lait] *a* poli(e); **it's not ~ to do that** ça ne se fait pas.
politely [pə'laitli] *ad* poliment.
politeness [pə'laitnis] *n* politesse *f*.
politic ['pɔlitik] *a* diplomatique.
political [pə'litikl] *a* politique.
political asylum *n* asile *m* politique.
politically [pə'litikli] *ad* politiquement.
politician [pɔli'tiʃən] *n* homme/femme politique, politicien/ne.

politics ['pɔlitiks] *npl* politique *f*.
polka ['pɔlkə] *n* polka *f*.
polka dot *n* pois *m*.
poll [pəul] *n* scrutin *m*, vote *m*; *(also:* **opinion ~)** sondage *m* (d'opinion) ♦ *vt* obtenir; **to go to the ~s** *(voters)* aller aux urnes; *(government)* tenir des élections.
pollen ['pɔlən] *n* pollen *m*.
pollen count *n* taux *m* de pollen.
pollination [pɔli'neiʃən] *n* pollinisation *f*.
polling ['pəuliŋ] *n (Brit POL)* élections *fpl*; *(TEL)* invitation *f* à émettre.
polling booth *n (Brit)* isoloir *m*.
polling day *n (Brit)* jour *m* des élections.
polling station *n (Brit)* bureau *m* de vote.
pollute [pə'lu:t] *vt* polluer.
pollution [pə'lu:ʃən] *n* pollution *f*.
polo ['pəuləu] *n* polo *m*.
poloneck ['pəuləunɛk] *n* col roulé ♦ *a* à col roulé.
poly ['pɔli] *n abbr (Brit) =* **polytechnic**.
polyester [pɔli'ɛstə*] *n* polyester *m*.
polygamy [pə'ligəmi] *n* polygamie *f*.
Polynesia [pɔli'ni:ziə] *n* Polynésie *f*.
Polynesian [pɔli'ni:ziən] *a* polynésien(ne) ♦ *n* Polynésien/ne.
polyp ['pɔlip] *n (MED)* polype *m*.
polystyrene [pɔli'stairi:n] *n* polystyrène *m*.
polytechnic [pɔli'tɛknik] *n (college)* I.U.T. *m*, Institut *m* Universitaire de Technologie.
polythene ['pɔliθi:n] *n* polyéthylène *m*.
polythene bag *n* sac *m* en plastique.
polyurethane [pɔli'juəriθein] *n* polyuréthane *m*.
pomegranate ['pɔmigrænit] *n* grenade *f*.
pommel ['pɔml] *n* pommeau *m* ♦ *vt =* **pummel**.
pomp [pɔmp] *n* pompe *f*, faste *f*, apparat *m*.
pompom ['pɔmpɔm], **pompon** ['pɔmpɔn] *n* pompon *m*.
pompous ['pɔmpəs] *a* pompeux(euse).
pond [pɔnd] *n* étang *m*; *(stagnant)* mare *f*.
ponder ['pɔndə*] *vi* réfléchir ♦ *vt* considérer, peser.
ponderous ['pɔndərəs] *a* pesant(e), lourd(e).
pong [pɔŋ] *(Brit col) n* puanteur *f* ♦ *vi* schlinguer.
pontiff ['pɔntif] *n* pontife *m*.
pontificate [pɔn'tifikeit] *vi (fig):* **to ~ (about)** pontifier (sur).
pontoon [pɔn'tu:n] *n* ponton *m*; *(Brit: CARDS)* vingt-et-un *m*.
pony ['pəuni] *n* poney *m*.
ponytail ['pəuniteil] *n* queue *f* de cheval.
pony trekking *n (Brit)* randonnée *f* équestre *or* à cheval.
poodle ['pu:dl] *n* caniche *m*.
pooh-pooh [pu:'pu:] *vt* dédaigner.
pool [pu:l] *n (of rain)* flaque *f*; *(pond)* mare *f*; *(artificial)* bassin *m*; *(also:* **swimming ~)** piscine *f*; *(sth shared)* fonds commun; *(money at cards)* cagnotte *f*; *(billiards)* poule *f*; *(COMM: consortium)* pool *m*; *(US: monopoly trust)* trust *m* ♦ *vt* mettre en commun; **typing ~**, *(US)* **secretary ~** pool *m* dactylographique; **to do the (football) ~s** *(Brit)* ≈ jouer au loto sportif.
poor [puə*] *a* pauvre; *(mediocre)* médiocre, faible, mauvais(e) ♦ *npl:* **the ~** les pauvres

mpl.

poorly ['puəlı] *ad* pauvrement; médiocrement ♦ *a* souffrant(e), malade.

pop [pɔp] *n (noise)* bruit sec; *(MUS)* musique *f* pop; *(col: drink)* soda *m; (US col: father)* papa *m* ♦ *vt (put)* fourrer, mettre (rapidement) ♦ *vi* éclater; *(cork)* sauter; **she ~ped her head out of the window** elle passa la tête par la fenêtre.

pop in *vi* entrer en passant.

pop out *vi* sortir.

pop up *vi* apparaître, surgir.

pop concert *n* concert *m* pop.

popcorn ['pɔpkɔ:n] *n* pop-corn *m.*

pope [pəup] *n* pape *m.*

poplar ['pɔplə*] *n* peuplier *m.*

poplin ['pɔplın] *n* popeline *f.*

popper ['pɔpə*] *n (Brit)* bouton-pression *m.*

poppy ['pɔpı] *n* coquelicot *m*; pavot *m.*

poppycock ['pɔpıkɔk] *n (col)* balivernes *fpl.*

popsicle ['pɔpsıkl] *n* ® *(US)* esquimau *m (glace).*

populace ['pɔpjuləs] *n* peuple *m.*

popular ['pɔpjulə*] *a* populaire; *(fashionable)* à la mode; **to be ~ (with)** *(person)* avoir du succès (auprès de); *(decision)* être bien accueilli(e) (par).

popularity [pɔpju'lærıtı] *n* popularité *f.*

popularize ['pɔpjuləraız] *vt* populariser; *(science)* vulgariser.

populate ['pɔpjuleıt] *vt* peupler.

population [pɔpju'leıʃən] *n* population *f.*

population explosion *n* explosion *f* démographique.

populous ['pɔpjuləs] *a* populeux(euse).

porcelain ['pɔ:slın] *n* porcelaine *f.*

porch [pɔ:tʃ] *n* porche *m.*

porcupine ['pɔ:kjupaın] *n* porc-épic *m.*

pore [pɔ:*] *n* pore *m* ♦ *vi:* **to ~ over** s'absorber dans, être plongé(e) dans.

pork [pɔ:k] *n* porc *m.*

pork chop *n* côte *f* de porc.

pornographic [pɔ:nə'græfık] *a* pornographique.

pornography [pɔ:'nɔgrəfı] *n* pornographie *f.*

porous ['pɔ:rəs] *a* poreux(euse).

porpoise ['pɔ:pəs] *n* marsouin *m.*

porridge ['pɔrıdʒ] *n* porridge *m.*

port [pɔ:t] *n (harbour)* port *m; (opening in ship)* sabord *m; (NAUT: left side)* bâbord *m; (wine)* porto *m; (COMPUT)* port *m*, accès *m* ♦ *cpd* portuaire, du port; **to ~** *(NAUT)* à bâbord; **~ of call** (port d')escale *f.*

portable ['pɔ:təbl] *a* portatif(ive).

portal ['pɔ:tl] *n* portail *m.*

portcullis [pɔ:t'kʌlıs] *n* herse *f.*

portend [pɔ:'tend] *vt* présager, annoncer.

portent ['pɔ:tent] *n* présage *m.*

porter ['pɔ:tə*] *n (for luggage)* porteur *m; (doorkeeper)* gardien/ne; portier *m.*

portfolio [pɔ:t'fəulıəu] *n* portefeuille *m; (of artist)* portfolio *m.*

porthole ['pɔ:thəul] *n* hublot *m.*

portico ['pɔ:tıkəu] *n* portique *m.*

portion ['pɔ:ʃən] *n* portion *f*, part *f.*

portly ['pɔ:tlı] *a* corpulent(e).

portrait ['pɔ:treıt] *n* portrait *m.*

portray [pɔ:'treı] *vt* faire le portrait de; *(in writing)* dépeindre, représenter.

portrayal [pɔ:'treıəl] *n* portrait *m*, représentation *f.*

Portugal ['pɔ:tjugl] *n* Portugal *m.*

Portuguese [pɔ:tju'gi:z] *a* portugais(e) ♦ *n (pl inv)* Portugais/e; *(LING)* portugais *m.*

Portuguese man-of-war *n (jellyfish)* galère *f.*

pose [pəuz] *n* pose *f; (pej)* affectation *f* ♦ *vi* poser; *(pretend):* **to ~ as** se poser en ♦ *vt* poser, créer; **to strike a ~** poser (pour la galerie).

poser ['pəuzə*] *n* question difficile *or* embarrassante; *(person)* = **poseur.**

poseur [pəu'zə:*] *n (pej)* poseur/euse.

posh [pɔʃ] *a (col)* chic *inv;* **to talk ~** parler d'une manière affectée.

position [pə'zıʃən] *n* position *f; (job)* situation *f* ♦ *vt* mettre en place *or* en position; **to be in a ~ to do sth** être en mesure de faire qch.

positive ['pɔzıtıv] *a* positif(ive); *(certain)* sûr(e), certain(e); *(definite)* formel(le), catégorique; *(clear)* indéniable, réel(le).

posse ['pɔsı] *n (US)* détachement *m.*

possess [pə'zes] *vt* posséder; **like one ~ed** comme un fou; **whatever can have ~ed you?** qu'est-ce qui vous a pris?

possession [pə'zeʃən] *n* possession *f;* **to take ~ of sth** prendre possession de qch.

possessive [pə'zesıv] *a* possessif(ive).

possessively [pə'zesıvlı] *ad* d'une façon possessive.

possessor [pə'zesə*] *n* possesseur *m.*

possibility [pɔsı'bılıtı] *n* possibilité *f;* éventualité *f;* **he's a ~ for the part** c'est un candidat possible pour le rôle.

possible ['pɔsıbl] *a* possible; *(solution)* envisageable, éventuel(le); **it is ~ to do it** il est possible de le faire; **as far as ~** dans la mesure du possible, autant que possible; **if ~** si possible; **as big as ~** aussi gros que possible.

possibly ['pɔsıblı] *ad (perhaps)* peut-être; **if you ~ can** si cela vous est possible; **I cannot ~ come** il m'est impossible de venir.

post [pəust] *n (Brit: mail)* poste *f; (: collection)* levée *f; (: letters, delivery)* courrier *m; (job, situation)* poste *m; (pole)* poteau *m; (trading ~)* comptoir (commercial) ♦ *vt (Brit: send by post, MIL)* poster; *(Brit: appoint):* **to ~ to** affecter à; *(notice)* afficher; **by ~** *(Brit)* par la poste; **by return of ~** *(Brit)* par retour du courrier; **to keep sb ~ed** tenir qn au courant.

post... [pəust] *prefix* post...; **~ 1990** *a* d'après 1990 ♦ *ad* après 1990.

postage ['pəustıdʒ] *n* affranchissement *m;* **~ paid** port payé; **~ prepaid** *(US)* franco (de port).

postage stamp *n* timbre-poste *m.*

postal ['pəustl] *a* postal(e).

postal order *n* mandat(-poste) *m.*

postbag ['pəustbæg] *n (Brit)* sac postal; *(postman's)* sacoche *f.*

postbox ['pəustbɔks] *n (Brit)* boîte *f* aux lettres.

postcard ['pəustka:d] *n* carte postale.

postcode ['pəustkəud] *n (Brit)* code postal.

postdate ['pəust'deıt] *vt (cheque)* postdater.

poster ['pəustə*] *n* affiche *f.*

poste restante [pəust'restɑ̃:nt] *n* (*Brit*) poste restante.

posterior [pɔs'tɪərɪə*] *n* (*col*) postérieur *m*, derrière *m*.

posterity [pɔs'terɪtɪ] *n* postérité *f*.

poster paint *n* gouache *f*.

post exchange (PX) *n* (*US MIL*) magasin *m* de l'armée.

post-free [pəust'fri:] *a* (*Brit*) franco (de port).

postgraduate [pəust'grædjuət] *n* ≈ étudiant/e de troisième cycle.

posthumous ['pɔstjuməs] *a* posthume.

posthumously ['pɔstjuməslɪ] *ad* après la mort de l'auteur, à titre posthume.

posting ['pəustɪŋ] *n* (*Brit*) affectation *f*.

postman ['pəustmən] *n* facteur *m*.

postmark ['pəustmɑ:k] *n* cachet *m* (de la poste).

postmaster ['pəustmɑ:stə*] *n* receveur *m* des postes.

Postmaster General *n* ≈ ministre *m* des Postes et Télécommunications.

postmistress ['pəustmɪstrɪs] *n* receveuse *f* des postes.

post-mortem [pəust'mɔ:təm] *n* autopsie *f*.

postnatal ['pəust'neɪtl] *a* post-natal(e).

post office *n* (*building*) poste *f*; (*organization*) postes *fpl*.

post office box (PO box) *n* boîte postale (B.P.).

post-paid ['pəust'peɪd] *a* (*Brit*) port payé.

postpone [pəs'pəun] *vt* remettre (à plus tard), reculer.

postponement [pəs'pəunmənt] *n* ajournement *m*, renvoi *m*.

postscript ['pəustskrɪpt] *n* post-scriptum *m*.

postulate ['pɔstjuleɪt] *vt* postuler.

posture ['pɔstʃə*] *n* posture *f*, attitude *f* ♦ *vi* poser.

postwar [pəust'wɔ:*] *a* d'après-guerre.

posy ['pəuzɪ] *n* petit bouquet.

pot [pɔt] *n* (*for cooking*) marmite *f*; casserole *f*; (*for plants, jam*) pot *m*; (*piece of pottery*) poterie *f*; (*col: marijuana*) herbe *f* ♦ *vt* (*plant*) mettre en pot; **to go to ~** aller à vau-l'eau; **~s of** (*Brit col*) beaucoup de, plein de.

potash ['pɔtæʃ] *n* potasse *f*.

potassium [pə'tæsɪəm] *n* potassium *m*.

potato, ~es [pə'teɪtəu] *n* pomme *f* de terre.

potato crisps, (*US*) **potato chips** *npl* chips *mpl*.

potato flour *n* fécule *f*.

potato peeler *n* épluche-legumes *m*.

potbellied ['pɔtbelɪd] *a* (*from overeating*) bedonnant(e); (*from malnutrition*) au ventre ballonné.

potency ['pəutnsɪ] *n* puissance *f*, force *f*; (*of drink*) degré *m* d'alcool.

potent ['pəutnt] *a* puissant(e); (*drink*) fort(e), très alcoolisé(e).

potentate ['pəutnteɪt] *n* potentat *m*.

potential [pə'tenʃl] *a* potentiel(le) ♦ *n* potentiel *m*; **to have ~** être prometteur(euse); ouvrir des possibilités.

potentially [pə'tenʃəlɪ] *ad* potentiellement; **it's ~ dangerous** ça pourrait se révéler dangereux, il y a possibilité de danger.

pothole ['pɔthəul] *n* (*in road*) nid *m* de poule;

potholer ['pɔthəulə*] *n* (*Brit*) spéléologue *m/f*.

potholing ['pɔthəulɪŋ] *n* (*Brit*): **to go ~** faire de la spéléologie.

potion ['pəuʃən] *n* potion *f*.

potluck [pɔt'lʌk] *n*: **to take ~** tenter sa chance.

potpourri [pəu'puri:] *n* pot-pourri *m*.

pot roast *n* rôti *m* à la cocotte.

potshot ['pɔtʃɔt] *n*: **to take ~s at** canarder.

potted ['pɔtɪd] *a* (*food*) en conserve; (*plant*) en pot; (*fig: shortened*) abrégé(e).

potter ['pɔtə*] *n* potier *m* ♦ *vi* (*Brit*): **to ~ around**, **~ about** bricoler; **~'s wheel** tour *m* de potier.

pottery ['pɔtərɪ] *n* poterie *f*; **a piece of ~** une poterie.

potty ['pɔtɪ] *a* (*Brit col: mad*) dingue ♦ *n* (*child's*) pot *m*.

potty-training ['pɔtɪtreɪnɪŋ] *n* apprentissage *m* de la propreté.

pouch [pautʃ] *n* (*ZOOL*) poche *f*; (*for tobacco*) blague *f*.

pouf(fe) [pu:f] *n* (*stool*) pouf *m*.

poultice ['pəultɪs] *n* cataplasme *m*.

poultry ['pəultrɪ] *n* volaille *f*.

poultry farm *n* élevage *m* de volaille.

poultry farmer *n* aviculteur *m*.

pounce [pauns] *vi*: **to ~ (on)** bondir (sur), fondre (sur) ♦ *n* bond *m*, attaque *f*.

pound [paund] *n* livre *f* (*weight* = 453g, 16 ounces; money = 100 pence); (*for dogs, cars*) fourrière *f* ♦ *vt* (*beat*) bourrer de coups, marteler; (*crush*) piler, pulvériser; (*with guns*) pilonner ♦ *vi* (*beat*) battre violemment, taper; **half a ~ (of)** une demi-livre (de); **a five-~ note** un billet de cinq livres.

pounding ['paundɪŋ] *n*: **to take a ~** (*fig*) prendre une raclée.

pound sterling *n* livre *f* sterling.

pour [pɔ:*] *vt* verser ♦ *vi* couler à flots; (*rain*) pleuvoir à verse; **to come ~ing in** (*water*) entrer à flots; (*letters*) arriver par milliers; (*cars, people*) affluer.

pour away , **pour off** *vt* vider.

pour in *vi* (*people*) affluer, se précipiter.

pour out *vi* (*people*) sortir en masse ♦ *vt* vider; déverser; (*serve: a drink*) verser.

pouring ['pɔ:rɪŋ] *a*: **~ rain** pluie torrentielle.

pout [paut] *n* moue *f* ♦ *vi* faire la moue.

poverty ['pɔvətɪ] *n* pauvreté *f*, misère *f*.

poverty-stricken ['pɔvətɪstrɪkn] *a* pauvre, déshérité(e).

poverty trap *n* (*Brit*) piège *m* de la pauvreté.

POW *n* abbr = **prisoner of war**.

powder ['paudə*] *n* poudre *f* ♦ *vt* poudrer; **to ~ one's nose** se poudrer; (*euphemism*) aller à la salle de bain; **~ed milk** lait *m* en poudre.

powder compact *n* poudrier *m*.

powder puff *n* houppette *f*.

powder room *n* toilettes *fpl* (pour dames).

powdery ['paudərɪ] *a* poudreux(euse).

power ['pauə*] *n* (*strength*) puissance *f*, force *f*; (*ability, POL: of party, leader*) pouvoir *m*; (*MATH*) puissance; (*of speech, thought*) faculté *f*; (*ELEC*) courant *m* ♦ *vt* faire marcher, actionner; **to do all in one's ~ to help sb** faire tout ce qui est en son pouvoir pour aider qn; **the world** ~s les grandes puissances; **to be in** ~ être au pouvoir.

powerboat ['pauəbəut] n (Brit) hors-bord m.

power cut n (Brit) coupure f de courant.

power-driven ['pauədrɪvn] a à moteur; (ELEC) électrique.

powered ['pauəd] a: ~ **by** actionné(e) par, fonctionnant à; **nuclear-~ submarine** sous-marin m (à propulsion) nucléaire.

power failure n panne f de courant.

powerful ['pauəful] a puissant(e).

powerhouse ['pauəhaus] n (fig: person) fonceur m; **a ~ of ideas** une mine d'idées.

powerless ['pauəlɪs] a impuissant(e).

power line n ligne f électrique.

power point n (Brit) prise f de courant.

power station n centrale f électrique.

power steering n direction assistée.

powwow ['pauwau] n conciliabule m.

pox [pɒks] n see **chicken**.

pp abbr (= per procurationem: by proxy) p.p.

p&p abbr (Brit: = postage and packing) frais mpl de port.

PPE n abbr (Brit scol) = philosophy, politics and economics.

PPS n abbr (= post postscriptum) PPS; (Brit: = parliamentary private secretary) parlementaire chargé de mission auprès d'un ministre.

PQ abbr (Canada) = Province of Quebec.

PR n abbr = **proportional representation**, **public relations** ♦ abbr (US POST) = Puerto Rico.

Pr. abbr (= prince) Pce.

practicability [præktɪkə'bɪlɪtɪ] n possibilité f de réalisation.

practicable ['præktɪkəbl] a (scheme) réalisable.

practical ['præktɪkl] a pratique.

practicality [præktɪ'kælɪtɪ] n (of plan) aspect m pratique; (of person) sens m pratique; **practicalities** npl détails mpl pratiques.

practical joke n farce f.

practically ['præktɪklɪ] ad (almost) pratiquement.

practice ['præktɪs] n pratique f; (of profession) exercice m; (at football etc) entraînement m; (business) cabinet m; clientèle f ♦ vt, vi (US) = **practise**; **in** ~ (in reality) en pratique; **out of** ~ rouillé(e); **2 hours' piano** ~ 2 heures de travail or d'exercices au piano; **target** ~ exercices de tir; **it's common** ~ c'est courant, ça se fait couramment; **to put sth into** ~ mettre qch en pratique.

practice match n match m d'entraînement.

practise, (US) **practice** ['præktɪs] vt (work at: piano, one's backhand etc) s'exercer à, travailler; (train for: skiing, running etc) s'entraîner à; (a sport, religion, method) pratiquer; (profession) exercer ♦ vi s'exercer, travailler; (train) s'entraîner; **to** ~ **for a match** s'entraîner pour un match.

practised ['præktɪst] a (Brit: person) expérimenté(e); (: performance) impeccable; (: liar) invétéré(e); **with a** ~ **eye** d'un œil exercé.

practising ['præktɪsɪŋ] a (Christian etc) pratiquant(e); (lawyer) en exercice;

(homosexual) déclaré.

practitioner [præk'tɪʃənə*] n praticien/ne.

pragmatic [præg'mætɪk] a pragmatique.

Prague [prɑːg] n Prague.

prairie ['prɛərɪ] n savane f; (US): **the** ~s la Prairie.

praise [preɪz] n éloge(s) m(pl), louange(s) f(pl) ♦ vt louer, faire l'éloge de.

praiseworthy ['preɪzwə:ðɪ] a digne de louanges.

pram [præm] n (Brit) landau m, voiture f d'enfant.

prance [prɑːns] vi (horse) caracoler.

prank [præŋk] n farce f.

prattle ['prætl] vi jacasser.

prawn [prɔːn] n crevette f (rose).

pray [preɪ] vi prier.

prayer [prɛə*] n prière f.

prayer book n livre m de prières.

pre... ['priː] prefix pré...; **pre-1970** a d'avant 1970 ♦ ad avant 1970.

preach [priːtʃ] vt, vi prêcher; **to** ~ **at sb** faire la morale à qn.

preacher ['priːtʃə*] n prédicateur m; (US: clergyman) pasteur m.

preamble [prɪ'æmbl] n préambule m.

prearranged [priːə'reɪndʒd] a organisé(e) or fixé(e) à l'avance.

precarious [prɪ'kɛərɪəs] a précaire.

precaution [prɪ'kɔːʃən] n précaution f.

precautionary [prɪ'kɔːʃənrɪ] a (measure) de précaution.

precede [prɪ'siːd] vt, vi précéder.

precedence ['prɛsɪdəns] n préséance f.

precedent ['prɛsɪdənt] n précédent m; **to establish** or **set a** ~ créer un précédent.

preceding [prɪ'siːdɪŋ] a qui précède (or précédait).

precept ['priːsɛpt] n précepte m.

precinct ['priːsɪŋkt] n (round cathedral) pourtour m, enceinte f; (US: district) circonscription f, arrondissement m; ~s npl (neighbourhood) alentours mpl, environs mpl; **pedestrian** ~ zone piétonne; **shopping** ~ (Brit) centre commercial.

precious ['prɛʃəs] a précieux(euse) ♦ ad (col): ~ **little** or **few** fort peu; **your** ~ **dog** (ironic) ton chien chéri, ton chéri chien.

precipice ['prɛsɪpɪs] n précipice m.

precipitate a [prɪ'sɪpɪtɪt] (hasty) précipité(e) ♦ vt [prɪ'sɪpɪteɪt] précipiter.

precipitation [prɪsɪpɪ'teɪʃən] n précipitation f.

precipitous [prɪ'sɪpɪtəs] a (steep) abrupt(e), à pic.

précis, pl **précis** ['preɪsiː, -z] n résumé m.

precise [prɪ'saɪs] a précis(e).

precisely [prɪ'saɪslɪ] ad précisément.

precision [prɪ'sɪʒən] n précision f.

preclude [prɪ'kluːd] vt exclure, empêcher; **to** ~ **sb from doing** empêcher qn de faire.

precocious [prɪ'kəuʃəs] a précoce.

preconceived [priːkən'siːvd] a (idea) préconçu(e).

preconception ['priːkən'sɛpʃən] n idée préconçue.

precondition ['priːkən'dɪʃən] n condition f nécessaire.

precursor [priː'kə:sə*] n précurseur m.

predate ['priː'deɪt] vt (precede) antidater.

predator ['prɛdətə*] n prédateur m, rapace m.
predatory ['prɛdətərɪ] a rapace.
predecessor ['pri:dɪsɛsə*] n prédécesseur m.
predestination [pri:dɛstɪ'neɪʃən] n prédestination f.
predetermine [pri:dɪ'tə:mɪn] vt déterminer à l'avance.
predicament [prɪ'dɪkəmənt] n situation f difficile.
predicate ['prɛdɪkɪt] n (LING) prédicat m.
predict [prɪ'dɪkt] vt prédire.
predictable [prɪ'dɪktəbl] a prévisible.
predictably [prɪ'dɪktəblɪ] ad (behave, react) de façon prévisible; ~ **she didn't arrive** comme on pouvait s'y attendre, elle n'est pas venue.
prediction [prɪ'dɪkʃən] n prédiction f.
predispose ['pri:dɪs'pəuz] vt prédisposer.
predominance [prɪ'dɔmɪnəns] n prédominance f.
predominant [prɪ'dɔmɪnənt] a prédominant(e).
predominantly [prɪ'dɔmɪnəntlɪ] ad en majeure partie; surtout.
predominate [prɪ'dɔmɪneɪt] vi prédominer.
pre-eminent [pri:'ɛmɪnənt] a prééminent(e).
pre-empt [pri:'ɛmt] vt (Brit) acquérir par droit de préemption; (fig) anticiper sur; **to ~ the issue** conclure avant même d'ouvrir les débats.
pre-emptive [pri:'ɛmtɪv] a: ~ **strike** attaque (or action) préventive.
preen [pri:n] vt: **to ~ itself** (bird) se lisser les plumes; **to ~ o.s.** s'admirer.
prefab ['pri:fæb] n bâtiment préfabriqué.
prefabricated [pri:'fæbrɪkeɪtɪd] a préfabriqué(e).
preface ['prɛfəs] n préface f.
prefect ['pri:fɛkt] n (Brit: in school) élève chargé de certaines fonctions de discipline; (in France) préfet m.
prefer [prɪ'fə:*] vt préférer; (LAW): **to ~ charges** procéder à une inculpation; **to ~ coffee to tea** préférer le café au thé.
preferable ['prɛfrəbl] a préférable.
preferably ['prɛfrəblɪ] ad de préférence.
preference ['prɛfrəns] n préférence f; **in ~ to sth** plutôt que qch, de préférence à qch.
preference shares npl (Brit) actions privilégiées.
preferential [prɛfə'rɛnʃəl] a préférentiel(le); ~ **treatment** traitement m de faveur.
preferred stock npl (US) = **preference shares**.
prefix ['pri:fɪks] n préfixe m.
pregnancy ['prɛgnənsɪ] n grossesse f.
pregnant ['prɛgnənt] a enceinte af; **3 months ~** enceinte de 3 mois.
prehistoric ['pri:hɪs'tɔrɪk] a préhistorique.
prehistory [pri:'hɪstərɪ] n préhistoire f.
prejudge [pri:'dʒʌdʒ] vt préjuger de.
prejudice ['prɛdʒudɪs] n préjugé m; (harm) tort m, préjudice m ♦ vt porter préjudice à; (bias): **to ~ sb in favour of/against** prévenir qn en faveur de/contre.
prejudiced ['prɛdʒudɪst] a (person) plein(e) de préjugés; (view) préconçu(e), partial(e); **to be ~ against sb/sth** avoir un parti-pris contre qn/qch.

prelate ['prɛlət] n prélat m.
preliminaries [prɪ'lɪmɪnərɪz] npl préliminaires mpl.
preliminary [prɪ'lɪmɪnərɪ] a préliminaire.
prelude ['prɛlju:d] n prélude m.
premarital ['pri:'mærɪtl] a avant le mariage.
premature ['prɛmətʃuə*] a prématuré(e); **to be ~ (in doing sth)** aller un peu (trop) vite (en faisant qch).
premeditated [pri:'mɛdɪteɪtɪd] a prémédité(e).
premeditation [pri:mɛdɪ'teɪʃən] n préméditation f.
premenstrual [pri:'mɛnstruəl] a prémenstruel(le).
premenstrual tension n irritabilité f avant les règles.
premier ['prɛmɪə*] a premier(ière), principal(e) ♦ n (POL) premier ministre.
première ['prɛmɪɛə*] n première f.
premise ['prɛmɪs] n prémisse f.
premises ['prɛmɪsɪz] npl locaux mpl; **on the ~** sur les lieux; sur place; **business ~** locaux commerciaux.
premium ['pri:mɪəm] n prime f; **to be at a ~** (fig: housing etc) être très demandé(e), être rarissime; **to sell at a ~** (shares) vendre au-dessus du pair.
premium bond n (Brit) bon m à lots.
premium deal n (COMM) offre spéciale.
premium gasoline n (US) super m.
premonition [prɛmə'nɪʃən] n prémonition f.
preoccupation [pri:ɔkju'peɪʃən] n préoccupation f.
preoccupied [pri:'ɔkjupaɪd] a préoccupé(e).
prep [prɛp] a abbr: ~ **school = preparatory school** ♦ n abbr (SCOL: = preparation) étude f.
prepackaged [pri:'pækɪdʒd] a préempaqueté(e).
prepaid [pri:'peɪd] a payé(e) d'avance.
preparation [prɛpə'reɪʃən] n préparation f; ~**s** (for trip, war) préparatifs mpl; **in ~ for** en vue de.
preparatory [prɪ'pærətərɪ] a préparatoire; ~ **to sth/to doing sth** en prévision de qch/avant de faire qch.
preparatory school n école primaire privée; (US) lycée privé.
prepare [prɪ'pɛə*] vt préparer ♦ vi: **to ~ for** se préparer à.
prepared [prɪ'pɛəd] a: ~ **for** préparé(e) à; ~ **to** prêt(e) à.
preponderance [prɪ'pɔndərns] n prépondérance f.
preposition [prɛpə'zɪʃən] n préposition f.
prepossessing [pri:pə'zɛsɪŋ] a avenant(e), engageant(e).
preposterous [prɪ'pɔstərəs] a absurde.
prep school n = **preparatory school**.
prerecord ['pri:rɪ'kɔ:d] vt: ~**ed broadcast** émission f en différé; ~**ed cassette** cassette enregistrée.
prerequisite [pri:'rɛkwɪzɪt] n condition f préalable.
prerogative [prɪ'rɔgətɪv] n prérogative f.
presbyterian [prɛzbɪ'tɪərɪən] a, n presbytérien(ne).
presbytery ['prɛzbɪtərɪ] n presbytère m.

preschool ['pri:'sku:l] a préscolaire; (child) d'âge préscolaire.

prescribe [prɪ'skraɪb] vt prescrire; ~d books (Brit SCOL) œuvres fpl au programme.

prescription [prɪ'skrɪpʃən] n prescription f; (MED) ordonnance f; to make up or (US) fill a ~ faire une ordonnance; "only available on ~" "uniquement sur ordonnance".

prescription charges npl (Brit) participation f fixe au coût de l'ordonnance.

prescriptive [prɪ'skrɪptɪv] a normatif(ive).

presence ['prezns] n présence f; ~ of mind présence d'esprit.

present ['preznt] a présent(e) ♦ n cadeau m; (also: ~ tense) présent m ♦ vt [prɪ'zent] présenter; (give): to ~ sb with sth offrir qch à qn; to be ~ at assister à; those ~ les présents; at ~ en ce moment; to give sb a ~ offrir un cadeau à qn; to ~ sb (to sb) présenter qn (à qn).

presentable [prɪ'zentəbl] a présentable.

presentation [prezn'teɪʃən] n présentation f; (gift) cadeau m, présent m; (ceremony) remise f du cadeau; on ~ of (voucher etc) sur présentation de.

present-day ['prezntdeɪ] a contemporain(e), actuel(le).

presenter [prɪ'zentə*] n (Brit RADIO, TV) présentateur/trice.

presently ['prezntlɪ] ad (soon) tout à l'heure, bientôt; (at present) en ce moment; (US: now) maintenant.

preservation [prezə'veɪʃən] n préservation f, conservation f.

preservative [prɪ'zə:vətɪv] n agent m de conservation.

preserve [prɪ'zə:v] vt (keep safe) préserver, protéger; (maintain) conserver, garder; (food) mettre en conserve ♦ n (for game, fish) réserve f; (often pl: jam) confiture f; (: fruit) fruits mpl en conserve.

preshrunk ['pri:'ʃrʌŋk] a irrétrécissable.

preside [prɪ'zaɪd] vi présider.

presidency ['prezɪdənsɪ] n présidence f.

president ['prezɪdənt] n président(e); (US: of company) président-directeur général, PDG m.

presidential [prezɪ'denʃl] a présidentiel(le).

press [pres] n (tool, machine, newspapers) presse f; (for wine) pressoir m; (crowd) cohue f, foule f ♦ vt (push) appuyer sur; (squeeze) presser, serrer; (clothes: iron) repasser; (pursue) talonner; (insist): to ~ sth on sb presser qn d'accepter qch; (urge, entreat): to ~ sb to do or into doing sth pousser qn à faire qch ♦ vi appuyer, peser; se presser; we are ~ed for time le temps nous manque; to ~ for sth faire pression pour obtenir qch; to ~ sb for an answer presser qn de répondre; to ~ charges against sb (LAW) engager des poursuites contre qn; to go to ~ (newspaper) aller à l'impression; to be in the ~ (being printed) être sous presse; (in the newspapers) être dans le journal.

press on vi continuer.

press agency n agence f de presse.

press clipping n coupure f de presse.

press conference n conférence f de presse.

press cutting n = **press clipping**.

press-gang ['presgæŋ] n recruteurs de la marine (jusqu'au 19ème siècle).

pressing ['presɪŋ] a urgent(e), pressant(e) ♦ n repassage m.

press release n communiqué m de presse.

press stud n (Brit) bouton-pression m.

press-up ['presʌp] n (Brit) traction f.

pressure ['preʃə*] n pression f; (stress) tension f ♦ vt = to put ~ on; to put ~ on sb (to do sth) faire pression sur qn (pour qu'il fasse qch).

pressure cooker n cocotte-minute f.

pressure gauge n manomètre m.

pressure group n groupe m de pression.

pressurize ['preʃəraɪz] vt pressuriser; (Brit fig): to ~ sb (into doing sth) faire pression sur qn (pour qu'il fasse qch).

pressurized ['preʃəraɪzd] a pressurisé(e).

Prestel ['prestel] n ® ≈ Minitel m ®.

prestige [pres'ti:ʒ] n prestige m.

prestigious [pres'tɪdʒəs] a prestigieux(euse).

presumably [prɪ'zju:məblɪ] ad vraisemblablement; ~ he did it c'est sans doute lui (qui a fait cela).

presume [prɪ'zju:m] vt présumer, supposer; to ~ to do (dare) se permettre de faire.

presumption [prɪ'zʌmpʃən] n supposition f, présomption f; (boldness) audace f.

presumptuous [prɪ'zʌmpʃəs] a présomptueux(euse).

presuppose [pri:sə'pəuz] vt présupposer.

pre-tax [pri:'tæks] a avant impôt(s).

pretence, (US) **pretense** [prɪ'tens] n (claim) prétention f; (pretext) prétexte m; she is devoid of all ~ elle n'est pas du tout prétentieuse; to make a ~ of doing faire semblant de faire; on or under the ~ of doing sth sous prétexte de faire qch.

pretend [prɪ'tend] vt (feign) feindre, simuler ♦ vi (feign) faire semblant; (claim): to ~ to sth prétendre à qch; to ~ to do faire semblant de faire.

pretense [prɪ'tens] n (US) = **pretence**.

pretension [prɪ'tenʃən] n (claim) prétention f; to have no ~s to sth/to being sth n'avoir aucune prétention à qch/à être qch.

pretentious [prɪ'tenʃəs] a prétentieux(euse).

preterite ['pretərɪt] n prétérit m.

pretext ['pri:tekst] n prétexte m; on or under the ~ of doing sth sous prétexte de faire qch.

pretty ['prɪtɪ] a joli(e) ♦ ad assez.

prevail [prɪ'veɪl] vi (win) l'emporter, prévaloir; (be usual) avoir cours; (persuade): to ~ (up)on sb to do persuader qn de faire.

prevailing [prɪ'veɪlɪŋ] a dominant(e).

prevalent ['prevələnt] a répandu(e), courant(e); (fashion) en vogue.

prevarication [prɪværɪ'keɪʃən] n (usage m de) faux-fuyants mpl.

prevent [prɪ'vent] vt: to ~ (from doing) empêcher (de faire).

preventable [prɪ'ventəbl] a évitable.

preventative [prɪ'ventətɪv] a préventif(ive).

prevention [prɪ'venʃən] n prévention f.

preventive [prɪ'ventɪv] a préventif(ive).

preview ['pri:vju:] n (of film) avant-première

f; (fig) aperçu m.

previous ['pri:vɪəs] a (last) précédent(e); (earlier) antérieur(e); (question, experience) préalable; **I have a ~ engagement** je suis déjà pris(e); **~ to doing** avant de faire.

previously ['pri:vɪəslɪ] ad précédemment, auparavant.

prewar [pri:'wɔ:*] a d'avant-guerre.

prey [preɪ] n proie f ♦ vi: **to ~ on** s'attaquer à; **it was ~ing on his mind** ça le rongeait or minait.

price [praɪs] n prix m; (BETTING: odds) cote f ♦ vt (goods) fixer le prix de; tarifer; **what is the ~ of ...?** combien coûte ...?, quel est le prix de ...?; **to go up** or **rise in ~** augmenter; **to put a ~ on sth** chiffrer qch; **to be ~ed out of the market** (article) être trop cher pour soutenir la concurrence; (producer, nation) ne pas pouvoir soutenir la concurrence; **what ~ his promises now?** (Brit) que valent maintenant toutes ses promesses?; **he regained his freedom, but at a ~** il a retrouvé sa liberté, mais cela lui a coûté cher.

price control n contrôle m des prix.

price-cutting ['praɪskʌtɪŋ] n réductions fpl de prix.

priceless ['praɪslɪs] a sans prix, inestimable; (col: amusing) impayable.

price list n tarif m.

price range n gamme f de prix; **it's within my ~** c'est dans mes prix.

price tag n étiquette f.

price war n guerre f des prix.

pricey ['praɪsɪ] a (col) chérot inv.

prick [prɪk] n piqûre f; (col!) bitte f (!); connard m (!) ♦ vt piquer; **to ~ up one's ears** dresser or tendre l'oreille.

prickle ['prɪkl] n (of plant) épine f; (sensation) picotement m.

prickly ['prɪklɪ] a piquant(e), épineux(euse); (fig: person) irritable.

prickly heat n fièvre f miliaire.

prickly pear n figue f de Barbarie.

pride [praɪd] n (feeling proud) fierté f; (: pej) orgueil m; (self-esteem) amour-propre m ♦ vt: **to ~ o.s. on** se flatter de; s'enorgueillir de; **to take (a) ~ in** être (très) fier(ère) de; **to take a ~ in doing** mettre sa fierté à faire; **to have ~ of place** (Brit) avoir la place d'honneur.

priest [pri:st] n prêtre m.

priestess ['pri:stɪs] n prêtresse f.

priesthood ['pri:sthud] n prêtrise f, sacerdoce m.

prig [prɪg] n poseur/euse, fat m.

prim [prɪm] a collet monté inv, guindé(e).

prima facie ['praɪmə'feɪʃɪ] a: **to have a ~ case** (LAW) avoir une affaire qui paraît fondée.

primarily ['praɪmərɪlɪ] ad principalement, essentiellement.

primary ['praɪmərɪ] a primaire; (first in importance) premier(ière), primordial(e) ♦ n (US: election) (élection f) primaire.

primary colour n couleur fondamentale.

primary products npl produits mpl de base.

primary school n (Brit) école primaire f.

primate n (REL) ['praɪmɪt] primat m; (ZOOL)

['praɪmeɪt] primate m.

prime [praɪm] a primordial(e), fondamental(e); (excellent) excellent(e) ♦ vt (gun, pump) amorcer; (fig) mettre au courant; **in the ~ of life** dans la fleur de l'âge.

prime minister n premier ministre.

primer ['praɪmə*] n (book) premier livre, manuel m élémentaire; (paint) apprêt m; (of gun) amorce f.

prime time n (RADIO, TV) heure(s) f(pl) de grande écoute.

primeval [praɪ'mi:vl] a primitif(ive).

primitive ['prɪmɪtɪv] a primitif(ive).

primrose ['prɪmrəuz] n primevère f.

primus (stove) ['praɪməs-] n ® (Brit) réchaud m de camping.

prince [prɪns] n prince m.

princess [prɪn'ses] n princesse f.

principal ['prɪnsɪpl] a principal(e) ♦ n (headmaster) directeur m, principal m; (in play) rôle principal; (money) principal m.

principality [prɪnsɪ'pælɪtɪ] n principauté f.

principally ['prɪnsɪplɪ] ad principalement.

principle ['prɪnsɪpl] n principe m; **in ~** en principe; **on ~** par principe.

print [prɪnt] n (mark) empreinte f; (letters) caractères mpl; (fabric) imprimé m; (ART) gravure f, estampe f; (PHOT) épreuve f ♦ vt imprimer; (publish) publier; (write in capitals) écrire en majuscules; **out of ~** épuisé(e).

print out vt (COMPUT) imprimer.

printed circuit board (PCB) n carte f à circuit imprimé.

printed matter n imprimés mpl.

printer ['prɪntə*] n imprimeur m; (machine) imprimante f.

printhead ['prɪnthed] n tête f d'impression.

printing ['prɪntɪŋ] n impression f.

printing press n presse f typographique.

print-out ['prɪntaut] n listing m.

print wheel n marguerite f.

prior ['praɪə*] a antérieur(e), précédent(e) ♦ n (REL) prieur m; **~ to doing** avant de faire; **without ~ notice** sans préavis; **to have a ~ claim to sth** avoir priorité pour qch.

priority [praɪ'ɔrɪtɪ] n priorité f; **to have** or **take ~ over sth/sb** avoir la priorité sur qch/qn.

priory ['praɪərɪ] n prieuré m.

prise [praɪz] vt: **to ~ open** forcer.

prism ['prɪzəm] n prisme m.

prison ['prɪzn] n prison f.

prison camp n camp m de prisonniers.

prisoner ['prɪznə*] n prisonnier/ière; **the ~ at the bar** l'accusé/e; **to take sb ~** faire qn prisonnier; **~ of war** prisonnier de guerre.

prissy ['prɪsɪ] a bégueule.

pristine ['prɪsti:n] a virginal(e).

privacy ['prɪvəsɪ] n intimité f, solitude f.

private ['praɪvɪt] a (not public) privé(e); (personal) personnel(le); (house, car, lesson) particulier(ière) ♦ n soldat m de deuxième classe; **"~"** (on envelope) "personnelle"; **in ~** en privé; **in (his) ~ life** dans sa vie privée; **he is a very ~ person** il est très secret; **to be in ~ practice** être médecin (or dentiste etc) non conventionné; **~ hearing** (LAW) audience f à huis-clos.

private enterprise n entreprise privée.

private eye n détective privé.

private limited company n (Brit) société f à participation restreinte (non cotée en bourse).

privately ['praɪvɪtlɪ] ad en privé; (within oneself) intérieurement.

private parts npl parties (génitales).

private property n propriété privée.

private school n école privée.

privation [praɪ'veɪʃən] n privation f.

privatize ['praɪvɪtaɪz] vt privatiser.

privet ['prɪvɪt] n troène m.

privilege ['prɪvɪlɪdʒ] n privilège m.

privileged ['prɪvɪlɪdʒd] a privilégié(e); **to be ~ to do sth** avoir le privilège de faire qch.

privy ['prɪvɪ] a: **to be ~ to** être au courant de.

privy council n conseil privé.

prize [praɪz] n prix m ♦ a (example, idiot) parfait(e); (bull, novel) primé(e) ♦ vt priser, faire grand cas de.

prize fight n combat professionnel.

prize giving n distribution f des prix.

prize money n argent m du prix.

prizewinner ['praɪzwɪnə*] n gagnant/e.

prizewinning ['praɪzwɪnɪŋ] a gagnant(e); (novel, essay etc) primé(e).

PRO n abbr = **public relations officer**.

pro [prəu] n (SPORT) professionnel/le; **the ~s and cons** le pour et le contre.

pro- [prəu] prefix (in favour of) pro-.

probability [prɔbə'bɪlɪtɪ] n probabilité f; **in all ~** très probablement.

probable ['prɔbəbl] a probable; **it is ~/hardly ~ that** ... il est probable/peu probable que ....

probably ['prɔbəblɪ] ad probablement.

probate ['prəubɪt] n (LAW) validation f, homologation f.

probation [prə'beɪʃən] n (in employment) (période f d')essai m; (LAW) liberté surveillée; (REL) noviciat m, probation f; **on ~** (employee) à l'essai; (LAW) en liberté surveillée.

probationary [prə'beɪʃənrɪ] a (period) d'essai.

probe [prəub] n (MED, SPACE) sonde f; (enquiry) enquête f, investigation f ♦ vt sonder, explorer.

probity ['prəubɪtɪ] n probité f.

problem ['prɔbləm] n problème m; **to have ~s with the car** avoir des ennuis avec la voiture; **what's the ~?** qu'y a-t-il?, quel est le problème?; **I had no ~ in finding her** je n'ai pas eu de mal à la trouver; **no ~!** pas de problème!

problematic [prɔblə'mætɪk] a problématique.

procedure [prə'si:dʒə*] n (ADMIN, LAW) procédure f; (method) marche f à suivre, façon f de procéder.

proceed [prə'si:d] vi (go forward) avancer; (go about it) procéder; (continue): **to ~ (with)** continuer, poursuivre; **to ~ to** aller à; passer à; **to ~ to do** se mettre à faire; **I am not sure how to ~** je ne sais pas exactement comment m'y prendre; **to ~ against sb** (LAW) intenter des poursuites contre qn.

proceeding [prə'si:dɪŋ] n procédé m, façon f d'agir.

proceedings [prə'si:dɪŋz] npl mesures fpl; (LAW) poursuites fpl; (meeting) réunion f, séance f; (records) compte rendu; actes mpl.

proceeds ['prəusi:dz] npl produit m, recette f.

process ['prəusɛs] n processus m; (method) procédé m ♦ vt traiter ♦ vi [prə'sɛs] (Brit formal: go in procession) défiler; **in ~** en cours; **we are in the ~ of doing** nous sommes en train de faire.

processed cheese n ≈ fromage fondu.

processing ['prəusɛsɪŋ] n traitement m.

procession [prə'sɛʃən] n défilé m, cortège m; **funeral ~** cortège funèbre, convoi m mortuaire.

proclaim [prə'kleɪm] vt déclarer, proclamer.

proclamation [prɔklə'meɪʃən] n proclamation f.

proclivity [prə'klɪvɪtɪ] n inclination f.

procrastination [prəukræstɪ'neɪʃən] n procrastination f.

procreation [prəukrɪ'eɪʃən] n procréation f.

procure [prə'kjuə*] vt (for o.s.) se procurer; (for sb) procurer.

procurement [prə'kjuəmənt] n achat m, approvisionnement m.

prod [prɔd] vt pousser ♦ n (push, jab) petit coup, poussée f.

prodigal ['prɔdɪgl] a prodigue.

prodigious [prə'dɪdʒəs] a prodigieux(euse).

prodigy ['prɔdɪdʒɪ] n prodige m.

produce n ['prɔdju:s] (AGR) produits mpl ♦ vt [prə'dju:s] produire; (to show) présenter; (cause) provoquer, causer; (THEATRE) monter, mettre en scène.

producer [prə'dju:sə*] n (THEATRE) metteur m en scène; (AGR, CINEMA) producteur m.

product ['prɔdʌkt] n produit m.

production [prə'dʌkʃən] n production f; (THEATRE) mise en scène; **to put into ~** (goods) entreprendre la fabrication de.

production agreement n (US) accord m de productivité.

production control n contrôle m de production.

production line n chaîne f (de fabrication).

production manager n directeur/trice de la production.

productive [prə'dʌktɪv] a productif(ive).

productivity [prɔdʌk'tɪvɪtɪ] n productivité f.

productivity agreement n (Brit) accord m de productivité.

productivity bonus n prime f de rendement.

Prof. [prɔf] abbr (= professor) Prof.

profane [prə'feɪn] a sacrilège; (lay) profane.

profess [prə'fɛs] vt professer; **I do not ~ to be an expert** je ne prétends pas être spécialiste.

professed [prə'fɛst] a (self-declared) déclaré(e).

profession [prə'fɛʃən] n profession f; **the ~s** les professions libérales.

professional [prə'fɛʃənl] n (SPORT) professionnel/le ♦ a professionnel(le); (work) de professionnel; **he's a ~ man** il exerce une profession libérale; **to take ~ advice** consulter un spécialiste.

professionalism [prə'fɛʃnəlɪzəm] n professionnalisme m.

professionally [prə'fɛʃnəlɪ] ad

professionnellement; (*SPORT*: *play*) en professionnel; **I only know him ~** je n'ai avec lui que des relations de travail.

professor [prə'fesə*] *n* professeur *m* (*titulaire d'une chaire*); (*US*: *teacher*) professeur *m*.

professorship [prə'fesəʃɪp] *n* chaire *f*.

proffer ['prɔfə*] *vt* (*hand*) tendre; (*remark*) faire; (*apologies*) présenter.

proficiency [prə'fɪʃənsɪ] *n* compétence *f*, aptitude *f*.

proficient [prə'fɪʃənt] *a* compétent(e), capable.

profile ['prəufaɪl] *n* profil *m*; **to keep a high/ low ~** (*fig*) rester *or* être très en évidence/ discret(ète).

profit ['prɔfɪt] *n* (*from trading*) bénéfice *m*; (*advantage*) profit *m* ♦ *vi*: **to ~ (by *or* from)** profiter (de); **~ and loss account** compte *m* de profits et pertes; **to make a ~** faire un *or* des bénéfice(s); **to sell sth at a ~** vendre qch à profit.

profitability [prɔfɪtə'bɪlɪtɪ] *n* rentabilité *f*.

profitable ['prɔfɪtəbl] *a* lucratif(ive), rentable; (*fig: beneficial*) avantageux(euse); (*: meeting*) fructueux(euse).

profit centre *n* centre *m* de profit.

profiteering [prɔfɪ'tɪərɪŋ] *n* (*pej*) mercantilisme *m*.

profit-making ['prɔfɪtmeɪkɪŋ] *a* à but lucratif.

profit margin *n* marge *f* bénéficiaire.

profit-sharing ['prɔfɪtʃɛərɪŋ] *n* intéressement *m* aux bénéfices.

profits tax *n* (*Brit*) impôt *m* sur les bénéfices.

profligate ['prɔflɪgɪt] *a* (*behaviour*, *act*) dissolu(e); (*person*) débauché(e); (*extravagant*): **~ (with)** prodigue (de).

pro forma ['prəu'fɔ:mə] *a*: **~ invoice** facture *f* pro-forma.

profound [prə'faund] *a* profond(e).

profuse [prə'fju:s] *a* abondant(e).

profusely [prə'fju:slɪ] *ad* abondamment; (*thank etc*) avec effusion.

profusion [prə'fju:ʒən] *n* profusion *f*, abondance *f*.

progeny ['prɔdʒɪnɪ] *n* progéniture *f*; descendants *mpl*.

programme, (*US*) **program** ['prəugræm] *n* programme *m*; (*RADIO*, *TV*) émission *f* ♦ *vt* programmer.

program(m)er ['prəugræmə*] *n* programmeur/euse.

program(m)ing ['prəugræmɪŋ] *n* programmation *f*.

program(m)ing language *n* langage *m* de programmation.

progress *n* ['prəugrɛs] progrès *m* ♦ *vi* [prə'grɛs] progresser, avancer; **in ~** en cours; **to make ~** progresser, faire des progrès, être en progrès; **as the match ~ed** au fur et à mesure que la partie avançait.

progression [prə'grɛʃən] *n* progression *f*.

progressive [prə'grɛsɪv] *a* progressif(ive); (*person*) progressiste.

progressively [prə'grɛsɪvlɪ] *ad* progressivement.

progress report *n* (*MED*) bulletin *m* de santé; (*ADMIN*) rapport *m* d'activité; rapport sur l'état (d'avancement) des travaux.

prohibit [prə'hɪbɪt] *vt* interdire, défendre; **to**

~ sb from doing sth défendre *or* interdire à qn de faire qch; **"smoking ~ed"** "défense de fumer".

prohibition [prəuɪ'bɪʃən] *n* prohibition *f*.

prohibitive [prə'hɪbɪtɪv] *a* (*price etc*) prohibitif(ive).

project *n* ['prɔdʒɛkt] (*plan*) projet *m*, plan *m*; (*venture*) opération *f*, entreprise *f*; (*gen SCOL: research*) étude *f*, dossier *m* ♦ *vb* [prə'dʒɛkt] *vt* projeter ♦ *vi* (*stick out*) faire saillie, s'avancer.

projectile [prə'dʒɛktaɪl] *n* projectile *m*.

projection [prə'dʒɛkʃən] *n* projection *f*; (*overhang*) saillie *f*.

projectionist [prə'dʒɛkʃənɪst] *n* (*CINEMA*) projectionniste *m/f*.

projection room *n* (*CINEMA*) cabine *f* de projection.

projector [prə'dʒɛktə*] *n* (*CINEMA etc*) projecteur *m*.

proletarian [prəulɪ'tɛərɪən] *a* prolétarien(ne) ♦ *n* prolétaire *m/f*.

proletariat [prəulɪ'tɛərɪət] *n* prolétariat *m*.

proliferate [prə'lɪfəreɪt] *vi* proliférer.

proliferation [prəlɪfə'reɪʃən] *n* prolifération *f*.

prolific [prə'lɪfɪk] *a* prolifique.

prologue ['prəulɔg] *n* prologue *m*.

prolong [prə'lɔŋ] *vt* prolonger.

prom [prɔm] *n* *abbr* = **promenade**, **promenade concert**; (*US*: *ball*) bal *m* d'étudiants.

promenade [prɔmə'nɑ:d] *n* (*by sea*) esplanade *f*, promenade *f*.

promenade concert *n* concert *m* (de musique classique).

promenade deck *n* (*NAUT*) pont *m* promenade.

prominence ['prɔmɪnəns] *n* proéminence *f*; importance *f*.

prominent ['prɔmɪnənt] *a* (*standing out*) proéminent(e); (*important*) important(e); **he is ~ in the field of ...** il est très connu dans le domaine de ....

prominently ['prɔmɪnəntlɪ] *ad* (*display*, *set*) bien en évidence; **he figured ~ in the case** il a joué un rôle important dans l'affaire.

promiscuity [prɔmɪs'kju:ɪtɪ] *n* (*sexual*) légèreté *f* de mœurs.

promiscuous [prə'mɪskjuəs] *a* (*sexually*) de mœurs légères.

promise ['prɔmɪs] *n* promesse *f* ♦ *vt*, *vi* promettre; **to make sb a ~** faire une promesse à qn; **to ~ (sb) to do sth** promettre (à qn) de faire qch; **a young man of ~** un jeune homme plein d'avenir; **to ~ well** *vi* promettre.

promising ['prɔmɪsɪŋ] *a* prometteur(euse).

promissory note ['prɔmɪsərɪ-] *n* billet *m* à ordre.

promontory ['prɔməntrɪ] *n* promontoire *m*.

promote [prə'məut] *vt* promouvoir; (*venture*, *event*) organiser, mettre sur pied; (*new product*) lancer; **the team was ~d to the second division** (*Brit FOOTBALL*) l'équipe est montée en 2e division.

promoter [prə'məutə*] *n* (*of event*) organisateur/trice; (*of cause etc*) partisan/e, défenseur *m*.

promotion [prə'məuʃən] *n* promotion *f*.

prompt |prɔmpt| *a* rapide ♦ *n* (*COMPUT*) message *m* (de guidage) ♦ *vt* inciter; (*cause*) entraîner, provoquer; (*THEATRE*) souffler (son rôle *or* ses répliques) à; **they're very ~** (*punctual*) ils sont ponctuels; **at 8 o'clock ~** à 8 heures précises; **he was ~ to accept** il a tout de suite accepté; **to ~ sb to do** inciter *or* pousser qn à faire.

prompter |'prɔmptə*| *n* (*THEATRE*) souffleur *m*.

promptly |'prɔmptlɪ| *ad* rapidement, sans délai; ponctuellement.

promptness |'prɔmptnɪs| *n* rapidité *f*; promptitude *f*; ponctualité *f*.

promulgate |'prɔmɔlgeɪt| *vt* promulguer.

prone |prəun| *a* (*lying*) couché(e) (face contre terre); (*liable*): **~ to** enclin(e) à; **to be ~ to illness** être facilement malade; **to be ~ to an illness** être sujet à une maladie; **she is ~ to burst into tears if** ... elle a tendance à tomber en larmes si ....

prong |prɔŋ| *n* pointe *f*; (*of fork*) dent *f*.

pronoun |'prəunaun| *n* pronom *m*.

pronounce |prə'nauns| *vt* prononcer ♦ *vi*: **to ~ (up)on** se prononcer sur; **they ~d him unfit to drive** ils l'ont déclaré inapte à la conduite.

pronounced |prə'naunst| *a* (*marked*) prononcé(e).

pronouncement |prə'naunsmənt| *n* déclaration *f*.

pronunciation |prənʌnsɪ'eɪʃən| *n* prononciation *f*.

proof |pru:f| *n* preuve *f*; (*test, of book, PHOT*) épreuve *f*; (*of alcohol*) degré *m* ♦ *a*: **~ against** à l'épreuve de ♦ *vt* (*Brit: tent, anorak*) imperméabiliser; **to be 70° ~** ≈ titrer 40 degrés.

proofreader |'pru:fri:də*| *n* correcteur/trice (d'épreuves).

Prop. *abbr* (*COMM*) = **proprietor**.

prop |prɔp| *n* support *m*, étai *m* ♦ *vt* (*also*: **~ up**) étayer, soutenir; (*lean*): **to ~ sth against** appuyer qch contre *or* à.

propaganda |prɔpə'gændə| *n* propagande *f*.

propagation |prɔpə'geɪʃən| *n* propagation *f*.

propel |prə'pɛl| *vt* propulser, faire avancer.

propeller |prə'pɛlə*| *n* hélice *f*.

propelling pencil |prə'pɛlɪŋ-| *n* (*Brit*) portemine *m inv*.

propensity |prə'pɛnsɪtɪ| *n* propension *f*.

proper |'prɔpə*| *a* (*suited, right*) approprié(e), bon(bonne); (*seemly*) correct(e), convenable; (*authentic*) vrai(e), véritable; (*col: real*) *n* + fini(e), vrai(e); **to go through the ~ channels** (*ADMIN*) passer par la voie officielle.

properly |'prɔpəlɪ| *ad* correctement, convenablement; (*really*) bel et bien.

proper noun *n* nom *m* propre.

property |'prɔpətɪ| *n* (*possessions*) biens *mpl*; (*house etc*) propriété *f*; (*land*) terres *fpl*, domaine *m*; (*CHEM etc: quality*) propriété *f*; **it's their ~** cela leur appartient, c'est leur propriété.

property developer *n* (*Brit*) promoteur immobilier.

property owner *n* propriétaire *m*.

property tax *n* impôt foncier.

prophecy |'prɔfɪsɪ| *n* prophétie *f*.

prophesy |'prɔfɪsaɪ| *vt* prédire ♦ *vi* prophétiser.

prophet |'prɔfɪt| *n* prophète *m*.

prophetic |prə'fɛtɪk| *a* prophétique.

proportion |prə'pɔːʃən| *n* proportion *f*; (*share*) part *f*; partie *f* ♦ *vt* proportionner; **to be in/out of ~ to** *or* **with sth** être à la mesure de/hors de proportion avec qch; **to see sth in ~** (*fig*) ramener qch à de justes proportions.

proportional |prə'pɔːʃənl|, **proportionate** |prə'pɔːʃənɪt| *a* proportionnel(le).

proportional representation (PR) *n* (*POL*) représentation proportionnelle.

proposal |prə'pəuzl| *n* proposition *f*, offre *f*; (*plan*) projet *m*; (*of marriage*) demande *f* en mariage.

propose |prə'pəuz| *vt* proposer, suggérer; (*have in mind*): **to ~ sth/to do** *or* **doing sth** envisager qch/de faire qch ♦ *vi* faire sa demande en mariage; **to ~ to do** avoir l'intention de faire.

proposer |prə'pəuzə*| *n* (*Brit: of motion etc*) auteur *m*.

proposition |prɔpə'zɪʃən| *n* proposition *f*; **to make sb a ~** faire une proposition à qn.

propound |prə'paund| *vt* proposer, soumettre.

proprietary |prə'praɪətərɪ| *a* de marque déposée; **~ article** article *m or* produit *m* de marque; **~ brand** marque déposée.

proprietor |prə'praɪətə*| *n* propriétaire *m/f*.

propriety |prə'praɪətɪ| *n* (*seemliness*) bienséance *f*, convenance *f*.

propulsion |prə'pʌlʃən| *n* propulsion *f*.

pro rata |prəu'rɑːtə| *ad* au prorata.

prosaic |prəu'zeɪɪk| *a* prosaïque.

Pros. Atty. *abbr* (*US*) = **prosecuting attorney**.

proscribe |prə'skraɪb| *vt* proscrire.

prose |prəuz| *n* prose *f*; (*SCOL: translation*) thème *m*.

prosecute |'prɔsɪkjuːt| *vt* poursuivre.

prosecuting attorney (Pros. Atty.) |'prɔsɪkjuːtɪŋ-| *n* (*US*) procureur *m*.

prosecution |prɔsɪ'kjuːʃən| *n* poursuites *fpl* judiciaires; (*accusing side*) accusation *f*.

prosecutor |'prɔsɪkjuːtə*| *n* procureur *m*; (*also*: **public ~**) ministère public.

prospect *n* |'prɔspɛkt| perspective *f*; (*hope*) espoir *m*, chances *fpl* ♦ *vt*, *vi* |prə'spɛkt| prospecter; **we are faced with the ~ of leaving** nous risquons de devoir partir; **there is every ~ of an early victory** tout laisse prévoir une victoire rapide.

prospecting |prə'spɛktɪŋ| *n* prospection *f*.

prospective |prə'spɛktɪv| *a* (*possible*) éventuel(le); (*future*) futur(e).

prospector |prə'spɛktə*| *n* prospecteur *m*; **gold ~** chercheur *m* d'or.

prospects |'prɔspɛkts| *npl* (*for work etc*) possibilités *fpl* d'avenir, débouchés *mpl*.

prospectus |prə'spɛktəs| *n* prospectus *m*.

prosper |'prɔspə*| *vi* prospérer.

prosperity |prɔ'spɛrɪtɪ| *n* prospérité *f*.

prosperous |'prɔspərəs| *a* prospère.

prostate |'prɔsteɪt| *n* (*also*: **~ gland**) prostate *f*.

prostitute |'prɔstɪtjuːt| *n* prostituée *f*; **male ~**

prostitué *m*.
prostitution |prɔstɪ'tju:ʃən| *n* prostitution *f*.
prostrate *a* |'prɔstreɪt| prosterné(e); *(fig)* prostré(e) ♦ *vt* |prɔ'streɪt|: **to ~ o.s. (before sb)** se prosterner (devant qn).
protagonist |prə'tægənɪst| *n* protagoniste *m*.
protect |prə'tɛkt| *vt* protéger.
protection |prə'tɛkʃən| *n* protection *f*; **to be under sb's ~** être sous la protection de qn.
protectionism |prə'tɛkʃənɪzəm| *n* protectionnisme *m*.
protection racket *n* racket *m*.
protective |prə'tɛktɪv| *a* protecteur(trice); **~ custody** *(LAW)* détention préventive.
protector |prə'tɛktə*| *n* protecteur/trice.
protégé |'prəʊtɛʒeɪ| *n* protégé *m*.
protégée |'prəʊtɛʒeɪ| *n* protégée *f*.
protein |'prəʊti:n| *n* protéine *f*.
pro tem |prəʊ'tɛm| *ad abbr* (= *pro tempore: for the time being*) provisoirement.
protest *n* |'prəʊtɛst| protestation *f* ♦ *vb* |prə'tɛst| *vi*: **to ~ against/about** protester contre/à propos de ♦ *vt* protester de.
Protestant |'prɔtɪstənt| *a*, *n* protestant(e).
protester, protestor |prə'tɛstə*| *n* *(in demonstration)* manifestant/e.
protest march *n* manifestation *f*.
protocol |'prəʊtəkɔl| *n* protocole *m*.
prototype |'prəʊtətaɪp| *n* prototype *m*.
protracted |prə'træktɪd| *a* prolongé(e).
protractor |prə'træktə*| *n* *(GEOM)* rapporteur *m*.
protrude |prə'tru:d| *vi* avancer, dépasser.
protuberance |prə'tju:bərəns| *n* protubérance *f*.
proud |praʊd| *a* fier(ère); *(pej)* orgueilleux(euse); **to be ~ to do sth** être fier de faire qch; **to do sb ~** *(col)* faire honneur à qn; **to do o.s. ~** *(col)* ne se priver de rien.
proudly |'praʊdlɪ| *ad* fièrement.
prove |pru:v| *vt* prouver, démontrer ♦ *vi*: **to ~ correct** *etc* s'avérer juste *etc*; **to ~ o.s.** montrer ce dont on est capable; **to ~ o.s./itself (to be) useful** *etc* se montrer *or* se révéler utile *etc*; **he was ~d right in the end** il s'est avéré qu'il avait raison.
proverb |'prɔvə:b| *n* proverbe *m*.
proverbial |prə'və:bɪəl| *a* proverbial(e).
provide |prə'vaɪd| *vt* fournir; **to ~ sb with sth** fournir qch à qn; **to be ~d with** *(person)* disposer de; *(thing)* être équipé(e) *or* muni(e) de.
provide for *vt fus* *(person)* subvenir aux besoins de; *(emergency)* prévoir.
provided |prə'vaɪdɪd| *cj*: **~ (that)** à condition que + *sub*.
Providence |'prɔvɪdəns| *n* la Providence.
providing |prə'vaɪdɪŋ| *cj* à condition que + *sub*.
province |'prɔvɪns| *n* province *f*.
provincial |prə'vɪnʃəl| *a* provincial(e).
provision |prə'vɪʒən| *n* *(supply)* provision *f*; *(supplying)* fourniture *f*; approvisionnement *m*; *(stipulation)* disposition *f*; **~s** *npl* *(food)* provisions *fpl*; **to make ~ for** *(one's future)* assurer; *(one's family)* assurer l'avenir de; **there's no ~ for this in the contract** le contrat ne prévoit pas cela.

provisional |prə'vɪʒənl| *a* provisoire ♦ *n*: **P~** *(Irish POL)* Provisional *m* *(membre de la tendance activiste de l'IRA)*.
provisional licence *n* *(Brit AUT)* permis *m* provisoire.
provisionally |prə'vɪʒnəlɪ| *ad* provisoirement.
proviso |prə'vaɪzəʊ| *n* condition *f*; **with the ~ that** à la condition (expresse) que.
Provo |'prɔvəʊ| *n abbr* *(col)* = **Provisional**.
provocation |prɔvə'keɪʃən| *n* provocation *f*.
provocative |prə'vɔkətɪv| *a* provocateur(trice), provocant(e).
provoke |prə'vəʊk| *vt* provoquer; **to ~ sb to sth/to do** *or* **into doing sth** pousser qn à qch/à faire qch.
provoking |prə'vəʊkɪŋ| *a* énervant(e), exaspérant(e).
provost |'prɔvəst| *n* *(Brit: of university)* principal *m*; *(Scottish)* maire *m*.
prow |praʊ| *n* proue *f*.
prowess |'praʊɪs| *n* prouesse *f*.
prowl |praʊl| *vi* *(also: ~ about, ~ around)* rôder ♦ *n*: **to be on the ~** rôder.
prowler |'praʊlə*| *n* rôdeur/euse.
proximity |prɔk'sɪmɪtɪ| *n* proximité *f*.
proxy |'prɔksɪ| *n* procuration *f*; **by ~** par procuration.
prude |pru:d| *n* prude *f*.
prudence |'pru:dns| *n* prudence *f*.
prudent |'pru:dnt| *a* prudent(e).
prudish |'pru:dɪʃ| *a* prude, pudibond(e).
prune |pru:n| *n* pruneau *m* ♦ *vt* élaguer.
pry |praɪ| *vi*: **to ~ into** fourrer son nez dans.
PS *n abbr* (= *postscript*) PS *m*.
psalm |sɑ:m| *n* psaume *m*.
PSAT *n abbr* *(US)* = *Preliminary Scholastic Aptitude Test*.
PSBR *n abbr* *(Brit:* = *public sector borrowing requirement)* besoins *mpl* d'emprunts des pouvoirs publics.
pseud |sju:d| *n* *(Brit col: intellectually)* pseudo-intello *m*; *(: socially)* snob *m/f*.
pseudo- |'sju:dəʊ| *prefix* pseudo-.
pseudonym |'sju:dənɪm| *n* pseudonyme *m*.
PST *abbr* *(US:* = *Pacific Standard Time)* heure d'hiver du Pacifique.
PSV *n abbr* *(Brit)* = **public service vehicle**.
psyche |'saɪkɪ| *n* psychisme *m*.
psychiatric |saɪkɪ'ætrɪk| *a* psychiatrique.
psychiatrist |saɪ'kaɪətrɪst| *n* psychiatre *m/f*.
psychiatry |saɪ'kaɪətrɪ| *n* psychiatrie *f*.
psychic |'saɪkɪk| *a* *(also: ~al)* *(méta)*psychique; *(person)* doué(e) de télépathie *or* d'un sixième sens.
psychoanalyse |saɪkəʊ'ænəlaɪz| *vt* psychanalyser.
psychoanalysis, *pl* **-lyses** |saɪkəʊə'næləsɪs, -si:z| *n* psychanalyse *f*.
psychoanalyst |saɪkəʊ'ænəlɪst| *n* psychanalyste *m/f*.
psychological |saɪkə'lɔdʒɪkl| *a* psychologique.
psychologist |saɪ'kɔlədʒɪst| *n* psychologue *m/f*.
psychology |saɪ'kɔlədʒɪ| *n* psychologie *f*.
psychopath |'saɪkəʊpæθ| *n* psychopathe *m/f*.
psychosis, *pl* **psychoses** |saɪ'kəʊsɪs, -si:z| *n* psychose *f*.
psychosomatic |'saɪkəʊsə'mætɪk| *a* psychosomatique.

psychotherapy [saɪkəu'θɛrəpɪ] *n* psycho-thérapie *f*.

psychotic [saɪ'kɔtɪk] *a, n* psychotique *(m/f)*.

PT *n abbr* (*Brit*: = *physical training*) EPS *f*.

Pt. *abbr* (*in place names*: = *Point*) Pte.

pt *abbr* = **pint, point**.

PTA *n abbr* = *Parent-Teacher Association*.

Pte. *abbr* (*Brit MIL*) = **private**.

PTO *abbr* (= *please turn over*) TSVP (= *tournez s'il vous plaît*).

PTV *n abbr* (*US*) = *pay television, public television*.

pub [pʌb] *n abbr* (= *public house*) pub *m*.

puberty ['pju:bətɪ] *n* puberté *f*.

pubic ['pju:bɪk] *a* pubien(ne), du pubis.

public ['pʌblɪk] *a* public(ique) ♦ *n* public *m*; **in ~ en public**; **the general ~** le grand public; **to be ~ knowledge** être de notoriété publique; **to go ~** (*COMM*) être coté(e) en Bourse.

public address system (PA) *n* (système *m* de) sonorisation *f*, sono *f* (*col*).

publican ['pʌblɪkən] *n* patron *m* or gérant *m* de pub.

publication [pʌblɪ'keɪʃən] *n* publication *f*.

public company *n* société *f* anonyme (*cotée en bourse*).

public convenience *n* (*Brit*) toilettes *fpl*.

public holiday *n* (*Brit*) jour férié.

public house *n* (*Brit*) pub *m*.

publicity [pʌb'lɪsɪtɪ] *n* publicité *f*.

publicize ['pʌblɪsaɪz] *vt* faire connaître, rendre public.

public limited company (plc) *n* ≈ société anonyme (SA) (*cotée en bourse*).

publicly ['pʌblɪklɪ] *ad* publiquement, en public.

public opinion *n* opinion publique.

public ownership *n*: **to be taken into ~** être nationalisé(e), devenir propriété de l'Etat.

public relations (PR) *n or npl* relations publiques (RP).

public relations officer *n* responsable *m/f* des relations publiques.

public school *n* (*Brit*) école privée; (*US*) école publique.

public sector *n* secteur public.

public service vehicle (PSV) *n* (*Brit*) véhicule affecté au transport de personnes.

public-spirited [pʌblɪk'spɪrɪtɪd] *a* qui fait preuve de civisme.

public transport, (*US*) **public transportation** *n* transports *mpl* en commun.

public utility *n* service public.

public works *npl* travaux publics.

publish ['pʌblɪʃ] *vt* publier.

publisher ['pʌblɪʃə*] *n* éditeur *m*.

publishing ['pʌblɪʃɪŋ] *n* (*industry*) édition *f*; (*of a book*) publication *f*.

publishing company *n* maison *f* d'édition.

puce [pju:s] *a* puce.

puck [pʌk] *n* (*elf*) lutin *m*; (*ICE HOCKEY*) palet *m*.

pucker ['pʌkə*] *vt* plisser.

pudding ['pudɪŋ] *n* (*Brit*: *sweet*) dessert *m*, entremets *m*; (*sausage*) boudin *m*: **rice ~** ≈ riz *m* au lait; **black ~**, (*US*) **blood ~** boudin (noir).

puddle ['pʌdl] *n* flaque *f* d'eau.

puerile ['pjuəraɪl] *a* puéril(e).

Puerto Rico ['pwə:təu'ri:kəu] *n* Porto Rico *f*.

puff [pʌf] *n* bouffée *f* ♦ *vt*: **to ~ one's pipe** tirer sur sa pipe; (*also*: **~ out**: *sails, cheeks*) gonfler ♦ *vi* sortir par bouffées; (*pant*) haleter; **to ~ out smoke** envoyer des bouffées de fumée.

puffed [pʌft] *a* (*col*: *out of breath*) tout(e) essoufflé(e).

puffin ['pʌfɪn] *n* macareux *m*.

puff pastry, (*US*) **puff paste** *n* pâte feuilletée.

puffy ['pʌfɪ] *a* bouffi(e), boursouflé(e).

pugnacious [pʌg'neɪʃəs] *a* pugnace, batailleur(euse).

pull [pul] *n* (*tug*): **to give sth a ~** tirer sur qch; (*of moon, magnet, the sea etc*) attraction *f*; (*fig*) influence *f* ♦ *vt* tirer; (*strain*: *muscle, tendon*) se claquer ♦ *vi* tirer; **to ~ a face** faire une grimace; **to ~ to pieces** mettre en morceaux; **to ~ one's punches** (*also fig*) ménager son adversaire; **to ~ one's weight** y mettre du sien; **to ~ o.s. together** se ressaisir; **to ~ sb's leg** (*fig*) faire marcher qn; **to ~ strings (for sb)** intervenir (en faveur de qn).

pull about *vt* (*Brit*: *handle roughly*: *object*) maltraiter; (*: person*) malmener.

pull apart *vt* séparer; (*break*) mettre en pièces, démantibuler.

pull down *vt* baisser, abaisser; (*house*) démolir; (*tree*) abattre.

pull in *vi* (*AUT*) se ranger; (*RAIL*) entrer en gare.

pull off *vt* enlever, ôter; (*deal etc*) conclure.

pull out *vi* démarrer, partir; (*withdraw*) se retirer; (*AUT*: *come out of line*) déboîter ♦ *vt* sortir; arracher; (*withdraw*) retirer.

pull over *vi* (*AUT*) se ranger.

pull round *vi* (*unconscious person*) revenir à soi; (*sick person*) se rétablir.

pull through *vi* s'en sortir.

pull up *vi* (*stop*) s'arrêter ♦ *vt* remonter; (*uproot*) déraciner, arracher; (*stop*) arrêter.

pulley ['pulɪ] *n* poulie *f*.

pull-out ['pulaut] *n* (*of forces etc*) retrait *m* ♦ *cpd* (*magazine, pages*) détachable.

pullover ['puləuvə*] *n* pull-over *m*, tricot *m*.

pulp [pʌlp] *n* (*of fruit*) pulpe *f*; (*for paper*) pâte *f* à papier; (*pej*: *also*: **~ magazines** *etc*) presse *f* à sensation or de bas étage; **to reduce sth to (a) ~** réduire qch en purée.

pulpit ['pulpɪt] *n* chaire *f*.

pulsate [pʌl'seɪt] *vi* battre, palpiter; (*music*) vibrer.

pulse [pʌls] *n* (*of blood*) pouls *m*; (*of heart*) battement *m*; (*of music, engine*) vibrations *fpl*; **to feel** *or* **take sb's ~** prendre le pouls à qn.

pulses ['pʌlsəz] *npl* (*CULIN*) légumineuses *fpl*.

pulverize ['pʌlvəraɪz] *vt* pulvériser.

puma ['pju:mə] *n* puma *m*.

pumice ['pʌmɪs] *n* (*also*: **~ stone**) pierre *f* ponce.

pummel ['pʌml] *vt* rouer de coups.

pump [pʌmp] *n* pompe *f*; (*shoe*) escarpin *m* ♦ *vt* pomper; (*fig*: *col*) faire parler; **to ~ sb for information** essayer de soutirer des

renseignements à qn.
pump up *vt* gonfler.
pumpkin ['pʌmpkɪn] *n* potiron *m*, citrouille *f*.
pun [pʌn] *n* jeu *m* de mots, calembour *m*.
punch [pʌntʃ] *n* (*blow*) coup *m* de poing; (*fig: force*) vivacité *f*, mordant *m*; (*tool*) poinçon *m*; (*drink*) punch *m* ♦ *vt* (*hit*): **to ~ sb/sth** donner un coup de poing à qn/sur qch; (*make a hole*) poinçonner, perforer; **to ~ a hole (in)** faire un trou (dans).
punch in *vi* (*US*) pointer (en arrivant).
punch out *vi* (*US*) pointer (en partant).
punch-drunk ['pʌntʃdrʌŋk] *a* (*Brit*) sonné(e).
punch(ed) card *n* carte perforée.
punch line *n* (*of joke*) conclusion *f*.
punch-up ['pʌntʃʌp] *n* (*Brit col*) bagarre *f*.
punctual ['pʌŋktjuəl] *a* ponctuel(le).
punctuality [pʌŋktju'ælɪtɪ] *n* ponctualité *f*.
punctually ['pʌŋktjuəlɪ] *ad* ponctuellement; **it will start ~ at 6** cela commencera à 6 heures précises.
punctuate ['pʌŋktjueɪt] *vt* ponctuer.
punctuation [pʌŋktju'eɪʃən] *n* ponctuation *f*.
punctuation mark *n* signe *m* de ponctuation.
puncture ['pʌŋktʃə*] *n* (*Brit*) crevaison *f* ♦ *vt* crever; **I have a ~** (*AUT*) j'ai (un pneu) crevé.
pundit ['pʌndɪt] *n* individu *m* qui pontifie, pontife *m*.
pungent ['pʌndʒənt] *a* piquant(e); (*fig*) mordant(e), caustique.
punish ['pʌnɪʃ] *vt* punir; **to ~ sb for sth/for doing sth** punir qn de qch/d'avoir fait qch.
punishable ['pʌnɪʃəbl] *a* punissable.
punishing ['pʌnɪʃɪŋ] *a* (*fig: exhausting*) épuisant(e) ♦ *n* punition *f*.
punishment ['pʌnɪʃmənt] *n* punition *f*, châtiment *m*; (*fig: col*): **to take a lot of ~** (*boxer*) encaisser; (*car, person etc*) être mis(e) à dure épreuve.
punk [pʌŋk] *n* (*person: also: ~ rocker*) punk *m/f*; (*music: also: ~ rock*) le punk; (*US col: hoodlum*) voyou *m*.
punt [pʌnt] *n* (*boat*) bachot *m* ♦ *vi* (*Brit: bet*) parier.
punter ['pʌntə*] *n* (*Brit: gambler*) parieur/euse; (: *col*) Monsieur tout le monde; type *m*.
puny ['pju:nɪ] *a* chétif(ive).
pup [pʌp] *n* chiot *m*.
pupil ['pju:pl] *n* élève *m/f*.
puppet ['pʌpɪt] *n* marionnette *f*, pantin *m*.
puppet government *n* gouvernement *m* fantoche.
puppy ['pʌpɪ] *n* chiot *m*, petit chien.
purchase ['pɜ:tʃɪs] *n* achat *m*; (*grip*) prise *f* ♦ *vt* acheter; **to get a ~ on** trouver appui sur.
purchase order *n* ordre *m* d'achat.
purchase price *n* prix *m* d'achat.
purchaser ['pɜ:tʃɪsə*] *n* acheteur/euse.
purchase tax *n* (*Brit*) taxe *f* à l'achat.
purchasing power ['pɜ:tʃɪsɪŋ-] *n* pouvoir *m* d'achat.
pure [pjuə*] *a* pur(e); **a ~ wool jumper** un pull en pure laine; **~ and simple** pur(e) et simple.
purebred ['pjuəbred] *a* de race.
purée ['pjuəreɪ] *n* purée *f*.
purely ['pjuəlɪ] *ad* purement.

purge [pɜ:dʒ] *n* (*MED*) purge *f*; (*POL*) épuration *f*, purge ♦ *vt* purger; (*fig*) épurer, purger.
purification [pjuərɪfɪ'keɪʃən] *n* purification *f*.
purify ['pjuərɪfaɪ] *vt* purifier, épurer.
purist ['pjuərɪst] *n* puriste *m/f*.
puritan ['pjuərɪtən] *n* puritain/e.
puritanical [pjuərɪ'tænɪkl] *a* puritain(e).
purity ['pjuərɪtɪ] *n* pureté *f*.
purl [pɜ:l] *n* maille *f* à l'envers ♦ *vt* tricoter à l'envers.
purloin [pɜ:'lɔɪn] *vt* dérober.
purple ['pɜ:pl] *a* violet(te); cramoisi(e).
purport [pɜ:'pɔ:t] *vi*: **to ~ to be/do** prétendre être/faire.
purpose ['pɜ:pəs] *n* intention *f*, but *m*; **on ~** exprès; **for illustrative ~s** à titre d'illustration; **for teaching ~s** dans un but pédagogique; **for the ~s of this meeting** pour cette réunion; **to no ~** en pure perte.
purpose-built ['pɜ:pəs'bɪlt] *a* (*Brit*) fait(e) sur mesure.
purposeful ['pɜ:pəsful] *a* déterminé(e), résolu(e).
purposely ['pɜ:pəslɪ] *ad* exprès.
purr [pɜ:*] *n* ronronnement *m* ♦ *vi* ronronner.
purse [pɜ:s] *n* porte-monnaie *m inv*, bourse *f*; (*US: handbag*) sac *m* (à main) ♦ *vt* serrer, pincer.
purser ['pɜ:sə*] *n* (*NAUT*) commissaire *m* du bord.
purse snatcher [-'snætʃə*] *n* (*US*) voleur *m* à l'arraché.
pursue [pə'sju:] *vt* poursuivre; (*pleasures*) rechercher; (*inquiry, matter*) approfondir.
pursuer [pə'sju:ə*] *n* poursuivant/e.
pursuit [pə'sju:t] *n* poursuite *f*; (*occupation*) occupation *f*, activité *f*; **scientific ~s** recherches *fpl* scientifiques; **in (the) ~ of sth** à la recherche de qch.
purveyor [pə'veɪə*] *n* fournisseur *m*.
pus [pʌs] *n* pus *m*.
push [puʃ] *n* poussée *f*; (*effort*) gros effort; (*drive*) énergie *f* ♦ *vt* pousser; (*button*) appuyer sur; (*thrust*): **to ~ sth (into)** enfoncer qch (dans); (*fig*) mettre en avant, faire de la publicité pour ♦ *vi* pousser; appuyer; **to ~ a door open/shut** pousser une porte (pour l'ouvrir/pour la fermer); **"~"** (*on door*) "pousser"; (*on bell*) "appuyer"; **to ~ for** (*better pay, conditions*) réclamer; **to be ~ed for time/money** être à court de temps/d'argent; **she is ~ing fifty** (*col*) elle frise la cinquantaine; **at a ~** (*Brit col*) à la limite, à la rigueur.
push aside *vt* écarter.
push in *vi* s'introduire de force.
push off *vi* (*col*) filer, ficher le camp.
push on *vi* (*continue*) continuer.
push over *vt* renverser.
push through *vt* (*measure*) faire voter.
push up *vt* (*total, prices*) faire monter.
push-bike ['puʃbaɪk] *n* (*Brit*) vélo *m*.
push-button ['puʃbʌtn] *n* bouton(-poussoir) *m*.
pushchair ['puʃtʃeə*] *n* (*Brit*) poussette *f*.
pusher ['puʃə*] *n* (*also*: **drug ~**) revendeur/euse (de drogue), ravitailleur/euse (en drogue).

pushing ['puʃɪŋ] *a* dynamique.
pushover ['puʃəuvə*] *n* (*col*): **it's a ~** c'est un jeu d'enfant.
push-up ['puʃʌp] *n* (*US*) traction *f*.
pushy ['puʃɪ] *a* (*pej*) arriviste.
puss, pussy(-cat) [pus, 'pusɪ(kæt)] *n* minet *m*.
put, *pt, pp* **put** |put| *vt* mettre; (*place*) poser, placer; (*say*) dire, exprimer; (*a question*) poser; (*estimate*) estimer; **to ~ sb in a good/bad mood** mettre qn de bonne/mauvaise humeur; **to ~ sb to bed** mettre qn au lit, coucher qn; **to ~ sb to a lot of trouble** déranger qn; **how shall I ~ it?** comment dirais-je?, comment dire?; **to ~ a lot of time into sth** passer beaucoup de temps à qch; **to ~ money on a horse** miser sur un cheval; **I ~ it to you that ...** (*Brit*) je (vous) suggère que ..., je suis d'avis que ...; **to stay ~** ne pas bouger.
put about *vi* (*NAUT*) virer de bord ♦ *vt* (*rumour*) faire courir.
put across *vt* (*ideas etc*) communiquer; faire comprendre.
put aside *vt* mettre de côté.
put away *vt* (*store*) ranger.
put back *vt* (*replace*) remettre, replacer; (*postpone*) remettre; (*delay, also: clock*) retarder; **this will ~ us back 10 years** cela nous ramènera dix ans en arrière.
put by *vt* (*money*) mettre de côté, économiser.
put down *vt* (*parcel etc*) poser, déposer; (*pay*) verser; (*in writing*) mettre par écrit, inscrire; (*suppress: revolt etc*) réprimer, faire cesser; (*attribute*) attribuer.
put forward *vt* (*ideas*) avancer, proposer; (*date, watch, clock*) avancer.
put in *vt* (*gas, electricity*) installer; (*application, complaint*) soumettre.
put in for *vt fus* (*job*) poser sa candidature pour; (*promotion*) solliciter.
put off *vt* (*light etc*) éteindre; (*postpone*) remettre à plus tard, ajourner; (*discourage*) dissuader.
put on *vt* (*clothes, lipstick etc*) mettre; (*light etc*) allumer; (*play etc*) monter; (*extra bus, train etc*) mettre en service; (*food, meal*) servir; (*weight*) prendre; (*assume: accent, manner*) prendre; (: *airs*) se donner, prendre; (*brake*) mettre; (*col: tease*) faire marcher; (*inform, indicate*): **to ~ sb on to sb/sth** indiquer qn/qch à qn.
put out *vt* mettre dehors; (*one's hand*) tendre; (*news, rumour*) faire courir, répandre; (*light etc*) éteindre; (*person: inconvenience*) déranger, gêner; (*Brit: dislocate*) se démettre ♦ *vi* (*NAUT*): **to ~ out to sea** prendre le large; **to ~ out from Plymouth** quitter Plymouth.
put through *vt* (*caller*) mettre en communication; (*call*) passer; **~ me through to Miss Blair** passez-moi Miss Blair.
put together *vt* mettre ensemble; (*assemble: furniture, toy etc*) monter, assembler; (*meal*) préparer.
put up *vt* (*raise*) lever, relever, remonter; (*pin up*) afficher; (*hang*) accrocher; (*build*) construire, ériger; (*a tent*) monter; (*in-*

crease) augmenter; (*accommodate*) loger; (*incite*): **to ~ sb up to doing sth** pousser qn à faire qch; **to ~ sth up for sale** mettre qch en vente.
put upon *vt fus*: **to be ~ upon** (*imposed on*) se laisser faire.
put up with *vt fus* supporter.
putrid ['pjuːtrɪd] *a* putride.
putt |pʌt| *vt* poter (la balle) ♦ *n* coup roulé.
putter ['pʌtə*] *n* (*GOLF*) putter *m*.
putting green ['pʌtɪŋ-] *n* green *m*.
putty ['pʌtɪ] *n* mastic *m*.
put-up ['putʌp] *a*: **~ job** affaire montée.
puzzle ['pʌzl] *n* énigme *f*, mystère *m*; (*jigsaw*) puzzle *m*; (*also:* **crossword ~**) problème *m* de mots croisés ♦ *vt* intriguer, rendre perplexe ♦ *vi* se creuser la tête; **to ~ over** chercher à comprendre; **to be ~d about sth** être perplexe au sujet de qch.
puzzling ['pʌzlɪŋ] *a* déconcertant(e), inexplicable.
PVC *n abbr* (= *polyvinyl chloride*) PVC *m*, polyvinyle *m*.
Pvt. *abbr* (*US MIL*) = **private**.
pw *abbr* (= *per week*) p.sem.
PX *n abbr* (*US MIL*) = **post exchange**.
pygmy ['pɪgmɪ] *n* pygmée *m/f*.
pyjamas [pɪ'dʒɑːməz] *npl* (*Brit*) pyjama *m*; **a pair of ~** un pyjama.
pylon ['paɪlən] *n* pylône *m*.
pyramid ['pɪrəmɪd] *n* pyramide *f*.
Pyrenean [pɪrə'niːən] *a* pyrénéen(ne), des Pyrénées.
Pyrenees [pɪrə'niːz] *npl*: **the ~** les Pyrénées *fpl*.
Pyrex ['paɪrɛks] *n* ® Pyrex *m* ® ♦ *cpd*: **~ dish** plat *m* en Pyrex.
python ['paɪθən] *n* python *m*.

Q

Q, q [kjuː] *n* (*letter*) Q, q *m*; **Q for Queen** Q comme Quintal.
Qatar |kæ'tɑː*| *n* Qatar *m*, Katar *m*.
QC *n abbr* (*Brit*: = *Queen's Counsel*) *titre donné à certains avocats*.
QED *abbr* (= *quod erat demonstrandum*) CQFD.
QM *n abbr* = **quartermaster**.
q.t. *n abbr* (*col*: = *quiet*): **on the ~** discrètement.
qty *abbr* (= *quantity*) qté.
quack [kwæk] *n* (*of duck*) coin-coin *m inv*; (*pej: doctor*) charlatan *m* ♦ *vi* faire coin-coin.
quad [kwɔd] *n abbr* = **quadruple, quadruplet, quadrangle**.
quadrangle ['kwɔdræŋgl] *n* (*MATH*) quadrilatère *m*; (*courtyard: abbr*: **quad**) cour *f*.
quadruped ['kwɔdruped] *n* quadrupède *m*.
quadruple [kwɔ'druːpl] *a, n* quadruple *m* ♦ *vt, vi* quadrupler.
quadruplet [kwɔ'druːplɪt] *n* quadruplé/e.

quagmire ['kwægmaɪə*] n bourbier m.

quail [kweɪl] n (ZOOL) caille f ♦ vi: **to ~ at** or **before** se décourager devant.

quaint [kweɪnt] a bizarre; (old-fashioned) désuet(ète); au charme vieillot, pittoresque.

quake [kweɪk] vi trembler ♦ n abbr = **earthquake.**

Quaker ['kweɪkə*] n quaker/esse.

qualification [kwɔlɪfɪ'keɪʃən] n (degree etc) diplôme m; (ability) compétence f, qualification f; (limitation) réserve f, restriction f; **what are your ~s?** qu'avez-vous comme diplômes?; quelles sont vos qualifications?

qualified ['kwɔlɪfaɪd] a diplômé(e); (able) compétent(e), qualifié(e); (limited) conditionnel(le), **it was a ~ success** ce fut un succès mitigé; **~ for/to do** qui a les diplômes requis pour/pour faire; qualifié pour/pour faire.

qualify ['kwɔlɪfaɪ] vt qualifier; (limit: statement) apporter des réserves à ♦ vi: **to ~ (as)** obtenir son diplôme (de); **to ~ (for)** remplir les conditions requises (pour); (SPORT) se qualifier (pour).

qualifying ['kwɔlɪfaɪɪŋ] a: **~ exam** examen m d'entrée; **~ round** éliminatoires fpl.

qualitative ['kwɔlɪtətɪv] a qualitatif(ive).

quality ['kwɔlɪtɪ] n qualité f ♦ cpd de qualité; **of good/poor ~** de bonne/mauvaise qualité.

quality control n contrôle m de qualité.

quality papers npl (Brit): **the ~** la presse d'information.

qualm [kwɑ:m] n doute m; scrupule m; **to have ~s about sth** avoir des doutes sur qch; éprouver des scrupules à propos de qch.

quandary ['kwɔndrɪ] n: **in a ~** devant un dilemme, dans l'embarras.

quango ['kwæŋgəu] n abbr (Brit: = quasi-autonomous non-governmental organization) commission nommée par le gouvernement.

quantitative ['kwɔntɪtətɪv] a quantitatif(ive).

quantity ['kwɔntɪtɪ] n quantité f; **in ~** en grande quantité.

quantity surveyor n (Brit) métreur vérificateur.

quarantine ['kwɔrəntiːn] n quarantaine f.

quarrel ['kwɔrl] n querelle f, dispute f ♦ vi se disputer, se quereller; **to have a ~ with sb** se quereller avec qn; **I've no ~ with him** je n'ai rien contre lui; **I can't ~ with that** je ne vois rien à redire à cela.

quarrelsome ['kwɔrəlsəm] a querelleur(euse).

quarry ['kwɔrɪ] n (for stone) carrière f; (animal) proie f, gibier m ♦ vt (marble etc) extraire.

quart [kwɔːt] n ≈ litre m.

quarter ['kwɔːtə*] n quart m; (of year) trimestre m; (district) quartier m; (US, Canada: 25 cents) (pièce f de) vingt-cinq cents mpl ♦ vt partager en quartiers or en quatre; (MIL) caserner, cantonner; **~s** npl logement m; (MIL) quartiers mpl, cantonnement m; **a ~ of an hour** un quart d'heure; **it's a ~ to 3**, (US) **it's a ~ of 3** il est 3 heures moins le quart; **it's a ~ past 3**, (US) **it's a ~ after 3** il est 3 heures et quart; **from all ~s** de tous côtés; **at close ~s** tout près.

quarter-deck ['kwɔːtədɛk] n (NAUT) plage f arrière.

quarter final n quart m de finale.

quarterly ['kwɔːtəlɪ] a trimestriel(le) ♦ ad tous les trois mois ♦ n (PRESS) revue trimestrielle.

quartermaster ['kwɔːtəmɑːstə*] n (MIL) intendant m militaire de troisième classe; (NAUT) maître m de manœuvre.

quartet(te) [kwɔː'tɛt] n quatuor m; (jazz players) quartette m.

quarto ['kwɔːtəu] a, n in-quarto (m) inv.

quartz [kwɔːts] n quartz m ♦ cpd de or en quartz; (watch, clock) à quartz.

quash [kwɔʃ] vt (verdict) annuler, casser.

quasi- ['kweɪzaɪ] prefix quasi- + noun; quasi, presque + adjective.

quaver ['kweɪvə*] n (Brit MUS) croche f ♦ vi trembler.

quay [kiː] n (also: **~side**) quai m.

queasy ['kwiːzɪ] a (stomach) délicat(e); **to feel ~** avoir mal au cœur.

Quebec [kwɪ'bɛk] n Québec m.

queen [kwiːn] n (gen) reine f; (CARDS etc) dame f.

queen mother n reine mère f.

queer [kwɪə*] a étrange, curieux(euse); (suspicious) louche; (Brit: sick): **I feel ~** je ne me sens pas bien ♦ n (col) homosexuel m.

quell [kwɛl] vt réprimer, étouffer.

quench [kwɛntʃ] vt (flames) éteindre; **to ~ one's thirst** se désaltérer.

querulous ['kwɛruləs] a (person) récriminateur(trice); (voice) plaintif(ive).

query ['kwɪərɪ] n question f; (doubt) doute m; (question mark) point m d'interrogation ♦ vt (disagree with, dispute) mettre en doute, questionner.

quest [kwɛst] n recherche f, quête f.

question ['kwɛstʃən] n question f ♦ vt (person) interroger; (plan, idea) mettre en question or en doute; **to ask sb a ~, to put a ~ to sb** poser une question à qn; **to bring** or **call sth into ~** remettre qch en question; **the ~ is ...** la question est de savoir ...; **it's a ~ of doing** il s'agit de faire; **there's some ~ of doing** il est question de faire; **beyond ~** sans aucun doute; **out of the ~** hors de question.

questionable ['kwɛstʃənəbl] a discutable.

questioner ['kwɛstʃənə*] n personne f qui pose une question (or qui a posé la question etc).

questioning ['kwɛstʃənɪŋ] a interrogateur(trice) ♦ n interrogatoire m.

question mark n point m d'interrogation.

questionnaire [kwɛstʃə'nɛə*] n questionnaire m.

queue [kjuː] (Brit) n queue f, file f ♦ vi faire la queue; **to jump the ~** passer avant son tour.

quibble ['kwɪbl] vi ergoter, chicaner.

quick [kwɪk] a rapide; (reply) prompt(e), rapide; (mind) vif(vive) ♦ ad vite, rapidement ♦ n: **cut to the ~** (fig) touché(e) au vif; **be ~!** dépêche-toi!; **to be ~ to act** agir tout de suite.

quicken ['kwɪkən] vt accélérer, presser; (rouse) stimuler ♦ vi s'accélérer, devenir plus rapide.

quicklime ['kwɪklaɪm] n chaux vive.

quickly |'kwıklı| *ad* (*fast*) vite, rapidement; (*immediately*) tout de suite.

quickness |'kwıknıs| *n* rapidité *f*, promptitude *f*; (*of mind*) vivacité *f*.

quicksand |'kwıksænd| *n* sables mouvants.

quickstep |'kwıkstɛp| *n* fox-trot *m*.

quick-tempered |kwık'tɛmpəd| *a* emporté(e).

quick-witted |kwık'wıtıd| *a* à l'esprit vif.

quid |kwıd| *n* (*pl inv*) (*Brit col*) livre *f*.

quid pro quo |'kwıdprəu'kwəu| *n* contrepartie *f*.

quiet |'kwaıət| *a* tranquille, calme; (*not noisy: engine*) silencieux(euse); (*reserved*) réservé(e); (*not busy: day, business*) calme; (*ceremony, colour*) discret(ète) ♦ *n* tranquillité *f*, calme *m* ♦ *vt, vi* (*US*) = **quieten**; **keep ~!** tais-toi!; **on the ~** en secret, discrètement; **I'll have a ~ word with him** je lui en parlerai discrètement.

quieten |'kwaıətn| (*also: ~ **down**) *vi* se calmer, s'apaiser ♦ *vt* calmer, apaiser.

quietly |'kwaıətlı| *ad* tranquillement, calmement; discrètement.

quietness |'kwaıətnıs| *n* tranquillité *f*, calme *m*; silence *m*.

quill |kwıl| *n* plume *f* (d'oie).

quilt |kwılt| *n* édredon *m*; (*continental ~*) couette *f*.

quilting |'kwıltıŋ| *n* ouatine *f*; molletonnage *m*.

quin |kwın| *n abbr* = **quintuplet**.

quince |kwıns| *n* coing *m*; (*tree*) cognassier *m*.

quinine |kwı'ni:n| *n* quinine *f*.

quintet(te) |kwın'tɛt| *n* quintette *m*.

quintuplet |kwın'tju:plıt| *n* quintuplé/e.

quip |kwıp| *n* remarque piquante *or* spirituelle, pointe *f* ♦ *vt*: ... **he ~ped** ... lança-t-il.

quire |'kwaıə*| *n* ≈ main *f* (de papier).

quirk |kwə:k| *n* bizarrerie *f*; **by some ~ of fate** par un caprice du hasard.

quit |kwıt|, *pt, pp* **quit** *or* **quitted** |kwıt| *vt* quitter ♦ *vi* (*give up*) abandonner, renoncer; (*resign*) démissionner; **to ~ doing** arrêter de faire; **~ stalling!** (*US col*) arrête de te dérober!; **notice to ~** (*Brit*) congé *m* (*signifié au locataire*).

quite |kwaıt| *ad* (*rather*) assez, plutôt; (*entirely*) complètement, tout à fait; **~ new** plutôt neuf; tout à fait neuf; **she's ~ pretty** elle est plutôt jolie; **I ~ understand** je comprends très bien; **~ a few of them** un assez grand nombre d'entre eux; **that's not ~ right** ce n'est pas tout à fait juste; **not ~ as many as last time** pas tout à fait autant que la dernière fois; **~ (so)!** exactement!

Quito |'ki:təu| *n* Quito.

quits |kwıts| *a*: **~ (with)** quitte (envers); **let's call it ~** restons-en là.

quiver |'kwıvə*| *vi* trembler, frémir ♦ *n* (*for arrows*) carquois *m*.

quiz |kwız| *n* (*on tv*) jeu-concours *m* (télévisé); (*in magazine etc*) test *m* de connaissances ♦ *vt* interroger.

quizzical |'kwızıkl| *a* narquois(e).

quoits |kwɔıts| *npl* jeu *m* du palet.

quorum |'kwɔ:rəm| *n* quorum *m*.

quota |'kwəutə| *n* quota *m*.

quotation |kwəu'teıʃən| *n* citation *f*; (*of*

**shares etc*) cote *f*, cours *m*; (*estimate*) devis *m*.

quotation marks *npl* guillemets *mpl*.

quote |kwəut| *n* citation *f* ♦ *vt* (*sentence, author*) citer; (*price*) donner, soumettre; (*shares*) coter ♦ *vi*: **to ~ from** citer; **to ~ for a job** établir un devis pour des travaux; **~s** *npl* (*col*) = **quotation marks**; **in ~s** entre guillemets; **~ ... unquote** (*in dictation*) ouvrez les guillemets ... fermez les guillemets.

quotient |'kwəuʃənt| *n* quotient *m*.

qv *abbr* (= *quod vide: which see*) voir.

qwerty keyboard |'kwə:tı-| *n* clavier *m* QWERTY.

R

R, r |ɑ:*| *n* (*letter*) R, r *m*; **R for Robert**, (*US*) **R for Roger** R comme Raoul.

R *abbr* (= *right*) dr; (= *river*) riv., fl.; (= *Réaumur* (*scale*)) R; (*US CINEMA*: = *restricted*) *interdit aux moins de 17 ans*; (*US POL*) = **republican**; (*Brit*) = *Rex, Regina*.

RA *abbr* = **rear admiral** ♦ *n abbr* (*Brit*) = *Royal Academy, Royal Academician*.

RAAF *n abbr* = *Royal Australian Air Force*.

Rabat |rə'bɑ:t| *n* Rabat.

rabbi |'ræbaı| *n* rabbin *m*.

rabbit |'ræbıt| *n* lapin *m* ♦ *vi*: **to ~ (on)** (*Brit*) parler à n'en plus finir.

rabbit hole *n* terrier *m* (de lapin).

rabbit hutch *n* clapier *m*.

rabble |'ræbl| *n* (*pej*) populace *f*.

rabid |'ræbıd| *a* enragé(e).

rabies |'reıbi:z| *n* rage *f*.

RAC *n abbr* (*Brit*: = *Royal Automobile Club*) ≈ ACF *m*.

raccoon |rə'ku:n| *n* raton *m* laveur.

race |reıs| *n* race *f*; (*competition, rush*) course *f* ♦ *vt* (*person*) faire la course avec; (*horse*) faire courir; (*engine*) emballer ♦ *vi* courir; (*engine*) s'emballer; **the human ~** la race humaine; **to ~ in/out** *etc* entrer/sortir *etc* à toute vitesse.

race car *n* (*US*) = **racing car**.

race car driver *n* (*US*) = **racing driver**.

racecourse |'reıskɔ:s| *n* champ *m* de courses.

racehorse |'reıshɔ:s| *n* cheval *m* de course.

race relations *npl* rapports *mpl* entre les races.

racetrack |'reıstræk| *n* piste *f*.

racial |'reıʃl| *a* racial(e).

racialism |'reıʃlızəm| *n* racisme *m*.

racialist |'reıʃlıst| *a, n* raciste (*m/f*).

racing |'reısıŋ| *n* courses *fpl*.

racing car *n* (*Brit*) voiture *f* de course.

racing driver *n* (*Brit*) pilote *m* de course.

racism |'reısızəm| *n* racisme *m*.

racist |'reısıst| *a, n* raciste (*m/f*).

rack |ræk| *n* (*also:* **luggage ~**) filet *m* à bagages; (*also:* **roof ~**) galerie *f* ♦ *vt* tourmenter; **magazine ~** porte-revues *m inv*;

shoe ~ étagère *f* à chaussures; **toast** ~ porte-toast *m*; **to** ~ **one's brains** se creuser la cervelle; **to go to** ~ **and ruin** (*building*) tomber en ruine; (*business*) péricliter.

rack up *vt* accumuler.

rack-and-pinion ['rækənd'pɪnjən] *n* (*TECH*) crémaillère *f*.

racket ['rækɪt] *n* (*for tennis*) raquette *f*; (*noise*) tapage *m*, vacarme *m*; (*swindle*) escroquerie *f*; (*organized crime*) racket *m*.

racketeer [rækɪ'tɪə*] *n* (*esp US*) racketteur *m*.

racoon [rə'kuːn] *n* = **raccoon**.

racquet ['rækɪt] *n* raquette *f*.

racy ['reɪsɪ] *a* plein(e) de verve; osé(e).

RADA [rɑːdə] *n abbr* (*Brit*) = Royal Academy of Dramatic Art.

radar ['reɪdɑː*] *n* radar *m* ♦ *cpd* radar *inv*.

radar trap *n* contrôle *m* radar.

radial ['reɪdɪəl] *a* (*also*: **~-ply**) à carcasse radiale.

radiance ['reɪdɪəns] *n* éclat *m*, rayonnement *m*.

radiant ['reɪdɪənt] *a* rayonnant(e); (*PHYSICS*) radiant(e).

radiate ['reɪdɪeɪt] *vt* (*heat*) émettre, dégager ♦ *vi* (*lines*) rayonner.

radiation [reɪdɪ'eɪʃən] *n* rayonnement *m*; (*radioactive*) radiation *f*.

radiation sickness *n* mal *m* des rayons.

radiator ['reɪdɪeɪtə*] *n* radiateur *m*.

radiator cap *n* bouchon *m* de radiateur.

radiator grill *n* (*AUT*) calandre *f*.

radical ['rædɪkl] *a* radical(e).

radii ['reɪdɪaɪ] *npl of* **radius**.

radio ['reɪdɪəu] *n* radio *f* ♦ *vi*: **to** ~ **to sb** envoyer un message radio à qn ♦ *vt* (*information*) transmettre par radio; (*one's position*) signaler par radio; (*person*) appeler par radio; **on the** ~ à la radio.

radioactive ['reɪdɪəu'æktɪv] *a* radioactif(ive).

radioactivity ['reɪdɪəuæk'tɪvɪtɪ] *n* radioactivité *f*.

radio announcer *n* annonceur *m*.

radio-controlled ['reɪdɪəukən'trəuld] *a* radioguidé(e).

radiographer [reɪdɪ'ɔgrəfə*] *n* radiologue *m/f* (*technicien*).

radiography [reɪdɪ'ɔgrəfɪ] *n* radiographie *f*.

radiologist [reɪdɪ'ɔlədʒɪst] *n* radiologue *m/f* (*médecin*).

radiology [reɪdɪ'ɔlədʒɪ] *n* radiologie *f*.

radio station *n* station *f* de radio.

radio taxi *n* radio-taxi *m*.

radiotelephone ['reɪdɪəu'telɪfəun] *n* radiotéléphone *m*.

radiotherapist ['reɪdɪəu'θerəpɪst] *n* radiothérapeute *m/f*.

radiotherapy ['reɪdɪəu'θerəpɪ] *n* radiothérapie *f*.

radish ['rædɪʃ] *n* radis *m*.

radium ['reɪdɪəm] *n* radium *m*.

radius, *pl* **radii** ['reɪdɪəs, -aɪ] *n* rayon *m*; (*ANAT*) radius *m*; **within a** ~ **of 50 miles** dans un rayon de 50 milles.

RAF *n abbr* (*Brit*) = Royal Air Force.

raffia ['ræfɪə] *n* raphia *m*.

raffish ['ræfɪʃ] *a* dissolu(e); canaille.

raffle ['ræfl] *n* tombola *f* ♦ *vt* mettre comme lot dans une tombola.

raft [rɑːft] *n* (*craft; also*: **life** ~) radeau *m*; (*logs*) train *m* de flottage.

rafter ['rɑːftə*] *n* chevron *m*.

rag [ræg] *n* chiffon *m*; (*pej*: *newspaper*) feuille *f*, torchon *m*; (*for charity*) attractions organisées par les étudiants au profit d'œuvres de charité ♦ *vt* (*Brit*) chahuter, mettre en boîte; **~s** *npl* haillons *mpl*; **in ~s** (*person*) en haillons; (*clothes*) en lambeaux.

rag-and-bone man [rægən'bəunmæn] *n* chiffonnier *m*.

ragbag ['rægbæg] *n* (*fig*) ramassis *m*.

rag doll *n* poupée *f* de chiffon.

rage [reɪdʒ] *n* (*fury*) rage *f*, fureur *f* ♦ *vi* (*person*) être fou(folle) de rage; (*storm*) faire rage, être déchaîné(e); **to fly into a** ~ se mettre en rage; **it's all the** ~ cela fait fureur.

ragged ['rægɪd] *a* (*edge*) inégal(e), qui accroche; (*cuff*) effiloché(e); (*appearance*) déguenillé(e).

raging ['reɪdʒɪŋ] *a* (*sea, storm*) en furie; (*fever, pain*) violent(e); ~ **toothache** rage *f* de dents; **in a** ~ **temper** dans une rage folle.

ragman ['rægmæn] *n* chiffonnier *m*.

rag trade *n* (*col*): **the** ~ la confection.

raid [reɪd] *n* (*MIL*) raid *m*; (*criminal*) hold-up *m inv*; (*by police*) descente *f*, rafle *f* ♦ *vt* faire un raid sur *or* un hold-up dans *or* une descente dans.

raider ['reɪdə*] *n* malfaiteur *m*.

rail [reɪl] *n* (*on stair*) rampe *f*; (*on bridge, balcony*) balustrade *f*; (*of ship*) bastingage *m*; (*for train*) rail *m*; **~s** *npl* rails *mpl*, voie ferrée; **by** ~ par chemin de fer, par le train.

railing(s) ['reɪlɪŋ(z)] *n(pl)* grille *f*.

railway ['reɪlweɪ], (*US*) **railroad** ['reɪlrəud] *n* chemin *m* de fer.

railway engine *n* locomotive *f*.

railway line *n* ligne *f* de chemin de fer.

railwayman ['reɪlweɪmən] *n* cheminot *m*.

railway station *n* gare *f*.

rain [reɪn] *n* pluie *f* ♦ *vi* pleuvoir; **in the** ~ sous la pluie; **it's ~ing** il pleut; **it's ~ing cats and dogs** il pleut à torrents.

rainbow ['reɪnbəu] *n* arc-en-ciel *m*.

raincoat ['reɪnkəut] *n* imperméable *m*.

raindrop ['reɪndrɔp] *n* goutte *f* de pluie.

rainfall ['reɪnfɔːl] *n* chute *f* de pluie; (*measurement*) hauteur *f* des précipitations.

rainproof ['reɪnpruːf] *a* imperméable.

rainstorm ['reɪnstɔːm] *n* pluie torrentielle.

rainwater ['reɪnwɔːtə*] *n* eau *f* de pluie.

rainy ['reɪnɪ] *a* pluvieux(euse).

raise [reɪz] *n* augmentation *f* ♦ *vt* (*lift*) lever; hausser; (*end: siege, embargo*) lever; (*build*) ériger; (*increase*) augmenter; (*a protest, doubt*) provoquer, causer; (*a question*) soulever; (*cattle, family*) élever; (*crop*) faire pousser; (*army, funds*) rassembler; (*loan*) obtenir; **to** ~ **one's glass to sb/sth** porter un toast en l'honneur de qn/qch; **to** ~ **one's voice** élever la voix; **to** ~ **sb's hopes** donner de l'espoir à qn; **to** ~ **a laugh/a smile** faire rire/sourire.

raisin ['reɪzn] *n* raisin sec.

Raj [rɑːdʒ] *n*: **the** ~ l'empire *m* (*aux Indes*).

rajah ['rɑːdʒə] *n* radja(h) *m*.

rake [reɪk] *n* (*tool*) râteau *m*; (*person*) débauché *m* ♦ *vt* (*garden*) ratisser; (*fire*) tisonner; (*with machine gun*) balayer ♦ *vi*: **to** ~ **through** (*fig: search*) fouiller (dans).

rake-off ['reikɔf] *n* (*col*) pourcentage *m*.

rakish ['reikiʃ] *a* dissolu(e); cavalier(ière).

rally ['ræli] *n* (*POL etc*) meeting *m*, rassemblement *m*; (*AUT*) rallye *m*; (*TENNIS*) échange *m* ♦ *vt* rassembler, rallier ♦ *vi* se rallier; (*sick person*) aller mieux; (*Stock Exchange*) reprendre.

rally round *vi* venir en aide ♦ *vt fus* se rallier à; venir en aide à.

rallying point ['ræliiŋ-] *n* (*MIL*) point *m* de ralliement.

RAM [ræm] *n abbr* (*COMPUT*) = **random access memory**.

ram [ræm] *n* bélier *m* ♦ *vt* enfoncer; (*soil*) tasser; (*crash into*) emboutir; percuter; éperonner.

ramble ['ræmbl] *n* randonnée *f* ♦ *vi* (*pej: also:* ~ **on**) discourir, pérorer.

rambler ['ræmblə*] *n* promeneur/euse, randonneur/euse; (*BOT*) rosier grimpant.

rambling ['ræmbliŋ] *a* (*speech*) décousu(e); (*house*) plein(e) de coins et de recoins; (*BOT*) grimpant(e).

RAMC *n abbr* (*Brit*) = *Royal Army Medical Corps*.

ramification [ræmifi'keiʃən] *n* ramification *f*.

ramp [ræmp] *n* (*incline*) rampe *f*; dénivellation *f*; (*in garage*) pont *m*.

rampage [ræm'peidʒ] *n*: **to be on the** ~ se déchaîner ♦ *vi*: **they went rampaging through the town** ils ont envahi les rues et ont tout saccagé sur leur passage.

rampant ['ræmpənt] *a* (*disease etc*) qui sévit.

rampart ['ræmpɑːt] *n* rempart *m*.

ramshackle ['ræmʃækl] *a* (*house*) délabré(e); (*car etc*) déglingué(e).

RAN *n abbr* = *Royal Australian Navy*.

ran [ræn] *pt of* **run**.

ranch [rɑːntʃ] *n* ranch *m*.

rancher ['rɑːntʃə*] *n* (*owner*) propriétaire *m* de ranch; (*ranch hand*) cowboy *m*.

rancid ['rænsid] *a* rance.

rancour, (*US*) **rancor** ['ræŋkə*] *n* rancune *f*, rancœur *f*.

random ['rændəm] *a* fait(e) or établi(e) au hasard; (*COMPUT, MATH*) aléatoire ♦ *n*: **at** ~ au hasard.

random access memory (RAM) *n* (*COMPUT*) mémoire vive, RAM *f*.

randy ['rændi] *a* (*Brit col*) excité(e); lubrique.

rang [ræŋ] *pt of* **ring**.

range [reindʒ] *n* (*of mountains*) chaîne *f*; (*of missile, voice*) portée *f*; (*of products*) choix *m*, gamme *f*; (*also:* **shooting** ~) champ *m* de tir; (*: indoor*) stand *m* de tir; (*also:* **kitchen** ~) fourneau *m* (de cuisine) ♦ *vt* (*place*) mettre en rang, placer; (*roam*) parcourir ♦ *vi*: **to** ~ **over** couvrir; **to** ~ **from ... to** aller de ... à; **price** ~ éventail *m* des prix; **do you have anything else in this price** ~? avez-vous autre chose dans ces prix?; **within (firing)** ~ à portée (de tir); ~**d left/right** (*text*) justifié à gauche/à droite.

ranger ['reindʒə*] *n* garde *m* forestier.

Rangoon [ræŋ'guːn] *n* Rangoon.

rank [ræŋk] *n* rang *m*; (*MIL*) grade *m*; (*Brit:*

also: **taxi** ~) station *f* de taxis ♦ *vi*: **to** ~ **among** compter or se classer parmi ♦ *vt*: **I** ~ **him sixth** je le place sixième ♦ *a* (*smell*) nauséabond(e); (*hypocrisy, injustice etc*) flagrant(e); **the** ~**s** (*MIL*) la troupe; **the** ~ **and file** (*fig*) la masse, la base; **to close** ~**s** (*MIL, fig*) serrer les rangs.

rankle ['ræŋkl] *vi* (*insult*) rester sur le cœur.

ransack ['rænsæk] *vt* fouiller (à fond); (*plunder*) piller.

ransom ['rænsəm] *n* rançon *f*; **to hold sb to** ~ (*fig*) exercer un chantage sur qn.

rant [rænt] *vi* fulminer.

ranting ['ræntiŋ] *n* invectives *fpl*.

rap [ræp] *n* petit coup sec; tape *f* ♦ *vt* frapper sur or à; taper sur.

rape [reip] *n* viol *m*; (*BOT*) colza *m* ♦ *vt* violer.

rape(seed) oil ['reip(siːd)-] *n* huile *f* de colza.

rapid ['ræpid] *a* rapide.

rapidity [rə'piditi] *n* rapidité *f*.

rapidly ['ræpidli] *ad* rapidement.

rapids ['ræpidz] *npl* (*GEO*) rapides *mpl*.

rapist ['reipist] *n* auteur *m* d'un viol.

rapport [ræ'pɔː*] *n* entente *f*.

rapt [ræpt] *a* (*attention*) extrême; **to be** ~ **in contemplation** être perdu(e) dans la contemplation.

rapture ['ræptʃə*] *n* extase *f*, ravissement *m*; **to go into** ~**s over** s'extasier sur.

rapturous ['ræptʃərəs] *a* extasié(e); frénétique.

rare [rɛə*] *a* rare; (*CULIN: steak*) saignant(e).

rarebit ['rɛəbit] *n see* **Welsh rarebit**.

rarefied ['rɛərifaid] *a* (*air, atmosphere*) raréfié(e).

rarely ['rɛəli] *ad* rarement.

raring ['rɛəriŋ] *a*: **to be** ~ **to go** (*col*) être très impatient(e) de commencer.

rarity ['rɛəriti] *n* rareté *f*.

rascal ['rɑːskl] *n* vaurien *m*.

rash [ræʃ] *a* imprudent(e), irréfléchi(e) ♦ *n* (*MED*) rougeur *f*, éruption *f*; **to come out in a** ~ avoir une éruption.

rasher ['ræʃə*] *n* fine tranche (de lard).

rasp [rɑːsp] *n* (*tool*) lime *f* ♦ *vt* (*speak: also:* ~ **out**) dire d'une voix grinçante.

raspberry ['rɑːzbəri] *n* framboise *f*.

raspberry bush *n* framboisier *m*.

rasping ['rɑːspiŋ] *a*: ~ **noise** grincement *m*.

rat [ræt] *n* rat *m*.

ratable ['reitəbl] *a* = **rateable**.

ratchet ['rætʃit] *n*: ~ **wheel** roue *f* à rochet.

rate [reit] *n* (*ratio*) taux *m*, pourcentage *m*; (*speed*) vitesse *f*, rythme *m*; (*price*) tarif *m* ♦ *vt* classer; évaluer; **to** ~ **sb/sth as** considérer qn/qch comme; **to** ~ **sb/sth among** classer qn/qch parmi; **to** ~ **sb/sth highly** avoir une haute opinion de qn/qch; **at a** ~ **of 60 kph** à une vitesse de 60 km/h; ~ **of exchange** taux or cours *m* du change; ~ **of flow** débit *m*; ~ **of return** (taux de) rendement *m*; **pulse** ~ fréquence *f* des pulsations.

rateable value *n* (*Brit*) valeur locative imposable.

ratepayer ['reitpeiə*] *n* (*Brit*) contribuable *m/f* (*payant les impôts locaux*).

rates ['reits] *npl* (*Brit*) impôts locaux.

rather ['rɑːðə*] ad (somewhat) assez, plutôt; (to some extent) un peu; **it's ~ expensive** c'est assez cher; (too much) c'est un peu cher; **there's ~ a lot** il y en a beaucoup; **I would or I'd ~ go** j'aimerais mieux or je préférerais partir; **I had ~ go** il vaudrait mieux que je parte; **I'd ~ not leave** j'aimerais mieux ne pas partir; **or ~** (more accurately) ou plutôt; **I ~ think he won't come** je crois bien qu'il ne viendra pas.

ratification [rætɪfɪ'keɪʃən] n ratification f.

ratify ['rætɪfaɪ] vt ratifier.

rating ['reɪtɪŋ] n classement m; cote f; (NAUT: category) classe f; (: sailor: Brit) matelot m; **~s** npl (RADIO, TV) indice(s) m(pl) d'écoute.

ratio ['reɪʃɪəu] n proportion f; **in the ~ of 100 to 1** dans la proportion de 100 contre 1.

ration ['ræʃən] n (gen pl) ration(s) f(pl) ♦ vt rationner.

rational ['ræʃənl] a raisonnable, sensé(e); (solution, reasoning) logique; (MED) lucide.

rationale [ræʃə'nɑːl] n raisonnement m; justification f.

rationalization [ræʃnəlaɪ'zeɪʃən] n rationalisation f.

rationalize ['ræʃnəlaɪz] vt rationaliser; (conduct) essayer d'expliquer or de motiver.

rationally ['ræʃnəlɪ] ad raisonnablement; logiquement.

rationing ['ræʃnɪŋ] n rationnement m.

rat poison n mort-aux-rats f inv.

rat race n foire f d'empoigne.

rattan [ræ'tæn] n rotin m.

rattle ['rætl] n cliquetis m; (louder) bruit m de ferraille; (object: of baby) hochet m; (: of sports fan) crécelle f ♦ vi cliqueter; faire un bruit de ferraille or du bruit ♦ vt agiter (bruyamment); (col: disconcert) décontenancer; (: annoy) embêter.

rattlesnake ['rætlsneɪk] n serpent m à sonnettes.

ratty ['rætɪ] a (col) en rogne.

raucous ['rɔːkəs] a rauque.

raucously ['rɔːkəslɪ] ad d'une voix rauque.

ravage ['rævɪdʒ] vt ravager.

ravages ['rævɪdʒɪz] npl ravages mpl.

rave [reɪv] vi (in anger) s'emporter; (with enthusiasm) s'extasier; (MED) délirer ♦ cpd: **~ review** (col) critique f dithyrambique.

raven ['reɪvən] n grand corbeau.

ravenous ['rævənəs] a affamé(e).

ravine [rə'viːn] n ravin m.

raving ['reɪvɪŋ] a: **~ lunatic** n fou furieux/folle furieuse.

ravings ['reɪvɪŋz] npl divagations fpl.

ravioli [rævɪ'əulɪ] n ravioli mpl.

ravish ['rævɪʃ] vt ravir.

ravishing ['rævɪʃɪŋ] a enchanteur(eresse).

raw [rɔː] a (uncooked) cru(e); (not processed) brut(e); (sore) à vif, irrité(e); (inexperienced) inexpérimenté(e); **~ deal** (col: bad bargain) sale coup m; (: unfair treatment): **to get a ~ deal** être traité(e) injustement.

Rawalpindi [rɔːl'pɪndɪ] n Rawalpindi.

raw material n matière première.

ray [reɪ] n rayon m; **~ of hope** lueur f d'espoir.

rayon ['reɪən] n rayonne f.

raze [reɪz] vt (also: **~ to the ground**) raser.

razor ['reɪzə*] n rasoir m.

razor blade n lame f de rasoir.

razzle(-dazzle) ['ræzl('dæzl)] n (Brit col): **to go on the ~** faire la bringue.

razzmatazz ['ræzmə'tæz] n (col) tralala m, tapage m.

R&B n abbr = rhythm and blues.

RC abbr = **Roman Catholic**.

RCAF n abbr = Royal Canadian Air Force.

RCMP n abbr = Royal Canadian Mounted Police.

RCN n abbr = Royal Canadian Navy.

RD abbr (US POST) = rural delivery.

Rd abbr = **road**.

R&D n abbr (= research and development) R-D f.

RDC n abbr (Brit) = rural district council.

RE n abbr (Brit) = religious education; (Brit MIL) = Royal Engineers.

re [riː] prep concernant.

reach [riːtʃ] n portée f, atteinte f; (of river etc) étendue f ♦ vt atteindre, arriver à ♦ vi s'étendre; (stretch out hand): **to ~ up/down/out** etc (for sth) lever/baisser/allonger etc le bras (pour prendre qch); **to ~ sb by phone** joindre qn par téléphone; **out of/within ~** (object) hors de/à portée; **within easy ~ (of)** (place) à proximité (de), proche (de).

react [riː'ækt] vi réagir.

reaction [riː'ækʃən] n réaction f.

reactionary [riː'ækʃənrɪ] a, n réactionnaire (m/f).

reactor [riː'æktə*] n réacteur m.

read, pt, pp read [riːd, rɛd] vi lire ♦ vt lire; (understand) comprendre, interpréter; (study) étudier; (subj: instrument etc) indiquer, marquer; **to take sth as read** (fig) considérer qch comme accepté; **do you ~ me?** (TEL) est-ce que vous me recevez?

read out vt lire à haute voix.

read over vt relire.

read through vt (quickly) parcourir; (thoroughly) lire jusqu'au bout.

read up vt, **read up on** vt fus étudier.

readable ['riːdəbl] a facile or agréable à lire.

reader ['riːdə*] n lecteur/trice; (book) livre m de lecture; (Brit: at university) maître m de conférences.

readership ['riːdəʃɪp] n (of paper etc) (nombre m de) lecteurs mpl.

readily ['rɛdɪlɪ] ad volontiers, avec empressement; (easily) facilement.

readiness ['rɛdɪnɪs] n empressement m; **in ~** (prepared) prêt(e).

reading ['riːdɪŋ] n lecture f; (understanding) interprétation f; (on instrument) indications fpl.

reading lamp n lampe f de bureau.

reading room n salle f de lecture.

readjust [riːə'dʒʌst] vt rajuster; (instrument) régler de nouveau ♦ vi (person): **to ~ (to)** se réadapter (à).

ready ['rɛdɪ] a prêt(e); (willing) prêt, disposé(e); (quick) prompt(e); (available) disponible ♦ n: **at the ~** (MIL) prêt à faire feu; (fig) tout(e) prêt(e); **~ for use** prêt à

l'emploi; **to be ~ to do sth** être prêt à faire qch; **to get ~** *vi* se préparer ♦ *vt* préparer.
ready cash *n* (argent *m*) liquide *m*.
ready-made ['rɛdɪ'meɪd] *a* tout(e) fait(e).
ready-mix ['rɛdɪmɪks] *n* (*for cakes etc*) préparation *f* en sachet.
ready reckoner *n* (*Brit*) barème *m*.
ready-to-wear ['rɛdɪtə'wɛə*] *a* (en) prêt-à-porter.
reagent [ri:'eɪdʒənt] *n* réactif *m*.
real [rɪəl] *a* réel(le); (*genuine*) véritable; (*proper*) vrai(e) ♦ *ad* (*US col*: *very*) vraiment; **in ~ life** dans la réalité.
real estate *n* biens fonciers *or* immobiliers.
realism ['rɪəlɪzəm] *n* réalisme *m*.
realist ['rɪəlɪst] *n* réaliste *m/f*.
realistic [rɪə'lɪstɪk] *a* réaliste.
reality [ri:'ælɪtɪ] *n* réalité *f*; **in ~** en réalité, en fait.
realization [rɪəlaɪ'zeɪʃən] *n* prise *f* de conscience; réalisation *f*.
realize ['rɪəlaɪz] *vt* (*understand*) se rendre compte de, prendre conscience de; (*a project*, COMM: *asset*) réaliser.
really ['rɪəlɪ] *ad* vraiment.
realm [rɛlm] *n* royaume *m*.
real-time ['ri:ltaɪm] *a* (COMPUT) en temps réel.
realtor ['rɪəltɔ:*] *n* (*US*) agent immobilier.
ream [ri:m] *n* rame *f* (*de papier*); **~s** (*fig*: *col*) des pages et des pages.
reap [ri:p] *vt* moissonner; (*fig*) récolter.
reaper ['ri:pə*] *n* (*machine*) moissonneuse *f*.
reappear [ri:ə'pɪə*] *vi* réapparaître, reparaître.
reappearance [ri:ə'pɪərəns] *n* réapparition *f*.
reapply [ri:ə'plaɪ] *vi*: **to ~ for** faire une nouvelle demande d'emploi concernant; reposer sa candidature à.
reappraisal [ri:ə'preɪzl] *n* réévaluation *f*.
rear [rɪə*] *a* de derrière, arrière *inv*; (AUT: *wheel etc*) arrière ♦ *n* arrière *m*, derrière *m* ♦ *vt* (*cattle*, *family*) élever ♦ *vi* (*also*: **~ up**: *animal*) se cabrer.
rear-engined ['rɪər'ɛndʒɪnd] *a* (AUT) avec moteur à l'arrière.
rearguard ['rɪəgɑ:d] *n* arrière-garde *f*.
rearm [ri:'ɑ:m] *vt*, *vi* réarmer.
rearmament [ri:'ɑ:məmənt] *n* réarmement *m*.
rearrange [ri:ə'reɪndʒ] *vt* réarranger.
rear-view ['rɪəvju:]: **~ mirror** *n* (AUT) rétroviseur *m*.
reason ['ri:zn] *n* raison *f* ♦ *vi*: **to ~ with sb** raisonner qn, faire entendre raison à qn; **the ~ for/why** la raison de/pour laquelle; **to have ~ to think** avoir lieu de penser; **it stands to ~ that** il va sans dire que; **she claims with good ~ that ...** elle affirme à juste titre que ...; **all the more ~ why** raison de plus pour + *infinitive or* pour que + *sub*.
reasonable ['ri:znəbl] *a* raisonnable; (*not bad*) acceptable.
reasonably ['ri:znəblɪ] *ad* (*to behave*) raisonnablement; (*fairly*) assez; **one can ~ assume that ...** on est fondé à *or* il est permis de supposer que ....
reasoned ['ri:znd] *a* (*argument*) raisonné(e).
reasoning ['ri:znɪŋ] *n* raisonnement *m*.
reassemble [ri:ə'sɛmbl] *vt* rassembler; (*ma-*

chine) remonter.
reassert [ri:ə'sɜ:t] *vt* réaffirmer.
reassurance [ri:ə'ʃuərəns] *n* assurance *f*, garantie *f*; (*comfort*) réconfort *m*.
reassure [ri:ə'ʃuə*] *vt* rassurer; **to ~ sb of** donner à qn l'assurance répétée de.
reassuring [ri:ə'ʃuərɪŋ] *a* rassurant(e).
reawakening [ri:ə'weɪknɪŋ] *n* réveil *m*.
rebate ['ri:beɪt] *n* (*on product*) rabais *m*; (*on tax etc*) dégrèvement *m*; (*repayment*) remboursement *m*.
rebel *n* ['rɛbl] rebelle *m/f* ♦ *vi* [rɪ'bɛl] se rebeller, se révolter.
rebellion [rɪ'bɛljən] *n* rébellion *f*, révolte *f*.
rebellious [rɪ'bɛljəs] *a* rebelle.
rebirth [ri:'bɜ:θ] *n* renaissance *f*.
rebound *vi* [rɪ'baund] (*ball*) rebondir ♦ *n* ['ri:baund] rebond *m*.
rebuff [rɪ'bʌf] *n* rebuffade *f* ♦ *vt* repousser.
rebuild [ri:'bɪld] *vt irg* reconstruire.
rebuke [rɪ'bju:k] *n* réprimande *f*, reproche *m* ♦ *vt* réprimander.
rebut [rɪ'bʌt] *vt* réfuter.
rebuttal [rɪ'bʌtl] *n* réfutation *f*.
recalcitrant [rɪ'kælsɪtrənt] *a* récalcitrant(e).
recall [rɪ'kɔ:l] *vt* rappeler; (*remember*) se rappeler, se souvenir de ♦ *n* rappel *m*; **beyond ~** *a* irrévocable.
recant [rɪ'kænt] *vi* se rétracter; (REL) abjurer.
recap ['ri:kæp] *n* récapitulation *f* ♦ *vt*, *vi* récapituler.
recapture [ri:'kæptʃə*] *vt* reprendre; (*atmosphere*) recréer.
recd. *abbr* = *received*.
recede [rɪ'si:d] *vi* s'éloigner; reculer; redescendre.
receding [rɪ'si:dɪŋ] *a* (*forehead*, *chin*) fuyant(e); **~ hairline** front dégarni.
receipt [rɪ'si:t] *n* (*document*) reçu *m*; (*for parcel etc*) accusé *m* de réception; (*act of receiving*) réception *f*; **~s** *npl* (COMM) recettes *fpl*; **to acknowledge ~ of** accuser réception de; **we are in ~ of ...** nous avons reçu ....
receivable [rɪ'si:vəbl] *a* (COMM) recevable; (*owing*) à recevoir.
receive [rɪ'si:v] *vt* recevoir; (*guest*) recevoir, accueillir; **"~d with thanks"** (COMM) "pour acquit".
receiver [rɪ'si:və*] *n* (TEL) récepteur *m*, combiné *m*; (RADIO) récepteur; (*of stolen goods*) receleur *m*; (COMM) administrateur *m* judiciaire.
recent ['ri:snt] *a* récent(e); **in ~ years** au cours de ces dernières années.
recently ['ri:sntlɪ] *ad* récemment; **as ~ as** pas plus tard que; **until ~** jusqu'à il y a peu de temps encore.
receptacle [rɪ'sɛptɪkl] *n* récipient *m*.
reception [rɪ'sɛpʃən] *n* réception *f*; (*welcome*) accueil *m*, réception.
reception centre *n* (*Brit*) centre *m* d'accueil.
reception desk *n* réception *f*.
receptionist [rɪ'sɛpʃənɪst] *n* réceptionniste *m/f*.
receptive [rɪ'sɛptɪv] *a* réceptif(ive).
recess [rɪ'sɛs] *n* (*in room*) renfoncement *m*; (*for bed*) alcôve *f*; (*secret place*) recoin *m*;

(POL etc: holiday) vacances fpl; (US: LAW: short break) suspension f d'audience; (SCOL: esp US) récréation f.

recession [rɪ'sɛʃən] n (ECON) récession f.

recharge [ri:'tʃɑːdʒ] vt (battery) recharger.

rechargeable [ri:'tʃɑːdʒəbl] a rechargeable.

recipe ['rɛsɪpɪ] n recette f.

recipient [rɪ'sɪpɪənt] n bénéficiaire m/f; (of letter) destinataire m/f.

reciprocal [rɪ'sɪprəkl] a réciproque.

reciprocate [rɪ'sɪprəkeɪt] vt retourner, offrir en retour ♦ vi en faire autant.

recital [rɪ'saɪtl] n récital m.

recite [rɪ'saɪt] vt (poem) réciter; (complaints etc) énumérer.

reckless ['rɛkləs] a (driver etc) imprudent(e); (spender etc) insouciant(e).

recklessly ['rɛkləslɪ] ad imprudemment; avec insouciance.

reckon ['rɛkən] vt (count) calculer, compter; (consider) considérer, estimer; (think): **I ~ (that)** ... je pense (que) ..., j'estime (que) ... ♦ vi: **he is somebody to be ~ed with** il ne faut pas le sous-estimer; **to ~ without sb/ sth** ne pas tenir compte de qn/qch.

reckon on vt fus compter sur, s'attendre à.

reckoning ['rɛknɪŋ] n compte m, calcul m; estimation f; **the day of ~** le jour du Jugement.

reclaim [rɪ'kleɪm] vt (land) amender; (: from sea) assécher; (: from forest) défricher; (demand back) réclamer (le remboursement or la restitution de).

reclamation [rɛklə'meɪʃən] n (of land) amendement m; assèchement m; défrichement m.

recline [rɪ'klaɪn] vi être allongé(e) or étendu(e).

reclining [rɪ'klaɪnɪŋ] a (seat) à dossier réglable.

recluse [rɪ'kluːs] n reclus/e, ermite m.

recognition [rɛkəg'nɪʃən] n reconnaissance f; **in ~ of** en reconnaissance de; **to gain ~** être reconnu(e); **transformed beyond ~** méconnaissable.

recognizable ['rɛkəgnaɪzəbl] a: **~ (by)** reconnaissable (à).

recognize ['rɛkəgnaɪz] vt: **to ~ (by/as)** reconnaître (à/comme étant).

recoil [rɪ'kɔɪl] vi (person): **to ~ (from)** reculer (devant) ♦ n (of gun) recul m.

recollect [rɛkə'lɛkt] vt se rappeler, se souvenir de.

recollection [rɛkə'lɛkʃən] n souvenir m; **to the best of my ~** autant que je m'en souvienne.

recommend [rɛkə'mɛnd] vt recommander; **she has a lot to ~ her** elle a beaucoup de choses en sa faveur.

recommendation [rɛkəmɛn'deɪʃən] n recommandation f.

recommended retail price (RRP) n (Brit) prix conseillé.

recompense ['rɛkəmpɛns] vt récompenser; (compensate) dédommager ♦ n récompense f; dédommagement m.

reconcilable ['rɛkənsaɪləbl] a (ideas) conciliable.

reconcile ['rɛkənsaɪl] vt (two people)

réconcilier; (two facts) concilier, accorder; **to ~ o.s. to** se résigner à.

reconciliation [rɛkənsɪlɪ'eɪʃən] n réconciliation f; conciliation f.

recondite [rɪ'kɔndaɪt] a abstrus(e), obscur(e).

recondition [ri:kən'dɪʃən] vt remettre à neuf; réviser entièrement.

reconnaissance [rɪ'kɔnɪsns] n (MIL) reconnaissance f.

reconnoitre, (US) **reconnoiter** [rɛkə'nɔɪtə*] (MIL) vt reconnaître ♦ vi faire une reconnaissance.

reconsider [ri:kən'sɪdə*] vt reconsidérer.

reconstitute [ri:'kɔnstɪtjuːt] vt reconstituer.

reconstruct [ri:kən'strʌkt] vt (building) reconstruire; (crime) reconstituer.

reconstruction [ri:kən'strʌkʃən] n reconstruction f; reconstitution f.

record n ['rɛkɔːd] rapport m, récit m; (of meeting etc) procès-verbal m; (register) registre m; (file) dossier m; (COMPUT) article m; (also: **police ~**) casier m judiciaire; (MUS: disc) disque m; (SPORT) record m ♦ vt [rɪ'kɔːd] (set down) noter; (relate) rapporter; (MUS: song etc) enregistrer; **in ~ time** dans un temps record inv; **public ~s** archives fpl; **to keep a ~ of** noter; **to keep the ~ straight** (fig) mettre les choses au point; **he is on ~ as saying that** ... il a déclaré en public que ...; **Italy's excellent ~** les excellents résultats obtenus par l'Italie; **off the ~** a officieux(euse) ♦ ad officieusement.

record card n (in file) fiche f.

recorded delivery letter n (Brit POST) ≈ lettre recommandée.

recorder [rɪ'kɔːdə*] n (LAW) avocat nommé à la fonction de juge; (MUS) flûte f à bec.

record holder n (SPORT) détenteur/trice du record.

recording [rɪ'kɔːdɪŋ] n (MUS) enregistrement m.

recording studio n studio m d'enregistrement.

record library n discothèque f.

record player n électrophone m.

recount [rɪ'kaunt] vt raconter.

re-count n ['ri:kaunt] (POL: of votes) nouveau décompte (des suffrages) ♦ vt [ri:'kaunt] recompter.

recoup [rɪ'kuːp] vt: **to ~ one's losses** récupérer ce qu'on a perdu, se refaire.

recourse [rɪ'kɔːs] n recours m; expédient m; **to have ~ to** recourir à, avoir recours à.

recover [rɪ'kʌvə*] vt récupérer ♦ vi (from illness) se rétablir; (from shock) se remettre; (country) se redresser.

re-cover [ri:'kʌvə*] vt (chair etc) recouvrir.

recovery [rɪ'kʌvərɪ] n récupération f; rétablissement m; redressement m.

recreate [ri:krɪ'eɪt] vt recréer.

recreation [rɛkrɪ'eɪʃən] n récréation f, détente f.

recreational [rɛkrɪ'eɪʃənl] a pour la détente, récréatif(ive).

recreational vehicle (RV) n (US) camping-car m.

recrimination [rɪkrɪmɪ'neɪʃən] n récrimination f.

recruit [rɪ'kruːt] n recrue f ♦ vt recruter.

recruiting office [rɪ'kruːtɪŋ-] n bureau m de

recrutement.
recruitment [rɪ'kru:tmənt] n recrutement m.
rectangle ['rɛktæŋgl] n rectangle m.
rectangular [rɛk'tæŋgjulə*] a rectangulaire.
rectify ['rɛktɪfaɪ] vt (error) rectifier, corriger; (omission) réparer.
rector ['rɛktə*] n (REL) pasteur m; (in Scottish universities) personnalité élue par les étudiants pour les représenter.
rectory ['rɛktərɪ] n presbytère m.
rectum ['rɛktəm] n (ANAT) rectum m.
recuperate [rɪ'kju:pəreɪt] vi (from illness) se rétablir.
recur [rɪ'kə:*] vi se reproduire; (idea, opportunity) se retrouver; (symptoms) réapparaître.
recurrence [rɪ'kə:rns] n répétition f; réapparition f.
recurrent [rɪ'kə:rnt] a périodique, fréquent(e).
recurring [rɪ'kə:rɪŋ] a (MATH) périodique.
red [rɛd] n rouge m; (POL: pej) rouge m/f ♦ a rouge; **in the ~** (account) à découvert; (business) en déficit.
red carpet treatment n réception f en grande pompe.
Red Cross n Croix-Rouge f.
redcurrant ['rɛdkʌrənt] n groseille f (rouge).
redden ['rɛdn] vt, vi rougir.
reddish ['rɛdɪʃ] a rougeâtre; (hair) plutôt roux(rousse).
redecorate [ri:'dɛkəreɪt] vt refaire à neuf, repeindre et retapisser.
redecoration [ri:dɛkə'reɪʃən] n remise f à neuf.
redeem [rɪ'di:m] vt (debt) rembourser; (sth in pawn) dégager; (fig, also REL) racheter.
redeemable [rɪ'di:məbl] a rachetable; remboursable, amortissable.
redeeming [rɪ'di:mɪŋ] a (feature) qui sauve, qui rachète (le reste).
redeploy [ri:dɪ'plɔɪ] vt (MIL) redéployer; (staff, resources) reconvertir.
redeployment [ri:dɪ'plɔɪmənt] n redéploiement m; reconversion f.
redevelop [ri:dɪ'vɛləp] vt rénover.
redevelopment [ri:dɪ'vɛləpmənt] n rénovation f.
red-haired [rɛd'hɛəd] a roux(rousse).
red-handed [rɛd'hændɪd] a: **to be caught ~** être pris(e) en flagrant délit or la main dans le sac.
redhead ['rɛdhɛd] n roux/rousse.
red herring n (fig) diversion f, fausse piste.
red-hot [rɛd'hɔt] a chauffé(e) au rouge, brûlant(e).
redirect [ri:daɪ'rɛkt] vt (mail) faire suivre.
redistribute [ri:dɪ'strɪbju:t] vt redistribuer.
red-letter day ['rɛdlɛtə-] n grand jour, jour mémorable.
red light n: **to go through a ~** (AUT) brûler un feu rouge.
red-light district n quartier réservé.
redness ['rɛdnɪs] n rougeur f; (of hair) rousseur f.
redo [ri:'du:] vt irg refaire.
redolent ['rɛdələnt] a: **~ of** qui sent; (fig) qui évoque.
redouble [ri:'dʌbl] vt: **to ~ one's efforts** redoubler d'efforts.

redraft [ri:'drɑ:ft] vt remanier.
redress [rɪ'drɛs] n réparation f ♦ vt redresser; **to ~ the balance** rétablir l'équilibre.
Red Sea n: **the ~** la mer Rouge.
redskin ['rɛdskɪn] n Peau-Rouge m/f.
red tape n (fig) paperasserie (administrative).
reduce [rɪ'dju:s] vt réduire; (lower) abaisser; **"~ speed now"** (AUT) "ralentir"; **to ~ sth by/to** réduire qch de/à; **to ~ sb to tears** faire pleurer qn.
reduced [rɪ'dju:st] a réduit(e); **"greatly ~ prices"** "gros rabais"; **at a ~ price** (goods) au rabais; (ticket etc) à prix réduit.
reduction [rɪ'dʌkʃən] n réduction f; (of price) baisse f; (discount) rabais m; réduction.
redundancy [rɪ'dʌndənsɪ] n (Brit) licenciement m, mise f au chômage; **compulsory ~** licenciement; **voluntary ~** départ m volontaire.
redundancy payment n (Brit) indemnité f de licenciement.
redundant [rɪ'dʌndnt] a (Brit: worker) licencié(e), mis(e) au chômage; (detail, object) superflu(e); **to be made ~** (worker) être licencié, être mis au chômage.
reed [ri:d] n (BOT) roseau m; (MUS: of clarinet etc) anche f.
reedy ['ri:dɪ] a (voice, instrument) ténu(e).
reef [ri:f] n (at sea) récif m, écueil m.
reek [ri:k] vi: **to ~ (of)** puer, empester.
reel [ri:l] n bobine f; (TECH) dévidoir m; (FISHING) moulinet m; (CINEMA) bande f ♦ vt (TECH) bobiner; (also: **~ up**) enrouler ♦ vi (sway) chanceler; **my head is ~ing** j'ai la tête qui tourne.
reel off vt (say) énumérer, débiter.
re-election [ri:ɪ'lɛkʃən] n réélection f.
re-enter [ri:'ɛntə*] vt (also SPACE) rentrer dans.
re-entry [ri:'ɛntrɪ] n (also SPACE) rentrée f.
re-export vt ['ri:ɪks'pɔ:t] réexporter ♦ n [ri:'ɛkspɔ:t] marchandise réexportée; (act) réexportation f.
ref [rɛf] n abbr (col: = referee) arbitre m.
ref. abbr (COMM: = with reference to) réf.
refectory [rɪ'fɛktərɪ] n réfectoire m.
refer [rɪ'fə:*] vt: **to ~ sth to** (dispute, decision) soumettre qch à; **to ~ sb to** (inquirer: for information) adresser or envoyer qn à; (reader: to text) renvoyer qn à; **he ~red me to the manager** il m'a dit de m'adresser au directeur.
refer to vt fus (allude to) parler de, faire allusion à; (apply to) s'appliquer à; (consult) se reporter à; **~ring to your letter** (COMM) en réponse à votre lettre.
referee [rɛfə'ri:] n arbitre m; (TENNIS) juge-arbitre m; (Brit: for job application) répondant/e ♦ vt arbitrer.
reference ['rɛfrəns] n référence f, renvoi m; (mention) allusion f, mention f; (for job application: letter) références; lettre f de recommandation; (: person) répondant/e; **with ~ to** en ce qui concerne; (COMM: in letter) me référant à; **"please quote this ~"** (COMM) "prière de rappeler cette référence".
reference book n ouvrage m de référence.
reference number n (COMM) numéro m de

référence.

referendum, pl **referenda** [rɛfə'rɛndəm. -də] n référendum m.

refill vt [ri:'fɪl] remplir à nouveau; (pen, lighter etc) recharger ♦ n ['ri:fɪl] (for pen etc) recharge f.

refine [rɪ'faɪn] vt (sugar, oil) raffiner; (taste) affiner.

refined [rɪ'faɪnd] a (person, taste) raffiné(e).

refinement [rɪ'faɪnmənt] n (of person) raffinement m.

refinery [rɪ'faɪnərɪ] n raffinerie f.

refit (NAUT) ['ri:fɪt] n remise f en état ♦ [ri:'fɪt] vt remettre en état.

reflate [ri:'fleɪt] vt (economy) relancer.

reflation [ri:'fleɪʃən] n relance f.

reflationary [ri:'fleɪʃənrɪ] a de relance.

reflect [rɪ'flɛkt] vt (light, image) réfléchir, refléter; (fig) refléter ♦ vi (think) réfléchir, méditer.

reflect on vt fus (discredit) porter atteinte à, faire tort à.

reflection [rɪ'flɛkʃən] n réflexion f; (image) reflet m; (criticism): ~ **on** critique f de; atteinte f à; **on** ~ réflexion faite.

reflector [rɪ'flɛktə*] n (also AUT) réflecteur m.

reflex ['ri:flɛks] a, n réflexe (m).

reflexive [rɪ'flɛksɪv] a (LING) réfléchi(e).

reform [rɪ'fɔ:m] n réforme f ♦ vt réformer.

reformat [ri:'fɔ:mæt] vt (COMPUT) reformater.

Reformation [rɛfə'meɪʃən] n: **the** ~ la Réforme.

reformatory [rɪ'fɔ:mətərɪ] n (US) centre m d'éducation surveillée.

reformed [rɪ'fɔ:md] a amendé(e), assagi(e).

reformer [rɪ'fɔ:mə*] n réformateur/trice.

refrain [rɪ'freɪn] vi: **to** ~ **from doing** s'abstenir de faire ♦ n refrain m.

refresh [rɪ'frɛʃ] vt rafraîchir; (subj: food, sleep etc) redonner des forces à.

refresher course [rɪ'frɛʃə-] n (Brit) cours m de recyclage.

refreshing [rɪ'frɛʃɪŋ] a rafraîchissant(e); (sleep) réparateur(trice); (fact, idea etc) qui réjouit par son originalité or sa rareté.

refreshment [rɪ'frɛʃmənt] n: **for some** ~ (eating) pour se restaurer or sustenter; **in need of** ~ (resting etc) ayant besoin de refaire ses forces; ~**(s)** rafraîchissement(s) m(pl).

refrigeration [rɪfrɪdʒə'reɪʃən] n réfrigération f.

refrigerator [rɪ'frɪdʒəreɪtə*] n réfrigérateur m, frigidaire m.

refuel [ri:'fjuəl] vt ravitailler en carburant ♦ vi se ravitailler en carburant.

refuge ['rɛfju:dʒ] n refuge m; **to take** ~ **in** se réfugier dans.

refugee [rɛfju'dʒi:] n réfugié/e.

refugee camp n camp m de réfugiés.

refund n ['ri:fʌnd] remboursement m ♦ vt [rɪ'fʌnd] rembourser.

refurbish [ri:'fɜ:bɪʃ] vt remettre à neuf.

refurnish [ri:'fɜ:nɪʃ] vt remeubler.

refusal [rɪ'fju:zəl] n refus m; **to have first** ~ **on sth** avoir droit de préemption sur qch.

refuse n ['rɛfju:s] ordures fpl, détritus mpl ♦ vt, vi [rɪ'fju:z] refuser; **to** ~ **to do sth** refuser de faire qch.

refuse collection n ramassage m d'ordures.

refuse collector n éboueur m.

refuse disposal n élimination f des ordures.

refute [rɪ'fju:t] vt réfuter.

regain [rɪ'geɪn] vt regagner; retrouver.

regal ['ri:gl] a royal(e).

regale [rɪ'geɪl] vt: **to** ~ **sb with sth** régaler qn de qch.

regalia [rɪ'geɪlɪə] n insignes mpl de la royauté.

regard [rɪ'ga:d] n respect m, estime f, considération f ♦ vt considérer; **to give one's** ~**s to** faire ses amitiés à; **"with kindest** ~**s"** "bien amicalement"; **as** ~**s, with** ~ **to** en ce qui concerne.

regarding [rɪ'ga:dɪŋ] prep en ce qui concerne.

regardless [rɪ'ga:dlɪs] ad quand même; ~ **of** sans se soucier de.

regatta [rɪ'gætə] n régate f.

regency ['ri:dʒənsɪ] n régence f.

regenerate [rɪ'dʒɛnəreɪt] vt régénérer ♦ vi se régénérer.

regent ['ri:dʒənt] n régent/e.

régime [reɪ'ʒi:m] n régime m.

regiment n ['rɛdʒɪmənt] régiment m ♦ vt ['rɛdʒɪmɛnt] imposer une discipline trop stricte à.

regimental [rɛdʒɪ'mɛntl] a d'un or du régiment.

regimentation [rɛdʒɪmɛn'teɪʃən] n réglementation excessive.

region ['ri:dʒən] n région f; **in the** ~ **of** (fig) aux alentours de.

regional ['ri:dʒənl] a régional(e).

regional development n aménagement m du territoire.

register ['rɛdʒɪstə*] n registre m; (also: **electoral** ~) liste électorale ♦ vt enregistrer, inscrire; (birth) déclarer; (vehicle) immatriculer; (luggage) enregistrer; (letter) envoyer en recommandé; (subj: instrument) marquer ♦ vi se faire inscrire; (at hotel) signer le registre; (make impression) être (bien) compris(e); **to** ~ **for a course** s'inscrire à un cours; **to** ~ **a protest** protester.

registered ['rɛdʒɪstəd] a (design) déposé(e); (Brit: letter) recommandé(e); (student, voter) inscrit(e).

registered company n société immatriculée.

registered nurse n (US) infirmier/ière diplômé(e) d'Etat.

registered office n siège social.

registered trademark n marque déposée.

registrar ['rɛdʒɪstrɑ:*] n officier m de l'état civil; secrétaire (général).

registration [rɛdʒɪs'treɪʃən] n (act) enregistrement m; inscription f; (AUT: also: ~ **number**) numéro m d'immatriculation.

registry ['rɛdʒɪstrɪ] n bureau m de l'enregistrement.

registry office n (Brit) bureau m de l'état civil; **to get married in a** ~ ≈ se marier à la mairie.

regret [rɪ'grɛt] n regret m ♦ vt regretter; **to** ~ **that** regretter que + sub; **we** ~ **to inform you that ...** nous sommes au regret de vous informer que ....

regretfully [rɪ'grɛtfəlɪ] ad à or avec regret.

regrettable [rɪ'grɛtəbl] a regrettable, fâcheux(euse).

regrettably [rɪ'grɛtəblɪ] ad (drunk, late) fâcheusement; ~, **he** ... malheureusement, il

regroup [ri:'gru:p] *vt* regrouper ♦ *vi* se regrouper.

regt *abbr* = **regiment**.

regular ['regjulə*] *a* régulier(ière); (*usual*) habituel(le), normal(e); (*listener, reader*) fidèle; (*soldier*) de métier; (*COMM: size*) ordinaire ♦ *n* (*client etc*) habitué/e.

regularity [regju'læriti] *n* régularité *f*.

regularly ['regjuləlı] *ad* régulièrement.

regulate ['regjuleit] *vt* régler.

regulation [regju'leiʃən] *n* (*rule*) règlement *m*; (*adjustment*) réglage *m* ♦ *cpd* réglementaire.

rehabilitation ['ri:əbili'teiʃən] *n* (*of offender*) réhabilitation *f*; (*of disabled*) rééducation *f*, réadaptation *f*.

rehash [ri:'hæʃ] *vt* (*col*) remanier.

rehearsal [ri'hə:səl] *n* répétition *f*; **dress ~** (*répétition*) générale.

rehearse [ri'hə:s] *vt* répéter.

rehouse [ri:'hauz] *vt* reloger.

reign [rein] *n* règne *m* ♦ *vi* régner.

reigning ['reiniŋ] *a* (*monarch*) régnant(e); (*champion*) actuel(le).

reimburse [ri:im'bə:s] *vt* rembourser.

rein [rein] *n* (*for horse*) rêne *f*; **to give sb free ~** (*fig*) donner carte blanche à qn.

reincarnation [ri:inkɑ:'neiʃən] *n* réincarnation *f*.

reindeer ['reindiə*] *n* (*pl inv*) renne *m*.

reinforce [ri:in'fɔ:s] *vt* renforcer.

reinforced concrete *n* béton armé.

reinforcement [ri:in'fɔ:smənt] *n* (*action*) renforcement *m*; **~s** *npl* (*MIL*) renfort(s) *m(pl)*.

reinstate [ri:in'steit] *vt* rétablir, réintégrer.

reinstatement [ri:in'steitmənt] *n* réintégration *f*.

reissue [ri:'ıʃju:] *vt* (*book*) rééditer; (*film*) ressortir.

reiterate [ri:'ıtəreit] *vt* réitérer, répéter.

reject *n* ['ri:dʒɛkt] (*COMM*) article *m* de rebut ♦ *vt* [ri'dʒɛkt] refuser; (*COMM: goods*) mettre au rebut; (*idea*) rejeter.

rejection [ri'dʒɛkʃən] *n* rejet *m*, refus *m*.

rejoice [ri'dʒɔɪs] *vi*: **to ~ (at** *or* **over)** se réjouir (de).

rejoinder [ri'dʒɔɪndə*] *n* (*retort*) réplique *f*.

rejuvenate [ri'dʒu:vəneit] *vt* rajeunir.

rekindle [ri:'kindl] *vt* rallumer; (*fig*) raviver.

relapse [ri'læps] *n* (*MED*) rechute *f*.

relate [ri'leit] *vt* (*tell*) raconter; (*connect*) établir un rapport entre ♦ *vi*: **to ~ to** (*connect*) se rapporter à; (*interact*) établir un rapport *or* une entente avec.

related [ri'leitid] *a* apparenté(e).

relating [ri'leitiŋ]: **~ to** *prep* concernant.

relation [ri'leiʃən] *n* (*person*) parent/e; (*link*) rapport *m*, lien *m*; **diplomatic/international ~s** relations diplomatiques/internationales; **in ~ to** en ce qui concerne; par rapport à; **to bear no ~ to** être sans rapport avec.

relationship [ri'leiʃənʃip] *n* rapport *m*, lien *m*; (*personal ties*) relations *fpl*, rapports; (*also*: **family ~**) lien de parenté; (*affair*) liaison *f*; **they have a good ~** ils s'entendent bien.

relative ['relətıv] *n* parent/e ♦ *a* relatif(ive); (*respective*) respectif(ive); **all her ~s** toute sa famille.

relatively ['relətıvlı] *ad* relativement.

relax [ri'læks] *vi* se relâcher; (*person: unwind*) se détendre; (*calm down*) se calmer ♦ *vt* relâcher; (*mind, person*) détendre.

relaxation [ri:læk'seiʃən] *n* relâchement *m*; détente *f*; (*entertainment*) distraction *f*.

relaxed [ri'lækst] *a* relâché(e); détendu(e).

relaxing [ri'læksiŋ] *a* délassant(e).

relay ['ri:lei] *n* (*SPORT*) course *f* de relais ♦ *vt* (*message*) retransmettre, relayer.

release [ri'li:s] *n* (*from prison, obligation*) libération *f*; (*of gas etc*) émission *f*; (*of film etc*) sortie *f*; (*record*) disque *m*; (*device*) déclencheur *m* ♦ *vt* (*prisoner*) libérer; (*book, film*) sortir; (*report, news*) rendre public, publier; (*gas etc*) émettre, dégager; (*free: from wreckage etc*) dégager; (*TECH: catch, spring etc*) déclencher; (*let go*) relâcher; lâcher; desserrer; **to ~ one's grip** *or* **hold** lâcher prise; **to ~ the clutch** (*AUT*) débrayer.

relegate ['relageit] *vt* reléguer; (*SPORT*): **to be ~d** descendre dans une division inférieure.

relent [ri'lent] *vi* se laisser fléchir.

relentless [ri'lentlis] *a* implacable.

relevance ['relavəns] *n* pertinence *f*; **~ of sth to sth** rapport *m* entre qch et qch.

relevant ['relavənt] *a* approprié(e); (*fact*) significatif(ive); (*information*) utile, pertinent(e); **~ to** ayant rapport à, approprié à.

reliability [rilaiə'biliti] *n* sérieux *m*; fiabilité *f*.

reliable [ri'laiəbl] *a* (*person, firm*) sérieux(euse), fiable; (*method, machine*) fiable.

reliably [ri'laiəbli] *ad*: **to be ~ informed** savoir de source sûre.

reliance [ri'laiəns] *n*: **~ (on)** (*trust*) confiance *f* (en); (*dependence*) besoin *m* (de), dépendance *f* (de).

reliant [ri'laiənt] *a*: **to be ~ on sth/sb** dépendre de qch/qn.

relic ['relik] *n* (*REL*) relique *f*; (*of the past*) vestige *m*.

relief [ri'li:f] *n* (*from pain, anxiety*) soulagement *m*; (*help, supplies*) secours *m(pl)*; (*of guard*) relève *f*; (*ART, GEO*) relief *m*; **by way of light ~** pour faire diversion.

relief map *n* carte *f* en relief.

relief road *n* (*Brit*) route *f* de délestage.

relieve [ri'li:v] *vt* (*pain, patient*) soulager; (*bring help*) secourir; (*take over from: gen*) relayer; (*: guard*) relever; **to ~ sb of sth** débarrasser qn de qch; **to ~ sb of his command** (*MIL*) relever qn de ses fonctions; **to ~ o.s.** (*euphemism*) se soulager, faire ses besoins.

religion [ri'lidʒən] *n* religion *f*.

religious [ri'lidʒəs] *a* religieux(euse); (*book*) de piété.

reline [ri:'lain] *vt* (*brakes*) refaire la garniture de.

relinquish [ri'liŋkwiʃ] *vt* abandonner; (*plan, habit*) renoncer à.

relish ['reliʃ] *n* (*CULIN*) condiment *m*; (*enjoyment*) délectation *f* ♦ *vt* (*food etc*)

savourer; **to ~ doing** se délecter à faire.
relive |ri:'lɪv| vt revivre.
reload |ri:'ləud| vt recharger.
relocate |ri:ləu'keɪt| vt (business) transférer ♦ vi se transférer, s'installer or s'établir ailleurs; **to ~ in** (déménager et) s'installer or s'établir à, se transférer à.
reluctance |rɪ'lʌktəns| n répugnance f.
reluctant |rɪ'lʌktənt| a peu disposé(e), qui hésite; **to be ~ to do sth** hésiter à faire qch.
reluctantly |rɪ'lʌktəntlɪ| ad à contrecœur, sans enthousiasme.
rely |rɪ'laɪ|: **to ~ on** vt fus compter sur; (be dependent) dépendre de.
remain |rɪ'meɪn| vi rester; **to ~ silent** garder le silence; **I ~, yours faithfully** (Brit: in letters) je vous prie d'agréer, Monsieur (etc), l'assurance de mes sentiments distingués.
remainder |rɪ'meɪndə*| n reste m; (COMM) fin f de série.
remaining |rɪ'meɪnɪŋ| a qui reste.
remains |rɪ'meɪnz| npl restes mpl.
remand |rɪ'mɑ:nd| n: **on ~** en détention préventive ♦ vt: **to ~ in custody** écrouer; renvoyer en détention provisoire.
remand home n (Brit) centre m d'éducation surveillée.
remark |rɪ'mɑ:k| n remarque f, observation f ♦ vt (faire) remarquer, dire; (notice) remarquer; **to ~ on sth** faire une or des remarque(s) sur qch.
remarkable |rɪ'mɑ:kəbl| a remarquable.
remarry |ri:'mærɪ| vi se remarier.
remedial |rɪ'mi:dɪəl| a (tuition, classes) de rattrapage.
remedy |'rɛmədɪ| n: **~ (for)** remède m (contre or à) ♦ vt remédier à.
remember |rɪ'mɛmbə*| vt se rappeler, se souvenir de; **I ~ seeing it, I ~ having seen it** je me rappelle l'avoir vu or que je l'ai vu; **she ~ed to do it** elle a pensé à le faire; **~ me to your wife** rappelez-moi au bon souvenir de votre femme.
remembrance |rɪ'mɛmbrəns| n souvenir m; mémoire f.
remind |rɪ'maɪnd| vt: **to ~ sb of sth** rappeler qch à qn; **to ~ sb to do** faire penser à qn à faire, rappeler à qn qu'il doit faire; **that ~s me!** j'y pense!
reminder |rɪ'maɪndə*| n rappel m; (note etc) pense-bête m.
reminisce |rɛmɪ'nɪs| vi: **to ~ (about)** évoquer ses souvenirs (de).
reminiscences |rɛmɪ'nɪsnsɪz| npl réminiscences fpl, souvenirs mpl.
reminiscent |rɛmɪ'nɪsnt| a: **~ of** qui rappelle, qui fait penser à.
remiss |rɪ'mɪs| a négligent(e); **it was ~ of me** c'était une négligence de ma part.
remission |rɪ'mɪʃən| n rémission f; (of debt, sentence) remise f; (of fee) exemption f.
remit |rɪ'mɪt| vt (send: money) envoyer.
remittance |rɪ'mɪtns| n envoi m, paiement m.
remnant |'rɛmnənt| n reste m, restant m; **~s** npl (COMM) coupons mpl; fins fpl de série.
remonstrate |'rɛmənstreɪt| vi: **to ~ (with sb about sth)** se plaindre (à qn de qch).
remorse |rɪ'mɔ:s| n remords m.
remorseful |rɪ'mɔ:sful| a plein(e) de remords.

remorseless |rɪ'mɔ:slɪs| a (fig) impitoyable.
remote |rɪ'məut| a éloigné(e), lointain(e); (person) distant(e); **there is a ~ possibility that ...** il est tout juste possible que ....
remote control n télécommande f.
remote-controlled |rɪ'məutkən'trəuld| a téléguidé(e).
remotely |rɪ'məutlɪ| ad au loin; (slightly) très vaguement.
remoteness |rɪ'məutnɪs| n éloignement m.
remould |'ri:məuld| n (Brit: tyre) pneu rechapé.
removable |rɪ'mu:vəbl| a (detachable) amovible.
removal |rɪ'mu:vəl| n (taking away) enlèvement m; suppression f; (Brit: from house) déménagement m; (from office: dismissal) renvoi m; (MED) ablation f.
removal man n (Brit) déménageur m.
removal van n (Brit) camion m de déménagement.
remove |rɪ'mu:v| vt enlever, retirer; (employee) renvoyer; (stain) faire partir; (doubt, abuse) supprimer; **first cousin once ~d** cousin/e au deuxième degré.
remover |rɪ'mu:və*| n (for paint) décapant m; (for varnish) dissolvant m; **make-up ~** démaquillant m; **~s** npl (Brit: company) entreprise f de déménagement.
remunerate |rɪ'mju:nəreɪt| vt rémunérer.
remuneration |rɪmju:nə'reɪʃən| n rémunération f.
rename |ri:'neɪm| vt rebaptiser.
rend, pt, pp **rent** |rɛnd, rɛnt| vt déchirer.
render |'rɛndə*| vt rendre; (CULIN: fat) clarifier.
rendering |'rɛndərɪŋ| n (MUS etc) interprétation f.
rendez-vous |'rɔndɪvu:| n rendez-vous m inv ♦ vi opérer une jonction, se rejoindre; (spaceship) effectuer un rendez-vous (dans l'espace); **to ~ with sb** rejoindre qn.
renegade |'rɛnɪgeɪd| n rénégat/e.
renew |rɪ'nju:| vt renouveler; (negotiations) reprendre; (acquaintance) renouer.
renewal |rɪ'nju:əl| n renouvellement m; reprise f.
renounce |rɪ'nauns| vt renoncer à; (disown) renier.
renovate |'rɛnəveɪt| vt rénover; (work of art) restaurer.
renovation |rɛnə'veɪʃən| n rénovation f; restauration f.
renown |rɪ'naun| n renommée f.
renowned |rɪ'naund| a renommé(e).
rent |rɛnt| pt, pp of **rend** ♦ n loyer m ♦ vt louer; (car, TV) louer, prendre en location; (also: **~ out**: car, TV) louer, donner en location.
rental |'rɛntl| n (for television, car) (prix m de) location f.
renunciation |rɪnʌnsɪ'eɪʃən| n renonciation f; (self-denial) renoncement m.
reopen |ri:'əupən| vt rouvrir.
reopening |ri:'əupnɪŋ| n réouverture f.
reorder |ri:'ɔ:də*| vt commander de nouveau; (rearrange) réorganiser.
reorganize |ri:'ɔ:gənaɪz| vt réorganiser.
Rep. abbr (US POL) = **representative**, **re-**

publican.
rep [rɛp] *n abbr* (*COMM*) = **representative**; (*THEATRE*) = **repertory**.
repair [rɪ'pɛə*] *n* réparation *f* ♦ *vt* réparer; **in good/bad** ~ en bon/mauvais état; **under** ~ en réparation.
repair kit *n* trousse *f* de réparations.
repair man *n* réparateur *m*.
repair shop *n* (*AUT etc*) atelier *m* de réparations.
repartee [rɛpɑː'tiː] *n* repartie *f*.
repast [rɪ'pɑːst] *n* (*formal*) repas *m*.
repatriate [riː'pætrɪeɪt] *vt* rapatrier.
repay [riː'peɪ] *vt irg* (*money*, *creditor*) rembourser; (*sb's efforts*) récompenser.
repayment [riː'peɪmənt] *n* remboursement *m*; récompense *f*.
repeal [rɪ'piːl] *n* (*of law*) abrogation *f*; (*of sentence*) annulation *f* ♦ *vt* abroger; annuler.
repeat [rɪ'piːt] *n* (*RADIO*, *TV*) reprise *f* ♦ *vt* répéter; (*pattern*) reproduire; (*promise*, *attack*, *also COMM: order*) renouveler; (*SCOL: a class*) redoubler ♦ *vi* répéter.
repeatedly [rɪ'piːtɪdlɪ] *ad* souvent, à plusieurs reprises.
repel [rɪ'pɛl] *vt* repousser.
repellent [rɪ'pɛlənt] *a* repoussant(e) ♦ *n*: **insect** ~ insectifuge *m*; **moth** ~ produit *m* antimite(s).
repent [rɪ'pɛnt] *vi*: **to** ~ (**of**) se repentir (de).
repentance [rɪ'pɛntəns] *n* repentir *m*.
repercussion [riːpə'kʌʃən] *n* (*consequence*) répercussion *f*.
repertoire ['rɛpətwɑː*] *n* répertoire *m*.
repertory ['rɛpətərɪ] *n* (*also*: ~ **theatre**) théâtre *m* de répertoire.
repertory company *n* troupe théâtrale permanente.
repetition [rɛpɪ'tɪʃən] *n* répétition *f*.
repetitious [rɛpɪ'tɪʃəs] *a* (*speech*) plein(e) de redites.
repetitive [rɪ'pɛtɪtɪv] *a* (*movement*, *work*) répétitif(ive); (*speech*) plein(e) de redites.
replace [rɪ'pleɪs] *vt* (*put back*) remettre, replacer; (*take the place of*) remplacer; (*TEL*): "~ **the receiver**" "raccrochez".
replacement [rɪ'pleɪsmənt] *n* replacement *m*; remplacement *m*; (*person*) remplaçant/e.
replacement part *n* pièce *f* de rechange.
replay ['riːpleɪ] *n* (*of match*) match rejoué; (*of tape*, *film*) répétition *f*.
replenish [rɪ'plɛnɪʃ] *vt* (*glass*) remplir (de nouveau); (*stock etc*) réapprovisionner.
replete [rɪ'pliːt] *a* rempli(e); (*well-fed*): ~ (**with**) rassasié(e) (de).
replica ['rɛplɪkə] *n* réplique *f*, copie exacte.
reply [rɪ'plaɪ] *n* réponse *f* ♦ *vi* répondre; **in** ~ (**to**) en réponse (à); **there's no** ~ (*TEL*) ça ne répond pas.
reply coupon *n* coupon-réponse *m*.
report [rɪ'pɔːt] *n* rapport *m*; (*PRESS etc*) reportage *m*; (*Brit: also*: **school** ~) bulletin *m* (scolaire); (*of gun*) détonation *f* ♦ *vt* rapporter, faire un compte rendu de; (*PRESS etc*) faire un reportage sur; (*bring to notice: occurrence*: *person*) signaler; (: *person*) dénoncer ♦ *vi* (*make a report*): **to** ~ (**on**) faire un rapport (sur); (*for newspaper*) faire un reportage (sur); (*present o.s.*): **to** ~ (**to sb**)

se présenter (chez qn); **it is** ~**ed that** on dit *or* annonce que; **it is** ~**ed from Berlin that** on nous apprend de Berlin que.
report card *n* (*US*, *Scottish*) bulletin *m* (scolaire).
reportedly [rɪ'pɔːtɪdlɪ] *ad*: **she is** ~ **living in Spain** elle habiterait en Espagne; **he** ~ **ordered them to ...** il leur aurait ordonné de ....
reported speech *n* (*LING*) discours indirect.
reporter [rɪ'pɔːtə*] *n* reporter *m*.
repose [rɪ'pəuz] *n*: **in** ~ en *or* au repos.
repossess ['riːpə'zɛs] *vt* saisir.
reprehensible [rɛprɪ'hɛnsɪbl] *a* répréhensible.
represent [rɛprɪ'zɛnt] *vt* représenter; (*explain*): **to** ~ **to sb that** expliquer à qn que.
representation [rɛprɪzɛn'teɪʃən] *n* représentation *f*; ~**s** *npl* (*protest*) démarche *f*.
representative [rɛprɪ'zɛntətɪv] *n* représentant/e; (*COMM*) représentant/e (de commerce); (*US POL*) député *m* ♦ *a*: ~ (**of**) représentatif(ive) (de), caractéristique (de).
repress [rɪ'prɛs] *vt* réprimer.
repression [rɪ'prɛʃən] *n* répression *f*.
repressive [rɪ'prɛsɪv] *a* répressif(ive).
reprieve [rɪ'priːv] *n* (*LAW*) grâce *f*; (*fig*) sursis *m*, délai *m* ♦ *vt* gracier; accorder un sursis *or* un délai à.
reprimand ['rɛprɪmɑːnd] *n* réprimande *f* ♦ *vt* réprimander.
reprint *n* ['riːprɪnt] réimpression *f* ♦ *vt* [riː'prɪnt] réimprimer.
reprisal [rɪ'praɪzl] *n* représailles *fpl*; **to take** ~**s** user de représailles.
reproach [rɪ'prəutʃ] *n* reproche *m* ♦ *vt*: **to** ~ **sb with sth** reprocher qch à qn; **beyond** ~ irréprochable.
reproachful [rɪ'prəutʃful] *a* de reproche.
reproduce [riːprə'djuːs] *vt* reproduire ♦ *vi* se reproduire.
reproduction [riːprə'dʌkʃən] *n* reproduction *f*.
reproductive [riːprə'dʌktɪv] *a* reproducteur(trice).
reproof [rɪ'pruːf] *n* reproche *m*.
reprove [rɪ'pruːv] *vt* (*action*) réprouver; (*person*): **to** ~ (**for**) blâmer (de).
reproving [rɪ'pruːvɪŋ] *a* réprobateur(trice).
reptile ['rɛptaɪl] *n* reptile *m*.
Repub. *abbr* (*US POL*) = **republican**.
republic [rɪ'pʌblɪk] *n* république *f*.
republican [rɪ'pʌblɪkən] *a*, *n* républicain(e).
repudiate [rɪ'pjuːdɪeɪt] *vt* (*ally*, *behaviour*) désavouer; (*accusation*) rejeter; (*wife*) répudier.
repugnant [rɪ'pʌgnənt] *a* répugnant(e).
repulse [rɪ'pʌls] *vt* repousser.
repulsion [rɪ'pʌlʃən] *n* répulsion *f*.
repulsive [rɪ'pʌlsɪv] *a* repoussant(e), répulsif(ive).
reputable ['rɛpjutəbl] *a* de bonne réputation; (*occupation*) honorable.
reputation [rɛpju'teɪʃən] *n* réputation *f*; **to have a** ~ **for** être réputé(e) pour; **he has a** ~ **for being awkward** il a la réputation de ne pas être commode.
repute [rɪ'pjuːt] *n* (bonne) réputation.
reputed [rɪ'pjuːtɪd] *a* réputé(e); **he is** ~ **to be rich/intelligent** *etc* on dit qu'il est riche/intelligent *etc*.

reputedly [rɪ'pjuːtɪdlɪ] *ad* d'après ce qu'on dit.

request [rɪ'kwɛst] *n* demande *f*; *(formal)* requête *f* ♦ *vt*: **to ~ (of** *or* **from sb)** demander (à qn); **at the ~ of** à la demande de.

request stop *n* *(Brit: for bus)* arrêt facultatif.

requiem ['rɛkwɪəm] *n* requiem *m*.

require [rɪ'kwaɪə*] *vt* *(need: subj: person)* avoir besoin de; *(: thing, situation)* nécessiter, demander; *(demand)* exiger, requérir; *(order)*: **to ~ sb to do sth/sth of sb** exiger que qn fasse qch/qch de qn; **if ~d** s'il le faut; **what qualifications are ~d?** quelles sont les qualifications requises?; **~d by law** requis par la loi.

required [rɪ'kwaɪəd] *a* requis(e), voulu(e).

requirement [rɪ'kwaɪəmənt] *n* exigence *f*; besoin *m*; condition *f* (requise).

requisite ['rɛkwɪzɪt] *n* chose *f* nécessaire ♦ *a* requis(e), nécessaire; **toilet ~s** accessoires *mpl* de toilette.

requisition [rɛkwɪ'zɪʃən] *n*: **~ (for)** demande *f* (de) ♦ *vt* *(MIL)* réquisitionner.

reroute [riː'ruːt] *vt* *(train etc)* dérouter.

resale ['riːseɪl] *n* revente *f*.

resale price maintenance (RPM) *n* *vente au détail à prix imposé*.

rescind [rɪ'sɪnd] *vt* annuler; *(law)* abroger; *(judgment)* rescinder.

rescue ['rɛskjuː] *n* sauvetage *m*; *(help)* secours *mpl* ♦ *vt* sauver; **to come to sb's ~** venir au secours de qn.

rescue party *n* équipe *f* de sauvetage.

rescuer ['rɛskjuə*] *n* sauveteur *m*.

research [rɪ'səːtʃ] *n* recherche(s) *f(pl)* ♦ *vt* faire des recherches sur ♦ *vi*: **to ~ (into sth)** faire des recherches (sur qch); **a piece of ~** un travail de recherche; **~ and development (R & D)** recherche-développement (R-D).

researcher [rɪ'səːtʃə*] *n* chercheur/euse.

research work *n* recherches *fpl*.

resell [riː'sɛl] *vt irg* revendre.

resemblance [rɪ'zɛmbləns] *n* ressemblance *f*; **to bear a strong ~ to** ressembler beaucoup à.

resemble [rɪ'zɛmbl] *vt* ressembler à.

resent [rɪ'zɛnt] *vt* éprouver du ressentiment de, être contrarié(e) par.

resentful [rɪ'zɛntful] *a* irrité(e), plein(e) de ressentiment.

resentment [rɪ'zɛntmənt] *n* ressentiment *m*.

reservation [rɛzə'veɪʃən] *n* *(booking)* réservation *f*; *(doubt)* réserve *f*; *(protected area)* réserve; *(Brit AUT: also:* **central ~)** bande médiane; **to make a ~ (in a hotel/a restaurant/on a plane)** réserver *or* retenir une chambre/une table/une place; **with ~s** *(doubts)* avec certaines réserves.

reservation desk *n* *(US: in hotel)* réception *f*.

reserve [rɪ'zəːv] *n* réserve *f*; *(SPORT)* remplaçant/e ♦ *vt* *(seats etc)* réserver, retenir; **~s** *npl* *(MIL)* réservistes *mpl*; **in ~** en réserve.

reserve currency *n* monnaie *f* de réserve.

reserved [rɪ'zəːvd] *a* réservé(e).

reserve price *n* *(Brit)* mise *f* à prix, prix *m* de départ.

reserve team *n* *(Brit SPORT)* deuxième équipe *f*.

reservist [rɪ'zəːvɪst] *n* *(MIL)* réserviste *m*.

reservoir ['rɛzəvwɑː*] *n* réservoir *m*.

reset [riː'sɛt] *vt irg* remettre; *(clock, watch)* mettre à l'heure; *(COMPUT)* remettre à zéro.

reshape [riː'ʃeɪp] *vt* *(policy)* réorganiser.

reshuffle [riː'ʃʌfl] *n*: **Cabinet ~** *(POL)* remaniement ministériel.

reside [rɪ'zaɪd] *vi* résider.

residence ['rɛzɪdəns] *n* résidence *f*; **to take up ~** s'installer; **in ~** *(queen etc)* en résidence; *(doctor)* résidant(e).

residence permit *n* *(Brit)* permis *m* de séjour.

resident ['rɛzɪdənt] *n* résident/e ♦ *a* résidant(e).

residential [rɛzɪ'dɛnʃəl] *a* de résidence; *(area)* résidentiel(le).

residue ['rɛzɪdjuː] *n* reste *m*; *(CHEM, PHYSICS)* résidu *m*.

resign [rɪ'zaɪn] *vt* *(one's post)* se démettre de ♦ *vi*: **to ~ (from)** démissionner (de); **to ~ o.s. to** *(endure)* se résigner à.

resignation [rɛzɪg'neɪʃən] *n* démission *f*; résignation *f*; **to tender one's ~** donner sa démission.

resigned [rɪ'zaɪnd] *a* résigné(e).

resilience [rɪ'zɪlɪəns] *n* *(of material)* élasticité *f*; *(of person)* ressort *m*.

resilient [rɪ'zɪlɪənt] *a* *(person)* qui réagit, qui a du ressort.

resin ['rɛzɪn] *n* résine *f*.

resist [rɪ'zɪst] *vt* résister à.

resistance [rɪ'zɪstəns] *n* résistance *f*.

resistant [rɪ'zɪstənt] *a*: **~ (to)** résistant(e) (à).

resolute ['rɛzəluːt] *a* résolu(e).

resolution [rɛzə'luːʃən] *n* résolution *f*; **to make a ~** prendre une résolution.

resolve [rɪ'zɔlv] *n* résolution *f* ♦ *vt* *(decide)*: **to ~ to do** résoudre *or* décider de faire; *(problem)* résoudre.

resolved [rɪ'zɔlvd] *a* résolu(e).

resonance ['rɛzənəns] *n* résonance *f*.

resonant ['rɛzənənt] *a* résonnant(e).

resort [rɪ'zɔːt] *n* *(town)* station *f* (de vacances); *(recourse)* recours *m* ♦ *vi*: **to ~ to** avoir recours à; **seaside/winter sports ~** station balnéaire/de sports d'hiver; **in the last ~** en dernier ressort.

resound [rɪ'zaund] *vi*: **to ~ (with)** retentir (de).

resounding [rɪ'zaundɪŋ] *a* retentissant(e).

resource [rɪ'sɔːs] *n* ressource *f*; **~s** *npl* ressources; **natural ~s** ressources naturelles; **to leave sb to his** *(or* **her)** **own ~s** *(fig)* livrer qn à lui-même *(or* elle-même).

resourceful [rɪ'sɔːsful] *a* plein(e) de ressource, débrouillard(e).

resourcefulness [rɪ'sɔːsfəlnɪs] *n* ressource *f*.

respect [rɪs'pɛkt] *n* respect *m*; *(point, detail)*: **in some ~s** à certains égards ♦ *vt* respecter; **~s** *npl* respects, hommages *mpl*; **to have** *or* **show ~ for sb/sth** respecter qn/qch; **out of ~ for** par respect pour; **with ~ to** en ce qui concerne; **in ~ of** sous le rapport de, quant à; **in this ~** sous ce rapport, à cet égard; **with due ~ I** ... malgré le respect que je vous dois, je ....

respectability |rɪspɛktə'bɪlɪtɪ| n respectabilité f.

respectable |rɪs'pɛktəbl| a respectable; (quite good: result etc) honorable; (player) assez bon(bonne).

respectful |rɪs'pɛktful| a respectueux(euse).

respective |rɪs'pɛktɪv| a respectif(ive).

respectively |rɪs'pɛktɪvlɪ| ad respectivement.

respiration |rɛspɪ'reɪʃən| n respiration f.

respirator |'rɛspɪreɪtə*| n respirateur m.

respiratory |'rɛspərətərɪ| a respiratoire.

respite |'rɛspaɪt| n répit m.

resplendent |rɪs'plɛndənt| a resplendissant(e).

respond |rɪs'pɒnd| vi répondre; (to treatment) réagir.

respondent |rɪs'pɒndənt| n (LAW) défendeur/deresse.

response |rɪs'pɒns| n réponse f; (to treatment) réaction f; **in ~ to** en réponse à.

responsibility |rɪspɒnsɪ'bɪlɪtɪ| n responsabilité f; **to take ~ for sth/sb** accepter la responsabilité de qch/d'être responsable de qn.

responsible |rɪs'pɒnsɪbl| a (liable): **~ (for)** responsable (de); (person) digne de confiance; (job) qui comporte des responsabilités; **to be ~ to sb (for sth)** être responsable devant qn (de qch).

responsibly |rɪs'pɒnsɪblɪ| ad avec sérieux.

responsive |rɪs'pɒnsɪv| a qui n'est pas réservé(e) or indifférent(e).

rest |rɛst| n repos m; (stop) arrêt m, pause f; (MUS) silence m; (support) support m, appui m; (remainder) reste m, restant m ♦ vi se reposer; (be supported): **to ~ on** appuyer or reposer sur; (remain) rester ♦ vt (lean): **to ~ sth on/against** appuyer qch sur/contre; **the ~ of them** les autres; **to set sb's mind at ~** tranquilliser qn; **it ~s with him to** c'est à lui de; **~ assured that ...** soyez assuré que ....

restart |riː'stɑːt| vt (engine) remettre en marche; (work) reprendre.

restaurant |'rɛstərɒŋ| n restaurant m.

restaurant car n (Brit) wagon-restaurant m.

rest cure n cure f de repos.

restful |'rɛstful| a reposant(e).

rest home n maison f de repos.

restitution |rɛstɪ'tjuːʃən| n (act) restitution f; (reparation) réparation f.

restive |'rɛstɪv| a agité(e), impatient(e); (horse) rétif(ive).

restless |'rɛstlɪs| a agité(e); **to get ~** s'impatienter.

restlessly |'rɛstlɪslɪ| ad avec agitation.

restock |riː'stɒk| vt réapprovisionner.

restoration |rɛstə'reɪʃən| n restauration f; restitution f.

restorative |rɪ'stɒrətɪv| a reconstituant(e) ♦ n reconstituant m.

restore |rɪ'stɔː*| vt (building) restaurer; (sth stolen) restituer; (peace, health) rétablir.

restorer |rɪ'stɔːrə*| n (ART etc) restaurateur/trice (d'œuvres d'art).

restrain |rɪs'treɪn| vt (feeling) contenir; (person): **to ~ (from doing)** retenir (de faire).

restrained |rɪs'treɪnd| a (style) sobre; (manner) mesuré(e).

restraint |rɪs'treɪnt| n (restriction) contrainte f; (moderation) retenue f; (of style) sobriété f; **wage ~** limitations salariales.

restrict |rɪs'trɪkt| vt restreindre, limiter.

restricted area n (AUT) zone f à vitesse limitée.

restriction |rɪs'trɪkʃən| n restriction f, limitation f.

restrictive |rɪs'trɪktɪv| a restrictif(ive).

restrictive practices npl (INDUSTRY) pratiques fpl entravant la libre concurrence.

rest room n (US) toilettes fpl.

restructure |riː'strʌktʃə*| vt restructurer.

result |rɪ'zʌlt| n résultat m ♦ vi: **to ~ (from)** résulter (de); **to ~ in** aboutir à, se terminer par; **as a ~ it is too expensive** il en résulte que c'est trop cher; **as a ~ of** à la suite de.

resultant |rɪ'zʌltənt| a résultant(e).

resume |rɪ'zjuːm| vt (work, journey) reprendre; (sum up) résumer ♦ vi (work etc) reprendre.

résumé |'reɪzjuːmeɪ| n (summary) résumé m; (US: curriculum vitae) curriculum vitae m inv.

resumption |rɪ'zʌmpʃən| n reprise f.

resurgence |rɪ'sɜːdʒəns| n réapparition f.

resurrection |rɛzə'rɛkʃən| n résurrection f.

resuscitate |rɪ'sʌsɪteɪt| vt (MED) réanimer.

resuscitation |rɪsʌsɪ'teɪʃən| n réanimation f.

retail |'riːteɪl| n (vente f au) détail m ♦ cpd de or au détail ♦ vt vendre au détail ♦ vi: **to ~ at 10 francs** se vendre au détail à 10 francs.

retailer |'riːteɪlə*| n détaillant/e.

retail outlet n point m de vente.

retail price n prix m de détail.

retail price index n ≈ indice m des prix.

retain |rɪ'teɪn| vt (keep) garder, conserver; (employ) engager.

retainer |rɪ'teɪnə*| n (servant) serviteur m; (fee) acompte m, provision f.

retaliate |rɪ'tælɪeɪt| vi: **to ~ (against)** se venger (de); **to ~ (on sb)** rendre la pareille (à qn).

retaliation |rɪtælɪ'eɪʃən| n représailles fpl, vengeance f; **in ~ for** par représailles pour.

retaliatory |rɪ'tælɪətərɪ| a de représailles.

retarded |rɪ'tɑːdɪd| a retardé(e).

retch |rɛtʃ| vi avoir des haut-le-cœur.

retentive |rɪ'tɛntɪv| a: **~ memory** excellente mémoire.

rethink |'riː'θɪŋk| vt repenser.

reticence |'rɛtɪsns| n réticence f.

reticent |'rɛtɪsnt| a réticent(e).

retina |'rɛtɪnə| n rétine f.

retinue |'rɛtɪnjuː| n suite f, cortège m.

retire |rɪ'taɪə*| vi (give up work) prendre sa retraite; (withdraw) se retirer, partir; (go to bed) (aller) se coucher.

retired |rɪ'taɪəd| a (person) retraité(e).

retirement |rɪ'taɪəmənt| n retraite f.

retirement age n âge m de la retraite.

retiring |rɪ'taɪərɪŋ| a (person) réservé(e); (chairman etc) sortant(e).

retort |rɪ'tɔːt| n (reply) riposte f; (container) cornue f ♦ vi riposter.

retrace |riː'treɪs| vt reconstituer; **to ~ one's steps** revenir sur ses pas.

retract |rɪ'trækt| vt (statement, claws) rétracter; (undercarriage, aerial) rentrer,

escamoter ♦ *vi* se rétracter; rentrer.
retractable [rɪ'træktəbl] *a* escamotable.
retrain [ri:'trein] *vt* recycler ♦ *vi* se recycler.
retraining [ri:'treiniŋ] *n* recyclage *m*.
retread *vt* [ri:'tred] (*AUT: tyre*) rechaper ♦ ['ri:tred] *n* pneu rechapé.
retreat [rɪ'tri:t] *n* retraite *f* ♦ *vi* battre en retraite; (*flood*) reculer; **to beat a hasty ~** (*fig*) partir avec précipitation.
retrial [ri:'traiəl] *n* nouveau procès.
retribution [rɛtrɪ'bju:ʃən] *n* châtiment *m*.
retrieval [rɪ'tri:vəl] *n* récupération *f*; réparation *f*; recherche *f* et extraction *f*.
retrieve [rɪ'tri:v] *vt* (*sth lost*) récupérer; (*situation, honour*) sauver; (*error, loss*) réparer; (*COMPUT*) rechercher.
retriever [rɪ'tri:və*] *n* chien *m* d'arrêt.
retroactive [rɛtrəu'æktɪv] *a* rétroactif(ive).
retrograde ['rɛtrəgreɪd] *a* rétrograde.
retrospect ['rɛtrəspɛkt] *n*: **in ~** rétrospectivement, après coup.
retrospective [rɛtrə'spɛktɪv] *a* (*law*) rétroactif(ive) ♦ *n* (*ART*) rétrospective *f*.
return [rɪ'tə:n] *n* (*going or coming back*) retour *m*; (*of sth stolen etc*) restitution *f*; (*recompense*) récompense *f*; (*FINANCE: from land, shares*) rapport *m*; (*report*) relevé *m*, rapport ♦ *cpd* (*journey*) de retour; (*Brit: ticket*) aller et retour; (*match*) retour ♦ *vi* (*person etc: come back*) revenir; (: *go back*) retourner ♦ *vt* rendre; (*bring back*) rapporter; (*send back*) renvoyer; (*put back*) remettre; (*POL: candidate*) élire; **~s** *npl* (*COMM*) recettes *fpl*; bénéfices *mpl*; (: **~ed goods**) marchandises renvoyées; **many happy ~s (of the day)!** bon anniversaire!; **by ~ (of post)** par retour (du courrier); **in ~ (for)** en échange (de).
returnable [rɪ'tə:nəbl] *a* (*bottle etc*) consigné(e).
return key *n* (*COMPUT*) touche *f* de retour.
reunion [ri:'ju:nɪən] *n* réunion *f*.
reunite [ri:ju:'naɪt] *vt* réunir.
rev [rɛv] *n abbr* (= *revolution: AUT*) tour *m* ♦ *vb* (*also*: **~ up**) *vt* emballer ♦ *vi* s'emballer.
revaluation [ri:vælju'eɪʃən] *n* réévaluation *f*.
revamp ['ri:'væmp] *vt* (*house*) retaper; (*firm*) réorganiser.
rev counter *n* (*Brit*) compte-tours *m inv*.
Rev(d). *abbr* = **reverend**.
reveal [rɪ'vi:l] *vt* (*make known*) révéler; (*display*) laisser voir.
revealing [rɪ'vi:lɪŋ] *a* révélateur(trice); (*dress*) au décolleté généreux *or* suggestif.
reveille [rɪ'vælɪ] *n* (*MIL.*) réveil *m*.
revel ['rɛvl] *vi*: **to ~ in sth/in doing** se délecter de qch/à faire.
revelation [rɛvə'leɪʃən] *n* révélation *f*.
reveller ['rɛvlə*] *n* fêtard *m*.
revelry ['rɛvlrɪ] *n* festivités *fpl*.
revenge [rɪ'vɛndʒ] *n* vengeance *f*; (*in game etc*) revanche *f* ♦ *vt* venger; **to take ~** se venger.
revengeful [rɪ'vɛndʒful] *a* vengeur(eresse); vindicatif(ive).
revenue ['rɛvənju:] *n* revenu *m*.
reverberate [rɪ'və:bəreɪt] *vi* (*sound*) retentir, se répercuter; (*light*) se réverbérer.
reverberation [rɪvə:bə'reɪʃən] *n* répercussion

f; réverbération *f*.
revere [rɪ'vɪə*] *vt* vénérer, révérer.
reverence ['rɛvərəns] *n* vénération *f*, révérence *f*.
reverend *a* vénérable; **the R~ John Smith** (*Anglican*) le révérend John Smith; (*Catholic*) l'abbé John Smith; (*Protestant*) le pasteur John Smith.
reverent ['rɛvərənt] *a* respectueux(euse).
reverie ['rɛvərɪ] *n* rêverie *f*.
reversal [rɪ'və:sl] *n* (*of opinion*) revirement *m*.
reverse [rɪ'və:s] *n* contraire *m*, opposé *m*; (*back*) dos *m*, envers *m*; (*AUT: also*: **~ gear**) marche *f* arrière ♦ *a* (*order, direction*) opposé(e), inverse ♦ *vt* (*turn*) renverser, retourner; (*change*) renverser, changer complètement; (*LAW: judgment*) réformer ♦ *vi* (*Brit AUT*) faire marche arrière; **to go into ~** faire marche arrière; **in ~ order** en ordre inverse.
reversed charge call *n* (*Brit TEL*) communication *f* en PCV.
reverse video *n* vidéo *m* inverse.
reversible [rɪ'və:səbl] *a* (*garment*) réversible; (*procedure*) révocable.
reversing lights [rɪ'və:sɪŋ-] *npl* (*Brit AUT*) feux *mpl* de marche arrière *or* de recul.
reversion [rɪ'və:ʃən] *n* retour *m*.
revert [rɪ'və:t] *vi*: **to ~ to** revenir à, retourner à.
review [rɪ'vju:] *n* revue *f*; (*of book, film*) critique *f* ♦ *vt* passer en revue; faire la critique de; **to come under ~** être révisé(e).
reviewer [rɪ'vju:ə*] *n* critique *m*.
revile [rɪ'vaɪl] *vt* injurier.
revise [rɪ'vaɪz] *vt* (*manuscript*) revoir, corriger; (*opinion*) réviser, modifier; (*study: subject, notes*) réviser; **~d edition** édition revue et corrigée.
revision [rɪ'vɪʒən] *n* révision *f*; (*revised version*) version corrigée.
revitalize [ri:'vaɪtəlaɪz] *vt* revitaliser.
revival [rɪ'vaɪvəl] *n* reprise *f*; rétablissement *m*; (*of faith*) renouveau *m*.
revive [rɪ'vaɪv] *vt* (*person*) ranimer; (*custom*) rétablir; (*hope, courage*) redonner; (*play, fashion*) reprendre ♦ *vi* (*person*) reprendre connaissance; (*hope*) renaître; (*activity*) reprendre.
revoke [rɪ'vəuk] *vt* révoquer; (*promise, decision*) revenir sur.
revolt [rɪ'vəult] *n* révolte *f* ♦ *vi* se révolter, se rebeller.
revolting [rɪ'vəultɪŋ] *a* dégoûtant(e).
revolution [rɛvə'lu:ʃən] *n* révolution *f*; (*of wheel etc*) tour *m*, révolution.
revolutionary [rɛvə'lu:ʃənrɪ] *a*, *n* révolutionnaire (*m/f*).
revolutionize [rɛvə'lu:ʃənaɪz] *vt* révolutionner.
revolve [rɪ'vɔlv] *vi* tourner.
revolver [rɪ'vɔlvə*] *n* revolver *m*.
revolving [rɪ'vɔlvɪŋ] *a* (*chair*) pivotant(e); (*light*) tournant(e).
revolving credit *n* crédit *m* à renouvellement automatique.
revolving door *n* (*porte f à*) tambour *m*.
revue [rɪ'vju:] *n* (*THEATRE*) revue *f*.
revulsion [rɪ'vʌlʃən] *n* dégoût *m*, répugnance *f*.

reward [rɪ'wɔ:d] *n* récompense *f* ♦ *vt*: **to ~ (for)** récompenser (de).

rewarding [rɪ'wɔ:dɪŋ] *a* (*fig*) qui (en) vaut la peine, gratifiant(e); **financially ~** financièrement intéressant(e).

rewind [ri:'waɪnd] *vt irg* (*watch*) remonter; (*ribbon etc*) réembobiner.

rewire [ri:'waɪə*] *vt* (*house*) refaire l'installation électrique de.

reword [ri:'wɔ:d] *vt* formuler *or* exprimer différemment.

rewrite [ri:'raɪt] *vt irg* récrire.

Reykjavik ['reɪkjəvi:k] *n* Reykjavik.

RFD *abbr* (*US POST*) = *rural free delivery.*

Rh *abbr* (= *rhesus*) Rh.

rhapsody ['ræpsədɪ] *n* (*MUS*) rhapsodie *f*; (*fig*) éloge délirant.

rhesus factor ['ri:səs-] *n* (*MED*) facteur *m* rhésus.

rhetoric ['rɛtərɪk] *n* rhétorique *f*.

rhetorical [rɪ'tɔrɪkl] *a* rhétorique.

rheumatic [ru:'mætɪk] *a* rhumatismal(e).

rheumatism ['ru:mətɪzəm] *n* rhumatisme *m*.

rheumatoid arthritis ['ru:mətɔɪd-] *n* polyarthrite *f* chronique.

Rhine [raɪn] *n*: **the ~** le Rhin.

rhinestone ['raɪnstəun] *n* faux diamant.

rhinoceros [raɪ'nɔsərəs] *n* rhinocéros *m*.

Rhodes [rəudz] *n* Rhodes *f*.

Rhodesia [rəu'di:ʒə] *n* Rhodésie *f*.

Rhodesian [rəu'di:ʒən] *a* rhodésien(ne) ♦ *n* Rhodésien/ne.

rhododendron [rəudə'dɛndrn] *n* rhododendron *m*.

Rhone [rəun] *n*: **the ~** le Rhône.

rhubarb ['ru:bɑ:b] *n* rhubarbe *f*.

rhyme [raɪm] *n* rime *f*; (*verse*) vers *mpl* ♦ *vi*: **to ~ (with)** rimer (avec); **without ~ or reason** sans rime ni raison.

rhythm ['rɪðm] *n* rythme *m*.

rhythmic(al) ['rɪðmɪk(l)] *a* rythmique.

rhythmically ['rɪðmɪklɪ] *ad* avec rythme.

RI *n abbr* (*Brit*) = *religious instruction* ♦ *abbr* (*US POST*) = *Rhode Island.*

rib [rɪb] *n* (*ANAT*) côte *f* ♦ *vt* (*mock*) taquiner.

ribald ['rɪbəld] *a* paillard(e).

ribbed [rɪbd] *a* (*knitting*) à côtes; (*shell*) strié(e).

ribbon ['rɪbən] *n* ruban *m*; **in ~s** (*torn*) en lambeaux.

rice [raɪs] *n* riz *m*.

ricefield ['raɪsfi:ld] *n* rizière *f*.

rice pudding *n* riz *m* au lait.

rich [rɪtʃ] *a* riche; (*gift, clothes*) somptueux(euse); **the ~** *npl* les riches *mpl*; **~es** *npl* richesses *fpl*; **to be ~ in sth** être riche en qch.

richly ['rɪtʃlɪ] *ad* richement; (*deserved, earned*) largement, grandement.

richness ['rɪtʃnɪs] *n* richesse *f*.

rickets ['rɪkɪts] *n* rachitisme *m*.

rickety ['rɪkɪtɪ] *a* branlant(e).

rickshaw ['rɪkʃɔ:] *n* pousse(-pousse) *m inv*.

ricochet ['rɪkəʃeɪ] *n* ricochet *m* ♦ *vi* ricocher.

rid, *pt*, *pp* **rid** [rɪd] *vt*: **to ~ sb of** débarrasser qn de; **to get ~ of** se débarrasser de.

riddance ['rɪdns] *n*: **good ~!** bon débarras!

ridden ['rɪdn] *pp* of **ride**.

riddle ['rɪdl] *n* (*puzzle*) énigme *f* ♦ *vt*: **to be**

~d with être criblé(e) de.

ride [raɪd] *n* promenade *f*, tour *m*; (*distance covered*) trajet *m* ♦ *vb* (*pt* **rode**, *pp* **ridden** [rəud, 'rɪdn]) *vi* (*as sport*) monter (à cheval), faire du cheval; (*go somewhere: on horse, bicycle*) aller (à cheval *or* bicyclette *etc*); *vt* (*a certain horse*) monter; (*distance*) parcourir, faire; **we rode all day/all the way** nous sommes restés toute la journée en selle/avons fait tout le chemin en selle *or* à cheval; **to ~ a horse/bicycle/camel** monter à cheval/à bicyclette/à dos de chameau; **can you ~ a bike?** est-ce que tu sais monter à bicyclette?; **to ~ at anchor** (*NAUT*) être à l'ancre; **horse/car ~** promenade *or* tour à cheval/en voiture; **to go for a ~** faire une promenade (en voiture *or* à bicyclette *etc*); **to take sb for a ~** (*fig*) faire marcher qn; rouler qn.

ride out *vt*: **to ~ out the storm** (*fig*) surmonter les difficultés.

rider ['raɪdə*] *n* cavalier/ière; (*in race*) jockey *m*; (*on bicycle*) cycliste *m/f*; (*on motorcycle*) motocycliste *m/f*; (*in document*) annexe *f*, clause additionnelle.

ridge [rɪdʒ] *n* (*of hill*) faîte *m*; (*of roof, mountain*) arête *f*; (*on object*) strie *f*.

ridicule ['rɪdɪkju:l] *n* ridicule *m*; dérision *f* ♦ *vt* ridiculiser, tourner en dérision; **to hold sb/sth up to ~** tourner qn/qch en ridicule.

ridiculous [rɪ'dɪkjuləs] *a* ridicule.

riding ['raɪdɪŋ] *n* équitation *f*.

riding school *n* manège *m*, école *f* d'équitation.

rife [raɪf] *a* répandu(e); **~ with** abondant(e) en.

riffraff ['rɪfræf] *n* racaille *f*.

rifle ['raɪfl] *n* fusil *m* (à canon rayé) ♦ *vt* vider, dévaliser.

rifle through *vt fus* fouiller dans.

rifle range *n* champ *m* de tir; (*indoor*) stand *m* de tir.

rift [rɪft] *n* fente *f*, fissure *f*; (*fig: disagreement*) désaccord *m*.

rig [rɪg] *n* (*also: oil ~: on land*) derrick *m*; (*: at sea*) plate-forme pétrolière ♦ *vt* (*election etc*) truquer.

rig out *vt* (*Brit*) habiller; (*: pej*) fringuer, attifer.

rig up *vt* arranger, faire avec des moyens de fortune.

rigging ['rɪgɪŋ] *n* (*NAUT*) gréement *m*.

right [raɪt] *a* (*true*) juste, exact(e); (*correctly chosen: answer, road etc*) bon(bonne); (*suitable*) approprié(e), convenable; (*just*) juste, équitable; (*morally good*) bien *inv*; (*not left*) droit(e) ♦ *n* (*title, claim*) droit *m*; (*not left*) droite *f* ♦ *ad* (*answer*) correctement; (*not on the left*) à droite ♦ *vt* redresser ♦ *excl* bon!; **the ~ time** (*precise*) l'heure exacte; (*not wrong*) la bonne heure; **to be ~** (*person*) avoir raison; (*answer*) être juste *or* correct(e); **to get sth ~** ne pas se tromper sur qch; **let's get it ~ this time!** essayons de ne pas nous tromper cette fois-ci!; **you did the ~ thing** vous avez bien fait; **to put a mistake ~** (*Brit*) rectifier une erreur; **~ now** en ce moment même; tout de suite; ~ **before/after** juste avant/après; ~ **against the wall** tout contre le mur; ~ **ahead** tout droit; droit devant; ~ **in the middle** en plein milieu; ~ **away** immédiatement; **to go** ~ **to the end of sth** aller jusqu'au bout de qch; **by** ~**s** en toute justice; **on the** ~ à droite; ~ **and wrong** le bien et le mal; **to be in the** ~ avoir raison; **film** ~**s** droits d'adaptation cinématographique; ~ **of way** droit m de passage; (*AUT*) priorité f.

right angle n angle droit.

righteous ['raɪtʃəs] a droit(e), vertueux(euse); (*anger*) justifié(e).

righteousness ['raɪtʃəsnɪs] n droiture f, vertu f.

rightful ['raɪtful] a (*heir*) légitime.

rightfully ['raɪtfəlɪ] ad à juste titre, légitimement.

right-handed [raɪt'hændɪd] a (*person*) droitier(ière).

right-hand man ['raɪthænd-] n bras droit (*fig*).

right-hand side ['raɪthænd-] n côté droit.

rightly ['raɪtlɪ] ad bien, correctement; (*with reason*) à juste titre; **if I remember** ~ (*Brit*) si je me souviens bien.

right-minded ['raɪt'maɪndɪd] a sensé(e), sain(e) d'esprit.

rights issue n (*STOCK EXCHANGE*) émission préférentielle or de droit de souscription.

right wing n (*MIL, SPORT*) aile droite; (*POL*) droite f ♦ a: **right-wing** (*POL*) de droite.

right-winger [raɪt'wɪŋə*] n (*POL*) membre m de la droite; (*SPORT*) ailier droit.

rigid ['rɪdʒɪd] a rigide; (*principle*) strict(e).

rigidity [rɪ'dʒɪdɪtɪ] n rigidité f.

rigidly ['rɪdʒɪdlɪ] ad rigidement; (*behave*) inflexiblement.

rigmarole ['rɪgmərəul] n galimatias m, comédie f.

rigor ['rɪgə*] n (*US*) = **rigour.**

rigor mortis ['rɪgə'mɔ:tɪs] n rigidité f cadavérique.

rigorous ['rɪgərəs] a rigoureux(euse).

rigorously ['rɪgərəslɪ] ad rigoureusement.

rigour, (*US*) **rigor** ['rɪgə*] n rigueur f.

rig-out ['rɪgaut] n (*Brit col*) tenue f.

rile [raɪl] vt agacer.

rim [rɪm] n bord m; (*of spectacles*) monture f; (*of wheel*) jante f.

rimless ['rɪmlɪs] a (*spectacles*) à monture invisible.

rind [raɪnd] n (*of bacon*) couenne f; (*of lemon etc*) écorce f.

ring [rɪŋ] n anneau m; (*on finger*) bague f; (*also*: **wedding** ~) alliance f; (*for napkin*) rond m; (*of people, objects*) cercle m; (*of spies*) réseau m; (*of smoke etc*) rond; (*arena*) piste f, arène f; (*for boxing*) ring m; (*sound of bell*) sonnerie f; (*telephone call*) coup m de téléphone ♦ vb (*pt* **rang,** *pp* **rung** [ræŋ, rʌŋ]) vi (*person, bell*) sonner; (*also*: ~ **out**: *voice, words*) retentir; (*TEL*) téléphoner ♦ vt (*Brit TEL*: *also*: ~ **up**) téléphoner à; **to** ~ **the bell** sonner; **to give sb a** ~ (*TEL*) passer un coup de téléphone or de fil à qn; **that has the** ~ **of truth about it** cela sonne vrai; **the name doesn't** ~ **a bell (with me)** ce nom ne me dit rien.

ring back vt, vi (*Brit TEL*) rappeler.

ring off vi (*Brit TEL*) raccrocher.

ring binder n classeur m à anneaux.

ring finger n annulaire m.

ringing ['rɪŋɪŋ] n (*of bell*) tintement m; (*louder, also of telephone*) sonnerie f; (*in ears*) bourdonnement m.

ringing tone n (*Brit TEL*) sonnerie f.

ringleader ['rɪŋliːdə*] n (*of gang*) chef m, meneur m.

ringlets ['rɪŋlɪts] npl anglaises fpl.

ring road n (*Brit*) route f de ceinture.

rink [rɪŋk] n (*also*: **ice** ~) patinoire f; (*for roller-skating*) skating m.

rinse [rɪns] n rinçage m ♦ vt rincer.

Rio (de Janeiro) ['riːəu(dədʒə'nɪərəu)] n Rio de Janeiro.

riot ['raɪət] n émeute f, bagarres fpl ♦ vi manifester avec violence; **a** ~ **of colours** une débauche or orgie de couleurs; **to run** ~ se déchaîner.

rioter ['raɪətə*] n émeutier/ière, manifestant/e.

riotous ['raɪətəs] a tapageur(euse); tordant(e).

riotously ['raɪətəslɪ] ad: ~ **funny** tordant(e).

riot police n forces fpl de police intervenant en cas d'émeute; **hundreds of** ~ des centaines de policiers casqués et armés.

RIP abbr (= *rest in peace*) RIP.

rip [rɪp] n déchirure f ♦ vt déchirer ♦ vi se déchirer.

rip up vt déchirer.

ripcord ['rɪpkɔːd] n poignée f d'ouverture.

ripe [raɪp] a (*fruit*) mûr(e); (*cheese*) fait(e).

ripen ['raɪpn] vt mûrir ♦ vi mûrir; se faire.

ripeness ['raɪpnɪs] n maturité f.

rip-off ['rɪpɔf] n (*col*): **it's a** ~! c'est du vol manifeste!

riposte [rɪ'pɔst] n riposte f.

ripple ['rɪpl] n ride f, ondulation f; égrènement m, cascade f ♦ vi se rider, onduler ♦ vt rider, faire onduler.

rise [raɪz] n (*slope*) côte f, pente f; (*hill*) élévation f; (*increase*: *in wages*: *Brit*) augmentation f; (: *in prices, temperature*) hausse f, augmentation; (*fig*) ascension f ♦ vi (*pt* **rose,** *pp* **risen** [rəuz, rɪzn]) s'élever, monter; (*prices*) augmenter, monter; (*waters, river*) monter; (*sun, wind, person: from chair, bed*) se lever; (*also*: ~ **up**: *rebel*) se révolter; se rebeller; ~ **to power** montée f au pouvoir; **to give** ~ **to** donner lieu à; **to** ~ **to the occasion** se montrer à la hauteur.

rising ['raɪzɪŋ] a (*increasing*: *number, prices*) en hausse; (*tide*) montant(e); (*sun, moon*) levant(e) ♦ n (*uprising*) soulèvement m, insurrection f.

rising damp n humidité f (montant des fondations).

risk [rɪsk] n risque m, danger m; (*deliberate*) risque ♦ vt risquer; **to take** or **run the** ~ **of doing** courir le risque de faire; **at** ~ en danger; **at one's own** ~ à ses risques et périls; **it's a fire/health** ~ cela présente un risque d'incendie/pour la santé; **I'll** ~ **it** je vais risquer le coup.

risk capital n capital-risques m.

risky ['rɪskɪ] a risqué(e).

risqué ['riːskeɪ] a (*joke*) risqué(e).

rissole ['rɪsəul] n croquette f.
rite [raɪt] n rite m; **the last ~s** les derniers sacrements.
ritual ['rɪtjuəl] a rituel(le) ♦ n rituel m.
rival ['raɪvl] n rival/e; (in business) concurrent/e ♦ a rival(e); qui fait concurrence ♦ vt être en concurrence avec; **to ~ sb/sth in** rivaliser avec qn/qch de.
rivalry ['raɪvlrɪ] n rivalité f; concurrence f.
river ['rɪvə*] n rivière f; (major, also fig) fleuve m ♦ cpd (port, traffic) fluvial(e); **up/down ~** en amont/aval.
riverbank ['rɪvəbæŋk] n rive f, berge f.
riverbed ['rɪvəbed] n lit m (de rivière or de fleuve).
riverside ['rɪvəsaɪd] n bord m de la rivière or du fleuve.
rivet ['rɪvɪt] n rivet m ♦ vt riveter; (fig) river, fixer.
riveting ['rɪvɪtɪŋ] a (fig) fascinant(e).
Riviera [rɪvɪ'eərə] n: **the (French) ~** la Côte d'Azur; **the Italian ~** la Riviera (italienne).
Riyadh [rɪ'jɑːd] n Riyad.
RN n abbr (Brit) = **Royal Navy**; (US) = **registered nurse**.
RNA n abbr (= ribonucleic acid) ARN m.
RNLI n abbr (Brit: = Royal National Lifeboat Institution) ≈ SNSM f.
RNZAF n abbr = Royal New Zealand Air Force.
RNZN n abbr = Royal New Zealand Navy.
road [rəud] n route f; (in town) rue f; (fig) chemin, voie f; **main ~** grande route; **major ~** route principale or à priorité; **minor ~** voie secondaire; **it takes four hours by ~** il y a quatre heures de route; **"~ up"** (Brit) "attention travaux".
roadblock ['rəudblɔk] n barrage routier.
road haulage n transports routiers.
roadhog ['rəudhɔg] n chauffard m.
road map n carte routière.
road safety n sécurité routière.
roadside ['rəudsaɪd] n bord m de la route, bas-côté m ♦ cpd (situé(e) etc) au bord de la route; **by the ~** au bord de la route.
roadsign ['rəudsaɪn] n panneau m de signalisation.
roadsweeper ['rəudswiːpə*] n (Brit: person) balayeur/euse.
road transport n transports routiers.
road user n usager m de la route.
roadway ['rəudweɪ] n chaussée f.
roadworks ['rəudwəːks] npl travaux mpl (de réfection des routes).
roadworthy ['rəudwəːðɪ] a en bon état de marche.
roam [rəum] vi errer, vagabonder ♦ vt parcourir, errer par.
roar [rɔː*] n rugissement m; (of crowd) hurlements mpl; (of vehicle, thunder, storm) grondement m ♦ vi rugir; hurler; gronder; **to ~ with laughter** éclater de rire.
roaring ['rɔːrɪŋ] a: **a ~ fire** une belle flambée; **a ~ success** un succès fou; **to do a ~ trade** faire des affaires d'or.
roast [rəust] n rôti m ♦ vt (meat) (faire) rôtir.
roast beef n rôti m de bœuf, rosbif m.
rob [rɔb] vt (person) voler; (bank) dévaliser; **to ~ sb of sth** voler or dérober qch à qn;

(fig: deprive) priver qn de qch.
robber ['rɔbə*] n bandit m, voleur m.
robbery ['rɔbərɪ] n vol m.
robe [rəub] n (for ceremony etc) robe f; (also: **bath~**) peignoir m ♦ vt revêtir (d'une robe).
robin ['rɔbɪn] n rouge-gorge m.
robot ['rəubɔt] n robot m.
robotics [rə'bɔtɪks] n robotique m.
robust [rəu'bʌst] a robuste; (material, appetite) solide.
rock [rɔk] n (substance) roche f, roc m; (boulder) rocher m; roche; (Brit: sweet) ≈ sucre m d'orge ♦ vt (swing gently: cradle) balancer; (child) bercer; (shake) ébranler, secouer ♦ vi (se) balancer; être ébranlé(e) or secoué(e); **on the ~s** (drink) avec des glaçons; (ship) sur les écueils; (marriage etc) en train de craquer; **to ~ the boat** (fig) jouer les trouble-fête.
rock and roll n rock m, rock'n'roll m.
rock-bottom ['rɔk'bɔtəm] n (fig) niveau le plus bas ♦ a (fig: prices) sacrifié(e); **to reach** or **touch ~** (price, person) tomber au plus bas.
rock climber n varappeur/euse.
rock climbing n varappe f.
rockery ['rɔkərɪ] n (jardin m de) rocaille f.
rocket ['rɔkɪt] n fusée f; (MIL) fusée, roquette f ♦ vi (prices) monter en flèche.
rocket launcher n lance-roquettes m inv.
rock face n paroi rocheuse.
rock fall n chute f de pierres.
rocking chair ['rɔkɪŋ-] n fauteuil m à bascule.
rocking horse ['rɔkɪŋ-] n cheval m à bascule.
rocky ['rɔkɪ] a (hill) rocheux(euse); (path) rocailleux(euse); (unsteady: table) branlant(e).
Rocky Mountains npl: **the ~** les (montagnes fpl) Rocheuses fpl.
rod [rɔd] n (metallic) tringle f; (TECH) tige f; (wooden) baguette f; (also: **fishing ~**) canne f à pêche.
rode [rəud] pt of **ride**.
rodent ['rəudnt] n rongeur m.
rodeo ['rəudɪəu] n rodéo m.
roe [rəu] n (species: also: **~ deer**) chevreuil m; (of fish: also: **hard ~**) œufs mpl de poisson; **soft ~** laitance f.
roe deer n chevreuil m; chevreuil femelle.
rogue [rəug] n coquin/e.
roguish ['rəugɪʃ] a coquin(e).
role [rəul] n rôle m.
roll [rəul] n rouleau m; (of banknotes) liasse f; (also: **bread ~**) petit pain; (register) liste f; (sound: of drums etc) roulement m; (movement: of ship) roulis m ♦ vt rouler; (also: **~ up**: string) enrouler; (also: **~ out**: pastry) étendre au rouleau ♦ vi rouler; (wheel) tourner; **cheese ~** ≈ sandwich m au fromage (dans un petit pain).
roll about, **roll around** vi rouler çà et là; (person) se rouler par terre.
roll by vi (time) s'écouler, passer.
roll in vi (mail, cash) affluer.
roll over vi se retourner.
roll up vi (col: arrive) arriver, s'amener ♦ vt (carpet, cloth, map) rouler; (sleeves) retrousser; **to ~ o.s. up into a ball** se rouler

en boule.
roll call n appel m.
rolled gold [rəuld-] a plaqué or inv.
roller ['rəulə*] n rouleau m; (wheel) roulette f.
roller blind n (Brit) store m.
roller coaster n montagnes fpl russes.
roller skates npl patins mpl à roulettes.
rollicking ['rɔlıkıŋ] a bruyant(e) et joyeux(euse); (play) bouffon(ne); **to have a ~ time** s'amuser follement.
rolling ['rəulıŋ] a (landscape) onduleux(euse).
rolling mill n laminoir m.
rolling pin n rouleau m à pâtisserie.
rolling stock n (RAIL) matériel roulant.
roll-on-roll-off ['rəulɔn'rəulɔf] a (Brit: ferry) transroulier(ière).
roly-poly ['rəulı'pəulı] n (Brit CULIN) roulé m à la confiture.
ROM [rɔm] n abbr (COMPUT: = read-only memory) mémoire morte, ROM f.
Roman ['rəumən] a romain(e) ♦ n Romain/e.
Roman Catholic a, n catholique (m/f).
romance [rə'mæns] n histoire f (or film m or aventure f) romanesque; (charm) poésie f; (love affair) idylle f.
Romanesque [rəumə'nɛsk] a roman(e).
Romania [rəu'meɪnɪə] n Roumanie f.
Romanian [rəu'meɪnɪən] a roumain(e) ♦ n Roumain/e; (LING) roumain m.
Roman numeral n chiffre romain.
romantic [rə'mæntɪk] a romantique; (play, attachment) sentimental(e).
romanticism [rə'mæntɪsɪzəm] n romantisme m.
Romany ['rɔmənɪ] a de bohémien ♦ n bohémien/ne; (LING) romani m.
Rome [rəum] n Rome.
romp [rɔmp] n jeux bruyants ♦ vi (also: ~ about) s'ébattre, jouer bruyamment; **to ~ home** (horse) arriver bon premier.
rompers ['rɔmpəz] npl barboteuse f.
rondo ['rɔndəu] n (MUS) rondeau m.
roof [ru:f] n toit m; (of tunnel, cave) plafond m ♦ vt couvrir (d'un toit); **the ~ of the mouth** la voûte du palais.
roof garden n toit-terrasse m.
roofing ['ru:fıŋ] n toiture f.
roof rack n (AUT) galerie f.
rook [ruk] n (bird) freux m; (CHESS) tour f ♦ vt (col: cheat) rouler, escroquer.
room [ru:m] n (in house) pièce f; (also: bed~) chambre f (à coucher); (in school etc) salle f; (space) place f; **~s** npl (lodging) meublé m; "**~s to let**", (US) "**~s for rent**" "chambres à louer"; **is there ~ for this?** est-ce qu'il y a de la place pour ceci?; **to make ~ for sb** faire de la place à qn; **there is ~ for improvement** on peut faire mieux.
rooming house ['ru:mıŋ-] n (US) maison f de rapport.
roommate ['ru:mmeɪt] n camarade m/f de chambre.
room service n service m des chambres (dans un hôtel).
room temperature n température ambiante; "**serve at ~**" (wine) "servir chambré".
roomy ['ru:mı] a spacieux(euse); (garment) ample.
roost [ru:st] n juchoir m ♦ vi se jucher.

rooster ['ru:stə*] n coq m.
root [ru:t] n (BOT, MATH) racine f; (fig: of problem) origine f, fond m ♦ vi (plant) s'enraciner; **to take ~** (plant, idea) prendre racine.
root about vi (fig) fouiller.
root for vt fus (col) applaudir.
root out vt extirper.
rope [rəup] n corde f; (NAUT) cordage m ♦ vt (box) corder; (climbers) encorder; **to ~ sb in** (fig) embringuer qn; **to know the ~s** (fig) être au courant, connaître les ficelles.
rope ladder n échelle f de corde.
rosary ['rəuzərı] n chapelet m.
rose [rəuz] pt of **rise** ♦ n rose f; (also: ~bush) rosier m; (on watering can) pomme f ♦ a rose.
rosé ['rəuzeı] n rosé m.
rosebed ['rəuzbɛd] n massif m de rosiers.
rosebud ['rəuzbʌd] n bouton m de rose.
rosebush ['rəuzbuʃ] n rosier m.
rosemary ['rəuzmərı] n romarin m.
rosette [rəu'zɛt] n rosette f; (larger) cocarde f.
ROSPA ['rɔspə] n abbr (Brit) = Royal Society for the Prevention of Accidents.
roster ['rɔstə*] n: **duty ~** tableau m de service.
rostrum ['rɔstrəm] n tribune f (pour un orateur etc).
rosy ['rəuzı] a rose; **a ~ future** un bel avenir.
rot [rɔt] n (decay) pourriture f; (fig: pej) idioties fpl, balivernes fpl ♦ vt, vi pourrir; **to stop the ~** (Brit fig) rétablir la situation; **dry ~** pourriture sèche (du bois); **wet ~** pourriture (du bois).
rota ['rəutə] n liste f, tableau m de service; **on a ~ basis** par roulement.
rotary ['rəutərı] a rotatif(ive).
rotate [rəu'teɪt] vt (revolve) faire tourner; (change round: crops) alterner; (: jobs) faire à tour de rôle ♦ vi (revolve) tourner.
rotating [rəu'teɪtɪŋ] a (movement) tournant(e).
rotation [rəu'teɪʃən] n rotation f; **in ~** à tour de rôle.
rote [rəut] n: **by ~** machinalement, par cœur.
rotor ['rəutə*] n rotor m.
rotten ['rɔtn] a (decayed) pourri(e); (dishonest) corrompu(e); (col: bad) mauvais(e), moche; **to feel ~** (ill) être mal fichu(e).
rotting ['rɔtıŋ] a pourrissant(e).
rotund [rəu'tʌnd] a rondelet(te); arrondi(e).
rouble, (US) **ruble** ['ru:bl] n rouble m.
rouge [ru:ʒ] n rouge m (à joues).
rough [rʌf] a (cloth, skin) rêche, rugueux(euse); (terrain) accidenté(e); (path) rocailleux(euse); (voice) rauque, rude; (person, manner: coarse) rude, fruste; (: violent) brutal(e); (district, weather) mauvais(e); (plan) ébauché(e); (guess) approximatif(ive) ♦ n (GOLF) rough m; **the sea is ~ today** la mer est agitée aujourd'hui; **to have a ~ time (of it)** en voir de dures; **~ estimate** approximation f; **to ~ it** vivre à la dure; **to play ~** jouer avec brutalité; **to sleep ~** (Brit) coucher à la dure; **to feel ~** (Brit) être mal fichu(e).

rough out vt (draft) ébaucher.

roughage ['rʌfɪdʒ] n fibres fpl diététiques.

rough-and-ready ['rʌfən'redɪ] a (accommodation, method) rudimentaire.

rough-and-tumble ['rʌfən'tʌmbl] n agitation f.

roughcast ['rʌfkɑːst] n crépi m.

rough copy, rough draft n brouillon m.

roughen ['rʌfn] vt (a surface) rendre rude or rugueux (euse).

rough justice n justice f sommaire.

roughly ['rʌflɪ] ad (handle) rudement, brutalement; (make) grossièrement; (approximately) à peu près, en gros; ~ **speaking** en gros.

roughness ['rʌfnɪs] n (of cloth, skin) rugosité f; (of person) rudesse f; brutalité f.

roughshod ['rʌfʃɔd] ad: **to ride** ~ **over** ne tenir aucun compte de.

rough work n (at school etc) brouillon m.

roulette [ruːˈlet] n roulette f.

Roumania etc [ruːˈmeɪnɪə] = **Romania** etc.

round [raund] a rond(e) ♦ n rond m, cercle m; (Brit: of toast) tranche f; (duty: of policeman, milkman etc) tournée f; (: of doctor) visites fpl; (game: of cards, in competition) partie f; (BOXING) round m; (of talks) série f ♦ vt (corner) tourner; (bend) prendre; (cape) doubler ♦ prep autour de ♦ ad: **right** ~, **all** ~ tout autour; **the long way** ~ (par) le chemin le plus long; **all the year** ~ toute l'année; **in** ~ **figures** en chiffres ronds; **it's just** ~ **the corner** c'est juste après le coin; (fig) c'est tout près; **to ask sb** ~ inviter qn (chez soi); **I'll be** ~ **at 6 o'clock** je serai là à 6 heures; **to go** ~ faire le tour or un détour; **to go** ~ **to sb's (house)** aller chez qn; **to go** ~ **an obstacle** contourner un obstacle; **go** ~ **the back** passez par derrière; **to go** ~ **a house** visiter une maison, faire le tour d'une maison; **enough to go** ~ assez pour tout le monde; **she arrived** ~ **(about) noon** (Brit) elle est arrivée vers midi; ~ **the clock** 24 heures sur 24; **to go the** ~**s** (disease, story) circuler; **the daily** ~ (fig) la routine quotidienne; ~ **of ammunition** cartouche f; ~ **of applause** ban m, applaudissements mpl; ~ **of drinks** tournée f; ~ **of sandwiches** (Brit) sandwich m.

round off vt (speech etc) terminer.

round up vt rassembler; (criminals) effectuer une rafle de; (prices) arrondir (au chiffre supérieur).

roundabout ['raundəbaut] n (Brit AUT) rond-point m (à sens giratoire); (at fair) manège m (de chevaux de bois) ♦ a (route, means) détourné(e).

rounded ['raundɪd] a arrondi(e); (style) harmonieux (euse).

rounders ['raundəz] npl (game) ≈ balle f au camp.

roundly ['raundlɪ] ad (fig) tout net, carrément.

round-shouldered ['raund'ʃəuldəd] a au dos rond.

roundsman ['raundzmən] n (Brit) livreur m.

round trip n (voyage m) aller et retour m.

roundup ['raundʌp] n rassemblement m; (of criminals) rafle f; **a** ~ **of the latest news** un rappel des derniers événements.

rouse [rauz] vt (wake up) réveiller; (stir up) susciter; provoquer; éveiller.

rousing ['rauzɪŋ] a (welcome) enthousiaste.

rout [raut] n (MIL) déroute f ♦ vt mettre en déroute.

route [ruːt] n itinéraire m; (of bus) parcours m; (of trade, shipping) route f; **"all** ~**s"** (AUT) "toutes directions"; **the best** ~ **to London** le meilleur itinéraire pour aller à Londres; **en** ~ **for** en route pour.

route map n (Brit: for journey) croquis m d'itinéraire; (for trains etc) carte f du réseau.

routine [ruːˈtiːn] a (work) ordinaire, courant(e); (procedure) d'usage ♦ n routine f; (THEATRE) numéro m; **daily** ~ occupations journalières.

roving ['rəuvɪŋ] a (life) vagabond(e).

roving reporter n reporter volant.

row [rəu] n (line) rangée f; (of people, seats, KNITTING) rang m; (behind one another: of cars, people) file f; [rau] (noise) vacarme m; (dispute) dispute f, querelle f; (scolding) réprimande f, savon m ♦ vi (in boat) ramer; (as sport) faire de l'aviron; [rau] se disputer, se quereller ♦ vt (boat) faire aller à la rame or à l'aviron; **in a** ~ (fig) d'affilée; **to have a** ~ se disputer, se quereller.

rowboat ['rəubəut] n (US) canot m (à rames).

rowdiness ['raudɪnɪs] n tapage m, chahut m; (fighting) bagarre f.

rowdy ['raudɪ] a chahuteur(euse); bagarreur(euse) ♦ n voyou m.

rowdyism ['raudɪɪzəm] n tendances fpl à la violence; actes mpl de violence.

rowing ['rəuɪŋ] n canotage m; (as sport) aviron m.

rowing boat n (Brit) canot m (à rames).

rowlock ['rɔlək] n (Brit) dame f de nage, tolet m.

royal ['rɔɪəl] a royal(e).

Royal Air Force (RAF) n (Brit) armée de l'air britannique.

royal blue a bleu roi inv.

royalist ['rɔɪəlɪst] a, n royaliste (m/f).

Royal Navy (RN) n (Brit) marine de guerre britannique.

royalty ['rɔɪəltɪ] n (royal persons) (membres mpl de la) famille royale; (payment: to author) droits mpl d'auteur; (: to inventor) royalties fpl.

RP n abbr (Brit: = received pronunciation) prononciation f standard.

rpm abbr (= revolutions per minute) t/mn (= tours/minute).

RR abbr (US) = **railroad**.

R&R n abbr (US MIL) = rest and recreation.

RSA n abbr (Brit) = Royal Society of Arts, Royal Scottish Academy.

RSPB n abbr (Brit): = Royal Society for the Protection of Birds) ≈ LPO f.

RSPCA n abbr (Brit): = Royal Society for the Prevention of Cruelty to Animals) ≈ SPA f.

RSVP abbr (= répondez s'il vous plaît) RSVP.

Rt Hon. abbr (Brit: = Right Honourable) titre donné aux députés de la Chambre des communes.

Rt Rev. abbr (= Right Reverend) très révérend.

rub [rʌb] n (with cloth) coup m de chiffon or de torchon; (on person) friction f ♦ vt frotter; frictionner; **to ~ sb up** or (US) **~ sb the wrong way** prendre qn à rebrousse-poil.
rub down vt (body) frictionner; (horse) bouchonner.
rub in vt (ointment) faire pénétrer.
rub off vi partir; **to ~ off on** déteindre sur.
rub out vt effacer ♦ vi s'effacer.
rubber ['rʌbə*] n caoutchouc m; (Brit: eraser) gomme f (à effacer).
rubber band n élastique m.
rubber plant n caoutchouc m (plante verte).
rubber ring n (for swimming) bouée f (de natation).
rubber stamp n tampon m.
rubber-stamp [rʌbə'stæmp] vt (fig) approuver sans discussion.
rubbery ['rʌbərɪ] a caoutchouteux(euse).
rubbish ['rʌbɪʃ] n (from household) ordures fpl; (fig: pej) choses fpl sans valeur; camelote f; (nonsense) bêtises fpl, idioties fpl ♦ vt (Brit col) dénigrer, rabaisser; **what you've just said is ~** tu viens de dire une bêtise.
rubbish bin n (Brit) boîte f à ordures, poubelle f.
rubbish dump n (in town) décharge publique, dépotoir m.
rubbishy ['rʌbɪʃɪ] a (Brit col) qui ne vaut rien, moche.
rubble ['rʌbl] n décombres mpl; (smaller) gravats mpl.
ruble ['ru:bl] n (US) = **rouble**.
ruby ['ru:bɪ] n rubis m.
RUC n abbr (Brit) = Royal Ulster Constabulary.
rucksack ['rʌksæk] n sac m à dos.
ructions ['rʌkʃənz] npl grabuge m.
rudder ['rʌdə*] n gouvernail m.
ruddy ['rʌdɪ] a (face) coloré(e); (col: damned) sacré(e), fichu(e).
rude [ru:d] a (impolite: person) impoli(e); (: word, manners) grossier(ière); (shocking) indécent(e), inconvenant(e); **to be ~ to sb** être grossier envers qn.
rudely ['ru:dlɪ] ad impoliment; grossièrement.
rudeness ['ru:dnɪs] n impolitesse f; grossièreté f.
rudiment ['ru:dɪmənt] n rudiment m.
rudimentary [ru:dɪ'mɛntərɪ] a rudimentaire.
rueful ['ru:ful] a triste.
ruff [rʌf] n fraise f, collerette f.
ruffian ['rʌfɪən] n brute f, voyou m.
ruffle ['rʌfl] vt (hair) ébouriffer; (clothes) chiffonner; (water) agiter; (fig: person) émouvoir, faire perdre son flegme à.
rug [rʌg] n petit tapis; (Brit: for knees) couverture f.
rugby ['rʌgbɪ] n (also: ~ **football**) rugby m.
rugged ['rʌgɪd] a (landscape) accidenté(e); (features, kindness, character) rude; (determination) farouche.
rugger ['rʌgə*] n (Brit col) rugby m.
ruin ['ru:ɪn] n ruine f ♦ vt ruiner; (spoil: clothes) abîmer; **~s** npl ruine(s); **in ~s** en ruine.
ruination [ru:ɪ'neɪʃən] n ruine f.
ruinous ['ru:ɪnəs] a ruineux(euse).

rule [ru:l] n règle f; (regulation) règlement m; (government) autorité f, gouvernement m; (dominion etc): **under British ~** sous l'autorité britannique ♦ vt (country) gouverner; (person) dominer; (decide) décider ♦ vi commander; décider; (LAW): **to ~ against/in favour of/on** statuer contre/en faveur de/sur; **to ~ that** (umpire, judge etc) décider que; **it's against the ~s** c'est contraire au règlement; **by ~ of thumb** à vue de nez; **as a ~** normalement, en règle générale.
rule out vt exclure; **murder cannot be ~d out** l'hypothèse d'un meurtre ne peut être exclue.
ruled [ru:ld] a (paper) réglé(e).
ruler ['ru:lə*] n (sovereign) souverain/e; (leader) chef m (d'État); (for measuring) règle f.
ruling ['ru:lɪŋ] a (party) au pouvoir; (class) dirigeant(e) ♦ n (LAW) décision f.
rum [rʌm] n rhum m ♦ a (Brit col) bizarre.
Rumania etc [ru:'meɪnɪə] = **Romania** etc.
rumble ['rʌmbl] n grondement m; gargouillement m ♦ vi gronder; (stomach, pipe) gargouiller.
rumbustious [rʌm'bʌstʃəs], (US)
rumbunctious [rʌm'bʌŋkʃəs] a (person) exubérant(e).
rummage ['rʌmɪdʒ] vi fouiller.
rumour, (US) **rumor** ['ru:mə*] n rumeur f, bruit m (qui court) ♦ vt: **it is ~ed that** le bruit court que.
rump [rʌmp] n (of animal) croupe f; (also: ~ **steak**) romsteck m.
rumple ['rʌmpl] vt (hair) ébouriffer; (clothes) chiffonner, friper.
rumpus ['rʌmpəs] n (col) tapage m, chahut m; (quarrel) prise f de bec; **to kick up a ~** faire toute une histoire.
run [rʌn] n (race etc) course f; (outing) tour m or promenade f (en voiture); (journey) parcours m, trajet m; (series) suite f, série f; (THEATRE) série de représentations; (SKI) piste f; (in tights, stockings) maille filée, échelle f ♦ vb (pt **ran**, pp **run** [ræn, rʌn]) vt (business) diriger; (competition, course) organiser; (hotel, house) tenir; (COMPUT: program) exécuter; (force through: rope, pipe): **to ~ sth through** faire passer qch à travers; (to pass: hand, finger): **to ~ sth over** promener or passer qch sur; (water, bath) faire couler ♦ vi courir; (pass: road etc) passer; (work: machine, factory) marcher; (bus, train) circuler; (continue: play) se jouer, être à l'affiche; (: contract) être valide or en vigueur; (slide: drawer etc) glisser; (flow: river, bath) couler; (colours, washing) déteindre; (in election) être candidat, se présenter; **to go for a ~** aller courir or faire un peu de course à pied; (in car) faire un tour or une promenade (en voiture); **to break into a ~** se mettre à courir; **a ~ of luck** une série de coups de chance; **to have the ~ of sb's house** avoir la maison de qn à sa disposition; **there was a ~ on** (meat, tickets) les gens se sont rués sur; **in the long ~** à longue échéance; à la longue; en fin de compte; **in the short ~** à

brève échéance, à court terme; **on the ~** en fuite; **to make a ~ for it** s'enfuir; **I'll ~ you to the station** je vais vous emmener *or* conduire à la gare; **to ~ errands** faire des commissions; **the train ~s between Gatwick and Victoria** le train assure le service entre Gatwick et Victoria; **the bus ~s every 20 minutes** il y a un autobus toutes les 20 minutes; **it's very cheap to ~** (*car, machine*) c'est très économique; **to ~ on petrol** *or* (*US*) **gas/on diesel/off batteries** marcher à l'essence/au diesel/sur piles; **to ~ for president** être candidat à la présidence; **their losses ran into millions** leurs pertes se sont élevées à plusieurs millions; **to be ~ off one's feet** (*Brit*) ne plus savoir où donner de la tête.

run about *vi* (*children*) courir çà et là.

run across *vt fus* (*find*) trouver par hasard.

run away *vi* s'enfuir.

run down *vi* (*clock*) s'arrêter (faute d'avoir été remonté) ♦ *vt* (*AUT*) renverser; (*Brit: reduce: production*) réduire progressivement; (*: factory/shop*) réduire progressivement la production/l'activité de; (*criticize*) critiquer, dénigrer; **to be ~ down** être fatigué(e) *or* à plat.

run in *vt* (*Brit: car*) roder.

run into *vt fus* (*meet: person*) rencontrer par hasard; (*: trouble*) se heurter à; (*collide with*) heurter; **to ~ into debt** contracter des dettes.

run off *vi* s'enfuir ♦ *vt* (*water*) laisser s'écouler.

run out *vi* (*person*) sortir en courant; (*liquid*) couler; (*lease*) expirer; (*money*) être épuisé(e).

run out of *vt fus* se trouver à court de; **I've ~ out of petrol** *or* (*US*) **gas** je suis en panne d'essence.

run over *vt* (*AUT*) écraser ♦ *vt fus* (*revise*) revoir, reprendre.

run through *vt fus* (*instructions*) reprendre, revoir.

run up *vt* (*debt*) laisser accumuler; **to ~ up against** (*difficulties*) se heurter à.

runaway ['rʌnəweɪ] *a* (*horse*) emballé(e); (*truck*) fou(folle); (*inflation*) galopant(e).

rundown ['rʌndaun] *n* (*Brit: of industry etc*) réduction progressive.

rung [rʌŋ] *pp of* **ring** ♦ *n* (*of ladder*) barreau *m*.

run-in ['rʌnɪn] *n* (*col*) accrochage *m*, prise *f* de bec.

runner ['rʌnə*] *n* (*in race: person*) coureur/euse; (*: horse*) partant *m*; (*on sledge*) patin *m*; (*for drawer etc*) coulisseau *m*; (*carpet: in hall etc*) chemin *m*.

runner bean *n* (*Brit*) haricot *m* (à rames).

runner-up [rʌnər'ʌp] *n* second/e.

running ['rʌnɪŋ] *n* (*in race etc*) course *f*; (*of business*) direction *f*; (*of event*) organisation *f*; (*of machine etc*) marche *f*, fonctionnement *m* ♦ *a* (*water*) courant(e); (*commentary*) suivi(e); **6 days ~** 6 jours de suite; **to be in/out of the ~ for sth** être/ne pas être sur les rangs pour qch.

running costs *npl* (*of business*) frais *mpl* de gestion; (*of car*): **the ~ are high** elle revient cher.

running head *n* (*TYP, WORD PROCESSING*) titre courant.

running mate *n* (*US POL*) candidat *m* à la vice-présidence.

runny ['rʌnɪ] *a* qui coule.

run-off ['rʌnɔf] *n* (*in contest, election*) deuxième tour *m*; (*extra race etc*) épreuve *f* supplémentaire.

run-of-the-mill ['rʌnəvðə'mɪl] *a* ordinaire, banal(e).

runt [rʌnt] *n* (*also pej*) avorton *m*.

run-through ['rʌnθruː] *n* répétition *f*, essai *m*.

run-up ['rʌnʌp] *n* (*Brit*): **~ to sth** période *f* précédant qch.

runway ['rʌnweɪ] *n* (*AVIAT*) piste *f* (d'envol *or* d'atterrissage).

rupee [ruː'piː] *n* roupie *f*.

rupture ['rʌptʃə*] *n* (*MED*) hernie *f* ♦ *vt*: **to ~ o.s.** se donner une hernie.

rural ['ruərl] *a* rural(e).

ruse [ruːz] *n* ruse *f*.

rush [rʌʃ] *n* course précipitée; (*of crowd*) ruée *f*, bousculade *f*; (*hurry*) hâte *f*, bousculade; (*current*) flot *m*; (*BOT*) jonc *m*; (*for chair*) paille *f* ♦ *vt* transporter *or* envoyer d'urgence; (*attack: town etc*) prendre d'assaut; (*Brit col: overcharge*) estamper; faire payer ♦ *vi* se précipiter; **don't ~ me!** laissez-moi le temps de souffler!; **to ~ sth off** (*do quickly*) faire qch à la hâte; (*send*) envoyer d'urgence; **is there any ~ for this?** est-ce urgent?; **we've had a ~ of orders** nous avons reçu une avalanche de commandes; **I'm in a ~ (to do)** je suis vraiment pressé (de faire); **gold ~** ruée vers l'or.

rush through *vt fus* (*work*) exécuter à la hâte ♦ *vt* (*COMM: order*) exécuter d'urgence.

rush hour *n* heures *fpl* de pointe *or* d'affluence.

rush job *n* travail urgent.

rush matting *n* natte *f* de paille.

rusk [rʌsk] *n* biscotte *f*.

Russia ['rʌʃə] *n* Russie *f*.

Russian ['rʌʃən] *a* russe ♦ *n* Russe *m/f*; (*LING*) russe *m*.

rust [rʌst] *n* rouille *f* ♦ *vi* rouiller.

rustic ['rʌstɪk] *a* rustique ♦ *n* (*pej*) rustaud(e).

rustle ['rʌsl] *vi* bruire, produire un bruissement ♦ *vt* (*paper*) froisser; (*US: cattle*) voler.

rustproof ['rʌstpruːf] *a* inoxydable.

rustproofing ['rʌstpruːfɪŋ] *n* traitement *m* antirouille.

rusty ['rʌstɪ] *a* rouillé(e).

rut [rʌt] *n* ornière *f*; (*ZOOL*) rut *m*; **to be in a ~** (*fig*) suivre l'ornière, s'encroûter.

rutabaga [ruːtə'beɪgə] *n* (*US*) rutabaga *m*.

ruthless ['ruːθlɪs] *a* sans pitié, impitoyable.

ruthlessness ['ruːθlɪsnɪs] *n* dureté *f*, cruauté *f*.

RV *abbr* (= *revised version*) traduction anglaise de la Bible de 1885 ♦ *n abbr* (*US*) = **recreational vehicle**.

rye [raɪ] *n* seigle *m*.

rye bread *n* pain *m* de seigle.

S

S, s [ɛs] n (letter) S, s m; (US scol.: = satisfactory) ≈ assez bien; **S for Sugar** S comme Suzanne.

S abbr (= south, small) S; (= saint) St.

SA n abbr = **South Africa, South America**.

Sabbath ['sæbəθ] n (Jewish) sabbat m; (Christian) dimanche m.

sabbatical [sə'bætɪkl] a: ~ **year** année f sabbatique.

sabotage ['sæbətɑːʒ] n sabotage m ♦ vt saboter.

saccharin(e) ['sækərɪn] n saccharine f.

sachet ['sæʃeɪ] n sachet m.

sack [sæk] n (bag) sac m ♦ vt (dismiss) renvoyer, mettre à la porte; (plunder) piller, mettre à sac; **to give sb the** ~ renvoyer qn, mettre qn à la porte; **to get the** ~ être renvoyé(e) or mis(e) à la porte.

sackful ['sækful] n: a ~ **of** un (plein) sac de.

sacking ['sækɪŋ] n toile f à sac; (dismissal) renvoi m.

sacrament ['sækrəmənt] n sacrement m.

sacred ['seɪkrɪd] a sacré(e).

sacrifice ['sækrɪfaɪs] n sacrifice m ♦ vt sacrifier; **to make** ~s **(for sb)** se sacrifier or faire des sacrifices (pour qn).

sacrilege ['sækrɪlɪdʒ] n sacrilège m.

sacrosanct ['sækrəʊsæŋkt] a sacro-saint(e).

sad [sæd] a (unhappy) triste; (deplorable) triste, fâcheux(euse).

sadden ['sædn] vt attrister, affliger.

saddle ['sædl] n selle f ♦ vt (horse) seller; **to be** ~d **with sth** (col) avoir qch sur les bras.

saddlebag ['sædlbæg] n sacoche f.

sadism ['seɪdɪzəm] n sadisme m.

sadist ['seɪdɪst] n sadique m/f.

sadistic [sə'dɪstɪk] a sadique.

sadly ['sædlɪ] ad tristement; (regrettably) malheureusement.

sadness ['sædnɪs] n tristesse f.

sae abbr (Brit: = stamped addressed envelope) enveloppe affranchie pour la réponse.

safari [sə'fɑːrɪ] n safari m.

safari park n réserve f.

safe [seɪf] a (out of danger) hors de danger, en sécurité; (not dangerous) sans danger; (cautious) prudent(e); (sure: bet etc) assuré(e) ♦ n coffre-fort m; ~ **from** à l'abri de; ~ **and sound** sain(e) et sauf(sauve); **(just) to be on the** ~ **side** pour plus de sûreté, par précaution; **to play** ~ ne prendre aucun risque; **it is** ~ **to say that** ... on peut dire sans crainte que ...; ~ **journey!** bon voyage!

safe-breaker ['seɪfbreɪkə*] n (Brit) perceur m de coffre-fort.

safe-conduct [seɪf'kɒndʌkt] n sauf-conduit m.

safe-cracker ['seɪfkrækə*] n = **safe-breaker**.

safe-deposit ['seɪfdɪpɒzɪt] n (vault) dépôt m de coffres-forts; (box) coffre-fort m.

safeguard ['seɪfgɑːd] n sauvegarde f, protection f ♦ vt sauvegarder, protéger.

safekeeping ['seɪf'kiːpɪŋ] n bonne garde.

safely ['seɪflɪ] ad sans danger, sans risque; (without mishap) sans accident; **I can** ~ **say** ... je peux dire à coup sûr ....

safety ['seɪftɪ] n sécurité f; ~ **first!** la sécurité d'abord!

safety belt n ceinture f de sécurité.

safety curtain n rideau m de fer.

safety net n filet m de sécurité.

safety pin n épingle f de sûreté or de nourrice.

safety valve n soupape f de sûreté.

saffron ['sæfrən] n safran m.

sag [sæg] vi s'affaisser, fléchir; pendre.

saga ['sɑːgə] n saga f; (fig) épopée f.

sage [seɪdʒ] n (herb) sauge f; (man) sage m.

Sagittarius [sædʒɪ'tɛərɪəs] n le Sagittaire; **to be** ~ être du Sagittaire.

sago ['seɪgəʊ] n sagou m.

Sahara [sə'hɑːrə] n: **the** ~ **(Desert)** le (désert du) Sahara m.

Sahel [sæ'hɛl] n Sahel m.

said [sɛd] pt, pp of **say**.

Saigon [saɪ'gɒn] n Saigon.

sail [seɪl] n (on boat) voile f; (trip): **to go for a** ~ faire un tour en bateau ♦ vt (boat) manœuvrer, piloter ♦ vi (travel: ship) avancer, naviguer; (: passenger) aller or se rendre (en bateau); (set off) partir, prendre la mer; (SPORT) faire de la voile; **they** ~ed **into Le Havre** ils sont entrés dans le port du Havre.

sail through vi, vt fus (fig) réussir haut la main.

sailboat ['seɪlbəʊt] n (US) bateau m à voiles, voilier m.

sailing ['seɪlɪŋ] n (SPORT) voile f; **to go** ~ faire de la voile.

sailing boat n bateau m à voiles, voilier m.

sailing ship n grand voilier.

sailor ['seɪlə*] n marin m, matelot m.

saint [seɪnt] n saint(e).

saintly ['seɪntlɪ] a saint(e), plein(e) de bonté.

sake [seɪk] n: **for the** ~ **of** (out of concern for) pour, dans l'intérêt de; (out of consideration for) par égard pour; (in order to achieve) pour plus de, par souci de; **arguing for arguing's** ~ discuter pour (le plaisir de) discuter; **for the** ~ **of argument** à titre d'exemple; **for heaven's** ~! pour l'amour du ciel!

salad ['sæləd] n salade f; **tomato** ~ salade de tomates.

salad bowl n saladier m.

salad cream n (Brit) (sorte f de) mayonnaise f.

salad dressing n vinaigrette f.

salad oil n huile f de table.

salami [sə'lɑːmɪ] n salami m.

salaried ['sælərɪd] a (staff) salarié(e), qui touche un traitement.

salary ['sælərɪ] n salaire m, traitement m.

salary scale n échelle f des traitements.

sale [seɪl] n vente f; (at reduced prices) soldes mpl; **"for** ~**"** "à vendre"; **on** ~ en vente; **on**

~ **or return** vendu(e) avec faculté de retour;
closing-down or (US) **liquidation** ~
liquidation f (avant fermeture); ~ **and lease
back** n cession-bail f.

saleroom ['seɪlruːm] n salle f des ventes.

sales assistant n (Brit) vendeur/euse.

sales clerk n (US) vendeur/euse.

sales conference n réunion f de vente.

sales drive n campagne commerciale,
animation f des ventes.

sales force n (ensemble m du) service des
ventes.

salesman ['seɪlzmən] n vendeur m; (representative) représentant m de commerce.

sales manager n directeur commercial.

salesmanship ['seɪlzmənʃɪp] n art m de la
vente.

sales tax n (US) taxe f à l'achat.

saleswoman ['seɪlzwumən] n vendeuse f.

salient ['seɪlɪənt] a saillant(e).

saline ['seɪlaɪn] a salin(e).

saliva [sə'laɪvə] n salive f.

sallow ['sæləu] a cireux(euse).

sally forth, **sally out** vi partir plein(e)
d'entrain.

salmon ['sæmən] n (pl inv) saumon m.

salmon trout n truite saumonée.

saloon [sə'luːn] n (US) bar m; (Brit AUT)
berline f; (ship's lounge) salon m.

Salop ['sæləp] n abbr (Brit) = Shropshire.

SALT [sɔːlt] n abbr (= Strategic Arms Limitation Talks/Treaty) SALT m.

salt [sɔːlt] n sel m ♦ vt saler ♦ cpd de sel;
(CULIN) salé(e); **an old** ~ un vieux loup de
mer.

salt away vt mettre de côté.

salt cellar n salière f.

salt-free ['sɔːlt'friː] a sans sel.

saltwater ['sɔːlt'wɔːtə*] a (fish etc) (d'eau) de
mer.

salty ['sɔːltɪ] a salé(e).

salubrious [sə'luːbrɪəs] a salubre.

salutary ['sæljutərɪ] a salutaire.

salute [sə'luːt] n salut m ♦ vt saluer.

salvage ['sælvɪdʒ] n (saving) sauvetage m;
(things saved) biens sauvés or récupérés ♦ vt
sauver, récupérer.

salvage vessel n bateau m de sauvetage.

salvation [sæl'veɪʃən] n salut m.

Salvation Army n Armée f du Salut.

salver ['sælvə*] n plateau m de métal.

salvo ['sælvəu] n salve f.

Samaritan [sə'mærɪtən] n: **the** ~**s**
(organization) ≈ S.O.S. Amitié.

same [seɪm] a même ♦ pronoun: **the** ~ le(la)
même, les mêmes; **the** ~ **book as** le même
livre que; **on the** ~ **day** le même jour; **at
the** ~ **time** en même temps; **all** or **just the**
~ tout de même, quand même; **they're one
and the** ~ (person/thing) c'est une seule et
même personne/chose; **to do the** ~ faire de
même, en faire autant; **to do the** ~ **as sb**
faire comme qn; **and the** ~ **to you!** et à
vous de même!; (after insult) toi-même!; ~
here! moi aussi!; **the** ~ **again!** (in bar etc)
la même chose!

sample ['sɑːmpl] n échantillon m; (MED)
prélèvement m ♦ vt (food, wine) goûter; **to
take a** ~ prélever un échantillon; **free** ~

échantillon gratuit.

sanatorium, pl **sanatoria** [sænə'tɔːrɪəm, -rɪə]
n sanatorium m.

sanctify ['sæŋktɪfaɪ] vt sanctifier.

sanctimonious [sæŋktɪ'məunɪəs] a
moralisateur(trice).

sanction ['sæŋkʃən] n sanction f ♦ vt
cautionner, sanctionner; **to impose economic
~s on** or **against** prendre des sanctions
économiques contre.

sanctity ['sæŋktɪtɪ] n sainteté f, caractère sacré.

sanctuary ['sæŋktjuərɪ] n (holy place)
sanctuaire m; (refuge) asile m; (for wild
life) réserve f.

sand [sænd] n sable m ♦ vt sabler; (also: ~
down: wood etc) poncer.

sandal ['sændl] n sandale f.

sandbag ['sændbæg] n sac m de sable.

sandblast ['sændblɑːst] vt décaper à la sableuse.

sandbox ['sændbɔks] n (US: for children) tas
m de sable.

sandcastle ['sændkɑːsl] n château m de sable.

sand dune n dune f de sable.

sandpaper ['sændpeɪpə*] n papier m de verre.

sandpit ['sændpɪt] n (Brit: for children) tas m
de sable.

sands [sændz] npl plage f (de sable).

sandstone ['sændstəun] n grès m.

sandstorm ['sændstɔːm] n tempête f de sable.

sandwich ['sændwɪtʃ] n sandwich m ♦ vt
(also: ~ **in**) intercaler; ~**ed between** pris en
sandwich entre; **cheese/ham** ~ sandwich au
fromage/jambon.

sandwich board n panneau m publicitaire
(porté par un homme-sandwich).

sandwich course n (Brit) cours m de
formation professionnelle.

sandy ['sændɪ] a sablonneux(euse); couvert(e)
de sable; (colour) sable inv, blond roux inv.

sane [seɪn] a (person) sain(e) d'esprit;
(outlook) sensé(e), sain(e).

sang [sæŋ] pt of **sing**.

sanguine ['sæŋgwɪn] a optimiste.

sanitarium, pl **sanitaria** [sænɪ'tɛərɪəm, -rɪə] n
(US) = **sanatorium**.

sanitary ['sænɪtərɪ] a (system, arrangements)
sanitaire; (clean) hygiénique.

sanitary towel, (US) **sanitary napkin** n
serviette f hygiénique.

sanitation [sænɪ'teɪʃən] n (in house)
installations fpl sanitaires; (in town) système
m sanitaire.

sanitation department n (US) service m de
voirie.

sanity ['sænɪtɪ] n santé mentale; (common
sense) bon sens.

sank [sæŋk] pt of **sink**.

San Marino ['sænmə'riːnəu] n Saint-Marin m.

Santa Claus [sæntə'klɔːz] n le Père Noël.

Santiago [sæntɪ'ɑːgəu] n (also: ~ **de Chile**)
Santiago (du Chili).

sap [sæp] n (of plants) sève f ♦ vt (strength)
saper, miner.

sapling ['sæplɪŋ] n jeune arbre m.

sapphire ['sæfaɪə*] n saphir m.

sarcasm ['sɑːkæzm] n sarcasme m, raillerie f.

sarcastic [sɑː'kæstɪk] a sarcastique.

sarcophagus, pl **sarcophagi** [saː'kɔfəgəs, -gaɪ] n sarcophage m.
sardine [saː'diːn] n sardine f.
Sardinia [saː'dɪnɪə] n Sardaigne f.
Sardinian [saː'dɪnɪən] a sarde ♦ n Sarde m/f; (LING) sarde m.
sardonic [saː'dɔnɪk] a sardonique.
sari ['saːrɪ] n sari m.
sartorial [saː'tɔːrɪəl] a vestimentaire.
SAS n abbr (Brit MIL: = Special Air Service) ≈ GIGN m.
SASE n abbr (US: = self-addressed stamped envelope) enveloppe affranchie pour la réponse.
sash [sæʃ] n écharpe f.
sash window n fenêtre f à guillotine.
SAT n abbr (US) = Scholastic Aptitude Test.
Sat. abbr (= Saturday) sa.
sat [sæt] pt, pp of **sit**.
Satan ['seɪtn] n Satan m.
satanic [sə'tænɪk] a satanique, démoniaque.
satchel ['sætʃl] n cartable m.
sated ['seɪtɪd] a repu(e); blasé(e).
satellite ['sætəlaɪt] a, n satellite (m).
satiate ['seɪʃɪeɪt] vt rassasier.
satin ['sætɪn] n satin m ♦ a en or de satin, satiné(e); **with a ~ finish** satiné(e).
satire ['sætaɪə*] n satire f.
satirical [sə'tɪrɪkl] a satirique.
satirist ['sætɪrɪst] n (writer) auteur m satirique; (cartoonist) caricaturiste m/f.
satirize ['sætɪraɪz] vt faire la satire de, satiriser.
satisfaction [sætɪs'fækʃən] n satisfaction f.
satisfactory [sætɪs'fæktərɪ] a satisfaisant(e).
satisfy ['sætɪsfaɪ] vt satisfaire, contenter; (convince) convaincre, persuader; **to ~ the requirements** remplir les conditions; **to ~ sb (that)** convaincre qn (que); **to ~ o.s. of sth** vérifier qch, s'assurer de qch.
satisfying ['sætɪsfaɪɪŋ] a satisfaisant(e).
saturate ['sætʃəreɪt] vt: **to ~ (with)** saturer (de).
saturation [sætʃə'reɪʃən] n saturation f.
Saturday ['sætədɪ] n samedi m; for phrases see also **Tuesday**.
sauce [sɔːs] n sauce f.
saucepan ['sɔːspən] n casserole f.
saucer ['sɔːsə*] n soucoupe f.
saucy ['sɔːsɪ] a impertinent(e).
Saudi Arabia ['saudɪ-] n Arabie f Saoudite or Séoudite.
Saudi (Arabian) ['saudɪ-] a saoudien(ne) ♦ n Saoudien(ne).
sauna ['sɔːnə] n sauna m.
saunter ['sɔːntə*] vi: **to ~ to** aller en flânant or se balader jusqu'à.
sausage ['sɔsɪdʒ] n saucisse f; (salami etc) saucisson m.
sausage roll n friand m.
sauté ['səuteɪ] a (CULIN: potatoes) sauté(e); (: onions) revenu(e) ♦ vt faire sauter; faire revenir.
savage ['sævɪdʒ] a (cruel, fierce) brutal(e), féroce; (primitive) primitif(ive), sauvage ♦ n sauvage m/f ♦ vt attaquer férocement.
savagery ['sævɪdʒrɪ] n sauvagerie f, brutalité f, férocité f.
save [seɪv] vt (person, belongings) sauver;

(money) mettre de côté, économiser; (time) (faire) gagner; (food) garder; (COMPUT) sauvegarder; (avoid: trouble) éviter ♦ vi (also: ~ **up**) mettre de l'argent de côté ♦ n (SPORT) arrêt m (du ballon) ♦ prep sauf, à l'exception de; **it will ~ me an hour** ça me fera gagner une heure; **to ~ face** sauver la face; **God ~ the Queen!** vive la Reine!
saving ['seɪvɪŋ] n économie f ♦ a: **the ~ grace of** ce qui rachète; **~s** npl économies fpl; **to make ~s** faire des économies.
savings account n compte m d'épargne.
savings bank n caisse f d'épargne.
saviour, (US) **savior** ['seɪvjə*] n sauveur m.
savour, (US) **savor** ['seɪvə*] n saveur f, goût m ♦ vt savourer.
savo(u)ry ['seɪvərɪ] a savoureux(euse); (dish: not sweet) salé(e).
savvy ['sævɪ] n (col) jugeote f.
saw [sɔː] pt of **see** ♦ n (tool) scie f ♦ vt (pt **sawed,** pp **sawed** or **sawn** [sɔːn]) scier; **to ~ sth up** débiter qch à la scie.
sawdust ['sɔːdʌst] n sciure f.
sawmill ['sɔːmɪl] n scierie f.
sawn-off ['sɔːnɔf], (US) **sawed-off** ['sɔːdɔf] a: **~ shotgun** carabine f à canon scié.
saxophone ['sæksəfəun] n saxophone m.
say [seɪ] n: **to have one's ~** dire ce qu'on a à dire; **to have a ~** avoir voix au chapitre ♦ vt (pt, pp **said** [sed]) dire; **could you ~ that again?** pourriez-vous répéter ceci?; **to ~ yes/no** dire oui/non; **she said (that) I was to give you this** elle m'a chargé de vous remettre ceci; **my watch ~s 3 o'clock** ma montre indique 3 heures, il est 3 heures à ma montre; **shall we ~ Tuesday?** disons mardi?; **that doesn't ~ much for him** ce n'est pas vraiment à son honneur; **when all is said and done** en fin de compte, en définitive; **there is something** or **a lot to be said for it** cela a des avantages; **that is to ~** c'est-à-dire; **to ~ nothing of** sans compter; **~ that ... mettons** or **disons que ...; that goes without ~ing** cela va sans dire, cela va de soi.
saying ['seɪɪŋ] n dicton m, proverbe m.
SBA n abbr (US: = Small Business Administration) organisme d'aide aux PME.
SC n abbr (US) = **supreme court** ♦ abbr (US POST) = South Carolina.
s/c abbr = **self-contained**.
scab [skæb] n croûte f; (pej) jaune m.
scabby ['skæbɪ] a croûteux(euse).
scaffold ['skæfəld] n échafaud m.
scaffolding ['skæfəldɪŋ] n échafaudage m.
scald [skɔːld] n brûlure f ♦ vt ébouillanter.
scalding ['skɔːldɪŋ] a (also: ~ **hot**) brûlant(e), bouillant(e).
scale [skeɪl] n (of fish) écaille f; (MUS) gamme f; (of ruler, thermometer etc) graduation f, échelle (graduée); (of salaries, fees etc) barème m; (of map, also size, extent) échelle ♦ vt (mountain) escalader; (fish) écailler; **pay ~** échelle des salaires; **~ of charges** tarif m (des consultations or prestations etc); **on a large ~** sur une grande échelle, en grand; **to draw sth to ~** dessiner qch à l'échelle; **small-~ model** modèle réduit.
scale down vt réduire.
scale drawing n dessin m à l'échelle.

scale model n modèle m à l'échelle.

scales [skeɪlz] npl balance f; (larger) bascule f.

scallion ['skæljən] n oignon m; (US: shallot) échalote f; (: leek) poireau m.

scallop ['skɔləp] n coquille f Saint-Jacques.

scalp [skælp] n cuir chevelu ♦ vt scalper.

scalpel ['skælpl] n scalpel m.

scalper ['skælpə*] n (US col: of tickets) revendeur m de billets.

scamp [skæmp] vt bâcler.

scamper ['skæmpə*] vi: to ~ away, ~ off détaler.

scampi ['skæmpɪ] npl langoustines (frites), scampi mpl.

scan [skæn] vt scruter, examiner; (glance at quickly) parcourir; (poetry) scander; (TV, RADAR) balayer ♦ n (MED) scanographie f.

scandal ['skændl] n scandale m; (gossip) ragots mpl.

scandalize ['skændəlaɪz] vt scandaliser, indigner.

scandalous ['skændələs] a scandaleux(euse).

Scandinavia [skændɪ'neɪvɪə] n Scandinavie f.

Scandinavian [skændɪ'neɪvɪən] a scandinave ♦ n Scandinave m/f.

scanner ['skænə*] n (RADAR, MED) scanner m, scanographe m.

scant [skænt] a insuffisant(e).

scantily ['skæntɪlɪ] ad: ~ clad or dressed vêtu(e) du strict minimum.

scanty ['skæntɪ] a peu abondant(e), insuffisant(e), maigre.

scapegoat ['skeɪpgəut] n bouc m émissaire.

scar [skɑː] n cicatrice f ♦ vt laisser une cicatrice or une marque à.

scarce [skɛəs] a rare, peu abondant(e).

scarcely ['skɛəslɪ] ad à peine, presque pas; ~ anybody pratiquement personne; I can ~ believe it j'ai du mal à le croire.

scarcity ['skɛəsɪtɪ] n rareté f, manque m, pénurie f.

scarcity value n valeur f de rareté.

scare [skɛə*] n peur f, panique f ♦ vt effrayer, faire peur à; to ~ sb stiff faire une peur bleue à qn; bomb ~ alerte f à la bombe.

scare away, scare off vt faire fuir.

scarecrow ['skɛəkrəu] n épouvantail m.

scared ['skɛəd] a: to be ~ avoir peur.

scaremonger ['skɛəmʌŋgə*] n alarmiste m/f.

scarf, pl **scarves** [skɑːf, skɑːvz] n (long) écharpe f; (square) foulard m.

scarlet ['skɑːlɪt] a écarlate.

scarlet fever n scarlatine f.

scarves [skɑːvz] npl of **scarf**.

scary ['skɛərɪ] a (col) qui fiche la frousse.

scathing ['skeɪðɪŋ] a cinglant(e), acerbe; to be ~ about sth être très critique vis-à-vis de qch.

scatter ['skætə*] vt éparpiller, répandre; (crowd) disperser ♦ vi se disperser.

scatterbrained ['skætəbreɪnd] a écervelé(e), étourdi(e).

scattered ['skætəd] a épars(e), dispersé(e).

scatty ['skætɪ] a (Brit col) loufoque.

scavenge ['skævəndʒ] vi (person): to ~ (for) faire les poubelles (pour trouver); to ~ for food (hyenas etc) se nourrir de charognes.

scavenger ['skævəndʒə*] n éboueur m.

SCE n abbr = Scottish Certificate of Education.

scenario [sɪ'nɑːrɪəu] n scénario m.

scene [siːn] n (THEATRE, fig etc) scène f; (of crime, accident) lieu(x) m(pl), endroit m; (sight, view) spectacle m, vue f; behind the ~s (also fig) dans les coulisses; to make a ~ (col: fuss) faire une scène or toute une histoire; to appear on the ~ (also fig) faire son apparition, arriver; the political ~ la situation politique.

scenery ['siːnərɪ] n (THEATRE) décor(s) m(pl); (landscape) paysage m.

scenic ['siːnɪk] a scénique; offrant de beaux paysages or panoramas.

scent [sɛnt] n parfum m, odeur f; (fig: track) piste f; (sense of smell) odorat m ♦ vt parfumer; (smell, also fig) flairer; to put or throw sb off the ~ (fig) mettre or lancer qn sur une mauvaise piste.

sceptic, (US) **skeptic** ['skɛptɪk] n sceptique m/f.

sceptical, (US) **skeptical** ['skɛptɪkl] a sceptique.

scepticism, (US) **skepticism** ['skɛptɪsɪzəm] n scepticisme m.

sceptre, (US) **scepter** ['sɛptə*] n sceptre m.

schedule ['ʃɛdjuːl, (US) 'skɛdjuːl] n programme m, plan m; (of trains) horaire m; (of prices etc) barème m, tarif m ♦ vt prévoir; as ~d comme prévu; on ~ à l'heure (prévue); à la date prévue; to be ahead of/behind ~ avoir de l'avance/du retard; we are working to a very tight ~ notre programme de travail est très serré or intense; everything went according to ~ tout s'est passé comme prévu.

scheduled ['ʃɛdjuːld, (US) 'skɛdjuːld] a (date, time) prévu(e), indiqué(e); (visit, event) programmé(e), prévu; (train, bus, stop, flight) régulier(ière).

schematic [skɪ'mætɪk] a schématique.

scheme [skiːm] n plan m, projet m; (method) procédé m; (dishonest plan, plot) complot m, combine f; (arrangement) arrangement m, classification f; (pension ~ etc) régime m ♦ vt, vi comploter, manigancer; colour ~ combinaison f de(s) couleurs.

scheming ['skiːmɪŋ] a rusé(e), intrigant(e) ♦ n manigances fpl, intrigues fpl.

schism ['skɪzəm] n schisme m.

schizophrenia [skɪtsə'friːnɪə] n schizophrénie f.

schizophrenic [skɪtsə'frɛnɪk] a schizophrène.

scholar ['skɔlə*] n érudit/e.

scholarly ['skɔləlɪ] a érudit(e), savant(e).

scholarship ['skɔləʃɪp] n érudition f; (grant) bourse f (d'études).

school [skuːl] n (gen) école f; (in university) faculté f; (secondary school) collège m, lycée m; (of fish) banc m ♦ cpd scolaire ♦ vt (animal) dresser.

school age n âge m scolaire.

schoolbook ['skuːlbuk] n livre m scolaire or de classe.

schoolboy ['skuːlbɔɪ] n écolier m; collégien m, lycéen m.

schoolchild, pl **-children** ['skuːltʃaɪld, -'tʃɪldrən] n écolier/ière, collégien/ne, lycéen/

ne.

schooldays ['sku:ldeɪz] *npl* années *fpl* de scolarité.

schoolgirl ['sku:lgə:l] *n* écolière *f*; collégienne *f*, lycéenne *f*.

schooling ['sku:lɪŋ] *n* instruction *f*, études *fpl*.

school-leaving age ['sku:l'li:vɪŋ-] *n* âge *m* de fin de scolarité.

schoolmaster ['sku:lmɑ:stə*] *n* (*primary*) instituteur *m*; (*secondary*) professeur *m*.

schoolmistress ['sku:lmɪstrɪs] *n* (*primary*) institutrice *f*; (*secondary*) professeur *m*.

school report *n* (*Brit*) bulletin *m* (scolaire).

schoolroom ['sku:lru:m] *n* (salle *f* de) classe *f*.

schoolteacher ['sku:lti:tʃə*] *n* (*primary*) instituteur/trice; (*secondary*) professeur *m*.

schooner ['sku:nə*] *n* (*ship*) schooner *m*, goélette *f*; (*glass*) grand verre (à xérès).

sciatica [saɪ'ætɪkə] *n* sciatique *f*.

science ['saɪəns] *n* science *f*; **the ~s** les sciences; (*SCOL*) les matières *fpl* scientifiques.

science fiction *n* science-fiction *f*.

scientific [saɪən'tɪfɪk] *a* scientifique.

scientist ['saɪəntɪst] *n* scientifique *m/f*; (*eminent*) savant *m*.

sci-fi ['saɪfaɪ] *n abbr* (*col*: = *science fiction*) SF *f*.

Scilly Isles ['sɪlɪ'aɪlz] *npl*, **Scillies** ['sɪlɪz] *npl*: **the ~** les Sorlingues *fpl*, les iles *fpl* Scilly.

scintillating ['sɪntɪleɪtɪŋ] *a* scintillant(e), étincelant(e); (*wit etc*) brillant(e).

scissors ['sɪzəz] *npl* ciseaux *mpl*; **a pair of ~** une paire de ciseaux.

sclerosis [sklɪ'rəʊsɪs] *n* sclérose *f*.

scoff [skɒf] *vt* (*Brit col: eat*) avaler, bouffer ♦ *vi*: **to ~ (at)** (*mock*) se moquer (de).

scold [skəʊld] *vt* gronder, attraper, réprimander.

scolding ['skəʊldɪŋ] *n* réprimande *f*.

scone [skɒn] *n* sorte de petit pain rond au lait.

scoop [sku:p] *n* pelle *f* (à main); (*for ice cream*) boule *f* à glace; (*PRESS*) reportage exclusif *or* à sensation.

scoop out *vt* évider, creuser.

scoop up *vt* ramasser.

scooter ['sku:tə*] *n* (*motor cycle*) scooter *m*; (*toy*) trottinette *f*.

scope [skəʊp] *n* (*capacity: of plan, undertaking*) portée *f*, envergure *f*; (*: of person*) compétence *f*, capacités *fpl*; (*opportunity*) possibilités *fpl*; **within the ~ of** dans les limites de; **there is plenty of ~ for improvement** (*Brit*) cela pourrait être beaucoup mieux.

scorch [skɔ:tʃ] *vt* (*clothes*) brûler (légèrement), roussir; (*earth, grass*) dessécher, brûler.

scorched earth policy *n* politique *f* de la terre brûlée.

scorcher ['skɔ:tʃə*] *n* (*col: hot day*) journée *f* torride.

scorching ['skɔ:tʃɪŋ] *a* torride, brûlant(e).

score [skɔ:*] *n* score *m*, décompte *m* des points; (*MUS*) partition *f*; (*twenty*) vingt ♦ *vt* (*goal, point*) marquer; (*success*) remporter; (*cut: leather, wood, card*) entailler, inciser ♦ *vi* marquer des points; (*FOOTBALL*) marquer un but; (*keep score*) compter les points; **on that ~** sur ce chapitre, à cet égard; **to have an old ~ to settle with sb** (*fig*) avoir un (vieux) compte à régler avec qn; **~s of** (*fig*) des tas de; **to ~ well/6 out of 10** obtenir un bon résultat/6 sur 10.

score out *vt* rayer, barrer, biffer.

scoreboard ['skɔ:bɔ:d] *n* tableau *m*.

scorecard ['skɔ:kɑ:d] *n* (*SPORT*) carton *m*, feuille *f* de marque.

scorer ['skɔ:rə*] *n* (*FOOTBALL*) auteur *m* du but; buteur *m*; (*keeping score*) marqueur *m*.

scorn [skɔ:n] *n* mépris *m*, dédain *m* ♦ *vt* mépriser, dédaigner.

scornful ['skɔ:nful] *a* méprisant(e), dédaigneux(euse).

Scorpio ['skɔ:pɪəʊ] *n* le Scorpion; **to be ~** être du Scorpion.

scorpion ['skɔ:pɪən] *n* scorpion *m*.

Scot [skɒt] *n* Ecossais/e.

Scotch [skɒtʃ] *n* whisky *m*, scotch *m*.

scotch [skɒtʃ] *vt* faire échouer; enrayer; étouffer.

Scotch tape *n* ® scotch *m* ®, ruban adhésif.

scot-free ['skɒt'fri:] *a*: **to get off ~** s'en tirer sans être puni(e) (*or* sans payer); s'en sortir indemne.

Scotland ['skɒtlənd] *n* Écosse *f*.

Scots [skɒts] *a* écossais(e).

Scotsman ['skɒtsmən] *n* Ecossais *m*.

Scotswoman ['skɒtswumən] *n* Ecossaise *f*.

Scottish ['skɒtɪʃ] *a* écossais(e).

scoundrel ['skaundrl] *n* vaurien *m*.

scour ['skauə*] *vt* (*clean*) récurer; frotter; décaper; (*search*) battre, parcourir.

scourer ['skauərə*] *n* tampon abrasif *or* à récurer; (*powder*) poudre *f* à récurer.

scourge [skə:dʒ] *n* fléau *m*.

scout [skaut] *n* (*MIL*) éclaireur *m*; (*also:* **boy ~**) scout *m*.

scout around *vi* chercher.

scowl [skaul] *vi* se renfrogner, avoir l'air maussade; **to ~ at** regarder de travers.

scrabble ['skræbl] *vi* (*claw*): **to ~ (at)** gratter; **to ~ about** *or* **around for sth** chercher qch à tâtons ♦ *n*: **S~** ® Scrabble *m* ®.

scraggy ['skrægɪ] *a* décharné(e), efflanqué(e), famélique.

scram [skræm] *vi* (*col*) ficher le camp.

scramble ['skræmbl] *n* bousculade *f*, ruée *f* ♦ *vi* avancer tant bien que mal (à quatre pattes *or* en grimpant); **to ~ for** se bousculer *or* se disputer pour (avoir); **to go scrambling** (*SPORT*) faire du trial.

scrambled eggs *npl* œufs brouillés.

scrap [skræp] *n* bout *m*, morceau *m*; (*fight*) bagarre *f*; (*also:* **~ iron**) ferraille *f* ♦ *vt* jeter, mettre au rebut; (*fig*) abandonner, laisser tomber; **~s** *npl* (*waste*) déchets *mpl*; **to sell sth for ~** vendre qch à la casse *or* à la ferraille.

scrapbook ['skræpbuk] *n* album *m*.

scrap dealer *n* marchand *m* de ferraille.

scrape [skreɪp] *vt, vi* gratter, racler ♦ *n*: **to get into a ~** s'attirer des ennuis.

scrape through *vi* (*in exam etc*) réussir de justesse.

scraper ['skreɪpə*] *n* grattoir *m*, racloir *m*.

scrap heap *n* tas *m* de ferraille; (*fig*): **on the**

~ au rancart *or* rebut.

scrap merchant *n* (*Brit*) marchand *m* de ferraille.

scrap metal *n* ferraille *f*.

scrap paper *n* papier *m* brouillon.

scrappy ['skræpɪ] *a* fragmentaire, décousu(e).

scrap yard *n* parc *m* à ferrailles; (*for cars*) cimetière *m* de voitures.

scratch [skrætʃ] *n* égratignure *f*, rayure *f*; éraflure *f*; (*from claw*) coup *m* de griffe ♦ *a*: ~ **team** équipe de fortune *or* improvisée ♦ *vt* (*record*) rayer; (*paint etc*) érafler; (*with claw, nail*) griffer; (*COMPUT*) effacer ♦ *vi* (se) gratter; **to start from** ~ partir de zéro; **to be up to** ~ être à la hauteur.

scrawl [skrɔ:l] *n* gribouillage *m* ♦ *vi* gribouiller.

scrawny ['skrɔ:nɪ] *a* décharné(e).

scream [skri:m] *n* cri perçant, hurlement *m* ♦ *vi* crier, hurler; **to be a** ~ (*col*) être impayable; **to** ~ **at sb to do sth** crier *or* hurler à qn de faire qch.

scree [skri:] *n* éboulis *m*.

screech [skri:tʃ] *n* cri strident, hurlement *m*; (*of tyres, brakes*) crissement *m*, grincement *m* ♦ *vi* hurler; crisser, grincer.

screen [skri:n] *n* écran *m*, paravent *m*; (*CINEMA*, *TV*) écran; (*fig*) écran, rideau *m* ♦ *vt* masquer, cacher; (*from the wind etc*) abriter, protéger; (*film*) projeter; (*candidates etc*) filtrer; (*for illness*): **to** ~ **sb for sth** faire subir un test de dépistage de qch à qn.

screen editing *n* (*COMPUT*) édition *f or* correction *f* sur écran.

screening ['skri:nɪŋ] *n* (*of film*) projection *f*; (*MED*) test *m* (*or* tests) de dépistage; (*for security*) filtrage *m*.

screen memory *n* (*COMPUT*) mémoire *f* écran.

screenplay ['skri:npleɪ] *n* scénario *m*.

screen test *n* bout *m* d'essai.

screw [skru:] *n* vis *f*; (*propeller*) hélice *f* ♦ *vt* visser; (*col!: woman*) baiser (!); **to** ~ **sth to the wall** visser qch au mur; **to have one's head** ~ed **on** (*fig*) avoir la tête sur les épaules.

screw up *vt* (*paper, material*) froisser; (*col: ruin*) bousiller; **to** ~ **up one's face** faire la grimace.

screwdriver ['skru:draɪvə*] *n* tournevis *m*.

screwy ['skru:ɪ] *a* (*col*) dingue, cinglé(e).

scribble ['skrɪbl] *n* gribouillage *m* ♦ *vt* gribouiller, griffonner; **to** ~ **sth down** griffonner qch.

scribe [skraɪb] *n* scribe *m*.

script [skrɪpt] *n* (*CINEMA etc*) scénario *m*, texte *m*; (*in exam*) copie *f*; (*writing*) (écriture *f*) script *m*.

scripted ['skrɪptɪd] *a* (*RADIO*, *TV*) préparé(e) à l'avance.

Scripture ['skrɪptʃə*] *n* Écriture Sainte.

scriptwriter ['skrɪptraɪtə*] *n* scénariste *m/f*, dialoguiste *m/f*.

scroll [skrəul] *n* rouleau *m* ♦ *vt* (*COMPUT*) faire défiler (sur l'écran).

scrotum ['skrəutəm] *n* scrotum *m*.

scrounge [skraundʒ] (*col*) *vt*: **to** ~ **sth** (**off** *or* **from sb**) se faire payer qch (par qn), em-

prunter qch (à qn) ♦ *vi*: **to** ~ **on sb** vivre aux crochets de qn.

scrounger ['skraundʒə*] *n* parasite *m*.

scrub [skrʌb] *n* (*clean*) nettoyage *m* (à la brosse); (*land*) broussailles *fpl* ♦ *vt* (*floor*) nettoyer à la brosse; (*pan*) récurer; (*washing*) frotter; (*reject*) annuler.

scrubbing brush ['skrʌbɪŋ-] *n* brosse dure.

scruff [skrʌf] *n*: **by the** ~ **of the neck** par la peau du cou.

scruffy ['skrʌfɪ] *a* débraillé(e).

scrum(mage) ['skrʌm(ɪdʒ)] *n* mêlée *f*.

scruple ['skru:pl] *n* scrupule *m*; **to have no** ~s **about doing sth** n'avoir aucun scrupule à faire qch.

scrupulous ['skru:pjuləs] *a* scrupuleux(euse).

scrupulously ['skru:pjuləslɪ] *ad* scrupuleusement; **to be** ~ **honest** être d'une honnêteté scrupuleuse.

scrutinize ['skru:tɪnaɪz] *vt* scruter, examiner minutieusement.

scrutiny ['skru:tɪnɪ] *n* examen minutieux; **under the** ~ **of sb** sous la surveillance de qn.

scuba ['sku:bə] *n* scaphandre *m* (autonome).

scuba diving *n* plongée sous-marine (autonome).

scuff [skʌf] *vt* érafler.

scuffle ['skʌfl] *n* échauffourée *f*, rixe *f*.

scull [skʌl] *n* aviron *m*.

scullery ['skʌlərɪ] *n* arrière-cuisine *f*.

sculptor ['skʌlptə*] *n* sculpteur *m*.

sculpture ['skʌlptʃə*] *n* sculpture *f*.

scum [skʌm] *n* écume *f*, mousse *f*; (*pej: people*) rebut *m*, lie *f*.

scupper ['skʌpə*] *vt* (*Brit*) saborder.

scurrilous ['skʌrɪləs] *a* haineux(euse), virulent(e); calomnieux(euse).

scurry ['skʌrɪ] *vi* filer à toute allure; **to** ~ **off** détaler, se sauver.

scurvy ['skə:vɪ] *n* scorbut *m*.

scuttle ['skʌtl] *n* (*NAUT*) écoutille *f*; (*also:* **coal** ~) seau *m* (à charbon) ♦ *vt* (*ship*) saborder ♦ *vi* (*scamper*): **to** ~ **away**, ~ **off** détaler.

scythe [saɪð] *n* faux *f*.

SD *abbr* (*US POST*) = South Dakota.

SDI *n abbr* (= *Strategic Defense Initiative*) IDS *f*.

SDLP *n abbr* (*Brit POL*) = Social Democratic and Labour Party.

SDP *n abbr* (*Brit POL*) = Social Democratic Party.

sea [si:] *n* mer *f* ♦ *cpd* marin(e), de (la) mer, maritime; **on the** ~ (*boat*) en mer; (*town*) au bord de la mer; **by** *or* **beside the** ~ (*holiday*) au bord de la mer; (*village*) près de la mer; **by** ~ par mer, en bateau; **out to** ~ au large; (**out**) **at** ~ en mer; **heavy** *or* **rough** ~(**s**) grosse mer, mer agitée; **a** ~ **of faces** (*fig*) une multitude de visages; **to be all at** ~ (*fig*) nager complètement.

sea bed *n* fond *m* de la mer.

sea bird *n* oiseau *m* de mer.

seaboard ['si:bɔ:d] *n* côte *f*.

sea breeze *n* brise *f* de mer.

seafarer ['si:fɛərə*] *n* marin *m*.

seafaring ['si:fɛərɪŋ] *a* (*life*) de marin; ~ **people** les gens *mpl* de mer.

seafood ['si:fu:d] *n* fruits *mpl* de mer.

sea front n bord m de mer.
seagoing ['si:gəuɪŋ] a (ship) de haute mer.
seagull ['si:gʌl] n mouette f.
seal [si:l] n (animal) phoque m; (stamp) sceau m, cachet m; (impression) cachet, estampille f ♦ vt sceller; (envelope) coller; (: with seal) cacheter; (decide: sb's fate) décider (de); (: bargain) conclure; ~ **of approval** approbation f.
seal off vt (close) condamner; (forbid entry to) interdire l'accès de.
sea level n niveau m de la mer.
sealing wax ['si:lɪŋ-] n cire f à cacheter.
sea lion n lion m de mer.
sealskin ['si:lskɪn] n peau f de phoque.
seam [si:m] n couture f; (of coal) veine f, filon m; **the hall was bursting at the ~s** la salle était pleine à craquer.
seaman ['si:mən] n marin m.
seamanship ['si:mənʃɪp] n qualités fpl de marin.
seamless ['si:mlɪs] a sans couture(s).
seamy ['si:mɪ] a louche, mal famé(e).
seance ['seɪɔns] n séance f de spiritisme.
seaplane ['si:pleɪn] n hydravion m.
seaport ['si:pɔ:t] n port m de mer.
search [sə:tʃ] n (for person, thing) recherche(s) f(pl); (of drawer, pockets) fouille f; (LAW: at sb's home) perquisition f ♦ vt fouiller; (examine) examiner minutieusement; scruter ♦ vi: **to ~ for** chercher; **in ~ of** à la recherche de; "**~ and replace**" (COMPUT) "rechercher et remplacer".
search through vt fus fouiller.
searcher ['sə:tʃə*] n chercheur/euse.
searching ['sə:tʃɪŋ] a (look, question) pénétrant(e); (examination) minutieux(euse).
searchlight ['sə:tʃlaɪt] n projecteur m.
search party n expédition f de secours.
search warrant n mandat m de perquisition.
searing ['sɪərɪŋ] a (heat) brûlant(e); (pain) aigu(ë).
seashore ['si:ʃɔ:*] n rivage m, plage f, bord m de (la) mer; **on the ~** sur le rivage.
seasick ['si:sɪk] a: **to be ~** avoir le mal de mer.
seaside ['si:saɪd] n bord m de la mer.
seaside resort n station f balnéaire.
season ['si:zn] n saison f ♦ vt assaisonner, relever; **to be in/out of ~** être/ne pas être de saison; **the busy ~** (for shops) la période de pointe; (for hotels etc) la pleine saison; **the open ~** (HUNTING) saison f de la chasse.
seasonal ['si:znl] a saisonnier(ière).
seasoned ['si:znd] a (wood) séché(e); (fig: worker, actor, troops) expérimenté(e); **a ~ campaigner** un vieux militant, un vétéran.
seasoning ['si:znɪŋ] n assaisonnement m.
season ticket n carte f d'abonnement.
seat [si:t] n siège m; (in bus, train: place) place f; (PARLIAMENT) siège; (buttocks) postérieur m; (of trousers) fond m ♦ vt faire asseoir, placer; (have room for) avoir des places assises pour, pouvoir accueillir; **are there any ~s left?** est-ce qu'il reste des places?; **to take one's ~** prendre place; **to be ~ed** être assis; **please be ~ed** veuillez vous asseoir.
seat belt n ceinture f de sécurité.

seating capacity ['si:tɪŋ-] n nombre m de places assises.
seating room ['si:tɪŋ-] n places assises.
SEATO ['si:təu] n abbr (= Southeast Asia Treaty Organization) OTASE f (= Organisation du traité de l'Asie du Sud-Est).
sea water n eau f de mer.
seaweed ['si:wi:d] n algues fpl.
seaworthy ['si:wə:ðɪ] a en état de naviguer.
SEC n abbr (US: = Securities and Exchange Commission) ≈ COB f (= Commission des opérations de Bourse).
sec. abbr (= second) sec.
secateurs [sɛkə'tə:z] npl sécateur m.
secede [sɪ'si:d] vi faire sécession.
secluded [sɪ'klu:dɪd] a retiré(e), à l'écart.
seclusion [sɪ'klu:ʒən] n solitude f.
second ['sɛkənd] num deuxième, second(e) ♦ ad (in race etc) en seconde position ♦ n (unit of time) seconde f; (in series, position) deuxième m/f, second/e; (Brit SCOL) ≈ licence f avec mention bien or assez bien; (AUT: also: ~ **gear**) seconde f; (COMM: imperfect) article m de second choix ♦ vt (motion) appuyer; [sɪ'kɔnd] (employee) détacher, mettre en détachement; **Charles the S~** Charles II; **just a ~!** une seconde!, un instant!; (stopping sb) pas si vite!; ~ **floor** (Brit) deuxième (étage) m; (US) premier (étage) m; **to ask for a ~ opinion** (MED) demander l'avis d'un autre médecin; **to have ~ thoughts (about doing sth)** changer d'avis (à propos de faire qch); **on ~ thoughts** or (US) **thought** à la réflexion.
secondary ['sɛkəndərɪ] a secondaire.
secondary picket n piquet m (de grève) secondaire.
secondary school n collège m, lycée m.
second-best [sɛkənd'bɛst] n deuxième choix m; **as a ~** faute de mieux.
second-class ['sɛkənd'klɑ:s] a de deuxième classe ♦ ad: **to send sth ~** envoyer qch à tarif réduit; **to travel ~** voyager en seconde; ~ **citizen** citoyen/ne de deuxième classe.
second cousin n cousin/e issu(e) de germains.
seconder ['sɛkəndə*] n personne f qui appuie une motion.
secondhand ['sɛkənd'hænd] a d'occasion; ♦ ad (buy) d'occasion; **to hear sth ~** apprendre qch indirectement.
second hand n (on clock) trotteuse f.
second-in-command ['sɛkəndɪnkə'mɑ:nd] n (MIL) commandant m en second; (ADMIN) adjoint/e, sous-chef m.
secondly ['sɛkəndlɪ] ad deuxièmement.
secondment [sɪ'kɔndmənt] n (Brit) détachement m.
second-rate ['sɛkənd'reɪt] a de deuxième ordre, de qualité inférieure.
secrecy ['si:krəsɪ] n secret m; **in ~** en secret, dans le secret.
secret ['si:krɪt] a secret(ète) ♦ n secret m; **in ~ ad** en secret, secrètement, en cachette; **to keep sth ~ from sb** cacher qch à qn, ne pas révéler qch à qn; **keep it ~** n'en parle à personne; **to make no ~ of sth** ne pas cacher qch.
secret agent n agent secret.

secretarial [sɛkrɪ'tɛərɪəl] a de secrétaire, de secrétariat.

secretariat [sɛkrɪ'tɛərɪət] n secrétariat m.

secretary ['sɛkrətərɪ] n secrétaire m/f; (COMM) secrétaire général; **S~ of State** (US POL) ≈ ministre m des Affaires étrangères; (Brit POL): **S~ of State (for)** ministre m (de).

secrete [sɪ'kriːt] vt (ANAT, BIOL, MED) sécréter; (hide) cacher.

secretion [sɪ'kriːʃən] n sécrétion f.

secretive ['siːkrətɪv] a réservé(e); (pej) cachottier(ière), dissimulé(e).

secretly ['siːkrɪtlɪ] ad en secret, secrètement, en cachette.

sect [sɛkt] n secte f.

sectarian [sɛk'tɛərɪən] a sectaire.

section ['sɛkʃən] n coupe f, section f; (department) section; (COMM) rayon m; (of document) section, article m, paragraphe m ♦ vt sectionner; **the business** etc ~ (PRESS) la page des affaires etc.

sectional ['sɛkʃənl] a (drawing) en coupe.

sector ['sɛktə*] n secteur m.

secular ['sɛkjulə*] a profane; laïque; séculier(ière).

secure [sɪ'kjuə*] a (free from anxiety) sans inquiétude, sécurisé(e); (firmly fixed) solide, bien attaché(e) (or fermé(e) etc); (in safe place) en lieu sûr, en sûreté ♦ vt (fix) fixer, attacher; (get) obtenir, se procurer; (COMM: loan) garantir; **to make sth** ~ bien fixer or attacher qch; **to** ~ **sth for sb** obtenir qch pour qn, procurer qch à qn.

secured creditor n créancier/ière privilégié(e).

security [sɪ'kjuərɪtɪ] n sécurité f, mesures fpl de sécurité; (for loan) caution f, garantie f; **securities** npl (STOCK EXCHANGE) valeurs fpl, titres mpl; **to increase** or **tighten** ~ renforcer les mesures de sécurité; ~ **of tenure** stabilité f d'un emploi, titularisation f.

security forces npl forces fpl de sécurité.

security guard n garde chargé de la sécurité; (transporting money) convoyeur m de fonds.

security risk n menace f pour la sécurité de l'état (or d'une entreprise etc).

secy abbr (= secretary) secr.

sedan [sə'dæn] n (US AUT) berline f.

sedate [sɪ'deɪt] a calme; posé(e) ♦ vt donner des sédatifs à.

sedation [sɪ'deɪʃən] n (MED) sédation f; **to be under** ~ être sous calmants.

sedative ['sɛdɪtɪv] n calmant m, sédatif m.

sedentary ['sɛdntrɪ] a sédentaire.

sediment ['sɛdɪmənt] n sédiment m, dépôt m.

sedition [sɪ'dɪʃən] n sédition f.

seduce [sɪ'djuːs] vt séduire.

seduction [sɪ'dʌkʃən] n séduction f.

seductive [sɪ'dʌktɪv] a séduisant(e), séducteur(trice).

see [siː] vb (pt saw, pp seen [sɔː, siːn]) vt (gen) voir; (accompany): **to** ~ **sb to the door** reconduire or raccompagner qn jusqu'à la porte ♦ vi voir ♦ n évêché m; **to** ~ **that** (ensure) veiller à ce que + sub, faire en sorte que + sub, s'assurer que; **there was nobody to be** ~**n** il n'y avait pas un chat; **let me** ~ (show me) fais(-moi) voir; (let me think) voyons (un peu); **to go and** ~ **sb** aller voir qn; ~ **for yourself** voyez vous-même; **I don't know what she** ~**s in him** je ne sais pas ce qu'elle lui trouve; **as far as I can** ~ pour autant que je puisse en juger; ~ **you !** au revoir!, à bientôt!; ~ **you soon/later/tomorrow!** à bientôt/plus tard/demain!

see about vt fus (deal with) s'occuper de.

see off vt accompagner (à la gare or à l'aéroport etc).

see through vt mener à bonne fin ♦ vt fus voir clair dans.

see to vt fus s'occuper de, se charger de.

seed [siːd] n graine f; (fig) germe m; (TENNIS) tête f de série; **to go to** ~ monter en graine; (fig) se laisser aller.

seedless ['siːdlɪs] a sans pépins.

seedling ['siːdlɪŋ] n jeune plant m, semis m.

seedy ['siːdɪ] a (shabby) minable, miteux(euse).

seeing ['siːɪŋ] cj: ~ **(that)** vu que, étant donné que.

seek [siːk], pt, pp **sought** [siːk, sɔːt] vt chercher, rechercher; **to** ~ **advice/help from sb** demander conseil/de l'aide à qn.

seek out vt (person) chercher.

seem [siːm] vi sembler, paraître; **there** ~**s to be ...** il semble qu'il y a ..., on dirait qu'il y a ...; **it** ~**s (that) ...** il semble que ...; **what** ~**s to be the trouble?** qu'est-ce qui ne va pas?.

seemingly ['siːmɪŋlɪ] ad apparemment.

seen [siːn] pp of **see**.

seep [siːp] vi suinter, filtrer.

seer [sɪə*] n prophète/prophétesse, voyant/e.

seersucker ['sɪəsʌkə*] n cloqué m, étoffe cloquée.

seesaw ['siːsɔː] n (jeu m de) bascule f.

seethe [siːð] vi être en effervescence; **to** ~ **with anger** bouillir de colère.

see-through ['siːθruː] a transparent(e).

segment ['sɛgmənt] n segment m.

segregate ['sɛgrɪgeɪt] vt séparer, isoler.

segregation [sɛgrɪ'geɪʃən] n ségrégation f.

Seine [seɪn] n: **the** ~ la Seine.

seismic ['saɪzmɪk] a sismique.

seize [siːz] vt (grasp) saisir, attraper; (take possession of) s'emparer de; (LAW) saisir.

seize up vi (TECH) se gripper.

seize (up)on vt fus saisir, sauter sur.

seizure ['siːʒə*] n (MED) crise f, attaque f; (LAW) saisie f.

seldom ['sɛldəm] ad rarement.

select [sɪ'lɛkt] a choisi(e), d'élite; (hotel, restaurant, club) chic inv, sélect inv ♦ vt sélectionner, choisir; **a** ~ **few** quelques privilégiés.

selection [sɪ'lɛkʃən] n sélection f, choix m.

selection committee n comité m de sélection.

selective [sɪ'lɛktɪv] a sélectif(ive); (school) à recrutement sélectif.

selector [sɪ'lɛktə*] n (person) sélectionneur/euse; (TECH) sélecteur m.

self [sɛlf] n (pl **selves** [sɛlvz]): **the** ~ le moi inv ♦ prefix auto-.

self-addressed ['sɛlfə'drɛst] a: ~ **envelope** enveloppe f à mon (or votre etc) nom.

self-adhesive [sɛlfəd'hiːzɪv] a autocollant(e).

self-assertive [sɛlfə'sɜːtɪv] *a* autoritaire.

self-assurance [sɛlfə'ʃuərəns] *n* assurance *f*.

self-assured [sɛlfə'ʃuəd] *a* sûr(e) de soi, plein(e) d'assurance.

self-catering [sɛlf'keɪtərɪŋ] *a* (*Brit: flat*) avec cuisine, où l'on peut faire sa cuisine; (: *holiday*) en appartement (*or* chalet *etc*) loué.

self-centred, (*US*) **self-centered** [sɛlf'sɛntəd] *a* égocentrique.

self-cleaning [sɛlf'kliːnɪŋ] *a* autonettoyant(e).

self-coloured, (*US*) **self-colored** [sɛlf'kʌləd] *a* uni(e).

self-confessed [sɛlfkən'fɛst] *a* (*alcoholic etc*) déclaré(e), qui ne s'en cache pas.

self-confidence [sɛlf'kɒnfɪdns] *n* confiance *f* en soi.

self-conscious [sɛlf'kɒnʃəs] *a* timide, qui manque d'assurance.

self-contained [sɛlfkən'teɪnd] *a* (*Brit: flat*) avec entrée particulière, indépendant(e).

self-control [sɛlfkən'trəul] *n* maîtrise *f* de soi.

self-defeating [sɛlfdɪ'fiːtɪŋ] *a* qui a un effet contraire à l'effet recherché.

self-defence, (*US*) **self-defense** [sɛlfdɪ'fɛns] *n* légitime défense *f*.

self-discipline [sɛlf'dɪsɪplɪn] *n* discipline personnelle.

self-employed [sɛlfɪm'plɔɪd] *a* qui travaille à son compte.

self-esteem [sɛlfɪ'stiːm] *n* amour-propre *m*.

self-evident [sɛlf'ɛvɪdnt] *a* évident(e), qui va de soi.

self-explanatory [sɛlfɪk'splænətrɪ] *a* qui se passe d'explication.

self-governing [sɛlf'gʌvənɪŋ] *a* autonome.

self-help ['sɛlf'hɛlp] *n* initiative personnelle, efforts personnels.

self-importance [sɛlfɪm'pɔːtns] suffisance *f*.

self-indulgent [sɛlfɪn'dʌldʒənt] *a* qui ne se refuse rien.

self-inflicted [sɛlfɪn'flɪktɪd] *a* volontaire.

self-interest [sɛlf'ɪntrɪst] *n* intérêt personnel.

selfish ['sɛlfɪʃ] *a* égoïste.

selfishness ['sɛlfɪʃnɪs] *n* égoïsme *m*.

selfless ['sɛlflɪs] *a* désintéressé(e).

selflessly ['sɛlflɪslɪ] *ad* sans penser à soi.

self-made man ['sɛlfmeɪd-] *n* self-made man *m*.

self-pity [sɛlf'pɪtɪ] *n* apitoiement *m* sur soi-même.

self-portrait [sɛlf'pɔːtreɪt] *n* autoportrait *m*.

self-possessed [sɛlfpə'zɛst] *a* assuré(e).

self-preservation [sɛlfprɛzə'veɪʃən] *n* instinct *m* de conservation.

self-raising [sɛlf'reɪzɪŋ], (*US*) **self-rising** [sɛlf'raɪzɪŋ] *a*: ~ **flour** farine *f* pour gâteaux (*avec levure incorporée*).

self-reliant [sɛlfrɪ'laɪənt] *a* indépendant(e).

self-respect [sɛlfrɪs'pɛkt] *n* respect *m* de soi, amour-propre *m*.

self-respecting [sɛlfrɪs'pɛktɪŋ] *a* qui se respecte.

self-righteous [sɛlf'raɪtʃəs] *a* satisfait(e) de soi, pharisaïque.

self-rising [sɛlf'raɪzɪŋ] *a* (*US*) = **self-raising**.

self-sacrifice [sɛlf'sækrɪfaɪs] *n* abnégation *f*.

self-same ['sɛlfseɪm] *a* même.

self-satisfied [sɛlf'sætɪsfaɪd] *a* content(e) de soi, suffisant(e).

self-sealing [sɛlf'siːlɪŋ] *a* (*envelope*) autocollant(e).

self-service [sɛlf'sɜːvɪs] *a*, *n* libre-service (*m*), self-service (*m*).

self-styled ['sɛlfstaɪld] *a* soi-disant *inv*.

self-sufficient [sɛlfsə'fɪʃənt] *a* indépendant(e).

self-supporting [sɛlfsə'pɔːtɪŋ] *a* financièrement indépendant(e).

self-taught [sɛlf'tɔːt] *a* autodidacte.

self-test ['sɛlftɛst] *n* (*COMPUT*) test *m* automatique.

sell, *pt*, *pp* **sold** [sɛl, səuld] *vt* vendre ♦ *vi* se vendre; **to** ~ **at** *or* **for 10 F** se vendre 10 F; **to** ~ **sb an idea** (*fig*) faire accepter une idée à qn.

sell off *vt* liquider.

sell out *vi*: **to** ~ **out (to)** (*COMM*) vendre son fonds *or* son affaire (à) ♦ *vt* vendre tout son stock de; **the tickets are all sold out** il ne reste plus de billets.

sell up *vi* vendre son fonds *or* son affaire.

sell-by date ['sɛlbaɪ-] *n* date *f* limite de vente.

seller ['sɛlə*] *n* vendeur/euse, marchand/e; ~'s **market** marché *m* à la hausse.

selling price ['sɛlɪŋ-] *n* prix *m* de vente.

sellotape ['sɛləuteɪp] *n* ® (*Brit*) papier collant, scotch *m* ®.

sellout ['sɛlaut] *n* trahison *f*, capitulation *f*; (*of tickets*): **it was a** ~ tous les billets ont été vendus.

selves [sɛlvz] *npl of* **self**.

semantic [sɪ'mæntɪk] *a* sémantique.

semantics [sɪ'mæntɪks] *n* sémantique *f*.

semaphore ['sɛməfɔː*] *n* signaux *mpl* à bras; (*RAIL*) sémaphore *m*.

semblance ['sɛmblns] *n* semblant *m*.

semen ['siːmən] *n* sperme *m*.

semester [sɪ'mɛstə*] *n* (*esp US*) semestre *m*.

semi... ['sɛmɪ] *prefix* semi-, demi-; à demi, à moitié ♦ *n*: **semi** = **semidetached (house)**.

semi-breve ['sɛmɪbriːv] *n* (*Brit*) ronde *f*.

semicircle ['sɛmɪsəːkl] *n* demi-cercle *m*.

semicircular ['sɛmɪ'sə:kjulə*] *a* en demi-cercle, semi-circulaire.

semicolon [sɛmɪ'kəulən] *n* point-virgule *m*.

semiconductor [sɛmɪkən'dʌktə*] *n* semiconducteur *m*.

semiconscious [sɛmɪ'kɒnʃəs] *a* à demi conscient(e).

semidetached (house) [sɛmɪdɪ'tætʃt-] *n* (*Brit*) maison jumelée *or* jumelle.

semifinal [sɛmɪ'faɪnl] *n* demi-finale *f*.

seminar ['sɛmɪnɑː*] *n* séminaire *m*.

seminary ['sɛmɪnərɪ] *n* (*REL*: *for priests*) séminaire *m*.

semiprecious [sɛmɪ'prɛʃəs] *a* semi-précieux(euse).

semiquaver ['sɛmɪkweɪvə*] *n* (*Brit*) double croche *f*.

semiskilled [sɛmɪ'skɪld] *a*: ~ **worker** *n* ouvrier/ière spécialisé(e).

semitone ['sɛmɪtəun] *n* (*MUS*) demi-ton *m*.

semolina [sɛmə'liːnə] *n* semoule *f*.

SEN *n abbr* (*Brit*) = *State Enrolled Nurse*.

Sen., sen. *abbr* = **senator, senior**.

senate ['sɛnɪt] *n* sénat *m*.

senator ['sɛnɪtə*] *n* sénateur *m*.

send, *pt*, *pp* **sent** [sɛnd, sɛnt] *vt* envoyer; **to** ~ **by post** *or* (*US*) **mail** envoyer *or* expédier par la poste; **to ~ sb for sth** envoyer qn chercher qch; **to ~ word that ...** faire dire que ...; **she ~s (you) her love** elle vous adresse ses amitiés; **to ~ sb to Coventry** (*Brit*) mettre qn en quarantaine; **to ~ sb to sleep** endormir qn; **to ~ sb into fits of laughter** faire rire qn aux éclats; **to ~ sth flying** envoyer valser qch.

send away *vt* (*letter, goods*) envoyer, expédier.

send away for *vt fus* commander par correspondance, se faire envoyer.

send back *vt* renvoyer.

send for *vt fus* envoyer chercher; faire venir; (*by post*) se faire envoyer, commander par correspondance.

send in *vt* (*report, application, resignation*) remettre.

send off *vt* (*goods*) envoyer, expédier; (*Brit SPORT: player*) expulser *or* renvoyer du terrain.

send on *vt* (*Brit: letter*) faire suivre; (*luggage etc: in advance*) (faire) expédier à l'avance.

send out *vt* (*invitation*) envoyer (par la poste); (*emit: light, heat, signals*) émettre.

send round *vt* (*letter, document etc*) faire circuler.

send up *vt* (*person, price*) faire monter; (*Brit: parody*) mettre en boîte, parodier.

sender ['sɛndə*] *n* expéditeur/trice.

send-off ['sɛndɔf] *n:* **a good ~** des adieux chaleureux.

Senegal [sɛnɪ'gɔːl] *n* Sénégal *m*.

Senegalese ['sɛnɪgə'liːz] *a* sénégalais(e) ♦ *n* (*pl inv*) Sénégalais/e.

senile ['siːnaɪl] *a* sénile.

senility [sɪ'nɪlɪtɪ] *n* sénilité *f*.

senior ['siːnɪə*] *a* (*older*) aîné(e), plus âgé(e); (*of higher rank*) supérieur(e) ♦ *n* aîné/e; (*in service*) personne *f* qui a plus d'ancienneté; **P. Jones ~** P. Jones père.

senior citizen *n* personne âgée.

senior high school *n* (*US*) ≈ lycée *m*.

seniority [siːnɪ'ɔrɪtɪ] *n* priorité *f* d'âge, ancienneté *f*; (*in rank*) supériorité *f* (hiérarchique).

sensation [sɛn'seɪʃən] *n* sensation *f*; **to create a ~** faire sensation.

sensational [sɛn'seɪʃənl] *a* qui fait sensation; (*marvellous*) sensationnel(le).

sense [sɛns] *n* sens *m*; (*feeling*) sentiment *m*; (*meaning*) signification *f*; (*wisdom*) bon sens ♦ *vt* sentir, pressentir; **~s** *npl* raison *f*; **it makes ~** c'est logique; **~ of humour** sens de l'humour; **there is no ~ in (doing) that** cela n'a pas de sens; **to come to one's ~s** (*regain consciousness*) reprendre conscience; (*become reasonable*) revenir à la raison; **to take leave of one's ~s** perdre la tête.

senseless ['sɛnslɪs] *a* insensé(e), stupide; (*unconscious*) sans connaissance.

sensibility [sɛnsɪ'bɪlɪtɪ] *n* sensibilité *f*; **sensibilities** *npl* susceptibilité *f*.

sensible ['sɛnsɪbl] *a* sensé(e), raisonnable; (*shoes etc*) pratique.

sensitive ['sɛnsɪtɪv] *a:* **~ (to)** sensible (à); **he is very ~ about it** c'est un point très sensible (chez lui).

sensitivity [sɛnsɪ'tɪvɪtɪ] *n* sensibilité *f*.

sensual ['sɛnsjuəl] *a* sensuel(le).

sensuous ['sɛnsjuəs] *a* voluptueux(euse), sensuel(le).

sent [sɛnt] *pt, pp of* **send**.

sentence ['sɛntns] *n* (*LING*) phrase *f*; (*LAW: judgment*) condamnation *f*, sentence *f*; (*: punishment*) peine *f* ♦ *vt:* **to ~ sb to death/ to 5 years** condamner qn à mort/à 5 ans; **to pass ~ on sb** prononcer une peine contre qn.

sentiment ['sɛntɪmənt] *n* sentiment *m*; (*opinion*) opinion *f*, avis *m*.

sentimental [sɛntɪ'mɛntl] *a* sentimental(e).

sentimentality ['sɛntɪmɛn'tælɪtɪ] *n* sentimentalité *f*, sensiblerie *f*.

sentry ['sɛntrɪ] *n* sentinelle *f*, factionnaire *m*.

sentry duty *n:* **to be on ~** être de faction.

Seoul [səul] *n* Séoul.

separable ['sɛprəbl] *a* séparable.

separate *a* ['sɛprɪt] séparé(e), indépendant(e), différent(e) ♦ *vb* ['sɛpəreɪt] *vt* séparer ♦ *vi* se séparer; **~ from** distinct(e) de; **under ~ cover** (*COMM*) sous pli séparé; **to ~ into** diviser en.

separately ['sɛprɪtlɪ] *ad* séparément.

separates ['sɛprɪts] *npl* (*clothes*) coordonnés *mpl*.

separation [sɛpə'reɪʃən] *n* séparation *f*.

Sept. *abbr* (= *September*) sept.

September [sɛp'tɛmbə*] *n* septembre *m*; *for phrases see also* **July**.

septic ['sɛptɪk] *a* septique; (*wound*) infecté(e); **to go ~** s'infecter.

septicaemia [sɛptɪ'siːmɪə] *n* septicémie *f*.

septic tank *n* fosse *f* septique.

sequel ['siːkwl] *n* conséquence *f*; séquelles *fpl*; (*of story*) suite *f*.

sequence ['siːkwəns] *n* ordre *m*, suite *f*; **in ~** par ordre, dans l'ordre, les uns après les autres; **~ of tenses** concordance *f* des temps.

sequential [sɪ'kwɛnʃəl] *a:* **~ access** (*COMPUT*) accès séquentiel.

sequin ['siːkwɪn] *n* paillette *f*.

Serbo-Croat ['sɜːbəu'krəuæt] *n* (*LING*) serbo-croate *m*.

serenade [sɛrə'neɪd] *n* sérénade *f* ♦ *vt* donner une sérénade à.

serene [sɪ'riːn] *a* serein(e), calme, paisible.

serenity [sə'rɛnɪtɪ] *n* sérénité *f*, calme *m*.

sergeant ['sɑːdʒənt] *n* sergent *m*; (*POLICE*) brigadier *m*.

sergeant major *n* sergent-major *m*.

serial ['sɪərɪəl] *n* feuilleton *m* ♦ *a* (*COMPUT: interface, printer*) série *inv*; (*: access*) séquentiel(le).

serialize ['sɪərɪəlaɪz] *vt* publier (*or* adapter) en feuilleton.

serial number *n* numéro *m* de série.

series ['sɪərɪz] *n* série *f*; (*PUBLISHING*) collection *f*.

serious ['sɪərɪəs] *a* sérieux(euse); (*accident etc*) grave; **are you ~ (about it?)** parlez-vous sérieusement?

seriously ['sɪərɪəslɪ] *ad* sérieusement, gravement; **to take sth/sb ~** prendre qch/qn au sérieux.

seriousness ['sɪərɪəsnɪs] *n* sérieux *m*, gravité *f*.

sermon ['sɜːmən] *n* sermon *m*.

serrated [sɪ'reɪtɪd] *a* en dents de scie.

serum ['sɪərəm] *n* sérum *m*.

servant ['sɜːvənt] *n* domestique *m/f*; (*fig*) serviteur/servante.

serve [sɜːv] *vt* (*employer etc*) servir, être au service de; (*purpose*) servir à; (*customer, food, meal*) servir; (*apprenticeship*) faire, accomplir; (*prison term*) faire; purger ♦ *vi* (*also TENNIS*) servir; (*be useful*): **to ~ as/for/to do** servir de/à/à faire ♦ *n* (*TENNIS*) service *m*; **are you being ~d?** est-ce qu'on s'occupe de vous?; **to ~ on a committee/jury** faire partie d'un comité/jury; **it ~s him right** c'est bien fait pour lui; **it ~s my purpose** cela fait mon affaire.

serve out , serve up *vt* (*food*) servir.

service ['sɜːvɪs] *n* (*gen*) service *m*; (*AUT: maintenance*) révision *f*; (*REL*) office *m* ♦ *vt* (*car, washing machine*) réviser; **the S~s** *npl* les forces armées; **to be of ~ to sb, to do sb a ~** rendre service à qn; **to put one's car in for ~** donner sa voiture à réviser; **dinner ~** service de table.

serviceable ['sɜːvɪsəbl] *a* pratique, commode.

service area *n* (*on motorway*) aire *f* de services.

service charge *n* (*Brit*) service *m*.

service industries *npl* les industries *fpl* de service, les services *mpl*.

serviceman ['sɜːvɪsmən] *n* militaire *m*.

service station *n* station-service *f*.

serviette [sɜːvɪ'ɛt] *n* (*Brit*) serviette *f* (de table).

servile ['sɜːvaɪl] *a* servile.

session ['sɛʃən] *n* (*sitting*) séance *f*; (*SCOL*) année *f* scolaire (*or* universitaire); **to be in ~** siéger, être en session *or* en séance.

set [sɛt] *n* série *f*, assortiment *m*; (*of tools etc*) jeu *m*; (*RADIO, TV*) poste *m*; (*TENNIS*) set *m*; (*group of people*) cercle *m*, milieu *m*; (*CINEMA*) plateau *m*; (*THEATRE: stage*) scène *f*; (: *scenery*) décor *m*; (*MATH*) ensemble *m*; (*HAIRDRESSING*) mise *f* en plis ♦ *a* (*fixed*) fixe, déterminé(e); (*ready*) prêt(e) ♦ *vb* (*pt, pp* **set**) *vt* (*place*) mettre, poser, placer; (*fix, establish*) fixer; (: *record*) établir; (*assign: task, homework*) donner; (*adjust*) régler; (*decide: rules etc*) fixer, choisir; (*TYP*) composer ♦ *vi* (*sun*) se coucher; (*jam, jelly, concrete*) prendre; **to be ~ on doing** être résolu(e) à faire; **to be all ~ to do** être (fin) prêt(e) pour faire; **to be (dead) ~ against** être (totalement) opposé à; **he's ~ in his ways** il n'est pas très souple, il tient à ses habitudes; **to ~ to music** mettre en musique; **to ~ on fire** mettre le feu à; **to ~ free** libérer; **to ~ sth going** déclencher qch; **to ~ sail** partir, prendre la mer; **a ~ phrase** une expression toute faite, une locution; **a ~ of false teeth** un dentier; **a ~ of dining-room furniture** une salle à manger.

set about *vt fus* (*task*) entreprendre, se mettre à; **to ~ about doing sth** se mettre à faire qch.

set aside *vt* mettre de côté.

set back *vt* (*in time*): **to ~ back (by)** retarder (de); (*place*): **a house ~ back from the road** une maison située en retrait de la route.

set in *vi* (*infection, bad weather*) s'installer; (*complications*) survenir, surgir; **the rain has ~ in for the day** c'est parti pour qu'il pleuve toute la journée.

set off *vi* se mettre en route, partir ♦ *vt* (*bomb*) faire exploser; (*cause to start*) déclencher; (*show up well*) mettre en valeur, faire valoir.

set out *vi*: **to ~ out to do** entreprendre de faire; avoir pour but *or* intention de faire ♦ *vt* (*arrange*) disposer; (*state*) présenter, exposer; **to ~ out (from)** partir (de).

set up *vt* (*organization*) fonder, constituer; (*monument*) ériger; **to ~ up shop** (*fig*) s'établir, s'installer.

setback ['sɛtbæk] *n* (*hitch*) revers *m*, contretemps *m*; (*in health*) rechute *f*.

set menu *n* menu *m*.

set square *n* équerre *f*.

settee [sɛ'tiː] *n* canapé *m*.

setting ['sɛtɪŋ] *n* cadre *m*; (*of jewel*) monture *f*.

setting lotion *n* lotion *f* pour mise en plis.

settle ['sɛtl] *vt* (*argument, matter, account*) régler; (*problem*) résoudre; (*MED: calm*) calmer; (*colonize: land*) coloniser ♦ *vi* (*bird, dust etc*) se poser; (*sediment*) se déposer; (*also*: **~ down**) s'installer, se fixer; (: *become calmer*) se calmer; se ranger; **to ~ to sth** se mettre sérieusement à qch; **to ~ for sth** accepter qch, se contenter de qch; **to ~ on sth** opter *or* se décider pour qch; **that's ~d then** alors, c'est d'accord!; **to ~ one's stomach** calmer les maux d'estomac.

settle in *vi* s'installer.

settle up *vi*: **to ~ up with sb** régler (ce que l'on doit à) qn.

settlement ['sɛtlmənt] *n* (*payment*) règlement *m*; (*agreement*) accord *m*; (*colony*) colonie *f*; (*village etc*) établissement *m*; hameau *m*; **in ~ of our account** (*COMM*) en règlement de notre compte.

settler ['sɛtlə*] *n* colon *m*.

setup ['sɛtʌp] *n* (*arrangement*) manière *f* dont les choses sont organisées; (*situation*) situation *f*, allure *f* des choses.

seven ['sɛvn] *num* sept.

seventeen [sɛvn'tiːn] *num* dix-sept.

seventh ['sɛvnθ] *num* septième.

seventy ['sɛvntɪ] *num* soixante-dix.

sever ['sɛvə*] *vt* couper, trancher; (*relations*) rompre.

several ['sɛvərl] *a, pronoun* plusieurs (*m/fpl*); **~ of us** plusieurs d'entre nous; **~ times** plusieurs fois.

severance ['sɛvərəns] *n* (*of relations*) rupture *f*.

severance pay *n* indemnité *f* de licenciement.

severe [sɪ'vɪə*] *a* sévère, strict(e); (*serious*) grave, sérieux(euse); (*hard*) rigoureux(euse), dur(e); (*plain*) sévère, austère.

severely [sɪ'vɪəlɪ] *ad* sévèrement; (*wounded, ill*) gravement.

severity [sɪ'vɛrɪtɪ] *n* sévérité *f*; gravité *f*; rigueur *f*.

sew, *pt* **sewed**, *pp* **sewn** [səu, səud, səun] *vt*,

vi coudre.
 sew up *vt* (re)coudre; **it is all sewn up**
 (fig) c'est dans le sac *or* dans la poche.
sewage ['suːɪdʒ] *n* vidange(s) *f(pl)*.
sewer ['suːə*] *n* égout *m*.
sewing ['səʊɪŋ] *n* couture *f*.
sewing machine *n* machine *f* à coudre.
sewn [səʊn] *pp of* **sew**.
sex [sɛks] *n* sexe *m*; **to have ~ with** avoir des
 rapports (sexuels) avec.
sex act *n* acte sexuel.
sexism ['sɛksɪzəm] *n* sexisme *m*.
sexist ['sɛksɪst] *a* sexiste.
sextet [sɛks'tɛt] *n* sextuor *m*.
sexual ['sɛksjuəl] *a* sexuel(le); **~ assault**
 attentat *m* à la pudeur; **~ intercourse**
 rapports sexuels.
sexy ['sɛksɪ] *a* sexy *inv*.
Seychelles [seɪ'ʃɛl(z)] *npl*: **the ~** les Seychelles *fpl*.
SF *n abbr* (= *science fiction*) SF *f*.
SG *n abbr* (*US*) = **Surgeon General**.
Sgt *abbr* (= *sergeant*) Sgt.
shabbiness ['ʃæbɪnɪs] *n* aspect miteux;
 mesquinerie *f*.
shabby ['ʃæbɪ] *a* miteux(euse); (*behaviour*)
 mesquin(e), méprisable.
shack [ʃæk] *n* cabane *f*, hutte *f*.
shackles ['ʃæklz] *npl* chaînes *fpl*, entraves *fpl*.
shade [ʃeɪd] *n* ombre *f*; (*for lamp*) abat-jour
 m inv; (*of colour*) nuance *f*, ton *m*; (*US:
 window ~*) store *m*; (*small quantity*): **a ~ of**
 un soupçon de ♦ *vt* abriter du soleil, om-
 brager; **~s** *npl* (*US: sunglasses*) lunettes *fpl*
 de soleil; **in the ~** à l'ombre; **a ~ smaller** un
 tout petit peu plus petit.
shadow ['ʃædəʊ] *n* ombre *f* ♦ *vt* (*follow*) filer;
 without *or* **beyond a ~ of doubt** sans l'ombre d'un doute.
shadow cabinet *n* (*Brit POL*) cabinet
 parallèle formé par le parti qui n'est pas au
 pouvoir.
shadowy ['ʃædəʊɪ] *a* ombragé(e); (*dim*)
 vague, indistinct(e).
shady ['ʃeɪdɪ] *a* ombragé(e); (*fig: dishonest*)
 louche, véreux(euse).
shaft [ʃɑːft] *n* (*of arrow, spear*) hampe *f*;
 (*AUT, TECH*) arbre *m*; (*of mine*) puits *m*; (*of
 lift*) cage *f*; (*of light*) rayon *m*, trait *m*;
 ventilator ~ conduit *m* d'aération *or* de
 ventilation.
shaggy ['ʃægɪ] *a* hirsute; en broussaille.
shake [ʃeɪk] *vb* (*pt* **shook**, *pp* **shaken** [ʃuk,
 'ʃeɪkn]) *vt* secouer; (*bottle, cocktail*) agiter;
 (*house, confidence*) ébranler ♦ *vi* trembler ♦
 n secousse *f*; **to ~ one's head** (*in refusal
 etc*) dire *or* faire non de la tête; (*in dismay*)
 secouer la tête; **to ~ hands with sb** serrer
 la main à qn.
shake off *vt* secouer; (*fig*) se débarrasser
 de.
shake up *vt* secouer.
shake-up ['ʃeɪkʌp] *n* grand remaniement.
shakily ['ʃeɪkɪlɪ] *ad* (*reply*) d'une voix tremblante; (*walk*) d'un pas mal assuré; (*write*)
 d'une main tremblante.
shaky ['ʃeɪkɪ] *a* (*hand, voice*) tremblant(e);
 (*building*) branlant(e), peu solide; (*memory*)
 chancelant(e); (*knowledge*) incertain(e).

shale [ʃeɪl] *n* schiste argileux.
shall [ʃæl] *auxiliary vb*: **I ~ go** j'irai.
shallot [ʃə'lɔt] *n* (*Brit*) échalote *f*.
shallow ['ʃæləʊ] *a* peu profond(e); (*fig*)
 superficiel(le), qui manque de profondeur.
sham [ʃæm] *n* frime *f*; (*jewellery, furniture*)
 imitation *f* ♦ *a* feint(e), simulé(e) ♦ *vt* feindre, simuler.
shambles ['ʃæmblz] *n* confusion *f*, pagaïe *f*,
 fouillis *m*; **the economy is (in) a complete ~**
 l'économie est dans la confusion la plus
 totale.
shame [ʃeɪm] *n* honte *f* ♦ *vt* faire honte à; **it is
 a ~ (that/to do)** c'est dommage (que + *sub/*
 de faire); **what a ~!** quel dommage!; **to put
 sb/sth to ~** (*fig*) faire honte à qn/qch.
shamefaced ['ʃeɪmfeɪst] *a* honteux(euse),
 penaud(e).
shameful ['ʃeɪmful] *a* honteux(euse),
 scandaleux(euse).
shameless ['ʃeɪmlɪs] *a* éhonté(e), effronté(e);
 (*immodest*) impudique.
shampoo [ʃæm'puː] *n* shampooing *m* ♦ *vt*
 faire un shampooing à; **~ and set**
 shampooing et mise *f* en plis.
shamrock ['ʃæmrɔk] *n* trèfle *m* (*emblème
 national de l'Irlande*).
shandy ['ʃændɪ] *n* bière panachée.
shan't [ʃɑːnt] = **shall not**.
shanty town ['ʃæntɪ-] *n* bidonville *m*.
SHAPE [ʃeɪp] *n abbr* (= *Supreme Headquarters Allied Powers, Europe*) quartier
 général des forces alliées en Europe.
shape [ʃeɪp] *n* forme *f* ♦ *vt* façonner, modeler;
 (*clay, stone*) donner forme à; (*statement*)
 formuler; (*sb's ideas, character*) former;
 (*sb's life*) déterminer; (*course of events*)
 influer sur le cours de ♦ *vi* (*also: ~ up*:
 events) prendre tournure; (: *person*) faire
 des progrès, s'en sortir; **to take ~** prendre
 forme *or* tournure; **in the ~ of a heart** en
 forme de cœur; **I can't bear gardening in
 any ~ or form** je déteste le jardinage sous
 quelque forme que ce soit; **to get o.s. into ~**
 (re)trouver la forme.
-shaped [ʃeɪpt] *suffix*: **heart-~** en forme de
 cœur.
shapeless ['ʃeɪplɪs] *a* informe, sans forme.
shapely ['ʃeɪplɪ] *a* bien proportionné(e),
 beau(belle).
share [ʃɛə*] *n* (*thing received, contribution*)
 part *f*; (*COMM*) action *f* ♦ *vt* partager; (*have
 in common*) avoir en commun; **to ~ out
 (among** *or* **between)** partager (entre); **to ~
 in** (*joy, sorrow*) prendre part à; (*profits*)
 participer à, avoir part à; (*work*) partager.
share capital *n* capital social.
share certificate *n* certificat *m or* titre *m*
 d'action.
shareholder ['ʃɛəhəʊldə*] *n* actionnaire *m/f*.
share index *n* indice *m* de la Bourse.
shark [ʃɑːk] *n* requin *m*.
sharp [ʃɑːp] *a* (*razor, knife*) tranchant(e),
 bien aiguisé(e); (*point*) aigu(ë); (*nose, chin*)
 pointu(e); (*outline*) net(te); (*curve, bend*)
 brusque; (*cold, pain*) vif(vive); (*MUS*) dièse;
 (*voice*) coupant(e); (*person: quick-witted*)
 vif(vive), éveillé(e); (: *unscrupulous*)
 malhonnête ♦ *n* (*MUS*) dièse *m* ♦ *ad*: **at 2**

o'clock ~ à 2 heures pile *or* tapantes; **turn ~ left** tournez immédiatement à gauche; **to be ~ with sb** être brusque avec qn; **look ~!** dépêche-toi!

sharpen ['ʃɑːpn] *vt* aiguiser; (*pencil*) tailler; (*fig*) aviver.

sharpener ['ʃɑːpnə*] *n* (*also:* **pencil ~**) taille-crayon(s) *m inv*; (*also:* **knife ~**) aiguisoir *m*.

sharp-eyed [ʃɑːp'aɪd] *a* à qui rien n'échappe.

sharply ['ʃɑːplɪ] *ad* (*abruptly*) brusquement; (*clearly*) nettement; (*harshly*) sèchement, vertement.

sharp-tempered [ʃɑːp'tɛmpəd] *a* prompt(e) à se mettre en colère.

sharp-witted [ʃɑːp'wɪtɪd] *a* à l'esprit vif, malin(igne).

shatter ['ʃætə*] *vt* fracasser, briser, faire voler en éclats; (*fig: upset*) bouleverser; (*: ruin*) briser, ruiner ♦ *vi* voler en éclats, se briser, se fracasser.

shattered ['ʃætəd] *a* (*overwhelmed, grief-stricken*) bouleversé(e); (*col: exhausted*) éreinté(e).

shatterproof ['ʃætəpruːf] *a* incassable.

shave [ʃeɪv] *vt* raser ♦ *vi* se raser ♦ *n*: **to have a ~** se raser.

shaven [ʃeɪvn] *a* (*head*) rasé(e).

shaver ['ʃeɪvə*] *n* (*also:* **electric ~**) rasoir *m* électrique.

shaving ['ʃeɪvɪŋ] *n* (*action*) rasage *m*; **~s** *npl* (*of wood etc*) copeaux *mpl*.

shaving brush *n* blaireau *m*.

shaving cream *n* crème *f* à raser.

shaving soap *n* savon *m* à barbe.

shawl [ʃɔːl] *n* châle *m*.

she [ʃiː] *pronoun* elle; **there ~ is** la voilà; **~-elephant** *etc* éléphant *etc* femelle; *NB: for ships, countries follow the gender of your translation.*

sheaf, *pl* **sheaves** [ʃiːf, ʃiːvz] *n* gerbe *f*.

shear [ʃɪə*] *vt* (*pt* **~ed**, *pp* **~ed** *or* **shorn** [ʃɔːn]) (*sheep*) tondre.
 shear off *vt* tondre; (*branch*) élaguer.

shears ['ʃɪəz] *npl* (*for hedge*) cisaille(s) *f(pl)*.

sheath [ʃiːθ] *n* gaine *f*, fourreau *m*, étui *m*; (*contraceptive*) préservatif *m*.

sheathe [ʃiːð] *vt* gainer; (*sword*) rengainer.

sheath knife *n* couteau *m* à gaine.

sheaves [ʃiːvz] *npl* of **sheaf**.

shed [ʃɛd] *n* remise *f*, resserre *f*; (*INDUSTRY, RAIL*) hangar *m* ♦ *vt* (*pt*, *pp* **shed**) (*leaves, fur etc*) perdre; (*tears*) verser, répandre; **to ~ light on** (*problem, mystery*) faire la lumière sur.

she'd [ʃiːd] = **she had**, **she would**.

sheen [ʃiːn] *n* lustre *m*.

sheep [ʃiːp] *n* (*pl inv*) mouton *m*.

sheepdog ['ʃiːpdɔg] *n* chien *m* de berger.

sheep farmer *n* éleveur *m* de moutons.

sheepish ['ʃiːpɪʃ] *a* penaud(e), timide.

sheepskin ['ʃiːpskɪn] *n* peau *f* de mouton.

sheepskin jacket *n* canadienne *f*.

sheer [ʃɪə*] *a* (*utter*) pur(e), pur et simple; (*steep*) à pic, abrupt(e); (*almost transparent*) extrêmement fin(e) ♦ *ad* à pic, abruptement; **by ~ chance** par pur hasard.

sheet [ʃiːt] *n* (*on bed*) drap *m*; (*of paper*) feuille *f*; (*of glass, metal*) feuille, plaque *f*.

sheet feed *n* (*on printer*) alimentation *f* en papier (feuille à feuille).

sheet lightning *n* éclair *m* en nappe(s).

sheet metal *n* tôle *f*.

sheet music *n* partition(s) *f(pl)*.

sheik(h) [ʃeɪk] *n* cheik *m*.

shelf, *pl* **shelves** [ʃɛlf, ʃɛlvz] *n* étagère *f*, rayon *m*; **set of shelves** rayonnage *m*.

shelf life *n* (*COMM*) durée *f* de conservation (avant la vente).

shell [ʃɛl] *n* (*on beach*) coquillage *m*; (*of egg, nut etc*) coquille *f*; (*explosive*) obus *m*; (*of building*) carcasse *f* ♦ *vt* (*crab, prawn etc*) décortiquer; (*peas*) écosser; (*MIL*) bombarder (d'obus).
 shell out *vi* (*col*): **to ~ out (for)** casquer (pour).

she'll [ʃiːl] = **she will**, **she shall**.

shellfish ['ʃɛlfɪʃ] *n* (*pl inv*) (*crab etc*) crustacé *m*; (*scallop etc*) coquillage *m*; (*pl: as food*) crustacés; coquillages.

shelter ['ʃɛltə*] *n* abri *m*, refuge *m* ♦ *vt* abriter, protéger; (*give lodging to*) donner asile à ♦ *vi* s'abriter, se mettre à l'abri; **to take ~ (from)** s'abriter (de).

sheltered ['ʃɛltəd] *a* (*life*) retiré(e), à l'abri des soucis; (*spot*) abrité(e).

shelve [ʃɛlv] *vt* (*fig*) mettre en suspens *or* en sommeil.

shelves ['ʃɛlvz] *npl* of **shelf**.

shelving ['ʃɛlvɪŋ] *n* (*shelves*) rayonnage(s) *m(pl)*.

shepherd ['ʃɛpəd] *n* berger *m* ♦ *vt* (*guide*) guider, escorter.

shepherdess ['ʃɛpədɪs] *n* bergère *f*.

shepherd's pie *n* ≈ hachis *m* Parmentier.

sherbet ['ʃɜːbət] *n* (*Brit: powder*) poudre acidulée; (*US: water ice*) sorbet *m*.

sheriff ['ʃɛrɪf] *n* shérif *m*.

sherry ['ʃɛrɪ] *n* xérès *m*, sherry *m*.

she's [ʃiːz] = **she is**, **she has**.

Shetland ['ʃɛtlənd] *n* (*also:* **the ~s, the ~ Isles** *or* **Islands**) les îles *fpl* Shetland.

shield [ʃiːld] *n* bouclier *m* ♦ *vt*: **to ~ (from)** protéger (de *or* contre).

shift [ʃɪft] *n* (*change*) changement *m*; (*of workers*) équipe *f*, poste *m* ♦ *vt* déplacer, changer de place; (*remove*) enlever ♦ *vi* changer de place, bouger; **the wind has ~ed to the south** le vent a tourné au sud; **a ~ in demand** (*COMM*) un déplacement de la demande.

shift key *n* (*on typewriter*) touche *f* de majuscule.

shiftless ['ʃɪftlɪs] *a* fainéant(e).

shift work *n* travail *m* par roulement; **to do ~** travailler par roulement.

shifty ['ʃɪftɪ] *a* sournois(e); (*eyes*) fuyant(e).

shilling ['ʃɪlɪŋ] *n* (*Brit*) shilling *m* (= *12 old pence; 20 in a pound*).

shilly-shally ['ʃɪlɪʃælɪ] *vi* tergiverser, atermoyer.

shimmer ['ʃɪmə*] *n* miroitement *m*, chatoiement *m* ♦ *vi* miroiter, chatoyer.

shin [ʃɪn] *n* tibia *m* ♦ *vi*: **to ~ up/down a tree** grimper dans un/descendre d'un arbre.

shindig ['ʃɪndɪg] *n* (*col*) bamboula *f*.

shine [ʃaɪn] *n* éclat *m*, brillant *m* ♦ *vb* (*pt*, *pp* **shone** [ʃɔn]) *vi* briller ♦ *vt* faire briller *or* reluire; (*torch*): **to ~ on** braquer sur.

shingle ['ʃɪŋgl] *n* (*on beach*) galets *mpl*; (*on roof*) bardeau *m*.

shingles ['ʃɪŋglz] *n* (*MED*) zona *m*.

shining ['ʃaɪnɪŋ] *a* brillant(e).

shiny ['ʃaɪnɪ] *a* brillant(e).

ship [ʃɪp] *n* bateau *m*; (*large*) navire *m* ♦ *vt* transporter (par mer); (*send*) expédier (par mer); (*load*) charger, embarquer; **on board ~** à bord.

shipbuilder ['ʃɪpbɪldə*] *n* constructeur *m* de navires.

shipbuilding ['ʃɪpbɪldɪŋ] *n* construction navale.

ship canal *n* canal *m* maritime *or* de navigation.

ship chandler [-'tʃɑːndlə*] *n* fournisseur *m* maritime, shipchandler *m*.

shipment ['ʃɪpmənt] *n* cargaison *f*.

shipowner ['ʃɪpəunə*] *n* armateur *m*.

shipper ['ʃɪpə*] *n* affréteur *m*, expéditeur *m*.

shipping ['ʃɪpɪŋ] *n* (*ships*) navires *mpl*; (*traffic*) navigation *f*.

shipping agent *n* agent *m* maritime.

shipping company *n* compagnie *f* de navigation.

shipping lane *n* couloir *m* de navigation.

shipping line *n* = **shipping company**.

shipshape ['ʃɪpʃeɪp] *a* en ordre impeccable.

shipwreck ['ʃɪprɛk] *n* épave *f*; (*event*) naufrage *m* ♦ *vt*: **to be ~ed** faire naufrage.

shipyard ['ʃɪpjɑːd] *n* chantier naval.

shire ['ʃaɪə*] *n* (*Brit*) comté *m*.

shirk [ʃəːk] *vt* esquiver, se dérober à.

shirt [ʃəːt] *n* chemise *f*; **in ~ sleeves** en bras de chemise.

shirty ['ʃəːtɪ] *a* (*Brit col*) de mauvais poil.

shit [ʃɪt] *excl* (*col!*) merde (*!*).

shiver ['ʃɪvə*] *n* frisson *m* ♦ *vi* frissonner.

shoal [ʃəul] *n* (*of fish*) banc *m*.

shock [ʃɔk] *n* (*impact*) choc *m*, heurt *m*; (*ELEC*) secousse *f*, décharge *f*; (*emotional*) choc; (*MED*) commotion *f*, choc ♦ *vt* (*scandalize*) choquer, scandaliser; (*upset*) bouleverser; **suffering from ~** (*MED*) commotionné(e); **it gave us a ~** ça nous a fait un choc; **it came as a ~ to hear that ...** nous avons appris avec stupeur que ...

shock absorber *n* amortisseur *m*.

shocking ['ʃɔkɪŋ] *a* choquant(e), scandaleux(euse); (*weather, handwriting*) épouvantable.

shockproof ['ʃɔkpruːf] *a* anti-choc *inv*.

shock therapy, shock treatment *n* (*MED*) (traitement *m* par) électrochoc(s) *m(pl)*.

shod [ʃɔd] *pt, pp of* **shoe**; **well-~** bien chaussé(e).

shoddy ['ʃɔdɪ] *a* de mauvaise qualité, mal fait(e).

shoe [ʃuː] *n* chaussure *f*, soulier *m*; (*also*: **horse~**) fer *m* à cheval; (*also*: **brake ~**) mâchoire *f* de frein ♦ *vt* (*pt, pp* **shod** [ʃɔd]) (*horse*) ferrer.

shoebrush ['ʃuːbrʌʃ] *n* brosse *f* à chaussures.

shoehorn ['ʃuːhɔːn] *n* chausse-pied *m*.

shoelace ['ʃuːleɪs] *n* lacet *m* (de soulier).

shoemaker ['ʃuːmeɪkə*] *n* cordonnier *m*, fabricant *m* de chaussures.

shoe polish *n* cirage *m*.

shoeshop ['ʃuːʃɔp] *n* magasin *m* de chaussures.

shoestring ['ʃuːstrɪŋ] *n*: **on a ~** (*fig*) avec un budget dérisoire; avec des moyens très restreints.

shoetree ['ʃuːtriː] *n* embauchoir *m*.

shone [ʃɔn] *pt, pp of* **shine**.

shoo [ʃuː] *excl* (allez,) ouste! ♦ *vt* (*also*: **~ away, ~ off**) chasser.

shook [ʃuk] *pt of* **shake**.

shoot [ʃuːt] *n* (*on branch, seedling*) pousse *f*; (*shooting party*) partie *f* de chasse ♦ *vb* (*pt, pp* **shot** [ʃɔt]) *vt* (*game: Brit*) chasser; tirer; abattre; (*person*) blesser (*or* tuer) d'un coup de fusil (*or* de revolver); (*execute*) fusiller; (*CINEMA*) tourner ♦ *vi* (*with gun, bow*): **to ~ (at)** tirer (sur); (*FOOTBALL*) shooter, tirer; **to ~ past sb** passer en flèche devant qn; **to ~ in/out** entrer/sortir comme une flèche.

shoot down *vt* (*plane*) abattre.

shoot up *vi* (*fig*) monter en flèche.

shooting ['ʃuːtɪŋ] *n* (*shots*) coups *mpl* de feu; (*attack*) fusillade *f*; (*: murder*) homicide *m* (à l'aide d'une arme à feu); (*HUNTING*) chasse *f*; (*CINEMA*) tournage *m*.

shooting range *n* stand *m* de tir.

shooting star *n* étoile filante.

shop [ʃɔp] *n* magasin *m*; (*workshop*) atelier *m* ♦ *vi* (*also*: **go ~ping**) faire ses courses *or* ses achats; **repair ~** atelier de réparations; **to talk ~** (*fig*) parler boutique.

shop around *vi* faire le tour des magasins (pour comparer les prix); (*fig*) se renseigner avant de choisir *or* decider.

shop assistant *n* (*Brit*) vendeur/euse.

shop floor *n* (*Brit: fig*) ouvriers *mpl*.

shopkeeper ['ʃɔpkiːpə*] *n* marchand/e, commerçant/e.

shoplift ['ʃɔplɪft] *vi* voler à l'étalage.

shoplifter ['ʃɔplɪftə*] *n* voleur/euse à l'étalage.

shoplifting ['ʃɔplɪftɪŋ] *n* vol *m* à l'étalage.

shopper ['ʃɔpə*] *n* personne *f* qui fait ses courses, acheteur/euse.

shopping ['ʃɔpɪŋ] *n* (*goods*) achats *mpl*, provisions *fpl*.

shopping bag *n* sac *m* (à provisions).

shopping centre *n* centre commercial.

shop-soiled ['ʃɔpsɔɪld] *a* défraîchi(e), qui a fait la vitrine.

shop steward *n* (*Brit INDUSTRY*) délégué/e syndical(e).

shop window *n* vitrine *f*.

shore [ʃɔː*] *n* (*of sea, lake*) rivage *m*, rive *f* ♦ *vt*: **to ~ (up)** étayer; **on ~** à terre.

shore leave *n* (*NAUT*) permission *f* à terre.

shorn [ʃɔːn] *pp of* **shear**; **~ of** dépouillé(e) de.

short [ʃɔːt] *a* (*not long*) court(e); (*soon finished*) court, bref(brève); (*person, step*) petit(e); (*curt*) brusque, sec(sèche); (*insufficient*) insuffisant(e) ♦ *n* (*also*: **~ film**) court métrage; **to be ~ of sth** être à court de *or* manquer de qch; **to be in ~ supply** manquer, être difficile à trouver; **I'm 3 ~** il m'en manque 3; **in ~** bref; en bref; **~ of doing** à moins de faire; **everything ~ of** tout sauf; **it is ~ for** c'est l'abréviation *or* le diminutif de; **a ~ time ago** il y a peu de temps; **in the ~ term** à court terme; **to cut ~** (*speech, visit*) abréger, écourter; (*person*) couper la parole à; **to fall ~ of** ne pas être à la hauteur de; **to stop ~** s'arrêter net; **to stop ~ of** ne pas aller jusqu'à.

shortage ['ʃɔːtɪdʒ] *n* manque *m*, pénurie *f*.

shortbread ['ʃɔːtbred] *n* ≈ sablé *m*.

short-change [ʃɔːt'tʃeɪndʒ] *vt*: **to ~ sb** ne pas rendre assez à qn.

short-circuit [ʃɔːt'sɜːkɪt] *n* court-circuit *m* ♦ *vt* court-circuiter ♦ *vi* se mettre en court-circuit.

shortcoming ['ʃɔːtkʌmɪŋ] *n* défaut *m*.

short(crust) pastry ['ʃɔːt(krʌst)-] *n* (*Brit*) pâte brisée.

shortcut ['ʃɔːtkʌt] *n* raccourci *m*.

shorten ['ʃɔːtn] *vt* raccourcir; (*text, visit*) abréger.

shortening ['ʃɔːtnɪŋ] *n* (*CULIN*) matière grasse.

shortfall ['ʃɔːtfɔːl] *n* déficit *m*.

shorthand ['ʃɔːthænd] *n* (*Brit*) sténo(graphie) *f*; **to take sth down in ~** prendre qch en sténo.

shorthand notebook *n* bloc *m* sténo.

shorthand typist *n* (*Brit*) sténodactylo *m/f*.

short list *n* (*Brit: for job*) liste *f* des candidats sélectionnés.

short-lived ['ʃɔːt'lɪvd] *a* de courte durée.

shortly ['ʃɔːtlɪ] *ad* bientôt, sous peu.

shortness ['ʃɔːtnɪs] *n* brièveté *f*.

shorts [ʃɔːts] *npl* (*also*: **a pair of ~**) un short.

short-sighted [ʃɔːt'saɪtɪd] *a* (*Brit*) myope; (*fig*) qui manque de clairvoyance.

short-staffed [ʃɔːt'stɑːft] *a* à court de personnel.

short story *n* nouvelle *f*.

short-tempered [ʃɔːt'tempəd] *a* qui s'emporte facilement.

short-term ['ʃɔːttɜːm] *a* (*effect*) à court terme.

short time *n*: **to work ~**, **to be on ~** (*INDUSTRY*) être en chômage partiel, travailler à horaire réduit.

short wave *n* (*RADIO*) ondes courtes.

shot [ʃɒt] *pt, pp of* **shoot** ♦ *n* coup *m* (de feu); (*shotgun pellets*) plombs *mpl*; (*person*) tireur *m*; (*try*) coup, essai *m*; (*injection*) piqûre *f*; (*PHOT*) photo *f*; **to fire a ~ at sb/sth** tirer sur qn/qch; **to have a ~ at (doing)** essayer de faire qch; **like a ~** comme une flèche; (*very readily*) sans hésiter; **to get ~ of sb/sth** (*col*) se débarrasser de qn/qch; **a big ~** (*col*) un gros bonnet.

shotgun ['ʃɒtgʌn] *n* fusil *m* de chasse.

should [ʃud] *auxiliary vb*: **I ~ go now** je devrais partir maintenant; **he ~ be there now** il devrait être arrivé maintenant; **I ~ go if I were you** si j'étais vous j'irais; **I ~ like to** j'aimerais bien, volontiers; **~ he phone ...** si jamais il téléphone ....

shoulder ['ʃəʊldə*] *n* épaule *f*; (*Brit: of road*): **hard ~** accotement *m* ♦ *vt* (*fig*) endosser, se charger de; **to look over one's ~** regarder derrière soi (en tournant la tête); **to rub ~s with sb** (*fig*) côtoyer qn; **to give sb the cold ~** (*fig*) battre froid à qn.

shoulder bag *n* sac *m* à bandoulière.

shoulder blade *n* omoplate *f*.

shoulder strap *n* bretelle *f*.

shouldn't ['ʃudnt] = **should not**.

shout [ʃaut] *n* cri *m* ♦ *vt* crier ♦ *vi* crier,

pousser des cris; **to give sb a ~** appeler qn.

shout down *vt* huer.

shouting ['ʃautɪŋ] *n* cris *mpl*.

shove [ʃʌv] *vt* pousser; (*col: put*): **to ~ sth in** fourrer *or* ficher qch dans ♦ *n* poussée *f*; **he ~d me out of the way** il m'a écarté en me poussant.

shove off *vi* (*NAUT*) pousser au large; (*fig: col*) ficher le camp.

shovel ['ʃʌvl] *n* pelle *f* ♦ *vt* pelleter, enlever (*or enfourner*) à la pelle.

show [ʃəʊ] *n* (*of emotion*) manifestation *f*, démonstration *f*; (*semblance*) semblant *m*, apparence *f*; (*exhibition*) exposition *f*, salon *m*; (*THEATRE*) spectacle *m*, représentation *f*; (*CINEMA*) séance *f* ♦ *vb* (*pt* **~ed**, *pp* **shown** [ʃəʊn]) *vt* montrer; (*courage etc*) faire preuve de, manifester; (*exhibit*) exposer ♦ *vi* se voir, être visible; **to ~ sb to his seat/to the door** accompagner qn jusqu'à sa place/la porte; **to ~ a profit/ loss** (*COMM*) indiquer un bénéfice/une perte; **it just goes to ~ that ...** ça prouve bien que ...; **to ask for a ~ of hands** demander que l'on vote à main levée; **to be on ~** être exposé(e); **it's just for ~** c'est juste pour l'effet; **who's running the ~ here?** (*col*) qui est-ce qui commande ici?

show in *vt* faire entrer.

show off *vi* (*pej*) crâner ♦ *vt* (*display*) faire valoir; (*pej*) faire étalage de.

show out *vt* reconduire à la porte.

show up *vi* (*stand out*) ressortir; (*col: turn up*) se montrer ♦ *vt* démontrer; (*unmask*) démasquer, dénoncer.

show business *n* le monde du spectacle.

showcase ['ʃəʊkeɪs] *n* vitrine *f*.

showdown ['ʃəʊdaun] *n* épreuve *f* de force.

shower ['ʃauə*] *n* (*also*: **~ bath**) douche *f*; (*rain*) averse *f*; (*of stones etc*) pluie *f*, grêle *f*; (*US: party*) réunion organisée pour la remise de cadeaux ♦ *vi* prendre une douche, se doucher ♦ *vt*: **to ~ sb with** (*gifts etc*) combler qn de; (*abuse etc*) accabler qn de; (*missiles*) bombarder qn de; **to have** *or* **take a ~** prendre une douche, se doucher.

shower cap *n* bonnet *m* de douche.

showerproof ['ʃauəpruːf] *a* imperméable.

showery ['ʃauərɪ] *a* (*weather*) pluvieux(euse).

showground ['ʃəʊgraund] *n* champ *m* de foire.

showing ['ʃəʊɪŋ] *n* (*of film*) projection *f*.

show jumping *n* concours *m* hippique.

showman ['ʃəʊmən] *n* (*at fair, circus*) forain *m*; (*fig*) comédien *m*.

showmanship ['ʃəʊmənʃɪp] *n* art *m* de la mise en scène.

shown [ʃəʊn] *pp of* **show**.

show-off ['ʃəʊɔf] *n* (*col: person*) crâneur/euse, m'as-tu-vu/e.

showpiece ['ʃəʊpiːs] *n* (*of exhibition etc*) joyau *m*, clou *m*; **that hospital is a ~** cet hôpital est un modèle du genre.

showroom ['ʃəʊrum] *n* magasin *m or* salle *f* d'exposition.

showy ['ʃəʊɪ] *a* tapageur(euse).

shrank [ʃræŋk] *pt of* **shrink**.

shrapnel ['ʃræpnl] *n* éclats *mpl* d'obus.

shred [ʃred] *n* (*gen pl*) lambeau *m*, petit morceau *m*; (*fig: of truth, evidence*) parcelle *f*

♦ *vt* mettre en lambeaux, déchirer; (*documents*) détruire; (*CULIN*) râper; couper en lanières.

shredder ['ʃrɛdə*] *n* (*for vegetables*) râpeur *m*; (*for documents, papers*) déchiqueteuse *f*.

shrewd [ʃru:d] *a* astucieux(euse), perspicace.

shrewdness ['ʃru:dnɪs] *n* perspicacité *f*.

shriek [ʃri:k] *n* cri perçant *or* aigu, hurlement *m* ♦ *vt, vi* hurler, crier.

shrift [ʃrɪft] *n*: **to give sb short ~** expédier qn sans ménagements.

shrill [ʃrɪl] *a* perçant(e), aigu(ë), strident(e).

shrimp [ʃrɪmp] *n* crevette grise.

shrine [ʃraɪn] *n* châsse *f*; (*place*) lieu *m* de pèlerinage.

shrink, pt shrank, pp shrunk [ʃrɪŋk, ʃræŋk, ʃrʌŋk] *vi* rétrécir; (*fig*) se réduire; se contracter ♦ *vt* (*wool*) (faire) rétrécir ♦ *n* (*col: pej*) psychanalyste *m/f*; **to ~ from (doing) sth** reculer devant (la pensée de faire) qch.

shrinkage ['ʃrɪŋkɪdʒ] *n* (*of clothes*) rétrécissement *m*.

shrink-wrap ['ʃrɪŋkræp] *vt* emballer sous film plastique.

shrivel ['ʃrɪvl] (*also: ~ up*) *vt* ratatiner, flétrir ♦ *vi* se ratatiner, se flétrir.

shroud [ʃraud] *n* linceul *m* ♦ *vt*: **~ed in mystery** enveloppé(e) de mystère.

Shrove Tuesday ['ʃrəuv-] *n* (le) Mardi gras.

shrub [ʃrʌb] *n* arbuste *m*.

shrubbery ['ʃrʌbərɪ] *n* massif *m* d'arbustes.

shrug [ʃrʌg] *n* haussement *m* d'épaules ♦ *vt, vi*: **to ~ (one's shoulders)** hausser les épaules.

shrug off *vt* faire fi de; (*cold, illness*) se débarrasser de.

shrunk [ʃrʌŋk] *pp of* **shrink**.

shrunken ['ʃrʌŋkn] *a* ratatiné(e).

shudder ['ʃʌdə*] *n* frisson *m*, frémissement *m* ♦ *vi* frissonner, frémir.

shuffle ['ʃʌfl] *vt* (*cards*) battre; **to ~ (one's feet)** traîner les pieds.

shun [ʃʌn] *vt* éviter, fuir.

shunt [ʃʌnt] *vt* (*RAIL: direct*) aiguiller; (*: divert*) détourner ♦ *vi*: **to ~ (to and fro)** faire la navette.

shunting ['ʃʌntɪŋ] *n* (*RAIL*) triage *m*.

shunting yard *n* voies *fpl* de garage *or* de triage.

shush [ʃuʃ] *excl* chut!

shut, pt, pp shut [ʃʌt] *vt* fermer ♦ *vi* (se) fermer.

shut down *vt* fermer définitivement; (*machine*) arrêter ♦ *vi* fermer définitivement.

shut off *vt* couper, arrêter.

shut out *vt* (*person, cold*) empêcher d'entrer; (*noise*) éviter d'entendre; (*block: view*) boucher; (*: memory of sth*) chasser de son esprit.

shut up *vi* (*col: keep quiet*) se taire ♦ *vt* (*close*) fermer; (*silence*) faire taire.

shutdown ['ʃʌtdaun] *n* fermeture *f*.

shutter ['ʃʌtə*] *n* volet *m*; (*PHOT*) obturateur *m*.

shuttle ['ʃʌtl] *n* navette *f*; (*also: ~ service*) (service *m* de) navette *f* ♦ *vi* (*vehicle, person*) faire la navette ♦ *vt* (*passengers*) transporter par un système de navette.

shuttlecock ['ʃʌtlkɔk] *n* volant *m* (*de badminton*).

shy [ʃaɪ] *a* timide; **to fight ~ of** se dérober devant; **to be ~ of doing sth** hésiter à faire qch, ne pas oser faire qch ♦ *vi*: **to ~ away from doing sth** (*fig*) craindre de faire qch.

shyness ['ʃaɪnɪs] *n* timidité *f*.

Siam [saɪ'æm] *n* Siam *m*.

Siamese [saɪə'mi:z] *a*: **~ cat** chat siamois; **~ twins** (frères *mpl*) siamois, (sœurs *fpl*) siamoises.

Siberia [saɪ'bɪərɪə] *n* Sibérie *f*.

siblings ['sɪblɪŋz] *npl* (*formal*) enfants *mpl* d'un même couple.

Sicilian [sɪ'sɪlɪən] *a* sicilien(ne) ♦ *n* Sicilien/ne.

Sicily ['sɪsɪlɪ] *n* Sicile *f*.

sick [sɪk] *a* (*ill*) malade; (*vomiting*): **to be ~** vomir; (*humour*) noir(e), macabre; **to feel ~** avoir envie de vomir, avoir mal au cœur; **to fall ~** tomber malade; **to be (off) ~** être absent(e) pour cause de maladie; **a ~ person** un(e) malade; **to be ~ of** (*fig*) en avoir assez de.

sick bay *n* infirmerie *f*.

sicken ['sɪkn] *vt* écœurer ♦ *vi*: **to be ~ing for sth** (*cold, flu etc*) couver qch.

sickening ['sɪknɪŋ] *a* (*fig*) écœurant(e), révoltant(e), répugnant(e).

sickle ['sɪkl] *n* faucille *f*.

sick leave *n* congé *m* de maladie.

sickly ['sɪklɪ] *a* maladif(ive), souffreteux(euse); (*causing nausea*) écœurant(e).

sickness ['sɪknɪs] *n* maladie *f*; (*vomiting*) vomissement(s) *m(pl)*.

sickness benefit *n* (prestations *fpl* de l') assurance-maladie *f*.

sick pay *n* indemnité *f* de maladie.

sickroom ['sɪkru:m] *n* infirmerie *f*.

side [saɪd] *n* côté *m*; (*of animal*) flanc *m*; (*of lake, road*) bord *m*; (*of mountain*) versant *m*; (*fig: aspect*) côté, aspect *m*; (*team: SPORT*) équipe *f* ♦ *cpd* (*door, entrance*) latéral(e) ♦ *vi*: **to ~ with sb** prendre le parti de qn, se ranger du côté de qn; **by the ~ of** au bord de; **~ by ~** côte à côte; **the right/wrong ~** le bon/mauvais côté, l'endroit/l'envers *m*; **they are on our ~** ils sont avec nous; **from all ~s** de tous côtés; **to take ~s (with)** prendre parti (pour); **a ~ of beef** ≈ un quartier de bœuf.

sideboard ['saɪdbɔ:d] *n* buffet *m*.

sideboards ['saɪdbɔ:dz] (*Brit*), **sideburns** ['saɪdbə:nz] *npl* (*whiskers*) pattes *fpl*.

sidecar ['saɪdkɑ:*] *n* side-car *m*.

side dish *n* (plat *m* d')accompagnement *m*.

side drum *n* (*MUS*) tambour plat, caisse claire.

side effect *n* (*MED*) effet *m* secondaire.

sidekick ['saɪdkɪk] *n* (*col*) sous-fifre *m*.

sidelight ['saɪdlaɪt] *n* (*AUT*) veilleuse *f*.

sideline ['saɪdlaɪn] *n* (*SPORT*) (ligne *f* de) touche *f*; (*fig*) activité *f* secondaire.

sidelong ['saɪdlɔŋ] *a*: **to give sb a ~ glance** regarder qn du coin de l'œil.

side plate *n* petite assiette.

side road *n* petite route, route transversale.

sidesaddle ['saɪdsædl] *ad* en amazone.

side show *n* attraction *f*.

sidestep ['saɪdstɛp] *vt* (*question*) éluder;

(problem) éviter ♦ *vi (BOXING etc)* esquiver.
side street *n* rue transversale.
sidetrack ['saɪdtræk] *vt (fig)* faire dévier de son sujet.
sidewalk ['saɪdwɔ:k] *n (US)* trottoir *m*.
sideways ['saɪdweɪz] *ad* de côté.
siding ['saɪdɪŋ] *n (RAIL)* voie *f* de garage.
sidle ['saɪdl] *vi:* **to ~ up (to)** s'approcher furtivement (de).
siege [si:dʒ] *n* siège *m*; **to lay ~ to** assiéger.
siege economy *n* économie *f* de (temps de) siège.
Sierra Leone [sɪ'ɛrəlɪ'əun] *n* Sierra Leone *f*.
sieve [sɪv] *n* tamis *m*, passoire *f* ♦ *vt* tamiser, passer (au tamis).
sift [sɪft] *vt* passer au tamis *or* au crible; *(fig)* passer au crible ♦ *vi (fig):* **to ~ through** passer en revue.
sigh [saɪ] *n* soupir *m* ♦ *vi* soupirer, pousser un soupir.
sight [saɪt] *n (faculty)* vue *f;* · *(spectacle)* spectacle *m*; *(on gun)* mire *f* ♦ *vt* apercevoir; **in ~** visible; *(fig)* en vue; **out of ~** hors de vue; **at ~** *(COMM)* à vue; **at first ~** à première vue, au premier abord; **I know her by ~** je la connais de vue; **to catch ~ of sb/sth** apercevoir qn/qch; **to lose ~ of sb/ sth** perdre qn/qch de vue; **to set one's ~s on sth** jeter son dévolu sur qch.
sighted ['saɪtɪd] *a* qui voit; **partially ~** qui a un certain degré de vision.
sightseeing ['saɪtsi:ɪŋ] *n* tourisme *m*; **to go ~** faire du tourisme.
sightseer ['saɪtsi:ə*] *n* touriste *m/f*.
sign [saɪn] *n (gen)* signe *m*; *(with hand etc)* signe, geste *m*; *(notice)* panneau *m*, écriteau *m*; *(also:* **road ~**) panneau de signalisation ♦ *vt* signer; **as a ~ of** en signe de; **it's a good/bad ~** c'est bon/mauvais signe; **plus/ minus ~** signe plus/moins; **there's no ~ of a change of mind** rien ne laisse présager un revirement; **he was showing ~s of improvement** il commençait visiblement à faire des progrès; **to ~ one's name** signer.
sign away *vt (rights etc)* renoncer officiellement à.
sign in *vi* signer le registre (en arrivant).
sign off *vi (RADIO, TV)* terminer l'émission.
sign on *vi (MIL)* s'engager; *(as unem- ployed)* s'inscrire au chômage; *(enrol):* **to ~ on for a course** s'inscrire pour un cours ♦ *vt (MIL)* engager; *(employee)* embaucher.
sign out *vi* signer le registre (en partant).
sign over *vt:* **to ~ sth over to sb** céder qch par écrit à qn.
sign up *(MIL) vt* engager ♦ *vi* s'engager.
signal ['sɪgnl] *n* signal *m* ♦ *vi (AUT)* mettre son clignotant ♦ *vt (person)* faire signe à; *(message)* communiquer par signaux; **to ~ a left/right turn** *(AUT)* indiquer *or* signaler que l'on tourne à gauche/droite; **to ~ to sb (to do sth)** faire signe à qn (de faire qch).
signal box *n (RAIL)* poste *m* d'aiguillage.
signalman [sɪgnlmən] *n (RAIL)* aiguilleur *m*.
signatory ['sɪgnətərɪ] *n* signataire *m/f*.
signature ['sɪgnətʃə*] *n* signature *f*.
signature tune *n* indicatif musical.
signet ring ['sɪgnət-] *n* chevalière *f*.
significance [sɪg'nɪfɪkəns] *n* signification *f*;

importance *f*; **that is of no ~** ceci n'a pas d'importance.
significant [sɪg'nɪfɪkənt] *a* significatif(ive); *(important)* important(e), considérable.
significantly [sɪg'nɪfɪkəntlɪ] *ad (improve, in- crease)* sensiblement; *(smile)* d'un air entendu, éloquemment; **~, ...** fait significatif, ...
signify ['sɪgnɪfaɪ] *vt* signifier.
sign language *n* langage *m* par signes.
signpost ['saɪnpəust] *n* poteau indicateur.
silage ['saɪlɪdʒ] *n (fodder)* fourrage vert; *(method)* ensilage *m*.
silence ['saɪləns] *n* silence *m* ♦ *vt* faire taire, réduire au silence.
silencer ['saɪlənsə*] *n (on gun, Brit AUT)* silencieux *m*.
silent ['saɪlnt] *a* silencieux(euse); *(film)* muet(te); **to keep** *or* **remain ~** garder le silence, ne rien dire.
silently ['saɪlntlɪ] *ad* silencieusement.
silent partner *n (COMM)* bailleur *m* de fonds, commanditaire *m*.
silhouette [sɪlu:'ɛt] *n* silhouette *f* ♦ *vt:* **~d against** se profilant sur, se découpant contre.
silicon ['sɪlɪkən] *n* silicium *m*.
silicon chip ['sɪlɪkən-] *n* puce *f* électronique.
silicone ['sɪlɪkəun] *n* silicone *f*.
silk [sɪlk] *n* soie *f* ♦ *cpd* de *or* en soie.
silky ['sɪlkɪ] *a* soyeux(euse).
sill [sɪl] *n (also:* **window~**) rebord *m* (de la fenêtre); *(of door)* seuil *m*; *(AUT)* bas *m* de marche.
silly ['sɪlɪ] *a* stupide, sot(te), bête; **to do something ~** faire une bêtise.
silo ['saɪləu] *n* silo *m*.
silt [sɪlt] *n* vase *f*; limon *m*.
silver ['sɪlvə*] *n* argent *m*; *(money)* monnaie *f* (en pièces d'argent); *(also:* **~ware**) argenterie *f* ♦ *cpd* d'argent, en argent.
silver paper *(Brit)*, **silver foil** *n* papier *m* d'argent *or* d'étain.
silver-plated [sɪlvə'pleɪtɪd] *a* plaqué(e) argent.
silversmith *n* orfèvre *m/f*.
silverware ['sɪlvəwɛə*] *n* argenterie *f*.
silver wedding (anniversary) *n* noces *fpl* d'argent.
silvery ['sɪlvrɪ] *a* argenté(e).
similar ['sɪmɪlə*] *a:* **~ (to)** semblable (à).
similarity [sɪmɪ'lærɪtɪ] *n* ressemblance *f*, similarité *f*.
similarly ['sɪmɪləlɪ] *ad* de la même façon, de même.
simile ['sɪmɪlɪ] *n* comparaison *f*.
simmer ['sɪmə*] *vi* cuire à feu doux, mijoter.
simmer down *vi (fig: col)* se calmer.
simper ['sɪmpə*] *vi* minauder.
simpering ['sɪmpərɪŋ] *a* stupide.
simple ['sɪmpl] *a* simple; **the ~ truth** la vérité pure et simple.
simple interest *n (MATH, COMM)* intérêts *mpl* simples.
simple-minded [sɪmpl'maɪndɪd] *a* simplet(te), simple d'esprit.
simpleton ['sɪmpltən] *n* nigaud/e, niais/e.
simplicity [sɪm'plɪsɪtɪ] *n* simplicité *f*.
simplification [sɪmplɪfɪ'keɪʃən] *n* sim- plification *f*.
simplify ['sɪmplɪfaɪ] *vt* simplifier.

simply ['sɪmplɪ] *ad* simplement; (*without fuss*) avec simplicité.

simulate ['sɪmjuleɪt] *vt* simuler, feindre.

simulation [sɪmju'leɪʃən] *n* simulation *f*.

simultaneous [sɪml'teɪnɪəs] *a* simultané(e).

simultaneously [sɪml'teɪnɪəslɪ] *ad* simultanément.

sin [sɪn] *n* péché *m* ♦ *vi* pécher.

Sinai ['saɪneɪaɪ] *n* Sinaï *m*.

since [sɪns] *ad*, *prep* depuis ♦ *cj* (*time*) depuis que; (*because*) puisque, étant donné que, comme; ~ **then** depuis ce moment-là; ~ **Monday** depuis lundi; **(ever)** ~ **I arrived** depuis mon arrivée, depuis que je suis arrivé.

sincere [sɪn'sɪə*] *a* sincère.

sincerely [sɪn'sɪəlɪ] *ad* sincèrement; **Yours** ~ (*at end of letter*) veuillez agréer, Monsieur (*or Madame*), l'expression de mes sentiments distingués *or* les meilleurs.

sincerity [sɪn'serɪtɪ] *n* sincérité *f*.

sine [saɪn] *n* (*MATH*) sinus *m*.

sinew ['sɪnju:] *n* tendon *m*; ~**s** *npl* muscles *mpl*.

sinful ['sɪnful] *a* coupable.

sing, *pt* **sang**, *pp* **sung** [sɪŋ, sæŋ, sʌŋ] *vt*, *vi* chanter.

Singapore [sɪŋgə'pɔ:*] *n* Singapour *m*.

singe [sɪndʒ] *vt* brûler légèrement; (*clothes*) roussir.

singer ['sɪŋə*] *n* chanteur/euse.

Singhalese [sɪŋhə'li:z] *a* = **Sinhalese**.

singing ['sɪŋɪŋ] *n* (*of person, bird*) chant *m*; façon *f* de chanter; (*of kettle, bullet, in ears*) sifflement *m*.

single ['sɪŋgl] *a* seul(e), unique; (*unmarried*) célibataire; (*not double*) simple ♦ *n* (*Brit: also:* ~ **ticket**) aller *m* (simple); (*record*) 45 tours *m*; **not a** ~ **one was left** il n'en est pas resté un(e) seul(e); **every** ~ **day** chaque jour sans exception.

single out *vt* choisir; distinguer.

single bed *n* lit à une place.

single-breasted ['sɪŋglbrestɪd] *a* droit(e).

single file *n*: **in** ~ en file indienne.

single-handed [sɪŋgl'hændɪd] *ad* tout(e) seul(e), sans (aucune) aide.

single-minded [sɪŋgl'maɪndɪd] *a* résolu(e), tenace.

single parent *n* parent unique (*or* célibataire).

unique.

single room *n* chambre *f* à un lit *or* pour une personne.

singles ['sɪŋglz] *npl* (*TENNIS*) simple *m*; (*US: single people*) célibataires *m/fpl*.

singlet ['sɪŋglɪt] *n* tricot *m* de corps.

singly ['sɪŋglɪ] *ad* séparément.

singsong ['sɪŋsɒŋ] *a* (*tone*) chantant(e) ♦ *n* (*songs*): **to have a** ~ chanter quelque chose (ensemble).

singular ['sɪŋgjulə*] *a* singulier(ière); (*odd*) singulier, étrange; (*LING*) (au) singulier, du singulier ♦ *n* (*LING*) singulier *m*; **in the feminine** ~ au féminin singulier.

singularly ['sɪŋgjuləlɪ] *ad* singulièrement; étrangement.

Sinhalese [sɪnhə'li:z] *a* cingalais(e).

sinister ['sɪnɪstə*] *a* sinistre.

sink [sɪŋk] *n* évier *m* ♦ *vb* (*pt* **sank**, *pp* **sunk**

[sæŋk, sʌŋk]) *vt* (*ship*) (faire) couler, faire sombrer; (*foundations*) creuser; (*piles etc*): **to** ~ **sth into** enfoncer qch dans ♦ *vi* couler, sombrer; (*ground etc*) s'affaisser; **he sank into a chair/the mud** il s'est enfoncé dans un fauteuil/la boue; **a** ~**ing feeling** un serrement de cœur.

sink in *vi* s'enfoncer, pénétrer; (*explanation*): **it took a long time to** ~ **in** il a fallu longtemps pour que ça rentre.

sinking fund ['sɪŋkɪŋ-] *n* fonds *mpl* d'amortissement.

sink unit *n* bloc-évier *m*.

sinner ['sɪnə*] *n* pécheur/eresse.

Sino- ['saɪnəʊ] *prefix* sino-.

sinuous ['sɪnjuəs] *a* sinueux(euse).

sinus ['saɪnəs] *n* (*ANAT*) sinus *m inv*.

sip [sɪp] *n* petite gorgée ♦ *vt* boire à petites gorgées.

siphon ['saɪfən] *n* siphon *m* ♦ *vt* (*also:* ~ **off**) siphonner; (: *fig: funds*) transférer; (: *illegally*) détourner.

sir [sə*] *n* monsieur *m*; **S~ John Smith** sir John Smith; **yes** ~ oui Monsieur; **Dear S~** (*in letter*) Monsieur.

siren ['saɪərn] *n* sirène *f*.

sirloin ['sə:lɔɪn] *n* aloyau *m*.

sirloin steak *n* bifteck *m* dans l'aloyau.

sirocco [sɪ'rɒkəʊ] *n* sirocco *m*.

sisal ['saɪsəl] *n* sisal *m*.

sissy ['sɪsɪ] *n* (*col: coward*) poule mouillée.

sister ['sɪstə*] *n* sœur *f*; (*nun*) religieuse *f*, (bonne) sœur; (*Brit: nurse*) infirmière *f* en chef ♦ *cpd*: ~ **organization** organisation *f* sœur; ~ **ship** sister(-)ship *m*.

sister-in-law ['sɪstərɪnlɔ:] *n* belle-sœur *f*.

sit, *pt*, *pp* **sat** [sɪt, sæt] *vi* s'asseoir; (*assembly*) être en séance, siéger; (*for painter*) poser; (*dress etc*) tomber ♦ *vt* (*exam*) passer, se présenter à; **to** ~ **on a committee** faire partie d'un comité; **to** ~ **tight** ne pas bouger.

sit about, sit around *vi* être assis(e) *or* rester à ne rien faire.

sit back *vi* (*in seat*) bien s'installer, se carrer.

sit down *vi* s'asseoir; **to be** ~**ting down** être assis(e).

sit in *vi*: **to** ~ **in on a discussion** assister à une discussion.

sit up *vi* s'asseoir; (*not go to bed*) rester debout, ne pas se coucher.

sitcom ['sɪtkɔm] *n abbr* (*TV*: = *situation comedy*) série *f* comique.

sit-down ['sɪtdaun] *a*: **a** ~ **strike** une grève sur le tas; **a** ~ **meal** un repas assis.

site [saɪt] *n* emplacement *m*, site *m*; (*also: building* ~) chantier *m* ♦ *vt* placer.

sit-in ['sɪtɪn] *n* (*demonstration*) sit-in *m inv*, occupation *f* de locaux.

siting ['saɪtɪŋ] *n* (*location*) emplacement *m*.

sitter ['sɪtə*] *n* (*for painter*) modèle *m*; (*also: baby*~) baby-sitter *m/f*.

sitting ['sɪtɪŋ] *n* (*of assembly etc*) séance *f*; (*in canteen*) service *m*.

sitting member *n* (*POL*) parlementaire *m/f* en exercice.

sitting room *n* salon *m*.

sitting tenant *n* (*Brit*) locataire occupant(e).

situate ['sɪtjueɪt] *vt* situer.

situated ['sɪtjueɪtɪd] *a* situé(e).

situation [sɪtju'eɪʃən] *n* situation *f*; **"~s vacant/wanted"** (*Brit*) "offres/demandes d'emploi".

situation comedy *n* (*THEATRE*) comédie *f* de situation.

six [sɪks] *num* six.

sixteen [sɪks'ti:n] *num* seize.

sixth ['sɪksθ] *a* sixième; **the upper/lower ~** (*Brit SCOL*) la terminale/la première.

sixty ['sɪkstɪ] *num* soixante.

size [saɪz] *n* dimensions *fpl*; (*of person*) taille *f*; (*of estate, area*) étendue *f*; (*of problem*) ampleur *f*; (*of company*) importance *f*; (*of clothing*) taille; (*of shoes*) pointure *f*; (*glue*) colle *f*; **I take ~ 14** (*of dress etc*) ≈ je prends du 42 *or* la taille 42; **the small/large ~** (*of soap powder etc*) le petit/grand modèle; **it's the ~ of** ... c'est de la taille (*or* grosseur) de ..., c'est grand (*or* gros) comme ...; **cut to ~** découpé(e) aux dimensions voulues.

size up *vt* juger, jauger.

sizeable ['saɪzəbl] *a* assez grand(e) *or* gros(se); assez important(e).

sizzle ['sɪzl] *vi* grésiller.

SK *abbr* (*Canada*) = Saskatchewan.

skate [skeɪt] *n* patin *m*; (*fish: pl inv*) raie *f* ♦ *vi* patiner.

skate over, skate around *vt* (*problem, issue*) éluder.

skateboard ['skeɪtbɔ:d] *n* skateboard *m*, planche *f* à roulettes.

skater ['skeɪtə*] *n* patineur/euse.

skating ['skeɪtɪŋ] *n* patinage *m*.

skating rink *n* patinoire *f*.

skeleton ['skɛlɪtn] *n* squelette *m*; (*outline*) schéma *m*.

skeleton key *n* passe-partout *m*.

skeleton staff *n* effectifs réduits.

skeptic *etc* ['skɛptɪk] (*US*) = **sceptic** *etc*.

sketch [skɛtʃ] *n* (*drawing*) croquis *m*, esquisse *f*; (*THEATRE*) sketch *m*, saynète *f* ♦ *vt* esquisser, faire un croquis *or* une esquisse de.

sketch book *n* carnet *m* à dessin.

sketch pad *n* bloc *m* à dessin.

sketchy ['skɛtʃɪ] *a* incomplet(ète), fragmentaire.

skew [skju:] *n* (*Brit*): **on the ~** de travers, en biais.

skewer ['skju:ə*] *n* brochette *f*.

ski [ski:] *n* ski *m* ♦ *vi* skier, faire du ski.

ski boot *n* chaussure *f* de ski.

skid [skɪd] *n* dérapage *m* ♦ *vi* déraper; **to go into a ~** déraper.

skid mark *n* trace *f* de dérapage.

skier ['ski:ə*] *n* skieur/euse.

skiing ['ski:ɪŋ] *n* ski *m*; **to go ~** (aller) faire du ski.

ski instructor *n* moniteur/trice de ski.

ski jump *n* (*ramp*) tremplin *m*; (*event*) saut *m* à skis.

skilful, (*US*) **skillful** ['skɪlful] *a* habile, adroit(e).

ski lift *n* remonte-pente *m inv*.

skill [skɪl] *n* (*ability*) habileté *f*, adresse *f*, talent *m*; (*art, craft*) technique(s) *f(pl)*, compétences *fpl*.

skilled [skɪld] *a* habile, adroit(e); (*worker*) qualifié(e).

skillet ['skɪlɪt] *n* poêlon *m*.

skillful *etc* ['skɪlful] (*US*) = **skilful** *etc*.

skil(l)fully ['skɪlfəlɪ] *ad* habilement, adroitement.

skim [skɪm] *vt* (*milk*) écrémer; (*soup*) écumer; (*glide over*) raser, effleurer ♦ *vi*: **to ~ through** (*fig*) parcourir.

skimmed milk *n* lait écrémé.

skimp [skɪmp] *vt* (*work*) bâcler, faire à la va-vite; (*cloth etc*) lésiner sur.

skimpy ['skɪmpɪ] *a* étriqué(e); maigre.

skin [skɪn] *n* peau *f* ♦ *vt* (*fruit etc*) éplucher; (*animal*) écorcher; **wet** *or* **soaked to the ~** trempé(e) jusqu'aux os.

skin-deep ['skɪn'di:p] *a* superficiel(le).

skin diver *n* plongeur/euse sous-marin(e).

skin diving *n* plongée sous-marine.

skinflint ['skɪnflɪnt] *n* grippe-sou *m*.

skin graft *n* greffe *f* de peau.

skinny ['skɪnɪ] *a* maigre, maigrichon(ne).

skin test *n* cuti(-réaction) *f*.

skintight ['skɪntaɪt] *a* (*dress etc*) collant(e), ajusté(e).

skip [skɪp] *n* petit bond *or* saut; (*container*) benne *f* ♦ *vi* gambader, sautiller; (*with rope*) sauter à la corde ♦ *vt* (*pass over*) sauter; **to ~ school** (*esp US*) faire l'école buissonnière.

ski pants *npl* pantalon *m* de ski.

ski pole *n* bâton *m* de ski.

skipper ['skɪpə*] *n* (*NAUT, SPORT*) capitaine *m* ♦ *vt* (*boat*) commander; (*team*) être le chef de.

skipping rope ['skɪpɪŋ-] *n* (*Brit*) corde *f* à sauter.

ski resort *n* station *f* de sports d'hiver.

skirmish ['skə:mɪʃ] *n* escarmouche *f*, accrochage *m*.

skirt [skə:t] *n* jupe *f* ♦ *vt* longer, contourner.

skirting board *n* (*Brit*) plinthe *f*.

ski run *n* piste *f* de ski.

ski suit *n* combinaison *f* de ski.

skit [skɪt] *n* sketch *m* satirique.

ski tow *n* = **ski lift**.

skittle ['skɪtl] *n* quille *f*; **~s** (*game*) (jeu *m* de) quilles *fpl*.

skive [skaɪv] *vi* (*Brit col*) tirer au flanc.

skulk [skʌlk] *vi* rôder furtivement.

skull [skʌl] *n* crâne *m*.

skullcap ['skʌlkæp] *n* calotte *f*.

skunk [skʌŋk] *n* mouffette *f*; (*fur*) sconse *m*.

sky [skaɪ] *n* ciel *m*; **to praise sb to the ~** porter qn aux nues.

sky-blue [skaɪ'blu:] *a* bleu ciel *inv*.

sky-high ['skaɪ'haɪ] *ad* très haut ♦ *a*: **prices are ~** les prix sont exorbitants.

skylark ['skaɪlɑ:k] *n* (*bird*) alouette *f* (des champs).

skylight ['skaɪlaɪt] *n* lucarne *f*.

skyline ['skaɪlaɪn] *n* (*horizon*) (ligne *f* d')horizon *m*; (*of city*) ligne des toits.

skyscraper ['skaɪskreɪpə*] *n* gratte-ciel *m inv*.

slab [slæb] *n* plaque *f*; dalle *f*; (*of wood*) bloc *m*; (*of meat, cheese*) tranche épaisse.

slack [slæk] *a* (*loose*) lâche, desserré(e); (*slow*) stagnant(e); (*careless*) négligent(e), peu sérieux(euse) *or* consciencieux(euse); (*COMM: market*) peu actif(ive); (: *demand*) faible; (*period*) creux(euse) ♦ *n* (*in rope etc*) mou *m*; **business is ~** les affaires vont mal.

slacken ['slækn] (*also:* **~ off**) *vi* ralentir, diminuer ♦ *vt* relâcher.

slacks [slæks] *npl* pantalon *m*.

slag [slæg] *n* scories *fpl*.

slag heap *n* crassier *m*.

slain [sleɪn] *pp of* **slay**.

slake [sleɪk] *vt* (*one's thirst*) étancher.

slalom ['slɑːləm] *n* slalom *m*.

slam [slæm] *vt* (*door*) (faire) claquer; (*throw*) jeter violemment, flanquer; (*criticize*) éreinter, démolir ♦ *vi* claquer.

slander ['slɑːndə*] *n* calomnie *f*; (*LAW*) diffamation *f* ♦ *vt* calomnier; diffamer.

slanderous ['slɑːndrəs] *a* calomnieux(euse); diffamatoire.

slang [slæŋ] *n* argot *m*.

slant [slɑːnt] *n* inclinaison *f*; (*fig*) angle *m*, point *m* de vue.

slanted ['slɑːntɪd] *a* tendancieux(euse).

slanting ['slɑːntɪŋ] *a* en pente, incliné(e); couché(e).

slap [slæp] *n* claque *f*, gifle *f*; (*on the back*) tape *f* ♦ *vt* donner une claque *or* une gifle (*or* une tape) à ♦ *ad* (*directly*) tout droit, en plein.

slapdash ['slæpdæʃ] *a* (*work*) fait(e) sans soin *or* à la va-vite; (*person*) insouciant(e), négligent(e).

slapstick ['slæpstɪk] *n* (*comedy*) grosse farce, style *m* tarte à la crème.

slap-up ['slæpʌp] *a* (*Brit*): **a ~ meal** un repas extra *or* fameux.

slash [slæʃ] *vt* entailler, taillader; (*fig: prices*) casser.

slat [slæt] *n* (*of wood*) latte *f*, lame *f*.

slate [sleɪt] *n* ardoise *f* ♦ *vt* (*fig: criticize*) éreinter, démolir.

slaughter ['slɔːtə*] *n* carnage *m*, massacre *m*; (*of animals*) abattage *m* ♦ *vt* (*animal*) abattre; (*people*) massacrer.

slaughterhouse ['slɔːtəhaus] *n* abattoir *m*.

Slav [slɑːv] *a* slave.

slave [sleɪv] *n* esclave *m/f* ♦ *vi* (*also:* **~ away**) trimer, travailler comme un forçat; **to ~ (away) at sth/at doing sth** se tuer à qch/à faire qch.

slave labour *n* travail *m* d'esclave; **it's just ~** (*fig*) c'est de l'esclavage.

slaver ['slævə*] *vi* (*dribble*) baver.

slavery ['sleɪvərɪ] *n* esclavage *m*.

Slavic ['slævɪk] *a* slave.

slavish ['sleɪvɪʃ] *a* servile.

Slavonic [slə'vɔnɪk] *a* slave.

slay, *pt* **slew,** *pp* **slain** [sleɪ, sluː, sleɪn] *vt* (*literary*) tuer.

sleazy ['sliːzɪ] *a* miteux(euse), minable.

sledge [slɛdʒ] *n* luge *f*.

sledgehammer ['slɛdʒhæmə*] *n* marteau *m* de forgeron.

sleek [sliːk] *a* (*hair, fur*) brillant(e), luisant(e); (*car, boat*) aux lignes pures *or* élégantes.

sleep [sliːp] *n* sommeil *m* ♦ *vi* (*pt, pp* **slept** [slɛpt]) dormir; (*spend night*) dormir, coucher ♦ *vt*: **we can ~ 4** on peut coucher *or* loger 4 personnes; **to go to ~** s'endormir; **to have a good night's ~** passer une bonne

nuit; **to put to ~** (*patient*) endormir; (*animal: euphemism: kill*) piquer; **to ~ lightly** avoir le sommeil léger; **to ~ with sb** (*euphemism*) coucher avec qn.

sleep in *vi* (*lie late*) faire la grasse matinée; (*oversleep*) se réveiller trop tard.

sleeper ['sliːpə*] *n* (*person*) dormeur/euse; (*Brit RAIL: on track*) traverse *f*; (*: train*) train *m* de voitures-lits; (*: carriage*) wagon-lits *m*, voiture-lits *f*; (*: berth*) couchette *f*.

sleepily ['sliːpɪlɪ] *ad* d'un air endormi.

sleeping ['sliːpɪŋ] *a* qui dort, endormi(e).

sleeping bag *n* sac *m* de couchage.

sleeping car *n* wagon-lits *m*, voiture-lits *f*.

sleeping partner *n* (*Brit COMM*) = **silent partner**.

sleeping pill *n* somnifère *m*.

sleepless ['sliːplɪs] *a*: **a ~ night** une nuit blanche.

sleeplessness ['sliːplɪsnɪs] *n* insomnie *f*.

sleepwalker ['sliːpwɔːkə*] *n* somnambule *m/f*.

sleepy ['sliːpɪ] *a* qui a envie de dormir; (*fig*) endormi(e); **to be** *or* **feel ~** avoir sommeil, avoir envie de dormir.

sleet [sliːt] *n* neige fondue.

sleeve [sliːv] *n* manche *f*; (*of record*) pochette *f*.

sleeveless ['sliːvlɪs] *a* (*garment*) sans manches.

sleigh [sleɪ] *n* traîneau *m*.

sleight [slaɪt] *n*: **~ of hand** tour *m* de passe-passe.

slender ['slɛndə*] *a* svelte, mince; (*fig*) faible, ténu(e).

slept [slɛpt] *pt, pp of* **sleep**.

sleuth [sluːθ] *n* (*col*) détective (privé).

slew [sluː] *vi* (*also:* **~ round**) virer, pivoter ♦ *pt of* **slay**.

slice [slaɪs] *n* tranche *f*; (*round*) rondelle *f* ♦ *vt* couper en tranches (*or* en rondelles); **~d bread** pain *m* en tranches.

slick [slɪk] *a* brillant(e) en apparence; mielleux(euse) ♦ *n* (*also:* **oil ~**) nappe *f* de pétrole, marée noire.

slid [slɪd] *pt, pp of* **slide**.

slide [slaɪd] *n* (*in playground*) toboggan *m*; (*PHOT*) diapositive *f*; (*Brit:* **hair ~**) barrette *f*; (*microscope ~*) (lame *f*) porte-objet *m*; (*in prices*) chute *f*, baisse *f* ♦ *vb* (*pt, pp* **slid** [slɪd]) *vt* (faire) glisser ♦ *vi* glisser; **to let things ~** (*fig*) laisser les choses aller à la dérive.

slide projector *n* (*PHOT*) projecteur *m* de diapositives.

slide rule *n* règle *f* à calcul.

sliding ['slaɪdɪŋ] *a* (*door*) coulissant(e); **~ roof** (*AUT*) toit ouvrant.

sliding scale *n* échelle *f* mobile.

slight [slaɪt] *a* (*slim*) mince, menu(e); (*frail*) frêle; (*trivial*) faible, insignifiant(e); (*small*) petit(e), léger(ère) (*before n*) ♦ *n* offense *f*, affront *m* ♦ *vt* (*offend*) blesser, offenser; **the ~est** le (*or* la) moindre; **not in the ~est** pas le moins du monde, pas du tout.

slightly ['slaɪtlɪ] *ad* légèrement, un peu; **~ built** fluet(te).

slim [slɪm] *a* mince ♦ *vi* maigrir, suivre un régime amaigrissant.

slime [slaɪm] *n* vase *f*; substance visqueuse.

slimming [slɪmɪŋ] *n* amaigrissement *m* ♦ *a* (*diet, pills*) amaigrissant(e), pour maigrir.

slimy ['slaɪmɪ] *a* visqueux(euse), gluant(e); (*covered with mud*) vaseux(euse).

sling [slɪŋ] *n* (*MED*) écharpe *f* ♦ *vt* (*pt, pp* **slung** [slʌŋ]) lancer, jeter; **to have one's arm in a** ~ avoir le bras en écharpe.

slink, *pt, pp* **slunk** [slɪŋk, slʌŋk] *vi*: **to** ~ **away** *or* **off** s'en aller furtivement.

slip [slɪp] *n* faux pas; (*mistake*) erreur *f*, bévue *f*; (*underskirt*) combinaison *f*; (*of paper*) petite feuille, fiche *f* ♦ *vt* (*slide*) glisser ♦ *vi* (*slide*) glisser; (*move smoothly*): **to** ~ **into/out of** se glisser *or* se faufiler dans/hors de; (*decline*) baisser; **to let a chance** ~ **by** laisser passer une occasion; **to** ~ **sth on/off** enfiler/enlever qch; **it** ~**ped from her hand** cela lui a glissé des mains; **to give sb the** ~ fausser compagnie à qn; **a** ~ **of the tongue** un lapsus.

slip away *vi* s'esquiver.

slip in *vt* glisser.

slip out *vi* sortir.

slip-on ['slɪpɔn] *a* facile à enfiler; ~ **shoes** mocassins *mpl*.

slipped disc [slɪpt-] *n* déplacement *m* de vertèbres.

slipper ['slɪpə*] *n* pantoufle *f*.

slippery ['slɪpərɪ] *a* glissant(e); (*fig: person*) insaisissable.

slip road *n* (*Brit: to motorway*) bretelle *f* d'accès.

slipshod ['slɪpʃɔd] *a* négligé(e), peu soigné(e).

slip-up ['slɪpʌp] *n* bévue *f*.

slipway ['slɪpweɪ] *n* cale *f* (de construction *or* de lancement).

slit [slɪt] *n* fente *f*; (*cut*) incision *f*; (*tear*) déchirure *f* ♦ *vt* (*pt, pp* **slit**) fendre; couper; inciser; déchirer; **to** ~ **sb's throat** trancher la gorge à qn.

slither ['slɪðə*] *vi* glisser, déraper.

sliver ['slɪvə*] *n* (*of glass, wood*) éclat *m*; (*of cheese, sausage*) petit morceau.

slob [slɔb] *n* (*col*) rustaud/e.

slog [slɔg] *n* (*Brit*) gros effort; tâche fastidieuse ♦ *vi* travailler très dur.

slogan ['sləʊgən] *n* slogan *m*.

slop [slɔp] *vi* (*also:* ~ **over**) se renverser; déborder ♦ *vt* répandre; renverser.

slope [sləʊp] *n* pente *f*; (*side of mountain*) versant *m*; (*slant*) inclinaison *f* ♦ *vi*: **to** ~ **down** être *or* descendre en pente; **to** ~ **up** monter.

sloping ['sləʊpɪŋ] *a* en pente, incliné(e); (*handwriting*) penché(e).

sloppy ['slɔpɪ] *a* (*work*) peu soigné(e), bâclé(e); (*appearance*) négligé(e), débraillé(e); (*film etc*) sentimental(e).

slosh [slɔʃ] *vi* (*col*): **to** ~ **about** *or* **around** (*children*) patauger; (*liquid*) clapoter.

sloshed [slɔʃt] *a* (*col: drunk*) bourré(e).

slot [slɔt] *n* fente *f*; (*fig: in timetable, RADIO, TV*) créneau *m*, plage *f* ♦ *vt*: **to** ~ **into** encastrer *or* insérer dans ♦ *vi*: **to** ~ **into** s'encastrer *or* s'insérer dans.

sloth [sləʊθ] *n* (*vice*) paresse *f*; (*ZOOL*) paresseux *m*.

slot machine *n* (*Brit: vending machine*) distributeur *m* (automatique), machine *f* à sous;

(*for gambling*) appareil *m or* machine à sous.

slot meter *n* (*Brit*) compteur *m* à pièces.

slouch [slautʃ] *vi* avoir le dos rond, être voûté(e).

slouch about, **slouch around** *vi* traîner à ne rien faire.

slovenly ['slʌvənlɪ] *a* sale, débraillé(e), négligé(e).

slow [sləʊ] *a* lent(e); (*watch*): **to be** ~ retarder ♦ *ad* lentement ♦ *vt, vi* (*also:* ~ **down**, ~ **up**) ralentir; " ~ " (*road sign*) "ralentir"; **at a** ~ **speed** à petite vitesse; **to be** ~ **to act/decide** être lent à agir/décider; **my watch is 20 minutes** ~ ma montre retarde de 20 minutes; **business is** ~ les affaires marchent au ralenti; **to go** ~ (*driver*) rouler lentement; (*in industrial dispute*) faire la grève perlée.

slow-acting [sləʊˈæktɪŋ] *a* qui agit lentement, à action lente.

slowly ['sləʊlɪ] *ad* lentement.

slow motion *n*: **in** ~ au ralenti.

slowness ['sləʊnɪs] *n* lenteur *f*.

sludge [slʌdʒ] *n* boue *f*.

slug [slʌg] *n* limace *f*; (*bullet*) balle *f*.

sluggish ['slʌgɪʃ] *a* mou(molle), lent(e); (*business, sales*) stagnant(e).

sluice [slu:s] *n* écluse *f*; (*also:* ~ **gate**) vanne *f* ♦ *vt*: **to** ~ **down** *or* **out** laver à grande eau.

slum [slʌm] *n* taudis *m*.

slumber ['slʌmbə*] *n* sommeil *m*.

slump [slʌmp] *n* baisse soudaine, effondrement *m*; crise *f* ♦ *vi* s'effondrer, s'affaisser.

slung [slʌŋ] *pt, pp of* **sling**.

slunk [slʌŋk] *pt, pp of* **slink**.

slur [slə:*] *n* bredouillement *m*; (*smear*): ~ (**on**) atteinte *f* (à); insinuation *f* (contre) ♦ *vt* mal articuler; **to be a** ~ **on** porter atteinte à.

slurred [slə:d] *a* (*pronunciation*) inarticulé(e), indistinct(e).

slush [slʌʃ] *n* neige fondue.

slush fund *n* caisse noire, fonds secrets.

slushy ['slʌʃɪ] *a* (*snow*) fondu(e); (*street*) couvert(e) de neige fondue; (*Brit: fig*) à l'eau de rose.

slut [slʌt] *n* souillon *f*.

sly [slaɪ] *a* rusé(e); sournois(e); **on the** ~ en cachette.

smack [smæk] *n* (*slap*) tape *f*; (*on face*) gifle *f* ♦ *vt* donner une tape à; gifler; (*child*) donner la fessée à ♦ *vi*: **to** ~ **of** avoir des relents de, sentir ♦ *ad* (*col*): **it fell** ~ **in the middle** c'est tombé en plein milieu *or* en plein dedans; **to** ~ **one's lips** se lécher les babines.

smacker ['smækə*] *n* (*col: kiss*) bisou *m or* bise *f* sonore; (*: Brit: pound note*) livre *f*; (*: US: dollar bill*) dollar *m*.

small [smɔ:l] *a* petit(e); (*letter*) minuscule ♦ *n*: **the** ~ **of the back** le creux des reins; **to get** *or* **grow** ~**er** diminuer; **to make** ~**er** (*amount, income*) diminuer; (*object, garment*) rapetisser; **a** ~ **shopkeeper** un petit commerçant.

small ads *npl* (*Brit*) petites annonces. ·

small arms *npl* armes individuelles.

small change *n* petite *or* menue monnaie.

smallholder ['smɔ:lhəʊldə*] *n* (*Brit*) petit cultivateur.

smallholding ['smɔːlhəuldɪŋ] n (Brit) petite ferme.

small hours npl: **in the ~** au petit matin.

smallish ['smɔːlɪʃ] a plutôt or assez petit(e).

small-minded [smɔː'maɪndɪd] a mesquin(e).

smallpox ['smɔːlpɔks] n variole f.

small print n (in contract etc) clause(s) imprimée(s) en petits caractères.

small-scale ['smɔːlskeɪl] a (map, model) à échelle réduite, à petite échelle; (business, farming) peu important(e), modeste.

small talk n menus propos.

small-time ['smɔːltaɪm] a (farmer etc) petit(e); **a ~ thief** un voleur à la petite semaine.

smarmy ['smɑːmɪ] a (Brit pej) flagorneur(euse), lécheur(euse).

smart [smɑːt] a élégant(e), chic inv; (clever) intelligent(e); (pej) futé(e); (quick) vif(vive), prompt(e) ♦ vi faire mal, brûler; **the ~ set** le beau monde; **to look ~** être élégant(e); **my eyes are ~ing** j'ai les yeux irrités or qui me piquent.

smarten up ['smɑːtn-] vi devenir plus élégant(e), se faire beau(belle) ♦ vt rendre plus élégant(e).

smash [smæʃ] n (also: **~-up**) collision f, accident m; (sound) fracas m ♦ vt casser, briser, fracasser; (opponent) écraser; (hopes) ruiner, détruire; (SPORT: record) pulvériser ♦ vi se briser, se fracasser; s'écraser.
  smash up vt (car) bousiller; (room) tout casser dans.

smash hit n (grand) succès.

smashing ['smæʃɪŋ] a (col) formidable.

smattering ['smætərɪŋ] n: **a ~ of** quelques notions de.

smear [smɪə*] n tache f, salissure f; trace f; (MED) frottis m; (insult) calomnie f ♦ vt enduire; (fig) porter atteinte à; **his hands were ~ed with oil/ink** il avait les mains maculées de cambouis/d'encre.

smear campaign n campagne f de dénigrement.

smear test n (Brit MED) frottis m.

smell [smɛl] n odeur f; (sense) odorat m ♦ vb (pt, pp **smelt** or **smelled** [smɛlt, smɛld]) vt sentir ♦ vi faire mal, brûler; **to ~ (of)** sentir; (pej) sentir mauvais; **it ~s good** ça sent bon.

smelly ['smɛlɪ] a qui sent mauvais, malodorant(e).

smelt [smɛlt] pt, pp of **smell** ♦ vt (ore) fondre.

smile [smaɪl] n sourire m ♦ vi sourire.

smiling ['smaɪlɪŋ] a souriant(e).

smirk [smə:k] n petit sourire suffisant or affecté.

smith [smɪθ] n maréchal-ferrant m; forgeron m.

smithy ['smɪðɪ] n forge f.

smitten ['smɪtn] a: **~ with** pris(e) de; frappé(e) de.

smock [smɔk] n blouse f, sarrau m.

smog [smɔg] n brouillard mêlé de fumée.

smoke [sməuk] n fumée f ♦ vt, vi fumer; **to have a ~** fumer une cigarette; **do you ~?** est-ce que vous fumez?; **to go up in ~** (house etc) brûler; (fig) partir en fumée.

smoked ['sməukt] a (bacon, glass) fumé(e).

smokeless fuel ['sməuklɪs-] n combustible non polluant.

smokeless zone ['sməuklɪs-] n (Brit) zone f où l'usage du charbon est réglementé.

smoker ['sməukə*] n (person) fumeur/euse; (RAIL) wagon m fumeurs.

smoke screen n rideau m or écran m de fumée; (fig) paravent m.

smoke shop n (US) (bureau m de) tabac m.

smoking ['sməukɪŋ] n: **"no ~"** (sign) "défense de fumer"; **he's given up ~** il a arrêté de fumer.

smoking compartment, (US) **smoking car** n wagon m fumeurs.

smoking room n fumoir m.

smoky ['sməukɪ] a enfumé(e).

smolder ['sməuldə*] vi (US) = **smoulder**.

smooth [smuːð] a lisse; (sauce) onctueux(euse); (flavour, whisky) moelleux(euse); (cigarette) doux(douce); (movement) régulier(ière), sans à-coups or heurts; (landing, take-off) en douceur; (flight) sans secousses; (person) doucereux(euse), mielleux(euse) ♦ vt lisser, défroisser; (also: **~ out**: creases, difficulties) faire disparaître.
  smooth over vt: **to ~ things over** (fig) arranger les choses.

smoothly ['smuːðlɪ] ad (easily) facilement, sans difficulté(s); **everything went ~** tout s'est bien passé.

smother ['smʌðə*] vt étouffer.

smoulder, (US) **smolder** ['sməuldə*] vi couver.

smudge [smʌdʒ] n tache f, bavure f ♦ vt salir, maculer.

smug [smʌg] a suffisant(e), content(e) de soi.

smuggle ['smʌgl] vt passer en contrebande or en fraude; **to ~ in/out** (goods etc) faire entrer/sortir clandestinement or en fraude.

smuggler ['smʌglə*] n contrebandier/ière.

smuggling ['smʌglɪŋ] n contrebande f.

smut [smʌt] n (grain of soot) grain m de suie; (mark) tache f de suie; (in conversation etc) obscénités fpl.

smutty ['smʌtɪ] a (fig) grossier(ière), obscène.

snack [snæk] n casse-croûte m inv; **to have a ~** prendre un en-cas, manger quelque chose (de léger).

snack bar n snack(-bar) m.

snag [snæg] n inconvénient m, difficulté f.

snail [sneɪl] n escargot m.

snake [sneɪk] n serpent m.

snap [snæp] n (sound) claquement m, bruit sec; (photograph) photo f, instantané m; (game) sorte de jeu de bataille ♦ a subit(e); fait(e) sans réfléchir ♦ vt faire claquer; (break) casser net; (photograph) prendre un instantané de ♦ vi se casser net or avec un bruit sec; (fig: person) craquer; **to ~ at sb** (subj: person) parler d'un ton brusque à qn; (: dog) essayer de mordre qn; **to ~ open/shut** s'ouvrir/se refermer brusquement; **to ~ one's fingers at** (fig) se moquer de; **a cold ~** (of weather) un refroidissement soudain de la température.
  snap off vt (break) casser net.
  snap up vt sauter sur, saisir.

snap fastener n bouton-pression m.

snappy ['snæpɪ] a prompt(e); (slogan) qui a du punch; **make it ~!** (col: hurry up) grouille-toi!, magne-toi!

snapshot ['snæpʃɔt] n photo f, instantané m.

snare [snɛə*] n piège m ♦ vt attraper, prendre au piège.

snarl [snɑːl] n grondement m or grognement m féroce ♦ vi gronder ♦ vt: **to get ~ed up** (wool, plans) s'emmêler; (traffic) se bloquer.

snatch [snætʃ] n (fig) vol m; (Brit: small amount): **~es of** des fragments mpl or bribes fpl de ♦ vt saisir (d'un geste vif); (steal) voler ♦ vi: **don't ~!** doucement!; **to ~ a sandwich** manger or avaler un sandwich à la hâte; **to ~ some sleep** arriver à dormir un peu.

snatch up vt saisir, s'emparer de.

sneak [sniːk] vi: **to ~ in/out** entrer/sortir furtivement or à la dérobée ♦ vt: **to ~ a look at sth** regarder furtivement qch.

sneakers ['sniːkəz] npl chaussures fpl de tennis or basket.

sneaking ['sniːkɪŋ] a: **to have a ~ feeling** or **suspicion that ...** avoir la vague impression que ....

sneaky ['sniːkɪ] a sournois(e).

sneer [snɪə*] n ricanement m ♦ vi ricaner, sourire d'un air sarcastique; **to ~ at sb/sth** se moquer de qn/qch avec mépris.

sneeze [sniːz] n éternuement m ♦ vi éternuer.

snide [snaɪd] a sarcastique, narquois(e).

sniff [snɪf] n reniflement m ♦ vi renifler ♦ vt renifler, flairer; (glue, drug) sniffer, respirer.

sniff at vt fus: **it's not to be ~ed at** il ne faut pas cracher dessus, ce n'est pas à dédaigner.

snigger ['snɪgə*] n ricanement m; rire moqueur ♦ vi ricaner; pouffer de rire.

snip [snɪp] n petit bout; (bargain) (bonne) occasion or affaire ♦ vt couper.

sniper ['snaɪpə*] n (marksman) tireur embusqué.

snippet ['snɪpɪt] n bribes fpl.

snivelling ['snɪvlɪŋ] a larmoyant(e), pleurnicheur(euse).

snob [snɔb] n snob m/f.

snobbery ['snɔbərɪ] n snobisme m.

snobbish ['snɔbɪʃ] a snob inv.

snooker ['snuːkə*] n sorte de jeu de billard.

snoop ['snuːp] vi: **to ~ on sb** espionner qn; **to ~ about somewhere** fourrer son nez quelque part.

snooper ['snuːpə*] n fureteur/euse.

snooty ['snuːtɪ] a snob inv, prétentieux(euse).

snooze [snuːz] n petit somme ♦ vi faire un petit somme.

snore [snɔː*] vi ronfler ♦ n ronflement m.

snoring ['snɔːrɪŋ] n ronflement(s) m(pl).

snorkel ['snɔːkl] n (of swimmer) tuba m.

snort [snɔːt] n grognement m ♦ vi grogner; (horse) renâcler ♦ vt (col: drugs) sniffer.

snotty ['snɔtɪ] a morveux(euse).

snout [snaut] n museau m.

snow [snəu] n neige f ♦ vi neiger ♦ vt: **to be ~ed under with work** être débordé(e) de travail.

snowball ['snəubɔːl] n boule f de neige.

snowbound ['snəubaund] a enneigé(e), bloqué(e) par la neige.

snow-capped ['snəukæpt] a (peak, mountain) couvert(e) de neige.

snowdrift ['snəudrɪft] n congère f.

snowdrop ['snəudrɔp] n perce-neige m.

snowfall ['snəufɔːl] n chute f de neige.

snowflake ['snəufleɪk] n flocon m de neige.

snowman ['snəumæn] n bonhomme m de neige.

snowplough, (US) **snowplow** ['snəuplau] n chasse-neige m inv.

snowshoe ['snəuʃuː] n raquette f (pour la neige).

snowstorm ['snəustɔːm] n tempête f de neige.

snowy ['snəuɪ] a neigeux(euse); (covered with snow) enneigé(e).

SNP n abbr (Brit POL) = Scottish National Party.

snub [snʌb] vt repousser, snober ♦ n rebuffade f.

snub-nosed [snʌb'nəuzd] a au nez retroussé.

snuff [snʌf] n tabac m à priser ♦ vt (also: ~ out: candle) moucher.

snug [snʌg] a douillet(te), confortable; **it's a ~ fit** c'est bien ajusté(e).

snuggle ['snʌgl] vi: **to ~ down in bed/up to sb** se pelotonner dans son lit/contre qn.

SO abbr (BANKING) = **standing order.**

so [səu] ad (degree) si, tellement; (manner: thus) ainsi, de cette façon ♦ cj donc, par conséquent; **~ as to do** afin de or pour faire; **~ that** (purpose) afin de + infinitive, pour que or afin que + sub; (result) si bien que, de (telle) sorte que; **~ that's the reason!** c'est donc (pour) ça!; **~ do I, ~ am I** etc moi etc aussi; **~ it is!, ~ it does!** c'est vrai!; **if ~** si oui; **I hope ~** je l'espère; **10 or ~** 10 à peu près or environ; **quite ~!** exactement!, c'est bien ça!; **even ~** quand même, tout de même; **~ far** jusqu'ici, jusqu'à maintenant; (in past) jusque-là; **~ long!** à bientôt!, au revoir!; **~ many** tant de; **~ much** tant ♦ a tant de; **~ to speak** pour ainsi dire; **~ (what)?** (col) (bon) et alors?, et après?

soak [səuk] vt faire or laisser tremper ♦ vi tremper; **to be ~ed through** être trempé jusqu'aux os.

soak in vi pénétrer, être absorbé(e).

soak up vt absorber.

soaking ['səukɪŋ] a (also: ~ wet) trempé(e).

so and so n un tel/une telle.

soap [səup] n savon m.

soapflakes ['səupfleɪks] npl paillettes fpl de savon.

soap opera n feuilleton télévisé (quotidienneté réaliste ou embellie).

soap powder n lessive f, détergent m.

soapsuds ['səupsʌdz] npl mousse f de savon.

soapy ['səupɪ] a savonneux(euse).

soar [sɔː*] vi monter (en flèche), s'élancer; **~ing prices** prix qui grimpent.

sob [sɔb] n sanglot m ♦ vi sangloter.

s.o.b. n abbr (US col!: = son of a bitch) salaud m (!).

sober ['səubə*] a qui n'est pas (or plus) ivre; (sedate) sérieux(euse), sensé(e); (moderate) mesuré(e); (colour, style) sobre, discret(ète).

sober up vt dégriser ♦ vi se dégriser.

sobriety [sə'braɪətɪ] n (not being drunk) sobriété f; (seriousness, sedateness) sérieux m.

Soc. *abbr* (= *society*) Soc.
so-called ['səu'kɔːld] *a* soi-disant *inv*.
soccer ['sɔkə*] *n* football *m*.
soccer pitch *n* terrain *m* de football.
soccer player *n* footballeur *m*.
sociable ['səuʃəbl] *a* sociable.
social ['səuʃl] *a* social(e) ♦ *n* (petite) fête.
social climber *n* arriviste *m/f*.
social club *n* amicale *f*, foyer *m*.
Social Democrat *n* social-démocrate *m/f*.
social insurance *n* (*US*) sécurité sociale.
socialism ['səuʃəlɪzəm] *n* socialisme *m*.
socialist ['səuʃəlɪst] *a*, *n* socialiste (*m/f*).
socialite ['səuʃəlaɪt] *n* personnalité mondaine.
socialize ['səuʃəlaɪz] *vi* voir *or* rencontrer des gens, se faire des amis; **to ~ with** fréquenter; lier connaissance *or* parler avec.
socially ['səuʃəlɪ] *ad* socialement, en société.
social science *n* sciences humaines.
social security *n* aide sociale.
social welfare *n* sécurité sociale.
social work *n* assistance sociale.
social worker *n* assistant*e* social(e).
society [sə'saɪətɪ] *n* société *f*; (*club*) société, association *f*; (*also*: **high ~**) (haute) société, grand monde ♦ *cpd* (*party*) mondain(e).
socio-economic ['səusɪəui:kə'nɔmɪk] *a* socio-économique.
sociological [səusɪə'lɔdʒɪkl] *a* sociologique.
sociologist [səusɪ'ɔlədʒɪst] *n* sociologue *m/f*.
sociology [səusɪ'ɔlədʒɪ] *n* sociologie *f*.
sock [sɔk] *n* chaussette *f* ♦ *vt* (*col*: *hit*) flanquer un coup à; **to pull one's ~s up** (*fig*) se secouer (les puces).
socket ['sɔkɪt] *n* cavité *f*; (*ELEC*: *also*: **wall ~**) prise *f* de courant; (*: for light bulb*) douille *f*.
sod [sɔd] *n* (*of earth*) motte *f*; (*Brit col!*) con *m* (!); salaud *m* (!).
soda ['səudə] *n* (*CHEM*) soude *f*; (*also*: **~ water**) eau *f* de Seltz; (*US*: *also*: **~ pop**) soda *m*.
sodden ['sɔdn] *a* trempé(e); détrempé(e).
sodium ['səudɪəm] *n* sodium *m*.
sodium chloride *n* chlorure *m* de sodium.
sofa ['səufə] *n* sofa *m*, canapé *m*.
Sofia ['səufɪə] *n* Sofia.
soft [sɔft] *a* (*not rough*) doux(douce); (*not hard*) mou(molle); (*not loud*) doux, léger(ère); (*kind*) doux, gentil(le); (*weak*) indulgent(e); (*stupid*) stupide, débile.
soft-boiled ['sɔftbɔɪld] *a* (*egg*) à la coque.
soft drink *n* boisson non alcoolisée.
soft drugs *npl* drogues douces.
soften ['sɔfn] *vt* (r)amollir; adoucir; atténuer ♦ *vi* se ramollir; s'adoucir; s'atténuer.
softener ['sɔfnə*] *n* (*water ~*) adoucisseur *m*; (*fabric ~*) produit assouplissant.
soft fruit *n* (*Brit*) baies *fpl*.
soft furnishings *npl* tissus *mpl* d'ameublement.
soft-hearted [sɔft'hɑːtɪd] *a* au cœur tendre.
softly ['sɔftlɪ] *ad* doucement; légèrement; gentiment.
softness ['sɔftnɪs] *n* douceur *f*.
soft sell *n* promotion *f* de vente discrète.
soft toy *n* jouet *m* en peluche.
software ['sɔftwɛə*] *n* logiciel *m*, software *m*.
software package *n* progiciel *m*.

SOGAT ['səugæt] *n abbr* (*Brit*: = *Society of Graphical and Allied Trades*) syndicat des ouvriers du livre.
soggy ['sɔgɪ] *a* trempé(e); détrempé(e).
soil [sɔɪl] *n* (*earth*) sol *m*, terre *f* ♦ *vt* salir; (*fig*) souiller.
soiled [sɔɪld] *a* sale; (*COMM*) défraîchi(e).
sojourn ['sɔdʒəːn] *n* (*formal*) séjour *m*.
solace ['sɔlɪs] *n* consolation *f*, réconfort *m*.
solar ['səulə*] *a* solaire.
solarium, *pl* **solaria** [sə'lɛərɪəm, -rɪə] *n* solarium *m*.
solar plexus [-'plɛksəs] *n* (*ANAT*) plexus *m* solaire.
sold [səuld] *pt*, *pp* of **sell**.
solder ['səuldə*] *vt* souder (*au fil à souder*) ♦ *n* soudure *f*.
soldier ['səuldʒə*] *n* soldat *m*, militaire *m* ♦ *vi*: **to ~ on** persévérer, s'accrocher; **toy ~** petit soldat.
sold out *a* (*COMM*) épuisé(e).
sole [səul] *n* (*of foot*) plante *f*; (*of shoe*) semelle *f*; (*fish*: *pl inv*) sole *f* ♦ *a* seul(e), unique; **the ~ reason** la seule et unique raison.
solely ['səullɪ] *ad* seulement, uniquement; **I will hold you ~ responsible** je vous en tiendrai pour seul responsable.
solemn ['sɔləm] *a* solennel(le); sérieux(euse), grave.
sole trader *n* (*COMM*) chef *m* d'entreprise individuelle.
solicit [sə'lɪsɪt] *vt* (*request*) solliciter ♦ *vi* (*prostitute*) racoler.
solicitor [sə'lɪsɪtə*] *n* (*Brit*: *for wills etc*) ≈ notaire *m*; (*: in court*) ≈ avocat *m*.
solid ['sɔlɪd] *a* (*not hollow*) plein(e), compact(e), massif(ive); (*strong, sound, reliable, not liquid*) solide; (*meal*) consistant(e), substantiel(le); (*vote*) unanime ♦ *n* solide *m*; **to be on ~ ground** être sur la terre ferme; (*fig*) être en terrain sûr; **we waited 2 ~ hours** nous avons attendu deux heures entières.
solidarity [sɔlɪ'dærɪtɪ] *n* solidarité *f*.
solidify [sə'lɪdɪfaɪ] *vi* se solidifier ♦ *vt* solidifier.
solidity [sə'lɪdɪtɪ] *n* solidité *f*.
solid-state ['sɔlɪdsteɪt] *a* (*ELEC*) à circuits intégrés.
soliloquy [sə'lɪləkwɪ] *n* monologue *m*.
solitaire [sɔlɪ'tɛə*] *n* (*gem*, *Brit*: *game*) solitaire *m*; (*US*: *card game*) réussite *f*.
solitary ['sɔlɪtərɪ] *a* solitaire.
solitary confinement *n* (*LAW*) isolement *m* (cellulaire).
solitude ['sɔlɪtjuːd] *n* solitude *f*.
solo ['səuləu] *n* solo *m*.
soloist ['səuləuɪst] *n* soliste *m/f*.
Solomon Islands ['sɔləmən-] *npl*: **the ~** les (îles *fpl*) Salomon *fpl*.
solstice ['sɔlstɪs] *n* solstice *m*.
soluble ['sɔljubl] *a* soluble.
solution [sə'luːʃən] *n* solution *f*.
solve [sɔlv] *vt* résoudre.
solvency ['sɔlvənsɪ] *n* (*COMM*) solvabilité *f*.
solvent ['sɔlvənt] *a* (*COMM*) solvable ♦ *n* (*CHEM*) (dis)solvant *m*.
solvent abuse *n* usage *m* de solvants

hallucinogènes.

Som. *abbr* (*Brit*) = *Somerset.*

Somali [sə'mɑːlɪ] *a* somali(e), somalien(ne) ♦ *n* Somali/e, Somalien/ne.

Somalia [sə'mɑːlɪə] *n* (République *f* de) Somalie *f*.

sombre, (*US*) **somber** ['sɔmbə*] *a* sombre, morne.

some [sʌm] *a* (*a few*) quelques; (*certain*) certains(certaines); (*a certain number or amount*) *see phrases below*; (*unspecified*) un(e) ... (quelconque) ♦ *pronoun* quelques uns(unes); un peu ♦ *ad*: ~ **10 people** quelque 10 personnes, 10 personnes environ; ~ **children came** des enfants sont venus; ~ **people say that ...** certains disent que ...; **have ~ tea/ice-cream/water** prends du thé/ de la glace/de l'eau; **there's ~ milk in the fridge** il y a du lait *or* un peu de lait dans le frigo; ~ **(of it) was left** il en est resté un peu; **could I have ~ of that cheese?** pourriez-vous me donner un peu de ce fromage?; **I've got ~** (*i.e. books etc*) j'en ai (quelques uns); (*i.e. milk, money etc*) j'en ai (un peu); **would you like ~?** est-ce que vous en voulez?, en voulez-vous?; **after ~ time** après un certain temps; **at ~ length** assez longuement; **in ~ form or other** sous une forme ou une autre, sous une forme quelconque.

somebody ['sʌmbədɪ] *pronoun* quelqu'un; ~ **or other** quelqu'un, je ne sais qui.

someday ['sʌmdeɪ] *ad* un de ces jours, un jour ou l'autre.

somehow ['sʌmhau] *ad* d'une façon ou d'une autre; (*for some reason*) pour une raison ou une autre.

someone ['sʌmwʌn] *pronoun* = **somebody.**

someplace ['sʌmpleɪs] *ad* (*US*) = **somewhere.**

somersault ['sʌməsɔːlt] *n* culbute *f*, saut périlleux ♦ *vi* faire la culbute *or* un saut périlleux; (*car*) faire un tonneau.

something ['sʌmθɪŋ] *pronoun* quelque chose *m*; ~ **interesting** quelque chose d'intéressant; ~ **to do** quelque chose à faire; **he's ~ like me** il est un peu comme moi; **it's ~ of a problem** il y a là un problème.

sometime ['sʌmtaɪm] *ad* (*in future*) un de ces jours, un jour ou l'autre; (*in past*): ~ **last month** au cours du mois dernier.

sometimes ['sʌmtaɪmz] *ad* quelquefois, parfois.

somewhat ['sʌmwɔt] *ad* quelque peu, un peu.

somewhere ['sʌmwɛə*] *ad* quelque part; ~ **else** ailleurs, autre part.

son [sʌn] *n* fils *m*.

sonar ['səunɑː*] *n* sonar *m*.

sonata [sə'nɑːtə] *n* sonate *f*.

song [sɔŋ] *n* chanson *f*.

songbook ['sɔŋbuk] *n* chansonnier *m*.

songwriter ['sɔŋraɪtə*] *n* auteur-compositeur *m*.

sonic ['sɔnɪk] *a* (*boom*) supersonique.

son-in-law ['sʌnɪnlɔː] *n* gendre *m*, beau-fils *m*.

sonnet ['sɔnɪt] *n* sonnet *m*.

sonny ['sʌnɪ] *n* (*col*) fiston *m*.

soon [suːn] *ad* bientôt; (*early*) tôt; ~ **afterwards** peu après; **quite ~** sous peu; **how ~** **can you do it?** combien de temps vous faut-il pour le faire, au plus pressé?; **how ~ can you come back?** quand *or* dans combien de temps pouvez-vous revenir, au plus tôt; **see you ~!** à bientôt!; *see also* **as.**

sooner ['suːnə*] *ad* (*time*) plus tôt; (*preference*): **I would ~ do** j'aimerais autant *or* je préférerais faire; ~ **or later** tôt ou tard; **no ~ said than done** sitôt dit, sitôt fait; **the ~ the better** le plus tôt sera le mieux; **no ~ had we left than ...** à peine étions-nous partis que ....

soot [sut] *n* suie *f*.

soothe [suːð] *vt* calmer, apaiser.

soothing ['suːðɪŋ] *a* (*ointment etc*) lénitif(ive), lénifiant(e); (*tone, words etc*) apaisant(e); (*drink, bath*) relaxant(e).

SOP *n abbr* = *standard operating procedure.*

sop [sɔp] *n*: **that's only a ~** c'est pour nous (*or les etc*) amadouer.

sophisticated [sə'fɪstɪkeɪtɪd] *a* raffiné(e), sophistiqué(e); (*system etc*) très perfectionné(e), sophistiqué.

sophistication [səfɪstɪ'keɪʃən] *n* raffinement *m*; (*niveau m de*) perfectionnement *m*.

sophomore ['sɔfəmɔː*] *n* (*US*) étudiant/e de seconde année.

soporific [sɔpə'rɪfɪk] *a* soporifique ♦ *n* somnifère *m*.

sopping ['sɔpɪŋ] *a* (*also:* ~ **wet**) tout(e) trempé(e).

soppy ['sɔpɪ] *a* (*pej*) sentimental(e).

soprano [sə'prɑːnəu] *n* (*voice*) soprano *m*; (*singer*) soprano *m/f*.

sorbet ['sɔːbeɪ] *n* sorbet *m*.

sorcerer ['sɔːsərə*] *n* sorcier *m*.

sordid ['sɔːdɪd] *a* sordide.

sore [sɔː*] *a* (*painful*) douloureux(euse), sensible; (*offended*) contrarié(e), vexé(e) ♦ *n* plaie *f*; **to have a ~ throat** avoir mal à la gorge; **it's a ~ point** (*fig*) c'est un point délicat.

sorely ['sɔːlɪ] *ad* (*tempted*) fortement.

sorrel ['sɔrəl] *n* oseille *f*.

sorrow ['sɔrəu] *n* peine *f*, chagrin *m*.

sorrowful ['sɔrəuful] *a* triste.

sorry ['sɔrɪ] *a* désolé(e); (*condition, excuse, tale*) triste, déplorable; (*sight*) désolant(e); ~! pardon!, excusez-moi!; **to feel ~ for sb** plaindre qn; **I'm ~ to hear that ...** je suis désolé(e) *or* navré(e) d'apprendre que ...; **to be ~ about sth** regretter qch.

sort [sɔːt] *n* genre *m*, espèce *f*, sorte *f*; (*make: of coffee, car etc*) marque *f* ♦ *vt* (*also:* ~ **out**: *papers*) trier; classer; ranger; (: *letters etc*) trier; (: *problems*) résoudre, régler; (*COMPUT*) trier; **what ~ do you want?** quelle sorte *or* quel genre voulez-vous?; **what ~ of car?** quelle marque de voiture?; **I'll do nothing of the ~!** je ne ferai rien de tel!; **it's ~ of awkward** (*col*) c'est plutôt gênant.

sortie ['sɔːtɪ] *n* sortie *f*.

sorting office ['sɔːtɪŋ-] *n* (*POST*) bureau *m* de tri.

SOS *n abbr* (= *save our souls*) SOS *m*.

so-so ['səusəu] *ad* comme ci comme ça.

soufflé ['suːfleɪ] *n* soufflé *m*.

sought [sɔːt] *pt, pp* of **seek.**

sought-after ['sɔːtɑːftə*] *a* recherché(e).

soul [səul] n âme f; **the poor ~ had nowhere to sleep** le pauvre n'avait nulle part où dormir; **I didn't see a ~** je n'ai vu (absolument) personne.

soul-destroying ['səuldıstrɔıŋ] a démoralisant(e).

soulful ['səulful] a plein(e) de sentiment.

soulless ['səullıs] a sans cœur, inhumain(e).

soul mate n âme f sœur.

soul-searching ['səulsə:tʃıŋ] n: **after much ~, I decided ...** j'ai longuement réfléchi avant de décider ....

sound [saund] a (healthy) en bonne santé, sain(e); (safe, not damaged) solide, en bon état; (reliable, not superficial) sérieux(euse), solide; (sensible) sensé(e); ♦ ad: **~ asleep** dormant d'un profond sommeil ♦ n (noise) son m; bruit m; (GEO) détroit m, bras m de mer ♦ vt (alarm) sonner; (also: **~ out**: opinions) sonder ♦ vi sonner, retentir; (fig: seem) sembler (être); **to be of ~ mind** être sain(e) d'esprit; **I don't like the ~ of it** ça ne me dit rien qui vaille; **to ~ one's horn** (AUT) klaxonner, actionner son avertisseur; **to ~ like** ressembler à; **it ~s as if ...** il semblerait que ..., j'ai l'impression que ....
   sound off vi (col): **to ~ off (about)** la ramener (sur).

sound barrier n mur m du son.

sound effects npl bruitage m.

sound engineer n ingénieur m du son.

sounding ['saundıŋ] n (NAUT etc) sondage m.

sounding board n (MUS) table f d'harmonie; (fig): **to use sb as a ~ for one's ideas** essayer ses idées sur qn.

soundly ['saundlı] ad (sleep) profondément; (beat) complètement, à plate couture.

soundproof ['saundpru:f] vt insonoriser ♦ a insonorisé(e).

soundtrack ['saundtræk] n (of film) bande f sonore.

sound wave n (PHYSICS) onde f sonore.

soup [su:p] n soupe f, potage m; **in the ~** (fig) dans le pétrin.

soup course n potage m.

soup kitchen n soupe f populaire.

soup plate n assiette creuse or à soupe.

soupspoon ['su:pspu:n] n cuiller f à soupe.

sour ['sauə*] a aigre, acide; (milk) tourné(e), aigre; (fig) acerbe, aigre; revêche; **to go or turn ~** (milk, wine) tourner; (fig: relationship, plans) mal tourner; **it's ~ grapes** c'est du dépit.

source [sɔ:s] n source f; **I have it from a reliable ~ that** je sais de source sûre que.

south [sauθ] n sud m ♦ a sud inv, du sud ♦ ad au sud, vers le sud; **(to the) ~ of** au sud de; **to travel ~** aller en direction du sud; **the S~ of France** le Sud de la France, le Midi.

South Africa n Afrique f du Sud.

South African a sud-africain(e) ♦ n Sud-Africain/e.

South America n Amérique f du Sud.

South American a sud-américain(e) ♦ n Sud-Américain/e.

southbound ['sauθbaund] a en direction du sud; (carriageway) sud inv.

south-east [sauθ'i:st] n sud-est m.

South-east Asia n le Sud-Est asiatique.

southerly ['sʌðəlı] a du sud; au sud.

southern ['sʌðən] a (du) sud; méridional(e); **with a ~ aspect** orienté(e) or exposé(e) au sud; **the ~ hemisphere** l'hémisphère sud or austral.

South Pole n Pôle m Sud.

South Sea Islands npl: **the ~** l'Océanie f.

South Seas npl: **the ~** les mers fpl du Sud.

southward(s) ['sauθwəd(z)] ad vers le sud.

south-west [sauθ'west] n sud-ouest m.

souvenir [su:və'nıə*] n souvenir m (objet).

sovereign ['sɔvrın] a, n souverain(e).

sovereignty ['sɔvrıntı] n souveraineté f.

soviet ['səuvıət] a soviétique.

Soviet Union n: **the ~** l'Union f soviétique.

sow n [sau] truie f ♦ vt [səu] (pt ~ed, pp sown [səun]) semer.

soya ['sɔıə], (US) **soy** [sɔı] n: **~ bean** graine f de soja; **~ sauce** sauce f au soja.

spa [spa:] n (town) station f thermale; (US: also: **health ~**) établissement m de cure de rajeunissement.

space [speıs] n (gen) espace m; (room) place f; espace; (length of time) laps m de temps ♦ cpd spatial(e) ♦ vt (also: **~ out**) espacer; **to clear a ~ for sth** faire de la place pour qch; **in a confined ~** dans un espace réduit or restreint; **in a short ~ of time** dans peu de temps; **(with)in the ~ of an hour** en l'espace d'une heure.

space bar n (on typewriter) barre f d'espacement.

spacecraft ['speıskra:ft] n engin spatial.

spaceman ['speısmæn] n astronaute m, cosmonaute m.

spaceship ['speısʃıp] n engin or vaisseau spatial.

space shuttle n navette spatiale.

spacesuit ['speıssu:t] n combinaison spatiale.

spacewoman ['speıswumən] n astronaute f, cosmonaute f.

spacing ['speısıŋ] n espacement m; **single/double ~** (TYP etc) interligne m simple/double.

spacious ['speıʃəs] a spacieux(euse), grand(e).

spade [speıd] n (tool) bêche f, pelle f; (child's) pelle; **~s** npl (CARDS) pique m.

spadework ['speıdwə:k] n (fig) gros m du travail.

spaghetti [spə'getı] n spaghetti mpl.

Spain [speın] n Espagne f.

span [spæn] pt of **spin** ♦ n (of bird, plane) envergure f; (of arch) portée f; (in time) espace m de temps, durée f ♦ vt enjamber, franchir; (fig) couvrir, embrasser.

Spaniard ['spænjəd] n Espagnol/e.

spaniel ['spænjəl] n épagneul m.

Spanish ['spænıʃ] a espagnol(e), d'Espagne ♦ n (LING) espagnol m; **the ~** npl les Espagnols; **~ omelette** omelette f à l'espagnole.

spank [spæŋk] vt donner une fessée à.

spanner ['spænə*] n (Brit) clé f (de mécanicien).

spar [spa:*] n espar m ♦ vi (BOXING) s'entraîner.

spare [speə*] a de réserve, de rechange; (surplus) de or en trop, de reste ♦ n (part) pièce f de rechange, pièce détachée ♦ vt (do *without)* se passer de; *(afford to give)* donner, accorder, passer; *(refrain from hurting)* épargner; *(refrain from using)* ménager; **to ~** *(surplus)* en surplus, de trop; **there are 2 going ~** *(Brit)* il y en a 2 de disponible; **to ~ no expense** ne pas reculer devant la dépense; **can you ~ the time?** est-ce que vous avez le temps?; **there is no time to ~** il n'y a pas de temps à perdre; **I've a few minutes to ~** je dispose de quelques minutes.

spare part *n* pièce *f* de rechange, pièce détachée.

spare room *n* chambre *f* d'ami.

spare time *n* moments *mpl* de loisir.

spare tyre *n* (*AUT*) pneu *m* de rechange.

spare wheel *n* (*AUT*) roue *f* de secours.

sparing ['spɛərɪŋ] *a*: **to be ~ with** ménager.

sparingly ['spɛərɪŋlɪ] *ad* avec modération.

spark [spɑːk] *n* étincelle *f*; *(fig)* étincelle, lueur *f*.

spark(ing) plug ['spɑːk(ɪŋ)-] *n* bougie *f*.

sparkle ['spɑːkl] *n* scintillement *m*, étincellement *m*, éclat *m* ♦ *vi* étinceler, scintiller; *(bubble)* pétiller.

sparkling ['spɑːklɪŋ] *a* étincelant(e), scintillant(e); *(wine)* mousseux(euse), pétillant(e).

sparrow ['spærəu] *n* moineau *m*.

sparse [spɑːs] *a* clairsemé(e).

spartan ['spɑːtən] *a* *(fig)* spartiate.

spasm ['spæzəm] *n* (*MED*) spasme *m*; *(fig)* accès *m*.

spasmodic [spæz'mɔdɪk] *a* *(fig)* intermittent(e).

spastic ['spæstɪk] *n* handicapé/e moteur.

spat [spæt] *pt, pp of* **spit** ♦ *n* (*US*) prise *f* de bec.

spate [speɪt] *n* *(fig)*: **~ of** avalanche *f or* torrent *m* de; **in ~** *(river)* en crue.

spatial ['speɪʃl] *a* spatial(e).

spatter ['spætə*] *n* éclaboussure(s) *f(pl)* ♦ *vt* éclabousser ♦ *vi* gicler.

spatula ['spætjulə] *n* spatule *f*.

spawn [spɔːn] *vt* pondre; *(pej)* engendrer ♦ *vi* frayer ♦ *n* frai *m*.

SPCA *n abbr* (*US: = Society for the Prevention of Cruelty to Animals*) ≈ SPA *f*.

SPCC *n abbr* (*US: = Society for the Prevention of Cruelty to Children*).

speak, *pt* **spoke,** *pp* **spoken** [spiːk, spəuk, 'spəukn] *vt* *(language)* parler; *(truth)* dire ♦ *vi* parler; *(make a speech)* prendre la parole; **to ~ to sb/of *or* about sth** parler à qn/de qch; **~ing!** *(on telephone)* c'est moi-même!; **to ~ one's mind** dire ce que l'on pense; **it ~s for itself** c'est évident; **~ up!** parle plus fort!; **he has no money to ~ of** il n'a pas d'argent.

speak for *vt fus*: **to ~ for sb** parler pour qn; **that picture is already spoken for** *(in shop)* ce tableau est déjà réservé.

speaker ['spiːkə*] *n* *(in public)* orateur *m*; *(also:* **loud~**) haut-parleur *m*; (*POL*): **the S~** le président de la Chambre des communes *(Brit) or* des représentants *(US)*; **are you a Welsh ~?** parlez-vous gallois?

speaking ['spiːkɪŋ] *a* parlant(e); **French-~ people** les francophones; **to be on ~ terms**

se parler.

spear [spɪə*] *n* lance *f* ♦ *vt* transpercer.

spearhead ['spɪəhɛd] *n* fer *m* de lance; (*MIL*) colonne *f* d'attaque ♦ *vt* *(attack etc)* mener.

spearmint ['spɪəmɪnt] *n* (*BOT etc*) menthe verte.

spec [spɛk] *n* (*Brit col*): **on ~** à tout hasard; **to buy on ~** acheter avec l'espoir de faire une bonne affaire.

special ['spɛʃl] *a* spécial(e) ♦ *n* *(train)* train spécial; **take ~ care** soyez particulièrement prudents; **nothing ~** rien de spécial; **today's ~** *(at restaurant)* le plat du jour.

special agent *n* agent secret.

special correspondent *n* envoyé spécial.

special delivery *n* (*POST*): **by ~** en exprès.

specialist ['spɛʃəlɪst] *n* spécialiste *m/f*; **heart ~** cardiologue *m/f*.

speciality [spɛʃɪ'ælɪtɪ] *n* spécialité *f*.

specialize ['spɛʃəlaɪz] *vi*: **to ~ (in)** se spécialiser (dans).

specially ['spɛʃlɪ] *ad* spécialement, particulièrement.

special offer *n* (*COMM*) réclame *f*.

species ['spiːʃiːz] *n* *(pl inv)* espèce *f*.

specific [spə'sɪfɪk] *a* *(not vague)* précis(e), explicite; *(particular)* particulier(ière); (*BOT, CHEM etc*) spécifique; **to be ~ to** être particulier à, être le *or* un caractère *(or* les caractères) spécifique(s) de.

specifically [spə'sɪfɪklɪ] *ad* explicitement, précisément; *(intend, ask, design)* expressément, spécialement; *(exclusively)* exclusivement, spécifiquement.

specification [spɛsɪfɪ'keɪʃən] *n* spécification *f*; stipulation *f*; **~s** *npl* *(of car, building etc)* spécification.

specify ['spɛsɪfaɪ] *vt* spécifier, préciser; **unless otherwise specified** sauf indication contraire.

specimen ['spɛsɪmən] *n* spécimen *m*, échantillon *m*; (*MED*) prélèvement *m*.

specimen copy *n* spécimen *m*.

specimen signature *n* spécimen *m* de signature.

speck [spɛk] *n* petite tache, petit point; *(particle)* grain *m*.

speckled ['spɛkld] *a* tacheté(e), moucheté(e).

specs [spɛks] *npl* *(col)* lunettes *fpl*.

spectacle ['spɛktəkl] *n* spectacle *m*.

spectacle case *n* *(Brit)* étui *m* à lunettes.

spectacles ['spɛktəklz] *npl* *(Brit)* lunettes *fpl*.

spectacular [spɛk'tækjulə*] *a* spectaculaire ♦ *n* *(CINEMA etc)* superproduction *f*.

spectator [spɛk'teɪtə*] *n* spectateur/trice.

spectra ['spɛktrə] *npl of* **spectrum**.

spectre, *(US)* **specter** ['spɛktə*] *n* spectre *m*, fantôme *m*.

spectrum, *pl* **spectra** ['spɛktrəm, -rə] *n* spectre *m*; *(fig)* gamme *f*.

speculate ['spɛkjuleɪt] *vi* spéculer; *(try to guess)*: **to ~ about** s'interroger sur.

speculation [spɛkju'leɪʃən] *n* spéculation *f*; conjectures *fpl*.

speculative ['spɛkjulətɪv] *a* spéculatif(ive).

speculator ['spɛkjuleɪtə*] *n* spéculateur/trice.

speech [spiːtʃ] *n* *(faculty)* parole *f*; *(talk)* discours *m*, allocution *f*; *(manner of speaking)* façon *f* de parler, langage *m*; *(language)* langage *m*; *(enunciation)* élocution f.

speech day n (Brit SCOL) distribution f des prix.

speech impediment n défaut m d'élocution.

speechless ['spi:tʃlɪs] a muet(te).

speech therapy n orthophonie f.

speed [spi:d] n vitesse f; (promptness) rapidité f ♦ vi (pt, pp **sped** [spɛd]): **to ~ along/by** etc aller/passer etc à toute vitesse; (AUT: exceed ~ limit) faire un excès de vitesse; **at ~** (Brit) rapidement; **at full** or **top ~** à toute vitesse or allure; **at a ~ of 70 km/h** à une vitesse de 70 km/h; **shorthand/ typing ~s** nombre m de mots à la minute en sténographie/dactylographie; **a five-~ gearbox** une boîte cinq vitesses.

speed up, pt, pp **~ed up** vi aller plus vite, accélérer ♦ vt accélérer.

speedboat ['spi:dbəut] n vedette f, hors-bord m inv.

speedily ['spi:dɪlɪ] ad rapidement, promptement.

speeding ['spi:dɪŋ] n (AUT) excès m de vitesse.

speed limit n limitation f de vitesse, vitesse maximale permise.

speedometer [spɪ'dɔmɪtə*] n compteur m (de vitesse).

speed trap n (AUT) piège m de police pour contrôle de vitesse.

speedway n (SPORT) piste f de vitesse pour motos; (: also: ~ **racing**) épreuve(s) f(pl) de vitesse de motos.

speedy [spi:dɪ] a rapide, prompt(e).

speleologist [spɛlɪ'ɔlədʒɪst] n spéléologue m/f.

spell [spɛl] n (also: **magic ~**) sortilège m, charme m; (period of time) (courte) période ♦ vt (pt, pp **spelt** or **~ed** [spɛlt, spɛld]) (in writing) écrire, orthographier; (aloud) épeler; (fig) signifier; **to cast a ~ on sb** jeter un sort à qn; **he can't ~** il fait des fautes d'orthographe; **how do you ~ your name?** comment écrivez-vous votre nom?; **can you ~ it for me?** pouvez-vous me l'épeler?

spellbound ['spɛlbaund] a envoûté(e), subjugué(e).

spelling ['spɛlɪŋ] n orthographe f.

spelt [spɛlt] pt, pp of **spell**.

spend, pt, pp **spent** [spɛnd, spɛnt] vt (money) dépenser; (time, life) passer; (devote): **to ~ time/money/effort on sth** consacrer du temps/de l'argent/de l'énergie à qch.

spending ['spɛndɪŋ] n dépenses fpl; **government ~** les dépenses publiques.

spending money n argent m de poche.

spending power n pouvoir m d'achat.

spendthrift ['spɛndθrɪft] n dépensier/ière.

spent [spɛnt] pt, pp of **spend** ♦ a (patience) épuisé(e), à bout; (cartridge, bullets) vide; **~ matches** vieilles allumettes.

sperm [spə:m] n spermatozoïde m; (semen) sperme m.

sperm whale n cachalot m.

spew [spju:] vt vomir.

sphere [sfɪə*] n sphère f; (fig) sphère, domaine m.

spherical ['sfɛrɪkl] a sphérique.

sphinx [sfɪŋks] n sphinx m.

spice [spaɪs] n épice f ♦ vt épicer.

spick-and-span ['spɪkən'spæn] a impeccable.

spicy ['spaɪsɪ] a épicé(e), relevé(e); (fig) piquant(e).

spider ['spaɪdə*] n araignée f; **~'s web** toile f d'araignée.

spiel [spi:l] n laïus m inv.

spike [spaɪk] n pointe f; (ELEC) pointe de tension; **~s** npl (SPORT) chaussures fpl à pointes.

spike heel n (US) talon m aiguille.

spiky ['spaɪkɪ] a (bush, branch) épineux(euse); (animal) plein(e) de piquants.

spill, pt, pp **spilt** or **~ed** [spɪl, -t, -d] vt renverser; répandre ♦ vi se répandre; **to ~ the beans** (col) vendre la mèche; (: confess) lâcher le morceau.

spill out vi sortir à flots, se répandre.

spill over vi déborder.

spin [spɪn] n (revolution of wheel) tour m; (AVIAT) (chute f en) vrille f; (trip in car) petit tour, balade f ♦ vb (pt **spun, span**, pp **spun** [spʌn, spæn]) vt (wool etc) filer; (wheel) faire tourner; (Brit: clothes) essorer ♦ vi tourner, tournoyer; **to ~ a yarn** débiter une longue histoire; **to ~ a coin** (Brit) jouer à pile ou face.

spin out vt faire durer.

spinach ['spɪnɪtʃ] n épinard m; (as food) épinards.

spinal ['spaɪnl] a vertébral(e), spinal(e).

spinal column n colonne vertébrale.

spinal cord n moelle épinière.

spindly ['spɪndlɪ] a grêle, filiforme.

spin-dry ['spɪn'draɪ] vt essorer.

spin-dryer [spɪn'draɪə*] n (Brit) essoreuse f.

spine [spaɪn] n colonne vertébrale; (thorn) épine f, piquant m.

spine-chilling ['spaɪntʃɪlɪŋ] a terrifiant(e).

spineless ['spaɪnlɪs] a invertébré(e); (fig) mou(molle), sans caractère.

spinner ['spɪnə*] n (of thread) fileur/euse.

spinning ['spɪnɪŋ] n (of thread) filage m; (by machine) filature f.

spinning top n toupie f.

spinning wheel n rouet m.

spin-off ['spɪnɔf] n sous-produit m; avantage inattendu.

spinster ['spɪnstə*] n célibataire f; vieille fille.

spiral ['spaɪərl] n spirale f ♦ a en spirale ♦ vi (fig: prices etc) monter en flèche; **the inflationary ~** la spirale inflationniste.

spiral staircase n escalier m en colimaçon.

spire ['spaɪə*] n flèche f, aiguille f.

spirit ['spɪrɪt] n (soul) esprit m, âme f; (ghost) esprit, revenant m; (mood) esprit, état m d'esprit; (courage) courage m, énergie f; **~s** npl (drink) spiritueux mpl, alcool m; **in good ~s** de bonne humeur; **in low ~s** démoralisé(e); **community ~** solidarité f; **public ~** civisme m.

spirit duplicator n duplicateur m à alcool.

spirited ['spɪrɪtɪd] a vif(vive), fougueux(euse), plein(e) d'allant.

spirit level n niveau m à bulle.

spiritual ['spɪrɪtjuəl] a spirituel(le); religieux(euse) ♦ n (also: **Negro ~**) spiritual m.

spiritualism ['spɪrɪtjuəlɪzəm] n spiritisme m.

spit [spɪt] *n* (*for roasting*) broche *f*; (*spittle*) crachat *m*; (*saliva*) salive *f* ♦ *vi* (*pt, pp* **spat** [spæt]) cracher; (*sound*) crépiter.

spite [spaɪt] *n* rancune *f*, dépit *m* ♦ *vt* contrarier, vexer; **in ~ of** en dépit de, malgré.

spiteful ['spaɪtful] *a* malveillant(e), rancunier(ière).

spitroast ['spɪt'rəust] *vt* faire rôtir à la broche.

spitting ['spɪtɪŋ] *n*: "**~ prohibited**" "défense de cracher" ♦ *a*: **to be the ~ image of sb** être le portrait tout craché de qn.

spittle ['spɪtl] *n* salive *f*; bave *f*; crachat *m*.

spiv [spɪv] *n* (*Brit col*) chevalier *m* d'industrie, aigrefin *m*.

splash [splæʃ] *n* éclaboussement *m*; (*of colour*) tache *f* ♦ *excl* (*sound*) plouf! ♦ *vt* éclabousser ♦ *vi* (*also*: **~ about**) barboter, patauger.

splashdown ['splæʃdaun] *n* amerrissage *m*.

splay [spleɪ] *a*: **~footed** marchant les pieds en dehors.

spleen [spliːn] *n* (*ANAT*) rate *f*.

splendid ['splendɪd] *a* splendide, superbe, magnifique.

splendour, (*US*) **splendor** ['splendə*] *n* splendeur *f*, magnificence *f*.

splice [splaɪs] *vt* épisser.

splint [splɪnt] *n* attelle *f*, éclisse *f*.

splinter ['splɪntə*] *n* (*wood*) écharde *f*; (*metal*) éclat *m* ♦ *vi* se fragmenter.

splinter group *n* groupe dissident.

split [splɪt] *n* fente *f*, déchirure *f*; (*fig: POL*) scission *f* ♦ *vb* (*pt, pp* **split**) *vt* fendre, déchirer; (*party*) diviser; (*work, profits*) partager, répartir ♦ *vi* (*break*) se fendre, se briser; (*divide*) se diviser; **let's ~ the difference** coupons la poire en deux; **to do the ~s** faire le grand écart.

split up *vi* (*couple*) se séparer, rompre; (*meeting*) se disperser.

split-level ['splɪtlevl] *a* (*house*) à deux *or* plusieurs niveaux.

split peas *npl* pois cassés.

split personality *n* double personnalité *f*.

split second *n* fraction *f* de seconde.

splitting ['splɪtɪŋ] *a*: **a ~ headache** un mal de tête atroce.

splutter ['splʌtə*] *vi* bafouiller; postillonner.

spoil, *pt, pp* **spoilt** *or* **~ed** [spɔɪl, -t, -d] *vt* (*damage*) abîmer; (*mar*) gâcher; (*child*) gâter; (*ballot paper*) rendre nul ♦ *vi*: **to be ~ing for a fight** chercher la bagarre.

spoils [spɔɪlz] *npl* butin *m*.

spoilsport ['spɔɪlspɔːt] *n* trouble-fête *m/f inv*, rabat-joie *m inv*.

spoilt [spɔɪlt] *pt, pp of* **spoil** ♦ *a* (*child*) gâté(e); (*ballot paper*) nul(le).

spoke [spəuk] *pt of* **speak** ♦ *n* rayon *m*.

spoken ['spəukn] *pp of* **speak**.

spokesman ['spəuksmən], **spokeswoman** [-wumən] *n* porte-parole *m inv*.

sponge [spʌndʒ] *n* éponge *f*; (*CULIN: also*: **~ cake**) ≈ biscuit *m* de Savoie ♦ *vt* éponger ♦ *vi*: **to ~ on** *or* (*US*) **off** vivre aux crochets de.

sponge bag *n* (*Brit*) trousse *f* de toilette.

sponge cake *n* ≈ biscuit *m* de Savoie.

sponger ['spʌndʒə*] *n* (*pej*) parasite *m*.

spongy ['spʌndʒɪ] *a* spongieux(euse).

sponsor ['sponsə*] *n* sponsor *m*, personne *f* (*ou* organisme *m*) qui assure le parrainage; (*of new member*) parrain *m*/marraine *f* ♦ *vt* (*programme, competition etc*) parrainer, patronner, sponsoriser; (*POL: bill*) présenter; (*new member*) parrainer; **I ~ed him at 3p a mile** (*in fund-raising race*) je me suis engagé à lui donner 3p par mile.

sponsorship ['sponsəʃɪp] *n* patronage *m*, parrainage *m*.

spontaneity [spontə'neɪɪtɪ] *n* spontanéité *f*.

spontaneous [spon'teɪnɪəs] *a* spontané(e).

spooky ['spuːkɪ] *a* qui donne la chair de poule.

spool [spuːl] *n* bobine *f*.

spoon [spuːn] *n* cuiller *f*.

spoon-feed ['spuːnfiːd] *vt* nourrir à la cuiller; (*fig*) mâcher le travail à.

spoonful ['spuːnful] *n* cuillerée *f*.

sporadic [spə'rædɪk] *a* sporadique.

sport [spɔːt] *n* sport *m*; (*amusement*) divertissement *m*; (*person*) chic type/chic fille ♦ *vt* arborer; **indoor/outdoor ~s** sports en salle/de plein air; **to say sth in ~** dire qch pour rire.

sporting ['spɔːtɪŋ] *a* sportif(ive); **to give sb a ~ chance** donner sa chance à qn.

sport jacket *n* (*US*) = **sports jacket**.

sports car *n* voiture *f* de sport.

sports ground *n* terrain *m* de sport.

sports jacket *n* veste *f* de sport.

sportsman ['spɔːtsmən] *n* sportif *m*.

sportsmanship ['spɔːtsmənʃɪp] *n* esprit sportif, sportivité *f*.

sports page *n* page *f* des sports.

sportswear ['spɔːtsweə*] *n* vêtements *mpl* de sport.

sportswoman ['spɔːtswumən] *n* sportive *f*.

sporty ['spɔːtɪ] *a* sportif(ive).

spot [spot] *n* tache *f*; (*dot: on pattern*) pois *m*; (*pimple*) bouton *m*; (*place*) endroit *m*, coin *m*; (*also*: **~ advertisement**) message *m* publicitaire; (*small amount*): **a ~ of** un peu de ♦ *vt* (*notice*) apercevoir, repérer; **on the ~** sur place, sur les lieux; (*immediately*) sur le champ; **to put sb on the ~** (*fig*) mettre qn dans l'embarras; **to come out in ~s** se couvrir de boutons, avoir une éruption de boutons.

spot check *n* contrôle intermittent.

spotless ['spotlɪs] *a* immaculé(e).

spotlight ['spotlaɪt] *n* projecteur *m*; (*AUT*) phare *m* auxiliaire.

spot-on [spot'ɔn] *a* (*Brit col*) en plein dans le mille.

spot price *n* prix *m* sur place.

spotted ['spotɪd] *a* tacheté(e), moucheté(e); à pois; **~ with** tacheté(e) de.

spotty ['spotɪ] *a* (*face*) boutonneux(euse).

spouse [spauz] *n* époux/épouse.

spout [spaut] *n* (*of jug*) bec *m*; (*of liquid*) jet *m* ♦ *vi* jaillir.

sprain [spreɪn] *n* entorse *f*, foulure *f* ♦ *vt*: **to ~ one's ankle** se fouler *or* se tordre la cheville.

sprang [spræŋ] *pt of* **spring**.

sprawl [sprɔːl] *vi* s'étaler ♦ *n*: **urban ~** expansion urbaine; **to send sb ~ing** envoyer qn rouler par terre.

spray [spreɪ] *n* jet *m* (en fines gouttelettes);

spread — *(container)* vaporisateur *m*, bombe *f*; *(of flowers)* petit bouquet ♦ *vt* vaporiser, pulvériser; *(crops)* traiter ♦ *cpd* *(deodorant etc)* en bombe *or* atomiseur.

spread [sprɛd] *n* *(distribution)* répartition *f*; *(CULIN)* pâte *f* à tartiner; *(PRESS, TYP: two pages)* double page *f* ♦ *vb* ♦ *(pt, pp* **spread**) *vt* *(paste, contents)* étendre, étaler; *(rumour, disease)* répandre, propager; *(repayments)* échelonner, étaler; *(wealth)* répartir ♦ *vi* s'étendre; se répandre; se propager; **middle-age** ~ embonpoint *m* (pris avec l'âge).

spread-eagled ['sprɛdi:gld] *a*: **to be** *or* **lie** ~ être étendu(e) bras et jambes écartés.

spreadsheet ['sprɛdʃi:t] *n* *(COMPUT)* tableur *m*.

spree [spri:] *n*: **to go on a** ~ faire la fête.

sprig [sprɪg] *n* rameau *m*.

sprightly ['spraɪtlɪ] *a* alerte.

spring [sprɪŋ] *n* *(leap)* bond *m*, saut *m*; *(coiled metal)* ressort *m*; *(bounciness)* élasticité *f*; *(season)* printemps *m*; *(of water)* source *f* ♦ *vb* *(pt* **sprang**, *pp* **sprung** [spræŋ, sprʌŋ]) *vi* bondir, sauter ♦ *vt*: **to** ~ **a leak** *(pipe etc)* se mettre à fuir; **he sprang the news on me** il m'a annoncé la nouvelle de but en blanc; **in** ~, **in the** ~ au printemps; **to** ~ **from** provenir de; **to** ~ **into action** passer à l'action; **to walk with a** ~ **in one's step** marcher d'un pas souple.

spring up *vi* *(problem)* se présenter, surgir.

springboard ['sprɪŋbɔ:d] *n* tremplin *m*.

spring-clean [sprɪŋ'kli:n] *n* *(also:* ~**ing**) grand nettoyage de printemps.

spring onion *n* *(Brit)* ciboule *f*, cive *f*.

springtime ['sprɪŋtaɪm] *n* printemps *m*.

springy ['sprɪŋɪ] *a* élastique, souple.

sprinkle ['sprɪŋkl] *vt* *(pour)* répandre; verser; **to** ~ **water** *etc* **on,** ~ **with water** *etc* asperger d'eau *etc*; **to** ~ **sugar** *etc* **on,** ~ **with sugar** *etc* saupoudrer de sucre *etc*; ~**d with** *(fig)* parsemé(e) de.

sprinkler ['sprɪŋklə*] *n* *(for lawn etc)* arroseur *m*; *(to put out fire)* diffuseur *m* d'extincteur automatique d'incendie.

sprinkling ['sprɪŋklɪŋ] *n* *(of water)* quelques gouttes *fpl*; *(of salt)* pincée *f*; *(of sugar)* légère couche *f*.

sprint [sprɪnt] *n* sprint *m* ♦ *vi* sprinter.

sprinter ['sprɪntə*] *n* sprinteur/euse.

sprite [spraɪt] *n* lutin *m*.

sprocket ['sprɔkɪt] *n* *(on printer etc)* picot *m*.

sprout [spraut] *vi* germer, pousser.

sprouts [sprauts] *npl* *(also:* **Brussels** ~) choux *mpl* de Bruxelles.

spruce [spru:s] *n* épicéa *m* ♦ *a* net(te), pimpant(e).

spruce up *vt* *(smarten up: room etc)* apprêter; **to** ~ **o.s. up** se faire beau(belle).

sprung [sprʌŋ] *pp* *of* **spring**.

spry [spraɪ] *a* alerte, vif(vive).

SPUC *n abbr* = *Society for the Protection of Unborn Children.*

spud [spʌd] *n* *(col: potato)* patate *f*.

spun [spʌn] *pt, pp of* **spin.**

spur [spə:*] *n* éperon *m*; *(fig)* aiguillon *m* ♦ *vt* *(also:* ~ **on**) éperonner; aiguillonner; **on the** ~ **of the moment** sous l'impulsion du moment.

spurious ['spjuərɪəs] *a* faux(fausse).

spurn [spə:n] *vt* repousser avec mépris.

spurt [spə:t] *n* jet *m*; *(of energy)* sursaut *m* ♦ *vi* jaillir, gicler; **to put in** *or* **on a** ~ *(runner)* piquer un sprint; *(fig: in work etc)* donner un coup de collier.

sputter ['spʌtə*] *vi* = **splutter.**

spy [spaɪ] *n* espion/ne ♦ *vi*: **to** ~ **on** espionner, épier ♦ *vt* *(see)* apercevoir ♦ *cpd* *(film, story)* d'espionnage.

spying ['spaɪɪŋ] *n* espionnage *m*.

Sq. *abbr* *(in address)* = **square.**

sq. *abbr* *(MATH etc)* = **square.**

squabble ['skwɔbl] *n* querelle *f*, chamaillerie *f* ♦ *vi* se chamailler.

squad [skwɔd] *n* *(MIL, POLICE)* escouade *f*, groupe *m*; *(FOOTBALL)* contingent *m*; **flying** ~ *(POLICE)* brigade volante.

squad car *n* *(Brit POLICE)* voiture *f* de police.

squadron ['skwɔdrn] *n* *(MIL)* escadron *m*; *(AVIAT, NAUT)* escadrille *f*.

squalid ['skwɔlɪd] *a* sordide, ignoble.

squall [skwɔ:l] *n* rafale *f*, bourrasque *f*.

squalor ['skwɔlə*] *n* conditions *fpl* sordides.

squander ['skwɔndə*] *vt* gaspiller, dilapider.

square [skwɛə*] *n* carré *m*; *(in town)* place *f*; *(US: block of houses)* îlot *m*, pâté *m* de maisons; *(instrument)* équerre *f* ♦ *a* carré(e); *(honest)* honnête, régulier(ière); *(col: ideas, tastes)* vieux jeu *inv*, qui retarde ♦ *vt* *(arrange)* régler; arranger; *(MATH)* élever au carré; *(reconcile)* concilier ♦ *vi* *(agree)* cadrer, s'accorder; **all** ~ quitte; à égalité; **a** ~ **meal** un repas convenable; **2 metres** ~ (de) 2 mètres sur 2; **1** ~ **metre** 1 mètre carré; **we're back to** ~ **one** *(fig)* on se retrouve à la case départ.

square up *vi* *(Brit: settle)* régler; **to** ~ **up with sb** régler ses comptes avec qn.

square bracket *n* *(TYP)* crochet *m*.

squarely ['skwɛəlɪ] *ad* carrément; *(honestly, fairly)* honnêtement, équitablement.

square root *n* racine carrée.

squash [skwɔʃ] *n* *(Brit: drink)*: **lemon/orange** ~ citronnade/orangeade *f*; *(SPORT)* squash *m*; *(vegetable)* courge *f* ♦ *vt* écraser.

squat [skwɔt] *a* petit(e) et épais(se), ramassé(e) ♦ *vi* s'accroupir; *(on property)* squatter, squattériser.

squatter ['skwɔtə*] *n* squatter *m*.

squawk [skwɔ:k] *vi* pousser un *or* des gloussement(s).

squeak [skwi:k] *n* *(of hinge, wheel etc)* grincement *m*; *(of shoes)* craquement *m*; *(of mouse etc)* petit cri aigu ♦ *vi* grincer, crier.

squeal [skwi:l] *vi* pousser un *or* des cri(s) aigu(s) *or* perçant(s).

squeamish ['skwi:mɪʃ] *a* facilement dégoûté(e); facilement scandalisé(e).

squeeze [skwi:z] *n* pression *f*; *(also:* **credit** ~) encadrement *m* du crédit, restrictions *fpl* de crédit ♦ *vt* presser; *(hand, arm)* serrer ♦ *vi*: **to** ~ **past/under sth** se glisser avec (beaucoup de) difficulté devant/sous qch; **a** ~ **of lemon** quelques gouttes de citron.

squeeze out *vt* exprimer; *(fig)* soutirer.

squelch [skwɛltʃ] *vi* faire un bruit de succion; patauger.

squib [skwɪb] n pétard m.

squid [skwɪd] n calmar m.

squiggle ['skwɪgl] n gribouillis m.

squint [skwɪnt] vi loucher ♦ n: **he has a ~** il louche, il souffre de strabisme; **to ~ at sth** regarder qch du coin de l'œil; (quickly) jeter un coup d'œil à qch.

squire ['skwaɪə*] n (Brit) propriétaire terrien.

squirm [skwə:m] vi se tortiller.

squirrel ['skwɪrəl] n écureuil m.

squirt [skwə:t] n jet m ♦ vi jaillir, gicler.

Sr abbr = **senior, sister** (REL).

SRC n abbr (Brit: = Students' Representative Council) ≈ CROUS m.

Sri Lanka [srɪ'læŋkə] n Sri Lanka m or f.

SRN n abbr (Brit) = State Registered Nurse.

SRO abbr (US) = standing room only.

SS abbr (= steamship) S/S.

SSA n abbr (US: = Social Security Administration) organisme de sécurité sociale.

SST n abbr (US) = supersonic transport.

ST abbr (US: = Standard Time) heure officielle.

St abbr (= saint) St; (= street) R.

stab [stæb] n (with knife etc) coup m (de couteau etc); (col: try): **to have a ~ at (doing) sth** s'essayer à (faire) qch ♦ vt poignarder; **to ~ sb to death** tuer qn à coups de couteau.

stabbing ['stæbɪŋ] n: **there's been a ~** quelqu'un a été attaqué à coups de couteau ♦ a (pain, ache) lancinant(e).

stability [stə'bɪlɪtɪ] n stabilité f.

stabilization [steɪbəlaɪ'zeɪʃən] n stabilisation f.

stabilize ['steɪbəlaɪz] vt stabiliser ♦ vi se stabiliser.

stabilizer ['steɪbəlaɪzə*] n stabilisateur m.

stable ['steɪbl] n écurie f ♦ a stable; **riding ~s** centre m d'équitation.

staccato [stə'kɑ:təu] ad staccato ♦ a (MUS) piqué(e); (noise, voice) saccadé(e).

stack [stæk] n tas m, pile f ♦ vt empiler, entasser; **there's ~s of time** (Brit col) on a tout le temps.

stadium ['steɪdɪəm] n stade m.

staff [stɑ:f] n (work force) personnel m; (Brit SCOL: also: **teaching ~**) professeurs mpl, enseignants mpl, personnel enseignant; (servants) domestiques mpl; (MIL) état-major m; (stick) perche f, bâton m ♦ vt pourvoir en personnel.

staffroom ['stɑ:fru:m] n salle f des professeurs.

Staffs abbr (Brit) = Staffordshire.

stag [stæg] n cerf m; (Brit STOCK EXCHANGE) loup m.

stage [steɪdʒ] n scène f; (profession): **the ~** le théâtre; (point) étape f, stade m; (platform) estrade f ♦ vt (play) monter, mettre en scène; (demonstration) organiser; (fig: recovery etc) effectuer; **in ~s** par étapes, par degrés; **to go through a difficult ~** traverser une période difficile; **in the early ~s** au début; **in the final ~s** à la fin.

stagecoach ['steɪdʒkəutʃ] n diligence f.

stage door n entrée f des artistes.

stage fright n trac m.

stagehand ['steɪdʒhænd] n machiniste m.

stage-manage ['steɪdʒmænɪdʒ] vt (fig) orchestrer.

stage manager n régisseur m.

stagger ['stægə*] vi chanceler, tituber ♦ vt (person) stupéfier; bouleverser; (hours, holidays) étaler, échelonner.

staggering ['stægərɪŋ] a (amazing) stupéfiant(e), renversant(e).

stagnant ['stægnənt] a stagnant(e).

stagnate [stæg'neɪt] vi stagner, croupir.

stagnation [stæg'neɪʃən] n stagnation f.

stag party n enterrement m de vie de garçon.

staid [steɪd] a posé(e), rassis(e).

stain [steɪn] n tache f; (colouring) colorant m ♦ vt tacher; (wood) teindre.

stained glass window n vitrail m.

stainless ['steɪnlɪs] a (steel) inoxydable.

stain remover n détachant m.

stair [stɛə*] n (step) marche f; **~s** npl escalier m; **on the ~s** dans l'escalier.

staircase ['stɛəkeɪs], **stairway** ['stɛəweɪ] n escalier m.

stairwell ['stɛəwɛl] n cage f d'escalier.

stake [steɪk] n pieu m, poteau m; (BETTING) enjeu m ♦ vt risquer, jouer; (also: ~ **out**: area) marquer, délimiter; **to be at ~** être en jeu; **to have a ~ in sth** avoir des intérêts (en jeu) dans qch; **to ~ a claim (to sth)** revendiquer (qch).

stalactite ['stæləktaɪt] n stalactite f.

stalagmite ['stæləgmaɪt] n stalagmite f.

stale [steɪl] a (bread) rassis(e); (beer) éventé(e); (smell) de renfermé.

stalemate ['steɪlmeɪt] n pat m; (fig) impasse f.

stalk [stɔ:k] n tige f ♦ vt traquer ♦ vi: **to ~ in/out** etc entrer/sortir etc avec raideur.

stall [stɔ:l] n (Brit: in street, market etc) éventaire m, étal m; (in stable) stalle f ♦ vt (AUT) caler ♦ vi (AUT) caler; (fig) essayer de gagner du temps; **~s** npl (Brit: in cinema, theatre) orchestre m; **a newspaper/flower ~** un kiosque à journaux/de fleuriste.

stallholder ['stɔ:lhəuldə*] n (Brit) marchand/e en plein air.

stallion ['stæljən] n étalon m (cheval).

stalwart ['stɔ:lwət] n partisan m fidèle.

stamen ['steɪmɛn] n étamine f.

stamina ['stæmɪnə] n vigueur f, endurance f.

stammer ['stæmə*] n bégaiement m ♦ vi bégayer.

stamp [stæmp] n timbre m; (mark, also fig) empreinte f; (on document) cachet m ♦ vi (also: ~ **one's foot**) taper du pied ♦ vt tamponner, estamper; (letter) timbrer; **~ed addressed envelope (s.a.e.)** enveloppe affranchie pour la réponse.

stamp out vt (fire) piétiner; (crime) éradiquer; (opposition) éliminer.

stamp album n album m de timbres(-poste).

stamp collecting n philatélie f.

stamp duty n (Brit) droit m de timbre.

stampede [stæm'pi:d] n ruée f; (of cattle) débandade f.

stamp machine n distributeur m de timbres-poste.

stance [stæns] n position f.

stand [stænd] n (position) position f; (MIL) résistance f; (structure) guéridon m; support m; (COMM) étalage m, stand m; (SPORT)

tribune *f*; (*also*: **music** ~) pupitre *m* ♦ *vb* (*pt, pp* **stood** [stud]) *vi* être *or* se tenir (debout); (*rise*) se lever, se mettre debout; (*be placed*) se trouver ♦ *vt* (*place*) mettre, poser; (*tolerate, withstand*) supporter; **to make a** ~ prendre position; **to take a** ~ **on an issue** prendre position sur un problème; **to** ~ **for parliament** (*Brit*) se présenter aux élections (*comme candidat à la députation*); **to** ~ **guard** *or* **watch** (*MIL*) monter la garde; **it** ~s **to reason** c'est logique; cela va de soi; **as things** ~ dans l'état actuel des choses; **to** ~ **sb a drink/meal** payer à boire/à manger à qn; **I can't** ~ **him** je ne peux pas le voir.
stand aside *vi* s'écarter.
stand by *vi* (*be ready*) se tenir prêt(e) ♦ *vt fus* (*opinion*) s'en tenir à.
stand down *vi* (*withdraw*) se retirer; (*LAW*) renoncer à ses droits.
stand for *vt fus* (*signify*) représenter, signifier; (*tolerate*) supporter, tolérer.
stand in for *vt fus* remplacer.
stand out *vi* (*be prominent*) ressortir.
stand up *vi* (*rise*) se lever, se mettre debout.
stand up for *vt fus* défendre.
stand up to *vt fus* tenir tête à, résister à.
stand-alone ['stændǝlǝun] *a* (*COMPUT*) autonome.
standard ['stændǝd] *n* (*reference*) norme *f*; (*level*) niveau *m*; (*flag*) étendard *m* ♦ *a* (*size etc*) ordinaire, normal(e); (*model, feature*) standard *inv*; (*practice*) courant(e); (*text*) de base ~s *npl* (*morals*) morale *f*, principes *mpl*; **to be** *or* **come up to** ~ être du niveau voulu *or* à la hauteur; **to apply a double** ~ avoir *or* appliquer deux poids deux mesures; ~ **of living** niveau de vie.
standardization [stændǝdaɪ'zeɪʃǝn] *n* standardisation *f*.
standardize ['stændǝdaɪz] *vt* standardiser.
standard lamp *n* (*Brit*) lampadaire *m*.
standard time *n* heure légale.
stand-by ['stændbaɪ] *n* remplaçant/e ♦ *a* (*provisions*) de réserve; (*generator*) de secours; (*ticket, passenger*) sans garantie; **to be on** ~ se tenir prêt(e) (à intervenir); (*doctor*) être de garde.
stand-in ['stændɪn] *n* remplaçant/e; (*CINEMA*) doublure *f*.
standing ['stændɪŋ] *a* debout *inv*; (*permanent: rule*) immuable; (*army*) de métier; (*grievance*) constant(e), de longue date ♦ *n* réputation *f*, rang *m*, standing *m*; (*duration*): **of 6 months'** ~ qui dure depuis 6 mois; **of many years'** ~ qui dure *or* existe depuis longtemps; **he was given a** ~ **ovation** on s'est levé pour l'acclamer; **it's a** ~ **joke** c'est un vieux sujet de plaisanterie; **a man of some** ~ un homme estimé.
standing committee *n* commission permanente.
standing order *n* (*Brit: at bank*) virement permanent; ~s *npl* (*MIL*) règlement *m*.
standing room *n* places *fpl* debout.
stand-offish [stænd'ɔfɪʃ] *a* distant(e), froid(e).
standpat ['stændpæt] *a* (*US*) inflexible, rigide.
standpipe ['stændpaɪp] *n* colonne *f* d'alimentation.

standpoint ['stændpɔɪnt] *n* point *m* de vue.
standstill ['stændstɪl] *n*: **at a** ~ à l'arrêt; (*fig*) au point mort; **to come to a** ~ s'immobiliser, s'arrêter.
stank [stæŋk] *pt of* **stink**.
stanza ['stænzǝ] *n* strophe *f*; couplet *m*.
staple ['steɪpl] *n* (*for papers*) agrafe *f*; (*chief product*) produit *m* de base ♦ *a* (*food, crop, industry etc*) de base, principal(e) ♦ *vt* agrafer.
stapler ['steɪplǝ*] *n* agrafeuse *f*.
star [stɑː*] *n* étoile *f*; (*celebrity*) vedette *f* ♦ *vi*: **to** ~ (**in**) être la vedette (de) ♦ *vt* (*CINEMA*) avoir pour vedette; **4-**~ **hotel** hôtel *m* 4 étoiles; **2-**~ **petrol** (*Brit*) essence *f* ordinaire; **4-**~ **petrol** (*Brit*) super *m*.
star attraction *n* grande attraction.
starboard ['stɑːbǝd] *n* tribord *m*; **to** ~ à tribord.
starch [stɑːtʃ] *n* amidon *m*.
starched ['stɑːtʃt] *a* (*collar*) amidonné(e), empesé(e).
starchy ['stɑːtʃɪ] *a* riche en féculents; (*person*) guindé(e).
stardom ['stɑːdǝm] *n* célébrité *f*.
stare [stɛǝ*] *n* regard *m* fixe ♦ *vi*: **to** ~ **at** regarder fixement.
starfish ['stɑːfɪʃ] *n* étoile *f* de mer.
stark [stɑːk] *a* (*bleak*) désolé(e), morne; (*simplicity, colour*) austère; (*reality, poverty*) nu(e) ♦ *ad*: ~ **naked** complètement nu(e).
starlet ['stɑːlɪt] *n* (*CINEMA*) starlette *f*.
starlight ['stɑːlaɪt] *n*: **by** ~ à la lumière des étoiles.
starling ['stɑːlɪŋ] *n* étourneau *m*.
starlit ['stɑːlɪt] *a* étoilé(e); illuminé(e) par les étoiles.
starry ['stɑːrɪ] *a* étoilé(e).
starry-eyed [stɑːrɪ'aɪd] *a* (*innocent*) ingénu(e).
star-studded ['stɑːstʌdɪd] *a*: **a** ~ **cast** une distribution prestigieuse.
start [stɑːt] *n* commencement *m*, début *m*; (*race*) départ *m*; (*sudden movement*) sursaut *m*; (*advantage*) avance *f* ♦ *vt* commencer; (*found: business, newspaper*) lancer, créer ♦ *vi* partir, se mettre en route; (*jump*) sursauter; **to** ~ **doing sth** se mettre à faire qch; **at the** ~ au début; **for a** ~ d'abord, pour commencer; **to make an early** ~ partir *or* commencer de bonne heure; **to** ~ (**off**) **with** ... (*firstly*) d'abord ...; (*at the beginning*) au commencement ....
start off *vi* commencer; (*leave*) partir.
start over *vi* (*US*) recommencer.
start up *vi* commencer; (*car*) démarrer ♦ *vt* déclencher; (*car*) mettre en marche.
starter ['stɑːtǝ*] *n* (*AUT*) démarreur *m*; (*SPORT: official*) starter *m*; (: *runner, horse*) partant *m*; (*Brit CULIN*) entrée *f*.
starting handle ['stɑːtɪŋ-] *n* (*Brit*) manivelle *f*.
starting point ['stɑːtɪŋ-] *n* point *m* de départ.
starting price ['stɑːtɪŋ-] *n* prix initial.
startle ['stɑːtl] *vt* faire sursauter; donner un choc à.
startling ['stɑːtlɪŋ] *a* surprenant(e), saisissant(e).
star turn *n* (*Brit*) vedette *f*.

starvation [stɑːˈveɪʃən] *n* faim *f*, famine *f*; **to die of** ~ mourir de faim *or* d'inanition.

starve [stɑːv] *vi* mourir de faim; être affamé(e) ♦ *vt* affamer; **I'm starving** je meurs de faim.

state [steɪt] *n* état *m*; (*pomp*): **in** ~ en grande pompe ♦ *vt* (*declare*) déclarer, affirmer; (*specify*) indiquer, spécifier; **to be in a** ~ être dans tous ses états; ~ **of emergency** état d'urgence; ~ **of mind** état d'esprit; **the** ~ **of the art** l'état actuel de la technologie (*or* des connaissances).

state control *n* contrôle *m* de l'État.

stated [ˈsteɪtɪd] *a* fixé(e), prescrit(e).

State Department *n* (*US*) Département *m* d'État, ≈ ministère *m* des Affaires étrangères.

state education *n* (*Brit*) enseignement public.

stateless [ˈsteɪtlɪs] *a* apatride.

stately [ˈsteɪtlɪ] *a* majestueux(euse), imposant(e).

statement [ˈsteɪtmənt] *n* déclaration *f*; (*LAW*) déposition *f*; (*ECON*) relevé *m*; **official** ~ communiqué officiel; ~ **of account, bank** ~ relevé de compte.

state-owned [ˈsteɪtəʊnd] *a* étatisé(e).

States [steɪts] *npl*: **the** ~ les États-Unis *mpl*.

state secret *n* secret *m* d'État.

statesman [ˈsteɪtsmən] *n* homme *m* d'État.

statesmanship [ˈsteɪtsmənʃɪp] *n* qualités *fpl* d'homme d'état.

static [ˈstætɪk] *n* (*RADIO*) parasites *mpl*; (*also:* ~ **electricity**) électricité *f* statique ♦ *a* statique.

station [ˈsteɪʃən] *n* gare *f*; (*MIL, POLICE*) poste *m* (militaire *or* de police *etc*); (*rank*) condition *f*, rang *m* ♦ *vt* placer, poster; **action** ~**s** postes de combat; **to be** ~**ed in** (*MIL*) être en garnison à.

stationary [ˈsteɪʃnərɪ] *a* à l'arrêt, immobile.

stationer [ˈsteɪʃənə*] *n* papetier/ière; ~**'s (shop)** papeterie *f*.

stationery [ˈsteɪʃnərɪ] *n* papier *m* à lettres, petit matériel de bureau.

station master *n* (*RAIL*) chef *m* de gare.

station wagon *n* (*US*) break *m*.

statistic [stəˈtɪstɪk] *n* statistique *f*.

statistical [stəˈtɪstɪkl] *a* statistique.

statistics [stəˈtɪstɪks] *n* (*science*) statistique *f*.

statue [ˈstætjuː] *n* statue *f*.

statuesque [stætjuˈɛsk] *a* sculptural(e).

statuette [stætjuˈɛt] *n* statuette *f*.

stature [ˈstætʃə*] *n* stature *f*; (*fig*) envergure *f*.

status [ˈsteɪtəs] *n* position *f*, situation *f*; (*prestige*) prestige *m*; (*ADMIN, official position*) statut *m*.

status quo [-ˈkwəʊ] *n*: **the** ~ le statu quo.

status symbol *n* marque *f* de standing, signe extérieur de richesse.

statute [ˈstætjuːt] *n* loi *f*; ~**s** *npl* (*of club etc*) statuts *mpl*.

statute book *n* ≈ code *m*, textes *mpl* de loi.

statutory [ˈstætjutrɪ] *a* statutaire, prévu(e) par un article de loi; ~ **meeting** assemblée constitutive *or* statutaire.

staunch [stɔːntʃ] *a* sûr(e), loyal(e) ♦ *vt* étancher.

stave [steɪv] *n* (*MUS*) portée *f* ♦ *vt*: **to** ~ **off** (*attack*) parer; (*threat*) conjurer.

stay [steɪ] *n* (*period of time*) séjour *m*; (*LAW*): ~ **of execution** sursis *m* à statuer ♦ *vi* rester; (*reside*) loger; (*spend some time*) séjourner; **to** ~ **put** ne pas bouger; **to** ~ **with friends** loger chez des amis; **to** ~ **the night** passer la nuit.

stay behind *vi* rester en arrière.

stay in *vi* (*at home*) rester à la maison.

stay on *vi* rester.

stay out *vi* (*of house*) ne pas rentrer; (*strikers*) rester en grève.

stay up *vi* (*at night*) ne pas se coucher.

staying power [ˈsteɪɪŋ-] *n* endurance *f*.

STD *n abbr* (*Brit*: = *subscriber trunk dialling*) l'automatique *m*; (= *sexually transmitted disease*) MST *f*.

stead [stɛd] *n* (*Brit*): **in sb's** ~ à la place de qn; **to stand sb in good** ~ être très utile *or* servir beaucoup à qn.

steadfast [ˈstɛdfɑːst] *a* ferme, résolu(e).

steadily [ˈstɛdɪlɪ] *ad* régulièrement; fermement; d'une voix *etc* ferme.

steady [ˈstɛdɪ] *a* stable, solide, ferme; (*regular*) constant(e), régulier(ière); (*person*) calme, pondéré(e) ♦ *vt* assurer, stabiliser; (*voice*) assurer; **to** ~ **oneself** reprendre son aplomb.

steak [steɪk] *n* (*meat*) bifteck *m*, steak *m*; (*fish*) tranche *f*.

steakhouse [ˈsteɪkhaʊs] *n* ≈ grill-room *m*.

steal [stiːl] *vt* **stole**, *pp* **stolen** [stiːl, stəʊl, ˈstəʊln] *vt, vi* voler.

steal away, steal off *vi* s'esquiver.

stealth [stɛlθ] *n*: **by** ~ furtivement.

stealthy [ˈstɛlθɪ] *a* furtif(ive).

steam [stiːm] *n* vapeur *f* ♦ *vt* passer à la vapeur; (*CULIN*) cuire à la vapeur ♦ *vi* fumer; (*ship*): **to** ~ **along** filer; **under one's own** ~ (*fig*) par ses propres moyens; **to run out of** ~ (*fig: person*) caler; être à bout; **to let off** ~ (*fig: col*) se défouler.

steam up *vi* (*window*) se couvrir de buée; **to get** ~**ed up about sth** (*fig: col*) s'exciter à propos de qch.

steam engine *n* locomotive *f* à vapeur.

steamer [ˈstiːmə*] *n* (bateau *m* à) vapeur *m*; (*CULIN*) ≈ couscoussier *m*.

steam iron *n* fer *m* à repasser à vapeur.

steamroller [ˈstiːmrəʊlə*] *n* rouleau compresseur.

steamy [ˈstiːmɪ] *a* embué(e), humide.

steed [stiːd] *n* (*literary*) coursier *m*.

steel [stiːl] *n* acier *m* ♦ *cpd* d'acier.

steel band *n* steel band *m*.

steel industry *n* sidérurgie *f*.

steel mill *n* aciérie *f*, usine *f* sidérurgique.

steelworks [ˈstiːlwɜːks] *n* aciérie *f*.

steely [ˈstiːlɪ] *a* (*determination*) inflexible; (*eyes, gaze*) d'acier.

steep [stiːp] *a* raide, escarpé(e); (*price*) très élevé(e), excessif(ive) ♦ *vt* (faire) tremper.

steeple [ˈstiːpl] *n* clocher *m*.

steeplechase [ˈstiːpltʃeɪs] *n* steeple-(chase) *m*.

steeplejack [ˈstiːpldʒæk] *n* réparateur *m* de clochers et de hautes cheminées.

steeply [ˈstiːplɪ] *ad* en pente raide.

steer [stɪə*] *n* bœuf *m* ♦ *vt* diriger, gouverner;

(lead) guider ♦ *vi* tenir le gouvernail; **to ~ clear of sb/sth** *(fig)* éviter qn/qch.
steering ['stɪərɪŋ] *n* *(AUT)* conduite *f*.
steering column *n* *(AUT)* colonne *f* de direction.
steering committee *n* comité *m* d'organisation.
steering wheel *n* volant *m*.
stellar ['stɛlə*] *a* stellaire.
stem [stɛm] *n* *(of plant)* tige *f*; *(of leaf, fruit)* queue *f*; *(of glass)* pied *m* ♦ *vt* contenir, endiguer, juguler.
  stem from *vt fus* provenir de, découler de.
stench [stɛntʃ] *n* puanteur *f*.
stencil ['stɛnsl] *n* stencil *m*; pochoir *m* ♦ *vt* polycopier.
stenographer [stɛ'nɔgrəfə*] *n* *(US)* sténographe *m/f*.
stenography [stɛ'nɔgrəfɪ] *n* *(US)* sténo(graphie) *f*.
step [stɛp] *n* pas *m*; *(stair)* marche *f*; *(action)* mesure *f*, disposition *f* ♦ *vi*: **to ~ forward** faire un pas en avant, avancer; **~s** *npl* *(Brit)* = **stepladder**; **~ by ~** pas à pas; *(fig)* petit à petit; **to be in ~ (with)** *(fig)* aller dans le sens (de); **to be out of ~ (with)** *(fig)* être déphasé(e) (par rapport à).
  step down *vi* *(fig)* se retirer, se désister.
  step in *vi* *(fig)* intervenir.
  step off *vt fus* descendre de.
  step over *vt fus* enjamber.
  step up *vt* augmenter; intensifier.
stepbrother ['stɛpbrʌðə*] *n* demi-frère *m*.
stepchild ['stɛptʃaɪld] *n* beau-fils/belle-fille.
stepdaughter ['stɛpdɔ:tə*] *n* belle-fille *f*.
stepfather ['stɛpfɑ:ðə*] *n* beau-père *m*.
stepladder ['stɛplædə*] *n* *(Brit)* escabeau *m*.
stepmother ['stɛpmʌðə*] *n* belle-mère *f*.
stepping stone ['stɛpɪŋ-] *n* pierre *f* de gué; *(fig)* tremplin *m*.
stepsister ['stɛpsɪstə*] *n* demi-sœur *f*.
stepson ['stɛpsʌn] *n* beau-fils *m*.
stereo ['stɛrɪəu] *n* *(system)* stéréo *f*; *(record player)* chaine *f* stéréo ♦ *a* *(also:* **~phonic)** stéréophonique; **in ~** en stéréo.
stereotype ['stɪərɪətaɪp] *n* stéréotype *m* ♦ *vt* stéréotyper.
sterile ['stɛraɪl] *a* stérile.
sterility [stɛ'rɪlɪtɪ] *n* stérilité *f*.
sterilization [stɛrɪlaɪ'zeɪʃən] *n* stérilisation *f*.
sterilize ['stɛrɪlaɪz] *vt* stériliser.
sterling ['stə:lɪŋ] *a* sterling *inv*; *(silver)* de bon aloi, fin(e); *(fig)* à toute épreuve, excellent(e) ♦ *n* *(currency)* livre *f* sterling *inv*; **a pound ~** une livre sterling.
sterling area *n* zone *f* sterling *inv*.
stern [stə:n] *a* sévère ♦ *n* *(NAUT)* arrière *m*, poupe *f*.
sternum ['stə:nəm] *n* sternum *m*.
steroid ['stɪərɔɪd] *n* stéroïde *m*.
stethoscope ['stɛθəskəup] *n* stéthoscope *m*.
stevedore ['sti:vədɔ:*] *n* docker *m*, débardeur *m*.
stew [stju:] *n* ragoût *m* ♦ *vt, vi* cuire à la casserole; **~ed tea** thé trop infusé; **~ed fruit** fruits cuits *or* en compote.
steward ['stju:əd] *n* *(AVIAT, NAUT, RAIL)* steward *m*; *(in club etc)* intendant *m*; *(also:* **shop ~)** délégué syndical.

stewardess ['stju:ədɛs] *n* hôtesse *f*.
stewing steak ['stju:ɪŋ-], *(US)* **stew meat** *n* bœuf *m* à braiser.
St. Ex. *abbr* = **stock exchange**.
stg *abbr* = **sterling**.
stick [stɪk] *n* bâton *m*; *(of chalk etc)* morceau *m* ♦ *vb* *(pt, pp* **stuck** [stʌk]) *vt* *(glue)* coller; *(thrust)*: **to ~ sth into** piquer *or* planter *or* enfoncer qch dans; *(col: put)* mettre, fourrer; *(: tolerate)* supporter ♦ *vi* *(adhere)* coller; *(remain)* rester; *(get jammed: door, lift)* se bloquer; **to get hold of the wrong end of the ~** *(Brit fig)* comprendre de travers; **to ~ to** *(one's word, promise)* s'en tenir à; *(principles)* rester fidèle à.
  stick around *vi* *(col)* rester (dans les parages).
  stick out *vi* dépasser, sortir ♦ *vt*: **to ~ it out** *(col)* tenir le coup.
  stick up *vi* dépasser, sortir.
  stick up for *vt fus* défendre.
sticker ['stɪkə*] *n* auto-collant *m*.
sticking plaster ['stɪkɪŋ-] *n* sparadrap *m*, pansement adhésif.
stickleback ['stɪklbæk] *n* épinoche *f*.
stickler ['stɪklə*] *n*: **to be a ~ for** être pointilleux(euse) sur.
stick-up ['stɪkʌp] *n* *(col)* braquage *m*, hold-up *m*.
sticky ['stɪkɪ] *a* poisseux(euse); *(label)* adhésif(ive).
stiff [stɪf] *a* *(gen)* raide, rigide; *(door, brush)* dur(e); *(difficult)* difficile, ardu(e); *(cold)* froid(e), distant(e); *(strong, high)* fort(e), élevé(e); **to be** *or* **feel ~** *(person)* avoir des courbatures; **to have a ~ back** avoir mal au dos; **~ neck** torticolis *m*; **~ upper lip** *(Brit: fig)* flegme *m* *(typiquement britannique)*.
stiffen ['stɪfn] *vt* raidir, renforcer ♦ *vi* se raidir; se durcir.
stiffness ['stɪfnɪs] *n* raideur *f*.
stifle ['staɪfl] *vt* étouffer, réprimer.
stifling ['staɪflɪŋ] *a* *(heat)* suffocant(e).
stigma, *pl* *(BOT, MED, REL)* **~ta** *(fig)* **~s** ['stɪgmə, stɪg'mɑ:tə] *n* stigmate *m*.
stile [staɪl] *n* échalier *m*.
stiletto [stɪ'lɛtəu] *n* *(Brit: also:* **~ heel)** talon *m* aiguille.
still [stɪl] *a* *(motionless)* immobile; *(calm)* calme, tranquille; *(Brit: orange drink etc)* non gazeux(euse) ♦ *ad* *(up to this time)* encore, toujours; *(even)* encore; *(nonetheless)* quand même, tout de même ♦ *n* *(CINEMA)* photo *f*; **to stand ~** rester immobile, ne pas bouger; **keep ~!** ne bouge pas!; **he ~ hasn't arrived** il n'est pas encore arrivé, il n'est toujours pas arrivé.
stillborn ['stɪlbɔ:n] *a* mort-né(e).
still life *n* nature morte.
stilt [stɪlt] *n* échasse *f*; *(pile)* pilotis *m*.
stilted ['stɪltɪd] *a* guindé(e), emprunté(e).
stimulant ['stɪmjulənt] *n* stimulant *m*.
stimulate ['stɪmjuleɪt] *vt* stimuler.
stimulating ['stɪmjuleɪtɪŋ] *a* stimulant(e).
stimulation ['stɪmjuleɪʃən] *n* stimulation *f*.
stimulus, *pl* **stimuli** ['stɪmjuləs, 'stɪmjulaɪ] *n* stimulant *m*; *(BIOL, PSYCH)* stimulus *m*.
sting [stɪŋ] *n* piqûre *f*; *(organ)* dard *m*; *(col: confidence trick)* arnaque *m* ♦ *vt* *(pt, pp*

stung |stʌŋ|) piquer ♦ *vi* piquer; **my eyes are ~ing** j'ai les yeux qui piquent.

stingy |'stɪndʒɪ| *a* avare, pingre, chiche.

stink |stɪŋk| *n* puanteur *f* ♦ *vi* (*pt* **stank**, *pp* **stunk** |stæŋk, stʌŋk|) puer, empester.

stinker |'stɪŋkə*| *n* (*col*: *problem*, *exam*) vacherie *f*; (: *person*) dégueulasse *m/f*.

stinking |'stɪŋkɪŋ| *a* (*fig*: *col*) infect(e); **~ rich** bourré(e) de pognon.

stint |stɪnt| *n* part *f* de travail ♦ *vi*: **to ~ on** lésiner sur, être chiche de.

stipend |'staɪpɛnd| *n* (*of vicar etc*) traitement *m*.

stipendiary |staɪ'pɛndɪərɪ| *a*: **~ magistrate** juge *m* de tribunal d'instance.

stipulate |'stɪpjuleɪt| *vt* stipuler.

stipulation |stɪpju'leɪʃən| *n* stipulation *f*, condition *f*.

stir |stə:*| *n* agitation *f*, sensation *f* ♦ *vt* remuer ♦ *vi* remuer, bouger; **to give sth a ~** remuer qch; **to cause a ~** faire sensation.

stir up *vt* exciter.

stirring |stə:rɪŋ| *a* excitant(e); émouvant(e).

stirrup |'stɪrəp| *n* étrier *m*.

stitch |stɪtʃ| *n* (*SEWING*) point *m*; (*KNITTING*) maille *f*; (*MED*) point de suture; (*pain*) point de côté ♦ *vt* coudre, piquer; suturer.

stoat |stəut| *n* hermine *f* (*avec son pelage d'été*).

stock |stɔk| *n* réserve *f*, provision *f*; (*COMM*) stock *m*; (*AGR*) cheptel *m*, bétail *m*; (*CULIN*) bouillon *m*; (*FINANCE*) valeurs *fpl*, titres *mpl*; (*RAIL*: *also*: **rolling ~**) matériel roulant; (*descent*, *origin*) souche *f* ♦ *a* (*fig*: *reply etc*) courant(e); classique ♦ *vt* (*have in stock*) avoir, vendre; **well-~ed** bien approvisionné(e) *or* fourni(e); **in ~** en stock, en magasin; **out of ~** épuisé(e); **to take ~** (*fig*) faire le point; **~s and shares** valeurs (mobilières), titres; **government ~** fonds *mpl* publics.

stock up *vi*: **to ~ up (with)** s'approvisionner (en).

stockade |stɔ'keɪd| *n* palissade *f*.

stockbroker |'stɔkbrəukə*| *n* agent *m* de change.

stock control *n* (*COMM*) gestion *f* des stocks.

stock cube *n* (*Brit CULIN*) bouillon-cube *m*.

stock exchange *n* Bourse *f* (des valeurs).

stockholder |'stɔkhəuldə*| *n* actionnaire *m/f*.

Stockholm |'stɔkhəum| *n* Stockholm.

stocking |'stɔkɪŋ| *n* bas *m*.

stock-in-trade |'stɔkɪn'treɪd| *n* (*fig*): **it's his ~** c'est sa spécialité.

stockist |'stɔkɪst| *n* (*Brit*) stockiste *m*.

stock market *n* (*Brit*) Bourse *f*, marché financier.

stock phrase *n* cliché *m*.

stockpile |'stɔkpaɪl| *n* stock *m*, réserve *f* ♦ *vt* stocker, accumuler.

stockroom |'stɔkru:m| *n* réserve *f*, magasin *m*.

stocktaking |'stɔkteɪkɪŋ| *n* (*Brit COMM*) inventaire *m*.

stocky |'stɔkɪ| *a* trapu(e), râblé(e).

stodgy |'stɔdʒɪ| *a* bourratif(ive), lourd(e).

stoic |'stəuɪk| *n* stoïque *m/f*.

stoical |'stəuɪkl| *a* stoïque.

stoke |stəuk| *vt* garnir, entretenir; chauffer.

stoker |'stəukə*| *n* (*RAIL*, *NAUT etc*) chauffeur *m*.

stole |stəul| *pt of* **steal** ♦ *n* étole *f*.

stolen |'stəuln| *pp of* **steal**.

stolid |'stɔlɪd| *a* impassible, flegmatique.

stomach |'stʌmək| *n* estomac *m*; (*abdomen*) ventre *m* ♦ *vt* supporter, digérer.

stomach ache *n* mal *m* à l'estomac *or* au ventre.

stomach pump *n* pompe stomacale.

stomach ulcer *n* ulcère *m* à l'estomac.

stomp |stɔmp| *vi*: **to ~ in/out** entrer/sortir d'un pas bruyant.

stone |stəun| *n* pierre *f*; (*pebble*) caillou *m*, galet *m*; (*in fruit*) noyau *m*; (*MED*) calcul *m*; (*Brit*: *weight*) = 6.348 *kg*; 14 *pounds* ♦ *cpd* de or en pierre ♦ *vt* dénoyauter; **within a ~'s throw of the station** à deux pas de la gare.

Stone Age *n*: **the ~** l'âge *m* de pierre.

stone-cold |'stəun'kəuld| *a* complètement froid(e).

stoned |stəund| *a* (*col*: *drunk*) bourré(e); (: *on drugs*) défoncé(e).

stone-deaf |'stəun'dɛf| *a* sourd(e) comme un pot.

stonemason |'stəunmeɪsn| *n* tailleur *m* de pierre(s).

stonework |'stəunwə:k| *n* maçonnerie *f*.

stony |'stəunɪ| *a* pierreux(euse), rocailleux(euse).

stood |stud| *pt*, *pp of* **stand**.

stool |stu:l| *n* tabouret *m*.

stoop |stu:p| *vi* (*also*: **have a ~**) être voûté(e); (*bend*) se baisser, se courber; (*fig*): **to ~ to sth/doing sth** s'abaisser jusqu'à qch/jusqu'à faire qch.

stop |stɔp| *n* arrêt *m*; (*short stay*) halte *f*; (*in punctuation*) point *m* ♦ *vt* arrêter; (*break off*) interrompre; (*also*: **put a ~ to**) mettre fin à; (*prevent*) empêcher ♦ *vi* s'arrêter; (*rain*, *noise etc*) cesser, s'arrêter; **to ~ doing sth** cesser *or* arrêter de faire qch; **to ~ sb (from) doing sth** empêcher qn de faire qch; **to ~ dead** *vi* s'arrêter net; **~ it!** arrête!

stop by *vi* s'arrêter (au passage).

stop off *vi* faire une courte halte.

stop up *vt* (*hole*) boucher.

stopcock |'stɔpkɔk| *n* robinet *m* d'arrêt.

stopgap |'stɔpgæp| *n* (*person*) bouche-trou *m*; (*also*: **~ measure**) mesure *f* intérimaire.

stoplights |'stɔplaɪts| *npl* (*AUT*) signaux *mpl* de stop, feux *mpl* arrière.

stopover |'stɔpəuvə*| *n* halte *f*; (*AVIAT*) escale *f*.

stoppage |'stɔpɪdʒ| *n* arrêt *m*; (*of pay*) retenue *f*; (*strike*) arrêt de travail.

stopper |'stɔpə*| *n* bouchon *m*.

stop press *n* nouvelles *fpl* de dernière heure.

stopwatch |'stɔpwɔtʃ| *n* chronomètre *m*.

storage |'stɔ:rɪdʒ| *n* emmagasinage *m*; (*of nuclear waste etc*) stockage *m*; (*in house*) rangement *m*; (*COMPUT*) mise *f* en mémoire *or* réserve.

storage heater *n* (*Brit*) radiateur *m* électrique par accumulation.

store |stɔ:*| *n* provision *f*, réserve *f*; (*depot*) entrepôt *m*; (*Brit*: *large shop*) grand magasin; (US: *shop*) magasin *m* ♦ *vt* emmagasiner; (*nuclear waste etc*) stocker; (*in filing system*) classer, ranger; (*COMPUT*) mettre en mémoire; **~s** *npl* provisions; **who knows what is in ~ for us?** qui sait ce que l'avenir nous réserve *or* ce qui nous attend?; **to set great/little ~ by sth** faire grand cas/ peu de cas de qch.

store up *vt* mettre en réserve, emmagasiner.

storehouse ['stɔ:haus] *n* entrepôt *m*.

storekeeper ['stɔ:ki:pə*] *n* (*US*) commerçant/ e.

storeroom ['stɔ:ru:m] *n* réserve *f*, magasin *m*.

storey, (*US*) **story** ['stɔ:rɪ] *n* étage *m*.

stork [stɔ:k] *n* cigogne *f*.

storm [stɔ:m] *n* tempête *f*; (*also*: **electric ~**) orage *m* ♦ *vi* (*fig*) fulminer ♦ *vt* prendre d'assaut.

storm cloud *n* nuage *m* d'orage.

storm door *n* double-porte (extérieure).

stormy ['stɔ:mɪ] *a* orageux(euse).

story ['stɔ:rɪ] *n* histoire *f*; récit *m*; (*PRESS*: *article*) article *m*; (: *subject*) affaire *f*; (*US*) = **storey**.

storybook ['stɔ:rɪbuk] *n* livre *m* d'histoires *or* de contes.

storyteller ['stɔ:rɪtɛlə*] *n* conteur/euse.

stout [staut] *a* solide; (*brave*) intrépide; (*fat*) gros(se), corpulent(e) ♦ *n* bière brune.

stove [stəuv] *n* (*for cooking*) fourneau *m*; (: *small*) réchaud *m*; (*for heating*) poêle *m*; **gas/electric ~** (*cooker*) cuisinière *f* à gaz/ électrique.

stow [stəu] *vt* ranger; cacher.

stowaway ['stəuəweɪ] *n* passager/ère clandestin(e).

straddle ['strædl] *vt* enjamber, être à cheval sur.

strafe [strɑ:f] *vt* mitrailler.

straggle ['strægl] *vi* être (*or* marcher) en désordre; **~d along the coast** disséminé(e) tout au long de la côte.

straggler ['stræglə*] *n* traînard/e.

straggling ['stræglɪŋ], **straggly** ['stræglɪ] *a* (*hair*) en désordre.

straight [streɪt] *a* droit(e); (*frank*) honnête, franc(franche); (*plain*, *uncomplicated*) simple; (*THEATRE*: *part*, *play*) sérieux(euse); (*col*: *not bent*) normal(e); réglo *inv* ♦ *ad* (*tout*) droit; (*drink*) sec, sans eau ♦ *n*: **the ~** (*SPORT*) la ligne droite; **to put** *or* **get ~** mettre en ordre, mettre de l'ordre dans; **let's get this ~** mettons les choses au point; **10 ~ wins** 10 victoires d'affilée; **to go ~ home** rentrer directement à la maison; **~ away**, **~ off** (*at once*) tout de suite; **~ off**, **~ out** sans hésiter.

straighten ['streɪtn] *vt* (*also*: **~ out**) redresser; **to ~ things out** arranger les choses.

straight-faced [streɪt'feɪst] *a* impassible ♦ *ad* en gardant son sérieux.

straightforward [streɪt'fɔ:wəd] *a* simple; (*frank*) honnête, direct(e).

strain [streɪn] *n* (*TECH*) tension *f*; pression *f*; (*physical*) effort *m*; (*mental*) tension (nerveuse); (*MED*) entorse *f*; (*streak*, *trace*) tendance *f*; élément *m*; (*breed*) variété *f*; (*of*

virus) souche *f*; **~s** *npl* (*of music*) accents *mpl*, accords *mpl* ♦ *vt* tendre fortement; mettre à l'épreuve; (*filter*) passer, filtrer ♦ *vi* peiner, fournir un gros effort; **he's been under a lot of ~** il a traversé des moments très difficiles, il est très éprouvé nerveusement.

strained [streɪnd] *a* (*laugh etc*) forcé(e), contraint(e); (*relations*) tendu(e).

strainer ['streɪnə*] *n* passoire *f*.

strait [streɪt] *n* (*GEO*) détroit *m*; **to be in dire ~s** (*fig*) être dans une situation désespérée.

straitjacket ['streɪtdʒækɪt] *n* camisole *f* de force.

strait-laced [streɪt'leɪst] *a* collet monté *inv*.

strand [strænd] *n* (*of thread*) fil *m*, brin *m* ♦ *vt* (*boat*) échouer.

stranded ['strændɪd] *a* en rade, en plan.

strange [streɪndʒ] *a* (*not known*) inconnu(e); (*odd*) étrange, bizarre.

strangely ['streɪndʒlɪ] *ad* étrangement, bizarrement.

stranger ['streɪndʒə*] *n* (*unknown*) inconnu/e; (*from somewhere else*) étranger/ère; **I'm a ~ here** je ne suis pas d'ici.

strangle ['stræŋgl] *vt* étrangler.

stranglehold ['stræŋglhəuld] *n* (*fig*) emprise totale, mainmise *f*.

strangulation [stræŋgju'leɪʃən] *n* strangulation *f*.

strap [stræp] *n* lanière *f*, courroie *f*, sangle *f*; (*of slip*, *dress*) bretelle *f* ♦ *vt* attacher (avec une courroie *etc*).

straphanging ['stræphæŋɪŋ] *n* (fait *m* de) voyager debout (dans le métro *etc*).

strapless ['stræplɪs] *a* (*bra*, *dress*) sans bretelles.

strapping ['stræpɪŋ] *a* bien découplé(e), costaud(e).

Strasbourg ['stræzbə:g] *n* Strasbourg.

strata ['strɑ:tə] *npl of* **stratum**.

stratagem ['strætɪdʒəm] *n* stratagème *m*.

strategic [strə'ti:dʒɪk] *a* stratégique.

strategist ['strætɪdʒɪst] *n* stratège *m*.

strategy ['strætɪdʒɪ] *n* stratégie *f*.

stratosphere ['strætəsfɪə*] *n* stratosphère *f*.

stratum, *pl* **strata** ['strɑ:təm, 'strɑ:tə] *n* strate *f*, couche *f*.

straw [strɔ:] *n* paille *f*; **that's the last ~!** ça c'est le comble!

strawberry ['strɔ:bərɪ] *n* fraise *f*; (*plant*) fraisier *m*.

stray [streɪ] *a* (*animal*) perdu(e), errant(e) ♦ *vi* s'égarer; **~ bullet** balle perdue.

streak [stri:k] *n* raie *f*, bande *f*, filet *m*; (*fig: of madness etc*): **a ~ of** une *or* des tendance(s) à ♦ *vt* zébrer, strier ♦ *vi*: **to ~ past** passer à toute allure; **to have ~s in one's hair** s'être fait faire des mèches; **a winning/losing ~** une bonne/mauvaise série *or* période.

streaky ['stri:kɪ] *a* zébré(e), strié(e).

streaky bacon *n* (*Brit*) ≈ lard *m* (maigre).

stream [stri:m] *n* (*brook*) ruisseau *m*; (*current*) courant *m*, flot *m*; (*of people*) défilé ininterrompu, flot ♦ *vt* (*SCOL*) répartir par niveau ♦ *vi* ruisseler; **to ~ in/out** entrer/ sortir à flots; **against the ~** à contre courant; **on ~** (*new power plant etc*) en service.

streamer ['stri:mə*] *n* serpentin *m*, banderole *f*.

stream feed *n* (*on photocopier etc*) alimentation *f* en continu.

streamline ['stri:mlaɪn] *vt* donner un profil aérodynamique à; (*fig*) rationaliser.

streamlined ['stri:mlaɪnd] *a* (*AVIAT*) fuselé(e), profilé(e); (*AUT*) aérodynamique; (*fig*) rationalisé(e).

street [stri:t] *n* rue *f*; **the back ~s** les quartiers pauvres; **to be on the ~s** (*homeless*) être à la rue *or* sans abri; (*as prostitute*) faire le trottoir.

streetcar ['stri:tkɑ:*] *n* (*US*) tramway *m*.

street lamp *n* réverbère *m*.

street lighting *n* éclairage public.

street map, street plan *n* plan *m* des rues.

street market *n* marché *m* à ciel ouvert.

streetwise ['stri:twaɪz] *a* (*col*) futé(e), réaliste.

strength [strɛŋθ] *n* force *f*; (*of girder, knot etc*) solidité *f*; (*of chemical solution*) titre *m*; (*of wine*) degré *m* d'alcool; **on the ~ of** en vertu de; **at full ~** au grand complet; **below ~** à effectifs réduits.

strengthen ['strɛŋθn] *vt* renforcer; (*muscle*) fortifier.

strenuous ['strɛnjuəs] *a* vigoureux(euse), énergique; (*tiring*) ardu(e), fatigant(e).

stress [strɛs] *n* (*force, pressure*) pression *f*; (*mental strain*) tension (nerveuse); (*accent*) accent *m*; (*emphasis*) insistance *f* ♦ *vt* insister sur, souligner; **to lay great ~ on sth** insister beaucoup sur qch; **to be under ~** être stressé(e).

stressful ['strɛsful] *a* (*job*) stressant(e).

stretch [strɛtʃ] *n* (*of sand etc*) étendue *f*; (*of time*) période *f* ♦ *vi* s'étirer; (*extend*): **to ~ to** *or* **as far as** s'étendre jusqu'à; (*be enough: money, food*): **to ~ to** aller pour ♦ *vt* tendre, étirer; (*spread*) étendre; (*fig*) pousser (au maximum); **at a ~** sans discontinuer, sans interruption; **to ~ a muscle** se distendre un muscle; **to ~ one's legs** se dégourdir les jambes.

stretch out *vi* s'étendre ♦ *vt* (*arm etc*) allonger, tendre; (*to spread*) étendre; **to ~ out for sth** allonger la main pour prendre qch.

stretcher ['strɛtʃə*] *n* brancard *m*, civière *f*.

stretcher-bearer ['strɛtʃəbɛərə*] *n* brancardier *m*.

stretch marks *npl* (*on skin*) vergetures *fpl*.

strewn [stru:n] *a*: **~ with** jonché(e) de.

stricken ['strɪkən] *a* très éprouvé(e); dévasté(e); **~ with** frappé(e) *or* atteint(e) de.

strict [strɪkt] *a* strict(e); **in ~ confidence** tout à fait confidentiellement.

strictly ['strɪktlɪ] *ad* strictement; **~ confidential** strictement confidentiel(le); **~ speaking** à strictement parler.

strictness ['strɪktnɪs] *n* sévérité *f*.

stride [straɪd] *n* grand pas, enjambée *f* ♦ *vi* (*pt* **strode**, *pp* **stridden** [strəud, 'strɪdn]) marcher à grands pas; **to take in one's ~** (*fig: changes etc*) accepter sans sourciller.

strident ['straɪdnt] *a* strident(e).

strife [straɪf] *n* conflit *m*, dissensions *fpl*.

strike [straɪk] *n* grève *f*; (*of oil etc*) découverte *f*; (*attack*) raid *m* ♦ *vb* (*pt, pp* **struck** [strʌk]) *vt* frapper; (*oil etc*) trouver, découvrir; (*make: agreement, deal*) conclure ♦ *vi* faire grève; (*attack*) attaquer; (*clock*) sonner; **to go on** *or* **come out on ~** se mettre en grève, faire grève; **to ~ a match** frotter une allumette; **to ~ a balance** (*fig*) trouver un juste milieu.

strike back *vi* (*MIL, fig*) contre-attaquer.

strike down *vt* (*fig*) terrasser.

strike off *vt* (*from list*) rayer; (*: doctor etc*) radier.

strike out *vt* rayer.

strike up *vt* (*MUS*) se mettre à jouer; **to ~ up a friendship with** se lier d'amitié avec.

strikebreaker ['straɪkbreɪkə*] *n* briseur *m* de grève.

striker ['straɪkə*] *n* gréviste *m/f*; (*SPORT*) buteur *m*.

striking ['straɪkɪŋ] *a* frappant(e), saisissant(e).

string [strɪŋ] *n* ficelle *f*, fil *m*; (*row: of beads*) rang *m*; (*: of onions, excuses*) chapelet *m*; (*: of people, cars*) file *f*; (*MUS*) corde *f*; (*COMPUT*) chaîne *f* ♦ *vt* (*pt, pp* **strung** [strʌŋ]): **to ~ out** échelonner; **to ~ together** enchaîner; **the ~s** (*MUS*) les instruments *mpl* à cordes; **to get a job by pulling ~s** obtenir un emploi en faisant jouer le piston; **with no ~s attached** (*fig*) sans conditions.

string bean *n* haricot vert.

string(ed) instrument *n* (*MUS*) instrument *m* à cordes.

stringent ['strɪndʒənt] *a* rigoureux(euse); (*need*) impérieux(euse).

string quartet *n* quatuor *m* à cordes.

strip [strɪp] *n* bande *f*; (*SPORT*): **wearing the Celtic ~** en tenue du Celtic ♦ *vt* déshabiller; (*fig*) dégarnir, dépouiller; (*also: ~ down: machine*) démonter ♦ *vi* se déshabiller.

strip cartoon *n* bande dessinée.

stripe [straɪp] *n* raie *f*, rayure *f*.

striped ['straɪpt] *a* rayé(e), à rayures.

strip light *n* (*Brit*) (tube *m* au) néon *m*.

stripper ['strɪpə*] *n* strip-teaseuse *f*.

striptease ['strɪpti:z] *n* strip-tease *m*.

strive, *pt* **strove**, *pp* **striven** [straɪv, strəuv, 'strɪvn] *vi*: **to ~ to do** s'efforcer de faire.

strode [strəud] *pt of* **stride**.

stroke [strəuk] *n* coup *m*; (*MED*) attaque *f*; (*caress*) caresse *f*; (*SWIMMING: style*) (sorte *f* de) nage *f*; (*of piston*) course *f* ♦ *vt* caresser; **at a ~** d'un (seul) coup; **on the ~ of 5** à 5 heures sonnantes; **a ~ of luck** un coup de chance; **a 2-~ engine** un moteur à 2 temps.

stroll [strəul] *n* petite promenade ♦ *vi* flâner, se promener nonchalamment; **to go for a ~** aller se promener *or* faire un tour.

stroller ['strəulə*] *n* (*US*) poussette *f*.

strong [strɒŋ] *a* (*gen*) fort(e); (*healthy*) vigoureux(euse); (*object, material*) solide; (*distaste, desire*) vif(vive); (*drugs, chemicals*) puissant(e) ♦ *ad*: **to be going ~** (*company*) marcher bien; (*person*) être toujours solide; **they are 50 ~** ils sont au nombre de 50.

strong-arm ['strɒŋɑ:m] *a* (*tactics, methods*) musclé(e).

strongbox ['strɔŋbɔks] n coffre-fort m.

strong drink n boisson alcoolisée.

stronghold ['strɔŋhəuld] n bastion m.

strong language n grossièretés fpl.

strongly ['strɔŋlɪ] ad fortement, avec force; vigoureusement; solidement; **I feel ~ about it** c'est une question qui me tient particulièrement à cœur; (negatively) j'y suis profondément opposé(e).

strongman ['strɔŋmæn] n hercule m, colosse m; (fig) homme m à poigne.

strongroom ['strɔŋruːm] n chambre forte.

strove [strəuv] pt of **strive**.

struck [strʌk] pt, pp of **strike**.

structural ['strʌktʃrəl] a structural(e); (CONSTR) de construction; affectant les parties portantes.

structurally ['strʌktʃrəlɪ] ad du point de vue de la construction.

structure ['strʌktʃə*] n structure f; (building) construction f.

struggle ['strʌgl] n lutte f ♦ vi lutter, se battre; **to have a ~ to do sth** avoir beaucoup de mal à faire qch.

strum [strʌm] vt (guitar) gratter de.

strung [strʌŋ] pt, pp of **string**.

strut [strʌt] n étai m, support m ♦ vi se pavaner.

strychnine ['strɪkniːn] n strychnine f.

stub [stʌb] n bout m; (of ticket etc) talon m ♦ vt: **to ~ one's toe (on sth)** se heurter le doigt de pied (contre qch).

stub out vt écraser.

stubble ['stʌbl] n chaume m; (on chin) barbe f de plusieurs jours.

stubborn ['stʌbən] a têtu(e), obstiné(e), opiniâtre.

stubby ['stʌbɪ] a trapu(e); gros(se) et court(e).

stucco ['stʌkəu] n stuc m.

stuck [stʌk] pt, pp of **stick** ♦ a (jammed) bloqué(e), coincé(e); **to get ~** se bloquer or coincer.

stuck-up [stʌk'ʌp] a prétentieux(euse).

stud [stʌd] n clou m (à grosse tête); (collar ~) bouton m de col; (of horses) écurie f, haras m; (also: ~ **horse**) étalon m ♦ vt (fig): **~ded with** parsemé(e) or criblé(e) de.

student ['stjuːdənt] n étudiant/e ♦ cpd estudiantin(e); universitaire; d'étudiant; **law/medical ~** étudiant en droit/médecine.

student driver n (US) (conducteur/trice) débutant(e).

students' union n (Brit: association) ≈ union f des étudiants; (: building) ≈ foyer m des étudiants.

studied ['stʌdɪd] a étudié(e), calculé(e).

studio ['stjuːdɪəu] n studio m, atelier m.

studio flat, (US) **studio apartment** n studio m.

studious ['stjuːdɪəs] a studieux(euse), appliqué(e); (studied) étudié(e).

studiously ['stjuːdɪəslɪ] ad (carefully) soigneusement.

study ['stʌdɪ] n étude f; (room) bureau m ♦ vt étudier ♦ vi étudier, faire ses études; **to make a ~ of sth** étudier qch, faire une étude de qch; **to ~ for an exam** préparer un examen.

stuff [stʌf] n (gen) chose(s) f(pl), truc m; (belongings) affaires fpl, trucs; (substance) substance f ♦ vt rembourrer; (CULIN) farcir; (animal: for exhibition) empailler; **my nose is ~ed up** j'ai le nez bouché; **get ~ed!** (col!) va te faire foutre! (!); **~ed toy** jouet m en peluche.

stuffing ['stʌfɪŋ] n bourre f, rembourrage m; (CULIN) farce f.

stuffy ['stʌfɪ] a (room) mal ventilé(e) or aéré(e); (ideas) vieux jeu inv.

stumble ['stʌmbl] vi trébucher.

stumble across vt fus (fig) tomber sur.

stumbling block ['stʌmblɪŋ-] n pierre f d'achoppement.

stump [stʌmp] n souche f; (of limb) moignon m ♦ vt: **to be ~ed** sécher, ne pas savoir que répondre.

stun [stʌn] vt (subj: blow) étourdir; (: news) abasourdir, stupéfier.

stung [stʌŋ] pt, pp of **sting**.

stunk [stʌŋk] pp of **stink**.

stunning ['stʌnɪŋ] a étourdissant(e); (fabulous) stupéfiant(e), sensationnel(le).

stunt [stʌnt] n tour m de force; truc m publicitaire; (AVIAT) acrobatie f ♦ vt retarder, arrêter.

stunted ['stʌntɪd] a rabougri(e).

stuntman ['stʌntmæn] n cascadeur m.

stupefaction [stjuːpɪ'fækʃən] n stupéfaction f, stupeur f.

stupefy ['stjuːpɪfaɪ] vt étourdir; abrutir; (fig) stupéfier.

stupendous [stjuː'pɛndəs] a prodigieux(euse), fantastique.

stupid ['stjuːpɪd] a stupide, bête.

stupidity [stjuː'pɪdɪtɪ] n stupidité f, bêtise f.

stupidly ['stjuːpɪdlɪ] ad stupidement, bêtement.

stupor ['stjuːpə*] n stupeur f.

sturdy ['stɜːdɪ] a robuste, vigoureux(euse), solide.

sturgeon ['stɜːdʒən] n esturgeon m.

stutter ['stʌtə*] n bégaiement m ♦ vi bégayer.

sty [staɪ] n (of pigs) porcherie f.

stye [staɪ] n (MED) orgelet m.

style [staɪl] n style m; (of dress etc) genre m; (distinction) allure f, cachet m, style; **in the latest ~** à la dernière mode; **hair ~** coiffure f.

stylish ['staɪlɪʃ] a élégant(e), chic inv.

stylist ['staɪlɪst] n (hair ~) coiffeur/euse; (literary ~) styliste m/f.

stylized ['staɪlaɪzd] a stylisé(e).

stylus, pl **styli** or **styluses** ['staɪləs, -laɪ] n (of record player) pointe f de lecture.

suave [swɑːv] a doucereux(euse), onctueux(euse).

sub [sʌb] n abbr = **submarine, subscription**.

sub... [sʌb] prefix sub..., sous-.

subcommittee ['sʌbkəmɪtɪ] n sous-comité m.

subconscious [sʌb'kɔnʃəs] a subconscient(e) ♦ n subconscient m.

subcontinent [sʌb'kɔntɪnənt] n: **the (Indian) ~** le sous-continent indien.

subcontract n ['sʌb'kɔntrækt] contrat m de sous-traitance ♦ vt [sʌbkən'trækt] sous-traiter.

subcontractor ['sʌbkən'træktə*] n sous-traitant m.

subdivide [sʌbdɪ'vaɪd] vt subdiviser.

subdivision ['sʌbdɪvɪʒən] n subdivision f.
subdue [səb'dju:] vt subjuguer, soumettre.
subdued [səb'dju:d] a contenu(e), atténué(e); (light) tamisé(e); (person) qui a perdu de son entrain.
sub-editor ['sʌb'ɛdɪtə*] n (Brit) secrétaire m/f de (la) rédaction.
subject n ['sʌbdʒɪkt] sujet m; (SCOL) matière f ♦ vt [səb'dʒɛkt]: **to ~ to** soumettre à; exposer à; **to be ~ to** (law) être soumis(e) à; (disease) être sujet(te) à; **~ to confirmation in writing** sous réserve de confirmation écrite; **to change the ~** changer de conversation.
subjection [səb'dʒɛkʃən] n soumission f, sujétion f.
subjective [səb'dʒɛktɪv] a subjectif(ive).
subject matter n sujet m; contenu m.
sub judice [sʌb'dju:dɪsɪ] a (LAW) devant les tribunaux.
subjugate ['sʌbdʒugeɪt] vt subjuguer.
subjunctive [səb'dʒʌŋkɪv] a subjonctif(ive) ♦ n subjonctif m.
sublet [sʌb'lɛt] vt sous-louer.
sublime [sə'blaɪm] a sublime.
subliminal [sʌb'lɪmɪnl] a subliminal(e).
submachine gun ['sʌbmə'ʃi:n-] n fusil-mitrailleur m.
submarine [sʌbmə'ri:n] n sous-marin m.
submerge [səb'mə:dʒ] vt submerger; immerger ♦ vi plonger.
submersion [səb'mə:ʃən] n submersion f; immersion f.
submission [səb'mɪʃən] n soumission f; (to committee etc) présentation f.
submissive [səb'mɪsɪv] a soumis(e).
submit [səb'mɪt] vt soumettre ♦ vi se soumettre.
subnormal [sʌb'nɔ:ml] a au-dessous de la normale; (person) arriéré(e).
subordinate [sə'bɔ:dɪnət] a, n subordonné(e).
subpoena [səb'pi:nə] (LAW) n citation f, assignation f ♦ vt citer or assigner (à comparaître).
subroutine [sʌbru:'ti:n] n (COMPUT) sous-programme m.
subscribe [səb'skraɪb] vi cotiser; **to ~ to** (opinion, fund) souscrire à; (newspaper) s'abonner à; être abonné(e) à.
subscriber [səb'skraɪbə*] n (to periodical, telephone) abonné/e.
subscript ['sʌbskrɪpt] n (TYP) indice inférieur.
subscription [səb'skrɪpʃən] n (to fund) souscription f; (to magazine etc) abonnement m; (membership dues) cotisation f; **to take out a ~ to** s'abonner à.
subsequent ['sʌbsɪkwənt] a ultérieur(e), suivant(e); **~ to** prep à la suite de.
subsequently ['sʌbsɪkwəntlɪ] ad par la suite.
subservient [səb'sə:vɪənt] a obséquieux(euse).
subside [səb'saɪd] vi s'affaisser; (flood) baisser; (wind) tomber.
subsidence [səb'saɪdns] n affaissement m.
subsidiary [səb'sɪdɪərɪ] n subsidiaire, accessoire; (Brit SCOL: subject) complémentaire ♦ n filiale f.
subsidize ['sʌbsɪdaɪz] vt subventionner.
subsidy ['sʌbsɪdɪ] n subvention f.
subsist [səb'sɪst] vi: **to ~ on sth** (arriver à) vivre avec or subsister avec qch.
subsistence [səb'sɪstəns] n existence f, subsistance f.
subsistence allowance n indemnité f de séjour.
subsistence level n niveau m de vie minimum.
substance ['sʌbstəns] n substance f; (fig) essentiel m; **a man of ~** un homme jouissant d'une certaine fortune; **to lack ~** être plutôt mince (fig).
substandard [sʌb'stændəd] a (goods) de qualité inférieure, qui laisse à désirer; (housing) inférieur(e) aux normes requises.
substantial [səb'stænʃl] a substantiel(le); (fig) important(e).
substantially [səb'stænʃəlɪ] ad considérablement; en grande partie.
substantiate [səb'stænʃɪeɪt] vt étayer, fournir des preuves à l'appui de.
substitute ['sʌbstɪtju:t] n (person) remplaçant/e; (thing) succédané m ♦ vt: **to ~ sth/sb for** substituer qch/qn à, remplacer par qch/qn.
substitute teacher n (US) suppléant/e.
substitution [sʌbstɪ'tju:ʃən] n substitution f.
subterfuge ['sʌbtəfju:dʒ] n subterfuge m.
subterranean [sʌbtə'reɪnɪən] a souterrain(e).
subtitle ['sʌbtaɪtl] n (CINEMA) sous-titre m.
subtle ['sʌtl] a subtil(e).
subtlety ['sʌtlɪ] n subtilité f.
subtly ['sʌtlɪ] ad subtilement.
subtotal [sʌb'təutl] n total partiel.
subtract [səb'trækt] vt soustraire, retrancher.
subtraction [səb'trækʃən] n soustraction f.
subtropical [sʌb'trɒpɪkl] a subtropical(e).
suburb ['sʌbə:b] n faubourg m; **the ~s** la banlieue.
suburban [sə'bə:bən] a de banlieue, suburbain(e).
suburbia [sə'bə:bɪə] n la banlieue.
subvention [səb'vɛnʃən] n (subsidy) subvention f.
subversion [səb'və:ʃən] n subversion f.
subversive [səb'və:sɪv] a subversif(ive).
subway ['sʌbweɪ] n (US) métro m; (Brit) passage souterrain.
sub-zero [sʌb'zɪərəu] a au-dessous de zéro.
succeed [sək'si:d] vi réussir ♦ vt succéder à; **to ~ in doing** réussir à faire.
succeeding [sək'si:dɪŋ] a suivant(e), qui suit (or suivent or suivront etc).
success [sək'sɛs] n succès m; réussite f.
successful [sək'sɛsful] a qui a du succès; (candidate) choisi(e), agréé(e); (business) prospère, qui réussit; (attempt) couronné(e) de succès; **to be ~ (in doing)** réussir (à faire).
successfully [sək'sɛsfəlɪ] ad avec succès.
succession [sək'sɛʃən] n succession f; **in ~** successivement; **3 years in ~** 3 ans de suite.
successive [sək'sɛsɪv] a successif(ive); **on 3 ~ days** 3 jours de suite or consécutifs.
successor [sək'sɛsə*] n successeur m.
succinct [sək'sɪŋkt] a succinct(e), bref(brève).
succulent ['sʌkjulənt] a succulent(e) ♦ n (BOT): **~s** plantes grasses.
succumb [sə'kʌm] vi succomber.
such [sʌtʃ] a tel(telle); (of that kind): **~ a**

book un livre de ce genre *or* pareil, un tel livre; ~ **books** des livres de ce genre *or* pareils, de tels livres; *(so much)*: ~ **courage** un tel courage ♦ *ad* si; ~ **a long trip** un si long voyage; ~ **good books** de si bons livres; ~ **a long trip that** un voyage si *or* tellement long que; ~ **a lot of** tellement *or* tant de; **making** ~ **a noise that** faisant un tel bruit que *or* tellement de bruit que; ~ **a long time ago** il y a si *or* tellement longtemps; ~ **as** *(like)* tel(telle) que, comme; **a noise** ~ **as to** un bruit de nature à; ~ **books as I have** les quelques livres que j'ai; **as** ~ *ad* en tant que tel(telle), à proprement parler.

such-and-such ['sʌtʃənsʌtʃ] *a* tel(telle) ou tel(telle).

suchlike ['sʌtʃlaɪk] *pronoun (col)*: **and** ~ et le reste.

suck [sʌk] *vt* sucer; *(breast, bottle)* téter; *(subj: pump, machine)* aspirer.

sucker ['sʌkə*] *n (BOT, ZOOL, TECH)* ventouse *f*; *(col)* naïf/ïve, poire *f*.

suckle ['sʌkl] *vt* allaiter.

suction ['sʌkʃən] *n* succion *f*.

suction pump *n* pompe aspirante.

Sudan [su'dɑːn] *n* Soudan *m*.

Sudanese [suːdə'niːz] *a* soudanais(e) ♦ *n* Soudanais/e.

sudden ['sʌdn] *a* soudain(e), subit(e); **all of a** ~ soudain, tout à coup.

suddenly ['sʌdnlɪ] *ad* brusquement, tout à coup, soudain.

suds [sʌdz] *npl* eau savonneuse.

sue [suː] *vt* poursuivre en justice, intenter un procès à ♦ *vi*: **to** ~ **(for)** intenter un procès (pour); **to** ~ **for divorce** engager une procédure de divorce; **to** ~ **sb for damages** poursuivre qn en dommages-intérêts.

suede [sweɪd] *n* daim *m*, cuir suédé ♦ *cpd* de daim.

suet ['suɪt] *n* graisse *f* de rognon *or* de bœuf.

Suez Canal ['suːɪz-] *n* canal *m* de Suez.

Suff. *abbr (Brit)* = **Suffolk**.

suffer ['sʌfə*] *vt* souffrir, subir; *(bear)* tolérer, supporter, subir ♦ *vi* souffrir; **to** ~ **from** *(illness)* souffrir de, avoir; **to** ~ **from the effects of alcohol/a fall** se ressentir des effets de l'alcool/des conséquences d'une chute.

sufferance ['sʌfərns] *n*: **he was only there on** ~ sa présence était seulement tolérée.

sufferer ['sʌfərə*] *n* malade *m/f*; victime *m/f*.

suffering ['sʌfərɪŋ] *n* souffrance(s) *f(pl)*.

suffice [sə'faɪs] *vi* suffire.

sufficient [sə'fɪʃənt] *a* suffisant(e); ~ **money** suffisamment d'argent.

sufficiently [sə'fɪʃəntlɪ] *ad* suffisamment, assez.

suffix ['sʌfɪks] *n* suffixe *m*.

suffocate ['sʌfəkeɪt] *vi* suffoquer; étouffer.

suffocation [sʌfə'keɪʃən] *n* suffocation *f*; *(MED)* asphyxie *f*.

suffrage ['sʌfrɪdʒ] *n* suffrage *m*; droit *m* de suffrage *or* de vote.

suffuse [sə'fjuːz] *vt* baigner, imprégner; **the room was** ~**d with light** la pièce baignait dans la lumière *or* était imprégnée de lumière.

sugar ['ʃugə*] *n* sucre *m* ♦ *vt* sucrer.

sugar beet *n* betterave sucrière.

sugar bowl *n* sucrier *m*.

sugar cane *n* canne *f* à sucre.

sugar-coated ['ʃugə'kəutɪd] *a* dragéifié(e).

sugar lump *n* morceau *m* de sucre.

sugar refinery *n* raffinerie *f* de sucre.

sugary ['ʃugərɪ] *a* sucré(e).

suggest [sə'dʒest] *vt* suggérer, proposer; *(indicate)* laisser supposer, suggérer; **what do you** ~ **I do?** que vous me suggérez de faire?

suggestion [sə'dʒestʃən] *n* suggestion *f*.

suggestive [sə'dʒestɪv] *a* suggestif(ive).

suicidal [suɪ'saɪdl] *a* suicidaire.

suicide ['suɪsaɪd] *n* suicide *m*; **to commit** ~ se suicider.

suicide attempt, suicide bid *n* tentative *f* de suicide.

suit [suːt] *n (man's)* costume *m*, complet *m*; *(woman's)* tailleur *m*, ensemble *m*; *(CARDS)* couleur *f*; *(law~)* procès *m* ♦ *vt* aller à; convenir à; *(adapt)*: **to** ~ **sth to** adapter *or* approprier qch à; **to be** ~**ed to sth** *(suitable for)* être adapté(e) *or* approprié(e) à qch; **well** ~**ed** *(couple)* faits l'un pour l'autre, très bien assortis; **to bring a** ~ **against sb** intenter un procès contre qn; **to follow** ~ *(fig)* faire de même.

suitable ['suːtəbl] *a* qui convient; approprié(e), adéquat(e); **would tomorrow be** ~**?** est-ce que demain vous conviendrait?; **we found somebody** ~ nous avons trouvé la personne qui'il nous faut.

suitably ['suːtəblɪ] *ad* comme il se doit (*or* se devait *etc*), convenablement.

suitcase ['suːtkeɪs] *n* valise *f*.

suite [swiːt] *n (of rooms, also MUS)* suite *f*; *(furniture)*: **bedroom/dining room** ~ (ensemble *m* de) chambre *f* à coucher/salle *f* à manger; **a three-piece** ~ un salon (canapé et deux fauteuils).

suitor ['suːtə*] *n* soupirant *m*, prétendant *m*.

sulfate ['sʌlfeɪt] *n (US)* = **sulphate**.

sulfur *etc* ['sʌlfə*] *(US)* = **sulphur** *etc*.

sulk [sʌlk] *vi* bouder.

sulky ['sʌlkɪ] *a* boudeur(euse), maussade.

sullen ['sʌlən] *a* renfrogné(e), maussade; morne.

sulphate, *(US)* **sulfate** ['sʌlfeɪt] *n* sulfate *m*; **copper** ~ sulfate de cuivre.

sulphur, *(US)* **sulfur** ['sʌlfə*] *n* soufre *m*.

sulphuric, *(US)* **sulfuric** [sʌl'fjuərɪk] *a*: ~ **acid** acide *m* sulfurique.

sultan ['sʌltən] *n* sultan *m*.

sultana [sʌl'tɑːnə] *n (fruit)* raisin (sec) de Smyrne.

sultry ['sʌltrɪ] *a* étouffant(e).

sum [sʌm] *n* somme *f*; *(SCOL etc)* calcul *m*. **sum up** *vt* résumer; *(evaluate rapidly)* récapituler ♦ *vi* résumer.

Sumatra [su'mɑːtrə] *n* Sumatra.

summarize ['sʌmənaɪz] *vt* résumer.

summary ['sʌmərɪ] *n* résumé *m* ♦ *a (justice)* sommaire.

summer ['sʌmə*] *n* été *m* ♦ *cpd* d'été, estival(e); **in (the)** ~ en été, pendant l'été.

summer camp *n (US)* colonie *f* de vacances.

summerhouse ['sʌməhaus] *n (in garden)*

pavillon *m*.
summertime ['sʌmətaɪm] *n* (*season*) été *m*.
summer time *n* (*by clock*) heure *f* d'été.
summery ['sʌmərɪ] *a* estival(e); d'été.
summing-up [sʌmɪŋ'ʌp] *n* résumé *m*, récapitulation *f*.
summit ['sʌmɪt] *n* sommet *m*; (*also*: ~ **conference**) (conférence *f* au) sommet *m*.
summon ['sʌmən] *vt* appeler, convoquer; **to ~ a witness** citer *or* assigner un témoin.
summon up *vt* rassembler, faire appel à.
summons ['sʌmənz] *n* citation *f*, assignation *f* ♦ *vt* citer, assigner; **to serve a ~ on sb** remettre une assignation à qn.
sump [sʌmp] *n* (*Brit AUT*) carter *m*.
sumptuous ['sʌmptjuəs] *a* somptueux(euse).
Sun. *abbr* (= *Sunday*) dim.
sun [sʌn] *n* soleil *m*; **in the ~** au soleil; **to catch the ~** prendre le soleil; **everything under the ~** absolument tout.
sunbathe ['sʌnbeɪð] *vi* prendre un bain de soleil.
sunbeam ['sʌnbiːm] *n* rayon *m* de soleil.
sunbed ['sʌnbed] *n* lit pliant; (*with sun lamp*) lit à ultra-violets.
sunburn ['sʌnbəːn] *n* coup *m* de soleil.
sunburnt ['sʌnbəːnt], **sunburned** ['sʌnbəːnd] *a* bronzé(e), hâlé(e); (*painfully*) brûlé(e) par le soleil.
sun cream *n* crème *f* (anti-)solaire.
sundae ['sʌndeɪ] *n* sundae *m*, coupe glacée.
Sunday ['sʌndɪ] *n* dimanche *m*; *for phrases see also* **Tuesday**.
Sunday school *n* ≈ catéchisme *m*.
sundial ['sʌndaɪəl] *n* cadran *m* solaire.
sundown ['sʌndaun] *n* coucher *m* du soleil.
sundries ['sʌndrɪz] *npl* articles divers.
sundry ['sʌndrɪ] *a* divers(e), différent(e); **all and ~** tout le monde, n'importe qui.
sunflower ['sʌnflauə*] *n* tournesol *m*.
sung [sʌŋ] *pp of* **sing**.
sunglasses ['sʌnglɑːsɪz] *npl* lunettes *fpl* de soleil.
sunk [sʌŋk] *pp of* **sink**.
sunken ['sʌŋkn] *a* (*rock, ship*) submergé(e); (*eyes, cheeks*) creux(euse); (*bath*) encastré(e).
sunlamp ['sʌnlæmp] *n* lampe *f* à rayons ultra-violets.
sunlight ['sʌnlaɪt] *n* (lumière *f* du) soleil *m*.
sunlit ['sʌnlɪt] *a* ensoleillé(e).
sunny ['sʌnɪ] *a* ensoleillé(e); (*fig*) épanoui(e), radieux(euse); **it is ~** il fait (du) soleil, il y a du soleil.
sunrise ['sʌnraɪz] *n* lever *m* du soleil.
sun roof *n* (*AUT*) toit ouvrant.
sunset ['sʌnsɛt] *n* coucher *m* du soleil.
sunshade ['sʌnʃeɪd] *n* (*lady's*) ombrelle *f*; (*over table*) parasol *m*.
sunshine ['sʌnʃaɪn] *n* (lumière *f* du) soleil *m*.
sunspot ['sʌnspɔt] *n* tache *f* solaire.
sunstroke ['sʌnstrəuk] *n* insolation *f*, coup *m* de soleil.
suntan ['sʌntæn] *n* bronzage *m*.
suntanned ['sʌntænd] *a* bronzé(e).
suntan oil *n* huile *f* solaire.
suntrap ['sʌntræp] *n* coin très ensoleillé.
super ['suːpə*] *a* (*col*) formidable.
superannuation [suːpərænjuˈeɪʃən] *n*

cotisations *fpl* pour la pension.
superb [suːˈpəːb] *a* superbe, magnifique.
supercilious [suːpəˈsɪlɪəs] *a* hautain(e), dédaigneux(euse).
superficial [suːpəˈfɪʃəl] *a* superficiel(le).
superficially [suːpəˈfɪʃəlɪ] *ad* superficiellement.
superfluous [suˈpəːfluəs] *a* superflu(e).
superhuman [suːpəˈhjuːmən] *a* surhumain(e).
superimpose ['suːpərɪmˈpəuz] *vt* superposer.
superintend [suːpərɪnˈtɛnd] *vt* surveiller.
superintendent [suːpərɪnˈtɛndənt] *n* directeur/trice; (*POLICE*) ≈ commissaire *m*.
superior [suˈpɪərɪə*] *a* supérieur(e); (*COMM: goods, quality*) de qualité supérieure; (*smug*) condescendant(e), méprisant(e) ♦ *n* supérieur/e; **Mother S~** (*REL*) Mère supérieure.
superiority [supɪərɪˈɔrɪtɪ] *n* supériorité *f*.
superlative [suˈpəːlətɪv] *a* sans pareil(le), suprême ♦ *n* (*LING*) superlatif *m*.
superman ['suːpəmæn] *n* surhomme *m*.
supermarket ['suːpəmɑːkɪt] *n* supermarché *m*.
supernatural [suːpəˈnætʃərəl] *a* surnaturel(le).
superpower ['suːpəpauə*] *n* (*POL*) superpuissance *f*.
supersede [suːpəˈsiːd] *vt* remplacer, supplanter.
supersonic ['suːpəˈsɔnɪk] *a* supersonique.
superstition [suːpəˈstɪʃən] *n* superstition *f*.
superstitious [suːpəˈstɪʃəs] *a* superstitieux(euse).
superstore ['suːpəstɔː*] *n* (*Brit*) hypermarché *m*, grand surface.
supertanker ['suːpətæŋkə*] *n* pétrolier géant, superpétrolier *m*.
supertax ['suːpətæks] *n* tranche supérieure de l'impôt.
supervise ['suːpəvaɪz] *vt* (*children etc*) surveiller; (*organization, work*) diriger.
supervision [suːpəˈvɪʒən] *n* surveillance *f*; direction *f*; **under medical ~** sous contrôle du médecin.
supervisor ['suːpəvaɪzə*] *n* surveillant/e; (*in shop*) chef *m* de rayon; (*SCOL*) directeur/trice de thèse.
supervisory ['suːpəvaɪzərɪ] *a* de surveillance.
supine ['suːpaɪn] *a* couché(e) *or* étendu(e) sur le dos.
supper ['sʌpə*] *n* dîner *m*; (*late*) souper *m*; **to have ~** souper.
supplant [səˈplɑːnt] *vt* supplanter.
supple ['sʌpl] *a* souple.
supplement *n* ['sʌplɪmənt] supplément *m* ♦ *vt* [sʌplɪ'mɛnt] ajouter à, compléter.
supplementary [sʌplɪˈmɛntərɪ] *a* supplémentaire.
supplementary benefit *n* (*Brit*) allocation *f* supplémentaire d'aide sociale.
supplier [səˈplaɪə*] *n* fournisseur *m*.
supply [səˈplaɪ] *vt* (*goods*): **to ~ sth (to sb)** fournir qch (à qn); (*people, organization*): **to ~ sb (with sth)** approvisionner *or* ravitailler qn (en qch); fournir qn (en qch), fournir qch à qn; (*system, machine*): **to ~ sth (with sth)** alimenter qch (en qch); (*a need*) répondre à ♦ *n* provision *f*, réserve *f*; (*supplying*) approvisionnement *m*; (*TECH*) alimentation;

supplies *npl* (*food*) vivres *mpl*; (*MIL*) subsistances *fpl*; **office supplies** fournitures *fpl* de bureau; **to be in short ~** être rare, manquer; **the electricity/water/gas ~** l'alimentation en électricité/eau/gaz; **~ and demand** l'offre *f* et la demande; **it comes supplied with an adaptor** il (*or* elle) est pourvu(e) d'un adaptateur.

supply teacher *n* (*Brit*) suppléant/e.

support [sə'pɔːt] *n* (*moral, financial etc*) soutien *m*, appui *m*; (*TECH*) support *m*, soutien ♦ *vt* soutenir, supporter; (*financially*) subvenir aux besoins de; (*uphold*) être pour, être partisan de, appuyer; (*SPORT: team*) être pour; **to ~ o.s.** (*financially*) gagner sa vie.

supporter [sə'pɔːtə*] *n* (*POL etc*) partisan/e; (*SPORT*) supporter *m*.

supporting [sə'pɔːtɪŋ] *a* (*THEATRE etc: role*) secondaire; (: *actor*) qui a un rôle secondaire.

suppose [sə'pəuz] *vt, vi* supposer; imaginer; **to be ~d to do/be** être censé(e) faire/être; **I don't ~ she'll come** je suppose qu'elle ne viendra pas, cela m'étonnerait qu'elle vienne.

supposedly [sə'pəuzɪdlɪ] *ad* soi-disant.

supposing [sə'pəuzɪŋ] *cj* si, à supposer que + *sub*.

supposition [sʌpə'zɪʃən] *n* supposition *f*, hypothèse *f*.

suppository [sə'pɔzɪtrɪ] *n* suppositoire *m*.

suppress [sə'prɛs] *vt* (*revolt, feeling*) réprimer; (*publication*) supprimer; (*scandal*) étouffer.

suppression [sə'prɛʃən] *n* suppression *f*, répression *f*.

suppressor [sə'prɛsə*] *n* (*ELEC etc*) dispositif *m* antiparasite.

supremacy [su'prɛməsɪ] *n* suprématie *f*.

supreme [su'priːm] *a* suprême.

Supreme Court *n* (*US*) Cour *f* suprême.

Supt. *abbr* (*POLICE*) = **superintendent**.

surcharge ['sɔːtʃɑːdʒ] *n* surcharge *f*; (*extra tax*) surtaxe *f*.

sure [ʃuə*] *a* (*gen*) sûr(e); (*definite, convinced*) sûr, certain(e) ♦ *ad* (*col: esp US*): **that ~ is pretty, that's ~ pretty** c'est drôlement joli(e); **~!** (*of course*) bien sûr!; **~ enough** effectivement; **I'm not ~ how/ why/when** je ne sais pas très bien comment/ pourquoi/quand; **to be ~ of o.s.** être sûr de soi; **to make ~ of** s'assurer de; vérifier.

sure-footed [ʃuə'futɪd] *a* au pied sûr.

surely ['ʃuəlɪ] *ad* sûrement; certainement; **~ you don't mean that!** vous ne parlez pas sérieusement!

surety ['ʃuərətɪ] *n* caution *f*; **to go** *or* **stand ~ for sb** se porter caution pour qn.

surf [sɔːf] *n* ressac *m*.

surface ['sɔːfɪs] *n* surface *f* ♦ *vt* (*road*) poser le revêtement de ♦ *vi* remonter à la surface; faire surface; **on the ~** (*fig*) au premier abord.

surface area *n* superficie *f*, aire *f*.

surface mail *n* courrier *m* par voie de terre (*or* maritime).

surfboard ['sɔːfbɔːd] *n* planche *f* de surf.

surfeit ['sɔːfɪt] *n*: **a ~ of** un excès de; une indigestion de.

surfer ['sɔːfə*] *n* surfiste *m/f*.

surfing ['sɔːfɪŋ] *n* surf *m*.

surge [sɔːdʒ] *n* vague *f*, montée *f*; (*ELEC*) pointe *f* de courant ♦ *vi* déferler; **to ~ forward** se précipiter (en avant).

surgeon ['sɔːdʒən] *n* chirurgien *m*.

Surgeon General *n* (*US*) chef *m* du service fédéral de la santé publique.

surgery ['sɔːdʒərɪ] *n* chirurgie *f*; (*Brit: room*) cabinet *m* (de consultation); (: *session*) consultation *f*; (: *of MP etc*) permanence *f* (*où le député etc reçoit les électeurs etc*); **to undergo ~** être opéré(e).

surgery hours *npl* (*Brit*) heures *fpl* de consultation.

surgical ['sɔːdʒɪkl] *a* chirurgical(e).

surgical spirit *n* (*Brit*) alcool *m* à 90°.

surly ['sɔːlɪ] *a* revêche, maussade.

surmise [sɔː'maɪz] *vt* présumer, conjecturer.

surmount [sɔː'maunt] *vt* surmonter.

surname ['sɔːneɪm] *n* nom *m* de famille.

surpass [sɔː'pɑːs] *vt* surpasser, dépasser.

surplus ['sɔːpləs] *n* surplus *m*, excédent *m* ♦ *a* en surplus, de trop; **it is ~ to our requirements** cela dépasse nos besoins; **~ stock** surplus *m*.

surprise [sə'praɪz] *n* (*gen*) surprise *f*; (*astonishment*) étonnement *m* ♦ *vt* surprendre; étonner; **to take by ~** (*person*) prendre au dépourvu; (*MIL: town, fort*) prendre par surprise.

surprising [sə'praɪzɪŋ] *a* surprenant(e), étonnant(e).

surprisingly [sə'praɪzɪŋlɪ] *ad* (*easy, helpful*) étonnamment, étrangement; (**somewhat**) **~, he agreed** curieusement, il a accepté.

surrealism [sə'rɪəlɪzəm] *n* surréalisme *m*.

surrealist [sə'rɪəlɪst] *a, n* surréaliste (*m/f*).

surrender [sə'rɛndə*] *n* reddition *f*, capitulation *f* ♦ *vi* se rendre, capituler ♦ *vt* (*claim, right*) renoncer à.

surrender value *n* valeur *f* de rachat.

surreptitious [sʌrəp'tɪʃəs] *a* subreptice, furtif(ive).

surrogate ['sʌrəgɪt] *n* (*Brit: substitute*) substitut *m* ♦ *a* de substitution, de remplacement; **a food ~** un succédané alimentaire; **~ coffee** ersatz *m* or succédané *m* de café.

surrogate mother *n* mère porteuse *or* de substitution.

surround [sə'raund] *vt* entourer; (*MIL etc*) encercler.

surrounding [sə'raundɪŋ] *a* environnant(e).

surroundings [sə'raundɪŋz] *npl* environs *mpl*, alentours *mpl*.

surtax ['sɔːtæks] *n* surtaxe *f*.

surveillance [sɔː'veɪləns] *n* surveillance *f*.

survey *n* ['sɔːveɪ] enquête *f*, étude *f*; (*in house buying etc*) inspection *f*, (rapport *m* d')expertise *f*; (*of land*) levé *m*; (*comprehensive view: of situation etc*) vue *f* d'ensemble ♦ *vt* [sɔː'veɪ] passer en revue; enquêter sur; inspecter; (*building*) expertiser; (*land*) faire le levé de.

surveying [sɔː'veɪɪŋ] *n* arpentage *m*.

surveyor [sɔː'veɪə*] *n* (*of building*) expert *m*; (*of land*) (arpenteur *m*) géomètre *m*.

survival [sə'vaɪvl] *n* survie *f*; (*relic*) vestige *m*

♦ *cpd (course, kit)* de survie.
survive [sə'vaɪv] *vi* survivre; *(custom etc)* subsister ♦ *vt* survivre à, réchapper de; *(person)* survivre à.
survivor [sə'vaɪvə*] *n* survivant/e.
susceptible [sə'sɛptəbl] *a*: ~ **(to)** sensible (à); *(disease)* prédisposé(e) (à).
suspect *a, n* ['sʌspɛkt] suspect(e) ♦ *vt* [səs'pɛkt] soupçonner, suspecter.
suspend [səs'pɛnd] *vt* suspendre.
suspended sentence *n* condamnation *f* avec sursis.
suspender belt [səs'pɛndə*-] *n (Brit)* porte-jarretelles *m inv*.
suspenders [səs'pɛndəz] *npl (Brit)* jarretelles *fpl*; *(US)* bretelles *fpl*.
suspense [səs'pɛns] *n* attente *f*; *(in film etc)* suspense *m*.
suspense account *n* compte *m* d'attente.
suspension [səs'pɛnʃən] *n (gen, AUT)* suspension *f*; *(of driving licence)* retrait *m* provisoire.
suspension bridge *n* pont suspendu.
suspicion [səs'pɪʃən] *n* soupçon(s) *m(pl)*; **to be under** ~ être considéré(e) comme suspect(e), être suspecté(e); **arrested on** ~ **of murder** arrêté sur présomption de meurtre.
suspicious [səs'pɪʃəs] *a (suspecting)* soupçonneux(euse), méfiant(e); *(causing suspicion)* suspect(e); **to be** ~ **of** or **about sb/sth** avoir des doutes à propos de qn/sur qch, trouver qn/qch suspect(e).
suss out ['sʌs'aʊt] *vt (Brit col: discover)* supputer; (: *understand)* piger.
sustain [səs'teɪn] *vt* supporter; soutenir; corroborer; *(suffer)* subir; recevoir.
sustained [səs'teɪnd] *a (effort)* soutenu(e), prolongé(e).
sustenance ['sʌstɪnəns] *n* nourriture *f*; moyens *mpl* de subsistance.
suture ['su:tʃə*] *n* suture *f*.
SW *abbr* (= *short wave)* OC.
swab [swɔb] *n (MED)* tampon *m*; prélèvement *m* ♦ *vt (NAUT: also:* ~ **down)** nettoyer.
swagger ['swægə*] *vi* plastronner, parader.
swallow ['swɔləu] *n (bird)* hirondelle *f*; *(of food etc)* gorgée *f* ♦ *vt* avaler; *(fig)* gober.
swallow up *vt* engloutir.
swam [swæm] *pt of* **swim**.
swamp [swɔmp] *n* marais *m*, marécage *m* ♦ *vt* submerger.
swampy ['swɔmpɪ] *a* marécageux(euse).
swan [swɔn] *n* cygne *m*.
swank [swæŋk] *vi (col)* faire de l'épate.
swan song *n (fig)* chant *m* du cygne.
swap [swɔp] *n* échange *m*, troc *m* ♦ *vt*: **to** ~ **(for)** échanger (contre), troquer (contre).
swarm [swɔ:m] *n* essaim *m* ♦ *vi* essaimer; fourmiller, grouiller.
swarthy ['swɔ:ðɪ] *a* basané(e), bistré(e).
swashbuckling ['swɔʃbʌklɪŋ] *a (film)* de cape et d'épée.
swastika ['swɔstɪkə] *n* croix gammée.
swat [swɔt] *vt* écraser ♦ *n (Brit: also:* **fly** ~) tapette *f*.
swathe [sweɪð] *vt*: **to** ~ **in** *(bandages, blankets)* emmitoufler de.
swatter ['swɔtə*] *n (also:* **fly** ~) tapette *f*.

sway [sweɪ] *vi* se balancer, osciller; tanguer ♦ *vt (influence)* influencer ♦ *n (rule, power)*: ~ **(over)** emprise *f* (sur); **to hold** ~ **over sb** avoir de l'emprise sur qn.
Swaziland ['swɑ:zɪlænd] *n* Swaziland *m*.
swear, *pt* **swore,** *pp* **sworn** [swɛə*, swɔ:*, swɔ:n] *vi* jurer; **to** ~ **to sth** jurer de qch; **to** ~ **an oath** prêter serment.
swear in *vt* assermenter.
swearword ['swɛəwə:d] *n* gros mot, juron *m*.
sweat [swɛt] *n* sueur *f*, transpiration *f* ♦ *vi* suer; **in a** ~ en sueur.
sweatband ['swɛtbænd] *n (SPORT)* bandeau *m*.
sweater ['swɛtə*] *n* tricot *m*, pull *m*.
sweatshirt ['swɛtʃə:t] *n* sweat-shirt *m*.
sweatshop ['swɛtʃɔp] *n* atelier *m* où les ouvriers sont exploités.
sweaty ['swɛtɪ] *a* en sueur, moite *or* mouillé(e) de sueur.
Swede [swi:d] *n* Suédois/e.
swede [swi:d] *n (Brit)* rutabaga *m*.
Sweden ['swi:dn] *n* Suède *f*.
Swedish ['swi:dɪʃ] *a* suédois(e) ♦ *n (LING)* suédois *m*.
sweep [swi:p] *n* coup de balai; *(curve)* grande courbe; *(range)* champ *m*; *(also:* **chimney** ~) ramoneur *m* ♦ *vb (pt, pp* **swept** [swɛpt]) *vt* balayer; *(fashion, craze)* se répandre dans ♦ *vi* avancer majestueusement *or* rapidement; s'élancer; s'étendre.
sweep away *vt* balayer; entraîner; emporter.
sweep past *vi* passer majestueusement *or* rapidement.
sweep up *vt, vi* balayer.
sweeping ['swi:pɪŋ] *a (gesture)* large; circulaire; *(changes, reforms)* radical(e); **a** ~ **statement** une généralisation hâtive.
sweepstake ['swi:psteɪk] *n* sweepstake *m*.
sweet [swi:t] *n (Brit)* dessert *m*; *(candy)* bonbon *m* ♦ *a* doux(douce); *(not savoury)* sucré(e); *(fresh)* frais(fraîche), pur(e); *(kind)* gentil(le); *(cute)* mignon(ne) ♦ *ad*: **to smell** ~ sentir bon; **to taste** ~ avoir un goût sucré; ~ **and sour** *a* aigre-doux(douce).
sweetbread ['swi:tbrɛd] *n* ris *m* de veau.
sweetcorn ['swi:tkɔ:n] *n* maïs doux.
sweeten ['swi:tn] *vt* sucrer; *(fig)* adoucir.
sweetener ['swi:tnə*] *n (CULIN)* édulcorant *m*.
sweetheart ['swi:thɑ:t] *n* amoureux/euse.
sweetly ['swi:tlɪ] *ad (smile)* gentiment; *(sing, play)* mélodieusement.
sweetness ['swi:tnɪs] *n* douceur *f*; *(of taste)* goût sucré.
sweet pea *n* pois *m* de senteur.
sweet potato *n* patate douce.
sweetshop ['swi:tʃɔp] *n (Brit)* confiserie *f*.
sweet tooth *n*: **to have a** ~ aimer les sucreries.
swell [swɛl] *n (of sea)* houle *f* ♦ *a (col: excellent)* chouette ♦ *vb (pt* ~**ed,** *pp* **swollen** *or* ~**ed** ['swəulən]) *vt* augmenter; grossir ♦ *vi* grossir, augmenter; *(sound)* s'enfler; *(MED)* enfler.
swelling ['swɛlɪŋ] *n (MED)* enflure *f*; grosseur *f*.
sweltering ['swɛltərɪŋ] *a* étouffant(e), op-

pressant(e).

swept [swɛpt] *pt, pp of* **sweep**.

swerve [swɜ:v] *vi* faire une embardée *or* un écart; dévier.

swift [swɪft] *n* (*bird*) martinet *m* ♦ *a* rapide, prompt(e).

swiftly ['swɪftlɪ] *ad* rapidement, vite.

swiftness ['swɪftnɪs] *n* rapidité *f*.

swig [swɪg] *n* (*col: drink*) lampée *f*.

swill [swɪl] *n* pâtée *f* ♦ *vt* (*also:* ~ **out**, ~ **down**) laver à grande eau.

swim [swɪm] *n:* **to go for a** ~ aller nager *or* se baigner ♦ *vb* (*pt* **swam**, *pp* **swum** [swæm, swʌm]) *vi* nager; (*SPORT*) faire de la natation; (*fig: head, room*) tourner ♦ *vt* traverser (à la nage); (*distance*) faire (à la nage); **to** ~ **a length** nager une longueur; **to go** ~**ming** aller nager.

swimmer ['swɪmə*] *n* nageur/euse.

swimming ['swɪmɪŋ] *n* nage *f*, natation *f*.

swimming baths *npl* (*Brit*) piscine *f*.

swimming cap *n* bonnet *m* de bain.

swimming costume *n* (*Brit*) maillot *m* (de bain).

swimming pool *n* piscine *f*.

swimming trunks *npl* maillot *m* de bain.

swimsuit ['swɪmsu:t] *n* maillot *m* (de bain).

swindle ['swɪndl] *n* escroquerie *f* ♦ *vt* escroquer.

swindler ['swɪndlə*] *n* escroc *m*.

swine [swaɪn] *n* (*pl inv*) pourceau *m*, porc *m*; (*col!*) salaud *m* (*!*).

swing [swɪŋ] *n* balançoire *f*; (*movement*) balancement *m*, oscillations *fpl*; (*MUS*) swing *m*; rythme *m* ♦ *vb* (*pt, pp* **swung** [swʌŋ]) *vt* balancer, faire osciller; (*also:* ~ **round**) tourner, faire virer ♦ *vi* se balancer, osciller; (*also:* ~ **round**) virer, tourner; **a** ~ **to the left** (*POL*) un revirement en faveur de la gauche; **to be in full** ~ battre son plein; **to get into the** ~ **of things** se mettre dans le bain; **the road** ~**s south** la route prend la direction sud.

swing bridge *n* pont tournant.

swing door *n* (*Brit*) porte battante.

swingeing ['swɪndʒɪŋ] *a* (*Brit*) écrasant(e); considérable.

swinging ['swɪŋɪŋ] *a* rythmé(e); entraînant(e); (*fig*) dans le vent; ~ **door** (*US*) porte battante.

swipe [swaɪp] *n* grand coup; gifle *f* ♦ *vt* (*hit*) frapper à toute volée; gifler; (*col: steal*) piquer.

swirl [swɜ:l] *n* tourbillon *m* ♦ *vi* tourbillonner, tournoyer.

swish [swɪʃ] *a* (*Brit col: smart*) rupin(e) ♦ *vi* (*whip*) siffler; (*skirt, long grass*) bruire.

Swiss [swɪs] *a* suisse ♦ *n* (*pl inv*) Suisse/esse.

Swiss French *a* suisse romand(e).

Swiss German *a* suisse-allemand(e).

Swiss roll *n* gâteau roulé.

switch [swɪtʃ] *n* (*for light, radio etc*) bouton *m*; (*change*) changement *m*, revirement *m* ♦ *vt* (*change*) changer; (*exchange*) intervertir; (*invert*): **to** ~ (**round** *or* **over**) changer de place.

switch off *vt* éteindre; (*engine*) arrêter.

switch on *vt* allumer; (*engine, machine*) mettre en marche; (*Brit: water supply*) ouvrir.

switchback ['swɪtʃbæk] *n* (*Brit*) montagnes *fpl* russes.

switchblade ['swɪtʃbleɪd] *n* (*also:* ~ **knife**) couteau *m* à cran d'arrêt.

switchboard ['swɪtʃbɔ:d] *n* (*TEL*) standard *m*.

switchboard operator *n* (*TEL*) standardiste *m/f*.

Switzerland ['swɪtsələnd] *n* Suisse *f*.

swivel ['swɪvl] *vi* (*also:* ~ **round**) pivoter, tourner.

swollen ['swəulən] *pp of* **swell** ♦ *a* (*ankle etc*) enflé(e).

swoon [swu:n] *vi* se pâmer.

swoop [swu:p] *n* (*by police etc*) rafle *f*, descente *f*; (*of bird etc*) descente *f* en piqué ♦ *vi* (*also:* ~ **down**) descendre en piqué, piquer.

swop [swɔp] *n, vt* = **swap**.

sword [sɔ:d] *n* épée *f*.

swordfish ['sɔ:dfɪʃ] *n* espadon *m*.

swore [swɔ:*] *pt of* **swear**.

sworn [swɔ:n] *pp of* **swear**.

swot [swɔt] *vt, vi* bûcher, potasser.

swum [swʌm] *pp of* **swim**.

swung [swʌŋ] *pt, pp of* **swing**.

sycamore ['sɪkəmɔ:*] *n* sycomore *m*.

sycophant ['sɪkəfænt] *n* flagorneur/euse.

sycophantic [sɪkə'fæntɪk] *a* flagorneur(euse).

Sydney ['sɪdnɪ] *n* Sydney.

syllable ['sɪləbl] *n* syllabe *f*.

syllabus ['sɪləbəs] *n* programme *m*; **on the** ~ au programme.

symbol ['sɪmbl] *n* symbole *m*.

symbolic(al) [sɪm'bɔlɪk(l)] *a* symbolique.

symbolism ['sɪmbəlɪzəm] *n* symbolisme *m*.

symbolize ['sɪmbəlaɪz] *vt* symboliser.

symmetrical [sɪ'metrɪkl] *a* symétrique.

symmetry ['sɪmɪtrɪ] *n* symétrie *f*.

sympathetic [sɪmpə'θetɪk] *a* (*showing pity*) compatissant(e); (*understanding*) bienveillant(e), compréhensif(ive); ~ **towards** bien disposé(e) envers.

sympathetically [sɪmpə'θetɪklɪ] *ad* avec compassion (*or* bienveillance).

sympathize ['sɪmpəθaɪz] *vi:* **to** ~ **with sb** (*in grief*) être de tout cœur avec qn, compatir à la douleur de qn; (*in predicament*) partager les sentiments de qn; **to** ~ **with** (*sb's feelings*) comprendre.

sympathizer ['sɪmpəθaɪzə*] *n* (*POL*) sympathisant/e.

sympathy ['sɪmpəθɪ] *n* compassion *f*; **in** ~ **with** en accord avec; (*strike*) en *or* par solidarité avec; **with our deepest** ~ en vous priant d'accepter nos sincères condoléances.

symphonic [sɪm'fɔnɪk] *a* symphonique.

symphony ['sɪmfənɪ] *n* symphonie *f*.

symphony orchestra *n* orchestre *m* symphonique.

symposium [sɪm'pəuzɪəm] *n* symposium *m*.

symptom ['sɪmptəm] *n* symptôme *m*; indice *m*.

symptomatic [sɪmptə'mætɪk] *a* symptomatique.

synagogue ['sɪnəgɔg] *n* synagogue *f*.

synchromesh [sɪŋkrəu'meʃ] *n* (*AUT*) synchronisation *f*.

synchronize ['sɪŋkrənaɪz] *vt* synchroniser ♦ *vi:* **to** ~ **with** se produire en même temps que.

syncopated ['sɪŋkəpeɪtɪd] a syncopé(e).

syndicate ['sɪndɪkɪt] n syndicat m, coopérative f; (PRESS) agence f de presse.

syndrome ['sɪndrəʊm] n syndrome m.

synonym ['sɪnənɪm] n synonyme m.

synonymous [sɪ'nɒnɪməs] a: ~ (with) synonyme (de).

synopsis, pl **synopses** [sɪ'nɒpsɪs, -siːz] n résumé m, synopsis m or f.

syntax ['sɪntæks] n syntaxe f.

synthesis, pl **syntheses** ['sɪnθəsɪs, -siːz] n synthèse f.

synthesizer ['sɪnθəsaɪzə*] n (MUS) synthétiseur m.

synthetic [sɪn'θetɪk] a synthétique ♦ n matière f synthétique; ~s npl textiles artificiels.

syphilis ['sɪfɪlɪs] n syphilis f.

syphon ['saɪfən] n, vb = **siphon**.

Syria ['sɪrɪə] n Syrie f.

Syrian ['sɪrɪən] a syrien(ne) ♦ n Syrien/ne.

syringe [sɪ'rɪndʒ] n seringue f.

syrup ['sɪrəp] n sirop m; (Brit: also: **golden** ~) mélasse raffinée.

syrupy ['sɪrəpɪ] a sirupeux(euse).

system ['sɪstəm] n système m; (order) méthode f; (ANAT) organisme m.

systematic [sɪstə'mætɪk] a systématique; méthodique.

system disk n (COMPUT) disque m système.

systems analyst n analyste-programmeur m/f.

T

T, t [tiː] n (letter) T, t m; **T for Tommy** T comme Thérèse.

TA n abbr (Brit) = Territorial Army.

ta [tɑː] excl (Brit col) merci!

tab [tæb] n abbr = **tabulator** ♦ n (loop on coat etc) attache f; (label) étiquette f; **to keep ~s on** (fig) surveiller.

tabby ['tæbɪ] n (also: ~ **cat**) chat/te tigré(e).

tabernacle ['tæbənækl] n tabernacle m.

table ['teɪbl] n table f ♦ vt (Brit: motion etc) présenter; **to lay** or **set the ~** mettre le couvert or la table; **to clear the ~** débarrasser la table; **league ~** (Brit FOOTBALL, RUGBY) classement m (du championnat); **~ of contents** table des matières.

tablecloth ['teɪblklɒθ] n nappe f.

table d'hôte [tɑːbl'dəʊt] a (meal) à prix fixe.

table lamp n lampe décorative.

tableland ['teɪbllænd] n plateau m.

tablemat ['teɪblmæt] n (for plate) napperon m, set m; (for hot dish) dessous-de-plat m inv.

table salt n sel fin or de table.

tablespoon ['teɪblspuːn] n cuiller f de service; (also: ~**ful**: as measurement) cuillerée f à soupe.

tablet ['tæblɪt] n (MED) comprimé m; (: for

sucking) pastille f; (for writing) bloc m; (of stone) plaque f; ~ **of soap** (Brit) savonnette f.

table tennis n ping-pong m, tennis m de table.

table wine n vin m de table.

tabloid ['tæblɔɪd] n (newspaper) tabloïde m; **the ~s** les journaux mpl populaires.

taboo [tə'buː] a, n tabou (m).

tabulate ['tæbjuleɪt] vt (data, figures) mettre sous forme de table(s).

tabulator ['tæbjuleɪtə*] n tabulateur m.

tachograph ['tækəgrɑːf] n tachygraphe m.

tachometer [tæ'kɒmɪtə*] n tachymètre m.

tacit ['tæsɪt] a tacite.

taciturn ['tæsɪtəːn] a taciturne.

tack [tæk] n (nail) petit clou; (stitch) point m de bâti; (NAUT) bord m, bordée f ♦ vt clouer; bâtir ♦ vi tirer un or des bord(s); **to change ~** virer de bord; **on the wrong ~** (fig) sur la mauvaise voie; **to ~ sth on to (the end of)** sth (of letter, book) rajouter qch à la fin de qch.

tackle ['tækl] n matériel m, équipement m; (for lifting) appareil m de levage; (FOOTBALL, RUGBY) plaquage m ♦ vt (difficulty) s'attaquer à; (FOOTBALL, RUGBY) plaquer.

tacky ['tækɪ] a collant(e); pas sec(sèche); (col: shabby) moche.

tact [tækt] n tact m.

tactful ['tæktful] a plein(e) de tact.

tactfully ['tæktfəlɪ] ad avec tact.

tactical ['tæktɪkl] a tactique; ~ **error** erreur f de tactique.

tactics ['tæktɪks] n, npl tactique f.

tactless ['tæktlɪs] a qui manque de tact.

tactlessly ['tæktlɪslɪ] ad sans tact.

tadpole ['tædpəʊl] n têtard m.

taffy ['tæfɪ] n (US) (bonbon m au) caramel m.

tag [tæg] n étiquette f; **price/name ~** étiquette (portant le prix/le nom).

tag along vi suivre.

Tahiti [tɑː'hiːtɪ] n Tahiti m.

tail [teɪl] n queue f; (of shirt) pan m ♦ vt (follow) suivre, filer; **to turn ~** se sauver à toutes jambes; see also **head**.

tail away, **tail off** vi (in size, quality etc) baisser peu à peu.

tailback ['teɪlbæk] n (Brit) bouchon m.

tail coat n habit m.

tail end n bout m, fin f.

tailgate ['teɪlgeɪt] n (AUT) hayon m arrière.

tail light n (AUT) feu m arrière.

tailor ['teɪlə*] n tailleur m (artisan) ♦ vt: **to ~ sth (to)** adapter qch exactement (à); ~**'s (shop)** (boutique f de) tailleur m.

tailoring ['teɪlərɪŋ] n (cut) coupe f.

tailor-made ['teɪlə'meɪd] a fait(e) sur mesure; (fig) conçu(e) spécialement.

tailwind ['teɪlwɪnd] n vent m arrière inv.

taint [teɪnt] vt (meat, food) gâter; (fig: reputation) salir.

tainted ['teɪntɪd] a (food) gâté(e); (water, air) infecté(e); (fig) souillé(e).

Taiwan ['taɪ'wɑːn] n Taiwan (no article).

take [teɪk] vb (pt **took**, pp **taken** [tʊk, 'teɪkn]) vt prendre; (gain: prize) remporter; (require: effort, courage) demander; (tolerate) accepter, supporter; (*hold: passengers etc*) contenir; (*accompany*) emmener, accompagner; (*bring, carry*) apporter, emporter; (*exam*) passer, se présenter à; (*conduct: meeting*) présider ♦ *vi* (*dye, fire etc*) prendre ♦ *n* (*CINEMA*) prise *f* de vues; **to ~ sth from** (*drawer etc*) prendre qch dans; (*person*) prendre qch à; **I ~ it that** je suppose que; **I took him for a doctor** je l'ai pris pour un docteur; **to ~ sb's hand** prendre qn par la main; **to ~ for a walk** (*child, dog*) emmener promener; **to be taken ill** tomber malade; **to ~ it upon o.s. to do sth** prendre sur soi de faire qch; **~ the first (street) on the left** prenez la première à gauche; **it won't ~ long** ça ne prendra pas longtemps; **I was quite taken with her/it** elle/cela m'a beaucoup plu.

take after *vt fus* ressembler à.

take apart *vt* démonter.

take away *vt* emporter; (*remove*) enlever; (*subtract*) soustraire ♦ *vi*: **to ~ away from** diminuer.

take back *vt* (*return*) rendre, rapporter; (*one's words*) retirer.

take down *vt* (*building*) démolir; (*dismantle: scaffolding*) démonter; (*letter etc*) prendre, écrire.

take in *vt* (*deceive*) tromper, rouler; (*understand*) comprendre, saisir; (*include*) couvrir, inclure; (*lodger*) prendre; (*orphan, stray dog*) recueillir; (*dress, waistband*) reprendre.

take off *vi* (*AVIAT*) décoller ♦ *vt* (*remove*) enlever; (*imitate*) imiter, pasticher.

take on *vt* (*work*) accepter, se charger de; (*employee*) prendre, embaucher; (*opponent*) accepter de se battre contre.

take out *vt* sortir; (*remove*) enlever; (*licence*) prendre, se procurer; **to ~ sth out of** enlever qch de; prendre qch dans; **don't ~ it out on me!** ne t'en prends pas à moi!

take over *vt* (*business*) reprendre ♦ *vi*: **to ~ over from sb** prendre la relève de qn.

take to *vt fus* (*person*) se prendre d'amitié pour; (*activity*) prendre goût à; **to ~ to doing sth** prendre l'habitude de faire qch.

take up *vt* (*one's story, a dress*) reprendre; (*occupy: time, space*) prendre, occuper; (*engage in: hobby etc*) se mettre à; (*accept: offer, challenge*) accepter; (*absorb: liquids*) absorber ♦ *vi*: **to ~ up with sb** se lier d'amitié avec qn.

takeaway ['teɪkəweɪ] *a* (*Brit: food*) à emporter.

take-home pay ['teɪkhəum-] *n* salaire net.

taken ['teɪkən] *pp of* **take**.

takeoff ['teɪkɔf] *n* (*AVIAT*) décollage *m*.

takeout ['teɪkaut] *a* (*US*) = **takeaway**.

takeover ['teɪkəuvə*] *n* (*COMM*) rachat *m*.

takeover bid *n* offre publique d'achat, OPA *f*.

takings ['teɪkɪŋz] *npl* (*COMM*) recette *f*.

talc [tælk] *n* (*also*: **~um powder**) talc *m*.

tale [teɪl] *n* (*story*) conte *m*, histoire *f*; (*account*) récit *m*; (*pej*) histoire; **to tell ~s** (*fig*) rapporter.

talent ['tælnt] *n* talent *m*, don *m*.

talented ['tæləntɪd] *a* doué(e), plein(e) de talent.

talent scout *n* découvreur *m* de vedettes (*or* joueurs *etc*).

talk [tɔ:k] *n* propos *mpl*; (*gossip*) racontars *mpl* (*pej*); (*conversation*) discussion *f*; (*interview*) entretien *m*; (*a speech*) causerie *f*, exposé *m* ♦ *vi* (*chatter*) bavarder; **~s** *npl* (*POL etc*) entretiens *mpl*; conférence *f*; **to give a ~** faire un exposé; **to ~ about** parler de; (*converse*) s'entretenir *or* parler de; **~ing of films, have you seen ...?** à propos de films, avez-vous vu ...?; **to ~ sb out of/into doing** persuader qn de ne pas faire/de faire; **to ~ shop** parler métier *or* affaires.

talk over *vt* discuter (de).

talkative ['tɔ:kətɪv] *a* bavard(e).

talker ['tɔ:kə*] *n* causeur/euse; (*pej*) bavard/e.

talking point ['tɔ:kɪŋ-] *n* sujet *m* de conversation.

talking-to ['tɔ:kɪŋtu] *n*: **to give sb a good ~** passer un savon à qn.

talk show *n* (*TV, RADIO*) causerie (télévisée *or* radiodiffusée).

tall [tɔ:l] *a* (*person*) grand(e); (*building, tree*) haut(e); **to be 6 feet ~** ≈ mesurer 1 mètre 80; **how ~ are you?** combien mesurez-vous?

tallboy ['tɔ:lbɔɪ] *n* (*Brit*) grande commode.

tallness ['tɔ:lnɪs] *n* grande taille; hauteur *f*.

tall story *n* histoire *f* invraisemblable.

tally ['tælɪ] *n* compte *m* ♦ *vi*: **to ~ (with)** correspondre (à); **to keep a ~ of sth** tenir le compte de qch.

talon ['tælən] *n* griffe *f*; (*of eagle*) serre *f*.

tambourine [tæmbə'ri:n] *n* tambourin *m*.

tame [teɪm] *a* apprivoisé(e); (*fig: story, style*) insipide.

tamper ['tæmpə*] *vi*: **to ~ with** toucher à (*en cachette ou sans permission*).

tampon ['tæmpən] *n* tampon *m* hygiénique *or* périodique.

tan [tæn] *n* (*also*: **sun~**) bronzage *m* ♦ *vt, vi* bronzer, brunir ♦ *a* (*colour*) brun roux *inv*; **to get a ~** bronzer.

tandem ['tændəm] *n* tandem *m*.

tang [tæŋ] *n* odeur (*or* saveur) piquante.

tangent ['tændʒənt] *n* (*MATH*) tangente *f*; **to go off at a ~** (*fig*) changer complètement de direction.

tangerine [tændʒə'ri:n] *n* mandarine *f*.

tangible ['tændʒəbl] *a* tangible; **~ assets** biens réels.

Tangier [tæn'dʒɪə*] *n* Tanger *m*.

tangle ['tæŋgl] *n* enchevêtrement *m* ♦ *vt* enchevêtrer; **to get in(to) a ~** s'emmêler.

tango ['tæŋgəu] *n* tango *m*.

tank [tæŋk] *n* réservoir *m*; (*for processing*) cuve *f*; (*for fish*) aquarium *m*; (*MIL*) char *m* d'assaut, tank *m*.

tankard ['tæŋkəd] *n* chope *f*.

tanker ['tæŋkə*] *n* (*ship*) pétrolier *m*, tanker *m*; (*truck*) camion-citerne *m*; (*RAIL*) wagon-citerne *m*.

tanned [tænd] *a* bronzé(e).

tannin ['tænɪn] *n* tanin *m*.

tanning ['tænɪŋ] *n* (*of leather*) tannage *m*.

tannoy ['tænɔɪ] *n* ® (*Brit*) haut-parleur *m*; **over the ~** par haut-parleur.

tantalizing ['tæntəlaɪzɪŋ] *a* (*smell*) extrêmement appétissant(e); (*offer*) terriblement tentant(e).

tantamount ['tæntəmaunt] *a:* ~ **to** qui équivaut à.

tantrum ['tæntrəm] *n* accès *m* de colère; **to throw a** ~ piquer une colère.

Tanzania [tænzə'nɪə] *n* Tanzanie *f*.

Tanzanian [tænzə'nɪən] *a* tanzanien(ne) ♦ *n* Tanzanien/ne.

tap [tæp] *n* (*on sink etc*) robinet *m*; (*gentle blow*) petite tape ♦ *vt* frapper *or* taper légèrement; (*resources*) exploiter, utiliser; (*telephone*) mettre sur écoute; **on** ~ (*beer*) en tonneau; (*fig: resources*) disponible.

tap-dancing ['tæpdɑːnsɪŋ] *n* claquettes *fpl*.

tape [teɪp] *n* ruban *m*; (*also:* **magnetic** ~) bande *f* (magnétique) ♦ *vt* (*record*) enregistrer (au magnétophone *or* sur bande); **on** ~ (*song etc*) enregistré(e).

tape deck *n* platine *f* d'enregistrement.

tape measure *n* mètre *m* à ruban.

taper ['teɪpə*] *n* cierge *m* ♦ *vi* s'effiler.

tape-record ['teɪprɪkɔːd] *vt* enregistrer (au magnétophone *or* sur bande).

tape recorder *n* magnétophone *m*.

tape recording *n* enregistrement *m* (au magnétophone).

tapered ['teɪpəd], **tapering** ['teɪpərɪŋ] *a* fuselé(e), effilé(e).

tapestry ['tæpɪstrɪ] *n* tapisserie *f*.

tape-worm ['teɪpwəːm] *n* ver *m* solitaire, ténia *m*.

tapioca [tæpɪ'əukə] *n* tapioca *m*.

tappet ['tæpɪt] *n* (*AUT*) poussoir *m* (de soupape).

tar [tɑː] *n* goudron *m*; **low-/middle-**~ **cigarettes** cigarettes *fpl* à faible/moyenne teneur en goudron.

tarantula [tə'ræntjulə] *n* tarentule *f*.

tardy ['tɑːdɪ] *a* tardif(ive).

target ['tɑːgɪt] *n* cible *f*; (*fig: objective*) objectif *m*; **to be on** ~ (*project*) progresser comme prévu.

target practice *n* exercices *mpl* de tir (à la cible).

tariff ['tærɪf] *n* (*COMM*) tarif *m*; (*taxes*) tarif douanier.

tariff barrier *n* barrière douanière.

tarmac ['tɑːmæk] *n* (*Brit: on road*) macadam *m*; (*AVIAT*) aire *f* d'envol ♦ *vt* (*Brit*) goudronner.

tarnish ['tɑːnɪʃ] *vt* ternir.

tarpaulin [tɑː'pɔːlɪn] *n* bâche goudronnée.

tarragon ['tærəgən] *n* estragon *m*.

tart [tɑːt] *n* (*CULIN*) tarte *f*; (*Brit col: pej: woman*) poule *f* ♦ *a* (*flavour*) âpre, aigrelet(te).

tart up *vt* (*col*): **to** ~ **o.s. up** se faire beau(belle); (*: pej*) s'attifer.

tartan ['tɑːtn] *n* tartan *m* ♦ *a* écossais(e).

tartar ['tɑːtə*] *n* (*on teeth*) tartre *m*.

tartar sauce *n* sauce *f* tartare.

task [tɑːsk] *n* tâche *f*; **to take to** ~ prendre à partie.

task force *n* (*MIL, POLICE*) détachement spécial.

taskmaster ['tɑːskmɑːstə*] *n:* **he's a hard** ~ il est très exigeant dans le travail.

Tasmania [tæz'meɪnɪə] *n* Tasmanie *f*.

tassel ['tæsl] *n* gland *m*; pompon *m*.

taste [teɪst] *n* goût *m*; (*fig: glimpse, idea*) idée

f, aperçu *m* ♦ *vt* goûter ♦ *vi*: **to** ~ **of** (*fish etc*) avoir le *or* un goût de; **it** ~**s like fish** ça a un *or* le goût de poisson, on dirait du poisson; **what does it** ~ **like?** quel goût ça a?; **you can** ~ **the garlic (in it)** on sent bien l'ail; **can I have a** ~ **of this wine?** puis-je goûter un peu de ce vin?; **to have a** ~ **of sth** goûter (à) qch; **to have a** ~ **for sth** aimer qch, avoir un penchant pour qch; **to be in good/bad** *or* **poor** ~ être de bon/mauvais goût.

taste bud *n* papille *f*.

tasteful ['teɪstful] *a* de bon goût.

tastefully ['teɪstfəlɪ] *ad* avec goût.

tasteless ['teɪstlɪs] *a* (*food*) qui n'a aucun goût; (*remark*) de mauvais goût.

tasty ['teɪstɪ] *a* savoureux(euse), délicieux(euse).

tattered ['tætəd] *a see* **tatters**.

tatters ['tætəz] *npl:* **in** ~ (*also:* **tattered**) en lambeaux.

tattoo [tə'tuː] *n* tatouage *m*; (*spectacle*) parade *f* militaire ♦ *vt* tatouer.

tatty ['tætɪ] *a* (*Brit col*) défraîchi(e), en piteux état.

taught [tɔːt] *pt, pp of* **teach**.

taunt [tɔːnt] *n* raillerie *f* ♦ *vt* railler.

Taurus ['tɔːrəs] *n* le Taureau; **to be** ~ être du Taureau.

taut [tɔːt] *a* tendu(e).

tavern ['tævən] *n* taverne *f*.

tawdry ['tɔːdrɪ] *a* (d'un mauvais goût) criard.

tawny ['tɔːnɪ] *a* fauve (*couleur*).

tax [tæks] *n* (*on goods etc*) taxe *f*; (*on income*) impôts *mpl*, contributions *fpl* ♦ *vt* taxer; imposer; (*fig: strain: patience etc*) mettre à l'épreuve; **before/after** ~ avant/après l'impôt; **free of** ~ exonéré(e) d'impôt.

taxable ['tæksəbl] *a* (*income*) imposable.

tax allowance *n* part *f* du revenu non imposable, abattement *m* à la base.

taxation [tæk'seɪʃən] *n* taxation *f*; impôts *mpl*, contributions *fpl*; **system of** ~ système fiscal.

tax avoidance *n* évasion fiscale.

tax collector *n* percepteur *m*.

tax disc *n* (*Brit AUT*) vignette *f* (automobile).

tax evasion *n* fraude fiscale.

tax exemption *n* exonération fiscale, exemption *f* d'impôts.

tax exile *n* personne qui s'expatrie pour fuir une fiscalité excessive.

tax-free ['tæksfriː] *a* exempt(e) d'impôts.

tax haven *n* paradis fiscal.

taxi ['tæksɪ] *n* taxi *m* ♦ *vi* (*AVIAT*) rouler (lentement) au sol.

taxidermist ['tæksɪdəːmɪst] *n* empailleur/euse (*d'animaux*).

taxi driver *n* chauffeur *m* de taxi.

taximeter ['tæksɪmiːtə*] *n* taximètre *m*.

tax inspector *n* (*Brit*) percepteur *m*.

taxi rank (*Brit*), **taxi stand** *n* station *f* de taxis.

tax payer *n* contribuable *m/f*.

tax rebate *n* ristourne *f* d'impôt.

tax relief *n* dégrèvement *or* allègement fiscal, réduction *f* d'impôt.

tax return *n* déclaration *f* d'impôts *or* de revenus.

tax year n année fiscale.

TB n abbr = **tuberculosis**.

TD n abbr (US) = **Treasury Department**; (. FOOTBALL) = **touchdown**.

tea [ti:] n thé m; (Brit: snack: for children) goûter m; **high** ~ (Brit) collation combinant goûter et dîner.

tea bag n sachet m de thé.

tea break n (Brit) pause-thé f.

teacake ['ti:keɪk] n (Brit) ≈ petit pain aux raisins.

teach, pt, pp **taught** [ti:tʃ, tɔ:t] vt: **to** ~ **sb sth**, ~ **sth to sb** apprendre qch à qn; (in school etc) enseigner qch à qn ♦ vi enseigner; **it taught him a lesson** (fig) ça lui a servi de leçon.

teacher ['ti:tʃə*] n (in secondary school) professeur m; (in primary school) instituteur/trice; **French** ~ professeur de français.

teacher training college n (for primary schools) ≈ école normale d'instituteurs; (for secondary schools) collège m de formation pédagogique (pour l'enseignement secondaire).

teaching ['ti:tʃɪŋ] n enseignement m.

teaching aids npl supports mpl pédagogiques.

teaching hospital n (Brit) C.H.U. m, centre m hospitalo-universitaire.

teaching staff n (Brit) enseignants mpl.

tea cosy n couvre-théière m.

teacup ['ti:kʌˌ¹] n tasse f à thé.

teak [ti:k] n teck m ♦ a en or de teck.

tea leaves npl feuilles fpl de thé.

team [ti:m] n équipe f; (of animals) attelage m.

team up vi: **to** ~ **up (with)** faire équipe (avec).

team games npl jeux mpl d'équipe.

teamwork ['ti:mwə:k] n travail m d'équipe.

tea party n thé m (réception).

teapot ['ti:pɔt] n théière f.

tear n [tɛə*] déchirure f; [tɪə*] larme f ♦ vb [tɛə*] (pt **tore**, pp **torn** [tɔ:*, tɔ:n]) vt déchirer ♦ vi se déchirer; **in** ~**s** en larmes; **to burst into** ~**s** fondre en larmes; **to** ~ **to pieces** or **to bits** or **to shreds** mettre en pièces; (fig) démolir.

tear along vi (rush) aller à toute vitesse.

tear apart vt (also fig) déchirer.

tear away vt: **to** ~ **o.s. away (from sth)** (fig) s'arracher (de qch).

tear out vt (sheet of paper, cheque) arracher.

tear up vt (sheet of paper etc) déchirer, mettre en morceaux or pièces.

tearaway ['tɛərəweɪ] n (col) casse-cou m inv.

teardrop ['tɪədrɔp] n larme f.

tearful ['tɪəful] a larmoyant(e).

tear gas n gaz m lacrymogène.

tearoom ['ti:ru:m] n salon m de thé.

tease [ti:z] n taquin/e ♦ vt taquiner; (unkindly) tourmenter.

tea set n service m à thé.

teashop ['ti:ʃɔp] n (Brit) pâtisserie-salon de thé f.

teaspoon ['ti:spu:n] n petite cuiller; (also: ~**ful**: as measurement) ≈ cuillerée f à café.

tea strainer n passoire f (à thé).

teat [ti:t] n tétine f.

teatime ['ti:taɪm] n l'heure f du thé.

tea towel n (Brit) torchon m (à vaisselle).

tea urn n fontaine f à thé.

tech [tɛk] n abbr (col) = **technology**, **technical college**.

technical ['tɛknɪkl] a technique.

technical college n C.E.T. m, collège m d'enseignement technique.

technicality [tɛknɪ'kælɪtɪ] n technicité f; (detail) détail m technique; **on a legal** ~ à cause de (or grâce à) l'application à la lettre d'une subtilité juridique; pour vice de forme.

technically ['tɛknɪklɪ] ad techniquement.

technician [tɛk'nɪʃən] n technicien/ne.

technique [tɛk'ni:k] n technique f.

technocrat ['tɛknəkræt] n technocrate m/f.

technological [tɛknə'lɔdʒɪkl] a technologique.

technologist [tɛk'nɔlədʒɪst] n technologue m/f.

technology [tɛk'nɔlədʒɪ] n technologie f.

teddy (bear) ['tɛdɪ-] n ours m (en peluche).

tedious ['ti:dɪəs] a fastidieux(euse).

tedium ['ti:dɪəm] n ennui m.

tee [ti:] n (GOLF) tee m.

teem [ti:m] vi: **to** ~ **(with)** grouiller (de); **it is** ~**ing (with rain)** il pleut à torrents.

teenage ['ti:neɪdʒ] a (fashions etc) pour jeunes, pour adolescents.

teenager ['ti:neɪdʒə*] n jeune m/f, adolescent/e.

teens [ti:nz] npl: **to be in one's** ~ être adolescent(e).

tee-shirt ['ti:ʃə:t] n = **T-shirt**.

teeter ['ti:tə*] vi chanceler, vaciller.

teeth [ti:θ] npl of **tooth**.

teethe [ti:ð] vi percer ses dents.

teething ring ['ti:ðɪŋ-] n anneau m (pour bébé qui perce ses dents).

teething troubles ['ti:ðɪŋ-] npl (fig) difficultés initiales.

teetotal ['ti:'təutl] a (person) qui ne boit jamais d'alcool.

teetotaller, (US) **teetotaler** ['ti:'təutlə*] n personne f qui ne boit jamais d'alcool.

TEFL ['tɛfl] n abbr = Teaching of English as a Foreign Language.

Teheran [tɛə'rɑ:n] n Téhéran.

tel. abbr (= telephone) tél.

Tel Aviv ['tɛlə'vi:v] n Tel Aviv.

telecast ['tɛlɪkɑ:st] vt télédiffuser, téléviser.

telecommunications ['tɛlɪkəmju:nɪ'keɪʃənz] n télécommunications fpl.

telegram ['tɛlɪgræm] n télégramme m.

telegraph ['tɛlɪgrɑ:f] n télégraphe m.

telegraphic [tɛlɪ'græfɪk] a télégraphique.

telegraph pole n poteau m télégraphique.

telegraph wire n fil m télégraphique.

telepathic [tɛlɪ'pæθɪk] a télépathique.

telepathy [tə'lɛpəθɪ] n télépathie f.

telephone ['tɛlɪfəun] n téléphone m ♦ vt (person) téléphoner à; (message) téléphoner; **to have a** ~, (Brit) **to be on the** ~ (subscriber) être abonné(e) au téléphone; **to be on the** ~ (be speaking) être au téléphone.

telephone booth, (Brit) **telephone box** n cabine f téléphonique.

telephone call n appel m téléphonique, communication f téléphonique.

telephone directory n annuaire m (du téléphone).

telephone exchange n central m (téléphonique).

telephone kiosk n (Brit) cabine f téléphonique.

telephone number n numéro m de téléphone.

telephone operator téléphoniste m/f, standardiste m/f.

telephone tapping n mise f sur écoute.

telephonist [tə'lefənɪst] n (Brit) téléphoniste m/f.

telephoto ['tɛlɪ'fəutəu] a: ~ **lens** téléobjectif m.

teleprinter ['tɛlɪprɪntə*] n téléscripteur m.

Teleprompter ['tɛlɪprɔmptə*] n ® (US) prompteur m.

telescope ['tɛlɪskəup] n télescope m ♦ vi se télescoper ♦ vt télescoper.

telescopic [tɛlɪ'skɔpɪk] a télescopique; (umbrella) à manche télescopique.

Teletex ['tɛlətɛks] n ® (TEL) Télétex m ®.

televiewer ['tɛlɪvjuːə*] n téléspectateur/trice.

televise ['tɛlɪvaɪz] vt téléviser.

television ['tɛlɪvɪʒən] n télévision f.

television licence n (Brit) redevance f (de l'audio-visuel).

television programme n émission f de télévision.

television set n poste m de télévision, téléviseur m.

telex ['tɛlɛks] n télex m ♦ vt (message) envoyer par télex; (person) envoyer un télex à ♦ vi envoyer un télex.

tell, pt, pp **told** [tɛl, təuld] vt dire; (relate: story) raconter; (distinguish): **to ~ sth from** distinguer qch de ♦ vi (talk): **to ~ (of)** parler (de); (have effect) se faire sentir, se voir; **to ~ sb to do sth** dire à qn de faire; **to ~ sb about sth** (place, object etc) parler de qch à qn; (what happened etc) raconter qch à qn; **to ~ the time** (know how to) savoir lire l'heure; **can you ~ me the time?** pourriez-vous me dire l'heure?; **(I) ~ you what** ... écoute, ...; **I can't ~ them apart** je n'arrive pas à les distinguer.

tell off vt réprimander, gronder.

tell on vt fus (inform against) dénoncer, rapporter contre.

teller ['tɛlə*] n (in bank) caissier/ière.

telling ['tɛlɪŋ] a (remark, detail) révélateur(trice).

telltale ['tɛlteɪl] a (sign) éloquent(e), révélateur(trice).

telly ['tɛlɪ] n abbr (Brit col: = television) télé f.

temerity [tə'mɛrɪtɪ] n témérité f.

temp [tɛmp] abbr (Brit col: = temporary) n intérimaire m/f ♦ vi travailler comme intérimaire.

temper ['tɛmpə*] n (nature) caractère m; (mood) humeur f; (fit of anger) colère f ♦ vt (moderate) tempérer, adoucir; **to be in a ~** être en colère; **to lose one's ~** se mettre en colère; **to keep one's ~** rester calme.

temperament ['tɛmprəmənt] n (nature) tempérament m.

temperamental [tɛmprə'mɛntl] a ca-

pricieux(euse).

temperance ['tɛmpərns] n modération f; (in drinking) tempérance f.

temperate ['tɛmprət] a modéré(e); (climate) tempéré(e).

temperature ['tɛmprətʃə*] n température f; **to have** or **run a ~** avoir de la fièvre.

temperature chart n (MED) feuille f de température.

tempered ['tɛmpəd] a (steel) trempé(e).

tempest ['tɛmpɪst] n tempête f.

tempestuous [tɛm'pɛstjuəs] a (fig) orageux(euse); (: person) passionné(e).

tempi ['tɛmpiː] npl of **tempo**.

template ['tɛmplɪt] n patron m.

temple ['tɛmpl] n (building) temple m; (ANAT) tempe f.

templet ['tɛmplɪt] n = **template**.

tempo, ~**s** or **tempi** ['tɛmpəu, 'tɛmpiː] n tempo m; (fig: of life etc) rythme m.

temporal ['tɛmpərl] a temporel(le).

temporarily ['tɛmpərərɪlɪ] ad temporairement; provisoirement.

temporary ['tɛmpərərɪ] a temporaire, provisoire; (job, worker) temporaire; ~ **secretary** (secrétaire f) intérimaire f; **a ~ teacher** un professeur remplaçant or suppléant.

temporize ['tɛmpəraɪz] vi atermoyer; transiger.

tempt [tɛmpt] vt tenter; **to ~ sb into doing** induire qn à faire; **to be ~ed to do sth** être tenté(e) de faire qch.

temptation [tɛmp'teɪʃən] n tentation f.

tempting ['tɛmptɪŋ] a tentant(e).

ten [tɛn] num dix ♦ n: ~**s of thousands** des dizaines fpl de milliers.

tenable ['tɛnəbl] a défendable.

tenacious [tə'neɪʃəs] a tenace.

tenacity [tə'næsɪtɪ] n ténacité f.

tenancy ['tɛnənsɪ] n location f; état m de locataire.

tenant ['tɛnənt] n locataire m/f.

tend [tɛnd] vt s'occuper de; (sick etc) soigner ♦ vi: **to ~ to do** avoir tendance à faire; (colour): **to ~ to** tirer sur.

tendency ['tɛndənsɪ] n tendance f.

tender ['tɛndə*] a tendre; (delicate) délicat(e); (sore) sensible; (affectionate) tendre, doux(douce) ♦ n (COMM: offer) soumission f; (money): **legal ~** cours légal ♦ vt offrir; **to ~ one's resignation** donner or remettre sa démission; **to put in a ~ (for)** faire une soumission (pour); **to put work out to ~** (Brit) mettre un contrat en adjudication.

tenderize ['tɛndəraɪz] vt (CULIN) attendrir.

tenderly ['tɛndəlɪ] ad tendrement.

tenderness ['tɛndənɪs] n tendresse f; (of meat) tendreté f.

tendon ['tɛndən] n tendon m.

tenement ['tɛnəmənt] n immeuble m (de rapport).

Tenerife [tɛnə'riːf] n Ténérife f.

tenet ['tɛnət] n principe m.

tenner ['tɛnə*] n (Brit col) billet m de dix livres.

tennis ['tɛnɪs] n tennis m ♦ cpd (club, match, racket, player) de tennis.

tennis ball n balle f de tennis.
tennis court n (court m de) tennis m.
tennis elbow n (MED) synovite f du coude.
tennis shoes npl (chaussures fpl de) tennis mpl.
tenor ['tɛnə*] n (MUS) ténor m; (of speech etc) sens général.
tenpin bowling ['tɛnpɪn-] n (Brit) bowling m (à 10 quilles).
tense [tɛns] a tendu(e); (person) tendu, crispé(e) ♦ n (LING) temps m ♦ vt (tighten: muscles) tendre.
tenseness ['tɛnsnɪs] n tension f.
tension ['tɛnʃən] n tension f.
tent [tɛnt] n tente f.
tentacle ['tɛntəkl] n tentacule m.
tentative ['tɛntətɪv] a timide, hésitant(e); (conclusion) provisoire.
tenterhooks ['tɛntəhuks] npl: on ~ sur des charbons ardents.
tenth [tɛnθ] num dixième.
tent peg n piquet m de tente.
tent pole n montant m de tente.
tenuous ['tɛnjuəs] a ténu(e).
tenure ['tɛnjuə*] n (of property) bail m; (of job) période f de jouissance; statut m de titulaire.
tepid ['tɛpɪd] a tiède.
term [tə:m] n (limit) terme m; (word) terme, mot m; (SCOL) trimestre m; (LAW) session f ♦ vt appeler; ~s npl (conditions) conditions fpl; (COMM) tarif m; ~ of imprisonment peine f de prison; his ~ of office la période où il était en fonction; in the short/long ~ à court/long terme; "easy ~s" (COMM) "facilités de paiement"; to come to ~s with (problem) faire face à; to be on good ~s with bien s'entendre avec, être en bons termes avec.
terminal ['tə:mɪnl] a terminal(e); (disease) dans sa phase terminale ♦ n (ELEC) borne f; (for oil, ore etc, also COMPUT) terminal m; (also: air ~) aérogare f; (Brit: also: coach ~) gare routière.
terminate ['tə:mɪneɪt] vt mettre fin à ♦ vi: to ~ in finir en or par.
termination [tə:mɪ'neɪʃən] n fin f; cessation f; (of contract) résiliation f; ~ of pregnancy (MED) interruption f de grossesse.
termini ['tə:mɪnaɪ] npl of **terminus**.
terminology [tə:mɪ'nɔlədʒɪ] n terminologie f.
terminus, pl **termini** ['tə:mɪnəs, 'tə:mɪnaɪ] n terminus m inv.
termite ['tə:maɪt] n termite m.
Ter(r). abbr = **terrace**.
terrace ['tɛrəs] n terrasse f; (Brit: row of houses) rangée f de maisons (attenantes les unes aux autres); **the ~s** (Brit SPORT) les gradins mpl.
terraced ['tɛrəst] a (garden) en terrasses; (in a row: house, cottage etc) attenant(e) aux maisons voisines.
terracotta ['tɛrə'kɔtə] n terre cuite.
terrain [tɛ'reɪn] n terrain m (sol).
terrible ['tɛrɪbl] a terrible, atroce; (weather, work) affreux(euse), épouvantable.
terribly ['tɛrɪblɪ] ad terriblement; (very badly) affreusement mal.
terrier ['tɛrɪə*] n terrier m (chien).

terrific [tə'rɪfɪk] a fantastique, incroyable, terrible; (wonderful) formidable, sensationnel(le).
terrify ['tɛrɪfaɪ] vt terrifier.
territorial [tɛrɪ'tɔ:rɪəl] a territorial(e).
territorial waters npl eaux territoriales.
territory ['tɛrɪtərɪ] n territoire m.
terror ['tɛrə*] n terreur f.
terrorism ['tɛrərɪzəm] n terrorisme m.
terrorist ['tɛrərɪst] n terroriste m/f.
terrorize ['tɛrəraɪz] vt terroriser.
terse [tə:s] a (style) concis(e); (reply) laconique.
tertiary ['tə:ʃərɪ] a tertiaire; ~ **education** (Brit) enseignement m postscolaire.
Terylene ['tɛrɪli:n] n ® (Brit) tergal m ®.
TESL ['tɛsl] n abbr = Teaching of English as a Second Language.
test [tɛst] n (trial, check) essai m; (: of goods in factory) contrôle m; (of courage etc) épreuve f; (MED) examens mpl; (CHEM) analyses fpl; (exam: of intelligence etc) test m (d'aptitude); (: in school) interrogation f de contrôle; (also: **driving** ~) (examen du) permis m de conduire ♦ vt essayer; contrôler; mettre à l'épreuve; examiner; analyser; tester; faire subir une interrogation (de contrôle) à; **to put sth to the** ~ mettre qch à l'épreuve.
testament ['tɛstəmənt] n testament m; **the Old/New T~** l'Ancien/le Nouveau Testament.
test ban n (also: **nuclear** ~) interdiction f des essais nucléaires.
test case n (LAW, fig) affaire-test f.
test flight n vol m d'essai.
testicle ['tɛstɪkl] n testicule m.
testify ['tɛstɪfaɪ] vi (LAW) témoigner, déposer; **to** ~ **to sth** (LAW) attester qch; (gen) témoigner de qch.
testimonial [tɛstɪ'məunɪəl] n (Brit: reference) recommandation f; (gift) témoignage m d'estime.
testimony ['tɛstɪmənɪ] n (LAW) témoignage m, déposition f.
testing ['tɛstɪŋ] a (situation, period) difficile.
testing ground n banc m d'essai.
test match n (CRICKET, RUGBY) match international.
test paper n (SCOL) interrogation écrite.
test pilot n pilote m d'essai.
test tube n éprouvette f.
test-tube baby ['tɛstjuːb-] n bébé-éprouvette m.
testy ['tɛstɪ] a irritable.
tetanus ['tɛtənəs] n tétanos m.
tetchy ['tɛtʃɪ] a hargneux(euse).
tether ['tɛðə*] vt attacher ♦ n: **at the end of one's** ~ à bout (de patience).
text [tɛkst] n texte m.
textbook ['tɛkstbuk] n manuel m.
textile ['tɛkstaɪl] n textile m.
texture ['tɛkstʃə*] n texture f; (of skin, paper etc) grain m.
TGIF abbr (col) = thank God it's Friday.
TGWU n abbr (Brit: = Transport and General Workers' Union) syndicat de transporteurs.
Thai [taɪ] a thaïlandais(e) ♦ n Thaïlandais/e; (LING) thaï m.
Thailand ['taɪlænd] n Thaïlande f.

thalidomide [θəˈlɪdəmaɪd] n Ⓡ thalidomide f Ⓡ.

Thames [tɛmz] n: **the** ~ la Tamise.

than [ðæn, ðən] cj que; (with numerals): **more** ~ **10/once** plus de 10/d'une fois; **I have more/less** ~ **you** j'en ai plus/moins que toi; **she has more apples** ~ **pears** elle a plus de pommes que de poires; **it is better to phone** ~ **to write** il vaut mieux téléphoner (plutôt) qu'écrire; **no sooner did he leave** ~ **the phone rang** il venait de partir quand le téléphone a sonné.

thank [θæŋk] vt remercier, dire merci à; ~ **you (very much)** merci (beaucoup); ~ **heavens,** ~ **God** Dieu merci.

thankful [ˈθæŋkful] a: ~ **(for)** reconnaissant(e) (de); ~ **for/that** (relieved) soulagé(e) de/que.

thankfully [ˈθæŋkfəlɪ] ad avec reconnaissance; avec soulagement; ~ **there were few victims** il y eut fort heureusement peu de victimes.

thankless [ˈθæŋklɪs] a ingrat(e).

thanks [θæŋks] npl remerciements mpl ♦ excl merci!; ~ **to** prep grâce à.

Thanksgiving (Day) [ˈθæŋksgɪvɪŋ-] n jour m d'action de grâce.

that [ðæt, ðət] cj que ♦ a (pl those) ce(cet + vowel or h mute), f cette; (not "this"): ~ **book** ce livre-là ♦ pronoun (pl those) ce; (not "this one") cela, ça; (the one) celui(celle); (relative: subject) qui; (: object) que, prep + lequel(laquelle); (with time): **on the day** ~ **he came** le jour où il est venu ♦ ad: ~ **high** aussi haut; si haut; **it's about** ~ **high** c'est à peu près de cette hauteur; ~ **one** celui-là(celle-là); ~ **one over there** celui-là (or celle-là) là-bas; **what's** ~? qu'est-ce que c'est?; **who's** ~? qui est-ce?; **is** ~ **you?** c'est toi?; ~'s **what he said** c'est or voilà ce qu'il a dit; ~ **is** ... c'est-à-dire ..., à savoir ...; **all** ~ tout cela, tout ça; **I can't work** ~ **much** je ne peux pas travailler autant que cela; **at** or **with** ~, **she** ... là-dessus, elle ...; **do it like** ~ fais-le comme ça; **not** ~ **I know of** pas à ma connaissance.

thatched [θætʃt] a (roof) de chaume; ~ **cottage** chaumière f.

thaw [θɔ:] n dégel m ♦ vi (ice) fondre; (food) dégeler ♦ vt (food) (faire) dégeler; **it's ~ing** (weather) il dégèle.

the [ði:, ðə] definite article le, f la, (l' + vowel or h mute), pl les (NB: à + le(s) = au(x); de + le = du; de + les = des); (in titles): **Richard** ~ **Second** Richard Deux ♦ ad: ~ **more he works** ~ **more he earns** plus il travaille, plus il gagne d'argent; ~ **sooner** ~ **better** le plus tôt sera le mieux; ~ **rich and** ~ **poor** les riches et les pauvres.

theatre, (US) **theater** [ˈθɪətə*] n théâtre m.

theatre-goer [ˈθɪətəgəuə*] n habitué/e du théâtre.

theatrical [θɪˈætrɪkl] a théâtral(e); ~ **company** troupe f de théâtre.

theft [θeft] n vol m (larcin).

their [ðɛə*] a leur, pl leurs.

theirs [ðɛəz] pronoun le(la) leur, les leurs; **it is** ~ c'est à eux; **a friend of** ~ un de leurs amis.

them [ðɛm, ðəm] pronoun (direct) les; (indirect) leur; (stressed, after prep) eux(elles); **I see** ~ je les vois; **give** ~ **the book** donne-leur le livre; **give me a few of** ~ donnez m'en quelques uns (or quelques unes).

theme [θi:m] n thème m.

theme song n chanson principale.

themselves [ðəmˈselvz] pl pronoun (reflexive) se; (emphatic) eux-mêmes(elles-mêmes); **between** ~ entre eux(elles).

then [ðɛn] ad (at that time) alors, à ce moment-là; (next) puis, ensuite; (and also) et puis ♦ cj (therefore) alors, dans ce cas ♦ a: **the** ~ **president** le président d'alors or de l'époque; **by** ~ (past) à ce moment-là; (future) d'ici là; **from** ~ **on** dès lors; **before** ~ avant; **until** ~ jusqu'à ce moment-là, jusque-là; **and** ~ **what?** et puis après?; **what do you want me to do ~?** (afterwards) que veux-tu que je fasse ensuite?; (in that case) bon alors, qu'est-ce que je fais?

theologian [θɪəˈləudʒən] n théologien/ne.

theological [θɪəˈlɔdʒɪkl] a théologique.

theology [θɪˈɔlədʒɪ] n théologie f.

theorem [ˈθɪərəm] n théorème m.

theoretical [θɪəˈretɪkl] a théorique.

theorize [ˈθɪəraɪz] vi élaborer une théorie; (pej) faire des théories.

theory [ˈθɪərɪ] n théorie f.

therapeutic(al) [θɛrəˈpju:tɪk(l)] a thérapeutique.

therapist [ˈθɛrəpɪst] n thérapeute m/f.

therapy [ˈθɛrəpɪ] n thérapie f.

there [ðɛə*] ad là, là-bas; ~, ~! allons, allons!; **it's** ~ c'est là; **he went** ~ il y est allé; ~ **is,** ~ **are** il y a; ~ **he is** le voilà; ~ **has been** il y a eu; **on/in** ~ là-dessus/-dedans; **back** ~ là-bas; **down** ~ là-bas en bas; **over** ~ là-bas; **through** ~ par là; **to go** ~ **and back** faire l'aller et retour.

thereabouts [ˈðɛərəˈbauts] ad (place) par là, près de là; (amount) environ, à peu près.

thereafter [ðɛərˈɑ:ftə*] ad par la suite.

thereby [ˈðɛəbaɪ] ad ainsi.

therefore [ˈðɛəfɔ:*] ad donc, par conséquent.

there's [ˈðɛəz] = **there is, there has**.

thereupon [ðɛərəˈpɔn] ad (at that point) sur ce; (formal: on that subject) à ce sujet.

thermal [ˈθə:ml] a thermique; ~ **paper/printer** papier m/imprimante f thermique.

thermodynamics [ˈθə:mədaɪˈnæmɪks] n thermodynamique f.

thermometer [θəˈmɔmɪtə*] n thermomètre m.

thermonuclear [ˈθə:məuˈnju:klɪə*] a thermonucléaire.

Thermos [ˈθə:məs] n Ⓡ (also: ~ **flask**) thermos m or f inv Ⓡ.

thermostat [ˈθə:məustæt] n thermostat m.

thesaurus [θɪˈsɔ:rəs] n dictionnaire m synonymique.

these [ði:z] pl pronoun ceux-ci(celles-ci) ♦ pl a ces; (not "those"): ~ **books** ces livres-ci.

thesis, pl **theses** [ˈθi:sɪs, ˈθi:si:z] n thèse f.

they [ðeɪ] pl pronoun ils(elles); (stressed) eux(elles); ~ **say that** ... (it is said that) on dit que ....

they'd [ðeɪd] = **they had, they would**.

they'll [ðeɪl] = **they shall, they will.**
they're [ðɛə*] = **they are.**
they've [ðeɪv] = **they have.**
thick [θɪk] *a* épais(se); (*crowd*) dense; (*stupid*) bête, borné(e) ♦ *n*: **in the ~ of** au beau milieu de, en plein cœur de; **it's 20 cm ~** ça a 20 cm d'épaisseur.
thicken ['θɪkn] *vi* s'épaissir ♦ *vt* (*sauce etc*) épaissir.
thicket ['θɪkɪt] *n* fourré *m*, hallier *m*.
thickly ['θɪklɪ] *ad* (*spread*) en couche épaisse; (*cut*) en tranches épaisses; **~ populated** à forte densité de population.
thickness ['θɪknɪs] *n* épaisseur *f*.
thickset [θɪk'sɛt] *a* trapu(e), costaud(e).
thickskinned [θɪk'skɪnd] *a* (*fig*) peu sensible.
thief, *pl* **thieves** [θi:f, θi:vz] *n* voleur/euse.
thieving ['θi:vɪŋ] *n* vol *m* (*larcin*).
thigh [θaɪ] *n* cuisse *f*.
thighbone ['θaɪbəun] *n* fémur *m*.
thimble ['θɪmbl] *n* dé *m* (à coudre).
thin [θɪn] *a* mince; (*person*) maigre; (*soup*) peu épais(se); (*hair, crowd*) clairsemé(e); (*fog*) léger(ère) ♦ *vt* (*hair*) éclaircir; (*also:* **~ down**: *sauce, paint*) délayer ♦ *vi* (*fog*) s'éclaircir; (*also:* **~ out**: *crowd*) se disperser; **his hair is ~ning** il se dégarnit.
thing [θɪŋ] *n* chose *f*; (*object*) objet *m*; (*contraption*) truc *m*; **~s** *npl* (*belongings*) affaires *fpl*; **first ~ (in the morning)** à la première heure, tout de suite (le matin); **last ~ (at night), he ...** juste avant de se coucher, il ...; **the ~ is ...** c'est que ...; **for one ~** d'abord; **the best ~ would be to** le mieux serait de; **how are ~s?** comment ça va?; **she's got a ~ about ...** elle déteste ...; **poor ~!** le (*or* la) pauvre!
think, *pt, pp* **thought** [θɪŋk, θɔ:t] *vi* penser, réfléchir ♦ *vt* penser, croire; (*imagine*) s'imaginer; **to ~ of** penser à; **what do you ~ of it?** qu'en pensez-vous?; **what did you ~ of them?** qu'avez-vous pensé d'eux?; **to ~ about sth/sb** penser à qch/qn; **I'll ~ about it** je vais y réfléchir; **to ~ of doing** avoir l'idée de faire; **I ~ so/not** je crois *or* pense que oui/non; **to ~ well of** avoir une haute opinion de; **~ again!** attention, réfléchis bien!; **to ~ aloud** penser tout haut.
   think out *vt* (*plan*) bien réfléchir à; (*solution*) trouver.
   think over *vt* bien réfléchir à; **I'd like to ~ things over** (*offer, suggestion*) j'aimerais bien y réfléchir un peu.
   think through *vt* étudier dans tous les détails.
   think up *vt* inventer, trouver.
thinking ['θɪŋkɪŋ] *n*: **to my (way of) ~** selon moi.
think tank *n* groupe *m* de réflexion.
thinly ['θɪnlɪ] *ad* (*cut*) en tranches fines; (*spread*) en couche mince.
thinness ['θɪnnɪs] *n* minceur *f*; maigreur *f*.
third [θɜ:d] *num* troisième ♦ *n* troisième *m/f*; (*fraction*) tiers *m*; (*Brit* SCOL: *degree*) ≈ licence *f* avec mention passable; **a ~ of** le tiers de.
third-degree burns ['θɜ:dɪgri:-] *npl* brûlures *fpl* au troisième degré.
thirdly ['θɜ:dlɪ] *ad* troisièmement.

third party insurance *n* (*Brit*) assurance *f* au tiers.
third-rate ['θɜ:d'reɪt] *a* de qualité médiocre.
Third World *n*: **the ~** le Tiers-Monde.
thirst [θɜ:st] *n* soif *f*.
thirsty ['θɜ:stɪ] *a* qui a soif, assoiffé(e); **to be ~** avoir soif.
thirteen [θɜ:'ti:n] *num* treize.
thirtieth ['θɜ:tɪɪθ] *num* trentième.
thirty ['θɜ:tɪ] *num* trente.
this [ðɪs] *a* (*pl* **these**) ce(cet + *vowel or h mute*), *f* cette; (*not "that"*): **~ book** ce livre-ci ♦ *pronoun* (*pl* **these**) ce; ceci; (*not "that one"*) celui-ci(celle-ci) ♦ *ad*: **~ high** aussi haut; si haut; **it's about ~ high** c'est à peu près de cette hauteur; **who is ~?** qui est-ce?; **what is ~?** qu'est-ce que c'est?; **~ is Mr Brown** (*in photo*) voici M. Brown; (*in introduction*) je vous présente M. Brown; (*on telephone*) (c'est) M. Brown à l'appareil; **~ is what he said** voici ce qu'il a dit; **~ time** cette fois-ci; **~ time last year** l'année dernière à la même époque; **~ way** (*in this direction*) par ici; (*in this fashion*) de cette façon, ainsi; **they were talking of ~ and that** ils parlaient de choses et d'autres.
thistle ['θɪsl] *n* chardon *m*.
thong [θɒŋ] *n* lanière *f*.
thorn [θɔ:n] *n* épine *f*.
thorny ['θɔ:nɪ] *a* épineux(euse).
thorough ['θʌrə] *a* (*search*) minutieux(euse); (*knowledge, research*) approfondi(e); (*work*) consciencieux(euse); (*cleaning*) à fond.
thoroughbred ['θʌrəbrɛd] *n* (*horse*) pur-sang *m inv.*
thoroughfare ['θʌrəfɛə*] *n* rue *f*; **"no ~"** (*Brit*) "passage interdit".
thoroughly ['θʌrəlɪ] *ad* minutieusement; en profondeur; à fond; **he ~ agreed** il était tout à fait d'accord.
thoroughness ['θʌrənɪs] *n* soin (méticuleux).
those [ðəuz] *pl pronoun* ceux-là(celles-là) ♦ *pl a* ces; (*not "these"*): **~ books** ces livres-là.
though [ðəu] *cj* bien que + *sub*, quoique + *sub* ♦ *ad* pourtant; **even ~** quand bien même + *conditional*; **it's not easy, ~** pourtant, ce n'est pas facile.
thought [θɔ:t] *pt, pp of* **think** ♦ *n* pensée *f*; (*opinion*) avis *m*; (*intention*) intention *f*; **after much ~** après mûre réflexion; **I've just had a ~** je viens de penser à quelque chose; **to give sth some ~** réfléchir à qch.
thoughtful ['θɔ:tful] *a* pensif(ive); (*considerate*) prévenant(e).
thoughtfully ['θɔ:tfəlɪ] *ad* pensivement; avec prévenance.
thoughtless ['θɔ:tlɪs] *a* étourdi(e); qui manque de considération.
thoughtlessly ['θɔ:tlɪslɪ] *ad* inconsidérément.
thousand ['θauzənd] *num* mille; **one ~** mille; **~s of** des milliers de.
thousandth ['θauzəntθ] *num* millième.
thrash [θræʃ] *vt* rouer de coups; donner une correction à; (*defeat*) battre à plate(s) couture(s).
   thrash about *vi* se débattre.
   thrash out *vt* débattre de.
thrashing ['θræʃɪŋ] *n*: **to give sb a ~** = **to thrash sb.**

thread [θrɛd] n fil m; (of screw) pas m, filetage m ♦ vt (needle) enfiler; **to ~ one's way between** se faufiler entre.

threadbare ['θrɛdbɛə*] a râpé(e), élimé(e).

threat [θrɛt] n menace f; **to be under ~ of** être menacé(e) de.

threaten ['θrɛtn] vi (storm) menacer ♦ vt: **to ~ sb with sth/to do** menacer qn de qch/de faire.

threatening ['θrɛtnɪŋ] a menaçant(e).

three [θriː] num trois.

three-dimensional [θriːdɪ'mɛnʃənl] a à trois dimensions; (film) en relief.

threefold ['θriːfəuld] ad: **to increase ~** tripler.

three-piece ['θriːpiːs]: **~ suit** n complet m (avec gilet); **~ suite** n salon m comprenant un canapé et deux fauteuils assortis.

three-ply [θriː'plaɪ] a (wood) à trois épaisseurs; (wool) trois fils inv.

three-quarters [θriː'kwɔːtəz] npl trois-quarts mpl; **~ full** aux trois-quarts plein.

three-wheeler [θriː'wiːlə*] n (car) voiture f à trois roues.

thresh [θrɛʃ] vt (AGR) battre.

threshing machine ['θrɛʃɪŋ-] n batteuse f.

threshold ['θrɛʃhəuld] n seuil m; **to be on the ~ of** (fig) être au seuil de.

threshold agreement n (ECON) accord m d'indexation des salaires.

threw [θruː] pt of **throw**.

thrift [θrɪft] n économie f.

thrifty ['θrɪftɪ] a économe.

thrill [θrɪl] n frisson m, émotion f ♦ vi tressaillir, frissonner ♦ vt (audience) électriser; **to be ~ed** (with gift etc) être ravi(e).

thriller ['θrɪlə*] n film m (or roman m or pièce f) à suspense.

thrilling ['θrɪlɪŋ] a (book, play etc) saisissant(e); (news, discovery) excitant(e).

thrive, pt **thrived**, **throve**, pp **thrived**, **thriven** [θraɪv, θrəuv, 'θrɪvn] vi pousser or se développer bien; (business) prospérer; **he ~s on it** cela lui réussit.

thriving ['θraɪvɪŋ] a vigoureux(euse); (industry etc) prospère.

throat [θrəut] n gorge f; **to have a sore ~** avoir mal à la gorge.

throb [θrɔb] n (of heart) pulsation f; (of engine) vibration f; (of pain) élancement m ♦ vi (heart) palpiter; (engine) vibrer; (pain) lanciner; (wound) causer des élancements; **my head is ~bing** j'ai des élancements dans la tête.

throes [θrəuz] npl: **in the ~ of** au beau milieu de; **en proie à; in the ~ of death** à l'agonie.

thrombosis [θrɔm'bəusɪs] n thrombose f.

throne [θrəun] n trône m.

throng ['θrɔŋ] n foule f ♦ vt se presser dans.

throttle ['θrɔtl] n (AUT) accélérateur m ♦ vt étrangler.

through [θruː] prep à travers; (time) pendant, durant; (by means of) par, par l'intermédiaire de; (owing to) à cause de ♦ a (ticket, train, passage) direct(e) ♦ ad à travers; **(from) Monday ~ Friday** (US) de lundi à vendredi; **to let sb ~** laisser passer qn; **to put sb ~ to sb** (TEL) passer qn à qn; **to be ~** (TEL) avoir la communication; (have finished) avoir fini; **"no ~ traffic"** (US) "passage interdit"; **"no ~ way"** (Brit) "impasse".

throughout [θruː'aut] prep (place) partout dans; (time) durant tout(e) le(la) ♦ ad partout.

throughput ['θruːput] n (of goods, materials) quantité de matières premières utilisée; (COMPUT) débit m.

throve [θrəuv] pt of **thrive**.

throw [θrəu] n jet m; (SPORT) lancer m ♦ vt (pt **threw**, pp **thrown** [θruː, θrəun]) lancer, jeter; (SPORT) lancer; (rider) désarçonner; (fig) décontenancer; (pottery) tourner; **to ~ a party** donner une réception.

throw about, **throw around** vt (litter etc) éparpiller.

throw away vt jeter.

throw off vt se débarrasser de.

throw out vt jeter dehors; (reject) rejeter.

throw together vt (clothes, meal etc) assembler à la hâte; (essay) bâcler.

throw up vi vomir.

throwaway ['θrəuəweɪ] a à jeter.

throwback ['θrəubæk] n: **it's a ~ to** ça nous etc ramène à.

throw-in ['θrəuɪn] n (SPORT) remise f en jeu.

thru [θruː] prep, a, ad (US) = **through**.

thrush [θrʌʃ] n (ZOOL) grive f; (MED: esp in children) muguet m; (: Brit: in women) muguet vaginal.

thrust [θrʌst] n (TECH) poussée f ♦ vt (pt, pp **thrust**) pousser brusquement; (push in) enfoncer.

thrusting ['θrʌstɪŋ] a dynamique; qui se met trop en avant.

thud [θʌd] n bruit sourd.

thug [θʌg] n voyou m.

thumb [θʌm] n (ANAT) pouce m ♦ vt (book) feuilleter; **to ~ a lift** faire de l'auto-stop, arrêter une voiture; **to give sb/sth the ~s up** (approve) donner le feu vert à qn/qch.

thumb index n répertoire m (à onglets).

thumbnail ['θʌmneɪl] n ongle m du pouce.

thumbnail sketch n croquis m.

thumbtack ['θʌmtæk] n (US) punaise f (clou).

thump [θʌmp] n grand coup; (sound) bruit sourd ♦ vt cogner sur ♦ vi cogner, frapper.

thunder ['θʌndə*] n tonnerre m ♦ vi tonner; (train etc): **to ~ past** passer dans un grondement or un bruit de tonnerre.

thunderbolt ['θʌndəbəult] n foudre f.

thunderclap ['θʌndəklæp] n coup m de tonnerre.

thunderous ['θʌndərəs] a étourdissant(e).

thunderstorm ['θʌndəstɔːm] n orage m.

thunderstruck ['θʌndəstrʌk] a (fig) abasourdi(e).

thundery ['θʌndərɪ] a orageux(euse).

Thur(s). abbr (= Thursday) jeu.

Thursday ['θəːzdɪ] n jeudi m; for phrases see also **Tuesday**.

thus [ðʌs] ad ainsi.

thwart [θwɔːt] vt contrecarrer.

thyme [taɪm] n thym m.

thyroid ['θaɪrɔɪd] n thyroïde f.

tiara [tɪ'ɑːrə] n (woman's) diadème m.

Tibet [tɪ'bɛt] n Tibet m.

Tibetan [tɪ'bɛtən] a tibétain(e) ♦ n Tibétain/e;

(*LING*) tibétain *m*.

tibia ['tɪbɪə] *n* tibia *m*.

tic [tɪk] *n* tic (nerveux).

tick [tɪk] *n* (*sound: of clock*) tic-tac *m*; (*mark*) coche *f*; (*ZOOL*) tique *f*; (*Brit col*): **in a** ~ dans un instant; (*Brit col: credit*): **to buy sth on** ~ acheter qch à crédit ♦ *vi* faire tic-tac ♦ *vt* cocher; **to put a** ~ **against sth** cocher qch.

tick off *vt* cocher; (*person*) réprimander, attraper.

tick over *vi* (*Brit: engine*) tourner au ralenti; (: *fig*) aller *or* marcher doucettement.

ticker tape ['tɪkəteɪp] *n* bande *f* de téléscripteur; (*US: in celebrations*) ≈ serpentin *m*.

ticket ['tɪkɪt] *n* billet *m*; (*for bus, tube*) ticket *m*; (*in shop: on goods*) étiquette *f*; (: *from cash register*) reçu *m*, ticket; (*for library*) carte *f*; (*US POL*) liste électorale (*soutenue par un parti*); **to get a (parking)** ~ (*AUT*) attraper une contravention (pour stationnement illégal).

ticket agency *n* (*THEATRE*) agence *f* de spectacles.

ticket collector *n* contrôleur/euse.

ticket holder *n* personne munie d'un billet.

ticket inspector *n* contrôleur/euse.

ticket office *n* guichet *m*, bureau *m* de vente des billets.

tickle ['tɪkl] *n* chatouillement *m* ♦ *vt* chatouiller; (*fig*) plaire à; faire rire.

ticklish ['tɪklɪʃ] *a* (*person*) chatouilleux(euse); (*which tickles: blanket*) qui chatouille; (: *cough*) qui irrite.

tidal ['taɪdl] *a* à marée.

tidal wave *n* raz-de-marée *m inv*.

tidbit ['tɪdbɪt] *n* (*esp US*) = **titbit**.

tiddlywinks ['tɪdlɪwɪŋks] *n* jeu *m* de puce.

tide [taɪd] *n* marée *f*; (*fig: of events*) cours *m* ♦ *vt*: **to** ~ **sb over** dépanner qn; **high/low** ~ marée haute/basse.

tidily ['taɪdɪlɪ] *ad* avec soin, soigneusement.

tidiness ['taɪdɪnɪs] *n* bon ordre; goût *m* de l'ordre.

tidy ['taɪdɪ] *a* (*room*) bien rangé(e); (*dress, work*) net(nette), soigné(e); (*person*) ordonné(e), qui a de l'ordre; (: *in character*) soigneux(euse); (*mind*) méthodique ♦ *vt* (*also:* ~ **up**) ranger; **to** ~ **o.s. up** s'arranger.

tie [taɪ] *n* (*string etc*) cordon *m*; (*Brit: also: neck*~) cravate *f*; (*fig: link*) lien *m*; (*SPORT: draw*) égalité *f* de points; match nul; (: *match*) rencontre *f*; (*US RAIL*) traverse *f* ♦ *vt* (*parcel*) attacher; (*ribbon*) nouer ♦ *vi* (*SPORT*) faire match nul; finir à égalité de points; **"black/white** ~**"** "smoking/habit de rigueur"; **family** ~**s** liens de famille; **to** ~ **sth in a bow** faire un nœud à *or* avec qch; **to** ~ **a knot in sth** faire un nœud à qch.

tie down *vt* attacher; (*fig*): **to** ~ **sb down to** contraindre qn à accepter.

tie in *vi*: **to** ~ **in (with)** (*correspond*) correspondre (à).

tie on *vt* (*Brit: label etc*) attacher (avec une ficelle).

tie up *vt* (*parcel*) ficeler; (*dog, boat*) atta-

cher; (*arrangements*) conclure; **to be** ~**d up** (*busy*) être pris *or* occupé.

tie-break(er) ['taɪbreɪk(ə*)] *n* (*TENNIS*) tie-break *m*; (*in quiz*) question *f* subsidiaire.

tie-on ['taɪɔn] *a* (*Brit: label*) qui s'attache.

tie-pin ['taɪpɪn] *n* (*Brit*) épingle *f* de cravate.

tier [tɪə*] *n* gradin *m*; (*of cake*) étage *m*.

Tierra del Fuego [tɪ'ɛrədel'fweɪgəu] *n* Terre *f* de Feu.

tie tack *n* (*US*) épingle *f* de cravate.

tiff [tɪf] *n* petite querelle.

tiger ['taɪgə*] *n* tigre *m*.

tight [taɪt] *a* (*rope*) tendu(e), raide; (*clothes*) étroit(e), très juste; (*budget, programme, bend*) serré(e); (*control*) strict(e), sévère; (*col: drunk*) ivre, rond(e) ♦ *ad* (*squeeze*) très fort; (*shut*) à bloc, hermétiquement; **to be packed** ~ (*suitcase*) être bourré(e); (*people*) être serré(e); **everybody hold** ~! accrochez-vous bien!

tighten ['taɪtn] *vt* (*rope*) tendre; (*screw*) resserrer; (*control*) renforcer ♦ *vi* se tendre; se resserrer.

tight-fisted [taɪt'fɪstɪd] *a* avare.

tightly ['taɪtlɪ] *ad* (*grasp*) bien, très fort.

tight-rope ['taɪtrəup] *n* corde *f* raide.

tight-rope walker *n* funambule *m/f*.

tights [taɪts] *npl* (*Brit*) collant *m*.

tigress ['taɪgrɪs] *n* tigresse *f*.

tilde ['tɪldə] *n* tilde *m*.

tile [taɪl] *n* (*on roof*) tuile *f*; (*on wall or floor*) carreau *m* ♦ *vt* (*floor, bathroom etc*) carreler.

tiled [taɪld] *a* en tuiles; carrelé(e).

till [tɪl] *n* caisse (enregistreuse) ♦ *vt* (*land*) cultiver ♦ *prep, cj* = **until**.

tiller ['tɪlə*] *n* (*NAUT*) barre *f* (du gouvernail).

tilt [tɪlt] *vt* pencher, incliner ♦ *vi* pencher, être incliné(e) ♦ *n* (*slope*) inclinaison *f*; **to wear one's hat at a** ~ porter son chapeau incliné sur le côté; **(at) full** ~ à toute vitesse.

timber ['tɪmbə*] *n* (*material*) bois *m* de construction; (*trees*) arbres *mpl*.

time [taɪm] *n* temps *m*; (*epoch: often pl*) époque *f*, temps; (*by clock*) heure *f*; (*moment*) moment *m*; (*occasion, also MATH*) fois *f*; (*MUS*) mesure *f* ♦ *vt* (*race*) chronométrer; (*programme*) minuter; (*remark etc*) choisir le moment de; **a long** ~ un long moment, longtemps; **for the** ~ **being** pour le moment; **from** ~ **to** ~ de temps en temps; ~ **after** ~, ~ **and again** bien des fois; **in** ~ (*soon enough*) à temps; (*after some time*) avec le temps, à la longue; (*MUS*) en mesure; **in a week's** ~ dans une semaine; **in no** ~ en un rien de temps; **on** ~ à l'heure; **to be 30 minutes behind/ahead of** ~ avoir 30 minutes de retard/d'avance; **by the** ~ **he arrived** quand il est arrivé, le temps qu'il arrive (*sub*); **5** ~**s 5** 5 fois 5; **what** ~ **is it?** quelle heure est-il?; **what** ~ **do you make it?** quelle heure avez-vous?; **to have a good** ~ bien s'amuser; **we** (*or* **they** *etc*) **had a hard** ~ ça a été difficile *or* pénible; ~**'s up!** c'est l'heure!; **I've no** ~ **for it** (*fig*) cela m'agace; **he'll do it in his own (good)** ~ (*without being hurried*) il le fera quand il en aura le temps; **he'll do it in** *or* (*US*) **on his own** ~ (*out of working hours*) il le fera à ses heures perdues; **to be behind the ~s** retarder (sur son temps).

time-and-motion study ['taɪmənd'məuʃən-] n étude f des cadences.

time bomb n bombe f à retardement.

time clock n horloge pointeuse.

time-consuming ['taɪmkənsju:mɪŋ] a qui prend beaucoup de temps.

time difference n décalage m horaire.

time-honoured, (US) **time-honored** ['taɪmɔnəd] a consacré(e).

timekeeper ['taɪmki:pə*] n (SPORT) chronomètre m.

time lag n (Brit) décalage m; (: in travel) décalage horaire.

timeless ['taɪmlɪs] a éternel(le).

time limit n limite f de temps, délai m.

timely ['taɪmlɪ] a opportun(e).

time off n temps m libre.

timer ['taɪmə*] n (in kitchen) compte-minutes m inv; (TECH) minuteur m.

time-saving ['taɪmseɪvɪŋ] a qui fait gagner du temps.

time scale n délais mpl.

time-sharing ['taɪmʃɛərɪŋ] n (COMPUT) temps partagé.

time sheet n feuille f de présence.

time signal n signal m horaire.

time switch n (Brit) minuteur m; (: for lighting) minuterie f.

timetable ['taɪmteɪbl] n (RAIL) indicateur m/ horaire m; (SCOL) emploi m du temps; (programme of events etc) programme m.

time zone n fuseau m horaire.

timid ['tɪmɪd] a timide; (easily scared) peureux(euse).

timidity [tɪ'mɪdɪtɪ] n timidité f.

timing ['taɪmɪŋ] n minutage m; chronométrage m; **the ~ of his resignation** le moment choisi pour sa démission.

timing device n (on bomb) mécanisme m de retardement.

timpani ['tɪmpənɪ] npl timbales fpl.

tin [tɪn] n étain m; (also: ~ **plate**) fer-blanc m; (Brit: can) boîte f (de conserve); (: for baking) moule m (à gâteau); **a ~ of paint** un pot de peinture.

tin foil n papier m d'étain.

tinge [tɪndʒ] n nuance f ♦ vt: **~d with** teinté(e) de.

tingle ['tɪŋgl] n picotement m; frisson m ♦ vi picoter.

tinker ['tɪŋkə*] n rétameur ambulant; (gipsy) romanichel m.

tinker with vt fus bricoler, rafistoler.

tinkle ['tɪŋkl] vi tinter ♦ n (col): **to give sb a ~** passer un coup de fil à qn.

tin mine n mine f d'étain.

tinned [tɪnd] a (Brit: food) en boîte, en conserve.

tinny ['tɪnɪ] a métallique.

tin opener [-'əupnə*] n (Brit) ouvre-boîte(s) m.

tinsel ['tɪnsl] n guirlandes fpl de Noël (argentées).

tint [tɪnt] n teinte f; (for hair) shampooing colorant ♦ vt (hair) faire un shampooing colorant à.

tinted ['tɪntɪd] a (hair) teint(e); (spectacles, glass) teinté(e).

tiny ['taɪnɪ] a minuscule.

tip [tɪp] n (end) bout m; (protective: on umbrella etc) embout m; (gratuity) pourboire m; (Brit: for coal) terril m; (: for rubbish) décharge f; (advice) tuyau m ♦ vt (waiter) donner un pourboire à; (tilt) incliner; (overturn: also: ~ **over**) renverser; (empty: also: ~ **out**) déverser; (predict: winner etc) pronostiquer; **he ~ped out the contents of the box** il a vidé le contenu de la boîte.

tip off vt prévenir, avertir.

tip-off ['tɪpɔf] n (hint) tuyau m.

tipped ['tɪpt] a (Brit: cigarette) (à bout) filtre inv; **steel-~** à bout métallique, à embout de métal.

Tipp-Ex ['tɪpɛks] n ® (Brit) Tipp-Ex m ®.

tipple ['tɪpl] (Brit) vi picoler ♦ n: **to have a ~** boire un petit coup.

tipsy ['tɪpsɪ] a un peu ivre, éméché(e).

tiptoe ['tɪptəu] n: **on ~** sur la pointe des pieds.

tiptop ['tɪptɔp] a: **in ~ condition** en excellent état.

tire ['taɪə*] n (US) = **tyre** ♦ vt fatiguer ♦ vi se fatiguer.

tire out vt épuiser.

tired ['taɪəd] a fatigué(e); **to be/feel/look ~** être/se sentir/avoir l'air fatigué; **to be ~ of** en avoir assez de, être las(lasse) de.

tiredness ['taɪədnɪs] n fatigue f.

tireless ['taɪəlɪs] a infatigable, inlassable.

tiresome ['taɪəsəm] a ennuyeux(euse).

tiring ['taɪərɪŋ] a fatigant(e).

tissue ['tɪʃu:] n tissu m; (paper handkerchief) mouchoir m en papier, kleenex m ®.

tissue paper n papier m de soie.

tit [tɪt] n (bird) mésange f; (col: breast) nichon m; **to give ~ for tat** rendre coup pour coup.

titanium [tɪ'teɪnɪəm] n titane m.

titbit ['tɪtbɪt] n (food) friandise f; (before meal) amuse-gueule m inv; (news) potin m.

titillate ['tɪtɪleɪt] vt titiller, exciter.

titivate ['tɪtɪveɪt] vt pomponner.

title ['taɪtl] n titre m; (LAW: right): **~ (to)** droit m (à).

title deed n (LAW) titre (constitutif) de propriété.

title page n page f de titre.

title role n rôle principal.

titter ['tɪtə*] vi rire (bêtement).

tittle-tattle ['tɪtltætl] n bavardages mpl.

titular ['tɪtjulə*] a (in name only) nominal(e).

tizzy ['tɪzɪ] n: **to be in a ~** être dans tous ses états.

T-junction ['ti:'dʒʌŋkʃən] n croisement m en T.

TM n abbr = **trademark, transcendental meditation**.

TN abbr (US POST) = Tennessee.

TNT n abbr (= trinitrotoluene) TNT m.

to [tu:, tə] prep à; (towards) vers; envers ♦ with vb (simple infinitive): **~ go/eat** aller/ manger; (following another vb): **to want/try ~ do** vouloir faire/essayer de faire; (purpose, result) pour, afin de; **to give sth ~ sb** donner qch à qn; **give it ~ me** donne-le-moi; **the key ~ the front door** la clé de la porte d'entrée; **it belongs ~ him** cela lui appartient, c'est à lui; **the main thing is ~ ...** l'important est de ...; **to go ~ France/ Portugal** aller en France/au Portugal; **the road ~ Edinburgh** la route d'Édimbourg; **I went ~ Claude's** je suis allé chez Claude; **to go ~ town/school** aller en ville/à l'école; **8 apples ~ the kilo** 8 pommes le kilo; **it's 25 ~ 3** il est 3 heures moins 25; **pull/push the door ~** tirez/poussez la porte; **to go ~ and fro** aller et venir; **he did it ~ help you** il l'a fait pour t'aider; **I don't want ~** je ne veux pas; **I have things ~ do** j'ai des choses à faire; **ready ~ go** prêt à partir.

toad [təud] n crapaud m.

toadstool ['təudstu:l] n champignon (vénéneux).

toady ['təudɪ] vi flatter bassement.

toast [təust] n (CULIN) pain grillé, toast m; (drink, speech) toast ♦ vt (CULIN) faire griller; (drink to) porter un toast à; **a piece or slice of ~** un toast.

toaster ['təustə*] n grille-pain m inv.

toastmaster ['təustmɑ:stə*] n animateur m pour réceptions.

toast rack n porte-toast m inv.

tobacco [tə'bækəu] n tabac m; **pipe ~** tabac à pipe.

tobacconist [tə'bækənɪst] n marchand/e de tabac; **~'s (shop)** (bureau m de) tabac m.

Tobago [tə'beɪgəu] n see **Trinidad**.

toboggan [tə'bɔgən] n toboggan m; (child's) luge f.

today [tə'deɪ] ad, n (also fig) aujourd'hui (m); **what day is it ~?** quel jour sommes-nous aujourd'hui?; **what date is it ~?** quelle est la date aujourd'hui?; **~ is the 4th of March** aujourd'hui nous sommes le 4 mars; **a week ago ~** il y a huit jours aujourd'hui.

toddler ['tɔdlə*] n enfant m/f qui commence à marcher, bambin m.

toddy ['tɔdɪ] n grog m.

to-do [tə'du:] n (fuss) histoire f, affaire f.

toe [təu] n doigt m de pied, orteil m; (of shoe) bout m ♦ vt: **to ~ the line** (fig) obéir, se conformer; **big ~** gros orteil; **little ~** petit orteil.

toehold ['təuhəuld] n prise f.

toenail ['təuneɪl] n ongle m de l'orteil.

toffee ['tɔfɪ] n caramel m.

toffee apple n (Brit) pomme caramélisée.

toga ['təugə] n toge f.

together [tə'gɛðə*] ad ensemble; (at same time) en même temps; **~ with** prep avec.

togetherness [tə'gɛðənɪs] n camaraderie f; intimité f.

toggle switch ['tɔgl-] n (COMPUT) interrupteur m à bascule.

Togo ['təugəu] n Togo m.

togs [tɔgz] npl (col: clothes) fringues fpl.

toil [tɔɪl] n dur travail, labeur m ♦ vi travailler dur; peiner.

toilet ['tɔɪlət] n (Brit: lavatory) toilettes fpl, cabinets mpl ♦ cpd (bag, soap etc) de toilette; **to go to the ~** aller aux toilettes.

toilet bag n (Brit) nécessaire m de toilette.

toilet bowl n cuvette f des W.-C.

toilet paper n papier m hygiénique.

toiletries ['tɔɪlətrɪz] npl articles mpl de toilette.

toilet roll n rouleau m de papier hygiénique.

toilet water n eau f de toilette.

to-ing and fro-ing ['tu:ɪŋən'frəuɪŋ] n (Brit) allées et venues fpl.

token ['təukən] n (sign) marque f, témoignage m; (voucher) bon m, coupon m; (fee, strike) symbolique; **by the same ~** (fig) de même; **book/record ~** (Brit) chèque-livre/-disque m.

Tokyo ['təukjəu] n Tokyo.

told [təuld] pt, pp of **tell**.

tolerable ['tɔlərəbl] a (bearable) tolérable; (fairly good) passable.

tolerably ['tɔlərəblɪ] ad: **~ good** tolérable.

tolerance ['tɔlərns] n (also TECH) tolérance f.

tolerant ['tɔlərnt] a: **~ (of)** tolérant(e) (à l'égard de).

tolerate ['tɔləreɪt] vt supporter; (MED, TECH) tolérer.

toleration [tɔlə'reɪʃən] n tolérance f.

toll [təul] n (tax, charge) péage m ♦ vi (bell) sonner; **the accident ~ on the roads** le nombre des victimes de la route.

tollbridge ['təulbrɪdʒ] n pont m à péage.

tomato, **~es** [tə'mɑ:təu] n tomate f.

tomb [tu:m] n tombe f.

tombola [tɔm'bəulə] n tombola f.

tomboy ['tɔmbɔɪ] n garçon manqué.

tombstone ['tu:mstəun] n pierre tombale.

tomcat ['tɔmkæt] n matou m.

tomorrow [tə'mɔrəu] ad, n (also fig) demain (m); **the day after ~** après-demain; **a week ~** demain en huit; **~ morning** demain matin.

ton [tʌn] n tonne f (Brit: = 1016 kg; US = 907 kg; metric = 1000 kg); (NAUT: also: **register ~**) tonneau m (= 2.83 cu.m.); **~s of** (col) des tas de.

tonal ['təunl] a tonal(e).

tone [təun] n ton m; (of radio, Brit TEL) tonalité f ♦ vi s'harmoniser.

tone down vt (colour, criticism) adoucir; (sound) baisser.

tone up vt (muscles) tonifier.

tone-deaf [təun'dɛf] a qui n'a pas d'oreille.

toner ['təunə*] n (for photocopier) encre f.

Tonga [tɔŋə] n îles fpl Tonga.

tongs [tɔŋz] npl pinces fpl; (for coal) pincettes fpl; (for hair) fer m à friser.

tongue [tʌŋ] n langue f; **~ in cheek** ad ironiquement.

tongue-tied ['tʌŋtaɪd] a (fig) muet(te).

tongue-twister ['tʌŋtwɪstə*] n phrase f très difficile à prononcer.

tonic ['tɔnɪk] n (MED) tonique m; (MUS) tonique f; (also: **~ water**) tonic m.

tonight [tə'naɪt] ad, n cette nuit; (this evening) ce soir; **(I'll) see you ~!** à ce soir!

tonnage ['tʌnɪdʒ] n (NAUT) tonnage m.

tonne [tʌn] n (Brit: metric ton) tonne f.

tonsil ['tɔnsl] n amygdale f; **to have one's ~s out** se faire opérer des amygdales.

tonsillitis [tɔnsɪ'laɪtɪs] n amygdalite f; **to have ~** avoir une angine or une amygdalite.

too [tu:] ad (excessively) trop; (also) aussi; **it's ~ sweet** c'est trop sucré; **I went ~** moi aussi, j'y suis allé; **~ much** ad trop ♦ a trop de; **~ many** a trop de; **~ bad!** tant pis!

took [tuk] pt of **take**.

tool [tu:l] *n* outil *m*; *(fig)* instrument *m* ♦ *vt* travailler, ouvrager.

tool box *n* boîte *f* à outils.

tool kit *n* trousse *f* à outils.

toot [tu:t] *n* coup *m* de sifflet *(or de klaxon)* ♦ *vi* siffler; *(with car-horn)* klaxonner.

tooth, *pl* **teeth** [tu:θ, ti:θ] *n (ANAT, TECH)* dent *f*; **to have a ~ out** *or (US)* **pulled** se faire arracher une dent; **to brush one's teeth** se laver les dents; **by the skin of one's teeth** *(fig)* de justesse.

toothache ['tu:θeɪk] *n* mal *m* de dents; **to have ~** avoir mal aux dents.

toothbrush ['tu:θbrʌʃ] *n* brosse *f* à dents.

toothpaste ['tu:θpeɪst] *n* (pâte *f*) dentifrice *m*.

toothpick ['tu:θpɪk] *n* cure-dent *m*.

tooth powder *n* poudre *f* dentifrice.

top [tɔp] *n (of mountain, head)* sommet *m*; *(of page, ladder)* haut *m*; *(of list, queue)* commencement *m*; *(of box, cupboard, table)* dessus *m*; *(lid: of box, jar)* couvercle *m*; *(: of bottle)* bouchon *m*; *(toy)* toupie *f*; *(DRESS: blouse etc)* haut; *(of pyjamas)* veste *f* ♦ *a* du haut; *(in rank)* premier(ière); *(best)* meilleur(e) ♦ *vt (exceed)* dépasser; *(be first in)* être en tête de; **the ~ of the milk** *(Brit)* la crème du lait; **at the ~ of the stairs/ page/street** en haut de l'escalier/de la page/ de la rue; **on ~ of** sur; *(in addition to)* en plus de; **from ~ to toe** *(Brit)* de la tête aux pieds; **at the ~ of the list** en tête de liste; **at the ~ of one's voice** à tue-tête; **at ~ speed** à toute vitesse; **over the ~** *(col: behaviour etc)* qui dépasse les limites.

top up, *(US)* **top off** *vt* remplir.

topaz ['təupæz] *n* topaze *f*.

topcoat ['tɔpkəut] *n* pardessus *m*.

topflight ['tɔpflaɪt] *a* excellent(e).

top floor *n* dernier étage.

top hat *n* haut-de-forme *m*.

top-heavy [tɔp'hɛvɪ] *a (object)* trop lourd(e) du haut.

topic ['tɔpɪk] *n* sujet *m*, thème *m*.

topical ['tɔpɪkl] *a* d'actualité.

topless ['tɔplɪs] *a (bather etc)* aux seins nus; **~ swimsuit** monokini *m*.

top-level ['tɔplɛvl] *a (talks)* à l'échelon le plus élevé.

topmost ['tɔpməust] *a* le(la) plus haut(e).

topography [tə'pɔgrəfɪ] *n* topographie *f*.

topping ['tɔpɪŋ] *n (CULIN)* couche *f* de crème, fromage etc qui recouvre un plat.

topple ['tɔpl] *vt* renverser, faire tomber ♦ *vi* basculer; tomber.

top-ranking ['tɔpræŋkɪŋ] *a* très haut placé(e).

TOPS [tɔps] *n abbr (Brit: = Training Opportunities Scheme) programme de recyclage professionnel.*

top-secret ['tɔp'si:krɪt] *a* ultra-secret(ète).

top-security ['tɔpsə'kjuərɪtɪ] *a (Brit)* de haute sécurité.

topsy-turvy ['tɔpsɪ'tə:vɪ] *a, ad* sens dessus-dessous.

top-up ['tɔpʌp] *n*: **would you like a ~?** je vous en remets *or* rajoute?

torch [tɔ:tʃ] *n* torche *f*; *(Brit: electric)* lampe *f* de poche.

tore [tɔ:*] *pt* of **tear**.

torment *n* ['tɔ:mɛnt] tourment *m* ♦ *vt*

[tɔ:'mɛnt] tourmenter; *(fig: annoy)* agacer.

torn [tɔ:n] *pp* of **tear** ♦ *a*: **~ between** *(fig)* tiraillé(e) entre.

tornado, **~es** [tɔ:'neɪdəu] *n* tornade *f*.

torpedo, **~es** [tɔ:'pi:dəu] *n* torpille *f*.

torpedo boat *n* torpilleur *m*.

torpor ['tɔ:pə*] *n* torpeur *f*.

torque [tɔ:k] *n* couple *m* de torsion.

torrent ['tɔrnt] *n* torrent *m*.

torrential [tɔ'rɛnʃl] *a* torrentiel(le).

torrid ['tɔrɪd] *a* torride; *(fig)* ardent(e).

torso ['tɔ:səu] *n* torse *m*.

tortoise ['tɔ:təs] *n* tortue *f*.

tortoiseshell ['tɔ:təʃɛl] *a* en écaille.

tortuous ['tɔ:tjuəs] *a* tortueux(euse).

torture ['tɔ:tʃə*] *n* torture *f* ♦ *vt* torturer.

torturer ['tɔ:tʃərə*] *n* tortionnaire *m*.

Tory ['tɔ:rɪ] *a (Brit POL)* tory *(pl* tories), conservateur(trice) ♦ *n* tory *m/f*, conservateur/trice.

toss [tɔs] *vt* lancer, jeter; *(Brit: pancake)* faire sauter; *(head)* rejeter en arrière ♦ *n (movement: of head etc)* mouvement soudain; *(of coin)* tirage *m* à pile ou face; **to ~ a coin** jouer à pile ou face; **to ~ up for sth** *(Brit)* jouer qch à pile ou face; **to ~ and turn** *(in bed)* se tourner et se retourner; **to win/lose the ~** gagner/perdre à pile ou face; *(SPORT)* gagner/perdre le tirage au sort.

tot [tɔt] *n (Brit: drink)* petit verre; *(child)* bambin *m*.

tot up *vt (Brit: figures)* additionner.

total ['təutl] *a* total(e) ♦ *n* total *m* ♦ *vt (add up)* faire le total de, totaliser; *(amount to)* s'élever à; **in ~** au total.

totalitarian [təutælɪ'tɛərɪən] *a* totalitaire.

totality [təu'tælɪtɪ] *n* totalité *f*.

totally ['təutəlɪ] *ad* totalement.

tote bag [təut-] *n* fourre-tout *m inv*.

totem pole ['təutəm-] *n* mât *m* totémique.

totter ['tɔtə*] *vi* chanceler; *(object, government)* être chancelant(e).

touch [tʌtʃ] *n* contact *m*, toucher *m*; *(sense, also skill: of pianist etc)* toucher; *(fig: note, also FOOTBALL)* touche *f* ♦ *vt (gen)* toucher; *(tamper with)* toucher à; **the personal ~** la petite note personnelle; **to put the finishing ~es to sth** mettre la dernière main à qch; **a ~ of** *(fig)* un petit peu de; une touche de; **in ~ with** en contact ou rapport avec; **to get in ~ with** prendre contact avec; **I'll be in ~** je resterai en contact; **to lose ~** *(friends)* se perdre de vue; **to be out of ~ with events** ne pas être au courant de ce qui se passe.

touch on *vt fus (topic)* effleurer, toucher.

touch up *vt (paint)* retoucher.

touch-and-go ['tʌtʃən'gəu] *a* incertain(e); **it was ~ whether we did it** nous avons failli ne pas le faire.

touchdown ['tʌtʃdaun] *n* atterrissage *m*; *(on sea)* amerrissage *m*; *(US FOOTBALL)* touché-en-but *m*.

touched [tʌtʃt] *a* touché(e); *(col)* cinglé(e).

touching ['tʌtʃɪŋ] *a* touchant(e), attendrissant(e).

touchline ['tʌtʃlaɪn] *n (SPORT)* (ligne *f* de) touche *f*.

touch-type ['tʌtʃtaɪp] *vi* taper au toucher.

touchy ['tʌtʃɪ] *a (person)* susceptible.

tough [tʌf] *a* dur(e); (*resistant*) résistant(e), solide; (*meat*) dur, coriace; (*journey*) pénible; (*task, problem, situation*) difficile; (*rough*) dur ♦ *n* (*gangster etc*) dur *m*; ~ **luck!** pas de chance!; tant pis!

toughen ['tʌfn] *vt* rendre plus dur(e) (*or* plus résistant(e) *or* plus solide).

toughness ['tʌfnɪs] *n* dureté *f*; résistance *f*; solidité *f*.

toupee ['tu:peɪ] *n* postiche *m*.

tour ['tuə*] *n* voyage *m*; (*also:* **package** ~) voyage organisé; (*of town, museum*) tour *m*, visite *f*; (*by artist*) tournée *f* ♦ *vt* visiter; **to go on a ~ of** (*museum, region*) visiter; **to go on** ~ partir en tournée.

touring ['tuərɪŋ] *n* voyages *mpl* touristiques, tourisme *m*.

tourism ['tuərɪzm] *n* tourisme *m*.

tourist ['tuərɪst] *n* touriste *m/f* ♦ *ad* (*travel*) en classe touriste ♦ *cpd* touristique; **the ~ trade** le tourisme.

tourist office *n* syndicat *m* d'initiative.

tournament ['tuənəmənt] *n* tournoi *m*.

tourniquet ['tuənɪkeɪ] *n* (*MED*) garrot *m*.

tour operator ['tuər'ɔpəreɪtə*] *n* (*Brit*) organisateur *m* de voyages, tour-opérateur *m*.

tousled ['tauzld] *a* (*hair*) ébouriffé(e).

tout [taut] *vi:* **to ~ for** essayer de racoler; **to ~ sth (around)** (*Brit*) essayer de placer *or* (re)vendre qch ♦ *n* (*Brit: ticket* ~) revendeur *m* de billets.

tow [təu] *n:* **to give sb a ~** (*AUT*) remorquer qn ♦ *vt* remorquer; **"on ~"**, (*US*) **"in ~"** (*AUT*) "véhicule en remorque".

toward(s) [tə'wɔ:d(z)] *prep* vers; (*of attitude*) envers, à l'égard de; (*of purpose*) pour; ~ **noon/the end of the year** vers midi/la fin de l'année; **to feel friendly ~ sb** être bien disposé envers qn.

towel ['tauəl] *n* serviette *f* (de toilette); (*also:* **tea** ~) torchon *m*; **to throw in the ~** (*fig*) jeter l'éponge.

towelling ['tauəlɪŋ] *n* (*fabric*) tissu-éponge *m*.

towel rail, (*US*) **towel rack** *n* porte-serviettes *m inv*.

tower ['tauə*] *n* tour *f* ♦ *vi* (*building, mountain*) se dresser (majestueusement); **to ~ above** *or* **over sb/sth** dominer qn/qch.

tower block *n* (*Brit*) tour *f* (d'habitation).

towering ['tauərɪŋ] *a* très haut(e), imposant(e).

towline ['təulaɪn] *n* (câble *m* de) remorque *f*.

town [taun] *n* ville *f*; **to go to ~** aller en ville; (*fig*) y mettre le paquet; **in the ~** dans la ville, en ville; **to be out of ~** (*person*) être en déplacement.

town centre *n* centre *m* de la ville, centre-ville *m*.

town clerk *n* ≈ secrétaire *m/f* de mairie.

town council *n* conseil municipal.

town hall *n* ≈ mairie *f*.

town plan *n* plan *m* de ville.

town planner *n* urbaniste *m/f*.

town planning *n* urbanisme *m*.

townspeople ['taunzpi:pl] *npl* citadins *mpl*.

towpath ['təupɑ:θ] *n* (chemin *m* de) halage *m*.

towrope ['təurəup] *n* (câble *m* de) remorque *f*.

tow truck *n* (*US*) dépanneuse *f*.

toxic ['tɔksɪk] *a* toxique.

toxin ['tɔksɪn] *n* toxine *f*.

toy [tɔɪ] *n* jouet *m*.

toy with *vt fus* jouer avec; (*idea*) caresser.

toyshop ['tɔɪʃɔp] *m* magasin *m* de jouets.

trace [treɪs] *n* trace *f* ♦ *vt* (*draw*) tracer, dessiner; (*follow*) suivre la trace de; (*locate*) retrouver; **without ~** (*disappear*) sans laisser de traces; **there was no ~ of it** il n'y en avait pas trace.

trace element *n* oligo-élément *m*.

trachea [trə'kɪə] *n* (*ANAT*) trachée *f*.

tracing paper ['treɪsɪŋ-] *n* papier-calque *m*.

track [træk] *n* (*mark*) trace *f*; (*path: gen*) chemin *m*, piste *f*; (*: of bullet etc*) trajectoire *f*; (*: of suspect, animal*) piste *f*; (*RAIL*) voie ferrée, rails *mpl*; (*on tape, COMPUT, SPORT*) piste; (*on record*) plage *f* ♦ *vt* suivre la trace *or* la piste de; **to keep ~ of** suivre; **to be on the right ~** (*fig*) être sur la bonne voie.

track down *vt* (*prey*) trouver et capturer; (*sth lost*) finir par retrouver.

tracked [trækt] *a* (*AUT*) à chenille.

tracker dog ['trækə-] *n* (*Brit*) chien policier.

track events *npl* (*SPORT*) épreuves *fpl* sur piste.

tracking station ['trækɪŋ-] *n* (*SPACE*) centre *m* d'observation de satellites.

track record *n:* **to have a good ~** (*fig*) avoir fait ses preuves.

track suit *n* survêtement *m*.

tract [trækt] *n* (*GEO*) étendue *f*, zone *f*; (*pamphlet*) tract *m*; **respiratory ~** (*ANAT*) système *m* respiratoire.

traction ['trækʃən] *n* traction *f*.

tractor ['træktə*] *n* tracteur *m*.

tractor feed *n* (*on printer*) entraînement *m* par ergots.

trade [treɪd] *n* commerce *m*; (*skill, job*) métier *m* ♦ *vi* faire du commerce; **to ~ with/in** faire du commerce avec/le commerce de; **foreign ~** commerce extérieur; **Department of T~ and Industry (DTI)** (*Brit*) ministère *m* du Commerce et de l'Industrie.

trade in *vt* (*old car etc*) faire reprendre.

trade barrier *n* barrière commerciale.

trade deficit *n* déficit extérieur.

Trade Descriptions Act *n* (*Brit*) *loi contre les appellations et la publicité mensongères.*

trade discount *n* remise *f* au détaillant.

trade fair *n* foire(-exposition) commerciale.

trade-in ['treɪdɪn] *n* reprise *f*.

trade-in price *n* prix *m* à la reprise.

trademark ['treɪdmɑ:k] *n* marque *f* de fabrique.

trade mission *n* mission commerciale.

trade name *n* marque déposée.

trader ['treɪdə*] *n* commerçant/e, négociant/e.

trade secret *n* secret *m* de fabrication.

tradesman ['treɪdzmən] *n* (*shopkeeper*) commerçant.

trade union *n* syndicat *m*.

trade unionist [-'ju:njənɪst] *n* syndicaliste *m/f*.

trade wind *n* alizé *m*.

trading ['treɪdɪŋ] *n* affaires *fpl*, commerce *m*.

trading estate *n* (*Brit*) zone industrielle.

trading stamp *n* timbre-prime *m*.

tradition [trə'dɪʃən] *n* tradition *f*; ~**s** *npl*

coutumes *fpl*, traditions.
traditional [trə'dɪʃənl] *a* traditionnel(le).
traffic ['træfɪk] *n* trafic *m*; (*cars*) circulation *f* ♦ *vi*: **to ~ in** (*pej: liquor, drugs*) faire le trafic de.
traffic circle *n* (*US*) rond-point *m*.
traffic island *n* refuge *m* (pour piétons).
traffic jam *n* embouteillage *m*.
trafficker ['træfɪkə*] *n* trafiquant/e.
traffic lights *npl* feux *mpl* (de signalisation).
traffic offence *n* (*Brit*) infraction *f* au code de la route.
traffic sign *n* panneau *m* de signalisation.
traffic violation *n* (*US*) = **traffic offence**.
traffic warden *n* contractuel/le.
tragedy ['trædʒədɪ] *n* tragédie *f*.
tragic ['trædʒɪk] *a* tragique.
trail [treɪl] *n* (*tracks*) trace *f*, piste *f*; (*path*) chemin *m*, piste; (*of smoke etc*) traînée *f* ♦ *vt* traîner, tirer; (*follow*) suivre ♦ *vi* traîner; **to be on sb's ~** être sur la piste de qn.
 trail away, trail off *vi* (*sound, voice*) s'évanouir; (*interest*) disparaître.
 trail behind *vi* traîner, être à la traîne.
trailer ['treɪlə*] *n* (*AUT*) remorque *f*; (*US*) caravane *f*; (*CINEMA*) bande-annonce *f*.
trailer truck *n* (*US*) (camion *m*) semi-remorque *m*.
train [treɪn] *n* train *m*; (*in underground*) rame *f*; (*of dress*) traîne *f*; (*Brit: series*): **~ of events** série *f* d'événements ♦ *vt* (*apprentice, doctor etc*) former; (*sportsman*) entraîner; (*dog*) dresser; (*memory*) exercer; (*point: gun etc*): **to ~ sth on** braquer qch sur ♦ *vi* recevoir sa formation; s'entraîner; **one's ~ of thought** le fil de sa pensée; **to go by ~** voyager par le train *or* en train; **to ~ sb to do sth** apprendre à qn à faire qch; (*employee*) former qn à faire qch.
train attendant *n* (*US*) employé/e des wagons-lits.
trained [treɪnd] *a* qualifié(e), qui a reçu une formation; dressé(e).
trainee [treɪ'ni:] *n* stagiaire *m/f*; (*in trade*) apprenti/e.
trainer ['treɪnə*] *n* (*SPORT*) entraîneur/euse; (*of dogs etc*) dresseur/euse; **~s** *npl* (*shoes*) chaussures *fpl* de sport.
training ['treɪnɪŋ] *n* formation *f*; entraînement *m*; dressage *m*; **in ~** (*SPORT*) à l'entraînement; (*fit*) en forme.
training college *n* école professionnelle; (*for teachers*) ≈ école normale.
training course *n* cours *m* de formation professionnelle.
training shoes *npl* chaussures *fpl* de sport.
traipse [treɪps] *vi* (se) traîner, déambuler.
trait [treɪt] *n* trait *m* (de caractère).
traitor ['treɪtə*] *n* traître *m*.
trajectory [trə'dʒɛktərɪ] *n* trajectoire *f*.
tram [træm] *n* (*Brit: also:* **~car**) tram(way) *m*.
tramline ['træmlaɪn] *n* ligne *f* de tram(way).
tramp [træmp] *n* (*person*) vagabond/e, clochard/e; (*col: pej: woman*): **to be a ~** être coureuse ♦ *vi* marcher d'un pas lourd ♦ *vt* (*walk through: town, streets*) parcourir à pied.
trample ['træmpl] *vt*: **to ~** (**underfoot**)

piétiner; (*fig*) bafouer.
trampoline ['træmpəliːn] *n* trampolino *m*.
trance [trɑːns] *n* transe *f*; (*MED*) catalepsie *f*; **to go into a ~** entrer en transe.
tranquil ['træŋkwɪl] *a* tranquille.
tranquillity [træŋ'kwɪlɪtɪ] *n* tranquillité *f*.
tranquillizer ['træŋkwɪlaɪzə*] *n* (*MED*) tranquillisant *m*.
transact [træn'zækt] *vt* (*business*) traiter.
transaction [træn'zækʃən] *n* transaction *f*; **~s** *npl* (*minutes*) actes *mpl*; **cash ~** transaction au comptant.
transatlantic ['trænzət'læntɪk] *a* transatlantique.
transcend [træn'sɛnd] *vt* transcender; (*excel over*) surpasser.
transcendental [trænsɛn'dɛntl] *a*: **~ meditation** méditation transcendantale.
transcribe [træn'skraɪb] *vt* transcrire.
transcript ['trænskrɪpt] *n* transcription *f* (*texte*).
transcription [træn'skrɪpʃən] *n* transcription *f*.
transept ['trænsɛpt] *n* transept *m*.
transfer *n* ['trænsfə*] (*gen, also SPORT*) transfert *m*; (*POL: of power*) passation *f*; (*of money*) virement *m*; (*picture, design*) décalcomanie *f*; (*: stick-on*) autocollant *m* ♦ *vt* [træns'fə:*] transférer; passer; virer; décalquer; **to ~ the charges** (*Brit TEL*) téléphoner en P.C.V.; **by bank ~** par virement bancaire.
transferable [træns'fɜːrəbl] *a* transmissible, transférable; **"not ~"** "personnel".
transfix [træns'fɪks] *vt* transpercer; (*fig*): **~ed with fear** paralysé(e) par la peur.
transform [træns'fɔːm] *vt* transformer.
transformation [trænsfə'meɪʃən] *n* transformation *f*.
transformer [træns'fɔːmə*] *n* (*ELEC*) transformateur *m*.
transfusion [træns'fjuːʒən] *n* transfusion *f*.
transgress [træns'grɛs] *vt* transgresser.
transient ['trænzɪənt] *a* transitoire, éphémère.
transistor [træn'zɪstə*] *n* (*ELEC*; *also*: **~ radio**) transistor *m*.
transit ['trænzɪt] *n*: **in ~** en transit.
transit camp *n* camp *m* de transit.
transition [træn'zɪʃən] *n* transition *f*.
transitional [træn'zɪʃənl] *a* transitoire.
transitive ['trænzɪtɪv] *a* (*LING*) transitif(ive).
transit lounge *n* (*AVIAT*) salle *f* de transit.
transitory ['trænzɪtərɪ] *a* transitoire.
translate [trænz'leɪt] *vt*: **to ~ (from/into)** traduire (du/en).
translation [trænz'leɪʃən] *n* traduction *f*; (*SCOL: as opposed to prose*) version *f*.
translator [trænz'leɪtə*] *n* traducteur/trice.
translucent [trænz'luːsnt] *a* translucide.
transmission [trænz'mɪʃən] *n* transmission *f*.
transmit [trænz'mɪt] *vt* transmettre; (*RADIO, TV*) émettre.
transmitter [trænz'mɪtə*] *n* émetteur *m*.
transparency [træns'pɛərnsɪ] *n* (*Brit PHOT*) diapositive *f*.
transparent [træns'pærnt] *a* transparent(e).
transpire [træns'paɪə*] *vi* (*become known*): **it finally ~d that** ... on a finalement appris que ...; (*happen*) arriver.
transplant *vt* [træns'plɑːnt] transplanter;

(*seedlings*) repiquer ♦ *n* ['trænspɑːnt] (*MED*) transplantation *f*; **to have a heart** ~ subir une greffe du cœur.

transport *n* ['trænspɔːt] transport *m* ♦ *vt* [træns'pɔːt] transporter; **public** ~ transports en commun; **Department of T~** (*Brit*) ministère *m* des Transports.

transportation ['trænspɔː'teɪʃən] *n* (moyen *m* de) transport *m*; (*of prisoners*) transportation *f*; **Department of T~** (*US*) ministère *m* des Transports.

transport café *n* (*Brit*) ≈ restaurant *m* de routiers.

transpose [træns'pəuz] *vt* transposer.

transship [træns'ʃɪp] *vt* transborder.

transverse ['trænzvɜːs] *a* transversal(e).

transvestite [trænz'vɛstaɪt] *n* travesti.e.

trap [træp] *n* (*snare*, *trick*) piège *m*; (*carriage*) cabriolet *m* ♦ *vt* prendre au piège; (*immobilize*) bloquer; (*jam*) coincer; **to set** *or* **lay a** ~ (**for sb**) tendre un piège (à qn); **to shut one's** ~ (*col*) la fermer.

trap door *n* trappe *f*.

trapeze [trə'piːz] *n* trapèze *m*.

trapper ['træpə*] *n* trappeur *m*.

trappings ['træpɪŋz] *npl* ornements *mpl*; attributs *mpl*.

trash [træʃ] *n* (*pej*: *goods*) camelote *f*; (: *nonsense*) sottises *fpl*; (*US*: *rubbish*) ordures *fpl*.

trash can *n* (*US*) boîte *f* à ordures.

trauma ['trɔːmə] *n* traumatisme *m*.

traumatic [trɔː'mætɪk] *a* traumatisant(e).

travel ['trævl] *n* voyage(s) *m(pl)* ♦ *vi* voyager; (*move*) aller, se déplacer ♦ *vt* (*distance*) parcourir; **this wine doesn't** ~ **well** ce vin voyage mal.

travel agency *n* agence *f* de voyages.

travel agent *n* agent *m* de voyages.

travel brochure *n* brochure *f* touristique.

traveller, (*US*) **traveler** ['trævlə*] *n* voyageur/euse; (*COMM*) représentant *m* de commerce.

traveller's cheque, (*US*) **traveler's check** *n* chèque *m* de voyage.

travelling, (*US*) **traveling** ['trævlɪŋ] *n* voyage(s) *m(pl)* ♦ *a* (*circus*, *exhibition*) ambulant(e) ♦ *cpd* (*bag*, *clock*) de voyage; (*expenses*) de déplacement.

travel(l)ing salesman *n* voyageur *m* de commerce.

travelogue ['trævəlɔg] *n* (*book*, *talk*) récit *m* de voyage; (*film*) documentaire *m* de voyage.

travel sickness *n* mal *m* de la route (*or* de mer *or* de l'air).

traverse ['trævəs] *vt* traverser.

travesty ['trævəstɪ] *n* parodie *f*.

trawler ['trɔːlə*] *n* chalutier *m*.

tray [treɪ] *n* (*for carrying*) plateau *m*; (*on desk*) corbeille *f*.

treacherous ['trɛtʃərəs] *a* traître(sse); **road conditions are** ~ l'état des routes est dangereux.

treachery ['trɛtʃərɪ] *n* traîtrise *f*.

treacle ['triːkl] *n* mélasse *f*.

tread [trɛd] *n* pas *m*; (*sound*) bruit *m* de pas; (*of tyre*) chape *f*, bande *f* de roulement ♦ *vi* (*pt* **trod**, *pp* **trodden** [trɔd, 'trɔdn]) marcher.

tread on *vt fus* marcher sur.

treadle ['trɛdl] *n* pédale *f* (*de machine*).

treas. *abbr* = **treasurer**.

treason ['triːzn] *n* trahison *f*.

treasure ['trɛʒə*] *n* trésor *m* ♦ *vt* (*value*) tenir beaucoup à; (*store*) conserver précieusement.

treasure hunt *n* chasse *f* au trésor.

treasurer ['trɛʒərə*] *n* trésorier/ière.

treasury ['trɛʒərɪ] *n* trésorerie *f*; **the T~**, (*US*) **the T~ Department** ≈ le ministère des Finances.

treasury bill *n* bon *m* du Trésor.

treat [triːt] *n* petit cadeau, petite surprise ♦ *vt* traiter; **it was a** ~ ça m'a (*or* nous a *etc*) vraiment fait plaisir; **to** ~ **sb to sth** offrir qch à qn; **to** ~ **sth as a joke** prendre qch à la plaisanterie.

treatise ['triːtɪz] *n* traité *m* (*ouvrage*).

treatment ['triːtmənt] *n* traitement *m*; **to have** ~ **for sth** (*MED*) suivre un traitement pour qch.

treaty ['triːtɪ] *n* traité *m*.

treble ['trɛbl] *a* triple ♦ *n* (*MUS*) soprano *m* ♦ *vt*, *vi* tripler.

treble clef *n* clé *f* de sol.

tree [triː] *n* arbre *m*.

tree-lined ['triːlaɪnd] *a* bordé(e) d'arbres.

treetop ['triːtɔp] *n* cime *f* d'un arbre.

tree trunk *n* tronc *m* d'arbre.

trek [trɛk] *n* voyage *m*; randonnée *f*; (*tiring walk*) tirée *f* ♦ *vi* (*as holiday*) faire de la randonnée.

trellis ['trɛlɪs] *n* treillis *m*, treillage *m*.

tremble ['trɛmbl] *vi* trembler.

trembling ['trɛmblɪŋ] *n* tremblement *m* ♦ *a* tremblant(e).

tremendous [trɪ'mɛndəs] *a* énorme, formidable; (*excellent*) fantastique, formidable.

tremendously [trɪ'mɛndəslɪ] *ad* énormément, extrêmement + *adjective*; formidablement.

tremor ['trɛmə*] *n* tremblement *m*; (*also*: **earth** ~) secousse *f* sismique.

trench [trɛntʃ] *n* tranchée *f*.

trench coat *n* trench-coat *m*.

trench warfare *n* guerre *f* de tranchées.

trend [trend] *n* (*tendency*) tendance *f*; (*of events*) cours *m*; (*fashion*) mode *f*; ~ **towards/away from doing** tendance à faire/à ne pas faire; **to set the** ~ donner le ton; **to set a** ~ lancer une mode.

trendy ['trendɪ] *a* (*idea*) dans le vent; (*clothes*) dernier cri *inv*.

trepidation [trɛpɪ'deɪʃən] *n* vive agitation.

trespass ['trespəs] *vi*: **to** ~ **on** s'introduire sans permission dans; (*fig*) empiéter sur; **"no ~ing"** "propriété privée", "défense d'entrer".

trespasser ['trespəsə*] *n* intrus/e; **"~s will be prosecuted"** "interdiction d'entrer sous peine de poursuites".

tress [tres] *n* boucle *f* de cheveux.

trestle ['tresl] *n* tréteau *m*.

trestle table *n* table *f* à tréteaux.

trial ['traɪəl] *n* (*LAW*) procès *m*, jugement *m*; (*test: of machine etc*) essai *m*; (*hardship*) épreuve *f*; (*worry*) souci *m*; ~**s** *npl* (*SPORT*) épreuves éliminatoires; **horse** ~**s** concours *m* hippique; ~ **by jury** jugement par jury; **to be sent for** ~ être traduit(e) en justice; **to be on** ~ passer en jugement; **by** ~ **and error** par tâtonnements.

trial balance n (COMM) balance f de vérification.

trial basis n: **on a ~** pour une période d'essai.

trial run n essai m.

triangle ['traɪæŋgl] n (MATH, MUS) triangle m.

triangular [traɪ'æŋgjulə*] a triangulaire.

tribal ['traɪbl] a tribal(e).

tribe [traɪb] n tribu f.

tribesman ['traɪbzmən] n membre m de la tribu.

tribulation [trɪbju'leɪʃən] n tribulation f, malheur m.

tribunal [traɪ'bju:nl] n tribunal m.

tributary ['trɪbjutərɪ] n (river) affluent m.

tribute ['trɪbju:t] n tribut m, hommage m; **to pay ~ to** rendre hommage à.

trice [traɪs] n: **in a ~** en un clin d'œil.

trick [trɪk] n ruse f; (clever act) astuce f; (joke) tour m; (CARDS) levée f ♦ vt attraper, rouler; **to play a ~ on sb** jouer un tour à qn; **to ~ sb into doing sth** persuader qn par la ruse de faire qch; **to ~ sb out of sth** obtenir qch de qn par la ruse; **it's a ~ of the light** c'est une illusion d'optique causée par la lumière; **that should do the ~** (col) ça devrait faire l'affaire.

trickery ['trɪkərɪ] n ruse f.

trickle ['trɪkl] n (of water etc) filet m ♦ vi couler en un filet or goutte à goutte; **to ~ in/out** (people) entrer/sortir par petits groupes.

trick question n question-piège f.

trickster ['trɪkstə*] n arnaqueur/euse, filou m.

tricky ['trɪkɪ] a difficile, délicat(e).

tricycle ['traɪsɪkl] n tricycle m.

trifle ['traɪfl] n bagatelle f; (CULIN) ≈ diplomate m ♦ ad: **a ~ long** un peu long ♦ vi: **to ~ with** traiter à la légère.

trifling ['traɪflɪŋ] a insignifiant(e).

trigger ['trɪgə*] n (of gun) gâchette f.
     trigger off vt déclencher.

trigonometry [trɪgə'nɔmətrɪ] n trigonométrie f.

trilby ['trɪlbɪ] n (Brit: also: **~ hat**) chapeau mou, feutre m.

trill [trɪl] n (of bird, MUS) trille m.

trilogy ['trɪlədʒɪ] n trilogie f.

trim [trɪm] a net(te); (house, garden) bien tenu(e); (figure) svelte ♦ n (haircut etc) légère coupe; (embellishment) finitions fpl; (on car) garnitures fpl ♦ vt couper légèrement; (decorate): **to ~ (with)** décorer (de); (NAUT: a sail) gréer; **to keep in (good) ~** maintenir en (bon) état.

trimmings ['trɪmɪŋz] npl décorations fpl; (extras: gen CULIN) garniture f.

Trinidad and Tobago ['trɪnɪdæd-] n Trinité et Tobago f.

Trinity ['trɪnɪtɪ] n: **the ~** la Trinité.

trinket ['trɪŋkɪt] n bibelot m; (piece of jewellery) colifichet m.

trio ['tri:əu] n trio m.

trip [trɪp] n voyage m; (excursion) excursion f; (stumble) faux pas ♦ vi faire un faux pas, trébucher; (go lightly) marcher d'un pas léger; **on a ~** en voyage.
     trip up vi trébucher ♦ vt faire un croc-en-jambe à.

tripartite [traɪ'pɑːtaɪt] a triparti(e).

tripe [traɪp] n (CULIN) tripes fpl; (pej: rubbish) idioties fpl.

triple ['trɪpl] a triple ♦ ad: **~ the distance/the speed** trois fois la distance/la vitesse.

triplets ['trɪplɪts] npl triplés/ées.

triplicate ['trɪplɪkət] n: **in ~** en trois exemplaires.

tripod ['traɪpɔd] n trépied m.

Tripoli ['trɪpəlɪ] n Tripoli.

tripper ['trɪpə*] n (Brit) touriste m/f; excursionniste m/f.

tripwire ['trɪpwaɪə*] n fil m de déclenchement.

trite [traɪt] a banal(e).

triumph ['traɪʌmf] n triomphe m ♦ vi: **to ~ (over)** triompher (de).

triumphal [traɪ'ʌmfl] a triomphal(e).

triumphant [traɪ'ʌmfənt] a triomphant(e).

trivia ['trɪvɪə] npl futilités fpl.

trivial ['trɪvɪəl] a insignifiant(e); (commonplace) banal(e).

triviality [trɪvɪ'ælɪtɪ] n caractère insignifiant; banalité f.

trivialize ['trɪvɪəlaɪz] vt rendre banal(e).

trod [trɔd] pt of **tread**.

trodden [trɔdn] pp of **tread**.

trolley ['trɔlɪ] n chariot m.

trolley bus n trolleybus m.

trollop ['trɔləp] n prostituée f.

trombone [trɔm'bəun] n trombone m.

troop [tru:p] n bande f, groupe m ♦ vi: **to ~ in/out** entrer/sortir en groupe; **~ing the colour** (Brit: ceremony) le salut au drapeau.

troop carrier n (plane) avion m de transport de troupes; (NAUT: also: **troopship**) transport m (navire).

trooper ['tru:pə*] n (MIL) soldat m de cavalerie; (US: policeman) ≈ gendarme m.

troops [tru:ps] npl (MIL) troupes fpl; (: men) hommes mpl, soldats mpl.

troopship ['tru:pʃɪp] n transport m (navire).

trophy ['trəufɪ] n trophée m.

tropic ['trɔpɪk] n tropique m; **in the ~s** sous les tropiques; **T~ of Cancer/Capricorn** tropique du Cancer/Capricorne.

tropical ['trɔpɪkl] a tropical(e).

trot [trɔt] n trot m ♦ vi trotter; **on the ~** (Brit: fig) d'affilée.
     trot out vt (excuse, reason) débiter; (names, facts) réciter les uns après les autres.

trouble ['trʌbl] n difficulté(s) f(pl), problème(s) m(pl); (worry) ennuis mpl, soucis mpl; (bother, effort) peine f; (POL) conflit(s) m(pl), troubles mpl; (MED): **stomach etc ~** troubles gastriques etc ♦ vt déranger, gêner; (worry) inquiéter ♦ vi: **to ~ to do** prendre la peine de faire; **~s** npl (POL etc) troubles mpl; **to be in ~** avoir des ennuis; (ship, climber etc) être en difficulté; **to have ~ doing sth** avoir du mal à faire qch; **to go to the ~ of doing** se donner le mal de faire; **it's no ~!** je vous en prie!; **please don't ~ yourself** je vous en prie, ne vous dérangez pas!; **the ~ is ...** le problème, c'est que ...; **what's the ~?** qu'est-ce qui ne va pas?

troubled ['trʌbld] a (person) inquiet(ète); (epoch, life) agité(e).

trouble-free ['trʌblfri:] a sans problèmes or

ennuis.

troublemaker ['trʌblmeɪkəʳ] *n* élément perturbateur, fauteur *m* de troubles.

troubleshooter ['trʌblʃuːtəʳ] *n* (*in conflict*) conciliateur *m*.

troublesome ['trʌblsəm] *a* ennuyeux(euse), gênant(e).

trouble spot *n* point chaud (*fig*).

trough [trɔf] *n* (*also:* **drinking ~**) abreuvoir *m*; (*also:* **feeding ~**) auge *f*; (*channel*) chenal *m*; **~ of low pressure** (*METEOROLOGY*) dépression *f*.

trounce [trauns] *vt* (*defeat*) battre à plates coutures.

troupe [truːp] *n* troupe *f*.

trouser press *n* presse-pantalon *m inv*.

trousers ['trauzəz] *npl* pantalon *m*; **short ~** (*Brit*) culottes courtes.

trouser suit *n* (*Brit*) tailleur-pantalon *m*.

trousseau, *pl* **~x** *or* **~s** ['truːsəu, -z] *n* trousseau *m*.

trout [traut] *n* (*pl inv*) truite *f*.

trowel ['trauəl] *n* truelle *f*.

truant ['truːənt] *n*: **to play ~** (*Brit*) faire l'école buissonnière.

truce [truːs] *n* trêve *f*.

truck [trʌk] *n* camion *m*; (*RAIL*) wagon *m* à plate-forme; (*for luggage*) chariot *m* (à bagages).

truck driver *n* camionneur *m*.

trucker ['trʌkəʳ] *n* (*esp US*) camionneur *m*.

truck farm *n* (*US*) jardin maraîcher.

trucking ['trʌkɪŋ] *n* (*esp US*) transport routier.

trucking company *n* (*US*) entreprise *f* de transport (routier).

truculent ['trʌkjulənt] *a* agressif(ive).

trudge [trʌdʒ] *vi* marcher lourdement, se traîner.

true [truː] *a* vrai(e); (*accurate*) exact(e); (*genuine*) vrai, véritable; (*faithful*) fidèle; (*wall*) d'aplomb; (*beam*) droit(e); (*wheel*) dans l'axe; **to come ~** se réaliser; **~ to life** réaliste.

truffle ['trʌfl] *n* truffe *f*.

truly ['truːlɪ] *ad* vraiment, réellement; (*truthfully*) sans mentir; (*faithfully*) fidèlement; **yours ~** (*in letter*) je vous prie d'agréer, Monsieur (*or* Madame *etc*), l'expression de mes sentiments respectueux.

trump [trʌmp] *n* atout *m*; **to turn up ~s** (*fig*) faire des miracles.

trump card *n* atout rɪ; (*fig*) carte maîtresse *f*.

trumped-up [trʌmpt'ʌp] *a* inventé(e) (de toutes pièces).

trumpet ['trʌmpɪt] *n* trompette *f*.

truncated [trʌŋ'keɪtɪd] *a* tronqué(e).

truncheon ['trʌntʃən] *n* bâton *m* (d'agent de police); matraque *f*.

trundle ['trʌndl] *vt, vi*: **to ~ along** rouler bruyamment.

trunk [trʌŋk] *n* (*of tree, person*) tronc *m*; (*of elephant*) trompe *f*; (*case*) malle *f*; (*US AUT*) coffre *m*.

trunk call *n* (*Brit TEL*) communication interurbaine.

trunk road *n* (*Brit*) ≈ (route) nationale.

trunks [trʌŋks] *npl* (*also:* **swimming ~**) maillot *m or* slip *m* de bain.

truss [trʌs] *n* (*MED*) bandage *m* herniaire ♦ *vt:* **to ~ (up)** (*CULIN*) brider.

trust [trʌst] *n* confiance *f*; (*LAW*) fidéicommis *m*; (*COMM*) trust *m* ♦ *vt* (*rely on*) avoir confiance en; (*entrust*): **to ~ sth to sb** confier qch à qn; (*hope*): **to ~ (that)** espérer (que); **to take sth on ~** accepter qch sans garanties (*or* sans preuves); **in ~** (*LAW*) par fidéicommis.

trust company *n* société *f* fiduciaire.

trusted ['trʌstɪd] *a* en qui l'on a confiance.

trustee [trʌs'tiː] *n* (*LAW*) fidéicommissaire *m/f*; (*of school etc*) administrateur/trice.

trustful ['trʌstful] *a* confiant(e).

trust fund *n* fonds *m* en fidéicommis.

trusting ['trʌstɪŋ] *a* confiant(e).

trustworthy ['trʌstwəːðɪ] *a* digne de confiance.

trusty ['trʌstɪ] *a* fidèle.

truth, **~s** [truːθ, truːðz] *n* vérité *f*.

truthful ['truːθful] *a* (*person*) qui dit la vérité; (*description*) exact(e), vrai(e).

truthfully ['truːθfəlɪ] *ad* sincèrement, sans mentir.

truthfulness ['truːθfəlnɪs] *n* véracité *f*.

try [traɪ] *n* essai *m*, tentative *f*; (*RUGBY*) essai ♦ *vt* (*LAW*) juger; (*test: sth new*) essayer, tester; (*strain*) éprouver ♦ *vi* essayer; **to ~ to do** essayer de faire; (*seek*) chercher à faire; **to ~ one's (very) best** *or* **one's (very) hardest** faire de son mieux; **to give sth a ~** essayer qch.

try on *vt* (*clothes*) essayer; **to ~ it on** (*fig*) tenter le coup, bluffer.

try out *vt* essayer, mettre à l'essai.

trying ['traɪɪŋ] *a* pénible.

tsar [zɑːʳ] *n* tsar *m*.

T-shirt ['tiːʃəːt] *n* tee-shirt *m*.

T-square ['tiːskwɛəʳ] *n* équerre *f* en T.

TT *a abbr* (*Brit col*) = **teetotal** ♦ *abbr* (*US POST*) = *Trust Territory*.

tub [tʌb] *n* cuve *f*; baquet *m*; (*bath*) baignoire *f*.

tuba ['tjuːbə] *n* tuba *m*.

tubby ['tʌbɪ] *a* rondelet(te).

tube [tjuːb] *n* tube *m*; (*Brit: underground*) métro *m*; (*for tyre*) chambre *f* à air; (*col: television*): **the ~** la télé.

tubeless ['tjuːblɪs] *a* (*tyre*) sans chambre à air.

tuber ['tjuːbəʳ] *n* (*BOT*) tubercule *m*.

tuberculosis [tjubɜːkju'ləusɪs] *n* tuberculose *f*.

tube station *n* (*Brit*) station *f* de métro.

tubing ['tjuːbɪŋ] *n* tubes *mpl*; **a piece of ~** un tube.

tubular ['tjuːbjuləʳ] *a* tubulaire.

TUC *n abbr* (*Brit*: = *Trades Union Congress*) confédération *f* des syndicats britanniques.

tuck [tʌk] *n* (*SEWING*) pli *m*, rempli *m* ♦ *vt* (*put*) mettre.

tuck away *vt* cacher, ranger.

tuck in *vt* rentrer; (*child*) border ♦ *vi* (*eat*) manger de bon appétit; attaquer le repas.

tuck up *vt* (*child*) border.

tuck shop *n* boutique *f* à provisions (*dans une école*).

Tue(s). *abbr* (= *Tuesday*) ma.

Tuesday ['tjuːzdɪ] *n* mardi *m*; **(the date) today is ~ 23rd March** nous sommes aujourd'hui le mardi 23 mars; **on ~** mardi; **on ~s** le mardi; **every ~** tous les mardis, chaque mardi; **every other ~** un mardi sur deux; **last/next ~** mardi dernier/prochain; **~ next** mardi qui vient; **the following ~** le mardi suivant; **a week/fortnight on ~, ~ week/fortnight** dans huit/quinze; **the ~ before last** l'autre mardi; **the ~ after next** mardi en huit; **~ morning/lunchtime/ afternoon/ evening** mardi matin/midi/après-midi/soir; **~ night** mardi soir; (*overnight*) la nuit de mardi (à mercredi); **~'s newspaper** le journal de mardi.

tuft [tʌft] n touffe f.

tug [tʌg] n (*ship*) remorqueur m ♦ vt tirer (sur).

tug-of-war [tʌgəv'wɔː*] n lutte f à la corde.

tuition [tjuː'ɪʃən] n (*Brit*: *lessons*) leçons fpl; (*US*: *fees*) frais mpl de scolarité.

tulip ['tjuːlɪp] n tulipe f.

tumble ['tʌmbl] n (*fall*) chute f, culbute f ♦ vi tomber, dégringoler; (*somersault*) faire une or des culbute(s) ♦ vt renverser, faire tomber; **to ~ to sth** (*col*) réaliser qch.

tumbledown ['tʌmbldaun] a délabré(e).

tumble dryer n (*Brit*) séchoir m (à linge) à air chaud.

tumbler ['tʌmblə*] n verre (droit), gobelet m.

tummy ['tʌmɪ] n (*col*) ventre m.

tumour, (*US*) **tumor** ['tjuːmə*] n tumeur f.

tumult ['tjuːmʌlt] n tumulte m.

tumultuous [tjuː'mʌltjuəs] a tumultueux(euse).

tuna ['tjuːnə] n (*pl inv*) (*also*: **~ fish**) thon m.

tune [tjuːn] n (*melody*) air m ♦ vt (*MUS*) accorder; (*RADIO, TV, AUT*) régler, mettre au point; **to be in/out of ~** (*instrument*) être accordé/désaccordé; (*singer*) chanter juste/faux; **to be in/out of ~ with** (*fig*) être en accord/désaccord avec; **she was robbed to the ~ of £10,000** (*fig*) on lui a volé la jolie somme de 10 000 livres.

tune in vi (*RADIO, TV*): **to ~ in (to)** se mettre à l'écoute (de).

tune up vi (*musician*) accorder son instrument.

tuneful ['tjuːnful] a mélodieux(euse).

tuner ['tjuːnə*] n (*radio set*) radio-préamplificateur m; **piano ~** accordeur m de pianos.

tuner amplifier n radio-ampli m.

tungsten ['tʌŋstn] n tungstène m.

tunic ['tjuːnɪk] n tunique f.

tuning ['tjuːnɪŋ] n réglage m.

tuning fork n diapason m.

Tunis ['tjuːnɪs] n Tunis.

Tunisia [tjuː'nɪzɪə] n Tunisie f.

Tunisian [tjuː'nɪzɪən] a tunisien(ne) ♦ n Tunisien/ne.

tunnel ['tʌnl] n tunnel m; (*in mine*) galerie f ♦ vi creuser un tunnel (or une galerie).

tunny ['tʌnɪ] n thon m.

turban ['təːbən] n turban m.

turbid ['təːbɪd] a boueux(euse).

turbine ['təːbaɪn] n turbine f.

turbojet [təːbəu'dʒɛt] n turboréacteur m.

turboprop [təːbəu'prɔp] n (*engine*) turbopropulseur m.

turbot ['təːbət] n (*pl inv*) turbot m.

turbulence ['təːbjuləns] n (*AVIAT*) turbulence f.

turbulent ['təːbjulənt] a turbulent(e); (*sea*) agité(e).

tureen [tə'riːn] n soupière f.

turf [təːf] n gazon m; (*clod*) motte f (de gazon) ♦ vt gazonner; **the T~** le turf, les courses fpl.

turf out vt (*col*) jeter; jeter dehors.

turf accountant n (*Brit*) bookmaker m.

turgid ['təːdʒɪd] a (*speech*) pompeux(euse).

Turin ['tjuərɪn] n Turin.

Turk [təːk] n Turc/Turque.

Turkey ['təːkɪ] n Turquie f.

turkey ['təːkɪ] n dindon m, dinde f.

Turkish ['təːkɪʃ] a turc(turque) ♦ n (*LING*) turc m.

Turkish bath n bain turc.

Turkish delight n loukoum m.

turmeric ['təːmərɪk] n curcuma m.

turmoil ['təːmɔɪl] n trouble m, bouleversement m.

turn [təːn] n tour m; (*in road*) tournant m; (*tendency: of mind, events*) tournure f; (*performance*) numéro m; (*MED*) crise f, attaque f ♦ vt (*collar, steak*) retourner; (*milk*) faire tourner; (*change*): **to ~ sth into** changer qch en; (*shape: wood, metal*) tourner ♦ vi tourner; (*person: look back*) se (re)tourner; (*reverse direction*) faire demi-tour; (*change*) changer; (*become*) devenir; **to ~ into** se changer en, se transformer en; **a good ~** un service; **a bad ~** un mauvais tour; **it gave me quite a ~** ça m'a fait un coup; **"no left ~"** (*AUT*) "défense de tourner à gauche"; **it's your ~** c'est (à) votre tour; **in ~** à son tour; à tour de rôle; **to take ~s** se relayer; **to take ~s at** faire à tour de rôle; **at the ~ of the year/ century** à la fin de l'année/du siècle; **to take a ~ for the worse** (*situation, events*) empirer; **his health** or **he has taken a ~ for the worse** son état s'est aggravé.

turn about vi faire demi-tour; faire un demi-tour.

turn away vi se détourner, tourner la tête ♦ vt (*reject: person*) renvoyer; (*: business*) refuser.

turn back vi revenir, faire demi-tour.

turn down vt (*refuse*) rejeter, refuser; (*reduce*) baisser; (*fold*) rabattre.

turn in vi (*col: go to bed*) aller se coucher ♦ vt (*fold*) rentrer.

turn off vi (*from road*) tourner ♦ vt (*light, radio etc*) éteindre; (*engine*) arrêter.

turn on vt (*light, radio etc*) allumer; (*engine*) mettre en marche.

turn out vt (*light, gas*) éteindre; (*produce: goods, novel, good pupils*) produire ♦ vi (*appear, attend: troops, doctor etc*) être présent(e); **to ~ out to be ...** s'avérer ..., se révéler ....

turn over vi (*person*) se retourner ♦ vt (*object*) retourner; (*page*) tourner.

turn round vi faire demi-tour; (*rotate*) tourner.

turn up vi (*person*) arriver, se pointer; (*lost object*) être retrouvé(e) ♦ vt (*collar*) remonter; (*increase: sound, volume etc*) mettre plus fort.

turnabout ['tə:nəbaut], **turnaround** ['tə:nəraund] *n* volte-face *f inv*.

turncoat ['tə:nkəut] *n* rénégat/e.

turned-up ['tə:ndʌp] *a* (*nose*) retroussé(e).

turning ['tə:nɪŋ] *n* (*in road*) tournant *m*; **the first ~ on the right** la première (rue *or* route) à droite.

turning circle *n* (*Brit*) rayon *m* de braquage.

turning point *n* (*fig*) tournant *m*, moment décisif.

turning radius *n* (*US*) = **turning circle**.

turnip ['tə:nɪp] *n* navet *m*.

turnout ['tə:naut] *n* (nombre *m* de personnes dans l')assistance *f*.

turnover ['tə:nəuvə*] *n* (COMM: *amount of money*) chiffre *m* d'affaires; (: *of goods*) roulement *m*; (CULIN) sorte de chausson; **there is a rapid ~ in staff** le personnel change souvent.

turnpike ['tə:npaɪk] *n* (*US*) autoroute *f* à péage.

turnstile ['tə:nstaɪl] *n* tourniquet *m* (*d'entrée*).

turntable ['tə:nteɪbl] *n* (*on record player*) platine *f*.

turn-up ['tə:nʌp] *n* (*Brit*: *on trousers*) revers *m*.

turpentine ['tə:pəntaɪn] *n* (*also*: **turps**) (essence *f* de) térébenthine *f*.

turquoise ['tə:kwɔɪz] *n* (*stone*) turquoise *f* ♦ *a* turquoise *inv*.

turret ['tʌrɪt] *n* tourelle *f*.

turtle ['tə:tl] *n* tortue marine.

turtleneck (sweater) ['tə:tlnɛk-] *n* pullover *m* à col montant.

Tuscany ['tʌskənɪ] *n* Toscane *f*.

tusk [tʌsk] *n* défense *f* (*d'éléphant*).

tussle ['tʌsl] *n* bagarre *f*, mêlée *f*.

tutor ['tju:tə*] *n* (*Brit SCOL*) directeur/trice d'études; (*private teacher*) précepteur/trice.

tutorial [tju:'tɔ:rɪəl] *n* (SCOL) (séance *f* de) travaux *mpl* pratiques.

tuxedo [tʌk'si:dəu] *n* (*US*) smoking *m*.

TV [ti:'vi:] *n abbr* (= *television*) télé *f*, TV *f*.

twaddle ['twɔdl] *n* balivernes *fpl*.

twang [twæŋ] *n* (*of instrument*) son vibrant; (*of voice*) ton nasillard ♦ *vi* vibrer ♦ *vt* (*guitar*) pincer les cordes de.

tweak [twi:k] *vt* (*nose*) tordre; (*ear, hair*) tirer.

tweed [twi:d] *n* tweed *m*.

tweezers ['twi:zəz] *npl* pince *f* à épiler.

twelfth [twɛlfθ] *num* douzième.

Twelfth Night *n* la fête des Rois.

twelve [twɛlv] *num* douze; **at ~ (o'clock)** à midi; (*midnight*) à minuit.

twentieth ['twɛntɪɪθ] *num* vingtième.

twenty ['twɛntɪ] *num* vingt.

twerp [twə:p] *n* (*col*) imbécile *m/f*.

twice [twaɪs] *ad* deux fois; **~ as much** deux fois plus; **~ a week** deux fois par semaine; **she is ~ your age** elle a deux fois ton âge.

twiddle ['twɪdl] *vt, vi*: **to ~ (with)** sth tripoter qch; **to ~ one's thumbs** (*fig*) se tourner les pouces.

twig [twɪg] *n* brindille *f* ♦ *vt, vi* (*col*) piger.

twilight ['twaɪlaɪt] *n* crépuscule *m*; (*morning*) aube *f*; **in the ~** dans la pénombre.

twill [twɪl] *n* sergé *m*.

twin [twɪn] *a, n* jumeau(elle) ♦ *vt* jumeler.

twin(-bedded) room ['twɪn('bɛdɪd)-] *n* chambre *f* à deux lits.

twin beds *npl* lits *mpl* jumeaux.

twin-carburettor ['twɪnkɑ:bju'rɛtə*] *a* à double carburateur.

twine [twaɪn] *n* ficelle *f* ♦ *vi* (*plant*) s'enrouler.

twin-engined [twɪn'ɛndʒɪnd] *a* bimoteur; **~ aircraft** bimoteur *m*.

twinge [twɪndʒ] *n* (*of pain*) élancement *m*; (*of conscience*) remords *m*.

twinkle ['twɪŋkl] *n* scintillement *m*; pétillement *m* ♦ *vi* scintiller; (*eyes*) pétiller.

twin town *n* ville jumelée.

twirl [twə:l] *n* tournoiement *m* ♦ *vt* faire tournoyer ♦ *vi* tournoyer.

twist [twɪst] *n* torsion *f*, tour *m*; (*in wire, flex*) tortillon *m*; (*bend: in road*) tournant *m*; (*in story*) coup *m* de théâtre ♦ *vt* tordre; (*weave*) entortiller; (*roll around*) enrouler; (*fig*) déformer ♦ *vi* s'entortiller; s'enrouler; (*road*) serpenter; **to ~ one's ankle/wrist** (MED) se tordre la cheville/le poignet.

twisted ['twɪstɪd] *a* (*wire, rope*) entortillé(e); (*ankle, wrist*) tordu(e), foulé(e); (*fig: logic, mind*) tordu.

twit [twɪt] *n* (*col*) crétin/e.

twitch [twɪtʃ] *n* saccade *f*; (*nervous*) tic *m* ♦ *vi* se convulser; avoir un tic.

two [tu:] *num* deux; **~ by ~**, **in ~s** par deux; **to put ~ and ~ together** (*fig*) faire le rapport.

two-door [tu:'dɔ:*] *a* (AUT) à deux portes.

two-faced [tu:'feɪst] *a* (*pej: person*) faux(fausse).

twofold ['tu:fəuld] *ad*: **to increase ~** doubler ♦ *a* (*increase*) de cent pour cent; (*reply*) en deux parties.

two-piece ['tu:'pi:s] *n* (*also*: **~ suit**) (costume *m*) deux-pièces *m inv*; (*also*: **~ swimsuit**) (maillot *m* de bain) deux-pièces.

two-seater [tu:'si:tə*] *n* (*plane*) (avion *m*) bi-place *m*; (*car*) voiture *f* à deux places.

twosome ['tu:səm] *n* (*people*) couple *m*.

two-stroke ['tu:strəuk] *n* (*also*: **~ engine**) moteur *m* à deux temps ♦ *a* à deux temps.

two-tone ['tu:'təun] *a* (*in colour*) à deux tons.

two-way ['tu:weɪ] *a* (*traffic*) dans les deux sens; **~ radio** émetteur-récepteur *m*.

TX *abbr* (*US POST*) = **Texas**.

tycoon [taɪ'ku:n] *n*: **(business) ~** gros homme d'affaires.

type [taɪp] *n* (*category*) genre *m*, espèce *f*; (*model*) modèle *m*; (*example*) type *m*; (TYP) type, caractère *m* ♦ *vt* (*letter etc*) taper (à la machine); **what ~ do you want?** quel genre voulez-vous?; **in bold/italic ~** en caractères gras/en italiques.

typecast ['taɪpkɑ:st] *a* condamné(e) à toujours jouer le même rôle.

typeface ['taɪpfeɪs] *n* police *f* (de caractères).

typescript ['taɪpskrɪpt] *n* texte dactylographié.

typeset ['taɪpsɛt] *vt* composer (*en imprimerie*).

typesetter ['taɪpsɛtə*] *n* compositeur *m*.

typewriter ['taɪpraɪtə*] *n* machine *f* à écrire.

typewritten ['taɪprɪtn] *a* dactylographié(e).

typhoid ['taɪfɔɪd] *n* typhoïde *f*.

typhoon [taɪ'fu:n] *n* typhon *m*.

typhus ['taɪfəs] *n* typhus *m*.

typical ['tɪpɪkl] a typique, caractéristique.
typify ['tɪpɪfaɪ] vt être caractéristique de.
typing ['taɪpɪŋ] n dactylo(graphie) f.
typing error n faute f de frappe.
typing pool n pool m de dactylos.
typist ['taɪpɪst] n dactylo m/f.
typo ['taɪpəʊ] n abbr (col: = typographical error) coquille f.
typography [tɪ'pɒgrəfɪ] n typographie f.
tyranny ['tɪrənɪ] n tyrannie f.
tyrant ['taɪərnt] n tyran m.
tyre, (US) **tire** ['taɪə*] n pneu m.
tyre pressure n pression f (de gonflage).
Tyrol [tɪ'rəʊl] n Tyrol m.
Tyrolean [tɪrə'li:ən], **Tyrolese** [tɪrə'li:z] a tyrolien(ne) ♦ n Tyrolien/ne.
Tyrrhenian Sea [tɪ'ri:nɪən-] n: **the ~** la mer Tyrrhénienne.
tzar [zɑ:*] n = **tsar.**

U

U, u [ju:] n (letter) U, u m; **U for Uncle** U comme Ursule.
U n abbr (Brit CINEMA: = universal) ≈ tous publics.
UAW n abbr (US: = United Automobile Workers) syndicat des ouvriers de l'automobile.
UB40 n abbr (Brit: = unemployment benefit form 40) numéro de référence d'un formulaire d'inscription au chômage: par extension, le bénéficiaire.
U-bend ['ju:bɛnd] n (Brit AUT) coude m, virage m en épingle à cheveux; (in pipe) coude.
ubiquitous [ju:'bɪkwɪtəs] a doué(e) d'ubiquité, omniprésent(e).
UCCA ['ʌkə] n abbr (Brit) = Universities Central Council on Admissions.
UDA n abbr (Brit) = Ulster Defence Association.
UDC n abbr (Brit) = Urban District Council.
udder ['ʌdə*] n pis m, mamelle f.
UDI n abbr (Brit POL) = unilateral declaration of independence.
UDR n abbr (Brit) = Ulster Defence Regiment.
UEFA [ju:'eɪfə] n abbr (= Union of European Football Associations) UEFA f.
UFO ['ju:fəʊ] n abbr (= unidentified flying object) ovni m (= objet volant non identifié).
Uganda [ju:'gændə] n Ouganda m.
Ugandan [ju:'gændən] a ougandais(e) ♦ n Ougandais/e.
UGC n abbr (Brit: = University Grants Committee) commission d'attribution des dotations aux universités.
ugh [ə:h] excl pouah!
ugliness ['ʌglɪnɪs] n laideur f.
ugly ['ʌglɪ] a laid(e), vilain(e); (fig) répugnant(e).

UHF abbr (= ultra-high frequency) UHF.
UHT a abbr (= ultra-heat treated): **~ milk** n lait UHT or longue conservation.
UK n abbr = **United Kingdom.**
ulcer ['ʌlsə*] n ulcère m; **mouth ~** aphte f.
Ulster ['ʌlstə*] n Ulster m.
ulterior [ʌl'tɪərɪə*] a ultérieur(e); **~ motive** arrière-pensée f.
ultimate ['ʌltɪmət] a ultime, final(e); (authority) suprême ♦ n: **the ~ in luxury** le summum du luxe.
ultimately ['ʌltɪmətlɪ] ad (in the end) en fin de compte; (at last) finalement; (eventually) par la suite.
ultimatum, pl **~s** or **ultimata** [ʌltɪ'meɪtəm, -tə] n ultimatum m.
ultrasonic [ʌltrə'sɒnɪk] a ultrasonique.
ultrasound ['ʌltrəsaund] n (MED) ultrason m.
ultraviolet ['ʌltrə'vaɪəlɪt] a ultraviolet(te).
umbilical [ʌmbɪ'laɪkl] a: **~ cord** cordon ombilical.
umbrage ['ʌmbrɪdʒ] n: **to take ~** prendre ombrage, se froisser.
umbrella [ʌm'brɛlə] n parapluie m; (fig): **under the ~ of** sous les auspices de; chapeauté(e) par.
umpire ['ʌmpaɪə*] n arbitre m; (TENNIS) juge m de chaise ♦ vt arbitrer.
umpteen [ʌmp'ti:n] a je ne sais combien de; **for the ~th time** pour la nième fois.
UMW n abbr (= United Mineworkers of America) syndicat des mineurs.
UN n abbr = **United Nations.**
unabashed [ʌnə'bæʃt] a nullement intimidé(e).
unabated [ʌnə'beɪtɪd] a non diminué(e).
unable [ʌn'eɪbl] a: **to be ~ to** ne (pas) pouvoir, être dans l'impossibilité de; (not capable) être incapable de.
unabridged [ʌnə'brɪdʒd] a complet(ète), intégral(e).
unacceptable [ʌnək'sɛptəbl] a (behaviour) inadmissible; (price, proposal) inacceptable.
unaccompanied [ʌnə'kʌmpənɪd] a (child, lady) non accompagné(e); (singing, song) sans accompagnement.
unaccountably [ʌnə'kauntəblɪ] ad inexplicablement.
unaccounted [ʌnə'kauntɪd] a: **two passengers are ~ for** on est sans nouvelles de deux passagers.
unaccustomed [ʌnə'kʌstəmd] a inaccoutumé(e), inhabituel(le); **to be ~ to sth** ne pas avoir l'habitude de qch.
unacquainted [ʌnə'kweintɪd] a: **to be ~ with** ne pas connaître.
unadulterated [ʌnə'dʌltəreɪtɪd] a pur(e), naturel(le).
unaffected [ʌnə'fɛktɪd] a (person, behaviour) naturel(le); (emotionally): **to be ~ by** ne pas être touché(e) par.
unafraid [ʌnə'freɪd] a: **to be ~** ne pas avoir peur.
unaided [ʌn'eɪdɪd] a sans aide, tout(e) seul(e).
unanimity [ju:nə'nɪmɪtɪ] n unanimité f.
unanimous [ju:'nænɪməs] a unanime.
unanimously [ju:'nænɪməslɪ] ad à l'unanimité.
unanswered [ʌn'ɑ:nsəd] a (question, letter)

sans réponse.

unappetizing [ʌn'æpɪtaɪzɪŋ] *a* peu appétissant(e).

unappreciative [ʌnə'priːʃɪətɪv] *a* indifférent(e).

unarmed [ʌn'ɑːmd] *a (person)* non armé(e); *(combat)* sans armes.

unashamed [ʌnə'ʃeɪmd] *a* sans honte; impudent(e).

unassisted [ʌnə'sɪstɪd] *a* non assisté(e) ♦ *ad* sans aide, tout(e) seul(e).

unassuming [ʌnə'sjuːmɪŋ] *a* modeste, sans prétentions.

unattached [ʌnə'tætʃt] *a* libre, sans attaches.

unattended [ʌnə'tɛndɪd] *a (car, child, luggage)* sans surveillance.

unattractive [ʌnə'træktɪv] *a* peu attrayant(e).

unauthorized [ʌn'ɔːθəraɪzd] *a* non autorisé(e), sans autorisation.

unavailable [ʌnə'veɪləbl] *a (article, room, book)* (qui n'est) pas disponible; *(person)* (qui n'est) pas libre.

unavoidable [ʌnə'vɔɪdəbl] *a* inévitable.

unavoidably [ʌnə'vɔɪdəblɪ] *ad* inévitablement.

unaware [ʌnə'wɛə*] *a*: **to be ~ of** ignorer, ne pas savoir, être inconscient(e) de.

unawares [ʌnə'wɛəz] *ad* à l'improviste, au dépourvu.

unbalanced [ʌn'bælənst] *a* déséquilibré(e).

unbearable [ʌn'bɛərəbl] *a* insupportable.

unbeatable [ʌn'biːtəbl] *a* imbattable.

unbeaten [ʌn'biːtn] *a* invaincu(e); *(record)* non battu(e).

unbecoming [ʌnbɪ'kʌmɪŋ] *a (unseemly: language, behaviour)* malséant(e), inconvenant(e); *(unflattering: garment)* peu seyant(e).

unbeknown(st) [ʌnbɪ'nəun(st)] *ad*: **~ to** à l'insu de.

unbelief [ʌnbɪ'liːf] *n* incrédulité *f*.

unbelievable [ʌnbɪ'liːvəbl] *a* incroyable.

unbelievingly [ʌnbɪ'liːvɪŋlɪ] *ad* avec incrédulité.

unbend [ʌn'bɛnd] *vb (irg) vi* se détendre ♦ *vt (wire)* redresser, détordre.

unbending [ʌn'bɛndɪŋ] *a (fig)* inflexible.

unbias(s)ed [ʌn'baɪəst] *a* impartial(e).

unblemished [ʌn'blɛmɪʃt] *a* impeccable.

unblock [ʌn'blɔk] *vt (pipe)* déboucher; *(road)* dégager.

unborn [ʌn'bɔːn] *a* à naître.

unbounded [ʌn'baundɪd] *a* sans bornes, illimité(e).

unbreakable [ʌn'breɪkəbl] *a* incassable.

unbridled [ʌn'braɪdld] *a* débridé(e), déchaîné(e).

unbroken [ʌn'brəukən] *a* intact(e); *(line)* continu(e); *(record)* non battu(e).

unbuckle [ʌn'bʌkl] *vt* déboucler.

unburden [ʌn'bəːdn] *vt*: **to ~ o.s.** s'épancher, se livrer.

unbutton [ʌn'bʌtn] *vt* déboutonner.

uncalled-for [ʌn'kɔːldfɔː*] *a* déplacé(e), injustifié(e).

uncanny [ʌn'kænɪ] *a* étrange, troublant(e).

unceasing [ʌn'siːsɪŋ] *a* incessant(e), continu(e).

unceremonious [ʌnsɛrɪ'məunɪəs] *a (abrupt, rude)* brusque.

uncertain [ʌn'səːtn] *a* incertain(e); **we were ~ whether** ... nous ne savions pas vraiment si ...; **in no ~ terms** sans équivoque possible.

uncertainty [ʌn'səːtntɪ] *n* incertitude *f*, doutes *mpl*.

unchallenged [ʌn'tʃælɪndʒd] *a (gen)* incontesté(e); *(information)* non contesté(e); **to go ~** ne pas être contesté.

unchanged [ʌn'tʃeɪndʒd] *a* inchangé(e).

uncharitable [ʌn'tʃærɪtəbl] *a* peu charitable.

uncharted [ʌn'tʃɑːtɪd] *a* inexploré(e).

unchecked [ʌn'tʃɛkt] *a* non réprimé(e).

uncivilized [ʌn'sɪvɪlaɪzd] *a* non civilisé(e); *(fig)* barbare.

uncle ['ʌŋkl] *n* oncle *m*.

unclear [ʌn'klɪə*] *a* (qui n'est) pas clair(e) *or* évident(e); **I'm still ~ about what I'm supposed to do** je ne sais pas encore exactement ce que je dois faire.

uncoil [ʌn'kɔɪl] *vt* dérouler ♦ *vi* se dérouler.

uncomfortable [ʌn'kʌmfətəbl] *a* inconfortable; *(uneasy)* mal à l'aise, gêné(e); *(situation)* désagréable.

uncomfortably [ʌn'kʌmfətəblɪ] *ad* inconfortablement; d'un ton *etc* gêné *or* embarrassé; désagréablement.

uncommitted [ʌnkə'mɪtɪd] *a (attitude, country)* non engagé(e).

uncommon [ʌn'kɔmən] *a* rare, singulier(ière), peu commun(e).

uncommunicative [ʌnkə'mjuːnɪkətɪv] *a* réservé(e).

uncomplicated [ʌn'kɔmplɪkeɪtɪd] *a* simple, peu compliqué(e).

uncompromising [ʌn'kɔmprəmaɪzɪŋ] *a* intransigeant(e), inflexible.

unconcerned [ʌnkən'səːnd] *a (unworried)*: **to be ~ (about)** ne pas s'inquiéter (de).

unconditional [ʌnkən'dɪʃənl] *a* sans conditions.

uncongenial [ʌnkən'dʒiːnɪəl] *a* peu agréable.

unconnected [ʌnkə'nɛktɪd] *a (unrelated)*: **~ (with)** sans rapport (avec).

unconscious [ʌn'kɔnʃəs] *a* sans connaissance, évanoui(e); *(unaware)* inconscient(e) ♦ *n*: **the ~** l'inconscient *m*; **to knock sb ~** assommer qn.

unconsciously [ʌn'kɔnʃəslɪ] *ad* inconsciemment.

unconstitutional ['ʌnkɔnstɪ'tjuːʃənl] *a* anticonstitutionnel(le).

uncontested [ʌnkən'tɛstɪd] *a (champion)* incontesté(e); *(POL: seat)* non disputé(e).

uncontrollable [ʌnkən'trəuləbl] *a (child, dog)* indiscipliné(e); *(emotion)* irrépressible.

uncontrolled [ʌnkən'trəuld] *a (laughter, price rises)* incontrôlé(e).

unconventional [ʌnkən'vɛnʃənl] *a* non conventionnel(le).

unconvinced [ʌnkən'vɪnst] *a*: **to be ~** ne pas être convaincu(e).

unconvincing [ʌnkən'vɪnsɪŋ] *a* peu convaincant(e).

uncork [ʌn'kɔːk] *vt* déboucher.

uncorroborated [ʌnkə'rɔbəreɪtɪd] *a* non confirmé(e).

uncouth [ʌn'kuːθ] *a* grossier(ière), fruste.

uncover [ʌn'kʌvə*] *vt* découvrir.

unctuous ['ʌŋktjuəs] *a* onctueux(euse),

mielleux(euse).

undamaged [ʌn'dæmɪdʒd] *a* (*goods*) intact(e), en bon état; (*fig: reputation*) intact.

undaunted [ʌn'dɔ:ntɪd] *a* non intimidé(e), inébranlable.

undecided [ʌndɪ'saɪdɪd] *a* indécis(e), irrésolu(e).

undelivered [ʌndɪ'lɪvəd] *a* non remis(e), non livré(e).

undeniable [ʌndɪ'naɪəbl] *a* indéniable, incontestable.

under ['ʌndə*] *prep* sous; (*less than*) (de) moins de; au-dessous de; (*according to*) selon, en vertu de ♦ *ad* au-dessous; en dessous; **from ~ sth** de dessous *or* de sous qch; **~ there** là-dessous; **in ~ 2 hours** en moins de 2 heures; **~ anaesthetic** sous anesthésie; **~ discussion** en discussion; **~ the circumstances** étant donné les circonstances; **~ repair** en (cours de) réparation.

under... ['ʌndə*] *prefix* sous-.

under-age [ʌndər'eɪdʒ] *a* qui n'a pas l'âge réglementaire.

underarm ['ʌndərɑ:m] *ad* par en-dessous ♦ *a* (*throw*) par en-dessous; (*deodorant*) pour les aisselles.

undercapitalised ['ʌndə'kæpɪtəlaɪzd] *a* sous-capitalisé(e).

undercarriage ['ʌndəkærɪdʒ] *n* (*Brit AVIAT*) train *m* d'atterrissage.

undercharge [ʌndə'tʃɑ:dʒ] *vt* ne pas faire payer assez à.

underclothes ['ʌndəkləʊðz] *npl* sous-vêtements *mpl*; (*women's only*) dessous *mpl*.

undercoat ['ʌndəkəʊt] *n* (*paint*) couche *f* de fond.

undercover [ʌndə'kʌvə*] *a* secret(ète), clandestin(e).

undercurrent ['ʌndəkʌrnt] *n* courant sous-jacent.

undercut [ʌndə'kʌt] *vt irg* vendre moins cher que.

underdeveloped ['ʌndədɪ'vɛləpt] *a* sous-développé(e).

underdog ['ʌndədɒg] *n* opprimé *m*.

underdone [ʌndə'dʌn] *a* (*food*) pas assez cuit(e).

under-employment ['ʌndərɪm'plɔɪmənt] *n* sous-emploi *m*.

underestimate ['ʌndər'ɛstɪmeɪt] *vt* sous-estimer, mésestimer.

underexposed ['ʌndərɪks'pəʊzd] *a* (*PHOT*) sous-exposé(e).

underfed [ʌndə'fɛd] *a* sous-alimenté(e).

underfoot [ʌndə'fʊt] *ad* sous les pieds.

undergo [ʌndə'gəʊ] *vt irg* subir; (*treatment*) suivre; **the car is ~ing repairs** la voiture est en réparation.

undergraduate [ʌndə'grædjuɪt] *n* étudiant/e (qui prépare la licence) ♦ *cpd*: **~ courses** cours *mpl* préparant à la licence.

underground ['ʌndəgraund] *a* souterrain(e); (*fig*) clandestin(e) ♦ *n* (*Brit*) métro *m*; (*POL*) clandestinité *f*.

undergrowth ['ʌndəgrəʊθ] *n* broussailles *fpl*, sous-bois *m*.

underhand(ed) [ʌndə'hænd(ɪd)] *a* (*fig*) sournois(e), en dessous.

underinsured [ʌndərɪn'ʃuəd] *a* sous-assuré(e).

underlie [ʌndə'laɪ] *vt irg* être à la base de; **the underlying cause** la cause sous-jacente.

underline [ʌndə'laɪn] *vt* souligner.

underling ['ʌndəlɪŋ] *n* (*pej*) sous-fifre *m*, subalterne *m*.

undermanning [ʌndə'mænɪŋ] *n* pénurie *f* de main-d'œuvre.

undermentioned [ʌndə'mɛnʃənd] *a* mentionné(e) ci-dessous.

undermine [ʌndə'maɪn] *vt* saper, miner.

underneath [ʌndə'ni:θ] *ad* (en) dessous ♦ *prep* sous, au-dessous de.

undernourished [ʌndə'nʌrɪʃt] *a* sous-alimenté(e).

underpaid [ʌndə'peɪd] *a* sous-payé(e).

underpants ['ʌndəpænts] *npl* caleçon *m*, slip *m*.

underpass ['ʌndəpɑ:s] *n* (*Brit*) passage souterrain; (*: on motorway*) passage inférieur.

underpin [ʌndə'pɪn] *vt* (*argument, case*) étayer.

underplay [ʌndə'pleɪ] *vt* (*Brit*) minimiser.

underpopulated [ʌndə'pɒpjuleɪtɪd] *a* sous-peuplé(e).

underprice [ʌndə'praɪs] *vt* vendre à un prix trop bas.

underprivileged [ʌndə'prɪvɪlɪdʒd] *a* défavorisé(e), déshérité(e).

underrate [ʌndə'reɪt] *vt* sous-estimer, mésestimer.

underscore [ʌndə'skɔ:*] *vt* souligner.

underseal [ʌndə'si:l] *vt* (*Brit*) traiter contre la rouille.

undersecretary ['ʌndə'sɛkrətərɪ] *n* sous-secrétaire *m*.

undersell [ʌndə'sɛl] *vt* (*competitors*) vendre moins cher que.

undershirt ['ʌndəʃə:t] *n* (*US*) tricot *m* de corps.

undershorts ['ʌndəʃɔ:ts] *npl* (*US*) caleçon *m*, slip *m*.

underside ['ʌndəsaɪd] *n* dessous *m*.

undersigned ['ʌndəsaɪnd] *a, n* soussigné(e) (*m/f*).

underskirt ['ʌndəskə:t] *n* (*Brit*) jupon *m*.

understaffed [ʌndə'stɑ:ft] *a* qui manque de personnel.

understand [ʌndə'stænd] *vb* (*irg: like* **stand**) *vt, vi* comprendre; **I ~ that** ... je me suis laissé dire que ...; je crois comprendre que ...; **to make o.s. understood** se faire comprendre.

understandable [ʌndə'stændəbl] *a* compréhensible.

understanding [ʌndə'stændɪŋ] *a* compréhensif(ive) ♦ *n* compréhension *f*; (*agreement*) accord *m*; **to come to an ~ with sb** s'entendre avec qn; **on the ~ that** ... à condition que ....

understate [ʌndə'steɪt] *vt* minimiser.

understatement ['ʌndəsteɪtmənt] *n*: **that's an ~** c'est (bien) peu dire, le terme est faible.

understood [ʌndə'stud] *pt, pp of* **understand** ♦ *a* entendu(e); (*implied*) sous-entendu(e).

understudy ['ʌndəstʌdɪ] *n* doublure *f*.

undertake [ʌndə'teɪk] *vt irg* (*job, task*) entreprendre; (*duty*) se charger de; **to ~ to do**

sth s'engager à faire qch.

undertaker ['ʌndəteɪkə*] *n* entrepreneur *m* des pompes funèbres, croque-mort *m*.

undertaking ['ʌndəteɪkɪŋ] *n* entreprise *f*; (*promise*) promesse *f*.

undertone ['ʌndətəʊn] *n* (*low voice*): **in an ~** à mi-voix; (*of criticism etc*) nuance cachée.

undervalue [ʌndə'vælju:] *vt* sous-estimer.

underwater [ʌndə'wɔ:tə*] *ad* sous l'eau ♦ *a* sous-marin(e).

underwear ['ʌndəweə*] *n* sous-vêtements *mpl*; (*women's only*) dessous *mpl*.

underweight [ʌndə'weɪt] *a* d'un poids insuffisant; (*person*) (trop) maigre.

underworld ['ʌndəwɔ:ld] *n* (*of crime*) milieu *m*, pègre *f*.

underwrite [ʌndə'raɪt] *vt* (*FINANCE*) garantir; (*INSURANCE*) souscrire.

underwriter ['ʌndəraɪtə*] *n* (*INSURANCE*) souscripteur *m*.

undeserving [ʌndɪ'zɜ:vɪŋ] *a*: **to be ~ of** ne pas mériter.

undesirable [ʌndɪ'zaɪərəbl] *a* peu souhaitable; indésirable.

undeveloped [ʌndɪ'vɛləpt] *a* (*land, resources*) non exploité(e).

undies ['ʌndɪz] *npl* (*col*) dessous *mpl*, lingerie *f*.

undiluted ['ʌndaɪ'lu:tɪd] *a* pur(e), non dilué(e).

undiplomatic ['ʌndɪplə'mætɪk] *a* peu diplomatique, maladroit(e).

undischarged ['ʌndɪs'tʃɑ:dʒd] *a*: **~ bankrupt** failli(e) non réhabilité(e).

undisciplined [ʌn'dɪsɪplɪnd] *a* indiscipliné(e).

undisguised ['ʌndɪs'gaɪzd] *a* (*dislike, amusement etc*) franc(franche).

undisputed ['ʌndɪs'pju:tɪd] *a* incontesté(e).

undistinguished ['ʌndɪs'tɪŋgwɪʃt] *a* médiocre, quelconque.

undisturbed [ʌndɪs'tɜ:bd] *a* (*sleep*) tranquille, paisible; **to leave ~** ne pas déranger.

undivided [ʌndɪ'vaɪdɪd] *a*: **can I have your ~ attention?** puis-je avoir toute votre attention?

undo [ʌn'du:] *vt irg* défaire.

undoing [ʌn'du:ɪŋ] *n* ruine *f*, perte *f*.

undone [ʌn'dʌn] *pp of* **undo**; **to come ~** se défaire.

undoubted [ʌn'daʊtɪd] *a* indubitable, certain(e).

undoubtedly [ʌn'daʊtɪdlɪ] *ad* sans aucun doute.

undress [ʌn'drɛs] *vi* se déshabiller ♦ *vt* déshabiller.

undrinkable [ʌn'drɪŋkəbl] *a* (*unpalatable*) imbuvable; (*poisonous*) non potable.

undue [ʌn'dju:] *a* indu(e), excessif(ive).

undulating ['ʌndjʊleɪtɪŋ] *a* ondoyant(e), onduleux(euse).

unduly [ʌn'dju:lɪ] *ad* trop, excessivement.

undying [ʌn'daɪɪŋ] *a* éternel(le).

unearned [ʌn'ɜ:nd] *a* (*praise, respect*) immérité(e); **~ income** rentes *fpl*.

unearth [ʌn'ɜ:θ] *vt* déterrer; (*fig*) dénicher.

unearthly [ʌn'ɜ:θlɪ] *a* surnaturel(le); (*hour*) indu(e), impossible.

uneasy [ʌn'i:zɪ] *a* mal à l'aise, gêné(e); (*worried*) inquiet(ète); **to feel ~ about**

doing sth se sentir mal à l'aise à l'idée de faire qch.

uneconomic(al) ['ʌni:kə'nɔmɪk(l)] *a* peu économique; peu rentable.

uneducated [ʌn'ɛdjukeɪtɪd] *a* sans éducation.

unemployed [ʌnɪm'plɔɪd] *a* sans travail, au chômage ♦ *n*: **the ~** les chômeurs *mpl*.

unemployment [ʌnɪm'plɔɪmənt] *n* chômage *m*.

unemployment benefit, (*US*) **unemployment compensation** *n* allocation *f* de chômage.

unending [ʌn'ɛndɪŋ] *a* interminable.

unenviable [ʌn'ɛnvɪəbl] *a* peu enviable.

unequal [ʌn'i:kwəl] *a* inégal(e).

unequalled, (*US*) **unequaled** [ʌn'i:kwəld] *a* inégalé(e).

unequivocal [ʌnɪ'kwɪvəkl] *a* (*answer*) sans équivoque; (*person*) catégorique.

unerring [ʌn'ɜ:rɪŋ] *a* infaillible, sûr(e).

UNESCO [ju:'nɛskəʊ] *n abbr* (= *United Nations Educational, Scientific and Cultural Organization*) UNESCO *f*.

unethical [ʌn'ɛθɪkl] *a* (*methods*) immoral(e); (*doctor's behaviour*) qui ne respecte pas l'éthique.

uneven [ʌn'i:vn] *a* inégal(e); irrégulier(ière).

uneventful [ʌnɪ'vɛntful] *a* tranquille, sans histoires.

unexceptional [ʌnɪk'sɛpʃənl] *a* banal(e), quelconque.

unexciting [ʌnɪk'saɪtɪŋ] *a* pas passionnant(e).

unexpected [ʌnɪk'spɛktɪd] *a* inattendu(e), imprévu(e).

unexpectedly [ʌnɪk'spɛktɪdlɪ] *ad* contre toute attente; (*arrive*) à l'improviste.

unexplained [ʌnɪk'spleɪnd] *a* inexpliqué(e).

unexploded [ʌnɪk'spləʊdɪd] *a* non explosé(e) *or* éclaté(e).

unfailing [ʌn'feɪlɪŋ] *a* inépuisable; infaillible.

unfair [ʌn'feə*] *a*: **~ (to)** injuste (envers); **it's ~ that** ... il n'est pas juste que ....

unfair dismissal *n* licenciement abusif.

unfairly [ʌn'feəlɪ] *ad* injustement.

unfaithful [ʌn'feɪθful] *a* infidèle.

unfamiliar [ʌnfə'mɪlɪə*] *a* étrange, inconnu(e); **to be ~ with sth** mal connaître qch.

unfashionable [ʌn'fæʃnəbl] *a* (*clothes*) démodé(e); (*district*) déshérité(e), pas à la mode.

unfasten [ʌn'fɑ:sn] *vt* défaire; détacher.

unfathomable [ʌn'fæðəməbl] *a* insondable.

unfavourable, (*US*) **unfavorable** [ʌn'feɪvrəbl] *a* défavorable.

unfavo(u)rably [ʌn'feɪvrəblɪ] *ad*: **to look ~ upon** ne pas être favorable à.

unfeeling [ʌn'fi:lɪŋ] *a* insensible, dur(e).

unfinished [ʌn'fɪnɪʃt] *a* inachevé(e).

unfit [ʌn'fɪt] *a* (*physically*) pas en forme; (*incompetent*): **~ (for)** impropre (à); (*work, service*) inapte (à).

unflagging [ʌn'flægɪŋ] *a* infatigable, inlassable.

unflappable [ʌn'flæpəbl] *a* imperturbable.

unflattering [ʌn'flætərɪŋ] *a* (*dress, hairstyle*) qui n'avantage pas; (*remark*) peu flatteur(euse).

unflinching [ʌn'flɪntʃɪŋ] *a* stoïque.

unfold [ʌn'fəuld] *vt* déplier; *(fig)* révéler, exposer ♦ *vi* se dérouler.
unforeseeable [ʌnfɔː'siːəbl] *a* imprévisible.
unforeseen ['ʌnfɔː'siːn] *a* imprévu(e).
unforgettable [ʌnfə'gɛtəbl] *a* inoubliable.
unforgivable [ʌnfə'gɪvəbl] *a* impardonnable.
unformatted [ʌn'fɔːmætɪd] *a* (*disk, text*) non formaté(e).
unfortunate [ʌn'fɔːtʃnət] *a* malheureux(euse); (*event, remark*) malencontreux(euse).
unfortunately [ʌn'fɔːtʃnətlɪ] *ad* malheureusement.
unfounded [ʌn'faundɪd] *a* sans fondement.
unfriendly [ʌn'frɛndlɪ] *a* froid(e), inamical(e).
unfulfilled [ʌnful'fɪld] *a* (*ambition, prophecy*) non réalisé(e); (*desire*) insatisfait(e); (*promise*) non tenu(e); (*terms of contract*) non rempli(e); (*person*) qui n'a pas su se réaliser.
unfurl [ʌn'fɔːl] *vt* déployer.
unfurnished [ʌn'fəːnɪʃt] *a* non meublé(e).
ungainly [ʌn'geɪnlɪ] *a* gauche, dégingandé(e).
ungodly [ʌn'gɔdlɪ] *a* impie; **at an ~ hour** à une heure indue.
ungrateful [ʌn'greɪtful] *a* qui manque de reconnaissance, ingrat(e).
unguarded [ʌn'gɑːdɪd] *a:* **~ moment** moment *m* d'inattention.
unhappily [ʌn'hæpɪlɪ] *ad* tristement; (*unfortunately*) malheureusement.
unhappiness [ʌn'hæpɪnɪs] *n* tristesse *f*, peine *f*.
unhappy [ʌn'hæpɪ] *a* triste, malheureux(euse); (*unfortunate: remark etc*) malheureux(euse); (*not pleased*): **~ with** mécontent(e) de, peu satisfait(e) de.
unharmed [ʌn'hɑːmd] *a* indemne, sain(e) et sauf(sauve).
unhealthy [ʌn'hɛlθɪ] *a* (*gen*) malsain(e); (*person*) maladif(ive).
unheard-of [ʌn'həːdɔv] *a* inouï(e), sans précédent.
unhelpful [ʌn'hɛlpful] *a* (*person*) peu serviable; (*advice*) peu utile.
unhesitating [ʌn'hɛzɪteɪtɪŋ] *a* (*loyalty*) spontané(e); (*reply, offer*) immédiat(e).
unhook [ʌn'huk] *vt* décrocher; dégrafer.
unhurt [ʌn'həːt] *a* indemne, sain(e) et sauf(sauve).
unhygienic ['ʌnhaɪ'dʒiːnɪk] *a* antihygiénique.
UNICEF ['juːnɪsɛf] *n abbr* (= *United Nations International Children's Emergency Fund*) UNICEF *m*, FISE *m*.
unicorn ['juːnɪkɔːn] *n* licorne *f*.
unidentified [ʌnaɪ'dɛntɪfaɪd] *a* non identifié(e).
uniform ['juːnɪfɔːm] *n* uniforme *m* ♦ *a* uniforme.
uniformity [juːnɪ'fɔːmɪtɪ] *n* uniformité *f*.
unify ['juːnɪfaɪ] *vt* unifier.
unilateral [juːnɪ'lætərəl] *a* unilatéral(e).
unimaginable [ʌnɪ'mædʒɪnəbl] *a* inimaginable, inconcevable.
unimaginative [ʌnɪ'mædʒɪnətɪv] *a* sans imagination.
unimpaired [ʌnɪm'pɛəd] *a* intact(e).
unimportant [ʌnɪm'pɔːtənt] *a* sans importance.
unimpressed [ʌnɪm'prɛst] *a* pas im-

pressionné(e).
uninhabited [ʌnɪn'hæbɪtɪd] *a* inhabité(e).
uninhibited [ʌnɪn'hɪbɪtɪd] *a* sans inhibitions; sans retenue.
uninjured [ʌn'ɪndʒəd] *a* indemne.
unintelligent [ʌnɪn'tɛlɪdʒənt] *a* inintelligent(e).
unintentional [ʌnɪn'tɛnʃənəl] *a* involontaire.
unintentionally [ʌnɪn'tɛnʃnəlɪ] *ad* sans le vouloir.
uninvited [ʌnɪn'vaɪtɪd] *a* (*guest*) qui n'a pas été invité(e).
uninviting [ʌnɪn'vaɪtɪŋ] *a* (*place*) peu attirant(e); (*food*) peu appétissant(e).
union ['juːnjən] *n* union *f*; (*also*: **trade ~**) syndicat *m* ♦ *cpd* du syndicat, syndical(e).
unionize ['juːnjənaɪz] *vt* syndiquer.
Union Jack *n* drapeau du *Royaume-Uni*.
Union of Soviet Socialist Republics (USSR) *n* Union *f* des républiques socialistes soviétiques (URSS).
union shop *n* *entreprise où tous les travailleurs doivent être syndiqués*.
unique [juː'niːk] *a* unique.
unisex ['juːnɪsɛks] *a* unisexe.
unison ['juːnɪsn] *n*: **in ~** à l'unisson, en chœur.
unit ['juːnɪt] *n* unité *f*; (*section: of furniture etc*) élément *m*, bloc *m*; (*team, squad*) groupe *m*, service *m*; **production ~** atelier *m* de fabrication; **sink ~** bloc-évier *m*.
unit cost *n* coût *m* unitaire.
unite [juː'naɪt] *vt* unir ♦ *vi* s'unir.
united [juː'naɪtɪd] *a* uni(e); unifié(e); (*efforts*) conjugué(e).
United Arab Emirates *npl* Émirats Arabes Unis.
United Kingdom (UK) *n* Royaume-Uni *m* (R.U.).
United Nations (Organization) (UN, UNO) *n* (Organisation *f* des) Nations unies (ONU).
United States (of America) (US, USA) *n* États-Unis *mpl*.
unit price *n* prix *m* unitaire.
unit trust *n* (*Brit COMM*) fonds commun de placement, FCP *m*.
unity ['juːnɪtɪ] *n* unité *f*.
Univ. *abbr* = **university**.
universal [juːnɪ'vɔːsl] *a* universel(le).
universe ['juːnɪvɔːs] *n* univers *m*.
university [juːnɪ'vɔːsɪtɪ] *n* université *f* ♦ *cpd* (*student, professor*) d'université; (*education, year, degree*) universitaire.
unjust [ʌn'dʒʌst] *a* injuste.
unjustifiable ['ʌndʒʌstɪ'faɪəbl] *a* injustifiable.
unjustified [ʌn'dʒʌstɪfaɪd] *a* injustifié(e); (*text*) non justifié(e).
unkempt [ʌn'kɛmpt] *a* mal tenu(e), débraillé(e); mal peigné(e).
unkind [ʌn'kaɪnd] *a* peu gentil(le), méchant(e).
unkindly [ʌn'kaɪndlɪ] *ad* (*treat, speak*) avec méchanceté.
unknown [ʌn'nəun] *a* inconnu(e); **~ to me** sans que je le sache; **~ quantity** (*MATH, fig*) inconnue *f*.
unladen [ʌn'leɪdn] *a* (*ship, weight*) à vide.
unlawful [ʌn'lɔːful] *a* illégal(e).

unleash [ʌn'liːʃ] *vt* détacher; (*fig*) déchaîner, déclencher.

unleavened [ʌn'lɛvnd] *a* sans levain.

unless [ʌn'lɛs] *cj*: ~ **he leaves** à moins qu'il (ne) parte; ~ **we leave** à moins de partir, à moins que nous (ne) partions; ~ **otherwise stated** sauf indication contraire; ~ **I am mistaken** si je ne me trompe.

unlicensed [ʌn'laɪsnst] *a* (*Brit*) non patenté(e) pour la vente des spiritueux.

unlike [ʌn'laɪk] *a* dissemblable, différent(e) ♦ *prep* à la différence de, contrairement à.

unlikelihood [ʌn'laɪklɪhud] *a* improbabilité *f*.

unlikely [ʌn'laɪklɪ] *a* (*result, event*) improbable; (*explanation*) invraisemblable.

unlimited [ʌn'lɪmɪtɪd] *a* illimité(e).

unlisted ['ʌn'lɪstɪd] *a* (*US TEL*) sur la liste rouge; (*STOCK EXCHANGE*) non coté(e) en bourse.

unlit [ʌn'lɪt] *a* (*room*) non éclairé(e).

unload [ʌn'ləud] *vt* décharger.

unlock [ʌn'lɔk] *vt* ouvrir.

unlucky [ʌn'lʌkɪ] *a* malchanceux(euse); (*object, number*) qui porte malheur; **to be ~** (*person*) ne pas avoir de chance.

unmanageable [ʌn'mænɪdʒəbl] *a* (*unwieldy: tool, vehicle*) peu maniable; (*: situation*) inextricable.

unmanned [ʌn'mænd] *a* sans équipage.

unmannerly [ʌn'mænəlɪ] *a* mal élevé(e), impoli(e).

unmarked [ʌn'mɑːkt] *a* (*unstained*) sans marque; ~ **police car** voiture de police banalisée.

unmarried [ʌn'mærɪd] *a* célibataire.

unmask [ʌn'mɑːsk] *vt* démasquer.

unmatched [ʌn'mætʃt] *a* sans égal(e).

unmentionable [ʌn'mɛnʃnəbl] *a* (*topic*) dont on ne parle pas; (*word*) qui ne se dit pas.

unmerciful [ʌn'məːsɪful] *a* sans pitié.

unmistakable [ʌnmɪs'teɪkəbl] *a* indubitable; qu'on ne peut pas ne pas reconnaître.

unmitigated [ʌn'mɪtɪgeɪtɪd] *a* non mitigé(e), absolu(e), pur(e).

unnamed [ʌn'neɪmd] *a* (*nameless*) sans nom; (*anonymous*) anonyme.

unnatural [ʌn'nætʃrəl] *a* non naturel(le); contre nature.

unnecessary [ʌn'nɛsəsərɪ] *a* inutile, superflu(e).

unnerve [ʌn'nəːv] *vt* faire perdre son sang-froid à.

unnoticed [ʌn'nəutɪst] *a* inaperçu(e).

UNO ['juːnəu] *n abbr* = **United Nations Organization.**

unobservant [ʌnəb'zəːvnt] *a* pas observateur(trice).

unobtainable [ʌnəb'teɪnəbl] *a* (*TEL*) impossible à obtenir.

unobtrusive [ʌnəb'truːsiv] *a* discret(ète).

unoccupied [ʌn'ɔkjupaɪd] *a* (*seat, table, also MIL*) libre; (*house*) inoccupé(e).

unofficial [ʌnə'fɪʃl] *a* non officiel(le); (*strike*) ≈ non sanctionné(e) par la centrale.

unopposed [ʌnə'pəuzd] *a* sans opposition.

unorthodox [ʌn'ɔːθədɔks] *a* peu orthodoxe.

unpack [ʌn'pæk] *vi* défaire sa valise, déballer ses affaires.

unpaid [ʌn'peɪd] *a* (*bill*) impayé(e); (*holiday*)

non-payé(e), sans salaire; (*work*) non rétribué(e); (*worker*) bénévole.

unpalatable [ʌn'pælətəbl] *a* (*truth*) désagréable (à entendre).

unparalleled [ʌn'pærəlɛld] *a* incomparable, sans égal.

unpatriotic ['ʌnpætrɪ'ɔtɪk] *a* (*person*) manquant de patriotisme; (*speech, attitude*) antipatriotique.

unplanned [ʌn'plænd] *a* (*visit*) imprévu(e); (*baby*) non prévu(e).

unpleasant [ʌn'plɛznt] *a* déplaisant(e), désagréable.

unplug [ʌn'plʌg] *vt* débrancher.

unpolluted [ʌnpə'luːtɪd] *a* non pollué(e).

unpopular [ʌn'pɔpjulə*] *a* impopulaire; **to make o.s. ~ (with)** se rendre impopulaire (auprès de).

unprecedented [ʌn'prɛsɪdəntɪd] *a* sans précédent.

unpredictable [ʌnprɪ'dɪktəbl] *a* imprévisible.

unprejudiced [ʌn'prɛdʒudɪst] *a* (*not biased*) impartial(e); (*having no prejudices*) qui n'a pas de préjugés.

unprepared [ʌnprɪ'pɛəd] *a* (*person*) qui n'est pas suffisamment préparé(e); (*speech*) improvisé(e).

unprepossessing ['ʌnpriːpə'zɛsɪŋ] *a* peu avenant(e).

unpretentious [ʌnprɪ'tɛnʃəs] *a* sans prétention(s).

unprincipled [ʌn'prɪnsɪpld] *a* sans principes.

unproductive [ʌnprə'dʌktɪv] *a* improductif(ive); (*discussion*) stérile.

unprofessional [ʌnprə'fɛʃənl] *a* (*conduct*) contraire à la déontologie.

unprofitable [ʌn'prɔfɪtəbl] *a* non rentable.

unprovoked [ʌnprə'vəukt] *a* (*attack*) sans provocation.

unpunished [ʌn'pʌnɪʃt] *a* impuni(e).

unqualified [ʌn'kwɔlɪfaɪd] *a* (*teacher*) non diplômé(e), sans titres; (*success*) sans réserve, total(e).

unquestionably [ʌn'kwɛstʃənəblɪ] *ad* incontestablement.

unquestioning [ʌn'kwɛstʃənɪŋ] *a* (*obedience, acceptance*) inconditionnel(le).

unravel [ʌn'rævl] *vt* démêler.

unreal [ʌn'rɪəl] *a* irréel(le).

unrealistic ['ʌnrɪə'lɪstɪk] *a* (*idea*) irréaliste; (*estimate*) peu réaliste.

unreasonable [ʌn'riːznəbl] *a* qui n'est pas raisonnable; **to make ~ demands on sb** exiger trop de qn.

unrecognizable [ʌn'rɛkəgnaɪzəbl] *a* pas reconnaissable.

unrecognized [ʌn'rɛkəgnaɪzd] *a* (*talent, genius*) méconnu(e).

unrecorded [ʌnrə'kɔːdɪd] *a* non enregistré(e).

unrefined [ʌnrə'faɪnd] *a* (*sugar, petroleum*) non raffiné(e).

unrehearsed [ʌnrɪ'həːst] *a* (*THEATRE etc*) qui n'a pas été répété(e); (*spontaneous*) spontané(e).

unrelated [ʌnrɪ'leɪtɪd] *a* sans rapport; sans lien de parenté.

unrelenting [ʌnrɪ'lɛntɪŋ] *a* implacable; acharné(e).

unreliable [ʌnrɪ'laɪəbl] *a* sur qui (*or* quoi) on

ne peut pas compter, peu fiable.

unrelieved [ʌnrɪ'li:vd] *a* (*monotony*) constant(e), uniforme.

unremitting [ʌnrɪ'mɪtɪŋ] *a* inlassable, infatigable, acharné(e).

unrepeatable [ʌnrɪ'pi:təbl] *a* (*offer*) unique, exceptionnel(le).

unrepentant [ʌnrɪ'pentənt] *a* impénitent(e).

unrepresentative ['ʌnreprɪ'zentətɪv] *a*: ~ (**of**) peu représentatif(ive) (de).

unreserved [ʌnrɪ'zɜːvd] *a* (*seat*) non réservé(e); (*approval, admiration*) sans réserve.

unresponsive [ʌnrɪs'pɒnsɪv] *a* insensible.

unrest [ʌn'rest] *n* agitation *f*, troubles *mpl*.

unrestricted [ʌnrɪ'strɪktɪd] *a* illimité(e); **to have ~ access to** avoir librement accès *or* accès en tout temps à.

unrewarded [ʌnrɪ'wɔːdɪd] *a* pas récompensé(e).

unripe [ʌn'raɪp] *a* pas mûr(e).

unrivalled, (*US*) **unrivaled** [ʌn'raɪvəld] *a* sans égal, incomparable.

unroll [ʌn'rəul] *vt* dérouler.

unruffled [ʌn'rʌfld] *a* (*person*) imperturbable; (*hair*) qui n'est pas ébouriffé(e).

unruly [ʌn'ru:lɪ] *a* indiscipliné(e).

unsafe [ʌn'seɪf] *a* (*machine, wiring*) dangereux(euse); (*method*) hasardeux(euse); **~ to drink/eat** non potable/comestible.

unsaid [ʌn'sed] *a*: **to leave sth ~** passer qch sous silence.

unsaleable, (*US*) **unsalable** [ʌn'seɪləbl] *a* invendable.

unsatisfactory ['ʌnsætɪs'fæktərɪ] *a* qui laisse à désirer.

unsavoury, (*US*) **unsavory** [ʌn'seɪvərɪ] *a* (*fig*) peu recommandable, répugnant(e).

unscathed [ʌn'skeɪðd] *a* indemne.

unscientific ['ʌnsaɪən'tɪfɪk] *a* non scientifique.

unscrew [ʌn'skru:] *vt* dévisser.

unscrupulous [ʌn'skru:pjuləs] *a* sans scrupules.

unsecured ['ʌnsɪ'kjuəd] *a*: **~ creditor** créancier/ière sans garantie.

unseemly [ʌn'si:mlɪ] *a* inconvenant(e).

unseen [ʌn'si:n] *a* (*person*) invisible; (*danger*) imprévu(e).

unselfish [ʌn'selfɪʃ] *a* désintéressé(e).

unsettled [ʌn'setld] *a* (*restless*) perturbé(e); (*unpredictable*) instable; incertain(e); (*not finalized*) non résolu(e).

unsettling [ʌn'setlɪŋ] *a* qui a un effet perturbateur.

unshak(e)able [ʌn'ʃeɪkəbl] *a* inébranlable.

unshaven [ʌn'ʃeɪvn] *a* non *or* mal rasé(e).

unsightly [ʌn'saɪtlɪ] *a* disgracieux(euse), laid(e).

unskilled [ʌn'skɪld] *a*: **~ worker** manœuvre *m*.

unsociable [ʌn'səuʃəbl] *a* (*person*) peu sociable; (*behaviour*) qui manque de sociabilité.

unsocial [ʌn'səuʃl] *a* (*hours*) en dehors de l'horaire normal.

unsold [ʌn'səuld] *a* invendu(e), non vendu(e).

unsolicited [ʌnsə'lɪsɪtɪd] *a* non sollicité(e).

unsophisticated [ʌnsə'fɪstɪkeɪtɪd] *a* simple, naturel(le).

unsound [ʌn'saund] *a* (*health*) chancelant(e);

(*floor, foundations*) peu solide; (*policy, advice*) peu judicieux(euse).

unspeakable [ʌn'spi:kəbl] *a* indicible; (*awful*) innommable.

unspoken [ʌn'spəukn] *a* (*word*) qui n'est pas prononcé(e); (*agreement, approval*) tacite.

unsteady [ʌn'stedɪ] *a* mal assuré(e), chancelant(e), instable.

unstinting [ʌn'stɪntɪŋ] *a* (*support*) total(e), sans réserve; (*generosity*) sans limites.

unstuck [ʌn'stʌk] *a*: **to come ~** se décoller; (*fig*) faire fiasco.

unsubstantiated ['ʌnsəb'stænʃɪeɪtɪd] *a* (*rumour*) qui n'est pas confirmé(e); (*accusation*) sans preuve.

unsuccessful [ʌnsək'sesful] *a* (*attempt*) infructueux(euse); (*writer, proposal*) qui n'a pas de succès; (*marriage*) malheureux(euse), qui ne réussit pas; **to be ~** (*in attempting sth*) ne pas réussir; ne pas avoir de succès; (*application*) ne pas être retenu(e).

unsuccessfully [ʌnsək'sesfəlɪ] *ad* en vain.

unsuitable [ʌn'su:təbl] *a* qui ne convient pas, peu approprié(e); inopportun(e).

unsuited [ʌn'su:tɪd] *a*: **to be ~ for** *or* **to** être inapte *or* impropre à.

unsupported [ʌnsə'pɔ:tɪd] *a* (*claim*) non soutenu(e); (*theory*) qui n'est pas corroboré(e).

unsure [ʌn'ʃuə*] *a* pas sûr(e); **to be ~ of o.s.** ne pas être sûr de soi, manquer de confiance en soi.

unsuspecting [ʌnsə'spektɪŋ] *a* qui ne se méfie pas.

unsweetened [ʌn'swi:tnd] *a* non sucré(e).

unswerving [ʌn'swɜ:vɪŋ] *a* inébranlable.

unsympathetic ['ʌnsɪmpə'θetɪk] *a* hostile; (*unpleasant*) antipathique; **~ to** indifférent(e) à.

untangle [ʌn'tæŋgl] *vt* démêler, débrouiller.

untapped [ʌn'tæpt] *a* (*resources*) inexploité(e).

untaxed [ʌn'tækst] *a* (*goods*) non taxé(e); (*income*) non imposé(e).

unthinkable [ʌn'θɪŋkəbl] *a* impensable, inconcevable.

untidy [ʌn'taɪdɪ] *a* (*room*) en désordre; (*appearance*) désordonné(e), débraillé(e); (*person*) sans ordre, désordonné; débraillé; (*work*) peu soigné(e).

untie [ʌn'taɪ] *vt* (*knot, parcel*) défaire; (*prisoner, dog*) détacher.

until [ən'tɪl] *prep* jusqu'à; (*after negative*) avant ♦ *cj* jusqu'à ce que + *sub*, en attendant que + *sub*; (*in past, after negative*) avant que + *sub*; **~ now** jusqu'à présent, jusqu'ici; **~ then** jusque-là; **from morning ~ night** du matin au soir *or* jusqu'au soir.

untimely [ʌn'taɪmlɪ] *a* inopportun(e); (*death*) prématuré(e).

untold [ʌn'təuld] *a* incalculable; indescriptible.

untouched [ʌn'tʌtʃt] *a* (*not used etc*) tel(le) quel(le), intact(e); (*safe: person*) indemne; (*unaffected*): **~ by** indifférent(e) à.

untoward [ʌntə'wɔ:d] *a* fâcheux(euse), malencontreux(euse).

untrammelled [ʌn'træmld] *a* sans entraves.

untranslatable [ʌntrænz'leɪtəbl] *a* intraduisible.

untrue [ʌn'truː] a (*statement*) faux(fausse).

untrustworthy [ʌn'trʌstwəːðɪ] a (*person*) pas digne de confiance, peu sûr(e).

unusable [ʌn'juːzəbl] a inutilisable.

unused [ʌn'juːzd] a (*new*) neuf(neuve); [ʌn'juːst]: **to be ~ to** sth/**to doing** sth ne pas avoir l'habitude de qch/de faire qch.

unusual [ʌn'juːʒuəl] a insolite, exceptionnel(le), rare.

unusually [ʌn'juːʒuəlɪ] ad exceptionnellement, particulièrement.

unveil [ʌn'veɪl] vt dévoiler.

unwanted [ʌn'wɔntɪd] a non désiré(e).

unwarranted [ʌn'wɔrəntɪd] a injustifié(e).

unwary [ʌn'wɛərɪ] a imprudent(e).

unwavering [ʌn'weɪvərɪŋ] a inébranlable.

unwelcome [ʌn'wɛlkəm] a importun(e); **to feel ~** se sentir de trop.

unwell [ʌn'wɛl] a indisposé(e), souffrant(e); **to feel ~** ne pas se sentir bien.

unwieldy [ʌn'wiːldɪ] a difficile à manier.

unwilling [ʌn'wɪlɪŋ] a: **to be ~ to do** ne pas vouloir faire.

unwillingly [ʌn'wɪlɪŋlɪ] ad à contrecœur, contre son gré.

unwind [ʌn'waɪnd] vb (*irg*) vt dérouler ♦ vi (*relax*) se détendre.

unwise [ʌn'waɪz] a imprudent(e), peu judicieux(euse).

unwitting [ʌn'wɪtɪŋ] a involontaire.

unworkable [ʌn'wəːkəbl] a (*plan etc*) inexploitable.

unworthy [ʌn'wəːðɪ] a indigne.

unwrap [ʌn'ræp] vt défaire; ouvrir.

unwritten [ʌn'rɪtn] a (*agreement*) tacite.

unzip [ʌn'zɪp] vt ouvrir (la fermeture éclair de).

up [ʌp] prep: **to go/be ~** sth monter/être sur qch ♦ ad en haut; en l'air ♦ vi (*col*): **she ~ped and left** elle a fichu le camp sans plus attendre ♦ vt (*col: price etc*) augmenter; ~ **there** là-haut; **~ above** au-dessus; ~ **to** jusqu'à; "**this side ~**" "haut"; **to be ~** (*out of bed*) être levé(e), être debout *inv*; **to be ~ (by)** (*of price, value*) avoir augmenté (de); **when the year was ~** (*finished*) à la fin de l'année; **time's ~** c'est l'heure; **it is ~ to you** c'est à vous de décider, ça ne tient qu'à vous; **what is he ~ to?** qu'est-ce qu'il peut bien faire?; **he is not ~ to it** il n'en est pas capable; **he's well ~ in** or **on** ... (*Brit: knowledgeable*) il s'y connaît en ...; **~ with Leeds United!** vive Leeds United!; **what's ~?** (*col*) qu'est-ce qui ne va pas?; **what's ~ with him?** (*col*) qu'est-ce qui lui arrive?; **~s and downs** *npl* (*fig*) hauts et bas *mpl*.

up-and-coming [ʌpənd'kʌmɪŋ] a plein(e) d'avenir or de promesses.

upbeat ['ʌpbiːt] n (*MUS*) levé m; (*in economy, prosperity*) amélioration f ♦ a (*optimistic*) optimiste.

upbraid [ʌp'breɪd] vt morigéner.

upbringing ['ʌpbrɪŋɪŋ] n éducation f.

update [ʌp'deɪt] vt mettre à jour.

upend [ʌp'ɛnd] vt mettre debout.

upgrade [ʌp'greɪd] vt (*person*) promouvoir; (*job*) revaloriser; (*property, equipment*) moderniser.

upheaval [ʌp'hiːvl] n bouleversement m;

branle-bas m; crise f.

uphill [ʌp'hɪl] a qui monte; (*fig: task*) difficile, pénible ♦ ad (*face, look*) en amont, vers l'amont; (*go, move*) vers le haut, en haut; **to go ~** monter.

uphold [ʌp'həʊld] vt irg maintenir; soutenir.

upholstery [ʌp'həʊlstərɪ] n rembourrage m; (*of car*) garniture f.

upkeep ['ʌpkiːp] n entretien m.

up-market [ʌp'mɑːkɪt] a (*product*) haut de gamme *inv*.

upon [ə'pɔn] prep sur.

upper ['ʌpə*] a supérieur(e); du dessus ♦ n (*of shoe*) empeigne f.

upper class n: **the ~** ≈ la haute bourgeoisie ♦ a: **upper-class** (*district*) élégant(e), huppé(e); (*accent, attitude*) caractéristique des classes supérieures.

upper hand n: **to have the ~** avoir le dessus.

uppermost ['ʌpəməʊst] a le(la) plus haut(e); en dessus; **it was ~ in my mind** j'y pensais avant tout autre chose.

Upper Volta [-'vɔltə] n Haute Volta.

upright ['ʌpraɪt] a droit(e); vertical(e); (*fig*) droit, honnête ♦ n montant m.

uprising ['ʌpraɪzɪŋ] n soulèvement m, insurrection f.

uproar ['ʌprɔː*] n tumulte m, vacarme m.

uproot [ʌp'ruːt] vt déraciner.

upset n ['ʌpsɛt] dérangement m ♦ vt [ʌp'sɛt] (*irg: like* set) (*glass etc*) renverser; (*plan*) déranger; (*person: offend*) contrarier; (*: grieve*) faire de la peine à; bouleverser ♦ a [ʌp'sɛt] contrarié(e); peiné(e); (*stomach*) détraqué(e), dérangé(e); **to get ~** (*sad*) devenir triste; (*offended*) se vexer; **to have a stomach ~** (*Brit*) avoir une indigestion.

upset price n (*US, Scottish*) mise f à prix, prix m de départ.

upsetting [ʌp'sɛtɪŋ] a (*offending*) vexant(e); (*annoying*) ennuyeux(euse).

upshot ['ʌpʃɔt] n résultat m; **the ~ of it all was that** ... il a résulté de tout cela que ....

upside down ['ʌpsaɪd-] ad à l'envers.

upstairs [ʌp'stɛəz] ad en haut ♦ a (*room*) du dessus, d'en haut ♦ n: **there's no ~** il n'y a pas d'étage.

upstart ['ʌpstɑːt] n parvenu/e.

upstream [ʌp'striːm] ad en amont.

upsurge ['ʌpsəːdʒ] n (*of enthusiasm etc*) vague f.

uptake ['ʌpteɪk] n: **he is quick/slow on the ~** il comprend vite/est lent à comprendre.

uptight [ʌp'taɪt] a (*col*) très tendu(e), crispé(e).

up-to-date ['ʌptə'deɪt] a moderne; très récent(e).

upturn ['ʌptəːn] n (*in economy*) reprise f.

upturned ['ʌptəːnd] a (*nose*) retroussé(e).

upward ['ʌpwəd] a ascendant(e); vers le haut.

upward(s) ['ʌpwəd(z)] ad vers le haut; **and ~** et plus, et au-dessus.

URA n abbr (*US*) = *Urban Renewal Administration*.

Ural Mountains ['juərəl-] *npl*: **the ~** (*also*: **the Urals**) les monts *mpl* Oural, l'Oural m.

uranium [juə'reɪnɪəm] n uranium m.

Uranus [juə'reɪnəs] n Uranus f.

urban ['ə:bən] *a* urbain(e).

urbane [ə:'beɪn] *a* urbain(e), courtois(e).

urbanization ['ə:bənaɪ'zeɪʃən] *n* urbanisation *f*.

urchin ['ə:tʃɪn] *n* gosse *m*, garnement *m*; **sea ~** oursin *m*.

urge [ə:dʒ] *n* besoin (impératif), envie (pressante) ♦ *vt* (*caution etc*) recommander avec insistance; (*person*): **to ~ sb to do** presser qn de faire, recommander avec insistance à qn de faire.

urge on *vt* pousser, presser.

urgency ['ə:dʒənsɪ] *n* urgence *f*; (*of tone*) insistance *f*.

urgent ['ə:dʒənt] *a* urgent(e); (*plea, tone*) pressant(e).

urgently ['ə:dʒəntlɪ] *ad* d'urgence, de toute urgence; (*need*) sans délai.

urinal ['juərɪnl] *n* (*Brit*) urinoir *m*.

urinate ['juərɪneɪt] *vi* uriner.

urine ['juərɪn] *n* urine *f*.

urn [ə:n] *n* urne *f*; (*also*: **tea ~**) fontaine *f* à thé.

Uruguay ['juərəgwaɪ] *n* Uruguay *m*.

Uruguayan [juərə'gwaɪən] *a* uruguayen(ne) ♦ *n* Uruguayen/ne.

US *n abbr* = **United States**.

us [ʌs] *pronoun* nous.

USA *n abbr* = **United States of America**; (*MIL*) = *United States Army*.

usable ['ju:zəbl] *a* utilisable.

USAF *n abbr* = *United States Air Force*.

usage ['ju:zɪdʒ] *n* usage *m*.

USCG *n abbr* = *United States Coast Guard*.

USDA *n abbr* = *United States Department of Agriculture*.

USDAW ['ʌzdɔ:] *n abbr* (*Brit*: = *Union of Shop, Distributive and Allied Workers*) syndicat du commerce de détail et de la distribution.

USDI *n abbr* = *United States Department of the Interior*.

use *n* [ju:s] emploi *m*, utilisation *f*; usage *m* ♦ *vt* [ju:z] se servir de, utiliser, employer; **she ~d to do it** elle le faisait (autrefois), elle avait coutume de le faire; **in ~** en usage; **out of ~** hors d'usage; **to be of ~** servir, être utile; **to make ~ of sth** utiliser qch; **ready for ~** prêt à l'emploi; **to be of ~** être utile; **it's no ~** ça ne sert à rien; **to have the ~ of** avoir l'usage de; **what's this ~d for?** à quoi est-ce que ça sert?; **to be ~d to** avoir l'habitude de, être habitué(e) à; **to get ~d to** s'habituer à.

use up *vt* finir, épuiser; (*food*) consommer.

used [ju:zd] *a* (*car*) d'occasion.

useful ['ju:sful] *a* utile; **to come in ~** être utile.

usefulness ['ju:sfəlnɪs] *n* utilité *f*.

useless ['ju:slɪs] *a* inutile.

user ['ju:zə*] *n* utilisateur/trice, usager *m*.

user-friendly ['ju:zə'frendlɪ] *a* convivial(e), facile d'emploi.

USES *n abbr* = *United States Employment Service*.

usher ['ʌʃə*] *n* placeur *m* ♦ *vt*: **to ~ sb in** faire entrer qn.

usherette [ʌʃə'ret] *n* (*in cinema*) ouvreuse *f*.

USIA *n abbr* = *United States Information Agency*.

USM *n abbr* = *United States Mail, United States Mint*.

USN *n abbr* = *United States Navy*.

USPHS *n abbr* = *United States Public Health Service*.

USPO *n abbr* = *United States Post Office*.

USS *abbr* = *United States Ship* (or *Steamer*).

USSR *n abbr* = **Union of Soviet Socialist Republics**.

usu. *abbr* = **usually**.

usual ['ju:ʒuəl] *a* habituel(le); **as ~** comme d'habitude.

usually ['ju:ʒuəlɪ] *ad* d'habitude, d'ordinaire.

usurer ['ju:ʒərə*] *n* usurier/ière.

usurp [ju:'zə:p] *vt* usurper.

UT *abbr* (*US POST*) = *Utah*.

utensil [ju:'tensl] *n* ustensile *m*; **kitchen ~s** batterie *f* de cuisine.

uterus ['ju:tərəs] *n* utérus *m*.

utilitarian [ju:tɪlɪ'teərɪən] *a* utilitaire.

utility [ju:'tɪlɪtɪ] *n* utilité *f*; (*also*: **public ~**) service public.

utility room *n* buanderie *f*.

utilization [ju:tɪlaɪ'zeɪʃən] *n* utilisation *f*.

utilize ['ju:tɪlaɪz] *vt* utiliser; exploiter.

utmost ['ʌtməust] *a* extrême, le(la) plus grand(e) ♦ *n*: **to do one's ~** faire tout son possible; **of the ~ importance** d'une importance capitale, de la plus haute importance.

utter ['ʌtə*] *a* total(e), complet(ète) ♦ *vt* prononcer, proférer; émettre.

utterance ['ʌtrns] *n* paroles *fpl*.

utterly ['ʌtəlɪ] *ad* complètement, totalement.

U-turn ['ju:'tə:n] *n* demi-tour *m*; (*fig*) volte-face *f inv*.

V

V, v [vi:] *n* (*letter*) V, v *m*; **V for Victor** V comme Victor.

v *abbr* (= *verse*, = *vide*: *see*) v.; (= *versus*) c.; (= *volt*) V.

VA *abbr* (*US POST*) = *Virginia*.

vac [væk] *n abbr* (*Brit col*) = **vacation**.

vacancy ['veɪkənsɪ] *n* (*Brit*: *job*) poste vacant; (*room*) chambre *f* disponible; **"no vacancies"** "complet".

vacant ['veɪkənt] *a* (*post*) vacant(e); (*seat etc*) libre, disponible; (*expression*) distrait(e).

vacant lot *n* terrain inoccupé; (*for sale*) terrain à vendre.

vacate [və'keɪt] *vt* quitter.

vacation [və'keɪʃən] *n* (*esp US*) vacances *fpl*; **to take a ~** prendre des vacances; **on ~** en vacances.

vacation course *n* cours *mpl* de vacances.

vaccinate ['væksɪneɪt] *vt* vacciner.

vaccination [væksɪ'neɪʃən] *n* vaccination *f*.

vaccine ['væksi:n] *n* vaccin *m*.

vacuum ['vækjum] *n* vide *m*.
vacuum bottle *n* (*US*) = **vacuum flask**.
vacuum cleaner *n* aspirateur *m*.
vacuum flask *n* (*Brit*) bouteille *f* thermos ®.
vacuum-packed ['vækjum'pækt] *a* emballé(e) sous vide.
vagabond ['vægəbɔnd] *n* vagabond/e; (*tramp*) chemineau *m*, clochard/e.
vagary ['veɪgərɪ] *n* caprice *m*.
vagina [və'dʒaɪnə] *n* vagin *m*.
vagrancy ['veɪgrənsɪ] *n* vagabondage *m*.
vagrant ['veɪgrənt] *n* vagabond/e, mendiant/e.
vague [veɪg] *a* vague, imprécis(e); (*blurred: photo, memory*) flou(e); **I haven't the ~st idea** je n'en ai pas la moindre idée.
vaguely ['veɪglɪ] *ad* vaguement.
vain [veɪn] *a* (*useless*) vain(e); (*conceited*) vaniteux(euse); **in ~** en vain.
valance ['vælɔns] *n* (*of bed*) tour *m* de lit.
valedictory [vælɪ'dɪktərɪ] *a* d'adieu.
valentine ['væləntaɪn] *n* (*also:* ~ **card**) carte *f* de la Saint-Valentin.
valet ['vælɪt] *n* valet *m* de chambre.
valet parking *n* parcage *m* par les soins du personnel (de l'hôtel *etc*).
valet service *n* (*for clothes*) pressing *m*; (*for car*) nettoyage complet.
valiant ['væliənt] *a* vaillant(e), courageux(euse).
valid ['vælɪd] *a* valide, valable; (*excuse*) valable.
validate ['vælɪdeɪt] *vt* (*contract, document*) valider; (*argument, claim*) prouver la justesse de, confirmer.
validity [və'lɪdɪtɪ] *n* validité *f*.
valise [və'liːz] *n* sac *m* de voyage.
valley ['vælɪ] *n* vallée *f*.
valour, (*US*) **valor** ['vælə*] *n* courage *m*.
valuable ['væljuəbl] *a* (*jewel*) de grande valeur; (*time*) précieux(euse); **~s** *npl* objets *mpl* de valeur.
valuation [vælju'eɪʃən] *n* évaluation *f*, expertise *f*.
value ['væljuː] *n* valeur *f* ♦ *vt* (*fix price*) évaluer, expertiser; (*cherish*) tenir à; **you get good ~ (for money) in that shop** vous en avez pour votre argent dans ce magasin; **to lose (in) ~** (*currency*) baisser; (*property*) se déprécier; **to gain (in) ~** (*currency*) monter; (*property*) prendre de la valeur; **to be of great ~ to sb** (*fig*) être très utile à qn.
value added tax (VAT) *n* (*Brit*) taxe *f* à la valeur ajoutée (TVA).
valued ['væljuːd] *a* (*appreciated*) estimé(e).
valuer ['væljuə*] *n* expert *m* (en estimations).
valve [vælv] *n* (*in machine*) soupape *f*; (*on tyre*) valve *f*; (*in radio*) lampe *f*.
vampire ['væmpaɪə*] *n* vampire *m*.
van [væn] *n* (*AUT*) camionnette *f*; (*Brit RAIL*) fourgon *m*.
V and A *n abbr* (*Brit*) = *Victoria and Albert Museum*.
vandal ['vændl] *n* vandale *m/f*.
vandalism ['vændəlɪzəm] *n* vandalisme *m*.
vandalize ['vændəlaɪz] *vt* saccager.
vanguard ['vængɑːd] *n* avant-garde *m*.
vanilla [və'nɪlə] *n* vanille *f* ♦ *cpd* (*ice cream*) à la vanille.
vanish ['vænɪʃ] *vi* disparaître.

vanity ['vænɪtɪ] *n* vanité *f*.
vanity case *n* sac *m* de toilette.
vantage ['vɑːntɪdʒ] *n*: ~ **point** bonne position.
vaporize ['veɪpəraɪz] *vt* vaporiser ♦ *vi* se vaporiser.
vapour, (*US*) **vapor** ['veɪpə*] *n* vapeur *f*; (*on window*) buée *f*.
vapo(u)r trail *n* (*AVIAT*) traînée *f* de condensation.
variable ['vɛərɪəbl] *a* variable; (*mood*) changeant(e) ♦ *n* variable *f*.
variance ['vɛərɪəns] *n*: **to be at ~ (with)** être en désaccord (avec); (*facts*) être en contradiction (avec).
variant ['vɛərɪənt] *n* variante *f*.
variation [vɛərɪ'eɪʃən] *n* variation *f*; (*in opinion*) changement *m*.
varicose ['værɪkəus] *a*: ~ **veins** varices *fpl*.
varied ['vɛərɪd] *a* varié(e), divers(e).
variety [və'raɪətɪ] *n* variété *f*; (*quantity*): **a wide ~ of** ... une quantité *or* un grand nombre de ... (différent(e)s *or* divers(es)); **for a ~ of reasons** pour diverses raisons.
variety show *n* (spectacle *m* de) variétés *fpl*.
various ['vɛərɪəs] *a* divers(e), différent(e); (*several*) divers, plusieurs; **at ~ times** (*different*) en diverses occasions; (*several*) à plusieurs reprises.
varnish ['vɑːnɪʃ] *n* vernis *m*; (*for nails*) vernis (à ongles) ♦ *vt* vernir; **to ~ one's nails** se vernir les ongles.
vary ['vɛərɪ] *vt, vi* varier, changer; **to ~ with** *or* **according to** varier selon.
varying ['vɛərɪɪŋ] *a* variable.
vase [vɑːz] *n* vase *m*.
vasectomy [væ'sɛktəmɪ] *n* vasectomie *f*.
vaseline ['væsɪliːn] *n* ® vaseline *f*.
vast [vɑːst] *a* vaste, immense; (*amount, success*) énorme.
vastly ['vɑːstlɪ] *ad* infiniment, extrêmement.
vastness ['vɑːstnɪs] *n* immensité *f*.
VAT [væt] *n abbr* (*Brit*) = **value added tax**.
vat [væt] *n* cuve *f*.
Vatican ['vætɪkən] *n*: **the ~** le Vatican.
vault [vɔːlt] *n* (*of roof*) voûte *f*; (*tomb*) caveau *m*; (*in bank*) salle *f* des coffres; chambre forte; (*jump*) saut *m* ♦ *vt* (*also:* ~ **over**) sauter (d'un bond).
vaunted ['vɔːntɪd] *a*: **much-~** tant célébré(e).
VC *n abbr* = **vice-chairman**; (*Brit*: = *Victoria Cross*) *distinction militaire*.
VCR *n abbr* = **video cassette recorder**.
VD *n abbr* = **venereal disease**.
VDU *n abbr* = **visual display unit**.
veal [viːl] *n* veau *m*.
veer [vɪə*] *vi* tourner; virer.
veg. [vɛdʒ] *n abbr* (*Brit col*) = **vegetable(s)**.
vegetable ['vɛdʒtəbl] *n* légume *m* ♦ *a* végétal(e).
vegetable garden *n* (jardin *m*) potager *m*.
vegetarian [vɛdʒɪ'tɛərɪən] *a, n* végétarien(ne).
vegetate ['vɛdʒɪteɪt] *vi* végéter.
vegetation [vɛdʒɪ'teɪʃən] *n* végétation *f*.
vehemence ['viːɪməns] *n* véhémence *f*, violence *f*.
vehement ['viːɪmənt] *a* violent(e), impétueux(euse); (*impassioned*) ardent(e).
vehicle ['viːɪkl] *n* véhicule *m*.
vehicular [vɪ'hɪkjulə*] *a*: **"no ~ traffic"**

"interdit à tout véhicule".

veil [veɪl] *n* voile *m* ♦ *vt* voiler; **under a ~ of secrecy** (*fig*) dans le plus grand secret.

veiled [veɪld] *a* voilé(e).

vein [veɪn] *n* veine *f*; (*on leaf*) nervure *f*; (*fig: mood*) esprit *m*.

vellum ['vɛləm] *n* (*writing paper*) vélin *m*.

velocity [vɪ'lɔsɪtɪ] *n* vitesse *f*, vélocité *f*.

velvet ['vɛlvɪt] *n* velours *m*.

vending machine ['vɛndɪŋ-] *n* distributeur *m* automatique.

vendor ['vɛndə*] *n* vendeur/euse; **street ~** marchand ambulant.

veneer [və'nɪə*] *n* placage *m* de bois; (*fig*) vernis *m*.

venerable ['vɛnərəbl] *a* vénérable.

venereal [vɪ'nɪərɪəl] *a*: **~ disease (VD)** maladie vénérienne.

Venetian [vɪ'niːʃən] *a*: **~ blind** store vénitien.

Venezuela [vɛnɛ'zweɪlə] *n* Venezuela *m*.

Venezuelan [vɛnɛ'zweɪlən] *a* vénézuélien(ne) ♦ *n* Vénézuélien/ne.

vengeance ['vɛndʒəns] *n* vengeance *f*; **with a ~** (*fig*) vraiment, pour de bon.

vengeful ['vɛndʒful] *a* vengeur(geresse).

Venice ['vɛnɪs] *n* Venise.

venison ['vɛnɪsn] *n* venaison *f*.

venom ['vɛnəm] *n* venin *m*.

venomous ['vɛnəməs] *a* venimeux(euse).

vent [vɛnt] *n* conduit *m* d'aération; (*in dress, jacket*) fente *f* ♦ *vt* (*fig: one's feelings*) donner libre cours à.

ventilate ['vɛntɪleɪt] *vt* (*room*) ventiler, aérer.

ventilation [vɛntɪ'leɪʃən] *n* ventilation *f*, aération *f*.

ventilation shaft *n* conduit *m* de ventilation *or* d'aération.

ventilator ['vɛntɪleɪtə*] *n* ventilateur *m*.

ventriloquist [vɛn'trɪləkwɪst] *n* ventriloque *m/f*.

venture ['vɛntʃə*] *n* entreprise *f* ♦ *vt* risquer, hasarder ♦ *vi* s'aventurer, se risquer; **a business ~** une entreprise commerciale; **to ~ to do sth** se risquer à faire qch.

venture capital *n* capital-risques *m*.

venue ['vɛnjuː] *n* (*of conference etc*) lieu *m* de la réunion (*or* manifestation *etc*); (*of match*) lieu de la rencontre.

Venus ['viːnəs] *n* (*planet*) Vénus *f*.

veracity [və'ræsɪtɪ] *n* véracité *f*.

veranda(h) [və'rændə] *n* véranda *f*.

verb [vəːb] *n* verbe *m*.

verbal ['vəːbl] *a* verbal(e); (*translation*) littéral(e).

verbally ['vəːbəlɪ] *ad* verbalement.

verbatim [vəː'beɪtɪm] *a, ad* mot pour mot.

verbose [vəː'bəus] *a* verbeux(euse).

verdict ['vəːdɪkt] *n* verdict *m*; **~ of guilty/not guilty** verdict de culpabilité/de non-culpabilité.

verge [vəːdʒ] *n* bord *m*; **"soft ~s"** (*Brit*) "accotements non stabilisés"; **on the ~ of doing** sur le point de faire.

verge on *vt fus* approcher de.

verger ['vəːdʒə*] *n* (*REL*) bedeau *m*.

verification [vɛrɪfɪ'keɪʃən] *n* vérification *f*.

verify ['vɛrɪfaɪ] *vt* vérifier.

veritable ['vɛrɪtəbl] *a* véritable.

vermin ['vəːmɪn] *npl* animaux *mpl* nuisibles; (*insects*) vermine *f*.

vermouth ['vəːməθ] *n* vermouth *m*.

vernacular [və'nækjulə*] *n* langue *f* vernaculaire, dialecte *m*.

versatile ['vəːsətaɪl] *a* polyvalent(e).

verse [vəːs] *n* vers *mpl*; (*stanza*) strophe *f*; (*in bible*) verset *m*; **in ~** en vers.

versed [vəːst] *a*: **(well-)~ in** versé(e) dans.

version ['vəːʃən] *n* version *f*.

versus ['vəːsəs] *prep* contre.

vertebra, *pl* **~e** ['vəːtɪbrə, -briː] *n* vertèbre *f*.

vertebrate ['vəːtɪbrɪt] *n* vertébré *m*.

vertical ['vəːtɪkl] *a* vertical(e) ♦ *n* verticale *f*.

vertically ['vəːtɪklɪ] *ad* verticalement.

vertigo ['vəːtɪgəu] *n* vertige *m*; **to suffer from ~** avoir des vertiges.

verve [vəːv] *n* brio *m*; enthousiasme *m*.

very ['vɛrɪ] *ad* très ♦ *a*: **the ~ book which** le livre même que; **the ~ thought (of it)** ... rien que d'y penser ...; **at the ~ end** tout à la fin; **the ~ last** le tout dernier; **at the ~ least** au moins; **~ well** très bien; **~ little** très peu; **~ much** beaucoup.

vespers ['vɛspəz] *npl* vêpres *fpl*.

vessel ['vɛsl] *n* (*ANAT*, *NAUT*) vaisseau *m*; (*container*) récipient *m*.

vest [vɛst] *n* (*Brit*) tricot *m* de corps; (*US*) gilet *m* ♦ *vt*: **to ~ sb with sth, to ~ sth in sb** investir qn de qch.

vested interest *n*: **to have a ~ in doing** avoir tout intérêt à faire; **~s** *npl* (*COMM*) droits acquis.

vestibule ['vɛstɪbjuːl] *n* vestibule *m*.

vestige ['vɛstɪdʒ] *n* vestige *m*.

vestry ['vɛstrɪ] *n* sacristie *f*.

Vesuvius [vɪ'suːvɪəs] *n* Vésuve *m*.

vet [vɛt] *n abbr* (= *veterinary surgeon*) vétérinaire *m/f* ♦ *vt* examiner minutieusement; (*text*) revoir; (*candidate*) se renseigner soigneusement sur, soumettre à une enquête approfondie.

veteran ['vɛtərn] *n* vétéran *m*; (*also*: **war ~**) ancien combattant ♦ *a*: **she's a ~ campaigner for** ... cela fait très longtemps qu'elle lutte pour ....

veteran car *n* voiture *f* d'époque.

veterinarian [vɛtrɪ'nɛərɪən] *n* (*US*) = **veterinary surgeon**.

veterinary ['vɛtrɪnərɪ] *a* vétérinaire.

veterinary surgeon *n* (*Brit*) vétérinaire *m/f*.

veto ['viːtəu] *n* (*pl* **~es**) veto *m* ♦ *vt* opposer son veto à; **to put a ~ on** mettre (*or* opposer) son veto à.

vex [vɛks] *vt* fâcher, contrarier.

vexed [vɛkst] *a* (*question*) controversé(e).

VFD *n abbr* (*US*) = *voluntary fire department*.

VG *n abbr* (*Brit*: *SCOL etc*: = *very good*) tb (= *très bien*).

VHF *abbr* (= *very high frequency*) VHF.

VI *abbr* (*US POST*) = *Virgin Islands*.

via ['vaɪə] *prep* par, via.

viability [vaɪə'bɪlɪtɪ] *n* viabilité *f*.

viable ['vaɪəbl] *a* viable.

viaduct ['vaɪədʌkt] *n* viaduc *m*.

vibrant ['vaɪbrnt] *a* (*sound, colour*) vibrant(e).

vibrate [vaɪ'breɪt] *vi*: **to ~ (with)** vibrer (de); (*resound*) retentir (de).

vibration [vaɪ'breɪʃən] *n* vibration *f*.

vicar ['vɪkə*] *n* pasteur *m* (*de l'Église an-*

glicane).

vicarage ['vɪkərɪdʒ] *n* presbytère *m*.
vicarious [vɪ'kɛərɪəs] *a* (*pleasure, experience*) indirect(e).
vice [vaɪs] *n* (*evil*) vice *m*; (*TECH*) étau *m*.
vice- [vaɪs] *prefix* vice-.
vice-chairman [vaɪs'tʃɛəmən] *n* vice-président/e.
vice-chancellor [vaɪs't ʃɑ:nsələ*] *n* (*Brit*) ≈ président/e d'université.
vice-president [vaɪs'prɛzɪdənt] *n* vice-président/e.
vice squad *n* ≈ brigade mondaine.
vice versa ['vaɪsɪ'vɜːsə] *ad* vice versa.
vicinity [vɪ'sɪnɪtɪ] *n* environs *mpl*, alentours *mpl*.
vicious ['vɪʃəs] *a* (*remark*) cruel(le), méchant(e); (*blow*) brutal(e); **a ~ circle** un cercle vicieux.
viciousness ['vɪʃəsnɪs] *n* méchanceté *f*, cruauté *f*; brutalité *f*.
vicissitudes [vɪ'sɪsɪtjuːdz] *npl* vicissitudes *fpl*.
victim ['vɪktɪm] *n* victime *f*; **to be the ~ of** être victime de.
victimization ['vɪktɪmaɪ'zeɪʃən] *n* brimades *fpl*; représailles *fpl*.
victimize ['vɪktɪmaɪz] *vt* brimer; exercer des représailles sur.
victor ['vɪktə*] *n* vainqueur *m*.
Victorian [vɪk'tɔːrɪən] *a* victorien(ne).
victorious [vɪk'tɔːrɪəs] *a* victorieux(euse).
victory ['vɪktərɪ] *n* victoire *f*; **to win a ~ over sb** remporter une victoire sur qn.
video ['vɪdɪəʊ] *n* (~ *film*) vidéo *f*; (*also:* ~ **cassette**) vidéocassette *f*; (*also:* ~ **cassette recorder**) magnétoscope *m* ♦ *cpd* vidéo *inv*.
video cassette *n* vidéocassette *f*.
video cassette recorder *n* magnétoscope *m*.
video recording *n* enregistrement *m* (en) vidéo.
video tape *n* bande *f* vidéo *inv*; (*cassette*) vidéocassette *f*.
vie [vaɪ] *vi*: **to ~ with** lutter avec, rivaliser avec.
Vienna [vɪ'ɛnə] *n* Vienne.
Vietnam, Viet Nam ['vjɛt'næm] *n* Viet-Nam *or* Vietnam *m*.
Vietnamese [vjɛtnə'miːz] *a* vietnamien(ne) ♦ *n* (*pl inv*) Vietnamien/ne; (*LING*) vietnamien *m*.
view [vjuː] *n* vue *f*; (*opinion*) avis *m*, vue ♦ *vt* (*situation*) considérer; (*house*) visiter; **on ~** (*in museum etc*) exposé(e); **in full ~ of sb** sous les yeux de qn; **to be within ~ (of sth)** être à portée de vue (de qch); **an overall ~ of the situation** une vue d'ensemble de la situation; **in my ~** à mon avis; **in ~ of the fact that** étant donné que; **with a ~ to doing sth** dans l'intention de faire qch.
viewdata ['vjuːdeɪtə] *n* (*Brit*) télétexte *m* (*version téléphonique*).
viewer ['vjuːə*] *n* (*viewfinder*) viseur *m*; (*small projector*) visionneuse *f*; (*TV*) téléspectateur/trice.
viewfinder ['vjuːfaɪndə*] *n* viseur *m*.
viewpoint ['vjuːpɔɪnt] *n* point *m* de vue.
vigil ['vɪdʒɪl] *n* veille *f*; **to keep ~** veiller.
vigilance ['vɪdʒɪləns] *n* vigilance *f*.
vigilance committee *n* comité *m*

d'autodéfense.
vigilant ['vɪdʒɪlənt] *a* vigilant(e).
vigorous ['vɪɡərəs] *a* vigoureux(euse).
vigour, (*US*) **vigor** ['vɪɡə*] *n* vigueur *f*.
vile [vaɪl] *a* (*action*) vil(e); (*smell*) abominable; (*temper*) massacrant(e).
vilify ['vɪlɪfaɪ] *vt* calomnier, vilipender.
villa ['vɪlə] *n* villa *f*.
village ['vɪlɪdʒ] *n* village *m*.
villager ['vɪlɪdʒə*] *n* villageois/e.
villain ['vɪlən] *n* (*scoundrel*) scélérat *m*; (*criminal*) bandit *m*; (*in novel etc*) traître *m*.
VIN *n abbr* (*US*) = *vehicle identification number.*
vindicate ['vɪndɪkeɪt] *vt* défendre avec succès; justifier.
vindication [vɪndɪ'keɪʃən] *n*: **in ~ of** pour justifier.
vindictive [vɪn'dɪktɪv] *a* vindicatif(ive), rancunier(ière).
vine [vaɪn] *n* vigne *f*; (*climbing plant*) plante grimpante.
vinegar ['vɪnɪɡə*] *n* vinaigre *m*.
vine grower *n* viticulteur *m*.
vine-growing ['vaɪnɡrəʊɪŋ] *a* viticole ♦ *n* viticulture *f*.
vineyard ['vɪnjɑːd] *n* vignoble *m*.
vintage ['vɪntɪdʒ] *n* (*year*) année *f*, millésime *m*; **the 1970 ~** le millésime 1970.
vintage car *n* voiture ancienne.
vintage wine *n* vin *m* de grand cru.
vinyl ['vaɪnl] *n* vinyle *m*.
viola [vɪ'əʊlə] *n* alto *m*.
violate ['vaɪəleɪt] *vt* violer.
violation [vaɪə'leɪʃən] *n* violation *f*; **in ~ of** (*rule, law*) en infraction à, en violation de.
violence ['vaɪələns] *n* violence *f*; (*POL etc*) incidents violents.
violent ['vaɪələnt] *a* violent(e); **a ~ dislike of sb/sth** une aversion profonde pour qn/qch.
violently ['vaɪələntlɪ] *ad* violemment; (*ill, angry*) terriblement.
violet ['vaɪələt] *a* (*colour*) violet(te) ♦ *n* (*plant*) violette *f*.
violin [vaɪə'lɪn] *n* violon *m*.
violinist [vaɪə'lɪnɪst] *n* violoniste *m/f*.
VIP *n abbr* (= *very important person*) VIP *m*.
viper ['vaɪpə*] *n* vipère *f*.
virgin ['vɜːdʒɪn] *n* vierge *f* ♦ *a* vierge; **she is a ~** elle est vierge; **the Blessed V~** la Sainte Vierge.
virginity [vɜː'dʒɪnɪtɪ] *n* virginité *f*.
Virgo ['vɜːɡəʊ] *n* la Vierge; **to be ~** être de la Vierge.
virile ['vɪraɪl] *a* viril(e).
virility [vɪ'rɪlɪtɪ] *n* virilité *f*.
virtual ['vɜːtjʊəl] *a* (*COMPUT, PHYSICS*) virtuel(le); (*in effect*) **it's a ~ impossibility** c'est pratiquement impossible; **the ~ leader** le chef dans la pratique.
virtually ['vɜːtjʊəlɪ] *ad* (*almost*) pratiquement; **it is ~ impossible** c'est quasiment impossible.
virtue ['vɜːtjuː] *n* vertu *f*; (*advantage*) mérite *m*, avantage *m*; **by ~ of** par le fait de.
virtuoso [vɜːtjʊ'əʊzəʊ] *n* virtuose *m/f*.
virtuous ['vɜːtjʊəs] *a* vertueux(euse).
virulent ['vɪrʊlənt] *a* virulent(e).
virus ['vaɪərəs] *n* virus *m*.

visa ['viːzə] *n* visa *m*.
vis-à-vis [viːzəˈviː] *prep* vis-à-vis de.
viscount ['vaɪkaʊnt] *n* vicomte *m*.
viscous ['vɪskəs] *a* visqueux(euse), gluant(e).
vise [vaɪs] *n* (*US TECH*) = **vice**.
visibility [vɪzɪ'bɪlɪtɪ] *n* visibilité *f*.
visible ['vɪzəbl] *a* visible; ~ **exports/imports** exportations/importations *fpl* visibles.
visibly ['vɪzəblɪ] *ad* visiblement.
vision ['vɪʒən] *n* (*sight*) vue *f*, vision *f*; (*foresight, in dream*) vision.
visionary ['vɪʒənrɪ] *n* visionnaire *m/f*.
visit ['vɪzɪt] *n* visite *f*; (*stay*) séjour *m* ♦ *vt* (*person*) rendre visite à; (*place*) visiter; **on a private/official** ~ en visite privée/officielle.
visiting ['vɪzɪtɪŋ] *a* (*speaker, team*) invité(e), de l'extérieur.
visiting card *n* carte *f* de visite.
visiting hours *npl* heures *fpl* de visite.
visiting professor *n* ≈ professeur associé.
visitor ['vɪzɪtə*] *n* visiteur/euse; (*in hotel*) client/e.
visitors' book *n* livre *m* d'or; (*in hotel*) registre *m*.
visor ['vaɪzə*] *n* visière *f*.
VISTA ['vɪstə] *n abbr* (= *Volunteers in Service to America*) programme d'assistance bénévole aux régions pauvres.
vista ['vɪstə] *n* vue *f*, perspective *f*.
visual ['vɪzjʊəl] *a* visuel(le).
visual aid *n* support visuel (pour l'enseignement).
visual display unit (VDU) *n* console *f* de visualisation, visuel *m*.
visualize ['vɪzjʊəlaɪz] *vt* se représenter; (*foresee*) prévoir.
visually ['vɪzjʊəlɪ] *ad* visuellement; ~ **handicapped** handicapé(e) visuel(le).
vital ['vaɪtl] *a* vital(e); **of** ~ **importance (to sb/sth)** d'une importance capitale (pour qn/qch).
vitality [vaɪ'tælɪtɪ] *n* vitalité *f*.
vitally ['vaɪtəlɪ] *ad* extrêmement.
vital statistics *npl* (*of population*) statistiques *fpl* démographiques; (*col: woman's*) mensurations *fpl*.
vitamin ['vɪtəmɪn] *n* vitamine *f*.
vitiate ['vɪʃɪeɪt] *vt* vicier.
vitreous ['vɪtrɪəs] *a* (*china*) vitreux(euse); (*enamel*) vitrifié(e).
vitriolic [vɪtrɪ'ɔlɪk] *a* (*fig*) venimeux(euse).
viva ['vaɪvə] *n* (*also:* ~ **voce**) (*examen*) oral.
vivacious [vɪ'veɪʃəs] *a* animé(e), qui a de la vivacité.
vivacity [vɪ'væsɪtɪ] *n* vivacité *f*.
vivid ['vɪvɪd] *a* (*account*) frappant(e); (*light, imagination*) vif(vive).
vividly ['vɪvɪdlɪ] *ad* (*describe*) d'une manière vivante; (*remember*) de façon précise.
vivisection [vɪvɪ'sɛkʃən] *n* vivisection *f*.
vixen ['vɪksn] *n* renarde *f*; (*pej: woman*) mégère *f*.
viz *abbr* (= *vide licet: namely*) à savoir, c. à d.
VLF *abbr* = *very low frequency*.
V-neck ['viːnɛk] *n* décolleté *m* en V.
VOA *n abbr* (= *Voice of America*) voix *f* de l'Amérique (*émissions de radio à destination de l'étranger*).

vocabulary [vəu'kæbjulərɪ] *n* vocabulaire *m*.
vocal ['vəukl] *a* vocal(e); (*articulate*) qui n'hésite pas à s'exprimer, qui sait faire entendre ses opinions; ~**s** *npl* voix *fpl*.
vocal chords *npl* cordes vocales.
vocalist ['vəukəlɪst] *n* chanteur/euse.
vocation [vəu'keɪʃən] *n* vocation *f*.
vocational [vəu'keɪʃənl] *a* professionnel(le); ~ **guidance/training** orientation/formation professionnelle.
vociferous [və'sɪfərəs] *a* bruyant(e).
vodka ['vɔdkə] *n* vodka *f*.
vogue [vəug] *n* mode *f*; (*popularity*) vogue *f*; **to be in** ~ être en vogue or à la mode.
voice [vɔɪs] *n* voix *f*; (*opinion*) avis *m* ♦ *vt* (*opinion*) exprimer, formuler; **in a loud/soft** ~ à voix haute/basse; **to give** ~ **to** exprimer.
void [vɔɪd] *n* vide *m* ♦ *a* (*invalid*) nul(le); (*empty*): ~ **of** vide de, dépourvu(e) de.
voile [vɔɪl] *n* voile *m* (*tissu*).
vol. *abbr* (= *volume*) vol.
volatile ['vɔlətaɪl] *a* volatil(e); (*fig*) versatile.
volcanic [vɔl'kænɪk] *a* volcanique.
volcano, ~es [vɔl'keɪnəu] *n* volcan *m*.
volition [və'lɪʃən] *n*: **of one's own** ~ de son propre gré.
volley ['vɔlɪ] *n* (*of gunfire*) salve *f*; (*of stones etc*) pluie *f*, volée *f*; (*TENNIS etc*) volée *f*.
volleyball ['vɔlɪbɔːl] *n* volley(-ball) *m*.
volt [vəult] *n* volt *m*.
voltage ['vəultɪdʒ] *n* tension *f*, voltage *m*; **high/low** ~ haute/basse tension.
voluble ['vɔljubl] *a* volubile.
volume ['vɔljuːm] *n* volume *m*; (*of tank*) capacité *f*; ~ **one/two** (*of book*) tome un/deux; **his expression spoke** ~**s** son expression en disait long.
volume control *n* (*RADIO, TV*) bouton *m* de réglage du volume.
volume discount *n* (*COMM*) remise *f* sur la quantité.
voluminous [və'luːmɪnəs] *a* volumineux(euse).
voluntarily ['vɔləntrɪlɪ] *ad* volontairement; bénévolement.
voluntary ['vɔləntərɪ] *a* volontaire; (*unpaid*) bénévole.
voluntary liquidation *n* (*COMM*) dépôt *m* de bilan.
voluntary redundancy *n* (*Brit*) départ *m* volontaire (*en cas de licenciements*).
volunteer [vɔlən'tɪə*] *n* volontaire *m/f* ♦ *vi* (*MIL*) s'engager comme volontaire; **to** ~ **to do** se proposer pour faire.
voluptuous [və'lʌptjuəs] *a* voluptueux(euse).
vomit ['vɔmɪt] *n* vomissure *f* ♦ *vt, vi* vomir.
vote [vəut] *n* vote *m*, suffrage *m*; (*cast*) voix *f*, vote; (*franchise*) droit *m* de vote ♦ *vt* (*bill*) voter; (*chairman*) élire ♦ *vi* voter; **to put sth to the** ~, **to take a** ~ **on sth** mettre qch aux voix, procéder à un vote sur qch; ~ **for** or **in favour of/against** voter pour/contre; **to** ~ **to do sth** voter en faveur de faire qch; ~ **of censure** motion *f* de censure; ~ **of thanks** discours *m* de remerciement.
voter ['vəutə*] *n* électeur/trice.
voting ['vəutɪŋ] *n* scrutin *m*.
voting paper *n* (*Brit*) bulletin *m* de vote.
voting right *n* droit *m* de vote.
vouch [vautʃ] *vt*: **to** ~ **for** *vt fus* se porter

garant de.

voucher ['vautʃə*] *n* (*for meal, petrol*) bon *m*; (*receipt*) reçu *m*; **travel** ~ bon *m* de transport.

vow [vau] *n* vœu *m*, serment *m* ♦ *vi* jurer; **to take** *or* **make a** ~ **to do sth** faire le vœu de faire qch.

vowel ['vauəl] *n* voyelle *f*.

voyage ['vɔɪɪdʒ] *n* voyage *m* par mer, traversée *f*.

VP *n abbr* = **vice-president**.

vs *abbr* (= *versus*) c.

VSO *n abbr* (*Brit*: = *Voluntary Service Overseas*) ≈ coopération civile.

VT *abbr* (*US POST*) = *Vermont*.

vulgar ['vʌlɡə*] *a* vulgaire.

vulgarity [vʌl'ɡærɪtɪ] *n* vulgarité *f*.

vulnerability [vʌlnərə'bɪlɪtɪ] *n* vulnérabilité *f*.

vulnerable ['vʌlnərəbl] *a* vulnérable.

vulture ['vʌltʃə*] *n* vautour *m*.

W

W, w ['dʌblju:] *n* (*letter*) W, w *m*; **W for William** W comme William.

W *abbr* (= *west*) O; (*ELEC*: = *watt*) W.

WA *abbr* (*US POST*) = *Washington*.

wad [wɔd] *n* (*of cotton wool, paper*) tampon *m*; (*of banknotes etc*) liasse *f*.

wadding ['wɔdɪŋ] *n* rembourrage *m*.

waddle ['wɔdl] *vi* se dandiner.

wade [weɪd] *vi*: **to** ~ **through** marcher dans, patauger dans ♦ *vt* passer à gué.

wafer ['weɪfə*] *n* (*CULIN*) gaufrette *f*; (*REL*) pain *m* d'hostie; (*COMPUT*) tranche *f* (de silicium).

wafer-thin ['weɪfə'θɪn] *a* ultra-mince, mince comme du papier à cigarette.

waffle ['wɔfl] *n* (*CULIN*) gaufre *f*; (*col*) rabâchage *m*; remplissage *m* ♦ *vi* parler pour ne rien dire; faire du remplissage.

waffle iron *n* gaufrier *m*.

waft [wɔft] *vt* porter ♦ *vi* flotter.

wag [wæɡ] *vt* agiter, remuer ♦ *vi* remuer; **the dog** ~**ged its tail** le chien a remué la queue.

wage [weɪdʒ] *n* (*also*: ~**s**) salaire *m*, paye *f* ♦ *vt*: **to** ~ **war** faire la guerre; **a day's** ~**s** un jour de salaire.

wage claim *n* demande *f* d'augmentation de salaire.

wage differential *n* éventail *m* des salaires.

wage earner *n* salarié/e; (*breadwinner*) soutien *m* de famille.

wage freeze *n* blocage *m* des salaires.

wage packet *n* (*Brit*) (enveloppe *f* de) paye *f*.

wager ['weɪdʒə*] *n* pari *m* ♦ *vt* parier.

waggle ['wæɡl] *vt*, *vi* remuer.

wag(g)on ['wæɡən] *n* (*horse-drawn*) chariot *m*; (*Brit RAIL*) wagon *m* (de marchandises).

wail [weɪl] *n* gémissement *m*; (*of siren*) hurlement *m* ♦ *vi* gémir; hurler.

waist [weɪst] *n* taille *f*, ceinture *f*.

waistcoat ['weɪskəut] *n* (*Brit*) gilet *m*.

waistline ['weɪstlaɪn] *n* (tour *m* de) taille *f*.

wait [weɪt] *n* attente *f* ♦ *vi* attendre; **to** ~ **for sb/sth** attendre qn/qch; **to keep sb** ~**ing** faire attendre qn; ~ **a minute!** un instant!; **"repairs while you** ~**"** "réparations minute"; **I can't** ~ **to ...** (*fig*) je meurs d'envie de ...; **to lie in** ~ **for** guetter.

wait behind *vi* rester (à attendre).

wait on *vt fus* servir.

wait up *vi* attendre, ne pas se coucher; **don't** ~ **up for me** ne m'attendez pas pour aller vous coucher.

waiter ['weɪtə*] *n* garçon *m* (de café), serveur *m*.

waiting ['weɪtɪŋ] *n*: **"no** ~**"** (*Brit AUT*) "stationnement interdit".

waiting list *n* liste *f* d'attente.

waiting room *n* salle *f* d'attente.

waitress ['weɪtrɪs] *n* serveuse *f*.

waive [weɪv] *vt* renoncer à, abandonner.

waiver ['weɪvə*] *n* dispense *f*.

wake [weɪk] *vb* (*pt* **woke**, ~**d**, *pp* **woken**, ~**d** [wəuk, 'wəukn]) *vt* (*also*: ~ **up**) réveiller ♦ *vi* (*also*: ~ **up**) se réveiller ♦ *n* (*for dead person*) veillée *f* mortuaire; (*NAUT*) sillage *m*; **to** ~ **up to sth** (*fig*) se rendre compte de qch; **in the** ~ **of** (*fig*) à la suite de; **to follow in sb's** ~ (*fig*) marcher sur les traces de qn.

waken ['weɪkn] *vt*, *vi* = **wake**.

Wales [weɪlz] *n* pays *m* de Galles.

walk [wɔːk] *n* promenade *f*; (*short*) petit tour; (*gait*) démarche *f*; (*pace*): **at a quick** ~ d'un pas rapide; (*path*) chemin *m*; (*in park etc*) allée *f* ♦ *vi* marcher; (*for pleasure, exercise*) se promener ♦ *vt* (*distance*) faire à pied; (*dog*) promener; **10 minutes'** ~ **from** à 10 minutes de marche de; **to go for a** ~ se promener; faire un tour; **I'll** ~ **you home** je vais vous raccompagner chez vous; **from all** ~**s of life** de toutes conditions sociales.

walk out *vi* (*go out*) sortir; (*as protest*) partir (en signe de protestation); (*strike*) se mettre en grève; **to** ~ **out on sb** quitter qn.

walker ['wɔːkə*] *n* (*person*) marcheur/euse.

walkie-talkie ['wɔːkɪ'tɔːkɪ] *n* talkie-walkie *m*.

walking ['wɔːkɪŋ] *n* marche *f* à pied; **it's within** ~ **distance** on peut y aller à pied.

walking holiday *n* vacances passées à faire de la randonnée.

walking shoes *npl* chaussures *fpl* de marche.

walking stick *n* canne *f*.

walk-on ['wɔːkɔn] *a* (*THEATRE*: *part*) de figurant/e.

walkout ['wɔːkaut] *n* (*of workers*) grève-surprise *f*.

walkover ['wɔːkəuvə*] *n* (*col*) victoire *f or* examen *m etc* facile.

walkway ['wɔːkweɪ] *n* promenade *f*, cheminement piéton.

wall [wɔːl] *n* mur *m*; (*of tunnel, cave*) paroi *f*; **to go to the** ~ (*fig: firm etc*) faire faillite.

wall in *vt* (*garden etc*) entourer d'un mur.

wall cupboard *n* placard mural.

walled [wɔːld] *a* (*city*) fortifié(e).

wallet ['wɔlɪt] *n* portefeuille *m*.

wallflower ['wɔːlflauə*] *n* giroflée *f*; **to be a** ~ (*fig*) faire tapisserie.

wall hanging n tenture (murale), tapisserie f.

wallop ['wɔləp] vt (Brit col) taper sur, cogner.

wallow ['wɔləʊ] vi se vautrer; **to ~ in one's grief** se complaire à sa douleur.

wallpaper ['wɔ:lpeɪpə*] n papier peint.

wall-to-wall ['wɔ:ltə'wɔ:l] a: **~ carpeting** moquette f.

wally [wɔlɪ] n (col) imbécile m/f.

walnut ['wɔ:lnʌt] n noix f; (tree) noyer m.

walrus, pl ~ or **~es** ['wɔ:lrəs] n morse m.

waltz [wɔ:lts] n valse f ♦ vi valser.

wan [wɔn] a pâle; triste.

wand [wɔnd] n (also: **magic ~**) baguette f (magique).

wander ['wɔndə*] vi (person) errer, aller sans but; (thoughts) vagabonder; (river) serpenter ♦ vt errer dans.

wanderer ['wɔndərə*] n vagabond/e.

wandering ['wɔndrɪŋ] a (tribe) nomade; (minstrel, actor) ambulant(e).

wane [weɪn] vi (moon) décroître; (reputation) décliner.

wangle ['wæŋgl] (Brit col) vt se débrouiller pour avoir; carotter ♦ n combine f, magouille f.

want [wɔnt] vt vouloir; (need) avoir besoin de; (lack) manquer de ♦ n (poverty) pauvreté f, besoin m; **~s** npl (needs) besoins mpl; **for ~ of** par manque de, faute de; **to ~ to do** vouloir faire; **to ~ sb to do** vouloir que qn fasse; **you're ~ed on the phone** on vous demande au téléphone; **"cook ~ed"** "on demande un cuisinier".

want ads npl (US) petites annonces.

wanting ['wɔntɪŋ] a: **to be ~ (in)** manquer (de); **to be found ~** ne pas être à la hauteur.

wanton ['wɔntn] a capricieux(euse); dévergondé(e).

war [wɔ:*] n guerre f; **to go to ~** se mettre en guerre.

warble ['wɔ:bl] n (of bird) gazouillis m ♦ vi gazouiller.

war cry n cri m de guerre.

ward [wɔ:d] n (in hospital) salle f; (POL) section électorale; (LAW: child) pupille m/f.
ward off vt parer, éviter.

warden ['wɔ:dn] n (Brit: of institution) directeur/trice; (of park, game reserve) gardien/ne; (Brit: also: **traffic ~**) contractuel/le.

warder ['wɔ:də*] n (Brit) gardien m de prison.

wardrobe ['wɔ:drəʊb] n (cupboard) armoire f; (clothes) garde-robe f; (THEATRE) costumes mpl.

warehouse ['wɛəhaʊs] n entrepôt m.

wares [wɛəz] npl marchandises fpl.

warfare ['wɔ:fɛə*] n guerre f.

war game n jeu m de stratégie militaire.

warhead ['wɔ:hɛd] n (MIL) ogive f.

warily ['wɛərɪlɪ] ad avec prudence, avec précaution.

warlike ['wɔ:laɪk] a guerrier(ière).

warm [wɔ:m] a chaud(e); (person, greeting, welcome, applause) chaleureux(euse); (supporter) ardent(e), enthousiaste; **it's ~** il fait chaud; **I'm ~** j'ai chaud; **to keep sth ~** tenir qch au chaud; **with my ~est thanks/**

congratulations avec mes remerciements/ mes félicitations les plus sincères.

warm up vi (person, room) se réchauffer; (water) chauffer; (athlete, discussion) s'échauffer ♦ vt réchauffer; chauffer; (engine) faire chauffer.

warm-blooded ['wɔ:m'blʌdɪd] a (ZOOL) à sang chaud.

war memorial n monument m aux morts.

warm-hearted [wɔ:m'hɑ:tɪd] a affectueux(euse).

warmly ['wɔ:mlɪ] ad chaudement; chaleureusement.

warmonger ['wɔ:mʌŋgə*] n belliciste m/f.

warmongering ['wɔ:mʌŋgrɪŋ] n propagande f belliciste, bellicisme m.

warmth [wɔ:mθ] n chaleur f.

warm-up ['wɔ:mʌp] n (SPORT) période f d'échauffement.

warn [wɔ:n] vt avertir, prévenir; **to ~ sb not to do sth** or **against doing sth** prévenir qn de ne pas faire qch.

warning ['wɔ:nɪŋ] n avertissement m; (notice) avis m; **without (any) ~** (suddenly) inopinément; (without notifying) sans prévenir; **gale ~** (METEOROLOGY) avis de grand vent.

warning light n avertisseur lumineux.

warning triangle n (AUT) triangle m de présignalisation.

warp [wɔ:p] n (TEXTILES) chaîne f ♦ vi (wood) travailler, se voiler or gauchir ♦ vt voiler; (fig) pervertir.

warpath ['wɔ:pɑ:θ] n: **to be on the ~** (fig) être sur le sentier de la guerre.

warped [wɔ:pt] a (wood) gauchi(e); (fig) perverti(e).

warrant ['wɔrnt] n (guarantee) garantie f; (LAW: to arrest) mandat m d'arrêt; (: to search) mandat de perquisition ♦ vt (justify, merit) justifier.

warrant officer n (MIL) adjudant m; (NAUT) premier-maître m.

warranty ['wɔrəntɪ] n garantie f; **under ~** (COMM) sous garantie.

warren ['wɔrən] n (of rabbits) terriers mpl, garenne f.

warring ['wɔ:rɪŋ] a (nations) en guerre; (interests etc) contradictoire, opposé(e).

warrior ['wɔrɪə*] n guerrier/ière.

Warsaw ['wɔ:sɔ:] n Varsovie.

warship ['wɔ:ʃɪp] n navire m de guerre.

wart [wɔ:t] n verrue f.

wartime ['wɔ:taɪm] n: **in ~** en temps de guerre.

wary ['wɛərɪ] a prudent(e); **to be ~ about** or **of doing sth** hésiter beaucoup à faire qch.

was [wɔz] pt of **be**.

wash [wɔʃ] vt laver; (sweep, carry: sea etc) emporter, entraîner; (: ashore) rejeter ♦ vi se laver ♦ n (paint) badigeon m; (washing programme) lavage m; (of ship) sillage m; **to give sth a ~** laver qch; **to have a ~** se laver, faire sa toilette; **he was ~ed overboard** il a été emporté par une vague.

wash away vt (stain) enlever au lavage; (subj: river etc) emporter.

wash down vt laver; laver à grande eau.

wash off vi partir au lavage.

wash up vi faire la vaisselle; (US: have a wash) se débarbouiller.
washable ['wɔʃəbl] a lavable.
washbasin ['wɔʃbeɪsn] n lavabo m.
washcloth ['wɔʃklɔθ] n (US) gant m de toilette.
washer ['wɔʃə*] n (TECH) rondelle f, joint m.
wash-hand basin ['wɔʃhænd-] n (Brit) lavabo m.
washing ['wɔʃɪŋ] n (Brit: linen etc) lessive f.
washing line n (Brit) corde f à linge.
washing machine n machine f à laver.
washing powder n (Brit) lessive f (en poudre).
Washington ['wɔʃɪŋtən] n (city, state) Washington m.
washing-up [wɔʃɪŋ'ʌp] n vaisselle f.
washing-up liquid n (Brit) produit m pour la vaisselle.
wash-out ['wɔʃaut] n (col) désastre m.
washroom ['wɔʃrum] n toilettes fpl.
wasn't ['wɔznt] = was not.
Wasp, WASP [wɔsp] n abbr (US col: = White Anglo-Saxon Protestant) surnom, souvent péjoratif, donné à l'américain de souche anglo-saxonne, aisé et de tendance conservatrice.
wasp [wɔsp] n guêpe f.
waspish ['wɔspɪʃ] a irritable.
wastage ['weɪstɪdʒ] n gaspillage m; (in manufacturing, transport etc) déchet m.
waste [weɪst] n gaspillage m; (of time) perte f; (rubbish) déchets mpl; (also: **household** ~) ordures fpl ♦ a (material) de rebut; (energy, heat) perdu(e); (food) inutilisé(e); (land, ground: in city) à l'abandon; (: in country) inculte, en friche ♦ vt gaspiller; (time, opportunity) perdre; ~s npl étendue f désertique; **it's a ~ of money** c'est de l'argent jeté en l'air; **to go to** ~ être gaspillé(e); **to lay** ~ (destroy) dévaster.
waste away vi dépérir.
wastebin ['weɪstbɪn] n (Brit) corbeille f à papier; (in kitchen) boîte f à ordures.
waste disposal (unit) n (Brit) broyeur m d'ordures.
wasteful ['weɪstful] a gaspilleur(euse); (process) peu économique.
waste ground n (Brit) terrain m vague.
wasteland ['weɪstlənd] n terres fpl à l'abandon; (in town) terrain(s) m(pl) vague(s).
wastepaper basket ['weɪstpeɪpə-] n corbeille f à papier.
waste pipe n (tuyau m de) vidange f.
waste products n (INDUSTRY) déchets mpl (de fabrication).
watch [wɔtʃ] n montre f; (act of watching) surveillance f; guet m; (guard: MIL) sentinelle f; (: NAUT) homme m de quart; (NAUT: spell of duty) quart m ♦ vt (look at) observer; (: match, programme) regarder; (spy on, guard) surveiller; (be careful of) faire attention à ♦ vi regarder; (keep guard) monter la garde; **to keep a close** ~ **on sb/sth** surveiller qn/qch de près; ~ **what you're doing** fais attention à ce que tu fais.
watch out vi faire attention.

watchband ['wɔtʃbænd] n (US) bracelet m de montre.
watchdog ['wɔtʃdɔg] n chien m de garde; (fig) gardien/ne.
watchful ['wɔtʃful] a attentif(ive), vigilant(e).
watchmaker ['wɔtʃmeɪkə*] n horloger/ère.
watchman ['wɔtʃmən] n gardien m; (also: **night** ~) veilleur m de nuit.
watch stem n (US) remontoir m.
watch strap n bracelet m de montre.
watchword ['wɔtʃwə:d] n mot m de passe.
water ['wɔ:tə*] n eau f ♦ vt (plant) arroser ♦ vi (eyes) larmoyer; **a drink of** ~ un verre d'eau; **in British** ~s dans les eaux territoriales Britanniques; **to pass** ~ uriner; **to make sb's mouth** ~ mettre l'eau à la bouche de qn.
water down vt (milk) couper d'eau; (fig: story) édulcorer.
water closet n (Brit) w.-c. mpl, waters mpl.
watercolour, (US) **watercolor** ['wɔ:təkʌlə*] n aquarelle f; ~s npl couleurs fpl pour aquarelle.
water-cooled ['wɔ:təku:ld] a à refroidissement par eau.
watercress ['wɔ:təkrɛs] n cresson m (de fontaine).
waterfall ['wɔ:təfɔ:l] n chute f d'eau.
waterfront ['wɔ:təfrʌnt] n (seafront) front m de mer; (at docks) quais mpl.
water heater n chauffe-eau m.
water hole n mare f.
water ice n (Brit) sorbet m.
watering can ['wɔ:tərɪŋ-] n arrosoir m.
water level n niveau m de l'eau; (of flood) niveau des eaux.
water lily n nénuphar m.
waterline ['wɔ:təlaɪn] n (NAUT) ligne f de flottaison.
waterlogged ['wɔ:təlɔgd] a détrempé(e); imbibé(e) d'eau.
water main n canalisation f d'eau.
watermark ['wɔ:təma:k] n (on paper) filigrane m.
watermelon ['wɔ:təmɛlən] n pastèque f.
water polo n water-polo m.
waterproof ['wɔ:təpru:f] a imperméable.
water-repellent ['wɔ:tərɪpɛlnt] a hydrofuge.
watershed ['wɔ:təʃɛd] n (GEO) ligne f de partage des eaux; (fig) moment m critique, point décisif.
water-skiing ['wɔ:təski:ɪŋ] n ski m nautique.
water softener n adoucisseur m d'eau.
water tank n réservoir m d'eau.
watertight ['wɔ:tətaɪt] a étanche.
water vapour n vapeur f d'eau.
waterway ['wɔ:təweɪ] n cours m d'eau navigable.
waterworks ['wɔ:təwə:ks] npl station f hydraulique.
watery ['wɔ:təri] a (colour) délavé(e); (coffee) trop faible.
watt [wɔt] n watt m.
wattage ['wɔtɪdʒ] n puissance f or consommation f en watts.
wattle ['wɔtl] n clayonnage m.
wave [weɪv] n vague f; (of hand) geste m, signe m; (RADIO) onde f; (in hair) ondulation f; (fig: of enthusiasm, strikes etc) vague ♦ vi

faire signe de la main; (*flag*) flotter au vent ♦ *vt* (*handkerchief*) agiter; (*stick*) brandir; (*hair*) onduler; **to ~ goodbye to sb** dire au revoir de la main à qn; **short/medium** (*RADIO*) ondes courtes/moyennes; **long ~** (*RADIO*) grandes ondes; **the new ~** (*CINEMA, MUS*) la nouvelle vague.

wave aside, wave away *vt* (*person*): **to ~ sb aside** faire signe à qn de s'écarter; (*fig: suggestion, objection*) rejeter, repousser; (: *doubts*) chasser.

waveband ['weɪvbænd] *n* bande *f* de fréquences.

wavelength ['weɪvlɛŋθ] *n* longueur *f* d'ondes.

waver ['weɪvə*] *vi* vaciller; (*voice*) trembler; (*person*) hésiter.

wavy ['weɪvɪ] *a* ondulé(e); onduleux(euse).

wax [wæks] *n* cire *f*; (*for skis*) fart *m* ♦ *vt* cirer; (*car*) lustrer ♦ *vi* (*moon*) croître.

waxen [wæksn] *a* cireux(euse).

waxworks ['wækswɔːks] *npl* personnages *mpl* de cire; musée *m* de cire.

way [weɪ] *n* chemin *m*, voie *f*; (*path, access*) passage *m*; (*distance*) distance *f*; (*direction*) chemin, direction *f*; (*manner*) façon *f*, manière *f*; (*habit*) habitude *f*, façon; (*condition*) état *m*; **which ~? — this ~** par où *or* de quel côté? — par ici; **to crawl one's ~ to ...** ramper jusqu'à ...; **to lie one's ~ out of it** s'en sortir par un mensonge; **to lose one's ~** perdre son chemin; **on the ~ (to)** en route (pour); **to be on one's ~** être en route; **to be in the ~** bloquer le passage; (*fig*) gêner; **to keep out of sb's ~** éviter qn; **it's a long ~ away** c'est loin d'ici; **the village is rather out of the ~** le village est plutôt à l'écart *or* isolé; **to go out of one's ~ to do** (*fig*) se donner beaucoup de mal pour faire; **to be under ~** (*work, project*) être en cours; **to make ~ (for sb/sth)** faire place (à qn/qch), s'écarter pour laisser passer (qn/qch); **to get one's own ~** arriver à ses fins; **put it the right ~ up** (*Brit*) mettez-le dans le bon sens; **to be the wrong ~ round** être à l'envers, ne pas être dans le bon sens; **in a bad ~** il va mal; **in a ~** d'un côté; **in some ~s** à certains égards; **in the ~ of** en fait de, comme; **by ~ of** (*through*) en passant par, via; (*as a sort of*) en guise de; **"~ in"** (*Brit*) "entrée"; **"~ out"** (*Brit*) "sortie"; **the ~ back** le chemin du retour; **this ~ and that** par-ci par-là; **"give ~"** (*Brit AUT*) "cédez la priorité"; **no ~!** (*col*) pas question!

waybill ['weɪbɪl] *n* (*COMM*) récépissé *m*.

waylay [weɪˈleɪ] *vt irg* attaquer; (*fig*): **I got waylaid** quelqu'un m'a accroché.

wayside ['weɪsaɪd] *n* bord *m* de la route; **to fall by the ~** (*fig*) abandonner; (*morally*) quitter le droit chemin.

way station *n* (*US: RAIL*) petite gare; (: *fig*) étape *f*.

wayward ['weɪwəd] *a* capricieux(euse), entêté(e).

WC *n abbr* (*Brit: = water closet*) w.-c. *mpl*, waters *mpl*.

WCC *n abbr* (= *World Council of Churches*) COE *m* (= *Conseil œcuménique des Églises*).

we [wiː] *pl pronoun* nous.

weak [wiːk] *a* faible; (*health*) fragile; (*beam etc*) peu solide; (*tea, coffee*) léger(ère); **to grow ~(er)** s'affaiblir, faiblir.

weaken ['wiːkn] *vi* faiblir ♦ *vt* affaiblir.

weak-kneed ['wiːk'niːd] *a* (*fig*) lâche, faible.

weakling ['wiːklɪŋ] *n* gringalet *m*; faible *m/f*.

weakly ['wiːklɪ] *a* chétif(ive) ♦ *ad* faiblement.

weakness ['wiːknɪs] *n* faiblesse *f*; (*fault*) point *m* faible.

wealth [wɛlθ] *n* (*money, resources*) richesse(s) *f(pl)*; (*of details*) profusion *f*.

wealth tax *n* impôt *m* sur la fortune.

wealthy ['wɛlθɪ] *a* riche.

wean [wiːn] *vt* sevrer.

weapon ['wɛpən] *n* arme *f*.

wear [wɛə*] *n* (*use*) usage *m*; (*deterioration through use*) usure *f*; (*clothing*): **sports/baby~** vêtements *mpl* de sport/pour bébés; **town/evening ~** tenue *f* de ville/de soirée ♦ *vb* (*pt* **wore**, *pp* **worn** [wɔː*, wɔːn]) *vt* (*clothes*) porter; (*beard etc*) avoir; (*damage: through use*) user ♦ *vi* (*last*) faire de l'usage; (*rub etc through*) s'user; **~ and tear** usure *f*; **to ~ a hole in sth** faire (à la longue) un trou dans qch.

wear away *vt* user, ronger ♦ *vi* s'user, être rongé(e).

wear down *vt* user; (*strength*) épuiser.

wear off *vi* disparaître.

wear on *vi* se poursuivre; passer.

wear out *vt* user; (*person, strength*) épuiser.

wearable ['wɛərəbl] *a* mettable.

wearily ['wɪərɪlɪ] *ad* avec lassitude.

weariness ['wɪərɪnɪs] *n* épuisement *m*, lassitude *f*.

wearisome ['wɪərɪsəm] *a* (*tiring*) fatigant(e); (*boring*) ennuyeux(euse).

weary ['wɪərɪ] *a* (*tired*) épuisé(e); (*dispirited*) las(lasse); abattu(e) ♦ *vt* lasser ♦ *vi*: **to ~ of** se lasser de.

weasel ['wiːzl] *n* (*ZOOL*) belette *f*.

weather ['wɛðə*] *n* temps *m* ♦ *vt* (*wood*) faire mûrir; (*tempest, crisis*) essuyer, être pris(e) dans; survivre à, tenir le coup durant; **what's the ~ like?** quel temps fait-il?; **under the ~** (*fig: ill*) mal fichu(e).

weather-beaten ['wɛðəbiːtn] *a* (*person*) hâlé(e); (*building*) dégradé(e) par les intempéries.

weather cock *n* girouette *f*.

weather forecast *n* prévisions *fpl* météorologiques, météo *f*.

weatherman ['wɛðəmæn] *n* météorologue *m*.

weatherproof ['wɛðəpruːf] *a* (*garment*) imperméable; (*building*) étanche.

weather report *n* bulletin *m* météo, météo *f*.

weather vane *n* = **weather cock**.

weave, *pt* **wove**, *pp* **woven** [wiːv, wəuv, 'wəuvn] *vt* (*cloth*) tisser; (*basket*) tresser ♦ *vi* (*fig: pt, pp ~d: move in and out*) se faufiler.

weaver ['wiːvə*] *n* tisserand/e.

weaving ['wiːvɪŋ] *n* tissage *m*.

web [wɛb] *n* (*of spider*) toile *f*; (*on foot*) palmure *f*; (*fabric, also fig*) tissu *m*.

webbed ['wɛbd] *a* (*foot*) palmé(e).

webbing ['wɛbɪŋ] *n* (*on chair*) sangles *fpl*.

wed [wɛd] *vt* (*pt, pp* **wedded**) épouser ♦ *n*:

the newly-~s les jeunes mariés.
Wed. *abbr* (= *Wednesday*) me.
we'd [wi:d] = **we had, we would.**
wedded ['wɛdɪd] *pt, pp of* **wed.**
wedding [wɛdɪŋ] *n* mariage *m*.
wedding anniversary *n* anniversaire *m* de mariage; **silver/golden ~** noces *fpl* d'argent/d'or.
wedding day *n* jour *m* du mariage.
wedding dress *n* robe *f* de mariage.
wedding present *n* cadeau *m* de mariage.
wedding ring *n* alliance *f*.
wedge [wɛdʒ] *n* (*of wood etc*) coin *m*; (*under door etc*) cale *f*; (*of cake*) part *f* ♦ *vt* (*fix*) caler; (*push*) enfoncer, coincer.
wedge-heeled shoes ['wɛdʒhi:ld-] *npl* chaussures *fpl* à semelles compensées.
wedlock ['wɛdlɔk] *n* (union *f* du) mariage *m*.
Wednesday ['wɛdnzdɪ] *n* mercredi *m*; *for phrases see also* **Tuesday.**
wee [wi:] *a* (*Scottish*) petit(e); tout(e) petit(e).
weed [wi:d] *n* mauvaise herbe ♦ *vt* désherber.
weed-killer ['wi:dkɪlə*] *n* désherbant *m*.
weedy ['wi:dɪ] *a* (*man*) gringalet.
week [wi:k] *n* semaine *f*; **once/twice a ~** une fois/deux fois par semaine; **in two ~s' time** dans quinze jours; **Tuesday ~, a ~ on Tuesday** mardi en huit.
weekday ['wi:kdeɪ] *n* jour *m* de semaine; (*COMM*) jour ouvrable; **on ~s** en semaine.
weekend [wi:k'ɛnd] *n* week-end *m*.
weekend case *n* sac *m* de voyage.
weekly ['wi:klɪ] *ad* une fois par semaine, chaque semaine ♦ *a, n* hebdomadaire (*m*).
weep, *pt, pp* **wept** [wi:p, wɛpt] *vi* (*person*) pleurer; (*MED: wound etc*) suinter.
weeping willow ['wi:pɪŋ-] *n* saule pleureur.
weft [wɛft] *n* (*TEXTILES*) trame *f*.
weigh [weɪ] *vt, vi* peser; **to ~ anchor** lever l'ancre; **to ~ the pros and cons** peser le pour et le contre.
weigh down *vt* (*branch*) faire plier; (*fig: with worry*) accabler.
weigh out *vt* (*goods*) peser.
weigh up *vt* examiner.
weighbridge ['weɪbrɪdʒ] *n* pont-bascule *m*.
weighing machine ['weɪɪŋ-] *n* balance *f*, bascule *f*.
weight [weɪt] *n* poids *m* ♦ *vt* alourdir; (*fig: factor*) pondérer; **sold by ~** vendu au poids; **to put on/lose ~** grossir/maigrir; **~s and measures** poids et mesures.
weighting ['weɪtɪŋ] *n:* **~ allowance** indemnité *f* de résidence.
weightlessness ['weɪtlɪsnɪs] *n* apesanteur *f*.
weight lifter [-'lɪftə*] *n* haltérophile *m*.
weighty ['weɪtɪ] *a* lourd(e).
weir [wɪə*] *n* barrage *m*.
weird [wɪəd] *a* bizarre; (*eerie*) surnaturel(le).
welcome ['wɛlkəm] *a* bienvenu(e) ♦ *n* accueil *m* ♦ *vt* accueillir; (*also:* **bid ~**) souhaiter la bienvenue à; (*be glad of*) se réjouir de; **to be ~** être le(la) bienvenu(e); **to make sb ~** faire bon accueil à qn; **you're ~ to try** vous pouvez essayer si vous voulez; **you're ~!** (*after thanks*) de rien, il n'y a pas de quoi.
welcoming ['wɛlkəmɪŋ] *a* accueillant(e); (*speech*) d'accueil.

weld [wɛld] *n* soudure *f* ♦ *vt* souder.
welder ['wɛldə*] *n* (*person*) soudeur *m*.
welding ['wɛldɪŋ] *n* soudure *f* (autogène).
welfare ['wɛlfɛə*] *n* bien-être *m*.
welfare state *n* Etat-providence *m*.
welfare work *n* travail social.
well [wɛl] *n* puits *m* ♦ *ad* bien ♦ *a:* **to be ~** aller bien ♦ *excl* eh bien!; bon!; enfin!; **~ done!** bravo!; **I don't feel ~** je ne me sens pas bien; **get ~ soon!** remets-toi vite!; **to do ~** in sth bien réussir en *or* dans qch; **to think ~ of sb** penser du bien de qn; **as ~** (*in addition*) aussi, également; **you might as ~ tell me** tu ferais aussi bien de me le dire; **as ~ as** aussi bien que *or* de; en plus de; **~, as I was saying** ... donc, comme je disais ....
well up *vi* (*tears, emotions*) monter.
we'll [wi:l] = **we will, we shall.**
well-behaved ['wɛlbɪ'heɪvd] *a* sage, obéissant(e).
well-being ['wɛl'bi:ɪŋ] *n* bien-être *m*.
well-bred ['wɛl'brɛd] *a* bien élevé(e).
well-built ['wɛl'bɪlt] *a* (*house*) bien construit(e); (*person*) bien bâti(e).
well-chosen ['wɛl'tʃəuzn] *a* (*remarks, words*) bien choisi(e), pertinent(e).
well-developed ['wɛldɪ'vɛləpt] *a* (*girl*) bien fait(e).
well-disposed ['wɛl'dɪspəuzd] *a:* **~ to(wards)** bien disposé(e) envers.
well-dressed ['wɛl'drɛst] *a* bien habillé(e), bien vêtu(e).
well-earned ['wɛl'ə:nd] *a* (*rest*) bien mérité(e).
well-groomed ['wɛl'gru:md] *a* très soigné(e) de sa personne.
well-heeled ['wɛl'hi:ld] *a* (*col: wealthy*) fortuné(e), riche.
well-informed ['wɛlɪn'fɔ:md] *a* (*having knowledge of sth*) bien renseigné(e); (*having general knowledge*) cultivé(e).
Wellington ['wɛlɪŋtən] *n* Wellington.
wellingtons ['wɛlɪŋtənz] *npl* (*also:* **wellington boots**) bottes *fpl* de caoutchouc.
well-kept ['wɛl'kɛpt] *a* (*house, grounds*) bien tenu(e), bien entretenu(e); (*secret*) bien gardé(e); (*hair, hands*) soigné(e).
well-known ['wɛl'nəun] *a* (*person*) bien connu(e).
well-mannered ['wɛl'mænəd] *a* bien élevé(e).
well-meaning ['wɛl'mi:nɪŋ] *a* bien intentionné(e).
well-nigh ['wɛl'naɪ] *ad:* **~ impossible** pratiquement impossible.
well-off ['wɛl'ɔf] *a* aisé(e), assez riche.
well-read ['wɛl'rɛd] *a* cultivé(e).
well-spoken ['wɛl'spəukn] *a* (*person*) qui parle bien; (*words*) bien choisi(e).
well-stocked ['wɛl'stɔkt] *a* bien approvisionné(e).
well-timed ['wɛl'taɪmd] *a* opportun(e).
well-to-do ['wɛltə'du:] *a* aisé(e), assez riche.
well-wisher ['wɛlwɪʃə*] *n* ami/e, admirateur/trice; **scores of ~s had gathered** de nombreux amis et admirateurs s'étaient rassemblés; **letters from ~s** des lettres d'encouragement.
Welsh [wɛlʃ] *a* gallois(e) ♦ *n* (*LING*) gallois *m*; **the ~** *npl* les Gallois.

Welshman, Welshwoman ['wɛlʃmən, -wumən] n Gallois/e.

Welsh rarebit n croûte f au fromage.

welter ['wɛltə*] n fatras m.

went [wɛnt] pt of **go**.

wept [wɛpt] pt, pp of **weep**.

were [wɜ:*] pt of **be**.

we're [wɪə*] = **we are**.

weren't [wɜ:nt] = **were not**.

werewolf, pl **-wolves** ['wɪəwulf, -wulvz] n loup-garou m.

west [wɛst] n ouest m ♦ a ouest inv, de or à l'ouest ♦ ad à or vers l'ouest; **the W~** l'Occident m, l'Ouest.

westbound ['wɛstbaund] a (traffic) en direction de l'ouest; (carriageway) ouest inv.

West Country n: **the ~** le sud-ouest de l'Angleterre.

westerly ['wɛstəlɪ] a (situation) à l'ouest; (wind) d'ouest.

western ['wɛstən] a occidental(e), de or à l'ouest ♦ n (CINEMA) western m.

westernized ['wɛstənaɪzd] a occidentalisé(e).

West German a ouest-allemand(e) ♦ n Allemand/e de l'Ouest.

West Germany n Allemagne f de l'Ouest.

West Indian a antillais(e) ♦ n Antillais/e.

West Indies [-'ɪndɪz] npl: **the ~** les Antilles fpl.

westward(s) ['wɛstwəd(z)] ad vers l'ouest.

wet [wɛt] a mouillé(e); (damp) humide; (soaked) trempé(e); (rainy) pluvieux(euse) ♦ vt: **to ~ one's pants** or **o.s.** mouiller sa culotte, faire pipi dans sa culotte; **to get ~** se mouiller; **"~ paint"** "attention peinture fraîche".

wet blanket n (fig) rabat-joie m inv.

wetness ['wɛtnɪs] n humidité f.

wet suit n combinaison f de plongée.

we've [wi:v] = **we have**.

whack [wæk] vt donner un grand coup à.

whacked [wækt] a (Brit col: tired) crevé(e).

whale [weɪl] n (ZOOL) baleine f.

whaler ['weɪlə*] n (ship) baleinier m.

wharf, pl **wharves** [wɔ:f, wɔ:vz] n quai m.

what [wɔt] excl quoi!, comment! ♦ a quel(le) ♦ pronoun (interrogative) que, prep + quoi; (relative, indirect: object) ce que; (: subject) ce qui; **~ are you doing?** que fais-tu?, qu'est-ce que tu fais?; **~ has happened?** que s'est-il passé?, qu'est-ce qui s'est passé?; **~'s in there?** qu'y a-t-il là-dedans?, qu'est-ce qu'il y a là-dedans?; **for ~ reason?** pour quelle raison?; **I saw ~ you did/is on the table** j'ai vu ce que vous avez fait/ce qui est sur la table; **I don't know ~ to do** je ne sais pas que or quoi faire; **~ a mess!** quel désordre!; **~ is his address?** quelle est son adresse?; **~ will it cost?** combien est-ce que ça coûtera?; **~ is it called?** comment est-ce que ça s'appelle?; **~ I want is a cup of tea** ce que je veux, c'est une tasse de thé; **~ about doing ...?** et si on faisait ...?; **~ about me?** et moi?

whatever [wɔt'ɛvə*] a: **~ book** quel que soit le livre que (or qui) + sub; n'importe quel livre ♦ pronoun: **do ~ is necessary** faites (tout) ce qui est nécessaire; **~ happens** quoi qu'il arrive; **no reason ~** or **whatsoever** pas

la moindre raison; **nothing ~** or **whatsoever** rien du tout.

wheat [wi:t] n blé m, froment m.

wheatgerm ['wi:tdʒɜ:m] n germe m de blé.

wheatmeal ['wi:tmi:l] n farine bise.

wheedle ['wi:dl] vt: **to ~ sb into doing sth** cajoler or enjôler qn pour qu'il fasse qch; **to ~ sth out of sb** obtenir qch de qn par des cajoleries.

wheel [wi:l] n roue f; (AUT: also: **steering ~**) volant m; (NAUT) gouvernail m ♦ vt pousser, rouler ♦ vi (also: **~ round**) tourner.

wheelbarrow ['wi:lbærəu] n brouette f.

wheelbase ['wi:lbeɪs] n empattement m.

wheelchair ['wi:ltʃɛə*] n fauteuil roulant.

wheel clamp n (AUT) sabot m (de Denver).

wheeler-dealer ['wi:lə'di:lə*] n (pej) combinard/e, affairiste m/f.

wheeling ['wi:lɪŋ] n: **~ and dealing** (pej) manigances fpl, magouilles fpl.

wheeze [wi:z] n respiration bruyante (d'asthmatique) ♦ vi respirer bruyamment.

when [wɛn] ad quand ♦ cj quand, lorsque; (whereas) alors que; **on the day ~ I met him** le jour où je l'ai rencontré.

whenever [wɛn'ɛvə*] ad quand donc ♦ cj quand; (every time that) chaque fois que; **I go ~ I can** j'y vais quand or chaque fois que je le peux.

where [wɛə*] ad, cj où; **this is ~** c'est là que; **~ are you from?** d'où venez vous?

whereabouts ['wɛərəbauts] ad où donc ♦ n: **sb's ~** l'endroit où se trouve qn.

whereas [wɛər'æz] cj alors que.

whereby [wɛə'baɪ] ad (formal) par lequel (or laquelle etc).

whereupon [wɛərə'pɔn] ad sur quoi, et sur ce.

wherever [wɛər'ɛvə*] ad où donc ♦ cj où que + sub; **sit ~ you like** asseyez-vous (là) où vous voulez.

wherewithal ['wɛəwɪðɔ:l] n: **the ~ (to do sth)** les moyens mpl (de faire qch).

whet [wɛt] vt aiguiser.

whether ['wɛðə*] cj si; **I don't know ~ to accept or not** je ne sais pas si je dois accepter ou non; **it's doubtful ~** il est peu probable que; **~ you go or not** que vous y alliez ou non.

whey [weɪ] n petit-lait m.

which [wɪtʃ] a (interrogative) quel(le), pl quels(quelles); **~ one of you?** lequel(laquelle) d'entre vous?; **tell me ~ one you want** dis-moi lequel tu veux or celui que tu veux ♦ pronoun (interrogative) lequel(laquelle), pl lesquels(lesquelles); (indirect) celui(celle) qui (or que); (relative: subject) qui; (: object) que, prep + lequel(laquelle) (NB: à + lequel = auquel; de + lequel = duquel); **~ do you want?** lequel or laquelle etc veux-tu?; **I don't mind ~** peu importe lequel; **the apple ~ you ate/~ is on the table** la pomme que vous avez mangée/ qui est sur la table; **the chair on ~** la chaise sur laquelle; **the book of ~** le livre dont or duquel; **he said he knew, ~ is true/I feared** il a dit qu'il le savait, ce qui est vrai/ce que je craignais; **after ~** après quoi; **in ~ case** auquel cas; **by ~ time** ... heure (or moment) à laquelle(auquel) ..., et à ce moment-là ....

whichever [wɪtʃ'ɛvə*] *a*: **take ~ book you prefer** prenez le livre que vous préférez, peu importe lequel; **~ book you take** quel que soit le livre que vous preniez; **~ way you de** quelque façon que vous + *sub*.

whiff [wɪf] *n* bouffée *f*; **to catch a ~ of sth** sentir l'odeur de qch.

while [waɪl] *n* moment *m* ♦ *cj* pendant que; (*as long as*) tant que; (*as, whereas*) alors que; (*though*) quoique + *sub*; **for a ~** pendant quelque temps; **in a ~** dans un moment; **all the ~** pendant tout ce temps-là; **we'll make it worth your ~** nous vous récompenserons de votre peine.
  while away *vt* (*time*) (faire) passer.

whilst [waɪlst] *cj* = **while**.

whim [wɪm] *n* caprice *m*.

whimper ['wɪmpə*] *n* geignement *m* ♦ *vi* geindre.

whimsical ['wɪmzɪkl] *a* (*person*) capricieux(euse); (*look*) étrange.

whine [waɪn] *n* gémissement *m* ♦ *vi* gémir, geindre; pleurnicher.

whip [wɪp] *n* fouet *m*; (*for riding*) cravache *f*; (*POL: person*) chef *m* de file (*assurant la discipline dans son groupe parlementaire*) ♦ *vt* fouetter; (*snatch*) enlever (*or* sortir) brusquement.
  whip up *vt* (*cream*) fouetter; (*col: meal*) préparer en vitesse; (*stir up: support*) stimuler; (: *feeling*) attiser, aviver.

whiplash ['wɪplæʃ] *n* (*MED: also:* **~ injury**) coup *m* du lapin.

whipped cream [wɪpt-] *n* crème fouettée.

whipping boy ['wɪpɪŋ-] *n* (*fig*) bouc *m* émissaire.

whip-round ['wɪpraund] *n* (*Brit*) collecte *f*.

whirl [wə:l] *n* tourbillon *m* ♦ *vt* faire tourbillonner; faire tournoyer ♦ *vi* tourbillonner.

whirlpool ['wə:lpu:l] *n* tourbillon *m*.

whirlwind ['wə:lwɪnd] *n* tornade *f*.

whirr [wə:*] *vi* bruire; ronronner; vrombir.

whisk [wɪsk] *n* (*CULIN*) fouet *m* ♦ *vt* fouetter, battre; **to ~ sb away** *or* **off** emmener qn rapidement.

whiskers ['wɪskəz] *npl* (*of animal*) moustaches *fpl*; (*of man*) favoris *mpl*.

whisky, (*Irish, US*) **whiskey** ['wɪskɪ] *n* whisky *m*.

whisper ['wɪspə*] *n* chuchotement *m*; (*fig: of leaves*) bruissement *m*; (*rumour*) rumeur *f* ♦ *vt, vi* chuchoter; **to ~ sth to sb** chuchoter qch à (l'oreille de) qn.

whispering ['wɪspərɪŋ] *n* chuchotement(s) *m(pl)*.

whist [wɪst] *n* (*Brit*) whist *m*.

whistle ['wɪsl] *n* (*sound*) sifflement *m*; (*object*) sifflet *m* ♦ *vi* siffler ♦ *vt* siffler, siffloter.

whistle-stop ['wɪslstɔp] *a*: **to make a ~ tour of** (*POL*) faire la tournée électorale des petits patelins de.

Whit [wɪt] *n* la Pentecôte.

white [waɪt] *a* blanc(blanche); (*with fear*) blême ♦ *n* blanc *m*; (*person*) blanc/blanche; **to turn** *or* **go ~** (*person*) pâlir, blêmir; (*hair*) blanchir; **the ~s** (*washing*) le linge blanc; **tennis ~s** tenue *f* de tennis.

whitebait ['waɪtbeɪt] *n* blanchaille *f*.

white coffee *n* (*Brit*) café *m* au lait, (café) crème *m*.

white-collar worker ['waɪtkɔlə-] *n* employé/e de bureau.

white elephant *n* (*fig*) objet dispendieux et superflu.

white goods *npl* (*appliances*) (gros) électroménager *m*; (*linen etc*) linge *m* de maison.

white-hot [waɪt'hɔt] *a* (*metal*) incandescent(e).

white lie *n* pieux mensonge.

whiteness ['waɪtnɪs] *n* blancheur *f*.

white noise *n* son *m* blanc.

whiteout ['waɪtaut] *n* jour blanc.

white paper *n* (*POL*) livre blanc.

whitewash ['waɪtwɔʃ] *n* (*paint*) lait *m* de chaux ♦ *vt* blanchir à la chaux; (*fig*) blanchir.

whiting ['waɪtɪŋ] *n* (*pl inv*) (*fish*) merlan *m*.

Whit Monday *n* le lundi de Pentecôte.

Whitsun ['wɪtsn] *n* la Pentecôte.

whittle ['wɪtl] *vt*: **to ~ away, ~ down** (*costs*) réduire, rogner.

whizz [wɪz] *vi* aller (*or* passer) à toute vitesse.

whizz kid *n* (*col*) petit prodige.

WHO *n abbr* (= *World Health Organization*) OMS *f* (= · *Organisation mondiale de la Santé*).

who [hu:] *pronoun* qui.

whodunit [hu:'dʌnɪt] *n* (*col*) roman policier.

whoever [hu:'ɛvə*] *pronoun*: **~ finds it** celui(celle) qui le trouve (, qui que ce soit), quiconque le trouve; **ask ~ you like** demandez à qui vous voulez; **~ he marries** qui que ce soit *or* quelle que soit la personne qu'il épouse; **~ told you that?** qui a bien pu vous dire ça?, qui donc vous a dit ça?

whole [həul] *a* (*complete*) entier(ière), tout(e); (*not broken*) intact(e), complet(ète) ♦ *n* (*total*) totalité *f*; (*sth not broken*) tout *m*; **the ~ lot (of it)** tout; **the ~ lot (of them)** tous (sans exception); **the ~ of the time** tout le temps; **the ~ of the town** la ville tout entière; **~ villages were destroyed** des villages entiers ont été détruits; **on the ~, as a ~** dans l'ensemble.

wholehearted [həul'hɑ:tɪd] *a* sans réserve(s), sincère.

wholemeal ['həulmi:l] *a* (*Brit: flour, bread*) complet(ète).

whole note *n* (*US*) ronde *f*.

wholesale ['həulseɪl] *n* (vente *f* en) gros *m* ♦ *a* de gros; (*destruction*) systématique.

wholesaler ['həulseɪlə*] *n* grossiste *m/f*.

wholesome ['həulsəm] *a* sain(e); (*advice*) salutaire.

wholewheat ['həulwi:t] *a* = **wholemeal**.

wholly ['həulɪ] *ad* entièrement, tout à fait.

whom [hu:m] *pronoun* que, *prep* + qui (*check syntax of French verb used*); (*interrogative*) qui; **those to ~ I spoke** ceux à qui j'ai parlé.

whooping cough ['hu:pɪŋ-] *n* coqueluche *f*.

whoosh [wuʃ] *n, vi*: **the skiers ~ed past, the skiers came by with a ~** les skieurs passèrent dans un glissement rapide.

whopper ['wɔpə*] *n* (*col: lie*) gros bobard; (: *large thing*) monstre *m*, phénomène *m*.

whopping ['wɔpɪŋ] a (col: big) énorme.

whore [hɔ:*] n (col: pej) putain f.

whose [hu:z] a: ~ **book is this?** à qui est ce livre?; ~ **pencil have you taken?** à qui est le crayon que vous avez pris?, c'est le crayon de qui que vous avez pris?; **the man** ~ **son you rescued** l'homme dont or de qui vous avez sauvé le fils; **the girl** ~ **sister you were speaking to** la fille à la sœur de qui or laquelle vous parliez ♦ pronoun: ~ **is this?** à qui est ceci?; **I know** ~ **it is** je sais à qui c'est.

Who's Who ['hu:z'hu:] n ≈ Bottin Mondain.

why [waɪ] ad (gen) ♦ excl eh bien!, tiens!; **the reason** ~ la raison pour laquelle; ~ **is he late?** pourquoi est-il en retard?

whyever [waɪ'ɛvə*] ad pourquoi donc, mais pourquoi.

WI n abbr (Brit: = Women's Institute) amicale de femmes au foyer ♦ abbr (GEO) = **West Indies**; (US POST) = Wisconsin.

wick [wɪk] n mèche f (de bougie).

wicked ['wɪkɪd] a foncièrement mauvais(e), inique; (mischievous: grin, look) espiègle, malicieux(euse); (terrible: prices, weather) épouvantable.

wicker ['wɪkə*] n osier m; (also: ~**work**) vannerie f.

wicket ['wɪkɪt] n (CRICKET) guichet m; espace compris entre les deux guichets.

wicket keeper n (CRICKET) gardien m de guichet.

wide [waɪd] a large; (region, knowledge) vaste, très étendu(e); (choice) grand(e) ♦ ad: **to open** ~ ouvrir tout grand; **to shoot** ~ tirer à côté; **it is 3 metres** ~ cela fait 3 mètres de large.

wide-angle lens ['waɪdæŋgl-] n objectif m grand-angulaire.

wide-awake [waɪdə'weɪk] a bien éveillé(e).

wide-eyed [waɪd'aɪd] a aux yeux écarquillés; (fig) naïf(ïve), crédule.

widely ['waɪdlɪ] ad (different) radicalement; (spaced) sur une grande étendue; (believed) généralement; **to be** ~ **read** (author) être beaucoup lu(e); (reader) avoir beaucoup lu, être cultivé(e).

widen ['waɪdn] vt élargir.

wideness ['waɪdnɪs] n largeur f.

wide open a grand(e) ouvert(e).

wide-ranging [waɪd'reɪndʒɪŋ] a (survey, report) vaste; (interests) divers(e).

widespread ['waɪdspred] a (belief etc) très répandu(e).

widow ['wɪdəu] n veuve f.

widowed ['wɪdəud] a (qui est devenu(e)) veuf(veuve).

widower ['wɪdəuə*] n veuf m.

width [wɪdθ] n largeur f; **it's 7 metres in** ~ cela fait 7 mètres de large.

widthways ['wɪdθweɪz] ad en largeur.

wield [wi:ld] vt (sword) manier; (power) exercer.

wife, pl **wives** [waɪf, waɪvz] n femme (mariée), épouse f.

wig [wɪg] n perruque f.

wigging ['wɪgɪŋ] n (Brit col) savon m, engueulade f.

wiggle ['wɪgl] vt agiter, remuer ♦ vi (loose

screw etc) branler; (worm) se tortiller.

wiggly ['wɪglɪ] a (line) ondulé(e).

wild [waɪld] a sauvage; (sea) déchaîné(e); (idea, life) fou(folle); extravagant(e); (col: angry) hors de soi, furieux(euse); (: enthusiastic): **to be** ~ **about** être fou(folle) or dingue de ♦ n: **the** ~ la nature; ~**s** npl régions fpl sauvages.

wild card n (COMPUT) caractère m de remplacement.

wildcat ['waɪldkæt] n chat m sauvage.

wildcat strike n grève f sauvage.

wilderness ['wɪldənɪs] n désert m, région f sauvage.

wildfire ['waɪldfaɪə*] n: **to spread like** ~ se répandre comme une traînée de poudre.

wild-goose chase [waɪld'gu:s-] n (fig) fausse piste.

wildlife ['waɪldlaɪf] n faune f (et flore f) sauvage(s).

wildly ['waɪldlɪ] ad (applaud) frénétiquement; (hit, guess) au hasard; (happy) follement.

wiles [waɪlz] npl ruses fpl, artifices mpl.

wilful, (US) **willful** ['wɪlful] a (person) obstiné(e); (action) délibéré(e); (crime) prémédité(e).

will [wɪl] auxiliary vb: **he** ~ **come** il viendra; **you won't lose it,** ~ **you?** vous ne le perdrez pas, n'est-ce pas?; **that** ~ **be the postman** c'est probablement or ça doit être le facteur; ~ **you sit down** voulez-vous vous asseoir; **the car won't start** la voiture ne veut pas démarrer ♦ vt (pt, pp ~**ed**) exhorter par la pensée; **he** ~**ed himself to go on** par un suprême effort de volonté, il continua ♦ n volonté f; (LAW) testament m; **to do sth of one's own free** ~ faire qch de son propre gré; **against one's** ~ à contre-cœur.

willful ['wɪlful] a (US) = **wilful**.

willing ['wɪlɪŋ] a de bonne volonté, serviable ♦ n: **to show** ~ faire preuve de bonne volonté; **he's** ~ **to do it** il est disposé à le faire, il veut bien le faire.

willingly ['wɪlɪŋlɪ] ad volontiers.

willingness ['wɪlɪŋnɪs] n bonne volonté.

will-o'-the wisp ['wɪləðə'wɪsp] n (also fig) feu follet m.

willow ['wɪləu] n saule m.

will power n volonté f.

willy-nilly ['wɪlɪ'nɪlɪ] ad bon gré mal gré.

wilt [wɪlt] vi dépérir.

Wilts [wɪlts] abbr (Brit) = Wiltshire.

wily ['waɪlɪ] a rusé(e).

wimp [wɪmp] n (col) mauviette f.

win [wɪn] n (in sports etc) victoire f ♦ vb (pt, pp **won** [wʌn]) vt (battle, money) gagner; (prize, contract) remporter; (popularity) acquérir ♦ vi gagner.

win over , (Brit)

win round vt gagner, se concilier.

wince [wɪns] n tressaillement m ♦ vi tressaillir.

winch [wɪntʃ] n treuil m.

Winchester disk ['wɪntʃɪstə-] n (COMPUT) disque m Winchester.

wind n [wɪnd] (also MED) vent m ♦ vb [waɪnd] (pt, pp **wound** [waund]) vt enrouler; (wrap) envelopper; (clock, toy) remonter; (take breath away: [wɪnd]) couper le souffle à ♦ vi (*road, river*) serpenter; **the ~(s)** (*MUS*) les instruments *mpl* à vent; **into** *or* **against the** ~ contre le vent; **to get ~ of sth** (*fig*) avoir vent de qch; **to break** ~ avoir des gaz.

wind down *vt* (*car window*) baisser; (*fig: production, business*) réduire progressivement.

wind up *vt* (*clock*) remonter; (*debate*) terminer, clôturer.

windbreak ['wɪndbreɪk] *n* brise-vent *m inv*.

windcheater ['wɪndtʃiːtə*], (*US*) **windbreaker** ['wɪndbreɪkə*] *n* anorak *m*.

winder ['waɪndə*] *n* (*Brit: on watch*) remontoir *m*.

windfall ['wɪndfɔːl] *n* coup *m* de chance.

winding ['waɪndɪŋ] *a* (*road*) sinueux(euse); (*staircase*) tournant(e).

wind instrument *n* (*MUS*) instrument *m* à vent.

windmill ['wɪndmɪl] *n* moulin *m* à vent.

window ['wɪndəu] *n* fenêtre *f*; (*in car, train, also:* ~**pane**) vitre *f*; (*in shop etc*) vitrine *f*.

window box *n* jardinière *f*.

window cleaner *n* (*person*) laveur/euse de vitres.

window dressing *n* arrangement *m* de la vitrine.

window envelope *n* enveloppe *f* à fenêtre.

window frame *n* châssis *m* de fenêtre.

window ledge *n* rebord *m* de la fenêtre.

window pane *n* vitre *f*, carreau *m*.

window-shopping ['wɪndəuʃɔpɪŋ] *n*: **to go** ~ faire du lèche-vitrines.

windowsill ['wɪndəusɪl] *n* (*inside*) appui *m* de la fenêtre; (*outside*) rebord *m* de la fenêtre.

windpipe ['wɪndpaɪp] *n* gosier *m*.

windscreen ['wɪndskriːn], (*US*) **windshield** ['wɪndʃiːld] *n* pare-brise *m inv*.

windscreen washer *n* lave-glace *m inv*.

windscreen wiper *n* essuie-glace *m inv*.

windswept ['wɪndswept] *a* balayé(e) par le vent.

wind tunnel *n* soufflerie *f*.

windy ['wɪndɪ] *a* venté(e), venteux(euse); **it's** ~ il y a du vent.

wine [waɪn] *n* vin *m* ♦ *vt*: **to** ~ **and dine sb** offrir un dîner bien arrosé à qn.

wine cellar *n* cave *f* à vins.

wine glass *n* verre *m* à vin.

wine list *n* carte *f* des vins.

wine merchant *n* marchand/e de vins.

wine tasting *n* dégustation *f* (de vins).

wine waiter *n* sommelier *m*.

wing [wɪŋ] *n* aile *f*; (*in air force*) groupe *m* d'escadrilles; ~**s** *npl* (*THEATRE*) coulisses *fpl*.

winger ['wɪŋə*] *n* (*SPORT*) ailier *m*.

wing mirror *n* (*Brit*) rétroviseur latéral.

wing nut *n* papillon *m*, écrou *m* à ailettes.

wingspan ['wɪŋspæn] *n*, **wingspread** ['wɪŋspred] *n* envergure *f*.

wink [wɪŋk] *n* clin *m* d'œil ♦ *vi* faire un clin d'œil; (*blink*) cligner des yeux.

winkle ['wɪŋkl] *n* bigorneau *m*.

winner ['wɪnə*] *n* gagnant/e.

winning ['wɪnɪŋ] *a* (*team*) gagnant(e); (*goal*) décisif(ive); (*charming*) charmeur(euse).

winning post *n* poteau *m* d'arrivée.

winnings ['wɪnɪŋz] *npl* gains *mpl*.

winsome ['wɪnsəm] *a* avenant(e), engageant(e).

winter ['wɪntə*] *n* hiver *m* ♦ *vi* hiverner.

winter sports *npl* sports *mpl* d'hiver.

wintry ['wɪntrɪ] *a* hivernal(e).

wipe [waɪp] *n* coup *m* de torchon (*or* de chiffon *or* d'éponge) ♦ *vt* essuyer; **to wipe a** ~ donner un coup de torchon à qch; **to** ~ **one's nose** se moucher.

wipe off *vt* essuyer.

wipe out *vt* (*debt*) régler; (*memory*) oublier; (*destroy*) anéantir.

wipe up *vt* essuyer.

wire ['waɪə*] *n* fil *m* (de fer); (*ELEC*) fil électrique; (*TEL*) télégramme *m* ♦ *vt* (*fence*) grillager; (*house*) faire l'installation électrique de; (*also:* ~ **up**) brancher.

wire brush *n* brosse *f* métallique.

wire cutters *npl* cisaille *f*.

wireless ['waɪəlɪs] *n* (*Brit*) télégraphie *f* sans fil; (*set*) T.S.F. *f*.

wire netting *n* treillis *m* métallique, grillage *m*.

wire-tapping ['waɪə'tæpɪŋ] *n* écoute *f* téléphonique.

wiring ['waɪərɪŋ] *n* (*ELEC*) installation *f* électrique.

wiry ['waɪərɪ] *a* noueux(euse), nerveux(euse).

wisdom ['wɪzdəm] *n* sagesse *f*; (*of action*) prudence *f*.

wisdom tooth *n* dent *f* de sagesse.

wise [waɪz] *a* sage, prudent(e), judicieux(euse); **I'm none the** ~**r** je ne suis pas plus avancé(e) pour autant.

wise up *vi* (*col*): **to** ~ **up to** commencer à se rendre compte de.

...wise [waɪz] *suffix*: **time**~ en ce qui concerne le temps, question temps.

wisecrack ['waɪzkræk] *n* sarcasme *m*.

wish [wɪʃ] *n* (*desire*) désir *m*; (*specific desire*) souhait *m*, vœu *m* ♦ *vt* souhaiter, désirer, vouloir; **best** ~**es** (*on birthday etc*) meilleurs vœux; **with best** ~**es** (*in letter*) bien amicalement; **give her my best** ~**es** faites-lui mes amitiés; **to** ~ **sb goodbye** dire au revoir à qn; **he** ~**ed me well** il me souhaitait de réussir; **to** ~ **to do/sb to do** désirer *or* vouloir faire/que qn fasse; **to** ~ **for** souhaiter; **to** ~ **sth on sb** souhaiter qch à qn.

wishful ['wɪʃful] *a*: **it's** ~ **thinking** c'est prendre ses désirs pour des réalités.

wishy-washy ['wɪʃɪ'wɔʃɪ] *a* (*col: person*) qui manque de caractère, falot(e); (*: ideas, thinking*) faiblard(e).

wisp [wɪsp] *n* fine mèche (*de cheveux*); (*of smoke*) mince volute *f*; **a** ~ **of straw** un fétu de paille.

wistful ['wɪstful] *a* mélancolique.

wit [wɪt] *n* (*gen pl: intelligence*) intelligence *f*, esprit *m*; (*presence of mind*) présence *f* d'esprit; (*wittiness*) esprit; (*person*) homme/femme d'esprit; **to be at one's** ~**s' end** (*fig*) ne plus savoir que faire; **to have one's** ~**s about one** avoir toute sa présence d'esprit, ne pas perdre la tête; **to** ~ *ad* à savoir.

witch [wɪtʃ] *n* sorcière *f*.

witchcraft ['wɪtʃkrɑːft] *n* sorcellerie *f*.

witch doctor *n* sorcier *m*.

witch-hunt ['wɪtʃhʌnt] *n* chasse *f* aux sorcières.

with [wɪð, wɪθ] *prep* avec; **red ~ anger** rouge de colère; **to shake ~ fear** trembler de peur; **the man ~ the grey hat** l'homme au chapeau gris; **to stay overnight ~ friends** passer la nuit chez des amis; **to be ~ it** (*fig*) être dans le vent; **I am ~ you** (*I understand*) je vous suis.

withdraw [wɪθ'drɔ:] *vb (irg) vt* retirer ♦ *vi* se retirer; (*go back on promise*) se rétracter; **to ~ into o.s.** se replier sur soi-même.

withdrawal [wɪθ'drɔ:əl] *n* retrait *m*; (*MED*) état *m* de manque.

withdrawal symptoms *npl:* **to have ~** être en état de manque, présenter les symptômes *mpl* de sevrage.

withdrawn [wɪθ'drɔ:n] *pp* of **withdraw** ♦ *a* (*person*) renfermé(e).

wither ['wɪðə*] *vi* se faner.

withered ['wɪðəd] *a* fané(e), flétri(e); (*limb*) atrophié(e).

withhold [wɪθ'həuld] *vt irg* (*money*) retenir; (*decision*) remettre; (*permission*): **to ~ (from)** refuser (à); (*information*): **to ~ (from)** cacher (à).

within [wɪð'ɪn] *prep* à l'intérieur de ♦ *ad* à l'intérieur; **~ sight of** en vue de; **~ a mile of** à moins d'un mille de; **~ the week** avant la fin de la semaine; **~ an hour from now** d'ici une heure; **to be ~ the law** être légal(e) *or* dans les limites de la légalité.

without [wɪð'aut] *prep* sans; **~ anybody knowing** sans que personne le sache; **to go** *or* **do ~ sth** se passer de qch.

withstand [wɪθ'stænd] *vt irg* résister à.

witness ['wɪtnɪs] *n* (*person*) témoin *m*; (*evidence*) témoignage *m* ♦ *vt* (*event*) être témoin de; (*document*) attester l'authenticité de; **to bear ~ to sth** témoigner de qch; **~ for the prosecution/defence** témoin à charge/à décharge; **to ~ to sth/having seen sth** témoigner de qch/d'avoir vu qch.

witness box, (*US*) **witness stand** *n* barre *f* des témoins.

witticism ['wɪtɪsɪzəm] *n* mot *m* d'esprit.

witty ['wɪtɪ] *a* spirituel(le), plein(e) d'esprit.

wives [waɪvz] *npl* of **wife**.

wizard ['wɪzəd] *n* magicien *m*.

wizened ['wɪznd] *a* ratatiné(e).

wk *abbr* = **week**.

Wm. *abbr* = **William**.

WO *n abbr* = **warrant officer**.

wobble ['wɔbl] *vi* trembler; (*chair*) branler.

wobbly ['wɔblɪ] *a* tremblant(e); branlant(e).

woe [wəu] *n* malheur *m*.

woke [wəuk] *pt* of **wake**.

woken ['wəukn] *pp* of **wake**.

wolf, *pl* **wolves** [wulf, wulvz] *n* loup *m*.

woman, *pl* **women** ['wumən, 'wɪmɪn] *n* femme *f* ♦ *cpd:* **~ doctor** femme *f* médecin; **~ friend** amie *f*; **~ teacher** professeur *m* femme; **young ~** jeune femme; **women's page** (*PRESS*) page *f* des lectrices.

womanize ['wumənaɪz] *vi* jouer les séducteurs.

womanly ['wumənlɪ] *a* féminin(e).

womb [wu:m] *n* (*ANAT*) utérus *m*.

women ['wɪmɪn] *npl* of **woman**.

Women's (Liberation) Movement *n* (*also:* **women's lib**) mouvement *m* de libération de la femme, MLF *m*.

won [wʌn] *pt, pp* of **win**.

wonder ['wʌndə*] *n* merveille *f*, miracle *m*; (*feeling*) émerveillement *m* ♦ *vi:* **to ~ whether** se demander si; **to ~ at** s'étonner de; s'émerveiller de; **to ~ about** songer à; **it's no ~ that** il n'est pas étonnant que + *sub*.

wonderful ['wʌndəful] *a* merveilleux(euse).

wonderfully ['wʌndəfəlɪ] *ad* (+ *adjective*) merveilleusement; (+ *vb*) à merveille.

wonky ['wɔŋkɪ] *a* (*Brit col*) qui ne va *or* ne marche pas très bien.

won't [wəunt] = **will not**.

woo [wu:] *vt* (*woman*) faire la cour à.

wood [wud] *n* (*timber, forest*) bois *m* ♦ *cpd* de bois, en bois.

wood carving *n* sculpture *f* en *or* sur bois.

wooded ['wudɪd] *a* boisé(e).

wooden ['wudn] *a* en bois; (*fig*) raide; inexpressif(ive).

woodland ['wudlənd] *n* forêt *f*, région boisée.

woodpecker ['wudpɛkə*] *n* pic *m* (*oiseau*).

wood pigeon *n* ramier *m*.

woodwind ['wudwɪnd] *n* (*MUS*) bois *m*; **the ~** (*MUS*) les bois.

woodwork ['wudwə:k] *n* menuiserie *f*.

woodworm ['wudwə:m] *n* ver *m* du bois.

woof [wuf] *n* (*of dog*) aboiement *m* ♦ *vi* aboyer; **~, ~!** oua, oua!

wool [wul] *n* laine *f*; **to pull the ~ over sb's eyes** (*fig*) en faire accroire à qn.

woollen, (*US*) **woolen** ['wulən] *a* de laine; (*industry*) lainier(ière) ♦ *n:* **~s** lainages *mpl*.

woolly, (*US*) **wooly** ['wulɪ] *a* laineux(euse); (*fig: ideas*) confus(e).

word [wə:d] *n* mot *m*; (*spoken*) mot, parole *f*; (*promise*) parole; (*news*) nouvelles *fpl* ♦ *vt* rédiger, formuler; **~ for ~** (*repeat*) mot pour mot; (*translate*) mot à mot; **what's the ~ for "pen" in French?** comment dit-on "pen" en français?; **to put sth into ~s** exprimer qch; **in other ~s** en d'autres termes; **to have a ~ with sb** toucher un mot à qn; **to have ~s with sb** (*quarrel with*) avoir des mots avec qn; **to break/keep one's ~** manquer à/tenir sa parole; **I'll take your ~ for it** je vous crois sur parole; **to send ~ of** prévenir de; **to leave ~ (with sb/for sb) that** ... laisser un mot (à qn/pour qn) disant que ....

wording ['wə:dɪŋ] *n* termes *mpl*, langage *m*; libellé *m*.

word-perfect ['wə:d'pə:fɪkt] *a:* **he was ~ (in his speech** *etc*), **his speech** *etc* **was ~** il savait son discours *etc* sur le bout du doigt.

word processing *n* traitement *m* de texte.

word processor *n* machine *f* de traitement de texte.

wordwrap ['wə:dræp] *n* (*COMPUT*) retour *m* (automatique) à la ligne.

wordy ['wə:dɪ] *a* verbeux(euse).

wore [wɔ:*] *pt* of **wear**.

work [wə:k] *n* travail *m*; (*ART, LITERATURE*) œuvre *f* ♦ *vi* travailler; (*mechanism*) marcher, fonctionner; (*plan etc*) marcher; (*medicine*) agir ♦ *vt* (*clay, wood etc*) travailler; (*mine etc*) exploiter; (*machine*) faire marcher *or* fonctionner; **to go to ~** aller travailler; **to set to ~, to start ~** se mettre à l'œuvre; **to be at ~ (on sth)** travailler (sur qch); **to be out of ~** être au chômage; **to ~ hard** travailler dur; **to ~ loose** se défaire, se desserrer.

work on *vt fus* travailler à; (*principle*) se baser sur.

work out *vi* (*plans etc*) marcher; (SPORT) s'entraîner ♦ *vt* (*problem*) résoudre; (*plan*) élaborer; **it ~s out at £100** ça fait 100 livres.

workable ['wɔːkəbl] *a* (*solution*) réalisable.

workaholic [wɔːkə'hɒlɪk] *n* bourreau *m* de travail.

workbench ['wɔːkbɛntʃ] *n* établi *m*.

worked up *a*: **to get ~** se mettre dans tous ses états.

worker ['wɔːkə*] *n* travailleur/euse, ouvrier/ière; **office ~** employé/e de bureau.

work force *n* main-d'œuvre *f*.

work-in ['wɔːkɪn] *n* (*Brit*) occupation *f* d'usine *etc* (*sans arrêt de la production*).

working ['wɔːkɪŋ] *a* (*day, tools etc, conditions*) de travail; (*wife*) qui travaille; (*partner, population*) actif(ive); **in ~ order** en état de marche; **a ~ knowledge of English** une connaissance toute pratique de l'anglais.

working capital *n* (COMM) fonds *mpl* de roulement.

working class *n* classe ouvrière ♦ *a*: **working-class** ouvrier(ière), de la classe ouvrière.

working man *n* travailleur *m*.

working model *n* modèle opérationnel.

working party *n* (*Brit*) groupe *m* de travail.

working week *n* semaine *f* de travail.

work-in-progress ['wɔːkɪn'prəʊgrɛs] *n* (COMM) en-cours *m inv*; (: *value*) valeur *f* des en-cours.

workload ['wɔːkləʊd] *n* charge *f* de travail.

workman ['wɔːkmən] *n* ouvrier *m*.

workmanship ['wɔːkmənʃɪp] *n* métier *m*, habileté *f*; facture *f*.

workmate ['wɔːkmeɪt] *n* collègue *m/f*.

workout ['wɔːkaut] *n* (SPORT) séance *f* d'entraînement.

work permit *n* permis *m* de travail.

works [wɔːks] *n* (*Brit*: *factory*) usine *f* ♦ *npl* (*of clock, machine*) mécanisme *m*; **road ~** travaux *mpl* (d'entretien des routes).

works council *n* comité *m* d'entreprise.

work sheet *n* (COMPUT) feuille *f* de programmation.

workshop ['wɔːkʃɔp] *n* atelier *m*.

work station *n* poste *m* de travail.

work study *n* étude *f* du travail.

work-to-rule ['wɔːktə'ruːl] *n* (*Brit*) grève *f* du zèle.

world [wɔːld] *n* monde *m* ♦ *cpd* (*champion*) du monde; (*power, war*) mondial(e); **all over the ~** dans le monde entier, partout dans le monde; **to think the ~ of sb** (*fig*) ne jurer que par qn; **what in the ~ is he doing?** qu'est-ce qu'il peut bien être en train de faire?; **to do sb a ~ of good** faire le plus grand bien à qn; **W~ War One/Two** Première/Deuxième guerre mondiale; **out of**

this ~ *a* extraordinaire.

World Cup *n*: **the ~** (FOOTBALL) la Coupe du monde.

world-famous [wɔːld'feɪməs] *a* de renommée mondiale.

worldly ['wɔːldlɪ] *a* de ce monde.

world-wide ['wɔːld'waɪd] *a* universel(le) ♦ *ad* dans le monde entier.

worm [wɔːm] *n* ver *m*.

worn [wɔːn] *pp of* **wear** ♦ *a* usé(e).

worn-out ['wɔːnaut] *a* (*object*) complètement usé(e); (*person*) épuisé(e).

worried ['wʌrɪd] *a* inquiet(ète); **to be ~ about sth** être inquiet au sujet de qch.

worrier ['wʌrɪə*] *n* inquiet/ète.

worrisome ['wʌrɪsəm] *a* inquiétant(e).

worry ['wʌrɪ] *n* souci *m* ♦ *vt* inquiéter ♦ *vi* s'inquiéter, se faire du souci; **to ~ about** *or* **over sth/sb** se faire du souci pour *or* à propos de qch/qn.

worrying ['wʌrɪŋ] *a* inquiétant(e).

worse [wɔːs] *a* pire, plus mauvais(e) ♦ *ad* plus mal ♦ *n* pire *m*; **to get ~** (*condition, situation*) empirer, se dégrader; **a change for the ~** une détérioration; **he is none the ~ for it** il ne s'en porte pas plus mal; **so much the ~ for you!** tant pis pour vous!

worsen ['wɔːsn] *vt, vi* empirer.

worse off *a* moins à l'aise financièrement; (*fig*): **you'll be ~ this way** ça ira moins bien de cette façon; **he is now ~ than before** il se retrouve dans une situation pire qu'auparavant.

worship ['wɔːʃɪp] *n* culte *m* ♦ *vt* (*God*) rendre un culte à; (*person*) adorer; **Your W~** (*Brit*: *to mayor*) Monsieur le Maire; (: *to judge*) Monsieur le Juge.

worshipper ['wɔːʃɪpə*] *n* adorateur/trice; (*in church*) fidèle *m/f*.

worst [wɔːst] *a* le(la) pire, le(la) plus mauvais(e) ♦ *ad* le plus mal ♦ *n* pire *m*; **at ~** au pis aller; **if the ~ comes to the ~** si le pire doit arriver.

worsted ['wustɪd] *n*: **(wool) ~** laine peignée.

worth [wɔːθ] *n* valeur *f* ♦ *a*: **to be ~** valoir; **how much is it ~?** ça vaut combien?; **it's ~ it** cela en vaut la peine; **50 pence ~ of apples** (pour) 50 pence de pommes.

worthless ['wɔːθlɪs] *a* qui ne vaut rien.

worthwhile ['wɔːθ'waɪl] *a* (*activity*) qui en vaut la peine; (*cause*) louable; **a ~ book** un livre qui vaut la peine d'être lu.

worthy ['wɔːðɪ] *a* (*person*) digne; (*motive*) louable; **~ of** digne de.

would [wud] *auxiliary vb*: **she ~ come** elle viendrait; **he ~ have come** il serait venu; **~ you like a biscuit?** voulez-vous *or* voudriez-vous un biscuit?; **~ you close the door, please?** voulez-vous fermer la porte, s'il vous plaît; **he ~ go there on Mondays** il y allait le lundi; **you WOULD say that, ~n't you!** bien évidemment tu dis ça!; c'est bien de toi de dire ça!; **she ~n't leave** elle a refusé de partir.

would-be ['wudbiː] *a* (*pej*) soi-disant.

wound *vb* [waund] *pt, pp of* **wind** ♦ *n, vt* [wuːnd] *n* blessure *f* ♦ *vt* blesser; **~ed in the leg** blessé à la jambe.

wove [wəuv] *pt of* **weave**.

woven ['wəʊvn] *pp of* **weave.**

WP *n abbr* = **word processing, word processor** ♦ *abbr* (*Brit col*) = *weather permitting.*

WPC *n abbr* (*Brit*) = *woman police constable.*

wpm *abbr* (= *words per minute*) mots/minute.

WRAC *n abbr* (*Brit:* = *Women's Royal Army Corps*) *auxiliaires féminines de l'armée de terre.*

WRAF *n abbr* (*Brit:* = *Women's Royal Air Force*) *auxiliaires féminines de l'armée de l'air.*

wrangle ['ræŋgl] *n* dispute *f* ♦ *vi* se disputer.

wrap [ræp] *n* (*stole*) écharpe *f*; (*cape*) pèlerine *f* ♦ *vt* (*also:* ~ **up**) envelopper; **under** ~**s** (*fig: plan, scheme*) secret(ète).

wrapper ['ræpə*] *n* (*Brit: of book*) couverture *f*; (*on chocolate etc*) papier *m*.

wrapping paper ['ræpɪŋ-] *n* papier *m* d'emballage; (*for gift*) papier cadeau. —

wrath [rɒθ] *n* courroux *m*.

wreak [riːk] *vt* (*destruction*) entraîner; **to** ~ **havoc** faire des ravages; **to** ~ **vengeance on** se venger de, exercer sa vengeance sur.

wreath, ~**s** [riːθ, riːðz] *n* couronne *f*.

wreck [rɛk] *n* (*sea disaster*) naufrage *m*; (*ship*) épave *f*; (*pej: person*) loque (humaine) ♦ *vt* démolir; (*ship*) provoquer le naufrage de; (*fig*) briser, ruiner.

wreckage ['rɛkɪdʒ] *n* débris *mpl*; (*of building*) décombres *mpl*; (*of ship*) naufrage *m*.

wrecker ['rɛkə*] *n* (*US: breakdown van*) dépanneuse *f*.

WREN [rɛn] *n abbr* (*Brit*) *membre du WRNS.*

wren [rɛn] *n* (*ZOOL*) roitelet *m*.

wrench [rɛntʃ] *n* (*TECH*) clé *f* (à écrous); (*tug*) violent mouvement de torsion; (*fig*) arrachement *m* ♦ *vt* tirer violemment sur, tordre; **to** ~ **sth from** arracher qch (violemment) à *or* de.

wrest [rɛst] *vt*: **to** ~ **sth from sb** arracher *or* ravir qch à qn.

wrestle ['rɛsl] *vi*: **to** ~ (**with sb**) lutter (avec qn); **to** ~ **with** (*fig*) se débattre avec, lutter contre.

wrestler ['rɛslə*] *n* lutteur/euse.

wrestling ['rɛslɪŋ] *n* lutte *f*; (*also:* **all-in** ~: *Brit*) catch *m*.

wrestling match *n* rencontre *f* de lutte (*or* de catch).

wretch [rɛtʃ] *n* pauvre malheureux/euse; **little** ~**!** (*often humorous*) petit(e) misérable!

wretched ['rɛtʃɪd] *a* misérable; (*col*) maudit(e).

wriggle ['rɪgl] *n* tortillement *m* ♦ *vi* se tortiller.

wring, *pt, pp* **wrung** [rɪŋ, rʌŋ] *vt* tordre; (*wet clothes*) essorer; (*fig*): **to** ~ **sth out of** arracher qch à.

wringer ['rɪŋə*] *n* essoreuse *f*.

wringing ['rɪŋɪŋ] *a* (*also:* ~ **wet**) tout mouillé(e), trempé(e).

wrinkle ['rɪŋkl] *n* (*on skin*) ride *f*; (*on paper etc*) pli *m* ♦ *vt* rider, plisser ♦ *vi* se plisser.

wrinkled ['rɪŋkld] *a*, **wrinkly** ['rɪŋklɪ] *a* (*fabric, paper*) froissé(e), plissé(e); (*surface*) plissé; (*skin*) ridé(e), plissé.

wrist [rɪst] *n* poignet *m*.

wristband ['rɪstbænd] *n* (*Brit: of shirt*) poignet *m*; (: *of watch*) bracelet *m*.

wrist watch *n* montre-bracelet *f*.

writ [rɪt] *n* acte *m* judiciaire; **to issue a** ~ **against sb, serve a** ~ **on sb** assigner qn en justice.

write, *pt* **wrote,** *pp* **written** [raɪt, rəʊt, 'rɪtn] *vt, vi* écrire; **to** ~ **sb a letter** écrire une lettre à qn.

write away *vi*: **to** ~ **away for** (*information*) (écrire pour) demander; (*goods*) (écrire pour) commander.

write down *vt* noter; (*put in writing*) mettre par écrit.

write off *vt* (*debt*) passer aux profits et pertes; (*depreciate*) amortir; (*smash up: car etc*) démolir complètement.

write out *vt* écrire; (*copy*) recopier.

write up *vt* rédiger.

write-off ['raɪtɒf] *n* perte totale; **the car is a** ~ la voiture est bonne pour la casse.

write-protect ['raɪtprə'tɛkt] *vt* (*COMPUT*) protéger contre l'écriture.

writer ['raɪtə*] *n* auteur *m*, écrivain *m*.

write-up ['raɪtʌp] *n* (*review*) critique *f*.

writhe [raɪð] *vi* se tordre.

writing ['raɪtɪŋ] *n* écriture *f*; (*of author*) œuvres *fpl*; **in** ~ par écrit; **in my own** ~ écrit(e) de ma main.

writing case *n* nécessaire *m* de correspondance.

writing desk *n* secrétaire *m*.

writing paper *n* papier *m* à lettres.

written ['rɪtn] *pp of* **write.**

WRNS *n abbr* (*Brit:* = *Women's Royal Naval Service*) *auxiliaires féminines de la marine.*

wrong [rɒŋ] *a* faux(fausse); (*incorrectly chosen: number, road etc*) mauvais(e); (*not suitable*) qui ne convient pas; (*wicked*) mal; (*unfair*) injuste ♦ *ad* faux ♦ *n* tort *m* ♦ *vt* faire du tort à, léser; **to be** ~ (*answer*) être faux(fausse); (*in doing/saying*) avoir tort (de dire/faire); **you are** ~ **to do it** tu as tort de le faire; **it's** ~ **to steal, stealing is** ~ c'est mal de voler; **you are** ~ **about that, you've got it** ~ tu te trompes; **to be in the** ~ avoir tort; **what's** ~**?** qu'est-ce qui ne va pas?; **there's nothing** ~ tout va bien; **what's** ~ **with the car?** qu'est-ce qu'elle a, la voiture?; **to go** ~ (*person*) se tromper; (*plan*) mal tourner; (*machine*) se détraquer.

wrongful ['rɒŋful] *a* injustifié(e); ~ **dismissal** (*INDUSTRY*) licenciement abusif.

wrongly ['rɒŋlɪ] *ad* à tort; (*answer, do, count*) mal, incorrectement; (*treat*) injustement.

wrong number *n* (*TEL*): **you have the** ~ vous vous êtes trompé de numéro.

wrong side *n* (*of cloth*) envers *m*.

wrote [rəʊt] *pt of* **write.**

wrought [rɔːt] *a*: ~ **iron** fer forgé.

wrung [rʌŋ] *pt, pp of* **wring.**

WRVS *n abbr* (*Brit:* = *Women's Royal Voluntary Service*) *auxiliaires féminines bénévoles au service de la collectivité.*

wry [raɪ] *a* désabusé(e).

wt. *abbr* (= *weight*) pds.

WV *abbr* (*US POST*) = *West Virginia.*

WY *abbr* (*US POST*) = *Wyoming.*

WYSIWYG ['wɪzɪwɪg] *abbr* (*COMPUT:* = *what you see is what you get*) ce que vous voyez est ce que vous aurez.

X, x [ɛks] *n* (*letter*) X, x *m*; (*Brit CINEMA*: *old*) film interdit aux moins de 18 ans; **X for Xmas** X comme Xavier.

Xerox ['zɪərɔks] ® *n* (*also*: ~ **machine**) photocopieuse *f*; (*photocopy*) photocopie *f* ♦ *vt* photocopier.

XL *abbr* (= *extra large*) XL.

Xmas ['ɛksməs] *n abbr* = **Christmas**.

X-rated ['ɛks'reɪtɪd] *a* (*US*: *film*) interdit(e) aux moins de 18 ans.

X-ray [ɛks'reɪ] *n* rayon *m* X; (*photograph*) radio(graphie) *f* ♦ *vt* radiographier.

xylophone ['zaɪləfəun] *n* xylophone *m*.

Y

Y, y [waɪ] *n* (*letter*) Y, y *m*; **Y for Yellow**, (*US*) **Y for Yoke** Y comme Yvonne.

yacht [jɔt] *n* voilier *m*; (*motor*, *luxury* ~) yacht *m*.

yachting ['jɔtɪŋ] *n* yachting *m*, navigation *f* de plaisance.

yachtsman ['jɔtsmən] *n* yacht(s)man *m*.

yam [jæm] *n* igname *f*.

Yank [jæŋk], **Yankee** ['jæŋkɪ] *n* (*pej*) Amerloque *m/f*, Ricain/e.

yank [jæŋk] *vt* tirer d'un coup sec.

yap [jæp] *vi* (*dog*) japper.

yard [jɑːd] *n* (*of house etc*) cour *f*; (*US*: *garden*) jardin *m*; (*measure*) yard *m* (= *914 mm; 3 feet*); **builder's** ~ chantier *m*.

yardstick ['jɑːdstɪk] *n* (*fig*) mesure *f*, critère *m*.

yarn [jɑːn] *n* fil *m*; (*tale*) longue histoire *f*.

yawn [jɔːn] *n* bâillement *m* ♦ *vi* bâiller.

yawning ['jɔːnɪŋ] *a* (*gap*) béant(e).

yd *abbr* = **yard**.

yeah [jɛə] *ad* (*col*) ouais.

year [jɪə*] *n* an *m*, année *f*; (*SCOL etc*) année; **every** ~ tous les ans, chaque année; **this** ~ cette année; **a** *or* **per** ~ par an; ~ **in**, ~ **out** année après année; **to be 8 ~s old** avoir 8 ans; **an eight-~-old child** un enfant de huit ans.

yearbook ['jɪəbuk] *n* annuaire *m*.

yearly ['jɪəlɪ] *a* annuel(le) ♦ *ad* annuellement; **twice** ~ deux fois par an.

yearn [jɔːn] *vi*: **to** ~ **for sth/to do** aspirer à qch/à faire, languir après qch.

yearning ['jɔːnɪŋ] *n* désir ardent, envie *f*.

yeast [jiːst] *n* levure *f*.

yell [jɛl] *n* hurlement *m*, cri *m* ♦ *vi* hurler.

yellow ['jɛləu] *a*, *n* jaune (*m*).

yellow fever *n* fièvre *f* jaune.

yellowish ['jɛləuɪʃ] *a* qui tire sur le jaune, jaunâtre (*péj*).

Yellow Sea *n*: **the** ~ la mer Jaune.

yelp [jɛlp] *n* jappement *m*; glapissement *m* ♦ *vi* japper; glapir.

Yemen ['jɛmən] *n* Yémen *m*.

yen [jɛn] *n* (*currency*) yen *m*; (*craving*): ~ **for/to do** grand(e) envie *f* or désir *m* de/de faire.

yeoman ['jəumən] *n*: **Y~ of the Guard** hallebardier *m* de la garde royale.

yes [jɛs] *ad* oui; (*answering negative question*) si ♦ *n* oui *m*; **to say** ~ **(to)** dire oui (à).

yesterday ['jɛstədɪ] *ad*, *n* hier (*m*); ~ **morning/evening** hier matin/soir; **the day before** ~ avant-hier; **all day** ~ toute la journée d'hier.

yet [jɛt] *ad* encore; déjà ♦ *cj* pourtant, néanmoins; **it is not finished** ~ ce n'est pas encore fini *or* toujours pas fini; **must you go just** ~**?** dois-tu déjà partir?; **the best** ~ le meilleur jusqu'ici *or* jusque-là; **as** ~ jusqu'ici, encore; **a few days** ~ encore quelques jours; ~ **again** une fois de plus.

yew [juː] *n* if *m*.

YHA *n abbr* (*Brit*) = *Youth Hostels Association*.

Yiddish ['jɪdɪʃ] *n* yiddish *m*.

yield [jiːld] *n* production *f*, rendement *m*; (*FINANCE*) rapport *m* ♦ *vt* produire, rendre, rapporter; (*surrender*) céder ♦ *vi* céder; (*US AUT*) céder la priorité; **a** ~ **of 5%** un rendement de 5%.

YMCA *n abbr* (= *Young Men's Christian Association*) ≈ union chrétienne de jeunes gens (UCJG).

yob(bo) ['jɔb(əu)] *n* (*Brit col*) loubar(d) *m*.

yodel ['jəudl] *vi* faire des tyroliennes, jodler.

yoga ['jəugə] *n* yoga *m*.

yog(h)ourt, yog(h)urt ['jəugət] *n* yaourt *m*.

yoke [jəuk] *n* joug *m* ♦ *vt* (*also*: ~ **together**: *oxen*) accoupler.

yolk [jəuk] *n* jaune *m* (d'œuf).

yonder ['jɔndə*] *ad* là(-bas).

Yorks [jɔːks] *abbr* (*Brit*) = *Yorkshire*.

you [juː] *pronoun* tu; (*polite form*) vous; (*pl*) vous; (*complement*) te, t' + *vowel*; vous; (*stressed*) toi; vous; (*impersonal: one*) on; **if I was** *or* **were** ~ si j'étais vous, à votre place; **fresh air does** ~ **good** l'air frais (vous) fait du bien; ~ **never know** on ne sait jamais.

you'd [juːd] = **you had, you would**.

you'll [juːl] = **you will, you shall**.

young [jʌŋ] *a* jeune ♦ *npl* (*of animal*) petits *mpl*; (*people*): **the** ~ les jeunes, la jeunesse; **a** ~ **man** un jeune homme; **a** ~ **lady** (*unmarried*) une jeune fille, une demoiselle; (*married*) une jeune femme *or* dame; **my** ~**er brother** mon frère cadet; **the** ~**er generation** la jeune génération.

youngish ['jʌŋɪʃ] *a* assez jeune.

youngster ['jʌŋstə*] *n* jeune *m/f*; (*child*) enfant *m/f*.

your [jɔː*] *a* ton(ta), tes *pl*; (*polite form*, *pl*) votre, vos *pl*.

you're [juə*] = **you are**.

yours [jɔ:z] *pronoun* le(la) tien(ne), les tiens(tiennes); (*polite form, pl*) le(la) vôtre, les vôtres; **is it ~?** c'est à toi (*or* à vous)?; **a friend of ~** un(e) de tes (*or* de vos) amis.

yourself [jɔ:'sɛlf] *pronoun* (*reflexive*) te; (*: polite form*) vous; (*after prep*) toi; vous; (*emphatic*) toi-même; vous-même; **you ~ told me** c'est vous qui me l'avez dit, vous me l'avez dit vous-même.

yourselves [jɔ:'sɛlvz] *pl pronoun* vous; (*emphatic*) vous-mêmes.

youth [ju:θ] *n* jeunesse *f*; (*young man*) (*pl ~s* [ju:ðz]) jeune homme *m*; **in my ~** dans ma jeunesse, quand j'étais jeune.

youth club *n* centre *m* de jeunes.

youthful ['ju:θful] *a* jeune; (*enthusiasm etc*) juvénile; (*misdemeanour*) de jeunesse.

youthfulness ['ju:θfəlnɪs] *n* jeunesse *f*.

youth hostel *n* auberge *f* de jeunesse.

youth movement *n* mouvement *m* de jeunes.

you've [ju:v] = **you have**.

yowl [jaul] *n* hurlement *m*; miaulement *m* ♦ *vi* hurler; miauler.

YTS *n abbr* (*Brit*: = *Youth Training Scheme*) ≈ TUC *m*.

Yugoslav ['ju:gəuslɑ:v] *a* yougoslave ♦ *n* Yougoslave *m/f*.

Yugoslavia ['ju:gəu'slɑ:vɪə] *n* Yougoslavie *f*.

Yugoslavian ['ju:gəu'slɑ:vɪən] *a* yougoslave.

Yule [ju:l]: **~ log** *n* bûche *f* de Noël.

yuppie ['jʌpɪ] *n* yuppie *m/f*.

YWCA *n abbr* (= *Young Women's Christian Association*) union chrétienne féminine.

Z

Z, z [zɛd, (*US*) zi:] *n* (*letter*) Z, z *m*; **Z for Zebra** Z comme Zoé.

Zaire [zɑ:'i:ə*] *n* Zaïre *m*.

Zambia ['zæmbɪə] *n* Zambie *f*.

Zambian ['zæmbɪən] *a* zambien(ne) ♦ *n* Zambien/ne.

zany ['zeɪnɪ] *a* farfelu(e), loufoque.

zap [zæp] *vt* (*COMPUT*) effacer.

zeal [zi:l] *n* (*revolutionary etc*) ferveur *f*; (*keenness*) ardeur *f*, zèle *m*.

zealot ['zɛlət] *n* fanatique *m/f*.

zealous ['zɛləs] *a* fervent(e); ardent(e), zélé(e).

zebra ['zi:brə] *n* zèbre *m*.

zebra crossing *n* (*Brit*) passage *m* pour piétons.

zenith ['zɛnɪθ] *n* (*ASTRONOMY*) zénith *m*; (*fig*) zénith, apogée *m*.

zero ['zɪərəu] *n* zéro *m* ♦ *vi*: **to ~ in on** (*target*) se diriger droit sur; **5° below ~** 5 degrés au-dessous de zéro.

zero hour *n* l'heure *f* H.

zero-rated ['zi:rəur'eɪtɪd] *a* (*Brit*) exonéré(e) de TVA.

zest [zɛst] *n* entrain *m*, élan *m*; (*of lemon etc*) zeste *m*.

zigzag ['zɪgzæg] *n* zigzag *m* ♦ *vi* zigzaguer, faire des zigzags.

Zimbabwe [zɪm'bɑ:bwɪ] *n* Zimbabwe *m*.

Zimbabwean [zɪm'bɑ:bwɪən] *a* zimbabwéen(ne) ♦ *n* Zimbabwéen/ne.

zinc [zɪŋk] *n* zinc *m*.

Zionism ['zaɪənɪzəm] *n* sionisme *m*.

Zionist ['zaɪənɪst] *a* sioniste ♦ *n* Sioniste *m/f*.

zip [zɪp] *n* (*also*: **~ fastener**, (*US*) **~per**) fermeture *f* éclair ® *or* à glissière; (*energy*) entrain *m* ♦ *vt* (*also*: **~ up**) fermer (avec une fermeture éclair ®).

zip code *n* (*US*) code postal.

zither ['zɪðə*] *n* cithare *f*.

zodiac ['zəudiæk] *n* zodiaque *m*.

zombie ['zɔmbɪ] *n* (*fig*): **like a ~** avec l'air d'un zombie, comme un automate.

zone [zəun] *n* zone *f*.

zoo [zu:] *n* zoo *m*.

zoological [zuə'lɔdʒɪkl] *a* zoologique.

zoologist [zu'ɔlədʒɪst] *n* zoologiste *m/f*.

zoology [zu:'ɔlədʒɪ] *n* zoologie *f*.

zoom [zu:m] *vi*: **to ~ past** passer en trombe; **to ~ in (on sb/sth)** (*PHOT, CINEMA*) zoomer (sur qn/qch).

zoom lens *n* zoom *m*, objectif *m* à focale variable.

zucchini [zu:'ki:nɪ] *n(pl)* (*US*) courgette(s) *f(pl)*.

Zulu ['zu:lu:] *a* zoulou ♦ *n* Zoulou *m/f*.

Zurich ['zjuərɪk] *n* Zurich.